INTERNATIONAL MONETARY FUND

International
Financial Statistics

Yearbook 2006

INTERNATIONAL FINANCIAL STATISTICS
Vol. LIX, 2006
Prepared by the IMF Statistics Department
Robert W. Edwards, Director

For information related to this publication, please:
     fax the Statistics Department at (202) 589-9810,
     or write Statistics Department
          International Monetary Fund
          Washington, D.C. 20431
     or e-mail your query to **StatisticsQuery@imf.org**
For copyright inquiries, please fax the Editorial Division at (202) 623-6579.
For purchases only, please contact Publication Services (see information below).

International Financial Statistics (IFS) is a standard source of statistics on all aspects of international and domestic finance. *IFS* publishes, for most countries of the world, current data on exchange rates, international liquidity, international banking, money and banking, interest rates, prices, production, international transactions (including balance of payments and international investment position), government finance, and national accounts. Information is presented in tables for specific countries and in tables for area and world aggregates. *IFS* is published monthly and annually.

Address orders to:
International Monetary Fund
Attention: Publication Services
Washington, D.C. 20431
U.S.A.
Telephone: (202) 623-7430
Telefax: (202) 623-7201
E-mail: publications@imf.org
Internet: http://www.imf.org

ISSN 0250-7463
ISBN 1-58906-577-8

POSTMASTER: Send address changes to International Financial Statistics, Publication Services, 700 19th St., N.W., Washington, D.C. 20431. Postage for periodicals paid at Washington, D.C. USPS 049-610

Recycled paper

CONTENTS

"Country" in this publication does not always refer to a territorial entity that is a state as understood by international law and practice; the term also covers the euro area, the Eastern Caribbean Currency Union, and some nonsovereign territorial entities, for which statistical data are provided internationally on a separate basis.

SELECTION OF STATISTICAL PUBLICATIONS

International Financial Statistics (IFS)

Acknowledged as a standard source of statistics on all aspects of international and domestic finance, *IFS* publishes, for most countries of the world, current data on exchange rates, international liquidity, international banking, money and banking, interest rates, prices, production, international transactions (including balance of payments and international investment position), government finance, and national accounts. Information is presented in tables for specific countries and in tables for area and world aggregates. *IFS* is published monthly and annually. *Price:* Subscription price is US$695 a year (US$445 to university faculty and students) for twelve monthly issues and the yearbook. Single copy price is US$89 for a monthly issue and US$145 for a yearbook issue.

Balance of Payments Statistics Yearbook (BOPSY)

Issued in three parts, this annual publication contains balance of payments and international investment position data. Part 1 provides detailed tables on balance of payments statistics for approximately 167 countries and international investment position data for 93 countries. Part 2 presents tables of regional and world totals of major balance of payments components. Part 3 contains descriptions of methodologies, compilation practices, and data sources used by reporting countries Price: US$129.

Direction of Trade Statistics (DOTS)

Quarterly issues of this publication provide, for about 156 countries, tables with current data (or estimates) on the value of imports from and exports to their most important trading partners. In addition, similar summary tables for the world, industrial countries, and developing countries are included. The yearbook provides, for the most recent seven years, detailed trade data by country for approximately 186 countries, the world, and major areas. *Price:* Subscription price is US$209 a year (US$179 to university faculty and students) for the quarterly issues and the yearbook. Price for a quarterly issue only is US$34, the yearbook only is US$92, and a guide only is US$12.50.

Government Finance Statistics Yearbook (GFSY)

This annual publication provides detailed data on transactions in revenue, expense, net acquisition of assets and liabilities, other economic flows, and balances of assets and liabilities of general government and its subsectors. The data are compiled according to the framework of the 2001 *Government Finance Statistics Manual,* which provides for several summary measures of government fiscal performance. *Price:* US$94.

CD-ROM Subscriptions

International Financial Statistics (IFS), Balance of Payments Statistics (BOPS), Direction of Trade Statistics (DOTS), and *Government Finance Statistics (GFS)* are available on CD-ROM by annual subscription. The CD-ROMs incorporate a Windows-based browser facility, as well as a flat file of the database in scientific notation. *Price of each subscription:* US$520 a year for single-user PC license (US$295 for university faculty and students). Network and redistribution licenses are negotiated on a case-by-case basis. Please contact Publication Services for information.

Subscription Packages

Combined Subscription Package

The combined subscription package includes all issues of *IFS, DOTS, BOPSY, GFSY,* and *Staff Papers,* the Fund's economic journal. *Combined subscription price:* US$1,195 a year (US$889 for university faculty and students). Expedited delivery available at additional cost; please inquire.

Combined Statistical Yearbook Subscription

This subscription comprises *BOPSY, GFSY, IFSY,* and *DOTSY* at a combined rate of US$415. Because of different publication dates of the four yearbooks, it may take up to one year to service an order. Expedited delivery available at additional cost; please inquire.

IFS on the Internet

The Statistics Department of the Fund is pleased to make available to subscribers the *International Financial Statistics (IFS)* database through an easy-to-use online service. The *IFS* database contains time series data beginning in 1948. The browser software provides a familiar and easy-to-use Windows interface for browsing the database, selecting series of interest, displaying the selected series in a spreadsheet format, and saving the selected series for transfer to other software systems, such as Microsoft Excel®. Single user license price for the *IFS Online Service* is $575, and $345 for academic users. Dependent on certain criteria, a range of scaled discounts is available. For full details of qualification for these discounts and online payment, please visit http://www.imfstatistics.org or email us directly at publications@imf.org.

Address orders to

Publication Services, IMF, Washington, DC 20431, USA
Telephone: (202) 623-7430 Telefax: (202) 623-7201 E-mail: publications@imf.org
Internet: http://www.imf.org

Note: Prices include the cost of delivery by surface mail. Expedited delivery is available for an additional charge.

country, lines **w**, **x**, and **y** are presented. Notes on the tables in the monthly issues for these countries describe the current exchange rate systems and identify the exchange rates shown.

European Currency Unit (ECU) and the Euro

For periods before January 1999, the exchange rate sections in tables for members of the European Union (EU)—Austria, Belgium, Denmark, Finland, France, Germany, Greece, Ireland, Italy, Luxembourg, the Netherlands, Portugal, Spain, Sweden, and the United Kingdom—Norway and the United States contain a time series on the value of the European currency unit (ECU).

The ECU was issued by the European Monetary Institute (EMI)—successor to the European Monetary Cooperation Fund on January 1, 1994—against gold and foreign exchange deposits by the central banks of the EU member states. The ECU was defined as a basket of currencies of the EU member countries. The share of each currency in the basket was based on the gross national product and foreign trade of the country issuing that currency. The equivalent of the ECU was calculated—first in U.S. dollars and then in the currencies of the member countries—by using representative market exchange rates for the U.S. dollar, as reported by the member countries. In *IFS,* series **ea** and **ec** refer to end-of-period values of national currency units per ECU and ECUs per unit of national currency, respectively; series **eb** and **ed** are the arithmetic averages of values within the period.

On January 1, 1999, the euro replaced the ECU, at a rate of one euro per one ECU. Irrevocable conversion factors for the euro, adopted for the eleven countries in the euro area, fixed the central rates between the euro and the currencies participating in the exchange rate mechanism. The irrevocable fixed factors, legally mandated to have six significant digits, are the following: Austria (S 13.7603), Belgium (BF 40.3399), Finland (Fmk 5.94573), France (F 6.55957), Germany (DM 1.95583), Ireland (IR£0.787564), Italy (Lit 1936.27), Luxembourg (Lux F 40.3399), the Netherlands (f. 2.20371), Portugal (Esc 200.482), and Spain (Pta 166.386).

An accord established compulsory intervention rates for the Danish krone (± 2.25 percent around the euro central rate) and the Greek drachma (± 15 percent around the euro central rate) from January 1, 1999 onwards. Greece joined the euro area on January 1, 2001, adopting the euro as its currency, with a conversion factor of 340.750 drachmas per euro.

In addition, from January 1, 1999 onwards, the member countries of the Bank of Central African States and the Central Bank of West African States changed the peg of their currencies from the French franc to the euro, at a rate of CFAF 655.957 per euro. A few other countries also have pegged their currencies to the euro.

On January 1, 2002, euro banknotes and coins were issued. National currencies continued to be accepted in trade for a short transition period that ended in all member countries by the end of February 2002. The statistical treatment of euro banknotes and coins and outstanding national currencies is described in the section *European Economic and Monetary Union* in Section 5—Money and Banking.

Effective Exchange Rates

The country tables, euro area tables, and world tables provide measures of effective exchange rates, compiled by the IMF's Research Department, Policy Development and Review Department, Statistics Department, and area departments.

A **nominal** effective exchange rate index represents the ratio (expressed on the base 2000=100) of an index of a currency's period-average exchange rate to a weighted geometric average of exchange rates for the currencies of selected countries and the euro area. A **real effective** exchange rate index represents a nominal effective exchange rate index adjusted for relative movements in national price or cost indicators of the home country, selected countries, and the euro area.

Line ahx

For ease of comparison between the nominal effective exchange rate index and the real effective exchange rate index, the average exchange rate expressed in terms of U.S. dollars per unit of each of the national currencies (line **ah**) is also given as an index form based on 2000=100 (line **ahx**). In both cases of the indices, an increase in the index reflects an appreciation. Because of certain data-related limits, particularly where Fund estimates have been used, data users need to exercise considerable caution in interpreting movements in nominal and real effective exchange rates.

The Fund publishes calculated effective exchange rates data only for countries that have given their approval. Please note that similar indices that are calculated by country authorities could cause different results.

Lines neu and reu

The nominal effective exchange rate index (line **neu**) and the real effective exchange rate index (line **reu**) are published in the country tables for approximately 18 industrial countries and the euro area, for which data are available for normalized unit labor costs in manufacturing.

For the nominal effective exchange rate index, weights are derived from trade in manufactured goods among industrial countries over the period 1999–01. For the real effective exchange rate index for these countries (excluding Australia and New Zealand) and the euro area (excluding Ireland and Portugal), data are compiled from the nominal effective exchange rate index and from a cost indicator of relative normalized unit labor costs in manufacturing. The **reu** and **neu** indices are discussed more fully in the world table section of this introduction.

A selection of other measures of real effective exchange rates for these countries and the euro area, using alternative measures of costs and prices, is shown in the world table *Real Effective Exchange Rates Indices.*

Lines nec and rec

The country tables for selected other countries include a nominal effective exchange rate index in line **nec**. This index is based on a methodology that takes account of each country's trade in both *manufactured* goods and *primary* products with its partner, or competitor, countries.

For *manufactured* goods, trade by type of good and market is distinguished in the database. So it is possible to allow at a disaggregated level for competition among various exporters in a foreign market (i.e., third-market competition) as well as that arising from bilateral trade links.

For *primary* products, the weights assigned depend principally on a country's role as a global supplier or buyer of the product. Trade in crude petroleum, petroleum, and other energy products is excluded. For some countries that depend heavily on tourism, bilateral exports of tourism services averaged over 1999–01 are also included in calculating the competitiveness weights.

From January 2006 onwards, the line **nec** index is weighted based on disaggregate trade data for manufactured goods and primary products covering the three-year period 1999–01. Before that, the weights are for the three-year span 1989–91. The series based on the old weights and the new weights are linked by splicing at December 1995, and the reference base is shifted to 2000=100.

INTRODUCTION

Table of Contents

1. Overview

The Fund's principal statistical publication, *International Financial Statistics (IFS)*, has been published monthly since January 1948. In 1961, the monthly was supplemented by a yearbook, and in 1991 and 2000, respectively, *IFS* was introduced on CD-ROM and the Internet.

IFS contains country tables for most Fund members, as well as for Anguilla, Aruba, the Central African Economic and Monetary Community (CEMAC), the Eastern Caribbean Currency Union (ECCU), the euro area, Montserrat, the Netherlands Antilles, the West African Economic Monetary Union (WAEMU), and some nonsovereign territorial entities for which statistics are provided internationally on a separate basis. Also, selected series are drawn from the country tables and published in area and world tables. The country tables normally include data on a country's exchange rates, Fund position, international liquidity, money and banking accounts, interest rates, prices, production, labor, international transactions, government accounts, national accounts, and population. Selected series, including data on Fund accounts, international reserves, and international trade, are drawn from the country tables and published in world tables as well.

The monthly printed issue of *IFS* reports current monthly, quarterly, and annual data, while the yearbook reports 12 observations of annual data. Most annual data on the CD-ROM and Internet begin in 1948; quarterly and monthly data generally begin in 1957; most balance of payments data begin in 1970.

The following sections describe conceptual and technical aspects of various data published in *IFS*. The reader will find more detailed descriptions—about coverage, deviations from the standard methodologies, and discontinuities in the data—in the footnotes in the individual country and world tables in the monthly and yearbook issues of *IFS*, in the Print_Me file on the CD-ROM, and in the PDF pages on the Internet. (Where references are made in this introduction to notes in monthly issues, they refer to notes files on the CD-ROM and Internet as well.)

2. Exchange Rates and Exchange Rate Arrangements

Exchange rates in *IFS* are classified into three broad categories, reflecting the role of the authorities in determining the rates and/or the multiplicity of the exchange rates in a country. The three categories are the **market rate**, describing an exchange rate determined largely by market forces; the **official rate**, describing an exchange rate determined by the authorities—sometimes in a flexible manner; and the **principal**, **secondary**, or **tertiary rate**, for countries maintaining multiple exchange arrangements.

In *IFS*, exchange rates are expressed in time series of national currency units per SDR (the unit of account for the Fund) and national currency units per U.S. dollar, or vice versa.

The exchange rates in SDRs are classified and coded as follows:

Series **aa** shows the end-of-period national currency value of the SDR, and series **ac** shows the end-of-period SDR value of the national currency unit.

Series **sa**, **sb**, **sc**, and **sd**—provided on the country table for the United States—show the SDR value of U.S. dollars. Series **sa** and **sc** refer to end-of-period values of U.S. dollars per SDR and SDRs per U.S. dollar, respectively, while series **sb** and **sd** are geometric averages of values within the period.

The exchange rates in U.S. dollars are classified and coded as follows:

Series **ae** shows end-of-period national currency units per U.S. dollar, and series **ag** shows end-of-period U.S. dollars per unit of national currency.

Series **rf** shows period-average national currency units per U.S. dollar, and series **rh** shows period-average U.S. dollars per unit of national currency. Series **rf** and **rh** data are the monthly average of market rates or official rates of the reporting country. If those are not available, they are the monthly average rates in New York. Or if the latter are not available, they are estimates based on simple averages of the end-of-month market rates quoted in the reporting country.

The country tables contain two of the U.S. dollar series—either **ae** and **rf** or **ag** and **rh**—depending on the form in which the exchange rate is quoted.

Reciprocal relationships are the following:

The end-of-period rates **aa** and **ac**, **ae** and **ag**, and **sa** and **sc** are reciprocals of each other. The period-average SDR rates in terms of the U.S. dollar (**sb** and **sd**) are also reciprocals of each other, because they are calculated as geometric averages. Other period average rates (**rf** and **rh**) are calculated as arithmetic averages and are not reciprocals.

The relationship between trade figures in *IFS* and exchange rates is the following:

All trade figures in *IFS* are converted from national currency values to U.S. dollars and from U.S. dollar values to national currency, using series **rf**. Conversions are based on the data available for the shortest period, and these data are summed to obtain data for longer periods. Conversion is based on longer period rates of only the difference, if any, between the longer period data and the sum of the shorter period data. The country table notes in the monthly issues identify the exchange rates used.

For members maintaining dual or multiple exchange rate systems, which often reflect wide ranges of exchange rates in effect in a

The real effective exchange rate index in line **rec** is derived from the nominal effective exchange rate index, adjusted for relative changes in consumer prices. Consumer price indices, often available monthly, are used as a measure of domestic costs and prices for these countries. This practice typically reflects the use of consumer prices by the reference and partner, or competitor, countries in compiling these indices.

For countries where multiple exchange rates are in effect, Fund staff estimates of weighted average exchange rates are used in many cases. A weighted average exchange rate is constructed as an average of the various exchange rates, with the weights reflecting the share of trade transacted at each rate. For countries where a weighted average exchange rate cannot be calculated, the principal rate, generally line **ahx**, is used.

The notes to the country tables in the monthly issues provide information about exceptions in the choice of the consumer price index (generally line 64) and the period average exchange rate index (generally line **ahx**). For a relatively small number of countries, notes in the country tables in the monthly issues indicate 1) where alternative price indices, such as the wholesale/producer price index or a weighted average of several price indices, are used; 2) where data constraints have made it necessary to use weighting schemes based on aggregate bilateral non-oil trade data; and 3) where trade in services (such as tourism) has been taken into account.

The world table section of this introduction provides a description of the effective exchange rates tables. In addition, a Fund working paper entitled "A Primer on the IMF's Information Notice System" (WP/97/71), distributed in May 1997, provides background on the concepts and methodology underlying the effective exchange rates. Another Fund working paper "New Rates from New Weights" (WP/05/99), provides background on the methodology underlying the new weights.

SDR Value

Before July 1974, the value of the SDR (unit of account for the Fund) was fixed in terms of U.S. dollars. Over time, the value changed as follows: SDR 1 = U.S. dollar 1 through November 1971; SDR 1 = U.S. dollar 1.08571 from December 1971 through January 1973; and SDR 1 = U.S. dollar 1.20635 from February 1973 through June 1974.

Since July 1974, the Fund has determined the value of the SDR daily on the basis of a basket of currencies, with each currency being assigned a weight in the determination of that value. The currencies in the basket are valued at their market exchange rates for the U.S. dollar. The U.S. dollar equivalents of each currency are summed to yield the rate of the SDR in terms of the U.S. dollar. The rates for the SDR in terms of other currencies are derived from the market exchange rates of these currencies for the U.S. dollar and the U.S. dollar rate for the SDR.

Although the method of calculating the U.S. dollar/SDR exchange rate has remained the same, the currencies' number and weight have changed over time. Their amount in the SDR basket is reviewed every five years.

From July 1974 through June 1978, the currencies in the basket were of the countries that averaged more than 1 percent share in world exports of goods and services from 1968–72. This established a basket of 16 currencies. Each currency's relative weight was broadly proportionate to the country's exports but modified for the U.S. dollar to reflect its real weight in the world economy. To preserve the continuity of valuation, the amount of each of the 16 currencies was such that on June 28, 1974 the value of SDR 1 = U.S. dollar 1.20635.

From July 1978 through December 1980, the composition of the basket was changed on the basis of updated data for 1972–76. The

weights of some currencies were also changed. The amount of each of the 16 currencies in the revised basket was such as to ensure that the value of the SDR in terms of any currency on June 30, 1978 was exactly the same in the revised valuation as in the previous valuation.

Since January 1, 1981, the value of the SDR has been determined based on the currencies of the five member countries having the largest exports of goods and services during the five-year period ending one year before the date of the latest revision to the valuation basket. Broadly reflecting the currencies' relative importance in international trade and finance, the weights are based on the value of the exports of goods and services of the members issuing these currencies and the balances of their currencies officially held by members of the Fund.

From January 1981 through December 1985, the currencies and currency weights of the five members having the largest exports of goods and services during 1975–79 were the U.S. dollar, 42 percent; deutsche mark, 19 percent; French franc, Japanese yen, and pound sterling, 13 percent each.

From January 1986 through December 1990, reflecting the period 1980–84, the weights had changed to U.S. dollar, 42 percent; deutsche mark, 19 percent; Japanese yen, 15 percent; French franc and pound sterling, 12 percent each.

From January 1991 through December 1995, reflecting the period 1985–89, the weights were U.S. dollar, 40 percent; deutsche mark, 21 percent; Japanese yen, 17 percent; French franc and pound sterling, 11 percent each.

On January 1, 1996, the weights were U.S. dollar, 39 percent; deutsche mark, 21 percent; Japanese yen, 18 percent; French franc and pound sterling, 11 percent each.

On January 1, 1999, the currency amount of deutsche mark and French francs were replaced with equivalent amounts of euros, based on the fixed conversion rates between those currencies and the euro, announced on December 31, 1998 by the European Council. The weights in the SDR basket were changed to U.S. dollar, 39 percent; euro, 32 percent (in replacement of the 21 percent for the deutsche mark and 11 percent for the French franc), Japanese yen, 18 percent; and pound sterling, 11 percent.

On January 1, 2001, the weights had changed to U.S. dollar, 45 percent; euro, 29 percent; Japanese yen, 15 percent; and pound sterling, 11 percent.

As of January 1, 2006, the value of the SDR has been determined based on the four currencies included in the valuation basket in the following proportions: U.S. dollar, 44 percent; euro, 34 percent; Japanese yen and pound sterling, 11 percent each.

World Tables on Exchange Rates

Tables A, B, C, and D on exchange rates, described below, are presented in *IFS*. Daily exchange rates are not yet provided on the CD-ROM or Internet.

Table A of exchange rates gives the monthly, quarterly, and annual SDR rates in terms of U.S. dollars and reciprocals of these rates.

Table B reports for the latest available month the daily rates and the monthly averages, both in terms of currency units per U.S. dollar (**af**) and U.S. dollars per currency unit (**ah**) of (1) 16 major currencies, other than the U.S. dollar, as quoted in the markets of these countries, (2) the SDR, and (3) the euro.

Table C gives daily rates of currencies in terms of national currency units per SDR for the latest available month.

Table D provides, in terms of national currency units per SDR, end-of-period rates for the currencies of Fund members—including

Hong Kong (Special Administrative Region as of 1997)—and the Netherlands Antilles.

Method of Deriving IFS Exchange Rates

For countries that have introduced new currencies, the rates shown in *IFS* for the period before the introduction of the most recent currency may be used as conversion factors—they may be used to convert national currency data in *IFS* to U.S. dollar or SDR data. In such cases, the factors are constructed by chain linking the exchange rates of the old and the new currencies. The basis used is the value of the new currency relative to the old currency, as established by the issuing agency at the time the new currency was introduced. Footnotes about the introduction of new currencies are to be found on individual country tables in the monthly issues of *IFS*.

For countries that are members of the euro area, the exchange rates shown are expressed in national currency units per SDR or per U.S. dollar through 1998, and in euros per SDR or per U.S. dollar thereafter.

A detailed description of the derivation of the exchange rates in *IFS*, as well as technical issues associated with these rates, is contained in the *IFS Supplement on Exchange Rates*, No. 9 (1985).

3. Fund Accounts

Data on members' Fund accounts are presented in the Fund Position section in the country tables and in 12 world tables. Details about Fund Accounts terms and concepts and the time series in the country and world tables follow:

Terms and Concepts in Fund Accounts

Quota

When a country joins the Fund, it is assigned a quota that fits into the structure of existing quotas. Quotas are considered in the light of the member's economic characteristics relative to those of other members of comparable size. The size of the member's quota determines, among other things, the member's voting power, the size of its potential access to Fund resources, and its share in allocations of SDRs.

Quotas are reviewed at intervals of not more than five years. The reviews take account of changes in the relative economic positions of members and the growth of the world economy. Initial subscriptions, and normally subscriptions associated with increases in quotas, are paid mainly in the member's own currency, and a smaller portion, not exceeding 25 percent, is paid in reserve assets (SDRs or other members' currencies that are acceptable to the Fund).

General Resources Account

The General Resources Account (GRA) resources consist of the currencies of Fund member countries, SDRs, and gold. These resources are received in the form of subscriptions (which are equal to quotas), borrowings, charges on the use of the Fund's resources, income from investments, and interest on the Fund's holdings of SDRs. Subscriptions are the main source of funds.

Borrowing Arrangements

Borrowings are regarded as a temporary source of funds. The Fund has the authority to borrow the currency of any member from any source with the consent of the issuer.

General Arrangements to Borrow

The Fund's first borrowings were made under the General Arrangements to Borrow (GAB). The Arrangements were established in 1962 initially for four years but, through successive extensions, have been continuously in force since then. The original Arrangements permitted the Fund to borrow the currencies of ten industrial country members (those forming the Group of Ten) to finance purchases by any of these ten countries.

The Fund also had an agreement with Switzerland, under which Switzerland undertook to consider making loans to the Fund to finance additional purchases by members that made purchases financed by the GAB.

The revised GAB, that became effective in December 1983, permits the Fund under certain circumstances to extend GAB resources to members that are not GAB participants, authorizes participation of the Swiss National Bank, and permits certain borrowing arrangements between the Fund and nonparticipating members to be associated with the GAB. The GAB decision was amended on December 22, 1992 to take account of Switzerland's membership in the Fund.

Temporary Arrangements

The Fund has also entered into borrowing arrangements to finance purchases under its temporary lending facilities.

Oil Facilities: The Fund arranged in 1974 and 1975 to borrow from the principal oil exporting countries and other countries with strong external positions to finance two special facilities—the 1974 and 1975 Oil Facilities. Under these facilities, repayments were completed in May 1983.

Supplementary Financing Facility: In 1977 the Fund initiated bilateral borrowing arrangements with 14 countries or their institutions to finance commitments under the Supplementary Financing Facility. This facility was established in 1979, and its funds were fully committed by March 1981.

Policy on Enlarged Access: The first borrowing agreement under the Policy on Enlarged Access to the Fund's resources was reached in March 1981 between the Fund and the Saudi Arabian Monetary Agency.

Others: Since then, additional agreements have been entered into with central banks and official agencies of a number of countries, and with international agencies. In December 1986 the Fund entered into a borrowing arrangement with the government of Japan, under which resources were made available for use by the Fund in support of members' adjustment programs, including under the Enlarged Access Policy.

All of the above borrowing arrangements were disbursed and used by December 1991, except for the GAB, which remains intact. Meanwhile, in December 1987 the Fund, as "Trustee," was authorized to enter into borrowing arrangements with official lenders from a wide range of countries to finance loans under the Enhanced Structural Adjustment Facility, renamed Poverty Reduction and Growth Facility in November 1999.

New Arrangements to Borrow

The New Arrangements to Borrow (NAB), which became effective on November 17, 1998, is a set of credit arrangements between the Fund and 25 members and institutions to provide supplementary resources to the Fund. These resources are to forestall or cope with an impairment of the international monetary system or to deal with an exceptional situation that poses a threat to the stability of that system. The NAB does not replace the GAB, which remains in force.

The total amount of resources available to the Fund under the NAB and GAB combined will be up to SDR 34 billion, double the amount available under the GAB alone. By strengthening the Fund's

Fund from time to time. The policy was discontinued in November 1992 because of the effectiveness of the increases in quotas under the Ninth Review, which increased the Fund's ordinary resources by 50 percent.

Systemic Transformation Facility (STF): The STF could be accessed between April 1993 and December 1995. It was to help member countries facing balance of payments difficulties owing to severe disruptions of their traditional trade and payments arrangements. The disruptions had arisen during a shift from significant reliance on trading at nonmarket prices to multilateral, market-based trade. Countries eligible to draw on the STF included most of those belonging to the former Council for Mutual Economic Assistance, the Baltic countries, Russia, and other countries of the former Soviet Union (BRO), and a number of other countries experiencing similar transformation.

Access

Except for access to the credit tranches and the Extended Facility, which are now subject to common ceilings, access to resources under one policy or facility is independent of access under any other policies or facilities.

All requests for purchases other than those in the reserve tranche are subject to examination by the Fund to determine whether the proposed use of purchases would be consistent with the provisions of the Articles of Agreement and Fund policies. These provisions call for adequate safeguards to ensure that the member will adopt the policies, take measures to overcome its balance of payments difficulties, and meet scheduled repurchases, thereby ensuring the revolving nature of the Fund's resources.

Repurchases

Because the Fund's resources revolve to finance temporary balance of payments deficits, members that purchase from the Fund must subsequently repurchase their currencies with the currencies of other members or SDRs. A member is required to repurchase Fund holdings of its currency that are subject to charges. These holdings include those that result from purchases of currencies or SDRs, other than reserve tranche purchases, and all adjusted Fund holdings that are more than 100 percent of the member's quota.

Members may repurchase at any time the Fund's holdings of their currencies that are subject to charges. However, if their balance of payments and reserve positions improve, they are expected to repurchase the Fund's holdings of their currencies from purchases.

In any event, they must make repurchases—irrespective of their balance of payments positions—in installments within limits of 3 1/4 to 5 years for purchases under the credit tranche policies, the Compensatory Financing Facility, and the Buffer Stock Financing Facility; 4 1/2 to 10 years for purchases under the Extended Facility and Systemic Transformation Facility financed by ordinary resources; and 3 1/2 to 7 years for purchases under the Policy on Enlarged Access to resources.

Positions in the Fund

The Fund normally determines the currencies that are used in transactions and operations with members. Each quarter, the Fund prepares a financial transactions plan, in which it indicates the amounts of particular currencies and SDRs to be used during the relevant period. The Fund selects the currencies of members with strong balance of payments and reserve positions. It also seeks to promote, over time, balanced **"positions in the Fund."**

The effects of Fund transactions and operations are summarized in the Fund's **holdings of members' currencies** and in two other measures, namely, **reserve position in the Fund** and total **Fund credit and loans outstanding**. (See world table in the monthly printed copy of *IFS* and the yearbook, entitled Fund Accounts: Position to Date, and also the Fund Position section in the country tables.)

These measures are defined as follows:

The Fund's **holdings of a member's currency** reflect, among other things, the transactions and operations of the Fund in that currency. This concept is used in calculating the amounts that a member can draw on the Fund under tranche policies and in respect to certain of its obligations to the Fund.

A member's **reserve position in the Fund** (time series .1c.s), which has the characteristics of a reserve asset, comprises the reserve tranche position and creditor position under the various borrowing arrangements. A reserve tranche position arises from (1) the payment of part of a member's subscription in reserve assets and (2) the Fund's net use of the member's currency. Normally, a member's reserve tranche position is equal to its quota less the adjusted Fund holdings of its currency, less subscriptions receivable, less the balances held in the administrative accounts of the Fund to the extent they are not above 0.1 percent of a member's quota, if positive.

Total Fund credit and loans outstanding (.2tl.) represents the sum of (1) the use of Fund credit within the GRA and (2) outstanding loans under the SAF, PRGF, and the Trust Fund.

Use of Fund credit within the General Resources Account (.2egs) is the sum of a member's outstanding purchases and the Fund's net operational receipts and expenditures in that currency that increase the adjusted Fund holdings above quota. It measures the amount that a member is obligated to repurchase.

Outstanding purchases (.2kk.) are equal to purchases other than reserve tranche purchases, less repurchases, less other members' purchases of that member's currency, and less any other use by the Fund of that member's currency (except administrative expenditures) that the member wishes to attribute to specific outstanding purchases.

Use of Fund credit within the Special Disbursement Account (SDA) relates to outstanding loans under the structural adjustment facility (SAF) and that portion of the enhanced structural adjustment facility (ESAF) loans not financed from the ESAF Trust Account. The SDA is the vehicle for receiving and investing profits from the sale of the IMF's gold (i.e., the net proceeds in excess of the book value of SDR 35 a fine ounce), and for making transfers to other accounts for special purposes authorized in the Articles, in particular for financial assistance to low-income members of the IMF.

Structural Adjustment Facility and Poverty Reduction and Growth Facility

The Structural Adjustment Facility (SAF), established in March 1986, provides additional balance of payments assistance in the form of loans on concessional terms. This assistance is for low-income developing countries that were eligible for International Development Association (IDA) resources, that face protracted balance of payments problems, and that are in need of such assistance.

Resources of the SAF comprise Trust Fund reflows, the interest income on SAF loans, investment income from the resources available for the facility, and amounts not used for the Supplementary Financing Facility (SFF) Subsidy Account, which may be transferred back to the SDA.

The Enhanced Structural Adjustment Facility (ESAF) was established in December 1987 and renamed Poverty Reduction and Growth Facility (PRGF), effective November 22, 1999. It provides ability to support the adjustment efforts of its members and to address their balance of payments difficulties, the NAB is an important element of the Fund's capacity to respond to potential systemic problems. The NAB will be in effect for five years, beginning on November 17, 1998, and may be renewed.

Financing Policies and Facilities

Purchases (.2kk.)

The principal way the Fund makes its resources available to members is to sell to them currencies of other members or SDRs in exchange for their own currencies. Such transactions change the composition, but not the overall size, of the Fund's resources. A member to whom the Fund sells currencies or SDRs is said to make "purchases" (also referred to as "drawings") from the Fund.

The purpose of making the Fund's resources available to members is to meet their balance of payments needs. The Fund's resources are provided through permanent policies for general balance of payments purposes (the tranche policies), permanent facilities for specific purposes (the Buffer Stock Financing Facility, the Extended Fund Facility, the Compensatory and Contingency Financing Facility, and the Supplemental Reserve Facility (SRF)), and temporary facilities (the Oil Facilities, the Supplementary Financing Facility, the Policy on Enlarged Access to the Fund's resources, and the Systemic Transformation Facility (STF)).

Permanent Policies

Reserve Tranche: A member's reserve tranche is the excess of its quota in the Fund over the adjusted Fund holdings of its currency in the GRA. Adjusted Fund holdings of a member's currency are equal to the actual holdings of the currency less holdings arising from outstanding purchases under the Fund's policies and facilities, which are subject to exclusion under Article XXX(c). Reserve tranche purchases, like all other purchases, may be made only to meet a balance of payments need. However, for reserve tranche purchases the Fund does not challenge a member's statement of need. As the reserve tranche is considered a reserve deposit in the Fund, a member using its reserve tranche is not considered to be using Fund credit.

Credit Tranche Policy: The credit tranche policy is often referred to as the Fund's basic financing policy. Credit under this policy is viewed as being available in tranches, each tranche being equivalent to 25 percent of quota. Credit tranche purchases may be made outright or under a stand-by arrangement. The latter, which is like a line of credit, assures the member that during a given period it will be able to use the Fund's resources up to a specified amount, so long as it is observing the terms of the arrangement.

Permanent Facilities

Buffer Stock Financing Facility: The Buffer Stock Financing Facility, established in June 1969, is to assist members with a balance of payments need related to their participation in arrangements to finance approved international buffer stocks of primary products.

Extended Fund Facility (EFF): The EFF, established in September 1974, is to make resources available for longer periods and in larger amounts than under the credit tranche policies. It is to assist members that are experiencing balance of payments difficulties owing to structural imbalances in production, trade, and prices, or that are unable to pursue active development policies because of their weak balance of payments positions.

Compensatory and Contingency Financing Facility (CCFF): The CCFF superseded the Compensatory Financing Facility (CFF) in August 1988. The CCFF keeps the essential elements of the CFF and adds a mechanism for contingency financing to support adjustment programs approved by the Fund.

The CFF, established in February 1963, was to assist members, particularly primary producing countries, experiencing balance of payments difficulties attributable to shortfalls in earnings from merchandise exports. Such difficulties were also attributable to invisibles both temporary and due largely to factors beyond their control.

In May 1981 the Fund decided to extend financial assistance to members facing balance of payments difficulties produced by an excess in the cost of their cereal imports. This assistance was integrated with support available under the compensatory financing facility for temporary shortfalls in export receipts.

Supplemental Reserve Facility (SRF): The SRF, established in December 1997, is to financially assist a member country experiencing exceptional balance of payments difficulties caused by a large short-term financing need. This need resulted from a sudden and disruptive loss of market confidence reflected in pressure on the capital account and the member's reserves.

Financing under the SRF, available in the form of additional resources under a Stand-By or Extended Arrangement, may be committed for up to one year and be generally available in two or more tranches. Purchases under the SRF are included as part of either the Stand-By or the Extended Fund Facility, as indicated in the footnote to the world table "Financing Components of Members' Outstanding Obligations to the Fund."

Access

Under the present guidelines on access limits, adopted on October 24, 1994, member access to the Fund's general resources in the credit tranches and the Extended Facility is subject to an annual limit of 100 percent of quota, and a cumulative limit of 300 percent of quota. This is net of scheduled repurchases and excluding purchases under the Compensatory Financing Facility and the Buffer Stock Financing Facility.

Within these limits, the amount of access in individual cases will vary according to the circumstances of the member. In exceptional circumstances, the Fund may approve Stand-By or Extended Arrangements that provide for amounts over these access limits. The guidelines and access limits are intended to be temporary and are reviewed periodically.

Temporary Facilities

Oil Facilities: The oil facilities, set up in June 1974 and April 1975, were to assist members with balance of payments difficulties owing to the rise in oil prices. Purchases under the facilities were completed in May 1976.

Supplementary Financing Facility (SFF): The SFF, established in February 1979, was to assist members facing payments difficulties that were large in relation to their economies and their Fund quotas. Resources under the facility, which were borrowed and therefore not part of the Fund's ordinary resources, were made available only in connection with an upper credit tranche stand-by arrangement and an extended arrangement. The facility was fully committed by March 1981.

Enlarged Access Policy: The Policy on Enlarged Access to the Fund's resources, which continued the policies of the Supplementary Financing Facility following the full commitment of the latter's resources, became operational in May 1981. Under this policy, resources were provided only under stand-by and extended arrangements. The amount of assistance available to a member under the policy was determined according to guidelines adopted by the additional assistance in the form of loans on concessional terms to low-income developing countries that were eligible for assistance from the SAF.

In contrast to the uniform access limit of 70 percent of quota for SAF loans, individual access limits for PRGF loans are determined on the basis of balance of payments need and the strength of adjustment efforts. The maximum access limit is set at 250 percent of quota, with a provision for higher access in exceptional cases. Repayment of each loan must be made in 10 equal semiannual installments starting 5 1/2 years and finishing 10 years after the date of the disbursement. Outstanding SAF and PRGF loans do not affect a member's access to the Fund's general resources, which remain available under the terms of those policies.

Resources available for disbursement under PRGF arrangements include (1) the resources of the PRGF Trust (previously the ESAF Trust, established in December 1987), which comprise special loans and contributions and are held separately from the property and assets of all other accounts of the Fund, including other administered accounts, (2) amounts available from the SDA that have not been used under SAF arrangements, and (3) amounts made available by associated lenders.

Trust Fund and Supplementary Financing Facility Subsidy Account

The Fund is Trustee for two additional accounts, whose resources are legally separate from the resources of the Fund. These are the Trust Fund and the Supplementary Financing Facility (SFF) Subsidy Account.

The Trust Fund, established in May 1976, provides balance of payments assistance on concessional terms to eligible members and also distributes funds directly to developing members. The resources of the Trust Fund are derived from profits from the sale of about 25 million ounces of the Fund's gold holdings during 1976–80, from income on the investment of these profits, from contributions by members, and from low-interest borrowings.

The SFF Subsidy Account, established in December 1980, reduced the cost for low-income developing countries for using the supplementary financing facility. The SFF Subsidy Account consists of transfers from reflows of Trust Fund loans, donations, loans, and the interest income received from investment of resources held pending disbursement.

SDRs

SDRs are unconditional reserve assets created by the Fund to supplement existing reserve assets. SDRs are allocated to Fund members that participate in the Fund's Operations Division for SDRs and Administered Accounts in proportion to their quotas. Six SDR allocations totaling SDR 21.4 billion have been made by the Fund (in January 1970, January 1971, January 1972, January 1979, January 1980, and January 1981).

The Fund cannot allocate SDRs to itself but receives them from members through various financial transactions and operations. Entities authorized to conduct transactions in SDRs are the Fund itself, participants in the Fund's Operations Division for SDRs and Administered Accounts, and prescribed "other holders."

The SDR can be used for a wide range of transactions and operations, including for acquiring other members' currencies, settling financial obligations, making donations, and extending loans. SDRs may also be used in swap arrangements and as security for the performance of financial obligations. Forward as well as spot transactions may be conducted in SDRs.

World Tables on Fund Accounts

Twelve world tables on Fund Accounts are presented in *IFS*, as described below. The tables on Fund accounts arrangements, position to date, financing components, and borrowing agreements are not yet available on the CD-ROM or Internet.

The world table Fund Accounts: Arrangements reports the current status of stand-by, extended, and poverty reduction and growth (previously, the enhanced structural adjustment) arrangements.

The table Fund Accounts: Position to Date reports latest monthly data on members' Fund positions, including quota, reserve position in the Fund, total Fund credit and loans outstanding, Fund holdings of currencies, and positions in the SDR Department.

The table Financing Components of Members' Outstanding Obligations to the Fund reports latest monthly data on the sources of financing of Fund credit and loans outstanding.

The tables Purchases (.2kk.) and Repurchases (.2lk.) relate to transactions within the General Resources Account (GRA). Purchases exclude reserve tranche purchases.

The table Fund Accounts: Borrowing Agreements reports the current status of the Fund's borrowing activities.

The tables Loan Disbursements (.2kl.) and Repayments of Loans (.2ll.) relate to the Structural Adjustment Facility (SAF), Poverty Reduction and Growth Facility (PRGF; which was previously named Enhanced Structural Adjustment Facility-ESAF), and Trust Fund loans.

The table Total Fund Credit and Loans Outstanding (.2tl.) relates to the outstanding use of Fund resources under the GRA and to outstanding loans under the SAF, PRGF, and Trust Fund.

The table Use of Fund Credit: GRA (.2egs) relates to the outstanding use of the Fund resources under the GRA.

The table SDRs (.1b.s) shows holdings of SDRs by members and includes a foot table showing SDR holdings by all participants, the IMF, other holders, and the world.

The table Reserve Position in the Fund (.1c.s) relates to members' claims on the Fund.

Pamphlet on Fund Accounts

A more detailed description of the Fund accounts is contained in the IMF's *Financial Organization and Operations of the IMF*, Pamphlet No. 45, sixth edition, 2001.

4. International Liquidity

Data on international liquidity are presented in the country tables and in world tables on reserves. The international liquidity section in the country tables comprises lines for total reserves minus gold, gold holdings, other foreign assets and foreign liabilities of the monetary authorities, and foreign accounts of other financial institutions. The euro area section for international liquidity covers assets of the European Central Bank (ECB) and the national central banks (NCBs) of the countries that have adopted the euro (details below).

Total Reserves (Minus Gold) and Gold Holdings

Total Reserves Minus Gold (line 1 l.d) is the sum of the items Foreign Exchange, Reserve Position in the Fund, and the U.S. dollar value of SDR holdings by monetary authorities. Monetary authorities comprise central banks and, to the extent that they perform monetary authorities' functions, currency boards, exchange stabilization funds, and treasuries.

Official Gold Holdings (lines 1ad and 1and) are expressed in millions of fine troy ounces and valued, according to national practice, in U.S. dollars.

Under Total Reserves Minus Gold, the line for Foreign Exchange (1d.d) includes monetary authorities' claims on nonresidents in the form of foreign banknotes, bank deposits, treasury bills, short- and long-term government securities, ECUs (for periods before January 1999), and other claims usable in the event of balance of payments need.

For *IFS* yearbook users, this background information on foreign exchange is particularly useful: Before December 1971, when the U.S. dollar was at par with the SDR, foreign exchange data were compiled and expressed in terms of U.S. dollars at official par values. Conversions from national currencies to U.S. dollars from December 1971 through January 1973 were calculated at the cross rates reflecting the parities and central rates agreed to in December 1971. From February 1973 through June 1974, foreign exchange was valued at the cross rates of parities or central rates for countries having effective parities or central rates, and at market rates for the Canadian dollar, Irish pound, Italian lira, Japanese yen, and pound sterling. Beginning in July 1974, foreign exchange is valued at end-of-month market rates or, in the absence of market rate quotations, at other prevailing official rates.

Total Reserves for the Euro Area

Until December 31, 1998, member countries of the European Union (Austria, Belgium, Denmark, Finland, France, Germany, Greece, Ireland, Italy, Luxembourg, the Netherlands, Portugal, Spain, Sweden, and the United Kingdom) held ECU deposits with the European Monetary Cooperation Fund (EMCF) and/or its successor, the European Monetary Institute. The reserves data for each country excluded, from gold and foreign exchange holdings, the deposits of gold and foreign exchange with the EMCF, but the data included, in foreign exchange holdings, the equivalent amounts of ECU deposits.

These deposits were transferred from the EMCF to the EMI upon its creation on January 1, 1994, and to the European Central Bank (ECB) when it succeeded the EMI on June 1, 1998. Each national central bank (NCB) deposited gold and foreign exchange with the ECB. On January 1, 1999, the euro replaced the ECU at a rate of one euro per one ECU.

Total reserves for the euro area and individual euro area countries are based on the statistical definition of international reserves adopted by the ECB's Statistics Committee in December 1998. Defined on a euro area-wide residency basis, they include reserve assets denominated only in currencies of non-euro area countries. All positions with residents of other euro area countries and with the ECB are excluded from reserve assets.

For the euro area countries, Total Reserves minus Gold (line 1 l.d) is defined in broad accordance with the fifth edition of the *Balance of Payments Manual*. It includes the monetary authorities' holdings of SDRs, reserve position in the Fund, and foreign exchange, including financial derivative claims on non-euro area countries. It excludes claims among euro area countries and all euro-denominated claims on non-euro area countries. Total reserves of the euro area comprise the reserve holdings of the NCBs and ECB. Definitions of reserves at the national and euro area levels are harmonized.

Other Foreign Assets, Foreign Liabilities

Time series, where significant, are also provided in international liquidity sections on other foreign assets and foreign liabilities of monetary authorities.

Other Assets (line 3..d) usually comprises claims on nonresidents that are of limited usability in the event of balance of payments need, such as balances under bilateral payments agreements and holdings of inconvertible currencies. (Claims on nonresidents under Other Assets (line 3..d) are included in line 11.)

Other Liabilities (line 4..d) comprises foreign liabilities of the monetary authorities other than use of Fund credit (GRA), SAF, PRGF, and Trust Fund loans outstanding. Positions with the Fund are reported separately, in SDRs, in the Fund position section of the country tables.

Foreign Accounts of Other Financial Institutions

Where significant, foreign accounts of financial institutions other than the monetary authorities are reported. The measures provided are normally U.S. dollar equivalents of time series reported in the appropriate money and banking sections as follows: line 7a.d is derived from line 21; line 7b.d is derived from line 26c plus line 26cl; line 7e.d is derived from line 41; and line 7f.d is derived from line 46c plus line 46cl. Sometimes the measures are reported directly in U.S. dollars and may differ slightly in coverage.

In addition for some countries, summary data are provided on the foreign accounts of special or international license banks that operate locally but are not presently covered in the money and banking section. Their foreign assets are reported as line 7k.d, and their foreign liabilities as line 7m.d, when available (although 7m.d is not shown separately if it is equal to line 7k.d).

World Tables on Reserves

World tables on reserves report all country table time series on reserves, other than gold at national valuation, and present totals for countries, country groups, and the world.

Also provided is a table on total reserves, with gold valued at SDR 35 per ounce. A foot table to that table reports total reserves of all countries, including gold valued both at SDR 35 per ounce and at market prices. And the yearbook includes a world table on the ratio of nongold reserves (line 1 l.d) to imports (line 71..d), expressed in terms of the number of weeks of imports covered by the stock of nongold reserves.

Except for the world table on gold holdings in physical terms, world tables on reserves are expressed in SDRs. Foreign exchange holdings are expressed in SDRs by converting the U.S. dollar values shown in the country tables on the basis of the end-period U.S. dollar/SDR rate.

Similarly, a foot table to the world table on gold indicates gold holdings valued at SDR 35 per ounce and at market prices for all countries, the IMF, the ECB, the Bank for International Settlements (BIS), and the world. A simple addition of the gold held by all of these holders would involve double-counting, because most of the gold deposited with the BIS is also included in countries' official gold reserves. *IFS* therefore reports BIS gold holdings net of gold deposits, and negative figures for BIS gold holdings are balanced by forward operations. This foot table also provides data on the U.S. dollar price of gold on the London market, the U.S. dollar/SDR rate, and the end-period derived market price of gold in terms of SDRs.

5. Money and Banking

Statistics on the accounts of monetary and other financial institutions are given in money and banking sections 10 through 50 in the country tables and in world tables, described in the world table section of this introduction.

Monetary Authorities

Monetary authorities' data (section 10) in *IFS* generally consolidate the accounts of the central bank with the accounts of other institutions that undertake monetary functions. These functions include issuing currency, holding international reserves, and conducting Fund account transactions. Data on monetary authorities measure the stock of reserve money comprising currency in circulation, deposits of the deposit money banks, and deposits of other residents, apart from the central government, with the monetary authorities.

Major aggregates of the accounts on the asset side are foreign assets (line 11) and domestic assets (line 12*). Domestic assets are broken down into Claims on Central Government (line 12a), Claims on Deposit Money Banks (line 12e), and, if sizable, Claims on State and Local Governments (line 12b); Claims on Nonfinancial Public Enterprises (line 12c); Claims on the Private Sector (line 12d); Claims on Other Banking Institutions (line 12f), and Claims on Nonbank Financial Institutions (line 12g).

In some countries, where insufficient data are available to provide disaggregations of claims on governmental bodies other than the central government, a classification of Claims on Official Entities (line 12bx) is used. In addition, in countries where insufficient data are available to provide disaggregations of claims on other banking institutions and nonbank financial institutions, a classification of Claims on Other Financial Institutions (line 12f) is used.

The principal liabilities of monetary authorities consist of Reserve Money (line 14); Other Liabilities to Deposit Money Banks (line 14n), comprising liabilities of the central bank to deposit money banks that are excluded from Reserve Money; Liabilities of the Central Bank: Securities (line 16ac); Foreign Liabilities (line 16c); Central Government Deposits (line 16d); and Capital Accounts (line 17a).

Deposit Money Banks

Deposit money banks comprise commercial banks and other financial institutions that accept transferable deposits, such as demand deposits. Deposit money banks' data (section 20) measure the stock of deposit money.

Major aggregates of the accounts on the assets side are Reserves (line 20), comprising domestic currency holdings and deposits with the monetary authorities; Claims on Monetary Authorities: Securities (line 20c), comprising holdings of securities issued by the central bank; Other Claims on Monetary Authorities (line 20n), comprising claims on the central bank that are excluded from Reserves; Foreign Assets (line 21); and Claims on Other Resident Sectors (lines 22*), as described in the preceding section on monetary authorities (lines 12*).

The principal liabilities consist of Demand Deposits (line 24); Time, Savings, and Foreign Currency Deposits (line 25); Money Market Instruments (line 26aa); Bonds (line 26ab); Foreign Liabilities (line 26c); Central Government Deposits (line 26d); Credit from Monetary Authorities (line 26g); Liabilities to Other Banking Institutions (line 26i); Liabilities to Nonbank Financial Institutions (line 26j); and Capital Accounts (line 27a).

Monetary Survey

Monetary authorities' and deposit money banks' data are consolidated into a monetary survey (section 30). The survey measures the stock of narrow Money (line 34), comprising transferable deposits and currency outside deposit money banks, and the Quasi-Money (line 35) liabilities of these institutions, comprising time, savings, and foreign currency deposits.

Standard relationships between the monetary survey lines and the component lines in sections 10 and 20 are as follows:

Foreign Assets (Net) (line 31n) equals the sum of foreign asset lines 11 and 21, less the sum of foreign liability lines 16c and 26c.

Claims on Central Government (Net) (line 32an) equals claims on central government (the sum of lines 12a and 22a), less central government deposits (the sum of lines 16d and 26d), plus, where applicable, the counterpart entries of lines 24..i and 24..r (private sector demand deposits with the postal checking system and with the Treasury).

Claims on State and Local Governments (line 32b) equals the sum of lines 12b and 22b. Note that, for some countries, lack of sufficient data to perform the standard classifications of claims on governmental bodies excluding the central government has resulted in the use of the alternative classification "claims on official entities" (line 32bx), which is the sum of lines 12bx and 22bx. These series may therefore include state and local governments, public financial institutions, and nonfinancial public enterprises.

Claims on Nonfinancial Public Enterprises (line 32c) equals the sum of lines 12c and 22c.

Claims on Private Sector (line 32d) equals the sum of lines 12d and 22d.

Claims on Other Banking Institutions (line 32f) equals the sum of lines 12f and 22f.

Claims on Nonbank Financial Institutions (line 32g) equals the sum of lines 12g and 22g.

Domestic Credit (line 32) is the sum of lines 32an, 32b, 32c, 32d, 32f, and 32g even when, owing to their small size, data for lines 32b, 32c, 32f, and 32g are not published separately. Thus, the data for line 32 may be larger than the sum of its published components.

Money (line 34) equals the sum of currency outside deposit money banks (line 14a) and demand deposits other than those of the central government (lines 14d, 14e, 14f, 14g, and 24) plus, where applicable, lines 24..i and 24..r.

Quasi-Money (line 35) equals the sum of lines 15 and 25, comprising time, savings, and foreign currency deposits of resident sectors other than central government.

The data in line 34 are frequently referred to as M1, while the sum of lines 34 and 35 gives a broader measure of money similar to that which is frequently called M2.

Money Market Instruments (line 36aa) equals the sum of lines 16aa and 26aa.

Bonds (line 36ab) equals the sum of lines 16ab and 26ab.

Liabilities of Central Bank: Securities (line 36ac) equals the outstanding stock of securities issued by the monetary authorities (line 16ac) less the holdings of these securities by deposit money banks (line 20c).

Restricted Deposits (line 36b) equals the sum of lines 16b and 26b.

Long-Term Foreign Liabilities (line 36cl) equals the sum of lines 16cl and 26cl.

Counterpart Funds (line 36e) equals the sum of lines 16e and 26e.

Central Government Lending Funds (line 36f) equals the sum of lines 16f and 26f.

Liabilities to Other Banking Institutions (line 36i) is equal to line 26i.

Liabilities to Nonbank Financial Institutions (line 36j) is equal to line 26j.

Capital Accounts (line 37a) equals the sum of lines 17a and 27a.

These monetary survey lines give the full range of *IFS* standard lines. Some of them are not applicable to every country, whereas others may not be published separately in sections 10 and 20, because the data are small. Unpublished lines are included in Other Items (Net) (lines 17r and 27r) but are classified in the appropriate monetary survey aggregates in section 30.

Exceptions to the standard calculations of monetary survey aggregates are indicated in the notes to the country tables in the monthly issues. Exceptions also exist in the standard presentation of the consolidation of financial institutions, e.g., for Japan, Nicaragua, the United Kingdom, and the United States.

Other Banking Institutions

Section 40 contains data on the accounts of other banking institutions. This subsector comprises institutions that do not accept transferable deposits but that perform financial intermediation by accepting other types of deposits or by issuing securities or other liabilities that are close substitutes for deposits. This subsector covers such institutions as savings and mortgage loan institutions, post-office savings institutions, building and loan associations, finance companies that accept deposits or deposit substitutes, development banks, and offshore banking institutions.

The major aggregates in this section are claims on the various sectors of the economy (lines 42*), as described in the preceding paragraphs, and quasi-monetary liabilities (line 45), largely in the form of time and savings deposits.

Banking Survey

Where reasonably complete data are available for other banking institutions, a banking survey (section 50) is published. It consolidates data for other banking institutions with the monetary survey and thus provides a broader measure of monetary liabilities.

The sectoral classification of assets in the banking survey follows the classification used in the monetary survey, as outlined in the description for that section.

Nonbank Financial Institutions

For a few countries, data are shown on the accounts of nonbank financial institutions, such as insurance companies, pension funds, and superannuation funds. Given the nature of their liabilities, these institutions generally exert minimal impact on the liquidity of a given economy. However, they can play a significant role in distributing credit from the financial sector to the rest of the economy.

European Economic and Monetary Union (Euro Area)

Stage Three of the European Economic and Monetary Union (EMU), beginning in January 1999, created a monetary union among European countries. New definitions of statistics aggregates were created, resulting in a major break in data series for all participating countries. The euro area, an official descriptor of the monetary union, is defined by its membership as of a specified date. The 11 original members were Austria, Belgium, Finland, France, Germany, Ireland, Italy, Luxembourg, Netherlands, Portugal, and Spain. Greece joined in January 2001. In 2002, euro banknotes and coins were issued, and national currency banknotes and coins withdrawn.

The main features of the euro area monetary statistics are described as follows:

Creation of the Eurosystem

In Stage Three of the EMU, the "Eurosystem"—the European Central Bank (ECB) and the national central banks (NCBs) of the euro area member states—executes a single monetary policy for the euro area. The new common currency unit is the euro. Until 2002, national currency circulated, and various types of transactions were denominated in either euros or national currency.

The monetary statistics standards for the euro area countries underwent comprehensive revisions. The revisions permitted compilation of consolidated monetary accounts for the euro area and provided the data needed to execute the single monetary policy. Statistical standards are based on the *European System of Accounts 1995* (*1995 ESA*) and additional standards prescribed by ECB regulation. Statistics are collected under a "layered approach," whereby monetary statistics compiled at the country level are forwarded to the ECB for consolidation into euro area totals. NCBs are required to compile monetary statistics according to a single set of standards and a common format for submission of data to the ECB.

Denomination in Euros

Beginning with data for 1999, monetary data for euro area countries presented in *IFS* are denominated in euros, except for Greece whose data are denominated in euros beginning in January 2001. Data for the consolidated euro area table are in euros for all time periods.

Residency Principles

Statistics are compiled on the basis of both national residency criteria, described in the fifth edition of the *Balance of Payments Manual*, and euro area-wide residency criteria, based on the EU membership as of a specified date.

In the application of the latter criteria, all institutional units located in euro area countries are treated as resident, and all units outside the euro area as nonresident. For example, claims on government under the national criteria include only claims on the government of the country, whereas claims on government under the euro area-wide residency criteria include claims on the governments of all euro area countries. Under the euro area-wide residency criteria, the ECB is a resident unit, whereas under the national residency criteria, it is a foreign unit for all countries. Under ECB statistical reporting requirements—concerning the consolidated balance sheet of the monetary financial institutions sector—the ECB is to be classified as a resident unit of the country where it is physically located (Germany).

The monetary statistics in the tables for each euro area country are presented on both national and euro area-wide residency bases.

Euro Banknotes and Coins

On January 1, 2002, euro banknotes and coins were issued. The existing national currencies continued to be accepted in trade for a short transition period that ended in all member countries by the end of February 2002, at the latest. The national currencies and coins can be redeemed with the national authorities for extended periods, or indefinitely, as set by national policy. The changeover to euro banknotes and coins was smooth, and the stock of outstanding national currencies rapidly decreased by 86 percent between January 1 and February 28, 2002. The national currencies still outstanding at the end of each reporting period remained part of the euro area monetary aggregates until year-end 2002. Euro area monetary aggregates are net of banknotes and coins held by monetary financial institutions (other depository corporations) in the euro area.

The euro banknotes are issued by the Eurosystem as a whole, comprising the ECB and the national central banks of the euro area countries. Banknotes are put into circulation by each NCB as demanded and are physically identical regardless of the issuing NCB. According to the accounting regime chosen by the Eurosystem, although the ECB does not put banknotes into circulation, a share of 8 percent of the total value of euro banknotes put into circulation is allocated to the balance sheet of the ECB each month. The balance of the remaining 92 percent is allocated among the NCBs on a monthly basis, whereby each NCB of the Eurosystem records on its balance sheet as "banknotes issued" a share proportional to its share in the ECB's capital. This allocation procedure is referred to as the capital share mechanism–CSM.

For each NCB, the difference between the value of the euro banknotes allocated according to the CSM and the value of euro banknotes it puts into circulation is classified as an "Intra-Eurosystem claim/liability related to banknote issue." Each NCB will have a single claim/liability vis-à-vis the Eurosystem, calculated monthly. Similarly, the ECB will always have an Intra-Eurosystem claim equal to its 8 percent share of banknotes issued.

On the country pages for the euro area countries, Intra-Eurosystem claims/liabilities related to banknote issue are classified by the IMF as part of monetary authorities' Claims on Banking Institutions (line 12e.u)/Liabilities to Banking Institutions (line 14c.u). Intra-Eurosystem claims/liabilities related to banknote issue are also recorded within the memo item Net Claims on Eurosystem (line 12e.s). In contrast, in the Monetary Authorities (Eurosystem) section on the euro area page, the Intra-Eurosystem claims/liabilities of the Eurosystem members are recorded as part of Other Items (Net) (line 17r), where they effectively net to zero.

Euro coins are issued by national authorities. The ECB approves the volume of coins to be issued by each country. All have a common design on the obverse and a national design on the reverse. All revenues associated with coin issuance are retained by national authorities without application to an accounting allocation mechanism such as is used for banknotes.

The euro also has been adopted officially by several small jurisdictions within Europe—Andorra, Monaco, San Marino, and the Vatican. It is also used as the principal currency in several areas that were formerly part of Yugoslavia.

TARGET

Effective with data beginning end-November 2000, changes in the operating procedures of the TARGET (Trans-European Automated Real-Time Gross Settlement Express Transfer) euro clearing system affect monetary authorities' Foreign Assets (line 11), Foreign Liabilities (line 16c), Claims on Banking Institutions (line 12e.u), and Liabilities to Banking Institutions (line 14c.u). (See Recording of TARGET System Positions in the following section.)

Monetary Authorities—Euro Area

In *IFS* country tables, the term monetary authorities refers to the national central bank and other institutional units that perform monetary authorities' functions and are included in the central bank subsector (currency boards, exchange stabilization funds, etc). For the euro area member countries, upon joining the union, the monetary authority consists of the NCB, as defined by its membership within the Eurosystem.

At the Eurosystem level, monetary authority refers to the ECB and the NCBs of the euro area member countries, based on the actual date of membership.

For purposes of comparison with pre-euro area data, "of which" lines show positions with residents of the country.

Beginning in January 1999, Foreign Assets (line 11) and Foreign Liabilities (line 16c) include only positions with non-euro area countries. All positions with residents of other euro area countries, including the ECB, are classified as domestic positions in the data based on euro area residency.

Claims on General Government (line 12a.u) includes claims on the central government and other levels of government, including the social security system. It also includes claims on general government in other euro area countries.

Claims on Banking Institutions (NCBs and Other Monetary Financial Institutions or MFIs) (line 12e.u) and Liabilities to Banking Institutions (NCBs and Other MFIs) (line 14c.u) include all positions with NCBs and Other MFIs in all euro area countries. Before January 1999, positions with NCBs and Other MFIs in other euro area countries were in Foreign Assets and Foreign Liabilities. Other MFIs are monetary institutions other than the NCB and ECB. Other MFIs were previously called deposit money banks (DMBs) and other banking institutions (OBIs). Beginning in January 1999, other MFIs is defined to include money market funds.

Claims on Other Resident Sectors (line 12d) comprises claims on nonbank financial institutions, public nonfinancial corporations, and the private sector.

Net Claims on Eurosystem (line 12e.s) equals gross claims on, less gross liabilities to, the ECB and other NCBs within the Eurosystem. This item comprises euro-denominated claims equivalent to the transfer of foreign currency reserves to the ECB, Intra-Eurosystem claims/liabilities related to banknote issuance, net claims or liabilities within the TARGET clearing system (see description below), and other positions such as contra-entries to the NCBs' holdings of assets acquired in conjunction with open-market or intervention operations. NCBs' issues of securities other than shares and money market paper held by other NCBs, which are not separately identifiable, are included in Liabilities to Banking Institutions (line 14c.u). Before January 1999, positions with the EMI or ECB and other euro area NCBs are included in Foreign Assets and Foreign Liabilities.

Currency Issued (line14a): Until 2002, this line covers national currency in circulation. Beginning in 2002, this series is redefined to include euro banknotes issued by each NCB, euro coins issued by each euro area country, and national currency not yet withdrawn. The amount of euro banknotes recorded as issued by each NCB is the legal allocation recorded on its balance sheet according to the accounting regime (CSM) described above in **Euro Banknotes and Coins.** That amount does not correspond to either the actual amount of euro banknotes put into circulation by the NCB or the actual circulation of euro banknotes within the domestic territory. The actual amount of euro banknotes put into circulation by the NCB is included within Memo: Currency Put into Circulation (line 14m). In addition, this item includes euro coin issued and the national currency not yet withdrawn.

Capital Accounts (line 17a) includes general provisions.

Recording of TARGET System Positions

Effective November 2000, external positions of members of the TARGET (Trans-European Automated Real-Time Gross Settlement Express Transfer) euro clearing system with each other are affected by changes in TARGET's operating procedures. Previously, from January 1999 to October 2000, TARGET positions are on a gross bilateral basis between all members, which results in large external asset and liability positions between the TARGET members. From November 2000 onward, multilateral netting by novation procedures results in each member recording only a single TARGET position vis-à-vis the ECB, which is generally a much smaller value than recorded under the previous arrangement.

This change affects Monetary Authorities' Foreign Assets (line 11) and Foreign Liabilities (line 16c) of all TARGET members. It also affects Monetary Authorities' Claims on Banking Institutions (line 12e.u) and Liabilities to Banking Institutions (line 14c.u) of the euro area TARGET members. The non-euro area TARGET members are not permitted to hold a net liability position against TARGET as a whole; therefore, after November 2000, they do not have any TARGET-related Foreign Liabilities.

Banking Institutions—Euro Area

For comparison with pre-euro area data, "of which" lines show positions with residents of the country.

Beginning in January 1999, this section covers the accounts of other MFIs (monetary financial institutions)—monetary institutions other than the NCB and ECB. Other MFIs were previously called deposit money banks (DMBs) and other banking institutions (OBIs). Beginning in January 1999, other MFIs is defined to include money market funds.

Claims on Monetary Authorities (line 20) comprises banking institutions' holdings of euro banknotes and coins, holdings of national currency, deposits with the NCB, and loans to the NCB.

Claims on Banking Institutions (including ECB) in Other Euro Area Countries (line 20b.u) and Liabilities to Banking Institutions (including ECB) in Other Euro Area Countries (line 26h.u) comprise all positions with the ECB, NCBs, and Other MFIs in other euro area countries. These positions are classified as domestic under the euro area residency criteria. Before January 1999, these accounts were classified under Foreign Assets and Foreign Liabilities. Claims include holdings of currencies issued in other euro area countries.

Beginning in January 1999, Foreign Assets (line 21) and Foreign Liabilities (line 26c) include only positions with non-euro area countries. All positions with residents of other euro area countries, including the ECB, are classified as domestic positions.

Claims on General Government (line 22a.u) includes claims on central government and other levels of government in all euro area countries.

Claims on Other Resident Sectors (line 22d.u) comprises claims on nonbank financial institutions, public nonfinancial corporations, and the private sectors in all euro area countries.

Demand Deposits (line 24.u) includes demand deposits in all currencies by other resident sectors in all euro area countries.

Other Deposits (line 25.u) includes deposits with fixed maturity, deposits redeemable at notice, securities repurchase agreements, and subordinated debt in the form of deposits by other resident sectors of all euro area countries. Before January 1999, subordinated debt was included in Other Items (Net) (line 27r).

Money Market Fund Shares (line 26m.u) include shares/units issued by money market funds.

Bonds and Money Market Instruments (line 26n.u) include subordinated debt in the form of securities, other bonds, and money market paper.

Credit from Monetary Authorities (line 26g) comprises banking institutions' borrowing from the NCBs.

Other Items (Net) (line 27r) includes holdings of shares issued by other MFIs.

Banking Survey (Based on National Residency)—Euro Area

This section consolidates the accounts of the monetary authorities and banking institutions based on national residency criteria.

Foreign Assets (Net) (line 31n) includes positions with nonresidents of the country. Positions with the ECB for all euro area countries are classified in Foreign Assets under the national residency criteria.

Claims on General Government (Net) (line 32an) includes claims on general government minus deposits of central government. Deposits of other levels of government are included in liabilities to other resident sectors.

Until 2002, Currency Issued (line 34a.n) covers national currency in circulation. Beginning in 2002, this series is redefined to include euro banknotes issued by each NCB, euro coins issued by each euro area country, and the amount of national currency not yet withdrawn. Under the accounting regime used by the Eurosystem, the allocation of euro banknotes issued by each NCB is the legal allocation recorded on its balance sheet according to the accounting regime (CSM) described above in **Euro Banknotes and Coins**. The allocation does not correspond to either the actual amount of euro banknotes placed in circulation by the NCB or the actual circulation of banknotes within the domestic territory.

Other Items (Net) (line 37r) includes other MFIs' holdings of shares issued by other MFIs.

Banking Survey (Based on Euro Area-Wide Residency)

This section consolidates the accounts of the monetary authorities and banking institutions based on euro area-wide residency criteria.

Foreign Assets (Net) (line 31n.u) includes all positions with nonresidents of the euro area. Positions with residents of all euro area countries, including the ECB, are classified as domestic positions.

Claims on General Government (Net) (line 32anu) includes claims on central government and all other levels of government of all euro area countries minus deposits of central government of all euro area countries. Deposits of other levels of government are included in liabilities to other resident sectors.

Until 2002, Currency Issued (line 34a.u) covers national currency in circulation. Beginning in 2002, this series is redefined to include euro banknotes issued by each NCB, euro coins issued by each euro area country, and the amount of national currency not yet withdrawn. Under the accounting regime used by the Eurosystem, the allocation of euro banknotes issued by each NCB is the legal allocation recorded on its balance sheet according to the accounting regime (CSM) described above in **Euro Banknotes and Coins**. The allocation does not correspond to either the actual amount of euro banknotes placed in circulation by the NCB or the actual circulation of banknotes within the domestic territory.

Other Items (Net) (line 37r.u) includes other MFIs' holdings of shares issued by other MFIs.

6. Interest Rates

Data are presented in the Interest Rates section in the country tables and in the world tables on national and international interest rates.

Discount Rate/Bank Rate (line 60) is the rate at which the central banks lend or discount eligible paper for deposit money banks, typically shown on an end-of-period basis.

Money Market Rate (line 60b) is the rate on short-term lending between financial institutions.

Treasury Bill Rate (line 60c) is the rate at which short-term securities are issued or traded in the market.

Deposit Rate (line 60l) usually refers to rates offered to resident customers for demand, time, or savings deposits. Often, rates for time and savings deposits are classified according to maturity and amounts deposited. In addition, deposit money banks and similar deposit-taking institutions may offer short- and medium-term instruments at specified rates for specific amounts and maturities; these are frequently termed "certificates of deposit." For countries where savings deposits are important, a Savings Rate (line 60k) is also published.

Lending Rate (line 60p) is the bank rate that usually meets the short- and medium-term financing needs of the private sector. This rate is normally differentiated according to creditworthiness of borrowers and objectives of financing.

Government Bond Yield (line 61*) refers to one or more series representing yields to maturity of government bonds or other bonds that would indicate longer term rates.

Interest rates for foreign-currency-denominated instruments are also published for countries where such instruments are important.

Quarterly and annual interest rate data are arithmetic averages of monthly interest rates reported by the countries.

The country notes in the monthly issues carry a brief description of the nature and characteristics of the rates reported and of the financial instrument to which they relate.

A typical series from each of these groups is included in the world tables on national interest rates.

Euro Area Interest Rates

The Eurosystem Marginal Lending Facility Rate (line 60) is the rate at which other monetary financial institutions (MFIs) obtain overnight liquidity from NCBs, against eligible assets. The terms and conditions of the lending are identical throughout the euro area. The Eurosystem Refinancing Rate (line 60r), Interbank Rate (Overnight) (line 60a), and Interbank Rate (Three-Month) (line 60b) are also provided on the euro area table.

A new set of harmonized MFI interest rate statistics is compiled for the euro area MFIs, covering euro-denominated deposits and loans vis-à-vis nonfinancial sectors (other than government) resident in the euro area. The ECB *Manual on MFI Interest Rate Statistics* (ECB: October 2003) describes compilation procedures for interest rates on household and corporate customers' deposits and lending—both for stocks and new business. Interest rates on new business cover all business during the reference month in which new agreements with customers resulted from a first-time contract or new negotiation of existing deposits and loans. The two series for interest rates on bad loans and loans for debt restructuring are not included within the MFI interest rate statistics.

Deposit Rate, Households–Stock (line 60lhs) is the volume-weighted average interest paid on outstanding amounts of euro-denominated deposits from households with an agreed maturity up to and including two years. Deposit Rate, Households–New Business (line 60lhn) is the comparable rate for new business with an agreed maturity up to and including one year. Deposit Rate, Corporations–Stock (line 60lcs) is the volume-weighted average interest paid on outstanding amounts of euro-denominated deposits from nonfinancial corporations with an agreed maturity up to and including two years. Deposit Rate, Corporations–New Business (line 60lcn) is the rate for new business with an agreed maturity up to and including one year. Repos (Repurchase Agreements) (line 60lcr) is the counterpart of cash received against securities/gold sold under a firm commitment to repurchase the securities/gold at a fixed rate on a specified date. The repo series includes holdings by households and nonfinancial corporations. At the euro area level, about 40 percent of repos are held by households. Repos are not applicable for most countries. Data are available only for France, Italy, Greece, Spain, and the euro area.

Lending Rate, Households–Stock (line 60phs) is the volume-weighted average interest charged on outstanding amounts of euro-denominated loans to households with an agreed maturity up to and including one year. Lending Rate, Households–New Business (line 60pns) is the rate for new business loans at a floating rate or up to and including a one-year interest rate fixation. Lending Rate, Households–House Purchase, Stock (line 60phm) is the volume-weighted average interest charged on outstanding amounts of euro-denominated loans to households for purchasing or improving housing with a maturity of five years or more. Lending Rate, Households–House Purchase, New Business (line 60phn) is the rate for new business for loans with fixed interest rates between five and ten years. Lending Rate, Corporations–Stock (line 60pcs) is the volume-weighted average interest charged on outstanding amounts of euro-denominated loans to nonfinancial corporations with an agreed maturity up to and including one year. Lending Rate, Corporations–New Business (line 60pcn) is the rate for new business for loans over 1 million euros at a floating rate or up to and including a one-year interest rate fixation.

World Table on International Interest Rates

The world table on international interest rates reports London interbank offer rates on deposits denominated in SDRs, U.S. dollars, euros, French francs, deutsche mark, Japanese yen, and Swiss francs and Paris interbank offer rates on deposits denominated in pounds sterling. Monthly data are averages of daily rates. The table includes the premium or discount on three-month forward rates of currencies of the major industrial countries against the U.S. dollar.

This table also reports the SDR interest rate and the rate of remuneration. Monthly data are arithmetic averages of daily rates. Interest is paid on holdings of SDRs, and charges are levied on participants' cumulative allocations. Interest and charges accrue daily at the same rate and are settled quarterly in SDRs. As a result, participants who have SDR holdings above their net cumulative allocations receive net interest, and those with holdings below their net cumulative allocations pay net charges. Other official holders of SDRs—including the Fund's General Resources Account—receive interest on their holdings and pay no charges because they receive no allocations.

The Fund also pays quarterly remuneration to members on their creditor positions arising from the use of their currencies in Fund transactions and operations. This is determined by the positive difference between the remuneration norm and the average daily balances of the member's currency in the General Resources Account.

Effective August 1, 1983, the weekly SDR interest rate has been based on the combined market interest rate. That rate is calculated by applying to the specific amounts of the five currencies included in the SDR valuation basket, converted into SDR equivalents, the market rates on specified short-term money market instruments quoted in the five countries.

As of January 1, 1991, the interest rates used in this calculation are market yield for three-month U.S. treasury bills, three-month interbank deposit rate (line 60bs) in Germany, three-month rate for treasury bills (line 60cs) in France, three-month rate on certificates of deposit (line 60bs) in Japan, and market yield for three-month U.K. treasury bills (line 60cs). These series are shown in the table.

The combined market rate is calculated each Friday and enters into effect each Monday. The interest rate on the SDR is 100 percent of the combined market rate, rounded to two nearest decimal places. The rate of remuneration, effective February 2, 1987, is 100 percent of the rate of interest on the SDR.

7. Prices, Production, and Labor

This section (lines 62 through 67) covers domestic prices, production, and labor market indicators. The index series are compiled from reported versions of national indices and, for some production and labor series, from absolute data.

There is a wide variation between countries and over time in the selection of base years, depending upon the availability of comprehensive benchmark data that permit an adequate review of weighting patterns. The series are linked by using ratio splicing at the first annual overlap, and the linked series are shifted to a common base period 2000=100.

For industrial production, the data are seasonally adjusted if an appropriate adjusted series is available. Seasonally adjusted series are indicated in the descriptor and also described in the country notes in the monthly issues.

Share Prices

Indices shown for Share Prices (line 62) generally relate to common shares of companies traded on national or foreign stock exchanges. Monthly indices are obtained as simple arithmetic averages of the daily or weekly indices, although in some cases mid-month or end-of-month quotations are included.

All reported indices are adjusted for changes in quoted nominal capital of companies. Indices are, in general, base-weighted arithmetic averages with market value of outstanding shares as weights.

Producer Price Index or Wholesale Price Index

Indices shown for Producer or Wholesale Prices (line 63) are designed to monitor changes in prices of items at the first important commercial transaction. Where a choice is available, preference is given to the Producer Price Index (PPI), because the concept, weighting pattern, and coverage are likely to be more consistent with national accounts and industrial production statistics. In principle, the PPI should include service industries, but in practice it is limited to the domestic agricultural and industrial sectors. The prices should be farm-gate prices for the agricultural sector and ex-factory prices for the industrial sector.

The Wholesale Price Index (WPI), when used, covers a mixture of prices of agricultural and industrial goods at various stages of production and distribution, inclusive of imports and import duties. Preference is given to indices that provide broad coverage of the economy. The indices are computed using the Laspeyres formula, unless otherwise indicated in the country notes in the monthly issues.

Subindices are occasionally included for the PPI or the WPI.

Consumer Price Index

Indices shown for Consumer Prices (line 64) are the most frequently used indicators of inflation and reflect changes in the cost of acquiring a fixed basket of goods and services by the average consumer. Preference is given to series having wider geographical coverage and relating to all income groups, provided they are no less current than more narrowly defined series.

Because the weights are usually derived from household expenditure surveys (which may be conducted infrequently), information on the year to which the weights refer is provided in the country table notes in the monthly issues. The notes also provide information on any limitations in the coverage of commodities for pricing, income groups, or their expenditures in the chosen index. The Laspeyres formula is used unless otherwise indicated in the country notes.

For the European Union (EU) countries, a harmonized index of consumer prices (HICP) (line 64h) is shown. It is compiled according to methodological and sampling standards set by the European Commission. Owing to institutional differences among the EU member countries, the HICP excludes expenditure on certain types of goods and services. Examples are medical care and services of owner-occupied dwellings.

Wage Rates or Earnings

Indices shown for Wages Rates or Earnings (line 65) represent wage rates or earnings per worker employed per specified time period. Where establishment surveys are the source, the indices are likely to have the same coverage as the Industrial Production Index (line 66) and the Industrial Employment Index (line 67). Preference is given to data for earnings that include payments in kind and family allowances and that cover salaried employees as well as wage earners. The indices either are computed from absolute wage data or are as reported directly to the Fund.

Industrial Production

Indices shown for Industrial Production (line 66) are included as indicators of current economic activity. For some countries the indices are supplemented by indicators (such as data on tourism) relevant to a particular country.

Generally, the coverage of industrial production indices comprises mining and quarrying, manufacturing and electricity, and gas and water, according to the UN International Standard Industrial Classification (ISIC). The indices are generally compiled using the Laspeyres formula.

For many developing countries the indices refer to the production of a major primary commodity, such as crude petroleum. For most of the OECD countries, Industrial Production data are sourced from the OECD database, as indicated in the country notes. It should be noted that there may be differences for annual data between seasonal adjusted and unadjusted series. These differences are the result of OECD calculation methodology, which is based on two different calculation methods, namely the frequency method and the proxy method. The frequency method is the annual average of the adjusted 12 months data while the proxy method uses the annual data of the unadjusted series for the seasonally adjusted series.

Labor

Labor market indicators refer to the levels of the Labor Force (line 67d), Employment (line 67e), Unemployment (line 67c), and the Unemployment Rate (line 67r). Data on labor market statistics cover the economically active civilian population. They are provided by the International Labor Organization (ILO), which publishes these data in its *Yearbook of Labour Statistics* and its Laborsta database, http://laborsta.ilo.org. The concept of employment and unemployment conforms to the recommendations adopted by the ILO: Thirteenth International Conference of Labor Statisticians, Geneva, 1992. In addition, indices of employment in the industrial sector (line 67) are provided for 49 countries. For the euro area, EUROSTAT provides the data. Supplemental sources are also available on the industrial countries' websites.

8. International Transactions

Summary statistics on the international transactions of a country are given in lines 70 through 79. A section on external trade statistics (lines 70 through 76) provides data on the values (lines 70 and 71), volumes (lines 72 and 73), unit values (lines 74 and 75), and prices (line 76) for exports and imports. A section follows on balance of payments statistics (lines 78 through 79).

External Trade

Merchandise Exports f.o.b. (line 70) and Imports c.i.f. (line 71) are, in general, customs statistics reported under the general trade system, in accordance with the recommendations of the UN International Merchandise Trade Statistics: Concepts and Definitions, 1998. For some countries, data relate to the special trade system. The difference between general and special trade lies mainly in the treatment of the recording of the movement of goods through customs-bonded storage areas (warehouses, free areas, etc.).

Many countries use customs data on exports and imports as the primary source for the recording of exports and imports of goods in the balance of payments. However, customs data and the entries for goods in the balance of payments may not be equal, owing to differences in definition. These differences may relate to the following:

- the coverage of transactions (e.g., the goods item in the balance of payments often includes adjustments for certain goods transactions that may not be recorded by customs authorities, e.g., parcel post),
- the time of recording of transactions (e.g., in the balance of payments, transactions are to be recorded when change of ownership occurs, rather than the moment goods cross the customs border, which generally determines when goods are recorded in customs based trade statistics), and
- some classification differences (e.g., in the balance of payments, repair on goods is part of goods transactions).

The data for Merchandise Imports f.o.b. (line 71.v) are obtained directly from statistical authorities.

Details of commodity exports are presented for commodities that are traded in the international markets and have an impact on world market prices.

Data for petroleum exports are presented only for 12 oil exporting countries. For a number of these countries, data estimated by Fund staff are derived from available data for the volume of production. They are also derived from estimates for prices that are, in part, taken from *Petroleum Intelligence Weekly* and other international sources. The country table notes in the monthly issues provide details of these estimates.

For a number of countries where data are uncurrent or unavailable, additional lines show data, converted from U.S. dollars to national currency, from the Fund's *Direction of Trade Statistics* quarterly publication (*DOTS*). Exports and imports data published in *DOTS* include reported data, updated where necessary with estimates for the current periods. The introduction of *DOTS* gives a description of the nature of the estimates.

Indices for Volume of Exports (line 72) and Volume of Imports (line 73) are either Laspeyres or Paasche. For nine countries, as indicated in the country notes, export volume indices are calculated from reported volume data for individual commodities weighted by reported values.

Indices for Unit Value of Exports (line 74) and Unit Value of Imports (line 75) are Laspeyres, with weights derived from the data for transactions. For about seven countries, also as indicated in the country notes, export unit values are calculated from reported value and volume data for individual commodities. The country indices are unit value indices, except for a few, which are components of wholesale price indices or based on specific price quotations.

Indices for export and import prices are compiled from survey data for wholesale prices or directly from the exporter or importer (called "direct pricing"). They are shown in line 76, where available. Indices based on direct pricing are generally considered preferable to unit value indices, because problems of unit value bias are reduced.

A more detailed presentation of trade statistics is presented in the *IFS Supplement on Trade Statistics*, No. 15 (1988).

Balance of Payments Statistics

The balance of payments lines are presented on the basis of the methodology and presentation of the fifth edition of the *Balance of Payments Manual (BPM5)*. Published by the IMF in 1993, the *BPM5* was supplemented and amended by the *Financial Derivatives, a Supplement to the Fifth Edition (1993) of the Balance of Payments Manual*, published in 2000. Before 1995, issues of the *IFS Yearbook* presented balance of payments data based on the fourth edition of the manual (*BPM4*).

Lines for Balance of Payments Statistics

In *IFS*, balance of payments data are shown in an analytic presentation (i.e., the components are classified into five major data categories, which the Fund regards as useful for analyzing balance of payments developments in a uniform manner). In the analytic presentation, the components are arrayed to highlight the financing items (the reserves and related items). The standard presentation, as described in the *BPM5*, provides structural framework within which balance of payments statistics are compiled. Both analytic and standard presentations are published in the *Balance of Payments Statistics Yearbook*.

Current Account, n.i.e. (line 78ald) is the sum of the balance on goods, services and income (line 78aid), plus current transfers, n.i.e.: credit (line 78ajd), plus current transfers: debit (line 78akd) (i.e., line 78aid, plus line 78ajd, plus line 78akd).

Goods: Exports f.o.b. (line 78aad) and Goods: Imports f.o.b. (line 78abd) are both measured on the "free-on-board" (f.o.b.) basis—that is, by the value of the goods at the border of the exporting economy. For imports, this excludes the cost of freight and insurance incurred beyond the border of the exporting economy. The goods item covers general merchandise, goods for processing, repairs on goods, goods procured in ports by carriers, and nonmonetary gold.

Trade Balance (line 78acd) is the balance of exports f.o.b. and imports f.o.b. (line 78aad plus line 78abd). A positive trade balance shows that merchandise exports are larger than merchandise imports, whereas a negative trade balance shows that merchandise imports are larger than merchandise exports.

Services: Credit (line 78add) and Services: Debit (line 78aed) comprise services in transportation, travel, communication, construction, insurance, finance, computer and information, royalties and license fees, other business, personal, cultural and recreational, and government, n.i.e.

Balance on Goods and Services (line 78afd) is the sum of the balance on goods (line 78acd), plus services: credit (line 78add), plus services: debit (line 78aed) (i.e., line 78acd, plus line 78add, plus line 78aed).

Income: Credit (line 78agd) and Income: Debit (line 78ahd) comprise (1) investment income (consisting of direct investment income, portfolio investment income, and other investment income), and (2) compensation of employees.

Balance on Gds., Serv., & Inc. (i.e., Balance on Goods, Services, and Income) (line 78aid) is the sum of the balance on goods and services (line 78afd), plus income: credit (line 78agd), plus income: debit (line 78ahd) (i.e., line 78afd, plus line 78agd, plus line 78ahd).

Current Transfers, n.i.e.: Credit (line 78ajd) comprise all current transfers received by the reporting economy, except those made to the economy to finance its "overall balance" (see line 78cbd description below); therefore, the label "n.i.e." The latter are included in Exceptional Financing (line 79ded) (see below). (Note: Some of the capital and financial account lines shown below are also labeled "n.i.e." This means that Exceptional Financing items have been excluded from specific capital and financial account components.) Current transfers comprise (1) general government transfers and (2) other sector transfers, including workers' remittances.

Current Transfers: Debit (line 78akd) comprise all current transfers paid by the reporting economy.

Capital Account, n.i.e. (line 78bcd) is the balance on the capital account (capital account, n.i.e.: credit, plus capital account: debit). Capital account, n.i.e.: credit (line 78bad) covers (1) transfers linked to the acquisition of a fixed asset and (2) the disposal of nonproduced, nonfinancial assets. It does not include debt forgiveness, which is classified under Exceptional Financing. Capital account: debit (line 78bbd) covers (1) transfers linked to the disposal of fixed assets, and (2) acquisition of nonproduced, nonfinancial assets.

Financial Account, n.i.e. (line 78bjd) is the net sum of direct investment (line 78bdd plus line 78bed), portfolio investment (line 78bfd plus line 78bgd), financial derivatives (line 78bwd plus line 78bxd), and other investment (line 78bhd plus line 78bid).

Direct Investment Abroad (line 78bdd) and Direct Investment in Rep. Econ., n.i.e. (Direct Investment in the Reporting Economy, n.i.e.) (line 78bed) represent the flows of direct investment capital out of the reporting economy and those into the reporting economy, respectively. Direct investment includes equity capital, reinvested earnings, other capital, and financial derivatives associated with various intercompany transactions between affiliated enterprises. Excluded are flows of direct investment capital into the reporting economy for exceptional financing, such as debt-for-equity swaps. Direct investment abroad is usually shown with a negative figure, reflecting an increase in net outward investment by residents, with a corresponding net payment outflow from the reporting economy. Direct investment in the reporting economy is generally shown with a positive figure, reflecting an increase in net inward investment by nonresidents, with a corresponding net payment inflow into the reporting economy.

Portfolio Investment Assets (line 78bfd) and Portfolio Investment Liab., n.i.e. (Portfolio Investment Liabilities) (line 78bgd) include transactions with nonresidents in financial securities of any maturity (such as corporate securities, bonds, notes, and money market instruments) other than those included in direct investment, exceptional financing, and reserve assets.

Equity Securities Assets (line 78bkd) and Equity Securities Liabilities (line 78bmd) include shares, stocks, participation, and similar documents (such as American depository receipts) that usually denote ownership of equity.

Debt Securities Assets (line 78bld) and Debt Securities Liabilities (line 78bnd) cover (1) bonds, debentures, notes, etc., and (2) money market or negotiable debt instruments.

Financial Derivatives Assets (line 78bwd) and Financial Derivatives Liabilities (line 78bxd) cover financial instruments that are linked to other specific financial instruments, indicators, or commodities, and through which specific financial risks (such as interest rate risk, foreign exchange risk, equity and commodity price risks, credit risk, etc.) can, in their own right, be traded in financial markets. The *IFS* presents gross asset and liability information. However, owing to the unique nature of financial derivatives, and the manner in which some institutions record transactions, some countries can provide only net transactions data. While such net data could be included under assets, in the *IFS* it has been decided to include these net transactions, and net positions when reported, under liabilities, because one common source of demand for these instruments is from entities that are hedging cash flows associated with debt liabilities.

Other Investment Assets (line 78bhd) and Other Investment Liabilities, n.i.e. (line 78bid) include all financial transactions not covered in direct investment, portfolio investment, financial derivatives, or reserve assets. Major categories are transactions in currency and deposits, loans, and trade credits.

Net Errors and Omissions (line 78cad) is a residual category needed to ensure that all debit and credit entries in the balance of payments statement sum to zero. It reflects statistical inconsistencies in the recording of the credit and debit entries. In the *IFS* presentation, net errors and omissions is equal to, and opposite in sign to, the total value of the following items: the current account balance (line 78ald), the capital account balance (line 78bcd), the financial account balance (line 78bjd), and reserves and reserve related items (line 79dad). The item is intended as an offset to the overstatement or understatement of the recorded components. Thus, if the balance of those components is a credit, the item for net errors and omissions will be shown as a debit of equal value, and vice versa.

Overall Balance (line 78cbd) is the sum of the balances on the current account (line 78ald), the capital account (line 78bcd), the financial account (line 78bjd), and net errors and omissions (line 78cad) (i.e., line 78ald, plus line 78bcd, plus line 78bjd, plus line 78cad).

Reserves and Related Items (line 79dad) is the sum of transactions in reserve assets (line 79dbd), exceptional financing (line 79ded), and use of Fund credit and loans (line 78dcd) (i.e., line 79dbd, plus line 79ded, plus line 79dcd).

Reserve Assets (line 79dbd) consists of external assets readily available to and controlled by monetary authorities primarily for direct financing of payments imbalances and for indirect regulating of the magnitude of such imbalances through exchange market intervention. Reserve assets comprise monetary gold, special drawing rights, reserve position in the Fund, foreign exchange assets (consisting of currency and deposits and securities), and other claims.

Use of Fund Credit and Loans (line 79dcd) includes purchases and repurchases in the credit tranches of the Fund's General Resource Account, and net borrowings under the Structural Adjustment Facility (SAF), the Poverty Reduction and Growth Facility (PRGF), which was previously named the Enhanced Structural Adjustment Facility (ESAF), and the Trust Fund.

Exceptional Financing (line 79ded) includes any other transactions undertaken by the authorities to finance the "overall balance," as an alternative to, or in conjunction with, the use of reserve assets and the use of Fund credit and loans from the Fund.

A more detailed presentation of balance of payments data for use in cross-country comparisons is published in the *Balance of Payments Statistics Yearbook*.

Lines for International Investment Position

The international investment position (IIP) data are presented in lines 79aad through 79ljd. An economy's IIP is a balance sheet of the stock of external financial assets and liabilities. The coverage of the various components of IIP is similar to that of the corresponding components under the balance of payments. The IIP at the end of a specific period reflects not only the sum of balance of payments transactions over time, but also price changes, exchange rate changes, and other adjustments.

Countries in the early stages of IIP compilation are encouraged to submit partial IIP statements. In general, these partial statements include data on the monetary authorities (including international reserves) and at least one other sector. No totals are shown for partial IIP statements.

9. Government Finance

Section 80 presents summary statistics on government finance. The summary statistics cover operations of the budgetary central government or of the consolidated central government (i.e., operations of budgetary central government, extrabudgetary units, and social security funds). The coverage of consolidated central government may not necessarily include all existing extrabudgetary units and/or social security funds.

Unless otherwise stated in individual country notes in the monthly issues, data are as reported for *IFS*. In some cases, data are derived from unpublished worksheets and are therefore not attributed to a specific source.

Quarterly and monthly data, when available, may not add up to the annual data, owing to differences in coverage and/or methodology. The country notes in the monthly issues will indicate these differences.

More extensive data for use in cross-country comparisons are published in the *Government Finance Statistics Yearbook (GFSY)* and are based on *A Manual on Government Finance Statistics*. When countries do not report data for *IFS* but provide data for the *GFSY*, these data are published in *IFS*.

The data for lines 80 through 87 are flows and are on a cash basis, as follows:

The Deficit or Surplus (line 80) is calculated as the difference between Revenue and, if applicable, Grants Received (lines 81 and 81z) on the one hand and Expenditure and Lending Minus Repayments (lines 82 and 83) on the other. The deficit/surplus is also equal, with the opposite sign, to the sum of the net borrowing by the government plus the net decrease in government cash, deposits, and securities held for liquidity purposes.

Revenue (line 81) comprises all nonrepayable government receipts, whether requited or unrequited, other than grants; revenue is shown net of refunds and other adjustment transactions.

Grants Received (line 81z) comprises all unrequited, nonrepayable, noncompulsory receipts from other governments—domestic or foreign—and international institutions. Grants are grouped with revenue because, like revenue, they provide the means whereby expenditure can be made without incurring a debt for future repayment.

Expenditure (line 82) comprises all nonrepayable payments by government, whether requited or unrequited and whether for current or capital purposes.

Lending Minus Repayments (line 83) comprises government acquisition of claims on others—both loans and equities—for public policy purposes and is net of repayments of lending and sales of equities previously purchased. Line 83 includes both domestic and foreign lending minus repayments. In determining the deficit or surplus, lending minus repayments is grouped with expenditure, because it is presumed to represent a means of pursuing government policy objectives and not to be an action undertaken to manage government liquidity.

The total of the financing items equals the deficit or surplus with a reverse sign. Total Financing is classified according to the residence of the lender. Where this information is not available, the distinction is based on the currency in which the debt instruments are denominated.

For some countries, Total Financing is broken down between Net Borrowing and Use of Cash Balances. Net Borrowing covers the net change in government liabilities to all other sectors. It represents mainly other sectors' direct loans or advances to government or their holding of government securities acquired from the government itself or in transactions with others. Where possible, data for Domestic and Foreign Net Borrowing are classified according to the residence of the lender.

Use of Cash Balances (line 87) is intended to measure changes over a period—resulting from transactions but not revaluations—in government holdings of currency and deposits with the monetary system. It corresponds to changes in *IFS* lines 16d and 26d. All currency issues are regarded as liabilities of the monetary authorities, rather than government debt. And any proceeds reaching the government are regarded as coming from the monetary authorities.

Data for outstanding Debt (lines 88 and 89) relate to the direct and assumed debt of the central government and exclude loans guaranteed by the government. The distinction between Domestic and Foreign Debt (lines 88a and 89a) is based on residence of the lender, where possible, but otherwise on the currency in which the debt instruments are denominated (lines 88b and 89b).

The euro area table and the tables of the individual euro area countries also present Deficit or Surplus (line 80g) and Debt (line 88g) data for the general government, expressed as percent of harmonized Gross Domestic Product. Both indicators are defined according to the convergence criteria on public finance as laid down in the Maastricht Treaty. Deficit or Surplus corresponds to net lending/borrowing. The data are not comparable with central government Deficit or Surplus (line 80) and Debt (line 88), owing to differences in coverage as well as in definition.

10. National Accounts and Population

The summary data for national accounts are compiled according to the *System of National Accounts (SNA)*. Gross Domestic Product (GDP) is presented in *IFS* as the sum of final expenditures, following the presentation of the *1993 SNA*, as well as the *European System of Accounts (1995 ESA)*.

The national accounts lines shown in the country tables are as follows:

Household Consumption Expenditure, including Nonprofit Institutions Serving Households (NPISHs) (line 96f), Government Consumption Expenditure (line 91f), Gross Fixed Capital Formation (line 93e), Changes in Inventories (line 93i) (formerly Increase/Decrease(-) in Stocks), Exports of Goods and Services (line 90c), and Imports of Goods and Services (line 98c).

Household Consumption Expenditure, including Nonprofit Institutions Serving Households (NPISHs) (line 96f) consists of the expenditure incurred by resident households and resident NPISHs on individual consumption goods and services. Government Consumption Expenditure (line 91f) consists of expenditure incurred by general government on both individual-consumption goods and services and collective-consumption services.

Gross Fixed Capital Formation (line 93e) is measured by the total value of a producer's acquisitions, less disposals, of fixed assets during the accounting period, plus certain additions to the value of nonproduced assets (such as subsoil assets or major improvements in the quantity, quality, or productivity of land). Changes in Inventories (line 93i) (including work-in-progress) consist of changes in (1) stocks of outputs that are still held by the units that produced them before the outputs are further processed, sold, delivered to other units, or used in other ways and (2) stocks of products acquired from other units that are intended to be used for intermediate consumption or for resale without further processing.

Exports of Goods and Services (line 90c) consist of sales, barter, gifts, or grants of goods and services from residents to nonresidents. Imports of Goods and Services (line 98c) consist of purchases, barter, or receipts of gifts or grants of goods and services by residents from nonresidents. Gross Domestic Product (GDP) (line 99b) is the sum of consumption expenditure (of households, NPISHs, and general government), gross fixed capital formation, changes in inventories, and exports of goods and services, less the value of imports of goods and services.

Net Primary Income from Abroad (line 98.n) is the difference between the total values of the primary incomes receivable from, and payable to, nonresidents. Gross National Income (line 99a) is derived by adding net primary income from abroad to GDP.

Gross National Income (GNI) (line 99a) is derived by adding Net Primary Income from Abroad (line 98.n) to GDP. Gross National Disposable Income (GNDI) (line 99i) is derived by adding Net Current Transfers from Abroad (line 98t) to GNI, and Gross Saving (line 99s) is derived by deducting final consumption expenditure (lines 96f + 91f) from GNDI. Consumption of Fixed Capital (line 99cf) is shown for countries that provide these data.

The country table notes in the monthly issues provide information on which countries have implemented the *1993 SNA* or the *1995 ESA*.

The national accounts lines generally do not explicitly show the statistical discrepancies between aggregate GDP compiled from expenditure flows as against GDP compiled from the production or income accounts (or from a mixture of these accounts). Hence, in some cases, the components of GDP that are shown in *IFS* may not add up exactly to the total.

For countries that publish quarterly seasonally adjusted data, the data in *IFS* in the monthly issues are also on a seasonally adjusted basis (codes ending with c or r). For the United States, Japan, Australia, South Africa, Argentina, and Mexico, quarterly data are shown at annual rates, which the country authorities provide as such.

Lines 99b.p and 99b.r are measures of GDP volume at reference year value levels. In the past, these series used a common reference year (e.g., 1990) for publication. With the June 1999 issue, these series are published on the same reference year(s) as reported by the national compilers. The code *p* indicates data that are not seasonally adjusted, whereas code *r* indicates data that are seasonally adjusted.

Lines 99bvp and 99bvr are GDP volume indices that are presented on a standard 2000 reference year and are derived from the GDP volume series reported by national compilers. For this calculation the data series provided by national compilers are linked together (if there is more than one series) to form a single time series. The earliest overlapping year from the different reference year series is used to calculate the link factors.

The GDP Deflator (lines 99bip or 99bir) are not direct measurements of prices but are derived implicitly: the GDP series at current prices is divided by constant price GDP series referenced to 2000. The latter series is constructed by multiplying the 2000 current price GDP level by the GDP volume index (2000=100). The deflator is expressed in index form with 2000=100.

Data on Population are provided by the Population Division of the Department of Economic and Social Affairs of the United Nations. These data represent mid-year estimates and are revised every two years.

11. World Tables

Besides the world tables on exchange rates, members' Fund positions and transactions, international reserves, and interest rates—discussed earlier in this introduction—*IFS* also brings together country data on money, consumer prices, values and unit values of countries' exports and imports, and wholesale prices and unit values (expressed in U.S. dollars) of principal world trade commodities. Tables on balance of payments may be found in the *IFS* yearbook and also in the *Balance of Payments Statistics Yearbook, Part 2*.

Tables showing totals or averages of country series may report data for selected countries only.

Country Groups

Countries whose data are included in **world/all countries**' totals and averages are arrayed into two main groups—industrial countries and developing countries. The **industrial** countries' group also shows separate data for the euro area. The **developing** countries group is further subdivided into area subgroups for Africa, Asia, Europe, the Middle East, and the Western Hemisphere.

The country composition of the world is all countries for which the topic series are available in the *IFS* files. Consequently, the country coverage of some areas, mainly Africa and Asia, differs from topic to topic, and area and world totals or averages may be biased to some extent toward the larger reporting countries.

Data for subgroups oil exporting countries and non-oil developing countries are shown as memorandum items. Oil exporting countries are defined as those countries whose oil exports (net of any imports of crude oil) both represent a minimum of two thirds of their total exports and are at least equivalent to approximately 1 percent of world exports of oil. The calculations presently used to determine which countries meet the above criteria are based on 1976–78 averages.

Area and World Indices

Area and world indices are obtained as weighted averages of country indices. (Refer to *IFS* World Tables Methodologies.)

Weights are normally updated at about five-year intervals—following international practice—to reflect changes in the importance of each country's data with the data of all other countries. The standard weight base years used are 1953, 1958, 1963, 1970, 1975, 1980, 1984–86, 1990, 1995, and 2000. The corresponding time spans to which the weights are applied are 1948–55, 1955–60, 1960–68, 1968–73, 1973–78, 1978–83, 1983–88, 1988–93, 1993–98, and 1998 onward.

Separate averages are calculated for each time span, and the index series are linked by the splicing at overlap years and shifted to the reference base 2000=100.

Calculation of Area Totals and Averages

The calculation of area totals and averages in the world tables takes account of the problem that data for some countries are not current and may have gaps. Area estimates are made when data are available for countries whose combined weights represent at least 60 percent of the total country weights.

Area totals or averages are estimated by assuming that the rate of change in the unreported country data is the same as the rate of change in the weighted total or average of the reported country data for that area. These estimates are made for the area totals and averages only; separate country estimates are not calculated.

Tables	Calculation Method	Weights Used	Publication*
Consumer Prices	Weighted geometric average	PPP value of GDP	MYC
Producer prices\wholesale prices	Weighted geometric average	PPP value of GDP	Y
Industrial Production	Weighted geometric average	Value added in industry	MYC
Wages	Weighted geometric average	Value added in industry	Y
Employment	Weighted geometric average	Value added in industry	Y
GDP volume	Weighted geometric average	PPP value of GDP	Y
GDP deflator	Weighted geometric average	PPP value of GDP	Y
Gross capital formation as percent of GDP	Weighted arithmetic average	PPP value of GDP	Y
Final consumption expenditure as percent of GDP	Weighted arithmetic average	PPP value of GDP	Y
Exports, f.o.b.	Summation	No weights required	MYC
Imports, c.i.f.	Summation	No weights required	MYC
Export unit value	Weighted arithmetic average	Exports value in U.S. dollars	MYC
Import unit value	Weighted arithmetic average	Imports value in U.S. dollars	MYC
Terms of trade	Export unit values are divided by import unit values	No weights required	Y

*M: Monthly; Y: Yearbook; C: CD-Rom.

The world totals and averages are made from the calculated and estimated data for the two main groups—industrial countries and developing countries. A world total or average will only be calculated when totals or averages are available for both these country groups.

Calculation of Individual World Tables

International Reserves: Country series on international reserves begin generally with their appropriate dates and are complete monthly time series; therefore, earlier period estimates are not required. When current data of a few countries of an area are not reported, the area total is estimated by carrying forward the last reported country figure.

Money (and Reserve Money and Money plus Quasi-Money, which are available in the yearbook): Percent changes are based on end-of-year data (over a 12-month period for Money). When there is more than one version or definition of money over time, different time series are chained through a ratio splicing technique. When actual stock data needed for the growth rate calculation are missing, no percent change is shown in the world table.

Ratio of Reserve Money to Money plus Quasi-Money (available in the yearbook): The measures of money used in calculating this ratio are end-of-year data.

Income Velocity of Money plus Quasi-Money: The measure of income in this table is *IFS* data on GDP. The data for money plus quasi-money are annual averages of the highest frequency data available. The ratio is then converted into an index number with a base year of 1995.

Real Effective Exchange Rate Indices: This table shows three real effective exchange rate indices for industrial countries. Two of these comprise alternative measures of costs and prices derived from Relative Unit Labor Costs (line 65um) and Relative Normalized Unit Labor Costs (line reu). They have been applied to the weighting scheme, based on aggregated data for trade in manufactured goods, averaged over the period 1999–01. The weights reflect both the relative importance of a country's trading partners in its direct bilateral trade relations and that resulting from competition in third markets. The measure is expressed as an index 2000=100 in accord with all indices published in *IFS*.

One of the two indices—the index Based on Relative Normalized Unit Labor Costs (line reu)—is also shown in the country tables (except for Ireland), with the Nominal Effective Exchange Rate Index (line neu) from which the measures are drawn.

The third real effective exchange rate index—Based on Relative Consumer Prices (line rec)—is provided as a measure of domestic cost and price developments. It covers trade in manufactured goods and primary products for trading partners—and competitors. It uses the same methodology used to compile nominal and real effective exchange rates for nonindustrial countries, as discussed in the exchange rate and exchange rate arrangements section of this introduction.

Beginning with the October 1992 issue of *IFS*, the data published are from a revised database. The database underwent a comprehensive review and update of the underlying data sources and a change in the method of normalization of output per hour. The method uses the Hodrick-Prescott filter, which smoothes a time series by removing short-run fluctuations while retaining changes of a larger amplitude.

The footnotes to this world table in the monthly issues discuss the data sources used to derive the cost and price indicators for the real effective exchange rates.

Producer/Wholesale Prices (world table available in the yearbook): Data are those prices reported in lines 63* in the country tables. The percent changes are calculated from the index number series.

Consumer Prices: Data are those prices reported in lines 64* in the country tables. The percent changes are calculated from the index number series.

Industrial Production: This table presents non-seasonally adjusted indices on industrial production for 22 industrial countries, together with an aggregate index for the group. The data are those shown in the country tables as either Industrial Production (lines 66..*) or Manufacturing Production (lines 66ey*), the asterisk representing a wildcard.

Wages (world table available in the yearbook): This table presents indices computed either from absolute wage data or from the wage indices reported to the Fund for the industrial sector for 21 industrial countries. The data are those shown in the country tables as Wage Rates or Earnings (line 65).

Employment (world table available in the yearbook): This table presents indices computed from indices of employment or number of persons employed as reported by the countries for the industrial sector for 20 industrial countries. The data are those shown in the country tables as Employment (lines 67 or 67ey).

Exports and *Imports:* Data are published in U.S. dollars, as reported, if available, by the countries. Otherwise, monthly data in national currency, published in the country tables (lines 70... and 71...), are converted to U.S. dollars using the exchange rate **rf**. For quarterly and annual data, conversions are made using the trade-weighted average of the monthly exchange rates.

Export Unit Values/Export Prices and *Import Unit Values/Import Prices:* Data are the index numbers reported in the country tables expressed in U.S. dollars at rate **rf**. The country indices are typically unit value data (lines 74 and 75). However, for some countries, they are components of wholesale price indices or are derived from specific price quotations (lines 76, 76.x, and 76aa). World estimates are made when data are available for countries whose combined weights represent at least 60 percent of the total country weights.

Terms of Trade (world table available in the yearbook): Data are index numbers computed from the export and import unit value indices and shown in the appropriate world table. The percent changes are calculated from the index number series. The country coverage within the areas for the export and import unit values is not identical, leading to a small degree of asymmetry in the terms of trade calculation.

Balance of Payments (world tables available in the yearbook): For a precise definition of the concepts used in these tables, the reader is referred to the section in this introduction on international transactions. The concepts and definitions are further described in the fifth edition of the *Balance of Payments Manual*, as supplemented and amended by *Financial Derivatives, a Supplement to the Fifth Edition of the Balance of Payments Manual.*

Trade Balance is the series reported in line 78acd of the country tables. Current Account Balance, Excluding Exceptional Financing is the series reported in line 78ald of the country tables. Capital and Financial Account, Including Net Errors and Omissions but Excluding Reserve Assets, Use of Fund Credit, and Exceptional Financing are the sum of the series reported in lines 78bcd, 78bjd, and 78cad of the country tables. Overall Balance Excluding Reserve Assets, Use of Fund Credit, and Exceptional Financing is the series reported in line 78cbd (calculated as the sum of lines 78ald, 78bcd, 78bjd, and 78cad) of the country tables. Note that in some cases, data published in the country pages may be more current than those in the Balance of Payments

world tables due to an earlier cutoff date for calculating these world tables.

GDP Volume Measures (world table available in the yearbook): Data are derived from those series reported in lines 99bvp and 99bvr in the country tables. The percent changes are calculated from index numbers.

GDP Deflator (world table available in the yearbook): Data are derived from those series reported in lines 99bip in the country tables. The percent changes are calculated from index numbers.

Gross Capital Formation as Percentage of GDP (world table available in the yearbook): Data are the percent share of gross capital formation in GDP at current market prices. Gross capital formation comprises Gross Fixed Capital Formation and Increase/Decrease (-) in Stocks (lines 93e and 93i, respectively).

Final Consumption Expenditure as a Percentage of GDP (world table available in the yearbook): Data are the percent share of final consumption expenditure in GDP at current market prices, which comprises Government Consumption and Private Consumption (91f and 96f, respectively).

Commodity Prices: Data are obtained primarily from the Commodities and Special Issues Division of the IMF's Research Department, from *Commodity Price Data* of the World Bank, from *Monthly Commodity Price Bulletin* of the UNCTAD, and from a number of countries that produce commodities that are significantly traded in the international markets. Data derived from the last source are reported in the country tables. The market price series (lines 76) are expressed as U.S. dollars per quantity units and refer to values often used in the respective commodity markets. For comparison purposes, indices of unit values (lines 74) at base 2000=100 are provided. The accompanying notes to the table (located in the back of the printed copies) provide information specific to each commodity series, including data sources, grades, and quotation frequency.

12. Country Codes and *IFS* Line Numbers

Each *IFS* time series carries a unique identification code. For publication purposes, the code has been truncated to a three-digit country code and to a five-digit subject code, referred to as the *IFS* line number.

Line numbers apply uniformly across countries—that is, a given line number measures the same economic variable for each country, subject to data availability. The line numbers take the form of two numerics followed by three alphabetic codes (NNaaa). The two numerics are the section and subsection codes, the first two alphabetic codes are the classification codes, and the last alphabetic code is the qualification code. Any of these positions may be blank: for publication purposes, blanks in the first or final positions are omitted, whereas embedded blanks are represented by a period. The line numbers are part of the descriptor stub in the country tables.

Data expressed in units of money (values or prices) are ordinarily expressed in national currency and in natural form, that is, without seasonal adjustment. For these data the qualification code is blank.

Transformation of these data is denoted by various qualification codes. For data that are not seasonally adjusted, qualification codes are *d* for U.S. dollar values, *s* for SDR values, and *p* for constant national currency values. For data that are seasonally adjusted for *IFS*, codes are *f* for U.S. dollar values, *u* for SDR values, and *b* for national currency values. For data that are seasonally adjusted by national compilers, codes are *c* for national currency values and *r* for constant national currency values.

The qualification codes are also used to distinguish separate groups of deposit money banks or other financial institutions when data for separate groups are given.

13. Symbols, Conventions, and Abbreviations

The abbreviation "ff.," often used on the title page of the printed copies of *IFS*, means "following."

Entries printed in bold on the country pages of the monthly book refer to updates and revisions made since the publication of the preceding issue of *IFS*.

Italic midheadings in the middle of the pages of the monthly book and yearbook identify the units in which data are expressed and whether data are stocks (end of period), flows (transactions during a period), or averages (for a period).

(—) Indicates that a figure is zero or less than half a significant digit or that data do not exist.

(....) Indicates a lack of statistical data that can be reported or calculated from underlying observations.

(†) Marks a break in the comparability of data, as explained in the relevant notes in the monthly and yearbook. In these instances, data after the symbol do not form a consistent series with those for earlier dates. The break symbols not explained in the country table notes can show a point of splice, where series having different base years are linked. A case would be the series described in the section of this introduction on prices, production, and labor. They can also point out a change in magnitude for high-inflation countries, as described in the section on electronic products.

(e) In superscript position after the figure marks an observation that is an estimate.

(f) In superscript position after the figure marks an observation that is forecast.

(p) In superscript position after the figure marks that data are in whole or in part provisional or preliminary.

Standard source codes, listed in the footnotes, refer with some exceptions to the following data sources:

(A) Annual report of the central bank

(B) Bulletin of the central bank

(C) Customs department of a country

(E) OECD

(L) International Labor Organization

(M) Ministry or other national source

(N) National bureau or other national source

(S) Statistical office

(U) United Nations

(V) Eurostat

The CD-ROM supports text messages to indicate breaks in the data. The time series observations with footnotes are highlighted in bold blue type within the *IFS* Data Viewer. When the cursor is moved over the footnoted cell, a small window will be displayed with the footnoted text. These footnotes/comments provide meaningful information about the specific observation, e.g., butt splicing, ratio splicing, extrapolation, estimations, etc.

Because of space limits in the phototypesetting of descriptor stubs on the country tables and table headings of world tables, abbreviations are sometimes necessary. While most are self-explanatory, the following abbreviation in the descriptors and table headings should be noted:

n.i.e. = Not included elsewhere.

Of which: Currency Outside DMBs = Of which: Currency Outside Deposit Money Banks.

Househ.Cons.Expend.,incl.NPISHs = Household Consumption Expenditure, including Nonprofit Institutions Serving Households.

Use of Fund Credit (GRA) = Use of Fund Credit (General Resources Account).

Data relating to fiscal years are allocated to calendar years to which most of their months refer. Fiscal years ending June 30 are allocated to that calendar year. For instance, the fiscal year from July 1, 1999 to June 30, 2000 is shown as calendar year 2000.

For countries that have reported semiannual transactions data, the data for the first half of a year may be given in the monthly book in the column for the second quarter of that year. And those for the second half may be given in the column for the fourth quarter. In these instances, no data are shown in the columns for the first and third quarters.

14. CD-ROM and Internet Account Subscriptions

The *IFS* is available on CD-ROM and the Internet. It contains:

(1) all time series appearing on *IFS* country tables;

(2) all series published in the *IFS* world tables, except for the daily exchange rates appearing in the Exchange Rates tables;

(3) the following exchange rate series as available for all Fund members, plus Aruba and the Netherlands Antilles: aa, ac, ae, af, ag, ah, b, c, de, dg, ea, eb, ec, ed, g, rb, rd, rf, rh, sa, sb, sc, sd, wa, wc, we, wf, wg, wh, xe, xf, ye, yf, nec, rec, aat, aet, rbt, rft, neu, reu, and ahx (for an explanation of series af, ah, de, dg, rb, and rd, see *IFS Supplement on Exchange Rates*, No. 9 (1985));

(4) Fund accounts time series, denominated in SDR terms, for all countries for which data are available, though some series are not published in the *IFS* monthly book (2af, 2al , 2ap, 2aq, 2as, 2at 2ej, 2ek, 2en, 2eo, 2f.s, 1c.s, 2tl, 2egs, 2eb, 2h.s, 1bd, 1b.s, 2dus, 2krs, 2ees, 2kxs, 2eu, 2ey, 2eg, 2ens, 2ehs, 2eqs, 2ers, 2ets, 2kk, 2lk, 2kl, 2ll, 1ch, and 1cj) and in percentages (2tlp, 2fz, and 1bf); and

(5) balance of payments series (78aad to 79ded) for all countries for which data are available, though some series are not published in the *IFS* monthly book.

All series in *IFS* contain publication code F except for the euro data lines that contain the code W.

A partner country code may sometimes be included in the control field. When it exists, it usually is shown in the *IFS* printed copy either in the italic midheading (see Real Effective Exchange Rate Indices table) or in the notes (see Commodity Prices table notes). Occasionally, the partner country code attached to a commodity price refers to a market (e.g., the London Metals Exchange) rather than the country of origin.

In the yearbook, data expressed in national currency for countries that have undergone periods of high inflation (e.g., Brazil, Democratic Republic of Congo, and Turkey) are presented in different magnitudes on the same printed line. Users may refer to midheaders on country pages for an indication of the magnitude changes. The practice of expressing different magnitudes on the same line was adopted to prevent early-period data from disappearing from the printed tables. On the CD-ROM and the Internet (CSV format), the data are stored in a scientific notation with six significant digits for all time periods. Therefore, historical as well as current data may be viewed when using the display choices available on the CD-ROM and the Internet.

WORLD
and
AREA TABLES

Exchange Rates

	Jan.	Feb.	Mar.	Apr.	May	June	July	Aug.	Sep.	Oct.	Nov.	Dec.	I	II	III	IV	Year
sa US Dollars per SDR (End of Period)
1989	1.31093	1.32150	1.29271	1.29566	1.24362	1.24639	1.28749	1.24652	1.27981	1.27782	1.28771	1.31416	1.29271	1.24639	1.27981	1.31416	1.31416
1990	1.32559	1.31681	1.30083	1.30247	1.31200	1.32388	1.36564	1.38595	1.39256	1.43078	1.42677	1.42266	1.30083	1.32388	1.39256	1.42266	1.42266
1991	1.43476	1.42053	1.34632	1.34081	1.34084	1.31452	1.33400	1.33698	1.36800	1.36652	1.38072	1.43043	1.34632	1.31452	1.36800	1.43043	1.43043
1992	1.39733	1.38091	1.37174	1.36976	1.39632	1.43117	1.44416	1.48286	1.47284	1.40595	1.37896	1.37500	1.37174	1.43117	1.47284	1.37500	1.37500
1993	1.38188	1.37610	1.39773	1.42339	1.42847	1.40360	1.39072	1.40758	1.41840	1.39293	1.38389	1.37356	1.39773	1.40360	1.41840	1.37356	1.37356
1994	1.38067	1.39930	1.41260	1.42138	1.41733	1.44837	1.44327	1.44770	1.46738	1.48454	1.45674	1.45985	1.41260	1.44837	1.46738	1.45985	1.45985
1995	1.47670	1.49440	1.56050	1.57303	1.57591	1.56876	1.55954	1.49249	1.50632	1.49455	1.48615	1.48649	1.56050	1.56876	1.50632	1.48649	1.48649
1996	1.45169	1.46868	1.46121	1.45006	1.44219	1.44334	1.46554	1.45766	1.43937	1.44623	1.44462	1.43796	1.46121	1.44334	1.43937	1.43796	1.43796
1997	1.39466	1.38494	1.38689	1.36553	1.39179	1.38814	1.35862	1.36358	1.36521	1.38362	1.36184	1.34925	1.38689	1.38814	1.36521	1.34925	1.34925
1998	1.34536	1.35023	1.33589	1.34666	1.33536	1.33154	1.32949	1.34222	1.37132	1.40835	1.38017	1.40803	1.33589	1.33154	1.37132	1.40803	1.40803
1999	1.38977	1.36556	1.35784	1.35123	1.34196	1.33587	1.36421	1.36986	1.38769	1.38072	1.36963	1.37251	1.35784	1.33587	1.38769	1.37251	1.37251
2000	1.35288	1.33928	1.34687	1.31921	1.32002	1.33728	1.31335	1.30480	1.29789	1.27934	1.28197	1.30291	1.34687	1.33728	1.29789	1.30291	1.30291
2001	1.29779	1.29248	1.26065	1.26579	1.25423	1.24565	1.25874	1.28823	1.28901	1.27808	1.26608	1.25673	1.26065	1.24565	1.28901	1.25673	1.25673
2002	1.24204	1.24163	1.24691	1.26771	1.29066	1.33046	1.32248	1.32751	1.32269	1.32163	1.32408	1.35952	1.24691	1.33046	1.32269	1.35952	1.35952
2003	1.37654	1.37085	1.37379	1.38391	1.41995	1.40086	1.39195	1.37727	1.42979	1.43178	1.44878	1.48597	1.37379	1.40086	1.42979	1.48597	1.48597
2004	1.48131	1.48007	1.48051	1.45183	1.46882	1.46622	1.45776	1.46073	1.46899	1.49878	1.53590	1.55301	1.48051	1.46622	1.46899	1.55301	1.55301
2005	1.52484	1.53199	1.51083	1.51678	1.47495	1.45661	1.45186	1.45984	1.44946	1.44580	1.42414	1.42927	1.51083	1.45661	1.44946	1.42927	1.42927
2006	1.44540	1.43503	1.44085	1.47106	1.49418	1.47937							1.44085	1.47937			
sb US Dollars per SDR (Period Average, geometric)
1989	1.32525	1.31652	1.30486	1.29975	1.26560	1.24062	1.27158	1.26166	1.24703	1.27221	1.27724	1.30191	1.31552	1.26843	1.26005	1.28372	1.28176
1990	1.31850	1.32659	1.30170	1.30135	1.31832	1.31442	1.34402	1.37719	1.39049	1.42846	1.44481	1.42654	1.31556	1.31134	1.37042	1.43325	1.35675
1991	1.42291	1.44058	1.38077	1.35123	1.34351	1.31934	1.32155	1.33571	1.35355	1.36201	1.38487	1.40799	1.41453	1.33796	1.33687	1.38483	1.36816
1992	1.40925	1.39042	1.36599	1.37060	1.38810	1.41173	1.44375	1.45645	1.45767	1.43476	1.38701	1.38883	1.38844	1.39004	1.45261	1.40336	1.40838
1993	1.37705	1.37168	1.38045	1.41266	1.41561	1.40969	1.39025	1.40151	1.41756	1.40746	1.38903	1.38404	1.37639	1.41265	1.40306	1.39347	1.39633
1994	1.37343	1.38750	1.40197	1.40425	1.41500	1.42736	1.45706	1.45439	1.46377	1.47720	1.47121	1.45201	1.38759	1.41550	1.45840	1.46676	1.43170
1995	1.46580	1.47826	1.53602	1.57620	1.55819	1.56369	1.55763	1.51069	1.48396	1.49828	1.49474	1.48532	1.49305	1.56601	1.51712	1.49277	1.51695
1996	1.46779	1.46625	1.46181	1.45086	1.44464	1.44290	1.45003	1.45830	1.44811	1.43968	1.45295	1.43817	1.46528	1.44613	1.45214	1.44359	1.45176
1997	1.41537	1.38421	1.37811	1.37150	1.38518	1.39032	1.37726	1.35396	1.35939	1.36989	1.37399	1.35418	1.39256	1.38231	1.36350	1.36599	1.37602
1998	1.34310	1.35002	1.34421	1.34312	1.34373	1.33354	1.33092	1.32668	1.36482	1.40747	1.39199	1.40211	1.34577	1.34013	1.34070	1.40051	1.35654
1999	1.40441	1.38073	1.36265	1.35485	1.34869	1.34004	1.33924	1.36415	1.37613	1.38943	1.37626	1.37280	1.38249	1.34785	1.35975	1.37948	1.36732
2000	1.37068	1.34485	1.34286	1.33915	1.31082	1.33062	1.32348	1.30836	1.29409	1.28650	1.28276	1.29440	1.35274	1.32681	1.30859	1.28788	1.31879
2001	1.30203	1.29353	1.27989	1.26764	1.26217	1.25028	1.25125	1.27495	1.28593	1.27882	1.26827	1.26279	1.29179	1.26001	1.27062	1.26995	1.27304
2002	1.25276	1.24463	1.25009	1.25669	1.27713	1.30065	1.33033	1.32103	1.32182	1.31765	1.33109	1.34003	1.24915	1.27803	1.32269	1.32960	1.29484
2003	1.36538	1.37045	1.37004	1.36908	1.40825	1.41481	1.39832	1.38494	1.39628	1.43198	1.43391	1.46743	1.36861	1.39658	1.39042	1.43959	1.39883
2004	1.49108	1.49645	1.47301	1.46088	1.45118	1.46565	1.47273	1.46495	1.46450	1.47952	1.51377	1.54036	1.48982	1.46100	1.46620	1.51103	1.48201
2005	1.52868	1.51752	1.52527	1.51043	1.49728	1.46737	1.44970	1.46691	1.46601	1.44540	1.42714	1.43121	1.52222	1.49169	1.46087	1.43458	1.47734
2006	1.44694	1.43561	1.43904	1.45121	1.48877	1.47800							1.44053	1.47266			
sc SDRs per US Dollar (End of Period)
1989	.76282	.75672	.77357	.77181	.80410	.80232	.77670	.80223	.78137	.78258	.77657	.76094	.77357	.80232	.78137	.76094	.76094
1990	.75438	.75941	.76874	.76777	.76219	.75536	.73226	.72153	.71810	.69892	.70089	.70291	.76874	.75536	.71810	.70291	.70291
1991	.69698	.70396	.74277	.74582	.74580	.76074	.74962	.74795	.73100	.73179	.72426	.69909	.74277	.76074	.73100	.69909	.69909
1992	.71565	.72416	.72900	.73006	.71617	.69873	.69244	.67437	.67896	.71127	.72518	.72727	.72900	.69873	.67896	.72727	.72727
1993	.72365	.72669	.71545	.70255	.70005	.71245	.71905	.71044	.70502	.71791	.72260	.72804	.71545	.71245	.70502	.72804	.72804
1994	.72429	.71465	.70792	.70354	.70555	.69043	.69075	.67361	.68646	.68500	.70792	.69043	.68149	.68500	.68500
1995	.67719	.66916	.64082	.63572	.63455	.63745	.64121	.67002	.66387	.66910	.67288	.67273	.64082	.63745	.66387	.67273	.67273
1996	.68885	.68088	.68436	.68963	.69339	.69284	.68234	.68603	.69475	.69145	.69222	.69543	.68436	.69284	.69475	.69543	.69543
1997	.71702	.72205	.72104	.73232	.71850	.72039	.73604	.73336	.73249	.72274	.73430	.74115	.72104	.72039	.73249	.74115	.74115
1998	.74330	.74061	.74856	.74258	.74886	.75101	.75217	.74503	.72922	.71005	.72455	.71021	.74856	.75101	.72922	.71021	.71021
1999	.71954	.73230	.73646	.74007	.74518	.74857	.73000	.72062	.72426	.73013	.72859	.72859	.73646	.74857	.72062	.72859	.72859
2000	.73917	.74667	.74246	.75803	.75757	.74779	.76141	.76640	.77048	.78165	.78005	.76751	.74246	.74779	.77048	.76751	.76751
2001	.77054	.77371	.79324	.79002	.79731	.80280	.79445	.77626	.77579	.78243	.78984	.79572	.79324	.80280	.77579	.79572	.79572
2002	.80513	.80403	.80198	.78883	.77480	.75162	.75615	.75329	.75603	.75664	.75524	.73555	.80198	.75162	.75603	.73555	.73555
2003	.72646	.72947	.72791	.72259	.70425	.71385	.71842	.72608	.70614	.69843	.69024	.67296	.72791	.71385	.70614	.67296	.67296
2004	.67508	.67564	.67544	.68879	.68082	.68203	.68599	.68459	.68074	.66721	.65108	.64391	.67544	.68203	.68074	.64391	.64391
2005	.65581	.65275	.66189	.65929	.67799	.68652	.68877	.68501	.68991	.69166	.70218	.69966	.66189	.68652	.68991	.69966	.69966
2006	.69185	.69685	.69404	.67978	.66926	.67596							.69404	.67596			
sd SDRs per US Dollar (Period Average, geometric)
1989	.75458	.75958	.76637	.76938	.79014	.80605	.78642	.79261	.80191	.78603	.78294	.76810	.76016	.78838	.79362	.77899	.78018
1990	.75844	.75381	.76823	.76843	.75854	.76079	.74404	.72612	.71917	.70006	.69213	.70100	.76014	.76258	.72970	.69772	.73706
1991	.70279	.69417	.72423	.74007	.74432	.75795	.75669	.74867	.73880	.73421	.72209	.71023	.70694	.74741	.74802	.72211	.73091
1992	.70960	.71921	.73207	.72961	.72041	.70835	.69264	.68660	.68603	.69698	.72098	.72003	.72024	.71940	.68842	.71258	.71004
1993	.72619	.72903	.72440	.70788	.70641	.70938	.71930	.71352	.70544	.71050	.71993	.72252	.72654	.70789	.71276	.71763	.71616
1994	.72810	.72072	.71328	.71213	.70671	.70059	.68631	.68757	.68317	.67696	.67971	.68870	.72068	.70646	.68568	.68177	.69847
1995	.68222	.67647	.65104	.63444	.64200	.63951	.64200	.66195	.67387	.66743	.66901	.67326	.66977	.63937	.65914	.66990	.65922
1996	.68130	.68201	.68408	.68925	.69221	.69305	.68964	.68573	.69056	.69460	.68825	.69533	.68246	.69150	.68864	.69272	.68882
1997	.70653	.72243	.72563	.72913	.72193	.71926	.72608	.73857	.73562	.72999	.72781	.73845	.71810	.72344	.73341	.73207	.72673
1998	.74455	.74073	.74393	.74453	.74420	.74988	.75136	.75376	.73270	.71114	.71840	.71321	.73431	.74620	.74588	.71424	.73722
1999	.71204	.72425	.73387	.73809	.74146	.74624	.74669	.73306	.72668	.71972	.72661	.72844	.72333	.74192	.73543	.72491	.73136
2000	.72957	.74358	.74467	.74674	.76288	.75153	.75559	.76431	.77275	.77730	.77957	.77256	.73924	.75369	.76418	.77647	.75827
2001	.76803	.77308	.78132	.78887	.79229	.79982	.79920	.78435	.77765	.78197	.78847	.79189	.77412	.79364	.78702	.78744	.78552
2002	.79824	.80345	.79994	.79574	.78301	.76885	.75169	.75698	.75653	.75893	.75127	.74625	.80054	.78245	.75506	.75213	.77230
2003	.73239	.72969	.72990	.73042	.71010	.70681	.71515	.72205	.71619	.69833	.69739	.68146	.73067	.71618	.71922	.69467	.71517
2004	.67066	.66825	.67888	.68452	.68909	.68229	.67901	.68262	.68283	.67589	.66060	.64920	.67123	.68449	.68204	.66198	.67494
2005	.65416	.65897	.65562	.66206	.66788	.68149	.68980	.68171	.68212	.69185	.70070	.69871	.65694	.67048	.68454	.69709	.67726
2006	.69111	.69657	.69491	.68908	.67169	.67659							.69420	.67912			

Exchange Rates

		1994	1995	1996	1997	1998	1999	2000	2001	2002	2003	2004	2005
							Market, Official, or Principal Rate						
							National Currency Units per SDR: End of Period (aa)						
Industrial Countries													
US dollar	111	1.4599	1.4865	1.4380	1.3493	1.4080	1.3725	1.3029	1.2567	1.3595	1.4860	1.5530	1.4293
Canadian dollar	156	2.0479	2.0294	1.9694	1.9282	2.1550	1.9809	1.9546	2.0015	2.1475	1.9205	1.8692	1.6644
Australian dollar	193	1.8793	1.9953	1.8053	2.0672	2.2936	2.0993	2.3518	2.4613	2.4011	1.9813	1.9936	1.9480
Japanese yen	158	145.61	152.86	166.80	175.34	162.77	140.27	149.70	165.64	163.01	159.15	161.70	168.61
New Zealand dollar	196	2.2721	2.2754	2.0368	2.3195	2.6723	2.6364	2.9598	3.0246	2.5822	2.2861	2.1618	2.0975
EMU Euro	163	....	....	....	....	....	1.36623	1.40023	1.42600	1.29639	1.17654	1.14016	1.21155
Austrian schilling	122	16.013	14.996	15.751	17.045	16.540	....	....	....	....	....	....	....
Belgium franc	124	46.478	43.725	46.022	49.814	48.682	....	....	....	....	....	....	....
Finnish markka	172	6.9244	6.4790	6.6777	7.3139	7.1753	....	....	....	....	....	....	....
French franc	132	7.8044	7.2838	7.5306	8.0794	7.9161	....	....	....	....	....	....	....
Deutsche mark	134	2.2610	2.1309	2.2357	2.4180	2.3556	....	....	....	....	....	....	....
Greek drachma	174	350.51	352.36	355.20	381.31	397.87	450.79	476.37	....	....	....	....	....
Irish pound	178	.94360	.92587	.85537	.94327	.94670	....	....	....	....	....	....	....
Italian lira	136	2,379.2	2,355.7	2,200.9	2,373.6	2,327.6	....	....	....	....	....	....	....
Luxembourg franc	137	46.478	43.725	46.022	49.814	48.682	....	....	....	....	....	....	....
Netherlands guilder	138	2.5330	2.3849	2.5072	2.7217	2.6595	....	....	....	....	....	....	....
Portuguese escudo	182	232.25	222.10	224.88	247.35	241.94	....	....	....	....	....	....	....
Spanish peseta	184	192.32	180.47	188.77	204.68	200.79	....	....	....	....	....	....	....
Danish krone	128	8.880	8.244	8.548	9.210	8.992	10.155	10.450	10.568	9.628	8.853	8.491	9.039
Icelandic krona	176	99.708	96.964	96.185	97.389	97.605	99.576	110.356	129.380	109.550	105.489	94.796	90.015
Norwegian krone	142	9.8715	9.3931	9.2641	9.8707	10.7010	11.0343	11.5288	11.3251	9.4700	9.9263	9.3802	9.6762
Swedish krona	144	10.8927	9.8973	9.8802	10.6280	11.3501	11.7006	12.4232	13.4062	11.9978	10.6829	10.2725	11.3747
Swiss franc	146	1.9146	1.7102	1.9361	1.9636	1.9382	2.1955	2.1322	2.1079	1.8854	1.8380	1.7574	1.8785
Pound sterling	112	.93430	.95903	.84686	.81585	.84643	.84912	.87315	.86647	.84348	.83262	.80409	.83005
Developing Countries													
Africa													
Algerian dinar	612	62.6166	77.5576	80.7931	78.8150	84.9790	95.1346	98.1649	97.7982	108.3856	107.9004	112.7698	104.8797
Angolan kwanza	614	.7434	.0085	.2905	.3540	.9807	† 7.6585	21.9121	40.1517	79.7581	117.5127	133.5399	115.4557
Benin, CFA franc	638	† 780.44	728.38	753.06	807.94	791.61	† 896.19	918.49	935.39	850.37	771.76	747.90	794.73
Botswana pula	616	3.9670	4.1944	5.2404	5.1400	6.2774	6.3572	6.9861	8.7760	7.4331	6.6014	6.6482	7.8791
Burkina Faso, CFA franc	748	† 780.44	728.38	753.06	807.94	791.61	† 896.19	918.49	935.39	850.37	771.76	747.90	794.73
Burundi franc	618	360.78	413.37	462.63	551.56	710.64	860.83	1,014.76	1,090.92	1,451.07	1,618.31	1,717.35	1,425.93
Cameroon, CFA franc	622	† 780.44	728.38	753.06	807.94	791.61	† 896.19	918.49	935.39	850.37	771.76	747.90	794.73
Cape Verde escudo	624	118.45	115.14	122.46	129.85	132.71	150.65	154.40	157.24	142.95	129.74	125.73	133.60
Cent.African Rep.,CFA franc	626	† 780.44	728.38	753.06	807.94	791.61	† 896.19	918.49	935.39	850.37	771.76	747.90	794.73
Chad, CFA franc	628	† 780.44	728.38	753.06	807.94	791.61	† 896.19	918.49	935.39	850.37	771.76	747.90	794.73
Comorian franc	632	† 585.32	546.28	564.79	605.95	593.70	672.14	688.87	701.54	637.78	578.82	560.92	596.05
Congo, Dem.Rep., congo franc	636	47.445	.220	1.662	1.430	† 3.450	6.176	65.146	394.111	519.528	† 553.554	689.673	616.414
Congo, Rep., CFA franc	634	† 780.44	728.38	753.06	807.94	791.61	† 896.19	918.49	935.39	850.37	771.76	747.90	794.73
Côte d'Ivoire,CFA franc	662	† 780.44	728.38	753.06	807.94	791.61	† 896.19	918.49	935.39	850.37	771.76	747.90	794.73
Djibouti franc	611	259.45	264.18	255.56	239.79	250.24	243.92	231.55	223.35	241.62	264.09	276.00	254.01
Eq. Guinea, CFA franc	642	† 780.44	728.38	753.06	807.94	791.61	† 896.19	918.49	935.39	850.37	771.76	747.90	794.73
Eritrean nafka	643	8.6861	9.3946	9.2403	† 9.6134	10.6967	13.1761	13.2897	17.3397	19.2117	20.4878	21.4121	21.9750
Ethiopian birr	644	8.6861	9.3946	9.2403	9.2613	10.5644	11.1640	10.8324	10.7555	11.6659	12.8100	13.4365	12.4078
Gabon, CFA franc	646	† 780.44	728.38	753.06	807.94	791.61	† 896.19	918.49	935.39	850.37	771.76	747.90	794.73
Gambian dalasi	648	13.983	14.330	14.225	14.207	15.476	15.849	19.397	21.279	31.802	46.005	46.083	40.212
Ghanaian cedi	652	1,536.68	2,154.33	2,522.74	3,066.48	3,274.49	4,852.02	9,182.45	9,201.70	11,472.74	13,154.28	14,061.36	13,050.41
Guinean franc	656	1,432.15	1,483.49	1,494.23	1,544.82	1,827.67	2,382.68	2,452.43	2,498.79	2,620.18	2,964.24	3,516.29	6,442.84
Guinea-Bissau, CFA franc	654	345.18	501.49	772.88	807.94	791.61	896.19	918.49	935.39	850.37	771.76	747.90	794.73
Kenya shilling	664	65.458	83.153	79.118	84.568	87.165	100.098	101.674	98.779	104.781	113.140	120.117	103.432
Lesotho loti	666	5.1730	5.4220	6.7332	6.5675	8.2511	8.4471	9.8611	15.2397	11.7463	9.8668	8.7434	9.0401
Liberian dollar	668	1.4599	1.4865	1.4380	1.3493	† 60.8973	54.2141	55.6994	62.2081	88.3688	75.0415	84.6390	80.7538
Malagasy ariary	674	1,130.2	1,017.6	1,244.8	1,426.1	1,521.3	1,796.1	1,706.9	1,666.7	1,749.6	1,812.3	2,903.2	† 3,087.0
Malawi kwacha	676	22.3337	22.7479	22.0340	28.6416	61.7894	63.7362	104.3318	84.5705	118.4665	161.3258	169.1899	176.9159
Mali, CFA franc	678	† 780.44	728.38	753.06	807.94	791.61	† 896.19	918.49	935.39	850.37	771.76	747.90	794.73
Mauritanian ouguiya	682	187.40	203.81	204.84	227.15	289.74	308.81	328.72	331.93	365.32	394.67	....	....
Mauritian rupee	684	26.077	26.258	25.842	30.041	34.896	34.955	36.327	38.197	39.694	38.766	43.802	43.831
Moroccan dirham	686	13.080	12.589	12.653	13.107	13.031	13.845	13.836	14.528	13.822	13.002	12.762	13.220
Mozambique, metical	688	9,709.5	16,187.9	16,359.7	15,574.4	17,411.7	18,254.4	† 22,332.5	29,307.5	32,430.4	35,450.3	29,350.8	34,564.0
Namibia dollar	728	5.17298	5.42197	6.73325	6.56747	8.25106	8.44711	9.86107	15.23974	11.74625	9.86684	8.74345	9.04013
Niger, CFA franc	692	† 780.44	728.38	753.06	807.94	791.61	† 896.19	918.49	935.39	850.37	771.76	747.90	794.73
Nigerian naira	694	32.113	32.534	31.471	29.530	† 30.816	134.437	142.734	141.948	171.843	202.835	205.541	184.376
Rwanda franc	714	201.39	445.67	437.37	411.31	450.75	479.24	560.67	572.84	695.88	849.07	878.35	791.41
São Tomé & Príncipe dobra	716	1,730.37	2,611.58	4,074.04	9,403.91	9,694.29	10,019.32	11,218.90	11,335.34	12,496.49	14,051.18	15,691.55	17,050.76
Senegal, CFA franc	722	† 780.44	728.38	753.06	807.94	791.61	† 896.19	918.49	935.39	850.37	771.76	747.90	794.73
Seychelles rupee	718	7.2345	7.2345	7.2345	6.9218	7.6699	7.3671	8.1642	7.2226	6.8474	8.1434	8.5131	7.8601
Sierra Leonean leone	724	894.90	1,402.35	1,307.24	1,799.00	2,239.84	3,123.90	2,171.52	2,716.13	2,979.70	3,807.32	4,321.94	4,191.36
South African rand	199	5.1730	5.4220	6.7332	6.5675	8.2511	8.4471	9.8611	15.2397	11.7463	9.8668	8.7434	9.0401
Sudanese pound	732	58.3940	78.2363	208.4000	232.3489	334.8307	353.6958	335.3039	328.5469	355.7592	386.5900	389.2309	329.5039
Swaziland lilangeni	734	5.1730	5.4220	6.7332	6.5675	8.2511	8.4471	9.8611	15.2397	11.7463	9.8668	8.7434	9.0401
Tanzanian shilling	738	764.16	818.10	856.51	842.70	958.87	1,094.34	1,046.58	1,151.54	1,327.30	1,580.51	1,619.73	1,665.83
Togo, CFA franc	742	780.44	728.38	753.06	807.94	791.61	† 896.19	918.49	935.39	850.37	771.76	747.90	794.73
Tunisian dinar	744	1.4470	1.4134	1.4358	1.5483	1.5502	1.7191	1.8049	1.8453	1.8137	1.7955	1.8627	1.9487
Uganda shilling	746	1,352.9	1,500.5	1,480.5	1,538.3	1,918.7	2,067.1	2,301.8	2,170.9	2,518.6	2,875.8	2,700.0	2,596.8
Zambian kwacha	754	993.095	1,421.278	1,844.457	1,908.973	3,236.948	3,612.707	5,417.278	4,813.779	5,892.703	6,903.044	7,409.892	5,015.280
Zimbabwe dollar	698	12.24	13.84	15.59	25.11	52.62	52.35	71.75	69.17	74.82	1,224.03	8,897.61	111,432.45
Asia													
Afghanistan,afghani	512	.730	1.486	4.314	4.048	4.224	† 64.221	....	59.392	† 61.008	† 72.612	74.886	71.978
Bangladesh taka	513	58.759	60.574	61.041	61.323	68.289	69.998	70.357	71.634	78.716	87.348	94.333	94.632
Bhutan,ngultrum	514	45.810	52.295	51.666	52.999	59.813	59.690	60.911	60.549	65.298	67.768	67.688	64.410
Cambodian riel	522	3,759.1	3,754.9	3,901.2	4,657.6	5,308.3	5,174.4	5,087.9	4,895.0	5,342.9	5,920.1	6,254.0	5,877.2

Exchange Rates

2006, International Monetary Fund : *International Financial Statistics Yearbook*

		1994	1995	1996	1997	1998	1999	2000	2001	2002	2003	2004	2005
						Market, Official, or Principal Rate							
						National Currency Units per SDR: End of Period (aa)							
Asia(Cont.)													
Chinese yuan	924	† 12.3302	12.3637	11.9325	11.1715	11.6567	11.3637	10.7847	10.4017	11.2532	12.2989	12.8535	11.5345
Fiji dollar	819	2.0570	2.1248	1.9900	2.0902	2.7965	2.6981	2.8479	2.9017	2.8072	2.5589	2.5547	2.4939
Hong Kong dollar	532	11.2963	11.4935	11.1241	10.4513	10.9066	10.6658	10.1575	9.7987	10.6015	11.5356	12.0723	11.0804
Indian rupee	534	45.810	52.295	51.666	52.999	59.813	59.690	60.911	60.549	65.298	67.768	67.688	64.410
Indonesian rupiah	536	3,211.7	3,430.8	3,426.7	6,274.0	11,299.4	9,724.2	12,501.4	13,070.0	12,154.1	12,578.7	14,427.5	14,049.7
Kiribati, Aust.dollar	826	1.8793	1.9953	1.8053	2.0672	2.2936	2.0993	2.3518	2.4613	2.4011	1.9813	1.9936	1.9480
Korean won	542	1,151.4	1,151.6	1,213.9	2,287.0	1,695.3	1,561.9	1,647.5	1,650.7	1,612.7	1,772.2	1,607.5	1,445.8
Lao P.D. Rep., kip	544	1,049.63	† 1,372.03	1,344.49	3,554.60	6,017.92	10,431.08	10,707.31	11,926.37	14,519.67	15,553.65	16,114.81	15,354.65
Macao pataca	546	11.6352	11.8391	11.4571	10.7690	11.2359	10.9868	10.4672	10.0932	10.9208	11.8832	12.4388	11.4157
Malaysian ringgit	548	3.73722	3.77866	3.63660	5.25115	5.35051	5.21554	4.95106	4.77557	5.16618	5.64669	5.90144	5.40264
Maldivian rufiyaa	556	17.182	17.496	16.925	15.881	16.573	16.154	15.335	16.086	17.402	19.020	19.879	18.295
Mongolian togrog	948	604.509	704.031	997.240	1,097.156	1,270.043	1,471.839	1,429.292	1,384.916	1,529.460	1,735.613	1,877.589	1,745.139
Myanmar kyat	518	8.5085	8.5085	8.5085	8.5085	8.5085	8.5085	8.5085	8.5085	8.5085	8.5085	8.5085	8.5085
Nepalese rupee	558	72.817	83.243	82.007	85.408	95.288	94.326	96.806	96.108	106.450	110.021	111.506	105.837
Pakistan rupee	564	44.963	50.912	57.691	59.434	64.608	† 71.075	75.607	76.489	79.578	85.020	91.820	85.513
Papua New Guinea kina	853	1.7205	1.9846	1.9366	2.3630	2.9518	3.6995	4.0028	4.7281	5.4643	4.9532	4.8532	4.4250
Philippine peso	566	35.647	38.967	37.801	53.936	54.996	55.330	65.143	64.601	72.185	82.574	87.383	75.847
Samoa tala	862	3.5789	3.7566	3.5004	3.7324	4.2385	4.1428	4.3532	4.4628	4.3729	4.1277	4.1513	3.9504
Singapore dollar	576	2.1324	2.1023	2.0129	2.2607	2.3380	2.2866	2.2560	2.3262	2.3608	2.5273	2.5373	2.3786
Solomon Islands dollar	813	4.8597	5.1668	5.2081	6.4067	6.8417	6.9671	6.6441	6.9935	10.1381	11.1309	11.6592	10.8278
Sri Lanka rupee	524	72.963	80.341	81.540	82.689	96.164	99.054	107.594	117.075	131.500	143.750	162.453	145.953
Thai baht	578	36.628	37.445	36.826	† 63.748	51.662	51.428	56.374	55.575	58.665	58.831	60.662	58.643
Tongan pa'anga	866	1.8371	1.8883	1.7438	1.8377	2.2749	2.2066	2.5754	2.7736	3.0299	3.0020	2.9689	2.9439
Vanuatu vatu	846	163.62	169.07	159.28	167.73	182.73	176.90	186.07	184.41	181.05	166.15	165.44	160.55
Vietnamese dong	582	16,132.8	16,373.7	16,031.8	16,585.0	19,557.5	19,253.6	18,910.4	18,956.5	20,940.7	23,249.5	24,501.8	22,748.3
Europe													
Albanian lek	914	139.547	140.087	148.211	201.227	197.941	185.454	185.847	171.606	181.822	158.375	143.871	148.044
Armenian dram	911	591.98	597.57	625.61	667.85	735.03	718.88	719.44	706.04	795.17	841.06	754.51	643.44
Azerbaijan manat	912	1.2210	1.3200	1.1786	1.0492	1.0954	1.2018	1.1896	1.2002	1.3304	1.4631	1.5229	1.3129
Belarusian rubel	913	15.474	17.095	22.288	41.476	309.767	439.203	1,537.434	1,985.633	2,610.278	3,203.751	3,370.032	3,075.789
Bosnia & Herzegovina conv.marka.	963	....	....	....	2.418	2.356	2.672	2.739	2.789	2.536	2.301	2.230	2.370
Bulgarian lev	918	.0964	.1051	.7008	2.3969	2.3586	2.6721	2.7386	2.7891	2.5627	2.3012	2.2300	2.3696
Croatian kuna	960	8.21706	7.90233	7.96572	8.50446	8.79667	10.49648	10.62568	10.50129	9.71478	9.09192	8.75414	8.90953
Cyprus pound	423	.69523	.67867	.67567	.70935	.70152	.78862	.80357	.81712	.74344	.69134	.66004	.69234
Czech Republic koruna	935	40.947	39.544	39.302	46.733	42.037	49.382	49.267	45.568	40.977	38.121	34.733	35.143
Estonian kroon	939	18.088	17.038	17.888	19.343	18.882	21.359	21.915	22.234	20.306	18.440	17.815	18.896
Georgian lari	915	....	1.8284	1.8348	1.7594	2.5345	2.6489	2.5732	2.5889	2.8414	3.0834	2.8342	2.5620
Hungarian forint	944	161.591	207.321	237.163	274.572	308.401	346.586	370.978	350.665	306.110	308.963	279.992	305.263
Kazakhstani tenge	916	79.21	95.06	105.40	101.94	117.99	189.68	188.27	188.76	210.18	214.31	201.89	191.49
Kyrgyz som	917	15.55	16.65	24.01	23.44	41.36	62.35	62.94	59.97	62.67	65.67	64.64	59.03
Latvian lats	941	.80000	.79825	.79951	.79606	.80117	.80017	.79868	.80179	.80755	.80391	.80135	.84756
Lithuanian litas	946	5.839	5.946	5.752	5.397	5.632	5.490	5.212	5.027	4.502	4.104	3.936	4.159
Macedonian denar	962	59.264	56.456	59.547	74.776	72.987	82.816	86.420	86.930	79.665	72.887	69.990	74.120
Maltese lira	181	.53738	.52384	.51712	.52717	.53141	.56558	.57038	.56812	.54220	.50895	.49470	.51841
Moldovan lev	921	6.2336	6.6877	6.7215	6.2882	11.7185	15.9077	16.1343	16.4517	18.7913	19.6445	19.3522	18.3404
Polish zloty	964	3.5579	3.6687	4.1349	4.7467	4.9337	5.6936	5.3982	5.0097	5.2189	5.5587	4.6641	4.6613
Romanian leu	968	.258	.383	.580	1.083	1.542	2.506	3.378	3.971	4.554	4.844	4.514	† 4.442
Russian ruble	922	5.1825	6.8973	7.9951	8.0415	† 29.0758	37.0578	36.6899	37.8778	43.2115	43.7685	43.0940	41.1380
Slovak koruna	936	45.660	43.954	45.864	46.930	51.975	58.011	61.744	60.910	54.430	49.000	44.255	45.662
Slovenian tolar	961	184.609	187.283	203.443	228.266	226.974	270.069	296.252	315.371	300.550	281.394	273.707	289.327
Tajik somoni	923	.058	.436	.472	1.008	1.377	1.971	† 2.866	3.205	4.079	4.393	4.716	4.573
Turkish new lira	186	.0565	.0887	.1550	.2774	.4428	.7431	.8774	1.8224	2.2346	2.0754	2.0803	† 1.9224
Ukrainian hryvnia	926	1.5212	2.6668	† 2.7163	2.5622	4.8253	7.1594	7.0807	6.6588	7.2495	7.9224	8.2393	7.2178
Middle East													
Bahrain, Kingdom of, dinar	419	.54890	.55892	.54067	.50732	.52942	.51606	.48989	.47253	.51118	.55873	.58393	.53741
Egyptian pound	469	4.9504	5.0392	4.8718	4.5713	4.7704	4.6734	4.8077	5.6427	6.1178	9.1435	9.5221	8.1929
Iranian rial	429	2,534.26	2,597.64	2,515.19	2,366.94	2,465.36	2,405.04	2,948.39	2,200.47	† 10,810.87	12,292.11	13,655.62	12,993.49
Iraqi dinar	433	.45381	.46209	.44700	.41942	.43770	.42665	.40502	.39066	.42262	....	....	....
Israeli new sheqel	436	4.4058	4.6601	4.6748	4.7709	5.8588	5.7000	5.2651	5.5497	6.4400	6.5071	6.6904	6.5789
Jordan dinar	439	1.02336	1.05392	1.01951	.95662	.99829	.97311	.92376	.89102	.96390	1.05355	1.10108	1.01335
Kuwaiti dinar	443	.43813	.44436	.43123	.41139	.42461	.41749	.39793	.38691	.40726	.43792	.45767	.41735
Lebanese pound	446	2,404.4	2,372.4	2,231.7	2,060.3	2,123.3	2,069.1	1,964.1	1,894.5	2,049.5	2,240.1	2,341.2	2,154.6
Libyan dinar	672	.63412	.63412	.63412	.63412	.63412	.63412	.70403	.81699	1.64474	1.93237	1.93237	1.93237
Rial Omani	449	.56131	.57156	.55290	.51879	.54139	.52773	.50097	.48321	.52274	.57136	.59713	.54955
Qatar riyal	453	5.3139	5.4108	5.2342	4.9113	5.1252	4.9959	4.7426	4.5745	4.9487	5.4089	5.6530	5.2025
Saudi Arabian riyal	456	5.4744	5.5743	5.3924	5.0597	5.2801	5.1469	4.8859	4.7127	5.0982	5.5724	5.8238	5.3526
Syrian pound	463	16.387	16.686	16.141	15.145	15.805	15.406	14.625	14.107	15.261	16.680	17.433	16.044
U.A.Emirates dirham	466	5.3591	5.4569	5.2788	4.9551	5.1710	5.0405	4.7849	4.6153	4.9928	5.4572	5.7034	5.2490
Yemen,Rep.,Yemeni rial	474	17.533	† 74.384	† 182.492	176.023	199.447	218.366	215.749	217.754	243.368	273.879	288.658	278.822
Western Hemisphere													
Anguilla, E.Caribbean dollar	312	3.9416	4.0135	3.8825	3.6430	3.8017	3.7058	3.5179	3.3932	3.6707	4.0121	4.1931	3.8590
Antigua & Barbuda,E.Car.dollar	311	3.9416	4.0135	3.8825	3.6430	3.8017	3.7058	3.5179	3.3932	3.6707	4.0121	4.1931	3.8590
Argentine peso	213	1.45912	1.48649	1.43724	1.34858	1.40733	1.37182	1.30226	1.25610	4.51361	4.31674	4.59536	4.30496
Aruban florin	314	2.6131	2.6608	2.5739	2.4152	2.5204	2.4568	2.3322	2.2495	2.4335	2.6599	2.7799	2.5584
Bahamian dollar	313	1.4599	1.4865	1.4380	1.3493	1.4080	1.3725	1.3029	1.2567	1.3595	1.4860	1.5530	1.4293
Barbados dollar	316	2.9197	2.9730	2.8759	2.6985	2.8161	2.7450	2.6058	2.5135	2.7190	2.9719	3.1060	2.8585
Belize dollar	339	2.9197	2.9730	2.8759	2.6985	2.8161	2.7450	2.6058	2.5135	2.7190	2.9719	3.1060	2.8585
Bolivia, boliviano	218	6.85400	7.33583	7.45582	7.23873	7.94833	8.22133	8.32559	8.57090	10.18280	11.63515	12.50173	11.49133
Brazilian real	223	† 1.23503	1.44635	1.49462	1.50630	1.70189	2.45542	2.54667	2.91612	4.80250	4.29208	4.12107	....
Chilean peso	228	589.91	605.19	611.09	593.41	667.08	727.53	746.15	824.67	968.49	890.72	869.42	734.94
Colombian peso	233	1,213.53	1,468.13	1,445.62	1,745.36	2,122.63	2,571.77	2,849.49	2,892.15	3,894.74	4,132.22	3,746.02	3,264.77
Costa Rican colon	238	240.98	289.72	316.51	329.61	382.17	409.27	414.35	429.39	514.88	621.92	712.23	709.89

Exchange Rates

Market, Official, or Principal Rate
National Currency Units per SDR: End of Period (aa)

		1994	1995	1996	1997	1998	1999	2000	2001	2002	2003	2004	2005
Western Hemisphere(Cont.)													
Dominica, E.Caribbean dollar........	321	3.9416	4.0135	3.8825	3.6430	3.8017	3.7058	3.5179	3.3932	3.6707	4.0121	4.1931	3.8590
Dominican peso............................	243	19.071	20.015	20.220	19.383	22.230	22.014	21.725	21.551	28.813	55.352	48.313	49.852
Ecuadoran sucre...........................	248	3,312.4	4,345.8	5,227.0	5,974.5	9,609.8	27,783.7	32,572.8	31,418.3	33,988.0	37,149.3	38,825.3	35,731.8
Salvadoran colon.........................	253	12.7737	13.0142	12.5893	11.8127	12.3273	12.0163	11.4070	10.9964	11.8958	13.0022	13.5888	12.5061
Grenada, E.Caribbean dollar..........	328	3.9416	4.0135	3.8825	3.6430	3.8017	3.7058	3.5179	3.3932	3.6707	4.0121	4.1931	3.8590
Guatemalan quetzal......................	258	8.2460	8.9810	8.5782	8.3342	9.6425	10.7342	10.0731	10.0544	10.6140	11.9482	12.0334	10.8772
Guyana dollar...............................	336	208.029	208.852	203.112	194.292	228.453	247.738	240.713	238.150	260.688	288.650	310.214	286.211
Haitian gourde.............................	263	18.9001	24.0215	21.7028	23.3569	23.2390	24.6577	29.3470	33.1009	51.1305	62.5369	57.8214	61.4590
Honduran lempira.........................	268	13.7227	15.3751	18.5057	17.6673	19.4415	19.9067	19.7270	20.0068	23.0076	26.3733	28.9369	27.0063
Jamaica dollar..............................	343	48.4692	58.8894	50.1351	49.0326	52.1744	56.6719	59.1715	59.4257	69.0115	89.9266	95.4325	92.0174
Mexican peso................................	273	7.7737	11.3605	11.2893	10.9064	13.8902	13.0585	12.4717	11.4894	14.0201	16.6964	17.4943	15.4042
Montserrat, E.Caribbean dollar......	351	3.9416	4.0135	3.8825	3.6430	3.8017	3.7058	3.5179	3.3932	3.6707	4.0121	4.1931	3.8590
Netherlands Antilles guilder...........	353	2.6131	2.6608	2.5739	2.4152	2.5204	2.4568	2.3322	2.2495	2.4335	2.6599	2.7799	2.5584
Nicaraguan gold córdoba..............	278	10.382	11.840	12.832	13.486	15.761	16.907	17.012	17.394	19.946	23.109	25.359	24.506
Panamanian balboa......................	283	1.4599	1.4865	1.4380	1.3493	1.4080	1.3725	1.3029	1.2567	1.3595	1.4860	1.5530	1.4293
Paraguayan guarani......................	288	2,809.8	2,942.7	3,033.6	3,184.2	3,999.1	4,568.9	4,595.2	5,884.0	9,657.5	9,086.6	9,706.3	8,747.1
Peruvian new sol...........................	293	3.18247	3.43379	3.73870	3.68345	4.44937	4.81751	4.59536	4.32818	4.77735	5.14591	5.09620	4.90240
St.Kitts & Nevis, E.C. dollar...........	361	3.9416	4.0135	3.8825	3.6430	3.8017	3.7058	3.5179	3.3932	3.6707	4.0121	4.1931	3.8590
St.Lucia, E.Caribbean dollar...........	362	3.9416	4.0135	3.8825	3.6430	3.8017	3.7058	3.5179	3.3932	3.6707	4.0121	4.1931	3.8590
St. Vinc. & Grens., E. Carib. dollar..	364	3.9416	4.0135	3.8825	3.6430	3.8017	3.7058	3.5179	3.3932	3.6707	4.0121	4.1931	3.8590
Surinamese dollar.........................	366	† .598	.605	.577	.541	.565	1.355	2.838	2.738	3.419	† 3.901	† 4.216	3.916
Trinidad & Tobago dollar...............	369	8.6616	8.9146	8.9074	8.5001	9.2881	8.6467	8.2078	7.9051	8.5648	9.3615	9.7838	9.0191
Uruguayan peso............................	298	8.1766	10.5704	12.5289	13.5465	15.2307	15.9417	16.3059	18.5594	36.9789	43.5389	40.9218	34.4454
Venezuelan bolivar.......................	299	† 248.175	431.082	685.188	680.359	794.833	889.730	911.711	958.885	1,905.027	2,374.580	2,978.673	3,068.643

Fund Accounts: Position to Date

(As of June 30, 2006 and Expressed in Millions of SDRs)

		Quota	Reserve Position in the Fund	Total Fund Credit and Loans Outstanding				Fund Holdings of Currency		SDR Department		
				Total Amount	Percent of Quota	Outstanding Purchases (GRA)	Outstanding Loans	Amount	Percent of Quota	Net Cumulative Allocation	Holdings of SDR	
											Amount	Percent of Allocation
		(1)	(2)	(3)	(4)	(5)	(6)	(7)	(8)	(9)	(10)	(11)
All Countries	010	213,478.4	23,889.8	19,146.6	9.0	15,251.6	3,895.0	204,845.3	96.0	21,433.3	17,395.6	81.2
Industrial Countries	110	130,566.6	17,624.8	—	—	—	—	112,944.2	86.5	14,595.3	12,501.0	85.7
United States	111	37,149.3	5,344.3	—	—	—	—	31,805.6	85.6	4,899.5	5,825.2	118.9
Canada	156	6,369.2	738.3	—	—	—	—	5,630.9	88.4	779.3	635.0	81.5
Australia	193	3,236.4	403.2	—	—	—	—	2,833.5	87.6	470.5	135.0	28.7
Japan	158	13,312.8	1,848.8	—	—	—	—	11,464.9	86.1	891.7	1,827.5	204.9
New Zealand	196	894.6	102.5	—	—	—	—	792.2	88.5	141.3	23.4	16.6
Austria	122	1,872.3	258.2	—	—	—	—	1,614.1	86.2	179.0	104.1	58.2
Belgium	124	4,605.2	612.4	—	—	—	—	3,992.8	86.7	485.2	210.0	43.3
Denmark	128	1,642.8	134.6	—	—	—	—	1,508.2	91.8	178.9	43.5	24.3
Finland	172	1,263.8	174.7	—	—	—	—	1,089.1	86.2	142.7	98.5	69.0
France	132	10,738.5	1,423.4	—	—	—	—	9,315.3	86.7	1,079.9	623.2	57.7
Germany	134	13,008.2	1,785.5	—	—	—	—	11,222.8	86.3	1,210.8	1,341.0	110.8
Greece	174	823.0	111.5	—	—	—	—	711.5	86.4	103.5	20.1	19.4
Iceland	176	117.6	18.6	—	—	—	—	99.0	84.2	16.4	.1	.4
Ireland	178	838.4	109.3	—	—	—	—	729.1	87.0	87.3	62.4	71.5
Italy	136	7,055.5	957.3	—	—	—	—	6,098.2	86.4	702.4	177.2	25.2
Luxembourg	137	279.1	38.5	—	—	—	—	240.6	86.2	17.0	11.8	69.8
Netherlands	138	5,162.4	692.8	—	—	—	—	4,469.6	86.6	530.3	513.0	96.7
Norway	142	1,671.7	122.6	—	—	—	—	1,549.1	92.7	167.8	205.4	122.4
Portugal	182	867.4	117.6	—	—	—	—	749.9	86.5	53.3	73.6	138.1
San Marino	135	17.0	4.1	—	—	—	—	12.9	75.9	—	.7	—
Spain	184	3,048.9	406.9	—	—	—	—	2,642.0	86.7	298.8	217.7	72.9
Sweden	144	2,395.5	297.4	—	—	—	—	2,098.1	87.6	246.5	123.4	50.0
Switzerland	146	3,458.5	393.5	—	—	—	—	3,065.0	88.6	—	20.4	—
United Kingdom	112	10,738.5	1,528.9	—	—	—	—	9,209.7	85.8	1,913.1	208.8	10.9
Developing Countries	200	82,911.8	6,264.9	19,146.6	23.1	15,251.6	3,895.0	91,901.1	110.8	6,838.1	4,894.5	71.6
Africa	605	11,498.1	274.1	2,234.1	19.4	659.6	1,574.5	11,884.2	103.4	1,382.5	391.9	28.3
Algeria	612	1,254.7	85.1	—	—	—	—	1,169.6	93.2	128.6	.7	.5
Angola	614	286.3	—	—	—	—	....	286.4	100.1	—	.2	—
Benin	638	61.9	2.2	.9	1.4	—	.9	59.7	96.5	9.4	.1	.7
Botswana	616	63.0	7.1	—	—	—	—	55.9	88.7	4.4	36.2	830.4
Burkina Faso	748	60.2	7.4	13.8	22.9	—	13.8	52.9	87.8	9.4	—	.2
Burundi	618	77.0	.4	40.7	52.9	—	40.7	76.6	99.5	13.7	.3	1.9
Cameroon	622	185.7	.7	5.3	2.9	—	5.3	185.0	99.6	24.5	3.1	12.6
Cape Verde	624	9.6	—	8.6	90.0	—	8.6	9.6	99.9	.6	—	5.6
Central African Rep.	626	55.7	.2	30.4	54.6	12.5	17.9	68.1	122.2	9.3	3.0	32.3
Chad	628	56.0	.3	50.4	90.0	—	50.4	55.7	99.5	9.4	—	—
Comoros	632	8.9	.5	—	—	—	—	8.4	93.9	.7	—	.8
Congo, Dem. Rep. of	636	533.0	—	553.5	103.8	—	553.5	533.0	100.0	86.3	1.8	2.1
Congo, Republic of	634	84.6	.5	17.1	20.2	—	17.1	84.1	99.4	9.7	.3	2.8
Côte d'Ivoire	662	325.2	.6	116.9	35.9	—	116.9	324.6	99.8	37.8	.6	1.5
Djibouti	611	15.9	1.1	12.5	78.9	—	12.5	14.8	93.1	1.2	.2	19.3
Equatorial Guinea	642	32.6	—	—	—	—	—	32.6	100.0	5.8	.4	7.6
Eritrea	643	15.9	—	—	—	—	—	15.9	100.0	—	—	—
Ethiopia	644	133.7	7.2	—	—	—	—	126.5	94.6	11.2	—	.4
Gabon	646	154.3	.2	44.4	28.8	44.4	—	198.5	128.6	14.1	.3	2.4
Gambia, The	648	31.1	1.5	13.2	42.4	—	13.2	29.6	95.2	5.1	.9	17.1
Ghana	652	369.0	—	79.1	21.4	—	79.1	369.0	100.0	63.0	.2	.3
Guinea	656	107.1	.1	54.8	51.2	—	54.8	107.0	99.9	17.6	2.6	14.8
Guinea-Bissau	654	14.2	—	6.6	46.8	—	6.6	14.2	100.0	1.2	.4	30.2
Kenya	664	271.4	12.8	105.2	38.8	—	105.2	258.6	95.3	37.0	.1	.3
Lesotho	666	34.9	3.6	24.5	70.2	—	24.5	31.3	89.8	3.7	.2	6.1
Liberia	668	71.3	—	223.4	313.3	200.5	22.9	271.8	381.2	21.0	—	—
Madagascar	674	122.2	—	11.3	9.3	—	11.3	122.2	100.0	19.3	—	.2
Malawi	676	69.4	2.3	48.2	69.5	10.8	37.4	78.0	112.3	11.0	.7	6.8
Mali	678	93.3	9.3	4.0	4.3	—	4.0	84.0	90.1	15.9	.1	.5
Mauritania	682	64.4	—	—	—	—	—	64.4	100.0	9.7	.2	2.2
Mauritius	684	101.6	11.8	—	—	—	—	89.8	88.4	15.7	18.2	115.3
Morocco	686	588.2	70.4	—	—	—	—	517.8	88.0	85.7	46.7	54.5
Mozambique	688	113.6	—	6.5	5.7	—	6.5	113.6	100.0	—	.1	—
Namibia	728	136.5	.1	—	—	—	—	136.4	100.0	—	—	—
Niger	692	65.8	8.6	17.6	26.8	—	17.6	57.2	86.9	9.4	.1	1.1
Nigeria	694	1,753.2	.1	—	—	—	—	1,753.1	100.0	157.2	.4	.3
Rwanda	714	80.1	—	2.9	3.6	—	2.9	80.1	100.0	13.7	15.2	110.7
São Tomé & Príncipe	716	7.4	—	2.5	33.3	—	2.5	7.4	100.0	.6	.2	39.9
Senegal	722	161.8	1.6	17.3	10.7	—	17.3	160.2	99.0	24.5	.5	2.2
Seychelles	718	8.8	—	—	—	—	—	8.8	100.0	.4	—	1.8
Sierra Leone	724	103.7	—	137.6	132.7	—	137.6	103.7	100.0	17.5	21.2	121.5
Somalia	726	44.2	—	112.0	253.4	96.7	15.3	140.9	318.8	13.7	—	—
South Africa	199	1,868.5	.9	—	—	—	—	1,867.7	100.0	220.4	222.9	101.2
Sudan	732	169.7	—	353.9	208.5	294.6	59.2	464.3	273.6	52.2	—	—
Swaziland	734	50.7	6.6	—	—	—	—	44.1	87.1	6.4	2.5	38.6
Tanzania	738	198.9	10.0	8.4	4.2	—	8.4	188.9	95.0	31.4	—	—
Togo	742	73.4	.3	7.6	10.4	—	7.6	73.1	99.5	11.0	—	.2
Tunisia	744	286.5	20.2	—	—	—	—	266.3	92.9	34.2	.7	2.2
Uganda	746	180.5	—	6.0	3.3	—	6.0	180.5	100.0	29.4	.3	1.1
Zambia	754	489.1	—	22.0	4.5	—	22.0	489.1	100.0	68.3	10.0	14.7
Zimbabwe	698	353.4	.3	75.0	21.2	—	75.0	353.1	99.9	10.2	—	—

Fund Accounts: Position to Date

(As of June 30, 2006 and Expressed in Millions of SDRs)

| | Quota | Reserve Position in the Fund | Total Fund Credit and Loans Outstanding | | | | Fund Holdings of Currency | | SDR Department | Holdings of SDR | |
			Total Amount	Percent of Quota	Outstanding Purchases (GRA)	Outstanding Loans	Amount	Percent of Quota	Net Cumulative Allocation	Amount	Percent of Allocation
	(1)	(2)	(3)	(4)	(5)	(6)	(7)	(8)	(9)	(10)	(11)
Asia.............................. 505	**22,046.8**	**2,194.5**	**4,356.1**	**19.8**	**2,884.9**	**1,471.2**	**22,737.7**	**103.1**	**2,043.7**	**1,517.6**	**74.3**
Afghanistan, I.R. of......... 512	161.9	—	—	—	—	—	161.9	100.0	26.7	.1	.4
Bangladesh................... 513	533.3	.2	283.1	53.1	—	283.1	533.1	100.0	47.1	.7	1.5
Bhutan......................... 514	6.3	1.0	—	—	—	—	5.3	83.8	—	.3	—
Brunei Darussalam......... 516	215.2	24.6	—	—	—	—	190.8	88.7	—	10.7	—
Cambodia..................... 522	87.5	—	—	—	—	—	87.5	100.0	15.4	—	.1
China,P.R.: Mainland..... 924	6,369.2	758.3	—	—	—	—	5,611.0	88.1	236.8	938.5	396.3
China,P.R.:Hong Kong..... 532	....	....	....	....	....	—	....	....	....	....	....
Fiji............................. 819	70.3	15.4	—	—	—	—	54.9	78.1	7.0	5.7	82.6
India........................... 534	4,158.2	516.1	—	—	—	—	3,642.1	87.6	681.2	.3	—
Indonesia.................... 536	2,079.3	145.5	2,473.2	118.9	2,473.2	—	4,407.0	211.9	239.0	11.4	4.8
Kiribati....................... 826	5.6	—	—	—	—	....	5.6	100.0	—	—	—
Korea......................... 542	1,633.6	189.1	—	—	—	—	1,444.6	88.4	72.9	33.3	45.7
Lao People's Dem.Rep.... 544	52.9	—	19.3	36.5	—	19.3	52.9	100.0	9.4	9.8	104.3
Malaysia...................... 548	1,486.6	175.9	—	—	—	—	1,310.7	88.2	139.0	139.9	100.6
Maldives...................... 556	8.2	1.6	4.1	50.0	4.1	—	10.7	131.1	.3	.3	115.4
Marshall Islands,Rep...... 867	3.5	—	—	—	—	—	3.5	100.0	—	—	—
Micronesia, Fed.Sts........ 868	5.1	—	—	—	—	—	5.1	100.0	—	1.3	—
Mongolia..................... 948	51.1	.1	22.2	43.4	—	22.2	51.0	99.7	—	.1	—
Myanmar..................... 518	258.4	—	—	—	—	—	258.4	100.0	43.5	.2	.4
Nepal.......................... 558	71.3	—	14.3	20.0	—	14.3	71.3	100.0	8.1	6.1	75.0
Pakistan...................... 564	1,033.7	—	1,008.0	97.5	44.2	963.8	1,077.8	104.3	170.0	147.2	86.6
Palau.......................... 565	3.1	.1	—	—	—	—	3.1	100.0	—	—	—
Papua New Guinea........ 853	131.6	.4	—	—	—	—	131.2	99.7	9.3	—	.2
Philippines................... 566	879.9	87.5	209.2	23.8	209.2	—	1,001.5	113.8	116.6	.6	.5
Samoa........................ 862	11.6	.7	—	—	—	—	10.9	94.1	1.1	2.5	217.7
Singapore.................... 576	862.5	100.7	—	—	—	—	761.9	88.3	16.5	204.4	1,240.4
Solomon Islands............ 813	10.4	.6	—	—	—	—	9.9	94.7	.7	—	.9
Sri Lanka..................... 524	413.4	47.9	192.6	46.6	154.2	38.4	519.8	125.7	70.9	1.4	2.0
Thailand...................... 578	1,081.9	124.6	—	—	—	—	957.3	88.5	84.7	.6	.7
Timor-Leste.................. 537	8.2	—	—	—	—	—	8.2	100.0	—	—	—
Tonga......................... 866	6.9	1.7	—	—	—	—	5.2	75.2	—	.3	—
Vanuatu...................... 846	17.0	2.5	—	—	—	—	14.5	85.3	—	1.0	—
Vietnam...................... 582	329.1	—	130.2	39.6	—	130.2	329.1	100.0	47.7	.9	2.0
Europe...................... 170	**17,270.1**	**709.2**	**10,061.2**	**58.3**	**9,446.1**	**615.1**	**26,007.2**	**150.6**	**374.1**	**248.0**	**66.3**
Albania....................... 914	48.7	3.4	63.1	129.6	1.2	61.9	46.6	95.6	—	7.6	—
Armenia....................... 911	92.0	—	115.8	125.8	—	115.8	92.0	100.0	—	8.3	—
Azerbaijan, Republic of... 912	160.9	—	101.9	63.3	17.6	84.3	178.5	110.9	—	9.5	—
Belarus....................... 913	386.4	—	—	—	—	—	386.4	100.0	—	—	—
Bosnia & Herzegovina..... 963	169.1	—	28.0	16.5	28.0	—	197.1	116.5	20.5	.3	1.6
Bulgaria...................... 918	640.2	33.1	272.4	42.5	272.4	—	879.5	137.4	—	.7	—
Croatia........................ 960	365.1	.2	—	—	—	—	364.9	100.0	44.2	.1	.3
Cyprus........................ 423	139.6	16.0	—	—	—	—	123.6	88.5	19.4	2.9	14.8
Czech Republic............. 935	819.3	91.1	—	—	—	—	728.2	88.9	—	9.8	—
Estonia........................ 939	65.2	—	—	—	—	—	65.2	100.0	—	.1	—
Georgia....................... 915	150.3	—	159.3	106.0	—	159.3	150.3	100.0	—	1.2	—
Hungary...................... 944	1,038.4	121.3	—	—	—	—	917.1	88.3	47.0	—	—
Kazakhstan.................. 916	365.7	—	—	—	—	—	365.7	100.0	—	.8	—
Kyrgyz Republic............ 917	88.8	—	116.4	131.1	—	116.4	88.8	100.0	—	10.3	—
Latvia......................... 941	126.8	.1	—	—	—	—	126.8	100.0	—	.1	—
Lithuania..................... 946	144.2	—	—	—	—	—	144.2	100.0	—	.1	—
Macedonia, FYR............ 962	68.9	—	40.5	58.8	30.8	9.7	99.7	144.7	8.4	.7	8.4
Malta.......................... 181	102.0	40.3	—	—	—	—	61.7	60.5	11.3	33.0	292.2
Moldova...................... 921	123.2	—	70.0	56.8	31.8	38.2	155.0	125.8	—	.1	—
Poland........................ 964	1,369.0	110.7	—	—	—	—	1,258.4	91.9	—	57.1	—
Romania...................... 968	1,030.2	—	120.6	11.7	120.6	—	1,150.8	111.7	76.0	.4	.6
Russia........................ 922	5,945.4	154.1	—	—	—	—	5,791.3	97.4	—	4.7	—
Serbia & Montenegro...... 965	467.7	—	487.5	104.2	487.5	—	955.2	204.2	56.7	27.7	48.9
Slovak Republic............ 936	357.5	—	—	—	—	—	357.5	100.0	—	.9	—
Slovenia...................... 961	231.7	26.3	—	—	—	—	205.4	88.6	25.4	8.3	32.5
Tajikistan..................... 923	87.0	—	29.4	33.8	—	29.4	87.0	100.0	—	3.8	—
Turkey........................ 186	964.0	112.8	7,765.0	805.5	7,765.0	—	8,616.3	893.8	112.3	12.2	10.8
Turkmenistan............... 925	75.2	—	—	—	—	—	75.2	100.0	—	—	—
Ukraine....................... 926	1,372.0	—	691.4	50.4	691.4	—	2,063.4	150.4	—	.5	—
Uzbekistan................... 927	275.6	—	—	—	—	—	275.6	100.0	—	—	—
Middle East................ 405	**16,162.9**	**1,929.9**	**620.8**	**3.8**	**457.1**	**163.8**	**14,690.9**	**90.9**	**986.5**	**1,816.8**	**184.2**
Bahrain, Kingdom of...... 419	135.0	71.2	—	—	—	—	63.8	47.3	6.2	2.6	42.3
Egypt.......................... 469	943.7	—	—	—	—	—	943.7	100.0	135.9	76.2	56.0
Iran, I.R. of.................. 429	1,497.2	—	—	—	—	—	1,497.2	100.0	244.1	275.2	112.7
Iraq............................ 433	1,188.4	171.1	297.1	25.0	297.1	—	1,314.4	110.6	68.5	292.6	427.3
Israel.......................... 436	928.2	105.2	—	—	—	—	823.0	88.7	106.4	13.2	12.5
Jordan........................ 439	170.5	.2	138.6	81.3	138.6	—	308.9	181.2	16.9	.6	3.7
Kuwait........................ 443	1,381.1	158.1	—	—	—	—	1,223.0	88.6	26.7	133.3	498.3
Lebanon...................... 446	203.0	18.8	—	—	—	—	184.2	90.7	4.4	22.5	512.8
Libya.......................... 672	1,123.7	395.5	—	—	—	—	728.2	64.8	58.8	507.6	863.7
Oman.......................... 449	194.0	18.1	—	—	—	—	176.0	90.7	6.3	10.7	171.4
Qatar.......................... 453	263.8	30.4	—	—	—	—	233.4	88.5	12.8	26.1	203.8
Saudi Arabia................. 456	6,985.5	891.0	—	—	—	—	6,094.5	87.2	195.5	406.5	207.9

Fund Accounts: Position to Date

(As of June 30, 2006 and Expressed in Millions of SDRs)

		Quota	Reserve Position in the Fund	Total Fund Credit and Loans Outstanding				Fund Holdings of Currency		SDR Department		
				Total Amount	Percent of Quota	Outstanding Purchases (GRA)	Outstanding Loans	Amount	Percent of Quota	Net Cumulative Allocation	Holdings of SDR	
											Amount	Percent of Allocation
		(1)	(2)	(3)	(4)	(5)	(6)	(7)	(8)	(9)	(10)	(11)
Middle East(Cont.)												
Syrian Arab Republic	463	293.6	—	—	—	—	—	293.6	100.0	36.6	36.6	100.0
United Arab Emirates	466	611.7	70.3	—	—	—	—	542.0	88.6	38.7	7.6	19.5
Yemen, Republic of	474	243.5	—	185.1	76.0	21.3	163.8	264.8	108.8	28.7	5.5	19.1
Western Hemisphere	**205**	**15,933.9**	**1,157.3**	**1,874.4**	**11.8**	**1,803.8**	**70.5**	**16,581.1**	**104.1**	**2,051.3**	**920.2**	**44.9**
Antigua and Barbuda	311	13.5	—	—	—	—	—	13.5	100.0	—	—	—
Argentina	213	2,117.1	.2	—	—	—	—	2,116.9	100.0	318.4	191.7	60.2
Bahamas, The	313	130.3	6.3	—	—	—	—	124.0	95.2	10.2	—	.3
Barbados	316	67.5	5.4	—	—	—	—	62.1	92.0	8.0	—	.2
Belize	339	18.8	4.2	—	—	—	—	14.6	77.5	—	1.8	—
Bolivia	218	171.5	8.9	9.7	5.6	9.7	—	172.3	100.5	26.7	27.0	101.1
Brazil	223	3,036.1	—	—	—	—	—	3,036.5	100.0	358.7	12.2	3.4
Chile	228	856.1	99.5	—	—	—	—	756.6	88.4	121.9	36.7	30.1
Colombia	233	774.0	285.8	—	—	—	—	488.2	63.1	114.3	123.9	108.4
Costa Rica	238	164.1	20.0	—	—	—	—	144.1	87.8	23.7	.1	.3
Dominica	321	8.2	—	7.6	92.3	2.2	5.4	10.4	126.8	.6	—	1.6
Dominican Republic	243	218.9	—	349.2	159.5	349.2	—	568.1	259.5	31.6	46.9	148.4
Ecuador	248	302.3	17.2	30.2	10.0	30.2	—	315.3	104.3	32.9	.8	2.5
El Salvador	253	171.3	—	—	—	—	—	171.3	100.0	25.0	25.0	100.0
Grenada	328	11.7	—	7.0	60.2	5.5	1.6	17.2	146.9	.9	.1	15.9
Guatemala	258	210.2	—	—	—	—	—	210.2	100.0	27.7	4.2	15.2
Guyana	336	90.9	—	27.8	30.6	—	27.8	90.9	100.0	14.5	1.4	9.6
Haiti	263	81.9	.1	22.0	26.9	20.5	1.5	102.3	124.9	13.7	6.9	50.6
Honduras	268	129.5	8.6	20.3	15.7	—	20.3	120.9	93.3	19.1	.2	.9
Jamaica	343	273.5	—	—	—	—	—	273.5	100.0	40.6	.2	.4
Mexico	273	2,585.8	300.8	—	—	—	—	2,285.0	88.4	290.0	316.5	109.1
Nicaragua	278	130.0	—	13.9	10.7	—	13.9	130.0	100.0	19.5	—	.1
Panama	283	206.6	11.9	13.3	6.5	13.3	—	208.1	100.7	26.3	.8	3.0
Paraguay	288	99.9	21.5	—	—	—	—	78.4	78.5	13.7	89.7	654.6
Peru	293	638.4	—	26.8	4.2	26.8	—	665.2	104.2	91.3	.5	.5
St. Kitts and Nevis	361	8.9	.1	—	—	—	—	8.8	99.1	—	—	—
St. Lucia	362	15.3	—	—	—	—	—	15.3	100.0	.7	1.5	207.2
St. Vincent & Grens	364	8.3	.5	—	—	—	—	7.8	94.0	.4	—	1.6
Suriname	366	92.1	6.1	—	—	—	—	86.0	93.4	7.8	1.0	12.4
Trinidad and Tobago	369	335.6	38.4	—	—	—	—	297.2	88.6	46.2	2.5	5.3
Uruguay	298	306.5	—	1,346.6	439.3	1,346.6	—	1,653.1	539.3	50.0	26.8	53.7
Venezuela, Rep. Bol	299	2,659.1	321.9	—	—	—	—	2,337.2	87.9	316.9	1.8	.6
Memorandum Items												
Oil Exporting Ctys	**999**	**20,991.7**	**2,287.1**	**2,770.3**	**13.2**	**2,770.3**	**—**	**21,475.7**	**102.3**	**1,493.0**	**1,673.8**	**112.1**
Non-Oil Develop.Ctys	**201**	**61,920.1**	**3,977.9**	**16,376.3**	**26.4**	**12,481.3**	**3,895.0**	**70,425.4**	**113.7**	**5,345.1**	**3,220.8**	**60.3**

Financing Components of Members' Outstanding Obligations to the Fund

(As of June 30, 2006 and Expressed in Millions of SDRs)

			Outstanding Purchases (GRA)									Outstanding Loans			
		Total Fund Credit and Loans Outstanding	Ordinary Resources					Borrower Resources				SAF Arrangements	PRGF Arrangements		Trust Fund
			Total Amount	CCFF	STF	Stand-by/ Credit Tranche	Extended Fund Facility	SFF	EAR	GAB	NAB	SDA Resources	SDA Resources	PRGF Trust Resources	Administered Accounts
		(1)	(2)	(3)	(4)	(5)	(6)	(7)	(8)	(9)	(10)	(11)	(12)	(13)	(14)
All Countries	010	19,146.6	15,251.6	82.8	—	10,297.2	4,507.7	94.4	269.9	—	—	8.8	—	3,797.6	88.6
Industrial Countries	110	—		....						—	—	....	....		....
Developing Countries	200	19,146.6	15,251.6	82.8	—	10,297.2	4,507.7	94.4	269.9	—	—	8.8	—	3,797.6	88.6
Africa	605	2,234.1	659.6	82.8	....	147.3	65.6	94.4	269.9	—	—	8.8	—	1,477.0	88.6
Algeria	612	—	—	....	....	....	....	....	....	—	—	....	....	—	....
Angola	614	—	—	....	....	....	....	....	—	—	....	....		—	....
Benin	638	.9	—	....	....	....	....	....	—	—	....	—		.9	—
Botswana	616	—	—	....						—	—	....	....	—	....
Burkina Faso	748	13.8	—	—		....				—	—	—	—	13.8	—
Burundi	618	40.7	—	—		....				—	—	—	—	40.7	—
Cameroon	622	5.3	—	—		—				—	—	—	—	5.3	—
Cape Verde	624	8.6	—	—	....					—	—	—	—	8.6	....
Central African Rep.	626	30.4	12.5	—	....	12.5	....			—	—	—	—	17.9	—
Chad	628	50.4	—	—		—				—	—	—	—	50.4	—
Comoros	632	—	—	....						—	—	—	—	—	—
Congo, Dem. Rep. of	636	553.5	—	—		—				—	—	—	—	553.5	—
Congo, Republic of	634	17.1	—	—		—				—	—	—	—	17.1	—
Côte d'Ivoire	662	116.9	—	—		—				—	—	—	—	116.9	—
Djibouti	611	12.5	—	—		—				—	—	—	—	12.5	....
Equatorial Guinea	642	—	—	....						—	—	—	—	—	....
Eritrea	643	—	—							—	—	—	—	—	—
Ethiopia	644	—	—							—	—	—	—	—	....
Gabon	646	44.4	44.4	—	....	41.7	2.8	—	—	—	—	—	—	—	....
Gambia, The	648	13.2	—	—		—		—	—	—	—	—	—	13.2	—
Ghana	652	79.1	—	—	....	—				—	—	—	—	79.1	—
Guinea	656	54.8	—	—			....			—	—	—	—	54.8	—
Guinea-Bissau	654	6.6	—	—		—				—	—	—	—	6.6	....
Kenya	664	105.2	—	—		—				—	—	—	—	105.2	—
Lesotho	666	24.5	—	—		—				—	—	—	—	24.5	—
Liberia	668	223.4	200.5	34.7	—	45.2	....	36.3	84.3	—	—	—	....	—	22.9
Madagascar	674	11.3	—	—		—				—	—	—	—	11.3	—
Malawi	676	48.2	10.8	—		10.8				—	—	—	—	37.4	—
Mali	678	4.0	—	—	....	....				—	—	—	—	4.0	—
Mauritania	682	—	—	—		—				—	—	—	—	—	—
Mauritius	684	—	—	—		—				—	—	—	—	—	—
Morocco	686	—	—	—		—				—	—	—	—	—	—
Mozambique	688	6.5	—	....	....	—		....		—	—	—	—	6.5	....
Namibia	728	—	—	—		—				—	—	—	—	—	—
Niger	692	17.6	—	—		—				—	—	—	—	17.6	—
Nigeria	694	—	—	....	....	—				—	—	....	....	—	....
Rwanda	714	2.9	—	—		—				—	—	—	—	2.9	....
São Tomé & Príncipe	716	2.5	—	—		—				—	—	—	—	2.5	—
Senegal	722	17.3	—	—		—				—	—	—	—	17.3	....
Seychelles	718	—	—	—	....	....				—	—	—	—	—	....
Sierra Leone	724	137.6	—	—		—				—	—	—	—	137.6	—
Somalia	726	112.0	96.7	28.5	....	12.6	....		55.5	—	—	8.8	—	—	6.5
South Africa	199	—	—	—		—				—	—	—	....	....	....
Sudan	732	353.9	294.6	19.6	....	24.5	62.9	58.1	130.1	—	—	—	—	—	59.2
Swaziland	734	—	—	—		—				—	—	....	....	—	—
Tanzania	738	8.4	—	—		—				—	—	—	—	8.4	—
Togo	742	7.6	—	—		—				—	—	—	—	7.6	—
Tunisia	744	—	—	—		—				—	—	....	....	—	....
Uganda	746	6.0	—	—		—				—	—	—	—	6.0	—
Zambia	754	22.0	—	—		—				—	—	—	—	22.0	—
Zimbabwe	698	75.0	—	—		—				—	—	—	—	75.0	—
Asia	505	4,356.1	2,884.9	—	—	137.7	2,747.3	—	—	—	—	....	....	1,471.2	—
Afghanistan, I.R. of	512	—	—	—		—				—	—	....	....	—	—
Bangladesh	513	283.1	—	—		—				—	—	—	—	283.1	—
Bhutan	514	—	—	—	....					—	—	....	....	—	—
Brunei Darussalam	516	—	—	—	....					—	—	....	....	—	—
Cambodia	522	—	—	—		—				—	—	—	—	—	—
China, People's Rep.	924	—	—	—		—				—	—	....	....	—	—
Fiji	819	—	—	—		—				—	—	—	—	—	—
India	534	—	—	—		—				—	—	—	—	—	—
Indonesia	536	2,473.2	2,473.2	—	—	—	2,473.2	....		—	—	—	—	....	....
Kiribati	826	—	—	—		—				—	—	—	—	—	—
Korea	542	—	—	—		—				—	—	—	—	—	—
Lao People's Dem.Rep.	544	19.3	—	—		—				—	—	—	—	19.3	—
Malaysia	548	—	—	—		—				—	—	—	—	—	—
Maldives	556	4.1	4.1	....	....	4.1	....			—	—	—	—	—	—
Marshall Islands,Rep.	867	—	—	....	....					—	—	....	....	—	—
Micronesia, Fed.Sts.	868	—	—	—		—				—	—	....	....	—	—
Mongolia	948	22.2	—	—		—				—	—	—	—	22.2	—
Myanmar	518	—	—	—		—				—	—	....	....	—	—
Nepal	558	14.3	—	—		—				—	—	—	—	14.3	—
Pakistan	564	1,008.0	44.2	—	....	—	44.2			—	—	—	—	963.8	—

Financing Components of Members' Outstanding Obligations to the Fund

(As of June 30, 2006 and Expressed in Millions of SDRs)

		Total Fund Credit and Loans Outstanding		Outstanding Purchases (GRA)								Outstanding Loans			
				Ordinary Resources				Borrower Resources				SAF Arrangements	PRGF Arrangements		Trust Fund
			Total Amount	CCFF	STF	Stand-by/ Credit Tranche	Extended Fund Facility	SFF	EAR	GAB	NAB	SDA Resources	SDA Resources	PRGF Trust Resources	Administered Accounts
		(1)	(2)	(3)	(4)	(5)	(6)	(7)	(8)	(9)	(10)	(11)	(12)	(13)	(14)
Asia(Cont.)															
Palau	565	—	—	—	....	—	—	....	—	—	—	—	....	....	—
Papua New Guinea	853	—	—	—	....	—	—	....	—	—	—	—	....	....	—
Philippines	566	209.2	209.2	—	....	—	209.2	....	—	—	—	—	....	....	—
Samoa	862	—	—	—	....	—	—	....	—	—	—	—	....	....	—
Singapore	576	—	—	—	....	—	—	....	—	—	—	—	....	....	....
Solomon Islands	813	—	—	—	....	—	—	....	—	—	—	—	....	....	....
Sri Lanka	524	192.6	154.2	—	—	133.6	20.6	—	—	—	—	—	—	38.4	—
Thailand	578	—	—	—	....	—	....	—	—	—	—	—	....	....	—
Tonga	866	—	—	—	....	—	—	....	—	—	—	—	....	....	—
Vanuatu	846	—	—	—	....	—	....	....	—	—	—	—	....	....	—
Vietnam	582	130.2	—	—	—	—	—	—	—	—	—	—	....	130.2	—
Europe	170	**10,061.2**	**9,446.1**	—	—	7,950.0	1,496.1	—	—	—	—	—	—	**615.1**	—
Albania	914	63.1	1.2	—	—	—	1.2	—	—	—	—	—	—	61.9	—
Armenia	911	115.8	—	—	—	—	—	—	—	—	—	—	—	115.8	—
Azerbaijan, Republic of	912	101.9	17.6	—	—	—	17.6	—	—	—	—	—	—	84.3	—
Belarus	913	—	—	—	—	—	—	....	—	—	—	—	....	....	—
Bosnia & Herzegovina	963	28.0	28.0	—	—	28.0	—	—	—	—	—	—	—	—	—
Bulgaria	918	272.4	272.4	—	—	6.5	265.9	—	—	—	—	—	—	—	—
Croatia	960	—	—	—	—	—	—	—	—	—	—	—	....	....	—
Cyprus	423	—	—	—	—	—	—	—	—	—	—	—	....	....	—
Czech Republic	935	—	—	—	—	—	—	—	—	—	—	—	....	....	—
Estonia	939	—	—	—	—	—	—	—	—	—	—	—	—	—	—
Georgia	915	159.3	—	—	—	—	—	—	—	—	—	—	—	159.3	—
Hungary	944	—	—	—	—	—	—	—	—	—	—	—	....	....	—
Kazakhstan	916	—	—	—	—	—	—	—	—	—	—	—	....	....	—
Kyrgyz Republic	917	116.4	—	—	—	—	—	—	—	—	—	—	—	116.4	—
Latvia	941	—	—	—	—	—	—	—	—	—	—	—	—	—	—
Lithuania	946	—	—	—	—	—	—	—	—	—	—	—	—	—	—
Macedonia, FYR	962	40.5	30.8	—	—	30.0	.8	—	—	—	—	—	—	9.7	—
Malta	181	—	—	—	....	—	....	....	—	—	—	—	....	....	....
Moldova	921	70.0	31.8	—	—	—	31.8	—	—	—	—	—	—	38.2	—
Poland	964	—	—	—	—	—	—	—	—	—	—	—	....	....	—
Romania	968	120.6	120.6	—	—	120.6	—	—	—	—	—	—	....	....	—
Russia	922	—	—	—	—	—	—	—	—	—	—	—	—	—	—
Serbia & Montenegro	965	487.5	487.5	—	—	—	487.5	—	—	—	—	—	....	....	—
Slovak Republic	936	—	—	—	—	—	—	—	—	—	—	—	....	....	—
Slovenia	961	—	—	—	....	—	—	—	—	—	—	—	....	....	—
Tajikistan	923	29.4	—	—	—	—	—	—	—	—	—	—	—	29.4	—
Turkey	186	7,765.0	7,765.0	—	....	7,765.0	....	—	—	—	—	—	—	—	—
Turkmenistan	925	—	—	—	—	—	—	—	—	—	—	—	—	—	—
Ukraine	926	691.4	691.4	—	—	—	691.4	—	—	—	—	—	—	—	—
Uzbekistan	927	—	—	—	—	—	—	—	—	—	—	—	—	—	—
Middle East	405	**620.8**	**457.1**	—	....	298.4	158.6	....	....	—	—	—	—	**163.8**	—
Bahrain, Kingdom of	419	—	—	....	....	....	....	....	....	—	—	—	....	....	....
Egypt	469	—	—	....	....	—	....	....	....	—	—	—	....	....	....
Iran, I.R. of	429	—	—	—	....	—	—	....	....	—	—	—	....	....	....
Iraq	433	297.1	297.1	—	....	297.1	—	....	....	—	—	—	....	....	....
Israel	436	—	—	....	....	—	—	....	....	—	—	—	....	....	....
Jordan	439	138.6	138.6	—	....	1.3	137.3	....	....	—	—	—	....	....	....
Kuwait	443	—	—	....	....	....	....	....	....	—	—	—	....	....	....
Lebanon	446	—	—	....	....	....	....	....	....	—	—	—	....	....	....
Libya	672	—	—	....	....	....	....	....	....	—	—	—	....	....	....
Oman	449	—	—	....	....	—	—	....	....	—	—	—	....	....	....
Qatar	453	—	—	....	....	—	—	....	....	—	—	—	....	....	....
Saudi Arabia	456	—	—	....	....	—	—	....	....	—	—	—	....	....	....
Syrian Arab Republic	463	—	—	....	....	—	—	....	....	—	—	—	....	....	....
United Arab Emirates	466	—	—	....	....	—	—	....	....	—	—	—	....	....	....
Yemen, Republic of	474	185.1	21.3	—	....	—	21.3	....	....	—	—	—	....	163.8	—
Western Hemisphere	205	**1,874.4**	**1,803.8**	—	....	1,763.8	40.1	—	—	—	—	—	—	**70.5**	—
Antigua and Barbuda	311	—	—	—	....	....	....	....	—	—	—	—	....	....	—
Argentina	213	—	—	—	....	—	—	—	—	—	—	—	....	....	—
Bahamas, The	313	—	—	—	....	....	....	....	—	—	—	—	....	....	—
Barbados	316	—	—	—	....	—	....	....	—	—	—	—	....	....	—
Belize	339	—	—	—	....	....	....	....	—	—	—	—	....	....	—
Bolivia	218	9.7	9.7	—	....	9.7	....	—	—	—	—	—	....	....	—
Brazil	223	—	—	—	....	—	....	—	—	—	—	—	—	—	—
Chile	228	—	—	—	....	—	....	—	—	—	—	—	—	—	—
Colombia	233	—	—	—	....	—	—	—	—	—	—	—	....	....	—
Costa Rica	238	—	—	—	....	—	—	—	—	—	—	—	....	....	—
Dominica	321	7.6	2.2	—	....	2.2	—	—	—	—	—	—	....	5.4	—
Dominican Republic	243	349.2	349.2	—	....	349.2	—	—	—	—	—	—	....	....	—
Ecuador	248	30.2	30.2	—	....	30.2	....	—	—	—	—	—	....	....	—
El Salvador	253	—	—	—	....	—	....	—	—	—	—	—	....	....	—
Grenada	328	7.0	5.5	—	....	5.5	—	—	—	—	—	—	....	1.6	—
Guatemala	258	—	—	—	....	—	....	—	—	—	—	—	....	....	—

Financing Components of Members' Outstanding Obligations to the Fund

(As of June 30, 2006 and Expressed in Millions of SDRs)

	Total Fund Credit and Loans Outstanding	Outstanding Purchases (GRA)									Outstanding Loans			
			Ordinary Resources				Borrower Resources				SAF Arrangements	PRGF Arrangements		Trust Fund
		Total Amount	CCFF	STF	Stand-by/ Credit Tranche	Extended Fund Facility	SFF	EAR	GAB	NAB	SDA Resources	SDA Resources	PRGF Trust Resources	Administered Accounts
	(1)	(2)	(3)	(4)	(5)	(6)	(7)	(8)	(9)	(10)	(11)	(12)	(13)	(14)
Western Hemisphere(C														
Guyana........................ 336	27.8	—	—	....	20.5	—	—	—	—	—	—	....	27.8	—
Haiti.............................. 263	22.0	20.5	—	....	20.5	—	—	—	—	—	—	....	1.5	—
Honduras...................... 268	20.3	—	—	....	—	—	—	—	—	—	....	—	20.3	—
Jamaica......................... 343	—	—	—	....	—	—	—	—	—	—	....	....	....	....
Mexico.......................... 273	—	—	—	....	—	—	—	—	—	—	....	....	....	....
Nicaragua...................... 278	13.9	—	—	....	—	....	....	....	—	—	....	....	13.9	....
Panama......................... 283	13.3	13.3	—	....	—	13.3	....	....	—	—	....	....	....	....
Paraguay....................... 288	—	—	....	....	—	—	....	....	—	—	....	....	....	....
Peru.............................. 293	26.8	26.8	....	....	—	26.8	....	—	—	—	....	....	....	....
St. Kitts and Nevis.......... 361	—	—	....	....	—	....	....	....	—	—	—	....	....	....
St. Lucia........................ 362	—	—	—	....	—	....	....	....	—	—	....	....	....	....
St. Vincent & Grens........ 364	—	—	....	....	—	....	....	....	—	—	....	....	....	....
Suriname....................... 366	—	—	....	....	....	....	....	—	—	—	....	....	....	....
Trinidad and Tobago....... 369	—	—	—	....	—	....	....	—	—	—	....	....	....	....
Uruguay........................ 298	1,346.6	1,346.6	—	....	1,346.6	....	....	—	—	—	....	....	....	....
Venezuela, Rep. Bol........ 299	—	....	....	....	....	....	....	—	—	—	....	....	....	....
Memorandum Items														
Oil Exporting Ctys...... 999	2,770.3	2,770.3	—	—	297.1	2,473.2	....	—	—	—	....	....	....	....
Non-Oil Develop.Ctys. 201	16,376.3	12,481.3	82.8	—	10,000.1	2,034.5	94.4	269.9	—	—	8.8	—	3,797.6	88.6

Purchases

2kk

Expressed in Millions of SDRs

		1994	1995	1996	1997	1998	1999	2000	2001	2002	2003	2004	2005
World	001	4,979.5	16,967.9	5,271.0	16,112.9	20,586.2	10,010.1	7,178.0	23,761.6	25,237.0	20,323.1	4,170.7	2,288.6
Developing Countries	200	4,979.5	16,967.9	5,271.0	16,112.9	20,586.2	10,010.1	7,178.0	23,761.6	25,237.0	20,323.1	4,170.7	2,288.6
Africa	605	761.5	1,038.5	556.9	370.1	313.6	266.9	35.6	—	27.0	9.6	47.2	—
Algeria	612	587.5	312.8	512.2	337.6	253.3	223.5	—	—	—	—	—	—
Angola	614	—	—	—	—	—	—	—	—	—	—	—	—
Benin	638	—	—	—	—	—	—	—	—	—	—	—	—
Burkina Faso	748	—	—	—	—	—	—	—	—	—	—	—	—
Burundi	618	—	—	—	—	—	—	—	—	9.6	9.6	—	—
Cameroon	622	21.9	8.5	19.7	—	—	—	—	—	—	—	—	—
Cape Verde	624	—	—	—	—	—	—	—	—	—	—	—	—
Central African Rep.	626	10.7	—	—	—	—	—	—	—	—	—	5.6	—
Chad	628	10.3	—	—	—	—	—	—	—	—	—	—	—
Comoros	632	—	—	—	—	—	—	—	—	—	—	—	—
Congo, Dem. Rep. of	636	—	—	—	—	—	—	—	—	—	—	—	—
Congo, Republic of	634	12.5	—	—	—	7.2	—	10.6	—	—	—	—	—
Côte d'Ivoire	662	—	—	—	—	—	—	—	—	—	—	—	—
Djibouti	611	—	—	2.9	1.1	2.3	1.0	—	—	—	—	—	—
Equatorial Guinea	642	—	—	—	—	—	—	—	—	—	—	—	—
Ethiopia	644	—	—	—	—	—	—	—	—	—	—	—	—
Gabon	646	44.7	37.5	22.1	16.6	—	—	13.2	—	—	—	41.7	—
Gambia, The	648	—	—	—	—	—	—	—	—	—	—	—	—
Ghana	652	—	—	—	—	—	—	—	—	—	—	—	—
Guinea	656	—	—	—	—	—	—	—	—	—	—	—	—
Guinea-Bissau	654	—	—	—	—	—	2.1	1.4	—	—	—	—	—
Kenya	664	—	—	—	—	—	—	—	—	—	—	—	—
Lesotho	666	—	—	—	—	—	—	—	—	—	—	—	—
Liberia	668	—	—	—	—	—	—	—	—	—	—	—	—
Madagascar	674	—	—	—	—	—	—	—	—	—	—	—	—
Malawi	676	12.7	—	—	—	—	—	—	—	17.4	—	—	—
Mali	678	—	—	—	—	—	—	—	—	—	—	—	—
Mauritania	682	—	—	—	—	—	—	—	—	—	—	—	—
Mauritius	684	—	—	—	—	—	—	—	—	—	—	—	—
Morocco	686	—	—	—	—	—	—	—	—	—	—	—	—
Mozambique	688	—	—	—	—	—	—	—	—	—	—	—	—
Niger	692	11.1	—	—	—	—	—	—	—	—	—	—	—
Nigeria	694	—	—	—	—	—	—	—	—	—	—	—	—
Rwanda	714	—	8.9	—	14.9	—	—	—	—	—	—	—	—
São Tomé & Príncipe	716	—	—	—	—	—	—	—	—	—	—	—	—
Senegal	722	30.9	—	—	—	—	—	—	—	—	—	—	—
Seychelles	718	—	—	—	—	—	—	—	—	—	—	—	—
Sierra Leone	724	—	—	—	—	11.6	15.6	10.4	—	—	—	—	—
Somalia	726	—	—	—	—	—	—	—	—	—	—	—	—
South Africa	199	—	—	—	—	—	—	—	—	—	—	—	—
Sudan	732	—	—	—	—	—	—	—	—	—	—	—	—
Swaziland	734	—	—	—	—	—	—	—	—	—	—	—	—
Tanzania	738	—	—	—	—	—	—	—	—	—	—	—	—
Togo	742	—	—	—	—	—	—	—	—	—	—	—	—
Tunisia	744	—	—	—	—	—	—	—	—	—	—	—	—
Uganda	746	—	—	—	—	—	—	—	—	—	—	—	—
Zambia	754	—	651.7	—	—	—	—	—	—	—	—	—	—
Zimbabwe	698	19.1	19.1	—	—	39.2	24.7	—	—	—	—	—	—
Asia	505	220.2	167.3	109.2	12,801.7	11,259.8	2,236.4	1,267.6	784.7	1,197.6	1,396.9	—	107.5
Afghanistan, I.R. of	512	—	—	—	—	—	—	—	—	—	—	—	—
Bangladesh	513	—	—	—	—	98.1	—	—	—	—	—	—	—
Bhutan	514	—	—	—	—	—	—	—	—	—	—	—	—
Cambodia	522	—	—	—	—	—	—	—	—	—	—	—	—
China, People's Rep.	924	—	—	—	—	—	—	—	—	—	—	—	—
Fiji	819	—	—	—	—	—	—	—	—	—	—	—	—
India	534	—	—	—	—	—	—	—	—	—	—	—	—
Indonesia	536	—	—	—	2,201.5	4,254.3	1,011.0	851.2	309.7	1,101.0	1,376.2	—	—
Kiribati	826	—	—	—	—	—	—	—	—	—	—	—	—
Korea	542	—	—	—	8,200.0	5,850.0	362.5	—	—	—	—	—	—
Lao People's Dem.Rep.	544	—	—	—	—	—	—	—	—	—	—	—	—
Malaysia	548	—	—	—	—	—	—	—	—	—	—	—	—
Maldives	556	—	—	—	—	—	—	—	—	—	—	—	4.1
Micronesia, Fed.Sts.	868	—	—	—	—	—	—	—	—	—	—	—	—
Mongolia	948	—	—	—	—	—	—	—	—	—	—	—	—
Myanmar	518	—	—	—	—	—	—	—	—	—	—	—	—
Nepal	558	—	—	—	—	—	—	—	—	—	—	—	—
Pakistan	564	123.2	134.0	107.2	91.5	19.0	409.6	150.0	315.0	—	—	—	—
Palau	565	—	—	—	—	—	—	—	—	—	—	—	—
Papua New Guinea	853	—	33.3	2.0	—	—	—	28.9	56.7	—	—	—	—
Philippines	566	36.5	—	—	508.8	538.3	253.3	237.6	—	—	—	—	—
Samoa	862	—	—	—	—	—	—	—	—	—	—	—	—
Solomon Islands	813	—	—	—	—	—	—	—	—	—	—	—	—
Sri Lanka	524	—	—	—	—	—	—	—	103.4	96.7	20.7	—	103.4
Thailand	578	—	—	—	1,800.0	500.0	200.0	—	—	—	—	—	—
Vietnam	582	60.5	—	—	—	—	—	—	—	—	—	—	—

Purchases

2kk		1994	1995	1996	1997	1998	1999	2000	2001	2002	2003	2004	2005
							Expressed in Millions of SDRs						
Europe	170	**3,177.1**	**5,337.2**	**3,488.2**	**2,272.3**	**5,312.9**	**1,944.9**	**3,253.3**	**9,456.6**	**10,327.5**	**1,696.3**	**1,028.3**	**1,801.0**
Albania	914	—	—	—	8.8	—	—	—	—	—	—	—	—
Armenia	911	16.9	30.4	—	—	—	—	—	—	—	—	—	—
Azerbaijan, Republic of	912	—	67.9	53.8	20.5	15.8	68.6	—	—	—	—	—	—
Belarus	913	—	120.1	—	—	—	—	—	—	—	—	—	—
Bosnia & Herzegovina	963	—	30.3	—	—	24.2	29.0	27.2	14.0	31.6	24.0	12.0	—
Bulgaria	918	232.5	—	80.0	355.2	228.9	209.2	209.2	104.6	84.0	104.0	52.0	—
Croatia	960	78.5	65.4	—	28.8	—	—	—	—	—	—	—	—
Cyprus	423	—	—	—	—	—	—	—	—	—	—	—	—
Czech Republic	935	—	—	—	—	—	—	—	—	—	—	—	—
Estonia	939	—	20.9	—	—	—	—	—	—	—	—	—	—
Georgia	915	27.8	50.0	—	—	—	—	—	—	—	—	—	—
Hungary	944	—	—	—	—	—	—	—	—	—	—	—	—
Kazakhstan	916	136.1	92.8	92.8	—	154.7	—	—	—	—	—	—	—
Kyrgyz Republic	917	—	—	—	—	—	—	—	—	—	—	—	—
Latvia	941	32.0	—	—	—	—	—	—	—	—	—	—	—
Lithuania	946	46.6	41.4	31.1	41.4	—	—	—	—	—	—	—	—
Macedonia, FYR	962	12.4	24.8	9.9	—	—	13.8	1.1	—	—	12.0	8.0	10.5
Moldova	921	49.5	42.4	22.5	15.0	—	50.0	—	—	—	—	—	—
Poland	964	640.3	—	—	—	—	—	—	—	—	—	—	—
Romania	968	245.1	37.7	—	120.6	—	53.0	86.8	52.0	82.7	165.3	—	—
Russia	922	1,078.3	3,594.3	2,587.9	1,467.3	4,600.0	471.4	—	—	—	—	—	—
Serbia & Montenegro	965	—	—	—	—	—	—	116.9	100.0	200.0	200.0	162.5	125.0
Slovak Republic	936	96.5	—	—	—	—	—	—	—	—	—	—	—
Tajikistan	923	—	—	15.0	7.5	7.5	—	—	—	—	—	—	—
Turkey	186	235.5	225.0	—	—	—	583.2	2,622.1	8,895.2	9,929.2	1,191.0	793.8	1,665.5
Ukraine	926	249.3	788.0	536.0	207.3	281.8	466.6	190.1	290.8	—	—	—	—
Uzbekistan	927	—	106.0	59.3	—	—	—	—	—	—	—	—	—
Middle East	405	**65.6**	**75.8**	**166.2**	**154.0**	**32.7**	**77.4**	**15.2**	**37.0**	**71.6**	**—**	**297.1**	**—**
Bahrain, Kingdom of	419	—	—	—	—	—	—	—	—	—	—	—	—
Egypt	469	—	—	—	—	—	—	—	—	—	—	—	—
Iran, I.R. of	429	—	—	—	—	—	—	—	—	—	—	297.1	—
Iraq	433	—	—	—	—	—	—	—	—	—	—	—	—
Israel	436	—	—	—	—	—	—	—	—	—	—	—	—
Jordan	439	65.6	75.8	82.2	96.7	23.7	55.4	15.2	30.5	71.6	—	—	—
Lebanon	446	—	—	—	—	—	—	—	—	—	—	—	—
Syrian Arab Republic	463	—	—	—	—	—	—	—	—	—	—	—	—
Yemen, Republic of	474	—	—	84.0	57.4	9.0	22.0	—	6.5	—	—	—	—
Western Hemisphere	205	**755.1**	**10,349.1**	**950.6**	**514.7**	**3,667.2**	**5,484.5**	**2,606.3**	**13,483.5**	**13,613.3**	**17,220.2**	**2,798.0**	**380.1**
Antigua and Barbuda	311	—	—	—	—	—	—	—	—	—	—	—	—
Argentina	213	612.0	1,559.0	548.2	321.0	—	—	1,587.8	8,168.5	—	4,004.5	2,341.0	—
Barbados	316	—	—	—	—	—	—	—	—	—	—	—	—
Belize	339	—	—	—	—	—	—	—	—	—	64.3	37.5	9.7
Bolivia	218	—	—	—	—	—	—	—	—	—	—	—	—
Brazil	223	—	—	—	—	3,419.0	4,450.1	—	5,277.2	12,274.0	12,635.4	—	—
Chile	228	—	—	—	—	—	—	—	—	—	—	—	—
Colombia	233	—	—	—	—	—	—	—	—	—	—	—	—
Costa Rica	238	—	—	—	—	—	—	—	—	—	—	—	—
Dominica	321	—	—	—	—	—	—	—	—	2.1	.9	—	—
Dominican Republic	243	—	—	—	—	39.7	—	—	—	—	87.6	43.8	148.9
Ecuador	248	98.9	—	—	—	—	—	113.3	37.8	75.6	60.4	—	—
El Salvador	253	—	—	—	—	—	—	—	—	—	—	—	—
Grenada	328	—	—	—	—	—	—	—	—	—	2.9	2.9	—
Guatemala	258	—	—	—	—	—	—	—	—	—	—	—	—
Guyana	336	—	—	—	—	—	—	—	—	—	—	—	20.5
Haiti	263	—	16.4	—	—	15.2	—	—	—	—	—	—	—
Honduras	268	—	—	—	—	47.5	—	—	—	—	—	—	—
Jamaica	343	34.4	7.0	—	—	—	—	—	—	—	—	—	—
Mexico	273	—	8,758.0	—	—	—	1,034.4	905.1	—	—	—	—	—
Nicaragua	278	—	—	—	—	—	—	—	—	—	—	—	—
Panama	283	9.9	8.7	52.4	33.2	30.0	—	—	—	—	—	—	—
Paraguay	288	—	—	—	—	—	—	—	—	—	—	—	—
Peru	293	—	—	—	160.5	—	—	—	—	—	—	—	—
St. Kitts and Nevis	361	—	—	—	—	1.6	—	—	—	—	—	—	—
St. Lucia	362	—	—	—	—	—	—	—	—	—	—	—	—
St. Vincent & Grens.	364	—	—	—	—	—	—	—	—	—	—	—	—
Suriname	366	—	—	—	—	—	—	—	—	—	—	—	—
Trinidad and Tobago	369	—	—	—	—	—	—	—	—	—	—	—	—
Uruguay	298	—	—	—	—	114.2	—	—	—	1,261.7	364.2	372.8	201.1
Venezuela, Rep. Bol.	299	—	—	350.0	—	—	—	—	—	—	—	—	—
Memorandum Items													
Oil Exporting Ctys	999	587.5	312.8	862.2	2,539.1	4,507.6	1,234.5	851.2	309.7	1,101.0	1,376.2	297.1	—
Non-Oil Develop.Ctys	201	4,392.0	16,655.1	4,408.7	13,573.8	16,078.6	8,775.6	6,326.9	23,452.0	24,136.0	18,946.9	3,873.6	2,288.6

Repurchases

Expressed in Millions of SDRs

		1994	1995	1996	1997	1998	1999	2000	2001	2002	2003	2004	2005
World	001	4,572.0	6,650.9	5,071.9	5,681.3	6,694.2	19,398.8	15,249.4	13,274.9	15,113.1	18,892.1	13,829.0	29,100.2
Developing Countries	200	4,572.0	6,650.9	5,071.9	5,681.3	6,694.2	19,398.8	15,249.4	13,274.9	15,113.1	18,892.1	13,829.0	29,100.2
Africa	605	423.3	1,522.4	269.2	730.0	827.9	407.3	198.2	241.1	426.4	348.1	318.7	549.8
Algeria	612	136.5	112.5	93.8	254.6	320.8	262.8	70.2	110.5	229.6	313.7	250.8	414.0
Burkina Faso	748	—	—	—	—	—	—	—	—	—	—	—	—
Burundi	618	—	—	—	—	—	—	—	—	—	—	19.3	—
Cameroon	622	3.9	4.0	4.0	8.2	12.0	13.3	14.1	2.5	—	—	—	—
Central African Rep	626	.4	—	—	2.7	5.6	2.4	—	—	—	—	—	—
Chad	628	—	—	—	3.9	5.2	1.3	—	—	—	—	—	—
Comoros	632	—	—	—	—	—	—	—	—	—	—	—	—
Congo, Dem. Rep. of	636	3.0	.9	22.7	—	.4	.7	—	—	157.1	—	—	—
Congo, Republic of	634	2.0	1.5	—	1.6	7.8	3.1	—	.9	3.6	2.7	5.3	5.3
Côte d'Ivoire	662	53.5	56.8	32.8	16.1	—	—	—	—	—	—	—	—
Djibouti	611	—	—	—	—	—	.7	1.7	1.6	1.8	1.3	.1	—
Equatorial Guinea	642	—	—	—	—	—	—	—	—	—	—	—	—
Ethiopia	644	—	—	—	—	—	—	—	—	—	—	—	—
Gabon	646	16.1	34.5	3.8	2.6	16.7	17.9	7.4	8.7	10.1	10.1	16.7	16.7
Gambia, The	648	—	—	—	—	—	—	—	—	—	—	—	—
Ghana	652	27.1	13.1	16.8	34.5	24.6	—	—	—	—	—	—	—
Guinea	656	—	—	—	—	—	—	—	—	—	—	—	—
Guinea-Bissau	654	—	—	—	—	—	—	—	—	.3	1.6	1.5	.2
Kenya	664	—	—	—	—	—	—	—	—	—	—	—	—
Lesotho	666	—	—	—	—	—	—	—	—	—	—	—	—
Liberia	668	—	.1	—	—	—	—	.2	.3	.2	—	—	—
Madagascar	674	4.5	.6	—	—	—	—	—	—	—	—	—	—
Malawi	676	1.2	—	—	—	6.4	6.4	—	—	—	—	—	2.2
Mali	678	4.8	1.0	—	—	—	—	—	—	—	—	—	—
Mauritania	682	—	—	—	—	—	—	—	—	—	—	—	—
Mauritius	684	—	—	—	—	—	—	—	—	—	—	—	—
Morocco	686	106.1	66.2	32.5	2.3	—	—	—	—	—	—	—	—
Niger	692	2.0	—	—	4.2	5.6	1.4	—	—	—	—	—	—
Nigeria	694	—	—	—	—	—	—	—	—	—	—	—	—
Rwanda	714	—	—	—	—	—	4.5	6.7	7.4	5.2	—	—	—
Senegal	722	2.5	—	—	11.6	15.5	3.9	—	—	—	—	—	—
Sierra Leone	724	42.6	—	—	—	—	—	—	37.5	—	—	—	—
Somalia	726	—	—	—	—	—	—	—	—	—	—	—	—
South Africa	199	—	—	—	307.2	307.2	—	—	—	—	—	—	—
Sudan	732	—	23.0	24.5	25.5	42.2	27.6	41.1	41.1	17.0	18.7	21.1	—
Swaziland	734	—	—	—	—	—	—	—	—	—	—	—	—
Tanzania	738	—	—	—	—	—	—	—	—	—	—	—	—
Togo	742	2.4	2.0	.2	—	—	—	—	—	—	—	—	—
Tunisia	744	—	10.2	32.1	36.6	36.6	36.6	30.4	24.7	—	—	—	—
Uganda	746	—	—	—	—	—	—	—	—	—	—	—	—
Zambia	754	14.6	1,196.2	—	—	—	—	—	—	—	—	—	—
Zimbabwe	698	—	—	5.9	18.5	21.6	24.8	26.4	5.9	1.5	—	3.9	111.5
Asia	505	1,066.0	1,113.8	1,262.8	831.0	2,514.2	8,330.4	375.5	6,943.9	3,419.1	2,110.8	1,417.5	1,056.9
Afghanistan, I.R. of	512	—	—	—	—	—	—	—	—	—	—	—	—
Bangladesh	513	—	—	—	—	—	—	—	—	49.1	49.1	—	—
Bhutan	514	—	—	—	—	—	—	—	—	—	—	—	—
Cambodia	522	—	—	—	—	1.0	1.0	1.0	1.0	1.0	1.0	—	—
China, People's Rep	924	—	—	—	—	—	—	—	—	—	—	—	—
Fiji	819	—	—	—	—	—	—	—	—	—	—	—	—
India	534	821.7	796.5	881.4	495.5	304.9	246.4	38.5	—	—	—	—	—
Indonesia	536	—	—	—	—	—	—	—	1,375.9	1,834.6	979.3	678.1	774.8
Korea	542	—	—	—	—	2,050.0	7,900.0	—	4,462.5	—	—	—	—
Lao People's Dem.Rep	544	—	—	—	—	—	—	—	—	—	—	—	—
Malaysia	548	—	—	—	—	—	—	—	—	—	—	—	—
Mongolia	948	—	6.3	6.9	.6	—	—	—	—	—	—	—	—
Myanmar	518	—	—	—	—	—	—	—	—	—	—	—	—
Nepal	558	—	—	—	—	—	—	—	—	—	—	—	—
Pakistan	564	34.1	61.2	167.0	138.8	39.7	107.6	161.2	80.8	167.4	351.7	309.4	—
Papua New Guinea	853	21.4	10.7	—	—	3.0	16.7	14.7	1.0	—	3.8	40.4	41.4
Philippines	566	188.7	239.1	207.5	156.9	58.2	39.5	6.1	6.1	313.0	434.4	318.8	214.9
Samoa	862	—	—	—	—	—	—	—	—	—	—	—	—
Solomon Islands	813	—	—	—	—	—	—	—	—	—	—	—	—
Sri Lanka	524	—	—	—	—	—	—	—	—	—	—	69.8	25.8
Thailand	578	—	—	—	—	—	—	150.0	1,012.5	1,050.0	287.5	—	—
Vietnam	582	—	—	—	39.3	57.4	19.2	4.0	4.0	4.0	4.0	1.0	—
Europe	170	1,325.2	2,010.7	1,047.8	687.5	1,522.7	4,309.1	3,841.5	4,763.9	6,767.4	3,120.3	4,981.4	8,403.9
Albania	914	—	.8	5.7	5.8	.9	—	—	4.4	4.4	—	—	—
Armenia	911	—	—	—	—	.4	9.6	12.0	5.6	5.6	7.0	5.6	1.4
Azerbaijan, Republic of	912	—	—	—	—	—	11.7	39.0	30.9	35.8	45.3	25.7	16.2
Belarus	913	—	—	—	—	17.9	42.5	42.1	23.4	23.4	23.4	11.7	5.8
Bosnia & Herzegovina	963	—	18.4	1.4	.7	—	15.2	15.2	6.1	17.6	36.3	32.1	26.7
Bulgaria	918	48.0	162.3	154.9	64.4	134.7	90.7	105.3	236.2	195.2	76.6	89.2	300.1
Croatia	960	6.2	3.9	3.1	1.6	6.5	22.9	21.8	24.2	97.2	—	—	—
Cyprus	423	—	—	—	—	—	—	—	—	—	—	—	—
Czech Republic	935	780.7	—	—	—	—	—	—	—	—	—	—	—
Estonia	939	—	1.0	7.7	14.1	18.7	2.9	3.9	3.9	10.7	—	—	—
Georgia	915	—	—	—	—	.7	15.7	19.7	9.3	9.3	11.6	9.3	2.3
Hungary	944	114.7	522.9	140.0	—	118.7	—	—	—	—	—	—	—
Kazakhstan	916	—	—	—	4.6	70.0	128.5	335.1	—	—	—	—	—

Repurchases

Expressed in Millions of SDRs

2lk		1994	1995	1996	1997	1998	1999	2000	2001	2002	2003	2004	2005
Europe(Cont.)													
Kyrgyz Republic	917	—	—	2.7	7.1	8.5	5.4	5.4	5.4	5.4	4.0	—	—
Latvia	941	—	1.9	17.5	26.7	18.3	11.1	7.6	7.6	7.6	7.6	3.8	—
Lithuania	946			16.9	31.1	20.6	12.1	20.7	26.7	31.1	59.1	13.4	16.8
Macedonia, FYR	962	1.2	.7	.6	.3	1.7	12.4	14.7	6.0	5.9	11.0	8.3	1.8
Moldova	921	—		5.1	14.6	47.2	47.9	18.6	11.3	13.8	15.8	14.6	14.6
Poland	964	219.4	918.6	—		—							
Romania	968	89.6	245.8	245.4	98.4	92.3	102.0	72.9	91.7	75.7	79.6	115.3	102.8
Russia	922			359.5	359.5	673.9	3,101.1	2,189.5	2,997.9	1,147.6	1,356.1	1,117.4	2,293.8
Serbia & Montenegro	965	—	—	—							—	158.5	139.7
Slovak Republic	936	61.9	132.3	85.6	37.6	49.8	38.1	96.5	—			—	—
Slovenia	961	3.6	2.2	1.8	.9	—	—						
Tajikistan	923				—	—	3.8	7.5	9.4	7.5	1.9		
Turkey	186	—	—	—	20.1	164.6	210.2	65.6	867.6	4,916.4	1,223.9	3,158.2	5,266.5
Ukraine	926	—	—	—	—	77.3	407.0	643.5	361.2	140.7	144.5	201.8	202.8
Uzbekistan	927	—	—	—	—		18.4	49.4	35.1	16.6	16.6	16.6	12.5
Middle East	405	**48.4**	**135.2**	**163.2**	**49.4**	**6.8**	**50.7**	**77.9**	**81.7**	**74.6**	**76.3**	**72.8**	**59.9**
Egypt	469	22.5	62.7	58.6	10.9	—	—	—	—	—	—	—	—
Iran, I.R. of	429	—	—	—	—	—	—	—	—	—	—	—	—
Iraq	433	—	—	—	—	—	—	—	—	—	—	—	—
Israel	436	—	67.0	89.3	22.3	—	—	—	—	—	—	—	—
Jordan	439	25.9	5.6	15.3	16.2	6.8	26.0	23.8	40.2	61.0	71.4	66.1	52.2
Syrian Arab Republic	463	—		—		—							
Yemen, Republic of	474						24.8	54.1	41.4	13.6	4.8	6.7	7.8
Western Hemisphere	205	**1,709.2**	**1,868.8**	**2,329.0**	**3,383.4**	**1,822.5**	**6,301.3**	**10,756.2**	**1,244.3**	**4,425.6**	**13,236.7**	**7,038.6**	**19,029.7**
Argentina	213	289.7	319.3	296.5	347.8	484.2	602.5	970.2	927.6	573.6	4,105.8	3,714.1	2,417.3
Barbados	316		11.9	18.4	6.5	—	—	—	—	—	—	—	—
Belize	339	—				—							12.1
Bolivia	218	—				—							
Brazil	223	93.5	32.3	48.2	23.7	15.5	1,445.9	5,074.2	—	3,588.3	8,898.6	2,939.8	16,116.7
Chile	228	147.0	199.5										
Colombia	233	—			—								
Costa Rica	238	13.8	29.1	15.8	.5	—	—	—	—	—	—	—	—
Dominica	321	—				—							.3
Dominican Republic	243	5.6	22.4	41.0	45.3	21.1	—	—	—	19.9	19.9	—	—
Ecuador	248	14.9	19.0	15.8	2.0	49.5	49.5	—	—	—	24.8	75.6	132.0
El Salvador	253	—			—								
Grenada	328	—			—								
Guatemala	258	—			—								
Guyana	336	15.3	15.6	8.1	6.7	1.4	—	—	—	—	—	—	—
Haiti	263	14.8	.3			6.0	8.2	2.2	—	7.6	7.6	—	—
Honduras	268	11.2	28.8	26.1	6.4	—	—	—	—	23.8	23.8	—	—
Jamaica	343	60.9	62.9	49.5	25.1	12.5	13.9	14.5	14.5	14.5	11.4	5.4	.6
Mexico	273	841.0	754.1	1,413.6	2,499.2	783.7	3,726.7	4,164.3	—	—	—	—	—
Nicaragua	278	2.1	8.5	6.4	—								
Panama	283	.9	25.6	35.8	18.8	9.9	17.2	39.3	26.2	6.2	6.7	6.7	6.7
Paraguay	288	—			—								
Peru	293	—	—	—	53.6	107.1	107.1	107.1	120.5	133.9	80.3	26.8	26.8
St. Kitts and Nevis	361	—	—	—	—	—	—	—	—	.8	.8		
St. Lucia	362	—	—	—	—	—	—	—	—				
St. Vincent & Grens	364	—	—	—	—	—	—	—	—				
Trinidad and Tobago	369	50.4	28.7	17.3	13.3	3.1	—	—	—	—	—	—	—
Uruguay	298	7.4	6.5	8.0	6.0	—	—	—	—	57.1	57.1	270.3	317.3
Venezuela, Rep. Bol.	299	140.6	304.2	328.5	328.5	328.5	330.3	384.4	155.6				
Memorandum Items													
Oil Exporting Ctys	999	277.1	416.7	422.3	583.2	649.3	593.1	454.7	1,642.0	2,064.2	1,292.9	928.8	1,188.8
Non-Oil Develop.Ctys	201	4,295.0	6,234.2	4,649.6	5,098.1	6,044.9	18,805.7	14,794.7	11,633.0	13,048.9	17,599.2	12,900.1	27,911.4

Loan Disbursements

Expressed in Millions of SDRs

		1994	1995	1996	1997	1998	1999	2000	2001	2002	2003	2004	2005
World	001	910.4	1,431.4	708.6	730.6	896.0	736.8	492.5	872.6	1,344.5	848.4	812.4	404.0
Developing Countries	200	910.4	1,431.4	708.6	730.6	896.0	736.8	492.5	872.6	1,344.5	848.4	812.4	404.0
Africa	605	467.1	1,247.8	404.3	348.3	532.6	334.8	364.8	467.0	922.9	275.5	399.5	218.5
Benin	638	18.1	9.1	13.6	4.5	—	7.2	6.8	8.1	4.0	6.7	1.4	.9
Burkina Faso	748	17.7	17.7	6.6	13.3	13.3	12.2	5.6	16.8	11.2	3.4	3.4	10.3
Burundi	618	—	—	—	—	—	—	—	—	—	—	26.4	14.3
Cameroon	622	—	—	—	27.0	54.0	45.0	52.0	15.9	31.8	15.9	—	2.7
Cape Verde	624	—	—	—	—	—	—	—	—	2.5	2.5	1.2	2.5
Central African Rep.	626	—	—	—	—	8.2	8.2	—	8.0	—	—	—	—
Chad	628	—	8.3	16.5	8.3	8.3	8.3	10.4	13.4	13.4	5.2	—	4.2
Comoros	632	1.4	—	—	—	—	—	—	—	—	—	—	—
Congo, Dem. Rep. of	636	—	—	—	—	—	—	—	—	420.0	53.4	53.4	26.7
Congo, Republic of	634	—	—	13.9	—	—	—	—	—	—	—	7.9	7.9
Côte d'Ivoire	662	119.1	119.1	95.3	—	123.9	—	—	—	58.5	—	—	—
Djibouti	611	—	—	—	—	—	2.7	2.7	3.6	4.5	—	—	—
Equatorial Guinea	642	1.8	—	—	—	—	—	—	—	—	—	—	—
Ethiopia	644	14.1	—	14.7	—	14.7	—	—	34.8	34.2	10.4	20.9	—
Gambia, The	648	—	—	—	—	3.4	3.4	6.9	6.9	2.9	—	—	—
Ghana	652	—	27.4	27.4	—	82.2	44.3	26.8	52.6	52.6	52.7	26.4	26.4
Guinea	656	8.7	20.3	—	23.6	23.6	7.9	—	20.7	12.9	—	—	—
Guinea-Bissau	654	—	1.6	2.1	4.5	2.4	—	5.1	—	—	—	—	—
Kenya	664	22.6	—	24.9	—	—	—	33.6	—	—	25.0	—	50.0
Lesotho	666	3.8	—	—	—	—	—	—	7.0	7.0	3.5	7.0	—
Liberia	668	—	—	—	—	—	—	—	—	—	—	—	—
Madagascar	674	—	—	13.6	13.6	—	13.6	38.0	22.7	11.3	11.3	34.9	11.3
Malawi	676	5.6	7.6	15.3	7.6	12.8	7.6	6.4	—	—	6.4	—	5.4
Mali	678	29.5	29.5	20.7	20.7	10.3	17.1	6.8	18.2	6.8	12.9	1.3	1.3
Mauritania	682	17.0	14.3	14.3	14.3	—	6.1	6.1	18.2	12.1	.9	—	—
Mauritius	684	—	—	—	—	—	—	—	—	—	—	—	—
Morocco	686	—	—	—	—	—	—	—	—	—	—	—	—
Mozambique	688	14.7	—	12.6	25.2	25.2	21.0	45.2	8.4	8.4	8.4	1.6	3.2
Niger	692	—	—	9.7	19.3	19.3	19.3	8.5	8.5	16.9	16.9	8.4	11.8
Rwanda	714	—	—	—	—	11.9	21.4	19.0	9.5	.6	.6	1.1	1.1
São Tomé & Príncipe	716	—	—	—	—	—	—	1.9	—	—	—	—	.4
Senegal	722	16.7	54.7	23.8	35.7	35.7	14.3	14.3	23.3	9.0	3.5	3.5	3.5
Sierra Leone	724	95.6	13.1	10.2	5.1	—	—	—	46.8	28.0	14.0	28.0	14.0
Somalia	726	—	—	—	—	—	—	—	—	—	—	—	—
Sudan	732	—	—	—	—	—	—	—	—	—	—	—	—
Swaziland	734	—	—	—	—	—	—	—	—	—	—	—	—
Tanzania	738	—	—	25.7	61.4	35.7	58.8	40.0	40.0	40.0	17.8	5.6	5.6
Togo	742	10.9	21.7	—	10.9	10.9	—	—	—	—	—	—	—
Uganda	746	36.7	36.8	43.5	43.5	36.8	25.7	8.9	8.9	1.5	4.0	2.0	4.0
Zambia	754	—	833.4	—	10.0	—	10.0	20.0	74.8	132.7	—	165.1	11.0
Zimbabwe	698	33.4	33.4	—	—	—	—	—	—	—	—	—	—
Asia	505	358.9	100.1	132.2	125.2	113.7	52.2	14.3	194.3	325.6	460.6	278.4	67.3
Afghanistan, I.R. of	512	—	—	—	—	—	—	—	—	—	—	—	—
Bangladesh	513	—	—	—	—	—	—	—	—	—	49.5	99.0	67.3
Cambodia	522	14.0	28.0	—	—	—	8.4	8.4	16.7	16.7	8.4	—	—
China,P.R.: Mainland	924	—	—	—	—	—	—	—	—	—	—	—	—
India	534	—	—	—	—	—	—	—	—	—	—	—	—
Lao People's Dem.Rep.	544	5.9	11.7	5.9	5.9	—	—	—	4.5	9.1	4.5	—	—
Maldives	556	—	—	—	—	—	—	—	—	—	—	—	—
Mongolia	948	14.8	—	5.6	5.6	—	5.9	5.9	4.1	—	8.1	—	—
Myanmar	518	—	—	—	—	—	—	—	—	—	—	—	—
Nepal	558	5.6	—	—	—	—	—	—	—	—	7.1	7.1	—
Pakistan	564	202.2	—	—	113.7	113.7	37.9	—	86.2	258.4	344.6	172.3	—
Papua New Guinea	853	—	—	—	—	—	—	—	—	—	—	—	—
Philippines	566	—	—	—	—	—	—	—	—	—	—	—	—
Samoa	862	—	—	—	—	—	—	—	—	—	—	—	—
Solomon Islands	813	—	—	—	—	—	—	—	—	—	—	—	—
Sri Lanka	524	56.0	—	—	—	—	—	—	—	—	38.4	—	—
Thailand	578	—	—	—	—	—	—	—	—	—	—	—	—
Vietnam	582	60.4	60.4	120.8	—	—	—	—	82.8	41.4	—	—	—
Europe	170	25.0	37.4	105.4	178.4	146.2	107.7	58.9	87.4	83.5	83.0	79.7	87.1
Albania	914	15.5	7.1	—	—	5.9	15.5	14.3	9.4	4.0	8.0	8.0	8.0
Armenia	911	—	—	33.8	16.9	37.8	20.9	—	10.0	20.0	20.0	19.0	6.6
Azerbaijan, Republic of	912	—	—	—	55.6	14.6	11.7	—	8.1	8.1	25.7	—	12.9
Georgia	915	—	—	55.5	55.5	27.8	33.3	—	27.0	22.5	—	14.0	28.0
Kyrgyz Republic	917	9.5	30.3	16.1	32.3	10.8	19.6	14.3	11.7	11.7	21.3	19.1	12.1
Macedonia, FYR	962	—	—	—	18.2	9.1	—	1.7	—	—	—	—	—
Moldova	921	—	—	—	—	—	—	9.2	9.2	9.2	—	—	—
Tajikistan	923	—	—	—	—	40.3	6.7	19.3	12.0	8.0	8.0	19.6	19.6
Middle East	405	—	—	—	44.0	44.0	62.0	—	88.8	—	—	—	—
Egypt	469	—	—	—	—	—	—	—	—	—	—	—	—
Yemen, Republic of	474	—	—	—	44.0	44.0	62.0	—	88.8	—	—	—	—
Western Hemisphere	205	59.4	46.1	66.8	34.8	59.4	180.1	54.5	35.2	12.5	29.2	54.8	31.1
Bolivia	218	30.4	16.8	33.7	16.8	33.6	16.8	11.2	19.0	—	—	—	—
Dominica	321	—	—	—	—	—	—	—	—	—	—	2.4	.6	2.4
El Salvador	253	—	—	—	—	—	—	—	—	—	—	—	—
Grenada	328	—	—	—	—	—	—	—	—	—	—	—	—
Guyana	336	9.0	9.0	17.9	17.9	9.0	9.0	7.0	—	5.6	6.0	6.0	18.5

Loan Disbursements

2kl		1994	1995	1996	1997	1998	1999	2000	2001	2002	2003	2004	2005
						Expressed in Millions of SDRs							
Western Hemisphere(Cont.)													
Haiti...................................	263	—	—	15.2	—	—	—	—	—	—	—	20.3	10.2
Honduras.............................	268	—	20.3	—	—	—	76.0	16.2	16.2	—	—	—	—
Nicaragua.............................	278	20.0	—	—	—	16.8	78.3	20.2	—	7.0	20.9	27.9	—
Memorandum Items													
Non-Oil Develop.Ctys..............	201	910.4	1,431.4	708.6	730.6	896.0	736.8	492.5	872.6	1,344.5	848.4	812.4	404.0

Repayments of Loans

211

Expressed in Millions of SDRs

		1994	1995	1996	1997	1998	1999	2000	2001	2002	2003	2004	2005
World	001	**223.4**	**373.8**	**484.5**	**606.0**	**620.9**	**595.2**	**605.1**	**789.6**	**906.6**	**842.2**	**933.3**	**887.9**
Developing Countries	200	**223.4**	**373.8**	**484.5**	**606.0**	**620.9**	**595.2**	**605.1**	**789.6**	**906.6**	**842.2**	**933.3**	**887.9**
Africa	605	**145.2**	**230.6**	**300.0**	**338.4**	**350.0**	**324.5**	**320.6**	**501.5**	**625.9**	**532.6**	**593.4**	**563.4**
Benin	638	.6	1.3	1.3	3.1	3.9	6.5	9.5	11.4	11.3	11.4	8.5	6.0
Burkina Faso	748	—	—	.6	1.3	2.1	3.9	7.5	10.1	10.8	12.6	13.5	11.7
Burundi	618	4.3	6.0	6.0	6.0	6.8	5.6	3.8	3.8	2.1	—	—	—
Cameroon	622	—	—	—	—	—	—	—	—	—	8.1	18.9	27.0
Central African Rep.	626	2.9	4.9	4.3	2.7	3.9	1.2	.6	—	—	—	1.6	3.3
Chad	628	1.2	4.6	4.3	4.3	3.1	2.1	.6	2.5	5.8	12.4	9.5	10.4
Comoros	632	—	—	—	.2	.2	.3	.5	.5	.3	.3	.1	—
Congo, Dem. Rep. of	636	—	—	2.4	—	.2	—	—	—	142.9	—	—	—
Congo, Republic of	634	—	—	—	—	—	—	—	—	2.8	2.8	2.8	2.8
Côte d'Ivoire	662	—	—	—	—	—	6.0	29.8	52.4	66.7	75.0	85.5	61.7
Djibouti	611	—	—	—	—	—	—	—	—	—	—	—	.5
Equatorial Guinea	642	.4	.7	.8	2.2	2.1	1.8	2.0	2.0	.9	.6	.2	—
Ethiopia	644	—	—	—	—	2.8	7.1	9.9	9.9	12.8	10.0	8.7	5.9
Gambia, The	648	2.7	4.1	5.1	5.1	4.1	3.1	1.7	.7	—	—	7.6	1.4
Ghana	652	30.5	57.8	69.4	85.9	77.7	55.4	28.1	51.4	11.0	15.1	29.6	36.3
Guinea	656	4.1	5.8	5.8	7.5	6.9	5.2	6.1	9.3	8.7	10.5	13.2	17.4
Guinea-Bissau	654	.3	.8	.8	.8	.5	.5	.2	.5	.9	1.9	2.1	1.9
Kenya	664	9.7	25.8	41.9	48.9	46.1	43.7	32.2	18.6	14.0	14.0	9.5	5.0
Lesotho	666	1.1	1.8	2.3	3.1	3.6	4.3	3.9	3.4	2.9	1.8	.4	—
Liberia	668	.7	—	—	—	.4	.4	.3	.2	—	—	—	—
Madagascar	674	3.9	9.1	11.6	12.9	10.3	9.0	3.8	1.3	2.7	5.4	5.4	8.1
Malawi	676	2.8	6.5	10.2	12.3	12.3	10.0	6.9	5.5	5.7	7.2	9.2	10.2
Mali	678	2.0	3.6	5.1	5.1	8.1	8.6	13.0	16.9	21.0	21.1	21.7	18.2
Mauritania	682	4.2	5.9	6.8	5.4	5.1	6.8	8.3	10.3	12.5	13.6	12.0	9.7
Mauritius	684	—	—	—	—	—	—	—	—	—	—	—	—
Morocco	686	—	—	—	—	—	—	—	—	—	—	—	—
Mozambique	688	7.3	9.5	22.5	11.0	18.1	22.8	22.2	21.0	17.1	14.8	15.3	20.5
Niger	692	5.1	6.7	8.1	6.7	4.7	3.0	1.3	1.0	2.9	6.8	9.7	9.7
Rwanda	714	—	—	.9	1.8	1.8	1.8	1.8	.9	—	1.2	3.6	6.7
São Tomé & Príncipe	716	.1	.2	.2	.2	.2	.1	—	—	—	—	—	.1
Senegal	722	17.4	26.8	30.6	34.0	28.9	20.0	17.1	21.1	20.8	27.9	33.3	31.2
Sierra Leone	724	13.8	2.3	2.3	—	—	9.1	19.1	21.7	24.3	24.8	15.7	5.7
Somalia	726	—	—	—	—	—	—	—	—	—	—	—	—
Sudan	732	—	3.0	—	5.2	—	—	—	—	—	—	—	—
Swaziland	734	—	—	—	—	—	—	—	—	—	—	—	—
Tanzania	738	10.7	12.8	15.0	22.5	27.8	21.4	19.3	17.1	17.3	17.4	27.5	38.3
Togo	742	2.3	5.4	7.7	8.4	8.4	6.9	7.1	8.1	7.3	9.8	10.9	7.6
Uganda	746	17.1	18.8	34.1	41.8	45.8	37.6	37.1	32.4	31.7	34.1	37.5	35.6
Zambia	754	—	6.6	—	—	—	—	—	166.7	167.7	168.7	169.7	170.7
Zimbabwe	698	—	—	—	—	14.0	20.4	27.0	1.0	.9	3.2	10.2	—
Asia	505	**62.0**	**123.6**	**152.1**	**230.4**	**224.9**	**222.7**	**226.5**	**223.3**	**169.9**	**171.4**	**151.2**	**103.3**
Afghanistan, I.R. of	512	—	—	—	—	—	—	—	—	—	—	—	—
Bangladesh	513	38.4	40.3	58.9	86.3	77.6	70.9	69.0	50.3	17.3	2.9	—	—
Cambodia	522	—	—	—	—	—	1.4	4.2	8.4	8.4	8.4	7.0	5.9
China, People's Rep.	924	—	—	—	—	—	—	—	—	—	—	—	—
India	534	—	—	—	—	—	—	—	—	—	—	—	—
Lao People's Dem.Rep.	544	—	1.2	2.1	3.5	4.7	5.9	5.9	7.3	7.0	6.5	5.3	4.1
Mongolia	948	—	—	—	—	.9	2.8	4.8	5.4	5.9	6.1	4.9	4.0
Myanmar	518	—	—	—	—	—	—	—	—	—	—	—	—
Nepal	558	3.7	5.2	5.2	5.2	4.8	4.3	3.4	3.4	3.4	2.2	.6	—
Pakistan	564	10.9	54.6	54.6	87.4	76.5	64.7	62.3	62.3	40.4	74.6	79.6	53.1
Papua New Guinea	853	—	—	—	—	—	—	—	—	—	—	—	—
Philippines	566	—	—	—	—	—	—	—	—	—	—	—	—
Samoa	862	—	—	—	—	—	—	—	—	—	—	—	—
Solomon Islands	813	—	—	—	—	—	—	—	—	—	—	—	—
Sri Lanka	524	8.9	22.3	31.2	48.0	60.4	72.7	64.9	56.0	39.2	22.4	5.6	—
Thailand	578	—	—	—	—	—	—	—	—	—	—	—	—
Vietnam	582	—	—	—	—	—	—	12.1	30.2	48.3	48.3	48.3	36.2
Europe	170	**—**	**—**	**—**	**—**	**—**	**2.5**	**8.8**	**18.6**	**63.3**	**82.2**	**101.7**	**114.5**
Albania	914	—	—	—	—	—	2.5	5.5	6.2	6.2	6.8	6.4	6.2
Armenia	911	—	—	—	—	—	—	—	1.7	8.4	11.8	17.7	21.9
Azerbaijan, Republic of	912	—	—	—	—	—	—	—	—	2.0	11.1	14.6	16.4
Georgia	915	—	—	—	—	—	—	—	2.8	13.9	22.2	27.8	34.4
Kyrgyz Republic	917	—	—	—	—	—	—	3.3	8.0	12.8	17.6	21.7	20.9
Macedonia, FYR	962	—	—	—	—	—	—	—	—	.9	4.5	5.5	5.5
Tajikistan	923	—	—	—	—	—	—	—	—	19.0	8.1	8.1	9.4
Middle East	405	**—**	**—**	**—**	**—**	**—**	**—**	**—**	**—**	**—**	**—**	**8.8**	**21.2**	**30.0**
Egypt	469	—	—	—	—	—	—	—	—	—	—	—	—
Yemen, Republic of	474	—	—	—	—	—	—	—	—	—	8.8	21.2	30.0
Western Hemisphere	205	**16.3**	**19.6**	**32.4**	**37.2**	**46.0**	**45.5**	**49.1**	**46.2**	**47.5**	**47.1**	**65.7**	**76.6**
Bolivia	218	10.4	17.2	21.8	24.9	29.9	24.5	22.4	22.9	21.2	20.5	27.4	24.7
Dominica	321	.5	.6	.6	.4	.2	—	—	—	—	—	—	—
El Salvador	253	—	—	—	—	—	—	—	—	—	—	—	—
Grenada	328	—	—	—	—	—	—	—	—	—	—	—	—
Guyana	336	—	—	8.3	11.9	14.5	16.3	19.0	12.5	12.5	12.5	13.4	11.6
Haiti	263	5.3	1.8	1.8	—	—	—	—	—	3.0	3.0	3.0	3.0
Honduras	268	—	—	—	—	1.4	2.7	3.7	6.8	6.8	5.4	10.1	18.3

Repayments of Loans

		1994	1995	1996	1997	1998	1999	2000	2001	2002	2003	2004	2005
						Expressed in Millions of SDRs							
2II													
Western Hemisphere(Cont.)													
Memorandum Items													
Non-Oil Develop.Ctys.............	201	223.4	373.8	484.5	606.0	620.9	595.2	605.1	789.6	906.6	842.2	933.3	887.9
Nicaragua................................	278	—	—	—	—	—	2.0	4.0	4.0	4.0	5.7	11.9	19.0

Total Fund Credit & Loans Outstdg.

2tl

		1994	1995	1996	1997	1998	1999	2000	2001	2002	2003	2004	2005
		Expressed in Millions of SDRs											
World	001	30,260.9	41,636.1	42,058.6	52,614.7	66,781.7	57,534.1	49,350.2	59,920.0	70,481.7	71,919.0	62,139.8	34,714.3
Developing Countries	200	30,260.9	41,636.1	42,058.6	52,614.7	66,781.7	57,534.1	49,350.2	59,920.0	70,481.7	71,919.0	62,139.8	34,714.3
Africa	605	6,531.6	7,065.3	7,457.3	7,107.3	6,775.7	6,645.5	6,527.1	6,251.5	6,149.0	5,553.4	5,088.1	4,174.2
Algeria	612	793.8	994.1	1,412.5	1,495.5	1,428.0	1,388.7	1,318.5	1,208.0	978.4	664.7	414.0	—
Angola	614												
Benin	638	48.8	56.6	68.9	70.3	66.4	67.1	64.4	61.1	53.9	49.2	42.0	36.9
Burkina Faso	748	32.8	50.5	56.5	68.5	79.6	87.9	86.1	92.7	93.0	83.9	73.8	72.4
Burundi	618	40.1	34.2	28.2	22.2	15.4	9.8	6.0	2.1	9.6	19.3	26.4	40.7
Cameroon	622	29.9	34.4	50.1	68.9	110.9	142.7	180.5	194.0	225.8	233.6	214.7	190.3
Cape Verde	624	—	—	—	—	—	—	—	—	2.5	4.9	6.2	8.6
Central African Rep.	626	28.3	23.5	19.2	13.8	12.5	17.1	16.5	24.5	24.5	24.5	28.4	25.1
Chad	628	29.3	33.0	45.2	45.3	45.3	50.2	60.0	70.9	78.5	71.3	61.8	55.5
Comoros	632	2.3	2.3	2.3	2.1	1.9	1.6	1.1	.7	.4	.1	—	—
Congo, Dem. Rep. of	636	327.3	326.4	301.3	301.3	300.7	300.0	300.0	300.0	420.0	473.4	526.8	553.5
Congo, Republic of	634	14.0	12.5	26.4	24.8	24.3	21.1	31.7	30.8	24.4	18.9	18.7	18.5
Côte d'Ivoire	662	224.8	287.1	349.6	333.5	457.3	451.4	421.6	369.2	361.1	286.0	200.5	138.8
Djibouti	611	—	—	2.9	4.0	6.3	9.3	10.3	12.3	15.1	13.8	13.6	13.1
Equatorial Guinea	642	13.4	12.7	11.9	9.8	7.6	5.8	3.8	1.7	.8	.2	—	—
Ethiopia	644	49.4	49.4	64.2	64.2	76.1	69.0	59.1	84.0	105.4	105.8	118.0	112.1
Gabon	646	61.4	65.0	83.3	97.2	80.5	62.6	68.4	59.6	49.5	39.4	64.4	47.6
Gambia, The	648	23.9	19.8	14.7	9.6	8.9	9.3	14.4	20.6	23.5	23.5	15.9	14.6
Ghana	652	479.7	436.2	377.3	257.0	236.9	225.8	224.5	225.7	267.3	304.9	301.6	291.7
Guinea	656	48.6	63.1	57.3	73.4	90.0	92.7	86.6	98.1	102.2	91.7	78.5	61.1
Guinea-Bissau	654	3.2	4.0	5.3	9.0	11.0	12.6	19.0	18.4	17.2	13.8	10.2	9.0
Kenya	664	277.3	251.5	234.5	185.6	139.5	95.8	97.2	78.6	64.6	75.6	66.1	111.1
Lesotho	666	27.6	25.8	23.5	20.4	16.8	12.5	8.5	12.1	16.2	17.9	24.5	24.5
Liberia	668	225.8	225.7	225.7	225.7	225.3	224.8	224.4	223.9	223.7	223.7	223.7	223.6
Madagascar	674	58.6	48.9	50.8	51.5	41.2	45.8	80.0	101.4	110.0	115.9	145.4	148.6
Malawi	676	76.9	78.0	83.1	78.4	72.6	63.8	63.4	57.9	69.6	68.8	59.5	52.6
Mali	678	74.1	99.0	114.6	130.2	132.4	140.9	134.7	136.0	121.8	113.6	93.2	76.4
Mauritania	682	58.8	67.1	74.6	83.4	78.3	77.6	75.4	83.2	82.9	70.2	58.2	48.5
Mauritius	684	—	—	—	—	—	—	—	—	—	—	—	—
Morocco	686	101.1	34.8	2.3	—	—	—	—	—	—	—	—	—
Mozambique	688	145.2	135.8	125.9	140.1	147.2	145.4	168.5	155.9	147.2	140.8	127.0	109.8
Namibia	728												
Niger	692	41.8	35.0	36.6	45.0	54.1	49.6	56.8	64.3	78.3	88.4	87.2	89.3
Nigeria	694	—	—	—	—	—	—	—	—	—	—	—	—
Rwanda	714	8.8	17.7	16.8	29.9	40.1	55.3	65.9	67.1	62.5	61.8	59.4	53.9
São Tomé & Príncipe	716	.7	.6	.4	.2	.1	—	1.9	1.9	1.9	1.9	1.9	2.2
Senegal	722	205.4	233.3	226.5	216.5	207.8	198.2	195.4	197.6	185.8	161.3	131.5	103.8
Seychelles	718	—	—	—	—	—	—	—	—	—	—	—	—
Sierra Leone	724	100.2	110.9	118.8	123.9	135.4	142.0	133.2	120.8	124.5	113.8	126.0	134.4
Somalia	726	112.0	112.0	112.0	112.0	112.0	112.0	112.0	112.0	112.0	112.0	112.0	112.0
South Africa	199	614.4	614.4	614.4	307.2	—	—	—	—	—	—	—	—
Sudan	732	671.6	645.7	621.2	590.5	548.4	520.8	479.7	438.6	421.6	402.9	381.7	362.6
Swaziland	734	—	—	—	—	—	—	—	—	—	—	—	—
Tanzania	738	145.5	132.7	143.4	182.4	190.2	227.6	248.3	271.2	293.9	294.3	272.3	239.6
Togo	742	56.0	70.4	62.5	64.9	67.4	60.4	53.3	45.3	38.0	28.2	17.4	9.8
Tunisia	744	207.3	197.1	165.0	128.4	91.8	55.2	24.7	—	—	—	—	—
Uganda	746	262.6	280.6	290.1	291.7	282.7	270.8	242.6	219.1	188.9	158.8	123.3	91.7
Zambia	754	551.2	833.4	833.4	843.4	843.4	853.4	873.4	781.6	746.6	577.9	573.3	413.6
Zimbabwe	698	257.5	310.0	304.1	285.5	289.2	268.8	215.4	208.4	206.1	202.9	188.8	77.3
Asia	505	5,816.8	4,846.9	3,673.4	15,538.9	24,173.2	17,908.7	18,588.5	12,400.3	10,334.5	9,909.9	8,619.6	7,523.3
Afghanistan, I.R. of	512	—	—	—	—	—	—	—	—	—	—	—	—
Bangladesh	513	473.4	433.1	374.2	287.9	308.4	237.6	168.6	118.3	51.9	49.5	148.5	215.8
Bhutan	514	—	—	—	—	—	—	—	—	—	—	—	—
Cambodia	522	20.3	48.3	48.3	48.3	47.2	53.1	56.2	63.5	70.8	69.7	62.7	56.8
China, People's Rep.	924	—	—	—	—	—	—	—	—	—	—	—	—
Fiji	819	—	—	—	—	—	—	—	—	—	—	—	—
India	534	2,763.2	1,966.6	1,085.3	589.8	284.9	38.5	—	—	—	—	—	—
Indonesia	536	—	—	—	2,201.5	6,455.8	7,466.8	8,318.0	7,251.7	6,518.1	6,915.1	6,237.0	5,462.2
Kiribati	826	—	—	—	—	—	—	—	—	—	—	—	—
Korea	542	—	—	—	8,200.0	12,000.0	4,462.5	4,462.5	—	—	—	—	—
Lao People's Dem.Rep.	544	32.2	42.8	46.6	49.0	44.3	38.4	32.5	29.7	31.8	29.9	24.6	20.5
Malaysia	548	—	—	—	—	—	—	—	—	—	—	—	—
Maldives	556	—	—	—	—	—	—	—	—	—	—	—	4.1
Mongolia	948	37.9	31.6	30.3	35.2	34.3	37.5	38.6	37.3	31.3	33.4	28.5	24.5
Myanmar	518	—	—	—	—	—	—	—	—	—	—	—	—
Nepal	558	37.7	32.5	27.2	22.0	17.2	12.9	9.5	6.2	2.8	7.7	14.3	14.3
Pakistan	564	1,096.8	1,115.0	1,000.5	979.5	996.0	1,271.2	1,197.7	1,455.8	1,506.4	1,424.6	1,207.9	1,044.0
Palau	565	—	—	—	—	—	—	—	—	—	—	—	—
Papua New Guinea	853	10.7	33.3	35.3	35.3	32.4	15.7	29.9	85.5	85.5	81.8	41.4	—
Philippines	566	728.6	489.5	281.9	633.8	1,114.0	1,327.7	1,559.2	1,553.1	1,240.2	805.8	486.9	272.1
Samoa	862	—	—	—	—	—	—	—	—	—	—	—	—
Solomon Islands	813	—	—	—	—	—	—	—	—	—	—	—	—
Sri Lanka	524	422.8	400.5	369.2	321.2	260.8	188.1	123.2	170.6	228.0	264.7	189.3	266.8
Thailand	578	—	—	—	1,800.0	2,300.0	2,500.0	2,350.0	1,337.5	287.5	—	—	—
Tonga	866	—	—	—	—	—	—	—	—	—	—	—	—
Vietnam	582	193.4	253.8	374.6	335.3	277.9	258.7	242.6	291.2	280.2	227.9	178.6	142.3

Total Fund Credit & Loans Outstdg.

2006, International Monetary Fund : *International Financial Statistics Yearbook*

2tl		1994	1995	1996	1997	1998	1999	2000	2001	2002	2003	2004	2005
						Expressed in Millions of SDRs							
Europe	170	**8,036.4**	**11,400.3**	**13,945.3**	**15,708.5**	**19,644.9**	**17,385.4**	**16,847.3**	**21,608.7**	**25,189.0**	**23,765.9**	**19,790.8**	**13,160.5**
Albania	914	37.1	43.4	37.7	40.7	45.8	58.7	67.5	66.3	59.6	60.8	62.4	64.3
Armenia	911	16.9	47.3	81.0	97.9	135.3	146.6	134.7	137.4	143.3	144.4	140.1	123.4
Azerbaijan, Republic of	912	—	67.9	121.7	197.7	228.1	296.7	257.7	234.9	205.1	174.5	134.2	114.5
Belarus	913	70.1	190.2	190.2	190.2	172.3	129.7	87.6	64.3	40.9	17.5	5.8	—
Bosnia & Herzegovina	963	—	32.5	31.0	30.3	54.5	68.4	80.4	88.4	102.4	90.1	70.0	43.4
Bulgaria	918	644.4	482.1	407.2	698.0	792.3	910.7	1,014.6	883.0	771.8	799.2	762.0	461.8
Croatia	960	87.1	148.6	145.4	172.7	166.1	143.2	121.4	97.2	—	—	—	—
Cyprus	423												
Czech Republic	935												
Estonia	939	41.9	61.8	54.2	40.0	21.3	18.4	14.5	10.7				
Georgia	915	27.8	77.7	133.2	188.7	215.8	233.3	213.7	228.7	228.0	194.3	171.3	162.5
Hungary	944	781.6	258.7	118.7	118.7	—	—	—	—	—	—	—	—
Kazakhstan	916	198.0	290.8	383.6	379.0	463.7	335.1	—	—	—	—	—	—
Kyrgyz Republic	917	53.3	83.6	97.1	122.2	124.4	138.7	144.3	142.7	136.3	135.9	133.2	124.5
Latvia	941	109.8	107.9	90.4	63.7	45.4	34.3	26.7	19.1	11.4	3.8	—	—
Lithuania	946	134.6	176.0	190.1	200.5	179.8	167.8	147.1	120.3	89.3	30.2	16.8	—
Macedonia, FYR	962	14.0	38.1	47.4	65.3	72.7	74.1	62.3	56.3	49.6	46.0	40.3	43.5
Moldova	921	112.5	154.9	172.3	172.7	125.6	127.7	118.3	116.3	111.8	95.9	81.4	66.8
Poland	964	918.6	—	—	—	—	—	—	—	—	—	—	—
Romania	968	906.4	698.3	453.0	475.2	382.8	333.8	347.7	308.0	314.9	400.6	285.4	182.6
Russia	922	2,875.6	6,469.8	8,698.2	9,805.9	13,732.0	11,102.3	8,912.8	5,914.8	4,767.3	3,411.2	2,293.8	—
Serbia & Montenegro	965	—	—	—	—	—	—	116.9	216.9	416.9	616.9	621.0	606.3
Slovak Republic	936	439.8	307.5	222.0	184.4	134.6	96.5	—	—	—	—	—	—
Slovenia	961	4.9	2.7	.9	—	—	—	—	—	—	—	—	—
Tajikistan	923	—	—	15.0	22.5	70.3	73.2	85.0	87.7	69.2	67.2	78.7	88.9
Turkey	186	235.5	460.5	460.5	440.4	275.8	648.8	3,205.3	11,232.9	16,245.7	16,212.8	13,848.3	10,247.3
Ukraine	926	249.3	1,037.3	1,573.3	1,780.6	1,985.0	2,044.6	1,591.2	1,520.7	1,380.0	1,235.5	1,033.7	830.9
Uzbekistan	927	—	106.0	165.2	165.2	165.2	146.8	97.5	62.3	45.7	29.1	12.5	—
Middle East	405	**409.7**	**350.3**	**353.3**	**502.0**	**571.8**	**660.5**	**597.8**	**641.8**	**638.8**	**553.7**	**756.8**	**666.9**
Bahrain, Kingdom of	419	—	—	—	—	—	—	—	—	—	—	—	—
Egypt	469	132.2	69.5	10.9	—	—	—	—	—	—	—	—	—
Iran, I.R. of	429	—	—	—	—	—	—	—	—	—	—	297.1	297.1
Iraq	433	—	—	—	—	—	—	—	—	—	—	—	—
Israel	436	178.6	111.7	22.3	—	—	—	—	—	—	—	—	—
Jordan	439	98.9	169.2	236.1	316.6	333.4	362.9	354.3	344.5	355.0	283.6	217.5	165.3
Syrian Arab Republic	463	—	—	—	—	—	—	—	—	—	—	—	—
Yemen, Republic of	474	—	—	84.0	185.4	238.4	297.6	243.5	297.3	283.8	270.1	242.2	204.5
Western Hemisphere	205	**9,466.4**	**17,973.3**	**16,629.2**	**13,758.1**	**15,616.2**	**14,934.0**	**6,789.5**	**19,017.6**	**28,170.4**	**32,136.0**	**27,884.5**	**9,189.4**
Antigua and Barbuda	311	—	—	—	—	—	—	—	—	—	—	—	—
Argentina	213	2,884.7	4,124.4	4,376.0	4,349.3	3,865.1	3,262.6	3,880.3	11,121.1	10,547.5	10,446.2	9,073.0	6,655.7
Barbados	316	36.8	24.9	6.5	—	—	—	—	—	—	—	—	—
Belize	339												
Bolivia	218	180.5	180.1	192.0	183.9	187.6	180.0	168.8	164.8	143.7	187.5	197.7	170.6
Brazil	223	127.5	95.2	47.0	23.3	3,426.8	6,431.0	1,356.8	6,633.9	15,319.6	19,056.5	16,116.7	—
Chile	228	199.5	—	—	—	—	—	—	—	—	—	—	—
Colombia	233												
Costa Rica	238	45.5	16.3	.5	—	—	—	—	—	2.1	5.3	5.9	8.1
Dominica	321	1.7	1.1	.6	.2	—	—	—	—	19.9	87.6	131.3	280.2
Dominican Republic	243	129.9	107.5	66.5	21.1	39.7	39.7	39.7	39.7	—	—	—	—
Ecuador	248	135.7	116.7	100.9	98.9	49.5	—	113.3	151.1	226.7	262.3	186.8	54.7
El Salvador	253												
Grenada	328	—	—	—	—	—	—	—	—	—	2.9	5.9	5.9
Guatemala	258												
Guyana	336	122.3	115.6	117.1	116.4	109.5	102.2	90.1	77.7	70.7	64.2	56.7	63.6
Haiti	263	3.8	18.2	31.6	31.6	40.8	32.6	30.4	30.4	19.7	9.1	6.1	23.5
Honduras	268	74.8	66.4	40.3	33.9	80.0	153.3	165.8	175.1	144.6	115.4	125.7	117.6
Jamaica	343	217.6	161.7	112.2	87.1	74.7	60.8	46.3	31.9	17.4	6.0	.6	—
Mexico	273	2,644.2	10,648.1	9,234.5	6,735.2	5,951.5	3,259.2	—	—	—	—	—	—
Nicaragua	278	34.9	26.4	20.0	20.0	36.8	113.2	129.3	125.3	128.3	143.5	159.5	140.5
Panama	283	91.3	74.4	91.0	105.4	125.5	108.3	69.1	42.9	36.7	30.0	23.3	16.7
Paraguay	288												
Peru	293	642.7	642.7	642.7	749.6	642.5	535.4	428.3	307.8	173.9	93.6	66.9	40.1
St. Kitts and Nevis	361	—	—	—	—	1.6	1.6	1.6	1.6	.8	—	—	—
St. Lucia	362	—	—	—	—	—	—	—	—	—	—	—	—
St. Vincent & Grens	364	—	—	—	—	—	—	—	—	—	—	—	—
Suriname	366	—	—	—	—	—	—	—	—	—	—	—	—
Trinidad and Tobago	369	62.4	33.8	16.5	3.1	—	—	—	—	—	—	—	—
Uruguay	298	20.5	14.0	6.0	—	114.2	114.2	114.2	114.2	1,318.8	1,625.9	1,728.4	1,612.2
Venezuela, Rep. Bol.	299	1,810.2	1,506.0	1,527.4	1,198.9	870.4	540.0	155.6	—	—	—	—	—
Memorandum Items													
Oil Exporting Ctys.	999	2,603.9	2,500.0	2,940.0	4,895.9	8,754.2	9,395.6	9,792.1	8,459.7	7,496.5	7,579.8	6,948.1	5,759.3
Non-Oil Develop.Ctys.	201	27,657.0	39,136.1	39,118.6	47,718.8	58,027.5	48,138.5	39,558.2	51,460.3	62,985.2	64,339.1	55,191.7	28,955.0

Use of Fund Credit (GRA)

		1994	1995	1996	1997	1998	1999	2000	2001	2002	2003	2004	2005
						Expressed in Millions of SDRs							
World	001	25,611.7	35,929.2	36,127.5	46,559.0	60,451.0	51,061.9	42,990.5	53,477.2	63,601.1	65,032.1	55,373.8	28,432.1
Developing Countries	200	25,611.7	35,929.2	36,127.5	46,559.0	60,451.0	51,061.9	42,990.5	53,477.2	63,601.1	65,032.1	55,373.8	28,432.1
Africa	605	3,863.9	3,380.4	3,668.1	3,308.2	2,793.9	2,653.5	2,490.9	2,249.7	1,850.3	1,511.8	1,240.3	671.3
Algeria	612	793.8	994.1	1,412.5	1,495.5	1,428.0	1,388.7	1,318.5	1,208.0	978.4	664.7	414.0	—
Burkina Faso	748												
Burundi	618	—	—	—	—	—	—	—	—	9.6	19.3	—	—
Cameroon	622	29.9	34.4	50.1	41.9	29.9	16.6	2.5	—	—	—	—	—
Central African Rep.	626	10.7	10.7	10.7	8.0	2.4	—	—	—	—	—	5.6	5.6
Chad	628	10.3	10.3	10.3	6.5	1.3	—	—	—	—	—		
Comoros	632												
Congo, Dem. Rep. of	636	181.8	180.9	158.2	158.2	157.8	157.1	157.1	157.1	—	—	—	—
Congo, Republic of	634	14.0	12.5	12.5	10.9	10.4	7.2	17.8	16.9	13.3	10.6	5.3	—
Côte d'Ivoire	662	105.7	48.9	16.1	—	—	—	—	—	—	—		
Djibouti	611	—	—	2.9	4.0	6.3	6.6	4.8	3.2	1.4	.1		
Equatorial Guinea	642												
Ethiopia	644												
Gabon	646	61.4	65.0	83.3	97.2	80.5	62.6	68.4	59.6	49.5	39.4	64.4	47.6
Gambia, The	648												
Ghana	652	89.0	75.9	59.0	24.6	—	—	—	—	—	—		
Guinea	656												
Guinea-Bissau	654	—	—	—	—	—	2.1	3.6	3.6	3.3	1.7	.2	—
Kenya	664												
Lesotho	666												
Liberia	668	201.6	201.5	201.5	201.5	201.5	201.5	201.3	201.0	200.8	200.8	200.8	200.7
Madagascar	674	.6	—	—	—	—	—	—	—	—	—		
Malawi	676	12.7	12.7	12.7	12.7	6.4	—	—	—	17.4	17.4	17.4	15.2
Mali	678	1.0	—	—	—	—	—	—	—	—	—		
Mauritania	682												
Mauritius	684												
Morocco	686	101.1	34.8	2.3	—	—	—	—	—	—	—	—	—
Niger	692	11.1	11.1	11.1	6.9	1.4	—	—	—	—	—		
Nigeria	694												
Rwanda	714	—	8.9	8.9	23.8	23.8	19.3	12.6	5.2	—	—		
Senegal	722	30.9	30.9	30.9	19.3	3.9	—	—	—	—	—		
Sierra Leone	724	—	—	—	—	11.6	27.1	37.5	—	—	—		
Somalia	726	96.7	96.7	96.7	96.7	96.7	96.7	96.7	96.7	96.7	96.7	96.7	96.7
South Africa	199	614.4	614.4	614.4	307.2	—	—	—	—	—	—		
Sudan	732	604.2	581.3	556.8	531.3	489.1	461.5	420.4	379.4	362.4	343.6	322.5	303.4
Swaziland	734	—	—	—	—	—	—	—	—	—	—		
Tanzania	738	—	—	—	—	—	—	—	—	—	—		
Togo	742	2.2	.2	—	—	—	—	—	—	—	—		
Tunisia	744	207.3	197.1	165.0	128.4	91.8	55.2	24.7	—	—	—		
Uganda	746	—	—	—	—	—	—	—	—	—	—		
Zambia	754	544.6	—	—	—	—	—	—	—	—	—		
Zimbabwe	698	139.0	158.1	152.2	133.6	151.3	151.2	124.9	119.0	117.5	117.5	113.6	2.1
Asia	505	4,178.6	3,232.1	2,078.5	14,049.2	22,794.7	16,700.7	17,592.7	11,433.5	9,212.1	8,498.2	7,080.7	6,020.5
Afghanistan, I.R. of	512	—	—	—	—	—	—	—	—	—	—		
Bangladesh	513	—	—	—	—	98.1	98.1	98.1	98.1	49.1	—	—	—
Bhutan	514	—	—	—	—	—	—	—	—	—	—		
Cambodia	522	6.3	6.3	6.3	6.3	5.2	4.2	3.1	2.1	1.0	—	—	—
China, People's Rep.	924	—	—	—	—	—	—	—	—	—	—		
Fiji	819	—	—	—	—	—	—	—	—	—	—		
India	534	2,763.2	1,966.6	1,085.3	589.8	284.9	38.5	—	—	—	—	—	—
Indonesia	536	—	—	—	2,201.5	6,455.8	7,466.8	8,318.0	7,251.7	6,518.1	6,915.1	6,237.0	5,462.2
Korea	542	—	—	—	8,200.0	12,000.0	4,462.5	4,462.5	—	—	—	—	—
Lao People's Dem.Rep.	544	—	—	—	—	—	—	—	—	—	—		—
Malaysia	548	—	—	—	—	—	—	—	—	—	—		
Maldives	556	—	—	—	—	—	—	—	—	—	—		4.1
Mongolia	948	13.8	7.5	.6	—	—	—	—	—	—	—		
Myanmar	518	—	—	—	—	—	—	—	—	—	—		
Nepal	558	—	—	—	—	—	—	—	—	—	—		
Pakistan	564	523.2	595.9	536.1	488.8	468.0	770.0	758.8	993.0	825.6	473.9	164.5	53.7
Palau	565	—	—	—	—	—	—	—	—	—	—		
Papua New Guinea	853	10.7	33.3	35.3	35.3	32.4	15.7	29.9	85.5	85.5	81.8	41.4	—
Philippines	566	728.6	489.5	281.9	633.8	1,114.0	1,327.7	1,559.2	1,553.1	1,240.2	805.8	486.9	272.1
Samoa	862	—	—	—	—	—	—	—	—	—	—		
Solomon Islands	813	—	—	—	—	—	—	—	—	—	—		
Sri Lanka	524	—	—	—	—	—	—	—	103.4	200.0	220.7	150.9	228.4
Thailand	578	—	—	—	1,800.0	2,300.0	2,500.0	2,350.0	1,337.5	287.5	—	—	—
Vietnam	582	133.0	133.0	133.0	93.7	36.3	17.1	13.1	9.1	5.0	1.0	—	—
Europe	170	8,002.9	11,329.4	13,769.1	15,353.9	19,144.1	16,779.5	16,191.3	20,883.9	24,444.0	23,020.1	19,067.0	12,464.1
Albania	914	13.1	12.3	6.6	9.7	8.8	8.8	8.8	4.4	—	—		
Armenia	911	16.9	47.3	47.3	47.3	46.8	37.3	25.3	19.7	14.1	7.0	1.4	—
Azerbaijan, Republic of	912	—	67.9	121.7	142.2	157.9	214.8	175.8	144.9	109.2	63.9	38.2	22.0
Belarus	913	70.1	190.2	190.2	190.2	172.3	129.7	87.6	64.3	40.9	17.5	5.8	—
Bosnia & Herzegovina	963	—	32.5	31.0	30.3	54.5	68.4	80.4	88.4	102.4	90.1	70.0	43.4
Bulgaria	918	644.4	482.1	407.2	698.0	792.3	910.7	1,014.6	883.0	771.8	799.2	762.0	461.8
Croatia	960	87.1	148.6	145.4	172.7	166.1	143.2	121.4	97.2	—	—	—	—
Cyprus	423	—	—	—	—	—	—	—	—	—	—		
Czech Republic	935	—	—	—	—	—	—	—	—	—	—		
Estonia	939	41.9	61.8	54.2	40.0	21.3	18.4	14.5	10.7	—	—	—	—
Georgia	915	27.8	77.7	77.7	77.7	77.0	61.3	41.6	32.4	23.1	11.6	2.3	—

Use of Fund Credit (GRA)

		1994	1995	1996	1997	1998	1999	2000	2001	2002	2003	2004	2005
						Expressed in Millions of SDRs							
Europe(Cont.)													
Hungary	944	781.6	258.7	118.7	118.7	—	—	—	—	—	—	—	—
Kazakhstan	916	198.0	290.8	383.6	379.0	463.7	335.1	—	—	—	—	—	—
Kyrgyz Republic	917	43.9	43.9	41.2	34.1	25.5	20.2	14.8	9.4	4.0	—	—	—
Latvia	941	109.8	107.9	90.4	63.7	45.4	34.3	26.7	19.1	11.4	3.8	—	—
Lithuania	946	134.6	176.0	190.1	200.5	179.8	167.8	147.1	120.3	89.3	30.2	16.8	—
Macedonia, FYR	962	14.0	38.1	47.4	47.1	45.4	46.8	33.3	27.3	21.5	22.4	22.2	30.9
Moldova	921	112.5	154.9	172.3	172.7	125.6	127.7	109.1	97.8	84.1	68.2	53.6	39.1
Poland	964	918.6	—	—	—	—	—	—	—	—	—	—	—
Romania	968	906.4	698.3	453.0	475.2	382.8	333.8	347.7	308.0	314.9	400.6	285.4	182.6
Russia	922	2,875.6	6,469.8	8,698.2	9,805.9	13,732.0	11,102.3	8,912.8	5,914.8	4,767.3	3,411.2	2,293.8	—
Serbia & Montenegro	965	—	—	—	—	—	—	116.9	216.9	416.9	616.9	621.0	606.3
Slovak Republic	936	439.8	307.5	222.0	184.4	134.6	96.5	—	—	—	—	—	—
Slovenia	961	4.9	2.7	.9	—	—	—	—	—	—	—	—	—
Tajikistan	923	—	—	15.0	22.5	30.0	26.3	18.8	9.4	1.9	—	—	—
Turkey	186	235.5	460.5	460.5	440.4	275.8	648.8	3,205.3	11,232.9	16,245.7	16,212.8	13,848.3	10,247.3
Ukraine	926	249.3	1,037.3	1,573.3	1,780.6	1,985.0	2,044.6	1,591.2	1,520.7	1,380.0	1,235.5	1,033.7	830.9
Uzbekistan	927	—	106.0	165.2	165.2	165.2	146.8	97.5	62.3	45.7	29.1	12.5	—
Middle East	405	**409.7**	**350.3**	**353.3**	**458.0**	**483.8**	**510.5**	**447.8**	**403.1**	**400.0**	**323.7**	**548.1**	**488.1**
Egypt	469	132.2	69.5	10.9	—	—	—	—	—	—	—	—	—
Iran, I.R. of	429	—	—	—	—	—	—	—	—	—	—	—	—
Iraq	433	—	—	—	—	—	—	—	—	—	—	297.1	297.1
Israel	436	178.6	111.7	22.3	—	—	—	—	—	—	—	—	—
Jordan	439	98.9	169.2	236.1	316.6	333.4	362.9	354.3	344.5	355.0	283.6	217.5	165.3
Syrian Arab Republic	463	—	—	—	—	—	—	—	—	—	—	—	—
Yemen, Republic of	474	—	—	84.0	141.4	150.4	147.6	93.5	58.6	45.0	40.2	33.5	25.7
Western Hemisphere	205	**9,156.6**	**17,636.9**	**16,258.5**	**13,389.8**	**15,234.5**	**14,417.7**	**6,267.8**	**18,506.9**	**27,694.7**	**31,678.3**	**27,437.7**	**8,788.1**
Argentina	213	2,884.7	4,124.4	4,376.0	4,349.3	3,865.1	3,262.6	3,880.3	11,121.1	10,547.5	10,446.2	9,073.0	6,655.7
Barbados	316	36.8	24.9	6.5	—	—	—	—	—	—	—	—	—
Belize	339	—	—	—	—	—	—	—	—	—	—	—	—
Bolivia	218	—	—	—	—	—	—	—	—	—	64.3	101.8	99.4
Brazil	223	127.5	95.2	47.0	23.3	3,426.8	6,431.0	1,356.8	6,633.9	15,319.6	19,056.5	16,116.7	—
Chile	228	199.5	—	—	—	—	—	—	—	—	—	—	—
Colombia	233	—	—	—	—	—	—	—	—	—	—	—	—
Costa Rica	238	45.5	16.3	.5	—	—	—	—	—	—	—	—	—
Dominica	321	—	—	—	—	—	—	—	—	2.1	3.0	3.0	2.7
Dominican Republic	243	129.9	107.5	66.5	21.1	39.7	39.7	39.7	39.7	19.9	87.6	131.3	280.2
Ecuador	248	135.7	116.7	100.9	98.9	49.5	—	113.3	151.1	226.7	262.3	186.8	54.7
El Salvador	253	—	—	—	—	—	—	—	—	—	—	—	—
Grenada	328	—	—	—	—	—	—	—	—	—	2.9	5.9	5.9
Guatemala	258	—	—	—	—	—	—	—	—	—	—	—	—
Guyana	336	31.8	16.2	8.1	1.4	—	—	—	—	—	—	—	—
Haiti	263	.3	16.4	16.4	16.4	25.6	17.4	15.2	15.2	7.6	—	—	20.5
Honduras	268	61.3	32.5	6.4	—	47.5	47.5	47.5	47.5	23.8	—	—	—
Jamaica	343	217.6	161.7	112.2	87.1	74.7	60.8	46.3	31.9	17.4	6.0	.6	—
Mexico	273	2,644.2	10,648.1	9,234.5	6,735.2	5,951.5	3,259.2	—	—	—	—	—	—
Nicaragua	278	14.9	6.4	—	—	—	—	—	—	—	—	—	—
Panama	283	91.3	74.4	91.0	105.4	125.5	108.3	69.1	42.9	36.7	30.0	23.3	16.7
Paraguay	288	—	—	—	—	—	—	—	—	—	—	—	—
Peru	293	642.7	642.7	642.7	749.6	642.5	535.4	428.3	307.8	173.9	93.6	66.9	40.1
St. Kitts and Nevis	361	—	—	—	—	1.6	1.6	1.6	1.6	.8	—	—	—
St. Lucia	362	—	—	—	—	—	—	—	—	—	—	—	—
St. Vincent & Grens	364	—	—	—	—	—	—	—	—	—	—	—	—
Trinidad and Tobago	369	62.4	33.8	16.5	3.1	—	—	—	—	—	—	—	—
Uruguay	298	20.5	14.0	6.0	—	114.2	114.2	114.2	114.2	1,318.8	1,625.9	1,728.4	1,612.2
Venezuela, Rep. Bol	299	1,810.2	1,506.0	1,527.4	1,198.9	870.4	540.0	155.6	—	—	—	—	—
Memorandum Items													
Oil Exporting Ctys	999	**2,603.9**	**2,500.0**	**2,940.0**	**4,895.9**	**8,754.2**	**9,395.6**	**9,792.1**	**8,459.7**	**7,496.5**	**7,579.8**	**6,948.1**	**5,759.3**
Non-Oil Develop.Ctys	201	**23,007.7**	**33,429.1**	**33,187.5**	**41,663.2**	**51,696.8**	**41,666.3**	**33,198.5**	**45,017.5**	**56,104.6**	**57,452.2**	**48,425.7**	**22,672.8**

Total Reserves minus Gold

1I s		1994	1995	1996	1997	1998	1999	2000	2001	2002	2003	2004	2005
						Millions of SDRs: End of Period							
All Countries	010	860,302	991,320	1,145,667	1,265,422	1,248,489	1,371,098	1,551,989	1,706,715	1,855,803	2,122,157	2,487,131	2,962,546
Industrial Countries	110	433,940	487,827	548,944	577,832	546,026	588,314	652,817	687,710	730,566	818,814	902,443	934,058
United States	111	43,350	50,307	44,536	43,659	50,223	44,080	43,442	45,860	49,990	50,401	48,866	37,840
Canada	156	8,416	10,124	14,202	13,209	16,553	20,493	24,639	27,024	27,204	24,376	22,169	23,062
Australia	193	7,730	8,003	10,073	12,485	10,398	15,455	13,906	14,287	15,218	21,662	23,054	29,345
Japan	158	86,214	123,277	150,663	162,793	153,030	209,045	272,392	314,431	339,227	446,368	536,952	583,707
New Zealand	196	2,540	2,967	4,140	3,299	2,986	3,246	3,033	2,836	3,650	4,095	4,473	6,222
Euro Area (incl. ECB)	163	....	....	....	....	....	187,088	185,988	186,965	181,678	149,983	136,147	129,240
Austria	122	11,523	12,600	15,901	14,628	15,932	† 11,017	10,990	9,954	7,123	5,700	5,060	4,785
Belgium	124	9,505	10,883	11,789	11,999	12,977	† 7,969	7,671	8,965	8,720	7,395	6,672	5,766
Finland	172	7,303	6,753	4,810	6,238	6,885	† 5,989	6,122	6,352	6,830	7,076	7,932	7,408
France	132	17,986	18,065	18,635	22,922	31,471	† 28,926	28,428	25,263	20,864	20,314	22,739	19,418
Germany	134	52,994	57,185	57,844	57,504	52,573	† 44,472	43,664	40,903	37,639	34,115	31,437	31,582
Greece	174	9,924	9,943	12,171	9,335	12,399	13,204	10,303	† 4,101	5,945	2,935	767	354
Ireland	178	4,189	5,806	5,706	4,837	6,674	† 3,880	4,114	4,445	3,983	2,745	1,823	545
Italy	136	22,102	23,482	31,954	41,311	21,227	† 16,336	19,623	19,431	21,039	20,434	17,939	17,852
Luxembourg	137	52	50	51	47		† 56	59	84	112	188	192	169
Netherlands	138	23,655	22,680	18,615	18,429	15,211	† 7,203	7,401	7,189	7,034	7,515	6,598	6,384
Portugal	182	10,627	10,663	11,070	11,606	11,239	† 6,140	6,838	7,692	8,223	3,954	3,332	2,434
Spain	184	28,459	23,199	40,284	50,694	39,245	† 24,127	23,784	23,539	25,403	13,317	7,977	6,771
Denmark	128	6,203	7,411	9,834	14,174	10,841	16,238	11,596	13,615	19,849	24,970	25,166	† 23,040
Iceland	176	201	207	316	284	303	349	298	269	324	533	674	725
Norway	142	13,033	15,148	18,441	17,343	13,528	17,346	21,181	18,522	23,538	25,048	28,530	32,874
San Marino	135	121	134	150	136	121	105	104	106	135	170	229	248
Sweden	144	15,929	16,180	13,288	8,023	10,013	10,943	11,407	11,112	12,598	13,245	14,249	15,437
Switzerland	146	23,790	24,496	26,727	28,926	29,254	26,463	24,769	25,467	29,536	32,068	35,735	25,396
United Kingdom	112	28,094	28,265	27,745	23,952	22,877	† 24,260	29,759	27,205	27,620	25,895	26,199	26,923
Developing Countries	200	426,363	503,494	596,723	687,590	702,463	782,784	899,171	1,019,005	1,125,237	1,303,343	1,584,688	2,028,488
Africa	605	16,201	17,727	22,107	32,239	29,362	30,703	42,148	51,814	53,615	61,644	82,083	113,103
CEMAC (Incl. BEAC hqtrs.)	758	....	....	....	....	....	....	965	859	1,177	1,220	2,003	3,599
Cameroon	622	† 2	3	2	1	1	3	163	264	463	430	534	664
Central African Republic	626	144	157	162	132	103	99	102	94	91	89	96	97
Chad	628	52	96	114	101	85	69	85	97	161	126	143	158
Congo, Rep. of	634	34	40	63	44	1	29	170	55	23	23	77	512
Equatorial Guinea	642	—	—	—	4	1	2	18	56	65	160	608	1,471
Gabon	646	120	100	173	209	11	13	146	8	103	132	286	468
WAEMU (Incl. BCEAO hqtrs.)	759	....	1,708	1,905	2,126	2,247	2,136	2,520	3,008	4,012	4,528	4,668	4,319
Benin	638	† 177	133	182	188	186	291	352	460	453	483	412	460
Burkina Faso	748	163	234	235	256	265	215	187	207	231	506	431	307
Côte d'Ivoire	662	140	356	421	458	608	459	513	811	1,371	877	1,091	925
Guinea Bissau	654	13	14	8	25	25	26	51	55	76	22	47	56
Mali	678	† 152	217	300	308	286	255	293	278	437	641	554	598
Niger	692	76	64	55	39	38	29	62	85	98	175	166	175
Senegal	722	123	183	200	286	306	294	295	356	469	748	893	833
Togo	742	65	88	62	88	84	89	117	101	151	138	232	136
Algeria	612	1,832	1,349	2,945	5,964	4,862	3,297	9,228	14,388	17,092	22,292	27,847	39,393
Angola	614	....	143	384	294	144	361	920	582	276	427	885	2,237
Botswana	616	3,015	3,159	3,496	4,206	4,219	4,538	4,849	4,693	4,026	3,593	3,645	4,414
Burundi	618	140	141	97	84	47	35	25	14	43	45	42	70
Cape Verde	624	29	25	19	14	6	31	22	36	59	63	90	122
Comoros	632	30	30	35	30	28	27	33	50	59	63	67	60
Congo, Dem. Rep. of	636	83	99	57	....	....	....	....	....	....	....		
Djibouti	611	51	49	54	49	47	51	52	56	54	67	60	62
Eritrea	643	....	27	57	148	16	25	20	32	22	17	22	20
Ethiopia	644	373	519	509	371	363	334	235	345	649	643	964	785
Gambia, The	648	67	71	71	71	76	81	84	84	79	40	54	69
Ghana	652	400	469	576	399	268	331	178	237	397	910	1,047	1,226
Guinea	656	60	58	61	90	168	145	114	159	126	....	71	67
Kenya	664	382	238	519	584	556	577	689	847	786	997	978	1,259
Lesotho	666	255	307	320	424	408	364	321	308	299	310	323	364
Liberia	668	3	19	—	—	—	—	—	—	2	5	12	18
Madagascar	674	49	73	168	209	122	166	219	317	267	279	324	337
Malawi	676	29	74	153	105	181	180	186	161	119	82	82	111
Mauritania	682	27	57	98	149	144	163	215	226	291	280	....	....
Mauritius	684	512	581	623	514	397	533	689	665	903	1,061	1,034	937
Morocco	686	2,981	2,423	2,638	2,959	3,150	4,145	3,702	6,743	7,453	9,321	10,519	11,326
Mozambique	688	122	131	239	383	432	477	555	568	590	631	728	737
Namibia	728	139	149	135	186	185	223	199	186	238	219	222	218
Nigeria	694	949	971	2,834	5,619	5,043	3,971	7,607	8,321	5,393	4,797	10,918	19,786
Rwanda	714	35	67	74	114	120	127	146	169	179	144	203	284
São Tomé & Príncipe	716	....	3	3	9	7	† 8	9	12	13	17	13	19
Seychelles	718	21	18	15	20	15	22	34	30	51	45	22	39
Sierra Leone	724	28	23	18	29	31	29	38	41	62	45	81	119
South Africa	199	1,154	1,897	655	3,557	3,094	4,629	4,669	4,810	4,343	4,371	8,462	12,999
Sudan	732	54	110	74	60	64	138	† 190	94	324	570	1,047	1,714
Swaziland	734	203	201	177	219	255	274	270	216	203	187	208	171
Tanzania	738	227	182	306	461	426	565	748	920	1,125	1,372	1,478	1,433
Tunisia	744	1,001	1,080	1,320	1,466	1,314	1,648	1,390	1,583	1,685	1,982	2,534	3,059

Total Reserves minus Gold

		1994	1995	1996	1997	1998	1999	2000	2001	2002	2003	2004	2005
							Millions of SDRs: End of Period						
1l s													
Africa(Cont.)													
Uganda	746	220	309	367	470	515	556	620	782	687	727	842	940
Zambia	754	184	150	155	177	49	33	188	146	394	167	217	392
Zimbabwe	698	278	401	416	119	93	195	148	51	61	....	....	....
Asia *	505	262,647	291,127	343,989	384,346	413,548	482,890	547,597	631,296	717,624	840,155	1,039,344	1,304,423
Bangladesh	513	2,150	1,574	1,276	1,172	1,353	1,168	1,140	1,015	1,238	1,735	2,043	1,936
Bhutan	514	83	† 88	132	140	182	213	244	257	261	247	257	327
Brunei Darussalam	516	....	....	....	....	....	377	313	311	322	324	325	346
Cambodia	522	81	129	185	221	230	286	385	467	571	549	607	667
China, P.R.: Mainland	924	36,246	50,708	74,438	105,809	105,955	114,919	129,155	171,560	214,140	274,670	395,683	574,779
China, P.R.: Hong Kong	532	33,737	37,268	44,374	68,782	63,671	70,117	82,540	88,448	82,306	79,652	79,549	86,928
China, P.R.: Macao	546	1,347	1,518	1,684	1,877	1,749	2,082	2,550	2,792	2,795	2,923	3,500	4,680
Fiji	819	187	235	297	267	274	312	316	292	264	285	308	220
India	534	13,493	12,056	14,027	18,298	19,418	23,801	29,090	36,500	49,772	66,581	81,515	92,302
Indonesia	536	8,311	9,222	12,692	12,293	16,131	19,268	21,876	21,680	22,781	23,528	22,506	23,081
Korea	542	17,563	21,983	23,670	15,096	36,913	53,907	73,781	81,762	89,256	104,500	128,136	147,150
Lao P. D. Rep	544	42e	62	118	83	80	74	107	104	141	140	144	164
Malaysia	548	17,415	15,994	18,783	15,407	18,153	22,286	21,744	23,491	24,539	29,490	42,422	48,877
Maldives	556	21	32	53	73	84	93	94	74	98	107	131	130
Micronesia, Fed. States of	868	....	47	62	64	72	68	87	78	86	60	35	35
Mongolia	948	56	79	75	130	67	99	137	164	257	159	152	301
Myanmar	518	289	377	159	185	224	193	171	319	346	370	433	539
Nepal	558	475	395	397	464	537	616	726	826	749	823	942	1,049
Pakistan	564	2,007	1,166	381	886	730	1,101	1,162	2,896	5,942	7,363	6,310	7,020
Papua New Guinea	853	66	176	406	269	137	149	220	336	236	333	407	502
Philippines	566	4,136	4,303	6,995	5,409	6,587	9,668	10,047	10,723	9,804	9,189	8,446	11,143
Samoa	862	35	37	42	48	44	50	49	45	46	56	62	65
Singapore	576	39,851	46,213	53,442	52,836	53,215	55,987	61,502	59,977	60,331	64,433	72,267	81,016
Solomon Islands	813	12	11	23	27	35	37	25	15	13	25	52	67
Sri Lanka	524	1,401	1,404	1,364	1,500	1,406	1,192	797	1,024	1,200	1,524	1,373	1,855
Thailand	578	20,093	24,206	26,239	19,403	20,472	24,818	24,573	25,745	27,985	27,643	31,335	35,466
Tonga	866	24	19	21	20	20	18	19	19	18	27	36	33
Vanuatu	846	30	32	31	28	32	30	30	30	27	29	40	47
Vietnam	582	....	890	1,207	1,472	1,422	2,423	2,622	2,924	3,031	4,189	4,534	6,333
*of which:													
Taiwan Province of China	528	63,331	60,754	61,224	61,888	64,161	77,376	81,926	97,245	118,907	139,055	155,658	177,216
Europe	170	30,530	57,652	61,672	71,931	72,769	78,853	97,249	111,317	138,280	169,358	213,502	297,234
Albania	914	140	162	195	229	273	356	473	589	617	679	874	982
Armenia	911	22	67	108	170	230	232	244	255	313	343	371	528
Azerbaijan, Republic of	912	1	81	147	345	318	490	522	577	530	540	692	824
Belarus	913	† 69	254	326	292	499	214	269	311	455	400	483	795
Bosnia & Herzegovina	963	....	....	....	60	124	330	381	972	972	1,208	1,550	1,771
Bulgaria	918	686	832	336	1,565	1,907	2,107	2,421	2,619	3,242	4,234	5,651	5,626
Croatia	960	962	1,275	1,609	1,882	2,000	2,204	2,705	3,742	4,329	5,512	5,639	6,157
Cyprus	423	1,003	751	1,072	1,031	980	1,335	1,336	1,804	2,223	2,192	2,518	2,932
Czech Republic	935	4,209	9,312	8,590	7,214	8,908	9,330	9,992	11,412	17,326	18,016	18,196	20,521
Estonia	939	304	390	443	562	576	622	707	653	736	924	1,151	1,360
Georgia	915	....	131	131	148	87	96	84	127	145	128	247	331
Hungary	944	4,614	8,055	6,760	6,232	6,618	7,981	8,588	8,536	7,612	8,572	10,243	12,971
Kazakhstan	916	574	764	900	1,258	1,038	1,078	1,224	1,589	1,880	2,851	5,456	4,257
Kyrgyz Republic	917	18	54	66	126	116	167	183	210	212	245	340	399
Latvia	941	373	340	455	563	569	635	653	914	913	964	1,231	1,562
Lithuania	946	360	509	537	749	1,001	871	1,007	1,287	1,728	2,269	2,262	2,603
Macedonia, FYR	962	102	173	167	190	217	313	330	593	531	604	583	860
Malta	181	1,267	1,079	1,126	1,103	1,181	1,303	1,128	1,326	1,625	1,836	1,759	1,803
Moldova	921	123	173	217	271	102	135	171	182	198	203	303	418
Poland	964	4,002	9,939	12,409	15,125	19,407	19,202	20,387	20,409	21,073	21,924	22,745	28,591
Romania	968	1,429	1,062	1,462	2,819	2,036	1,112	1,896	3,121	4,505	5,411	9,412	13,904
Russia	922	2,727	9,676	7,842	9,557	5,541	6,162	18,623	25,895	32,404	49,244	77,790	123,064
Slovak Republic	936	1,158	2,263	2,378	2,394	2,037	2,456	3,087	3,295	6,479	7,859	9,284	10,425
Slovenia	961	1,027	1,225	1,598	2,457	2,584	2,308	2,453	3,445	5,134	5,718	5,662	5,651
Tajikistan	923	....	....	....	27	38	40	71	74	66	75	101	118
Turkey	186	4,911	8,370	11,430	13,829	13,841	17,010	17,260	15,022	19,910	22,875	22,968	35,388
Ukraine	926	446	707	1,363	1,735	541	762	1,038	2,352	3,120	4,530	5,990	13,374
Middle East	405	45,585	50,058	60,551	73,304	72,440	78,426	92,099	98,269	97,426	100,614	107,692	135,040
Bahrain, Kingdom of	419	801	861	917	956	766	997	1,200	1,340	1,269	1,197	1,250	....
Egypt	469	9,234	10,886	12,099	13,833	12,872	10,553	10,068	10,285	9,741	9,145	9,191	14,419
Israel	436	4,653	5,462	7,938	15,069	16,104	16,470	17,869	18,603	17,714	17,709	17,446	19,632
Jordan	439	1,159	1,327	1,223	1,631	1,243	1,916	2,557	2,437	2,925	3,496	3,391	3,673
Kuwait	443	2,398	2,395	2,444	2,558	2,803	3,515	5,436	7,875	6,773	5,099	5,307	6,201
Lebanon	446	2,661	3,050	4,125	4,429	4,656	5,665	4,562	3,990	5,328	8,425	7,556	8,317
Libya	672	....	....	....	....	5,163	5,304	9,564	11,777	10,524	13,179	16,541	27,642
Oman	449	1,128	1,232	1,364	1,534	1,376	2,016	1,827	1,882	2,334	2,418	2,316	3,049
Qatar	453	451	500	477	608	741	950	889	1,045	1,152	1,981	2,187	3,178
Saudi Arabia	456	5,054	5,800	† 9,959	11,026	10,099	12,384	15,032	14,001	15,160	15,222	17,573	18,562
United Arab Emirates	466	4,561	5,026	5,602	6,205	6,447	7,778	10,379	11,256	11,195	10,154	11,932	14,700
Yemen, Republic of	474	175	416	707	892	707	1,072	2,226	2,911	3,244	3,356	3,648	4,279
Western Hemisphere	205	71,399	86,929	108,404	125,770	114,344	111,912	120,078	126,309	118,292	131,572	142,066	178,689
ECCU (incl. ECCB hqtrs.)	309	179	211	203	228	256	268	297	357	374	366	408	420
Anguilla	312	6	9	10	12	13	15	16	19	19	22	19	28
Antigua and Barbuda	311	31	40	33	38	42	51	49	63	64	77	77	89
Dominica	321	11	15	16	18	20	23	23	25	33	32	27	34
Grenada	328	21	25	25	32	33	37	44	51	65	56	78	66

Total Reserves minus Gold

1l s

Western Hemisphere(Cont.)		1994	1995	1996	1997	1998	1999	2000	2001	2002	2003	2004	2005
						Millions of SDRs: End of Period							
Montserrat	351	5	6	6	8	18	10	8	10	11	10	9	10
St. Kitts and Nevis	361	22	23	23	27	33	36	35	45	48	44	51	50
St. Lucia	362	40	42	39	45	50	54	61	71	69	72	85	81
St. Vincent & Grens	364	21	20	21	23	28	31	42	49	39	34	48	49
Argentina	213	9,814	9,612	12,590	16,542	17,579	19,127	19,301	11,580	7,715	9,525	12,160	19,016
Aruba	314	122	146	130	128	158	160	160	234	250	199	190	191
Bahamas, The	313	121	121	119	168	246	299	268	254	280	330	434	410
Barbados	316	134	147	201	196	260	220	363	549	492	497	373	422
Belize	339	24	25	41	44	31	52	94	89	84	57	31	50
Bolivia	218	309	444	664	805	674	710	711	705	427	482	562	929
Brazil	223	25,393	33,440	40,560	37,670	30,241	25,352	24,935	28,438	27,718	33,050	33,960	37,484
Chile	228	8,965	9,512	10,412	13,024	11,271	10,650	11,539	11,442	11,284	10,659	10,299	11,845
Colombia	233	5,474	5,616	6,846	7,265	6,144	5,834	6,843	8,079	7,894	7,257	8,624	10,346
Costa Rica	238	612	704	696	935	755	1,064	1,011	1,058	1,105	1,238	1,237	1,618
Dominican Republic	243	173	246	244	290	356	506	481	875	345	170	514	1,290
Ecuador	248	1,263	1,095	1,292	1,551	1,150	1,197	727	668	526	547	689	1,199
El Salvador	253	445	510	652	969	1,146	1,326	1,360	1,268	1,083	1,206	1,129	1,205
Guatemala	258	591	472	605	824	948	866	1,340	1,824	1,691	1,907	2,206	2,563
Guyana	336	169	181	229	234	196	195	234	229	209	186	149	176
Haiti	263	35	129	150	153	183	192	140	113	60	42	74	93
Honduras	268	117	176	173	430	581	916	1,008	1,126	1,121	962	1,269	1,628
Jamaica	343	504	458	612	506	504	404	809	1,512	1,210	804	1,189	1,518
Mexico	273	4,301	11,333	13,514	21,343	22,584	23,156	27,253	35,601	37,215	39,675	41,301	51,813
Netherlands Antilles	353	123	137	131	159	176	193	200	240	299	251	267	323
Nicaragua	278	97	92	137	280	249	371	375	302	330	338	430	509
Panama	283	482	526	603	851	678	600	555	869	870	680	406	847
Paraguay	288	706	735	730	619	614	713	585	568	463	652	752	908
Peru	293	4,790	5,531	7,356	8,140	6,794	6,361	6,427	6,900	6,869	6,579	7,841	9,515
Suriname	366	27	89	67	81	75	28	48	95	78	71	83	88
Trinidad and Tobago	369	241	241	378	524	556	689	1,064	1,517	1,491	1,649	2,040	3,398
Uruguay	298	663	774	870	1,154	1,472	1,516	1,903	2,464	566	1,402	1,615	2,151
Venezuela, Rep. Bol	299	5,526	4,227	8,198	10,656	8,466	8,945	10,046	7,352	6,243	10,791	11,832	16,735
Memorandum Items													
Oil Exporting Countries	999	43,434	43,740	60,123	70,933	70,503	77,143	102,277	110,344	108,620	118,610	138,196	182,298
Non-Oil Developing Countries.	201	382,929	459,754	536,601	616,657	631,959	705,641	796,894	908,662	1,016,617	1,184,733	1,446,492	1,846,190

Nongold Reserves/Imports

		1994	1995	1996	1997	1998	1999	2000	2001	2002	2003	2004	2005
1rl s							*Weeks of Imports*						
World.................................	001	**15.5**	**15.2**	**16.2**	**15.7**	**16.4**	**16.9**	**16.0**	**17.6**	**20.0**	**21.4**	**21.5**	**21.0**
Industrial Countries.................	110	**11.9**	**11.5**	**12.1**	**11.1**	**10.7**	**10.7**	**10.2**	**10.8**	**12.1**	**12.8**	**12.4**	**10.8**
United States.....................	111	4.8	5.0	4.1	3.4	3.9	3.0	2.3	2.5	2.9	3.0	2.6	1.6
Canada.............................	156	4.1	4.7	6.1	4.6	5.9	6.6	6.8	7.8	8.5	7.7	6.4	5.2
Australia..........................	193	11.0	10.1	11.5	13.3	11.8	15.9	13.2	14.6	14.8	18.8	17.0	17.4
Japan..............................	158	23.8	28.4	32.3	33.7	39.9	47.9	48.6	58.9	71.1	90.1	95.4	84.3
New Zealand......................	196	16.2	16.4	21.0	15.9	17.5	16.2	14.8	13.9	17.2	17.1	15.6	17.6
Euro Area													
Austria............................	122	15.8	14.7	17.7	15.8	17.1	11.3	10.8	9.2	6.9	5.0	3.8	7.5
Belgium...........................	124	5.5	5.3	5.4	5.4	5.8	3.5	2.9	3.3	3.1	2.4	1.9	1.3
Finland............................	172	23.9	18.6	12.3	14.7	15.6	13.5	12.2	12.9	14.4	13.1	12.6	9.5
France.............................	132	5.8	5.0	4.9	5.9	7.9	7.0	6.2	5.5	4.7	4.2	4.1	3.0
Germany..........................	134	10.4	9.5	9.4	9.1	8.2	6.7	6.0	5.5	5.4	4.4	3.5	3.0
Greece.............................	174	35.2	28.7	30.7	23.5	30.9	32.8	23.9	9.0	13.5	5.1	1.2	.5
Ireland............................	178	12.3	13.6	11.9	8.7	10.9	5.9	5.4	5.7	5.5	4.0	2.4	.6
Italy...............................	136	9.9	8.8	11.5	13.8	7.1	5.3	5.6	5.4	6.0	5.3	4.1	3.4
Luxembourg......................	137	.5	.4	.4	.4	....	.4	.4	.5	.7	1.1	.9	.7
Netherlands......................	138	12.7	9.9	7.7	7.3	5.9	2.7	2.5	2.4	2.6	2.5	1.9	1.5
Portugal...........................	182	29.5	24.7	23.5	23.2	21.4	11.0	12.1	12.8	15.2	7.5	5.5	3.4
Spain..............................	184	23.4	15.8	24.7	29.0	21.6	11.9	10.5	10.0	11.0	4.9	2.5	1.7
Denmark...........................	128	12.9	12.5	16.3	22.4	17.1	26.0	17.7	20.2	28.7	34.3	30.4	23.0
Iceland............................	176	10.3	9.1	11.6	10.0	8.9	9.9	7.8	7.8	10.1	14.8	15.3	11.8
Norway............................	142	36.2	35.5	38.7	34.1	26.4	36.2	41.7	36.7	47.7	49.0	47.9	44.6
Sweden............................	144	23.3	19.3	14.8	8.6	10.7	11.4	10.5	11.3	13.2	12.2	11.4	10.3
Switzerland.......................	146	28.2	24.6	26.8	28.6	29.0	25.0	22.1	21.6	25.3	25.9	26.2	15.8
United Kingdom..................	112	9.4	8.2	7.2	5.5	5.3	5.4	6.0	5.5	5.8	5.3	4.7	4.1
Developing Countries...............	200	**22.2**	**21.9**	**23.3**	**24.0**	**28.0**	**29.9**	**27.3**	**30.7**	**34.5**	**37.0**	**36.7**	**37.2**
Africa............................	605	**14.8**	**13.5**	**16.2**	**21.4**	**20.4**	**21.7**	**27.1**	**30.3**	**33.6**	**34.0**	**37.0**	**40.5**
CEMAC													
Cameroon..........................	622	.1	.2	.1	—	—	.2	7.4	9.3	17.5	16.5	17.9	20.2
Central African Republic..............	626	78.4	69.8	85.4	66.1	51.7	54.1	59.2	57.7	53.3	53.4	51.3	43.9
Chad...............................	628	22.3	20.3	25.8	21.2	17.5	15.6	18.2	9.4	6.9	12.3	15.4	13.8
Congo, Rep. of.....................	634	4.1	4.6	3.1	3.4	.1	2.4	15.7	3.3	1.5	1.3	3.5	18.7
Equatorial Guinea.................	642	.5	—	.1	.8	.1	.4	2.7	4.5	9.1	10.1	31.9	53.3
Gabon.............................	646	12.0	8.7	13.5	13.3	.7	1.1	9.9	.6	7.6	9.9	18.0	24.8
WAEMU													
Benin..............................	638	31.1	13.8	20.8	19.3	18.5	27.8	42.0	48.3	44.2	41.9	37.2	38.2
Burkina Faso......................	748	35.4	39.7	27.2	30.5	26.5	27.0	19.4	26.6	29.5	57.1	36.9	17.7
Côte d'Ivoire......................	662	5.5	9.4	10.9	11.6	14.9	10.1	12.5	21.9	39.5	21.0	21.1	14.7
Guinea Bissau.....................	654	5.9	7.9	6.9	19.8	29.5	36.3	58.3	58.3	92.1	26.3	39.6	34.6
Mali...............................	678	19.5	21.7	29.0	29.2	27.5	22.1	24.6	18.3	33.4	39.7	33.7	28.7
Niger..............................	692	17.5	13.2	9.1	7.4	5.9	5.0	10.6	13.5	14.9	21.7	17.0	14.1
Senegal............................	722	9.1	10.0	10.4	15.0	15.4	13.4	13.1	13.4	16.3	24.2	25.3	18.6
Togo...............................	742	22.1	11.4	6.9	9.6	10.4	13.0	16.3	12.7	18.4	12.6	33.5	17.1
Algeria............................	612	15.2	10.3	24.2	51.5	37.9	25.7	68.2	94.6	101.0	139.1	123.8	146.1
Botswana..........................	616	139.5	127.8	151.7	130.7	129.4	146.3	133.1	169.5	170.6	107.0	85.1	82.0
Burundi...........................	618	47.4	46.5	57.1	48.4	21.6	21.1	11.6	6.6	23.6	22.2	19.4	19.5
Cape Verde........................	624	10.5	7.6	6.1	4.3	1.9	9.0	6.4	10.1	15.1	13.9	18.8	20.6
Comoros...........................	632	43.5	37.0	....	....	....	....	....	....	....	....	....	....
Congo, Dem. Rep. of...............	636	16.4	8.8	3.9	....	....	....	....	....	....	....	....	....
Djibouti...........................	611	19.5	21.2	22.4	23.4	21.8	24.1	....	....	....	....	....	....
Ethiopia...........................	644	27.4	35.0	27.2	....	17.5	15.5	12.6	12.5	28.3	23.5	25.2	14.1
Gambia, The.......................	648	24.0	30.3	20.6	28.7	24.2	30.1	30.4	41.1	37.8	19.7	19.0	21.6
Ghana.............................	652	14.4	19.0	20.4	12.0	7.6	6.8	4.1	4.9	10.3	21.9	20.8	17.9
Guinea............................	656	6.5	5.5	7.0	10.2	22.9	18.7	12.6	17.3	13.4	....	8.3	5.8
Kenya.............................	664	13.9	6.1	13.2	12.5	12.7	14.5	15.0	17.3	17.1	20.7	17.4	15.2
Lesotho............................	666	22.8	24.1	24.0	29.0	31.3	30.0	26.9	26.9	25.7	21.4	18.2	19.1
Madagascar........................	674	8.5	10.4	24.0	29.4	12.8	15.9	14.9	21.7	31.3	19.4	17.8	16.1
Malawi............................	676	4.5	12.1	18.4	9.5	25.8	19.0	23.7	18.7	12.1	8.1	7.1	7.5
Mauritania.........................	682	5.1	....	....	....	....	....	....	....	....	....	....	....
Mauritius..........................	684	20.1	22.7	20.4	16.5	14.0	16.9	22.3	21.9	29.6	34.7	30.1	22.0
Morocco...........................	686	27.4	18.7	20.3	21.8	22.4	29.8	21.7	39.9	44.4	50.5	47.6	41.4
Mozambique.......................	688	9.1	14.4	23.6	36.4	40.1	29.9	32.5	34.9	25.4	27.8	29.9	22.6
Namibia...........................	728	7.5	7.1	6.0	7.4	8.2	9.9	8.7	7.9	11.4	8.5	7.4	6.6
Nigeria............................	694	10.9	9.1	32.9	41.5	40.1	33.0	59.1	46.9	50.5	34.2	62.2	96.7
Rwanda............................	714	22.0	21.7	21.6	26.8	30.9	36.3	47.0	44.2	62.5	45.5	57.6	48.9
São Tomé & Príncipe...............	716	....	9.1	11.7	40.1	....	....	....	....	....	....	....	....
Seychelles.........................	718	7.6	6.1	3.0	4.0	2.9	3.6	6.6	4.0	8.6	8.5	3.6	5.3
Sierra Leone.......................	724	14.0	13.5	6.6	21.6	24.1	25.4	17.1	14.7	16.7	11.4	22.7	25.7
South Africa.......................	199	3.8	4.8	1.6	7.6	7.7	12.4	10.7	11.1	10.5	8.2	12.8	15.5
Sudan..............................	732	3.3	7.0	3.6	2.7	2.5	6.9	8.3	2.7	9.4	15.3	20.7	18.9
Swaziland..........................	734	18.4	15.4	12.4	14.4	17.1	18.3	17.4	12.4	15.2	9.5	8.8	6.0
Tanzania...........................	738	11.5	8.4	16.5	24.2	21.4	25.9	33.3	35.1	47.9	49.9	47.5	40.1
Tunisia............................	744	11.5	10.6	12.8	12.9	11.5	13.9	11.0	10.9	12.5	14.0	16.0	17.3
Uganda............................	746	19.1	22.6	23.1	25.0	26.8	29.6	27.3	32.1	43.7	44.9	33.6	36.9
Zambia............................	754	20.9	16.7	13.8	15.2	3.3	2.9	12.8	7.3	22.2	8.2	8.7	10.6
Zimbabwe..........................	698	9.4	11.6	8.2	2.7	2.5	6.6	5.4	2.0	2.5	....	....	....

Nongold Reserves/Imports

1rl s		1994	1995	1996	1997	1998	1999	2000	2001	2002	2003	2004	2005
							Weeks of Imports						
Asia *	505	**24.5**	**22.5**	**24.5**	**25.3**	**34.1**	**35.7**	**30.8**	**36.9**	**41.8**	**44.6**	**44.7**	**44.8**
Bangladesh	513	35.5	18.7	14.4	11.9	14.2	10.8	9.2	7.9	11.1	14.1	13.1	11.2
Bhutan	514	68.9	60.4	77.4	71.6	99.9	83.5	94.3	88.3	93.9	76.6	50.4	....
Cambodia	522	....	....	....	13.9	14.9	16.4	18.3	21.0	24.1	24.5	23.6	39.1
China, P.R.: Mainland	924	23.8	29.7	40.1	52.1	55.3	49.5	38.9	46.0	51.3	51.4	57.0	64.7
China, P.R.: Hong Kong	532	15.8	14.9	16.7	23.1	25.3	27.9	26.3	28.7	28.0	26.5	23.7	21.6
China, P.R.: Macao	546	48.1	57.5	63.0	63.3	65.5	72.9	76.6	76.5	78.1	82.0	81.3	88.9
Fiji	819	17.1	20.4	22.5	19.4	27.8	24.7	26.0	24.0	20.8	18.8	19.5	10.2
India	534	38.2	26.9	27.6	31.0	33.1	36.2	38.3	47.3	62.3	70.9	67.6	51.0
Indonesia	536	19.7	17.5	22.1	16.8	33.5	41.3	34.0	45.7	51.5	55.8	39.1	44.1
Korea	542	13.0	12.6	11.8	7.3	29.0	32.1	31.1	37.9	41.5	45.2	46.1	41.9
Lao People's Democratic Rep.	544	5.6	8.1	12.8	8.3	10.6	10.0	13.5	12.9	23.1	20.7	23.0	15.1
Malaysia	548	22.2	15.9	17.9	13.7	22.8	24.3	18.0	20.8	21.7	27.8	32.5	31.8
Maldives	556	7.3	9.3	13.1	14.7	17.4	16.4	16.4	12.3	17.7	17.6	16.5	13.0
Mongolia	948	18.5	14.7	12.7	19.5	9.7	13.8	15.1	16.8	26.3	15.3	12.0	18.9
Myanmar	518	24.6	21.6	8.7	6.3	6.1	5.9	4.8	7.2	10.4	13.7	15.9	20.8
Nepal	558	31.2	22.9	21.2	19.2	31.6	30.9	31.2	36.6	37.3	36.2	40.7	41.9
Pakistan	564	17.1	7.9	2.4	5.4	5.7	7.7	7.2	18.6	37.4	43.6	28.4	20.6
Papua New Guinea	853	3.3	9.4	17.4	11.1	8.1	9.0	13.0	20.5	13.5	18.8	19.6	21.6
Philippines	566	13.9	11.7	15.3	9.8	15.3	21.2	18.4	20.1	18.6	18.0	16.1	17.6
Samoa	862	32.4	30.3	31.5	34.5	33.0	30.7	36.7	24.6	25.5	33.9	32.0	25.6
Singapore	576	29.5	28.7	30.4	28.0	37.2	36.0	31.0	33.8	36.6	38.9	33.6	30.1
Solomon Islands	813	6.4	5.4	14.3	12.8	17.0	23.9	17.0	12.3	14.7	28.6	49.2	34.5
Sri Lanka	524	22.3	20.9	18.8	18.0	17.4	14.5	8.6	11.2	13.9	17.7	13.9	15.6
Thailand	578	28.0	26.4	27.1	21.7	34.9	35.2	26.9	27.2	30.6	28.2	26.8	22.3
Tonga	866	26.7	19.3	21.3	19.6	21.7	17.5	18.6	17.1	14.7	22.1	27.4	22.2
Vanuatu	846	25.3	26.4	23.4	20.7	24.8	22.0	23.3	21.7	21.2	21.7	25.1	25.0
Vietnam	582	....	....	8.1	8.9	9.1	14.7	11.4	11.9	11.3	13.0	11.8	12.9
*of which:													
Taiwan Province of China	528	56.2	45.3	45.2	38.1	44.8	49.8	39.7	59.2	74.5	84.4	74.8	72.1
Europe	170	**10.7**	**15.4**	**13.8**	**14.3**	**15.3**	**18.2**	**18.4**	**19.4**	**23.2**	**24.2**	**24.2**	**26.8**
Albania	914	17.6	17.6	15.6	24.9	23.7	22.0	29.4	29.0	29.0	28.2	30.6	27.9
Armenia	911	4.3	7.7	9.5	13.3	18.7	20.7	18.8	19.1	22.4	20.7	22.2	22.2
Azerbaijan, Republic of	912	.1	9.4	11.4	30.5	21.6	33.8	30.2	26.3	22.5	15.9	15.9	14.5
Belarus	913	1.7	3.5	3.5	2.4	4.3	2.3	2.1	2.5	3.5	2.7	2.4	3.5
Bulgaria	918	12.2	11.4	3.7	21.0	28.2	27.6	25.2	23.6	28.7	30.0	31.5	23.0
Croatia	960	13.2	13.4	15.5	14.5	17.7	20.2	23.2	26.7	28.5	30.0	27.5	24.7
Cyprus	423	25.2	15.7	20.1	19.6	19.5	26.3	23.5	30.1	40.7	39.5	35.9	34.7
Czech Republic	935	17.5	27.3	21.9	17.6	21.5	22.6	20.0	19.5	28.6	25.9	20.5	19.9
Estonia	939	13.8	12.6	11.4	11.2	10.7	12.9	11.3	9.9	10.8	11.0	11.2	10.0
Georgia	915	....	25.7	14.3	11.0	7.2	11.8	8.0	11.0	12.9	8.7	10.8	9.9
Hungary	944	24.5	40.5	28.0	20.7	18.9	20.4	18.2	16.5	14.2	13.9	13.9	14.8
Kazakhstan	916	12.2	15.5	15.9	20.5	17.6	21.0	16.4	16.1	20.2	26.2	34.5	18.2
Kyrgyz Republic	917	4.3	8.1	5.9	12.5	10.1	19.9	22.4	29.3	25.6	26.4	29.2	26.9
Latvia	941	22.7	14.5	14.7	14.5	13.1	15.4	13.9	17.0	15.9	14.2	14.1	13.6
Lithuania	946	11.6	13.1	10.3	10.5	13.7	13.4	13.1	13.9	16.2	18.1	14.7	12.5
Macedonia, FYR	962	5.2	7.8	7.7	7.5	8.3	12.6	10.7	22.9	18.8	20.2	16.1	19.8
Malta	181	39.4	28.3	30.1	30.3	32.4	32.7	22.5	31.8	40.5	41.8	37.1	35.9
Moldova	921	13.3	15.9	15.1	16.2	7.3	16.5	14.9	13.3	13.5	11.2	13.8	13.5
Poland	964	14.2	26.4	25.0	25.1	30.6	29.9	28.2	26.5	27.0	24.9	20.9	21.1
Romania	968	15.3	8.0	9.6	17.5	12.6	7.6	9.8	13.1	17.8	17.4	23.3	25.5
Russia	922	3.7	10.9	7.8	8.5	6.4	10.1	25.7	28.6	34.2	45.5	58.6	66.4
Slovak Republic	936	12.9	19.0	15.6	15.6	10.9	14.7	15.6	13.9	26.2	25.6	24.6	21.4
Slovenia	961	10.7	10.0	12.7	18.4	18.7	16.3	16.4	22.2	33.2	31.9	26.0	21.5
Turkey	186	16.0	18.1	19.6	20.0	22.1	29.8	21.5	23.7	28.3	26.9	19.2	26.6
Ukraine	926	3.1	3.5	5.8	7.1	2.7	4.6	5.0	9.7	13.0	15.2	16.7	27.5
Middle East	405	**27.0**	**26.9**	**29.1**	**32.0**	**33.2**	**34.4**	**34.5**	**32.6**	**32.7**	**32.8**	**29.7**	**28.2**
Bahrain	419	16.2	17.9	16.0	16.7	15.7	19.3	17.6	20.3	17.9	16.3	15.6	....
Egypt	469	68.6	71.6	69.4	73.5	58.3	47.0	48.7	52.7	54.9	63.4	57.7	54.0
Israel	436	14.0	14.3	18.8	34.3	40.2	35.4	38.5	34.3	35.3	37.7	32.9	31.0
Jordan	439	26.0	27.7	21.3	27.9	23.8	36.8	37.7	32.7	40.7	47.0	33.7	26.0
Kuwait	443	27.2	23.8	21.8	21.8	23.8	32.9	51.5	65.4	53.2	35.9	33.9	26.4
Lebanon	446	77.7	43.0	40.9	41.6	48.2	65.1	49.6	35.7	58.4	90.8	64.9	66.0
Libya	672	72.7	75.8	71.5	67.2	69.2	91.0	173.6	175.0	169.2	235.2	211.2	285.3
Oman	449	21.9	22.4	22.3	21.4	17.7	30.8	24.6	21.2	27.5	28.4	21.1	25.7
Qatar	453	17.7	11.4	12.4	12.8	15.9	27.1	18.5	18.2	20.1	31.3	29.4	29.4
Saudi Arabia	456	16.5	16.0	26.9	27.0	24.7	31.6	33.7	29.3	33.2	31.9	31.7	24.7
United Arab Emirates	466	16.5	18.5	18.5	14.5	19.1	16.7	20.1	19.7	18.6	15.1	15.6	14.2
Yemen, Republic of	474	6.3	20.4	26.0	31.1	23.9	38.1	64.9	77.1	82.6	70.6	....	....
Western Hemisphere	205	**24.4**	**26.7**	**28.9**	**26.6**	**24.0**	**23.7**	**20.8**	**21.6**	**23.5**	**27.7**	**25.6**	**25.2**
ECCU													
Anguilla	312	13.1	20.5	12.5	13.8	13.2	11.3	11.2	16.2	19.5	22.5	17.4	15.9
Antigua and Barbuda	311	7.0	8.9	6.8	7.1	8.0	8.8	8.2	11.0	11.4	14.0	13.9	10.9
Dominica	321	8.3	9.8	9.2	10.3	10.9	11.9	10.3	12.3	20.3	19.4	15.2	15.5
Grenada	328	13.7	15.5	12.2	12.8	12.2	12.4	12.1	15.2	21.5	16.9	22.7	....
St. Kitts and Nevis	361	12.9	13.1	11.4	12.8	16.3	16.8	12.0	15.5	17.0	16.4	....	....
St. Lucia	362	9.9	10.7	9.3	9.6	11.2	10.9	11.5	13.0	15.8	13.8	15.0	11.0
St. Vincent & Grens	364	12.5	11.4	11.9	8.6	10.5	11.0	17.6	18.6	15.5	13.2	17.3	15.0
Argentina	213	34.5	36.9	39.6	38.1	41.0	53.5	51.7	37.2	60.7	53.2	43.8	49.3
Aruba	314	....	19.9	16.9	14.6	14.2	14.6	13.0	18.2	21.0	18.1	17.6	13.8
Bahamas, The	313	8.7	7.5	6.5	7.1	9.6	12.1	8.8	8.7	11.5	14.5	22.1	14.4
Barbados	316	16.6	14.8	18.1	13.8	18.8	14.2	21.3	33.0	33.5	33.9	21.3	19.5
Belize	339	6.9	7.6	11.9	10.8	7.8	10.0	12.2	11.3	11.4	8.0	4.8	6.3

Nongold Reserves/Imports

1rl s		1994	1995	1996	1997	1998	1999	2000	2001	2002	2003	2004	2005
Western Hemisphere(Cont.)						*Weeks of Imports*							
Bolivia	218	19.4	24.1	30.4	30.5	24.9	28.9	26.3	27.0	17.1	23.1	24.6	29.5
Brazil	223	53.3	47.7	53.4	41.8	36.2	34.9	28.6	31.7	39.4	50.2	41.3	35.9
Chile	228	57.6	46.2	40.6	43.9	41.5	47.5	42.2	42.9	46.7	42.5	33.4	27.0
Colombia	233	35.0	31.3	37.4	33.1	30.7	39.1	40.2	41.1	43.9	40.4	41.6	36.3
Costa Rica	238	12.3	13.3	12.0	13.2	8.9	12.0	10.7	10.5	10.9	12.5	12.1	12.3
Dominican Republic	243	3.8	5.2	4.4	4.2	4.6	6.0	4.4	8.4	3.5	2.2	6.7	11.6
Ecuador	248	26.5	20.4	22.6	22.0	15.1	28.3	13.2	8.1	5.8	6.3	6.8	8.7
El Salvador	253	15.0	13.8	18.2	22.8	26.9	30.1	24.3	21.4	19.6	21.3	18.7	16.7
Guatemala	258	16.1	11.1	14.4	15.0	14.9	13.6	17.6	21.3	19.0	21.9	22.8	21.6
Guyana	336	25.4	26.5	28.7	25.7	23.8	25.5	27.3	25.6	25.7	24.9	18.5	16.6
Haiti	263	10.6	15.3	16.9	16.6	16.8	13.4	9.1	7.3	3.8	2.7	4.6	4.8
Honduras	268	8.4	8.3	7.0	14.0	16.8	24.4	23.9	25.0	26.6	22.7	26.2	26.2
Jamaica	343	17.2	12.6	15.4	11.3	12.2	9.9	16.6	29.4	24.2	17.1	25.5	25.3
Mexico	273	3.9	11.5	10.8	13.0	12.6	11.1	10.1	13.2	14.9	17.2	16.1	16.6
Netherlands Antilles	353	5.3	....	....	....	6.3	7.9	4.7	5.5	9.3	7.4	7.0	7.0
Nicaragua	278	8.5	7.3	8.9	13.6	12.2	14.2	14.1	11.1	13.3	13.9	15.7	14.6
Panama	283	15.2	16.2	16.2	19.9	14.6	12.2	11.1	19.2	20.6	17.0	9.1	15.1
Paraguay	288	22.1	18.1	17.0	14.0	15.5	26.7	18.1	17.0	19.6	24.4	19.6	23.4
Peru	293	54.3	46.0	58.3	55.5	50.2	55.7	49.0	....	....	....	....	....
Suriname	366	4.9	11.8	10.0	10.0	10.0	3.5	6.3	45.5	40.2	31.2	31.0	23.2
Trinidad and Tobago	369	16.2	10.9	13.2	12.3	13.6	17.9	21.8	27.7	28.9	32.7	33.9	50.0
Uruguay	298	18.1	20.9	19.6	21.7	28.3	32.2	37.2	52.6	20.4	49.5	41.9	41.2
Venezuela, Rep. Bol	299	45.7	25.8	62.0	51.2	39.2	45.4	42.0	26.2	34.0	90.1	57.3	51.8
Memorandum Items													
Oil Exporting Countries	999	24.9	21.8	28.9	27.9	31.6	34.6	38.8	39.8	41.4	43.4	40.7	42.6
Non-Oil Developing Countries	201	21.9	21.9	22.8	23.6	27.6	29.5	26.2	29.8	33.9	36.4	36.3	36.7

SDRs

		1994	1995	1996	1997	1998	1999	2000	2001	2002	2003	2004	2005
							Millions of SDRs: End of Period						
All Countries	010	**15,761.5**	**19,773.2**	**18,521.4**	**20,532.2**	**20,379.7**	**18,456.7**	**18,489.0**	**19,556.8**	**19,672.7**	**19,914.6**	**20,301.5**	**20,055.5**
Industrial Countries	110	**12,485.9**	**14,998.5**	**14,521.1**	**15,511.5**	**15,844.0**	**14,726.0**	**14,411.1**	**15,967.8**	**15,791.9**	**15,305.9**	**15,282.8**	**12,430.8**
United States	111	6,876.43	7,424.77	7,171.50	7,431.46	7,530.17	7,538.96	8,088.47	8,580.44	8,948.51	8,504.64	8,774.97	5,744.05
Canada	156	786.44	791.85	812.37	834.27	779.52	383.75	440.64	488.96	528.84	563.95	595.19	627.61
Australia	193	49.93	36.77	25.39	13.81	12.59	52.64	71.79	86.80	100.26	114.27	125.50	135.11
Japan	158	1,426.99	1,821.07	1,837.31	1,955.05	1,891.04	1,935.45	1,870.15	1,891.67	1,856.76	1,861.31	1,827.75	1,808.24
New Zealand	196	.23	.57	.27	.24	1.23	4.97	10.03	12.82	15.89	18.95	21.99	24.08
Euro Area													
Austria	122	193.81	121.69	135.69	124.77	105.87	105.91	102.74	185.33	136.05	121.94	103.10	102.59
Belgium	124	123.44	331.14	346.49	362.69	433.25	197.10	235.81	375.70	407.85	434.12	225.28	219.90
Finland	172	222.66	241.63	201.58	241.71	247.53	211.33	106.46	186.27	147.03	130.98	106.72	113.27
France	132	248.31	642.76	682.07	719.88	786.19	252.67	308.90	391.74	457.85	512.32	563.26	614.38
Germany	134	763.32	1,346.21	1,326.24	1,324.95	1,326.57	1,427.29	1,352.90	1,426.43	1,456.23	1,307.13	1,326.98	1,323.65
Greece	174	.22	.01	.41	.24	.32	3.76	9.19	7.71	11.13	14.43	17.41	20.33
Ireland	178	101.30	107.16	114.87	123.08	137.14	29.23	36.97	43.46	48.60	52.99	57.33	61.64
Italy	136	85.76	.03	20.44	49.57	78.65	122.49	182.43	236.45	79.32	104.85	93.14	159.88
Luxembourg	137	7.22	7.46	7.75	8.04	8.72	1.78	3.22	5.00	6.72	8.29	9.83	11.43
Netherlands	138	441.92	616.41	566.17	586.49	643.85	742.39	501.12	598.28	512.89	523.45	500.82	500.95
Portugal	182	48.32	56.96	68.19	79.43	95.95	32.12	41.22	49.42	55.82	61.13	66.25	71.98
Spain	184	174.50	276.78	313.87	351.26	408.08	189.78	222.63	279.19	260.06	278.04	213.96	232.11
Denmark	128	124.63	106.76	116.72	248.72	245.96	249.94	50.51	223.49	75.87	54.58	28.77	78.13
Iceland	176	.08	.02	.03	.01	.01	.01	.04	.09	.11	.03	.08	.03
Norway	142	266.73	311.47	247.19	257.87	294.08	297.97	235.35	282.06	232.07	225.42	232.31	214.85
San Marino	135	.11	.18	.25	.33	.42	.08	.20	.34	.43	.49	.56	.66
Sweden	144	46.40	296.83	198.91	276.70	292.37	227.78	165.25	157.08	132.03	133.13	134.80	123.47
Switzerland	146	161.95	181.27	87.84	170.49	192.32	344.72	124.71	225.00	54.24	24.72	45.50	41.86
United Kingdom	112	335.21	278.72	239.48	350.44	332.17	373.87	250.39	234.07	267.29	254.68	211.29	200.59
Developing Countries	200	**3,275.6**	**4,774.7**	**4,000.4**	**5,020.7**	**4,535.7**	**3,730.7**	**4,077.9**	**3,589.0**	**3,880.8**	**4,608.8**	**5,018.8**	**7,624.7**
Africa	605	**119.0**	**134.0**	**117.1**	**122.2**	**280.2**	**394.4**	**404.6**	**463.5**	**481.7**	**491.1**	**468.6**	**401.7**
CEMAC (incl. BEAC hqtrs.)	758	1.13	1.35	.35	.08	.24	6.50	6.19	5.26	4.13	2.32	16.35	3.88
Cameroon	622	.03	.03	.11	—	.01	1.90	5.93	.01	.87	.99	.43	1.49
Central African Rep.	626	.01	.02	.01	—	.01	.04	—	.01	.01	.01	1.58	.08
Chad	628	—	.02	.16	.01	.01	.02	—	—	.01	—	.04	.05
Congo, Rep. of	634	.03	.02	.01	.01	—	.08	.03	.15	2.38	.43	4.66	1.70
Equatorial Guinea	642	.01	.01	.01	—	.01	—	.09	.79	.44	.03	.44	.44
Gabon	646	.17	—	.02	—	.01	—	.05	.04	—	—	4.03	.08
WAEMU (incl. BCEAO hqtrs.)	759	6.90	10.20	5.78	2.28	1.33	6.62	2.18	8.15	8.94	10.93	6.41	2.48
Benin	638	.02	.08	.21	.04	.05	.15	.05	.30	.09	.13	.02	.12
Burkina Faso	748	5.55	5.52	1.78	1.63	.54	.53	.31	.41	.30	.21	.11	.14
Côte d'Ivoire	662	.11	1.24	.82	.02	.12	2.48	.97	.58	.86	.18	.13	.45
Guinea Bissau	654	—	.01	.01	.04	.02	.06	.03	.16	.30	.80	.44	.40
Mali	678	.14	.31	.21	.05	.06	.42	.08	.30	.03	.61	.04	.19
Niger	692	.29	.20	1.33	.12	.14	.98	.02	.25	.50	1.80	.60	.21
Senegal	722	.75	2.57	1.18	.35	.36	1.83	.71	5.96	6.68	7.10	4.71	.96
Togo	742	.05	.27	.25	.01	.05	.17	—	.18	.19	.10	.01	.01
Algeria	612	15.66	.78	3.47	.54	1.09	1.38	2.34	9.14	10.18	38.19	.80	2.44
Angola	614	.10	.11	.11	.12	.12	.13	.13	.14	.14	.14	.15	.15
Botswana	616	25.39	27.06	28.71	30.36	32.41	28.05	29.89	31.53	32.63	33.52	34.42	35.58
Burundi	618	.14	.05	.08	.05	.07	.07	.03	.04	.12	.09	.23	.19
Cape Verde	624	.05	.02	.04	.02	.04	.01	.04	.01	—	—	.02	.02
Comoros	632	.03	.07	.04	.10	—	.12	.13	.02	.03	—	—	—
Congo, Dem. Rep. of	636	—	—	—	—	—	—	—	—	6.12	5.35	3.54	.96
Djibouti	611	.11	.06	.10	.55	.27	.06	.28	.10	.76	.09	.64	.02
Eritrea	643	—	—	—	—	—	—	—	—	—	—	—	—
Ethiopia	644	.28	.17	.01	.09	.06	.05	—	.15	.11	.06	.33	.13
Gambia, The	648	.18	.09	.20	.09	.30	.49	.17	.01	.01	.02	.48	.11
Ghana	652	2.88	1.64	1.55	2.50	42.41	13.28	.41	3.19	2.71	31.49	13.34	.77
Guinea	656	3.79	5.01	.54	1.97	1.02	.94	.19	.63	1.22	.15	—	.01
Kenya	664	.47	.19	.54	.50	.42	1.71	.21	.78	.61	1.37	.39	.01
Lesotho	666	.33	.24	.92	.89	.86	.85	.51	.46	.44	.42	.40	.31
Liberia	668	—	—	—	—	—	—	—	—	—	—	—	—
Madagascar	674	.02	.02	.04	.05	.03	.11	.04	.09	.03	.02	.12	.03
Malawi	676	4.25	.59	.94	.07	4.84	.29	.36	.67	.07	.32	.77	.74
Mauritania	682	—	.04	.99	.26	.01	—	.28	.16	.15	.09	.02	.10
Mauritius	684	21.34	21.68	22.15	22.48	22.84	16.07	16.45	16.81	17.04	17.24	17.53	17.97
Morocco	686	18.04	17.25	5.17	.88	2.34	62.06	91.64	98.14	90.01	75.62	77.41	55.09
Mozambique	688	.03	.03	.04	.04	.04	.05	.05	.05	.05	.05	.05	.16
Namibia	728	.01	.01	.01	.01	.01	.02	.02	.02	.02	.02	.02	.02
Nigeria	694	—	.45	.43	.44	.52	.14	.24	.53	.11	.15	.27	.29
Rwanda	714	1.75	13.65	12.71	19.64	17.36	10.54	.87	9.82	7.48	20.03	19.45	18.13
São Tomé & Príncipe	716	.01	.03	.01	—	—	—	—	—	.01	.02	—	.03
Seychelles	718	.02	.02	.02	.03	.03	.03	.01	.02	.01	—	—	—
Sierra Leone	724	6.18	11.48	5.32	8.29	7.36	15.17	4.03	.30	17.69	23.20	32.82	22.93
Somalia	726	—	—	—	—	—	—	—	—	—	—	—	—
South Africa	199	.85	3.29	.82	6.81	131.67	209.60	222.40	222.56	222.77	222.79	222.82	222.87
Sudan	732	—	—	—	—	—	—	—	—	.13	.23	—	.04
Swaziland	734	5.89	5.90	5.93	5.94	5.96	2.42	2.44	2.45	2.46	2.47	2.47	2.48
Tanzania	738	—	.05	.10	.08	.25	.20	.11	.39	.08	.34	.05	.49
Tunisia	744	1.84	4.72	11.05	12.09	2.07	19.33	2.97	1.34	1.98	1.65	6.01	1.53

SDRs

1b s		1994	1995	1996	1997	1998	1999	2000	2001	2002	2003	2004	2005
Africa(Cont.)					*Millions of SDRs: End of Period*								
Uganda	746	2.10	.30	.74	3.98	3.54	1.69	2.72	1.48	2.18	3.22	.43	.80
Zambia	754	—	8.17	1.41	.79	.57	.05	17.13	53.25	51.73	.32	16.00	11.00
Zimbabwe	698	.05	.52	6.78	.22	.28	.79	.18	—	.01	—	—	.02
Asia	505	**647.5**	**875.4**	**925.4**	**1,530.8**	**1,298.9**	**906.1**	**927.8**	**973.6**	**1,045.2**	**1,226.6**	**1,342.6**	**1,442.8**
Afghanistan, Islamic Rep. of	512	.96	—	—	—	—	—	—	—	—	.40	.04	.03
Bangladesh	513	24.64	107.28	76.19	21.65	9.14	.66	.33	.95	1.65	2.16	.80	.65
Bhutan	514	.40	.44	.47	.50	.54	.13	.17	.21	.23	.25	.27	.30
Brunei Darussalam	516			.54	1.58	2.75	3.75	5.04	6.24	6.99	7.85	8.81	10.17
Cambodia	522	10.89	10.21	9.51	8.77	6.95	3.78	.14	.41	.40	.14	.05	.17
China, P.R.: Mainland	924	369.13	391.58	427.15	446.53	480.10	539.58	612.71	676.82	734.19	741.33	803.01	875.38
Fiji	819	7.39	7.67	7.99	8.29	8.62	4.10	4.47	4.81	5.02	5.18	5.35	5.59
India	534	1.41	93.33	85.12	57.38	59.02	3.04	1.22	4.15	5.03	1.91	3.24	3.15
Indonesia	536	.27	.87	1.53	369.98	221.52	.27	24.50	12.64	13.66	2.49	1.58	4.91
Kiribati	826	.01	.01	.01	.01	.01	.01	.01	.01	.01	.01	.01	.01
Korea	542	52.30	65.74	82.34	43.60	8.12	.50	2.70	2.66	8.68	14.18	21.14	30.54
Lao P. D. Rep.	544	7.46	9.49	7.17	9.31	4.32	.05	.07	2.72	4.47	12.87	9.90	9.86
Malaysia	548	92.71	101.64	115.28	129.88	145.77	60.80	80.81	99.58	111.36	119.95	128.18	137.16
Maldives	556	.03	.05	.06	.08	.10	.14	.20	.25	.28	.30	.32	.32
Marshall Islands, Rep. of	867	—	—	—	—	—	—	—	—	—	—	—	—
Micronesia, Fed. States of	868	.866	.907	.944	.982	1.024	1.060	1.106	1.149	1.176	1.196	1.217	1.247
Mongolia	948	1.98	1.70	.30	.52	.34	.12	.01	.01	.03	.03	.03	.01
Myanmar	518	.10	.06	.06	.06	.23	.12	.11	.44	.06	.07	.03	.16
Nepal	558	.09	.01	.01	.08	.02	.23	.01	.07	.01	.54	6.23	6.15
Pakistan	564	.21	9.90	9.18	7.98	.65	.17	10.92	3.09	1.57	166.87	157.76	151.02
Palau	565	—	—	—	—	—	—	—	—	—	—	—	—
Papua New Guinea	853	.07	.47	.04	.06	.04	.53	9.34	6.93	4.46	2.48	.47	.02
Philippines	566	16.65	5.36	1.67	1.28	1.36	5.11	1.48	11.15	7.48	1.19	.65	.59
Samoa	862	1.99	2.04	2.10	2.14	2.19	2.24	2.29	2.34	2.38	2.40	2.43	2.46
Singapore	576	24.13	33.05	42.48	52.25	64.91	89.23	105.32	119.56	130.19	139.61	188.86	199.57
Solomon Islands	813	.01	—	.01	—	—	.01	—	.01	—	—	—	—
Sri Lanka	524	.24	.62	1.34	.31	.89	.70	.31	.68	1.72	.42	.12	1.06
Thailand	578	21.84	30.46	41.50	357.56	277.86	188.06	63.43	4.19	3.09	.24	.66	.43
Tonga	866	.49	.04	.08	.11	.15	.03	.10	.15	.19	.22	.24	.28
Vanuatu	846	.22	.29	.36	.44	.53	.60	.70	.79	.84	.89	.93	.99
Vietnam	582	11.03	2.20	11.91	9.44	1.79	1.06	.25	11.59	.03	1.46	.29	.61
Europe	170	**373.6**	**636.8**	**511.5**	**784.2**	**730.0**	**568.0**	**558.1**	**480.8**	**276.4**	**294.6**	**251.4**	**225.1**
Albania	914	.20	.10	.52	.46	43.39	56.06	58.33	64.87	60.02	60.98	64.90	8.75
Armenia	911	.19	29.82	28.86	27.63	19.89	29.64	16.54	8.15	22.14	12.67	7.70	7.12
Azerbaijan, Republic of	912	—	.84	14.48	4.14	.08	5.15	5.07	1.98	.51	12.14	9.36	9.74
Belarus	913	.01	3.05	.10	—	.30	.30	.14	.31	.19	.02	.01	.02
Bosnia and Herzegovina	963	—	5.05	1.84	—	3.71	5.59	8.18	4.86	2.31	2.29	.32	.23
Bulgaria	918	10.39	20.08	8.31	8.37	21.38	59.53	64.97	1.80	.55	45.54	8.45	.70
Croatia	960	3.09	94.40	87.31	109.00	164.19	138.07	113.01	85.49	1.10	.03	.03	.18
Cyprus	423	.11	.03	.03	.25	.20	.40	.77	1.13	1.53	1.99	2.51	2.92
Czech Republic	935		.12	—	—	—		.16	.68	3.36	6.28	3.41	8.24
Estonia	939	1.09	.20	.12	.01	.05	.99	.01	.03	.05	.05	.05	.05
Georgia	915	1.61	1.12	.05	.10	3.69	6.13	2.51	3.15	2.13	3.31	7.22	.71
Hungary	944	1.08	.58	.35	.13	.52	3.19	8.97	16.36	24.07	31.20	37.56	44.62
Kazakhstan	916	69.54	154.87	240.19	327.15	275.08	164.24	.01	—	.76	.78	.79	.81
Kyrgyz Republic	917	.65	9.59	5.14	.70	.24	3.71	.54	1.05	.47	6.94	12.80	3.69
Latvia	941	.21	1.49	1.56	1.50	.21	2.24	—	.07	.05	.09	.10	.10
Lithuania	946	10.38	12.22	7.09	7.95	11.50	3.19	1.01	14.67	39.31	.04	.06	.05
Macedonia, FYR	962	.01	.15	.03	.28	.76	.87	.50	1.77	4.50	.19	.49	.55
Malta	181	35.62	37.64	39.75	41.91	44.36	22.49	24.51	26.39	28.94	29.84	30.77	32.10
Moldova	921	14.62	8.81	5.45	.89	.50	.23	.26	.59	.20	.03	.05	.01
Poland	964	1.02	1.51	3.08	3.99	5.02	8.13	13.60	20.54	29.04	36.89	45.17	54.43
Romania	968	38.14	37.72	2.82	76.95	.83	7.34	.75	5.42	1.69	.18	.36	.38
Russia	922	2.11	78.53	3.13	90.68	.05	.41	.41	2.29	.88	.49	.55	3.95
Serbia & Montenegro	965	—	—	—	—	—	—	15.22	6.81	.70	.26	.03	21.16
Slovak Republic	936	58.89	39.00	11.24	19.59	1.19	.57	.37	.53	.85	.86	.88	.90
Slovenia	961	.04	.04	.09	.05	.17	1.17	2.83	4.00	5.13	6.18	7.18	8.13
Tajikistan	923	—	—	2.21	9.06	2.05	.04	6.02	3.86	1.34	.57	.85	3.80
Turkey	186	.82	1.93	.98	.58	.97	.06	21.88	3.56	23.01	20.46	9.02	11.07
Turkmenistan	925	—	—	—	—	—	—	—	—	—	—	—	—
Ukraine	926	123.73	97.06	46.72	52.70	129.53	47.86	191.19	199.80	20.81	14.27	.75	.70
Uzbekistan	927	—	.81	.03	.09	.16	.41	.30	.61	.79	.07	.02	.01
Middle East	405	**1,090.4**	**1,165.0**	**1,397.5**	**1,556.0**	**1,424.9**	**829.9**	**1,041.1**	**1,076.7**	**1,211.3**	**1,316.5**	**1,741.1**	**1,776.5**
Bahrain, Kingdom of	419	11.01	11.28	11.68	11.90	12.15	.03	1.03	.84	.77	.68	.58	1.68
Egypt	469	59.19	69.51	85.57	83.92	113.80	30.07	36.94	27.68	67.24	127.01	106.38	70.70
Iran, I.R. of	429	97.91	89.88	239.76	244.62	1.12	101.26	267.49	267.40	267.96	268.41	273.91	274.66
Iraq	433	—	—	—	—	—	—	—	—	—	—	296.12	293.58
Israel	436	.24	.38	.95	.03	.20	.11	.83	1.37	3.36	6.39	9.77	13.04
Jordan	439	.46	.82	.57	.14	.55	.19	.47	.93	.63	.75	1.08	.43
Kuwait	443	55.02	61.28	68.15	74.14	82.51	53.74	69.79	85.90	97.74	107.51	117.07	128.70
Lebanon	446	11.35	12.34	13.34	14.33	15.44	16.38	18.21	19.37	20.10	20.64	21.19	22.00
Libya	672	324.75	349.69	373.87	398.47	425.79	372.59	412.77	441.19	448.87	461.97	475.41	494.88
Oman	449	6.17	7.49	8.84	10.10	11.47	1.33	3.12	5.02	6.53	7.81	8.98	10.32
Qatar	453	19.88	21.21	22.52	23.76	25.11	10.67	15.85	17.90	19.98	21.75	23.45	25.41
Saudi Arabia	456	415.98	448.24	481.28	512.14	545.95	110.45	146.57	192.27	243.89	289.75	334.08	384.64
Syrian Arab Rep.	463	—	—	.01	.01	.05	.05	.01	.32	.02	.04	36.58	36.58
United Arab Emirates	466	54.99	55.91	57.60	58.36	59.19	4.55	3.08	1.76	1.13	.48	3.49	6.73
Yemen, Republic of	474	33.49	37.01	33.34	124.06	131.55	128.48	64.96	14.71	33.04	3.29	33.03	13.18

SDRs

1b s		1994	1995	1996	1997	1998	1999	2000	2001	2002	2003	2004	2005
							Millions of SDRs: End of Period						
Western Hemisphere	205	**1,045.1**	**1,963.5**	**1,049.0**	**1,027.6**	**801.7**	**1,032.3**	**1,146.4**	**594.5**	**866.3**	**1,279.9**	**1,215.1**	**3,778.5**
ECCU (incl. ECCB hqtrs.)	309	3.36	3.47	3.60	3.67	3.80	3.89	3.91	4.02	4.07	4.11	1.56	1.55
Antigua and Barbuda	311	—	—	—	—	—	.01	.01	.01	.01	.01	.01	.01
Dominica	321	—	—	—	—	—	.01	—	—	—	—	.03	.01
Grenada	328	.02	.02	.04	—	.03	—	—	—	—	—	.01	.01
St. Kitts and Nevis	361	—	—	—	—	—	—	—	.01	—	—	—	—
St. Lucia	362	1.36	1.39	1.42	1.45	1.48	1.50	1.43	1.46	1.48	1.49	1.50	1.52
St. Vincent & Grens	364	.09	.08	.07	.07	.07	.06	.06	.03	.02	—	—	—
Argentina	213	385.68	362.67	277.42	123.58	187.73	100.34	562.21	8.49	69.28	678.68	564.49	3,104.08
Bahamas, The	313	.01	.02	.01	.02	.02	.02	.09	.09	.08	.01	.02	.01
Barbados	316	.03	.03	.02	.02	.02	.01	.02	.04	.04	.01	.01	.01
Belize	339	.37	.47	.61	.71	.82	1.01	1.20	1.37	1.48	1.56	1.64	1.76
Bolivia	218	16.99	26.88	26.81	26.81	26.81	27.27	27.29	27.32	27.35	27.13	26.56	26.75
Brazil	223	.30	.68	.66	.37	1.24	7.32	.27	8.42	202.07	1.54	2.67	20.19
Chile	228	.45	2.07	1.33	.96	5.86	13.48	18.89	23.02	26.87	30.72	33.88	36.63
Colombia	233	116.38	118.83	122.83	127.64	139.34	95.18	103.32	107.81	113.15	115.19	116.51	120.71
Costa Rica	238	.12	.04	.01	.02	.05	.59	.33	.07	.06	.04	.09	.03
Dominican Republic	243	2.53	.35	.29	.23	.19	.21	.27	.35	.21	.09	1.02	.39
Ecuador	248	2.97	2.11	1.87	.41	.20	1.70	.24	1.85	1.38	.67	36.09	15.24
El Salvador	253	.07	24.99	24.99	24.98	24.98	24.98	24.98	24.98	24.98	24.98	24.98	24.98
Guatemala	258	11.38	10.60	10.15	9.44	8.65	8.36	7.52	6.73	6.06	5.53	5.14	4.58
Guyana	336	.05	.09	.07	.14	.17	.92	7.02	1.96	3.43	3.26	4.60	.34
Haiti	263	—	.36	.03	.06	.39	.62	.05	.41	.37	.23	.12	8.61
Honduras	268	.15	.10	.06	.06	.05	.68	.08	.25	.35	.08	.06	.20
Jamaica	343	.02	.31	.05	.17	.46	.53	.07	1.19	.66	.04	.05	—
Mexico	273	121.13	1,074.05	178.69	490.13	239.65	575.45	281.23	283.47	288.02	291.64	299.23	311.57
Nicaragua	278	.01	—	.02	.03	.15	.16	.05	.26	.02	.04	.32	.22
Panama	283	.03	.55	.03	.37	.10	1.20	.27	1.10	.78	.56	.56	.76
Paraguay	288	67.63	70.58	73.30	76.08	79.14	74.81	78.49	81.33	83.25	84.63	86.04	88.21
Peru	293	.31	.50	.22	.17	1.48	.28	1.15	1.39	.55	.27	.23	.34
Suriname	366	—	7.75	8.22	8.23	8.25	2.00	1.77	1.56	1.42	1.32	1.21	1.06
Trinidad and Tobago	369	.08	.15	.03	.10	.08	—	.06	.16	.29	.74	1.73	2.60
Uruguay	298	.02	2.39	2.75	.03	.53	.71	.36	1.47	4.16	2.52	.78	4.37
Venezuela, Rep. Bol	299	316.94	255.38	316.98	135.27	73.73	92.89	27.69	7.92	8.41	6.98	5.48	3.32
Memorandum Items													
Oil Exporting Countries	999	**1,307.6**	**1,291.2**	**1,574.4**	**1,827.8**	**1,448.0**	**749.3**	**973.4**	**1,041.7**	**1,118.5**	**1,205.5**	**1,540.6**	**1,629.9**
Non-Oil Developing Countries.	201	**1,968.0**	**3,483.5**	**2,426.0**	**3,192.9**	**3,087.7**	**2,981.4**	**3,104.5**	**2,547.4**	**2,762.4**	**3,403.3**	**3,478.1**	**5,994.9**

SDR Holdings

Millions of SDRs: End of Period

		1994	1995	1996	1997	1998	1999	2000	2001	2002	2003	2004	2005
World	001	21,476.9	21,484.5	21,495.2	21,508.2	21,522.1	21,534.8	21,527.5	21,539.5	21,525.8	21,521.2	21,468.7	21,470.4
All Participants	969	15,761.5	19,773.2	18,521.4	20,532.2	20,379.7	18,456.7	18,489.0	19,556.8	19,672.7	19,914.6	20,301.5	20,055.5
IMF	992	5,510.08	652.47	1,726.32	634.78	687.34	2,459.29	2,413.89	1,543.19	1,201.69	1,087.86	841.50	1,128.50
Other Holders	970	205.33	1,058.87	1,247.41	341.26	455.05	618.86	624.58	439.53	651.43	518.69	325.66	286.44

Reserve Position in the Fund

		1994	1995	1996	1997	1998	1999	2000	2001	2002	2003	2004	2005
						Millions of SDRs: End of Period							
All Countries.............	010	31,725.6	36,673.2	38,005.3	47,078.0	60,630.9	54,785.6	47,377.7	56,861.3	66,064.6	66,507.8	55,786.2	28,561.2
Industrial Countries........	110	27,417.0	31,643.8	32,609.8	41,336.5	53,919.2	46,775.8	39,699.5	46,960.1	53,717.1	52,584.4	43,581.8	21,010.4
United States................	111	8,240.8	9,854.7	10,733.8	13,393.4	17,124.1	13,092.9	11,377.3	14,219.0	16,166.5	15,164.9	12,584.7	5,622.4
Canada..................	156	629.18	836.15	852.79	1,167.32	1,632.72	2,307.95	1,925.85	2,278.39	2,633.36	2,588.94	2,149.58	980.30
Australia.................	193	346.86	337.62	334.89	538.98	892.26	1,189.43	953.89	1,123.59	1,422.89	1,381.33	1,098.71	543.00
Japan.......................	158	5,912.26	5,448.95	4,639.25	6,777.41	6,813.09	4,773.53	4,032.09	4,018.95	5,298.43	5,204.18	4,371.38	2,013.20
New Zealand............	196	100.82	110.33	126.63	131.92	252.82	308.59	245.68	308.25	337.91	433.07	305.45	115.26
Euro Area													
Austria..................	122	363.86	458.91	562.40	713.73	969.69	698.68	531.46	662.48	705.16	770.73	602.32	275.67
Belgium..................	124	556.33	675.81	747.30	875.80	1,348.36	1,668.38	1,303.84	1,631.74	1,759.41	1,812.32	1,478.63	777.89
Finland..................	172	196.13	259.51	292.84	414.15	594.98	464.32	381.84	438.98	476.83	522.09	405.99	198.27
France..................	132	1,626.73	1,853.88	1,874.51	2,119.18	3,161.79	3,949.93	3,470.99	3,893.91	4,249.92	4,241.98	3,453.00	2,013.94
Germany..................	134	2,760.48	3,504.97	3,802.51	4,406.90	5,698.26	4,676.60	4,191.00	4,695.84	4,924.84	5,152.31	4,419.30	2,436.60
Greece..................	174	113.69	113.69	113.69	113.69	191.49	284.98	227.82	284.31	322.45	334.26	270.60	117.72
Ireland..................	178	151.93	197.47	226.07	252.15	413.56	302.94	252.37	267.68	345.25	386.68	269.23	123.25
Italy..................	136	1,392.80	1,320.60	1,289.87	1,660.68	3,075.29	2,583.58	2,230.13	2,559.73	2,874.12	2,795.77	2,384.59	1,230.20
Luxembourg..............	137	23.61	22.94	23.56	21.75	59.37	54.37	55.47	78.95	104.75	120.26	89.66	40.65
Netherlands.............	138	802.16	1,169.12	1,275.26	1,625.48	2,112.77	1,879.77	1,524.06	1,871.66	2,095.25	2,055.01	1,717.59	833.83
Portugal................	182	230.80	302.98	320.31	313.36	442.12	274.96	242.38	299.42	329.07	360.82	283.34	141.61
Spain..................	184	759.53	1,064.90	1,110.30	1,409.46	1,557.82	1,111.18	907.54	1,055.08	1,170.75	1,253.37	1,014.29	525.99
Denmark................	128	294.59	400.00	421.81	467.92	827.45	582.07	440.12	566.83	721.95	686.33	542.81	216.00
Iceland................	176	10.48	10.48	10.49	10.49	10.50	18.58	18.58	18.58	18.58	18.58	18.58	18.59
Norway................	142	440.93	636.16	643.80	725.52	899.13	621.23	448.09	577.34	729.81	669.50	559.24	210.92
San Marino............	135	2.35	2.35	2.35	2.35	2.35	4.10	4.10	4.10	4.10	4.10	4.10	4.10
Sweden................	144	451.42	451.43	451.43	589.10	899.90	862.95	683.33	827.12	1,050.33	988.12	842.47	371.96
Switzerland...........	146	643.21	981.22	1,064.90	1,407.48	1,828.05	1,218.12	963.67	1,258.68	1,410.04	1,383.44	1,153.85	571.23
United Kingdom........	112	1,366.1	1,629.5	1,689.1	2,198.2	3,111.3	3,846.7	3,287.9	4,019.5	4,565.4	4,256.3	3,562.4	1,627.8
Developing Countries.......	200	4,308.6	5,029.4	5,395.4	5,741.5	6,711.7	8,009.8	7,678.1	9,901.1	12,347.5	13,923.4	12,204.4	7,550.8
Africa..................	605	157.6	151.0	152.0	150.5	159.4	335.5	290.0	289.5	291.5	306.0	296.5	279.7
CEMAC (incl. BEAC hqtrs.).....	758	1.23	1.28	1.35	1.39	1.43	1.52	1.59	1.65	1.70	1.80	1.81	1.90
Cameroon..............	622	.34	.36	.37	.41	.45	.50	.52	.54	.58	.64	.65	.70
Central African Rep......	626	.09	.09	.10	.10	.10	.10	.11	.11	.12	.16	.16	.16
Chad..................	628	.28	.28	.28	.28	.28	.28	.28	.28	.28	.28	.28	.28
Congo, Rep. of..........	634	.47	.50	.54	.54	.54	.54	.54	.54	.54	.54	.54	.54
Equatorial Guinea........	642	—	—	—	—	—	—	—	—	—	—	—	—
Gabon................	646	.05	.05	.07	.07	.07	.11	.15	.18	.18	.18	.18	.22
WAEMU (incl. BCEAO hqtrs.).....	759	28.07	28.19	28.33	28.46	28.54	28.62	28.71	28.86	29.05	29.29	29.49	29.81
Benin................	638	2.10	2.13	2.16	2.18	2.18	2.19	2.19	2.19	2.19	2.19	2.19	2.19
Burkina Faso..........	748	7.20	7.22	7.22	7.22	7.22	7.22	7.22	7.23	7.26	7.28	7.31	7.33
Côte d'Ivoire..........	662	.09	.09	.11	.17	.19	.24	.28	.31	.45	.57	.59	.64
Guinea Bissau..........	654	—	—	—	—	—	—	—	—	—	—	—	—
Mali................	678	8.73	8.73	8.76	8.76	8.78	8.78	8.78	8.83	8.83	8.88	8.97	9.14
Niger................	692	8.56	8.56	8.56	8.56	8.56	8.56	8.56	8.56	8.56	8.56	8.56	8.61
Senegal..............	722	1.14	1.20	1.27	1.33	1.35	1.37	1.40	1.44	1.45	1.48	1.53	1.57
Togo................	742	.25	.25	.25	.25	.25	.25	.28	.30	.31	.33	.33	.33
Algeria................	612	.01	.01	.01	.01	.01	85.08	85.08	85.08	85.08	85.08	85.08	85.08
Angola................	614	—	—	—	—	—	—	—	—	—	—	—	—
Botswana..............	616	16.34	19.28	19.91	18.13	27.61	22.59	17.74	22.28	23.80	30.32	20.50	7.41
Burundi................	618	5.86	5.86	5.86	5.86	5.86	5.86	5.86	.36	.36	.36	.36	.36
Cape Verde............	624	—	—	—	—	—	—	—	—	—	—	—	.02
Comoros..............	632	.52	.54	.54	.54	.54	.54	.54	.54	.54	.54	.54	.54
Congo, Dem. Rep. of......	636	—	—	—	—	—	—	—	—	—	—	—	—
Djibouti................	611						1.10	1.10	1.10	1.10	1.10	1.10	1.10
Eritrea................	643	—	.01	.01	.01	.01	.01	.01	.01	.01	.01	.01	.01
Ethiopia................	644	7.01	7.03	7.05	7.08	7.10	7.10	7.10	7.12	7.17	7.19	7.19	7.19
Gambia, The..........	648	1.48	1.48	1.48	1.48	1.48	1.48	1.48	1.48	1.48	1.48	1.48	1.48
Ghana................	652	17.38	17.38	17.38	17.38	17.38	41.13	—	—	—	—	—	—
Guinea................	656	.07	.07	.08	.08	.08	.08	.08	.08	.08	.08	.08	.08
Kenya................	664	12.31	12.31	12.32	12.36	12.42	12.43	12.45	12.54	12.58	12.68	12.70	12.74
Lesotho................	666	3.51	3.51	3.51	3.52	3.53	3.53	3.54	3.54	3.54	3.54	3.56	3.60
Liberia................	668	.03	.03	.03	.03	.03	.03	.03	.03	.03	.03	.03	.03
Madagascar............	674	.01	.02	.02	.03	.03	.03	.03	.03	.03	.03	.03	.03
Malawi................	676	2.22	2.22	2.22	2.22	2.24	2.24	2.24	2.27	2.28	2.29	2.29	2.29
Mauritania............	682	—	—	—	—	—	—	—	—	—	—	—	—
Mauritius..............	684	7.33	7.34	7.37	7.37	7.38	14.47	14.47	14.47	14.48	21.88	21.88	17.51
Morocco..............	686	30.31	30.31	30.32	30.32	30.32	70.44	70.44	70.44	70.44	70.44	70.44	70.44
Mozambique..........	688	.01	.01	.01	.01	.01	.01	.01	.01	.01	.01	.01	.01
Namibia..............	728	.01	.02	.03	.03	.04	.04	.04	.04	.05	.05	.06	.07
Nigeria................	694	.07	.07	.07	.07	.07	.09	.14	.14	.14	.14	.14	.14
Rwanda................	714	9.79	—	—	—	—	—	—	—	—	—	—	—
São Tomé & Príncipe......	716	—	—	—	—	—	—	—	—	—	—	—	—
Seychelles............	718	.80	.80	.80	.80	—	—	—	—	—	—	—	—
Sierra Leone..........	724	.02	.02	.02	.02	.02	.02	.02	.02	.02	.02	.02	.02
Somalia................	726	—	—	—	—	—	—	—	—	—	—	—	—
South Africa..........	199	.05	.06	.10	.10	.11	.11	.27	.35	.42	.50	.57	.69
Sudan................	732	.01	.01	.01	.01	.01	.01	.01	.01	.01	.01	.01	.01
Swaziland............	734	3.00	3.00	3.00	3.00	3.00	6.55	6.55	6.55	6.55	6.55	6.56	6.56
Tanzania..............	738	9.98	9.98	9.98	9.98	9.98	9.98	9.98	9.98	9.99	10.00	10.00	10.00
Tunisia................	744	.04	.04	.04	.04	.04	20.17	20.17	20.17	20.17	20.20	20.22	20.22

Reserve Position in the Fund

Millions of SDRs: End of Period

1c s		1994	1995	1996	1997	1998	1999	2000	2001	2002	2003	2004	2005
Africa(Cont.)													
Uganda	746	—	—	—	—	—	—	—	—	—	—	—	—
Zambia	754	.02	.02	.02	.02	.02	.02	.02	.02	.02	.02	.02	.02
Zimbabwe	698	.07	.10	.11	.15	.19	.27	.31	.33	.33	.33	.33	.33
Asia	505	**2,173.8**	**2,848.4**	**3,142.2**	**3,201.8**	**3,680.0**	**3,643.0**	**3,355.3**	**4,013.9**	**4,910.5**	**5,359.9**	**4,815.8**	**2,608.2**
Afghanistan, Islamic Rep. of	512	4.93	4.93	4.93	4.93	4.93	4.93	4.93	4.93	4.93	—	—	—
Bangladesh	513	.07	.09	.11	.11	.16	.19	.19	.19	.19	.19	.21	.23
Bhutan	514	.57	.57	.57	.57	.57	1.02	1.02	1.02	1.02	1.02	1.02	1.02
Brunei Darussalam	516	—	—	35.26	35.26	35.26	35.28	35.28	35.28	51.79	58.29	58.29	32.27
Cambodia	522	—	—	—	—	—	—	—	—	—	—	—	—
China, P.R.: Mainland	924	517.31	817.78	970.97	1,682.40	2,523.33	1,684.72	1,462.33	2,060.54	2,738.22	2,555.95	2,138.08	973.02
China, P.R.: Hong Kong	532	—	—	—	—	31.34	—	—	—	—	—	—	—
Fiji	819	9.99	10.00	10.05	10.08	10.12	14.94	14.98	15.00	15.07	15.19	15.26	15.31
India	534	212.63	212.63	212.63	212.63	212.79	488.57	488.64	488.78	488.88	887.01	917.09	630.97
Indonesia	536	213.99	270.00	298.00	—	.05	145.47	145.48	145.48	145.50	145.50	145.50	145.50
Kiribati	826	—	—	—	—	—	—	—	—	.02	.01	—	—
Korea	542	363.61	438.49	474.30	443.72	.06	208.60	208.64	208.83	383.99	507.66	507.68	213.97
Lao P. D. Rep.	544	—	—	—	—	—	—	—	—	—	—	—	—
Malaysia	548	273.70	456.34	478.20	444.68	444.68	608.16	608.16	608.16	581.22	586.19	499.76	199.43
Maldives	556	.88	.88	.88	.88	.88	1.55	1.55	1.55	1.55	1.55	1.55	1.55
Marshall Islands, Rep. of	867	—	—	—	—	—	—	—	—	—	—	—	—
Micronesia, Fed. States of	868	.001	.001	.001	.001	.001	.001	.001	.001	.001	.001	.001	.001
Mongolia	948	—	—	—	—	—	.02	.04	.06	.08	.10	.12	.14
Myanmar	518	—	—	—	—	—	—	—	—	—	—	—	—
Nepal	558	5.73	5.73	5.73	5.73	5.73	5.73	5.75	5.75	5.75	5.77	—	—
Pakistan	564	.06	.06	.06	.06	.06	.10	.10	.11	.12	—	—	—
Palau	565	—	—	—	—	—	—	—	—	—	.12	.12	.12
Papua New Guinea	853	.05	.05	.05	.05	.05	.05	.18	.30	.40	.43	.44	
Philippines	566	87.10	87.10	87.10	87.10	87.10	87.10	87.10	87.18	87.28	87.36	87.43	87.49
Samoa	862	.66	.67	.67	.68	.68	.68	.68	.68	.69	.69	.69	.69
Singapore	576	172.84	199.85	204.73	248.42	297.65	303.44	237.71	297.50	351.29	379.27	283.42	121.84
Solomon Islands	813	.54	.54	.54	.54	.54	.54	.54	.54	.55	.55	.55	.55
Sri Lanka	524	20.25	20.25	20.25	20.25	20.25	47.71	47.74	47.79	47.82	47.86	47.86	47.86
Thailand	578	285.15	318.69	333.47	.02	.02	.02	.02	.02	.02	75.02	106.56	131.59
Tonga	866	1.20	1.21	1.21	1.21	1.22	1.70	1.71	1.71	1.71	1.71	1.71	1.71
Vanuatu	846	2.49	2.49	2.49	2.50	2.50	2.50	2.50	2.50	2.50	2.50	2.50	2.50
Vietnam	582	.01	.01	.01	.01	.01	.01	.01	.01	.01	.01	.01	.01
Europe	170	**262.8**	**264.6**	**268.2**	**269.2**	**302.8**	**653.1**	**665.3**	**1,099.4**	**1,418.3**	**1,662.6**	**1,377.5**	**854.9**
Albania	914	—	—	—	—	—	3.4	3.4	3.4	3.4	3.4	3.4	3.4
Armenia	911	.01	.01	.01	—	—	—	—	—	—	—	—	—
Azerbaijan, Republic of	912	.01	.01	.01	.01	.01	.01	.01	.01	.01	.01	.01	.01
Belarus	913	.02	.02	.02	.02	.02	.02	.02	.02	.02	.02	.02	.02
Bosnia and Herzegovina	963	—	—	—	—	—	—	—	—	—	—	—	—
Bulgaria	918	32.63	32.63	32.63	32.63	32.63	32.69	32.74	32.78	32.78	32.78	32.85	33.00
Croatia	960	—	—	.03	.07	.11	.14	.16	.16	.16	.16	.16	.16
Cyprus	423	25.45	25.45	25.45	25.45	25.45	35.36	35.37	35.37	49.11	66.82	47.28	21.73
Czech Republic	935	—	—	—	—	—	—	2.35	120.45	173.45	314.61	263.97	126.56
Estonia	939	.01	.01	.01	.01	.01	.01	.01	.01	.01	.01	.01	.01
Georgia	915	.01	.01	.01	.01	.01	.01	.01	.01	.01	.01	.01	.01
Hungary	944	56.10	56.10	56.10	56.10	56.10	176.78	201.78	321.95	437.47	454.95	346.26	134.56
Kazakhstan	916	.01	.01	.01	.01	.01	.01	.01	.01	.01	.01	.01	.01
Kyrgyz Republic	917	.01	—	—	—	—	—	—	—	—	—	—	—
Latvia	941	.01	.01	.01	.01	.01	.01	.06	.06	.06	.06	.06	.06
Lithuania	946	.01	.01	.01	.01	.02	.02	.02	.02	.02	.02	.02	.02
Macedonia, FYR	962	—	—	—	—	—	—	—	—	—	—	—	—
Malta	181	25.44	27.26	30.66	31.64	31.64	40.26	40.26	40.26	40.26	40.26	40.26	40.26
Moldova	921	.01	.01	.01	.01	.01	.01	.01	.01	—	.01	.01	.01
Poland	964	77.13	77.13	77.13	77.13	77.13	172.26	172.26	366.84	478.86	537.97	451.33	209.17
Romania	968	—	—	—	—	—	—	—	—	—	—	—	—
Russia	922	.84	.77	.93	.93	.93	.93	.93	1.14	1.18	1.43	1.83	137.04
Serbia & Montenegro	965	—	—	—	—	—	—	—	—	—	—	—	—
Slovak Republic	936	—	—	—	—	—	—	—	—	—	—	—	—
Slovenia	961	12.87	12.88	12.88	12.88	46.46	78.40	63.19	64.16	88.77	97.34	77.26	36.12
Tajikistan	923	—	—	—	—	—	—	—	—	—	—	—	—
Turkey	186	32.27	32.28	32.28	32.28	32.28	112.77	112.78	112.78	112.78	112.78	112.78	112.78
Turkmenistan	925	.01	—	—	—	—	—	—	—	—	—	—	—
Ukraine	926	.01	—	—	.01	.01	—	—	—	—	—	—	—
Uzbekistan	927	.01	.01	.01	.01	.01	.01	.01	.01	.01	.01	.01	.01
Middle East	405	**1,396.5**	**1,399.0**	**1,401.7**	**1,393.2**	**1,500.1**	**2,325.2**	**2,365.1**	**3,474.4**	**4,345.6**	**4,828.7**	**4,019.9**	**2,492.5**
Bahrain, Kingdom of	419	42.19	43.70	45.09	46.70	48.51	62.37	64.86	67.18	68.62	69.70	70.84	71.20
Egypt	469	53.75	53.75	53.75	53.75	53.75	120.08	120.08	—	—	—	—	—
Iran, I.R. of	429	—	—	—	—	—	—	—	—	—	—	—	—
Iraq	433	—	—	—	—	—	—	—	—	—	—	171.10	171.10
Israel	436	—	—	—	.01	.01	65.51	89.91	157.36	304.01	354.79	298.26	141.17
Jordan	439	—	—	—	—	—	.01	.05	.05	.05	.05	.09	.14
Kuwait	443	142.59	138.95	136.53	167.55	244.76	368.30	373.80	476.07	528.29	522.74	458.94	208.82
Lebanon	446	18.83	18.83	18.83	18.83	18.83	18.83	18.83	18.83	18.83	18.83	18.83	18.83
Libya	672	318.98	318.98	318.98	318.98	318.98	395.51	395.51	395.51	395.51	395.51	395.51	395.51
Oman	449	35.98	34.47	33.97	31.15	31.15	49.80	49.80	64.96	73.41	77.57	63.68	24.24
Qatar	453	30.65	29.73	29.23	26.40	26.40	44.73	44.73	79.11	99.59	103.46	86.36	34.66
Saudi Arabia	456	604.3	574.7	560.9	532.5	523.8	987.5	1,042.7	2,035.5	2,621.4	3,046.8	2,253.1	1,333.7

Reserve Position in the Fund

		1994	1995	1996	1997	1998	1999	2000	2001	2002	2003	2004	2005
1c s							*Millions of SDRs: End of Period*						
Middle East(Cont.)													
Syrian Arab Rep.	463	.01	.01	.01	.01	.01	.01	.01	.01	.01	.01	.01	.01
United Arab Emirates	466	149.12	185.81	204.37	197.37	233.89	212.55	164.82	179.79	235.83	239.30	203.16	93.04
Yemen, Republic of	474	.01	.01	.01	.01	.01	.01	.01	.01	.01	.01	.01	—
Western Hemisphere	205	318.0	366.5	431.4	726.8	1,069.3	1,053.0	1,002.5	1,024.0	1,381.6	1,766.2	1,694.7	1,315.5
ECCU (incl. ECCB hqtrs.)	309	.53	.53	.53	.53	.53	.58	.59	.59	.59	.60	.60	.60
Antigua and Barbuda	311	—	—	—	—	—	—	—	—	—	.01	.01	.01
Dominica	321	.01	.01	.01	.01	.01	.01	.01	.01	.01	.01	.01	.01
Grenada	328	—	—	—	—	—	—	—	—	—	—	—	—
St. Kitts and Nevis	361	.01	.01	.01	.01	.01	.07	.08	.08	.08	.08	.08	.08
St. Lucia	362	—	—	—	—	—	—	—	—	—	.01	.01	.01
St. Vincent & Grens	364	.50	.50	.50	.50	.50	.50	.50	.50	.50	.50	.50	.50
Argentina	213	—	—	—	—	—	—	—	—	.02	.06	.16	.20
Bahamas, The	313	6.24	6.24	6.24	6.24	6.24	6.24	6.24	6.24	6.24	6.25	6.26	6.26
Barbados	316	.03	.03	.03	.03	.03	4.68	4.68	4.71	4.85	5.02	5.15	5.30
Belize	339	2.91	2.91	2.91	2.91	2.91	4.24	4.24	4.24	4.24	4.24	4.24	4.24
Bolivia	218	8.87	8.87	8.87	8.87	8.87	8.87	8.87	8.87	8.87	8.87	8.87	8.87
Brazil	223	—	—	—	—	—	—	—	—	—	—	—	—
Chile	228	.02	.02	35.03	232.03	429.63	299.43	248.82	245.66	360.93	392.29	287.04	131.39
Colombia	233	86.75	135.26	165.06	263.41	408.28	285.80	285.80	285.80	285.80	285.80	285.80	285.80
Costa Rica	238	8.73	8.73	8.73	8.73	8.73	20.00	20.00	20.00	20.00	20.00	20.00	20.00
Dominican Republic	243	—	—	—	—	—	—	—	—	—	—	—	—
Ecuador	248	17.13	17.15	17.15	17.15	17.15	17.15	17.15	17.15	17.15	17.15	17.15	17.15
El Salvador	253	—	—	—	—	—	—	—	—	—	—	—	—
Guatemala	258	—	—	—	—	—	—	—	—	—	—	—	—
Guyana	336	—	—	—	—	—	—	—	—	—	—	—	—
Haiti	263	.05	.05	.05	.05	.05	.05	.06	.06	.07	.07	.07	.07
Honduras	268	—	—	—	—	—	8.63	8.63	8.63	8.63	8.63	8.63	8.63
Jamaica	343	—	—	—	—	—	—	—	—	—	—	—	—
Mexico	273	—	.03	.12	.12	.21	.27	.32	.39	226.46	526.53	578.31	415.76
Nicaragua	278	—	—	—	—	—	—	—	—	—	—	—	—
Panama	283	11.86	11.86	11.86	11.86	11.86	11.86	11.86	11.86	11.86	11.86	11.86	11.86
Paraguay	288	14.53	14.53	14.53	14.53	14.53	21.48	21.48	21.48	21.48	21.48	21.48	21.48
Peru	293	—	—	—	—	—	6.13	6.13	6.13	6.13	6.12	6.12	6.12
Suriname	366	—	—	—	—	—	—	—	—	—	—	—	—
Trinidad and Tobago	369	.01	.01	.01	.01	.02	.02	.02	24.57	76.37	129.32	111.09	49.90
Uruguay	298	15.38	15.38	15.38	15.38	15.38	35.68	35.68	35.68	—	—	—	—
Venezuela, Rep. Bol.	299	144.95	144.95	144.95	144.95	144.95	321.90	321.90	321.90	321.90	321.90	321.90	321.90
Memorandum Items													
Oil Exporting Countries	999	1,640.7	1,697.7	1,727.0	1,418.9	1,524.0	2,610.9	2,623.9	3,783.6	4,506.7	4,938.0	4,184.4	2,813.7
Non-Oil Developing Countries	201	2,667.9	3,331.8	3,668.4	4,322.6	5,187.6	5,398.9	5,054.2	6,117.6	7,840.8	8,985.5	8,020.0	4,737.0

Foreign Exchange

		1994	1995	1996	1997	1998	1999	2000	2001	2002	2003	2004	2005
						Millions of SDRs: End of Period							
All Countries	010	812,812	934,871	1,089,138	1,197,810	1,167,476	1,297,849	1,486,120	1,630,290	1,770,063	2,035,731	2,411,038	2,913,929
Industrial Countries	110	394,037	441,184	501,813	520,984	476,263	526,812	598,707	624,782	661,057	750,924	843,578	900,617
United States	111	28,233	33,028	26,631	22,834	25,568	23,448	23,976	23,061	24,875	26,731	27,507	26,474
Canada	156	7,000	8,496	12,537	11,208	14,141	17,801	22,272	24,257	24,042	21,223	19,424	21,454
Australia	193	7,334	7,628	9,713	11,932	9,493	14,213	12,880	13,077	13,694	20,166	21,829	28,666
Japan	158	78,875	116,007	144,187	154,060	144,326	202,336	266,490	308,521	332,072	439,302	530,753	579,886
New Zealand	196	2,439	2,856	4,013	3,167	2,731	2,933	2,778	2,515	3,297	3,643	4,146	6,083
Euro Area (incl. ECB)	163	....	....	....	....	....	166,111	167,802	165,440	158,741	126,628	116,474	117,092
Austria	122	10,966	12,020	15,203	13,789	14,856	10,212	10,355	9,106	6,281	4,807	4,355	4,407
Belgium	124	8,826	9,876	10,696	10,761	11,195	† 6,104	6,131	6,957	6,553	5,149	4,968	4,768
Finland	172	6,885	6,252	4,315	5,582	6,043	5,313	5,634	5,727	6,206	6,423	7,419	7,097
France	132	16,111	15,568	16,078	20,083	27,523	24,724	24,648	20,978	16,156	15,560	18,723	16,789
Germany	134	49,470	52,334	52,716	51,772	45,548	† 38,368	38,120	34,781	31,258	27,656	25,691	27,822
Greece	174	9,810	9,829	12,057	9,221	12,207	12,915	10,066	† 3,809	5,612	2,586	479	216
Ireland	178	3,935	5,501	5,365	4,462	6,123	3,548	3,824	4,134	3,589	2,305	1,496	360
Italy	136	20,623	22,161	30,643	39,601	18,073	† 13,630	17,210	16,635	18,086	17,534	15,461	16,462
Luxembourg	137	21	20	20	18	....	—	—	—	—	60	93	117
Netherlands	138	22,411	20,895	16,773	16,217	12,455	4,581	5,376	4,719	4,426	4,937	4,379	5,049
Portugal	182	10,348	10,303	10,681	11,214	10,701	† 5,833	6,554	7,343	7,838	3,532	2,982	2,220
Spain	184	27,525	21,857	38,860	48,933	37,229	22,826	22,654	22,205	23,972	11,785	6,749	6,013
Denmark	128	5,784	6,904	9,295	13,457	9,767	15,406	11,105	12,825	19,052	24,229	24,595	† 22,746
Iceland	176	190	197	305	274	292	330	280	250	305	515	655	706
Norway	142	12,325	14,201	17,550	16,360	12,335	16,427	20,498	17,663	22,576	24,153	27,739	32,448
San Marino	135	118	131	147	133	118	101	99	102	130	165	224	243
Sweden	144	15,431	15,432	12,637	7,157	8,820	9,852	10,559	10,137	11,416	12,123	13,272	14,941
Switzerland	146	22,985	23,333	25,574	27,348	27,234	24,900	23,681	23,984	28,072	30,660	34,536	24,783
United Kingdom	112	26,392	26,357	25,816	21,403	19,434	† 20,040	26,221	22,951	22,787	21,384	22,426	25,095
Developing Countries	200	418,776	493,686	587,325	676,826	691,213	771,037	887,413	1,005,508	1,109,006	1,284,807	1,567,460	2,013,313
Africa	605	15,924	17,441	21,838	31,966	28,922	29,969	41,453	51,057	52,842	60,846	81,313	112,421
CEMAC (Incl. BEAC hqtrs.)	758	....	....	....	....	....	....	957	852	1,172	1,216	1,985	3,593
Cameroon	622	† 1	2	1	—	—	1	156	263	462	429	533	662
Central African Republic	626	144	157	161	132	103	99	102	94	91	89	94	97
Chad	628	52	96	114	100	85	69	85	97	161	126	142	157
Congo, Rep. of	634	34	39	63	44	—	28	170	54	20	22	72	510
Equatorial Guinea	642	—	—	—	4	1	2	18	56	65	160	608	1,471
Gabon	646	120	100	173	209	11	13	146	8	103	132	281	467
WAEMU (Incl. BCEAO hqtrs.)	759	....	1,669	1,871	2,095	2,217	2,101	2,490	2,971	3,974	4,488	4,632	4,286
Benin	638	† 175	131	180	185	183	289	349	457	451	481	410	457
Burkina Faso	748	150	221	226	247	257	207	179	200	223	499	423	299
Côte d'Ivoire	662	140	355	420	458	607	457	511	810	1,369	877	1,090	924
Guinea Bissau	654	13	14	8	25	25	26	51	55	75	21	47	55
Mali	678	† 143	208	291	299	277	246	284	268	428	631	545	589
Niger	692	67	55	45	31	29	19	53	76	89	165	157	166
Senegal	722	121	179	198	285	304	290	293	348	461	739	886	831
Togo	742	64	87	61	88	83	89	117	100	150	137	231	136
Algeria	612	1,816	1,348	2,942	5,963	4,861	3,211	9,141	14,293	16,997	22,169	27,761	39,305
Angola	614	....	143	383	294	144	361	920	582	276	427	885	2,237
Botswana	616	2,973	3,112	3,448	4,158	4,159	4,488	4,802	4,639	3,970	3,530	3,591	4,371
Burundi	618	134	135	91	78	41	29	19	14	43	45	42	69
Cape Verde	624	29	25	19	14	6	31	22	36	59	63	90	122
Comoros	632	30	29	35	29	27	26	32	49	58	63	66	59
Congo, Dem. Rep. of	636	83	99	57	....	....	....	....	....	....	....	....	....
Djibouti	611	50	48	53	49	47	50	51	55	52	66	59	61
Eritrea	643	....	27	57	148	16	25	20	32	22	17	22	20
Ethiopia	644	366	512	502	364	356	327	228	337	641	636	956	777
Gambia, The	648	65	70	69	70	74	79	82	83	77	38	52	67
Ghana	652	380	450	557	379	208	276	178	234	394	879	1,034	1,226
Guinea	656	56	53	60	88	167	144	113	159	125	....	71	66
Kenya	664	369	225	506	571	543	563	676	834	772	983	965	1,246
Lesotho	666	251	304	316	419	404	360	317	304	295	306	319	360
Liberia	668	3	19	—	—	—	—	—	—	2	5	12	18
Madagascar	674	49	73	167	209	122	165	219	317	267	279	324	337
Malawi	676	23	71	150	103	174	177	184	158	116	80	79	108
Mauritania	682	27	57	97	149	144	163	215	226	291	279	....	....
Mauritius	684	483	552	594	484	367	502	658	634	871	1,022	995	902
Morocco	686	2,933	2,375	2,603	2,928	3,117	4,013	3,540	6,574	7,293	9,175	10,371	11,200
Mozambique	688	122	131	239	383	432	476	555	567	590	631	728	737
Namibia	728	139	149	135	186	185	223	199	186	238	219	222	218
Nigeria	694	949	971	2,834	5,619	5,043	3,971	7,606	8,320	5,392	4,797	10,918	19,786
Rwanda	714	24	53	62	94	102	116	145	159	172	124	183	266
São Tomé & Príncipe	716	....	3	3	9	7	8	9	12	13	17	13	19
Seychelles	718	20	17	14	19	15	22	34	30	51	45	22	39
Sierra Leone	724	22	12	13	20	24	14	34	41	45	22	48	96
South Africa	199	1,153	1,894	654	3,550	2,963	4,419	4,446	4,587	4,120	4,148	8,238	12,775
Sudan	732	54	110	74	60	64	138	† 190	94	324	570	1,047	1,714
Swaziland	734	195	192	168	210	246	265	261	207	194	178	199	162
Tanzania	738	217	172	296	451	415	555	738	910	1,114	1,361	1,468	1,423
Tunisia	744	999	1,075	1,309	1,454	1,312	1,608	1,367	1,561	1,662	1,960	2,508	3,037

Foreign Exchange

Foreign Exchange

		1994	1995	1996	1997	1998	1999	2000	2001	2002	2003	2004	2005
						Millions of SDRs: End of Period							
1d s													
Africa(Cont.)													
Uganda	746	218	308	367	466	512	554	617	781	685	724	842	940
Zambia	754	184	142	153	176	49	33	171	93	342	166	201	381
Zimbabwe	698	277	400	410	118	92	194	148	51	61	....	....	....
Asia	505	259,826	287,403	339,922	379,613	408,569	478,341	543,314	626,309	711,668	833,569	1,033,186	1,300,372
Bangladesh	513	2,125	1,467	1,200	1,150	1,344	1,168	1,140	1,013	1,236	1,732	2,042	1,935
Bhutan	514	82	† 87	131	139	181	212	243	256	260	245	255	326
Brunei Darussalam	516	....	....	....	....	....	338	273	270	263	258	258	303
Cambodia	522	70	119	175	213	223	283	385	467	570	549	607	667
China, P.R.: Mainland	924	35,360	49,498	73,040	103,680	102,952	112,695	127,080	168,823	210,668	271,372	392,742	572,930
China, P.R.: Hong Kong	532	33,737	37,268	44,374	68,782	63,639	70,117	82,540	88,448	82,306	79,652	79,549	86,928
China, P.R.: Macao	546	1,347	1,518	1,684	1,877	1,749	2,082	2,550	2,792	2,795	2,923	3,500	4,680
Fiji	819	170	217	279	249	255	293	297	272	244	265	287	199
India	534	13,279	11,750	13,729	18,028	19,146	23,309	28,601	36,007	49,278	65,692	80,594	91,668
Indonesia	536	8,097	8,951	12,393	11,923	15,910	19,122	21,706	21,522	22,621	23,380	22,359	22,931
Korea	542	17,147	21,479	23,114	14,608	36,905	53,697	73,570	81,551	88,863	103,978	127,607	146,906
Lao P. D. Rep.	544	34e	52	111	74	75	74	107	101	136	127	134	154
Malaysia	548	17,048	15,436	18,190	14,833	17,562	21,617	21,055	22,784	23,846	28,784	41,794	48,540
Maldives	556	20	31	52	72	83	91	92	72	96	105	129	128
Micronesia, Fed. States of	868	....	46	61	63	71	66	86	77	85	59	34	34
Mongolia	948	54	77	74	130	66	99	137	164	257	159	152	301
Myanmar	518	289	377	159	185	223	193	171	318	346	370	433	539
Nepal	558	469	389	392	458	531	610	720	820	743	816	935	1,043
Pakistan	564	2,006	1,156	372	878	729	1,101	1,151	2,893	5,940	7,196	6,152	6,869
Papua New Guinea	853	66	175	406	269	137	149	211	329	232	330	406	502
Philippines	566	4,032	4,211	6,906	5,320	6,498	9,576	9,958	10,625	9,710	9,101	8,358	11,055
Samoa	862	32	34	40	45	41	47	46	42	43	53	58	61
Singapore	576	39,654	45,980	53,194	52,535	52,852	55,595	61,159	59,560	59,849	63,914	71,795	80,695
Solomon Islands	813	11	10	22	26	34	37	24	15	13	24	51	66
Sri Lanka	524	1,381	1,384	1,343	1,480	1,385	1,143	749	975	1,150	1,476	1,325	1,806
Thailand	578	19,786	23,857	25,864	19,045	20,194	24,630	24,509	25,741	27,982	27,568	31,228	35,334
Tonga	866	23	18	20	19	19	16	17	17	17	25	34	31
Vanuatu	846	27	30	28	25	29	27	27	27	24	26	36	44
Vietnam	582	....	888	1,195	1,462	1,420	2,422	2,622	2,912	3,031	4,187	4,534	6,332
Europe	170	29,893	56,750	60,892	70,878	71,736	77,632	96,025	109,737	136,585	167,400	211,873	296,154
Albania	914	140	162	195	228	229	296	411	521	554	615	806	970
Armenia	911	22	37	79	142	210	202	228	247	290	331	363	521
Azerbaijan, Republic of	912	1	80	132	341	318	485	517	575	529	528	683	814
Belarus	913	† 69	251	326	292	499	214	269	311	455	400	483	795
Bosnia & Herzegovina	963	....	....	....	60	120	324	373	967	970	1,206	1,550	1,771
Bulgaria	918	643	779	295	1,524	1,853	2,015	2,324	2,584	3,208	4,155	5,610	5,592
Croatia	960	959	1,181	1,522	1,773	1,835	2,066	2,592	3,657	4,327	5,512	5,639	6,157
Cyprus	423	978	726	1,047	1,006	954	1,300	1,300	1,768	2,172	2,123	2,468	2,908
Czech Republic	935	4,209	9,312	8,590	7,214	8,908	9,330	9,990	11,290	17,150	17,695	17,929	20,386
Estonia	939	303	390	443	562	576	621	707	653	736	924	1,151	1,360
Georgia	915	....	129	131	148	84	90	81	124	143	125	239	330
Hungary	944	4,557	7,999	6,703	6,175	6,562	7,801	8,377	8,197	7,150	8,086	9,860	12,792
Kazakhstan	916	504	609	660	931	763	914	1,223	1,589	1,879	2,850	5,455	4,256
Kyrgyz Republic	917	17	45	61	125	116	164	183	209	212	238	327	395
Latvia	941	373	339	453	562	569	633	653	914	913	964	1,231	1,562
Lithuania	946	350	497	530	741	989	867	1,006	1,273	1,689	2,269	2,262	2,603
Macedonia, FYR	962	102	173	167	190	217	312	329	591	527	604	582	859
Malta	181	1,206	1,014	1,056	1,029	1,105	1,240	1,064	1,259	1,556	1,766	1,688	1,730
Moldova	921	109	164	211	270	101	135	170	181	198	203	303	418
Poland	964	3,923	9,860	12,329	15,044	19,325	19,021	20,201	20,021	20,565	21,350	22,249	28,327
Romania	968	1,391	1,024	1,459	2,742	2,036	1,105	1,895	3,116	4,504	5,410	9,411	13,903
Russia	922	2,724	9,596	7,838	9,465	5,540	6,161	18,622	25,891	32,402	49,242	77,788	122,923
Slovak Republic	936	1,100	2,224	2,366	2,375	2,036	2,455	3,087	3,295	6,478	7,858	9,283	10,424
Slovenia	961	1,014	1,212	1,585	2,444	2,537	2,229	2,387	3,377	5,040	5,615	5,578	5,606
Tajikistan	923	....	....	....	18	36	40	65	70	64	75	101	114
Turkey	186	4,878	8,336	11,397	13,796	13,808	16,897	17,126	14,906	19,775	22,741	22,846	35,264
Ukraine	926	322	610	1,316	1,682	411	715	847	2,152	3,099	4,515	5,989	13,373
Middle East	405	43,098	47,494	57,752	70,355	69,515	75,271	88,693	93,718	91,869	94,469	101,931	130,771
Bahrain, Kingdom of	419	748	806	860	898	706	935	1,135	1,272	1,200	1,126	1,178	....
Egypt	469	9,121	10,762	11,960	13,696	12,704	10,403	9,911	10,258	9,673	9,018	9,084	14,349
Israel	436	4,653	5,462	7,937	15,069	16,103	16,404	17,778	18,444	17,407	17,348	17,138	19,478
Jordan	439	1,159	1,326	1,223	1,631	1,243	1,915	2,556	2,436	2,924	3,495	3,390	3,673
Kuwait	443	2,200	2,195	2,240	2,317	2,476	3,092	4,992	7,314	6,147	4,469	4,731	5,863
Lebanon	446	2,630	3,019	4,093	4,396	4,622	5,630	4,525	3,951	5,289	8,386	7,516	8,276
Libya	672	....	....	....	....	4,418	4,536	8,756	10,940	9,679	12,322	15,670	26,752
Oman	449	1,086	1,190	1,321	1,493	1,334	1,965	1,774	1,812	2,254	2,333	2,244	3,015
Qatar	453	400	449	425	558	689	895	828	948	1,033	1,856	2,077	3,118
Saudi Arabia	456	4,033	4,777	† 8,917	9,981	9,030	11,286	13,843	11,773	12,295	11,886	14,986	16,844
United Arab Emirates	466	4,357	4,784	5,340	5,949	6,154	7,561	10,211	11,075	10,958	9,914	11,725	14,600
Yemen, Republic of	474	141	379	674	768	575	944	2,161	2,896	3,211	3,353	3,615	4,266
Western Hemisphere	205	70,034	84,597	106,922	124,014	112,471	109,824	117,927	124,688	116,042	128,524	139,156	173,595
ECCU (incl. ECCB hqtrs.)	309	175	207	198	224	252	263	292	352	369	361	406	418
Anguilla	312	6	9	10	12	13	15	16	19	19	22	22	28
Antigua and Barbuda	311	31	40	33	38	42	51	49	63	64	77	77	89
Dominica	321	11	15	16	18	20	23	23	25	33	32	27	34
Grenada	328	21	25	25	32	33	37	44	51	65	56	78	66
Montserrat	351	5	6	6	8	18	10	8	10	11	10	9	10
St. Kitts and Nevis	361	22	23	23	27	33	36	35	45	48	44	50	50

Foreign Exchange

1d s		1994	1995	1996	1997	1998	1999	2000	2001	2002	2003	2004	2005
Western Hemisphere(Cont.)						*Millions of SDRs: End of Period*							
St. Lucia	362	38	41	38	44	49	53	59	69	68	70	84	80
St. Vincent & Grens	364	21	19	20	23	27	30	42	48	39	34	48	48
Argentina	213	9,428	9,249	12,313	16,419	17,392	19,027	18,738	11,572	7,646	8,846	11,595	15,912
Aruba	314	122	146	130	128	158	160	160	234	250	199	190	191
Bahamas, The	313	115	114	113	162	240	293	262	248	274	324	428	404
Barbados	316	134	147	201	196	260	215	358	545	487	492	368	417
Belize	339	20	22	37	40	28	47	89	84	79	51	25	44
Bolivia	218	283	408	628	770	638	674	675	669	391	446	526	893
Brazil	223	25,392	33,439	40,559	37,670	30,239	25,345	24,935	28,430	27,516	33,048	33,957	37,463
Chile	228	8,965	9,510	10,376	12,791	10,835	10,337	11,272	11,173	10,896	10,236	9,978	11,677
Colombia	233	5,270	5,362	6,559	6,874	5,596	5,454	6,454	7,686	7,495	6,856	8,222	9,939
Costa Rica	238	603	695	687	926	746	1,043	991	1,038	1,084	1,218	1,217	1,598
Dominican Republic	243	170	246	243	290	356	505	481	875	344	170	513	1,289
Ecuador	248	1,243	1,076	1,273	1,534	1,133	1,178	709	649	507	529	635	1,167
El Salvador	253	445	485	627	944	1,121	1,301	1,335	1,243	1,058	1,181	1,104	1,180
Guatemala	258	580	462	595	814	940	858	1,333	1,817	1,685	1,901	2,201	2,559
Guyana	336	169	181	229	234	196	195	227	227	206	183	145	176
Haiti	263	35	128	150	153	183	192	140	112	60	41	73	84
Honduras	268	117	176	173	430	581	907	999	1,118	1,112	954	1,260	1,619
Jamaica	343	504	458	612	505	503	403	809	1,511	1,209	804	1,189	1,518
Mexico	273	4,179	10,259	13,335	20,853	22,344	22,581	26,972	35,317	36,700	38,857	40,423	51,085
Netherlands Antilles	353	123	137	131	159	176	193	200	240	299	251	267	323
Nicaragua	278	97	92	137	280	249	371	375	302	330	338	430	509
Panama	283	471	513	591	838	666	587	542	856	857	668	394	834
Paraguay	288	624	650	642	529	520	616	486	465	358	546	645	798
Peru	293	4,790	5,530	7,356	8,139	6,792	6,361	6,426	6,899	6,869	6,579	7,840	9,515
Suriname	366	27	82	59	73	67	20	40	87	71	64	76	81
Trinidad and Tobago	369	241	241	378	523	556	689	1,064	1,493	1,415	1,519	1,927	3,345
Uruguay	298	648	756	852	1,138	1,457	1,480	1,867	2,427	562	1,399	1,614	2,146
Venezuela, Rep. Bol.	299	5,064	3,826	7,736	10,376	8,247	8,530	9,696	7,022	5,912	10,462	11,505	16,410
Memorandum Items													
Oil Exporting Countries	999	40,486	40,751	56,821	67,686	67,531	73,782	98,679	105,518	102,995	112,466	132,471	177,855
Non-Oil Developing Countries.	201	378,290	452,935	530,504	609,140	623,681	697,254	788,733	899,990	1,006,011	1,172,341	1,434,988	1,835,458

Gold (Million Fine Troy Ounces)

1ad

		1994	1995	1996	1997	1998	1999	2000	2001	2002	2003	2004	2005
						Millions of Ounces: End of Period							
All Countries............	010	915.67	907.34	905.50	888.64	968.41	967.07	952.44	942.98	931.18	913.29	900.58	881.69
Industrial Countries........	110	768.05	754.97	748.16	732.47	808.67	810.43	796.51	783.55	769.85	754.29	740.60	723.78
United States..........	111	261.73	261.70	261.66	261.64	261.61	261.67	261.61	262.00	262.00	261.55	261.59	261.55
Canada................	156	3.89	3.41	3.09	3.09	2.49	1.81	1.18	1.05	.60	.11	.11	.11
Australia..............	193	7.90	7.90	7.90	2.56	2.56	2.56	2.56	2.56	2.56	2.56	2.56	2.57
Japan.................	158	24.23	24.23	24.23	24.23	24.23	24.23	24.55	24.60	24.60	24.60	24.60	24.60
New Zealand...........	196												
Euro Area (incl. ECB)........	163	....	....	....	....	....	402.76	399.54	401.88	399.02	393.54	390.00	375.86
Austria...............	122	18.34	11.99	10.75	7.87	9.64	13.10	12.14	11.17	10.21	10.21	9.89	9.73
Belgium..............	124	25.04	20.54	15.32	15.32	9.52	8.30	8.30	8.30	8.29	8.29	8.29	7.32
Finland...............	172	2.00	1.60	1.60	1.60	2.00	1.58	1.58	1.58	1.58	1.58	1.58	1.58
France................	132	81.85	81.85	81.85	81.89	102.37	97.25	97.25	97.25	97.25	97.25	95.98	90.85
Germany..............	134	95.18	95.18	95.18	95.18	118.98	111.52	111.52	111.13	110.79	110.58	110.38	110.21
Greece...............	174	3.45	3.46	3.47	3.64	3.62	4.24	4.26	3.94	3.94	3.45	3.46	3.47
Ireland...............	178	.36	.36	.36	.36	.45	.18	.18	.18	.18	.18	.18	.18
Italy.................	136	66.67	66.67	66.67	66.67	83.36	78.83	78.83	78.83	78.83	78.83	78.83	78.83
Luxembourg...........	137	.31	.31	.31	.31	....	.08	.08	.08	.08	.08	.07	.07
Netherlands...........	138	34.77	34.77	34.77	27.07	33.83	31.57	29.32	28.44	27.38	25.00	25.00	22.34
Portugal..............	182	16.07	16.07	16.07	16.07	20.09	19.51	19.51	19.51	19.03	16.63	14.86	13.42
Spain.................	184	15.62	15.63	15.63	15.63	19.54	16.83	16.83	16.83	16.83	16.83	16.83	14.72
Denmark...............	128	1.63	1.65	1.66	1.69	2.14	2.14	2.14	2.14	2.14	2.14	2.14	2.14
Iceland...............	176	.05	.05	.05	.05	.06	.06	.06	.06	.06	.06	.06	.06
Norway...............	142	1.18	1.18	1.18	1.18	1.18	1.18	1.18	1.18	1.18	1.18	—	—
San Marino...........	135	—	—	—	—	—	—	—	—	—	—	—	—
Sweden...............	144	6.07	4.70	4.70	4.72	4.72	5.96	5.96	5.96	5.96	5.96	5.96	5.41
Switzerland............	146	83.28	83.28	83.28	83.28	83.28	83.28	77.79	70.68	61.62	52.51	43.54	41.48
United Kingdom........	112	18.44	18.43	18.43	18.42	23.00	20.55	15.67	11.42	10.09	10.07	10.04	9.99
Developing Countries........	200	147.63	152.37	157.35	156.17	159.74	156.64	155.93	159.44	161.33	159.00	159.97	157.92
Africa..............	605	12.69	13.84	13.49	14.09	13.98	14.01	15.69	15.22	15.34	13.18	13.24	13.27
CEMAC (incl. BEAC hqtrs.).......	758	....	.23	.23	.23	.23	.23	.23	.23	.23	.23	.23	.23
Cameroon..........	622	.03	.03	.03	.03	.03	.03	.03	.03	.03	.03	.03	.03
Central African Republic....	626	.01	.01	.01	.01	.01	.01	.01	.01	.01	.01	.01	.01
Chad..............	628	.01	.01	.01	.01	.01	.01	.01	.01	.01	.01	.01	.01
Congo, Rep. of........	634	.01	.01	.01	.01	.01	.01	.01	.01	.01	.01	.01	.01
Equatorial Guinea......	642	—	—	—	—	—	—	—	—	—	—	—	—
Gabon.............	646	.01	.01	.01	.01	.01	.01	.01	.01	.01	.01	.01	.01
WAEMU (incl. BCEAO hqtrs.).....	759	....	.80	.86	.90	.96	1.01	1.06	1.12	1.17	1.17	1.17	1.17
Benin..............	638	.01	—	—	—	—	—	—	—	—	—	—	—
Burkina Faso........	748	.01	—	—	—	—	—	—	—	—	—	—	—
Côte d'Ivoire........	662	.04	—	—	—	—	—	—	—	—	—	—	—
Guinea Bissau.......	654	—	—	—	—	—	—	—	—	—	—	—	—
Mali..............	678	.02	—	—	—	—	—	—	—	—	—	—	—
Niger.............	692	.01	—	—	—	—	—	—	—	—	—	—	—
Senegal...........	722	.03	—	—	—	—	—	—	—	—	—	—	—
Togo.............	742	.01	—	—	—	—	—	—	—	—	—	—	—
Algeria.............	612	5.58	5.58	5.58	5.58	5.58	5.58	5.58	5.58	5.58	5.58	5.58	5.58
Burundi.............	618	.02	.02	.02	.02	.02	.02	.02	—	—	—	—	—
Cape Verde..........	624	—	—	—	—	—	—	—	—	—	—	—	—
Comoros............	632	—	—	—	—	—	—	—	—	—	—	—	—
Congo, Dem. Rep. of...	636	.03	.03	....	.05	....	....	....	....	....	....	....	....
Eritrea.............	643	....	....	....	.10	.16	.08	.04	.04	—	—	—	—
Ethiopia............	644	.11	.11	.30	.30	.30	.30	.20	.20	.25	—	—	—
Ghana.............	652	.28	.28	.28	.28	.28	.28	.28	.28	.28	.28	.28	.28
Guinea.............	656	....	....	....	....	....	....	.07	.03	.27	....	.01	—
Kenya.............	664	.08	.08	.08	.08	—	—	—	—	—	—	—	—
Malawi............	676	.01	.01	.01	.01	.01	.01	.01	.01	.01	.01	.01	.01
Mauritania..........	682	.01	.01	.01	.01	.01	.01	.01	.01	.01	.01	....	....
Mauritius...........	684	.06	.06	.06	.06	.06	.06	.06	.06	.06	.06	.06	.06
Morocco............	686	.70	.70	.70	.70	.70	.70	.71	.71	.71	.71	.71	.71
Mozambique.........	688	....	....	....	.07	.07	.06	.07	.05	.06	.02	.06	.10
Namibia............	728	—	—	—	—	—	—	—	—	—	—	—	—
Nigeria.............	694	.69	.69	.69	.69	.69	.69	.69	.69	.69	.69	.69	.69
Rwanda............	714	....	....	—	—	—	—	—	—	—	—	—	—
South Africa.........	199	4.20	4.25	3.79	3.99	4.00	3.94	5.90	5.72	5.58	3.98	3.98	3.99
Tunisia.............	744	.22	.22	.22	.22	.22	.22	.22	.22	.22	.22	.22	.22
Zambia.............	754	....	—	—	—	—	—	—	—	—	—	—	—
Zimbabwe...........	698	.47	.76	.64	.77	.62	.73	.47	.20	.14	....	....	....
Asia...............	505	53.70	55.38	56.53	56.75	56.41	56.11	57.27	61.62	65.50	65.03	64.04	61.87
Bangladesh..........	513	.09	.09	.09	.10	.11	.11	.11	.11	.11	.11	.11	.11
Brunei Darussalam......	516	....	....	....	....	....	—	—	—	—	—	—	—
Cambodia...........	522	—	—	—	—	.40	.40	.40	.40	.40	.40	.40	.40
China, P.R.: Mainland........	924	12.70	12.70	12.70	12.70	12.70	12.70	12.70	16.10	19.29	19.29	19.29	19.29
China, P.R.: Hong Kong	532	.07	.07	.07	.07	.07	.07	.07	.07	.07	.07	.07	.07
China, P.R.: Macao......	546	—	—	—	—	—	—	—	—	—	—	—	—
Fiji................	819	—	—	—	—	—	—	—	—	—	—	—	.01
India...............	534	11.80	12.78	12.78	12.74	11.49	11.50	11.50	11.50	11.50	11.50	11.50	11.50
Indonesia...........	536	3.10	3.10	3.10	3.10	3.10	3.10	3.10	3.10	3.10	3.10	3.10	3.10
Korea..............	542	.33	.33	.33	.33	.43	.44	.44	.44	.44	.45	.45	.46
Lao People's Democratic Rep.......	544	.02	.02	.02	.02	.02	.12	.02	.07	.07	.12	.12	.15
Malaysia............	548	2.39	2.39	2.39	2.35	2.35	1.18	1.17	1.17	1.17	1.17	1.17	1.17
Maldives............	556	—	—	—	—	—	—	—	—	—	—	—	—

Gold (Million Fine Troy Ounces)

		1994	1995	1996	1997	1998	1999	2000	2001	2002	2003	2004	2005
	1ad						*Millions of Ounces: End of Period*						
Asia(Cont.)													
Micronesia, Fed. States of	868	....	—	—	—	—	—	—	—	—	—	—	—
Mongolia	948	.03	.10	.15	.08	.03	—	.08	.18	.14	.02	.03	—
Myanmar	518	.25	.23	.23	.23	.23	.23	.23	.23	.23	.23	.23	.23
Nepal	558	.15	.15	.15	.15	.15	.15	.15	.15	.15	.15	.15	.13
Pakistan	564	2.05	2.05	2.06	2.07	2.08	2.09	2.09	2.09	2.09	2.10	2.10	2.10
Papua New Guinea	853	.06	.01	.06	.06	.06	.06	.06	.06	.06	.06	.06	.06
Philippines	566	2.89	3.58	4.65	4.99	5.43	6.20	7.23	7.98	8.73	8.22	7.12	4.97
Sri Lanka	524	.06	.06	.06	.06	.06	.06	† .34	.26	.22	.17	.17	.17
Thailand	578	2.47	2.47	2.47	2.47	2.47	2.47	2.37	2.48	2.50	2.60	2.70	2.70
Europe	170	22.00	23.38	28.05	30.81	31.12	30.05	29.46	30.90	29.82	29.66	29.89	30.13
Albania	914	.05	.06	.12	.12	.12	.12	.11	.11	.08	.07	.07	.07
Armenia	911	.01	.03	.03	.04	.04	.04	.04	.04	.04	—	—	—
Azerbaijan, Republic of	912	—	—	.01	—	—	—	—	—	—	—	—	—
Belarus	913	—	—	....	....	—	—	....	....	.20	.10	.20	.40
Bosnia & Herzegovina	963	....	....	....	—	—	—	—	—	—	—	—	—
Bulgaria	918	1.03	1.03	1.03	1.29	1.29	1.28	1.28	1.29	1.28	1.28	1.28	1.28
Croatia	960	—	—	—	—	—	—	—	—	—	—	—	—
Cyprus	423	.46	.46	.44	.46	.46	.46	.46	.46	.46	.47	.47	.47
Czech Republic	935	2.10	1.99	1.99	1.04	.29	.45	.45	.44	.44	.44	.44	.44
Estonia	939	.01	.01	.01	.01	.01	.01	.01	.01	.01	.01	.01	.01
Georgia	915	....	—	—	—	—	—	—	—	—	—	—	—
Hungary	944	.11	.11	.10	.10	.10	.10	.10	.10	.10	.10	.10	.10
Kazakhstan	916	.99	1.36	1.80	1.81	1.75	1.80	1.84	1.84	1.71	1.74	1.83	1.92
Kyrgyz Republic	917	....	.14	.12	.08	.08	.08	.08	.08	.08	.08	.08	.08
Latvia	941	.25	.25	.25	.25	.25	.25	.25	.25	.25	.25	.25	.25
Lithuania	946	.19	.19	.19	.19	.19	.19	.19	.19	.19	.19	.19	.19
Macedonia, FYR	962	.05	.05	.08	.08	.10	.10	.11	.19	.20	.09	.20	.22
Malta	181	.11	.04	.04	.01	.01	.01	—	.01	—	—	—	—
Moldova	921	—	—	—	—	—	—	—	—	—	—	—	—
Poland	964	.47	.47	.47	.90	3.31	3.31	3.31	3.31	3.31	3.31	3.31	3.31
Romania	968	2.63	2.70	2.82	3.02	3.22	3.32	3.37	3.38	3.39	3.38	3.38	3.37
Russia	922	8.42	9.41	13.49	16.30	14.74	13.33	12.36	13.60	12.46	12.55	12.44	12.44
Slovak Republic	936	1.29	1.29	1.29	1.29	1.29	1.29	1.29	1.13	1.13	1.13	1.13	1.13
Slovenia	961	—	—	—	—	—	—	—	.24	.24	.24	.24	.16
Tajikistan	923	....	....	....	.01	.01	.01	.01	.01	—	.01	.03	.04
Turkey	186	3.82	3.75	3.75	3.75	3.75	3.74	3.74	3.73	3.73	3.73	3.73	3.73
Ukraine	926	.04	.05	.03	.06	.11	.16	.45	.48	.50	.50	.51	.53
Middle East	405	31.41	30.96	31.55	31.35	35.97	35.20	35.12	35.12	34.84	34.44	34.46	34.44
Bahrain, Kingdom of	419	.15	.15	.15	.15	.15	.15	.15	.15	.15	.15	.15	.15
Egypt	469	2.43	2.43	2.43	2.43	2.43	2.43	2.43	2.43	2.43	2.43	2.43	2.43
Iran, I.R. of	429	4.74	4.84	....	....	....	....	....	....	....	....	....	....
Israel	436	.01	.01	.01	.01	—	—	—	—	—	—	—	—
Jordan	439	.79	.79	.80	.81	.83	.49	.40	.41	.41	.41	.41	.41
Kuwait	443	2.54	2.54	2.54	2.54	2.54	2.54	2.54	2.54	2.54	2.54	2.54	2.54
Lebanon	446	9.22	9.22	9.22	9.22	9.22	9.22	9.22	9.22	9.22	9.22	9.22	9.22
Libya	672	....	....	....	....	4.62	4.62	4.62	4.62	4.62	4.62	4.62	4.62
Oman	449	.29	.29	.29	.29	.29	.29	.29	.29	—	—	—	—
Qatar	453	.81	.27	.27	.05	.05	.02	.02	.02	.02	.02	.04	.02
Saudi Arabia	456	4.60	4.60	4.60	4.60	4.60	4.60	4.60	4.60	4.60	4.60	4.60	4.60
Syrian Arab Rep.	463	.83	.83	.83	.83	.83	.83	.83	.83	.83	.83	.83	.83
United Arab Emirates	466	.80	.80	.80	.80	.80	.40	.40	.40	.40	—	—	—
Yemen, Republic of	474	.05	.05	.05	.05	.05	.05	.05	.05	.05	.05	.05	.05
Western Hemisphere	205	27.83	28.81	27.72	23.18	22.26	21.27	18.38	16.57	15.83	16.69	18.34	18.20
Argentina	213	4.37	4.37	4.37	.36	.36	.34	.02	.01	.01	.01	1.77	1.76
Aruba	314	.10	.10	.10	.10	.10	.10	.10	.10	.10	.10	.10	.10
Bahamas, The	313	—	—	—	—	—	—	—	—	—	—	—	—
Barbados	316	—	—	—	—	—	—	—	—	—	—	—	—
Bolivia	218	.89	.89	.94	.94	.94	.94	.94	.94	.91	.91	.91	.91
Brazil	223	3.71	4.58	3.69	3.03	4.60	3.17	1.89	.46	.44	.45	.45	.44
Chile	228	1.86	1.86	1.86	1.86	1.22	1.22	.07	.07	.01	.01	.01	.01
Colombia	233	.29	.27	.25	.36	.36	.33	.33	.33	.33	.33	.33	.33
Costa Rica	238	.03	.03	—	—	—	—	—	—	—	—	—	—
Dominican Republic	243	.02	.02	.02	.02	.02	.02	.02	.02	.02	.02	.02	.02
Ecuador	248	.41	.41	.41	.41	.41	† .85	.85	.85	.85	.85	.85	.85
El Salvador	253	.47	.47	.47	.47	.47	.47	.47	.47	.47	.47	.42	.33
Guatemala	258	.21	.21	.21	.21	.22	.22	.22	.22	.22	.22	.22	.22
Haiti	263	.02	.02	.02	.02	.02	—	—	—	—	—	—	—
Honduras	268	.02	.02	.02	.02	.02	.02	.02	.02	.02	.02	.02	.02
Jamaica	343	—	—	—	—	—	—	—	—	—	—	—	—
Mexico	273	.43	.51	.26	.19	.22	.16	.25	.23	.22	.17	.14	.11
Netherlands Antilles	353	.55	.55	.55	.55	.42	.42	.42	.42	.42	.42	.42	.42
Nicaragua	278	.01	.02	.02	.02	.02	.02	.01	.01	.01	.01	—	—
Paraguay	288	.03	.03	.03	.03	.03	.03	.03	.03	.03	.03	—	—
Peru	293	1.12	1.12	1.11	1.11	1.10	1.10	1.10	1.11	1.11	1.11	1.11	1.11
Suriname	366	.05	.09	.13	.19	.13	.25	.26	.27	.02	.02	.02	.03
Trinidad and Tobago	369	.05	.05	.05	.06	.06	.06	.06	.06	.06	.06	.06	.06
Uruguay	298	1.70	1.72	1.74	1.76	1.78	1.80	1.08	.01	.01	.01	.01	.01
Venezuela, Rep. Bol.	299	11.46	11.46	11.46	11.46	9.76	9.76	10.24	10.94	10.56	11.47	11.49	11.48

Gold (Million Fine Troy Ounces)

		1994	1995	1996	1997	1998	1999	2000	2001	2002	2003	2004	2005
1ad						*Millions of Ounces: End of Period*							
Memorandum Items													
Oil Exporting Countries...........	999	38.75	38.31	38.89	38.67	41.59	41.16	41.64	42.34	41.67	42.18	42.23	42.19
Non-Oil Developing Countries.	201	108.88	114.07	118.46	117.50	118.15	115.48	114.29	117.10	119.66	116.82	117.75	115.73
Gold Holdings at SDR 35 per Ounce (1a.s)						*Millions of SDRs: End of Period*							
World..............................	001	39,059	38,911	38,762	38,072	37,739	37,692	37,180	36,847	36,433	35,803	35,375	34,689
All Countries........................	010	32,049	31,757	31,693	31,102	33,894	33,847	33,335	33,004	32,591	31,965	31,520	30,859
of which: ECB........................	168	....	....	....	....	....	841	841	863	863	863	863	810
IMF....................................	992	3,620	3,620	3,620	3,620	3,620	3,620	3,620	3,620	3,620	3,620	3,620	3,620
EMI.....................................	977	3,146	3,278	3,219	3,131	....	....	....	....	....	....	....	....
BIS.....................................	993	244	255	230	218	224	224	224	222	222	218	234	209
Gold Holdings at Market Prices (1ams)						*Millions of SDRs: End of Period*							
World..............................	001	292,970	289,247	284,388	233,962	220,395	227,738	223,763	231,623	262,434	287,237	285,054	355,733
All Countries........................	010	240,389	236,070	232,522	191,131	197,943	204,510	200,625	207,471	234,760	256,446	253,992	316,462
of which: ECB........................	168	....	....	....	....	....	5,082	5,062	5,425	6,216	6,923	6,954	8,307
IMF....................................	992	27,156	26,913	26,562	22,248	21,143	21,875	21,789	22,758	26,078	29,045	29,173	37,127
EMI.....................................	977	23,594	24,369	23,618	19,240	....	....	....	....	....	....	....	....
BIS.....................................	993	1,831	1,896	1,687	1,343	1,309	1,353	1,349	1,394	1,596	1,746	1,888	2,144
Gold Prices and SDR Rates:						*End of Period*							
US Dollars per Oz.(London)(c..)........	112	383.25	386.75	369.25	290.20	287.80	290.25	274.45	276.50	342.75	417.25	438.00	513.00
US Dollars per SDR (sa.)..................	111	1.4599	1.4865	1.4380	1.3493	1.4080	1.3725	1.3029	1.2567	1.3595	1.4860	1.5530	1.4293
SDRs per Ounce (g..)......................	112	262.53	260.18	256.79	215.08	204.40	211.47	210.64	220.02	252.11	280.79	282.03	358.92

Total Reserves

1 s (w/ Gold at SDR 35 per Oz)

Millions of SDRs: End of Period

		1994	1995	1996	1997	1998	1999	2000	2001	2002	2003	2004	2005
All Countries	010	892,351	1,023,077	1,177,360	1,296,525	1,282,383	1,404,945	1,585,324	1,739,720	1,888,394	2,154,122	2,518,651	2,993,406
Industrial Countries	110	460,821	514,251	575,129	603,469	574,330	616,679	680,695	715,134	757,511	845,214	928,364	959,390
United States	111	52,510	59,467	53,694	52,817	59,379	53,238	52,598	55,030	59,160	59,555	58,022	46,994
Canada	156	8,552	10,243	14,310	13,317	16,640	20,556	24,680	27,061	27,225	24,380	22,173	23,066
Australia	193	8,007	8,279	10,350	12,575	10,487	15,545	13,996	14,377	15,307	21,751	23,143	29,434
Japan	158	87,062	124,125	151,511	163,641	153,878	209,893	273,251	315,292	340,088	447,229	537,813	584,568
New Zealand	196	2,540	2,967	4,140	3,299	2,986	3,246	3,033	2,836	3,650	4,095	4,473	6,222
Euro Area (incl. ECB)	163	....	....	....	....	....	201,185	199,971	201,031	195,644	163,757	149,796	142,395
Austria	122	12,165	13,020	16,277	14,903	22,661	† 11,475	11,414	10,345	7,480	6,057	5,406	5,125
Belgium	124	10,382	11,601	12,326	12,535	13,310	† 8,260	7,961	9,255	9,010	7,686	6,962	6,022
Finland	172	7,374	6,809	4,866	6,294	6,955	† 6,044	6,178	6,408	6,885	7,131	7,987	7,464
France	132	20,851	20,930	21,500	25,788	35,054	† 32,330	31,832	28,667	24,268	23,718	26,098	22,597
Germany	134	56,325	60,517	61,176	60,835	56,737	† 48,376	47,567	44,793	41,516	37,986	35,301	35,440
Greece	174	10,045	10,064	12,292	9,462	12,526	13,352	10,452	† 4,239	6,083	3,056	888	476
Ireland	178	4,201	5,818	5,719	4,849	6,690	† 3,886	4,120	4,451	3,989	2,751	1,829	551
Italy	136	24,435	25,815	34,287	43,644	24,144	† 19,095	22,382	22,190	23,798	23,193	20,698	20,611
Luxembourg	137	63	61	62	58	....	† 59	61	87	114	191	195	171
Netherlands	138	24,872	23,897	19,832	19,376	16,395	† 8,308	8,427	8,184	7,993	8,390	7,472	7,166
Portugal	182	11,189	11,225	11,632	12,169	11,942	† 6,823	7,520	8,375	8,889	4,536	3,852	2,904
Spain	184	29,006	23,746	40,831	51,241	39,929	† 24,716	24,373	24,128	25,992	13,906	8,566	7,286
Denmark	128	6,260	7,468	9,892	14,233	10,916	16,313	11,671	13,690	19,924	25,045	25,241	† 23,115
Iceland	176	202	209	317	286	305	351	301	271	326	535	676	727
Norway	142	13,074	15,190	18,482	17,385	13,570	17,387	21,223	18,564	23,579	25,089	28,530	32,874
San Marino	135	121	134	150	136	121	105	104	106	135	170	229	248
Sweden	144	16,141	16,344	13,452	8,188	10,178	11,151	11,616	11,330	12,807	13,453	14,458	15,626
Switzerland	146	26,704	27,411	29,642	31,840	32,169	29,378	27,492	27,941	31,693	33,906	37,259	26,847
United Kingdom	112	28,739	28,910	28,390	24,596	23,682	† 24,979	30,308	27,604	27,973	26,248	26,551	27,273
Developing Countries	200	431,529	508,827	602,231	693,056	708,053	788,266	904,629	1,024,585	1,130,883	1,308,908	1,590,287	2,034,016
Africa	605	16,645	18,212	22,579	32,732	29,852	31,194	42,697	52,347	54,152	62,105	82,547	113,567
CEMAC (Incl. BEAC hqtrs.)	758	....	....	....	....	....	....	973	867	1,185	1,228	2,011	3,607
Cameroon	622	† 3	4	3	2	2	4	164	265	464	431	535	665
Central African Republic	626	144	158	162	133	104	100	103	95	91	89	96	98
Chad	628	52	96	115	101	86	70	85	98	161	126	143	158
Congo, Rep. of	634	35	40	64	45	1	29	171	55	24	24	77	512
Equatorial Guinea	642	—	—	—	4	1	2	18	56	65	160	608	1,471
Gabon	646	120	100	173	210	11	14	146	8	103	133	286	468
WAEMU (Incl. BCEAO hqtrs.)	759	....	1,736	1,935	2,157	2,281	2,172	2,557	3,047	4,053	4,569	4,709	4,360
Benin	638	† 177	133	182	188	186	291	352	460	453	483	412	460
Burkina Faso	748	163	234	235	256	265	215	187	207	231	506	431	307
Côte d'Ivoire	662	141	356	421	458	608	459	513	811	1,371	877	1,091	925
Guinea Bissau	654	13	14	8	25	25	26	51	55	76	22	47	56
Mali	678	† 152	217	300	308	286	255	293	278	437	641	554	598
Niger	692	76	64	55	39	38	29	62	85	98	175	166	175
Senegal	722	124	183	200	286	306	294	295	356	469	748	893	833
Togo	742	65	88	62	88	84	89	117	101	151	138	232	136
Algeria	612	2,027	1,544	3,141	6,159	5,057	3,493	9,424	14,583	17,288	22,487	28,042	39,588
Angola	614	....	143	384	294	144	361	920	582	276	427	885	2,237
Botswana	616	3,015	3,159	3,496	4,206	4,219	4,538	4,849	4,693	4,026	3,593	3,645	4,414
Burundi	618	141	142	98	84	47	36	26	14	43	45	42	70
Cape Verde	624	29	25	19	14	6	31	22	36	59	63	90	122
Comoros	632	30	30	35	30	28	27	33	50	59	63	67	60
Congo, Dem. Rep. of	636	84	100	....	....	....	....	....	....	....	....	....	....
Djibouti	611	51	49	54	49	47	51	52	56	54	67	60	62
Eritrea	643	....	....	....	151	22	28	21	33	22	17	22	20
Ethiopia	644	377	523	520	382	374	345	242	352	657	643	964	785
Gambia, The	648	67	71	71	71	76	81	84	84	79	40	54	69
Ghana	652	410	479	586	408	277	340	188	247	407	920	1,057	1,236
Guinea	656	....	....	....	....	....	....	116	160	135	....	71	67
Kenya	664	385	241	522	587	556	577	689	847	786	997	978	1,259
Lesotho	666	255	307	320	424	408	364	321	308	299	310	323	364
Liberia	668	3	19	—	—	—	—	—	—	2	5	12	18
Madagascar	674	49	73	168	209	122	166	219	317	267	279	324	337
Malawi	676	30	74	154	106	182	180	187	162	119	83	83	111
Mauritania	682	28	58	99	149	144	164	215	227	292	280	....	....
Mauritius	684	514	583	625	516	399	535	691	667	905	1,064	1,036	940
Morocco	686	3,006	2,447	2,663	2,984	3,174	4,170	3,727	6,768	7,478	9,346	10,544	11,350
Mozambique	688	....	....	....	† 386	435	479	557	569	593	632	731	741
Namibia	728	139	149	135	186	185	223	199	186	238	219	222	218
Nigeria	694	973	995	2,858	5,643	5,067	3,995	7,631	8,345	5,417	4,821	10,942	19,810
Rwanda	714	....	....	74	114	120	127	146	169	179	144	203	284
São Tomé & Príncipe	716	—	3	3	9	7	8	9	12	13	17	13	19
Seychelles	718	21	18	15	20	15	22	34	30	51	45	22	39
Sierra Leone	724	28	23	18	29	31	29	38	41	62	45	81	119
South Africa	199	1,301	2,046	787	3,697	3,234	4,767	4,875	5,011	4,538	4,510	8,601	13,139
Sudan	732	54	110	74	60	64	138	† 190	94	324	570	1,047	1,714
Swaziland	734	203	201	177	219	255	274	270	216	203	187	208	171
Tanzania	738	227	182	306	461	426	565	748	920	1,125	1,372	1,478	1,433
Tunisia	744	1,009	1,087	1,327	1,474	1,322	1,655	1,398	1,590	1,692	1,990	2,542	3,067
Uganda	746	220	309	367	470	515	556	620	782	687	727	842	940
Zambia	754	....	150	155	177	49	33	188	146	394	167	217	392
Zimbabwe	698	294	427	439	146	115	221	165	58	66	....	....	....

Total Reserves

1 s (w/ Gold at SDR 35 per Oz)		1994	1995	1996	1997	1998	1999	2000	2001	2002	2003	2004	2005
							Millions of SDRs: End of Period						
Asia *	505	264,527	293,065	345,968	386,332	415,522	484,854	549,602	633,453	719,917	842,431	1,041,586	1,306,588
Bangladesh	513	2,153	1,577	1,279	1,176	1,357	1,172	1,144	1,018	1,242	1,739	2,047	1,940
Bhutan	514	83	† 88	132	140	182	213	244	257	261	247	257	327
Brunei Darussalam	516	....	....	....	....	....	377	313	311	322	324	325	346
Cambodia	522	81	129	185	221	244	300	399	481	585	563	621	681
China, P.R.: Mainland	924	36,691	51,152	74,883	106,253	106,400	115,364	129,600	172,124	214,815	275,345	396,358	575,454
China, P.R.: Hong Kong	532	33,739	37,270	44,376	68,784	63,673	70,119	82,542	88,450	82,308	79,654	79,551	86,931
China, P.R.: Macao	546	1,347	1,518	1,684	1,877	1,749	2,082	2,550	2,792	2,795	2,923	3,500	4,680
Fiji	819	187	235	297	267	274	312	316	292	264	285	308	220
India	534	13,907	12,504	14,474	18,744	19,820	24,203	29,493	36,902	50,174	66,984	81,917	92,704
Indonesia	536	8,419	9,330	12,801	12,402	16,240	19,376	21,984	21,789	22,889	23,637	22,615	23,190
Korea	542	17,574	21,995	23,682	15,107	36,928	53,922	73,797	81,778	89,272	104,516	128,152	147,166
Lao People's Democratic Rep.	544	42e	62	118	83	80	74	107	104	141	140	144	164
Malaysia	548	17,498	16,077	18,867	15,489	18,235	22,328	21,784	23,532	24,580	29,531	42,462	48,918
Maldives	556	21	32	53	73	84	93	94	74	98	107	131	130
Micronesia, Fed. States of	868	....	47	62	64	72	68	87	78	86	60	35	35
Mongolia	948	57	82	80	133	68	99	140	170	262	159	153	301
Myanmar	518	298	386	167	193	232	202	179	327	354	378	441	547
Nepal	558	480	400	403	469	542	621	731	831	754	828	947	1,053
Pakistan	564	2,078	1,238	453	958	803	1,174	1,235	2,970	6,015	7,436	6,383	7,093
Papua New Guinea	853	68	176	408	271	139	152	222	339	239	335	410	505
Philippines	566	4,237	4,428	7,158	5,583	6,777	9,885	10,300	11,003	11,110	9,477	8,695	11,317
Samoa	862	35	37	42	48	44	50	49	45	46	56	62	65
Singapore	576	39,851	46,213	53,442	52,836	53,215	55,987	61,502	59,977	60,331	64,433	72,267	81,016
Solomon Islands	813	12	11	23	27	35	37	25	15	13	25	52	67
Sri Lanka	524	1,404	1,407	1,366	1,502	1,408	1,194	† 809	1,033	1,207	1,530	1,379	1,861
Thailand	578	20,179	24,293	26,326	19,490	20,559	24,905	24,655	25,832	28,073	27,734	31,430	35,561
Tonga	866	24	19	21	20	20	18	19	19	18	27	36	33
Vanuatu	846	30	32	31	28	32	30	30	30	27	29	40	47
*of which:													
Taiwan Province of China	528	63,806	61,229	61,699	62,362	64,636	77,851	82,400	97,720	119,381	139,532	156,134	177,693
Europe	170	31,300	58,470	62,654	73,010	73,858	79,905	98,280	112,398	139,324	170,396	214,548	298,288
Albania	914	142	164	199	233	277	360	476	593	620	682	877	985
Armenia	911	22	68	109	171	232	234	246	257	314	343	371	528
Azerbaijan, Republic of	912	1	81	147	346	318	490	522	577	530	540	692	824
Belarus	913	† 69	254	....	....	....	....	....	....	462	404	490	809
Bosnia & Herzegovina	963	....	....	....	60	124	330	381	972	972	1,208	1,550	1,771
Bulgaria	918	722	868	372	1,610	1,952	2,152	2,466	2,664	3,286	4,278	5,696	5,670
Croatia	960	962	1,275	1,609	1,882	2,000	2,204	2,705	3,742	4,329	5,512	5,639	6,157
Cyprus	423	1,019	767	1,088	1,048	996	1,352	1,353	1,821	2,239	2,208	2,534	2,949
Czech Republic	935	4,282	9,382	8,659	7,251	8,918	9,346	10,008	11,427	17,342	18,031	18,212	20,536
Estonia	939	304	390	443	562	576	622	707	653	736	924	1,152	1,360
Georgia	915	....	131	131	148	87	96	84	127	145	128	247	331
Hungary	944	4,618	8,059	6,763	6,235	6,622	7,985	8,592	8,539	7,615	8,575	10,247	12,974
Kazakhstan	916	608	811	963	1,321	1,099	1,141	1,288	1,654	1,939	2,912	5,520	4,324
Kyrgyz Republic	917	....	59	70	129	119	170	186	213	215	248	343	402
Latvia	941	382	349	464	572	578	644	662	923	922	973	1,240	1,570
Lithuania	946	366	516	544	755	1,007	877	1,013	1,294	1,735	2,276	2,268	2,609
Macedonia, FYR	962	104	175	169	193	221	317	333	600	538	607	590	867
Malta	181	1,271	1,081	1,128	1,103	1,181	1,303	1,129	1,326	1,625	1,836	1,759	1,803
Moldova	921	123	173	217	271	102	135	171	182	198	203	303	418
Poland	964	4,018	9,955	12,426	15,156	19,522	19,318	20,502	20,525	21,189	22,040	22,861	28,706
Romania	968	1,521	1,157	1,561	2,925	2,149	1,228	2,014	3,240	4,624	5,529	9,530	14,022
Russia	922	3,021	10,005	8,314	10,127	6,056	6,628	19,056	26,370	32,840	49,683	78,226	123,499
Slovak Republic	936	1,204	2,308	2,423	2,439	2,083	2,501	3,132	3,335	6,519	7,898	9,323	10,465
Slovenia	961	1,027	1,225	1,598	2,457	2,584	2,308	2,453	3,454	5,143	5,727	5,671	5,656
Tajikistan	923	....	....	....	27	38	40	71	74	66	76	103	119
Turkey	186	5,045	8,501	11,561	13,960	13,972	17,141	17,391	15,153	20,041	23,005	23,098	35,519
Ukraine	926	447	708	1,364	1,737	545	768	1,054	2,369	3,137	4,547	6,008	13,392
Middle East	405	46,685	51,142	61,655	74,401	73,698	79,658	93,328	99,498	98,645	101,819	108,899	136,246
Bahrain, Kingdom of	419	806	866	922	962	772	1,003	1,205	1,345	1,275	1,202	1,255	....
Egypt	469	9,319	10,971	12,184	13,919	12,957	10,638	10,153	10,370	9,826	9,230	9,276	14,504
Israel	436	4,653	5,462	7,938	15,069	16,104	16,470	17,869	18,603	17,714	17,709	17,446	19,632
Jordan	439	1,187	1,355	1,251	1,659	1,272	1,933	2,571	2,451	2,939	3,510	3,406	3,688
Kuwait	443	2,487	2,484	2,533	2,647	2,892	3,603	5,525	7,964	6,862	5,188	5,396	6,290
Lebanon	446	2,983	3,372	4,448	4,752	4,979	5,988	4,885	4,312	5,651	8,748	7,879	8,640
Libya	672	....	....	....	....	5,325	5,466	9,726	11,939	10,686	13,341	16,703	27,804
Oman	449	1,138	1,242	1,374	1,544	1,386	2,027	1,837	1,892	2,334	2,418	2,316	3,049
Qatar	453	479	528	506	620	752	954	893	1,049	1,157	1,987	2,198	3,185
Saudi Arabia	456	5,214	5,961	† 10,120	11,187	10,260	12,545	15,193	14,162	15,321	15,383	17,734	18,723
United Arab Emirates	466	4,589	5,054	5,630	6,233	6,474	7,792	10,393	11,270	11,209	10,154	11,932	14,700
Yemen, Republic of	474	176	418	709	893	709	1,074	2,228	2,913	3,246	3,358	3,649	4,280
Western Hemisphere	205	72,373	87,938	109,374	126,581	115,123	112,656	120,722	126,890	118,846	132,157	142,708	179,327
ECCU (incl. ECCB hqtrs.)	309	179	211	203	228	256	268	297	357	374	366	408	420
Anguilla	312	6	9	10	12	13	15	16	19	19	22	22	28
Antigua and Barbuda	311	31	40	33	38	42	51	49	63	64	77	77	89
Dominica	321	11	15	16	18	20	23	23	25	33	32	27	34
Grenada	328	21	25	25	32	33	37	44	51	65	56	78	66
Montserrat	351	5	6	6	8	18	10	8	10	11	10	9	10
St. Kitts and Nevis	361	22	23	23	27	33	36	35	45	48	44	51	50
St. Lucia	362	40	42	39	45	50	54	61	71	69	72	85	81
St. Vincent & Grens	364	21	20	21	23	28	31	42	49	39	34	48	49
Argentina	213	9,967	9,765	12,743	16,555	17,592	19,139	19,301	11,580	7,716	9,525	12,222	19,077

Total Reserves

1 s (w/ Gold at SDR 35 per Oz) Western Hemisphere(Cont.)		1994	1995	1996	1997	1998	1999	2000	2001	2002	2003	2004	2005
		Millions of SDRs: End of Period											
Aruba	314	125	149	134	131	161	164	163	237	253	202	194	195
Bahamas, The	313	121	121	119	168	246	299	268	254	280	330	434	410
Barbados	316	134	147	201	196	260	220	363	549	492	497	373	422
Belize	339	24	25	41	44	31	52	94	89	84	57	31	50
Bolivia	218	340	475	697	838	707	743	744	738	459	514	594	961
Brazil	223	25,523	33,600	40,689	37,776	30,401	25,463	25,001	28,454	27,734	33,065	33,975	37,499
Chile	228	9,030	9,577	10,477	13,089	11,313	10,692	11,542	11,444	11,284	10,660	10,299	11,845
Colombia	233	5,484	5,626	6,855	7,278	6,157	5,846	6,855	8,091	7,906	7,269	8,636	10,357
Costa Rica	238	613	705	696	935	755	1,064	1,011	1,058	1,105	1,238	1,238	1,618
Dominican Republic	243	173	247	244	290	357	506	482	876	345	171	515	1,290
Ecuador	248	1,278	1,109	1,307	1,566	1,165	† 1,226	756	698	555	576	718	1,229
El Salvador	253	461	527	668	986	1,162	1,342	1,377	1,285	1,100	1,223	1,144	1,217
Guatemala	258	599	480	612	831	956	874	1,348	1,832	1,699	1,914	2,214	2,571
Guyana	336	169	181	229	234	196	195	234	229	209	186	149	176
Haiti	263	36	130	151	154	184	192	140	113	60	42	74	93
Honduras	268	118	177	174	431	582	917	1,009	1,127	1,122	963	1,269	1,629
Jamaica	343	504	458	612	506	504	404	809	1,512	1,210	804	1,189	1,518
Mexico	273	4,316	11,351	13,523	21,350	22,592	23,162	27,262	35,609	37,223	39,681	41,306	51,816
Netherlands Antilles	353	142	156	151	178	191	208	215	254	314	266	282	338
Nicaragua	278	97	92	138	281	249	372	375	303	330	338	430	509
Panama	283	482	526	603	851	678	600	555	869	870	680	406	847
Paraguay	288	707	736	731	621	615	714	587	569	464	653	752	908
Peru	293	4,829	5,570	7,395	8,179	6,832	6,399	6,466	6,939	6,908	6,618	7,880	9,554
Suriname	366	29	93	72	88	80	37	57	104	79	72	84	89
Trinidad and Tobago	369	243	243	380	526	558	691	1,066	1,520	1,494	1,652	2,042	3,400
Uruguay	298	723	834	931	1,215	1,535	1,579	1,940	2,465	566	1,402	1,616	2,151
Venezuela, Rep. Bol	299	5,927	4,628	8,599	11,057	8,807	9,287	10,404	7,735	6,612	11,192	12,234	17,137
Memorandum Items													
Oil Exporting Countries	999	44,790	45,081	61,484	72,286	71,959	78,583	103,734	111,826	110,079	120,086	139,674	183,775
Non-Oil Developing Countries.	201	386,739	463,746	540,747	620,770	636,094	709,683	800,894	912,760	1,020,805	1,188,822	1,450,613	1,850,240
(with Gold at SDR 35 per Ounce) (1..s)						*Millions of SDRs: End of Period*							
All Countries	010	892,351	1,023,077	1,177,360	1,296,525	1,282,383	1,404,945	1,585,324	1,739,720	1,888,394	2,154,122	2,518,651	2,993,406
(with Gold at Market Prices) (1m.s)						*Millions of SDRs: End of Period*							
All Countries	010	1,100,691	1,227,390	1,378,189	1,456,554	1,446,432	1,575,608	1,752,613	1,914,186	2,090,563	2,378,603	2,741,124	3,279,008

Reserve Money

		1994	1995	1996	1997	1998	1999	2000	2001	2002	2003	2004	2005
						Percent Change over Previous Year							
Industrial Countries													
United States	111	8.7	4.4	4.7	8.0	6.1	19.8	−6.0	7.7	7.5	5.2	4.3	4.5
Canada	156	2.3	1.4	4.3	3.3	6.6	24.3	−7.4	4.2	5.5	1.0	4.6	3.3
Australia	193	8.2	5.0	61.2	−20.3	5.7	−5.1	−.7	18.8	2.2	1.9	3.3	8.4
Japan	158	2.9	7.8	8.5	7.3	3.7	44.5	−19.9	19.4	11.8	12.0	3.8	.9
New Zealand	196	11.6	7.1	−2.7	4.9	6.3	76.1	−24.4	9.2	8.6	2.1	−11.4	66.7
Euro Area													
Austria	122	4.5	−1.0	6.9	−.7	....	....	....	....	....	....	....	....
Belgium	124	−6.7	9.2	3.7	2.3	56.2	....	....	....	....	....	....	....
Finland	172	51.1	1.6	−32.8	−7.7	−1.8	....	....	....	....	....	....	....
France	132	.1	8.7	2.2	3.0	22.4	....	....	....	....	....	....	....
Germany	134	−1.6	2.0	4.8	−.9	1.1	....	....	....	....	....	....	....
Greece	174	35.6	3.2	12.1	11.3	34.8	25.1	−16.1	....	....	....	....	....
Ireland	178	4.3	26.6	1.1	18.9	....	....	....	....	....	....	....	....
Italy	136	−5.0	−6.3	2.4	7.4	−29.0	....	....	....	....	....	....	....
Luxembourg	137	—	−11.5	17.1	−.2	....	....	....	....	....	....	....	....
Netherlands	138	6.0	−12.3	−4.4	10.2	5.4	....	....	....	....	....	....	....
Portugal	182	−58.8	−2.5	11.2	−1.3	.6	....	....	....	....	....	....	....
Spain	184	10.1	4.5	3.3	6.8	3.4	....	....	....	....	....	....	....
Denmark	128	.7	13.5	33.3	31.1	−22.6	98.8	−22.7	−5.6	10.9	8.7	−7.3	15.6
Iceland	176	3.0	−18.1	26.4	11.4	2.2	55.7	−11.8	−11.7	13.4	−36.0	140.4	−8.9
Norway	142	3.3	5.2	53.0	−11.5	−11.0	50.2	−16.3	−.8	49.2	−28.5	....	....
Sweden	144	22.4	−14.9	−33.1	−25.8	3.8	17.0	−5.0	9.6	−.7	.5	1.3	1.7
Switzerland	146	.6	−2.4	5.1	−2.3	7.7	17.0	−10.6	12.5	−6.8	7.9	−3.1	2.5
United Kingdom	112	5.3	7.0	3.5	7.1	4.5	18.6	−.3	.6	4.4	7.9	14.0	2.1
Developing Countries													
Africa													
CEMAC	758	....	....	....	....	....	....	....	5.6	14.3	1.3	17.7	27.0
Cameroon	622	39.3	−21.0	28.3	40.2	10.2	8.2	34.2	22.3	27.7	−11.3	16.5	−1.7
Central African Republic	626	84.2	4.5	7.7	−12.4	−20.2	7.7	9.3	−6.2	−6.0	−8.0	15.3	17.4
Chad	628	23.5	58.2	31.5	−4.2	−10.2	−6.3	16.3	17.4	34.4	−10.3	7.3	32.7
Congo, Rep. of	634	35.4	8.3	8.6	11.6	−20.7	34.2	103.1	−23.4	−8.6	7.2	20.4	69.0
Equatorial Guinea	642	78.0	99.1	14.6	9.8	−19.9	95.3	48.9	85.6	4.6	142.5	25.1	77.9
Gabon	646	129.4	−4.2	28.8	1.7	−8.5	−7.9	36.2	−4.2	1.1	14.4	21.3	35.5
WAEMU	759	19.5	9.0	2.6	11.2	7.4	3.5	11.6	23.7	20.6	−1.9	1.4	3.7
Benin	638	1.4	−26.1	9.2	19.9	−4.4	75.7	40.7	23.2	−13.1	2.4	−18.9	32.4
Burkina Faso	748	−.8	24.0	4.7	23.5	−3.6	−14.1	.1	.2	−24.2	170.0	−26.4	−16.3
Côte d'Ivoire	662	56.3	11.6	6.7	11.8	19.1	−7.7	2.0	34.3	40.0	−42.0	20.6	1.7
Guinea Bissau	654	32.3	32.1	38.7	125.8	−13.3	34.5	87.5	15.9	30.5	−67.8	58.6	35.3
Mali	678	−19.4	10.3	18.3	7.7	−5.6	12.7	26.5	11.9	46.6	32.0	−15.1	14.8
Niger	692	−24.0	13.0	−5.9	−21.3	−35.7	32.0	3.9	48.6	−4.7	83.9	11.0	7.2
Senegal	722	49.2	4.1	−14.2	3.3	6.8	15.9	5.8	34.3	12.2	52.5	10.3	−1.9
Togo	742	2.4	28.8	−12.6	.8	10.9	14.3	21.1	−6.4	5.9	−20.9	31.1	−19.6
Algeria	612	−5.3	7.6	19.9	16.6	13.1	11.4	22.4	41.4	25.5	43.6	11.3	6.6
Angola	614	....	....	3,397.1	92.0	49.8	419.9	217.7	146.6	117.7	76.0	55.9	66.4
Botswana	616	11.7	41.3	23.3	30.2	−1.0	22.0	−7.6	44.1	−13.7	27.9	32.0	15.7
Burundi	618	26.5	−.8	19.1	1.9	2.7	35.6	−2.6	11.1	23.2	10.9	37.2	32.7
Cape Verde	624	−38.9	22.7	−6.3	.5	9.3	6.7	15.8	7.6	15.3	2.8	6.9	14.3
Comoros	632	14.3	−10.2	36.3	−12.4	−10.8	19.1	25.9	70.6	18.9	−1.5	−1.6	−1.4
Congo, Dem. Rep. of	636	3,264.3	650.3	524.2	106.5	2,690.2	420.3	−38.5	112.7	21.2	29.3	65.3	15.6
Djibouti	611	5.5	−12.6	−3.7	−2.1	−2.0	4.4	−.8	5.4	9.0	31.2	−5.1	.7
Eritrea	643	....	....	86.1	88.5	−34.8	38.3	7.7	−3.4	16.9	13.5	6.2	7.5
Ethiopia	644	10.3	12.6	−16.5	8.8	−12.2	−4.9	38.7	−9.0	34.8	15.1	89.5	9.0
Gambia, The	648	−3.9	25.4	.5	26.8	7.2	14.5	16.8	21.0	34.1	62.7	11.0	11.9
Ghana	652	78.9	35.1	44.8	33.4	16.7	38.4	54.5	41.0	46.2	28.1	17.9	6.8
Guinea	656	−10.0	12.3	−1.4	27.2	4.9	....	....	14.9	21.7	17.8	35.8	14.5
Kenya	664	22.8	31.0	8.2	2.1	−.4	6.0	−.7	−1.0	11.9	−1.1	14.6	2.6
Lesotho	666	6.6	32.4	5.0	12.3	38.9	32.8	−6.6	−25.4	.3	6.6	6.1	33.1
Liberia	668	5.4	31.3	17.9	8.0	1.9	4.4	41.3	11.8	6.3	8.9	62.3	27.0
Madagascar	674	71.9	29.7	48.7	1.1	6.5	26.1	11.8	29.5	4.4	−.2	19.0	11.6
Malawi	676	41.3	89.6	38.5	.2	38.6	32.1	5.8	33.8	26.7	27.6	30.7	14.7
Mauritania	682	−3.7	−5.7	−49.5	−13.1	−7.5	4.5	4.9	5.4	3.2	−.3	....	....
Mauritius	684	5.1	14.6	−5.2	−2.2	9.4	7.8	11.8	10.4	14.9	66.3	16.4	17.1
Morocco	686	6.2	5.2	7.6	7.9	7.1	13.3	3.2	21.4	3.6	16.2	12.6	9.5
Mozambique	688	66.4	31.7	26.6	16.1	−3.7	17.5	25.7	53.0	17.3	21.9	20.4	17.6
Namibia	728	60.2	11.2	22.3	19.9	3.6	43.6	−6.3	8.3	7.3	11.7	13.9	10.8
Nigeria	694	31.3	20.5	6.1	4.5	16.7	21.7	48.2	34.1	13.1	42.9	−5.3	−9.7
Rwanda	714	9.3	38.7	22.6	11.4	−8.8	14.8	−8.3	22.2	−.9	11.5	32.4	59.4
São Tomé and Príncipe	716	....	....	81.1	144.9	10.1	−15.2	29.3	74.7	14.3	64.8	−25.6	58.3
Seychelles	718	47.7	20.8	13.7	18.7	−49.3	9.4	3.1	7.2	26.7	−19.4	82.5	3.4
Sierra Leone	724	25.4	12.1	23.9	109.0	−20.4	39.0	9.2	29.4	24.9	22.4	12.6	24.3
South Africa	199	17.8	29.8	13.6	11.5	5.5	23.3	4.7	14.6	13.6	11.8	14.8	11.8
Sudan	732	39.9	76.7	81.8	34.3	29.4	35.1	46.7	4.5	21.3	27.3	28.2	38.7
Swaziland	734	17.6	2.5	−7.4	5.4	−8.4	11.6	−4.5	−6.4	29.6	30.6	33.2	2.9
Tanzania	738	48.7	39.1	6.6	8.7	14.7	21.5	9.4	5.0	19.1	12.6	23.5	27.7
Tunisia	744	7.2	9.4	35.8	8.1	−11.8	30.5	−11.4	17.9	−3.1	7.5	16.7	11.2
Uganda	746	48.1	13.7	11.6	9.1	20.0	15.1	21.8	13.4	10.7	11.0	20.5	13.2
Zambia	754	48.0	−14.6	35.4	48.2	16.8	28.5	53.4	45.7	43.0	19.2	32.3	5.8
Zimbabwe	698	23.6	2.5	65.9	37.8	29.9	60.9	16.0	164.9	171.2	394.8	217.6	454.1

Reserve Money

		1994	1995	1996	1997	1998	1999	2000	2001	2002	2003	2004	2005
						Percent Change over Previous Year							
Asia													
Bangladesh	513	29.6	−9.3	8.7	9.4	13.4	12.7	14.5	24.1	3.3	6.9	8.0	25.6
Bhutan	514	−33.4	67.1	8.3	9.3	55.4	25.7	21.1	2.3	13.3	19.9	10.2	38.1
Brunei Darussalam	516	....	....	....	....	....	....	−4.3	2.4	5.2	.8	12.3	5.6
Cambodia	522	25.4	10.0	43.0	21.2	47.2	15.9	24.9	17.1	45.7	8.5	23.9	−1.0
China, P.R.: Mainland	924	31.0	20.6	29.5	13.9	2.3	7.3	8.5	9.2	13.3	17.1	11.4	9.3
China, P.R.: Hong Kong	532	9.7	3.9	5.0	6.4	2.2	19.6	−8.1	6.7	7.1	18.9	.8	−3.7
Fiji	819	1.7	8.8	1.9	5.0	6.3	56.8	−18.9	19.3	9.5	31.9	−14.3	2.2
India	534	21.7	12.6	9.5	11.2	12.4	11.4	7.7	10.2	9.3	13.8	16.3	14.9
Indonesia	536	25.2	17.8	35.8	38.3	77.8	38.8	24.3	16.0	−.9	12.8	24.4	31.0
Korea	542	9.2	16.3	−12.2	−12.5	−8.1	37.6	−.9	16.3	15.7	7.3	−4.8	11.5
Lao People's Democratic Rep	544	22.3	13.4	24.0	43.8	87.7	71.0	59.1	7.3	31.2	23.2	16.2	18.0
Malaysia	548	36.2	24.7	35.2	28.4	−56.4	26.3	−9.4	−3.3	6.4	6.9	10.0	5.1
Maldives	556	13.8	1.1	17.8	15.7	11.0	6.9	4.5	9.8	19.1	−2.0	26.2	6.0
Mongolia	948	103.8	29.0	36.4	23.1	18.3	50.4	20.2	6.8	21.9	14.5	17.0	19.7
Myanmar	518	23.1	27.8	32.0	29.5	26.8	18.7	34.5	51.6	34.9	46.1	29.3	24.5
Nepal	558	11.7	8.6	9.9	61.1	−9.3	10.3	19.3	12.0	−.1	2.9	15.3	9.2
Pakistan	564	15.7	17.9	−3.6	14.3	13.0	13.0	−2.1	28.3	8.8	16.5	20.0	10.0
Papua New Guinea	853	11.3	15.3	91.3	−34.3	20.7	73.3	−16.4	5.5	13.5	−.1	30.2	7.4
Philippines	566	7.9	12.4	32.5	−6.1	2.0	36.7	−10.6	−11.1	16.3	9.3	4.2	23.6
Samoa	862	3.2	4.4	20.5	19.1	−45.7	21.4	8.8	−4.8	20.3	10.7	15.8	3.4
Singapore	576	6.2	9.4	6.7	5.6	−13.3	28.6	−13.7	8.5	−.3	3.4	5.7	7.2
Solomon Islands	813	30.9	23.0	30.4	−6.2	46.0	−.3	14.6	−3.3	16.5	27.3	72.9	20.9
Sri Lanka	524	20.5	15.5	8.8	−2.1	10.9	8.2	4.7	7.0	12.3	11.9	20.9	....
Thailand	578	15.0	22.6	12.6	17.2	−6.5	28.5	−18.6	5.7	13.6	11.8	12.4	5.1
Tonga	866	−4.5	−17.7	43.0	12.3	10.3	7.5	12.6	29.7	20.7	−9.4	59.6	−14.9
Vanuatu	846	−6.8	30.4	−4.2	−.2	5.2	22.3	1.9	−.4	—	8.0	10.3	10.8
Vietnam	582	....	....	20.1	12.5	8.7	50.5	25.0	16.7	12.4	27.4	16.1	23.6
Europe													
Albania	914	....	28.1	14.0	48.1	−1.1	21.6	17.8	18.1	7.7	−2.0	11.2	11.0
Armenia	911	842.0	92.0	42.8	24.8	4.9	....	34.4	11.1	38.4	6.6	12.9	55.5
Azerbaijan, Republic of	912	642.9	179.8	17.6	41.4	−24.3	15.9	29.1	1.5	14.0	23.5	64.7	6.3
Belarus	913	....	287.9	78.1	107.6	162.9	178.5	124.4	103.9	32.1	51.1	41.9	73.7
Bosnia and Herzegovina	963	....	....	....	....	38.8	241.7	19.2	164.6	−8.9	12.5	24.2	22.6
Bulgaria	918	55.9	52.0	91.5	826.7	10.2	17.6	11.1	30.4	8.0	16.1	40.2	12.4
Croatia	960	109.6	43.1	30.0	18.0	12.3	28.6	15.1	36.6	27.9	24.0	19.9	20.6
Cyprus	423	12.5	−4.3	−8.8	−.8	16.2	14.8	10.8	7.6	24.8	4.8	8.0	2.6
Czech Republic	935	34.4	53.6	.5	.1	22.5	8.9	6.9	4.9	−49.6	7.3	3.6	7.6
Estonia	939	11.6	19.9	22.2	37.7	6.4	26.7	14.9	−9.8	−1.5	14.6	24.0	33.0
Georgia	915	....	....	36.3	32.6	−6.3	18.8	27.0	10.4	19.7	14.3	46.9	16.2
Hungary	944	−1.6	17.8	−8.5	29.9	20.6	26.2	17.3	1.7	5.5	10.2	11.7	8.4
Kazakhstan	916	623.4	113.5	26.8	36.8	−29.4	55.7	6.0	30.6	18.6	52.2	82.4	14.8
Kyrgyz Republic	917	....	....	23.9	21.1	7.6	30.7	11.7	11.5	42.7	32.6	21.8	24.9
Latvia	941	19.5	1.6	23.0	31.2	6.7	11.6	7.7	13.3	18.4	6.3	18.6	44.3
Lithuania	946	44.2	35.0	2.2	32.4	28.8	−4.0	−3.3	8.3	20.8	26.6	7.1	27.6
Macedonia, FYR	962	71.7	30.6	−3.2	22.7	5.6	29.6	46.6	8.1	3.8	7.8	−.3	29.6
Malta	181	31.7	−12.2	−4.2	1.5	3.0	6.9	3.5	3.7	11.5	−5.2	4.6	.6
Moldova	921	128.9	41.3	9.5	32.9	−6.7	40.3	30.9	27.9	31.1	16.6	39.8	....
Poland	964	22.6	45.0	20.5	34.0	16.9	−1.3	−7.8	30.5	−2.6	6.9	4.9	5.5
Romania	968	87.5	56.2	51.4	136.5	20.8	92.4	54.7	59.9	54.7	20.0	72.6	57.9
Russia	922	203.5	107.8	27.3	27.6	28.1	65.6	67.2	29.1	31.2	54.1	24.1	22.4
Slovak Republic	936	23.9	30.8	28.7	18.2	−5.6	20.0	4.0	22.6	1.7	−7.3	.8	21.8
Slovenia	961	56.9	25.2	15.6	23.0	19.7	21.3	1.9	35.5	−1.8	5.4	3.9	5.5
Turkey	186	119.5	79.5	91.5	99.9	80.4	97.5	46.2	78.5	17.6	18.6	33.5	41.8
Ukraine	926	407.4	132.8	39.9	49.0	16.6	41.3	43.9	42.5	33.6	30.1	34.1	53.9
Middle East													
Bahrain	419	−4.1	34.5	−11.1	12.6	−21.7	45.5	−.6	14.4	13.9	34.8	4.4	25.4
Egypt	469	12.5	9.3	4.2	11.1	19.3	1.6	18.7	17.0	8.7	39.7	18.6	4.3
Iran, I.R. of	429	34.2	48.0	27.1	23.0	18.0	17.1	16.7	6.4	26.7	14.4	14.5	22.3
Israel	436	−6.7	−26.8	34.9	119.3	14.4	23.8	.6	.7	−15.8	−7.5	−22.7	−11.4
Jordan	439	5.1	6.4	−13.4	−2.8	−4.7	12.1	.8	−5.7	3.9	16.9	3.2	18.4
Kuwait	443	.1	−6.6	.8	−10.1	5.0	30.0	−8.3	−2.5	13.2	16.9	13.4	2.3
Lebanon	446	76.7	21.2	21.2	50.0	−5.5	5.5	6.6	37.2	10.1	121.7	3.3	−2.1
Libya	672	15.9	7.7	9.0	6.6	−1.0	−5.3	−.9	10.0	2.6	11.2	46.3	45.0
Oman	449	4.1	3.6	6.4	8.5	7.1	−1.1	8.8	8.8	30.3	5.8	−8.2	42.2
Qatar	453	−6.9	5.0	6.1	9.7	3.1	12.2	6.7	11.6	17.0	14.9	31.1	37.1
Saudi Arabia	456	4.5	−2.3	−1.4	7.6	−1.2	23.5	−4.0	−4.1	9.3	5.1	11.4	10.8
Syrian Arab Rep	463	8.6	4.7	7.6	4.8	5.0	7.3	15.2	16.9	16.0	10.2	25.2	....
United Arab Emirates	466	25.7	13.1	8.1	.5	.2	30.5	36.5	6.0	−1.9	12.3	29.5	19.3
Yemen, Republic of	474	35.5	19.8	6.9	−12.5	11.2	20.8	14.0	14.0	9.2	21.1	14.4	21.4
Western Hemisphere													
ECCU	309	2.8	10.7	−5.9	6.8	17.5	6.4	4.3	13.9	8.3	10.7	13.9	−5.3
Anguilla	312	−2.1	33.7	14.6	12.5	12.2	11.2	2.7	28.6	1.3	26.2	3.2	15.9
Antigua and Barbuda	311	15.0	17.5	−17.3	4.6	13.1	14.0	−2.5	20.1	5.3	27.0	3.4	6.0
Dominica	321	−9.4	17.4	−.7	2.8	11.6	12.4	−2.7	−.8	42.5	−3.4	−6.7	4.9
Grenada	328	6.4	8.5	.3	12.5	6.4	6.0	10.4	11.2	18.7	9.0	39.9	−22.7
Montserrat	351	19.5	9.0	3.0	26.1	115.2	−44.0	−24.9	14.9	13.4	6.1	−8.3	−1.8
St. Kitts and Nevis	361	7.2	−1.5	−3.3	6.6	19.7	12.9	7.9	10.4	16.4	−2.7	21.9	−8.6
St. Lucia	362	−4.6	11.5	−4.4	1.7	13.9	3.3	3.8	16.4	2.1	12.3	19.8	−11.6
St. Vincent & Grens	364	−3.3	−5.4	−2.6	9.1	20.8	16.8	20.6	9.5	−10.6	4.3	6.0	1.9
Argentina	213	8.5	−15.4	2.1	13.6	2.6	.8	−8.8	17.9	69.8	66.3	20.7	1.2
Aruba	314	−6.4	18.0	−14.3	−4.2	40.5	6.3	−11.5	32.4	13.7	−5.7	4.9	1.3
Bahamas, The	313	12.0	2.8	−2.6	14.5	19.7	20.8	−2.2	10.4	11.7	6.4	31.7	−8.1
Barbados	316	−1.9	15.7	34.2	−9.6	9.0	4.2	11.9	15.2	39.2	19.8	−29.0	.6

Reserve Money

Western Hemisphere(Cont.)

		1994	1995	1996	1997	1998	1999	2000	2001	2002	2003	2004	2005
								Percent Change over Previous Year					
Belize.............................	339	−2.0	13.4	2.9	5.2	7.8	21.9	22.7	27.1	−22.9	4.1	12.3	16.7
Bolivia...........................	218	4.3	23.3	15.7	20.1	−20.8	11.3	10.4	12.1	1.5	13.6	17.9	52.1
Brazil.............................	223	2,241.7	11.9	22.8	34.2	−11.1	7.8	4.8	19.0	150.0	−4.2	10.8	7.9
Chile..............................	228	17.7	21.3	11.5	7.2	9.8	4.5	−7.0	8.9	−3.0	13.1	22.0	28.8
Colombia........................	233	28.2	6.8	17.7	16.5	−17.1	39.7	9.1	9.9	20.3	16.4	15.4	18.0
Costa Rica......................	238	29.6	16.2	21.9	16.9	11.2	7.4	−4.7	−25.9	4.3	29.8	26.4	22.6
Dominican Republic.........	243	.5	16.4	10.9	18.9	22.4	15.0	10.3	28.9	−8.7	108.2	5.7	23.9
Ecuador..........................	248	2.5	−9.5	7.0	7.2	−3.9	−15.0	−42.7	11.4	−8.8	16.6	9.6	41.3
El Salvador.....................	253	22.2	12.4	10.0	13.3	8.3	10.2	−9.7	−29.2	−22.4	52.7	−19.7	3.9
Guatemala......................	258	4.5	3.5	12.8	22.9	−3.9	2.8	19.3	16.2	18.4	11.1	18.0	7.5
Guyana...........................	336	31.4	19.1	5.9	17.1	11.8	−3.9	14.0	10.9	10.0	10.3	9.1	11.3
Haiti...............................	263	23.8	14.7	−4.1	11.1	.3	29.0	25.9	16.9	23.9	31.4	18.2	3.7
Honduras........................	268	47.0	23.9	43.5	91.9	16.1	11.6	9.3	9.8	26.2	6.6	38.7	30.9
Jamaica..........................	343	34.3	29.7	4.0	15.2	22.1	−4.2	7.8	−6.4	−3.2	24.5	11.8	.5
Mexico...........................	273	21.2	33.4	23.1	48.4	33.7	36.2	10.3	5.0	16.9	15.0	12.0	11.7
Netherlands Antilles........	353	−6.5	19.9	−14.3	15.6	9.9	−5.9	8.2	36.3	24.9	−6.0	19.8	7.7
Nicaragua.......................	278	52.5	23.6	34.6	32.5	19.7	5.7	4.7	41.7	10.8	19.2	15.7	15.5
Panama..........................	283	−1.8	2.8	39.8	2.8	3.3	−1.5	4.9	.4	−2.0	−.3	4.4	12.9
Paraguay........................	288	27.3	26.2	−1.9	7.3	6.5	9.1	−1.0	6.1	2.7	50.9	17.4	4.5
Peru...............................	293	31.0	31.2	37.8	38.7	5.7	15.6	2.0	4.6	8.3	−6.2	5.2	30.3
Suriname........................	366	207.8	227.0	−10.3	−.4	65.0	47.4	155.0	14.5	31.6	−8.3	20.7	9.8
Trinidad and Tobago.......	369	56.9	−.7	8.9	16.1	20.9	3.7	3.1	10.7	−1.4	6.4	−3.2	53.9
Uruguay..........................	298	32.4	30.5	32.5	25.0	14.4	21.2	9.4	26.2	.7	60.6	−18.0	12.5
Venezuela, Rep. Bol........	299	64.0	31.7	96.9	73.9	18.2	33.0	14.8	12.0	19.5	47.2	45.3	40.2

Money

		1994	1995	1996	1997	1998	1999	2000	2001	2002	2003	2004	2005
							Percent Change over Previous Year						
Industrial Countries													
United States	111	−.1	−2.2	−.8	.9	.7	8.1	−5.2	9.3	−.4	5.9	5.6	.5
Canada	156	6.6	10.2	12.7	9.2	5.7	10.9	13.0	12.7	5.8	5.8	9.8	6.8
Australia	193	10.9	6.5	14.0	13.3	6.1	9.8	9.1	21.3	25.7	10.2	5.4	10.2
Japan	158	4.2	13.1	9.7	8.6	5.0	11.7	3.5	13.7	23.5	4.5	4.0	5.6
New Zealand	196	6.1	8.4	2.1	7.2	8.7	18.3	7.2	19.7	6.5	8.4	.4	3.1
Euro Area													
Austria	122	8.6	14.8	4.7	4.7	....	....	....	....	....	....	....	....
Belgium	124	1.5	4.9	4.2	3.1	....	....	....	....	....	....	....	....
Finland	172	8.9	14.0	16.4	5.5	4.8	....	....	....	....	....	....	....
Germany	134	4.9	7.1	12.3	2.1	10.4	....	....	....	....	....	....	....
Greece	174	23.5	13.6	10.9	14.4	11.9	34.3	−4.0	....	....	....	....	....
Ireland	178	12.5	64.1	8.8	−17.4	25.2	....	....	....	....	....	....	....
Italy	136	3.9	.4	4.9	6.5	11.1	....	....	....	....	....	....	....
Netherlands	138	1.7	13.5	12.1	7.8	....	....	....	....	....	....	....	....
Portugal	182	6.6	10.9	12.1	12.9	17.0	....	....	....	....	....	....	....
Spain	184	7.1	2.9	7.1	14.0	15.8	....	....	....	....	....	....	....
Denmark	128	−1.4	4.6	11.5	5.7	4.8	5.8	1.1	7.5	3.8	8.9	14.4	19.9
Iceland	176	10.7	9.6	8.5	16.4	20.3	21.1	2.6	−2.0	23.9	30.8	23.5	23.5
Norway	142	4.4	1.1	9.5	6.2	19.3	5.6	7.6	16.7	8.2	4.8	....	....
Switzerland	146	4.0	6.1	27.4	9.0	6.8	9.5	−2.1	8.5	10.2	24.1	−5.6	6.5
United Kingdom	112	.8	16.7	9.3	25.7	9.5	11.0	14.1	11.4	10.0	10.2	12.7	12.5
Developing Countries													
Africa													
CEMAC	758	....	....	....	....	....	....	....	2.7	14.2	−3.1	12.6	20.5
Cameroon	622	35.1	−11.6	−1.6	34.9	14.5	10.8	17.4	12.8	14.3	−5.2	7.6	.4
Central African Rep.	626	74.0	7.6	4.9	−8.1	−18.3	12.6	3.2	−2.6	−4.4	−9.8	14.4	16.4
Chad	628	31.5	42.7	33.5	−4.7	−8.0	−3.1	17.7	21.8	27.3	−3.1	2.5	32.2
Congo, Rep. of	634	40.4	.3	13.6	8.7	−13.6	27.8	68.2	−23.1	13.9	−13.3	18.6	42.1
Equatorial Guinea	642	135.5	58.4	50.1	−4.3	9.7	89.8	34.8	26.0	51.7	56.2	49.0	37.4
Gabon	646	41.9	12.3	26.0	8.1	−5.1	−5.1	19.3	3.7	4.4	−.5	12.3	36.4
WAEMU	759	54.9	13.6	6.1	8.4	7.9	4.4	6.5	13.3	15.1	1.1	2.5	8.9
Benin	638	67.3	−13.2	17.2	2.0	−4.7	46.9	35.0	10.0	−8.6	10.9	−17.2	33.3
Burkina Faso	748	38.9	25.5	7.0	17.5	−2.6	−1.9	5.3	−3.0	−7.1	85.4	−16.3	−7.0
Côte d'Ivoire	662	61.7	18.2	2.3	11.7	12.9	−1.7	−3.7	14.8	32.1	−34.6	13.6	7.5
Guinea Bissau	654	58.1	46.9	51.0	236.3	−12.1	22.4	63.7	7.8	22.3	−64.8	43.6	20.3
Mali	678	47.9	13.8	21.3	6.5	4.5	−.6	9.4	29.6	28.9	26.4	−7.2	12.8
Niger	692	15.4	9.2	−9.5	−19.4	−18.5	15.4	11.8	35.3	−8.2	56.4	21.7	5.7
Senegal	722	54.4	3.7	8.5	−.1	15.7	10.8	5.5	14.9	5.8	47.6	6.7	8.4
Togo	742	104.6	37.7	−7.8	1.9	6.9	9.9	22.2	−8.7	−8.1	4.3	24.7	−3.2
Algeria	612	7.8	7.1	13.4	14.6	20.9	8.9	17.3	18.5	15.2	14.6	33.2	11.1
Angola	614	....	....	3,392.6	107.5	39.8	326.2	342.0	168.1	134.0	106.4	39.1	59.2
Botswana	616	11.1	7.2	14.7	9.1	45.8	17.3	6.9	23.9	9.7	11.7	46.6	−5.4
Burundi	618	28.3	−3.3	12.5	10.5	1.3	41.9	−1.0	16.8	25.5	19.0	26.3	17.1
Cape Verde	624	8.2	16.6	10.6	21.6	−2.0	17.3	11.4	2.6	8.8	1.3	6.0	17.6
Comoros	632	9.8	−5.3	8.1	−18.6	−5.5	16.4	21.0	62.5	10.4	−2.1	−5.7	8.6
Congo, Dem. Rep. of	636	5,635.4	407.2	....	....	....	....	....	....	41.0	24.6	62.4	18.8
Djibouti	611	3.3	−1.6	−2.9	−9.6	−9.9	3.5	−7.8	2.6	24.0	20.7	10.7	.6
Eritrea	643	....	....	29.9	36.1	18.0	46.4	13.4	28.1	18.8	15.9	12.6	16.7
Ethiopia	644	21.4	2.7	−2.7	20.2	−4.7	14.8	9.6	4.8	19.4	12.3	20.0	16.4
Gambia, The	648	−11.7	15.7	−3.8	38.8	−.5	14.3	37.4	14.4	56.1	63.5	8.2	6.9
Ghana	652	50.3	33.4	31.7	46.0	20.9	15.8	38.2	46.3	59.9	33.2	28.2	7.0
Guinea	656	−3.2	8.5	−.2	21.3	8.7	....	....	12.0	21.6	31.1	28.0	21.9
Kenya	664	5.2	6.6	14.6	17.4	4.5	16.7	8.8	5.9	18.7	29.5	8.4	10.3
Lesotho	666	12.3	10.5	19.3	22.7	24.9	−2.6	8.2	24.7	11.5	6.7	3.4	15.1
Liberia	668	7.6	42.4	6.7	−1.4	128.8	14.9	−11.5	6.7	38.8	16.6	35.3	30.7
Madagascar	674	56.5	15.2	17.3	22.9	10.9	20.2	13.2	30.3	7.5	4.2	19.4	1.1
Malawi	676	50.5	44.0	24.7	16.5	63.4	33.5	38.9	13.5	26.5	27.1	44.8	21.7
Mauritania	682	−5.4	−8.1	−10.9	8.3	5.3	6.3	22.7	14.8	4.3	11.4	....	....
Mauritius	684	19.4	8.0	2.7	8.0	9.2	3.5	10.8	16.2	17.5	12.4	16.6	10.1
Morocco	686	11.1	6.0	5.8	7.2	7.8	11.6	7.9	15.3	9.0	9.8	9.9	14.3
Mozambique	688	50.5	35.0	20.0	25.1	14.5	24.6	22.3	17.6	14.5	23.8	16.2	29.5
Namibia	728	20.8	8.1	56.8	4.0	27.8	22.0	28.5	9.4	9.5	14.0	21.4	−1.3
Nigeria	694	43.4	16.3	13.5	16.8	19.0	22.5	62.1	25.7	15.9	29.5	8.6	15.9
Rwanda	714	15.6	41.1	11.7	22.7	−.8	7.0	6.7	1.0	10.4	17.0	21.4	29.4
São Tomé and Príncipe	716	....	....	66.5	107.8	−3.3	5.3	23.5	54.3	13.7	49.9	6.2	95.9
Seychelles	718	−3.0	2.9	34.4	44.8	19.3	38.4	−1.1	12.6	17.9	11.7	−21.9	13.9
Sierra Leone	724	10.0	29.5	6.6	57.1	7.3	49.4	4.4	35.4	30.6	18.4	17.6	23.1
South Africa	199	....	....	....	....	....	....	....	....	....	11.1	11.6	19.5
Swaziland	734	7.3	16.6	16.5	16.2	1.9	32.3	−.3	14.2	10.3	28.4	11.9	19.8
Tanzania	738	33.3	29.9	4.9	9.9	10.5	16.0	9.9	10.2	25.2	16.1	18.2	33.7
Tunisia	744	10.7	9.6	13.0	13.0	7.5	16.0	9.9	10.1	−1.7	5.4	10.6	13.7
Uganda	746	36.5	15.4	10.3	13.7	19.5	12.6	16.8	12.8	21.0	12.3	8.6	19.6
Zambia	754	44.8	61.1	19.4	31.0	16.8	23.6	51.2	34.2	24.5	29.4	22.9	14.1
Zimbabwe	698	18.2	52.4	23.1	53.7	23.5	34.7	53.3	142.8	170.0	485.1	228.6	552.6
Asia													
Bangladesh	513	24.3	16.7	4.7	7.7	7.4	12.7	18.4	10.7	5.1	7.6	17.8	18.3
Bhutan	514	27.1	26.6	56.8	4.5	21.2	41.7	5.8	23.1	43.8	−2.9	19.0	11.4
Brunei Darussalam	516	....	....	....	....	....	....	−.9	3.6	9.8	3.0	9.0	1.3
Cambodia	522	−1.1	38.1	18.1	17.0	41.2	−2.1	1.4	13.0	33.4	15.1	23.2	14.7
China, P.R.: Mainland	924	27.2	17.3	19.4	26.3	11.2	21.4	16.1	13.1	14.9	18.7	13.9	11.6

Money

							Percent Change over Previous Year						

34 x

Asia(Cont.)

		1994	1995	1996	1997	1998	1999	2000	2001	2002	2003	2004	2005
China, P.R.: Hong Kong	532	.1	.3	15.3	−3.8	−4.6	15.4	—	14.3	14.0	34.8	14.9	−15.2
China, P.R.: Macao	546	....	....	....	....	....	−2.6	−7.8	19.6	7.3	38.4	52.9	−4.8
Fiji	819	−6.0	13.0	18.7	−2.3	10.6	39.8	−13.7	4.6	14.7	26.1	13.4	17.9
India	534	27.4	11.1	14.1	12.6	11.7	16.9	10.6	10.0	12.5	16.2	20.7	18.9
Indonesia	536	23.7	15.6	10.0	32.8	25.3	28.8	37.7	8.8	7.4	17.0	15.1	10.2
Korea	542	11.9	19.6	1.7	−11.4	1.6	24.7	5.9	13.8	18.0	3.7	4.5	12.9
Lao People's Dem. Rep	544	17.4	9.5	12.5	5.8	111.4	29.6	57.3	8.0	57.9	42.5	44.3	17.2
Malaysia	548	16.8	13.2	23.7	11.8	−29.7	28.4	7.7	3.7	9.5	16.0	11.2	8.7
Maldives	556	22.2	5.2	17.9	13.0	16.0	14.6	11.3	−6.1	14.3	11.5	19.7	22.5
Micronesia, Fed.Sts.	868	....	....	−1.7	10.2	−1.1	−6.5	−5.5	13.0	−7.3	14.1	4.9	6.1
Mongolia	948	78.2	29.0	42.7	25.1	8.5	39.0	13.9	19.4	20.2	13.4	4.4	21.2
Myanmar	518	33.8	28.1	33.4	31.0	28.2	22.6	34.5	50.8	44.0	17.5	25.4	31.3
Nepal	558	20.6	9.9	5.9	44.2	−11.2	21.1	14.4	....	....	....	....	....
Pakistan	564	15.1	12.8	7.5	32.5	4.6	8.6	10.1	10.1	15.9	24.1	21.6	36.7
Papua New Guinea	853	3.4	14.0	52.0	−5.5	10.3	21.0	2.2	3.2	21.0	8.3	29.9	35.6
Philippines	566	11.3	21.7	19.8	14.2	7.4	38.3	−1.3	.4	22.0	8.6	9.2	9.2
Samoa	862	8.1	29.1	−.2	22.5	−10.7	20.7	16.1	−6.9	10.1	23.6	5.7	28.7
Singapore	576	2.3	8.3	6.7	1.7	−1.0	14.2	6.9	8.5	−.7	8.1	14.0	4.4
Solomon Islands	813	31.4	5.0	15.7	7.4	−.2	25.7	−5.8	−1.5	3.5	29.6	12.9	44.4
Sri Lanka	524	18.7	6.7	4.0	9.8	12.1	12.8	9.1	3.2	14.0	16.0	16.6	....
Thailand	578	12.8	13.1	5.3	5.5	−2.4	43.5	−12.5	11.6	14.0	15.8	8.4	7.4
Tonga	866	−5.5	−13.9	3.8	2.6	4.7	22.1	10.6	26.2	32.0	12.7	15.7	1.2
Vanuatu	846	.9	10.1	3.5	1.8	14.4	.2	6.1	−.5	44.3	5.7	4.9	9.7
Vietnam	582	....	....	25.1	19.5	13.1	51.2	33.1	23.5	11.5	25.3	26.1	22.2

Europe

		1994	1995	1996	1997	1998	1999	2000	2001	2002	2003	2004	2005
Albania	914	....	52.8	52.6	1.4	−8.7	23.0	20.4	15.3	6.7	−5.2	19.4	31.7
Armenia	911	907.3	124.3	32.4	10.6	19.6	−.9	36.7	8.3	49.2	6.9	7.4	52.6
Azerbaijan, Republic of	912	468.3	130.5	30.4	36.1	−25.6	17.5	12.9	7.6	16.2	27.0	30.6	14.9
Belarus	913	....	273.2	56.7	115.5	139.1	188.4	117.8	84.7	45.4	63.7	48.0	53.8
Bosnia & Herzegovina	963	....	....	....	....	11.9	199.4	28.0	89.7	13.1	4.3	15.2	16.9
Bulgaria	918	....	....	217.1	556.4	13.9	9.0	18.8	25.8	11.0	19.9	28.2	20.8
Croatia	960	112.2	24.6	37.9	21.0	−1.4	1.7	30.1	31.5	30.2	9.8	2.0	12.3
Cyprus	423	4.9	6.2	6.8	7.8	3.7	42.1	−2.1	−.5	1.1	30.6	7.6	18.1
Czech Republic	935	50.2	6.7	4.7	−7.3	−3.4	10.8	11.4	17.0	17.0	16.6	17.4	34.5
Estonia	939	20.9	29.8	37.6	24.0	−6.3	32.1	20.5	19.5	9.3	13.0	17.4	22.1
Georgia	915	....	....	36.0	29.8	−9.5	9.4	33.5	5.9	14.9	14.1	58.4	26.8
Hungary	944	8.0	3.8	22.5	23.5	17.2	19.3	11.3	16.8	18.7	10.3	.4	24.8
Kazakhstan	916	576.0	108.2	20.9	8.2	−21.3	73.4	14.7	14.3	41.5	25.4	57.7	16.4
Kyrgyz Republic	917	....	....	16.6	7.8	2.9	31.0	9.6	20.7	38.1	38.3	22.9	36.1
Latvia	941	31.1	.8	20.3	33.3	6.0	6.3	19.6	13.0	21.3	17.7	22.3	34.1
Lithuania	946	41.8	40.9	3.5	41.5	9.0	−5.3	7.5	18.9	23.5	26.5	18.4	8.1
Macedonia, FYR	962	....	....	−3.6	16.2	9.1	32.4	13.1	−50.1	148.2	2.1	2.1	5.0
Malta	181	9.1	7.6	−1.9	—	7.2	10.6	2.6	6.7	7.0	89.6	7.0	....
Moldova	921	116.5	68.8	12.4	30.6	−18.0	38.9	36.7	23.6	42.4	24.0	38.3	....
Poland	964	39.7	36.4	39.8	17.9	16.2	23.1	−6.4	14.0	19.9	18.3	9.4	19.7
Romania	968	104.9	54.0	57.0	66.3	17.4	34.2	56.2	38.8	37.3	28.3	35.0	60.6
Russia	922	187.0	120.7	27.2	55.6	15.0	53.3	66.9	35.5	25.6	45.6	30.5	35.5
Slovak Republic	936	6.2	20.9	15.8	−4.4	−11.4	4.2	21.5	21.3	8.5	44.6	14.3	15.6
Slovenia	961	35.1	24.8	18.4	18.1	25.2	26.6	6.1	19.9	47.1	12.8	27.9	12.7
Tajikistan	923	....	....	....	....	....	17.6	46.9	25.4	34.4	28.3	8.5	—
Turkey	186	81.5	68.3	129.5	69.1	63.1	93.6	57.3	46.3	36.7	43.1	26.4	52.2
Ukraine	926	444.0	151.7	34.9	43.3	14.1	36.4	47.1	43.1	35.2	31.9	28.3	46.9

Middle East

		1994	1995	1996	1997	1998	1999	2000	2001	2002	2003	2004	2005
Bahrain, Kingdom of	419	−5.5	−3.6	.8	3.7	5.1	16.6	4.6	23.8	17.3	26.9	4.8	23.4
Egypt	469	10.7	8.5	7.2	9.4	20.3	.8	5.3	7.9	13.0	23.4	16.0	15.6
Iran, I.R. of	429	41.6	32.5	33.6	19.9	22.7	21.5	24.7	23.0	23.6	18.9	14.9	22.8
Israel	436	7.7	15.1	20.4	11.3	12.3	20.4	2.5	21.8	1.5	11.7	23.6	15.4
Jordan	439	1.3	−.2	−11.8	6.1	−.8	9.5	14.2	3.8	8.5	24.5	10.9	28.2
Kuwait	443	1.1	5.2	4.9	.4	−8.3	19.9	7.0	11.8	25.9	26.4	21.5	17.4
Lebanon	446	25.7	8.6	12.4	10.0	6.3	10.2	5.7	−1.0	8.5	10.9	6.4	−2.6
Libya	672	13.0	6.2	1.2	5.2	.4	4.7	4.5	1.2	12.9	3.8	17.0	31.8
Oman	449	4.7	−.3	6.8	9.2	−8.0	1.1	7.5	27.7	10.0	4.7	12.8	24.3
Qatar	453	−8.1	−4.9	4.4	6.3	2.1	−.9	6.5	17.3	20.5	79.3	29.4	53.2
Saudi Arabia	456	3.4	−.2	6.1	6.1	−.6	11.7	5.7	8.4	12.7	10.2	18.2	7.8
Syrian Arab Republic	463	8.2	8.7	8.6	6.7	8.0	11.1	17.7	13.9	17.8	27.0	1.3	....
United Arab Emirates	466	5.6	8.6	6.9	13.9	9.5	8.9	12.6	15.8	19.2	23.8	38.7	29.2
Yemen, Republic of	474	35.1	17.5	−4.5	6.3	8.1	15.2	19.3	14.5	8.2	13.4	12.4	13.3

Western Hemisphere

		1994	1995	1996	1997	1998	1999	2000	2001	2002	2003	2004	2005
ECCU	309	9.3	14.6	−2.1	6.4	14.9	9.0	.7	4.3	6.1	14.8	25.4	8.4
Anguilla	312	9.2	37.8	5.7	1.8	5.1	9.7	21.8	−11.0	13.1	13.9	24.3	4.0
Antigua and Barbuda	311	15.5	26.7	−6.2	2.1	25.1	−1.0	−1.7	8.4	−2.4	17.4	22.9	20.9
Dominica	321	−3.9	21.6	6.0	−1.9	7.9	26.6	−19.4	.4	23.2	.9	6.3	22.7
Grenada	328	12.3	6.2	1.3	4.6	14.2	9.1	4.9	4.9	17.0	13.6	46.8	−17.6
Montserrat	351	24.2	−4.4	−4.1	54.0	14.8	−22.4	−15.3	4.2	2.8	27.9	4.3	−12.4
St. Kitts and Nevis	361	−1.9	17.4	3.5	−.8	20.6	5.2	7.5	−6.0	11.5	24.1	29.3	−1.2
St. Lucia	362	3.8	11.6	−5.6	5.7	6.8	12.0	−.3	−.3	1.9	21.3	30.4	16.4
St. Vincent & Grenadines	364	21.7	−2.9	6.5	25.2	13.4	24.1	12.9	10.1	2.6	6.0	13.8	11.3
Argentina	213	15.7	1.6	14.6	12.8	—	1.6	−9.1	−20.1	78.4	51.9	30.2	27.4
Aruba	314	16.8	.5	.9	5.7	15.6	7.8	1.1	17.5	20.4	16.7	−2.5	.4
Bahamas, The	313	9.1	6.8	.5	15.7	14.7	26.1	6.7	−3.9	5.7	9.0	18.5	15.2
Barbados	316	8.3	−17.0	46.4	−1.1	23.4	20.7	23.5	1.3	2.3	31.0	6.5	9.6
Belize	339	5.7	7.8	5.5	1.3	12.3	33.0	15.7	32.1	−13.5	22.4	9.4	5.6
Bolivia	218	29.3	21.1	21.7	19.0	7.1	−5.8	8.8	18.7	−.4	19.3	18.6	58.0

Money

		1994	1995	1996	1997	1998	1999	2000	2001	2002	2003	2004	2005
34 x							*Percent Change over Previous Year*						
Western Hemisphere(Cont.)													
Brazil	223	2,195.4	25.7	29.9	22.3	7.5	13.6	18.9	12.1	29.1	4.0	17.6	10.3
Chile	228	15.8	22.3	16.4	19.9	−4.6	15.8	7.2	11.4	9.1	11.5	16.0	13.5
Colombia	233	29.0	20.2	23.4	17.4	−7.9	24.2	25.9	9.6	16.9	15.5	15.4	18.7
Costa Rica	238	37.9	−6.0	16.9	54.3	17.1	28.6	19.8	13.2	16.4	15.1	7.9	25.2
Dominican Republic	243	7.5	17.3	22.3	19.3	6.2	21.8	−1.1	16.4	6.1	64.5	5.7	22.0
Ecuador	248	....	....	....	....	....	....	....	....	....	10.6	26.4	19.5
El Salvador	253	4.0	8.8	14.3	.6	8.0	15.1	−6.7	9.6	−9.0	9.9	4.8	8.0
Guatemala	258	40.1	9.9	13.5	29.9	13.5	13.6	21.8	11.8	8.4	18.0	6.7	16.5
Guyana	336	10.4	16.7	14.5	10.0	−1.6	23.0	10.4	1.2	7.8	14.2	14.0	7.7
Haiti	263	31.8	31.6	−13.1	18.7	.3	26.6	9.5	15.1	27.3	20.2	11.3	18.3
Honduras	268	36.1	21.7	29.4	41.0	12.7	18.2	8.2	3.6	14.8	21.3	16.0	20.4
Jamaica	343	25.7	38.0	14.4	2.8	6.4	22.8	6.3	13.0	9.7	6.1	18.5	12.5
Mexico	273	.8	2.4	38.7	32.2	21.2	25.8	14.2	13.3	14.2	14.0	8.5	16.4
Netherlands Antilles	353	13.8	7.9	−4.3	—	2.6	3.3	2.1	14.3	15.2	−5.3	12.8	11.9
Nicaragua	278	36.2	13.2	25.9	24.7	23.6	23.5	8.3	32.8	3.1	24.9	14.2	20.3
Panama	283	13.5	1.3	3.3	18.3	13.0	1.6	2.9	10.3	2.0	10.1	10.8	18.4
Paraguay	288	30.0	28.2	.5	10.4	5.2	9.2	18.2	7.1	.6	37.3	26.3	20.9
Peru	293	28.9	34.2	19.7	69.1	26.3	16.2	−5.4	1.8	2.8	−3.2	11.1	11.0
Suriname	366	245.6	178.2	−2.0	20.2	34.6	51.5	104.3	38.2	38.4	4.2	23.2	11.5
Trinidad and Tobago	369	19.5	4.7	6.1	21.1	5.8	12.3	6.6	19.6	15.8	−1.4	8.4	58.7
Uruguay	298	40.4	32.3	24.8	16.7	14.1	3.1	−3.5	−4.2	3.8	34.3	15.9	33.5
Venezuela, Rep. Bol	299	139.2	38.0	149.2	77.0	4.7	24.5	25.3	15.5	18.2	73.7	46.6	53.7

Money plus Quasi-Money

		1994	1995	1996	1997	1998	1999	2000	2001	2002	2003	2004	2005
							Percent Change over Previous Year						
Industrial Countries													
United States	111	.1	5.6	6.1	6.6	10.1	8.2	6.9	14.0	4.3	2.5	3.1	5.9
Canada	156	8.0	6.2	5.0	8.6	2.3	5.7	13.9	6.5	5.6	7.0	10.2	7.9
Australia	193	10.0	8.5	10.6	7.3	8.4	11.7	3.7	13.2	5.6	13.3	11.7	7.7
Japan	158	3.1	2.7	2.3	3.1	4.1	3.4	1.1	2.2	3.4	1.8	1.6	2.0
New Zealand	196	7.6	9.3	16.1	5.2	1.8	5.0	2.3	6.8	7.7	10.6	5.1	12.2
Euro Area													
Austria	122	5.4	5.0	2.8	2.2	....	....	....	....	....	....	....	....
Belgium	124	2.8	4.9	6.3	7.1	....	....	....	....	....	....	....	....
Finland	172	1.4	6.0	−2.9	2.5	3.7	....	....	....	....	....	....	....
France	132	3.3	8.7	—	6.6	....	....	....	....	....	....	....	....
Germany	134	2.6	4.4	7.4	2.4	5.9	....	....	....	....	....	....	....
Ireland	178	10.1	52.8	15.6	19.5	17.8	....	....	....	....	....	....	....
Italy	136	1.8	2.3	2.2	−5.8	.6	....	....	....	....	....	....	....
Netherlands	138	.3	6.0	5.6	6.7	....	....	....	....	....	....	....	....
Portugal	182	9.1	8.3	5.6	6.8	5.9	....	....	....	....	....	....	....
Spain	184	7.1	6.6	2.6	1.4	7.1	....	....	....	....	....	....	....
Denmark	128	−10.0	6.2	8.1	6.8	3.3	−.9	−5.2	3.6	4.2	6.0	11.0	16.1
Iceland	176	2.0	2.5	6.2	9.4	15.2	17.3	10.7	14.9	15.0	22.4	13.5	29.8
Norway	142	5.0	3.8	6.9	1.4	15.5	1.7	8.7	8.8	7.6	3.4	....	....
Sweden	144	....	....	....	....	....	....	....	....	3.7	4.1	2.4	12.2
Switzerland	146	4.2	4.6	9.6	6.6	5.1	13.3	−16.9	3.9	5.7	8.4	2.9	6.8
United Kingdom	112	7.7	20.3	14.5	25.5	6.8	19.1	11.1	8.6	5.0	9.8	10.1	13.8
Developing Countries													
Africa													
CEMAC	758	....	....	....	....	....	....	....	6.4	14.9	1.7	10.3	17.9
Cameroon	622	26.5	−6.2	−10.1	18.6	7.8	13.3	19.1	15.1	15.9	1.3	6.4	4.9
Central African Republic	626	78.5	4.3	4.9	−7.7	−16.1	11.1	2.4	−1.1	−4.3	−8.0	14.2	16.5
Chad	628	31.4	48.7	27.9	−4.1	−7.7	−2.6	18.5	22.0	26.6	−3.1	3.5	31.3
Congo, Rep. of	634	28.2	−.1	15.7	9.5	−12.8	19.9	58.5	−22.8	13.1	−2.4	17.4	37.1
Equatorial Guinea	642	139.5	48.9	42.8	9.3	15.6	68.7	36.2	35.1	53.1	56.7	33.5	34.7
Gabon	646	37.4	10.1	17.2	11.3	−1.8	−3.0	18.3	7.5	5.7	−1.2	11.4	27.5
WAEMU	759	39.8	14.1	7.6	7.3	3.5	5.0	7.2	11.8	15.6	3.0	5.2	8.3
Benin	638	47.9	−1.8	13.0	4.6	−3.6	34.8	26.0	12.2	−7.0	10.8	−9.3	26.3
Burkina Faso	748	29.4	22.3	5.2	17.7	1.0	2.6	6.2	1.6	.6	60.6	−8.3	−4.8
Côte d'Ivoire	662	46.8	18.1	3.9	8.2	6.0	−1.7	−1.9	12.0	30.0	−26.3	9.6	7.7
Guinea Bissau	654	48.5	43.0	48.3	119.4	−11.1	21.5	60.8	7.3	22.8	−64.7	42.8	21.3
Mali	678	39.2	7.3	24.5	8.9	4.2	1.0	12.2	19.6	27.9	26.4	−2.6	9.8
Niger	692	6.7	3.8	−6.6	−21.3	−18.5	15.4	12.4	31.4	−.5	42.5	19.7	7.0
Senegal	722	38.7	7.4	11.7	3.7	8.5	13.1	10.7	13.6	8.2	31.5	12.2	8.2
Togo	742	44.3	22.3	−6.3	−5.8	.1	8.4	15.2	−2.6	−2.2	10.9	18.1	2.2
Algeria	612	13.0	9.2	14.4	18.6	18.9	13.7	13.2	24.8	36.8	16.0	11.3	10.3
Angola	614	....	....	4,105.6	71.9	57.6	564.8	309.0	160.6	158.6	63.9	37.0	60.5
Botswana	616	12.8	12.3	18.8	28.6	39.4	26.3	1.4	31.2	−.5	17.6	13.9	10.6
Burundi	618	33.3	−11.2	24.3	9.4	−3.7	47.3	4.3	15.7	29.5	15.9	17.8	19.0
Cape Verde	624	12.2	18.2	9.7	10.9	2.8	14.9	13.7	9.9	13.6	9.0	11.1	14.5
Comoros	632	7.3	−6.1	9.8	−4.2	−14.2	18.5	14.5	46.7	9.2	−1.2	−5.0	3.2
Congo, Dem. Rep. of	636	6,968.9	357.6	....	....	....	....	....	....	40.0	32.3	72.9	25.5
Djibouti	611	3.7	5.3	−7.4	−4.5	−4.1	−3.8	1.1	7.5	15.7	17.8	13.9	11.3
Eritrea	643	....	....	21.0	28.1	20.5	36.1	17.3	32.6	20.6	15.1	11.6	10.7
Ethiopia	644	23.2	9.0	9.0	19.8	−1.1	13.7	13.1	9.7	15.9	12.4	19.3	18.6
Gambia, The	648	−3.8	14.2	5.8	23.0	10.2	12.1	34.8	19.4	35.3	43.4	18.3	13.1
Ghana	652	52.6	43.2	39.2	44.1	17.5	25.4	54.2	31.7	48.9	34.2	27.4	9.3
Guinea	656	−3.4	11.3	3.6	18.2	6.4	....	....	12.9	19.7	33.2	36.5	33.4
Kenya	664	23.2	29.0	25.3	20.2	2.9	6.5	4.9	2.8	11.7	11.9	13.7	10.0
Lesotho	666	10.9	9.8	17.1	14.8	15.5	−5.1	1.4	17.2	8.8	6.0	3.3	9.1
Liberia	668	11.7	29.5	−11.9	3.5	106.0	11.6	18.3	12.7	4.9	9.5	45.7	34.1
Madagascar	674	52.6	16.2	16.0	20.8	6.2	19.2	17.2	23.8	8.0	8.8	25.2	2.2
Malawi	676	36.5	56.2	40.0	2.1	67.8	28.0	45.5	23.7	22.6	27.5	29.7	16.2
Mauritania	682	−.5	−5.1	−5.1	8.0	4.1	2.1	16.1	17.3	8.9	10.5	....	....
Mauritius	684	12.2	18.6	7.5	16.4	11.2	15.1	9.2	10.9	12.7	8.7	21.0	19.5
Morocco	686	10.2	7.0	6.6	8.0	6.0	10.2	8.4	14.1	6.4	8.7	7.8	14.0
Mozambique	688	50.4	47.7	19.1	23.9	17.8	31.8	38.3	28.2	21.1	18.3	5.8	27.3
Namibia	728	30.9	22.6	24.1	8.1	10.5	19.5	13.2	6.2	8.0	9.6	16.1	9.8
Nigeria	694	34.5	19.4	16.2	16.0	22.3	33.1	48.1	27.0	21.6	24.1	14.0	16.2
Rwanda	714	−3.7	69.5	8.6	29.1	3.5	7.9	15.6	11.2	12.6	15.4	30.0	18.0
São Tomé and Príncipe	716	....	....	84.5	116.4	2.8	7.7	24.9	40.1	25.0	53.0	2.9	90.8
Seychelles	718	18.8	14.4	14.3	16.2	15.8	18.8	4.6	11.9	11.1	5.9	.9	4.0
Sierra Leone	724	8.8	19.6	29.7	47.1	11.3	37.8	12.1	33.7	29.6	21.9	20.1	31.3
South Africa	199	....	....	....	....	....	....	....	....	....	14.8	8.8	19.9
Swaziland	734	10.9	3.9	16.3	19.4	12.9	15.6	−6.6	10.7	13.2	14.4	10.3	9.7
Tanzania	738	35.3	33.0	8.4	12.9	10.8	18.6	14.8	17.1	25.1	16.6	19.2	38.2
Tunisia	744	8.1	6.6	13.3	16.5	5.4	18.9	14.1	10.7	4.4	6.4	11.3	11.0
Uganda	746	35.8	13.9	19.3	19.2	19.4	22.9	13.6	18.1	9.2	25.0	17.9	16.5
Zambia	754	59.2	55.5	35.0	25.1	25.6	27.7	73.8	13.6	31.0	25.0	32.0	1.9
Zimbabwe	698	35.1	25.5	33.3	41.2	11.3	35.9	68.9	128.5	191.7	430.0	229.3	532.7
Asia													
Bangladesh	513	19.3	12.2	10.7	9.8	11.4	15.4	19.3	14.7	13.3	13.1	16.3	17.2
Bhutan	514	23.3	35.6	9.0	58.9	13.9	32.0	17.4	7.9	27.9	1.0	19.9	11.9
Brunei Darussalam	516	....	....	....	....	....	....	47.7	−12.0	1.9	4.0	16.0	−4.5
Cambodia	522	35.6	43.6	40.4	16.6	15.7	17.3	26.9	20.4	31.1	14.9	30.4	16.1

Money plus Quasi-Money

		1994	1995	1996	1997	1998	1999	2000	2001	2002	2003	2004	2005
						Percent Change over Previous Year							
China, P.R.: Mainland	924	31.5	29.5	25.3	20.7	14.9	14.7	12.3	15.0	18.3	19.6	14.4	17.9
China, P.R.: Hong Kong	532	11.7	10.6	12.5	8.7	11.1	8.3	9.3	−.3	.5	6.3	7.3	3.4
Fiji	819	2.5	4.5	.9	−8.7	−.5	13.6	−1.5	−3.1	7.8	25.0	10.5	15.1
India	534	20.3	11.0	18.7	17.7	18.2	17.1	15.2	14.3	16.8	13.0	16.7	15.6
Indonesia	536	20.2	27.5	27.1	25.3	62.8	12.2	16.6	12.8	4.8	7.9	8.5	16.4
Korea	542	18.7	15.6	15.8	14.1	27.0	27.4	25.4	13.2	11.0	6.7	−.6	3.1
Lao People's Democratic Rep.	544	31.9	16.4	26.7	65.8	113.3	78.4	46.0	13.7	37.6	20.1	21.6	5.1
Malaysia	548	11.5	18.5	25.6	16.0	.2	12.1	10.0	2.4	4.6	8.1	11.7	6.3
Maldives	556	24.0	15.4	26.1	23.3	23.0	3.5	4.2	9.1	19.5	14.5	32.8	11.7
Micronesia, Federal States of	868	....	....	−5.8	3.8	.7	3.4	−1.0	6.0	−12.0	−3.7	−.1	1.6
Mongolia	948	80.0	32.6	17.2	42.2	−1.7	31.6	17.6	27.9	42.0	49.6	20.5	37.1
Myanmar	518	35.6	36.5	38.9	28.8	34.2	29.7	42.4	43.9	34.6	1.4	32.4	27.3
Nepal	558	18.1	15.6	12.2	29.2	11.1	21.6	18.8	....	....	....	....	....
Pakistan	564	17.4	13.8	20.1	19.9	7.9	4.3	12.1	11.7	16.8	17.5	20.5	16.5
Papua New Guinea	853	−1.3	13.7	30.7	7.7	2.5	9.2	5.0	1.6	7.3	−4.4	14.8	29.5
Philippines	566	26.7	23.9	23.7	23.1	8.6	16.9	8.1	3.6	10.4	3.6	9.9	6.4
Samoa	862	13.9	24.4	6.3	15.2	2.5	15.7	16.3	6.1	10.2	14.0	8.3	15.6
Singapore	576	14.4	8.5	9.8	10.3	30.2	8.5	−2.0	5.9	−.3	8.1	6.2	6.2
Solomon Islands	813	25.1	9.2	15.3	6.7	2.5	7.0	.6	−13.6	6.0	25.4	17.5	38.8
Sri Lanka	524	19.7	35.8	11.3	15.6	13.2	13.4	12.9	13.6	13.4	15.3	19.6	....
Thailand	578	10.7	17.7	10.6	19.6	10.1	3.8	4.9	5.5	3.8	4.8	5.4	5.9
Tonga	866	6.6	.7	5.3	7.8	14.7	11.9	18.8	14.9	7.8	14.4	13.2	13.2
Vanuatu	846	2.9	13.4	10.1	−.4	12.6	−9.2	5.5	5.7	−1.7	−.8	9.9	11.4
Vietnam	582	....	....	25.7	24.3	23.5	66.4	35.4	27.3	13.3	33.1	31.0	30.9
Europe													
Albania	914	....	51.8	43.8	28.5	20.6	22.3	12.0	19.9	5.9	7.6	13.1	14.2
Armenia	911	740.4	64.3	35.1	29.2	36.7	14.0	38.6	4.3	34.0	10.4	22.3	27.8
Azerbaijan, Republic of	912	1,116.5	25.4	17.1	41.4	−17.4	20.1	73.4	−10.6	14.6	30.8	46.1	21.8
Belarus	913	....	158.4	52.4	111.4	276.0	132.7	219.3	62.3	50.3	56.8	45.6	41.3
Bosnia & Herzegovina	963	....	....	....	....	22.0	27.5	11.3	90.0	9.4	9.5	22.4	18.7
Bulgaria	918	77.5	40.5	123.9	351.4	11.8	13.4	30.8	26.0	12.3	20.2	24.0	24.5
Croatia	960	74.6	40.4	49.2	38.4	13.0	−1.8	29.1	45.7	9.6	10.7	8.2	10.7
Cyprus	423	12.5	11.4	10.5	11.0	8.3	20.8	9.7	13.4	9.0	4.0	5.6	10.2
Czech Republic	935	20.4	29.3	6.4	1.7	3.4	2.6	16.0	11.2	−2.1	7.4	4.4	8.4
Estonia	939	30.4	27.5	36.8	37.8	4.2	23.7	25.7	23.0	11.2	10.9	15.8	41.9
Georgia	915	....	....	40.2	42.8	−.8	20.6	39.2	19.6	17.9	22.8	42.4	26.5
Hungary	944	14.2	20.9	22.2	19.7	15.6	15.7	12.6	16.2	14.1	12.5	8.9	13.3
Kazakhstan	916	576.0	108.2	20.9	8.2	−14.1	84.4	45.0	20.8	30.1	29.5	69.3	24.8
Kyrgyz Republic	917	....	....	14.8	32.2	17.5	33.7	11.7	11.3	33.9	33.4	32.1	10.0
Latvia	941	50.3	−21.4	19.6	37.0	6.7	8.3	27.0	19.8	19.9	22.1	26.7	38.3
Lithuania	946	63.0	28.9	−3.5	34.1	14.5	7.7	16.5	21.4	16.9	18.2	24.1	32.9
Macedonia, FYR	962	−57.1	11.7	−1.0	23.5	13.0	32.0	21.4	32.1	15.7	15.8	16.1	15.2
Malta	181	14.9	11.8	8.6	8.0	8.1	9.8	4.0	8.4	10.4	−6.2	2.4	4.2
Moldova	921	115.7	65.3	14.8	34.5	−8.3	42.9	41.7	35.8	38.6	30.4	39.8	....
Poland	964	38.2	35.0	31.0	29.1	25.2	19.4	11.8	15.0	−2.8	5.7	6.9	12.2
Romania	968	138.1	70.1	67.4	105.0	48.9	44.9	38.0	46.2	38.2	23.3	39.9	33.9
Russia	922	216.5	112.6	29.6	28.8	37.6	56.7	58.0	36.3	33.8	38.5	33.7	36.3
Slovak Republic	936	17.4	18.4	16.2	8.4	5.0	11.6	15.2	11.9	4.0	10.0	6.8	3.6
Slovenia	961	44.7	29.8	23.3	23.3	19.5	15.1	18.0	30.4	12.3	6.2	7.6	7.5
Turkey	186	145.3	103.6	117.3	97.5	89.7	100.3	40.5	86.2	29.1	14.6	22.1	25.2
Ukraine	926	567.9	115.5	35.1	33.9	22.2	40.6	44.5	42.9	42.3	46.9	32.8	53.9
Middle East													
Bahrain	419	6.0	7.4	3.1	7.8	16.8	4.1	10.2	9.2	10.3	6.4	4.1	22.0
Egypt	469	11.2	9.9	10.8	10.8	10.8	5.7	11.6	13.2	12.6	21.3	14.4	11.3
Iran, I.R. of	429	33.3	30.1	32.5	23.7	20.4	21.5	22.4	27.6	24.9	24.5	23.0	22.8
Israel	436	24.6	21.7	25.0	15.0	19.7	15.5	8.0	9.5	6.9	−.1	3.6	11.2
Jordan	439	3.3	5.7	−.9	7.6	6.3	15.5	7.6	8.1	8.6	16.6	10.5	21.4
Kuwait	443	5.4	9.4	−.6	3.9	−.8	1.6	6.3	12.8	4.8	7.8	12.1	12.3
Lebanon	446	25.3	16.4	26.4	19.6	16.1	11.7	9.8	7.5	8.1	13.0	10.1	4.5
Libya	672	14.0	9.6	1.0	−3.7	3.8	7.4	3.1	4.3	6.1	6.5	13.8	29.0
Oman	449	6.7	7.7	8.1	24.5	4.8	6.4	6.0	9.2	5.2	2.5	4.0	21.3
Qatar	453	9.1	1.1	5.6	9.9	8.0	11.4	10.7	—	11.8	15.8	20.5	43.3
Saudi Arabia	456	3.0	3.4	7.3	5.2	3.6	6.8	4.5	5.1	15.2	8.5	17.3	13.2
Syrian Arab Rep.	463	12.2	9.2	10.2	8.2	10.5	13.4	19.0	23.5	18.5	7.8	15.3	....
United Arab Emirates	466	7.9	10.2	6.9	9.0	4.2	11.5	15.3	23.2	11.0	15.5	23.8	30.5
Yemen, Republic of	474	32.5	50.7	8.1	11.2	11.8	13.8	25.3	18.8	17.5	19.7	14.6	14.4
Western Hemisphere													
ECCU	309	8.1	13.8	2.3	8.1	13.4	13.6	9.2	6.4	7.6	8.7	11.6	8.0
Anguilla	312	11.8	25.6	3.4	9.0	20.1	9.2	17.9	12.4	13.0	8.2	20.6	31.5
Antigua and Barbuda	311	8.1	21.1	−3.3	7.2	15.9	26.8	6.3	5.2	5.6	16.0	6.1	9.0
Dominica	321	3.8	22.6	7.1	3.2	6.3	9.8	−2.2	6.1	9.9	6.5	4.7	4.0
Grenada	328	12.3	9.9	8.4	10.1	11.9	13.8	14.5	10.7	8.7	6.4	19.9	−4.3
Montserrat	351	21.3	−1.8	−7.7	14.9	15.0	−7.7	−7.9	2.8	−.5	11.7	8.5	3.5
St. Kitts and Nevis	361	1.4	15.5	1.6	14.3	11.0	3.7	27.9	1.1	7.3	14.6	16.6	4.3
St. Lucia	362	7.5	9.6	4.6	3.9	10.8	8.7	5.3	5.1	2.2	8.1	8.5	13.8
St. Vincent & Grens	364	6.3	4.5	6.1	12.1	14.9	17.0	5.1	8.0	5.1	3.1	10.0	6.5
Argentina	213	17.6	−2.8	18.8	25.5	10.5	4.1	1.5	−19.4	19.7	29.6	21.4	21.5
Aruba	314	13.9	4.2	4.3	4.0	13.6	10.2	2.0	6.4	10.5	9.0	2.6	6.4
Bahamas, The	313	8.7	8.5	5.6	23.5	16.2	10.6	9.3	4.9	3.0	3.7	9.2	10.8
Barbados	316	8.9	4.9	19.3	8.8	7.6	12.1	9.4	2.4	15.8	6.8	12.2	9.2
Belize	339	8.4	18.2	7.6	11.5	5.9	15.8	12.4	12.3	−1.7	4.7	8.6	7.5
Bolivia	218	24.2	7.7	24.2	16.7	12.9	5.7	.4	2.2	−6.9	13.9	2.2	22.2
Brazil	223	1,279.7	34.6	12.3	19.4	9.8	6.9	3.9	12.5	24.1	3.6	19.4	18.9
Chile	228	11.7	24.3	20.1	24.4	13.2	13.1	9.1	5.7	7.5	.6	17.5	19.1

Money plus Quasi-Money

Western Hemisphere(Cont.)		1994	1995	1996	1997	1998	1999	2000	2001	2002	2003	2004	2005
						Percent Change over Previous Year							
Colombia	233	39.7	21.7	24.4	41.9	20.9	13.7	14.7	16.0	13.6	9.9	18.1	19.2
Costa Rica	238	22.0	4.8	47.6	16.4	26.3	29.0	18.4	10.4	20.9	16.7	33.8	24.7
Dominican Republic	243	12.1	17.8	18.4	24.2	16.6	23.7	17.4	26.9	10.3	63.1	9.0	14.3
Ecuador	248	....	....	....	....	....	....	....	....	....	18.9	24.2	20.9
El Salvador	253	40.4	11.9	13.8	10.6	9.0	8.8	2.0	3.7	−3.1	2.3	1.6	2.7
Guatemala	258	12.0	15.8	13.8	18.4	19.4	12.5	35.5	18.1	11.8	15.0	9.4	14.0
Guyana	336	12.5	24.4	19.4	10.1	6.7	10.8	8.4	8.7	5.7	7.8	8.7	7.7
Haiti	263	31.4	27.1	1.1	24.8	9.7	23.0	20.1	14.1	22.8	39.0	5.2	17.8
Honduras	268	30.3	29.2	41.2	50.5	22.9	24.7	24.4	17.5	13.7	15.8	20.7	20.4
Jamaica	343	40.6	31.8	10.9	13.3	7.7	12.2	13.0	8.6	12.0	10.5	14.0	9.2
Mexico	273	20.1	31.9	27.0	33.0	17.4	18.7	−4.5	12.5	4.7	11.1	11.5	8.4
Netherlands Antilles	353	8.7	7.5	−3.5	2.1	4.0	5.6	2.8	14.8	11.5	7.3	11.5	10.1
Nicaragua	278	65.9	35.1	40.6	52.5	32.1	18.8	9.4	41.0	13.3	12.6	17.2	9.8
Panama	283	15.5	7.9	6.1	15.0	13.0	8.5	10.0	9.6	−.3	4.8	8.4	8.3
Paraguay	288	23.6	15.7	14.1	7.7	9.9	18.2	4.8	16.4	3.1	7.6	14.2	7.7
Peru	293	37.2	29.3	37.2	30.8	17.3	14.5	−.4	2.1	5.1	−2.4	3.1	16.8
Suriname	366	204.7	181.5	38.5	19.0	37.8	37.9	80.5	28.2	116.7	19.9	31.0	10.9
Trinidad and Tobago	369	16.7	4.0	5.8	11.3	14.5	4.2	11.7	6.9	5.7	−.7	14.1	29.4
Uruguay	298	42.1	39.0	36.6	28.4	19.3	13.1	7.2	19.0	28.2	12.5	−1.7	.3
Venezuela, Rep. Bol.	299	68.9	36.6	70.2	61.1	15.4	20.7	23.1	15.3	15.8	57.6	46.9	54.1

Ratio of Reserve Money to Money plus Quasi-Money

39abi		1994	1995	1996	1997	1998	1999	2000	2001	2002	2003	2004	2005
							Percent						
Industrial Countries													
United States	111	10.8	10.7	10.6	10.7	10.3	11.4	10.1	9.5	9.8	10.0	10.2	10.0
Canada	156	7.0	6.7	6.6	6.3	6.6	7.7	6.3	6.2	6.2	5.8	5.5	5.3
Australia	193	8.6	8.3	12.2	9.0	8.8	7.5	7.2	7.5	7.3	6.5	6.0	6.1
Japan	158	9.3	9.7	10.3	10.7	10.7	14.9	11.8	13.8	14.9	16.5	16.8	16.6
New Zealand	196	2.8	2.8	2.3	2.3	2.4	4.0	3.0	3.1	3.1	2.8	2.4	3.6
Euro Area													
Austria	122	10.3	9.7	10.1	9.8	....	....	....	....	....	....	....	....
Belgium	124	7.0	7.3	7.1	6.8	....	....	....	....	....	....	....	....
Finland	172	19.1	18.3	12.6	11.4	10.8	....	....	....	....	....	....	....
France	132	17.8	17.8	18.1	17.5	....	....	....	....	....	....	....	....
Germany	134	13.6	13.3	13.0	12.6	12.0	....	....	....	....	....	....	....
Ireland	178	13.2	10.9	9.6	9.5	....	....	....	....	....	....	....	....
Italy	136	17.6	16.2	16.2	18.5	13.0	....	....	....	....	....	....	....
Netherlands	138	11.7	9.7	8.8	9.1	....	....	....	....	....	....	....	....
Portugal	182	8.8	7.9	8.3	7.7	7.3	....	....	....	....	....	....	....
Denmark	128	4.6	4.9	6.0	7.4	5.5	11.1	9.0	8.2	8.8	9.0	7.5	7.5
Iceland	176	12.5	10.0	11.9	12.1	10.8	14.3	11.4	8.7	8.6	4.5	9.5	6.7
Norway	142	8.7	8.9	12.7	11.1	8.5	12.6	9.7	8.9	12.3	8.5	....	....
Sweden	144	27.6	21.9	13.7	9.4	9.1	10.0	8.8	9.8	9.4	9.1	9.0	8.2
Switzerland	146	9.0	8.4	8.0	7.4	7.5	7.8	8.4	9.1	8.0	8.0	7.5	7.2
United Kingdom	112	5.2	4.6	4.2	3.6	3.5	3.5	3.1	2.9	2.9	2.8	2.9	2.6
Developing Countries													
Africa													
CEMAC	758	....	....	....	....	....	....	49.0	48.7	48.4	48.2	51.4	55.4
Cameroon	622	26.2	22.0	31.4	37.1	38.0	36.2	40.8	43.4	47.8	41.8	45.8	42.9
Central African Republic	626	83.8	84.0	86.3	82.0	78.0	75.7	80.8	76.6	75.3	75.3	76.0	76.5
Chad	628	75.4	80.2	82.4	82.3	80.1	77.1	75.6	72.8	77.3	71.6	74.2	75.0
Congo, Rep. of	634	54.0	58.5	54.9	55.9	50.8	56.9	72.9	72.4	58.6	64.3	65.9	81.3
Equatorial Guinea	642	56.4	75.4	60.5	60.8	42.2	48.8	53.4	73.3	50.1	77.5	72.7	96.0
Gabon	646	41.1	35.7	39.3	35.9	33.4	31.7	36.5	32.6	31.2	36.1	39.3	41.7
WAEMU	759	42.3	40.4	38.6	40.0	41.5	40.9	42.6	47.2	49.3	46.9	45.2	43.3
Benin	638	43.2	32.5	31.4	36.0	35.7	46.5	51.9	57.0	53.3	49.2	44.1	46.2
Burkina Faso	748	51.7	52.4	52.2	54.8	52.3	43.8	41.3	40.7	30.7	51.6	41.4	36.4
Côte d'Ivoire	662	38.2	36.1	37.1	38.3	43.0	40.4	42.0	50.4	54.3	42.7	47.0	44.4
Guinea Bissau	654	65.3	60.3	56.4	58.1	56.7	62.7	73.1	79.0	84.0	76.5	85.0	94.8
Mali	678	48.8	50.2	47.7	47.2	42.8	47.7	53.8	50.3	57.7	60.2	52.5	54.9
Niger	692	46.9	51.1	51.5	51.5	40.6	46.4	42.9	48.5	46.4	59.9	55.5	55.6
Senegal	722	40.5	39.2	30.1	30.0	29.5	30.3	28.9	34.2	35.4	41.1	40.4	36.6
Togo	742	38.4	40.5	37.8	36.1	40.1	42.3	44.4	42.7	46.2	33.0	36.6	28.8
Algeria	612	32.3	31.9	33.4	32.8	31.2	30.6	33.1	37.5	34.4	42.6	42.6	41.2
Angola	614	....	71.9	59.8	66.8	63.5	49.6	38.6	36.5	30.7	33.0	37.6	38.9
Botswana	616	36.6	46.1	47.9	48.5	34.4	33.2	30.3	33.2	28.8	31.3	36.3	38.0
Burundi	618	40.0	44.7	42.8	39.9	42.6	39.2	36.6	35.1	33.4	31.9	37.2	41.5
Cape Verde	624	41.2	42.7	36.5	33.1	35.2	32.7	33.3	32.6	33.1	31.2	30.0	30.0
Comoros	632	52.4	50.1	62.2	56.9	59.1	59.4	65.3	75.9	82.7	82.4	85.4	81.6
Congo, Dem. Rep. of	636	40.3	66.1	62.1	19.3	81.1	63.6	5.9	64.3	55.7	54.4	52.0	47.9
Djibouti	611	19.6	16.2	16.9	17.3	17.7	19.2	18.9	18.5	17.4	19.4	16.2	14.6
Eritrea	643	....	41.6	64.0	94.2	51.0	51.8	47.6	34.6	33.6	33.1	31.5	30.6
Ethiopia	644	55.3	57.1	43.7	39.7	35.2	29.5	36.1	30.0	34.9	35.7	56.7	52.2
Gambia, The	648	38.3	42.1	40.0	41.2	40.1	40.9	35.4	35.9	35.6	40.4	37.9	37.5
Ghana	652	42.6	40.2	41.8	38.7	38.4	42.4	42.5	45.5	44.7	42.6	39.4	38.5
Guinea	656	58.1	58.6	55.8	60.1	59.2	....	63.0	64.2	65.2	57.7	57.4	49.3
Kenya	664	38.4	39.0	33.7	28.6	27.7	27.5	26.1	25.1	25.2	22.2	22.4	20.9
Lesotho	666	24.0	29.0	26.0	25.4	30.5	42.8	39.4	25.1	23.1	23.2	23.9	29.1
Liberia	668	70.2	71.2	95.2	99.3	49.1	46.0	54.9	54.5	55.2	54.9	61.2	57.9
Madagascar	674	39.6	44.1	56.6	47.3	47.5	50.2	47.9	50.1	48.5	44.5	42.3	46.1
Malawi	676	46.9	56.9	56.3	55.3	45.7	47.2	34.3	37.1	38.3	38.4	38.7	38.2
Mauritania	682	80.1	79.6	42.4	34.1	30.3	31.0	28.0	25.2	23.8	21.5	....	....
Mauritius	684	8.4	8.1	7.1	6.0	5.9	5.5	5.6	5.6	5.7	8.6	8.3	8.2
Morocco	686	27.3	26.8	27.1	27.1	27.4	28.1	26.8	28.5	27.7	29.7	31.0	29.8
Mozambique	688	38.7	34.5	36.7	34.4	28.1	25.0	22.8	27.2	26.3	27.1	30.9	28.5
Namibia	728	8.4	7.6	7.5	8.3	7.8	9.3	7.7	7.9	7.8	8.0	7.8	7.9
Nigeria	694	56.8	57.3	52.4	47.2	45.0	41.1	41.2	43.5	40.4	46.6	38.7	30.1
Rwanda	714	53.0	43.4	48.9	42.2	37.2	39.6	31.4	34.5	30.3	29.3	29.8	40.3
São Tomé and Príncipe	716	....	51.4	50.5	57.1	61.2	48.2	49.9	62.2	56.9	61.3	44.3	36.8
Seychelles	718	38.4	40.6	40.4	41.2	18.1	16.6	16.4	15.7	17.9	13.6	24.6	24.5
Sierra Leone	724	56.5	53.0	50.6	71.9	51.4	51.8	50.5	48.9	47.1	47.3	44.3	42.0
South Africa	199	7.2	8.2	8.1	7.9	7.3	7.9	7.2	7.2	8.9	8.6	9.1	8.5
Sudan	732	78.3	90.6	107.8	94.7	80.2	70.9	68.1	46.5	36.9	30.8	25.8	23.4
Swaziland	734	20.6	20.3	16.2	14.3	11.6	11.2	11.4	9.7	11.1	12.6	15.3	14.3
Tanzania	738	39.7	41.6	40.9	39.4	40.8	41.8	39.8	35.7	34.0	32.8	34.0	31.4
Tunisia	744	20.8	21.4	25.6	23.8	19.9	21.8	16.9	18.0	16.7	16.9	17.7	17.8
Uganda	746	44.9	44.8	41.9	38.3	37.4	37.9	39.1	40.6	35.9	33.8	36.7	35.6
Zambia	754	47.5	26.1	26.2	31.0	28.8	29.0	25.6	32.9	35.9	34.2	34.3	35.6
Zimbabwe	698	27.6	22.5	28.1	27.4	32.0	37.9	26.0	30.1	28.0	26.2	25.2	22.1
Asia													
Bangladesh	513	29.0	23.4	23.0	22.9	23.3	22.8	21.9	23.7	21.6	20.4	18.9	20.3
Bhutan	514	53.7	66.2	65.8	45.2	61.7	58.7	60.6	57.5	51.0	60.4	55.6	68.6
Brunei Darussalam	516	....	....	....	....	....	18.1	11.7	13.7	14.1	13.7	13.3	14.7
Cambodia	522	63.2	48.5	49.3	51.3	65.2	64.5	63.4	61.7	68.6	64.8	61.5	52.5

Ratio of Reserve Money to Money plus Quasi-Money

		1994	1995	1996	1997	1998	1999	2000	2001	2002	2003	2004	2005
39abi							*Percent*						
Asia(Cont.)													
China, P.R.: Mainland	924	36.7	34.2	35.3	33.3	29.7	27.8	26.8	25.5	24.4	23.9	23.3	21.6
China, P.R.: Hong Kong	532	9.8	9.2	8.6	8.4	7.7	8.5	7.2	7.7	8.2	9.2	8.6	8.0
Fiji	819	16.0	16.6	16.8	19.3	20.6	28.5	23.5	28.9	29.4	31.0	24.0	21.3
India	534	32.6	33.1	30.5	28.9	27.4	26.1	24.4	23.5	22.0	22.2	22.1	22.0
Indonesia	536	10.9	10.1	10.8	11.9	13.0	16.1	17.1	17.6	16.7	17.4	20.0	22.5
Korea	542	18.9	19.0	14.4	11.1	8.0	8.7	6.8	7.0	7.3	7.4	7.1	7.6
Lao People's Democratic Rep.	544	44.7	43.6	42.6	37.0	32.5	31.2	34.0	32.1	30.6	31.4	30.0	33.7
Malaysia	548	17.7	18.6	20.0	22.1	9.6	10.9	8.9	8.4	8.6	8.5	8.4	8.3
Maldives	556	76.9	67.4	63.0	59.0	53.3	55.0	55.2	55.6	55.4	47.4	45.1	42.8
Mongolia	948	37.8	36.8	42.8	37.0	44.5	50.9	52.0	43.4	37.3	28.6	27.7	24.2
Myanmar	518	73.8	69.1	65.6	66.0	62.3	57.0	53.8	56.8	56.9	82.0	80.0	78.2
Nepal	558	39.6	37.2	36.5	45.5	37.1	33.6	33.8	....	....	....	....	....
Pakistan	564	39.6	41.0	32.9	31.4	32.8	35.6	31.1	35.7	33.2	32.9	32.8	31.0
Papua New Guinea	853	12.7	12.9	18.8	11.5	13.5	21.5	17.1	17.7	18.8	19.6	22.2	18.4
Philippines	566	28.4	25.8	27.7	21.1	19.8	23.2	19.2	16.5	17.3	18.3	17.3	20.1
Samoa	862	43.5	36.5	41.4	42.8	22.7	23.8	22.3	20.0	21.8	21.2	22.6	20.2
Singapore	576	16.6	16.7	16.2	15.6	10.3	12.3	10.8	11.1	11.1	10.6	10.5	10.6
Solomon Islands	813	19.7	22.2	25.0	22.0	31.3	29.2	33.3	37.3	41.0	41.6	61.2	53.4
Sri Lanka	524	35.6	30.3	29.6	25.1	24.6	23.5	21.8	20.5	20.3	19.7	19.9	....
Thailand	578	10.2	10.6	10.8	10.6	9.0	11.1	8.6	8.6	9.5	10.1	10.8	10.7
Tonga	866	26.2	21.4	29.1	30.3	29.2	28.0	26.6	30.0	33.6	26.6	37.6	28.2
Vanuatu	846	11.1	12.8	11.1	11.2	10.4	14.0	13.6	12.8	13.0	14.1	14.2	14.1
Vietnam	582	....	58.2	55.6	50.3	44.3	40.0	36.9	33.9	33.6	32.2	28.5	26.9
Europe													
Albania	914	59.4	50.1	39.7	45.8	37.5	37.3	39.2	38.7	39.3	35.8	35.2	34.2
Armenia	911	61.2	71.6	75.7	73.1	56.1	49.2	47.7	50.8	52.5	50.7	46.8	56.9
Azerbaijan, Republic of	912	31.2	69.7	69.9	69.9	64.1	61.8	46.0	52.3	52.0	49.1	55.4	48.3
Belarus	913	25.3	38.0	44.4	43.6	30.5	36.5	25.7	32.3	28.4	27.3	26.6	32.8
Bosnia & Herzegovina	963	....	....	....	11.4	12.9	34.7	37.2	51.7	43.1	44.3	44.9	46.4
Bulgaria	918	20.3	21.9	18.8	38.5	38.0	39.4	33.5	34.7	33.3	32.2	36.4	32.9
Croatia	960	27.0	27.5	23.9	20.4	20.3	26.6	23.7	22.2	25.9	29.1	32.2	35.1
Cyprus	423	25.9	22.2	18.4	16.4	17.6	16.7	16.9	16.0	18.4	18.5	18.9	17.6
Czech Republic	935	24.3	28.9	27.3	26.9	31.8	33.8	31.1	29.4	15.1	15.1	15.0	14.9
Estonia	939	49.6	46.7	41.7	41.7	42.5	43.6	39.8	29.2	25.9	26.7	28.6	26.8
Georgia	915	....	82.7	80.4	74.6	70.5	69.5	63.4	58.5	59.3	55.2	57.0	52.3
Hungary	944	27.3	26.6	19.9	21.6	22.6	24.6	25.7	22.5	20.8	20.4	20.9	20.0
Kazakhstan	916	42.3	43.3	45.5	57.5	47.2	39.9	29.2	31.5	28.8	33.8	36.4	33.5
Kyrgyz Republic	917	....	73.6	79.5	72.8	66.7	65.2	65.2	65.3	69.6	69.2	63.8	72.5
Latvia	941	38.6	49.9	51.3	49.1	49.2	50.7	43.0	40.6	40.1	34.9	32.7	34.1
Lithuania	946	41.6	43.5	46.1	45.5	51.2	45.6	37.8	33.7	34.8	37.3	32.2	30.9
Macedonia, FYR	962	34.4	40.2	39.4	39.1	36.5	35.9	43.3	35.5	31.8	29.6	25.4	28.6
Malta	181	37.2	29.3	25.8	24.3	23.1	22.5	22.4	21.4	21.6	21.9	22.3	21.6
Moldova	921	73.3	62.6	59.7	59.1	60.1	59.0	54.5	51.3	48.5	43.4	43.4	....
Poland	964	25.4	27.3	25.1	26.0	24.3	20.1	16.6	18.8	18.8	19.1	18.7	17.6
Romania	968	35.8	32.9	29.7	34.3	27.8	36.9	41.4	45.3	50.7	49.3	60.9	71.8
Russia	922	48.1	47.0	46.2	45.7	42.6	44.9	47.6	45.0	44.2	49.2	45.6	41.0
Slovak Republic	936	16.2	17.9	19.8	21.6	19.4	20.9	18.9	20.7	20.2	17.0	16.1	18.9
Slovenia	961	12.9	12.4	11.6	11.6	11.6	12.3	10.6	11.0	9.6	9.5	9.2	9.0
Turkey	186	22.9	20.2	17.8	18.0	17.1	16.9	17.6	16.8	15.3	15.9	17.3	19.6
Ukraine	926	43.1	46.6	48.2	53.6	51.1	51.4	51.2	51.0	47.9	42.4	42.8	42.8
Middle East													
Bahrain	419	12.9	16.2	13.9	14.5	9.7	13.6	12.3	12.9	13.3	16.8	16.9	17.3
Egypt	469	32.3	32.2	30.2	30.3	32.7	31.4	33.4	34.6	33.4	38.4	39.8	37.3
Iran, I.R. of	429	40.1	45.6	43.8	43.5	42.7	41.1	39.2	32.7	33.1	30.5	28.3	28.2
Israel	436	15.6	9.4	10.1	19.3	18.4	19.7	18.4	16.9	13.3	12.3	9.2	7.3
Jordan	439	51.9	52.2	45.6	41.2	36.9	35.8	33.5	29.3	28.0	28.1	26.2	25.6
Kuwait	443	7.5	6.4	6.5	5.6	5.9	7.6	6.5	5.7	6.1	6.6	6.7	6.1
Lebanon	446	19.4	20.2	19.4	24.3	19.8	18.7	18.1	23.1	23.6	46.3	43.4	40.7
Libya	672	59.9	58.9	63.6	70.4	67.1	59.2	56.8	60.0	58.0	60.5	77.8	87.5
Oman	449	21.1	20.3	20.0	17.4	17.8	16.6	17.0	16.9	20.9	21.6	19.1	22.4
Qatar	453	11.0	11.4	11.5	11.5	11.4	11.0	10.6	11.9	12.4	12.3	13.4	12.8
Saudi Arabia	456	24.1	22.8	20.9	21.4	20.4	23.6	21.6	19.8	18.7	18.2	17.3	16.9
Syrian Arab Rep.	463	56.9	54.5	53.2	51.6	49.0	46.3	44.9	42.4	41.5	42.5	46.1	....
United Arab Emirates	466	22.4	22.9	23.2	21.4	20.6	24.1	28.5	24.5	21.7	21.1	22.0	20.2
Yemen, Republic of	474	90.6	72.0	71.3	56.1	55.8	59.2	53.9	51.7	48.1	48.7	48.6	51.5
Western Hemisphere													
ECCU	309	19.1	18.8	17.1	16.8	17.5	16.4	15.6	16.7	16.8	17.2	17.5	15.3
Anguilla	312	12.1	12.9	14.2	14.7	13.7	14.0	12.2	14.0	12.5	14.6	12.5	11.0
Antigua and Barbuda	311	18.7	18.2	15.5	15.2	14.8	13.3	12.2	13.9	13.9	15.2	14.8	14.4
Dominica	321	18.6	17.8	16.6	16.5	17.3	17.7	17.6	16.5	21.4	19.4	17.3	17.4
Grenada	328	19.4	19.1	17.7	18.1	17.2	16.0	15.4	15.5	16.9	17.4	20.3	16.3
Montserrat	351	20.2	22.4	25.0	27.5	51.4	31.2	25.4	28.4	32.4	30.7	26.0	24.6
St. Kitts and Nevis	361	22.7	19.3	18.4	17.2	18.5	20.2	17.0	18.6	20.2	17.1	17.9	15.7
St. Lucia	362	18.6	18.9	17.3	16.9	17.4	16.5	16.3	18.0	18.0	18.7	20.7	16.0
St. Vincent & Grens.	364	23.0	20.8	19.1	18.6	19.6	19.6	22.4	22.8	19.4	19.6	18.9	18.1
Argentina	213	30.4	26.5	22.8	20.6	19.1	18.5	16.7	24.4	34.6	44.3	44.0	36.7
Aruba	314	19.5	22.1	18.1	16.7	20.7	19.9	17.3	21.5	22.1	19.1	19.6	18.6
Bahamas, The	313	13.2	12.5	11.5	10.7	11.0	12.0	10.7	11.3	12.3	12.6	15.2	12.6
Barbados	316	15.7	17.3	19.5	16.2	16.4	15.2	15.6	17.5	21.0	23.6	14.9	13.8
Belize	339	22.3	21.4	20.4	19.3	19.6	20.6	22.5	25.5	20.0	19.9	20.6	22.3
Bolivia	218	22.9	26.3	24.5	25.2	17.7	18.6	20.5	22.4	24.5	24.4	28.1	35.0
Brazil	223	29.0	24.1	26.3	29.6	24.0	24.2	24.4	25.8	52.0	48.1	44.6	40.5
Chile	228	18.8	18.3	17.0	14.7	14.2	13.1	11.2	11.5	10.4	11.7	12.1	13.1

Ratio of Reserve Money to Money plus Quasi-Money

Western Hemisphere(Cont.)		1994	1995	1996	1997	1998	1999	2000	2001	2002	2003	2004	2005
							Percent						
Colombia	233	44.7	39.2	37.0	30.4	20.9	25.6	24.4	23.1	24.5	25.9	25.3	25.1
Costa Rica	238	51.9	57.5	47.5	47.7	42.0	34.9	28.1	18.9	16.3	18.1	17.1	16.8
Dominican Republic	243	41.5	41.0	38.4	36.8	38.6	35.9	33.7	34.3	28.4	36.2	35.1	38.1
Ecuador	248	42.8	36.1	36.0	35.9	32.2	25.5	13.6	14.1	8.7	8.5	7.5	8.8
El Salvador	253	24.5	24.6	23.8	24.3	24.2	24.5	21.7	14.8	11.9	17.7	14.0	14.1
Guatemala	258	50.3	45.0	44.6	46.3	37.3	34.1	30.0	29.5	31.2	30.2	32.5	30.7
Guyana	336	39.0	37.3	33.1	35.2	36.9	32.0	33.7	34.4	35.8	36.6	38.0	38.0
Haiti	263	55.4	50.0	47.4	42.2	38.6	40.4	42.3	43.4	43.8	41.4	46.5	40.9
Honduras	268	32.0	30.7	31.2	39.8	37.6	33.6	29.5	27.6	30.7	28.2	32.4	35.3
Jamaica	343	38.1	37.5	35.1	35.7	40.5	34.6	33.0	28.4	24.6	27.7	27.1	25.0
Mexico	273	8.9	9.1	8.8	9.8	11.1	12.8	14.8	13.8	15.4	15.9	16.0	16.5
Netherlands Antilles	353	14.9	16.7	14.8	16.7	17.7	15.8	16.6	19.7	22.1	19.3	20.8	20.3
Nicaragua	278	50.7	46.4	44.4	38.5	34.9	31.1	29.7	29.9	29.2	30.9	30.5	32.1
Panama	283	5.0	4.8	6.3	5.6	5.1	4.7	4.4	4.1	4.0	3.8	3.7	3.8
Paraguay	288	29.3	32.0	27.5	27.4	26.6	24.5	23.1	21.1	21.0	29.5	30.3	29.4
Peru	293	38.8	39.4	39.5	41.9	37.8	38.2	39.1	40.0	41.3	39.6	40.5	45.2
Suriname	366	61.4	71.3	46.2	38.6	46.3	49.5	69.9	62.4	37.9	29.0	26.7	26.5
Trinidad and Tobago	369	22.7	21.6	22.3	23.2	24.5	24.4	22.5	23.3	21.7	23.3	19.8	23.5
Uruguay	298	31.6	29.6	28.8	28.0	26.9	28.8	29.4	31.2	24.5	35.0	29.2	32.7
Venezuela, Rep. Bol.	299	31.9	30.8	35.6	38.4	39.4	43.4	40.5	39.3	40.6	37.9	37.5	34.1

Income Velocity of Money plus Quasi-Money

Index Numbers: 2000=100

		1994	1995	1996	1997	1998	1999	2000	2001	2002	2003	2004	2005
Industrial Countries													
United States	111	109.6	108.5	108.1	107.7	103.1	101.0	100.0	90.5	89.6	91.7	95.2	95.6
Canada	156	106.8	105.8	104.0	101.1	102.4	104.0	100.0	96.6	95.4	93.8	90.4	88.9
Australia	193	114.8	111.5	107.3	105.3	102.6	96.4	100.0	93.9	95.0	89.1	85.4	84.9
Japan	158	114.5	113.0	112.5	111.3	104.9	99.9	100.0	97.0	92.5	91.1	90.6	90.0
New Zealand	196	110.4	107.6	97.2	95.8	95.8	96.8	100.0	100.8	97.7	94.3	96.0	89.5
Euro Area													
Austria	122	....	....	....	....	....	....	....	....	....	....	....	....
Belgium	124	....	....	....	....	....	....	....	....	....	....	....	....
Finland	172	....	....	....	....	....	....	....	....	....	....	....	....
France	132	....	....	....	....	....	....	....	....	....	....	....	....
Germany	134	....	....	....	....	....	....	....	....	....	....	....	....
Greece	174	104.4	104.4	101.8	102.3	104.0	94.0	100.0	....	....	....	....	....
Ireland	178	....	....	....	....	....	....	....	....	....	....	....	....
Italy	136	....	....	....	....	....	....	....	....	....	....	....	....
Luxembourg	137	....	....	....	....	....	....	....	....	....	....	....	....
Netherlands	138	....	....	....	....	....	....	....	....	....	....	....	....
Portugal	182	....	....	....	....	....	....	....	....	....	....	....	....
Spain	184	....	....	....	....	....	....	....	....	....	....	....	....
Denmark	128	90.0	88.4	85.7	84.5	84.5	88.9	100.0	99.7	98.3	95.1	89.2	81.3
Iceland	176	113.4	114.0	115.2	116.0	111.8	102.6	100.0	98.2	89.2	75.5	73.6	61.6
Norway	142	85.4	88.3	90.5	96.5	85.2	91.2	100.0	95.5	88.4	88.7	....	....
Sweden	144	114.4	114.7	109.4	106.1	103.2	101.5	100.0	105.1	105.0	104.6	106.9	99.0
Switzerland	146	107.0	103.5	94.9	90.6	88.4	79.5	100.0	97.8	94.3	87.8	87.6	84.1
United Kingdom	112	174.5	153.3	142.3	120.2	119.5	105.7	100.0	96.3	96.4	93.0	89.5	81.9
Developing Countries													
Africa													
CEMAC													
Cameroon	622	83.3	102.4	126.2	115.9	113.8	108.3	100.0	93.8	86.3	....	....	....
Central African Republic	626	69.8	78.9	69.7	80.2	99.7	96.8	100.0	106.6	112.3	116.9	103.6	94.4
Chad	628	129.1	95.1	85.1	98.4	117.4	113.8	100.0	103.6	90.4	107.2	152.1	139.5
Congo, Rep. of	634	89.3	96.0	102.1	97.3	95.5	100.3	100.0	115.6	105.1	105.4	99.5	96.5
Equatorial Guinea	642	48.7	38.3	42.5	91.4	74.3	65.0	100.0	98.7	69.5	52.9	61.7	65.6
Gabon	646	107.2	103.5	104.8	101.6	89.0	90.3	100.0	84.2	86.9	89.3	87.0	....
WAEMU	759	....	95.9	98.1	101.9	107.5	106.0	100.0	96.2	87.4	....	....	....
Benin	638	100.5	124.9	123.3	129.1	146.5	115.0	100.0	97.2	111.7	106.6	121.3	104.0
Burkina Faso	748	107.3	98.9	104.4	95.3	108.5	106.3	100.0	111.2	120.2	83.3	97.9	113.7
Côte d'Ivoire	662	76.5	76.0	81.3	92.6	96.3	100.5	100.0	93.1	74.2	100.8	92.2	89.3
Guinea Bissau	654	662.4	457.0	337.4	184.6	155.2	144.8	100.0	88.6	70.2	194.4	145.3	128.2
Mali	678	88.4	114.3	96.7	98.3	103.2	107.3	100.0	97.7	79.2	67.8	70.3	68.7
Niger	692	54.0	62.6	73.1	97.4	135.1	118.8	100.0	83.8	92.2	66.9	56.2	56.8
Senegal	722	109.3	115.1	109.6	111.2	111.6	105.2	100.0	94.3	90.8	74.4	66.5	67.4
Togo	742	86.9	100.1	117.0	130.3	123.6	118.2	100.0	103.7	111.7	104.6	90.9	95.1
Algeria	612	82.2	101.5	113.8	103.8	88.9	89.4	100.0	82.9	63.7	63.1	....	....
Angola	614	....	46.5	67.2	81.9	75.8	76.6	100.0	82.5	69.0	101.9	122.2	113.2
Botswana	616	122.3	121.0	118.0	114.6	93.4	78.9	100.0	95.9	98.9	91.1	88.0	91.1
Burundi	618	94.5	98.4	83.3	99.2	120.3	93.0	100.0	93.0	76.3	72.6	71.6	69.3
Ethiopia	644	98.6	108.1	111.0	110.5	110.7	105.7	100.0	92.8	95.6	91.8	94.6	91.2
Kenya	664	92.5	83.3	75.5	74.0	80.1	80.6	100.0	103.1	93.5	91.8	90.1	92.5
Lesotho	666	81.6	84.8	86.7	87.9	79.3	94.6	100.0	94.0	97.0	100.0	106.2	102.7
Madagascar	674	84.0	106.7	110.8	102.0	108.3	104.4	100.0	91.8	85.6	88.8	85.3	103.3
Malawi	676	70.4	91.8	107.3	131.8	99.2	109.8	100.0	96.5	94.2	85.6	79.6	81.2
Mauritius	684	110.3	102.2	107.4	102.5	104.6	98.1	100.0	99.0	94.7	95.3	88.0	78.3
Morocco	686	123.3	116.4	123.5	113.9	116.1	105.8	100.0	94.8	92.5	89.8	88.1	79.7
Mozambique	688	110.1	115.8	153.7	151.0	151.3	127.6	100.0	105.4	110.2	109.5	121.4	112.5
Namibia	728	122.0	109.5	104.3	107.7	109.3	100.7	100.0	108.1	....	....	....	....
Nigeria	694	71.3	129.1	158.6	142.3	114.0	98.7	100.0	76.9	72.9	75.3	78.6	98.3
Rwanda	714	72.1	87.0	100.2	102.2	109.8	105.7	100.0	96.1	93.3	88.7	79.5	74.3
Seychelles	718	152.3	131.0	118.5	115.3	112.7	98.5	100.0	91.5	87.2	81.6	82.4	78.7
Sierra Leone	724	157.7	162.1	164.8	107.8	122.1	101.7	100.0	90.0	85.3	82.7	85.8	75.8
South Africa	199	116.8	116.1	114.5	111.1	105.2	100.9	100.0	96.7	119.7	112.1	113.6	104.1
Swaziland	734	74.3	87.0	85.9	83.7	83.4	81.6	100.0	101.7	104.0	104.2	102.3	102.1
Tanzania	738	77.6	76.6	88.2	97.6	104.3	101.6	100.0	97.2	88.6	86.0	83.5	69.4
Tunisia	744	119.5	120.9	119.2	112.2	114.9	105.7	100.0	97.5	97.1	98.2	96.5	91.8
Uganda	746	143.4	145.7	133.5	124.7	111.6	109.5	100.0	98.6	84.1	83.8	75.0	76.7
Zimbabwe	698	103.1	90.1	93.9	79.3	100.0	117.4	100.0	94.4	77.5	47.5	62.2	53.5
Asia													
Bangladesh	513	119.4	119.9	118.1	116.9	116.3	110.5	100.0	93.3	88.7	86.3	82.2	77.6
Bhutan	514	164.2	141.8	152.8	116.5	116.7	103.4	100.0	....	....	....	....	....
Brunei Darussalam	516	....	....	....	....	....	141.8	100.0	114.3	114.7	119.1	115.2	138.7
Cambodia	522	203.8	168.9	131.0	123.8	123.8	120.8	100.0	91.8	75.4	71.4	63.4	65.5
China, P.R.: Mainland	924	151.4	146.6	136.7	124.1	113.9	103.9	100.0	95.9	88.8	83.7	96.4	93.0
China, P.R.: Hong Kong	532	141.9	136.6	133.8	136.6	116.4	105.3	100.0	99.1	96.8	88.1	85.9	88.8
Fiji	819	80.3	78.9	84.3	93.8	102.5	104.8	100.0	108.6	107.0	93.2	91.4	....
India	534	118.8	125.6	121.8	115.2	111.5	107.0	100.0	94.7	87.1	86.8	84.1	82.2
Indonesia	536	118.9	110.9	102.3	96.2	90.0	92.3	100.0	107.4	113.4	114.8	118.2	121.9
Korea	542	182.3	184.9	179.6	172.2	133.7	114.8	100.0	95.0	94.1	93.4	101.1	101.6
Lao People's Democratic Rep.	544	110.1	122.1	116.3	89.5	80.8	110.4	100.0	101.0	86.0	79.1	85.1	93.2
Malaysia	548	121.6	116.8	106.1	101.5	101.8	96.4	100.0	95.2	98.6	99.5	101.4	105.0
Maldives	556	133.7	131.9	118.0	108.0	93.3	98.3	100.0	95.5	85.6	80.8	68.3	60.2
Nepal	558	141.2	134.4	136.1	118.7	114.5	107.1	100.0	....	....	....	....	....

Income Velocity of Money plus Quasi-Money

39adi		1994	1995	1996	1997	1998	1999	2000	2001	2002	2003	2004	2005
						Index Numbers: 2000=100							
Asia(Cont.)													
Pakistan	564	85.1	89.3	84.5	80.8	82.6	86.9	100.0	98.2	88.9	82.8	78.9	80.1
Philippines	566	130.6	118.7	109.4	99.2	100.4	95.9	100.0	104.5	103.3	108.6	111.2	116.5
Singapore	576	122.7	124.7	124.1	122.7	91.3	85.7	100.0	90.7	93.9	88.7	93.9	94.5
Solomon Islands	813	90.6	97.9	98.3	97.3	107.9	107.5	100.0	118.8	117.3	....	....	....
Sri Lanka	524	116.5	98.9	102.3	102.6	106.4	99.3	100.0	98.5	97.7	94.3	90.8	....
Thailand	578	137.6	134.8	134.2	115.2	102.3	98.8	100.0	98.9	101.2	105.0	109.2	112.7
Vietnam	582	222.7	225.5	213.2	197.7	184.3	122.6	100.0	85.6	84.1	72.4	64.2	57.6
Europe													
Albania	914	161.0	132.2	125.9	100.3	106.4	100.1	100.0	92.3	92.7	94.1	92.0	....
Armenia	911	112.3	190.8	178.8	168.4	146.3	132.7	100.0	109.3	94.6	102.2	98.1	90.3
Belarus	913	45.3	119.6	124.0	112.2	57.1	105.8	100.0	115.9	117.3	104.7	98.3	88.6
Bosnia & Herzegovina	963	....	....	....	109.7	102.3	99.5	100.0	57.4	55.8	53.2	....	....
Bulgaria	918	46.2	55.1	49.3	108.0	124.3	116.3	100.0	88.2	85.4	75.9	67.8	59.7
Croatia	960	238.1	190.8	140.3	116.2	114.3	119.8	100.0	74.5	74.4	73.6	73.0	71.0
Cyprus	423	126.5	128.6	120.6	114.3	113.5	100.7	100.0	94.8	90.8	93.4	94.1	91.1
Czech Republic	935	94.7	90.8	96.6	102.2	108.7	110.1	100.0	96.9	103.2	101.7	105.4	103.0
Estonia	939	131.5	141.6	134.3	119.6	130.6	110.6	100.0	91.4	92.0	90.4	86.7	71.2
Hungary	944	87.6	93.2	93.6	96.9	99.0	96.7	100.0	97.2	96.2	94.3	94.9	89.3
Kazakhstan	916	109.3	121.6	129.8	142.2	170.5	117.5	100.0	101.0	86.8	84.7	65.9	66.4
Kyrgyz Republic	917	....	65.8	83.1	82.4	78.1	83.3	100.0	101.6	77.4	64.6	55.0	53.1
Latvia	941	90.0	130.5	130.1	110.0	113.0	114.1	100.0	91.7	84.4	76.7	70.2	61.0
Lithuania	946	88.5	103.8	135.8	123.5	121.5	110.2	100.0	87.3	79.9	73.8	65.4	56.0
Macedonia, FYR	962	153.2	158.7	166.8	142.4	132.1	107.3	100.0	74.9	67.5	60.1	54.6	....
Malta	181	97.2	96.8	93.5	102.4	99.9	96.0	100.0	94.3	88.9	96.0	93.8	94.2
Moldova	921	140.2	116.0	121.6	103.4	115.3	109.0	100.0	87.6	74.8	70.2	58.2	....
Poland	964	115.2	127.8	122.3	115.6	107.6	100.0	100.0	91.0	97.0	95.7	98.0	92.7
Romania	968	107.6	91.7	82.7	93.7	93.0	93.7	100.0	99.4	93.3	98.7	88.0	75.5
Russia	922	101.1	111.2	120.7	109.3	89.1	104.3	100.0	89.8	81.3	71.8	68.8	64.2
Slovak Republic	936	106.0	104.2	99.3	102.3	106.8	103.3	100.0	96.9	101.5	100.7	105.4	110.5
Slovenia	961	138.1	138.1	129.0	118.9	110.4	107.6	100.0	85.6	85.0	86.9	86.9	84.8
Turkey	186	144.9	142.8	125.1	123.6	118.0	87.3	100.0	76.9	92.7	104.8	102.7	92.8
Ukraine	926	68.6	144.1	159.5	136.4	122.6	110.9	100.0	84.0	65.3	52.6	51.1	40.9
Middle East													
Bahrain	419	111.8	109.3	110.6	106.7	89.0	91.6	100.0	91.1	87.9	94.0	103.5	99.5
Egypt	469	90.7	96.2	97.6	98.8	99.6	100.9	100.0	93.2	87.4	79.4	80.6	80.1
Iran, I.R. of	429	85.8	94.0	94.8	90.3	84.3	92.1	100.0	90.7	100.2	96.3	99.3	....
Israel	436	128.2	122.9	115.3	113.4	104.7	98.8	100.0	92.9	89.6	91.3	91.9	87.4
Jordan	439	105.5	110.8	116.5	113.2	116.3	103.7	100.0	98.1	96.3	87.7	....	....
Kuwait	443	79.0	79.4	92.8	87.2	75.5	86.2	100.0	81.9	86.7	95.5	101.7	....
Libya	672	69.1	67.6	76.3	92.1	79.9	82.5	100.0	98.5	124.7	144.5	154.3	159.5
Oman	449	111.3	110.5	113.1	94.2	80.0	83.8	100.0	91.9	89.0	93.1	101.8	104.2
Qatar	453	64.8	70.8	74.6	84.7	71.2	77.2	100.0	99.9	99.3	103.1	102.7	....
Saudi Arabia	456	96.0	98.5	101.7	101.1	86.3	89.2	100.0	92.4	82.7	86.7	86.3	94.2
Syrian Arab Rep.	463	108.7	112.3	123.4	123.0	118.0	107.8	100.0	85.4	76.7	73.8	....	....
Yemen, Republic of	474	58.2	64.2	84.4	91.0	78.1	95.4	100.0	88.4	83.9	81.0	....	....
Western Hemisphere													
ECCU	309	131.5	119.6	122.4	119.6	112.4	104.9	100.0	94.5	88.8	....	....	....
Anguilla	312	149.9	120.5	123.0	126.4	118.9	115.8	100.0	90.7	82.4	79.2	81.7	....
Antigua and Barbuda	311	148.1	120.7	136.7	137.1	126.3	104.6	100.0	100.1	97.2	88.4	90.5	....
Dominica	321	122.0	102.6	102.6	103.1	102.7	96.5	100.0	92.5	80.8	77.8	81.0	....
Grenada	328	122.6	117.4	116.8	114.2	112.2	106.1	100.0	87.2	82.7	84.6	69.5	....
Montserrat	351	186.0	179.3	208.3	115.0	91.8	93.8	100.0	97.0	106.8	95.5	95.4	94.6
St. Kitts and Nevis	361	127.8	119.2	125.1	123.2	115.7	118.5	100.0	102.8	98.1	89.1	84.7	....
St. Lucia	362	110.7	111.3	109.6	107.4	106.5	103.1	100.0	92.3	92.6	90.0	88.4	86.1
St. Vincent & Grens.	364	125.9	132.9	132.1	123.4	116.1	103.6	100.0	95.4	94.8	95.8	94.4	....
Argentina	213	153.3	158.1	140.4	120.3	111.2	101.3	100.0	117.4	114.0	105.8	103.7	101.5
Aruba	314	....	98.5	98.6	105.2	100.7	94.6	100.0	96.0	87.5	84.4	87.3	....
Barbados	316	122.4	125.3	112.1	113.2	113.6	105.9	100.0	97.1	81.6	83.4	77.4	....
Belize	339	136.3	123.2	118.4	108.3	107.7	98.9	100.0	92.9	100.8	101.9	99.1	....
Bolivia	218	99.5	107.8	101.0	96.1	95.7	93.1	100.0	101.3	114.6	110.0	120.1	111.3
Brazil	223	69.8	96.0	103.0	96.4	92.2	91.9	100.0	96.8	87.5	97.7	92.9	85.7
Chile	228	151.6	145.5	133.7	119.5	111.1	99.9	100.0	101.5	100.5	109.9	106.2	99.4
Colombia	233	130.9	134.4	128.9	109.7	104.8	99.4	100.0	93.0	88.3	90.3	85.8	79.9
Costa Rica	238	117.2	142.1	112.5	117.1	112.7	108.7	100.0	99.5	92.4	91.2	79.3	74.9
Dominican Republic	243	138.1	135.4	127.3	118.8	116.1	103.7	100.0	85.5	86.3	68.5	95.7	96.6
Ecuador	248	178.2	180.6	177.2	183.4	168.1	112.3	100.0	122.9	96.1	90.4	81.1	....
El Salvador	253	104.8	110.1	105.0	102.5	101.5	96.8	100.0	101.3	108.3	110.6	115.3	....
Guatemala	258	141.5	139.4	137.3	131.1	126.2	122.4	100.0	93.2	92.1	86.9	87.1	85.9
Haiti	263	103.7	93.0	121.6	112.8	120.0	107.2	100.0	96.8	86.5	79.2	88.2	89.7
Honduras	268	169.0	170.0	153.3	130.8	122.3	107.3	100.0	94.3	90.6	87.2	82.3	78.4
Jamaica	343	107.6	103.0	110.4	106.1	105.8	100.6	100.0	101.3	99.4	103.7	103.9	....
Mexico	273	76.8	75.3	81.5	77.0	79.4	79.9	100.0	94.1	96.8	95.9	96.3	96.4
Nicaragua	278	199.3	177.2	146.9	109.9	98.3	96.8	100.0	78.3	71.9	68.9	68.0	71.0
Panama	283	129.4	122.6	124.4	117.0	112.3	108.5	100.0	92.7	96.6	97.2	98.4	....
Paraguay	288	107.6	110.0	107.9	105.9	107.9	94.0	100.0	89.7	99.0	111.6	....	....
Peru	293	165.0	156.5	129.2	113.5	102.0	93.4	100.0	99.5	99.9	108.9	117.1	110.6
Trinidad and Tobago	369	93.2	96.9	99.9	93.1	86.3	93.2	100.0	100.1	95.4	114.8	109.3	106.3
Uruguay	298	127.7	127.7	124.8	121.9	116.8	104.6	100.0	85.5	70.4	75.7	92.6	100.1
Venezuela, Rep. Bol.	299	69.9	80.8	102.1	90.3	93.3	91.7	100.0	96.9	101.5	80.1	83.8	....

National Interest Rates

		1994	1995	1996	1997	1998	1999	2000	2001	2002	2003	2004	2005
							Central Bank Discount Rates (60) *(End of period in percent per annum)*						

		1994	1995	1996	1997	1998	1999	2000	2001	2002	2003	2004	2005
Industrial Countries													
United States	111	4.75	5.25	5.00	5.00	4.50	5.00	6.00	1.25	.75	† 2.00	3.15	5.15
Canada	156	7.43	5.79	3.25	4.50	5.25	5.00	6.00	2.50	3.00	3.00	2.75	3.50
Australia	193	5.75	5.75	....	....	....	....	....	....	....	....	....	....
Japan	158	1.75	.50	.50	.50	.50	.50	.50	.10	.10	.10	.10	.10
New Zealand	196	9.75	9.80	8.80	9.70	5.60	5.00	6.50	4.75	5.75	5.00	6.50	7.25
Euro Area	163	....	....	....	....	....	4.00	5.75	4.25	3.75	3.00	3.00	3.25
Austria	122	4.50	3.00	2.50	2.50	2.50	....	....	....	....	....	....	....
Belgium	124	4.50	3.00	2.50	2.75	2.75	....	....	....	....	....	....	....
Finland	172	5.25	4.88	4.00	4.00	3.50	....	....	....	....	....	2.25	....
Germany	134	4.50	3.00	2.50	2.50	2.50	....	....	....	....	....	....	....
Greece	174	20.50	18.00	16.50	14.50	....	† 11.81	8.10	....	....	....	....	....
Ireland	178	6.25	6.50	6.25	6.75	4.06	....	....	....	....	....	....	....
Italy	136	7.50	9.00	7.50	5.50	3.00	....	....	....	....	....	....	....
Portugal	182	8.88	8.50	6.70	5.31	3.00	....	....	....	....	....	....	....
Spain	184	7.38	9.00	6.25	4.75	3.00	....	....	....	....	....	....	....
Denmark	128	5.00	4.25	3.25	3.50	3.50	3.00	4.75	3.25	2.86	2.00	2.00	2.25
Iceland	176	4.70	5.93	5.70	6.55	† 8.50	10.00	12.40	12.00	8.20	7.70	10.25	....
Norway	142	6.75	6.75	6.00	5.50	10.00	7.50	9.00	8.50	8.50	4.25	3.75	4.25
Sweden	144	7.00	7.00	3.50	2.50	2.00	1.50	2.00	2.00	† 4.50	3.00	2.00	1.50
Switzerland	146	3.50	1.50	1.00	1.00	1.00	.50	† 3.20	1.59	.50	.11	.54	.73
Developing Countries													
Africa													
CEMAC	758	† 7.75	8.60	7.75	7.50	7.00	7.30	7.00	6.50	6.30	6.00	6.00	5.50
Cameroon	622	† 7.75	8.60	7.75	7.50	7.00	7.30	7.00	6.50	6.30	6.00	6.00	5.50
Central African Rep.	626	† 7.75	8.60	7.75	7.50	7.00	7.60	7.00	6.50	6.30	6.00	6.00	5.50
Chad	628	† 7.75	8.60	7.75	7.50	7.00	7.60	7.00	6.50	6.30	6.00	6.00	5.50
Congo, Republic of	634	† 7.75	8.60	7.75	7.50	7.00	7.60	7.00	6.50	6.30	6.00	6.00	5.50
Equatorial Guinea	642	† 7.75	8.60	7.75	7.50	7.00	7.60	7.00	6.50	6.30	6.00	6.00	5.50
Gabon	646	† 7.75	8.60	7.75	7.50	7.00	7.60	7.00	6.50	6.30	6.00	6.00	5.50
WAEMU	759	....	6.00	6.00	6.00	6.00	6.00	6.00	6.00	6.00	4.50	4.00	4.00
Benin	638	6.00	6.00	6.00	6.00	6.00	6.00	6.00	6.00	6.00	4.50	4.00	4.00
Burkina Faso	748	6.00	6.00	6.00	6.00	6.00	6.00	6.00	6.00	6.00	4.50	4.00	4.00
Côte d'Ivoire	662	6.00	6.00	6.00	6.00	6.00	6.00	6.00	6.00	6.00	4.50	4.00	4.00
Guinea-Bissau	654	6.00	6.00	6.00	6.00	6.00	6.00	6.00	6.00	6.00	4.50	4.00	4.00
Mali	678	6.00	6.00	6.00	6.00	6.00	6.00	6.00	6.00	6.00	4.50	4.00	4.00
Niger	692	6.00	6.00	6.00	6.00	6.00	6.00	6.00	6.00	6.00	4.50	4.00	4.00
Senegal	722	6.00	6.00	6.00	6.00	6.00	6.00	6.00	6.00	6.00	4.50	4.00	4.00
Togo	742	6.00	6.00	6.00	6.00	6.00	6.00	6.00	6.00	6.00	4.50	4.00	4.00
Algeria	612	21.00	† 14.00	13.00	11.00	9.50	8.50	6.00	6.00	5.50	4.50	4.00	4.00
Angola	614	....	160.00	2.00	48.00	58.00	120.00	150.00	150.00	150.00	150.00	95.00	95.00
Botswana	616	13.50	13.00	13.00	12.00	12.75	13.75	14.25	14.25	15.25	14.25	14.25	14.50
Burundi	618	10.00	10.00	10.00	12.00	12.00	12.00	14.00	14.00	15.50	14.50	14.50	14.50
Comoros	632	....	....	....	....	....	† 6.36	5.63	5.89	4.79	3.82	3.55	3.59
Congo, Dem. Rep. of	636	145.00	125.00	238.00	13.00	22.00	120.00	120.00	140.00	24.00	8.00	....	....
Ethiopia	644	12.00	12.00	....	....	....	....	....	....	....	....	....	....
Gambia, The	648	13.50	14.00	14.00	14.00	12.00	10.50	10.00	13.00	18.00	29.00	28.00	14.00
Ghana	652	33.00	45.00	45.00	45.00	37.00	27.00	27.00	27.00	24.50	21.50	18.50	15.50
Guinea	656	17.00	18.00	18.00	15.00	....	....	11.50	16.25	16.25	16.25	16.25	22.25
Kenya	664	21.50	24.50	26.88	32.27	17.07	26.46	....	....	....	....	....	....
Lesotho	666	13.50	15.50	17.00	15.60	19.50	19.00	15.00	13.00	16.19	15.00	13.00	13.00
Madagascar	674	....	....	....	....	....	15.00	....	....	....	....	....	....
Malawi	676	40.00	50.00	27.00	23.00	43.00	47.00	50.23	46.80	40.00	35.00	25.00	25.00
Mauritius	684	13.80	11.40	11.82	10.46	17.19	....	....	....	....	....	....	....
Morocco	686	7.17	....	....	....	6.04	5.42	5.00	4.71	3.79	3.25	3.25	3.25
Mozambique	688	69.70	57.75	32.00	12.95	9.95	9.95	9.95	9.95	9.95	9.95	9.95	9.95
Namibia	728	15.50	17.50	17.75	16.00	18.75	11.50	11.25	9.25	12.75	7.75	7.50	7.00
Nigeria	694	13.50	13.50	13.50	13.50	13.50	18.00	14.00	20.50	16.50	15.00	15.00	13.00
Rwanda	714	11.00	16.00	16.00	10.75	11.38	11.19	11.69	13.00	13.00	14.50	14.50	12.50
São Tomé & Príncipe	716	32.00	50.00	35.00	55.00	29.50	17.00	17.00	15.50	15.50	14.50	14.50	18.20
Seychelles	718	12.50	12.83	11.00	11.00	5.50	5.50	5.50	5.50	5.50	4.67	3.51	3.87
South Africa	199	13.00	15.00	17.00	16.00	† 19.32	12.00	12.00	9.50	13.50	8.00	7.50	7.00
Swaziland	734	12.00	15.00	16.75	15.75	18.00	12.00	11.00	9.50	13.50	8.00	7.50	7.00
Tanzania	738	67.50	47.90	19.00	16.20	17.60	20.20	10.70	8.70	9.18	12.34	14.42	19.33
Tunisia	744	8.88	8.88	7.88	....	....	....	....	....	....	....	....	....
Uganda	746	15.00	13.30	15.85	14.08	9.10	15.75	18.86	8.88	13.08	25.62	16.15	14.36
Zambia	754	20.50	40.20	47.00	17.70	....	32.93	25.67	40.10	27.87	14.35	16.68	14.81
Zimbabwe	698	29.50	29.50	27.00	31.50	† 39.50	74.41	57.84	57.20	29.65	300.00	110.00	540.00
Asia													
Bangladesh	513	5.50	6.00	7.00	8.00	8.00	7.00	7.00	6.00	6.00	5.00	5.00	5.00
China,P.R.: Mainland	924	10.08	10.44	9.00	8.55	4.59	3.24	3.24	3.24	2.70	2.70	3.33	3.33
China,P.R.:Hong Kong	532	5.75	6.25	6.00	7.00	6.25	7.00	8.00	3.25	2.75	2.50	3.75	5.75
Fiji	819	6.00	6.00	6.00	1.88	2.50	2.50	8.00	1.75	1.75	1.75	2.25	2.75
India	534	12.00	12.00	12.00	9.00	9.00	8.00	8.00	6.50	6.25	6.00	6.00	6.00
Indonesia	536	12.44	13.99	12.80	20.00	38.44	12.51	14.53	17.62	12.93	8.31	7.43	12.75
Korea	542	5.00	5.00	5.00	5.00	3.00	3.00	3.00	2.50	2.50	2.50	2.00	2.00
Lao People's Dem.Rep.	544	30.00	32.08	35.00	....	35.00	34.89	35.17	35.00	20.00	20.00	20.00	20.00
Malaysia	548	4.51	6.47	7.28	....	....	....	8.65	8.60	9.90	11.50	15.75	4.40
Mongolia	948	180.00	150.00	109.00	45.50	23.30	11.40	8.65	8.60	9.90	11.50	15.75	4.40
Myanmar	518	11.00	12.50	15.00	15.00	15.00	12.00	10.00	10.00	10.00	10.00	10.00	10.00
Nepal	558	11.00	11.00	11.00	9.00	9.00	9.00	7.50	6.50	5.50	5.50	5.50	6.00

National Interest Rates

		1994	1995	1996	1997	1998	1999	2000	2001	2002	2003	2004	2005
						Central Bank Discount Rates (60) *(End of period in percent per annum)*							

		1994	1995	1996	1997	1998	1999	2000	2001	2002	2003	2004	2005
Asia(Cont.)													
Pakistan	564	† 15.00	17.00	20.00	18.00	16.50	13.00	13.00	10.00	7.50	7.50	7.50	9.00
Papua New Guinea	853	6.55	† 18.00	14.86	9.49	17.07	16.66	9.79	11.73	11.71	† 15.50	12.67	9.67
Philippines	566	8.30	10.83	11.70	14.64	12.40	7.89	13.81	8.30	4.19	5.53	8.36	5.70
Sri Lanka	524	17.00	17.00	17.00	17.00	17.00	16.00	25.00	....	18.00	15.00	15.00	15.00
Thailand	578	9.50	10.50	10.50	12.50	12.50	4.00	4.00	3.75	3.25	2.75	3.50	5.50
Vanuatu	846	....	....	....	....	7.00	7.00	7.00	6.50	6.50	6.50	6.50	6.25
Vietnam	582	....	....	18.90	10.80	12.00	6.00	6.00	4.80	4.80	5.00	5.00	5.00
Europe													
Albania	914	25.00	20.50	24.00	32.00	23.44	18.00	10.82	7.00	8.50	6.50	5.25	5.00
Armenia	911	210.00	77.80	26.00	65.10	....	....	....	....	....	....	....	....
Azerbaijan, Republic of	912	200.00	80.00	20.00	12.00	14.00	10.00	10.00	10.00	7.00	7.00	7.00	9.00
Belarus	913	480.00	66.00	8.30	8.90	9.60	23.40	† 80.00	48.00	38.00	28.00	17.00	11.00
Bulgaria	918	72.00	34.00	180.00	† 6.65	5.08	4.46	4.63	4.65	3.31	2.83	2.37	† 2.05
Croatia	960	8.50	8.50	6.50	5.90	5.90	7.90	5.90	5.90	4.50	4.50	4.50	4.50
Cyprus	423	6.50	6.50	† 7.50	7.00	7.00	7.00	7.00	5.50	5.00	4.50	5.50	4.25
Czech Republic	935	8.50	11.30	12.40	14.75	9.50	5.25	5.25	4.50	2.75	2.00	2.50	2.00
Hungary	944	25.00	28.00	23.00	20.50	17.00	14.50	11.00	9.75	8.50	12.50	9.50	6.00
Kazakhstan	916	230.00	† 52.50	35.00	18.50	25.00	18.00	14.00	9.00	7.50	7.00	7.00	8.00
Latvia	941	25.00	24.00	9.50	4.00	4.00	4.00	3.50	3.50	3.00	3.00	4.00	4.00
Macedonia, FYR	962	33.00	15.00	9.20	8.90	8.90	8.90	7.90	10.70	10.70	6.50	6.50	6.50
Malta	181	5.50	5.50	5.50	5.50	5.50	4.75	4.75	4.25	3.75	† 3.00	3.00	3.25
Poland	964	28.00	25.00	22.00	24.50	18.25	19.00	21.50	14.00	7.75	5.75	7.00	4.50
Russia	922	....	160.00	48.00	28.00	60.00	55.00	25.00	25.00	21.00	16.00	13.00	12.00
Slovak Republic	936	12.00	9.75	8.80	8.80	8.80	8.80	8.80	† 7.75	6.50	6.00	4.00	3.00
Slovenia	961	17.00	11.00	11.00	11.00	11.00	9.00	11.00	12.00	10.50	7.25	5.00	5.00
Tajikistan	923	....	....	....	76.00	36.40	20.10	20.60	20.00	† 24.75	† 15.00	10.00	9.00
Turkey	186	55.00	50.00	50.00	67.00	67.00	60.00	60.00	60.00	55.00	43.00	38.00	23.00
Ukraine	926	252.00	110.00	40.00	35.00	60.00	45.00	27.00	12.50	7.00	7.00	9.00	9.50
Middle East													
Egypt	469	14.00	13.50	13.00	12.25	12.00	12.00	12.00	11.00	10.00	10.00	10.00	10.00
Israel	436	17.01	14.19	15.30	13.72	13.47	11.20	8.21	5.67	9.18	5.20	3.90	4.44
Jordan	439	8.50	8.50	8.50	7.75	9.00	8.00	6.50	5.00	4.50	2.50	3.75	6.50
Kuwait	443	7.00	7.25	7.25	7.50	7.00	6.75	7.25	4.25	3.25	3.25	4.75	6.00
Lebanon	446	16.49	19.01	25.00	30.00	30.00	25.00	20.00	20.00	20.00	20.00	20.00	12.00
Libya	672	....	....	....	....	3.00	5.00	5.00	5.00	5.00	5.00	4.00	4.00
Syrian Arab Republic	463	5.00	5.00	5.00	5.00	5.00	5.00	5.00	5.00	5.00	....	....	....
Western Hemisphere													
ECCU	309	9.00	9.00	9.00	8.00	8.00	8.00	8.00	7.00	7.00	6.50	6.50	6.50
Anguilla	312	9.00	9.00	9.00	8.00	8.00	8.00	8.00	7.00	7.00	6.50	6.50	6.50
Antigua and Barbuda	311	9.00	9.00	9.00	8.00	8.00	8.00	8.00	7.00	7.00	6.50	6.50	6.50
Dominica	321	9.00	9.00	9.00	8.00	8.00	8.00	8.00	7.00	7.00	6.50	6.50	6.50
Grenada	328	9.00	9.00	9.00	8.00	8.00	8.00	8.00	7.00	7.00	6.50	6.50	6.50
Montserrat	351	9.00	9.00	9.00	8.00	8.00	8.00	8.00	7.00	7.00	6.50	6.50	6.50
St. Kitts and Nevis	361	9.00	9.00	9.00	8.00	8.00	8.00	8.00	7.00	7.00	6.50	6.50	6.50
St. Lucia	362	9.00	9.00	9.00	8.00	8.00	8.00	8.00	7.00	7.00	6.50	6.50	6.50
St. Vincent & Grens	364	9.00	9.00	9.00	8.00	8.00	8.00	8.00	7.00	7.00	6.50	6.50	6.50
Aruba	314	9.50	9.50	9.50	9.50	9.50	6.50	6.50	6.50	6.50	5.00	5.00	5.00
Bahamas, The	313	6.50	6.50	6.50	6.50	6.50	5.75	5.75	5.75	5.75	5.75	5.75	5.25
Barbados	316	9.50	12.50	12.50	9.00	9.00	10.00	10.00	7.50	7.50	7.50	7.50	10.00
Belize	339	12.00	12.00	12.00	12.00	12.00	12.00	12.00	12.00	12.00	12.00	12.00	12.00
Bolivia	218	....	....	16.50	13.25	14.10	12.50	10.00	8.50	12.50	7.50	6.00	5.25
Brazil	223	....	....	25.34	45.09	39.41	21.37	† 18.52	21.43	30.42	23.92	24.55	25.34
Chile	228	13.89	7.96	11.75	7.96	9.12	7.44	8.73	6.50	3.00	2.45	2.25	4.50
Colombia	233	44.90	40.42	35.05	31.32	42.28	23.05	18.28	13.25	10.00	12.00	11.25	10.75
Costa Rica	238	37.75	38.50	35.00	31.00	37.00	34.00	31.50	28.75	31.25	26.00	26.00	27.00
Ecuador	248	44.88	59.41	46.38	37.46	61.84	64.40	† 13.16	16.44	14.55	11.19	9.86	9.61
Guyana	336	20.25	17.25	12.00	11.00	11.25	13.25	11.75	8.75	6.25	5.50	6.00	6.00
Netherlands Antilles	353	5.00	6.00	6.00	6.00	6.00	6.00	6.00	6.00	6.00	....	....	....
Nicaragua	278	10.50	....	....	....	....	....	....	....	....	....	....	....
Paraguay	288	19.15	20.50	15.00	20.00	20.00	20.00	20.00	20.00	20.00	20.00	20.00	20.00
Peru	293	16.08	18.44	18.16	15.94	18.72	17.80	14.00	5.00	4.50	3.25	3.75	4.00
Trinidad and Tobago	369	13.00	13.00	13.00	13.00	13.00	13.00	13.00	13.00	7.25	7.00	7.00	8.00
Uruguay	298	182.30	178.70	160.30	95.50	73.70	66.39	57.26	71.66	316.01	46.27	10.00	10.00
Venezuela, Rep. Bol	299	48.00	49.00	45.00	45.00	60.00	38.00	38.00	37.00	40.00	28.50	28.50	28.50

National Interest Rates

		1994	1995	1996	1997	1998	1999	2000	2001	2002	2003	2004	2005
						Money Market Rates (60b)							
						(Period averages in percent per annum)							
Industrial Countries													
United States	111	4.20	5.84	5.30	5.46	5.35	4.97	6.24	3.89	1.67	1.13	1.35	3.21
Canada	156	5.05	6.92	4.32	3.26	4.87	4.74	5.52	4.11	2.45	2.93	2.25	2.66
Australia	193	5.18	† 7.50	7.20	5.50	4.99	† 4.78	5.90	5.06	4.55	4.81	5.25	5.46
Japan	158	2.20	1.21	.47	.48	.37	.06	.11	.06	.01	—	—	—
New Zealand	196	6.13	8.91	9.38	7.38	6.86	4.33	6.12	5.76	5.40	5.33	5.77	6.76
Euro Area	163	6.53	6.82	5.09	4.38	3.96	2.97	4.39	4.26	3.32	2.34	2.11	2.19
Austria	122	5.03	4.36	3.19	3.27	3.36	....	....	....	....	....	....	....
Belgium	124	5.72	4.80	3.24	3.46	3.58	....	....	....	....	....	....	....
Finland	172	5.35	5.75	3.63	3.23	3.57	2.96	4.39	4.26	3.32	2.33	2.11	2.18
France	132	5.69	6.35	3.73	3.24	3.39	....	....	....	....	....	....	....
Germany	134	5.35	4.50	3.27	3.18	3.41	2.73	4.11	4.37	3.28	2.32	2.05	2.09
Greece	174	24.60	16.40	13.80	12.80	13.99	....	....	....	....	....	....	....
Ireland	178	† 5.75	5.45	5.74	6.43	3.23	3.14	4.84	3.31	2.88	2.08	2.13	2.40
Italy	136	8.51	10.46	8.82	6.88	4.99	2.95	4.39	4.26	3.32	2.33	2.10	2.18
Luxembourg	137	5.16	4.26	3.29	3.36	3.48	....	....	....	....	....	....	....
Netherlands	138	5.14	4.22	2.89	3.07	3.21	....	....	....	....	....	....	....
Portugal	182	10.62	8.91	7.38	5.78	4.34	2.71	....	....	....	....	....	....
Spain	184	7.81	8.98	7.65	5.49	4.34	2.72	4.11	4.36	3.28	2.31	2.04	2.09
Denmark	128	6.30	6.19	3.98	3.71	4.27	3.37	4.98	....	3.56	2.38	2.16	2.20
Iceland	176	4.96	6.58	6.96	7.38	8.12	9.24	11.61	14.51	11.21	5.14	6.22	....
Norway	142	5.70	5.54	4.97	3.77	6.03	6.87	6.72	7.38	7.05	4.45	2.17	2.26
Sweden	144	7.36	8.54	6.28	4.21	4.24	3.14	3.81	4.09	4.19	3.29	....	....
Switzerland	146	3.85	2.89	1.78	1.35	1.22	.93	† 3.50	1.65	.44	.09	.55	.63
United Kingdom	112	4.88	6.08	5.96	6.61	7.21	5.20	5.77	5.08	3.89	3.59	4.29	4.70
Developing Countries													
Africa													
WAEMU	759	....	4.95	4.95	4.95	4.95	4.95	4.95	4.95	4.95	4.95	4.95	4.95
Benin	638	4.95	4.95	4.95	4.95	4.95	4.95	4.95	4.95	4.95	4.95	4.95	4.95
Burkina Faso	748	4.95	4.95	4.95	4.95	4.95	4.95	4.95	4.95	4.95	4.95	4.95	4.95
Côte d'Ivoire	662	4.95	4.95	4.95	4.95	4.95	4.95	4.95	4.95	4.95	4.95	4.95	4.95
Guinea-Bissau	654	4.95	4.95	4.95	4.95	4.95	4.95	4.95	4.95	4.95	4.95	4.95	4.95
Mali	678	4.95	4.95	4.95	4.95	4.95	4.95	4.95	4.95	4.95	4.95	4.95	4.95
Niger	692	4.95	4.95	4.95	4.95	4.95	4.95	4.95	4.95	4.95	4.95	4.95	4.95
Senegal	722	4.95	4.95	4.95	4.95	4.95	4.95	4.95	4.95	4.95	4.95	4.95	4.95
Togo	742	4.95	4.95	4.95	4.95	4.95	4.95	4.95	4.95	4.95	4.95	4.95	4.95
Algeria	612	19.80	† 19.75	18.09	13.00	10.00	9.99	6.45	2.84	3.13	1.91	1.09	2.01
Ghana	652	....	....	....	....	....	....	....	....	....	24.71	15.73	14.70
Madagascar	674	....	29.00	10.00	....	12.00	17.25	16.00	9.00	9.00	10.50	16.50	16.50
Mauritius	684	10.23	10.35	9.96	9.43	8.99	10.01	7.66	7.25	6.20	3.22	1.33	2.45
Morocco	686	12.29	10.06	8.42	7.89	6.30	5.64	5.41	4.44	2.99	3.22	2.39	2.78
Mozambique	688	....	....	....	....	....	9.92	16.12	† 25.00	20.40	13.34	9.87	6.35
Namibia	728	10.25	13.08	15.00	15.41	17.14	13.17	9.19	9.53	10.46	10.03	6.93	6.87
South Africa	199	10.24	13.07	15.54	15.59	17.11	13.06	9.54	† 8.49	11.11	10.93	7.15	6.62
Swaziland	734	7.01	8.52	9.77	10.35	10.63	8.86	5.54	5.06	7.31	6.98	4.12	3.47
Tunisia	744	8.81	8.81	8.64	6.88	6.89	5.99	5.88	6.04	5.93	5.14	5.00	5.00
Zimbabwe	698	30.90	29.64	26.18	25.15	37.22	53.13	64.98	21.52	32.35	110.05	129.58	....
Asia													
China,P.R.:Hong Kong	532	5.44	6.00	5.13	4.50	5.50	5.75	7.13	2.69	1.50	.07	.13	4.25
China,P.R.:Macao	546	5.91	6.01	5.60	7.54	5.41	5.70	6.29	2.11	1.48	.11	.27	4.09
Fiji	819	4.10	3.95	2.43	1.91	1.27	1.27	2.58	.79	.92	.86	.90	1.28
India	534	7.14	15.57	11.04	5.29	....	....	....	....	....	....	....	....
Indonesia	536	9.74	13.64	13.96	27.82	62.79	23.58	10.32	15.03	13.54	7.76	5.38	6.78
Korea	542	12.45	12.57	12.44	13.24	14.98	5.01	5.16	4.69	4.21	4.00	3.65	3.33
Malaysia	548	4.20	5.60	6.92	7.61	8.46	3.38	2.66	2.79	2.73	2.74	2.70	2.72
Maldives	556	5.00	6.80	6.80	6.80	6.80	6.80	6.80	....	....	....	....	....
Pakistan	564	8.36	11.52	11.40	12.10	10.76	9.04	8.57	8.49	5.53	2.14	2.70	6.83
Papua New Guinea	853	....	....	....	....	....	....	9.54	11.05	9.11	13.58	7.79	4.36
Philippines	566	13.99	11.93	12.77	16.16	13.90	10.16	10.84	9.75	7.15	6.97	7.05	7.31
Singapore	576	3.68	2.56	2.93	4.35	5.00	2.04	2.57	1.99	.96	.74	1.04	2.28
Sri Lanka	524	18.54	41.87	24.33	18.42	15.74	16.69	17.30	21.24	12.33	9.68	8.87	10.15
Thailand	578	7.25	10.96	9.23	14.59	13.02	1.77	1.95	2.00	1.76	1.31	1.23	2.62
Vanuatu	846	6.00	6.00	6.00	6.00	8.65	6.99	5.58	5.50	5.50	5.50	5.50	5.50
Europe													
Armenia	911	....	....	48.56	36.41	27.84	23.65	18.63	19.40	12.29	7.51	4.18	3.17
Bulgaria	918	66.43	53.09	119.88	66.43	2.48	2.93	3.02	3.74	2.47	1.95	1.95	2.03
Croatia	960	26.93	21.13	17.60	9.71	11.16	10.21	6.78	3.42	1.75	3.31	5.11	3.10
Cyprus	423	....	....	6.85	4.82	4.80	5.15	5.96	4.93	3.42	3.35	4.01	3.27
Czech Republic	935	12.65	10.93	12.67	17.50	10.08	5.58	5.42	4.69	2.63	2.08	2.56	2.17
Estonia	939	5.67	4.94	3.53	6.45	11.66	5.39	† 5.68	5.31	3.88	2.92	2.50	2.38
Georgia	915	....	....	43.39	26.58	43.26	34.61	18.17	† 17.52	27.69	16.88	11.87	7.71
Kyrgyz Republic	917	....	....	....	....	43.98	43.71	24.26	11.92	....	....	....	3.24
Latvia	941	37.18	22.39	13.08	3.76	4.42	4.72	2.97	5.23	3.01	2.86	3.25	2.49
Lithuania	946	69.48	26.73	20.26	9.55	† 6.12	6.26	3.60	3.37	2.21	1.79	1.53	1.97
Moldova	921	....	....	....	28.10	30.91	32.60	20.77	11.04	5.13	11.51	13.19	5.87
Poland	964	23.32	25.82	20.63	22.43	20.59	13.58	18.16	16.23	9.39	5.76	6.03	5.34
Russia	922	....	190.43	47.65	20.97	50.56	14.79	7.14	10.10	8.19	3.77	3.33	2.68
Slovak Republic	936	....	....	....	....	....	....	8.08	7.76	6.33	6.08	3.82	3.02

National Interest Rates

		1994	1995	1996	1997	1998	1999	2000	2001	2002	2003	2004	2005
						Money Market Rates (60b) *(Period averages in percent per annum)*							
Europe(Cont.)													
Slovenia......................	961	29.08	12.18	13.98	9.71	7.45	6.87	6.95	6.90	4.93	5.59	4.40	3.73
Turkey.........................	186	136.47	72.30	76.24	70.32	74.60	73.53	56.72	91.95	49.51	36.16	21.42	14.73
Ukraine.......................	926	....	....	....	22.05	40.41	44.98	18.34	16.57	5.50	7.90	6.34	4.16
Middle East													
Bahrain, Kingdom of.....	419	5.18	6.24	5.69	....	5.69	5.58	6.89	3.85	2.02	1.24	1.74	3.64
Jordan.........................	439	....	....	....	....	....	5.19	5.28	4.63	3.49	2.58	2.18	3.59
Kuwait.........................	443	6.31	7.43	6.98	7.05	7.24	6.32	6.82	4.62	2.99	2.47	2.14	2.83
Libya...........................	672	....	....	....	....	4.00	4.00	4.00	4.00	4.00	4.00	4.00	....
Western Hemisphere													
ECCU............................	309	5.25	5.25	5.25	5.25	5.25	5.25	5.25	† 5.64	6.32	6.07	4.67	4.01
Anguilla....................	312	5.25	5.25	5.25	5.25	5.25	5.25	5.25	† 5.64	6.32	6.07	4.67	4.01
Antigua and Barbuda..	311	5.25	5.25	5.25	5.25	5.25	5.25	5.25	† 5.64	6.32	6.07	4.67	4.01
Dominica...................	321	5.25	5.25	5.25	5.25	5.25	5.25	5.25	† 5.64	6.32	6.07	4.67	4.01
Grenada....................	328	5.25	5.25	5.25	5.25	5.25	5.25	5.25	† 5.64	6.32	6.07	4.67	4.01
Montserrat................	351	5.25	5.25	5.25	5.25	5.25	5.25	5.25	† 5.64	6.32	6.07	4.67	4.01
St. Kitts and Nevis......	361	5.25	5.25	5.25	5.25	5.25	5.25	5.25	† 5.64	6.32	6.07	4.67	4.01
St. Lucia....................	362	5.25	5.25	5.25	5.25	5.25	5.25	5.25	† 5.64	6.32	6.07	4.67	4.01
St. Vincent & Grens.....	364	5.25	5.25	5.25	5.25	5.25	5.25	5.25	† 5.64	6.32	6.07	4.67	4.01
Argentina....................	213	7.66	9.46	6.23	6.63	6.81	6.99	8.15	24.90	41.35	3.74	1.96	4.11
Bolivia.........................	218	....	22.42	20.27	13.97	12.57	13.49	7.40	6.99	8.41	4.07	4.05	3.53
Brazil...........................	223	4,820.64	53.37	27.45	25.00	29.50	26.26	17.59	17.47	19.11	23.37	16.24	19.12
Chile............................	228	....	....	....	....	....	....	10.09	6.81	4.08	2.72	1.88	3.48
Colombia......................	233	....	22.40	28.37	23.83	35.00	18.81	10.87	10.43	6.06	6.95	7.01	6.18
Dominican Republic.......	243	....	....	14.70	13.01	16.68	15.30	18.28	13.47	14.50	24.24	36.76	12.57
El Salvador...................	253	....	....	....	10.43	9.43	10.68	6.93	5.28	4.40	3.86	4.36	5.18
Guatemala....................	258	....	....	....	7.77	6.62	9.23	9.33	10.58	9.11	6.65	6.16	6.54
Mexico.........................	273	16.47	† 60.92	33.61	21.91	26.89	24.10	16.96	12.89	8.17	6.83	7.15	9.59
Panama........................	283									2.22	1.50	1.90	3.13
Paraguay......................	288	18.64	20.18	16.35	12.48	20.74	17.26	10.70	13.45	13.19	13.02	1.33	2.29
Uruguay.......................	298	39.82	36.81	28.47	23.43	20.48	13.96	14.82	22.10	86.10	20.76	3.57	1.25
Venezuela, Rep. Bol.......	299	....	....	16.70	12.47	18.58	7.48	8.14	13.33	28.87	13.23	4.38	2.62

National Interest Rates

		1994	1995	1996	1997	1998	1999	2000	2001	2002	2003	2004	2005
		Treasury Bill Rates (60c)											

(Period averages in percent per annum)

Industrial Countries													
United States	111	4.27	5.51	5.02	5.07	4.82	4.66	5.84	3.45	1.61	1.01	1.38	3.17
Canada	156	5.54	6.89	4.21	3.26	4.73	4.72	5.49	3.77	2.59	2.87	2.22	2.73
Australia	193	5.69	† 7.64	7.02	5.29	4.84	4.76	5.98	4.80	....	....	....	....
New Zealand	196	6.69	8.82	9.09	7.53	7.10	4.58	6.39	5.56	5.52	5.21	5.85	6.53
Belgium	124	5.57	4.67	3.19	3.38	3.51	2.72	4.02	4.16	3.17	2.23	1.97	2.02
France	132	5.79	6.58	3.84	3.35	3.45	2.72	4.23	4.26	3.28	2.27	....	....
Germany	134	5.05	4.40	3.30	3.32	3.42	2.88	4.32	3.66	2.97	1.98	2.00	2.03
Greece	174	17.50	14.20	11.20	11.38	10.30	8.30	† 6.22	4.08	3.50	2.34	2.27	2.33
Iceland	176	4.95	7.22	6.97	7.04	7.40	8.61	11.12	11.03	8.01	4.93	6.04	....
Ireland	178	5.87	6.19	5.36	6.03	5.37	....	....	....	....	....	....	....
Italy	136	9.17	10.85	8.46	6.33	4.59	3.01	4.53	4.05	3.26	2.19	2.08	2.17
Portugal	182	....	7.75	5.75	4.43	....	....	....	....	....	....	....	....
Spain	184	8.11	9.79	7.23	5.02	3.79	3.01	4.61	3.92	3.34	2.21	2.17	2.19
Sweden	144	7.40	8.75	5.79	4.11	4.19	3.12	3.95	4.00	4.07	3.03	2.11	1.72
Switzerland	146	3.97	2.78	1.72	1.45	1.32	1.17	2.93	2.68	.94	.16	.37	.71
United Kingdom	112	5.15	6.33	5.78	6.48	6.82	5.04	5.80	4.77	3.86	3.55	4.43	4.55
Developing Countries													
Africa													
Algeria	612	16.50	....	....	....	† 9.96	10.05	7.95	5.69	1.80	1.25	.15	1.30
Ethiopia	644	12.00	12.00	7.22	3.97	3.48	3.65	2.74	3.06	1.30	† 1.31	.56	.25
Ghana	652	27.72	35.38	41.64	42.77	34.33	26.37	36.28	40.96	25.11	27.25	16.57	14.89
Kenya	664	23.32	18.29	22.25	22.87	22.83	13.87	12.05	12.60	8.95	3.51	3.17	8.43
Lesotho	666	9.44	12.40	13.89	14.83	15.47	12.45	9.06	9.49	11.34	11.96	8.52	7.23
Madagascar	674	....	....	....	....	....	....	....	10.28	....	11.94	12.95	18.84
Malawi	676	27.68	46.30	30.83	18.31	32.98	42.85	39.52	42.41	41.75	39.32	28.58	24.36
Mozambique	688	....	....	....	....	....	....	16.97	24.77	29.55	15.31	12.37	9.10
Namibia	728	11.35	13.91	15.25	15.69	17.24	13.28	10.26	9.29	11.00	10.51	7.78	7.09
Nigeria	694	12.87	12.50	12.25	12.00	12.26	17.82	15.50	17.50	19.03	14.79	14.34	7.63
Seychelles	718	12.50	12.28	11.55	10.50	8.13	5.00	5.00	5.00	5.00	4.61	3.17	3.34
Sierra Leone	724	12.19	14.73	29.25	12.71	22.10	32.42	26.22	13.74	15.15	15.68	26.14	22.98
South Africa	199	10.93	13.53	15.04	15.26	16.53	12.85	10.11	9.68	11.16	10.67	7.53	6.91
Swaziland	734	8.35	10.87	13.68	14.37	13.09	11.19	8.30	7.16	8.59	10.61	7.94	7.08
Tanzania	738	35.09	40.33	15.30	9.59	11.83	10.05	9.78	4.14	3.55	6.26	8.35	10.67
Uganda	746	12.52	8.75	11.71	10.59	7.77	7.43	13.19	11.00	5.85	16.87	9.02	8.51
Zambia	754	74.21	39.81	52.78	29.48	24.94	36.19	31.37	44.28	34.54	29.97	12.60	16.32
Zimbabwe	698	29.22	27.98	24.53	22.07	32.78	50.48	64.78	17.60	28.51	52.72	125.68	185.11
Asia													
China,P.R.:Hong Kong	532	5.66	5.55	4.45	7.50	5.04	4.94	5.69	1.69	1.35	−.08	.07	3.65
Fiji	819	2.69	3.15	2.98	2.60	2.00	2.00	3.63	1.51	1.66	1.06	1.56	1.94
Lao People's Dem.Rep.	544	....	20.46	....	....	23.66	30.00	29.94	22.70	21.41	24.87	20.37	18.61
Malaysia	548	3.68	5.50	6.41	6.41	6.86	3.53	2.86	2.79	2.73	2.79	2.40	2.48
Nepal	558	6.50	9.90	11.51	2.52	3.70	4.30	5.30	5.00	3.80	3.85	2.40	2.20
Pakistan	564	11.26	12.49	13.61	† 15.74	....	....	8.38	10.71	6.08	1.93	2.48	7.18
Papua New Guinea	853	† 7.82	17.40	14.44	9.94	21.18	22.70	17.00	12.36	10.93	18.69	8.85	3.81
Philippines	566	12.71	11.76	12.34	12.89	15.00	10.00	9.91	9.73	5.49	5.87	7.32	6.13
Singapore	576	1.94	1.05	1.38	2.32	2.12	1.12	2.18	1.69	.81	.64	.96	2.04
Solomon Islands	813	11.25	12.50	12.75	12.88	6.00	6.00	7.05	8.23	6.87	5.85	6.00	4.53
Sri Lanka	524	12.68	16.81	† 17.40	....	12.59	12.51	14.02	17.57	12.47	8.09	7.71	9.03
Vietnam	582	....	....	....	....	....	....	5.42	5.49	5.92	5.83	....	6.13
Europe													
Albania	914	....	13.84	17.81	32.59	27.49	17.54	10.80	7.72	9.49	8.81	6.79	5.52
Armenia	911	....	37.81	† 43.95	57.54	46.99	55.10	24.40	† 20.59	14.75	11.91	5.27	4.05
Azerbaijan, Republic of	912	....	....	....	12.23	14.10	18.31	16.73	16.51	14.12	8.00	4.62	7.52
Bulgaria	918	57.72	48.27	114.31	78.35	6.02	5.43	4.21	4.57	4.29	2.81	2.64	....
Cyprus	423	6.00	6.00	6.05	5.38	5.59	5.59	6.01	....	....	3.56	....	....
Czech Republic	935	6.98	8.99	11.91	11.21	10.51	5.71	5.37	5.06	2.72	2.04	2.57	1.96
Georgia	915	....	....	....	....	....	....	....	29.93	43.42	44.26	19.16	....
Hungary	944	26.93	32.04	23.96	20.13	17.83	14.68	11.03	10.79	8.91	8.22	11.32	6.95
Kazakhstan	916	214.34	48.98	28.91	15.15	23.59	15.63	6.59	5.28	5.20	5.86	3.28	3.28
Kyrgyz Republic	917	143.13	34.90	40.10	35.83	43.67	47.19	32.26	19.08	10.15	7.21	4.94	4.40
Latvia	941	....	28.24	16.27	4.73	5.27	6.23	† 4.85	5.63	3.52	3.24	....	....
Lithuania	946	....	26.82	20.95	8.64	10.69	11.14	† 9.27	5.68	3.72	2.61	....	....
Malta	181	4.29	4.65	4.99	5.08	5.41	5.15	4.89	4.93	4.03	3.29	2.94	3.18
Moldova	921	....	52.90	39.01	23.63	30.54	28.49	22.20	14.24	5.89	15.08	11.89	3.70
Poland	964	28.81	25.62	20.32	21.58	19.09	13.14	16.62	....	....	....	....	....
Romania	968	....	....	51.09	85.72	63.99	74.21	51.86	42.18	27.03	....	....	....
Russia	922	....	168.04	86.07	23.43	....	....	12.12	12.45	12.72	5.35	....	....
Slovenia	961	....	....	....	....	....	8.63	10.94	10.88	8.73	6.53	4.17	3.66
Turkey	186	....	....	....	....	....	....	25.18	85.33	59.50	34.90	22.08	....
Middle East													
Bahrain, Kingdom of	419	4.81	6.07	5.49	5.68	5.53	5.46	6.56	3.78	1.75	1.13	1.56	....
Egypt	469	....	....	....	8.80	8.80	9.00	9.10	7.20	5.50	6.90	9.90	8.57
Israel	436	11.77	14.37	15.34	13.39	11.33	11.41	8.81	6.50	7.38	7.00	4.78	4.34
Kuwait	443	6.32	7.35	6.93	6.98	....	....	....	....	....	....	....	....
Lebanon	446	15.09	19.40	15.19	13.42	12.70	11.57	11.18	11.18	10.90	....	5.25	5.22
Western Hemisphere													
Antigua and Barbuda	311	7.00	7.00	7.00	7.00	7.00	7.00	7.00	7.00	7.00	7.00	7.00	7.00
Bahamas, The	313	1.88	3.01	4.45	4.35	3.84	1.97	1.03	1.94	2.50	1.78	.56	.14
Barbados	316	7.26	8.01	6.85	3.61	5.61	5.83	5.29	3.14	2.10	1.41	1.20	4.62
Belize	339	4.27	4.10	3.78	3.51	3.83	5.91	5.91	5.91	4.59	3.22	3.22	3.22

National Interest Rates

		1994	1995	1996	1997	1998	1999	2000	2001	2002	2003	2004	2005
						Treasury Bill Rates (60c)							
						(Period averages in percent per annum)							
Western Hemisphere(Cont.)													
Bolivia..............................	218	17.89	24.51	19.93	13.65	12.33	14.07	10.99	11.48	12.41	9.92	7.41	4.96
Brazil...............................	223	....	49.93	25.73	24.79	28.57	26.39	18.51	20.06	19.43	22.10	17.14	18.76
Dominica...........................	321	6.40	6.40	6.40	6.40	6.40	6.40	6.40	6.40	6.40	6.40	6.40	6.40
Grenada............................	328	6.50	6.50	6.50	6.50	6.50	6.50	6.50	† 7.00	7.00	6.50	5.50	5.50
Guyana.............................	336	17.66	17.51	11.35	8.91	8.33	11.31	9.88	7.78	4.94	3.04	3.62	3.79
Haiti.................................	263	....	....	....	14.13	16.21	7.71	12.33	13.53	7.56	20.50	12.24	8.29
Jamaica.............................	343	42.98	27.65	37.95	21.14	25.65	20.75	18.24	16.71	15.54	25.94	15.47	13.39
Mexico..............................	273	14.10	48.44	31.39	19.80	24.76	21.41	15.24	11.31	7.09	6.23	6.82	9.20
Netherlands Antilles..............	353	4.48	5.46	5.66	5.77	5.82	6.15	6.15	6.15	4.96	2.80	3.86	3.52
St. Kitts and Nevis...............	361	6.50	6.50	6.50	6.50	6.50	6.50	6.50	7.50	7.50	7.17	7.00	7.00
St. Lucia............................	362	7.00	7.00	7.00	7.00	7.00	7.00	7.00	6.80	6.80	6.33	6.40	4.73
St. Vincent & Grens...............	364	6.50	6.50	6.50	6.50	6.50	6.50	6.50	7.00	7.00	5.73	4.60	4.85
Trinidad and Tobago.............	369	10.00	8.41	10.44	9.83	11.93	10.40	10.56	8.55	4.83	4.71	4.77	4.86
Uruguay............................	298	44.60	39.40	29.20	23.18	....	....	....	....	....	32.53	14.75	4.14

National Interest Rates

		1994	1995	1996	1997	1998	1999	2000	2001	2002	2003	2004	2005
						Deposit Rates (60l) except for United States (60lc) *(Period averages in percent per annum)*							
Industrial Countries													
United States	111	4.63	5.92	5.39	5.62	5.47	5.33	6.46	3.69	1.73	1.15	1.56	3.51
Canada	156	3.98	5.28	3.00	1.90	3.08	2.88	3.48	2.25	.83	1.10	.78	.79
Australia	193	4.92	6.11	5.71	4.32	3.71	3.47	4.20	3.20	3.07	3.26	3.63	3.70
Japan	158	1.70	.90	.30	.30	.27	.12	.07	.06	.04	.04	.08	.27
New Zealand	196	6.38	8.49	8.49	7.26	6.78	4.56	6.36	5.35	5.33	5.10	5.77	6.68
Euro Area	163	....	....	4.08	3.41	3.20	2.45	3.45	3.49	2.80	....	....	....
Austria	122	2.31	2.19	1.71	1.50	† 2.65	2.21	....	....	....	....	....	....
Belgium	124	4.86	4.04	2.66	2.88	3.01	2.42	3.58	3.40	2.60	1.65	....	....
Finland	172	3.27	3.19	2.35	2.00	....	1.22	1.63	1.94	1.49	....	1.03	....
France	132	4.50	4.50	3.67	3.50	3.21	2.69	2.63	3.00	3.00	2.69	2.25	2.15
Germany	134	4.47	3.85	2.83	2.69	2.88	2.43	3.40	3.56	2.65	....	....	....
Greece	174	18.92	15.75	13.51	10.11	10.70	8.69	6.13	3.32	2.76	2.48	2.29	2.23
Ireland	178	.33	.44	.29	.46	.43	.10	.10	.10	.10	.04	.01	.01
Italy	136	6.20	6.45	6.49	4.83	3.16	1.61	1.84	1.96	1.43	.95	....	....
Luxembourg	137	5.00	5.00	3.54	3.46	3.31	....	....	....	....	....	....	....
Netherlands	138	† 4.70	4.40	3.54	3.18	3.10	2.74	2.89	3.10	2.77	2.49	2.31	2.34
Portugal	182	8.37	8.38	6.32	4.56	3.37	2.40	....	....	....	....	....	....
Spain	184	6.70	7.68	6.12	3.96	2.92	1.85	2.95	3.08	2.50	....	....	....
Denmark	128	† 3.53	3.85	2.80	2.65	3.08	2.43	3.15	3.30	† 2.40	2.40	....	....
Iceland	176	3.03	3.69	4.25	4.72	4.50	4.82	7.11	6.94	4.69	4.81	4.85	....
Norway	142	5.21	4.95	4.15	3.63	7.24	5.38	6.73	† 6.43	6.46	2.12	1.48	1.83
Sweden	144	4.91	6.16	2.47	2.50	1.91	1.65	2.15	2.10	2.26	1.51	1.00	.79
Switzerland	146	3.63	1.28	1.34	1.00	.69	1.24	† 3.00	1.68	.43	.17	.39	.76
United Kingdom	112	3.66	4.11	3.05	3.63	4.48	....	....	....	....	....	....	....
Developing Countries													
Africa													
CEMAC	758	5.50	5.50	5.00	5.00	5.00	5.00	5.00	5.00	5.00	5.00	5.00	4.75
Cameroon	622	8.08	5.50	5.38	5.04	5.00	5.00	5.00	5.00	5.00	5.00	5.00	4.92
Central African Rep.	626	8.08	5.50	5.46	5.00	5.00	5.00	5.00	5.00	5.00	5.00	5.00	4.92
Chad	628	8.08	5.50	5.46	5.00	5.00	5.00	5.00	5.00	5.00	5.00	5.00	4.92
Congo, Republic of	634	8.08	5.50	5.46	5.00	5.00	5.00	5.00	5.00	5.00	5.00	5.00	4.92
Equatorial Guinea	642	8.08	5.50	5.46	5.00	5.00	5.00	5.00	5.00	5.00	5.00	5.00	4.92
Gabon	646	8.08	5.50	5.46	5.00	5.00	5.00	5.00	5.00	5.00	5.00	5.00	4.92
WAEMU	759	....	3.50	3.50	3.50	3.50	3.50	3.50	3.50	3.50	3.50	3.50	3.50
Benin	638	3.50	3.50	3.50	3.50	3.50	3.50	3.50	3.50	3.50	3.50	3.50	3.50
Burkina Faso	748	3.50	3.50	3.50	3.50	3.50	3.50	3.50	3.50	3.50	3.50	3.50	3.50
Côte d'Ivoire	662	3.50	3.50	3.50	3.50	3.50	3.50	3.50	3.50	3.50	3.50	3.50	3.50
Guinea-Bissau	654	3.50	3.50	3.50	3.50	3.50	3.50	3.50	3.50	3.50	3.50	3.50	3.50
Mali	678	3.50	3.50	3.50	3.50	3.50	3.50	3.50	3.50	3.50	3.50	3.50	3.50
Niger	692	3.50	3.50	3.50	3.50	3.50	3.50	3.50	3.50	3.50	3.50	3.50	3.50
Senegal	722	3.50	3.50	3.50	3.50	3.50	3.50	3.50	3.50	3.50	3.50	3.50	3.50
Togo	742	3.50	3.50	3.50	3.50	3.50	3.50	3.50	3.50	3.50	3.50	3.50	3.50
Algeria	612	12.00	† 16.00	14.50	9.75	8.50	7.50	7.50	6.25	5.25	5.25	2.50	1.75
Angola	614	....	125.92	147.13	29.25	36.88	† 36.57	† 39.58	47.91	48.69	26.17	15.44	13.40
Botswana	616	10.59	9.79	9.68	9.51	8.43	9.10	9.42	10.09	10.45	9.95	9.85	9.25
Cape Verde	624	4.00	† 5.00	5.00	5.04	5.27	4.76	4.34	4.67	4.86	3.93	3.46	3.38
Comoros	632	....	....	....	....	....	† 11.42	3.00	3.00	3.17	3.50	3.50	3.00
Congo, Dem. Rep. of	636	60.00	60.00	60.00	....	....	....	....	....	....	....	....	....
Djibouti	611	....	....	....	....	....	....	....	2.81	1.23	.82	.80	.85
Ethiopia	644	11.50	11.46	9.42	7.00	6.00	6.32	6.00	6.00	3.79	3.35	3.38	3.46
Gambia, The	648	12.58	12.50	12.50	12.50	12.50	12.50	12.50	12.50	12.71	16.42	22.00	17.33
Ghana	652	23.15	28.73	34.50	35.76	32.05	23.56	28.60	30.85	16.21	14.32	13.63	10.16
Guinea	656	18.00	17.50	....	....	6.38	5.67	7.50	8.03	7.40	6.50	8.85	14.35
Kenya	664	....	13.60	17.59	16.72	18.40	9.55	8.10	6.64	5.49	4.13	† 2.43	5.08
Lesotho	666	8.43	13.34	12.73	11.81	10.73	7.45	4.92	4.83	5.19	5.16	4.24	3.95
Liberia	668	6.34	6.37	....	6.43	6.22	6.25	6.18	5.94	6.25	5.29	3.84	3.43
Madagascar	674	19.50	18.50	19.00	14.38	8.00	15.33	15.00	12.00	12.00	11.50	15.19	18.75
Malawi	676	25.00	37.27	26.33	10.21	19.06	33.21	33.25	34.96	28.08	25.13	13.73	10.92
Mauritania	682	....	....	....	....	....	....	....	....	....	8.00	....	....
Mauritius	684	11.04	12.23	10.77	9.08	9.28	10.92	9.61	9.78	9.88	9.53	8.15	7.25
Morocco	686	....	....	....	....	7.26	6.39	5.16	5.04	4.54	3.78	3.61	3.52
Mozambique	688	33.38	38.84	18.14	25.43	8.22	7.86	9.70	† 15.01	17.99	12.15	9.91	7.80
Namibia	728	9.18	10.84	12.56	12.70	12.94	10.82	7.39	6.79	7.81	8.76	6.35	6.24
Nigeria	694	13.09	13.53	13.06	7.17	10.11	12.81	11.69	15.26	16.67	14.22	13.70	10.53
Rwanda	714	....	....	10.92	9.46	8.50	7.95	8.94	9.22	8.00	8.14	....	7.95
São Tomé & Príncipe	716	35.00	35.00	31.00	36.75	38.29	27.00	† 21.00	15.00	15.00	11.79	11.49	....
Seychelles	718	8.85	9.22	9.90	9.20	7.53	5.13	4.77	4.92	4.93	3.99	3.55	3.72
Sierra Leone	724	11.63	7.03	13.96	9.91	7.12	9.50	9.25	7.67	8.23	8.42	10.14	11.07
South Africa	199	11.11	13.54	14.91	15.38	16.50	12.24	9.20	† 9.37	10.77	9.76	6.55	6.04
Swaziland	734	7.54	9.44	11.08	12.00	11.92	9.86	6.53	6.15	8.02	7.59	4.63	4.01
Tanzania	738	....	24.63	13.59	7.83	7.75	7.75	† 7.39	4.81	3.29	3.05	4.20	4.70
Uganda	746	9.99	7.61	10.62	11.84	11.36	8.73	9.84	8.47	5.56	9.85	7.74	8.79
Zambia	754	46.14	30.24	42.13	34.48	13.08	20.27	20.24	23.41	23.33	21.95	11.51	11.19
Zimbabwe	698	26.75	25.92	21.58	18.60	29.06	38.51	50.17	13.95	18.38	35.92	103.21	91.08
Asia													
Bangladesh	513	6.40	6.04	7.28	8.11	8.42	8.74	8.56	8.50	8.17	7.82	7.11	8.09
Bhutan	514	8.00	8.00	8.25	8.25	8.25	8.25	8.25	7.50	7.00	5.00	4.50	4.50
Brunei Darussalam	516	....	....	....	....	....	....	....	....	....	1.06	1.04	1.01
Cambodia	522	....	8.71	8.80	8.03	7.80	7.33	6.83	4.36	2.49	2.02	1.79	1.92

National Interest Rates

		1994	1995	1996	1997	1998	1999	2000	2001	2002	2003	2004	2005
						Deposit Rates (60l)							
						except for United States (60lc)							
						(Period averages in percent per annum)							

		1994	1995	1996	1997	1998	1999	2000	2001	2002	2003	2004	2005
Asia(Cont.)													
China,P.R.: Mainland	924	10.98	10.98	7.47	5.67	3.78	2.25	2.25	2.25	1.98	1.98	2.25	2.25
China,P.R.:Hong Kong	532	3.54	5.63	4.64	5.98	6.62	4.50	4.80	2.38	.35	.07	.03	1.26
China,P.R.:Macao	546	4.21	5.93	5.23	6.22	7.00	5.30	5.33	2.59	.63	....	.08	1.58
Fiji	819	3.15	3.18	3.38	3.08	2.17	1.24	.90	.78	.62	.51	.38	.38
Indonesia	536	12.53	16.72	17.26	20.01	39.07	25.74	12.50	15.48	15.50	10.59	6.44	8.08
Korea	542	8.50	8.83	7.50	† 10.81	13.29	7.95	7.94	5.79	4.95	4.25	3.87	3.72
Lao People's Dem.Rep.	544	12.00	14.00	16.00	....	17.79	13.42	12.00	6.50	6.00	6.58	7.85	4.75
Malaysia	548	4.89	5.93	7.09	7.78	8.51	4.12	3.36	3.37	3.21	3.07	3.00	3.00
Maldives	556	....	....	6.80	6.80	6.80	6.93	6.88	6.97	7.50	7.50	† 6.50	6.50
Micronesia, Fed.Sts.	868	....	5.33	4.58	4.21	3.98	3.72	4.59	3.17	1.47	1.02	1.02	1.62
Mongolia	948	115.71	74.62	44.75	36.37	27.51	23.42	16.80	14.30	13.22	14.00	14.15	13.00
Myanmar	518	9.00	9.75	12.50	12.50	12.50	11.00	9.75	9.50	9.50	9.50	9.50	9.50
Nepal	558	8.75	....	9.63	9.79	8.92	7.31	5.96	4.75	....	....	2.65	2.25
Papua New Guinea	853	5.09	† 7.30	7.13	4.13	8.36	8.13	8.46	5.46	3.18	4.38	1.73	.85
Philippines	566	10.54	8.39	9.68	10.19	12.11	8.17	8.31	8.74	4.61	5.22	6.18	5.56
Samoa	862	5.50	5.50	5.50	5.50	6.50	6.50	6.46	5.53	5.10	5.10	5.10	5.10
Singapore	576	3.00	3.50	3.41	3.47	4.60	1.68	1.71	1.54	.91	.51	.41	.44
Solomon Islands	813	9.00	8.38	6.46	2.42	2.33	2.88	2.54	1.35	.75	.75	.92	.98
Sri Lanka	524	13.10	12.13	12.36	11.25	9.56	9.12	9.17	11.01	9.22	6.00	5.07	10.23
Thailand	578	8.46	11.58	10.33	10.52	10.65	4.73	3.29	2.54	1.98	1.33	1.00	1.88
Tonga	866	4.64	4.72	5.53	5.57	5.63	5.42	5.36	5.47	5.47	5.47	5.85	5.90
Vanuatu	846	5.06	3.00	4.50	3.73	3.29	1.60	1.27	1.25	1.00	1.21	1.71	2.00
Vietnam	582	....	....	....	8.51	9.23	7.37	3.65	5.30	6.45	6.62	....	7.15
Europe													
Albania	914	19.83	† 15.30	16.78	27.28	22.56	12.95	8.30	7.73	8.54	8.38	6.61	5.09
Armenia	911	....	63.18	32.19	26.08	24.94	27.35	18.08	14.90	9.60	6.87	4.90	5.81
Azerbaijan, Republic of	912	....	....	....	....	....	12.08	12.90	8.46	8.66	9.54	9.18	8.52
Belarus	913	89.60	100.82	32.36	15.64	14.33	23.80	37.55	34.18	26.85	17.44	12.72	9.23
Bosnia & Herzegovina	963	....	....	....	....	51.88	9.07	14.67	....	† 4.53	4.03	3.72	3.56
Bulgaria	918	51.14	35.94	74.68	46.83	3.00	3.21	3.10	2.88	2.77	2.89	3.01	3.04
Croatia	960	6.52	5.53	5.59	4.30	4.62	4.31	3.74	3.23	1.89	1.53	1.87	1.71
Cyprus	423	5.75	5.75	† 7.00	6.50	6.50	6.50	6.50	4.65	4.20	3.30	3.99	3.48
Czech Republic	935	7.07	6.96	6.79	7.71	8.08	4.48	3.42	2.87	2.00	1.33	1.28	1.17
Estonia	939	11.51	8.74	6.05	6.19	8.07	4.19	3.76	4.03	2.74	2.40	2.16	2.13
Georgia	915	....	....	31.05	13.73	17.00	14.58	10.17	7.75	9.82	9.28	7.24	7.55
Hungary	944	20.31	† 24.36	18.57	16.94	14.42	11.94	9.49	8.40	7.41	10.98	9.09	5.17
Kyrgyz Republic	917	....	....	36.73	39.59	35.76	35.58	18.38	12.50	5.91	4.98	6.70	5.76
Latvia	941	31.68	14.79	11.71	5.90	5.33	5.04	4.38	5.24	3.23	3.02	3.27	2.78
Lithuania	946	48.43	20.05	13.95	7.89	5.98	4.94	3.86	3.00	1.70	1.27	1.22	....
Macedonia, FYR	962	117.56	24.07	12.75	11.64	11.68	11.40	11.18	9.97	9.56	7.97	6.54	6.60
Malta	181	4.50	4.50	4.50	4.56	4.64	4.66	4.86	4.84	4.30	3.44	2.63	2.71
Moldova	921	....	....	25.43	23.47	21.68	27.54	24.87	20.93	14.20	12.55	15.12	13.22
Poland	964	† 33.40	26.78	20.02	19.36	18.19	11.22	14.17	11.80	6.21	3.71	3.75	2.79
Russia	922	....	101.96	55.05	† 16.77	17.05	13.68	6.51	4.85	4.96	4.48	3.79	3.99
Slovak Republic	936	9.32	9.01	9.30	13.44	16.25	14.37	8.45	6.46	6.65	5.33	4.14	† 2.44
Slovenia	961	28.10	15.38	15.08	13.19	10.54	7.24	10.05	9.81	8.24	5.95	3.82	3.18
Tajikistan	923	....	....	....	23.93	9.82	5.24	1.26	5.19	† 9.21	9.67	9.75	9.75
Turkey	186	87.79	76.02	80.74	79.49	80.11	78.43	47.16	74.70	50.49	37.68	24.26	20.40
Ukraine	926	208.63	70.29	33.63	18.21	22.25	20.70	13.72	10.99	7.93	6.98	7.80	8.57
Middle East													
Bahrain, Kingdom of	419	4.00	5.70	5.18	5.28	4.74	4.80	5.82	2.71	1.34	1.48	1.54	3.14
Egypt	469	11.83	10.92	10.54	9.84	9.36	9.22	9.46	9.46	9.33	8.23	7.73	7.23
Israel	436	12.19	14.08	14.48	13.07	10.99	11.34	8.63	6.18	6.03	6.65	3.62	3.24
Jordan	439	7.09	7.68	8.50	9.10	8.21	8.30	6.97	5.81	4.43	3.14	2.49	2.91
Kuwait	443	5.70	6.53	6.05	5.93	6.32	5.76	5.89	4.47	3.15	2.42	2.65	3.47
Lebanon	446	14.80	16.30	15.54	13.37	13.61	12.50	11.21	10.85	11.03	8.69	7.37	8.15
Oman	449	4.34	6.53	6.85	7.30	8.46	8.12	7.63	4.50	2.89	2.37	2.32	3.30
Qatar	453	4.84	6.19	6.50	6.63	6.56	6.50	....	....	....	....	....	....
Saudi Arabia	456	5.10	6.18	5.47	5.79	6.21	6.14	6.67	3.92	2.23	1.63	1.73	3.75
Syrian Arab Republic	463	4.00	4.00	4.00	4.00	4.00	4.00	4.00	4.00	4.00	3.33	1.92	1.00
Western Hemisphere													
ECCU	309	3.87	4.06	4.16	4.20	4.30	4.35	4.46	4.37	4.04	4.43	3.76	4.08
Anguilla	312	3.47	3.64	3.74	3.77	3.79	3.78	3.52	3.54	3.25	4.59	4.83	4.91
Antigua and Barbuda	311	4.19	4.02	4.33	4.36	4.34	4.45	5.18	4.49	4.36	4.86	4.12	3.72
Dominica	321	4.50	4.20	4.30	4.27	4.23	4.38	3.87	3.98	3.91	3.66	3.26	3.31
Grenada	328	3.61	3.67	3.74	3.93	4.16	4.30	4.24	4.23	3.59	3.39	3.32	2.88
Montserrat	351	3.25	3.24	3.29	3.02	2.74	3.14	3.35	3.35	3.08	3.06	2.29	2.52
St. Kitts and Nevis	361	3.99	4.52	4.27	4.27	4.22	4.31	4.32	4.23	4.01	4.49	4.54	4.53
St. Lucia	362	3.83	4.43	4.50	4.65	4.80	4.76	4.80	4.88	4.27	5.47	3.05	2.85
St. Vincent & Grens	364	3.89	4.34	4.14	4.21	4.27	4.46	4.54	4.56	4.35	4.56	3.30	2.88
Argentina	213	8.08	11.90	7.36	6.97	7.56	8.05	8.34	16.16	39.25	10.16	2.61	3.76
Aruba	314	4.40	4.30	4.20	4.40	....	† 6.17	6.20	5.84	5.56	5.33	4.26	3.94
Bahamas, The	313	4.30	4.20	5.14	5.23	5.36	4.57	4.08	4.25	4.25	3.95	3.83	3.22
Barbados	316	4.32	5.11	5.20	4.58	4.20	4.40	4.97	4.04	2.70	2.56	2.54	3.18
Belize	339	8.55	9.37	9.08	9.19	8.76	8.12	7.69	6.35	6.28	6.93	7.42	7.71
Bolivia	218	18.43	18.87	19.16	14.73	12.82	12.26	10.98	9.82	9.58	11.41	7.42	4.93
Brazil	223	5,175.24	52.25	26.45	24.35	28.00	26.02	17.20	17.86	19.14	21.97	15.42	17.63
Chile	228	15.12	13.73	13.48	12.02	14.92	8.56	9.20	6.19	3.80	2.73	1.94	3.93
Colombia	233	29.42	32.34	31.15	24.13	32.58	21.33	12.15	12.44	8.94	7.80	7.80	7.01
Costa Rica	238	17.72	23.88	17.29	13.03	12.76	14.31	13.38	11.77	11.46	10.41	9.51	10.14
Dominican Republic	243	13.70	14.94	13.91	13.40	17.65	16.07	17.65	15.61	16.54	20.50	21.12	13.86

National Interest Rates

Deposit Rates (60l)
except for United States (60lc)
(Period averages in percent per annum)

Western Hemisphere(Cont.)		1994	1995	1996	1997	1998	1999	2000	2001	2002	2003	2004	2005
Ecuador	248	33.65	43.31	41.50	28.09	39.39	† 10.03	8.46	6.58	5.47	5.53	4.08	3.53
El Salvador	253	13.57	14.37	13.98	11.77	10.32	10.75	9.31	....	....	....	....	....
Guatemala	258	9.69	7.87	7.65	† 5.83	5.44	7.96	10.17	8.75	6.92	4.78	4.19	4.35
Guyana	336	11.42	12.90	10.49	8.56	8.10	9.08	8.71	7.63	4.53	3.18	2.67	2.60
Haiti	263	....	....	....	10.74	13.06	7.39	11.85	13.66	8.24	13.99	10.79	3.39
Honduras	268	11.56	11.97	16.70	21.28	18.58	19.97	15.93	14.48	13.74	11.48	11.09	10.90
Jamaica	343	36.41	23.21	25.16	13.95	15.61	13.48	11.62	9.64	8.58	8.46	7.98	7.50
Mexico	273	15.03	39.82	26.40	16.36	15.45	11.60	8.26	6.23	3.76	3.09	2.70	3.46
Netherlands Antilles	353	4.05	3.75	3.67	3.66	3.58	3.59	3.63	3.65	3.62	3.48	2.92	2.78
Nicaragua	278	11.70	11.15	12.35	12.41	10.77	† 11.83	10.80	11.56	7.79	5.55	4.72	4.03
Panama	283	6.11	7.18	7.20	7.03	6.76	6.92	7.07	6.83	4.97	3.98	2.23	2.70
Paraguay	288	23.12	21.16	17.16	13.00	† 16.21	19.75	15.72	16.22	22.86	15.83	5.11	1.66
Peru	293	22.35	15.70	14.90	15.01	15.11	16.27	13.29	9.92	4.19	3.83	2.98	3.43
Suriname	366	7.45	21.00	17.83	17.25	16.00	15.60	15.48	11.86	9.00	8.28	8.34	7.97
Trinidad and Tobago	369	6.91	....	....	6.91	7.95	8.51	8.15	7.66	4.76	2.91	2.79	2.20
Uruguay	298	55.78	57.68	42.43	29.57	22.76	21.49	18.26	21.60	† 62.58	29.69	6.20	2.84
Venezuela, Rep. Bol.	299	39.02	24.72	27.58	14.70	34.84	21.28	16.30	15.51	29.00	17.21	12.60	11.63

National Interest Rates

		1994	1995	1996	1997	1998	1999	2000	2001	2002	2003	2004	2005
							Lending Rates (60p)						
							(Period averages in percent per annum)						
Industrial Countries													
United States	111	7.14	8.83	8.27	8.44	8.35	7.99	9.23	6.92	4.68	4.12	4.34	6.19
Canada	156	6.88	8.65	6.06	4.96	6.60	6.44	7.27	5.81	4.21	4.69	4.00	4.42
Australia	193	9.23	10.70	10.50	8.89	8.15	7.99	9.27	8.66	8.16	8.41	8.85	9.06
Japan	158	4.13	3.51	2.66	2.45	2.32	2.16	2.07	1.97	1.86	1.82	1.77	1.68
New Zealand	196	9.69	12.09	12.27	11.35	11.22	8.49	10.22	9.88	9.83	9.81	10.38	11.53
Euro Area	163	....	....	8.88	7.58	6.73	5.65	6.60	6.83	6.14	....	....	....
Austria	122	....	....	....	....	6.42	5.64	....	....	....	....	....	....
Belgium	124	9.42	8.42	7.17	7.06	7.25	6.71	7.98	8.46	7.71	6.89	6.70	6.72
Finland	172	7.91	7.75	6.16	5.29	5.35	4.71	5.61	5.79	4.82	....	3.69	....
France	132	7.89	8.12	6.77	6.34	6.55	6.36	6.70	6.98	6.60	6.60	6.60	....
Germany	134	11.48	10.94	10.02	9.13	9.02	8.81	9.63	10.01	9.70	....	....	....
Greece	174	27.44	23.05	20.96	18.92	18.56	15.00	12.32	8.59	7.41	6.79	....	....
Ireland	178	6.13	6.56	5.85	6.57	6.22	3.34	4.77	4.84	3.83	2.85	2.57	2.65
Italy	136	11.22	12.47	12.06	9.75	7.88	5.58	6.26	6.53	5.78	5.03	....	5.31
Luxembourg	137	6.58	6.50	5.50	5.50	5.27	....	....	....	....	....	....	....
Netherlands	138	8.29	7.21	5.90	6.13	6.50	† 3.46	4.79	5.00	3.96	3.00	2.75	2.77
Portugal	182	15.01	13.80	11.73	9.15	7.24	5.19	....	....	....	....	....	....
Spain	184	8.95	10.05	8.50	6.08	5.01	3.95	5.18	5.16	4.31	....	....	....
Denmark	128	† 9.95	10.33	8.70	7.73	7.90	7.13	8.08	8.20	† 7.10	....	....	....
Iceland	176	10.57	11.58	12.43	12.89	12.78	13.30	16.80	17.95	15.37	11.95	12.02	....
Norway	142	8.38	7.60	6.68	6.00	9.80	7.61	8.93	8.69	8.71	4.73	4.04	4.04
Sweden	144	10.64	11.11	7.38	7.01	5.94	5.53	5.83	5.55	5.64	4.79	4.00	3.31
Switzerland	146	5.51	5.48	4.97	4.47	4.07	3.90	4.29	4.30	3.93	3.27	3.20	3.12
United Kingdom	112	5.48	6.69	5.96	6.58	7.21	5.33	5.98	5.08	4.00	3.69	4.40	4.65
Developing Countries													
Africa													
CEMAC	758	16.00	16.00	22.00	22.00	22.00	22.00	22.00	18.00	18.00	18.00	18.00	17.00
Cameroon	622	17.50	16.00	22.00	22.00	22.00	22.00	22.00	20.67	18.00	18.00	18.00	17.67
Central African Rep.	626	17.50	16.00	22.00	22.00	22.00	22.00	22.00	20.67	18.00	18.00	18.00	17.67
Chad	628	17.50	16.00	22.00	22.00	22.00	22.00	22.00	20.67	18.00	18.00	18.00	17.67
Congo, Republic of	634	17.50	16.00	22.00	22.00	22.00	22.00	22.00	20.67	18.00	18.00	18.00	17.67
Equatorial Guinea	642	17.50	16.00	22.00	22.00	22.00	22.00	22.00	20.67	18.00	18.00	18.00	17.67
Gabon	646	17.50	16.00	22.00	22.00	22.00	22.00	22.00	20.67	18.00	18.00	18.00	17.67
Algeria	612	16.00	† 19.00	19.00	12.50	11.00	10.00	10.00	9.50	8.50	8.00	8.00	8.00
Angola	614	....	206.25	217.88	37.75	45.00	† 80.30	† 103.16	95.97	97.34	96.12	82.33	67.72
Botswana	616	13.92	14.42	14.50	13.95	13.65	14.78	15.48	15.75	16.21	16.33	15.75	15.74
Burundi	618	14.20	15.26	....	....	....	15.24	15.77	16.82	19.47	18.23	18.25	19.11
Cape Verde	624	10.67	12.00	12.00	12.06	12.51	12.03	11.94	12.85	13.17	12.73	12.69	12.29
Comoros	632	....	....	....	....	....	† 13.67	12.00	12.00	12.00	11.83	11.00	11.00
Congo, Dem. Rep. of	636	398.25	293.88	247.00	134.58	29.00	124.58	165.00	167.92	66.79	....	....	....
Djibouti	611	....	....	....	....	....	....	....	11.46	11.30	11.30	11.25	11.15
Ethiopia	644	14.33	15.08	13.92	10.50	10.50	10.58	10.89	10.87	8.66	† 7.00	7.00	7.00
Gambia, The	648	25.00	25.04	25.50	25.50	25.38	24.00	24.00	24.00	24.00	29.33	36.50	34.92
Guinea	656	22.00	21.50	....	....	19.56	19.88	19.38	....	....	....	....	....
Guinea-Bissau	654	36.33	32.92	51.75	....	....	....	....	....	....	....	....	....
Kenya	664	36.24	28.80	33.79	30.25	29.49	22.38	22.34	19.67	18.45	16.57	† 12.53	12.88
Lesotho	666	14.25	16.38	17.71	18.03	20.06	19.06	17.11	16.55	17.11	16.02	12.38	11.72
Liberia	668	14.53	15.57	....	16.83	† 21.74	16.72	20.53	22.14	20.21	17.06	18.10	17.03
Madagascar	674	30.50	37.50	32.75	30.00	27.00	28.00	26.50	25.25	25.25	24.25	25.50	27.00
Malawi	676	31.00	47.33	45.33	28.25	37.67	53.58	53.13	56.17	50.54	48.92	36.83	33.08
Mauritania	682	....	....	....	....	....	....	....	....	....	21.00	....	....
Mauritius	684	18.92	20.81	20.81	18.92	19.92	21.63	20.77	21.10	21.00	21.00	21.00	21.04
Morocco	686	10.00	....	....	....	13.50	13.50	13.31	13.25	13.13	12.56	11.50	....
Mozambique	688	....	....	....	....	24.35	19.63	19.04	† 22.73	26.71	24.69	22.08	19.47
Namibia	728	17.05	18.51	19.16	20.18	20.72	18.48	15.28	14.53	13.84	14.70	11.39	10.61
Nigeria	694	20.48	20.23	19.84	17.80	18.18	20.29	21.27	23.44	24.77	20.71	19.18	17.95
Rwanda	714	....	....	....	....	....	....	....	....	....	....	....	....
São Tomé & Príncipe	716	30.00	52.00	38.00	51.50	55.58	40.33	† 39.67	37.00	37.08	32.68	29.77	....
Seychelles	718	15.72	15.76	16.22	14.88	14.39	12.01	11.45	11.14	11.09	11.08	10.13	9.98
Sierra Leone	724	27.33	28.83	32.12	23.87	23.83	26.83	26.25	24.27	22.17	20.00	22.08	24.58
South Africa	199	15.58	17.90	19.52	20.00	21.79	18.00	14.50	13.77	15.75	14.96	11.29	10.63
Swaziland	734	14.25	17.05	18.67	19.50	19.50	17.42	14.00	13.25	15.25	14.63	11.29	10.63
Tanzania	738	39.00	42.83	† 33.97	26.27	22.89	21.89	† 21.58	20.26	16.43	14.48	13.92	15.12
Uganda	746	....	20.16	20.29	21.37	20.86	21.55	22.92	22.66	19.10	18.94	20.60	19.80
Zambia	754	70.56	45.53	53.78	46.69	31.80	40.52	38.80	46.23	45.20	40.57	30.73	28.21
Zimbabwe	698	34.86	34.73	34.23	32.55	42.06	55.39	68.21	38.02	36.48	97.29	278.92	235.68
Asia													
Bangladesh	513	14.50	14.00	14.00	14.00	14.00	14.13	15.50	15.83	16.00	16.00	14.75	14.00
Bhutan	514	16.00	16.00	16.00	16.00	16.00	16.00	16.00	15.75	15.25	15.00	15.00	14.00
Brunei Darussalam	516	....	....	....	....	6.50	5.50	5.50	5.50	5.50	5.50	5.50	† 5.50
Cambodia	522	....	18.70	18.80	18.40	18.33	17.56	17.34	16.50	16.23	18.47	17.62	17.33
China,P.R.: Mainland	924	10.98	12.06	10.08	8.64	6.39	5.85	5.85	5.85	5.31	5.31	5.58	5.58
China,P.R.:Hong Kong	532	8.50	8.75	8.50	9.50	9.00	8.50	9.50	5.13	5.00	5.00	5.00	7.75
China,P.R.:Macao	546	7.95	9.90	9.56	9.73	10.97	9.46	9.89	7.99	6.11	6.00	6.01	7.05
Fiji	819	11.28	11.06	11.33	11.03	9.66	8.77	8.40	8.34	8.05	7.60	7.17	6.78
India	534	14.75	15.46	15.96	13.83	13.54	12.54	12.29	12.08	11.92	11.46	10.92	10.75
Indonesia	536	17.76	18.85	19.22	21.82	32.15	27.66	18.46	18.55	18.95	16.94	14.12	14.05
Korea	542	8.50	9.00	8.84	† 11.88	15.28	9.40	8.55	7.71	6.77	6.24	5.90	5.59
Lao People's Dem.Rep.	544	24.00	† 25.67	27.00	....	29.28	32.00	32.00	26.17	29.33	30.50	29.25	26.83
Malaysia	548	8.76	8.73	9.94	10.63	12.13	8.56	7.67	7.13	6.53	6.30	6.05	5.95
Maldives	556	....	....	15.00	15.00	15.00	12.50	13.00	13.00	13.54	14.00	† 13.00	13.00

National Interest Rates

		1994	1995	1996	1997	1998	1999	2000	2001	2002	2003	2004	2005
							Lending Rates (60p) *(Period averages in percent per annum)*						
Asia(Cont.)													
Micronesia, Fed.Sts.	868	....	15.00	15.00	15.00	15.00	15.17	15.33	15.33	15.28	15.00	15.38	16.38
Mongolia	948	279.22	134.37	87.91	82.05	46.77	39.29	32.75	30.24	28.38	26.31	25.38	23.56
Myanmar	518	16.50	16.50	16.50	16.50	16.50	16.13	15.25	15.00	15.00	15.00	15.00	15.00
Nepal	558	....	....	12.88	14.54	14.00	11.33	9.46	7.67	....	....	8.50	8.13
Papua New Guinea	853	9.16	13.14	13.30	10.45	17.70	18.90	17.54	16.21	13.89	13.36	13.25	11.47
Philippines	566	15.06	14.68	14.84	16.28	16.78	11.78	10.91	12.40	9.14	9.47	10.08	10.18
Samoa	862	12.00	12.00	12.00	12.00	11.50	11.50	11.00	9.93	9.75	9.75	9.75	9.75
Singapore	576	5.88	6.37	6.26	6.32	7.44	5.80	5.83	5.66	5.37	5.31	5.30	5.30
Solomon Islands	813	15.72	16.59	17.78	15.71	14.84	14.50	15.49	15.72	16.42	16.33	16.07	16.08
Sri Lanka	524	18.13	18.04	18.26	14.69	15.03	14.72	16.16	19.39	13.17	10.34	9.47	7.00
Thailand	578	10.90	13.25	13.40	13.65	14.42	8.98	7.83	7.25	6.88	5.94	5.50	5.79
Tonga	866	† 10.36	10.47	10.92	11.15	11.25	11.37	11.34	11.34	11.40	11.34	11.59	11.38
Vanuatu	846	16.00	10.50	10.50	10.50	10.96	10.29	9.85	8.81	7.41	5.90	7.61	7.47
Vietnam	582	....	....	20.10	14.42	14.40	12.70	10.55	9.42	9.06	9.48	....	11.03
Europe													
Albania	914	23.67	† 19.65	23.96	....	....	21.62	22.10	19.65	15.30	14.27	11.76	13.08
Armenia	911	....	111.86	66.36	54.23	48.49	38.85	31.57	26.69	21.14	20.83	18.63	17.98
Azerbaijan, Republic of	912	....	....	....	....	....	19.48	19.66	19.71	17.37	15.46	15.72	17.03
Belarus	913	148.50	175.00	62.33	31.80	26.99	51.04	67.67	46.97	36.88	23.98	16.91	11.36
Bosnia & Herzegovina	963	....	....	....	....	73.50	24.29	30.50	....	† 12.70	10.87	10.28	9.61
Bulgaria	918	72.58	58.98	123.48	83.96	13.30	12.79	11.52	11.11	9.35	8.82	8.77	7.87
Croatia	960	22.91	20.24	22.52	15.47	15.75	14.94	12.07	9.55	† 12.84	11.58	11.75	11.19
Cyprus	423	8.83	8.50	8.50	8.08	8.00	8.00	8.00	† 7.52	7.15	6.95	7.66	7.07
Czech Republic	935	13.12	12.80	12.54	13.20	12.81	8.68	7.16	7.20	6.72	5.95	6.03	5.78
Estonia	939	24.65	19.01	14.87	11.76	15.06	11.09	7.43	7.78	6.70	5.51	5.66	4.93
Georgia	915	....	....	58.24	50.64	46.00	33.42	32.75	27.25	31.83	32.27	31.23	21.63
Hungary	944	27.40	32.61	27.31	21.77	19.28	16.34	12.60	12.12	10.17	9.60	12.82	8.54
Kyrgyz Republic	917	....	....	65.02	49.38	73.44	60.86	51.90	37.33	24.81	19.13	29.27	26.60
Latvia	941	55.86	34.56	25.78	15.25	14.29	14.20	11.87	11.17	7.97	5.38	7.45	6.11
Lithuania	946	62.30	27.08	21.56	14.39	12.21	13.09	12.14	9.63	6.84	5.84	5.74	....
Macedonia, FYR	962	159.82	45.95	21.58	21.42	21.03	20.45	18.93	19.35	18.36	16.00	12.44	12.17
Malta	181	8.50	† 7.38	7.77	7.99	8.09	7.70	7.28	6.90	6.04	5.85	5.32	5.51
Moldova	921	....	....	36.67	33.33	30.83	35.54	33.78	28.69	23.52	19.29	20.94	19.26
Poland	964	32.83	† 33.45	26.08	24.96	24.49	16.94	20.01	18.36	12.03	7.30	7.56	6.83
Russia	922	....	320.31	146.81	† 32.04	41.79	39.72	24.43	17.91	15.71	12.98	11.40	10.68
Slovak Republic	936	14.56	16.85	13.92	18.65	21.17	21.07	14.89	11.24	10.25	8.46	9.07	† 6.68
Slovenia	961	38.87	23.36	22.60	20.02	16.09	12.38	15.77	15.05	13.17	10.75	8.65	7.80
Tajikistan	923	....	....	....	75.52	50.89	26.24	25.59	21.05	† 14.20	16.57	20.32	23.27
Ukraine	926	250.28	122.70	79.88	49.12	54.50	54.95	41.53	32.28	25.35	17.89	17.40	16.17
Middle East													
Bahrain, Kingdom of	419	10.83	11.83	12.45	12.33	11.92	11.86	11.73	10.81	8.50	8.38	7.99	7.90
Egypt	469	16.51	16.47	15.58	13.79	13.02	12.97	13.22	13.29	13.79	13.53	13.38	13.14
Israel	436	17.45	20.22	20.68	18.71	16.18	16.36	12.87	10.03	9.89	10.65	7.44	6.39
Jordan	439	10.45	10.66	11.25	12.25	12.61	12.33	11.80	10.94	10.18	9.30	8.26	7.61
Kuwait	443	7.61	8.37	8.77	8.80	8.93	8.56	8.87	7.88	6.48	5.42	5.64	7.50
Lebanon	446	23.88	24.69	25.21	20.29	....	19.48	18.15	17.19	16.58	13.43	10.81	10.64
Libya	672	....	....	....	....	....	7.00	7.00	7.00	7.00	7.00	6.08	6.13
Oman	449	8.57	9.38	9.23	9.30	10.09	10.32	10.06	9.23	8.55	8.23	7.57	7.01
Syrian Arab Republic	463	9.00	9.00	9.00	9.00	9.00	9.00	9.00	9.00	9.00	8.00	7.54	8.00
Qatar	453	8.86	....	....	....	....	....	....	....	....	....	....	....
Western Hemisphere													
ECCU	309	11.71	11.94	11.74	11.77	11.60	11.91	11.98	11.55	11.47	13.34	10.93	11.42
Anguilla	312	12.84	12.60	11.95	11.37	11.16	11.31	11.32	10.74	10.35	11.42	10.99	10.82
Antigua and Barbuda	311	13.15	12.70	12.26	11.98	12.20	12.07	12.17	11.62	11.39	12.82	11.96	11.49
Dominica	321	11.61	11.50	11.43	11.43	11.17	11.27	11.40	11.68	11.14	10.97	8.94	10.36
Grenada	328	11.03	11.08	9.99	11.24	11.73	11.62	11.60	10.19	11.31	12.05	10.18	10.13
Montserrat	351	13.06	12.63	12.37	12.37	12.15	11.52	11.52	11.52	11.34	12.10	10.95	10.56
St. Kitts and Nevis	361	10.94	10.89	10.92	11.16	11.42	11.21	11.11	11.08	10.89	12.22	10.25	10.09
St. Lucia	362	11.06	12.62	12.82	12.68	11.40	12.79	13.06	12.97	12.59	15.00	11.07	10.27
St. Vincent & Grens.	364	11.73	11.07	11.23	11.29	11.31	11.55	11.46	11.63	11.56	11.83	9.69	9.38
Argentina	213	10.06	17.85	10.51	9.24	10.64	11.04	11.09	27.71	51.68	19.15	6.78	6.16
Aruba	314	10.60	10.60	10.30	10.00	....	† 13.14	12.07	12.10	13.08	11.50	11.58	11.53
Bahamas, The	313	6.88	6.75	6.75	6.75	6.75	6.75	6.38	6.00	6.00	6.00	6.00	5.54
Barbados	316	9.08	10.00	10.00	9.83	9.75	9.40	10.19	9.58	8.50	8.50	8.33	9.17
Belize	339	14.78	15.69	16.30	16.29	16.50	16.27	16.01	15.45	14.83	14.35	13.94	14.26
Bolivia	218	55.57	51.02	55.97	50.05	39.41	35.37	34.60	20.06	20.63	17.66	14.47	16.62
Brazil	223	....	....	....	78.19	86.36	80.44	56.83	57.62	62.88	67.00	54.93	55.38
Chile	228	20.34	18.16	17.37	15.67	20.17	12.62	14.84	11.89	7.76	6.18	5.13	6.68
Colombia	233	40.47	42.72	41.99	34.22	42.24	† 25.77	18.79	20.72	16.33	15.19	15.08	14.56
Costa Rica	238	33.03	36.70	26.27	22.48	22.47	25.74	24.89	23.83	26.42	25.58	23.43	24.66
Dominican Republic	243	28.68	30.68	23.73	21.01	25.64	25.05	26.80	24.26	26.06	31.39	32.63	24.11
Ecuador	248	43.99	55.67	54.50	43.02	49.55	† 16.53	16.26	15.46	15.08	13.08	9.65	9.34
El Salvador	253	19.03	19.08	18.57	16.05	14.98	15.46	13.96	....	....	....	....	....
Guatemala	258	22.93	21.16	22.72	† 18.64	16.56	19.51	20.88	18.96	16.86	14.98	13.81	13.03
Guyana	336	18.36	19.22	17.79	17.04	16.77	17.11	17.01	17.01	16.33	14.99	14.54	14.54
Haiti	263	....	....	....	21.00	23.62	22.88	25.09	28.63	25.67	30.58	34.08	27.38
Honduras	268	24.68	26.95	29.74	32.07	30.69	30.15	26.82	23.76	22.69	20.80	19.88	18.83
Jamaica	343	49.46	43.58	39.83	32.86	31.59	27.01	23.35	20.61	18.50	18.89	18.14	17.36
Mexico	273	19.30	59.43	36.39	22.14	26.36	23.74	16.93	12.80	8.20	6.91	7.22	9.90
Netherlands Antilles	353	12.73	12.93	13.21	13.29	13.58	13.60	9.98	10.44	10.14	11.26	10.56	9.60
Nicaragua	278	20.14	19.89	20.72	21.02	21.63	† 17.57	18.14	18.55	18.30	15.55	13.49	12.10
Panama	283	10.15	11.10	10.62	10.63	10.82	10.05	† 10.48	10.97	10.58	9.93	8.82	8.67

National Interest Rates

		1994	1995	1996	1997	1998	1999	2000	2001	2002	2003	2004	2005
							Lending Rates (60p)						
							(Period averages in percent per annum)						
Western Hemisphere(Cont.)													
Paraguay..	288	† 35.47	33.94	31.88	27.79	30.49	30.21	26.78	28.25	38.66	49.99	33.54	29.91
Peru...	293	53.56	27.16	26.07	29.96	30.80	30.79	27.91	20.43	14.73	14.21	14.49	14.97
Suriname..	366	15.38	40.18	35.78	33.13	27.50	27.33	28.95	25.73	22.18	21.04	20.44	18.06
Trinidad and Tobago.......................	369	15.98	15.17	15.79	15.33	17.33	17.04	16.50	15.67	12.48	11.17	9.31	9.10
Uruguay..	298	89.28	93.05	85.93	67.19	54.39	50.03	46.06	48.56	† 118.38	58.94	23.68	13.61
Venezuela, Rep. Bol........................	299	54.66	39.74	39.41	23.69	46.35	32.13	25.20	22.45	36.58	25.19	18.50	16.81

National Interest Rates

		1994	1995	1996	1997	1998	1999	2000	2001	2002	2003	2004	2005
						Government Bond Yields (61) *(Average yields to maturity in percent per annum)*							
Industrial Countries													
United States	111	7.08	6.58	6.44	6.35	5.26	5.64	6.03	5.02	4.61	4.02	4.27	4.29
Canada	156	8.63	8.28	7.50	6.42	5.47	5.69	5.89	5.78	5.66	5.28	5.08	4.39
Australia	193	9.04	9.17	8.17	6.89	5.50	6.08	6.26	5.63	5.82	5.36	5.61	5.32
Japan	158	3.71	2.53	2.23	1.69	1.10	† 1.77	1.75	1.33	1.25	1.01	1.50	1.36
New Zealand	196	7.48	7.94	8.04	7.21	6.47	6.13	6.85	6.12	6.28	5.51	5.98	5.98
Euro Area	163	8.18	8.73	7.23	5.96	4.70	4.65	5.44	5.03	4.92	4.16	4.14	3.44
Austria	122	6.69	6.47	5.30	4.79	4.29	4.09	....	....	....	....	....	....
Belgium	124	7.82	7.45	6.45	5.74	4.72	4.81	5.58	5.13	4.96	4.18	4.15	3.41
Finland	172	9.03	8.78	....	....	....	4.72	5.48	5.04	4.98	4.14	4.11	3.35
France	132	7.35	7.59	6.39	5.63	4.72	4.69	5.45	5.05	4.93	4.18	4.15	3.46
Germany	134	6.67	6.50	5.63	5.08	4.39	4.26	5.24	4.70	4.61	3.81	3.75	3.18
Greece	174	....	....	....	....	8.48	6.30	6.10	5.30	5.12	4.27	4.26	3.59
Ireland	178	8.19	8.30	7.48	6.49	4.99	....	....	....	....	....	....	....
Italy	136	10.56	12.21	9.40	6.86	4.90	4.73	5.58	5.19	5.03	4.25	4.26	3.56
Luxembourg	137	6.38	6.05	5.21	5.39	5.29	....	....	....	....	....	....	....
Netherlands	138	7.20	7.20	6.49	5.81	4.87	4.92	5.51	5.17	5.00	4.18	4.10	3.37
Portugal	182	10.83	10.34	7.25	5.48	4.09	....	....	....	....	....	....	....
Spain	184	9.69	11.04	8.18	5.84	4.55	4.30	5.36	4.87	4.62	3.52	3.59	3.05
Denmark	128	7.41	7.58	6.04	5.08	4.59	4.30	5.54	....	4.57	3.53	3.32	3.01
Iceland	176	5.02	7.18	5.61	5.49	4.73	4.28	5.35	5.33	5.23	4.41	3.88	....
Norway	142	7.13	6.82	5.94	5.13	5.35	5.38	6.38	6.31	6.33	4.50	3.60	3.28
Sweden	144	9.52	10.24	8.06	6.61	4.99	4.98	5.37	5.11	5.30	4.64	4.42	3.38
Switzerland	146	5.23	3.73	3.63	3.08	† 2.71	3.62	3.55	3.56	2.40	2.78	2.38	1.96
United Kingdom	112	8.05	8.26	8.10	7.09	5.45	4.70	4.68	4.78	4.83	4.64	4.77	4.39
Developing Countries													
Africa													
Botswana	616	....	....	....	....	....	....	....	....	....	10.46	10.07	9.49
Ethiopia	644	13.00	13.00	13.00	....	....	....	....	....	....	† 3.05	3.91	3.98
Ghana	652	....	....	....	....	....	....	....	....	....	....	21.50	20.54
Malawi	676	23.50	38.58	42.67	39.25	....	....	....	....	....	....	....	....
Namibia	728	14.63	16.11	15.48	14.70	15.10	14.90	13.81	11.39	12.86	12.72	† 11.88	10.68
Seychelles	718	14.38	13.25	13.25	11.63	8.96	8.58	8.22	8.13	8.25	5.96	6.58	6.00
South Africa	199	14.83	16.11	15.48	14.70	15.12	14.90	13.79	11.41	11.50	9.62	9.53	8.07
Asia													
Fiji	819	6.49	6.69	7.41	7.08	6.49	6.17	5.57	4.79	4.28	3.27	2.56	2.76
Korea	542	12.30	12.40	10.90	11.70	12.80	8.72	8.50	6.66	6.47	4.93	4.45	4.66
Malaysia	548	5.11	6.51	6.39	6.87	7.66	5.63	5.11	3.54	3.47	3.60	4.09	3.57
Myanmar	518	10.50	10.50	13.13	14.00	14.00	† 11.00	9.00	9.00	9.00	9.00	9.00	9.00
Nepal	558	9.00	3.00	9.00	9.00	9.00	8.75	8.50	8.50	8.25	7.50	6.63	6.50
Pakistan	564	7.07	6.63	6.06	5.43	4.79	4.16	....	....	....	....	....	....
Papua New Guinea	853	....	....	....	....	....	....	....	....	....	....	....	8.00
Philippines	566	13.25	14.25	13.99	13.01	† 17.99	12.33	11.77	13.40	8.69	8.72	10.27	8.66
Samoa	862	13.50	13.50	13.50	13.50	13.50	13.50	13.50	13.50	13.50	13.50	13.50	13.50
Solomon Islands	813	13.00	13.00	11.50	11.75	12.50	12.88	13.00	13.00	13.00	13.00	13.00	13.00
Sri Lanka	524	....	....	....	....	....	....	....	....	....	....	....	....
Thailand	578	10.75	10.75	10.75	10.75	10.25	6.69	6.95	5.82	5.07	3.76	5.09	5.13
Vanuatu	846	8.00	8.00	8.00	8.00	8.00	8.50	8.50	8.50	8.50	8.50	8.50	8.50
Europe													
Armenia	911	....	....	....	....	....	....	25.51	23.15	17.44	15.71	8.21	5.18
Bulgaria	918	56.86	49.76	....	....	10.10	10.05	7.38	6.70	6.75	....	....	3.34
Czech Republic	935	....	....	....	....	....	....	6.72	4.84	3.17	3.77	3.33	3.19
Slovak Republic	936	....	....	....	....	....	....	8.34	8.06	6.91	4.99	5.02	3.52
Western Hemisphere													
Honduras	268	23.11	27.24	35.55	29.59	20.34	16.04	14.79	15.28	11.97	11.26	11.67	11.32
Jamaica	343	26.82	26.85	26.87	26.85	....	....	....	....	....	....	....	....
Mexico	273	....	51.74	32.81	21.44	....	20.11	† 15.81	† 10.28	10.13	8.98	9.54	9.42
Netherlands Antilles	353	7.48	8.02	8.25	8.67	8.60	8.75	8.77	9.00	8.20	6.72	7.09	6.46
Venezuela, Rep. Bol.	299	54.73	53.38	49.09	25.41	47.88	† 31.12	21.03	22.12	38.51	32.15	15.57	12.93

International Interest Rates

London Interbank Offer Rates on SDR Deposits
(99260lsa, 60lsb, 60lsc)
(Period averages in percent per annum)

		1994	1995	1996	1997	1998	1999	2000	2001	2002	2003	2004	2005
Three-Month	992	3.86	4.60	3.72	3.91	....	....	....	....	....	....	....	....
Six-Month	992	3.97	4.63	3.79	4.00	....	....	....	....	....	....	....	....
One-Year	992	4.22	4.72	3.95	4.14	....	....	....	....	....	....	....	....

London Interbank Offer Rates on US Dollar Deposits
(11160lda, 60ldb, 60ldc, 60ldd, 60lde, 60ldf)
(Period averages in percent per annum)

		1994	1995	1996	1997	1998	1999	2000	2001	2002	2003	2004	2005
Overnight	111	4.24	5.90	5.35	5.54	....	....	....	3.98	1.75	1.19	1.40	3.25
Seven-Day	111	4.31	5.93	5.40	5.58	5.53	5.16	6.36	3.95	1.76	1.20	1.44	3.30
One-Month	111	4.46	5.97	5.44	5.64	5.60	5.25	6.41	3.88	1.76	1.21	1.50	3.38
Three-Month	111	4.74	6.04	5.51	5.76	5.59	5.41	6.53	3.78	1.79	1.22	1.62	3.56
Six-Month	111	5.07	6.10	5.59	5.86	5.56	5.53	6.65	3.73	1.87	1.23	1.79	3.76
One-Year	111	5.59	6.24	5.78	6.08	5.53	5.71	6.83	3.86	2.19	1.36	2.12	4.02

London Interbank Offer Rates on Three-Month Deposits (60ea)
(Pound sterling rates relate to Paris market)
(Period averages in percent per annum)

		1994	1995	1996	1997	1998	1999	2000	2001	2002	2003	2004	2005
Euro	163	....	....	....	....	....	2.96	4.41	4.26	3.32	2.33	2.11	2.18
French Franc	132	5.88	6.68	3.94	3.48	3.64	....	....	....	....	....	....	....
Deutsche Mark	134	5.36	4.53	3.31	3.37	3.60	....	....	....	....	....	....	....
Netherlands Guilder	138	5.23	4.47	3.03	3.37	3.55	....	....	....	....	....	....	....
Swiss Franc	146	4.16	3.09	2.05	1.71	1.60	1.39	3.10	2.94	1.18	.33	.47	.80
Japanese Yen	158	2.31	1.27	.63	.63	.71	.22	.28	.15	.08	.06	.05	.06
Pound Sterling	112	5.54	6.73	6.09	6.90	7.39	5.54	6.19	5.04	4.06	3.73	4.64	4.76

London Interbank Offer Rates on Six-Month Deposits (60eb)
(Pound sterling rates relate to Paris market)
(Period averages in percent per annum)

		1994	1995	1996	1997	1998	1999	2000	2001	2002	2003	2004	2005
Euro	163	....	....	....	....	....	3.05	4.54	4.15	3.35	2.30	2.15	2.24
French Franc	132	5.95	6.61	4.02	3.54	3.68	....	....	....	....	....	....	....
Deutsche Mark	134	5.35	4.57	3.31	3.42	3.66	....	....	....	....	....	....	....
Netherlands Guilder	138	5.25	4.55	3.08	3.46	3.64	....	....	....	....	....	....	....
Japanese Yen	158	2.36	1.26	.71	.65	.71	.24	.31	.15	.09	.07	.06	.07
Swiss Franc	146	4.23	3.16	2.09	1.78	1.68	1.55	3.26	2.87	1.24	.38	.59	.87
Pound Sterling	112	5.80	6.91	6.13	7.04	7.32	5.62	6.31	5.02	4.16	3.76	4.77	4.76

Discounts (-) or Premiums (60f) on Three-Month Forward Exchange Rates
(End of period in percent per annum based on end-of-period quotation of the currencies against the US dollar)

		1994	1995	1996	1997	1998	1999	2000	2001	2002	2003	2004	2005
Canada	156	−3.99	−.23	22.78	....	....	....	....	....	....	....	....	....
Australia	193	−3.58	−4.07	−2.02	−.74	−2.49	.49	−.65	−2.13	−4.72	−5.68	−3.05	−4.74
Japan	158	3.69	4.86	5.12	5.45	6.25	6.25	5.75	2.78	5.27	1.31	9.30	4.81
Austria	122	−1.13	−1.67	2.34	1.99	2.32	....	....	....	....	....	....	....
Belgium	124	1.10	1.43	2.44	2.17	1.90	....	....	....	....	....	....	....
Denmark	128	.20	.80	1.85	1.74	.99	2.36	.97	−1.78	−1.72	−1.09	.50	2.06
Finland	172	.43	1.14	2.32	2.12	1.85	....	....	....	....	....	....	....
Germany	134	1.24	1.81	2.26	2.10	1.89	....	....	....	....	....	....	....
Italy	136	−.87	−4.64	−1.00	−2.62	.51	....	....	....	....	....	....	....
Norway	142	.09	−1.08	.89	1.98	1.12	.32	−.99	−4.44	−4.84	−.60	.66	2.36
Spain	184	−3.67	−7.31	.79	4.81	3.50	....	....	....	....	....	....	....
Sweden	144	−1.66	−.36	−.37	−.58	.84	2.54	4.07	2.36	1.99	−1.71	−.48	2.69
Switzerland	146	1.98	3.30	2.50	4.21	3.34	4.65	3.30	−.17	.81	1.26	1.63	3.13
United Kingdom	112	.41	−.72	2.39	−3.86	−.89	−1.02	1.31	−.66	−3.08	−1.55	−4.61	−1.23

SDR Interest Rate (99260s) and Rate of Remuneration (99260r)
(Period averages in percent per annum)

		1994	1995	1996	1997	1998	1999	2000	2001	2002	2003	2004	2005
SDR Interest Rate	992	4.2858	4.5847	3.8998	4.0719	4.1052	3.4759	4.4397	3.4258	2.2416	1.6491	1.8358	2.6041
United States (3-Mo.T-Bill Rate)	111	4.35	5.65	5.14	5.20	4.90	4.77	6.00	3.48	1.63	1.02	1.39	3.21
United Kingdom (3-Mo.T-Bill Rate)	112	5.18	6.40	5.89	6.62	7.23	5.14	5.83	4.79	3.96	3.55	4.44	4.59
France (3-Mo.T-Bill Rate)	132	5.79	6.58	3.84	3.35	3.45	2.72	4.23	4.26	3.28	2.27	....	....
Germany (3-Mo. Interbank Rate)	134	5.31	4.48	3.27	3.30	3.52	2.94	4.37	4.25	3.30	2.32	2.09	2.17
Japan (3-Mo.Certif. of Deposits)	158	2.24	1.22	.59	.62	.72	.15	.23	....	....	....	....	....
Rate of Remuneration	992	4.2858	4.5847	3.8998	4.0719	4.1052	3.4759	4.4397	3.4258	2.2416	1.6491	1.8358	2.6041

Real Effective Exchange Rate Indices

		1994	1995	1996	1997	1998	1999	2000	2001	2002	2003	2004	2005

(2000=100)
Based on Relative Unit Labor Costs (65um.110)

Industrial Countries

		1994	1995	1996	1997	1998	1999	2000	2001	2002	2003	2004	2005
United States	111	87.3	81.0	82.0	87.2	90.6	89.7	100.0	104.0	102.9	92.7	84.4	84.6
Canada	156	99.8	99.9	103.6	106.3	103.1	102.5	100.0	99.9	97.2	107.4	114.1	120.7
Japan	158	110.8	111.8	93.4	88.7	85.7	96.3	100.0	92.4	83.0	78.1	77.6	75.1
Euro Area	163	126.1	132.9	132.2	119.5	115.5	110.7	100.0	99.2	103.1	115.0	121.4	120.2
Austria	122	124.1	119.4	114.1	106.5	104.5	100.9	100.0	100.0	98.9	101.8	95.4	100.0
Belgium	124	116.9	120.8	113.4	103.9	104.5	102.5	100.0	101.9	104.5	109.2	113.0	114.9
Finland	172	112.1	127.1	120.2	114.7	114.1	110.0	100.0	104.4	105.5	109.6	113.6	115.7
France	132	116.5	117.0	115.8	108.0	109.9	107.1	100.0	98.1	98.5	103.1	104.9	103.3
Germany *	134	112.5	123.5	121.1	112.1	106.9	106.3	100.0	98.4	100.4	102.9	101.8	97.5
Ireland	178	180.5	165.2	165.7	153.9	128.5	112.8	100.0	103.3	96.0	100.0	105.1	104.6
Italy	136	97.3	89.2	102.0	105.1	104.6	103.8	100.0	102.5	107.6	116.3	125.0	129.5
Netherlands	138	107.7	110.3	106.3	102.8	104.4	103.0	100.0	103.6	106.9	114.0	115.6	115.4
Spain	184	95.3	94.2	98.1	97.1	99.4	100.3	100.0	102.6	105.3	108.9	112.0	112.6
Denmark	128	100.8	103.8	109.2	102.6	103.8	104.6	100.0	99.8	102.6	107.8	114.7	115.1
Norway	142	80.3	85.0	86.4	91.5	92.3	97.0	100.0	103.1	115.3	114.5	114.1	121.1
Sweden	144	93.4	100.2	113.5	105.1	105.7	103.5	100.0	97.5	94.0	96.0	92.4	91.2
Switzerland	146	95.8	101.2	99.1	95.7	100.0	99.0	100.0	104.2	109.9	111.7	115.0	116.2
United Kingdom	112	68.0	68.7	72.8	88.9	96.6	96.7	100.0	96.6	98.8	92.5	95.6	95.8

(2000=100)
Based on Relative Consumer Prices (..rec)

		1994	1995	1996	1997	1998	1999	2000	2001	2002	2003	2004	2005
United States	111	88.2	85.2	87.2	91.3	97.8	96.8	100.0	105.6	105.4	98.7	94.1	92.7
Canada	156	111.1	107.5	108.1	107.0	100.7	99.5	100.0	97.1	96.3	107.0	112.8	119.7
Japan	158	106.5	108.2	90.7	85.3	85.3	94.8	100.0	89.1	83.0	84.5	84.5	79.4
Euro Area	163	123.1	129.3	128.0	115.4	117.1	112.7	100.0	101.0	105.5	118.8	122.9	121.2
Austria	122	109.1	113.2	110.4	105.7	105.2	103.3	100.0	100.1	100.9	104.1	105.6	105.7
Belgium	124	112.6	116.7	113.6	106.6	106.4	104.6	100.0	100.6	102.2	106.9	108.5	109.4
Finland	172	106.9	116.5	110.8	105.7	106.2	105.2	100.0	100.4	102.0	106.9	107.0	104.8
France	132	112.2	115.2	114.6	108.7	108.9	105.8	100.0	99.6	101.2	106.6	108.4	107.9
Germany *	134	117.5	122.7	117.9	110.9	111.0	107.4	100.0	100.0	101.0	106.2	107.7	106.9
Ireland	178	110.4	111.1	113.0	112.6	108.8	104.8	100.0	103.4	109.3	120.3	123.1	123.5
Italy	136	103.6	96.6	107.1	106.3	106.7	105.3	100.0	101.4	103.8	110.2	112.1	111.0
Netherlands	138	109.4	114.0	111.4	105.0	106.5	105.3	100.0	103.1	106.7	113.1	113.9	113.3
Spain	184	103.6	105.4	107.6	102.6	103.0	102.4	100.0	101.8	104.1	109.2	111.3	112.9
Denmark	128	103.7	108.1	106.9	103.3	104.9	104.4	100.0	101.0	103.0	108.2	109.3	108.4
Norway	142	102.9	105.9	105.2	105.7	103.0	102.5	100.0	103.5	112.3	110.9	110.6	111.1
Sweden	144	107.5	107.3	115.6	109.1	105.5	102.5	100.0	91.6	94.1	100.2	101.2	96.9
Switzerland	146	109.1	116.3	112.7	103.6	104.7	102.8	100.0	102.6	106.3	106.4	105.6	104.0
United Kingdom	112	80.3	77.4	78.8	91.7	97.6	97.3	100.0	97.8	98.7	96.0	101.8	101.3

(2000=100)
Based on Relative Normalized Unit Labor Costs (..reu)

		1994	1995	1996	1997	1998	1999	2000	2001	2002	2003	2004	2005
United States	111	87.4	80.5	82.2	86.5	91.6	90.6	100.0	103.8	105.8	96.7	88.6	90.0
Canada	156	102.2	101.6	103.1	107.0	101.3	101.0	100.0	98.7	93.7	97.9	100.5	104.0
Japan	158	105.2	110.3	93.9	89.4	83.4	94.3	100.0	89.4	80.2	77.1	77.9	74.6
Euro Area	163	125.6	133.1	134.3	121.0	117.9	112.8	100.0	101.9	105.2	116.4	121.0	120.3
Austria	122	124.9	122.0	116.0	109.1	107.3	104.9	100.0	98.8	98.7	99.9	100.8	100.8
Belgium	124	113.7	118.9	113.8	109.0	109.0	105.0	100.0	101.7	104.9	109.4	111.9	113.5
Finland	172	112.4	125.5	117.4	110.8	110.2	106.5	100.0	103.3	103.6	107.2	110.6	110.7
France	132	116.1	118.1	114.4	108.4	107.5	105.4	100.0	97.2	98.0	101.2	102.7	101.5
Germany *	134	110.5	119.9	118.7	111.2	108.8	106.4	100.0	100.1	99.3	102.0	100.8	98.4
Ireland	178	163.6	153.1	145.3	135.9	122.6	113.2	100.0	102.0	102.8	107.1	108.5	107.3
Italy	136	95.9	89.3	102.7	104.7	103.5	103.6	100.0	103.6	106.6	113.8	120.3	123.9
Netherlands	138	107.4	111.4	108.0	102.3	104.1	103.2	100.0	102.8	105.9	111.3	113.6	112.9
Spain	184	102.1	101.4	104.2	101.2	103.0	102.5	100.0	102.8	106.6	112.5	116.0	117.3
Denmark	128	102.2	106.5	105.0	102.0	104.2	103.8	100.0	102.1	104.7	110.6	111.5	111.5
Norway	142	83.3	88.5	90.9	94.3	95.4	99.2	100.0	107.2	120.9	120.4	118.3	126.2
Sweden	144	96.9	98.2	110.7	107.5	105.8	101.8	100.0	92.0	91.1	94.0	96.4	94.3
Switzerland	146	93.5	100.1	100.4	96.7	102.2	101.5	100.0	105.8	111.6	112.8	114.5	115.3
United Kingdom	112	74.4	72.5	75.1	89.0	94.7	95.9	100.0	99.5	99.5	94.0	98.7	97.6

* Data refer to the former
Federal Republic of Germany

Production and Labor Indices

		1994	1995	1996	1997	1998	1999	2000	2001	2002	2003	2004	2005

Industrial Production

Index Numbers (2000=100): (66..i)

	code	1994	1995	1996	1997	1998	1999	2000	2001	2002	2003	2004	2005
Industrial Countries	110	83.6	85.9	87.7	91.9	93.1	95.5	100.0	97.0	96.6	97.6	101.1	103.0
United States	111	73.8	† 77.4	80.7	86.6	91.7	95.8	100.0	96.5	96.6	97.2	101.1	104.5
Canada	156	....	78.6	79.5	84.0	86.9	92.1	100.0	96.0	97.6	98.6	102.5	105.2
Australia	193	85.8	87.1	90.5	92.1	94.6	95.1	100.0	† 101.4	104.6	104.7	104.9	106.1
Japan	158	92.0	95.5	97.7	101.2	94.5	94.8	100.0	93.7	92.6	95.4	100.5	101.7
New Zealand	196	75.4	95.0	97.2	97.5	94.4	96.3	100.0	100.3	105.4	106.5	110.4	107.7
Euro Area													
Austria	122	70.9	74.5	75.2	80.0	86.6	91.8	100.0	102.8	103.6	105.6	112.3	117.4
Belgium	124	81.8	86.5	86.9	91.0	94.1	94.9	100.0	99.0	100.3	101.1	104.3	103.9
Finland	172	64.0	69.1	71.3	77.3	84.3	89.0	100.0	99.8	102.0	103.2	108.4	105.8
France	132	97.7	87.0	86.7	90.4	93.9	96.1	100.0	101.2	100.0	99.6	102.0	102.2
Germany	134	86.7	† 87.4	87.6	90.3	93.6	94.8	100.0	100.2	99.2	99.6	102.6	106.1
Greece	174	85.4	† 87.1	86.8	88.8	96.0	95.2	100.0	97.5	97.4	97.0	98.1	97.2
Ireland	178	41.2	† 49.6	53.6	63.0	75.5	86.6	100.0	110.0	117.9	123.5	123.8	127.6
Italy	136	88.0	92.9	91.3	94.9	96.0	95.9	100.0	99.0	97.4	96.9	96.3	95.5
Luxembourg	137	79.7	† 81.3	81.4	86.1	86.0	95.9	100.0	103.1	105.2	110.7	117.8	125.2
Netherlands	138	90.5	90.9	93.0	93.3	95.6	96.8	100.0	100.6	101.5	100.1	102.6	101.4
Portugal	182	77.7	84.7	89.1	91.4	96.6	99.5	100.0	103.1	102.7	102.6	100.0	100.3
Spain	184	80.0	83.9	82.7	88.5	93.4	95.8	100.0	98.5	98.7	100.0	101.6	102.3
Denmark	128	83.2	86.5	87.6	92.0	94.7	94.9	100.0	102.0	103.0	102.3	102.0	103.8
Norway	142	85.2	90.4	95.0	98.4	97.4	97.1	100.0	98.7	99.6	95.5	97.4	96.9
Sweden	144	91.3	82.3	83.5	88.0	91.8	94.0	100.0	99.5	100.7	103.3	106.5	108.3
Switzerland	146	80.6	82.2	82.2	86.0	89.1	92.2	100.0	99.3	94.2	94.5	98.4	100.9
United Kingdom	112	91.6	† 93.2	94.5	95.8	96.0	98.1	100.0	98.5	96.6	96.3	97.0	95.3

Wages

Index Numbers (2000=100): (65, 65ey, 65..c)

	code	1994	1995	1996	1997	1998	1999	2000	2001	2002	2003	2004	2005
Industrial Countries	110	86.5	88.9	91.4	93.7	95.5	97.6	100.0	102.0	103.6	105.6	107.4	109.6
United States	111	84.0	86.2	89.0	91.7	93.9	96.7	100.0	103.1	106.8	109.9	112.7	115.7
Canada	156	89.7	90.9	93.6	94.3	96.2	97.5	100.0	101.6	104.4	107.8	110.7	112.7
Australia	193	78.4	82.4	85.6	89.1	92.8	95.3	100.0	104.9	110.3	116.5	120.9	127.6
Japan	158	94.5	96.5	98.3	99.7	99.5	99.7	100.0	99.4	97.2	96.8	96.4	96.7
New Zealand	196	90.0	91.3	93.1	95.2	97.0	98.5	100.0	101.9	104.1	106.5	108.9	112.0
Euro Area													
Austria	122	95.8	100.0	† 90.9	92.9	95.2	98.0	100.0	102.2	104.8	106.8	108.5	111.4
Belgium	124	87.5	89.3	91.1	93.0	95.3	97.9	100.0	102.8	105.4	107.4	109.8	112.5
Finland	172	81.1	84.7	88.2	90.4	93.6	96.1	100.0	104.5	108.2	112.6	116.8	121.0
France	132	86.3	87.0	88.5	91.0	93.6	95.7	100.0	104.5	108.4	112.8	116.1	119.2
Germany	134	83.3	87.0	91.1	92.7	94.6	97.2	100.0	103.3	106.5	108.0	110.0	111.3
Greece	174	....	....	....	....	....	96.9	100.0	101.5	105.9	124.3	130.4	132.5
Ireland	178	77.4	79.1	81.1	85.0	88.5	93.7	100.0	109.1	115.2	122.6	128.7	133.6
Italy	136	84.6	87.2	90.0	93.2	95.8	98.0	100.0	101.8	104.5	107.2	110.5	113.9
Netherlands	138	85.7	86.6	88.1	90.8	93.7	96.4	100.0	103.9	107.7	110.6	112.3	113.3
Spain	184	80.7	84.6	89.1	92.7	95.3	97.7	100.0	103.8	108.1	112.7	118.8	122.1
Denmark	128	79.3	82.3	85.4	88.8	92.6	96.5	100.0	104.2	108.3	112.3	115.7	119.1
Iceland	176	96.8	100.0	75.1	81.2	87.5	92.9	100.0	109.6	115.5	121.7	129.0	138.3
Norway	142	....	....	....	....	91.3	96.1	100.0	104.5	110.0	115.2	120.0	124.1
Sweden	144	78.2	82.4	87.8	91.7	95.0	96.7	100.0	102.9	106.4	109.4	112.3	115.7
Switzerland	146	94.9	96.2	97.4	97.8	98.5	98.8	100.0	102.5	104.3	105.8	106.7	107.8
United Kingdom	112	77.9	80.4	83.2	86.8	91.3	95.7	100.0	104.5	108.2	111.9	116.7	121.5

Employment

Index Numbers (2000=100): (67, 67ey, 67..c, 67e, 67eyc)

	code	1994	1995	1996	1997	1998	1999	2000	2001	2002	2003	2004	2005
Industrial Countries	110	96.7	97.5	97.7	98.4	99.2	99.5	100.0	99.0	96.7	95.5	95.8	96.6
United States	111	86.7	89.0	90.8	93.2	95.5	97.9	100.0	100.0	98.9	98.6	99.7	101.3
Canada	156	83.8	85.4	87.4	90.6	93.6	95.5	100.0	99.5	100.1	99.8	97.2	95.3
Australia	193	97.8	98.8	99.0	100.5	97.2	95.5	100.0	96.7	97.8	95.8	96.4	94.7
Japan	158	113.6	111.5	109.0	107.8	105.9	102.8	100.0	97.0	92.2	89.4	88.4	88.5
New Zealand	196	100.8	104.7	103.6	100.6	102.8	99.2	100.0	103.1	103.2	99.1	102.5	99.1
Euro Area													
Austria	122	98.0	97.9	97.2	97.5	98.1	99.2	100.0	100.5	100.7	101.6	99.4	103.3
Finland	172	86.4	92.5	93.0	93.8	96.2	98.8	100.0	100.7	99.4	95.2	92.9	93.3
France	132	100.8	100.9	99.7	98.9	99.0	98.6	100.0	100.9	99.1	96.9	94.4	92.4
Germany	134	98.6	98.5	98.3	97.8	98.0	99.4	100.0	100.6	99.8	98.8	105.9	105.6
Greece	174	92.7	93.5	94.7	94.3	98.3	98.2	100.0	99.9	102.1	104.6	105.5	106.9
Ireland	178	80.2	85.1	89.2	94.4	97.1	96.2	100.0	101.0	96.3	92.5	89.8	88.5
Italy	136	102.4	100.7	99.6	98.9	99.8	100.0	100.0	100.8	101.9	103.7	104.5	105.6
Luxembourg	137	....	....	....	....	....	94.7	100.0	105.6	109.0	111.0	113.9	117.4
Netherlands	138	76.7	86.3	88.4	91.1	94.4	97.6	100.0	103.7	104.4	103.8	102.4	102.1
Spain	184	81.0	83.2	85.6	88.2	91.2	95.5	100.0	102.0	112.3	115.3	118.3	126.1
Denmark	128	93.9	95.8	96.5	98.4	98.8	99.5	100.0	100.1	99.6	98.9	99.9	100.4
Norway	142	89.7	91.6	93.9	96.7	99.1	99.5	100.0	100.4	100.7	100.0	100.3	100.9
Sweden	144	95.6	100.8	101.6	100.5	100.9	100.1	100.0	97.6	93.8	90.9	89.4	86.1
Switzerland	146	107.1	105.7	103.0	100.4	99.9	99.0	100.0	101.4	98.7	95.5	93.8	94.0
United Kingdom	112	90.1	91.3	92.6	94.9	96.5	98.2	100.0	101.2	101.6	101.8	102.7	103.6

Producer Prices/Wholesale Prices

		1994	1995	1996	1997	1998	1999	2000	2001	2002	2003	2004	2005
		Percent Change over Previous Year; Calculated from Indices											
World	001	25.9	14.9	6.4	4.7	3.7	4.7	7.9	3.6	2.4	3.8	6.1	6.0
Industrial Countries	110	1.2	3.3	.8	.5	−1.4	.2	4.4	.9	−1.3	2.6	4.0	5.0
United States	111	1.3	3.6	2.3	−.1	−2.5	.8	5.8	1.1	−2.3	5.3	6.2	7.3
Canada	156	6.1	7.4	.4	.9	−.1	1.6	5.1	1.1	.1	−1.4	3.2	1.5
Australia	193	.8	4.2	.3	1.2	−4.0	−.9	7.1	3.1	.2	.5	4.0	6.0
Japan	158	−1.7	−.8	−1.6	.7	−1.5	−1.5	.1	−2.3	−2.1	−.8	1.2	1.7
New Zealand	196	1.3	.8	.6	.4	.7	1.0	7.6	6.0	.2	−.8	1.7	5.4
Euro Area	163	....	....	.4	1.1	−.8	−.4	5.3	2.2	−.1	1.5	2.1	4.1
Austria	122	1.3	.3	—	.4	−.5	−.8	4.0	1.5	−.4	1.6	4.9	2.1
Belgium	124	1.6	3.3	2.2	3.7	−1.9	—	10.6	2.2	−.6	−.2	3.4	3.8
Finland	172	1.3	.7	−.9	1.6	−1.4	−.1	8.3	−.3	−1.2	−.1	1.6	3.6
France	132	1.2	6.1	−2.7	−.6	−.9	−1.3	4.4	1.2	−.2	.9	2.1	3.1
Germany	134	.6	1.7	−1.2	1.2	−.4	−1.0	3.3	3.0	−.4	1.7	1.6	4.6
Greece	174	....	....	5.7	3.4	2.9	2.4	5.3	3.6	2.3	2.4	3.5	5.9
Ireland	178	.9	2.2	.5	−.5	1.5	1.1	6.1	2.9	.2	−5.6	1.7	....
Italy	136	3.7	7.9	1.9	1.3	.1	−.3	6.0	1.9	−.2	1.6	2.7	4.0
Luxembourg	137	1.5	3.9	−3.1	1.5	2.4	−3.1	4.8	−.2	−.8	1.2	9.0	8.1
Netherlands	138	.5	1.5	2.0	1.8	−.2	1.0	4.8	3.0	.8	1.4	3.9	2.8
Portugal	182	....	....	....	....	....	....	....	2.8	.4	.8	2.7	4.1
Spain	184	4.3	6.4	1.7	1.0	−.7	.7	5.4	1.7	.7	1.4	3.4	4.9
Denmark	128	1.2	2.9	1.1	1.9	−.6	.5	5.9	2.0	.1	.2	2.2	4.1
Norway	142	1.3	2.6	2.2	1.4	.6	3.1	6.9	−4.7	−5.6	3.6	11.8	16.6
Sweden	144	4.8	7.7	−1.8	1.2	−.6	1.1	5.8	3.2	.5	−.8	2.3	5.1
Switzerland	146	−.5	−.1	−1.8	−.7	−1.2	−1.0	.9	.5	−.5	—	1.2	.8
United Kingdom	112	2.5	4.0	2.6	.9	—	.4	1.5	−.3	—	1.5	2.5	2.8
Developing Countries	200	87.4	39.4	17.3	12.8	13.9	12.9	14.2	8.5	9.1	6.0	9.8	7.7
Africa	605	7.4	9.1	6.7	5.2	4.7	3.5	6.2	5.4	8.5	1.3	1.9	3.3
Central African Rep	626	....	....	....	....	—	1.2	6.4	8.9	8.6	3.8	−.5	2.2
Morocco	686	2.3	6.5	4.4	−1.6	2.8	−1.7	4.2	−.4	2.2	−4.5	....	....
South Africa	199	8.3	9.5	6.9	7.1	3.5	5.8	9.2	8.5	14.2	1.7	.7	3.1
Tunisia	744	3.4	5.7	3.7	2.4	3.2	.4	3.3	1.8	3.0	3.2	2.6	4.3
Zambia	754	70.6	72.0	....	....	....	....	....	....	....	....	....	....
Zimbabwe	698	22.3	20.8	17.1	12.9	31.5	57.2	....	....	....	....	....	....
Asia	505	7.3	8.8	4.6	5.1	19.1	2.2	6.5	4.7	2.2	4.7	7.4	6.8
China, P.R.: Hong Kong	532	2.1	2.7	−.1	−.3	−1.8	−1.6	.2	−1.6	−2.7	−.3	2.3	.7
India	534	10.5	9.3	4.5	4.5	5.9	3.5	6.6	4.8	2.5	5.4	6.6	4.7
Indonesia	536	5.4	11.4	7.9	9.0	101.8	10.5	12.5	13.0	4.4	3.4	7.4	15.3
Korea	542	2.7	4.7	3.2	3.8	12.2	−2.1	2.0	−.5	−.3	2.2	6.1	2.1
Malaysia	548	4.9	5.5	2.3	2.6	10.8	−3.3	3.1	−5.0	4.5	5.7	9.2	6.6
Pakistan	564	19.7	12.8	11.1	11.2	2.3	7.3	4.0	4.6	3.0	6.5	8.4	8.7
Philippines	566	4.1	4.2	4.1	3.5	10.9	7.0	12.5	17.0	2.9	8.1	7.5	10.0
Singapore	576	−.4	—	.1	−1.2	−3.0	2.1	10.1	−1.6	−1.5	2.0	5.1	9.7
Sri Lanka	524	5.0	8.8	20.5	6.9	6.2	−.4	1.7	11.7	10.7	3.0	12.6	11.5
Thailand	578	4.0	8.2	1.8	5.1	12.2	−4.7	3.9	2.5	1.7	4.0	6.7	9.1
Europe	170	199.2	130.8	42.9	33.4	17.4	39.7	34.8	19.9	13.2	−4.4	15.7	11.6
Armenia	911	....	....	....	....	14.6	47.6	−.4	1.1	3.6	8.9	−13.3	7.7
Belarus	913	2,170.8	499.1	34.7	87.5	72.5	355.8	185.6	71.8	40.4	37.5	24.1	12.1
Bulgaria	918	1,146.3	55.7	132.7	971.2	17.0	2.8	17.5	3.7	1.3	4.9	6.0	6.9
Croatia	960	77.6	.7	1.4	2.3	−1.2	2.6	12.1	1.1	1.8	−.3	3.4	3.1
Cyprus	423	3.3	3.6	2.1	2.8	.5	1.2	7.2	1.6	1.4	2.9	4.7	3.5
Czech Republic	935	5.3	7.5	4.8	4.9	4.9	1.0	4.9	2.8	−.5	−.3	5.6	3.0
Estonia	939	....	25.6	14.8	8.4	4.2	−1.2	4.9	4.4	.4	.2	2.9	2.1
Georgia	915	....	....	....	....	....	14.3	5.8	3.7	6.0	....	....	....
Hungary	944	12.3	28.5	21.8	20.3	11.3	5.1	11.7	4.8	−1.4	2.4	3.5	3.7
Kazakhstan	916	....	....	23.9	15.5	.8	18.9	38.0	.3	.2	9.3	16.7	23.7
Kyrgyz Republic	917	215.3	21.8	23.0	26.3	7.9	56.3	29.8	9.1	5.6	5.6	8.8	3.1
Latvia	941	16.8	11.9	13.7	4.1	1.9	−4.0	.6	1.7	.9	3.2	8.6	7.8
Lithuania	946	44.7	28.3	17.3	4.3	−7.4	1.4	17.5	−3.7	−3.6	−.3	7.7	13.2
Poland	964	30.1	25.5	13.2	12.2	7.2	5.5	7.7	1.7	1.2	2.7	7.0	.9
Romania	968	140.5	35.1	49.9	156.9	33.2	44.5	53.4	38.1	23.1	19.5	19.1	10.6
Russia	922	337.0	236.5	50.8	15.0	7.0	58.9	46.5	18.2	10.4	16.4	23.4	20.5
Slovak Republic	936	10.0	9.0	4.1	4.5	3.3	3.8	9.8	6.6	2.1	8.3	3.4	4.7
Slovenia	961	17.7	12.8	6.7	6.1	6.0	2.1	7.6	9.0	5.1	2.5	4.3	2.7
Turkey	186	121.3	86.0	75.9	81.8	71.8	53.1	51.4	61.6	50.1	−58.8	14.6	5.9
Ukraine	926	1,143.8	487.9	51.9	7.7	13.2	31.1	20.9	8.6	3.1	7.8	20.4	16.8
Middle East	405	16.0	24.6	14.3	5.5	4.5	7.9	7.4	2.2	5.3	8.0	10.0	7.7
Egypt	469	4.6	6.3	8.3	4.2	1.4	.9	1.8	1.0	6.4	14.4	17.1	5.3
Iran, I.R. of	429	37.6	60.6	32.9	10.7	11.9	19.2	18.9	5.9	8.2	10.6	12.6	12.4
Israel	436	7.9	10.7	8.6	6.3	4.2	7.1	3.6	−.1	3.9	4.3	5.4	6.2
Jordan	439	4.8	−2.4	2.0	1.6	.6	−2.4	−3.6	−1.5	1.6	2.6	6.0	9.5
Kuwait	443	−.2	1.4	5.2	−1.3	−1.6	−1.2	.4	2.0	3.3	1.9	.4	4.5
Saudi Arabia	456	1.8	7.3	−.3	—	−1.9	.4	.4	−.1	—	.9	3.1	2.9
Syrian Arab Rep	463	14.2	6.9	3.2	2.5	−.6	−1.8	−5.7	−5.0	7.4	....	....	....
Western Hemisphere	205	246.4	35.8	18.2	11.1	8.4	12.4	13.5	7.6	17.6	17.9	9.8	6.6
Argentina	213	.4	4.3	2.9	−1.1	−3.4	−4.0	3.7	−2.0	78.3	19.6	7.7	8.4
Brazil	223	2,311.6	57.5	6.3	8.1	3.5	16.6	18.1	12.6	16.7	27.6	10.5	7.3
Chile	228	7.7	7.6	6.2	1.6	1.9	5.2	11.4	7.8	6.8	6.6	2.5	5.4
Colombia	233	17.2	18.1	15.0	15.4	17.3	9.8	13.2	9.4	5.3	9.1	5.2	3.1
Costa Rica	238	13.1	23.9	16.0	11.6	8.8	10.1	11.0	9.3	8.0	10.6	15.5	13.7
Ecuador	248	....	....	31.2	31.2	31.2	102.7	164.3	−.2	6.8	7.3	9.1	14.6
El Salvador	253	....	....	....	....	....	....	6.5	1.0	−2.0	3.0	6.7	8.4
Mexico	273	6.1	38.6	33.9	17.5	16.0	14.2	7.8	5.0	5.1	7.5	9.3	4.2

Producer Prices/Wholesale Prices

		1994	1995	1996	1997	1998	1999	2000	2001	2002	2003	2004	2005
							Percent Change over Previous Year; Calculated from Indices						
Western Hemisphere(Cont.)													
Panama...	283	2.0	3.0	2.1	−2.2	−3.9	2.7	8.8	−3.2	−3.0	1.7	4.4	5.6
Paraguay..	288	....	....	....	1.2	14.9	5.3	14.7	5.8	19.9	26.5	5.8	9.0
Peru..	293	17.9	10.5	9.4	7.4	7.3	4.9	4.3	1.4	−1.0	1.7	5.2	2.3
Trinidad and Tobago.....................	369	5.4	3.6	2.9	1.9	1.4	1.7	1.3	.9	.6	.9	3.5	2.3
Uruguay...	298	34.2	37.7	25.0	16.4	9.3	−.9	6.8	6.6	31.9	38.9	14.7	−2.6
Venezuela, Rep. Bol......................	299	78.2	57.7	103.2	29.8	22.2	16.2	15.2	15.5	37.3	51.4	30.5	17.9
Memorandum Items													
Oil Exporting Countries...........	999	20.1	26.7	22.4	10.4	45.0	10.9	11.4	8.7	8.0	9.6	10.2	11.9
Non-Oil Developing Countries.	201	100.6	41.4	16.5	13.2	9.8	13.2	14.6	8.5	9.2	5.4	9.8	7.1

Indices

		1994	1995	1996	1997	1998	1999	2000	2001	2002	2003	2004	2005
							Index Numbers: 2000=100						
World...	001	66.7	76.6	81.4	85.3	88.5	92.7	100.0	103.6	106.2	110.2	117.0	124.0
Industrial Countries...............	110	92.7	95.8	96.5	97.0	95.6	95.8	100.0	100.9	99.5	102.1	106.2	111.5
Developing Countries.............	200	36.9	51.5	60.4	68.1	77.6	87.6	100.0	108.5	118.3	125.4	137.7	148.3
Africa..	605	70.9	77.4	82.6	86.9	91.0	94.2	100.0	105.4	114.4	115.9	118.1	122.0
Asia...	505	64.5	70.2	73.4	77.1	91.9	93.9	100.0	104.7	107.0	112.0	120.3	128.5
Europe.......................................	170	10.3	23.7	33.9	45.2	53.1	74.2	100.0	119.9	135.7	129.7	150.1	167.5
Middle East..............................	405	55.0	68.5	78.3	82.6	86.3	93.1	100.0	102.2	107.6	116.3	127.9	137.8
Western Hemisphere...............	205	40.6	55.1	65.1	72.3	78.4	88.1	100.0	107.6	126.5	149.1	163.6	174.5

Consumer Prices

		1994	1995	1996	1997	1998	1999	2000	2001	2002	2003	2004	2005
		Percent Change over Previous Year; Calculated from Indices											
World	001	26.66	15.33	8.69	6.13	5.78	5.40	4.38	4.09	3.42	3.51	3.42	3.61
Industrial Countries	110	2.35	2.44	2.24	2.04	1.41	1.42	2.38	2.18	1.47	1.89	2.02	2.32
United States	111	2.61	2.81	2.93	2.34	1.55	2.19	3.38	2.83	1.59	2.27	2.68	3.39
Canada	156	.19	2.17	1.58	1.62	.99	1.72	2.75	2.53	2.25	2.77	1.83	2.23
Australia	193	1.89	4.64	2.61	.25	.85	1.47	4.48	4.38	3.00	2.77	2.34	2.67
Japan	158	.71	−.13	.14	1.73	.66	−.34	−.67	−.73	−.92	−.25	−.01	−.29
New Zealand	196	2.40	3.74	2.30	1.17	1.29	−.12	2.62	2.63	2.68	1.75	2.29	3.04
Euro Area	163	....	....	2.15	1.58	1.09	1.12	2.34	2.11	2.25	2.07	2.14	2.19
Austria	122	2.96	2.25	1.84	1.33	.90	.56	2.35	2.66	1.81	1.36	2.05	2.30
Belgium	124	2.38	1.47	2.06	1.63	.95	1.12	2.54	2.47	1.64	1.59	2.09	2.78
Finland	172	1.09	.99	.62	1.20	1.40	1.16	3.37	2.57	1.56	.88	.19	.86
France	132	1.66	1.78	2.01	1.20	.67	.50	1.69	1.66	1.92	2.08	2.13	1.77
Germany	134	2.74	1.72	1.45	1.88	.94	.57	1.47	1.98	1.37	1.05	1.67	1.95
Greece	174	10.92	8.94	8.20	5.54	4.77	2.64	3.17	3.40	3.57	3.54	2.89	3.56
Ireland	178	2.37	2.52	1.74	1.40	2.43	1.64	5.56	4.87	4.67	3.48	2.19	2.43
Italy	136	4.03	5.24	3.97	2.04	1.96	1.66	2.54	2.79	2.47	2.67	2.21	1.99
Luxembourg	137	2.20	1.92	1.39	1.37	.96	1.00	3.15	2.67	2.07	2.05	2.23	2.49
Netherlands	138	2.80	2.10	2.02	2.16	1.98	2.21	3.03	4.20	3.26	2.10	1.24	1.67
Portugal	182	5.21	4.12	3.12	2.16	2.72	2.30	2.85	4.39	3.55	3.28	2.36	2.29
Spain	184	4.72	4.67	3.56	1.97	1.83	2.31	3.43	3.59	3.07	3.03	3.03	3.37
Denmark	128	1.99	2.10	2.11	2.20	1.85	2.48	2.92	2.35	2.43	2.09	1.16	1.81
Iceland	176	1.55	1.65	2.30	1.75	1.72	3.22	5.16	6.39	5.17	2.06	2.80	4.16
Norway	142	1.40	2.46	1.26	2.58	2.26	2.33	3.09	3.02	1.29	2.48	.47	1.52
Sweden	144	2.16	2.46	.53	.66	−.27	.46	.90	2.41	2.16	1.93	.37	.45
Switzerland	146	.86	1.80	.82	.52	.02	.82	1.54	.99	.64	.64	.80	1.17
United Kingdom	112	2.48	3.41	2.45	3.13	3.42	1.56	2.93	1.82	1.63	2.91	2.96	2.83
Developing Countries	200	65.00	33.41	17.26	11.46	11.52	10.21	6.76	6.38	5.74	5.44	5.09	5.13
Africa	605	32.53	32.72	24.20	13.05	7.97	9.81	11.50	12.29	8.84	6.58	4.68	6.44
Cameroon	622	35.09	9.07	3.92	4.79	3.17	1.87	1.23	4.42	2.83	.62	.23	2.01
Central African Rep.	626	24.57	19.19	3.72	1.61	−1.89	−1.41	3.20	3.83	2.33	4.13	−2.07	2.88
Chad	628	41.72	9.23	11.33	5.57	4.26	−8.03	3.82	12.43	5.19	−1.75	−5.36	3.00
Gabon	646	36.12	9.65	.69	3.97	1.45	−1.94	.50	2.14	.04	2.24	.39	.07
WAEMU	759	29.97	12.05	3.41	3.00	3.69	.19	1.78	4.03	2.93	1.34	.54	5.11
Benin	638	38.53	14.46	4.91	3.47	5.75	.33	4.17	3.98	2.49	1.49	.87	5.36
Burkina Faso	748	25.18	7.39	6.17	2.31	5.05	−1.07	−.30	5.01	2.18	2.03	−.40	6.42
Côte d'Ivoire	662	26.08	14.30	2.48	4.02	4.69	.79	2.46	4.28	3.11	3.35	1.44	3.89
Guinea Bissau	654	15.18	45.37	50.73	49.10	6.50	−.70	8.64	3.35	3.30	−3.50	.88	3.33
Mali	678	23.18	13.44	6.81	−.36	4.04	−1.20	−.68	5.19	5.03	−1.35	−3.10	6.40
Niger	692	36.04	10.56	5.29	2.93	4.55	−2.30	2.90	4.01	2.63	−1.61	.26	7.80
Senegal	722	32.29	7.86	2.75	1.58	1.16	.83	.73	3.07	2.23	−.03	.51	1.70
Togo	742	39.16	16.43	4.69	8.25	.97	−.07	1.89	3.91	3.07	−.96	.39	6.80
Algeria	612	29.05	29.78	18.69	5.73	4.95	2.64	.34	4.23	1.42	2.58	3.56	1.64
Angola	614	948.81	2,671.79	4,145.11	219.18	107.28	248.20	325.00	169.73	95.60	98.22	43.54	22.40
Botswana	616	10.54	10.51	10.08	8.72	6.66	7.75	8.60	6.59	8.01	9.19	6.93	8.65
Burundi	618	14.85	19.26	26.44	31.11	12.50	3.40	24.31	9.24	−1.32	10.70	7.85	13.52
Cape Verde	624	3.45	8.35	5.96	8.56	4.39	4.36	−2.48	3.35	1.88	1.19	−1.89	.42
Congo, Dem. Rep. of	636	23,773	542	492	199	29	285	550	314	38	13	4	21
Ethiopia	644	7.59	10.02	−5.07	2.40	2.58	7.94	.66	−8.24	1.65	17.76	3.26	11.61
Gambia, The	648	1.71	6.98	1.10	2.78	3.49	2.16	.19	4.42	8.61	17.03	14.21	3.17
Ghana	652	24.87	59.46	46.56	27.89	14.62	12.41	25.19	32.91	14.82	26.67	12.62	15.12
Kenya	664	28.81	1.55	8.86	11.36	6.72	5.74	9.98	5.74	1.96	9.82	11.62	10.31
Lesotho	666	8.21	9.27	9.33	7.33	7.33	7.33	6.13	−9.62	33.81	6.67	5.02	3.44
Madagascar	674	38.94	49.06	19.77	4.49	6.21	9.93	12.03	6.94	15.93	−1.22	13.81	18.51
Malawi	676	34.65	83.33	37.60	9.14	29.75	44.80	29.58	22.70	14.74	9.58	11.43	15.41
Mauritania	682	4.13	6.54	4.68	4.63	8.03	4.07	3.25	4.71	3.90	5.15	10.37	12.13
Mauritius	684	7.32	6.03	6.55	6.83	6.81	6.91	4.20	5.39	6.40	3.91	4.74	4.91
Morocco	686	5.14	6.12	2.99	1.04	2.75	.68	1.89	.62	2.80	1.17	1.49	.98
Mozambique	688	63.18	54.43	48.49	7.37	1.48	2.86	12.72	9.05	16.78	13.43	12.66	7.17
Namibia	728	....	....	....	....	....	....	....	....	....	7.15	4.15	2.26
Nigeria	694	57.03	72.81	29.29	8.21	10.32	4.76	8.79	18.79	13.02	14.05	19.42	13.51
Rwanda	714	41.04	41.04	7.41	12.02	6.21	−2.41	4.29	2.98	2.25	7.15	12.03	9.13
Seychelles	718	1.74	−.24	−1.10	.62	2.58	6.35	6.27	5.97	.20	3.29	3.84	.91
Sierra Leone	724	24.20	25.99	23.14	14.95	35.53	34.09	−.84	2.09	−3.29	7.60	14.19	12.05
South Africa	199	8.94	8.68	7.35	8.60	6.88	5.18	5.34	5.70	9.16	5.86	1.39	3.40
Sudan	732	115.40	68.38	132.82	46.65	17.11	15.99	5.69	5.85	8.30	7.70	8.40	8.50
Tanzania	738	33.09	28.38	20.98	16.09	12.80	7.89	5.92	5.13	.98	3.54	.03	8.63
Tunisia	744	4.73	6.24	3.73	3.65	3.13	2.69	2.93	1.98	2.72	2.71	3.63	2.02
Uganda	746	9.73	8.59	7.22	6.93	−.02	6.60	2.83	2.00	−.32	7.84	3.31	8.15
Zambia	754	54.60	34.93	43.07	24.42	24.46	26.79	26.03	21.39	22.23	21.40	17.97	18.32
Zimbabwe	698	22.26	22.59	21.43	18.74	31.82	58.52	55.86	76.71	140.08	....	....	....
Asia	505	14.69	11.80	7.66	4.65	8.03	2.16	1.50	2.39	1.94	1.96	3.47	3.56
Bangladesh	513	5.31	10.20	2.38	5.39	8.40	6.11	2.21	2.01	3.33	5.66	9.17	7.04
Bhutan	514	6.99	9.50	8.79	6.51	10.58	6.78	4.01	3.41	2.46	2.10	4.60	5.29
Cambodia	522	....	1.06	10.07	3.17	14.81	4.01	−.79	−.60	3.23	1.21	3.94	5.65
China, P.R.: Mainland	924	24.24	16.90	8.32	2.81	−.84	−1.41	.26	.46	−.77	1.16	3.99	1.82
China, P.R.: Hong Kong	532	8.79	9.04	6.33	5.80	2.83	−3.95	−3.74	−1.61	−3.04	−2.58	−.38	.91
China, P.R.: Macao	546	6.25	8.56	4.82	3.49	.17	−3.20	−1.61	−1.99	−2.64	−1.56	.98	4.40
Fiji	819	.82	2.17	3.05	3.37	5.71	1.97	1.09	4.27	.76	4.17	2.83	2.37
India	534	10.21	10.22	8.98	7.16	13.23	4.67	4.01	3.68	4.39	3.81	3.77	4.25
Indonesia	536	8.52	9.43	7.97	6.23	58.39	20.49	3.72	11.50	11.88	6.59	6.24	10.45
Korea	542	6.26	4.48	4.93	4.43	7.51	.81	2.26	4.10	2.69	3.55	3.61	2.72
Lao People's Dem. Rep.	544	6.78	19.59	13.02	27.51	90.98	128.42	25.08	7.81	10.63	15.49	10.46	7.17

Consumer Prices

		1994	1995	1996	1997	1998	1999	2000	2001	2002	2003	2004	2005
					Percent Change over Previous Year; Calculated from Indices								
Asia(Cont.)													
Malaysia	548	3.72	3.45	3.49	2.66	5.27	2.74	1.53	1.42	1.81	1.06	1.45	2.99
Maldives	556	3.38	5.49	6.24	7.58	−1.41	2.95	−1.18	.68	.93	−2.87	6.41	3.29
Mongolia	948	87.58	.04	46.89	36.56	9.36	7.56	11.60	6.28	.92	5.13	8.24	12.72
Myanmar	518	24.10	25.19	16.28	29.70	51.49	18.40	−.11	21.10	57.07	36.59	4.53	9.37
Nepal	558	8.35	7.62	9.22	4.01	11.24	7.45	2.48	2.69	3.03	5.71	2.84	6.84
Pakistan	564	12.37	12.34	10.37	11.38	6.23	4.14	4.37	3.15	3.29	2.91	7.44	9.06
Papua New Guinea	853	2.85	17.28	11.62	3.96	13.57	14.93	15.60	9.30	11.80	14.71	2.16	1.70
Philippines	566	8.36	6.71	7.51	5.59	9.27	5.95	3.95	6.80	3.00	3.45	5.98	7.63
Samoa	862	12.08	−2.90	5.37	6.86	2.22	.27	.97	3.84	8.05	.12	16.34	1.85
Singapore	576	3.10	1.72	1.38	2.00	−.27	.02	1.36	1.00	−.39	.51	1.66	.47
Solomon Islands	813	13.26	9.63	11.77	8.08	12.40	8.02	7.06	6.89	10.16	9.96	6.73	7.17
Sri Lanka	524	8.45	7.67	15.94	9.57	9.36	4.69	6.18	14.16	9.55	6.31	7.58	11.64
Thailand	578	5.09	5.80	5.83	5.60	8.07	.30	1.57	1.64	.62	1.80	2.77	4.54
Tonga	866	1.01	1.46	3.00	2.12	3.27	4.46	6.31	8.30	10.36	11.64	10.98	8.32
Vanuatu	846	2.30	2.23	.91	2.83	3.28	2.00	2.46	3.65	1.96	3.02	1.44	....
Vietnam	582	....	....	5.68	3.21	7.27	4.12	−1.71	−.43	3.83	3.10	7.80	8.25
Europe	170	190.28	120.65	44.85	34.37	29.51	50.22	25.28	21.21	15.34	11.33	8.44	8.54
Albania	914	22.57	7.79	12.73	33.18	20.64	.39	.05	3.11	7.77	.48	2.28	2.37
Armenia	911	4,962.22	175.97	18.70	13.91	8.67	.66	−2.78	2.75	−1.76	2.69	8.06	.64
Azerbaijan, Republic of	912	1,664.53	411.74	19.90	3.67	−.80	−8.52	1.86	1.48	2.83	2.17	6.78	9.48
Belarus	913	2,221.02	709.35	52.71	63.94	72.87	293.68	168.62	61.13	42.54	28.40	18.11	10.34
Bulgaria	918	96.06	62.05	121.61	1,058.37	18.67	2.57	10.32	7.36	5.81	2.16	6.35	5.04
Croatia	960	107.15	4.04	4.34	4.13	6.43	3.70	5.42	4.63	1.71	1.47	2.07	3.34
Cyprus	423	4.70	2.62	2.98	3.61	2.23	1.63	4.14	1.98	2.80	4.14	2.29	2.56
Czech Republic	935	9.87	9.47	8.82	8.45	10.68	2.10	3.93	4.71	1.79	.11	2.83	1.85
Estonia	939	47.65	28.78	23.05	10.58	8.21	3.30	4.03	5.74	3.57	1.34	3.05	4.09
Georgia	915	....	162.72	39.36	7.09	3.54	19.19	4.06	4.65	5.56	4.78	5.70	8.23
Hungary	944	18.87	28.30	23.60	18.28	14.23	10.00	9.80	9.22	5.27	4.64	6.78	3.55
Kazakhstan	916	1,877.37	176.16	39.18	17.41	7.15	8.30	13.18	8.35	5.84	6.44	6.88	7.58
Kyrgyz Republic	917	....	....	31.95	23.44	10.46	37.03	18.70	6.92	2.13	2.97	4.11	4.35
Latvia	941	35.93	24.98	17.61	8.44	4.66	2.36	2.65	2.49	1.94	2.92	6.19	6.76
Lithuania	946	72.15	39.66	24.62	8.88	5.07	.75	1.01	1.30	.30	−1.18	1.20	2.66
Macedonia, FYR	962	126.58	16.37	2.47	1.29	.54	−1.28	6.61	5.20	2.31	1.10	1.05	.04
Malta	181	4.13	4.43	2.05	3.11	2.39	2.13	2.37	2.93	2.19	1.30	2.79	3.01
Moldova	921	....	9.91	23.51	11.80	7.66	39.27	31.29	9.76	5.30	11.75	12.53	13.11
Poland	964	33.25	28.07	19.82	15.08	11.73	7.28	10.06	5.49	1.90	.79	3.58	2.11
Romania	968	136.76	32.24	38.83	154.76	59.10	45.80	45.67	34.47	22.54	15.27	11.88	8.99
Russia	922	307.63	197.47	47.74	14.77	27.67	85.74	20.78	21.46	15.79	13.66	10.88	12.68
Slovak Republic	936	13.41	9.92	5.78	6.14	6.67	10.57	12.04	7.33	3.32	8.55	7.55	2.71
Slovenia	961	20.99	13.41	9.85	8.36	7.91	6.15	8.88	8.42	7.47	5.58	3.59	2.48
Turkey	186	106.26	88.11	80.35	85.73	84.64	64.87	54.92	54.40	44.96	25.30	8.60	8.18
Ukraine	926	891.19	376.75	80.33	15.94	10.58	22.68	28.20	11.96	.76	5.21	9.04	13.52
Middle East	405	13.78	21.36	12.82	7.61	7.11	7.50	4.98	3.63	5.29	6.53	7.36	6.34
Bahrain, Kingdom of	419	.82	2.70	−.45	2.43	−.37	−1.29	−.70	−1.21	−.50	1.59	2.35	2.60
Egypt	469	8.15	15.74	7.19	4.63	3.87	3.08	2.68	2.27	2.74	4.51	11.27	4.87
Iran, I.R. of	429	31.45	49.66	28.94	17.35	17.87	20.07	14.48	11.27	14.34	16.47	14.76	13.43
Israel	436	12.34	10.05	11.27	9.00	5.43	5.20	1.14	1.10	5.64	.72	−.42	1.33
Jordan	439	3.52	2.35	6.50	3.04	3.09	.61	.67	1.77	1.83	1.63	3.36	3.51
Kuwait	443	2.53	2.69	3.56	.66	.15	2.99	2.51	1.30	.89	.96	1.25	4.10
Oman	449	.41	2.46	.90	−.52	−.83	.43	−1.14	−1.06	−.66	−.42	.36	1.22
Qatar	453	1.32	2.96	7.26	2.60	2.92	2.16	1.68	1.44	.24	2.27	6.80	8.81
Saudi Arabia	456	.56	4.87	1.22	.06	−.36	−1.35	−1.13	−1.11	.23	.59	.33	.72
Syrian Arab Republic	463	15.33	7.98	8.25	1.89	−.80	−3.70	−3.85	3.00	.97	....	....	....
Yemen, Republic of	474	49.39	55.08	30.73	2.18	5.98	8.66	4.59	11.91	12.23	10.83	....	....
Western Hemisphere	205	211.30	40.34	21.34	13.09	9.88	8.95	8.15	6.34	9.09	10.81	6.74	6.36
Anguilla	312	3.51	1.39	3.58	.11	2.64	2.64	−35.82	2.25	.56	3.03	4.40	4.84
Dominica	321	.02	1.32	1.68	2.44	1.00	1.19	.86	1.52	.24	1.55	1.99	1.74
Grenada	328	3.77	1.87	2.03	1.24	1.41	.57	2.14	1.67	1.07	....	....	....
St. Kitts and Nevis	361	1.44	2.96	1.98	8.99	3.46	3.45	1.98	2.15	2.05	2.23	2.30	1.80
St. Lucia	362	2.53	5.63	.92	−.01	3.20	3.48	3.64	5.40	−.26	1.03	1.47	3.91
St. Vincent & Grenadines	364	1.01	1.74	4.41	.44	2.14	1.03	.20	.82	.81	.25	2.94	3.74
Argentina	213	4.18	3.38	.16	.53	.92	−1.17	−.94	−1.07	25.87	13.44	4.42	9.64
Aruba	314	6.31	3.36	3.23	3.00	1.87	2.28	4.04	3.11	3.44	3.29	2.53	3.40
Bahamas, The	313	1.41	2.07	1.52	.79	1.86	1.44	1.04	2.92	.90	3.36	.54	1.56
Barbados	316	.08	1.88	2.39	7.71	−1.27	1.56	2.44	2.58	.13	1.62	1.42	6.06
Belize	339	2.59	2.89	6.40	1.05	−.87	−1.21	.61	1.16	2.21	2.61	3.09	3.64
Bolivia	218	7.87	10.19	12.43	4.71	7.67	2.16	4.60	1.60	.92	3.34	4.44	5.40
Brazil	223	2,075.89	66.01	15.76	6.93	3.20	4.86	7.04	6.84	8.45	14.71	6.60	6.88
Chile	228	11.44	8.24	7.36	6.14	5.11	3.34	3.84	3.57	2.49	2.81	1.05	3.05
Colombia	233	23.84	20.96	20.24	18.47	18.68	10.88	9.22	7.97	6.35	7.13	5.90	5.05
Costa Rica	238	13.53	23.19	17.52	13.23	11.67	10.05	10.99	11.23	9.16	9.45	12.32	13.80
Dominican Republic	243	8.26	12.54	5.40	8.30	4.83	6.47	7.72	8.88	5.22	27.45	51.46	4.19
Ecuador	248	27.44	22.89	24.37	30.64	36.10	52.24	96.09	37.68	12.48	7.93	2.74	2.41
El Salvador	253	10.59	10.03	9.79	4.49	2.55	.51	2.27	3.75	1.87	2.12	4.45	4.69
Guatemala	258	10.86	8.41	11.06	9.23	6.97	4.86	5.98	7.63	8.03	5.48	7.39	8.42
Guyana	336	....	12.21	7.09	3.56	4.59	7.54	6.15	2.63	5.34	5.98	4.67	6.34
Haiti	263	39.33	27.61	20.58	20.56	10.63	8.67	13.71	14.17	9.85	39.28	22.81	15.83
Honduras	268	21.73	29.46	23.84	20.17	13.71	11.65	11.06	9.67	7.70	7.67	8.11	8.81
Mexico	273	6.97	35.00	34.38	20.63	15.93	16.59	9.50	6.36	5.03	4.55	4.69	3.99
Netherlands Antilles	353	1.78	2.80	3.60	3.26	1.13	.37	5.81	1.79	.42	2.03	1.38	3.38
Nicaragua	278	6.71	10.94	11.62	9.22	13.04	11.22	11.55	7.36	3.99	5.15	8.44	9.42
Panama	283	1.27	.99	1.26	1.32	.56	1.25	1.50	.31	1.01	.10	.40	3.26
Paraguay	288	20.57	13.43	9.80	6.95	11.55	6.75	8.98	7.27	10.51	14.23	4.33	6.79

Consumer Prices

		1994	1995	1996	1997	1998	1999	2000	2001	2002	2003	2004	2005
		Percent Change over Previous Year; Calculated from Indices											
Western Hemisphere(Cont.)													
Peru...............................	293	23.74	11.13	11.54	8.56	7.25	3.47	3.76	1.98	.19	2.26	3.66	1.62
Suriname........................	366	368.48	235.56	−.70	7.15	18.98	98.93	59.40	38.64	15.49	22.97	9.95	9.95
Trinidad and Tobago.....	369	8.81	5.18	3.40	3.63	5.61	3.44	3.56	5.54	4.14	3.81	3.72	6.89
Uruguay..........................	298	44.74	42.25	28.34	19.82	10.81	5.66	4.76	4.36	13.97	19.38	9.16	4.70
Venezuela, Rep. Bol.......	299	60.82	59.92	99.88	50.04	35.78	23.57	16.21	12.53	22.43	31.09	21.75	15.95
Memorandum Items													
Oil Exporting Countries..........	999	20.15	25.15	20.44	11.77	27.63	14.31	6.15	8.54	9.76	9.78	8.65	9.57
Non-Oil Developing Countries.	201	71.65	34.46	16.87	11.42	9.67	9.76	6.82	6.14	5.31	4.98	4.70	4.66

Indices

		1994	1995	1996	1997	1998	1999	2000	2001	2002	2003	2004	2005
		Index Numbers: 2000=100											
World.......................................	001	64.6	74.5	81.0	85.9	90.9	95.8	100.0	104.1	107.6	111.4	115.2	119.4
Industrial Countries.................	110	88.9	91.0	93.1	95.0	96.3	97.7	100.0	102.2	103.7	105.6	107.8	110.3
Developing Countries..............	200	43.7	58.3	68.4	76.2	85.0	93.7	100.0	106.4	112.5	118.6	124.6	131.0
Africa.......................................	605	40.6	53.9	66.9	75.6	81.7	89.7	100.0	112.3	122.2	130.2	136.3	145.1
Asia..	505	70.9	79.2	85.3	89.3	96.4	98.5	100.0	102.4	104.4	106.4	110.1	114.0
Europe.....................................	170	9.6	21.1	30.5	41.0	53.1	79.8	100.0	121.2	139.8	155.6	168.8	183.2
Middle East.............................	405	56.1	68.1	76.9	82.7	88.6	95.3	100.0	103.6	109.1	116.2	124.8	132.7
Western Hemisphere..............	205	40.1	56.3	68.3	77.2	84.9	92.5	100.0	106.3	116.0	128.5	137.2	145.9

Exports, f.o.b.

		1994	1995	1996	1997	1998	1999	2000	2001	2002	2003	2004	2005
							Billions of US Dollars						
World	001	4,139.7	4,946.5	5,169.0	5,539.9	5,453.7	5,646.4	6,381.1	6,135.1	6,435.3	7,474.4	9,086.9	10,239.8
Industrial Countries	110	2,766.9	3,289.8	3,383.0	3,644.9	3,673.9	3,739.7	4,004.6	3,874.4	3,995.6	4,572.1	5,368.7	5,750.4
United States	111	513	585	625	689	682	696	782	729	693	725	819	907
Canada	156	165	192	202	214	214	238	277	260	252	273	304	359
Australia	193	48	53	60	63	56	56	64	63	65	72	86	106
Japan	158	397	443	411	421	388	419	479	403	417	472	566	595
New Zealand	196	12.2	13.6	14.4	14.2	12.0	12.5	13.3	13.7	14.4	16.5	20.3	21.7
Euro Area													
Austria	122	45.0	57.6	57.8	58.6	62.7	† 64.1	64.2	66.7	70.9	87.6	109.0	46.4
Belgium	124	144	176	175	172	179	† 179	188	190	216	256	307	336
Finland	172	29.7	39.6	38.4	39.3	43.0	† 41.8	45.5	42.8	44.7	52.5	60.9	65.2
France	132	236	287	288	290	306	† 302	300	297	312	365	424	440
Germany	134	430	524	524	512	543	† 543	550	571	615	752	912	978
Greece	174	8.8	11.0	11.9	11.1	10.7	10.5	10.7	9.5	10.3	13.2	15.0	15.5
Ireland	178	34.1	44.6	48.7	53.5	64.5	† 71.2	77.1	83.0	87.4	92.4	104.2	109.6
Italy	136	191	234	252	240	246	† 235	240	244	254	299	353	373
Luxembourg	137	7	8	7	7	8	† 8	8	8	8	10	12	13
Netherlands	138	156	196	197	195	201	† 200	213	216	221	259	318	346
Portugal	182	18.0	23.2	24.6	24.0	† 24.8	† 25.2	23.3	24.4	25.5	30.6	33.0	32.2
Spain	184	72.9	91.0	102.0	104.4	109.2	† 110.0	113.3	115.2	123.5	156.0	182.1	191.0
Denmark	128	43.1	51.5	51.5	49.1	48.8	50.4	50.4	51.1	56.3	65.3	75.6	83.7
Iceland	176	1.62	1.80	1.64	1.85	2.05	2.00	1.89	2.02	2.23	2.39	2.90	2.94
Norway	142	34.7	42.0	49.6	48.5	40.4	45.5	60.1	59.2	59.7	67.5	81.7	101.9
Sweden	144	61.3	79.8	84.9	82.9	85.0	84.8	87.7	78.2	82.9	102.4	123.3	130.2
Switzerland	146	66	78	76	72	75	76	75	78	87	101	118	126
United Kingdom	112	204	242	262	281	272	268	282	267	276	304	342	371
Developing Countries	200	1,372.84	1,656.65	1,786.02	1,895.00	1,779.75	1,906.71	2,376.43	2,260.67	2,439.69	2,902.22	3,718.15	4,489.43
Africa	605	79.49	94.45	107.08	108.60	92.08	100.43	125.16	118.22	121.96	149.30	196.54	248.66
Algeria	612	8.9	10.3	13.2	....	....	....	....	....	18.8	24.6	32.3	46.5
Angola	614	3.0	3.6	5.1	5.0	3.5	5.2	7.9	6.5	8.3	9.5	13.5	23.1
Benin	638	.40	.42	.65	.42	.41	.42	.39	.37	.45	.56	.67	.29
Botswana	616	1.85	2.14	2.54	2.84	1.95	....	2.68	2.31	2.32	3.02	3.60	4.29
Burkina Faso	748	.107	.276	.233	.232	.319	.216	.241	.227	.247	.320	.479	.590
Burundi	618	.12	.11	.04	.09	.06	.05	.05	.04	.03	.04	.05	.09
Cameroon	622	1.5	1.6	1.6	1.7	1.7	1.6	1.8	1.7	1.8	2.2	2.5	2.5
Cape Verde	624	—	.01	.01	.01	.01	.01	.01	.01	.01	.01	.02	.02
Central African Rep	626	.15	.17	.15	.16	.15	.15	.16	.14	.15	.12	.13	.14
Chad	628	.15	.24	.24	.24	.26	.24	.18	.19	.18	.60	2.25	3.23
Congo, Rep. of	634	.96	1.17	1.35	1.67	1.37	1.56	2.49	2.06	2.28	2.68	3.44	5.00
Côte d'Ivoire	662	2.7	3.8	4.4	4.5	4.6	4.7	3.9	3.9	5.3	5.8	6.9	7.2
Equatorial Guinea	642	.06	.09	.18	.50	.44	.71	1.10	1.83	2.12	2.80	4.70	6.95
Ethiopia	644	.37	.42	.42	.59	.56	.47	.49	.46	.48	.50	.68	.88
Gabon	646	2.4	2.7	3.2	3.0	1.9	2.4	2.6	2.5	2.4	2.8	3.5	4.7
Gambia, The	648	.035	.016	.021	.015	.021	.012	.015	.010	.013	.008	.010	.009
Ghana	652	1.4	1.7	1.7	1.6	1.8	1.7	1.7	....	....	2.3	2.5	2.5
Guinea	656	.52	.70	.71	.69	.69	.64	.67	.73	.71	.61	.73	.91
Guinea-Bissau	654	.086	.044	.028	.048	.027	.051	.062	.063	.054	.065	.088	.080
Kenya	664	1.6	1.9	2.1	2.1	2.0	1.7	1.7	1.9	2.1	2.4	2.7	3.3
Lesotho	666	.14	.16	.19	.20	.19	.17	.22	.28	.36	.47	.71	.68
Madagascar	674	.37	.37	.46	.41	.54	.58	.82	.93	.49	.86	.98	.75
Malawi	676	.34	.41	.48	.54	.43	.45	.38	.45	.41	.53	.48	.50
Mali	678	.33	.44	.43	.56	.56	.57	.55	.73	.87	.93	1.03	1.15
Mauritius	684	1.35	1.54	1.80	1.59	1.65	1.59	1.56	1.63	1.80	1.90	1.99	2.14
Morocco	686	5.6	6.9	6.9	7.0	7.2	7.4	7.4	7.1	7.8	8.8	9.9	10.5
Namibia	728	1.31	1.41	1.42	1.34	1.23	1.23	1.32	1.18	1.07	1.26	1.83	1.99
Niger	692	.23	.29	.33	.27	.33	.29	.28	.27	.28	.35	.38	.41
Rwanda	714	.03	.05	.06	.09	.06	.06	.05	.08	.06	.06	.10	.13
Senegal	722	.79	.99	.99	.90	.97	1.03	.92	1.00	1.07	1.26	1.47	1.60
Seychelles	718	.05	.05	.14	.11	.12	.15	.19	.22	.23	.27	.29	.40
Sierra Leone	724	.12	.04	.05	.02	.01	.01	.01	.03	.05	.09	.14	.16
South Africa	199	25.3	27.9	29.2	31.0	† 26.4	26.7	30.0	29.3	29.7	36.5	46.1	51.7
Sudan	732	.5	.6	.6	.6	.6	.8	1.8	1.7	1.9	2.5	3.8	4.8
Swaziland	734	.79	.87	.86	.96	.98	.94	.91	1.07	1.03	1.64	1.94	2.01
Tanzania	738	.52	.68	.78	.75	.59	.54	.66	.78	.90	1.13	1.34	1.48
Togo	742	.33	.38	.44	.42	.42	.39	.36	.36	.43	.62	.37	.36
Tunisia	744	4.7	5.5	5.5	5.6	5.7	5.9	5.9	6.6	6.9	8.0	9.7	10.5
Uganda	746	.41	.46	.59	.55	.50	.52	.46	.46	.44	.56	.88	.82
Zambia	754	1.06	1.03	1.04	.91	1.03	1.06	.67	.99	.93	.98	1.46	1.72
Zimbabwe	698	1.88	2.11	2.41	2.39	2.11	1.89	1.93	1.21	1.40	1.40	1.52	1.49
Asia *	505	768.46	932.70	972.99	1,041.79	987.72	1,054.30	1,269.78	1,182.42	1,299.15	1,536.92	1,956.37	2,277.52
Bangladesh	513	2.7	3.2	3.3	3.8	3.8	3.9	4.8	4.8	4.6	5.3	6.6	7.2
Bhutan	514	.1	.1	.1	.1	.1	.1	.1	.1	.1	.1	.2	....
Cambodia	522	....	....	....	1	1	1	1	1	1	2	2	1
China, P.R.: Mainland	924	121	149	151	183	184	195	249	266	326	438	593	762
China, P.R.: Hong Kong	532	151	174	181	188	174	174	202	190	200	224	259	289
China, P.R.: Macao	546	1.87	2.00	2.00	2.15	2.14	2.20	2.54	2.30	2.36	2.58	2.81	2.48
Fiji	819	.45	.54	.59	.52	.45	.48	.48	.44	.55	.68	.68	.72
India	534	25.0	30.6	33.1	35.0	33.4	35.7	42.4	43.4	50.4	59.0	75.6	95.2
Indonesia	536	40.1	45.4	49.8	56.3	50.4	51.2	65.4	56.4	58.1	61.1	71.6	47.9
Korea	542	96	125	130	136	132	144	172	150	162	194	254	284
Lao People's Dem. Rep	544	.3	.3	.3	.4	.4	.3	.3	.3	.3	.4	.4	.5
Malaysia	548	58.8	73.9	78.3	78.7	73.3	84.6	98.2	88.0	93.3	99.4	125.7	140.9

Exports, f.o.b.

		1994	1995	1996	1997	1998	1999	2000	2001	2002	2003	2004	2005
							Billions of US Dollars						
Asia *(Cont.)													
Maldives	556	—	—	.1	.1	.1	.1	.1	.1	.1	.1	.1	.1
Mongolia	948	.4	.5	.4	.6	.3	.5	.5	.5	.5	.6	.9	1.1
Myanmar	518	.80	.86	.75	.87	1.08	1.14	1.65	2.38	3.05	2.48	2.38	3.81
Nepal	558	.362	.345	.385	.406	.474	.602	.804	.737	.568	.662	.756	.830
Pakistan	564	7.4	8.0	9.3	8.7	8.5	8.4	9.0	9.2	9.9	11.9	13.4	16.1
Papua New Guinea	853	2.6	2.6	2.5	2.1	1.8	1.9	2.1	1.8	1.6	2.2	2.6	3.2
Philippines	566	13.3	17.5	20.4	24.9	29.4	36.6	39.8	32.7	36.5	36.2	39.7	39.9
Samoa	862	.004	.009	.010	.015	.015	.020	.014	.016	.014	.015	.011	.012
Singapore	576	96.8	118.3	125.0	125.0	109.9	114.7	137.8	121.8	125.2	144.2	198.6	229.6
Solomon Islands	813	.142	.168	.162	.157	.118	.126	.065	.047	.057	.074	.097	.102
Sri Lanka	524	3.21	3.80	4.10	4.64	4.81	4.59	5.43	4.82	4.70	5.13	5.76	6.35
Thailand	578	45	56	56	57	54	58	69	65	68	80	96	110
Tonga	866	.0138	.0141	.0114	.0100	.0072	.0122	.0086	.0066	.0144	.0176	.0150	.0130
Vanuatu	846	.025	.028	.030	.035	.034	.026	.026	.020	.019	.027	.037	.040
Vietnam	582	....	....	7	9	9	12	14	15	17	20	26	32
* of which:													
Taiwan Province of China	528	92.9	111.6	115.7	121.1	110.5	121.5	147.8	122.5	130.5	143.9	173.9	197.8
Europe	170	**202.12**	**254.73**	**276.10**	**284.90**	**279.87**	**278.80**	**340.82**	**359.34**	**396.49**	**510.32**	**686.54**	**835.77**
Albania	914	.1	.2	.2	.1	.2	.4	.3	.3	.3	.4	.6	.7
Armenia	911	.22	.27	.29	.23	.22	.23	.29	.34	.51	.69	.72	.95
Azerbaijan, Republic of	912	.7	.6	.6	.8	.6	.9	1.7	2.3	2.2	2.6	3.6	4.3
Belarus	913	3	5	6	7	7	6	7	7	8	10	14	16
Bulgaria	918	4	5	7	5	4	4	5	5	6	8	10	12
Croatia	960	4.4	4.5	4.6	4.0	4.5	4.3	4.4	4.7	4.9	6.2	8.0	8.8
Cyprus	423	.97	1.23	1.40	1.10	1.06	1.00	.95	.98	.77	.83	1.08	1.30
Czech Republic	935	† 16	† 22	22	23	26	26	29	33	38	49	67	78
Estonia	939	† 1.3	1.7	1.8	2.1	2.5	2.4	3.2	3.3	3.4	4.5	5.9	7.7
Georgia	915	—	—	—	—	—	—	—	—	—	—	1	1
Hungary	944	10.4	12.8	15.6	19.0	23.0	25.0	28.0	30.5	34.5	42.5	54.9	61.8
Kazakhstan	916	3.2	5.3	5.9	6.5	5.3	5.9	8.8	8.6	9.7	12.9	20.1	27.8
Kyrgyz Republic	917	.3	.4	.5	.6	.5	.5	.5	.5	.5	.6	.7	.7
Latvia	941	1	1	1	2	2	2	2	2	2	3	4	5
Lithuania	946	2	2	3	3	3	3	4	4	5	7	9	12
Macedonia, FYR	962	1.1	1.2	1.1	1.2	1.3	1.2	1.3	1.2	1.1	1.4	1.7	2.0
Malta	181	1.57	1.91	1.73	1.63	1.83	1.98	2.44	1.96	2.23	2.47	2.64	2.33
Moldova	921	1	1	1	1	1	—	—	1	1	1	1	1
Poland	964	17	23	24	26	27	27	32	36	41	54	74	89
Romania	968	6.2	7.9	8.1	8.4	8.3	8.5	10.4	11.4	13.9	17.6	23.5	27.7
Russia	922	† 68	83	91	89	75	76	106	102	107	136	183	244
Slovak Republic	936	7	9	9	8	11	10	12	13	14	22	28	32
Slovenia	961	7	8	8	8	9	9	9	9	10	13	16	18
Turkey	186	18	22	23	26	27	27	28	31	35	47	62	72
Ukraine	926	10	13	14	14	13	12	15	16	18	23	33	34
Middle East	405	**143.05**	**157.92**	**184.57**	**187.70**	**150.29**	**183.39**	**292.15**	**268.89**	**288.29**	**347.05**	**440.74**	**605.81**
Bahrain, Kingdom of	419	3.6	4.1	4.7	4.4	3.3	4.4	6.2	5.6	5.8	6.6	7.5	10.0
Egypt	469	3.5	3.4	3.5	3.9	3.1	3.6	4.7	4.1	4.7	6.3	7.5	10.7
Iran, I.R. of	429	19	18	22	18	13	21	28	24	28	34	44	58
Israel	436	17	19	21	23	23	26	31	29	29	32	39	43
Jordan	439	1.42	1.77	1.82	1.83	1.79	1.83	1.90	2.29	2.77	3.08	3.92	4.30
Kuwait	443	11.3	12.8	14.9	14.2	9.6	12.2	19.4	16.2	15.4	20.7	28.6	44.9
Lebanon	446	.5	.7	.7	.6	.7	.7	.7	.9	1.0	1.5	1.7	1.8
Libya	672	9	8	8	7	7	8	13	11	10	15	21	30
Oman	449	5.5	6.1	7.3	7.6	5.5	7.2	11.3	11.1	11.2	11.7	13.3	18.7
Qatar	453	3.2	3.7	4.4	5.6	5.0	7.2	....	....	11.0	13.4	18.7	26.5
Qatar	453	3.2	3.7	4.4	5.6	5.0	7.2	....	....	11.0	13.4	18.7	26.5
Saudi Arabia	456	43	50	61	61	39	51	77	68	72	93	126	181
Syrian Arab Rep.	463	3.0	3.6	4.0	3.9	2.9	3.5	† 19.3	21.6	28.1	23.6	22.2	....
United Arab Emirates	466	....	....	....	....	....	....	50	49	52	67	83	113
Yemen, Republic of	474	1	2	3	3	1	2	4	3	3	4	....	....
Western Hemisphere	205	**183.18**	**222.03**	**250.82**	**277.13**	**275.60**	**294.14**	**353.30**	**339.09**	**342.25**	**372.30**	**458.20**	**554.60**
Anguilla	312	.0009	.0005	.0016	.0016	.0032	.0026	.0040	.0032	.0043	.0042	.0057	.0147
Argentina	213	16	21	24	26	26	23	26	27	26	30	35	40
Aruba	314	....	—	—	—	—	—	.2	.1	.1	.1	.1	.1
Bahamas, The	313	.2	.2	.2	.2	.3	.5	.6	.4	.4	.4	.4	.5
Barbados	316	.18	.24	.28	.28	.25	.26	.27	.26	.24	.25	.28	.36
Belize	339	.13	.14	.15	.16	.16	.17	.21	.16	.16	.19	.21	.21
Bolivia	218	1.0	1.1	1.1	1.2	1.1	1.1	1.2	1.3	1.3	1.6	2.1	2.7
Brazil	223	44	47	48	53	51	48	55	58	60	73	96	118
Chile	228	11.6	16.0	16.6	17.9	16.3	17.2	19.2	18.3	18.2	21.7	32.2	40.6
Colombia	233	8.5	10.1	10.6	11.5	10.9	11.6	13.0	12.3	11.9	13.1	16.2	21.1
Costa Rica	238	2.9	3.5	3.8	4.3	5.5	6.7	5.8	5.0	5.3	6.1	6.3	7.0
Dominica	321	—	—	.1	.1	.1	.1	.1	—	—	—	—	—
Dominican Republic	243	.64	.87	.95	1.02	.88	.81	.97	.80	.83	1.04	1.25	1.40
Ecuador	248	3.8	4.3	5.2	5.3	4.2	4.5	4.9	4.7	5.0	6.2	7.8	10.1
El Salvador	253	.8	1.0	1.0	1.4	1.3	1.2	1.3	1.2	1.2	1.3	1.4	1.6
Grenada	328	.02	.02	.02	.02	.03	.05	.07	.06	.06	.04	.03	....
Guadeloupe	329	.15	.16	....	....	....	....	....	....	....	....	....	....
Guatemala	258	1.6	2.0	2.1	2.4	2.6	2.5	2.7	2.5	2.5	2.6	2.9	3.5
Guyana	336	.44	.47	.58	.59	.55	.52	.50	.49	.50	.51	.59	.55
Haiti	263	.082	.110	.090	.212	.320	.334	.318	.274	.280	.347	.391	.470
Honduras	268	.8	1.2	1.3	1.4	1.5	1.2	1.4	1.3	1.3	1.3	1.5	1.7
Jamaica	343	1.21	1.43	1.38	1.38	1.31	1.24	1.29	1.22	1.11	1.18	1.39	1.50

Exports, f.o.b.

		1994	1995	1996	1997	1998	1999	2000	2001	2002	2003	2004	2005
						Billions of US Dollars							
Western Hemisphere(Cont.)													
Martinique..................................	349	.18	.22	....	....	....	....	....	....	....	....	....	....
Mexico.......................................	273	61	80	96	110	117	136	166	159	161	165	189	214
Netherlands Antilles....................	353	1.4	....	....	....	1.2	1.5	2.0	2.4	1.6	1.2	1.4	1.6
Nicaragua...................................	278	.3	.5	.5	.6	.6	.5	.6	.6	.6	.6	.8	.9
Panama.......................................	283	.58	.63	....	.72	.78	.82	.86	.91	.85	.86	.94	1.08
Paraguay.....................................	288	.8	.9	1.0	1.1	1.0	.7	.9	1.0	1.0	1.2	1.6	1.7
Peru..	293	4.4	5.5	5.9	6.8	5.8	6.1	7.0	7.0	7.7	9.1	12.6	17.2
St. Lucia......................................	362	.1	.1	.1	.1	.1	.1	—	.1	—	.1	....	....
St. Vincent & Grens.....................	364	.05	.04	.05	.05	.05	.05	.05	.04	.04	.04	.03	.04
Suriname.....................................	366	.45	.48	.54	.56	.51	.46	.51	.20	.16	.19	.23	.27
Trinidad and Tobago....................	369	1.9	2.5	2.5	2.5	2.3	2.8	4.3	4.3	3.9	5.2	6.4	8.5
Uruguay......................................	298	1.9	2.1	2.4	2.7	2.8	2.2	2.3	2.1	1.9	2.2	2.9	3.4
Venezuela, Rep. Bol.....................	299	16	18	23	22	17	20	31	25	26	24	34	52
Memorandum Items													
Euro Area....................................	163	....	....	....	....	791.46	† 953.81	966.50	967.61	1,021.22	1,255.05	1,479.81	1,538.16
Oil Exporting Countries...........	999	187.50	209.68	248.53	254.74	201.45	238.67	363.06	319.32	329.81	398.32	522.16	684.81
Non-Oil Developing Countries.	201	1,186.37	1,448.55	1,538.71	1,641.71	1,580.28	1,669.78	2,014.47	1,941.88	2,110.17	2,504.37	3,196.79	3,806.18

Imports, c.i.f.

		1994	1995	1996	1997	1998	1999	2000	2001	2002	2003	2004	2005
		Billions of US Dollars											
World	001	4,228.1	5,046.5	5,299.2	5,644.7	5,575.9	5,797.2	6,573.3	6,332.7	6,570.7	7,652.1	9,343.7	10,488.0
Industrial Countries	110	2,768.1	3,267.1	3,386.1	3,636.5	3,739.8	3,931.0	4,339.6	4,160.6	4,266.7	4,928.3	5,855.0	6,434.7
United States	111	689	771	822	899	944	1,059	1,259	1,179	1,200	1,303	1,526	1,732
Canada	156	155	168	175	201	206	220	245	227	227	245	280	332
Australia	193	53	61	65	66	65	69	72	64	73	89	109	125
Japan	158	275	336	349	339	280	311	380	349	337	383	455	515
New Zealand	196	11.9	14.0	14.7	14.5	12.5	14.3	13.9	13.3	15.0	18.6	23.2	26.2
Euro Area													
Austria	122	55.3	66.4	67.3	64.8	68.2	† 69.6	69.0	70.4	72.8	88.3	108.9	47.2
Belgium	124	130	160	164	157	165	† 165	177	179	198	235	286	319
Finland	172	23.2	28.1	29.3	29.8	32.3	† 31.6	33.9	32.1	33.6	41.6	50.7	58.2
France	132	235	281	282	272	290	† 295	311	302	312	370	443	483
Germany	134	385	464	459	446	471	† 474	495	486	490	605	718	777
Greece	174	21.4	26.8	29.7	27.9	29.4	28.7	29.2	29.9	31.2	44.4	51.6	49.8
Ireland	178	25.9	33.1	35.9	39.2	44.6	† 47.2	51.5	51.3	51.5	53.3	61.4	69.1
Italy	136	169	206	208	210	218	† 220	238	236	246	297	355	385
Luxembourg	137	8	10	10	9	10	† 11	11	11	12	14	17	17
Netherlands	138	141	177	181	178	188	† 188	199	196	194	233	284	309
Portugal	182	27.3	33.3	35.2	35.1	† 38.5	† 39.8	38.2	39.4	38.3	40.8	49.2	53.4
Spain	184	92.2	113.3	121.8	122.7	133.1	† 144.4	152.9	153.6	163.5	208.5	257.6	287.6
Denmark	128	36.6	45.7	45.0	44.4	46.3	44.5	44.4	44.1	48.9	56.2	66.9	74.5
Iceland	176	1.47	1.76	2.03	1.99	2.49	2.50	2.59	2.25	2.27	2.79	3.55	4.56
Norway	142	27.3	33.0	35.6	35.7	37.5	34.2	34.4	33.0	34.9	39.5	48.1	54.8
Sweden	144	52.0	64.7	66.9	65.7	68.6	68.8	73.3	64.3	67.6	84.2	100.8	111.2
Switzerland	146	64	77	74	71	74	75	76	77	82	96	110	120
United Kingdom	112	226	265	287	307	314	318	334	321	335	381	452	483
Developing Countries	200	1,459.98	1,779.41	1,913.07	2,008.20	1,836.15	1,866.25	2,233.69	2,172.12	2,303.96	2,723.74	3,488.61	4,053.26
Africa	605	83.06	101.36	101.83	105.65	105.53	101.00	105.42	111.63	112.73	140.03	179.34	207.44
Algeria	612	9.2	10.1	9.1	....	....	....	....	....	12.0	12.4	18.2	20.0
Benin	638	.43	.75	.65	.68	.74	.75	.75	.57	.62	.72	.89	.89
Botswana	616	1.64	1.91	1.72	2.26	2.39	2.21	2.47	1.81	1.67	2.59	3.46	4.00
Burkina Faso	748	.35	.45	.65	.59	.73	.57	.65	.51	.55	.69	.94	1.29
Burundi	618	.22	.23	.13	.12	.16	.12	.15	.14	.13	.16	.18	.27
Cameroon	622	1.1	.9	1.1	1.2	1.5	1.3	1.5	1.9	1.9	2.0	2.4	2.5
Cape Verde	624	.21	.25	.23	.24	.23	.25	.23	.23	.28	.35	.39	.44
Central African Rep.	626	.14	.17	.14	.14	.15	.13	.12	.11	.12	.13	.15	.16
Chad	628	.18	.37	.33	.33	.36	.32	.32	.68	1.65	.79	.75	.85
Congo, Rep. of	634	.63	.67	1.55	.93	.68	.85	.74	1.10	1.09	1.34	1.76	2.04
Côte d'Ivoire	662	1.9	2.9	2.9	2.8	3.0	3.3	2.8	2.4	2.5	3.2	4.2	4.7
Equatorial Guinea	642	.04	.05	.29	.33	.32	.43	.45	.81	.51	1.22	1.54	2.05
Ethiopia	644	1.03	1.15	1.40	....	1.52	1.54	1.26	1.81	1.62	2.12	3.09	4.13
Gabon	646	.76	.88	.96	1.10	1.10	.84	.99	.86	.95	1.04	1.28	1.40
Gambia, The	648	.21	.18	.26	.17	.23	.19	.19	.13	.15	.16	.23	.24
Ghana	652	2.1	1.9	2.1	2.3	2.6	3.5	3.0	3.2	2.7	3.2	4.1	5.1
Guinea-Bissau	654	.164	.133	.087	.089	.063	.051	.060	.062	.058	.065	.096	.120
Kenya	664	2.1	3.0	2.9	3.3	3.2	2.8	3.1	3.2	3.2	3.7	4.6	6.1
Lesotho	666	.85	.99	1.00	1.02	.96	.87	.81	.75	.82	1.12	1.43	1.41
Madagascar	674	.44	.54	.52	.50	.69	.74	1.00	.96	.60	1.11	1.47	1.55
Malawi	676	.49	.47	.62	.78	.52	.67	.53	.56	.70	.79	.93	1.10
Mali	678	.59	.77	.77	.74	.76	.82	.81	.99	.93	1.25	1.33	1.55
Mauritius	684	1.93	1.98	2.29	2.19	2.07	2.25	2.09	1.99	2.16	2.36	2.77	3.16
Morocco	686	8.3	10.0	9.7	9.5	10.3	9.9	11.5	11.0	11.9	14.3	17.8	20.3
Mozambique	688	1	1	1	1	1	1	1	1	2	2	2	2
Namibia	728	1.41	1.62	1.67	1.75	1.65	1.61	1.55	1.55	1.47	1.98	2.42	2.45
Niger	692	.33	.37	.45	.37	.47	.41	.40	.41	.47	.62	.79	.92
Nigeria	694	6.6	† 8.2	6.4	9.5	9.2	8.6	8.7	11.6	7.5	10.9	14.2	15.2
Rwanda	714	.12	.24	.26	.30	.28	.25	.21	.25	.20	.25	.28	.43
Senegal	722	1.02	1.41	1.44	1.33	1.46	1.56	1.52	1.73	2.03	2.39	2.85	3.33
Seychelles	718	.21	.23	.38	.34	.38	.43	.34	.48	.42	.41	.50	.55
Sierra Leone	724	.15	.13	.21	.09	.09	.08	.15	.18	.26	.30	.29	.34
South Africa	199	23	31	30	33	† 29	27	30	28	29	41	53	62
Sudan	732	1.2	† 1.2	1.5	1.6	1.9	1.4	1.6	2.3	2.4	2.9	4.1	6.8
Swaziland	734	.84	1.01	1.06	1.07	1.09	1.07	1.05	1.14	.94	1.52	1.92	2.10
Tanzania	738	1.5	1.7	1.4	1.3	1.5	1.6	1.5	1.7	1.7	2.1	2.5	2.7
Togo	742	.22	.59	.66	.65	.59	.49	.48	.52	.58	.84	.56	.59
Tunisia	744	6.6	7.9	7.7	7.9	8.4	8.5	8.6	9.5	9.5	10.9	12.8	13.2
Uganda	746	.87	1.06	1.19	1.32	1.41	1.34	1.54	1.59	1.11	1.25	2.02	1.90
Zambia	754	.67	.69	.84	.82	1.10	.82	.99	1.31	1.25	1.57	2.02	2.75
Zimbabwe	698	2.24	2.66	3.81	3.11	2.70	2.13	1.86	1.72	1.75	1.71	2.20	2.75
Asia *	505	812.73	999.96	1,050.54	1,066.38	886.65	965.75	1,205.58	1,117.64	1,214.48	1,454.52	1,875.98	2,164.10
Bangladesh	513	4.6	6.5	6.6	6.9	7.0	7.7	8.4	8.3	7.9	9.5	12.6	12.9
Bhutan	514	.1	.1	.1	.1	.1	.2	.2	.2	.2	.2	.4	....
Cambodia	522	....	....	....	1	1	1	1	1	2	2	2	1
China, P.R.: Mainland	924	116	132	139	142	140	166	225	244	295	413	561	660
China, P.R.: Hong Kong	532	162	193	199	209	185	180	213	201	208	232	271	300
China, P.R.: Macao	546	2.13	2.04	2.00	2.08	1.95	2.04	2.25	2.39	2.53	2.76	3.48	3.91
Fiji	819	.83	.89	.99	.97	.72	.90	.83	.79	.90	1.17	1.27	1.61
India	534	26.8	34.7	37.9	41.4	43.0	47.0	51.5	50.4	56.5	72.6	97.4	134.6
Indonesia	536	32.0	40.6	42.9	51.3	35.3	33.3	43.6	31.0	31.3	32.6	46.5	38.9
Korea	542	102	135	150	145	93	120	160	141	152	179	224	261
Lao People's Dem. Rep.	544	.6	.6	.7	.7	.6	.5	.5	.5	.4	.5	.5	.8
Malaysia	548	59.6	77.7	78.4	79.0	58.3	65.4	82.0	73.9	79.9	81.9	105.3	114.4

Imports, c.i.f.

		1994	1995	1996	1997	1998	1999	2000	2001	2002	2003	2004	2005
							Billions of US Dollars						
Asia *(Cont.)													
Maldives	556	.2	.3	.3	.3	.4	.4	.4	.4	.4	.5	.6	.7
Mongolia	948	.2	.4	.4	.5	.5	.5	.6	.6	.7	.8	1.0	1.2
Myanmar	518	.89	1.35	1.37	2.06	2.69	2.32	2.40	2.88	2.35	2.09	2.20	1.93
Nepal	558	1.16	1.33	1.40	1.69	1.25	1.42	1.57	1.47	1.42	1.75	1.87	1.86
Pakistan	564	8.9	11.5	12.1	11.6	9.3	10.2	10.9	10.2	11.2	13.0	17.9	25.4
Papua New Guinea	853	1.52	1.45	1.74	1.70	1.23	1.19	1.15	1.07	1.24	1.37	1.68	1.73
Philippines	566	22.6	28.3	34.1	38.6	31.5	32.6	37.0	34.9	37.2	39.5	42.3	47.0
Samoa	862	.081	.095	.100	.097	.097	.115	.090	.120	.128	.129	.155	.187
Singapore	576	103	125	131	132	105	111	135	116	116	128	174	200
Solomon Islands	813	.142	.154	.118	.148	.150	.111	.098	.082	.065	.068	.085	.144
Sri Lanka	524	4.78	5.19	5.42	5.84	5.93	5.87	6.28	5.97	6.10	6.67	7.97	8.83
Thailand	578	54	71	72	63	43	50	62	62	65	76	94	118
Tonga	866	.069	.077	.075	.073	.069	.073	.069	.072	.089	.094	.105	.110
Vanuatu	846	.089	.095	.098	.094	.093	.098	.087	.090	.090	.105	.128	.140
Vietnam	582	....	....	11	12	12	12	16	16	19	25	31	36
* of which:													
Taiwan Province of China	528	85.5	103.7	101.3	113.9	104.9	111.0	139.9	107.3	112.8	127.4	168.1	182.6
Europe	170	217.16	289.23	333.45	353.96	348.20	308.81	358.34	374.66	421.93	540.40	712.58	822.98
Albania	914	.6	.7	.9	.6	.8	1.2	1.1	1.3	1.5	1.9	2.3	2.6
Armenia	911	.39	.67	.86	.89	.90	.80	.88	.87	.99	1.28	1.35	1.77
Azerbaijan, Republic of	912	.8	.7	1.0	.8	1.1	1.0	1.2	1.4	1.7	2.6	3.5	4.2
Belarus	913	3	6	7	9	9	7	9	8	9	12	16	17
Bulgaria	918	4	6	7	5	5	5	7	7	8	11	14	18
Croatia	960	5.5	7.4	7.8	9.1	8.3	7.8	7.9	9.1	10.7	14.2	16.6	18.6
Cyprus	423	3.02	3.69	3.98	3.70	3.69	3.62	3.85	3.92	3.86	4.29	5.66	6.28
Czech Republic	935	† 18	† 26	29	29	30	29	34	38	43	54	72	77
Estonia	939	† 1.7	2.4	2.9	3.5	3.9	3.4	4.2	4.3	4.8	6.5	8.3	10.1
Georgia	915	—	1	1	1	1	1	1	1	1	1	2	2
Hungary	944	14.3	15.4	18.1	21.1	25.7	27.9	32.0	33.7	37.8	47.6	59.6	65.3
Kazakhstan	916	3.6	3.8	4.2	4.3	4.3	3.7	5.0	6.4	6.6	8.4	12.8	17.4
Kyrgyz Republic	917	.3	.5	.8	.7	.8	.6	.6	.5	.6	.7	.9	1.1
Latvia	941	1	2	2	3	3	3	3	4	4	5	7	9
Lithuania	946	2	3	4	5	5	5	5	6	8	10	12	15
Macedonia, FYR	962	1.5	1.7	1.6	1.8	1.9	1.8	2.1	1.7	2.0	2.3	2.9	3.2
Malta	181	2.44	2.94	2.80	2.55	2.67	2.85	3.40	2.73	2.84	3.40	3.83	3.73
Moldova	921	1	1	1	1	1	1	1	1	1	1	2	2
Poland	964	21	29	37	42	46	46	49	50	55	68	88	101
Romania	968	7.1	10.3	11.4	11.3	11.8	10.4	13.1	15.6	17.9	24.0	32.7	40.5
Russia	922	† 55	69	75	79	64	44	49	59	67	84	107	138
Slovak Republic	936	7	9	11	11	14	12	13	16	17	24	30	36
Slovenia	961	7	9	9	9	10	10	10	10	11	14	18	20
Turkey	186	23	36	44	49	46	41	55	41	50	66	96	99
Ukraine	926	11	15	18	17	15	12	14	16	17	23	29	36
Middle East	405	128.15	143.67	155.57	160.58	159.58	162.49	180.85	197.08	210.54	237.14	292.34	356.07
Bahrain, Kingdom of	419	3.7	3.7	4.3	4.0	3.6	3.7	4.6	4.3	5.0	5.7	6.5	7.9
Egypt	469	10.2	11.8	13.0	13.2	16.2	16.0	14.0	12.8	12.6	11.1	12.9	19.9
Iran, I.R. of	429	14	14	16	14	14	13	14	18	21	28	35	42
Israel	436	25.2	29.6	31.6	30.8	29.3	33.2	31.4	35.4	35.5	36.3	42.9	47.1
Jordan	439	3.4	3.7	4.3	4.1	3.8	3.7	4.6	4.9	5.1	5.7	8.1	10.5
Kuwait	443	6.7	7.8	8.4	8.2	8.6	7.6	7.2	7.9	9.0	11.0	12.6	17.5
Lebanon	446	2.6	5.5	7.5	7.5	7.1	6.2	6.2	7.3	6.4	7.2	9.4	9.4
Libya	672	4.3	4.1	4.4	4.6	5.5	4.2	3.7	4.4	4.4	4.3	6.3	7.2
Oman	449	3.91	4.25	4.58	5.03	5.68	4.67	5.04	5.80	6.01	6.57	8.87	8.83
Qatar	453	1.93	3.40	2.87	3.32	3.41	2.50	....	....	4.05	4.90	6.00	8.04
Saudi Arabia	456	23	28	28	29	30	28	30	31	32	37	45	56
Syrian Arab Rep.	463	5.5	4.7	5.4	4.0	3.9	3.8	† 16.7	19.6	21.0	21.1	29.1	....
United Arab Emirates	466	21	21	23	30	25	33	35	37	43	52	62	77
Yemen, Republic of	474	2	2	2	2	2	2	2	2	3	4	....	....
Western Hemisphere	205	222.22	251.61	280.37	331.90	349.21	336.55	391.64	382.11	355.83	366.88	448.51	527.94
Anguilla	312	.0364	.0324	.0599	.0616	.0714	.0919	.0945	.0777	.0699	.0768	.1025	.1299
Argentina	213	22	20	24	30	31	26	25	20	9	14	22	29
Aruba	314	....	.6	.6	.6	.8	.8	.8	.8	.8	.8	.9	1.0
Bahamas, The	313	1.1	1.2	1.4	1.7	1.9	1.8	2.1	1.9	1.7	1.8	1.6	2.1
Barbados	316	.61	.77	.83	1.00	1.01	1.11	1.16	1.09	1.04	1.13	1.41	1.60
Belize	339	.26	.26	.26	.29	.30	.37	.52	.52	.52	.55	.52	.59
Bolivia	218	1.2	1.4	1.6	1.9	2.0	1.8	1.8	1.7	1.8	1.6	1.8	2.3
Brazil	223	36	54	57	63	61	52	59	59	50	51	66	78
Chile	228	11.8	15.9	19.2	20.8	19.9	16.0	18.5	17.4	17.1	19.4	24.9	32.6
Colombia	233	11.9	13.9	13.7	15.4	14.6	10.7	11.5	12.8	12.7	13.9	16.7	21.2
Costa Rica	238	3.8	4.1	4.3	5.0	6.2	6.4	6.4	6.6	7.2	7.7	8.3	9.8
Dominica	321	.1	.1	.1	.1	.1	.1	.1	.1	.1	.1	.1	.2
Dominican Republic	243	3.4	3.6	4.1	4.8	5.6	6.0	7.4	6.8	6.9	6.1	6.2	8.3
Ecuador	248	3.6	4.2	4.3	5.0	5.6	3.0	3.7	5.4	6.4	6.7	8.2	10.3
El Salvador	253	2.2	2.9	2.7	3.0	3.1	3.1	3.8	3.9	3.9	4.4	4.9	5.4
Grenada	328	.12	.12	.15	.17	.20	.21	.25	....	....	.26	.28	....
Guadeloupe	329	1.48	1.89	....	....	....	....	....	....	....	....	....	....
Guatemala	258	2.8	3.3	3.1	3.9	4.7	4.6	5.2	5.6	6.3	6.7	7.8	8.8
Guyana	336	.51	.53	.60	.64	....	....	....	.58	.58	.58	.65	.79
Haiti	263	.252	.653	.665	.648	.797	1.025	1.036	1.013	1.130	1.188	1.306	1.454
Honduras	268	1.1	1.6	1.8	2.1	2.5	2.7	2.9	2.9	3.0	3.3	3.9	4.6
Jamaica	343	2.22	2.82	2.97	3.13	3.04	2.90	3.30	3.36	3.53	3.64	3.77	4.46
Martinique	349	1.63	1.96	....	....	....	....	....	....	....	....	....	....

Imports, c.i.f.

		1994	1995	1996	1997	1998	1999	2000	2001	2002	2003	2004	2005
						Billions of US Dollars							
Western Hemisphere(Cont.)													
Mexico..................................	273	83	76	94	115	131	149	183	176	177	179	207	232
Netherlands Antilles....................	353	1.8	....	....	....	2.1	1.7	2.9	2.8	2.3	2.6	3.1	3.5
Nicaragua................................	278	.9	1.0	1.2	1.4	1.5	1.9	1.8	1.8	1.8	1.9	2.2	2.6
Panama..................................	283	2.40	2.51	2.78	3.00	3.40	3.52	3.38	2.96	2.98	3.09	3.59	4.18
Paraguay.................................	288	2.4	3.1	3.2	3.1	2.9	1.9	2.2	2.2	1.7	2.1	3.1	2.9
Peru......................................	293	6.7	9.3	9.4	10.3	9.9	8.2	8.9	....	....	....	....	....
St. Lucia..................................	362	.3	.3	.3	.3	.3	.4	.4	.4	.3	.4	.5	.6
St. Vincent & Grens...................	364	.13	.14	.13	.19	.19	.20	.16	.17	.18	.20	.23	.24
Suriname.................................	366	.42	.59	.50	.57	.55	.56	.52	.14	.14	.18	.22	.28
Trinidad and Tobago....................	369	1.1	1.7	2.1	3.0	3.0	2.7	3.3	3.6	3.6	3.9	4.9	5.1
Uruguay..................................	298	2.8	2.9	3.3	3.7	3.8	3.4	3.5	3.1	2.0	2.2	3.1	3.9
Venezuela, Rep. Bol....................	299	9.2	12.6	9.9	14.6	15.8	14.1	16.2	18.3	13.0	9.3	16.7	24.0
Memorandum Items													
Euro Area...............................	163	....	....	....	....	709.27	† 906.95	923.39	922.48	967.08	1,195.33	1,420.86	1,509.25
Oil Exporting Countries...........	999	132.35	154.74	155.72	178.50	163.25	158.98	178.65	181.02	185.65	211.17	274.30	318.06
Non-Oil Developing Countries.	201	1,328.61	1,626.03	1,759.11	1,831.23	1,674.29	1,708.84	2,057.18	1,993.07	2,120.49	2,515.27	3,217.70	3,739.17

Export Unit Values/Export Prices

		1994	1995	1996	1997	1998	1999	2000	2001	2002	2003	2004	2005
		Indices of Unit Values (Prices) In Terms of US Dollars: 2000=100											
World.........................	001	110.1	120.9	118.7	111.4	105.3	103.7	100.0	96.2	96.9	106.8	116.3	123.0
Industrial Countries...............	110	110.9	122.4	119.8	111.4	108.0	105.6	100.0	97.2	97.9	109.2	119.0	124.6
United States....................	111	98.9	103.9	104.5	103.1	99.7	98.4	100.0	99.2	98.2	99.7	103.6	106.9
Canada..........................	156	92.1	98.9	100.2	98.2	97.4	105.7	100.0	97.7	93.2	103.8	114.8	129.0
Australia........................	193	106.8	116.3	117.7	113.6	100.9	96.2	100.0	98.2	100.0	109.9	129.1	152.9
Japan...........................	158	116.3	123.6	111.9	102.5	96.0	99.2	100.0	91.4	87.6	90.9	96.0	96.1
New Zealand....................	196	113.3	123.3	124.7	116.5	98.6	98.9	100.0	100.9	99.4	111.4	128.6	138.3
Euro Area													
Belgium........................	124	109.0	125.9	123.0	112.1	110.4	105.2	100.0	99.3	103.5	120.4	134.9	142.0
Finland........................	172	113.3	145.1	139.1	120.5	117.0	107.1	100.0	92.8	92.3	106.0	117.2	119.6
France..........................	132	† 143.8	158.7	150.0	128.5	123.2	114.0	100.0	107.7	109.0	130.7	141.4	140.4
Germany.......................	134	128.3	148.5	138.4	120.5	118.1	111.5	100.0	99.0	101.5	118.3	128.9	129.7
Greece.........................	174	114.8	132.5	137.5	123.2	116.4	121.7	100.0	104.9	111.5	133.4	154.1	160.1
Ireland.........................	178	109.8	119.8	118.9	113.9	109.8	110.0	100.0	98.3	103.2	114.7	115.4	!19.1
Italy............................	136	96.6	104.5	115.1	107.6	109.1	107.1	100.0	100.6	107.3	129.6	148.6	158.7
Netherlands....................	138	114.4	131.9	126.0	115.6	110.1	102.8	100.0	99.6	99.4	115.9	126.3	131.7
Portugal........................	182	133.0	144.2	131.6	119.2	116.3	109.3	100.0	92.9	96.3	112.0	....	....
Spain..........................	184	115.3	131.9	131.2	117.2	114.9	108.9	100.0	97.6	101.7	120.1	133.4	139.9
Denmark........................	128	114.4	130.4	128.4	114.9	111.8	107.9	100.0	98.9	102.4	121.7	135.8	142.4
Iceland (1995=100)............	176	88.2	100.0	95.8	90.9	....	....	100.0					
Norway.........................	142	76.1	87.4	92.6	85.6	71.2	77.9	100.0	93.1	93.3	104.3	126.8	160.9
Sweden.........................	144	108.3	130.5	132.0	117.0	111.8	106.5	100.0	90.1	93.8	110.3	121.2	124.1
Switzerland.....................	146	115.0	130.2	125.8	111.1	111.5	109.3	100.0	101.3	107.1	123.5	137.2	139.4
United Kingdom.................	112	108.8	116.1	115.5	114.9	110.6	105.8	100.0	93.6	97.4	108.0	121.5	125.5
Developing Countries.............	200	107.0	115.2	114.5	110.5	96.0	97.1	100.0	92.7	93.4	98.7	107.1	117.4
Africa............................	605	116.7	121.0	118.3	115.9	106.7	101.0	100.0	94.5	96.6	120.8	142.1	149.5
Burkina Faso (1995=100)........	748	76.3	100.0	95.4	....	....	....	....	....	....	....	....	....
Kenya..........................	664	98.6	116.8	111.6	127.2	125.2	100.6	100.0	....	....	....	....	....
Mauritius.......................	684	107.0	117.3	126.4	111.3	111.4	105.4	100.0	91.7	97.0	109.8	122.7	124.0
Morocco........................	686	103.8	124.1	128.5	118.5	114.5	110.2	100.0	94.4	99.1	116.0	126.9	....
Rwanda.........................	714	60.2	100.0	91.1	102.8	50.6	....	....	....	....	....	....	....
South Africa....................	199	120.3	119.0	114.3	113.4	102.1	98.7	100.0	94.3	95.8	122.1	146.6	156.2
Asia.............................	505	112.7	121.0	118.0	113.8	99.4	98.4	100.0	92.2	90.0	92.2	97.8	102.7
China, P.R.: Hong Kong.............	532	106.4	109.8	109.6	107.7	103.6	100.6	100.0	97.6	95.0	93.8	94.8	96.3
India...........................	534	113.6	107.5	102.6	116.8	106.8	101.0	100.0	94.3	91.9	103.9	116.3	....
Indonesia.......................	536	90.3	103.1	109.0	103.6	80.8	64.9	100.0	89.9	95.5	102.7	120.4	81.4
Korea...........................	542	150.6	161.8	140.5	127.9	102.0	99.6	100.0	86.9	83.1	85.1	91.5	92.7
Pakistan........................	564	96.7	117.7	114.2	115.0	117.2	109.4	100.0	93.9	89.9	96.2	103.0	103.5
Papua New Guinea...............	853	87.3	99.0	99.4	97.2	81.2	80.3	100.0	89.4	85.5	101.0	126.1	....
Philippines......................	566	134.9	139.7	145.3	134.1	104.6	120.2	100.0	82.8	75.9	78.9	76.3	....
Samoa..........................	862	117.2	....	....	....	....	....	....	....	....	....	....	....
Singapore.......................	576	113.2	119.9	119.4	111.7	† 97.2	96.2	100.0	92.5	† 90.5	89.7	92.7	96.0
Sri Lanka.......................	524	89.1	98.6	102.1	104.5	109.9	100.6	100.0	96.2	90.7	96.4	100.4	103.4
Thailand........................	578	100.2	109.5	119.1	117.0	103.7	100.5	100.0	101.3	96.2	104.9	117.9	129.8
Europe..........................	170	111.3	126.2	121.6	114.8	112.9	106.5	100.0	99.6	102.4	114.6	130.5	137.3
Hungary.........................	944	114.9	128.7	125.0	117.3	115.4	108.3	100.0	100.7	106.3	121.7	132.5	133.6
Latvia..........................	941	91.0	112.1	114.1	110.9	108.1	104.9	100.0	99.1	103.4	120.8	145.0	152.9
Poland..........................	964	110.0	125.6	122.5	113.6	114.2	108.1	100.3	102.0	106.4	117.9	138.3	150.6
Turkey..........................	186	† 113.9	128.3	122.6	116.8	112.1	104.5	100.0	97.4	95.7	105.3	† 122.0	129.3
Middle East......................	405	68.9	75.3	85.2	80.9	58.7	74.0	100.0	89.0	92.7	102.8	128.7	165.5
Israel...........................	436	98.0	102.7	† 102.7	101.8	98.8	99.9	100.0	† 96.4	96.4	100.6	105.8	114.3
Jordan..........................	439	95.9	111.4	117.0	113.6	107.3	104.6	100.0	101.4	101.7	101.9	113.7	131.0
Saudi Arabia....................	456	63.6	70.2	83.0	78.5	50.7	73.4	100.0	104.3	103.0	117.4	143.1	205.8
Syrian Arab Rep.................	463	80.0	100.0	105.6	83.3	....	....	....	....	....	....	....	....
Western Hemisphere..............	205	101.3	108.9	114.8	114.3	99.8	107.3	100.0	94.3	109.3	117.4	112.3	127.2
Argentina.......................	213	105.0	111.0	118.3	114.2	102.3	90.9	100.0	96.6	93.0	101.9	111.4	112.8
Bolivia..........................	218	131.5	141.1	138.4	98.2	86.8	85.4	100.0	91.5	80.5	90.4	121.9	141.8
Brazil..........................	223	99.0	102.9	106.4	112.7	98.6	93.3	100.0	94.8	90.7	101.1	111.8	132.4
Colombia.......................	233	102.9	111.6	104.3	115.0	102.4	95.4	100.0	89.1	85.4	87.3	96.2	110.9
Dominican Republic..............	243	88.8	102.1	95.1	105.6	85.3	....	....	....	....	....	....	....
Ecuador........................	248	73.0	75.4	29.1	28.7	21.6	78.1	100.0	87.8	94.3	106.6	117.8	150.2
Guatemala (1990=100)..........	258	68.7	....	....	....	....	....	....	....	....	....	....	....
Honduras.......................	268	98.4	132.4	118.6	135.6	138.2	102.9	100.0	101.0	95.2	82.4	102.2	135.3
Peru............................	293	88.5	107.2	106.8	103.6	83.9	82.7	100.0	84.8	88.0	98.5	125.6	173.5
Memorandum Items													
Oil Exporting Countries..........	999	69.9	78.1	88.0	83.5	58.6	69.5	100.0	86.7	91.9	102.0	128.4	165.8
Non-Oil Developing Countries.	201	113.1	121.3	118.8	114.9	102.5	101.9	100.0	93.7	93.7	98.1	103.4	108.7

Import Unit Values/Import Prices

Indices of Unit Values (Prices) In Terms of US Dollars: 2000=100

		1994	1995	1996	1997	1998	1999	2000	2001	2002	2003	2004	2005
World	001	**105.4**	**116.1**	**114.7**	**108.5**	**101.6**	**99.7**	**100.0**	**96.3**	**95.8**	**104.6**	**114.5**	**121.6**
Industrial Countries	110	**106.2**	**116.9**	**115.0**	**107.9**	**102.2**	**100.4**	**100.0**	**96.3**	**96.2**	**106.0**	**115.8**	**122.5**
United States	111	96.2	100.6	101.6	99.1	93.1	93.9	100.0	96.5	94.1	96.9	102.3	110.0
Canada	156	98.6	101.8	102.1	101.2	94.3	95.7	100.0	98.7	98.2	101.9	107.9	115.9
Australia	193	111.4	117.0	116.9	110.7	101.6	102.0	100.0	94.3	94.5	103.8	111.1	116.6
Japan	158	99.1	107.6	102.1	98.6	86.7	90.4	100.0	90.9	86.8	93.1	103.9	115.4
New Zealand	196	109.4	121.1	123.3	117.5	98.8	100.0	100.0	93.6	96.4	106.9	116.4	124.0
Euro Area													
Belgium	124	103.3	120.8	119.2	109.5	105.9	102.8	100.0	99.5	102.2	119.8	136.1	142.8
Finland	172	109.7	131.2	126.6	113.3	106.2	102.3	100.0	94.3	96.3	114.8	130.8	139.6
France	132	† 133.7	149.0	142.7	124.4	118.0	108.6	100.0	99.5	98.9	118.7	127.6	127.0
Germany	134	118.8	138.2	129.0	114.9	110.7	104.2	100.0	97.1	97.2	110.4	120.3	123.2
Ireland	178	108.8	121.2	119.1	113.4	109.0	106.7	100.0	100.0	101.1	111.1	119.6	120.7
Italy	136	98.0	108.9	115.1	106.0	102.4	99.5	100.0	99.7	104.4	124.8	143.8	157.0
Netherlands	138	112.6	127.8	122.8	112.6	107.9	103.4	100.0	101.2	101.1	117.5	130.9	132.6
Portugal	182	124.8	137.7	130.0	115.1	109.4	106.0	100.0	88.9	91.0	110.3	....	....
Spain	184	112.7	126.4	124.9	111.9	107.2	102.5	100.0	96.2	98.0	115.9	130.6	137.4
Denmark	128	109.9	127.7	125.7	114.2	112.6	108.1	100.0	98.2	101.6	119.2	132.4	137.4
Iceland (1995=100)	176	88.9	100.0	99.9	94.3	....	....	....	....	....	....	....	....
Norway	142	129.4	144.9	141.2	126.5	117.6	109.0	100.0	98.2	102.8	116.1	126.5	132.4
Sweden	144	103.4	119.2	122.3	109.5	104.2	102.7	100.0	92.7	98.6	116.2	131.2	138.4
Switzerland	146	119.5	135.0	129.1	115.9	112.9	106.5	100.0	100.1	104.8	121.5	135.3	142.1
United Kingdom	112	105.7	116.0	114.5	112.1	107.6	103.5	100.0	94.3	95.8	103.6	115.6	119.6
Developing Countries	200	**102.6**	**112.9**	**113.1**	**109.8**	**99.1**	**96.7**	**100.0**	**96.4**	**93.9**	**99.0**	**108.9**	**117.7**
Africa	605	**109.9**	**118.0**	**111.2**	**107.2**	**98.2**	**99.7**	**100.0**	**94.3**	**94.2**	**112.4**	**131.2**	**137.5**
Kenya	664	81.8	102.8	101.1	105.0	104.8	97.8	100.0	....	....	....	....	....
Mauritius	684	107.7	117.8	122.1	106.5	99.1	100.2	100.0	97.0	98.8	113.2	138.3	160.9
Morocco	686	130.0	137.4	142.5	125.9	109.1	106.8	100.0	97.4	98.1	108.9	121.5	....
South Africa	199	107.3	114.0	105.0	103.8	96.0	96.3	100.0	93.2	92.4	113.9	135.2	143.5
Asia	505	**104.9**	**113.3**	**113.8**	**108.6**	**96.4**	**95.2**	**100.0**	**95.3**	**92.8**	**96.2**	**104.6**	**111.9**
China, P.R.: Hong Kong	532	105.9	111.2	109.8	107.2	101.9	99.6	100.0	96.8	93.0	92.9	95.5	98.3
India	534	95.6	99.9	104.2	102.7	91.3	96.5	100.0	96.4	103.7	108.0	139.5	....
Korea	542	110.1	116.8	112.0	104.7	87.4	87.3	100.0	91.0	87.5	95.6	107.3	117.3
Pakistan	564	90.3	98.5	95.5	96.8	85.8	92.6	100.0	94.0	94.8	108.5	121.8	137.6
Philippines	566	174.0	173.6	178.8	162.1	120.1	117.3	100.0	79.9	83.3	82.6	80.5	....
Singapore	576	106.7	114.9	114.2	106.8	93.0	93.3	100.0	96.5	95.9	98.9	103.6	110.7
Thailand	578	83.9	94.7	107.2	104.1	95.7	92.2	100.0	108.6	101.4	106.0	120.3	139.6
Europe	170	**104.1**	**119.6**	**118.8**	**109.8**	**106.4**	**100.6**	**100.0**	**99.8**	**100.9**	**113.1**	**125.9**	**134.4**
Czechoslovakia (1990=100)	934	....	....	....	....	....	....	....	....	....	....	....	....
Hungary	944	112.1	123.4	122.7	113.8	110.5	105.4	100.0	100.9	106.1	122.1	133.9	137.9
Poland	964	109.0	122.8	122.5	114.9	110.6	103.9	100.5	100.3	101.0	116.0	129.1	141.2
Turkey	186	† 105.3	123.0	115.6	105.6	101.2	95.7	100.0	99.7	98.5	106.3	† 119.6	127.9
Middle East	405	**102.3**	**110.1**	**109.4**	**104.0**	**102.1**	**99.5**	**100.0**	**97.9**	**94.1**	**99.1**	**109.7**	**117.9**
Israel	436	102.8	111.5	† 110.7	105.7	99.9	97.0	100.0	† 98.6	98.5	104.4	112.0	120.2
Jordan	439	84.8	95.7	103.2	100.9	100.1	97.7	100.0	102.3	105.1	115.3	130.2	148.0
Syrian Arab Rep.	463	89.0	100.0	105.9	90.7	....	....	....	....	....	....	....	....
Western Hemisphere	205	**82.8**	**102.4**	**103.9**	**116.4**	**105.5**	**98.5**	**100.0**	**99.6**	**91.5**	**92.6**	**104.6**	**122.0**
Argentina	213	109.7	115.7	114.3	111.7	106.0	100.0	100.0	97.3	94.0	94.1	101.3	105.4
Brazil	223	67.6	93.9	98.9	113.6	105.3	95.8	100.0	99.5	86.8	86.2	101.6	130.6
Colombia	233	113.4	121.2	122.5	119.4	110.3	102.4	100.0	98.2	95.7	95.0	103.7	113.8
Venezuela, Rep. Bol.	299	82.3	104.3	94.4	98.3	101.4	102.2	100.0	104.5	100.1	112.2	123.1	125.5
Memorandum Items													
Oil Exporting Countries	999	**92.5**	**106.7**	**97.5**	**98.5**	**104.7**	**104.8**	**100.0**	**100.3**	**91.3**	**98.2**	**111.5**	**114.5**
Non-Oil Developing Countries.	201	**102.9**	**113.1**	**113.5**	**110.1**	**98.9**	**96.5**	**100.0**	**96.3**	**93.9**	**99.0**	**108.9**	**117.8**

Terms of Trade

		1994	1995	1996	1997	1998	1999	2000	2001	2002	2003	2004	2005
		\multicolumn{12}{c}{Percent Change over Previous Year; Calculated from Indices}											
World	001	−.2	−.3	−.6	−.8	.9	.3	−3.8	−.1	1.3	.9	−.4	−.5
Industrial Countries	110	.1	.3	−.6	−.9	2.4	−.5	−4.9	1.0	.8	1.2	−.2	−1.0
United States	111	.4	.5	−.5	1.1	2.9	−2.1	−4.6	2.8	1.5	−1.3	−1.7	−4.0
Canada	156	.7	4.1	1.0	−1.1	6.3	7.0	−9.5	−1.1	−4.1	7.4	4.5	4.6
Australia	193	−.4	3.7	1.3	1.9	−3.2	−5.0	6.1	4.1	1.7	.1	9.7	12.8
Japan	158	2.9	−2.1	−4.5	−5.2	6.5	−.9	−8.9	.6	.3	−3.3	−5.3	−9.9
New Zealand	196	−.6	−1.7	−.7	−2.0	.7	−1.0	1.2	7.8	−4.3	1.1	6.0	1.0
Euro Area													
Belgium	124	−.7	−1.2	−1.1	−.8	1.8	−1.8	−2.3	−.2	1.5	−.8	−1.4	.3
Finland	172	1.8	7.1	−.7	−3.1	3.6	−5.0	−4.5	−1.6	−2.5	−3.7	−2.9	−4.4
France	132	1.0	−1.0	−1.2	−1.8	1.1	.5	−4.7	8.3	1.7	—	.6	−.2
Germany	134	−2.8	−.4	−.2	−2.2	1.8	.3	−6.6	1.9	2.5	2.6	—	−1.8
Greece	174	−.5	3.0	5.6	−.4	−3.4	1.2	8.4	−2.4	.8	−.9	1.9	−4.7
Ireland	178	−3.7	−1.9	.9	.6	.3	2.3	−3.0	−1.7	3.8	1.2	−6.5	2.1
Italy	136	−.4	−2.7	4.3	1.5	5.1	1.0	−7.1	.9	1.8	1.1	−.5	−2.2
Netherlands	138	.2	1.6	−.6	.1	−.7	−2.5	.6	−1.5	−.1	.3	−2.3	2.9
Portugal	182	1.3	−1.7	−3.3	2.3	2.6	−3.0	−2.9	4.4	1.5	−4.2	....	....
Spain	184	−1.5	2.0	.7	−.4	2.4	−.8	−6.0	1.5	2.2	−.1	−1.5	−.3
Denmark	128	−.1	−1.9	—	−1.6	−1.2	.5	.2	.7	—	1.4	.5	1.0
Iceland	176	−1.2	.8	−4.2	.6	....	....	....	....	....	....	....	....
Norway	142	−4.0	2.5	8.8	3.1	−10.5	18.1	39.9	−5.1	−4.4	−1.0	11.6	21.1
Sweden	144	.4	4.6	−1.4	−1.1	.5	−3.4	−3.6	−2.8	−2.1	−.2	−2.7	−2.9
Switzerland	146	4.3	.2	1.0	−1.6	3.1	3.9	−2.6	1.1	1.1	−.6	−.3	−3.3
United Kingdom	112	−1.3	−2.7	.8	1.6	.2	−.6	−2.1	−.8	2.6	2.5	.8	−.2
Developing Countries	200	−1.3	−2.2	−.7	−.6	−3.7	3.7	−.4	−3.9	3.6	.2	−1.4	1.5
Africa	605	.4	−3.3	3.6	1.7	.5	−6.8	−1.3	.1	2.4	4.8	.8	.4
Burkina Faso	748	−20.3	10.2	−5.7	....	....	....	....	....	....	....	....	....
Kenya	664	12.2	−5.7	−2.8	9.7	−1.5	−13.8	−2.8	....	....	....	....	....
Mauritius	684	−2.4	.2	3.9	.9	7.5	−6.4	−4.9	−5.5	3.8	−1.1	−8.5	−13.2
Morocco	686	−13.3	13.1	−.1	4.3	11.6	−1.7	−3.1	−3.1	4.3	5.5	−2.0	....
South Africa	199	4.2	−6.9	4.3	.4	−2.6	−3.7	−2.4	1.2	2.3	3.5	1.1	.4
Togo	742	18.8	18.8	337.7	−15.5	−13.7	−32.7	3.4	−62.3	−19.3	−20.0	21.2	−27.5
Asia	505	−1.2	−.6	−2.8	1.1	−1.7	.3	−3.2	−3.3	.3	−1.2	−2.4	−1.9
China, P.R.: Hong Kong	532	−1.2	−1.7	1.0	.7	1.2	−.7	−1.0	.8	1.3	−1.2	−1.7	−1.3
India	534	5.1	−9.5	−8.4	15.5	2.9	−10.5	−4.5	−2.2	−9.4	8.6	−13.3	....
Korea	542	3.4	1.3	−9.4	−2.6	−4.5	−2.2	−12.3	−4.5	−.5	−6.3	−4.2	−7.3
Pakistan	564	—	11.5	.2	−.8	14.9	−13.5	−15.3	−.1	−5.0	−6.5	−4.6	−11.1
Philippines	566	−.6	3.8	1.0	1.8	5.2	17.6	−2.4	3.6	−12.1	4.9	−.7	....
Singapore	576	−3.1	−1.7	.2	—	—	−1.5	−2.9	−4.1	−1.6	−3.9	−1.4	−2.9
Sri Lanka	524	−1.0	−.6	2.1	4.1	13.4	−4.5	−6.9	−1.6	2.5	....	....	....
Thailand	578	.3	−3.2	−3.9	1.2	−3.7	.7	−8.3	−6.8	1.8	4.3	−1.0	−5.2
Europe	170	.6	−1.3	−3.0	2.2	1.5	−.3	−5.5	−.2	1.7	−.1	2.3	−1.5
Hungary	944	.9	1.8	−2.3	1.3	1.3	−1.6	−2.7	−.2	.4	−.5	−.7	−2.1
Poland	964	2.3	1.4	−2.2	−1.2	4.4	.8	−4.1	2.0	3.4	−3.5	5.4	−.4
Turkey	186	−9.4	−3.6	1.7	4.3	.1	−1.3	−8.5	−2.3	−.6	2.0	3.0	−.9
Middle East	405	−2.1	1.6	13.8	−.1	−26.1	29.4	34.5	−9.1	8.4	5.2	13.1	19.7
Israel	436	−3.5	−3.3	.7	3.8	2.6	4.2	−2.9	−2.2	—	−1.4	−2.0	.7
Jordan	439	7.7	2.8	−2.5	−.7	−4.8	—	−6.7	−.9	−2.3	−8.7	−1.2	1.3
Syrian Arab Rep.	463	−4.8	11.2	−.4	−7.8	....	....	....	....	....	....	....	....
Western Hemisphere	205	−3.7	−13.1	3.8	−11.1	−3.7	15.0	−8.2	−5.3	26.2	6.1	−15.3	−2.8
Argentina	213	1.5	.3	7.8	−1.2	−5.5	−5.9	10.0	−.7	−.4	9.5	1.5	−2.6
Brazil	223	−15.6	−25.2	−1.8	−7.8	−5.5	3.9	2.7	−4.7	9.7	12.2	−6.1	−7.9
Colombia	233	20.0	1.4	−7.6	13.2	−3.5	.3	7.3	−9.3	−1.6	3.0	1.0	5.0
Memorandum Items													
Oil Exporting Countries	999	−5.3	−3.2	23.4	−6.0	−34.1	18.6	50.7	−13.6	16.5	3.2	10.8	25.8
Non-Oil Developing Countries	201	−1.0	−2.5	−2.4	−.4	−.7	2.0	−5.3	−2.7	2.5	−.6	−4.2	−2.8

Indices

		1994	1995	1996	1997	1998	1999	2000	2001	2002	2003	2004	2005
		\multicolumn{12}{c}{Index Numbers: 2000=100}											
World	001	104.5	104.2	103.5	102.7	103.6	104.0	100.0	99.9	101.2	102.1	101.6	101.1
Industrial Countries	110	104.4	104.8	104.1	103.2	105.7	105.1	100.0	101.0	101.8	103.0	102.8	101.7
Developing Countries	200	104.3	102.0	101.3	100.6	96.9	100.4	100.0	96.1	99.5	99.7	98.3	99.8
Africa	605	106.1	102.6	106.3	108.1	108.7	101.3	100.0	100.1	102.6	107.5	108.3	108.7
Asia	505	107.4	106.8	103.7	104.8	103.1	103.3	100.0	96.7	97.0	95.8	93.5	91.8
Europe	170	106.9	105.5	102.3	104.6	106.1	105.8	100.0	99.8	101.5	101.3	103.7	102.1
Middle East	405	67.3	68.4	77.8	77.8	57.5	74.3	100.0	90.9	98.6	103.7	117.3	140.4
Western Hemisphere	205	122.4	106.4	110.5	98.3	94.7	108.9	100.0	94.7	119.4	126.7	107.3	104.2

Balance of Payments

		1994	1995	1996	1997	1998	1999	2000	2001	2002	2003	2004	2005
							Trade Balance *Expressed in Millions of US Dollars*						
All Countries	010	95,114	119,948	102,205	116,439	66,165	39,231	9,332	–4,442	32,308	67,370	49,323	....
Industrial Countries	110	94,660	122,051	93,487	95,650	24,296	–115,544	–246,719	–214,313	–215,901	–258,522	–350,645	....
United States	111	–163,781	–172,330	–189,100	–196,164	–244,736	–343,716	–449,785	–424,085	–478,807	–544,044	–661,930	–777,861
Canada	156	14,834	25,855	31,091	18,565	15,922	28,292	45,047	45,716	36,498	40,177	50,226	53,791
Australia	193	–3,277	–4,223	–635	1,849	–5,332	–9,761	–4,841	1,736	–5,517	–15,335	–18,142	–13,672
Japan	158	144,191	131,787	83,585	101,600	122,389	123,325	116,716	70,214	93,829	106,395	132,134	93,958
New Zealand	196	1,408	971	523	903	912	–371	680	1,471	166	–457	–1,427	....
Euro Area													
Austria	122	–7,914	–6,656	–7,315	–4,274	–3,684	–3,629	–2,737	–1,269	3,588	1,141	3,048	3,427
Belgium	124	....	....	....	....	....	....	....	....	9,518	10,957	9,708	1,978
Belgium-Luxembourg	126	6,901	9,555	8,690	7,703	6,981	7,027	2,591	3,707	....	....	....	....
Finland	172	7,723	12,437	11,314	11,544	12,490	12,168	13,684	12,659	12,882	12,947	12,840	10,145
France	132	7,249	10,998	14,936	26,899	24,940	16,939	–3,618	2,837	7,638	3,426	–8,666	–32,144
Germany	134	51,028	63,910	69,379	70,119	76,117	68,778	55,464	87,414	125,755	144,739	187,563	189,241
Greece	174	–11,273	–14,425	–15,505	–15,375	....	–17,951	–20,239	–19,087	–21,455	–25,606	–31,621	–34,253
Ireland	178	9,366	13,557	15,754	18,625	25,390	23,587	25,010	27,263	33,447	36,882	39,506	37,649
Italy	136	31,568	38,729	54,118	39,878	35,631	23,437	9,549	15,540	13,412	11,477	10,911	405
Luxembourg	137	....	....	....	....	....	....	....	....	–2,064	–2,936	–3,441	–4,181
Netherlands	138	18,686	23,812	22,767	20,937	20,430	15,947	17,800	19,187	18,565	35,749	42,946	44,324
Portugal	182	–8,321	–8,910	–9,849	–10,499	–12,876	–14,427	–14,532	–13,906	–13,311	–14,178	–18,644	–20,855
Spain	184	–14,892	–18,665	–16,066	–14,216	–21,639	–31,813	–37,087	–34,518	–34,632	–45,155	–66,730	–85,592
Denmark	128	7,441	6,528	7,532	5,369	3,886	6,658	6,641	7,418	7,662	9,697	9,527	....
Iceland	176	272	206	19	5	–351	–307	–474	–75	150	–210	–519	–1,480
Norway	142	7,496	8,685	12,972	11,648	2,061	10,723	25,975	26,472	24,340	28,162	33,619	50,138
Sweden	144	9,558	15,978	18,636	17,999	17,632	15,714	15,215	13,832	16,631	18,933	23,415	19,701
Switzerland	146	3,346	3,260	1,869	2,738	933	850	2,071	1,640	6,647	6,958	15,737	4,850
United Kingdom	112	–16,947	–19,006	–21,228	–20,203	–36,127	–47,012	–49,850	–58,477	–70,843	–78,242	–110,704	–119,371
Developing Countries	200	454	–2,103	8,718	20,789	41,869	154,775	256,051	209,871	248,209	325,892	399,968	....
Africa	605	3,660	3,266	16,676	11,352	–4,629	6,143	28,141	18,580	14,622	21,914	24,812	....
Algeria	612	....	....	....	....	....	....	....	....	....	....	....	....
Angola	614	1,563	2,255	3,055	2,410	1,464	2,047	4,881	3,355	4,568	4,028	7,643	....
Botswana	616	510	555	750	895	78	785	902	710	676	897	....	....
Burundi	618	–92	–63	–60	–9	–59	–42	–59	–69	–74	–93	....	....
Cape Verde	624	–181	–217	–184	–172	–186	–213	–187	–194	–236	–291	....	....
Comoros	632	–34	–42	....	....	....	....	....	....	....	....	....	....
Congo, Dem. Rep. of	636	....	....	....	....	....	....	....	....	....	....	....	....
Djibouti	611	–181	–171	....	....	....	....	....	....	....	....	....	....
Eritrea	643	–411	–368	–455	–469	–480	–489	–435	....	....	....	....	....
Ethiopia	644	–554	–670	–585	–413	–799	–920	–645	–1,170	–975	–1,399	–2,090	....
Gambia, The	648	–57	–40	–98	–87	....	....	....	....	....	....	....	....
Ghana	652	–342	–257	–381	–654	–901	–1,274	–830	–1,101	–692	–714	–1,513	....
Guinea	656	–170	–39	111	118	121	54	79	169	40	–35	37	....
Kenya	664	–238	–750	–515	–886	–1,012	–975	–1,262	–1,347	–996	–1,143	–1,598	....
Lesotho	666	–667	–825	–812	–828	–673	–607	–516	–400	–405	–519	–595	....
Liberia	668	....	....	....	....	....	....	....	....	....	....	....	....
Madagascar	674	–96	–122	–120	–178	–154	–158	–174	–27	–117	–254	....	....
Malawi	676	–160	–63	–78	–158	39	–127	–59	–44	–151	....	....	....
Mauritania	682	47	184	134	107	40	....	....	....	....	....	....	....
Mauritius	684	–397	–241	–326	–436	–264	–392	–392	–218	–211	–303	–575	....
Morocco	686	–2,107	–2,482	–2,193	–1,864	–2,319	–2,448	–3,235	–3,022	–3,061	–4,345	–6,487	....
Mozambique	688	–767	–536	–478	–454	–491	–806	–682	–271	–667	–604	–346	–497
Namibia	728	–86	–130	–127	–272	–173	–204	–1	–202	–211	–464	–283	....
Nigeria	694	2,948	3,513	9,679	5,706	–240	4,288	10,415	6,895	4,738	12,130	12,561	....
Rwanda	714	–524	–162	–157	–185	–169	–185	–155	–152	–166	–159	–160	....
São Tomé & Príncipe	716	....	....	....	....	–12	–18	–22	–21	–23	....	....	....
Seychelles	718	–135	–161	–170	–190	–212	–224	–117	–205	–140	–91	–116	....
Sierra Leone	724	–73	–127	–180	–56	–57	–81	–124	–136	–195	–200	–98	....
Somalia	726	....	....	....	....	....	....	....	....	....	....	....	....
South Africa	199	4,398	2,379	2,859	2,319	1,991	4,008	4,698	5,255	4,756	3,431	–281	–1,878
Sudan	732	–522	–510	–719	–828	–1,137	–476	440	304	–345	6	192	–1,122
Swaziland	734	–50	–197	–204	–104	–106	–131	–136	–82	91	118	24	....
Tanzania	738	–790	–657	–449	–449	–776	–872	–704	–820	–615	–824	–906	....
Tunisia	744	–1,567	–1,989	–1,761	–1,955	–2,152	–2,141	–2,253	–2,369	–2,123	–2,269	–2,434	....
Uganda	746	–251	–367	–348	–450	–656	–506	–500	–500	–571	–682	–757	–921
Zambia	754	....	....	....	54	–153	–98	–221	....	....	....	....	....
Zimbabwe	698	158	....	....	....	....	....	....	....	....	....	....	....
CEMAC													
Cameroon	622	402	627	....	....	....	....	....	....	....	....	....	....
Central African Rep.	626	15	....	....	....	....	....	....	....	....	....	....	....
Chad	628	–77	....	....	....	....	....	....	....	....	....	....	....
Congo, Republic of	634	346	632	1,068	1,013	809	1,037	2,037	1,374	1,598	1,011	....	....
Equatorial Guinea	642	25	–31	–117	....	....	....	....	....	....	....	....	....
Gabon	646	1,589	1,847	2,373	2,002	744	1,588	2,523	1,766	1,614	2,136	....	....
WAEMU													
Benin	638	–54	–203	–32	–153	–158	–214	–124	–180	–231	–278	....	....
Burkina Faso	748	–129	....	....	....	....	....	–312	–286	....	....	....	....
Côte d'Ivoire	662	1,289	1,376	1,824	1,793	1,720	1,895	1,486	1,528	2,819	2,557	2,734	....
Guinea-Bissau	654	–21	–35	–35	–14	....	....	....	1	–4	—	....	....

Balance of Payments

Trade Balance
Expressed in Millions of US Dollars

		1994	1995	1996	1997	1998	1999	2000	2001	2002	2003	2004	2005
Africa(Cont.)													
Mali	678	−114	−115	−119	16	−2	−35	−47	−10	163	−60	....	....
Niger	692	−44	−18	−26	−28	−70	−49	−41	−59	−92	−137	....	....
Senegal	722	−203	−250	−276	−271	−313	−346	−417	−425	−537	−809	....	....
Togo	742	−37	−129	−127	−108	−133	−98	−123	−159	−151	−157	....	....
Asia*	505	**−6,535**	**−13,372**	**−21,348**	**31,712**	**137,475**	**136,772**	**117,858**	**115,084**	**136,325**	**152,569**	**153,652**	**....**
Afghanistan, I.R. of	512	....	....	....	....	....	....	....	....	....	....		
Bangladesh	513	−1,416	−2,324	−2,275	−1,711	−1,574	−2,077	−1,654	−2,049	−1,678	−2,442	−3,006	....
Bhutan	514	....	....	....	....	....	....	....	....	....	....		
Brunei Darussalam	516	....	....	....	....	....	....	....	....	....	....		
Cambodia	522	−255	−332	−428	−328	−1,270	−651	−831	−941	−564	−533	−718	....
China,P.R.: Mainland	924	7,290	18,050	19,535	46,222	46,614	35,982	34,474	34,017	44,167	44,652	58,982	134,189
China,P.R.:Hong Kong	532	....	....	....	....	−7,833	−3,159	−8,193	−8,331	−5,053	−5,779	−9,312	−7,627
China,P.R.: Macao	546	....	....	....						−920	−1,093	−1,841	....
Fiji	819	−229	−242	−168	−283	−186	−116	....	....				
French Terr.: French Polynesia	887	....	....	....	....	....	....			−962	−1,381	−1,260	−1,373
French Terr.: New Caledonia	839									−609	−625	−464	−588
India	534	−4,150	−6,719	−10,052	−10,028	−10,752	−8,679	−10,640	−6,418	−3,559	−8,870	....	....
Indonesia	536	7,901	6,533	5,948	10,075	18,429	20,643	25,042	22,696	23,513	24,844	20,151	22,368
Kiribati	826	−21	....										
Korea	542	−3,017	−4,365	−15,077	−3,256	41,665	28,463	16,954	13,488	14,777	21,952	37,569	33,473
Lao People's Dem.Rep	544	−214	−316	−321	−283	−165	−190	−205	−217	....	....	....	....
Malaysia	548	1,577	−103	3,848	3,510	17,505	22,644	20,827	18,383	18,135	25,711	27,493	....
Maldives	556	−120	−151	−186	−217	−216	−262	−233	−236	−212	−262	−386	....
Mongolia	948	34	25	−36	115	−62	−56	−73	−101	−156	−200	−29	....
Myanmar	518	−613	−831	−940	−1,143	−1,401	−887	−504	78	399	798	928	....
Nepal	558	−790	−961	−1,106	−1,278	−757	−882	−814	−765	−793	−963	−1,049	....
Pakistan	564	−2,239	−2,891	−3,656	−2,399	−1,984	−1,847	−1,157	−610	−596	−109	−3,396	−6,178
Papua New Guinea	853	1,326	1,408	1,017	677	695	856	1,095	881	....	....		
Philippines	566	−7,850	−8,944	−11,342	−11,127	−28	4,959	3,814	−743	407	−5,455	−6,381	....
Samoa	862	−65	−72	−81	−85	−77	−98	....	....	....	....	−143	−175
Singapore	576	1,354	6,452	7,186	6,509	13,411	12,442	12,723	15,709	17,581	28,130	31,239	....
Solomon Islands	813	—	14	11	−28	−18	55	....	....				
Sri Lanka	524	−1,085	−985	−800	−640	−505	−769	−1,044	−560	−796	−872	−1,443	....
Thailand	578	−3,726	−7,968	−9,488	1,572	16,238	14,013	11,701	8,543	9,081	11,175	10,785	3,162
Tonga	866	....	....	....	....	....	....	....	−57	−55	....		
Vanuatu	846	−50	−51	−51	−44	−42	−59	−50	−58	−58	−65	−75	−93
Vietnam	582	....	....	−2,775	−1,247	−989	972	375	481	−1,054	−2,528	−2,256	....
*of which:													
Taiwan Prov.of China	528	11,849	13,235	17,543	13,882	10,316	14,705	13,674	19,718	24,191	24,890	16,128	17,932
Europe	170	**−3,043**	**−15,441**	**−27,497**	**−41,429**	**−44,615**	**−13,516**	**3,562**	**9,511**	**5,019**	**5,185**	**19,486**	**....**
Albania	914	−460	−475	−678	−535	−604	−663	−814	−1,027	−1,155	−1,336	−1,592	−1,821
Armenia	911	−178	−403	−469	−559	−577	−474	−463	−420	−369	−434	−458	−588
Azerbaijan, Republic of	912	....	−373	−694	−567	−1,046	−408	319	614	482	−98	161	3,299
Belarus	913	−490	−666	−1,149	−1,407	−1,501	−570	−884	−807	−914	−1,256	−2,066	−527
Bosnia & Herzegovina	963	....	....	....	−3,116	−3,297	−2,764	−2,958	−3,340	−4,159	−4,570	−4,954	
Bulgaria	918	−17	121	188	380	−381	−1,081	−1,176	−1,580	−1,594	−2,519	−3,643	−5,399
Croatia	960	−1,278	−3,228	−3,488	−5,383	−4,072	−3,299	−3,203	−4,101	−5,648	−7,908	−8,350	−9,291
Cyprus	423	−1,736	−2,085	−2,183	−2,071	−2,426	−2,309	−2,606	−2,577	−2,847	−3,130	−4,059	−4,292
Czech Republic	935	−1,408	−3,685	−5,706	−4,938	−2,647	−1,902	−3,095	−3,078	−2,240	−2,519	−1,046	1,735
Estonia	939	−356	−666	−1,019	−1,124	−1,115	−878	−781	−775	−1,118	−1,567	−2,019	−1,845
Faroe Islands	816	....	....	....	....	69	17	−38	37	66	−90	....	....
Georgia	915	....	....	....	−786	−695	−534	−512	−550	−483	−636	−916	−1,214
Hungary	944	−3,716	−1,459	−1,673	−1,328	−1,885	−2,170	−2,913	−2,237	−2,119	−3,279	−3,006	−1,917
Kazakhstan	916	....	114	−335	−276	−801	344	2,168	983	1,987	3,679	6,785	10,322
Kyrgyz Republic	917	−86	−122	−252	−15	−221	−89	4	31	−74	−133	−171	....
Latvia	941	−301	−580	−798	−848	−1,130	−1,027	−1,044	−1,335	−1,479	−2,003	−2,781	−2,966
Lithuania	946	−205	−698	−896	−1,147	−1,518	−1,405	−1,104	−1,108	−1,315	−1,704	−2,383	−2,843
Macedonia, FYR	962	....	....	−317	−388	−515	−496	−690	−526	−804	−848	−1,112	....
Malta	181	−603	−810	−838	−721	−673	−663	−754	−566	−357	−686	−847	−1,108
Moldova	921	−54	−70	−260	−348	−388	−137	−294	−315	−378	−623	−754	−1,191
Poland	964	−575	−1,646	−7,287	−9,822	−12,836	−15,072	−12,307	−7,661	−7,249	−5,725	−5,622	−2,694
Romania	968	−411	−1,577	−2,470	−1,980	−2,625	−1,092	−1,684	−2,969	−2,611	−4,537	−6,665	....
Russia	922	16,928	19,816	21,591	14,913	16,429	36,014	60,172	48,121	46,335	59,860	85,825	118,266
Slovak Republic	936	61	−229	−2,283	−2,084	−2,351	−1,109	−895	....	−2,166	−649	....	....
Slovenia	961	−336	−954	−826	−775	−792	−1,235	−1,139	−619	−248	−622	−1,258	−1,270
Tajikistan	923	....	....	....	....	....	....	....	....	−124	−120	−135	−323
Turkey	186	−4,134	−13,114	−10,264	−15,048	−14,052	−10,185	−21,959	−3,733	−7,283	−14,010	−23,924	....
Turkmenistan	925	....	....	304	−231	....	....	....	....	....	....		
Ukraine	926	−2,575	−2,702	−4,296	−4,205	−2,584	244	779	198	710	518	3,741	−1,135
Uzbekistan	927	....	....	....	....	....	....	....	....	....	....		
Middle East	405	**22,132**	**24,044**	**40,115**	**38,025**	**−4,856**	**38,178**	**108,246**	**75,562**	**74,463**	**107,010**	**148,925**	**....**
Bahrain, Kingdom of	419	120	626	665	605	−28	894	1,849	1,610	1,190	1,402	1,485	....
Egypt	469	−5,953	−7,597	−8,390	−8,632	−10,214	−9,928	−8,321	−6,935	−5,762	−4,201	−6,576	....
Iran, I.R. of	429	6,817	5,586	7,402	4,258	−1,168	7,597	13,138	....	....	....	....	....
Iraq	433	....	....	....	....	....	....	....	....	....	....		
Israel	436	−5,486	−7,271	−7,140	−5,284	−3,505	−4,751	−3,540	−3,747	−4,436	−3,063	−2,948	−4,034
Jordan	439	−1,579	−1,518	−2,001	−1,813	−1,602	−1,460	−2,174	−2,007	−1,731	−1,996	−3,378	....
Kuwait	443	4,685	5,579	6,997	6,534	1,903	5,516	13,027	9,192	7,242	11,912	19,301	....
Lebanon	446	....	....	....	....	....	....	....	....	−4,962	−5,223	−7,105	....

Balance of Payments

		1994	1995	1996	1997	1998	1999	2000	2001	2002	2003	2004	2005

Trade Balance
Expressed in Millions of US Dollars

		1994	1995	1996	1997	1998	1999	2000	2001	2002	2003	2004	2005
Middle East(Cont.)													
Libya	672	945	2,302	2,085	2,249	396	2,974	9,379	6,160	2,443	7,464	8,657	....
Oman	449	1,849	2,015	3,142	3,012	307	2,938	6,725	5,763	5,536	5,584	5,472	....
Qatar	453	....	....	....	....	....	....	....	....	....	....	....	....
Saudi Arabia	456	21,261	24,358	35,323	34,317	11,272	25,006	49,777	39,366	42,840	59,376	84,947	123,308
Syrian Arab Republic	463	−1,275	−146	−338	454	−178	216	1,423	1,424	2,210	1,332	−374	....
United Arab Emirates	466	....	....	....	....	....	....	....	....	....	....	....	....
West Bank and Gaza	487	....	−1,909	−2,364	−2,443	−2,411	−2,618	−2,303	−1,467	....	....	....	....
Yemen, Republic of	474	274	149	−31	−133	−785	358	1,313	766	689	377	817	2,256
Western Hemisphere	205	**−15,760**	**−600**	**773**	**−18,872**	**−41,506**	**−12,803**	**−1,757**	**−8,866**	**17,780**	**39,214**	**53,093**	**....**
Argentina	213	−4,139	2,357	1,760	−2,123	−3,097	−795	2,452	7,385	17,178	16,805	13,239	....
Aruba	314	−311	−425	−308	−387	−353	−604	−56	55	−531	−344	−274	−53
Bahamas, The	313	−815	−931	−1,014	−1,116	−1,374	−1,270	−1,518	−1,387	−1,327	−1,332	−1,340	....
Barbados	316	−355	−446	−456	−599	−651	−714	−744	−681	−702	−801	−971	....
Belize	339	−75	−66	−58	−90	−105	−114	−197	−209	−187	−207	−174	....
Bolivia	218	−30	−182	−236	−477	−656	−488	−364	−295	100	421	479
Brazil	223	10,861	−3,157	−5,453	−6,652	−6,603	−1,261	−698	2,650	13,121	24,794	33,641	44,757
Chile	228	732	1,381	−1,072	−1,428	−2,040	2,427	2,119	1,844	2,386	3,685	9,195	10,180
Colombia	233	−2,229	−2,546	−2,092	−2,638	−2,450	1,775	2,648	579	238	555	1,346	1,594
Costa Rica	238	−606	−323	−249	−498	−399	580	−210	−820	−1,267	−1,131	−1,463	....
Dominican Republic	243	−1,451	−1,391	−1,674	−1,995	−2,617	−2,904	−3,742	−3,503	−3,673	−2,156	−1,952	−3,481
Ecuador	248	149	−66	921	491	−1,132	1,588	1,395	−397	−998	−71	321	....
El Salvador	253	−1,170	−1,462	−1,242	−1,143	−1,306	−1,356	−1,740	−1,933	−1,865	−2,275	−2,619	....
Guatemala	258	−997	−875	−643	−940	−1,409	−1,445	−1,657	−2,282	−2,972	−3,116	−3,760	....
Guyana	336	−41	−41	23	—	−8	4	−47	−56	−24	−17	−14	....
Haiti	263	−111	−429	−416	−354	−527	−674	−755	−750	−706	−783	....	....
Honduras	268	−250	−141	−287	−294	−323	−753	−658	−834	−829	−965	−1,267	....
Jamaica	343	−551	−829	−994	−1,132	−1,131	−1,187	−1,442	−1,618	−1,871	−1,943	−1,945	....
Mexico	273	−18,464	7,089	6,531	623	−7,834	−5,613	−8,337	−9,617	−7,633	−5,780	−8,811	−7,559
Netherlands Antilles	353	−921	−1,035	−1,129	−975	−1,048	−1,117	−986	−1,114	−1,027	−1,003	−1,168	....
Nicaragua	278	−429	−385	−527	−728	−749	−1,071	−921	−910	−918	−972	−1,089	....
Panama	283	−250	−589	−644	−685	−1,296	−1,340	−1,143	−696	−1,035	−1,202	−1,588	−1,358
Paraguay	288	−243	−270	−587	−865	−393	−441	−537	−614	−280	−275	−391	....
Peru	293	−1,075	−2,241	−1,991	−1,678	−2,437	−655	−411	−195	292	836	2,792	5,163
Suriname	366	99	123	−2	36	−27	44	153	140	47	30	42	22
Trinidad and Tobago	369	741	588	382	−529	−741	64	969	718	238	1,293	....	....
Uruguay	298	−706	−563	−687	−704	−772	−897	−927	−775	48	183	31	....
Venezuela, Rep. Bol.	299	7,625	7,013	13,770	8,954	952	6,471	16,664	7,456	13,421	16,483	21,430	31,532
ECCU													
Anguilla	312	−37	−46	−51	−53	−60	−78	−79	−65	−57	....	....	....
Antigua and Barbuda	311	−242	−238	−271	−275	−283	−315	−293	−283	−291	....	....	....
Dominica	321	−47	−53	−64	−65	−53	−66	−76	−71	−59	....	....	....
Grenada	328	−94	−105	−122	−122	−137	−110	−138	−133	−139	....	....	....
Montserrat	351	−27	−22	5	−20	−18	−18	−18	−16	−21	....	....	....
St. Kitts and Nevis	361	−70	−81	−93	−85	−87	−90	−121	−112	−113	....	....	....
St. Lucia	362	−166	−155	−181	−222	−225	−251	−249	−218	−207	....	....	....
St. Vincent & Grens	364	−67	−57	−75	−105	−120	−127	−93	−109	−117	....	....	....
Memorandum Items													
Oil Exporting Ctys	999	60,101	66,000	100,394	92,797	41,350	96,254	190,410	139,433	138,341	185,759	238,692	....
Non-Oil Develop.Ctys	201	−59,647	−68,104	−91,676	−72,008	519	58,521	65,641	70,438	109,868	140,133	161,276	....

Balance of Payments

2006, International Monetary Fund : *International Financial Statistics Yearbook*

Current Account Balance
Excluding Exceptional Financing
Expressed in Millions of US Dollars

		1994	1995	1996	1997	1998	1999	2000	2001	2002	2003	2004	2005
All Countries	010	−65,128	−67,096	−57,809	−17,247	−104,660	−132,165	−168,925	−161,545	−141,360	−46,443	−33,657	....
Industrial Countries	110	1,121	31,839	25,287	62,219	−54,719	−184,672	−305,479	−258,814	−292,659	−294,232	−361,473	....
United States	111	−121,642	−113,664	−124,857	−140,906	−214,037	−300,082	−415,996	−389,455	−475,208	−519,680	−668,074	−804,961
Canada	156	−13,024	−4,328	3,378	−8,233	−7,839	1,765	19,622	16,281	12,604	10,315	21,157	26,555
Australia	193	−16,953	−19,278	−15,649	−12,240	−18,338	−22,212	−15,306	−7,854	−16,468	−29,696	−40,101	−42,084
Japan	158	130,255	111,044	65,792	96,814	118,749	114,604	119,660	87,798	112,447	136,215	172,059	165,783
New Zealand	196	−2,384	−3,003	−3,891	−4,304	−2,157	−3,515	−2,661	−1,435	−2,467	−3,569	−6,456	....
Euro Area													
Austria	122	−2,992	−5,448	−4,890	−5,221	−5,258	−6,655	−4,864	−3,636	565	−638	765	3,848
Belgium	124	....	....	....	....	....	....	....	....	11,611	12,736	12,155	6,563
Belgium-Luxembourg	126	12,571	14,232	13,762	13,914	12,168	14,086	11,381	9,392	....	....	....	....
Finland	172	1,110	5,231	5,003	6,633	7,340	8,045	8,975	8,704	10,148	7,119	9,698	4,983
France	132	7,415	10,840	20,561	37,801	37,699	41,509	18,581	28,759	10,997	11,803	−6,808	−33,289
Germany	134	−30,887	−29,886	−14,118	−9,539	−15,122	−26,794	−31,955	482	41,049	45,797	101,794	115,519
Greece	174	−146	−2,864	−4,554	−4,860		−7,295	−9,820	−9,400	−9,582	−12,804	−13,476	−17,879
Ireland	178	1,577	1,721	2,049	1,866	1,016	245	−516	−690	−1,101	89	−1,423	−3,945
Italy	136	13,209	25,076	39,999	32,403	19,998	8,111	−5,781	−652	−9,369	−19,406	−15,137	−26,814
Luxembourg	137	....	....	....	....	....	....	....	....	2,410	1,867	3,562	3,560
Netherlands	138	17,294	25,773	21,502	25,077	13,031	15,684	7,264	9,810	11,017	29,690	54,414	40,187
Portugal	182	−2,196	−132	−5,023	−6,756	−8,507	−10,414	−11,748	−11,355	−9,947	−9,207	−12,962	−17,007
Spain	184	−6,389	−1,967	−2,234	−830	−7,251	−17,860	−23,076	−23,579	−22,592	−31,737	−54,865	−83,136
Denmark	128	3,189	1,855	3,090	921	−2,008	3,047	2,262	4,848	3,460	6,963	5,941	....
Iceland	176	116	52	−131	−128	−555	−589	−847	−336	146	−543	−1,231	−2,617
Norway	142	3,760	5,233	10,969	10,036	6	8,378	25,851	26,171	24,473	28,876	34,711	49,488
Sweden	144	743	4,940	5,892	7,406	4,639	5,982	6,617	6,696	12,784	22,844	27,485	23,643
Switzerland	146	16,729	20,703	19,916	25,317	25,194	28,578	33,562	22,483	24,930	44,925	58,294	49,710
United Kingdom	112	−10,234	−14,291	−11,278	−2,952	−6,630	−39,289	−36,684	−31,847	−24,570	−26,192	−42,973	−57,616
Developing Countries	200	−66,249	−98,936	−83,096	−79,466	−49,941	52,507	136,554	97,269	151,300	247,789	327,815	....
Africa	605	−8,378	−13,557	2,178	−5,111	−18,563	−9,071	12,037	3,358	650	10,389	11,418	....
Algeria	612	....	....	....	....	....	....	....	....	....	....	....	....
Angola	614	−340	−295	3,266	−884	−1,867	−1,710	796	−1,431	−150	−720	686	....
Botswana	616	222	300	495	721	170	583	545	618	143	483	....	....
Burundi	618	−17	10	−40	—	−51	−23	−53	−39	−10	−37	....	....
Cape Verde	624	−46	−62	−35	−30	−59	−74	−58	−56	−72	−77	....	....
Comoros	632	−7	−19	....	....	....	....	....	....	....	....	....	....
Congo, Dem. Rep. of	636	....	....	....	....	....	....	....	....	....	....	....	....
Djibouti	611	−46	−23	....	....	....	....	....	....	....	....	....	....
Eritrea	643	124	−32	−60	5	−293	−209	−105	....	....	....	....	....
Ethiopia	644	125	39	80	−40	−333	−465	13	−373	−137	−136	−668	....
Gambia, The	648	8	−8	−48	−24	....	....	....	....	....	....	....	....
Ghana	652	−255	−144	−307	−403	−522	−964	−387	−325	−32	255	−236	....
Guinea	656	−248	−216	−177	−91	−184	−214	−155	−102	−200	−188	−175	....
Kenya	664	98	−400	−73	−457	−475	−90	−199	−341	−137	68	−378	....
Lesotho	666	108	−323	−303	−269	−280	−221	−151	−95	−127	−135	−76	....
Liberia	668	....	....	....	....	....	....	....	....	....	....	....	....
Madagascar	674	−277	−276	−291	−266	−301	−252	−283	−170	−298	−439	....	....
Malawi	676	−181	−78	−147	−276	−4	−158	−73	−60	−201	....	....	....
Mauritania	682	−70	22	91	48	77	....	....	....	....	....	....	....
Mauritius	684	−232	−22	34	−89	3	−124	−37	276	249	93	−107	....
Morocco	686	−723	−1,296	−58	−169	−146	−171	−501	1,606	1,472	1,552	922	....
Mozambique	688	−467	−445	−421	−296	−429	−912	−764	−657	−869	−816	−607	−761
Namibia	728	85	176	116	90	162	158	293	58	128	336	573	....
Nigeria	694	−2,128	−2,578	3,507	552	−4,244	506	7,429	2,478	1,083	9,504	12,264	....
Rwanda	714	−72	57	−9	−62	−83	−141	−94	−102	−126	−85	−6	....
São Tomé & Príncipe	716	....	....	....	....	−10	−16	−19	−21	−23	....	....	....
Seychelles	718	24	−3	−59	−73	−118	−127	−51	−123	−131	−16	−28	....
Sierra Leone	724	−89	−118	−151	−55	−33	−99	−112	−98	−73	−80	−74	....
Somalia	726	....	....	....	....	....	....	....	....	....	....	....	....
South Africa	199	30	−2,493	−1,678	−2,227	−2,199	−675	−191	153	684	−2,323	−7,442	−10,079
Sudan	732	−602	−500	−827	−828	−957	−465	−557	−618	−1,008	−955	−871	−3,013
Swaziland	734	2	−30	−52	−3	−93	−35	−75	−57	58	116	114	....
Tanzania	738	−711	−646	−511	−630	−920	−835	−499	−457	−217	−393	−437	....
Tunisia	744	−537	−774	−478	−595	−675	−442	−821	−840	−746	−730	−555	....
Uganda	746	−208	−339	−252	−367	−503	−711	−825	−368	−360	−352	−188	−267
Zambia	754	....	....	....	−383	−573	−447	−584	....	....	....	....	....
Zimbabwe	698	−425	....	....	....	....	....	....	....	....	....	....	....
CEMAC													
Cameroon	622	−56	90	....	....	....	....	....	....	....	....	....	....
Central African Rep.	626	−25	....	....	....	....	....	....	....	....	....	....	....
Chad	628	−38	....	....	....	....	....	....	....	....	....	....	....
Congo, Republic of	634	−793	−625	−651	−156	−241	−231	648	−28	−34	−3	....	....
Equatorial Guinea	642	—	−123	−344	....	....	....	....	....	....	....	....	....
Gabon	646	317	465	889	531	−596	390	1,001	517	336	575	....	....
WAEMU													
Benin	638	−23	−213	−57	−170	−151	−191	−111	−160	−239	−349	....	....
Burkina Faso	748	15	....	....	....	....	....	−392	−381	....	....	....	....
Côte d'Ivoire	662	−14	−492	−162	−155	−290	−120	−241	−61	768	295	303	....

Balance of Payments

Current Account Balance
Excluding Exceptional Financing
Expressed in Millions of US Dollars

		1994	1995	1996	1997	1998	1999	2000	2001	2002	2003	2004	2005
Africa(Cont.)													
Guinea-Bissau	654	−48	−51	−60	−30	....	....	....	−27	−9	−6	....	....
Mali	678	−163	−284	−261	−178	−208	−253	−255	−310	−149	−271	....	....
Niger	692	−126	−152	−109	−133	−152	−137	−104	−92	−165	−219	....	....
Senegal	722	−187	−244	−201	−185	−247	−320	−332	−245	−317	−437	....	....
Togo	742	−56	−122	−154	−117	−140	−127	−140	−169	−140	−162	....	....
Asia*	505	−3,504	−38,588	−39,095	18,465	114,737	113,080	89,685	94,371	136,010	175,876	193,096	....
Afghanistan, I.R. of	512	....	....	....	....	....	....	....	....	....	....	....	....
Bangladesh	513	200	−824	−991	−286	−35	−364	−306	−535	739	132	−279	....
Bhutan	514	....	....	....	....	....	....	....	....	....	....	....	....
Brunei Darussalam	516	....	....	....	....	....	....	....	....	....	....	....	....
Cambodia	522	−157	−186	−185	−210	−1,110	−433	−499	−558	−129	−159	−240	....
China,P.R.: Mainland	924	6,908	1,618	7,243	36,963	31,472	21,115	20,518	17,401	35,422	45,875	68,659	160,818
China,P.R.:Hong Kong	532	....	....	....	....	2,507	10,248	6,993	9,786	12,412	16,470	15,728	20,284
China,P.R.: Macao	546	....	....	....	....	....	....	....	....	2,739	3,179	4,163	....
Fiji	819	−113	−113	14	−34	−60	13	....	....	....	....	....	....
French Terr.: French Polynesia	887	....	....	....	....	....	....	....	....	6	−119	186	21
French Terr.: New Caledonia	839	....	....	....	....	....	....	....	....	−107	−37	281	31
India	534	−1,676	−5,563	−5,956	−2,965	−6,903	−3,228	−4,601	1,410	7,059	6,853	....	....
Indonesia	536	−2,792	−6,431	−7,663	−4,889	4,097	5,783	7,992	6,901	7,824	8,387	1,562	929
Kiribati	826	1	....	....	....	....	....	....	....	....	....	....	....
Korea	542	−4,024	−8,665	−23,210	−8,384	40,371	24,522	12,251	8,033	5,394	11,950	28,174	16,559
Lao People's Dem.Rep.	544	−284	−346	−347	−306	−150	−121	−8	−82	....	....	....	....
Malaysia	548	−4,520	−8,644	−4,462	−5,935	9,529	12,604	8,488	7,287	7,190	13,381	14,871	....
Maldives	556	−11	−18	−7	−35	−22	−79	−51	−59	−36	−32	−134	....
Mongolia	948	46	39	−101	55	−129	−112	−156	−154	−158	−148	−25	....
Myanmar	518	−130	−261	−283	−416	−499	−285	−212	−154	97	−19	112	....
Nepal	558	−352	−356	−327	−388	−67	−256	−299	−339	56	120	52	....
Pakistan	564	−1,812	−3,349	−4,436	−1,712	−2,248	−920	−85	1,878	3,854	3,573	−817	−3,463
Papua New Guinea	853	402	492	189	−192	−29	95	345	282	....	....	....	....
Philippines	566	−2,950	−1,980	−3,953	−4,351	1,546	7,219	6,258	1,323	4,383	1,396	2,080	....
Samoa	862	6	9	12	9	20	−19	....	....	....	....	−17	−29
Singapore	576	11,400	14,708	13,853	14,913	18,270	14,773	11,936	14,383	15,727	26,951	27,897	....
Solomon Islands	813	−3	8	15	−38	8	21	....	....	....	....	....	....
Sri Lanka	524	−757	−770	−683	−395	−228	−561	−1,044	−237	−268	−106	−677	....
Thailand	578	−8,085	−13,582	−14,691	−3,021	14,242	12,428	9,313	6,192	7,014	7,953	6,857	−3,719
Tonga	866	....	....	....	....	....	....	....	−11	−3	....	....	....
Vanuatu	846	−20	−18	−27	−19	−9	−33	−14	−15	−39	−47	−52	−64
Vietnam	582	....	....	−2,020	−1,528	−1,074	1,177	1,106	682	−604	−1,878	−926	....
of which:													
Taiwan Prov.of China	528	6,498	5,474	10,923	7,051	3,438	7,992	8,901	18,093	25,628	29,257	18,493	16,116
Europe	170	4,665	−5,569	−15,043	−29,986	−26,380	−3,559	14,893	15,760	4,569	−3,579	592	....
Albania	914	−157	−12	−107	−272	−65	−155	−156	−217	−408	−407	−358	−571
Armenia	911	−104	−218	−291	−307	−418	−307	−278	−200	−148	−189	−162	−193
Azerbaijan, Republic of	912	....	−401	−931	−916	−1,365	−600	−168	−52	−768	−2,021	−2,589	167
Belarus	913	−444	−458	−516	−859	−1,017	−194	−338	−394	−311	−424	−1,043	469
Bosnia & Herzegovina	963	....	....	....	....	−345	−501	−396	−736	−1,190	−1,637	−1,784	−2,087
Bulgaria	918	−32	−26	16	427	−62	−652	−704	−984	−827	−1,855	−1,417	−3,133
Croatia	960	554	−1,592	−1,049	−2,825	−1,468	−1,408	−471	−727	−1,917	−2,132	−1,911	−2,541
Cyprus	423	74	−205	−468	−418	291	−170	−488	−322	−458	−331	−923	−962
Czech Republic	935	−820	−1,374	−4,128	−3,622	−1,308	−1,466	−2,690	−3,273	−4,265	−5,785	−6,538	−2,495
Estonia	939	−166	−158	−398	−562	−478	−295	−299	−325	−779	−1,115	−1,458	−1,445
Faroe Islands	816	....	....	....	....	224	176	99	146	126	−7	....	....
Georgia	915	....	....	....	−514	−276	−198	−269	−212	−221	−375	−426	−751
Hungary	944	−4,054	−1,650	−1,766	−2,080	−3,391	−3,775	−4,004	−3,205	−4,693	−7,231	−8,639	−7,962
Kazakhstan	916	....	−213	−751	−799	−1,225	−171	366	−1,390	−1,024	−273	455	−486
Kyrgyz Republic	917	−84	−235	−425	−139	−412	−252	−124	−57	−80	−99	−101	....
Latvia	941	201	−16	−280	−345	−650	−654	−371	−626	−624	−910	−1,766	−1,959
Lithuania	946	−94	−614	−723	−981	−1,298	−1,194	−675	−574	−721	−1,278	−1,725	−1,771
Macedonia, FYR	962	....	....	−288	−275	−270	−32	−72	−244	−358	−149	−415	−725
Malta	181	−132	−361	−406	−202	−221	−122	−470	−165	12	−280	−515	....
Moldova	921	−82	−88	−195	−275	−335	−79	−108	−37	−75	−140	−53	−308
Poland	964	954	854	−3,264	−5,744	−6,901	−12,487	−9,981	−5,375	−5,009	−4,599	−10,522	−4,364
Romania	968	−455	−1,780	−2,579	−2,104	−2,917	−1,297	−1,355	−2,229	−1,525	−3,311	−6,382	....
Russia	922	7,844	6,965	10,847	−80	219	24,616	46,839	33,935	29,116	35,410	58,592	84,249
Slovak Republic	936	671	390	−2,090	−1,961	−2,126	−1,155	−694	....	−1,955	−282	....	....
Slovenia	961	575	−75	55	50	−118	−698	−548	31	335	−85	−670	−362
Tajikistan	923	....	....	....	....	....	....	....	....	−15	−5	−57	−19
Turkey	186	2,631	−2,338	−2,437	−2,638	1,984	−1,344	−9,819	3,390	−1,521	−8,037	−15,543	....
Turkmenistan	925	....	....	—	−580	....	....	....	....	....	....	....	....
Ukraine	926	−1,163	−1,152	−1,184	−1,335	−1,296	1,658	1,481	1,402	3,174	2,891	6,909	2,531
Uzbekistan	927	....	....	....	....	....	....	....	....	....	....	....	....
Middle East	405	−7,734	−3,380	8,502	3,820	−28,593	9,261	67,951	37,118	26,781	58,235	104,172	....
Bahrain, Kingdom of	419	−256	237	260	−31	−777	−37	830	227	−50	201	415	....
Egypt	469	31	−254	−192	−711	−2,566	−1,635	−971	−388	622	3,743	3,922	....
Iran, I.R. of	429	4,956	3,358	5,232	2,213	−2,139	6,555	12,481	....	....	....	....	....
Iraq	433	....	....	....	....	....	....	....	....	....	....	....	....
Israel	436	−3,447	−4,790	−5,248	−3,458	−1,257	−1,689	−1,285	−1,648	−1,300	814	1,845	2,385
Jordan	439	−398	−259	−222	29	14	405	59	−4	537	1,179	−18	....

Balance of Payments

		1994	1995	1996	1997	1998	1999	2000	2001	2002	2003	2004	2005

Current Account Balance
Excluding Exceptional Financing
Expressed in Millions of US Dollars

		1994	1995	1996	1997	1998	1999	2000	2001	2002	2003	2004	2005
Middle East(Cont.)													
Kuwait	443	3,243	5,016	7,107	7,935	2,215	5,010	14,672	8,324	4,251	9,416	18,884	....
Lebanon	446	....	....	....	....	....	....	....	....	−4,385	−5,463	−4,805	....
Libya	672	26	1,650	1,220	1,550	−351	2,136	7,740	3,417	117	3,642	3,705	....
Oman	449	−805	−801	243	−166	−3,164	−460	3,129	1,885	1,367	880	443	....
Qatar	453	....	....	....	....	....	....	....	....	....	....	....	....
Saudi Arabia	456	−10,473	−5,318	679	305	−13,132	411	14,317	9,353	11,873	28,048	51,926	87,131
Syrian Arab Republic	463	−791	263	40	461	58	201	1,061	1,221	1,440	728	205	....
United Arab Emirates	466	....	....	....	....	....	....	....	....	....	....	....	....
West Bank and Gaza	487	....	−984	−1,424	−1,548	−1,213	−1,327	−1,023	−641	....	....	....	....
Yemen, Republic of	474	178	144	39	−69	−472	358	1,337	667	538	149	225	1,215
Western Hemisphere	**205**	**−51,298**	**−37,842**	**−39,638**	**−66,654**	**−91,143**	**−57,204**	**−48,012**	**−53,337**	**−16,710**	**6,868**	**18,538**	**....**
Argentina	213	−10,979	−5,118	−6,770	−12,138	−14,482	−11,943	−8,981	−3,291	8,668	7,982	3,281	....
Aruba	314	81	—	−69	−196	−19	−429	211	321	−335	−150	14	−259
Bahamas, The	313	−42	−146	−263	−472	−995	−324	−633	−645	−423	−474	−203	....
Barbados	316	134	43	70	−50	−63	−148	−146	−111	−168	−170	−337	....
Belize	339	−40	−17	−7	−32	−60	−68	−156	−190	−183	−207	−182	....
Bolivia	218	−90	−303	−404	−554	−666	−488	−446	−274	−352	76	337	467
Brazil	223	−1,153	−18,136	−23,248	−30,491	−33,829	−25,400	−24,225	−23,215	−7,637	4,177	11,711	14,199
Chile	228	−1,586	−1,350	−3,083	−3,660	−3,918	99	−898	−1,100	−580	−964	1,586	703
Colombia	233	−3,667	−4,516	−4,641	−5,751	−4,858	671	780	−1,089	−1,359	−974	−938	−1,930
Costa Rica	238	−244	−358	−264	−481	−521	−666	−707	−713	−916	−929	−831	....
Dominican Republic	243	−283	−183	−213	−163	−338	−429	−1,027	−741	−798	1,036	1,142	−143
Ecuador	248	−898	−1,000	−55	−457	−2,099	918	921	−695	−1,399	−472	−157	....
El Salvador	253	−18	−262	−169	−98	−91	−239	−431	−150	−405	−764	−612	....
Guatemala	258	−625	−572	−452	−634	−1,039	−1,026	−1,050	−1,253	−1,235	−1,039	−1,188	....
Guyana	336	−125	−135	−33	−63	−56	−50	−82	−96	−66	−47	−30	....
Haiti	263	−23	−87	−138	−48	29	−60	−85	−95	−48	−13	....	....
Honduras	268	−343	−201	−335	−272	−395	−625	−262	−339	−264	−314	−413	....
Jamaica	343	82	−99	−143	−332	−334	−216	−367	−759	−1,074	−773	−509	....
Mexico	273	−29,662	−1,576	−2,537	−7,695	−16,017	−13,943	−18,652	−17,668	−13,541	−8,637	−7,195	−5,723
Netherlands Antilles	353	−98	128	−254	−65	−137	−277	−51	−211	−59	7	−92	....
Nicaragua	278	−911	−722	−825	−841	−687	−928	−792	−796	−767	−749	−772	....
Panama	283	16	−471	−201	−507	−1,016	−1,159	−673	−170	−96	−503	−1,127	−818
Paraguay	288	−274	−92	−353	−650	−160	−165	−163	−266	93	132	20	....
Peru	293	−2,701	−4,625	−3,646	−3,367	−3,321	−1,464	−1,526	−1,144	−1,063	−935	−11	1,030
Suriname	366	59	73	−64	−68	−155	−29	32	−84	−131	−159	−138	−144
Trinidad and Tobago	369	218	294	105	−614	−644	31	544	416	76	985	....	....
Uruguay	298	−438	−213	−233	−287	−476	−508	−566	−488	322	−56	−103	....
Venezuela, Rep. Bol.	299	2,541	2,014	8,914	3,732	−4,432	2,112	11,853	1,983	7,599	11,448	13,830	25,359
ECCU													
Anguilla	312	−11	−9	−20	−19	−19	−51	−54	−36	−35	....	....	....
Antigua and Barbuda	311	−6	−1	−59	−47	−47	−57	−66	−64	−103	....	....	....
Dominica	321	−38	−41	−51	−42	−23	−36	−53	−49	−38	....	....	....
Grenada	328	−27	−41	−56	−68	−82	−53	−84	−99	−116	....	....	....
Montserrat	351	−12	−2	16	−2	3	−1	−7	−6	−8	....	....	....
St. Kitts and Nevis	361	−24	−45	−65	−62	−46	−82	−66	−106	−124	....	....	....
St. Lucia	362	−48	−33	−58	−78	−60	−97	−79	−75	−104	....	....	....
St. Vincent & Grens	364	−57	−41	−36	−84	−92	−73	−29	−41	−42	....	....	....
Memorandum Items													
Oil Exporting Ctys	999	−5,062	−4,163	24,206	18,434	−21,253	26,380	108,864	61,102	52,889	97,918	144,815	....
Non-Oil Develop.Ctys	201	−61,187	−94,772	−107,302	−97,900	−28,689	26,127	27,690	36,167	98,410	149,871	183,001	....

Balance of Payments

Capital and Financial Account
Including Net Errors and Omissions, but Excluding Reserve Assets,
Use of Fund Credit, and Exceptional Financing
Expressed in Millions of US Dollars

		1994	1995	1996	1997	1998	1999	2000	2001	2002	2003	2004	2005
All Countries	010	126,265	184,839	219,346	82,976	83,586	255,715	328,224	285,726	365,487	511,822	649,704	....
Industrial Countries	110	34,311	46,293	51,649	−38,467	47,487	224,453	350,772	285,549	358,956	460,640	506,959	....
United States	111	116,293	123,411	118,190	141,918	220,768	291,355	416,291	394,381	478,901	518,151	665,270	790,861
Canada	156	12,632	7,039	2,119	5,840	12,836	4,168	−15,902	−14,109	−12,789	−13,570	−23,992	−25,219
Australia	193	15,993	19,674	18,120	15,113	16,298	28,918	13,941	8,950	16,590	36,573	41,267	49,340
Japan	158	−104,990	−52,433	−30,652	−90,247	−124,914	−38,348	−70,705	−47,311	−66,314	50,938	−11,205	−143,458
New Zealand	196	3,117	3,387	5,663	2,862	1,671	3,704	2,518	1,248	3,554	4,352	7,084	....
Euro Area													
Austria	122	3,826	6,839	5,965	2,168	8,740	4,484	4,119	1,748	−2,288	−1,385	−2,614	−4,727
Belgium	124									−11,646	−14,461	−13,129	−8,299
Belgium-Luxembourg	126	−12,351	−13,990	−13,169	−12,858	−14,263	−15,954	−12,340	−7,950	....	....	....	....
Finland	172	3,603	−5,603	−8,038	−4,329	−7,044	−8,032	−8,624	−8,294	−10,262	−7,627	−8,792	−5,181
France	132	−4,968	−10,128	−20,321	−31,861	−17,883	−42,957	−21,014	−34,325	−14,962	−10,529	10,916	24,242
Germany	134	28,850	37,111	12,921	5,782	19,138	12,679	26,733	−5,948	−43,028	−46,481	−103,601	−118,120
Greece	174	6,455	2,841	8,769	345	....	9,730	12,393	3,701	11,445	8,081	10,199	17,775
Ireland	178	−1,752	618	−2,101	−2,974	2,196	−2,218	477	1,085	809	−1,979	−11	2,040
Italy	136	−11,634	−22,272	−28,092	−19,254	−41,470	−16,162	9,028	64	12,538	20,521	12,294	25,784
Luxembourg	137									−2,375	−1,759	−3,554	−3,608
Netherlands	138	−16,794	−27,684	−27,197	−27,786	−15,370	−20,295	−7,044	−10,161	−11,149	−30,507	−55,427	−42,634
Portugal	182	765	−168	5,746	8,001	9,016	10,630	12,118	12,208	10,965	2,752	11,099	15,266
Spain	184	6,426	−4,447	26,514	12,585	−7,102	−4,935	20,196	22,238	26,282	16,248	48,453	81,216
Denmark	128	−5,041	643	474	5,611	−2,231	6,517	−7,783	−1,531	2,085	−2,289	−7,366	....
Iceland	176	−266	−48	284	84	587	674	773	287	−85	850	1,433	2,688
Norway	142	−3,507	−4,658	−4,499	−11,234	−6,390	−2,394	−22,165	−28,517	−18,749	−28,548	−29,484	−44,920
Sweden	144	1,639	−6,604	−12,278	−14,118	−1,386	−4,101	−6,446	−7,744	−12,119	−20,768	−28,585	−23,394
Switzerland	146	−15,720	−20,673	−17,394	−23,163	−24,015	−31,263	−37,776	−21,861	−22,381	−41,521	−56,676	−67,402
United Kingdom	112	11,735	13,438	10,626	−952	6,373	38,253	41,985	27,391	23,935	23,600	43,380	59,348
Developing Countries	200	91,954	138,546	167,697	121,442	36,099	31,262	−22,548	177	6,532	51,181	142,745	....
Africa	605	−1,679	−2,029	−9,873	3,846	4,966	−327	−6,225	−1,626	−8,178	−6,376	13,174	....
Algeria	612	....	....	....	....	....	....	....	....	....	....	....	....
Angola	614	−688	−944	−505	279	755	1,667	−478	645	−206	982	−346	....
Botswana	616	−86	−93	16	−86	−126	−189	−178	−448	−83	−312	....	....
Burundi	618	52	26	5	−40	−27	−26	−42	−35	−37	−64	....	....
Cape Verde	624	68	30	57	30	69	123	30	39	82	21	....	....
Comoros	632	12	9	....	....	....	....	....	....	....	....	....	....
Congo, Dem. Rep. of	636	....	....	....	....	....	....	....	....	....	....	....	....
Djibouti	611	47	−1	....	....	....	....	....	....	....	....	....	....
Eritrea	643	−69	29	117	115	133	210	40	....	....	....	....	....
Ethiopia	644	−126	−145	−544	−388	−28	229	−203	−407	−998	−143	−281	....
Gambia, The	648	−2	9	62	31	....	....	....	....	....	....	....	....
Ghana	652	508	326	282	481	549	828	17	203	18	248	222	....
Guinea	656	124	144	117	−40	26	139	92	−14	120	−41	116	....
Kenya	664	−36	259	460	472	558	56	192	351	121	357	387	....
Lesotho	666	13	421	419	410	396	180	169	261	−51	69	81	....
Liberia	668	....	....	....	....	....	....	....	....	....	....	....	....
Madagascar	674	1	−54	197	250	1	148	123	−83	15	74	....	....
Malawi	676	195	3	26	292	−170	191	165	−8	291	....	....	....
Mauritania	682	−35	−28	−87	−20	−34	....	....	....	....	....	....	....
Mauritius	684	189	131	14	54	−69	314	268	−328	92	129	80	....
Morocco	686	1,206	−599	−615	−820	−494	102	−665	−746	−1,524	−1,398	−186	....
Mozambique	688	−99	58	−3	−183	37	586	347	172	−570	852	748	564
Namibia	728	−10	−152	−93	−23	−106	−307	−477	−417	−338	−665	−710	....
Nigeria	694	190	−195	−4,268	−536	1,371	−4,043	−4,340	−2,255	−5,772	−10,764	−3,773	....
Rwanda	714	78	−5	29	93	76	69	−37	32	105	97	107	....
São Tomé & Príncipe	716	....	....	....	....	4	14	14	20	16	....	....	....
Seychelles	718	−51	−29	−3	28	44	28	−52	76	−58	−105	−157	....
Sierra Leone	724	30	119	128	75	35	83	122	128	53	51	79	....
Somalia	726	....	....	....	....	....	....	....	....	....	....	....	....
South Africa	199	342	3,404	−82	6,593	2,244	2,591	670	−175	−1,006	1,969	13,767	15,845
Sudan	732	621	563	864	846	1,030	580	681	467	1,253	1,282	1,653	3,628
Swaziland	734	−5	53	44	30	144	61	68	—	−83	−160	−133	....
Tanzania	738	292	288	257	332	410	756	497	406	544	788	637	....
Tunisia	744	1,063	871	920	981	538	1,180	616	1,129	886	1,113	1,532	....
Uganda	746	145	288	243	326	462	255	361	459	185	349	311	348
Zambia	754	....	....	....	−549	−98	−207	64	....	....	....	....	....
Zimbabwe	698	339	....	....	....	....	....	....	....	....	....	....	....
CEMAC													
Cameroon	622	−495	−74	....	....	....	....	....	....	....	....	....	....
Central African Rep	626	38	....	....	....	....	....	....	....	....	....	....	....
Chad	628	43	....	....	....	....	....	....	....	....	....	....	....
Congo, Republic of	634	639	45	−665	−527	−788	−425	−891	−652	−679	−159	....	....
Equatorial Guinea	642	−18	112	339	....	....	....	....	....	....	....	....	....
Gabon	646	−490	−693	−974	−643	−128	−826	−721	−775	−558	−675	....	....
WAEMU													
Benin	638	41	−42	−92	70	65	103	91	92	−22	249	....	....
Burkina Faso	748	−22	....	....	....	....	....	200	194	....	....	....	....

Balance of Payments

		1994	1995	1996	1997	1998	1999	2000	2001	2002	2003	2004	2005

Capital and Financial Account

Including Net Errors and Omissions, but Excluding Reserve Assets,
Use of Fund Credit, and Exceptional Financing
Expressed in Millions of US Dollars

Africa(Cont.)

		1994	1995	1996	1997	1998	1999	2000	2001	2002	2003	2004	2005
Côte d'Ivoire	662	−7	238	−686	−322	−359	−588	−367	−25	−1,047	−1,082	−1,083	....
Guinea-Bissau	654	−7	10	17	15	....	....	....	14	14	36	....	....
Mali	678	98	232	290	169	162	240	317	263	287	408	....	....
Niger	692	50	134	96	105	136	135	139	114	152	175	....	....
Senegal	722	210	212	−1	90	−1	52	101	51	69	164	....	....
Togo	742	−41	−72	129	130	123	159	176	167	170	153	....	....
Asia*	**505**	**63,498**	**77,623**	**96,568**	**−13,185**	**−75,983**	**−21,957**	**−32,153**	**1,565**	**21,598**	**57,881**	**144,550**	**....**
Afghanistan, I.R. of	512	....	....	....	....	....	....	....	....	....	....	....	
Bangladesh	513	492	312	577	151	324	175	275	392	−242	757	782	....
Bhutan	514	....	....	....	....	....	....	....	....	....	....	....	
Brunei Darussalam	516	....	....	....	....	....	....	....	....	....	....	....	
Cambodia	522	193	212	257	244	1,099	422	520	574	230	159	342	....
China,P.R.: Mainland	924	23,545	20,851	24,462	−1,106	−25,224	−12,463	−9,825	30,046	39,795	70,711	137,494	46,523
China,P.R.:Hong Kong	532	....	....	....	....	−9,297	−220	3,051	−5,102	−14,789	−15,476	−12,442	−18,906
China,P.R.: Macao	546	....	....	....	....	....	....	....	....	−2,446	−2,655	−3,065	
Fiji	819	135	206	65	9	65	−58	....	....	....	....	....	
French Terr.: French Polynesia	887	....	....	....	....	....	....	....	....	−6	119	−186	−21
French Terr.: New Caledonia	839	....	....	....	....	....	....	....	....	107	37	−281	−31
India	534	12,067	4,831	9,914	8,286	9,974	9,892	10,670	7,280	11,793	18,813	....	....
Indonesia	536	3,576	8,004	12,166	−3,248	−7,534	−3,867	−4,066	−6,916	−2,866	−4,740	−1,241	−1,272
Kiribati	826	−7	....	....	....	....	....	....	....	....	....	....	
Korea	542	8,638	15,704	24,626	−14,596	−14,441	8,738	11,539	5,245	6,375	13,842	10,501	3,306
Lao People's Dem.Rep	544	106	196	188	−64	−104	−212	52	79	....	....	....	
Malaysia	548	1,360	6,881	6,975	2,061	489	−7,892	−9,497	−6,287	−3,533	−3,201	7,003	....
Maldives	556	17	35	36	57	42	88	47	29	76	58	178	
Mongolia	948	−40	−7	13	−49	76	93	71	75	171	−1	−22	
Myanmar	518	176	229	258	447	560	239	188	333	−51	58	−18	
Nepal	558	414	371	358	557	347	34	222	40	−369	−19	−153	....
Pakistan	564	3,155	2,145	3,656	2,249	−862	−1,596	−2,542	319	230	−665	−534	3,938
Papua New Guinea	853	−572	−531	14	15	−192	30	−241	−153	....	....	....	
Philippines	566	5,277	3,215	8,291	1,257	−267	−3,569	−6,634	−1,027	−4,494	−1,475	−3,667	....
Samoa	862	−10	−7	−5	2	−15	26	....	....	....	....	25	28
Singapore	576	−6,664	−6,067	−6,454	−6,798	−15,281	−10,585	−5,185	−15,250	−14,400	−20,276	−15,809	....
Solomon Islands	813	1	−9	3	47	9	−26	....	....	....	....	....	
Sri Lanka	524	1,065	1,009	692	702	451	466	683	−71	5	−259	−258	....
Thailand	578	12,254	20,741	16,859	−15,229	−16,938	−11,040	−11,120	−3,916	−1,478	−7,435	−1,148	9,136
Tonga	866	....	....	....	....	....	....	....	13	10	....	....	
Vanuatu	846	14	24	22	17	3	10	−5	4	21	38	47	54
Vietnam	582	....	....	2,298	1,856	1,111	133	−996	−476	1,052	4,024	1,861	....
*of which:													
Taiwan Prov.of China	528	−1,876	−9,405	−9,821	−7,779	1,389	10,601	−6,424	−740	8,036	7,835	8,102	3,940
Europe	**170**	**−18,319**	**24,509**	**3,599**	**33,469**	**9,054**	**13,571**	**2,353**	**−7,744**	**23,686**	**48,378**	**72,419**	**....**
Albania	914	164	32	163	312	118	262	276	364	443	505	644	719
Armenia	911	101	248	245	357	419	312	295	216	211	263	194	380
Azerbaijan, Republic of	912	....	458	846	1,055	1,305	733	493	125	803	2,145	2,906	−7
Belarus	913	127	380	302	924	697	214	464	316	408	342	1,228	49
Bosnia & Herzegovina	963	....	....	....	....	−15	−87	132	1,203	630	1,565	1,995	2,422
Bulgaria	918	−184	470	−754	718	−32	748	841	1,357	1,542	2,585	3,147	3,847
Croatia	960	−278	1,632	2,066	3,216	1,629	1,866	1,126	2,125	2,731	3,533	1,979	3,564
Cyprus	423	173	−158	408	371	−374	809	480	933	143	1,295	1,665	
Czech Republic	935	4,294	8,827	3,302	1,863	3,199	3,105	3,533	5,060	10,883	6,228	6,800	6,374
Estonia	939	184	241	505	778	516	414	427	283	849	1,285	1,729	1,830
Faroe Islands	816	....	....	....	....	....	....	....	....	....	....	....	
Georgia	915	....	....	....	452	172	184	275	239	32	326	521	734
Hungary	944	3,579	7,033	529	1,906	4,342	6,110	5,056	3,121	2,901	7,567	10,620	12,866
Kazakhstan	916	....	512	910	1,348	782	424	204	1,774	1,559	1,806	3,544	−1,459
Kyrgyz Republic	917	89	154	405	185	355	226	91	44	100	146	245	....
Latvia	941	−145	−17	491	447	712	819	374	941	636	990	2,169	2,483
Lithuania	946	207	783	718	1,206	1,725	1,015	833	933	1,183	1,891	1,620	2,489
Macedonia, FYR	962	....	....	193	157	313	174	352	329	236	204	443	....
Malta	181	514	54	321	209	412	360	248	420	276	424	308	943
Moldova	921	95	−88	92	87	−18	−37	103	12	28	124	203	404
Poland	964	52	8,981	7,088	8,785	12,825	12,643	10,605	4,948	5,657	5,805	11,323	12,510
Romania	968	626	1,300	1,997	3,563	2,274	1,536	2,263	3,764	3,316	4,324	12,571	....
Russia	922	−26,957	−15,291	−28,065	−6,438	−21,597	−26,319	−32,916	−22,669	−17,553	−7,148	−11,701	−19,281
Slovak Republic	936	535	1,401	2,460	2,060	1,649	1,932	1,614	....	5,639	1,790	....	....
Slovenia	961	72	315	535	1,238	276	617	726	1,254	1,482	395	373	568
Tajikistan	923	....	....	....	....	....	....	....	....	17	33	61	25
Turkey	186	−2,428	6,998	6,981	5,981	−1,543	6,698	5,885	−16,278	1,307	12,124	19,851	....
Turkmenistan	925	....	....	8	978	....	....	....	....	....	....	....	
Ukraine	926	−37	−472	581	632	−2,161	−1,842	−908	−409	−1,943	−718	−4,386	8,194
Uzbekistan	927	....	....	....	....	....	....	....	....	....	....	....	
Middle East	**405**	**6,898**	**8,716**	**2,974**	**7,040**	**24,710**	**−4,759**	**−50,069**	**−29,798**	**−21,304**	**−52,134**	**−82,735**	**....**
Bahrain, Kingdom of	419	208	−68	−267	134	761	62	−630	−104	85	−157	−257	....
Egypt	469	−1,195	−1,573	−1,533	75	1,179	−2,979	−1,059	−956	−1,426	−4,150	−4,506	....
Iran, I.R. of	429	−4,048	−572	−2,791	−5,910	1,148	−6,104	−11,398	....	....	....	....	
Iraq	433	....	....	....	....	....	....	....	....	....	....	....	

Balance of Payments

Capital and Financial Account
Including Net Errors and Omissions, but Excluding Reserve Assets,
Use of Fund Credit, and Exceptional Financing
Expressed in Millions of US Dollars

		1994	1995	1996	1997	1998	1999	2000	2001	2002	2003	2004	2005
Middle East(Cont.)													
Israel	436	1,337	5,169	6,325	10,401	1,095	1,563	1,606	2,036	231	−1,009	−3,763	−1,502
Jordan	439	133	87	34	245	−550	347	634	−240	393	170	196	....
Kuwait	443	−3,193	−5,157	−7,132	−7,929	−1,957	−4,092	−12,404	−5,419	−5,224	−11,240	−18,258	....
Lebanon	446	....	....	....	....	....	....	....	....	2,166	1,460	4,465	....
Libya	672	248	51	1	4	−75	−1,448	−1,282	−2,124	161	−626	2,027	....
Oman	449	144	369	−55	699	2,393	664	−866	−871	−1,058	−224	39	....
Qatar	453	....	....	....	....	....	....	....	....	....	....	....	....
Saudi Arabia	456	10,327	6,533	5,062	342	12,414	2,404	−11,652	−11,262	−9,137	−26,440	−47,428	−87,596
Syrian Arab Republic	463	1,357	576	947	−12	376	58	−247	−201	−390	−33	212	....
United Arab Emirates	466	....	....	....	....	....	....	....	....	....	....	....	....
West Bank and Gaza	487	....	984	1,646	1,706	1,160	1,292	1,107	603	....	....	....	
Yemen, Republic of	474	−900	−672	−475	4,087	−109	−284	258	−114	−113	182	148	−781
Western Hemisphere	205	41,557	29,726	74,429	90,273	73,352	44,734	63,547	37,780	−9,269	3,433	−4,662	....
Argentina	213	10,305	2,807	10,028	15,469	18,572	13,955	7,804	−18,114	−22,070	−17,059	−10,274	....
Aruba	314	−84	43	43	177	70	432	−226	−238	375	114	−13	237
Bahamas, The	313	51	143	256	529	1,115	390	572	614	483	584	387	....
Barbados	316	−96	—	17	67	57	184	323	333	144	237	180	....
Belize	339	36	21	27	33	46	93	208	187	174	199	151	....
Bolivia	218	1	395	672	654	791	515	407	238	9	−137	−265	−49
Brazil	223	7,751	31,105	31,930	22,240	17,527	8,635	32,206	19,797	−3,630	−591	−5,112	13,368
Chile	228	4,737	2,488	5,676	6,979	1,727	−846	1,214	501	765	607	−1,778	1,008
Colombia	233	3,849	4,512	6,371	6,028	3,460	−983	81	2,314	1,497	786	3,408	3,656
Costa Rica	238	141	574	194	288	16	896	365	577	879	703	798	....
Dominican Republic	243	−228	329	173	254	350	581	978	1,255	244	−1,584	−597	815
Ecuador	248	123	−459	−71	−65	1,314	−1,862	−6,618	437	1,179	542	492	....
El Salvador	253	131	410	334	460	394	447	385	−27	282	1,080	572	....
Guatemala	258	632	420	666	863	1,275	901	1,692	1,727	1,256	1,589	1,797	....
Guyana	336	119	92	45	62	43	71	122	122	81	57	75	....
Haiti	263	−26	225	87	78	5	86	28	89	−20	8	....	....
Honduras	268	273	160	257	454	239	436	106	265	245	116	781	....
Jamaica	343	276	126	414	162	378	80	886	1,624	832	342	1,203	....
Mexico	273	12,463	−14,735	13,533	26,857	19,187	18,193	25,778	24,983	20,900	18,454	11,299	12,688
Netherlands Antilles	353	22	−67	182	59	162	202	−79	429	111	20	98	....
Nicaragua	278	−608	−242	77	548	285	533	336	304	366	280	375	....
Panama	283	−378	139	467	850	911	1,350	596	804	240	234	731	1,493
Paraguay	288	575	137	306	435	177	−136	−177	216	−218	100	250	....
Peru	293	4,254	4,034	4,526	5,421	2,080	602	1,395	1,576	2,073	1,496	2,467	381
Suriname	366	−24	49	62	87	163	25	−23	162	112	166	214	163
Trinidad and Tobago	369	−32	−210	133	807	724	131	−103	86	39	−576	....	....
Uruguay	298	547	440	386	687	831	398	733	792	−4,219	1,013	407	....
Venezuela, Rep. Bol.	299	−3,485	−3,458	−2,676	−638	1,027	−1,054	−5,895	−3,812	−12,027	−5,994	−11,675	−19,934
ECCU													
Anguilla	312	11	9	22	21	21	53	55	40	37	....	....	
Antigua and Barbuda	311	14	14	48	50	56	68	60	80	110	....	....	
Dominica	321	34	49	53	43	27	47	53	53	46	....	....	
Grenada	328	32	47	56	75	86	58	91	104	147	....	....	
Montserrat	351	14	3	−16	5	10	−9	3	8	10	....	....	
St. Kitts and Nevis	361	24	48	64	65	57	85	62	118	134	....	....	
St. Lucia	362	45	39	52	83	70	101	84	87	109	....	....	
St. Vincent & Grens	364	58	39	36	85	100	77	43	50	36	....	....	
Memorandum Items													
Oil Exporting Ctys	999	−1,265	548	−7,091	−23,281	7,383	−22,858	−70,414	−48,075	−46,234	−74,309	−101,408	....
Non-Oil Develop.Ctys	201	93,219	137,998	174,788	144,723	28,716	54,120	47,866	48,252	52,765	125,490	244,153	....

Balance of Payments

		1994	1995	1996	1997	1998	1999	2000	2001	2002	2003	2004	2005
Overall Balance Excluding Reserves Assets, Use of Fund Credit, and Exceptional Financing *Expressed in Millions of US Dollars*													
All Countries	010	61,137	117,743	161,537	65,729	−21,298	123,374	159,199	124,035	224,002	465,385	616,053	....
Industrial Countries	110	35,432	78,133	76,936	23,752	−7,232	39,781	45,292	26,734	66,296	166,408	145,486	
United States	111	−5,350	9,747	−6,667	1,012	6,731	−8,727	295	4,927	3,692	−1,529	−2,804	−14,100
Canada	156	−392	2,711	5,498	−2,393	4,996	5,933	3,720	2,172	−185	−3,255	−2,836	1,335
Australia	193	−960	396	2,471	2,873	−2,040	6,705	−1,365	1,096	122	6,877	1,166	7,256
Japan	158	25,265	58,611	35,141	6,567	−6,164	76,256	48,955	40,487	46,134	187,153	160,854	22,325
New Zealand	196	733	384	1,772	−1,442	−486	188	−143	−187	1,086	783	629	....
Euro Area													
Austria	122	834	1,391	1,075	−3,053	3,482	−2,172	−746	−1,888	−1,723	−2,023	−1,849	−880
Belgium	124	....	....	....	....	....	....	....	....	−35	−1,725	−974	−1,736
Belgium-Luxembourg	126	219	243	593	1,056	−2,095	−1,867	−959	1,442	....	....	....	....
Finland	172	4,714	−372	−3,036	2,304	296	13	351	410	−113	−508	906	−197
France	132	2,448	712	239	5,940	19,815	−1,448	−2,433	−5,567	−3,965	1,274	4,108	−9,047
Germany	134	−2,036	7,226	−1,196	−3,757	4,016	−14,115	−5,222	−5,466	−1,979	−684	−1,807	−2,601
Greece	174	6,309	−23	4,215	−4,515		2,435	2,573	−5,699	1,863	−4,722	−3,277	−104
Ireland	178	−176	2,339	−52	−1,109	3,212	−1,973	−39	395	−292	−1,890	−1,435	−1,906
Italy	136	1,575	2,804	11,907	13,150	−21,472	−8,051	3,247	−588	3,169	1,115	−2,844	−1,030
Luxembourg	137	....	....	....	....	....	....	....	....	35	108	8	−48
Netherlands	138	500	−1,911	−5,695	−2,709	−2,339	−4,611	219	−351	−132	−817	−1,013	−2,448
Portugal	182	−1,430	−300	723	1,245	508	216	371	852	1,017	−6,455	−1,863	−1,741
Spain	184	36	−6,414	24,280	11,755	−14,354	−22,795	−2,880	−1,341	3,690	−15,489	−6,412	−1,919
Denmark	128	−1,851	2,498	3,563	6,532	−4,239	9,564	−5,521	3,317	5,546	4,674	−1,426	....
Iceland	176	−150	4	153	−44	32	86	−74	−48	61	307	202	71
Norway	142	253	575	6,470	−1,198	−6,384	5,984	3,686	−2,346	5,723	328	5,227	4,567
Sweden	144	2,381	−1,664	−6,386	−6,712	3,254	1,881	170	−1,048	665	2,076	−1,100	249
Switzerland	146	1,009	29	2,521	2,154	1,179	−2,685	−4,214	622	2,549	3,405	1,618	−17,691
United Kingdom	112	1,500	−853	−653	−3,904	−257	−1,036	5,300	−4,456	−635	−2,592	407	1,732
Developing Countries	200	25,705	39,610	84,601	41,977	−14,066	83,593	113,907	97,300	157,706	298,977	470,567	....
Africa	605	−10,057	−15,586	−7,695	−1,265	−13,597	−9,398	5,811	1,732	−7,528	4,013	24,592	....
Algeria	612	....	....	....	....	....	....	....	....	....	....	....	....
Angola	614	−1,028	−1,239	2,761	−604	−1,112	−43	318	−786	−356	263	340	
Botswana	616	135	207	511	635	44	394	367	170	61	171	....	....
Burundi	618	35	37	−35	−41	−78	−49	−95	−74	−47	−101	....	....
Cape Verde	624	22	−32	22	—	11	49	−28	−17	10	−56	....	....
Comoros	632	5	−10	....	....	....	....	....	....	....	....	....	....
Congo, Dem. Rep. of	636	....	....	....	....	....	....	....	....	....	....	....	....
Djibouti	611	1	−24	....	....	....	....	....	....	....	....	....	....
Eritrea	643	54	−3	57	120	−160	1	−64	....	....	....	....	
Ethiopia	644	—	−105	−465	−429	−360	−236	−190	−781	−1,134	−280	−949	....
Gambia, The	648	6	1	15	7	....	....	....	....	....	....	....	
Ghana	652	253	183	−25	77	28	−136	−369	−121	−14	504	−13	....
Guinea	656	−124	−72	−60	−131	−158	−76	−63	−117	−80	−229	−59	....
Kenya	664	62	−142	387	15	83	−34	−7	10	−16	425	9	....
Lesotho	666	121	98	117	141	116	−41	18	166	−178	−66	5	....
Liberia	668	....	....	....	....	....	....	....	....	....	....	....	
Madagascar	674	−276	−330	−94	−16	−299	−104	−160	−253	−283	−365	....	....
Malawi	676	14	−75	−122	16	−174	33	91	−68	90	....	....	....
Mauritania	682	−105	−6	4	28	43	....	....	....	....	....	....	
Mauritius	684	−44	109	48	−35	−65	190	231	−52	341	222	−27	....
Morocco	686	483	−1,895	−673	−988	−640	−69	−1,166	861	−52	154	736	....
Mozambique	688	−566	−387	−424	−478	−393	−326	−416	−485	−1,439	35	141	−197
Namibia	728	75	24	23	68	56	−149	−184	−359	−210	−329	−137	....
Nigeria	694	−1,938	−2,774	−761	15	−2,873	−3,538	3,089	223	−4,689	−1,260	8,491	....
Rwanda	714	6	53	20	31	−7	−72	−131	−70	−21	12	101	....
São Tomé & Príncipe	716	....	....	....	....	−6	−3	−5	−1	−7	....	....	....
Seychelles	718	−28	−32	−62	−45	−74	−99	−103	−47	−189	−122	−185	....
Sierra Leone	724	−59	1	−22	20	2	−16	10	30	−20	−29	5	....
Somalia	726	....	....	....	....	....	....	....	....	....	....	....	
South Africa	199	372	911	−1,761	4,366	45	1,916	480	−22	−322	−354	6,324	5,766
Sudan	732	19	63	38	18	73	115	124	−151	245	327	782	615
Swaziland	734	−4	24	−8	28	50	26	−6	−57	−26	−44	−19	....
Tanzania	738	−419	−359	−254	−297	−509	−79	−1	−51	327	395	200	....
Tunisia	744	527	97	442	386	−138	738	−205	288	140	383	977	....
Uganda	746	−62	−51	−9	−41	−41	−455	−464	91	−175	−3	123	82
Zambia	754	....	....	....	−932	−671	−654	−520	....	....	....	....	....
Zimbabwe	698	−86	....	....	....	....	....	....	....	....	....	....	
CEMAC													
Cameroon	622	−551	15	....	....	....	....	....	....	....	....	....	
Central African Rep.	626	13	....	....	....	....	....	....	....	....	....	....	
Chad	628	6	....	....	....	....	....	....	....	....	....	....	
Congo, Republic of	634	−155	−581	−1,316	−682	−1,029	−656	−243	−681	−713	−161	....	....
Equatorial Guinea	642	−18	−12	−5	....	....	....	....	....	....	....	....	
Gabon	646	−173	−228	−86	−112	−723	−436	280	−258	−222	−101	....	....
WAEMU													
Benin	638	18	−255	−149	−100	−87	−89	−20	−69	−261	−100	....	....
Burkina Faso	748	−7	....	....	....	....	....	−192	−187	....	....	....	....
Côte d'Ivoire	662	−20	−254	−848	−477	−650	−708	−608	−86	−278	−787	−781	....

Balance of Payments

Overall Balance

Excluding Reserves Assets, Use of Fund Credit, and Exceptional Financing

Expressed in Millions of US Dollars

		1994	1995	1996	1997	1998	1999	2000	2001	2002	2003	2004	2005
Africa(Cont.)													
Guinea-Bissau	654	−55	−41	−43	−15	....	....	....	−13	6	29	....	....
Mali	678	−65	−52	29	−10	−46	−13	63	−47	138	137	....	....
Niger	692	−76	−18	−13	−28	−16	−2	35	22	−12	−44	....	....
Senegal	722	23	−33	−201	−95	−248	−268	−231	−194	−247	−273	....	....
Togo	742	−97	−194	−25	13	−17	32	37	−2	30	−9	....	....
Asia*	505	**59,994**	**39,035**	**57,473**	**5,280**	**38,754**	**91,123**	**57,532**	**95,936**	**157,607**	**233,758**	**337,645**	....
Afghanistan, I.R. of	512	....	....	....	....	....	....	....	....	....	....	....	....
Bangladesh	513	691	−512	−414	−135	288	−189	−31	−144	497	889	503	....
Bhutan	514	....	....	....	....	....	....	....	....	....	....	....	....
Brunei Darussalam	516	....	....	....	....	....	....	....	....	....	....	....	....
Cambodia	522	36	26	72	34	−11	−11	21	16	101	—	102	....
China,P.R.: Mainland	924	30,453	22,469	31,705	35,857	6,248	8,652	10,693	47,447	75,217	116,586	206,153	207,342
China,P.R.:Hong Kong	532	....	....	....	....	−6,789	10,028	10,044	4,684	−2,377	994	3,286	1,378
China,P.R.: Macao	546	....	....	....	....	....	....	....	....	293	524	1,098	....
Fiji	819	23	93	78	−25	5	−45	....	....	....	....	....	....
French Terr.: French Polynesia	887	....	....	....	....	....	....	....	....	—	—	—	—
French Terr.: New Caledonia	839	....	....	....	....	....	....	....	....	—	—	—	—
India	534	10,391	−733	3,958	5,321	3,071	6,664	6,069	8,690	18,853	25,667	....	....
Indonesia	536	784	1,573	4,503	−8,137	−3,437	1,916	3,926	−15	4,958	3,647	321	−343
Kiribati	826	−6	....	....	....	....	....	....	....	....	....	....	....
Korea	542	4,614	7,039	1,416	−22,979	25,930	33,260	23,790	13,278	11,769	25,791	38,675	19,864
Lao People's Dem.Rep.	544	−178	−151	−158	−369	−254	−333	43	−4	....	....	....	....
Malaysia	548	−3,160	−1,763	2,513	−3,875	10,018	4,712	−1,009	1,000	3,657	10,181	21,875	....
Maldives	556	5	17	28	22	20	9	−4	−30	40	26	44	....
Mongolia	948	6	32	−87	7	−53	−19	−86	−79	13	−149	−46	....
Myanmar	518	46	−32	−25	31	60	−46	−23	180	45	39	94	....
Nepal	558	63	15	31	169	280	−223	−77	−300	−313	101	−102	....
Pakistan	564	1,343	−1,204	−780	538	−3,110	−2,516	−2,627	2,197	4,084	2,908	−1,351	475
Papua New Guinea	853	−170	−39	202	−177	−221	125	104	129	....	....	....	....
Philippines	566	2,327	1,235	4,338	−3,094	1,279	3,650	−376	296	−111	−79	−1,587	....
Samoa	862	−4	2	7	11	6	7	....	....	....	....	8	−1
Singapore	576	4,736	8,641	7,399	8,114	2,989	4,188	6,751	−867	1,327	6,675	12,087	....
Solomon Islands	813	−2	−1	18	9	17	−5	....	....	....	....	....	....
Sri Lanka	524	308	239	9	307	224	−95	−361	−308	−262	−365	−935	....
Thailand	578	4,169	7,159	2,167	−18,250	−2,696	1,388	−1,806	2,276	5,537	518	5,710	5,417
Tonga	866	....	....	....	....	....	....	....	2	7	....	....	....
Vanuatu	846	−6	5	−5	−2	−7	−23	−19	−10	−18	−9	−5	−9
Vietnam	582	....	....	278	328	37	1,310	110	206	448	2,146	935	....
*of which:													
Taiwan Prov.of China	528	4,622	−3,931	1,102	−728	4,827	18,593	2,477	17,353	33,664	37,092	26,595	20,056
Europe	170	**−13,654**	**18,940**	**−11,444**	**3,483**	**−17,550**	**9,835**	**17,146**	**7,869**	**28,129**	**44,805**	**73,017**	....
Albania	914	7	21	56	40	52	107	120	147	36	98	286	148
Armenia	911	−3	30	−45	50	1	5	17	17	63	73	33	187
Azerbaijan, Republic of	912	....	58	−85	139	−59	133	326	73	34	124	317	161
Belarus	913	−317	−78	−214	65	−319	20	125	−79	97	−81	185	518
Bosnia & Herzegovina	963	....	....	....	....	−360	−588	−264	467	−560	−72	210	334
Bulgaria	918	−216	445	−739	1,145	−94	96	137	373	715	730	1,730	714
Croatia	960	277	40	1,017	390	161	458	656	1,398	815	1,401	68	1,022
Cyprus	423	247	−363	−60	−47	−83	639	−8	611	389	−188	371	703
Czech Republic	935	3,474	7,453	−825	−1,758	1,890	1,639	844	1,787	6,618	442	263	3,879
Estonia	939	17	84	106	216	37	119	128	−42	69	169	271	386
Faroe Islands	816												
Georgia	915	....	....	....	−62	−103	−14	6	28	−190	−49	96	−16
Hungary	944	−475	5,384	−1,237	−175	951	2,335	1,052	−84	−1,792	336	1,981	4,904
Kazakhstan	916	....	299	159	548	−443	253	570	385	535	1,534	3,999	−1,945
Kyrgyz Republic	917	5	−81	−20	46	−57	−26	−33	−13	20	47	145	....
Latvia	941	57	−33	211	102	63	165	3	314	12	79	403	524
Lithuania	946	113	168	−5	224	427	−179	158	359	463	613	−104	718
Macedonia, FYR	962	....	....	−95	−119	43	142	279	86	−122	55	28	....
Malta	181	383	−307	−85	7	191	238	−222	255	288	144	−207	218
Moldova	921	13	−175	−103	−188	−353	−116	−5	−25	−47	−16	150	96
Poland	964	1,006	9,835	3,824	3,041	5,924	156	624	−427	648	1,206	801	8,146
Romania	968	171	−480	−582	1,459	−643	239	908	1,535	1,791	1,013	6,189	....
Russia	922	−19,113	−8,326	−17,218	−6,518	−21,378	−1,704	13,923	11,266	11,563	28,262	46,890	64,968
Slovak Republic	936	1,205	1,791	370	99	−478	777	920	....	3,684	1,508	....	....
Slovenia	961	647	240	590	1,288	158	−81	178	1,285	1,817	310	−297	206
Tajikistan	923	....	....	....	....	....	....	....	....	2	28	4	6
Turkey	186	203	4,660	4,544	3,343	441	5,354	−3,934	−12,888	−214	4,087	4,308	....
Turkmenistan	925	....	....	8	398	....	....	....	....	....	....	....	....
Ukraine	926	−1,200	−1,624	−603	−703	−3,457	−184	573	993	1,231	2,173	2,523	10,725
Uzbekistan	927	....	....	....	....	....	....	....	....	....	....	....	....
Middle East	405	**−837**	**5,337**	**11,476**	**10,860**	**−3,882**	**4,503**	**17,882**	**7,320**	**5,476**	**6,100**	**21,437**	....
Bahrain, Kingdom of	419	−48	169	−6	103	−17	25	200	123	35	44	158	....
Egypt	469	−1,164	−1,827	−1,725	−635	−1,387	−4,614	−2,030	−1,345	−804	−407	−584	....
Iran, I.R. of	429	908	2,786	2,441	−3,697	−991	451	1,083	....	....	....	....	....
Iraq	433	....	....	....	....	....	....	....	....	....	....	....	....
Israel	436	−2,111	379	1,078	6,943	−161	−127	321	388	−1,068	−195	−1,918	883
Jordan	439	−265	−171	−188	275	−536	752	693	−244	930	1,348	179	....

Balance of Payments

Overall Balance

Excluding Reserves Assets, Use of Fund Credit, and Exceptional Financing

Expressed in Millions of US Dollars

		1994	1995	1996	1997	1998	1999	2000	2001	2002	2003	2004	2005
Middle East(Cont.)													
Kuwait	443	50	−141	−25	6	258	918	2,268	2,905	−973	−1,824	626	....
Lebanon	446	....	....	....	....	....	....	....	....	−2,219	−4,002	−340	....
Libya	672	274	1,701	1,221	1,553	−426	688	6,458	1,293	278	3,016	5,732	....
Oman	449	−661	−432	187	533	−771	205	2,263	1,015	309	656	482	....
Qatar	453	....	....	....	....	....	....	....	....	....	....	....	....
Saudi Arabia	456	−146	1,215	5,741	647	−718	2,815	2,665	−1,909	2,736	1,608	4,498	−464
Syrian Arab Republic	463	566	839	987	449	434	259	814	1,020	1,050	695	417	....
United Arab Emirates	466	....	....	....	....	....	....	....	....	....	....	....	....
West Bank and Gaza	487	....	—	221	158	−53	−35	84	−39	....	....	....	....
Yemen, Republic of	474	−722	−528	−436	4,018	−581	74	1,594	553	425	330	373	434
Western Hemisphere	205	−9,741	−8,116	34,792	23,619	−17,791	−12,470	15,534	−15,558	−25,979	10,301	13,876	....
Argentina	213	−675	−2,311	3,258	3,331	4,090	2,013	−1,176	−21,405	−13,402	−9,077	−6,993	....
Aruba	314	−3	43	−26	−18	51	3	−15	83	40	−36	2	−22
Bahamas, The	313	9	−3	−8	57	119	65	−61	−31	60	110	183	....
Barbados	316	38	42	86	17	−6	36	178	222	−24	67	−157	....
Belize	339	−4	4	21	1	−14	25	52	−3	−8	−8	−32	....
Bolivia	218	−90	92	268	101	125	27	−39	−36	−343	−62	73	418
Brazil	223	6,598	12,969	8,682	−8,251	−16,302	−16,765	7,981	−3,418	−11,266	3,586	6,599	27,566
Chile	228	3,151	1,139	2,593	3,318	−2,191	−747	317	−599	185	−357	−191	1,711
Colombia	233	182	−4	1,729	278	−1,398	−312	862	1,225	139	−188	2,470	1,726
Costa Rica	238	−103	216	−69	−193	−504	230	−341	−136	−37	−226	−34	....
Dominican Republic	243	−511	146	−40	91	11	151	−48	515	−554	−548	545	672
Ecuador	248	−775	−1,459	−126	−521	−784	−944	−5,697	−258	−221	70	335	....
El Salvador	253	113	148	165	363	303	208	−45	−178	−123	316	−40	....
Guatemala	258	6	−152	214	230	235	−125	643	474	21	550	608	....
Guyana	336	−6	−43	12	−2	−13	22	40	26	15	10	45	....
Haiti	263	−50	138	−50	30	34	26	−57	−5	−68	−5	....	....
Honduras	268	−70	−41	−79	182	−155	−188	−157	−74	−19	−198	368	....
Jamaica	343	358	27	271	−170	44	−136	518	865	−242	−432	694	....
Mexico	273	−17,199	−16,312	10,997	19,162	3,170	4,250	7,126	7,314	7,359	9,817	4,104	6,965
Netherlands Antilles	353	−76	60	−72	−6	25	−75	−130	218	52	27	6	....
Nicaragua	278	−1,519	−964	−748	−293	−402	−395	−456	−492	−401	−470	−398	....
Panama	283	−362	−331	267	343	−105	191	−77	634	144	−269	−396	675
Paraguay	288	301	45	−47	−216	17	−301	−339	−50	−126	233	270	....
Peru	293	1,553	−590	880	2,055	−1,241	−862	−130	432	1,010	561	2,456	1,411
Suriname	366	34	123	−2	19	8	−4	10	78	−19	7	76	20
Trinidad and Tobago	369	186	84	238	194	80	162	441	502	116	409	....	....
Uruguay	298	109	228	152	400	355	−110	166	304	−3,897	958	304	....
Venezuela, Rep. Bol.	299	−944	−1,444	6,238	3,094	−3,405	1,058	5,958	−1,829	−4,428	5,454	2,155	5,425
ECCU													
Anguilla	312	—	—	1	2	2	2	—	4	2	....	....	....
Antigua and Barbuda	311	8	14	−11	3	9	10	−6	16	8	....	....	....
Dominica	321	−3	8	2	1	4	11	—	3	8	....	....	....
Grenada	328	5	6	—	7	4	5	7	6	31	....	....	....
Montserrat	351	2	1	—	3	14	−11	−4	2	2	....	....	....
St. Kitts and Nevis	361	−1	2	−1	4	11	3	−4	12	10	....	....	....
St. Lucia	362	−3	6	−6	5	10	4	5	12	5	....	....	....
St. Vincent & Grens	364	—	−1	—	1	8	4	14	9	−6	....	....	....
Memorandum Items													
Oil Exporting Ctys	999	−6,327	−3,615	17,115	−4,847	−13,869	3,522	38,450	13,027	6,656	23,609	43,407	....
Non-Oil Develop.Ctys	201	32,033	43,226	67,486	46,823	−197	80,071	75,456	84,273	151,050	275,368	427,160	....

Balance of Payments

		1994	1995	1996	1997	1998	1999	2000	2001	2002	2003	2004	2005

Exports of Goods and Services
As percent of GDP

		1994	1995	1996	1997	1998	1999	2000	2001	2002	2003	2004	2005
Industrial Countries													
United States	111	9.9	10.7	10.9	11.3	10.7	10.4	10.9	9.9	9.3	9.3	9.8	10.2
Canada	156	33.8	37.2	38.2	39.3	41.2	43.0	45.5	43.4	41.4	37.9	38.2	37.9
Australia	193	17.8	18.8	19.0	20.1	19.4	18.4	21.4	22.0	20.3	17.7	17.8	19.1
Japan	158	9.3	9.4	10.1	11.3	11.4	10.7	11.4	11.0	11.8	12.4	13.9	14.9
New Zealand	196	30.5	29.4	28.2	27.6	28.9	29.4	34.1	34.9	32.7	28.9	28.6	....
Euro Area													
Austria	122	36.0	37.5	38.9	42.3	43.5	44.9	49.5	51.9	52.5	51.8	54.7	55.7
Belgium	124	....	....	....	....	....	....	....	....	82.2	80.5	83.3	86.7
Belgium-Luxembourg	126	....	....	....	....	....	....	....	....				
Finland	172	35.4	36.6	37.2	38.7	38.4	37.6	43.0	40.0	38.7	37.4	38.2	39.1
France	132	22.4	23.1	23.2	25.7	26.3	26.2	28.5	28.1	27.0	25.6	25.8	26.1
Germany	134	23.1	23.9	24.9	27.4	28.7	29.0	33.0	34.5	35.3	35.6	38.0	40.3
Greece	174	14.5	13.2	12.3	12.2	....	19.9	25.4					
Ireland	178	69.3	74.5	75.2	76.9	110.5	86.5	95.7	96.5	92.9	83.2	82.5	78.6
Italy	136	23.3	26.3	25.2	25.8	25.5	24.5	27.1	27.1	25.7	24.5	25.3	26.5
Luxembourg	137	....	....	....	....	....	....	....	....	132.2	125.7	139.5	149.6
Netherlands	138	52.7	57.6	58.0	61.6	61.0	60.2	66.1	63.5	60.7	60.6	64.1	67.3
Portugal	182	28.8	30.8	30.2	31.3	31.8	28.1	29.9	29.2	28.5	28.6	29.3	29.1
Spain	184	21.4	22.4	23.7	26.3	27.3	26.7	29.0	28.5	27.3	26.4	26.1	25.6
Denmark	128	36.1	36.1	36.5	36.5	36.3	40.1	46.1	47.1	47.2	45.0	45.5	....
Iceland	176	35.3	36.3	37.0	36.4	35.0	33.8	34.1	39.5	38.5	34.9	34.6	31.6
Norway	142	38.2	37.9	40.8	41.4	37.6	39.3	46.6	45.4	41.2	40.3	42.6	45.0
Sweden	144	34.3	38.1	37.2	40.5	41.3	42.4	44.5	44.3	44.4	43.6	46.8	49.8
Switzerland	146	39.2	39.2	40.3	45.9	44.8	45.7	50.7	49.7	47.5	46.7	50.5	52.3
United Kingdom	112	26.6	28.3	29.4	28.7	26.9	26.5	28.0	27.4	26.3	25.5	25.2	26.1
Developing Countries													
Africa													
Algeria	612	....	....	....	....	....	....	....	....	....	....	....	....
Angola	614		76.8	82.2	67.3	56.3	86.3	89.7	75.4	85.7	....	....	....
Botswana	616	50.1	54.7	55.7	62.4	48.5	64.2	55.4	44.6	49.8	47.2	....	....
Burundi	618	8.9	12.9	5.9	9.5	7.7	7.4	7.5	6.7	5.9	7.2	....	....
Cape Verde	624	15.0	17.0	20.1	27.3	22.7	22.0	27.1	29.6	31.3	34.0	....	....
Comoros	632	20.5	20.4	....	....	....	....	....	....	....	....	....	....
Congo, Dem. Rep. of	636	....	....	....	....	....	....	....	....	....	....	....	....
Djibouti	611	....	....	....	....	....	....	....	....	....	....	....	....
Eritrea	643	....	....	....	....	....	....	....	....	....	....	....	....
Ethiopia	644	12.9	13.9	13.3	14.5	15.1	15.3	15.7	15.6	....	....	....	....
Gambia, The	648	71.5	....	....	....	....	....	....	....	....	....	....	....
Ghana	652	25.5	24.5	24.9	24.0	....	....	....	....	....	....	....	....
Guinea	656	....	....	....	....	....	....	....	....	....	....	....	....
Kenya	664	37.1	32.6	32.6	28.1	24.8	25.5	21.8	22.8	24.1	23.7	26.1	....
Lesotho	666	21.7	21.3	24.3	27.6	27.7	23.7	29.5	41.8	56.1	49.3	56.4	....
Liberia	668	....	....	....	....	....	....	....	....	....	....	....	....
Madagascar	674	22.0	23.7	20.1	22.2	22.2	24.5	30.6	28.2	16.1	20.6	....	....
Malawi	676	29.1	33.6	23.9	21.7	32.1	28.0	25.1	27.5	24.4	....	....	....
Mauritania	682	42.4	47.6	47.3	42.8	39.9	....	....	....	....	....	....	....
Mauritius	684	56.5	58.1	62.7	59.6	62.0	61.2	57.2	62.8	62.0	56.3	54.1	....
Morocco	686	24.9	27.3	26.3	28.5	27.8	30.1	31.4	33.0	33.8	32.5	33.2	....
Mozambique	688	15.4	18.0	16.5	14.7	13.4	14.2	18.0	26.4	28.2	27.2	....	....
Namibia	728	48.6	49.5	49.9	47.4	47.2	44.9	45.7	46.5	....	....	....	....
Nigeria	694	23.6	13.7	13.1	11.9	7.5	38.5	42.8	44.9	39.0	46.9	41.9	....
Rwanda	714	4.3	5.8	6.0	7.7	5.6	6.0	7.1	9.2	7.5	7.7	11.0	....
São Tomé & Príncipe	716	....	....	....	....	....	....	....	....	....	....	....	....
Seychelles	718	62.4	65.4	66.3	65.6	60.9	68.0	79.1	83.0	77.7	....	....	....
Sierra Leone	724	23.7	14.7	11.6	5.6	7.5	4.3	8.7	10.1	10.5	17.9	20.1	....
Somalia	726	....	....	....	....	....	....	....	....	....	....	....	....
South Africa	199	22.1	22.8	24.7	24.6	25.8	25.3	27.8	30.1	32.9	28.0	26.7	27.1
Sudan	732	10.3	8.2	8.2	6.2	....	....	....	....	....	....	....	....
Swaziland	734	78.9	74.7	71.9	73.4	78.6	73.1	81.6	90.7	95.9	96.4	....	....
Tanzania	738	20.8	24.1	21.1	15.7	13.7	13.2	14.2	16.1	16.3	18.1	19.3	....
Tunisia	744	44.2	44.3	41.6	43.2	42.8	42.3	44.3	47.7	45.3	43.9	47.2	....
Uganda	746	10.2	11.0	12.8	11.5	10.8	11.3	11.5	12.0	11.8	13.3	14.4	....
Zambia	754	....	....	....	31.2	....	....	....	....	....	....	....	....
Zimbabwe	698	34.0	....	....	....	....	....	....	....	....	....	....	....
CEMAC													
Cameroon	622	26.2	23.3	....	....	....	....	....	....	....	....	....	....
Central African Rep.	626	21.0	....	....	....	....	....	....	....	....	....	....	....
Chad	628	16.1	....	....	....	....	....	....	....	....	....	....	....
Congo, Republic of	634	58.0	64.9	68.7	75.8	75.5	71.9	81.0	78.2	80.7	43.4	....	....
Equatorial Guinea	642	54.6	56.6	65.8	....	....	....	....	....	....	....	....	....
Gabon	646	61.7	59.4	62.2	60.2	46.1	63.9	70.9	64.2	54.3	55.3	....	....
WAEMU													
Benin	638	33.8	28.3	27.7	23.8	22.7	24.0	22.4	20.8	21.4	20.0	....	....
Burkina Faso	748	12.8	....	....	....	....	....	9.2	9.2	....	....	....	....
Côte d'Ivoire	662	44.4	43.4	46.2	43.0	40.8	41.8	41.2	42.1	50.1	45.9	47.7	....
Guinea-Bissau	654	6.1	6.6	8.5	20.3	....	....	....	33.8	29.9	29.7	....	....
Mali	678	22.9	19.5	18.8	23.7	21.8	23.1	24.1	28.9	31.6	26.8	....	....

Balance of Payments

Exports of Goods and Services
As percent of GDP

		1994	1995	1996	1997	1998	1999	2000	2001	2002	2003	2004	2005
Africa(Cont.)													
Niger	692	18.1	16.9	18.2	16.7	17.8	15.9	19.4	18.6	16.2	17.2	....	....
Senegal	722	31.7	30.9	27.0	27.3	27.7	28.1	27.9	28.8	28.5	26.5	....	....
Togo	742	40.6	30.2	33.8	30.2	31.3	29.2	31.9	32.9	35.6	38.5	....	....
Asia*													
Afghanistan, I.R. of	512	....	....	....	....	....	....	....	....	....	....	....	....
Bangladesh	513	10.5	11.7	11.6	13.4	13.7	13.9	15.9	15.0	14.7	15.6	16.5	....
Bhutan	514	....	....	....	....	....	....	....	....	....	....	....	....
Brunei Darussalam	516	....	....	....	....	....	....	....	....	....	....	....	....
Cambodia	522	19.5	28.2	23.0	26.1	94.4	48.8	65.1	75.8	55.0	55.6	61.6	....
China,P.R.: Mainland	924	22.0	21.0	20.9	22.9	21.7	22.1	25.9	25.1	28.0	33.0	33.9	37.6
China,P.R.:Hong Kong	532	....	....	....	....	125.6	128.8	144.1	139.3	149.6	171.1	190.2	197.9
China,P.R.: Macao	546	....	....	....	....	....	....	....	....	104.3	103.3	105.3	....
Fiji	819	56.1	54.4	60.9	56.8	56.4	57.2	....	....	....	....	....	....
French Terr.: French Polynesia	887	....	....	....	....	....	....	....	....	....	....	....	....
French Terr.: New Caledonia	839	....	....	....	....	....	....	....	....	....	....	....	....
India	534	9.8	10.4	10.6	10.7	10.8	11.3	12.8	12.9	14.0	14.0	....	....
Indonesia	536	25.5	26.2	25.0	29.3	57.5	39.9	42.8	38.3	32.9	29.4	32.7	35.3
Kiribati	826	....	....	....	....	....	....	....	....	....	....	....	....
Korea	542	26.4	28.6	27.5	32.0	45.7	38.6	40.4	37.5	35.1	37.9	44.0	42.5
Lao People's Dem.Rep.	544	25.4	22.9	22.8	24.3	37.9	32.2	29.2	27.2	....	....	....	....
Malaysia	548	88.9	93.8	91.3	93.1	115.6	121.3	124.4	116.4	113.6	114.1	121.2	....
Maldives	556	76.6	79.7	81.9	79.1	79.0	73.7	73.2	74.3	77.3	84.3	106.7	....
Mongolia	948	41.6	38.7	39.4	54.5	51.7	54.0	59.4	56.2	59.1	61.8	72.6	....
Myanmar	518	1.4	1.2	1.0	.8	.7	.5	.5	.6	.3	.2	.2	....
Nepal	558	23.5	24.4	26.1	26.5	23.0	25.3	24.0	20.7	17.3	18.0	18.2	....
Pakistan	564	17.4	17.3	17.9	16.9	15.6	15.2	14.3	15.8	16.6	17.8	16.9	17.3
Papua New Guinea	853	52.8	61.8	57.5	51.9	55.6	63.3	66.8	68.4	....	....	....	....
Philippines	566	31.6	36.2	40.4	49.0	56.7	51.2	54.4	48.3	48.7	48.5	49.4	....
Samoa	862	23.6	32.2	33.3	32.7	37.0	34.6	....	....	....	....	29.4	....
Singapore	576	171.3	187.5	180.9	174.9	172.2	182.8	192.8	190.1	190.6	208.2	221.9	....
Solomon Islands	813	60.1	57.6	53.2	55.5	54.9	58.1	....	....	....	....	....	....
Sri Lanka	524	33.8	35.4	35.0	36.5	35.3	35.5	39.1	39.2	36.1	35.9	36.3	....
Thailand	578	38.9	41.8	39.3	48.0	58.9	58.2	66.6	65.9	64.2	65.7	70.5	73.5
Tonga	866	....	....	....	....	....	....	20.2	28.8	....	....	....	
Vanuatu	846	48.1	46.3	50.1	48.1	58.1	56.0	64.2	59.3	44.2	45.6	....	....
Vietnam	582	....	....	38.5	43.6	44.0	48.9	55.0	54.6	56.1	59.3	....	....
*of which:													
Taiwan Prov.of China	528	....	....	....	....	....	....	....	....	....	....	....	....
Europe													
Albania	914	11.3	12.3	12.4	10.3	10.8	15.8	19.0	20.5	20.5	20.8	....	....
Armenia	911	35.3	23.3	23.1	20.2	19.0	20.8	23.4	25.5	29.4	32.2	27.5	27.3
Azerbaijan, Republic of	912	....	32.5	25.0	29.0	22.7	28.0	40.2	41.5	42.8	42.0	48.8	66.3
Belarus	913	....	50.0	46.2	55.6	46.6	52.7	73.3	68.6	63.8	64.9	67.7	61.4
Bosnia & Herzegovina	963	....	....	....	....	27.3	26.5	33.4	32.5	29.1	31.2	....	....
Bulgaria	918	53.5	51.7	63.2	60.6	47.0	44.7	55.6	53.2	51.8	53.7	57.0	60.0
Croatia	960	48.4	35.8	39.6	39.4	39.4	40.8	46.9	48.6	46.0	50.3	49.9	49.1
Cyprus	423	48.6	50.2	51.0	51.7	49.6	51.5	55.0	56.0	51.4	47.9	47.9	....
Czech Republic	935	51.4	51.0	48.6	51.5	54.2	55.3	63.2	65.5	60.5	61.8	71.1	71.6
Estonia	939	72.1	68.5	62.9	73.0	75.2	70.8	87.3	83.2	74.1	74.2	78.5	83.5
Faroe Islands	816	....	....	....	....	....	....	....	....	....	....	....	....
Georgia	915	....	....	....	16.4	18.4	19.5	21.9	25.3	29.3	31.9	31.4	....
Hungary	944	25.9	44.2	48.3	54.8	61.8	64.2	73.7	72.8	64.4	62.7	66.4	67.9
Kazakhstan	916	....	34.7	34.6	36.4	32.1	39.4	56.8	47.3	50.2	50.1	52.3	54.9
Kyrgyz Republic	917	33.6	30.0	30.8	38.2	36.4	42.2	41.8	36.7	39.9	38.8	42.6	....
Latvia	941	41.5	42.7	46.8	46.8	47.1	40.0	41.2	41.2	40.6	41.8	43.7	47.3
Lithuania	946	55.3	49.9	52.2	53.1	45.7	39.1	44.6	49.8	53.0	51.4	52.3	58.1
Macedonia, FYR.	962	....	....	29.5	35.7	40.2	39.8	45.6	40.7	36.0	36.2	....	....
Malta	181	96.0	92.4	85.3	75.3	77.9	81.7	91.7	79.9	82.3	78.6	75.4	70.6
Moldova	921	....	61.3	54.9	54.8	46.8	52.1	49.8	49.7	52.8	53.5	51.9	52.4
Poland	964	25.3	25.7	23.8	25.2	25.0	22.9	27.0	27.0	28.7	33.3	37.8	37.4
Romania	968	23.9	26.5	27.3	28.2	22.6	27.7	32.7	33.4	35.4	34.7	35.9	....
Russia	922	27.2	29.7	26.3	24.9	32.0	43.2	44.1	37.0	35.0	35.3	34.6	35.1
Slovak Republic	936	58.0	56.5	52.3	55.7	58.7	59.3	69.1	....	70.4	76.5	....	....
Slovenia	961	60.1	51.1	51.2	53.0	52.8	48.7	55.4	57.2	57.4	56.0	60.1	64.8
Tajikistan	923	....	....	....	....	....	....	....	....	....	....	....	....
Turkey	186	22.3	21.6	25.1	27.4	27.2	24.7	25.7	34.6	29.8	29.3	30.1	....
Turkmenistan	925	....	....	....	....	....	....	....	....	....	....	....	....
Ukraine	926	45.3	46.2	45.7	40.6	42.1	54.0	62.4	55.5	55.1	57.8	63.6	53.5
Uzbekistan	927	....	....	....	....	....	....	....	....	....	....	....	....
Middle East													
Bahrain, Kingdom of	419	79.7	82.0	88.0	79.1	64.6	78.9	90.0	83.3	82.3	83.1	83.4	....
Egypt	469	23.4	22.0	20.8	19.6	14.8	16.3	17.2	17.8	19.5	28.1	33.9	....
Iran, I.R. of	429	26.6	17.8	16.4	11.7	7.9	8.9	9.0	....	....	....	....	....
Iraq	433	....	....	....	....	....	....	....	....	....	....	....	....
Israel	436	31.0	30.7	29.9	30.5	31.4	36.1	39.7	35.1	37.2	38.8	44.1	45.9
Jordan	439	49.1	51.7	52.9	49.3	45.8	43.4	41.9	42.2	48.1	48.4	....	....
Kuwait	443	51.1	52.4	52.3	52.9	43.9	45.8	57.8	52.6	44.6	54.0	60.2	....
Lebanon	446	....	....	....	....	....	....	....	....	....	....	....	....
Libya	672	27.1	29.4	28.5	26.7	19.7	24.1	39.9	39.3	53.6	61.6	57.8	....

Balance of Payments

		1994	1995	1996	1997	1998	1999	2000	2001	2002	2003	2004	2005
Exports of Goods and Services													
As percent of GDP													
Middle East(Cont.)													
Oman	449	43.0	44.0	49.8	50.0	41.9	48.7	59.2	57.9	57.5	56.5	57.2	....
Qatar	453	....	....	....	....	....	....	....	....	....	....	....	....
Saudi Arabia	456	34.2	37.6	40.3	39.4	29.8	34.8	43.7	39.9	41.2	46.1	52.7	58.3
Syrian Arab Republic	463	11.5	11.3	9.7	8.5	6.8	7.5	8.5	8.8	9.1	7.6	....	....
United Arab Emirates	466	....	....	....	....	....	....	....	....	....	....	....	....
West Bank and Gaza	487	....	....	....	....	....	....	....	....	....	....	....	....
Yemen, Republic of	474	7.5	17.1	31.4	36.5	27.0	35.3	42.1	36.9	36.9	37.5	....	....
Western Hemisphere													
Argentina	213	7.5	9.7	10.4	10.6	10.5	9.9	11.0	11.6	28.4	26.4	26.0	....
Aruba	314	....	150.9	181.6	166.1	123.5	134.2	190.2	179.7	130.0	154.2	185.9	....
Bahamas, The	313	56.0	57.6	....	....	....	....	....	....	....	....	....	....
Barbados	316	57.6	59.4	60.8	56.6	54.4	52.6	53.1	52.1	49.8	....	....	....
Belize	339	47.8	48.0	48.2	50.6	47.4	56.7	52.9	49.1	50.4	50.4	48.9	....
Bolivia	218	19.7	18.4	17.7	17.8	15.9	15.8	17.5	18.7	19.7	24.2	29.4	32.2
Brazil	223	9.0	7.5	6.8	7.3	7.5	10.3	10.7	13.3	15.2	16.5	18.1	16.9
Chile	228	25.6	27.1	26.7	26.3	25.5	28.8	31.0	32.7	33.5	36.2	40.3	41.4
Colombia	233	13.3	13.3	13.5	13.3	13.6	16.2	18.8	18.3	17.5	19.8	20.1	19.9
Costa Rica	238	31.4	38.0	40.8	41.7	48.8	52.2	48.6	41.6	42.4	46.8	46.4	....
Dominican Republic	243	38.1	37.3	36.7	37.3	37.2	37.7	38.3	34.1	33.0	45.8	43.5	28.9
Ecuador	248	....	....	....	....	....	....	....	....	....	....	....	....
El Salvador	253	20.2	21.5	21.3	26.2	25.4	25.5	27.9	26.0	26.6	26.8	27.2	....
Guatemala	258	17.3	19.3	17.7	17.9	18.0	19.0	20.0	18.6	17.0	16.6	16.9	....
Guyana	336	107.1	101.2	101.0	98.6	95.7	98.7	94.3	92.3	91.2	89.5	94.9	....
Haiti	263	3.3	8.2	6.4	11.7	12.6	13.0	13.7	12.7	13.1	16.6	....	....
Honduras	268	39.2	41.3	47.1	46.5	46.1	41.1	41.3	37.9	38.1	38.8	40.7	....
Jamaica	343	62.1	58.6	50.9	45.7	43.7	44.9	45.5	41.3	38.0	43.0	44.2	....
Mexico	273	16.9	31.2	32.1	30.3	30.7	30.8	31.0	27.6	26.8	27.8	29.6	29.8
Netherlands Antilles	353	....	....	....	....	....	....	....	....	....	....	....	....
Nicaragua	278	16.4	20.8	21.8	26.6	26.4	25.7	28.0	27.1	28.4	31.5	36.3	....
Panama	283	87.9	87.9	79.5	83.2	75.2	62.3	67.4	67.6	61.9	58.6	62.4	....
Paraguay	288	48.2	53.3	45.7	41.4	48.6	37.3	37.9	35.7	43.4	45.7	....	....
Peru	293	12.2	12.3	13.1	14.2	13.3	14.9	16.0	15.8	16.3	17.7	21.2	24.8
Suriname	366	60.5	74.9	57.9	53.2	44.7	47.5	55.1	65.0	42.8	53.6	83.4	....
Trinidad and Tobago	369	42.5	52.5	48.9	52.2	48.5	50.2	59.4	55.3	51.4	56.0	....	....
Uruguay	298	18.6	18.2	18.8	19.4	18.5	17.0	18.2	17.6	21.8	27.6	30.3	....
Venezuela, Rep. Bol	299	30.3	26.8	35.8	29.3	20.9	22.8	29.6	22.8	29.9	33.6	36.6	....
ECCU													
Anguilla	312	102.4	93.0	90.6	94.0	107.0	83.1	80.2	84.3	78.8	....	....	....
Antigua and Barbuda	311	87.3	81.4	74.5	76.3	75.1	73.2	70.4	....	....	....	....	....
Dominica	321	46.7	50.6	51.6	56.0	58.4	58.6	53.3	45.0	48.0	....	....	....
Grenada	328	48.3	44.8	44.7	44.1	47.3	57.6	57.4	....	....	....	....	....
Montserrat	351	55.1	61.3	116.2	54.0	37.8	60.8	48.7	43.0	40.6	....	....	....
St. Kitts and Nevis	361	56.8	51.6	52.1	50.9	50.5	47.9	45.6	45.0	44.2	....	....	....
St. Lucia	362	65.1	68.7	62.1	62.0	61.8	54.9	56.1	51.5	48.8	....	....	....
St. Vincent & Grens	364	46.6	51.3	53.3	50.1	49.7	53.1	53.1	50.3	49.0	....	....	....

Balance of Payments

		1994	1995	1996	1997	1998	1999	2000	2001	2002	2003	2004	2005
							Imports of Goods and Services						
							As percent of GDP						
Industrial Countries													
United States	111	11.3	12.0	12.2	12.6	12.6	13.3	14.8	13.5	13.4	13.8	15.1	16.0
Canada	156	32.7	34.0	34.3	37.4	39.4	39.4	39.8	37.8	37.0	34.3	34.2	34.1
Australia	193	19.1	20.1	19.1	19.7	21.2	21.0	22.5	21.5	21.5	20.5	20.8	21.1
Japan	158	7.3	8.0	9.7	10.2	9.5	9.1	9.9	10.3	10.5	10.7	11.8	13.3
New Zealand	196	28.6	28.2	27.8	27.2	28.6	30.3	33.0	31.9	31.6	28.4	29.2	....
Euro Area													
Austria	122	36.3	38.4	40.0	43.8	44.1	45.7	50.1	51.6	50.6	50.6	52.8	53.0
Belgium	124	....	....	....	....	....	....	....	....	77.6	76.5	79.6	85.1
Belgium-Luxembourg	126	....	....	....	....	....	....	....	....	....	....	....	....
Finland	172	29.5	28.8	29.7	30.6	29.6	29.0	33.6	31.5	30.2	30.7	32.6	35.2
France	132	20.6	21.3	21.2	22.7	23.5	23.8	27.3	26.0	25.3	24.5	25.7	27.2
Germany	134	22.9	23.5	24.1	26.4	27.5	28.4	32.9	32.7	31.1	31.6	33.0	35.3
Greece	174	20.4	21.0	20.6	21.1	....	28.5	36.0	....	....	....	....	....
Ireland	178	59.7	63.5	64.2	64.8	96.0	73.3	83.0	81.8	76.2	67.7	67.6	65.9
Italy	136	19.7	22.2	20.3	21.8	22.2	22.5	26.1	25.7	24.8	24.0	24.5	26.4
Luxembourg	137	....	....	....	....	....	....	....	....	105.5	101.3	112.7	119.0
Netherlands	138	47.2	51.7	52.1	55.3	55.4	55.7	62.0	59.3	56.7	54.0	56.3	59.1
Portugal	182	36.9	37.8	37.9	40.2	42.1	38.3	41.1	39.1	36.4	35.1	36.9	37.7
Spain	184	21.4	22.6	23.2	25.7	27.6	28.6	32.0	30.8	29.2	28.5	29.9	30.7
Denmark	128	30.2	31.8	31.4	33.1	34.4	35.4	40.3	40.6	41.5	38.8	40.4	....
Iceland	176	30.2	32.6	36.4	35.7	39.4	38.5	41.0	40.3	36.8	38.0	40.2	45.0
Norway	142	32.0	31.7	31.7	33.1	35.8	31.9	29.3	28.4	27.4	26.8	28.4	27.6
Sweden	144	30.3	32.4	31.1	34.0	35.7	37.2	39.5	38.5	37.6	36.8	38.5	42.0
Switzerland	146	34.2	34.6	36.1	40.6	40.1	40.3	44.0	44.2	40.3	39.5	40.8	45.4
United Kingdom	112	27.3	28.8	29.8	28.6	27.8	28.2	30.0	30.1	29.3	28.3	28.6	30.0
Developing Countries													
Africa													
Algeria	612	....	....	....	....	....	....	....	....	....	....		
Angola	614	—	70.5	68.4	68.0	72.5	92.7	62.9	74.9	71.1	....	....	
Botswana	616	40.8	46.3	42.4	48.7	52.5	51.4	42.8	35.6	38.2	35.6		
Burundi	618	24.9	25.9	15.9	13.5	18.5	15.2	21.2	22.1	23.6	29.4		
Cape Verde	624	56.2	60.0	55.0	58.2	58.9	59.5	60.4	62.3	67.6	67.2		
Comoros	632	46.9	46.0	....	....	....	....	....	....	....	....		
Congo, Dem. Rep. of	636	....	....	....	....	....	....	....	....	....	....		
Djibouti	611	....	....	....	....	....	....	....	....	....	....		
Eritrea	643	....	....	....	....	....	....	....	....	....	....		
Ethiopia	644	23.8	26.3	22.6	20.7	28.8	30.2	25.6	34.3	....	....		
Gambia, The	648	82.5	....	....	....	....	....	....	....	....	....		
Ghana	652	36.8	32.8	34.3	37.9	....	....	....	....	....	....		
Guinea	656	....	....	....	....	....	....	....	....	....	....		
Kenya	664	34.4	39.1	37.3	35.6	32.4	31.2	29.6	30.7	28.8	28.1	31.8	....
Lesotho	666	104.7	112.2	111.8	106.6	103.2	91.0	89.6	95.4	117.1	101.4	102.2	
Liberia	668	....	....	....	....	....	....	....	....	....	....		
Madagascar	674	29.4	31.2	25.1	30.5	30.2	32.2	39.2	32.4	22.8	30.2		
Malawi	676	52.6	47.2	33.9	34.5	37.2	42.8	36.1	37.5	41.1	....		
Mauritania	682	53.1	48.1	53.4	48.2	47.9	....	....	....	....	....		
Mauritius	684	65.2	60.7	63.5	64.3	63.6	66.1	59.1	58.5	59.0	55.1	56.4	....
Morocco	686	30.9	34.0	29.6	31.8	31.9	33.9	37.6	36.2	36.9	36.5	39.7	....
Mozambique	688	56.2	46.1	35.3	29.4	28.6	36.8	38.9	43.7	50.5	44.9	....	....
Namibia	728	57.6	59.9	60.5	59.1	56.1	54.5	49.0	52.4	....	....	....	
Nigeria	694	22.9	14.2	8.7	10.6	10.2	33.5	24.5	36.0	34.0	29.1	25.0	....
Rwanda	714	63.3	29.1	26.5	25.5	21.1	23.5	23.5	25.1	24.7	23.7	27.1	
São Tomé & Príncipe	716	....	....	....	....	....	....	....	....	....	....		
Seychelles	718	55.1	62.5	75.7	76.6	76.7	84.5	78.7	95.7	82.6	....		
Sierra Leone	724	32.5	29.9	35.5	14.1	19.0	28.0	39.3	34.3	35.9	40.9	31.9	....
Somalia	726	....	....	....	....	....	....	....	....	....	....		
South Africa	199	19.8	22.1	23.2	23.4	24.5	22.7	24.9	26.2	29.2	26.2	27.4	28.5
Sudan	732	21.9	14.9	18.9	15.7	....	....	....	....	....	....		
Swaziland	734	91.0	93.4	97.9	91.3	99.6	91.6	97.1	105.9	96.1	92.6	....	
Tanzania	738	40.2	40.7	33.4	25.5	28.1	25.6	22.6	24.4	22.6	26.9	28.3	....
Tunisia	744	48.4	48.9	43.5	46.0	46.1	44.5	47.9	52.1	49.5	47.6	50.0	....
Uganda	746	22.3	24.6	27.1	25.9	29.9	23.4	24.5	25.5	26.6	27.0	27.3	
Zambia	754	....	....	....	34.1	....	....	....	....	....	....		
Zimbabwe	698	36.5	....	....	....	....	....	....	....	....	....		
CEMAC													
Cameroon	622	22.7	18.4	....	....	....	....	....	....	....	....		
Central African Rep.	626	28.7	....	....	....	....	....	....	....	....	....		
Chad	628	34.9	....	....	....	....	....	....	....	....	....		
Congo, Republic of	634	90.9	63.6	60.0	60.2	72.0	58.6	36.8	54.6	53.2	27.9	....	
Equatorial Guinea	642	50.7	117.9	174.2	....	....	....	....	....	....	....		
Gabon	646	38.3	35.8	32.7	36.5	46.6	40.8	33.6	35.9	35.3	31.1	....	
WAEMU													
Benin	638	39.6	41.2	31.7	33.0	31.1	34.2	30.0	29.8	31.6	30.2	....	....
Burkina Faso	748	22.7	....	....	....	....	....	25.6	23.0	....	....		
Côte d'Ivoire	662	34.2	38.1	37.5	35.3	34.5	33.6	34.2	34.4	34.2	35.7	38.6	....
Guinea-Bissau	654	12.8	20.0	25.7	31.7	....	....	....	46.2	42.2	42.5	....	....
Mali	678	43.5	36.4	33.4	33.0	31.1	33.1	34.7	38.1	33.3	34.3	....	....

Balance of Payments

Balance of Payments

		1994	1995	1996	1997	1998	1999	2000	2001	2002	2003	2004	2005
Imports of Goods and Services													
As percent of GDP													
Africa(Cont.)													
Niger	692	29.7	24.1	25.4	24.4	26.8	23.5	27.6	27.1	25.7	28.2	....	....
Senegal	722	39.1	37.3	32.8	33.6	34.3	35.1	37.2	37.8	38.9	38.5	....	....
Togo	742	49.9	43.6	46.8	41.3	44.3	39.3	45.3	49.6	50.1	53.3	....	....
Asia*													
Afghanistan, I.R. of	512	....	....	....	....	....	....	....	....	....	....	....	....
Bangladesh	513	16.0	20.0	18.7	19.0	18.6	20.0	21.3	21.3	19.5	21.7	23.4	....
Bhutan	514	....	....	....	....	....	....	....	....	....	....	....	....
Brunei Darussalam	516	....	....	....	....	....	....	....	....	....	....	....	....
Cambodia	522	31.7	39.9	36.7	36.4	136.3	67.2	85.0	95.0	62.8	64.2	69.6	....
China,P.R.: Mainland	924	20.6	19.3	18.8	18.2	17.1	19.1	23.2	22.8	25.2	30.5	31.3	32.0
China,P.R.:Hong Kong	532	....	....	....	....	125.1	123.6	139.6	134.6	141.3	161.9	181.3	185.5
China,P.R.: Macao	546	....	....	....	....	....	....	....	....	63.7	61.2	58.0	....
Fiji	819	59.5	58.3	59.3	57.8	58.5	56.1	....	....	....	....	....	....
French Terr.: French Polynesia	887	....	....	....	....	....	....	....	....	....	....	....	....
French Terr.: New Caledonia	839	....	....	....	....	....	....	....	....	....	....	....	....
India	534	11.7	13.2	14.2	13.9	14.1	13.8	15.6	14.7	15.0	15.9	....	....
Indonesia	536	24.7	26.9	26.1	29.1	46.1	30.7	33.9	30.8	26.3	24.0	28.2	31.6
Kiribati	826	....	....	....	....	....	....	....	....	....	....	....	....
Korea	542	27.5	30.0	31.3	33.2	33.3	32.4	37.7	35.5	33.9	35.5	39.7	39.9
Lao People's Dem.Rep.	544	43.5	42.1	41.1	40.7	46.9	39.8	33.4	31.9	....	....	....	....
Malaysia	548	90.5	97.8	89.9	92.2	93.5	96.3	104.5	98.0	96.3	93.1	99.9	....
Maldives	556	72.4	78.3	78.5	78.9	76.0	78.4	72.3	73.0	71.2	77.3	112.4	....
Mongolia	948	42.8	39.7	47.1	48.9	64.2	66.8	74.7	73.2	79.0	80.2	84.2	....
Myanmar	518	2.0	1.9	1.6	1.4	1.1	.7	.6	.5	.3	.2	.2	....
Nepal	558	36.1	38.5	39.6	39.6	31.5	34.0	33.5	31.0	30.7	32.3	32.5	....
Pakistan	564	23.3	24.1	26.6	22.7	20.3	19.7	17.2	18.0	17.2	18.3	23.2	26.4
Papua New Guinea	853	35.3	39.3	44.5	48.9	49.7	52.4	50.6	52.0	....	....	....	....
Philippines	566	40.6	45.0	49.9	61.3	60.8	48.3	52.5	52.2	49.5	57.5	58.2	....
Samoa	862	49.2	57.6	55.4	57.4	56.2	61.1	....	....	....	....	54.3	....
Singapore	576	156.4	171.5	165.7	162.0	151.4	165.7	177.9	172.0	169.1	176.3	192.4	....
Solomon Islands	813	77.6	63.5	58.5	71.4	59.8	52.0	....	....	....	....	....	....
Sri Lanka	524	45.6	45.9	43.9	43.6	41.1	43.3	49.6	45.3	42.8	42.1	45.4	....
Thailand	578	44.1	49.0	45.9	48.0	43.4	45.9	58.4	59.9	58.1	59.5	66.3	75.7
Tonga	866	....	....	....	....	....	....	....	70.2	74.3	....	....	....
Vanuatu	846	50.4	48.3	48.0	44.9	52.4	62.4	60.1	64.3	54.8	55.2	....	....
Vietnam	582	....	....	50.0	50.6	49.6	47.4	55.6	54.9	61.2	67.6	....	....
*of which:													
Taiwan Prov.of China	528	....	....	....	....	....	....	....	....	....	....	....	....
Europe													
Albania	914	37.6	33.7	36.9	37.4	34.4	32.0	40.6	43.4	46.6	46.2	....	....
Armenia	911	67.0	56.4	55.6	58.1	53.6	49.8	50.5	46.2	46.6	50.1	42.3	40.5
Azerbaijan, Republic of	912	....	53.4	56.0	53.0	54.5	41.9	38.4	37.3	50.0	65.5	72.7	55.7
Belarus	913	....	54.6	50.2	61.6	53.3	54.8	77.6	72.7	67.1	68.7	73.5	60.4
Bosnia & Herzegovina	963	....	....	....	....	98.4	90.1	87.8	87.0	84.8	85.7	....	....
Bulgaria	918	53.5	49.6	60.1	55.3	47.0	50.6	60.9	61.9	58.9	63.4	68.5	77.2
Croatia	960	47.1	48.4	49.7	57.5	48.7	49.2	52.1	54.4	56.7	58.1	57.3	56.3
Cyprus	423	47.9	50.5	54.0	53.6	53.1	50.7	56.4	54.4	52.4	47.7	51.0	....
Czech Republic	935	53.7	54.4	54.7	57.1	55.4	56.5	66.2	68.0	62.6	64.1	71.6	69.6
Estonia	939	82.5	76.1	73.7	83.8	85.1	76.2	90.7	85.4	81.4	82.2	86.9	89.9
Faroe Islands	816	....	....	....	....	....	....	....	....	....	....	....	....
Georgia	915	....	....	....	40.2	37.1	38.8	39.0	40.0	42.4	46.5	47.9	....
Hungary	944	34.5	44.6	47.9	53.9	63.3	66.9	77.5	74.3	66.7	67.2	69.2	69.1
Kazakhstan	916	....	35.5	37.6	39.0	37.1	38.4	49.2	49.2	50.3	44.6	43.6	45.7
Kyrgyz Republic	917	44.9	48.7	56.5	46.2	56.8	56.5	47.9	37.7	44.9	45.5	51.3	....
Latvia	941	40.1	44.8	54.2	54.6	59.6	49.5	48.7	51.1	50.7	54.6	59.6	62.3
Lithuania	946	61.4	61.0	61.8	63.4	57.2	49.2	50.9	55.2	58.5	57.3	59.3	65.1
Macedonia, FYR	962	....	....	40.2	50.0	56.3	52.2	63.5	56.6	57.8	54.6	....	....
Malta	181	106.8	105.5	98.7	82.6	83.4	86.7	101.4	85.0	81.2	82.6	82.4	81.3
Moldova	921	....	69.8	73.7	74.3	72.4	67.4	75.4	73.5	77.9	87.2	81.7	93.9
Poland	964	23.0	24.3	26.3	29.5	30.0	31.0	33.4	30.6	31.9	35.7	39.6	37.7
Romania	968	25.9	31.9	35.4	34.9	30.3	32.0	37.9	41.1	41.1	42.2	45.1	....
Russia	922	23.6	26.4	22.1	22.7	27.5	27.0	23.5	24.2	24.4	23.9	22.3	21.6
Slovak Republic	936	53.3	54.9	63.1	65.2	69.2	64.5	71.4	....	77.4	77.8	....	....
Slovenia	961	57.9	53.0	52.1	53.7	54.2	52.8	58.9	57.8	55.9	56.0	61.3	65.2
Tajikistan	923	....	....	....	....	....	....	....	....	....	....	....	....
Turkey	186	20.1	23.7	27.1	29.6	27.5	26.2	31.0	30.9	29.5	30.8	33.8	....
Turkmenistan	925	....	....	....	....	....	....	....	....	....	....	....	....
Ukraine	926	49.0	49.4	48.2	43.6	45.0	48.2	57.4	53.9	50.7	55.2	56.0	52.7
Uzbekistan	927	....	....	....	....	....	....	....	....	....	....	....	....
Middle East													
Bahrain, Kingdom of	419	74.0	70.5	76.2	69.5	63.9	63.0	64.4	60.5	66.6	64.6	64.2	....
Egypt	469	30.3	28.5	27.0	27.6	24.9	23.9	23.4	23.3	23.2	27.6	34.4	....
Iran, I.R. of	429	21.2	14.2	12.7	10.5	9.1	6.4	5.3	....	....	....	....	....
Iraq	433	....	....	....	....	....	....	....	....	....	....	....	....
Israel	436	39.5	39.4	37.9	35.8	34.5	39.2	40.3	38.2	41.1	40.2	44.8	46.5
Jordan	439	72.3	72.8	78.2	71.6	65.6	61.3	68.6	67.4	67.6	70.0	....	....
Kuwait	443	44.8	46.5	41.4	42.4	51.1	39.4	30.8	36.4	36.6	35.7	33.2	....
Lebanon	446	....	....	....	....	....	....	....	....	....	....	....	....
Libya	672	26.1	22.6	23.8	21.8	21.3	17.4	14.7	20.6	46.8	35.8	34.1	....

Balance of Payments

Imports of Goods and Services
As percent of GDP

		1994	1995	1996	1997	1998	1999	2000	2001	2002	2003	2004	2005
Middle East(Cont.)													
Oman	449	35.6	36.5	36.4	39.2	50.4	38.3	32.0	36.1	36.9	37.9	42.8	....
Qatar	453	....	....	....	....	....	....	....	....	....	....	....	
Saudi Arabia	456	29.2	31.5	31.5	31.7	30.4	27.7	28.1	26.2	26.3	25.5	26.7	25.6
Syrian Arab Republic	463	13.8	10.9	9.9	7.7	6.8	7.1	6.7	7.0	7.0	6.6	....	....
United Arab Emirates	466	....	....	....	....	....	....	....	....	....	....	....	....
West Bank and Gaza	487	....	....	....	....	....	....	....	....	....	....	....	....
Yemen, Republic of	474	8.6	19.5	36.6	45.4	48.0	37.7	34.6	36.0	37.7	40.2	....	....
Western Hemisphere													
Argentina	213	10.6	10.1	11.1	12.8	13.0	11.6	11.6	10.3	13.1	14.5	18.4	....
Aruba	314	....	152.8	185.5	177.0	124.4	154.2	173.7	157.2	137.4	155.4	177.7	....
Bahamas, The	313	53.7	58.5	....	....	....	....	....	....	....	....	....	....
Barbados	316	49.6	56.3	56.6	58.8	56.9	58.3	58.6	56.5	55.7	....	....	....
Belize	339	55.1	52.5	50.0	57.2	56.6	65.9	72.4	68.9	67.7	67.4	60.5	....
Bolivia	218	22.6	23.4	23.4	26.0	25.9	24.0	24.7	24.3	26.2	25.3	26.8	29.6
Brazil	223	8.0	9.0	8.5	9.3	9.4	11.8	12.0	14.3	13.4	12.6	13.3	12.3
Chile	228	24.6	25.7	28.1	28.2	28.7	26.5	29.1	31.2	31.0	32.0	31.3	33.1
Colombia	233	17.4	17.3	16.9	17.2	17.6	15.5	17.2	19.4	18.9	20.9	20.5	20.3
Costa Rica	238	34.0	40.3	42.7	44.5	50.0	45.5	45.8	42.1	45.8	48.4	49.3	....
Dominican Republic	243	42.3	39.9	40.6	41.2	44.3	43.9	46.3	40.9	40.7	45.4	41.9	31.7
Ecuador	248	....	....	....	....	....	....	....	....	....	....	....	....
El Salvador	253	35.2	38.1	34.3	37.8	37.5	37.8	42.9	41.8	41.3	43.2	44.4	....
Guatemala	258	24.6	25.4	22.4	23.6	26.0	27.4	28.9	28.9	29.4	29.3	31.1	....
Guyana	336	121.9	113.9	99.7	100.9	101.3	102.8	104.3	103.0	97.7	93.9	99.2	....
Haiti	263	11.4	34.3	26.3	27.5	27.7	30.6	36.9	37.0	38.3	48.6	....	....
Honduras	268	48.4	46.8	55.2	53.3	53.5	55.5	54.2	53.1	52.1	53.8	58.8	....
Jamaica	343	62.6	64.3	59.3	54.6	52.1	51.8	56.1	56.5	56.4	60.0	59.7	....
Mexico	273	22.0	28.7	30.2	30.5	32.9	32.6	33.0	29.8	28.7	29.5	31.7	31.6
Netherlands Antilles	353	....	....	....	....	....	....	....	....	....	....	....	....
Nicaragua	278	32.8	36.1	41.4	50.6	49.8	57.6	54.5	52.3	53.9	57.5	62.6	....
Panama	283	86.9	89.7	80.5	85.8	81.2	67.9	69.9	66.0	62.4	58.6	64.6	....
Paraguay	288	53.4	57.7	52.4	50.4	52.6	41.9	42.6	42.3	44.6	46.1	....	....
Peru	293	15.7	17.9	17.8	18.4	18.8	17.5	18.1	17.8	17.5	17.8	18.3	19.3
Suriname	366	50.9	65.5	65.7	60.3	60.9	50.7	51.9	61.7	51.3	64.0	91.3	....
Trinidad and Tobago	369	29.8	39.6	38.0	56.3	53.8	44.4	45.5	44.8	45.8	40.7	....	....
Uruguay	298	19.9	18.5	19.4	20.2	20.0	19.1	20.9	20.0	20.2	24.4	27.8	....
Venezuela, Rep. Bol.	299	22.5	21.8	21.0	21.9	22.8	19.1	18.2	19.4	18.6	17.0	20.2	....
ECCU													
Anguilla	312	103.6	122.5	123.6	115.7	130.6	138.1	143.6	122.7	112.9	....	....	....
Antigua and Barbuda	311	84.4	88.9	86.5	82.3	79.0	81.4	75.1	....	....	....	....	....
Dominica	321	62.4	66.6	69.6	70.5	66.4	67.5	67.5	62.3	61.1	....	....	....
Grenada	328	61.2	60.9	65.6	67.1	72.2	69.9	75.1	....	....	....	....	....
Montserrat	351	81.3	81.1	109.0	100.3	106.7	115.2	108.6	118.4	118.8	....	....	....
St. Kitts and Nevis	361	67.2	75.0	78.9	71.2	67.2	72.3	75.5	70.6	73.4	....	....	....
St. Lucia	362	71.3	71.1	68.5	71.6	67.7	67.0	63.8	58.8	59.7	....	....	....
St. Vincent & Grens	364	70.6	65.7	66.5	78.1	78.6	73.5	60.9	61.1	60.2	....	....	....

Balance of Payments

		1994	1995	1996	1997	1998	1999	2000	2001	2002	2003	2004	2005

Current Account Balance
Excluding Exceptional Financing
As percent of GDP

		1994	1995	1996	1997	1998	1999	2000	2001	2002	2003	2004	2005
Industrial Countries													
United States	111	−1.7	−1.5	−1.6	−1.7	−2.4	−3.2	−4.2	−3.8	−4.5	−4.7	−5.7	−6.4
Canada	156	−2.3	−.7	.6	−1.3	−1.3	.3	2.7	2.3	1.7	1.2	2.1	2.4
Australia	193	−4.9	−5.2	−3.8	−2.9	−4.9	−5.5	−3.9	−2.1	−4.0	−5.7	−6.3	−5.9
Japan	158	2.7	2.1	1.4	2.3	3.1	2.6	2.6	2.1	2.9	3.2	3.8	3.6
New Zealand	196	−4.6	−4.9	−5.8	−6.4	−3.9	−6.1	−5.1	−2.7	−4.1	−4.4	−6.5	....
Euro Area													
Austria	122	−1.5	−2.3	−2.1	−2.5	−2.5	−3.1	−2.5	−1.9	.3	−.2	.3	1.3
Belgium	124	....	....	....	....	....	....	....	....	4.6	4.1	3.4	1.8
Belgium-Luxembourg	126	....	....	....	....	....	....	....	....				
Finland	172	1.1	4.0	3.9	5.4	5.6	6.2	7.4	7.1	7.7	4.4	5.2	2.6
France	132	.5	.7	1.3	2.7	2.6	2.9	1.4	2.1	.8	.7	−.3	−1.6
Germany	134	−1.4	−1.2	−.6	−.4	−.7	−1.2	−1.7	—	2.0	1.9	3.7	4.1
Greece	174	−.1	−2.4	−3.7	−4.0	....	−5.8	−8.5					
Ireland	178	2.9	2.6	2.8	2.3	1.2	.3	−.5	−.7	−.9	.1	−.8	−2.0
Italy	136	1.3	2.2	3.2	2.7	1.6	.7	−.5	−.1	−.8	−1.3	−.9	−1.5
Luxembourg	137	....	....	....	....	....	....	....	....	10.7	6.4	10.6	9.8
Netherlands	138	5.0	6.2	5.1	6.5	3.2	3.8	1.9	2.4	2.5	5.5	9.0	6.4
Portugal	182	−2.5	−.1	−4.6	−6.6	−8.0	−8.6	−10.4	−9.8	−7.8	−5.9	−7.3	−9.3
Spain	184	−1.3	−.3	−.4	−.1	−1.2	−2.9	−4.0	−3.9	−3.3	−3.6	−5.3	−7.4
Denmark	128	2.1	1.0	1.7	.5	−1.2	1.8	1.4	3.0	2.0	3.3	2.4	....
Iceland	176	1.9	.8	−1.8	−1.7	−6.7	−6.8	−9.8	−4.3	1.7	−5.0	−9.4	−16.6
Norway	142	3.0	3.5	6.9	6.4	—	5.3	15.5	15.4	12.9	13.0	13.6	16.7
Sweden	144	.3	2.0	2.2	3.0	1.9	2.4	2.7	3.0	5.2	7.5	7.8	6.6
Switzerland	146	6.2	6.6	6.6	9.7	9.4	10.8	13.6	9.0	9.0	13.9	16.3	13.5
United Kingdom	112	−1.0	−1.3	−.9	−.2	−.5	−2.7	−2.5	−2.2	−1.6	−1.5	−2.0	−2.6
Developing Countries													
Africa													
Algeria	612	....	....	....	....	....	....	....	....	....	....	....	....
Angola	614	—	−5.9	50.1	−11.6	−28.7	−27.8	8.7	−16.0	−1.5	....	....	....
Botswana	616	5.4	6.8	11.6	14.8	3.6	12.5	10.1	10.4	2.5	6.2	....	....
Burundi	618	−1.6	1.0	−4.6	—	−5.8	−2.9	−7.5	−5.9	−1.6	−6.3	....	....
Cape Verde	624	−11.2	−12.6	−6.9	−6.0	−11.1	−12.4	−10.8	−9.9	−11.5	−9.5	....	....
Comoros	632	−3.7	−8.4	....	....	....	....	....	....	....	....	....	....
Congo, Dem. Rep. of	636	....	....	....	....	....	....	....	....	....	....	....	....
Djibouti	611	....	....	....	....	....	....	....	....	....	....	....	....
Eritrea	643	....	....	....	....	....	....	....	....	....	....	....	....
Ethiopia	644	2.4	.7	1.3	−.6	−5.3	−7.6	.2	−6.0	....	....	....	....
Gambia, The	648	2.7	....	....	....	....	....	....	....	....	....	....	....
Ghana	652	−4.7	−2.2	−4.4	−5.9	....	....	....	....	....	....	....	....
Guinea	656	....	....	....	....	....	....	....	....	....	....	....	....
Kenya	664	1.4	−4.4	−.8	−4.3	−4.1	−.8	−1.6	−2.6	−1.0	.5	−2.4	....
Lesotho	666	12.9	−34.6	−32.1	−26.3	−31.5	−24.2	−17.6	−12.5	−18.1	−12.7	−5.6	....
Liberia	668	....	....	....	....	....	....	....	....	....	....	....	....
Madagascar	674	−9.3	−8.7	−7.3	−7.5	−8.0	−6.8	−7.3	−3.8	−6.8	−8.0	....	....
Malawi	676	−15.1	−5.6	−6.5	−10.4	−.2	−8.9	−4.2	−3.5	−10.4	....	....	....
Mauritania	682	−7.0	2.1	8.4	4.5	7.9	....	....	....	....	....	....	....
Mauritius	684	−6.5	−.5	.8	−2.1	.1	−2.9	−.8	6.1	5.2	1.7	−1.7	....
Morocco	686	−2.4	−3.9	−.2	−.5	−.4	−.5	−1.5	4.7	4.1	3.5	1.8	....
Mozambique	688	−21.2	−19.4	−14.5	−8.6	−10.9	−22.4	−19.9	−17.8	−21.4	−16.5	....	....
Namibia	728	2.6	5.0	3.3	2.5	4.8	4.7	8.7	1.9	....	....	....	....
Nigeria	694	−5.1	−2.9	2.7	.4	−3.2	1.4	15.2	5.7	2.3	17.1	19.1	....
Rwanda	714	−6.1	4.5	−.6	−3.3	−4.1	−7.5	−5.2	−5.9	−7.2	−4.8	−.3	....
São Tomé & Príncipe	716	....	....	....	....	....	....	....	....	....	....	....	....
Seychelles	718	4.9	−.6	−11.8	−12.9	−19.4	−20.5	−8.3	−20.0	−18.7	....	....	....
Sierra Leone	724	−9.8	−13.6	−16.0	−6.5	−4.9	−14.8	−17.7	−12.1	−7.8	−8.1	−6.9	....
Somalia	726	....	....	....	....	....	....	....	....	....	....	....	....
South Africa	199	—	−1.6	−1.2	−1.5	−1.6	−.5	−.1	.1	.6	−1.4	−3.5	−4.2
Sudan	732	−10.4	−6.0	−10.1	−8.1	....	....	....	....	....	....	....	....
Swaziland	734	.2	−2.2	−3.9	−.2	−6.9	−2.6	−5.4	−4.5	4.9	6.0	....	....
Tanzania	738	−15.8	−12.3	−7.9	−8.2	−11.0	−9.7	−5.5	−4.8	−2.2	−3.8	−3.9	....
Tunisia	744	−3.4	−4.3	−2.4	−3.1	−3.4	−2.1	−4.2	−4.2	−3.5	−2.9	−2.0	....
Uganda	746	−4.0	−5.6	−4.1	−5.6	−7.9	−11.8	−14.4	−6.3	−6.0	−5.4	−2.4	....
Zambia	754	....	....	....	−9.8	....	....	....	....	....	....	....	....
Zimbabwe	698	−6.2	....	....	....	....	....	....	....	....	....	....	....
CEMAC													
Cameroon	622	−.8	1.0	....	....	....	....	....	....	....	....	....	....
Central African Rep.	626	−2.9	....	....	....	....	....	....	....	....	....	....	....
Chad	628	−3.2	....	....	....	....	....	....	....	....	....	....	....
Congo, Republic of	634	−44.8	−29.5	−25.6	−6.7	−12.2	−9.7	20.0	−1.0	−1.1	−.1	....	....
Equatorial Guinea	642	−.3	−74.2	−125.7	....	....	....	....	....	....	....	....	....
Gabon	646	7.6	9.4	15.5	9.8	−12.9	9.0	20.3	11.9	6.8	9.5	....	....
WAEMU													
Benin	638	−1.5	−9.8	−2.4	−7.5	−6.2	−7.7	−4.7	−6.4	−8.5	−9.8	....	....
Burkina Faso	748	.7	....	....	....	....	....	−15.2	−13.5	....	....	....	....
Côte d'Ivoire	662	−.2	−4.9	−1.5	−1.3	−2.3	−1.0	−2.3	−.6	6.6	2.1	1.9	....
Guinea-Bissau	654	−7.5	−11.3	−18.0	−10.8	....	....	....	−13.5	−4.2	−2.7	....	....
Mali	678	−9.2	−10.4	−9.3	−6.6	−7.1	−8.6	−9.5	−10.2	−4.5	−6.3	....	....

Balance of Payments

		1994	1995	1996	1997	1998	1999	2000	2001	2002	2003	2004	2005
						Current Account Balance Excluding Exceptional Financing *As percent of GDP*							
Africa(Cont.)													
Niger	692	−8.9	−8.0	−5.4	−7.2	−7.3	−6.8	−6.3	−5.2	−8.1	−9.1	....	....
Senegal	722	−4.8	−5.0	−4.0	−4.0	−4.9	−6.2	−7.1	−5.0	−5.9	−6.3	....	....
Togo	742	−5.7	−7.9	−9.4	−6.9	−8.8	−8.1	−10.5	−13.0	−9.7	−9.0	....	....
Asia*													
Afghanistan, I.R. of	512	....	....	....	....	....	....	....	....	....	....		
Bangladesh	513	.6	−2.2	−2.5	−.7	−.1	−.8	−.7	−1.2	1.6	.3	−.5	....
Bhutan	514	....	....	....	....	....	....	....	....	....	....	....	
Brunei Darussalam	516	....	....	....	....	....	....	....	....	....	....	....	
Cambodia	522	−5.6	−5.4	−5.3	−6.1	−35.5	−12.3	−13.6	−14.0	−3.0	−3.5	−4.6	....
China,P.R.: Mainland	924	1.3	.2	.9	4.1	3.3	2.1	1.9	1.5	2.7	3.1	3.5	7.2
China,P.R.:Hong Kong	532	....	....	....	....	1.5	6.3	4.1	5.9	7.6	10.4	9.5	11.4
China,P.R.: Macao	546	....	....	....	....	....	....	....	....	40.1	40.1	40.3	....
Fiji	819	−6.2	−5.7	.6	−1.6	−3.6	.7	....	....	....	....	....	....
French Terr.: French Polynesia	887	....	....	....	....	....	....	....	....	....	....	....	
French Terr.: New Caledonia	839	....	....	....	....	....	....	....	....	....	....	....	
India	534	−.5	−1.5	−1.5	−.7	−1.6	−.7	−1.0	.3	1.4	1.2	....	
Indonesia	536	−1.6	−3.2	−3.4	−2.3	4.3	4.1	4.8	4.2	3.9	3.5	.6	.3
Kiribati	826	....	....	....	....	....	....	....	....	....	....		
Korea	542	−1.0	−1.7	−4.2	−1.6	11.7	5.5	2.4	1.7	1.0	2.0	4.1	2.1
Lao People's Dem.Rep	544	−18.4	−19.5	−18.5	−17.5	−11.7	−8.3	−.5	−4.7	....	....	....	
Malaysia	548	−6.1	−9.7	−4.4	−5.9	13.2	15.9	9.4	8.3	7.5	12.9	12.6	....
Maldives	556	−3.1	−4.6	−1.7	−6.8	−4.0	−13.4	−8.2	−9.4	−5.6	−4.6	−20.8	
Mongolia	948	4.7	3.0	−8.3	4.8	−12.3	−11.4	−15.1	−13.6	−13.2	−11.0	−1.5	
Myanmar	518	−.2	−.2	−.2	−.2	−.2	−.1	−.1	—	—	—	....	
Nepal	558	−8.7	−8.4	−7.4	−8.0	−1.5	−5.1	−5.6	−6.2	1.0	2.0	.8	....
Pakistan	564	−3.5	−5.7	−7.5	−2.9	−3.8	−1.5	−.1	2.8	5.2	4.3	−.9	−3.1
Papua New Guinea	853	7.4	10.2	3.7	−3.9	−.8	2.8	9.9	9.2	....	....	....	
Philippines	566	−4.6	−2.7	−4.8	−5.3	2.4	9.5	8.2	1.9	5.7	1.8	2.4	....
Samoa	862	2.9	4.7	5.4	3.7	9.0	−8.2	....	....	....	....	−4.7	....
Singapore	576	16.1	17.5	15.0	15.6	22.3	17.9	12.9	16.8	17.8	29.1	25.9	....
Solomon Islands	813	−1.1	2.3	3.6	−9.3	2.3	5.6	....	....	....	....		
Sri Lanka	524	−6.5	−5.9	−4.9	−2.6	−1.4	−3.6	−6.4	−1.5	−1.6	−.6	−3.4	....
Thailand	578	−5.6	−8.1	−8.1	−2.0	12.7	10.1	7.6	5.4	5.5	5.6	4.2	−2.1
Tonga	866	....	....	....	....	....	....	....	−8.3	−2.3	....	....	
Vanuatu	846	−9.2	−7.7	−11.0	−7.6	−3.7	−13.2	−5.6	−6.2	−16.7	−17.0	....	
Vietnam	582	....	....	−8.2	−5.7	−3.9	4.1	3.5	2.1	−1.7	−4.7	....	
*of which:													
Taiwan Prov.of China	528	....	....	....	....	....	....	....	....	....	....		
Europe													
Albania	914	−8.1	−.5	−3.6	−12.6	−2.4	−4.5	−4.2	−5.3	−9.1	−7.3	....	
Armenia	911	−16.0	−17.0	−18.2	−18.7	−22.1	−16.6	−14.6	−9.4	−6.2	−6.7	−4.5	−3.9
Azerbaijan, Republic of	912	....	−16.6	−29.3	−23.1	−30.7	−13.1	−3.2	−.9	−12.3	−27.8	−29.8	1.3
Belarus	913	....	−4.3	−3.6	−6.1	−6.7	−1.6	−3.2	−3.2	−2.1	−2.4	−4.5	1.6
Bosnia & Herzegovina	963	....	....	....	....	−8.4	−10.2	−8.4	−14.7	−21.2	−23.3	....	
Bulgaria	918	−.3	−.2	.2	4.1	−.5	−5.0	−5.6	−7.2	−5.3	−9.3	−5.8	−11.8
Croatia	960	3.8	−8.5	−5.3	−13.9	−6.8	−7.1	−2.6	−3.7	−8.3	−7.2	−5.4	−6.6
Cyprus	423	1.0	−2.2	−5.1	−4.8	3.1	−1.8	−5.3	−3.4	−4.4	−2.5	−6.0	....
Czech Republic	935	−2.0	−2.5	−6.7	−6.3	−2.1	−2.4	−4.7	−5.3	−5.7	−6.3	−6.0	−2.0
Estonia	939	−6.9	−4.2	−8.6	−11.4	−8.6	−5.3	−5.5	−5.4	−11.1	−12.1	−13.0	−11.0
Faroe Islands	816	....	....	....	....	....	....	....	....	....	....		
Georgia	915	....	....	....	−14.6	−7.6	−7.1	−8.8	−6.6	−6.5	−9.4	−8.2	....
Hungary	944	−9.8	−3.7	−3.9	−4.6	−7.2	−7.9	−8.5	−6.1	−7.2	−8.7	−8.6	−7.3
Kazakhstan	916	....	−1.2	−3.7	−3.8	−5.8	−1.0	2.0	−6.5	−4.4	−.9	1.1	−.9
Kyrgyz Republic	917	−7.6	−15.7	−23.3	−7.8	−25.1	−20.2	−9.1	−3.7	−5.0	−5.2	−4.6	....
Latvia	941	5.0	−.3	−5.0	−5.6	−9.8	−9.0	−4.7	−7.5	−6.7	−8.1	−12.9	−12.4
Lithuania	946	−2.2	−9.6	−9.0	−10.0	−11.7	−11.0	−5.9	−4.7	−5.1	−6.9	−7.7	−6.9
Macedonia, FYR	962	....	....	−6.5	−7.4	−7.5	−.9	−2.0	−7.1	−9.4	−3.2	....	
Malta	181	−4.8	−11.1	−12.2	−5.5	−5.7	−3.1	−12.0	−4.2	.3	−5.7	−9.6	−13.0
Moldova	921	....	−6.1	−11.5	−14.3	−19.7	−6.7	−8.4	−2.5	−4.5	−7.1	−2.0	−10.5
Poland	964	1.0	.6	−2.1	−3.7	−4.0	−7.4	−5.8	−2.8	−2.5	−2.1	−4.2	−1.5
Romania	968	−1.5	−5.0	−7.3	−6.0	−6.9	−3.6	−3.7	−5.5	−3.3	−5.6	−8.5	....
Russia	922	2.8	2.2	2.8	—	.1	12.6	18.0	11.1	8.4	8.2	10.0	11.0
Slovak Republic	936	4.3	2.0	−10.0	−9.3	−9.6	−5.7	−3.4	....	−8.0	−.9	....	
Slovenia	961	4.0	−.4	.3	.3	−.6	−3.2	−2.8	.2	1.5	−.3	−2.1	−1.1
Tajikistan	923	....	....	....	....	....	....	....	....	....	....		
Turkey	186	2.0	−1.4	−1.3	−1.4	1.0	−.7	−4.9	2.3	−.8	−3.4	−5.1	....
Turkmenistan	925	....	....	....	....	....	....	....	....	....	....		
Ukraine	926	−3.2	−3.1	−2.7	−2.7	−3.1	5.3	4.7	3.7	7.5	5.8	10.6	3.1
Uzbekistan	927	....	....	....	....	....	....	....	....	....	....		
Middle East													
Bahrain, Kingdom of	419	−4.6	4.1	4.3	−.5	−12.6	−.6	10.4	2.9	−.6	2.1	3.8	....
Egypt	469	.1	−.4	−.3	−.9	−3.0	−1.8	−1.0	−.4	.7	5.2	5.0	....
Iran, I.R. of	429	6.6	3.2	3.7	1.3	−1.1	2.6	3.8	....	....	....	....	
Iraq	433	....	....	....	....	....	....	....	....	....	....		
Israel	436	−4.5	−5.3	−5.3	−3.3	−1.2	−1.6	−1.1	−1.4	−1.2	.7	1.6	1.9
Jordan	439	−6.5	−3.8	−3.2	.4	.2	5.0	.7	—	5.7	11.8	....	
Kuwait	443	13.0	18.4	22.6	26.1	8.5	16.6	39.8	24.4	11.2	20.4	33.9	....
Lebanon	446	....	....	....	....	....	....	....	....	....	....		

Balance of Payments

Current Account Balance
Excluding Exceptional Financing
As percent of GDP

		1994	1995	1996	1997	1998	1999	2000	2001	2002	2003	2004	2005
Middle East(Cont.)													
Libya	672	.1	6.5	4.4	5.0	−1.3	7.0	22.6	12.0	.6	14.8	12.0	....
Oman	449	−6.2	−5.8	1.6	−1.0	−22.5	−2.9	15.8	9.5	6.7	4.0	1.8	....
Qatar	453	....	....	....	....	....	....	....	....	....	....	....	28.1
Saudi Arabia	456	−7.8	−3.7	.4	.2	−9.0	.3	7.6	5.1	6.3	13.1	20.7	28.1
Syrian Arab Republic	463	−1.8	.5	.1	.7	.1	.3	1.3	1.4	1.6	.8	....	....
United Arab Emirates	466	....	....	....	....	....	....	....	....	....	....	....	....
West Bank and Gaza	487	....	....	....	....	....	....	....	....	....	....	....	....
Yemen, Republic of	474	.7	1.1	.5	−1.0	−7.6	4.8	14.0	7.0	5.2	1.3	....	....
Western Hemisphere													
Argentina	213	−4.3	−2.0	−2.5	−4.1	−4.8	−4.2	−3.2	−1.2	8.5	6.2	2.1	....
Aruba	314	....	—	−5.0	−12.8	−1.1	−24.9	11.3	16.9	−17.5	−7.5	.7	....
Bahamas, The	313	−1.4	−4.8	....	....	....	....	....	....	....	....	....	....
Barbados	316	7.7	2.3	3.5	−2.3	−2.6	−6.0	−5.6	−4.3	−6.5	....	....	....
Belize	339	−6.9	−2.8	−1.0	−4.9	−8.7	−9.3	−18.7	−21.9	−19.7	−21.2	−17.6	....
Bolivia	218	−1.5	−4.5	−5.5	−7.0	−7.8	−5.9	−5.3	−3.4	−4.5	.9	3.9	4.8
Brazil	223	−.2	−2.6	−3.0	−3.8	−4.3	−4.7	−4.0	−4.6	−1.7	.8	1.9	1.8
Chile	228	−2.8	−1.9	−4.1	−4.4	−4.9	.1	−1.2	−1.6	−.9	−1.3	1.7	.6
Colombia	233	−4.6	−4.9	−4.8	−5.4	−4.9	.8	.9	−1.3	−1.7	−1.2	−1.0	−1.6
Costa Rica	238	−2.3	−3.1	−2.2	−3.7	−3.7	−4.2	−4.4	−4.3	−5.4	−5.3	−4.5	....
Dominican Republic	243	−2.1	−1.2	−1.3	−.9	−1.7	−2.0	−4.4	−3.0	−3.2	5.3	5.3	−.4
Ecuador	248	....	....	....	....	....	....	....	....	....	....	....	....
El Salvador	253	−.2	−2.8	−1.6	−.9	−.8	−1.9	−3.3	−1.1	−2.8	−5.1	−3.9	....
Guatemala	258	−4.8	−3.9	−2.9	−3.6	−5.4	−5.6	−5.4	−6.0	−5.3	−4.2	−4.4	....
Guyana	336	−22.9	−21.7	−4.6	−8.4	−7.7	−7.3	−11.5	−13.4	−9.1	−6.3	−3.8	....
Haiti	263	−1.1	−3.7	−4.6	−1.5	.8	−1.5	−2.3	−2.7	−1.5	−.5	....	....
Honduras	268	−10.0	−5.1	−8.2	−5.8	−7.5	−11.5	−4.4	−5.3	−4.0	−4.5	−5.5	....
Jamaica	343	1.7	−1.7	−2.2	−4.5	−4.3	−2.8	−4.7	−9.3	−12.7	−9.4	−5.8	....
Mexico	273	−7.0	−.6	−.8	−1.9	−3.8	−2.9	−3.2	−2.8	−2.1	−1.4	−1.1	−.7
Netherlands Antilles	353	....	....	....	....	....	....	....	....	....	....	....	....
Nicaragua	278	−30.6	−22.7	−24.8	−24.8	−19.2	−24.8	−20.1	−19.3	−19.1	−18.1	−17.0	....
Panama	283	.2	−5.4	−2.2	−5.0	−9.3	−10.1	−5.8	−1.4	−.8	−3.9	−7.9	....
Paraguay	288	−3.5	−1.0	−3.7	−6.8	−1.9	−2.1	−2.1	−3.9	1.7	2.2	....	....
Peru	293	−6.0	−8.6	−6.5	−5.7	−5.9	−2.8	−2.9	−2.1	−1.9	−1.5	—	1.3
Suriname	366	9.7	10.6	−7.3	−7.3	−16.4	−3.3	3.6	−10.9	−13.8	−15.6	−12.4	....
Trinidad and Tobago	369	4.4	5.5	1.8	−10.7	−10.6	.4	6.7	4.7	.9	9.4	....	....
Uruguay	298	−2.5	−1.1	−1.1	−1.3	−2.1	−2.4	−2.8	−2.6	2.6	−.5	−.8	....
Venezuela, Rep. Bol.	299	4.3	2.6	12.6	4.3	−4.9	2.2	10.1	1.6	8.2	13.7	12.7	....
ECCU													
Anguilla	312	−18.6	−15.5	−31.1	−26.1	−24.6	−59.2	−63.0	−40.9	−39.9	....	....	....
Antigua and Barbuda	311	−1.3	−.1	−11.0	−8.2	−7.5	−8.8	−9.9	....	....	....	....	....
Dominica	321	−17.5	−18.5	−21.7	−17.2	−8.9	−13.4	−19.5	−18.4	−14.9	....	....	....
Grenada	328	−10.3	−14.8	−18.9	−21.6	−23.2	−14.0	−20.5	....	....	....	....	....
Montserrat	351	−22.4	−3.3	32.1	−4.8	9.1	−4.0	−18.7	−16.2	−21.3	....	....	....
St. Kitts and Nevis	361	−11.4	−19.8	−26.6	−22.4	−16.1	−27.1	−20.1	−31.0	−35.4	....	....	....
St. Lucia	362	−9.3	−6.0	−10.2	−13.5	−9.5	−14.5	−11.5	−11.4	−15.4	....	....	....
St. Vincent & Grens	364	−23.8	−15.3	−12.7	−28.7	−29.1	−21.9	−8.8	−11.9	−11.7	....	....	....

GDP Volume Measures

		1994	1995	1996	1997	1998	1999	2000	2001	2002	2003	2004	2005
		\multicolumn{12}{c}{*Percent Change over Previous Year; Calculated from Indices*}										
World..	001	**4.40**	**4.04**	**4.19**	**4.09**	**2.49**	**3.71**	**4.61**	**2.34**	**2.73**	**3.75**	**4.88**	**3.87**
Industrial Countries.................	110	**2.86**	**2.72**	**2.60**	**3.21**	**2.52**	**3.47**	**3.66**	**1.25**	**1.32**	**1.96**	**3.18**	**2.59**
United States.............................	111	4.02	2.50	3.70	4.50	4.18	4.45	3.66	.75	1.60	2.70	4.22	3.52
Canada......................................	156	4.80	2.81	1.62	4.22	4.10	5.53	5.26	1.92	3.28	1.71	3.09	2.74
Australia....................................	193	5.20	3.54	4.33	3.99	5.04	4.43	3.33	2.24	4.13	3.07	3.55	2.46
Japan..	158	−1.19	1.41	2.14	1.10	−1.93	−.24	2.79	.39	.14	2.12	2.71	3.13
New Zealand..............................	196	5.78	3.90	3.19	2.98	1.15	5.19	2.48	3.78	4.47	3.87	3.43	2.05
Euro Area...................................	163	....	....	1.34	2.20	2.74	.45	3.25	3.64	.84	.61	1.75	1.58
Austria......................................	122	2.66	1.91	2.62	1.84	3.56	3.34	3.34	.81	.99	1.40	2.44	1.92
Belgium.....................................	124	3.23	4.35	1.16	3.34	.33	4.71	3.86	1.05	1.50	.91	2.59	1.25
Finland......................................	172	3.94	4.35	3.79	6.19	4.96	3.38	4.98	1.03	2.20	2.44	3.62	2.09
France.......................................	132	2.08	2.35	1.08	2.21	2.11	4.62	4.02	1.85	1.03	1.09	2.32	1.19
Germany....................................	134	2.66	1.89	.99	1.80	2.03	2.01	3.21	1.24	.06	−.19	1.63	.89
Greece.......................................	174	2.00	2.10	2.36	3.64	3.36	3.60	4.13	5.25	3.83	4.75	4.68	3.66
Ireland......................................	178	5.76	9.73	7.99	10.83	8.61	11.57	9.22	6.18	6.11	4.44	4.47	4.66
Italy..	136	2.15	2.83	.72	1.89	1.44	1.93	3.58	1.80	.34	.04	1.07	−.04
Luxembourg................................	137	3.82	15.98	1.52	5.94	6.49	−3.32	9.49	1.60	....	....	....	....
Netherlands...............................	138	6.70	16.86	3.41	4.28	3.92	4.68	3.94	1.93	.08	.34	1.95	1.53
Portugal....................................	182	2.47	2.92	3.19	3.47	3.49	8.45	3.92	2.02	.76	−1.12	1.18	.37
Spain..	184	2.38	4.97	2.41	3.87	1.67	7.65	5.04	3.54	2.68	3.00	3.09	3.43
Denmark....................................	128	5.53	3.07	2.83	3.20	2.16	2.56	3.53	.70	.47	.69	1.87	3.05
Iceland......................................	176	4.03	.08	5.22	4.67	5.77	4.30	4.15	3.83	−1.05	3.01	8.20	5.59
Norway......................................	142	5.26	4.36	5.25	5.19	2.63	2.13	2.84	2.73	1.11	1.13	3.08	2.26
Sweden.....................................	144	3.90	3.91	1.34	2.33	3.66	4.53	4.33	1.07	2.00	1.69	3.74	2.70
Switzerland................................	146	1.07	.38	.52	1.91	2.79	1.31	3.61	1.04	.31	−.27	2.07	1.86
United Kingdom..........................	112	4.31	2.93	2.75	3.04	3.34	3.02	3.81	2.35	2.06	2.67	3.26	1.86
Developing Countries...............	200	**6.63**	**5.95**	**6.49**	**5.35**	**2.46**	**4.02**	**5.87**	**3.81**	**4.62**	**6.17**	**7.17**	**5.57**
Africa......................................	605	**1.73**	**2.54**	**5.57**	**2.89**	**3.13**	**2.75**	**3.47**	**4.18**	**2.97**	**3.96**	**4.19**	**4.44**
Benin...	638	2.02	6.05	4.32	5.73	3.96	5.34	4.86	6.25	4.42	3.88	3.38	3.50
Botswana...................................	616	4.05	3.23	5.54	5.61	8.06	4.13	16.95	9.11	1.58	9.54	3.39	8.37
Burkina Faso..............................	748	2.09	6.48	9.87	6.83	8.48	3.75	1.59	6.78	4.55	8.02	4.59	7.09
Burundi......................................	618	−3.08	−7.02	−8.61	.38	4.49	−1.00	−.90	2.10	4.50	−1.20	4.40	.90
Cameroon...................................	622	−2.64	3.30	5.00	5.00	....	....	....	....	....	....	....	....
Congo, Dem. Rep. of...................	636	−3.87	.72	−1.10	−5.43	−1.76	−4.23	−6.97	.94	....	....	....	....
Congo, Rep. of...........................	634	−5.47	2.19	4.29	−.47	3.75	−3.22	8.00	....	....	....	....	....
Côte d'Ivoire..............................	662	2.05	7.08	6.89	6.62	5.99	....	....	....	....	....	....	....
Gambia, The..............................	648	−3.40	5.31	.78	1.59	6.50	6.40	5.52	5.78	....	....	....	....
Ghana..	652	3.27	4.02	4.60	4.18	....	....	....	....	....	....	....	....
Guinea-Bissau............................	654	4.97	.97	4.78	6.55	−28.17	7.64	7.43	.10	−7.01	.55	....	....
Kenya..	664	2.63	4.41	4.15	3.00	.28	−3.60	7.06	4.38	.40	2.77	4.34	....
Lesotho......................................	666	3.40	4.39	9.97	8.14	−4.65	.23	1.33	3.21	3.50	3.09	3.15	1.21
Madagascar................................	674	−.07	1.71	2.14	3.69	3.94	4.68	4.74	6.01	−12.67	9.78	5.28	4.65
Malawi.......................................	676	−11.61	15.01	8.15	6.35	2.35	1.25	−8.39	−4.15	2.08	3.90	5.08	2.08
Mali..	678	2.65	6.63	3.59	....	....	....	....	....	....	....	....	....
Mauritius...................................	684	4.16	4.26	5.47	5.71	6.12	2.73	9.03	2.56	1.92	4.27	5.43	2.59
Morocco.....................................	686	10.64	−6.56	11.80	−2.23	7.67	−.08	.96	6.29	3.19	5.52	4.25	1.71
Mozambique...............................	688	6.98	3.31	6.76	11.07	12.63	7.54	1.94	13.10	8.71	7.94	7.29	7.70
Namibia.....................................	728	7.32	4.11	3.19	4.23	3.29	3.42	3.27	....	....	....	....	....
Niger...	692	4.00	2.61	3.42	2.75	10.42	−.57	−1.41	7.10	3.00	5.32	.90	....
Nigeria.......................................	694	1.25	2.17	3.86	3.23	2.31	2.82	3.71	4.22	4.09	3.78	....	....
Rwanda......................................	714	−82.27	99.39	29.43	46.18	24.86	20.67	1.32	6.44	2.18	6.89	25.83	22.22
Senegal......................................	722	2.87	5.17	5.15	3.12	5.90	6.35	3.19	4.59	.64	6.66	5.59	....
Seychelles..................................	718	−.81	−.83	4.92	4.59	5.50	2.90	1.40	.95	....	....	....	....
Sierra Leone...............................	724	−1.95	−8.00	6.09	−17.60	−.84	−8.12	3.81	18.17	27.46	9.29	7.36	7.53
South Africa...............................	199	3.23	3.12	4.31	2.65	.52	2.36	4.15	2.74	3.69	2.98	4.47	4.87
Swaziland...................................	734	3.36	3.79	3.89	3.83	3.26	3.53	2.03	1.77	....	....	....	....
Togo..	742	14.98	7.85	8.84	14.38	−2.30	2.48	−.78	−.18	4.14	2.70	3.00	....
Tunisia.......................................	744	3.18	2.35	7.15	5.44	4.78	6.05	4.69	4.92	1.66	5.56	6.04	4.22
Uganda......................................	746	−13.62	8.81	16.98	8.54	19.59	26.39	19.54	12.19	8.97	14.17	−2.69	3.94
Zambia.......................................	754	−3.51	−2.27	6.50	3.50	....	....	....	....	....	....	....	....
Zimbabwe...................................	698	5.80	.16	10.45	2.78	2.70	−3.76	−7.81	−2.54	−4.35	−10.45	−4.06	....
Asia..	505	**9.62**	**8.17**	**8.26**	**6.12**	**2.25**	**6.25**	**6.95**	**5.59**	**6.68**	**8.13**	**8.14**	**....**
Bangladesh................................	513	4.08	4.92	4.62	5.39	5.23	4.87	5.95	5.27	4.42	5.26	6.27	5.38
China, P.R.: Mainland.................	924	12.63	9.00	9.75	8.59	7.81	7.18	8.39	7.21	8.91	10.20	9.90	....
China, P.R.: Hong Kong...............	532	5.61	3.92	4.22	5.12	−5.46	4.00	9.97	.64	1.84	3.20	8.60	7.27
India...	534	7.25	7.34	7.84	4.80	6.51	6.06	4.36	5.76	3.77	8.45	7.53	8.06
Indonesia...................................	536	7.54	8.22	7.82	4.70	−13.13	.79	4.92	3.83	4.38	4.72	5.05	5.60
Korea..	542	8.54	9.17	7.00	4.65	−6.85	9.49	8.49	3.84	6.97	3.10	4.73	3.96
Lao People's Democratic Rep.......	544	9.51	7.05	6.89	6.91	3.99	7.28	5.79	5.76	5.92	5.80	6.89	7.28
Malaysia....................................	548	9.21	9.83	10.00	7.32	−7.36	6.14	8.86	.32	4.35	5.48	7.23	5.16
Maldives....................................	556	7.51	7.37	9.09	10.41	9.79	7.23	4.77	3.45	6.53	8.54	9.52	−5.19
Mongolia....................................	948	2.31	6.33	2.35	4.00	3.53	3.22	1.06	1.05	4.00	5.57	10.72	6.24
Myanmar....................................	518	7.48	6.95	6.44	5.74	5.77	10.92	6.23	11.34	12.03	13.84	....	....
Nepal...	558	8.27	2.73	5.69	5.01	3.34	4.54	6.09	4.74	−.32	2.74	3.48	....
Pakistan.....................................	564	3.90	5.14	4.99	−.10	2.55	3.66	4.26	1.86	3.22	4.95	6.39	7.78
Papua New Guinea......................	853	5.95	−3.45	6.60	−6.34	4.68	1.86	−2.49	−.12	−.16	2.90	2.90	2.95
Philippines.................................	566	4.39	4.68	5.85	5.19	−.58	3.40	4.01	3.40	5.54	4.92	5.00	4.83
Samoa.......................................	862	−2.54	6.56	7.27	.80	2.39	2.28	7.03	6.23	1.21	−1.01	3.20	....
Singapore...................................	576	11.40	8.04	8.17	8.56	−.76	6.83	9.64	−2.28	4.04	2.93	8.72	6.38
Sri Lanka....................................	524	5.63	5.45	3.76	6.30	4.74	4.33	6.02	−1.54	3.96	6.02	5.45	6.02

GDP Volume Measures

		1994	1995	1996	1997	1998	1999	2000	2001	2002	2003	2004	2005
					Percent Change over Previous Year; Calculated from Indices								
Asia(Cont.)													
Thailand	578	8.99	9.24	5.90	−1.37	−10.51	4.45	4.75	2.17	5.32	7.03	6.17	4.46
Tonga	866	4.79	....	....	....	....	....	....	....	....	....	....	....
Vanuatu	846	2.54	3.17	8.74	4.91	4.31	−3.18	2.67	−2.71	−4.91	2.43	....	....
Europe	170	.10	7.87	4.61	4.01	2.65	.58	5.04	.18	4.43	4.88	6.83	5.63
Belarus	913	−11.70	−10.40	2.80	11.40	8.40	3.40	5.80	4.73	5.05	7.04	11.45	9.24
Bulgaria	918	1.82	2.86	−9.40	−5.58	4.01	2.30	5.39	4.07	4.89	4.45	5.73	5.54
Croatia	960	.64	1.69	4.26	6.76	2.52	−.86	2.86	4.44	5.58	5.34	3.80	4.28
Kazakhstan	916	....	−8.17	.50	1.69	−1.86	2.69	9.81	13.53	9.81	9.29	9.60	9.47
Cyprus	423	5.90	9.92	1.80	2.30	4.97	4.81	5.04	4.11	2.11	1.92	3.92	3.75
Czech Republic	935	2.22	12.51	4.16	−.73	−1.15	1.21	3.89	2.64	1.49	3.21	4.69	5.95
Estonia	939	−1.64	4.53	4.40	11.10	4.44	.31	7.85	6.46	7.24	6.69	7.81	9.78
Hungary	944	2.95	1.49	1.32	4.57	4.86	4.15	6.00	4.33	3.82	3.38	5.22	4.12
Kyrgyz Republic	917	−20.10	−5.40	7.08	9.92	2.12	3.58	5.54	5.32	—	6.99	7.05	−.61
Latvia	941	2.20	−.90	3.79	8.28	4.72	4.70	6.91	8.04	6.47	7.20	8.54	10.19
Lithuania	946	−9.77	3.29	4.68	7.01	7.28	−1.70	4.65	6.44	6.75	10.50	6.98	7.47
Malta	181	3.00	9.33	3.99	4.85	3.43	4.06	6.30	−.42	1.72	−2.57	−.55	2.35
Poland	964	5.20	17.14	6.24	7.09	4.98	4.52	4.19	1.12	1.40	3.84	5.27	3.24
Romania	968	3.93	7.14	3.95	−6.05	−4.82	−1.15	2.15	5.75	5.12	5.22	8.45	....
San Marino	135	....	....	....	....	7.52	9.00	2.20	7.67	−1.67	....	....	....
Slovak Republic	936	6.21	5.84	6.15	4.61	4.21	1.47	2.83	3.23	4.12	4.16	5.42	6.12
Slovenia	961	5.33	4.11	3.73	4.84	3.87	5.42	4.10	2.66	3.45	2.65	4.17	3.87
Turkey	186	−5.46	7.19	7.00	7.53	3.09	−4.71	7.15	−7.32	7.79	5.95	8.93	7.38
Middle East	405	2.23	3.25	5.32	3.80	4.15	1.99	5.21	2.68	3.84	5.76	4.92	
Bahrain	419	−.25	3.93	4.10	3.11	4.78	4.32	5.28	4.64	5.18	6.78	5.85	6.90
Egypt	469	3.97	4.64	4.99	5.49	7.54	6.11	5.38	3.52	3.19	3.11	4.17	4.94
Iran, I.R. of	429	−.35	2.65	7.10	3.38	2.74	1.93	5.14	3.67	7.52	7.11	5.08	....
Israel	436	6.76	7.05	5.36	3.62	3.69	2.34	7.67	−.26	−1.20	1.73	4.44	5.17
Jordan	439	4.99	6.18	2.07	3.32	3.01	3.06	4.10	4.90	4.82	3.25	....	....
Kuwait	443	8.63	1.38	.60	2.49	3.65	−1.79	4.69	.73	5.11	13.38	6.20	....
Oman	449	3.85	4.83	2.89	6.18	2.70	−.23	5.49	7.51	2.57	2.01	5.64	....
Saudi Arabia	456	.67	.20	3.38	2.59	2.83	−.75	4.86	.55	.13	7.66	5.27	6.56
Syrian Arab Rep	463	7.65	5.75	7.34	2.49	7.60	−2.00	.63	3.37	3.23	....	....	....
Yemen Republic	474	3.00	12.19	8.03	6.26	6.83	2.43	4.65	4.66	3.90	4.01	....	....
Western Hemisphere	205	4.97	1.63	3.59	5.20	2.18	.24	3.99	.64	−.36	1.91	5.84	4.22
ECCU	309	3.00	.65	2.67	3.24	3.99	4.09	2.82	−1.30	.19	....	....	....
Antigua and Barbuda	311	6.33	−4.18	6.60	5.23	3.27	3.66	....	....	....	....	....	....
Anguilla	312	7.13	−4.15	3.48	9.20	5.17	8.65	−.33	3.36	−3.09	2.87	15.88	7.80
Argentina	213	5.84	−2.85	5.53	8.11	3.85	−3.39	−.79	−4.41	−10.89	8.84	9.03	9.18
Bahamas, The	313	1.95	1.08	....	....	....	....	....	....	....	....	....	....
Barbados	316	4.47	2.51	3.14	3.30	4.37	3.61	2.28	−2.60	.46	2.04	4.76	3.88
Belize	339	.19	.66	1.42	3.59	3.70	8.74	13.00	4.61	4.72	9.17	4.62	3.10
Bolivia	218	4.67	4.68	4.36	4.95	5.03	.43	2.51	1.68	2.49	2.94	3.92	4.06
Brazil	223	5.85	4.22	2.66	3.27	.13	.79	4.36	1.31	1.93	.54	4.94	2.28
Chile	228	5.71	10.63	7.40	6.61	3.23	−.76	4.49	3.38	2.18	3.92	6.16	6.35
Colombia	233	5.15	5.20	2.06	3.43	.57	−4.20	2.92	1.47	1.93	3.86	4.79	5.20
Costa Rica	238	4.73	3.92	.89	5.58	8.40	8.22	1.80	1.08	2.89	6.40	4.14	5.95
Dominica	321	1.43	1.97	3.51	2.51	3.15	.64	.64	−3.75	−4.06	1.96	3.50	....
Dominican Republic	243	2.95	5.94	7.35	8.14	8.30	6.13	7.87	2.30	5.03	−.40	2.67	9.25
Ecuador	248	4.70	1.75	2.40	4.05	2.12	−6.30	2.80	5.12	3.41	2.66	6.95	6.67
El Salvador	253	6.37	6.72	1.71	4.25	3.75	3.45	2.15	1.65	2.23	1.81	1.54	....
Guatemala	258	4.04	4.95	2.94	4.37	5.01	3.84	3.61	2.33	2.25	2.13	2.75	3.16
Guyana	336	8.48	5.05	7.93	6.18	−1.68	2.96	−1.36	2.28	1.13	−.63	2.51	....
Haiti	263	−8.29	4.43	2.70	2.71	2.18	2.71	.87	−1.04	−.26	.37	−3.52	1.79
Honduras	268	−1.30	4.08	3.58	4.99	2.90	−1.89	5.75	2.61	2.72	3.48	5.02	4.05
Jamaica	343	.98	2.45	.25	−1.08	−1.14	1.05	.71	1.52	1.11	2.26	.94	....
Mexico	273	4.42	−6.17	5.15	6.77	5.03	3.76	6.59	−.03	.77	1.44	4.00	2.96
Montserrat	351	.89	−7.74	−21.33	−20.02	−10.04	−12.75	−2.99	−2.57	3.34	17.16	−11.60	−2.96
Nicaragua	278	3.34	5.91	6.34	3.97	3.71	7.04	4.10	2.96	.75	2.52	5.14	3.98
Panama	283	7.41	1.75	2.81	6.46	7.34	3.92	2.72	.57	2.23	4.21	7.56	6.38
Paraguay	288	3.09	4.71	1.27	2.59	−.41	.48	−.35	2.72	−2.32	2.55	....	....
Peru	293	12.82	8.58	2.49	6.84	−.68	.89	2.92	.18	4.94	3.96	4.81	6.67
St. Kitts and Nevis	361	5.10	3.14	6.68	7.41	.95	3.64	4.32	1.99	.95	2.20	6.42	....
St. Lucia	362	1.32	1.66	2.87	3.43	5.91	2.50	−1.41	−5.14	1.64	3.17	6.34	....
St. Vincent & Grenadines	364	−2.00	7.57	1.45	3.66	5.12	4.16	1.85	1.06	2.72	4.01	3.40	....
Suriname	366	3.25	1.10	.57	6.47	2.32	−1.61	−.07	4.55	3.04	5.30	4.61	....
Trinidad and Tobago	369	3.56	3.96	7.04	7.69	8.12	8.02	6.90	4.17	6.85	12.62	6.38	7.00
Uruguay	298	7.28	−1.45	5.58	5.05	4.54	−2.85	−1.44	−3.38	−11.03	2.18	11.82	6.56
Venezuela, Rep. Bol	299	−2.35	3.95	−.20	6.37	.29	−5.97	3.69	3.39	−8.86	−7.72	17.33	....
Memorandum Items													
Oil Exporting Countries	999	3.09	4.74	5.53	4.31	−4.41	.16	4.79	3.33	2.90	4.19	6.63	....
Non-Oil Developing Countries	201	7.08	6.10	6.61	5.48	3.36	4.44	5.99	3.86	4.81	6.39	7.22	5.55

GDP Volume Measures

		1994	1995	1996	1997	1998	1999	2000	2001	2002	2003	2004	2005
Indices							*Index Numbers: 2000=100*						
World..	001	79.7	82.9	86.4	89.9	92.2	95.6	100.0	102.3	105.1	109.1	114.4	118.8
Industrial Countries................	110	83.6	85.9	88.1	90.9	93.2	96.5	100.0	101.2	102.6	104.6	107.9	110.7
Developing Countries.............	200	74.6	79.0	84.1	88.6	90.8	94.5	100.0	103.8	108.6	115.3	123.6	130.5
Africa....................................	605	81.9	84.0	88.6	91.2	94.1	96.6	100.0	104.2	107.3	111.5	116.2	121.3
Asia.......................................	505	69.3	74.9	81.1	86.1	88.0	93.5	100.0	105.6	112.6	121.8	131.7	....
Europe...................................	170	78.6	84.7	88.7	92.2	94.7	95.2	100.0	100.2	104.6	109.7	117.2	123.8
Middle East...........................	405	79.3	81.9	86.2	89.5	93.2	95.1	100.0	102.7	106.6	112.8	118.3	....
Western Hemisphere.............	205	84.8	86.2	89.2	93.9	95.9	96.2	100.0	100.6	100.3	102.2	108.2	112.7

GDP Deflators

		1994	1995	1996	1997	1998	1999	2000	2001	2002	2003	2004	2005
					Percent Change over Previous Year; Calculated from Indices								
World	001	**19.0**	**9.8**	**6.6**	**5.2**	**4.4**	**3.4**	**4.1**	**3.7**	**3.6**	**3.6**	**5.6**	**3.5**
Industrial Countries	110	**2.1**	**1.9**	**1.8**	**1.5**	**1.2**	**1.1**	**1.6**	**1.8**	**1.6**	**1.6**	**1.8**	**1.9**
United States	111	2.1	2.0	1.9	1.7	1.1	1.4	2.2	2.4	1.7	2.0	2.6	2.8
Canada	156	1.1	2.3	1.6	1.2	−.4	1.7	4.0	1.0	1.0	3.4	3.0	3.3
Australia	193	.7	1.8	2.1	1.3	.5	.5	4.1	4.0	2.6	3.2	3.4	4.5
Japan	158	1.7	—	−.2	.8	.1	−1.3	−1.6	−1.2	−1.6	−1.9	−1.5	−1.8
New Zealand	196	1.8	2.6	1.6	.7	.7	.8	3.1	3.8	−.1	2.7	3.6	2.4
Euro Area	163	....	....	3.1	−.1	3.1	1.1	1.5	2.8	5.1	2.1	1.9	1.6
Austria	122	2.7	2.0	1.0	—	.3	.6	1.8	1.8	1.3	1.0	1.7	2.0
Belgium	124	2.1	2.1	.6	1.2	1.5	1.0	1.7	1.8	1.8	1.7	2.3	2.2
Finland	172	1.8	4.8	−.4	2.2	3.7	−.3	3.0	3.2	1.0	−.3	.5	1.6
France	132	1.5	1.0	1.7	1.1	2.3	−1.4	1.4	2.0	2.4	1.9	1.7	1.9
Germany	134	2.4	1.9	.5	.3	.6	.4	−.7	1.2	1.4	1.0	.8	.5
Greece	174	11.2	9.8	7.4	6.8	5.2	2.8	6.0	1.7	3.8	3.5	3.4	3.7
Ireland	178	1.7	3.0	2.0	4.3	5.7	5.6	5.5	5.7	5.0	2.0	2.2	3.1
Italy	136	3.6	5.0	5.2	2.5	2.6	1.3	2.0	3.0	3.4	3.1	2.9	2.1
Netherlands	138	−1.4	−9.1	1.3	2.6	1.9	14.3	4.1	5.1	3.8	2.5	.9	1.6
Portugal	182	6.1	5.0	3.1	2.8	4.0	9.7	3.0	3.7	3.9	2.7	2.8	2.7
Spain	184	3.9	4.9	3.5	2.4	3.1	2.0	3.5	4.2	4.4	4.0	4.1	4.4
Denmark	128	1.5	1.3	2.0	2.0	1.2	1.7	3.0	2.5	2.3	1.9	2.2	2.6
Iceland	176	2.1	3.0	2.0	5.2	5.0	3.2	3.6	8.6	5.6	.5	2.3	2.9
Norway	142	−.1	2.9	4.1	2.9	−.7	6.6	15.9	1.1	−1.6	2.6	5.6	8.4
Sweden	144	2.7	3.6	1.0	1.7	.6	.9	1.4	2.1	1.6	2.0	.8	1.1
Switzerland	146	1.5	.8	−.1	−.1	−.3	.7	.8	.6	1.6	1.2	.5	.6
United Kingdom	112	1.6	2.7	3.5	2.9	2.7	2.2	1.3	2.2	3.1	3.1	2.6	2.2
Developing Countries	200	**47.9**	**22.0**	**13.8**	**10.6**	**9.2**	**6.4**	**7.6**	**6.2**	**6.2**	**6.1**	**10.9**	**5.6**
Africa	605	**16.9**	**31.4**	**23.0**	**12.3**	**6.4**	**14.1**	**19.8**	**12.2**	**9.4**	**10.6**	**10.3**	**5.1**
Benin	638	35.0	15.1	6.9	3.7	5.2	.4	4.5	2.7	2.3	1.7	−.2	4.6
Botswana	616	16.4	7.6	9.8	18.3	5.2	2.5	9.8	15.3	1.0	−1.0	6.5	5.7
Burkina Faso	748	25.7	5.8	1.0	.7	6.0	−3.1	−1.7	5.8	4.0	3.0	3.1	3.2
Burundi	618	17.7	−.5	15.2	29.8	11.7	15.0	13.2	5.4	1.7	11.6	11.2	14.2
Cameroon	622	24.4	11.6	5.5	3.7	....	....	....	....	....	....	....	....
Congo, Dem. Rep. of	636	....	467.9	638.7	184.9	30.3	441.7	516.2	369.4	....	....	....	....
Ethiopia	644	2.6	12.7	.9	3.7	10.2	3.3	2.9	−6.3	−7.0	14.5	....	....
Ghana	652	30.2	43.2	39.8	19.5	....	....	....	....	....	....	....	....
Guinea-Bissau	654	82.7	−2.3	4.5	12.6	4.0	5.4	3.3	−5.0	4.6	−2.8	....	....
Kenya	664	17.0	11.3	9.0	14.4	11.1	11.1	21.6	1.6	.9	7.0	6.9	....
Lesotho	666	7.6	9.3	8.9	7.7	9.3	12.8	5.8	6.7	8.5	6.0	6.3	4.3
Madagascar	674	41.6	45.1	17.8	7.3	8.5	9.8	7.1	7.3	15.3	2.8	14.3	18.3
Malawi	676	32.2	77.2	51.2	17.9	23.3	39.9	44.7	24.5	17.3	11.5	14.7	16.2
Mali	678	33.9	30.1	1.7	....	....	....	....	....	....	....	....	....
Mauritius	684	6.5	5.4	7.1	5.1	6.9	5.2	2.1	7.1	5.8	5.9	6.0	3.7
Morocco	686	1.1	8.1	1.1	1.9	.4	.5	1.5	1.8	.6	−.1	1.5	1.4
Mozambique	688	55.4	50.3	48.2	9.6	4.8	3.4	6.3	19.5	16.5	8.9	9.3	9.6
Namibia	728	15.7	5.7	14.5	7.1	8.6	6.5	8.9	....	....	....	....	....
Niger	692	16.9	17.3	5.4	2.0	2.4	2.0	−4.0	2.8	6.3	−1.9	−.3	....
Nigeria	694	28.8	111.6	37.5	.8	−4.2	12.1	44.6	−6.3	10.6	23.7	....	....
Rwanda	714	228.9	2.6	−3.4	−10.0	−10.9	−14.0	8.0	.4	7.0	2.7	−7.5	−9.7
Senegal	722	30.2	7.5	1.2	2.1	2.8	.3	2.0	2.5	3.5	1.0	−4.9	....
Seychelles	718	2.0	−.8	−1.5	8.2	7.2	.9	4.8	1.5	....	....	....	....
Sierra Leone	724	25.1	33.6	24.3	16.8	27.0	25.0	6.1	1.8	−3.7	8.2	16.0	7.9
South Africa	199	9.6	10.3	8.1	8.1	7.7	7.1	8.8	7.7	10.5	4.4	5.6	4.7
Swaziland	734	17.2	17.2	10.6	12.0	9.0	9.2	12.2	10.7	....	....	....	....
Tanzania	738	31.4	26.9	19.7	20.8	13.9	10.2	7.7	7.7	7.4	7.1	8.5	7.6
Togo	742	34.7	30.6	.6	2.5	−2.8	1.1	−1.7	1.2	1.1	1.1	−.4	....
Tunisia	744	4.5	5.4	4.4	4.0	3.0	3.1	3.2	2.8	2.4	1.9	3.1	1.4
Uganda	746	51.1	6.4	−6.5	2.8	−8.0	−11.9	−9.7	−4.0	−2.1	2.8	2.2	14.6
Zambia	754	56.7	37.0	23.7	25.7	....	....	....	....	....	....	....	....
Zimbabwe	698	24.9	9.5	25.8	16.1	36.9	65.3	56.1	121.3	150.4	263.0	349.5	....
Asia	505	**13.4**	**11.3**	**6.6**	**4.5**	**7.6**	**1.2**	**2.8**	**3.8**	**2.1**	**2.9**	**11.7**	**....**
Bangladesh	513	3.8	7.3	4.2	3.1	5.3	4.7	1.9	1.6	3.2	4.5	4.2	5.0
Bhutan	514	10.7	3.6	9.7	14.0	8.8	8.1	4.8	5.5	4.3	3.9	3.3	....
China, P.R.: Mainland	924	20.2	15.0	6.4	.9	−2.2	−2.4	−.3	2.9	.5	2.4	19.8	....
China, P.R.: Hong Kong	532	6.9	2.5	5.7	5.6	.2	−5.8	−5.6	−1.8	−3.5	−6.3	−3.6	−.2
Fiji	819	.6	1.0	3.7	2.6	7.4	7.1	−2.6	3.0	2.3	4.6	3.0	....
India	534	9.4	9.0	7.4	6.7	7.9	5.7	3.2	2.8	3.6	4.0	4.0	4.1
Indonesia	536	7.8	9.9	8.7	12.6	75.3	14.2	20.4	16.7	6.0	4.4	6.3	13.7
Korea	542	7.8	7.4	5.1	4.6	5.8	−.1	.7	3.5	2.8	2.7	2.7	−.4
Lao People's Democratic Rep.	544	6.4	20.6	12.9	19.3	85.2	127.1	25.1	8.6	10.6	4.4	22.5	7.3
Malaysia	548	3.9	3.6	3.7	3.5	8.5	—	4.8	−2.9	3.7	3.5	6.3	4.6
Maldives	556	8.6	6.0	3.5	2.2	−3.2	1.7	1.1	.6	.6	−.4	2.4	4.0
Mongolia	948	65.1	35.5	10.6	29.9	−5.8	10.7	9.6	10.7	2.8	10.4	15.3	10.3
Myanmar	518	22.1	19.6	23.0	33.7	35.9	22.7	9.7	24.8	41.5	20.5	....	....
Nepal	558	7.4	7.1	7.5	7.3	3.8	8.8	4.6	3.4	3.1	4.9	5.1	....
Pakistan	564	12.7	13.7	8.2	14.6	7.5	5.9	23.8	7.7	2.4	4.4	7.8	9.8
Papua New Guinea	853	7.2	16.0	2.9	11.2	5.3	11.1	13.1	6.9	12.3	8.0	4.0	....
Philippines	566	10.0	7.6	7.7	6.2	10.5	8.0	8.3	4.7	3.4	3.8	7.2	6.4
Samoa	862	19.2	−6.9	4.5	11.7	3.2	2.3	2.5	3.5	4.8	7.8	3.7	....
Singapore	576	2.7	2.1	1.0	.4	−2.3	−4.6	4.2	−1.8	−.7	−.9	3.5	.6

GDP Deflators

		1994	1995	1996	1997	1998	1999	2000	2001	2002	2003	2004	2005
						Percent Change over Previous Year; Calculated from Indices							
Asia(Cont.)													
Sri Lanka	524	9.3	8.4	12.1	8.6	8.4	4.4	6.7	12.4	8.4	5.0	9.3	9.9
Thailand	578	5.2	5.6	4.0	4.1	9.2	−4.0	1.3	2.1	.8	1.6	3.3	4.6
Vanuatu	846	2.4	3.4	−5.4	3.2	4.8	3.2	1.2	4.3	.7	.7	....	....
Europe	**170**	**61.3**	**51.0**	**37.8**	**54.9**	**33.2**	**29.4**	**26.0**	**22.6**	**17.4**	**10.8**	**7.5**	**4.2**
Belarus	913	1,945.1	661.5	53.7	71.6	76.6	316.8	185.3	79.5	44.9	30.7	22.7	16.6
Bulgaria	918	72.7	62.8	120.8	948.3	23.7	3.7	6.7	6.7	3.8	2.3	4.8	3.8
Croatia	960	107.7	10.6	5.3	7.4	8.4	3.8	4.7	4.0	3.6	3.9	3.3	3.2
Cyprus	423	5.3	3.0	1.8	2.8	2.4	2.3	3.7	3.2	2.2	5.0	2.4	2.8
Czech Republic	935	13.4	10.2	8.7	8.3	11.2	2.8	1.4	4.9	2.8	2.6	3.4	—
Estonia	939	39.7	31.4	24.3	10.4	8.9	4.5	5.4	5.6	4.4	2.1	3.1	6.2
Hungary	944	19.5	26.7	21.2	18.5	12.6	8.4	9.9	8.3	8.7	6.7	4.1	2.5
Kazakhstan	916	....	152.1	28.4	16.6	4.9	23.7	12.4	7.4	1.8	15.8	20.2	14.8
Kyrgyz Republic	917	180.9	42.0	35.3	19.3	9.1	37.7	27.0	7.3	2.0	4.0	5.1	6.8
Latvia	941	36.2	15.1	14.9	7.0	4.6	4.4	4.2	1.7	3.6	3.6	6.8	9.0
Lithuania	946	61.6	46.4	20.6	14.0	5.0	−.6	1.0	−.5	.2	−1.1	2.8	5.9
Malta	181	6.2	1.9	.8	12.9	1.9	1.4	1.9	2.6	2.3	4.0	.7	2.2
Poland	964	37.4	27.9	17.9	13.9	11.1	6.1	7.3	3.5	2.2	.4	4.0	2.8
Romania	968	139.0	35.3	45.3	147.2	55.3	47.7	44.2	37.4	23.4	24.0	15.0	....
San Marino	135	....	....	....	....	1.8	1.6	2.6	2.8	2.3	....	....	....
Slovak Republic	936	13.4	9.9	4.3	6.7	5.2	6.5	8.5	5.0	4.6	4.7	6.0	2.4
Slovenia	961	22.6	24.6	11.1	8.4	6.8	6.4	5.4	8.7	7.9	5.8	3.2	1.0
Turkey	186	106.5	87.2	77.8	81.5	75.7	55.6	50.2	54.5	44.3	22.3	9.9	5.4
Middle East	**405**	**14.0**	**18.4**	**14.2**	**7.6**	**−.1**	**15.1**	**14.9**	**3.5**	**11.5**	**7.7**	**13.4**	**....**
Bahrain	419	7.3	1.1	.2	.9	−7.1	2.6	14.4	−4.9	1.3	6.5	8.3	9.7
Egypt	469	7.0	11.4	7.1	6.3	3.9	.9	4.9	1.9	2.4	6.9	11.6	5.4
Iran, I.R. of	429	31.0	38.7	24.7	14.0	9.5	30.1	26.4	11.6	28.3	11.8	20.6	....
Israel	436	13.8	8.9	11.3	9.2	6.5	6.5	1.5	1.9	4.4	—	−.2	.6
Jordan	439	4.8	4.6	2.1	1.2	6.0	−.1	−.3	1.1	1.6	2.9	....	....
Kuwait	443	−6.0	8.5	15.5	−4.7	−17.2	18.1	17.8	−8.3	5.5	4.8	12.3	....
Oman	449	−.4	1.9	7.6	−2.4	−13.4	11.8	19.9	−6.6	−.7	5.1	7.7	....
Saudi Arabia	456	1.0	5.8	7.1	2.0	−14.0	11.2	11.6	−3.4	2.9	5.7	10.8	16.0
Syrian Arab Rep	463	13.6	6.7	12.7	5.3	−1.5	5.7	9.7	2.1	3.0	....	....	....
Yemen Republic	474	26.1	48.3	31.4	12.8	−10.1	35.6	25.4	.3	7.4	11.0	....	....
Western Hemisphere	**205**	**219.0**	**38.6**	**20.7**	**11.2**	**7.9**	**7.8**	**9.0**	**5.7**	**11.3**	**12.0**	**9.5**	**6.6**
ECCU	309	3.6	2.8	2.0	2.3	2.5	1.8	1.3	1.8	1.0	....	....	....
Antigua and Barbuda	311	3.0	3.0	2.7	2.2	3.3	1.3	....	....	....	....	....	....
Argentina	213	2.8	3.2	−.1	−.5	−1.7	−1.8	1.0	−1.1	30.6	10.5	9.1	8.9
Anguilla	312	24.1	5.3	2.0	2.6	7.4	−2.2	2.2	−1.3	5.9	1.2	7.4	....
Bahamas, The	313	4.9	−.5	....	....	....	....	....	....	....	....	....	....
Barbados	316	.8	4.8	3.5	6.4	3.4	.9	1.0	2.1	−3.2	7.1	−.7	....
Belize	339	3.6	6.1	2.0	−1.5	1.5	−2.2	.6	−.2	1.8	−3.0	.9	....
Bolivia	218	8.0	11.4	11.6	5.7	7.1	2.4	5.2	1.9	2.8	6.2	7.4	8.8
Brazil	223	2,240.4	77.6	17.4	8.3	4.9	5.7	8.4	7.4	10.2	15.0	8.2	7.2
Chile	228	16.4	7.9	2.7	4.3	1.9	2.4	4.6	3.8	4.2	5.8	7.0	4.8
Colombia	233	22.9	18.9	16.9	16.8	14.8	12.6	12.1	6.2	5.9	8.1	7.1	5.5
Costa Rica	238	15.5	22.2	15.8	14.9	12.1	15.0	7.0	8.6	9.2	8.3	11.8	11.1
Dominica	321	5.3	1.1	3.5	1.2	2.6	2.5	.6	2.0	.1	.6	5.3	....
Dominican Republic	243	9.1	8.9	3.7	7.2	5.2	4.2	4.9	6.0	6.1	30.0	48.2	5.6
Ecuador	248	17.8	6.9	2.8	6.8	−3.6	−23.5	−7.0	25.5	11.8	9.0	4.1	....
El Salvador	253	10.6	10.2	6.8	3.5	3.9	.3	3.2	3.4	1.4	2.5	4.3	....
Guatemala	258	11.7	8.7	8.9	8.3	9.5	5.1	6.8	7.6	8.1	6.1	6.8	9.0
Guyana	336	17.6	11.4	4.0	1.4	3.0	8.5	9.2	.3	2.6	4.7	5.9	....
Haiti	263	69.6	9.2	28.8	12.7	14.2	7.0	11.1	11.6	10.0	26.9	21.5	17.6
Honduras	268	28.9	24.9	22.9	22.3	11.6	11.6	9.7	8.0	6.3	7.7	8.5	10.3
Jamaica	343	32.6	23.1	18.5	10.1	8.6	5.6	11.5	8.4	8.7	12.8	13.1	....
Montserrat	351	21.7	2.5	36.3	−20.7	2.0	8.1	1.2	2.4	6.0	−14.7	22.5	5.8
Mexico	273	8.3	37.9	30.7	17.7	15.4	15.1	12.1	5.8	7.0	8.5	7.6	5.4
Nicaragua	278	80.1	13.4	9.6	9.8	14.0	9.2	8.6	7.2	3.2	5.3	10.0	10.3
Panama	283	−.7	.5	4.7	1.6	1.0	.8	−1.2	1.0	1.7	1.1	2.1	....
Paraguay	288	21.0	13.0	10.5	3.0	12.4	2.5	11.9	1.7	16.4	18.3	....	....
Peru	293	26.2	12.9	10.5	7.5	6.2	3.9	3.6	1.4	.6	2.3	5.7	3.5
St. Kitts and Nevis	361	6.3	4.5	—	4.8	3.3	2.4	3.5	1.9	1.5	1.8	4.3	....
St. Lucia	362	2.8	8.4	.1	−1.5	3.6	2.7	3.5	2.3	1.0	1.8	.2	....
St. Vincent & Grenadines	364	2.9	2.5	3.9	1.0	2.8	.2	−.4	1.9	1.7	.2	4.9	....
Suriname	366	439.0	273.9	12.5	.7	−.7	104.7	54.7	35.3	30.3	12.8	9.1	....
Trinidad and Tobago	369	15.6	4.0	1.9	−3.7	−1.9	4.3	12.0	2.8	−5.8	6.1	2.1	17.6
Uruguay	298	39.0	41.0	26.4	19.3	9.4	4.2	4.0	5.3	18.7	18.4	7.5	1.7
Venezuela, Rep. Bol	299	62.9	51.8	115.5	33.9	18.9	26.2	29.5	8.0	33.0	34.9	30.9	....
Memorandum Items													
Oil Exporting Countries	999	18.4	24.9	23.9	12.4	27.8	18.8	23.3	8.8	13.8	11.0	13.7	....
Non-Oil Developing Countries	201	52.1	21.7	12.6	10.4	7.1	5.1	6.0	5.9	5.4	5.6	10.6	4.9

GDP Deflators

		1994	1995	1996	1997	1998	1999	2000	2001	2002	2003	2004	2005
Indices						Index Numbers: 2000=100							
World....................................	001	72.3	79.3	84.6	89.0	92.9	96.0	100.0	103.7	107.4	111.2	117.5	121.5
Industrial Countries................	110	91.4	93.1	94.7	96.2	97.3	98.5	100.0	101.8	103.5	105.1	107.1	109.1
Developing Countries..............	200	52.1	63.5	72.3	80.0	87.4	92.9	100.0	106.2	112.8	119.7	132.7	140.1
Africa....................................	605	37.9	49.7	61.2	68.7	73.1	83.5	100.0	112.2	122.7	135.6	149.6	157.3
Asia.......................................	505	72.1	80.2	85.5	89.4	96.1	97.3	100.0	103.8	106.0	109.1	121.8	....
Europe...................................	170	14.3	21.6	29.7	46.0	61.3	79.4	100.0	122.6	144.0	159.5	171.5	178.6
Middle East...........................	405	52.1	61.6	70.4	75.7	75.6	87.0	100.0	103.5	115.4	124.3	140.9	....
Western Hemisphere..............	205	42.4	58.8	71.0	78.9	85.1	91.8	100.0	105.7	117.7	131.8	144.3	153.9

Gross Capital Formation as Percentage of GDP

		1994	1995	1996	1997	1998	1999	2000	2001	2002	2003	2004	2005
							Percentages						
World	001	**23.90**	**24.22**	**23.86**	**24.00**	**23.64**	**23.50**	**23.79**	**23.13**	**22.75**	**23.32**	**24.11**	....
Industrial Countries	110	**20.69**	**20.83**	**20.82**	**21.16**	**21.30**	**21.45**	**21.64**	**20.54**	**19.71**	**19.71**	**20.33**	**20.74**
United States	111	18.64	18.61	19.00	19.77	20.25	20.63	20.78	19.14	18.40	18.46	19.61	20.06
Canada	156	18.86	18.74	18.20	20.73	20.48	20.13	20.26	19.38	19.92	20.15	20.63	21.15
Australia	193	24.11	23.47	23.24	22.70	24.67	25.24	23.84	22.06	24.03	25.87	25.76	26.21
Japan	158	28.36	28.45	29.11	28.23	25.89	25.18	25.18	24.68	23.06	22.88	22.95	....
New Zealand	196	22.27	23.32	22.82	21.88	20.32	22.27	21.57	22.21	21.89	23.50	24.50	24.49
Euro Area	163	19.98	20.21	19.33	19.62	21.23	21.42	22.54	20.97	20.02	20.08	20.40	20.93
Austria	122	22.81	23.35	22.75	22.98	23.15	23.36	23.38	22.53	20.74	21.74	21.28	20.77
Belgium	124	20.29	20.01	19.57	20.41	20.31	21.10	21.83	20.52	19.23	19.09	19.99	21.37
Finland	172	17.21	17.97	16.98	18.94	19.92	19.40	20.47	20.42	19.26	18.81	19.37	20.21
France	132	18.40	18.64	17.72	17.45	18.77	19.24	20.47	20.07	18.97	18.83	19.47	20.16
Germany	134	22.47	22.22	21.11	21.11	21.61	21.49	21.78	19.49	17.20	17.23	17.19	17.17
Greece	174	18.75	18.92	19.79	20.08	21.35	22.53	23.39	23.46	23.56	25.28	25.19	23.75
Ireland	178	16.13	18.11	19.59	21.48	23.37	24.39	25.04	23.42	22.29	23.23	24.63	27.05
Italy	136	18.75	19.83	19.17	19.36	19.62	20.06	20.70	20.58	21.13	20.67	20.84	20.91
Luxembourg	137	22.94	19.60	20.19	22.24	23.34	23.94	23.15	24.43	21.55	21.26	20.42	21.43
Netherlands	138	20.29	21.02	21.70	22.26	22.75	22.86	22.03	21.48	19.69	19.03	19.54	19.17
Portugal	182	23.91	24.41	24.39	25.73	26.50	27.68	27.56	26.97	25.11	22.71	22.81	22.22
Spain	184	21.47	21.90	21.73	22.08	23.27	25.14	26.28	26.34	26.60	27.45	28.28	29.68
Denmark	128	17.63	19.51	19.04	20.81	21.54	19.84	21.18	20.36	20.41	19.64	20.20	20.91
Iceland	176	17.29	17.62	20.49	19.70	23.99	21.70	22.90	21.27	17.40	19.72	23.42	28.62
Norway	142	21.78	22.89	21.49	23.81	27.27	23.73	20.95	19.63	19.25	18.45	19.94	20.62
Sweden	144	16.39	17.02	16.43	16.07	17.13	17.35	18.29	17.55	16.60	16.37	16.22	17.07
Switzerland	146	23.52	23.37	22.53	22.12	23.39	22.41	23.19	23.63	21.67	20.97	20.36	20.71
United Kingdom	112	16.50	17.01	16.76	17.04	18.19	17.94	17.49	17.26	16.84	16.45	16.94	17.08
Developing Countries	200	**28.33**	**28.88**	**28.06**	**27.93**	**26.65**	**26.13**	**26.56**	**26.45**	**26.67**	**27.96**	**28.98**	....
Africa	605	**18.97**	**19.12**	**18.00**	**17.60**	**18.69**	**18.33**	**17.70**	**18.18**	**18.71**	**19.70**	**21.55**	....
Algeria	612	31.46	31.57	25.08	23.29	27.34	26.25	23.05	27.09	30.42	29.80	....	....
Benin	638	17.80	21.42	17.55	18.54	18.16	18.34	18.67	19.67	18.45	20.30	20.75	18.93
Botswana	616	27.33	25.68	23.73	25.95	30.04	36.78	28.49	39.41	41.46	39.95	43.21	34.78
Burkina Faso	748	24.30	21.36	22.36	24.65	21.91	20.51	21.11	19.64	18.64	20.68	18.21	21.53
Burundi	618	8.70	9.29	12.28	7.20	6.80	7.53	7.55	7.29	10.06	10.72	11.26	15.52
Cameroon	622	14.08	13.69	15.08	16.15	....	....	....	....	....	....	....	....
Central African Rep.	626	11.71	14.12	7.28	10.08	11.01	12.96	11.07	10.19	9.62	6.41	6.82	9.78
Congo, Dem. Rep. of	636	3.46	11.05	14.29	8.15	6.54	9.64	11.04	8.10	9.29	13.80	19.61	....
Congo, Rep. of	634	46.16	50.58	29.15	24.92	49.35	38.56	23.26	35.57	25.92	26.32	25.35	25.33
Côte d'Ivoire	662	12.54	14.95	13.24	13.50	11.58	13.24	10.49	10.91	8.94	9.57	....	....
Ethiopia	644	15.16	16.44	19.10	17.00	17.20	16.00	15.35	16.50	....	....	....	....
Gabon	646	21.87	23.67	23.34	29.59	37.28	28.04	26.14	30.53	28.41	23.90	25.40	....
Ghana	652	23.95	20.02	21.47	24.55	....	....	....	....	....	....	....	....
Guinea-Bissau	654	12.94	18.15	19.77	13.06	6.16	10.78	15.12	18.44	22.48	19.39	....	....
Kenya	664	19.29	21.80	20.33	18.50	17.30	16.15	17.41	19.18	16.31	17.41	18.28	....
Malawi	676	28.66	17.16	11.92	11.33	13.05	14.82	14.50	14.94	11.69	12.47	11.25	11.00
Mali	678	24.37	25.29	18.70	22.54	19.70	18.54	19.66	24.30	18.45	24.62	....	....
Mauritania	682	19.12	20.38	17.76	17.05	13.79	16.03	15.68	16.52	....	....	....	....
Mauritius	684	19.54	17.92	15.90	20.08	19.74	17.64	20.11	13.49	15.40	13.87	24.52	22.79
Morocco	686	21.32	20.67	19.58	20.70	22.16	23.13	23.70	22.89	22.70	24.10	25.04	25.96
Mozambique	688	24.82	30.63	21.83	20.58	24.22	36.68	33.54	25.89	29.83	27.44	....	....
Namibia	728	21.71	21.70	23.12	20.17	25.75	23.28	19.92	23.79	....	....	....	....
Niger	692	17.06	12.59	15.57	15.88	16.20	10.22	19.09	12.04	19.04	17.83	....	....
Nigeria	694	9.32	5.81	6.11	7.01	6.72	5.33	5.41	7.66	8.93	12.05	16.16	....
Rwanda	714	9.98	13.41	14.37	13.80	14.81	17.23	17.53	18.41	16.92	18.43	....	....
Senegal	722	19.83	21.07	20.84	20.17	24.33	24.47	21.97	22.21	21.53	22.26	23.36	....
Seychelles	718	27.08	30.34	32.14	34.36	36.11	....	....	....	....	....	....	....
Sierra Leone	724	8.67	5.49	10.02	4.35	5.50	3.48	6.46	5.63	5.84	13.90	....	....
South Africa	199	16.87	18.17	17.29	16.64	17.00	16.38	15.91	15.29	16.05	16.94	17.64	18.23
Swaziland	734	21.50	19.95	20.69	20.60	22.39	18.75	19.90	18.30	18.21	12.91	....	....
Togo	742	14.90	14.60	12.75	10.97	16.23	11.81	15.40	16.60	16.39	19.45	....	....
Tunisia	744	24.64	24.70	25.01	26.44	26.90	26.32	27.35	27.92	25.68	25.10	24.37	23.37
Uganda	746	14.53	17.14	17.07	16.77	18.63	19.93	18.90	19.64	20.49	21.87	....	....
Zambia	754	8.24	15.95	12.84	14.57	16.39	17.56	18.67	20.04	22.98	26.13	....	....
Zimbabwe	698	28.98	14.77	19.04	18.22	20.89	15.54	15.33	7.64	5.22	7.68	10.18	....
Asia	505	**34.18**	**34.91**	**33.31**	**32.44**	**29.37**	**29.71**	**30.24**	**30.72**	**31.30**	**33.24**	**34.06**	....
Bangladesh	513	18.40	19.12	19.99	20.72	21.63	22.19	23.02	23.09	23.15	23.41	24.02	24.43
Bhutan	514	47.44	46.84	44.68	34.10	38.22	43.07	43.77	....	....	....	....	....
China, P.R.: Mainland	924	41.25	40.81	39.32	38.00	37.40	37.14	36.38	38.00	39.21	42.35	43.15	....
China, P.R.: Hong Kong	532	31.22	34.06	31.58	34.01	28.86	24.85	27.52	25.33	22.85	21.92	21.83	20.53
Fiji	819	13.49	13.85	11.39	11.72	16.01	14.43	12.44	14.86	....	....	....	....
India	534	23.38	26.53	21.77	22.57	21.38	25.36	23.57	23.68	24.70	25.40	27.20	....
Indonesia	536	31.06	31.93	30.69	31.75	16.77	11.37	22.25	22.03	20.93	25.31	23.20	22.24
Korea	542	36.95	37.67	38.87	35.97	25.00	29.12	31.00	29.33	29.08	29.96	30.36	30.24
Malaysia	548	41.20	43.64	41.48	42.97	26.67	22.38	27.30	23.92	24.00	21.59	22.74	19.94
Myanmar	518	12.37	14.24	12.25	12.50	12.38	13.43	12.45	11.57	10.15	11.02	12.05	....
Nepal	558	22.41	25.20	27.33	25.34	24.84	20.48	24.31	24.05	24.08	25.83	26.69	....
Pakistan	564	19.54	18.54	18.98	17.92	17.71	15.57	17.37	17.19	16.77	16.94	17.33	16.84
Papua New Guinea	853	21.37	21.94	22.75	21.06	17.91	16.37	21.89	22.95	21.19	19.33	18.26	....
Philippines	566	24.06	22.45	24.02	24.78	20.34	18.75	21.17	18.97	17.66	16.83	16.79	15.14
Singapore	576	33.10	34.17	35.81	39.25	32.27	31.98	32.41	26.45	23.73	15.60	19.42	18.58

Gross Capital Formation as Percentage of GDP

		1994	1995	1996	1997	1998	1999	2000	2001	2002	2003	2004	2005
							Percentages						
Asia(Cont.)													
Sri Lanka	524	27.03	25.73	24.25	24.39	25.49	27.29	28.04	22.00	21.16	22.07	24.98	26.46
Thailand	578	40.25	42.09	41.82	33.66	20.45	20.50	22.84	24.10	23.80	24.92	27.09	31.61
Vanuatu	846	28.84	32.66	24.80	18.84	17.69	20.28	22.15	19.96	21.18	19.91	....	....
Europe	170	**23.62**	**23.94**	**24.12**	**24.21**	**24.43**	**23.29**	**24.26**	**21.88**	**22.16**	**22.83**	**24.32**	**23.98**
Armenia	911	23.45	18.42	20.01	19.07	19.14	18.35	18.64	19.76	21.67	24.26	24.88	29.69
Belarus	913	32.94	24.75	23.52	26.84	26.71	23.71	25.40	23.76	22.18	26.61	30.49	29.62
Bulgaria	918	9.39	15.65	8.12	9.88	16.88	17.92	18.29	20.67	19.81	21.74	23.45	28.00
Cyprus	423	25.43	22.11	21.91	19.57	19.51	17.32	18.67	16.75	18.97	17.32	20.53	20.49
Czech Republic	935	29.75	32.52	33.02	30.55	28.55	26.94	28.77	28.88	27.92	27.11	27.81	26.37
Estonia	939	27.05	26.64	27.01	30.43	30.34	24.91	27.79	29.17	31.79	32.00	31.21	31.83
Hungary	944	22.19	22.60	25.50	26.57	28.85	28.72	29.89	26.43	25.03	24.44	25.36	23.67
Kazakhstan	916	26.83	22.55	16.89	16.25	16.58	17.08	18.21	27.67	29.20	26.55	26.26	27.74
Kyrgyz Republic	917	9.01	18.34	25.20	21.45	15.16	17.76	19.76	15.49	17.61	11.83	14.49	14.38
Malta	181	30.66	31.98	28.63	21.43	20.03	19.30	26.49	19.37	14.86	17.44	17.96	22.79
Moldova	921	28.83	24.88	24.25	23.81	25.87	22.88	23.95	23.28	21.66	21.36	26.36	29.79
Poland	964	17.62	18.72	20.88	23.43	25.06	25.24	24.84	20.78	18.64	18.77	19.98	18.93
Romania	968	24.81	24.27	25.85	20.63	17.75	16.08	19.47	22.56	21.68	21.85	22.32	23.00
Slovak Republic	936	20.97	24.84	34.75	34.54	34.00	27.57	25.92	29.58	29.01	24.62	26.01	28.42
Slovenia	961	20.94	22.89	22.73	23.87	25.08	27.46	26.79	24.14	23.36	24.71	26.33	25.32
Turkey	186	21.48	25.47	24.55	25.11	24.18	23.35	24.51	16.78	21.32	22.78	25.71	24.77
Ukraine	926	35.33	26.68	22.67	21.45	20.82	17.44	19.72	21.81	20.19	22.01	21.17	22.17
Middle East	405	**21.38**	**23.19**	**24.76**	**24.63**	**25.24**	**23.14**	**23.09**	**23.01**	**24.22**	**24.49**	**24.04**	....
Egypt	469	16.57	17.21	16.61	18.16	21.50	21.62	19.55	18.26	18.26	17.01	16.94	17.70
Iran, I.R. of	429	22.74	29.20	35.88	35.75	32.84	29.74	32.98	32.86	35.10	36.29	36.02	....
Israel	436	25.27	26.41	25.68	24.12	22.49	22.83	21.58	21.18	18.69	17.04	17.43	18.46
Jordan	439	34.17	32.96	30.52	25.73	21.82	21.57	22.36	21.06	20.13	20.79	....	....
Kuwait	443	16.16	14.76	15.11	13.64	18.45	14.56	7.67	8.71	17.09	14.61	14.19	....
Libya	672	16.33	12.16	15.50	12.36	11.96	11.19	13.37	12.71	15.03	....	....	....
Oman	449	15.74	14.98	13.70	17.65	23.98	14.85	11.93	12.64	12.51	15.60	18.73	....
Qatar	453	24.52	35.08	35.77	35.43	31.97	18.88	20.15	23.32	31.45	35.58	30.03	....
Saudi Arabia	456	19.85	19.79	18.10	18.30	22.42	21.14	18.71	18.88	19.67	19.82	18.14	16.24
Syrian Arab Rep	463	29.96	27.23	23.60	20.85	20.55	18.77	17.27	20.77	20.36	23.14	....	....
United Arab Emirates	466	29.36	28.52	26.41	28.10	30.08	....	....	....	....	....	....	....
Yemen, Republic of	474	20.73	21.82	23.29	25.17	32.75	23.75	17.16	17.20	16.20	16.84	....	....
Western Hemisphere	205	**21.55**	**21.48**	**21.37**	**23.07**	**22.89**	**20.68**	**21.05**	**20.13**	**18.80**	**18.94**	**20.77**	**20.82**
Antigua and Barbuda	311	32.40	36.91	39.67	41.32	....	....	....	....	....	....	....	....
Argentina	213	19.97	18.52	19.64	20.86	21.00	17.88	17.52	15.61	10.98	14.59	18.87	21.18
Bahamas, The	313	21.17	23.21	....	....	....	....	....	....	....	....	....	....
Barbados	316	13.31	14.08	12.67	15.40	....	....	....	....	....	....	....	....
Belize	339	20.56	21.71	20.36	20.17	19.07	24.60	31.70	24.87	23.99	20.69	19.80	....
Bolivia	218	14.37	15.24	16.24	19.63	23.61	18.77	18.14	14.27	16.29	13.33	11.18	13.22
Brazil	223	22.15	22.29	20.92	21.50	21.12	20.16	21.54	21.20	19.76	19.76	21.32	20.57
Chile	228	24.29	26.18	27.38	27.72	26.90	20.90	21.86	22.09	21.66	21.95	21.35	22.99
Colombia	233	25.50	25.72	22.05	20.79	19.61	12.77	13.58	14.14	15.15	17.07	....	....
Costa Rica	238	20.05	18.24	15.96	18.08	20.46	17.03	16.91	20.26	22.62	20.63	22.88	25.54
Dominica	321	25.69	31.30	28.78	31.35	27.25	27.70	28.06	23.90	20.64	25.06	27.41	....
Dominican Republic	243	19.37	17.88	18.03	19.01	23.95	22.74	23.51	19.90	21.14	15.81	16.98	15.01
El Salvador	253	19.69	20.04	15.19	15.12	17.55	16.43	16.93	16.67	16.19	16.67	15.56	....
Grenada	328	35.80	32.08	34.83	35.90	36.11	39.89	43.81	36.16	32.86	41.78	35.59	....
Guatemala	258	15.68	15.05	12.69	13.68	17.40	17.35	17.84	17.78	19.11	18.81	19.82	19.26
Honduras	268	37.63	31.56	31.13	32.17	30.93	34.67	30.72	29.57	25.62	26.64	30.38	29.88
Jamaica	343	27.15	28.76	29.11	29.25	25.81	24.45	26.82	29.13	31.74	29.86	....	....
Mexico	273	21.72	19.82	23.11	25.86	24.32	23.47	23.73	20.88	20.65	20.55	22.09	21.79
Nicaragua	278	20.37	22.00	25.77	31.16	31.03	38.35	30.98	28.25	26.07	25.86	27.12	29.36
Panama	283	24.48	27.65	26.74	25.68	27.21	25.79	24.14	17.64	15.75	19.00	19.32	....
Paraguay	288	23.36	23.93	23.40	23.55	22.93	23.04	21.85	19.78	19.09	19.82	....	....
Peru	293	22.25	24.83	22.85	24.13	23.66	21.16	20.24	18.80	18.79	18.81	18.50	18.48
St. Vincent & Grenadines	364	28.51	30.05	28.16	30.81	35.81	34.55	27.28	29.78	30.05	33.87	34.90	....
Suriname	366	34.16	29.67	66.90	60.16	84.13	57.06	51.71	57.87	64.56	66.99	....	....
Trinidad and Tobago	369	20.20	20.78	24.28	30.11	33.38	21.01	17.03	19.44	....	....	....	....
Uruguay	298	15.87	15.41	15.24	15.22	15.87	15.14	13.96	13.77	11.52	12.59	13.08	13.16
Venezuela, Rep. Bol.	299	14.16	18.11	16.55	27.67	30.66	26.52	24.17	27.52	21.16	15.56	21.05	....
Memorandum Items													
Oil Exporting Countries	999	**24.05**	**25.67**	**25.75**	**27.20**	**22.64**	**19.01**	**22.62**	**23.37**	**23.56**	**24.98**	**24.77**	....
Non-Oil Developing Countries.	201	**28.94**	**29.35**	**28.39**	**28.03**	**27.14**	**27.00**	**27.04**	**26.83**	**27.05**	**28.32**	**29.48**	....

Final Consumption Expenditure as Percentage of GDP

		1994	1995	1996	1997	1998	1999	2000	2001	2002	2003	2004	2005
							Percentages						
World................................	001	**76.10**	**75.88**	**76.02**	**75.66**	**75.86**	**76.31**	**75.98**	**76.68**	**76.56**	**76.26**	**75.47**	....
Industrial Countries................	110	**79.01**	**78.73**	**78.73**	**78.20**	**78.45**	**78.96**	**79.18**	**80.06**	**80.81**	**81.12**	**80.83**	**80.92**
United States........................	111	82.68	82.62	82.23	81.45	81.58	82.18	83.09	84.49	85.65	86.10	85.71	85.76
Canada..............................	156	80.36	78.42	78.12	77.57	77.73	75.82	73.46	75.01	75.77	75.78	75.17	74.84
Australia............................	193	77.04	77.84	77.04	76.93	77.12	77.64	77.12	77.34	77.09	76.87	77.00	76.03
Japan................................	158	69.62	70.15	70.64	70.75	71.93	73.69	73.34	74.55	75.69	75.37	75.39	75.41
New Zealand........................	196	75.83	75.87	76.58	77.69	79.39	78.50	76.75	75.46	76.39	76.28	76.56	78.03
Euro Area............................	163	78.00	77.53	77.95	77.31	77.26	76.83	78.91	77.37	77.37	77.77	77.54	77.66
Austria..............................	122	77.61	77.15	77.93	76.81	75.59	74.99	74.18	74.36	74.27	74.76	74.50	74.27
Belgium............................	124	75.67	75.67	76.44	75.23	75.42	74.72	74.62	75.27	75.38	76.34	75.98	76.28
Finland.............................	172	76.35	74.48	75.61	73.08	71.30	71.40	69.83	70.65	72.13	74.31	74.37	74.91
France..............................	132	80.73	80.22	80.77	79.65	78.68	78.66	78.63	78.78	79.32	80.16	80.28	80.80
Germany............................	134	77.38	77.31	77.99	77.64	77.03	77.65	77.87	78.50	78.27	78.72	77.87	77.84
Greece..............................	174	86.73	88.40	88.19	87.27	87.00	86.01	87.52	83.99	83.86	82.37	83.66	83.48
Ireland.............................	178	74.97	70.93	69.74	66.67	64.70	60.81	59.91	59.62	58.78	59.07	58.87	60.29
Italy................................	136	77.86	76.37	76.16	76.79	77.30	78.08	78.37	78.05	77.91	78.78	78.47	79.14
Luxembourg........................	137	65.64	59.20	59.58	60.44	60.21	55.33	53.70	56.70	56.18	57.52	57.85	56.27
Netherlands........................	138	73.59	73.30	73.02	72.07	72.57	72.93	72.42	72.73	73.79	74.01	73.20	72.63
Portugal............................	182	86.55	85.27	85.37	84.95	85.95	82.38	83.20	82.93	83.09	83.97	85.05	86.55
Spain...............................	184	78.68	78.08	77.75	77.07	76.66	76.73	76.85	76.11	75.43	74.79	75.50	75.54
Denmark............................	128	77.13	76.40	76.06	75.52	76.35	75.12	72.78	73.00	73.76	74.28	74.89	74.37
Iceland.............................	176	79.12	80.25	80.43	79.77	80.48	83.04	84.44	79.80	81.01	83.39	82.26	84.90
Norway..............................	142	72.04	70.87	69.49	67.90	70.84	68.77	61.71	63.30	67.09	68.13	65.91	62.15
Sweden..............................	144	79.42	76.50	77.33	76.80	76.68	76.50	75.82	75.99	76.69	77.03	75.62	75.22
Switzerland.........................	146	70.91	71.49	72.35	72.33	71.70	71.95	71.10	72.01	71.94	72.48	72.31	72.79
United Kingdom....................	112	84.18	83.05	83.30	82.50	82.39	83.43	84.24	85.08	85.96	86.11	85.70	86.46
Developing Countries...............	200	**72.10**	**71.96**	**72.28**	**72.16**	**72.53**	**72.89**	**71.87**	**72.34**	**71.10**	**70.01**	**68.59**	....
Africa...............................	605	**83.53**	**83.05**	**82.56**	**83.56**	**85.14**	**80.85**	**78.00**	**81.23**	**80.41**	**81.02**	**80.87**	**81.80**
Algeria..............................	612	74.05	72.57	67.72	67.99	72.79	68.38	55.49	58.28	59.57	55.95	....	....
Benin................................	638	89.94	87.64	85.97	85.81	87.25	87.73	85.64	88.87	90.29	89.78	88.43	88.06
Botswana...........................	616	62.42	63.66	61.40	56.51	57.48	62.79	55.57	42.99	46.66	49.89	49.76	50.53
Burkina Faso........................	748	85.35	89.77	92.93	89.53	91.97	94.31	95.22	94.17	93.96	92.04	92.59	90.77
Burundi.............................	618	107.06	105.06	97.61	97.39	104.49	100.86	105.92	107.85	107.37	108.27	107.15	111.91
Cameroon...........................	622	73.86	76.02	75.67	73.47	....	....	....	....	....	....	....	....
Central African Rep.................	626	89.91	91.91	96.87	91.97	94.72	91.80	93.84	95.20	94.56	93.35	98.45	96.18
Congo, Dem. Rep. of................	636	93.36	84.21	77.52	90.34	94.73	90.13	89.16	93.14	87.82	93.31	83.21	....
Congo, Rep. of......................	634	71.33	47.89	61.96	59.64	50.49	48.46	33.31	44.21	43.80	42.81	45.30	39.43
Côte d'Ivoire........................	662	77.64	79.66	76.00	76.79	80.20	77.81	81.18	80.59	75.16	79.69	80.05	79.27
Ethiopia............................	644	94.97	93.31	93.50	103.50	92.20	98.80	101.00	99.00	91.92	92.46	95.07	94.50
Gabon..............................	646	54.71	52.69	49.05	49.02	61.03	65.19	71.67	....	....	....	....	....
Ghana..............................	652	87.40	88.30	88.14	92.19	....	....	....	....	....	....	....	....
Guinea-Bissau......................	654	107.50	102.75	102.79	96.87	113.96	97.11	116.63	107.16	109.39	110.54	110.54	110.54
Kenya..............................	664	77.57	84.11	83.97	88.87	90.32	89.63	93.34	94.73	95.13	93.84	91.95	....
Madagascar.........................	674	96.66	96.63	93.65	96.35	95.07	93.11	93.54	89.27	95.64	97.13	92.89	....
Malawi.............................	676	94.85	96.82	98.15	100.95	92.35	100.45	95.71	94.19	106.22	110.19	114.05	131.90
Mali................................	678	95.73	91.69	95.97	86.81	89.57	91.49	90.93	84.93	83.21	81.74	87.70	82.48
Mauritania.........................	682	91.61	80.13	88.34	88.40	94.17	92.25	94.21	86.09	....	....	....	....
Mauritius...........................	684	76.96	76.84	76.01	75.49	75.05	76.71	74.42	73.38	74.81	75.25	77.85	83.40
Morocco............................	686	87.74	89.03	88.06	86.45	86.12	85.43	87.71	87.11	86.69	86.17	88.32	89.39
Mozambique........................	688	111.74	109.16	101.83	98.92	93.18	90.97	91.52	85.89	73.43	80.40	78.24	77.81
Namibia............................	728	83.31	86.79	87.96	90.87	89.10	89.42	90.01	87.64	....	....	....	....
Niger...............................	692	92.99	94.32	91.52	91.64	92.81	97.41	88.94	95.68	90.46	99.82	96.54	96.37
Nigeria.............................	694	85.53	84.25	88.92	88.65	102.78	66.91	54.34	83.17	80.19	82.65	81.40	....
Rwanda.............................	714	127.43	107.26	105.80	104.08	102.90	100.04	98.72	97.42	99.97	100.84	97.61	101.42
Senegal.............................	722	93.70	90.85	91.24	89.15	89.19	85.53	87.00	91.95	....	....	....	....
Seychelles..........................	718	75.30	76.39	77.07	77.71	81.26	87.29	73.80	99.47	80.96	87.05	88.73	88.65
Sierra Leone........................	724	91.80	95.00	91.65	98.27	94.63	96.10	96.00	103.35	94.34	88.97	....	....
South Africa........................	199	81.86	80.91	81.55	82.57	82.10	81.63	81.13	80.99	80.20	81.82	82.48	83.72
Swaziland...........................	734	96.51	98.68	105.31	96.66	96.70	99.70	95.46	86.73	88.57	91.03	89.22	91.22
Togo................................	742	94.43	98.79	100.15	100.13	96.75	98.36	98.02	100.03	98.13	97.50	90.14	90.29
Tunisia..............................	744	78.30	79.21	76.49	76.02	76.45	75.94	76.30	76.66	78.60	78.77	78.41	79.27
Uganda.............................	746	96.72	98.74	103.40	93.18	91.62	92.50	94.11	94.56	94.53	92.28	91.37	90.69
Zambia.............................	754	92.58	87.81	94.71	90.63	96.08	101.14	91.70	82.72	82.34	81.25	....	....
Zimbabwe..........................	698	72.94	83.60	80.90	90.62	81.58	84.51	87.50	94.69	95.76	94.51	95.49	....
Asia.................................	505	**65.85**	**65.81**	**66.67**	**66.19**	**66.34**	**67.65**	**67.09**	**66.84**	**65.98**	**64.36**	**63.21**	....
Bangladesh.........................	513	86.90	86.87	85.10	84.10	82.59	82.29	82.12	82.00	81.84	81.37	80.47	79.84
Bhutan.............................	514	62.35	57.91	64.98	75.37	77.31	74.98	72.59	....	....	....	....	....
China, P.R.: Mainland...............	924	57.39	57.49	58.54	58.19	58.74	60.14	61.13	59.79	58.20	55.45	54.30	....
China, P.R.: Hong Kong.............	532	67.55	70.39	69.87	69.35	70.59	69.89	68.03	70.18	68.86	68.84	69.30	67.00
Fiji.................................	819	78.68	80.58	78.88	79.12	76.83	68.13	75.87	75.86	....	....	....	....
India................................	534	76.31	75.30	76.70	75.78	77.74	77.53	76.62	76.74	74.66	73.55	71.83	....
Indonesia...........................	536	67.80	69.41	69.92	68.52	73.47	80.55	68.18	68.46	73.21	75.42	75.84	73.66
Korea...............................	542	63.74	63.47	64.27	64.22	62.13	64.23	66.08	68.11	68.62	66.98	65.05	66.75
Malaysia............................	548	60.40	60.29	57.14	56.11	51.33	52.57	52.75	57.69	57.74	57.54	56.00	56.53
Myanmar...........................	518	88.25	86.63	88.54	88.21	88.25	86.90	87.65	88.49	89.76	88.97	87.89	....
Nepal...............................	558	85.33	85.19	86.17	86.04	86.23	86.39	84.83	85.02	87.98	88.41	87.78	....
Pakistan............................	564	83.21	84.17	88.52	86.77	83.33	86.05	83.88	83.88	83.32	82.46	81.61	87.79
Papua New Guinea..................	853	64.87	60.72	66.25	79.84	76.87	73.40	61.17	63.97	75.90	65.12	63.69	....
Philippines.........................	566	85.15	85.47	85.40	85.79	87.60	85.69	82.70	82.88	80.93	80.29	78.96	79.34
Singapore..........................	576	52.10	49.77	49.71	48.93	48.63	50.91	51.69	56.10	58.88	57.83	54.23	52.59

Final Consumption Expenditure as Percentage of GDP

		1994	1995	1996	1997	1998	1999	2000	2001	2002	2003	2004	2005
							Percentages						
Asia(Cont.)													
Sri Lanka..............	524	84.78	84.71	84.68	82.68	80.29	80.49	82.57	84.23	85.56	84.10	84.11	82.80
Thailand..............	578	63.73	63.07	63.96	64.74	65.21	67.46	67.46	68.61	68.32	67.87	67.79	68.74
Vanuatu..............	846	76.87	73.94	76.77	79.71	77.57	80.83	80.69	79.35	84.42	85.38	....	....
Europe......................	**170**	**78.58**	**79.53**	**79.90**	**80.60**	**81.11**	**82.22**	**81.70**	**81.91**	**79.61**	**80.76**	**79.25**	**80.53**
Armenia..............	911	105.83	117.45	111.65	114.74	111.15	108.28	108.94	104.84	99.07	93.49	92.65	86.82
Belarus..............	913	79.90	79.64	80.56	77.38	77.71	78.15	76.39	79.18	80.52	78.51	74.33	72.81
Bulgaria..............	918	91.23	85.94	86.47	85.54	82.89	87.85	87.06	86.90	86.81	87.75	86.80	88.60
Cyprus..............	423	74.23	78.42	81.44	82.63	82.01	81.49	81.75	81.84	82.49	82.83	82.65	83.34
Czech Republic..............	935	72.93	71.80	72.94	74.78	72.58	74.25	74.31	73.66	74.13	75.10	72.67	71.54
Estonia..............	939	84.26	83.03	84.64	81.00	80.35	80.33	77.09	76.55	77.56	77.44	74.96	72.01
Hungary..............	944	84.28	77.45	74.04	72.40	72.58	74.00	74.15	75.15	77.31	79.92	78.19	78.48
Kazakhstan..............	916	82.57	81.88	83.88	86.38	88.16	80.67	74.25	73.42	70.85	67.90	65.02	63.10
Kyrgyz Republic..............	917	97.29	94.55	100.62	86.22	106.10	96.77	85.73	82.30	86.15	94.74	94.22	104.00
Malta..............	181	79.51	81.68	85.30	86.37	85.37	85.91	84.20	86.08	83.69	86.08	88.99	88.60
Moldova..............	921	75.43	82.89	94.34	97.35	100.89	90.01	103.02	101.11	103.25	110.25	103.95	108.41
Poland..............	964	80.23	79.13	80.56	80.50	79.77	80.67	81.58	82.89	84.79	83.80	82.01	81.38
Romania..............	968	77.26	81.32	82.57	86.44	90.28	88.75	86.16	85.19	84.02	85.66	86.74	87.52
Slovak Republic..............	936	73.41	72.66	75.77	74.95	76.67	76.79	76.55	78.51	78.17	77.24	76.71	76.04
Slovenia..............	961	76.87	78.92	78.22	76.87	76.36	76.74	76.68	76.60	75.26	75.36	74.87	75.03
Turkey..............	186	81.61	81.10	78.84	80.30	81.87	87.42	85.59	86.27	80.25	80.08	79.17	82.37
Ukraine..............	926	67.83	76.40	79.88	81.61	81.46	77.03	75.25	76.57	75.43	75.42	71.31	76.96
Middle East..............................	**405**	**73.91**	**73.61**	**72.19**	**72.72**	**78.16**	**73.78**	**69.84**	**71.63**	**69.75**	**67.76**	**64.77**	**....**
Egypt..............	469	84.86	85.00	87.31	88.10	88.00	86.64	87.06	86.59	86.09	85.65	83.43	83.95
Iran, I.R. of..............	429	62.15	63.04	59.76	61.16	69.34	64.53	61.53	62.13	57.86	57.71	56.93	....
Israel..............	436	89.02	87.91	87.71	86.03	85.10	84.91	83.81	86.39	89.68	88.59	87.80	86.91
Jordan..............	439	89.71	88.17	94.78	96.54	97.66	96.30	104.35	104.02	100.94	101.52	....	....
Kuwait..............	443	74.97	74.85	71.80	73.10	88.78	78.94	65.40	75.14	74.90	67.12	58.83	....
Libya..............	672	82.74	81.08	79.74	82.70	89.55	82.16	67.26	76.43	74.20	62.28	45.96	32.51
Oman..............	449	76.04	76.54	72.26	70.88	83.48	73.51	60.24	66.21	66.93	65.78	66.89	....
Qatar..............	453	64.37	63.92	60.29	52.45	56.90	46.77	34.89	35.30	35.69	33.97	32.48	....
Saudi Arabia..............	456	72.17	70.52	68.43	68.49	74.38	67.32	62.54	65.31	62.92	58.18	54.06	49.46
Syrian Arab Rep..............	463	82.37	79.66	82.66	80.53	79.82	80.91	75.78	72.69	71.76	73.93	....	....
United Arab Emirates..............	466	63.06	64.41	61.41	63.10	69.90	....	....	....	....	....	....	....
Yemen Republic..............	474	97.34	97.82	85.73	83.69	88.23	78.61	75.25	81.95	83.35	87.39	....	....
Western Hemisphere................	**205**	**80.07**	**79.36**	**79.18**	**78.94**	**80.31**	**80.71**	**79.73**	**81.07**	**79.34**	**78.45**	**76.39**	**76.60**
Antigua and Barbuda..............	311	66.07	71.83	74.83	69.61	66.63	63.01	67.17	57.33	59.17	57.40	57.68	....
Argentina..............	213	83.11	81.91	81.03	81.39	81.55	83.87	83.12	83.07	74.13	74.64	74.00	73.25
Bahamas, The..............	313	84.02	83.45	....	....	....	....	....	....	....	....	....	....
Barbados..............	316	72.17	81.70	80.28	84.07	83.63	86.12	88.07	86.66	88.69	88.65	92.17	....
Belize..............	339	86.23	86.15	88.75	90.55	91.80	90.90	86.90	91.26	93.02	92.24	93.36	....
Bolivia..............	218	91.16	89.39	88.46	88.62	89.28	91.63	90.90	91.02	89.72	87.47	83.89	....
Brazil..............	223	77.50	79.48	80.99	80.87	81.06	81.38	79.97	79.79	78.17	76.64	74.02	75.05
Chile..............	228	71.98	71.39	74.31	74.40	76.37	76.83	76.28	76.38	75.93	73.90	69.75	68.74
Colombia..............	233	80.38	80.63	83.49	84.99	86.17	86.58	84.21	86.19	86.07	83.28	....	....
Costa Rica..............	238	85.52	84.57	87.51	85.76	82.19	77.15	80.23	82.72	82.63	81.24	80.26	79.67
Dominica..............	321	90.40	84.70	89.22	83.22	80.68	81.18	86.17	93.28	92.44	87.02	86.06	....
Dominican Republic..............	243	86.09	85.71	84.95	85.03	83.89	84.06	85.37	87.35	86.71	84.85	82.55	88.54
El Salvador..............	253	95.55	96.08	97.67	96.54	94.74	95.92	98.11	99.13	98.60	99.68	101.36	....
Grenada..............	328	77.13	84.05	86.12	87.04	88.68	72.82	74.36	85.29	91.23	88.18	97.68	....
Guatemala..............	258	91.55	91.12	92.09	91.96	90.69	91.00	90.92	92.40	93.24	93.84	94.48	95.05
Guyana..............	336	63.58	62.30	62.15	64.58	....	....	....	78.34	74.59	76.04	78.56	....
Haiti..............	263	101.21	121.61	98.80	102.14	99.31	....	....	....	....	....	....	....
Honduras..............	268	72.39	72.82	73.99	73.46	76.73	80.28	83.15	86.86	89.60	89.08	88.42	90.61
Jamaica..............	343	79.10	81.53	82.39	83.57	84.16	83.82	84.58	87.07	88.20	88.01	85.90	....
Mexico..............	273	83.11	77.52	74.83	74.24	77.82	78.15	78.21	81.39	81.21	81.07	79.95	79.81
Nicaragua..............	278	96.20	93.55	93.46	93.64	92.75	94.23	96.24	97.44	100.23	101.00	99.50	100.26
Panama..............	283	62.53	61.03	72.01	69.92	74.71	75.40	73.10	75.57	79.08	75.95	77.38	....
Paraguay..............	288	95.22	92.47	92.81	92.66	94.00	90.70	92.90	96.32	93.81	94.64	....	....
Peru..............	293	81.13	80.85	82.10	80.29	81.72	81.17	81.68	82.89	82.09	81.19	78.87	76.32
St. Kitts and Nevis..............	361	70.67	77.18	80.81	76.38	73.78	88.81	80.38	71.39	80.08	68.45	69.15	....
St. Lucia..............	362	77.81	76.86	81.91	84.22	81.71	82.35	84.32	86.21	89.58	94.48	93.39	83.88
St. Vincent & Grenadines..............	364	95.77	84.34	85.08	97.25	93.15	86.07	80.97	81.04	81.27	83.38	87.74	....
Suriname..............	366	30.57	26.73	59.64	73.36	....	....	....	....	74.82	66.75	65.17	....
Trinidad and Tobago..............	369	66.96	64.70	65.35	73.10	71.94	73.23	69.10	69.82	74.82	66.75	65.17	....
Uruguay..............	298	84.74	84.70	84.95	84.77	84.86	86.12	87.72	87.92	86.52	85.90	84.56	84.64
Venezuela, Rep. Bol..............	299	77.28	76.59	68.26	65.05	71.10	69.73	64.20	69.15	66.55	67.63	62.84	....
Memorandum Items													
Oil Exporting Countries...........	**999**	**70.39**	**70.66**	**68.74**	**68.28**	**75.05**	**72.25**	**63.32**	**66.98**	**66.98**	**66.49**	**64.49**	**....**
Non-Oil Developing Countries.	**201**	**72.34**	**72.15**	**72.79**	**72.71**	**72.23**	**72.97**	**72.91**	**73.00**	**71.60**	**70.44**	**69.08**	**....**

Commodity Prices

Market Prices (lines 76) and Unit Values (lines 74) Country of Origin and, for Market Prices, Pricing Point in Parentheses

		1994	1995	1996	1997	1998	1999	2000	2001	2002	2003	2004	2005
Aluminum (US $/MT)													
All Origins (London) *	156	1,475.64	1,805.02	1,506.81	1,599.28	1,357.58	1,359.99	1,551.50	1,446.74	1,351.08	1,432.83	1,718.52	1,900.52
Bananas (US $/MT)													
Latin America (US Ports) *	248	439.79	445.10	469.58	522.56	492.19	373.92	422.27	584.70	527.61	375.19	524.84	576.77
Barley (US $/MT)													
Canada (Winnepeg) *	156	72.65	104.01	119.67	97.24	85.05	75.94	77.23	93.94	108.97	104.72	98.99	95.08
Beef (US cents/pound)													
Australia-NZ (US Ports) *	193	105.82	86.50	80.97	84.17	78.30	83.14	87.79	96.54	95.40	89.74	113.91	118.73
Argentina (frozen)	213	111.55	102.34	82.14	87.83	114.38	100.56	99.28	80.58	....	....	....	....
Butter (US cents/pound)													
New Zealand	196	84.44	99.29	103.19	83.72	80.42	68.96	63.99	67.76	57.10	68.30	87.46	93.64
Coal (US $/MT)													
Australia	193	32.30	39.37	38.07	35.10	29.23	25.89	26.25	32.31	27.06	27.95	56.73	51.02
Australia	193	37.35	40.08	43.14	41.43	37.37	31.60	29.13	33.28	34.14	32.82	43.49	71.11
South Africa	199	28.56	35.23	33.52	31.35	26.84	24.27	26.57	33.86	26.01	29.97	54.69	46.06
Cocoa Beans (US $/MT)													
New York and London *	652	1,395.68	1,432.54	1,455.25	1,618.74	1,676.00	1,135.05	903.91	1,088.38	1,779.04	1,753.07	1,550.74	1,544.66
Coconut Oil (US $/MT)													
Philippines (New York) *	566	610.82	672.38	769.06	663.21	655.03	758.59	457.73	314.23	414.78	461.75	673.30	619.63
Philippines	566	559.83	616.30	719.91	623.44	598.64	716.07	445.89	294.47	373.28	425.55	602.24	570.33
Coffee (US cents/pound)													
Other Milds (New York) *	386	148.53	149.41	120.25	185.02	132.40	101.67	85.05	61.91	60.37	64.05	80.09	114.33
Brazil (New York)	223	143.32	145.98	120.29	166.80	121.81	88.92	79.80	50.50	45.03	50.78	69.24	101.41
Brazil	223	115.51	123.88	100.21	143.38	106.24	79.56	73.16	43.74	34.95	43.16	56.27	84.43
Uganda (New York) *	799	119.82	126.83	82.84	80.70	83.93	67.65	42.16	27.32	30.82	38.38	37.28	53.37
Copper (US $/MT)													
United Kingdom (London) *	112	2,305.53	2,932.04	2,293.39	2,275.19	1,653.71	1,572.53	1,814.52	1,580.17	1,560.29	1,779.36	2,863.47	3,676.50
Copra (US $/MT)													
Philippines (Europ. Ports)	566	416.84	438.50	488.98	433.75	411.03	462.27	308.92	195.55	265.93	299.45	451.13	413.71
Cotton (US cents/pound)													
Liverpool Index *	111	79.72	98.30	80.54	79.23	65.53	53.13	59.05	48.00	46.26	63.44	62.01	55.17
DAP (US $/MT)													
US Gulf Coast	111	172.79	216.59	213.16	199.92	203.42	177.78	154.22	147.73	157.53	179.41	221.25	247.03
Fish (US $/kilogram)													
Norway *	142	5.01	4.78	4.11	3.73	3.72	3.57	3.65	2.89	2.94	2.99	3.34	4.06
Fish Meal (US $/MT)													
Any Origin (Hamburg) *	293	403.17	521.48	629.27	645.95	709.00	433.11	452.10	530.05	645.54	650.20	692.88	744.23
Iceland	176	452.21	528.38	611.03	673.15	724.26	493.31	468.77	....	....	....	....	....
Gasoline (US cents/gallon)													
US Gulf Coast	111	47.90	50.92	59.65	58.53	41.30	51.84	83.37	73.41	72.05	87.17	117.03	158.83
Gold (US $/troy ounce)													
United Kingdom (London)	112	384.12	384.16	387.82	331.00	294.14	278.87	279.17	271.05	310.04	363.53	409.23	444.84
Groundnuts (US $/MT)													
Nigeria (London) *	694	921.03	816.67	810.11	874.21	795.10	762.64	785.51	753.25	654.93	855.90	910.00	769.11
Groundnut Oil (US $/MT)													
Any Origin (Europe) *	694	1,022.64	990.92	897.33	1,010.42	908.58	786.67	712.43	671.80	687.97	1,250.63	1,159.42	1,060.44
Hides (US cents/pound)													
United States (Chicago) *	111	86.81	88.14	87.32	88.25	76.69	72.15	80.22	84.60	80.75	68.30	67.13	65.64
Iron Ore (US cents/DMTU)													
Brazil (North Sea Ports) *	223	26.47	28.38	30.00	30.15	31.00	27.59	28.79	30.03	29.33	31.95	37.90	65.00
Jute (US $/MT)													
Bangladesh (Chitta.-Chalna)	513	295.67	365.67	454.25	302.00	259.08	275.67	278.83	329.58	290.75	241.96	280.63	290.00
Lamb (US cents/pound)													
New Zealand (London) *	196	125.66	113.26	145.44	150.28	116.00	115.84	112.85	130.25	146.04	159.81	165.77	160.92
Lead (US $/MT)													
United Kingdom (London) *	112	548.72	629.30	774.13	623.06	526.92	501.77	454.17	476.36	452.25	514.21	881.95	974.37
Linseed Oil (US $/MT)													
Any Origin	001	516.74	657.50	565.83	571.24	707.71	512.54	399.39	382.25	520.21	678.20	872.75	....
Maize (US $/MT)													
United States (US Gulf Pts) *	111	107.78	123.45	164.52	117.17	101.62	90.29	88.22	89.61	99.33	105.19	111.78	98.41
Thailand	578	162.64	204.19	302.33	280.57	153.70	173.23	304.96	111.77	181.77	184.60	145.85	258.92
Natural Gas (US $/000 M³)													
Russian Federation	922	83.25	97.06	99.00	96.13	80.82	65.05	124.34	139.44	95.99	125.51	135.18	212.94
Indonesia	536	69.12	74.83	82.11	79.13	57.95	70.33	110.14	98.24	93.14	104.80	123.95	147.96
United States	111	68.94	61.36	96.82	88.57	75.16	81.40	155.07	142.53	120.99	197.83	212.69	319.03
Newsprint (US $/short ton)													
Finland	172	401.99	605.05	650.84	470.85	453.66	....	....	....	....	....	....	....
Nickel (US $/MT)													
United Kingdom(N.Europ.Ports)*	156	6,331.93	8,223.56	7,504.09	6,924.72	4,623.59	6,002.51	8,630.52	5,969.63	6,783.31	9,630.29	13,821.01	14,777.82
Olive Oil (US $/MT)													
United Kingdom *	112	3,148.84	4,499.51	5,965.18	4,236.48	3,227.05	3,650.44	2,980.12	2,667.28	2,900.51	3,796.77	4,630.94	5,519.16
Oranges (US $/MT)													
French Import Price *	132	411.34	531.47	491.67	458.96	442.40	438.23	363.21	595.50	564.53	683.05	854.55	842.28
Palm Kernel Oil(US $/MT)													
Malaysia (Rotterdam)	548	627.75	677.67	727.97	651.83	686.93	695.03	448.72	308.86	416.47	458.49	640.71	627.15
Palm Oil (US $/MT)													
Malaysia (N.W.Europe)*	548	437.27	537.62	467.15	490.43	600.85	377.28	261.14	238.40	356.75	410.37	434.72	367.69
Malaysia	548	484.21	623.66	509.38	506.51	603.02	424.93	295.36	248.32	359.56	425.80	441.23	384.51
Pepper (US cents/pound)													
Singapore	576	139.41	171.86	167.71	286.88	322.29	309.58	196.93	112.28	104.49	127.71	116.45	112.68

Commodity Prices

		1994	1995	1996	1997	1998	1999	2000	2001	2002	2003	2004	2005
		Market Prices (lines 76) and Unit Values (lines 74) Country of Origin and, for Market Prices, Pricing Point in Parentheses											
Petroleum, spot (US$/barrel)													
Average crude price *	001	15.95	17.20	20.37	19.27	13.07	17.98	28.23	24.33	24.95	28.89	37.76	53.35
Dubai Fateh *	466	14.83	16.13	18.54	18.10	12.09	17.08	26.09	22.71	23.73	26.73	33.46	49.20
U.K. Brent *	112	15.83	17.06	20.45	19.12	12.72	17.70	28.31	24.41	25.00	28.85	38.30	54.44
West Texas Intermediate *	111	17.18	18.43	22.13	20.59	14.42	19.17	30.32	25.87	26.12	31.10	41.45	56.44
Phosphate Rock (US $/MT)													
Morocco (Casablanca)	686	33.00	35.00	39.00	40.83	43.00	44.00	43.75	41.84	41.00	40.50	40.98	42.00
Potash (US $/MT)													
Canada (Vancouver)	156	105.72	117.76	116.93	116.53	116.89	121.64	122.50	118.08	113.32	113.28	124.56	158.18
Poultry (US cents/pound)													
United States (Georgia) *	111	55.29	55.48	62.31	60.99	63.16	59.97	59.45	63.63	63.08	66.21	75.73	73.90
Plywood (US cents/sheet)													
Philippines (Tokyo)	566	599.50	584.44	529.52	484.96	374.56	440.56	448.23	409.65	402.75	436.08	464.83	508.61
Pulp (US $/MT)													
Sweden (North Sea Ports)	144	552.46	853.45	574.12	554.87	508.77	500.14	664.63	518.71	452.21	521.42	634.49	636.20
Rice (US $/MT)													
Thailand (Bangkok) *	578	269.46	320.80	338.06	302.47	305.42	248.97	203.69	172.71	191.83	199.46	245.78	287.81
Thailand	578	484.96	314.89	366.64	372.75	320.89	285.42	265.83	205.82	222.40	248.76	269.97	308.58
Rubber (US cents/pound)													
Malaysia (Singapore) *	548	51.07	71.68	63.59	46.16	32.73	28.83	30.30	26.09	34.70	49.12	59.17	68.12
Malaysia	548	49.75	72.17	64.55	47.04	33.06	29.03	31.38	27.40	32.70	45.22	54.17	61.43
Thailand	578	44.08	63.83	59.01	43.29	30.41	25.95	27.03	23.51	28.28	40.74	51.30	56.87
Shrimp (US $/pound)													
United States (U.S. Gulf Ports)*	111	13.86	15.72	14.39	15.78	16.55	14.93	17.22	12.95	12.06	11.51	10.39	9.87
Silver (US cents/troy ounce)													
United States (New York)	111	528.4	519.2	518.3	489.2	553.4	525.0	499.9	438.6	462.5	491.1	669.1	733.8
Sisal (US $/MT)													
East Africa (Europe)	639	604.58	710.42	868.25	777.50	821.33	695.75	628.67	699.00	659.92	698.42	862.08	885.00
Sorghum (US $/MT)													
United States (US Gulf Ports)	111	103.87	118.97	150.03	109.62	98.04	84.39	88.00	95.23	101.75	106.54	109.80	96.22
Soybeans (US $/MT)													
United States (Rotterdam) *	111	229.58	224.17	277.42	280.67	223.17	174.92	183.00	168.75	188.75	233.25	276.83	223.17
Soybean Meal (US $/MT)													
United States (Rotterdam) *	111	198.83	198.58	266.42	279.83	174.58	152.42	187.08	180.75	183.92	214.58	257.17	205.92
Soybean Oil (US $/MT)													
All Origins (Dutch Ports) *	111	603.04	584.69	544.23	525.84	562.49	392.40	351.81	347.00	409.84	500.29	590.45	495.75
Sugar (US cents/pound)													
EU Import Price *	112	28.20	31.21	31.15	28.38	27.13	26.84	25.16	23.88	24.91	27.09	30.38	30.18
Free Market *	001	12.11	13.28	11.96	11.40	8.92	6.27	8.08	8.23	6.24	6.92	7.55	10.07
U.S. Import Price *	111	22.03	23.06	22.36	21.93	22.06	21.14	19.40	21.34	20.94	21.50	20.57	21.07
Philippines	566	15.36	19.72	19.30	22.28	19.21	21.14	16.14	17.64	18.14	18.99	13.12	13.30
Sunflower Oil (US $/MT)													
EU (NW European ports) *	112	723.53	631.71	560.39	556.89	665.23	466.46	379.33	436.11	605.83	650.00	734.41	1,144.54
Superphosphate (US $/MT)													
United States (US Gulf Ports)	111	132.11	149.63	175.83	171.91	173.67	154.50	137.72	126.88	133.07	149.34	186.31	201.48
Swine Meat (US cents/pound)													
United States (Iowa) *	111	56.41	62.80	92.49	72.86	45.62	44.41	59.29	61.43	47.26	53.40	71.01	67.69
Tea (US cents/kg)													
Average Auction (London) *	112	183.32	164.16	177.17	237.19	238.56	232.36	248.12	198.12	179.19	194.33	198.15	216.38
Sri Lanka	524	184.77	199.64	252.46	268.48	286.82	229.90	239.43	233.78	226.30	237.99	246.38	262.39
Timber (US $/cubic meter)													
Hardwood Logs													
Malaysia, Sarawak *	548	316.32	257.68	252.15	237.74	162.86	187.02	190.06	159.87	162.40	187.11	197.40	202.18
Hardwood Sawnwood													
Malaysia *	548	821.44	740.19	740.89	662.33	484.16	601.11	599.18	488.26	518.38	550.20	582.77	650.17
Softwood Logs													
United States *	111	201.23	193.84	204.07	185.31	159.10	164.55	180.78	157.73	145.92	145.57	173.68	181.54
Softwood Sawnwood													
United States *	111	299.55	300.62	309.91	294.13	279.81	300.55	284.81	282.83	273.25	284.30	323.98	328.34
Tin (US $/MT)													
Any Origin (London) *	112	5,459.98	6,197.36	6,158.88	5,640.48	5,536.23	5,391.40	5,435.90	4,489.44	4,061.00	4,889.65	8,480.94	7,385.25
Malaysia	548	5,318.29	6,180.62	6,168.86	5,339.01	5,517.63	5,374.75	5,549.34	4,446.94	4,135.67	4,931.50	8,313.21	7,337.91
Bolivia	218	5,405.45	6,187.31	6,306.34	3,846.06	3,711.16	3,638.32	3,712.68	3,387.58	2,759.03	3,165.37	5,574.95	5,101.68
Thailand	578	5,479.86	6,105.92	6,140.62	5,628.33	5,417.60	5,269.51	5,337.70	4,299.91	4,066.90	4,809.93	8,456.79	7,535.08
Tobacco (US $/MT)													
United States (All Markets)	111	2,641.66	2,643.44	3,056.73	3,531.81	3,336.12	3,101.45	2,988.17	2,989.02	2,733.62	....	....	
Uranium (US $/pound)													
Restricted *	001	9.42	11.67	15.60	12.10	10.39	10.02	8.29	8.62	9.83	11.24	18.05	27.93
Urea (US $/MT)													
Ukraine	926	....	187.21	179.00	114.00	83.08	66.40	101.12	95.32	94.36	138.90	175.29	219.02
Wheat (US $/MT)													
Australia	193	128.75	189.78	214.17	168.79	144.97	129.36	124.72	144.03	152.78	165.55	167.05	163.43
United States (US Gulf Pts) *	111	149.78	176.96	207.14	159.67	126.10	112.05	114.00	126.80	148.53	146.14	156.88	152.44
Argentina	213	129.50	145.46	179.98	153.15	125.12	113.83	110.55	120.56	121.22	152.45	140.04	128.27
Wool (US cents/kilogram)													
Australia-NZ(UK) 48's *	112	399.59	497.14	428.88	442.79	336.39	276.47	280.98	332.43	565.65	658.99	553.20	530.61
Australia-NZ(UK) 64's *	112	745.33	775.31	651.59	759.84	552.81	619.25	733.54	623.44	644.41	702.04	713.28	677.73
Australia (greasy wool)	193	323.18	395.82	325.53	358.97	274.66	238.06	252.51	257.03	368.84	425.87	397.07	377.67
Zinc (US $/MT)													
United Kingdom (London) *	112	998.22	1,031.09	1,024.98	1,314.90	1,024.29	1,075.80	1,127.70	886.82	778.90	827.97	1,048.04	1,380.55
Bolivia	218	988.05	1,037.23	1,013.71	781.46	603.80	630.35	672.84	549.21	462.51	438.64	614.92	786.50

Commodity Prices

		1994	1995	1996	1997	1998	1999	2000	2001	2002	2003	2004	2005
All Primary Commodities	001	79.0	86.1	92.1	88.1	68.4	75.3	100.0	90.9	91.1	103.0	130.4	168.4
Non-Fuel Primary Commodities	001	115.4	125.8	123.8	120.0	102.9	95.4	100.0	95.1	96.7	103.4	122.5	135.1
Food	001	119.8	126.6	137.4	125.6	111.7	97.6	100.0	100.1	103.6	108.9	124.5	124.1
Beverages	001	153.4	154.2	131.4	172.2	149.6	117.8	100.0	83.9	97.7	102.5	105.6	127.8
Agricultural Raw Materials	001	119.7	123.7	119.2	113.5	94.6	95.8	100.0	95.1	96.7	100.4	105.9	107.6
Metals	001	100.9	122.1	108.3	109.6	90.1	89.1	100.0	90.2	87.7	98.4	134.0	169.3
Energy	001	58.8	64.0	74.5	70.4	49.2	64.1	100.0	88.5	88.0	102.8	134.7	186.9
World Bank LMICs	200	128.8	140.8	132.5	135.4	114.2	101.6	100.0	90.9	95.7	105.1	123.7	140.2
Aluminum (US $/MT)													
All Origins (London) *	156	95.1	116.3	97.1	103.1	87.5	87.7	100.0	93.2	87.1	92.4	110.8	122.5
Bananas (US $/MT)													
Latin America (US Ports) *	248	104.1	105.4	111.2	123.7	116.6	88.5	100.0	138.5	124.9	88.9	124.3	136.6
Barley (US $/MT)													
Canada (Winnepeg) *	156	94.1	134.7	154.9	125.9	110.1	98.3	100.0	121.6	141.1	135.6	128.2	123.1
Beef (US cents/pound)													
Australia-NZ (US Ports) *	193	120.5	98.5	92.2	95.9	89.2	94.7	100.0	110.0	108.7	102.2	129.8	135.2
Argentina (frozen)	213	112.4	103.1	82.7	88.5	115.2	101.3	100.0	81.2	....	....	....	....
Butter (US cents/pound)													
New Zealand	196	132.0	155.2	161.3	130.8	125.7	107.8	100.0	105.9	89.2	106.7	136.7	146.3
Coal (US $/MT)													
Australia	193	123.0	150.0	145.0	133.7	111.4	98.6	100.0	123.1	103.1	106.5	216.1	194.4
Australia	193	128.2	137.6	148.1	142.2	128.3	108.5	100.0	114.3	117.2	112.7	149.3	244.1
South Africa	199	107.5	132.6	126.1	118.0	101.0	91.4	100.0	127.5	97.9	112.8	205.8	173.4
Cocoa Beans (US $/MT)													
New York and London *	652	154.4	158.5	161.0	179.1	185.4	125.6	100.0	120.4	196.8	193.9	171.6	170.9
Coconut Oil (US $/MT)													
Philippines (New York) *	566	133.4	146.9	168.0	144.9	143.1	165.7	100.0	68.6	90.6	100.9	147.1	135.4
Philippines	566	125.6	138.2	161.5	139.8	134.3	160.6	100.0	66.0	83.7	95.4	135.1	127.9
Coffee (US cents/pound)													
Other Milds (New York) *	386	174.6	175.7	141.4	217.6	155.7	119.6	100.0	72.8	71.0	75.3	94.2	134.4
Brazil (New York)	223	179.6	182.9	150.7	209.0	152.6	111.4	100.0	63.3	56.4	63.6	86.8	127.1
Brazil	223	157.9	169.3	137.0	196.0	145.2	108.8	100.0	59.8	47.8	59.0	76.9	115.4
Uganda (New York) *	799	284.2	300.8	196.5	191.4	199.1	160.5	100.0	64.8	73.1	91.0	88.4	126.6
Copper (US $/MT)													
United Kingdom (London) *	112	127.1	161.6	126.4	125.4	91.1	86.7	100.0	87.1	86.0	98.1	157.8	202.6
Copra (US $/MT)													
Philippines (Europ. Ports)	566	134.9	141.9	158.3	140.4	133.1	149.6	100.0	63.3	86.1	96.9	146.0	133.9
Cotton (US cents/pound)													
Liverpool Index *	111	135.0	166.5	136.4	134.2	111.0	90.0	100.0	81.3	78.3	107.4	105.0	93.4
DAP (US $/MT)													
US Gulf Coast	111	112.0	140.4	138.2	129.6	131.9	115.3	100.0	95.8	102.1	116.3	143.5	160.2
Fish (US $/kilogram)													
Norway *	142	137.5	131.0	112.8	102.2	102.0	97.9	100.0	79.3	80.6	82.1	91.7	111.5
Fish Meal (US $/MT)													
Any Origin (Hamburg) *	293	89.2	115.3	139.2	142.9	156.8	95.8	100.0	117.2	142.8	143.8	153.3	164.6
Iceland	176	96.5	112.7	130.3	143.6	154.5	105.2	100.0	....	....	....	....	....
Gasoline (US cents/gallon)													
US Gulf Coast	111	57.5	61.1	71.5	70.2	49.5	62.2	100.0	88.0	86.4	104.6	140.4	190.5
Gold (US $/troy ounce)													
United Kingdom (London)	112	137.6	137.6	138.9	118.6	105.4	99.9	100.0	97.1	111.1	130.2	146.6	159.3
Groundnuts (US $/MT)													
Nigeria (London) *	694	117.3	104.0	103.1	111.3	101.2	97.1	100.0	95.9	83.4	109.0	115.8	97.9
Groundnut Oil (US $/MT)													
Any Origin (Europe) *	694	143.5	139.1	126.0	141.8	127.5	110.4	100.0	94.3	96.6	175.5	162.7	148.8
Hides (US cents/pound)													
United States (Chicago) *	111	108.2	109.9	108.8	110.0	95.6	89.9	100.0	105.5	100.7	85.1	83.7	81.8
Iron Ore (US cents/DMTU)													
Brazil (North Sea Ports) *	223	91.9	98.6	104.2	104.7	107.7	95.8	100.0	104.3	101.9	111.0	131.6	225.8
Jute (US $/MT)													
Bangladesh (Chitta.-Chalna)	513	106.0	131.1	162.9	108.3	92.9	98.9	100.0	118.2	104.3	86.8	100.6	104.0
Lamb (US cents/pound)													
New Zealand (London) *	196	111.3	100.4	128.9	133.2	102.8	102.7	100.0	115.4	129.4	141.6	146.9	142.6
Lead (US $/MT)													
United Kingdom (London) *	112	120.8	138.6	170.4	137.2	116.0	110.5	100.0	104.9	99.6	113.2	194.2	214.5
Linseed Oil (US $/MT)													
Any Origin	001	129.4	164.6	141.7	143.0	177.2	128.3	100.0	95.7	130.3	169.8	218.5	....
Maize (US $/MT)													
United States (US Gulf Pts) *	111	122.2	139.9	186.5	132.8	115.2	102.4	100.0	101.6	112.6	119.2	126.7	111.5
Thailand	578	53.3	67.0	99.1	92.0	50.4	56.8	100.0	36.7	59.6	60.5	47.8	84.9
Natural Gas (US $/000 M³)													
Russian Federation	922	67.0	78.1	79.6	77.3	65.0	52.3	100.0	112.1	77.2	100.9	108.7	171.3
Indonesia	536	62.8	67.9	74.5	71.8	52.6	63.8	100.0	89.2	84.6	95.1	112.5	134.3
United States	111	44.5	39.6	62.4	57.1	48.5	52.5	100.0	91.9	78.0	127.6	137.2	205.7
Newsprint (US $/short ton)													
Finland (1995=100)	172	66.4	100.0	107.6	77.8	75.0	....	....	....	....	....	....	....
Nickel (US $/MT)													
United Kingdom(N.Europ.Ports)*	156	73.4	95.3	86.9	80.2	53.6	69.5	100.0	69.2	78.6	111.6	160.1	171.2
Olive Oil (US $/MT)													
United Kingdom *	112	105.7	151.0	200.2	142.2	108.3	122.5	100.0	89.5	97.3	127.4	155.4	185.2
Oranges (US $/MT)													
French Import Price *	132	113.3	146.3	135.4	126.4	121.8	120.7	100.0	164.0	155.4	188.1	235.3	231.9

Commodity Prices

		1994	1995	1996	1997	1998	1999	2000	2001	2002	2003	2004	2005
						Indices of Market Prices (lines 76) and of Unit Values (lines 74)							
						2000=100							
Palm Kernel Oil(US $/MT)													
Malaysia (Rotterdam)....................	548	139.9	151.0	162.2	145.3	153.1	154.9	100.0	68.8	92.8	102.2	142.8	139.8
Palm Oil (US $/MT)													
Malaysia (N.W.Europe)*...............	548	167.4	205.9	178.9	187.8	230.1	144.5	100.0	91.3	136.6	157.1	166.5	140.8
Malaysia....................................	548	163.9	211.1	172.5	171.5	204.2	143.9	100.0	84.1	121.7	144.2	149.4	130.2
Pepper (US cents/pound)													
Malaysia (New York)...................	548	70.8	87.3	85.2	145.7	163.7	157.2	100.0	57.0	53.1	64.6	59.1	57.2
Singapore...................................	576	70.8	87.3	85.2	145.7	163.7	157.2	100.0	57.0	53.1	64.8	59.1	57.2
Petroleum,spot (US$/barrel)													
Average crude price *...................	001	56.5	60.9	72.2	68.2	46.3	63.7	100.0	86.2	88.4	102.3	133.7	189.0
Dubai Fateh *.............................	466	56.9	61.8	71.1	69.4	46.3	65.5	100.0	87.1	91.0	102.5	128.3	188.6
U.K. Brent *.............................	112	55.9	60.3	72.3	67.5	44.9	62.5	100.0	86.2	88.3	101.9	135.3	192.3
West Texas Intermediate *..........	111	56.7	60.8	73.0	67.9	47.6	63.2	100.0	85.3	86.1	102.6	136.7	186.2
Phosphate Rock (US $/MT)													
Morocco (Casablanca).................	686	75.4	80.0	89.1	93.3	98.3	100.6	100.0	95.6	93.7	92.6	93.7	96.0
Potash (US $/MT)													
Canada (Vancouver).....................	156	86.3	96.1	95.5	95.1	95.4	99.3	100.0	96.4	92.5	92.5	101.7	129.1
Poultry (US cents/pound)													
United States (Georgia) *.............	111	93.0	93.3	104.8	102.6	106.2	100.9	100.0	107.0	106.1	111.4	127.4	124.3
Plywood (US cents/sheet)													
Philippines (Tokyo)......................	566	133.7	130.4	118.1	108.2	83.6	98.3	100.0	91.4	89.9	97.3	103.7	113.5
Pulp (US $/MT)													
Sweden (North Sea Ports).............	144	83.1	128.4	86.4	83.5	76.5	75.3	100.0	78.0	68.0	78.5	95.5	95.7
Rice (US $/MT)													
Thailand (Bangkok) *..................	578	132.3	157.5	166.0	148.5	149.9	122.2	100.0	84.8	94.2	97.9	120.7	141.3
Thailand....................................	578	182.4	118.5	137.9	140.2	120.7	107.4	100.0	77.4	83.7	93.6	101.6	116.1
Rubber (US cents/pound)													
Malaysia (Singapore) *.................	548	168.5	236.6	209.9	152.3	108.0	95.2	100.0	86.1	114.5	162.1	195.3	224.8
Malaysia....................................	548	158.5	230.0	205.7	149.9	105.3	92.5	100.0	87.3	104.2	144.1	172.6	195.7
Thailand....................................	578	163.1	236.2	218.3	160.1	112.5	96.0	100.0	87.0	104.6	150.7	189.8	210.4
Shrimp (US $/pound)													
United States(U.S. Gulf Ports)*.......	111	80.5	91.3	83.6	91.7	96.2	86.7	100.0	75.2	70.1	66.9	60.4	57.3
Silver (US cents/troy ounce)													
United States (New York).............	111	105.7	103.9	103.7	97.9	110.7	105.0	100.0	87.7	92.5	98.2	133.8	146.8
Sisal (US $/MT)													
East Africa (Europe)......................	639	96.2	113.0	138.1	123.7	130.6	110.7	100.0	111.2	105.0	111.1	137.1	140.8
Sorghum (US $/MT)													
United States (US Gulf Ports).........	111	118.0	135.2	170.5	124.6	111.4	95.9	100.0	108.2	115.6	121.1	124.8	109.3
Soybeans (US $/MT)													
United States (Rotterdam) *..........	111	125.5	122.5	151.6	153.4	121.9	95.6	100.0	92.2	103.1	127.5	151.3	121.9
Soybean Meal (US $/MT)													
United States (Rotterdam) *..........	111	106.3	106.1	142.4	149.6	93.3	81.5	100.0	96.6	98.3	114.7	137.5	110.1
Soybean Oil (US $/MT)													
All Origins (Dutch Ports) *.............	111	171.4	166.2	154.7	149.5	159.9	111.5	100.0	98.6	116.5	142.2	167.8	140.9
Sugar (US cents/pound)													
EU Import Price *...........................	112	112.1	124.0	123.8	112.8	107.8	106.7	100.0	94.9	99.0	107.6	120.7	119.9
Free Market *.............................	001	149.9	164.4	148.0	141.1	110.4	77.5	100.0	101.9	77.2	85.7	93.4	124.7
U.S. Import Price *........................	111	113.6	118.9	115.3	113.1	113.8	109.0	100.0	110.0	108.0	110.8	106.1	108.6
Philippines.................................	566	95.1	122.2	119.6	138.0	119.0	130.9	100.0	109.3	112.4	117.6	81.3	82.4
Sunflower Oil (US $/MT)													
EU (NW European ports) *.............	112	190.7	166.5	147.7	146.8	175.4	123.0	100.0	115.0	159.7	171.4	193.6	301.7
Superphosphate (US $/MT)													
United States (US Gulf Ports)........	111	95.9	108.7	127.7	124.8	126.1	112.2	100.0	92.1	96.6	108.4	135.3	146.3
Swine Meat (US cents/pound)													
United States (Iowa) *..................	111	95.1	105.9	156.0	122.9	76.9	74.9	100.0	103.6	79.7	90.1	119.8	114.2
Tea (US cents/kg)													
Average Auction (London) *..........	112	73.9	66.2	71.4	95.6	96.1	93.6	100.0	79.9	72.2	78.3	79.9	87.2
Sri Lanka...................................	524	77.2	83.4	105.4	112.1	119.8	96.0	100.0	97.6	94.5	99.4	102.9	109.6
Timber (US $/cubic meter)													
Hardwood Logs													
Malaysia, Sarawak *.....................	548	166.4	135.6	132.7	125.1	85.7	98.4	100.0	84.1	85.4	98.4	103.9	106.4
Hardwood Sawnwood													
Malaysia *..................................	548	137.1	123.5	123.7	110.5	80.8	100.3	100.0	81.5	86.5	91.8	97.3	108.5
Softwood Logs													
United States *............................	111	111.3	107.2	112.9	102.5	88.0	91.0	100.0	87.2	80.7	80.5	96.1	100.4
Softwood Sawnwood													
United States *............................	111	105.2	105.6	108.8	103.3	98.2	105.5	100.0	99.3	95.9	99.8	113.8	115.3
Tin (US $/MT)													
Any Origin (London) *..................	112	100.4	114.0	113.3	103.8	101.8	99.2	100.0	82.6	74.7	90.0	156.0	135.9
Malaysia....................................	548	95.8	111.4	111.2	96.2	99.4	96.9	100.0	80.1	74.5	88.9	149.8	132.2
Bolivia......................................	218	145.6	166.7	169.9	103.6	100.0	98.0	100.0	91.2	74.3	85.3	150.2	137.4
Thailand....................................	578	102.7	114.4	115.0	105.4	101.5	98.7	100.0	80.6	76.2	90.1	158.4	141.2
Tobacco (US $/MT)													
United States (All Markets)...........	111	88.4	88.5	102.3	118.2	111.6	103.8	100.0	100.0	91.5	....	....	....
Uranium (US $/pound)													
Restricted *...............................	001	113.7	140.8	188.3	146.0	125.4	120.9	100.0	104.0	118.6	135.6	217.8	337.1
Urea (US $/MT)													
Ukraine.....................................	926	....	185.1	177.0	112.7	82.2	65.7	100.0	94.3	93.3	137.4	173.4	216.6
Wheat (US $/MT)													
Australia....................................	193	103.2	152.2	171.7	135.3	116.2	103.7	100.0	115.5	122.5	132.7	133.9	131.0
United States (US Gulf Pts) *........	111	131.4	155.2	181.7	140.1	110.6	98.3	100.0	111.2	130.3	128.2	137.6	133.7
Argentina.................................	213	117.1	131.6	162.8	138.5	113.2	103.0	100.0	109.1	109.7	137.9	126.7	116.0

Commodity Prices

		1994	1995	1996	1997	1998	1999	2000	2001	2002	2003	2004	2005
						Indices of Market Prices (lines 76) and of Unit Values (lines 74)							
							2000=100						
Wool (US cents/kilogram)													
Australia-NZ(UK) 48's *	**112**	142.2	176.9	152.6	157.6	119.7	98.4	100.0	118.3	201.3	234.5	196.9	188.8
Australia-NZ(UK) 64's *	**112**	101.6	105.7	88.8	103.6	75.4	84.4	100.0	85.0	87.8	95.7	97.2	92.4
Australia (greasy wool)................	**193**	128.0	156.8	128.9	142.2	108.8	94.3	100.0	101.8	146.1	168.7	157.2	149.6
Zinc (US $/MT)													
United Kingdom (London) *	**112**	88.5	91.4	90.9	116.6	90.8	95.4	100.0	78.6	69.1	73.4	92.9	122.4
Bolivia..............................	**218**	146.8	154.2	150.7	116.1	89.7	93.7	100.0	81.6	68.7	65.2	91.4	116.9

COUNTRY TABLES

Albania 914

		1994	1995	1996	1997	1998	1999	2000	2001	2002	2003	2004	2005
Exchange Rates						*Leks per SDR: End of Period*							
Market Rate..................................	aa	139.55	140.09	148.21	201.23	197.94	185.45	185.85	171.61	181.82	158.37	143.87	148.04
						Leks per US Dollar: End of Period (ae) Period Average (rf)							
Market Rate..................................	ae	95.59	94.24	103.07	149.14	140.58	135.12	142.64	136.55	133.74	106.58	92.64	103.58
Market Rate..................................	rf	94.62	92.70	104.50	148.93	150.63	137.69	143.71	143.48	140.15	121.86	102.78	99.87
Fund Position						*Millions of SDRs: End of Period*							
Quota..	2f.s	35.30	35.30	35.30	35.30	35.30	48.70	48.70	48.70	48.70	48.70	48.70	48.70
SDRs...	1b.s	.20	.10	.52	.46	43.39	56.06	58.33	64.87	60.02	60.98	64.90	8.75
Reserve Position in the Fund...........	1c.s	.01	.01	.01	.01	.01	3.36	3.36	3.36	3.36	3.35	3.35	3.35
Total Fund Cred.&Loans Outstg.......	2tl	37.13	43.40	37.70	40.74	45.77	58.69	67.47	66.25	59.63	60.83	62.43	64.27
International Liquidity					*Millions of US Dollars Unless Otherwise Indicated: End of Period*								
Total Reserves minus Gold.............	1l.d	204.80	241.05	280.86	308.93	384.22	488.30	615.65	739.90	838.78	1,009.42	1,357.60	1,404.09
SDRs...................................	1b.d	.30	.14	.75	.62	61.10	76.95	76.00	81.52	81.60	90.61	100.79	12.50
Reserve Position in the Fund.........	1c.d	.01	.01	.01	.01	.01	4.60	4.37	4.22	4.56	4.99	5.21	4.80
Foreign Exchange.....................	1d.d	204.50	240.90	280.10	308.30	323.12	406.75	535.27	654.17	752.62	913.83	1,251.60	1,386.79
Gold (Million Fine Troy Ounces)........	1ad	.05	.06	.12	.12	.12	.12	.11	.11	.08	.07	.07	.07
Gold (National Valuation)...............	1and	20.85	24.30	42.50	33.40	33.70	34.50	30.40	30.70	27.68	28.86	30.25	35.49
Monetary Authorities						*Billions of Leks: End of Period*							
Foreign Assets.............................	11	22.65	46.76	57.02	85.21	91.04	71.08	92.34	104.90	114.63	109.77	127.56	147.82
Claims on Central Government........	12a	69.33	45.69	52.14	85.48	77.56	74.72	82.49	74.14	78.58	74.30	65.63	68.74
Claims on Banks...........................	12e	3.42	3.31	3.37	7.44	7.00	6.69	6.63	6.73	10.72	.42	.28	.21
Reserve Money...........................	14	42.07	53.88	61.39	90.93	89.89	109.31	128.78	152.14	163.89	160.55	178.60	198.25
of which: Currency Outside Banks..	14a	27.63	41.91	47.81	72.73	68.32	81.34	99.24	119.08	130.78	125.19	138.10	149.68
Other Liabilities to Banks...............	14n	—	—	—	—	2.44	.79	5.23	—	—	1.21	2.26	.51
Foreign Liabilities........................	16c	59.41	33.65	36.81	53.85	55.11	24.15	20.48	18.94	19.65	11.45	10.53	10.86
Central Government Deposits..........	16d	3.75	4.27	3.25	5.62	5.39	5.85	7.62	4.20	5.90	8.82	7.97	10.26
Capital Accounts.........................	17a	14.26	10.61	16.83	31.43	38.56	14.82	21.52	20.92	27.49	14.31	3.43	6.75
Other Items (Net)........................	17r	−24.08	−6.64	−4.99	−3.00	−15.14	−1.85	−2.10	−10.36	−12.98	−11.85	−9.33	−9.86
Banking Institutions						*Billions of Leks: End of Period*							
Reserves.....................................	20	11.93	10.30	12.90	16.44	21.57	28.15	30.16	33.81	32.02	35.21	40.69	49.92
Other Claims on Monetary Author....	20n	—	—	—	1.40	2.44	.79	5.15	† —	—	1.20	2.26	.51
Foreign Assets.............................	21	16.94	23.47	35.44	38.96	49.97	57.97	65.05	83.36	81.33	77.60	71.38	88.24
Claims on Central Government........	22a	86.55	108.52	142.51	108.30	125.45	147.34	156.15	† 170.30	175.98	205.43	221.68	224.73
Claims on Nonfin.Pub.Enterprises....	22c	3.25	3.09	3.41	2.83	2.83	1.67	1.48	1.68	1.16	1.13	1.24	1.20
Claims on Private Sector...............	22d	7.20	8.35	10.89	13.01	14.86	18.22	24.41	34.94	46.17	58.14	76.86	128.75
Demand Deposits.........................	24	11.14	17.35	42.59	18.94	15.41	21.67	24.81	23.94	21.90	19.54	34.73	77.99
Time and Savings Deposits............	25a	18.70	28.12	30.24	70.55	115.53	136.66	140.46	162.25	171.99	204.78	218.58	198.98
Foreign Currency Deposits............	25b	13.30	20.08	33.91	36.33	40.26	53.21	63.60	88.13	91.96	98.91	115.80	152.71
Foreign Liabilities........................	26c	1.82	1.14	1.22	2.02	2.87	4.83	6.83	12.05	15.49	17.22	15.55	17.33
Central Government Deposits..........	26d	68.05	75.92	80.41	25.80	1.05	.80	1.46	2.25	.82	.86	.65	.29
Credit from Monetary Authorities.....	26g	.65	—	1.69	3.64	4.73	1.44	5.81	† 1.05	3.98	.66	.83	.76
Capital Accounts.........................	27a	10.37	12.01	16.70	21.85	26.46	27.00	34.17	34.43	38.13	38.52	42.83	51.41
Other Items (Net)........................	27r	1.84	−.89	−1.60	1.81	10.80	8.52	5.27	−.02	−7.60	−1.77	−14.84	−6.14
Banking Survey						*Billions of Leks: End of Period*							
Foreign Assets (Net).....................	31n	−21.63	35.44	54.42	68.30	83.03	100.07	130.08	157.28	160.83	158.71	172.86	207.87
Domestic Credit...........................	32	94.52	85.46	125.30	178.20	214.27	235.30	255.45	† 274.61	295.18	329.32	356.79	412.86
Claims on Central Govt. (Net).......	32an	84.07	74.02	111.00	162.37	196.57	215.41	229.55	† 237.99	247.85	270.05	278.69	282.91
Claims on Nonfin.Pub.Enterprises....	32c	3.25	3.09	3.41	2.83	2.83	1.67	1.48	1.68	1.16	1.13	1.24	1.20
Claims on Private Sector...............	32d	7.20	8.35	10.89	13.01	14.86	18.22	24.41	34.94	46.17	58.14	76.86	128.75
Money.......................................	34	38.77	59.25	90.41	91.67	83.73	103.00	124.04	143.03	152.67	144.73	172.83	227.68
Quasi-Money...............................	35	32.01	48.20	64.15	106.88	155.80	189.87	204.06	250.39	263.94	303.70	334.37	351.68
Capital Accounts...........................	37a	24.62	22.62	33.53	53.29	65.02	41.83	55.69	55.36	65.62	52.83	46.26	58.16
Other Items (Net)........................	37r	−22.50	−9.17	−7.60	−4.63	−6.60	1.25	1.81	† −16.81	−26.23	−13.23	−23.80	−16.79
Money plus Quasi-Money...............	35l	70.77	107.45	154.55	198.55	239.53	292.87	328.10	393.41	416.62	448.43	507.20	579.36
Interest Rates						*Percent Per Annum*							
Bank Rate (End of Period)................	60	25.00	20.50	24.00	32.00	23.44	18.00	10.82	7.00	8.50	6.50	5.25	5.00
Treasury Bill Rate...........................	60c	....	13.84	17.81	32.59	27.49	17.54	10.80	7.72	9.49	8.81	6.79	5.52
Deposit Rate...............................	60l	19.83	† 15.30	16.78	27.28	22.56	12.95	8.30	7.73	8.54	8.38	6.61	5.09
Lending Rate..............................	60p	23.67	† 19.65	23.96	....	....	21.62	22.10	19.65	15.30	14.27	11.76	13.08
Prices and Labor						*Index Numbers (2000=100): Period Averages*							
Producer Prices............................	63	....	....	....	....	93.3	95.3	100.0	94.6	100.7	106.9	118.4	....
Consumer Prices...........................	64	51.0	55.0	62.0	82.5	99.6	100.0	100.0	† 103.1	111.1	111.7	114.2	116.9
Wages:Average Monthly Earnings....	65	31.9	42.8	57.7	63.9	67.0	84.9	100.0	115.1	131.4	142.5	163.1	179.2
						Number in Thousands: Period Averages							
Labor Force................................	67d	1,423	1,309	1,274	1,301	1,320	1,305	1,283	1,101	1,092	1,089	1,090	1,086
Employment................................	67e	1,162	1,138	1,116	1,108	1,085	1,065	1,068	921	920	926	931	931
Unemployment.............................	67c	262	171	158	194	235	240	215	181	172	163	159	155
Unemployment Rate (%).................	67r	18.0	12.9	12.3	14.9	17.7	18.4	16.8	16.4	15.8	15.2	14.4	14.3
Intl. Transactions & Positions						*Millions of Leks*							
Exports.....................................	70	13,387	18,712	22,001	21,044	31,104	48,430	37,037	44,095	47,490	54,487	62,121	65,766
Imports, c.i.f................................	71	57,019	66,145	98,060	95,021	126,271	159,465	157,109	190,155	210,368	225,982	236,073	261,710

Albania 914

		1994	1995	1996	1997	1998	1999	2000	2001	2002	2003	2004	2005
Balance of Payments		*Millions of US Dollars: Minus Sign Indicates Debit*											
Current Account, n.i.e.	78ald	−157.3	−11.5	−107.3	−272.2	−65.1	−155.4	−156.3	−217.3	−407.5	−406.8	−357.9	−571.5
Goods: Exports f.o.b.	78aad	141.3	204.9	243.7	158.6	208.0	275.0	255.7	304.5	330.2	447.2	603.3	656.3
Goods: Imports f.o.b.	78abd	−601.0	−679.7	−922.0	−693.6	−811.7	−938.0	−1,070.0	−1,331.6	−1,485.4	−1,783.5	−2,194.9	−2,477.6
Trade Balance	78acd	−459.7	−474.8	−678.3	−535.0	−603.6	−663.0	−814.3	−1,027.1	−1,155.1	−1,336.3	−1,591.6	−1,821.3
Services: Credit	78add	79.1	98.8	129.2	63.8	86.6	269.4	447.8	534.3	585.0	719.7	1,003.5	1,164.6
Services: Debit	78aed	−132.5	−156.5	−189.4	−115.2	−129.3	−163.1	−429.3	−444.1	−590.2	−802.6	−1,054.8	−1,382.9
Balance on Goods & Services	78afd	−513.1	−532.5	−738.5	−586.4	−646.3	−556.7	−795.8	−936.9	−1,160.3	−1,419.2	−1,642.9	−2,039.6
Income: Credit	78agd	55.1	72.0	83.7	61.4	86.1	85.5	115.9	162.5	148.3	194.8	203.7	226.7
Income: Debit	78ahd	−41.3	−28.4	−11.9	−11.8	−8.7	−10.2	−9.3	−13.5	−20.6	−24.4	−28.3	−52.6
Balance on Gds, Serv. & Inc.	78aid	−499.3	−488.9	−666.7	−536.8	−569.0	−481.4	−689.2	−787.9	−1,032.6	−1,248.8	−1,467.5	−1,865.5
Current Transfers, n.i.e.: Credit	78ajd	347.5	521.2	595.9	299.8	560.8	508.9	629.0	647.5	683.7	924.2	1,200.2	1,519.2
Current Transfers: Debit	78akd	−5.5	−43.8	−36.5	−35.2	−56.9	−182.9	−96.1	−76.9	−58.6	−82.3	−90.6	−225.1
Capital Account, n.i.e.	78bcd	—	389.4	4.8	2.0	31.0	22.6	78.0	117.7	121.2	157.0	132.4	122.9
Capital Account, n.i.e.: Credit	78bad	—	389.4	4.8	2.0	31.0	22.6	78.0	117.7	121.2	157.0	132.4	122.9
Capital Account: Debit	78bbd	—	—	—	—	—	—	—	—	—	—	....	....
Financial Account, n.i.e.	78bjd	40.2	−411.0	61.5	151.4	15.4	33.7	188.4	110.0	213.4	200.6	396.3	392.6
Direct Investment Abroad	78bdd	—	....	—	—	—	—	—	—	—	—	−13.6	−4.1
Dir. Invest. in Rep. Econ., n.i.e.	78bed	53.0	70.0	90.1	47.5	45.0	41.2	143.0	207.3	135.0	178.0	341.3	262.5
Portfolio Investment Assets	78bfd	—	....	....	—	—	—	−25.0	−23.5	−36.8	−22.5	−3.6	−5.7
Equity Securities	78bkd	—	....	....	....	....	—	—	—	—	—	....	....
Debt Securities	78bld	—	....	....	....	....	—	−25.0	−23.5	−36.8	−22.5	−3.6	−5.7
Portfolio Investment Liab., n.i.e.	78bgd	—	....	....	....	....	—	—	—	—	....	....	....
Equity Securities	78bmd	—	....	....	....	....	—	—	—	—	....	....	....
Debt Securities	78bnd	—	....	....	....	....	....	—	—	....	....	....	....
Financial Derivatives Assets	78bwd	....	....	....	....	....	....	....	....	....	....	....	....
Financial Derivatives Liabilities	78bxd	....	....	....	....	....	....	....	....	....	....	....	....
Other Investment Assets	78bhd	−97.3	−97.0	−138.6	59.8	−126.9	−130.1	−40.2	−197.2	−2.7	−71.6	−113.8	6.6
Monetary Authorities	78bod	....	—	—	—	—	—	....	−1.8	2.2	.3	....	—
General Government	78bpd	....	—	—	—	—	—	—	—	—	—	—	—
Banks	78bqd	−22.9	−68.4	−110.5	81.5	−91.2	−96.8	−2.5	−132.3	42.2	−45.3	−112.1	8.5
Other Sectors	78brd	−74.4	−28.6	−28.1	−21.7	−35.7	−33.3	−37.7	−63.1	−47.1	−26.7	−1.7	−1.9
Other Investment Liab., n.i.e.	78bid	84.5	−384.0	110.0	44.1	97.3	122.6	110.6	123.4	118.0	116.7	186.1	133.2
Monetary Authorities	78bsd	—	−9.1	10.4	16.0	10.4	8.9	−.2	−.3	.5	−1.0	−1.2	−1.5
General Government	78btd	74.6	−404.5	61.3	40.3	81.3	97.9	90.8	86.1	118.2	96.6	106.4	50.4
Banks	78bud	2.6	−3.3	4.0	−.6	3.5	16.0	5.2	42.1	10.9	19.8	.3	20.7
Other Sectors	78bvd	7.3	32.9	34.3	−11.6	2.0	−.2	14.8	−4.5	−11.6	1.4	80.6	63.6
Net Errors and Omissions	78cad	123.9	53.7	96.9	158.4	71.1	206.2	9.8	136.3	108.5	147.4	115.3	203.8
Overall Balance	78cbd	6.8	20.6	55.9	39.5	52.4	107.1	119.9	146.7	35.6	98.1	286.1	147.8
Reserves and Related Items	79dad	−6.8	−20.6	−55.9	−39.5	−52.4	−107.1	−119.9	−146.7	−35.6	−98.1	−286.1	−147.8
Reserve Assets	79dbd	−55.2	−30.5	−47.6	−43.7	−60.0	−124.7	−132.0	−145.1	−28.6	−99.6	−288.4	−150.7
Use of Fund Credit and Loans	79dcd	22.3	9.9	−8.3	4.2	6.8	17.5	12.1	−1.6	−8.5	1.5	2.4	3.0
Exceptional Financing	79ded	26.1	....	....	—	.8	.1	—	—	1.5	—	—	—
Government Finance		*Millions of Leks: Year Ending December 31*											
Deficit (-) or Surplus	80	....	−20,157	−34,689	−41,053	−38,972	....	....	....	....	....	....	....
Revenue	81	....	49,068	47,551	53,205	89,145	....	....	....	....	....	....	....
Grants Received	81z	....	598	722	2,304	9,005	....	....	....	....	....	....	....
Expenditure	82	....	69,687	83,553	97,472	137,254	....	....	....	....	....	....	....
Lending Minus Repayments	83	....	136	−591	−910	−132	....	....	....	....	....	....	....
Financing													
Domestic	84a	....	15,919	27,680	36,815	27,464	....	....	....	....	....	....	....
Foreign	85a	....	4,238	7,009	4,238	11,509	....	....	....	....	....	....	....
Debt: Domestic	88a	....	53,876	82,654	120,527	149,439	....	....	....	....	....	....	....
Foreign	89a	....	25,434	42,668	55,432	64,405	....	....	....	....	....	....	....
National Accounts		*Billions of Leks*											
Househ.Cons.Expend.,incl.NPISHs	96f	....	....	211,984	287,801	346,775	334,801	372,012	423,351	456,752	509,022	....	....
Government Consumption Expend	91f	....	....	30,539	34,871	40,222	43,703	47,020	56,154	63,666	68,806	....	....
Gross Fixed Capital Formation	93e	....	....	52,935	49,547	58,184	81,633	112,958	151,156	143,914	160,209	....	....
Changes in Inventories	93i	....	....	91,343	34,287	64,147	91,067	104,500	77,039	130,188	116,273	....	....
Exports of Goods and Services	90c	....	....	38,782	33,739	44,376	74,588	93,453	107,524	122,044	141,290	....	....
Imports of Goods and Services (-)	98c	....	....	110,934	118,365	141,738	151,910	199,036	227,507	291,847	312,931	....	....
Gross Domestic Product (GDP)	99b	184,393	229,793	314,879	322,186	412,327	474,291	530,907	587,716	624,718	682,669	755,320	....
GDP Volume 1986 Prices	99b.p	13,331	15,107	16,482	15,325	16,547	17,748	19,125	20,180	....	....	....	....
GDP Volume (2000=100)	99bvp	69.7	79.0	86.2	80.1	86.5	92.8	100.0	105.5	....	....	....	....
GDP Deflator (2000=100)	99bip	49.8	54.8	68.8	75.7	89.8	96.3	100.0	104.9	....	....	....	....
		Milliions: Midyear Estimates											
Population	99z	3.17	3.13	3.10	3.08	3.07	3.06	3.06	3.07	3.08	3.09	3.11	3.13

Algeria 612

		1994	1995	1996	1997	1998	1999	2000	2001	2002	2003	2004	2005
Exchange Rates						*Dinars per SDR: End of Period*							
Official Rate	aa	62.617	77.558	80.793	78.815	84.979	95.135	98.165	97.798	108.386	107.900	112.770	104.880
					Dinars per US Dollar: End of Period (ae) Period Average (rf)								
Official Rate	ae	42.893	52.175	56.186	58.414	60.353	69.314	75.343	77.820	79.723	72.613	72.614	73.380
Official Rate	rf	35.059	47.663	54.749	57.707	58.739	66.574	75.260	77.215	79.682	77.395	72.061	73.276
					Index Numbers (2000=100): Period Averages								
Nominal Effective Exchange Rate	nec	159.52	105.29	94.60	101.49	106.27	100.38	100.00	103.37	97.55	88.89	88.77	86.30
Real Effective Exchange Rate	rec	117.61	98.57	100.25	108.20	113.48	104.89	100.00	103.04	95.18	86.12	86.68	83.29
Fund Position					*Millions of SDRs: End of Period*								
Quota	2f.s	914	914	914	914	914	1,255	1,255	1,255	1,255	1,255	1,255	1,255
SDRs	1b.s	16	1	3	1	1	1	2	9	10	38	1	2
Reserve Position in the Fund	1c.s	—	—	—	—	—	85	85	85	85	85	85	85
Total Fund Cred.&Loans Outstg.	2tl	794	994	1,413	1,496	1,428	1,389	1,319	1,208	978	665	414	—
International Liquidity				*Millions of US Dollars Unless Otherwise Indicated: End of Period*									
Total Reserves minus Gold	1l.d	2,674	2,005	4,235	8,047	6,846	4,526	12,024	18,081	23,238	33,125	43,246	56,303
SDRs	1b.d	23	1	5	1	2	2	3	11	14	57	1	3
Reserve Position in the Fund	1c.d	—	—	—	—	—	117	111	107	116	126	132	122
Foreign Exchange	1d.d	2,651	2,004	4,230	8,046	6,844	4,407	11,910	17,963	23,108	32,942	43,113	56,178
Gold (Million Fine Troy Ounces)	1ad	5.58	5.58	5.58	5.58	5.58	5.58	5.58	5.58	5.58	5.58	5.58	5.58
Gold (National Valuation)	1and	285	290	281	264	275	268	255	246	266	290	303	279
Monetary Authorities:Other Assets	3..d	1	4	3	9	7	19	9	9	10	10	15	20
Other Liab.	4..d	466	363	291	414	387	364	208	182	248	303	240	277
Deposit Money Banks: Assets	7a.d	1,046	638	576	396	456	402	376	416	624	765	1,060	1,248
Liabilities	7b.d	4,200	2,749	2,088	1,216	1,068	1,015	720	767	927	1,111	1,583	1,148
Monetary Authorities					*Billions of Dinars: End of Period*								
Foreign Assets	11	120.39	111.71	252.88	485.04	423.47	329.89	919.47	1,445.97	1,868.63	2,419.76	3,173.29	4,171.91
Claims on Central Government	12a	255.57	243.40	180.87	177.67	174.59	163.48	168.20	144.67	133.77	141.97	122.11	118.13
Claims on Deposit Money Banks	12e	50.45	188.59	255.13	219.06	226.25	310.80	170.54	—	—	—	—	—
Reserve Money	14	237.22	255.17	305.91	356.63	403.47	449.46	550.23	777.84	976.36	1,402.27	1,560.07	1,663.06
of which: Currency Outside DMBs	14a	222.99	249.77	290.88	337.62	390.78	440.26	484.95	577.34	664.69	781.34	874.31	921.02
Foreign Liabilities	16c	69.68	96.06	130.45	142.06	144.70	157.34	145.08	132.30	125.80	93.72	64.12	20.36
Central Government Deposits	16d	9.25	9.80	4.41	21.93	75.32	4.46	324.61	420.96	438.55	606.08	1,037.91	2,104.62
Other Items (Net)	17r	110.26	182.67	248.11	361.16	200.82	192.89	238.28	259.54	461.70	459.66	633.30	501.99
Deposit Money Banks					*Billions of Dinars: End of Period*								
Reserves	20	7.32	5.58	12.79	18.77	15.85	13.37	42.74	182.94	339.61	624.51	679.40	694.20
Foreign Assets	21	44.88	33.30	32.38	23.11	27.50	27.89	28.32	32.35	49.75	55.53	76.96	91.56
Claims on Central Government	22a	204.63	155.64	141.43	273.15	410.39	459.49	600.38	591.50	841.87	805.90	794.16	865.03
Claims on Nonfin.Pub.Enterprises	22c	208.00	461.00	637.71	632.59	601.86	760.48	530.06	549.31	706.45	791.37	865.19	895.16
Claims on Private Sector	22d	96.75	103.47	137.85	108.56	128.86	173.89	245.31	289.05	559.37	586.56	672.86	881.62
Demand Deposits	24	196.45	210.78	234.03	254.83	334.52	352.71	460.27	551.88	647.57	719.59	1,139.21	1,220.36
Time Deposits	25	247.68	280.46	325.96	409.95	474.19	578.57	617.87	836.18	1,411.11	1,655.92	1,484.72	1,621.48
Foreign Liabilities	26c	35.14	22.58	20.79	15.71	25.48	30.87	26.66	35.18	37.28	38.76	65.34	63.63
Long-Term Foreign Liabilities	26cl	145.02	120.88	96.51	55.30	39.00	39.46	27.61	24.50	36.62	41.88	49.63	20.59
Central Government Deposits	26d	38.82	44.53	97.53	84.36	55.74	56.66	33.51	26.90	69.93	51.14	66.51	99.13
Central Govt. Lending Funds	26f	13.61	13.79	12.30	12.90	13.69	13.22	20.95	11.13	36.24	59.76	44.30	54.52
Credit from Monetary Authorities	26g	50.69	190.29	259.13	219.06	226.25	310.80	170.54	—	—	—	—	—
Other Items (Net)	27r	−165.83	−124.31	−84.09	4.07	15.58	52.82	89.39	159.39	258.31	296.81	238.85	347.86
Post Office: Checking Deposits	24..i	48.50	53.74	57.96	71.68	81.05	87.43	89.09	97.00	100.64	117.19	120.33	144.83
Treasury: Checking Deposits	24..r	7.89	4.82	6.22	7.43	7.33	9.38	7.07	9.44	8.80	12.94	37.98	131.22
Monetary Survey					*Billions of Dinars: End of Period*								
Foreign Assets (Net)	31n	60.45	26.37	134.02	350.38	280.79	169.57	776.05	1,310.85	1,755.31	2,342.80	3,120.79	4,179.48
Domestic Credit	32	774.38	968.93	1,061.39	1,164.93	1,273.45	1,593.76	1,282.87	1,234.07	1,843.47	1,799.73	1,510.78	833.74
Claims on Central Govt. (Net)	32an	468.54	403.29	284.55	423.65	542.30	658.66	506.61	394.74	576.60	420.79	−29.84	−944.54
Claims on Nonfin.Pub.Enterprises	32c	208.00	461.00	637.71	632.59	601.86	760.48	530.06	549.31	706.45	791.37	865.19	895.16
Claims on Private Sector	32d	96.79	103.50	137.88	108.63	129.18	174.48	245.99	289.80	560.12	587.25	673.50	882.45
Money	34	485.65	520.29	589.99	675.96	817.26	889.78	1,044.02	1,237.38	1,425.97	1,634.50	2,176.40	2,418.20
Quasi-Money	35	247.68	280.46	325.96	409.95	474.19	578.57	617.87	836.18	1,411.11	1,655.92	1,484.72	1,621.48
Long-Term Foreign Liabilities	36cl	145.02	120.88	96.51	55.30	39.00	39.46	27.61	24.50	36.62	41.88	49.63	20.59
Central Govt. Lending Funds	36f	13.61	13.79	12.30	12.90	13.69	13.22	20.95	11.13	36.24	59.76	44.30	54.52
Other Items (Net)	37r	−57.13	59.89	170.65	361.21	210.10	242.26	348.47	435.72	688.84	750.47	876.52	898.44
Money plus Quasi-Money	35l	733.33	800.74	915.95	1,085.91	1,291.46	1,468.36	1,661.89	2,073.56	2,837.08	3,290.42	3,661.13	4,039.67
Interest Rates					*Percent Per Annum*								
Discount Rate	60	21.00	† 14.00	13.00	11.00	9.50	8.50	6.00	6.00	5.50	4.50	4.00	4.00
Money Market Rate	60b	19.80	† 19.75	18.09	13.00	10.00	9.99	6.45	2.84	3.13	1.91	1.09	2.01
Treasury Bill Rate	60c	16.50	....	....	....	† 9.96	10.05	7.95	5.69	1.80	1.25	.15	1.30
Deposit Rate	60l	12.00	† 16.00	14.50	9.75	8.50	7.50	7.50	6.25	5.25	5.25	2.50	1.75
Lending Rate	60p	16.00	† 19.00	19.00	12.50	11.00	10.00	10.00	9.50	8.50	8.00	8.00	8.00
Prices, Production, Labor					*Index Numbers (2000=100): Period Averages*								
Producer Prices	63	....	....	....	91.0	94.7	97.8	100.0	104.0	107.2	111.3	116.2	120.2
Consumer Prices	64	56.8	73.7	87.5	92.5	97.1	99.7	100.0	104.2	105.7	108.4	112.3	114.1
Industrial Production	66	103.9	102.8	95.2	91.8	98.4	98.7	100.0	99.8	100.9	102.1	102.5	103.9
Crude Petroleum Production	66aa	86.1	85.3	90.4	90.8	92.5	96.1	100.0	97.8	103.4	138.4	149.9	161.9
					Number in Thousands: Period Averages								
Labor Force	67d	6,810	7,560	7,810	8,070	8,326	8,583	8,850	9,075	9,303	8,762	9,470	9,659
Employment	67e	5,154	5,436	5,625	5,815	5,993	6,077	6,240	6,597	6,900	6,684	7,798	8,182
Unemployment	67c	1,656	2,124	2,185	2,255	2,333	2,506	2,610	2,478	2,403	2,078	1,672	1,475
Unemployment Rate (%)	67r	24.4	28.1	28.0	28.0	28.0	29.2	29.5	27.3	25.9	23.7	17.7	15.3

Algeria   612

2006, International Monetary Fund : *International Financial Statistics Yearbook*

		1994	1995	1996	1997	1998	1999	2000	2001	2002	2003	2004	2005
Intl. Transactions & Positions							*Millions of Dinars*						
Exports...............................	70	311,319	488,924	723,781	801,786	599,666	833,838	1,658,048	1,477,355	1,497,940	1,792,700	2,255,787	3,252,735
Imports, c.i.f.................................	71	328,498	481,394	497,668	501,361	552,146	609,950	690,208	767,517	953,737	958,181	1,309,270	1,468,457
Volume of Exports							*2000=100*						
Petroleum..................................	72a	81.5	81.5	90.2	85.4	90.5	93.8	100.0	98.5	108.1	....	....	....
Crude Petroleum.........................	72aa	72.2	73.0	85.6	81.0	88.9	90.5	100.0	95.1	118.8	157.8	191.1	210.0
Refined Petroleum......................	72ab	96.7	95.5	98.3	93.0	93.8	99.9	100.0	104.7	92.4	92.5	73.8	70.6
Export Prices							*2000=100: Index of Prices in US Dollars*						
Crude Petroleum......................	76aad	57.2	61.7	76.1	68.3	45.5	62.9	100.0	87.1	88.5	102.1	135.3	191.6
Government Finance						*Millions of Dinars: Year Ending December 31*							
Deficit (-) or Surplus........................	80	† −65,354	−28,243	75,258	66,126	−108,134	−16,493	398,856	171,015	10,449	....	....	....
Revenue.........................	81	† 434,199	600,847	825,157	926,668	774,511	950,496	1,578,161	1,505,526	1,603,198	....	....	....
Expenditure.......................	82	† 493,626	625,965	749,009	863,196	875,739	961,682	1,178,122	1,321,028	1,550,646	....	....	....
Lending Minus Repayments...........	83	5,927	3,125	890	−2,654	6,906	5,307	1,183	13,483	42,103	....	....	....
Financing													
Net Borrowing: Domestic..............	84a	−120,023	−147,866	−178,249	....	....	....	....	....	....	....	....	....
Foreign........	85a	141,376	172,158	100,937	....	....	....	....	....	....	....	....	....
Use of Cash Balances....................	87	44,001	3,951	2,054	....	....	....	....	....	....	....	....	....
National Accounts							*Billions of Dinars*						
Househ.Cons.Expend.,incl.NPISHs....	96f	837.5	1,114.8	1,335.0	1,430.3	1,556.7	1,670.7	1,714.2	1,847.1	1,970.6	2,108.8	....	....
Government Consumption Expend...	91f	263.9	340.2	405.4	459.8	503.6	543.6	560.1	624.6	683.2	758.2	....	....
Gross Fixed Capital Formation..........	93e	407.5	541.8	639.4	638.1	728.8	789.8	879.4	965.5	1,102.2	1,218.7	....	....
Changes in Inventories....................	93i	60.4	91.2	5.2	9.3	45.2	60.2	65.6	183.8	253.0	308.2	....	....
Exports of Goods and Services..........	90c	342.6	533.0	781.7	837.2	652.3	911.6	1,734.8	1,550.9	1,587.7	1,988.7	....	....
Imports of Goods and Services (-).....	98c	424.5	616.1	596.7	594.7	656.1	737.6	855.2	930.7	1,142.6	1,258.6	....	....
Gross Domestic Product (GDP).........	99b	1,487.4	2,005.0	2,570.0	2,780.2	2,830.5	3,238.2	4,098.8	4,241.8	4,454.8	5,124.0	....	....
							Millions: Midyear Estimates						
Population...............................	99z	27.74	28.27	28.76	29.20	29.62	30.03	30.46	30.91	31.38	31.87	32.36	32.85

Angola 614

		1994	1995	1996	1997	1998	1999	2000	2001	2002	2003	2004	2005
Exchange Rates		*Kwanzas per Thousands SDRs through 1994; per SDR Thereafter: End of Period*											
Market Rate...............................	aa	.7434	.0085	.2905	.3540	.9807	† 7.6585	21.9121	40.1517	79.7581	117.5127	133.5399	115.4557
		Kwanzas per Thous.US$ through 1994; per US$ Thereafter: End of Period: (ae) Period Average (rf)											
Market Rate...............................	ae	.5093	.0057	.2020	.2624	.6965	† 5.5799	16.8178	31.9494	58.6664	79.0815	85.9878	80.7795
Market Rate...............................	rf	.0595	.0028	.1280	.2290	.3928	2.7907	10.0405	22.0579	43.5302	74.6063	83.5414	87.1591
Fund Position		*Millions of SDRs: End of Period*											
Quota...............................	2f.s	207.30	207.30	207.30	207.30	207.30	286.30	286.30	286.30	286.30	286.30	286.30	286.30
SDRs...............................	1b.s	.10	.11	.11	.12	.12	.13	.13	.14	.14	.14	.15	.15
Reserve Position in the Fund............	1c.s	—	—	—	—	—	—	—	—	—	—	—	—
Total Fund Cred.&Loans Outstg........	2tl	—	—	—	—	—	—	—	—	—	—	—	—
International Liquidity		*Millions of US Dollars Unless Otherwise Indicated: End of Period*											
Total Reserves minus Gold..............	1l.d	....	212.83	551.62	396.43	203.45	496.10	1,198.21	731.87	375.55	634.20	1,374.05	3,196.85
SDRs...............................	1b.d	.15	.16	.16	.16	.17	.18	.17	.17	.19	.21	.23	.21
Reserve Position in the Fund..........	1c.d	—	—	—	—	—	—	—	—	—	—	—	—
Foreign Exchange.....................	1d.d	....	212.67	551.46	396.27	203.28	495.93	1,198.04	731.69	375.35	633.99	1,373.82	3,196.64
Monetary Authorities: Other Assets..	3..d	....	143.95	6.86	1.98	.85	—	—	—	—	1.60	4.25	4.29
Other Liab..	4..d	....	1,901.59	348.01	329.78	444.98	90.53	212.42	247.35	107.88	30.36	28.82	30.53
Banking Institutions: Assets...........	7a.d	....	264.62	523.49	833.30	682.25	747.42	878.08	1,168.78	1,453.84	1,283.96	1,364.52	1,758.22
Liabilities..........	7b.d	....	69.68	61.07	137.31	199.46	119.12	49.14	157.42	126.89	90.07	109.17	138.84
Monetary Authorities		*Millions of Kwanzas: End of Period*											
Foreign Assets...............................	11	....	2.1	112.8	104.0	141.7	† 2,768.2	20,151.3	23,382.7	22,031.9	50,153.4	118,236.8	258,323.8
Claims on Central Government........	12a	....	4.3	36.2	82.3	330.2	† 4,033.1	1,062.1	559.1	26,425.9	25,528.9	23,235.5	24,774.6
Claims on Nonfin.Pub.Enterprises..	12c	....	2.9	2.5	3.7	2.5	† 32.4	156.4	272.3	371.3	787.2	741.0	1,113.2
Claims on Private Sector..............	12d	....	—	—	—	—	† 9.0	43.2	247.2	392.2	704.8	2,403.8	2,201.9
Claims on Banking Institutions.........	12e	....	—	—	48.8	61.5	† 76.7	252.6	330.4	287.2	1.0	1.0	1.0
Reserve Money.......................	14	....	2.6	89.9	172.6	258.6	† 1,956.0	6,215.2	15,325.7	33,365.3	58,722.7	91,560.2	152,324.1
of which: Currency Outside Banks..	14a	....	1.2	42.2	101.6	165.7	† 665.4	2,968.6	8,215.3	20,878.5	35,407.9	45,933.1	59,692.6
Time & Foreign Currency Deposits..	15	....	2.4	58.5	6.8	7.2	† 13.5	41.3	—	146.6	240.7	1,920.1	1,460.7
Liabs. of Central Bank: Securities.....	16ac	....	—	—	.3	—	† 7.0	190.0	3,292.0	5,277.6	11,778.2	11,215.7	28,768.1
Foreign Liabilities........................	16c	....	10.8	70.3	86.5	309.9	† 505.1	3,572.4	7,902.8	6,328.8	2,401.0	2,477.9	2,466.3
Central Government Deposits...........	16d	....	.3	21.3	—	.2	† 2,878.4	14,251.9	1,213.0	5,717.2	12,592.5	54,439.6	146,691.7
Capital Accounts.......................	17a	....	−1.2	18.4	15.1	23.2	† −636.4	−351.9	1,363.0	3,240.8	12,210.7	7,203.3	−16,015.8
Other Items (Net)..........................	17r	....	−5.6	−106.8	−42.4	−63.3	† 2,195.7	−2,253.3	−4,304.8	−4,567.7	−20,770.5	−24,198.6	−29,280.6
Banking Institutions		*Millions of Kwanzas: End of Period*											
Reserves...............................	20	....	1.1	47.7	82.3	92.4	† 1,044.9	2,964.2	7,509.5	16,099.8	25,389.6	48,901.0	96,539.8
Claims on Mon.Author.:Securities..	20c	....	—	—	—	—	† 7.0	175.0	3,292.0	5,277.6	11,778.2	11,073.3	23,178.4
Foreign Assets...........................	21	....	1.5	105.7	218.6	475.2	† 4,170.6	14,767.4	37,341.8	85,291.6	101,537.7	117,332.1	142,028.2
Claims on Central Government........	22a	....	.3	1.0	5.9	55.3	† 12.0	3.3	40.4	2,017.1	15,981.2	47,304.8	94,241.2
Claims on Local Government...........	22b	....	—	—	—	—	† .4	10.0	23.1	3.7	947.6	1,361.9	235.1
Claims on Nonfin. Pub. Enterprises..	22c	....	—	—	—	.2	† 61.1	186.7	601.6	1,061.5	4,126.9	7,484.1	11,296.4
Claims on Private Sector................	22d	....	.7	26.5	90.6	90.0	† 432.9	1,802.7	7,106.2	22,849.1	52,359.3	86,066.9	135,126.9
Demand Deposits.......................	24	....	1.2	51.8	93.3	106.6	† 516.0	2,037.0	5,449.5	10,961.0	33,630.1	49,970.9	92,991.6
Time, Savings,& Fgn.Currency Dep...	25	....	.4	78.0	194.5	344.9	† 2,720.5	10,741.5	27,697.1	74,981.0	108,606.3	145,725.9	236,874.0
of which: Fgn. Currency Deposits...	25b	....	.4	67.7	170.1	330.7	† 2,626.3	10,696.1	26,833.9	73,081.0	104,739.3	140,699.1	218,955.5
Money Market Instruments..............	26aa	....	—	—	—	—	† —	—	321.3	649.2	2,361.6	25,552.1	40,076.3
Foreign Liabilities........................	26c	....	.4	12.3	36.0	138.9	† 664.7	826.4	5,029.4	7,444.4	7,123.2	9,387.6	11,215.7
Central Government Deposits...........	26d	....	—	5.2	6.8	28.9	† 462.8	2,538.1	8,856.9	20,633.7	22,841.4	40,432.0	61,480.8
Credit from Monetary Authorities.....	26g	....	—	—	48.0	58.0	† 500.6	1,180.8	—	—	—	—	—
Capital Accounts.......................	27a	....	.2	16.1	23.9	100.6	† 703.7	2,905.2	8,901.6	17,980.4	36,889.9	53,295.3	70,613.7
Other Items (Net)..........................	27r	....	1.4	17.7	−5.1	−64.9	† 160.6	−319.7	−341.2	−49.4	667.8	−4,839.7	−10,606.2
Banking Survey		*Millions of Kwanzas: End of Period*											
Foreign Assets (Net).......................	31n	....	−7.6	135.9	200.1	168.0	† 5,768.9	30,520.0	47,792.3	93,550.3	142,166.9	223,703.3	386,669.9
Domestic Credit.........................	32	....	7.9	39.9	175.7	449.0	† 1,239.7	−13,525.7	−1,220.1	26,769.9	65,001.8	73,726.5	60,816.8
Claims on Central Govt.(Net)......	32an	....	4.3	10.8	81.4	356.3	† 703.9	−15,724.7	−9,470.4	2,092.1	6,076.2	−24,331.2	−89,156.7
Claims on Local Government..........	32b	....	—	—	—	—	† .4	10.0	23.1	3.7	947.6	1,361.9	235.1
Claims on Nonfin.Pub.Enterprises...	32c	....	2.9	2.5	3.7	2.7	† 93.5	343.1	873.9	1,432.8	4,914.1	8,225.1	12,409.6
Claims on Private Sector.............	32d	....	.7	26.5	90.6	90.0	† 441.9	1,845.8	7,353.4	23,241.4	53,064.0	88,470.7	137,328.8
Money......................	34	....	2.7	93.9	194.9	272.4	† 1,206.5	5,332.8	14,298.7	33,459.2	69,074.5	96,058.5	152,909.9
Quasi-Money............................	35	....	2.8	136.5	201.3	352.1	† 2,734.0	10,782.7	27,697.1	75,127.6	108,847.0	147,646.0	238,334.7
Money Market Instruments..............	36aa	....	—	—	.3	—	† —	—	321.3	649.2	2,361.6	25,552.1	40,076.3
Liabs. of Central Banks: Securities....	36ac	....	—	—	.3	—	† —	15.0	—	—	—	142.4	5,589.7
Capital Accounts.......................	37a	....	−1.0	34.5	38.9	123.8	† 67.3	2,553.4	10,264.6	21,221.2	49,100.7	60,498.6	54,597.9
Other Items (Net).......................	37r	....	−4.2	−89.1	−59.6	−131.3	† 3,000.8	−1,689.6	−6,009.3	−10,137.0	−22,215.0	−32,467.8	−44,021.8
Money plus Quasi-Money..............	35l	....	5.5	230.4	396.2	624.6	† 3,940.5	16,115.5	41,995.8	108,586.8	177,921.5	243,704.5	391,244.6
Interest Rates		*Percent Per Annum*											
Discount Rate (End of Period)...........	60	....	160.00	2.00	48.00	58.00	120.00	150.00	150.00	150.00	150.00	95.00	95.00
Deposit Rate...........................	60l	....	125.92	147.13	29.25	36.88	† 36.57	† 39.58	47.91	48.69	26.17	15.44	13.40
Lending Rate...........................	60p	....	206.25	217.88	37.75	45.00	† 80.30	† 103.16	95.97	97.34	96.12	82.33	67.72
Prices		*Index Numbers (2000=100): Period Averages*											
Consumer Prices...........................	64	....	† —	1.0	3.3	6.8	23.5	100.0	269.7	527.6	1,045.8	1,501.2	1,837.5
Consumer Prices (2000=1 Million)...	64.a	8.7	240.6	10,213.9	32,600.4	....	....	....	....	....	....	....	....
Intl. Transactions & Positions		*Millions of US Dollars*											
Exports, f.o.b...............................	70..d	3,018.0	3,642.0	5,095.0	5,007.0	3,543.0	5,157.0	7,921.0	6,534.0	8,328.0	9,508.0	13,475.0	23,120.0
Imports, f.o.b...............................	71.vd	1,454.0	1,468.0	2,040.0	2,597.0	2,079.0	3,109.0	3,040.0	3,179.0	3,760.0	5,480.0	5,832.0	8,150.0

Angola 614

		1994	1995	1996	1997	1998	1999	2000	2001	2002	2003	2004	2005
Balance of Payments						*Millions of US Dollars: Minus Sign Indicates Debit*							
Current Account, n.i.e.	78ald	−339.8	−295.0	3,266.4	−883.5	−1,867.1	−1,710.4	795.7	−1,430.9	−150.1	−719.6	686.2	....
Goods: Exports f.o.b.	78aad	3,016.6	3,722.7	5,095.0	5,006.8	3,542.9	5,156.5	7,920.7	6,534.3	8,327.9	9,508.2	13,475.0	....
Goods: Imports f.o.b.	78abd	−1,454.1	−1,467.7	−2,040.5	−2,597.0	−2,079.4	−3,109.1	−3,039.5	−3,179.2	−3,760.1	−5,480.1	−5,831.8	
Trade Balance	78acd	1,562.5	2,255.0	3,054.5	2,409.8	1,463.5	2,047.5	4,881.2	3,355.1	4,567.8	4,028.1	7,643.2	
Services: Credit	78add	150.2	113.1	267.7	138.5	121.8	153.0	267.3	202.5	206.8	201.1	322.8	....
Services: Debit	78aed	−1,562.9	−2,051.4	−2,423.3	−2,605.4	−2,635.2	−2,594.6	−2,699.5	−3,518.1	−3,322.0	−3,321.1	−4,802.7	....
Balance on Goods & Services	78afd	149.8	316.7	898.9	−57.1	−1,049.8	−394.1	2,449.0	39.5	1,452.6	908.0	3,163.3	
Income: Credit	78agd	13.0	15.9	43.3	112.1	34.5	24.1	34.4	23.0	17.7	12.3	33.0	
Income: Debit	78ahd	−747.7	−783.2	−1,516.7	−1,033.1	−1,003.3	−1,396.2	−1,715.2	−1,584.0	−1,652.3	−1,738.7	−2,516.6	
Balance on Gds, Serv. & Inc.	78aid	−584.9	−450.6	−574.4	−978.1	−2,018.6	−1,766.2	768.2	−1,521.5	−182.1	−818.5	679.6	
Current Transfers, n.i.e.: Credit	78ajd	333.2	312.2	3,949.4	176.4	238.2	154.5	123.5	208.3	142.3	186.2	124.4	
Current Transfers: Debit	78akd	−88.1	−156.7	−108.6	−81.8	−86.7	−98.7	−96.0	−117.8	−110.3	−87.3	−117.9	
Capital Account, n.i.e.	78bcd	—	—	—	11.2	8.4	6.8	18.3	3.9	....	....	—	
Capital Account, n.i.e.: Credit	78bad	—	—	—	11.2	8.4	6.8	18.3	3.9	....	....	—	
Capital Account: Debit	78bbd												
Financial Account, n.i.e.	78bjd	−443.4	−924.8	−654.5	449.9	368.3	1,739.6	−445.6	950.0	−356.7	1,370.5	−628.2	....
Direct Investment Abroad	78bdd	—	—	—	—	—	—	—	—	−28.7	−23.6	−35.2	
Dir. Invest. in Rep. Econ., n.i.e.	78bed	170.3	472.4	180.6	411.7	1,114.0	2,471.5	878.6	2,145.5	1,672.1	3,504.7	1,444.3	
Portfolio Investment Assets	78bfd	—	—	—	—	—	—	—	....	....	1.0	−2.7	
Equity Securities	78bkd	—	—	—	—	—	—	—	—	....		−3.3	
Debt Securities	78bld	—	—	—	—	—	—	—	....	....	1.0	.6	
Portfolio Investment Liab., n.i.e.	78bgd	—	—	—	—	—	—	—	—			—	
Equity Securities	78bmd	—	—	—	—	—	—	—	—			—	
Debt Securities	78bnd	—	—	—	—	—	—	—	—			—	
Financial Derivatives Assets	78bwd	....	....			....		....	....				
Financial Derivatives Liabilities	78bxd	....	....										
Other Investment Assets	78bhd	214.1	−168.4	−327.6	−330.7	−40.8	−186.1	−702.1	−516.6	−1,321.0	120.0	−1,951.5	
Monetary Authorities	78bod	....	....		....	....		....	....		....	....	
General Government	78bpd	—	—	—	....	—	—	—	—	....	....	....	
Banks	78bqd	—	−4.4	−48.8	—	—	—	—	—	−1,112.6	75.0	−68.2	
Other Sectors	78brd	214.1	−164.1	−278.8	−330.7	−40.8	−186.1	−702.1	−516.6	−208.4	45.0	−1,883.3	
Other Investment Liab., n.i.e.	78bid	−827.8	−1,228.8	−507.4	368.9	−704.8	−545.7	−622.1	−678.9	−679.1	−2,231.5	−83.0	
Monetary Authorities	78bsd	−185.9	−114.3	−143.9	—	−303.0	−272.2	17.3	−62.0	−142.7	−38.0	−2.2	
General Government	78btd	−792.6	−778.1	−202.7	−69.0	−478.6	−180.5	−665.3	−483.1	−352.0	309.5	−161.1	
Banks	78bud	—	—	−1.6	4.8	2.4	3.5	—	—	52.1	−10.5	18.4	
Other Sectors	78bvd	150.7	−336.4	−159.2	433.2	74.4	−96.5	25.9	−133.8	−236.6	−2,492.5	61.9	
Net Errors and Omissions	78cad	−244.5	−19.4	149.2	−181.8	378.5	−78.9	−50.6	−308.6	150.5	−388.2	282.3	
Overall Balance	78cbd	−1,027.7	−1,239.3	2,761.0	−604.3	−1,112.0	−42.9	317.8	−785.6	−356.3	262.8	340.3	
Reserves and Related Items	79dad	1,027.7	1,239.3	−2,761.0	604.3	1,112.0	42.9	−317.8	785.6	356.3	−262.8	−340.3	
Reserve Assets	79dbd	14.2	−30.7	−330.3	162.6	318.0	−530.1	−631.3	466.3	356.3	−262.8	−780.3	
Use of Fund Credit and Loans	79dcd	—	—	—	—	—	—	—	—	—			
Exceptional Financing	79ded	1,013.5	1,270.0	−2,430.7	441.7	794.0	573.0	313.4	319.3	....	....	440.0	....
International Investment Position						*Millions of US Dollars*							
Assets	79aad	....	....	....	....	....	....	....	....		2,884.0	5,370.3	....
Direct Investment Abroad	79abd	....	....	....	....	....	....	....	....		23.6	23.9	
Portfolio Investment	79acd	....	....	....	....	....	....	....	....		—	49.8	....
Equity Securities	79add	....	....	....	....	....	....	....	....		—	—	
Debt Securities	79aed	....	....	....	....	....	....	....	....		—	—	
Financial Derivatives	79ald	....	....	....	....	....	....	....	....		—	—	
Other Investment	79afd	....	....	....	....	....	....	....	....		2,226.4	3,926.6	....
Monetary Authorities	79agd	....	....	....	....	....	....	....	....		....	....	
General Government	79ahd	....	....	....	....	....	....	....	....		—	—	
Banks	79aid	....	....	....	....	....	....	....	....		1,213.4	1,281.4	
Other Sectors	79ajd	....	....	....	....	....	....	....	....		1,013.0	2,645.2	
Reserve Assets	79akd	....	....	....	....	....	....	....	....		634.0	1,370.0	
Liabilities	79lad	....	....	....	....	....	....	....	....		20,518.8	22,427.4	
Dir. Invest. in Rep. Economy	79lbd	....	....	....	....	....	....	....	....		11,987.5	13,436.7	
Portfolio Investment	79lcd	....	....	....	....	....	....	....	....		—	—	....
Equity Securities	79ldd	....	....	....	....	....	....	....	....		—	—	
Debt Securities	79led	....	....	....	....	....	....	....	....		—	—	
Financial Derivatives	79lld	....	....	....	....	....	....	....	....		—	—	
Other Investment	79lfd	....	....	....	....	....	....	....	....		8,531.3	8,990.7	
Monetary Authorities	79lgd	....	....	....	....	....	....	....	....		22.0	23.8	
General Government	79lhd	....	....	....	....	....	....	....	....		6,974.4	7,366.9	
Banks	79lid	....	....	....	....	....	....	....	....		90.8	109.2	....
Other Sectors	79ljd	....	....	....	....	....	....	....	....		1,444.1	1,490.9	....
National Accounts						*Millions of Kwanzas*							
Gross Domestic Product (GDP)	99b	620.2	13.7	835.5	1,752.0	2,556.0	17,171.0	91,666.0	197,111.0	426,428.0	1,031,435.0	1,693,564.0	2,518,898.0
GDP Volume 1992 Prices	99b.p	2.7	3.0	3.4	3.6	3.8	3.9	4.0	4.2	4.9	5.1	5.6	6.5
GDP Deflator (2000=100)	99bip	1.0	—	1.1	2.1	3.0	19.4	100.0	204.2	382.5	894.6	1,322.1	1,699.6
GDP Volume (2000=100)	99bvp	67.3	74.4	83.9	89.1	94.0	96.5	100.0	105.3	121.6	125.8	139.7	161.7
						Millions: Midyear Estimates							
Population	99z	11.94	12.28	12.60	12.90	13.19	13.50	13.84	14.21	14.62	15.05	15.49	15.94

Anguilla 312

		1994	1995	1996	1997	1998	1999	2000	2001	2002	2003	2004	2005
Exchange Rates		*E. Caribbean Dollars per SDR: End of Period (aa) E. Caribbean Dollars per US Dollar: End of Period (ae)*											
Official Rate	aa	3.9416	4.0135	3.8825	3.6430	3.8017	3.7058	3.5179	3.3932	3.6707	4.0121	4.1931	3.8590
Official Rate	ae	2.7000	2.7000	2.7000	2.7000	2.7000	2.7000	2.7000	2.7000	2.7000	2.7000	2.7000	2.7000
International Liquidity		*Millions of US Dollars Unless Otherwise Indicated: End of Period*											
Total Reserves minus Gold	1l.d	9.14	12.78	14.45	16.31	18.15	19.91	20.30	24.19	26.20	33.28	34.25	39.70
Foreign Exchange	1d.d	9.14	12.78	14.45	16.31	18.15	19.91	20.30	24.19	26.20	33.28	34.25	39.70
Monetary Authorities: Other Liab.	4..d	—	—	—	—	—	—	—	—	—	—	—	—
Deposit Money Banks: Assets	7a.d	49.34	66.99	74.43	76.65	108.01	89.54	93.14	103.52	129.83	131.97	203.60	234.46
Liabilities	7b.d	38.01	37.47	48.60	49.21	64.12	69.08	75.46	71.52	78.48	90.94	114.14	95.49
Monetary Authorities		*Millions of E. Caribbean Dollars: End of Period*											
Foreign Assets	11	24.69	34.53	39.00	44.05	49.01	53.83	54.89	65.51	70.87	89.92	90.20	107.36
Claims on Central Government	12a	—	.05	—	—	—	—	—	5.01	.43	—	—	—
Claims on Deposit Money Banks	12e	.01	.01	.01	.02	.01	.01	.02	.02	.01	.03	2.35	.01
Reserve Money	14	24.69	33.00	37.82	42.56	47.77	53.11	54.53	70.13	71.05	89.65	92.51	107.21
of which: Currency Outside DMBs	14a	5.04	7.06	7.32	7.17	8.45	8.72	8.76	8.98	8.25	8.98	9.51	9.58
Foreign Liabilities	16c	—	—	—	—	—	—	—	—	—	—	—	—
Central Government Deposits	16d	.01	1.58	1.19	1.51	1.26	.72	.39	.40	.27	.30	.05	.16
Other Items (Net)	17r	—	—	—	—	—	—	—	—	—	—	—	—
Deposit Money Banks		*Millions of E. Caribbean Dollars: End of Period*											
Reserves	20	19.20	21.48	30.84	34.40	35.75	44.51	49.27	61.27	62.79	81.50	82.95	97.41
Foreign Assets	21	133.21	180.87	200.95	206.96	291.63	241.76	251.47	279.51	350.54	356.31	549.72	633.04
Claims on Central Government	22a	.73	1.12	.35	1.62	1.76	—	—	—	—	—	.17	59.23
Claims on Local Government	22b	—	—	—	—	—	1.85	12.51	16.11	21.68	23.32	53.53	17.18
Claims on Nonfin.Pub.Enterprises	22c	—	—	—	—	7.90	7.89	7.61	7.38	8.20	5.17	3.45	3.62
Claims on Private Sector	22d	193.34	204.82	219.31	245.12	261.08	337.06	424.83	457.66	479.17	540.38	589.89	711.12
Claims on Nonbank Financial Insts.	22g	.35	.75	.80	1.63	.82	.65	.63	.93	1.04	1.64	6.95	4.91
Demand Deposits	24	7.73	10.53	11.26	11.13	11.44	13.11	17.84	14.70	18.46	21.53	28.42	29.85
Time, Savings,& Fgn.Currency Dep	25	191.60	239.14	246.94	270.47	327.55	357.56	420.57	479.01	541.47	584.36	703.73	935.84
Foreign Liabilities	26c	102.62	101.16	131.21	132.86	173.11	186.53	203.74	193.09	211.90	245.53	308.17	257.83
Central Government Deposits	26d	26.32	31.83	38.22	41.06	45.57	45.87	55.34	62.72	69.07	70.78	77.58	92.53
Credit from Monetary Authorities	26g	.01	—	.02	—	1.82	.01	3.52	.02	.02	2.22	2.36	.02
Capital Accounts	27a	21.09	25.82	31.76	37.96	47.13	54.80	62.46	87.72	103.73	110.39	131.63	153.02
Other Items (Net)	27r	−2.54	.56	−7.15	−3.76	−7.70	−24.16	−17.14	−14.40	−21.22	−26.48	34.77	57.42
Monetary Survey		*Millions of E. Caribbean Dollars: End of Period*											
Foreign Assets (Net)	31n	55.27	114.24	108.74	118.15	167.53	109.06	102.62	151.93	209.51	200.71	331.75	482.57
Domestic Credit	32	168.09	173.32	181.05	205.80	224.72	300.85	389.86	423.97	441.18	499.44	576.36	703.37
Claims on Central Govt. (Net)	32an	−25.60	−32.25	−39.06	−40.95	−45.06	−46.59	−55.72	−58.11	−68.90	−71.07	−77.46	−33.46
Claims on Local Government	32b	—	—	—	—	—	1.85	12.51	16.11	21.68	23.32	53.53	17.18
Claims on Nonfin.Pub.Enterprises	32c	—	—	—	—	7.90	7.89	7.61	7.38	8.20	5.17	3.45	3.62
Claims on Private Sector	32d	193.34	204.82	219.31	245.12	261.08	337.06	424.83	457.66	479.17	540.38	589.89	711.12
Claims on Nonbank Financial Inst.	32g	.35	.75	.80	1.63	.82	.65	.63	.93	1.04	1.64	6.95	4.91
Money	34	12.78	17.60	18.61	18.94	19.91	21.84	26.61	23.68	26.79	30.51	37.93	39.43
Quasi-Money	35	191.60	239.14	246.94	270.47	327.55	357.56	420.57	479.01	541.47	584.36	703.73	935.84
Capital Accounts	37a	21.09	25.82	31.76	37.96	47.13	54.80	62.46	87.72	103.73	110.39	131.63	153.02
Other Items (Net)	37r	−2.11	5.00	−7.52	−3.42	−2.34	−24.29	−17.15	−14.52	−21.29	−25.11	34.82	57.65
Money plus Quasi-Money	35l	204.38	256.74	265.54	289.41	347.46	379.40	447.18	502.69	568.25	614.87	741.66	975.27
Money (National Definitions)		*Millions of E. Caribbean Dollars: End of Period*											
M1	59ma	10.77	15.05	15.50	14.85	17.51	18.53	20.13	20.35	19.51	24.48	26.06	29.82
M2	59mb	199.48	249.45	258.80	283.19	340.99	369.78	432.13	484.25	545.58	587.13	697.71	912.77
Interest Rates		*Percent Per Annum*											
Discount Rate (End of Period)	60	9.00	9.00	9.00	8.00	8.00	8.00	8.00	7.00	7.00	6.50	6.50	6.50
Money Market Rate	60b	5.25	5.25	5.25	5.25	5.25	5.25	5.25	† 5.64	6.32	6.07	4.67	4.01
Savings Rate	60k	4.60	4.96	5.00	5.00	5.00	5.00	5.00	5.00	5.00	† 3.23	3.81	3.51
Deposit Rate	60l	3.47	3.64	3.74	3.77	3.79	3.78	3.52	3.54	3.25	4.59	4.83	4.91
Deposit Rate (Fgn. Currency)	60l.f	....	....	....	....	....	....	....	....	....	4.65	4.71	4.93
Lending Rate	60p	12.84	12.60	11.95	11.37	11.16	11.31	11.32	10.74	10.35	11.42	10.99	10.82
Prices, Tourism, Labor		*Index Numbers (2000=100): Period Averages*											
Consumer Prices	64	140.7	142.6	147.7	147.9	151.8	155.8	100.0	102.3	102.8	105.9	110.6	116.0
Number of Tourists	66t	399.2	352.0	342.5	394.4	400.8	106.8	100.0	36.5	33.5	51.1	....	....
		Number in Thousands: Period Averages											
Employment	67e	....	....	....	....	....	6.2	....	5.6	5.5	....	....	....
Intl. Transactions & Positions		*Millions of E. Caribbean Dollars*											
Exports	70	2.4	1.4	4.3	4.2	8.6	7.1	10.9	8.6	11.7	11.5	15.5	39.8
Imports	71	98.2	87.4	161.8	166.3	192.7	248.1	255.2	209.8	188.7	207.4	276.7	350.7

Anguilla 312

Balance of Payments		1994	1995	1996	1997	1998	1999	2000	2001	2002	2003	2004	2005
		Millions of US Dollars: Minus Sign Indicates Debit											
Current Account, n.i.e.	78ald	−11.46	−9.47	−20.26	−18.74	−19.07	−51.05	−54.47	−35.87	−35.38	....	....	....
Goods: Exports f.o.b.	78aad	1.67	1.23	1.76	1.60	3.50	2.90	4.43	3.57	4.38	....	....	....
Goods: Imports f.o.b.	78abd	−39.09	−47.00	−52.86	−54.26	−63.01	−80.86	−83.29	−68.50	−61.63	....	....	....
Trade Balance	78acd	−37.41	−45.78	−51.10	−52.66	−59.51	−77.96	−78.86	−64.93	−57.26			
Services: Credit	78add	61.43	55.56	57.22	66.01	79.44	68.80	64.94	70.43	65.53			
Services: Debit	78aed	−24.78	−27.81	−27.59	−28.96	−38.19	−38.30	−40.86	−39.12	−38.53			
Balance on Goods & Services	78afd	−.76	−18.03	−21.47	−15.61	−18.26	−47.46	−54.77	−33.62	−30.26			
Income: Credit	78agd	1.47	2.06	2.27	3.28	1.56	3.67	3.97	1.86	1.56			
Income: Debit	78ahd	−10.78	−9.60	−8.48	−7.07	−5.43	−6.87	−6.67	−5.39	−6.82			
Balance on Gds, Serv. & Inc.	78aid	−10.06	−25.57	−27.67	−19.40	−22.13	−50.65	−57.47	−37.14	−35.52			
Current Transfers, n.i.e.: Credit	78ajd	5.28	21.51	12.63	7.20	9.30	8.25	11.15	9.83	8.54			
Current Transfers: Debit	78akd	−6.68	−5.42	−5.22	−6.54	−6.24	−8.64	−8.14	−8.57	−8.40			
Capital Account, n.i.e.	78bcd	6.80	5.40	5.23	2.51	5.60	7.96	9.75	8.81	6.80			
Capital Account, n.i.e.: Credit	78bad	8.11	6.71	6.54	3.87	6.95	9.31	11.10	10.11	8.12			
Capital Account: Debit	78bbd	−1.31	−1.31	−1.31	−1.35	−1.35	−1.35	−1.35	−1.30	−1.32			
Financial Account, n.i.e.	78bjd	−1.50	−.95	35.73	19.20	11.60	58.75	41.05	20.23	17.26			
Direct Investment Abroad	78bdd	—											
Dir. Invest. in Rep. Econ., n.i.e.	78bed	11.14	17.58	33.23	21.24	28.06	38.01	38.18	32.72	36.53			
Portfolio Investment Assets	78bfd	—	−.18	—	—	—	—	—	—	−.85			
Equity Securities	78bkd	....	....	....	....	....	....	....	....	....			
Debt Securities	78bld	....	....	....	....	....	....	....	....	....			
Portfolio Investment Liab., n.i.e.	78bgd	—	—	—	—	−.23	—	—	1.15	.01			
Equity Securities	78bmd	....	....	....	....	....	....	....	....	....			
Debt Securities	78bnd	....	....	....	....	....	....	....	....	....			
Financial Derivatives Assets	78bwd	....	....	....	....	....	....	....	....	....			
Financial Derivatives Liabilities	78bxd	....	....	....	....	....	....	....	....	....			
Other Investment Assets	78bhd	−.44	−.75	−1.23	−.61	−.56	−1.29	−.66	−3.49	−.57			
Monetary Authorities	78bod	....	....	....	....	....	....	....	....	....			
General Government	78bpd	....	....	....	....	....	....	....	....	....			
Banks	78bqd	....	....	....	....	....	....	....	....	....			
Other Sectors	78brd	....	....	....	....	....	....	....	....	....			
Other Investment Liab., n.i.e.	78bid	−12.20	−17.60	3.73	−1.43	−15.67	22.03	3.53	−10.15	−17.86			
Monetary Authorities	78bsd	....	....	....	....	....	....	....	....	....			
General Government	78btd	....	....	....	....	....	....	....	....	....			
Banks	78bud	....	....	....	....	....	....	....	....	....			
Other Sectors	78bvd	....	....	....	....	....	....	....	....	....			
Net Errors and Omissions	78cad	6.16	5.03	−19.26	−1.12	3.70	−13.90	4.05	10.73	13.07			
Overall Balance	78cbd	—	—	1.44	1.86	1.84	1.76	.39	3.90	1.75			
Reserves and Related Items	79dad	—	—	−1.44	−1.86	−1.84	−1.76	−.39	−3.90	−1.75			
Reserve Assets	79dbd	—	—	−1.44	−1.86	−1.84	−1.76	−.39	−3.90	−1.75			
Use of Fund Credit and Loans	79dcd	....	....	....	....	....	....	....	....	....			
Exceptional Financing	79ded	....	....	....	....	....	....	....	....	....			
National Accounts		*Millions of E. Caribbean Dollars*											
Gross Domestic Product (GDP)	99b	199.9	201.8	213.0	238.6	269.6	286.5	291.7	297.5	305.4	317.8	395.5	....
GDP Volume 1990 Prices	99b.p	149.6	143.4	148.4	162.1	170.5	185.2	184.6	190.8	184.9	190.2	220.4	237.6
GDP Volume (2000=100)	99bvp	81.1	77.7	80.4	87.8	92.3	100.3	100.0	103.4	100.2	103.0	119.4	128.7
GDP Deflator (2000=100)	99bip	84.5	89.0	90.8	93.2	100.1	97.9	100.0	98.7	104.5	105.7	113.6	....
		Millions: Midyear Estimates											
Population	99z	.010	.010	.011	.011	.011	.011	.011	.011	.012	.012	.012	.012

Antigua and Barbuda 311

		1994	1995	1996	1997	1998	1999	2000	2001	2002	2003	2004	2005
Exchange Rates		E. Caribbean Dollars per SDR: End of Period (aa) E. Caribbean Dollars per US Dollar: End of Period (ae)											
Official Rate............................	aa	3.9416	4.0135	3.8825	3.6430	3.8017	3.7058	3.5179	3.3932	3.6707	4.0121	4.1931	3.8590
Official Rate............................	ae	2.7000	2.7000	2.7000	2.7000	2.7000	2.7000	2.7000	2.7000	2.7000	2.7000	2.7000	2.7000
		Index Numbers (2000=100): Period Averages											
Official Rate............................	ahx	100.0	100.0	100.0	100.0	100.0	100.0	100.0	100.0	100.0	100.0	100.0	100.0
Nominal Effective Exchange Rate.....	nec	98.3	95.3	96.9	98.9	100.8	99.4	100.0	102.5	102.2	98.9	96.2	96.0
Real Effective Exchange Rate...........	rec	102.7	99.1	100.9	100.9	104.2	102.0	100.0	103.3	104.7	102.4	100.2	99.9
Fund Position		Millions of SDRs: End of Period											
Quota...................................	2f.s	8.50	8.50	8.50	8.50	8.50	13.50	13.50	13.50	13.50	13.50	13.50	13.50
SDRs.....................................	1b.s	—	—	—	—	—	.01	.01	.01	.01	.01	.01	.01
Reserve Position in the Fund...........	1c.s	—	—	—	—	—	—	—	—	—	.01	.01	.01
Total Fund Cred.&Loans Outstg........	2tl	—	—	—	—	—	—	—	—	—	—	—	—
International Liquidity		Millions of US Dollars: End of Period											
Total Reserves minus Gold..............	1l.d	45.81	59.44	47.74	50.70	59.37	69.73	63.56	79.72	87.65	113.77	120.14	127.32
SDRs..............................	1b.d	.01	.01	.01	.01	.01	.01	.01	.01	.01	.01	.01	.01
Reserve Position in the Fund..........	1c.d	—	—	—	—	—	—	—	—	—	.01	.01	.01
Foreign Exchange..........................	1d.d	45.80	59.43	47.73	50.69	59.36	69.72	63.55	79.71	87.64	113.75	120.12	127.30
Monetary Authorities: Other Liab.....	4..d	—	—	—	—	—	—	—	—	—	—	—	—
Deposit Money Banks: Assets..........	7a.d	77.30	77.54	72.02	58.79	71.34	160.10	172.17	187.34	259.14	297.26	331.95	561.61
Liabilities...................	7b.d	60.72	46.57	78.47	103.51	114.42	129.49	181.85	148.54	208.93	163.61	181.78	191.44
Monetary Authorities		Millions of E. Caribbean Dollars: End of Period											
Foreign Assets...........................	11	123.95	159.27	129.36	137.41	161.22	189.29	172.76	216.59	238.44	309.95	327.27	347.09
Claims on Central Government........	12a	39.13	32.70	29.30	28.65	26.77	25.30	36.48	34.92	26.39	26.63	22.23	22.17
Claims on Deposit Money Banks......	12e	1.33	1.18	1.03	.95	.90	.74	.62	.49	.40	.33	.26	.02
Reserve Money.............................	14	164.26	193.00	159.61	166.91	188.77	215.20	209.74	251.86	265.20	336.85	348.42	369.22
of which: Currency Outside DMBs..	14a	65.87	77.22	68.06	66.55	79.78	85.01	84.63	78.13	88.20	98.86	113.34	122.14
Foreign Liabilities........................	16c	—	—	—	—	—	—	—	—	—	—	—	—
Central Government Deposits...........	16d	.14	.15	.08	.11	.12	.12	.13	.14	.04	.06	1.34	.06
Other Items (Net).........................	17r	—	—	—	—	—	—	—	—	—	—	—	—
Deposit Money Banks		Millions of E. Caribbean Dollars: End of Period											
Reserves.....................................	20	96.82	116.90	93.87	99.01	115.73	130.99	117.01	190.80	172.61	215.82	244.86	242.23
Foreign Assets.............................	21	208.72	209.36	194.46	158.72	192.61	432.28	464.85	505.83	699.67	802.59	896.28	1,516.35
Claims on Central Government........	22a	124.62	162.83	161.20	192.52	224.83	269.28	283.05	270.51	293.64	289.37	290.74	282.32
Claims on Local Government............	22b	.23	.72	.52	.72	1.43	—	—	.48	.57	.55	.21	.45
Claims on Nonfin.Pub.Enterprises...	22c	9.53	33.78	33.25	32.44	53.94	77.60	87.36	82.26	75.55	75.53	88.63	95.59
Claims on Private Sector.................	22d	613.83	706.86	850.34	1,027.00	1,103.30	1,196.01	1,308.10	1,348.71	1,413.70	1,491.61	1,508.11	1,665.65
Claims on Nonbank Financial Insts...	22g	21.50	7.78	6.73	6.75	9.34	16.43	8.24	10.13	8.89	47.31	54.76	60.38
Demand Deposits..........................	24	161.74	211.25	202.53	209.64	265.73	256.97	251.51	286.40	267.50	318.87	399.97	498.23
Time, Savings,& Fgn.Currency Dep...	25	649.27	773.57	756.28	824.64	929.91	1,274.88	1,382.59	1,444.39	1,554.36	1,798.06	1,836.94	1,940.51
Foreign Liabilities.........................	26c	163.95	125.73	211.88	279.48	308.92	349.62	491.00	401.05	564.11	441.76	490.82	516.88
Central Government Deposits...........	26d	53.83	65.10	72.77	71.32	69.60	57.57	54.26	55.31	63.45	58.24	82.41	81.70
Credit from Monetary Authorities.....	26g	1.29	1.17	1.03	4.31	15.63	13.60	10.97	31.50	3.14	4.70	9.71	.02
Capital Accounts..........................	27a	99.96	107.12	112.55	130.99	147.70	164.56	157.96	174.91	195.26	194.02	231.51	288.75
Other Items (Net).........................	27r	−54.80	−45.70	−16.67	−3.21	−36.31	5.40	−79.68	15.16	16.80	107.15	32.23	536.88
Monetary Survey		Millions of E. Caribbean Dollars: End of Period											
Foreign Assets (Net)......................	31n	168.72	242.91	111.94	16.66	44.91	271.95	146.61	321.38	374.00	670.79	732.73	1,346.56
Domestic Credit............................	32	754.86	879.42	1,008.49	1,216.65	1,349.89	1,526.93	1,668.85	1,691.55	1,755.25	1,872.71	1,880.92	2,044.80
Claims on Central Govt. (Net)........	32an	109.78	130.28	117.65	149.73	181.88	236.89	265.15	249.99	256.55	257.70	229.22	222.73
Claims on Local Government..........	32b	.23	.72	.52	.72	1.43	—	—	.48	.57	.55	.21	.45
Claims on Nonfin.Pub.Enterprises...	32c	9.53	33.78	33.25	32.44	53.94	77.60	87.36	82.26	75.55	75.53	88.63	95.59
Claims on Private Sector...............	32d	613.83	706.86	850.34	1,027.00	1,103.30	1,196.01	1,308.10	1,348.71	1,413.70	1,491.61	1,508.11	1,665.65
Claims on Nonbank Financial Inst...	32g	21.50	7.78	6.73	6.75	9.34	16.43	8.24	10.13	8.89	47.31	54.76	60.38
Money......................................	34	227.79	288.56	270.67	276.25	345.56	342.02	336.14	364.54	355.71	417.74	513.32	620.39
Quasi-Money................................	35	649.27	773.57	756.28	824.64	929.91	1,274.88	1,382.59	1,444.39	1,554.36	1,798.06	1,836.94	1,940.51
Capital Accounts...........................	37a	99.96	107.12	112.55	130.99	147.70	164.56	157.96	174.91	195.26	194.02	231.51	288.75
Other Items (Net).........................	37r	−53.44	−46.92	−19.08	1.43	−28.38	17.42	−61.23	29.10	23.92	133.68	31.89	541.72
Money plus Quasi-Money................	35l	877.06	1,062.12	1,026.95	1,100.89	1,275.47	1,616.89	1,718.74	1,808.93	1,910.07	2,215.80	2,350.26	2,560.90
Money (National Definitions)		Millions of E. Caribbean Dollars: End of Period											
M1...	59ma	194.92	259.58	233.18	242.39	298.70	302.59	284.33	307.13	308.01	369.52	444.54	525.35
M2...	59mb	823.10	998.77	948.94	1,030.10	1,187.53	1,311.71	1,386.99	1,453.58	1,545.09	1,871.10	2,042.92	2,184.05
Interest Rates		Percent Per Annum											
Discount Rate (End of Period)..........	60	9.00	9.00	9.00	8.00	8.00	8.00	8.00	7.00	7.00	6.50	6.50	6.50
Money Market Rate.......................	60b	5.25	5.25	5.25	5.25	5.25	5.25	5.25	† 5.64	6.32	6.07	4.67	4.01
Treasury Bill Rate.........................	60c	7.00	7.00	7.00	7.00	7.00	7.00	7.00	7.00	7.00	7.00	7.00	7.00
Savings Rate................................	60k	8.00	8.00	8.00	8.00	8.00	8.00	8.00	8.00	8.00	† 3.56	3.43	3.38
Deposit Rate................................	60l	4.19	4.02	4.33	4.36	4.34	4.45	5.18	4.49	4.36	4.86	4.12	3.72
Deposit Rate (Fgn. Currency)..........	60l.f	....	....	....	....	....	....	....	....	....	4.64	2.80	3.21
Lending Rate...............................	60p	13.15	12.70	12.26	11.98	12.20	12.07	12.17	11.62	11.39	12.82	11.96	11.49
Intl. Transactions & Positions		Millions of US Dollars											
Exports......................................	70..d	44.4	53.1	37.7	37.9	36.2	37.8	50.0	39.0	39.0	45.0	47.0	57.0
Imports, c.i.f................................	71..d	341.5	345.7	365.3	370.4	385.2	414.1	402.0	377.0	400.0	422.0	451.0	610.0

Antigua and Barbuda   311

		1994	1995	1996	1997	1998	1999	2000	2001	2002	2003	2004	2005
Balance of Payments		*Millions of US Dollars: Minus Sign Indicates Debit*											
Current Account, n.i.e.	78ald	−6.34	−.52	−59.44	−47.37	−46.77	−57.26	−65.78	−64.41	−102.56	....	....	....
Goods: Exports f.o.b.	78aad	45.23	53.15	38.88	38.80	37.38	37.43	49.71	38.62	44.80	....	....	....
Goods: Imports f.o.b.	78abd	−287.50	−291.04	−309.94	−313.86	−320.84	−352.70	−342.39	−321.17	−335.64	....	....	....
Trade Balance	78acd	−242.27	−237.89	−271.06	−275.06	−283.46	−315.27	−292.68	−282.55	−290.84	....	....	....
Services: Credit	78add	391.23	348.46	363.64	404.49	428.52	439.21	416.39	402.67	391.84	....	....	....
Services: Debit	78aed	−134.42	−147.89	−157.43	−164.43	−169.09	−177.27	−154.32	−171.89	−174.68	....	....	....
Balance on Goods & Services	78afd	14.53	−37.32	−64.84	−35.00	−24.02	−53.33	−30.61	−51.77	−73.67	....	....	....
Income: Credit	78agd	4.26	5.21	5.79	3.71	12.89	11.70	15.52	18.69	12.56	....	....	....
Income: Debit	78ahd	−30.81	−32.07	−32.01	−25.86	−33.92	−35.14	−60.04	−40.47	−47.06	....	....	....
Balance on Gds, Serv. & Inc.	78aid	−12.03	−64.18	−91.06	−57.16	−45.06	−76.77	−75.13	−73.55	−108.17	....	....	....
Current Transfers, n.i.e.: Credit	78ajd	15.15	78.04	35.19	19.90	12.42	23.61	18.43	22.52	22.97	....	....	....
Current Transfers: Debit	78akd	−9.47	−14.38	−3.56	−10.12	−14.13	−4.10	−9.09	−13.38	−17.36	....	....	....
Capital Account, n.i.e.	78bcd	5.91	6.99	4.36	9.17	156.33	17.62	39.33	11.93	13.92	....	....	....
Capital Account, n.i.e.: Credit	78bad	6.53	6.99	4.36	9.17	156.33	17.62	39.33	11.93	13.92	....	....	....
Capital Account: Debit	78bbd	−.62	—	—	—	—	—	—	—	—	....	....	....
Financial Account, n.i.e.	78bjd	−19.88	−10.66	54.98	50.54	−56.72	52.10	42.07	60.05	84.65	....	....	....
Direct Investment Abroad	78bdd	—	—	—	—	—	—	—	—	—	....	....	....
Dir. Invest. in Rep. Econ., n.i.e.	78bed	24.79	31.49	19.35	22.94	22.77	32.09	28.11	43.93	47.71	....	....	....
Portfolio Investment Assets	78bfd	−1.38	1.19	−.78	—	—	−.09	−.01	−.05	−2.92	....	....	....
Equity Securities	78bkd	....	....	....	....	....	....	....	....	....	....	....	....
Debt Securities	78bld	....	....	....	....	....	....	....	....	....	....	....	....
Portfolio Investment Liab., n.i.e.	78bgd	—	−1.28	−.81	—	−.29	2.78	2.35	−2.46	.74	....	....	....
Equity Securities	78bmd	....	....	....	....	....	....	....	....	....	....	....	....
Debt Securities	78bnd	....	....	....	....	....	....	....	....	....	....	....	....
Financial Derivatives Assets	78bwd	....	....	....	....	....	....	....	....	....	....	....	....
Financial Derivatives Liabilities	78bxd	....	....	....	....	....	....	....	....	....	....	....	....
Other Investment Assets	78bhd	−23.89	−31.34	−6.68	−2.40	−20.41	74.74	−.39	−3.74	−10.83	....	....	....
Monetary Authorities	78bod	....	....	....	....	....	....	....	....	....	....	....	....
General Government	78bpd	....	....	....	....	....	....	....	....	....	....	....	....
Banks	78bqd	....	....	....	....	....	....	....	....	....	....	....	....
Other Sectors	78brd	....	....	....	....	....	....	....	....	....	....	....	....
Other Investment Liab., n.i.e.	78bid	−19.40	−10.71	43.90	29.99	−58.79	−57.41	12.00	22.36	49.94	....	....	....
Monetary Authorities	78bsd	—	—	—	—	—	—	—	—	—	....	....	....
General Government	78btd	....	....	....	....	....	....	....	....	....	....	....	....
Banks	78bud	....	....	....	....	....	....	....	....	....	....	....	....
Other Sectors	78bvd	....	....	....	....	....	....	....	....	....	....	....	....
Net Errors and Omissions	78cad	28.39	17.78	−11.16	−9.38	−43.96	−2.07	−21.78	8.44	11.72	....	....	....
Overall Balance	78cbd	8.08	13.59	−11.26	2.96	8.88	10.39	−6.16	16.00	7.73	....	....	....
Reserves and Related Items	79dad	−8.08	−13.59	11.26	−2.96	−8.89	−10.39	6.16	−16.00	−7.73	....	....	....
Reserve Assets	79dbd	−8.08	−13.59	11.26	−2.96	−8.89	−10.39	6.16	−16.00	−7.73	....	....	....
Use of Fund Credit and Loans	79dcd	—	—	—	—	—	—	—	—	—	....	....	....
Exceptional Financing	79ded	....	....	....	....	....	....	....	....	....	....	....	....
National Accounts		*Millions of E. Caribbean Dollars*											
Househ.Cons.Expend.,incl.NPISHs.	96f	633.8	672.5	784.0	774.0	750.6	711.3	780.1	644.4	637.1	755.2	833.7	....
Government Consumption Expend.	91f	258.2	284.8	307.7	318.1	364.9	396.4	420.0	435.0	504.5	413.8	441.0	....
Gross Fixed Capital Formation	93e	437.4	491.9	578.8	614.6	720.6	793.8	862.4	937.2	989.4	1,055.6	1,103.6	....
Exports of Goods and Services	90c	1,190.0	1,084.3	1,086.8	1,190.2	1,245.6	1,259.8	1,260.3	1,195.3	1,162.4	1,252.9	1,367.3	....
Imports of Goods and Services (-)	98c	1,169.2	1,201.0	1,298.3	1,328.1	1,407.5	1,403.3	1,536.2	1,329.1	1,363.9	1,440.8	1,535.8	....
Gross Domestic Product (GDP)	99b	1,350.2	1,332.7	1,459.0	1,568.8	1,674.2	1,758.1	1,786.6	1,882.9	1,929.4	2,036.7	2,209.8	....
Net Primary Income from Abroad	98.n	−71.7	−72.5	−70.8	−72.8	−80.6	−80.8	−84.7	−66.9	−111.9	−113.1	−136.2	....
Gross National Income (GNI)	99a	1,278.6	1,260.2	1,388.2	1,496.0	1,593.6	1,677.3	1,701.9	1,815.9	1,817.5	1,923.6	2,073.6	....
Net Current Transf.from Abroad	98t	2.4	187.3	85.4	33.1	−2.0	55.7	1.7	24.7	15.2	33.7	33.2	....
Gross Nat'l Disposable Inc.(GNDI)	99i	1,281.0	1,447.5	1,473.6	1,529.1	1,591.7	1,733.0	1,703.6	1,840.6	1,832.7	1,957.3	2,106.8	....
Gross Saving	99s	389.0	490.0	381.9	437.0	476.2	625.4	503.6	761.2	691.1	788.3	832.1	....
GDP Volume 1990 Prices	99b.p	1,219.1	1,168.2	1,245.3	1,310.5	1,353.4	1,403.0	....	....	....	....	....	....
GDP Volume (1995=100)	99bvp	104.4	100.0	106.6	112.2	115.9	120.1	....	....	....	....	....	....
GDP Deflator (1995=100)	99bip	97.1	100.0	102.7	104.9	108.4	109.8	....	....	....	....	....	....
		Millions: Midyear Estimates											
Population	99z	.07	.07	.07	.07	.07	.08	.08	.08	.08	.08	.08	....

Argentina 213

		1994	1995	1996	1997	1998	1999	2000	2001	2002	2003	2004	2005
Exchange Rates						*Pesos per SDR: End of Period*							
Official Rate....................	aa	1.45912	1.48649	1.43724	1.34858	1.40733	1.37182	1.30226	1.25610	4.51361	4.31674	4.59536	4.30496
					Pesos per US Dollar: End of Period (ae) Period Average (rf)								
Official Rate....................	ae	.99950	1.00000	.99950	.99950	.99950	.99950	.99950	.99950	3.32000	2.90500	2.95900	3.01200
Official Rate....................	rf	.99901	.99975	.99966	.99950	.99950	.99950	.99950	.99950	3.06326	2.90063	2.92330	2.90366
Fund Position						*Millions of SDRs: End of Period*							
Quota............................	2f.s	1,537.1	1,537.1	1,537.1	1,537.1	1,537.1	2,117.1	2,117.1	2,117.1	2,117.1	2,117.1	2,117.1	2,117.1
SDRs............................	1b.s	385.7	362.7	277.4	123.6	187.7	100.3	562.2	8.5	69.3	678.7	564.5	3,104.1
Reserve Position in the Fund...........	1c.s	—	—	—	—	—	—	—	—	—	.1	.2	.2
Total Fund Cred.&Loans Outstg.......	2tl	2,884.7	4,124.4	4,376.0	4,349.3	3,865.1	3,262.6	3,880.3	11,121.1	10,547.5	10,446.2	9,073.0	6,655.7
International Liquidity					*Millions of US Dollars Unless Otherwise Indicated: End of Period*								
Total Reserves minus Gold..............	1l.d	14,327	14,288	18,104	22,320	24,752	26,252	25,147	14,553	10,489	14,153	18,884	27,179
SDRs..........................	1b.d	563	539	399	167	264	138	733	11	94	1,008	877	4,437
Reserve Position in the Fund..........	1c.d	—	—	—	—	—	—	—	—	—	—	—	—
Foreign Exchange.....................	1d.d	13,764	13,749	17,705	22,153	24,488	26,114	24,414	14,542	10,395	13,145	18,007	22,742
Gold (Million Fine Troy Ounces).......	1ad	4.374	4.374	4.374	.361	.360	.338	.019	.009	.009	.009	1.770	1.760
Gold (National Valuation)...............	1and	1,651	1,679	1,611	120	124	121	7	3	3	4	769	908
Monetary Authorities:Other Assets...	3..d	57	22	30	42	30	13	3	—	—	—	—	—
Other Liab................	4..d	—	—	—	—	—	—	—	5	18	34	4	10
Deposit Money Banks: Assets...........	7a.d	5,587	6,302	10,011	17,732	16,895	15,007	17,911	7,179	3,627	3,350	2,878	2,877
Liabilities...............	7b.d	10,995	13,649	15,820	21,048	21,440	22,831	24,170	16,297	12,717	9,334	7,290	5,513
Other Banking Insts.: Assets...........	7e.d	26	31	25	24	17	74	42	35	15	21	8	10
Liabilities...................	7f.d	39	62	84	148	395	434	405	263	45	17	28	13
Monetary Authorities						*Millions of Pesos: End of Period*							
Foreign Assets........................	11	† 16,035	15,989	19,745	22,806	26,249	27,322	26,925	15,321	35,236	40,733	58,444	85,145
Claims on Central Government.......	12a	† 8,361	8,499	8,223	7,867	7,170	6,350	7,468	20,495	57,231	62,584	65,538	55,537
Claims on Deposit Money Banks.......	12e	† 22,463	24,129	2,106	1,794	2,070	2,160	1,930	6,019	24,794	25,098	24,897	16,579
Claims on Other Banking Insts.........	12f	† 4	3	3	—	—	—	—	—	81	91	116	14
Reserve Money.......................	14	† 16,267	13,769	14,060	15,975	16,392	16,524	15,077	17,768	30,165	50,158	60,525	61,256
of which: Currency Outside DMBs..	14a	† 11,229	11,161	11,736	13,331	13,503	13,736	12,571	9,081	16,430	26,649	33,872	43,764
Foreign Liabilities.....................	16c	† 4,211	6,131	6,293	5,868	5,442	4,478	5,056	13,982	48,286	45,652	41,915	28,867
Central Government Deposits...........	16d	† 764	1,677	2,242	325	1,343	935	1,769	4,366	67	259	161	1,899
Capital Accounts.....................	17a	† 3,279	3,583	4,053	4,059	4,604	4,415	4,659	3,542	7,012	5,993	7,206	8,251
Other Items (Net)...................	17r	† 22,342	23,461	3,430	6,242	7,708	9,480	9,762	2,177	31,811	26,445	39,187	57,001
Deposit Money Banks						*Millions of Pesos: End of Period*							
Reserves............................	20	† 5,203	2,637	2,358	2,673	2,905	3,101	2,826	8,429	13,507	23,061	26,439	17,470
Foreign Assets........................	21	† 5,587	6,302	10,011	17,732	16,895	15,007	17,911	7,179	12,196	9,830	8,559	8,722
Claims on Central Government........	22a	† 6,094	10,299	13,013	14,513	17,433	18,982	18,859	20,518	82,709	92,425	101,437	98,472
Claims on State and Local Govts.....	22b	† 5,008	5,247	5,273	5,950	5,827	8,924	9,585	9,133	11,366	2,503	1,828	1,396
Claims on Official Entities...........	22bx	† 493	463	565	612	285	276	278	443	259	617	591	610
Claims on Private Sector..................	22d	† 51,372	50,780	54,093	63,131	70,525	68,431	65,843	54,159	47,249	39,926	46,092	60,693
Demand Deposits.....................	24	† 5,133	5,458	7,305	8,151	7,986	8,099	7,267	6,763	11,843	16,292	22,055	27,512
Time, Savings,& Fgn.Currency Dep...	25	† 37,109	35,352	42,710	56,038	64,162	67,315	70,677	57,078	59,022	70,224	81,485	95,654
Foreign Liabilities......................	26c	† 10,995	13,649	15,820	21,048	21,440	22,831	24,170	16,297	42,768	27,392	21,679	16,712
Central Government Deposits...........	26d	† 3,014	2,467	3,054	3,990	4,525	3,602	4,474	2,150	5,255	8,691	13,491	13,656
Credit from Monetary Authorities.....	26g	† 2,184	2,650	1,375	409	393	308	78	4,478	28,879	28,352	29,239	17,415
Capital Accounts.....................	27a	† 13,519	13,771	15,065	15,806	16,674	16,437	16,726	15,816	25,033	20,964	23,045	26,342
Other Items (Net)...................	27r	† 1,802	2,381	−18	−830	−1,311	−3,868	−8,092	−2,722	−5,513	−3,553	−6,049	−9,928
Monetary Survey						*Millions of Pesos: End of Period*							
Foreign Assets (Net)......................	31n	† 6,416	2,510	7,643	13,623	16,262	15,021	15,610	−7,778	−43,622	−22,481	3,409	48,287
Domestic Credit........................	32	† 67,554	71,148	75,874	87,759	95,372	98,427	95,790	98,231	193,573	189,196	201,950	201,167
Claims on Central Govt. (Net).......	32an	† 10,677	14,654	15,940	18,066	18,735	20,795	20,084	34,496	134,619	146,059	153,323	138,453
Claims on State and Local Govts....	32b	† 5,008	5,247	5,273	5,950	5,827	8,924	9,585	9,133	11,366	2,503	1,828	1,396
Claims on Official Entities..............	32bx	† 493	463	565	612	285	276	278	443	259	617	591	610
Claims on Private Sector..............	32d	† 51,372	50,780	54,093	63,131	70,525	68,431	65,843	54,159	47,249	39,926	46,092	60,693
Claims on Other Banking Insts.......	32f	† 4	3	3	—	—	—	—	—	81	91	116	14
Money................................	34	† 16,362	16,619	19,042	21,482	21,489	21,836	19,838	15,844	28,272	42,940	55,927	71,275
Quasi-Money..........................	35	† 37,109	35,352	42,710	56,038	64,162	67,315	70,677	57,078	59,022	70,224	81,485	95,654
Capital Accounts......................	37a	† 16,798	17,354	19,118	19,864	21,279	20,852	21,386	19,358	32,045	26,956	30,252	34,593
Other Items (Net).....................	37r	† 3,701	4,333	2,647	3,997	4,704	3,446	−501	−1,827	30,612	26,594	37,695	47,932
Money plus Quasi-Money..............	35l	† 53,471	51,971	61,752	77,520	85,651	89,150	90,515	72,922	87,294	113,164	137,412	166,929
Other Banking Institutions						*Millions of Pesos: End of Period*							
Reserves............................	40	† 20	14	7	6	7	15	15	89	141	169	79	126
Foreign Assets........................	41	† 26	31	25	24	17	74	42	35	49	61	25	31
Claims on Central Government........	42a	† 35	37	84	96	114	89	56	18	941	677	525	173
Claims on Local and State Govts......	42b	† 2	2	—	2	—	—	—	—	6	—	—	—
Claims on Official Entities...............	42bx	† —	—	—	—	—	—	—	2	—	—	—	—
Claims on Private Sector...............	42d	† 838	725	846	1,103	1,681	2,147	2,067	1,821	676	532	879	1,378
Claims on Deposit Money Banks......	42e	† 10	13	20	18	22	27	27	22	15	25	27	27
Time, Savings,& Fgn.Currency Dep...	45	† 501	284	348	320	333	295	344	223	192	215	203	286
Foreign Liabilities......................	46c	† 39	62	84	148	395	434	405	263	153	51	82	39
Credit from Monetary Authorities.....	46g	† 4	3	3	—	—	—	—	—	81	91	116	14
Capital Accounts......................	47a	† 236	210	190	233	367	468	557	667	1,052	981	834	819
Other Items (Net).....................	47r	† 151	263	357	547	746	1,155	902	833	351	126	300	578

Argentina 213

		1994	1995	1996	1997	1998	1999	2000	2001	2002	2003	2004	2005
Banking Survey						*Millions of Pesos: End of Period*							
Foreign Assets (Net)........................	51n	† 6,403	2,480	7,585	13,499	15,884	14,661	15,247	−8,006	−43,726	−22,472	3,352	48,279
Domestic Credit.............................	52	† 68,424	71,908	76,802	88,959	97,167	100,663	97,913	100,072	195,116	190,315	203,239	202,704
Claims on Central Govt. (Net).......	52an	† 10,711	14,691	16,024	18,163	18,850	20,884	20,140	34,514	135,560	146,736	153,848	138,626
Claims on State and Local Govts....	52b	† 5,009	5,249	5,273	5,951	5,827	8,924	9,585	9,133	11,372	2,503	1,828	1,396
Claims on Official Entities..............	52bx	† 493	463	565	612	285	276	278	445	259	618	591	611
Claims on Private Sector...............	52d	† 52,210	51,505	54,939	64,234	72,206	70,578	67,910	55,979	47,924	40,458	46,971	62,071
Liquid Liabilities...........................	55l	† 53,952	52,241	62,094	77,835	85,977	89,430	90,844	73,056	87,345	113,210	137,536	167,088
Capital Accounts...........................	57a	† 17,034	17,564	19,308	20,098	21,646	21,320	21,942	20,024	33,098	27,937	31,086	35,412
Other Items (Net).........................	57r	† 3,841	4,584	2,984	4,526	5,428	4,573	374	−1,015	30,947	26,696	37,968	48,483
Interest Rates							*Percent Per Annum*						
Money Market Rate......................	60b	7.66	9.46	6.23	6.63	6.81	6.99	8.15	24.90	41.35	3.74	1.96	4.11
Money Market Rate (Fgn. Cur.)........	60b.f	....	8.40	5.91	6.39	6.55	6.07	7.53	12.76	13.01	1.64	2.03	2.86
Deposit Rate.................................	60l	8.08	11.90	7.36	6.97	7.56	8.05	8.34	16.16	39.25	10.16	2.61	3.76
Deposit Rate (Fgn. Currency)...........	60l.f	5.68	8.19	6.10	5.87	6.40	6.42	7.03	9.81	4.44	.86	.38	.43
Lending Rate.................................	60p	10.06	17.85	10.51	9.24	10.64	11.04	11.09	27.71	51.68	19.15	6.78	6.16
Lending Rate (Fgn. Currency)...........	60p.f	8.17	13.88	9.12	7.84	8.95	9.07	9.67	17.67	....	....	....	....
Prices, Production, Labor						*Index Numbers (2000=100): Period Averages*							
Share Prices.................................	62	114.6	84.0	111.4	149.0	110.6	96.9	100.0	72.6	79.4	145.4	219.6	296.7
Producer Prices..............................	63	97.9	102.1	105.1	104.0	100.5	96.4	100.0	98.0	174.6	208.9	225.0	243.9
Consumer Prices............................	64	97.2	100.5	† 100.7	101.2	102.1	100.9	100.0	98.9	124.5	141.3	147.5	161.7
Wages: Monthly(Mfg)('95=100).......	65ey	101.7	100.0	100.7	....	....	....	....	....	....	....	....	....
Manufacturing Prod., Seas.Adj........	66eyc	103.0	96.6	99.1	108.4	110.6	101.4	100.0	74.4	67.0	78.6	89.9	97.7
Crude Petroleum Production............	66aa	86.4	93.2	99.5	108.1	109.8	104.1	100.0	100.3	98.0	96.0	90.2	85.9
						Number in Thousands: Period Averages							
Labor Force..................................	67d	11,923	12,306	12,526	12,971	13,077	13,455	13,780	13,914	14,336	14,989	15,435	15,518
Employment..................................	67e	10,520	10,301	10,453	11,231	11,495	11,641	11,760	11,401	11,827	12,470	13,388	13,801
Unemployment.............................	67c	1,402	2,006	2,074	1,740	1,582	1,814	2,019	2,513	2,509	2,519	2,047	1,718
Unemployment Rate (%)................	67r	12.0	16.0	16.6	13.4	12.1	13.5	14.7	18.1	17.5	16.8	13.6	11.6
Intl. Transactions & Positions							*Millions of US Dollars*						
Exports.......................................	70..d	15,839	20,963	23,811	26,431	26,434	23,309	26,341	26,543	25,650	29,566	34,550	40,013
Wheat......................................	70d.d	657	1,005	1,066	1,347	1,308	1,002	1,218	1,302	1,097	941	1,367	1,284
Imports, c.i.f................................	71..d	21,590	20,122	23,762	30,450	31,377	25,508	25,280	20,320	8,990	13,834	22,445	28,688
Imports, f.o.b...............................	71.vd	20,077	18,726	22,190	28,554	29,532	24,103	23,889	19,158	8,473	13,118	21,311	27,301
							2000=100						
Volume of Exports........................	72	57.3	71.7	76.4	87.9	98.1	97.4	100.0	104.3	105.1	110.5	117.8	134.5
Wheat......................................	72d	47.0	62.5	53.5	78.7	95.5	79.9	100.0	97.9	82.1	55.9	90.6	....
Volume of Imports........................	73	77.8	68.8	82.2	107.8	117.2	100.0	100.0	82.6	37.9	58.2	87.4	107.7
					2000=100: Indices of Unit Values in US Dollars								
Unit Value of Exports/Export Prices...	74..d	105.0	111.0	118.3	114.2	102.3	90.9	100.0	96.6	93.0	101.9	111.4	112.8
Frozen Beef................................	74kad	112.4	103.1	82.7	88.5	115.2	101.3	100.0	81.2	....	....	....	....
Corned Beef (1990=100)..............	74kdd	116.7	....	....	....	....	....	....	....	....	....	....	....
Wheat......................................	74d.d	117.1	131.6	162.8	138.5	113.2	103.0	100.0	109.1	109.7	137.9	126.7	116.0
Unit Value of Imports/Import Prices..	75..d	109.7	115.7	114.3	111.7	106.0	100.0	100.0	97.3	94.0	94.1	101.3	105.4

		1994	1995	1996	1997	1998	1999	2000	2001	2002	2003	2004	2005
Balance of Payments		*Millions of US Dollars: Minus Sign Indicates Debit*											
Current Account, n.i.e.	78ald	−10,979	−5,118	−6,770	−12,138	−14,482	−11,943	−8,981	−3,291	8,668	7,982	3,281	....
Goods: Exports f.o.b.	78aad	16,023	21,162	24,043	26,431	26,434	23,309	26,341	26,543	25,651	29,939	34,550	....
Goods: Imports f.o.b.	78abd	−20,162	−18,804	−22,283	−28,554	−29,531	−24,103	−23,889	−19,158	−8,473	−13,134	−21,311	....
Trade Balance	78acd	−4,139	2,357	1,760	−2,123	−3,097	−795	2,452	7,385	17,178	16,805	13,239	....
Services: Credit	78add	3,364	3,826	4,405	4,599	4,854	4,719	4,936	4,627	3,295	4,224	5,221	....
Services: Debit	78aed	−7,143	−7,262	−7,952	−8,984	−9,298	−8,830	−9,219	−8,490	−4,885	−5,622	−6,870	....
Balance on Goods & Services	78afd	−7,918	−1,079	−1,787	−6,508	−7,542	−4,906	−1,832	3,522	15,588	15,407	11,590	....
Income: Credit	78agd	3,480	4,368	4,444	5,487	6,134	6,075	7,420	5,847	3,021	3,084	3,439	....
Income: Debit	78ahd	−7,039	−9,004	−9,909	−11,632	−13,538	−13,565	−14,968	−13,085	−10,506	−11,054	−12,389	....
Balance on Gds, Serv. & Inc.	78aid	−11,477	−5,715	−7,252	−12,653	−14,946	−12,396	−9,380	−3,715	8,103	7,437	2,640	....
Current Transfers, n.i.e.: Credit	78ajd	839	870	752	831	802	790	792	856	798	922	1,104	....
Current Transfers: Debit	78akd	−342	−273	−270	−316	−338	−337	−393	−431	−234	−377	−463	....
Capital Account, n.i.e.	78bcd	18	14	51	66	73	149	106	157	406	70	43	....
Capital Account, n.i.e.: Credit	78bad	27	25	72	112	92	161	121	165	410	77	47	....
Capital Account: Debit	78bbd	−10	−11	−21	−46	−19	−12	−15	−8	−4	−7	−4	....
Financial Account, n.i.e.	78bjd	12,400	5,466	11,582	17,674	18,936	14,448	7,853	−14,971	−20,686	−15,864	−10,448	....
Direct Investment Abroad	78bdd	−1,013	−1,497	−1,601	−3,653	−2,325	−1,730	−901	−161	627	−774	−351	....
Dir. Invest. in Rep. Econ., n.i.e.	78bed	3,635	5,609	6,949	9,160	7,291	23,988	10,418	2,166	2,149	1,652	4,274	....
Portfolio Investment Assets	78bfd	−1,486	−2,882	−2,381	−1,570	−1,906	−2,005	−1,252	212	477	−95	−77	....
Equity Securities	78bkd	−763	−401	−594	−838	−839	167	−1,455	−931	13	−34	−72	....
Debt Securities	78bld	−723	−2,481	−1,787	−733	−1,067	−2,173	203	1,143	464	−61	−5	....
Portfolio Investment Liab., n.i.e.	78bgd	10,947	5,196	11,975	12,595	10,693	−4,780	−1,331	−9,715	−5,117	−7,663	−9,341	....
Equity Securities	78bmd	4,220	1,552	867	2,319	−210	−10,773	−3,227	31	−116	65	−86	....
Debt Securities	78bnd	6,727	3,643	11,108	10,276	10,903	5,993	1,896	−9,746	−5,001	−7,728	−9,255	....
Financial Derivatives Assets	78bwd	....	....	....	....	....	....	....	....	....	....	....	....
Financial Derivatives Liabilities	78bxd	....	....	....	....	....	....	....	....	....	....	....	....
Other Investment Assets	78bhd	−3,227	−8,108	−5,225	−7,116	−173	−2,862	−1,368	−1,907	−8,896	−4,403	−2,316	....
Monetary Authorities	78bod	—	—	—	—	—	—	—	—	—	—	—	....
General Government	78bpd	378	−671	54	−99	111	−1,553	1,056	232	307	−78	−161	....
Banks	78bqd	−297	−603	−3,039	−5,337	613	995	−2,348	8,960	1,896	447	240	....
Other Sectors	78brd	−3,308	−6,834	−2,240	−1,681	−897	−2,304	−76	−11,099	−11,099	−4,773	−2,395	....
Other Investment Liab., n.i.e.	78bid	3,544	7,148	1,865	8,259	5,356	1,838	2,287	−5,566	−9,925	−4,581	−2,636	....
Monetary Authorities	78bsd	−16	−94	−214	−11	−10	−13	−16	1,130	−341	−634	53	....
General Government	78btd	535	1,903	−151	311	1,924	1,203	440	1,007	−2,207	−98	−1,054	....
Banks	78bud	1,098	3,250	443	3,843	621	1,133	898	−6,775	−2,178	−2,917	−916	....
Other Sectors	78bvd	1,927	2,089	1,788	4,116	2,822	−486	964	−928	−5,199	−932	−719	....
Net Errors and Omissions	78cad	−2,113	−2,674	−1,605	−2,272	−437	−642	−154	−3,300	−1,790	−1,265	131	....
Overall Balance	78cbd	−675	−2,311	3,258	3,331	4,090	2,013	−1,176	−21,405	−13,402	−9,077	−6,993	....
Reserves and Related Items	79dad	675	2,311	−3,258	−3,331	−4,090	−2,013	1,176	21,405	13,402	9,077	6,993	....
Reserve Assets	79dbd	−685	82	−3,875	−3,293	−3,436	−1,186	403	12,070	4,526	−3,497	−5,283	....
Use of Fund Credit and Loans	79dcd	455	1,924	367	−38	−654	−826	773	9,335	−739	−151	−2,038	....
Exceptional Financing	79ded	904	305	250	—	—	—	—	—	9,616	12,725	14,314	....
International Investment Position		*Millions of US Dollars*											
Assets	79aad	89,673	102,834	117,398	133,241	140,617	150,380	153,633	132,797	131,982	144,844	153,163	....
Direct Investment Abroad	79abd	9,148	10,696	12,374	16,034	18,335	20,118	21,141	21,283	20,618	21,500	21,476	....
Portfolio Investment	79acd	19,154	22,539	26,548	28,900	30,270	34,410	35,190	1,225	843	939	1,016	....
Equity Securities	79add	68	108	102	217	51	31	43	43	30	64	73	....
Debt Securities	79aed	19,087	22,431	26,447	28,683	30,219	34,379	35,147	1,182	813	875	943	....
Financial Derivatives	79ald	—	—	—	—	—	—	—	—	—	—	—	....
Other Investment	79afd	44,775	53,097	58,331	65,333	65,498	68,374	69,652	95,365	99,951	107,278	110,148	....
Monetary Authorities	79agd	—	—	—	—	—	—	—	—	—	—	—	....
General Government	79ahd	5,252	6,136	6,091	6,075	5,957	7,524	6,377	6,600	6,108	6,330	6,719	....
Banks	79aid	5,377	5,980	9,019	14,355	13,742	12,747	15,095	5,888	3,141	2,694	2,442	....
Other Sectors	79ajd	34,147	40,981	43,221	44,902	45,799	48,103	48,179	82,877	90,702	98,254	100,987	....
Reserve Assets	79akd	16,595	16,502	20,144	22,974	26,513	27,479	27,651	14,923	10,570	15,128	20,523	....
Liabilities	79lad	104,654	129,292	153,039	183,069	198,491	210,367	213,540	190,722	133,701	145,892	149,410	....
Dir. Invest. in Rep. Economy	79lbd	22,428	27,991	33,589	42,084	47,898	62,088	67,769	79,504	43,146	48,571	50,280	....
Portfolio Investment	79lcd	42,043	50,327	66,863	82,209	86,298	83,187	78,437	34,265	21,794	30,456	36,200	....
Equity Securities	79ldd	10,102	11,597	13,730	19,070	14,297	8,389	3,636	2,206	862	2,127	2,371	....
Debt Securities	79led	31,941	38,730	53,132	63,140	72,000	74,798	74,802	32,059	20,932	28,329	33,829	....
Financial Derivatives	79lld	—	—	—	—	—	—	—	—	—	—	—	....
Other Investment	79lfd	40,182	50,974	52,588	58,777	64,296	65,093	67,333	76,953	68,761	66,865	62,930	....
Monetary Authorities	79lgd	4,281	6,184	6,331	5,898	5,462	4,493	5,067	13,980	14,466	15,512	14,132	....
General Government	79lhd	20,510	23,225	22,054	20,587	22,766	23,334	22,932	23,548	23,035	23,843	24,309	....
Banks	79lid	7,988	11,238	11,681	15,524	16,146	17,279	18,177	11,402	8,725	6,601	4,385	....
Other Sectors	79ljd	7,403	10,327	12,522	16,768	19,923	19,987	21,158	28,023	22,534	20,910	20,103	....
Government Finance		*Millions of Pesos: Year Ending December 31*											
Deficit (-) or Surplus	80	−1,885.7	† −1,426.0	−5,233.6	−4,357.3	−4,148.3	−8,125.7	−6,817.6	−8,739.9	−3,463.8	445.9	9,424.4	....
Revenue	81	15,591.8	† 38,060.9	35,501.0	41,944.1	42,921.1	41,132.2	42,437.9	39,268.4	42,345.7	57,254.9	73,902.0	....
Exp. & Lending Minus Repay	82z	17,477.5	† 39,486.9	40,734.6	46,301.4	47,069.4	49,257.9	49,255.5	48,008.3	45,809.5	56,809.0	64,477.6	....
Expenditure	82	....	40,574.5	41,066.1	46,174.3	47,108.3	49,214.2	49,365.9	48,032.9	45,774.8	56,827.3	63,291.4	....
Lending Minus Repayments	83	....	−1,087.6	−331.5	127.1	−38.9	43.7	−110.4	−24.6	34.7	−18.3	1,186.2	....
Total Financing	84	1,885.7	† 1,426.0	5,233.6	4,357.3	4,148.2	8,125.7	6,817.6	8,739.9	3,463.8	−445.9	−9,424.4	....
Net Borrowing: Domestic	84a	863.2	....	−1,622.4	2,008.2	−576.8	−2,276.1	−1,924.6	....	....	....	....	....
Foreign	85a	1,256.8	....	....	....	....	....	....	....	....	....	....	....
Use of Cash Balances	87	−234.3	† −2,371.3	−344.1	1,262.1	−1,585.9	556.5	−533.9	−2,239.6	9,991.0	−532.1	−6,867.6	....

Argentina 213

		1994	1995	1996	1997	1998	1999	2000	2001	2002	2003	2004	2005
National Accounts							*Millions of Pesos*						
Househ.Cons.Expend.,incl.NPISHs....	**96f**	180,007	176,909	186,487	203,029	206,434	198,870	197,044	185,164	193,482	237,567	281,167	326,276
Government Consumption Expend...	**91f**	33,948	34,446	34,023	35,325	37,353	38,909	39,175	38,038	38,245	42,997	49,826	63,360
Gross Fixed Capital Formation.........	**93e**	51,331	46,285	49,211	56,727	59,595	51,074	46,020	38,099	37,387	56,904	85,652	114,133
Changes in Inventories...................	**93i**	79	1,493	4,251	4,350	3,180	−378	3,766	3,854	−3,076	−2,041	−1,262	−1,481
Exports of Goods and Services.........	**90c**	19,364	24,897	28,301	30,834	31,046	27,751	30,937	30,977	86,553	93,869	113,067	130,958
Imports of Goods and Services (-).....	**98c**	27,289	25,998	30,124	37,406	38,659	32,702	32,738	27,435	40,010	53,385	81,142	101,306
Gross Domestic Product (GDP).........	**99b**	257,440	258,032	272,150	292,859	298,948	283,523	284,204	268,697	312,580	375,910	447,307	531,939
Net Primary Income from Abroad.....	**98.n**	−3,697	−4,669	−5,502	−6,218	−7,406	−7,464	−7,470	−7,744	−19,402	−22,429	−26,293	−18,349
Gross National Income (GNI)...........	**99a**	253,743	253,363	266,648	286,641	291,542	276,059	276,734	260,953	293,179	353,481	421,350	513,545
GDP Vol. 1993 Prices......................	**99b.p**	250,308	243,186	256,626	277,441	288,123	278,369	276,173	263,997	235,236	256,024	279,141	304,764
GDP Volume (2000=100)................	**99bvp**	90.6	88.1	92.9	100.5	104.3	100.8	100.0	95.6	85.2	92.7	101.1	110.4
GDP Deflator (2000=100)................	**99bip**	99.9	103.1	103.1	102.6	100.8	99.0	100.0	98.9	129.1	142.7	155.7	169.6
							Millions: Midyear Estimates						
Population...............................	**99z**	34.40	34.83	35.27	35.69	36.10	36.50	36.90	37.27	37.64	38.01	38.37	38.75

Armenia, Republic of   911

		1994	1995	1996	1997	1998	1999	2000	2001	2002	2003	2004	2005
Exchange Rates						*Dram per SDR: End of Period*							
Official Rate............................	aa	591.98	597.57	625.61	667.85	735.03	718.88	719.44	706.04	795.17	841.06	754.51	643.44
						Dram per US Dollar: End of Period (ae) Period Average (rf)							
Official Rate............................	ae	405.51	402.00	435.07	494.98	522.03	523.77	552.18	561.81	584.89	566.00	485.84	450.19
Official Rate............................	rf	288.65	405.91	414.04	490.85	504.92	535.06	539.53	555.08	573.35	578.76	533.45	457.69
						Index Numbers (2000=100): Period Averages							
Nominal Effective Exchange Rate.....	nec	26.48	42.80	82.37	77.37	81.54	91.03	100.00	102.03	98.38	89.10	91.86	106.51
Real Effective Exchange Rate...........	rec	36.06	65.83	92.00	90.86	96.97	97.87	100.00	98.94	91.40	82.63	87.40	97.61
Fund Position						*Millions of SDRs: End of Period*							
Quota.......................................	2f.s	67.50	67.50	67.50	67.50	67.50	92.00	92.00	92.00	92.00	92.00	92.00	92.00
SDRs..	1b.s	.19	29.82	28.86	27.63	19.89	29.64	16.54	8.15	22.14	12.67	7.70	7.12
Reserve Position in the Fund............	1c.s	.01	.01	.01	—	—	—	—	—	—	—	—	—
Total Fund Cred.&Loans Outstg........	2tl	16.88	47.25	81.00	97.88	135.25	146.62	134.66	137.35	143.29	144.44	140.13	123.42
International Liquidity						*Millions of US Dollars Unless Otherwise Indicated: End of Period*							
Total Reserves minus Gold..............	1l.d	32.28	99.58	155.65	228.75	324.00	318.56	318.32	320.82	425.02	510.19	575.87	755.04
SDRs.....................................	1b.d	.28	44.33	41.50	37.28	28.00	40.68	21.55	10.24	30.10	18.83	11.96	10.18
Reserve Position in the Fund.........	1c.d	.01	.01	.01	.01	.01	—	—	—	—	—	—	—
Foreign Exchange......................	1d.d	31.99	55.24	114.14	191.46	295.99	277.88	296.77	310.58	394.92	491.36	563.90	744.86
Gold (Million Fine Troy Ounces)........	1ad	.0100	.0300	.0340	.0361	.0432	.0436	.0446	.0449	.0449	—	—	—
Gold (National Valuation)...............	1and	2.44	10.46	12.82	10.72	12.37	12.69	12.17	12.41	15.68	—	—	—
Monetary Authorities:Other Assets...	3..d	.20	.10	.52	.25	.10	.05	.11	.01	.01	.03	.08	.12
Other Liab...	4..d	2.05	1.19	5.09	5.05	2.54	1.59	2.89	6.51	12.81	15.63	22.90	20.78
Deposit Money Banks: Assets..........	7a.d	22.03	24.28	18.14	33.28	33.12	70.34	96.07	100.98	125.99	180.76	252.21	211.34
Liabilities...................	7b.d	12.98	24.59	50.74	73.39	96.10	111.50	119.90	105.29	93.10	102.07	128.88	158.46
Monetary Authorities						*Millions of Dram: End of Period*							
Foreign Assets...........................	11	14,162	44,278	73,523	118,657	175,652	173,521	182,551	187,222	257,770	288,786	279,433	339,966
Claims on General Government........	12a	9,536	10,624	27,971	16,491	18,083	18,471	10,296	10,190	3,437	1,047	5,887	5,573
Claims on Private Sector.................	12d	—	—	—	—	—	30	179	684	683	38	43	22
Claims on Deposit Money Banks......	12e	3,629	3,781	3,346	3,345	3,253	1,698	3,332	3,905	10,392	8,700	12,857	11,700
Reserve Money...........................	14	15,002	28,806	41,140	51,333	53,863	53,853	72,389	80,418	111,272	118,642	133,895	208,160
of which: Currency Outside DMBs..	14a	10,056	24,601	34,784	37,596	41,370	42,610	59,486	65,037	88,553	91,997	98,569	144,311
Time,Savings,& Fgn.Currency Dep...	15	781	556	116	187	491	346	1	1	1	43	155	113
Liabs. of Central Bank: Securities.....	16ac	—	—	—	—	—	—	—	—	—	—	—	21,215
Foreign Liabilities......................	16c	10,823	28,715	52,890	67,863	100,741	106,234	98,480	100,633	121,433	130,334	116,857	88,769
General Government Deposits.........	16d	1,433	423	8,733	8,165	9,851	10,165	2,004	1,922	13,148	32,554	42,735	22,939
Capital Accounts........................	17a	596	1,691	7,214	13,733	16,609	12,079	21,412	22,026	33,427	19,926	918	−12,634
Other Items (Net)........................	17r	−1,309	−1,509	−5,254	−2,788	15,431	11,043	2,073	−2,999	−6,997	−2,928	3,661	28,699
Deposit Money Banks						*Millions of Dram: End of Period*							
Reserves..................................	20	3,164	3,987	6,083	13,681	12,033	11,082	12,593	14,717	22,092	25,478	34,083	61,971
Claims on Mon.Author.:Securities....	20c	—	—	—	—	—	—	—	—	—	—	—	21,215
Foreign Assets...........................	21	8,933	9,759	7,894	16,472	17,287	36,843	53,048	56,732	73,691	102,308	122,534	95,145
Claims on General Government........	22a	335	354	5,865	9,198	15,436	12,268	16,890	18,250	26,313	29,179	33,138	38,968
of which: Claims on Local Govts.....	22ab	—	—	—	—	2	5	—	—	—	—	—	—
Claims on Other Sectors.................	22d	20,718	37,946	37,181	48,486	70,791	86,188	102,406	91,826	93,478	97,088	136,602	182,271
Claims on Nonbank Financial Insts...	22g	—	—	—	—	11,369	4,352	7,137	5,398	4,492	6,559	6,269	6,547
Demand Deposits.........................	24	3,188	5,375	4,968	6,372	11,216	9,553	11,743	12,073	26,400	30,618	33,283	57,095
Time,Savings,& Fgn.Currency Dep....	25	10,310	9,617	14,424	26,005	42,868	56,881	80,258	80,854	96,578	110,503	153,375	163,385
Money Market Instruments..............	26aa	—	—	—	—	24	201	—	90	—	562	3,406	519
Foreign Liabilities......................	26c	5,262	9,884	22,074	36,328	50,168	58,399	66,207	59,151	54,453	57,770	62,616	71,338
General Government Deposits.........	26d	1,324	1,748	2,533	2,469	3,662	5,205	15,881	17,121	16,662	12,278	13,540	16,438
of which: Local Govt. Deposits.......	26db	790	857	222	577	349	209	70	58	105	—	—	—
Credit from Monetary Authorities.....	26g	1,367	4,093	3,539	3,710	3,257	1,701	3,342	3,973	10,601	8,870	13,094	11,899
Capital Accounts........................	27a	3,646	7,579	12,315	17,835	28,685	36,366	38,151	38,166	35,479	55,148	68,842	98,501
Other Items (Net)........................	27r	8,053	13,750	−2,831	−4,882	−12,966	−17,574	−23,507	−24,504	−20,108	−15,137	−15,531	−13,059
Monetary Survey						*Millions of Dram: End of Period*							
Foreign Assets (Net)........................	31n	7,010	15,438	6,453	30,938	42,030	45,731	70,912	84,171	155,576	202,990	222,494	275,005
Domestic Credit...........................	32	27,832	46,753	59,753	63,544	102,167	105,941	119,023	107,305	98,594	89,080	125,665	194,002
Claims on General Govt. (Net)........	32an	7,113	8,807	22,570	15,055	20,005	15,368	9,301	9,396	−60	−14,605	−17,249	5,163
Claims on Other Sectors...............	32d	20,718	37,946	37,181	48,486	70,791	86,218	102,586	92,511	94,161	97,126	136,645	182,292
Claims on Nonbank Financial Insts.	32g	—	—	3	3	11,372	4,354	7,137	5,398	4,492	6,559	6,269	6,547
Money......................................	34	13,410	30,078	39,830	44,055	52,678	52,227	71,395	77,297	115,307	123,272	132,414	202,056
Quasi-Money..............................	35	11,091	10,173	14,540	26,192	43,360	57,227	80,259	80,855	96,579	110,546	153,530	163,498
Money Market Instruments..............	36aa	—	—	—	—	24	201	—	90	—	562	3,406	519
Liabs. of Central Bank: Securities......	36ac												
Capital Accounts........................	37a	4,242	9,270	19,530	31,568	45,295	48,445	59,562	60,192	68,906	75,074	69,760	85,867
Other Items (Net)........................	37r	6,099	12,670	−7,694	−7,333	2,840	−6,428	−21,280	−26,958	−26,623	−17,384	−10,951	17,067
Money plus Quasi-Money...............	35l	24,501	40,251	54,371	70,247	96,037	109,454	151,653	158,151	211,886	233,818	285,943	365,554
Interest Rates						*Percent Per Annum*							
Discount Rate (End of Period)...........	60	210.00	77.80	26.00	65.10	....	....	....	....	....	....	....	....
Refinancing Rate (End of Period)......	60a	210.00	52.00	60.00	54.00	39.00	† 43.00	25.00	15.00	13.50	7.00	3.75	3.50
Money Market Rate.......................	60b	....	....	48.56	36.41	27.84	23.65	18.63	19.40	12.29	7.51	4.18	3.17
Treasury Bill Rate........................	60c	....	37.81	† 43.95	57.54	46.99	55.10	24.40	† 20.59	14.75	11.91	5.27	4.05
Deposit Rate...............................	60l	....	63.18	32.19	26.08	24.94	27.35	18.08	14.90	9.60	6.87	4.90	5.81
Lending Rate...............................	60p	....	111.86	66.36	54.23	48.49	38.85	31.57	26.69	21.14	20.83	18.63	17.98
Government Bond Yield..................	61	....	....	....	....	....	....	25.51	23.15	17.44	15.71	8.21	5.18

Armenia, Republic of 911

		1994	1995	1996	1997	1998	1999	2000	2001	2002	2003	2004	2005
Prices, Production, Labor		\multicolumn{12}{c}{*Index Numbers (2000=100): Period Averages*}										
Producer Prices	63	....	....	....	59.3	68.0	100.4	100.0	101.1	104.7	114.0	98.8	106.4
Consumer Prices	64	25.2	69.5	82.5	† 94.0	102.2	† 102.9	100.0	102.8	100.9	103.7	112.0	† 112.7
Wages:Avg. Month.Earn	65	7.9	27.3	39.8	54.0	71.8	86.9	100.0	110.7	124.2	157.4	201.1	241.3
Industrial Production	66	....	57.2	6.0	6.5	6.8	94.3	100.0	102.9	113.5	35.2	44.1	54.2
		\multicolumn{12}{c}{*Number in Thousands: Period Averages*}										
Employment	67e	1,487.6	1,476.4	1,435.6	1,372.2	1,337.3	1,298.2	1,277.7	1,264.9	1,106.4	1,107.6	1,110.9	....
Unemployment	67c	91.8	131.7	159.3	174.4	133.8	175.0	153.9	138.4	127.3	118.6	108.6	....
Unemployment Rate (%)	67r	8.5	10.4	15.2	15.1	13.3	15.0	15.7	14.1	13.1	14.2	....	....
Intl. Transactions & Positions		\multicolumn{12}{c}{*Millions of US Dollars*}										
Exports	70..d	215.50	270.90	290.30	232.55	220.50	232.20	294.20	342.80	505.16	685.60	715.03	950.40
Imports, c.i.f.	71..d	393.80	673.90	855.80	892.30	902.40	799.70	881.90	874.30	987.20	1,279.50	1,350.98	1,767.90
Imports, f.o.b.	71.vd	343.80	625.40	757.50	779.40	794.10	703.60	776.20	751.90	863.60	1,115.80	1,199.67	1,545.20
Balance of Payments		\multicolumn{12}{c}{*Millions of US Dollars: Minus Sign Indicates Debit*}										
Current Account, n.i.e.	78ald	−103.78	−218.37	−290.68	−306.51	−417.96	−307.05	−278.34	−199.60	−147.90	−189.42	−161.62	−193.24
Goods: Exports f.o.b.	78aad	215.35	270.90	290.44	233.64	228.89	247.31	309.92	353.11	513.79	696.14	738.31	1,004.86
Goods: Imports f.o.b.	78abd	−393.63	−673.87	−759.63	−793.10	−806.29	−721.35	−773.41	−773.34	−882.56	−1,130.20	−1,196.27	−1,592.78
Trade Balance	78acd	−178.28	−402.97	−469.19	−559.46	−577.40	−474.04	−463.49	−420.23	−368.77	−434.06	−457.96	−587.92
Services: Credit	78add	13.67	28.60	77.71	96.60	130.34	135.81	136.94	186.54	183.86	207.41	246.68	331.80
Services: Debit	78aed	−40.70	−52.27	−128.52	−159.38	−208.71	−197.87	−192.75	−204.34	−224.53	−275.74	−317.39	−391.05
Balance on Goods & Services	78afd	−205.31	−426.64	−520.00	−622.24	−655.77	−536.10	−519.30	−438.03	−409.44	−502.39	−528.67	−647.17
Income: Credit	78agd	....	54.63	78.04	138.95	103.91	93.57	103.74	103.75	136.56	165.98	310.76	365.47
Income: Debit	78ahd	−4.02	−14.61	−33.31	−40.44	−43.51	−38.64	−50.84	−39.30	−48.37	−71.49	−274.11	−320.73
Balance on Gds, Serv. & Inc.	78aid	−209.33	−386.62	−475.27	−523.73	−595.37	−481.17	−466.40	−373.58	−321.25	−407.90	−492.02	−602.43
Current Transfers, n.i.e.: Credit	78ajd	106.33	169.95	198.99	252.41	203.02	200.57	208.52	200.79	199.68	245.02	389.11	474.02
Current Transfers: Debit	78akd	−.78	−1.70	−14.40	−35.19	−25.61	−26.45	−20.46	−26.81	−26.33	−26.54	−58.71	−64.82
Capital Account, n.i.e.	78bcd	5.74	8.05	13.40	10.88	9.74	12.55	28.31	30.12	68.06	89.95	34.31	50.90
Capital Account, n.i.e.: Credit	78bad	5.74	8.05	13.40	10.88	9.74	16.85	29.49	32.57	70.18	92.15	40.20	53.72
Capital Account: Debit	78bbd	....	....	....	....	—	−4.30	−1.18	−2.45	−2.12	−2.20	−5.89	−2.82
Financial Account, n.i.e.	78bjd	89.94	227.48	216.76	334.82	390.43	286.18	249.88	175.18	147.80	174.47	161.07	325.96
Direct Investment Abroad	78bdd	....	....	....	....	....	....	....	....	....	−.36	−2.25	−6.72
Dir. Invest. in Rep. Econ., n.i.e.	78bed	8.00	25.32	17.57	51.94	220.83	122.04	104.19	69.87	110.74	120.88	218.80	258.24
Portfolio Investment Assets	78bfd	....	....	−.01	−.14	.63	.06	−19.10	−5.76	3.38	.05	−.48	−2.72
Equity Securities	78bkd	....	....	−.01	−.03	.53	.01	−3.01	−.53	−.86	.05	−.11	−.20
Debt Securities	78bld	....	....	....	−.11	.10	.05	−16.09	−5.23	4.24	—	−.37	−2.52
Portfolio Investment Liab., n.i.e.	78bgd	....	....	7.23	15.90	−16.57	1.58	.25	.04	−1.85	.22	−2.39	1.13
Equity Securities	78bmd	....	....	1.88	.46	.72	−.32	.40	.50	−.41	.05	1.37	1.33
Debt Securities	78bnd	....	....	5.35	15.44	−17.29	1.90	−.15	−.46	−1.44	.17	−3.76	−.20
Financial Derivatives Assets	78bwd	....	....	....	....	....	....	....	....	—	—	....	....
Financial Derivatives Liabilities	78bxd	....	....	....	....	....	....	....	....	—	—	....	....
Other Investment Assets	78bhd	35.89	−8.60	35.34	40.76	19.97	2.97	−9.49	−18.33	−88.05	−63.58	−142.31	−36.30
Monetary Authorities	78bod	....	−8.58	−.08	1.36	.07	.06	−.10	.04	.03	−.11	−1.46	2.55
General Government	78bpd	−6.24	....	....	....	−43.27	15.56	11.33	12.76	−6.80	2.18	−19.89	−58.71
Banks	78bqd	.27	−.02	7.33	−17.57	6.17	−34.42	−14.11	−19.70	−38.21	−52.70	−62.89	42.10
Other Sectors	78brd	41.86	....	28.09	56.97	57.00	21.77	−6.61	−11.43	−43.07	−12.95	−58.07	−22.24
Other Investment Liab., n.i.e.	78bid	46.05	210.76	156.63	226.36	165.57	159.53	174.03	129.36	123.58	117.26	89.70	112.33
Monetary Authorities	78bsd	−9.18	.53	4.68	−.04	−2.92	−.93	1.59	3.97	4.44	.25	5.26	.87
General Government	78btd	55.26	151.20	44.21	122.86	35.01	80.16	44.28	62.30	45.15	24.67	38.46	36.06
Banks	78bud	−.03	.03	26.18	29.04	23.99	11.19	8.78	−3.70	2.67	10.50	32.84	24.16
Other Sectors	78bvd	....	59.00	81.56	74.50	109.49	69.11	119.38	66.79	71.32	81.84	13.14	51.24
Net Errors and Omissions	78cad	4.83	12.35	15.06	10.83	18.39	13.11	17.05	11.01	−4.77	−1.63	−.95	3.02
Overall Balance	78cbd	−3.27	29.51	−45.46	50.02	.60	4.79	16.90	16.71	63.19	73.37	32.81	186.64
Reserves and Related Items	79dad	3.27	−29.51	45.46	−50.02	−.60	−4.79	−16.90	−16.71	−63.19	−73.37	−32.81	−186.64
Reserve Assets	79dbd	−21.24	−76.22	−60.35	−73.48	−52.13	−20.79	−19.75	−20.06	−82.25	−47.35	−26.40	−161.89
Use of Fund Credit and Loans	79dcd	24.50	46.71	49.04	23.46	51.53	16.00	−15.91	3.35	8.07	1.78	−6.41	−24.75
Exceptional Financing	79ded	....	....	56.77	....	....	—	—	18.77	—	10.99	−27.81	....
International Investment Position		\multicolumn{12}{c}{*Millions of US Dollars*}										
Assets	79aad	....	....	....	381.90	417.38	489.43	529.43	544.14	685.05	786.86	978.28	1,130.39
Direct Investment Abroad	79abd	....	....	....	—	—	—	.01	.02	.36	.39	2.67	10.27
Portfolio Investment	79acd	....	....	....	.61	.18	.12	19.27	8.91	4.53	4.46	4.62	5.94
Equity Securities	79add	....	....	....	.50	.10	.09	3.09	3.61	4.47	4.39	4.49	3.29
Debt Securities	79aed	....	....	....	.11	.08	.03	16.18	5.30	.06	.07	.13	2.65
Financial Derivatives	79ald	....	....	....	—	—	—	—	—	—	—	—	−.01
Other Investment	79agd	....	....	....	141.82	124.09	185.77	196.02	204.06	247.98	277.95	421.04	440.41
Monetary Authorities	79agd	....	....	....	.18	.10	.04	.14	.17	.62	.71	2.49	.13
General Government	79ahd	....	....	....	18.00	61.27	45.71	35.96	23.19	29.99	27.80	47.69	106.65
Banks	79aid	....	....	....	37.77	33.85	70.12	83.37	98.52	131.32	180.68	248.52	201.70
Other Sectors	79ajd	....	....	....	85.87	28.87	69.90	76.55	82.18	86.05	68.76	122.34	131.93
Reserve Assets	79akd	....	....	....	239.47	293.10	303.53	314.13	331.15	432.18	504.06	549.95	673.78
Liabilities	79lad	....	....	....	949.92	1,332.15	1,607.72	1,829.71	1,978.23	2,197.45	2,363.71	2,669.87	2,889.89
Dir. Invest. in Rep. Economy	79lbd	....	....	....	103.44	312.67	421.36	513.09	579.85	684.48	793.38	1,005.08	1,279.34
Portfolio Investment	79lcd	....	....	....	21.18	3.44	4.47	4.79	5.92	5.83	6.38	4.26	4.50
Equity Securities	79ldd	....	....	....	.44	1.09	.75	1.09	1.55	2.93	2.94	4.22	4.50
Debt Securities	79led	....	....	....	20.74	2.35	3.72	3.70	4.37	2.90	3.44	.04	—
Financial Derivatives	79lld	....	....	....	....	....	....	....	....	....	....	....	....
Other Investment	79lfd	....	....	....	825.30	1,016.04	1,181.90	1,311.83	1,392.46	1,507.14	1,563.95	1,660.53	1,606.05
Monetary Authorities	79lgd	....	....	....	137.49	192.94	202.80	178.35	179.12	207.68	230.25	240.57	197.24
General Government	79lhd	....	....	....	496.80	538.29	611.83	694.23	757.71	853.16	860.23	942.49	903.15
Banks	79lid	....	....	....	112.51	96.73	111.51	118.48	114.97	94.83	94.62	129.35	152.40
Other Sectors	79ljd	....	....	....	78.50	188.08	255.75	320.77	340.66	351.47	378.85	348.12	353.26

Armenia, Republic of   911

National Accounts		1994	1995	1996	1997	1998	1999	2000	2001	2002	2003	2004	2005
							Millions of Dram						
Househ.Cons.Expend.,incl.NPISHs....	96f	176,885	555,056	664,002	832,638	956,322	951,565	1,001,704	1,100,035	1,213,754	1,353,059	1,573,592	1,709,417
Government Consumption Expend...	91f	21,086	58,336	74,265	90,220	105,589	117,591	121,791	132,708	136,071	165,831	194,095	238,831
Gross Fixed Capital Formation..........	93e	37,855	84,365	118,254	130,336	154,925	162,134	190,130	208,025	287,369	373,615	455,305	657,718
Changes in Inventories....................	93i	6,012	11,859	14,029	23,015	27,900	19,085	2,149	24,304	7,839	20,490	19,361	8,422
Exports of Goods and Services..........	90c	73,569	124,965	153,665	163,065	181,552	204,976	241,078	299,477	399,975	522,366	522,485	604,045
Imports of Goods and Services (-).....	98c	136,747	324,775	370,208	468,722	504,820	491,769	521,272	542,653	634,733	812,890	803,769	896,009
Gross Domestic Product (GDP).........	99b	187,065	522,256	661,209	804,336	955,385	987,444	1,031,338	1,175,877	1,362,472	1,624,643	1,907,945	2,243,953
Statistical Discrepancy....................	99bs	8,404	12,451	7,203	33,783	33,917	23,862	−4,241	−46,020	−47,803	2,172	−53,123	−78,470
							Millions: Midyear Estimates						
Population................................	99z	3.29	3.23	3.18	3.14	3.12	3.10	3.08	3.06	3.05	3.04	3.03	3.02

Aruba 314

		1994	1995	1996	1997	1998	1999	2000	2001	2002	2003	2004	2005
Exchange Rates						*Aruban Florins per SDR: End of Period*							
Official Rate	aa	2.6131	2.6608	2.5739	2.4152	2.5204	2.4568	2.3322	2.2495	2.4335	2.6599	2.7799	2.5584
					Aruban Florins per US Dollar: End of Period (ae) Period Average (rf)								
Official Rate	ae	1.7900	1.7900	1.7900	1.7900	1.7900	1.7900	1.7900	1.7900	1.7900	1.7900	1.7900	1.7900
Official Rate	rf	1.7900	1.7900	1.7900	1.7900	1.7900	1.7900	1.7900	1.7900	1.7900	1.7900	1.7900	1.7900
International Liquidity						*Millions of US Dollars: End of Period*							
Total Reserves minus Gold	1l.d	177.59	216.67	187.62	172.33	222.19	219.91	208.01	293.71	339.73	295.22	295.42	273.51
Foreign Exchange	1d.d	177.59	216.67	187.62	172.33	222.19	219.91	208.01	293.71	339.73	295.22	295.42	273.51
Gold (Million Fine Troy Ounces)	1ad	.100	.100	.100	.100	.100	.100	.100	.100	.100	.100	.100	.100
Gold (National Valuation)	1and	25.630	26.307	27.978	27.978	22.878	22.900	22.900	30.751	38.118	46.404	48.663	56.996
Deposit Money Banks: Assets	7a.d	222.37	207.98	233.69	257.38	269.57	280.49	299.19	297.19	303.20	354.35	329.04	324.76
Liabilities	7b.d	150.87	161.08	190.85	217.10	190.79	191.93	221.36	228.81	259.06	302.95	268.50	276.20
Monetary Authorities						*Millions of Aruban Florins: End of Period*							
Foreign Assets	11	363.77	434.93	385.91	358.55	438.67	434.74	417.17	580.79	676.35	611.51	615.92	591.61
Reserve Money	14	233.57	275.54	236.23	226.35	318.08	338.01	299.00	395.80	449.93	424.46	445.26	450.86
of which: Currency Outside DMBs	14a	87.56	93.70	94.87	101.52	104.91	122.44	121.48	125.96	127.84	126.13	130.66	144.12
Central Government Deposits	16d	71.70	99.97	92.55	68.27	65.56	55.64	57.84	96.97	112.16	67.29	48.28	6.91
Capital Accounts	17a	56.02	66.40	70.48	76.12	71.71	65.95	80.62	90.81	124.84	140.68	143.41	157.37
Other Items (Net)	17r	2.48	−6.98	−13.35	−12.19	−16.67	−24.87	−20.28	−2.80	−10.59	−20.92	−21.03	−23.53
Deposit Money Banks						*Millions of Aruban Florins: End of Period*							
Reserves	20	147.44	181.48	154.97	119.11	209.55	224.24	181.36	245.95	314.01	293.31	306.59	302.13
Foreign Assets	21	398.05	372.29	418.30	460.71	482.53	502.08	535.55	531.96	542.73	634.29	588.99	581.31
Claims on Central Government	22a	67.94	36.88	59.43	59.50	55.91	61.44	43.47	62.37	65.86	83.70	84.89	125.30
Claims on Private Sector	22d	946.52	1,017.98	1,121.78	1,185.47	1,248.15	1,376.10	1,502.35	1,581.67	1,783.64	2,012.89	2,090.13	2,283.76
Demand Deposits	24	350.09	343.90	346.37	366.07	433.80	458.88	471.23	553.43	705.49	856.30	826.72	808.37
Time and Savings Deposits	25	755.64	795.31	853.93	881.59	991.61	1,105.88	1,133.42	1,138.99	1,188.42	1,230.30	1,313.76	1,455.89
Bonds	26ab	....	....	12.75	—	5.00	5.00	5.00	5.00	5.00	5.00	5.00	5.00
Foreign Liabilities	26c	270.06	288.33	341.61	388.62	341.52	343.55	396.23	409.58	463.71	542.28	480.62	494.40
Central Government Deposits	26d	37.90	22.95	16.33	15.89	11.28	7.93	9.02	6.41	31.19	59.73	65.18	142.36
Capital Accounts	27a	70.34	85.62	105.49	112.89	105.78	109.64	127.57	146.19	135.59	164.04	233.36	243.86
Other Items (Net)	27r	75.91	72.51	78.00	59.73	107.15	133.00	120.26	162.36	176.82	166.54	145.96	142.62
Monetary Survey						*Millions of Aruban Florins: End of Period*							
Foreign Assets (Net)	31n	478.10	517.80	461.50	428.18	578.01	593.16	554.17	700.60	746.91	700.92	722.78	675.56
Domestic Credit	32	904.86	931.93	1,072.33	1,160.81	1,227.22	1,373.97	1,478.96	1,540.66	1,706.14	1,969.56	2,061.56	2,259.79
Claims on Central Govt. (Net)	32an	−41.66	−86.05	−49.45	−24.66	−20.93	−2.13	−23.39	−41.01	−77.50	−43.33	−28.56	−23.96
Claims on Private Sector	32d	946.52	1,017.98	1,121.78	1,185.47	1,248.15	1,376.10	1,502.35	1,581.67	1,783.64	2,012.89	2,090.13	2,283.76
Money	34	441.45	443.70	447.47	473.18	547.00	589.73	596.51	701.05	844.41	985.61	960.83	964.98
Quasi-Money	35	756.17	804.74	855.08	881.76	991.78	1,106.06	1,133.60	1,139.18	1,189.11	1,230.99	1,314.45	1,456.67
Bonds	36ab	....	....	12.75	—	5.00	5.00	5.00	5.00	5.00	5.00	5.00	5.00
Other Items (Net)	37r	185.34	201.30	218.52	234.04	261.45	266.35	298.02	396.02	414.52	448.88	504.05	508.69
Money plus Quasi-Money	35l	1,197.62	1,248.44	1,302.55	1,354.94	1,538.78	1,695.79	1,730.11	1,840.23	2,033.52	2,216.59	2,275.29	2,421.66
Interest Rates						*Percent Per Annum*							
Discount Rate	60	9.5	9.5	9.5	9.5	9.5	6.5	6.5	6.5	6.5	5.0	5.0	5.0
Deposit Rate	60l	4.4	4.3	4.2	4.4	....	† 6.2	6.2	5.8	5.6	5.3	4.3	3.9
Lending Rate	60p	10.6	10.6	10.3	10.0	....	† 13.1	12.1	12.1	13.1	11.5	11.6	11.5
Prices and Tourism						*Index Numbers (2000=100): Period Averages*							
Consumer Prices	64	83.9	86.8	89.6	92.2	94.0	† 96.1	100.0	103.1	106.7	110.2	113.0	116.8
Number of Tourists	66ta	80.7	85.8	88.9	90.1	89.8	94.7	100.0	95.9	89.1	89.0	101.0	101.6
Number of Tourist Nights	66tb	80.7	85.2	89.5	92.3	93.2	98.0	100.0	98.0	92.7	97.1	107.5	108.5
Intl. Transactions & Positions						*Millions of US Dollars*							
Exports	70..d	....	14.7	12.5	24.1	29.1	29.2	173.0	148.9	128.4	83.4	79.6	106.6
Imports, c.i.f	71..d	....	566.5	578.3	614.5	814.7	782.1	835.2	841.4	841.4	847.8	875.2	1,031.1

Aruba 314

		1994	1995	1996	1997	1998	1999	2000	2001	2002	2003	2004	2005
Balance of Payments						*Millions of US Dollars: Minus Sign Indicates Debit*							
Current Account, n.i.e.	78ald	81.1	−.3	−69.1	−195.8	−18.8	−428.9	210.6	321.3	−334.6	−150.3	14.1	−258.8
Goods: Exports f.o.b.	78aad	1,296.8	1,347.2	1,735.7	1,728.7	1,164.8	1,391.1	2,526.4	2,424.0	1,488.0	2,052.0	2,723.5	3,483.7
Goods: Imports f.o.b.	78abd	−1,607.3	−1,772.5	−2,043.4	−2,115.9	−1,518.2	−1,995.2	−2,582.5	−2,369.2	−2,019.3	−2,396.3	−2,997.7	−3,536.3
Trade Balance	78acd	−310.6	−425.3	−307.7	−387.2	−353.4	−604.1	−56.1	54.8	−531.3	−344.3	−274.1	−52.6
Services: Credit	78add	624.2	645.1	769.9	815.8	892.1	921.5	1,007.8	987.9	996.8	1,047.7	1,243.6	1,304.0
Services: Debit	78aed	−228.7	−245.5	−515.9	−596.1	−553.1	−661.2	−645.8	−615.0	−607.7	−728.0	−794.0	−927.3
Balance on Goods & Services	78afd	85.0	−25.6	−53.6	−167.5	−14.4	−343.9	305.8	427.8	−142.2	−24.7	175.5	324.1
Income: Credit	78agd	9.6	16.4	19.2	20.7	40.5	40.2	53.1	50.0	34.3	34.4	36.1	39.9
Income: Debit	78ahd	−22.3	−24.6	−31.0	−37.9	−40.1	−76.5	−72.5	−98.2	−158.6	−75.9	−96.0	−496.0
Balance on Gds, Serv. & Inc.	78aid	72.3	−33.8	−65.5	−184.7	−14.0	−380.2	286.4	379.6	−266.5	−66.2	115.6	−132.0
Current Transfers, n.i.e.: Credit	78ajd	47.5	71.5	18.4	18.4	29.3	36.1	39.2	41.6	35.0	40.1	43.4	49.1
Current Transfers: Debit	78akd	−38.7	−37.9	−22.0	−29.5	−34.1	−84.9	−115.0	−99.9	−103.2	−124.1	−144.9	−175.9
Capital Account, n.i.e.	78bcd	−4.1	−.5	28.0	21.0	5.2	2.2	11.3	−1.0	21.3	100.4	18.4	18.4
Capital Account, n.i.e.: Credit	78bad	.3	3.1	28.7	21.6	10.2	7.3	16.3	9.0	28.5	122.9	30.5	26.6
Capital Account: Debit	78bbd	−4.4	−3.6	−.7	−.6	−5.0	−5.0	−5.0	−10.0	−7.2	−22.5	−12.1	−8.2
Financial Account, n.i.e.	78bjd	−75.4	41.6	10.7	158.9	64.2	449.6	−203.7	−228.1	339.0	−4.6	−37.9	191.6
Direct Investment Abroad	78bdd	—	....	−.3	1.7	−1.4	−.7	−6.1	−1.3	−.6	−6.2	.6	−5.2
Dir. Invest. in Rep. Econ., n.i.e.	78bed	−73.2	−5.5	84.5	195.9	83.6	468.5	−122.2	−260.4	331.3	155.9	143.1	118.9
Portfolio Investment Assets	78bfd	16.5	−16.6	−7.8	−1.6	−44.1	−53.7	−46.4	39.4	7.7	−24.8	−27.2	−11.6
Equity Securities	78bkd	—	....	....	....		−41.6	−45.3	5.9	−5.0	−19.6	−26.4	−1.7
Debt Securities	78bld	16.5	−16.6	−7.8	−1.6	−44.1	−12.1	−1.1	33.6	12.7	−5.3	−.8	−9.9
Portfolio Investment Liab., n.i.e.	78bgd	−25.8	....	1.6	−17.4	−3.4	32.3	43.8	17.1	56.8	66.5	60.7	21.3
Equity Securities	78bmd	—	....	....	....		−.1	2.7	−.1		.1		
Debt Securities	78bnd	−25.8	....	1.6	−17.4	−3.4	32.5	41.1	17.2	56.8	66.4	60.7	21.3
Financial Derivatives Assets	78bwd	....	....	....	....			—	—	.1		....	....
Financial Derivatives Liabilities	78bxd	....	....	....	....			—	—		—	....	....
Other Investment Assets	78bhd	5.8	12.5	−11.3	−49.7	29.2	6.9	14.0	3.3	−59.8	−81.7	−110.6	91.4
Monetary Authorities	78bod	....	....	....	....			—	—	—	—	....	....
General Government	78bpd	−.8	....	....	....		—	—	—	—	.2	—	—
Banks	78bqd	−3.7	15.6	−17.0	−30.7	−11.5	−3.2	27.9	−10.9	8.0	−68.3	48.6	−7.0
Other Sectors	78brd	10.4	−3.1	5.7	−19.0	40.7	10.1	−13.9	14.2	−67.8	−13.7	−159.2	98.4
Other Investment Liab., n.i.e.	78bid	1.3	51.2	−55.9	30.0	.4	−3.7	−86.8	−26.3	3.6	−114.4	−104.6	−23.2
Monetary Authorities	78bsd	—	....	....	....			—	—			....	....
General Government	78btd	.4	.6	−10.6	−8.9	22.2	−1.5	−21.5	−1.5	−1.3	−160.1	−12.5	−2.6
Banks	78bud	−8.7	10.7	17.0	37.3	−26.4	.4	27.7	6.5	23.7	72.7	−51.5	7.7
Other Sectors	78bvd	9.6	39.9	−62.3	1.6	4.6	−2.7	−93.0	−31.2	−18.8	−26.9	−40.6	−28.3
Net Errors and Omissions	78cad	−4.7	2.0	4.3	−2.5	.6	−20.0	−33.2	−9.4	14.6	18.2	6.9	26.6
Overall Balance	78cbd	−3.2	42.7	−26.1	−18.4	51.3	2.8	−15.0	82.8	40.2	−36.4	1.6	−22.2
Reserves and Related Items	79dad	3.2	−42.7	26.1	18.4	−51.3	−2.8	15.0	−82.8	−40.2	36.4	−1.6	22.2
Reserve Assets	79dbd	3.2	−42.7	26.1	18.4	−51.3	−2.8	15.0	−82.8	−40.2	36.4	−1.6	22.2
Use of Fund Credit and Loans	79dcd	—	....	....	....		....	....	....	....	....	....	....
Exceptional Financing	79ded	....	....	....	....	....	....	....	....	—	....	....	....
International Investment Position						*Millions of US Dollars*							
Assets	79aad	....	....	....	....	817.9	821.9	898.6	971.0	982.3	1,105.0	1,319.7	1,211.1
Direct Investment Abroad	79abd	....	....	....	....	—	—	—	—	—	—		
Portfolio Investment	79acd	....	....	....	....	245.8	230.9	300.2	281.6	260.8	317.7	339.9	347.9
Equity Securities	79add	....	....	....	....	151.6	138.7	182.8	171.6	153.7	209.4	227.0	245.8
Debt Securities	79aed	....	....	....	....	94.2	92.2	117.4	110.0	107.1	108.2	112.9	102.2
Financial Derivatives	79ald	....	....	....	....	—	—	—	—				
Other Investment	79afd	....	....	....	....	324.4	345.0	362.6	365.0	343.6	445.7	635.7	532.6
Monetary Authorities	79agd	....	....	....	....	—	—	—	—				
General Government	79ahd	....	....	....	....	—	—	—	—				
Banks	79aid	....	....	....	....	259.2	262.4	277.9	289.0	280.7	349.2	300.6	307.7
Other Sectors	79ajd	....	....	....	....	65.2	82.6	84.7	76.0	62.8	96.4	335.1	224.9
Reserve Assets	79akd	....	....	....	....	247.7	246.0	235.8	324.4	377.8	341.6	344.1	330.5
Liabilities	79lad	....	....	....	....	1,082.1	1,724.0	1,582.1	1,462.4	1,909.5	2,094.2	2,202.7	2,269.0
Dir. Invest. in Rep. Economy	79lbd	....	....	....	....	140.7	636.8	463.1	216.6	530.8	683.6	841.6	942.8
Portfolio Investment	79lcd	....	....	....	....	56.4	56.9	93.2	193.4	251.2	317.2	379.2	403.1
Equity Securities	79ldd	....	....	....	....	—	—	—	—				
Debt Securities	79led	....	....	....	....	56.4	56.9	93.2	193.4	251.2	317.2	379.2	403.1
Financial Derivatives	79lld	....	....	....	....	—							
Other Investment	79lfd	....	....	....	....	885.0	1,030.4	1,025.8	1,052.3	1,127.4	1,093.4	981.9	923.1
Monetary Authorities	79lgd					17.0	12.4	17.2	23.0	36.3	36.4	37.3	45.9
General Government	79lhd					360.4	348.2	317.9	310.4	328.0	185.4	180.8	158.3
Banks	79lid					190.8	191.2	218.9	225.4	247.2	320.0	268.5	276.2
Other Sectors	79ljd	....	....	....	....	316.8	478.6	471.8	493.5	515.9	551.7	495.2	442.7
National Accounts						*Millions of Aruban Florins*							
Exports of Goods and Services	90c	....	2,006.9	2,139.6	2,263.1	2,374.2	2,465.5	2,476.1	2,466.8	2,369.9	....	....	....
Government Consumption Expend.	91f	....	....	....	647.4	655.0	674.0	731.4	804.6	898.5	....	....	....
Gross Fixed Capital Formation	93e	....	....	....	773.6	851.7	899.1	787.0	742.8	765.9	....	....	....
Changes in Inventories	93i	....	....	....	56.0	93.3	53.1	30.8	20.2	32.4	....	....	....
Househ.Cons.Expend.,incl.NPISHs	96f	....	....	....	1,367.0	1,499.5	1,602.4	1,664.2	1,712.1	1,799.8	....	....	....
Imports of Goods and Services	98c	....	2,044.0	2,191.4	2,365.0	2,493.1	2,610.2	2,362.6	2,347.9	2,445.3	....	....	....
Gross Domestic Product (GDP)	99b	....	2,363.7	2,470.1	2,742.2	2,980.5	3,083.8	3,326.9	3,398.7	3,421.2	3,599.0	3,819.0	....
GDP at 1995 Prices	99b.p	....	2,363.7	2,390.0	2,579.2	2,751.7	2,783.8	2,886.3	2,866.3	2,792.4	2,836.0	2,936.0	....
GDP Volume (2000=100)	99bvp	....	81.9	82.8	89.4	95.3	96.4	100.0	99.3	96.7	98.3	101.7	....
GDP Deflator (2000=100)	99bip	....	86.8	89.7	92.2	94.0	96.1	100.0	102.9	106.3	110.1	112.8	....
						Millions: Midyear Estimates							
Population	99z	.08	.08	.09	.09	.09	.09	.09	.09	.10	.10	.10	....

Australia 193

		1994	1995	1996	1997	1998	1999	2000	2001	2002	2003	2004	2005
Exchange Rates		*SDRs per Australian Dollar: End of Period*											
Market Rate	ac	.5321	.5012	.5539	.4838	.4360	.4764	.4252	.4063	.4165	.5047	.5016	.5133
		US Dollars per Australian Dollar: End of Period (ag) Period Average (rh)											
Market Rate	ag	.7768	.7450	.7965	.6527	.6139	.6538	.5540	.5106	.5662	.7500	.7790	.7337
Market Rate	rh	.7317	.7415	.7829	.7441	.6294	.6453	.5823	.5176	.5439	.6519	.7366	.7638
		Index Numbers (2000=100): Period Averages											
Market Rate	ahx	125.6	127.3	134.4	127.8	108.1	110.8	100.0	88.9	93.4	111.9	126.5	131.2
Nominal Effective Exchange Rate	nec	107.2	103.8	113.3	114.9	106.9	107.1	100.0	93.6	96.5	106.9	114.9	117.8
Real Effective Exchange Rate	rec	107.3	104.9	114.4	113.8	104.1	104.5	100.0	95.9	100.6	112.6	121.2	124.8
Fund Position		*Millions of SDRs: End of Period*											
Quota	2f.s	2,333	2,333	2,333	2,333	2,333	3,236	3,236	3,236	3,236	3,236	3,236	3,236
SDRs	1b.s	50	37	25	14	13	53	72	87	100	114	125	135
Reserve Position in the Fund	1c.s	347	338	335	539	892	1,189	954	1,124	1,423	1,381	1,099	543
of which: Outstg.Fund Borrowing	2c	—	—	—	—	75	—	—	—	—	—	—	—
Total Fund Cred.&Loans Outstg.	2tl	—	—	—	—	—	—	—	—	—	—	—	—
International Liquidity		*Millions of US Dollars Unless Otherwise Indicated: End of Period*											
Total Reserves minus Gold	1l.d	11,285	11,896	14,485	16,845	14,641	21,212	18,118	17,955	20,689	32,189	35,803	41,941
SDRs	1b.d	73	55	37	19	18	72	94	109	136	170	195	193
Reserve Position in the Fund	1c.d	506	502	482	727	1,256	1,633	1,243	1,412	1,934	2,053	1,706	776
Foreign Exchange	1d.d	10,706	11,340	13,967	16,099	13,366	19,507	16,782	16,434	18,618	29,966	33,901	40,972
Gold (Million Fine Troy Ounces)	1ad	7.90	7.90	7.90	2.56	2.56	2.56	2.56	2.56	2.56	2.56	2.56	2.57
Gold (National Valuation)	1and	3,023	3,055	2,918	740	737	743	699	709	878	1,070	1,123	1,316
Monetary Authorities: Other Liab.	4..d	38	67	50	28	66	55	63	47	78	86	112	—
Banking Institutions: Assets	7a.d	13,369	16,808	22,217	23,424	23,148	29,906	28,703	31,014	26,640	45,869	56,152	54,176
Liabilities	7b.d	39,355	49,238	63,521	64,258	73,409	88,291	90,027	98,049	100,915	161,228	203,309	223,004
Monetary Authorities		*Millions of Australian Dollars: Average of Weekly Figures for Last Month of Period*											
Foreign Assets	11	18,344	20,080	22,581	28,325	27,632	38,596	39,820	44,335	44,568	55,222	53,835	65,855
Claims on Central Government	12a	13,445	17,700	30,608	18,373	23,702	14,683	18,833	20,267	21,276	11,871	18,250	23,958
Reserve Money	14	23,834	25,024	40,335	32,160	33,997	32,258	32,018	38,044	38,865	39,590	40,914	44,356
of which: Currency Outside Banks	14a	18,207	19,092	19,628	21,098	22,783	24,603	26,927	28,471	29,702	31,470	32,803	34,901
Foreign Liabilities	16c	49	90	63	43	108	84	114	92	137	115	143	—
Central Government Deposits	16d	941	3,076	4,123	2,703	4,214	9,485	12,076	9,815	9,704	8,529	13,120	26,803
Capital Accounts	17a	1,517	1,573	1,533	3,294	3,948	3,857	3,976	7,350	7,322	7,257	7,263	7,242
Other Items (Net)	17r	5,448	8,017	7,134	8,498	9,068	7,595	10,470	9,302	9,816	11,602	10,644	11,413
Banking Institutions		*Millions of Australian Dollars: Average of Weekly Figures for Last Month of Period*											
Reserves	20	5,498	5,830	13,378	8,789	9,052	5,052	4,228	8,532	† 8,205	7,254	7,305	8,573
Foreign Assets	21	17,210	22,562	27,893	35,887	37,706	45,742	51,810	60,740	† 47,050	61,158	72,083	73,840
Claims on Central Government	22a	28,457	28,072	25,635	19,991	20,182	23,153	13,371	11,756	† 7,421	−1,569	355	−4,247
Claims on State and Local Govts	22b	—	—	—	—	—	—	—	—	† 2,774	4,856	4,906	4,200
Claims on Nonfin.Pub. Enterprises	22c	3,233	3,591	3,909	4,659	6,550	11,104	10,593	12,131	† 2,042	2,488	1,395	1,620
Claims on Private Sector	22d	311,556	345,970	378,196	419,273	466,152	522,657	580,073	625,054	† 690,712	797,130	887,050	1,003,513
Claims on Nonbank Financial Insts.	22g	8,477	9,348	9,930	8,007	11,026	9,779	11,666	14,887	† 51,730	36,708	46,372	51,898
Demand Deposits	24	60,496	64,771	75,801	86,965	91,864	101,179	110,660	138,456	† 180,177	200,008	211,102	233,984
Time, Savings,& Fgn.Currency Dep.	25	197,542	215,949	236,124	247,668	271,109	305,051	309,634	339,526	† 324,661	374,291	433,012	460,067
Foreign Liabilities	26c	50,663	66,091	79,750	98,450	119,579	135,043	162,504	192,028	† 178,232	214,970	260,987	303,944
Central Government Deposits	26d	2,988	3,523	3,291	3,578	5,721	5,497	5,197	4,399	† 845	874	804	939
Capital Accounts	27a	—	—	—	—	—	—	—	—	† 69,335	78,829	86,185	91,618
Other Items (Net)	27r	62,741	65,038	63,975	59,947	62,395	70,717	83,746	58,690	† 56,684	39,054	27,377	48,844
Banking Survey		*Millions of Australian Dollars: Average of Weekly Figures for Last Month of Period*											
Foreign Assets (Net)	31n	−15,158	−23,540	−29,339	−34,282	−54,348	−50,789	−70,988	−87,045	† −86,751	−98,705	−135,213	−164,249
Domestic Credit	32	361,238	398,082	440,864	464,024	517,676	566,394	617,263	669,881	† 765,406	842,081	944,405	1,053,199
Claims on Central Govt. (Net)	32an	37,972	39,173	48,828	32,084	33,948	22,854	14,931	17,809	† 18,148	899	4,681	−8,031
Claims on State and Local Govts	32b	—	—	—	—	—	—	—	—	† 2,774	4,856	4,906	4,200
Claims on Nonfin.Pub. Enterprises	32c	3,233	3,591	3,909	4,659	6,550	11,104	10,593	12,131	† 2,042	2,488	1,395	1,620
Claims on Private Sector	32d	311,556	345,970	378,196	419,273	466,152	522,657	580,073	625,054	† 690,712	797,130	887,050	1,003,513
Claims on Nonbank Financial Insts.	32g	8,477	9,348	9,930	8,007	11,026	9,779	11,666	14,887	† 51,730	36,708	46,372	51,898
Money	34	78,820	83,953	95,715	108,431	115,010	126,260	137,808	167,125	† 210,119	231,553	243,950	268,904
Quasi-Money	35	197,542	215,949	236,124	247,668	271,109	305,051	309,634	339,526	† 324,661	374,291	433,012	460,067
Capital Accounts	37a	1,517	1,573	1,533	3,294	3,948	3,857	3,976	7,350	† 76,656	86,086	93,448	98,859
Other Items (Net)	37r	68,201	73,067	78,153	70,350	73,261	80,437	94,858	68,835	† 67,218	51,447	38,782	61,120
Money plus Quasi-Money	35l	276,361	299,903	331,839	356,098	386,119	431,311	447,442	506,651	† 534,781	605,844	676,962	728,971
Money (National Definitions)		*Millions of Australian Dollars: Average of Weekly Figures for Last Month of Period*											
Money Base	19ma	23,765	24,958	33,043	29,962	31,926	29,733	31,189	37,017	37,513	38,844	40,109	42,454
M1	59ma	78,761	83,898	95,465	108,136	114,736	125,832	137,620	166,941	149,064	160,944	168,847	182,193
M1, Seasonally Adjusted	59mac	76,044	81,077	92,798	104,771	111,429	122,719	134,212	162,812	145,580	157,381	165,324	178,499
M3	59mc	283,445	308,981	335,354	356,961	384,572	420,189	441,076	502,184	537,301	601,112	655,668	709,349
M3, Seasonally Adjusted	59mcc	280,064	305,581	332,275	353,460	381,481	417,398	437,767	497,583	532,420	594,969	648,468	701,205
Broad Money	59md	364,693	393,572	426,923	459,205	495,894	525,926	562,961	609,851	623,307	672,825	731,048	799,265
Broad Money, Seasonally Adjusted	59mdc	362,044	390,775	424,363	456,100	493,055	523,181	559,595	604,992	618,126	666,340	723,495	790,720
Interest Rates		*Percent Per Annum*											
Money Market Rate	60b	5.18	† 7.50	7.20	5.50	4.99	† 4.78	5.90	5.06	4.55	4.81	5.25	5.46
Treasury Bill Rate	60c	5.69	† 7.64	7.02	5.29	4.84	4.76	5.98	4.80	....	....	....	....
Deposit Rate	60l	4.92	6.11	5.71	4.32	3.71	3.47	4.20	3.20	3.07	3.26	3.63	3.70
Lending Rate	60p	9.23	10.70	10.50	8.89	8.15	7.99	9.29	8.66	8.16	8.41	8.85	9.06
Govt. Bond Yield: Short-Term	61a	8.19	8.42	7.53	6.00	5.02	5.55	6.18	4.97	5.30	4.90	5.30	5.27
Long-Term	61	9.04	9.17	8.17	6.89	5.50	6.08	6.26	5.63	5.82	5.36	5.61	5.32

		1994	1995	1996	1997	1998	1999	2000	2001	2002	2003	2004	2005
Prices, Production, Labor						*Index Numbers (2000=100): Period Averages*							
Share Prices	62	64.3	63.9	71.6	80.0	83.9	92.7	100.0	103.2	100.2	96.1	111.7	135.5
Prices: Manufacturing Output	63	92.7	96.6	96.9	98.1	94.2	† 93.3	100.0	103.1	103.3	103.8	107.9	114.3
Consumer Prices	64	86.9	90.9	93.3	93.5	94.3	95.7	100.0	104.4	107.5	110.5	113.1	116.1
Wages, Weekly Earnings	65	78.4	82.4	85.6	89.1	92.8	95.3	100.0	104.9	110.3	116.5	120.9	127.6
Industrial Production	66	85.8	87.1	90.5	92.1	94.6	95.1	100.0	† 101.4	104.6	104.7	104.9	106.1
Manufacturing Empl., Seas. Adj.	67eyc	97.8	98.8	99.0	100.5	97.2	95.5	100.0	96.7	97.8	95.8	96.4	94.7
						Number in Thousands: Period Averages							
Labor Force	67d	8,771	8,995	9,115	9,221	9,343	9,470	9,682	9,796	9,943	10,067	10,207	....
Employment	67e	7,942	8,256	8,364	8,444	8,618	8,785	9,043	9,157	9,334	9,481	9,677	....
Unemployment	67c	829	739	751	760	721	658	611	660	629	611	567	537
Unemployment Rate (%)	67r	9.5	8.2	8.2	8.3	7.8	7.0	6.3	6.7	6.3	5.9	5.5	5.1
Intl. Transactions & Positions						*Millions of Australian Dollars*							
Exports	70	64,904	71,657	76,978	84,786	88,977	86,895	110,464	122,664	119,483	109,811	117,577	138,716
Wheat	70d	2,283	1,765	3,987	4,407	3,514	3,311	3,813	4,330	4,136	2,426	4,192	2,978
Coal	70vr	6,700	7,380	7,758	8,784	9,823	8,391	9,340	12,482	12,843	10,890	13,302	21,814
Greasy Wool	70ha	2,394	2,242	2,108	2,446	1,715	1,494	2,103	2,304	2,482	1,790	1,973	1,864
Imports, c.i.f.	71	72,882	82,673	83,543	88,884	102,905	107,154	123,461	123,539	133,424	136,577	148,744	164,137
Imports, f.o.b.	71.v	68,087	77,467	78,402	83,364	96,723	101,446	116,840	117,357	126,457	129,884	140,956	155,626
						2000=100							
Volume of Exports	72	66.6	68.7	76.7	87.5	86.5	91.0	100.0	104.9	101.8	92.5	100.8	....
Wheat	72d	73.1	38.9	82.2	109.3	85.9	93.2	100.0	87.7	83.0	53.6	104.1	78.5
Coal	72vr	70.3	73.1	75.4	84.5	88.6	91.8	100.0	104.0	109.6	115.8	120.7	125.5
Greasy Wool	72ha	111.8	86.6	104.5	104.5	81.0	83.5	100.0	95.7	75.5	56.5	75.5	77.7
Volume of Imports	73	58.0	63.5	68.9	77.3	83.7	92.4	100.0	97.3	105.1	107.2	116.2	....
Export Prices	76	84.7	90.9	87.2	88.7	93.1	† 86.4	100.0	110.0	106.7	98.3	101.8	116.1
Wheat (1995=100)	76d	83.1	100.0	109.0	94.7	92.6	....	....	....	....	....	....	....
Coal (Unit Value)	74vr	102.1	108.1	110.2	111.3	118.7	97.9	100.0	128.5	125.5	100.7	118.0	186.1
Greasy Wool (Unit Value)	74ha	101.9	123.1	95.9	111.3	100.6	85.1	100.0	114.5	156.4	150.7	124.3	114.0
Import Prices	76.x	88.3	91.5	86.6	86.4	93.7	† 91.6	100.0	105.7	100.8	92.8	87.6	88.6
Balance of Payments						*Millions of US Dollars: Minus Sign Indicates Debit*							
Current Account, n.i.e.	78ald	−16,953	−19,278	−15,649	−12,240	−18,338	−22,212	−15,306	−7,854	−16,468	−29,696	−40,101	−42,084
Goods: Exports f.o.b.	78aad	47,371	53,220	60,397	64,893	55,884	56,096	64,025	63,625	65,013	70,526	87,096	106,505
Goods: Imports f.o.b.	78abd	−50,648	−57,443	−61,032	−63,044	−61,215	−65,857	−68,866	−61,890	−70,530	−85,861	−105,238	−120,177
Trade Balance	78acd	−3,277	−4,223	−635	1,849	−5,332	−9,761	−4,841	1,736	−5,517	−15,335	−18,142	−13,672
Services: Credit	78aad	14,401	16,398	18,864	18,727	16,416	17,690	19,062	17,444	18,680	22,138	26,366	28,350
Services: Debit	78aed	−15,481	−17,308	−18,778	−18,938	−17,794	−18,498	−18,666	−17,123	−18,095	−21,444	−27,043	−29,501
Balance on Goods & Services	78afd	−4,358	−5,133	−549	1,638	−6,710	−10,569	−4,444	2,057	−4,932	−14,641	−18,819	−14,823
Income: Credit	78agd	4,462	5,258	6,027	7,162	6,522	7,404	8,977	8,200	8,480	10,247	13,981	16,393
Income: Debit	78ahd	−16,829	−19,294	−21,220	−21,000	−17,868	−19,018	−19,791	−18,132	−19,953	−25,142	−34,994	−43,292
Balance on Gds, Serv. & Inc.	78aid	−16,726	−19,169	−15,741	−12,200	−18,056	−22,183	−15,258	−7,875	−16,404	−29,536	−39,833	−41,722
Current Transfers, n.i.e.: Credit	78ajd	2,204	2,364	2,699	2,765	2,651	3,003	2,622	2,242	2,310	2,767	3,145	3,262
Current Transfers: Debit	78akd	−2,431	−2,474	−2,606	−2,805	−2,933	−3,032	−2,669	−2,221	−2,373	−2,927	−3,414	−3,623
Capital Account, n.i.e.	78bcd	323	558	964	903	670	819	615	591	443	736	817	916
Capital Account, n.i.e.: Credit	78bad	908	1,250	1,674	1,606	1,315	1,535	1,406	1,320	1,298	1,664	....	....
Capital Account: Debit	78bbd	−586	−692	−710	−703	−646	−716	−791	−729	−855	−928	....	....
Financial Account, n.i.e.	78bjd	15,897	18,632	16,070	16,820	15,204	27,613	12,953	8,155	16,798	36,234	40,089	48,982
Direct Investment Abroad	78add	−2,817	−3,267	−7,052	−6,368	−3,346	422	−3,275	−11,967	−7,972	−16,626	−17,780	40,306
Dir. Invest. in Rep. Econ., n.i.e.	78bed	5,001	12,026	6,181	7,631	5,957	3,311	13,618	8,261	17,675	9,849	42,931	−37,217
Portfolio Investment Assets	78bfd	1,503	−2,842	−3,307	−79	−3,794	−10,487	−10,919	−10,053	−16,784	−9,217	−24,791	−17,505
Equity Securities	78bkd	−543	−1,175	−2,416	−567	−2,343	−6,710	−7,346	−4,936	−11,818	−3,905	−10,902	−4,952
Debt Securities	78bld	2,045	−1,668	−892	489	−1,451	−3,778	−3,573	−5,117	−4,966	−5,312	−13,889	−12,554
Portfolio Investment Liab., n.i.e.	78bgd	14,593	15,200	23,738	13,219	6,959	24,352	14,874	16,237	16,998	48,825	39,463	52,976
Equity Securities	78bmd	8,120	2,585	2,068	8,775	10,777	11,060	−726	7,159	276	11,587	−25,914	7,375
Debt Securities	78bnd	6,473	12,615	21,670	4,444	−3,818	13,292	15,601	9,078	16,722	37,238	65,376	45,602
Financial Derivatives Assets	78bwd	1,004	2,801	974	−470	−382	290	−1,165	2,215	2,015	7,581	18,068	14,754
Financial Derivatives Liabilities	78bxd	−632	−2,217	−681	1,092	−636	1,089	291	−1,754	−2,331	−7,738	−18,450	−15,292
Other Investment Assets	78bhd	−1,597	−3,223	−5,613	−6,735	−686	−2,987	−4,887	834	−3,708	−4,584	−6,099	−3,149
Monetary Authorities	78bod	—	—	−246	−414	−180	−327	133	275	411	110	—	—
General Government	78bpd	137	−57	−94	−840	−412	−214	−22	−153	−85	−104	−147	−274
Banks	78bqd	−2,438	−2,824	−4,618	−4,233	−608	−2,442	−1,745	−2,616	−3,593	−4,823	−6,227	−1,147
Other Sectors	78brd	704	−342	−656	−1,248	513	−5	−3,253	3,328	−441	232	276	−1,728
Other Investment Liab., n.i.e.	78bid	−1,158	154	1,829	8,530	11,131	11,624	4,416	4,382	10,905	8,145	6,747	14,110
Monetary Authorities	78bsd	−4	27	−29	−3	9	61	−70	3	7	37	7	14
General Government	78btd	157	133	103	−91	129	−228	75	−125	—	—	−27	—
Banks	78bud	−1,375	2,998	2,717	7,207	7,654	7,926	4,924	3,536	10,178	9,455	4,029	1,142
Other Sectors	78bvd	64	−3,004	−963	1,417	3,339	3,865	−514	969	720	−1,347	2,738	12,953
Net Errors and Omissions	78cad	−226	484	1,086	−2,610	424	485	372	204	−651	−397	362	−558
Overall Balance	78cbd	−960	396	2,471	2,873	−2,040	6,705	−1,365	1,096	122	6,877	1,166	7,256
Reserves and Related Items	79dad	960	−396	−2,471	−2,873	2,040	−6,705	1,365	−1,096	−122	−6,877	−1,166	−7,256
Reserve Assets	79dbd	960	−396	−2,471	−2,873	2,040	−6,705	1,365	−1,096	−122	−6,877	−1,166	−7,256
Use of Fund Credit and Loans	79dcd	—	—	—	—	—	—	—	—	—	—	—	—
Exceptional Financing	79ded	....	....	....	....	....	....	....	....	....	....	....	....

2006, International Monetary Fund : *International Financial Statistics Yearbook*

Australia 193

		1994	1995	1996	1997	1998	1999	2000	2001	2002	2003	2004	2005
International Investment Position						*Millions of US Dollars*							
Assets	79aad	119,962	133,885	161,821	173,545	185,349	232,599	231,688	258,480	284,613	404,600	500,755	479,722
Direct Investment Abroad	79abd	47,774	53,010	66,816	71,936	78,635	89,556	85,385	109,602	108,830	150,734	197,632	159,991
Portfolio Investment	79acd	29,375	35,658	42,023	42,451	48,651	72,847	75,990	79,667	91,716	130,334	166,719	183,812
Equity Securities	79add	22,538	27,029	31,518	32,947	36,652	57,043	59,024	59,889	65,020	92,808	114,325	124,689
Debt Securities	79aed	6,837	8,629	10,506	9,504	11,999	15,804	16,966	19,778	26,696	37,526	52,394	59,124
Financial Derivatives	79ald	8,924	7,679	6,733	8,058	9,282	10,756	12,593	14,780	19,576	33,139	38,078	27,355
Other Investment	79afd	19,581	22,589	28,847	34,006	33,404	37,485	38,903	35,767	42,924	57,136	61,398	65,307
Monetary Authorities	79agd	—	—	—	491	766	953	875	536	136	—	—	—
General Government	79ahd	1,201	1,208	1,377	4,044	4,283	4,677	4,223	4,155	4,508	5,682	5,934	5,895
Banks	79aid	9,232	11,905	16,989	18,892	18,470	21,626	21,183	22,160	28,219	40,073	48,948	47,225
Other Sectors	79ajd	9,148	9,476	10,481	10,578	9,886	10,229	12,622	8,916	10,060	11,381	6,516	12,188
Reserve Assets	79akd	14,308	14,949	17,402	17,094	15,377	21,956	18,817	18,664	21,567	33,258	36,927	43,257
Liabilities	79lad	309,880	335,211	388,362	360,313	380,429	451,510	428,585	433,878	513,693	742,251	899,159	890,719
Dir. Invest. in Rep. Economy	79lbd	95,519	104,074	116,724	101,043	105,944	120,589	111,138	111,739	141,599	199,881	267,419	210,650
Portfolio Investment	79lcd	162,325	181,223	218,728	203,158	208,590	254,691	241,859	247,051	273,016	401,242	482,453	531,384
Equity Securities	79ldd	46,544	51,314	61,123	60,297	72,987	100,761	84,902	89,081	87,307	138,851	146,411	175,219
Debt Securities	79led	115,780	129,909	157,605	142,861	135,603	153,930	156,958	157,969	185,709	262,391	336,041	356,165
Financial Derivatives	79lld	7,564	7,250	8,275	9,884	9,862	12,550	13,318	12,900	20,919	36,584	37,704	27,905
Other Investment	79lfd	44,472	42,665	44,636	46,227	56,034	63,679	62,270	62,189	78,158	104,544	111,583	120,780
Monetary Authorities	79lgd	46	71	45	33	36	100	18	19	28	81	91	93
General Government	79lhd	397	439	573	237	360	153	210	64	71	89	62	59
Banks	79lid	23,637	25,010	27,883	30,851	37,522	46,949	48,166	48,980	62,845	87,517	91,321	88,781
Other Sectors	79ljd	20,392	17,145	16,134	15,106	18,116	16,477	13,875	13,125	15,214	16,858	20,109	31,847
Government Finance						*Millions of Australian Dollars: Year Ending June 30*							
Deficit (-) or Surplus	80	–13,637	–11,641	–4,840	2,062	16,368	–3,398	6,801	4,194	–8,297	....	....	....
Revenue	81	104,559	114,234	125,092	134,579	142,036	† 151,934	163,767	161,200	164,432	....	....	....
Expenditure	82	121,561	127,358	135,130	139,857	140,877	† 149,023	156,883	156,296	165,946	....	....	....
Lending Minus Repayments	83	–3,365	–1,483	–5,198	–7,340	–15,209	† 6,309	83	710	6,783	....	....	....
Financing (by Residence of Lender)													
Domestic	84a	10,024	8,349	–3,123	–3,978	–11,213	....	....	....	....	....	....	....
Foreign	85a	3,612	3,292	7,963	1,916	–5,155	....	....	....	....	....	....	....
Debt: Domestic	88a	71,334	79,489	78,892	73,510	60,094	....	....	....	....	....	....	....
Foreign	89a	22,869	28,012	36,482	42,610	39,355	....	....	....	....	....	....	....
National Accounts						*Billions of Australian Dollars*							
Househ.Cons.Expend.,incl.NPISHs	96f.c	278.25	297.96	312.93	330.39	349.96	370.18	394.59	421.81	449.70	475.56	509.88	535.57
Government Consumption Expend	91f.c	87.52	91.61	97.71	101.52	107.28	113.14	121.96	128.83	136.44	145.93	156.53	169.14
Gross Fixed Capital Formation	93e.c	112.30	115.71	121.43	131.65	144.07	152.01	157.21	157.80	182.97	202.60	219.25	239.63
Changes in Inventories	93i.c	2.18	1.73	2.43	–4.22	2.17	5.08	2.46	–.76	–.26	6.53	3.64	3.32
Exports of Goods and Services	90c.c	84.29	93.95	101.13	112.35	115.05	114.10	143.37	156.96	153.83	142.37	154.03	176.48
Imports of Goods and Services (-)	98c.c	90.08	100.83	101.92	110.38	125.73	130.58	150.82	152.75	162.46	164.53	179.69	196.09
Gross Domestic Product (GDP)	99b.c	474.79	500.46	533.04	561.45	592.88	622.47	669.78	711.99	760.37	808.49	865.45	926.88
Net Primary Income from Abroad	98.nc	–16.75	–18.87	–19.40	–18.61	–18.11	–18.25	–18.53	–19.24	–21.11	–22.93	–28.60	–35.22
Gross National Income (GNI)	99a.c	458.05	481.59	513.64	542.84	574.77	604.22	651.25	692.75	739.26	785.56	836.86	891.67
Net Current Transf.from Abroad	98t.c	.75	1.14	.12	–.10	1.02	–1.39	1.29	–.16	–.64	.66	–.42	–1.21
Gross Nat'l Disposable Inc.(GNDI)	99i.c	458.80	482.73	513.76	542.74	575.79	602.83	652.54	692.60	738.62	786.23	836.44	890.46
Gross Saving	99s.c	93.03	93.16	103.13	110.84	118.55	119.52	135.98	141.96	152.49	164.74	170.03	185.75
Consumption of Fixed Capital	99cfc	77.93	80.59	82.57	86.51	92.13	97.60	104.12	111.75	119.03	125.12	131.47	138.18
GDP Vol. 2001/02 Ref.,Chained	99b.r	587.10	607.89	634.19	659.51	692.78	723.43	747.50	764.28	795.82	820.26	849.38	870.24
GDP Volume (2000=100)	99bvr	78.5	81.3	84.8	88.2	92.7	96.8	100.0	102.2	106.5	109.7	113.6	116.4
GDP Deflator (2000=100)	99bir	90.3	91.9	93.8	95.0	95.5	96.0	100.0	104.0	106.6	110.0	113.7	118.9
						Millions: Midyear Estimates							
Population	99z	17.73	17.94	18.16	18.39	18.62	18.85	19.07	19.29	19.51	19.73	19.94	20.16

Austria 122

		1994	1995	1996	1997	1998	1999	2000	2001	2002	2003	2004	2005
Exchange Rates						*Euros per SDR: End of Period*							
Market Rate	aa	16.013	14.996	15.751	17.045	16.540	1.3662	1.4002	1.4260	1.2964	1.1765	1.1402	1.2116
						Euros per US Dollar: End of Period (ae) Period Average (rf)							
Market Rate	ae	10.969	10.088	10.954	12.633	11.747	.9954	1.0747	1.1347	.9536	.7918	.7342	.8477
Market Rate	rf	11.422	10.081	10.587	12.204	12.379	.9386	1.0854	1.1175	1.0626	.8860	.8054	.8041
						Schillings per ECU: End of Period (ea) Period Average (eb)							
ECU Rate	ea	13.4923	13.2581	13.7253	13.9495	13.7058	....	....	....	....	....	....	....
ECU Rate	eb	13.5755	13.1880	13.4234	13.8403	13.8648	....	....	....	....	....	....	....
						Index Numbers (2000=100): Period Averages							
Official Rate (1995=100)	ahx	88.4	100.0	95.2	82.6	81.5	....	....	....	....	....	....	....
Nominal Effective Exchange Rate	neu	105.9	110.0	107.7	104.1	104.5	103.1	100.0	100.2	101.0	104.1	105.2	105.2
Real Effective Exchange Rate	reu	124.9	122.0	116.0	109.1	107.3	104.9	100.0	98.8	98.7	99.9	100.8	100.8
Fund Position						*Millions of SDRs: End of Period*							
Quota	2f.s	1,188	1,188	1,188	1,188	1,188	1,872	1,872	1,872	1,872	1,872	1,872	1,872
SDRs	1b.s	194	122	136	125	106	106	103	185	136	122	103	103
Reserve Position in the Fund	1c.s	364	459	562	714	970	699	531	662	705	771	602	276
of which: Outstg.Fund Borrowing	2c	—	—	—	—	38	—	—	—	—	—	—	—
International Liquidity						*Millions of US Dollars Unless Otherwise Indicated: End of Period*							
Total Res.Min.Gold (Eurosys.Def)	1l.d	16,822	18,730	22,865	19,736	22,432	† 15,120	14,319	12,509	9,683	8,470	7,858	6,839
SDRs	1b.d	283	181	195	168	149	145	134	233	185	181	160	147
Reserve Position in the Fund	1c.d	531	682	809	963	1,365	959	692	833	959	1,145	935	394
Foreign Exchange	1d.d	16,008	17,867	21,861	18,605	20,918	14,016	13,492	11,444	8,540	7,144	6,763	6,298
o/w:Fin.Deriv.Rel.to Reserves	1ddd	....	....	....	....	....				—	—	—	—
Other Reserve Assets	1e.d	....	....	....	....	....	—	—	—	—	—	—	—
Gold (Million Fine Troy Ounces)	1ad	18.34	11.99	10.75	7.87	9.64	13.10	12.14	11.17	10.21	10.21	9.89	9.73
Gold (Eurosystem Valuation)	1and	3,135	2,223	1,805	1,168	2,795	3,803	3,331	3,089	3,499	4,259	4,330	4,989
Memo:Euro Cl. on Non-EA Res	1dgd	....	....	....	....	....							
Non-Euro Cl. on EA Res	1dhd	....	....	....	....	....	2,146	1,453	985	3,588	4,389	3,742	3,165
Mon. Auth.: Other Foreign Assets	3..d	....	....	....	....	....							
Foreign Liabilities	4..d	18	19	8	107	....	† 1,584	845	925	613	472	8	11
Banking Insts.: Foreign Assets	7a.d	77,885	92,040	89,538	....	....	† 62,990	69,678	74,777	91,219	122,766	157,545	166,905
Foreign Liab	7b.d	84,321	99,148	102,739	....	....	† 49,417	49,932	58,520	56,534	70,378	81,780	85,734
Monetary Authorities						*Billions of Schillings through 1998; Billions of Euros Beginning 1999: End of Period*							
Fgn. Assets (Cl.on Non-EA Ctys)	11	217.4	237.0	268.3	263.4	....	21.95	20.48	19.01	16.44	13.69	11.56	11.87
Claims on General Government	12a.u	....	....	....	....	....	1.43	1.06	1.45	3.19	3.22	4.48	4.39
o/w: Claims on Gen.Govt.in Cty	12a	9.6	9.6	10.6	11.6	....	.22	.26	.40	.43	.59	.57	.57
Claims on Banking Institutions	12e.u	....	....	....	....	....	16.20	10.45	6.42	8.81	8.09	15.03	24.98
o/w: Claims on Bank.Inst.in Cty	12e	62.0	47.6	47.2	74.2	....	5.57	7.08	1.73	3.13	3.60	9.38	12.93
Claims on Other Resident Sectors	12d.u	....	....	....	....	....	2.33	2.42	2.32	2.58	2.43	2.68	3.19
o/w: Cl. on Oth.Res.Sect.in Cty	12d	....	....	....	....	....	.86	.90	.99	1.13	.94	1.03	1.07
Currency Issued	14a	158.3	168.6	176.7	178.8	....	13.92	14.54	10.69	11.01	12.29	14.11	15.90
Liabilities to Banking Insts	14c.u	....	....	....	....	....	16.21	8.76	6.87	11.04	7.40	12.99	20.68
o/w: Liabs to Bank.Inst.in Cty	14c	55.9	43.5	50.1	46.3	....	3.28	3.40	6.56	3.54	4.26	4.00	4.98
Demand Dep. of Other Res.Sect	14d.u	....	....	....	....	....	.01	.01	.01	.01	—	—	—
o/w:D.Dep.of Oth.Res.Sect.in Cty	14d	....	....	....	....	....	.01	.01	.01	.01	—	—	—
Other Dep. of Other Res.Sect	15..u	....	....	....	....	....							
o/w:O.Dep.of Oth.Res.Sect.in Cty	15	....	....	....	....	....							
Bonds & Money Mkt. Instruments	16n.u	....	....	....	....	....	—	—	—	—	—	—	—
Foreign Liab. (to Non-EA Ctys)	16c	.2	.2	.1	1.3	....	1.58	.91	1.05	.59	.37	.01	.01
Central Government Deposits	16d.u	....	....	....	....	....	.01	.01	.03	.02	.02	.01	—
o/w: Cent.Govt.Dep. in Cty	16d	.3	.2	.3	.2	....	.01	.01	.03	.02	.02	.01	—
Other Items (Net)	17r	74.4	81.6	98.9	122.5	....	10.18	10.18	10.56	8.36	7.36	6.64	7.83
Memo: Net Claims on Eurosystem	12e.s	....	....	....	....	....	−5.55	−3.84	3.04	−3.36	−.35	−4.96	−5.84
Currency Put into Circ	14m	....	....	....	....	....	....	....	....	18.41	15.35	11.23	7.20
Banking Institutions						*Billions of Schillings through 1998; Billions of Euros Beginning 1999: End of Period*							
Claims on Monetary Authorities	20	80.5	74.0	80.1	77.5	....	3.31	3.88	7.98	3.73	4.86	3.82	4.82
Claims on Bk.Inst.in Oth.EA Ctys	20b.u	....	....	....	....	....	31.09	38.65	44.68	39.15	43.61	47.05	57.86
Fgn. Assets (Cl.on Non-EA Ctys)	21	854.3	928.5	980.8	....	....	62.70	74.88	84.85	86.98	97.20	115.66	141.48
Claims on General Government	22a.u	....	....	....	....	....	52.90	51.69	48.80	49.72	49.55	54.42	55.86
o/w: Claims on Gen.Govt.in Cty	22a	805.6	† 833.1	823.9	783.4	....	49.85	48.51	43.72	41.85	39.98	41.79	38.91
Claims on Other Resident Sectors	22d.u	....	....	....	....	....	208.29	227.15	240.55	246.66	253.32	268.47	301.84
o/w: Cl. on Oth.Res.Sect.in Cty	22d	2,086.2	† 2,228.8	2,376.9	2,595.9	....	197.09	213.04	224.07	229.50	234.89	247.70	276.21
Demand Deposits	24..u	....	....	....	....	....	44.60	45.05	51.04	54.07	63.44	68.89	76.33
o/w:D.Dep.of Oth.Res.Sect.in Cty	24	201.1	244.0	255.2	273.5	....	42.15	42.69	48.41	51.45	60.66	66.08	72.40
Other Deposits	25..u	....	....	....	....	....	130.22	132.01	139.87	137.19	139.75	143.03	148.55
o/w:O.Dep.of Oth.Res.Sect.in Cty	25	1,721.0	1,770.9	1,812.1	1,840.7	....	123.21	124.96	132.12	129.78	130.51	132.85	137.41
Money Market Fund Shares	26m.u	....	....	....	....								
Bonds & Money Mkt. Instruments	26n.u	....	....	....	....	....	94.14	114.39	128.43	135.36	142.45	156.66	181.07
Foreign Liab. (to Non-EA Ctys)	26c	924.9	1,000.2	1,125.4	....	....	49.19	53.66	66.40	53.91	55.72	60.04	72.67
Central Government Deposits	26d.u	....	....	....	....	....	1.61	1.90	3.26	3.36	2.89	4.13	3.85
o/w: Cent.Govt.Dep. in Cty	26d	74.0	77.4	77.7	69.7	....	1.61	1.90	3.25	3.36	2.88	4.08	3.30
Credit from Monetary Authorities	26g	62.0	47.6	47.2	74.2	....	5.19	7.50	1.98	3.41	4.07	10.50	13.97
Liab. to Bk.Inst.in Oth. EA Ctys	26h.u	....	....	....	....	....	27.81	31.89	28.08	26.98	26.69	26.99	38.07
Capital Accounts	27a	226.6	238.4	254.7	275.7	....	25.50	27.25	29.30	30.93	33.96	38.36	53.08
Other Items (Net)	27r	78.3	89.0	81.6	....	....	−19.96	−17.40	−21.51	−18.98	−20.43	−19.18	−25.74

Austria 122

		1994	1995	1996	1997	1998	1999	2000	2001	2002	2003	2004	2005
Banking Survey (Nat'l Residency)		*Billions of Schillings through 1998; Billions of Euros Beginning 1999: End of Period*											
Foreign Assets (Net)	31n	146.6	165.1	123.6	....	....	42.55	56.15	71.50	78.90	93.62	110.31	130.32
Domestic Credit	32	2,827.2	† 2,993.8	3,133.4	3,321.0	....	246.41	260.79	265.88	269.53	273.50	287.00	313.45
Claims on General Govt. (Net)	32an	740.9	† 765.0	756.5	725.1	....	48.46	46.85	40.83	38.90	37.68	38.28	36.17
Claims on Other Resident Sectors	32d	2,086.2	† 2,228.8	2,376.9	2,595.9	....	197.96	213.94	225.05	230.63	235.83	248.72	277.28
Currency Issued	34a.n	158.3	168.6	176.7	178.8	....	13.92	14.54	10.69	11.01	12.29	14.11	15.90
Demand Deposits	34b.n	201.1	244.0	255.2	273.5	....	42.16	42.70	48.42	51.46	60.66	66.08	72.40
Other Deposits	35..n	1,721.0	1,770.9	1,812.1	1,840.7	....	123.21	124.96	132.12	129.78	130.51	132.85	137.41
Money Market Fund Shares	36m	....	....	....	....	....	—	—	—	—	—	—	—
Bonds & Money Mkt. Instruments	36n	538.7	596.8	607.9	630.2	....	94.14	114.39	128.43	135.36	142.45	156.66	181.07
o/w: Over Two Years	36na	....	....	....	....	....	87.95	104.01	118.57	128.15	135.12	147.76	166.11
Other Items (Net)	37r	354.7	378.6	405.1	....	....	15.54	20.35	17.73	20.82	21.21	27.62	36.99
Banking Survey (EA-Wide Residency)		*Billions of Euros: End of Period*											
Foreign Assets (Net)	31n.u	....	....	....	....	....	33.88	40.79	36.41	48.93	54.79	67.18	80.67
Domestic Credit	32..u	....	....	....	....	....	263.33	280.41	289.83	298.77	305.62	325.92	361.41
Claims on General Govt. (Net)	32anu	....	....	....	....	....	52.72	50.84	46.96	49.53	49.87	54.77	56.38
Claims on Other Resident Sect.	32d.u	....	....	....	....	....	210.62	229.57	242.87	249.24	255.75	271.15	305.03
Currency Issued	34a.u	....	....	....	....	....	13.92	14.54	10.69	11.01	12.29	14.11	15.90
Demand Deposits	34b.u	....	....	....	....	....	44.61	45.06	51.05	54.08	63.44	68.89	76.34
Other Deposits	35..u	....	....	....	....	....	130.22	132.01	139.87	137.19	139.75	143.03	148.55
o/w: Other Dep. Over Two Yrs.	35abu	....	....	....	....	....	49.83	50.09	50.65	49.07	51.34	52.92	53.38
Money Market Fund Shares	36m.u	....	....	....	....	....	—	—	—	—	—	—	—
Bonds & Money Mkt. Instruments	36n.u	....	....	....	....	....	94.14	114.39	128.43	135.36	142.45	156.66	181.07
o/w: Over Two Years	36nau	....	....	....	....	....	87.95	104.01	118.57	128.15	135.12	147.76	166.11
Other Items (Net)	37r.u	....	....	....	....	....	14.33	15.21	–3.79	10.05	2.48	10.41	20.22
Money (National Definitions)		*Billions of Schillings: End of Period*											
Central Bank Money	19mb	214.47	212.37	227.13	225.38	....	....	....	....	....	....	....	....
Extended Monetary Base	19mc	235.17	250.84	260.35	265.81	....	....	....	....	....	....	....	....
Money, M1	59ma	355.58	409.19	431.15	452.30	....	....	....	....	....	....	....	....
Interest Rates		*Percent Per Annum*											
Discount Rate (End of Period)	60	4.50	3.00	2.50	2.50	2.50	....	....	....	....	....	....	....
Money Market Rate	60b	5.03	4.36	3.19	3.27	3.36	....	....	....	....	....	....	....
Deposit Rate	60l	2.31	2.19	1.71	1.50	† 2.65	2.21	....	....	....	....	....	....
Households: Stocks, up to 2 years	60lhs	....	....	....	....	....	....	....	....	....	1.92	1.71	1.70
New Business, up to 1 year	60lhn	....	....	....	....	....	....	....	....	....	2.08	1.91	1.96
Corporations: Stocks, up to 2 years	60lcs	....	....	....	....	....	....	....	....	....	2.09	1.91	1.99
New Business, up to 1 year	60lcn	....	....	....	....	....	....	....	....	....	2.18	1.97	2.05
Lending Rate	60p	....	....	....	....	6.42	5.64	....	....	....	....	....	....
Households: Stocks, up to 1 year	60phs	....	....	....	....	....	....	....	....	....	8.37	7.53	7.11
New Bus., Floating & up to 1 year	60pns	....	....	....	....	....	....	....	....	....	5.50	5.28	5.00
House Purch., Stocks, Over 5 years	60phm	....	....	....	....	....	....	....	....	....	5.07	4.59	4.38
House Purch., New Bus., 5-10 yrs	60phn	....	....	....	....	....	....	....	....	....	5.03	4.92	4.60
Corporations: Stocks, up to 1 year	60pcs	....	....	....	....	....	....	....	....	....	4.27	3.86	3.68
New Bus., Over € 1 mil.,up to 1 yr	60pcn	....	....	....	....	....	....	....	....	....	3.29	2.88	2.89
Government Bond Yield	61	6.69	6.47	5.30	4.79	4.29	4.09	....	....	....	....	....	....
Prices, Production, Labor		*Index Numbers (2000=100): Period Averages*											
Share Prices (1995=100)	62	115.3	100.0	105.2	119.9	135.2	....	....	....	....	....	....	....
Wholesale Prices	63	96.8	97.1	† 97.1	97.4	96.9	96.1	100.0	† 101.5	101.1	102.7	107.8	† 110.1
Consumer Prices	64	91.3	93.3	† 95.0	96.3	97.2	97.7	100.0	† 102.7	104.5	105.9	108.1	† 110.6
Harmonized CPI	64h	....	94.0	95.7	96.8	97.6	98.1	100.0	102.3	104.0	† 105.4	107.4	109.7
Wages (1996=100)	65a	....	....	90.9	92.9	95.2	98.0	100.0	102.2	104.8	106.8	108.5	111.4
Industrial Production	66	70.9	74.5	75.2	80.0	86.6	91.8	100.0	102.8	103.6	105.6	112.3	117.4
Employment	67	98.0	97.9	97.2	97.5	98.1	99.2	100.0	100.5	100.7	101.6	99.4	103.3
		Number in Thousands: Period Averages											
Labor Force	67d	3,286	3,284	3,278	3,294	3,313	3,330	3,328	3,352	3,388	3,425	3,442	3,483
Employment	67e	3,742	3,759	3,710	3,056	3,075	3,109	3,134	3,148	3,155	3,185	3,199	3,230
Unemployment	67c	215	216	231	233	238	222	194	204	232	240	244	253
Unemployment Rate (%)	67r	6.5	6.6	7.0	7.1	7.2	6.7	5.8	6.1	6.9	7.0	7.1	7.3
Intl. Transactions & Positions		*Billions of Schillings through 1998; Billions of Euros Beginning 1999*											
Exports	70	511.89	580.01	612.19	715.02	774.74	† 60.27	69.69	74.45	75.05	77.44	87.67	37.33
Imports, c.i.f.	71	629.42	668.03	712.76	790.25	842.13	† 65.32	74.94	78.66	77.19	78.10	87.51	37.97

Austria 122

		1994	1995	1996	1997	1998	1999	2000	2001	2002	2003	2004	2005
Balance of Payments		*Millions of US Dollars: Minus Sign Indicates Debit*											
Current Account, n.i.e.	78ald	−2,992	−5,448	−4,890	−5,221	−5,258	−6,655	−4,864	−3,636	565	−638	765	3,848
Goods: Exports f.o.b.	78aad	45,175	57,695	57,937	58,662	63,299	64,422	64,684	66,900	73,667	89,622	112,068	117,233
Goods: Imports f.o.b.	78abd	−53,089	−64,352	−65,252	−62,936	−66,983	−68,051	−67,421	−68,169	−70,080	−88,480	−109,020	−113,806
Trade Balance	78acd	−7,914	−6,656	−7,315	−4,274	−3,684	−3,629	−2,737	−1,269	3,588	1,141	3,048	3,427
Services: Credit	78add	28,019	32,211	33,977	29,605	29,759	31,306	31,342	33,352	35,386	42,964	48,994	53,439
Services: Debit	78aed	−20,743	−27,703	−29,331	−28,569	−27,398	−29,421	−29,653	−31,437	−34,996	−41,261	−46,284	−48,622
Balance on Goods & Services	78afd	−639	−2,149	−2,669	−3,239	−1,323	−1,745	−1,048	646	3,978	2,845	5,758	8,245
Income: Credit	78agd	7,074	8,900	9,852	10,393	9,957	12,673	11,992	12,031	13,816	16,169	18,728	23,213
Income: Debit	78ahd	−8,344	−10,498	−10,291	−10,682	−11,958	−15,552	−14,456	−15,111	−15,406	−17,357	−20,965	−24,958
Balance on Gds, Serv. & Inc.	78aid	−1,909	−3,746	−3,107	−3,527	−3,325	−4,624	−3,512	−2,435	2,389	1,656	3,521	6,499
Current Transfers, n.i.e.: Credit	78ajd	1,370	2,972	3,145	2,912	2,940	2,925	2,914	3,267	3,815	4,388	5,314	6,256
Current Transfers: Debit	78akd	−2,453	−4,674	−4,928	−4,605	−4,874	−4,956	−4,267	−4,468	−5,639	−6,683	−8,070	−8,907
Capital Account, n.i.e.	78bcd	−68	−62	78	26	−347	−265	−432	−529	−378	8	−345	−237
Capital Account: n.i.e.: Credit	78bad	676	540	591	590	483	555	530	483	1,012	897	760	737
Capital Account: Debit	78bbd	−744	−602	−513	−564	−831	−820	−962	−1,013	−1,390	−888	−1,105	−974
Financial Account, n.i.e.	78bjd	4,311	7,365	5,325	1,666	9,535	4,789	3,407	1,795	−4,713	−2,464	−1,812	−1,439
Direct Investment Abroad	78bdd	−1,256	−1,134	−1,848	−1,984	−2,794	−3,306	−5,599	−3,132	−5,745	−7,143	−7,427	−9,205
Dir. Invest. in Rep. Econ., n.i.e.	78bed	2,117	1,901	4,485	2,624	4,661	3,008	8,523	5,906	319	7,098	4,022	8,796
Portfolio Investment Assets	78bfd	−4,475	−2,836	−8,296	−10,157	−11,210	−29,216	−27,145	−10,955	−22,992	−18,654	−32,965	−43,951
Equity Securities	78bkd	−842	−545	−1,146	−2,405	−5,280	−5,281	−15,387	35	−3,062	−2,762	−4,070	−5,809
Debt Securities	78bld	−3,633	−2,291	−7,150	−7,752	−5,930	−23,935	−11,757	−10,990	−19,930	−15,893	−28,895	−38,143
Portfolio Investment Liab., n.i.e.	78bmd	4,253	12,292	5,607	10,956	17,942	26,364	30,360	16,699	18,790	23,440	32,511	30,131
Equity Securities	78bmd	1,304	1,262	2,652	2,610	1,005	2,131	3,436	−4,538	2,772	2,431	7,401	5,867
Debt Securities	78bnd	2,949	11,030	2,955	8,345	16,937	24,232	26,924	21,237	16,018	21,009	25,110	24,264
Financial Derivatives Assets	78bwd	−85	−133	215	−191	303	−517	−441	−143	−495	−666	−18	282
Financial Derivatives Liabilities	78bxd	....	....	....	223	−99	100	254	95	8	−77	−813	−129
Other Investment Assets	78bhd	−2,545	−9,923	719	−5,208	−690	−11,592	−16,334	−8,680	11,978	−16,518	−21,509	−30,007
Monetary Authorities	78bod	−17	−131	131	—	−115	−3,561	1,760	538	−139	362	−147	−29
General Government	78bpd	−183	−231	324	−647	−512	331	−1,003	−286	775	−243	−539	−135
Banks	78bqd	−1,307	−10,848	2,292	−3,873	924	−5,242	−13,593	−6,790	12,057	−12,765	−17,143	−27,616
Other Sectors	78brd	−1,039	1,287	−2,027	−687	−988	−3,121	−3,498	−2,143	−715	−3,872	−3,680	−2,228
Other Investment Liab., n.i.e.	78bid	6,303	7,199	4,442	5,403	1,423	19,948	13,790	2,005	−6,576	10,056	24,388	42,644
Monetary Authorities	78bsd	—	—	—	—	−1	6,684	−647	−6,130	−1,443	959	12,470	8,772
General Government	78btd	1,558	467	−715	−319	526	101	157	1,417	−392	53	1,419	5,032
Banks	78bud	4,584	6,077	5,142	5,695	1,695	10,740	11,721	5,812	−9,146	7,528	9,034	25,879
Other Sectors	78bvd	160	655	15	27	−797	2,422	2,559	905	4,406	1,515	1,464	2,962
Net Errors and Omissions	78cad	−417	−464	562	476	−447	−40	1,143	482	2,803	1,070	−457	−2,922
Overall Balance	78cbd	834	1,391	1,075	−3,053	3,482	−2,172	−746	−1,888	−1,723	−2,023	−1,849	−750
Reserves and Related Items	79dad	−834	−1,391	−1,075	3,053	−3,482	2,172	746	1,888	1,723	2,023	1,849	750
Reserve Assets	79dbd	−834	−1,391	−1,075	3,053	−3,482	2,172	746	1,888	1,723	2,023	1,849	750
Use of Fund Credit and Loans	79dcd	—	—	—	—	—	—	—	—	—	—	—	—
Exceptional Financing	79ded	....	....	....	....	....	....	....	....	....	....	—	....
International Investment Position		*Millions of US Dollars*											
Assets	79aad	137,955	160,211	161,785	166,135	194,856	225,924	261,554	267,909	335,373	443,661	548,552	....
Direct Investment Abroad	79abd	9,390	11,707	11,868	15,159	18,726	20,458	26,262	29,934	44,076	58,295	71,058	....
Portfolio Investment	79acd	22,673	27,389	33,303	44,051	58,747	93,299	115,680	112,458	152,484	207,035	263,843	....
Equity Securities	79add	4,941	5,868	6,454	11,502	17,225	28,936	42,698	31,190	30,047	44,149	54,781	....
Debt Securities	79aed	17,732	21,521	26,849	32,549	41,522	64,363	72,982	81,268	122,437	162,885	209,062	....
Financial Derivatives	79ald	109	169	219	201	—	—	—	—	—	—	—	....
Other Investment	79afd	82,040	95,054	89,730	84,853	90,959	93,236	101,985	109,906	125,631	165,602	201,463	....
Monetary Authorities	79agd	—	—	—	12	189	4,355	2,383	1,765	2,220	2,172	2,486	....
General Government	79ahd	1,021	1,209	1,607	2,039	2,828	2,078	2,853	2,934	2,648	3,347	3,808	....
Banks	79aid	70,380	83,267	77,716	73,651	77,267	74,447	80,897	87,993	99,280	130,339	158,266	....
Other Sectors	79ajd	10,639	10,577	10,407	9,150	10,676	12,357	15,852	17,214	21,483	29,744	36,902	....
Reserve Assets	79akd	23,742	25,893	26,666	21,871	26,423	18,931	17,627	15,611	13,181	12,729	12,188	....
Liabilities	79lad	155,538	189,790	189,264	198,918	236,547	262,994	299,033	315,205	379,038	480,881	594,538	....
Dir. Invest. in Rep. Economy	79lbd	13,246	17,536	18,258	19,694	23,837	23,991	31,280	35,164	44,618	56,529	66,321	....
Portfolio Investment	79lcd	69,469	89,473	87,676	97,091	121,674	139,054	161,082	171,393	218,273	281,670	348,767	....
Equity Securities	79ldd	5,379	6,989	9,056	15,662	15,623	14,745	19,569	14,920	17,235	26,470	45,214	....
Debt Securities	79led	64,090	82,484	78,620	81,430	106,052	124,309	141,512	156,473	201,037	255,201	303,554	....
Financial Derivatives	79lld	119	129	110	12	—	—	—	—	—	—	—	....
Other Investment	79lfd	72,705	82,653	83,221	82,121	91,036	99,949	106,672	108,648	116,147	142,681	179,450	....
Monetary Authorities	79lgd	18	20	9	—	—	6,141	5,639	−562	−2,296	−1,368	12,262	....
General Government	79lhd	3,045	4,074	3,478	2,955	3,719	3,564	3,412	4,319	4,438	5,191	7,048	....
Banks	79lid	57,681	65,385	68,267	68,669	76,438	79,628	84,906	91,597	93,536	113,030	130,130	....
Other Sectors	79ljd	11,961	13,174	11,466	10,496	10,879	10,616	12,715	13,294	20,470	25,828	30,011	....

Government Finance

Federal Government

Billions of Schillings through 1998; Millions of Euros Beginning 1999: Year Ending December 31

		1994	1995	1996	1997	1998							
Deficit (-) or Surplus	80	−128.81	† −119.88	−99.71	....	....	....	....	....	....	....	....	....
Revenue	81	815.10	† 845.40	903.40	....	....	....	....	....	....	....	....	....
Grants Received	81z	4.03	† 23.93	16.36	....	....	....	....	....	....	....	....	....
Expenditure	82	917.14	† 981.20	1,009.89	....	....	....	....	....	....	....	....	....
Lending Minus Repayments	83	30.80	† 1.01	5.86	....	....	....	....	....	....	....	....	....
Financing													
Net Borrowing	84	121.24	† 113.75	127.56	....	....	....	....	....	....	....	....	....
Net Borrowing: Domestic	84a	89.13	....	....	....	....	....	....	....	....	....	....	....
Net Borrowing: Foreign	85a	47.25	....	....	....	....	....	....	....	....	....	....	....
Use of Cash Balances	87	7.57	† 6.13	−27.85	....	....	....	....	....	....	....	....	....
Debt: Domestic	88a	975.25	† 1,053.73	1,120.66	1,190.76	† 1,384.46	....	....	....	....	....	....	....
Debt: Foreign	89a	260.94	† 296.63	296.47	304.93	† 188.43	....	....	....	....	....	....	....

General Government

As Percent of Gross Domestic Product

Austria 122

National Accounts		1994	1995	1996	1997	1998	1999	2000	2001	2002	2003	2004	2005
		Billions of Schillings through 1998; Billions of Euros Beginning 1999											
Househ.Cons.Expend.,incl.NPISHs....	96f	1,344.7	† 1,378.1	1,452.8	1,474.6	1,502.9	† 112.0	117.4	121.6	123.9	127.7	133.0	137.6
Government Consumption Expend...	91f	459.5	485.3	497.6	482.2	498.2	† 38.0	38.7	38.9	40.1	41.4	42.7	44.5
Gross Fixed Capital Formation.........	93e	532.4	† 534.1	553.3	568.2	592.2	† 44.2	47.9	47.7	45.1	48.1	49.2	50.3
Changes in Inventories....................	93i	−2.3	29.9	16.0	17.3	20.8	† 2.5	1.3	1.0	.7	1.1	1.0	.7
Exports of Goods and Services..........	90c	781.1	847.0	897.5	1,012.2	1,104.2	† 85.3	95.6	103.3	107.7	109.6	121.7	133.1
Imports of Goods and Services (-).....	98c	798.8	† 853.8	917.4	1,006.5	1,066.2	† 81.9	92.7	97.9	97.2	101.5	111.7	121.4
Gross Domestic Product (GDP)........	99b	2,324.7	† 2,415.3	2,502.6	2,547.6	2,647.3	† 200.0	210.4	215.9	220.8	226.2	235.8	245.1
Net Primary Income from Abroad.....	98.n	−18.0	−34.7	−17.2	−26.8	−28.7	† −4.2	−4.0	−5.2	−2.7	−2.0	−2.8	−2.5
Gross National Income (GNI)............	99a	2,307.3	2,373.8	2,477.3	2,509.7	2,605.6	† 195.8	206.3	210.7	218.1	224.2	233.0	242.6
Net Current Transf.from Abroad.......	98t	....	....	....	....	....	† −3.4	−4.1	−3.1	−3.9	−4.7	....	....
Gross Nat'l Disposable Inc.(GNDI)....	99i	....	....	....	....	....	† 192.4	202.3	207.6	214.2	219.5	....	....
Gross Saving....................................	99s	....	....	....	....	....	† 41.4	45.1	45.9	49.6	49.8	....	....
Consumption of Fixed Capital..........	99cf	319.3	333.1	346.7	356.5	368.6	....	....	....	....	....	....	....
GDP Volume 2000 Ref., Chained.....	99b.p	2,458.0	2,504.9	2,570.5	2,617.8	2,711.0	† 203.6	210.4	212.1	214.2	217.2	222.5	226.8
GDP Volume (2000=100)................	99bvp	84.9	86.5	88.8	90.4	93.6	† 96.8	100.0	100.8	101.8	103.2	105.8	107.8
GDP Deflator (2000=100)................	99bip	94.6	† 96.4	97.4	97.3	97.7	† 98.2	100.0	101.8	103.1	104.2	106.0	108.1
		Millions: Midyear Estimates											
Population.................................	99z	8.00	8.05	8.08	8.09	8.09	8.09	8.10	8.11	8.13	8.15	8.17	8.19

Azerbaijan, Republic of   912

		1994	1995	1996	1997	1998	1999	2000	2001	2002	2003	2004	2005
Exchange Rates						*Manat per SDR: End of Period*							
Official Rate	aa	1.2210	1.3200	1.1786	1.0492	1.0954	1.2018	1.1896	1.2002	1.3304	1.4631	1.5229	1.3129
						Manat per US Dollar: End of Period (ae) Period Average (rf)							
Official Rate	ae	.8364	.8880	.8196	.7776	.7780	.8756	.9130	.9550	.9786	.9846	.9806	.9186
Official Rate	rf	.3140	.8827	.8603	.7971	.7738	.8240	.8948	.9313	.9722	.9821	.9827	.9454
Fund Position						*Millions of SDRs: End of Period*							
Quota	2f.s	117.00	117.00	117.00	117.00	117.00	160.90	160.90	160.90	160.90	160.90	160.90	160.90
SDRs	1b.s	—	.84	14.48	4.14	.08	5.15	5.07	1.98	.51	12.14	9.36	9.74
Reserve Position in the Fund	1c.s	.01	.01	.01	.01	.01	.01	.01	.01	.01	.01	.01	.01
Total Fund Cred.&Loans Outstg	2tl	—	67.86	121.68	197.73	228.14	296.73	257.73	234.90	205.11	174.47	134.18	114.48
International Liquidity						*Millions of US Dollars Unless Otherwise Indicated: End of Period*							
Total Reserves minus Gold	1l.d	2.03	120.88	211.28	466.09	447.33	672.59	679.61	724.98	720.47	802.84	1,075.08	1,177.74
SDRs	1b.d	—	1.25	20.82	5.59	.11	7.07	6.60	2.49	.70	18.03	14.53	13.91
Reserve Position in the Fund	1c.d	.01	.01	.01	.01	.01	.01	.01	.01	.01	.01	.02	.01
Foreign Exchange	1d.d	2.02	119.62	190.45	460.49	447.20	665.50	672.99	722.48	719.76	784.79	1,060.53	1,163.82
Gold (Million Fine Troy Ounces)	1ad	—	—	.01	—	—	—	—	—	—	—	—	—
Gold (National Valuation)	1and	—	—	2.38	1.38	1.37	—	—	—	—	—	—	—
Monetary Authorities:Other Assets	3..d	1.93	1.57	1.91	1.53	1.16	1.03	.05		.17	—	—	.13
Other Liab	4..d	2.87	1.75	1.33	1.37	13.28	12.34	12.01	.30	1.31	.87	.76	.95
Deposit Money Banks: Assets	7a.d	135.30	167.69	156.17	154.48	97.27	152.11	379.46	193.13	211.78	226.59	204.20	291.32
Liabilities	7b.d	41.05	33.95	75.89	53.16	56.08	69.32	96.54	92.58	110.60	109.46	90.12	179.19
Monetary Authorities						*Millions of Manat: End of Period*							
Foreign Assets	11	3.32	108.74	176.68	364.69	† 347.92	589.76	620.53	† 854.04	709.89	790.94	1,054.90	1,082.09
Claims on Central Government	12a	85.77	66.69	83.35	72.05	† 380.79	512.67	503.70	† 158.03	144.51	130.55	141.37	139.58
Claims on Nonfin.Pub.Enterprises	12c	.20	1.70	1.79	1.75	† .70	.69		† —	—	—	—	—
Claims on Private Sector	12d					† —				.07	.44	.51	.55
Claims on Deposit Money Banks	12e	28.34	210.48	178.73	173.09	† 150.03	149.25	140.25	† 20.20	17.28	47.32	62.94	73.32
Reserve Money	14	65.14	182.23	214.21	302.82	† 236.31	273.88	353.46	† 359.48	409.92	506.11	833.63	885.81
of which: Currency Outside DMBs	14a	55.23	120.48	173.09	234.10	† 185.21	227.17	269.96	† 293.80	333.75	408.18	477.79	547.41
Time, Savings,& Fgn.Currency Dep	15	.18	—	.01	.01	† —	—	—	† .41	2.01	10.69	.08	.20
Liabs. of Central Bank: Securities	16ac					† —			† —		.01	19.89	31.40
Foreign Liabilities	16c	2.40	91.13	144.50	208.52	† 260.25	367.41	317.55	† 282.21	274.16	256.11	205.08	151.18
Central Government Deposits	16d	47.17	89.54	66.89	73.53	† 363.44	567.47	511.26	† 297.62	122.52	118.10	121.45	191.41
Capital Accounts	17a	8.97	81.04	80.06	225.72	† 39.23	48.07	66.66	† 73.69	64.84	86.36	96.15	60.73
Other Items (Net)	17r	−6.23	−56.32	−65.13	−199.01	† −19.80	−4.47	15.53	† 18.86	−1.69	−8.14	−16.56	−25.18
Deposit Money Banks						*Millions of Manat: End of Period*							
Reserves	20	8.78	60.63	48.55	60.39	40.81	35.57	† 78.30	† 63.70	72.24	98.38	350.07	332.88
Claims on Mon.Author.: Securities	20c								† —			18.39	30.26
Foreign Assets	21	113.16	148.91	127.99	120.12	75.67	133.19	† 346.45	† 184.44	207.25	223.10	200.24	267.61
Claims on Central Government	22a	10.30	2.50	6.41	10.54	6.01	13.89	† 55.20	† 64.92	73.21	66.71	14.36	24.07
Claims on Nonfin.Pub.Enterprises	22c	124.71	280.72	343.96	327.10	331.77	344.44	† 163.52	† 99.32	93.70	98.38	161.88	274.12
Claims on Private Sector	22d	12.49	25.30	31.86	77.36	106.01	111.94	† 278.35	† 265.51	332.43	470.79	761.58	1,146.69
Claims on Nonbank Financial Insts	22g	.01	—	—	—	—	—	† .65	† .39	.11	20.13	20.77	23.07
Demand Deposits	24	18.74	50.26	50.02	64.76	40.60	43.17	† 43.64	† 43.75	58.55	91.64	175.10	202.80
Time,Savings,& Fgn.Currency Dep	25	134.87	91.11	83.75	130.34	132.49	165.21	† 454.66	† 348.71	392.38	520.28	853.06	1,083.53
Restricted Deposits	26b	—	—	—	—	—	—	† —	† 30.40	42.71	33.45	25.47	90.86
Foreign Liabilities	26c	34.33	30.15	62.20	41.34	43.63	60.69	† 88.14	† 88.41	108.23	107.77	88.37	164.61
Central Government Deposits	26d	20.32	19.64	44.46	6.04	16.45	16.99	† 37.08	† 10.25	5.18	12.53	62.09	39.46
Credit from Monetary Authorities	26g	11.31	178.65	156.47	167.60	123.17	118.58	† 130.84	† 19.29	17.26	47.21	62.80	67.23
Liab. to Nonbank Financial Insts	26j	.09	.57	1.49	1.37	1.11	.43	† —	† 3.17	5.47	21.12	45.63	90.51
Capital Accounts	27a	24.29	71.06	128.20	166.37	204.00	230.42	† 146.44	† 134.07	158.20	179.61	248.93	339.45
Other Items (Net)	27r	25.50	76.64	32.20	17.70	−1.18	3.53	† 21.66	† .23	−9.03	−36.11	−34.16	20.22
Monetary Survey						*Millions of Manat: End of Period*							
Foreign Assets (Net)	31n	79.75	136.37	97.97	234.96	† 119.71	294.85	† 561.28	† 667.86	534.75	650.15	961.69	1,033.92
Domestic Credit	32	166.00	267.73	356.01	409.24	† 445.39	399.16	† 453.08	† 280.30	516.34	656.37	916.94	1,377.18
Claims on Central Govt. (Net)	32an	28.58	−39.99	−21.60	3.02	† 6.91	−57.91	† 10.56	† −84.92	90.03	66.62	−27.80	−67.23
Claims on Nonfin.Pub.Enterprises	32c	124.92	282.41	345.75	328.85	† 332.47	345.13	† 163.52	† 99.32	93.70	98.38	161.88	274.12
Claims on Private Sector	32d	12.49	25.30	31.86	77.36	† 106.01	111.94	† 278.35	† 265.51	332.50	471.24	762.09	1,147.23
Claims on Nonbank Fin. Insts	32g	.01	—	—	—	† —	—	† .65	† .39	.11	20.13	20.77	23.07
Money	34	74.48	171.68	223.95	304.82	† 236.65	278.02	† 313.96	† 338.62	393.45	499.82	652.90	750.22
Quasi-Money	35	135.05	91.11	83.75	130.35	† 132.49	165.21	† 454.66	† 349.12	394.39	530.97	853.14	1,083.72
Liabs. of Central Bank: Securities	36ac	—	—	—	—	† —	—	—	† —	—	.01	1.50	1.15
Restricted Deposits	36b	—	—	—	—	† —	—	—	† 30.40	42.71	33.45	25.47	90.86
Liab. to Nonbank Financial Insts	36j	.09	.57	1.49	1.37	† 1.11	.43	† —	† 3.17	5.47	21.12	45.63	90.51
Capital Accounts	37a	33.27	152.10	208.26	392.09	† 243.23	278.49	† 213.11	† 207.76	223.03	265.97	345.08	400.18
Other Items (Net)	37r	2.87	−11.34	−63.47	−184.43	† −48.39	−28.14	† 32.63	† 19.08	−7.97	−44.82	−45.10	−5.54
Money plus Quasi-Money	35l	209.52	262.78	307.70	435.17	† 369.15	443.23	† 768.62	† 687.74	787.84	1,030.79	1,506.04	1,833.94
Money (National Definitions)						*Millions of Manat: End of Period*							
Reserve Money	19mb	....	147.26	197.08	267.86	211.42	251.32	308.38	336.12	374.38	463.20	640.04	687.76
M1	59ma	....	185.00	234.74	307.56	240.49	278.01	321.90	293.80	393.48	499.82	657.26	747.84
M2	59mb	....	191.52	240.84	311.25	243.70	280.86	332.22	337.50	406.42	518.44	683.60	791.82
Interest Rates						*Percent Per Annum*							
Refinancing Rate	60	200.00	80.00	20.00	12.00	14.00	10.00	10.00	10.00	7.00	7.00	7.00	9.00
Treasury Bill Rate	60c	....	....	....	12.23	14.10	18.31	16.73	16.51	14.12	8.00	4.62	7.52
Deposit Rate	60l	....	....	....	....	....	12.08	12.90	8.46	8.66	9.54	9.18	8.52
Deposit Rate (Foreign Currency)	60l.f	....	....	....	....	....	10.75	11.12	9.51	9.34	8.83	9.09	9.32
Lending Rate	60p	....	....	....	....	....	19.48	19.66	19.71	17.37	15.46	15.72	17.03
Lending Rate (Foreign Currency)	60p.f	....	....	....	....	....	16.27	17.98	18.67	18.69	18.64	19.68	19.14

		1994	1995	1996	1997	1998	1999	2000	2001	2002	2003	2004	2005
Prices and Labor						*Percent Change over Previous Period*							
Consumer Prices	64.xx	1,664.5	411.7	19.9	3.7	−.8	−8.5	1.9	1.5	2.8	2.2	6.8	9.5
						Number in Thousands: Period Averages							
Employment	67e	3,631.3	3,613.0	3,686.7	3,694.1	3,701.5	3,702.8	3,704.5	3,715.0	3,726.5	3,747.0	3,809.1	....
Unemployment	67c	23.6	28.3	31.9	38.3	42.3	45.2	43.7	48.5	51.0	54.4	56.0	....
Unemployment Rate (%)	67r	.7	.8	.9	1.0	1.1	1.2	1.2	1.3	1.3	1.4	1.4	....
Intl. Transactions & Positions						*Millions of US Dollars*							
Exports	70..d	652.7	637.2	631.2	781.3	606.2	929.7	1,745.2	2,314.3	2,167.4	2,590.4	3,615.4	4,347.2
Imports, cif	71..d	777.9	667.7	960.6	794.3	1,076.5	1,035.9	1,172.1	1,430.9	1,665.5	2,626.2	3,516.0	4,211.2
Balance of Payments						*Millions of US Dollars: Minus Sign Indicates Debit*							
Current Account, n.i.e.	78ald	....	−400.7	−931.2	−915.8	−1,364.5	−599.7	−167.8	−51.8	−768.4	−2,020.9	−2,589.2	167.3
Goods: Exports f.o.b.	78aad	....	612.3	643.7	808.3	677.8	1,025.2	1,858.3	2,078.9	2,304.9	2,624.6	3,743.0	7,649.0
Goods: Imports f.o.b.	78abd	....	−985.4	−1,337.6	−1,375.2	−1,723.9	−1,433.4	−1,539.0	−1,465.1	−1,823.3	−2,723.1	−3,581.7	−4,349.9
Trade Balance	78acd	....	−373.1	−693.9	−566.9	−1,046.2	−408.2	319.3	613.9	481.6	−98.5	161.3	3,299.1
Services: Credit	78add	....	172.4	149.3	341.8	331.7	256.8	259.8	289.8	362.1	432.0	492.0	683.0
Services: Debit	78aed	....	−304.6	−440.9	−726.0	−700.8	−485.1	−484.5	−664.9	−1,297.7	−2,046.5	−2,730.4	−2,653.0
Balance on Goods & Services	78afd	....	−505.4	−985.6	−951.1	−1,415.2	−636.5	94.6	238.8	−454.0	−1,713.0	−2,077.1	1,329.1
Income: Credit	78agd	....	9.9	15.1	22.8	38.3	11.0	55.9	41.5	37.1	52.6	65.3	201.8
Income: Debit	78ahd	....	−16.0	−27.2	−32.3	−51.6	−56.0	−391.4	−408.7	−421.8	−494.7	−765.9	−1,847.4
Balance on Gds, Serv., & Inc.	78aid	....	−511.4	−997.7	−960.6	−1,428.5	−681.5	−240.9	−128.4	−838.7	−2,155.0	−2,777.7	−316.6
Current Transfers, n.i.e.: Credit	78ajd	....	129.3	107.2	95.7	145.0	134.5	135.0	176.5	228.2	225.1	262.6	626.2
Current Transfers: Debit	78akd	....	−18.5	−40.7	−50.9	−80.9	−52.8	−62.0	−99.9	−157.9	−90.9	−74.1	−142.3
Capital Account, n.i.e.	78bcd	....	−1.6	—	−10.2	−.7	....	....	....	−28.7	−23.1	−4.1	40.9
Capital Account, n.i.e.: Credit	78bad	....	....	....	....	....	....	....	....	18.4	15.0	24.0	70.2
Capital Account: Debit	78bbd	....	−1.6	—	−10.2	−.7	....	....	....	−47.1	−38.1	−28.1	−29.3
Financial Account, n.i.e.	78bjd	....	400.3	822.5	1,092.1	1,326.0	690.2	493.4	126.0	918.0	2,279.7	2,960.2	78.0
Direct Investment Abroad	78bdd	....	....	....	....	....	....	−.8	....	−325.6	−933.3	−1,204.8	−1,220.8
Dir. Invest. in Rep. Econ., n.i.e.	78bed	....	330.1	627.3	1,114.8	1,023.0	510.3	129.9	226.5	1,392.4	3,285.0	3,556.1	1,679.9
Portfolio Investment Assets	78bfd	....	−1.7	—	1.1	—	....	....	....	−.4	—	−18.1	−47.8
Equity Securities	78bkd	....	....	....	....	....	....	....	....	....	....	1.9	—
Debt Securities	78bld	....	−1.7	—	1.1	—	....	....	....	−.4	—	−20.0	−47.8
Portfolio Investment Liab., n.i.e.	78bgd	....	—	—	—	.4	....	....	....	....	....	....	78.3
Equity Securities	78bmd	....	....	....	....	....	....	....	....	....	....	....	
Debt Securities	78bnd	....	—	—	—	.4	....	....	....	....	....	....	78.3
Financial Derivatives Assets	78bwd												
Financial Derivatives Liabilities	78bxd	....	....	....	....	....	....	....	....	....	....	—	—
Other Investment Assets	78bhd	....	−22.1	−216.8	−102.6	22.3	−81.0	−114.2	−394.0	−302.9	−169.2	−360.4	−1,365.3
Monetary Authorities	78bod	....	....	....	....	....	....	....	....	....	....	1.8	—
General Government	78bpd	....	....	....	....	....	....	....	−220.5	−200.7	−109.4	−123.5	−475.7
Banks	78bqd	....	−19.6	−136.9	5.3	62.4	−44.2	7.1	−77.7	−18.3	−16.7	20.1	−83.7
Other Sectors	78brd	....	−2.5	−79.8	−107.9	−40.1	−36.8	−121.2	−95.8	−83.9	−43.2	−258.8	−806.0
Other Investment Liab., n.i.e.	78bid	....	94.1	412.0	78.8	280.4	260.9	478.4	293.5	154.4	97.2	987.4	953.7
Monetary Authorities	78bsd	....	—	—	—	—	—	—	—	30.3	34.4	—	−1.0
General Government	78btd	....	30.0	—	70.8	75.6	161.6	246.2	138.6	17.2	32.4	34.8	37.5
Banks	78bud	....	−.3	26.5	−18.8	−1.7	−.1	−22.9	3.0	16.9	−.2	−16.4	46.7
Other Sectors	78bvd	....	64.3	385.5	26.8	206.5	99.3	255.0	151.9	90.0	30.5	969.0	870.4
Net Errors and Omissions	78cad	....	59.7	23.6	−27.0	−20.1	42.4	—	−.9	−86.7	−111.8	−49.9	−125.7
Overall Balance	78cbd	....	57.8	−85.0	139.2	−59.2	132.9	325.6	73.4	34.2	123.8	317.0	160.5
Reserves and Related Items	79dad	....	−57.8	85.0	−139.2	59.2	−132.9	−325.6	−73.4	−34.2	−123.8	−317.0	−160.5
Reserve Assets	79dbd	....	−161.6	7.1	−244.2	18.7	−228.5	−274.2	−44.1	5.0	−82.0	−257.2	−132.0
Use of Fund Credit and Loans	79dcd	....	103.8	77.9	105.0	40.5	95.6	−51.4	−29.3	−39.2	−41.8	−59.8	−28.5
Exceptional Financing	79ded	....	....	....	....	....	....	....	....	....	....	....	....
International Investment Position						*Millions of US Dollars*							
Assets	79aad	....	....	....	....	....	....	....	....	2,000.9	3,154.6	4,937.3	7,456.4
Direct Investment Abroad	79abd	....	....	....	....	....	—	.8	.8	326.4	1,259.7	2,464.5	3,685.3
Portfolio Investment	79acd	....	....	....	....	....	—	....	....	.4	.4	20.4	84.6
Equity Securities	79add	....	....	....	....	....	—	....	....	—	—	—	—
Debt Securities	79aed	....	....	....	....	....	—	....	....	—	.4	20.4	84.6
Financial derivatives	79ald	....	....	....	....	....	....	....	....	—	—	—	—
Other Investment	79afd	....	....	....	....	....	153.4	162.5	734.3	953.6	1,091.7	1,376.4	2,508.8
Monetary Authorities	79agd	....	....	....	....	....	....	....	....	—	—	—	—
General Government	79ahd	....	....	....	....	....	....	....	491.5	692.2	815.6	971.8	1,394.0
Banks	79aid	....	....	....	....	....	....	....	190.7	209.3	223.8	203.7	287.4
Other Sectors	79ajd	....	....	....	....	....	....	....	52.1	52.1	52.3	200.9	827.4
Reserve Assets	79akd	....	....	....	....	....	675.8	950.8	725.4	720.5	802.8	1,076.0	1,177.7
Liabilities	79lad	....	....	....	....	....	....	....	....	7,279.3	10,903.6	14,395.4	16,805.1
Dir. Invest. in Rep. Economy	79lbd	....	....	....	....	....	3,099.5	3,735.2	3,961.7	5,354.1	8,639.1	11,482.4	12,757.5
Portfolio Investment	79lcd	....	....	....	....	....	—	....	—	—	—	—	97.1
Equity Securities	79ldd	....	....	....	....	....	—	....	—	—	—	—	—
Debt Securities	79led	....	....	....	....	....	—	....	—	—	—	—	97.1
Financial Derivatives	79lld	....	....	....	....	....	....	....	—	—	—	—	—
Other Investment	79lfd	....	....	....	....	....	1,281.5	1,463.6	1,723.4	1,925.2	2,264.5	2,913.0	3,950.5
Monetary Authorities	79lgd	....	....	....	....	....	....	....	446.9	453.9	476.9	455.0	392.2
General Government	79lhd	....	....	....	....	....	....	....	56.8	87.3	131.4	237.0	351.9
Banks	79lid	....	....	....	....	....	....	....	98.2	115.2	112.5	96.1	101.6
Other Sectors	79ljd	....	....	....	....	....	....	....	1,121.5	1,268.8	1,543.7	2,124.9	3,104.8

Azerbaijan, Republic of 912

		1994	1995	1996	1997	1998	1999	2000	2001	2002	2003	2004	2005
Government Finance					*Millions of Manat: Year Ending December 31*								
Deficit(-)/ or Surplus........................	80	−41.85	−109.01	−81.20	−68.38	−124.60	−95.90	....	....	....	....	....	....
Total Revenue and Grants..............	81y	95.94	384.05	392.15	480.40	628.60	676.03	....	....	....	....	....	....
Revenue....................................	81	95.94	384.05	376.20	470.00	615.20	663.39	....	....	....	....	....	....
Grants.......................................	81z	—	—	15.95	10.40	13.39	12.64	....	....	....	....	....	....
Exp. & Lending Minus Repay..........	82z	137.79	493.06	473.35	548.78	753.19	771.93	....	....	....	....	....	....
Expenditure..............................	82	137.79	450.86	456.73	605.72	798.62	852.19	....	....	....	....	....	....
Lending Minus Repayments..........	83	—	42.19	16.61	−56.93	−45.43	−80.26	....	....	....	....	....	....
Total Financing...............................	80h	41.85	109.01	81.18	68.36	124.60	95.89	....	....	....	....	....	....
National Accounts						*Millions of Manat*							
Househ.Cons.Expend.,incl.NPISHs....	96f	....	1,895	2,514	2,548	3,015	3,171	3,473	3,703	3,813	4,286	4,761	4,758
Government Consumption Expend...	91f	....	177	211	202	259	279	280	292	752	885	1,100	1,161
Gross Fixed Capital Formation..........	93e	....	334	795	1,168	1,222	1,076	1,092	1,216	2,066	3,779	4,923	5,397
Changes in Inventories....................	93i	....	174	−3	−87	−74	−76	−116	−117	30	21	24	27
Exports of Goods and Services..........	90c	....	693	681	917	781	1,056	1,895	2,206	2,593	3,002	4,162	7,465
Imports of Goods and Services........	98c	....	1,140	1,528	1,675	1,876	1,580	1,811	1,984	3,034	4,684	6,203	6,694
Gross Domestic Product (GDP).........	99b	....	2,134	2,733	3,158	3,441	3,775	4,718	5,316	6,062	7,147	8,530	11,876
Statistical Discrepancy.....................	99bs	....	—	63	85	114	−151	−96	—	−158	−142	−237	−238
						Millions: Midyear Estimates							
Population..............................	99z	7.69	7.79	7.88	7.96	8.02	8.09	8.14	8.20	8.25	8.30	8.35	8.41

		1994	1995	1996	1997	1998	1999	2000	2001	2002	2003	2004	2005
Exchange Rates							_Bahamian Dollars per SDR: End of Period_							
Principal Rate..........aa=..........	wa	1.4599	1.4865	1.4380	1.3493	1.4080	1.3725	1.3029	1.2567	1.3595	1.4860	1.5530	1.4293
				Bahamian Dollars per US Dollar: End of Period (we and xe) Period Average (xf)									
Principal Rate..........ae=..........	we	1.0000	1.0000	1.0000	1.0000	1.0000	1.0000	1.0000	1.0000	1.0000	1.0000	1.0000	1.0000
Secondary Rate....................	xe	1.2250	1.2250	1.2250	1.2250	1.2250	1.2250	1.2250	1.2250	1.2250	1.2250	1.2250	1.2250
Secondary Rate....................	xf	1.2250	1.2250	1.2250	1.2250	1.2250	1.2250	1.2250	1.2250	1.2250	1.2250	1.2250	1.2250
					Index Numbers (2000=100): Period Averages								
Principal Rate....................	ahx	100.0	100.0	100.0	100.0	100.0	100.0	100.0	100.0	100.0	100.0	100.0	100.0
Nominal Effective Exchange Rate.....	nec	85.3	84.9	87.1	92.8	99.1	97.3	100.0	103.5	101.9	96.0	92.5	90.9
Real Effective Exchange Rate..........	rec	94.3	91.1	91.6	95.5	100.8	98.4	100.0	102.9	101.7	96.5	91.6	89.1
Fund Position							_Millions of SDRs: End of Period_							
Quota....................	2f.s	94.9	94.9	94.9	94.9	94.9	130.3	130.3	130.3	130.3	130.3	130.3	130.3
SDRs....................	1b.s	—	—	—	—	—	—	—	.1	.1	.1	—	—
Reserve Position in the Fund..........	1c.s	6.2	6.2	6.2	6.2	6.2	6.2	6.2	6.2	6.2	6.2	6.3	6.3
Total Fund Cred.&Loans Outstg........	2tl	—	—	—	—	—	—	—	—	—	—	—	—
International Liquidity					_Millions of US Dollars Unless Otherwise Indicated: End of Period_								
Total Reserves minus Gold..............	1l.d	176.6	179.2	171.4	227.0	346.5	410.5	349.6	319.3	380.6	491.1	674.4	586.3
SDRs....................	1b.d	—	—	—	—	—	—	—	.1	.1	.1	—	—
Reserve Position in the Fund..........	1c.d	9.1	9.3	9.0	8.4	8.8	8.6	8.1	7.8	8.5	9.3	9.7	8.9
Foreign Exchange....................	1d.d	167.5	169.9	162.4	218.6	337.7	401.9	341.4	311.3	372.1	481.8	664.7	577.3
Deposit Money Banks: Assets..........	7a.d	42,817	35,144	41,384	41,310	46,329	58,682	77,649	103,669	136,339	89,838	70,339	81,465
Liabilities....................	7b.d	43,219	35,542	41,796	41,662	47,053	59,127	78,346	104,136	136,804	90,451	70,878	81,960
Other Banking Insts.: Assets..........	7e.d	2,232	2,450	2,646	2,836	2,685	2,785	2,907	2,293	2,490	2,411	2,398	2,553
Liabilities....................	7f.d	1,802	1,881	2,084	2,384	2,498	2,626	2,644	2,036	2,130	2,077	1,825	2,047
Monetary Authorities							_Millions of Bahamian Dollars: End of Period_							
Foreign Assets....................	11	170	171	163	219	339	404	343	312	373	484	668	579
Claims on Central Government........	12a	144	149	153	141	62	73	129	190	182	115	150	150
Claims on Deposit Money Banks......	12e	—	—	—	1	—	—	—	—	—	—	—	—
Claims on Nonbank Financial Insts...	12g	3	4	3	4	5	8	9	8	8	8	8	8
Reserve Money....................	14	230	236	230	264	315	381	373	411	459	489	643	591
of which: Currency Outside DMBs..	14a	89	93	97	110	126	149	152	154	155	160	177	195
Central Government Deposits..........	16d	14	8	8	17	4	14	11	9	12	24	91	51
Capital Accounts....................	17a	77	78	80	84	87	90	98	95	97	96	96	104
Other Items (Net)....................	17r	−3	2	2	1	—	—	−1	−5	−5	−2	−4	−9
Deposit Money Banks							_Millions of Bahamian Dollars: End of Period_							
Reserves....................	20	123	128	118	146	183	226	208	250	292	318	457	384
Foreign Assets....................	21	42,817	35,144	41,384	41,310	46,329	58,682	77,649	103,669	136,339	89,838	70,339	81,465
Claims on Central Government........	22a	296	303	313	356	458	489	454	493	547	487	494	613
Claims on Official Entities................	22bx	73	77	82	79	128	158	126	133	203	347	314	266
Claims on Private Sector....................	22d	1,592	1,777	1,953	2,488	2,767	3,072	3,511	3,782	3,926	3,948	4,200	4,807
Claims on Other Banking Insts........	22f	20	18	16	27	29	25	33	54	65	65	105	107
Demand Deposits....................	24	309	336	334	398	460	588	630	605	644	714	860	1,002
Time, Savings,& Fgn.Currency Dep...	25	1,326	1,447	1,551	1,950	2,275	2,423	2,668	2,870	2,934	2,999	3,193	3,493
Bonds....................	26ab	10	9	8	6	6	8	6	8	9	5	1	—
Foreign Liabilities....................	26c	43,219	35,542	41,796	41,662	47,053	59,127	78,346	104,136	136,804	90,451	70,878	81,960
Central Government Deposits..........	26d	36	44	59	65	66	68	71	58	72	94	93	88
Credit from Monetary Authorities.....	26g	—	—	—	1	—	1	1	1	1	1	1	1
Liabilities to Other Banking Insts......	26i	27	40	43	43	42	34	37	48	43	43	38	49
Capital Accounts....................	27a	−26	2	25	250	−28	403	228	624	860	903	1,047	1,221
Other Items (Net)....................	27r	19	29	51	31	20	−1	−5	32	5	−206	−205	−172
Monetary Survey							_Millions of Bahamian Dollars: End of Period_							
Foreign Assets (Net)....................	31n	−231	−227	−248	−133	−385	−41	−355	−154	−92	−129	128	84
Domestic Credit....................	32	2,078	2,277	2,454	3,014	3,379	3,743	4,180	4,594	4,847	4,852	5,086	5,811
Claims on Central Govt. (Net)........	32an	390	401	399	415	450	481	501	617	646	485	460	624
Claims on Official Entities..............	32bx	73	77	82	79	128	158	126	133	203	347	314	266
Claims on Private Sector.............	32d	1,592	1,777	1,953	2,488	2,767	3,072	3,511	3,782	3,926	3,948	4,200	4,807
Claims on Other Banking Insts.......	32f	20	18	16	27	29	25	33	54	65	65	105	107
Claims on Nonbank Financial Inst..	32g	3	4	3	4	5	8	9	8	8	8	9	8
Money....................	34	416	445	447	517	593	748	798	767	811	884	1,047	1,207
Quasi-Money....................	35	1,326	1,447	1,551	1,950	2,275	2,423	2,668	2,870	2,934	2,999	3,193	3,493
Bonds....................	36ab	10	9	8	6	6	8	6	8	9	5	1	—
Liabilities to Other Banking Insts......	36i	27	40	43	43	42	34	37	48	43	43	38	49
Capital Accounts....................	37a	51	80	104	334	59	494	326	719	958	999	1,143	1,325
Other Items (Net)....................	37r	15	30	52	31	19	−5	−9	28	1	−207	−208	−179
Money plus Quasi-Money....................	35l	1,743	1,892	1,998	2,467	2,868	3,171	3,466	3,637	3,745	3,883	4,241	4,700
Other Banking Institutions							_Millions of Bahamian Dollars End of Period_							
Reserves....................	40	13	13	13	3	3	4	5	4	5	6	6	6
Foreign Assets....................	41	2,232	2,450	2,646	2,836	2,685	2,785	2,907	2,293	2,490	2,411	2,398	2,553
Claims on Central Government........	42a	22	22	22	3	3	4	4	3	3	4	4	5
Claims on Private Sector....................	42d	267	283	297	63	69	87	108	120	144	147	140	147
Claims on Deposit Money Banks......	42e	27	32	43	45	43	59	32	47	40	46	54	55
Demand Deposits....................	44	8	11	12	4	5	5	8	8	9	12	10	25
Time, Savings,& Fgn.Currency Dep...	45	243	248	260	39	41	66	78	71	84	97	94	89
Foreign Liabilities....................	46c	1,802	1,881	2,084	2,384	2,498	2,626	2,644	2,036	2,130	2,077	1,825	2,047
Central Government Deposits..........	46d	—	—	—	—	—	—	—	—	—	—	—	—
Credit from Monetary Authorities.....	46g	—	—	—	10	15	—	10	—	—	—	—	—
Credit from Deposit Money Banks...	46h	13	11	12	23	26	17	25	46	56	48	86	86
Capital Accounts....................	47a	323	317	285	252	231	253	318	359	404	381	613	545
Other Items (Net)....................	47r	172	333	369	239	−12	−27	−26	−52	−2	−1	−27	−27

		1994	1995	1996	1997	1998	1999	2000	2001	2002	2003	2004	2005
Banking Survey							*Millions of Bahamian Dollars: End of Period*						
Foreign Assets (Net)	51n	198	343	314	319	−198	119	−92	103	269	205	701	590
Domestic Credit	52	2,346	2,564	2,757	3,053	3,423	3,809	4,259	4,663	4,929	4,938	5,126	5,856
Claims on Central Govt. (Net)	52an	412	423	421	419	453	485	506	620	649	489	464	628
Claims on Official Entities	52bx	73	77	82	79	128	158	126	133	203	347	314	266
Claims on Private Sector	52d	1,859	2,060	2,250	2,551	2,837	3,159	3,619	3,902	4,070	4,095	4,339	4,954
Claims on Nonbank Financial Inst..	52g	3	4	3	4	5	8	9	8	8	8	9	8
Liquid Liabilities	55l	1,981	2,137	2,256	2,507	2,911	3,238	3,547	3,711	3,834	3,986	4,339	4,808
Bonds	56ab	10	9	8	6	6	8	6	8	9	5	1	
Capital Accounts	57a	374	397	389	586	290	747	644	1,077	1,362	1,380	1,756	1,870
Other Items (Net)	57r	179	363	417	274	18	−65	−30	−30	−7	−228	−269	−232
Interest Rates							*Percent Per Annum*						
Bank Rate (End of Period)	60	6.50	6.50	6.50	6.50	6.50	5.75	5.75	5.75	5.75	5.75	5.75	5.25
Treasury Bill Rate	60c	1.88	3.01	4.45	4.35	3.84	1.97	1.03	1.94	2.50	1.78	.56	.14
Savings Rate	60k	3.34	3.15	3.30	3.65	3.72	3.31	3.07	3.03	2.77	2.66	2.58	2.27
Deposit Rate	60l	4.30	4.20	5.14	5.23	5.36	4.57	4.08	4.25	4.25	3.95	3.83	3.22
Lending Rate	60p	6.88	6.75	6.75	6.75	6.75	6.38	6.00	6.00	6.00	6.00	6.00	5.54
Prices and Labor							*Index Numbers (2000=100): Period Averages*						
Consumer Prices	64	91.7	†93.6	95.0	95.8	97.6	99.0	100.0	102.9	103.8	107.3	107.9	109.6
Tourist Arrivals	66t	82.0	77.1	81.3	82.2	79.6	86.8	100.0	99.5	104.8	109.3	119.0	120.1
							Number in Thousands: Period Averages						
Labor Force	67d	137	....	....	....	296	....	....	....	....	174	....	....
Employment	67e	120	127	130	135	144	145	....	153	153	155	....	....
Unemployment	67c	18	16	17	15	12	12	....	11	15	19	....	....
Unemployment Rate (%)	67r	13.3	11.1	11.5	9.8	7.8	7.8	....	6.9	9.1	10.8	....	....
Intl. Transactions & Positions							*Millions of Bahamian Dollars*						
Exports	70	167	176	180	181	300	462	576	423	446	425	357	....
Imports, c.i.f.	71	1,056	1,243	1,366	1,666	1,873	1,757	2,074	1,912	1,728	1,762	1,586	....
Balance of Payments							*Millions of US Dollars: Minus Sign Indicates Debit*						
Current Account, n.i.e.	78ald	−42.2	−145.9	−263.3	−472.1	−995.4	−324.4	−632.9	−645.0	−423.3	−473.5	−203.5	....
Goods: Exports f.o.b.	78aad	198.5	225.4	273.3	295.0	362.9	406.8	464.8	416.9	422.1	426.5	471.2	....
Goods: Imports f.o.b.	78abd	−1,013.8	−1,156.7	−1,287.4	−1,410.7	−1,737.1	−1,677.2	−1,983.1	−1,804.2	−1,749.0	−1,758.5	−1,811.5	....
Trade Balance	78acd	−815.3	−931.3	−1,014.1	−1,115.7	−1,374.2	−1,270.4	−1,518.3	−1,387.3	−1,327.0	−1,332.0	−1,340.4	....
Services: Credit	78add	1,510.6	1,542.3	1,578.2	1,592.9	1,533.0	1,800.6	1,973.2	1,804.4	2,061.8	2,054.6	2,242.4	....
Services: Debit	78aed	−627.2	−639.1	−715.8	−836.0	−990.9	−933.6	−1,025.7	−973.2	−1,016.1	−1,092.4	−1,221.7	....
Balance on Goods & Services	78afd	68.1	−28.1	−151.7	−358.8	−832.1	−403.4	−570.8	−556.1	−281.3	−369.8	−319.7	....
Income: Credit	78agd	61.2	75.1	84.6	105.7	147.9	392.8	316.9	184.5	107.7	79.1	79.7	....
Income: Debit	78ahd	−198.8	−210.8	−233.4	−258.3	−345.4	−519.6	−457.1	−383.4	−292.1	−231.6	−214.3	....
Balance on Gds, Serv. & Inc.	78aid	−69.5	−163.8	−300.5	−511.4	−1,029.6	−530.2	−711.0	−755.0	−465.7	−522.2	−454.3	....
Current Transfers, n.i.e.: Credit	78ajd	33.1	25.1	45.9	50.0	45.0	218.3	88.5	120.9	55.4	59.8	264.7	....
Current Transfers: Debit	78akd	−5.8	−7.2	−8.7	−10.7	−10.8	−12.5	−10.5	−10.9	−13.0	−11.1	−13.9	....
Capital Account, n.i.e.	78bcd	−11.6	−12.5	−24.4	−12.9	−11.7	−14.5	−16.4	−21.3	−24.5	−37.4	−47.9	....
Capital Account, n.i.e.: Credit	78bad	—	—	—	—	—	—	—	....	....	....	—	....
Capital Account: Debit	78bbd	−11.6	−12.5	−24.4	−12.9	−11.7	−14.5	−16.4	−21.3	−24.5	−37.4	−47.9	....
Financial Account, n.i.e.	78bjd	66.8	104.6	181.1	412.0	817.7	616.1	429.9	264.6	405.0	535.5	359.4	....
Direct Investment Abroad	78bdd	.1	−.1	.3	−.4	−1.0	−.2	—	....	....	....	....	....
Dir. Invest. in Rep. Econ., n.i.e.	78bed	23.4	106.8	87.8	210.0	146.9	149.3	250.3	102.4	152.8	190.2	273.6	....
Portfolio Investment Assets	78bfd	....	....	....	....	....	....	....	....	....	....	....	....
Equity Securities	78bkd	....	....	....	....	....	....	....	....	....	....	....	....
Debt Securities	78bld	....	....	....	....	....	....	....	....	....	....	....	....
Portfolio Investment Liab., n.i.e.	78bgd	....	....	....	....	....	....	....	....	....	....	....	....
Equity Securities	78bmd	....	....	....	....	....	....	....	....	....	....	....	....
Debt Securities	78bnd	....	....	....	....	....	....	....	....	....	....	....	....
Financial Derivatives Assets	78bwd	....	....	....	....	....	....	....	....	....	....	....	....
Financial Derivatives Liabilities	78bxd	....	....	....	....	....	....	....	....	....	....	....	....
Other Investment Assets	78bhd	−7,455.9	7,436.6	−6,428.8	−80.7	−4,872.0	−12,487.1	−19,067.2	−25,411.7	−32,840.8	46,576.8	19,293.4	....
Monetary Authorities	78bod	—	—	—	—	—	—	—	....	....	....	—	....
General Government	78bpd	—	—	—	—	—	—	—	....	....	....	—	....
Banks	78bqd	−7,455.9	7,436.6	−6,428.8	−80.7	−4,872.0	−12,487.1	−19,067.2	−25,411.7	−32,840.8	46,576.8	19,293.4	....
Other Sectors	78brd	—	—	—	—	—	—	—	....	....	....	—	....
Other Investment Liab., n.i.e.	78bid	7,499.2	−7,438.7	6,521.8	283.1	5,543.8	12,954.1	19,246.9	25,573.9	33,093.1	−46,231.5	−19,207.6	....
Monetary Authorities	78bsd												
General Government	78btd	−5.8	−26.9	−25.2	19.2	−5.9	11.7	−11.2	−11.2	−35.1	52.6	−19.7	....
Banks	78bud	7,459.6	−7,417.9	6,451.8	141.9	4,901.8	12,578.9	19,039.1	25,532.1	33,024.4	−46,679.2	−19,358.0	....
Other Sectors	78bvd	45.4	6.1	95.2	122.0	647.9	363.5	218.9	63.8	103.8	395.1	170.1	....
Net Errors and Omissions	78cad	−3.9	50.9	99.0	129.5	308.6	−212.0	158.4	370.8	102.9	85.5	75.2	....
Overall Balance	78cbd	9.1	−2.9	−7.6	56.5	119.2	65.2	−61.0	−30.9	60.1	110.1	183.3	....
Reserves and Related Items	79dad	−9.1	2.9	7.6	−56.5	−119.2	−65.2	61.0	30.9	−60.1	−110.1	−183.3	....
Reserve Assets	79dbd	−9.1	2.9	7.6	−56.5	−119.2	−65.2	61.0	29.9	−60.1	−110.1	−183.3	....
Use of Fund Credit and Loans	79dcd	—	—	—	—	—	—	—	—	—	—	—	....
Exceptional Financing	79ded	....	....	....	....	....	....	....	1.0	....	....	—	....
Government Finance							*Millions of Bahamian Dollars: Year Ending December 31*						
Deficit (-) or Surplus	80	−20.0	−23.2	−64.0	−138.5	−80.4	−51.4	−8.0	−95.2	−134.3	−207.8	−197.0	....
Revenue	81	618.2	660.2	685.8	736.5	761.4	869.1	950.6	920.3	888.9	901.8	960.2	....
Grants Received	81z	....	....	.5	.5	—	—	—	—	—	—	—	....
Expenditure	82	604.5	657.3	720.2	840.0	806.4	885.2	924.8	956.0	1,018.2	1,067.6	1,119.7	....
Lending Minus Repayments	83	33.7	26.1	30.1	35.5	35.4	35.3	33.8	59.5	5.0	42.0	37.5	....
Financing													
Net Borrowing: Domestic	84a	47.3	10.1	95.1	133.4	72.1	38.0	10.4	40.8	42.1	29.5	210.8	....
Net borrowing: Foreign	85a	−9.6	14.8	−13.7	19.4	−3.1	11.6	5.5	32.3	103.4	197.1	−4.4	....
Use of Cash Balances	87	−17.7	−1.7	−17.5	−14.3	11.5	1.7	−8.0	22.1	−11.3	−18.8	−9.3	....
Debt: Domestic	88a	1,032.9	1,074.9	1,158.0	1,281.7	1,342.7	1,407.9	1,404.1	1,486.1	1,710.5	1,647.6	1,813.3	....
Debt: Foreign	89a	100.4	90.9	77.0	96.4	93.2	104.7	110.2	117.5	96.1	293.2	289.8	....

Bahamas, The   313

		1994	1995	1996	1997	1998	1999	2000	2001	2002	2003	2004	2005
National Accounts							*Millions of Bahamian Dollars*						
Househ.Cons.Expend.,incl.NPISHs....	96f	2,054.1	2,077.4	....	....	....	....	....	....	....	....	....	....
Government Consumption Expend...	91f	511.0	483.9	516.9	578.5	592.4	642.3	680.4	730.4	770.4	785.0	810.5	....
Gross Fixed Capital Formation.........	93e	614.0	698.5	....	....	....	....	....	....	....	....	....	....
Changes in Inventories....................	93i	32.4	13.8	....	....	....	....	....	....	....	....	....	....
Exports of Goods and Services.........	90c	1,569.3	1,680.1	1,733.7	1,750.2	1,793.5	2,130.8	2,351.1	2,163.5	2,370.7	2,322.1	2,471.4	....
Imports of Goods and Services (-).....	98c	1,633.3	1,819.6	2,036.7	2,491.4	2,639.9	2,826.5	3,172.1	3,000.4	2,862.7	2,981.3	3,290.9	....
Statistical Discrepancy.....................	99bs	−94.3	−64.7	−168.2	−88.2	−127.6	−195.2	−155.4	−163.0	−150.5	−120.0	−95.6	....
Gross Domestic Product (GDP).........	99b	3,053.1	3,069.4	....	....	....	....	....	....	....	....	....	....
Net Primary Income from Abroad.....	98.n	−89.3	−96.9	....	....	....	....	....	....	....	....	....	....
Gross National Income (GNI)...........	99a	2,963.8	2,972.5	....	....	....	....	....	....	....	....	....	....
Net Current Transf.from Abroad.....	98t	15.7	5.4	....	....	....	....	....	....	....	....	....	....
Gross Nat'l Disposable Inc.(GNDI)....	99i	2,979.5	2,977.9	....	....	....	....	....	....	....	....	....	....
Gross Saving.................................	99s	423.4	416.6	....	....	....	....	....	....	....	....	....	....
GDP Volume 1991 Prices.................	99b.p	2,716.8	2,746.1	....	....	....	....	....	....	....	....	....	....
GDP Volume (1995=100)................	99bvp	98.9	100.0	....	....	....	....	....	....	....	....	....	....
GDP Deflator (1995=100)...............	99bip	100.5	100.0	....	....	....	....	....	....	....	....	....	....
							Millions: Midyear Estimates						
Population..............................	99z	.27	.28	.28	.29	.29	.30	.30	.31	.31	.31	.32	.32

Bahrain, Kingdom of   419

		1994	1995	1996	1997	1998	1999	2000	2001	2002	2003	2004	2005
Exchange Rates						*SDRs per Dinar: End of Period*							
Official Rate	ac	1.8218	1.7892	1.8495	1.9711	1.8889	1.9377	2.0413	2.1163	1.9563	1.7898	1.7125	1.8608
				US Dollars per Dinar: End of Period (ag) Period Average (rh)									
Official Rate	ag	2.6596	2.6596	2.6596	2.6596	2.6596	2.6596	2.6596	2.6596	2.6596	2.6596	2.6596	2.6596
Official Rate	rh	2.6596	2.6596	2.6596	2.6596	2.6596	2.6596	2.6596	2.6596	2.6596	2.6596	2.6596	2.6596
				Index Numbers (2000=100): Period Averages									
Official Rate	ahx	100.0	100.0	100.0	100.0	100.0	100.0	100.0	100.0	100.0	100.0	100.0	100.0
Nominal Effective Exchange Rate	nec	88.6	84.4	86.4	91.8	95.7	95.3	100.0	103.8	101.8	93.8	89.1	88.4
Real Effective Exchange Rate	rec	97.6	92.9	92.5	98.6	100.9	98.0	100.0	101.8	100.7	93.2	88.7	88.1
Fund Position						*Millions of SDRs: End of Period*							
Quota	2f.s	82.8	82.8	82.8	82.8	82.8	135.0	135.0	135.0	135.0	135.0	135.0	135.0
SDRs	1b.s	11.0	11.3	11.7	11.9	12.1	—	1.0	.8	.8	.7	.6	1.7
Reserve Position in the Fund	1c.s	42.2	43.7	45.1	46.7	48.5	62.4	64.9	67.2	68.6	69.7	70.8	71.2
International Liquidity				*Millions of US Dollars Unless Otherwise Indicated: End of Period*									
Total Reserves minus Gold	1l.d	1,169.7	1,279.9	1,318.4	1,290.3	1,079.2	1,369.0	1,564.1	1,684.0	1,725.7	1,778.4	1,940.5	. . . .
SDRs	1b.d	16.1	16.8	16.8	16.1	17.1	—	1.3	1.1	1.1	1.0	.9	2.4
Reserve Position in the Fund	1c.d	61.6	65.0	64.8	63.0	68.3	85.6	84.5	84.4	93.3	103.6	110.0	101.8
Foreign Exchange	1d.d	1,092.0	1,198.2	1,236.8	1,211.2	993.8	1,283.4	1,478.3	1,598.5	1,631.4	1,673.8	1,829.6	. . . .
Monetary Agency	1dad	841.5	947.3	985.9	960.5	743.0	1,032.9	1,227.4	1,348.5	1,381.4	1,423.8	1,579.6	1,870.8
Government	1dbd	250.5	250.9	250.9	250.7	250.8	250.5	250.9	250.0	250.0	250.0	250.0	. . . .
Gold (Million Fine Troy Ounces)	1ad	.150	.150	.150	.150	.150	.150	.150	.150	.150	.150	.150	.150
Gold (National Valuation)	1and	6.6	6.6	6.6	6.6	6.6	6.6	6.6	6.6	6.6	6.6	6.6	6.6
Monetary Authorities: Other Liab.	4..d	—	—	—	—	—	—	—	—	—	—	—	—
Deposit Money Banks: Assets	7a.d	2,761.7	2,592.0	2,557.2	2,863.0	3,164.1	3,410.6	3,419.9	3,327.9	3,387.9	3,719.1	4,238.6	4,655.3
Liabilities	7b.d	1,486.2	1,136.4	1,042.3	1,583.2	1,522.1	2,305.3	1,672.9	1,480.6	1,536.0	1,949.3	2,856.7	2,810.4
OBU: Foreign Assets	7k.d	62,363	61,061	64,435	69,382	. . . .	. . . .	. . . .	. . . .	54,847	. . . .	. . . .	. . . .
Foreign Liabilities	7m.d	61,875	60,579	64,068	68,644	. . . .	. . . .	. . . .	. . . .	53,458	. . . .	. . . .	. . . .
Monetary Authorities						*Millions of Dinars: End of Period*							
Foreign Assets	11	417.2	481.5	478.0	514.7	509.5	518.5	592.1	634.5	653.1	672.8	734.0	841.3
Claims on Central Government	12a	41.9	14.7	16.7	43.7	40.4	12.4	20.7	41.7	113.5	116.3	127.4	131.9
Reserve Money	14	173.9	234.0	208.0	234.1	183.2	266.5	264.9	303.0	345.1	465.3	485.6	609.1
of which: Currency Outside DMBs	14a	105.5	103.3	102.9	104.6	93.3	113.0	120.7	122.9	142.0	155.8	173.7	190.8
Time and Savings Deposits	15	10.0	20.0	24.5	23.5	35.9	48.4	26.3	40.3	146.1	46.0	44.4	53.3
Foreign Liabilities	16c	—	—	—	—	—	—	—	—	—	—	—	—
Central Government Deposits	16d	120.3	131.4	124.5	122.2	137.5	124.4	133.0	125.1	128.1	130.6	133.5	137.0
Capital Accounts	17a	206.1	240.3	251.0	270.8	291.5	296.5	313.2	332.9	347.1	353.8	367.5	394.7
Other Items (Net)	17r	−51.1	−129.3	−113.0	−92.2	−98.2	−204.9	−124.7	−125.1	−199.8	−206.5	−169.6	−221.0
Deposit Money Banks						*Millions of Dinars: End of Period*							
Reserves	20	66.3	124.6	99.0	126.6	89.4	153.7	139.1	177.9	204.1	303.7	296.0	386.8
Foreign Assets	21	1,038.4	974.6	961.5	1,076.5	1,189.7	1,282.4	1,285.9	1,251.3	1,273.9	1,398.4	1,593.7	1,750.4
Claims on Central Government	22a	138.5	150.7	166.6	172.1	223.3	323.8	322.3	333.5	311.7	412.7	518.0	543.7
Claims on Private Sector	22d	915.0	947.8	954.7	1,074.3	1,164.2	1,302.5	1,380.5	1,411.3	1,606.6	1,754.2	2,172.7	2,622.9
Demand Deposits	24	239.2	229.2	232.4	243.1	272.3	313.2	325.1	429.1	505.2	665.6	687.4	871.7
Time and Savings Deposits	25	992.7	1,095.0	1,132.6	1,238.3	1,477.7	1,482.1	1,684.6	1,763.7	1,806.3	1,897.4	1,974.1	2,397.0
Foreign Liabilities	26c	558.8	427.3	391.9	595.3	572.3	866.8	629.0	556.7	577.6	732.9	1,074.1	1,056.7
Central Government Deposits	26d	416.7	358.0	433.3	443.1	409.9	431.0	436.7	426.3	439.4	513.2	665.1	649.7
Capital Accounts	27a	194.6	185.5	191.5	199.4	254.9	259.6	294.1	312.1	357.5	387.9	463.5	565.4
Other Items (Net)	27r	−243.7	−97.4	−200.0	−269.8	−320.4	−290.2	−241.7	−313.9	−289.7	−328.1	−283.7	−236.7
Monetary Survey						*Millions of Dinars: End of Period*							
Foreign Assets (Net)	31n	896.8	1,028.2	1,047.6	995.9	1,126.9	934.1	1,249.0	1,329.1	1,349.4	1,338.3	1,253.6	1,534.9
Domestic Credit	32	558.4	623.8	580.2	724.8	880.5	1,083.3	1,153.8	1,235.1	1,464.2	1,639.4	2,019.5	2,511.8
Claims on Central Govt. (Net)	32an	−356.6	−324.0	−374.5	−349.5	−283.7	−219.2	−226.7	−176.2	−142.3	−114.8	−153.2	−111.1
Claims on Private Sector	32d	915.0	947.8	954.7	1,074.3	1,164.2	1,302.5	1,380.5	1,411.3	1,606.6	1,754.2	2,172.7	2,622.9
Money	34	344.7	332.5	335.3	347.7	365.6	426.2	445.8	552.0	647.2	821.4	861.0	1,062.5
Quasi-Money	35	1,002.7	1,115.0	1,157.1	1,261.8	1,513.6	1,530.5	1,710.9	1,804.0	1,952.4	1,943.4	2,018.5	2,450.3
Other Items (Net)	37r	108.0	205.2	135.6	111.1	128.3	60.8	246.0	208.2	214.0	212.8	393.6	534.0
Money plus Quasi-Money	35l	1,347.4	1,447.5	1,492.4	1,609.5	1,879.2	1,956.7	2,156.7	2,356.0	2,599.6	2,764.8	2,879.5	3,512.7
Other Banking Institutions						*Millions of Dinars: End of Period*							
Reserves	40	. . . .	. . . .	. . . .	. . . .	. . . .	. . . .	. . . .	. . . .	. . . .	. . . .	. . . .	. . . .
Claims on Mon.Author.:Securities	40c	. . . .	. . . .	. . . .	. . . .	. . . .	. . . .	. . . .	. . . .	. . . .	. . . .	. . . .	. . . .
Foreign Assets	41	23,637.0	23,312.5	24,699.8	26,667.8	32,591.7	32,964.2	34,407.4	32,933.0	22,040.8	31,083.6	36,262.8	43,002.0
Claims on Central Government	42a	.2	.2	.3	.3	15.5	24.7	24.4	39.4	49.2	106.9	153.8	160.2
Claims on Local Government	42b	. . . .	. . . .	. . . .	. . . .								
Claims on Private Sector	42d	369.0	313.5	278.1	349.5	299.8	298.4	262.4	273.4	284.1	315.9	471.6	536.8
Other Claims on Dep.Money Banks	42e	. . . .	. . . .	. . . .	. . . .	. . . .	. . . .	. . . .	. . . .	. . . .	. . . .	. . . .	. . . .
Time and Saving Deposits	45	. . . .	. . . .	. . . .	. . . .								
Liquid Liabilities	45l	178.4	206.2	317.8	434.5	439.6	391.6	282.3	229.2	239.8	261.9	267.0	461.9
Money Market Instruments	46aa	. . . .	. . . .	. . . .	. . . .								
Foreign Liabilities	46c	23,613.8	22,799.6	23,993.5	25,852.6	31,798.4	32,042.1	33,712.0	32,206.7	21,286.7	30,244.7	35,282.2	41,487.5
Central Government Deposits	46d	174.5	369.3	375.4	243.7	190.0	177.5	185.6	228.2	197.6	269.2	332.7	355.5
Credit from Monetary Authorities	46g	. . . .	. . . .	. . . .	. . . .	. . . .	. . . .	. . . .	. . . .	. . . .	. . . .	. . . .	. . . .
Credit from Deposit Money Banks	46h	. . . .	. . . .	. . . .	. . . .	. . . .	. . . .	. . . .	. . . .	. . . .	. . . .	. . . .	. . . .
Capital Accounts	47a	. . . .	. . . .	. . . .	. . . .	. . . .	. . . .	. . . .	. . . .	. . . .	. . . .	. . . .	. . . .
Other Items (Net)	47r	. . . .	. . . .	. . . .	. . . .	. . . .	. . . .	. . . .	. . . .	. . . .	. . . .	. . . .	. . . .

Bahrain, Kingdom of   419

		1994	1995	1996	1997	1998	1999	2000	2001	2002	2003	2004	2005
Banking Survey						*Millions of Dinars: End of Period*							
Foreign Assets (Net)...........	51n	....	....	....	....	....	....	....	....	....	....	....	....
Domestic Credit.........................	52	....	....	....	....	....	....	....	....	....	....	....	....
Claims on Central Govt. (Net).......	52an	....	....	....	....	....	....	....	....	....	....	....	....
Claims on Local Government.........	52	....	....	....	....	....	....	....	....	....	....	....	....
Claims on Private Sector...............	52d	....	....	....	....	....	....	....	....	....	....	....	....
Liquid Liabilities......................	55l	....	....	....	....	....	....	....	....	....	....	....	....
Money Market Instruments..............	56a	....	....	....	....	....	....	....	....	....	....	....	....
Capital Accounts...........................	57a	....	....	....	....	....	....	....	....	....	....	....	....
Other Items (Net).........................	57r	....	....	....	....	....	....	....	....	....	....	....	....
Interest Rates						*Percent Per Annum*							
Money Market Rate........................	60b	5.2	6.2	5.7	....	5.7	5.6	6.9	3.9	2.0	1.2	1.7	3.6
Treasury Bill Rate........................	60c	4.8	6.1	5.5	5.7	5.5	5.5	6.6	3.8	1.8	1.1	1.6	....
Deposit Rate..............................	60l	4.0	5.7	5.2	5.3	4.7	4.8	5.8	2.7	1.3	1.5	1.5	3.1
Lending Rate................................	60p	10.8	11.8	12.5	12.3	11.9	11.9	11.7	10.8	8.5	8.4	8.0	7.9
Prices, Production, Labor						*Index Numbers (2000=100): Period Averages*							
Consumer Prices........................	64	97.8	100.4	100.0	† 102.4	102.0	100.7	100.0	98.8	98.3	99.9	102.2	104.9
Refined Petroleum Production..........	66ab	96.4	97.8	101.7	97.9	96.8	102.4	100.0	93.6	97.2	98.6	98.9	103.6
						Number in Thousands: Period Averages							
Labor Force..............................	67d	247	255	264	273	281	291	301	308	....	....	....	....
Employment...............................	67e	....	....	....	....	....	....	....	157	165	....	....	....
Unemployment.............................	67c	....	....	....	....	....	....	....	17	....	....	....	....
Unemployment Rate (%).............	67r	....	....	....	....	....	....	....	5.4	....	....	....	....
Intl. Transactions & Positions						*Millions of Dinars*							
Exports..................................	70	1,359.9	1,546.4	1,768.0	1,648.2	1,229.6	1,640.4	2,329.3	2,096.9	2,178.7	2,493.5	2,827.0	3,769.2
Imports, c.i.f...........................	71	1,409.2	1,397.1	1,606.6	1,513.6	1,340.9	1,390.3	1,742.2	1,619.0	1,884.7	2,127.1	2,438.2	2,987.8
Balance of Payments						*Millions of US Dollars: Minus Sign Indicates Debit*							
Current Account, n.i.e..................	78ald	−255.6	237.4	260.4	−31.1	−777.4	−37.0	830.1	227.1	−50.5	200.9	415.3	....
Goods: Exports f.o.b................	78aad	3,617.0	4,114.4	4,702.1	4,383.0	3,270.2	4,362.8	6,242.7	5,657.1	5,887.3	6,720.9	7,620.7	
Goods: Imports f.o.b................	78abd	−3,497.3	−3,488.3	−4,037.0	−3,778.2	−3,298.7	−3,468.4	−4,393.6	−4,047.1	−4,697.3	−5,319.1	−6,135.4	
Trade Balance.........................	78acd	119.7	626.1	665.2	604.8	−28.5	894.4	1,849.0	1,610.0	1,190.0	1,401.7	1,485.3	
Services: Credit......................	78add	818.6	683.2	666.2	637.2	724.7	858.9	933.5	950.4	1,068.0	1,260.1	1,558.2	
Services: Debit.......................	78aed	−621.8	−634.0	−612.8	−634.8	−651.9	−700.5	−738.5	−747.6	−926.6	−885.7	−933.5	
Balance on Goods & Services......	78afd	316.5	675.3	718.6	607.2	44.4	1,052.9	2,044.0	1,812.7	1,331.3	1,776.1	2,110.0	
Income: Credit.........................	78agd	3,112.5	4,086.9	3,815.1	4,271.0	4,764.0	5,118.5	6,327.9	3,794.4	1,678.9	1,266.6	2,544.3	
Income: Debit..........................	78ahd	−3,355.1	−4,145.8	−3,840.3	−4,507.1	−4,926.0	−5,388.9	−6,551.5	−4,115.9	−2,203.8	−1,759.6	−3,119.1	
Balance on Gds, Serv. & Inc.......	78aid	73.9	616.4	693.4	371.1	−117.6	782.5	1,820.4	1,491.2	806.4	1,283.1	1,535.2	
Current Transfers, n.i.e.: Credit.....	78ajd	101.1	120.7	126.3	232.7	65.2	36.7	22.4	22.9	14.7	—	—	
Current Transfers: Debit..............	78akd	−430.6	−499.7	−559.3	−634.8	−725.0	−856.2	−1,012.7	−1,286.9	−871.5	−1,082.2	−1,119.9	
Capital Account, n.i.e.................	78bcd	319.1	156.9	50.0	125.0	100.0	100.0	100.0	50.0	100.0	101.6	50.0	....
Capital Account, n.i.e.: Credit........	78bad	319.1	156.9	50.0	125.0	100.0	100.0	100.0	50.0	100.0	101.6	50.0	
Capital Account: Debit...............	78bbd	....	—	—	—	—	—	—	—	—	—	—	
Financial Account, n.i.e...............	78bjd	1,176.9	−1,726.7	−510.2	15.1	22.5	229.9	−29.8	−417.1	−1,234.1	493.1	−390.8	
Direct Investment Abroad..............	78bdd	−198.7	16.1	−304.8	−47.6	−180.8	−163.4	−9.6	−216.0	−190.0	−741.4	−1,035.6	
Dir. Invest. in Rep. Econ., n.i.e.......	78bed	208.2	430.6	2,048.2	329.3	179.5	453.7	363.6	80.4	217.0	516.7	865.3	
Portfolio Investment Assets............	78bfd	−454.0	−113.3	−779.9	−1,150.9	−1,206.7	−2,105.8	−88.3	−1,448.0	−5,140.0	−3,095.7	−3,892.6	
Equity Securities....................	78bkd	....	—	—	—	—	−119.9	−161.1	−389.0	−1,143.5	−489.0	−1,999.0	
Debt Securities......................	78bld	−454.0	−113.3	−779.9	−1,150.9	−1,206.7	−1,985.9	72.8	−1,059.0	−3,996.5	−2,606.7	−1,893.6	
Portfolio Investment Liab., n.i.e......	78bgd	....	—	—	—	194.8	112.8	282.5	−30.7	915.2	688.4	387.7	
Equity Securities....................	78bmd	....	—	—	—	—	—	—	1.2	366.0	238.5	20.9	
Debt Securities......................	78bnd	....	—	—	—	194.8	112.8	282.5	−31.9	549.2	449.9	366.8	
Financial Derivatives Assets...........	78bwd	....	....	....	....	....	....	....	....	....	....	....	
Financial Derivatives Liabilities.......	78bxd	....	....	....	....	....	....	....	....	....	....	....	
Other Investment Assets...............	78bhd	−4,527.1	1,124.5	−2,579.8	−4,342.1	−14,677.8	966.9	−3,833.9	5,623.2	33,425.4	−20,786.6	−9,779.9	....
Monetary Authorities..................	78bod	....	....	....	....	....	....	....	....	....	....	....	
General Government.................	78bpd	−8.0	−5.3	−8.0	−8.0	−5.1	−7.7	−5.9	−6.9	−7.2	−10.4	−5.1	
Banks.................................	78bqd	−4,519.1	1,129.8	−2,571.8	−4,334.1	−14,672.7	974.6	−3,828.0	5,629.1	33,427.2	−20,777.7	−9,777.2	
Other Sectors........................	78brd	....	....	....	....	....	....	....	1.0	5.3	1.6	2.3	
Other Investment Liab., n.i.e..........	78bid	6,148.4	−3,184.5	1,106.2	5,226.5	15,713.5	965.6	3,255.8	−4,426.0	−30,461.7	23,911.6	13,064.3	
Monetary Authorities..................	78bsd	....	....	....	....	....	....	....	....	....	....	....	
General Government.................	78btd	4.0	11.0	1.4	52.3	44.0	54.8	59.1	34.6	102.7	168.5	24.7	
Banks.................................	78bud	6,268.4	−2,901.9	1,056.3	5,175.5	15,394.5	875.7	3,249.2	−4,289.7	−29,734.7	23,793.4	13,004.7	
Other Sectors........................	78bvd	−123.9	−293.6	48.4	−1.3	275.0	35.1	−52.4	−170.9	−829.7	−50.3	35.0	
Net Errors and Omissions..............	78cad	−1,288.0	1,501.3	193.4	−6.3	638.3	−267.7	−650.3	213.5	1,217.8	−700.3	83.5	
Overall Balance......................	78cbd	−47.5	168.9	−6.4	102.8	−16.6	25.3	200.1	123.5	34.8	43.7	157.9	
Reserves and Related Items.............	79dad	47.5	−168.9	6.4	−102.8	16.6	−25.3	−200.1	−123.5	−34.8	−43.7	−157.9	....
Reserve Assets........................	79dbd	47.5	−168.9	6.4	−102.8	16.6	−25.3	−200.1	−123.5	−34.8	−43.7	−157.9	
Use of Fund Credit and Loans........	79dcd	—	—	—	—	—	—	—	—	—	—	—	
Exceptional Financing..................	79ded	....	....	....	....	....	....	....	....	....	....	....	

		1994	1995	1996	1997	1998	1999	2000	2001	2002	2003	2004	2005
International Investment Position							*Millions of US Dollars*							
Assets	79aad	66,735.3	65,872.8	69,518.6	75,156.1	91,569.9	92,887.3	97,291.7	93,445.4	65,165.3	89,831.1	104,355.3	....
Direct Investment Abroad	79abd	1,059.9	1,043.8	1,348.6	1,396.3	1,579.2	1,742.6	1,752.1	1,968.1	2,158.1	2,899.5	3,935.1	....
Portfolio Investment	79acd	6,647.5	6,760.6	7,538.9	8,696.9	10,268.2	12,373.7	12,719.2	14,166.7	19,338.0	22,433.7	25,968.9	....
Equity Securities	79add	—	—	—	—	1,342.6	1,462.4	1,840.2	2,229.2	3,372.7	3,861.7	5,502.0	....
Debt Securities	79aed	6,647.5	6,760.6	7,538.9	8,696.9	8,925.6	10,911.3	10,879.0	11,937.4	15,965.3	18,572.0	20,466.9	....
Financial Derivatives	79ald	—	—	—	—	—	—	—	—	—	—	—	....
Other Investment	79afd	57,917.8	56,788.0	59,359.8	63,693.9	78,366.6	77,392.1	81,245.7	75,615.6	42,183.1	62,959.2	72,750.0	....
Monetary Authorities	79agd	....	....	....	....	....	....	....	....	....	....	....	....
General Government	79ahd	....	....	....	....	....	....	....	....	....	....	....	....
Banks	79aid	57,917.8	56,788.0	59,359.8	63,693.9	78,366.6	77,392.1	81,220.0	75,590.9	42,163.7	62,941.4	72,718.6	....
Other Sectors	79ajd	....	....	....	....	....	....	25.7	24.7	19.4	17.8	31.3	....
Reserve Assets	79akd	1,110.1	1,280.4	1,271.3	1,369.0	1,355.9	1,379.0	1,574.7	1,695.1	1,486.1	1,538.6	1,701.4	....
Liabilities	79lad	64,529.6	62,081.9	65,187.8	70,744.5	86,515.4	88,016.3	92,136.4	87,929.8	59,426.0	84,599.9	98,690.3	....
Dir. Invest. in Rep. Economy	79lbd	1,972.8	2,403.4	4,451.6	4,780.9	4,960.3	5,414.0	5,905.8	5,986.1	6,203.1	6,719.8	7,354.0	....
Portfolio Investment	79lcd	—	—	—	—	194.8	307.6	615.9	585.3	1,500.5	2,188.9	2,576.6	....
Equity Securities	79ldd	—	—	—	—	—	—	25.8	27.1	393.0	631.5	652.4	....
Debt Securities	79led	—	—	—	—	194.8	307.6	590.1	558.2	1,107.4	1,557.4	1,924.2	....
Financial Derivatives	79lld	—	—	—	—	—	—	—	—	—	—	—	....
Other Investment	79lfd	62,556.8	59,678.5	60,736.2	65,963.7	81,360.3	82,294.6	85,614.7	81,358.4	51,722.4	75,691.2	88,759.7	....
Monetary Authorities	79lgd	—	—	—	—	—	—	—	—	—	—	—	....
General Government	79lhd	150.1	173.7	175.1	227.1	229.2	287.8	345.8	378.8	478.3	653.0	694.7	....
Banks	79lid	62,406.6	59,504.7	60,561.1	65,736.6	81,131.1	82,006.8	85,256.0	80,966.3	51,231.6	75,025.0	88,029.6	....
Other Sectors	79ljd	—	—	—	—	—	—	12.9	13.3	12.4	13.2	35.5	....
Government Finance							*Millions of Dinars: Year Ending December 31*							
Deficit (-) or Surplus	80	−58.3	−126.6	−55.0	−125.3	−116.5	−133.6	66.0	−31.0	....	....	....	
Revenue	81	476.3	526.6	615.5	633.1	516.6	653.5	1,065.9	969.3	....	....	....	
Grants Received	81z	37.6	37.6	18.8	46.9	37.6	37.6	18.8	37.6	....	....	....	
Expenditure	82	623.4	594.1	581.3	620.0	644.6	699.3	777.0	826.7	....	....	....	
Lending Minus Repayments	83	−51.2	96.7	108.0	185.3	26.1	125.4	241.7	211.2	....	....	....	
Financing													
Total Financing	80h	58.3	126.6	55.0	125.3	116.5	133.6	−66.0	30.9	....	....	....	
Domestic	84a	56.6	122.5	54.5	125.1	99.9	113.4	−87.6	19.1	....	....	....	
Foreign	85a	1.7	4.1	.5	.2	16.6	20.2	21.6	11.8	....	....	....	
Debt: Domestic	88a	318.8	314.0	297.0	319.5	404.5	482.0	747.9	773.6	....	....	....	
Foreign	89a	55.5	59.6	65.8	85.4	87.6	107.8	129.4	141.2	....	....	....	
National Accounts							*Millions of Dinars*							
Househ.Cons.Expend.,incl.NPISHs	96f	1,123.4	1,165.5	1,229.3	1,277.4	1,327.6	1,378.4	1,411.8	1,415.7	1,435.1	1,479.7	1,739.5	....
Government Consumption Expend	91f	440.0	458.5	464.3	465.1	482.8	518.2	526.0	550.6	588.7	672.3	705.6	....
Gross Fixed Capital Formation	93e	417.5	381.3	284.1	285.9	326.2	338.0	404.6	397.7	549.0	699.8	895.0	....
Changes in Inventories	93i	−6.5	−59.8	46.4	130.6	171.9	−141.2	−96.1	−34.2	137.5	114.0	45.6	....
Exports of Goods and Services	90c	1,667.8	1,803.9	2,018.5	1,887.6	1,502.1	1,963.4	2,680.3	2,454.2	2,580.3	2,883.3	3,412.8	....
Imports of Goods and Services (-)	98c	1,548.8	1,550.0	1,748.3	1,659.3	1,485.4	1,567.5	1,929.7	1,802.8	2,114.2	2,237.2	2,657.9	....
Gross Domestic Product (GDP)	99b	2,093.4	2,199.4	2,294.3	2,387.3	2,325.1	2,489.3	2,996.9	2,981.2	3,176.5	3,612.0	4,140.5	4,855.7
Net Primary Income from Abroad	98.n	−91.0	−22.2	−9.5	−88.8	−60.9	−101.6	−84.1	−120.8	−197.3	−196.0	−216.5	....
Gross National Income (GNI)	99a	2,002.4	2,177.2	2,284.8	2,298.5	2,264.3	2,387.7	2,912.8	2,860.4	2,979.2	3,416.0	3,924.0	....
Consumption of Fixed Capital	99cf	326.7	332.6	328.6	332.3	343.5	229.0	250.2	245.5	234.9	253.9	279.6	....
Net National Income	99e	1,675.7	1,844.6	1,956.2	1,966.2	1,920.8	2,158.7	2,662.6	2,614.9	2,744.3	3,162.1	3,644.4	....
GDP Volume 1989 Prices	99b.p	2,027.4	2,107.0	2,193.4	2,261.5	2,369.7	2,471.9	2,602.5	2,723.2	2,864.3	3,058.5	3,237.6	3,461.0
GDP Volume (2000=100)	99bvp	77.9	81.0	84.3	86.9	91.1	95.0	100.0	104.6	110.1	117.5	124.4	133.0
GDP Deflator (2000=100)	99bip	89.7	90.6	90.8	91.7	85.2	87.4	100.0	95.1	96.3	102.6	111.1	121.8
							Millions: Midyear Estimates							
Population	99z	.57	.58	.60	.62	.64	.66	.67	.68	.70	.71	.72	.73

Bangladesh 513

		1994	1995	1996	1997	1998	1999	2000	2001	2002	2003	2004	2005
Exchange Rates						*Taka per SDR: End of Period*							
Official Rate...............aa=..........	wa	58.759	60.574	61.041	61.323	68.289	69.998	70.357	71.634	78.716	87.348	94.333	94.632
						Taka per US Dollar: End of Period (we) Period Average (wf)							
Official Rate...............ae=..........	we	40.250	40.750	42.450	45.450	48.500	51.000	54.000	57.000	57.900	58.782	60.742	66.210
Official Rate...............rf=..........	wf	40.212	40.278	41.794	43.892	46.906	49.085	52.142	55.807	57.888	58.150	59.513	64.327
Fund Position						*Millions of SDRs: End of Period*							
Quota..........................	2f.s	392.5	392.5	392.5	392.5	392.5	533.3	533.3	533.3	533.3	533.3	533.3	533.3
SDRs...........................	1b.s	24.6	107.3	76.2	21.6	9.1	.7	.3	.9	1.7	2.2	.8	.7
Reserve Position in the Fund...	1c.s	.1	.1	.1	.1	.2	.2	.2	.2	.2	.2	.2	.2
Total Fund Cred.&Loans Outstg.......	2tl	473.4	433.1	374.2	287.9	308.4	237.6	168.6	118.3	51.9	49.5	148.5	215.8
International Liquidity					*Millions of US Dollars Unless Otherwise Indicated: End of Period*								
Total Reserves minus Gold..............	1l.d	3,138.7	2,339.7	1,834.6	1,581.5	1,905.4	1,603.6	1,486.0	1,275.0	1,683.2	2,577.9	3,172.4	2,767.2
SDRs..................................	1b.d	36.0	159.5	109.6	29.2	12.9	.9	.4	1.2	2.2	3.2	1.2	.9
Reserve Position in the Fund..........	1c.d	.1	.1	.2	.1	.2	.3	.2	.2	.2	.3	.3	.3
Foreign Exchange.....................	1d.d	3,102.6	2,180.1	1,724.9	1,552.1	1,892.3	1,602.5	1,485.3	1,273.6	1,680.7	2,574.4	3,170.9	2,766.0
Gold (Million Fine Troy Ounces)........	1ad	.094	.094	.094	.101	.105	.106	.109	.111	.112	.112	.113	.113
Gold (National Valuation)...............	1and	27.2	26.9	28.0	25.3	22.3	19.6	29.6	30.6	39.2	46.3	49.9	58.1
Monetary Authorities: Other Liab.....	4..d	124.0	171.8	160.9	127.5	257.4	137.6	151.9	289.5	186.6	226.8	307.5	265.2
Deposit Money Banks: Assets..........	7a.d	703.4	730.6	771.6	827.9	794.9	917.0	1,203.4	1,081.0	916.2	772.8	827.3	912.2
Liabilities..................	7b.d	283.7	327.0	399.7	510.7	437.3	463.7	571.4	673.5	633.6	444.8	349.8	441.4
Monetary Authorities						*Millions of Taka: End of Period*							
Foreign Assets......................	11	130,167	97,949	80,687	73,398	93,361	82,779	81,907	74,715	100,019	154,540	196,090	187,578
Claims on Central Government........	12a	5,697	22,783	38,576	36,371	47,968	72,915	81,529	130,336	86,210	56,217	91,521	178,455
Claims on Nonfin.Pub.Enterprises.....	12c	594	591	590	590	2,140	2,140	1,570	1,321	1,013	688	149	—
Claims on Private Sector...............	12d	—	—	—	—	—	7,594	7,707	9,324	10,802	12,005	12,593	12,997
Claims on Deposit Money Banks......	12e	26,275	29,139	34,551	36,220	40,993	48,641	51,472	52,925	55,307	56,468	59,324	60,218
Claims on Nonbank Financial Insts...	12g	13,153	11,555	11,521	11,493	11,724	12,617	12,507	11,477	11,467	8,736	10,898	10,441
Reserve Money......................	14	114,017	103,458	112,457	122,988	139,489	157,166	180,023	223,476	230,752	246,755	266,457	334,635
of which: Currency Outside DMBs..	14a	57,248	64,523	68,195	76,074	80,756	93,819	116,877	127,863	133,895	144,556	169,997	205,254
Other Liabilities to DMBs.................	14n	—	—	—	—	—	—	—	—	—	—	2,800	9,695
Liabs. of Central Bank: Securities....	16ac	4,000	2,755	7,361	—	—	—	—	—	—	—	—	—
Foreign Liabilities....................	16c	32,807	33,237	29,670	23,454	33,547	23,647	20,063	24,972	14,892	17,654	32,689	37,977
Central Government Deposits...........	16d	4,868	3,986	9	13	14	10	11	10	10	12	142	139
Central Govt. Lending Funds............	16f	18,977	14,128	11,263	8,452	18,209	22,120	10,516	9,129	10,728	10,971	9,457	10,550
Capital Accounts....................	17a	8,578	8,602	9,304	9,998	11,006	21,632	19,138	20,556	25,661	39,097	40,907	47,843
Other Items (Net)........................	17r	−7,360	−4,149	−4,139	−6,833	−6,079	2,111	6,941	1,955	−17,226	−25,834	18,124	8,850
Deposit Money Banks						*Millions of Taka: End of Period*							
Reserves..........................	20	56,221	43,333	45,882	48,678	64,661	63,584	65,494	96,995	94,687	104,787	104,238	140,338
Claims on Mon.Author.:Securities....	20c	3,994	2,741	7,358	—	—	—	—	—	—	—	—	—
Other Claims on Monetary Author.....	20n	—	—	—	—	—	—	—	—	—	—	2,800	9,695
Foreign Assets......................	21	28,313	29,770	32,753	37,628	38,554	46,766	64,985	61,619	53,048	45,429	50,250	60,395
Claims on Central Government........	22a	64,899	64,283	63,790	81,206	99,534	117,884	142,606	130,277	181,397	191,745	213,693	196,130
Claims on State & Local Govts.........	22b	622	800	816	809	1,388	1,279	1,417	1,392	999	749	581	435
Claims on Nonfin.Pub.Enterprises.....	22c	33,731	31,717	39,426	42,900	40,712	40,431	46,111	52,785	60,644	59,831	67,650	125,915
Claims on Private Sector...............	22d	220,332	318,484	359,202	411,731	465,130	509,760	577,077	667,883	779,577	852,312	991,035	1,153,482
Claims on Nonbank Financial Insts...	22g	14,644	18,114	20,234	19,231	20,312	25,019	26,986	31,433	30,250	35,840	61,324	53,162
Demand Deposits..........................	24	58,717	70,819	73,481	76,559	83,214	91,055	102,074	114,572	120,705	129,272	152,019	174,392
Time, Savings,& Fgn.Currency Dep...	25	277,489	305,996	347,091	383,813	433,586	504,965	603,882	701,196	814,259	935,128	1,083,528	1,265,769
Restricted Deposits....................	26b	21	23	45	31	38	54	634	364	279	283	252	266
Foreign Liabilities............................	26c	11,064	12,993	16,782	23,112	21,115	23,554	30,762	38,299	36,290	25,692	20,812	28,068
Central Government Deposits...........	26d	32,200	34,509	31,250	39,571	50,076	52,881	59,785	54,802	61,510	63,528	81,776	103,798
Central Govt. Lending Funds............	26f	5,423	6,443	5,869	7,164	7,174	6,391	6,065	5,431	5,832	6,125	5,283	6,511
Credit from Monetary Authorities.....	26g	28,781	30,843	37,623	39,047	43,789	44,463	47,049	48,551	48,137	48,898	54,221	64,023
Liab. to Nonbank Financial Insts.......	26j	—	—	—	—	366	50	35	—	—	—	6	5,324
Capital Accounts.....................	27a	21,068	27,738	30,511	33,528	35,989	43,684	52,904	60,044	65,477	76,461	89,950	108,226
Other Items (Net)........................	27r	−12,007	19,878	26,809	39,358	54,944	37,626	21,486	19,125	48,113	5,306	3,724	−16,825
Monetary Survey						*Millions of Taka: End of Period*							
Foreign Assets (Net)................	31n	114,609	81,489	66,989	64,460	77,253	82,344	96,067	73,064	101,884	156,624	192,840	181,928
Domestic Credit........................	32	316,604	429,832	502,896	564,747	638,818	736,748	837,714	981,416	1,100,839	1,154,583	1,367,526	1,627,080
Claims on Central Govt. (Net)........	32an	33,528	48,571	71,107	77,993	97,412	137,908	164,339	205,801	206,087	184,422	223,296	270,648
Claims on State & Local Govts........	32b	622	800	816	809	1,388	1,279	1,417	1,392	999	749	581	435
Claims on Nonfin.Pub.Enterprises...	32c	34,325	32,308	40,016	43,490	42,852	42,571	47,681	54,106	61,657	60,519	67,799	125,915
Claims on Private Sector...............	32d	220,332	318,484	359,202	411,731	465,130	517,354	584,784	677,207	790,379	864,317	1,003,628	1,166,479
Claims on Nonbank Financial Insts.	32g	27,797	29,669	31,755	30,724	32,036	37,636	39,493	42,910	41,717	44,576	72,222	63,603
Money............................	34	115,965	135,342	141,676	152,633	163,970	184,874	218,951	242,437	254,717	274,021	322,898	382,039
Quasi-Money........................	35	277,489	305,996	347,091	383,813	433,586	504,965	603,882	701,196	814,259	935,128	1,083,528	1,265,769
Restricted Deposits....................	36b	21	23	45	31	38	54	634	364	279	283	252	266
Central Govt. Lending Funds............	36f	24,400	20,571	17,132	15,616	25,383	28,511	16,581	14,560	16,560	17,096	14,740	17,061
Liab. to Nonbank Financial Insts.......	36j	—	—	—	—	366	50	35	—	—	—	6	5,324
Capital Accounts.....................	37a	29,646	36,340	39,815	43,526	46,995	65,316	72,042	80,600	91,138	115,558	130,857	156,069
Other Items (Net)........................	37r	−16,307	13,049	24,125	33,588	45,733	35,322	21,656	15,322	25,770	−30,879	8,085	−17,520
Money plus Quasi-Money..............	35l	393,454	441,338	488,767	536,446	597,556	689,839	822,833	943,633	1,068,976	1,209,149	1,406,426	1,647,808
Interest Rates						*Percent Per Annum*							
Discount Rate (End of Period)..........	60	5.50	6.00	7.00	8.00	8.00	7.00	7.00	6.00	6.00	5.00	5.00	5.00
Deposit Rate........................	60l	6.40	6.04	7.28	8.11	8.42	8.74	8.56	8.50	8.17	7.82	7.11	8.09
Lending Rate........................	60p	14.50	14.00	14.00	14.00	14.00	14.13	15.50	15.83	16.00	16.00	14.75	14.00

Bangladesh 513

		1994	1995	1996	1997	1998	1999	2000	2001	2002	2003	2004	2005
Prices, Production, Labor		Index Numbers (2000=100): Period Averages											
Share Prices................................	62	123.2	139.0	251.2	190.5	107.8	89.1	100.0	117.6	138.6	141.8	237.6	293.2
Consumer Prices............................	64	71.5	78.8	80.7	85.1	92.2	97.8	100.0	102.0	105.4	111.4	121.6	130.2
Industrial Production....................	66	68.7	73.4	78.0	85.2	88.7	91.8	100.0	102.6	110.1	115.4	126.8	....
					Number in Thousands: Period Averages								
Labor Force................................	67d	....	50,337	....	....	....	53,512	....	....	....	....	....	....
Employment................................	67e	....	....	54,597	....	....	....	51,764	....	....	44,322	....	....
Unemployment.............................	67c	....	....	1,417	....	....	....	1,750	....	....	2,002	....	....
Unemployment Rate.......................	67r	....	....	2.5	....	....	....	3.3	....	....	4.3	....	....
Intl. Transactions & Positions		Millions of Taka											
Exports..	70	107,013	127,782	137,944	166,087	179,614	192,571	249,860	269,150	264,295	306,090	393,862	465,466
Imports, c.i.f..................................	71	185,098	261,878	276,838	302,942	327,575	377,496	436,450	465,607	458,119	553,235	750,513	828,671
Imports, f.o.b.................................	71.v	166,246	235,502	248,932	265,565	298,386	342,064	394,340	421,415	....	....	....	
Balance of Payments		Millions of US Dollars: Minus Sign Indicates Debit											
Current Account, n.i.e....................	78ald	199.6	−823.9	−991.0	−286.3	−35.2	−364.4	−305.8	−535.4	739.3	131.6	−278.7	....
Goods: Exports f.o.b......................	78aad	2,934.4	3,733.3	4,009.3	4,839.9	5,141.4	5,458.3	6,399.2	6,084.7	6,102.4	7,050.1	8,150.7	....
Goods: Imports f.o.b......................	78abd	−4,350.5	−6,057.4	−6,284.6	−6,550.7	−6,715.7	−7,535.5	−8,052.9	−8,133.4	−7,780.1	−9,492.0	−11,157.1	....
Trade Balance............................	78acd	−1,416.1	−2,324.1	−2,275.3	−1,710.8	−1,574.3	−2,077.2	−1,653.7	−2,048.7	−1,677.8	−2,441.9	−3,006.5	....
Services: Credit............................	78add	589.8	698.2	604.8	687.3	723.9	777.7	815.1	752.2	848.7	1,011.7	1,083.0	....
Services: Debit............................	78aed	−1,025.0	−1,531.2	−1,166.0	−1,283.7	−1,237.1	−1,396.7	−1,620.2	−1,521.5	−1,405.7	−1,711.5	−1,931.4	....
Balance on Goods & Services......	78afd	−1,851.3	−3,157.1	−2,836.5	−2,307.2	−2,087.4	−2,696.3	−2,458.9	−2,818.0	−2,234.8	−3,141.7	−3,854.9	....
Income: Credit............................	78agd	150.5	270.1	129.4	86.6	91.5	94.3	78.4	76.6	56.8	56.5	102.6	....
Income: Debit............................	78ahd	−188.7	−201.8	−193.1	−198.0	−206.1	−258.5	−344.8	−361.9	−322.0	−361.3	−473.9	....
Balance on Gds, Serv. & Inc........	78aid	−1,889.6	−3,088.8	−2,900.2	−2,418.6	−2,202.1	−2,860.4	−2,725.3	−3,103.3	−2,500.1	−3,446.4	−4,226.2	....
Current Transfers, n.i.e.: Credit....	78ajd	2,091.4	2,266.7	1,912.8	2,136.5	2,172.9	2,501.4	2,426.5	2,572.8	3,245.4	3,586.2	3,960.4	....
Current Transfers: Debit..............	78akd	−2.2	−1.8	−4.0	−4.3	−5.9	−5.3	−7.0	−4.9	−6.0	−8.2	−12.9	....
Capital Account, n.i.e....................	78bcd	—	—	371.2	366.8	238.7	364.1	248.7	235.4	363.7	386.7	142.1	....
Capital Account, n.i.e.: Credit.......	78bad	—	—	371.2	366.8	238.7	364.1	248.7	235.4	363.7	386.7	142.1	....
Capital Account: Debit..................	78bbd	—	—	—	—	—	—	—	—	—	—	—	....
Financial Account, n.i.e.................	78bjd	748.8	178.8	92.4	−140.2	−116.0	−446.9	−256.0	262.1	−256.2	289.0	665.0	....
Direct Investment Abroad.............	78bdd	—	—	—	−3.1	−3.0	−.1	—	....	−2.7	−2.8	−4.1	....
Dir. Invest. in Rep. Econ., n.i.e.......	78bed	11.1	1.9	13.5	139.4	190.1	179.7	280.4	78.5	52.3	268.3	448.9	....
Portfolio Investment Assets...........	78bfd	—	—	—	—	—	−.2	—	.1	−1.2	—	—	....
Equity Securities......................	78bkd	—	—	—	—	—	−.2	—	−.2	−1.2	—	—	....
Debt Securities........................	78bld	—	—	—	—	—	—	—	.3	—	—	—	....
Portfolio Investment Liab., n.i.e....	78bgd	105.9	−15.2	−117.0	−9.9	−4.1	−1.1	1.3	−3.5	−1.4	1.6	4.3	....
Equity Securities......................	78bmd	105.9	−15.2	−117.0	−9.9	−4.2	−1.1	1.2	−3.5	−1.4	1.6	4.3	....
Debt Securities........................	78bnd	—	—	—	—	.1	—	.1	....	....	—	—	....
Financial Derivatives Assets..........	78bwd	—	—	—	—	—	—	—	....	....	....	....	....
Financial Derivatives Liabilities......	78bxd	—	—	—	—	—	—	—	....	....	....	....	....
Other Investment Assets................	78bhd	−1.6	−243.9	−426.7	−677.8	−859.7	−1,143.7	−1,246.8	−433.8	−560.4	−693.6	−495.1	....
Monetary Authorities....................	78bod	....	....	—	—	—	—	—	—	—	—	—	....
General Government....................	78bpd	−.1	—	—	—	—	—	—	—	—	—	—	....
Banks.......................................	78bqd	−1.5	−243.9	−41.1	−70.2	−38.1	−131.4	−315.7	151.7	143.7	136.2	−7.9	....
Other Sectors............................	78brd	—	—	−385.6	−607.6	−821.6	−1,012.3	−931.0	−585.5	−704.0	−829.8	−487.2	....
Other Investment Liab., n.i.e.........	78bid	633.4	436.1	622.6	411.2	560.7	518.4	709.1	620.7	257.1	715.5	711.0	....
Monetary Authorities....................	78bsd	15.0	58.3	−4.3	−25.5	126.6	−118.9	35.2	132.7	−99.9	37.9	55.1	....
General Government....................	78btd	718.5	374.2	511.3	294.1	404.6	524.7	537.9	413.7	138.2	728.2	664.9	....
Banks.......................................	78bud	−116.3	−34.2	83.0	118.4	2.6	30.7	105.7	29.0	58.4	−188.4	−35.4	....
Other Sectors............................	78bvd	16.2	37.9	32.7	24.2	26.9	82.0	30.4	45.3	160.4	137.9	26.4	....
Net Errors and Omissions................	78cad	−257.1	133.3	113.5	−75.5	201.0	258.0	282.4	−106.0	−349.3	81.1	−25.0	....
Overall Balance............................	78cbd	691.3	−511.7	−414.3	−135.1	288.5	−189.2	−30.7	−143.9	497.4	888.5	503.4	....
Reserves and Related Items.............	79dad	−691.3	511.7	414.3	135.1	−288.5	189.2	30.7	143.9	−497.4	−888.5	−503.4	....
Reserve Assets............................	79dbd	−636.2	572.8	499.9	253.8	−319.1	286.0	121.0	207.9	−411.8	−886.3	−649.8	....
Use of Fund Credit and Loans........	79dcd	−55.1	−61.0	−85.6	−118.7	30.6	−96.8	−90.3	−64.0	−85.6	−2.2	146.3	....
Exceptional Financing....................	79ded	—	—	—	....	—	....	—	....	....	....	—	....
International Investment Position		Millions of US Dollars											
Assets...	79aad	....	....	....	....	....	....	2,783.6	2,082.8	2,380.1	3,104.0	3,593.6	....
Direct Investment Abroad..............	79abd	....	—	—	—	—	—	68.3	85.3	88.3	95.5	94.7	
Portfolio Investment......................	79acd	....	—	—	—	—	—	.6	.7	1.0	1.0	.4	
Equity Securities..........................	79add	....	—	—	—	—	—	.6	.7	1.0	1.0	.4	
Debt Securities............................	79aed	....	—	—	—	—	—	—	—	—	—	—	
Financial Derivatives......................	79ald	....											
Other Investment..........................	79afd	....	730.6	771.6	827.9	794.9	917.0	1,203.4	691.1	568.4	383.5	390.9	
Monetary Authorities....................	79agd	....	—	—	—	—	—	—	—	—	—	—	
General Government....................	79ahd	....	—	—	—	—	—	—	—	—	—	—	
Banks.......................................	79aid	....	730.6	771.6	827.9	794.9	917.0	1,203.4	691.1	568.4	383.5	390.9	
Other Sectors............................	79ajd	....											
Reserve Assets............................	79akd	....	2,337.2	1,842.4	1,558.2	1,920.8	1,617.6	1,511.4	1,305.7	1,722.4	2,624.1	3,107.5	
Liabilities......................................	79lad	....	....	....	....	....	....	18,988.4	17,813.2	19,269.7	20,728.4	21,689.6	....
Dir. Invest. in Rep. Economy...........	79lbd	....	—	—	—	—	—	2,202.0	2,246.3	2,524.5	2,973.1	2,830.1	
Portfolio Investment......................	79lcd	....	—	—	—	—	—	22.2	17.2	16.7	21.6	87.3	
Equity Securities..........................	79ldd	....	—	—	—	—	—	19.8	15.2	14.7	19.6	85.4	
Debt Securities............................	79led	....	—	—	—	—	—	2.4	2.0	2.0	2.0	1.9	
Financial Derivatives......................	79lld	....	....	....	....	....	....						
Other Investment..........................	79lfd	....	17,018.2	15,509.7	15,462.1	14,569.4	15,267.0	16,764.2	15,549.7	16,728.4	17,733.8	18,772.1	
Monetary Authorities....................	79lgd	....	643.8	538.1	388.5	434.3	326.1	219.6	148.6	70.6	73.6	230.6	
General Government....................	79lhd	....	16,055.5	14,576.3	14,565.1	13,699.8	14,479.1	15,974.9	14,926.1	16,205.5	17,400.5	18,304.5	
Banks.......................................	79lid	....	318.8	395.3	508.5	435.4	461.8	569.7	475.0	452.3	259.8	237.0	
Other Sectors............................	79ljd	....	—	—	—	—	—	—	—	—	—	—	

Bangladesh   513

National Accounts		1994	1995	1996	1997	1998	1999	2000	2001	2002	2003	2004	2005
		Billions of Taka: Year Ending June 30											
Househ.Cons.Expend.,incl.NPISHs....	96f	1,110.6	1,254.4	1,342.2	1,440.8	1,558.6	1,707.1	1,838.5	1,964.9	2,099.3	2,285.0	2,495.2	2,734.8
Government Consumption Expend...	91f	66.1	70.6	73.3	78.9	94.7	100.8	108.4	114.3	136.6	160.7	184.1	207.2
Gross Fixed Capital Formation..........	93e	249.2	291.6	332.5	374.5	433.0	487.6	545.9	585.4	632.4	703.5	799.9	900.3
Changes in Inventories....................	93i	—	—	—	—	—	—	—	—	—	—	—	—
Exports of Goods and Services..........	90c	121.9	165.7	184.4	216.7	266.8	289.9	331.5	390.0	390.0	427.2	514.9	566.4
Imports of Goods and Services (-).....	98c	187.7	263.5	310.9	325.6	365.9	409.9	455.9	545.1	520.4	602.2	693.0	831.6
Gross Domestic Product (GDP).........	99b	1,354.1	1,525.2	1,663.2	1,807.0	2,001.8	2,197.0	2,370.9	2,535.5	2,732.0	3,005.8	3,329.7	3,684.8
Net Primary Income from Abroad.....	98.n	42.3	46.5	49.5	58.5	65.0	75.5	87.1	88.4	125.4	165.8	175.5	209.9
Gross National Income (GNI)...........	99a	1,396.5	1,571.7	1,712.8	1,865.5	2,066.7	2,272.5	2,458.0	2,623.9	2,857.4	3,171.6	3,505.3	3,894.7
Consumption of Fixed Capital..........	99cf	120.2	134.1	146.9	158.9	176.0	175.3	187.8	202.6	218.1	241.0	262.6	289.9
GDP Volume 1995/96 Prices...........	99b.p	1,515.1	1,589.8	1,663.2	1,752.9	1,844.5	1,934.3	2,049.3	2,157.4	2,252.6	2,371.0	2,519.7	2,655.1
GDP Volume (2000=100)...............	99bvp	73.9	77.6	81.2	85.5	90.0	94.4	100.0	105.3	109.9	115.7	123.0	129.6
GDP Deflator (2000=100)...............	99bip	77.3	82.9	86.4	89.1	93.8	98.2	100.0	101.6	104.8	109.6	114.2	120.0
		Millions: Midyear Estimates											
Population...............................	99z	113.95	116.45	118.95	121.43	123.90	126.40	128.92	131.46	134.03	136.62	139.21	141.82

		1994	1995	1996	1997	1998	1999	2000	2001	2002	2003	2004	2005
Exchange Rates		*Barbados Dollars per SDR: End of Period (aa) Barbados Dollars per US Dollar: End of Period (ae)*											
Official Rate........................	aa	2.9197	2.9730	2.8759	2.6985	2.8161	2.7450	2.6058	2.5135	2.7190	2.9719	3.1060	2.8585
Official Rate........................	ae	2.0000	2.0000	2.0000	2.0000	2.0000	2.0000	2.0000	2.0000	2.0000	2.0000	2.0000	2.0000
Fund Position		*Millions of SDRs: End of Period*											
Quota..............................	2f.s	48.90	48.90	48.90	48.90	48.90	67.50	67.50	67.50	67.50	67.50	67.50	67.50
SDRs...............................	1b.s	.03	.03	.02	.02	.02	.01	.02	.04	.04	.01	.04	.01
Reserve Position in the Fund...........	1c.s	.03	.03	.03	.03	.03	4.68	4.68	4.71	4.85	5.02	5.15	5.30
Total Fund Cred.&Loans Outstg.....	2tl	36.84	24.94	6.52	—	—	—	—	—	—	—	—	—
International Liquidity		*Millions of US Dollars Unless Otherwise Indicated: End of Period*											
Total Reserves minus Gold..............	1l.d	195.77	219.10	289.69	264.92	365.95	301.94	472.69	690.37	668.51	737.94	579.86	603.10
SDRs................................	1b.d	.04	.04	.03	.03	.03	.01	.02	.05	.06	.01	.06	.02
Reserve Position in the Fund........	1c.d	.04	.04	.04	.03	.04	6.42	6.09	5.92	6.60	7.46	8.00	7.57
Foreign Exchange.....................	1d.d	195.69	219.02	289.62	264.85	365.88	295.52	466.58	684.40	661.86	730.47	571.80	595.50
Monetary Authorities................	1dad	188.28	212.75	280.06	227.62	298.66	226.13	373.25	568.41	515.28	552.37	387.02	416.33
Government..........................	1dbd	7.41	6.27	9.56	37.23	67.22	69.39	93.33	115.99	146.58	178.10	184.78	179.17
Gold (Million Fine Troy Ounces).......	1ad	—	—	—	—	—	—	—	—	—	—	—	—
Gold (National Valuation)..............	1and	—	—	—	—	—	—	—	—	—	—	—	—
Monetary Authorities: Other Liab.....	4..d	38.33	28.20	16.59	12.02	7.83	6.99	.14	.11	.73	.59	.57	.37
Deposit Money Banks: Assets..........	7a.d	126.53	204.00	341.07	309.48	277.73	338.78	263.09	335.70	527.73	617.71	637.98	769.86
Liabilities.................	7b.d	173.11	274.86	402.14	382.40	400.97	450.04	373.02	440.94	607.94	566.85	623.63	863.25
Monetary Authorities		*Millions of Barbados Dollars: End of Period*											
Foreign Assets.......................	11	442.2	502.6	641.5	592.1	571.8	628.7	967.6	1,396.9	1,342.3	1,468.4	1,171.6	1,231.0
Claims on Central Government.......	12a	219.2	117.6	90.3	64.1	50.0	83.1	15.6	.6	.6	.6	52.7	199.7
Claims on Deposit Money Banks......	12e	—	6.0	—	—	23.5	15.0	—	—	—	—	—	—
Claims on Other Banking Insts........	12f	10.1	10.1	9.0	9.0	9.0	9.0	9.0	9.0	9.0	9.0	9.0	9.0
Reserve Money.......................	14	318.4	368.5	494.4	446.8	486.9	507.4	567.8	654.2	910.8	1,091.2	774.9	779.3
of which: Currency Outside DMBs..	14a	189.6	200.3	220.1	239.6	268.2	302.7	310.7	312.4	337.5	329.0	398.7	448.6
Foreign Liabilities.....................	16c	184.2	130.6	51.9	24.0	15.7	14.0	.3	.2	1.5	1.2	1.1	.7
Central Government Deposits..........	16d	212.0	197.8	255.5	266.7	244.5	261.6	471.5	757.7	474.4	405.7	471.7	695.2
Capital Accounts.....................	17a	35.5	35.9	35.1	33.7	34.6	34.1	32.9	32.2	33.9	35.9	37.0	41.0
Other Items (Net).....................	17r	−78.6	−96.4	−96.1	−106.0	−127.4	−81.3	−80.3	−37.8	−68.6	−56.0	−51.4	−76.6
Deposit Money Banks		*Millions of Barbados Dollars: End of Period*											
Reserves.............................	20	114.1	144.9	243.8	166.5	217.2	195.8	255.7	328.1	533.4	748.1	370.9	303.9
Foreign Assets.......................	21	253.1	408.0	682.1	619.0	555.5	677.6	526.2	671.4	1,055.5	1,235.4	1,276.0	1,539.7
Claims on Central Government........	22a	603.4	713.5	915.3	981.6	922.9	880.6	1,067.7	1,169.1	1,346.6	1,567.2	1,731.0	1,715.2
Claims on Private Sector................	22d	1,268.1	1,470.6	1,536.1	1,839.1	2,138.1	2,445.4	2,508.2	2,504.3	2,583.9	2,578.1	2,940.1	3,557.6
Claims on Other Banking Insts........	22f	159.3	39.4	41.2	91.6	108.5	94.1	109.2	111.5	178.4	180.6	338.7	465.7
Demand Deposits....................	24	309.6	208.4	370.0	350.1	493.3	615.6	825.7	837.1	842.3	1,211.7	1,247.7	1,355.6
Time, Savings,& Fgn.Currency Dep...	25	1,514.5	1,701.6	1,913.3	2,144.3	2,209.2	2,411.4	2,508.0	2,582.0	3,146.4	3,073.8	3,535.0	3,853.9
Foreign Liabilities.....................	26c	346.2	549.7	804.3	764.8	801.9	900.1	746.0	881.9	1,215.9	1,133.7	1,247.3	1,726.5
Central Government Deposits..........	26d	173.5	215.3	245.8	330.1	287.7	249.8	270.8	391.7	337.3	434.2	501.7	624.7
Credit from Monetary Authorities.....	26g	10.1	24.7	28.7	12.2	22.5	38.5	19.6	29.6	26.4	25.6	26.5	26.2
Capital Accounts.....................	27a	92.2	101.0	105.4	117.1	117.6	137.4	134.0	154.0	288.4	539.9	566.1	596.2
Other Items (Net).....................	27r	−48.2	−24.6	−48.9	−20.8	10.0	−59.4	−37.1	−91.9	−159.0	−109.4	−467.6	−601.0
Monetary Survey		*Millions of Barbados Dollars: End of Period*											
Foreign Assets (Net)......................	31n	164.8	230.3	467.4	422.2	309.7	392.2	747.5	1,186.2	1,180.4	1,568.9	1,199.2	1,043.5
Domestic Credit.......................	32	1,874.6	1,938.0	2,090.7	2,388.7	2,696.3	3,000.8	2,967.4	2,645.1	3,306.7	3,495.7	4,098.1	4,627.4
Claims on Central Govt. (Net)........	32an	437.0	417.9	504.4	449.0	440.8	452.3	341.0	20.4	535.4	728.0	810.3	595.0
Claims on Private Sector...............	32d	1,268.1	1,470.6	1,536.1	1,839.1	2,138.1	2,445.4	2,508.2	2,504.3	2,583.9	2,578.1	2,940.1	3,557.6
Claims on Other Banking Insts.......	32f	169.4	49.5	50.2	100.6	117.5	103.1	118.2	120.5	187.4	189.6	347.7	474.7
Money...............................	34	516.3	428.5	627.2	620.6	765.7	924.4	1,141.2	1,156.3	1,182.3	1,549.2	1,650.3	1,809.3
Quasi-Money..........................	35	1,514.5	1,701.6	1,913.3	2,144.3	2,209.2	2,411.4	2,508.0	2,582.0	3,146.4	3,073.8	3,535.0	3,853.9
Capital Accounts......................	37a	127.7	136.9	140.5	150.8	152.2	171.5	167.0	186.2	322.2	575.8	603.0	637.2
Other Items (Net).....................	37r	−119.1	−98.8	−122.8	−104.7	−121.1	−114.2	−101.3	−93.2	−163.7	−134.1	−490.9	−629.6
Money plus Quasi-Money..............	35l	2,030.8	2,130.1	2,540.5	2,764.9	2,974.9	3,335.8	3,649.2	3,738.3	4,328.7	4,623.0	5,185.2	5,663.2
Other Banking Institutions		*Millions of Barbados Dollars: End of Period*											
Claims on Central Government........	42a	.5	5.5	4.9	1.3	1.7	1.9	3.2	3.7	3.7	.6	5.3	7.9
Claims on Private Sector................	42d	417.5	424.7	443.0	381.8	433.4	378.6	423.0	446.4	442.3	440.6	451.4	474.9
Claims on Deposit Money Banks......	42e	2.1	6.3	14.8	19.5	14.0	13.9	53.6	21.3	57.4	43.5	36.6	97.8
Time Deposits........................	45	301.8	308.8	326.5	258.8	297.1	241.4	273.2	255.2	340.2	321.7	356.8	455.2
Central Government Deposits..........	46d	34.5	37.7	44.0	31.5	7.5	40.0	50.2	90.7	76.8	54.8	54.0	29.0
Credit from Deposit Money Banks.....	46h	46.8	49.2	43.8	70.7	92.6	63.4	94.9	54.3	15.4	52.2	31.7	11.7
Capital Accounts.....................	47a	5.1	5.1	5.1	7.9	10.9	18.9	18.9	18.9	18.9	18.9	18.9	18.9
Other Items (Net).....................	47r	32.0	35.8	43.3	33.7	40.9	30.7	42.6	52.4	52.1	37.2	32.0	65.8
Banking Survey		*Millions of Barbados Dollars: End of Period*											
Foreign Assets (Net)......................	51n	164.8	230.3	467.4	422.2	309.8	392.3	747.5	1,186.2	1,180.4	1,568.9	1,199.2	1,043.5
Domestic Credit.......................	52	2,088.7	2,281.0	2,444.5	2,639.6	3,006.4	3,238.1	3,225.1	2,884.0	3,488.6	3,692.5	4,153.1	4,606.4
Claims on Central Govt. (Net)........	52an	403.0	385.7	465.3	418.7	435.0	414.1	294.0	−66.6	462.4	673.8	761.6	573.9
Claims on Private Sector...............	52d	1,685.7	1,895.2	1,979.1	2,220.9	2,571.4	2,824.0	2,931.1	2,950.6	3,026.2	3,018.7	3,391.5	4,032.5
Liquid Liabilities......................	55l	2,332.5	2,438.9	2,867.0	3,023.6	3,271.9	3,577.0	3,920.1	3,992.9	4,667.7	4,944.5	5,541.9	6,118.4
Capital Accounts......................	57a	132.8	142.0	145.6	158.7	163.1	190.4	185.9	205.1	341.1	594.7	622.0	656.1
Other Items (Net).....................	57r	−211.8	−69.7	−100.6	−120.4	−118.9	−136.9	−133.4	−127.8	−339.7	−277.8	−811.5	−1,124.7
Interest Rates		*Percent Per Annum*											
Bank Rate (End of Period)...............	60	9.50	12.50	12.50	9.00	9.00	10.00	10.00	7.50	7.50	7.50	7.50	10.00
Treasury Bill Rate.....................	60c	7.26	8.01	6.85	3.61	5.61	5.83	5.29	3.14	2.10	1.41	1.20	4.62
Savings Rate..........................	60k	4.25	5.00	5.00	4.33	4.00	4.17	4.83	4.38	3.29	3.00	3.63	4.08
Deposit Rate.........................	60l	4.32	5.11	5.20	4.58	4.20	4.40	4.97	4.04	2.70	2.56	2.54	3.18
Lending Rate.........................	60p	9.08	10.00	10.00	9.83	9.75	9.40	10.19	9.58	8.50	8.50	8.33	9.17

Barbados 316

		1994	1995	1996	1997	1998	1999	2000	2001	2002	2003	2004	2005
Prices, Production, Labor					*Index Numbers (2000=100): Period Averages*								
Consumer Prices	64	† 86.7	88.3	90.4	97.4	96.1	97.6	100.0	† 102.6	102.7	104.4	105.9	112.3
Industrial Production	66	89.1	90.7	92.1	96.4	102.8	100.8	100.0	93.9	94.3	93.6	† 95.4	96.9
						Number in Thousands: Period Averages							
Labor Force	67d	135	137	136	136	136	137	139	145	143	145	146	....
Employment	67e	106	110	116	118	122	125	129	131	129	130	132	....
Unemployment	67c	28	27	20	20	17	14	13	14	15	16	14	....
Unemployment Rate (%)	67r	26.4	19.7	15.8	14.5	12.5	10.5	9.4	9.9	10.3	11.0	9.8	....
Intl. Transactions & Positions						*Millions of Barbados Dollars*							
Exports	70	363.0	477.8	561.2	565.9	503.1	527.6	544.7	518.7	483.0	499.5	556.5	718.9
Imports, c.i.f.	71	1,228.6	1,541.2	1,667.3	1,991.0	2,019.6	2,216.1	2,312.1	2,173.3	2,078.3	2,266.0	2,825.9	3,208.9
Balance of Payments					*Millions of US Dollars: Minus Sign Indicates Debit*								
Current Account, n.i.e.	78ald	133.6	42.6	69.7	−50.0	−63.0	−148.1	−145.5	−111.1	−168.1	−169.7	−337.2	....
Goods: Exports f.o.b.	78aad	190.0	245.4	286.7	289.0	270.1	275.3	286.4	271.2	253.0	264.2	293.1	....
Goods: Imports f.o.b.	78abd	−544.7	−691.1	−743.0	−887.7	−920.7	−989.4	−1,030.3	−952.3	−955.0	−1,065.6	−1,264.1	....
Trade Balance	78acd	−354.7	−445.8	−456.3	−598.7	−650.6	−714.1	−743.9	−681.1	−702.0	−801.4	−971.1	....
Services: Credit	78add	813.6	866.6	926.9	959.3	1,023.6	1,029.4	1,090.2	1,068.5	1,041.3	1,165.5	1,224.0	....
Services: Debit	78aed	−319.0	−363.2	−387.1	−409.5	−432.3	−458.3	−487.4	−498.5	−491.4	−518.9	−555.7	....
Balance on Goods & Services	78afd	140.0	57.7	83.6	−48.9	−59.3	−143.0	−141.1	−111.1	−152.0	−154.8	−302.8	....
Income: Credit	78agd	46.1	48.4	54.2	60.5	63.5	66.7	70.2	73.0	72.2	75.1	75.3	....
Income: Debit	78ahd	−86.8	−96.1	−106.3	−108.2	−119.4	−138.1	−152.5	−166.4	−174.0	−182.1	−197.3	....
Balance on Gds, Serv. & Inc.	78aid	99.3	10.0	31.4	−96.6	−115.2	−214.4	−223.4	−204.5	−253.8	−261.8	−424.8	....
Current Transfers, n.i.e.: Credit	78ajd	54.5	56.2	64.8	71.7	78.4	94.0	108.9	125.6	120.1	126.5	125.8	....
Current Transfers: Debit	78akd	−20.2	−23.6	−26.6	−25.1	−26.2	−27.7	−31.0	−32.3	−34.3	−34.5	−38.2	....
Capital Account, n.i.e.	78bcd	—	—	.4	—	.7	.7	1.8	1.3	—	—	—	....
Capital Account, n.i.e.: Credit	78bad	—	—	.4	—	.7	.7	1.8	1.3	—	—	—	....
Capital Account: Debit	78bbd	—	—	—	—	—	—	—	—	—	—	—	....
Financial Account, n.i.e.	78bjd	−5.9	−26.4	−22.8	19.9	55.1	120.3	289.2	284.8	118.6	202.6	134.5	....
Direct Investment Abroad	78bdd	−1.1	−3.3	−3.6	−1.2	−1.0	−1.3	−1.1	−1.1	−.5	−.5	−3.9	....
Dir. Invest. in Rep. Econ., n.i.e.	78bed	13.0	11.8	13.3	14.8	15.8	17.4	19.4	18.6	17.4	58.3	−12.1	....
Portfolio Investment Assets	78bfd	−1.9	−3.1	−17.5	−17.3	−29.1	−29.8	−29.2	−30.5	−24.8	−23.0	−58.5	....
Equity Securities	78bkd	−13.4	−7.6	−9.7	−11.3	−18.3	−16.3	−14.2	−14.8	−21.2	−23.2	−44.7	....
Debt Securities	78bld	11.5	4.6	−7.8	−6.0	−10.8	−13.5	−15.0	−15.7	−3.6	.2	−13.8	....
Portfolio Investment Liab., n.i.e.	78bgd	48.7	40.4	−1.6	−25.5	−25.6	44.9	100.3	150.2	−8.9	84.3	−9.7	....
Equity Securities	78bmd	—	—	—	−.1	−.1	−.1	—	—	1.1	94.7	.3	....
Debt Securities	78bnd	48.7	40.4	−1.6	−25.4	−25.6	45.0	100.3	150.2	−10.0	−10.4	−10.0	....
Financial Derivatives Assets	78bwd	....	....	....	....	....	....	....	....	....	....	....	....
Financial Derivatives Liabilities	78bxd	....	....	....	....	....	....	....	....	....	....	....	....
Other Investment Assets	78bhd	−88.9	−167.0	−210.9	−12.1	−12.6	−92.9	52.9	−56.7	−180.7	−82.9	30.1	....
Monetary Authorities	78bod	—	—	—	—	—	—	—	—	—	—	—	....
General Government	78bpd	−7.7	−9.3	−7.1	−14.1	−6.7	−4.4	−4.3	−5.4	−5.4	−4.3	−4.7	....
Banks	78bqd	−32.6	−87.5	−154.1	24.5	21.5	−72.5	66.9	−83.1	−201.3	−87.9	−26.0	....
Other Sectors	78brd	−48.6	−70.3	−49.8	−22.5	−27.4	−16.1	−9.7	31.8	26.1	9.3	60.8	....
Other Investment Liab., n.i.e.	78bid	24.3	94.9	197.4	61.1	107.5	182.1	146.9	204.4	315.9	166.5	188.6	....
Monetary Authorities	78bsd	−5.2	−8.5	−6.7	−6.7	—	—	—	—	—	—	—	....
General Government	78btd	−40.6	−34.3	9.8	7.9	23.8	5.0	18.6	11.5	−2.2	4.8	−23.2	....
Banks	78bud	16.6	101.4	127.3	−19.8	18.6	49.1	−77.0	67.9	167.0	−41.1	49.2	....
Other Sectors	78bvd	53.5	36.3	67.1	79.6	65.2	128.0	205.2	125.0	151.1	202.8	162.6	....
Net Errors and Omissions	78cad	−89.9	25.9	39.1	47.5	1.2	63.4	32.1	47.4	25.1	34.4	45.4	....
Overall Balance	78cbd	37.8	42.1	86.4	17.4	−6.1	36.3	177.6	222.4	−24.4	67.3	−157.3	....
Reserves and Related Items	79dad	−37.8	−42.1	−86.4	−17.4	6.1	−36.3	−177.6	−222.4	24.4	−67.3	157.3	....
Reserve Assets	79dbd	−59.1	−25.0	−61.1	−9.1	5.5	−37.0	−178.1	−222.9	23.9	−67.9	156.7	....
Use of Fund Credit and Loans	79dcd	—	−18.1	−26.8	−9.0	—	—	—	—	—	—	—	....
Exceptional Financing	79ded	21.3	1.0	1.5	.7	.6	.8	.5	.6	.5	.6	.6	....
Government Finance					*Millions of Barbados Dollars: Year Ending December 31*								
Deficit (-) or Surplus	80	−81.17	26.85	−129.65	−39.05	−39.21	−118.39	−76.69	−169.83	−308.41	−185.26	−125.98	−257.08
Total Revenue and Grants	81y	1,017.43	1,140.52	1,194.44	1,424.53	1,526.78	1,545.31	1,694.00	1,733.33	1,697.69	1,830.41	1,880.26	2,003.54
Revenue	81	1,017.43	1,140.52	1,194.44	1,424.53	1,526.78	1,545.31	1,694.00	1,733.33	1,697.69	1,830.41	1,880.26	2,003.54
Grants	81z	—	—	—	—	—	—	—	—	—	—	—	—
Exp. & Lending Minus Repay.	82z	1,098.60	1,113.67	1,324.09	1,463.58	1,565.99	1,663.70	1,770.69	1,903.16	2,006.10	2,015.67	2,006.24	2,260.62
Expenditure	82	1,070.34	1,125.78	1,324.26	1,458.02	1,573.67	1,660.81	1,767.40	1,882.54	2,004.96	2,013.57	2,004.53	2,174.79
Lending Minus Repayments	83	28.26	−12.10	−.17	5.56	−7.68	2.89	3.29	20.62	1.14	2.10	1.71	85.83
Statistical Discrepancy	80xx	−31.82	1.43	−47.48	−10.65	−14.08	28.95	−67.61	15.33	−212.55	−57.49	....	....
Total Financing	80h	112.99	−28.28	177.13	49.70	53.29	89.44	144.30	154.50	520.96	242.75	....	....
Domestic	84a	69.58	−19.30	162.93	83.98	104.99	6.69	−97.41	−162.97	551.49	90.76	....	....
Foreign	85a	43.41	−8.98	14.20	−34.28	−51.70	82.75	241.71	317.47	−30.53	151.99	....	....
Total Debt by Residence	88	2,492.2	2,479.9	2,721.1	2,737.1	2,796.2	2,897.5	3,232.7	3,692.7	3,950.7	4,043.3	4,135.8	4,912.9
Domestic	88a	1,777.8	1,762.2	1,967.0	2,036.9	2,121.4	2,108.6	2,204.1	2,333.4	2,605.4	2,710.1	2,803.2	3,386.1
Foreign	89a	714.4	717.7	754.1	700.2	674.9	788.9	1,028.6	1,359.4	1,345.3	1,333.1	1,332.6	1,526.9
National Accounts						*Millions of Barbados Dollars*							
Househ.Cons.Expend.,incl.NPISHs	96f	1,808	2,306	2,359	2,764	2,983	3,241	3,423	3,270	3,173	3,547	4,009	....
Government Consumption Expend	91f	707	752	848	927	982	1,027	1,084	1,143	1,219	1,249	1,176	....
Gross Capital Formation	93	464	527	506	676	....	....	....	....	....	....	....	....
Exports of Goods and Services	90c	1,980	2,177	2,380	2,438	2,522	2,546	2,583	2,591	2,480	2,753	2,790	....
Imports of Goods and Services (-)	98c	1,684	2,059	2,200	2,530	2,620	2,823	2,919	2,735	2,740	3,043	3,430	....
Gross Domestic Product (GDP)	99b	3,485	3,742	3,995	4,391	4,741	4,956	5,118	5,092	4,952	5,410	5,625	....
GDP Volume 1974 Prices	99b.p	825.8	846.5	873.1	901.9	941.3	975.3	997.5	971.6	976.1	996.0	1,043.4	1,083.9
GDP Volume (2000=100)	99bvp	82.8	84.9	87.5	90.4	94.4	97.8	100.0	97.4	97.9	99.8	104.6	108.7
GDP Deflator (2000=100)	99bip	82.3	86.2	89.2	94.9	98.2	99.0	100.0	102.1	98.9	105.9	105.1	....
						Millions: Midyear Estimates							
Population	99z	.26	.26	.26	.26	.26	.27	.27	.27	.27	.27	.27	.27

Belarus 913

		1994	1995	1996	1997	1998	1999	2000	2001	2002	2003	2004	2005
Exchange Rates						*Rubels per SDR: End of Period*							
Official Rate	aa	15.474	17.095	22.288	41.476	309.767	439.203	1,537.434	1,985.633	2,610.278	3,203.751	3,370.032	3,075.789
					Rubels per US Dollar: End of Period (ae) Period Average (rf)								
Official Rate	ae	10.600	11.500	15.500	30.740	106.000	320.000	1,180.000	1,580.000	1,920.000	2,156.000	2,170.000	2,152.000
Official Rate	rf	....	11.521	13.230	26.021	46.128	249.295	876.750	1,390.000	1,790.917	2,051.271	2,160.258	2,153.820
Fund Position						*Millions of SDRs: End of Period*							
Quota	2f.s	280.40	280.40	280.40	280.40	280.40	386.40	386.40	386.40	386.40	386.40	386.40	386.40
SDRs	1b.s	.01	3.05	.10	—	.30	.30	.14	.31	.19	.02	.01	.02
Reserve Position in the Fund	1c.s	.02	.02	.02	.02	.02	.02	.02	.02	.02	.02	.02	.02
Total Fund Cred.&Loans Outstg	2tl	70.10	190.20	190.20	190.20	172.27	129.74	87.62	64.26	40.89	17.52	5.84	—
International Liquidity						*Millions of US Dollars Unless Otherwise Indicated: End of Period*							
Total Reserves minus Gold	1l.d	† 100.99	377.02	469.15	393.70	702.76	294.27	350.50	390.68	618.81	594.81	749.37	1,136.62
SDRs	1b.d	.01	4.54	.14	—	.42	.42	.18	.40	.26	.03	.01	.03
Reserve Position in the Fund	1c.d	.03	.03	.03	.03	.03	.03	.03	.03	.03	.03	.03	.03
Foreign Exchange	1d.d	† 100.95	372.45	468.98	393.67	702.31	293.82	350.29	390.26	618.52	594.75	749.33	1,136.56
Monetary Authorities: Other Liab	4..d	7.53	11.88	144.97	61.87	78.90	77.31	94.29	137.08	253.69	275.63	75.80	14.62
Dep.Money Banks: Assets Conv	7axd	280.29	261.71	† 246.78	276.63	290.03	308.20	280.54	249.61	215.34	272.12	378.33	559.90
Assets Nonconv	7ayd	40.66	27.90	† 82.98	93.25	18.54	28.73	49.55	47.20	48.47	61.54	76.96	125.57
Dep.Money Banks: Liab. Conv	7bxd	51.69	88.05	† 84.25	89.30	134.49	108.07	99.16	142.17	202.86	329.25	536.17	763.63
Liab. Nonconv	7byd	36.49	31.68	† 58.55	70.10	4.71	7.78	14.90	45.92	70.48	66.34	79.92	72.06
Monetary Authorities						*Billions of Rubels: End of Period*							
Foreign Assets	11	1.23	4.59	7.41	12.33	76.46	98.36	423.56	706.18	1,439.90	1,946.82	2,056.50	3,009.20
Claims on Central Government	12a	1.68	4.88	8.59	14.45	54.93	153.75	302.80	504.35	190.42	643.26	432.56	533.66
Claims on Local Government	12b	—	—	—	—	—	—	—	—	—	—	—	—
Claims on Nonfin.Pub.Enterprises	12c	.01	.09	.11	.10	.02	.04	.02	—	8.17	12.07	15.07	.58
Claims on Private Sector	12d	.01	.04	.03	.07	.34	2.04	7.52	12.58	8.85	11.45	41.38	262.32
Claims on Banks	12e	1.43	2.32	6.72	17.05	51.23	60.23	107.08	180.56	255.45	332.13	564.54	818.34
Reserve Money	14	1.76	6.82	12.14	25.21	66.30	184.68	414.33	844.96	1,116.29	1,686.79	2,394.21	4,159.14
of which: Currency Outside DMBs	14a	.74	3.78	6.20	12.30	27.07	86.85	238.80	512.21	650.02	926.44	1,339.44	2,016.41
Time, Savings,& Fgn.Currency Dep	15	.02	.02	.02	.02	.08	.14	.31	.76		.19		
Foreign Liabilities	16c	1.26	3.39	6.49	9.79	70.72	81.72	245.98	344.17	593.81	650.39	184.16	31.46
Central Government Deposits	16d	.38	.34	1.11	2.01	6.49	15.07	41.74	35.10	22.57	126.68	233.75	208.96
Capital Accounts	17a	.30	.64	1.40	3.69	5.97	24.90	129.19	185.69	311.87	474.98	488.11	552.97
Other Items (Net)	17r	.64	.72	1.71	3.27	33.43	7.91	9.43	−7.02	−141.76	6.71	−190.18	−328.43
Deposit Money Banks						*Billions of Rubels: End of Period*							
Reserves	20	.95	2.84	† 5.69	11.89	35.69	92.00	158.12	324.84	389.80	675.58	1,132.30	2,098.85
Foreign Assets	21	3.69	3.33	† 5.11	11.37	67.89	107.82	389.51	468.96	506.52	719.35	987.98	1,475.14
Claims on Central Government	22a	.01	.64	† 2.27	6.08	21.96	53.80	176.94	302.61	550.20	849.63	1,018.86	1,575.51
Claims on Local Government	22b	—	—	† —	.02	.14	.36	.81	.47	81.52	194.24	83.72	295.44
Claims on Nonfin.Pub.Enterprises	22c	2.87	6.57	† 9.23	18.56	84.06	170.55	677.71	1,138.16	1,663.79	2,049.49	2,982.69	3,104.72
Claims on Private Sector	22d	3.13	7.36	† 12.30	30.29	113.00	279.70	802.50	1,400.76	2,320.55	4,283.53	6,885.68	10,034.22
Claims on Nonbank Financial Insts	22g	....	....	.30	.50	.48	1.28	1.31	7.94	11.65	21.70	49.57	60.82
Demand Deposits	24	1.88	6.13	† 9.24	21.05	52.49	140.71	259.60	425.66	714.29	1,308.43	1,968.51	3,073.06
Time, Savings,& Fgn. Currency Dep	25	4.24	7.89	† 11.61	23.90	136.24	271.89	1,104.98	1,678.72	2,569.99	3,935.86	5,675.19	7,600.55
Foreign Liabilities	26c	1.01	1.38	† 2.21	4.90	30.62	37.07	134.60	297.18	524.80	852.90	1,336.91	1,798.40
Central Government Deposits	26d	.24	1.00	† 2.85	5.80	20.99	44.72	177.91	443.51	347.22	314.73	775.91	1,734.23
Credit from Monetary Authorities	26g	1.24	2.12	† 6.49	15.93	48.37	53.47	84.39	142.49	152.10	180.33	511.31	733.17
Capital Accounts	27a	1.11	4.62	† 5.28	8.92	25.55	147.11	431.90	567.36	1,160.14	2,016.22	2,924.44	4,066.67
Other Items (Net)	27r	.93	−2.40	† −2.75	−1.79	8.96	10.53	13.53	88.82	55.48	185.05	−51.47	−361.38
Monetary Survey						*Billions of Rubels: End of Period*							
Foreign Assets (Net)	31n	2.64	3.16	† 3.82	9.01	43.01	87.38	432.49	533.79	827.80	1,162.88	1,523.41	2,654.49
Domestic Credit	32	7.08	18.23	† 28.90	62.27	247.45	601.73	1,749.98	2,888.25	4,465.35	7,623.97	10,499.86	13,924.07
Claims on Central Govt. (Net)	32an	1.07	4.17	† 6.91	12.72	49.41	147.76	260.09	328.35	370.82	1,051.49	441.75	165.98
Claims on Local Government	32b	—	—	† —	.02	.14	.36	.81	.47	81.52	194.24	83.72	295.44
Claims on Nonfin.Pub.Enterprises	32c	2.88	6.66	† 9.34	18.67	84.08	170.60	677.74	1,138.16	1,671.96	2,061.56	2,997.76	3,105.30
Claims on Private Sector	32d	3.13	7.40	† 12.34	30.36	113.34	281.74	810.03	1,413.34	2,329.40	4,294.98	6,927.06	10,296.54
Claims on Nonbank Financ. Insts	32g	....	....	.30	.50	.48	1.28	1.31	7.94	11.65	21.70	49.57	60.82
Money	34	2.69	10.03	† 15.71	33.85	80.93	233.42	508.43	939.18	1,365.67	2,235.62	3,308.72	5,090.35
Quasi-Money	35	4.25	7.91	† 11.63	23.93	136.32	272.03	1,105.28	1,679.48	2,569.99	3,936.05	5,675.19	7,600.55
Capital Accounts	37a	1.41	5.26	† 6.68	12.62	31.51	172.00	561.10	753.06	1,472.01	2,491.20	3,412.55	4,619.64
Other Items (Net)	37r	1.38	−1.80	† −1.30	.89	41.69	11.66	7.66	50.33	−114.51	123.98	−373.18	−731.98
Money plus Quasi-Money	35l	6.94	17.93	† 27.34	57.78	217.25	505.44	1,613.71	2,618.66	3,935.65	6,171.67	8,983.91	12,690.90
Money (National Definitions)						*Billions of Rubels: End of Period*							
Base Money	19ma	....	....	....	....	....	179.20	406.00	845.70	1,116.30	1,686.90	2,394.00	4,159.10
M1	59ma	....	....	....	....	....	217.90	469.20	889.60	1,259.10	2,002.50	3,111.40	4,945.79
M2	59mb	....	....	....	....	....	267.70	602.00	1,211.10	1,903.10	3,195.40	5,288.30	8,465.83
M2*	59mba	....	....	....	....	....	267.70	623.90	1,249.00	1,992.90	3,408.30	5,388.30	8,594.91
M3	59mc	....	....	....	....	....	496.90	1,571.50	2,610.20	3,923.70	6,132.30	8,839.00	12,570.59
Interest Rates						*Percent Per Annum*							
Refinancing Rate (End of Per.)	60	480.0	66.0	8.3	8.9	9.6	23.4	† 80.0	48.0	38.0	28.0	17.0	11.0
Deposit Rate	60l	89.6	100.8	32.4	15.6	14.3	23.8	37.6	34.2	26.9	17.4	12.7	9.2
Lending Rate	60p	148.5	175.0	62.3	31.8	27.0	51.0	67.7	47.0	36.9	24.0	16.9	11.4
Prices and Labor						*Percent Change over Previous Period*							
Producer Prices	63.xx	2,170.8	499.1	34.7	87.5	72.5	355.8	185.6	71.8	40.4	37.5	24.1	12.1
Consumer Prices	64.xx	2,221.0	709.3	52.7	63.9	72.9	293.7	168.6	61.1	42.5	28.4	18.1	10.3
Wages	65.xx	1,504.4	668.9	60.5	87.3	104.2	322.4	200.9	108.8	53.8	32.5	38.6	33.4
						Number in Thousands: Period Averages							
Employment	67e	4,701	4,410	4,365	4,370	4,417	4,442	4,441	4,417	4,381	4,339	4,316	4,332
Unemployment	67c	89	115	172	158	111	100	96	102	120	141	112	77
Unemployment Rate (%)	67r	1.8	2.5	3.8	3.5	2.4	2.2	2.1	2.3	2.7	3.1	2.5	1.7

Belarus 913

		1994	1995	1996	1997	1998	1999	2000	2001	2002	2003	2004	2005
Intl. Transactions & Positions							*Millions of US Dollars*						
Exports............................	70..d	2,510	4,803	5,652	7,301	7,070	5,909	7,326	7,451	8,021	9,946	13,774	15,979
Imports, c.i.f.......................	71..d	3,066	5,564	6,939	8,689	8,549	6,674	8,646	8,286	9,092	11,558	16,491	16,708
Balance of Payments						*Millions of US Dollars: Minus Sign Indicates Debit*							
Current Account, n.i.e.................	78ald	−443.8	−458.3	−515.9	−859.2	−1,016.5	−193.7	−338.4	−394.4	−311.2	−423.5	−1,042.9	469.1
Goods: Exports f.o.b.................	78aad	2,510.0	4,803.0	5,790.1	6,918.7	6,172.3	5,646.4	6,640.5	7,334.1	7,964.7	10,072.9	13,916.8	16,095.3
Goods: Imports f.o.b.................	78abd	−2,999.8	−5,468.7	−6,938.6	−8,325.7	−7,673.4	−6,216.4	−7,524.6	−8,140.8	−8,879.0	−11,328.5	−15,982.5	−16,622.6
Trade Balance..................	78acd	−489.8	−665.7	−1,148.5	−1,407.0	−1,501.1	−570.0	−884.1	−806.7	−914.3	−1,255.6	−2,065.7	−527.3
Services: Credit.................	78add	251.4	466.1	908.0	918.3	925.1	753.3	1,000.3	1,142.3	1,340.8	1,499.9	1,749.6	2,060.7
Services: Debit..................	78aed	−199.3	−283.7	−335.9	−364.8	−443.2	−438.8	−562.6	−841.3	−908.0	−915.0	−1,037.0	−1,237.0
Balance on Goods & Services..	78afd	−437.7	−483.3	−576.4	−853.0	−1,019.2	−255.5	−446.4	−505.7	−481.5	−670.7	−1,353.1	296.4
Income: Credit....................	78agd	.5	1.9	74.1	31.2	26.8	20.8	25.7	27.0	44.5	126.3	146.5	243.5
Income: Debit....................	78ahd	−29.3	−52.9	−104.9	−115.8	−119.7	−62.8	−72.4	−69.8	−73.1	−101.2	−121.0	−227.7
Balance on Gds, Serv. & Inc..	78aid	−466.5	−534.3	−607.2	−937.6	−1,112.1	−297.5	−493.1	−548.5	−510.1	−645.6	−1,327.6	312.2
Current Transfers, n.i.e.: Credit......	78ajd	50.9	107.2	135.5	106.1	120.9	137.0	177.1	202.6	260.4	291.7	378.7	280.0
Current Transfers: Debit..............	78akd	−28.2	−31.2	−44.2	−27.7	−25.3	−33.2	−22.4	−48.5	−61.5	−69.6	−94.0	−123.1
Capital Account, n.i.e................	78bcd	23.8	7.3	101.1	133.2	170.1	60.4	69.4	56.3	52.7	68.9	48.8	41.1
Capital Account, n.i.e.: Credit.......	78bad	23.8	7.3	257.2	248.0	261.3	131.1	125.6	132.3	119.8	133.2	128.3	135.4
Capital Account: Debit..............	78bbd	....	....	−156.1	−114.8	−91.2	−70.7	−56.2	−76.0	−67.1	−64.3	−79.5	−94.3
Financial Account, n.i.e..............	78bjd	144.6	204.0	378.7	738.1	354.8	399.5	140.1	265.0	482.5	231.9	872.5	147.2
Direct Investment Abroad.............	78bdd	....	....	....	−2.1	−2.3	−.8	−.2	−.3	206.2	−1.5	−1.3	−2.5
Dir. Invest. in Rep. Econ., n.i.e.....	78bed	10.5	14.7	104.5	351.6	203.2	444.0	118.8	95.8	247.1	171.8	169.4	305.0
Portfolio Investment Assets...........	78bfd	....	....	−17.7	−61.6	28.0	−15.4	−5.7	25.5	−2.4	.8	3.2	−2.9
Equity Securities...................	78bkd	....	....	....	−.6	.3	−7.3	.5	.7	6.9	−1.1	.6	—
Debt Securities...................	78bld	....	....	−17.7	−61.0	27.7	−8.1	−6.2	24.8	−9.3	1.9	2.6	−2.9
Portfolio Investment Liab., n.i.e......	78bgd	....	....	3.2	41.8	−13.4	−5.2	50.1	−45.4	−6.7	5.3	56.5	−38.6
Equity Securities...................	78bmd	....	....	....	....	2.7	....	.5	2.5	.7	3.3	.5	.6
Debt Securities...................	78bnd	....	....	3.2	41.8	−16.1	−5.2	49.6	−47.9	−7.4	2.0	56.0	−39.2
Financial Derivatives Assets...........	78bwd	....	....	....	....	....	....	....	....	....	....	....	1.9
Financial Derivatives Liabilities........	78bxd	....	....	....	....	....	....	....	....	....	....	....	−2.2
Other Investment Assets.............	78bhd	−232.5	−155.4	−131.5	49.9	199.4	−36.7	41.7	−139.2	−309.4	−61.0	−145.6	−461.8
Monetary Authorities..................	78bod	....	....	....	1.5	−.9	1.1	−.2	−99.3	−215.1	−10.0	231.5	72.8
General Government.................	78bpd	—	14.0	....	....	....	....	....	....	....	....	....	....
Banks................................	78bqd	−94.2	58.6	−40.2	−12.6	19.0	−16.4	8.4	17.5	19.1	−61.1	−120.5	−232.5
Other Sectors......................	78brd	−138.3	−228.0	−91.3	61.0	181.3	−21.4	33.5	−57.4	−113.4	10.1	−256.6	−302.1
Other Investment Liab., n.i.e.........	78bid	366.6	344.7	420.2	358.5	−60.1	13.6	−64.6	328.6	347.7	116.5	790.3	348.3
Monetary Authorities................	78bsd	−.3	3.7	133.1	−86.8	6.8	.7	−21.2	20.2	20.4	−135.3	−299.5	−65.7
General Government.................	78btd	239.4	81.7	33.4	62.4	24.7	−28.5	−37.2	44.9	9.3	−43.2	122.1	116.5
Banks................................	78bud	34.9	24.1	23.1	16.6	−20.3	−24.1	1.9	81.4	90.8	118.7	219.6	219.9
Other Sectors......................	78bvd	92.6	235.2	230.6	366.3	−71.3	65.5	−8.1	182.1	227.2	176.3	748.1	77.6
Net Errors and Omissions.............	78cad	−41.6	168.6	−178.1	53.0	172.3	−246.3	254.2	−5.4	−126.9	41.4	306.7	−139.3
Overall Balance...................	78cbd	−317.0	−78.4	−214.2	65.1	−319.3	19.9	125.3	−78.5	97.1	−81.4	185.1	518.1
Reserves and Related Items............	79dad	317.0	78.4	214.2	−65.1	319.3	−19.9	−125.3	78.5	−97.1	81.4	−185.1	−518.1
Reserve Assets.....................	79dbd	−58.6	−283.7	−78.6	75.3	54.6	34.6	−75.7	5.2	−100.9	13.8	−255.8	−539.2
Use of Fund Credit and Loans........	79dcd	—	177.8	—	—	−24.4	−58.1	−55.8	−29.8	−30.2	−32.3	−17.3	−8.9
Exceptional Financing...............	79ded	375.6	184.3	292.8	−140.4	289.1	3.6	6.2	103.1	33.9	99.8	88.0	30.0
International Investment Position							*Millions of US Dollars*						
Assets..	79aad	....	....	1,520.0	1,373.5	1,015.8	1,008.5	1,015.2	1,266.7	1,771.0	1,811.4	2,240.7	3,289.1
Direct Investment Abroad..............	79abd	....	....	184.6	101.9	28.9	24.3	23.8	20.1	3.7	6.2	8.2	13.9
Portfolio Investment..................	79acd	....	....	21.5	83.1	55.1	54.2	57.5	31.6	16.3	16.3	9.1	21.3
Equity Securities...................	79add	....	....	2.3	2.9	2.6	9.8	9.3	8.3	.8	1.8	.3	.3
Debt Securities....................	79aed	....	....	19.2	80.2	52.5	44.4	48.2	23.3	15.5	14.5	8.8	21.0
Financial Derivatives.................	79ald	....	....	....	....	....	....	....	....	....	....	2.0	....
Other Investment....................	79afd	....	....	844.8	794.9	592.8	625.4	577.1	855.6	1,273.2	1,289.9	1,451.2	1,957.3
Monetary Authorities.................	79agd	....	....	9.0	7.5	8.4	7.4	2.2	148.4	361.0	401.1	181.6	126.4
General Government.................	79ahd	....	....	—	—	—	—	—	—	—	—	—	—
Banks...............................	79aid	....	....	291.7	304.3	285.4	298.2	288.9	268.6	247.8	311.9	435.8	665.2
Other Sectors......................	79ajd	....	....	544.1	483.1	299.0	319.8	286.0	438.6	664.4	576.9	833.8	1,165.7
Reserve Assets.....................	79akd	....	....	469.1	393.6	339.0	304.6	356.8	359.4	477.8	499.0	770.2	1,296.6
Liabilities.............................	79lad	....	....	2,064.7	2,656.7	3,086.9	3,388.3	3,436.8	4,415.9	5,378.4	5,819.2	6,697.9	7,248.4
Dir. Invest. in Rep. Economy..........	79lbd	....	....	154.3	505.9	709.1	1,155.7	1,305.5	1,397.2	1,645.9	1,898.6	2,057.0	2,382.8
Portfolio Investment..................	79lcd	....	....	34.6	76.4	63.0	23.5	78.6	36.1	20.3	24.9	87.8	50.7
Equity Securities...................	79ldd	....	....	5.5	5.5	8.2	8.2	8.8	11.4	9.8	11.7	16.9	18.7
Debt Securities....................	79led	....	....	29.1	70.9	54.8	15.3	69.8	24.7	10.5	13.2	70.9	32.0
Financial Derivatives.................	79lld	....	....	....	....	....	....	....	....	....	....	3.7	7.1
Other Investment....................	79lfd	....	....	1,875.8	2,074.4	2,314.8	2,209.1	2,052.7	2,982.6	3,712.2	3,895.7	4,549.4	4,807.8
Monetary Authorities.................	79lgd	....	....	409.9	303.4	298.6	230.1	142.4	194.8	281.8	280.6	76.9	.6
General Government.................	79lhd	....	....	639.5	683.0	386.3	375.9	346.0	353.3	361.7	340.9	433.6	530.0
Banks...............................	79lid	....	....	142.8	159.4	139.1	112.4	114.1	188.1	273.4	395.6	616.1	835.8
Other Sectors......................	79ljd	....	....	683.6	928.6	1,490.8	1,490.7	1,450.2	2,246.4	2,795.3	2,878.6	3,422.8	3,441.4
Government Finance						*Billions of Rubels: Year Ending December 31*							
Deficit (-) or Surplus.................	80	−.33	−3.22	−3.46	−5.72	−5.99	−60.22	7.30	−235.68	....	....	....	....
Total Revenue and Grants............	81y	6.01	37.10	58.99	117.87	206.59	876.23	2,646.10	4,938.20	....	....	....	....
Revenue..............................	81	6.01	37.10	58.99	117.87	206.59	876.23	2,646.00	4,938.20	....	....	....	....
Grants..............................	81z	—	—	—	—	—	—	.10	....	....	....	....	....
Exp. & Lending Minus Repay.........	82z	6.34	40.33	62.46	123.59	212.58	936.45	2,638.80	5,173.88	....	....	....	....
Expenditure.........................	82	6.34	40.33	62.51	121.79	213.22	933.87	2,639.80	5,080.21	....	....	....	....
Lending Minus Repayments.........	83	—	—	−.06	1.80	−.64	2.58	−1.00	93.67	....	....	....	....
Total Financing......................	80h	.33	3.22	3.46	5.72	5.99	60.22	−7.30	235.68	....	....	....	....
Domestic............................	84a	−.13	2.79	3.69	4.11	7.97	84.65	42.90	−19.56	....	....	....	....
Foreign.............................	85a	.45	.43	−.22	1.61	−1.98	−24.43	−50.20	255.24	....	....	....	....
Total Debt by Residence...............	88	13.51	20.49	22.10	44.65	141.70	....	....	....	....	....	....	....
Domestic............................	88a	.51	3.04	7.42	14.63	33.56	....	....	....	....	....	....	....
Foreign.............................	89a	13.01	17.46	14.68	30.02	108.14	....	....	....	....	....	....	....

Belarus 913

National Accounts		1994	1995	1996	1997	1998	1999	2000	2001	2002	2003	2004	2005
							Billions of Rubels						
Househ.Cons.Expend.,incl.NPISHs....	96f	10.6	71.7	115.1	209.3	406.2	1,774.6	5,198.1	9,895.9	15,549.9	20,889.6	26,858.8	33,899.0
Government Consumption Expend...	91f	3.6	24.9	39.4	74.5	139.5	590.2	1,779.1	3,701.3	5,496.7	7,817.3	10,299.9	12,463.0
Gross Fixed Capital Formation..........	93e	5.9	30.0	40.4	92.6	182.1	796.7	2,301.9	3,893.0	5,746.4	9,288.5	13,568.6	17,783.2
Changes in Inventories....................	93i	−.1	.1	4.7	5.9	5.5	−79.3	18.0	187.5	50.2	441.0	1,674.7	1,080.4
Exports of Goods and Services..........	90c	12.7	60.3	88.9	219.6	414.6	1,791.5	5,912.4	11,750.9	16,705.0	23,816.1	33,937.6	39,097.8
Imports of Goods and Services (-).....	98c	15.0	65.6	96.7	240.8	448.7	1,865.0	6,230.0	12,516.1	17,610.5	25,224.4	37,119.0	38,446.8
Statistical Discrepancy....................	99bs	....	....	....	5.8	3.0	17.4	154.3	260.7	200.6	−463.3	771.2	−2,197.7
Gross Domestic Product (GDP)........	99b	17.8	121.4	191.8	366.8	702.2	3,026.1	9,133.8	17,173.2	26,138.3	36,564.8	49,991.8	63,678.9
Net Primary Income from Abroad.....	98.n	—	−.1	.2	−.5	−.4	2.8	−37.7	−60.1	−54.0	51.5	−40.2	....
Gross National Income (GNI)............	99a	17.8	121.4	192.0	366.3	701.8	3,028.9	9,096.1	17,113.1	26,084.3	36,616.3	49,951.6	....
Net Current Transf.from Abroad.......	98t	—	.8	1.2	2.1	4.5	31.2	116.0	217.9	309.9	460.5	616.3	....
Gross Nat'l Disposable Inc.(GNDI)....	99i	17.8	122.2	193.2	368.4	706.3	3,060.1	9,212.1	17,331.0	26,394.2	37,076.8	50,567.9	....
Gross Saving..................................	99s	3.6	25.5	38.7	84.5	160.7	695.3	2,234.9	3,733.8	5,347.6	8,369.9	13,409.2	....
GDP Volume 1995 Prices................	99b.p	135.6	121.4	124.8	139.0	150.7	155.8	164.8	....	....	....	....	....
GDP Volume 2000 Prices................	99b.p	....	....	....	....	....	....	9,133.8	9,565.4	10,048.0	10,755.7	11,987.2	13,095.3
GDP Volume (2000=100)...............	99bvp	† 82.2	73.6	75.7	84.3	91.4	94.5	100.0	104.7	110.0	117.8	131.2	143.4
GDP Deflator (2000=100)...............	99bip	.2	1.8	2.8	4.8	8.4	35.1	100.0	179.5	260.1	340.0	417.0	486.3
							Millions: Midyear Estimates						
Population.................................	99z	10.27	10.25	10.22	10.18	10.13	10.08	10.03	9.98	9.92	9.87	9.81	9.76

Belgium 124

		1994	1995	1996	1997	1998	1999	2000	2001	2002	2003	2004	2005
Exchange Rates					*Euros per SDR: End of Period*								
Market Rate.....................	aa	46.478	43.725	46.022	49.814	48.682	1.3662	1.4002	1.4260	1.2964	1.1765	1.1402	1.2116
				Euros per US Dollar: End of Period (we) Period Average (wf)									
Market Rate.....................	ae	31.838	29.415	32.005	36.920	34.575	.9954	1.0747	1.1347	.9536	.7918	.7342	.8477
Market Rate.....................	rf	33.456	29.480	30.962	35.774	36.299	.9386	1.0854	1.1175	1.0626	.8860	.8054	.8041
				Francs per ECU: End of Period (ea) Period Average (eb)									
ECU Rate.....................	ea	39.161	38.698	40.102	40.771	40.340	....	....	....	....	....	....	....
ECU Rate.....................	eb	39.662	38.537	39.290	40.529	40.623	....	....	....	....	....	....	....
				Index Numbers (2000=100): Period Averages									
Market Rate (1995=100)...............	ahx	88.2	100.0	95.1	82.4	81.2	....	....	....	....	....	....	....
Nominal Effective Exchange Rate.....	neu	108.4	114.1	111.1	105.4	105.7	104.0	100.0	100.5	101.6	105.7	106.8	106.9
Real Effective Exchange Rate...........	reu	113.7	118.9	113.8	109.0	109.0	105.0	100.0	101.7	104.9	109.4	111.9	113.5
Fund Position					*Millions of SDRs: End of Period*								
Quota.............................	2f.s	3,102	3,102	3,102	3,102	3,102	4,605	4,605	4,605	4,605	4,605	4,605	4,605
SDRs.............................	1b.s	123	331	346	363	433	197	236	376	408	434	225	220
Reserve Position in the Fund...........	1c.s	556	676	747	876	1,348	1,668	1,304	1,632	1,759	1,812	1,479	778
of which: Outstg.Fund Borrowing...	2c	—	—	—	—	140							
International Liquidity				*Millions of US Dollars Unless Otherwise Indicated: End of Period*									
Total Res.Min.Gold (Eurosys.Def)......	1l.d	13,876	16,177	16,953	16,190	18,272	† 10,938	9,994	11,266	11,855	10,989	10,361	8,241
SDRs.............................	1b.d	180	492	498	489	610	271	307	472	554	645	350	314
Reserve Position in the Fund.........	1c.d	812	1,005	1,075	1,182	1,899	2,290	1,699	2,051	2,392	2,693	2,296	1,112
Foreign Exchange.................	1d.d	12,884	14,680	15,380	14,519	15,763	† 8,377	7,988	8,743	8,909	7,651	7,715	6,815
o/w:Fin.Deriv.Rel.to Reserves.......	1ddd	....	....	....	....	....						119.86	−55.45
Other Reserve Assets.............	1e.d	....	....	....	....	....	—	—	—	—	—	—	—
Gold (Million Fine Troy Ounces)........	1ad	25.04	20.54	15.32	15.32	9.52	8.30	8.30	8.30	8.29	8.29	8.29	7.32
Gold (Eurosystem Valuation).........	1and	8,482	7,306	6,171	5,140	2,565	2,408	2,277	2,294	2,843	3,459	3,630	3,755
Memo:Euro Cl. on Non-EA Res........	1dgd	....	....	....	....	....	257	—	—	—	—	—	—
Non-Euro Cl. on EA Res.........	1dhd	....	....	....	....	....	139	427	704	313	405	569	556
Mon. Auth.: Other Foreign Assets....	3..d	115	113	100	91	97	†	—	—	—	—	—	—
Foreign Liabilities.................	4..d	477	629	144	81	382	† 7,341	1,081	1,719	1,141	1,646	1,957	825
Banking Insts.: Foreign Assets..........	7a.d	238,602	273,058	267,758	262,470	....	† 112,048	108,165	126,964	164,254	194,310	236,399	274,516
Foreign Liab..........	7b.d	263,337	302,856	293,657	280,033	....	† 181,820	163,882	176,325	199,014	236,307	274,681	328,341
Monetary Authorities			*Billions of Francs through 1998; Millions of Euros Beginning 1999: End of Period*										
Fgn. Assets (Cl.on Non-EA Ctys)......	11	729.1	692.6	741.4	793.7	712.1	13,303	12,737	15,024	13,675	11,321	10,531	10,687
Claims on General Government.......	12a.u	....	....	....	....	....	3,683	3,630	3,668	2,937	2,960	3,448	3,267
o/w: Claims on Gen.Govt.in Cty....	12a	79.3	86.3	91.0	94.1	47.0	1,123	1,220	1,158	805	666	681	851
Claims on Banking Institutions........	12e.u	....	....	....	....	....	25,795	17,312	9,699	18,118	30,707	42,768	52,746
o/w: Claims on Bank.Inst.in Cty...	12e	128.3	151.3	151.4	150.5	185.0	20,457	15,481	7,672	10,953	16,891	22,775	29,061
Claims on Other Resident Sectors....	12d.u	....	....	....	....	....	92	24	59	45	18	22	5
o/w: Cl. on Oth.Res.Sect.in Cty......	12d	....	....	....	....	....	3	3	2	2	2	2	2
Currency Issued.............................	14a	431.4	465.9	486.2	501.1	505.8	13,535	13,496	9,081	12,715	14,877	17,223	19,434
Liabilities to Banking Insts.................	14c.u	....	....	....	....	....	17,500	13,675	11,116	17,401	26,226	35,480	42,570
o/w: Liabs to Bank.Inst.in Cty...	14c	2.3	7.6	4.7	1.2	279.0	3,509	7,130	5,945	4,482	8,325	5,416	6,786
Demand Dep. of Other Res.Sect...	14d.u	....	....	....	....	....	19	12	7	6	9	6	6
o/w:D.Dep.of Oth.Res.Sect.in Cty...	14d	....	....	....	....	....	19	12	7	6	8	5	5
Other Dep. of Other Res.Sect...........	15..u	....	....	....	....	....	—	—	—	—	—	—	—
o/w:Oth.Dep.of Oth.Res.Sect.in Cty...	15	....	....	....	....	....	—	—	—	—	—	—	—
Bonds & Money Mkt. Instruments....	16n.u	....	....	....	....	....							
o/w: Held by Resid.of Cty...............	16n	—	—	230.0	230.0	—	....	....	....	....	....	....	....
Foreign Liab. (to Non-EA Ctys)........	16c	15.2	18.5	4.6	3.0	13.2	7,307	1,162	1,950	1,088	1,303	1,437	699
Central Government Deposits...........	16d.u	....	....	....	....	....	64	62	118	115	152	135	37
o/w: Cent.Govt.Dep. in Cty..........	16d	1.0	.5	.7	.1	.4	64	62	118	115	152	135	37
Capital Accounts.............................	17a	46.5	48.6	50.6	53.1	53.6	5,369	5,816	6,108	4,724	4,265	4,238	5,228
Other Items (Net).............................	17r	440.2	389.1	206.9	249.8	92.3	−921	−520	72	−1,272	−1,824	−1,750	−1,270
Memo: Net Claims on Eurosystem...	12e.s	....	....	....	....	....	−8,690	−5,103	−3,736	−6,655	−5,325	−11,469	−13,702
Currency Put into Circ...............	14m	....	....	....	....	....				7,887	3,807	126	−1,018
Banking Institutions			*Billions of Francs through 1998; Millions of Euros Beginning 1999: End of Period*										
Claims on Monetary Authorities.......	20	35.1	37.9	245.8	228.6	....	3,509	7,130	5,945	4,482	8,325	5,416	6,786
Claims on Bk.Inst.in Oth.EA Ctys...	20b.u	....	....	....	....	....	97,105	91,411	90,488	105,573	147,544	172,802	206,601
Fgn. Assets (Cl.on Non-EA Ctys).......	21	7,596.5	8,032.0	8,569.6	9,690.4	....	111,535	116,244	144,064	156,626	153,848	173,555	232,700
Claims on General Government.......	22a.u	....	....	....	....	....	175,991	160,255	180,779	166,928	172,616	178,590	183,000
o/w: Claims on Gen.Govt.in Cty....	22a	6,101.4	6,215.7	6,296.0	6,236.2	....	134,534	119,713	111,147	102,045	96,484	90,556	90,127
Claims on Other Resident Sectors.....	22d.u	....	....	....	....	....	218,724	225,662	230,712	234,954	241,277	250,701	276,529
o/w: Cl. on Oth.Res.Sect.in Cty...	22d	5,979.9	6,099.0	6,402.6	6,749.2	....	192,349	196,554	197,316	198,894	203,825	207,363	223,809
Demand Deposits.........................	24..u	....	....	....	....	....	53,554	58,499	61,397	62,067	67,348	78,158	90,396
o/w:D.Dep.of Oth.Res.Sect.in Cty...	24	1,111.3	1,152.7	1,200.0	1,237.0	....	50,428	53,682	56,546	57,877	62,071	72,713	81,172
Other Deposits.............................	25..u	....	....	....	....	....	188,347	182,139	199,536	212,803	230,923	251,408	267,848
o/w:Oth.Dep.of Oth.Res.Sect.in Cty...	25	4,706.0	4,936.3	5,490.4	5,915.4	....	157,750	154,139	167,216	176,584	193,039	208,015	221,380
Money Market Fund Shares...........	26m.u	....	....	....	....	....	1,029	804	1,191	1,609	1,815	1,994	1,980
Bonds & Money Mkt. Instruments....	26n.u	....	....	....	....	....	80,682	85,516	79,747	75,651	66,741	61,256	51,694
o/w: Held by Resid.of Cty...............	26n	3,703.8	3,691.3	3,593.6	3,291.5	....	....	....	....	....	....	....	....
Foreign Liab. (to Non-EA Ctys)........	26c	8,384.0	8,908.5	9,398.5	10,338.8	....	180,987	176,122	200,074	189,772	187,100	201,660	278,326
Central Government Deposits...........	26d.u	....	....	....	....	....	1,222	763	1,109	917	2,896	1,435	3,234
o/w: Cent.Govt.Dep. in Cty..........	26d	217.0	78.8	60.6	245.6	....	863	586	868	789	2,778	878	924
Credit from Monetary Authorities.....	26g	123.8	106.7	121.7	75.5	....	20,457	15,481	7,672	10,953	16,891	22,775	29,061
Liab. to Bk.Inst.in Oth. EA Ctys.......	26h.u	....	....	....	....	....	58,685	56,463	73,442	77,142	108,304	126,843	152,934
Capital Accounts.........................	27a	856.8	894.7	1,621.1	2,077.7	....	29,525	32,448	34,027	36,300	35,470	35,414	35,688
Other Items (Net).........................	27r	609.7	615.3	27.9	−277.3	....	−7,627	−7,532	−6,209	1,346	6,123	122	−5,546

Belgium 124

		1994	1995	1996	1997	1998	1999	2000	2001	2002	2003	2004	2005
Banking Survey (Nat'l Residency)					*Billions of Francs through 1998; Millions of Euros Beginning 1999: End of Period*								
Foreign Assets (Net)............	31n	−73.6	−202.4	−92.1	142.3	....	10,450	29,696	49,596	74,985	94,445	111,777	107,312
Domestic Credit....................	32	11,942.6	12,321.7	12,728.3	12,833.8	....	327,082	316,842	308,637	300,842	298,047	297,589	313,828
Claims on General Govt. (Net)......	32an	5,962.7	6,222.7	6,325.7	6,084.6	....	134,730	120,285	111,319	101,946	94,220	90,224	90,017
Claims on Other Resident Sectors.....	32d	5,979.9	6,099.0	6,402.6	6,749.2	....	192,352	196,557	197,318	198,896	203,827	207,365	223,811
Currency Issued....................	34a.n	431.4	465.9	486.2	501.1	505.8	13,535	13,496	9,081	12,715	14,877	17,223	19,434
Demand Deposits....................	34b.n	1,111.3	1,152.7	1,200.0	1,237.0	....	50,447	53,694	56,553	57,883	62,079	72,718	81,177
Other Deposits....................	35..n	4,706.0	4,936.3	5,490.4	5,915.4	....	157,750	154,139	167,216	176,584	193,039	208,015	221,380
Money Market Fund Shares..........	36m						1,029	804	1,191	1,609	1,815	1,994	1,980
Bonds & Money Mkt. Instruments....	36n	3,703.8	3,691.3	3,823.6	3,521.5	....	80,682	85,516	79,747	75,651	66,741	61,256	51,694
o/w: Over Two Years...............	36na	....	....	....	....	....	66,704	66,949	64,789	62,698	55,598	50,590	43,431
Capital Accounts..................	37a	903.3	943.3	1,671.7	2,130.8	....	34,894	38,264	40,135	41,024	39,735	39,652	40,916
Other Items (Net).................	37r	1,012.6	929.5	−36.0	−329.9	....	−808	626	4,310	10,360	14,209	8,509	4,557
Banking Survey (EA-Wide Residency)					*Millions of Euros: End of Period*								
Foreign Assets (Net)............	31n.u	....	....	....	....	....	−63,456	−48,303	−42,936	−20,559	−23,234	−19,011	−35,638
Domestic Credit..................	32..u	....	....	....	....	....	397,204	388,746	413,991	403,832	413,823	431,191	459,530
Claims on General Govt. (Net)....	32anu	....	....	....	....	....	178,388	163,060	183,220	168,833	172,528	180,468	182,996
Claims on Other Resident Sect......	32d.u	....	....	....	....	....	218,816	225,686	230,771	234,999	241,295	250,723	276,534
Currency Issued..................	34a.u	....	....	....	....	....	13,535	13,496	9,081	12,715	14,877	17,223	19,434
Demand Deposits..................	34b.u	....	....	....	....	....	53,573	58,511	61,404	62,073	67,357	78,164	90,402
Other Deposits..................	35..u	....	....	....	....	....	188,347	182,139	199,536	212,803	230,923	251,408	267,848
o/w: Other Dep. Over Two Yrs...	35abu	....	....	....	....	....	19,642	21,591	23,859	24,343	27,347	30,242	34,931
Money Market Fund Shares..........	36m.u	....	....	....	....	....	1,029	804	1,191	1,609	1,815	1,994	1,980
Bonds & Money Mkt. Instruments....	36n.u	....	....	....	....	....	80,682	85,516	79,747	75,651	66,741	61,256	51,694
o/w: Over Two Years...............	36nau	....	....	....	....	....	66,704	66,949	64,789	62,698	55,598	50,590	43,431
Capital Accounts.................	37a	....	....	....	....	....	34,894	38,264	40,135	41,024	39,735	39,652	40,916
Other Items (Net)................	37r.u	....	....	....	....	....	−38,315	−38,286	−20,039	−22,603	−30,856	−37,516	−48,384
Interest Rates					*Percent Per Annum*								
Discount Rate (End of Period).........	60	4.50	3.00	2.50	2.75	2.75	....	....	....	....	....	....	....
Money Market Rate.................	60b	5.72	4.80	3.24	3.46	3.58	....	....	....	....	....	....	....
Treasury Bill Rate................	60c	5.57	4.67	3.19	3.38	3.51	2.72	4.02	4.16	3.17	2.23	1.97	2.02
Deposit Rate......................	60l	4.86	4.04	2.66	2.88	3.01	2.42	3.58	3.40	2.60	1.65	....	....
Households: Stocks, up to 2 years..	60lhs	....	....	....	....	....	....	....	....	....	2.63	2.39	2.48
New Business, up to 1 year......	60lhn	....	....	....	....	....	....	....	....	....	2.06	1.83	1.95
Corporations: Stocks, up to 2 years	60lcs	....	....	....	....	....	....	....	....	....	2.36	2.12	2.10
New Business, up to 1 year........	60lcn	....	....	....	....	....	....	....	....	....	2.26	2.01	2.03
Lending Rate......................	60p	9.42	8.42	7.17	7.06	7.25	6.71	7.98	8.46	7.71	6.89	6.70	6.72
Households: Stocks, up to 1 year...	60phs	....	....	....	....	....	....	....	....	....	8.10	8.33	7.69
New Bus., Floating & up to 1 year	60pns	....	....	....	....	....	....	....	....	....	6.61	6.48	6.32
House Purch., Stocks, Over 5 years	60phm	....	....	....	....	....	....	....	....	....	5.54	5.19	4.67
House Purch., New Bus., 5-10 yrs	60phn	....	....	....	....	....	....	....	....	....	4.88	4.41	3.97
Corporations: Stocks, up to 1 year..	60pcs	....	....	....	....	....	....	....	....	....	4.32	4.11	3.82
New Bus., Over € 1 mil.,up to 1 yr	60pcn	....	....	....	....	....	....	....	....	....	3.13	2.80	2.77
Government Bond Yield.................	61	7.82	7.45	6.45	5.74	4.72	4.81	5.58	5.13	4.96	4.18	4.15	3.41
Prices, Production, Labor					*Index Numbers (2000=100): Period Averages*								
Industrial Share Prices................	62	106	100	....	....	....	....	....	....	....	....	....	....
Producer Prices													
Home and Import Goods...............	63	84.2	† 87.0	88.9	92.2	90.4	90.5	100.0	102.2	101.5	101.3	104.8	108.8
Industrial Production Prices...........	63b	89.3	† 91.4	91.9	93.4	92.3	91.9	100.0	100.8	102.2	102.8	107.4	109.8
Consumer Prices...................	64	90.8	92.1	† 94.0	95.5	96.4	97.5	100.0	102.5	104.2	105.8	108.0	† 111.0
Harmonized CPI...................	64h	....	92.4	94.0	95.4	96.3	97.4	100.0	102.4	104.0	† 105.6	107.6	110.3
Wages.............................	65	87.5	89.3	91.1	93.0	95.3	97.9	100.0	102.8	105.4	107.4	109.8	112.5
Industrial Production.............	66	81.8	86.5	86.9	91.0	94.1	94.9	100.0	99.0	100.3	101.1	104.3	103.9
					Number in Thousands: Period Averages								
Labor Force.......................	67d	4,160	4,185	4,196	4,214	4,241	4,382	4,401	....	4,402	4,070	....	....
Employment.......................	67e	3,755	3,795	3,792	3,839	3,857	† 4,007	4,092	4,051	4,070	4,070	4,139	....
Unemployment.....................	67c	589	597	588	570	541	508	474	470	499	538	379	....
Unemployment Rate (%).............	67r	13.9	14.1	13.8	13.3	12.6	11.7	10.9	10.8	11.2	12.3	12.8	....
Intl. Transactions & Positions													
(BLEU: Country Code (126)					*Billions of Francs*								
Exports...........................	70	4,579.0	4,996.1	5,133.1	5,916.2	....	....	....	....	....	....	....	....
Imports, c.i.f....................	71	4,192.0	4,568.4	4,729.1	5,554.4	....	....	....	....	....	....	....	....
					1995=100								
Volume of Exports.................	72	92.6	100.0	102.5	109.7	....	....	....	....	....	....	....	....
Volume of Imports.................	73	94.8	100.0	106.2	110.5	....	....	....	....	....	....	....	....
Unit Value of Exports.............	74	100.0	100.0	102.0	106.4	....	....	....	....	....	....	....	....
Unit Value of Imports.............	75	98.0	100.0	101.9	107.3	....	....	....	....	....	....	....	....
(For Belgium Only)					*Billions of Francs through 1998; Billions of Euros Beginning 1999*								
Exports...........................	70	4,792.7	5,177.8	5,430.2	6,142.9	6,491.3	† 168.10	203.94	212.55	228.58	225.95	246.71	269.83
Imports, c.i.f....................	71	4,339.7	4,702.0	5,065.8	5,619.2	5,967.9	† 154.62	192.18	199.49	209.73	207.69	229.61	256.14
					2000=100								
Volume of Exports.................	72	69.9	74.3	75.9	81.5	86.3	90.6	100.0	102.0	110.7	112.8	120.9	125.8
Volume of Imports.................	73	71.0	74.6	77.5	81.0	87.7	90.5	100.0	101.5	109.2	110.7	118.3	126.0
Unit Value of Exports.............	74	83.3	84.8	87.0	91.6	91.5	91.0	100.0	102.2	101.3	98.3	100.1	105.2
Unit Value of Imports.............	75	78.9	81.3	84.3	89.5	87.8	88.9	100.0	102.4	100.0	97.8	101.0	105.8

Belgium 124

		1994	1995	1996	1997	1998	1999	2000	2001	2002	2003	2004	2005
Balance of Payments						*Millions of US Dollars: Minus Sign Indicates Debit*							
(For Belgium-Luxembourg (126))													
Current Account, n.i.e.	78ald	12,571	14,232	13,762	13,914	12,168	14,086	11,381	9,392	....	....	....	....
Goods: Exports f.o.b.	78aad	122,795	155,219	154,695	149,497	153,558	161,263	164,677	163,498	....	....	....	....
Goods: Imports f.o.b.	78abd	−115,895	−145,664	−146,004	−141,794	−146,577	−154,237	−162,086	−159,790	....	....	....	....
Trade Balance	78acd	6,901	9,555	8,690	7,703	6,981	7,027	2,591	3,707	....	....	....	....
Services: Credit	78add	40,440	35,466	34,702	35,503	38,081	45,291	49,789	50,314	....	....	....	....
Services: Debit	78aed	−36,500	−33,134	−32,069	−31,664	−34,411	−39,167	−41,868	−43,316	....	....	....	....
Balance on Goods & Services	78afd	10,841	11,887	11,322	11,542	10,651	13,151	10,512	10,705	....	....	....	....
Income: Credit	78agd	89,403	74,798	62,884	58,237	65,251	71,892	75,673	78,906	....	....	....	....
Income: Debit	78ahd	−84,166	−67,990	−55,838	−51,882	−59,315	−66,125	−70,625	−75,999	....	....	....	....
Balance on Gds, Serv. & Inc.	78aid	16,078	18,695	18,368	17,896	16,588	18,918	15,560	13,612	....	....	....	....
Current Transfers, n.i.e.: Credit	78ajd	4,501	7,822	7,474	7,142	7,006	7,041	7,014	7,316	....	....	....	....
Current Transfers: Debit	78akd	−8,009	−12,285	−12,081	−11,124	−11,426	−11,872	−11,193	−11,535	....	....	....	....
Capital Account, n.i.e.	78bcd	....	378	179	403	−113	−54	−213	26	....	....	....	....
Capital Account, n.i.e.: Credit	78bad	....	734	673	783	323	449	222	480	....	....	....	....
Capital Account: Debit	78bbd	....	−356	−494	−379	−436	−503	−436	−454	....	....	....	....
Financial Account, n.i.e.	78bjd	−10,182	−12,912	−12,257	−12,091	−16,043	−13,470	−9,233	−7,978	....	....	....	....
Direct Investment Abroad	78bdd	−1,371	−11,603	−8,026	−7,252	−28,845	−130,012	−207,472	−86,091	....	....	....	....
Dir. Invest. in Rep. Econ., n.i.e.	78bed	8,514	10,689	14,064	11,998	22,690	142,703	214,941	73,635	....	....	....	....
Portfolio Investment Assets	78bfd	−40,963	−29,472	−48,409	−62,657	−100,234	−161,521	−122,814	−125,068	....	....	....	....
Equity Securities	78bkd	−10,649	−3,525	−3,582	−21,006	−29,087	−60,678	−103,290	−57,427	....	....	....	....
Debt Securities	78bld	−30,314	−25,946	−44,827	−41,651	−71,147	−100,842	−19,524	−67,642	....	....	....	....
Portfolio Investment Liab., n.i.e.	78bgd	17,445	4,649	36,666	54,047	59,253	135,837	132,547	140,588	....	....	....	....
Equity Securities	78bmd	22,489	6,505	34,243	47,207	58,418	92,372	82,908	97,662	....	....	....	....
Debt Securities	78bnd	−5,043	−1,856	2,423	6,840	835	43,466	49,639	42,926	....	....	....	....
Financial Derivatives Assets	78bwd	....	1,213	−970	−330	489	884	−3,653	−5,089	....	....	....	....
Financial Derivatives Liabilities	78bxd	....	630	483	444	302	1,142	1,252	942	....	....	....	....
Other Investment Assets	78bhd	11,269	−23,445	−14,977	−48,692	7,467	−58,713	−39,033	−70,053	....	....	....	....
Monetary Authorities	78bod	....	—	—	—	−147	−991	−342	13	....	....	....	....
General Government	78bpd	−294	−72	−372	−306	371	−1,848	−236	−137	....	....	....	....
Banks	78bqd	9,829	−16,926	9,164	−28,220	3,886	−12,806	−22,296	−58,086	....	....	....	....
Other Sectors	78brd	1,734	−6,447	−23,769	−20,166	3,357	−43,067	−16,159	−11,843	....	....	....	....
Other Investment Liab., n.i.e.	78bid	−5,076	34,426	8,913	40,352	22,836	56,210	14,999	63,158	....	....	....	....
Monetary Authorities	78bsd	—	223	−458	−50	193	23,578	−1,386	−3,903	....	....	....	....
General Government	78btd	−5,233	322	−40	−161	203	1,405	−1,279	415	....	....	....	....
Banks	78bud	64	42,121	6,469	31,211	18,087	6,702	7,139	67,159	....	....	....	....
Other Sectors	78bvd	93	−8,240	2,941	9,352	4,352	24,525	10,524	−513	....	....	....	....
Net Errors and Omissions	78cad	−2,169	−1,456	−1,091	−1,171	1,893	−2,430	−2,894	3	....	....	....	....
Overall Balance	78cbd	219	243	593	1,056	−2,095	−1,867	−959	1,442	....	....	....	....
Reserves and Related Items	79dad	−219	−243	−593	−1,056	2,095	1,867	959	−1,442	....	....	....	....
Reserve Assets	79dbd	−219	−243	−593	−1,056	2,095	1,867	959	−1,442	....	....	....	....
Use of Fund Credit and Loans	79dcd	—	—	—	—	—	—	—	—	....	....	....	....
Exceptional Financing	79ded	....	....	....	....	....	....	....	....	....	....	....	....
Balance of Payments						*Millions of US Dollars: Minus Sign Indicates Debit*							
(For Belgium Only)													
Current Account, n.i.e.	78ald	....	....	....	....	....	....	....	....	11,611	12,736	12,155	10,198
Goods: Exports f.o.b.	78aad	....	....	....	....	....	....	....	....	169,166	204,964	245,426	268,180
Goods: Imports f.o.b.	78abd	....	....	....	....	....	....	....	....	−159,648	−194,007	−235,718	−262,944
Trade Balance	78acd	....	....	....	....	....	....	....	....	9,518	10,957	9,708	5,236
Services: Credit	78add	....	....	....	....	....	....	....	....	37,822	44,647	52,597	55,488
Services: Debit	78aed	....	....	....	....	....	....	....	....	−35,863	−42,967	−48,990	−51,093
Balance on Goods & Services	78afd	....	....	....	....	....	....	....	....	11,477	12,637	13,314	9,631
Income: Credit	78agd	....	....	....	....	....	....	....	....	36,372	41,522	48,308	55,266
Income: Debit	78ahd	....	....	....	....	....	....	....	....	−31,897	−35,033	−42,755	−48,243
Balance on Gds, Serv. & Inc.	78aid	....	....	....	....	....	....	....	....	15,952	19,126	18,867	16,654
Current Transfers, n.i.e.: Credit	78ajd	....	....	....	....	....	....	....	....	5,275	6,513	7,941	9,404
Current Transfers: Debit	78akd	....	....	....	....	....	....	....	....	−9,616	−12,903	−14,653	−15,860
Capital Account, n.i.e.	78bcd	....	....	....	....	....	....	....	....	−585	−952	−429	−477
Capital Account, n.i.e.: Credit	78bad	....	....	....	....	....	....	....	....	219	267	399	397
Capital Account: Debit	78bbd	....	....	....	....	....	....	....	....	−803	−1,219	−828	−874
Financial Account, n.i.e.	78bjd	....	....	....	....	....	....	....	....	−6,483	1,381	5,698	7,338
Direct Investment Abroad	78bdd	....	....	....	....	....	....	....	....	−8,902	−26,720	−16,772	−7,839
Dir. Invest. in Rep. Econ., n.i.e.	78bed	....	....	....	....	....	....	....	....	18,081	35,970	42,882	27,314
Portfolio Investment Assets	78bfd	....	....	....	....	....	....	....	....	−5,707	−6,039	−35,563	−41,111
Equity Securities	78bkd	....	....	....	....	....	....	....	....	−3,551	−5,502	−8,042	−15,813
Debt Securities	78bld	....	....	....	....	....	....	....	....	−2,156	−537	−27,520	−25,298
Portfolio Investment Liab., n.i.e.	78bgd	....	....	....	....	....	....	....	....	20,149	6,628	5,070	−6,376
Equity Securities	78bmd	....	....	....	....	....	....	....	....	−467	3,182	4,092	5,430
Debt Securities	78bnd	....	....	....	....	....	....	....	....	20,616	3,446	978	−11,806
Financial Derivatives Assets	78bwd	....	....	....	....	....	....	....	....	−3,851	−7,195	−8,648	−8,661
Financial Derivatives Liabilities	78bxd	....	....	....	....	....	....	....	....	1,917	3,570	3,063	4,199
Other Investment Assets	78bhd	....	....	....	....	....	....	....	....	−43,583	−75,611	−64,698	−86,668
Monetary Authorities	78bod	....	....	....	....	....	....	....	....	186	−107	−853	−130
General Government	78bpd	....	....	....	....	....	....	....	....	−1	878	−403	10
Banks	78bqd	....	....	....	....	....	....	....	....	−40,292	−69,263	−64,840	−95,678
Other Sectors	78brd	....	....	....	....	....	....	....	....	−3,475	−7,120	1,398	9,131
Other Investment Liab., n.i.e.	78bid	....	....	....	....	....	....	....	....	15,413	70,779	80,365	126,480
Monetary Authorities	78bsd	....	....	....	....	....	....	....	....	6,695	6,663	15,366	5,639
General Government	78btd	....	....	....	....	....	....	....	....	−1,200	−632	−786	−296
Banks	78bud	....	....	....	....	....	....	....	....	6,681	57,497	57,694	120,771
Other Sectors	78bvd	....	....	....	....	....	....	....	....	3,238	7,250	8,092	367
Net Errors and Omissions	78cad	....	....	....	....	....	....	....	....	−4,579	−14,890	−18,398	−18,795
Overall Balance	78cbd	....	....	....	....	....	....	....	....	−35	−1,725	−974	−1,736
Reserves and Related Items	79dad	....	....	....	....	....	....	....	....	35	1,725	974	1,736

Belgium 124

		1994	1995	1996	1997	1998	1999	2000	2001	2002	2003	2004	2005
Balance of Payments(Cont.)													
Reserve Assets..............................	79dbd	....	....	....	....	....	....	....	....	35	1,725	974	1,736
Use of Fund Credit and Loans........	79dcd	....	....	....	....	....	....	....	....	—	—	—	—
Exceptional Financing...................	79ded	....	....	....	....	....	....	....	....	....	....	....	....
International Investment Position							*Millions of US Dollars*						
(For Belgium Only)													
Assets...	79aad	533,478	602,052	609,439	608,200	702,972	762,666	757,673	771,750	919,531	1,243,816	1,500,462	....
Direct Investment Abroad..............	79abd	69,541	80,690	87,311	94,734	134,982	151,795	179,773	181,459	223,940	313,938	369,230	....
Portfolio Investment......................	79acd	161,256	190,573	194,879	199,743	250,060	312,632	297,202	320,225	351,786	455,923	534,074	....
Equity Securities.......................	79add	59,804	63,767	64,571	64,661	94,142	125,274	124,687	110,226	104,971	146,643	172,164	....
Debt Securities..........................	79aed	101,453	126,806	130,308	135,081	155,918	187,358	172,515	209,999	246,816	309,280	361,910	....
Financial Derivatives....................	79ald	—	653	1,362	1,869	2,383	3,516	4,187	6,564	476	611	1,667	....
Other Investment.........................	79afd	279,199	306,655	302,837	290,473	295,043	281,414	264,269	249,933	328,630	458,896	581,502	....
Monetary Authorities.................	79agd	597	1,625	1,028	141	416	1,708	1,861	1,756	1,905	2,409	2,478	....
General Government...................	79ahd	1,947	7,952	7,277	6,333	6,375	5,425	5,025	4,815	405	834	753	....
Banks......................................	79aid	203,816	219,643	207,834	199,252	197,284	183,264	162,845	172,133	256,278	367,457	465,539	....
Other Sectors...........................	79ajd	72,839	77,435	86,698	84,748	90,968	91,017	94,539	71,228	70,042	88,197	112,733	....
Reserve Assets.............................	79akd	23,482	23,482	23,050	21,382	20,503	13,310	12,242	13,569	14,698	14,449	13,988	....
Liabilities....................................	79lad	495,611	554,101	542,475	528,266	604,018	617,628	615,340	653,214	815,099	1,116,151	1,387,974	....
Dir. Invest. in Rep. Economy..........	79lbd	105,881	112,960	123,883	128,728	180,492	179,924	195,219	203,537	255,745	357,137	471,071	....
Portfolio Investment......................	79lcd	103,808	106,724	97,497	89,423	91,255	112,113	126,455	127,152	167,594	223,877	259,902	....
Equity Securities.......................	79ldd	9,737	10,012	11,173	12,099	17,843	15,471	14,237	15,663	18,060	27,885	44,251	....
Debt Securities..........................	79led	94,071	96,713	86,324	77,324	73,412	96,643	112,218	111,489	149,534	195,992	215,652	....
Financial Derivatives....................	79lld	—	568	940	1,268	1,909	3,516	4,746	4,421	—	—	16	....
Other Investment.........................	79lfd	285,921	333,849	320,154	308,847	330,362	322,075	288,920	318,103	391,760	535,137	656,984	....
Monetary Authorities.................	79lgd	848	1,132	522	452	847	17,279	7,165	6,274	14,649	24,266	42,801	....
General Government...................	79lhd	942	864	694	385	411	1,808	651	888	4,394	4,784	5,094	....
Banks......................................	79lid	251,590	310,283	296,380	284,299	297,515	272,146	245,931	276,091	343,375	461,669	557,625	....
Other Sectors...........................	79ljd	32,540	21,571	22,559	23,711	31,589	30,841	35,173	34,850	29,342	44,417	51,464	....
Government Finance													
Central Government				*Billions of Francs through 1998; Millions of Euros Beginning 1999: Year Ending December 31*									
Deficit (-) or Surplus....................	80	−324.9	−259.1	† −210.2	−165.1	−162.1	† −3,644.0	−550.4	−1,856.9	−1,778.4	−728.4	−6,174.2	−2,274.7
Revenue......................................	81	3,476.4	3,567.5	† 3,685.2	3,820.1	3,986.1	† 39,405.1	42,181.4	42,278.1	45,189.6	50,387.4	47,914.0	45,633.6
Grants Received...........................	81z	5.7	11.1	† 5.0	20.3	6.8	....	....	....	....	....	....	....
Expenditure................................	82	3,821.3	3,885.6	† 3,909.5	4,032.3	4,152.3	† 43,049.1	42,731.8	44,135.0	46,968.0	51,115.8	54,088.2	47,908.3
Lending Minus Repayments...........	83	−14.3	−47.9	† −9.1	−26.8	2.7	....	....	....	....	....	....	....
Financing													
Net Borrowing: National Currency..	84a	360.1	380.1	† 612.9	104.7	273.1	† 7,990.6	2,283.1	3,763.1	4,767.8	3,556.7	7,297.0	3,087.2
Net borrowing: Foreign Currency....	85a	−152.4	−262.0	† −334.1	−1.0	−79.6	† −4,345.7	−1,727.9	−1,911.2	−2,989.8	−2,828.4	−1,122.9	−812.4
Use of Cash Balances...................	87	117.2	141.0	† −68.6	61.4	−31.4	....	....	....	....	....	....	....
Debt: National Currency................	88a	8,623.7	9,063.4	† 9,576.7	9,702.8	9,717.7	† 236,314.4	242,454.7	250,084.9	257,288.0	259,294.0	263,074.0	267,420.0
Debt: Foreign Currency.................	89a	1,349.5	1,085.3	† 734.0	784.4	701.7	† 10,441.3	8,606.9	7,079.8	5,464.0	3,724.0	2,444.0	1,740.0
General Government						*As Percent of Gross Domestic Product*							
National Accounts				*Billions of Francs through 1998; Billions of Euros Beginning 1999*									
Houseй.Cons.Expend.,incl.NPISHs.....	96f	4,286	4,537	4,643	4,797	4,935	† 127	134	139	142	147	153	159
Government Consumption Expend..	91f	1,668	1,806	1,875	1,915	1,917	† 51	54	56	60	63	66	69
Gross Fixed Capital Formation..........	93e	1,533	1,615	1,654	1,783	1,874	† 49	52	53	51	52	54	59
Changes in Inventories..................	93i	64	62	15	38	−28	† 1	3	—	—	1	3	4
Exports of Goods and Services..........	90c	5,282	5,681	5,941	6,599	6,850	† 179	213	220	221	222	242	260
Imports of Goods and Services (-).....	98c	4,965	5,320	5,601	6,210	6,463	† 169	206	210	208	210	230	253
Gross Domestic Product (GDP).........	99b	7,868	8,382	8,528	8,923	9,086	† 238	252	259	268	275	288	298
Net Primary Income from Abroad.....	98.n	182	168	166	173	194	† 5	6	4	3	4	3	3
Gross National Income (GNI)...........	99a	8,050	8,527	8,696	9,107	9,280	† 243	257	263	271	278	291	301
Net Current Transf.from Abroad.....	98t	−61	−56	−83	−83	−95	† −5	−7	−6	−6	−6	....	....
Gross Nat'l Disposable Inc.(GNDI)....	99i	7,989	8,268	8,434	8,852	9,185	† 238	250	257	265	272	....	....
Gross Saving................................	99s	2,035	2,101	2,057	2,252	2,331	† 61	64	63	65	65	....	....
Consumption of Fixed Capital..........	99cf	1,108	1,178	1,242	1,299	1,362	† 36	38	40	41	43	45	46
GDP Volume 1995 Prices.................	99b.p	7,980	8,162	8,231	8,551	8,728	† 222.8	....	....	....	....	....	....
GDP Volume 2000 Prices................	99b.p	....	....	....	....	....	† 242.4	251.7	254.4	258.2	260.6	267.3	270.6
GDP Volume (2000=100)...............	99bvp	84.0	87.7	88.7	91.6	91.9	† 96.3	100.0	101.0	102.6	103.5	106.2	107.5
GDP Deflator (2000=100)...............	99bip	92.2	94.1	94.7	95.9	97.3	† 98.3	100.0	101.8	103.6	105.4	107.8	110.2
							Millions: Midyear Estimates						
Population...............................	99z	10.10	10.14	10.17	10.21	10.24	10.27	10.30	10.33	10.36	10.38	10.40	10.42

Belize 339

		1994	1995	1996	1997	1998	1999	2000	2001	2002	2003	2004	2005
Exchange Rates		*Belize Dollars per SDR: End of Period (aa) Belize Dollars per US Dollar: End of Period (ae)*											
Official Rate	aa	2.9197	2.9730	2.8759	2.6985	2.8161	2.7450	2.6058	2.5135	2.7190	2.9719	3.1060	2.8585
Official Rate	ae	2.0000	2.0000	2.0000	2.0000	2.0000	2.0000	2.0000	2.0000	2.0000	2.0000	2.0000	2.0000
		Index Numbers (2000=100): Period Averages											
Official Rate	ahx	100.0	100.0	100.0	100.0	100.0	100.0	100.0	100.0	100.0	100.0	100.0	100.0
Nominal Effective Exchange Rate	nec	86.6	86.9	89.4	92.8	96.8	97.6	100.0	102.8	102.6	100.3	98.3	96.8
Real Effective Exchange Rate	rec	99.9	98.0	102.0	103.5	103.8	100.5	100.0	100.9	100.4	97.9	95.5	94.3
Fund Position		*Millions of SDRs: End of Period*											
Quota	2f.s	13.50	13.50	13.50	13.50	13.50	18.80	18.80	18.80	18.80	18.80	18.80	18.80
SDRs	1b.s	.37	.47	.61	.71	.82	1.01	1.20	1.37	1.48	1.56	1.64	1.76
Reserve Position in the Fund	1c.s	2.91	2.91	2.91	2.91	2.91	4.24	4.24	4.24	4.24	4.24	4.24	4.24
Total Fund Cred.&Loans Outstg	2tl	—	—	—	—	—	—	—	—	—	—	—	—
International Liquidity		*Millions of US Dollars Unless Otherwise Indicated: End of Period*											
Total Reserves minus Gold	1l.d	34.52	37.61	58.40	59.42	44.09	71.31	122.90	112.04	114.51	84.68	48.25	71.36
SDRs	1b.d	.54	.70	.88	.96	1.16	1.39	1.56	1.72	2.01	2.32	2.55	2.52
Reserve Position in the Fund	1c.d	4.25	4.33	4.19	3.93	4.10	5.82	5.52	5.33	5.76	6.30	6.58	6.06
Foreign Exchange	1d.d	29.72	32.58	53.34	54.53	38.82	64.10	115.82	104.99	106.74	76.07	39.12	62.78
Monetary Authorities: Other Liab.	4..d	6.21	5.31	1.77	3.64	1.61	1.04	.84	1.47	2.99	2.90	1.40	1.37
Deposit Money Banks: Assets	7a.d	24.27	26.21	38.45	35.84	37.94	45.64	71.64	69.17	58.95	62.09	67.05	73.82
Liabilities	7b.d	51.68	39.59	41.40	43.71	50.69	43.06	59.83	71.64	71.35	101.82	99.80	107.24
Other Banking Insts.: Assets	7e.d	—	—	—	—	—	—	—	—	—	—	—	—
Liabilities	7f.d	14.20	14.33	13.64	17.88	17.97	21.11	64.25	108.18	126.07	95.90	64.97	53.32
Monetary Authorities		*Millions of Belize Dollars: End of Period*											
Foreign Assets	11	68.94	75.24	116.85	118.89	88.23	142.90	245.85	224.15	229.98	169.43	96.57	142.78
Claims on Central Government	12a	67.54	81.72	110.78	89.86	94.89	67.38	62.49	78.03	63.59	165.37	165.13	181.66
Claims on Deposit Money Banks	12e	7.84	7.06	6.39	4.18	2.25	1.00	84.19	84.00	15.00	15.12	32.52	27.52
Reserve Money	14	102.50	116.21	119.64	125.81	135.57	165.22	202.80	257.79	198.86	207.09	232.65	271.60
of which: Currency Outside DMBs	14a	56.74	61.42	63.61	66.45	70.38	84.15	95.96	105.17	106.80	103.27	115.31	117.52
Foreign Liabilities	16c	12.41	10.62	3.54	7.29	3.22	2.08	1.67	2.94	5.99	5.79	2.79	2.74
Central Government Deposits	16d	17.88	19.42	65.93	47.31	21.48	25.87	91.92	31.48	83.08	123.06	48.09	84.03
Capital Accounts	17a	17.78	18.50	19.30	20.19	20.82	21.30	21.52	21.72	22.18	22.49	19.35	23.44
Other Items (Net)	17r	−6.24	−.73	25.62	12.35	4.29	−3.19	74.62	72.25	−1.54	−8.51	−8.65	−29.84
Deposit Money Banks		*Millions of Belize Dollars: End of Period*											
Reserves	20	45.13	53.77	54.71	58.68	64.85	59.02	101.45	103.28	84.42	100.36	114.69	137.81
Foreign Assets	21	48.53	52.42	76.90	71.68	75.89	91.27	143.27	138.34	117.90	124.18	134.10	147.64
Claims on Central Government	22a	52.99	63.88	39.77	61.92	58.39	80.11	87.12	87.87	62.98	54.98	81.55	67.33
Claims on Local Government	22b	.11	—	.05	.01	.23	1.38	1.16	2.17	2.49	3.27	5.43	4.38
Claims on Official Entities	22bx	.27	2.73	2.81	5.18	9.36	4.99	9.03	10.72	6.90	5.31	7.45	29.38
Claims on Private Sector	22d	405.27	436.44	478.03	540.03	610.72	641.14	679.71	771.03	884.12	1,010.75	1,124.92	1,182.58
Demand Deposits	24	86.81	93.32	99.12	99.03	115.85	141.86	185.99	225.05	214.13	295.42	321.98	330.89
Time, Savings,& Fgn.Currency Dep	25	316.35	388.84	421.56	486.98	504.93	552.39	612.72	631.29	665.59	638.57	690.29	750.87
Foreign Liabilities	26c	103.36	79.18	82.79	87.42	101.39	86.12	119.67	143.27	142.70	203.64	199.59	214.48
Central Government Deposits	26d	43.86	23.59	27.78	26.89	40.68	21.56	24.31	20.93	27.47	20.50	82.17	89.86
Credit from Monetary Authorities	26g	1.66	1.48	1.28	1.09	.88	.63	.41	.16	—	5.12	—	—
Capital Accounts	27a	31.04	39.40	43.54	49.77	51.73	69.71	71.33	89.16	112.06	154.42	192.03	227.62
Other Items (Net)	27r	−30.78	−16.57	−23.81	−13.69	4.00	5.64	7.31	3.55	−3.14	−18.82	−17.92	−44.60
Monetary Survey		*Millions of Belize Dollars: End of Period*											
Foreign Assets (Net)	31n	1.70	37.85	107.43	95.86	59.51	145.97	267.79	216.28	199.19	84.18	28.29	73.20
Domestic Credit	32	464.44	541.76	537.72	622.80	711.44	747.57	723.29	897.41	909.53	1,096.12	1,254.23	1,291.45
Claims on Central Govt. (Net)	32an	58.80	102.59	56.83	77.58	91.13	100.07	33.38	113.50	16.02	76.80	116.42	75.11
Claims on Local Government	32b	.11	—	.05	.01	.23	1.38	1.16	2.17	2.49	3.27	5.43	4.38
Claims on Official Entities	32bx	.27	2.73	2.81	5.18	9.36	4.99	9.03	10.72	6.90	5.31	7.45	29.38
Claims on Private Sector	32d	405.27	436.44	478.03	540.03	610.72	641.14	679.71	771.03	884.12	1,010.75	1,124.92	1,182.58
Money	34	144.18	155.47	164.02	166.17	186.65	248.24	287.32	379.65	328.47	402.17	439.93	464.59
Quasi-Money	35	316.35	388.84	421.56	486.98	504.93	552.39	612.72	631.29	665.59	638.57	690.29	750.87
Capital Accounts	37a	48.82	57.90	62.84	69.95	72.55	91.00	92.85	110.88	134.24	176.91	211.38	251.06
Other Items (Net)	37r	−43.20	−22.59	−3.28	−4.45	6.83	1.92	−1.82	−8.12	−19.59	−37.35	−59.09	−101.87
Money plus Quasi-Money	35l	460.53	544.31	585.58	653.15	691.58	800.62	900.04	1,010.93	994.07	1,040.74	1,130.23	1,215.46
Other Banking Institutions		*Millions of Belize Dollars: End of Period*											
Reserves	40	1.41	2.47	.93	3.17	1.58	11.35	10.17	20.68	8.36	5.85	5.34	9.72
Foreign Assets	41	—	—	—	—	—	—	—	—	—	—	7.88	8.30
Claims on Central Government	42a	—	—	—	—	—	—	—	—	—	—	28.04	.04
Claims on Official Entities	42bx	—	—	—	—	—	—	—	—	—	—	28.04	.04
Claims on Private Sector	42d	45.70	47.03	53.75	60.78	65.96	61.92	199.33	266.63	216.41	224.24	295.43	231.62
Foreign Liabilities	46c	28.41	28.66	27.29	35.77	35.93	42.22	128.50	216.35	252.14	191.81	129.94	106.63
Central Government Deposits	46d	1.23	1.40	1.07	1.20	2.71	27.06	6.10	3.35	8.81	85.36	222.18	289.92
Credit from Monetary Authorities	46g	3.35	4.07	6.30	6.02	5.77	5.36	4.45	85.27	16.57	11.10	33.64	2.85
Capital Accounts	47a	1.21	3.48	8.69	10.68	11.88	13.80	15.84	23.90	29.13	31.55	40.53	32.76
Other Items (Net)	47r	12.90	11.89	11.34	10.29	11.25	−15.17	54.61	−41.57	−81.88	−89.72	−89.61	−182.48
Banking Survey		*Millions of Belize Dollars: End of Period*											
Foreign Assets (Net)	51n	−26.70	9.20	80.14	60.09	23.58	103.75	139.29	−.07	−52.96	−107.63	−101.66	−33.44
Domestic Credit	52	508.91	587.39	590.40	682.38	774.70	782.43	916.52	1,160.69	1,117.13	1,235.00	1,363.39	1,241.48
Claims on Central Govt. (Net)	52an	57.57	101.20	55.76	76.38	88.42	73.01	27.29	110.15	7.21	−8.56	−97.88	−206.52
Claims on Local Government	52b	.11	—	.05	.01	.23	1.38	1.16	2.17	2.49	3.27	5.43	4.38
Claims on Official Entities	52bx	.27	2.73	2.81	5.18	9.36	4.99	9.03	10.72	6.90	5.31	35.49	29.42
Claims on Private Sector	52d	450.97	483.47	531.79	600.81	676.69	703.06	879.03	1,037.66	1,100.53	1,234.99	1,420.35	1,414.20
Liquid Liabilities	55l	459.12	541.85	584.65	649.98	690.00	789.27	889.87	990.25	985.71	1,034.89	1,124.89	1,205.73
Capital Accounts	57a	50.04	61.38	71.53	80.63	84.43	104.80	108.69	134.78	163.37	208.46	251.90	283.82
Other Items (Net)	57r	−26.95	−6.63	14.36	11.86	23.86	−7.89	57.24	35.58	−84.90	−115.97	−115.06	−281.51
Money (National Definitions)		*Millions of Belize Dollars: End of Period*											
M1	59ma	....	....	....	....	....	....	....	....	358.07	361.08	406.71	423.16
M2	59mb	....	....	....	....	....	....	....	....	1,063.42	1,101.14	1,248.23	1,329.95

		1994	1995	1996	1997	1998	1999	2000	2001	2002	2003	2004	2005
Interest Rates							*Percent Per Annum*						
Discount Rate (End of Period)..........	60	12.00	12.00	12.00	12.00	12.00	12.00	12.00	12.00	12.00	12.00	12.00	12.00
Treasury Bill Rate............................	60c	4.27	4.10	3.78	3.51	3.83	5.91	5.91	5.91	4.59	3.22	3.22	3.22
Savings Rate.................................	60k	5.32	5.30	5.30	5.35	5.43	5.42	5.43	5.44	5.10	5.05	5.08	5.09
Deposit Rate.................................	60l	8.55	9.37	9.08	9.19	8.76	8.12	7.69	6.35	6.28	6.93	7.42	7.71
Lending Rate.................................	60p	14.78	15.69	16.30	16.29	16.50	16.27	16.01	15.45	14.83	14.35	13.94	14.26
Prices and Labor							*Index Numbers (2000=100): Period Averages*						
Consumer Prices......................	64	91.8	94.4	100.4	101.5	100.6	99.4	100.0	101.2	103.4	106.1	109.4	113.3
							Number in Thousands: Period Averages						
Labor Force.................................	67d	70	....	75	81	86	89	....	94	94	102	108	111
Employment................................	67e	62	63	65	71	73	78	84	86	85	89	96	99
Unemployment.............................	67c	8	9	10	10	12	11	....	9	9	13	13	12
Unemployment Rate (%)...............	67r	11.1	12.5	13.8	12.7	14.3	12.8	11.1	9.1	10.0	12.9	11.6	11.0
Intl. Transactions & Positions							*Millions of Belize Dollars*						
Exports..	70	254.90	285.73	307.10	318.12	312.66	339.24	420.78	325.45	316.67	381.41	410.14	413.28
Imports, c.i.f...............................	71	519.86	514.43	510.97	572.42	590.32	739.82	1,048.57	1,033.65	1,049.03	1,104.17	1,028.21	1,185.83
Balance of Payments							*Millions of US Dollars: Minus Sign Indicates Debit*						
Current Account, n.i.e...................	78ald	−40.1	−17.2	−6.6	−31.9	−59.8	−67.8	−156.0	−189.9	−182.6	−207.4	−182.3	....
Goods: Exports f.o.b....................	78aad	156.5	164.6	171.3	193.4	186.2	261.5	281.8	269.1	309.7	315.5	306.9	....
Goods: Imports f.o.b....................	78abd	−231.9	−230.6	−229.5	−282.9	−290.9	−375.8	−478.4	−477.7	−496.9	−522.3	−480.8	....
Trade Balance...........................	78acd	−75.4	−66.1	−58.2	−89.5	−104.7	−114.3	−196.6	−208.7	−187.2	−206.8	−173.8	....
Services: Credit...........................	78add	121.1	132.8	137.9	137.8	140.5	153.8	158.2	157.3	156.9	178.6	199.2	....
Services: Debit............................	78aed	−88.0	−94.9	−91.3	−91.7	−99.0	−106.7	−124.5	−120.9	−130.5	−139.0	−145.7	....
Balance on Goods & Services.......	78afd	−42.2	−28.1	−11.7	−43.3	−63.3	−67.1	−162.9	−172.2	−160.7	−167.2	−120.3	....
Income: Credit............................	78agd	2.9	2.8	6.3	7.5	7.2	4.8	6.9	8.3	3.9	4.2	3.9	....
Income: Debit.............................	78ahd	−28.2	−25.1	−32.4	−30.8	−39.3	−45.0	−59.8	−75.2	−72.9	−89.7	−118.1	....
Balance on Gds, Serv. & Inc......	78aid	−67.5	−50.4	−37.8	−66.7	−95.4	−107.3	−215.8	−239.1	−229.6	−252.7	−234.4	....
Current Transfers, n.i.e.: Credit......	78ajd	34.4	38.3	34.2	38.2	38.4	41.9	61.1	51.0	49.1	47.7	54.3	....
Current Transfers: Debit...............	78akd	−6.9	−5.2	−3.1	−3.4	−2.8	−2.3	−1.3	−1.8	−2.1	−2.5	−2.2	....
Capital Account, n.i.e....................	78bcd	—	—	−2.2	−3.4	−1.9	.5	−2.5	.9	9.2	1.5	4.2	....
Capital Account, n.i.e.: Credit........	78bad	—	—	—	—	—	1.8	1.6	2.1	10.3	2.4	5.0	....
Capital Account: Debit..................	78bbd	—	—	−2.2	−3.4	−1.9	−1.3	−4.1	−1.3	−1.1	−.9	−.8	....
Financial Account, n.i.e..................	78bjd	3.6	−1.0	11.0	27.6	23.5	96.0	205.1	172.3	140.3	206.8	129.6	....
Direct Investment Abroad.............	78bdd	—	—	−5.7	−3.9	−4.5	—	—	—	—	−.4	−.1	....
Dir. Invest. in Rep. Econ., n.i.e......	78bed	15.4	21.1	16.6	12.0	17.7	53.6	23.3	59.9	24.3	−1.4	127.6	....
Portfolio Investment Assets...........	78bfd	—	—	—	—	....	—	—	—	—	−.2	−.2	....
Equity Securities......................	78bkd	—	—	—	—	....	—	—	—	—	−.2	−.2	....
Debt Securities........................	78bld	—	—	—	—	....	—	—	—	—	—	—	....
Portfolio Investment Liab., n.i.e......	78bgd	6.1	3.5	10.1	10.2	12.5	38.5	113.1	−14.9	126.6	75.5	75.7	....
Equity Securities......................	78bmd	—	—	—	—	....	—	—	—	—	—	—	....
Debt Securities........................	78bnd	6.1	3.5	10.1	10.2	12.5	38.5	113.1	−14.9	126.6	75.5	75.7	....
Financial Derivatives Assets...........	78bwd	....	....	—	—	....	....	....	—	.8	.7	.5	....
Financial Derivatives Liabilities.......	78bxd	....	....	—	—	....	....	....	—	—	—	—	....
Other Investment Assets...............	78bhd	−17.1	−14.1	−12.2	2.8	—	−13.8	−50.6	−1.7	3.3	−13.3	−7.4	....
Monetary Authorities..................	78bod	....	....	—	—	....	—	—	—	—	—	—	....
General Government...................	78bpd	—	—	—	—	....	−5.7	−11.1	−3.1	−4.0	−3.0	−3.0	....
Banks......................................	78bqd	−3.3	−1.7	−12.2	2.8	—	−6.2	−26.2	2.5	10.1	−3.0	−5.3	....
Other Sectors...........................	78brd	−13.8	−12.4	—	—	—	−1.9	−13.3	−1.1	−2.8	−7.3	.9	....
Other Investment Liab., n.i.e.........	78bid	−.8	−11.5	2.2	6.5	−2.2	17.7	119.2	129.0	−14.7	145.7	−66.5	....
Monetary Authorities..................	78bsd	—	—	—	—	—	−.6	41.8	−.6	−33.0	−2.6	−4.0	....
General Government...................	78btd	8.9	−2.6	19.7	11.5	8.8	17.6	56.8	122.6	−11.1	74.7	−53.0	....
Banks......................................	78bud	−9.3	−12.1	−6.3	4.8	7.2	−8.9	15.5	11.6	−1.4	30.2	.6	....
Other Sectors...........................	78bvd	−.3	3.2	−11.2	−9.8	−18.2	9.6	5.1	−4.6	30.8	43.4	−10.1	....
Net Errors and Omissions................	78cad	32.8	22.4	18.4	9.1	24.5	−4.0	5.1	14.0	24.9	−9.3	16.9	....
Overall Balance............................	78cbd	−3.6	4.1	20.6	1.4	−13.7	24.8	51.6	−2.8	−8.2	−8.4	−31.6	....
Reserves and Related Items..............	79dad	3.6	−4.1	−20.6	−1.4	13.7	−24.8	−51.6	2.8	8.2	8.4	31.6	....
Reserve Assets............................	79dbd	3.6	−4.1	−20.6	−1.4	13.7	−27.5	−51.9	2.5	6.0	30.8	31.6	....
Use of Fund Credit and Loans........	79dcd	—	—	—	—	—	—	—	—	—	—	—	....
Exceptional Financing...................	79ded	—	—	—	....	2.7	.3	.3	2.2	−22.5	—		....
Government Finance							*Thousands of Belize Dollars: Year Beginning April 1*						
Deficit (-) or Surplus......................	80	−70,802	−39,698	−15,671	−32,588f	....	....	....	....	....	....	....	....
Revenue.....................................	81	258,978	261,658	288,256	283,357f	....	....	....	....	....	....	....	....
Grants Received...........................	81z	13,264	1,079	4,076	41,191f	....	....	....	....	....	....	....	....
Expenditure................................	82	348,953	306,090	317,781	362,261f	....	....	....	....	....	....	....	....
Lending Minus Repayments...........	83	−5,909	−3,655	−9,778	−5,125f	....	....	....	....	....	....	....	....
Financing													
Domestic....................................	84a	45,433	41,604	−33,262	....	....	....	....	....	....	....	....	....
Foreign.......................................	85a	25,369	−1,906	48,933	....	....	....	....	....	....	....	....	....
Debt: Domestic............................	88a	145,985	167,747	168,330	....	....	....	....	....	....	....	....	....
Foreign.......................................	89a	285,800	282,610	329,798	....	....	....	....	....	....	....	....	....

Belize   339

National Accounts		1994	1995	1996	1997	1998	1999	2000	2001	2002	2003	2004	2005
		Millions of Belize Dollars											
Househ.Cons.Expend.,incl.NPISHs....	96f	823.8	891.1	956.9	994.9	1,067.1	1,133.5	1,231.8	1,357.4	1,456.8	1,519.8	1,632.8	....
Government Consumption Expend...	91f	177.6	177.1	181.4	190.2	197.5	197.9	214.8	228.3	266.8	289.6	300.9	....
Gross Fixed Capital Formation.........	93e	238.8	269.2	260.6	261.0	259.0	360.4	477.0	438.4	421.5	374.8	373.3	....
Changes in Inventories....................	93i	—	—	.5	3.0	3.8	−.1	50.7	−6.2	23.0	31.1	36.8	....
Exports of Goods and Services.........	90c	578.9	594.9	641.4	690.7	724.5	806.8	881.5	887.0	980.3	1,055.4	1,002.6	....
Imports of Goods and Services (-).....	98c	609.2	609.1	644.8	729.0	784.5	987.1	1,226.0	1,204.9	1,233.4	1,306.0	1,239.7	....
Gross Domestic Product (GDP).........	99b	1,161.3	1,240.0	1,282.6	1,308.8	1,377.6	1,464.7	1,664.7	1,737.6	1,853.0	1,961.6	2,071.2	....
Net Primary Income from Abroad.....	98.n	−59.9	−55.6	−64.4	−59.3	−70.3	−87.7	−128.3	−163.4	−165.8	−203.3	−242.5	....
Gross National Income (GNI)............	99a	1,101.4	1,184.4	1,218.2	1,249.5	1,307.3	1,377.0	1,536.4	1,574.2	1,687.2	1,758.3	1,828.7	....
Consumption of Fixed Capital..........	99cf	53.9	60.1	59.5	60.1	996.1	1,098.3	1,183.7	....	....	....	....	....
GDP Volume 2000 Prices.................	99b.p	1,235.3	1,243.5	1,261.2	1,306.5	1,354.8	1,473.2	1,664.7	1,741.5	1,823.7	1,990.9	2,083.0	2,147.6
GDP Volume (2000=100).................	99bvp	74.2	74.7	75.8	78.5	81.4	88.5	100.0	104.6	109.6	119.6	125.1	129.0
GDP Deflator (2000=100)................	99bip	94.0	99.7	101.7	100.2	101.7	99.4	100.0	99.8	101.6	98.5	99.4	....
		Millions: Midyear Estimates											
Population...............................	99z	.21	.21	.22	.23	.23	.24	.24	.25	.25	.26	.26	.27

Benin 638

		1994	1995	1996	1997	1998	1999	2000	2001	2002	2003	2004	2005
Exchange Rates						*Francs per SDR: End of Period*							
Official Rate	aa	† 780.44	728.38	753.06	807.94	791.61	† 896.19	918.49	935.39	850.37	771.76	747.90	794.73
					Francs per US Dollar: End of Period (ae) Period Average (rf)								
Official Rate	ae	† 534.60	490.00	523.70	598.81	562.21	† 652.95	704.95	744.31	625.50	519.36	481.58	556.04
Official Rate	rf	† 555.20	499.15	511.55	583.67	589.95	† 615.70	711.98	733.04	696.99	581.20	528.28	527.47
Fund Position						*Millions of SDRs: End of Period*							
Quota	2f.s	45.3	45.3	45.3	45.3	45.3	61.9	61.9	61.9	61.9	61.9	61.9	61.9
SDRs	1b.s	—	.1	.2	—	—	.2	.1	.3	.1	.1	—	.1
Reserve Position in the Fund	1c.s	2.1	2.1	2.2	2.2	2.2	2.2	2.2	2.2	2.2	2.2	2.2	2.2
Total Fund Cred.&Loans Outstg	2tl	48.8	56.6	68.9	70.3	66.4	67.1	64.4	61.1	53.9	49.2	42.0	36.9
International Liquidity					*Millions of US Dollars Unless Otherwise Indicated: End of Period*								
Total Reserves minus Gold	1l.d	† 258.2	197.9	261.8	253.1	261.5	400.1	458.1	578.1	615.7	717.9	640.0	656.8
SDRs	1b.d	—	.1	.3	.1	.1	.2	.1	.4	.1	.2	—	.2
Reserve Position in the Fund	1c.d	3.1	3.2	3.1	2.9	3.1	3.0	2.9	2.7	3.0	3.3	3.4	3.1
Foreign Exchange	1d.d	† 255.1	194.7	258.4	250.1	258.4	396.9	455.2	574.9	612.6	714.4	636.5	653.5
Gold (Million Fine Troy Ounces)	1ad	.011	—	—	—	—	—	—	—	—	—	—	—
Gold (National Valuation)	1and	4.1	—	—	—	—	—	—	—	—	—	—	—
Monetary Authorities: Other Liab	4..d	3.8	6.1	10.9	12.8	2.6	2.0	1.7	−2.5	2.8	6.3	26.6	14.8
Deposit Money Banks: Assets	7a.d	143.9	239.3	278.8	265.0	288.9	253.9	214.2	239.7	271.8	283.8	332.6	283.7
Liabilities	7b.d	30.4	50.2	102.0	53.1	89.5	107.3	88.2	99.0	100.3	151.5	172.7	184.4
Monetary Authorities						*Billions of Francs: End of Period*							
Foreign Assets	11	138.1	97.0	137.1	151.5	147.0	261.2	322.9	430.3	385.1	372.8	308.2	365.2
Claims on Central Government	12a	28.3	41.9	42.6	55.1	52.0	52.7	52.8	51.1	45.5	41.9	36.2	32.1
Claims on Deposit Money Banks	12e	—	—	2.0	1.0	—	—	—	—	—	—	—	—
Reserve Money	14	108.9	80.5	87.9	105.4	100.7	177.0	249.1	306.8	266.7	273.0	221.5	293.3
of which: Currency Outside DMBs	14a	77.3	50.6	68.9	80.8	70.4	160.3	211.8	222.3	167.9	190.3	129.9	193.3
Foreign Liabilities	16c	40.1	44.2	57.6	64.5	54.1	61.4	60.4	55.3	47.6	41.2	44.3	37.6
Central Government Deposits	16d	18.7	15.1	37.0	31.1	36.7	71.1	63.4	112.8	91.6	87.7	66.1	59.3
Other Items (Net)	17r	−1.4	−.9	−.8	6.6	7.5	4.4	2.9	6.5	24.8	12.7	12.5	7.1
Deposit Money Banks						*Billions of Francs: End of Period*							
Reserves	20	30.9	32.4	17.1	31.9	31.5	16.5	37.1	77.0	86.3	78.0	112.3	88.5
Foreign Assets	21	76.9	117.3	146.0	158.7	162.4	165.8	151.0	178.4	170.0	147.4	160.2	157.8
Claims on Central Government	22a	44.4	40.6	44.2	32.9	30.7	25.9	25.8	23.1	20.6	23.8	20.0	29.6
Claims on Private Sector	22d	75.0	80.4	102.4	71.7	100.1	161.7	194.0	192.8	222.2	293.8	312.1	375.1
Claims on Other Financial Insts	22f	1.0	1.0	—	—	—	—	—	—	—	—	—	—
Demand Deposits	24	106.3	107.8	114.8	107.5	108.4	104.2	146.7	167.2	191.3	208.8	198.6	225.3
Time Deposits	25	66.1	86.0	90.5	99.6	98.3	110.2	114.6	136.8	133.3	146.9	165.4	185.3
Foreign Liabilities	26c	14.9	24.1	52.8	31.0	49.6	67.6	59.8	72.9	61.4	76.2	81.2	99.1
Long-Term Foreign Liabilities	26cl	1.3	.5	.6	.8	.7	2.4	2.3	.9	1.4	2.5	2.0	3.5
Central Government Deposits	26d	35.0	34.0	35.1	39.8	56.1	74.4	79.4	84.5	95.0	81.9	97.0	108.1
Credit from Monetary Authorities	26g	—	—	4.0	1.0	—	—	—	—	—	—	—	—
Other Items (Net)	27r	4.5	19.3	12.0	15.5	11.6	10.9	5.2	9.2	16.9	26.8	60.3	29.7
Treasury Claims: Private Sector	22d.i	—	—	—	—	—	—	—	—	—	—	—	—
Post Office: Checking Deposits	24..i	2.0	2.8	5.3	4.4	4.7	5.1	5.8	9.6	7.3	7.4	8.1	29.9
Monetary Survey						*Billions of Francs: End of Period*							
Foreign Assets (Net)	31n	159.9	146.0	172.7	214.7	205.7	298.0	353.8	480.5	446.2	402.8	342.9	386.3
Domestic Credit	32	97.0	117.7	122.4	93.2	94.7	99.9	135.7	79.3	109.1	197.4	213.2	299.2
Claims on Central Govt. (Net)	32an	21.0	36.3	20.0	21.5	−5.4	−61.7	−58.3	−113.5	−113.2	−96.5	−98.8	−75.9
Claims on Private Sector	32d	75.0	80.4	102.4	71.7	100.1	161.7	194.0	192.8	222.2	293.8	312.1	375.1
Claims on Other Financial Insts	32f	1.0	1.0	—	—	—	—	—	—	—	—	—	—
Money	34	186.2	161.7	189.5	193.4	184.2	270.6	365.4	401.8	367.3	407.5	337.2	449.4
Quasi-Money	35	66.1	86.0	90.5	99.6	98.3	110.2	114.6	136.8	133.3	146.9	165.4	185.3
Long-Term Foreign Liabilities	36cl	1.3	.5	.6	.8	.7	2.4	2.3	.9	1.4	2.5	2.0	3.5
Other Items (Net)	37r	3.3	15.4	14.5	14.2	17.2	14.6	7.2	20.5	53.3	43.2	51.5	47.4
Money plus Quasi-Money	35l	252.3	247.7	280.0	293.0	282.5	380.8	480.0	538.5	500.6	554.4	502.6	634.7
Interest Rates						*Percent Per Annum*							
Bank Rate (End of Period)	60	6.00	6.00	6.00	6.00	6.00	6.00	6.00	6.00	6.00	4.50	4.00	4.00
Money Market Rate	60b	4.95	4.95	4.95	4.95	4.95	4.95	4.95	4.95	4.95	4.95	4.95	4.95
Deposit Rate	60l	3.50	3.50	3.50	3.50	3.50	3.50	3.50	3.50	3.50	3.50	3.50	3.50
Prices and Labor						*Index Numbers (2000=100): Period Averages*							
Consumer Prices	64	72.8	83.4	87.5	† 90.5	95.7	96.0	100.0	104.0	106.6	108.2	109.1	115.0
					Number in Thousands: Period Averages								
Labor Force	67d	....	....	3,211	....	....	....	....	....	....	....	....	....
Intl. Transactions & Positions						*Billions of Francs*							
Exports	70	220.90	209.60	334.70	243.40	240.40	259.50	279.40	273.90	312.10	322.80	355.00	153.25
Imports, c.i.f	71	239.35	372.20	334.70	397.90	434.00	464.58	400.64	456.51	502.45	515.05	470.97	471.93

		1994	1995	1996	1997	1998	1999	2000	2001	2002	2003	2004	2005
Balance of Payments						*Millions of US Dollars: Minus Sign Indicates Debit*							
Current Account, n.i.e.	78ald	−23.2	−213.1	−57.4	−169.9	−151.5	−191.4	−111.0	−160.5	−238.9	−348.6	....	....
Goods: Exports f.o.b.	78aad	397.9	419.9	527.7	424.0	414.3	421.5	392.4	373.5	447.8	540.8	....	....
Goods: Imports f.o.b.	78abd	−451.5	−622.5	−559.7	−576.9	−572.6	−635.2	−516.1	−553.0	−678.9	−818.7	....	....
Trade Balance	78acd	−53.6	−202.5	−32.0	−152.9	−158.3	−213.7	−123.7	−179.5	−231.1	−277.9		
Services: Credit	78add	142.2	194.3	126.1	116.0	142.3	176.9	136.1	147.1	152.2	172.3		
Services: Debit	78aed	−181.4	−272.2	−188.8	−172.3	−191.4	−215.3	−191.7	−191.9	−208.8	−253.9		
Balance on Goods & Services	78afd	−92.8	−280.4	−94.7	−209.2	−207.4	−252.2	−179.4	−224.3	−287.7	−359.5		
Income: Credit	78agd	18.8	23.5	36.5	25.4	31.1	29.1	31.2	29.4	25.2	26.3		
Income: Debit	78ahd	−21.7	−31.1	−57.5	−45.4	−44.5	−40.5	−43.5	−42.9	−51.0	−64.4		
Balance on Gds, Serv. & Inc.	78aid	−95.7	−288.0	−115.6	−229.2	−220.8	−263.6	−191.6	−237.7	−313.5	−397.6		
Current Transfers, n.i.e.: Credit	78ajd	98.5	105.4	92.4	77.8	102.0	87.1	91.3	87.3	93.2	56.6		
Current Transfers: Debit	78akd	−25.9	−30.5	−34.2	−18.5	−32.7	−14.9	−10.7	−10.0	−18.6	−7.5		
Capital Account, n.i.e.	78bcd	75.2	85.6	6.4	84.5	66.6	69.9	73.3	48.6	37.6	34.4		
Capital Account, n.i.e.: Credit	78bad	75.2	85.6	6.4	84.5	66.6	69.9	73.4	48.6	37.6	34.9		
Capital Account: Debit	78bbd	—	—	—	—	—	—	−.1	—	—	−.5		
Financial Account, n.i.e.	78bjd	−17.6	−126.3	−104.2	−21.3	−8.9	25.4	10.8	39.6	−61.4	32.1		
Direct Investment Abroad	78bdd	—	—	−21.9	−13.1	−5.2	−2.9	−11.3	−9.4	−5.7	−3.9		
Dir. Invest. in Rep. Econ., n.i.e.	78bed	13.6	13.3	35.5	27.0	38.0	40.7	67.5	50.9	17.9	48.3		
Portfolio Investment Assets	78bfd	−26.4	−64.2	−7.7	−7.8	1.2	−1.4	5.7	3.1	−3.6	−7.2		
Equity Securities	78bkd			1.4		.1	−.9	.9	−1.1	5.6	.3		
Debt Securities	78bld	−26.4	−64.2	−9.1	−7.7	1.1	−.5	4.7	4.2	−9.2	−7.5		
Portfolio Investment Liab., n.i.e.	78bgd	—	.3	2.5	2.0	1.2	2.0	.1	−.4	1.5	−.4		
Equity Securities	78bmd	—	.3	2.5	2.0	1.2	2.0	.1	−.4	1.5	−.4		
Debt Securities	78bnd	—	—	—	—	—	—	—	—	—	—		
Financial Derivatives Assets	78bwd	....	....	....	—	....	−.1	—	−.2	.1	−.2		
Financial Derivatives Liabilities	78bxd	—	—	—	—	—	8.6	—	—	—	—		
Other Investment Assets	78bhd	−52.2	−62.1	−4.0	−12.4	−9.6	−58.3	25.1	−34.4	−81.8	25.7		
Monetary Authorities	78bod	—	—	—	—	—	—	—	—	−.1	.1		
General Government	78bpd	11.9	−6.9	—	−.1	—	—	—	—	−.5	22.6		
Banks	78bqd	−50.8	−44.2	11.8	−41.1	12.4	−26.7	1.8	−46.6	−81.2	3.1		
Other Sectors	78brd	−13.3	−10.9	−15.8	28.8	−22.0	−31.6	23.4	12.2	10.2	−30.2		
Other Investment Liab., n.i.e.	78bid	47.4	−13.7	−108.6	−17.0	−34.4	36.8	−76.2	29.9	10.2	182.0		
Monetary Authorities	78bsd	.6	−2.7	5.2	4.7	−5.4	.3	−1.4	.8	−.8	4.5		
General Government	78btd	−28.1	−36.0	−129.4	−26.8	−29.7	−33.6	−49.2	−30.9	−46.8	−46.2		
Banks	78bud	9.8	−.4	4.5	−11.6	21.1	33.3	−21.0	12.7	−.9	32.4		
Other Sectors	78bvd	65.1	25.4	11.1	16.7	−20.4	36.8	−4.7	47.4	58.7	−20.9		
Net Errors and Omissions	78cad	−16.3	−1.0	6.3	6.7	7.1	7.3	6.7	3.6	2.1	182.0		
Overall Balance	78cbd	18.1	−254.9	−149.0	−100.0	−86.7	−88.7	−20.3	−68.7	−260.5	−100.0		
Reserves and Related Items	79dad	−18.1	254.9	149.0	100.0	86.7	88.7	20.3	68.7	260.5	100.0		
Reserve Assets	79dbd	−117.7	81.9	−78.3	−24.5	7.0	−40.2	−87.3	−147.4	88.8	−6.2		
Use of Fund Credit and Loans	79dcd	24.9	12.2	18.0	1.9	−5.3	1.1	−3.6	−4.1	−9.2	−6.6		
Exceptional Financing	79ded	74.6	160.7	209.3	122.6	85.0	127.8	111.2	220.2	180.9	112.8		
International Investment Position							*Millions of US Dollars*						
Assets	79aad	....	....	613.1	664.5	598.7	726.4	737.4	936.7	1,089.0	1,224.0		
Direct Investment Abroad	79abd	....	....	13.7	−2.3	5.3	5.6	10.5	12.6	16.2	19.7		
Portfolio Investment	79acd	....	....	75.9	75.2	94.4	81.4	67.6	65.0	83.4	95.5		
Equity Securities	79add	....	....	.2	—	2.5	1.7	3.2	3.2	1.7	1.4		
Debt Securities	79aed	....	....	75.8	75.2	91.9	79.7	64.4	61.8	81.7	94.1		
Financial Derivatives	79ald	....	....	.1	—	—	.1	—	.2	.3	.5		
Other Investment	79afd	....	....	261.6	338.4	236.9	239.2	200.5	279.1	398.5	390.3		
Monetary Authorities	79agd	....	....	—	—	—	—	—	—	—	—		
General Government	79ahd	....	....	.1	.1	.1	.1	.1	.1	.3	.2		
Banks	79aid	....	....	166.9	186.2	185.1	170.0	155.3	187.8	215.8	232.2		
Other Sectors	79ajd	....	....	94.6	152.2	51.7	69.2	45.1	91.3	182.4	157.9		
Reserve Assets	79akd	....	....	261.8	253.1	262.2	400.1	458.8	579.7	590.6	717.9		
Liabilities	79lad	....	....	1,802.5	1,628.9	1,776.1	1,748.1	1,842.2	1,884.0	2,126.6	2,253.6		
Dir. Invest. in Rep. Economy	79lbd	....	....	62.3	46.9	67.0	73.5	213.2	149.0	190.9	231.2		
Portfolio Investment	79lcd	....	....	81.7	62.2	91.2	95.1	16.3	11.4	17.7	15.9		
Equity Securities	79ldd	....	....	2.5	3.5	6.3	6.5	6.1	4.7	10.7	11.1		
Debt Securities	79led	....	....	79.2	58.7	84.9	88.6	10.2	6.6	7.1	4.7		
Financial Derivatives	79lld	....	....	.8	—	—	8.1	—	—	—	—		
Other Investment	79lfd	....	....	1,657.8	1,519.7	1,618.0	1,571.4	1,612.7	1,723.6	1,918.0	2,006.5		
Monetary Authorities	79lgd	....	....	115.1	109.1	102.1	99.6	89.3	82.2	75.0	80.0		
General Government	79lhd	....	....	1,368.5	1,165.8	1,288.4	1,204.2	1,291.5	1,310.0	1,470.6	1,585.0		
Banks	79lid	....	....	3.2	34.6	59.0	83.7	70.7	88.7	103.2	150.0		
Other Sectors	79ljd	....	....	171.0	210.2	168.4	183.9	161.2	242.6	269.1	191.6		
National Accounts							*Billions of Francs*						
Househ.Cons.Expend.,incl.NPISHs.	96f	659.3	792.7	875.2	961.2	1,073.8	1,144.6	1,227.3	1,403.8	1,525.8	1,595.1	1,627.4	1,758.4
Government Consumption Expend.	91f	138.7	156.5	163.2	174.9	190.0	199.7	211.1	224.3	241.1	261.0	258.7	274.9
Gross Fixed Capital Formation	93e	144.1	190.2	197.4	228.1	250.3	274.7	302.8	333.7	370.2	404.1	415.5	444.9
Changes in Inventories	93i	13.8	41.7	14.6	17.5	12.7	6.3	10.7	26.7	−9.2	15.7	27.0	−7.9
Exports of Goods and Services	90c	251.3	296.4	320.1	359.8	392.4	445.4	427.4	409.4	434.8	433.7	428.8	494.9
Imports of Goods and Services (-)	98c	320.1	394.5	362.6	417.5	470.7	538.3	499.6	565.9	605.8	642.2	612.7	656.2
Gross Domestic Product (GDP)	99b	887.3	1,083.0	1,207.8	1,323.9	1,448.4	1,532.4	1,679.6	1,832.1	1,956.9	2,067.5	2,132.8	2,309.1
Net Primary Income from Abroad	98.n	−14.5	−22.1	....	....	....	....	....	....	....	....	....	....
Gross National Income (GNI)	99a	816.6	980.8	....	....	....	....	....	....	....	....	....	....
GDP Volume 1985 Prices	99b.p	599.7	635.9	663.4	701.5	729.3	768.2	805.6	855.9	893.8	928.5	959.8	993.4
GDP Volume (2000=100)	99bvp	74.4	78.9	82.4	87.1	90.5	95.4	100.0	106.2	110.9	115.3	119.1	123.3
GDP Deflator (2000=100)	99bip	71.0	81.7	87.3	90.5	95.3	95.7	100.0	102.7	105.0	106.8	106.6	111.5
							Millions: Midyear Estimates						
Population	99z	6.00	6.20	6.40	6.59	6.78	6.98	7.20	7.43	7.67	7.92	8.18	8.44

Bhutan 514

		1994	1995	1996	1997	1998	1999	2000	2001	2002	2003	2004	2005
Exchange Rates						*Ngultrum per SDR: End of Period*							
Official Rate	aa	45.810	52.295	51.666	52.999	59.813	59.690	60.911	60.549	65.298	67.768	67.688	64.410
						Ngultrum per US Dollar: End of Period (ae) Period Average (rf)							
Official Rate	ae	31.380	35.180	35.930	39.280	42.480	43.490	46.750	48.180	48.030	45.605	43.585	45.065
Official Rate	rf	31.374	32.427	35.433	36.313	41.259	43.055	44.942	47.186	48.610	46.583	45.316	44.100
Fund Position						*Millions of SDRs: End of Period*							
Quota	2f.s	4.500	4.500	4.500	4.500	4.500	6.300	6.300	6.300	6.300	6.300	6.300	6.300
SDRs	1b.s	.405	.438	.471	.504	.541	.134	.174	.211	.235	.252	.270	.296
Reserve Position in the Fund	1c.s	.570	.570	.570	.570	.570	1.020	1.020	1.020	1.020	1.020	1.020	1.020
Total Fund Cred.&Loans Outstg.	2tl	—	—	—	—	—	—	—	—	—	—	—	—
International Liquidity						*Millions of US Dollars Unless Otherwise Indicated: End of Period*							
Total Reserves minus Gold	1l.d	121.40	† 130.46	190.07	188.72	256.80	292.29	317.63	323.36	354.95	366.60	398.62	467.43
SDRs	1b.d	.59	.65	.68	.68	.76	.18	.23	.27	.32	.37	.42	.42
Reserve Position in the Fund	1c.d	.83	.85	.82	.77	.80	1.40	1.33	1.28	1.39	1.52	1.58	1.46
Foreign Exchange	1d.d	119.98	† 128.96	188.57	187.27	255.24	290.70	316.08	321.81	353.24	364.71	396.62	465.55
of which: Convertible Currency	1dxd	116.56	† 127.17	150.95	155.27	189.55	214.66	236.69	230.94	258.16	286.30	271.65	359.49
Deposit Money Banks: Assets	7a.d	8.88	7.17	43.01	38.86	72.22	93.24	100.88	105.45	110.45	107.53	99.27	89.15
Liabilities	7b.d	—	—	—	—	—	—	—	20.20	—	—	—	—
Monetary Authorities						*Millions of Ngultrum End of Period*							
Foreign Assets	11	3,533	4,341	5,289	6,069	8,030	8,850	10,362	10,718	12,004	11,865	13,005	17,348
Claims on Central Government	12a		50	—	51					127	56	37	100
Claims on Deposit Money Banks	12e	7	3	308	3	1,193	1,188	893	293	194	303	895	768
Claims on Other Financial Insts.	12f	55	5	5	5								
Reserve Money	14	1,287	2,149	2,328	2,545	3,954	4,971	6,022	6,161	6,982	8,368	9,223	12,733
of which: Currency Outside DMBs	14a	348	433	423	721	769	969	1,270	1,610	1,648	1,802	2,072	2,405
Liabs.of Central Bank:Securities	16ac	600	550	1,000	681	560	487	410	410	1,100	—	200	100
Foreign Liabilities	16c	617	161	250	250	250							
Central Government Deposits	16d	30	29	334	28	1,207	1,234	918	338	141	357	1,088	835
Other Items (Net)	17r	1,062	1,510	1,690	2,624	3,252	3,344	3,905	4,102	4,101	3,499	3,428	4,548
of which: Valuation Adjustment	17rv	....	1,451	1,653	2,013	1,905	1,610	1,780	1,705	2,077	1,197	822	616
Deposit Money Banks						*Millions of Ngultrum End of Period*							
Reserves	20	829	1,850	1,490	2,338	2,475	3,215	4,375	4,519	5,385	6,342	6,410	9,325
Claims on Mon.Author.:Securities	20c	588	532	595	671	426	460	295	405	1,089	—	198	99
Foreign Assets	21	279	252	1,545	1,526	3,068	4,055	4,716	5,081	5,305	4,904	4,327	4,017
Claims on Central Government	22a	5	2	100	201	50	50	50	370	974	1,213	2,303	320
Claims on Nonfin.Pub.Enterprises	22c	561	535	484	449	411	372	333	315	252	252	233	1,228
Claims on Private Sector	22d	724	751	748	1,472	1,472	1,490	1,748	2,420	3,147	4,249	6,057	6,570
Demand Deposits	24	697	890	1,652	1,447	1,860	2,755	2,669	3,238	5,323	4,968	5,983	6,565
Time & Foreign Currency Deposits	25	1,351	1,926	1,465	3,458	3,782	4,741	5,996	5,868	6,732	7,076	8,546	9,600
Foreign Liabilities	26c	—	—	—	—	—	—	—	973				
Central Government Deposits	26d	140	344	459	209	322	914	631	1,288	1,415	1,951	1,829	2,300
Capital Accounts	27a	324	371	371	539	561	633	756	958	1,194	1,735	1,849	2,029
Other Items (Net)	27r	473	390	1,016	1,007	1,365	599	1,463	784	1,487	1,231	1,322	1,066
Monetary Survey						*Millions of Ngultrum: End of Period*							
Foreign Assets (Net)	31n	3,195	4,432	6,584	7,346	10,848	12,905	15,078	14,825	17,309	16,769	17,332	21,365
Domestic Credit	32	1,175	969	545	1,941	404	−236	581	1,479	2,943	3,462	5,714	5,083
Claims on Central Govt. (Net)	32an	−165	−321	−692	15	−1,480	−2,098	−1,499	−1,256	−456	−1,038	−577	−2,715
Claims on Nonfin.Pub.Enterprises	32c	561	535	484	449	411	372	333	315	252	252	233	1,228
Claims on Private Sector	32d	724	751	748	1,472	1,472	1,490	1,748	2,420	3,147	4,249	6,057	6,570
Claims on Other Financial Insts	32f	55	5	5	5								
Money	34	1,044	1,322	2,074	2,168	2,629	3,724	3,939	4,849	6,971	6,770	8,055	8,970
Quasi-Money	35	1,351	1,926	1,465	3,458	3,782	4,741	5,996	5,868	6,732	7,076	8,546	9,600
Liabs.of Central Bank:Securities	36ac	12	18	405	11	134	26	115	6	11	—	2	1
Other Items (Net)	37r	1,962	2,135	3,185	3,652	4,696	4,176	5,609	5,582	6,537	6,385	6,443	7,879
Money plus Quasi-Money	35l	2,395	3,249	3,540	5,626	6,410	8,465	9,935	10,716	13,703	13,846	16,601	18,570
Interest Rates						*Percent Per Annum*							
Deposit Rate	60l	8.0	8.0	8.3	8.3	8.3	8.3	8.3	7.5	7.0	5.0	4.5	4.5
Lending Rate	60p	16.0	16.0	16.0	16.0	16.0	16.0	16.0	15.8	15.3	15.0	15.0	14.0
Prices and Tourism						*Index Numbers (2000=100): Period Averages*							
Consumer Prices	64	64.2	70.3	76.4	81.4	90.0	96.1	† 100.0	103.4	106.0	108.2	113.2	119.1
Tourist Arrivals	66ta	52.5	63.0	67.9	71.6	81.6	94.7	100.0	84.6	74.1	82.8	122.4	180.3
Intl. Transactions & Positions						*Millions of Ngultrum: Year Ending June 30*							
Exports	70	2,082.7	3,350.1	3,553.8	4,274.2	4,455.6	4,988.0	4,615.8	4,994.7	5,478.6	6,190.1	8,271.1	....
Imports, c.i.f.	71	2,876.4	3,641.9	4,525.2	4,977.9	5,516.4	7,834.9	7,875.0	8,990.2	9,553.9	11,598.5	18,639.5	....
Government Finance						*Millions of Ngultrum: Year Ending June 30*							
Deficit (-) or Surplus	80	−45.1	7.8	238.6	−300.9	143.4	−304.9	−764.6	−2,490.8	−1,756.7p	....	....	....
Revenue	81	1,666.3	1,877.4	2,127.7	2,424.2	3,133.1	3,656.9	4,585.4	4,975.7	5,140.6p	....	....	....
Grants Received	81z	1,456.2	1,773.2	2,363.6	2,232.1	1,816.3	3,262.6	3,274.1	3,711.0	2,918.4p	....	....	....
Expenditure	82	2,891.0	3,655.6	4,152.6	4,630.6	4,588.4	7,284.0	8,334.2	10,716.5	9,813.7p	....	....	....
Lending Minus Repayments	83	276.6	−12.8	100.1	326.6	217.6	−59.6	289.9	461.0	2.0p	....	....	....
Financing													
Total Financing	84	45.1	−7.8	−238.6	300.9	−143.3	304.9	764.6	2,490.8	1,756.7p	....	....	....
Domestic	84a	21.0	−1.1	−211.8	176.6	−479.5	−248.8	158.0	1,434.1	1,047.1p	....	....	....
Foreign	85a	24.1	−6.7	−26.8	124.3	336.2	553.7	606.6	1,056.7	709.6p	....	....	....
Debt: Domestic	88a	64.9	28.4	107.4	—	—	—	—	—	....	....	....	....
Foreign	89a	2,733.3	2,634.0	3,962.1	4,084.9	4,661.2	6,205.3	7,721.8	15,723.8	....	....	....	....

Bhutan 514

		1994	1995	1996	1997	1998	1999	2000	2001	2002	2003	2004	2005
National Accounts						*Millions of Ngultrum: Calendar Year*							
Househ.Cons.Expend.,incl.NPISHs....	96f	3,770	3,428	5,171	7,138	9,322	10,067	11,329	....	....	....	....	....
Government Consumption Expend...	91f	1,585	2,400	2,502	3,651	3,308	4,271	4,422	....	....	....	....	....
Gross Fixed Capital Formation..........	93e	3,945	4,487	5,094	5,514	6,200	8,127	9,447	....	....	....	....	....
Changes in Inventories....................	93i	129	228	182	−632	45	108	49	....	....	....	....	....
Exports of Goods and Services..........	90c	2,508	3,712	3,979	4,771	5,148	5,714	6,456	....	....	....	....	....
Imports of Goods and Services (-).....	98c	3,349	4,190	5,120	6,128	7,686	9,164	10,004	....	....	....	....	....
Gross Domestic Product (GDP)........	99b	8,589	10,064	11,808	14,314	16,337	19,122	21,698	....	....	....	....	....
Net Primary Income from Abroad.....	98.n	−634	−1,208	−1,247	−1,141	−2,323	−3,083	−3,458	....	....	....	....	....
Gross National Income (GNI)............	99a	7,954	8,856	10,562	13,173	14,013	16,040	18,240	....	....	....	....	....
GDP at Factor Cost.........................	99ba	8,238	9,193	10,673	12,675	14,600	17,002	19,521	22,373	24,982	27,745	31,171	....
GDP at Fact.Cost,Vol.1980 Prices.....	99bap	2,713	2,921	....	....	....	....	....	....	....	....	....	....
GDP at Fact.Cost,Vol.2000 Prices.....	99bap	....	14,174	14,997	15,628	16,542	17,824	19,521	21,202	22,707	24,262	26,375	....
GDP Volume (2000=100)................	99bvp	67.4	† 72.6	76.8	80.1	84.7	91.3	100.0	108.6	116.3	124.3	135.1	....
GDP Deflator (2000=100)..............	99bip	62.6	64.9	71.2	81.1	88.3	95.4	100.0	105.5	110.0	114.4	118.2	....
						Millions: Midyear Estimates							
Population..............................	99z	1.71	1.73	1.76	1.80	1.85	1.89	1.94	1.98	2.03	2.07	2.12	2.16

		1994	1995	1996	1997	1998	1999	2000	2001	2002	2003	2004	2005
Exchange Rates						*Bolivianos per SDR: End of Period*							
Market Rate.................................	aa	6.8540	7.3358	7.4558	7.2387	7.9483	8.2213	8.3256	8.5709	10.1828	11.6351	12.5017	11.4913
						Bolivianos per US Dollar: End of Period (ae) Period Average (rf)							
Market Rate.................................	ae	4.6950	4.9350	5.1850	5.3650	5.6450	5.9900	6.3900	6.8200	7.4900	7.8300	8.0500	8.0400
Market Rate.................................	rf	4.6205	4.8003	5.0746	5.2543	5.5101	5.8124	6.1835	6.6069	7.1700	7.6592	7.9363	8.0661
						Index Numbers (2000=100): Period Averages							
Market Rate.................................	ahx	133.82	128.78	121.78	117.66	112.21	106.38	100.00	93.60	86.27	80.72	77.90	76.64
Nominal Effective Exchange Rate.....	nec	97.83	99.97	98.11	99.70	99.60	102.95	100.00	100.24	104.30	95.26	88.25	83.07
Real Effective Exchange Rate...........	rec	91.02	88.62	92.38	94.41	98.68	101.67	100.00	98.88	99.28	89.13	83.52	79.80
Fund Position						*Millions of SDRs: End of Period*							
Quota......................................	2f.s	126.2	126.2	126.2	126.2	126.2	171.5	171.5	171.5	171.5	171.5	171.5	171.5
SDRs..	1b.s	17.0	26.9	26.8	26.8	26.8	27.3	27.3	27.3	27.3	27.1	26.6	26.8
Reserve Position in the Fund...........	1c.s	8.9	8.9	8.9	8.9	8.9	8.9	8.9	8.9	8.9	8.9	8.9	8.9
Total Fund Cred.&Loans Outstg.......	2tl	180.5	180.1	192.0	183.9	187.6	180.0	168.8	164.8	143.7	187.5	197.7	170.6
International Liquidity						*Millions of US Dollars Unless Otherwise Indicated: End of Period*							
Total Reserves minus Gold..............	1l.d	451.0	660.0	955.0	1,086.6	948.5	974.9	926.4	886.4	580.5	716.8	872.4	1,327.6
SDRs......................................	1b.d	24.8	40.0	38.5	36.2	37.7	37.4	35.6	34.3	37.2	40.3	41.2	38.2
Reserve Position in the Fund........	1c.d	13.0	13.2	12.8	12.0	12.5	12.2	11.6	11.2	12.1	13.2	13.8	12.7
Foreign Exchange.........................	1d.d	413.2	606.8	903.7	1,038.5	898.3	925.3	879.3	840.9	531.2	663.3	817.3	1,276.7
Gold (Million Fine Troy Ounces).......	1ad	.893	.893	.939	.939	.939	.943	.939	.939	.911	.911	.911	.911
Gold (National Valuation)...............	1and	37.7	37.7	39.6	39.6	234.9	235.7	244.8	259.6	316.4	379.4	399.4	470.6
Monetary Authorities: Other Liab.....	4..d	503.9	545.9	419.3	370.1	323.9	297.1	283.0	237.3	56.9	52.4	49.0	49.7
Deposit Money Banks: Assets...........	7a.d	84.5	103.6	124.4	137.9	409.8	471.8	552.8	693.9	604.1	550.8	527.6	739.2
Liabilities..................	7b.d	476.8	544.0	540.9	721.4	879.7	744.6	461.3	214.7	181.1	107.2	119.2	152.6
Other Banking Insts.: Assets.............	7e.d	—	—	3.8	6.6	46.9	55.9	63.4	74.3	35.7	78.9	78.2	105.7
Liabilities..................	7f.d	4.1	—	2.5	2.4	8.1	13.3	16.5	15.0	19.1	28.3	51.7	48.1
Monetary Authorities						*Millions of Bolivianos: End of Period*							
Foreign Assets..............................	11	3,702	4,538	† 7,032	7,735	8,217	8,905	9,161	9,651	8,940	11,090	12,944	17,139
Claims on Central Government........	12a	5,009	4,328	† 3,889	3,475	3,598	4,123	4,731	5,436	6,492	7,253	7,866	8,025
Claims on State and Local Govts......	12b	18	—	† —									
Claims on Nonfin.Pub.Enterprises.....	12c	891	113	† 119	—	—	—	—	—	—	—	—	—
Claims on Private Sector.................	12d	—	—	† 2	2	2	2	3	4	3	4	2	3
Claims on Deposit Money Banks......	12e	2,405	3,032	† 3,394	3,427	3,444	3,506	2,873	3,028	2,671	2,750	2,458	2,297
Claims on Other Banking Insts........	12f	—	—	† 107	66	72	42	52	64			3	
Claims on Nonbank Financial Insts...	12g	108	119	† —	—	—	206	220	235	—	—	—	—
Reserve Money.............................	14	2,668	3,291	† 4,194	5,036	3,989	4,441	4,905	5,497	5,582	6,338	7,471	11,361
of which: Currency Outside DMBs..	14a	1,406	1,694	† 1,802	2,061	2,193	2,173	2,189	2,422	2,707	3,231	3,917	5,670
Time, Savings,& Fgn.Currency Dep...	15	1,682	897	† 547	452	451	994	542	624	441	581	708	656
of which: Fgn. Currency Deposits...	15b	1,235	522	† 573	442	446	990	530	597	435	571	673	496
Foreign Liabilities.........................	16c	2,698	2,970	† 3,606	3,317	3,320	3,259	3,214	3,031	1,889	2,592	2,865	2,360
Central Government Deposits..........	16d	2,589	3,565	† 4,460	3,591	3,489	3,642	3,679	3,750	3,237	3,659	4,288	4,122
Central Govt. Lending Funds............	16f	2,684	1,240	† 1,081	919	989	999	972	936	728	813	20	20
Capital Accounts...........................	17a	1,673	2,516	† 1,057	1,441	3,287	3,857	4,381	5,246	6,906	7,915	8,569	9,624
Other Items (Net).........................	17r	−1,861	−2,347	† −403	−52	−192	−407	−653	−667	−678	−803	−647	−677
Deposit Money Banks						*Millions of Bolivianos: End of Period*							
Reserves.....................................	20	1,133	1,450	† 2,788	3,588	1,426	1,459	1,797	1,827	1,753	1,789	1,990	2,240
Foreign Assets..............................	21	397	511	† 645	740	2,313	2,826	3,532	4,732	4,525	4,313	4,247	5,943
Claims on Central Government........	22a	103	572	† 1,522	1,590	1,322	924	1,053	1,530	1,919	1,765	2,025	1,959
Claims on State and Local Govts......	22b	—	—	† —									
Claims on Nonfin.Pub.Enterprises.....	22c	—	—	† —	5	1	2	2	39	28	53	66	30
Claims on Private Sector.................	22d	13,452	15,152	† 17,568	21,017	26,103	27,331	26,403	24,152	23,753	23,721	22,862	24,114
Claims on Other Banking Insts.........	22f	—	—	† —	—	11	10	—	6	54	2	3	4
Claims on Nonbank Financial Insts...	22g	—	—	† 153	131	309	291	263	407	451	482	467	514
Demand Deposits..........................	24	1,826	2,219	† 867	1,036	1,124	1,031	1,150	1,353	1,271	1,385	1,427	1,890
Time, Savings,& Fgn.Currency Dep...	25	7,809	8,887	† 13,542	15,916	18,237	19,203	19,424	19,130	17,651	19,779	19,172	21,230
of which: Fgn. Currency Deposits...	25b	7,568	8,700	† 13,201	15,546	17,799	18,737	18,947	18,601	17,229	19,190	17,851	18,849
Money Market Instruments..............	26aa	—	—	† —	—	70	68	891	1,576	2,235	34		
Foreign Liabilities.........................	26c	2,239	2,685	† 2,805	3,870	4,966	4,460	2,948	1,464	1,357	840	960	1,227
Central Government Deposits..........	26d	74	179	† 935	1,319	260	97	117	139	97	72	115	135
Credit from Monetary Authorities.....	26g	2,260	2,984	† 3,830	3,721	3,499	3,920	3,914	3,802	3,767	3,661	3,671	3,520
Liabilities to Other Banking Insts......	26i	—	—	† —	—	95	93	103	103	127	163	263	310
Liab. to Nonbank Financial Insts.......	26j	—	—	† —	310	520	894	927	2,069	2,332	2,158	2,042	1,944
Capital Accounts...........................	27a	1,899	2,043	† 2,352	2,821	3,822	4,626	5,252	5,732	6,608	6,978	6,713	6,889
Other Items (Net)..........................	27r	−1,023	−1,312	† −1,655	−1,921	−1,108	−1,550	−1,676	−2,676	−2,962	−2,944	−2,703	−2,342
Monetary Survey						*Millions of Bolivianos: End of Period*							
Foreign Assets (Net)........................	31n	−837	−606	† 1,266	1,288	2,244	4,012	6,532	9,888	10,219	11,971	13,366	19,496
Domestic Credit............................	32	16,917	16,541	† 17,964	21,377	27,669	29,192	28,931	27,984	29,366	29,548	28,892	30,392
Claims on Central Govt. (Net)........	32an	2,449	1,156	† 16	155	1,171	1,308	1,988	3,078	5,076	5,287	5,488	5,728
Claims on State and Local Govts.....	32b	18	—	† —									
Claims on Nonfin.Pub.Enterprises...	32c	891	113	† 119	5	1	2	2	39	28	53	66	30
Claims on Private Sector...............	32d	13,452	15,152	† 17,570	21,019	26,105	27,333	26,406	24,156	23,757	23,725	22,864	24,117
Claims on Other Banking Insts......	32f	—	—	† 107	66	83	52	52	70	54	2	6	4
Claims on Nonbank Financial Inst..	32g	108	119	† 153	131	309	497	483	642	451	482	467	514
Money.......................................	34	3,232	3,913	† 3,055	3,636	3,895	3,670	3,995	4,743	4,725	5,636	6,686	10,566
Quasi-Money................................	35	9,490	9,784	† 14,089	16,368	18,688	20,197	19,966	19,754	18,093	20,360	19,880	21,885
Money Market Instruments..............	36aa	—	—	† —	—	70	68	891	1,576	2,235	34	—	—
Central Govt. Lending Funds............	36f	2,684	1,240	† 1,081	919	989	999	972	936	728	813	20	20
Liabilities to Other Banking Insts......	36i	—	—	† —	—	95	93	103	103	127	163	263	310
Liab. to Nonbank Financial Insts.......	36j	—	—	† —	310	520	894	927	2,069	2,332	2,158	2,042	1,944
Capital Accounts...........................	37a	3,573	4,559	† 3,409	4,263	7,109	8,483	9,633	10,978	13,514	14,893	15,282	16,513
Other Items (Net)..........................	37r	−2,899	−3,560	† −2,405	−2,831	−1,452	−1,201	−1,025	−2,288	−2,169	−2,537	−1,915	−1,351
Money plus Quasi-Money................	35l	12,722	13,697	† 17,145	20,004	22,583	23,867	23,961	24,497	22,818	25,996	26,566	32,451

Bolivia 218

		1994	1995	1996	1997	1998	1999	2000	2001	2002	2003	2004	2005
Other Banking Institutions		*Millions of Bolivianos: End of Period*											
Reserves	40	1	—	† 160	192	80	84	135	178	400	177	174	276
Foreign Assets	41	—	—	† 20	35	265	335	405	507	268	618	629	850
Claims on Central Government	42a	3	3	† 106	91	118	14	150	529	497	785	900	629
Claims on State and Local Govts	42b	—	—	† —	—	—	—	—	—	—	—	—	—
Claims on Nonfin.Pub.Enterprises	42c	—	—	† —	—	—	—	—	—	4	—	—	—
Claims on Private Sector	42d	349	386	† 2,226	3,249	3,885	3,703	4,087	4,552	5,007	5,784	6,491	6,173
Claims on Deposit Money Banks	42e	—	—	† —	—	140	86	346	414	416	337	208	473
Claims on Nonbank Financial Insts	42g	—	—	† 4	4	26	57	88	164	35	58	90	58
Demand Deposits	44	—	—	† —	1	1	1	11	4	5	6	6	10
Time, Savings,& Fgn.Currency Dep	45	1	—	† 2,305	3,185	3,693	3,480	4,132	5,132	5,044	6,300	6,486	6,622
of which: Fgn. Currency Deposits	45b	1	—	† 2,251	3,114	3,619	3,429	4,075	5,073	4,981	6,210	6,294	6,164
Money Market Instruments	46aa	—	—	† —	—	—	—	68	208	364	—	—	—
Foreign Liabilities	46c	19	—	† 13	13	46	80	106	102	143	221	416	387
Central Government Deposits	46d	1	—	† 6	14	16	8	21	13	15	17	47	51
Credit from Monetary Authorities	46g	272	548	† 4	6	8	11	21	80	67	54	26	27
Credit from Deposit Money Banks	46h	—	—	† 86	100	72	55	39	47	29	30	31	29
Liabs. to Nonbank Financial Insts	46j	—	—	† 245	303	294	301	299	325	368	384	469	395
Capital Accounts	47a	21	−289	† 447	579	775	819	986	1,188	1,416	1,649	1,828	1,835
Other Items (Net)	47r	40	130	† −592	−630	−391	−476	−470	−756	−823	−902	−817	−899
Banking Survey		*Millions of Bolivianos: End of Period*											
Foreign Assets (Net)	51n	−857	−606	† 1,273	1,310	2,463	4,267	6,831	10,292	10,344	12,367	13,579	19,959
Domestic Credit	52	17,269	16,930	† 20,187	24,641	31,599	32,907	33,184	33,145	34,841	36,156	36,320	37,196
Claims on Central Govt. (Net)	52an	2,452	1,160	† 116	232	1,273	1,314	2,117	3,593	5,559	6,055	6,341	6,305
Claims on State and Local Govts	52b	18	—	† —	—	—	—	—	—	—	—	—	—
Claims on Nonfin.Pub.Enterprises	52c	891	113	† 119	5	1	2	2	39	32	53	66	30
Claims on Private Sector	52d	13,801	15,538	† 19,796	24,268	29,991	31,037	30,493	28,708	28,764	29,508	29,356	30,290
Claims on Nonbank Financial Inst	52g	108	119	† 157	135	335	554	572	806	486	540	557	571
Liquid Liabilities	55l	12,723	13,697	† 19,291	22,998	26,198	27,265	27,969	29,456	27,467	32,124	32,884	38,808
Money Market Instruments	56aa	—	—	† —	—	70	68	959	1,784	2,599	34	—	—
Central Govt. Lending Funds	56f	2,684	1,240	† 1,081	919	989	999	972	936	728	813	20	20
Liab. to Nonbank Financial Insts	56j	—	—	† 245	613	813	1,195	1,227	2,394	2,699	2,542	2,511	2,339
Capital Accounts	57a	3,593	4,270	† 3,856	4,842	7,884	9,302	10,619	12,166	14,930	16,542	17,110	18,348
Other Items (Net)	57r	−2,588	−2,882	† −3,014	−3,421	−1,892	−1,655	−1,730	−3,299	−3,239	−3,531	−2,625	−2,360
Money (National Definitions)		*Millions of Bolivianos: End of Period*											
Base Money	19ma	2,760	3,105	3,963	4,731	3,560	3,685	4,104	4,455	4,644	5,238	5,769	7,883
M1	59ma	1,890	2,333	2,580	3,061	3,276	3,153	3,287	3,709	3,908	4,532	5,258	7,486
M'1	59maa	3,232	3,913	4,768	5,738	6,342	5,893	6,406	7,533	8,115	9,206	9,372	11,542
M2	59mb	1,997	2,425	2,791	3,355	3,589	3,480	3,617	4,151	4,291	5,051	6,392	9,414
M'2	59mba	4,534	5,460	8,028	10,219	11,533	11,212	12,678	15,367	15,439	18,219	16,279	19,636
M3	59mc	2,132	2,520	2,983	3,526	3,766	3,646	3,798	4,295	4,408	5,220	6,764	10,263
M'3	59mca	11,767	12,880	18,430	22,039	25,118	25,777	27,264	29,160	28,473	29,912	30,194	34,371
M4	59md	2,136	2,523	3,106	3,532	3,782	3,646	3,803	4,332	4,432	5,261	6,824	10,351
M'4	59mda	12,036	13,330	18,948	22,408	25,552	26,162	28,013	31,341	29,971	31,832	32,785	36,308
Interest Rates		*Percent Per Annum*											
Discount Rate (End of Period)	60	....	....	16.50	13.25	14.10	12.50	10.00	8.50	12.50	7.50	6.00	5.25
Discount Rate (Fgn.Cur.)(End per)	60..f	....	....	9.89	8.58	9.30	9.04	7.41	5.69	5.58	6.38	7.46	7.25
Money Market Rate	60b	....	22.42	20.27	13.97	12.57	13.49	7.40	6.99	8.41	4.07	4.05	3.53
Money Market Rate (Fgn. Cur.)	60b.f	....	14.16	9.54	7.85	9.26	8.29	5.68	3.57	2.96	2.12	3.02	3.37
Treasury Bill Rate	60c	17.89	24.51	19.93	13.65	12.33	14.07	10.99	11.48	12.41	9.92	7.41	4.96
Treasury Bill Rate (Fgn.Currency)	60c.f	8.22	13.20	9.89	7.15	7.48	7.84	7.02	4.19	3.56	2.53	3.34	2.85
Savings Rate	60k	17.46	16.52	16.43	14.30	12.08	10.79	9.39	6.57	6.20	5.52	4.51	3.59
Savings Rate (Fgn.Currency)	60k.f	7.16	7.03	7.20	6.60	5.93	5.50	4.76	2.68	1.10	.73	.57	.55
Deposit Rate	60l	18.43	18.87	19.16	14.73	12.82	12.26	10.98	9.82	9.58	11.41	7.42	4.93
Deposit Rate (Fgn.Currency)	60l.f	9.89	10.36	10.13	8.32	7.96	8.78	7.84	5.21	2.82	2.01	1.98	1.87
Lending Rate	60p	55.57	51.02	55.97	50.05	39.41	35.37	34.60	20.06	20.63	17.66	14.47	16.62
Lending Rate (Fgn.Currency)	60p.f	16.46	16.86	17.64	16.48	15.66	16.03	15.68	14.46	12.11	10.30	10.00	11.33
Prices, Production, Labor		*Index Numbers (2000=100): Period Averages*											
Consumer Prices	64	67.0	73.8	83.0	86.9	93.6	95.6	100.0	101.6	102.5	106.0	110.7	116.6
Crude Petroleum Production	66aa	81.6	90.0	92.9	95.4	119.7	103.0	100.0	113.6	115.2	125.5	147.8	160.7
		Number in Thousands: Period Averages											
Labor Force	67d	....	1,317	1,413	3,645	....	....	3,824	....	....	....	....	....
Employment	67e	1,195	1,257	† 1,849	1,878	....	2,017	2,091	2,156	2,118	....	....	....
Unemployment	67c	39	47	† 74	71	....	157	169	200	202	....	....	....
Unemployment Rate (%)	67r	3.1	3.6	† 3.8	3.7	....	7.2	7.5	8.5	8.7	9.7	....	....
Intl. Transactions & Positions		*Millions of US Dollars*											
Exports	70..d	1,032.4	1,100.7	1,137.1	1,166.5	1,103.9	1,051.2	1,229.5	1,284.8	1,298.7	1,597.8	2,146.0	2,670.8
Tin	70q.d	91.1	88.6	85.5	75.1	59.9	65.3	70.5	52.6	53.2	66.0	131.7	112.4
Zinc	70t.d	105.3	151.3	153.4	119.3	92.3	91.4	101.3	71.6	66.5	73.2	90.0	118.0
Imports, c.i.f.	71..d	1,209.0	1,423.8	1,635.0	1,850.9	1,983.0	1,755.1	1,829.7	1,707.7	1,770.1	1,615.9	1,844.2	2,341.3
Imports, f.o.b.	71.vd	1,121.7	1,263.2	1,450.5	1,698.1	1,824.4	1,539.1	1,604.5	1,497.5	1,552.3	1,497.7	1,724.9	547.7
		2000=100											
Volume of Exports	72	89.4	95.6	97.6	101.6	96.2	87.7	100.0	107.3	129.1	145.3	173.4	194.5
Tin	72q	120.9	102.1	100.6	103.1	81.9	92.2	100.0	78.9	101.2	110.5	126.5	117.4
Zinc	72t	71.2	97.3	100.6	102.1	101.6	96.2	100.0	87.2	95.2	110.8	97.2	99.6
		2000=100: Indices of Unit Values in US Dollars											
Unit Value of Exports/Export Prices	74..d	131.5	141.1	138.4	98.2	86.8	85.4	100.0	91.5	80.5	90.4	121.9	141.8
Tin	74q.d	145.6	166.7	169.9	103.6	100.0	98.0	100.0	91.2	74.3	85.3	150.2	137.4
Zinc	74t.d	146.8	154.2	150.7	116.1	89.7	93.7	100.0	81.6	68.7	65.2	91.4	116.9

Bolivia   218

		1994	1995	1996	1997	1998	1999	2000	2001	2002	2003	2004	2005
Balance of Payments		\multicolumn{12}{c}{*Millions of US Dollars: Minus Sign Indicates Debit*}											
Current Account, n.i.e.	78ald	−90.2	−302.5	−404.3	−553.5	−666.1	−488.0	−446.3	−274.0	−351.9	75.6	337.5	466.6
Goods: Exports f.o.b.	78aad	985.1	1,041.4	1,132.0	1,166.6	1,104.0	1,051.2	1,246.1	1,284.8	1,298.7	1,597.8	2,146.0	2,670.8
Goods: Imports f.o.b.	78abd	−1,015.3	−1,223.7	−1,368.0	−1,643.6	−1,759.5	−1,539.0	−1,610.2	−1,580.0	−1,638.7	−1,497.4	−1,724.7	−2,191.5
Trade Balance	78acd	−30.2	−182.3	−236.0	−477.0	−655.5	−487.8	−364.1	−295.2	−340.0	100.5	421.3	479.3
Services: Credit	78add	196.0	192.4	180.9	247.2	251.2	259.4	224.0	235.9	256.6	363.9	416.4	455.5
Services: Debit	78aed	−337.5	−350.2	−363.4	−418.7	−440.5	−449.7	−467.7	−399.4	−433.3	−551.2	−606.7	−679.2
Balance on Goods & Services	78afd	−171.7	−340.1	−418.5	−648.5	−844.8	−678.1	−607.8	−458.7	−516.7	−86.9	231.1	255.6
Income: Credit	78agd	18.7	28.3	28.6	98.2	127.4	157.3	139.7	121.2	103.2	71.1	76.0	121.3
Income: Debit	78ahd	−201.2	−234.9	−236.8	−294.7	−289.3	−353.3	−365.0	−332.5	−307.9	−373.7	−460.6	−494.3
Balance on Gds, Serv. & Inc.	78aid	−354.2	−546.7	−626.7	−845.0	−1,006.7	−874.1	−833.1	−670.1	−721.4	−389.5	−153.6	−117.4
Current Transfers, n.i.e.: Credit	78ajd	269.2	248.0	226.2	300.3	352.3	414.7	420.0	431.6	407.8	510.9	542.6	648.5
Current Transfers: Debit	78akd	−5.2	−3.8	−3.8	−8.8	−11.7	−28.6	−33.2	−35.5	−38.4	−45.7	−51.5	−64.6
Capital Account, n.i.e.	78bcd	1.2	2.0	2.8	25.3	9.9	—	—	—	—	—	—	—
Capital Account, n.i.e.: Credit	78bad	1.2	2.0	2.8	25.3	9.9	—	—	—	—	—	—	—
Capital Account: Debit	78bbd	—	—	—	—	—	—	—	—	—	—	—	—
Financial Account, n.i.e.	78bjd	315.3	505.2	701.0	889.9	1,181.6	868.2	461.8	440.7	649.0	36.3	360.5	41.9
Direct Investment Abroad	78bdd	−2.2	−2.0	−2.1	−2.4	−2.8	−2.8	−2.8	−2.5	−2.5	−2.8	−2.8	−3.0
Dir. Invest. in Rep. Econ., n.i.e.	78bed	130.2	392.7	474.1	730.6	949.3	1,010.5	736.4	705.8	676.6	197.4	65.4	−276.6
Portfolio Investment Assets	78bfd	—	—	.3	−53.2	−74.5	−44.4	55.4	−23.0	−19.3	−68.2	−35.4	−153.4
Equity Securities	78bkd	—	—	—	—	—	—	—	—	—	—	1.2	3.9
Debt Securities	78bld	—	—	.3	−53.2	−74.5	−44.4	55.4	−23.0	−19.3	−68.2	−36.6	−157.4
Portfolio Investment Liab., n.i.e.	78bgd	—	—	—	—	—	−16.9	—	—	—	—	—	....
Equity Securities	78bmd	—	—	—	—	—	—	—	—	—	—	—	....
Debt Securities	78bnd	—	—	—	—	—	−16.9	—	—	—	—	—	....
Financial Derivatives Assets	78bwd	....	....	....	—	—	....	—	—	....	....	....	....
Financial Derivatives Liabilities	78bxd	....	....	....	—	—	....	....	....	....	....	....	....
Other Investment Assets	78bhd	−104.0	−38.4	12.2	−19.9	−13.2	−47.7	−146.1	−166.7	−193.4	−462.9	94.3	123.8
Monetary Authorities	78bod	....	....	....	—	−8.4	−9.2	−1.2	—	—	—	—	—
General Government	78bpd	—	—	−.2	—	—	—	−7.9	−15.7	−17.1	−17.7	−15.7	−12.1
Banks	78bqd	−104.0	−38.4	12.4	−19.9	66.1	−24.2	−94.4	−157.0	49.8	46.3	5.6	−131.7
Other Sectors	78brd	—	—	—	—	−70.9	−14.3	−42.6	6.1	−226.1	−491.5	104.4	267.6
Other Investment Liab., n.i.e.	78bid	291.3	152.9	216.5	234.8	322.8	−30.5	−181.1	−72.9	187.7	372.7	239.0	351.2
Monetary Authorities	78bsd	40.8	78.0	11.7	1.5	−46.0	−11.6	−23.7	−20.3	−18.1	−2.8	.1	.9
General Government	78btd	−16.9	−41.0	206.9	199.7	149.4	123.1	131.4	226.1	310.3	280.1	200.8	146.3
Banks	78bud	206.3	78.8	2.8	169.7	137.9	−138.1	−280.1	−247.7	−35.5	−80.9	20.1	−1.9
Other Sectors	78bvd	61.1	37.1	−4.9	−136.1	81.5	−3.9	−8.7	−31.0	−69.0	176.4	18.0	206.0
Net Errors and Omissions	78cad	−315.8	−112.3	−31.6	−260.7	−400.7	−353.2	−54.8	−202.7	−639.8	−173.5	−625.4	−90.7
Overall Balance	78cbd	−89.5	92.4	268.0	101.0	124.7	27.0	−39.4	−36.0	−342.7	−61.6	72.6	417.8
Reserves and Related Items	79dad	89.5	−92.4	−268.0	−101.0	−124.7	−27.0	39.4	36.0	342.7	61.6	−72.6	−417.8
Reserve Assets	79dbd	−26.4	−147.4	−310.1	−89.6	−133.0	−31.9	38.8	32.5	303.0	−152.0	−157.2	−463.4
Use of Fund Credit and Loans	79dcd	28.7	−1.1	17.1	−11.4	5.7	−10.9	−14.5	−5.3	−27.7	60.0	14.3	−39.2
Exceptional Financing	79ded	87.3	56.1	25.1	—	2.6	15.8	15.1	8.8	67.3	153.5	70.3	84.7
International Investment Position		\multicolumn{12}{c}{*Millions of US Dollars*}											
Assets	79aad	....	....	....	2,142.4	2,649.5	2,626.6	2,659.5	2,834.7	2,953.3	2,984.9	3,110.4	3,674.5
Direct Investment Abroad	79abd	....	....	....	21.9	24.4	26.9	29.4	31.9	34.4	83.4	84.2	87.2
Portfolio Investment	79acd	....	....	....	318.0	673.8	718.3	662.9	685.9	837.0	398.4	433.8	587.2
Equity Securities	79add	....	....	....	—	—	—	—	—	—	—	—	—
Debt Securities	79aed	....	....	....	318.0	673.8	718.3	662.9	685.9	837.0	398.4	433.8	587.2
Financial Derivatives	79ald	....	....	....	—	—	—	—	—	—	—	—	—
Other Investment	79afd	....	....	....	488.1	623.9	521.0	662.3	831.9	1,033.1	1,250.2	1,160.6	1,040.8
Monetary Authorities	79agd	....	....	....	164.7	247.8	124.5	123.7	124.9	134.3	152.1	164.4	170.4
General Government	79ahd	....	....	....	30.1	58.1	66.1	74.0	88.5	104.0	119.7	127.6	137.8
Banks	79aid	....	....	....	128.7	143.4	177.2	271.7	428.7	378.9	332.6	327.0	458.7
Other Sectors	79ajd	....	....	....	164.7	174.7	153.3	192.9	189.8	415.9	645.9	541.5	273.9
Reserve Assets	79akd	....	....	....	1,314.4	1,327.4	1,360.4	1,304.9	1,285.0	1,048.8	1,252.9	1,431.9	1,959.3
Liabilities	79lad	....	....	....	8,088.5	9,482.5	10,291.0	10,662.6	11,175.3	11,706.0	10,956.9	10,905.6	10,748.4
Dir. Invest. in Rep. Economy	79lbd	....	....	....	2,248.3	3,274.4	4,284.9	5,187.7	5,893.5	6,570.0	4,782.0	4,816.6	4,547.6
Portfolio Investment	79lcd	....	....	....	32.7	28.4	28.4	—	—	—	48.2	41.8	41.8
Equity Securities	79ldd	....	....	....	—	—	—	—	—	—	1.4	.9	.9
Debt Securities	79led	....	....	....	32.7	28.4	28.4	—	—	—	46.8	40.9	40.9
Financial Derivatives	79lld	....	....	....	—	—	—	—	—	—	1.4	.9	.9
Other Investment	79lfd	....	....	....	5,807.4	6,179.7	5,977.7	5,474.9	5,281.8	5,135.9	6,126.7	6,047.2	6,159.1
Monetary Authorities	79lgd	....	....	....	733.1	707.1	667.7	597.7	342.4	335.4	424.1	356.3	294.7
General Government	79lhd	....	....	....	3,304.7	3,490.1	3,454.8	3,434.5	3,774.3	3,773.7	4,455.2	4,409.5	4,403.0
Banks	79lid	....	....	....	849.1	1,002.4	854.2	579.5	312.3	301.0	306.4	318.5	312.5
Other Sectors	79ljd	....	....	....	920.5	980.1	1,001.0	863.2	852.9	725.8	941.0	963.0	1,148.9
Government Finance		\multicolumn{12}{c}{*Millions of Bolivianos: Year Ending December 31*}											
Deficit (-) or Surplus	80	−902	−697	−869	−1,783	−1,917	−1,969	−2,317	−3,915	−5,484	−4,543	....	....
Revenue	81	6,532	7,687	9,014	9,884	11,699	12,131	13,048	12,906	13,524	14,717	....	....
Expenditure	82	7,434	8,384	9,883	11,667	13,615	14,100	15,365	16,821	19,008	19,259	....	....
Financing													
Domestic	84a	165	−327	−355	602	646	860	1,314	2,373	2,023	721	....	....
Foreign	85a	737	1,024	1,224	1,181	1,271	1,109	1,003	1,543	3,461	3,821	....	....

Bolivia 218

		1994	1995	1996	1997	1998	1999	2000	2001	2002	2003	2004	2005
National Accounts							*Millions of Bolivianos*						
Househ.Cons.Expend.,incl.NPISHs....	96f	21,444	24,440	28,201	31,113	35,144	37,002	39,655	40,499	41,802	43,987	47,458	....
Government Consumption Expend...	91f	3,750	4,375	5,003	5,790	6,658	7,126	7,550	8,458	9,051	10,227	10,551	....
Gross Fixed Capital Formation.........	93e	4,104	5,007	6,072	7,899	10,841	9,197	9,289	7,491	8,871	7,906	8,183	9,625
Changes in Inventories....................	93i	−133	−93	23	276	212	−157	133	184	366	355	−449	726
Exports of Goods and Services..........	90c	5,987	7,269	8,476	8,791	9,223	8,129	9,490	10,743	12,263	15,848	21,682	27,381
Imports of Goods and Services (-).....	98c	7,516	8,764	10,238	12,226	15,256	13,141	14,188	13,585	15,710	16,322	18,330	24,701
Gross Domestic Product (GDP).........	99b	27,636	32,235	37,537	41,644	46,822	48,156	51,928	53,790	56,682	61,980	69,152	78,285
GDP Volume 1990 Prices.................	99b.p	18,034	18,877	19,701	20,677	21,717	21,809	22,356	22,733	23,298	23,983	24,924	25,935
GDP Volume (2000=100)................	99bvp	80.7	84.4	88.1	92.5	97.1	97.6	100.0	101.7	104.2	107.3	111.5	116.0
GDP Deflator (2000=100)...............	99bip	66.0	73.5	82.0	86.7	92.8	95.1	100.0	101.9	104.7	111.3	119.4	130.0
							Millions: Midyear Estimates						
Population................................	99z	7.32	7.48	7.65	7.81	7.98	8.15	8.32	8.49	8.66	8.84	9.01	9.18

Bosnia and Herzegovina   963

		1994	1995	1996	1997	1998	1999	2000	2001	2002	2003	2004	2005
Exchange Rates					*Convertible Marka per SDR: End of Period*								
Official Rate.............................	aa	....	....	....	2.418	2.356	2.672	2.739	2.789	2.536	2.301	2.230	2.370
					Convertible Marka per US Dollar: End of Period (ae) Period Average (rf)								
Official Rate.............................	ae	....	....	....	1.792	1.673	1.947	2.102	2.219	1.865	1.549	1.436	1.658
Official Rate.............................	rf	....	....	....	1.734	1.760	1.836	2.123	2.186	2.078	1.733	1.575	1.573
Fund Position					*Millions of SDRs: End of Period*								
Quota.................................	2f.s	—	121.2	121.2	121.2	121.2	169.1	169.1	169.1	169.1	169.1	169.1	169.1
SDRs.................................	1b.s	—	5.0	1.8	—	3.7	5.6	8.2	4.9	2.3	2.3	.3	.2
Reserve Position in the Fund...........	1c.s	—	—	—	—	—	—	—	—	—	—	—	—
Total Fund Cred.&Loans Outstg.......	2tl	—	32.5	31.0	30.3	54.5	68.4	80.4	88.4	102.4	90.1	70.0	43.4
International Liquidity					*Millions of US Dollars Unless Otherwise Indicated: End of Period*								
Total Reserves minus Gold..............	1l.d	....	....	....	80	175	452	497	1,221	1,321	1,796	2,408	2,531
SDRs............................	1b.d	—	8	3	—	5	8	11	6	3	3	1	—
Reserve Position in the Fund.........	1c.d	—	—	—	—	—	—	—	—	—	—	—	—
Foreign Exchange........................	1d.d	....	....	....	80	169	445	486	1,215	1,318	1,792	2,407	2,531
Monetary Authorities					*Millions of Convertible Marka End of Period*								
Foreign Assets.............................	11	....	....	....	144	292	881	1,044	2,737	2,492	2,808	3,485	4,224
Reserve Money.........................	14	....	....	....	170	236	807	961	2,544	2,318	2,608	3,239	3,970
of which: Currency Outside Banks..	14a	....	....	....	113	162	515	652	1,674	1,734	1,601	1,671	1,729
Foreign Liabilities........................	16c	....	....	....	73	128	183	220	276	261	208	157	104
Central Government Deposits...........	16d	....	....	....	—	7	9	10	49	27	19	45	38
Capital Accounts..........................	17a	....	....	....	1	30	34	58	121	181	215	227	245
Other Items (Net).........................	17r	....	....	....	−101	−109	−151	−207	−253	−295	−241	−182	−133
Deposit Money Banks					*Millions of Convertible Marka End of Period*								
Reserves.................................	20	....	....	....	71	90	275	287	872	595	1,005	1,567	2,238
Foreign Assets.............................	21	....	....	....	1,299	1,172	1,134	1,246	1,364	1,469	1,562	1,906	2,090
Claims on State Government...........	22ab	....	....	....	129	106	26	24	11	29	24	21	19
Claims on Local Government...........	22b	....	....	....	4	7	11	9	22	23	21	25	31
Claims on Other Resident Sectors.....	22d	....	....	....	3,835	4,193	4,129	4,368	3,306	4,220	5,076	5,882	7,496
Demand Deposits.........................	24	....	....	....	134	147	566	730	957	1,221	1,442	1,762	2,309
Time & Savings Deposits.................	25a	....	....	....	10	8	22	78	140	272	462	703	810
Foreign Currency Deposits..............	25b	....	....	....	907	1,219	1,039	970	1,827	1,786	1,914	2,586	3,124
Foreign Liabilities........................	26c	....	....	....	3,428	3,375	3,289	3,347	1,527	1,794	2,437	2,651	3,558
Central Government Deposits...........	26d	....	....	....	—	1	9	18	28	81	77	36	45
State Government Deposits..............	26da	....	....	....	331	288	183	158	318	365	471	490	591
Capital Accounts..........................	27a	....	....	....	1,043	1,305	1,257	1,096	1,119	1,214	1,305	1,472	1,713
Other Items (Net).........................	27r	....	....	....	−514	−775	−791	−462	−341	−395	−421	−302	−274
Monetary Survey					*Millions of Convertible Marka End of Period*								
Foreign Assets (Net)......................	31n	....	....	....	−2,058	−2,040	−1,457	−1,277	2,298	1,906	1,725	2,583	2,653
Domestic Credit............................	32	....	....	....	3,969	4,297	4,148	4,373	3,262	4,165	5,026	5,846	7,464
Claims on Central Govt. (Net)........	32an	....	....	....	—	−8	−18	−28	−77	−107	−95	−81	−82
Claims on State Government..........	32ab	....	....	....	129	106	26	24	11	29	24	21	19
Claims on Local Government.........	32b	....	....	....	4	7	11	9	22	23	21	25	31
Claims on Other Resident Sectors...	32d	....	....	....	3,835	4,193	4,129	4,368	3,306	4,220	5,076	5,882	7,496
Money..................................	34	....	....	....	343	384	1,149	1,471	2,790	3,154	3,289	3,788	4,428
Quasi-Money...............................	35	....	....	....	1,152	1,440	1,177	1,117	2,126	2,224	2,601	3,425	4,135
Capital Accounts..........................	37a	....	....	....	1,045	1,335	1,291	1,155	1,240	1,394	1,520	1,699	1,958
Other Items (Net).........................	37r	....	....	....	−629	−901	−926	−647	−596	−701	−660	−482	−404
Money plus Quasi-Money................	35l	....	....	....	1,495	1,824	2,326	2,588	4,916	5,378	5,891	7,213	8,562
Interest Rates					*Percent Per Annum*								
Deposit Rate................................	60l	....	....	....	....	51.88	9.07	14.67	....	† 4.53	4.03	3.72	3.56
Lending Rate...............................	60p	....	....	....	....	73.50	24.29	30.50	....	† 12.70	10.87	10.28	9.61
Intl. Transactions & Positions					*Millions of Convertible Marka*								
Exports..	70	....	....	....	....	1,043	1,376	2,265	2,256	2,089	2,363	....	....
Imports, f.o.b................................	71	....	....	....	....	5,120	6,048	6,583	7,331	8,048	8,223	....	....

Bosnia and Herzegovina   963

		1994	1995	1996	1997	1998	1999	2000	2001	2002	2003	2004	2005
Balance of Payments						*Millions of US Dollars: Minus Sign Indicates Debit*							
Current Account, n.i.e.	78ald	....	....	....	....	−344.9	−501.4	−396.1	−736.5	−1,189.7	−1,636.6	−1,784.3	−2,087.4
Goods: Exports f.o.b.	78aad	....	....	....	....	663.8	831.8	1,129.8	1,134.2	1,109.7	1,477.5	2,086.7	2,580.0
Goods: Imports f.o.b.	78abd	....	....	....	....	−3,779.4	−4,128.7	−3,894.2	−4,092.0	−4,449.4	−5,636.8	−6,656.4	−7,534.3
Trade Balance	78acd	....	....	....	....	−3,115.6	−3,296.9	−2,764.4	−2,957.8	−3,339.7	−4,159.3	−4,569.7	−4,954.3
Services: Credit	78add	....	....	....	....	460.2	463.7	450.0	496.8	524.2	716.3	894.2	1,012.5
Services: Debit	78aed	....	....	....	....	−270.0	−284.7	−263.1	−269.1	−305.1	−383.6	−432.2	−457.5
Balance on Goods & Services	78afd	....	....	....	....	−2,925.4	−3,117.9	−2,577.5	−2,730.1	−3,120.6	−3,826.7	−4,107.7	−4,399.3
Income: Credit	78agd	....	....	....	....	863.0	792.9	665.6	625.2	602.8	648.4	571.5	591.7
Income: Debit	78ahd	....	....	....	....	−53.7	−64.9	−75.6	−86.4	−93.9	−115.9	−115.3	−119.0
Balance on Gds, Serv. & Inc.	78aid	....	....	....	....	−2,116.1	−2,389.9	−1,987.6	−2,191.3	−2,611.7	−3,294.2	−3,651.5	−3,926.6
Current Transfers, n.i.e.: Credit	78ajd	....	....	....	....	1,857.5	1,974.9	1,666.8	1,527.7	1,523.9	1,780.8	2,040.6	2,023.4
Current Transfers: Debit	78akd	....	....	....	....	−86.3	−86.4	−75.4	−72.9	−101.9	−123.2	−173.4	−184.2
Capital Account, n.i.e.	78bcd	....	....	....	....	495.2	625.3	546.4	399.7	412.4	465.6	488.5	446.6
Capital Account, n.i.e.: Credit	78bad	....	....	....	....	495.2	625.3	546.4	399.7	412.4	465.6	488.5	446.6
Capital Account: Debit	78bbd	....	....	....	....	—	—	—	—	—	—	—	—
Financial Account, n.i.e.	78bjd	....	....	....	....	−626.1	−937.4	−241.3	724.1	107.1	770.1	887.9	1,331.8
Direct Investment Abroad	78bdd	....	....	....	....	—	—	—	—	—	—	−1.6	—
Dir. Invest. in Rep. Econ., n.i.e.	78bed	....	....	....	....	66.7	176.8	146.1	118.5	267.8	381.8	612.8	299.0
Portfolio Investment Assets	78bfd	....	....	....	....	—	—	—	—	—	—	—	....
Equity Securities	78bkd	....	....	....	....	—	—	—	—	—	—	....	....
Debt Securities	78bld	....	....	....	....	—	—	—	—	—	—	....	....
Portfolio Investment Liab., n.i.e.	78bgd	....	....	....	....	—	—	—	—	—	—	....	....
Equity Securities	78bmd	....	....	....	....	—	—	—	—	—	—	....	....
Debt Securities	78bnd	....	....	....	....	—	—	—	—	—	—	....	....
Financial Derivatives Assets	78bwd	....	....	....	....	—	—	—	—	—	—	—	....
Financial Derivatives Liabilities	78bxd	....	....	....	....	—	—	—	—	—	—	—	....
Other Investment Assets	78bhd	....	....	....	....	−679.1	−1,019.0	−675.0	648.9	−155.0	101.0	159.6	437.1
Monetary Authorities	78bod	....	....	....	....	....	....	....	....	....	....	....	....
General Government	78bpd	....	....	....	....	....	....	....	....	....	....	....	....
Banks	78bqd	....	....	....	....	17.3	−181.7	−91.6	−185.3	−49.1	−56.8	−223.0	−122.0
Other Sectors	78brd	....	....	....	....	−696.3	−837.3	−583.4	834.1	−105.9	157.8	382.5	559.1
Other Investment Liab., n.i.e.	78bid	....	....	....	....	−13.8	−95.2	287.7	−43.3	−5.7	287.4	117.2	595.6
Monetary Authorities	78bsd	....	....	....	....			1.3	27.2	−26.8	−.2	—	—
General Government	78btd	....	....	....	....	—	−36.9	−27.9	−24.4	−62.6	−96.3	−93.7	−90.4
Banks	78bud	....	....	....	....	−10.9	−58.0	308.6	−20.1	130.8	382.4	146.9	564.5
Other Sectors	78bvd	....	....	....	....	−3.0	−.3	5.7	−26.0	−47.2	1.4	63.9	121.6
Net Errors and Omissions	78cad	....	....	....	....	116.0	225.0	−172.9	79.6	110.5	328.8	618.4	643.2
Overall Balance	78cbd	....	....	....	....	−359.9	−588.4	−263.9	466.9	−559.8	−72.0	210.5	334.1
Reserves and Related Items	79dad	....	....	....	....	359.9	588.4	263.9	−466.9	559.8	72.0	−210.5	−334.1
Reserve Assets	79dbd	....	....	....	....	−84.0	−319.4	−76.5	−761.6	109.6	−196.6	−426.6	−458.4
Use of Fund Credit and Loans	79dcd	....	....	....	....	32.3	18.2	15.5	9.9	19.0	−17.1	−29.7	−39.4
Exceptional Financing	79ded	....	....	....	....	411.5	889.6	324.8	284.8	431.3	285.8	245.8	163.7
National Accounts						*Millions of Convertible Marka*							
Gross Domestic Product (GDP)	99b	....	....	4,192	6,367	7,244	8,990	10,050	10,960	11,650	12,170	....	....
						Millions: Midyear Estimates							
Population	99z	3.53	3.42	3.41	† 3.49	3.62	3.75	3.85	3.90	3.92	3.92	3.91	3.91

Botswana 616

		1994	1995	1996	1997	1998	1999	2000	2001	2002	2003	2004	2005
Exchange Rates						*Pula per SDR: End of Period*							
Official Rate	aa	3.9670	4.1944	5.2404	5.1400	6.2774	6.3572	6.9861	8.7760	7.4331	6.6014	6.6482	7.8791
						Pula per US Dollar: End of Period (ae) Period Average (rf)							
Official Rate	ae	2.7174	2.8217	3.6443	3.8095	4.4583	4.6318	5.3619	6.9832	5.4675	4.4425	4.2808	5.5127
Official Rate	rf	2.6846	2.7722	3.3242	3.6508	4.2259	4.6244	5.1018	5.8412	6.3278	4.9499	4.6929	5.1104
Fund Position						*Millions of SDRs: End of Period*							
Quota	2f.s	36.60	36.60	36.60	36.60	36.60	63.00	63.00	63.00	63.00	63.00	63.00	63.00
SDRs	1b.s	25.39	27.06	28.71	30.36	32.41	28.05	29.89	31.53	32.63	33.52	34.42	35.58
Reserve Position in the Fund	1c.s	16.34	19.28	19.91	18.13	27.61	22.59	17.74	22.28	23.80	30.32	20.50	7.41
Total Fund Cred.&Loans Outstg.	2tl												
International Liquidity						*Millions of US Dollars Unless Otherwise Indicated: End of Period*							
Total Reserves minus Gold	1l.d	4,401.47	4,695.48	5,027.66	5,675.00	5,940.67	6,228.83	6,318.21	5,897.25	5,473.92	5,339.78	5,661.43	6,309.06
SDRs	1b.d	37.07	40.22	41.28	40.96	45.63	38.50	38.94	39.62	44.36	49.81	53.46	50.85
Reserve Position in the Fund	1c.d	23.86	28.66	28.63	24.46	38.87	31.00	23.11	28.00	32.36	45.05	31.84	10.59
Foreign Exchange	1d.d	4,340.54	4,626.60	4,957.75	5,609.58	5,856.17	6,159.32	6,256.16	5,829.63	5,397.20	5,244.92	5,576.13	6,247.62
Monetary Authorities: Other Liab.	4..d	—	—	—	—	—	—	—	7.49	13.89	14.65	25.21	22.18
Banking Institutions: Assets	7a.d	63.42	69.60	124.51	211.33	317.73	290.52	267.62	354.83	329.65	436.17	415.56	542.92
Liabilities	7b.d	24.22	35.05	41.61	31.61	38.49	34.79	41.93	54.64	79.71	111.71	119.39	265.15
Monetary Authorities						*Millions of Pula: End of Period*							
Foreign Assets	11	10,567	12,115	18,356	21,637	26,502	28,867	33,900	† 40,993	29,767	23,578	24,109	34,494
Claims on Central Government	12a	—	—	—	—	—	—	—	† —	—	112	108	88
Claims on State and Local Govts.	12b	—	—	—	—	—	—	—	—	—	—	—	—
Claims on Nonfin.Pub.Enterprises.	12c	....	....	....	....	....	....	....	—	—	—	—	—
Claims on Private Sector	12d	....	....	....	....	....	....	....	24	28	—	39	45
Claims on Banking Institutions	12e	—	—	—	—	—	—	—	† —	—	—	12	—
Claims on Nonbank Financial Insts.	12g	....	....	....	....	....	....	....	—	—	—	—	—
Reserve Money	14	1,320	1,865	2,300	2,996	2,965	3,617	3,341	† 3,306	2,852	3,649	4,817	5,572
of which: Currency Outside Banks	14a	195	223	247	276	353	404	427	† 481	470	533	632	625
Other Liabs. to Banking Insts.	14n	—	—	—	—	—	—	—	† —	—	—	—	—
Time, Savings,&Fgn.Currency Dep.	15	46	48	47	63	26	172	183	† —	—	—	—	—
Liabs. of Central Bank: Securities	16ac	522	504	969	884	988	1,421	1,229	† 2,821	5,920	6,489	6,699	8,406
Restricted Deposits	16b	....	....	....	....	....	....	....	—	—	—	—	—
Foreign Liabilities	16c	—	—	—	—	—	—	—	† 52	76	65	108	122
Central Government Deposits	16d	6,705	6,460	7,204	15,364	18,955	20,199	24,219	† 28,342	16,977	10,916	9,649	13,312
Liab. to Nonbank Financial Insts.	16j	....	....	....	....	....	....	....	—	—	—	—	—
Capital Accounts	17a	2,935	2,941	6,108	1,888	3,229	3,415	4,384	† 6,668	4,107	2,759	3,055	7,203
Other Items (Net)	17r	−961	297	1,728	441	339	43	545	† −173	−138	−188	−61	13
Banking Institutions						*Millions of Pula: End of Period*							
Reserves	20	160	166	177	271	331	353	229	† 493	581	706	820	755
Claims on Mon.Author.:Securities	20c	493	832	1,192	1,572	1,322	1,718	1,197	† 2,024	1,946	2,464	3,144	4,968
Other Claims on Monetary Author.	20n	....	....	....	....	....	....	....	—	—	—	—	—
Foreign Assets	21	172	196	454	805	1,417	1,346	1,435	† 2,478	1,802	1,938	1,779	2,993
Claims on Central Government	22a	2	—	—	—	—	—	—	† 19	19	614	464	228
Claims on Local Government	22b	2	3	2	2	14	15	2	† 1	—	—	—	—
Claims on Nonfin.Pub.Enterprises.	22c	148	95	70	61	267	528	458	† 449	419	314	372	262
Claims on Private Sector	22d	1,600	1,560	1,626	1,775	2,461	3,518	4,344	† 5,295	6,607	7,428	9,182	9,986
Claims on Nonbank Financial Insts.	22g	....	....	....	....	....	....	....	53	72	80	70	91
Demand Deposits	24	579	607	704	762	1,160	1,371	1,470	† 1,869	2,054	2,290	2,989	3,206
Time, Savings,&Fgn.Currency Dep.	25	1,573	1,809	2,192	3,003	4,183	5,282	5,248	† 7,595	7,318	8,763	9,037	10,676
Money Market Instruments	26aa	....	....	....	....	....	....	....	—	—	—	—	—
Restricted Deposits	26b	....	....	....	....	....	....	....	—	—	—	—	—
Foreign Liabilities	26c	66	99	152	120	172	161	225	† 382	436	496	511	1,462
Central Government Deposits	26d	16	19	40	36	29	66	107	† 65	58	148	433	165
Credit from Monetary Authorities	26g	....	....	....	....	....	....	....	—	64	1	4	105
Liab. to Nonbank Financial Insts.	26j	....	....	....	....	....	....	....	118	114	114	605	633
Capital Accounts	27a	308	337	402	464	568	732	843	† 1,136	1,217	1,476	1,922	2,137
Other Items (Net)	27r	36	−19	31	101	−301	−135	−226	† −354	186	255	330	897
Banking Survey						*Millions of Pula: End of Period*							
Foreign Assets (Net)	31n	10,673	12,213	18,658	22,321	27,747	30,051	35,110	† 43,037	31,057	24,954	25,269	35,903
Domestic Credit	32	−4,969	−4,823	−5,546	−13,561	−16,242	−16,205	−19,520	† −22,567	−9,889	−2,516	152	−2,777
Claims on Central Govt. (Net)	32an	−6,719	−6,480	−7,244	−15,400	−18,984	−20,265	−24,325	† −28,388	−17,016	−10,338	−9,510	−13,161
Claims on Local Government	32b	2	3	2	2	14	15	2	† 1	—	—	—	—
Claims on Nonfin.Pub.Enterprises.	32c	148	95	70	61	267	528	458	† 449	419	314	372	262
Claims on Private Sector	32d	1,600	1,560	1,626	1,775	2,461	3,518	4,344	† 5,319	6,635	7,428	9,221	10,030
Claims on Nonbank Financial Insts.	32g	....	....	....	....	....	....	....	—	72	80	70	91
Money	34	774	829	951	1,038	1,513	1,775	1,897	† 2,354	2,581	2,882	4,225	3,998
Quasi-Money	35	1,619	1,856	2,239	3,066	4,209	5,454	5,432	† 7,595	7,318	8,763	9,037	10,676
Money Market Instruments	36aa	....	....	....	....	....	....	....	—	—	—	—	—
Liabs. of Central Bank: Securities	36ac	522	504	969	884	988	1,421	1,229	† 2,821	5,920	6,489	6,699	8,406
Restricted Deposits	36b	....	....	....	....	....	....	....	—	—	—	—	—
Liab. to Nonbank Financial Insts.	36j	....	....	....	....	....	....	....	118	114	114	605	633
Capital Accounts	37a	3,243	3,278	6,510	2,352	3,797	4,147	5,227	† 7,804	5,325	4,235	4,977	9,340
Other Items (Net)	37r	−1,382	−537	596	−1,004	−1,260	−1,759	−678	† −222	−90	−45	−121	73
Money plus Quasi-Money	35l	2,392	2,686	3,190	4,104	5,722	7,228	7,328	† 9,949	9,899	11,645	13,262	14,674
Money (National Definitions)						*Millions of Pula: End of Period*							
M1	59ma	785	818	886	969	1,320	1,533	1,514	2,356	2,581	2,881	4,224	3,968
M2	59mb	2,358	2,410	2,848	3,560	4,759	5,962	5,960	9,951	9,899	11,644	13,261	14,644
M3	59mc	2,880	3,537	4,489	5,316	6,679	8,486	8,400	12,772	15,819	18,134	19,960	23,050

Botswana 616

		1994	1995	1996	1997	1998	1999	2000	2001	2002	2003	2004	2005
Interest Rates						*Percent Per Annum*							
Bank Rate (End of Period)...............	60	13.50	13.00	13.00	12.00	12.75	13.75	14.25	14.25	15.25	14.25	14.25	14.50
Savings Rate..................................	60k	....	....	7.05	7.57	6.78	7.27	7.93	8.60	7.98	8.17	7.66	8.05
Deposit Rate.................................	60l	10.59	9.79	9.68	9.51	8.43	9.10	9.42	10.09	10.45	9.95	9.85	9.25
Deposit Rate (Fgn. Currency)............	60l.f	....	....	4.60	4.43	4.52	4.46	5.93	4.06	1.52	.96	1.36	2.17
Lending Rate..................................	60p	13.92	14.42	14.50	13.95	13.65	14.78	15.48	15.75	16.21	16.33	15.75	15.74
Government Bond Yield..................	61	....	....	....	....	....	....	....	....	....	10.46	10.07	9.49
Prices and Labor						*Index Numbers (2000=100): Period Averages*							
Consumer Prices...........................	64	60.6	66.9	† 73.7	80.1	85.5	92.1	100.0	106.6	115.1	125.7	134.4	146.1
						Number in Thousands: Period Averages							
Employment.................................	67e	231	233	238	230	242	257	265	271	279	....	....	....
Intl. Transactions & Positions						*Millions of Pula*							
Exports..	70	4,965.0	5,941.5	8,133.4	10,390.7	8,696.9	12,227.8	13,834.7	13,649.4	14,306.5	14,970.6	16,894.4	21,923.4
Imports, c.i.f................................	71	4,407.3	5,305.1	5,742.9	8,250.0	9,803.8	10,164.4	12,646.8	10,613.1	10,556.9	12,840.1	16,237.4	20,441.4
Balance of Payments						*Millions of US Dollars: Minus Sign Indicates Debit*							
Current Account, n.i.e...................	78ald	221.6	299.7	495.0	721.4	169.7	583.5	545.2	617.9	143.3	483.3	....	....
Goods: Exports f.o.b.....................	78aad	1,874.3	2,160.2	2,217.5	2,819.8	2,060.6	2,658.2	2,675.4	2,314.5	2,318.6	3,024.3		
Goods: Imports f.o.b.....................	78abd	−1,364.3	−1,605.4	−1,467.7	−1,924.5	−1,983.1	−1,873.5	−1,773.2	−1,604.1	−1,642.3	−2,127.2		
Trade Balance.............................	78acd	510.0	554.8	749.8	895.4	77.5	784.7	902.1	710.4	676.3	897.2		
Services: Credit............................	78add	186.1	260.4	163.0	210.2	254.9	331.2	324.8	340.3	489.6	664.2		
Services: Debit.............................	78aed	−312.0	−444.2	−343.6	−440.7	−522.4	−518.0	−547.5	−513.3	−509.7	−652.4		
Balance on Goods & Services.......	78afd	384.2	370.9	569.2	664.9	−190.0	597.9	679.4	537.3	656.2	908.9		
Income: Credit.............................	78agd	230.8	483.2	501.7	622.1	622.7	429.8	378.1	378.5	268.4	382.6		
Income: Debit..............................	78ahd	−455.1	−515.6	−754.8	−766.9	−503.1	−696.0	−729.5	−495.4	−993.6	−1,098.4		
Balance on Gds, Serv. & Inc..........	78aid	159.9	338.5	316.1	520.1	−70.5	331.7	328.1	420.4	−69.0	193.2		
Current Transfers, n.i.e.: Credit.....	78ajd	356.8	330.7	355.4	456.8	460.9	474.4	426.1	383.0	400.4	538.3		
Current Transfers: Debit................	78akd	−295.1	−369.5	−176.6	−255.5	−220.8	−222.6	−209.0	−185.5	−188.1	−248.2		
Capital Account, n.i.e....................	78bcd	19.2	14.4	6.2	16.9	31.8	20.6	38.1	5.8	15.7	22.5		
Capital Account, n.i.e.: Credit........	78bad	19.6	15.4	18.1	29.4	44.2	33.5	51.5	18.7	29.7	42.5		
Capital Account: Debit..................	78bbd	−.4	−.9	−11.9	−12.5	−12.4	−12.9	−13.3	−12.9	−14.0	−20.0		
Financial Account, n.i.e..................	78bjd	41.1	−33.9	42.4	5.6	−202.4	−231.0	−214.0	−509.4	−217.3	−378.8		
Direct Investment Abroad..............	78bdd	−9.5	−40.9	1.1	−4.1	−3.5	−1.5	−2.3	−370.9	−42.9	−206.1		
Dir. Invest. in Rep. Econ., n.i.e......	78bed	−14.2	70.4	71.2	100.1	95.3	36.7	57.2	22.1	403.4	418.0		
Portfolio Investment Assets...........	78bfd	—	−36.2	−35.5	−28.5	−42.8	−22.8	−34.1	−68.4	−420.2	−587.3		
Equity Securities..........................	78bkd	—	−30.8	−26.7	−33.1	−16.9	6.5	−3.4	−5.8	−325.5	−451.6		
Debt Securities............................	78bld	—	−5.4	−8.9	4.7	−25.9	−29.3	−30.7	−62.6	−94.8	−135.7		
Portfolio Investment Liab., n.i.e......	78bgd	−.1	5.5	28.9	10.8	−14.1	−7.5	−5.9	6.0	7.1	66.8		
Equity Securities..........................	78bmd	—	5.5	28.7	10.8	−14.1	−7.5	−5.9	6.0	7.1	10.2		
Debt Securities............................	78bnd	−.1	—	.2	—	—	—	—	—	—	56.6		
Financial Derivatives Assets...........	78bwd	....	−.2	—	—	—	—	—	—	—	—		
Financial Derivatives Liabilities.......	78bxd	....	.3	2.1	−15.4	5.2	−4.6	−3.0	—	—	—		
Other Investment Assets...............	78bhd	15.8	−88.7	−95.6	−166.6	−310.8	−274.7	−263.6	−152.7	−221.1	−220.7		
Monetary Authorities..................	78bod	....	....	....	....	....	....	....	....	....	....		
General Government....................	78bpd	19.7	−46.1	−28.7	−78.0	−101.1	−86.3	−90.4	−52.6	−80.8	−72.5		
Banks.......................................	78bqd	.4	−8.7	−35.1	−76.9	−139.7	−154.7	−135.0	−78.5	−112.9	−124.0		
Other Sectors............................	78brd	−4.3	−34.0	−31.8	−11.7	−70.0	−33.7	−38.3	−21.6	−27.3	−24.2		
Other Investment Liab., n.i.e..........	78bid	49.0	55.9	70.3	109.3	68.2	43.5	37.7	54.4	56.3	150.5		
Monetary Authorities..................	78bsd	—	—	—	—	—	—	—	—	—	—		
General Government....................	78btd	6.5	−12.3	−19.6	51.3	22.2	−16.1	−22.5	−21.1	−23.1	−13.5		
Banks.......................................	78bud	−2.8	−2.5	17.8	−3.4	−3.5	1.4	1.4	7.2	7.6	37.6		
Other Sectors............................	78bvd	45.3	70.7	72.1	61.4	49.5	58.1	58.9	68.3	71.9	126.4		
Net Errors and Omissions..............	78cad	−146.7	−73.6	−32.9	−108.8	45.1	21.1	−1.9	55.7	119.0	44.5		
Overall Balance...........................	78cbd	135.2	206.6	510.7	635.1	44.2	394.1	367.4	170.0	60.6	171.5		
Reserves and Related Items............	79dad	−135.2	−206.6	−510.7	−635.1	−44.2	−394.1	−367.4	−170.0	−60.6	−171.5		
Reserve Assets.............................	79dbd	−135.2	−206.6	−510.7	−635.1	−44.2	−394.1	−367.4	−170.0	−60.6	−171.5		
Use of Fund Credit and Loans........	79dcd	—	—	—	—	—	—	—	—	—	—		
Exceptional Financing...................	79ded	....	....	....	....	....	....	....	....	....	—		
International Investment Position						*Millions of US Dollars*							
Assets...	79aad	5,084.0	5,643.9	6,001.0	6,510.5	6,855.1	7,356.3	7,391.7	7,390.1	7,633.9	8,828.4	....	....
Direct Investment Abroad..............	79abd	484.5	650.1	576.7	404.5	257.5	596.9	516.6	865.8	1,023.7	1,446.6		
Portfolio Investment.....................	79acd	26.9	61.5	139.1	132.2	214.6	148.2	226.1	296.8	755.8	1,583.0		
Equity Securities..........................	79add	16.1	45.8	105.8	81.7	73.6	120.2	129.7	197.7	430.4	1,013.5		
Debt Securities............................	79aed	10.9	15.8	33.3	50.5	141.0	28.0	96.4	99.1	325.3	569.5		
Financial Derivatives.....................	79ald		.2		17.1	9.7							
Other Investment.........................	79afd	171.3	239.1	253.1	280.3	433.0	382.4	330.8	330.2	380.5	459.0		
Monetary Authorities..................	79agd	—	—	—	—	—	—	—	—	—	—		
General Government....................	79ahd	—	—	—	—	—	—	—	—	—	—		
Banks.......................................	79aid	63.3	69.5	99.9	186.2	291.5	289.9	250.9	274.3	361.9	413.6		
Other Sectors............................	79ajd	107.9	169.6	153.3	94.2	141.5	92.5	79.9	55.8	18.6	45.4		
Reserve Assets.............................	79akd	4,401.3	4,693.0	5,032.1	5,676.5	5,940.3	6,228.9	6,318.2	5,897.2	5,473.9	5,339.8		
Liabilities.....................................	79lad	2,005.3	1,995.1	1,941.9	2,151.9	2,248.7	2,514.8	3,056.6	2,338.7	1,987.2	2,492.2		
Dir. Invest. in Rep. Economy..........	79lbd	998.5	1,126.4	1,058.1	1,172.9	1,294.8	1,387.3	1,826.6	1,388.5	854.1	1,280.2		
Portfolio Investment.....................	79lcd	10.9	15.9	50.4	60.5	34.2	24.0	13.4	15.4	23.5	86.7		
Equity Securities..........................	79ldd	10.9	15.9	50.4	60.0	33.4	22.7	12.7	14.8	23.5	86.7		
Debt Securities............................	79led	—	—	—	.5	.8	1.3	.7	.5	—	—		
Financial Derivatives.....................	79lfd	—	.2	1.9	—	—	—	—	—	—	—		
Other Investment.........................	79lfd	996.0	852.6	831.5	918.5	919.7	1,103.5	1,216.5	934.9	1,109.7	1,125.3		
Monetary Authorities..................	79lgd	—	—	—	—	—	—	—	—	—	—		
General Government....................	79lhd	496.9	495.8	387.9	483.1	482.7	523.6	419.3	314.8	467.1	493.8		
Banks.......................................	79lid	38.9	35.1	27.4	23.7	16.8	15.3	25.3	25.5	31.1	—		
Other Sectors............................	79ljd	460.1	321.7	416.2	411.7	420.3	564.6	771.9	594.6	611.5	631.5		

Botswana 616

		1994	1995	1996	1997	1998	1999	2000	2001	2002	2003	2004	2005
Government Finance						*Millions of Pula: Year Beginning April 1*							
Deficit (-) or Surplus........................	80	195.60	269.90	1,302.40	875.19	−1,387.80	1,535.58	† 2,782.78	−931.23	−1,475.82	−133.89	. . . .	. . . .
Total Revenue and Grants...............	81y	4,472.50	5,464.40	7,394.80	8,281.29	7,677.62	11,963.09	† 13,975.10	12,585.86	14,227.61	16,135.93	. . . .	. . . .
Revenue......................................	81	4,396.80	5,427.30	7,311.80	8,169.20	7,539.93	11,837.04	† 13,920.76	12,527.87	13,999.19	16,074.57	. . . .	. . . .
Grants..	81z	75.70	37.10	83.00	112.09	137.69	126.05	† 54.34	57.99	228.42	61.36	. . . .	. . . .
Exp. & Lending Minus Repay...........	82z	4,276.90	5,194.50	6,092.40	7,406.10	9,065.42	10,427.51	† 11,192.32	13,517.09	15,703.43	16,269.82	. . . .	. . . .
Expenditure................................	82	4,389.10	5,181.60	6,283.50	7,188.10	9,199.78	10,608.94	† 11,102.91	13,404.19	15,693.45	17,191.18	. . . .	. . . .
Lending Minus Repayments...........	83	−112.20	12.90	−191.10	218.00	−134.36	−181.43	† 89.41	112.90	9.98	−921.36	. . . .	. . . .
Total Financing.............................	80h	−195.70	−269.80	−1,302.30	−875.14	1,387.80	−1,535.58	† −2,782.78	931.23	1,475.82	133.89	. . . .	. . . .
Total Net Borrowing.....................	84	69.50	89.80	−8,148.70	13,467.36	1,098.16	−216.47	† 899.26	−1,878.81	−6,256.77	−3,818.51	. . . .	. . . .
Use of Cash Balances...................	87	−265.20	−359.60	6,846.40	−14,342.50	289.64	−1,319.11	† −3,682.04	2,810.04	7,732.59	3,952.40	. . . .	. . . .
Total Debt by Currency...................	88	1,377.70	1,439.90	1,791.20	1,996.90	2,422.80	2,425.30	2,426.20	2,917.50	2,194.70	2,194.50	. . . .	. . . .
Domestic.....................................	88b	—	—	—	—	—	—	—	—	—	—	. . . .	. . . .
Foreign.......................................	89b	1,377.70	1,439.90	1,791.20	1,996.90	2,422.80	2,425.30	2,426.20	2,917.50	2,194.70	2,194.50	. . . .	. . . .
National Accounts						*Millions of Pula: Year Ending June 30*							
Househ.Cons.Expend.,incl.NPISHs....	96f	3,843.0	4,258.5	4,714.7	5,314.7	6,136.1	6,936.8	7,841.1	8,438.6	9,307.6	10,336.0	12,026.8	13,529.1
Government Consumption Expend...	91f	3,049.0	3,546.7	4,006.7	4,711.0	5,452.9	6,578.8	7,524.5	6,517.9	7,348.0	8,967.4	9,161.7	11,103.9
Gross Fixed Capital Formation..........	93e	2,813.8	3,135.2	3,632.4	4,275.9	5,170.1	6,263.3	6,751.1	6,898.2	7,743.2	8,735.7	9,017.8	9,937.2
Changes in Inventories...................	93i	204.3	13.7	−261.4	328.2	886.0	1,653.9	1,126.1	6,811.9	7,054.7	6,721.5	9,382.9	7,021.1
Exports of Goods and Services..........	90c	5,412.0	6,071.4	7,411.6	9,881.6	11,392.8	10,051.6	12,163.2	17,826.4	16,399.2	19,181.6	17,875.4	24,266.4
Imports of Goods and Services (-).....	98c	4,260.3	4,772.5	5,300.1	6,771.1	8,875.3	9,960.6	7,862.9	10,805.9	12,044.2	14,908.9	14,624.1	17,104.5
Gross Domestic Product (GDP).........	99b	11,041.3	12,261.7	14,203.9	17,740.3	20,162.7	21,523.8	27,649.0	34,787.1	35,693.4	38,688.3	42,580.4	48,753.1
Consumption of Fixed Capital..........	99cf	1,483.1	1,720.7	1,933.6	2,210.7	2,421.3	2,647.4	3,067.1	—	. . . .	. . . .	. . . .	. . . .
GDP Volume 1993/94 Prices............	99b.p	11,041.4	11,397.6	12,029.5	12,704.2	13,728.6	14,295.6	16,718.6	18,242.3	18,530.4	20,297.7	20,985.3	22,742.2
GDP Volume (2000=100)................	99bvp	66.0	68.2	72.0	76.0	82.1	85.5	100.0	109.1	110.8	121.4	125.5	136.0
GDP Deflator (2000=100)................	99bip	60.5	65.1	71.4	84.4	88.8	91.0	100.0	115.3	116.5	115.3	122.7	129.6
						Millions: Midyear Estimates							
Population...............................	99z	1.58	1.62	1.65	1.68	1.71	1.74	1.75	1.77	1.77	1.77	1.77	1.76

Brazil 223

		1994	1995	1996	1997	1998	1999	2000	2001	2002	2003	2004	2005
Exchange Rates						*Reais per SDR: End of Period*							
Principal Rate	aa	† 1.235	1.446	1.495	1.506	1.702	2.455	2.547	2.916	4.803	4.292	4.121	3.344
					Reais per US dollar: End of Period (ae)Period Average (rf)								
Principal Rate	ae	† .846	.973	1.039	1.116	1.209	1.789	1.955	2.320	3.533	2.888	2.654	2.340
Principal Rate	rf	† .639	.918	1.005	1.078	1.161	1.815	1.830	2.358	2.921	3.077	2.925	2.434
Fund Position						*Millions of SDRs: End of Period*							
Quota	2f.s	2,171	2,171	2,171	2,171	2,171	3,036	3,036	3,036	3,036	3,036	3,036	3,036
SDRs	1b.s	—	1	1	—	1	7	—	8	202	2	3	20
Reserve Position in the Fund	1c.s	—	—	—	—	—	—	—	—	—	—		
Total Fund Cred.&Loans Outstg	2tl	128	95	47	23	3,427	6,431	1,357	6,634	15,320	19,056	16,117	—
International Liquidity					*Millions of US Dollars Unless Otherwise Indicated: End of Period*								
Total Reserves minus Gold	1l.d	37,070	49,708	58,323	50,827	42,580	34,796	32,488	35,739	37,683	49,111	52,740	53,574
SDRs	1b.d	—	1	1	1	2	10	—	11	275	2	4	29
Reserve Position in the Fund	1c.d	—	—	—	—	—	—	—	—	—	—		
Foreign Exchange	1d.d	37,069	49,707	58,322	50,826	42,578	34,786	32,488	35,729	37,409	49,108	52,736	53,545
Other Liquid Foreign Assets	1e.d	319	365	467	503	585	618	—	—	—	—	—	—
Gold (Million Fine Troy Ounces)	1ad	3.71	4.58	3.69	3.03	4.60	3.17	1.89	.46	.44	.45	.45	.44
Gold (National Valuation)	1and	1,418	1,767	1,381	903	1,358	929	523	127	153	186	195	225
Monetary Authorities:Other Assets	3..d	1,851	4,077	5,050	4,935	5,456	5,334	6,110	—	—	—	—	—
Other Liab	4..d	6,888	5,614	3,239	2,948	8,284	5,288	2,419	1,255	4,735	9,435	4,523	2,304
Deposit Money Banks: Assets	7a.d	20,855	18,682	20,345	19,550	17,622	16,754	15,876	16,525	12,697	19,237	18,851	22,575
Liabilities	7b.d	36,771	42,494	51,432	54,756	51,207	42,286	40,953	40,215	31,545	30,578	29,990	31,939
Other Banking Insts.: Assets	7e.d	1,504	393	177	143	87	68	207	156	230	428	202	149
Liabilities	7f.d	2,224	2,247	3,211	4,398	9,406	6,282	7,975	8,532	8,873	9,651	8,749	7,127
Monetary Authorities						*Millions of Reais: End of Period*							
Foreign Assets	11	35,326	55,218	69,829	61,745	55,053	69,273	76,097	82,026	133,291	150,909	145,848	125,129
Claims on Central Government	12a	26,509	31,221	27,713	41,233	136,916	121,463	130,779	189,786	284,115	290,363	311,198	283,534
Claims on State and Local Govts	12b	—	—	—	—	—	—	—	—	—	—	—	—
Claims on Nonfin.Pub.Enterprises	12c	—	—	—	—	—	—	—	—	—	—	—	—
Claims on Private Sector	12d	3	5	5	5	—	—	—	—	—	—	—	—
Claims on Deposit Money Banks	12e	20,557	34,576	67,642	68,012	40,368	33,755	38,604	20,679	2,924	226	4,164	24,044
Claims on Other Banking Insts	12f	5	5	3	902	—	—	—	1,764	—	—	—	1,905
Claims on Nonbank Financial Insts	12g			6	7	1,926	2,036	1,373	1,456	1,070	606	—	—
Reserve Money	14	36,130	40,430	49,638	66,636	59,213	63,849	66,901	79,639	199,066	190,801	211,341	228,046
of which: Currency Outside DMBs	14a	8,700	12,517	15,316	18,141	21,186	25,977	28,641	32,627	42,351	43,065	52,020	58,271
Money Market Instruments	16aa									122	79	154	153
Liabs. of Central Bank: Securities	16ac	39,289	52,457	83,106	65,724	104,709	62,468	85,839	126,524	67,021	30,619	13,569	6,816
Restricted Deposits	16b	306	190	125	12	10	13	13	15	23	18	12	10
Foreign Liabilities	16c	5,970	5,594	3,435	3,324	15,834	25,239	8,184	22,249	90,301	109,044	78,443	5,392
Central Government Deposits	16d	12,094	22,239	25,143	41,135	50,403	75,779	88,380	82,516	89,151	120,264	158,817	209,672
Capital Accounts	17a	998	1,408	4,190	4,198	3,809	−4,496	−8,312	6,814	−12,032	8,788	13,648	−881
Other Items (Net)	17r	−12,387	−1,293	−438	−9,125	285	3,674	5,847	−22,045	−12,251	−17,509	−14,774	−14,596
Deposit Money Banks						*Millions of Reais: End of Period*							
Reserves	20	22,956	22,126	22,035	42,494	32,716	38,029	38,342	46,388	152,714	140,334	151,683	165,375
Claims on Mon.Author.:Securities	20c	5,192	6,578	18,932	11,603	54,196	40,140	52,257	61,525	36,467	19,021	9,223	4,077
Blocked Financial Assets	20d	—	—	—	—	—	—	—	—	—	—	—	—
Foreign Assets	21	17,602	18,159	21,130	21,810	21,285	29,959	31,032	38,331	44,850	55,565	50,039	52,842
Claims on Central Government	22a	8,963	28,869	48,056	111,023	127,933	185,809	218,079	263,553	271,926	318,731	334,285	382,589
Claims on State and Local Govts	22b	27,482	25,986	56,061	39,447	38,229	19,000	4,274	2,753	2,476	2,504	3,105	3,120
Claims on Nonfin.Pub.Enterprises	22c	10,245	12,399	18,736	5,716	12,996	15,481	3,710	1,544	2,321	2,160	3,043	4,930
Claims on Private Sector	22d	174,702	210,464	220,681	254,568	278,787	287,129	311,354	342,176	381,562	434,510	487,499	632,745
Claims on Other Banking Insts	22f	879	826	1,100	3,397	5,234	7,181	9,016	10,681	11,804	13,756	15,090	14,022
Claims on Nonbank Financial Insts	22g	—	—	—	—	5,910	985	794	3,676	484	147	156	38
Demand Deposits	24	13,979	14,034	14,320	27,912	29,064	36,258	45,057	50,388	64,680	65,879	75,207	85,626
Time and Savings Deposits	25	99,074	135,641	146,719	174,020	192,218	201,714	200,215	225,453	275,740	285,088	342,297	418,350
Money Market Instruments	26aa	3,320	4,744	7,029	10,283	12,684	13,377	22,880	32,739	20,140	34,560	33,104	39,090
Restricted Deposits	26b	18,868	24,707	26,237	28,952	33,331	35,564	39,059	41,835	48,564	55,088	58,491	66,997
Foreign Liabilities	26c	31,035	41,304	53,417	61,086	61,853	75,616	80,047	93,283	111,432	88,322	79,605	74,760
Central Government Deposits	26d	18,288	14,670	16,074	17,939	12,338	7,918	10,066	11,950	8,377	13,014	16,342	18,260
Credit from Monetary Authorities	26g	20,455	23,407	39,025	30,272	11,623	3,159	8,568	23,916	3,357	219	4,447	28,978
Liabilities to Other Banking Insts	26i	11,914	9,396	22,017	21,973	43,712	54,338	70,959	85,951	141,546	165,208	156,406	188,448
Liab. to Nonbank Financial Insts	26j	92	111	60	234	6,059	1,033	1,745	3,246	2,326	2,286	1,811	2,999
Capital Accounts	27a	44,094	57,704	74,127	95,976	117,477	135,963	136,846	166,080	192,483	227,739	250,025	288,478
Other Items (Net)	27r	6,902	−311	7,707	21,411	56,928	58,772	53,416	35,784	35,961	49,324	36,387	47,753
Monetary Survey						*Millions of Reais: End of Period*							
Foreign Assets (Net)	31n	15,923	26,479	34,107	19,145	−1,349	−1,623	18,897	4,825	−23,590	9,108	37,839	97,819
Domestic Credit	32	218,406	272,866	331,145	397,224	545,191	555,386	580,934	722,922	858,230	929,500	979,216	1,094,951
Claims on Central Govt. (Net)	32an	5,090	23,181	34,552	93,182	202,108	223,574	250,412	358,872	458,513	475,817	470,324	438,191
Claims on State and Local Govts	32b	27,482	25,986	56,061	39,447	38,229	19,000	4,274	2,753	2,476	2,504	3,105	3,120
Claims on Nonfin.Pub.Enterprises	32c	10,245	12,399	18,736	5,716	12,996	15,481	3,710	1,544	2,321	2,160	3,043	4,930
Claims on Private Sector	32d	174,705	210,469	220,686	254,573	278,787	287,129	311,354	342,176	381,562	434,510	487,499	632,745
Claims on Other Banking Insts	32f	884	831	1,103	4,299	5,234	7,181	9,016	12,445	11,804	13,756	15,090	15,927
Claims on Nonbank Financial Inst	32g	—	—	6	7	7,836	3,021	2,167	5,132	1,554	753	156	38
Money	34	25,540	32,094	41,683	50,999	54,824	62,294	74,078	83,060	107,209	111,542	131,152	144,677
Quasi-Money	35	99,074	135,641	146,719	174,020	192,218	201,714	200,215	225,453	275,740	285,088	342,297	418,350
Money Market Instruments	36aa	3,320	4,744	7,029	10,283	12,684	13,377	22,880	32,739	20,262	34,639	33,258	39,243
Liabs. of Central Bank: Securities	36ac	34,097	45,879	64,174	54,121	50,513	22,328	33,582	64,999	30,554	11,598	4,346	2,739
Restricted Deposits	36b	19,174	24,897	26,362	28,964	33,341	35,577	39,072	41,850	48,587	55,106	58,503	67,007
Liabilities to Other Banking Insts	36i	11,914	9,396	22,017	21,973	43,712	54,338	70,959	85,951	141,546	165,208	156,406	188,448
Liab. to Nonbank Financial Insts	36j	92	111	60	234	6,059	1,033	1,745	3,246	2,326	2,286	1,811	2,999
Capital Accounts	37a	45,092	59,112	78,317	100,174	121,286	131,467	128,534	172,894	180,450	236,528	263,672	287,597
Other Items (Net)	37r	−3,974	−12,529	−21,109	−24,399	29,204	31,635	28,766	17,556	27,966	36,613	25,611	41,710
Money plus Quasi-Money	35l	124,614	167,735	188,402	225,019	247,043	264,008	274,293	308,513	382,948	396,630	473,448	563,027

Brazil 223

		1994	1995	1996	1997	1998	1999	2000	2001	2002	2003	2004	2005
Other Banking Institutions						*Millions of Reais: End of Period*							
Reserves	40	1,526	611	768	1,174	5,427	224	547	245	393	3,066	4,461	1,420
Claims on Mon.Author.:Securities	40c	113	459	1,195	3,015	37,625	18,530	27,186	59,004	19,704	10,940	4,304	2,709
Blocked Financial Assets	40d	—	—	—	—	—	—	—	—	—	—	—	—
Foreign Assets	41	1,269	382	184	159	105	121	405	362	811	1,237	537	349
Claims on Central Government	42a	2,820	4,720	4,085	6,980	71,066	143,315	180,058	168,895	185,858	301,821	377,073	484,294
Claims on State and Local Govts	42b	918	1,890	1,164	2,441	7,013	4,773	3,133	2,917	3,902	4,786	5,939	6,040
Claims on Nonfin.Pub.Enterprises	42c	2,705	6,674	3,560	2,859	3,194	3,574	6,902	13,983	9,331	7,603	6,399	4,839
Claims on Private Sector	42d	28,158	30,305	29,298	33,356	37,441	54,610	87,037	80,607	99,298	105,748	133,437	161,540
Claims on Deposit Money Banks	42e	11,491	15,627	19,344	22,533	56,821	76,160	96,708	137,578	187,496	221,787	242,363	242,255
Claims on Nonbank Financial Insts	42g	—	—	—	—	434	179	783	592	1,945	756	138	85
Demand Deposits	44	—	—	—	—	—	—	—	—	—	—	—	—
Time and Savings Deposits	45	7,675	4,997	6,035	7,032	6,976	3,903	3,340	3,354	3,907	5,545	7,191	8,924
Money Market Instruments	46aa	178	138	525	485	137,513	204,315	271,162	319,921	313,565	451,461	542,887	648,447
Restricted Deposits	46b	190	301	304	249	529	626	820	625	575	505	509	569
Foreign Liabilities	46c	1,877	2,184	3,335	4,906	11,362	11,234	15,588	19,791	31,343	27,875	23,223	16,681
Central Government Deposits	46d	10,432	12,308	14,607	16,443	25,643	28,378	32,476	33,880	44,317	52,996	55,910	55,318
Credit from Monetary Authorities	46g	778	1,035	1,065	2,020	354	385	287	1,967	289	266	290	2,238
Credit from Deposit Money Banks	46h	958	1,162	1,152	3,804	1,667	1,362	1,144	1,856	1,818	3,379	3,504	6,349
Liab. to Nonbank Financial Insts	46j	—	—	—	—	74	51	28	1	262	52	69	405
Capital Accounts	47a	16,756	21,323	18,350	19,931	19,935	20,711	22,016	64,516	80,793	88,483	98,913	112,750
Other Items (Net)	47r	10,156	17,219	14,225	17,646	15,074	30,521	55,897	18,271	31,869	27,181	42,154	51,851
Banking Survey						*Millions of Reais: End of Period*							
Foreign Assets (Net)	51n	15,315	24,677	30,956	14,398	−12,606	−12,736	3,714	−14,603	−54,122	−17,531	15,153	81,487
Domestic Credit	52	241,692	303,315	353,542	422,118	633,462	726,280	817,355	943,589	1,102,441	1,283,463	1,431,202	1,680,504
Claims on Central Govt. (Net)	52an	−2,522	15,593	24,031	83,719	247,532	338,512	397,994	493,887	600,053	724,642	791,487	867,167
Claims on State and Local Govts	52b	28,400	27,875	57,225	41,889	45,242	23,774	7,408	5,669	6,378	7,290	9,044	9,160
Claims on Nonfin.Pub.Enterprises	52c	12,950	19,073	22,296	8,575	16,190	19,055	10,611	15,527	11,652	9,763	9,442	9,769
Claims on Private Sector	52d	202,863	240,774	249,984	287,929	316,228	341,739	398,392	422,782	480,860	540,258	620,936	794,285
Claims on Nonbank Financial Inst	52g	—	—	6	7	8,270	3,200	2,950	5,724	3,498	1,510	294	123
Liquid Liabilities	55l	130,475	171,812	193,431	230,740	235,331	252,159	266,630	286,934	364,889	366,635	418,783	491,832
Money Market Instruments	56aa	3,492	4,826	7,532	10,724	148,639	213,634	288,365	345,699	323,831	475,629	564,320	679,644
Liabs. of Central Bank: Securities	56ac	33,984	45,420	62,979	51,106	12,888	3,799	6,396	5,995	10,849	658	43	30
Restricted Deposits	56b	19,364	25,198	26,666	29,213	33,870	36,203	39,892	42,475	49,162	55,611	59,012	67,577
Liab. to Nonbank Financial Insts	56j	92	111	60	234	6,133	1,084	1,773	3,247	2,588	2,339	1,880	3,403
Capital Accounts	57a	61,848	80,435	96,667	120,105	141,221	152,178	150,550	237,410	261,243	325,011	362,585	400,346
Other Items (Net)	57r	7,752	190	−2,837	−5,606	42,773	54,487	67,462	7,226	35,757	40,050	39,733	119,158
Nonbank Financial Institutions						*Millions of Reais: End of Period*							
Reserves	40..n	3	6	31	14	3	4	4	5	98	7	11	11
Claims on Mon.Author.:Securities	40c.n	405	154	350	364	704	375	1,085	1,523	1,128	423	43	30
Blocked Financial Assets	40d.n	—	—	—	—	—	—	—	—	—	—	—	—
Foreign Assets	41..n	76	87	93	45	44	105	118	18	37	29	29	63
Claims on Central Government	42a.n	17	55	1,090	1,229	2,465	4,243	4,138	4,192	3,680	3,875	3,094	3,726
Claims on State and Local Govt	42b.n	360	348	408	103	617	43	38	66	133	207	399	466
Claims on Nonfin.Pub.Enterprises	42c.n	36	14	14	14	13	7	11	47	102	155	34	22
Claims on Private Sector	42d.n	11,219	15,678	10,208	11,366	11,458	12,509	16,397	15,206	14,023	13,488	17,387	23,689
Claims on Deposit Money Banks	42e.n	1,329	1,737	2,824	2,421	10,735	4,416	4,760	5,073	4,207	5,610	3,213	3,407
Claims on Other Banking Insts	42f.n	23	197	35	73	1,130	326	260	1,237	1,535	1,826	1,492	1,864
Money Market Instruments	46aan	1,181	3,901	5,482	8,307	9,247	7,033	7,428	6,253	6,721	9,933	12,530	48,595
Restricted Deposits	46b.n												
Foreign Liabilities	46c.n	1,529	2,293	2,994	3,728	4,224	5,115	4,862	4,073	4,625	3,395	1,112	899
Central Government Deposits	46d.n	—	—	1	1	3	36	37	104	14	22	34	41
Credit from Monetary Authorities	46g.n	—	—	—	—	—	—	—	98	75	129	—	—
Cred. from Deposit Money Banks	46h.n	—	—	—	—	6,488	1,071	838	3,651	360	196	177	47
Liabilities to Other Banking Insts	46i.n	1,517	1,619	3,670	4,093	5,617	5,036	3,063	2,024	2,886	3,144	2,104	2,220
Capital Accounts	47a.n	5,767	8,783	10,848	11,187	13,324	17,061	17,659	21,280	23,908	24,933	25,753	43,000
Other Items (Net)	47r.n	3,474	1,680	−7,942	−11,687	−11,735	−13,324	−7,076	−10,116	−13,648	−16,132	−16,009	−61,524
Money (National Definitions)						*Millions of Reais: End of Period*							
Base Money	19ma	17,685	21,682	19,796	31,828	39,184	48,430	47,686	53,256	73,302	73,219	88,733	101,247
Base Money (BA)	19maa	80,734	122,291	184,050	280,070	352,345	447,132	538,693	646,672	788,034	886,894	979,233	1,154,051
Base Money (B2)	19mab	101,902	156,428	231,898	318,599	374,282	458,567	540,894	649,254	789,960	887,675	980,140	1,155,131
M1	59ma	22,773	28,493	29,807	47,363	50,707	62,744	74,352	83,707	107,846	109,648	127,946	144,778
M2	59mb	132,558	178,755	188,735	239,777	254,965	274,770	283,785	321,612	397,503	412,895	493,497	582,464
M2A	59mba	60,443	72,380	60,084	63,353	63,170	271,790	356,298	....	....	....	....	....
M3	59mc	154,544	225,008	285,942	340,210	376,015	468,728	556,577	625,057	688,269	838,386	988,622	1,166,502
M3A	59mca	119,882	143,410	142,159	173,436	185,294	386,382	468,390	....	....	....	....	....
M4	59md	176,449	261,176	336,148	405,946	459,308	551,092	652,093	756,181	807,523	960,061	1,109,519	1,312,399
M4A	59mda	174,523	259,381	342,305	422,306	480,202	575,666	677,021	....	....	....	....	....
Interest Rates						*Percent Per Annum*							
Discount Rate (End of Period)	60	....	....	25.34	45.09	39.41	21.37	† 18.52	21.43	30.42	23.92	24.55	25.34
Money Market Rate	60b	4,820.64	53.37	27.45	25.00	29.50	26.26	17.59	17.47	19.11	23.37	16.24	19.12
Treasury Bill Rate	60c	....	49.93	25.73	24.79	28.57	26.39	18.51	20.06	19.43	22.10	17.14	18.76
Treasury Bill Rate (Fgn.Currency)	60c.f	....	17.78	15.13	11.60	15.04	....	....	11.46	....	....	....	....
Savings Rate	60k	4,206.04	40.26	16.39	16.62	14.48	12.31	8.44	8.66	9.27	11.26	8.09	9.21
Deposit Rate	60l	5,175.24	52.25	26.45	24.35	28.00	26.02	17.20	17.86	19.14	21.97	15.42	17.63
Lending Rate	60p	....	....	....	78.19	86.36	80.44	56.83	57.62	62.88	67.08	54.93	55.38

Brazil 223

		1994	1995	1996	1997	1998	1999	2000	2001	2002	2003	2004	2005
Prices and Labor						*Index Numbers (2000=100): Period Averages*							
Share Prices	62	20.8	24.4	37.0	64.3	57.0	71.0	100.0	87.0	71.7	91.8	139.8	174.5
Wholesale Prices	63	38.8	† 61.0	64.9	70.1	72.6	84.7	100.0	112.6	131.4	167.6	185.1	198.6
Consumer Prices	64	42.0	69.7	80.7	86.3	89.1	93.4	100.0	106.8	115.9	132.9	141.7	151.4
						Number in Thousands: Period Averages							
Labor Force	67d	....	74,138	72,997	75,213	76,886	79,315	77,467	83,952	86,917	88,803	....	....
Employment	67e	....	69,629	67,920	69,332	69,963	71,676	70,340	75,458	78,959	80,163	....	....
Unemployment	67c	....	4,510	5,076	5,882	6,923	7,639	7,127	7,853	7,958	8,640	....	....
Unemployment Rate (%)	67r	5.1	6.1	7.0	7.8	9.0	9.6	9.2	9.4	9.2	9.7	11.5	9.8
Intl. Transactions & Positions						*Millions of US Dollars*							
Exports	70..d	43,545	46,506	47,747	52,994	51,140	48,011	55,086	58,223	60,362	73,084	96,475	118,308
Coffee	70e.d	2,219	1,970	1,719	2,746	2,332	2,230	1,559	1,208	1,195	1,302	1,750	2,516
Imports, c.i.f.	71..d	36,192	54,137	56,792	63,291	61,135	51,909	59,053	58,640	49,716	50,845	66,432	77,585
Imports, f.o.b.	71.vd	33,079	49,972	53,346	59,747	57,763	49,295	55,839	55,572	47,237	48,291	62,835	73,560
						2000=100							
Volume of Exports	72	79.8	82.1	81.5	85.4	94.1	93.5	100.0	111.4	120.8	131.3	156.6	162.3
Coffee	72e	90.1	74.6	80.5	89.9	103.0	131.5	100.0	129.5	160.4	141.6	145.9	139.8
Volume of Imports	73	87.6	95.3	96.6	94.2	98.2	92.2	100.0	100.0	97.5	100.4	110.8	100.9
						2000=100: Indices of Unit Values in US Dollars							
Unit Value of Exports/Export Prices...	74..d	99.0	102.9	106.4	112.7	98.6	93.3	100.0	94.8	90.7	101.1	111.8	132.4
Coffee (Unit Value)	74e.d	157.9	169.3	137.0	196.0	145.2	108.8	100.0	59.8	47.8	59.0	76.9	115.4
Coffee (Wholesale Price)	76ebd	179.6	182.9	150.7	209.0	152.6	111.4	100.0	63.3	56.4	63.6	86.8	127.1
Unit Value of Imports/Import Prices..	75..d	67.6	93.9	98.9	113.6	105.3	95.8	100.0	99.5	86.8	86.2	101.6	130.6
Balance of Payments						*Millions of US Dollars: Minus Sign Indicates Debit*							
Current Account, n.i.e	78ald	−1,153	−18,136	−23,248	−30,491	−33,829	−25,400	−24,225	−23,215	−7,637	4,177	11,711	14,199
Goods: Exports f.o.b	78aad	44,102	46,506	47,851	53,189	51,136	48,011	55,086	58,223	60,362	73,084	96,475	118,308
Goods: Imports f.o.b	78abd	−33,241	−49,663	−53,304	−59,841	−57,739	−49,272	−55,783	−55,572	−47,240	−48,290	−62,835	−73,551
Trade Balance	78acd	10,861	−3,157	−5,453	−6,652	−6,603	−1,261	−698	2,650	13,121	24,794	33,641	44,757
Services: Credit	78add	4,908	6,135	4,655	5,989	7,631	7,189	9,498	9,322	9,551	10,447	12,584	16,095
Services: Debit	78aed	−10,254	−13,630	−12,714	−15,298	−16,676	−14,172	−16,660	−17,081	−14,509	−15,378	−17,261	−24,243
Balance on Goods & Services	78afd	5,515	−10,652	−13,512	−15,961	−15,648	−8,244	−7,860	−5,109	8,164	19,863	28,963	36,609
Income: Credit	78agd	2,202	3,457	5,350	5,344	4,914	3,936	3,621	3,280	3,295	3,339	3,199	3,194
Income: Debit	78ahd	−11,293	−14,562	−17,527	−21,688	−24,531	−22,780	−21,507	−23,023	−21,486	−21,891	−23,719	−29,162
Balance on Gds, Serv. & Inc	78aid	−3,576	−21,757	−25,689	−32,305	−35,265	−27,088	−25,746	−24,852	−10,026	1,311	8,443	10,642
Current Transfers, n.i.e.: Credit	78ajd	2,577	3,861	2,699	2,130	1,795	1,969	1,828	1,934	2,627	3,132	3,582	4,050
Current Transfers: Debit	78akd	−154	−240	−258	−316	−359	−281	−307	−296	−237	−265	−314	−493
Capital Account, n.i.e	78bcd	173	352	494	482	375	339	273	−36	433	498	339	663
Capital Account, n.i.e.: Credit	78bad	175	363	507	519	488	361	300	328	464	535	764	906
Capital Account: Debit	78bbd	−2	−11	−13	−37	−113	−22	−28	−364	−31	−37	−425	−243
Financial Account, n.i.e	78bjd	8,020	29,306	33,428	24,918	20,063	8,056	29,376	20,331	−3,909	−157	−3,307	13,800
Direct Investment Abroad	78bdd	−1,037	−1,384	467	−1,042	−2,721	−1,690	−2,282	2,258	−2,482	−249	−9,471	−2,517
Dir. Invest. in Rep. Econ., n.i.e	78bed	3,072	4,859	11,200	19,650	31,913	28,576	32,779	22,457	16,590	10,144	18,166	15,193
Portfolio Investment Assets	78bfd	−3,052	−936	−257	−335	−594	258	−1,696	−795	−321	179	−755	−1,771
Equity Securities	78bkd	—	−168	−49	−306	−553	−865	−1,953	−1,121	−389	−258	−121	−831
Debt Securities	78bld	−3,052	−768	−208	−29	−41	1,123	258	326	67	437	−633	−940
Portfolio Investment Liab., n.i.e	78bgd	47,784	10,171	21,089	10,393	19,013	3,542	8,651	872	−4,797	5,129	−3,996	6,655
Equity Securities	78bmd	7,280	2,775	5,785	5,099	−1,768	2,572	3,076	2,481	1,981	2,973	2,081	6,451
Debt Securities	78bnd	40,504	7,396	15,304	5,294	20,781	970	5,575	−1,609	−6,778	2,156	−6,076	204
Financial Derivatives Assets	78bwd	—	....	....	....	....	642	386	567	933	683	467	508
Financial Derivatives Liabilities	78bxd	—	....	....	....	....	−729	−583	−1,038	−1,289	−834	−1,145	−548
Other Investment Assets	78bhd	−4,368	−1,783	−3,327	2,251	−5,992	−4,399	−2,989	−6,586	−3,211	−9,483	−2,196	−3,792
Monetary Authorities	78bod	—	....	−44	−67	−84	1,668	−18	2,430	2	—	—	—
General Government	78bpd	—	....	....	2,146	60	−880	193	−1,085	−979	−1,101	−1,227	−2,329
Banks	78bqd	−4,077	−228	−4,610	5,133	3,383	−121	1,551	−3,561	4,335	−6,999	1,122	−45
Other Sectors	78brd	−291	−1,555	1,327	−4,961	−9,351	−5,066	−4,715	−4,370	−6,569	−1,383	−2,091	−1,418
Other Investment Liab., n.i.e	78bid	−34,379	18,379	4,256	−5,999	−21,556	−18,144	−4,890	2,596	−9,331	−5,724	−4,379	72
Monetary Authorities	78bsd	−545	−1,652	−3,773	−1,698	−1,704	−6,671	−201	−171	−156	−162	−163	−164
General Government	78btd	−35,609	....	—	....	....	934	1,540	−26	−493	−1,561	−2,633	−1,767
Banks	78bud	−1,439	7,071	6,450	−897	−8,550	−5,059	1,718	−741	−3,835	348	1,385	393
Other Sectors	78bvd	3,214	12,960	1,579	−3,404	−11,282	−7,348	−7,946	3,534	−4,847	−4,350	−2,967	1,610
Net Errors and Omissions	78cad	−442	1,447	−1,992	−3,160	−2,911	240	2,557	−498	−154	−933	−2,144	−1,096
Overall Balance	78cbd	6,598	12,969	8,682	−8,251	−16,302	−16,765	7,981	−3,418	−11,266	3,586	6,599	27,566
Reserves and Related Items	79dad	−6,598	−12,969	−8,682	8,251	16,302	16,765	−7,981	3,418	11,266	−3,586	−6,599	−27,566
Reserve Assets	79dbd	−7,215	−12,920	−8,326	8,284	6,990	7,783	2,260	−3,311	−314	−8,479	−2,238	−4,324
Use of Fund Credit and Loans	79dcd	−133	−49	−70	−33	4,773	4,059	−6,795	6,729	11,580	4,893	−4,362	−23,243
Exceptional Financing	79ded	750	—	−286	—	4,539	4,924	−3,446	—	—	—	—	—

		1994	1995	1996	1997	1998	1999	2000	2001	2002	2003	2004	2005
International Investment Position						*Millions of US Dollars*							
Assets	79aad	....	....	....	....	....	....	....	107,086	112,914	134,223	148,536	158,711
Direct Investment Abroad	79abd	....	....	....	....	....	....	....	49,689	54,423	54,892	69,196	71,788
Portfolio Investment	79acd	....	....	....	....	....	....	....	6,402	5,845	6,950	9,353	11,244
Equity Securities	79add	....	....	....	....	....	....	....	3,001	2,388	2,596	2,352	3,183
Debt Securities	79aed	....	....	....	....	....	....	....	3,401	3,457	4,354	7,001	8,061
Financial Derivatives	79ald	....	....	....	....	....	....	....	42	105	81	109	−18
Other Investment	79afd	....	....	....	....	....	....	....	15,087	14,705	23,004	16,943	21,897
Monetary Authorities	79agd	....	....	....	....	....	....	....	1,383	1,357	1,230	1,230	1,363
General Government	79ahd	....	....	....	....	....	....	....	—	—	—	—	2,329
Banks	79aid	....	....	....	....	....	....	....	5,521	4,052	10,850	6,832	8,120
Other Sectors	79ajd	....	....	....	....	....	....	....	8,183	9,296	10,924	8,882	10,086
Reserve Assets	79akd	....	....	....	....	....	....	....	35,866	37,837	49,296	52,935	53,799
Liabilities	79lad	....	....	....	....	....	....	....	372,052	343,450	406,759	446,229	499,268
Dir. Invest. in Rep. Economy	79lbd	....	....	....	....	....	....	....	121,948	100,847	132,799	161,259	195,562
Portfolio Investment	79lcd	....	....	....	....	....	....	....	151,741	137,355	166,095	184,758	232,627
Equity Securities	79ldd	....	....	....	....	....	....	....	36,910	27,249	53,138	77,261	125,532
Debt Securities	79led	....	....	....	....	....	....	....	114,831	110,106	112,957	107,497	107,096
Financial Derivatives	79lld	....	....	....	....	....	....	....	45	250	125	320	219
Other Investment	79lfd	....	....	....	....	....	....	....	98,317	104,999	107,740	99,892	70,859
Monetary Authorities	79lgd	....	....	....	....	....	....	....	9,250	21,729	28,965	25,577	412
General Government	79lhd	....	....	....	....	....	....	....	—	—	—	—	—
Banks	79lid	....	....	....	....	....	....	....	7,777	8,731	8,500	10,009	8,259
Other Sectors	79ljd	....	....	....	....	....	....	....	81,291	74,538	70,276	64,306	62,189
Government Finance						*Millions of Reais: End of Period*							
Deficit (-) or Surplus	80	−21,270	....	....	−63,664	−70,880	....	....	....	....	....	....	....
Revenue	81	108,280	....	....	213,409	237,116	....	....	....	....	....	....	....
Grants Received	81z	125	....	....	9	71	....	....	....	....	....	....	....
Expenditure	82	117,906	....	....	213,484	245,032	....	....	....	....	....	....	....
Lending Minus Repayments	83	11,769	....	....	63,597	63,034	....	....	....	....	....	....	....
National Accounts						*Thousands of Reais*							
Househ.Cons.Expend.,incl.NPISHs.	96f	208,256	386,910	486,813	545,698	566,192	606,701	670,702	725,760	781,174	882,983	975,245	1,075,343
Government Consumption Expend.	91f	62,388	126,652	144,001	158,502	174,847	185,828	209,953	230,741	270,965	309,631	332,332	378,745
Gross Fixed Capital Formation	93e	72,453	132,753	150,050	172,939	179,982	184,098	212,384	233,384	246,606	276,741	346,335	385,943
Changes in Inventories	93i	4,880	11,274	12,903	14,248	13,074	12,238	24,871	20,753	19,348	30,750	30,238	12,655
Exports of Goods and Services	90c	33,220	49,917	54,430	65,356	67,862	100,136	117,423	158,501	208,489	254,832	318,387	324,988
Imports of Goods and Services (-)	98c	31,993	61,314	69,311	86,000	87,769	115,154	134,079	170,403	180,554	198,754	235,917	240,075
Gross Domestic Product (GDP)	99b	349,205	646,192	778,887	870,743	914,188	973,846	1,101,255	1,198,736	1,346,028	1,556,182	1,766,621	1,937,598
Net Primary Income from Abroad	98.n	−5,913	−10,154	−12,228	−17,436	−21,241	−34,107	−32,597	−45,284	−51,944	−55,150	−58,491	−61,598
Gross National Income (GNI)	99a	343,292	636,038	766,659	853,307	892,947	939,739	1,068,658	1,153,452	1,294,084	1,501,032	1,708,130	1,876,000
GDP Volume 1990 Prices	99b.p	12,888	13,432	13,789	14,240	14,259	14,371	14,998	15,195	15,488	15,571	16,341	16,713
GDP Volume (2000=100)	99bvp	85.9	89.6	91.9	94.9	95.1	95.8	100.0	101.3	103.3	103.8	109.0	111.4
GDP Deflator (2000=100)	99bip	36.9	65.5	76.9	83.3	87.3	92.3	100.0	107.4	118.4	136.1	147.2	157.9
						Millions: Midyear Estimates							
Population	99z	158.98	161.38	163.82	166.30	168.81	171.34	173.86	176.38	178.89	181.41	183.91	186.40

Brunei Darussalam 516

		1994	1995	1996	1997	1998	1999	2000	2001	2002	2003	2004	2005
Exchange Rates						*Brunei Dollars per SDR: End of Period*							
Official Rate...............	aa	2.13240	2.10234	2.01286	2.26067	2.33803	2.28660	2.25599	2.32621	2.36081	2.52734	2.53731	2.37859
						Brunei Dollars per US Dollar: End of Period (ae) Period Average (rf)							
Official Rate...............	ae	1.46070	1.41430	1.39980	1.67550	1.66050	1.66600	1.73150	1.85100	1.73650	1.70080	1.63380	1.66420
Official Rate...............	rf	1.52744	1.41738	1.41004	1.48481	1.67360	1.69496	1.72396	1.79172	1.79059	1.74218	1.69023	1.66440
Fund Position						*Millions of SDRs: End of Period*							
Quota..................	2f.s	—	150.00	150.00	150.00	150.00	150.00	150.00	150.00	215.20	215.20	215.20	215.20
SDRs..................	1b.s	—	—	.54	1.58	2.75	3.75	5.04	6.24	6.99	7.85	8.81	10.17
Reserve Position in the Fund...........	1c.s	—	—	35.26	35.26	35.26	35.28	35.28	35.28	51.79	58.29	58.29	32.27
Total Fund Cred.&Loans Outstg.......	2tl	—	—	—	—	—	—	—	—	—	—	—	—
International Liquidity						*Millions of US Dollars Unless Otherwise Indicated: End of Period*							
Total Reserves minus Gold.............	1l.d	....	....	....	....	....	516.84	408.34	391.42	437.78	481.54	505.11	494.20
SDRs...........	1b.d	—	—	.77	2.13	3.87	5.15	6.57	7.85	9.50	11.67	13.69	14.54
Reserve Position in the Fund..........	1c.d	—	—	50.70	47.57	49.64	48.43	45.97	44.34	70.41	86.61	90.52	46.12
Foreign Exchange.................	1d.d	....	....	....	....	....	463.27	355.80	339.23	357.87	383.26	400.90	433.55
Gold (Million Fine Troy Ounces)........	1ad	....	....	....	....	....	—	—	—	—	—	—	—
Gold (National Valuation)...............	1and	....	....	....	....	....	—	—	—	—	—	—	—
Monetary Authorities: Other Assets..	3..d	....	....	....	....	....	13.7	13.2	12.4	13.5	13.8	14.4	14.1
Other Liabilities...............	4..d	....	....	....	....	....	13.9	13.4	12.6	13.3	13.6	14.0	13.7
Banking Institutions: Assets............	7a.d	....	....	....	....	....	2,018.0	3,223.4	2,764.7	2,694.0	3,229.8	4,433.9	4,982.0
Liabilities..........................	7b.d	....	....	....	....	....	71.1	69.9	187.3	180.1	108.8	90.5	299.1
Monetary Authorities						*Millions of Brunei Dollars: End of Period*							
Foreign Assets...................	11	....	....	....	....	....	759.8	757.1	729.7	806.4	830.4	832.6	851.8
Claims on Central Government........	12a	....	....	....	....	....	91.3	90.3	90.4	90.3	.3	.3	.3
Claims on Banking Institutions.........	12e	....	....	....	....	....	622.9	586.4	552.7	611.1	709.8	836.6	861.3
Reserve Money...................	14	....	....	....	....	....	1,088.4	1,041.9	1,066.5	1,122.3	1,131.6	1,271.1	1,341.7
of which: Currency Outside Banks..	14a	....	....	....	....	....	586.1	584.3	572.2	574.6	553.7	575.6	600.7
Foreign Liabilities.................	16c	....	....	....	....	....	23.1	23.2	23.3	23.2	23.2	22.9	22.9
Central Government Deposits...........	16d	....	....	....	....	....	80.6	197.6	197.8	257.5	291.0	291.6	295.3
Capital Accounts...................	17a	....	....	....	....	....	280.2	188.6	100.4	96.6	125.1	111.8	145.1
Other Items (Net)....................	17r	....	....	....	....	....	1.6	−17.5	−15.2	8.3	−30.3	−27.9	−91.6
Banking Institutions						*Millions of Brunei Dollars: End of Period*							
Reserves......................	20	....	....	....	....	....	464.6	455.9	515.9	525.1	583.5	684.8	774.1
Foreign Assets...................	21	....	....	....	....	....	3,362.0	5,581.3	5,117.5	4,678.2	5,493.2	7,244.1	8,291.1
Claims on Central Government........	22a	....	....	....	....	....	—	—	202.4	114.8	112.1	53.8	50.1
Claims on Nonfin.Pub.Enterprises...	22c	....	....	....	....	....	—	.4	.6	6.0	46.8	81.9	70.7
Claims on Private Sector.................	22d	....	....	....	....	....	4,692.0	5,203.3	5,382.3	5,616.1	5,807.9	6,178.7	6,392.0
Demand Deposits...................	24	....	....	....	....	....	2,203.8	2,179.7	2,291.7	2,570.7	2,685.5	2,955.3	2,974.8
Time, Savings,Fgn.Currency Dep......	25	....	....	....	....	....	3,216.5	6,105.1	4,939.1	4,803.2	5,024.7	6,057.2	5,580.4
Money Market Instruments..............	26aa	....	....	....	....	....	3.0	4.0	1.5	2.2	4.8	2.8	3.1
Foreign Liabilities.................	26c	....	....	....	....	....	118.4	121.0	346.7	312.8	185.0	147.8	497.8
Central Government Deposits...........	26d	....	....	....	....	....	1,505.9	1,103.9	1,901.2	1,621.0	2,313.9	3,279.8	4,559.9
Credit from Monetary Authorities.....	26g	....	....	....	....	....	622.5	585.7	552.3	610.7	709.3	836.4	857.8
Capital Accounts...................	27a	....	....	....	....	....	640.9	684.1	697.7	752.1	813.6	845.6	931.4
Other Items (Net)............................	27r	....	....	....	....	....	207.4	457.3	488.6	267.6	306.8	118.5	172.7
Banking Survey						*Millions of Brunei Dollars: End of Period*							
Foreign Assets (Net).......................	31n	....	....	....	....	....	3,980.2	6,194.2	5,477.3	5,148.6	6,115.5	7,906.0	8,622.2
Domestic Credit...........................	32	....	....	....	....	....	3,196.7	3,992.5	3,576.7	3,948.8	3,362.2	2,743.3	1,657.8
Claims on Central Govt. (Net)........	32an	....	....	....	....	....	−1,495.3	−1,211.2	−1,806.2	−1,673.3	−2,492.6	−3,517.3	−4,804.8
Claims on Nonfin.Pub.Enterprises...	32c	....	....	....	....	....	—	.4	.6	6.0	46.8	81.9	70.7
Claims on Private Sector.................	32d	....	....	....	....	....	4,692.0	5,203.3	5,382.3	5,616.1	5,807.9	6,178.7	6,392.0
Money...............................	34	....	....	....	....	....	2,789.9	2,764.1	2,863.9	3,145.2	3,239.2	3,530.8	3,575.6
Quasi-Money........................	35	....	....	....	....	....	3,216.5	6,105.1	4,939.1	4,803.2	5,024.7	6,057.2	5,580.4
Money Market Instruments..............	36aa	....	....	....	....	....	3.0	4.0	1.5	2.2	4.8	2.8	3.1
Capital Accounts...................	37a	....	....	....	....	....	921.1	872.8	798.1	848.7	938.6	957.3	1,076.4
Other Items (Net)....................	37r	....	....	....	....	....	246.4	440.8	451.3	298.1	270.4	101.1	44.6
Money plus Quasi-Money...............	35l	....	....	....	....	....	6,006.4	8,869.1	7,803.0	7,948.4	8,263.8	9,588.0	9,155.9
Money (National Definitions)						*Millions of Brunei Dollars: End of Period*							
M0....................	19mc	....	....	....	....	....	713.6	680.5	648.3	654.8	651.0	667.0	704.6
Money................................	59maa	....	....	....	....	....	2,917.4	2,860.2	2,940.0	3,225.5	2,685.5	2,955.3	2,974.8
Quasi Money.......................	59mab	....	....	....	....	....	3,876.7	6,516.7	5,274.6	4,796.5	5,194.5	6,104.8	5,580.4
Broad Money........................	59mba	....	....	....	....	....	6,794.2	9,377.0	8,214.7	8,021.9	7,880.0	9,060.0	8,555.2
Interest Rates						*Percent Per Annum*							
Deposit Rate........................	60l	....	....	....	....	....	....	....	....	....	1.065	1.044	1.006
Lending Rate................................	60p	....	....	....	....	6.500	5.500	5.500	5.500	5.500	5.500	5.500	† 5.500
Prices						*Index Numbers (2000=100): Period Averages*							
Consumer Prices........................	64	90.3	95.7	97.6	99.3	98.9	98.5	100.0	100.6	† 98.3	98.5	99.4	100.6
Intl. Transactions & Positions						*Millions of Brunei Dollars*							
Exports....................	70	3,290.5	3,388.3	3,682.7	3,970.5	3,194.3	4,325.1	6,733.5	6,521.8	6,628.7	7,704.3	8,562.7	....
Imports, c.i.f.............	71	2,760.5	2,959.6	3,513.8	3,157.6	2,335.8	2,250.7	1,907.8	2,045.8	2,786.6	2,311.8	2,412.5	....
National Accounts						*Millions of Brunei Dollars*							
Gross Domestic Product (GDP)........	99b	6,686.2	7,394.2	7,408.6	7,628.1	6,534.0	7,144.7	7,441.1	7,481.9	7,651.7	8,254.9	9,270.4	10,652.1
GDP Volume 1974 Prices.................	99b.p	3,795.1	3,910.6	3,951.5	4,093.8	3,930.6	4,031.4	4,145.3	4,271.6	4,392.3	4,559.7	4,638.4	....
GDP Deflator (2000=100)...............	99bip	98.1	105.3	104.4	103.8	92.6	98.7	100.0	97.6	97.0	100.9	111.3	....
						Millions: Midyear Estimates							
Population...............................	99z	.29	.29	.30	.31	.32	.33	.33	.34	.35	.36	.37	.37

Bulgaria 918

		1994	1995	1996	1997	1998	1999	2000	2001	2002	2003	2004	2005
Exchange Rates						*Leva per SDR: End of Period*							
Official Rate	aa	.0964	.1051	.7008	2.3969	2.3586	2.6721	2.7386	2.7891	2.5627	2.3012	2.2300	2.3696
						Leva per US Dollar: End of Period (ae) Period Average (rf)							
Official Rate	ae	.0660	.0707	.4874	1.7765	1.6751	1.9469	2.1019	2.2193	1.8850	1.5486	1.4359	1.6579
Official Rate	rf	.0541	.0672	.1779	1.6819	1.7604	1.8364	2.1233	2.1847	2.0770	1.7327	1.5751	1.5741
						Index Numbers (2000=100): Period Averages							
Nominal Effective Exchange Rate	nec	2,184.77	1,884.70	1,058.65	99.16	94.87	101.26	100.00	102.65	105.46	110.84	113.03	111.80
Real Effective Exchange Rate	rec	67.31	77.33	66.70	81.72	94.62	96.97	100.00	104.84	109.61	113.98	119.77	120.45
Fund Position						*Millions of SDRs: End of Period*							
Quota	2f.s	464.90	464.90	464.90	464.90	464.90	640.20	640.20	640.20	640.20	640.20	640.20	640.20
SDRs	1b.s	10.39	20.08	8.31	8.37	21.38	59.53	64.97	1.80	.55	45.54	8.45	.70
Reserve Position in the Fund	1c.s	32.63	32.63	32.63	32.63	32.63	32.69	32.74	32.78	32.78	32.78	32.85	33.00
Total Fund Cred.&Loans Outstg	2tl	644.41	482.12	407.25	698.02	792.27	910.74	1,014.62	883.00	771.75	799.16	761.95	461.83
International Liquidity					*Millions of US Dollars Unless Otherwise Indicated: End of Period*								
Total Reserves minus Gold	1l.d	1,001.80	1,236.45	483.57	2,111.52	2,684.71	2,892.12	3,154.93	3,290.77	4,407.06	6,291.01	8,776.25	8,040.54
SDRs	1b.d	15.16	29.84	11.95	11.29	30.10	81.70	84.65	2.26	.74	67.67	13.12	1.00
Reserve Position in the Fund	1c.d	47.63	48.50	46.92	44.03	45.95	44.87	42.66	41.19	44.56	48.71	51.02	47.17
Foreign Exchange	1d.d	939.00	1,158.10	424.70	2,056.20	2,608.65	2,765.54	3,027.63	3,247.32	4,361.76	6,174.64	8,712.10	7,992.37
Gold (Million Fine Troy Ounces)	1ad	1.031	1.031	1.031	1.288	1.293	1.284	1.284	1.285	1.282	1.282	1.281	1.280
Gold (National Valuation)	1and	309.37	309.37	309.37	† 362.57	371.67	329.65	305.33	289.56	339.98	413.76	445.90	† 654.22
Monetary Authorities:Other Liab	4..d	635.08	† 657.61	689.55	—	—	—	—	—	—	—	—	—
Deposit Money Banks: Assets	7a.d	1,659	† 1,063	973	1,360	1,469	1,492	1,942	2,102	2,018	1,939	3,126	3,272
Liabilities	7b.d	3,578	† 579	402	103	127	172	260	314	474	957	3,381	3,220
Monetary Authorities						*Millions of Leva: End of Period*							
Foreign Assets	11	124.6	† 154.0	618.0	4,666.1	5,243.1	6,353.5	7,379.7	7,888.2	8,795.0	10,192.8	13,079.2	14,270.4
Claims on Central Government	12a	54.2	† 100.7	410.9	1,632.1	1,665.9	2,203.2	2,560.9	2,314.6	1,926.4	1,838.9	1,693.5	1,094.4
Claims on Other Resident Sectors	12d	—	† .3	.5	.7	1.4	2.1	2.3	2.3	73.1	74.2	74.2	75.3
Claims on Banking Institutions	12e	54.8	† 40.7	238.8	213.9	143.5	125.9	73.1	36.1	24.2	6.8	6.8	5.0
Reserve Money	14	85.0	† 129.1	247.3	2,292.0	2,526.6	2,972.5	3,301.3	4,303.2	4,646.8	5,394.8	7,564.6	8,500.3
of which: Currency Outside Bls	14a	38.5	† 61.6	126.5	1,316.2	1,743.0	1,961.6	2,374.1	3,081.0	3,334.9	3,874.1	4,627.9	5,395.5
Other Liabs. to Banking Insts	14n	3.8	† 25.2	82.5	—	—	—	—	—	—	—	—	—
Other Deposits	15	—	† —	3.7	16.9	28.1	.4	973.6	712.2	855.7	1,384.7	870.4	833.1
Foreign Liabilities	16c	104.0	† 97.2	621.4	1,673.1	1,868.6	2,433.6	2,778.6	2,462.7	1,977.8	1,839.0	1,699.1	1,094.4
Central Government Deposits	16d	42.2	† 51.0	192.4	1,592.8	1,807.8	2,445.7	2,029.6	1,778.9	2,177.7	2,347.3	3,530.0	3,313.2
Capital Accounts	17a	91.3	† 102.2	307.3	961.7	916.3	1,019.5	1,190.6	1,229.8	1,371.3	1,455.7	1,487.9	1,985.5
Other Items (Net)	17r	−92.7	† −109.1	−186.5	−23.8	−93.6	−187.0	−257.6	−245.6	−210.5	−308.8	−298.2	−281.3
Banking Institutions						*Millions of Leva: End of Period*							
Reserves	20	43.5	† 67.6	118.6	800.2	643.8	745.3	598.1	864.4	1,071.2	1,388.2	2,428.4	2,954.4
Other Claims on Dep.Money Banks	20n	. . . .	25.2	82.5	—	—	—	—	—	—	—	—	—
Foreign Assets	21	109.5	† 75.2	474.2	2,416.7	2,459.9	2,904.5	4,081.9	4,665.3	3,803.1	3,002.7	4,488.9	5,423.9
Claims on Central Government	22a	283.6	† 226.1	615.1	2,168.4	1,526.3	1,202.7	1,068.0	1,338.0	1,945.5	2,024.0	2,211.6	2,679.0
Claims on Other General Govt	22b	2.8	† .1	—	—	17.0	30.3	30.6	39.6	12.5	27.0	28.3	60.3
Claims on Other Resident Sectors	22d	258.8	† 351.0	1,108.5	1,625.9	2,365.5	2,872.4	3,360.2	4,440.6	6,324.0	9,413.2	14,022.4	18,587.3
Demand Deposits	24	36.6	† 94.4	369.1	1,811.9	1,823.7	1,829.0	2,142.5	2,681.3	3,196.9	4,027.3	5,163.9	6,898.3
Other Deposits	25	342.9	† 432.1	818.0	2,676.7	2,912.6	3,497.1	4,085.9	5,670.0	6,395.9	7,351.2	9,620.2	12,600.1
Bonds	26n	. . . .	−.5	−3.7	—	—	—	—	8.5	36.9	103.7	187.9	398.0
Foreign Liabilities	26c	236.2	† 41.0	196.1	183.1	212.5	334.5	547.2	696.8	893.6	1,482.2	4,854.8	5,338.0
Central Government Deposits	26d	13.6	† 21.2	28.4	207.0	265.7	224.6	222.3	347.6	447.5	778.7	742.5	883.3
Credit from Central Bank	26g	28.7	† 34.5	106.1	58.0	7.5	.8	1.6	.3	.3	.3	.3	.3
Capital Accounts	27a	79.0	† 87.1	771.6	795.5	1,134.8	1,283.5	1,493.1	1,637.3	1,921.6	2,270.3	2,708.2	3,403.6
Other Items (Net)	27r	−38.8	† 35.4	113.4	1,279.1	655.8	585.8	646.3	306.0	263.5	−158.7	−98.3	183.4
Banking Survey						*Millions of Leva: End of Period*							
Foreign Assets (Net)	31n	−106.1	† 91.1	274.7	5,226.5	5,621.9	6,489.9	8,135.7	9,394.0	9,726.7	9,874.3	11,014.1	13,261.9
Domestic Credit	32	543.7	† 605.9	1,914.2	3,627.3	3,502.6	3,640.4	4,770.2	6,008.6	7,656.4	10,251.4	13,757.4	18,299.8
Claims on Central Govt. (Net)	32an	282.1	† 254.5	805.2	2,000.8	1,118.7	735.6	1,377.1	1,526.1	1,246.7	736.9	−367.5	−423.1
Claims on Other General Govt	32b	2.8	† .1	—	—	17.0	30.3	30.6	39.6	12.5	27.0	28.3	60.3
Claims on Other Resident Sectors	32d	258.8	† 351.3	1,109.1	1,626.5	2,366.8	2,874.5	3,362.5	4,442.9	6,397.2	9,487.4	14,096.6	18,662.6
Money	34	76.0	† 156.3	495.7	3,253.9	3,706.0	4,038.2	4,797.2	6,033.0	6,696.2	8,029.9	10,297.9	12,443.0
Quasi-Money	35	342.9	† 432.1	821.7	2,693.6	2,940.8	3,497.4	5,059.4	6,382.2	7,251.6	8,736.0	10,490.6	13,433.1
Bonds	36n	. . . .	† −.5	−3.7	—	—	—	—	8.5	36.9	103.7	187.9	398.0
Capital Accounts	37a	170.3	† 189.4	1,079.0	1,757.2	2,051.0	2,303.0	2,683.7	2,867.2	3,292.8	3,726.0	4,196.1	5,389.1
Other Items (Net)	37r	−151.6	† −80.3	−203.8	1,149.1	426.7	291.6	365.6	111.6	105.5	−470.0	−400.9	−101.4
Money plus Quasi-Money	35l	418.9	† 588.4	1,317.4	5,947.5	6,646.7	7,535.6	9,856.6	12,415.2	13,947.8	16,765.9	20,788.4	25,876.1
Money (National Definitions)						*Millions of Leva: End of Period*							
M3	59mc	. . . .	588.4	1,317.4	5,947.5	6,646.7	7,535.6	9,856.6	12,400.5	13,857.3	16,566.5	20,394.4	25,259.6
Interest Rates						*Percent Per Annum*							
Bank Rate (End of Period)	60	72.00	34.00	180.00	† 6.65	5.08	4.46	4.63	4.65	3.31	2.83	2.37	† 2.05
Money Market Rate	60b	66.43	53.09	119.88	66.43	2.48	2.93	3.02	3.74	2.47	1.95	1.95	2.03
Treasury Bill Yield	60c	57.72	48.27	114.31	78.35	6.02	5.43	4.21	4.57	4.29	2.81	2.64	. . . .
Deposit Rate	60l	51.14	35.94	74.68	46.83	3.00	3.21	3.10	2.88	2.77	2.89	3.01	3.04
Lending Rate	60p	72.58	58.98	123.48	83.96	13.30	12.79	11.52	11.11	9.35	8.82	8.77	7.87
Government Bond Yield	61	56.86	49.76	. . . .	. . . .	10.10	10.05	7.38	6.70	6.75	. . . .	. . . .	3.34
Prices, Production, Labor						*Index Numbers (2000=100): Period Averages*							
Producer Prices	63	1.8	† 2.8	6.6	70.7	82.8	85.1	100.0	103.7	105.0	110.2	116.8	124.8
Consumer Prices	64	1.8	2.9	6.4	74.5	88.4	90.6	100.0	107.4	113.6	116.0	123.4	129.6
Industrial Production	66	. . . .	. . . .	. . . .	. . . .	. . . .	. . . .	100.0	102.2	106.9	122.0	142.8	152.3
						Number in Thousands: Period Averages							
Labor Force	67d	2,521	2,265	2,721	2,679	2,527	2,489	2,323	2,563	2,520	3,283	3,322	3,316
Employment	67e	2,032	1,910	2,242	2,155	2,086	1,994	1,901	1,900	1,906	2,835	2,923	2,982
Unemployment	67c	488	424	479	524	465	611	567	663	592	449	405	334
Unemployment Rate (%)	67r	12.4	11.1	12.5	13.7	12.2	16.0	16.9	19.8	17.8	13.7	12.4	10.1

Bulgaria 918

		1994	1995	1996	1997	1998	1999	2000	2001	2002	2003	2004	2005
Intl. Transactions & Positions							*Millions of Leva*						
Exports...................................	70	216.2	359.7	859.8	8,281.4	7,391.1	7,302.6	10,247.1	11,176.1	11,857.9	13,041.9	15,617.1	18,514.6
Imports, c.i.f..........................	71	227.0	380.0	892.1	8,268.5	8,709.4	10,052.8	13,856.8	15,896.6	16,450.9	18,796.6	22,725.8	28,687.6
Balance of Payments							*Millions of US Dollars: Minus Sign Indicates Debit*						
Current Account, n.i.e..............	78ald	−31.8	−25.8	15.7	426.9	−61.9	−652.1	−703.7	−984.0	−826.7	−1,855.4	−1,417.3	−3,132.7
Goods: Exports f.o.b..............	78aad	3,935.1	5,345.0	4,890.2	4,939.6	4,193.5	4,006.4	4,824.6	5,112.9	5,692.1	7,540.6	9,847.6	11,739.7
Goods: Imports f.o.b..............	78abd	−3,951.9	−5,224.0	−4,702.6	−4,559.3	−4,574.2	−5,087.4	−6,000.2	−6,693.4	−7,286.6	−10,059.1	−13,490.9	−17,138.5
Trade Balance.....................	78acd	−16.8	121.0	187.6	380.3	−380.7	−1,081.0	−1,175.5	−1,580.5	−1,594.4	−2,518.5	−3,643.3	−5,398.7
Services: Credit....................	78add	1,256.9	1,431.4	1,366.0	1,337.4	1,787.8	1,788.4	2,175.2	2,123.4	2,364.9	3,166.3	4,004.3	4,256.2
Services: Debit.....................	78aed	−1,246.1	−1,277.9	−1,245.9	−1,171.0	−1,415.2	−1,474.1	−1,669.6	−1,721.3	−1,883.4	−2,572.6	−3,166.4	−3,446.1
Balance on Goods & Services.......	78afd	−6.0	274.5	307.7	546.7	−8.0	−766.7	−670.0	−1,178.4	−1,112.9	−1,924.8	−2,805.3	−4,588.7
Income: Credit.....................	78agd	84.6	149.7	181.0	210.8	306.3	265.4	320.8	352.0	319.7	327.8	1,489.5	1,467.3
Income: Debit......................	78ahd	−277.1	−581.9	−577.2	−567.4	−590.2	−450.5	−644.2	−656.0	−580.9	−954.0	−1,199.3	−1,155.6
Balance on Gds, Serv. & Inc.......	78aid	−198.5	−157.7	−88.5	190.1	−291.9	−951.9	−993.4	−1,482.3	−1,374.1	−2,551.0	−2,515.1	−4,277.0
Current Transfers, n.i.e.: Credit......	78ajd	357.1	256.8	231.8	275.5	261.5	328.7	354.1	598.5	653.6	865.5	1,294.7	1,361.4
Current Transfers: Debit.................	78akd	−190.4	−124.9	−127.6	−38.7	−31.5	−29.0	−64.3	−100.2	−106.2	−169.9	−196.8	−217.1
Capital Account, n.i.e..............	78bcd	763.3	—	65.9	—	—	−2.4	24.9	−.1	−.1	−.3	−.1	−1.3
Capital Account, n.i.e.: Credit.......	78bad	763.3	—	65.9	—	—	—	25.0	—	—	—	—	.1
Capital Account: Debit.............	78bbd	—	—	....	—	—	−2.4	−.1	−.1	−.1	−.3	−.1	−1.5
Financial Account, n.i.e............	78bjd	−1,018.7	326.6	−715.0	462.0	266.8	720.9	781.3	662.8	1,750.2	2,640.9	3,590.6	3,612.9
Direct Investment Abroad..........	78bdd	—	8.0	28.5	1.7	−.1	−17.1	−3.3	−9.7	−28.3	−26.5	217.1	−316.2
Dir. Invest. in Rep. Econ., n.i.e.......	78bed	105.4	90.4	109.0	504.8	537.3	818.8	1,001.5	812.9	904.7	2,096.7	2,560.0	2,614.1
Portfolio Investment Assets...........	78bfd	−222.0	9.7	−7.1	−13.7	−129.4	−207.4	−62.2	−40.3	218.3	−78.6	17.6	34.4
Equity Securities....................	78bkd	—	9.7	−7.1	−8.5	−10.6	—	−8.2	−33.5	−16.8	−15.7	−26.6	−3.5
Debt Securities.....................	78bld	−222.0	—	—	−5.2	−118.8	−207.4	−54.0	−6.8	235.1	−62.9	44.3	37.8
Portfolio Investment Liab., n.i.e......	78bgd	−9.8	−75.4	−122.2	146.5	−112.0	8.0	−114.7	105.1	−302.1	−132.9	−693.1	−969.1
Equity Securities....................	78bmd	—	—	2.0	52.0	19.3	1.9	4.9	−8.6	−22.9	−23.1	.3	92.1
Debt Securities.....................	78bnd	−9.8	−75.4	−124.2	94.5	−131.3	6.2	−119.6	113.7	−279.1	−109.8	−693.4	−1,061.2
Financial Derivatives Assets........	78bwd							—	—	—	—	—	—
Financial Derivatives Liabilities.......	78bxd	....	....	....	....	....	....	−1.8	17.5	6.7	−1.2	−5.7	−35.7
Other Investment Assets.............	78bhd	−209.2	404.2	−568.1	−53.9	222.3	−52.3	−332.1	−100.4	283.0	250.7	−922.6	214.5
Monetary Authorities..................	78bod							.9	−2.1	2.1	—	—	....
General Government................	78bpd	90.1	292.6	293.7	106.5	−19.8	−17.5	−9.1	−20.7	10.1	2.9	194.9	−21.0
Banks..............................	78bqd	−299.3	111.6	113.7	−440.6	102.9	25.7	−495.8	−129.8	263.1	263.0	−762.2	301.2
Other Sectors......................	78brd			−975.5	280.2	139.1	−60.5	171.9	52.2	7.6	−15.2	−355.3	−65.7
Other Investment Liab., n.i.e.........	78bid	−683.1	−110.3	−155.1	−123.4	−251.2	170.9	293.8	−122.3	667.9	532.7	2,417.3	2,071.0
Monetary Authorities..................	78bsd							—	—	—	—	—	—
General Government................	78btd	−951.0	−1.9	44.0	−82.1	−213.8	−104.9	−223.9	−310.0	−130.6	−100.0	−46.9	−76.1
Banks..............................	78bud	−39.2	−94.8	−179.7	−52.3	−65.2	10.1	108.4	102.9	256.3	365.5	1,143.1	1,123.6
Other Sectors......................	78bvd	307.1	−13.6	−19.4	11.0	27.8	265.8	409.3	84.8	542.2	267.2	1,321.1	1,023.5
Net Errors and Omissions.............	78cad	71.6	143.8	−105.3	256.4	−299.2	29.9	34.5	694.7	−208.3	−55.7	−443.1	235.5
Overall Balance....................	78cbd	−215.6	444.6	−738.7	1,145.3	−94.3	96.2	137.0	373.4	715.1	729.5	1,730.2	714.4
Reserves and Related Items.............	79dad	215.6	−444.6	738.7	−1,145.3	94.3	−96.2	−137.0	−373.4	−715.1	−729.5	−1,730.2	−714.4
Reserve Assets.....................	79dbd	−341.6	−233.7	750.9	−1,641.3	−461.4	−527.6	−408.9	−275.4	−586.2	−930.0	−1,829.4	−415.0
Use of Fund Credit and Loans.......	79dcd	262.4	−245.9	−108.7	396.9	129.4	161.9	136.0	−168.5	−142.3	36.4	−55.2	−436.2
Exceptional Financing..............	79ded	294.8	35.0	96.5	99.1	426.3	269.5	136.0	70.5	13.4	164.0	154.5	136.8
International Investment Position							*Millions of US Dollars*						
Assets.....................................	79aad	....	....	....	....	7,869.7	8,056.8	8,826.0	9,145.8	10,028.9	11,831.9	15,354.9	....
Direct Investment Abroad..............	79abd	....	....	....	....	74.5	10.9	87.0	96.7	125.0	47.1	−172.9	....
Portfolio Investment................	79acd	....	....	....	....	522.0	677.7	728.3	798.7	667.5	791.7	850.1	....
Equity Securities....................	79add	....	....	....	....	20.6	20.6	28.7	.4	.8	1.3	21.6	....
Debt Securities.....................	79aed	....	....	....	....	501.4	657.1	699.6	798.3	666.7	790.4	828.5	....
Financial Derivatives................	79ald	....	....	....	....	—	—	—	—	—	—	—	....
Other Investment..................	79afd	....	....	....	....	4,216.8	4,146.6	4,550.4	4,669.9	4,489.4	4,166.6	5,341.4	....
Monetary Authorities..................	79agd	....	....	....	....	3.0	.4	.4	.4	3.6	.5	16.0	....
General Government................	79ahd	....	....	....	....	2,348.2	2,389.9	2,416.7	2,446.7	2,461.1	2,135.9	1,963.3	....
Banks..............................	79aid	....	....	....	....	1,524.6	1,397.3	1,806.2	1,848.7	1,633.0	1,282.4	2,209.2	....
Other Sectors......................	79ajd	....	....	....	....	341.0	359.0	327.1	374.1	391.7	747.8	1,152.9	....
Reserve Assets.....................	79akd	....	....	....	....	3,056.4	3,221.6	3,460.3	3,580.5	4,747.0	6,826.5	9,336.3	....
Liabilities..................................	79lad	....	....	....	....	12,538.2	13,087.0	13,215.7	13,019.1	14,506.5	19,815.2	26,275.7	....
Dir. Invest. in Rep. Economy..........	79lbd	....	....	....	....	1,596.6	2,402.7	2,257.3	2,757.7	3,662.3	6,247.1	9,610.4	....
Portfolio Investment................	79lcd	....	....	....	....	5,173.1	5,195.4	5,193.6	5,073.2	4,667.0	4,554.3	3,929.1	....
Equity Securities....................	79ldd	....	....	....	....	113.4	97.9	99.9	95.3	76.4	25.8	26.0	....
Debt Securities.....................	79led	....	....	....	....	5,059.7	5,097.5	5,093.7	4,977.9	4,590.6	4,528.5	3,903.1	....
Financial Derivatives................	79lld	....	....	....	....	—	—	1.8	19.2	—	—	—	....
Other Investment..................	79lfd	....	....	....	....	5,768.5	5,488.9	5,763.0	5,169.0	6,177.2	9,013.8	12,736.2	....
Monetary Authorities..................	79lgd	....	....	....	....	1,116.3	1,250.8	1,322.9	1,110.0	1,049.3	1,187.5	1,183.3	....
General Government................	79lhd	....	....	....	....	3,170.9	2,525.3	2,336.1	2,111.1	2,195.1	3,842.2	4,043.1	....
Banks..............................	79lid	....	....	....	....	440.9	325.3	396.3	373.8	647.6	1,625.2	3,684.6	....
Other Sectors......................	79ljd	....	....	....	....	1,040.4	1,387.5	1,707.7	1,574.1	2,285.2	2,358.9	3,825.2	....

Bulgaria 918

		1994	1995	1996	1997	1998	1999	2000	2001	2002	2003	2004	2005
Government Finance		*Millions of Leva: Year Ending December 31*											
Deficit (-) or Surplus.........................	80	† −24.5	−46.2	−332.8	353.3	599.2	348.7	154.9	556.2	−9.8	255.4	1,329.0	2,741.5
Total Revenue and Grants..............	81y	† 209.3	315.5	703.3	5,662.1	7,530.6	8,219.9	9,340.1	10,268.4	10,637.4	12,057.2	14,385.0	16,472.2
Revenue..............................	81	† 209.3	314.6	699.1	5,558.0	7,380.3	8,015.0	9,124.7	9,874.4	10,229.5	11,760.6	14,355.5	15,900.2
Grants..................................	81z	† —	.9	4.2	104.1	150.3	204.9	215.4	394.0	407.9	296.7	29.5	571.9
Exp. & Lending Minus Repay..........	82z	† 233.8	361.7	1,036.1	5,308.8	6,931.4	7,871.1	9,185.2	9,712.2	10,647.2	11,801.8	13,056.0	13,730.7
Expenditure.................................	82	† 235.9	360.6	1,040.9	5,733.2	7,227.6	8,122.6	9,444.9	10,212.5	10,820.2	11,993.6	13,760.0	14,998.6
Lending Minus Repayments.........	83	† −2.1	1.1	−4.8	−424.4	−296.2	−251.5	−259.7	−500.3	−173.0	−191.8	−704.0	−1,268.0
Total Financing.............................	80h	† 24.5	46.2	332.8	−353.3	−599.3	−348.9	−154.9	−556.2	9.9	−255.4	−1,328.9	−2,741.1
Total Net Borrowing....................	84	† 53.0	58.7	295.5	1,261.0	−213.3	227.3	−434.0	−276.4	633.5	275.2	−302.1	−3,019.9
Net Domestic...........................	84a	† 44.6	65.5	331.3	1,204.3	−65.8	49.9	−3.9	−224.3	129.8	294.8	359.8	−584.8
Net Foreign..............................	85a	† 8.4	−6.8	−35.8	56.7	−147.5	177.4	−430.1	−52.1	503.7	−19.6	−661.9	−2,435.1
Use of Cash Balances...................	87	† −28.5	−12.5	37.3	−1,614.3	−386.0	−576.2	279.1	−279.8	−623.6	−530.6	−1,026.8	278.8
Total Debt by Residence..................	88	....	....	....	....	....	....	....	....	....	....	....	....
Domestic...............................	88a	† 275.1	345.4	1,052.8	....	....	....	....	....	....	....	....	....
Foreign....................................	89a	....	....	....	....	....	....	....	....	....	....	....	....
National Accounts		*Millions of Leva*											
Househ.Cons.Expend.,incl.NPISHs....	96f	389	622	1,313	12,724	15,144	16,964	18,506	20,642	22,238	23,759	26,098	29,375
Government Consumption Expend...	91f	90	134	210	2,188	3,440	3,937	4,786	5,177	5,832	6,555	7,125	7,789
Gross Fixed Capital Formation..........	93e	72	134	238	1,914	2,920	3,600	4,206	5,415	5,909	6,694	7,969	9,971
Changes in Inventories....................	93i	−23	4	−95	−191	865	662	688	726	497	816	1,006	1,774
Exports of Goods and Services........	90c	237	393	976	10,155	10,553	10,601	14,902	16,510	17,180	18,500	22,192	25,506
Imports of Goods and Services (-).....	98c	240	407	881	9,358	10,501	11,974	16,334	18,760	19,321	21,779	26,115	32,449
Gross Domestic Product (GDP)........	99b	526	880	1,761	17,433	22,421	23,790	26,753	29,709	32,335	34,547	38,275	41,948
Statistical Discrepancy....................	99bs	—	—	—	—	—	—	—	—	—	—	—	−18
Net Primary Income from Abroad.....	98.n	−11	−29	−69	−589	−510	−327	−671	−664	−489	−1,108	−1,038	−1,077
Gross National Income (GNI)..........	99a	515	852	1,692	16,844	21,911	23,464	26,082	29,045	31,777	33,439	37,238	40,871
Net Current Transf.from Abroad.......	98t	1	1	17	399	404	552	618	1,099	1,109	1,198	1,737	1,834
Gross Nat'l Disposable Inc.(GNDI)....	99i	516	853	1,709	17,242	22,315	24,016	26,701	30,144	32,944	34,637	38,975	42,705
Gross Saving..............................	99s	37	96	186	2,330	3,731	3,115	3,409	4,325	4,712	4,322	5,752	5,541
GDP Volume 1995 Prices..............	99b.p	856	880	798	753	783	801	845	879	922	963	1,018	1,074
GDP Volume (2000=100)...............	99bvp	101.3	104.2	94.4	89.2	92.7	94.9	100.0	104.1	109.2	114.0	120.5	127.2
GDP Deflator (2000=100)...............	99bip	1.9	3.2	7.0	73.1	90.4	93.7	100.0	106.7	110.7	113.3	118.7	123.2
		Millions: Midyear Estimates											
**Population...............................	99z	8.38	8.30	8.23	8.16	8.11	8.05	† 8.00	7.94	7.89	7.83	7.78	7.73

Burkina Faso 748

		1994	1995	1996	1997	1998	1999	2000	2001	2002	2003	2004	2005
Exchange Rates					*Francs per SDR: End of Period*								
Official Rate..................	aa	† 780.44	728.38	753.06	807.94	791.61	† 896.19	918.49	935.39	850.37	771.76	747.90	794.73
					Francs per US Dollar: End of Period (ae) Period Average (rf)								
Official Rate..................	ae	† 534.60	490.00	523.70	598.81	562.21	† 652.95	704.95	744.31	625.50	519.36	481.58	556.04
Official Rate..................	rf	† 555.20	499.15	511.55	583.67	589.95	† 615.70	711.98	733.04	696.99	581.20	528.28	527.47
Fund Position					*Millions of SDRs: End of Period*								
Quota................................	2f.s	44.2	44.2	44.2	44.2	44.2	60.2	60.2	60.2	60.2	60.2	60.2	60.2
SDRs.................................	1b.s	5.6	5.5	1.8	1.6	.5	.5	.3	.4	.3	.2	.1	.1
Reserve Position in the Fund............	1c.s	7.2	7.2	7.2	7.2	7.2	7.2	7.2	7.2	7.3	7.3	7.3	7.3
Total Fund Cred.&Loans Outstg........	2tl	32.8	50.5	56.5	68.5	79.6	87.9	86.1	92.7	93.0	83.9	73.8	72.4
International Liquidity				*Millions of US Dollars Unless Otherwise Indicated: End of Period*									
Total Reserves minus Gold..............	1l.d	237.2	347.4	338.6	344.8	373.3	295.0	243.6	260.5	313.4	752.2	669.1	438.4
SDRs.............................	1b.d	8.1	8.2	2.6	2.2	.8	.7	.4	.5	.4	.3	.2	.2
Reserve Position in the Fund..........	1c.d	10.5	10.7	10.4	9.7	10.2	9.9	9.4	9.1	9.9	10.8	11.3	10.5
Foreign Exchange......................	1d.d	218.6	328.4	325.6	332.9	362.4	284.4	233.8	250.9	303.1	741.1	657.6	427.7
Gold (Million Fine Troy Ounces)........	1ad	.011	—	—	—	—	—	—	—	—	—	—	—
Gold (National Valuation)........	1and	4.1	—	—	—	—	—	—	—	—	—	—	—
Monetary Authorities: Other Liab.....	4..d	14.9	4.1	5.8	29.0	43.9	29.3	37.8	22.6	20.1	41.9	41.3	28.2
Deposit Money Banks: Assets..........	7a.d	155.5	253.5	212.8	167.5	167.5	232.9	212.6	188.8	203.0	249.1	274.0	206.4
Liabilities...................	7b.d	39.7	58.7	44.0	54.5	67.0	129.1	105.3	119.5	111.2	176.4	186.2	198.5
Monetary Authorities					*Billions of Francs: End of Period*								
Foreign Assets.................................	11	126.8	170.2	177.3	206.5	209.9	192.6	171.7	193.9	196.0	390.7	322.2	243.8
Claims on Central Government........	12a	44.8	55.7	59.3	80.1	92.9	103.7	104.4	110.7	112.5	103.3	92.5	88.0
Claims on Deposit Money Banks......	12e	—	2.5	4.0	14.6	24.7	3.9	10.3	3.3	—	—	—	—
Claims on Other Financial Insts........	12f	.4	.3	.4	.7	1.1	1.1	1.1	1.1	1.1	1.0	1.2	1.1
Reserve Money............................	14	120.4	149.3	156.3	193.1	186.2	160.0	160.2	160.5	121.7	328.5	241.8	202.4
of which: Currency Outside DMBs..	14a	94.9	123.5	139.6	170.1	165.0	142.5	136.6	120.9	83.2	255.8	175.0	153.3
Foreign Liabilities........................	16c	33.6	38.8	45.6	72.7	87.7	97.9	105.7	103.6	91.7	86.5	75.1	73.3
Central Government Deposits..........	16d	19.5	37.4	37.3	29.5	48.4	45.0	22.9	41.4	79.9	65.3	83.3	50.9
Other Items (Net)........................	17r	−1.4	3.2	1.7	6.6	6.2	−1.6	−1.3	3.5	16.3	14.6	15.7	6.4
Deposit Money Banks					*Billions of Francs: End of Period*								
Reserves.......................................	20	20.9	17.7	9.1	15.7	14.4	19.8	18.1	35.4	30.1	61.8	65.8	46.2
Foreign Assets.................................	21	83.1	124.2	111.5	100.3	94.2	152.1	149.9	140.5	127.0	129.4	131.9	114.8
Claims on Central Government........	22a	35.3	27.3	26.1	28.1	32.7	26.1	21.4	15.0	20.6	31.3	36.0	18.1
Claims on Private Sector................	22d	72.3	79.0	89.9	163.2	180.9	186.5	217.6	247.9	293.6	338.6	380.3	472.7
Claims on Other Financial Insts........	22f	.3											
Demand Deposits......................	24	69.8	81.5	80.2	90.7	89.5	107.7	126.0	135.7	152.9	183.3	193.9	194.9
Time Deposits............................	25	62.6	71.0	70.7	83.7	94.3	108.5	117.5	131.7	152.6	184.6	205.5	203.8
Foreign Liabilities........................	26c	12.2	19.7	23.1	30.5	33.0	77.2	68.4	82.5	60.7	82.3	79.9	99.7
Long-Term Foreign Liabilities...........	26cl	9.0	9.1	—	2.1	4.7	7.1	5.8	6.4	8.8	9.3	9.8	10.6
Central Government Deposits..........	26d	59.0	61.3	54.6	57.5	58.0	60.5	60.1	57.1	74.0	78.9	86.4	90.6
Credit from Monetary Authorities.....	26g	—	2.5	—	14.6	25.2	4.4	10.3	3.3	—	—	—	—
Other Items (Net)........................	27r	−.7	3.1	7.9	28.3	17.6	19.2	18.8	22.1	22.2	22.8	38.5	52.0
Treasury Claims: Private Sector.......	22d.i	1.7	1.6	1.6	1.8	1.4	1.1	.4	.5	.9	1.3	.4	.3
Post Office: Checking Deposits.......	24..i	2.4	2.7	2.7	2.1	2.3	2.3	2.3	1.9	2.5	3.1	4.5	2.7
Monetary Survey					*Billions of Francs: End of Period*								
Foreign Assets (Net)......................	31n	164.2	236.0	220.1	203.5	183.4	169.6	147.5	148.4	170.5	351.3	299.1	185.5
Domestic Credit............................	32	77.0	66.3	86.5	187.3	203.5	214.2	263.7	278.0	276.4	333.1	344.8	441.2
Claims on Central Govt. (Net)........	32an	2.4	−14.6	−5.4	21.5	20.1	25.4	44.7	28.5	−19.2	−7.8	−37.2	−32.9
Claims on Private Sector................	32d	73.9	80.6	91.5	165.0	182.3	187.6	217.9	248.4	294.5	339.9	380.7	473.0
Claims on Other Financial Insts......	32f	.6	.3	.4	.7	1.1	1.1	1.1	1.1	1.1	1.0	1.2	1.1
Money......................................	34	170.3	213.7	228.7	268.9	261.9	256.9	270.4	262.3	243.7	452.0	378.2	351.8
Quasi-Money..............................	35	62.6	71.0	70.7	83.7	94.3	108.5	117.5	131.7	152.6	184.6	205.5	203.8
Long-Term Foreign Liabilities...........	36cl	9.0	9.1	—	2.1	4.7	7.1	5.8	6.4	8.8	9.3	9.8	10.6
Other Items (Net)..........................	37r	−.8	8.5	7.2	36.2	26.0	11.4	17.5	26.0	41.8	38.6	50.5	60.4
Money plus Quasi-Money...............	35l	232.9	284.7	299.4	352.5	356.2	365.3	387.9	394.0	396.3	636.5	583.7	555.6
Interest Rates					*Percent Per Annum*								
Bank Rate (End of Period)................	60	6.00	6.00	6.00	6.00	6.00	6.00	6.00	6.00	6.00	4.50	4.00	4.00
Money Market Rate........................	60b	4.95	4.95	4.95	4.95	4.95	4.95	4.95	4.95	4.95	4.95	4.95	4.95
Deposit Rate.................................	60l	3.50	3.50	3.50	3.50	3.50	3.50	3.50	3.50	3.50	3.50	3.50	3.50
Prices and Labor					*Index Numbers (2000=100): Period Averages*								
Consumer Prices...........................	64	82.7	88.9	94.3	† 96.5	101.4	100.3	100.0	105.0	107.3	109.5	109.0	116.0
					Number in Thousands: Period Averages								
Unemployment.............................	67c	27	14	13	9	9	8	7	....	....	....	....	....
Intl. Transactions & Positions					*Billions of Francs*								
Exports...	70	59.22	138.00	119.04	133.62	190.44	132.19	168.73	163.83	170.79	186.27	253.20	311.07
Imports, c.i.f.................................	71	193.70	227.00	330.96	342.35	430.33	350.77	468.19	373.30	381.70	398.30	497.91	678.21
					1995=100								
Unit Value of Exports.....................	74	84.8	100.0	97.8	....	....	....	....	....	....	....	....	....
Unit Value of Imports.....................	75	93.5	100.0	103.7	....	....	....	....	....	....	....	....	....

Burkina Faso 748

		1994	1995	1996	1997	1998	1999	2000	2001	2002	2003	2004	2005
Balance of Payments						*Millions of US Dollars: Minus Sign Indicates Debit*							
Current Account, n.i.e.	78ald	14.9	....	....	....	....	....	−392.0	−380.8	....	....	....	....
Goods: Exports f.o.b.	78aad	215.6	....	....	....	....	....	205.6	223.5	....	....	....	....
Goods: Imports f.o.b.	78abd	−344.3	....	....	....	....	....	−517.7	−509.3	....	....	....	....
Trade Balance	78acd	−128.7	....	....	....	....	....	−312.1	−285.8	....	....	....	....
Services: Credit	78add	56.3	....	....	....	....	....	31.4	36.5	....	....	....	....
Services: Debit	78aed	−138.3	....	....	....	....	....	−139.9	−141.2	....	....	....	....
Balance on Goods & Services	78afd	−210.7	....	....	....	....	....	−420.6	−390.5	....	....	....	....
Income: Credit	78agd	8.7	....	....	....	....	....	13.5	15.2	....	....	....	....
Income: Debit	78ahd	−38.1	....	....	....	....	....	−33.6	−39.7	....	....	....	....
Balance on Gds, Serv. & Inc.	78aid	−240.1	....	....	....	....	....	−440.7	−414.9	....	....	....	....
Current Transfers, n.i.e.: Credit	78ajd	308.0	....	....	....	....	....	87.6	72.0	....	....	....	....
Current Transfers: Debit	78akd	−53.0	....	....	....	....	....	−38.9	−37.9	....	....	....	....
Capital Account, n.i.e.	78bcd	—	....	....	....	....	....	175.9	165.2	....	....	....	....
Capital Account, n.i.e.: Credit	78bad	—	....	....	....	....	....	175.9	165.2	....	....	....	....
Capital Account: Debit	78bbd		....	....	....	....	....	—	—	....	....	....	....
Financial Account, n.i.e.	78bjd	−13.9	....	....	....	....	....	19.2	25.2	....	....	....	....
Direct Investment Abroad	78bdd	....	....	....	....	....	....	−.2	−.6	....	....	....	....
Dir. Invest. in Rep. Econ., n.i.e.	78bed	—	....	....	....	....	....	23.2	8.8	....	....	....	....
Portfolio Investment Assets	78bfd		....	....	....	....	....	6.2	10.0	....	....	....	....
Equity Securities	78bkd	....	....	....	....	....	....	.4	−2.1	....	....	....	....
Debt Securities	78bld		....	....	....	....	....	5.8	12.2	....	....	....	....
Portfolio Investment Liab., n.i.e.	78bgd	....	....	....	....	....	....	−2.6	.7	....	....	....	....
Equity Securities	78bmd	....	....	....	....	....	....	−2.6	.7	....	....	....	....
Debt Securities	78bnd	....	....	....	....	....	....	—	—	....	....	....	....
Financial Derivatives Assets	78bwd	....	....	....	....	....	....	—	—	....	....	....	....
Financial Derivatives Liabilities	78bxd	....	....	....	....	....	....	—	—	....	....	....	....
Other Investment Assets	78bhd	−139.2	....	....	....	....	....	−9.7	5.6	....	....	....	....
Monetary Authorities	78bod	....	....	....	....	....	....	....	....	....	....	....	....
General Government	78bpd	—	....	....	....	....	....	−2.1	−.5	....	....	....	....
Banks	78bqd	−135.2	....	....	....	....	....	−3.0	16.4	....	....	....	....
Other Sectors	78brd	−4.0	....	....	....	....	....	−4.6	−10.3	....	....	....	....
Other Investment Liab., n.i.e.	78bid	125.3	....	....	....	....	....	2.2	.6	....	....	....	....
Monetary Authorities	78bsd	—	....	....	....	....	....	5.7	.7	....	....	....	....
General Government	78btd	29.3	....	....	....	....	....	—	—	....	....	....	....
Banks	78bud	41.9	....	....	....	....	....	−13.7	−4.2	....	....	....	....
Other Sectors	78bvd	54.0	....	....	....	....	....	10.2	4.2	....	....	....	....
Net Errors and Omissions	78cad	−8.3	....	....	....	....	....	5.1	3.4	....	....	....	....
Overall Balance	78cbd	−7.3	....	....	....	....	....	−191.8	−187.0	....	....	....	....
Reserves and Related Items	79dad	7.3	....	....	....	....	....	191.8	187.0	....	....	....	....
Reserve Assets	79dbd	−17.4	....	....	....	....	....	30.6	−31.0	....	....	....	....
Use of Fund Credit and Loans	79dcd	25.5	....	....	....	....	....	−2.4	8.5	....	....	....	....
Exceptional Financing	79ded	−.7	....	....	....	....	....	163.6	209.6	....	....	....	....
International Investment Position								*Millions of US Dollars*					
Assets	79aad	....	....	....	....	....	....	457.2	428.8	....	....	....	....
Direct Investment Abroad	79abd	....	....	....	....	....	....	.4	.7	....	....	....	....
Portfolio Investment	79acd	....	....	....	....	....	....	84.0	51.8	....	....	....	....
Equity Securities	79add	....	....	....	....	....	....	1.3	3.1	....	....	....	....
Debt Securities	79aed	....	....	....	....	....	....	82.7	48.7	....	....	....	....
Financial Derivatives	79ald	....	....	....	....	....	....	—	—	....	....	....	....
Other Investment	79afd	....	....	....	....	....	....	130.1	115.8	....	....	....	....
Monetary Authorities	79agd	....	....	....	....	....	....	—	—	....	....	....	....
General Government	79ahd	....	....	....	....	....	....	3.7	7.2	....	....	....	....
Banks	79aid	....	....	....	....	....	....	125.0	102.2	....	....	....	....
Other Sectors	79ajd	....	....	....	....	....	....	1.3	6.3	....	....	....	....
Reserve Assets	79akd	....	....	....	....	....	....	242.6	260.5	....	....	....	....
Liabilities	79lad	....	....	....	....	....	....	1,815.3	1,513.9	....	....	....	....
Dir. Invest. in Rep. Economy	79lbd	....	....	....	....	....	....	27.8	15.9	....	....	....	....
Portfolio Investment	79lcd	....	....	....	....	....	....	4.3	2.9	....	....	....	....
Equity Securities	79ldd	....	....	....	....	....	....	1.5	1.6	....	....	....	....
Debt Securities	79led	....	....	....	....	....	....	2.8	1.3	....	....	....	....
Financial Derivatives	79lld	....	....	....	....	....	....	—	—	....	....	....	....
Other Investment	79lfd	....	....	....	....	....	....	1,783.2	1,495.1	....	....	....	....
Monetary Authorities	79lgd	....	....	....	....	....	....	149.5	119.3	....	....	....	....
General Government	79lhd	....	....	....	....	....	....	....	....	....	....	....	....
Banks	79lid	....	....	....	....	....	....	98.7	85.1	....	....	....	....
Other Sectors	79ljd	....	....	....	....	....	....	....	....	....	....	....	....
Government Finance						*Millions of Francs: Year Ending December 31*							
Deficit (-) or Surplus	80	−46,806	−37,971	−23,579	−50,500	−50,300	−63,800	−67,500	−61,796	−55,628	−88,796	−109,472	−123,152
Total Revenue and Grants	81y	189,669	225,178	223,280	279,200	303,100	377,600	363,000	313,231	335,183	434,302	462,158	496,719
Revenue	81	114,325	137,183	160,812	181,400	199,400	236,500	219,300	227,966	258,897	300,971	344,827	365,178
Grants	81z	75,344	87,995	62,468	97,800	103,700	141,100	143,700	85,265	76,286	133,331	117,331	131,541
Exp. & Lending Minus Repay	82z	225,115	244,859	229,859	323,200	347,900	432,100	431,500	387,948	422,519	508,231	576,983	631,942
Expenditure	82	227,449	247,053	231,552	325,700	348,500	431,800	428,400	389,841	422,606	484,727	582,370	645,111
Lending Minus Repayments	83	−2,334	−2,194	−1,693	−2,500	−600	300	3,100	−1,893	−87	23,504	−5,387	−13,169
Adjustment to Cash Basis	80x	−11,360	−18,290	−17,000	−6,500	−5,500	−9,300	1,000	12,921	31,708	−14,867	5,354	12,071
Total Financing	80h	46,806	37,971	23,579	50,500	50,300	63,800	67,500	61,796	55,628	88,796	109,472	123,152

Burkina Faso   748

		1994	1995	1996	1997	1998	1999	2000	2001	2002	2003	2004	2005
National Accounts						*Billions of Francs*							
Househ.Cons.Expend.,incl.NPISHs....	96f	726.6	887.4	1,041.0	1,074.0	1,300.9	1,301.6	1,306.4	1,482.4	1,616.7	1,784.9	1,953.8	2,105.0
Government Consumption Expend...	91f	281.1	306.9	330.9	347.6	378.1	428.4	438.5	467.1	498.5	519.3	546.4	604.6
Gross Fixed Capital Formation..........	93e	271.6	267.0	298.4	346.2	370.2	386.1	404.3	448.0	449.9	500.2	569.1	634.2
Changes in Inventories....................	93i	15.3	17.2	31.7	45.2	29.8	−9.8	−17.4	−41.5	−30.2	17.5	−77.3	8.4
Exports of Goods and Services.........	90c	149.4	168.0	139.8	154.5	211.9	176.7	168.7	190.1	202.1	218.3	289.9	311.1
Imports of Goods and Services (-).....	98c	263.4	316.0	365.4	380.1	465.5	448.6	468.2	476.1	485.6	536.6	581.5	678.2
Gross Domestic Product (GDP)........	99b	1,180.7	1,330.4	1,476.2	1,587.8	1,825.5	1,834.3	1,832.4	2,070.1	2,251.2	2,503.6	2,700.3	2,985.0
Net Primary Income from Abroad.....	98.n	92.5	115.8	111.7	102.4	118.7	93.9	90.3	93.3	100.2	136.2	133.3	114.1
Gross National Income (GNI)............	99a	1,273.2	1,446.2	1,587.9	1,690.2	1,944.2	1,928.2	1,922.6	2,163.3	2,351.4	2,639.8	2,833.6	3,099.1
GDP Volume 1985 Prices................	99b.p	968.6	1,031.4	1,133.2	1,210.6	1,313.2	1,362.4	1,384.0	1,477.9	1,545.1	1,669.0	1,745.6	1,869.3
GDP Volume (2000=100)...............	99bvp	70.0	74.5	81.9	87.5	94.9	98.4	100.0	106.8	111.6	120.6	126.1	135.1
GDP Deflator (2000=100)...............	99bip	92.1	97.4	98.4	99.1	105.0	101.7	100.0	105.8	110.0	113.3	116.8	120.6
						Millions: Midyear Estimates							
Population................................	99z	9.56	9.83	10.10	10.38	† 10.66	10.96	11.29	11.64	12.02	12.42	12.82	13.23

Burundi 618

		1994	1995	1996	1997	1998	1999	2000	2001	2002	2003	2004	2005
Exchange Rates							*Francs per SDR: End of Period*							
Official Rate	aa	360.78	413.37	462.63	551.56	710.64	860.83	1,014.76	1,090.92	1,451.07	1,618.31	1,717.35	1,425.93
					Francs per US Dollar: End of Period (ae) Period Average (rf)								
Official Rate	ae	246.94	277.92	322.35	408.38	505.16	628.58	778.20	864.20	1,071.23	1,093.00	1,109.51	997.78
Official Rate	rf	252.66	249.76	302.75	352.35	447.77	563.56	720.67	830.35	930.75	1,082.62	1,100.91	1,081.58
					Index Numbers (2000=100): Period Averages								
Official Rate	ahx	282.6	286.5	236.6	203.2	160.5	127.2	100.0	86.2	77.5	65.9	64.8	66.1
Nominal Effective Exchange Rate	nec	200.8	203.9	177.7	166.4	139.8	115.9	100.0	90.6	80.9	61.4	56.9	57.5
Real Effective Exchange Rate	rec	94.5	104.0	107.7	127.5	116.6	96.6	100.0	95.8	81.9	63.6	64.2	71.1
Fund Position							*Millions of SDRs: End of Period*							
Quota	2f.s	57.20	57.20	57.20	57.20	57.20	77.00	77.00	77.00	77.00	77.00	77.00	77.00
SDRs	1b.s	.14	.05	.08	.05	.07	.07	.03	.04	.12	.09	.23	.19
Reserve Position in the Fund	1c.s	5.86	5.86	5.86	5.86	5.86	5.86	5.86	.36	.36	.36	.36	.36
Total Fund Cred.&Loans Outstg	2tl	40.13	34.16	28.18	22.20	15.37	9.82	5.98	2.13	9.63	19.25	26.40	40.70
International Liquidity						*Millions of US Dollars Unless Otherwise Indicated: End of Period*								
Total Reserves minus Gold	1l.d	204.70	209.45	139.60	113.04	65.52	47.98	32.92	17.71	58.78	66.97	65.75	100.08
SDRs	1b.d	.21	.07	.11	.06	.09	.10	.04	.06	.16	.14	.35	.27
Reserve Position in the Fund	1c.d	8.56	8.71	8.43	7.91	8.25	8.04	7.64	.45	.49	.54	.56	.51
Foreign Exchange	1d.d	195.94	200.67	131.06	105.07	57.18	39.84	25.24	17.20	58.13	66.29	64.84	99.30
Gold (Million Fine Troy Ounces)	1ad	.017	.017	.017	.017	.017	.017	.017	.001	.001	.001	.001	.001
Gold (National Valuation)	1and	6.59	6.66	6.36	4.99	4.95	5.00	4.74	.27	.34	.40	.42	.49
Monetary Authorities: Other Liab	4..d	71.02	60.59	48.11	36.17	28.35	19.60	14.16	7.78	37.34	36.41	51.22	77.67
Deposit Money Banks: Assets	7a.d	19.00	17.00	24.00	12.00	5.00	13.00	18.00	14.00	18.00	39.33	49.59	59.17
Liabilities	7b.d	13.00	11.00	8.00	8.00	8.00	8.00	14.00	19.00	22.00	30.59	45.55	37.62
Other Banking Insts.: Assets	7e.d	—	—	—	—	—	—	—	—	—	—	—	—
Liabilities	7f.d	18.21	18.41	16.20	13.72	12.25	10.35	9.14	8.41	9.48	10.90	7.80	2.36
Monetary Authorities							*Millions of Francs: End of Period*							
Foreign Assets	11	54,230	61,439	48,407	49,620	37,711	33,642	33,702	20,573	64,415	75,336	77,622	114,195
Claims on Central Government	12a	8,698	10,504	12,443	20,702	27,498	41,685	59,106	69,082	75,991	103,781	129,673	154,371
Claims on Nonfin.Pub.Enterprises	12c	25	25	25	25	25	25	25	25	25	25	25	25
Claims on Private Sector	12d	420	1,486	1,563	1,181	1,220	703	827	1,191	1,414	1,578	1,817	2,231
Claims on Deposit Money Banks	12e	2,538	2,210	9,239	3,838	15,460	13,983	23,028	15,532	26,093	10,220	3,607	303
Claims on Other Financial Insts	12f	634	1,307	761	162	781	117	1,660	4,914	9,233	1,411	1,474	519
Reserve Money	14	22,292	22,114	26,346	26,854	27,566	37,387	36,398	40,431	49,820	55,246	75,771	100,516
of which: Currency Outside DMBs	14a	19,073	19,495	23,974	23,693	24,180	32,087	31,300	34,058	42,752	† 44,515	57,153	67,856
Nonfin.Pub.Ent. Deps	14e	649	577	371	749	860	710	1,044	347	449	1,158	1,218	1,348
Bonds	16ab	2,701	2,329	2,531	2,400	1,915	3,924	3,689	1,278	2,159	4,353	6,745	6,178
Restricted Deposits	16b	842	1,164	540	2,230	3,014	1,752	5,035	2,941	609	1,053	7,249	3,415
Stabilization Fund	16bb	4	74	16	20	—	4	47	51	19	15	22	180
Foreign Liabilities	16c	17,537	16,840	15,508	14,770	14,320	12,319	11,023	6,724	40,001	39,793	56,829	77,500
Central Government Deposits	16d	7,710	10,764	7,290	6,062	7,629	7,108	31,081	21,893	42,267	48,245	21,363	40,627
Capital Accounts	17a	12,744	15,926	17,531	20,418	20,262	22,482	24,206	22,068	24,087	25,568	28,714	31,788
Other Items (Net)	17r	2,714	7,762	2,675	2,773	7,987	5,179	6,870	15,932	18,210	18,079	17,526	11,440
Deposit Money Banks													
Commercial Banks							*Millions of Francs: End of Period*							
Reserves	20	2,171	1,290	1,716	2,852	2,839	4,754	3,625	6,289	† 6,720	† 9,308	17,712	30,923
Foreign Assets	21	4,773	4,760	7,907	4,898	2,650	8,427	14,352	12,334	† 16,878	† 42,990	55,018	59,039
Claims on Central Government	22a	5,311	6,799	8,824	10,524	10,879	9,888	220	4,361	† 6,387	† 3,107	11,024	26,476
Claims on Nonfin.Pub.Enterprises	22c	2,749	1,322	1,673	2,213	3,515	4,538	3,230	4,634	† 5,297	† 6,930	6,849	5,175
Claims on Private Sector	22d	34,022	29,162	35,886	39,516	52,948	69,385	101,356	110,418	† 143,552	† 158,978	161,388	159,742
Claims on Other Financial Insts	22f	142	284	1,748	106	106	105	265	273	† 1,350	† 96	91	86
Demand Deposits	24	19,095	18,730	18,038	22,235	22,180	34,296	34,860	44,244	† 55,838	† 72,107	91,079	104,871
Savings Deposits	25	14,951	10,681	16,373	17,038	15,955	26,144	30,976	35,126	† 48,691	† 53,090	52,364	65,208
Foreign Liabilities	26c	3,155	3,048	2,447	3,019	3,796	4,848	11,115	16,579	† 22,887	† 33,431	50,543	37,540
Central Government Deposits	26d	76	192	14	—	180	150	773	476	† 340	† 13,921	15,127	25,114
Credit from Monetary Authorities	26g	2,602	806	8,020	1,128	14,518	13,199	22,338	14,663	† 24,867	† 9,743	3,775	
Capital Accounts	27a	8,281	8,221	11,446	12,625	14,510	17,470	21,297	24,892	† 31,872	† 47,623	54,633	62,465
Other Items (Net)	27r	1,008	1,939	1,414	4,064	1,798	989	1,689	2,328	† −2,163	† −7,838	−15,439	−13,757
Other Monetary Institutions							*Millions of Francs: End of Period*							
Reserves	20..h	72	....	7	342	....	....	....	....	....	....	....	....
Claims on Central Government	22a.h	1,355	....	1,262	1,531	1,602	2,203	1,373	1,437	1,494	† 2,114	1,917	3,199
Claims on Nonfin.Pub.Enterprises	22c.h	1,071	....	† 1,896	1,312	....	....	....	....	....	....	....	....
Claims on Private Sector	22d.h	1,675	....	2,690	2,133	....	....	....	....	....	....	....	....
Claims on Other Financial Insts	22f.h	6	....	6	6	....	....	....	....	....	....	....	....
Demand Deposits	24..h	1,328	....	1,258	1,526	1,595	2,200	1,369	1,431	1,487	2,108	1,910	3,192
Time and Savings Deposits	25..h	2	....	2	2	2	2	2	2	2	2	2	2
Foreign Liabilities	26c.h	43	....	29	29	....	....	....	....	....	....	....	....
Central Government Deposits	26d.h	1,811	....	639	500	....	....	....	....	....	....	....	....
Cred.from Monetary Authorities	26g.h	303	....	1,195	1,172	....	....	....	....	....	....	....	....
Other Items (Net)	27r.h	115	....	−343	69	4	1	2	3	5	5	5	5
Monetary Survey							*Millions of Francs: End of Period*							
Foreign Assets (Net)	31n	38,267	46,311	38,330	36,699	22,244	24,902	25,916	9,604	† 18,405	† 45,102	25,268	58,194
Domestic Credit	32	48,316	39,933	61,466	73,341	90,764	121,389	136,209	173,966	† 202,135	† 215,853	277,768	286,083
Claims on Central Govt. (Net)	32an	7,578	6,347	15,225	26,695	32,169	46,517	28,846	52,510	† 41,265	† 46,835	106,124	118,305
Claims on Nonfin.Pub.Enterprises	32c	3,844	1,347	3,593	3,550	3,540	4,563	3,255	4,659	† 5,322	† 6,955	6,874	5,200
Claims on Private Sector	32d	36,117	30,648	40,138	42,830	54,168	70,087	102,183	111,609	† 144,965	† 160,556	163,204	161,974
Claims on Other Financial Insts	32f	776	1,591	2,510	267	887	222	1,925	5,188	† 10,583	† 1,507	1,565	605
Money	34	40,146	38,802	43,641	48,202	48,816	69,293	68,573	80,080	† 100,527	† 119,888	151,360	177,267
Quasi-Money	35	14,953	10,681	16,375	17,040	15,957	26,146	30,978	35,128	† 48,693	† 53,092	52,366	65,210
Other Items (Net)	37r	36,348	44,703	45,033	51,035	57,943	59,304	68,639	70,689	73,904	† 88,644	99,310	101,800
Money plus Quasi-Money	35l	55,098	49,482	60,017	65,242	64,773	95,439	99,551	115,209	† 149,220	† 172,980	203,726	242,477

Burundi 618

		1994	1995	1996	1997	1998	1999	2000	2001	2002	2003	2004	2005
Other Banking Institutions							*Millions of Francs: End of Period*						
Cash............................	40..f	132	123	191	† 478	102	291	† 799	178	† 145	† 255	126	1,922
Foreign Assets.....................	41..f	—	—	—	—	....	....	—	—	—	—	—	—
Claims on Central Government.......	42a.f	52	111	87	† 405	1,057	1,491	† 618	2,121	† 2,675	† 1,198	1,552	247
Claims on Private Sector..............	42d.f	12,577	13,319	14,304	† 15,376	16,637	18,068	† 21,256	25,902	† 29,972	† 20,466	18,544	16,672
Bonds.............................	46abf	3,347	2,324	3,224	† 2,829	2,561	2,980	† 3,981	5,198	† 4,873	† 1,521	234	757
Long-Term Foreign Liabilities..........	46clf	4,496	5,117	5,222	† 6,057	6,641	6,962	† 7,717	8,091	† 10,814	12,386	9,061	2,755
Central Govt. Lending Funds...........	46f.f	1,151	1,185	1,045	914	1,371	1,340	1,280	1,772	2,390	2,574	2,028	2,882
Credit from Monetary Authorities.....	46g.f	228	1,043	599	—	623	118	972	3,331	6,645	† 722	837	—
Credit from Depos. Money Banks.....	46h.f	—	4	375	—	1	—	† —	—	† —	† —	—	—
Capital Accounts.....................	47a.f	2,990	3,589	4,357	† 7,125	7,834	10,142	† 10,737	12,494	† 13,910	† 12,496	12,867	13,501
Other Items (Net).....................	47r.f	548	290	−242	† −667	−1,235	−1,692	† −2,015	−2,686	† −5,840	† −7,781	−4,804	−1,054
Banking Survey							*Millions of Francs: End of Period*						
Foreign Assets (Net)..................	51n	38,267	46,311	38,330	36,699	22,244	24,902	25,916	9,604	† 18,405	† 45,102	25,268	58,194
Domestic Credit......................	52	58,377	....	72,709	85,811	103,539	135,963	149,216	187,112	† 215,072	† 236,010	296,299	302,396
Claims on Central Govt. (Net).......	52an	5,840	....	14,674	26,625	32,526	47,248	† 29,464	54,631	† 43,940	† 48,033	107,676	118,551
Claims on Nonfin.Pub.Enterprises...	52c	3,844	1,347	3,593	3,550	3,540	4,563	3,255	4,659	† 5,322	† 6,955	6,874	5,200
Claims on Private Sector..............	52d	48,693	43,967	54,442	55,637	67,473	84,152	† 123,439	137,511	† 174,937	180,855	....	....
Liquid Liabilities.....................	55l	55,563	....	61,308	66,815	64,671	95,148	† 98,753	115,030	† 149,075	† 172,725	203,600	240,555
Other Items (Net).....................	57r	41,081	54,331	49,731	55,695	61,113	65,716	† 82,444	84,013	† 84,402	† 108,387	117,967	120,036
Interest Rates							*Percent Per Annum*						
Discount Rate (End of Period)..........	60	10.00	10.00	10.00	12.00	12.00	12.00	12.00	14.00	14.00	15.50	14.50	14.50	14.50
Lending Rate........................	60p	14.20	15.26	....	....	....	15.24	15.77	16.82	19.47	18.23	18.25	19.11
Prices							*Index Numbers (2000=100): Period Averages*						
Consumer Prices.....................	64	35.0	41.7	52.7	69.2	77.8	80.4	100.0	109.2	107.8	119.3	128.7	146.1
Intl. Transactions & Positions							*Millions of Francs*						
Exports................................	70	30,034	25,982	11,372	30,767	28,635	30,971	35,223	31,978	28,867	40,698	51,706	104,300
Imports, c.i.f.........................	71	56,511	58,186	37,332	43,250	70,274	66,308	106,059	115,249	121,050	169,742	194,054	286,959
Balance of Payments							*Millions of US Dollars: Minus Sign Indicates Debit*						
Current Account, n.i.e.....................	78ald	−16.9	10.4	−40.0	−.3	−51.4	−23.0	−53.2	−39.0	−10.2	−37.3	....	....
Goods: Exports f.o.b..................	78aad	80.7	112.9	40.4	87.5	64.0	55.0	49.1	39.2	31.0	37.5	....	....
Goods: Imports f.o.b..................	78abd	−172.6	−175.6	−100.0	−96.1	−123.5	−97.3	−107.9	−108.3	−104.8	−130.0	....	....
Trade Balance....................	78acd	−91.9	−62.7	−59.6	−8.6	−59.5	−42.3	−58.8	−69.1	−73.8	−92.5	....	....
Services: Credit.......................	78add	14.9	16.4	10.5	5.2	4.5	4.4	4.0	5.2	6.3	5.6	....	....
Services: Debit.......................	78aed	−93.9	−83.3	−38.4	−35.5	−41.6	−25.3	−42.8	−37.9	−43.2	−45.0	....	....
Balance on Goods & Services.......	78afd	−170.9	−129.6	−87.4	−38.8	−96.6	−63.2	−97.6	−101.8	−110.7	−131.9	....	....
Income: Credit......................	78agd	8.1	10.4	6.4	4.3	3.6	1.9	2.4	1.9	.9	1.3	....	....
Income: Debit........................	78ahd	−19.5	−22.9	−20.4	−16.8	−11.9	−11.3	−14.5	−15.8	−12.6	−18.6	....	....
Balance on Gds, Serv. & Inc.......	78aid	−182.3	−142.1	−101.4	−51.4	−104.9	−72.6	−109.7	−115.7	−122.4	−149.3	....	....
Current Transfers, n.i.e.: Credit......	78ajd	167.0	154.7	62.5	55.6	56.8	51.4	58.3	79.6	115.5	115.5	....	....
Current Transfers: Debit.................	78akd	−1.6	−2.1	−1.1	−4.5	−3.3	−1.8	−1.8	−2.9	−3.3	−3.5	....	....
Capital Account, n.i.e.....................	78bcd	−.2	−.8	−.3	−.1	—	—	—	—	−.5	−.9	....	....
Capital Account, n.i.e.: Credit........	78bad	—	—	—	—	—	—	—	—	—	—	....	....
Capital Account: Debit..................	78bbd	−.2	−.8	−.3	−.1	—	—	—	—	−.5	−.9	....	....
Financial Account, n.i.e.....................	78bjd	31.1	21.1	14.1	−12.3	−7.8	−6.5	−7.5	−4.0	−40.5	−50.0	....	....
Direct Investment Abroad..............	78bdd	−.1	−.6	—	—	—	.5	—	—	—	—	....	....
Dir. Invest. in Rep. Econ., n.i.e.......	78bed	—	2.0	—	—	—	.2	11.7	—	—	—	....	....
Portfolio Investment Assets...........	78bfd	—	—	—	—	—	—	—	—	—	....	....	....
Equity Securities.................	78bkd	—	—	—	—	—	—	—	—	—	....	....	....
Debt Securities..................	78bld	—	—	—	—	—	—	—	—	—	....	....	....
Portfolio Investment Liab., n.i.e.....	78bgd	—	—	—	—	—	—	—	—	—	....	....	....
Equity Securities.................	78bmd	—	—	—	—	—	—	—	—	—	....	....	....
Debt Securities..................	78bnd	—	—	—	—	—	—	—	—	—	....	....	....
Financial Derivatives Assets...........	78bwd	....	....	....	—	—	—	—	—	—	....	....	....
Financial Derivatives Liabilities.......	78bxd	....	....	....	—	—	—	—	—	—	....	....	....
Other Investment Assets..............	78bhd	−1.6	8.2	6.6	15.3	10.7	14.2	6.8	24.0	−4.3	−19.9	....	....
Monetary Authorities.................	78bod	....	....	—	—	—	—	—	—	—	—	....	....
General Government.................	78bpd	−.8	−.4	−.3	−.4	−.3	−.3	—	—	—	—	....	....
Banks..............................	78bqd	−8.8	.1	−10.4	8.5	5.0	−10.3	−8.2	2.4	−7.7	−22.2	....	....
Other Sectors......................	78brd	7.9	8.6	17.3	7.1	6.0	24.7	15.0	21.6	3.4	2.3	....	....
Other Investment Liab., n.i.e.........	78bid	32.9	11.5	7.6	−27.6	−18.5	−20.4	−25.9	−28.0	−36.2	−30.1	....	....
Monetary Authorities.................	78bsd	—	—	—	—	—	—	—	—	—	—	....	....
General Government.................	78btd	25.2	4.9	7.3	−34.0	−21.4	−23.4	−35.8	−34.6	−42.9	−41.0	....	....
Banks..............................	78bud	4.7	−.4	−2.0	1.6	1.7	1.9	8.7	6.6	6.8	10.0	....	....
Other Sectors......................	78bvd	3.0	7.0	2.2	4.8	1.1	1.1	1.2	.1	−.1	.9	....	....
Net Errors and Omissions................	78cad	21.1	5.9	−9.2	−27.8	−18.8	−19.0	−34.2	−31.2	3.9	−12.6	....	....
Overall Balance.....................	78cbd	35.2	36.7	−35.3	−40.5	−78.1	−48.6	−94.8	−74.3	−47.2	−100.9	....	....
Reserves and Related Items.............	79dad	−35.2	−36.7	35.3	40.5	78.1	48.6	94.8	74.3	47.2	100.9	....	....
Reserve Assets.....................	79dbd	−29.0	−27.6	44.0	−2.0	28.7	8.8	1.2	16.1	−46.9	−9.6	....	....
Use of Fund Credit and Loans........	79dcd	−6.1	−9.0	−8.7	−8.3	−9.3	−7.6	−5.0	−4.8	9.9	13.6	....	....
Exceptional Financing..................	79ded	....	....	....	50.8	58.6	47.4	98.7	63.0	84.3	97.0	....	....

Burundi 618

|---|---|---|---|---|---|---|---|---|---|---|---|---|---|
International Investment Position							*Millions of US Dollars*							
Assets	79aad	....	....	....	....	....	88.4	75.6	....	....	....	....	....
Direct Investment Abroad	79abd	....	....	....	—	—	–.4	—	—	—	—	....	....
Portfolio Investment	79acd	....	....	....	—	—	—	—	—	—	—	....	....
Equity Securities	79add	....	....	....	—	—	—	—	—	—	—	....	....
Debt Securities	79aed	....	....	....	—	—	—	—	—	—	—	....	....
Financial Derivatives	79ald	....	....	....	—	—	—	—	....	....	....	....	....
Other Investment	79afd	....	....	....	17.8	10.3	35.3	32.3	35.0	21.0	42.0	....	....
Monetary Authorities	79agd	....	....	....	....	—	—	—	—	—	—	....	....
General Government	79ahd	....	....	....	....	–.3	–.3	—	—	–.1	–.1	....	....
Banks	79aid	....	....	....	12.0	5.2	13.4	18.4	14.3	18.2	39.8	....	....
Other Sectors	79ajd	....	....	....	6.2	5.3	22.2	13.9	20.7	2.9	2.3	....	....
Reserve Assets	79akd	....	....	....	121.5	74.7	53.5	43.3	23.8	65.5	73.8	....	....
Liabilities	79lad	....	....	....	....	....	22.5	63.9	....	....	....	....	....
Dir. Invest. in Rep. Economy	79lbd	....	....	....	—	—	.2	10.8	—	—	—	....	....
Portfolio Investment	79lcd	....	....	....	—	—	—	—	—	—	—	....	....
Equity Securities	79ldd	....	....	....	—	—	—	—	—	—	—	....	....
Debt Securities	79led	....	....	....	—	—	—	—	—	—	—	....	....
Financial Derivatives	79lld	....	....	....	—	—	—	—	....	....	....	....	....
Other Investment	79lfd	....	....	....	34.6	43.6	22.3	53.0	8.0	43.3	77.0	....	....
Monetary Authorities	79lgd	....	....	....	....	21.6	13.4	7.8	2.7	13.0	28.5	....	....
General Government	79lhd	....	....	....	....	13.5	.2	29.8	–14.0	8.8	16.7	....	....
Banks	79lid	....	....	....	7.4	7.5	7.7	14.3	19.2	21.4	30.8	....	....
Other Sectors	79ljd	....	....	....	1.0	1.0	1.0	1.2	.1	.1	1.0	....	....
Government Finance							*Millions of Francs: Year Ending December 31*							
Deficit (-) or Surplus	80	–13,305.2	–6,638.4	–21,154.4	–10,390.4	–19,390.0	–26,831.3	–20,322.5	–38.2	–6,317.2	–32,871.2	–54,314.6	–53,330.3
Total Revenue and Grants	81y	68,493.8	58,743.4	47,086.9	59,150.3	85,639.4	99,076.1	114,215.4	161,346.9	185,911.5	200,319.3	218,892.5	304,883.2
Revenue	81	40,335.6	44,074.2	37,754.0	48,879.8	75,165.1	87,721.5	98,340.6	118,188.3	122,896.1	135,035.8	147,093.7	191,637.2
Grants	81z	28,158.2	14,669.2	9,332.9	10,270.5	10,474.3	11,354.6	15,874.8	43,158.6	63,015.4	65,283.5	71,798.8	113,246.0
Exp. & Lending Minus Repay	82z	81,799.0	65,381.8	68,241.3	69,540.7	105,029.4	125,907.4	134,537.9	161,385.1	192,228.7	233,190.5	273,207.1	358,213.5
Expenditure	82	81,898.7	65,152.6	67,556.6	70,716.6	106,295.2	126,713.5	138,304.1	166,072.2	193,740.2	235,124.6	274,423.8	360,254.8
Lending Minus Repayments	83	–99.7	229.2	684.7	–1,175.9	–1,265.8	–806.1	–3,766.2	–4,687.1	–1,511.5	–1,934.1	–1,216.7	–2,041.3
Total Financing	80h	13,305.2	6,638.4	21,154.4	18,271.9	19,390.0	26,831.1	20,322.4	38.2	6,317.2	32,871.2	54,314.6	53,330.3
Domestic	84a	4,675.6	–38.6	5,057.6	7,851.6	3,459.7	20,194.7	–30,359.2	3,254.6	–21,545.6	12,002.9	34,352.5	44,652.8
Foreign	85a	8,629.6	6,677.0	16,096.8	10,420.3	15,930.3	6,636.4	50,681.6	–3,216.4	27,862.8	20,868.3	19,962.1	8,677.5
Total Debt by Residence	88	278,631	323,864	380,437	465,172	605,411	740,305	912,989	968,564	1,269,334	1,487,783	1,620,827	1,433,443
Domestic	88a	13,502	17,695	27,357	39,989	49,659	64,528	68,072	80,294	95,081	117,255	163,072	195,224
Foreign	89a	265,129	306,169	353,080	424,239	555,752	675,777	852,509	888,270	1,174,253	1,370,528	1,457,755	1,238,219
National Accounts							*Millions of Francs*							
Househ.Cons.Expend.,incl.NPISHs.	96f	256,656	228,920	216,869	283,525	359,511	395,805	465,738	487,057	518,950	561,832	638,547	759,900
Government Consumption Expend.	91f	32,459	33,600	39,911	50,299	58,630	63,547	75,577	106,079	108,750	136,151	163,470	204,900
Gross Fixed Capital Formation	93e	23,446	23,419	32,712	21,975	24,000	34,314	38,564	40,073	55,787	69,131	84,139	133,800
Changes in Inventories	93i	53	–199	–400	2,700	3,200	—	—	—	3,000	—	176	—
Exports of Goods and Services	90c	24,029	32,298	15,426	33,760	32,018	34,507	39,761	38,236	35,967	48,686	60,201	76,100
Imports of Goods and Services (-)	98c	66,592	68,173	41,443	49,473	77,193	72,730	108,601	121,464	137,849	171,120	198,047	312,600
Gross Domestic Product (GDP)	99b	270,051	249,865	263,075	342,786	400,166	455,443	511,039	549,981	584,605	644,680	748,486	862,100
Net Primary Income from Abroad	98.n	–2,876	–3,152	–4,003	–4,416	–3,699	–5,315	–8,698	–11,545	–10,906	–18,778	–34,286	–35,200
Gross National Income (GNI)	99a	267,175	246,713	259,072	338,370	396,467	450,128	502,341	538,436	573,699	625,902	714,200	826,900
GDP Volume 1980 Prices	99b.p	123,698	115,013	105,113	105,512	110,249	109,147	108,164	110,436	115,405	114,020	119,037	120,108
GDP Volume (2000=100)	99bvp	114.4	106.3	97.2	97.5	101.9	100.9	100.0	102.1	106.7	105.4	110.1	111.0
GDP Deflator (2000=100)	99bip	46.2	46.0	53.0	68.8	76.8	88.3	100.0	105.4	107.2	119.7	133.1	151.9
							Millions: Midyear Estimates							
Population	99z	6.09	6.16	6.21	6.26	6.31	6.38	6.49	6.63	6.82	7.04	7.28	7.55

Cambodia 522

		1994	1995	1996	1997	1998	1999	2000	2001	2002	2003	2004	2005
Exchange Rates						*Riels per SDR: End of Period*							
Official Rate	aa	3,759.1	3,754.9	3,901.2	4,657.6	5,308.3	5,174.4	5,087.9	4,895.0	5,342.9	5,920.1	6,254.0	5,877.2
						Riels per US Dollar: End of Period (ae) Period Average (rf)							
Official Rate	ae	2,575.0	2,526.0	2,713.0	3,452.0	3,770.0	3,770.0	3,905.0	3,895.0	3,930.0	3,984.0	4,027.0	4,112.0
Official Rate	rf	2,545.3	2,450.8	2,624.1	2,946.3	3,744.4	3,807.8	3,840.8	3,916.3	3,912.1	3,973.3	4,016.3	4,092.5
Fund Position						*Millions of SDRs: End of Period*							
Quota	2f.s	65.00	65.00	65.00	65.00	65.00	87.50	87.50	87.50	87.50	87.50	87.50	87.50
SDRs	1b.s	10.89	10.21	9.51	8.77	6.95	3.78	.14	.41	.40	.14	.05	.17
Reserve Position in the Fund	1c.s	—	—	—	—	—	—	—	—	—	—	—	—
Total Fund Cred.&Loans Outstg	2tl	20.25	48.25	48.25	48.25	47.21	53.12	56.24	63.51	70.78	69.70	62.70	56.83
International Liquidity						*Millions of US Dollars Unless Otherwise Indicated: End of Period*							
Total Reserves minus Gold	1l.d	118.50	191.98	265.78	298.63	324.38	393.19	501.68	586.81	776.15	815.53	943.21	952.98
SDRs	1b.d	15.90	15.18	13.68	11.83	9.78	5.19	.18	.51	.55	.20	.08	.24
Reserve Position in the Fund	1c.d	—	—	—	—	—	—	—	—	—	—	—	—
Foreign Exchange	1d.d	102.60	176.80	252.10	286.80	314.60	388.00	501.50	586.30	775.60	815.33	943.13	952.74
Gold (Million Fine Troy Ounces)	1ad	—	—	—	—	.3998	.3998	.3998	.3998	.3998	.3998	.3998	.3998
Gold (National Valuation)	1and	—	—	—	—	114.85	116.27	109.21	110.75	137.54	166.40	175.00	205.60
Deposit Money Banks: Assets	7a.d	126.75	161.57	186.57	162.08	139.55	154.43	167.33	216.74	173.28	209.50	242.14	334.24
Liabilities	7b.d	63.93	65.78	59.55	58.03	59.51	56.88	44.23	50.27	41.61	79.88	72.72	80.98
Monetary Authorities						*Billions of Riels: End of Period*							
Foreign Assets	11	305.09	484.88	720.91	1,033.02	1,675.22	1,923.51	2,388.61	2,740.07	3,598.33	3,906.16	† 4,506.44	4,767.72
Claims on Central Government	12a	215.02	217.11	213.58	211.28	288.55	283.04	271.83	271.14	269.05	269.39	† 269.78	270.41
Claims on Private Sector	12d	2.70	—	—	—	—	—	—	—	—	—	† 2.54	2.40
Claims on Deposit Money Banks	12e	34.20	10.09	9.48	6.19	8.10	4.94	15.81	53.19	13.19	17.09	† 16.67	10.52
Reserve Money	14	285.91	314.53	449.83	545.33	802.61	929.87	1,161.01	1,359.61	1,980.66	2,149.95	† 2,664.50	2,637.15
of which: Currency Outside DMBs	14a	176.30	250.92	299.84	356.06	509.06	489.86	494.60	577.78	765.98	906.39	† 1,114.75	1,282.14
Restricted Deposits	16b	26.17	24.55	70.93	42.94	68.67	75.52	84.40	98.21	94.13	107.48	† 100.57	111.76
Foreign Liabilities	16c	76.12	181.17	188.23	224.73	250.59	274.88	286.14	310.89	378.19	412.63	† 392.12	333.99
Central Government Deposits	16d	70.12	62.36	81.86	153.49	106.11	176.26	268.08	346.16	429.09	488.04	† 525.61	677.15
Capital Accounts	17a	127.42	115.87	200.71	391.54	839.59	870.19	1,000.17	1,035.12	1,134.32	1,228.70	† 1,269.21	1,508.27
Other Items (Net)	17r	−28.74	13.60	−47.61	−107.53	−95.70	−115.22	−123.55	−85.58	−135.81	−194.17	† −156.59	−217.27
Deposit Money Banks						*Billions of Riels: End of Period*							
Reserves	20	88.75	88.15	178.43	199.15	346.00	503.74	737.13	866.85	1,270.85	1,329.73	† 1,569.14	1,420.05
Foreign Assets	21	326.39	408.14	506.15	559.51	526.10	582.19	653.43	844.19	680.99	834.64	† 975.09	1,374.40
Claims on Central Government	22a	.01	.31	.31	.31	.31	.31	.31	.01	40.91	90.81	† 90.20	56.10
Claims on Nonfin.Pub.Enterprises	22c	6.00	5.11	5.22	5.93	5.86	10.14	2.65	6.55	2.03	.01	† —	—
Claims on Private Sector	22d	234.39	293.40	434.55	636.79	654.60	763.23	898.46	936.11	1,058.91	1,336.62	† 1,813.97	2,201.88
Demand Deposits	24	20.94	27.29	29.09	28.70	34.21	42.09	45.04	31.94	47.30	29.47	† 33.12	34.45
Time and Savings Deposits	25a	17.80	5.07	7.85	13.21	19.77	31.71	45.89	55.50	74.31	81.87	† 97.33	112.71
Foreign Currency Deposits	25b	232.57	365.55	574.84	664.90	667.03	878.84	1,244.97	1,538.65	2,000.83	2,301.09	† 3,079.09	3,589.42
Restricted Deposits	26b	3.22	4.04	11.45	4.23	3.97	4.04	1.87	1.48	1.41	1.43	† 1.06	11.21
Foreign Liabilities	26c	164.61	166.15	161.56	200.32	224.37	214.45	172.73	195.82	163.54	318.26	† 292.84	333.01
Central Government Deposits	26d	1.75	7.14	4.38	4.26	4.20	4.15	.71	.01	—	.07	† 43.06	70.52
Credit from Monetary Authorities	26g	2.96	4.81	3.51	6.55	5.87	7.52	6.04	8.11	8.74	67.39	† —	—
Capital Accounts	27a	356.49	356.11	454.98	602.77	689.78	767.43	791.25	923.56	808.64	839.90	† 922.70	1,132.08
Other Items (Net)	27r	−144.79	−141.05	−123.00	−123.26	−116.42	−90.62	−16.53	−101.37	−51.09	−47.68	† −20.81	−230.97
Monetary Survey						*Billions of Riels: End of Period*							
Foreign Assets (Net)	31n	390.75	545.70	877.28	1,167.48	1,726.36	2,016.37	2,583.18	3,077.55	3,737.59	4,009.90	† 4,796.56	5,475.12
Domestic Credit	32	386.25	446.43	567.41	696.55	839.01	876.31	904.45	867.64	941.81	1,208.72	† 1,607.81	1,783.12
Claims on Central Govt. (Net)	32an	143.16	147.92	127.64	53.84	178.55	102.95	3.34	−75.02	−119.13	−127.92	† −208.69	−421.16
Claims on Nonfin.Pub.Enterprises	32c	6.00	5.11	5.22	5.93	5.86	10.14	2.65	6.55	2.03	.01	† —	—
Claims on Private Sector	32d	237.09	293.40	434.55	636.79	654.60	763.23	898.46	936.11	1,058.91	1,336.62	† 1,816.50	2,204.29
Money	34	201.68	278.49	328.93	384.76	543.27	531.95	539.64	609.72	813.28	935.86	† 1,152.88	1,322.79
Quasi-Money	35	250.37	370.62	582.69	678.11	686.80	910.55	1,290.87	1,594.15	2,075.14	2,382.96	† 3,176.42	3,702.13
Capital Accounts	37a	483.91	471.98	655.70	994.31	1,529.37	1,637.62	1,791.41	1,958.69	1,942.95	2,068.60	† 2,191.91	2,640.35
Other Items (Net)	37r	−158.95	−128.96	−122.63	−193.15	−194.15	−187.44	−134.30	−217.37	−151.98	−168.80	† −116.83	−407.02
Money plus Quasi-Money	35l	452.05	649.11	911.62	1,062.87	1,230.07	1,442.50	1,830.51	2,203.87	2,888.43	3,318.82	† 4,329.30	5,024.91
Interest Rates						*Percent Per Annum*							
Deposit Rate	60l	....	8.7	8.8	8.0	7.8	7.3	6.8	4.4	2.5	2.0	1.8	1.9
Lending Rate	60p	....	18.7	18.8	18.4	18.3	17.6	17.3	16.5	16.2	18.5	17.6	17.3
Prices and Labor						*Index Numbers (2000=100): Period Averages*							
Consumer Prices	64	73.6	74.3	81.8	84.4	96.9	100.8	100.0	† 99.4	102.6	103.8	107.9	114.0
						Number in Thousands: Period Averages							
Labor Force	67d	....	....	4,680	4,904	5,038	5,830	5,409	5,225	....	....	....	....
Intl. Transactions & Positions						*Millions of US Dollars*							
Exports	70..d	....	....	....	626	933	1,040	1,123	1,296	1,489	1,771	2,188	1,369
Imports, c.i.f	71..d	....	....	....	1,116	1,129	1,243	1,424	1,456	1,675	1,732	2,075	1,268

Cambodia 522

		1994	1995	1996	1997	1998	1999	2000	2001	2002	2003	2004	2005
Balance of Payments		\multicolumn{12}{c}{*Millions of US Dollars: Minus Sign Indicates Debit*}											
Current Account, n.i.e................	78ald	−156.6	−185.7	−184.9	−209.9	−175.3	−189.2	−137.6	−89.6	−109.0	−236.2	−185.1	−355.8
Goods: Exports f.o.b..................	78aad	489.9	855.2	643.6	736.0	802.0	1,130.3	1,397.1	1,571.2	1,769.8	2,086.8	2,588.9	2,910.3
Goods: Imports f.o.b..................	78abd	−744.4	−1,186.8	−1,071.8	−1,064.0	−1,165.8	−1,591.9	−1,935.7	−2,094.0	−2,360.5	−2,668.1	−3,269.5	−3,927.8
Trade Balance...................	78acd	−254.5	−331.6	−428.2	−328.0	−363.8	−461.5	−538.6	−522.8	−590.7	−581.3	−680.6	−1,017.6
Services: Credit....................	78add	54.5	114.0	162.8	160.4	177.3	293.9	428.5	524.6	604.2	545.3	801.3	1,106.5
Services: Debit....................	78aed	−139.6	−187.9	−214.8	−188.0	−222.1	−293.3	−329.2	−349.0	−377.2	−433.9	−513.0	−630.8
Balance on Goods & Services......	78afd	−339.6	−405.5	−480.2	−355.6	−408.6	−461.0	−439.3	−347.2	−363.8	−470.0	−392.3	−541.8
Income: Credit....................	78agd	2.1	9.7	12.6	16.0	47.9	51.4	67.1	57.5	50.6	43.7	48.6	67.7
Income: Debit....................	78ahd	−49.1	−66.9	−98.3	−58.5	−108.0	−150.0	−190.2	−195.4	−234.4	−223.0	−269.6	−321.8
Balance on Gds, Serv. & Inc......	78aid	−386.6	−462.7	−565.9	−398.1	−468.7	−559.5	−562.4	−485.1	−547.6	−649.3	−613.3	−795.9
Current Transfers, n.i.e.: Credit......	78ajd	230.0	277.9	383.4	188.5	299.0	377.9	432.0	403.8	447.9	425.3	443.7	460.8
Current Transfers: Debit..............	78akd	—	−.9	−2.4	−.3	−5.6	−7.6	−7.3	−8.3	−9.3	−12.1	−15.5	−20.7
Capital Account, n.i.e................	78bcd	73.2	78.0	75.8	65.2	−4.8	10.9	35.6	44.8	8.1	66.2	68.1	94.9
Capital Account, n.i.e.: Credit......	78bad	73.2	78.0	75.8	65.2	89.5	78.6	79.8	102.8	71.5	119.5	141.3	150.4
Capital Account: Debit...............	78bbd				—	−94.3	−67.7	−44.2	−58.0	−63.4	−53.3	−73.2	−55.5
Financial Account, n.i.e.............	78bjd	54.0	122.4	259.1	219.8	227.3	191.5	178.2	138.0	247.4	233.4	283.0	294.3
Direct Investment Abroad.............	78bdd	....	....	....	....	−19.8	−9.1	−6.6	−7.3	−6.0	−9.7	−10.3	−6.3
Dir. Invest. in Rep. Econ., n.i.e......	78bed	68.9	150.8	293.6	203.7	242.8	232.2	148.5	149.4	145.1	84.0	131.4	379.2
Portfolio Investment Assets...........	78bfd	....	....	....	....	−13.5	−7.8	−7.2	−7.7	−7.5	−7.7	−8.0	−7.2
Equity Securities..................	78bkd	....	....	....	....								
Debt Securities....................	78bld	....	....	....	....	−13.5	−7.8	−7.2	−7.7	−7.5	−7.7	−8.0	−7.2
Portfolio Investment Liab., n.i.e......	78bgd	....	....	....	....	....	....	....	....	....	....	....	....
Equity Securities..................	78bmd	....	....	....	....	....	....	....	....	....	....	....	....
Debt Securities....................	78bnd	....	....	....	....	....	....	....	....	....	....	....	....
Financial Derivatives Assets...........	78bwd	....	....	....	....	....	....	....	....	....	....	....	....
Financial Derivatives Liabilities.......	78bxd	....	....	....	....	....	....	....	....	....	....	....	....
Other Investment Assets............	78bhd	−46.8	−103.4	−118.0	−23.6	−72.8	−61.9	−176.3	−118.7	−129.9	−133.3	−24.5	−331.4
Monetary Authorities...............	78bod	....	....	....	....	....	....	....	....	....	....	....	....
General Government................	78bpd	....	....	....	....	....	....	....	....	....	....	....	....
Banks............................	78bqd	—	−39.8	−23.6	23.6	20.6	−16.8	−11.1	−45.4	39.8	−78.5	−34.2	−94.7
Other Sectors......................	78brd	−46.8	−63.6	−94.4	−47.2	−93.4	−45.1	−165.1	−73.4	−169.7	−54.9	9.7	−236.8
Other Investment Liab., n.i.e........	78bid	31.9	75.0	83.5	39.7	90.6	38.0	219.7	122.4	245.8	300.1	194.3	260.0
Monetary Authorities...............	78bsd	—	—	—	—	—	—	−5.5	−10.7	−10.9	—	—	—
General Government................	78btd	51.4	73.1	89.7	41.2	42.7	43.2	74.6	78.1	124.3	148.6	154.4	144.0
Banks............................	78bud	−19.5	1.9	−6.2	−1.5	1.5	−2.6	−6.7	.1	−8.6	34.3	−3.2	8.3
Other Sectors......................	78bvd					46.5	−2.5	157.3	54.9	141.0	117.2	43.0	107.8
Net Errors and Omissions..............	78cad	65.6	11.5	−78.0	−41.2	−23.0	37.1	21.4	−19.6	24.8	−27.7	−35.1	−22.0
Overall Balance.....................	78cbd	36.2	26.2	72.0	33.9	24.3	50.3	97.5	73.7	171.3	35.7	130.8	11.4
Reserves and Related Items............	79dad	−36.2	−26.2	−72.0	−33.9	−24.3	−50.3	−97.5	−73.7	−171.3	−35.7	−130.8	−11.4
Reserve Assets.....................	79dbd	−71.2	−73.2	−68.9	−34.3	−29.3	−65.1	−108.7	−90.2	−187.8	−41.2	−127.8	−9.8
Use of Fund Credit and Loans.......	79dcd	19.8	42.3	—	—	−1.4	8.3	4.0	9.3	9.3	−1.7	−10.3	−8.8
Exceptional Financing..................	79ded	15.2	4.7	−3.1	.4	6.5	6.5	7.2	7.2	7.2	7.2	7.2	7.2
International Investment Position		\multicolumn{12}{c}{*Millions of US Dollars*}											
Assets............................	79aad	....	....	....	....	1,805.8	1,991.5	2,337.1	2,612.8	3,018.5	3,301.1	3,498.4	3,842.4
Direct Investment Abroad.............	79abd	....	....	....	....	159.0	177.0	193.2	211.0	228.5	241.5	255.6	267.0
Portfolio Investment..................	79acd	....	....	....	....	164.8	181.7	198.8	217.4	236.8	253.8	270.3	286.4
Equity Securities..................	79add	....	....	....	....	148.3	163.5	178.9	195.7	213.1	228.5	243.3	257.8
Debt Securities....................	79aed	....	....	....	....	16.5	18.2	19.9	21.7	23.7	25.4	27.0	28.6
Financial Derivatives.................	79ald	....	....	....	....								
Other Investment....................	79afd	....	182.3	206.9	223.2	1,035.2	1,123.4	1,334.4	1,481.8	1,639.0	1,824.3	1,854.5	2,130.6
Monetary Authorities................	79agd	....	—	—	—								
General Government................	79ahd	....											
Banks............................	79aid	....	163.3	186.9	163.2	2.4	1.4	1.4	1.8	—	.4	2.5	.3
Other Sectors......................	79ajd	....	19.0	20.0	60.0	1,032.8	1,122.0	1,333.0	1,480.0	1,639.0	1,823.8	1,852.0	2,130.3
Reserve Assets.....................	79akd	....	192.1	504.1	575.2	446.9	509.5	610.7	702.6	914.2	981.5	1,118.0	1,158.3
Liabilities..........................	79lad	....	1,108.0	1,351.2	1,210.5	2,294.1	2,582.9	2,948.6	3,273.8	3,673.6	4,035.7	4,351.4	5,088.8
Dir. Invest. in Rep. Economy........	79lbd	....	498.1	677.6	580.4	1,199.1	1,431.3	1,579.8	1,729.2	1,874.3	1,958.3	2,089.7	2,490.8
Portfolio Investment..................	79lcd	....	—	—	—	—	—	—	—	—	—	—	—
Equity Securities..................	79ldd	....	—	—	—	—	—	—	—	—	—	—	—
Debt Securities....................	79led	....	—	—	—	—	—	—	—	—	—	—	—
Financial Derivatives.................	79lld	....	—	—	—	—	—	—	—	—	—	—	—
Other Investment....................	79lfd	....	609.9	673.6	630.1	1,095.0	1,151.5	1,368.7	1,544.6	1,799.2	2,077.4	2,261.6	2,598.0
Monetary Authorities................	79lgd	....	71.7	69.4	65.1	66.5	72.9	73.3	79.8	96.2	103.6	97.4	81.2
General Government................	79lhd	....	472.5	544.7	506.9	627.2	682.4	769.8	863.1	994.0	1,143.3	1,281.8	1,432.9
Banks............................	79lid	....	65.7	59.6	58.1	59.6	56.9	50.2	50.3	41.7	75.9	72.8	82.4
Other sectors......................	79ljd	....	—	—	—	341.8	339.3	475.5	551.4	667.4	754.6	809.7	1,001.4
Government Finance		\multicolumn{12}{c}{*Billions of Riels: Year Ending December 31*}											
Deficit (-) or Surplus..................	80	....	....	....	....	....	....	....	−439.86	−577.04	....	....	....
Revenue............................	81	....	....	....	....	....	....	....	1,521.19	1,729.37	....	....	....
Grants..............................	81z	....	....	....	....	....	....	....	500.73	452.97	....	....	....
Expenditure.........................	82	....	....	....	....	....	....	....	2,461.77	2,759.38	....	....	....
Financing													
Domestic............................	84a	....	....	....	....	....	....	....	51.22	−30.89	....	....	....
Foreign.............................	85a	....	....	....	....	....	....	....	388.64	607.94	....	....	....

Cambodia 522

		1994	1995	1996	1997	1998	1999	2000	2001	2002	2003	2004	2005
National Accounts							*Billions of Riels*						
Househ.Cons.Expend.,incl.NPISHs....	96f	6,571	7,812	8,749	8,932	10,887	11,732	12,211	12,949	13,715	14,880	17,513	20,872
Government Consumption Expend...	91f	493	493	529	553	563	661	737	828	913	975	961	1,048
Gross Fixed Capital Formation.........	93e	760	1,174	1,166	1,361	1,452	2,137	2,579	2,481	3,146	3,336	3,729	4,454
Changes in Inventories....................	93i	74	38	169	141	−80	196	−202	406	154	585	−25	535
Exports of Goods and Services.........	90c	1,833	2,630	2,334	3,411	3,661	5,423	7,020	8,214	9,300	10,481	13,636	16,504
Imports of Goods and Services (-).....	98c	2,748	3,929	4,030	4,598	5,202	7,174	8,698	9,568	10,718	12,337	15,201	18,736
Statistical Discrepancy.....................	99bs	−70	35	4	97	117	148	147	−31	−106	−100	30	66
Gross Domestic Product (GDP).........	99b	7,092	8,438	9,191	10,129	11,719	13,408	14,089	15,579	16,768	18,250	21,141	25,350
GDP Volume 2000 Prices.................	99b.p	9,277	9,883	10,411	10,999	11,545	12,994	14,089	15,169	16,108	17,493	19,234	21,812
GDP Volume (2000=100)...............	99bvp	65.8	70.1	73.9	78.1	81.9	92.2	100.0	107.7	114.3	124.2	136.5	154.8
GDP Deflator (2000=100)...............	99bip	76.4	85.4	88.3	92.1	101.5	103.2	100.0	102.7	104.1	104.3	109.9	116.2
						Millions: Midyear Estimates							
Population.................................	99z	11.06	11.37	11.66	11.94	† 12.21	12.48	12.74	13.01	13.27	13.53	13.80	14.07

Cameroon 622

		1994	1995	1996	1997	1998	1999	2000	2001	2002	2003	2004	2005
Exchange Rates						*Francs per SDR: End of Period*							
Official Rate	aa	† 780.44	728.38	753.06	807.94	791.61	† 896.19	918.49	935.39	850.37	771.76	747.90	794.73
						Francs per US Dollar: End of Period (ae) Period Average (rf)							
Official Rate	ae	† 534.60	490.00	523.70	598.81	562.21	† 652.95	704.95	744.31	625.50	519.36	481.58	556.04
Official Rate	rf	† 555.20	499.15	511.55	583.67	589.95	† 615.70	711.98	733.04	696.99	581.20	528.28	527.47
						Index Numbers (2000=100): Period Averages							
Official Rate	ahx	128.1	142.3	138.8	121.8	120.5	115.5	100.0	96.9	102.2	122.4	134.6	134.8
Nominal Effective Exchange Rate	nec	99.6	108.4	109.5	105.5	107.1	105.2	100.0	101.1	103.7	108.6	110.8	110.1
Real Effective Exchange Rate	rec	96.9	107.1	108.7	107.5	111.2	109.7	100.0	103.4	107.1	110.4	110.6	109.8
Fund Position						*Millions of SDRs: End of Period*							
Quota	2f.s	135.10	135.10	135.10	135.10	135.10	185.70	185.70	185.70	185.70	185.70	185.70	185.70
SDRs	1b.s	.03	.03	.11	—	.01	1.90	5.93	.01	.87	.99	.43	1.49
Reserve Position in the Fund	1c.s	.34	.36	.37	.41	.45	.50	.52	.54	.58	.64	.65	.70
Total Fund Cred.&Loans Outstg.	2tl	29.91	34.41	50.11	68.91	110.94	142.65	180.50	193.96	225.80	233.60	214.69	190.32
International Liquidity						*Millions of US Dollars Unless Otherwise Indicated: End of Period*							
Total Reserves minus Gold	1l.d	† 2.26	3.79	2.77	.86	1.29	4.43	212.00	331.83	629.66	639.64	829.31	949.38
SDRs	1b.d	.05	.04	.16	—	.02	2.61	7.73	.02	1.18	1.47	.67	2.13
Reserve Position in the Fund	1c.d	.49	.53	.53	.55	.63	.69	.67	.68	.79	.96	1.01	1.00
Foreign Exchange	1d.d	† 1.72	3.22	2.08	.31	.64	1.13	203.60	331.14	627.70	637.21	827.63	946.25
Gold (Million Fine Troy Ounces)	1ad	.030	.030	.030	.030	.030	.030	.030	.030	.030	.030	.030	.030
Gold (National Valuation)	1and	† 11.33	11.56	11.04	8.72	8.61	† 8.69	8.17	8.33	10.27	12.52	13.14	15.37
Monetary Authorities: Other Liab.	4..d	650.63	713.03	537.11	300.24	238.09	188.63	62.45	57.36	63.77	72.18	75.20	68.66
Deposit Money Banks: Assets	7a.d	135.55	131.07	90.23	105.23	122.82	163.34	163.10	153.17	248.67	317.31	391.47	418.48
Liabilities	7b.d	50.01	81.98	71.50	62.51	85.92	84.52	70.75	67.43	96.10	114.56	151.84	205.97
Monetary Authorities						*Billions of Francs: End of Period*							
Foreign Assets	11	7.37	7.53	7.25	5.70	5.57	8.57	155.21	253.18	400.27	338.70	405.71	536.44
Claims on Central Government	12a	340.51	338.23	340.59	338.61	358.64	403.25	434.19	499.81	518.28	490.23	442.91	333.12
Claims on Deposit Money Banks	12e	27.07	21.41	4.93	4.07	13.51	2.17	1.12	.15	—	—	—	—
Claims on Other Banking Insts.	12f	—	—	—	—	—	—	—	—	—	—	—	—
Reserve Money	14	180.77	142.77	183.17	256.74	282.83	305.91	410.67	502.29	641.32	568.66	662.67	651.14
of which: Currency Outside DMBs.	14a	136.33	102.29	95.32	180.28	205.76	237.40	264.96	296.14	333.74	298.02	324.04	273.48
Foreign Liabilities	16c	371.17	374.45	319.02	235.47	221.67	251.01	209.81	224.12	231.90	217.78	196.78	189.43
Central Government Deposits	16d	44.83	63.03	59.71	49.52	63.96	57.54	171.12	213.39	208.32	193.84	134.79	154.82
Capital Accounts	17a	22.17	20.38	21.00	22.19	21.45	25.24	26.74	27.89	26.06	23.87	23.21	24.05
Other Items (Net)	17r	−243.99	−233.45	−230.12	−215.54	−212.19	−224.75	−227.82	−214.54	−189.05	−175.21	−168.83	−149.88
Deposit Money Banks						*Billions of Francs: End of Period*							
Reserves	20	42.57	37.49	82.48	70.57	68.60	62.66	141.59	201.24	301.04	260.33	324.85	368.27
Foreign Assets	21	72.46	64.22	47.25	63.01	69.05	106.65	114.98	114.01	155.54	164.80	188.52	232.69
Claims on Central Government	22a	185.76	187.67	159.72	171.59	173.66	173.85	168.57	165.04	156.99	139.34	139.28	139.99
Claims on Nonfin.Pub.Enterprises	22c	39.45	42.06	36.26	39.76	53.95	54.35	89.19	82.95	84.92	97.12	80.69	77.71
Claims on Private Sector	22d	369.54	371.39	385.89	348.14	428.82	481.46	543.95	605.78	676.26	740.15	754.99	832.30
Claims on Other Banking Insts.	22f	.03	.19	.05	.06	.19	.08	—	.04	.01	—	.03	.04
Claims on Nonbank Financial Insts.	22g	4.43	8.83	9.16	11.95	14.57	5.41	4.56	7.20	10.87	8.11	11.43	4.18
Demand Deposits	24	223.09	213.97	213.45	237.72	271.06	294.49	361.99	410.94	473.35	462.88	492.14	550.03
Time and Savings Deposits	25	329.79	329.30	268.89	267.45	259.81	306.43	374.62	445.75	528.07	588.18	616.76	684.68
Bonds	26ab	3.85	3.85	.90	5.30	.90	.90	—	—	—	.28	.25	3.50
Foreign Liabilities	26c	17.44	36.08	34.84	34.74	43.80	47.21	39.18	47.73	58.15	47.36	63.07	101.69
Long-Term Foreign Liabilities	26cl	9.30	4.09	2.60	2.69	4.50	7.98	10.70	2.46	1.96	12.14	10.05	12.83
Central Government Deposits	26d	97.04	94.00	109.15	55.43	85.19	101.56	117.74	113.66	159.38	122.65	137.66	131.24
Credit from Monetary Authorities	26g	27.07	21.41	4.93	4.07	13.51	2.17	1.12	.15	—	—	—	—
Capital Accounts	27a	84.39	62.25	102.79	112.58	129.23	150.84	154.45	175.85	195.08	206.98	219.15	238.27
Other Items (Net)	27r	−77.72	−53.09	−16.75	−14.91	.84	−27.10	3.03	−20.28	−30.35	−30.62	−39.29	−67.08
Monetary Survey						*Billions of Francs: End of Period*							
Foreign Assets (Net)	31n	−318.07	−342.86	−301.96	−204.18	−195.36	−190.98	10.49	92.89	263.80	226.23	324.33	465.17
Domestic Credit	32	797.85	791.34	762.82	806.10	881.16	959.54	952.03	1,033.83	1,079.63	1,158.46	1,157.05	1,101.51
Claims on Central Govt. (Net)	32an	384.40	368.88	331.46	405.25	383.15	418.00	313.90	337.80	307.57	313.08	309.74	187.06
Claims on Nonfin.Pub.Enterprises	32c	39.45	42.06	36.26	39.76	53.95	54.35	89.19	82.95	84.92	97.12	80.69	77.71
Claims on Private Sector	32d	369.54	371.39	385.89	348.14	428.82	481.46	543.95	605.78	676.26	740.15	754.99	832.30
Claims on Other Banking Insts.	32f	.03	.19	.05	.06	.19	.08	—	.04	.01	—	.03	.04
Claims on Nonbank Financial Inst.	32g	4.43	8.83	9.16	12.89	15.06	5.64	4.99	7.26	10.87	8.11	11.60	4.41
Money	34	361.29	319.24	314.14	423.90	485.29	537.73	631.06	711.98	813.63	771.21	829.96	832.90
Quasi-Money	35	329.79	329.30	268.89	267.45	259.81	306.43	374.62	445.75	528.07	588.18	616.76	684.68
Bonds	36ab	3.85	3.85	.90	5.30	.90	.90	—	—	—	.28	.25	3.50
Other Items (Net)	37r	−215.15	−203.91	−123.08	−94.74	−60.19	−75.54	−43.16	−31.02	1.74	25.03	34.41	45.59
Money plus Quasi-Money	35l	691.08	648.55	583.03	691.35	745.09	844.17	1,005.69	1,157.74	1,341.70	1,359.38	1,446.72	1,517.58
Interest Rates						*Percent Per Annum*							
Discount Rate (End of Period)	60	† 7.75	8.60	7.75	7.50	7.00	7.30	7.00	6.50	6.30	6.00	6.00	5.50
Deposit Rate	60l	8.08	5.50	5.38	5.04	5.00	5.00	5.00	5.00	5.00	5.00	5.00	4.92
Lending Rate	60p	17.50	16.00	22.00	22.00	22.00	22.00	22.00	20.67	18.00	18.00	18.00	17.67
Prices and Production						*Index Numbers (2000=100): Period Averages*							
Consumer Prices	64	† 79.1	86.3	89.7	94.0	97.0	98.8	100.0	104.4	107.4	108.0	108.3	110.5
Industrial Production	66	....	....	83.9	92.2	97.1	106.8	100.0	100.6	102.6	106.5	112.1	....
Intl. Transactions & Positions						*Billions of Francs*							
Exports	70	825.20	811.02	821.61	982.81	985.80	985.70	1,305.10	1,282.10	1,256.00	1,305.40	1,309.10	1,313.70
Imports, c.i.f.	71	601.50	464.73	572.62	708.17	882.00	811.50	1,060.10	1,357.60	1,300.60	1,174.60	1,271.60	1,292.30

Cameroon 622

		1994	1995	1996	1997	1998	1999	2000	2001	2002	2003	2004	2005
Balance of Payments						*Millions of US Dollars: Minus Sign Indicates Debit*							
Current Account, n.i.e.	78ald	−56.1	89.9	....	....	....	....	....	....	....	....	....	....
Goods: Exports f.o.b.	78aad	1,454.2	1,735.9	....	....	....	....	....	....	....	....	....	....
Goods: Imports f.o.b.	78abd	−1,052.3	−1,109.0	....	....	....	....	....	....	....	....	....	....
Trade Balance	78acd	401.9	626.9	....	....	....	....	....	....	....	....	....	....
Services: Credit	78add	330.8	304.4	....	....	....	....	....	....	....	....	....	....
Services: Debit	78aed	−493.2	−498.6	....	....	....	....	....	....	....	....	....	....
Balance on Goods & Services	78afd	239.6	432.6	....	....	....	....	....	....	....	....	....	....
Income: Credit	78agd	19.9	12.4	....	....	....	....	....	....	....	....	....	....
Income: Debit	78ahd	−336.4	−424.6	....	....	....	....	....	....	....	....	....	....
Balance on Gds, Serv. & Inc.	78aid	−76.9	20.4	....	....	....	....	....	....	....	....	....	....
Current Transfers, n.i.e.: Credit	78ajd	83.8	100.7	....	....	....	....	....	....	....	....	....	....
Current Transfers: Debit	78akd	−63.0	−31.2	....	....	....	....	....	....	....	....	....	....
Capital Account, n.i.e.	78bcd	14.1	20.4	....	....	....	....	....	....	....	....	....	....
Capital Account, n.i.e.: Credit	78bad	14.1	21.1	....	....	....	....	....	....	....	....	....	....
Capital Account: Debit	78bbd	—	−.7	....	....	....	....	....	....	....	....	....	....
Financial Account, n.i.e.	78bjd	−626.4	43.3	....	....	....	....	....	....	....	....	....	....
Direct Investment Abroad	78bdd	−.4	−.6	....	....	....	....	....	....	....	....	....	....
Dir. Invest. in Rep. Econ., n.i.e.	78bed	−9.0	7.3	....	....	....	....	....	....	....	....	....	....
Portfolio Investment Assets	78bfd	−74.6	−26.2	....	....	....	....	....	....	....	....	....	....
Equity Securities	78bkd	6.4	—	....	....	....	....	....	....	....	....	....	....
Debt Securities	78bld	−81.1	−26.2	....	....	....	....	....	....	....	....	....	....
Portfolio Investment Liab., n.i.e.	78bgd	—	—	....	....	....	....	....	....	....	....	....	....
Equity Securities	78bmd	—	—	....	....	....	....	....	....	....	....	....	....
Debt Securities	78bnd	—	—	....	....	....	....	....	....	....	....	....	....
Financial Derivatives Assets	78bwd	....	....	....	....	....	....	....	....	....	....	....	....
Financial Derivatives Liabilities	78bxd	....	....	....	....	....	....	....	....	....	....	....	....
Other Investment Assets	78bhd	138.4	−146.8	....	....	....	....	....	....	....	....	....	....
Monetary Authorities	78bod	....	....	....	....	....	....	....	....	....	....	....	....
General Government	78bpd	—	—	....	....	....	....	....	....	....	....	....	....
Banks	78bqd	−27.9	6.6	....	....	....	....	....	....	....	....	....	....
Other Sectors	78brd	166.3	−153.4	....	....	....	....	....	....	....	....	....	....
Other Investment Liab., n.i.e.	78bid	−680.7	209.6	....	....	....	....	....	....	....	....	....	....
Monetary Authorities	78bsd	−181.3	666.9	....	....	....	....	....	....	....	....	....	....
General Government	78btd	−272.3	−457.0	....	....	....	....	....	....	....	....	....	....
Banks	78bud	−76.2	17.0	....	....	....	....	....	....	....	....	....	....
Other Sectors	78bvd	−150.9	−17.3	....	....	....	....	....	....	....	....	....	....
Net Errors and Omissions	78cad	117.0	−138.1	....	....	....	....	....	....	....	....	....	....
Overall Balance	78cbd	−551.3	15.4	....	....	....	....	....	....	....	....	....	....
Reserves and Related Items	79dad	551.3	−15.4	....	....	....	....	....	....	....	....	....	....
Reserve Assets	79dbd	.4	14.5	....	....	....	....	....	....	....	....	....	....
Use of Fund Credit and Loans	79dcd	25.3	6.7	....	....	....	....	....	....	....	....	....	....
Exceptional Financing	79ded	525.6	−36.6	....	....	....	....	....	....	....	....	....	....
Government Finance						*Billions of Francs: Year Ending June 30*							
Deficit (-) or Surplus	80	−99.05	† 8.25			83.71	7.16	....	....				
Revenue	81	385.90	† 536.54	....	....	862.31	867.46	....	....				
Grants Received	81z	—	† —	....	....	—	—	....	....				
Expenditure	82	483.49	† 525.27	....	....	777.60	859.80	....	....				
Lending Minus Repayments	83	1.46	† 3.02	....	....	1.00	.50	....	....				
Financing													
Domestic	84a	−13.09	† −13.17	....	....	−19.40	−14.90	....	....				
Foreign	85a	120.84	† 14.42	....	....	−63.10	8.50	....	....				
Adj. to Total Financing	84x	−8.70	† −9.50	....	....	−1.21	−.76	....	....				
Debt: Domestic	88a	1,179.18	† 1,419.89	....	....	1,391.38	1,224.04	....	....				
Foreign	89a	4,084.80	† 4,343.87	....	....	4,261.53	4,432.12	....	....				
National Accounts						*Billions of Francs: Year Ending June 30*							
Househ.Cons.Expend.,incl.NPISHs	96f	2,538.9	3,018.9	3,354.8	3,537.2	....	....	....	....	....	....	....	....
Government Consumption Expend.	91f	257.5	299.9	305.0	332.1	....	....	....	....	....	....	....	....
Gross Fixed Capital Formation	93e	533.0	597.5	729.3	850.5	....	....	....	....	....	....	....	....
Changes in Inventories	93i	—	—	—	—	....	....	....	....	....	....	....	....
Exports of Goods and Services	90c	768.5	1,068.3	1,116.3	1,335.8	....	....	....	....	....	....	....	....
Imports of Goods and Services (-)	98c	681.8	834.5	950.4	1,038.2	....	....	....	....	....	....	....	....
Gross Domestic Product (GDP)	99b	3,786.0	4,365.5	4,836.5	5,266.5	5,572.0	6,010.6	6,611.0	7,136.7	7,609.3	....	....	....
Net Primary Income from Abroad	98.n	−190.0	−168.5	−284.0	−299.0	....	....	....	....	....	....	....	....
Gross National Income (GNI)	99a	3,226.0	3,981.7	4,271.0	4,718.4	....	....	....	....	....	....	....	....
GDP Volume (1995=100)	99bvp	96.8	100.0	105.0	110.2	....	....	....	....	....	....	....	....
GDP Deflator (1995=100)	99bip	89.6	100.0	105.5	109.4	....	....	....	....	....	....	....	....
						Millions: Midyear Estimates							
Population	99z	12.98	13.30	13.62	13.94	14.25	14.55	14.86	15.16	15.45	15.75	16.04	16.32

		1994	1995	1996	1997	1998	1999	2000	2001	2002	2003	2004	2005
Exchange Rates		*Canadian Dollars per SDR: End of Period*											
Market Rate	aa	2.0479	2.0294	1.9694	1.9282	2.1550	1.9809	1.9546	2.0015	2.1475	1.9205	1.8692	1.6644
		Canadian Dollars per US Dollar: End of Period (ae) Period Average (rf)											
Market Rate	ae	1.4028	1.3652	1.3696	1.4291	1.5305	1.4433	1.5002	1.5926	1.5796	1.2924	1.2036	1.1645
Market Rate	rf	1.3656	1.3724	1.3635	1.3846	1.4835	1.4857	1.4851	1.5488	1.5693	1.4011	1.3010	1.2118
		Index Numbers (2000=100): Period Averages											
Market Rate	ahx	108.7	108.2	108.9	107.2	100.2	99.9	100.0	95.9	94.6	106.3	114.3	122.6
Nominal Effective Exchange Rate	neu	104.6	102.2	104.0	104.6	98.5	98.1	100.0	97.2	95.1	103.6	109.2	117.2
Real Effective Exchange Rate	reu	102.2	101.6	103.1	107.0	101.3	101.0	100.0	98.7	93.7	97.9	100.5	104.0
Fund Position		*Millions of SDRs: End of Period*											
Quota	2f.s	4,320	4,320	4,320	4,320	4,320	6,369	6,369	6,369	6,369	6,369	6,369	6,369
SDRs	1b.s	786	792	812	834	780	384	441	489	529	564	595	628
Reserve Position in the Fund	1c.s	629	836	853	1,167	1,633	2,308	1,926	2,278	2,633	2,589	2,150	980
of which: Outstg.Fund Borrowing	2c	—	—	—	—	204	—	—	—	—	—	—	—
International Liquidity		*Millions of US Dollars Unless Otherwise Indicated: End of Period*											
Total Reserves minus Gold	1l.d	12,286	15,049	20,422	17,823	23,308	28,126	32,102	33,962	36,984	36,222	34,429	32,962
SDRs	1b.d	1,148	1,177	1,168	1,126	1,098	527	574	614	719	838	924	897
Reserve Position in the Fund	1c.d	919	1,243	1,226	1,575	2,299	3,168	2,509	2,863	3,580	3,847	3,338	1,401
Foreign Exchange	1d.d	10,219	12,629	18,028	15,122	19,911	24,432	29,019	30,484	32,685	31,537	30,166	30,664
of which: US Dollars	1dxd	9,693	12,127	17,521	14,630	15,907	18,838	21,692	19,748	17,946	15,576	14,427	16,842
Gold (Million Fine Troy Ounces)	1ad	3.89	3.41	3.09	3.09	2.49	1.81	1.18	1.05	.60	.11	.11	.11
Gold (National Valuation)	1and	198	178	155	146	122	524	323	291	205	45	48	56
Monetary Authorities: Other Liab	4..d	355	349	139	99	64	187	65	67	134	85	107	123
Deposit Money Banks: Assets	7a.d	54,614	64,061	76,144	84,432	86,257	78,983	91,241	102,279	105,517	121,933	128,725	151,983
Liabilities	7b.d	80,507	77,143	87,951	108,978	111,723	92,325	94,728	109,353	116,856	127,166	133,561	169,872
Monetary Authorities		*Billions of Canadian Dollars: End of Period*											
Foreign Assets	11	17.51	20.79	28.18	25.68	35.86	40.72	48.24	54.16	58.47	46.82	41.45	38.39
Claims on Central Government	12a	30.41	30.09	31.03	31.81	32.41	41.68	36.98	40.08	41.89	43.22	46.82	50.94
Reserve Money	14	31.65	32.08	33.46	34.58	36.86	45.83	42.45	44.24	46.66	47.11	49.29	50.92
of which: Currency Outside DMBs	14a	27.30	27.99	28.78	30.15	32.32	38.72	36.34	38.66	41.13	42.35	44.54	46.54
Foreign Liabilities	16c	.50	.48	.19	.14	.10	.27	.10	.11	.21	.11	.13	.14
Central Government Deposits	16d	15.01	17.69	25.01	22.09	30.83	35.85	44.22	49.85	52.73	41.70	37.76	36.63
Other Items (Net)	17r	.76	.64	.56	.68	.47	.45	−1.55	.05	.76	1.12	1.08	1.65
Deposit Money Banks		*Billions of Canadian Dollars: End of Period*											
Reserves	20	5.04	4.67	5.24	4.79	4.89	8.56	6.87	6.07	5.96	5.10	5.41	5.45
Foreign Assets	21	73.94	83.18	97.07	109.86	122.21	104.96	127.50	148.80	152.19	147.45	145.09	162.40
Claims on Central Government	22a	78.33	84.20	81.50	72.55	71.89	70.75	85.79	100.16	100.04	103.31	98.71	105.06
Claims on Local Government	22b	13.15	13.01	12.91	14.80	15.24	15.95	16.37	17.58	23.10	22.65	25.25	31.41
Claims on Private Sector	22d	450.77	474.89	531.94	607.32	617.22	643.28	714.84	757.23	799.50	842.02	948.18	1,030.36
Demand Deposits	24	97.84	109.89	126.60	139.61	147.04	160.24	188.58	214.89	227.04	241.24	266.82	286.04
Savings & Fgn Currency Deposits	25	326.97	342.32	348.69	377.66	380.37	392.79	449.05	464.64	490.02	527.81	583.15	632.56
Foreign Liabilities	26c	105.94	97.52	113.51	146.31	160.94	122.40	129.33	157.69	170.59	149.85	145.06	180.84
Central Government Deposits	26d	2.78	6.19	4.22	6.63	5.89	11.59	4.17	4.12	2.26	3.48	2.45	2.46
Other Items (Net)	27r	87.70	104.04	135.63	139.12	137.21	156.48	180.24	188.49	190.87	198.15	225.16	232.77
Monetary Survey		*Billions of Canadian Dollars: End of Period*											
Foreign Assets (Net)	31n	−14.99	5.98	11.55	−10.91	−2.97	23.01	46.32	45.17	39.86	44.31	41.35	19.81
Domestic Credit	32	554.86	578.31	628.15	697.75	700.04	724.22	805.58	861.07	909.54	966.03	1,078.74	1,178.68
Claims on Central Govt. (Net)	32an	90.94	90.41	83.30	75.64	67.58	64.99	74.38	86.26	86.94	101.35	105.31	116.92
Claims on Local Government	32b	13.15	13.01	12.91	14.80	15.24	15.95	16.37	17.58	23.10	22.65	25.25	31.41
Claims on Private Sector	32d	450.77	474.89	531.94	607.32	617.22	643.28	714.84	757.23	799.50	842.02	948.18	1,030.36
Money	34	125.32	138.07	155.56	169.92	179.58	199.24	225.19	253.75	268.50	283.95	311.74	332.88
Quasi-Money	35	326.97	342.32	348.69	377.66	380.37	392.79	449.05	464.64	490.02	527.81	583.15	632.56
Other Items (Net)	37r	87.58	103.90	135.45	139.27	137.12	155.21	177.66	187.84	190.87	198.56	225.20	233.05
Money plus Quasi-Money	35l	452.29	480.40	504.25	547.57	559.95	592.03	674.24	718.40	758.52	811.77	894.89	965.44
Other Banking Institutions		*Billions of Canadian Dollars: End of Period*											
Reserves	40	14.94	16.77	16.57	15.45	16.93	19.56	20.98	12.55	12.72	14.32	14.26	14.46
Claims on Central Government	42a	6.74	7.41	7.58	5.18	5.47	6.49	1.35	3.30	3.12	4.15	5.03	5.19
Claims on State and Local Govts	42b	1.63	1.48	1.33	1.26	.94	.84	1.02	3.26	3.32	4.17	4.21	2.37
Claims on Private Sector	42d	141.24	140.10	144.18	132.09	133.94	135.34	103.52	113.07	121.40	133.48	146.50	164.09
Demand Deposits	44	8.96	8.37	8.69	7.87	8.07	8.11	.13	.19	.11	.11	.12	.13
Time and Savings Deposits	45	141.95	143.53	145.42	131.64	136.34	141.39	116.16	125.00	133.21	144.81	155.03	166.57
Money Market Instruments	46aa	1.01	1.29	3.07	1.63	2.06	2.57	.03	.04	.08	.11	.08	.10
Capital Accounts	47a	9.40	9.54	9.84	9.60	9.91	10.18	9.32	10.16	10.81	12.09	13.46	14.70
Other Items (Net)	47r	3.22	3.03	2.63	3.23	.91	−.03	1.22	−3.21	−3.66	−.99	1.32	4.60
Banking Survey		*Billions of Canadian Dollars: End of Period*											
Foreign Assets (Net)	51n	−14.99	5.98	11.55	−10.91	−2.97	23.01	46.32	45.17	39.86	44.31	41.35	19.81
Domestic Credit	52	704.47	727.30	781.23	836.28	840.38	866.88	911.47	980.70	1,037.37	1,107.83	1,234.48	1,350.33
Claims on Central Govt. (Net)	52an	97.68	97.83	90.88	80.82	73.05	71.48	75.73	89.56	90.06	105.50	110.35	122.10
Claims on State and Local Govts	52b	14.79	14.49	14.23	16.06	16.18	16.79	17.39	20.85	26.42	26.82	29.46	33.78
Claims on Private Sector	52d	592.01	614.99	676.11	739.40	751.15	778.62	818.35	870.30	920.89	975.51	1,094.68	1,194.45
Liquid Liabilities	55l	588.27	615.53	641.79	671.64	687.42	721.97	769.56	831.03	879.12	942.37	1,035.77	1,117.68
Money Market Instruments	56aa	1.01	1.29	3.07	1.63	2.06	2.57	.03	.04	.08	.11	.08	.10
Other Items (Net)	57r	100.21	116.47	147.92	152.11	147.94	165.35	188.21	194.79	198.02	209.66	239.98	252.35

Canada 156

		1994	1995	1996	1997	1998	1999	2000	2001	2002	2003	2004	2005
Nonbank Financial Institutions		*Billions of Canadian Dollars: End of Period*											
Reserves	40..n	2.42	3.63	3.72	3.78	3.86	† 4.57	6.00	6.89	5.96	9.21	8.86	10.04
Claims on Central Government	42a.n	25.50	29.43	28.56	30.05	31.33	† 32.20	29.22	29.83	32.34	33.84	32.34	31.12
Claims on State & Local Govts	42b.n	17.51	20.60	23.41	23.68	24.43	† 26.68	31.98	33.50	35.79	41.23	45.26	47.88
Claims on Private Sector	42d.n	126.46	131.93	137.89	154.64	164.51	† 196.09	211.66	223.16	228.52	243.79	268.68	301.77
Claims on Deposit Money Banks	42e.n	2.43	2.17	3.83	4.73	5.42	† 7.39	8.74	9.36	9.13	10.91	14.30	14.09
Money Market Instruments	46aan	8.50	8.89	10.57	16.71	18.80	† 29.01	27.13	18.78	19.77	16.36	17.03	17.98
Bonds	46abn	9.45	11.12	11.41	16.83	23.41	† 32.79	35.52	40.13	41.30	42.62	48.95	58.30
Cred. from Deposit Money Banks	46h.n	.30	.28	.21	.36	.36	† 3.34	5.04	5.54	6.71	4.47	4.13	6.18
Capital Accounts	47a.n	173.06	183.54	190.49	201.44	212.41	† 239.75	262.42	268.53	285.68	314.55	339.87	369.02
Other Items (Net)	47r.n	−16.99	−16.06	−15.27	−18.45	−25.44	† −37.96	−42.52	−30.24	−41.71	−39.03	−40.55	−46.58
Money (National Definitions)		*Billions of Canadian Dollars: End of Period*											
M1	59ma	60.99	65.53	77.92	86.50	93.62	101.18	116.10	133.86	140.20	153.74	171.11	189.75
M1, Seasonally Adjusted	59mac	59.21	63.70	75.80	84.08	90.86	98.04	112.25	129.41	136.04	149.80	167.23	185.93
Gross M1	59maa	58.58	64.33	74.04	84.92	90.78	99.65	115.44	132.09	141.34	154.86	172.57	190.83
Gross M1, Seasonally Adjusted	59maf	56.63	62.31	71.89	82.57	88.42	97.09	112.39	128.57	137.59	150.83	168.25	186.18
M1+	59mab	156.28	160.40	179.46	197.60	205.51	221.76	249.20	279.64	297.66	314.99	344.40	367.02
M1+, Seasonally Adjusted	59mag	153.21	157.27	175.96	193.65	201.25	217.01	243.80	273.63	291.45	308.77	337.99	360.44
M1++	59mad	225.55	227.23	242.06	254.87	257.61	275.29	303.38	345.98	373.95	401.87	444.19	476.84
M1++, Seasonally Adjusted	59mah	222.32	223.89	238.42	250.92	253.50	270.76	298.46	340.46	368.30	396.30	438.60	471.18
M2	59mb	428.43	446.24	455.91	450.30	454.58	478.68	510.99	541.84	568.81	602.47	639.70	674.07
M2, Seasonally Adjusted	59mbc	425.14	442.75	452.13	446.15	449.80	473.13	504.83	535.48	562.62	596.73	634.21	668.74
M2+	59mba	593.08	619.27	643.48	634.01	641.82	675.45	713.44	777.94	812.16	848.48	890.83	932.78
M2+, Seasonally Adjusted	59mbf	589.94	615.88	639.70	629.72	636.73	669.41	706.68	770.57	805.04	842.35	885.20	927.37
M2++	59mbb	730.59	763.71	824.68	875.62	924.40	976.00	1,053.91	1,134.03	1,177.60	1,222.97	1,290.88	1,371.45
M2++, Seasonally Adjusted	59mbg	727.21	760.20	820.91	871.67	919.66	970.42	1,047.89	1,127.75	1,172.00	1,217.99	1,286.02	1,366.55
M3	59mc	512.14	537.78	567.31	597.51	617.51	645.66	698.39	733.04	770.43	822.94	908.33	977.93
M3, Seasonally Adjusted	59mcc	507.59	532.64	561.40	590.70	609.83	637.21	689.28	723.92	762.30	815.53	901.32	971.18
Interest Rates		*Percent Per Annum*											
Bank Rate (End of Period)	60	7.43	5.79	3.25	4.50	5.25	5.00	6.00	2.50	3.00	3.00	2.75	3.50
Money Market Rate	60b	5.05	6.92	4.32	3.26	4.87	4.74	5.52	4.11	2.45	2.93	2.25	2.66
Corporate Paper Rate	60bc	5.66	7.22	4.35	3.61	5.05	4.94	5.71	3.87	2.66	2.94	2.31	2.84
Treasury Bill Rate	60c	5.54	6.89	4.21	3.26	4.73	4.72	5.49	3.77	2.59	2.87	2.22	2.73
Savings Rate	60k	.50	.50	.50	.50	.24	.10	.10	.10	.05	.05	.05	.05
Deposit Rate	60l	3.98	5.28	3.00	1.90	3.08	2.88	3.48	2.25	.83	1.10	.78	.79
Lending Rate	60p	6.88	8.65	6.06	4.96	6.60	6.44	7.27	5.81	4.21	4.69	4.00	4.42
Govt. Bond Yield: Med.-Term	61a	7.79	7.64	6.21	5.33	5.16	5.50	5.99	4.88	4.44	3.88	3.67	3.50
Long-Term	61	8.63	8.28	7.50	6.42	5.47	5.69	5.89	5.78	5.66	5.28	5.08	4.39
Prices, Production, Labor		*Index Numbers (2000=100): Period Averages*											
Industrial Share Prices	62	44.6	46.1	54.8	67.2	70.3	73.5	100.0	80.5	73.2	74.5	90.0	105.8
Prices: Industry Selling	63	86.1	92.5	92.9	93.7	93.7	95.2	100.0	† 101.1	101.2	99.8	102.9	104.5
Consumer Prices	64	89.8	† 91.8	93.2	94.7	95.7	97.3	100.0	102.5	104.8	107.7	109.7	112.2
Wages: Hourly Earnings (Mfg)	65ey	89.7	90.9	93.6	94.3	96.2	97.5	100.0	101.6	104.4	107.8	110.7	112.7
Industrial Production	66	....	78.6	79.5	84.0	86.9	92.1	100.0	96.0	97.6	98.6	102.5	105.2
Gold Production (1995=100)	66kr	97.8	100.0	....	....	....	93.6	95.5	100.0	99.5	100.1	99.8	....
Manufacturing Employment	67ey	83.8	85.4	87.4	90.6			100.0			97.2	95.3	

(Note: the row "Manufacturing Employment" and the following block straddle the header "Number in Thousands: Period Averages")

Labor etc.		*Number in Thousands: Period Averages*											
Labor Force	67d	14,832	14,928	15,145	15,354	15,632	15,721	15,999	16,246	16,690	17,047	17,183	....
Employment	67e	13,292	† 13,506	13,676	13,941	14,326	14,531	14,910	15,077	15,412	15,746	16,021	....
Unemployment	67c	1,541	† 1,422	1,469	1,414	1,305	1,182	1,083	1,164	1,269	1,286	1,235	1,173
Unemployment Rate (%)	67r	10.4	† 9.6	9.7	9.2	8.3	† 7.6	6.8	7.2	7.7	7.6	7.2	6.8
Intl. Transactions & Positions		*Millions of Canadian Dollars*											
Exports	70	225,908	263,697	274,884	296,928	317,903	354,108	410,994	402,172	396,020	381,655	395,897	434,874
Imports, f.o.b.	71.v	206,626	224,977	232,672	271,422	298,076	319,008	354,728	343,311	348,198	334,331	354,859	391,658
		2000=100											
Volume of Exports	72	59.8	65.8	69.8	† 75.6	82.0	91.2	100.0	95.9	96.5	95.6	101.9	105.5
Volume of Imports	73	58.9	63.5	66.9	† 79.3	86.1	95.8	100.0	94.4	96.0	99.7	108.7	118.2
Unit Value of Exports	74	84.7	91.4	92.0	† 91.6	97.3	105.7	100.0	101.9	98.4	97.9	100.6	105.3
Unit Value of Imports	75	90.7	94.1	93.7	† 94.3	94.2	95.7	100.0	103.0	103.8	96.1	94.5	94.6

Canada 156

Balance of Payments		1994	1995	1996	1997	1998	1999	2000	2001	2002	2003	2004	2005
		Millions of US Dollars: Minus Sign Indicates Debit											
Current Account, n.i.e.	78ald	−13,024	−4,328	3,378	−8,233	−7,839	1,765	19,622	16,281	12,604	10,315	21,157	26,555
Goods: Exports f.o.b.	78aad	166,990	193,373	205,443	219,063	220,539	248,494	289,022	271,849	263,908	285,068	330,106	374,308
Goods: Imports f.o.b.	78abd	−152,155	−167,517	−174,352	−200,498	−204,617	−220,203	−243,975	−226,132	−227,410	−244,891	−279,880	−320,517
Trade Balance	78acd	14,834	25,855	31,091	18,565	15,922	28,292	45,047	45,716	36,498	40,177	50,226	53,791
Services: Credit	78add	23,958	26,128	29,243	31,596	33,836	36,117	40,230	38,804	40,481	43,778	49,111	53,647
Services: Debit	78aed	−32,530	−33,473	−35,906	−38,013	−38,156	−40,573	−44,118	−43,843	−45,069	−52,227	−58,914	−64,956
Balance on Goods & Services	78afd	6,262	18,510	24,428	12,148	11,602	23,836	41,159	40,678	31,910	31,728	40,422	42,482
Income: Credit	78agd	15,443	18,888	19,204	23,998	21,830	22,158	24,746	16,822	19,444	21,215	28,905	39,832
Income: Debit	78ahd	−34,382	−41,609	−40,755	−44,878	−41,815	−44,777	−47,036	−42,238	−38,745	−42,380	−47,930	−55,340
Balance on Gds, Serv. & Inc.	78aid	−12,676	−4,211	2,877	−8,732	−8,383	1,216	18,868	15,262	12,609	10,563	21,397	26,974
Current Transfers, n.i.e.: Credit	78ajd	2,625	2,878	3,594	3,634	3,407	3,796	4,122	4,499	4,387	4,815	5,730	6,662
Current Transfers: Debit	78akd	−2,973	−2,995	−3,092	−3,135	−2,863	−3,247	−3,368	−3,480	−4,391	−5,063	−5,970	−7,082
Capital Account, n.i.e.	78bcd	7,498	4,950	5,833	5,429	3,336	3,400	3,581	3,721	3,145	2,982	3,424	4,881
Capital Account, n.i.e.: Credit	78bad	7,876	5,666	6,262	5,862	3,794	3,862	4,045	4,191	3,589	3,431	3,922	5,452
Capital Account: Debit	78bbd	−378	−716	−429	−433	−457	−462	−464	−471	−444	−449	−498	−570
Financial Account, n.i.e.	78bjd	5,159	−1,277	−9,277	3,394	4,944	−5,968	−14,500	−11,609	−14,360	−18,010	−31,258	−27,511
Direct Investment Abroad	78bdd	−9,303	−11,490	−13,107	−23,069	−34,112	−17,262	−44,487	−36,152	−26,818	−22,209	−42,528	−34,196
Dir. Invest. in Rep. Econ., n.i.e.	78bed	8,224	9,319	9,635	11,523	22,742	24,789	66,144	27,711	22,053	7,337	1,249	34,146
Portfolio Investment Assets	78bfd	−6,587	−5,328	−14,183	−8,568	−15,106	−15,579	−42,975	−24,374	−18,632	−13,829	−18,924	−42,728
Equity Securities	78bkd	−6,898	−4,570	−12,661	−3,777	−10,428	−13,910	−40,229	−23,120	−13,500	−5,816	−6,197	−18,164
Debt Securities	78bld	311	−759	−1,522	−4,792	−4,678	−1,669	−2,746	−1,254	−5,132	−8,013	−12,727	−24,565
Portfolio Investment Liab., n.i.e.	78bgd	17,155	18,402	13,718	11,692	16,590	2,653	10,259	24,166	11,869	13,876	41,586	6,978
Equity Securities	78bmd	4,718	−3,077	5,900	5,461	9,645	9,722	24,239	2,713	−914	9,947	27,145	7,565
Debt Securities	78bnd	12,437	21,479	7,818	6,230	6,945	−7,069	−13,980	21,454	12,783	3,929	14,441	−587
Financial Derivatives Assets	78bwd	....	....	....	....	....	....	....	....	....	....	....	....
Financial Derivatives Liabilities	78bxd	....	....	....	....	....	....	....	....	....	....	....	....
Other Investment Assets	78bhd	−20,378	−8,328	−21,064	−16,167	9,400	10,235	−4,195	−10,739	−7,938	−14,575	−7,899	−16,572
Monetary Authorities	78bod	....	....	....	....	....	....	....	....	....	....	....	....
General Government	78bpd	−436	−336	−119	−515	−579	−305	−232	−131	−19	339	−210	−395
Banks	78bqd	−12,575	−8,314	−13,847	−5,419	969	13,368	−7,301	−2,183	2,278	−15,172	−983	−16,285
Other Sectors	78brd	−7,366	322	−7,098	−10,233	9,010	−2,828	3,338	−8,425	−10,197	258	−6,706	108
Other Investment Liab., n.i.e.	78bid	16,049	−3,852	15,724	27,983	5,430	−10,804	754	7,779	5,106	11,390	−4,742	24,860
Monetary Authorities	78bsd	—	—	—	—	—	—	—	—	—	—	—	—
General Government	78btd	586	−484	−508	−321	−270	−318	−350	−237	−116	−527	−754	−138
Banks	78bud	15,233	−4,579	12,707	24,630	953	−16,273	−626	15,314	8,525	12,557	−1,000	23,946
Other Sectors	78bvd	230	1,211	3,525	3,673	4,747	5,788	1,730	−7,298	−3,303	−640	−2,989	1,053
Net Errors and Omissions	78cad	−26	3,366	5,563	−2,983	4,555	6,736	−4,984	−6,220	−1,574	1,457	3,842	−2,589
Overall Balance	78cbd	−392	2,711	5,498	−2,393	4,996	5,933	3,720	2,172	−185	−3,255	−2,836	1,335
Reserves and Related Items	79dad	392	−2,711	−5,498	2,393	−4,996	−5,933	−3,720	−2,172	185	3,255	2,836	−1,335
Reserve Assets	79dbd	392	−2,711	−5,498	2,393	−4,996	−5,933	−3,720	−2,172	185	3,255	2,836	−1,335
Use of Fund Credit and Loans	79dcd	—	—	—	—	—	—	—	—	—	—	—	—
Exceptional Financing	79ded	....	....	....	....	....	....	....	....	....	....	....	....
International Investment Position		*Millions of US Dollars*											
Assets	79aad	282,944	324,692	371,736	419,480	448,443	497,023	551,648	578,917	620,047	710,478	793,832	862,557
Direct Investment Abroad	79abd	104,302	118,105	132,329	152,969	171,780	201,434	237,639	250,692	274,350	312,167	369,777	392,675
Portfolio Investment	79acd	59,601	66,487	79,054	91,222	102,845	124,558	139,456	150,547	169,960	194,196	212,054	234,503
Equity Securities	79add	46,543	52,700	63,529	72,619	81,118	103,263	115,699	126,141	136,440	150,797	155,100	155,104
Debt Securities	79aed	13,057	13,787	15,525	18,603	21,728	21,294	23,757	24,407	33,520	43,400	56,954	79,400
Financial Derivatives	79ald	—	—	—	—	—	—	—	—	—	—	—	—
Other Investment	79afd	106,564	124,885	139,761	157,305	150,351	142,298	142,687	144,189	140,113	168,777	178,489	202,718
Monetary Authorities	79agd	—	—	—	—	—	—	—	—	—	—	—	—
General Government	79ahd	15,419	15,656	15,868	16,759	18,716	20,835	21,983	22,857	23,396	23,525	23,300	21,290
Banks	79aid	49,976	60,268	73,657	76,024	74,550	61,364	68,306	66,413	61,149	77,614	78,485	94,949
Other Sectors	79ajd	41,170	48,961	50,236	64,522	57,084	60,099	52,398	54,919	55,569	67,638	76,704	86,479
Reserve Assets	79akd	12,476	15,216	20,591	17,984	23,467	28,732	31,866	33,488	35,622	35,338	33,512	32,661
Liabilities	79lad	520,374	562,156	599,081	622,564	644,239	665,852	690,851	706,652	751,033	870,018	944,303	1,013,539
Dir. Invest. in Rep. Economy	79lbd	110,204	123,181	132,978	135,944	143,344	174,990	212,716	213,757	224,185	274,269	303,818	342,101
Portfolio Investment	79lcd	281,767	309,774	323,661	321,742	334,129	336,824	324,968	330,389	351,916	394,960	443,058	447,084
Equity Securities	79ldd	22,001	27,170	34,537	35,968	42,041	47,856	58,070	48,654	51,084	64,466	90,191	96,900
Debt Securities	79led	259,766	282,604	289,125	285,774	292,088	288,968	266,899	281,735	300,833	330,494	352,868	350,184
Financial Derivatives	79lld	—	—	—	—	—	—	—	—	—	—	—	—
Other Investment	79lfd	128,403	129,201	142,442	164,879	166,766	154,038	153,167	162,506	174,932	200,789	197,427	224,354
Monetary Authorities	79lgd	—	—	—	—	—	—	—	—	—	—	—	—
General Government	79lhd	4,568	4,059	3,334	2,790	2,648	2,530	2,011	1,609	1,638	1,299	608	471
Banks	79lid	83,691	79,735	92,486	115,623	118,008	100,131	98,443	113,639	123,359	141,643	146,120	173,047
Other Sectors	79ljd	40,145	45,407	46,622	46,466	46,110	51,377	52,713	47,257	49,935	57,847	50,698	50,837
Government Finance		*Billions of Canadian Dollars: Year Beginning April 1*											
Deficit (-) or Surplus	80	−36.70	−29.22	−15.55	5.33	3.10	9.14	13.39	14.38	....	....	....	....
Revenue	81	157.60	164.25	174.51	188.91	195.82	209.54	228.76	226.83	....	....	....	....
Grants Received	81z	.53	.52	.54	.52	.50	.56	.57	.61	....	....	....	....
Expenditure	82	196.04	199.90	190.91	186.95	193.92	201.68	213.48	212.61	....	....	....	....
Lending Minus Repayments	83	−1.20	−5.91	−.31	−2.85	−.70	−.72	2.46	.45	....	....	....	....
Financing													
Total Net Borrowing	84	35.59	40.04	19.43	−6.95	8.56	2.92	3.83	−15.55	....	....	....	....
Net Domestic	84a	42.91	29.10	22.10	−1.53	5.61	−12.75	−12.50	−20.44	....	....	....	....
Net Foreign	85a	−7.32	10.94	−2.67	−5.42	2.95	15.67	16.33	4.89	....	....	....	....
Use of Cash Balances	87	1.11	−10.81	−3.88	1.63	−11.66	−12.05	−17.22	1.17	....	....	....	....
Total Debt	88z	595.88	634.94	651.12	645.73	648.39	648.21	644.90	629.09	....	....	....	....
Domestic	88a	577.02	616.22	626.32	616.73	610.73	614.22	610.25	600.69	....	....	....	....
Foreign	89a	18.86	18.71	24.81	28.99	37.65	33.99	34.65	28.41	....	....	....	....

Canada 156

		1994	1995	1996	1997	1998	1999	2000	2001	2002	2003	2004	2005
National Accounts							*Billions of Canadian dollars*							
Househ.Cons.Expend.,incl.NPISHs....	96f.c	447.75	462.87	482.37	512.86	534.39	561.57	594.09	623.17	656.18	689.42	721.24	761.96
Government Consumption Expend...	91f.c	171.73	172.65	171.35	171.88	176.84	183.29	196.00	207.51	218.90	231.00	248.53	262.37
Gross Fixed Capital Formation..........	93e.c	144.96	143.00	149.94	174.84	181.62	193.83	209.94	219.85	227.19	237.19	258.96	280.02
Changes in Inventories....................	93i.c	.45	8.91	2.34	8.18	5.79	3.91	8.00	−5.24	2.87	7.56	7.22	9.47
Exports of Goods and Services.........	90c.c	262.13	302.48	321.25	348.60	377.35	418.54	484.33	482.07	474.30	459.56	492.58	518.26
Imports of Goods and Services (-).....	98c.c	253.01	276.62	287.55	331.27	360.26	386.03	428.93	418.81	423.99	409.99	438.35	464.03
Gross Domestic Product (GDP).........	99b.c	770.87	810.43	836.86	882.73	914.97	982.44	1,075.57	1,107.46	1,154.95	1,214.60	1,290.19	1,368.73
Net Primary Income from Abroad.....	98.nc	−27.99	−28.55	−28.33	−27.70	−30.04	−29.51	−22.37	−29.61	−27.39	−25.06	−22.48	−24.52
Gross National Income (GNI)............	99a.c	744.83	783.91	810.73	857.32	885.83	945.75	1,042.63	1,077.85	1,127.56	1,189.54	1,270.81	1,344.21
Gross Nat'l Disposable Inc.(GNDI)....	99i.c	744.36	783.75	811.42	858.02	886.60	946.88	1,044.10	1,079.53	1,128.92	1,190.09	1,270.04	1,343.99
Gross Saving....................................	99s.c	....	....	....	182.81	187.46	198.21	219.51	213.52	229.56	244.30	262.69	291.48
Consumption of Fixed Capital..........	99cfc	99.63	105.02	110.82	116.57	122.30	127.72	135.78	146.80	155.00	164.03	174.22	181.43
GDP Volume 1997 Ref., Chained.....	99b.r	810.70	833.46	846.95	882.73	918.91	969.75	1,020.79	1,040.39	1,074.52	1,092.89	1,126.63	1,157.45
GDP Volume (2000=100)...............	99bvr	79.4	81.6	83.0	86.5	90.0	95.0	100.0	101.9	105.3	107.1	110.4	113.4
GDP Deflator (2000=100)...............	99bir	90.2	92.3	93.8	94.9	94.5	96.1	100.0	101.0	102.0	105.5	108.7	112.2
							Millions: Midyear Estimates							
Population...............................	99z	29.01	29.30	29.59	29.86	30.13	30.40	30.69	30.99	31.31	31.64	31.96	32.27

		1994	1995	1996	1997	1998	1999	2000	2001	2002	2003	2004	2005
Exchange Rates						*Escudos per SDR: End of Period*							
Official Rate	aa	118.452	115.136	122.464	129.845	132.714	150.654	154.403	157.245	142.952	129.737	125.725	133.598
						Escudos per US Dollar: End of Period (ae) Period Average (rf)							
Official Rate	ae	81.140	77.455	85.165	96.235	94.255	109.765	118.506	125.122	105.149	87.308	80.956	93.473
Official Rate	rf	81.891	76.853	82.591	93.177	98.158	103.502	119.687	123.228	117.168	97.703	88.808	88.670
Fund Position						*Millions of SDRs: End of Period*							
Quota	2f.s	7.00	7.00	7.00	7.00	7.00	9.60	9.60	9.60	9.60	9.60	9.60	9.60
SDRs	1b.s	.05	.02	.04	.02	.04	.01	.04	.01	—	—	.02	.02
Reserve Position in the Fund	1c.s	—	—	—	—	—	—	—	—	—	—	—	.02
Total Fund Cred.&Loans Outstg.	2tl	—	—	—	—	—	—	—	—	2.46	4.92	6.15	8.64
International Liquidity						*Millions of US Dollars Unless Otherwise Indicated: End of Period*							
Total Reserves minus Gold	1l.d	42.08	36.89	27.57	19.32	8.32	42.62	28.26	45.43	79.80	93.61	139.53	173.97
SDRs	1b.d	.07	.03	.06	.03	.06	.02	.05	.02	—	—	.04	.02
Reserve Position in the Fund	1c.d	—	—	—	—	—	—	—	—	—	—	—	.02
Foreign Exchange	1d.d	42.01	36.86	27.50	19.29	8.26	42.59	28.21	45.40	79.79	93.60	139.49	173.92
Monetary Authorities: Other Liab.	4..d	.60	6.47	3.51	2.60	.94	1.09	1.35	1.36	1.42	.97	.70	.68
Deposit Money Banks: Assets	7a.d	31.60	10.62	32.35	23.89	33.41	30.10	42.45	42.95	44.76	52.87	66.53	117.96
Liabilities	7b.d	3.38	6.32	5.73	9.95	11.16	15.21	16.41	14.08	19.09	25.75	28.37	47.56
Monetary Authorities						*Millions of Escudos: End of Period*							
Foreign Assets	11	3,483.1	† 5,154.8	4,838.5	4,521.9	3,584.9	8,203.7	4,221.8	6,561.2	9,135.4	8,817.8	11,526.8	16,524.2
Claims on Central Government	12a	4,446.4	† 4,964.4	4,315.8	6,001.6	5,615.2	5,865.2	9,209.4	9,024.0	9,469.0	9,977.4	9,383.5	9,383.5
Claims on Local Government	12b	—	† —	—	—	—	—	—	—	—	—	—	—
Claims on Nonfin.Pub.Enterprises	12c	119.7	† 118.8	113.9	.1	—	86.8	82.3	82.3	72.3	72.3	60.5	53.8
Claims on Private Sector	12d	1,091.2	† 1,099.4	2,049.4	1,151.9	1,142.7	1,100.8	1,074.9	1,106.3	1,111.9	1,107.1	1,105.8	1,094.2
Claims on Deposit Money Banks	12e	592.1	† 632.7	630.3	519.8	361.6	331.4	1,098.9	438.4	274.5	409.8	44.0	27.3
Claims on Other Banking Insts.	12f	—	† —	—	—	—	—	—	—	—	—	—	—
Claims on Nonbank Financial Insts...	12g	....	—	—	—	5.5	5.5	—	—	—	32.8	29.5	15.2
Reserve Money	14	8,685.9	† 10,655.6	9,982.8	10,035.2	10,971.4	11,701.4	13,552.2	14,580.5	16,812.2	17,288.5	18,488.6	21,135.7
of which: Currency Outside DMBs.	14a	3,929.7	† 4,635.1	4,513.0	4,853.6	5,059.8	6,026.1	6,458.2	6,702.9	6,459.3	6,515.6	6,765.0	7,633.6
Time & Foreign Currency Deposits	15	173.9	† 101.4										
Foreign Liabilities	16c	48.7	† 500.9	298.8	249.8	88.8	119.7	159.6	170.0	500.7	722.9	829.8	1,217.6
Central Government Deposits	16d	—	† 245.9	230.8	944.7	516.6	2,446.1	607.7	675.1	1,199.7	948.5	1,184.6	2,896.5
Capital Accounts	17a	2,069.3	† 2,338.7	2,739.2	3,114.5	3,051.5	2,376.6	2,917.5	2,999.7	2,447.4	2,483.4	2,516.5	2,692.4
Other Items (Net)	17r	−1,245.3	† −1,872.4	−1,303.7	−2,149.0	−3,918.4	−1,050.4	−1,549.7	−1,213.1	−896.9	−1,026.2	−869.4	−843.9
Deposit Money Banks						*Millions of Escudos: End of Period*							
Reserves	20	4,803.9	† 5,987.1	5,472.5	5,701.4	5,820.3	5,648.0	7,111.0	7,869.1	9,760.4	10,796.5	11,695.1	13,546.7
Foreign Assets	21	2,563.7	† 822.3	2,754.7	2,299.1	3,149.0	3,303.5	5,031.1	5,373.5	4,706.1	4,615.9	5,386.0	11,026.5
Claims on Central Government	22a	6,046.7	† 7,557.0	8,944.3	10,357.8	10,347.4	10,036.0	14,472.6	14,961.6	17,677.1	18,157.5	19,139.3	21,698.7
Claims on Local Government	22b	76.2	† 97.1	109.1	.2	10.7	238.0	289.3	260.9	266.4	239.3	208.9	231.8
Claims on Nonfin.Pub.Enterprises	22c	432.7	† 545.0	378.5	24.2	21.4	425.3	73.3	132.9	157.8	107.6	100.5	421.7
Claims on Private Sector	22d	6,473.9	† 9,292.1	10,159.8	13,540.5	15,308.7	17,289.2	18,252.2	21,099.2	23,778.0	27,619.1	30,324.6	32,945.3
Claims on Nonbank Financial Insts.	22g								7.0	5.5	3.9	14.2	10.5
Demand Deposits	24	7,542.3	† 7,232.4	8,609.7	11,106.4	10,573.4	12,216.4	13,966.4	14,247.6	16,337.9	16,574.9	17,696.4	21,161.4
Time, Savings,& Fgn.Currency Dep...	25	10,394.4	† 12,974.5	14,251.9	14,386.0	15,557.7	17,494.4	20,301.7	23,826.3	28,050.8	32,342.0	37,084.8	41,697.8
Restricted Deposits	26b	203.8	† 257.6	491.7	398.1	710.0	242.6	502.8	210.4	187.4	192.5	236.9	223.4
Foreign Liabilities	26c	274.3	† 489.7	488.3	957.1	1,051.5	1,669.6	1,944.8	1,761.9	2,007.4	2,248.1	2,296.9	4,445.5
Central Government Deposits	26d	1,035.7	† 2,401.0	2,539.4	2,038.2	2,100.4	1,165.9	1,324.8	1,621.4	1,164.0	1,693.0	1,729.1	2,510.1
Counterpart Funds	26e	....	—	—	2.0	3.4	—	—	—	—	—	—	—
Credit from Monetary Authorities	26g	592.1	† 573.5	551.4	519.8	361.6	331.4	1,098.9	438.4	274.5	409.8	44.0	27.3
Liab. to Nonbank Financial Insts.	26j	20.3	† 181.1	298.7	125.6	36.2	306.0	257.0	276.3	188.4	184.6	162.2	388.2
Capital Accounts	27a	1,638.8	† 2,833.5	3,433.6	4,426.3	5,365.6	5,954.5	7,007.2	7,903.9	8,340.4	8,871.8	9,210.2	9,787.4
Other Items (Net)	27r	−1,304.6	† −2,642.8	−2,845.9	−2,036.3	−1,102.3	−2,440.8	−1,174.1	−582.0	−199.5	−976.9	−1,591.9	−359.9
Monetary Survey						*Millions of Escudos: End of Period*							
Foreign Assets (Net)	31n	5,723.8	† 4,986.5	6,806.0	5,614.0	5,593.6	9,717.9	7,148.5	10,002.8	11,333.5	10,462.7	13,786.1	21,887.6
Domestic Credit	32	17,651.1	† 21,026.9	23,300.6	28,093.4	29,834.6	31,434.8	41,521.5	44,377.7	50,174.3	54,675.5	57,453.1	60,448.2
Claims on Central Govt. (Net)	32an	9,457.4	† 9,874.5	10,489.9	13,376.5	13,345.6	12,289.2	21,749.5	21,689.1	24,782.4	25,493.4	25,609.1	25,675.6
Claims on Local Government	32b	76.2	† 97.1	109.1	.2	10.7	238.0	289.3	260.9	266.4	239.3	208.9	231.8
Claims on Nonfin.Pub.Enterprises	32c	552.4	† 663.8	492.4	24.3	21.4	512.1	155.6	215.2	230.1	179.9	161.0	475.5
Claims on Private Sector	32d	7,565.1	† 10,391.5	12,209.2	14,692.4	16,451.4	18,390.0	19,327.1	22,205.5	24,889.9	28,726.2	31,430.4	34,039.5
Claims on Other Banking Insts.	32f	—	† —	—	—	—	—	—	—	—	—	—	—
Claims on Nonbank Financial Inst..	32g	....	—	—	—	5.5	5.5	—	7.0	5.5	36.7	43.7	25.7
Money	34	11,472.0	† 11,867.5	13,122.7	15,960.0	15,633.2	18,332.6	20,425.3	20,951.3	22,798.3	23,090.9	24,482.8	28,796.6
Quasi-Money	35	10,568.3	† 13,075.9	14,251.9	14,386.0	15,557.7	17,494.4	20,301.7	23,826.3	28,050.8	32,342.0	37,084.8	41,697.8
Restricted Deposits	36b	203.8	† 257.6	491.7	398.1	710.0	242.6	502.8	210.4	187.4	192.5	236.9	223.4
Counterpart Funds	36e	....	—	—	2.0	3.4	—	—	—	—	—	—	—
Liab. to Nonbank Financial Insts.	36j	20.3	† 181.1	298.7	125.6	36.2	306.0	257.0	276.3	188.4	184.6	162.2	388.2
Capital Accounts	37a	3,708.1	† 5,172.2	6,172.8	7,540.8	8,417.1	8,331.1	9,924.7	10,903.6	10,787.8	11,355.2	11,726.7	12,479.8
Other Items (Net)	37r	−2,597.6	† −4,541.0	−4,231.2	−4,705.1	−4,929.4	−3,554.0	−2,741.5	−1,787.4	−505.0	−2,027.1	−2,454.2	−1,250.0
Money plus Quasi-Money	35l	22,040.3	† 24,943.4	27,374.6	30,346.0	31,190.9	35,827.0	40,727.0	44,777.6	50,849.1	55,432.9	61,567.6	70,494.4
Interest Rates						*Percent Per Annum*							
Deposit Rate	60l	4.00	† 5.00	5.00	5.04	5.27	4.76	4.34	4.67	4.86	3.93	3.46	3.38
Lending Rate	60p	10.67	12.00	12.00	12.06	12.06	11.94	12.03	12.51	13.17	12.73	12.69	12.29
Prices						*Index Numbers (2000=100): Period Averages*							
Consumer Prices	64	76	82	87	94	98	103	100	103	105	107	105	105
						Number in Thousands: Period Averages							
Unemployment	67c	1	1	....	....	....	....	....	....	....	....	....	....
Intl. Transactions & Positions						*Millions of Escudos*							
Exports	70	408	687	1,039	1,309	1,024	1,185	1,271	1,211	1,235	1,236	1,333	1,572
Imports, c.i.f.	71	17,113	19,394	19,355	21,936	22,395	25,484	27,517	28,803	32,269	34,235	34,309	38,913

Cape Verde 624

		1994	1995	1996	1997	1998	1999	2000	2001	2002	2003	2004	2005
Balance of Payments					*Millions of US Dollars: Minus Sign Indicates Debit*								
Current Account, n.i.e......................	78ald	−45.73	−61.62	−35.04	−29.72	−58.51	−74.18	−58.03	−55.73	−71.52	−77.25	....	....
Goods: Exports f.o.b..................	78aad	14.16	16.58	23.88	43.24	32.69	26.03	38.30	37.17	41.76	52.83	....	....
Goods: Imports f.o.b.....................	78abd	−195.26	−233.63	−207.52	−215.10	−218.81	−239.03	−225.66	−231.52	−278.02	−343.95	....	....
Trade Balance...................	78acd	−181.10	−217.05	−183.64	−171.87	−186.13	−213.00	−187.36	−194.35	−236.26	−291.11	....	....
Services: Credit...........................	78add	47.01	66.90	77.52	91.31	86.45	105.06	107.58	129.68	152.83	224.08	....	....
Services: Debit...........................	78aed	−34.52	−60.50	−70.03	−71.90	−90.59	−115.82	−100.24	−119.01	−142.08	−203.25	....	....
Balance on Goods & Services.......	78afd	−168.61	−210.65	−176.15	−152.46	−190.27	−223.76	−180.01	−183.68	−225.51	−270.29	....	....
Income: Credit............................	78agd	4.22	4.00	2.98	4.87	2.51	1.90	5.03	7.53	6.41	13.14	....	....
Income: Debit...........................	78ahd	−4.56	−6.57	−7.38	−8.46	−8.07	−10.41	−17.67	−12.66	−18.26	−29.79	....	....
Balance on Gds, Serv. & Inc.........	78aid	−168.95	−213.22	−180.55	−156.05	−195.83	−232.27	−192.66	−188.81	−237.36	−286.93	....	....
Current Transfers, n.i.e.: Credit......	78ajd	125.55	155.96	148.38	129.91	142.46	167.12	146.28	155.55	181.57	228.99	....	....
Current Transfers: Debit..................	78akd	−2.33	−4.36	−2.87	−3.58	−5.15	−9.04	−11.66	−22.47	−15.73	−19.30	....	....
Capital Account, n.i.e....................	78bcd	20.07	20.88	12.83	6.30	19.01	4.47	10.76	24.36	8.64	21.07	....	....
Capital Account, n.i.e.: Credit........	78bad	20.07	20.88	12.83	6.30	19.01	4.47	10.76	24.36	8.64	−.02	....	....
Capital Account: Debit..................	78bbd								....		21.09	....	....
Financial Account, n.i.e................	78bjd	39.60	44.51	46.00	44.06	36.99	127.77	31.53	38.53	80.67	5.55	....	....
Direct Investment Abroad..............	78bdd	−.42	−.57	−.26	−.05	....	−.42	−1.36	−.52	....	....	....	....
Dir. Invest. in Rep. Econ., n.i.e........	78bed	2.13	26.18	28.53	11.58	9.04	53.32	33.42	9.11	14.81	14.78	....	....
Portfolio Investment Assets............	78bfd	....	....	....	....	....	....	−.12	1.45	....	....	....	....
Equity Securities.....................	78bkd	....	....	....	....	....	....	....	1.56	....	....	....	....
Debt Securities...........................	78bld	....	....	....	....	....	....	−.12	−.11	....	....	....	....
Portfolio Investment Liab., n.i.e......	78bgd	....	....	....	....	....	2.98	....	....	....	....	....	....
Equity Securities.....................	78bmd	....	....	....	....	....	2.98	....	....	....	....	....	....
Debt Securities...........................	78bnd	....	....	....	....	....	....	....	....	....	....	....	....
Financial Derivatives Assets............	78bwd	....	....	....	....	....	....	....	....	....	....	....	....
Financial Derivatives Liabilities.......	78bxd											....	....
Other Investment Assets...............	78bhd	1.61	−1.67	−2.25	−1.79	−22.44	−13.91	−22.01	−3.30	−2.02	−7.24	....	....
Monetary Authorities..................	78bod	1.61	2.32	−2.34	−1.84	4.02	5.19	....	−.10	−.07	1.01	....	....
General Government...................	78bpd	—		....	....	−28.39	−18.54	−21.33			−4.29	....	....
Banks....................................	78bqd	—	−3.99	.09	.05	3.02	−.05	−.68	−1.64	−1.95	−3.95	....	....
Other Sectors...........................	78brd	—	—	....	....	−1.09	−.51	....	−1.56	....	−2.00	....	....
Other Investment Liab., n.i.e........	78bid	36.28	20.57	19.99	34.33	50.39	85.79	21.60	31.79	67.89		....	....
Monetary Authorities..................	78bsd	−1.21	−.93	−.12	−.12	−.01	.17	....	.03	2.97	....	....	....
General Government...................	78btd	22.74	17.57	22.88	19.79	28.49	42.98	9.68	2.98	9.58	−21.89	....	....
Banks....................................	78bud	1.11	2.38	.02	4.94	8.00	27.18	18.83	26.93	35.96	33.10	....	....
Other Sectors...........................	78bvd	13.64	1.55	−2.80	9.72	13.91	15.45	−6.91	1.85	19.37	−13.21	....	....
Net Errors and Omissions...............	78cad	8.31	−35.64	−1.34	−20.40	13.28	−8.74	49.31	−27.77	−7.67	−5.35	....	....
Overall Balance..................	78cbd	22.24	−31.87	22.46	.24	10.76	49.31	−27.77	−16.74	10.13	−55.98	....	....
Reserves and Related Items.............	79dad	−22.24	31.87	−22.46	−.24	−10.76	−49.31	27.77	16.74	−10.13	55.98	....	....
Reserve Assets.........................	79dbd	−20.78	30.93	−19.76	9.84	−8.50	−41.86	10.27	23.37	.17	9.92	....	....
Use of Fund Credit and Loans........	79dcd	—	—	—	—	—	—	—	—	3.19	3.52	....	....
Exceptional Financing..................	79ded	−1.46	.95	−2.70	−10.08	−2.26	−7.45	17.49	−6.63	−13.49	42.54	....	....
National Accounts							*Millions of Escudos*							
Househ.Cons.Expend.,incl.NPISHs....	96f	27,790	32,532	36,529	38,861	45,081	50,194	55,966	61,176	64,422	....	....	....
Government Consumption Expend...	91f	7,228	8,587	8,061	9,950	10,028	11,882	12,217	11,975	13,410	....	....	....
Gross Fixed Capital Formation..........	93e	14,625	14,618	15,689	17,795	16,194	21,223	19,653	21,985	26,151	....	....	....
Changes in Inventories...................	93i	239	763	−667	829	−116	1,920	165	−6	−89	....	....	....
Exports of Goods and Services........	90c	6,155	6,269	7,684	9,507	10,035	12,227	13,503	13,128	15,209	....	....	....
Imports of Goods and Services (-).....	98c	22,539	25,064	25,597	30,974	29,623	35,671	36,965	38,878	46,286	....	....	....
Gross Domestic Product (GDP)........	99b	33,497	37,705	41,698	45,968	51,599	61,774	64,539	69,380	72,817	79,527	84,200	91,900
GDP Volume 1980 Prices..............	99b.p	11,422	12,278	13,100	14,100	15,287	17,100	18,342	19,468	20,497	21,456	....	....
GDP Volume (2000=100)..............	99bvp	62.3	66.9	71.4	76.9	83.3	93.2	100.0	106.1	111.7	117.0	....	....
GDP Deflator (2000=100)..............	99bip	83.3	87.3	90.5	92.7	95.9	102.7	100.0	101.3	101.0	105.3	....	....
							Millions: Midyear Estimates							
Population...............................	99z	.38	.40	.41	.42	.43	.44	.45	.46	.47	.48	.50	.51

		1994	1995	1996	1997	1998	1999	2000	2001	2002	2003	2004	2005
Exchange Rates						*Francs per SDR: End of Period*							
Official Rate	aa	† 780.44	728.38	753.06	807.94	791.61	† 896.19	918.49	935.39	850.37	771.76	747.90	794.73
						Francs per US Dollar: End of Period (ae) Period Average (rf)							
Official Rate	ae	† 534.60	490.00	523.70	598.81	562.21	† 652.95	704.95	744.31	625.50	519.36	481.58	556.04
Official Rate	rf	† 555.20	499.15	511.55	583.67	589.95	† 615.70	711.98	733.04	696.99	581.20	528.28	527.47
Fund Position						*Millions of SDRs: End of Period*							
Quota	2f.s	410.10	410.10	410.10	410.10	410.10	568.90	568.90	568.90	568.90	568.90	568.90	568.90
SDRs	1b.s	1.13	1.35	.35	.08	.24	6.50	6.19	5.26	4.13	2.32	16.35	3.88
Reserve Position in the Fund	1c.s	1.23	1.28	1.35	1.39	1.43	1.52	1.59	1.65	1.70	1.80	1.81	1.90
Total Fund Cred.&Loans Outstg	2tl	176.40	181.00	236.12	259.81	281.17	299.45	360.80	381.52	403.55	387.88	387.94	337.11
International Liquidity						*Millions of US Dollars Unless Otherwise Indicated: End of Period*							
Total Reserves minus Gold	1l.d	....	....	....	....	....	....	1,256.72	1,079.10	1,600.67	1,812.80	3,110.41	5,143.90
SDRs	1b.d	1.64	2.01	.51	.11	.33	8.93	8.06	6.61	5.62	3.45	25.39	5.55
Reserve Position in the Fund	1c.d	1.80	1.91	1.94	1.87	2.01	2.09	2.07	2.07	2.31	2.68	2.81	2.71
Foreign Exchange	1d.d	....	....	....	....	....	....	1,246.59	1,070.41	1,592.75	1,806.67	3,082.21	5,135.64
Gold (Million Fine Troy Ounces)	1ad		.229	.229	.229	.229	.229	.229	.229	.229	.229	.229	.229
Gold (National Valuation)	1and	....	† 87.89	83.93	66.29	65.59	† 66.23	62.21	63.61	78.40	95.59	78.32	91.61
Monetary Authorities: Other Liab.	4..d	....	....	....	....	....	....	.49	.49	.56	.61	.63	.51
Deposit Money Banks: Assets	7a.d	....	....	....	....	....	....	.44	.30	.53	.53	.91	.92
Liabilities	7b.d	....	....	....	....	....	....	.13	.15	.28	.28	.31	.23
Monetary Authorities						*Billions of Francs: End of Period*							
Foreign Assets	11	....	....	....	....	....	....	929.77	849.75	1,049.72	991.10	1,535.59	2,911.10
Claims on Central Government	12a	....	....	....	....	....	....	864.55	1,070.37	1,090.21	1,037.75	1,002.31	886.11
Claims on Deposit Money Banks	12e	....	....	....	....	....	....	11.43	12.34	12.84	12.86	12.27	15.00
Claims on Other Banking Insts.	12f	....	....	....	....	....	....	4.00	3.00	—	—	—	—
Reserve Money	14	....	....	....	....	....	....	1,054.43	1,113.04	1,271.89	1,288.55	1,516.18	1,926.01
of which: Currency Outside DMBs	14a	....	....	....	....	....	....	690.21	760.84	814.94	770.56	855.81	980.37
Foreign Liabilities	16c	....	....	....	....	....	....	342.03	365.31	353.04	315.71	302.70	285.30
Central Government Deposits	16d	....	....	....	....	....	....	245.77	274.38	337.84	268.43	584.89	1,407.86
Capital Accounts	17a	....	....	....	....	....	....	229.01	235.80	233.13	232.73	228.63	225.52
Other Items (Net)	17r	....	....	....	....	....	....	−61.49	−53.06	−43.14	−63.71	−82.24	−32.48
Deposit Money Banks						*Billions of Francs: End of Period*							
Reserves	20	....	....	....	....	....	....	344.42	331.88	437.54	492.77	633.62	903.29
Foreign Assets	21	....	....	....	....	....	....	311.88	224.25	333.37	274.16	437.39	511.32
Claims on Central Government	22a	....	....	....	....	....	....	293.33	288.30	308.11	283.71	290.49	272.96
Claims on Nonfin.Pub.Enterprises	22c	....	....	....	....	....	....	144.46	141.79	135.29	150.33	133.97	141.05
Claims on Private Sector	22d	....	....	....	....	....	....	1,101.02	1,198.05	1,309.97	1,389.40	1,369.97	1,565.74
Claims on Other Banking Insts	22f	....	....	....	....	....	....	.82	.64	.65	.59	.62	.63
Claims on Nonbank Financial Insts	22g	....	....	....	....	....	....	29.95	30.37	37.69	33.55	41.07	36.03
Demand Deposits	24	....	....	....	....	....	....	807.44	776.84	944.44	928.62	1,059.25	1,317.62
Time and Savings Deposits	25	....	....	....	....	....	....	633.03	729.59	849.46	948.82	1,007.06	1,135.75
Bonds	26ab	....	....	....	....	....	....	2.65	2.25	1.85	1.34	1.53	5.14
Foreign Liabilities	26c	....	....	....	....	....	....	86.86	107.35	166.65	124.77	136.84	107.98
Long-Term Foreign Liabilities	26cl	....	....	....	....	....	....	8.04	5.90	10.70	22.92	10.65	20.30
Central Government Deposits	26d	....	....	....	....	....	....	301.53	257.65	303.63	249.50	287.39	455.68
Credit from Monetary Authorities	26g	....	....	....	....	....	....	11.43	12.34	12.84	12.86	12.27	15.00
Capital Accounts	27a	....	....	....	....	....	....	383.06	385.38	390.82	430.38	474.74	510.71
Other Items (Net)	27r	....	....	....	....	....	....	−8.16	−62.01	−117.77	−94.70	−82.57	−137.16
Monetary Survey						*Billions of Francs: End of Period*							
Foreign Assets (Net)	31n	....	....	....	....	....	....	804.72	595.44	852.70	801.85	1,522.80	3,008.84
Domestic Credit	32	....	....	....	....	....	....	1,891.26	2,200.56	2,240.44	2,377.40	1,966.33	1,039.21
Claims on Central Govt. (Net)	32an	....	....	....	....	....	....	610.57	826.64	756.84	803.53	420.52	−704.46
Claims on Nonfin.Pub.Enterprises	32c	....	....	....	....	....	....	144.46	141.79	135.29	150.33	133.97	141.05
Claims on Private Sector	32d	....	....	....	....	....	....	1,101.02	1,198.05	1,309.97	1,389.40	1,369.97	1,565.74
Claims on Other Banking Insts	32f	....	....	....	....	....	....	4.82	3.64	.65	.59	.62	.63
Claims on Nonbank Financial Inst.	32g	....	....	....	....	....	....	30.38	30.44	37.69	33.55	41.24	36.26
Money	34	....	....	....	....	....	....	1,517.45	1,558.00	1,778.79	1,724.41	1,941.80	2,340.34
Quasi-Money	35	....	....	....	....	....	....	633.03	729.59	849.46	948.82	1,007.06	1,135.75
Bonds	36ab	....	....	....	....	....	....	2.65	2.25	1.85	1.34	1.53	5.14
Other Items (Net)	37r	....	....	....	....	....	....	542.84	506.17	463.04	504.69	538.74	566.82
Money plus Quasi-Money	35l	....	....	....	....	....	....	2,150.48	2,287.59	2,628.25	2,673.23	2,948.86	3,476.09
Interest Rates						*Percent Per Annum*							
Discount Rate (End of Period)	60	† 7.75	8.60	7.75	7.50	7.00	7.30	7.00	6.50	6.30	6.00	6.00	5.50
Deposit Rate	60l	5.50	5.50	5.00	5.00	5.00	5.00	5.00	5.00	5.00	5.00	5.00	4.75
Lending Rate	60p	16.00	16.00	22.00	22.00	22.00	22.00	22.00	18.00	18.00	18.00	18.00	17.00

Central African Republic 626

		1994	1995	1996	1997	1998	1999	2000	2001	2002	2003	2004	2005
Exchange Rates						*Francs per SDR: End of Period*							
Official Rate	aa	† 780.44	728.38	753.06	807.94	791.61	† 896.19	918.49	935.39	850.37	771.76	747.90	794.73
						Francs per US Dollar: End of Period (ae) Period Average (rf)							
Official Rate	ae	† 534.60	490.00	523.70	598.81	562.21	† 652.95	704.95	744.31	625.50	519.36	481.58	556.04
Official Rate	rf	† 555.20	499.15	511.55	583.67	589.95	† 615.70	711.98	733.04	696.99	581.20	528.28	527.47
						Index Numbers (2000=100): Period Averages							
Official Rate	ahx	128.1	142.3	138.8	121.8	120.5	115.5	100.0	96.9	102.2	122.4	134.6	134.8
Nominal Effective Exchange Rate	nec	98.9	107.1	109.7	105.9	106.6	104.5	100.0	100.5	102.0	106.3	108.1	107.9
Real Effective Exchange Rate	rec	94.0	112.9	115.1	102.8	102.2	100.3	100.0	107.1	116.1	123.3	122.2	120.2
Fund Position						*Millions of SDRs: End of Period*							
Quota	2f.s	41.20	41.20	41.20	41.20	41.20	55.70	55.70	55.70	55.70	55.70	55.70	55.70
SDRs	1b.s	.01	.02	.01	—	.01	.04	—	.01	.01	.01	1.58	.08
Reserve Position in the Fund	1c.s	.09	.09	.10	.10	.10	.10	.11	.11	.12	.16	.16	.16
Total Fund Cred.&Loans Outstg.	2tl	28.34	23.48	19.22	13.80	12.47	17.09	16.48	24.48	24.48	24.48	28.40	25.11
International Liquidity						*Millions of US Dollars Unless Otherwise Indicated: End of Period*							
Total Reserves minus Gold	1l.d	210.01	233.64	232.24	178.56	145.70	136.28	133.26	118.75	123.24	132.41	148.32	139.22
SDRs	1b.d	.01	.02	.01	—	.01	.05	—	.01	.01	.01	2.46	.12
Reserve Position in the Fund	1c.d	.14	.14	.14	.13	.13	.13	.15	.14	.16	.24	.25	.23
Foreign Exchange	1d.d	209.86	233.48	232.09	178.43	145.56	136.10	133.11	118.60	123.06	132.17	145.62	138.87
Gold (Million Fine Troy Ounces)	1ad	.011	.011	.011	.011	.011	.011	.011	.011	.011	.011	.011	.011
Gold (National Valuation)	1and	† 4.21	4.29	4.10	3.24	3.20	† 3.23	3.03	3.09	3.81	4.65	4.88	5.71
Monetary Authorities: Other Liab.	4..d	12.57	12.79	12.43	11.87	12.90	17.24	16.36	16.85	17.14	18.64	21.14	19.55
Deposit Money Banks: Assets	7a.d	11.45	6.39	4.41	4.99	5.91	10.48	7.96	4.52	5.84	6.33	12.95	8.80
Liabilities	7b.d	12.10	7.93	7.35	6.36	7.43	8.81	9.39	8.10	9.64	15.10	16.83	15.10
Monetary Authorities						*Billions of Francs: End of Period*							
Foreign Assets	11	114.56	116.59	123.77	108.86	83.71	91.10	96.08	90.69	79.47	71.19	73.78	80.58
Claims on Central Government	12a	41.99	36.97	37.69	32.76	32.28	37.86	41.62	44.43	46.54	50.50	60.86	69.22
Claims on Deposit Money Banks	12e	—	1.60	1.24	.50	5.00	4.79	3.14	2.25	3.34	1.82	4.07	—
Claims on Other Banking Insts.	12f	—	—	—	—	—	—	—	—	—	—	—	—
Reserve Money	14	96.65	101.04	108.82	95.35	76.11	81.96	89.59	84.01	78.96	72.64	83.73	98.28
of which: Currency Outside DMBs	14a	88.53	98.97	104.00	92.96	75.25	81.12	88.62	82.57	77.43	70.37	81.34	89.86
Foreign Liabilities	16c	28.84	23.37	20.98	18.25	17.13	26.57	26.67	35.44	31.54	28.58	31.42	30.83
Central Government Deposits	16d	1.89	1.58	2.82	1.36	.91	3.45	2.36	6.00	.85	.87	2.17	1.56
Capital Accounts	17a	1.01	.83	.90	.65	.64	.97	1.32	1.72	1.58	1.74	1.71	1.56
Other Items (Net)	17r	28.16	28.35	29.18	26.51	26.20	20.81	20.90	10.21	16.43	19.68	19.68	17.57
Deposit Money Banks						*Billions of Francs: End of Period*							
Reserves	20	8.11	2.07	4.82	2.38	.86	.84	.96	1.44	1.53	2.27	2.39	8.42
Foreign Assets	21	6.12	3.13	2.31	2.99	3.32	6.84	5.61	3.37	3.66	3.29	6.24	4.89
Claims on Central Government	22a	5.07	4.35	3.33	4.47	3.50	3.96	10.68	11.79	8.32	8.06	5.68	9.27
Claims on Nonfin.Pub.Enterprises	22c	5.84	7.65	7.14	6.37	7.97	14.71	7.99	7.95	8.06	8.44	6.74	5.65
Claims on Private Sector	22d	18.70	23.16	23.25	24.17	27.95	27.77	30.90	34.52	41.32	40.98	49.65	48.46
Claims on Other Banking Insts.	22f	—	—	—	—	—	—	—	—	—	—	—	—
Claims on Nonbank Financial Insts.	22g	—	—	—	—	—	.92	.02	—	—	—	—	—
Demand Deposits	24	14.86	12.27	12.64	14.22	12.33	17.53	13.21	16.58	17.31	15.06	16.38	23.85
Time and Savings Deposits	25	11.89	8.98	9.42	9.14	9.97	9.69	9.08	10.54	10.19	11.08	12.51	14.72
Foreign Liabilities	26c	5.80	3.45	3.43	3.45	3.52	5.66	6.61	6.03	5.78	6.15	4.26	5.04
Long-Term Foreign Liabilities	26cl	.66	.44	.42	.36	.66	.10	.01	.01	.25	1.69	3.85	3.35
Central Government Deposits	26d	3.55	7.22	7.77	7.04	4.73	6.25	10.44	5.82	6.86	4.93	5.41	4.89
Credit from Monetary Authorities	26g	—	1.60	1.24	.50	5.00	4.79	3.14	2.25	3.34	1.82	4.07	—
Capital Accounts	27a	8.70	9.35	7.78	7.44	8.20	13.35	15.49	18.92	22.42	22.21	23.23	25.52
Other Items (Net)	27r	−1.62	−2.94	−1.85	−1.77	−.79	−2.31	−1.82	−1.08	−3.25	.09	.99	−.67
Monetary Survey						*Billions of Francs: End of Period*							
Foreign Assets (Net)	31n	85.38	92.47	101.25	89.79	65.73	65.62	68.40	52.58	45.55	38.05	40.48	46.26
Domestic Credit	32	66.15	63.33	60.82	59.38	66.06	75.53	78.41	86.88	96.55	102.18	115.35	126.15
Claims on Central Govt. (Net)	32an	41.61	32.52	30.44	28.84	30.14	32.13	39.51	44.41	47.16	52.76	58.96	72.04
Claims on Nonfin.Pub.Enterprises	32c	5.84	7.65	7.14	6.37	7.97	14.71	7.99	7.95	8.06	8.44	6.74	5.65
Claims on Private Sector	32d	18.70	23.16	23.25	24.17	27.95	27.77	30.90	34.52	41.32	40.98	49.65	48.46
Claims on Other Banking Insts.	32f	—	—	—	—	—	—	—	—	—	—	—	—
Claims on Nonbank Financial Inst.	32g	—	—	—	—	—	.92	.02	—	—	—	—	—
Money	34	103.40	111.24	116.64	107.19	87.58	98.64	101.83	99.15	94.74	85.44	97.72	113.70
Quasi-Money	35	11.89	8.98	9.42	9.14	9.97	9.69	9.08	10.54	10.19	11.08	12.51	14.72
Other Items (Net)	37r	36.25	35.58	36.00	32.84	34.25	32.81	35.90	29.77	37.17	43.72	45.61	43.98
Money plus Quasi-Money	35l	115.29	120.22	126.07	116.33	97.54	108.34	110.91	109.69	104.93	96.51	110.23	128.42
Interest Rates						*Percent Per Annum*							
Discount Rate (End of Period)	60	† 7.75	8.60	7.75	7.50	7.00	7.60	7.00	6.50	6.30	6.00	6.00	5.50
Deposit Rate	60l	8.08	5.50	5.46	5.00	5.00	5.00	5.00	5.00	5.00	5.00	5.00	4.92
Lending Rate	60p	17.50	16.00	22.00	22.00	22.00	22.00	22.00	20.67	18.00	18.00	18.00	17.67
Prices						*Index Numbers (2000=100): Period Averages*							
Wholesale Prices	63	....	....	....	92.9	92.9	94.0	100.0	108.9	118.3	122.8	122.1	124.9
Consumer Prices	64	79.7	95.0	98.6	100.2	98.3	96.9	100.0	103.8	106.3	110.6	108.4	111.5
Intl. Transactions & Positions						*Millions of Francs*							
Exports	70	83,900	85,300	75,100	94,850	89,309	90,136	114,414	104,299	102,292	70,325	66,036	73,846
Imports, c.i.f.	71	77,300	86,900	72,300	82,039	86,375	80,689	83,290	78,464	83,795	74,975	79,243	87,032

Central African Republic   626

		1994	1995	1996	1997	1998	1999	2000	2001	2002	2003	2004	2005
Balance of Payments		*Millions of US Dollars: Minus Sign Indicates Debit*											
Current Account, n.i.e.	78ald	−24.7	....	....	....	....	....	....	....	....	....	....	....
Goods: Exports f.o.b.	78aad	145.9	....	....	....	....	....	....	....	....	....	....	....
Goods: Imports f.o.b.	78abd	−130.6	....	....	....	....	....	....	....	....	....	....	....
Trade Balance	78acd	15.3	....	....	....	....	....	....	....	....	....	....	....
Services: Credit	78add	33.1	....	....	....	....	....	....	....	....	....	....	....
Services: Debit	78aed	−113.8	....	....	....	....	....	....	....	....	....	....	....
Balance on Goods & Services	78afd	−65.4	....	....	....	....	....	....	....	....	....	....	....
Income: Credit	78agd	—	....	....	....	....	....	....	....	....	....	....	....
Income: Debit	78ahd	−22.7	....	....	....	....	....	....	....	....	....	....	....
Balance on Gds, Serv. & Inc.	78aid	−88.1	....	....	....	....	....	....	....	....	....	....	....
Current Transfers, n.i.e.: Credit	78ajd	92.6	....	....	....	....	....	....	....	....	....	....	....
Current Transfers: Debit	78akd	−29.2	....	....	....	....	....	....	....	....	....	....	....
Capital Account, n.i.e.	78bcd	....	....	....	....	....	....	....	....	....	....	....	....
Capital Account, n.i.e.: Credit	78bad	....	....	....	....	....	....	....	....	....	....	....	....
Capital Account: Debit	78bbd	....	....	....	....	....	....	....	....	....	....	....	....
Financial Account, n.i.e.	78bjd	52.8	....	....	....	....	....	....	....	....	....	....	....
Direct Investment Abroad	78bdd	−7.2	....	....	....	....	....	....	....	....	....	....	....
Dir. Invest. in Rep. Econ., n.i.e.	78bed	3.6	....	....	....	....	....	....	....	....	....	....	....
Portfolio Investment Assets	78bfd	....	....	....	....	....	....	....	....	....	....	....	....
Equity Securities	78bkd	....	....	....	....	....	....	....	....	....	....	....	....
Debt Securities	78bld	....	....	....	....	....	....	....	....	....	....	....	....
Portfolio Investment Liab., n.i.e.	78bgd	....	....	....	....	....	....	....	....	....	....	....	....
Equity Securities	78bmd	....	....	....	....	....	....	....	....	....	....	....	....
Debt Securities	78bnd	....	....	....	....	....	....	....	....	....	....	....	....
Financial Derivatives Assets	78bwd	....	....	....	....	....	....	....	....	....	....	....	....
Financial Derivatives Liabilities	78bxd	....	....	....	....	....	....	....	....	....	....	....	....
Other Investment Assets	78bhd	8.1	....	....	....	....	....	....	....	....	....	....	....
Monetary Authorities	78bod	....	....	....	....	....	....	....	....	....	....	....	....
General Government	78bpd	....	....	....	....	....	....	....	....	....	....	....	....
Banks	78bqd	—	....	....	....	....	....	....	....	....	....	....	....
Other Sectors	78brd	8.1	....	....	....	....	....	....	....	....	....	....	....
Other Investment Liab., n.i.e.	78bid	48.3	....	....	....	....	....	....	....	....	....	....	....
Monetary Authorities	78bsd	—	....	....	....	....	....	....	....	....	....	....	....
General Government	78btd	43.9	....	....	....	....	....	....	....	....	....	....	....
Banks	78bud	5.9	....	....	....	....	....	....	....	....	....	....	....
Other Sectors	78bvd	−1.6	....	....	....	....	....	....	....	....	....	....	....
Net Errors and Omissions	78cad	−15.0	....	....	....	....	....	....	....	....	....	....	....
Overall Balance	78cbd	13.1	....	....	....	....	....	....	....	....	....	....	....
Reserves and Related Items	79dad	−13.1	....	....	....	....	....	....	....	....	....	....	....
Reserve Assets	79dbd	−56.0	....	....	....	....	....	....	....	....	....	....	....
Use of Fund Credit and Loans	79dcd	10.3	....	....	....	....	....	....	....	....	....	....	....
Exceptional Financing	79ded	32.6	....	....	....	....	....	....	....	....	....	....	....
National Accounts		*Billions of Francs*											
Househ.Cons.Expend.,incl.NPISHs.	96f	347	429	433	438	475	460	505	558	558	550	590	610
Government Consumption Expend.	91f	78	83	67	65	65	105	106	96	96	69	70	74
Gross Fixed Capital Formation	93e	56	73	35	43	47	80	72	70	67	42	46	70
Changes in Inventories	93i	−1	6	3	12	16	—	—	—	—	—	—	—
Exports of Goods and Services	90c	111	124	111	147	129	118	133	117	110	121	94	94
Imports of Goods and Services (-)	98c	118	157	132	158	162	148	165	154	139	119	129	136
Gross Domestic Product (GDP)	99b	473	557	516	547	571	615	651	686	692	662	670	711
Net Primary Income from Abroad	98.n	−9.9	−7.8	40.5	11.5	−6.8	−4.8	−9.1	−6.3	−6.3	−6.4	−3.3	....
Gross National Income (GNI)	99a	462.7	548.9	556.0	558.8	591.7	626.0	658.6	698.4	703.0	677.6	677.4	....
GDP Volume 1985 Prices	99b.p	380.4	404.7	390.7	416.9	440.9	456.5	462.2	474.0	475.8	453.6	466.5	476.0
GDP Volume (2000=100)	99bvp	82.3	87.5	84.5	90.2	95.4	98.8	100.0	102.5	102.9	98.1	100.9	103.0
GDP Deflator (2000=100)	99bip	88.2	97.7	93.7	93.2	91.9	95.7	100.0	102.8	103.2	103.6	102.0	106.1
		Millions: Midyear Estimates											
Population	99z	3.33	3.41	3.49	† 3.57	3.65	3.71	3.78	3.84	3.89	3.94	3.99	4.04

Chad 628

		1994	1995	1996	1997	1998	1999	2000	2001	2002	2003	2004	2005
Exchange Rates						*Francs per SDR: End of Period*							
Official Rate	aa	† 780.44	728.38	753.06	807.94	791.61	† 896.19	918.49	935.39	850.37	771.76	747.90	794.73
						Francs per US Dollar: End of Period (ae) Period Average (rf)							
Official Rate	ae	† 534.60	490.00	523.70	598.81	562.21	† 652.95	704.95	744.31	625.50	519.36	481.58	556.04
Official Rate	rf	† 555.20	499.15	511.55	583.67	589.95	† 615.70	711.98	733.04	696.99	581.20	528.28	527.47
Fund Position						*Millions of SDRs: End of Period*							
Quota	2f.s	41.30	41.30	41.30	41.30	41.30	56.00	56.00	56.00	56.00	56.00	56.00	56.00
SDRs	1b.s	—	.02	.16	.01	.01	.02	—	—	.01	—	.04	.05
Reserve Position in the Fund	1c.s	.28	.28	.28	.28	.28	.28	.28	.28	.28	.28	.28	.28
Total Fund Cred.&Loans Outstg	2tl	29.30	32.97	45.20	45.31	45.34	50.17	59.96	70.88	78.50	71.28	61.78	55.55
International Liquidity					*Millions of US Dollars Unless Otherwise Indicated: End of Period*								
Total Reserves minus Gold	1l.d	76.01	142.52	164.48	135.82	120.09	95.02	110.70	122.37	218.70	187.10	221.73	225.58
SDRs	1b.d	—	.03	.24	.01	.01	.03	—	—	.01	—	.07	.07
Reserve Position in the Fund	1c.d	.41	.42	.40	.38	.40	.39	.37	.35	.38	.42	.44	.40
Foreign Exchange	1d.d	75.60	142.07	163.84	135.44	119.68	94.60	110.33	122.02	218.31	186.68	221.23	225.10
Gold (Million Fine Troy Ounces)	1ad	.011	.011	.011	.011	.011	.011	.011	.011	.011	.011	.011	.011
Gold (National Valuation)	1and	† 4.21	4.29	4.10	3.24	3.24	† 3.23	3.03	3.09	3.81	4.65	4.88	5.71
Monetary Authorities: Other Liab.	4..d	.75	.44	1.10	16.61	12.47	18.56	21.07	18.28	18.42	21.03	21.41	19.52
Deposit Money Banks: Assets	7a.d	11.09	9.91	10.55	32.35	24.20	39.72	27.66	42.53	41.20	38.59	39.38	50.35
Liabilities	7b.d	22.36	17.37	8.83	14.78	8.59	14.56	12.96	15.53	29.48	34.04	53.09	59.46
Monetary Authorities						*Billions of Francs: End of Period*							
Foreign Assets	11	42.93	75.53	88.29	83.26	69.31	64.15	80.18	93.39	139.18	99.59	109.13	128.60
Claims on Central Government	12a	48.48	49.71	61.94	65.56	64.83	73.94	89.78	101.14	106.76	93.50	105.73	121.80
Claims on Deposit Money Banks	12e	.50	1.00	7.66	5.20	10.70	4.05	.50	4.50	1.50	10.43	7.81	15.00
Claims on Other Banking Insts.	12f	—	—	—	1.50	3.85	3.30	4.00	3.00				
Reserve Money	14	47.24	74.73	98.29	94.13	84.51	79.22	92.11	108.15	145.39	130.48	139.99	185.75
of which: Currency Outside DMBs..	14a	39.69	61.98	89.36	78.81	73.62	68.25	81.27	94.77	116.80	110.92	110.11	154.10
Foreign Liabilities	16c	23.27	24.23	34.62	46.55	42.91	57.08	69.92	79.91	78.28	65.93	56.51	55.00
Central Government Deposits	16d	3.61	10.78	6.99	3.40	9.87	3.27	6.16	9.86	13.57	6.15	17.84	18.73
Capital Accounts	17a	8.38	8.44	8.81	9.03	8.94	9.93	10.42	10.78	10.05	9.41	9.26	9.64
Other Items (Net)	17r	9.41	8.06	9.18	2.40	2.46	−4.06	−4.16	−6.66	.16	−8.45	−.94	−3.72
Deposit Money Banks						*Billions of Francs: End of Period*							
Reserves	20	6.17	10.08	7.39	12.77	10.13	10.35	9.89	12.89	28.59	19.54	29.87	31.65
Foreign Assets	21	5.93	4.86	5.52	19.37	13.61	25.94	19.50	31.65	25.77	20.04	18.96	28.00
Claims on Central Government	22a	7.98	8.19	2.22	2.49	1.88	1.60	3.08	7.40	8.81	12.49	23.71	17.76
Claims on Nonfin.Pub.Enterprises..	22c	7.13	7.25	17.24	20.77	19.95	15.05	19.49	21.97	22.51	29.88	18.88	40.79
Claims on Private Sector	22d	23.75	27.79	29.95	29.16	34.03	33.89	34.31	43.29	56.48	67.08	73.10	88.27
Claims on Other Banking Insts.	22f	—	—	—	—								
Claims on Nonbank Financial Insts.	22g	—	—	—	—	.36	.27	.02	.16	.14	1.13	.87	.56
Demand Deposits	24	18.73	20.68	22.98	27.11	25.38	27.80	31.60	43.43	59.79	60.23	65.31	77.78
Time and Savings Deposits	25	2.86	7.87	5.36	5.87	5.77	6.11	7.95	9.92	11.61	11.16	13.28	15.92
Bonds	26ab	—	—	—	—	.80	—	—	—	—	—	.66	1.64
Foreign Liabilities	26c	11.22	8.42	4.62	8.79	4.83	7.52	6.87	9.70	16.07	13.41	20.09	25.36
Long-Term Foreign Liabilities	26cl	.73	.09	—	.06	—	1.99	2.27	1.86	2.37	4.27	5.48	7.70
Central Government Deposits	26d	4.91	10.84	13.27	24.60	21.36	23.71	22.77	20.20	29.59	25.51	27.71	35.37
Credit from Monetary Authorities	26g	.50	1.00	7.66	5.20	10.70	4.05	.50	4.50	1.50	10.43	7.81	15.00
Capital Accounts	27a	11.95	11.57	13.45	15.52	15.83	17.83	27.35	39.23	27.68	30.59	35.64	36.72
Other Items (Net)	27r	.06	−2.30	−5.01	−2.60	−3.90	−1.91	−13.03	−11.47	−6.29	−5.43	−10.58	−8.47
Monetary Survey						*Billions of Francs: End of Period*							
Foreign Assets (Net)	31n	13.64	47.64	54.57	47.23	35.18	23.50	20.61	33.57	68.24	36.02	46.01	68.54
Domestic Credit	32	78.82	71.33	91.09	91.48	93.68	101.07	121.75	146.90	151.56	172.42	176.74	215.09
Claims on Central Govt. (Net)	32an	47.94	36.28	43.90	40.06	35.48	48.57	63.93	78.49	72.42	74.33	83.89	85.47
Claims on Nonfin.Pub.Enterprises...	32c	7.13	7.25	17.24	20.77	19.95	15.05	19.49	21.97	22.51	29.88	18.88	40.79
Claims on Private Sector	32d	23.75	27.79	29.95	29.16	34.03	33.89	34.31	43.29	56.48	67.08	73.10	88.27
Claims on Other Banking Insts.	32f	—	—	—	1.50	3.85	3.30	4.00	3.00	—	—	—	—
Claims on Nonbank Financial Inst.	32g	—	—	—	—	.36	.27	.02	.16	.14	1.13	.87	.56
Money	34	59.79	85.33	113.88	108.47	99.75	96.67	113.82	138.69	176.59	171.17	175.44	231.89
Quasi-Money	35	2.86	7.87	5.36	5.87	5.77	6.11	7.95	9.92	11.61	11.16	13.28	15.92
Bonds	36ab	—	—	—	—	.80	—	—	—	—	—	.66	1.64
Other Items (Net)	37r	29.80	25.76	26.43	24.36	23.33	21.79	20.58	31.86	31.59	26.11	33.37	34.18
Money plus Quasi-Money	35l	62.66	93.20	119.23	114.35	105.52	102.78	121.78	148.61	188.21	182.33	188.72	247.81
Interest Rates						*Percent Per Annum*							
Discount Rate (End of Period)	60	† 7.75	8.60	7.75	7.50	7.00	7.60	7.00	6.50	6.30	6.00	6.00	5.50
Deposit Rate	60l	8.08	5.50	5.46	5.00	5.00	5.00	5.00	5.00	5.00	5.00	5.00	4.92
Lending Rate	60p	17.50	16.00	22.00	22.00	22.00	22.00	22.00	20.67	18.00	18.00	18.00	17.67
Prices						*Index Numbers (2000=100): Period Averages*							
Consumer Prices	64	78.2	85.5	95.1	100.4	104.7	96.3	100.0	112.4	118.3	116.2	110.0	113.3
Intl. Transactions & Positions						*Millions of Francs*							
Exports	70	82,160	121,273	121,895	138,130	154,455	149,635	130,200	138,300	128,685	349,295	1,191,282	1,703,722
Imports, c.i.f	71	98,310	182,400	169,733	194,732	210,207	194,523	225,697	497,417	1,147,243	459,148	396,214	448,348

Chad   628

		1994	1995	1996	1997	1998	1999	2000	2001	2002	2003	2004	2005
Balance of Payments		*Millions of US Dollars: Minus Sign Indicates Debit*											
Current Account, n.i.e.	78ald	−37.7	....	....	....	....	....	....	....	....	....	....	....
Goods: Exports f.o.b.	78aad	135.3	....	....	....	....	....	....	....	....	....	....	....
Goods: Imports f.o.b.	78abd	−212.1	....	....	....	....	....	....	....	....	....	....	....
Trade Balance	78acd	−76.8	....	....	....	....	....	....	....	....	....	....	....
Services: Credit	78add	54.8	....	....	....	....	....	....	....	....	....	....	....
Services: Debit	78aed	−199.4	....	....	....	....	....	....	....	....	....	....	....
Balance on Goods & Services	78afd	−221.4	....	....	....	....	....	....	....	....	....	....	....
Income: Credit	78agd	5.0	....	....	....	....	....	....	....	....	....	....	....
Income: Debit	78ahd	−12.4	....	....	....	....	....	....	....	....	....	....	....
Balance on Gds, Serv. & Inc.	78aid	−228.7	....	....	....	....	....	....	....	....	....	....	....
Current Transfers, n.i.e.: Credit	78ajd	209.4	....	....	....	....	....	....	....	....	....	....	....
Current Transfers: Debit	78akd	−18.4	....	....	....	....	....	....	....	....	....	....	....
Capital Account, n.i.e.	78bcd	—	....	....	....	....	....	....	....	....	....	....	....
Capital Account, n.i.e.: Credit	78bad	—	....	....	....	....	....	....	....	....	....	....	....
Capital Account: Debit	78bbd	—	....	....	....	....	....	....	....	....	....	....	....
Financial Account, n.i.e.	78bjd	76.3	....	....	....	....	....	....	....	....	....	....	....
Direct Investment Abroad	78bdd	−.6	....	....	....	....	....	....	....	....	....	....	....
Dir. Invest. in Rep. Econ., n.i.e.	78bed	27.1	....	....	....	....	....	....	....	....	....	....	....
Portfolio Investment Assets	78bfd	—	....	....	....	....	....	....	....	....	....	....	....
Equity Securities	78bkd	—	....	....	....	....	....	....	....	....	....	....	....
Debt Securities	78bld	—	....	....	....	....	....	....	....	....	....	....	....
Portfolio Investment Liab., n.i.e.	78bgd	—	....	....	....	....	....	....	....	....	....	....	....
Equity Securities	78bmd	—	....	....	....	....	....	....	....	....	....	....	....
Debt Securities	78bnd	—	....	....	....	....	....	....	....	....	....	....	....
Financial Derivatives Assets	78bwd	....	....	....	....	....	....	....	....	....	....	....	....
Financial Derivatives Liabilities	78bxd	....	....	....	....	....	....	....	....	....	....	....	....
Other Investment Assets	78bhd	.6	....	....	....	....	....	....	....	....	....	....	....
Monetary Authorities	78bod	....	....	....	....	....	....	....	....	....	....	....	....
General Government	78bpd	—	....	....	....	....	....	....	....	....	....	....	....
Banks	78bqd	−4.8	....	....	....	....	....	....	....	....	....	....	....
Other Sectors	78brd	5.4	....	....	....	....	....	....	....	....	....	....	....
Other Investment Liab., n.i.e.	78bid	49.2	....	....	....	....	....	....	....	....	....	....	....
Monetary Authorities	78bsd	−.1	....	....	....	....	....	....	....	....	....	....	....
General Government	78btd	49.8	....	....	....	....	....	....	....	....	....	....	....
Banks	78bud	—	....	....	....	....	....	....	....	....	....	....	....
Other Sectors	78bvd	−.6	....	....	....	....	....	....	....	....	....	....	....
Net Errors and Omissions	78cad	−33.0	....	....	....	....	....	....	....	....	....	....	....
Overall Balance	78cbd	5.5	....	....	....	....	....	....	....	....	....	....	....
Reserves and Related Items	79dad	−5.5	....	....	....	....	....	....	....	....	....	....	....
Reserve Assets	79dbd	−30.7	....	....	....	....	....	....	....	....	....	....	....
Use of Fund Credit and Loans	79dcd	12.7	....	....	....	....	....	....	....	....	....	....	....
Exceptional Financing	79ded	12.4	....	....	....	....	....	....	....	....	....	....	....
Government Finance		*Millions of Francs: Year Ending December 31*											
Deficit (-) or Surplus	80	−82,198	−45,532	−97,696	−65,653	−65,161	−56,178	−47,612	3,653	....	....	....	....
Total Revenue and Grants	81y	87,592	98,502	110,407	128,747	115,415	107,489	136,732	145,106	....	....	....	....
Revenue	81	31,964	44,834	59,790	72,359	77,347	79,289	88,750	96,867	....	....	....	....
Grants	81z	55,628	53,668	50,617	56,388	38,068	28,200	47,982	48,239	....	....	....	....
Exp. & Lending Minus Repay.	82z	169,790	144,034	208,103	194,400	180,576	163,667	184,344	141,453	....	....	....	....
Expenditure	82	148,300	130,304	151,794	159,400	153,028	163,667	184,344	141,453	....	....	....	....
Lending Minus Repayments	83	21,490	13,730	56,309	35,000	27,548	—	—	—	....	....	....	....
Statistical Discrepancy	80xx	−1,341	31,313	22,600	46,377	13,208	32,642	−23,310	34,390	....	....	....	....
Total Financing	80h	80,857	76,845	120,296	112,030	78,369	88,820	24,302	30,737	....	....	....	....
Domestic	84a	−460	−5,817	14,546	28,432	5,041	32,650	9,658	1,141	....	....	....	....
Foreign	85a	81,317	82,662	105,750	83,598	73,328	56,170	14,644	29,596	....	....	....	....
Total Debt by Residence	88	423,574	435,728	489,035	546,857	525,691	642,939	800,014	862,293	....	....	....	....
Domestic	88a	6,503	5,481	4,236	7,108	7,310	24,000	65,113	66,300	....	....	....	....
Foreign	89a	417,071	430,247	484,799	539,749	518,381	618,939	734,901	795,993	....	....	....	....
National Accounts		*Billions of Francs*											
Gross Domestic Product (GDP)	99b	655.0	717.8	822.0	911.0	1,003.0	947.0	986.0	1,246.0	1,377.0	1,582.0	2,324.0	2,799.8
		Millions: Midyear Estimates											
Population	99z	6.83	7.03	7.25	7.47	7.70	7.95	8.22	8.51	8.81	9.13	9.45	9.75

Chile 228

		1994	1995	1996	1997	1998	1999	2000	2001	2002	2003	2004	2005
Exchange Rates					*Pesos per SDR: End of Period*								
Market Rate	aa	589.91	605.19	611.09	593.41	667.08	727.53	746.15	824.67	968.49	890.72	869.42	734.94
					Pesos per US Dollar: End of Period (ae) Period Average (rf)								
Market Rate	ae	404.09	407.13	424.97	439.81	473.77	530.07	572.68	656.20	712.38	599.42	559.83	514.21
Market Rate	rf	420.18	396.77	412.27	419.30	460.29	508.78	539.59	634.94	688.94	691.43	609.37	560.09
					Index Numbers (2000=100): Period Averages								
Market Rate	ahx	128.2	135.9	130.6	128.4	117.0	106.0	100.0	85.3	78.3	79.2	87.8	96.3
Nominal Effective Exchange Rate	nec	103.1	108.9	108.1	113.0	108.2	101.8	100.0	89.5	87.2	82.6	89.2	94.6
Real Effective Exchange Rate	rec	92.9	98.5	100.5	107.8	105.8	100.8	100.0	90.3	87.3	82.0	87.0	92.3
Fund Position					*Millions of SDRs: End of Period*								
Quota	2f.s	621.7	621.7	621.7	621.7	621.7	856.1	856.1	856.1	856.1	856.1	856.1	856.1
SDRs	1b.s	.5	2.1	1.3	1.0	5.9	13.5	18.9	23.0	26.9	30.7	33.9	36.6
Reserve Position in the Fund	1c.s	—	—	35.0	232.0	429.6	299.4	248.8	245.7	360.9	392.3	287.0	131.4
Total Fund Cred.&Loans Outstg	2tl	199.5	—	—	—	—	—	—	—	—	—	—	—
International Liquidity					*Millions of US Dollars Unless Otherwise Indicated: End of Period*								
Total Reserves minus Gold	1l.d	13,087.6	14,139.8	14,972.6	17,573.2	15,869.3	14,616.6	15,034.9	14,379.0	15,341.1	15,839.6	15,993.8	16,929.2
SDRs	1b.d	.7	3.1	1.9	1.3	8.3	18.5	24.6	28.9	36.5	45.7	52.6	52.3
Reserve Position in the Fund	1c.d	—	—	50.4	313.1	604.9	411.0	324.2	308.7	490.7	582.9	445.8	187.8
Foreign Exchange	1d.d	13,086.9	14,136.7	14,920.3	17,258.9	15,256.1	14,187.1	14,686.1	14,041.3	14,813.9	15,211.0	15,495.4	16,689.1
Gold (Million Fine Troy Ounces)	1ad	1.864	1.861	1.859	1.858	1.222	1.220	.074	.074	.008	.008	.008	.008
Gold (National Valuation)	1and	652.0	642.8	637.4	533.0	321.9	316.9	318.3	18.6	2.3	2.7	3.0	3.3
Monetary Authorities: Other Liab	4..d	2,573.3	1,596.2	7.9	353.6	330.6	488.6	316.9	286.1	243.5	244.4	269.0	318.8
Banking Institutions: Assets	7a.d	549.1	491.7	605.2	1,522.0	2,441.5	5,638.7	5,162.5	4,096.0	2,494.5	1,959.0	2,679.1	3,346.6
Liabilities	7b.d	—	—	—	2,151.7	2,267.5	1,505.2	1,214.0	5,627.1	6,009.7	8,163.1	10,361.4	12,665.9
Nonbank Financial Insts.: Assets	7e.d	199.3	51.6	148.5	384.7	1,779.6	4,628.5	3,912.0	4,724.8	5,877.6	11,749.5	16,484.5	22,656.1
Monetary Authorities					*Billions of Pesos: End of Period*								
Foreign Assets	11	5,999.0	6,439.5	7,230.9	† 8,062.0	7,784.1	8,097.1	8,770.8	† 9,616.6	11,006.6	9,673.9	9,147.6	8,918.4
Claims on Central Government	12a	3,597.8	3,805.1	3,817.6	† 3,863.8	3,890.8	4,099.6	4,546.3	† 5,049.0	5,069.6	4,088.2	3,324.1	2,234.4
Claims on State and Local Govts	12b	—	—	—	—	—	—	—	† —	—	—	—	—
Claims on Nonfin.Pub.Enterprises	12c	—	—	—	† —	—	—	—	† —	—	—	—	—
Claims on Private Sector	12d	188.0	200.8	224.8	† 837.6	846.3	863.5	878.5	† 880.8	892.6	924.3	934.7	947.0
Claims on Banking Institutions	12e	2,440.7	2,454.6	2,257.2	† 635.1	482.4	567.9	578.0	† 688.4	132.3	101.7	145.4	62.1
Claims on Nonbank Financial Insts	12g	....	....	....	....	....	....	....	....	....	....	....	....
Reserve Money	14	994.5	1,206.7	1,345.4	† 1,824.3	2,003.4	2,093.2	1,945.7	† 2,653.2	2,573.4	2,909.6	3,550.2	4,571.2
of which: Currency Outside Banks	14a	667.3	784.2	859.5	† 978.5	969.5	1,167.9	1,113.7	† 1,214.7	1,301.5	1,390.0	1,584.6	1,830.1
Other Liabs. to Banking Insts	14n	2,077.6	2,293.0	2,405.1	† 3,115.3	2,714.2	3,649.1	4,163.7	† —				
Time, Savings,& Fgn.Currency Dep	15	258.9	110.9	62.7	† 3.3	1.7	4.3	.4	† 20.1	21.8	20.4	19.0	8.8
Liabs. of Central Bank: Securities	16ac	4,967.7	5,658.2	6,862.5	† 7,424.9	7,304.3	7,144.8	7,987.6	† 12,414.1	13,313.6	12,417.9	11,170.3	9,928.9
Restricted Deposits	16b	....	....	....	....	....	....	....	....	....	....	....	....
Foreign Liabilities	16c	1,157.6	649.9	3.4	† 155.5	156.6	259.0	181.5	† 187.7	173.5	146.5	150.6	164.0
Central Government Deposits	16d	1,573.3	1,753.7	2,011.3	† 2,131.2	1,919.9	1,326.0	966.3	† 1,173.5	492.3	126.6	205.4	258.1
Liab. to Nonbank Financial Insts	16j												
Capital Accounts	17a	−113.3	374.1	268.3	† −1,319.0	−1,796.6	−1,535.9	−1,432.3	† −206.9	615.6	−819.4	−1,527.7	−2,752.0
Other Items (Net)	17r	1,309.0	853.5	571.8	† 62.9	700.2	687.8	960.5	† −7.1	−89.1	−13.4	−15.9	−16.9
Banking Institutions					*Billions of Pesos: End of Period*								
Reserves	20	713.0	719.9	750.9	† 664.8	911.5	916.0	880.3	† 948.6	931.2	1,512.7	1,962.4	2,729.8
Claims on Mon.Author.:Securities	20c	2,077.6	2,293.0	2,405.1	† 3,115.3	2,714.2	3,649.1	4,163.7	† 4,913.2	6,135.3	5,203.0	5,452.9	4,654.6
Other Claims on Monetary Author	20n	....	....	....	....	....	....	....	....	....	....	....	....
Foreign Assets	21	221.0	199.4	256.5	† 669.4	1,156.7	2,988.9	2,956.5	† 2,687.8	1,777.0	1,174.3	1,499.8	1,720.9
Claims on Central Government	22a	56.6	84.0	137.0	† 320.2	264.8	247.2	315.0	† 335.3	432.3	330.6	394.2	451.7
Claims on Local Government	22b	.4	.5	.5	† .4	.3	.3	.3	† .7	.7	.6	.6	.9
Claims on Nonfin.Pub.Enterprises	22c	124.6	95.4	88.7	† 133.5	550.0	128.2	73.3	† 247.5	61.3	160.8	161.6	229.7
Claims on Private Sector	22d	10,953.1	13,871.5	16,675.1	† 18,745.3	20,470.3	21,995.4	24,876.8	† 27,916.7	30,153.2	31,949.0	36,961.5	43,478.4
Claims on Nonbank Financial Insts	22g				† 697.9	617.2	760.7	407.4	† 829.8	240.0	436.4	567.1	615.8
Demand Deposits	24	1,212.7	1,515.5	1,816.9	† 2,101.0	1,967.1	2,233.3	2,531.3	† 2,847.6	3,129.3	3,551.0	4,148.2	4,676.8
Time, Savings,& Fgn.Currency Dep	25	6,250.2	8,021.0	9,788.5	† 12,497.1	14,702.0	16,537.2	18,110.9	† 18,933.2	20,297.9	19,931.5	23,509.2	28,342.2
Money Market Instruments	26aa	2,114.8	2,904.1	3,728.1	† 4,096.4	4,120.4	4,987.3	5,394.8	† 5,508.9	5,163.0	4,431.5	4,018.3	2,900.0
Restricted Deposits	26b	....	....	....	....	....	....	....	....	....	....	....	....
Foreign Liabilities	26c	1,720.7	1,613.0	1,544.4	† 946.4	1,074.3	797.9	695.2	† 3,692.5	4,281.2	4,893.1	5,800.6	6,513.0
Central Government Deposits	26d	490.2	708.7	686.2	† 816.5	664.3	898.9	774.4	† 1,090.4	1,170.7	1,258.9	1,461.3	2,679.3
Credit from Monetary Authorities	26g	443.3	361.7	326.5	† 228.4	176.8	119.9	140.3	† 561.5	262.8	699.0	1,062.5	419.7
Liabs. to Nonbank Financial Insts	26j	437.4	425.3	323.1	† 3,029.1	2,568.3	3,239.5	3,875.3	† 3,531.5	4,884.9	5,433.8	6,924.2	8,008.1
Capital Accounts	27a	2,334.5	3,133.0	3,743.7	† 2,509.0	2,848.2	3,075.7	3,492.9	† 3,781.1	4,069.5	4,343.8	4,669.0	5,134.8
Other Items (Net)	27r	−857.5	−1,418.6	−1,643.7	† −1,877.0	−1,436.5	−1,203.9	−1,341.8	† −2,067.1	−3,528.4	−3,775.4	−4,593.2	−4,792.3
Banking Survey					*Billions of Pesos: End of Period*								
Foreign Assets (Net)	31n	3,341.7	4,375.9	5,939.6	† 7,629.5	7,709.9	10,029.2	10,850.6	† 8,424.1	8,328.9	5,808.6	4,696.2	3,962.4
Domestic Credit	32	12,856.9	15,595.1	18,246.2	† 21,651.1	24,055.5	25,870.2	29,356.8	† 32,995.9	35,186.6	36,504.4	40,677.2	45,020.4
Claims on Central Govt. (Net)	32an	1,590.8	1,426.8	1,257.1	† 1,236.3	1,571.4	2,122.0	3,120.5	† 3,120.4	3,838.9	3,033.3	2,051.6	−251.4
Claims on Local Government	32b	.4	.5	.5	† .4	.3	.3	.3	† .7	.7	.6	.6	.9
Claims on Nonfin.Pub.Enterprises	32c	124.6	95.4	88.7	† 133.5	550.0	128.2	73.3	† 247.5	61.3	160.8	161.6	229.7
Claims on Private Sector	32d	11,141.1	14,072.3	16,899.9	† 19,582.9	21,316.6	22,859.0	25,755.3	† 28,797.4	31,045.7	32,873.3	37,896.3	44,425.4
Claims on Nonbank Financial Insts	32g	—	—	—	† 697.9	617.2	760.7	407.4	† 829.8	240.0	436.4	567.1	615.8
Money	34	1,880.2	2,300.0	2,677.0	† 3,079.5	2,936.5	3,401.2	3,645.2	† 4,062.3	4,430.8	4,941.0	5,732.8	6,506.9
Quasi-Money	35	6,509.1	8,131.9	9,851.2	† 12,500.4	14,703.8	16,541.4	18,111.3	† 18,953.2	20,319.7	19,951.9	23,528.2	28,351.0
Money Market Instruments	36aa	2,114.8	2,904.1	3,728.1	† 4,096.4	4,120.4	4,987.3	5,394.8	† 5,508.9	5,163.0	4,431.5	4,018.3	2,900.0
Liabs. of Central Bank: Securities	36ac	4,967.7	5,658.2	6,862.5	† 7,424.9	7,304.3	7,144.8	7,987.6	† 12,414.1	13,313.6	12,417.9	11,170.3	9,928.9
Restricted Deposits	36b												
Liabs. to Nonbank Financial Insts	36j	437.4	425.3	323.1	† 3,029.1	2,568.3	3,239.5	3,875.3	† 3,531.5	4,884.9	5,433.8	6,924.2	8,008.1
Capital Accounts	37a	2,221.2	3,507.1	4,012.0	† 1,190.0	1,051.6	1,539.8	2,060.6	† 3,574.2	4,685.1	3,524.4	3,141.2	2,382.8
Other Items (Net)	37r	−1,931.8	−2,955.7	−3,268.1	† −2,039.7	−919.4	−954.7	−867.5	† −6,624.3	−9,281.7	−8,387.4	−9,141.7	−9,094.9
Money plus Quasi-Money	35l	8,389.3	10,431.9	12,528.1	† 15,579.9	17,640.3	19,942.6	21,756.5	† 23,015.5	24,750.5	24,892.9	29,261.0	34,857.9

Chile 228

		1994	1995	1996	1997	1998	1999	2000	2001	2002	2003	2004	2005
Nonbank Financial Institutions						*Billions of Pesos End of Period*							
Reserves..................	40	....	....	....	....	....	....	....	—	—	—	—	—
Claims on Mon.Author.:Securities....	40c	3,462.9	3,883.0	4,538.6	4,937.3	5,521.9	5,670.3	6,566.5	† 6,958.9	6,224.2	5,646.4	4,252.2	4,072.8
Other Claims on Monetary Author....	40n	....	....	....	....	....	....	....	—	—	—	—	—
Foreign Assets..................	41	80.5	21.0	63.1	169.2	843.1	2,453.4	2,240.3	† 3,100.4	4,187.1	7,042.9	9,228.5	11,650.0
Claims on Central Government........	42a	108.3	195.7	384.5	428.7	505.2	655.9	790.0	† 1,172.1	1,428.8	1,641.1	2,073.8	2,229.5
Claims on State and Local Govts......	42b	....	....	....	....	....	....	....	—	—	—	—	—
Claims on Nonfin.Pub.Enterprises....	42c	....	....	....	....	....	....	....	—	—	—	—	—
Claims on Private Sector........	42d	3,452.3	3,582.9	3,478.7	3,510.9	2,691.5	2,866.7	3,116.8	† 3,740.1	4,134.7	6,279.1	7,370.5	7,920.9
Claims on Banking Institutions.........	42e	1,809.4	2,401.2	2,875.2	4,096.9	4,732.3	6,177.0	7,371.3	† 7,710.8	8,983.8	7,757.0	9,590.6	11,066.5
Restricted Deposits..................	46b	....	....	....	....	....	....	....	—	—	—	—	—
Foreign Liabilities..................	46c	14.3	118.0	138.1	148.5	160.9	194.9	242.8	† 263.4	294.6	329.3	378.1	415.7
Central Government Deposits...........	46d	....	....	....	....	....	....	....	—	—	—	—	—
Credit from Monetary Authorities.....	46g	....	....	....	....	....	....	....	—	—	—	—	—
Credit from Banking Institutions.......	46h	....	....	....	....	....	....	....	—	—	—	—	—
Capital Accounts..................	47a	.3	2.2	1.8	1.9	.4	.5	.5	† .1	.1	241.4	239.3	90.8
Insurance Technical Reserves..........	47d	8,983.3	10,228.8	11,553.9	13,404.0	14,552.2	18,092.5	20,342.9	† 22,955.9	25,226.9	28,935.2	33,271.7	37,806.2
Other Items (Net)..................	47r	−84.5	−265.2	−353.7	−411.5	−419.5	−464.5	−501.3	† −537.0	−563.0	−1,139.4	−1,373.5	−1,372.9
Money (National Definitions)						*Billions of Pesos End of Period*							
Base Money..................	19ma	878.9	1,068.5	1,211.3	1,395.2	1,396.8	1,786.9	1,713.4	1,894.1	1,983.2	2,094.4	2,329.2	2,928.1
M1..................	59ma	1,928.3	2,222.1	2,544.4	2,962.7	2,793.1	3,246.3	3,498.1	3,897.1	4,263.2	4,698.4	5,512.5	6,241.8
M1A..................	59maa	2,096.1	2,588.7	2,859.6	3,333.6	3,149.0	3,791.9	4,145.4	4,311.7	5,062.6	5,792.1	7,148.6	7,913.7
M2A..................	59mba	6,882.1	8,877.1	10,813.9	13,148.0	14,839.8	16,539.5	18,006.5	18,523.6	19,755.8	19,800.5	24,377.1	29,958.4
M3..................	59mc	8,203.5	10,401.0	12,503.2	15,029.2	16,708.2	18,514.5	20,165.2	20,830.0	22,091.2	22,049.5	26,562.7	32,204.5
M4..................	59md	13,271.7	16,037.0	19,286.8	23,141.3	24,681.1	26,574.7	29,385.2	30,013.0	30,486.0	30,649.2	33,991.6	38,732.2
M5..................	59me	13,283.5	16,042.3	19,286.8	23,141.3	24,681.1	26,574.7	29,385.2	30,013.0	30,486.0	30,861.1	34,627.2	39,735.2
M6..................	59mf	15,086.8	18,539.3	22,488.5	27,245.8	28,962.0	31,451.1	34,644.7	35,622.6	36,078.1	36,529.0	40,062.3	44,127.0
M7..................	59mg	15,703.7	19,149.4	23,022.7	27,806.9	30,088.7	33,189.8	36,821.5	38,330.8	38,945.4	39,231.9	42,837.1	47,266.8
Interest Rates						*Percent Per Annum*							
Discount Rate (End of Period)...........	60	13.89	7.96	11.75	7.96	9.12	7.44	8.73	6.50	3.00	2.45	2.25	4.50
Money Market Rate..................	60b	....	....	....	....	....	....	10.09	6.81	4.08	2.72	1.88	3.48
Savings Rate..................	60k	3.53	3.53	3.51	3.50	3.50	3.50	3.50	2.39	.69	.26	.22	.20
Deposit Rate..................	60l	15.12	13.73	13.48	12.02	14.92	8.56	9.20	6.19	3.80	2.73	1.94	3.93
Deposit Rate (Foreign Currency).......	60l.f	4.05	5.45	5.24	5.02	4.41	4.39	5.48	3.51	1.59	1.39	1.63	2.94
Lending Rate..................	60p	20.34	18.16	17.37	15.67	20.17	12.62	14.84	11.89	7.76	6.18	5.13	6.68
Lending Rate (Foreign Currency).......	60p.f	8.42	9.96	9.27	9.49	8.73	7.38	7.76	5.50	3.83	3.37	2.95	4.44
Prices, Production, Labor						*Index Numbers (2000=100): Period Averages*							
Industrial Share Prices..................	62	108.1	137.6	122.8	111.3	83.3	90.3	100.0	106.6	104.2	131.4	174.3	212.1
Prices: Home & Import Goods..........	63	72.1	77.5	82.4	83.7	85.3	89.8	100.0	107.8	115.2	122.8	125.8	132.6
Home Goods..................	63a	71.2	77.8	83.0	85.1	86.0	89.5	100.0	105.9	112.4	120.2	126.2	134.8
Consumer Prices..................	64	71.9	77.8	83.5	88.7	93.2	96.3	100.0	103.6	106.1	109.1	110.3	113.6
Wages, Hourly..................	65a	59.2	66.7	76.6	83.2	89.7	95.0	100.0	105.2	110.0	114.2	117.5	† 123.3
Manufacturing Production..............	66ey	84.5	88.6	91.9	96.4	96.5	96.5	100.0	101.9	† 102.6	108.0	116.6	123.1
Mining Production..................	66zx	51.6	57.2	70.2	76.6	81.6	94.8	100.0	101.6	98.0	104.4	114.7	113.5
Copper Production..................	66c	47.9	53.9	67.2	73.9	79.6	95.4	100.0	102.6	99.6	105.6	116.6	114.7
Employment..................	67	94.8	95.9	97.2	99.3	101.2	98.9	100.0	100.3	101.4	104.5	106.4	109.7
						Number in Thousands: Period Averages							
Labor Force..................	67d	5,300	5,274	5,601	5,684	5,852	5,934	5,871	5,949	6,000	6,128	6,358	....
Employment..................	67e	† 4,988	5,026	† 5,299	5,380	5,432	5,405	5,382	5,479	5,531	5,675	5,863	....
Unemployment..................	67c	† 427	402	350	344	384	572	536	535	529	515	546	507
Unemployment Rate (%)..................	67r	† 5.9	4.7	5.4	5.3	7.2	8.9	8.3	7.9	7.8	7.4	8.8	8.0
Intl. Transactions & Positions						*Millions of US Dollars*							
Exports..................	70..d	11,604	16,024	16,627	17,870	16,323	17,162	19,210	18,272	18,180	21,664	32,215	40,574
Imports, c.i.f..................	71..d	11,820	15,900	19,199	20,822	19,882	15,987	18,507	17,429	17,091	19,389	24,918	32,637
Imports, f.o.b..................	71.vd	10,872	14,643	17,699	19,298	18,363	14,735	17,091	16,428	15,794	17,979	23,020	30,394

Chile   228

		1994	1995	1996	1997	1998	1999	2000	2001	2002	2003	2004	2005
Balance of Payments		*Millions of US Dollars: Minus Sign Indicates Debit*											
Current Account, n.i.e.	78ald	−1,586	−1,350	−3,083	−3,660	−3,918	99	−898	−1,100	−580	−964	1,586	703
Goods: Exports f.o.b.	78aad	11,604	16,025	16,627	17,870	16,323	17,162	19,210	18,272	18,180	21,664	32,215	40,574
Goods: Imports f.o.b.	78abd	−10,872	−14,644	−17,699	−19,298	−18,363	−14,735	−17,091	−16,428	−15,794	−17,979	−23,020	−30,394
Trade Balance	78acd	732	1,381	−1,072	−1,428	−2,040	2,427	2,119	1,844	2,386	3,685	9,195	10,180
Services: Credit	78add	2,840	3,333	3,588	3,892	3,952	3,869	4,083	4,138	4,386	4,986	6,063	7,172
Services: Debit	78aed	−2,990	−3,657	−3,589	−4,028	−4,404	−4,606	−4,802	−4,983	−5,087	−5,631	−6,752	−7,760
Balance on Goods & Services	78afd	582	1,057	−1,073	−1,563	−2,492	1,690	1,400	999	1,684	3,039	8,507	9,591
Income: Credit	78agd	556	869	842	1,170	1,196	912	1,598	1,458	1,114	1,433	1,809	2,160
Income: Debit	78ahd	−3,056	−3,582	−3,359	−3,787	−3,085	−3,145	−4,453	−3,985	−3,960	−6,042	−9,808	−12,784
Balance on Gds, Serv. & Inc.	78aid	−1,917	−1,657	−3,590	−4,180	−4,381	−543	−1,456	−1,527	−1,163	−1,569	507	−1,033
Current Transfers, n.i.e.: Credit	78ajd	449	482	665	835	810	841	765	713	954	901	1,418	2,199
Current Transfers: Debit	78akd	−118	−175	−158	−315	−348	−198	−207	−286	−372	−296	−339	−464
Capital Account, n.i.e.	78bcd	—	—	—	—	—	—	—	—	83	—	5	—
Capital Account, n.i.e.: Credit	78bad	—	—	—	—	—	—	—	—	83	—	5	—
Capital Account: Debit	78bbd	—	—	—	—	—	—	—	—	—	—	—	—
Financial Account, n.i.e.	78bjd	5,294	2,357	5,660	6,742	1,966	237	787	1,362	1,634	1,265	−2,209	2,145
Direct Investment Abroad	78bdd	−911	−752	−1,133	−1,463	−1,483	−2,558	−3,987	−1,610	−343	−1,606	−1,527	−2,146
Dir. Invest. in Rep. Econ., n.i.e.	78bed	2,583	2,957	4,815	5,271	4,628	8,761	4,860	4,200	2,550	4,307	7,173	6,667
Portfolio Investment Assets	78bfd	−351	−14	−135	−989	−3,311	−5,795	766	−1,386	−3,316	−4,579	−4,674	−4,003
Equity Securities	78bkd	−351	−14	−43	−743	−2,518	−3,474	821	−2,094	−3,272	−4,734	−3,447	−3,800
Debt Securities	78bld	—	—	−92	−246	−792	−2,321	−55	708	−44	154	−1,227	−202
Portfolio Investment Liab., n.i.e.	78bgd	1,259	48	1,269	2,614	842	2,578	−127	1,525	999	2,054	1,122	1,470
Equity Securities	78bmd	1,259	−249	700	1,720	580	524	−427	−217	−320	318	8	1,635
Debt Securities	78bnd	—	297	569	894	262	2,054	300	1,742	1,319	1,736	1,114	−165
Financial Derivatives Assets	78bwd	—	—	—	—	—	....	....	....	1,788	1,840	639	1,244
Financial Derivatives Liabilities	78bxd	—	—	−22	165	−59	−6	2	−86	−1,912	−1,722	−723	−1,307
Other Investment Assets	78bhd	−152	−309	−855	−457	−1,953	−3,369	−2,065	−1,326	1,141	−571	−3,389	−2,047
Monetary Authorities	78bod	−57	10	—	—	—	—	—	—	—	−60	—	—
General Government	78bpd	—	—	—	—	—	—	—	—	—	1	—	—
Banks	78bqd	−26	57	−87	−547	−381	−1,642	653	145	635	299	−166	−557
Other Sectors	78brd	−70	−376	−768	90	−1,572	−1,727	−2,717	−1,471	505	−811	−3,223	−1,490
Other Investment Liab., n.i.e.	78bid	2,865	427	1,721	1,600	3,303	626	1,338	44	728	1,543	−829	2,267
Monetary Authorities	78bsd	−99	−402	−74	−24	−74	−66	36	−47	−2	−3	6	—
General Government	78btd	−99	−1,323	−545	−386	−171	−101	−128	−132	−294	−117	−115	−209
Banks	78bud	407	−322	−444	−1,498	−36	−36	−840	−278	771	1,302	1,606	170	1,253
Other Sectors	78bvd	2,656	2,474	2,784	3,508	3,584	1,633	1,707	−548	−279	57	−890	1,222
Net Errors and Omissions	78cad	−557	132	16	237	−239	−1,083	427	−861	−952	−658	426	−1,137
Overall Balance	78cbd	3,151	1,139	2,593	3,318	−2,191	−747	317	−599	185	−357	−191	1,711
Reserves and Related Items	79dad	−3,151	−1,139	−2,593	−3,318	2,191	747	−317	599	−185	357	191	−1,711
Reserve Assets	79dbd	−2,918	−740	−1,119	−3,318	2,191	747	−317	599	−185	357	191	−1,711
Use of Fund Credit and Loans	79dcd	−210	−298	—	—	—	—	—	—	—	—	—	—
Exceptional Financing	79ded	−22	−101	−1,475	—	—	—	—	—	—	—	—	—
International Investment Position		*Millions of US Dollars*											
Assets	79aad	....	....	....	32,134	36,815	46,699	47,007	47,245	49,839	60,998	75,955	91,237
Direct Investment Abroad	79abd	....	....	—	5,110	6,735	9,000	11,154	11,720	12,239	13,681	17,377	21,286
Portfolio Investment	79acd	....	....	—	1,176	4,717	11,402	9,876	10,562	13,019	21,374	28,512	37,027
Equity Securities	79add	....	....	—	902	3,411	7,670	6,911	7,870	10,682	18,753	24,281	32,725
Debt Securities	79aed	....	....	—	274	1,306	3,732	2,965	2,692	2,337	2,621	4,231	4,301
Financial Derivatives	79ald	....	....	....	—	—	—	—	406	268	535	995	1,023
Other Investment	79afd	....	....	598	7,575	9,071	11,344	10,863	10,148	8,961	9,557	13,056	14,939
Monetary Authorities	79agd	....	....	—	—	—	—	—	—	—	62	65	60
General Government	79ahd	....	....	—	—	—	—	—	—	—	—	—	—
Banks	79aid	....	....	598	1,055	1,284	2,741	2,486	2,341	1,706	1,403	1,573	2,130
Other Sectors	79ajd	....	....	—	6,520	7,787	8,603	8,377	7,807	7,255	8,091	11,418	12,749
Reserve Assets	79akd	....	....	15,660	18,273	16,292	14,952	15,114	14,410	15,352	15,852	16,016	16,962
Liabilities	79lad	....	....	....	66,973	71,588	80,230	82,219	81,218	80,906	98,494	106,169	123,451
Dir. Invest. in Rep. Economy	79lbd	....	....	—	34,523	37,630	43,498	45,753	43,482	42,311	54,082	60,540	73,620
Portfolio Investment	79lcd	....	....	6,417	9,172	7,966	10,611	9,187	10,121	10,527	14,632	16,192	18,174
Equity Securities	79ldd	....	....	5,223	7,111	5,704	6,451	4,701	3,590	2,304	3,974	4,622	7,021
Debt Securities	79led	....	....	1,194	2,061	2,262	4,159	4,486	6,532	8,223	10,658	11,571	11,153
Financial Derivatives	79lld	....	....	—	—	—	—	—	363	102	222	695	954
Other Investment	79lfd	....	....	21,367	23,279	25,992	26,122	27,278	27,252	27,966	29,558	28,741	30,703
Monetary Authorities	79lgd	....	....	189	166	92	26	62	15	13	10	17	17
General Government	79lhd	....	....	2,653	2,284	2,183	2,094	1,920	1,742	1,467	1,392	1,287	1,059
Banks	79lid	....	....	3,599	2,106	2,185	1,438	1,158	1,927	3,229	4,834	4,999	6,253
Other Sectors	79ljd	....	....	14,926	18,723	21,533	22,563	24,138	23,568	23,257	23,322	22,438	23,375
Government Finance		*Billions of Pesos: Year Ending December 31*											
Deficit (-) or Surplus	80	361.9	667.7	657.8	623.3	131.8	−502.4	56.4	....	....	....	....	....
Total Revenue and Grants	81y	4,822.8	5,747.7	6,626.3	7,358.9	7,726.9	7,737.8	8,976.1	....	....	....	....	....
Revenue	81	4,822.8	5,747.7	6,626.3	7,358.9	7,726.9	7,737.8	8,976.1	....	....	....	....	....
Grants	81z	—	—	—	—	—	—	—	....	....	....	....	....
Exp. & Lending Minus Repay	82z	4,460.9	5,080.1	5,968.5	6,735.6	7,595.1	8,240.2	8,919.7	....	....	....	....	....
Expenditure	82	4,482.0	5,137.1	5,982.8	6,695.3	7,575.8	8,235.4	8,853.3	....	....	....	....	....
Lending Minus Repayments	83	−21.1	−57.0	−14.3	40.3	19.3	4.8	66.4	....	....	....	....	....
Total Debt by Residence	88	5,477.7	5,056.4	4,719.1	4,588.0	4,657.6	5,159.4	5,606.9	....	....	....	....	....
Domestic	88a	3,305.6	3,432.1	3,392.0	3,476.5	3,491.6	3,684.3	4,129.2	....	....	....	....	....
Foreign	89a	2,172.1	1,624.3	1,327.1	1,111.5	1,165.9	1,475.1	1,477.7	....	....	....	....	....

Chile 228

National Accounts		1994	1995	1996	1997	1998	1999	2000	2001	2002	2003	2004	2005
							Billions of Pesos						
Househ.Cons.Expend.,incl.NPISHs....	96f	14,648.7	17,270.3	19,785.0	21,972.0	23,703.6	23,927.9	25,897.2	27,772.0	29,241.8	31,341.2	33,447.3	36,863.3
Government Consumption Expend...	91f	2,420.1	2,938.5	3,426.1	3,860.5	4,197.1	4,603.8	5,053.9	5,480.8	5,943.9	6,313.9	6,944.6	7,505.5
Gross Fixed Capital Formation..........	93e	5,649.2	7,117.9	8,240.7	9,414.2	9,545.7	7,740.1	8,410.7	9,456.7	9,879.1	10,769.3	11,724.8	14,285.3
Changes in Inventories....................	93i	110.3	294.9	312.9	211.8	281.7	22.8	457.4	159.6	157.0	414.4	638.3	555.4
Exports of Goods and Services..........	90c	6,544.1	8,295.4	8,520.5	9,404.2	9,608.6	10,992.3	12,820.2	14,501.0	15,773.5	18,665.0	23,597.3	27,003.9
Imports of Goods and Services (-).....	98c	6,158.5	7,672.6	9,047.9	10,140.1	10,801.9	10,148.4	12,064.1	13,833.3	14,653.5	16,549.4	18,446.6	21,664.4
Gross Domestic Product (GDP)..........	99b	23,714.7	28,309.2	31,237.3	34,722.6	36,534.9	37,138.5	40,575.3	43,536.8	46,341.8	50,954.4	57,905.7	64,549.1
Net Primary Income from Abroad......	98.n	−1,072.3	−1,106.4	−1,033.0	−1,104.5	−869.6	−1,132.6	−1,552.5	−1,588.0	−1,965.1	−3,166.6	−4,876.7	−5,924.7
Gross National Income (GNI)...........	99a	20,322.9	24,769.3	30,204.3	33,618.1	35,665.3	36,005.9	39,022.8	41,948.8	44,376.8	47,787.8	53,029.0	58,624.4
Consumption of Fixed Capital..........	99cf	1,957.3	2,269.8	4,122.4	4,424.2	4,644.6	5,007.2	5,257.3	5,706.9	6,184.2	6,579.1	7,562.5	....
Net National Income....................	99e	20,461.7	24,892.5	30,414.1	33,837.0	35,879.9	36,410.1	39,151.9	40,860.7	....	....	....	....
GDP Vol.1996 Prices......................	99b.p	26,289.6	29,084.5	31,237.3	33,300.7	34,376.6	34,115.0	35,646.5	36,850.3	37,655.1	39,130.1	41,541.8	44,178.9
GDP Volume (2000=100)...............	99bvp	73.8	81.6	87.6	93.4	96.4	95.7	100.0	103.4	105.6	109.8	116.5	123.9
GDP Deflator (2000=100)...............	99bip	79.2	85.5	87.9	91.6	93.4	95.6	100.0	103.8	108.1	114.4	122.5	128.4
						Millions: Midyear Estimates							
Population................................	99z	14.16	14.39	14.62	14.83	15.03	15.22	15.41	15.60	15.78	15.95	16.12	16.30

China, P.R.: Mainland   924

		1994	1995	1996	1997	1998	1999	2000	2001	2002	2003	2004	2005
Exchange Rates						*Yuan per SDR: End of Period*							
Market Rate..................aa=.........	wa	12.3302	12.3637	11.9325	11.1715	11.6567	11.3637	10.7847	10.4017	11.2532	12.2989	12.8535	11.5345
					Yuan per US Dollar: End of Period (we) Period Average (wf)								
Market Rate..................ae=.........	we	8.4462	8.3174	8.2982	8.2798	8.2787	8.2795	8.2774	8.2768	8.2773	8.2767	8.2765	8.0702
Market Rate..................rf=.........	wf	8.6187	8.3514	8.3142	8.2898	8.2790	8.2783	8.2785	8.2771	8.2770	8.2770	8.2768	8.1943
					Index Numbers (2000=100): Period Averages								
Nominal Effective Exchange Rate.....	nec	83.21	82.20	86.00	92.55	100.56	98.38	100.00	105.55	105.08	98.61	94.17	94.27
Real Effective Exchange Rate...........	rec	76.04	84.72	93.21	100.36	105.69	99.97	100.00	104.30	101.89	95.20	92.70	92.48
Fund Position						*Millions of SDRs: End of Period*							
Quota..	2f.s	3,385	3,385	3,385	3,385	3,385	4,687	4,687	6,369	6,369	6,369	6,369	6,369
SDRs...	1b.s	369	392	427	447	480	540	613	677	734	741	803	875
Reserve Position in the Fund............	1c.s	517	818	971	1,682	2,523	1,685	1,462	2,061	2,738	2,556	2,138	973
Total Fund Cred.&Loans Outstg........	2tl	—	—	—	—	—	—	—	—	—	—	—	—
International Liquidity					*Millions of US Dollars Unless Otherwise Indicated: End of Period*								
Total Reserves Minus Gold..............	1l.d	52,914	75,377	107,039	142,762	149,188	157,728	168,278	215,605	291,128	408,151	614,500	821,514
SDRs..	1b.d	539	582	614	602	676	741	798	851	998	1,102	1,247	1,251
Reserve Position in the Fund.........	1c.d	755	1,216	1,396	2,270	3,553	2,312	1,905	2,590	3,723	3,798	3,320	1,391
Foreign Exchange........................	1d.d	51,620	73,579	105,029	139,890	144,959	154,675	165,574	212,165	286,407	403,251	609,932	818,872
Gold (Million Fine Troy Ounces)........	1ad	12.7	12.7	12.7	12.7	12.7	12.7	12.7	16.1	19.3	19.3	19.3	19.3
Gold (National Valuation)................	1and	646	660	637	601	624	608	578	3,093	4,074	4,074	4,074	4,074
Banking Institutions: Liabilities.........	7b.d	44,890	50,370	55,990	59,035	54,685	† 47,057	49,536	37,477	47,317	53,221	64,588	62,868
Monetary Authorities						*Billions of Yuan: End of Period*							
Foreign Assets......................	11	445.13	666.95	956.22	1,345.21	1,376.17	1,485.75	1,558.28	1,986.04	2,324.29	3,114.18	4,696.01	6,343.99
Claims on General Government........	12a	168.77	158.28	158.28	158.28	158.28	158.28	158.28	282.13	286.38	290.10	296.96	289.24
Claims on Other Sectors...............	12d	72.83	68.01	65.87	17.10	10.38	10.15	11.02	19.55	20.67	20.63	13.63	6.67
Claims on Deposit Money Banks......	12e	1,045.10	1,151.03	1,451.84	1,435.79	1,305.75	1,537.39	1,351.92	1,131.16	998.26	1,061.95	937.64	781.77
Claims on Other Banking Insts.........	12f	26.99	18.16	11.77	207.23	296.28	383.31	860.04	854.73	† 230.51	136.33	104.79	487.43
Claims on Nonbank Financial Insts...	12g	....	....	....	....	....	....	....	....	724.03	725.60	886.51	1,322.61
Reserve Money......................	14	1,721.78	2,075.98	2,688.85	3,063.28	3,133.53	3,362.00	3,649.15	3,985.17	4,513.82	5,284.14	5,885.61	6,434.31
Of which Curr.Outside Banking Inst	14a	728.44	788.19	879.89	1,017.46	1,120.07	1,345.21	1,464.99	1,568.73	1,727.80	1,974.60	2,131.29	2,365.61
Bonds..	16ab	—	19.71	—	11.89	11.89	11.89	—	—	148.75	303.16	1,107.90	2,029.60
Foreign Liabilities........................	16c	—	—	—	22.29	20.14	39.90	39.39	50.91	42.31	48.26	56.23	64.16
General Government Deposits..........	16d	83.33	97.34	122.54	148.59	172.61	178.55	310.04	285.05	308.54	495.47	583.22	752.72
Capital Accounts...........................	17a	29.49	40.04	39.51	39.27	39.44	39.37	38.23	37.98	24.64	24.89	25.02	24.71
Other Items (Net).........................	17r	−75.78	−170.64	−206.92	−121.70	−230.76	−56.82	−97.26	−85.50	−453.93	−807.12	−722.45	−73.78
Banking Institutions						*Billions of Yuan: End of Period*							
Reserves..	20	768.59	1,006.41	1,387.00	1,645.68	1,511.15	1,610.78	1,619.32	1,817.14	2,041.32	2,428.93	3,739.81	4,028.35
Foreign Assets...............................	21	440.47	390.50	428.68	531.95	600.90	646.58	903.57	1,017.55	1,284.31	1,147.86	1,429.77	1,797.19
Claims on General Government.......	22a	47.82	105.73	182.30	151.98	498.79	607.94	739.31	1,104.51	1,355.36	1,523.22	1,849.78	1,983.21
Claims on Other Sectors................	22d	4,104.28	5,097.18	6,358.26	7,693.40	8,951.61	9,986.66	11,132.41	12,180.33	† 14,280.97	17,249.40	19,186.46	20,943.62
Claims on Nonbank Financial Insts...	22g	....	....	....	....	....	....	....	....	903.62	1,314.89	791.80	1,044.08
Demand Deposits...........................	24	1,238.99	1,520.16	1,876.49	2,381.03	2,648.57	3,235.62	3,846.88	4,414.01	5,356.21	6,431.42	7,442.32	8,314.92
Savings Deposits............................	25aa	2,051.60	2,804.55	3,637.34	4,363.52	5,020.57	5,580.51	5,975.44	6,785.08	7,954.16	9,463.32	11,955.54	14,105.10
Time Deposits...............................	25ab	194.31	332.42	504.19	673.85	830.19	947.68	1,126.11	1,418.01	1,643.38	2,094.04	2,538.22	3,310.00
Foreign Currency Deposits...............	25b	....	....	....	....	....	....	....	....	1,215.91	1,188.43	1,212.86	1,235.86
Other Deposits..............................	25e	292.13	377.70	401.74	315.07	383.55	496.20	586.97	679.86	804.18	1,021.00	1,062.62	1,536.78
Bonds...	26ab	21.30	18.91	29.98	354.18	520.38	635.46	742.89	844.80	1,010.24	1,165.40	1,520.35	2,037.88
Foreign Liabilities..........................	26c	379.15	418.95	464.61	488.80	452.72	† 389.61	410.03	310.19	391.66	440.50	534.57	507.36
Credit from Monetary Authorities.....	26g	1,034.44	1,119.78	1,423.29	1,403.85	1,206.98	828.92	913.44	964.67	1,243.39	1,086.14	980.29	784.48
Liabilities to Nonbank Fin. Insts.......	26j	....	....	....	....	....	....	....	....	856.73	995.55	951.54	1,012.70
Capital Accounts...........................	27a	343.25	351.58	411.37	428.59	658.27	626.34	739.67	765.98	877.22	1,072.93	1,179.14	1,403.24
Other Items (Net).........................	27r	−194.01	−344.23	−392.77	−385.88	−158.78	111.64	53.18	−63.07	−1,487.51	−1,294.43	−2,379.83	−4,451.87
Banking Survey						*Billions of Yuan: End of Period*							
Foreign Assets (Net)......................	31n	506.45	638.50	920.29	1,366.07	1,504.20	1,702.82	2,012.43	2,642.48	3,174.63	3,773.29	5,534.99	7,569.66
Domestic Credit.............................	32	4,310.37	5,331.86	6,642.17	7,954.34	9,546.87	10,701.30	11,873.21	13,487.60	17,262.47	20,628.36	22,441.91	24,836.71
Claims on General Govt. (Net).......	32an	133.26	166.67	218.04	161.67	484.47	587.67	587.55	1,101.59	1,333.19	1,317.85	1,563.52	1,519.73
Claims on Other Sectors...............	32d	4,177.11	5,165.19	6,424.13	7,710.50	8,961.99	9,996.82	11,143.43	12,199.89	† 14,301.64	17,270.02	19,200.09	20,950.29
Claims on Nonbank Financial Insts.	32g	....	....	....	....	....	....	....	....	1,627.64	2,040.49	1,678.30	2,366.69
Money...	34	1,967.43	2,308.35	2,756.38	3,480.65	3,869.05	4,697.64	5,454.10	6,168.85	7,088.18	8,411.86	9,581.54	10,690.32
Quasi-Money..................................	35	2,724.60	3,766.00	4,853.15	5,706.13	6,686.96	7,406.57	8,141.93	9,472.34	† 11,412.52	13,710.43	15,723.69	19,147.69
Foreign Currency Deposits...............	35b	....	....	....	....	....	....	....	....	1,215.91	1,188.43	1,212.86	1,235.86
Bonds...	36ab	21.30	38.62	29.98	356.31	526.40	642.69	742.12	844.23	1,079.66	1,173.93	1,678.71	2,388.23
Capital Accounts...........................	37a	372.74	391.62	450.88	467.86	697.71	665.70	777.90	803.96	901.86	1,097.82	1,204.15	1,427.94
Other Items (Net).........................	37r	−269.25	−534.23	−527.93	−690.53	−729.05	−1,008.46	−1,230.39	−1,159.30	† −1,261.02	−1,180.80	−1,424.06	−2,483.67
Money plus Quasi-Money...............	35l	4,692.03	6,074.35	7,609.53	9,186.78	10,556.01	12,104.21	13,596.02	15,641.19	18,500.70	22,122.28	25,305.23	29,838.01
Interest Rates						*Percent per Annum*							
Bank Rate......................................	60	10.08	10.44	9.00	8.55	4.59	3.24	3.24	3.24	2.70	2.70	3.33	3.33
Deposit Rate..................................	60l	10.98	10.98	7.47	5.67	3.78	2.25	2.25	2.25	1.98	1.98	2.25	2.25
Lending Rate..................................	60p	10.98	12.06	10.08	8.64	6.39	5.85	5.85	5.85	5.31	5.31	5.58	5.58
Prices, Production, Labor					*Percent Change over Corresponding Period of Previous Year*								
Consumer Prices.............................	64..x	24.2	16.9	8.3	2.8	−.8	−1.4	.3	.5	−.8	1.2	4.0	1.8
Industrial Production.......................	66..x	21.4	16.1	15.1	13.2	9.6	9.8	11.2	9.9	....	....	....	....
						Number in Thousands: Period Averages							
Employment..................................	67e	674,550	680,650	689,500	698,200	706,370	713,940	720,850	730,250	737,400	744,320	752,000	....
Unemployment..............................	67c	4,764	5,196	5,528	5,768	5,710	5,750	5,950	6,810	7,700	8,000	8,270	....
Unemployment Rate (%)..................	67r	2.8	2.9	3.0	3.0	3.1	3.1	3.1	3.6	4.0	4.3	4.2	....
Intl. Transactions & Positions						*Millions of US Dollars*							
Exports..	70..d	121,006	148,780	151,048	182,792	183,712	194,931	249,203	266,098	325,591	437,899	593,439	762,068
Imports, c.i.f..................................	71..d	115,614	132,084	138,833	142,370	140,237	165,699	225,094	243,553	295,171	413,062	560,683	660,159

China, P.R.: Mainland 924

Balance of Payments		1994	1995	1996	1997	1998	1999	2000	2001	2002	2003	2004	2005
		Millions of US Dollars: Minus Sign Indicates Debit											
Current Account, n.i.e.	78ald	6,908	1,618	7,243	36,963	31,472	21,115	20,518	17,401	35,422	45,875	68,659	160,818
Goods: Exports f.o.b.	78aad	102,561	128,110	151,077	182,670	183,529	194,716	249,131	266,075	325,651	438,270	593,393	762,484
Goods: Imports f.o.b.	78abd	−95,271	−110,060	−131,542	−136,448	−136,915	−158,734	−214,657	−232,058	−281,484	−393,618	−534,410	−628,295
Trade Balance	78acd	7,290	18,050	19,535	46,222	46,614	35,982	34,474	34,017	44,167	44,652	58,982	134,189
Services: Credit	78add	16,620	19,130	20,601	24,569	23,895	26,248	30,430	33,334	39,745	46,734	62,434	74,404
Services: Debit	78aed	−16,299	−25,223	−22,585	−27,967	−26,672	−31,589	−36,031	−39,267	−46,528	−55,306	−72,133	−83,795
Balance on Goods & Services	78afd	7,611	11,958	17,551	42,824	43,837	30,641	28,874	28,084	37,383	36,079	49,284	124,798
Income: Credit	78agd	5,737	5,191	7,318	5,710	5,584	8,330	12,550	9,388	8,344	16,095	20,544	38,959
Income: Debit	78ahd	−6,775	−16,965	−19,755	−16,715	−22,228	−22,800	−27,216	−28,563	−23,289	−23,933	−24,067	−28,324
Balance on Gds, Serv. & Inc	78aid	6,573	184	5,114	31,819	27,193	16,171	14,207	8,909	22,438	28,241	45,761	135,433
Current Transfers, n.i.e.: Credit	78ajd	1,269	1,827	2,368	5,477	4,661	5,368	6,861	9,125	13,795	18,482	24,326	27,735
Current Transfers: Debit	78akd	−934	−392	−239	−333	−382	−424	−550	−633	−811	−848	−1,428	−2,349
Capital Account, n.i.e	78bcd	—	—	—	−21	−47	−26	−35	−54	−50	−48	−69	4,102
Capital Account, n.i.e.: Credit	78bad	—	—	—	—	—	—	....	....	—	—	—	4,155
Capital Account: Debit	78bbd	—	—	—	−21	−47	−26	−35	−54	−50	−48	−69	−53
Financial Account, n.i.e.	78bjd	32,645	38,674	39,966	21,037	−6,275	5,204	1,958	34,832	32,341	52,774	110,729	58,862
Direct Investment Abroad	78bdd	−2,000	−2,000	−2,114	−2,563	−2,634	−1,775	−916	−6,884	−2,518	152	−1,805	−11,306
Dir. Invest. in Rep. Econ., n.i.e.	78bed	33,787	35,849	40,180	44,237	43,751	38,753	38,399	44,241	49,308	47,077	54,936	79,127
Portfolio Investment Assets	78bfd	−380	79	−628	−899	−3,830	−10,535	−11,307	−20,654	−12,095	2,983	6,486	−26,157
Equity Securities	78bkd	—	—	—	—	....	—	—	32	—	—	—	—
Debt Securities	78bld	−380	79	−628	−899	−3,830	−10,535	−11,307	−20,686	−12,095	2,983	6,486	−26,157
Portfolio Investment Liab., n.i.e.	78bgd	3,923	710	2,372	7,842	98	−699	7,317	1,249	1,752	8,444	13,203	21,224
Equity Securities	78bmd	....	....	....	5,657	765	612	6,912	849	2,249	7,729	10,923	20,346
Debt Securities	78bnd	3,923	710	2,372	2,185	−667	−1,311	405	400	−497	715	2,280	878
Financial Derivatives Assets	78bwd	....	....	....	....	....	....	....	....	....	....	....	....
Financial Derivatives Liabilities	78bxd	....	....	....	—	—	—	—	—	....	....	....	....
Other Investment Assets	78bhd	−1,189	−1,081	−1,126	−39,608	−35,041	−24,394	−43,864	20,813	−3,077	−17,922	1,980	−48,947
Monetary Authorities	78bod	....	....	....	−7,977	−2,417	−5,715	−7,261	−5,387	—	—	—	−4,354
General Government	78bpd	−1,136	−367	−1,102	—	....	....	....	....	....	....	....	....
Banks	78bqd	....	....	....	−12,572	2,841	6,075	−21,430	16,800	−10,258	−15,733	2,959	−23,656
Other Sectors	78brd	−53	−714	−24	−19,059	−35,465	−24,754	−15,173	9,400	7,181	−2,189	−979	−20,938
Other Investment Liab., n.i.e.	78bid	−1,496	5,116	1,282	12,028	−8,619	3,854	12,329	−3,933	−1,029	12,040	35,928	44,921
Monetary Authorities	78bsd	1,004	1,154	1,256	−2,037	−5,441	−3,936	—	—	—	—	—	1,778
General Government	78btd	5,178	6,021	4,995	—	—	3,233	3,153	1,124	40	−2,758	999	−360
Banks	78bud	−5,222	−4,045	−5,959	6,968	−3,150	−5,021	−8,281	−1,305	−1,725	10,269	13,375	9,186
Other Sectors	78bvd	−2,456	1,986	990	7,097	−28	9,578	17,457	−3,752	655	4,529	21,554	34,318
Net Errors and Omissions	78cad	−9,100	−17,823	−15,504	−22,122	−18,902	−17,641	−11,748	−4,732	7,504	17,985	26,834	−16,441
Overall Balance	78cbd	30,453	22,469	31,705	35,857	6,248	8,652	10,693	47,447	75,217	116,586	206,153	207,342
Reserves and Related Items	79dad	−30,453	−22,469	−31,705	−35,857	−6,248	−8,652	−10,693	−47,447	−75,217	−116,586	−206,153	−207,342
Reserve Assets	79dbd	−30,453	−22,469	−31,705	−35,857	−6,248	−8,652	−10,693	−47,447	−75,217	−116,586	−206,153	−207,342
Use of Fund Credit and Loans	79dcd	—	—	—	—	—	—	—	—	—	—	—	—
Exceptional Financing	79ded	....	....	....	....	—	—	....	....	—	....	....	—

International Investment Position													
		Millions of US Dollars											
Assets	79aad	....	....	....	....	....	....	....	....	....	....	925,430	1,218,172
Direct Investment Abroad	79abd	....	....	....	....	....	....	....	....	....	....	52,704	64,493
Portfolio Investment	79acd	....	....	....	....	....	....	....	....	....	....	92,028	116,739
Equity Securities	79add	....	....	....	....	....	....	....	....	....	....	....	....
Debt Securities	79aed	....	....	....	....	....	....	....	....	....	....	92,028	116,739
Financial Derivatives	79ald	....	....	....	....	....	....	....	....	....	....	....	....
Other Investment	79afd	....	....	....	....	....	....	....	....	....	....	162,124	211,247
Monetary Authorities	79agd	....	....	....	....	....	....	....	....	....	....	....	....
General Government	79ahd	....	....	....	....	....	....	....	....	....	....	....	....
Banks	79aid	....	....	....	....	....	....	....	....	....	....	....	....
Other Sectors	79ajd	....	....	....	....	....	....	....	....	....	....	....	....
Reserve Assets	79akd	....	....	....	....	....	....	....	....	....	....	618,574	825,693
Liabilities	79lad	....	....	....	....	....	....	....	....	....	....	805,105	930,692
Dir. Invest. in Rep. Economy	79lbd	....	....	....	....	....	....	....	....	....	....	536,954	610,162
Portfolio Investment	79lcd	....	....	....	....	....	....	....	....	....	....	56,623	76,617
Equity Securities	79ldd	....	....	....	....	....	....	....	....	....	....	43,290	63,636
Debt Securities	79led	....	....	....	....	....	....	....	....	....	....	13,332	12,981
Financial Derivatives	79lld	....	....	....	....	....	....	....	....	....	....	—	—
Other Investment	79lfd	....	....	....	....	....	....	....	....	....	....	211,529	243,913
Monetary Authorities	79lgd	....	....	....	....	....	....	....	....	....	....	....	....
General Government	79lhd	....	....	....	....	....	....	....	....	....	....	....	....
Banks	79lid	....	....	....	....	....	....	....	....	....	....	....	....
Other Sectors	79ljd	....	....	....	....	....	....	....	....	....	....	....	....

Government Finance													
		Billions of Yuan: Year Ending December 31											
Deficit (-) or Surplus	80	−94.07	−90.93	−86.70	−92.70	−125.57	−203.39	−277.03	−438.29	−309.78	−291.69	....	....
Total Revenue and Grants	81y	521.81	624.22	740.80	865.11	987.60	1,144.40	1,339.50	1,476.00	1,917.35	2,191.71	....	....
Exp. & Lending Minus Repay	82z	615.88	715.15	827.50	957.81	1,113.17	1,347.79	1,616.53	1,914.29	2,227.13	2,483.40	....	....
Financing													
Domestic	84a	63.64	69.96	55.35	56.44	95.25	188.26	260.49	256.90	319.33	315.69	....	....
Foreign	85a	3.06	−3.68	6.53	−.60	.56	−9.10	−.45	3.61	−9.53	4.61	....	....
Use of Cash Balances	87	−9.25	−8.13	−7.93	—	−3.58	−4.80	−10.56	....	....	....	....	....

China, P.R.: Mainland 924

		1994	1995	1996	1997	1998	1999	2000	2001	2002	2003	2004	2005
National Accounts							*Billions of Yuan*						
Househ.Cons.Expend.,incl.NPISHs....	96f	2,081.0	2,694.5	3,215.2	3,485.5	3,692.1	3,933.4	4,291.1	4,592.3	4,888.2	5,268.6	6,383.4	....
Government Consumption Expend...	91f	598.6	669.1	785.2	872.5	948.5	1,038.8	1,170.5	1,302.9	1,391.7	1,480.8	2,319.9	....
Gross Fixed Capital Formation.........	93e	1,685.6	2,030.1	2,333.6	2,515.4	2,763.1	2,947.6	3,262.4	3,681.3	4,191.8	5,130.4	6,511.7	....
Changes in Inventories....................	93i	240.4	357.7	353.1	330.3	191.5	122.6	−12.4	64.8	38.7	25.1	405.1	....
Exports (Net)..............................	90n	63.4	99.9	145.9	285.7	305.2	244.9	224.0	220.5	279.4	268.2	407.9	....
Gross Domestic Product (GDP)........	99b	4,669.1	5,851.1	6,833.0	7,489.4	7,900.3	8,267.3	8,934.1	9,859.3	10,789.8	12,173.0	16,028.0	18,232.1
Net Primary Income from Abroad.....	98.n	1,901.9	1,278.1	954.6	928.0	1,106.3	1,108.5	869.2	−161.3	−786.8	−1,991.6	−5,443.2	....
Gross National Income (GNI)...........	99a	6,571.0	7,129.1	7,787.6	8,417.4	9,006.6	9,375.8	9,803.3	9,698.0	10,003.0	10,181.4	10,584.8	....
GDP Volume 1995 Prices................	99b.p	5,491.4	5,985.8	6,569.6	7,133.8	7,690.7	8,242.6	8,934.1	9,577.8	10,430.9	11,494.4	12,632.6	....
GDP Volume (2000=100)...............	99bvp	61.5	67.0	73.5	79.8	86.1	92.3	100.0	107.2	116.8	128.7	141.4	....
GDP Deflator (2000=100)...............	99bip	85.0	97.7	104.0	105.0	102.7	100.3	100.0	102.9	103.4	105.9	126.9	....
							Millions: Midyear Estimates						
Population.................................	99z	1,207.6	1,219.3	1,231.0	1,242.4	1,253.5	1,264.1	1,274.0	1,283.2	1,291.8	1,300.0	1,308.0	1,315.8

China, P.R.: Hong Kong 532

		1994	1995	1996	1997	1998	1999	2000	2001	2002	2003	2004	2005
Exchange Rates		*Hong Kong Dollars per SDR: End of Period*											
Market Rate....................	aa	11.296	11.494	11.124	10.451	10.907	10.666	10.157	9.799	10.602	11.536	12.072	11.080
		Hong Kong Dollars per US Dollar: End of Period (ae) Period Average (rf)											
Market Rate....................	ae	7.738	7.732	7.736	7.746	7.746	7.771	7.796	7.797	7.798	7.763	7.774	7.753
Market Rate....................	rf	7.728	7.736	7.734	7.742	7.745	7.758	7.791	7.799	7.799	7.787	7.788	7.777
		Index Numbers (2000=100) Period Averages											
Nominal Effective Exchange Rate.....	nec	91.80	87.53	89.97	94.00	99.13	97.79	100.00	103.69	102.62	97.42	93.68	92.91
Fund Position		*Millions of SDRs: End of Period*											
Reserve Position in the Fund...........	1c.s	—	—	—	—	31.34	—	—	—	—	—	—	—
of which: Outstg.Fund Borrowing...	2c					31.34							
International Liquidity		*Billions of US Dollars Unless Otherwise Indicated: End of Period*											
Total Reserves minus Gold..............	1l.d	49.25	55.40	63.81	92.80	89.65	96.24	107.54	111.16	111.90	118.36	123.54	124.24
Reserve Position in the Fund..........	1c.d	—	—	—	—	.04	—	—	—	—	—	—	—
Foreign Exchange.........................	1d.d	49.25	55.40	63.81	† 92.80	† 89.61	96.24	107.54	111.16	111.90	118.36	123.54	124.24
Gold (Million Fine Troy Ounces)........	1ad	.068	.067	.067	.067	.067	.067	.067	.067	.067	.067	.067	.067
Gold (National Valuation)...............	1and	.026	.026	.025	.019	.019	.019	.018	.019	.023	.028	.029	.034
Banking Institutions: Assets.............	7a.d	614.80	655.58	608.62	600.63	501.17	475.78	450.48	405.22	394.41	440.28	508.07	512.64
Liabilities...................	7b.d	582.33	620.40	579.85	597.32	447.35	371.87	319.15	264.39	244.74	267.03	308.54	305.69
Monetary Authorities		*Billions of Hong Kong Dollars: End of Period*											
Foreign Assets.............................	11	297.27	376.59	463.89	549.97	672.68	691.27	803.69	822.50	832.87	868.65	904.91	884.91
Reserve Money..........................	14	79.88	82.96	87.12	92.71	94.77	† 234.39	215.40	229.74	246.11	292.67	294.87	283.98
of which: Currency Outside Banks..	14a	67.31	70.87	76.05	80.34	80.92	99.27	91.51	101.38	112.98	127.61	140.55	142.05
Foreign Liabilities.........................	16c	1.54	.03	.32	.04	.27	.04	19.82	42.08	1.67	1.01	.10	1.19
Government Deposits.....................	16d	131.24	125.92	145.90	237.63	424.56	392.21	417.16	380.60	301.67	252.30	280.09	297.09
Capital Accounts.........................	17a	125.77	160.13	172.86	190.21	242.22	290.86	307.10	302.59	327.17	384.88	423.59	443.15
Other Items (Net).........................	17r	−41.17	7.56	57.69	29.38	−89.15	−226.22	−155.79	−132.51	−43.75	−62.21	−93.75	−140.48
Banking Institutions		*Billions of Hong Kong Dollars: End of Period*											
Reserves..................................	20	12.57	12.09	11.07	12.37	13.85	32.67	14.34	12.53	11.91	41.18	28.36	15.51
Foreign Assets.............................	21	4,757.31	5,068.93	4,708.31	4,652.49	3,882.07	3,697.31	3,511.95	3,159.51	3,075.65	3,417.93	3,949.50	3,974.24
Claims on Government..................	22a	106.77	57.25	104.74	143.61	140.34	166.64	201.19	212.75	234.12	220.67	272.53	255.26
Claims on Other Sectors..................	22d	1,506.39	1,671.93	1,935.32	2,324.36	2,181.93	1,964.83	2,010.95	1,968.19	1,890.33	1,837.65	1,906.44	2,017.10
Demand Deposits........................	24	83.38	80.32	98.33	87.44	79.07	85.35	93.05	109.51	127.39	196.44	231.83	173.63
Time, Savings,& Fgn.Currency Dep...	25	1,534.82	1,713.81	1,923.57	2,113.05	2,374.65	2,560.47	2,816.59	2,781.96	2,768.92	2,874.11	3,060.47	3,235.28
Money Market Instruments..............	26aa	71.26	82.62	107.13	118.16	116.51	110.77	103.79	107.79	143.08	170.67	190.98	207.59
Foreign Liabilities........................	26c	4,506.08	4,796.95	4,485.74	4,626.87	3,465.16	2,889.78	2,488.13	2,061.42	1,908.48	2,072.93	2,398.47	2,369.83
Government Deposits.....................	26d	18.87	14.43	19.09	5.16	6.15	3.78	2.93	1.46	2.51	2.38	4.16	5.61
Capital Accounts.........................	27a	113.03	132.61	153.91	170.34	153.67	154.03	164.10	204.27	207.72	188.87	214.60	234.21
Other Items (Net).........................	27r	55.58	−10.56	−28.33	11.78	22.98	57.27	69.84	86.58	53.91	12.01	56.33	35.95
Banking Survey		*Billions of Hong Kong Dollars: End of Period*											
Foreign Assets (Net)......................	31n	546.96	648.53	686.14	575.54	1,089.32	1,498.76	1,807.70	1,878.52	1,998.37	2,212.64	2,455.84	2,488.14
Domestic Credit..........................	32	1,463.04	1,588.84	1,875.07	2,225.17	1,891.55	1,735.49	1,792.05	1,798.88	1,820.27	1,803.64	1,894.73	1,969.66
Claims on Government (net)...........	32an	−43.34	−83.10	−60.25	−99.18	−290.38	−229.34	−218.90	−169.31	−70.06	−34.00	−11.71	−47.44
Claims on Other Sectors..............	32d	1,506.39	1,671.93	1,935.32	2,324.36	2,181.93	1,964.83	2,010.95	1,968.19	1,890.33	1,837.65	1,906.44	2,017.10
Money..................................	34	150.70	151.19	174.38	167.78	159.99	184.62	184.56	210.88	240.37	324.06	372.38	315.69
Quasi-Money.............................	35	1,534.82	1,713.81	1,923.57	2,113.05	2,374.65	2,560.47	2,816.59	2,781.96	2,768.92	2,874.11	3,060.47	3,235.28
Money Market Instruments..............	36aa	71.26	82.62	107.13	118.16	116.51	110.77	103.79	107.79	143.08	170.67	190.98	207.59
Capital Accounts.........................	37a	238.81	292.75	326.77	360.55	395.89	444.89	471.20	506.86	534.90	573.75	638.19	677.36
Other Items (Net).........................	37r	14.40	−3.00	29.36	41.16	−66.17	−66.49	23.61	69.90	131.37	73.69	88.54	21.88
Money plus Quasi-Money..............	35l	1,685.52	1,865.00	2,097.95	2,280.84	2,534.64	2,745.08	3,001.15	2,992.84	3,009.29	3,198.17	3,432.85	3,550.97
Interest Rates		*Percent Per Annum*											
Discount Rate (End of Period)...........	60	5.75	6.25	6.00	7.00	6.25	7.00	8.00	3.25	2.75	2.50	3.75	5.75
Money Market Rate.......................	60b	5.44	6.00	5.13	4.50	5.50	5.75	7.13	2.69	1.50	.07	.13	4.25
Treasury Bill Rate.........................	60c	5.66	5.55	4.45	7.50	5.04	4.94	5.69	1.69	1.35	−.08	.07	3.65
Deposit Rate.............................	60l	3.54	5.63	4.64	5.98	6.62	4.50	4.80	2.38	.35	.07	.03	1.26
Lending Rate............................	60p	8.50	8.75	8.50	9.50	9.50	8.50	9.50	5.13	5.00	5.00	5.00	7.75
Prices, Production, Labor		*Index Numbers (2000=100): Period Averages*											
Share Prices...............................	62	59.4	56.2	71.6	83.4	58.8	79.1	100.0	78.4	65.2	64.1	80.5	89.4
Producer Prices...........................	63	100.9	103.7	103.6	† 103.3	101.4	99.8	100.0	98.4	95.7	95.4	97.6	98.3
Consumer Prices..........................	64	85.7	93.5	99.4	105.2	108.2	103.9	100.0	98.4	95.4	92.9	92.6	93.4
Wages:Avg.Earnings(Mfg)..............	65	72.4	80.2	† 86.3	93.4	99.3	98.6	100.0	102.1	100.9	97.9	97.3	99.1
Wage Rates (Manufacturing)............	65a	81.6	86.2	92.7	97.6	98.4	97.8	100.0	102.7	101.1	97.3	96.3	96.8
Manufacturing Production..............	66ey	121.9	123.1	118.5	† 117.6	107.4	100.5	100.0	95.6	86.3	78.3	80.6	....
		Number in Thousands: Period Averages											
Labor Force.............................	67d	2,972	3,001	3,094	3,216	3,359	....	3,383	3,427	3,488	3,501	3,529	....
Employment.............................	67e	2,873	2,905	† 3,073	3,164	3,122	3,112	3,207	3,252	3,232	3,219	3,288	....
Unemployment..........................	67c	56	96	87	71	154	208	167	175	256	277	241	201
Unemployment Rate (%).................	67r	1.9	3.2	† 2.8	2.2	4.7	6.3	5.0	5.1	7.3	7.9	6.8	5.6
Intl. Transactions & Positions		*Billions of US Dollars*											
Exports.....................................	70..d	151.40	173.75	180.75	188.06	174.00	173.89	201.86	189.89	200.09	223.76	259.26	289.34
Imports, c.i.f...............................	71..d	161.84	192.75	198.55	208.61	184.52	179.52	212.81	201.08	207.64	231.90	271.07	299.53
		2000=100											
Volume of Exports.......................	72	69.1	77.4	81.1	86.1	82.4	85.4	100.0	96.7	104.9	119.6	138.0	153.7
Volume of Imports.......................	73	71.6	81.4	84.9	91.0	84.5	84.7	100.0	98.0	105.7	119.1	135.9	147.5
Unit Value of Exports.....................	74	105.6	109.1	108.8	107.0	103.0	100.2	100.0	97.7	95.1	93.7	94.8	96.1
Unit Value of Imports.....................	75	105.1	110.4	109.0	106.5	101.3	99.2	100.0	96.9	93.1	92.8	95.5	98.1

China, P.R.: Hong Kong 532

		1994	1995	1996	1997	1998	1999	2000	2001	2002	2003	2004	2005
Balance of Payments					*Millions of US Dollars Minus Sign Indicates Debit*								
Current Account, n.i.e.	78ald	....	....	....	....	2,507	10,248	6,993	9,786	12,412	16,470	15,728	20,284
Goods: Exports f.o.b.	78aad	....	....	....	....	175,833	174,719	202,698	190,926	200,300	224,656	260,263	289,579
Goods: Imports f.o.b.	78abd	....	....	....	....	−183,666	−177,878	−210,891	−199,257	−205,353	−230,435	−269,575	−297,206
Trade Balance	78acd	....	....	....	....	−7,833	−3,159	−8,193	−8,331	−5,053	−5,779	−9,312	−7,627
Services: Credit	78add	....	....	....	....	33,840	35,624	40,430	41,135	44,600	46,555	55,157	62,175
Services: Debit	78aed	....	....	....	....	−25,079	−23,870	−24,698	−24,899	−25,964	−26,126	−31,138	−32,384
Balance on Goods & Services	78afd	....	....	....	....	928	8,595	7,538	7,905	13,583	14,651	14,708	22,164
Income: Credit	78agd	....	....	....	....	45,922	46,809	54,483	48,058	41,511	43,181	52,003	64,731
Income: Debit	78ahd	....	....	....	....	−42,747	−43,617	−53,359	−44,398	−40,787	−39,525	−48,997	−64,419
Balance on Gds, Serv. & Inc.	78aid	....	....	....	....	4,104	11,787	8,663	11,565	14,308	18,307	17,713	22,476
Current Transfers, n.i.e.: Credit	78ajd	....	....	....	....	669	570	538	605	777	529	626	742
Current Transfers: Debit	78akd	....	....	....	....	−2,265	−2,109	−2,208	−2,385	−2,673	−2,366	−2,611	−2,934
Capital Account, n.i.e.	78bcd	....	....	....	....	−2,382	−1,780	−1,546	−1,174	−2,011	−1,065	−329	−672
Capital Account, n.i.e.: Credit	78bad	....	....	....	....	377	103	57	41	31	132	1,152	952
Capital Account: Debit	78bbd	....	....	....	....	−2,759	−1,883	−1,602	−1,215	−2,042	−1,197	−1,480	−1,624
Financial Account, n.i.e.	78bjd	....	....	....	....	−8,476	1,061	4,165	−6,626	−19,751	−20,953	−20,094	−18,643
Direct Investment Abroad	78bdd	....	....	....	....	−16,985	−19,369	−59,352	−11,345	−17,463	−5,492	−45,715	−32,560
Dir. Invest. in Rep. Econ., n.i.e.	78bed	....	....	....	....	14,765	24,578	61,924	23,776	9,682	13,624	34,032	35,897
Portfolio Investment Assets	78bfd	....	....	....	....	25,492	−25,440	−22,022	−40,133	−37,702	−35,386	−43,214	−30,648
Equity Securities	78bkd	....	....	....	....	8,507	−30,337	−17,606	−22,682	−15,756	−9,951	−30,486	−25,452
Debt Securities	78bld	....	....	....	....	16,985	4,897	−4,416	−17,452	−21,946	−25,435	−12,728	−5,195
Portfolio Investment Liab., n.i.e.	78bgd	....	....	....	....	−3,407	58,525	46,508	−1,161	−1,084	1,386	3,882	9,076
Equity Securities	78bmd	....	....	....	....	−2,106	60,470	46,976	−855	1,391	5,771	1,979	10,874
Debt Securities	78bnd	....	....	....	....	−1,301	−1,944	−468	−305	−2,475	−4,385	1,902	−1,798
Financial Derivatives Assets	78bwd	....	....	....	....	10,837	21,224	8,445	17,971	20,035	30,005	20,605	17,561
Financial Derivatives Liabilities	78bxd	....	....	....	....	−7,538	−11,011	−8,240	−12,888	−13,424	−19,958	−14,912	−15,794
Other Investment Assets	78bhd	....	....	....	....	119,830	42,963	18,279	59,137	46,617	−28,671	−32,609	−7,628
Monetary Authorities	78bod	....	....	....	....	....	....	....	....	....	....	....	....
General Government	78bpd	....	....	....	....	....	....	....	....	....	....	....	....
Banks	78bqd	....	....	....	....	101,774	34,181	23,857	61,452	46,037	−18,154	−37,563	−2,462
Other Sectors	78brd	....	....	....	....	18,057	8,781	−5,578	−2,315	580	−10,517	4,954	−5,166
Other Investment Liab., n.i.e.	78bid	....	....	....	....	−151,470	−90,410	−41,375	−41,985	−26,412	23,539	57,838	5,452
Monetary Authorities	78bsd	....	....	....	....	....	....	....	....	....	....	....	....
General Government	78btd	....	....	....	....	....	....	....	....	....	....	....	....
Banks	78bud	....	....	....	....	−148,616	−85,768	−44,259	−42,888	−20,937	20,199	56,992	−3,249
Other Sectors	78bvd	....	....	....	....	−2,854	−4,642	2,884	903	−5,475	3,340	845	8,701
Net Errors and Omissions	78cad	....	....	....	....	1,561	499	431	2,699	6,973	6,542	7,980	409
Overall Balance	78cbd	....	....	....	....	−6,789	10,028	10,044	4,684	−2,377	994	3,286	1,378
Reserves and Related Items	79dad	....	....	....	....	6,789	−10,028	−10,044	−4,684	2,377	−994	−3,286	−1,378
Reserve Assets	79dbd	....	....	....	....	6,789	−10,028	−10,044	−4,684	2,377	−994	−3,286	−1,378
Use of Fund Credit and Loans	79dcd	....	....	....	....	....	....	....	....	....	....	....	....
Exceptional Financing	79ded	....	....	....	....	....	....	....	....	....	....	....	....
International Investment Position						*Millions of US Dollars*							
Assets	79aad	....	....	....	....	....	....	1,141,521	1,071,005	1,030,103	1,185,407	1,376,306	1,503,584
Direct Investment Abroad	79abd	....	....	....	235,763	223,811	321,635	388,380	352,602	309,430	339,649	403,120	470,488
Portfolio Investment	79acd	....	....	....	....	....	....	178,851	205,600	244,068	334,912	400,889	443,386
Equity Securities	79add	....	....	....	....	....	....	88,325	94,615	95,721	152,831	199,684	228,477
Debt Securities	79aed	....	....	....	....	....	....	90,526	110,984	148,347	182,081	201,205	214,909
Financial Derivatives	79ald	....	....	....	....	....	....	16,812	17,529	22,521	19,846	22,442	17,231
Other Investment	79afd	....	....	....	....	....	....	449,880	384,088	342,158	372,604	426,300	448,182
Monetary Authorities	79agd	....	....	....	....	....	....	....	....	....	....	....	....
General Government	79ahd	....	....	....	....	....	....	....	....	....	....	....	....
Banks	79aid	....	....	....	....	....	....	393,157	318,398	275,831	299,642	340,594	355,367
Other Sectors	79ajd	....	....	....	....	....	....	56,723	65,690	66,327	72,961	85,705	92,815
Reserve Assets	79akd	....	....	....	92,855	89,639	96,287	107,599	111,187	111,927	118,396	123,556	124,296
Liabilities	79lad	....	....	....	....	....	....	919,670	805,779	686,763	791,251	951,558	1,054,457
Dir. Invest. in Rep. Economy	79lbd	....	....	....	249,360	225,078	405,266	455,469	419,348	336,278	381,342	453,060	532,990
Portfolio Investment	79lcd	....	....	....	....	....	....	153,217	117,031	93,544	125,309	155,263	177,452
Equity Securities	79ldd	....	....	....	....	....	....	138,078	102,833	79,289	115,688	143,405	167,171
Debt Securities	79led	....	....	....	....	....	....	15,139	14,198	14,255	9,621	11,857	10,281
Financial Derivatives	79lld	....	....	....	....	....	....	12,517	12,059	21,198	19,598	21,136	17,067
Other Investment	79lfd	....	....	....	....	....	....	298,467	257,342	235,742	265,002	322,099	326,948
Monetary Authorities	79lgd	....	....	....	....	....	....	....	....	....	....	....	....
General Government	79lhd	....	....	....	....	....	....	....	....	....	....	....	....
Banks	79lid	....	....	....	....	....	....	279,017	231,182	213,161	236,968	296,511	286,074
Other Sectors	79ljd	....	....	....	....	....	....	19,451	26,160	22,581	28,034	25,588	40,874

China, P.R.: Hong Kong 532

National Accounts		1994	1995	1996	1997	1998	1999	2000	2001	2002	2003	2004	2005
						Billions of Hong Kong Dollars							
Househ.Cons.Expend.,incl.NPISHs....	96f	624	692	756	834	796	765	774	783	748	719	768	805
Government Consumption Expend...	91f	83	94	104	113	117	120	120	129	131	130	127	121
Gross Fixed Capital Formation.........	93e	306	334	378	452	389	325	347	333	286	261	275	289
Changes in Inventories....................	93i	21	46	10	12	−16	−11	14	−4	6	9	7	−5
Exports of Goods and Services.........	90c	1,404	1,598	1,683	1,743	1,610	1,625	1,888	1,802	1,910	2,112	2,457	2,735
Imports of Goods and Services (-).....	98c	1,391	1,647	1,701	1,788	1,603	1,559	1,829	1,743	1,804	1,997	2,342	2,563
Gross Domestic Product (GDP)........	99b	1,047	1,116	1,229	1,365	1,293	1,267	1,315	1,299	1,277	1,234	1,292	1,382
Net Primary Income from Abroad.....	98.n	2	9	−11	−2	25	25	9	29	6	28	23	2
Gross National Income (GNI)...........	99a	1,049	1,125	1,218	1,363	1,317	1,291	1,324	1,327	1,282	1,262	1,315	1,385
Net Current Transf.from Abroad.......	98t	....	....	....	−12	−12	−12	−13	−14	−15	−14	−15	−17
Gross Nat'l Disposable Inc.(GNDI)....	99i	....	....	....	1,351	1,305	1,280	1,311	1,313	1,268	1,248	1,300	1,367
Gross Saving.......................	99s	....	....	....	404	393	394	416	402	388	399	404	441
GDP Volume 1995 Prices...............	99b.p	1,068	1,110	1,157	1,216	1,150	1,196	1,315	1,323	1,347	1,391	1,510	1,620
GDP Volume (2000=100)..............	99bvp	81.2	84.4	88.0	92.5	87.4	90.9	100.0	100.6	102.5	105.8	114.9	123.2
GDP Deflator (2000=100)............	99bip	98.1	100.5	106.3	112.2	112.4	105.9	100.0	98.2	94.8	88.7	85.5	85.3
						Millions: Midyear Estimates							
Population...............................	99z	6.09	6.19	6.28	6.38	6.46	6.55	6.64	6.72	6.80	6.88	6.96	7.04

		1994	1995	1996	1997	1998	1999	2000	2001	2002	2003	2004	2005
Exchange Rates		*Patacas Per SDR: End of Period*											
Market Rate....................	aa	11.635	11.839	11.457	10.769	11.236	10.987	10.467	10.093	10.921	11.883	12.439	11.416
		Patacas per US Dollar: End of Period (ae) Period Average (rf)											
Market Rate....................	ae	7.970	7.965	7.968	7.982	7.980	8.005	8.034	8.031	8.033	7.997	8.010	7.987
Market Rate....................	rf	7.960	7.968	7.966	7.975	7.979	7.992	8.026	8.034	8.033	8.021	8.022	8.011
International Liquidity		*Billions of US Dollars Unless Otherwise Indicated: End of Period*											
Total Reserves minus Gold..............	1l.d	1.97	2.26	2.42	2.53	2.46	2.86	3.32	3.51	3.80	4.34	5.44	6.69
Foreign Exchange........................	1d.d	1.97	2.26	2.42	2.53	2.46	2.86	3.32	3.51	3.80	4.34	5.44	6.69
Gold (Million Fine Troy Ounces)........	1ad	—	—	—	—	—	—	—	—	—	—	—	—
Gold (National Valuation)..............	1and	—	—	—	—	—	—	—	—	—	—	—	—
Banking Institutions: Assets............	7a.d	6.08	6.77	10.83	10.75	† 12.63	7.83	8.58	9.30	10.65	11.72	12.88	17.48
Liabilities.................	7b.d	3.96	4.10	7.82	7.92	† 8.30	3.30	3.06	2.85	2.98	2.69	3.10	6.76
Monetary Authorities		*Millions of Patacas: End of Period*											
Foreign Assets......................	11	15,672.0	17,972.4	19,298.9	20,215.3	19,651.1	22,873.1	30,646.3	33,431.6	36,380.5	42,483.7	52,284.1	63,547.3
Claims on Government....................	12a	67.2	69.2	85.5	115.0	143.3	190.9	188.6	181.5	191.6	206.4	220.7	240.7
Claims on Deposit Money Banks......	12e	59.6	42.3	55.7	53.6	37.7	515.4	6,284.9	5,013.8	3,596.8	2,685.1	2,212.2	1,000.1
Reserve Money......................	14	2,405.7	2,735.1	2,909.6	3,047.8	3,239.1	3,957.9	3,665.3	3,871.6	4,208.8	4,885.1	5,591.5	6,016.0
of which: Currency Outside Banks..	14a	1,197.8	1,280.1	1,426.7	1,518.3	1,554.6	1,819.4	1,717.2	1,895.8	2,053.0	2,361.8	2,772.7	2,974.3
Liab. of Central Bank: Securities.......	16ac	8,686.3	11,242.7	11,207.2	10,942.6	11,803.9	15,086.4	17,530.0	16,927.7	15,837.5	17,076.1	18,157.0	20,326.5
Foreign Liabilities....................	16c	.9	.1	103.1	.1	.2	—	—	4.9	—	.1	1.9	—
Government Deposits....................	16d	4,246.0	3,160.3	4,555.6	5,744.6	3,835.0	3,450.8	14,320.4	15,662.8	17,596.8	20,643.9	27,891.0	35,349.2
Capital Accounts......................	17a	1,071.2	1,569.6	1,693.1	1,979.1	2,437.9	2,333.9	2,878.0	3,077.5	3,286.1	3,439.1	3,836.4	4,418.9
Other Items (Net)......................	17r	−611.2	−624.1	−1,028.6	−1,330.2	−1,483.8	−1,249.8	−1,274.0	−917.7	−760.4	−669.1	−760.7	−1,322.4
Banking Institutions		*Millions of Patacas: End of Period*											
Reserves......................	20	1,207.9	1,455.0	1,482.9	1,529.5	1,684.5	2,138.5	1,948.1	1,975.8	2,155.8	2,523.3	2,818.8	3,041.7
Claims on Mon.Author.: Securities...	20c	8,686.3	11,242.7	11,207.2	10,942.6	11,803.9	15,086.4	17,530.0	16,927.7	15,837.5	17,076.1	18,157.0	20,326.5
Foreign Assets......................	21	48,434.0	53,955.6	86,316.3	85,763.6	† 100,793.3	62,680.8	68,927.7	74,657.0	85,554.1	93,722.5	103,190.6	139,581.3
Claims on Government....................	22a	143.0	71.5	—	.3	2.2							
Claims on Nonfin.Pub. Enterprises.....	22c	....	....	....	....	....	....	....	1,438.7	2,008.4	1,951.8	1,947.2	1,947.2
Claims on Other Sectors..................	22d	39,707.3	41,694.5	44,492.5	48,890.5	† 42,808.1	42,111.3	39,127.6	34,897.7	32,321.9	31,895.7	34,768.2	42,765.0
Demand Deposits......................	24	4,038.6	4,337.6	4,289.2	3,790.7	† 3,954.1	3,543.7	3,228.2	4,020.9	4,297.8	6,427.8	10,668.0	9,814.6
Time & Savings Deposits.................	25	55,976.9	63,825.8	68,616.8	72,873.9	† 75,118.9	80,733.2	79,972.4	85,633.3	92,608.6	102,300.6	107,506.3	122,870.9
Foreign Liabilities....................	26c	31,533.0	32,685.2	62,316.5	63,178.3	† 66,239.9	26,433.7	24,598.4	22,861.4	23,974.1	21,488.8	24,797.9	53,966.0
Government Deposits....................	26d	1,161.6	1,439.4	1,677.6	2,275.6	4,244.5	2,784.9	4,447.9	3,943.1	4,468.7	4,686.0	5,477.1	7,074.2
Credit from Monetary Authorities.....	26g	59.6	42.3	55.7	53.6	37.7	515.4	6,284.9	5,013.8	3,596.8	2,685.1	2,212.2	1,000.1
Capital Accounts......................	27a	4,812.2	5,005.5	5,561.0	6,222.5	6,330.2	5,707.4	6,593.4	7,000.4	7,733.3	8,570.6	9,511.1	11,865.0
Other Items (Net)......................	27r	596.6	1,083.4	982.2	−1,268.1	1,166.7	2,298.8	2,408.5	1,424.0	1,198.2	1,010.7	709.1	1,070.8
Banking Survey		*Millions of Patacas: End of Period*											
Foreign Assets (Net)......................	31n	32,572.1	39,242.7	43,195.6	42,800.5	† 54,204.3	59,120.2	74,975.6	85,222.3	97,960.5	114,717.3	130,674.9	149,162.6
Domestic Credit......................	32	34,509.9	37,235.5	38,344.8	40,985.6	† 34,874.1	36,066.5	20,547.9	16,912.0	12,456.4	8,724.0	3,568.0	2,529.5
Claims on Government (net).........	32an	−5,197.4	−4,459.0	−6,147.7	−7,904.9	−7,934.0	−6,044.8	−18,579.7	−19,424.4	−21,873.9	−25,123.5	−33,147.4	−42,182.7
Claims on Nonfin.Pub. Enterprises..	32c	....	....	....	....	....	....	....	1,438.7	2,008.4	1,951.8	1,947.2	1,947.2
Claims on Other Sectors...............	32d	39,707.3	41,694.5	44,492.5	48,890.5	† 42,808.1	42,111.3	39,127.6	34,897.7	32,321.9	31,895.7	34,768.2	42,765.0
Money......................	34	5,236.4	5,617.7	5,715.9	5,309.0	† 5,508.7	5,363.1	4,945.4	5,916.7	6,350.8	8,789.6	13,440.7	12,788.9
Quasi-Money......................	35	55,976.9	63,825.8	68,616.8	72,873.9	† 75,118.9	80,733.2	79,972.4	85,633.3	92,608.6	102,300.6	107,506.3	122,870.9
Capital Accounts......................	37a	5,883.4	6,575.1	7,254.1	8,201.6	8,768.1	8,041.3	9,471.4	10,077.9	11,019.4	12,009.7	13,347.5	16,283.9
Other Items (Net)......................	37r	−14.6	459.3	−46.4	−2,598.3	−317.1	1,049.0	1,134.5	506.3	437.8	341.6	−51.6	−251.6
Money plus Quasi-Money.................	35l	61,213.3	69,443.5	74,332.7	78,182.9	† 80,627.6	86,096.3	84,917.8	91,550.0	98,959.4	111,090.2	120,947.0	135,659.8
Interest Rates		*Percent Per Annum*											
Interbank Rate (End of Period)........	60b	5.91	6.01	5.60	7.54	5.41	5.70	6.29	2.11	1.48	.11	.27	4.09
Deposit Rate......................	60l	4.21	5.93	5.23	6.22	7.00	5.30	5.33	2.59	.63	....	.08	1.58
Lending Rate......................	60p	7.95	9.90	9.56	9.73	10.97	9.46	9.89	7.99	6.11	6.00	6.01	7.05
Prices and Labor		*Index Numbers (2000=100): Period Averages*											
Consumer Prices......................	64	† 89.0	96.6	101.3	104.8	† 105.0	101.6	100.0	98.0	95.4	93.9	94.9	† 99.0
		Number in Thousands: Period Averages											
Labor Force......................	67d	177	187	202	202	206	209	210	217	214	216	229	248
Employment......................	67e	173	180	194	196	197	196	195	203	201	203	218	238
Unemployment......................	67c	4	7	9	7	10	13	14	14	13	13	11	10
Unemployment Rate (%).................	67r	2.5	3.6	4.3	3.2	4.6	6.3	6.8	6.4	6.3	6.0	4.8	4.1
Intl. Transactions & Positions		*Millions of US Dollars*											
Exports..............................	70..d	1,866.0	1,997.3	1,995.8	2,147.8	2,141.1	2,199.6	2,539.0	2,299.5	2,355.8	2,580.8	2,811.8	2,475.9
Imports, c.i.f.........................	71..d	2,126.2	2,041.6	1,999.8	2,081.8	1,954.9	2,039.5	2,254.7	2,386.3	2,529.8	2,755.2	3,477.9	3,913.4

		1994	1995	1996	1997	1998	1999	2000	2001	2002	2003	2004	2005
Balance of Payments						*Millions of US Dollars Minus Sign Indicates Debit*							
Current Account, n.i.e.	78ald	....	....	....	....	....	....	....	....	2,739	3,179	4,163	....
Goods: Exports f.o.b.	78aad	....	....	....	....	....	....	....	....	2,358	2,585	2,816	....
Goods: Imports f.o.b.	78abd	....	....	....	....	....	....	....	....	−3,277	−3,678	−4,657	....
Trade Balance	78acd	....	....	....	....	....	....	....	....	−920	−1,093	−1,841	....
Services: Credit	78add	....	....	....	....	....	....	....	....	4,758	5,605	8,063	....
Services: Debit	78aed	....	....	....	....	....	....	....	....	−1,071	−1,175	−1,337	....
Balance on Goods & Services	78afd	....	....	....	....	....	....	....	....	2,767	3,337	4,885	....
Income: Credit	78agd	....	....	....	....	....	....	....	....	449	394	381	....
Income: Debit	78ahd	....	....	....	....	....	....	....	....	−468	−547	−1,076	....
Balance on Gds, Serv. & Inc.	78aid	....	....	....	....	....	....	....	....	2,748	3,184	4,190	....
Current Transfers, n.i.e.: Credit	78ajd	....	....	....	....	....	....	....	....	90	103	98	....
Current Transfers: Debit	78akd	....	....	....	....	....	....	....	....	−99	−108	−124	....
Capital Account, n.i.e.	78bcd	....	....	....	....	....	....	....	....	139	88	274	....
Capital Account, n.i.e.: Credit	78bad	....	....	....	....	....	....	....	....	161	113	302	....
Capital Account: Debit	78bbd	....	....	....	....	....	....	....	....	−23	−25	−28	....
Financial Account, n.i.e.	78bjd	....	....	....	....	....	....	....	....	−1,086	−1,677	−1,667	....
Direct Investment Abroad	78bdd	....	....	....	....	....	....	....	....	−71	5	—	....
Dir. Invest. in Rep. Econ., n.i.e.	78bed	....	....	....	....	....	....	....	....	415	517	781	....
Portfolio Investment Assets	78bfd	....	....	....	....	....	....	....	....	−903	−1,191	−2,181	....
Equity Securities	78bkd	....	....	....	....	....	....	....	....	−290	−358	−487	....
Debt Securities	78bld	....	....	....	....	....	....	....	....	−613	−834	−1,694	....
Portfolio Investment Liab., n.i.e.	78bgd	....	....	....	....	....	....	....	....	1	—	—	....
Equity Securities	78bmd	....	....	....	....	....	....	....	....	1	—	—	....
Debt Securities	78bnd	....	....	....	....	....	....	....	....				
Financial Derivatives Assets	78bwd	....	....	....	....	....	....	....	....	118	−114	−584	....
Financial Derivatives Liabilities	78bxd	....	....	....	....	....	....	....	....	....	....	....	....
Other Investment Assets	78bhd	....	....	....	....	....	....	....	....	−878	−816	−235	....
Monetary Authorities	78bod	....	....	....	....	....	....	....	....	—	—	—	....
General Government	78bpd	....	....	....	....	....	....	....	....	−15	−12	−107	....
Banks	78bqd	....	....	....	....	....	....	....	....	−1,015	−760	−87	....
Other Sectors	78brd	....	....	....	....	....	....	....	....	152	−44	−40	....
Other Investment Liab., n.i.e.	78bid	....	....	....	....	....	....	....	....	232	−78	551	....
Monetary Authorities	78bsd	....	....	....	....	....	....	....	....	....	....	....	....
General Government	78btd	....	....	....	....	....	....	....	....	—	—	....	....
Banks	78bud	....	....	....	....	....	....	....	....	265	−119	430	....
Other Sectors	78bvd	....	....	....	....	....	....	....	....	−32	41	121	....
Net Errors and Omissions	78cad	....	....	....	....	....	....	....	....	−1,499	−1,066	−1,672	....
Overall Balance	78cbd	....	....	....	....	....	....	....	....	293	524	1,098	....
Reserves and Related Items	79dad	....	....	....	....	....	....	....	....	−293	−524	−1,098	....
Reserve Assets	79dbd	....	....	....	....	....	....	....	....	−293	−524	−1,098	....
Use of Fund Credit and Loans	79dcd	....	....	....	....	....	....	....	....	....	....	....	....
Exceptional Financing	79ded	....	....	....	....	....	....	....	....	....	....	....	....
Government Finance					*Millions of Patacas: Year Ending December 31*								
Deficit (-) or Surplus	80	....	....	25.4	882.2	−457.3	−452.8	777.3	....	....	....	....	....
Total Revenue and Grants	81y	....	....	9,491.9	10,934.6	10,098.8	10,749.4	9,809.6	....	....	....	....	....
Revenue	81	....	....	9,491.6	10,934.3	10,098.7	10,749.4	9,809.6	....	....	....	....	....
Grants	81z	....	....	.3	.3	.1	—	—	....	....	....	....	....
Exp. & Lending Minus Repay	82z	....	....	9,466.5	10,052.4	10,556.1	11,202.2	9,032.3	....	....	....	....	....
Expenditure	82	....	....	8,817.8	9,530.9	10,071.0	11,033.7	9,004.5	....	....	....	....	....
Lending Minus Repayments	83	....	....	648.7	521.5	485.1	168.5	27.8	....	....	....	....	....
National Accounts						*Millions of Patacas*							
Househ.Cons.Expend.,incl.NPISHs	96f	16,494.8	18,202.6	19,760.0	20,537.0	20,231.9	20,102.4	19,706.9	19,797.6	20,222.5	20,670.5	22,811.7	25,220.3
Government Consumption Expend	91f	4,159.2	4,791.5	5,335.9	5,877.4	6,182.2	6,918.8	6,045.1	6,108.2	6,322.9	6,830.0	7,093.2	7,941.3
Gross Fixed Capital Formation	93e	15,620.1	14,654.0	10,769.9	10,811.2	8,829.8	8,275.1	5,618.3	5,119.0	5,800.7	8,981.9	13,426.3	24,358.2
Changes in Inventories	93i	585.3	253.6	540.7	112.8	−71.8	83.3	73.7	18.8	240.2	318.5	600.9	607.2
Exports of Goods and Services	90c	38,418.4	43,232.5	44,063.2	44,552.6	41,756.6	41,119.1	49,179.5	51,038.3	57,166.0	65,691.5	87,273.5	89,023.1
Imports of Goods and Services (-)	98c	28,562.6	28,860.5	27,664.3	28,659.5	27,568.2	29,211.3	31,651.2	32,377.4	34,933.5	38,926.1	48,306.2	54,559.1
Gross Domestic Product (GDP)	99b	46,715.3	52,273.9	52,805.5	53,231.5	49,360.4	47,287.4	48,972.4	49,704.4	54,818.8	63,566.3	82,899.3	92,591.0
GDP Volume 1996 Prices	99b.p	53,754.6	55,526.3	55,293.5	55,139.1	52,618.8							
GDP Volume 2002 Prices	99b.p	....	....	....	....	46,862.1	45,756.8	48,386.4	49,784.0	54,818.8	62,583.6	80,282.3	85,628.9
GDP Volume (2000=100)	99bvp	98.9	102.2	101.8	101.5	† 96.8	94.6	100.0	102.9	113.3	129.3	165.9	177.0
GDP Deflator (2000=100)	99bip	96.4	104.4	105.9	107.1	104.1	102.1	100.0	98.6	98.8	100.4	102.0	106.8
						Millions: Midyear Estimates							
Population	99z	.41	.41	.42	.43	.43	.44	.44	.45	.45	.45	.46	.46

Colombia   233

		1994	1995	1996	1997	1998	1999	2000	2001	2002	2003	2004	2005
Exchange Rates						*Pesos per SDR: End of Period*							
Principal Rate..................	aa	1,213.53	1,468.13	1,445.62	1,745.36	2,122.63	2,571.77	2,849.49	2,892.15	3,894.74	4,132.22	3,746.02	3,264.77
					Pesos per US Dollar: End of Period (ae) Period Average (rf)								
Principal Rate..................	ae	831.27	987.65	1,005.33	1,293.58	1,507.52	1,873.77	2,187.02	2,301.33	2,864.79	2,780.82	2,412.10	2,284.22
Principal Rate..................	rf	844.84	912.83	1,036.69	1,140.96	1,426.04	1,756.23	2,087.90	2,299.63	2,504.24	2,877.65	2,628.61	2,320.83
					Index Numbers (2000=100): Period Averages								
Principal Rate..................	ahx	247.0	229.0	201.0	183.8	146.6	119.6	100.0	90.6	82.4	72.4	79.3	89.8
Nominal Effective Exchange Rate.....	nec	175.4	159.4	154.1	151.4	128.0	111.3	100.0	94.2	91.2	80.4	86.9	97.9
Real Effective Exchange Rate............	rec	112.3	113.9	120.4	128.1	120.2	109.1	100.0	96.9	95.3	84.9	92.8	105.3
Fund Position						*Millions of SDRs: End of Period*							
Quota..........................	2f.s	561	561	561	561	561	774	774	774	774	774	774	774
SDRs..........................	1b.s	116	119	123	128	139	95	103	108	113	115	117	121
Reserve Position in the Fund.......	1c.s	87	135	165	263	408	286	286	286	286	286	286	286
Total Fund Cred.&Loans Outstg........	2tl	—	—	—	—	—	—	—	—	—	—	—	—
International Liquidity						*Millions of US Dollars Unless Otherwise Indicated: End of Period*							
Total Reserves minus Gold..............	1l.d	7,991	8,349	9,845	9,803	8,651	8,008	8,916	10,154	10,732	10,784	13,394	14,787
SDRs........................	1b.d	170	177	177	172	196	131	135	135	154	171	181	173
Reserve Position in the Fund.........	1c.d	127	201	237	355	575	392	372	359	389	425	444	408
Foreign Exchange.................	1d.d	7,694	7,971	9,431	9,275	7,880	7,485	8,409	9,659	10,190	10,188	12,769	14,206
Gold (Million Fine Troy Ounces)........	1ad	.293	.267	.252	.358	.358	.328	.328	.327	.327	.327	.327	.327
Gold (National Valuation)................	1and	112	119	94	104	103	95	89	91	112	136	143	168
Monetary Authorities:Other Assets...	3..d	425	420	420	419	422	418	448	412	452	464	473	481
Other Liab........	4..d	383	473	355	249	237	212	187	184	133	129	60	66
Deposit Money Banks: Assets..........	7a.d	506	443	484	1,031	944	552	458	357	341	516	513	938
Liabilities.................	7b.d	1,854	2,136	2,654	3,316	2,868	1,712	1,365	1,120	1,122	793	1,346	2,031
Other Banking Insts.: Assets............	7e.d	169	134	257	199	162	211	133	164	121	132	539	1,071
Liabilities..................	7f.d	3,182	3,476	4,241	3,834	3,352	2,837	1,860	1,287	1,221	847	966	717
Monetary Authorities						*Billions of Pesos: End of Period*							
Foreign Assets........................	11	7,073.1	8,760.5	10,402.8	13,295.7	13,841.5	15,953.9	20,665.9	24,660.9	31,824.1	31,941.6	33,497.2	35,256.3
Claims on Central Government.........	12a	711.1	565.0	725.0	574.3	951.6	2,397.2	2,767.5	2,034.3	2,384.3	3,210.7	990.4	2,612.3
Claims on Nonfin.Pub.Enterprises.....	12c	—	—	—	—	—	—	—	—	—	—	—	—
Claims on Private Sector............	12d	52.2	81.6	105.8	128.3	538.8	541.4	397.6	203.0	200.8	181.6	205.4	321.0
Claims on Deposit Money Banks......	12e	66.3	239.9	62.6	416.3	905.8	2,508.5	1,536.3	919.2	1,807.4	3,206.1	1,992.4	3,492.0
Claims on Other Banking Insts........	12f	339.0	436.9	264.9	286.0	377.9	481.5	853.9	374.3	544.7	484.8	460.8	382.4
Claims on Nonbank Financial Insts...	12g			133.1	408.8	579.5	681.6	802.7	893.2	1,000.9	1,050.5	1,057.2	1,059.4
Reserve Money......................	14	5,902.5	6,301.1	7,415.6	8,640.7	7,165.0	10,012.5	10,922.4	12,003.0	14,441.8	16,816.9	19,402.1	22,902.3
of which: Currency Outside DMBs..	14a	2,373.3	2,994.3	3,536.0	4,453.0	4,997.3	6,505.9	7,676.6	8,653.6	10,188.5	12,196.6	13,948.7	16,500.9
Time, Savings,& Fgn.Currency Dep...	15	49.6	9.9	14.0	.8	120.4	101.3	7.9	2.0	1.3	1.0	.8	.8
Money Market Instruments..............	16aa	392.2	214.7	723.0	.5	15.8	—	—	—	—	—	—	—
Restricted Deposits..................	16b	.4	.4	.4	.3	.4	.3	.3	—	—	—	—	—
Foreign Liabilities..........................	16c	317.8	466.3	356.1	320.6	358.5	396.5	407.8	461.0	375.3	361.0	144.4	150.8
Central Government Deposits...........	16d	475.6	128.4	247.3	349.0	236.8	235.5	339.6	402.6	283.3	341.2	1,182.4	4,205.9
Capital Accounts......................	17a	1,388.1	3,110.2	3,231.1	6,120.0	9,644.1	12,089.9	15,696.9	16,963.9	23,484.6	23,470.6	18,494.2	16,838.0
Other Items (Net).....................	17r	−284.5	−147.1	−293.3	−322.6	−345.9	−271.8	−351.0	−747.5	−824.2	−915.2	−1,020.5	−974.5
Deposit Money Banks						*Billions of Pesos: End of Period*							
Reserves............................	20	2,937.1	2,736.3	2,890.2	3,544.7	2,157.1	3,242.9	3,008.2	3,201.2	4,112.9	4,459.2	5,287.1	6,212.9
Foreign Assets.......................	21	419.9	437.0	485.9	1,326.9	1,427.0	1,033.9	1,001.5	893.9	961.0	1,449.4	1,226.2	2,143.4
Claims on Central Government........	22a	430.9	463.7	617.1	1,441.0	2,454.1	2,167.1	5,525.5	9,616.7	13,179.7	16,569.7	22,406.9	27,441.3
Claims on Local Government.........	22b	1,009.7	1,407.0	1,715.4	3,214.1	3,498.4	3,577.6	3,373.2	3,746.1	3,783.4	3,582.4	3,306.5	3,579.2
Claims on Nonfin.Pub.Enterprises.....	22c	68.7	100.0	89.1	136.4	301.4	295.5	450.3	395.3	427.6	379.0	644.4	619.1
Claims on Private Sector.............	22d	11,266.6	15,162.0	18,547.0	26,167.9	33,048.8	31,334.5	32,452.5	36,215.7	40,461.1	44,158.2	49,015.1	59,623.4
Claims on Other Banking Insts........	22f	1,081.2	1,581.3	2,714.1	2,970.9	3,125.2	6,597.7	7,243.4	7,015.5	6,336.9	7,169.6	8,138.3	8,568.4
Demand Deposits..................	24	3,626.1	4,271.9	5,272.8	6,251.6	5,673.3	6,533.1	8,825.6	9,622.9	11,256.3	12,545.1	14,629.7	17,452.5
Time, Savings,& Fgn.Currency Dep...	25	6,447.3	8,005.4	10,036.5	16,709.5	23,452.4	25,587.6	27,956.5	33,498.9	37,454.3	39,933.3	47,809.7	57,133.7
Money Market Instruments..............	26aa	294.7	247.4	185.1	122.9	103.7	56.9	45.2	48.3	40.1	27.4	34.2	27.8
Bonds...........................	26ab	670.5	823.2	1,715.6	2,772.2	2,826.9	1,684.7	1,406.3	1,467.1	1,384.4	1,199.6	1,738.2	2,484.7
Restricted Deposits..................	26b	18.5	21.8	25.6	32.6	37.9	29.8	140.8	84.0	142.6	481.2	575.4	684.9
Foreign Liabilities......................	26c	1,537.2	2,107.6	2,664.2	4,267.7	4,333.4	3,205.0	2,984.3	2,807.6	3,156.9	2,227.4	3,217.0	4,638.8
Central Government Deposits...........	26d	1,015.3	1,319.0	1,666.7	2,333.0	2,457.4	2,243.1	2,615.1	3,526.4	3,443.9	5,393.3	4,932.0	4,314.6
Credit from Monetary Authorities.....	26g	122.9	119.4	104.0	73.3	934.0	2,471.6	1,538.5	904.9	1,908.4	3,106.7	1,992.1	3,491.6
Liabilities to Other Banking Insts......	26i	1,878.4	2,474.4	2,708.5	3,011.4	4,250.2	3,586.7	4,308.9	3,970.3	4,063.5	4,500.4	4,770.9	5,363.1
Capital Accounts..........................	27a	2,676.0	3,558.6	4,808.3	6,159.0	5,179.0	6,120.2	6,201.0	6,477.8	7,131.9	8,231.4	10,128.0	13,341.1
Other Items (Net).....................	27r	−1,072.8	−1,061.4	−2,128.5	−2,931.3	−3,236.2	−3,269.5	−2,967.8	−1,323.7	−719.6	121.8	197.2	−744.9
Monetary Survey						*Billions of Pesos: End of Period*							
Foreign Assets (Net)......................	31n	5,638.0	6,623.6	7,868.4	10,034.3	10,576.6	13,386.4	18,275.3	22,286.3	29,252.8	30,802.7	31,362.0	32,610.0
Domestic Credit.......................	32	13,468.5	18,350.1	22,997.5	32,645.6	42,181.5	45,595.6	50,911.8	56,565.0	64,592.1	71,052.2	80,110.6	95,686.0
Claims on Central Govt. (Net)........	32an	−348.9	−418.7	−571.9	−666.7	711.5	2,085.8	5,338.3	7,722.0	11,836.7	14,045.9	17,282.8	21,533.1
Claims on Local Government.........	32b	1,009.7	1,407.0	1,715.4	3,214.1	3,498.4	3,577.6	3,373.2	3,746.1	3,783.4	3,582.4	3,306.5	3,579.2
Claims on Nonfin.Pub.Enterprises.....	32c	68.7	100.0	89.1	136.4	301.4	295.5	450.3	395.3	427.6	379.0	644.4	619.1
Claims on Private Sector.............	32d	11,318.8	15,243.6	18,652.8	26,296.2	33,587.6	31,875.9	32,850.1	36,418.6	40,662.0	44,339.9	49,220.5	59,944.4
Claims on Other Banking Insts........	32f	1,420.2	2,018.2	2,979.0	3,256.9	3,503.1	7,079.3	8,097.3	7,389.8	6,881.6	7,654.5	8,599.1	8,950.8
Claims on Nonbank Financial Inst...	32g			133.1	408.8	579.5	681.6	802.7	893.2	1,000.9	1,050.5	1,057.2	1,059.4
Money..............................	34	6,722.4	8,078.5	9,966.0	11,697.9	10,772.0	13,376.7	16,837.0	18,450.6	21,576.4	24,916.9	28,764.9	34,140.7
Quasi-Money..........................	35	6,496.9	8,015.3	10,050.5	16,710.3	23,572.8	25,688.9	27,964.4	33,500.9	37,455.6	39,934.3	47,810.5	57,134.4
Money Market Instruments..............	36aa	686.9	462.1	908.1	123.4	119.5	56.9	45.2	48.3	40.1	27.4	34.2	27.8
Bonds...........................	36ab	670.5	823.2	1,715.6	2,772.2	2,826.9	1,684.7	1,406.3	1,467.1	1,384.4	1,199.6	1,738.2	2,484.7
Restricted Deposits..................	36b	18.9	22.2	26.0	32.9	38.3	30.2	141.2	84.0	142.6	481.2	575.4	684.9
Liabilities to Other Banking Insts......	36i	1,878.4	2,474.4	2,708.5	3,011.4	4,250.2	3,586.7	4,308.9	3,970.3	4,063.5	4,500.4	4,770.9	5,363.1
Capital Accounts..........................	37a	4,064.1	6,668.8	8,039.4	12,279.0	14,823.1	18,210.1	21,897.9	23,441.7	30,616.6	31,702.0	28,622.2	30,179.0
Other Items (Net).....................	37r	−1,431.6	−1,570.8	−2,548.2	−3,947.3	−3,644.7	−3,652.2	−3,413.8	−2,111.6	−1,434.2	−906.9	−843.8	−1,718.6
Money plus Quasi-Money..............	35l	13,219.3	16,093.8	20,016.5	28,408.2	34,344.8	39,065.6	44,801.4	51,951.5	59,032.0	64,851.2	76,575.4	91,275.1

Colombia   233

		1994	1995	1996	1997	1998	1999	2000	2001	2002	2003	2004	2005
Other Banking Institutions		*Billions of Pesos: End of Period*											
Reserves	40	702.0	988.1	1,282.4	1,103.8	334.8	641.8	481.5	269.9	131.6	188.2	199.6	194.3
Foreign Assets	41	140.2	132.0	258.5	256.7	244.9	394.2	289.8	411.0	339.6	370.7	1,289.0	2,447.0
Claims on Central Government	42a	273.7	131.1	155.7	265.2	1,306.3	3,607.2	3,519.3	3,519.0	3,956.9	4,801.2	5,392.5	4,962.8
Claims on Local Government	42b	783.2	1,294.4	1,472.6	1,256.2	870.9	649.1	630.1	465.1	398.8	521.4	445.5	300.1
Claims on Nonfin.Pub.Enterprises	42c	676.7	765.9	974.7	1,329.3	2,244.4	1,759.3	1,853.6	1,777.9	1,944.3	2,029.9	1,668.7	700.4
Claims on Private Sector	42d	10,207.6	13,978.3	17,955.1	19,457.4	18,014.6	18,975.6	13,836.5	11,240.7	10,202.0	7,947.1	9,360.8	7,815.6
Claims on Deposit Money Banks	42e	2,271.5	2,993.6	3,275.9	3,466.2	4,692.0	4,633.3	5,169.5	5,336.4	5,566.9	8,398.4	10,714.6	11,473.6
Demand Deposits	44	—	—	—	—	—	—	—	—	—	—	—	—
Time, Savings,& Fgn.Currency Dep	45	9,501.0	12,870.1	15,339.3	15,222.5	13,657.5	15,000.6	11,166.5	8,457.3	5,537.4	7,407.9	9,146.7	9,868.2
Money Market Instruments	46aa	89.4	35.0	15.1	13.1	16.9	1.5	1.6	1.4	1.3	—	—	—
Bonds	46ab	578.8	1,052.1	3,379.5	3,577.5	2,976.2	2,534.3	1,447.4	1,194.8	1,029.3	966.1	1,561.3	1,187.3
Restricted Deposits	46b	7.1	6.4	5.9	.7	.7	3.1	3.3	22.3	—	.4	.5	.4
Foreign Liabilities	46c	2,638.9	3,430.4	4,258.3	4,934.8	5,065.1	5,310.9	4,065.4	3,227.4	3,435.9	2,378.0	2,309.2	1,637.0
Central Government Deposits	46d	322.8	390.7	357.4	266.1	420.8	598.8	584.0	378.3	228.7	119.3	759.6	822.7
Credit from Monetary Authorities	46g	280.5	232.4	209.5	96.6	362.7	533.7	976.5	375.5	407.5	392.6	378.3	355.1
Credit from Deposit Money Banks	46h	1,112.2	1,632.2	1,617.5	2,176.8	2,505.6	5,695.9	6,519.5	7,440.2	8,065.0	8,140.6	9,014.3	9,048.6
Capital Accounts	47a	2,874.4	4,034.8	5,214.9	6,004.5	7,076.0	7,952.5	7,991.1	7,788.8	7,953.2	6,074.7	8,455.0	8,979.9
Other Items (Net)	47r	−2,350.2	−3,400.7	−5,022.6	−5,157.8	−4,373.4	−6,970.7	−6,974.7	−5,866.1	−4,118.1	−1,222.9	−2,554.2	−4,005.5
Banking Survey		*Billions of Pesos: End of Period*											
Foreign Assets (Net)	51n	3,139.3	3,325.2	3,868.6	5,356.2	5,756.4	8,469.6	14,499.7	19,469.8	26,156.5	28,795.3	30,341.8	33,420.0
Domestic Credit	52	23,666.7	32,110.9	40,219.2	51,430.7	60,693.8	62,908.8	62,070.2	65,799.6	73,983.9	78,578.0	87,619.4	99,691.2
Claims on Central Govt. (Net)	52an	−398.0	−678.3	−773.6	−667.6	1,597.0	5,094.2	8,273.6	10,862.6	15,564.9	18,727.8	21,915.7	25,673.2
Claims on Local Government	52b	1,792.9	2,701.4	3,188.0	4,470.3	4,369.3	4,226.8	4,003.3	4,211.3	4,182.2	4,103.8	3,752.0	3,879.3
Claims on Nonfin.Pub.Enterprises	52c	745.4	865.9	1,063.8	1,465.7	2,545.8	2,054.6	2,303.9	2,173.2	2,371.9	2,409.0	2,313.1	1,319.4
Claims on Private Sector	52d	21,526.4	29,221.9	36,608.0	45,753.6	51,602.2	50,851.5	46,686.7	47,659.3	50,864.0	52,286.9	58,581.4	67,760.0
Claims on Nonbank Financial Inst.	52g	—	—	133.1	408.8	579.5	681.6	802.7	893.2	1,000.9	1,050.5	1,057.2	1,059.4
Liquid Liabilities	55l	22,018.3	27,975.8	34,073.4	42,527.0	47,667.6	53,424.3	55,486.4	60,138.9	64,437.8	72,070.8	85,522.5	100,949.0
Money Market Instruments	56aa	776.3	497.1	923.2	136.5	136.4	58.4	46.8	49.7	41.3	27.5	34.2	27.8
Bonds	56ab	1,249.3	1,875.3	5,095.1	6,349.7	5,803.1	4,219.0	2,853.7	2,661.9	2,413.7	2,165.8	3,299.5	3,671.9
Restricted Deposits	56b	26.0	28.6	31.9	33.6	38.9	33.2	144.4	106.4	142.6	481.6	576.0	685.3
Capital Accounts	57a	6,938.5	10,703.6	13,254.3	18,283.5	21,899.1	26,162.6	29,889.0	31,230.5	38,569.8	37,776.8	37,077.2	39,159.0
Other Items (Net)	57r	−4,202.4	−5,644.3	−9,290.1	−10,543.4	−9,094.8	−12,519.0	−11,850.4	−8,917.9	−5,464.8	−5,149.0	−8,548.2	−11,381.7
Money (National Definitions)		*Billions of Pesos: End of Period*											
Reserve Money	19mb	5,634.4	6,267.1	6,627.6	8,287.1	6,923.1	9,739.6	10,710.4	11,647.9	14,107.4	16,441.5	19,260.2	22,804.0
M1	59ma	6,419.0	7,717.8	8,992.8	10,948.0	10,526.5	12,814.0	16,720.8	18,737.0	21,635.6	24,918.3	29,113.7	34,292.6
M2	59mb	22,569.1	28,961.3	34,815.5	43,794.6	48,558.1	53,670.5	56,178.6	62,158.4	66,672.2	74,758.4	88,342.4	104,090.5
M3	59mc	24,623.9	31,900.8	41,299.2	52,528.2	56,638.6	60,574.0	62,276.3	68,572.5	74,199.6	83,153.9	97,097.8	112,557.7
Interest Rates		*Percent Per Annum*											
Discount Rate (End of Period)	60	44.90	40.42	35.05	31.32	42.28	23.05	18.28	13.25	10.00	12.00	11.25	10.75
Money Market Rate	60b	....	22.40	28.37	23.83	35.00	18.81	10.87	10.43	6.06	6.95	7.01	6.18
Deposit Rate	60l	29.42	32.34	31.15	24.13	32.58	21.33	12.15	12.44	8.94	7.80	7.80	7.01
Lending Rate	60p	40.47	42.72	41.99	34.22	42.24	† 25.77	18.79	20.72	16.33	15.19	15.08	14.56
Prices, Production, Labor		*Index Numbers (2000=100): Period Averages*											
Share Prices	62	114.7	95.5	100.0	148.8	129.4	115.6	100.0	106.2	148.6	234.8	399.9	741.0
Producer Prices	63	43.7	51.6	† 59.4	68.6	80.4	88.3	100.0	109.4	115.2	125.7	132.2	136.3
Consumer Prices	64	40.4	48.8	† 58.7	69.6	82.6	91.6	100.0	108.0	114.8	123.0	130.3	136.9
Manufacturing Production	66ey	105.0	107.2	104.4	106.9	105.3	....	100.0	102.0	102.3	106.1	111.1	....
Vol.of Gold Produced(1990=100)	66kr	71.1	....	....	....	....	....	100.0	....	....	....	....	....
Crude Petroleum Prod	66aa	65.1	83.8	90.2	91.5	104.9	115.4	100.0	87.7	82.3	76.8	73.6	72.4
		Number in Thousands: Period Averages											
Labor Force	67d	5,261	....	6,190	6,488	6,653	7,056	7,436	† 19,617	19,704	20,409	20,256	....
Employment	67e	5,408	5,465	5,416	5,658	5,655	5,641	5,910	† 16,498	16,620	17,467	17,578	....
Unemployment	67c	442	522	735	782	998	1,415	1,526	† 2,942	3,098	2,878	2,767	2,406
Unemployment Rate (%)	67r	7.6	8.7	11.9	12.1	15.0	20.1	20.5	† 14.7	15.7	14.2	13.6	11.8
Intl. Transactions & Positions		*Millions of US Dollars*											
Exports	70..d	8,478.9	10,125.8	10,587.0	11,522.4	10,890.1	11,575.4	13,043.3	12,289.8	11,911.0	13,079.9	16,223.5	21,145.7
Coffee	70e.d	1,990.1	1,831.8	1,576.5	2,259.0	1,893.1	1,323.7	1,068.6	764.2	772.1	806.3	949.9	1,470.6
Imports, c.i.f.	71..d	11,882.9	13,852.9	13,683.6	15,377.7	14,634.7	10,658.6	11,538.5	12,833.6	12,711.1	13,888.5	16,745.7	21,204.4
Imports, f.o.b.	71.vd	11,039.3	12,921.1	12,793.6	14,408.9	13,726.4	9,990.0	10,783.8	12,009.8	11,911.2	13,029.7	15,629.2	19,798.8
Volume of Exports		*2000=100*											
Coffee	72e	128.3	106.6	115.6	119.7	122.5	109.0	100.0	109.7	113.2	111.6	114.7	118.5
Export Prices in Pesos	76	41.6	48.8	† 51.8	62.8	70.0	80.2	100.0	98.1	102.4	120.4	121.1	123.3
Import Prices in Pesos	76.x	45.9	53.0	† 60.8	65.2	75.3	86.1	100.0	108.2	114.8	131.0	130.5	126.5
Export Prices		*2000=100: Indices of Prices in US Dollars*											
Coffee	76e.d	129.0	158.7	128.5	196.6	142.9	116.5	100.0	69.4	63.0	64.0	80.0	114.4

Colombia 233

		1994	1995	1996	1997	1998	1999	2000	2001	2002	2003	2004	2005
Balance of Payments		*Millions of US Dollars: Minus Sign Indicates Debit*											
Current Account, n.i.e.	78ald	−3,667	−4,516	−4,641	−5,751	−4,858	671	765	−1,089	−1,358	−974	−938	−1,978
Goods: Exports f.o.b.	78aad	9,059	10,593	10,966	12,065	11,480	12,037	13,722	12,848	12,316	13,812	17,224	21,729
Goods: Imports f.o.b.	78abd	−11,288	−13,139	−13,058	−14,703	−13,930	−10,262	−11,090	−12,269	−12,077	−13,258	−15,878	−20,134
Trade Balance	78acd	−2,229	−2,546	−2,092	−2,638	−2,450	1,775	2,633	579	239	555	1,346	1,595
Services: Credit	78add	1,571	1,700	2,192	2,156	1,955	1,940	2,048	2,190	1,867	1,921	2,255	2,666
Services: Debit	78aed	−2,620	−2,873	−3,385	−3,656	−3,416	−3,144	−3,306	−3,602	−3,302	−3,360	−3,934	−4,767
Balance on Goods & Services	78afd	−3,277	−3,719	−3,285	−4,138	−3,911	572	1,375	−833	−1,196	−884	−333	−505
Income: Credit	78agd	702	678	716	920	949	923	1,054	919	717	553	671	1,076
Income: Debit	78ahd	−2,161	−2,274	−2,778	−3,246	−2,646	−2,278	−3,337	−3,529	−3,584	−3,951	−5,003	−6,637
Balance on Gds, Serv. & Inc.	78aid	−4,736	−5,315	−5,347	−6,464	−5,608	−784	−908	−3,443	−4,063	−4,283	−4,665	−6,067
Current Transfers, n.i.e.: Credit	78ajd	1,262	1,033	924	931	912	1,703	1,911	2,656	3,010	3,565	3,996	4,349
Current Transfers: Debit	78akd	−193	−234	−218	−217	−162	−248	−238	−302	−304	−256	−270	−260
Capital Account, n.i.e.	78bcd	—	—	—	—	—	—	—	—	—	—	—	—
Capital Account, n.i.e.: Credit	78bad	—	—	—	—	—	—	—	—	—	—	—	—
Capital Account: Debit	78bbd	—	—	—	—	—	—	—	—	—	—	—	—
Financial Account, n.i.e.	78bjd	3,393	4,560	6,683	6,587	3,307	−551	50	2,457	1,305	653	3,168	3,382
Direct Investment Abroad	78bdd	−149	−256	−328	−809	−796	−116	−325	−16	−857	−938	−142	−4,623
Dir. Invest. in Rep. Econ., n.i.e.	78bed	1,446	968	3,112	5,562	2,829	1,508	2,395	2,525	2,139	1,758	3,117	10,378
Portfolio Investment Assets	78bfd	−1,381	395	−586	−769	286	−1,345	−1,173	−3,460	2,030	−1,753	−1,565	−1,587
Equity Securities	78bkd	—	—	—	—	—	—	—	—	—	—	—	—
Debt Securities	78bld	−1,381	395	−586	−769	286	−1,345	−1,173	−3,460	2,030	−1,753	−1,565	−1,587
Portfolio Investment Liab., n.i.e.	78bgd	1,593	1,042	2,270	1,701	916	720	1,453	3,453	−933	130	1,136	−53
Equity Securities	78bmd	478	165	292	278	47	−27	17	−42	17	−52	130	86
Debt Securities	78bnd	1,115	877	1,978	1,424	869	747	1,436	3,495	−950	181	1,006	−138
Financial Derivatives Assets	78bwd	—	—	—	—	—	—	—	—	—	—	—	—
Financial Derivatives Liabilities	78bxd	—	—	—	295	−39	101	−125	−133	−111	−101	−190	−62
Other Investment Assets	78bhd	55	−3	−1,015	−1,656	−801	−789	−551	231	282	1,642	432	−181
Monetary Authorities	78bod	—	—	—	—	−7	5	−8	7	—	−4	−71	−3
General Government	78bpd	−31	−23	−20	−19	−15	−23	−40	−35	−30	−30	−51	−48
Banks	78bqd	−68	70	−41	−231	−177	118	145	102	57	−149	59	−474
Other Sectors	78brd	155	−50	−954	−1,407	−603	−889	−648	157	254	1,825	496	344
Other Investment Liab., n.i.e.	78bid	1,828	2,414	3,230	2,263	912	−630	−1,623	−143	−1,246	−85	380	−490
Monetary Authorities	78bsd	−177	51	14	−18	−22	−11	−15	−12	−13	−12	−68	5
General Government	78btd	−384	−80	−266	−54	347	910	340	226	−203	2,180	598	−1,063
Banks	78bud	727	588	417	487	−861	−1,208	−1,149	−331	−376	−577	619	426
Other Sectors	78bvd	1,663	1,854	3,066	1,848	1,448	−321	−799	−26	−654	−1,676	−769	142
Net Errors and Omissions	78cad	457	−48	−312	−559	153	−432	46	−143	192	134	240	321
Overall Balance	78cbd	182	−4	1,729	278	−1,398	−312	862	1,225	139	−188	2,470	1,726
Reserves and Related Items	79dad	−182	4	−1,729	−278	1,398	312	−862	−1,225	−139	188	−2,470	−1,726
Reserve Assets	79dbd	−182	4	−1,729	−278	1,398	312	−862	−1,225	−139	188	−2,470	−1,726
Use of Fund Credit and Loans	79dcd	—	—	—	—	—	—	—	—	—	—	—	—
Exceptional Financing	79ded	—	—	—	—	—	—	—	—	—	—	—	—
International Investment Position		*Millions of US Dollars*											
Assets	79aad	15,149	16,445	17,652	20,839	20,928	22,491	25,408	29,855	28,748	29,790	33,444	41,153
Direct Investment Abroad	79abd	744	1,028	1,096	1,893	2,648	2,703	2,989	2,952	3,553	4,390	4,357	8,876
Portfolio Investment	79acd	447	1,171	2,453	3,221	2,936	4,281	5,454	8,914	6,884	8,637	10,201	11,789
Equity Securities	79add	447	1,171	—	—	—	—	—	—	—	—	—	—
Debt Securities	79aed	—	—	2,453	3,221	2,936	4,281	5,454	8,914	6,884	8,637	10,201	11,789
Financial Derivatives	79ald	—	—	—	—	—	—	—	—	—	—	—	—
Other Investment	79afd	5,845	5,786	4,165	5,817	6,611	7,405	7,970	7,748	7,468	5,849	5,424	5,614
Monetary Authorities	79agd	40	40	477	472	473	473	501	502	503	530	607	617
General Government	79ahd	1,545	1,052	109	128	142	165	205	240	270	300	351	399
Banks	79aid	1,150	1,051	263	493	670	552	406	304	247	396	337	812
Other Sectors	79ajd	3,110	3,643	3,316	4,723	5,326	6,215	6,858	6,701	6,448	4,624	4,129	3,786
Reserve Assets	79akd	8,114	8,462	9,939	9,908	8,733	8,102	8,995	10,242	10,843	10,914	13,461	14,875
Liabilities	79lad	30,129	35,297	44,187	56,264	54,409	50,895	47,704	54,904	55,735	59,107	65,465	76,686
Dir. Invest. in Rep. Economy	79lbd	6,916	8,563	11,773	19,694	16,645	13,424	10,991	15,194	17,855	20,401	24,745	36,873
Portfolio Investment	79lcd	2,026	2,591	5,945	7,984	8,278	8,413	9,621	13,008	12,307	12,964	14,489	14,318
Equity Securities	79ldd	693	858	942	1,553	880	586	397	325	325	405	718	894
Debt Securities	79led	1,333	1,733	5,003	6,432	7,398	7,827	9,224	12,683	11,982	12,559	13,770	13,424
Financial Derivatives	79lld	—	—	—	295	256	357	253	139	57	12	—	—
Other Investment	79lfd	21,187	24,144	26,469	28,291	29,230	28,702	26,839	26,562	25,515	25,731	26,231	25,494
Monetary Authorities	79lgd	231	301	326	252	236	211	186	199	131	127	58	66
General Government	79lhd	5,102	5,144	4,723	4,516	5,000	5,864	6,580	6,878	6,876	9,357	10,027	8,806
Banks	79lid	4,518	5,169	5,546	6,002	4,949	3,884	2,712	2,332	1,959	1,326	1,947	2,366
Other Sectors	79ljd	11,336	13,530	15,874	17,520	19,045	18,743	17,362	17,153	16,549	14,920	14,200	14,256
Government Finance		*Billions of Pesos: Year Ending December 31*											
Deficit (-) or Surplus	80	−1,027.2	−1,939.8	−3,780.2	−4,504.0	−6,940.6	−8,888.9	−11,945.5	−11,169.7	−11,134.1	−11,128.2	−11,482.3	−14,257.8
Total Revenue and Grants	81y	7,656.1	9,521.2	12,007.3	15,282.6	16,880.2	20,144.0	23,285.3	28,941.6	31,459.1	35,798.3	40,629.2	46,255.5
Revenue	81	7,656.1	9,521.2	12,007.3	15,282.6	16,880.2	20,144.0	23,285.3	28,941.6	31,459.1	35,798.3	40,629.2	46,255.5
Grants	81z												
Exp. & Lending Minus Repay	82z	8,683.3	11,461.0	15,787.5	19,786.6	23,820.8	29,032.9	35,230.8	40,111.3	42,593.2	46,926.4	52,111.5	60,513.3
Expenditure	82	8,553.8	11,289.5	15,610.9	19,583.6	23,492.0	28,153.8	34,444.4	38,640.9	41,334.2	46,061.6	51,813.3	60,141.4
Lending Minus Repayments	83	129.5	171.5	176.6	203.0	328.8	879.1	786.4	1,470.4	1,259.0	864.8	298.2	371.9
Total Financing	80h	1,027.2	1,939.8	3,780.2	4,504.0	6,940.6	8,888.9	11,945.5	11,169.7	11,134.1	11,128.2	11,482.3	14,257.8
Domestic	84a	907.7	1,717.5	2,516.5	3,140.4	4,522.0	4,569.7	7,137.8	5,242.1	7,824.7	6,358.2	9,145.6	15,900.9
Foreign	85a	119.5	222.3	1,263.7	1,363.6	2,418.6	4,319.2	4,807.7	5,927.6	3,309.4	4,769.9	2,336.8	−1,643.1

Colombia 233

234

National Accounts		1994	1995	1996	1997	1998	1999	2000	2001	2002	2003	2004	2005
							Billions of Pesos						
Househ.Cons.Expend.,incl.NPISHs....	96f	44,510	55,462	65,966	79,194	92,501	97,631	110,217	123,241	135,272	147,878	....	....
Government Consumption Expend...	91f	9,774	12,622	18,123	24,246	28,548	33,588	37,057	39,268	39,847	42,423	....	....
Gross Fixed Capital Formation..........	93e	15,727	18,911	21,749	24,592	26,603	20,079	21,952	25,695	29,554	37,672	....	....
Changes in Inventories....................	93i	1,497	2,806	462	708	941	−725	1,793	967	1,268	1,344	....	....
Exports of Goods and Services..........	90c	10,129	12,272	15,308	18,063	21,083	27,807	37,606	38,477	39,380	48,486	55,717	61,587
Imports of Goods and Services (-).....	98c	14,127	17,701	20,993	25,261	29,363	26,983	33,926	39,308	42,113	49,557	54,615	60,668
Gross Domestic Product (GDP)........	99b	67,533	84,439	100,711	121,708	140,483	151,565	174,896	188,559	203,451	228,517	256,368	284,548
Net Primary Income from Abroad.....	98.n	−1,200	−1,442	−2,128	−2,706	−2,510	−2,663	−4,772	−6,013	−7,143	−9,917	....	....
Gross National Income (GNI)............	99a	66,333	82,997	98,583	119,002	137,973	148,902	170,124	182,545	196,308	218,600	....	....
Net Current Transf.from Abroad.......	98t	3,458	4,536	3,958	3,681	4,547	2,856	3,625	....	....	....	....	....
Gross Nat'l Disposable Inc.(GNDI)....	99i	69,791	87,534	102,541	123,147	142,128	151,758	172,107	....	....	....	....	....
Gross Saving................................	99s	15,506	19,450	18,453	19,707	20,556	20,540	22,136	....	....	....	....	....
GDP Volume 1994 Prices................	99b.p	67,533	71,046	72,507	74,994	75,421	72,251	74,364	75,458	76,917	79,884	83,714	88,063
GDP Volume (2000=100)...............	99bvp	90.8	95.5	97.5	100.8	101.4	97.2	100.0	101.5	103.4	107.4	112.6	118.4
GDP Deflator (2000=100)...............	99bip	42.5	50.5	59.1	69.0	79.2	89.2	100.0	106.2	112.5	121.6	130.2	137.4
							Millions: Midyear Estimates						
Population...............................	99z	37.82	38.54	39.26	39.98	40.70	41.41	42.12	42.83	43.53	44.22	44.92	45.60

Comoros 632

		1994	1995	1996	1997	1998	1999	2000	2001	2002	2003	2004	2005
Exchange Rates						*Francs per SDR: End of Period (aa)*							
Official Rate	aa	† 585.32	546.28	564.79	605.95	593.70	672.14	688.87	701.54	637.78	578.82	560.92	596.05
						Francs per US Dollar: End of Period (ae) Period Average (rf)							
Official Rate	ae	† 400.95	367.50	392.77	449.10	421.65	489.72	528.71	558.23	469.12	389.52	361.18	417.03
Official Rate	rf	416.40	374.36	383.66	437.75	442.46	461.77	533.98	549.78	522.74	435.90	396.21	395.60
Fund Position						*Millions of SDRs: End of Period*							
Quota	2f.s	6.50	6.50	6.50	6.50	6.50	8.90	8.90	8.90	8.90	8.90	8.90	8.90
SDRs	1b.s	.03	.07	.04	.10	—	.12	.13	.02	.03	—	—	—
Reserve Position in the Fund	1c.s	.52	.54	.54	.54	.54	.54	.54	.54	.54	.54	.54	.54
Total Fund Cred.&Loans Outstg	2tl	2.25	2.25	2.25	2.07	1.89	1.58	1.13	.68	.41	.14	—	—
International Liquidity						*Millions of US Dollars Unless Otherwise Indicated: End of Period*							
Total Reserves minus Gold	1l.d	44.03	44.48	50.55	40.48	39.14	37.15	43.21	62.32	79.94	94.30	103.74	85.80
SDRs	1b.d	.05	.11	.05	.13	.01	.16	.16	.02	.04	.01	—	—
Reserve Position in the Fund	1c.d	.76	.80	.78	.73	.76	.74	.70	.68	.73	.81	.84	.78
Foreign Exchange	1d.d	43.22	43.58	49.72	39.62	38.38	36.24	42.34	61.62	79.17	93.48	102.89	85.02
Gold (Million Fine Troy Ounces)	1ad	.001	.001	.001	.001	.001	.001	.001	.001	.001	.001	.001	.001
Gold (National Valuation)	1and	.22	.22	.21	.18	.17	.17	.16	.15	.20	.24	.25	.29
Deposit Money Banks: Assets	7a.d	.29	2.42	2.16	4.29	† 2.04	8.10	5.69	8.71	6.78	4.34	2.85	7.20
Liabilities	7b.d	.01	.25	.02	—	† 1.99	2.45	4.35	4.18	4.81	4.46	3.86	3.17
Monetary Authorities						*Millions of Francs: End of Period*							
Foreign Assets	11	17,729	16,422	19,950	18,305	† 16,582	18,294	23,017	34,879	38,796	37,860	37,571	35,948
Claims on Central Government	12a	3,483	3,589	3,569	3,646	† 3,806	3,814	3,858	3,654	3,930	3,120	3,457	4,554
Claims on Private Sector	12d	....	....	....	....	57	49	64	70	81	65	48	43
Claims on Other Banking Insts	12f	....	....	....	....	50	75	75	75	75	75	80	92
Reserve Money	14	9,756	8,760	11,936	10,454	† 9,326	11,104	13,980	23,851	28,358	27,940	27,505	27,130
of which: Currency Outside DMBs	14a	5,100	5,672	5,639	5,433	† 5,418	6,310	7,564	12,355	12,503	11,505	11,730	11,456
Foreign Liabilities	16c	1,428	1,421	1,393	1,385	† 1,183	1,171	915	1,393	397	223	163	186
Central Government Deposits	16d	1,743	1,278	1,723	1,515	† 542	518	508	712	582	1,126	1,270	860
Counterpart Funds	16e	....	....	....	....	56	49	49	49	49	49	50	—
Central Govt. Lending Funds	16f	....	....	....	....	504	314	316	1,374	1,191	465	550	954
Capital Accounts	17a	8,491	8,673	8,670	8,770	† 9,241	9,277	11,120	11,056	12,056	12,567	12,146	12,083
Other Items (Net)	17r	−206	−121	−203	−173	† −359	−199	126	245	250	−1,249	−526	−574
Deposit Money Banks						*Millions of Francs: End of Period*							
Reserves	20	3,082	1,631	4,719	4,024	† 5,195	3,796	5,257	8,806	12,547	13,214	13,156	11,854
Foreign Assets	21	115	889	848	1,927	† 859	3,966	3,009	4,864	3,182	1,690	1,029	3,001
Claims on Central Government	22a	—	—	415	94	† 358	554	300	301	300	300	781	601
Claims on Private Sector	22d	8,579	9,452	6,712	8,458	† 6,948	8,600	9,480	9,223	10,278	11,379	10,354	10,217
Demand Deposits	24	3,954	4,170	4,487	4,518	† 4,250	4,386	5,626	8,955	10,655	11,075	9,704	11,226
Time and Savings Deposits	25a	5,910	5,442	6,167	7,771	† 5,737	6,974	7,237	8,363	8,874	8,952	8,480	7,821
Foreign Currency Deposits	25b	....	....	....	....	21	62	63	125	110	151	356	26
Restricted Deposits	26b	....	....	....	....	260	618	111	482	1,348	767	1,276	1,267
Foreign Liabilities	26c	3	93	8	—	† 840	1,200	2,298	2,331	2,257	1,738	1,393	1,321
Central Government Deposits	26d	—	167	132	209	† 362	240	378	509	501	690	798	829
Credit From Monetary Authorities	26g	122	—	—	—	† —	—	—	—	—	—	—	—
Capital Accounts	27a	1,850	2,194	2,022	2,235	† 2,667	3,368	3,504	3,904	3,947	4,281	4,342	4,314
Other Items (Net)	27r	−63	−94	−122	−230	† −777	68	−1,171	−1,475	−1,384	−1,072	−1,029	−1,131
Monetary Survey						*Millions of Francs: End of Period*							
Foreign Assets (Net)	31n	16,413	15,797	19,397	18,847	† 15,418	19,889	22,813	36,019	39,324	37,587	37,045	37,442
Domestic Credit	32	12,497	12,450	10,213	10,474	† 10,315	12,342	12,891	12,103	13,590	13,133	12,671	13,827
Claims on Central Govt. (Net)	32an	3,822	2,925	3,422	2,016	† 3,260	3,610	3,272	2,733	3,148	1,604	2,170	3,465
Claims on Private Sector	32d	8,675	9,525	6,791	8,458	† 7,005	8,649	9,544	9,294	10,359	11,444	10,402	10,260
Claims on Other Banking Insts	32f	....	....	....	....	50	83	75	76	83	86	98	102
Money	34	12,714	12,000	13,021	10,603	† 10,015	11,662	14,115	22,937	25,323	24,793	23,368	25,383
Quasi-Money	35	5,910	5,442	6,167	7,771	† 5,758	7,036	7,300	8,487	8,984	9,102	8,836	7,847
Restricted Deposits	36b	....	....	....	....	260	618	111	482	1,348	767	1,276	1,267
Counterpart Funds	36e	....	....	....	....	56	49	49	49	49	49	50	—
Central Govt. Lending Funds	36f	....	....	....	....	504	314	316	1,374	1,191	465	550	954
Other Items (Net)	37r	10,286	10,765	10,422	10,947	† 9,139	12,553	13,813	14,793	16,020	15,545	15,636	15,820
Money plus Quasi-Money	35l	18,624	17,482	19,188	18,374	† 15,773	18,698	21,415	31,424	34,307	33,896	32,204	33,230
Other Banking Institutions						*Millions of Francs: End of Period*							
Reserves	40	1,340	1,250	856	88	† 475	1,060	947	1,484	2,013	1,578	1,479	1,867
Foreign Assets	41	4	2	5	—	† 89	96	9	10	11	11	9	9
Claims on Central Government	42a	11	—	—	—	† —	—	—	—	—	—	—	—
Claims on Private Sector	42d	1,985	2,200	3,029	4,022	† 4,038	3,329	3,334	2,928	2,293	2,594	2,690	2,212
Time Deposits	45	387	267	694	760	† 709	768	837	963	1,070	1,223	1,806	1,916
Central Government Deposits	46d	—	—	—	—	† 263	153	749	146	146	633	146	88
Long-Term Foreign Liabilities	46cl	1,838	1,964	1,588	1,633	† 845	688	527	364	197	104	—	—
Central Govt. Lending Funds	46f	230	296	317	306	† 883	896	280	809	979	394	619	542
Capital Accounts	47a	918	1,018	1,399	1,494	† 2,090	1,971	1,988	1,978	1,950	2,292	2,313	1,766
Other Items (Net)	47r	−33	−93	−108	−83	† −188	9	−91	161	−26	−463	−706	−223
Banking Survey						*Millions of Francs: End of Period*							
Foreign Assets (Net)	51n	14,579	13,835	17,814	17,214	† 14,662	19,297	22,295	35,666	39,138	37,494	37,055	37,451
Domestic Credit	52	14,493	14,650	13,242	14,496	† 14,040	15,435	15,401	14,809	15,654	15,009	15,116	15,850
Claims on Central Govt. (Net)	52an	3,833	2,925	3,422	2,016	† 2,997	3,457	2,523	2,587	3,002	971	2,024	3,378
Claims on Private Sector	52d	10,660	11,725	9,820	12,480	† 11,043	11,978	12,878	12,221	12,652	14,039	13,092	12,473
Liquid Liabilities	55l	17,704	16,525	19,002	19,114	† 16,166	18,522	21,360	30,812	33,257	33,113	32,220	33,286
Money	54	11,407	10,816	12,141	10,583	† 9,699	10,718	13,223	21,362	23,202	22,788	21,578	23,523
Quasi-Money	55	6,297	5,709	6,861	8,531	† 6,467	7,804	8,137	9,450	10,054	10,325	10,642	9,763
Restricted Deposits	56b	....	....	....	....	260	618	111	482	1,348	767	1,276	1,267
Counterpart Funds	56e	....	....	....	....	56	49	49	49	49	49	50	—
Central Govt. Lending Funds	56f	230	296	317	306	† 1,387	1,210	596	2,183	2,170	859	1,170	1,496
Other Items (Net)	57r	11,138	11,664	11,737	12,290	† 10,832	14,334	15,580	16,949	17,969	17,716	17,456	17,254

Comoros 632

		1994	1995	1996	1997	1998	1999	2000	2001	2002	2003	2004	2005
Interest Rates							*Percent Per Annum*						
Discount Rate	60	....	....	....	....	....	† 6.36	5.63	5.89	4.79	3.82	3.55	3.59
Deposit Rate	60l	....	....	....	....	....	† 11.42	3.00	3.00	3.17	3.50	3.50	3.00
Lending Rate	60p	....	....	....	....	....	† 13.67	12.00	12.00	12.00	11.83	11.00	11.00
Balance of Payments						*Millions of US Dollars: Minus Sign Indicates Debit*							
Current Account, n.i.e.	78ald	−7.22	−18.96	....	....	....	....	....	....	....	....	....	....
Goods: Exports f.o.b.	78aad	10.79	11.32	....	....	....	....	....	....	....	....	....	....
Goods: Imports f.o.b.	78abd	−44.94	−53.50	....	....	....	....	....	....	....	....	....	....
Trade Balance	78acd	−34.16	−42.18	....	....	....	....	....	....	....	....	....	....
Services: Credit	78add	28.84	34.51	....	....	....	....	....	....	....	....	....	....
Services: Debit	78aed	−45.59	−49.85	....	....	....	....	....	....	....	....	....	....
Balance on Goods & Services	78afd	−50.91	−57.53	....	....	....	....	....	....	....	....	....	....
Income: Credit	78agd	2.62	3.40	....	....	....	....	....	....	....	....	....	....
Income: Debit	78ahd	−2.69	−2.39	....	....	....	....	....	....	....	....	....	....
Balance on Gds, Serv. & Inc.	78aid	−50.98	−56.52	....	....	....	....	....	....	....	....	....	....
Current Transfers, n.i.e.: Credit	78ajd	49.95	41.06	....	....	....	....	....	....	....	....	....	....
Current Transfers: Debit	78akd	−6.19	−3.50	....	....	....	....	....	....	....	....	....	....
Capital Account, n.i.e.	78bcd	—	—	....	....	....	....	....	....	....	....	....	....
Capital Account, n.i.e.: Credit	78bad	—	—	....	....	....	....	....	....	....	....	....	....
Capital Account: Debit	78bbd	—	—	....	....	....	....	....	....	....	....	....	....
Financial Account, n.i.e.	78bjd	18.54	10.87	....	....	....	....	....	....	....	....	....	....
Direct Investment Abroad	78bdd	—	—	....	....	....	....	....	....	....	....	....	....
Dir. Invest. in Rep. Econ., n.i.e.	78bed	.18	.89	....	....	....	....	....	....	....	....	....	....
Portfolio Investment Assets	78bfd	—	—	....	....	....	....	....	....	....	....	....	....
Equity Securities	78bkd	—	—	....	....	....	....	....	....	....	....	....	....
Debt Securities	78bld	—	—	....	....	....	....	....	....	....	....	....	....
Portfolio Investment Liab., n.i.e.	78bgd	—	—	....	....	....	....	....	....	....	....	....	....
Equity Securities	78bmd	—	—	....	....	....	....	....	....	....	....	....	....
Debt Securities	78bnd	—	—	....	....	....	....	....	....	....	....	....	....
Financial Derivatives Assets	78bwd	....	....	....	....	....	....	....	....	....	....	....	....
Financial Derivatives Liabilities	78bxd	....	....	....	....	....	....	....	....	....	....	....	....
Other Investment Assets	78bhd	1.66	−1.83	....	....	....	....	....	....	....	....	....	....
Monetary Authorities	78bod	....	....	....	....	....	....	....	....	....	....	....	....
General Government	78bpd	—	—	....	....	....	....	....	....	....	....	....	....
Banks	78bqd	1.66	−1.83	....	....	....	....	....	....	....	....	....	....
Other Sectors	78brd	—	—	....	....	....	....	....	....	....	....	....	....
Other Investment Liab., n.i.e.	78bid	16.70	11.81	....	....	....	....	....	....	....	....	....	....
Monetary Authorities	78bsd	7.93	2.02	....	....	....	....	....	....	....	....	....	....
General Government	78btd	10.63	8.72	....	....	....	....	....	....	....	....	....	....
Banks	78bud	—	—	....	....	....	....	....	....	....	....	....	....
Other Sectors	78bvd	−1.86	1.06	....	....	....	....	....	....	....	....	....	....
Net Errors and Omissions	78cad	−6.33	−1.77	....	....	....	....	....	....	....	....	....	....
Overall Balance	78cbd	4.99	−9.86	....	....	....	....	....	....	....	....	....	....
Reserves and Related Items	79dad	−4.99	9.86	....	....	....	....	....	....	....	....	....	....
Reserve Assets	79dbd	−14.97	3.37	....	....	....	....	....	....	....	....	....	....
Use of Fund Credit and Loans	79dcd	1.89	—	....	....	....	....	....	....	....	....	....	....
Exceptional Financing	79ded	8.09	6.49	....	....	....	....	....	....	....	....	....	....
National Accounts						*Billions of Francs*							
Gross Domestic Product (GDP)	99b	80.4	84.1	....	....	....	....	....	....	....	....	....	....
						Millions: Midyear Estimates							
Population	99z	.59	.61	.62	.64	.66	.68	.70	.72	.74	.76	.78	.80

Congo, Democratic Republic of   636

		1994	1995	1996	1997	1998	1999	2000	2001	2002	2003	2004	2005
Exchange Rates		*Congo Francs per Thousand SDRs through 1994, per SDR Thereafter: End of Period*											
Market Rate.............................	aa	47.445	.220	1.662	1.430	† 3.450	6.176	65.146	394.111	519.528	† 553.554	689.673	616.414
		Congo Francs per Thousand US$ through 1994, per US$ Thereafter: End of Period (ae) Period Average (rf)											
Market Rate.............................	ae	32.500	.148	1.156	1.060	† 2.450	4.500	50.000	313.600	382.140	† 372.520	444.088	431.279
Market Rate.............................	rf	11.941	.070	.502	1.313	1.607	4.018	21.818	206.617	346.485	405.178	395.930	473.908
		Index Numbers (2000=100): Period Averages											
Market Rate.............................	ahx	—	100.0	13.8	4.1	924.1	363.6	100.0	12.9	4.0	3.4	3.5	2.9
Nominal Effective Exchange Rate.....	nec	596,184.6	20,984.5	3,124.1	1,033.3	893.5	582.4	100.0	15.9	4.6	3.6	3.2	2.6
Real Effective Exchange Rate...........	rec	50.6	46.5	47.7	47.6	49.2	133.7	100.0	77.7	36.6	31.7	28.5	27.8
Fund Position		*Millions of SDRs: End of Period*											
Quota.....................................	2f.s	291.00	291.00	291.00	291.00	291.00	291.00	291.00	291.00	533.00	533.00	533.00	533.00
SDRs.......................................	1b.s	—	—	—	—	—	—	—	—	6.12	5.35	3.54	.96
Reserve Position in the Fund...........	1c.s	—	—	—	—	—	—	—	—	—	—	—	—
Total Fund Cred.&Loans Outstg........	2tl	327.27	326.37	301.26	301.26	300.71	300.03	300.02	300.02	420.00	473.37	526.77	553.47
International Liquidity		*Millions of US Dollars Unless Otherwise Indicated: End of Period*											
Total Reserves minus Gold..............	1l.d	120.69	146.60	82.50	....	....	....	....	....	8.32	7.96	5.50	1.38
SDRs.....................................	1b.d	—	—	—	—	—	—	—	—	8.32	7.96	5.50	1.38
Reserve Position in the Fund.........	1c.d	—	—	—	—	—	—	—	—	—	—	—	—
Foreign Exchange......................	1d.d	120.69	146.60	82.50	....	....	....	....	....	....	....	....	....
Gold (Million Fine Troy Ounces)........	1ad	.028	.028	....	.054	....	....	....	....	....	....	....	....
Gold (National Valuation)................	1and	10.71	10.83	....	15.80	....	....	....	....	....	....	....	....
Monetary Authorities: Other Liab.....	4..d	280.95	331.50	244.16	205.15	5,841.57	5,423.52	−49.34	−38.34	139.49	185.94	202.71	169.40
Deposit Money Banks: Assets...........	7a.d	81.18	69.18	....	....	....	....	....	93.42	95.64	180.36	243.29	275.09
Liabilities..........	7b.d	31.29	16.75	35.04	....	....	....	....	48.77	41.96	84.01	95.11	79.57
Monetary Authorities		*Thousands of Congo Francs 1994–95; Millions Beginning 1996: End of Period*											
Foreign Assets.........................	11	† 5,148	25,276	† 107	67	1,834	4,125	2,571	20,163	28,663	36,414	110,243	65,906
Claims on Central Government........	12a	† 1,675	1,675	† 54	332	6,416	37,068	16,415	20,142	13,089	29,835	100,288	94,234
Claims on Nonfin.Pub.Enterprises.....	12c	† 5	323	† 7	6	149	272	301	1,895	—	—	—	—
Claims on Private Sector..................	12d	† 34	705	† 7	14	170	460	524	899	1,283	1,943	1,057	851
Claims on Deposit Money Banks......	12e	† 163	8,234	† 17	9	150	526	132	425	2,799	3,901	7,276	12,040
Claims on Other Banking Insts.........	12f	† 10	931	† —	—	—	—	3	—	—	—	—	—
Reserve Money..........................	14	† 2,355	17,668	† 110	228	6,353	33,057	20,314	43,205	52,376	67,728	111,923	129,401
of which: Currency Outside DMBs..	14a	† 2,771	16,839	† 83	152	5,145	29,445	18,180	36,110	49,757	63,148	101,467	119,937
Time & Foreign Currency Deposits....	15	† 707	1,522	† 8	9	195	436	470	2,524	5,333	3,964	6,071	7,191
Restricted Deposits........................	16b	† 1,005	4,870	† 38	29	703	1,526	1,224	6,936	3,650	3,459	4,688	4,553
Foreign Liabilities........................	16c	† 24,658	121,116	† 783	648	15,349	26,259	17,078	106,216	271,507	331,302	453,320	414,221
Central Government Deposits...........	16d	† 298	660	† 8	60	1,025	5,513	2,393	6,759	20,335	24,085	112,131	63,355
Counterpart Funds.......................	16e	† —	—	† —	—	—	—	—	—	—	—	—	—
Capital Accounts.........................	17a	† 4,124	24,842	† 128	449	4,760	6,104	4,150	17,043	−317,454	−360,408	−353,635	−344,821
Other Items (Net)........................	17r	† −25,179	−46,070	† −891	−995	−19,667	−30,445	−24,224	−138,495	10,085	1,965	−115,632	−100,869
Deposit Money Banks		*Congo Francs through 1993;*											
Reserves..................................	20	† 265	643	....	....	....	....	....	4,359	3,072	5,912	10,855	13,368
Foreign Assets..........................	21	† 2,638	10,260	....	....	....	....	....	29,295	36,548	67,188	108,043	118,639
Claims on Central Government........	22a	† 180	80	....	....	....	....	....	1,253	593	14,361	15,486	16,202
Claims on Nonfin.Pub.Enterprises.....	22c	† 76	170	....	....	....	....	....	395	827	228	1,799	444
Claims on Private Sector..................	22d	† 700	3,510	....	....	....	....	....	9,644	11,842	17,704	38,646	64,436
Claims on Other Banking Insts.........	22f	† —							903	—	1	32	4
Demand Deposits.......................	24	† 919	1,870	....	....	....	....	....	7,922	7,956	8,606	15,364	18,952
Time & Foreign Currency Deposits....	25	† 1,407	6,304	....	....	....	....	....	18,497	30,863	48,429	92,121	123,837
Restricted Deposits........................	26b	† 63	208	....	....	....	....	....	1,101	1,094	2,157	2,269	5,628
Foreign Liabilities........................	26c	† 1,017	2,484	....	....	....	....	....	15,295	16,036	31,295	42,235	34,317
Central Government Deposits...........	26d	† —	—	....	....	....	....	....	2,092	3,737	8,008	12,893	21,373
Counterpart Funds.......................	26e	† —	—	....	....	....	....	....					
Credit from Monetary Authorities.....	26g	† 163	8,234	† 17	9	150	526	132	622	1,533	3,218	8,309	15,209
Capital Accounts.........................	27a	† 201	4,125	....	....	....	....	....	9,860	12,445	16,717	19,234	26,592
Other Items (Net)........................	27r	† 253	−327	....	....	....	....	....	−9,541	−20,784	−13,035	−17,564	−32,815
Post Office: Checking Deposits.......	24..i	† —		....	....	....	....	....					
Monetary Survey		*Congo Francs through 1993;*											
Foreign Assets (Net).......................	31n	† −17,889	−88,064	....	....	....	....	....	−72,052	−222,333	−258,995	−277,269	−263,992
Domestic Credit...........................	32	† 2,383	6,733	....	....	....	....	....	26,224	3,561	31,982	32,285	91,442
Claims on Central Govt. (Net)........	32an	† 1,557	1,095	....	....	....	....	....	12,488	−10,391	12,104	−9,250	25,708
Claims on Nonfin.Pub.Enterprises...	32c	† 81	493	....	....	....	....	....	2,290	827	228	1,799	444
Claims on Private Sector...............	32d	† 735	4,214	....	....	....	....	....	10,543	13,125	19,648	39,703	65,286
Claims on Other Banking Insts.......	32f	† 10	931	....	....	....	....	....	903	—	1	32	4
Money....................................	34	† 3,725	18,895	....	....	....	....	....	41,064	57,893	72,110	117,078	139,097
Quasi-Money.............................	35	† 2,114	7,826	....	....	....	....	....	26,134	36,196	52,393	98,192	131,027
of which: Fgn. Currency Deposits...	35x	† 2,114	7,826	....	....	....	....	....	21,021	36,034	52,071	97,830	130,643
Restricted Deposits......................	36b	† 1,068	5,077	....	....	....	....	....	8,037	4,744	5,616	6,956	10,180
Counterpart Funds.......................	36e	† —	—	....	....	....	....	....					
Capital Accounts.........................	37a	† 4,324	28,967	....	....	....	....	....	26,903	−305,008	−343,691	−334,402	−318,229
Revaluation Accounts....................	37ar	† 1,203	88,808	† −534	....	....	....	−17,557	−105,946	—	—	−100,014	−51,290
Other Items (Net)........................	37r	† −12,223	−65,283	....	....	....	....	....	−41,500	−12,597	−13,441	−32,795	−83,336
Money plus Quasi-Money................	35l	† 5,839	26,721	....	....	....	....	....	67,198	94,089	124,503	215,270	270,124
Interest Rates		*Percent Per Annum*											
Discount Rate (End of Period)..........	60	145.0	125.0	238.0	13.0	22.0	120.0	120.0	140.0	24.0	8.0	....	....
Deposit Rate..............................	60l	60.0	60.0	60.0	....	....	....	....	....	....	....	....	....
Lending Rate..............................	60p	398.3	293.9	247.0	134.6	29.0	124.6	165.0	167.9	66.8	....	....	....
Prices		*Index Numbers (2000=100): Period Averages*											
Consumer Prices..........................	64	—	† .2	1.0	3.1	4.0	15.4	100.0	413.7	571.3	644.9	670.6	813.6
Intl. Transactions & Positions		*Millions of US Dollars*											
Exports......................................	70..d	....	1,563	1,547	1,449	1,422	809	824	901	1,132	1,374	1,850	2,190
Imports, c.i.f..............................	71..d	....	871	1,089	770	1,102	568	697	807	1,081	1,594	1,986	2,270

Congo, Democratic Republic of   636

		1994	1995	1996	1997	1998	1999	2000	2001	2002	2003	2004	2005
Government Finance		*Congo Francs through 1993; Thousands of Congo Francs 1994–95; Millions Beginning 1996: Year Ending December 31*											
Deficit (-) or Surplus........................	80	† −1,228	80	† −9	−63	....	....	....	....	....	....	....	....
Revenue.......................................	81	† 2,084	21,200	† 157	404	....	....	....	....	....	....	....	....
Grants Received...........................	81z	† 168	11,770	† 171	323	....	....	....	....	....	....	....	....
Expenditure................................	82	† 3,312	32,890	† 337	790	....	....	....	....	....	....	....	....
Lending Minus Repayments..........	83	† 168	—	† —	—	....	....	....	....	....	....	....	....
Financing													
Domestic..................................	84a	† 1,060	−80	† 9	63	....	....	....	....	....	....	....	....
Foreign...................................	85a	† 168	—	† —	—	....	....	....	....	....	....	....	....
Debt: Domestic.............................	88a	† 1,557	1,750	† 37	304	....	....	....	....	....	....	....	....
Foreign...............................	89a	† 116,448	921,660	† 7,019	11,871	....	....	....	....	....	....	....	....
National Accounts		*Thousands of Congo Francs through 1995; Millions of Congo Francs Beginning 1996*											
Househ.Cons.Expend.,incl.NPISHs....	96f	† 61,700	314,200	† 2,066	6,436	8,445	42,115	242,586	1,241,371	1,588,181	1,982,429	1,955,705	....
Government Consumption Expend...	91f	† 3,000	19,600	† 179	614	1,018	4,595	22,289	69,655	99,954	148,214	215,603	....
Gross Fixed Capital Formation..........	93e	† 5,200	38,300	† 450	666	731	2,251	31,114	107,279	165,080	286,759	481,185	....
Changes in Inventories....................	93i	† −2,800	5,500	† −36	−30	−77	2,746	1,677	6,733	13,455	28,321	30,567	....
Exports of Goods and Services..........	90c	† 16,900	112,900	† 896	1,876	2,494	3,427	19,427	199,468	468,482	616,491	913,996	....
Imports of Goods and Services (-)....	98c	† 14,700	94,100	† 659	1,758	2,621	3,310	20,027	216,960	412,853	778,694	987,507	....
Gross Domestic Product (GDP)........	99b	† 69,300	396,400	† 2,896	7,804	9,989	51,824	297,065	1,407,545	1,922,300	2,283,520	2,609,549	....
Net Primary Income from Abroad.....	98.n	† −500	−56,400	† −397	−360	−400	−2,060	−8,753	−112,581	−108,743	−72,409	−150,615	....
Gross National Income (GNI)............	99a	† 68,800	340,000	† 2,499	7,444	9,589	49,764	288,312	1,294,964	1,813,557	2,211,111	2,458,935	....
Consumption of Fixed Capital..........	99cf	† −2,100	−11,900	† −87	−234	−300	−1,555	−10,048	−2,642	....	....	....	....
Net National Income......................	99e	† 66,700	328,100	† 2,412	7,210	9,289	48,209	279,400	1,252,737	1,755,888	2,142,606	2,380,648	....
GDP Vol.1987 Prices......................	99b.p	† 181,300	182,600	† 181	171	168	161	150	151	....	....	....	....
GDP Volume (2000=100)...............	99bvp	121.3	122.1	120.8	114.2	112.2	107.5	100.0	100.9	....	....	....	....
GDP Deflator (2000=100)...............	99bip	—	.1	.8	2.3	3.0	16.2	100.0	469.4	....	....	....	....
		Millions: Midyear Estimates											
Population...............................	99z	43.69	45.00	46.12	47.10	48.00	48.96	50.05	51.31	52.71	54.23	55.85	57.55

Congo, Republic of   634

		1994	1995	1996	1997	1998	1999	2000	2001	2002	2003	2004	2005
Exchange Rates						*Francs per SDR: End of Period*							
Official Rate	aa	† 780.44	728.38	753.06	807.94	791.61	† 896.19	918.49	935.39	850.37	771.76	747.90	794.73
						Francs per US Dollar: End of Period (ae) Period Average (rf)							
Official Rate	ae	† 534.60	490.00	523.70	598.81	562.21	† 652.95	704.95	744.31	625.50	519.36	481.58	556.04
Official Rate	rf	† 555.20	499.15	511.55	583.67	589.95	† 615.70	711.98	733.04	696.99	581.20	528.28	527.47
Fund Position						*Millions of SDRs: End of Period*							
Quota	2f.s	57.90	57.90	57.90	57.90	57.90	84.60	84.60	84.60	84.60	84.60	84.60	84.60
SDRs	1b.s	.03	.02	.01	.01	—	.08	.03	.15	2.38	.43	4.66	1.70
Reserve Position in the Fund	1c.s	.47	.50	.54	.54	.54	.54	.54	.54	.54	.54	.54	.54
Total Fund Cred.&Loans Outstg	2tl	14.00	12.50	26.40	24.83	24.26	21.14	31.71	30.81	24.41	18.91	18.71	18.50
International Liquidity						*Millions of US Dollars Unless Otherwise Indicated: End of Period*							
Total Reserves minus Gold	1l.d	50.36	59.30	90.99	59.92	.84	39.35	222.01	68.91	31.63	34.80	119.60	731.83
SDRs	1b.d	.05	.03	.02	.01	.01	.11	.04	.19	3.23	.64	7.23	2.43
Reserve Position in the Fund	1c.d	.68	.75	.77	.72	.75	.74	.70	.67	.73	.80	.83	.77
Foreign Exchange	1d.d	49.63	58.52	90.20	59.19	.08	38.51	221.27	68.05	27.67	33.36	111.54	728.63
Gold (Million Fine Troy Ounces)	1ad	.011	.011	.011	.011	.011	.011	.011	.011	.011	.011	.011	.011
Gold (National Valuation)	1and	† 4.21	4.29	4.10	3.24	3.20	† 3.23	3.03	3.09	3.81	4.65	4.88	5.71
Monetary Authorities: Other Liab	4..d	17.20	18.62	16.48	13.53	35.97	25.10	24.66	22.97	27.65	28.74	32.04	39.09
Deposit Money Banks: Assets	7a.d	41.43	33.16	33.17	27.79	29.01	34.07	140.68	21.84	130.81	42.62	87.53	147.19
Liabilities	7b.d	50.04	28.91	25.81	14.13	41.82	39.17	17.98	17.79	68.69	39.94	57.27	16.15
Monetary Authorities						*Billions of Francs: End of Period*							
Foreign Assets	11	29.21	31.17	49.81	37.81	2.27	27.80	158.64	53.60	22.18	20.49	59.94	410.10
Claims on Central Government	12a	77.25	80.75	92.48	110.27	123.14	120.76	128.71	173.15	171.64	195.30	194.85	187.62
Claims on Deposit Money Banks	12e	1.54	4.26	3.70	5.01	7.16	6.20	6.45	2.44	—	.61	.39	—
Claims on Other Banking Insts	12f												
Reserve Money	14	85.97	93.09	101.08	112.80	89.44	120.07	243.82	186.79	170.80	183.09	220.39	372.36
of which: Currency Outside DMBs	14a	69.49	81.58	87.35	93.26	73.26	102.34	123.87	142.91	129.00	131.92	155.89	207.24
Foreign Liabilities	16c	20.12	18.23	28.51	28.17	39.43	35.33	46.51	45.91	38.05	29.52	29.42	36.44
Central Government Deposits	16d	22.34	15.87	24.01	19.59	11.33	12.77	21.03	12.90	13.25	13.25	17.47	196.48
Capital Accounts	17a	9.35	8.51	8.68	8.99	8.50	9.82	10.89	11.20	10.56	9.76	9.31	9.40
Other Items (Net)	17r	−29.78	−19.53	−16.30	−16.46	−16.13	−23.24	−28.45	−27.61	−33.28	−19.21	−21.42	−16.96
Deposit Money Banks						*Billions of Francs: End of Period*							
Reserves	20	12.05	7.41	8.99	15.08	13.85	12.72	105.99	30.07	29.34	37.44	52.33	136.15
Foreign Assets	21	22.15	16.25	17.37	16.64	16.31	22.25	99.17	16.25	81.82	22.13	42.15	81.84
Claims on Central Government	22a	30.76	28.91	29.45	25.74	28.74	20.12	26.43	15.07	24.86	16.81	23.08	10.63
Claims on Nonfin.Pub.Enterprises	22c	10.17	13.75	13.96	13.35	16.16	13.98	10.65	6.98	4.81	5.12	10.82	7.96
Claims on Private Sector	22d	75.62	85.68	98.09	106.53	112.01	158.00	109.59	101.03	60.62	75.06	73.02	77.12
Claims on Other Banking Insts	22f	.01	.02	.01	.30	.13	.78	.08	—	—	—	—	—
Claims on Nonbank Financial Insts	22g	.60	.84	1.05	1.16	1.33	.63	.05	.98	.98	1.57	1.20	1.06
Demand Deposits	24	60.57	49.16	61.08	68.85	68.39	76.68	171.74	81.36	129.77	89.50	110.72	159.98
Time and Savings Deposits	25	24.78	24.34	31.00	35.14	31.94	26.84	24.70	19.93	20.46	49.44	55.45	62.04
Foreign Liabilities	26c	26.75	14.04	13.51	8.45	23.51	25.57	12.67	13.24	42.97	20.74	27.08	8.46
Long-Term Foreign Liabilities	26cl	—	.13	.01	.01							.51	.52
Central Government Deposits	26d	6.10	11.03	12.65	10.95	17.44	25.53	56.16	11.83	15.48	15.14	11.28	47.33
Credit from Monetary Authorities	26g	1.54	4.26	3.70	5.01	7.16	6.20	6.45	2.44	—	.61	.39	—
Capital Accounts	27a	41.05	54.40	59.64	62.30	45.04	62.95	36.19	48.65	9.42	12.23	16.43	22.48
Other Items (Net)	27r	−9.42	−4.51	−12.65	−11.91	−4.96	4.70	44.04	−7.08	−15.66	−30.19	−19.88	13.94
Monetary Survey						*Billions of Francs: End of Period*							
Foreign Assets (Net)	31n	4.49	15.02	25.15	17.82	−44.36	−10.86	198.63	10.70	22.99	−7.64	45.09	446.52
Domestic Credit	32	165.98	183.04	198.39	226.80	252.73	275.96	198.32	272.48	239.75	265.46	274.22	40.57
Claims on Central Govt. (Net)	32an	79.58	82.75	85.27	105.46	123.10	102.58	77.94	163.49	173.34	183.73	189.17	−45.57
Claims on Nonfin.Pub.Enterprises	32c	10.17	13.75	13.96	13.35	16.16	13.98	10.65	6.98	4.81	5.12	10.82	7.96
Claims on Private Sector	32d	75.62	85.68	98.09	106.53	112.01	158.00	109.59	101.03	60.62	75.06	73.02	77.12
Claims on Other Banking Insts	32f	.01	.02	.01	.30	.13	.78	.08	—	—	—	—	—
Claims on Nonbank Financial Inst	32g	.60	.84	1.05	1.16	1.33	.63	.05	.98	.98	1.57	1.20	1.06
Money	34	134.49	134.85	153.18	166.56	143.98	184.03	309.58	238.08	271.24	235.15	278.79	396.19
Quasi-Money	35	24.78	24.34	31.00	35.14	31.94	26.84	24.70	19.93	20.46	49.44	55.45	62.04
Other Items (Net)	37r	11.20	38.87	39.37	42.92	32.45	54.23	62.67	25.16	−28.96	−27.42	−15.56	28.86
Money plus Quasi-Money	35l	159.27	159.19	184.17	201.70	175.92	210.87	334.28	258.01	291.69	284.59	334.24	458.23
Interest Rates						*Percent Per Annum*							
Discount Rate (End of Period)	60	† 7.75	8.60	7.75	7.50	7.00	7.60	7.00	6.50	6.30	6.00	6.00	5.50
Deposit Rate	60l	8.08	5.50	5.46	5.00	5.00	5.00	5.00	5.00	5.00	5.00	5.00	4.92
Lending Rate	60p	17.50	16.00	22.00	22.00	22.00	22.00	22.00	20.67	18.00	18.00	18.00	17.67
Prices and Production						*Index Numbers (2000=100): Period Averages*							
Consumer Prices	64	70.5	77.1	84.8	....	95.7	100.9	100.0	100.0	100.0	103.7	106.1	108.0	109.3
Crude Petroleum Production	66aa	71.0	72.8	81.6	91.1	96.4	100.3	100.0	92.1	91.3	85.4	21.2	93.6
Intl. Transactions & Positions						*Billions of Francs*							
Exports	70	532.40	585.30	688.10	973.70	806.90	960.50	1,772.20	1,506.40	1,589.10	1,555.90	1,819.00	2,637.10
Imports, c.i.f.	71	350.41	334.18	793.31	540.65	401.29	520.36	524.37	807.93	760.96	781.26	930.50	1,075.73
Imports, f.o.b.	71.v	340.20	324.50	770.20	524.90	329.40	429.80	321.30	....	....	....	....	....

Congo, Republic of   634

		1994	1995	1996	1997	1998	1999	2000	2001	2002	2003	2004	2005
Balance of Payments		*Millions of US Dollars: Minus Sign Indicates Debit*											
Current Account, n.i.e.	78ald	−793.4	−625.2	−650.9	−155.8	−240.6	−230.6	648.1	−28.4	−34.5	−2.6	....	....
Goods: Exports f.o.b.	78aad	958.9	1,286.6	1,654.9	1,661.5	1,367.8	1,560.1	2,491.8	2,055.3	2,288.8	1,461.1	....	....
Goods: Imports f.o.b.	78abd	−612.7	−654.2	−587.2	−648.8	−558.4	−522.7	−455.3	−681.3	−691.1	−449.9	....	....
Trade Balance	78acd	346.2	632.4	1,067.7	1,012.7	809.4	1,037.4	2,036.5	1,373.9	1,597.7	1,011.2	....	....
Services: Credit	78add	67.0	87.4	91.9	99.7	117.6	146.0	136.5	143.8	164.8	84.7	....	....
Services: Debit	78aed	−995.8	−691.7	−936.0	−748.5	−857.4	−868.6	−738.3	−852.2	−926.9	−544.9	....	....
Balance on Goods & Services	78afd	−582.7	28.2	223.5	363.9	69.6	314.9	1,434.7	665.6	835.6	551.0	....	....
Income: Credit	78agd	2.0	8.6	9.3	5.9	4.0	29.6	14.0	15.2	6.2	4.3	....	....
Income: Debit	78ahd	−291.1	−703.8	−914.7	−527.7	−311.1	−569.8	−819.3	−694.0	−866.4	−550.4	....	....
Balance on Gds, Serv. & Inc.	78aid	−871.8	−667.0	−681.9	−157.9	−237.6	−225.3	629.3	−13.2	−24.7	4.9	....	....
Current Transfers, n.i.e.: Credit	78ajd	111.3	52.0	54.5	9.0	10.0	14.9	38.9	18.3	12.9	9.6	....	....
Current Transfers: Debit	78akd	−33.0	−10.3	−23.5	−6.9	−13.0	−20.2	−20.1	−33.5	−22.7	−17.1	....	....
Capital Account, n.i.e.	78bcd	—	18.9	10.9	17.5	−.2	10.2	8.4	12.7	5.3	9.9	....	....
Capital Account, n.i.e.: Credit	78bad	—	18.9	11.6	17.5	—	10.3	8.9	13.3	5.3	9.9	....	....
Capital Account: Debit	78bbd	—	—	−.7	—	−.2	−.1	−.6	−.7	....	....	....	....
Financial Account, n.i.e.	78bjd	605.4	80.6	−663.4	−604.5	−715.9	−336.2	−821.8	−653.1	−464.3	−58.5	....	....
Direct Investment Abroad	78bdd	—	−1.6	.4	−3.5	8.1	−19.3	−3.8	−5.9	−4.2	.3	....	....
Dir. Invest. in Rep. Econ., n.i.e.	78bed	—	125.0	72.6	79.2	32.8	538.2	165.9	77.2	331.2	200.7	....	....
Portfolio Investment Assets	78bfd	—	−2.0	−1.0	−5.2	−13.5	−17.5	−4.5	−11.5	−7.0	−5.1	....	....
Equity Securities	78bkd	—	−2.5	−4.4	−3.8	−14.2	.6	−3.9	−10.2	−3.8	−5.1	....	....
Debt Securities	78bld	—	.5	3.4	−1.4	.8	−18.2	−.6	−1.3	−3.2		....	....
Portfolio Investment Liab., n.i.e.	78bgd	—	—	.1	.1	.7	−.2	−.1	....	....		....	....
Equity Securities	78bmd	—	—	—	.1	....	−.2	−.1	....	....		....	....
Debt Securities	78bnd	—	—	.1	—	.7	—	—	....	....		....	....
Financial Derivatives Assets	78bwd	....	....	....	....	....	....	....	....	....		....	....
Financial Derivatives Liabilities	78bxd	....	....	....	....	....	....	....	....	....		....	....
Other Investment Assets	78bhd	35.5	115.5	33.8	−19.9	49.5	84.3	−73.8	−41.1	−25.0	—	....	....
Monetary Authorities	78bod	....	....	....	....	....	....	....	....	....		....	....
General Government	78bpd	—	—	—	—	....	....	....	....	....		....	....
Banks	78bqd	33.9	13.1	−2.9	1.3	−5.5	−3.8	−20.4	27.1	31.9	....	....	....
Other Sectors	78brd	1.6	102.4	36.7	−21.1	55.0	88.1	−53.5	−68.2	−56.8	—	....	....
Other Investment Liab., n.i.e.	78bid	569.9	−156.3	−769.2	−655.2	−793.5	−921.7	−905.4	−671.8	−759.3	−254.4	....	....
Monetary Authorities	78bsd	—	1.1	−1.5	13.3	20.5	−6.2	1.4	−.4	−47.2	—	....	....
General Government	78btd	88.4	−457.9	−906.0	−586.4	−812.3	−459.6	−365.2	−606.8	−418.8	21.6	....	....
Banks	78bud	—	−25.4	−1.3	−8.7	14.8	13.6	−12.5	1.3	14.5	—	....	....
Other Sectors	78bvd	481.4	325.9	139.5	−73.4	−16.7	−469.5	−529.2	−65.9	−307.8	−276.0	....	....
Net Errors and Omissions	78cad	33.1	−54.9	−12.8	60.5	−72.0	−99.0	−77.6	−11.8	−219.7	−110.3	....	....
Overall Balance	78cbd	−154.9	−580.7	−1,316.1	−682.4	−1,028.6	−655.6	−242.8	−680.6	−713.1	−161.5	....	....
Reserves and Related Items	79dad	154.9	580.7	1,316.1	682.4	1,028.6	655.6	242.8	680.6	713.1	161.5	....	....
Reserve Assets	79dbd	−55.5	−4.3	−36.3	20.2	60.0	−40.9	−183.7	143.5	91.1	3.4	....	....
Use of Fund Credit and Loans	79dcd	15.0	−2.3	20.1	−2.1	−1.0	−4.2	13.6	−1.1	−8.2	−7.6	....	....
Exceptional Financing	79ded	195.4	587.3	1,332.2	664.3	969.6	700.7	413.0	538.3	630.3	165.7	....	....
Government Finance		*Billions of Francs: Year Ending December 31*											
Deficit (-) or Surplus	80	−129.9	−86.3	−24.5	−109.6	−226.0	−81.4	26.5	117.5p	....	....		....
Total Revenue and Grants	81y	230.6	260.4	362.1	401.6	266.8	394.1	611.3	642.4p	....	....		....
Revenue	81	220.2	249.7	357.8	400.2	263.2	387.8	604.5	637.4p	....	....		....
Grants	81z	10.4	10.7	4.3	1.4	3.6	6.3	6.8	5.0p	....	....		....
Exp. & Lending Minus Repay.	82z	360.5	346.6	386.6	511.2	492.8	475.5	584.8	524.9p	....	....		....
Expenditure	82	360.5	346.6	386.6	511.2	492.8	475.5	584.8	524.9p	....	....		....
Lending Minus Repayments	83	—	—	—	—	—	—	—	—p	....	....		....
Total Financing	80h	129.9	86.2	24.5	109.6	226.0	81.5	−26.5	....	....	....		....
Domestic	84a	12.9	15.9	−51.1	−77.3	39.7	−4.0	−71.8	....	....	....		....
Foreign	85a	117.0	70.3	75.6	186.9	186.3	85.4	45.3	....	....	....		....
Total Debt by Residence	88	....	....	....	....	....	4,112.3	3,681.5	....	....	....		....
Domestic	88a	....	....	....	....	....	390.0	433.6	....	....	....		....
Foreign	89a	2,875.4	2,839.4	3,318.7	3,468.4	3,770.4	3,722.4	3,247.9	....	....	....		....
National Accounts		*Billions of Francs*											
Househ.Cons.Expend.,incl.NPISHs.	96f	499.9	372.2	671.5	551.3	421.8	522.7	553.4	705.8	655.8	674.1	812.7	955.2
Government Consumption Expend.	91f	200.8	133.6	133.8	257.2	164.1	185.3	215.9	205.2	272.2	213.0	228.3	249.9
Gross Fixed Capital Formation	93e	439.6	521.8	364.9	329.3	557.6	512.4	534.2	682.9	599.2	555.6	623.2	804.0
Changes in Inventories	93i	13.8	12.4	13.9	8.6	15.0	51.0	3.0	50.0	−50.0	−10.2	−40.6	−30.0
Exports of Goods and Services	90c	557.6	682.9	894.8	1,024.9	837.2	1,046.3	1,853.0	1,541.9	1,622.8	1,331.6	1,714.3	2,619.3
Imports of Goods and Services (-)	98c	725.4	666.7	779.1	815.6	835.3	856.6	849.8	1,125.0	981.5	992.2	1,010.1	1,541.4
Gross Domestic Product (GDP)	99b	982.3	1,056.2	1,299.7	1,355.7	1,160.4	1,461.1	2,309.8	2,060.7	2,118.5	2,072.0	2,297.8	3,056.0
Net Primary Income from Abroad	98.n	−160.5	−352.9	−463.2	−304.5	−181.2	−332.6	−573.8	−497.5	−464.0	−340.6	−447.2	−592.1
Gross National Income (GNI)	99a	821.8	703.3	836.5	1,051.2	979.2	1,128.5	1,736.0	1,563.2	1,654.5	1,731.4	1,850.6	2,463.9
GDP Volume 1978 Prices	99b.p	401.3	410.1	....	....	....	....	....	....	....	....	....	....
GDP Volume (2000=100)	99bvp	86.9	† 88.8	92.6	92.2	95.7	92.6	100.0	....	....	....	....	....
GDP Deflator (2000=100)	99bip	48.9	51.5	60.7	63.7	52.5	82.3	100.0	....	....	....	....	....
		Millions: Midyear Estimates											
Population	99z	2.82	2.92	3.01	3.12	3.22	3.33	3.44	3.55	3.66	3.77	3.88	4.00

Costa Rica   238

		1994	1995	1996	1997	1998	1999	2000	2001	2002	2003	2004	2005
Exchange Rates					*Colones per SDR: End of Period*								
Market Rate..................................	aa	240.98	289.72	316.51	329.61	382.17	409.27	414.35	429.39	514.88	621.92	712.23	709.89
					Colones per US Dollar: End of Period (ae) Period Average (rf)								
Market Rate..................................	ae	165.07	194.90	220.11	244.29	271.42	298.19	318.02	341.67	378.72	418.53	458.61	496.68
Market Rate..................................	rf	157.07	179.73	207.69	232.60	257.23	285.68	308.19	328.87	359.82	398.66	437.94	477.79
					Index Numbers (2000=100): Period Averages								
Market Rate..................................	ahx	196.3	171.8	148.6	132.6	119.9	107.9	100.0	93.7	85.7	77.3	70.4	64.5
Nominal Effective Exchange Rate.....	nec	169.3	149.4	133.0	123.2	115.9	105.4	100.0	96.2	87.8	76.9	68.2	61.8
Real Effective Exchange Rate...........	rec	95.5	97.4	97.3	98.5	100.5	98.1	100.0	103.9	101.5	94.8	91.9	91.9
Fund Position					*Millions of SDRs: End of Period*								
Quota..	2f.s	119.00	119.00	119.00	119.00	119.00	164.10	164.10	164.10	164.10	164.10	164.10	164.10
SDRs..	1b.s	.12	.04	.01	.02	.05	.59	.33	.07	.06	.04	.09	.03
Reserve Position in the Fund...........	1c.s	8.73	8.73	8.73	8.73	8.73	20.00	20.00	20.00	20.00	20.00	20.00	20.00
Total Fund Cred.&Loans Outstg.......	2tl	45.46	16.32	.50	—	—	—	—	—	—	—	—	—
International Liquidity					*Millions of US Dollars Unless Otherwise Indicated: End of Period*								
Total Reserves minus Gold..............	1l.d	893.20	1,046.64	1,000.23	1,261.82	1,063.39	1,460.40	1,317.76	1,329.82	1,501.66	1,839.15	1,921.81	2,312.65
SDRs.......................................	1b.d	.18	.06	.01	.03	.07	.81	.43	.09	.09	.05	.13	.04
Reserve Position in the Fund..........	1c.d	12.74	12.97	12.55	11.77	12.29	27.45	26.06	25.13	27.19	29.72	31.06	28.59
Foreign Exchange......................	1d.d	880.28	1,033.61	987.67	1,250.02	1,051.04	1,432.14	1,291.27	1,304.59	1,474.38	1,809.38	1,890.61	2,284.02
Gold (Million Fine Troy Ounces).......	1ad	.034	.034	.002	.002	.002	.002	.002	.002	.002	.002	.002	.002
Gold (National Valuation)................	1and	....	....	....	.03	.02	.02	.02	.02	.02	.02	.02	.02
Monetary Authorities: Other Liab.....	4..d	1,294.60	1,217.58	1,115.12	1,047.67	1,078.46	1,013.79	917.51	811.13	671.21	574.96	283.21	186.68
Deposit Money Banks: Assets..........	7a.d	199.11	203.90	248.10	251.59	324.56	284.38	330.69	362.78	335.19	384.00	644.22	1,283.37
Liabilities...................	7b.d	102.24	166.96	200.85	293.53	333.73	387.96	529.25	651.69	727.40	901.48	1,008.60	1,046.53
Other Banking Insts.: Liabilities........	7f.d	3.58	....	....	....	....	....	....	....	....	....	....	....
Monetary Authorities					*Billions of Colones: End of Period*								
Foreign Assets............................	11	155.9	196.7	203.7	† 364.0	370.6	556.3	536.1	534.6	636.8	819.4	974.0	1,209.4
Claims on Central Government........	12a	71.5	100.2	283.4	† 359.7	416.8	312.1	234.5	82.8	83.6	90.2	100.5	112.1
Claims on Nonfin.Pub.Enterprises.....	12c	23.5	23.4	25.4	† 8.7	9.3	9.9	10.0	9.9	9.9	9.6	9.1	8.5
Claims on Deposit Money Banks......	12e	62.7	38.3	43.4	† 22.0	20.8	22.9	18.7	17.6	16.2	16.2	15.6	5.4
Claims on Other Banking Insts.........	12f	3.3	3.1	3.3	† 1.0	.9	.8	.7	.7	.6	.5	.5	.4
Reserve Money..........................	14	270.0	313.7	382.2	† 446.8	497.0	533.5	508.5	376.6	392.9	510.0	644.4	790.3
of which: Currency Outside DMBs..	14a	74.9	84.8	91.7	† 106.8	124.2	152.6	141.4	156.5	169.7	186.9	205.6	247.1
Time, Savings,& Fgn.Currency Dep...	15	4.8	4.7	8.2	† 4.2	4.3	3.7	3.2	3.3	1.8	—	—	—
Liabs. of Central Bank: Securities.....	16ac	78.9	128.5	46.8	† 196.4	184.2	379.4	406.9	496.2	696.5	906.8	930.3	1,245.2
Restricted Deposits........................	16b	—	—	—	† .3	.3	.3	.3	.3				
Foreign Liabilities.........................	16c	224.7	242.0	245.6	† 255.9	292.7	302.3	291.8	277.1	254.2	240.6	129.9	92.7
Central Government Deposits...........	16d	9.3	28.5	111.9	† 63.2	60.8	80.4	32.1	77.4	71.5	65.4	139.0	74.6
Counterpart Funds.......................	16e	—	—	—	† 8.6	10.8	2.5	2.3	5.0	.6	.6	.6	.6
Capital Accounts.........................	17a	26.8	29.0	126.9	† 126.5	105.8	−221.0	−280.4	−559.8	−675.7	−811.7	−870.2	−911.6
Other Items (Net).........................	17r	−297.5	−384.8	−362.4	† −346.5	−337.5	−179.1	−164.7	−30.6	5.3	24.3	125.7	44.0
of which: Valuation Adjustment.....	17rv	−335.0	−415.0	−401.3	† −353.0	−346.5	−196.6	−107.2	−41.9	−4.4	−2.3	−3.6	12.7
Deposit Money Banks					*Billions of Colones: End of Period*								
Reserves......................................	20	196.2	232.3	289.9	† 248.8	282.5	294.0	282.1	275.2	288.5	325.7	420.8	541.4
Claims on Mon.Author.:Securities....	20c	7.7	36.1	30.3	† 109.4	36.7	171.9	203.6	181.6	263.9	284.0	445.2	528.3
Foreign Assets.............................	21	32.9	39.7	54.6	† 61.5	88.1	84.8	105.2	124.0	126.9	160.7	295.4	637.4
Claims on Central Government........	22a	34.6	28.4	89.7	† 130.1	133.1	134.4	162.0	228.5	356.4	453.1	788.0	621.8
Claims on Nonfin.Pub.Enterprises.....	22c	2.8	2.4	2.5	† 7.3	7.0	9.8	23.4	11.1	11.5	11.1	16.7	20.0
Claims on Private Sector................	22d	222.9	223.0	329.9	† 434.3	670.6	914.3	1,180.0	1,493.3	1,824.4	2,176.4	2,613.9	3,428.8
Claims on Other Banking Insts.........	22f	2.6	.1	—	† 9.6	26.4	9.5	20.5	19.4	21.8	32.3	34.3	34.1
Demand Deposits.........................	24	86.6	67.0	84.9	† 243.7	279.6	350.5	479.7	542.3	662.6	779.0	837.6	1,058.8
Time, Savings,& Fgn.Currency Dep...	25	355.1	389.7	620.7	† 578.1	763.8	989.1	1,164.7	1,267.6	1,567.7	1,845.2	2,720.3	3,385.7
Bonds..	26ab				† 7.0	16.3	37.2	35.5	35.3	39.6	39.0	44.4	55.9
Restricted Deposits........................	26b	—	—	—	† .3	.1	—	—	.1	.1	.1	.2	.3
Foreign Liabilities.........................	26c	16.9	32.5	44.2	† 71.7	90.6	115.7	168.3	222.7	275.5	377.3	462.6	519.8
Central Government Deposits...........	26d	41.4	15.0	3.4	† —	—	—	—	—	—	—	—	—
Credit from Monetary Authorities.....	26g	45.8	14.5	11.0	† 9.2	7.9	7.5	4.9	7.7	4.6	2.8	1.0	1.8
Capital Accounts..........................	27a	31.8	63.7	95.5	† 185.6	229.1	306.7	370.6	486.8	589.6	738.7	852.0	1,093.8
Other Items (Net)...........................	27r	−78.0	−20.6	−62.7	† −94.6	−143.0	−187.8	−246.8	−229.3	−246.3	−338.8	−303.6	−304.3
Monetary Survey					*Billions of Colones: End of Period*								
Foreign Assets (Net).......................	31n	−52.8	−38.1	−31.5	† 97.8	75.4	223.2	181.2	158.8	234.1	362.2	677.0	1,234.3
Domestic Credit............................	32	310.5	336.9	618.9	† 887.5	1,203.4	1,310.4	1,599.0	1,768.2	2,236.7	2,707.9	3,424.1	4,151.2
Claims on Central Govt. (Net)........	32an	55.4	85.0	257.8	† 426.6	489.1	366.0	364.3	233.9	368.6	478.0	749.5	659.3
Claims on Nonfin.Pub.Enterprises...	32c	26.3	25.8	27.9	† 16.0	16.4	19.7	33.4	21.0	21.4	20.7	25.9	28.5
Claims on Private Sector...............	32d	222.9	223.0	329.9	† 434.3	670.6	914.3	1,180.0	1,493.3	1,824.4	2,176.4	2,613.9	3,428.8
Claims on Other Banking Insts.......	32f	5.9	3.1	3.3	† 10.6	27.3	10.3	21.3	20.1	22.4	32.8	34.8	34.6
Money..	34	161.6	151.9	177.5	† 354.6	415.4	534.1	639.7	724.2	843.1	970.1	1,046.7	1,310.4
Quasi-Money.................................	35	359.8	394.4	628.8	† 582.3	768.1	992.7	1,167.9	1,270.9	1,569.5	1,845.3	2,720.3	3,385.7
Bonds..	36ab	—	—	—	† 7.0	16.3	37.2	35.5	35.3	39.6	39.0	44.4	55.9
Liabs. of Central Bank: Securities.....	36ac	71.2	92.4	16.5	† 87.0	147.5	207.5	203.3	314.6	432.6	622.8	485.0	716.8
Restricted Deposits........................	36b	—	—	—	† .5	.4	.3	.3	.4	.1	.1	.2	.3
Counterpart Funds........................	36e	—	—	—	† 8.6	10.8	2.5	2.3	5.0	.6	.6	.6	.6
Capital Accounts..........................	37a	58.6	92.7	222.3	† 312.1	335.0	85.7	90.2	−73.0	−86.0	−73.0	−18.1	182.2
Other Items (Net)..........................	37r	−393.5	−432.7	−457.7	† −366.9	−414.6	−326.4	−359.1	−350.3	−328.7	−334.7	−178.1	−266.5
Money plus Quasi-Money.................	35l	521.4	546.3	806.3	† 936.9	1,183.5	1,526.8	1,807.6	1,995.1	2,412.6	2,815.4	3,767.0	4,696.1

Costa Rica   238

		1994	1995	1996	1997	1998	1999	2000	2001	2002	2003	2004	2005
Other Banking Institutions						*Billions of Colones: End of Period*							
Cash...	40	—	....	....	....	....	....	....	....	....	....	....	....
Claims on Central Government........	42a	.4	....	....	....	....	....	....	....	....	....	....	....
Claims on Official Entities................	42bx	—	....	....	....	....	....	....	....	....	....	....	....
Claims on Private Sector..................	42d	7.3	....	....	....	....	....	....	....	....	....	....	....
Demand Deposits...........................	44	—	....	....	....	....	....	....	....	....	....	....	....
Time, Savings,& Fgn.Currency Dep...	45	.5	....	....	....	....	....	....	....	....	....	....	....
Bonds..	46ab	2.1	....	....	....	....	....	....	....	....	....	....	....
Foreign Liabilities............................	46c	.6	....	....	....	....	....	....	....	....	....	....	....
Central Government Deposits..........	46d	—	....	....	....	....	....	....	....	....	....	....	....
Credit from Monetary Authorities.....	46g	2.4	....	....	....	....	....	....	....	....	....	....	....
Credit from Deposit Money Banks.....	46h	2.2	....	....	....	....	....	....	....	....	....	....	....
Capital Accounts............................	47a	.2	....	....	....	....	....	....	....	....	....	....	....
Other Items (Net)............................	47r	−.1	....	....	....	....	....	....	....	....	....	....	....
Banking Survey						*Billions of Colones: End of Period*							
Foreign Assets (net)........................	51n	−53.4	....	....	....	....	....	....	....	....	....	....	....
Domestic Credit..............................	52	312.3	....	....	....	....	....	....	....	....	....	....	....
Claims on Central Govt. (Net)....	52an	55.8	....	....	....	....	....	....	....	....	....	....	....
Claims on Official Entities..............	52bx	26.3	....	....	....	....	....	....	....	....	....	....	....
Claims on Private Sector................	52d	230.2	....	....	....	....	....	....	....	....	....	....	....
Liquid Liabilities.............................	55l	521.8	....	....	....	....	....	....	....	....	....	....	....
Bonds..	56ab	73.3	....	....	....	....	....	....	....	....	....	....	....
Capital Accounts............................	57a	58.8	....	....	....	....	....	....	....	....	....	....	....
Other Items (Net)...........................	57r	−395.0	....	....	....	....	....	....	....	....	....	....	....
Interest Rates						*Percent Per Annum*							
Discount Rate (End of Period)..........	60	37.75	38.50	35.00	31.00	37.00	34.00	31.50	28.75	31.25	26.00	26.00	27.00
Deposit Rate..................................	60l	17.72	23.88	17.29	13.03	12.76	14.31	13.38	11.77	11.46	10.41	9.51	10.14
Lending Rate..................................	60p	33.03	36.70	26.27	22.48	22.47	25.74	24.89	23.83	26.42	25.58	23.43	24.66
Prices and Labor						*Index Numbers (2000=100): Period Averages*							
Producer Prices..............................	63	46.9	58.1	67.4	75.2	81.8	90.1	100.0	109.3	118.0	130.5	150.7	171.3
Consumer Prices..............................	64	† 44.7	55.1	64.8	73.3	81.9	90.1	100.0	111.2	121.4	132.9	149.3	169.9
						Number in Thousands: Period Averages							
Labor Force....................................	67d	1,160	1,232	1,221	1,302	1,377	1,383	1,391	1,653	....	1,758	1,769	....
Employment...................................	67e	1,138	1,174	1,145	1,227	1,300	1,300	1,319	1,553	1,587	1,640	1,654	....
Unemployment...............................	67c	49	64	76	74	77	83	72	100	109	117	115	....
Unemployment Rate (%)...................	67r	4.2	5.2	6.2	5.7	5.6	6.0	5.2	6.1	6.4	6.7	6.5	....
Intl. Transactions & Positions						*Millions of US Dollars*							
Exports...	70..d	2,878.2	3,475.9	3,758.4	4,334.5	5,525.6	6,662.4	5,849.7	5,021.4	5,263.5	6,102.2	6,301.5	7,026.4
Imports, c.i.f..................................	71..d	3,788.5	4,090.0	4,326.6	4,969.6	6,238.7	6,354.6	6,388.5	6,568.6	7,187.9	7,663.2	8,268.0	9,812.0
Balance of Payments						*Millions of US Dollars: Minus Sign Indicates Debit*							
Current Account, n.i.e.....................	78ald	−244.0	−358.1	−263.7	−480.9	−520.8	−666.4	−706.8	−712.7	−916.1	−928.7	−831.5	....
Goods: Exports f.o.b......................	78aad	2,122.0	3,481.8	3,774.1	4,220.6	5,538.3	6,576.4	5,813.4	4,923.2	5,269.9	6,163.0	6,369.7	....
Goods: Imports f.o.b......................	78abd	−2,727.8	−3,804.4	−4,023.3	−4,718.2	−5,937.4	−5,996.1	−6,023.8	−5,743.3	−6,537.1	−7,294.4	−7,832.7	....
Trade Balance.............................	78acd	−605.8	−322.6	−249.2	−497.6	−399.0	580.3	−210.5	−820.1	−1,267.2	−1,131.4	−1,463.0	....
Services: Credit..............................	78add	1,195.0	969.1	1,053.5	1,128.6	1,343.4	1,666.1	1,936.3	1,900.6	1,869.9	2,027.0	2,240.4	....
Services: Debit...............................	78aed	−860.1	−913.0	−1,033.3	−988.4	−1,109.8	−1,195.1	−1,273.5	−1,168.9	−1,182.1	−1,188.4	−1,307.6	....
Balance on Goods & Services.......	78afd	−270.9	−266.5	−228.9	−357.4	−165.5	1,051.2	452.3	−88.4	−579.5	−292.7	−530.2	....
Income: Credit..............................	78agd	154.6	146.4	142.5	185.4	182.7	198.2	242.8	196.0	317.9	213.3	487.3	....
Income: Debit...............................	78ahd	−283.0	−371.9	−326.7	−434.4	−651.2	−2,019.8	−1,495.2	−975.6	−835.2	−1,061.9	−1,004.3	....
Balance on Gds, Serv. & Inc.......	78aid	−399.3	−492.0	−413.2	−606.4	−634.0	−770.4	−800.1	−867.9	−1,096.8	−1,141.4	−1,047.1	....
Current Transfers, n.i.e.: Credit......	78ajd	164.5	165.2	192.7	191.2	190.5	201.4	203.8	266.4	296.9	368.6	371.2	....
Current Transfers: Debit................	78akd	−9.2	−31.3	−43.2	−65.7	−77.3	−97.5	−110.5	−111.1	−116.2	−156.0	−155.5	....
Capital Account, n.i.e.....................	78bcd	—	—	28.2	....	....	—	8.9	12.4	5.7	26.1	9.4	....
Capital Account, n.i.e.: Credit........	78bad	—	—	28.2	....	....	—	8.9	12.4	5.7	26.1	9.4	....
Capital Account: Debit..................	78bbd	—	—	....	....	....	—	—	—	—	—	—	....
Financial Account, n.i.e...................	78bjd	−108.4	517.3	47.5	129.7	199.0	683.1	−34.6	320.4	844.8	594.3	707.7	....
Direct Investment Abroad..............	78bdd	−4.7	−5.5	−5.7	−4.4	−4.8	−5.0	−5.0	−11.1	−34.1	−26.9	−62.6	....
Dir. Invest. in Rep. Econ., n.i.e......	78bed	297.6	336.9	427.0	408.2	613.1	619.5	408.6	453.6	661.9	574.2	619.6	....
Portfolio Investment Assets.............	78bfd	—	−.4	....	−22.5	−33.9	−11.0	−18.5	−81.2	28.4	−91.6	53.1	....
Equity Securities..........................	78bkd	—	−.4	....	−22.5	−33.9	−28.1	−4.0	−21.9	4.6	−1.5	−6.6	....
Debt Securities............................	78bld	—	—	....	....	....	17.1	−14.4	−59.2	23.8	−90.1	59.8	....
Portfolio Investment Liab., n.i.e.......	78bgd	−1.2	−24.4	−21.5	−190.8	−296.0	−123.2	−67.5	−57.9	−125.8	−304.5	−25.4	....
Equity Securities..........................	78bmd	—	—	—	—	—	—	—	—	—	—	—	....
Debt Securities............................	78bnd	−1.2	−24.4	−21.5	−190.8	−296.0	−123.2	−67.5	−57.9	−125.8	−304.5	−25.4	....
Financial Derivatives Assets............	78bwd	....	....	....	....	....	....	....	....	....	....	....	....
Financial Derivatives Liabilities.......	78bxd	....	....	....	....	....	....	....	....	....	....	....	....
Other Investment Assets................	78bhd	−76.2	16.8	−159.3	−267.4	−95.6	156.1	−344.3	106.2	217.5	162.4	−110.6	....
Monetary Authorities..................	78bod	....	.1	−6.3	−.1	....	−.1	−.2	−.2	−.2	−27.6	−4.1	....
General Government...................	78bpd	−4.4	—	—	....	....	—	—	—	—	—	—	....
Banks.......................................	78bqd		−9.8	−17.8	43.3	−29.8	43.6	−76.3	54.4	.6	−35.2	−318.4	....
Other Sectors............................	78brd	−71.8	26.5	−135.2	−310.6	−65.8	112.7	−267.8	52.0	217.0	225.2	211.9	....
Other Investment Liab., n.i.e..........	78bid	−323.9	193.9	−192.9	206.7	16.2	46.8	−7.8	−89.2	96.9	280.8	233.5	....
Monetary Authorities..................	78bsd	−216.1	−94.4	−104.0	−118.6	−98.5	−93.7	−175.3	−135.2	−76.7	−47.4	−77.0	....
General Government...................	78btd	−106.2	12.9	−85.2	−64.1	−60.7	−77.9	−74.6	−65.3	−57.7	−86.5	−69.9	....
Banks.......................................	78bud	−18.8	23.0	48.7	73.7	37.3	49.0	142.9	144.6	59.2	173.2	106.8	....
Other Sectors............................	78bvd	17.2	252.4	−52.3	315.7	138.1	169.4	99.1	−33.4	172.1	241.5	273.7	....
Net Errors and Omissions................	78cad	249.1	57.1	118.7	157.8	−182.5	213.1	391.0	243.9	28.2	82.3	80.9	....
Overall Balance.............................	78cbd	−103.3	216.2	−69.3	−193.3	−504.3	229.7	−341.4	−136.0	−37.4	−226.1	−33.5	....
Reserves and Related Items.............	79dad	103.3	−216.2	69.3	193.3	504.3	−229.7	341.4	136.0	37.4	226.1	33.5	....
Reserve Assets.............................	79dbd	65.5	−179.2	77.3	−215.7	149.6	−481.0	152.9	−13.0	−163.0	−338.9	−80.3	....
Use of Fund Credit and Loans........	79dcd	−20.3	−44.4	−23.1	−.7	—	—	—	—	—	—	—	....
Exceptional Financing....................	79ded	58.1	7.4	15.0	409.7	354.7	251.3	188.4	149.0	200.4	564.9	113.8	....

Costa Rica 238

		1994	1995	1996	1997	1998	1999	2000	2001	2002	2003	2004	2005
International Investment Position							*Millions of US Dollars*						
Assets..	79aad	....	....	3,367.6	3,887.1	3,806.3	4,089.3	4,295.5	4,246.2	4,147.8	4,428.2	4,587.1	....
Direct Investment Abroad...............	79abd	....	....	60.0	65.7	71.4	77.6	86.1	97.4	128.9	153.9	212.7	....
Portfolio Investment......................	79acd	....	....	86.2	108.7	105.8	90.1	108.5	142.5	131.1	222.7	169.5	....
Equity Securities.......................	79add	....	....	19.0	41.5	38.6	40.0	44.0	7.4	2.7	4.3	10.9	....
Debt Securities..........................	79aed	....	....	67.2	67.2	67.2	50.1	64.5	135.1	128.3	218.4	158.6	....
Financial Derivatives.....................	79ald	....	....										....
Other Investment.........................	79afd	....	....	2,212.6	2,488.9	2,554.2	2,366.1	2,699.8	2,593.1	2,309.5	2,132.0	2,203.7	....
Monetary Authorities.................	79agd	....	....	132.6	132.7	132.7	132.8	133.0	133.2	133.3	160.9	165.0	....
General Government..................	79ahd	....	....	—	—	—	—	—	—	—	—	—	....
Banks.......................................	79aid	....	....	247.6	204.4	234.2	190.6	239.8	231.7	209.0	244.2	563.4	....
Other Sectors...........................	79ajd	....	....	1,832.3	2,151.9	2,187.3	2,042.6	2,327.0	2,228.3	1,967.2	1,727.0	1,475.2	....
Reserve Assets..............................	79akd	....	....	1,008.8	1,223.8	1,074.9	1,555.6	1,401.1	1,413.2	1,578.3	1,919.6	2,001.3	....
Liabilities......................................	79lad	....	....	5,369.5	6,053.5	6,672.8	7,433.2	7,561.5	8,057.4	8,716.1	9,567.9	9,668.8	....
Dir. Invest. in Rep. Economy..........	79lbd	....	....	836.1	1,221.5	1,759.0	2,364.7	2,709.1	3,182.8	3,739.3	4,258.3	4,443.6	....
Portfolio Investment......................	79lcd	....	....	674.2	773.1	699.6	794.9	744.5	844.3	921.8	863.6	632.6	....
Equity Securities.......................	79ldd	....	....										....
Debt Securities..........................	79led	....	....	674.2	773.1	699.6	794.9	744.5	844.3	921.8	863.6	632.6	....
Financial Derivatives.....................	79lld	....	....	—	—	—	—	—	—	—	—	—	....
Other Investment.........................	79lfd	....	....	3,859.2	4,058.9	4,214.2	4,273.7	4,107.8	4,030.3	4,055.1	4,446.0	4,592.6	....
Monetary Authorities.................	79lgd	....	....	659.5	548.4	559.0	493.8	419.5	318.6	262.7	335.7	259.3	....
General Government..................	79lhd	....	....	1,026.0	975.7	942.3	865.1	819.4	807.1	757.1	703.1	651.2	....
Banks.......................................	79lid	....	....	191.6	266.1	303.2	359.7	537.6	664.8	722.9	894.7	970.3	....
Other Sectors...........................	79ljd	....	....	1,982.1	2,268.7	2,409.7	2,555.1	2,331.3	2,239.8	2,312.3	2,512.5	2,711.9	....
Government Finance						*Millions of Colones: Year Ending December 31*							
Deficit (-) or Surplus.......................	80	−85,361	−84,575	−95,471	−81,769	−89,435	−98,989	−140,173	−144,246	−239,767	....	....	
Total Revenue and Grants..............	81y	191,247	253,699	302,497	363,540	444,486	547,435	599,101	704,131	781,797	....	....	
Revenue.......................................	81	191,247	253,699	302,497	363,540	444,486	547,435	599,101	704,131	781,797	....	....	
Grants..	81z	—	—	—	—	—	—	—	—	—	....	....	
Exp. & Lending Minus Repay..........	82z	276,608	338,274	397,968	445,309	533,921	646,424	739,274	848,377	1,021,564	....	....	
Expenditure.................................	82	276,608	338,274	397,968	445,309	533,921	646,424	739,274	848,377	1,021,564	....	....	
Lending Minus Repayments..........	83	—	—	—	—	—	—	—	—	—	....	....	
Total Financing.............................	80h	85,361	84,575	95,472	81,769	89,436	98,991	140,175	144,246	239,767	....	....	
Domestic......................................	84a	88,498	101,350	120,983	106,561	39,827	34,517	69,303	89,679	....	....	....	
Foreign..	85a	−3,138	−16,775	−25,511	−24,792	49,609	64,474	70,872	54,567	....	....	....	
Total Debt by Residence................	88	506,771	671,357	922,811	1,080,891	1,283,354	1,599,430	1,797,993	2,140,538	2,593,277	....	....	
Domestic Debt............................	88a	320,272	463,933	697,676	706,375	977,150	1,235,767	1,343,884	1,547,216	1,796,466	....	....	
Foreign Debt..............................	89a	186,499	207,424	225,135	374,516	306,204	363,663	454,109	593,322	796,811	....	....	
National Accounts							*Millions of Colones*						
Househ.Cons.Expend.,incl.NPISHs....	96f	1,189,292	1,496,157	1,822,342	2,168,885	2,510,880	2,916,434	3,290,353	3,689,866	4,109,780	4,661,108	5,371,385	6,297,746
Government Consumption Expend...	91f	228,887	284,636	330,455	390,087	469,886	565,207	652,654	772,575	898,116	1,011,166	1,150,736	1,323,175
Gross Fixed Capital Formation..........	93e	324,161	399,983	421,650	538,478	740,341	811,325	873,951	987,278	1,143,140	1,338,174	1,514,963	1,807,412
Changes in Inventories...................	93i	8,282	−15,918	−29,099	1,161	1,626	−42,745	−42,854	105,870	227,855	102,166	344,178	635,760
Exports of Goods and Services..........	90c	589,686	790,800	967,130	1,215,914	1,720,723	2,335,125	2,389,590	2,237,701	2,569,013	3,259,183	3,766,571	4,636,954
Imports of Goods and Services (-)....	98c	682,071	849,971	1,052,522	1,330,505	1,816,627	2,072,582	2,249,196	2,398,695	2,887,026	3,389,509	4,021,091	5,135,368
Gross Domestic Product (GDP).........	99b	1,658,236	2,105,687	2,459,957	2,984,020	3,626,830	4,512,763	4,914,498	5,394,595	6,060,878	6,982,288	8,126,742	9,565,678
Net Primary Income from Abroad.....	98.n	−21,837	−40,473	−38,353	−57,912	−120,500	−520,932	−385,150	−225,082	−218,906	−284,566	−341,040	−376,176
Gross National Income (GNI)............	99a	1,636,400	2,065,214	2,421,604	2,926,108	3,506,330	3,991,831	4,529,348	5,169,513	5,841,972	6,697,721	7,785,702	9,189,502
Consumption of Fixed Capital..........	99cf	92,123	115,025	138,579	168,727	201,867	256,097	284,228	319,941	368,135	420,566	501,284	590,038
GDP Volume 1991 Prices.................	99b.p	1,076,753	1,118,971	1,128,892	1,191,864	1,291,955	1,398,182	1,423,344	1,438,695	1,480,316	1,575,080	1,640,331	1,737,876
GDP Volume (2000=100).................	99bvp	75.6	78.6	79.3	83.7	90.8	98.2	100.0	101.1	104.0	110.7	115.2	122.1
GDP Deflator (2000=100)................	99bip	44.6	54.5	63.1	72.5	81.3	93.5	100.0	108.6	118.6	128.4	143.5	159.4
							Millions: Midyear Estimates						
Population................................	99z	3.39	3.47	3.56	3.65	3.75	3.84	3.93	4.01	4.10	4.18	4.25	4.33

Côte d'Ivoire   662

		1994	1995	1996	1997	1998	1999	2000	2001	2002	2003	2004	2005
Exchange Rates					*Francs per SDR: End of Period*								
Official Rate	aa	† 780.44	728.38	753.06	807.94	791.61	† 896.19	918.49	935.39	850.37	771.76	747.90	794.73
					Francs per US Dollar: End of Period (ae) Period Average (rf)								
Official Rate	ae	† 534.60	490.00	523.70	598.81	562.21	† 652.95	704.95	744.31	625.50	519.36	481.58	556.04
Official Rate	rf	† 555.20	499.15	511.55	583.67	589.95	† 615.70	711.98	733.04	696.99	581.20	528.28	527.47
					Index Numbers (2000=100): Period Averages								
Official Rate	ahx	128.1	142.3	138.8	121.8	120.5	115.5	100.0	96.9	102.2	122.4	134.6	134.8
Nominal Effective Exchange Rate	nec	96.3	102.6	103.6	100.0	104.9	105.8	100.0	102.0	105.4	112.1	115.0	113.6
Real Effective Exchange Rate	rec	88.9	102.3	102.2	100.0	106.9	106.0	100.0	103.4	107.6	115.0	116.6	116.4
Fund Position					*Millions of SDRs: End of Period*								
Quota	2f.s	238.2	238.2	238.2	238.2	238.2	325.2	325.2	325.2	325.2	325.2	325.2	325.2
SDRs	1b.s	.1	1.2	.8	—	.1	2.5	1.0	.6	.9	.2	.1	.4
Reserve Position in the Fund	1c.s	.1	.1	.1	.2	.2	.2	.3	.3	.4	.6	.6	.6
Total Fund Cred.&Loans Outstg	2tl	224.8	287.1	349.6	333.5	457.3	451.4	421.6	369.2	361.1	286.0	200.5	138.8
International Liquidity					*Millions of US Dollars Unless Otherwise Indicated: End of Period*								
Total Reserves minus Gold	1l.d	204.3	529.0	605.8	618.4	855.5	630.4	667.9	1,019.0	1,863.3	1,303.9	1,693.6	1,321.5
SDRs	1b.d	.2	1.8	1.2	—	.2	3.4	1.3	.7	1.2	.3	.2	.6
Reserve Position in the Fund	1c.d	.1	.1	.2	.2	.3	.3	.4	.4	.6	.8	.9	.9
Foreign Exchange	1d.d	204.0	527.0	604.4	618.1	855.0	626.6	666.2	1,017.9	1,861.5	1,302.7	1,692.5	1,320.0
Gold (Million Fine Troy Ounces)	1ad	.045	—	—	—	—	—	—	—	—	—	—	—
Gold (National Valuation)	1and	16.6	—	—	—	—	—	—	—	—	—	—	—
Monetary Authorities: Other Liab	4..d	1.7	9.6	7.8	10.6	14.4	8.1	.5	6.6	16.3	8.9	10.8	14.7
Deposit Money Banks: Assets	7a.d	202.1	352.6	268.5	266.8	311.3	351.9	252.5	222.3	364.6	290.1	351.2	413.1
Liabilities	7b.d	299.8	400.6	312.0	295.4	363.0	389.7	317.2	345.8	258.3	240.0	301.2	258.2
Monetary Authorities					*Billions of Francs: End of Period*								
Foreign Assets	11	109.2	259.2	317.2	370.3	481.0	412.0	475.1	766.6	1,165.5	677.6	819.5	762.1
Claims on Central Government	12a	433.2	382.6	439.8	449.3	572.3	596.4	538.3	491.1	497.6	432.6	360.3	313.7
Claims on Deposit Money Banks	12e	130.0	140.8	125.8	104.7	114.6	99.8	75.3	36.8	14.7	.5	—	9.4
Claims on Other Financial Insts	12f	5.1	12.3	14.4	13.4	14.7	14.2	12.7	9.7	7.9	5.2	—	—
Reserve Money	14	462.4	516.0	550.8	615.7	733.1	676.7	690.1	926.9	1,297.5	752.5	907.8	923.2
of which: Currency Outside DMBs	14a	392.6	451.4	473.2	571.8	652.1	615.5	620.7	774.7	1,146.7	568.6	671.5	751.4
Foreign Liabilities	16c	176.3	213.8	267.3	275.8	370.2	409.8	387.6	350.3	317.2	225.4	155.2	118.5
Central Government Deposits	16d	45.8	43.0	49.5	27.8	51.1	56.7	39.3	40.8	44.2	97.8	75.5	27.0
Other Items (Net)	17r	−6.9	22.0	29.5	18.4	28.2	−20.8	−15.6	−13.9	26.7	40.2	41.2	16.6
Deposit Money Banks					*Billions of Francs: End of Period*								
Reserves	20	66.6	58.1	74.7	45.4	67.2	60.7	64.7	96.1	106.4	172.4	221.1	151.4
Foreign Assets	21	108.0	172.8	140.6	159.8	175.0	229.8	178.0	165.5	228.1	150.7	169.1	229.7
Claims on Central Government	22a	314.9	371.1	413.4	415.9	412.6	382.8	325.4	302.5	292.8	300.5	277.6	283.3
Claims on Private Sector	22d	828.2	997.1	1,016.0	1,147.4	1,186.7	1,084.5	1,136.2	1,192.3	1,192.3	1,073.3	1,164.1	1,176.6
Claims on Other Financial Insts	22f	5.8	1.7	—	—	—	—	—	—	—	—	—	—
Demand Deposits	24	403.3	490.7	489.0	502.8	562.0	576.7	526.7	507.8	571.6	563.3	619.0	628.3
Time Deposits	25	412.1	485.3	519.6	527.7	485.1	477.7	489.3	515.3	641.1	618.6	632.2	683.9
Foreign Liabilities	26c	112.5	160.1	128.2	153.8	172.3	207.1	192.4	185.3	145.1	109.3	131.8	120.3
Long-Term Foreign Liabilities	26cl	47.8	36.2	35.2	23.1	31.7	47.4	31.3	72.1	16.4	15.3	13.3	23.3
Central Government Deposits	26d	171.1	183.1	243.3	278.9	325.7	234.4	267.3	287.6	262.3	214.6	214.3	185.2
Credit from Monetary Authorities	26g	134.4	152.2	124.3	104.7	116.0	91.0	76.8	37.0	14.7	.5	—	9.1
Other Items (Net)	27r	42.3	93.0	105.0	177.6	148.7	123.5	120.5	151.2	168.4	175.2	221.4	191.0
Treasury Claims: Private Sector	22d.i	26.7	19.0	22.7	22.0	—	16.0	13.4	21.2	16.3	14.2	9.8	13.6
Post Office: Checking Deposits	24..i	2.1	1.5	2.4	3.6	2.0	3.0	3.9	3.6	4.7	6.1	5.6	8.2
Monetary Survey					*Billions of Francs: End of Period*								
Foreign Assets (Net)	31n	−71.5	58.1	62.3	100.5	113.5	24.8	73.2	396.4	931.2	493.5	701.7	753.0
Domestic Credit	32	1,372.4	1,540.1	1,593.1	1,722.9	1,811.5	1,789.8	1,709.8	1,670.6	1,688.8	1,505.2	1,517.7	1,569.7
Claims on Central Govt. (Net)	32an	506.5	510.1	540.0	540.1	610.1	675.1	547.6	447.5	472.3	412.5	343.7	379.5
Claims on Private Sector	32d	854.9	1,016.0	1,038.7	1,169.4	1,186.7	1,100.5	1,149.5	1,213.5	1,208.6	1,087.5	1,174.0	1,190.2
Claims on Other Financial Insts	32f	10.9	13.9	14.4	13.4	14.7	14.2	12.7	9.7	7.9	5.2	—	—
Money	34	798.8	944.5	966.4	1,080.0	1,219.3	1,198.0	1,154.0	1,324.8	1,750.5	1,145.1	1,300.4	1,397.3
Quasi-Money	35	412.1	485.3	519.6	527.7	485.1	477.7	489.3	515.3	641.1	618.6	632.2	683.9
Long-Term Foreign Liabilities	36cl	47.8	36.2	35.2	23.1	31.7	47.4	31.3	72.1	16.4	15.3	13.3	23.3
Other Items (Net)	37r	42.1	132.0	134.2	192.6	188.9	91.6	108.5	154.9	212.0	219.7	273.6	218.3
Money plus Quasi-Money	35l	1,210.9	1,429.9	1,486.0	1,607.7	1,704.4	1,675.7	1,643.3	1,840.1	2,391.6	1,763.7	1,932.6	2,081.1
Interest Rates					*Percent Per Annum*								
Bank Rate (End of Period)	60	6.00	6.00	6.00	6.00	6.00	6.00	6.00	6.00	6.00	4.50	4.00	4.00
Money Market Rate	60b	4.95	4.95	4.95	4.95	4.95	4.95	4.95	4.95	4.95	4.95	4.95	4.95
Deposit Rate	60l	3.50	3.50	3.50	3.50	3.50	3.50	3.50	3.50	3.50	3.50	3.50	3.50
Prices, Production, Labor					*Index Numbers (2000=100): Period Averages*								
Consumer Prices	64	75.9	86.8	88.9	92.5	96.8	97.6	100.0	104.3	107.5	111.1	112.7	117.1
Industrial Production	66	68.8	74.8	84.8	94.9	105.5	108.5	100.0	96.1	92.2	85.1	81.6	96.1
					Number in Thousands: Period Averages								
Unemployment	67c	186	216	238	....	....	....	....	....	....	....	....	....
Unemployment Rate	67r	30.0	35.6	38.8	....	....	....	....	....	....	....	....	....
Intl. Transactions & Positions					*Billions of Francs*								
Exports	70	1,522.50	1,899.70	2,274.40	2,598.10	2,717.60	2,870.10	2,768.20	2,892.70	3,676.60	3,364.00	3,646.20	3,787.20
Imports, c.i.f	71	1,064.60	1,463.00	1,484.50	1,623.10	1,764.50	2,002.30	1,982.90	1,772.50	1,711.80	1,877.90	2,201.90	2,473.80

Côte d'Ivoire 662

		1994	1995	1996	1997	1998	1999	2000	2001	2002	2003	2004	2005
Balance of Payments		*Millions of US Dollars: Minus Sign Indicates Debit*											
Current Account, n.i.e.	78ald	−13.8	−492.4	−162.3	−154.7	−290.2	−119.5	−241.3	−61.3	768.2	294.6	302.6	....
Goods: Exports f.o.b.	78aad	2,895.9	3,805.9	4,446.1	4,451.2	4,606.4	4,661.5	3,888.0	3,945.9	5,274.8	5,787.7	6,902.1	....
Goods: Imports f.o.b.	78abd	−1,606.8	−2,430.3	−2,622.4	−2,658.4	−2,886.4	−2,766.0	−2,401.8	−2,417.7	−2,455.6	−3,230.9	−4,167.7	....
Trade Balance	78acd	1,289.1	1,375.5	1,823.7	1,792.8	1,720.0	1,895.5	1,486.2	1,528.2	2,819.3	2,556.8	2,734.4	....
Services: Credit	78add	507.7	530.9	565.7	579.6	614.5	586.5	482.4	577.8	585.3	664.3	748.3	....
Services: Debit	78aed	−1,011.1	−1,375.7	−1,440.3	−1,478.6	−1,524.1	−1,459.0	−1,226.9	−1,271.3	−1,544.7	−1,780.1	−2,012.9	....
Balance on Goods & Services	78afd	785.7	530.7	949.1	893.8	810.4	1,022.9	741.7	834.8	1,859.9	1,441.0	1,469.8	....
Income: Credit	78agd	133.8	189.5	170.7	161.2	169.0	162.6	141.6	137.3	141.2	170.6	179.3	....
Income: Debit	78ahd	−817.5	−976.1	−939.5	−829.2	−876.1	−919.2	−794.5	−723.1	−770.9	−830.1	−884.6	....
Balance on Gds, Serv. & Inc.	78aid	102.0	−255.8	180.2	225.8	103.4	266.3	88.8	249.0	1,230.2	781.5	764.5	....
Current Transfers, n.i.e.: Credit	78ajd	246.8	277.7	204.1	137.7	148.2	136.8	79.4	88.5	131.9	196.4	202.9	....
Current Transfers: Debit	78akd	−362.6	−514.3	−546.6	−518.3	−541.7	−522.6	−409.4	−398.7	−593.8	−683.3	−664.8	....
Capital Account, n.i.e.	78bcd	527.6	291.3	47.1	40.6	25.6	13.8	8.4	10.0	8.3	13.7	8.9	....
Capital Account, n.i.e.: Credit	78bad	527.6	291.3	49.8	50.5	35.9	17.4	9.9	11.5	9.1	14.1	11.5	....
Capital Account: Debit	78bbd	—	—	−2.7	−9.9	−10.3	−3.6	−1.4	−1.4	−.8	−.4	−2.7	....
Financial Account, n.i.e.	78bjd	−523.1	−88.6	−717.8	−323.0	−417.1	−580.6	−365.2	−69.8	−1,034.6	−1,041.7	−1,124.4	....
Direct Investment Abroad	78bdd	—	—	−.4	—	—	—	—	—	—	—	—	....
Dir. Invest. in Rep. Econ., n.i.e.	78bed	78.0	211.5	269.2	415.3	380.0	323.7	234.7	272.7	212.6	165.3	174.5	....
Portfolio Investment Assets	78bfd	−27.4	−8.4	−16.0	−26.9	−29.8	−31.9	−15.1	−15.8	−27.1	−41.7	−41.5	....
Equity Securities	78bkd	7.7	1.2	−1.6	.2	−1.7	−1.6	−1.3	−1.3	−2.0	−14.1	—	....
Debt Securities	78bld	−35.1	−9.6	−14.5	−27.1	−28.2	−30.3	−13.8	−14.5	−25.1	−27.5	−41.5	....
Portfolio Investment Liab., n.i.e.	78bgd	−.7	10.0	25.0	19.2	19.5	13.4	4.5	4.0	51.7	66.8	−1.3	....
Equity Securities	78bmd	1.1	1.2	10.2	8.6	8.6	5.6	1.2	2.4	3.6	15.8	−1.3	....
Debt Securities	78bnd	−1.8	8.8	14.9	10.6	10.8	7.8	3.4	1.6	48.1	51.1	—	....
Financial Derivatives Assets	78bwd	—	—	—	—	−3.2	−3.1	−2.6	−3.8	−6.0	−7.9	—	....
Financial Derivatives Liabilities	78bxd	—	—	−3.3	−3.1	—	—	—	—	1.9	2.6	—	....
Other Investment Assets	78bhd	−39.6	−323.2	−256.5	−304.8	−317.6	−350.6	−182.4	−129.1	−439.0	−341.7	−437.5	....
Monetary Authorities	78bod	—	—	....	....	....	—	—	—	—	—	—	....
General Government	78bpd	−11.9	−14.2	−22.3	−9.9	−7.7	−5.2	−4.5	−5.1	−7.8	−4.0	−8.3	....
Banks	78bqd	−95.3	−33.1	35.2	−25.7	−16.4	−49.1	2.8	37.7	−89.8	62.6	—	....
Other Sectors	78brd	67.5	−275.9	−269.4	−269.2	−293.5	−296.3	−180.7	−161.8	−341.5	−400.3	−429.1	....
Other Investment Liab., n.i.e.	78bid	−533.3	21.4	−735.8	−422.7	−465.9	−532.0	−404.3	−197.8	−828.6	−885.2	−818.7	....
Monetary Authorities	78bsd	−726.6	1.8	−1.2	4.3	3.1	−5.2	−.7	−14.4	10.5	−6.7	—	....
General Government	78btd	249.8	−105.8	−621.6	−473.6	−597.3	−583.6	−523.3	−487.3	−737.2	−678.8	−658.4	....
Banks	78bud	75.1	77.1	−38.5	64.9	37.3	42.0	23.1	46.1	−136.4	−9.6	—	....
Other Sectors	78bvd	−131.7	48.3	−74.5	−18.3	91.0	14.7	96.6	257.8	34.5	−190.1	−160.3	....
Net Errors and Omissions	78cad	−11.1	35.6	−15.4	−39.6	32.1	−21.5	−10.3	35.0	−20.3	−53.8	32.2	....
Overall Balance	78cbd	−20.3	−254.2	−848.4	−476.6	−649.6	−707.9	−608.3	−86.1	−278.4	−787.2	−780.8	....
Reserves and Related Items	79dad	20.3	254.2	848.4	476.6	649.6	707.9	608.3	86.1	278.4	787.2	780.8	....
Reserve Assets	79dbd	−194.5	−302.5	−113.4	−95.4	−179.8	109.8	−89.0	−386.6	−584.1	12.0	−15.1	....
Use of Fund Credit and Loans	79dcd	94.3	94.9	90.3	−22.3	168.8	−8.2	−38.8	−66.4	−13.5	−106.4	−127.1	....
Exceptional Financing	79ded	120.5	461.8	871.5	594.3	660.6	606.3	736.1	539.1	876.1	881.6	923.0	....
International Investment Position		*Millions of US Dollars*											
Assets	79aad	....	....	....	....	2,768.3	2,640.9	2,735.7	3,114.5	4,876.3	5,361.5	6,519.8	....
Direct Investment Abroad	79abd	....	....	....	....	—	—	—	—	—	—	—	....
Portfolio Investment	79acd	—	—	—	—	158.9	166.9	169.9	176.4	240.2	335.9	397.6	....
Equity Securities	79add	—	—	—	—	10.5	10.5	11.1	11.8	16.3	35.4	38.2	....
Debt Securities	79aed	—	—	—	—	148.4	156.3	158.7	164.6	223.9	300.5	359.5	....
Financial Derivatives	79ald	....	....	....	....	—	—	—	—	—	—	—	....
Other Investment	79afd	337.4	378.6	268.3	266.9	1,757.3	1,843.7	1,891.9	1,919.1	2,772.8	3,721.7	4,428.5	....
Monetary Authorities	79agd	....	....	....	....	—	—	—	—	—	—	—	....
General Government	79ahd	....	....	....	....	—	—	—	—	—	—	—	....
Banks	79aid	230.5	249.8	81.0	100.7	—	—	—	—	—	—	—	....
Other Sectors	79ajd	....	....	....	....	1,757.3	1,843.7	1,891.9	1,919.1	2,772.8	3,721.7	4,428.5	....
Reserve Assets	79akd	204.4	531.0	607.0	623.0	852.1	630.4	673.9	1,019.0	1,863.3	1,303.9	1,693.6	....
Liabilities	79lad	....	....	....	....	18,731.5	16,581.2	15,907.8	12,696.6	15,390.7	17,811.6	18,754.1	....
Dir. Invest. in Rep. Economy	79lbd	—	—	—	—	1,858.2	1,905.1	2,001.6	2,164.4	2,812.4	3,572.1	4,043.9	....
Portfolio Investment	79lcd	—	—	—	—	244.4	223.1	211.2	205.8	299.3	435.2	467.9	....
Equity Securities	79ldd	—	—	—	—	—	—	—	—	—	—	—	....
Debt Securities	79led	—	—	—	—	244.4	223.1	211.2	205.8	299.3	435.2	467.9	....
Financial Derivatives	79lld	....	....	....	....	—	—	—	—	—	—	—	....
Other Investment	79lfd	15,272.6	17,009.2	16,101.1	14,046.3	16,628.9	14,453.0	13,695.0	10,326.5	12,279.0	13,804.2	14,242.3	....
Monetary Authorities	79lgd	329.8	436.8	510.7	461.3	644.0	619.5	464.0	549.3	490.9	425.0	311.4	....
General Government	79lhd	....	....	....	....	14,790.1	12,756.1	12,027.6	8,518.3	10,291.1	11,841.9	12,386.6	....
Banks	79lid	743.5	522.9	266.2	295.4	437.8	429.2	454.9	511.8	507.1	562.8	493.3	....
Other Sectors	79ljd	....	....	....	....	757.0	648.2	663.2	832.3	990.0	974.5	1,051.0	....
Government Finance		*Billions of Francs: Year Ending December 31*											
Deficit (-) or Surplus	80	−280.1	−147.3	−57.7	23.2	−84.0	−11.0	....	....	....	....	....	....
Total Revenue and Grants	81y	878.7	1,142.2	1,274.5	1,374.2	1,442.7	1,482.1	....	....	....	....	....	....
Revenue	81	849.0	1,107.2	1,234.0	1,330.2	1,392.2	1,442.1	....	....	....	....	....	....
Grants	81z	29.7	35.0	40.5	44.1	50.5	40.0	....	....	....	....	....	....
Exp. & Lending Minus Repay.	82z	1,158.8	1,289.5	1,332.2	1,351.0	1,526.7	1,493.1	....	....	....	....	....	....
Expenditure	82	1,166.0	1,322.6	1,385.2	1,494.5	1,557.3	1,533.1	....	....	....	....	....	....
Lending Minus Repayments	83	−7.2	−33.1	−53.0	−143.5	−30.6	−40.0	....	....	....	....	....	....
Total Financing	80h	280.1	147.3	57.7	−23.2	84.0	11.0	....	....	....	....	....	....
Domestic	84a	−153.1	−61.6	−107.5	−85.0	36.3	−104.2	....	....	....	....	....	....
Foreign	85a	433.2	208.9	165.2	61.8	47.7	115.2	....	....	....	....	....	....
Total Debt by Residence	88	9,148.6	9,392.7	9,606.0	10,056.3	7,620.7	....	....	....	....	....	....	....
Domestic	88a	1,320.4	1,230.7	1,137.8	1,070.6	1,039.5	....	....	....	....	....	....	....
Foreign	89a	7,828.2	8,162.0	8,468.2	8,985.7	6,581.2	....	....	....	....	....	....	....

Côte d'Ivoire   662

National Accounts		1994	1995	1996	1997	1998	1999	2000	2001	2002	2003	2004	2005
							Billions of Francs						
Househ.Cons.Expend.,incl.NPISHs....	96f	2,749.2	3,379.0	3,502.3	4,535.0	4,916.0	4,868.0	5,076.6	5,241.7	4,834.1	5,225.9	5,384.7	5,707.2
Government Consumption Expend...	91f	555.0	594.0	714.4	713.2	1,132.0	1,150.0	1,050.0	1,100.5	1,290.6	1,279.2	1,162.0	1,055.2
Gross Fixed Capital Formation..........	93e	473.0	641.2	846.5	959.8	1,167.3	1,124.1	821.8	760.8	807.6	748.8	....	....
Changes in Inventories....................	93i	60.8	104.6	−112.0	−37.2	−294.3	−100.1	−30.0	98.0	−79.2	32.0	....	....
Exports of Goods and Services..........	90c	1,827.0	2,051.0	2,533.0	2,737.8	2,835.0	3,074.0	3,010.0	3,163.0	4,084.4	3,810.8	3,741.6	4,000.2
Imports of Goods and Services (-).....	98c	1,409.0	1,782.1	1,960.7	2,074.3	2,215.0	2,382.0	2,381.9	2,494.5	2,788.3	2,933.8	2,955.7	3,127.7
Gross Domestic Product (GDP).........	99b	4,256.0	4,987.7	5,548.2	6,834.4	7,541.1	7,734.1	7,546.5	7,869.5	8,149.3	8,162.9	8,178.5	8,530.5
GDP Volume 1986 Prices................	99b.p	3,306.0	3,540.0	3,783.8	4,034.3	4,276.1	....	....	....	....	....	....	....
							Millions: Midyear Estimates						
Population...............................	99z	14.34	14.76	15.17	15.59	16.00	16.38	16.73	17.05	17.34	17.60	17.87	18.15

Croatia 960

		1994	1995	1996	1997	1998	1999	2000	2001	2002	2003	2004	2005
Exchange Rates						*Kuna per SDR: End of Period*								
Official Rate	aa	8.217	7.902	7.966	8.504	8.797	10.496	10.626	10.501	9.715	9.092	8.754	8.910
					Kuna per US Dollar: End of Period (ae) Period Average (rf)									
Official Rate	ae	5.629	5.316	5.540	6.303	6.248	7.648	8.155	8.356	7.146	6.119	5.637	6.234
Official Rate	rf	5.996	5.230	5.434	6.101	6.362	7.112	8.277	8.340	7.869	6.704	6.036	5.947
					Index Numbers (2000=100): Period Averages									
Nominal Effective Exchange Rate	nec	104.67	111.86	111.53	111.79	109.46	102.04	100.00	103.06	104.90	105.94	108.41	109.44
Real Effective Exchange Rate	rec	102.57	105.02	103.94	104.40	109.21	105.51	100.47	100.00	103.72	104.87	105.43	107.58	109.74
Fund Position						*Millions of SDRs: End of Period*								
Quota	2f.s	261.6	261.6	261.6	261.6	261.6	365.1	365.1	365.1	365.1	365.1	365.1	365.1
SDRs	1b.s	3.1	94.4	87.3	109.0	164.2	138.1	113.0	85.5	1.1	—	—	.2
Reserve Position in the Fund	1c.s	—	—	—	.1	.1	.1	.2	.2	.2	.2	.2	.2
Total Fund Cred.&Loans Outstg	2tl	87.1	148.6	145.4	172.7	166.1	143.2	121.4	97.2	—	—	—	—
International Liquidity					*Millions of US Dollars Unless Otherwise Indicated: End of Period*									
Total Reserves minus Gold	1l.d	1,405.0	1,895.7	2,314.0	2,539.1	2,815.7	3,025.0	3,524.4	4,703.2	5,884.9	8,190.5	8,758.2	8,800.3
SDRs	1b.d	4.5	140.3	125.6	147.1	231.2	189.5	147.2	107.4	1.5	—	.1	.3
Reserve Position in the Fund	1c.d	—	—	—	.1	.2	.2	.2	.2	.2	.2	.2	.2
Foreign Exchange	1d.d	1,400.5	1,755.4	2,188.4	2,391.9	2,584.4	2,835.3	3,376.9	4,595.6	5,883.2	8,190.2	8,757.9	8,799.8
Gold (Million Fine Troy Ounces)	1ad	—	—	—	—	—	—	—	—	—	—	—	—
Gold (National Valuation)	1and	—	.2	—	.3	.5	.7	22.2	41.8	68.5	27.0	457.3	3.2	3.0
Monetary Authorities: Other Liab	4..d	.1	.2	.3	.5	.7	22.2	41.8	68.5	27.0	457.3	3.2	3.0
Deposit Money Banks: Assets	7a.d	1,258.3	1,748.8	2,265.4	2,567.9	2,042.9	1,621.4	2,416.9	3,926.2	3,635.4	5,782.9	7,726.1	5,706.6
Liabilities	7b.d	2,333.5	2,849.8	2,250.6	2,190.5	2,589.3	2,250.3	2,183.8	2,615.8	4,901.3	8,160.8	10,850.6	10,766.2
Monetary Authorities						*Millions of Kuna: End of Period*								
Foreign Assets	11	7,908.3	10,077.7	12,818.8	16,005.6	17,592.6	23,135.7	28,743.7	39,306.1	42,057.0	50,118.5	49,373.4	54,862.5
Claims on Central Government	12a	250.6	390.1	218.8	—	3.8	24.1	—	.5	1.4	3.3	1.4
Claims on Private Sector	12d	.7	.9	1.1	24.4	1.0	276.1	289.5	229.2	110.6	93.6	82.9	73.4
Claims on Deposit Money Banks	12e	223.8	220.2	213.9	33.5	1,043.7	1,139.4	329.9	18.5	17.9	972.0	408.9	4,215.6
Reserve Money	14	4,714.2	6,744.1	8,770.3	10,346.2	11,622.7	14,946.1	17,207.7	23,508.4	30,070.1	37,272.8	44,689.1	53,886.8
of which: Currency Outside DMBs	14a	2,658.2	3,365.1	4,366.2	5,319.6	5,730.1	5,958.9	6,636.7	8,507.4	9,680.9	10,573.1	10,955.6	12,163.8
DMBs' Fgn.Currency Deposits	14cf					1,668.4	4,636.2	5,490.5	5,705.1	7,042.3	6,686.6	10,764.7	13,495.9
Liabs. of Central Bank: Securities	16ac	375.1	168.3	665.7	722.0	2,242.9	2,887.2	4,207.3	6,372.3	6,212.4	4,920.2	—	—
Restricted Deposits	16b	40.3	212.2	243.2	101.1	119.1	380.6	315.0	325.4	49.0	12.6	12.4	55.9
Foreign Liabilities	16c	716.2	1,175.2	1,160.4	1,471.4	1,465.4	1,672.9	1,630.8	1,593.1	192.8	2,798.0	18.1	18.9
Central Government Deposits	16d	793.8	395.5	557.6	1,032.7	434.8	397.2	1,157.4	1,752.1	768.1	1,551.1	263.2	332.2
Capital Accounts	17a	2,066.0	2,019.4	1,900.1	2,361.8	2,902.1	4,535.5	5,216.6	6,425.2	5,354.7	5,039.0	5,096.5	5,357.4
Other Items (Net)	17r	−322.2	−25.8	−44.7	28.4	−146.0	−244.3	−371.6	−422.6	−461.3	−408.2	−210.8	−498.2
Deposit Money Banks						*Millions of Kuna: End of Period*								
Reserves	20	2,039.7	3,508.3	4,573.9	5,056.7	5,908.1	8,987.9	10,588.9	15,002.7	20,373.5	26,783.7	33,718.2	41,775.2
Claims on Mon. Author.:Securities	20c	378.6	163.3	669.5	673.3	2,233.9	2,793.8	4,136.7	6,221.7	5,805.9	4,951.7	—	—
Foreign Assets	21	7,082.5	9,296.6	12,549.6	16,185.8	12,763.1	12,400.0	19,710.4	32,807.7	25,977.8	35,382.9	43,551.0	35,572.5
Claims on Central Government	22a	17,837.0	17,188.1	16,693.4	15,238.8	14,864.2	16,264.4	19,055.5	20,059.8	21,917.7	21,543.6	21,051.3	28,877.2
Claims on Local Government	22b	112.9	147.1	145.4	308.8	654.0	905.6	1,174.9	1,280.0	1,422.4	1,563.1	1,787.9	1,767.2
Claims on Nonfin.Pub.Enterprises	22c	2,141.4	1,896.2	1,943.8	2,182.5	2,291.8	1,794.2	2,413.4	3,180.0	3,813.3	4,083.0	4,987.9	6,406.1
Claims on Private Sector	22d	25,344.4	30,674.5	31,600.7	46,100.9	56,650.9	52,699.9	56,775.7	69,823.7	90,982.7	104,728.2	118,932.1	139,167.5
Claims on Other Banking Insts	22f					.4	45.4	68.7	170.2	219.5	431.8	624.0	592.2
Claims on Nonbank Financial Insts	22g	62.1	100.8	140.2	246.8	193.9	154.0	161.7	281.4	915.3	761.8	893.9	1,161.8
Demand Deposits	24	3,969.7	4,870.0	7,007.5	8,423.8	7,808.9	7,891.5	11,386.0	15,180.6	21,166.2	23,315.0	23,591.3	26,653.3
Time, Savings,& Fgn.Currency Dep	25	10,828.8	16,257.4	25,204.1	36,876.9	43,654.7	42,363.6	54,552.7	82,050.0	85,055.7	94,406.1	104,222.1	114,752.8
Money Market Instruments	26aa	1.5	.2	.9	7.0	4.5	1.4	—	—	5.1	—	—	—
Bonds	26ab	207.0	130.5	127.2	126.6	149.7	435.4	478.2	317.8	211.2	598.4	1,163.5	1,077.0
Restricted Deposits	26b	12,087.7	10,662.4	8,223.6	5,852.3	4,196.0	3,434.2	2,549.6	1,600.8	1,680.5	1,709.0	2,054.6	2,036.4
Foreign Liabilities	26c	13,134.8	15,150.0	12,467.4	13,807.1	16,176.8	17,209.2	17,809.8	21,857.8	35,023.5	49,932.0	61,163.7	67,112.3
Central Government Deposits	26d	1,675.0	2,025.6	1,720.9	6,874.7	7,298.3	5,828.6	6,730.5	5,634.7	6,094.9	5,283.3	6,821.8	9,287.0
Credit from Monetary Authorities	26g	224.6	182.6	267.7	33.7	1,049.2	1,138.7	328.8	16.6	17.6	968.9	408.9	4,215.6
Capital Accounts	27a	13,883.6	15,392.4	15,441.8	17,023.6	19,786.8	21,975.4	24,953.1	25,455.1	26,323.2	27,389.5	28,666.4	32,665.7
Other Items (Net)	27r	−1,013.9	−1,695.9	−2,144.4	−3,032.2	−4,564.5	−4,232.7	−4,702.9	−3,286.2	−4,149.7	−3,372.5	−2,546.3	−2,480.4
Monetary Survey						*Millions of Kuna: End of Period*								
Foreign Assets (Net)	31n	1,139.8	3,049.2	11,740.6	16,912.9	12,713.5	16,653.6	29,013.5	48,662.9	32,818.4	32,771.3	31,742.6	23,303.8
Domestic Credit	32	43,280.3	47,976.5	48,464.9	56,194.8	66,937.0	65,937.9	72,051.5	87,637.5	112,518.9	126,372.0	141,278.1	168,427.7
Claims on Central Govt. (Net)	32an	15,618.1	15,157.1	14,633.7	7,331.4	7,134.9	10,062.7	11,167.6	12,673.0	15,055.2	14,710.6	13,969.6	19,259.4
Claims on Local Government	32b	112.9	147.1	145.4	308.8	654.0	905.6	1,174.9	1,280.0	1,422.4	1,563.1	1,787.9	1,767.2
Claims on Nonfin.Pub.Enterprises	32c	2,141.4	1,896.2	1,943.8	2,182.5	2,291.8	1,794.2	2,413.4	3,180.0	3,813.3	4,083.0	4,987.9	6,406.1
Claims on Private Sector	32d	25,345.1	30,675.3	31,601.8	46,125.3	56,651.9	52,976.0	57,065.2	70,052.9	91,093.2	104,821.7	119,015.0	139,240.9
Claims on Other Banking Insts	32f					10.5	45.4	68.7	170.2	219.5	431.8	624.0	592.2
Claims on Nonbank Financial Inst	32g	62.1	100.8	140.2	246.8	193.9	154.0	161.7	281.4	915.3	761.8	893.9	1,161.8
Money	34	6,648.8	8,283.6	11,419.6	13,814.3	13,621.1	13,858.9	18,030.2	23,703.6	30,869.8	33,888.7	34,562.1	38,817.1
Quasi-Money	35	10,828.8	16,257.4	25,204.1	36,876.9	43,654.7	42,363.6	54,552.7	82,050.0	85,055.7	94,406.1	104,222.1	114,752.8
Money Market Instruments	36aa	1.5	.2	.9	7.0	4.5	1.4	—	—	5.1	—	—	—
Bonds	36ab	207.0	130.5	127.2	126.6	149.7	435.4	478.2	317.8	211.2	598.4	1,163.5	1,077.0
Restricted Deposits	36b	12,128.0	10,874.6	8,466.8	5,953.4	4,315.1	3,814.8	2,864.6	1,926.2	1,729.5	1,721.6	2,067.0	2,092.3
Capital Accounts	37a	15,949.6	17,411.8	17,341.9	19,385.4	22,688.9	26,510.9	30,169.7	31,880.3	31,677.8	32,428.5	33,763.0	38,023.1
Other Items (Net)	37r	−1,343.4	−1,932.0	−2,354.7	−3,055.9	−4,783.5	−4,393.5	−5,030.4	−3,577.4	−4,211.7	−3,900.4	−2,756.9	−3,030.9
Money plus Quasi-Money	35l	17,477.6	24,541.0	36,623.7	50,691.2	57,275.8	56,222.5	72,582.9	105,753.6	115,925.5	128,294.7	138,784.2	153,570.0
Interest Rates						*Percent Per Annum*								
Discount Rate (End of Period)	60	8.50	8.50	6.50	5.90	5.90	7.90	5.90	5.90	4.50	4.50	4.50	4.50
Money Market Rate	60b	26.93	21.13	17.60	9.71	11.16	10.21	6.78	3.42	1.75	3.31	5.11	3.10
Deposit Rate	60l	6.52	5.53	5.59	4.30	4.62	4.31	3.74	3.23	1.89	1.53	1.87	1.71
Lending Rate	60p	22.91	20.24	22.52	15.47	15.75	14.94	12.07	9.55	† 12.84	11.58	11.75	11.19

Croatia 960

		1994	1995	1996	1997	1998	1999	2000	2001	2002	2003	2004	2005
Prices, Production, Labor		*Index Numbers (2000=100): Period Averages*											
Producer Prices	63	84.3	84.9	86.1	88.0	87.0	89.2	100.0	101.1	103.0	102.7	106.2	109.6
Consumer Prices	64	76.4	79.4	82.8	86.3	91.8	95.0	100.0	† 104.8	106.5	106.7	110.7	114.3
Wages	65	37.5	54.7	61.1	71.5	80.6	91.9	100.0	106.5	111.8	118.5	125.5	131.6
Industrial Production	66	87.1	87.3	90.1	96.4	99.8	98.4	100.0	106.0	111.8	116.4	120.6	126.7
Total Employment	67	107.2	105.7	99.2	97.8	103.4	100.4	100.0	100.5	101.3	103.9	105.1	104.8
		Number in Thousands: Period Averages											
Employment	67e	1,061	1,027	1,012	996	1,071	1,058	1,050	1,056	1,060	1,055	1,085	....
Unemployment	67c	243	241	261	278	288	322	358	380	390	330	250	....
Unemployment Rate (%)	67r	14.5	14.5	16.4	17.5	17.2	19.1	21.1	22.0	22.3	19.5	13.8	....
Intl. Transactions & Positions		*Millions of US Dollars*											
Exports	70..d	4,402.8	4,517.3	4,643.5	3,981.3	4,517.2	4,302.5	4,431.6	4,665.9	4,903.6	6,186.6	8,024.2	8,772.6
Imports, c.i.f.	71..d	5,529.9	7,351.5	7,783.8	9,101.5	8,275.6	7,798.6	7,886.5	9,147.1	10,722.0	14,209.0	16,589.2	18,560.4
Balance of Payments		*Millions of US Dollars: Minus Sign Indicates Debit*											
Current Account, n.i.e.	78ald	554.1	−1,591.8	−1,049.1	−2,825.4	−1,468.0	−1,408.1	−470.6	−727.4	−1,916.6	−2,132.3	−1,910.9	−2,541.2
Goods: Exports f.o.b.	78aad	4,402.8	4,517.3	4,677.5	4,021.1	4,580.6	4,394.7	4,567.2	4,759.3	5,003.9	6,308.0	8,209.9	8,991.6
Goods: Imports f.o.b.	78abd	−5,681.2	−7,744.8	−8,165.5	−9,404.1	−8,652.1	−7,693.3	−7,770.2	−8,860.0	−10,652.2	−14,216.0	−16,560.3	−18,282.5
Trade Balance	78acd	−1,278.4	−3,227.5	−3,488.0	−5,383.0	−4,071.5	−3,298.6	−3,203.1	−4,100.8	−5,648.3	−7,908.0	−8,350.4	−9,290.9
Services: Credit	78add	2,660.6	2,223.4	3,193.2	3,984.6	3,949.1	3,724.1	4,070.9	4,883.9	5,582.4	8,568.8	9,373.2	9,920.0
Services: Debit	78aed	−1,190.3	−1,361.1	−1,707.0	−2,273.9	−1,887.1	−2,097.8	−1,821.7	−1,949.2	−2,414.4	−2,981.8	−3,635.0	−3,399.9
Balance on Goods & Services	78afd	191.9	−2,365.2	−2,001.8	−3,672.3	−2,009.5	−1,672.3	−953.9	−1,166.0	−2,480.3	−2,321.0	−2,612.2	−2,770.8
Income: Credit	78agd	149.0	218.8	269.9	363.7	394.8	254.8	343.5	422.9	433.2	508.5	814.0	808.3
Income: Debit	78ahd	−313.2	−247.7	−339.7	−386.1	−559.1	−623.3	−740.6	−967.6	−960.0	−1,726.9	−1,598.3	−2,044.7
Balance on Gds, Serv. & Inc.	78aid	27.7	−2,394.1	−2,071.6	−3,694.7	−2,173.8	−2,040.8	−1,351.0	−1,710.8	−3,007.0	−3,539.4	−3,396.6	−4,007.3
Current Transfers, n.i.e.: Credit	78ajd	669.2	971.2	1,173.3	963.8	919.1	967.6	1,098.2	1,192.7	1,375.0	1,741.4	1,974.0	2,022.4
Current Transfers: Debit	78akd	−142.8	−168.9	−150.8	−94.5	−213.3	−335.0	−217.8	−209.3	−284.6	−334.4	−488.2	−556.3
Capital Account, n.i.e.	78bcd	—	—	16.2	21.3	19.1	24.9	20.6	133.6	443.4	83.9	28.5	60.8
Capital Account, n.i.e.: Credit	78bad	—	—	18.0	23.5	24.1	28.2	24.2	138.2	450.2	95.6	37.3	65.4
Capital Account: Debit	78bbd	—	—	−1.8	−2.2	−5.0	−3.4	−3.6	−4.6	−6.8	−11.7	−8.9	−4.6
Financial Account, n.i.e.	78bjd	16.4	1,135.3	2,996.3	3,020.8	1,610.3	2,868.6	1,790.2	2,200.7	2,993.1	4,783.1	3,010.2	4,720.1
Direct Investment Abroad	78bdd	−6.7	−5.5	−24.4	−186.1	−97.5	−56.2	−2.6	−154.5	−538.7	−107.8	−347.9	−176.4
Dir. Invest. in Rep. Econ., n.i.e.	78bed	116.9	114.3	510.8	532.8	932.3	1,463.7	1,085.3	1,337.7	1,212.8	2,132.9	1,261.5	1,625.5
Portfolio Investment Assets	78bfd	1.0	.3	6.2	11.2	−.1	−38.3	−22.7	−129.3	−626.5	143.9	−948.3	−579.8
Equity Securities	78bkd	1.0	.3	6.2	.2	−.1	−.3	−.2	.3	−69.4	−66.0	−40.1	−175.6
Debt Securities	78bld	—	—	—	11.0	—	−38.0	−22.5	−129.6	−557.2	210.0	−908.2	−404.2
Portfolio Investment Liab., n.i.e.	78bgd	9.9	4.5	622.0	565.7	15.1	571.1	730.3	730.4	187.3	820.4	1,209.4	−731.8
Equity Securities	78bmd	9.9	4.5	−6.8	15.9	1.3	−18.3	−.2	14.0	36.4	16.2	177.6	104.0
Debt Securities	78bnd	—	—	628.8	549.8	13.8	589.4	730.5	716.4	150.9	804.2	1,031.8	−835.9
Financial Derivatives Assets	78bwd	....	....	....	....	....	....	....	....	....	....	....	....
Financial Derivatives Liabilities	78bxd	....	....	....	....	....	....	....	....	....	....	....	....
Other Investment Assets	78bhd	−15.9	419.5	794.5	171.2	348.8	−15.4	−966.0	360.4	357.5	−2,526.6	−522.0	1,305.8
Monetary Authorities	78bod	....	....	....	....	....	....	....	....	....	....	....	....
General Government	78bpd	−.2	−15.5	−33.4	30.7	−22.3	15.1	−25.8	−19.2	−30.5	26.5	94.0	−58.2
Banks	78bqd	−189.3	−451.6	−589.2	−371.8	406.1	168.6	−899.1	−1,611.2	1,323.9	−2,304.4	−455.0	1,699.8
Other Sectors	78brd	173.6	886.6	1,417.1	512.3	−35.0	−199.1	−41.2	1,990.8	−936.0	−248.7	−160.9	−335.8
Other Investment Liab., n.i.e.	78bid	−88.8	602.2	1,087.2	1,926.0	411.7	943.7	965.9	55.9	2,400.7	4,320.1	2,357.5	3,276.8
Monetary Authorities	78bsd	—	—	—	—	—	—	21.6	18.5	25.6	−56.1	374.5	−442.7
General Government	78btd	−131.5	−47.2	268.8	95.7	−61.3	187.0	297.7	−192.5	413.6	586.4	506.9	285.8
Banks	78bud	52.6	492.5	226.2	670.3	135.7	38.4	−12.6	277.2	1,249.8	2,506.1	1,182.3	1,495.5
Other Sectors	78bvd	−9.9	156.9	592.2	1,160.0	337.3	696.7	662.4	−54.3	793.4	853.1	1,111.0	1,495.6
Net Errors and Omissions	78cad	−294.0	496.9	−946.1	173.7	−.9	−1,027.5	−684.6	−209.3	−705.4	−1,333.8	−1,059.6	−1,217.4
Overall Balance	78cbd	276.5	40.4	1,017.3	390.4	160.5	457.9	655.6	1,397.6	814.6	1,400.8	68.2	1,022.3
Reserves and Related Items	79dad	−276.5	−40.4	−1,017.3	−390.4	−160.5	−457.9	−655.6	−1,397.6	−814.6	−1,400.8	−68.2	−1,022.3
Reserve Assets	79dbd	−742.8	−443.2	−533.4	−428.0	−151.7	−426.4	−627.0	−1,366.7	−685.7	−1,400.8	−68.2	−1,022.3
Use of Fund Credit and Loans	79dcd	107.0	97.1	−4.5	37.5	−8.9	−31.5	−28.6	−30.8	−128.9	—	—	—
Exceptional Financing	79ded	359.3	305.7	−479.4	—	—	—	—	—	—	—	—	—
International Investment Position		*Millions of US Dollars*											
Assets	79aad	....	....	....	....	7,020.7	7,195.8	8,426.1	11,282.6	13,070.3	18,502.3	20,350.9	18,310.7
Direct Investment Abroad	79abd	....	....	....	....	1,002.4	881.7	875.1	966.6	1,825.9	2,057.7	2,220.0	2,167.1
Portfolio Investment	79acd	....	....	....	....	29.7	78.8	87.0	223.2	843.7	753.8	1,792.9	1,972.1
Equity Securities	79add	....	....	....	....	29.7	26.0	14.3	22.5	40.9	50.8	54.2	49.9
Debt Securities	79aed	....	....	....	....	—	52.9	72.7	200.7	802.9	703.0	1,738.8	1,922.2
Financial Derivatives	79ald	....	....	....	....	....	....	....	....	....	....	....	....
Other Investment	79afd	....	....	....	....	3,172.9	3,210.2	3,942.3	5,389.6	4,515.7	7,500.3	7,579.8	5,371.2
Monetary Authorities	79agd	....	....	....	....	—	—	—	—	—	.8	.8	.7
General Government	79ahd	....	....	....	....	70.0	49.7	72.5	88.9	126.4	108.9	21.4	74.8
Banks	79aid	....	....	....	....	1,978.6	1,657.7	2,510.9	3,988.0	2,966.1	5,788.8	5,985.3	3,799.4
Other Sectors	79ajd	....	....	....	....	1,124.3	1,502.8	1,358.9	1,312.7	1,423.2	1,601.8	1,572.4	1,496.2
Reserve Assets	79akd	....	....	....	....	2,815.7	3,025.0	3,521.8	4,703.3	5,884.9	8,190.5	8,758.2	8,800.3
Liabilities	79lad	....	....	....	....	12,434.0	12,475.3	14,293.3	15,291.9	21,304.7	33,165.1	41,522.3	39,256.5
Dir. Invest. in Rep. Economy	79lbd	....	....	....	....	1,939.7	2,566.9	3,568.0	4,239.0	6,909.7	10,496.1	12,877.6	11,531.5
Portfolio Investment	79lcd	....	....	....	....	2,417.2	2,751.5	3,355.4	3,964.8	4,460.0	6,076.5	7,834.0	6,102.9
Equity Securities	79ldd	....	....	....	....	87.3	128.3	108.8	145.4	180.8	215.4	385.7	307.3
Debt Securities	79led	....	....	....	....	2,329.8	2,623.2	3,246.6	3,819.4	4,279.2	5,861.1	7,448.3	5,795.7
Financial Derivatives	79lld	....	....	....	....	....	....	....	....	....	....	....	....
Other Investment	79lfd	....	....	....	....	8,077.1	7,156.9	7,369.8	7,088.1	9,935.0	16,592.5	20,810.6	21,622.1
Monetary Authorities	79lgd	....	....	....	....	233.9	217.9	198.8	189.9	24.2	457.0	3.2	3.1
General Government	79lhd	....	....	....	....	1,589.5	1,468.5	1,708.1	1,476.7	2,033.8	2,861.6	3,543.3	3,535.4
Banks	79lid	....	....	....	....	2,569.7	2,144.2	2,045.8	2,246.6	3,946.9	7,650.1	9,876.4	10,095.2
Other Sectors	79ljd	....	....	....	....	3,684.0	3,326.4	3,417.1	3,174.9	3,930.1	5,623.7	7,387.8	7,988.3

Croatia 960

		1994	1995	1996	1997	1998	1999	2000	2001	2002	2003	2004	2005
Government Finance						*Millions of Kuna: Year Ending December 31*							
Deficit (-) or Surplus..................	80	543.9	−715.4	−133.8	−1,160.2	1,256.7	−2,522.0	−6,107.9	−3,758.5	−3,872.0	....	....	....
Total Revenue and Grants.............	81y	22,817.3	27,485.1	30,813.1	33,702.4	42,376.2	40,277.9	41,774.7	49,156.8	69,870.2	....	....	....
Revenue.....................................	81	22,817.3	27,385.1	30,813.1	33,702.4	42,376.2	40,277.9	41,774.7	49,156.8	69,870.2	....	....	....
Grants..	81z	—	100.0	—	—	—	—	—	—	—	....	....	....
Exp. & Lending Minus Repay..........	82z	22,273.4	28,200.5	30,946.9	34,862.5	41,119.6	42,799.9	47,882.6	52,915.3	73,742.2	....	....	....
Expenditure..............................	82	22,282.8	28,475.6	30,971.2	34,395.2	41,390.4	47,379.6	49,567.5	56,386.7	72,186.2	....	....	....
Lending Minus Repayments.........	83	−9.3	−275.1	−24.3	467.4	−270.8	−4,579.7	−1,684.9	−3,471.4	1,556.0	....	....	....
Total Financing...............................	80h	−543.9	715.3	134.0	1,160.2	−1,256.7	2,521.9	6,107.8	3,758.5	3,872.0	....	....	....
Domestic....................................	84a	−591.2	29.3	−669.9	−1,825.7	−1,247.6	−2,093.1	−813.6	−353.9	1,597.7	....	....	....
Foreign......................................	85a	47.3	686.0	804.0	2,985.9	−9.1	4,615.0	6,921.4	4,112.4	2,274.3	....	....	....
Total Debt by Residence.................	88	....	27,739.7	29,814.0	32,760.0	....	....	....	....	....	....	....	....
Domestic.....................................	88a	17,284.7	16,405.4	16,533.7	14,501.6	13,697.5	13,944.0	14,549.8	21,944.3	23,596.6	....	....	....
Foreign..	89a	....	11,334.3	13,280.3	18,258.4	....	....	....	....	....	....	....	....
National Accounts						*Millions of Kuna:*							
Househ.Cons.Expend.,incl.NPISHs....	96f	46,575	64,043	67,046	79,023	82,741	83,336	109,500	99,611	—	115,081	122,100	130,576
Government Consumption Expend...	91f	25,738	27,756	27,475	30,189	34,968	37,550	37,829	36,399	36,399	38,374	39,724	46,691
Gross Fixed Capital Formation........	93e	12,210	15,398	22,089	29,936	32,066	33,025	33,281	36,984	44,114	56,662	62,525	65,391
Changes in Inventories...................	93i	2,982	1,916	1,599	4,143	982	−404	−2,421	2,665	6,822	5,508	5,384	6,284
Exports of Goods and Services.........	90c	40,086	37,951	43,402	50,873	54,547	54,930	64,864	80,246	81,375	90,927	98,330	107,824
Imports of Goods and Services (-).....	98c	40,149	43,402	53,631	70,351	67,700	65,335	72,430	90,265	98,089	109,721	115,273	123,338
Gross Domestic Product (GDP).........	99b	87,441	98,382	107,981	123,811	137,604	141,579	152,519	165,639	181,231	198,422	212,826	229,031
GDP Volume 1990 Prices.................	99b.p	193	196	205	219	....	....	....	....	....	....	....	....
GDP Volume 1997 Prices.................	99b.p	....	....	....	123,811	126,936	125,843	129,438	135,189	142,730	150,351	156,060	162,746
GDP Volume (2000=100).................	99bvp	84.5	85.9	89.6	† 95.7	98.1	97.2	100.0	104.4	110.3	116.2	120.6	125.7
GDP Deflator (2000=100)...............	99bip	67.8	75.1	79.0	84.9	92.0	95.5	100.0	104.0	107.8	112.0	115.7	119.4
						Millions: Midyear Estimates							
Population..............................	99z	4.66	4.67	4.65	4.62	4.57	4.53	4.51	4.50	4.51	4.52	4.54	4.55

		1994	1995	1996	1997	1998	1999	2000	2001	2002	2003	2004	2005
Exchange Rates						*SDRs per Pound: End of Period*							
Official Rate	ac	1.4384	1.4735	1.4800	1.4097	1.4255	1.2680	1.2444	1.2238	1.3451	1.4465	1.5151	1.4444
					US Dollars per Pound: End of Period (ag) Period Average (rh)								
Official Rate	ag	2.0998	2.1903	2.1282	1.9021	2.0071	1.7404	1.6214	1.5380	1.8287	2.1494	2.3529	2.0644
Official Rate	rh	2.0347	2.2113	2.1446	1.9476	1.9342	1.8400	1.6107	1.5559	1.6431	1.9356	2.1366	2.1571
					Index Numbers (2000=100): Period Averages								
Official Rate	ahx	126.3	137.3	133.1	120.9	120.1	114.5	100.0	96.6	102.0	120.2	132.7	133.9
Nominal Effective Exchange Rate	nec	93.7	97.4	98.5	97.7	103.2	103.7	100.0	102.5	105.9	111.7	114.3	114.6
Real Effective Exchange Rate	rec	103.8	104.9	103.7	101.8	105.4	103.3	100.0	101.0	104.1	111.0	113.0	112.9
Fund Position						*Millions of SDRs: End of Period*							
Quota	2f.s	100.0	100.0	100.0	100.0	100.0	139.6	139.6	139.6	139.6	139.6	139.6	139.6
SDRs	1b.s	.1		—	.2	.2	.4	.8	1.1	1.5	2.0	2.5	2.9
Reserve Position in the Fund	1c.s	25.5	25.5	25.5	25.5	25.5	35.4	35.4	35.4	49.1	66.8	47.3	21.7
Total Fund Cred.&Loans Outstg.	2tl	—	—	—	—	—	—	—	—	—	—	—	—
International Liquidity					*Millions of US Dollars Unless Otherwise Indicated: End of Period*								
Total Reserves minus Gold	1l.d	1,464.5	1,116.9	1,541.9	1,391.6	1,379.7	1,832.9	1,741.1	2,267.8	3,022.0	3,256.7	3,910.0	4,191.1
SDRs	1b.d	.2		—	.3	.3	.5	1.0	1.4	2.1	3.0	3.9	4.2
Reserve Position in the Fund	1c.d	37.2	37.8	36.6	34.3	35.8	48.5	46.1	44.4	66.8	99.3	73.4	31.1
Foreign Exchange	1d.d	1,427.2	1,079.0	1,505.3	1,356.9	1,343.6	1,783.8	1,694.0	2,221.9	2,953.2	3,154.5	3,832.7	4,155.9
Gold (Million Fine Troy Ounces)	1ad	.459	.460	.440	.462	.462	.464	.464	.464	.465	.465	.465	.465
Gold (National Valuation)	1and	15.6	16.7	170.2	133.9	132.9	142.6	127.6	127.6	149.2	196.2	204.1	238.1
Monetary Authorities: Other Liab.	4..d	55.7	89.6	56.4	73.2	57.1	49.7	24.5	40.5	15.5	15.9	15.5	14.7
Deposit Money Banks: Assets	7a.d	1,915.4	3,083.3	3,255.1	3,612.4	3,519.3	† 3,880.2	5,377.6	6,191.7	6,348.5	8,686.2	11,318.7	16,020.8
Liabilities	7b.d	2,697.5	3,738.3	4,302.8	4,694.4	4,790.3	† 5,273.4	6,579.1	7,683.4	8,621.3	10,328.7	12,705.9	16,690.1
Other Banking Insts.: Liabilities	7f.d	2,052.7	2,257.4	3,189.6	13,090.6	8,607.2	8,060.5	10,564.4	10,161.4	. . . .	. . . .	. . . .	. . . .
Monetary Authorities						*Millions of Pounds: End of Period*							
Foreign Assets	11	705.6	518.2	805.2	802.7	754.4	1,135.8	1,153.3	1,558.4	1,734.9	1,607.2	1,749.2	2,146.2
Claims on Central Government	12a	398.5	607.2	570.5	558.4	596.7	534.9	770.7	696.5	992.4	968.5	1,017.3	1,015.4
Claims on Deposit Money Banks	12e	12.4	22.4	6.5	.1	104.6	.1	3.1	—	—	8.0		
Reserve Money	14	872.4	834.6	761.5	755.5	878.0	1,008.3	1,117.0	1,201.5	1,498.8	1,571.4	1,697.2	1,741.9
of which: Currency Outside DMBs	14a	246.6	257.1	265.8	276.3	290.1	313.6	333.3	356.5	392.8	467.2	513.7	555.9
Foreign Liabilities	16c	26.6	40.9	26.5	38.5	28.4	28.5	15.1	26.3	8.5	7.4	6.6	7.1
Central Government Deposits	16d	175.2	227.3	342.9	339.5	325.7	316.4	451.2	559.5	598.8	755.2	858.2	824.4
Other Items (Net)	17r	42.4	45.1	251.3	227.7	223.6	317.4	343.8	467.6	621.3	249.7	204.6	588.3
Deposit Money Banks						*Millions of Pounds: End of Period*							
Reserves	20	612.4	555.1	479.7	452.9	455.4	† 681.3	761.0	941.3	1,481.3	1,128.6	1,178.6	1,422.2
Foreign Assets	21	912.2	1,407.7	1,529.5	1,899.1	1,753.4	† 2,229.5	3,316.6	4,025.8	3,471.6	4,041.2	4,810.6	7,760.5
Claims on Central Government	22a	566.5	463.7	722.1	834.5	854.0	† 983.3	902.4	1,409.2	1,415.9	1,765.4	1,716.0	1,995.6
Claims on Private Sector	22d	2,754.3	3,225.3	3,667.0	4,109.7	4,635.2	† 5,543.9	6,344.0	7,136.9	7,726.6	8,123.8	8,675.6	9,213.7
Demand Deposits	24	326.1	353.9	386.5	427.2	439.2	† 723.5	681.5	653.4	613.3	865.7	910.8	1,137.3
Time and Savings Deposits	25	2,785.4	3,131.2	3,487.3	3,890.0	4,243.3	† 4,971.3	5,575.0	6,462.9	7,143.6	7,159.9	7,536.0	8,189.0
Foreign Liabilities	26c	1,284.6	1,706.8	2,021.8	2,468.0	2,386.7	† 3,030.0	4,057.7	4,995.7	4,714.4	4,805.4	5,400.1	8,084.7
Central Government Deposits	26d	38.4	42.7	40.7	44.8	50.3	† 63.8	76.8	72.2	71.2	71.9	80.5	83.0
Credit from Monetary Authorities	26g	12.4	22.4	6.5	.1	5.6	† .1	3.1	—	—	8.0	—	—
Other Items (Net)	27r	398.5	394.8	455.5	466.2	573.1	† 649.4	929.9	1,329.1	1,552.9	2,148.1	2,453.3	2,897.9
Monetary Survey						*Millions of Pounds: End of Period*							
Foreign Assets (Net)	31n	306.6	178.3	286.4	195.4	92.7	† 306.7	397.1	562.2	483.6	835.7	1,153.1	1,814.9
Domestic Credit	32	3,579.3	4,108.1	4,670.8	5,229.1	5,847.5	† 6,840.1	7,661.5	8,794.1	9,642.6	10,208.8	10,638.8	11,494.4
Claims on Central Govt. (Net)	32an	751.5	800.9	908.9	1,008.6	1,074.8	† 1,137.9	1,145.1	1,474.1	1,738.3	1,906.8	1,794.6	2,103.6
Claims on Local Government	32b	42.9	46.8	55.6	65.4	79.3	† 90.9	92.4	127.5	132.6	142.4	133.2	140.6
Claims on Nonfin.Pub.Enterprises	32c	28.1	34.8	38.9	45.0	57.9	† 66.8	78.9	55.7	44.9	35.8	35.4	36.5
Claims on Private Sector	32d	2,756.8	3,225.7	3,667.4	4,110.0	4,635.6	† 5,544.6	6,344.7	7,136.9	7,726.6	8,123.8	8,675.6	9,213.7
Money	34	576.2	612.2	653.5	704.5	730.3	† 1,037.6	1,015.3	1,010.6	1,021.6	1,333.8	1,435.6	1,695.9
Quasi-Money	35	2,794.3	3,142.2	3,495.6	3,900.4	4,255.6	† 4,986.8	5,595.2	6,483.3	7,143.6	7,159.9	7,536.0	8,189.0
Other Items (Net)	37r	515.4	532.0	808.1	819.6	954.4	† 1,122.5	1,447.6	1,862.4	1,960.9	2,550.9	2,820.3	3,424.4
Money plus Quasi-Money	35l	3,370.5	3,754.4	4,149.1	4,604.9	4,985.9	† 6,024.4	6,610.5	7,493.9	8,165.2	8,493.6	8,971.6	9,885.0
Other Banking Institutions						*Millions of Pounds: End of Period*							
Reserves	40	27.0	25.1	20.6	32.3	39.6	35.2	76.3	90.1	. . . .	. . . .	. . . .	. . . .
Foreign Assets	41	977.1	1,030.2	1,498.4	6,901.6	4,290.9	4,647.4	6,527.0	6,615.8	. . . .	. . . .	. . . .	. . . .
Claims on Private Sector	42d	1,599.8	1,826.0	2,056.5	2,244.4	2,431.6	2,747.0	2,868.3	2,987.5	. . . .	. . . .	. . . .	. . . .
Liquid Liabilities	45l	1,685.0	1,897.6	2,095.8	2,327.6	2,582.7	2,754.2	3,072.8	3,428.0	. . . .	. . . .	. . . .	. . . .
Foreign Liabilities	46c	977.6	1,030.6	1,498.7	6,882.2	4,288.4	4,631.4	6,515.6	6,606.9	. . . .	. . . .	. . . .	. . . .
Capital Accounts	47a	41.9	39.9	42.9	43.8	48.6	80.0	90.3	92.5	. . . .	. . . .	. . . .	. . . .
Other Items (Net)	47r	−100.6	−86.8	−62.0	−75.2	−157.6	−36.0	−207.0	−434.1	. . . .	. . . .	. . . .	. . . .
Banking Survey						*Millions of Pounds: End of Period*							
Foreign Assets (Net)	51n	306.1	177.8	286.0	214.8	95.2	322.7	408.5	571.0	. . . .	. . . .	. . . .	. . . .
Domestic Credit	52	5,182.2	5,940.0	6,737.5	7,482.1	8,292.5	9,578.6	10,523.7	11,710.9	. . . .	. . . .	. . . .	. . . .
Claims on Central Govt. (Net)	52an	757.2	807.2	919.5	1,017.5	1,088.5	1,137.9	1,145.1	1,371.3	. . . .	. . . .	. . . .	. . . .
Claims on Local Government	52b	42.9	46.8	55.6	65.4	79.3	86.5	90.6	122.8	. . . .	. . . .	. . . .	. . . .
Claims on Nonfin.Pub.Enterprises	52c	28.1	34.8	38.9	45.0	57.9	63.3	75.8	92.4	. . . .	. . . .	. . . .	. . . .
Claims on Private Sector	52d	4,354.1	5,051.3	5,723.5	6,354.1	7,066.8	8,290.9	9,212.3	10,124.4	. . . .	. . . .	. . . .	. . . .
Monetary Liabilities	54	560.1	601.7	644.7	685.1	708.3	1,024.7	1,038.9	1,016.0	. . . .	. . . .	. . . .	. . . .
Quasi-Monetary Liabilities	55	4,468.6	5,026.2	5,580.0	6,214.4	6,822.0	7,722.7	8,644.1	9,885.2	. . . .	. . . .	. . . .	. . . .
Other Items (Net)	57r	459.6	489.9	798.7	797.4	857.5	1,184.3	1,398.7	1,654.7	. . . .	. . . .	. . . .	. . . .
Liquid Liabilities	55l	5,028.4	5,626.9	6,224.4	6,900.2	7,529.1	8,743.9	9,684.9	10,902.7	. . . .	. . . .	. . . .	. . . .
Interest Rates						*Percent Per Annum*							
Discount Rate (End of Period)	60	6.50	6.50	† 7.50	7.00	7.00	7.00	7.00	5.50	5.00	4.50	5.50	4.25
Money Market Rate	60b	. . . .	. . . .	6.85	4.82	4.80	5.15	5.96	4.93	3.42	3.35	4.01	3.27
Treasury Bill Rate	60c	6.00	6.00	6.05	5.38	5.59	5.59	6.01	. . . .	. . . .	3.56	. . . .	. . . .
Deposit Rate	60l	5.75	5.75	† 7.00	6.50	6.50	6.50	6.50	4.65	4.20	3.30	3.99	3.48
Lending Rate	60p	8.83	8.50	8.50	8.08	8.00	8.00	8.00	† 7.52	7.15	6.95	7.66	7.07

Cyprus 423

		1994	1995	1996	1997	1998	1999	2000	2001	2002	2003	2004	2005
Prices, Production, Labor						*Index Numbers (2000=100): Period Averages*							
Wholesale Prices	63	84.3	87.4	89.2	91.7	92.2	93.3	100.0	101.6	103.0	106.0	111.0	114.8
Wholesale Prices: Home Goods	63a	....	† 86.2	88.7	91.6	93.7	95.1	100.0	101.9	105.6	110.3	117.8	119.4
Consumer Prices	64	84.4	86.6	89.2	92.4	† 94.5	96.0	100.0	102.0	104.8	109.2	† 111.7	114.5
Harmonized CPI (2002=100)	64h	....	....	....	....	....	....	....	....	100.0	† 104.0	105.9	108.1
Industrial Production	66	93.1	94.6	91.8	91.5	94.1	† 95.7	† 100.0	101.8	105.8	107.8	109.9	110.1
Mining Production	66zx	81.0	74.6	76.4	76.5	90.2	† 96.3	† 100.0	95.4	105.4	110.1	111.1	115.9
						Number in Thousands: Period Averages								
Labor Force	67d	279	302	306	308	311	318	325	315	326	341	349	....
Employment	67e	271	284	286	286	289	279	294	310	315	327	336	....
Unemployment	67c	8	8	9	10	10	11	11	10	11	12	16	13
Unemployment Rate (%)	67r	2.7	2.6	3.1	3.4	3.4	3.6	3.4	3.0	3.2	3.5	3.6	5.2
Intl. Transactions & Positions							*Millions of Pounds*							
Exports	70	474.99	554.91	651.01	563.89	551.13	541.79	590.35	628.90	469.97	430.48	505.90	606.00
Imports, c.i.f.	71	1,481.66	1,670.41	1,857.53	1,899.37	1,904.84	1,970.92	2,401.96	2,526.73	2,352.68	2,211.99	2,645.64	2,920.22
Balance of Payments						*Millions of US Dollars: Minus Sign Indicates Debit*								
Current Account, n.i.e.	78ald	74.4	−205.1	−467.7	−418.1	291.4	−170.2	−488.1	−322.2	−457.8	−330.5	−923.4	−962.3
Goods: Exports f.o.b.	78aad	967.5	1,228.7	1,392.4	1,245.8	1,064.6	1,000.3	950.9	975.2	855.1	924.6	1,156.9	1,454.0
Goods: Imports f.o.b.	78abd	−2,703.0	−3,314.2	−3,575.7	−3,317.2	−3,490.4	−3,309.5	−3,556.6	−3,552.5	−3,702.6	−4,055.0	−5,216.2	−5,745.7
Trade Balance	78acd	−1,735.5	−2,085.5	−2,183.3	−2,071.4	−2,425.7	−2,309.2	−2,605.7	−2,577.3	−2,847.4	−3,130.4	−4,059.4	−4,291.8
Services: Credit	78add	2,646.7	3,377.6	3,309.8	3,305.1	3,594.7	3,947.0	4,068.1	4,340.0	4,511.7	5,376.8	6,219.5	6,488.3
Services: Debit	78aed	−862.1	−1,312.7	−1,407.2	−1,401.5	−1,497.6	−1,559.6	−1,585.3	−1,614.6	−1,764.2	−2,220.9	−2,636.9	−2,706.0
Balance on Goods & Services	78afd	49.2	−20.6	−280.7	−167.8	−328.6	78.1	−122.9	148.1	−99.9	25.5	−476.8	−509.4
Income: Credit	78agd	121.5	443.8	417.7	440.1	470.2	493.3	572.4	558.9	390.8	423.2	657.9	762.4
Income: Debit	78ahd	−211.1	−679.2	−643.8	−727.0	104.6	−844.7	−1,114.8	−1,083.3	−860.0	−940.1	−1,282.1	−1,308.0
Balance on Gds, Serv. & Inc.	78aid	−40.4	−256.0	−506.7	−454.7	246.2	−273.4	−665.3	−376.2	−569.1	−491.4	−1,100.9	−1,055.1
Current Transfers, n.i.e.: Credit	78ajd	125.0	61.9	52.8	48.8	94.0	145.5	236.8	147.3	271.9	402.4	594.2	631.1
Current Transfers: Debit	78akd	−10.2	−11.1	−13.7	−12.3	−48.9	−42.4	−59.6	−93.3	−160.6	−241.6	−416.7	−538.4
Capital Account, n.i.e.	78bcd	....	—	—	—	—	—	4.8	5.7	−5.4	20.3	125.3	86.8
Capital Account, n.i.e.: Credit	78bad	....	—	—	—	—	—	19.3	27.1	22.2	41.3	183.1	131.1
Capital Account: Debit	78bbd	....	—	—	—	—	—	−14.5	−21.5	−27.6	−21.0	−57.8	−44.3
Financial Account, n.i.e.	78bjd	185.7	−213.3	250.3	541.6	−420.2	844.9	530.3	965.1	939.6	9.1	1,198.9	1,717.3
Direct Investment Abroad	78bdd	−6.1	−15.7	−35.2	−27.9	−70.7	−182.6	−172.1	−249.1	−487.2	−502.4	−633.3	−428.0
Dir. Invest. in Rep. Econ., n.i.e.	78bed	75.2	243.1	233.7	546.5	345.4	813.1	854.9	944.7	1,086.5	906.1	1,107.8	1,151.0
Portfolio Investment Assets	78bfd	−244.6	−110.5	−142.8	−145.4	−160.3	−736.7	−453.4	−249.2	−1,094.3	−521.2	−1,770.3	−1,620.3
Equity Securities	78bkd	....						−94.5	−52.0	−543.5	161.9	−74.6	−18.4
Debt Securities	78bld	−244.6	−110.5	−142.8	−145.4	−160.3	−736.7	−358.9	−197.3	−550.8	−683.1	−1,695.8	−1,601.9
Portfolio Investment Liab., n.i.e.	78bgd	84.5	−27.4	69.7	254.7	355.1	493.6	169.7	517.7	552.6	802.5	2,979.0	1,566.5
Equity Securities	78bmd	....						29.1	88.9	−3.8	−.1	−13.9	13.2
Debt Securities	78bnd	84.5	−27.4	69.7	254.7	355.1	493.6	140.5	428.8	556.5	802.6	2,992.9	1,553.3
Financial Derivatives Assets	78bwd	....	....	....	....	....	....	—	—	−50.3	16.6	−23.6	−16.5
Financial Derivatives Liabilities	78bxd	....	....	....	....	....	....	3.2	—	—	—	−21.1	1.3
Other Investment Assets	78bhd	56.3	−1,162.6	−366.3	−1,529.9	−485.9	−408.1	−1,285.3	−1,478.4	1,420.5	−2,479.2	−2,999.1	−7,238.9
Monetary Authorities	78bod	....	—	—	—	—	—	—	—	—	—	159.0	—
General Government	78bpd	1.0	—	—	—	—	—	—	—	13.1	−20.8	−17.6	11.2
Banks	78bqd	55.3	—	—	—	—	—	—	—	1,414.3	−2,563.8	−3,067.6	−7,891.8
Other Sectors	78brd	....	−1,162.6	−366.3	−1,529.9	−485.9	−408.1	−1,285.3	−1,478.4	−6.9	105.4	−72.8	641.7
Other Investment Liab., n.i.e.	78bid	220.4	859.8	491.1	1,443.5	−403.8	865.6	1,413.4	1,479.4	−488.2	1,786.6	2,559.5	8,302.2
Monetary Authorities	78bsd	.4	—	—	—	—	—	—	—	−19.0	−2.5	−1.8	1.1
General Government	78btd	−228.6	—	—	—	—	—	—	—	−38.1	244.6	162.9	135.2
Banks	78bud	301.5	—	—	—	—	—	—	—	−539.9	1,590.5	2,467.9	7,595.0
Other Sectors	78bvd	147.1	859.8	491.1	1,443.5	−403.8	865.6	1,413.4	1,479.4	108.8	−46.0	−69.5	570.9
Net Errors and Omissions	78cad	−13.1	55.4	157.6	−170.5	46.2	−35.6	−55.2	−37.9	−87.4	113.5	−29.4	−139.1
Overall Balance	78cbd	246.9	−363.1	−59.8	−47.0	−82.5	639.0	−8.2	610.6	389.0	−187.6	371.4	702.7
Reserves and Related Items	79dad	−246.9	363.1	59.8	47.0	82.5	−639.0	8.2	−610.6	−389.0	187.6	−371.4	−702.7
Reserve Assets	79dbd	−246.9	363.1	59.8	47.0	82.5	−639.0	8.2	−610.6	−389.0	187.6	−371.4	−702.7
Use of Fund Credit and Loans	79dcd	—	—	—	—	—	—	—	—	—	—	—	—
Exceptional Financing	79ded	....	—	—	—	—	—	—	—	—	—	—	—
International Investment Position							*Millions of US Dollars*							
Assets	79aad	....	....	....	....	....	....	....	....	23,535.6	29,160.4	40,658.3	....
Direct Investment Abroad	79abd	....	....	....	....	....	....	....	....	1,279.0	2,050.1	2,926.3	....
Portfolio Investment	79acd	....	....	....	....	....	....	1,088.3	1,590.3	5,383.4	6,554.9	10,355.4	....
Equity Securities	79add	....	....	....	....	....	....	.3	129.3	1,122.5	1,206.2	1,930.1	....
Debt Securities	79aed	....	....	....	....	....	....	1,088.0	1,460.9	4,260.9	5,348.7	8,425.3	....
Financial Derivatives	79ald	....	....	....	....	....	....	....	....	2.7	4.9	43.1	....
Other Investment	79afd	....	....	....	....	....	....	3,951.0	4,269.6	13,686.1	17,074.5	23,214.9	....
Monetary Authorities	79agd	....	....	....	....	....	....	....	....	....	....	....	....
General Government	79ahd	....	....	....	....	....	....	....	....	43.2	48.6	60.7	....
Banks	79aid	....	....	....	....	....	....	3,951.0	4,268.9	9,048.9	11,848.0	16,474.5	....
Other Sectors	79ajd	....	....	....	....	....	....	....	....	4,594.0	5,177.9	6,679.6	....
Reserve Assets	79akd	....	....	....	....	....	....	1,869.9	2,396.4	3,184.5	3,476.0	4,118.7	....
Liabilities	79lad	....	....	....	....	....	....	....	....	22,299.7	28,535.1	38,582.2	....
Dir. Invest. in Rep. Economy	79lbd	....	....	....	....	....	....	....	....	4,912.3	6,728.0	8,554.9	....
Portfolio Investment	79lcd	....	....	....	....	....	....	979.3	1,445.1	2,086.0	3,145.4	7,352.6	....
Equity Securities	79ldd	....	....	....	....	....	....	....	....	235.5	150.5	178.3	....
Debt Securities	79led	....	....	....	....	....	....	979.3	1,445.1	1,850.5	2,995.0	7,174.2	....
Financial Derivatives	79lld	....	....	....	....	....	....	....	....	3.0	23.3	28.2	....
Other Investment	79lfd	....	....	....	....	....	....	8,691.0	9,367.7	15,298.4	18,638.3	22,646.5	....
Monetary Authorities	79lgd	....	....	....	....	....	....	.2	.2	43.7	45.0	46.1	....
General Government	79lhd	....	....	....	....	....	....	403.9	279.9	280.0	589.4	761.9	....
Banks	79lid	....	....	....	....	....	....	6,723.5	7,568.0	13,319.7	16,068.6	19,870.4	....
Other Sectors	79ljd	....	....	....	....	....	....	1,563.5	1,519.5	1,655.0	1,935.3	1,968.2	....

		1994	1995	1996	1997	1998	1999	2000	2001	2002	2003	2004	2005
Government Finance					*Millions of Pounds: Year Ending December 31*								
Deficit (-) or Surplus........................	80	−51.85	−39.90	−142.08	−231.22	−257.58	−201.27	−128.70	−129.41	−273.50	−416.20	....	....
Revenue...	81	1,140.55	1,266.90	1,321.30	1,373.39	1,473.17	1,590.06	1,857.50	2,081.20	2,122.30	2,400.60	....	....
Grants Received...........................	81z	3.97	3.90	2.35	1.64	.74	.94	2.50	2.50	2.80	5.20	....	....
Expenditure.................................	82	1,192.36	1,306.10	1,462.72	1,603.53	1,731.70	1,787.73	1,988.70	2,213.11	2,398.60	2,822.00	....	....
Lending Minus Repayments...........	83	4.01	4.60	3.01	2.72	−.21	4.54	—	—	—	—	....	....
Financing													
Net Borrowing: Domestic..............	84a	106.87	117.40	203.91	143.13	109.31	52.57	163.50	194.41	226.60	216.10	....	....
Foreign............................	85a	−65.02	−77.50	−61.83	88.08	148.28	148.70	−34.80	−65.00	46.90	200.10	....	....
Use of Cash Balances....................	87	10.00	—	—	—	−.01	—	—	—	—	—	....	....
Debt: Domestic.............................	88a	1,402.51	1,583.40	1,837.56	1,987.35	2,130.72	2,165.40	2,586.90	3,019.78	2,830.58	3,108.41	....	....
Foreign.................................	89a	556.65	479.27	402.95	515.33	664.77	850.68	820.82	760.56	844.75	1,059.15	....	....
National Accounts						*Millions of Pounds*							
Househ.Cons.Expend.,incl.NPISHs....	96f	2,111.0	2,686.3	2,830.2	2,964.6	3,165.6	3,325.1	3,712.8	3,927.3	4,083.4	4,288.5	4,677.4	5,036.0
Government Consumption Expend...	91f	608.1	566.9	671.7	772.0	822.2	923.9	929.7	1,067.9	1,171.2	1,356.5	1,318.9	1,413.9
Gross Fixed Capital Formation..........	93e	751.5	778.6	861.2	847.1	925.2	935.4	981.7	1,041.4	1,161.6	1,209.8	1,385.6	1,486.9
Changes in Inventories.....................	93i	180.0	138.6	80.8	38.0	23.3	−32.1	78.3	−19.1	47.1	−29.3	103.5	99.3
Exports of Goods and Services..........	90c	1,741.1	2,068.8	2,177.2	2,323.0	2,397.0	2,670.2	3,107.4	3,409.3	3,226.2	3,224.0	3,439.6	3,644.5
Imports of Goods and Services (-).....	98c	1,755.5	2,091.0	2,321.3	2,422.6	2,470.5	2,608.3	3,130.9	3,323.2	3,319.2	3,234.7	3,670.1	3,941.0
Gross Domestic Product (GDP)........	99b	3,663.2	4,148.2	4,299.8	4,522.1	4,862.8	5,214.2	5,679.0	6,103.6	6,370.3	6,814.8	7,254.9	7,739.6
Net Primary Income from Abroad.....	98.n	28.8	−76.5	−76.1	−111.9	328.6	−153.7	−305.0	−295.4	−261.5	−158.9	−294.6	−254.9
Gross National Income (GNI)...........	99a	3,692.0	4,071.7	4,223.7	4,410.2	5,191.4	5,060.5	5,374.0	5,808.2	6,108.8	6,655.9	6,960.3	7,484.7
Consumption of Fixed Capital..........	99cf	387.7	439.5	459.8	487.1	509.5	540.9	569.9	605.8	642.9	693.1	736.9	788.0
GDP Volume 1995 Prices.................	99b.p	3,773.7	4,148.2	4,222.9	4,319.9	4,534.7	4,752.7	4,992.3	5,197.6	5,307.2	5,408.9	5,621.0	5,831.8
GDP Volume (2000=100).................	99bvp	75.6	83.1	84.6	86.5	90.8	95.2	100.0	104.1	106.3	108.3	112.6	116.8
GDP Deflator (2000=100)................	99bip	85.3	87.9	89.5	92.0	94.3	96.4	100.0	103.2	105.5	110.8	113.5	116.7
						Millions: Midyear Estimates							
Population...............................	99z	.72	.73	.74	.75	.76	.78	.79	.80	.81	.82	.83	.84

Czech Republic 935

		1994	1995	1996	1997	1998	1999	2000	2001	2002	2003	2004	2005
Exchange Rates						*Koruny per SDR: End of Period*							
Official Rate....................	aa	40.947	39.544	39.302	46.733	42.037	49.382	49.267	45.568	40.977	38.121	34.733	35.143
					Koruny per US Dollar: End of Period (ae) Period Average (rf)								
Official Rate....................	ae	28.049	26.602	27.332	34.636	29.855	35.979	37.813	36.259	30.141	25.654	22.365	24.588
Official Rate....................	rf	28.785	26.541	27.145	31.698	32.281	34.569	38.598	38.035	32.739	28.209	25.700	23.957
					Index Numbers (2000=100): Period Averages								
Nominal Effective Exchange Rate.....	nec	102.59	102.59	104.28	100.27	100.78	99.50	100.00	104.35	116.55	117.27	118.13	125.32
Real Effective Exchange Rate..........	rec	82.66	85.45	91.05	92.08	100.30	98.50	100.00	106.39	118.71	117.26	118.49	125.22
Fund Position						*Millions of SDRs: End of Period*							
Quota................................	2f.s	589.6	589.6	589.6	589.6	589.6	819.3	819.3	819.3	819.3	819.3	819.3	819.3
SDRs.................................	1b.s	—	.1	—	—	—	—	.2	.7	3.4	6.3	3.4	8.2
Reserve Position in the Fund...........	1c.s	—	—	—	—	—	—	2.4	120.5	173.5	314.6	264.0	126.6
Total Fund Cred.&Loans Outstg.......	2tl	—	—	—	—	—	—	—	—	—	—	—	—
International Liquidity					*Millions of US Dollars Unless Otherwise Indicated: End of Period*								
Total Reserves minus Gold...............	1l.d	6,145	13,843	12,352	9,734	12,542	12,806	13,019	14,341	23,556	26,771	28,259	29,330
SDRs.................................	1b.d	—	—	—	—	—	—	—	1	5	9	5	12
Reserve Position in the Fund.........	1c.d	—	—	—	—	—	—	3	151	236	468	410	181
Foreign Exchange..................	1d.d	6,145	13,843	12,352	9,734	12,542	12,806	13,016	14,189	23,315	26,294	27,844	29,138
Gold (Million Fine Troy Ounces).......	1ad	2.098	1.990	1.985	1.041	.288	.446	.446	.444	.442	.442	.438	.435
Gold (National Valuation)................	1and	140	141	137	57	18	23	22	23	28	32	37	33
Monetary Authorities:Other Assets...	3..d	1,043	1,084	1,161	843	946	1,285	378	435	† 309	118	1,108	3,649
Other Liab...	4..d	1,791	1,802	658	696	381	849	366	407	† 157	120	1,053	3,538
Deposit Money Banks: Assets.......	7a.d	3,203	3,783	5,767	8,585	11,793	13,302	13,259	15,609	† 14,598	15,317	20,530	24,100
Liabilities..................	7b.d	2,464	6,428	9,048	9,124	10,799	9,678	8,419	7,714	† 7,664	10,094	10,275	9,793
Monetary Authorities						*Billions of Koruny: End of Period*							
Foreign Assets........................	11	205.53	400.83	373.08	368.28	403.23	507.82	507.43	536.61	† 720.12	690.65	657.63	811.71
Claims on Central Government........	12a	39.73	12.63	.32	—	—	—	—	11.65	† 10.69	9.68	13.18	4.05
Claims on Other Resident Sectors.....	12d	1.33	1.51	5.10	† 22.14	48.50	61.11	42.43	40.77	† 38.52	36.89	31.19	25.84
Claims on Banking Institutions.........	12e	77.71	74.84	84.88	100.49	74.91	50.47	37.10	20.52	† .13	.11	.08	29.06
Reserve Money.........................	14	223.23	342.77	344.40	† 344.60	422.24	459.78	491.57	515.76	† 260.14	279.08	289.06	310.97
of which: Currency Outside Bls.......	14a	83.58	104.27	118.90	118.74	127.16	157.90	171.82	180.38	† 197.81	221.36	236.77	263.79
Other Liabs. to Banking Insts...........	14n	....	....	....	....	....	....	....	....	455.20	439.50	402.86	377.61
Other Deposits........................	15	9.22	52.68	40.27	† .68	.79	.85	.70	.74	† .72	.66	.63	.61
Foreign Liabilities.....................	16c	50.25	47.93	17.98	24.11	11.38	30.55	13.83	14.74	† 4.73	3.09	23.55	86.99
Central Government Deposits..........	16d	51.86	41.15	43.09	† 68.46	63.07	62.44	57.97	84.25	† 82.26	73.28	92.15	178.49
Capital Accounts..................	17a	18.00	27.34	29.56	60.56	39.07	82.84	36.83	8.25	† −22.32	−40.40	−96.31	−75.86
Other Items (Net)..........................	17r	−28.26	−22.05	−11.91	−7.51	−9.92	−17.06	−13.93	−14.19	† −11.27	−17.88	−9.85	−8.13
Banking Institutions						*Billions of Koruny: End of Period*							
Reserves..............................	20	80.78	160.93	158.50	214.94	288.85	296.54	310.93	333.32	† 60.20	56.56	49.99	45.56
Other Claims on Monetary Author.....	20n	....	....	....	....	....	....	....	....	455.20	439.50	402.86	377.61
Foreign Assets........................	21	89.84	100.64	157.64	297.34	352.08	478.59	501.35	565.97	† 440.00	392.95	459.16	592.58
Claims on Central Government........	22a	94.64	130.94	103.86	62.05	73.66	93.76	117.90	270.78	† 433.78	520.96	437.97	403.54
Claims on Other General Govt........	22b	....	....	....	....	....	....	....	....	21.81	24.26	27.86	32.11
Claims on Other Resident Sectors.....	22d	904.27	1,036.60	1,153.91	† 1,250.40	1,176.26	1,098.47	1,029.89	916.37	† 720.70	782.47	886.84	1,076.87
Demand Deposits..................	24	307.64	310.89	317.46	297.24	275.68	288.88	326.53	402.50	† 626.31	741.80	787.24	897.31
Other Deposits..........................	25	426.43	601.90	663.78	755.75	809.54	797.54	945.94	1,022.98	† 890.51	880.24	899.91	924.83
Money Market Fund Shares.............	26m	....	....	....	....	....	....	....	....	....	....	48.19	59.20
Bonds................................	26n	21.21	46.68	60.88	81.58	113.38	189.74	93.39	76.74	† 48.58	51.58	26.81	60.06
Foreign Liabilities.....................	26c	69.12	170.99	247.29	316.01	322.40	348.22	318.35	279.70	† 231.01	258.96	229.79	240.80
Central Government Deposits..........	26d	90.33	92.38	88.19	51.87	55.31	54.59	50.83	80.54	† 101.89	48.63	46.60	66.07
Credit from Monetary Authorities.....	26g	77.71	74.01	79.82	96.93	52.76	33.68	18.27	4.66	† 2.74	.07	.07	29.19
Capital Accounts..................	27a	185.37	195.88	204.28	† 348.20	395.15	411.80	405.39	291.53	† 291.86	282.78	291.19	317.26
Other Items (Net)......................	27r	−8.29	−63.62	−87.77	−122.85	−133.39	−157.09	−198.63	−72.20	† −61.23	−47.41	−65.13	−66.45
Banking Survey						*Billions of Koruny: End of Period*							
Foreign Assets (Net)......................	31n	176.00	282.55	265.44	325.50	421.52	607.64	676.60	808.14	† 924.38	821.56	863.45	1,076.51
Domestic Credit......................	32	897.77	1,048.15	1,131.92	† 1,214.25	1,180.04	1,136.31	1,081.43	1,074.78	† 1,041.33	1,252.35	1,258.29	1,297.86
Claims on Central Govt. (Net)........	32an	−7.82	10.04	−27.10	† −58.28	−44.71	−23.27	9.10	117.65	† 260.31	408.72	312.40	163.05
Claims on Other General Govt.......	32b	....	....	....	....	....	....	....	....	21.81	24.26	27.86	32.11
Claims on Other Resident Sectors...	32d	905.59	1,038.12	1,159.02	† 1,272.53	1,224.76	1,159.58	1,072.33	957.13	† 759.22	819.36	918.03	1,102.70
Money................................	34	403.97	431.08	451.55	† 418.39	404.00	447.81	498.96	583.55	† 827.04	964.18	1,026.30	1,162.75
Quasi-Money..........................	35	435.65	654.58	704.05	† 756.44	810.33	798.39	946.64	1,023.72	† 891.23	880.90	900.54	925.44
Money Market Fund Shares.............	36m	....	....	....	....	....	....	....	....	....	....	48.19	59.20
Bonds................................	36n	21.21	46.68	60.88	81.58	113.38	189.74	93.39	76.74	† 48.58	51.58	26.81	60.06
Capital Accounts..................	37a	202.22	221.26	231.06	† 408.76	434.22	494.64	442.22	299.78	† 269.54	242.38	194.88	241.40
Other Items (Net)......................	37r	9.57	−24.86	−52.94	−125.41	−160.39	−186.63	−223.18	−100.87	† −70.62	−65.14	−74.98	−74.49
Money plus Quasi-Money...............	35l	839.62	1,085.66	1,155.59	† 1,174.83	1,214.33	1,246.20	1,445.60	1,607.27	† 1,718.27	1,845.08	1,926.84	2,088.19
Money (National Definitions)						*Billions of Koruny: End of Period*							
M1...	59ma	....	....	....	....	....	....	....	....	841.74	964.18	1,026.30	1,162.75
M2...	59mb	....	....	....	....	....	....	....	....	1,410.24	1,511.51	1,578.89	1,746.15
M3...	59mc	....	....	....	....	....	....	....	....	1,428.99	1,522.79	1,634.87	1,814.65
Interest Rates						*Percent Per Annum*							
Bank Rate (End of Period)..............	60	8.50	11.30	12.40	14.75	9.50	5.25	5.25	4.50	2.75	2.00	2.50	2.00
Money Market Rate.....................	60b	12.65	10.93	12.67	17.50	10.08	5.58	5.42	4.69	2.63	2.08	2.56	2.17
Treasury Bill Rate......................	60c	6.98	8.99	11.91	11.21	10.51	5.71	5.37	5.06	2.72	2.04	2.57	1.96
Deposit Rate.............................	60l	7.07	6.96	6.79	7.71	8.08	4.48	3.42	2.87	2.00	1.33	1.28	1.17
Lending Rate.............................	60p	13.12	12.80	12.54	13.20	12.81	8.68	7.16	7.20	6.72	5.95	6.03	5.78
Government Bond Yield..................	61	....	....	....	....	....	....	6.72	4.84	3.17	3.77	3.33	3.19

Czech Republic   935

		1994	1995	1996	1997	1998	1999	2000	2001	2002	2003	2004	2005
Prices, Production, Labor							*Index Numbers (2000=100): Period Averages*						
Producer Prices	63	76.1	81.8	85.8	89.9	94.4	95.3	100.0	102.8	102.3	102.0	107.7	111.0
Consumer Prices	64	66.1	72.1	78.5	85.2	94.2	96.2	100.0	104.7	106.6	106.7	109.7	111.7
Harmonized CPI (2002=100)	64h	....	....	....	....	....	....	....	....	100.0	† 99.9	102.5	104.1
Wages	65	51.4	61.0	72.2	79.3	86.7	94.0	100.0	108.7	116.5	124.3	132.5	139.7
Industrial Production	66	91.1	90.5	92.3	96.4	98.0	94.9	100.0	106.5	108.6	114.6	125.5	133.9
Industrial Employment	67	115.1	103.1	98.2	111.1	110.6	104.3	100.0	100.5	98.7	96.8	96.9	96.8
							Number in Thousands: Period Averages							
Labor Force	67d	....	....	5,199	5,215	5,233	5,236	5,181	5,171	5,139	....	5,133	....
Employment	67e	4,943	4,963	† 4,972	4,937	4,866	4,764	4,732	4,728	4,765	4,733	4,707	4,764
Unemployment	67c	202	181	206	248	336	454	455	418	457	523	457	410
Unemployment Rate (%)	67r	3.9	3.5	4.0	4.8	6.5	8.7	8.8	8.1	8.8	9.9	9.9	8.9
Intl. Transactions & Positions							*Millions of Koruny*							
Exports	70	466,403	574,722	594,630	722,501	850,240	908,756	1,121,099	1,269,634	1,254,394	1,370,930	1,722,657	1,875,220
Imports, c.i.f.	71	523,296	699,027	796,986	914,261	975,386	1,021,827	1,309,571	1,456,285	1,392,003	1,512,759	1,836,550	1,834,864
Imports, f.o.b.	71.v	501,549	670,445	752,343	861,770	926,559	973,169	1,241,924	1,386,319	1,325,717	1,440,723	1,749,095	1,829,561
Balance of Payments							*Millions of US Dollars: Minus Sign Indicates Debit*							
Current Account, n.i.e.	78ald	−820	−1,374	−4,128	−3,622	−1,308	−1,466	−2,690	−3,273	−4,265	−5,785	−6,538	−2,495
Goods: Exports f.o.b.	78aad	15,964	21,477	21,950	22,319	25,886	26,259	29,019	33,404	38,480	48,705	67,219	78,243
Goods: Imports f.o.b.	78abd	−17,372	−25,162	−27,656	−27,257	−28,532	−28,161	−32,114	−36,482	−40,720	−51,224	−68,265	−76,507
Trade Balance	78acd	−1,408	−3,685	−5,706	−4,938	−2,647	−1,902	−3,095	−3,078	−2,240	−2,519	−1,046	1,735
Services: Credit	78add	5,167	6,725	8,181	7,132	7,665	7,048	6,839	7,092	7,083	7,789	9,699	10,764
Services: Debit	78aed	−4,685	−4,882	−6,264	−5,389	−5,750	−5,850	−5,436	−5,567	−6,439	−7,320	−9,218	−9,954
Balance on Goods & Services	78afd	−926	−1,842	−3,789	−3,196	−731	−704	−1,692	−1,554	−1,597	−2,049	−565	2,546
Income: Credit	78agd	791	1,197	1,170	1,405	1,713	1,859	1,952	2,233	2,052	2,681	3,398	4,666
Income: Debit	78ahd	−812	−1,301	−1,892	−2,197	−2,806	−3,209	−3,323	−4,422	−5,632	−6,966	−9,535	−10,595
Balance on Gds, Serv. & Inc.	78aid	−947	−1,945	−4,512	−3,987	−1,825	−2,053	−3,063	−3,743	−5,177	−6,334	−6,702	−3,383
Current Transfers, n.i.e.: Credit	78ajd	298	664	617	866	1,067	1,310	948	959	1,465	1,663	1,830	3,175
Current Transfers: Debit	78akd	−171	−92	−233	−501	−550	−722	−575	−489	−553	−1,114	−1,666	−2,287
Capital Account, n.i.e.	78bcd	—	7	1	11	2	−2	−5	−9	−4	−3	−595	211
Capital Account, n.i.e.: Credit	78bad	—	12	1	17	14	18	6	2	7	7	218	239
Capital Account: Debit	78bbd	—	−5	—	−5	−12	−21	−11	−11	−11	−10	−813	−28
Financial Account, n.i.e.	78bjd	4,504	8,225	4,202	1,122	2,908	3,080	3,835	4,569	10,621	5,620	7,277	5,707
Direct Investment Abroad	78bdd	−116	−37	−155	−28	−125	−90	−43	−165	−211	−208	−1,037	−842
Dir. Invest. in Rep. Econ., n.i.e.	78bed	878	2,568	1,435	1,286	3,700	6,313	4,987	5,641	8,497	2,021	4,978	10,973
Portfolio Investment Assets	78bfd	−47	−325	−50	−159	−44	−1,882	−2,236	125	−2,373	−2,934	−2,565	−3,080
Equity Securities	78bkd	−47	−325	−50	3	119	−1,409	−1,167	247	−231	188	−1,206	−1,083
Debt Securities	78bld	....	....	....	−162	−163	−473	−1,069	−121	−2,142	−3,122	−1,359	−1,997
Portfolio Investment Liab., n.i.e.	78bgd	893	1,695	771	1,152	1,146	499	482	798	814	1,753	4,795	79
Equity Securities	78bmd	497	1,236	601	378	1,096	120	619	616	−265	1,104	738	−1,540
Debt Securities	78bnd	396	460	170	774	49	380	−137	181	1,079	649	4,057	1,619
Financial Derivatives Assets	78bwd	....	....	....	....	....	....	−129	−254	−476	257	−660	−82
Financial Derivatives Liabilities	78bxd	....	....	....	....	....	....	89	168	347	−114	514	−30
Other Investment Assets	78bhd	−2,437	−2,492	−2,370	−4,427	−1,552	−2,688	984	−1,199	4,015	2,279	−1,072	−4,322
Monetary Authorities	78bod	....	....	....	....			—	—	—	—	−7	−7
General Government	78bpd	−2,362	−2,138	48	16	20	28	76	180	651	278	941	583
Banks	78bqd	−163	−224	−2,317	−4,161	−1,652	−2,642	1,011	−1,299	3,844	1,469	−1,252	−4,599
Other Sectors	78brd	88	−130	−101	−281	80	−74	−102	−80	−480	533	−754	−299
Other Investment Liab., n.i.e.	78bid	5,333	6,816	4,571	3,298	−217	927	−300	−544	9	2,565	2,325	3,010
Monetary Authorities	78bsd	−47	40	−2	−11	−7	−57	—	1	−1	−2	27	204
General Government	78btd	2,821	1,657	−295	−360	−364	−185	−49	−129	−45	372	411	862
Banks	78bud	888	3,310	2,858	1,638	387	886	−974	−1,152	−282	1,214	−477	535
Other Sectors	78bvd	1,671	1,809	2,011	2,030	−234	283	723	735	338	981	2,365	1,409
Net Errors and Omissions	78cad	−210	596	−901	730	288	27	−296	499	266	611	118	456
Overall Balance	78cbd	3,474	7,453	−825	−1,758	1,890	1,639	844	1,787	6,618	442	263	3,879
Reserves and Related Items	79dad	−3,474	−7,453	825	1,758	−1,890	−1,639	−844	−1,787	−6,618	−442	−263	−3,879
Reserve Assets	79dbd	−2,357	−7,453	825	1,758	−1,890	−1,639	−844	−1,787	−6,618	−442	−263	−3,879
Use of Fund Credit and Loans	79dcd	−1,117	—	—	—	—	—	—	—	—	—	—	—
Exceptional Financing	79ded	....	—	—	—	....	....	....	—	—	—	—	—
International Investment Position							*Millions of US Dollars*							
Assets	79aad	20,471	29,396	30,629	29,779	36,426	37,465	38,304	42,609	52,419	59,926	69,276	74,181
Direct Investment Abroad	79abd	300	345	498	548	804	698	738	1,136	1,473	2,284	3,760	4,239
Portfolio Investment	79acd	433	755	1,372	1,032	1,202	2,900	4,772	5,106	9,102	13,408	16,644	17,435
Equity Securities	79add	334	693	748	417	449	1,843	2,439	1,894	2,869	1,845	3,404	4,386
Debt Securities	79aed	99	62	624	615	752	1,057	2,333	3,212	6,233	11,563	13,240	13,049
Financial Derivatives	79ald	—	—	—	—	—	—	168	435	1,036	941	1,775	1,682
Other Investment	79afd	13,494	14,273	16,323	18,425	21,804	21,042	19,488	21,469	17,098	16,336	18,648	21,269
Monetary Authorities	79agd	876	984	956	754	875	—	10	10	22	22	30	132
General Government	79ahd	6,278	5,987	5,931	5,923	5,902	5,843	5,839	5,813	3,301	3,102	2,172	1,562
Banks	79aid	2,944	3,469	5,622	8,308	11,263	11,841	10,305	12,116	9,349	8,859	10,853	14,520
Other Sectors	79ajd	3,396	3,833	3,814	3,440	3,763	3,358	3,335	3,530	4,427	4,353	5,593	5,054
Reserve Assets	79akd	6,243	14,023	12,435	9,774	12,617	12,825	13,139	14,464	23,710	26,957	28,449	29,555
Liabilities	79lad	18,088	27,182	33,151	32,863	40,361	40,548	43,378	49,340	65,598	80,485	106,163	109,025
Dir. Invest. in Rep. Economy	79lbd	4,547	7,350	8,572	9,234	14,375	17,552	21,644	27,092	38,669	45,287	57,259	59,459
Portfolio Investment	79lcd	2,910	4,696	5,298	4,880	5,564	4,602	4,353	4,974	6,673	8,717	17,036	17,806
Equity Securities	79ldd	1,331	2,642	3,398	3,028	3,793	2,724	3,059	3,551	4,250	5,488	9,339	8,968
Debt Securities	79led	1,579	2,054	1,900	1,853	1,771	1,878	1,294	1,423	2,423	3,229	7,697	8,838
Financial Derivatives	79lld	—	—	—	—	—	—	140	317	752	758	1,422	1,247
Other Investment	79lfd	10,631	15,136	19,280	18,749	20,422	18,394	17,242	16,957	19,504	25,724	30,445	30,513
Monetary Authorities	79lgd	62	98	85	64	64	6	5	6	5	5	42	243
General Government	79lhd	2,910	2,031	1,619	1,098	801	580	521	261	314	875	1,434	2,130
Banks	79lid	2,402	6,007	8,964	9,009	10,640	9,682	8,219	7,286	7,954	10,392	10,599	10,285
Other Sectors	79ljd	5,257	6,999	8,612	8,577	8,916	8,126	8,497	9,405	11,230	14,452	18,371	17,855

Czech Republic 935

		1994	1995	1996	1997	1998	1999	2000	2001	2002	2003	2004	2005
Government Finance		*Billions of Koruny: Year Ending December 31*											
Deficit (-) or Surplus........................	80	10.4	7.2	−1.8	−15.9	−29.2	−29.7	−46.1	−67.9	−45.6	−109.1	−93.7	−56.3
Total Revenue and Grants.............	81y	381.3	440.4	476.4	500.8	530.6	563.3	583.1	623.2	683.4	697.3	767.2	861.2
Revenue..	81	381.3	440.4	476.4	500.8	530.6	563.3	583.1	623.2	657.7	691.3	754.2	819.4
Grants...	81z	—	—	—	—	—	—	—	—	25.7	6.0	13.0	41.8
Exp. & Lending Minus Repay..........	82z	370.9	433.2	478.2	516.7	559.8	593.0	629.2	691.1	729.0	806.4	860.9	917.5
Expenditure.................................	82	373.1	433.9	480.6	521.2	561.6	593.8	629.5	688.2	746.2	806.1	862.5	922.8
Lending Minus Repayments.........	83	−2.2	−.7	−2.4	−4.5	−1.8	−.8	−.3	2.9	−17.3	.3	−1.6	−5.2
Total Financing...............................	80h	−10.4	−7.2	1.7	15.9	29.3	29.6	46.1	67.8	45.6	109.1	93.7	56.3
Domestic.......................................	84a	−10.4	−7.2	1.7	15.9	29.3	29.6	46.1	67.8	45.6	109.1	93.7	−6.6
Foreign...	85a	—	—	—	—	—	—	—	—	—	—	—	62.9
Total Debt by Residence..................	88	161.7	154.4	155.2	167.2	194.5	228.3	289.3	345.0	395.9	493.2	592.9	691.2
Domestic.......................................	88a	90.2	101.3	110.9	128.9	169.9	207.1	259.5	323.7	371.5	453.9	471.0	506.1
Foreign...	89a	71.5	53.1	44.3	38.3	24.6	21.2	29.8	21.3	24.4	39.3	121.9	185.1
National Accounts		*Billions of Koruny*											
Househ.Cons.Expend.,incl.NPISHs.....	96f	607.0	† 734.6	859.0	945.6	1,011.9	1,059.6	1,122.8	1,192.3	1,234.7	1,315.1	1,389.1	1,439.6
Government Consumption Expend...	91f	255.5	† 318.4	352.3	389.2	412.5	456.1	475.0	513.0	555.2	604.4	622.1	657.2
Gross Fixed Capital Formation..........	93e	339.8	† 463.5	521.0	534.4	554.6	550.6	594.9	638.6	643.3	685.6	743.8	773.9
Changes in Inventories....................	93i	12.2	† 13.4	27.4	11.0	5.6	−.6	23.6	30.0	30.9	7.3	25.8	−1.1
Exports of Goods and Services.........	90c	597.1	† 743.8	822.1	941.3	1,080.9	1,152.6	1,385.9	1,539.3	1,485.5	1,590.1	1,972.0	2,134.8
Imports of Goods and Services (-).....	98c	628.8	† 807.0	921.1	1,036.4	1,103.0	1,176.9	1,452.2	1,598.0	1,535.0	1,646.6	1,985.1	2,073.5
Gross Domestic Product (GDP).........	99b	1,182.8	1,466.7	1,660.6	1,785.1	1,962.5	2,041.4	2,150.1	2,315.3	2,414.7	2,555.8	2,767.7	2,931.1
Net Primary Income from Abroad.....	98.n	−.8	−3.0	−23.3	−28.2	−37.2	−49.1	−49.5	−79.0	−112.3	−111.0	−159.2	−134.5
Gross National Income (GNI)............	99a	1,181.9	1,459.5	1,635.9	1,755.9	1,927.4	1,994.7	2,096.9	2,231.5	2,298.4	2,441.3	2,632.9	2,771.8
Net Current Transf.from Abroad.......	98t	3.6	13.6	9.5	11.2	17.5	21.7	12.9	14.2	13.0	1.8	−.7	−4.6
Gross Nat'l Disposable Inc.(GNDI)....	99i	1,185.6	1,477.1	1,669.5	1,794.1	1,976.8	2,053.4	2,152.6	2,287.4	2,365.1	2,467.8	2,621.2	2,839.1
Gross Saving....................................	99s	323.0	424.8	454.9	441.0	525.5	512.1	542.4	570.4	553.3	532.2	588.2	707.6
GDP Volume 2000 Ref.,Chained......	99b.p	....	1,466.7	1,527.7	1,516.6	1,499.2	1,517.3	1,576.3	1,617.9	1,642.0	1,694.7	1,774.2	1,879.8
GDP Volume (2000=100)................	99bvp	82.7	† 93.0	96.9	96.2	95.1	96.3	100.0	102.6	104.2	107.5	112.6	119.3
GDP Deflator (2000=100)................	99bip	66.5	73.3	79.7	86.3	96.0	98.4	100.0	104.9	107.8	110.6	114.4	114.3
		Millions: Midyear Estimates											
Population.................................	99z	10.33	10.33	10.32	10.31	10.30	10.28	10.27	10.26	10.25	10.24	10.23	10.22

Denmark 128

		1994	1995	1996	1997	1998	1999	2000	2001	2002	2003	2004	2005
Exchange Rates							*Kroner per SDR: End of Period*						
Market Rate	aa	8.880	8.244	8.548	9.210	8.992	10.155	10.450	10.568	9.628	8.853	8.491	9.039
						Kroner per US Dollar: End of Period (ae) Period Average (rf)							
Market Rate	ae	6.083	5.546	5.945	6.826	6.387	7.399	8.021	8.410	7.082	5.958	5.468	6.324
Market Rate	rf	6.361	5.602	5.799	6.604	6.701	6.976	8.083	8.323	7.895	6.588	5.991	5.997
		Kroner per ECU through 1998; Kroner per Euro Beginning 1999: End of Period (ea) Period Average (eb)											
Euro Rate	ea	7.4823	7.2940	7.4466	7.5312	7.4488	† 7.4432	7.4631	7.4357	7.4243	7.4450	7.4334	7.4605
Euro Rate	ag	....	....	....	....	....	1.0046	.9305	.8813	1.0487	1.2630	1.3621	1.1797
Euro Rate	eb	7.5415	7.3271	7.3598	7.4830	7.4999	† 7.4356	7.4529	7.4521	7.4301	7.4306	7.4399	7.4518
Euro Rate	rh	....	....	....	....	....	1.0668	.9240	.8956	.9444	1.1308	1.2433	1.2458
					Index Numbers (2000=100): Period Averages								
Market Rate	ahx	127.0	144.0	139.0	122.2	120.4	115.7	100.0	96.9	102.4	122.6	134.7	134.6
Nominal Effective Exchange Rate	neu	105.5	110.5	108.9	105.2	106.1	104.5	100.0	101.3	102.3	106.2	107.4	107.2
Real Effective Exchange Rate	reu	102.2	106.5	105.0	102.0	104.2	103.8	100.0	102.1	104.7	110.6	111.5	111.5
Fund Position							*Millions of SDRs: End of Period*						
Quota	2f.s	1,069.9	1,069.9	1,069.9	1,069.9	1,069.9	1,642.8	1,642.8	1,642.8	1,642.8	1,642.8	1,642.8	1,642.8
SDRs	1b.s	124.6	106.8	116.7	248.7	246.0	249.9	50.5	223.5	75.9	54.6	28.8	78.1
Reserve Position in the Fund	1c.s	294.6	400.0	421.8	467.9	827.5	582.1	440.1	566.8	722.0	686.3	542.8	216.0
of which: Outstg.Fund Borrowing	2c	—	—	—	—	34.2	—	—	—	—	—	—	—
International Liquidity						*Millions of US Dollars Unless Otherwise Indicated: End of Period*							
Total Reserves minus Gold	1l.d	9,056	11,016	14,140	19,124	15,264	22,287	15,108	17,110	26,986	37,105	39,084	† 32,930
SDRs	1b.d	182	159	168	336	346	343	66	281	103	81	45	112
Reserve Position in the Fund	1c.d	430	595	607	631	1,165	799	573	712	982	1,020	843	309
Foreign Exchange	1d.d	8,444	10,262	13,366	18,157	13,753	21,145	14,469	16,117	25,901	36,004	38,196	† 32,510
Gold (Million Fine Troy Ounces)	1ad	1.629	1.646	1.662	1.687	2.143	2.141	2.141	2.141	2.140	2.140	2.140	2.140
Gold (National Valuation)	1and	703	714	590	545	677	531	569	557	703	872	970	† 1,098
Monetary Authorities: Other Liab.	4..d	253	397	275	124	196	297	381	421	400	481	266	† 379
Banking Institutions: Assets	7a.d	50,945	56,593	62,392	65,675	76,754	68,432	† 71,009	60,469	72,054	102,896	128,511	134,378
Liabilities	7b.d	30,141	33,246	40,172	50,347	61,484	63,340	62,554	58,799	75,582	110,390	129,545	128,275
Monetary Authorities							*Billions of Kroner: End of Period*						
Foreign Assets	11	63.18	69.34	86.25	129.49	101.85	169.06	† 120.86	152.26	199.74	227.62	219.35	216.15
Claims on Central Government	12a	20.05	14.83	15.47	15.19	15.50	14.80	† 14.97	16.47	18.33	17.15	15.44	10.34
Claims on Banking Institutions	12e	57.28	45.33	40.72	31.57	36.96	70.19	† 52.72	89.99	106.94	73.65	97.56	163.46
Claims on Other Banking Insts.	12f	24.99	19.97	21.26	20.24	22.95	24.56	....	....	....	....	....	....
Claims on Other Resident Sectors	12d	2.86	1.64	6.14	3.44	1.67	2.50	† 1.85	1.93	.23	.51	.47	.46
Reserve Money	14	63.15	71.69	95.55	125.31	97.00	192.86	† 58.28	54.99	60.96	66.28	61.45	71.04
of which: Currency Outside BIs	14a	28.93	30.59	30.94	33.25	34.49	36.86	† 37.43	39.21	38.98	40.99	43.72	47.27
Money Market Instruments	16m	....	....	....	....	....	....	51.87	113.62	160.66	157.28	160.38	207.58
Foreign Liabilities	16c	1.54	2.20	1.63	.88	1.25	2.43	† 3.37	3.89	3.70	3.09	1.76	2.56
Central Government Deposits	16d	56.91	35.44	31.65	30.73	34.03	36.49	† 35.32	40.56	47.06	40.89	58.08	53.50
Capital Accounts	17a	....	....	....	....	....	....	49.45	50.90	58.01	55.05	54.34	58.86
Other Items (Net)	17r	46.77	41.78	41.00	43.00	46.66	49.33	† −7.91	−3.32	−5.15	−3.67	−3.20	−3.15
Banking Institutions							*Billions of Kroner: End of Period*						
Reserves	20	32.69	39.57	51.62	70.63	54.20	96.26	† 23.82	17.37	32.47	18.91	27.70	25.79
Claims on Mon.Author.:Securities	20c	....	....	....	....	....	....	50.56	113.88	151.14	156.66	157.65	206.70
Foreign Assets	21	309.90	313.87	370.89	448.30	490.19	506.32	† 569.52	508.52	510.30	613.02	702.65	849.82
Claims on Central Government	22a	124.60	99.53	85.34	69.80	71.14	65.37	† 89.38	112.10	119.04	102.18	71.54	66.64
Claims on Other General Govt.	22b	....	....	....	....	....	....	57.95	61.17	66.27	75.03	83.06	89.81
Claims on Other Banking Insts.	22f	108.44	125.15	157.66	181.52	218.24	191.46	....	....	....	....	....	....
Claims on Other Resident Sectors	22d	297.74	312.89	331.06	357.73	405.37	420.62	† 1,750.73	1,904.42	1,999.09	2,122.47	2,318.41	2,653.98
Demand Deposits	24	248.31	259.86	287.09	304.47	321.44	336.34	† 346.55	373.20	391.63	427.72	492.54	595.76
Other Deposits	25	262.20	282.89	296.17	320.02	325.42	298.27	† 258.93	253.06	265.42	269.11	283.03	308.04
Money Market Instruments	26m	....	....	....	....	....	....	2.22	8.55	2.17	2.11	.20	1.93
Bonds	26n	....	....	....	....	....	....	1,173.61	1,268.87	1,363.06	1,417.13	1,513.98	1,756.33
Foreign Liabilities	26c	183.35	184.38	238.80	343.67	392.67	468.64	† 501.72	494.47	535.28	657.66	708.30	811.22
Central Government Deposits	26d	....	....	....	....	....	....	5.23	17.04	18.62	16.54	15.01	13.54
Credit from Monetary Authorities	26g	58.66	45.94	35.73	21.46	34.03	34.01	† 30.19	69.62	86.34	57.00	90.25	153.17
Capital Accounts	27a	79.54	75.37	77.42	82.25	87.64	91.43	† 221.46	212.55	207.06	235.80	241.96	275.83
Other Items (Net)	27r	41.31	42.58	61.35	56.11	77.93	51.34	† 2.28	20.12	8.69	5.16	15.37	−23.10
Banking Survey							*Billions of Kroner: End of Period*						
Foreign Assets (Net)	31n	188.19	196.62	216.70	233.24	198.12	204.31	† 185.29	162.42	171.06	179.88	211.94	252.18
Domestic Credit	32	528.22	545.50	592.83	629.40	714.58	697.55	† 1,874.33	2,038.48	2,137.28	2,259.90	2,415.82	2,754.18
Claims on Central Govt. (Net)	32an	87.74	78.91	69.16	54.26	52.62	43.68	† 63.80	70.96	71.69	61.89	13.89	9.93
Claims on Other General Govt.	32b	6.44	6.93	7.56	12.22	13.73	14.74	† 57.95	61.17	66.27	75.03	83.06	89.81
Claims on Other Banking Insts.	32f	133.43	145.13	178.91	201.75	241.19	216.02	....	....	....	....	....	....
Claims on Other Resident Sectors	32d	300.61	314.53	337.19	361.17	407.04	423.12	† 1,752.58	1,906.35	1,999.32	2,122.98	2,318.88	2,654.44
Money	34	279.05	291.98	325.52	344.05	360.74	381.77	† 385.98	414.85	430.82	469.15	536.62	643.62
Quasi-Money	35	262.20	282.89	296.17	320.02	325.42	298.27	† 258.93	253.06	265.42	269.11	283.03	308.05
Money Market Instruments	36m	....	....	....	....	....	....	3.53	8.30	11.70	2.73	2.93	2.82
Bonds	36n	....	....	....	....	....	....	1,148.73	1,244.30	1,340.38	1,394.52	1,492.32	1,732.34
Capital Accounts	37a	....	....	....	....	....	....	270.91	263.45	265.08	290.85	296.31	334.69
Other Items (Net)	37r	175.16	167.25	187.84	198.57	226.54	221.82	† −8.24	16.96	−5.08	13.38	16.19	−15.15
Money plus Quasi-Money	35l	541.25	574.87	621.69	664.08	686.16	680.04	† 644.91	667.91	696.24	738.27	819.65	951.66
Money (National Definitions)							*Billions of Kroner: End of Period*						
Broad Money	59mc	406.12	418.95	464.39	500.87	520.25	534.99	507.13	546.40	611.20	680.56	698.98	798.49
Interest Rates							*Percent Per Annum*						
Discount Rate (End of Period)	60	5.00	4.25	3.25	3.50	3.50	3.00	4.75	3.25	2.86	2.00	2.00	2.25
Money Market Rate	60b	6.30	6.19	3.98	3.71	4.27	3.37	4.98	....	3.56	2.38	2.16	2.20
Deposit Rate	60l	† 3.5	3.9	2.8	2.7	3.1	2.4	3.2	3.3	† 2.4	2.4	....	....
Lending Rate	60p	† 10.0	10.3	8.7	7.7	7.9	7.1	8.1	8.2	† 7.1	....	....	....
Government Bond Yield	61	7.41	7.58	6.04	5.08	4.59	4.30	5.54	....	4.57	3.53	3.32	3.01
Mortgage Bond Yield	61a	8.34	8.97	7.84	7.14	6.04	6.08	7.06	....	6.13	5.16	5.01	4.74

Denmark 128

		1994	1995	1996	1997	1998	1999	2000	2001	2002	2003	2004	2005
Prices, Production, Labor					*Index Numbers (2000=100): Period Averages*								
Share Prices: Industrial....................	62a	40	40	49	65	70	62	100	....	....	....	....	....
Shipping...........................	62b	33	30	37	66	68	77	100	....	....	....	....	....
Prices: Home & Import Goods.........	63	89.1	91.7	92.7	94.5	93.9	94.4	† 100.0	102.0	102.1	102.3	104.5	108.8
Home Goods................	63a	88.8	91.6	93.0	94.7	94.2	95.1	† 100.0	102.8	103.5	104.8	108.7	113.4
Consumer Prices........................	64	87.4	89.2	91.1	93.1	94.8	97.2	100.0	102.4	104.8	107.0	108.3	110.2
Harmonized CPI........................	64h	....	90.5	92.4	94.1	95.4	97.3	100.0	102.3	104.7	† 106.8	107.7	109.6
Wages: Hourly Earnings.................	65..c	79.3	82.3	85.4	88.8	92.6	96.5	100.0	104.2	108.3	112.3	115.7	119.1
Industrial Production.....................	66	83.2	86.5	87.6	92.0	94.7	94.9	100.0	102.0	103.0	102.3	102.0	103.8
Agricultural Production (1995=100).	66bx	101.1	100.0	100.2	101.0	104.6	104.8	....	....	....	....	....	....
					Number in Thousands: Period Averages								
Labor Force................................	67d	2,777	....	2,822	2,856	2,848	2,848	2,853	2,862	2,849	2,850	2,883	....
Employment..............................	67e	† 2,555	2,607	2,627	2,678	2,691	2,708	2,722	2,725	2,712	2,693	2,720	2,723
Unemployment............................	67c	343	288	246	220	183	158	151	135	138	160	166	153
Unemployment Rate (%).................	67r	12.2	10.3	8.8	7.9	6.6	5.7	5.4	4.8	4.9	5.7	5.9	5.6
Intl. Transactions & Positions					*Millions of Kroner*								
Exports..	70	273,163	288,186	298,562	324,271	326,504	351,916	408,239	424,670	442,754	429,272	452,400	502,534
Imports, c.i.f................................	71	231,794	256,094	260,977	293,063	309,787	310,586	358,871	367,032	384,710	369,701	400,125	447,284
					2000=100								
Volume of Exports.........................	72	69	† 78	80	84	86	92	100	103	109	107	110	117
Volume of Imports........................	73	69	† 81	82	88	93	93	100	102	108	106	113	123
Unit Value of Exports.....................	74	90	† 90	92	94	93	93	100	102	100	99	101	106
Unit Value of Imports.....................	75	86	† 88	90	93	93	93	100	101	99	97	98	102
Import Prices................................	76.x	90	92	92	94	93	93	100	101	100	99	100	104
Balance of Payments					*Millions of US Dollars: Minus Sign Indicates Debit*								
Current Account, n.i.e.....................	78ald	3,189	1,855	3,090	921	−2,008	3,047	2,262	4,848	3,460	6,963	5,941	....
Goods: Exports f.o.b.....................	78aad	41,741	50,348	50,735	48,103	47,908	49,787	50,084	50,466	55,473	64,537	75,050	....
Goods: Imports f.o.b.....................	78abd	−34,300	−43,821	−43,203	−42,734	−44,021	−43,128	−43,443	−43,048	−47,810	−54,840	−65,524	....
Trade Balance.........................	78acd	7,441	6,528	7,532	5,369	3,886	6,658	6,641	7,418	7,662	9,697	9,527	....
Services: Credit.............................	78add	13,661	15,307	16,502	14,044	15,212	19,982	23,721	25,134	26,667	31,672	36,304	....
Services: Debit..............................	78aed	−12,067	−14,040	−14,771	−13,727	−15,779	−18,402	−21,063	−22,121	−24,305	−28,254	−33,401	....
Balance on Goods & Services.......	78afd	9,035	7,795	9,263	5,685	3,319	8,238	9,300	10,431	10,024	13,116	12,430	....
Income: Credit.............................	78agd	22,743	28,433	37,626	18,774	10,401	9,090	11,883	10,737	9,265	11,180	12,784	....
Income: Debit..............................	78ahd	−27,385	−32,982	−42,235	−22,203	−14,247	−11,546	−15,907	−13,748	−12,805	−13,796	−15,114	....
Balance on Gds, Serv. & Inc.........	78aid	4,394	3,246	4,655	2,256	−527	5,782	5,276	7,420	6,484	10,499	10,100	....
Current Transfers, n.i.e.: Credit.......	78ajd	2,261	2,580	2,398	3,633	3,443	4,239	3,395	3,719	3,466	4,615	5,120	....
Current Transfers: Debit................	78akd	−3,466	−3,970	−3,963	−4,968	−4,924	−6,974	−6,410	−6,291	−6,489	−8,151	−9,279	....
Capital Account, n.i.e.....................	78bcd	....	....	....	128	50	128	−11	14	152	−7	13	....
Capital Account, n.i.e.: Credit........	78bad	....	....	....	128	81	372	320	300	411	344	511	....
Capital Account: Debit..................	78bbd	....	....	....	—	−31	−245	−332	−286	−258	−351	−498	....
Financial Account, n.i.e..................	78bjd	−5,647	−432	1,882	8,496	−1,489	7,414	−3,311	−5,712	3,819	−5,129	−19,023	....
Direct Investment Abroad..............	78bdd	−4,162	−2,969	−2,510	−4,355	−4,215	−17,819	−28,381	−13,154	−2,650	−856	9,930	....
Dir. Invest. in Rep. Econ., n.i.e.......	78bed	5,006	4,139	773	2,792	6,675	16,848	36,013	9,286	4,431	1,185	−8,804	....
Portfolio Investment Assets............	78bfd	−1,175	−1,171	−2,349	−6,239	−7,563	−9,721	−23,582	−14,772	−4,356	−21,930	−24,768	....
Equity Securities.........................	78bkd	....	....	....	....	....	−6,202	−13,944	−4,318	199	−3,467	−7,299	....
Debt Securities..........................	78bld	−1,175	−1,171	−2,349	....	....	−3,519	−9,638	−10,454	−4,555	−18,463	−17,469	....
Portfolio Investment Liab., n.i.e......	78bgd	−10,596	7,487	7,865	11,186	−2,598	7,014	5,783	10,510	4,843	6,010	10,055	....
Equity Securities.........................	78bmd	....	....	....	....	....	−18	2,341	861	591	1,389	1,562	....
Debt Securities..........................	78bnd	−10,596	7,487	7,865	....	....	7,031	3,442	9,649	4,253	4,621	8,493	....
Financial Derivatives Assets...........	78bwd	....	....	....	....	....	—	—	—	—	—	—	....
Financial Derivatives Liabilities.......	78bxd	....	....	....	....	....	320	326	694	390	−12	3,206	....
Other Investment Assets................	78bhd	12,136	−1,330	−9,339	−8,033	−1,797	−906	−2,025	9,054	−6,839	−9,314	−9,021	....
Monetary Authorities..................	78bod	....	....	....	....	....	−32	15	−13	−41	56	−13	....
General Government..................	78bpd	....	....	....	....	....	31	25	41	18	365	31	....
Banks.....................................	78bqd	12,136	−1,330	−9,339	....	....	329	−1,713	7,232	−6,062	−12,623	−14,576	....
Other Sectors...........................	78brd	....	....	....	−8,033	−1,797	−1,234	−352	1,794	−755	2,888	5,537	....
Other Investment Liab., n.i.e..........	78bid	−6,856	−6,589	7,442	13,145	8,009	11,677	8,554	−7,331	8,000	19,789	378	....
Monetary Authorities..................	78bsd	122	133	−108	....	....	158	113	61	−30	−27	−230	....
General Government..................	78btd	−4,058	−3,380	−1,563	....	....	−232	−329	−191	−158	−438	−177	....
Banks.....................................	78bud	414	15	9,343	....	....	7,659	10,466	−1,720	10,806	24,714	9,567	....
Other Sectors...........................	78bvd	−3,333	−3,357	−231	13,145	8,009	4,092	−1,696	−5,481	−2,619	−4,461	−8,782	....
Net Errors and Omissions................	78cad	606	1,075	−1,408	−3,012	−792	−1,024	−4,460	4,167	−1,887	2,846	11,644	....
Overall Balance.........................	78cbd	−1,851	2,498	3,563	6,532	−4,239	9,564	−5,521	3,317	5,546	4,674	−1,426	....
Reserves and Related Items..............	79dad	1,851	−2,498	−3,563	−6,532	4,239	−9,564	5,521	−3,317	−5,546	−4,674	1,426	....
Reserve Assets.............................	79dbd	1,851	−2,498	−3,563	−6,532	4,239	−9,564	5,521	−3,317	−5,546	−4,674	1,426	....
Use of Fund Credit and Loans........	79dcd	—	—	—	....	....	....	....	....	....	....	....	....
Exceptional Financing...................	79ded	....	....	....	....	....	....	....	....	....	....	....	....

Denmark 128

		1994	1995	1996	1997	1998	1999	2000	2001	2002	2003	2004	2005
International Investment Position							*Millions of US Dollars*							
Assets..	79aad	109,111	123,004	145,614	156,402	187,516	219,613	249,021	253,228	307,886	393,205	474,364	477,188
Direct Investment Abroad..............	79abd	19,892	24,702	27,589	28,128	34,664	44,841	65,890	78,252	86,679	102,596	111,678	118,403
Portfolio Investment......................	79acd	17,261	22,899	29,944	37,064	51,792	70,762	84,973	85,731	86,424	127,033	160,851	196,812
Equity Securities.........................	79add	8,877	10,819	16,149	22,414	32,623	50,132	56,480	47,978	35,796	52,118	65,428	88,657
Debt Securities...........................	79aed	8,384	12,081	13,794	14,650	19,169	20,630	28,493	37,753	50,628	74,915	95,423	108,154
Financial Derivatives....................	79ald	—	—	—	—	2,502	9,285	14,093	11,203	30,577	23,566	36,560	8,858
Other Investment..........................	79afd	62,798	63,469	73,513	71,931	82,423	72,054	69,009	59,937	76,433	101,816	125,174	119,058
Monetary Authorities..................	79agd	—	—	—	—	—	—	—	—	—	—	—	....
General Government...................	79ahd	2,795	2,524	2,187	2,051	2,524	2,621	3,396	3,363	4,196	4,968	5,414	....
Banks.......................................	79aid	46,359	49,766	55,177	56,255	64,534	54,775	51,786	45,066	59,508	82,220	103,729	....
Other Sectors............................	79ajd	13,645	11,179	16,149	13,624	15,365	14,658	13,827	11,508	12,729	14,627	16,031	....
Reserve Assets.............................	79akd	9,160	11,933	14,569	19,279	16,136	22,670	15,056	18,106	27,773	38,194	40,102	34,057
Liabilities...................................	79lad	151,734	170,934	187,737	197,480	235,320	241,569	272,052	279,551	339,698	421,714	503,500	473,234
Dir. Invest. in Rep. Economy..........	79lbd	18,083	23,801	22,205	22,268	31,055	41,225	66,459	75,438	82,809	100,191	109,170	101,908
Portfolio Investment......................	79lcd	72,826	88,713	101,607	106,505	117,215	105,272	104,119	112,507	127,484	159,180	197,683	209,989
Equity Securities.........................	79ldd	6,740	8,294	12,448	20,363	20,556	20,740	26,023	23,842	20,672	31,258	44,459	48,636
Debt Securities...........................	79led	66,086	80,418	89,158	86,141	96,658	84,532	78,095	88,665	106,812	127,923	153,225	161,353
Financial Derivatives....................	79lld	—	—	—	—	2,159	8,453	13,363	10,828	28,301	20,442	32,582	—
Other Investment..........................	79lfd	60,825	58,420	63,925	68,708	84,891	86,619	88,111	80,778	101,105	141,900	164,064	161,337
Monetary Authorities..................	79lgd	329	361	336	146	204	328	420	463	522	519	321	....
General Government...................	79lhd	3,123	1,983	1,178	732	1,265	949	468	647	551	89	83	....
Banks.......................................	79lid	27,289	29,210	35,159	42,631	53,475	52,813	60,547	58,685	75,829	110,902	129,869	....
Other Sectors............................	79ljd	30,084	26,866	27,252	25,198	29,948	32,530	26,675	20,983	24,202	30,389	33,791	....
Government Finance						*Millions of Kroner: Year Ending December 31*								
Deficit (-) or Surplus......................	80	−26,398	−23,692	−3,081	12,661	19,479	6,296	20,804f	....	....	....	....	....
Revenue.....................................	81	385,593	391,286	417,948	434,423	449,490	462,510	470,916f	....	....	....	....	....
Grants Received...........................	81z	5,546	3,873	3,771	4,583	4,826	4,665	5,507f	....	....	....	....	....
Expenditure................................	82	412,967	417,654	423,596	425,124	434,285	443,021	452,939f	....	....	....	....	....
Lending Minus Repayments............	83	4,570	1,195	1,202	1,222	554	17,857	2,677f	....	....	....	....	....
National Accounts							*Billions of Kroner*							
Househ.Cons.Expend.,incl.NPISHs....	96f	504.1	521.8	541.7	569.0	590.3	599.1	616.7	631.7	652.3	675.6	710.6	751.9
Government Consumption Expend...	91f	249.3	257.2	271.7	281.0	298.1	312.4	325.1	343.3	360.2	371.1	388.3	401.9
Gross Fixed Capital Formation..........	93e	168.0	187.4	198.7	220.6	237.9	240.1	261.1	264.0	268.9	274.2	290.5	320.4
Changes in Inventories..................	93i	4.2	11.5	4.9	13.7	12.7	.6	13.0	8.0	11.3	2.6	5.9	4.1
Exports of Goods and Services..........	90c	368.2	383.7	405.7	437.1	445.3	494.5	602.9	631.4	648.9	634.7	663.7	754.8
Imports of Goods and Services (-).....	98c	317.0	342.0	353.2	395.8	420.7	433.3	524.8	542.8	568.7	549.1	591.7	681.5
Gross Domestic Product (GDP).........	99b	976.9	1,019.5	1,069.5	1,125.6	1,163.6	1,213.5	1,294.0	1,335.6	1,372.7	1,409.2	1,467.3	1,551.5
Net Primary Income from Abroad.....	98.n	−14.4	−10.9	−13.7	−15.9	−13.1	−10.2	−27.4	−18.8	−16.2	−9.2	−4.7	2.7
Gross National Income (GNI)...........	99a	962.5	1,008.6	1,055.8	1,109.7	1,150.5	1,203.2	1,266.6	1,316.8	1,356.5	1,400.0	1,462.6	1,554.2
Net Current Transf.from Abroad.......	98t	−20.8	−21.5	−22.8	−18.5	−21.4	−27.8	−32.5	−28.0	−29.8	−30.7	−34.0	−31.7
Gross Nat'l Disposable Inc.(GNDI)....	99i	941.8	987.2	1,033.1	1,091.2	1,129.1	1,175.4	1,234.1	1,288.8	1,326.7	1,369.3	1,428.6	1,522.5
Gross Saving................................	99s	188.3	208.2	219.7	241.1	240.7	263.9	292.3	313.8	314.3	322.6	329.7	368.7
Consumption of Fixed Capital..........	99cf	152.0	158.0	167.1	176.9	184.5	195.1	204.4	214.4	223.0	227.9	237.4	246.3
GDP Volume 1995 Ref., Chained.....	99b.p	989.2	1,019.5	1,048.4	1,082.0	1,105.4	1,133.7	1,173.7	1,181.9	1,187.4	1,195.7	1,218.0	1,255.2
GDP Volume (2000=100)................	99bvp	84.3	86.9	89.3	92.2	94.2	96.6	100.0	100.7	101.2	101.9	103.8	106.9
GDP Deflator (2000=100)................	99bip	89.6	90.7	92.5	94.4	95.5	97.1	100.0	102.5	104.9	106.9	109.3	112.1
							Millions: Midyear Estimates							
Population..............................	99z	5.21	5.23	5.25	5.27	5.30	5.32	5.34	5.36	5.38	5.40	5.41	5.43

Djibouti 611

		1994	1995	1996	1997	1998	1999	2000	2001	2002	2003	2004	2005
Exchange Rates							*Francs per SDR: End of Period (aa)*						
Official Rate..................................	aa	259.45	264.18	255.56	239.79	250.24	243.92	231.55	223.35	241.62	264.09	276.00	254.01
						Francs per US Dollar: End of Period (ae) Period Average (rf)							
Official Rate..................................	ae	177.72	177.72	177.72	177.72	177.72	177.72	177.72	177.72	177.72	177.72	177.72	177.72
Official Rate..................................	rf	177.72	177.72	177.72	177.72	177.72	177.72	177.72	177.72	177.72	177.72	177.72	177.72
Fund Position							*Millions of SDRs: End of Period*						
Quota..	2f.s	11.50	11.50	11.50	11.50	11.50	15.90	15.90	15.90	15.90	15.90	15.90	15.90
SDRs...	1b.s	.11	.06	.10	.55	.27	.06	.28	.10	.76	.09	.64	.02
Reserve Position in the Fund............	1c.s	—	—	—	—	—	1.10	1.10	1.10	1.10	1.10	1.10	1.10
Total Fund Cred.&Loans Outstg........	2tl	—	—	2.88	3.98	6.30	9.28	10.29	12.32	15.06	13.75	13.63	13.08
International Liquidity						*Millions of US Dollars Unless Otherwise Indicated: End of Period*							
Total Reserves minus Gold..............	1l.d	73.76	72.16	76.97	66.57	66.45	70.61	67.80	70.31	73.71	100.13	93.94	89.26
SDRs...	1b.d	.16	.09	.15	.75	.38	.09	.36	.13	1.03	.14	.99	.02
Reserve Position in the Fund..........	1c.d	—	—	—	—	—	1.51	1.43	1.38	1.50	1.63	1.71	1.57
Foreign Exchange........................	1d.d	73.60	72.07	76.82	65.82	66.07	69.01	66.01	68.80	71.18	98.36	91.24	87.67
Deposit Money Banks: Assets..........	7a.d	211.53	209.96	173.31	167.22	169.95	178.25	166.03	201.85	251.41	296.17	372.84	430.64
Liabilities..........	7b.d	88.65	91.10	89.01	83.33	88.47	45.30	50.12	38.75	43.04	36.37	41.92	45.97
Other Banking Insts.: Liabilities........	7f.d	3.43	3.21	3.26	....	....	....	....	....	....	....	....	....
Monetary Authorities							*Millions of Francs: End of Period*						
Foreign Assets...............................	11	13,990	12,688	13,683	12,064	11,518	12,507	12,051	12,498	13,215	17,915	16,696	15,320
Claims on Central Government........	12a	534	534	1,275	1,487	2,176	2,928	2,832	3,234	3,177	4,331	4,620	4,550
Claims on Deposit Money Banks......	12e	40	42	44	44	44	—	—	—	—	—	—	—
Reserve Money................................	14	11,869	10,370	9,989	9,783	9,588	10,011	9,932	10,467	11,409	14,965	14,197	14,299
of which: Currency Outside DMBs..	14a	10,693	9,367	9,686	9,450	9,112	9,289	9,207	9,370	10,188	11,113	12,358	13,272
Central Government Deposits...........	16d	797	1,074	284	106	676	1,152	514	319	115	792	176	184
Capital Accounts.............................	17a	1,390	1,712	1,729	1,872	2,361	2,537	2,713	2,786	2,807	2,834	2,897	2,912
Other Items (Net)............................	17r	511	108	3,000	1,889	1,125	1,735	1,724	2,161	2,062	3,656	4,046	2,474
Deposit Money Banks							*Millions of Francs: End of Period*						
Reserves.......................................	20	1,148	1,065	638	778	575	743	718	1,056	1,221	3,854	1,888	1,164
Foreign Assets...............................	21	37,594	37,314	30,801	29,719	30,204	31,679	29,507	35,873	44,681	52,636	66,261	76,533
Claims on Central Government........	22a	2,525	2,144	1,569	1,678	724	214	111	74	1,478	1,318	1,069	1,333
Claims on Nonfin.Pub.Enterprises.....	22c	419	464	599	778	2,115	2,309	1,540	1,758	1,374	1,259	1,099	1,064
Claims on Private Sector................	22d	33,382	37,783	38,826	38,469	42,098	27,491	31,413	26,898	25,629	24,967	24,991	25,282
Demand Deposits............................	24	21,814	21,157	18,738	17,506	20,146	20,985	18,704	19,275	25,327	31,737	35,085	34,456
Time Deposits................................	25	23,030	26,841	23,185	23,943	24,845	21,747	24,697	27,924	29,922	34,207	40,311	49,981
Foreign Liabilities..........................	26c	15,755	16,191	15,819	14,810	15,723	8,051	8,908	6,886	7,650	6,464	7,450	8,170
Central Government Deposits...........	26d	2,089	727	568	605	877	233	87	31	3	12	54	507
Credit From Monetary Authorities....	26g	40	40	52	406	40	—	—	—	—	—	—	—
Capital Accounts.............................	27a	9,854	10,051	10,053	9,609	9,814	8,730	7,550	7,646	7,676	7,643	6,412	5,559
Other Items (Net)............................	27r	2,485	3,763	4,021	4,544	4,271	2,690	3,342	3,896	3,804	3,970	5,995	6,704
Monetary Survey							*Millions of Francs: End of Period*						
Foreign Assets (Net).......................	31n	35,815	33,794	27,904	25,959	24,336	33,720	29,979	38,410	47,230	59,918	71,057	79,339
Domestic Credit..............................	32	39,075	45,598	48,918	47,223	45,560	31,557	35,295	31,614	31,540	31,071	31,549	31,538
Claims on Central Govt. (Net).......	32an	5,180	7,233	9,384	7,873	1,347	1,757	2,342	2,958	4,537	4,845	5,459	5,192
Claims on Nonfin.Pub.Enterprises...	32c	419	464	599	778	2,115	2,309	1,540	1,758	1,374	1,259	1,099	1,064
Claims on Private Sector...............	32d	33,476	37,901	38,935	38,572	42,098	27,491	31,413	26,898	25,629	24,967	24,991	25,282
Money...	34	37,608	36,998	35,925	32,478	29,258	30,274	27,911	28,645	35,515	42,850	47,443	47,728
Quasi-Money..................................	35	23,030	26,841	23,185	23,943	24,845	21,747	24,697	27,924	29,922	34,207	40,311	49,981
Other Items (Net)............................	37r	14,254	15,553	17,715	16,817	15,805	13,256	12,665	13,455	13,333	13,932	14,851	13,168
Money plus Quasi-Money................	35l	60,638	63,839	59,110	56,421	54,103	52,021	52,608	56,569	65,437	77,057	87,754	97,709
Other Banking Institutions							*Millions of Francs: End of Period*						
Reserves.......................................	40	167	80	30	....	....	....	....	....	....	....	....	....
Claims on Private Sector................	42d	4,277	4,126	3,537	....	....	....	....	....	....	....	....	....
Long-Term Foreign Liabilities.........	46cl	610	570	580	....	....	....	....	....	....	....	....	....
Central Govt. Lending Funds...........	46f	1,542	1,533	1,180	....	....	....	....	....	....	....	....	....
Capital Accounts.............................	47a	1,557	1,817	1,696	....	....	....	....	....	....	....	....	....
Other Items (Net)............................	47r	735	286	111	....	....	....	....	....	....	....	....	....
Interest Rates							*Percent Per Annum*						
Deposit Rate..................................	60l	....	....	....	....	....	....	....	2.81	1.23	.82	.80	.85
Lending Rate..................................	60p	....	....	....	....	....	....	....	11.46	11.30	11.30	11.25	11.15
Intl. Transactions & Positions							*Millions of Francs*						
Exports...	70	2,151	2,414	2,439	1,917	2,195	2,168	....	....	....	....	....	....
Imports...	71	34,908	31,395	31,805	26,322	28,120	27,131	....	....	....	....	....	....
							1995=100						
Volume of Imports..........................	73	107.0	100.0	90.8	75.9	88.2	99.3	....	....	....	....	....	....
Import Prices.................................	76.x	100.6	100.0	110.5	102.1	103.8	95.3	....	....	....	....	....	....

Djibouti   611

		1994	1995	1996	1997	1998	1999	2000	2001	2002	2003	2004	2005
Balance of Payments				*Millions of US Dollars: Minus Sign Indicates Debit*									
Current Account, n.i.e.	**78ald**	−46.1	−23.0	....	....	....	....	....	....	....	....	....	....
Goods: Exports f.o.b.	**78aad**	56.4	33.5	....	....	....	....	....	....	....	....	....	....
Goods: Imports f.o.b.	**78abd**	−237.1	−205.0	....	....	....	....	....	....	....	....	....	....
Trade Balance	**78acd**	−180.7	−171.5	....	....	....	....	....	....	....	....	....	....
Services: Credit	**78add**	152.3	151.4	....	....	....	....	....	....	....	....	....	....
Services: Debit	**78aed**	−89.7	−87.2	....	....	....	....	....	....	....	....	....	....
Balance on Goods & Services	**78afd**	−118.1	−107.3	....	....	....	....	....	....	....	....	....	....
Income: Credit	**78agd**	23.7	25.9	....	....	....	....	....	....	....	....	....	....
Income: Debit	**78ahd**	−7.0	−8.7	....	....	....	....	....	....	....	....	....	....
Balance on Gds, Serv. & Inc.	**78aid**	−101.4	−90.0	....	....	....	....	....	....	....	....	....	....
Current Transfers, n.i.e.: Credit	**78ajd**	73.7	85.4	....	....	....	....	....	....	....	....	....	....
Current Transfers: Debit	**78akd**	−18.3	−18.4	....	....	....	....	....	....	....	....	....	....
Capital Account, n.i.e.	**78bcd**	—	—	....	....	....	....	....	....	....	....	....	....
Capital Account, n.i.e.: Credit	**78bad**	—	—	....	....	....	....	....	....	....	....	....	....
Capital Account: Debit	**78bbd**	—	—	....	....	....	....	....	....	....	....	....	....
Financial Account, n.i.e.	**78bjd**	39.0	−2.1	....	....	....	....	....	....	....	....	....	....
Direct Investment Abroad	**78bdd**	—	—	....	....	....	....	....	....	....	....	....	....
Dir. Invest. in Rep. Econ., n.i.e.	**78bed**	1.4	3.2	....	....	....	....	....	....	....	....	....	....
Portfolio Investment Assets	**78bfd**	—	—	....	....	....	....	....	....	....	....	....	....
Equity Securities	**78bkd**	—	—	....	....	....	....	....	....	....	....	....	....
Debt Securities	**78bld**	—	—	....	....	....	....	....	....	....	....	....	....
Portfolio Investment Liab., n.i.e.	**78bgd**	—	—	....	....	....	....	....	....	....	....	....	....
Equity Securities	**78bmd**	—	—	....	....	....	....	....	....	....	....	....	....
Debt Securities	**78bnd**	—	—	....	....	....	....	....	....	....	....	....	....
Financial Derivatives Assets	**78bwd**	....	....	....	....	....	....	....	....	....	....	....	....
Financial Derivatives Liabilities	**78bxd**	....	....	....	....	....	....	....	....	....	....	....	....
Other Investment Assets	**78bhd**	—	—	....	....	....	....	....	....	....	....	....	....
Monetary Authorities	**78bod**	....	....	....	....	....	....	....	....	....	....	....	....
General Government	**78bpd**	—	—	....	....	....	....	....	....	....	....	....	....
Banks	**78bqd**	—	—	....	....	....	....	....	....	....	....	....	....
Other Sectors	**78brd**	—	—	....	....	....	....	....	....	....	....	....	....
Other Investment Liab., n.i.e.	**78bid**	37.6	−5.4	....	....	....	....	....	....	....	....	....	....
Monetary Authorities	**78bsd**	—	—	....	....	....	....	....	....	....	....	....	....
General Government	**78btd**	12.0	−9.4	....	....	....	....	....	....	....	....	....	....
Banks	**78bud**	11.6	4.0	....	....	....	....	....	....	....	....	....	....
Other Sectors	**78bvd**	14.1	.1	....	....	....	....	....	....	....	....	....	....
Net Errors and Omissions	**78cad**	7.9	.7	....	....	....	....	....	....	....	....	....	....
Overall Balance	**78cbd**	.8	−24.5	....	....	....	....	....	....	....	....	....	....
Reserves and Related Items	**79dad**	−.8	24.5	....	....	....	....	....	....	....	....	....	....
Reserve Assets	**79dbd**	−3.4	7.3	....	....	....	....	....	....	....	....	....	....
Use of Fund Credit and Loans	**79dcd**	—	—	....	....	....	....	....	....	....	....	....	....
Exceptional Financing	**79ded**	2.6	17.2	....	....	....	....	....	....	....	....	....	....
				Millions: Midyear Estimates									
Population	**99z**	.60	.61	.63	.65	.67	.69	.71	.73	.75	.76	.78	.79

Dominica 321

		1994	1995	1996	1997	1998	1999	2000	2001	2002	2003	2004	2005
Exchange Rates		*E.Caribbean Dollars per SDR: End of Period (aa) E.Caribbean Dollars per US Dollar: End of Period (ae)*											
Official Rate	aa	3.9416	4.0135	3.8825	3.6430	3.8017	3.7058	3.5179	3.3932	3.6707	4.0121	4.1931	3.8590
Official Rate	ae	2.7000	2.7000	2.7000	2.7000	2.7000	2.7000	2.7000	2.7000	2.7000	2.7000	2.7000	2.7000
		Index Numbers (2000=100): Period Averages											
Nominal Effective Exchange Rate	nec	92.26	89.47	91.27	93.37	95.88	96.82	100.00	103.01	103.94	103.81	102.56	102.20
Real Effective Exchange Rate	rec	106.85	100.63	99.38	99.72	100.17	99.54	100.00	100.51	99.94	97.73	94.45	91.18
Fund Position		*Millions of SDRs: End of Period*											
Quota	2f.s	6.00	6.00	6.00	6.00	6.00	8.20	8.20	8.20	8.20	8.20	8.20	8.20
SDRs	1b.s	—	—	—	—	—	.01	—	—	—	—	.03	.01
Reserve Position in the Fund	1c.s	.01	.01	.01	.01	.01	.01	.01	.01	.01	.01	.01	.01
Total Fund Cred.&Loans Outstg	2tl	1.71	1.15	.59	.19	.03	—	—	—	2.05	5.33	5.95	8.08
International Liquidity		*Millions of US Dollars Unless Otherwise Indicated: End of Period*											
Total Reserves minus Gold	1l.d	15.41	22.12	22.89	23.89	27.67	31.57	29.37	31.22	45.50	47.74	42.32	49.17
SDRs	1b.d	—	—	—	—	—	.01	—	—	—	—	.05	.01
Reserve Position in the Fund	1c.d	.01	.01	.01	.01	.01	.01	.01	.01	.01	.01	.01	.01
Foreign Exchange	1d.d	15.40	22.11	22.88	23.88	27.65	31.55	29.36	31.21	45.48	47.72	42.25	49.15
Monetary Authorities: Other Liab	4..d	—	—	—	—	—	—	—	—	—	—	—	—
Deposit Money Banks: Assets	7a.d	26.62	28.14	38.81	43.08	51.84	60.28	44.68	51.24	77.01	101.93	149.15	129.86
Liabilities	7b.d	39.49	34.45	35.63	43.28	46.01	45.66	49.75	46.32	48.05	38.83	59.18	61.24
Monetary Authorities		*Millions of E. Caribbean Dollars: End of Period*											
Foreign Assets	11	41.74	60.65	62.71	64.67	74.87	85.34	79.41	84.38	122.96	129.09	114.98	133.53
Claims on Central Government	12a	26.20	19.78	14.82	13.34	11.34	11.13	11.44	10.75	17.14	30.55	32.12	38.37
Claims on Deposit Money Banks	12e	2.04	.01	.01	.01	.03	.03	.01	3.92	.01	.01	—	.03
Reserve Money	14	63.21	74.20	73.69	75.76	84.55	95.02	92.46	91.69	130.64	126.16	117.77	123.51
of which: Currency Outside DMBs	14a	24.49	29.16	28.53	28.21	29.13	34.09	35.45	34.61	35.51	34.18	37.60	38.96
Foreign Liabilities	16c	6.72	4.60	2.28	.68	.10	—	—	—	7.52	21.39	24.93	31.19
Central Government Deposits	16d	.04	.82	.76	.78	.78	.77	.63	1.50	2.60	1.12	11.28	3.58	16.39
Other Items (Net)	17r	—	.82	.82	.82	.82	.82	.82	.82	.86	.83	.83	.83	.84
Deposit Money Banks		*Millions of E. Caribbean Dollars: End of Period*											
Reserves	20	33.46	45.86	46.52	44.93	56.16	68.92	56.53	58.48	98.16	85.59	73.79	78.36
Foreign Assets	21	71.88	75.98	104.78	116.31	139.96	162.76	120.63	138.34	207.93	275.20	402.72	350.61
Claims on Central Government	22a	66.56	77.86	79.34	87.40	87.73	94.14	102.78	110.22	103.78	91.55	57.68	70.43
Claims on Local Government	22b	.23	.17	.17	.12	.09	.06	.05	.02	.01	.02	.05	.07
Claims on Nonfin.Pub.Enterprises	22c	29.07	29.13	19.27	21.77	23.05	24.25	27.82	24.29	23.37	22.21	21.63	19.46
Claims on Private Sector	22d	312.48	344.63	358.48	386.35	409.97	419.77	454.09	439.58	433.34	420.62	450.66	477.84
Claims on Nonbank Financial Insts	22g	.42	.46	1.57	1.48	1.52	1.22	3.11	2.86	2.05	2.39	2.43	2.88
Demand Deposits	24	54.24	66.57	72.79	71.41	78.28	101.85	74.24	75.54	100.26	102.68	107.95	139.53
Time, Savings,& Fgn.Currency Dep	25	260.18	319.08	342.74	358.88	379.83	398.90	413.50	444.86	474.59	513.27	535.11	529.54
Foreign Liabilities	26c	106.61	93.02	96.20	116.85	124.23	123.29	134.32	125.06	129.72	104.85	159.79	165.35
Central Government Deposits	26d	57.29	56.21	48.45	61.70	70.32	65.29	57.56	38.84	69.12	82.54	81.28	89.77
Credit from Monetary Authorities	26g	2.00	—	—	—	2.80	.85	5.30	—	—	—	—	—
Capital Accounts	27a	45.93	49.60	51.31	50.39	51.60	62.70	67.02	78.37	76.55	80.81	90.45	98.71
Other Items (Net)	27r	−12.14	−10.38	−1.35	−.87	11.42	18.25	13.07	11.11	18.40	13.44	34.36	−23.25
Monetary Survey		*Millions of E. Caribbean Dollars: End of Period*											
Foreign Assets (Net)	31n	.29	39.01	69.01	63.45	90.50	124.81	65.72	97.67	193.64	278.06	332.98	287.60
Domestic Credit	32	377.63	415.00	424.45	447.99	462.60	484.64	540.23	546.28	509.44	473.52	479.70	502.89
Claims on Central Govt. (Net)	32an	35.44	40.60	44.95	38.27	27.97	39.34	55.17	79.53	50.67	28.28	4.94	2.64
Claims on Local Government	32b	.23	.17	.17	.12	.09	.06	.05	.02	.01	.02	.05	.07
Claims on Nonfin.Pub.Enterprises	32c	29.07	29.13	19.27	21.77	23.05	24.25	27.82	24.29	23.37	22.21	21.63	19.46
Claims on Private Sector	32d	312.48	344.63	358.48	386.35	409.97	419.77	454.09	439.58	433.34	420.62	450.66	477.84
Claims on Nonbank Financial Inst	32g	.42	.46	1.57	1.48	1.52	1.22	3.11	2.86	2.05	2.39	2.43	2.88
Money	34	78.81	95.86	101.58	99.67	107.50	136.21	109.77	110.22	135.83	136.99	145.69	178.74
Quasi-Money	35	260.18	319.90	343.56	359.70	380.64	399.72	414.32	445.72	475.42	514.10	535.94	530.38
Capital Accounts	37a	48.26	51.97	53.61	52.55	53.86	64.89	69.11	80.38	78.72	83.19	92.94	101.00
Other Items (Net)	37r	−9.33	−13.72	−5.28	−.48	11.03	8.63	12.76	7.62	13.11	17.30	38.11	−19.64
Money plus Quasi-Money	35l	338.99	415.76	445.14	459.37	488.22	535.93	524.09	555.94	611.25	651.09	681.63	709.12
Money (National Definitions)		*Millions of E. Caribbean Dollars: End of Period*											
M1	59ma	62.29	72.88	71.43	74.70	85.45	106.82	90.33	91.58	106.65	107.88	111.20	143.04
M2	59mb	293.30	361.01	368.10	380.95	424.32	468.30	471.05	505.99	549.25	554.47	587.37	626.98
Interest Rates		*Percent Per Annum*											
Discount Rate (End of Period)	60	9.00	9.00	9.00	8.00	8.00	8.00	8.00	7.00	7.00	6.50	6.50	6.50
Money Market Rate	60b	5.25	5.25	5.25	5.25	5.25	5.25	5.25	† 5.64	6.32	6.07	4.67	4.01
Treasury Bill Rate	60c	6.40	6.40	6.40	6.40	6.40	6.40	6.40	6.40	6.40	6.40	6.40	6.40
Savings Rate	60k	5.46	5.50	5.50	5.50	5.50	5.50	5.50	5.50	5.00	† 3.38	3.41	3.49
Deposit Rate	60l	4.50	4.20	4.30	4.27	4.23	4.38	3.87	3.98	3.91	3.66	3.26	3.31
Lending Rate	60p	11.61	11.50	11.43	11.17	11.27	11.40	11.68	11.14	10.97	11.50	8.94	10.36
Prices		*Index Numbers (2000=100): Period Averages*											
Consumer Prices	64	91.9	93.1	94.7	97.0	† 98.0	99.2	100.0	101.5	101.8	103.3	105.4	107.2
Intl. Transactions & Positions		*Millions of E. Caribbean Dollars*											
Exports	70	127.30	121.81	138.46	143.01	169.81	150.45	144.67	118.03	115.20	108.01	108.75	110.61
Imports, c.i.f	71	260.10	316.66	350.85	326.45	356.99	373.23	400.24	355.02	314.05	345.46	392.03	446.43

Dominica 321

		1994	1995	1996	1997	1998	1999	2000	2001	2002	2003	2004	2005
Balance of Payments						*Millions of US Dollars: Minus Sign Indicates Debit*							
Current Account, n.i.e..................	78ald	−37.55	−40.73	−51.16	−42.25	−23.06	−35.77	−52.91	−49.09	−38.09	....	....	....
Goods: Exports f.o.b....................	78aad	48.33	50.27	52.91	53.77	63.19	56.01	54.75	44.41	42.93	....	....	....
Goods: Imports f.o.b....................	78abd	−95.76	−103.21	−117.20	−118.71	−116.35	−121.57	−130.39	−115.71	−102.35	....	....	....
Trade Balance....................	78acd	−47.43	−52.94	−64.29	−64.94	−53.16	−65.56	−75.64	−71.30	−59.42	....	....	....
Services: Credit...........................	78add	51.59	61.36	68.94	83.39	88.41	100.79	89.74	75.41	79.70	....	....	....
Services: Debit...........................	78aed	−37.76	−43.72	−47.17	−54.14	−55.83	−59.03	−52.69	−50.04	−53.72	....	....	....
Balance on Goods & Services......	78afd	−33.60	−35.30	−42.53	−35.70	−20.58	−23.79	−38.59	−45.93	−33.44	....	....	....
Income: Credit...........................	78agd	3.08	3.29	2.85	3.60	4.65	4.63	4.67	3.59	2.74	....	....	....
Income: Debit...........................	78ahd	−14.10	−16.59	−21.66	−20.51	−19.87	−30.17	−37.07	−24.23	−21.21	....	....	....
Balance on Gds, Serv. & Inc....	78aid	−44.62	−48.59	−61.33	−52.61	−35.80	−49.33	−70.98	−66.56	−51.91	....	....	....
Current Transfers, n.i.e.: Credit......	78ajd	14.86	16.26	17.83	17.44	19.92	20.46	25.09	24.77	20.56	....	....	....
Current Transfers: Debit.............	78akd	−7.79	−8.39	−7.66	−7.09	−7.18	−6.90	−7.02	−7.30	−6.74	....	....	....
Capital Account, n.i.e..................	78bcd	6.90	24.54	25.30	22.52	14.75	11.76	10.89	17.97	20.49	....	....	....
Capital Account, n.i.e.: Credit......	78bad	9.37	24.65	25.42	22.64	14.87	12.06	12.41	18.10	20.62	....	....	....
Capital Account: Debit...............	78bbd	−2.47	−.11	−.12	−.12	−.13	−.30	−1.52	−.13	−.13	....	....	....
Financial Account, n.i.e...............	78bjd	30.00	42.15	6.10	25.83	−2.23	38.37	43.38	24.95	8.94	....	....	....
Direct Investment Abroad..............	78bdd	—	—	—	—	—	—	—	—	—	....	....	....
Dir. Invest. in Rep. Econ., n.i.e.	78bed	22.60	54.09	17.80	21.11	6.51	17.96	10.82	11.90	11.44	....	....	....
Portfolio Investment Assets...........	78bfd	.01	−7.96	—	—	—	−9.81	−.40	.01	.01	....	....	....
Equity Securities........................	78bkd	....	....	....	....	....	....	....	....	....	....	....	....
Debt Securities...........................	78bld	....	....	....	....	....	....	....	....	....	....	....	....
Portfolio Investment Liab., n.i.e....	78bgd	—	—	.46	−.18	.53	39.47	11.21	−.24	12.10	....	....	....
Equity Securities........................	78bmd	....	....	....	....	....	....	....	....	....	....	....	....
Debt Securities...........................	78bnd	....	....	....	....	....	....	....	....	....	....	....	....
Financial Derivatives Assets...........	78bwd	....	....	....	....	....	....	....	....	....	....	....	....
Financial Derivatives Liabilities.......	78bxd	....	....	....	....	....	....	....	....	....	....	....	....
Other Investment Assets................	78bhd	−4.31	−3.60	−5.79	−3.01	−5.37	−3.92	−10.42	−5.03	−2.81	....	....	....
Monetary Authorities................	78bod	....	....	....	....	....	....	....	....	....	....	....	....
General Government..................	78bpd	....	....	....	....	....	....	....	....	....	....	....	....
Banks....................................	78bqd	....	....	....	....	....	....	....	....	....	....	....	....
Other Sectors............................	78brd	....	....	....	....	....	....	....	....	....	....	....	....
Other Investment Liab., n.i.e.........	78bid	11.71	−.38	−6.37	7.90	−3.90	−5.33	32.17	18.32	−11.81	....	....	....
Monetary Authorities................	78bsd	—	—	—	—	—	—	—	—	—	....	....	....
General Government..................	78btd	....	....	....	....	....	....	....	....	....	....	....	....
Banks....................................	78bud	....	....	....	....	....	....	....	....	....	....	....	....
Other Sectors............................	78bvd	....	....	....	....	−3.90	−5.33	32.17	18.32	−11.81	....	....	....
Net Errors and Omissions................	78cad	−2.71	−17.62	21.99	−5.46	14.09	−3.33	−.88	9.63	16.97	....	....	....
Overall Balance...........................	78cbd	−3.35	8.34	2.24	.64	3.54	11.02	.47	3.46	8.32	....	....	....
Reserves and Related Items............	79dad	3.35	−8.34	−2.24	−.64	−3.54	−11.03	−.48	−3.46	−8.32	....	....	....
Reserve Assets...........................	79dbd	4.15	−7.48	−1.43	−.09	−3.32	−10.99	−.48	−3.46	−11.03	....	....	....
Use of Fund Credit and Loans........	79dcd	−.80	−.86	−.81	−.55	−.22	−.04	—		2.71	....	....	....
Exceptional Financing....................	79ded	....	....	....	....	....	....	....	....	....	....	....	....
National Accounts						*Millions of E. Caribbean Dollars*							
Househ.Cons.Expend.,incl.NPISHs....	96f	404.9	381.4	440.2	407.5	412.2	427.6	470.3	517.5	490.4	480.5	523.8	....
Government Consumption Expend...	91f	117.4	123.2	128.9	143.1	153.0	159.3	160.6	152.8	147.3	135.1	139.7	....
Gross Fixed Capital Formation.........	93e	148.4	186.4	183.6	207.4	190.9	200.3	205.4	171.8	142.4	177.3	211.3	....
Exports of Goods and Services.........	90c	272.2	301.4	329.0	370.3	409.3	423.4	390.1	324.0	331.1	340.3	340.4	....
Imports of Goods and Services (-).....	98c	365.1	396.7	443.8	466.7	464.9	487.6	494.3	447.5	421.4	425.8	444.2	....
Gross Domestic Product (GDP).........	99b	577.8	595.6	637.9	661.6	700.5	722.8	732.2	718.6	689.9	707.5	771.0	....
Net Primary Income from Abroad....	98.n	−29.8	−35.9	−50.8	−45.7	−41.1	−69.1	−87.5	−55.7	−49.9	−32.7	−58.9	....
Gross National Income (GNI)...........	99a	548.0	559.7	587.1	616.0	659.4	653.9	644.7	662.9	640.0	677.0	712.1	....
Net Current Transf.from Abroad......	98t	19.1	21.2	27.5	28.0	34.4	36.6	48.8	47.2	37.3	34.5	43.0	....
Gross Nat'l Disposable Inc.(GNDI)....	99i	567.1	581.0	614.5	643.9	693.8	690.5	693.5	710.1	677.3	711.5	755.1	....
Gross Saving..............................	99s	44.8	76.4	45.5	93.3	128.6	103.7	62.6	39.8	39.6	118.7	91.6	....
GDP Volume 1990 Prices.................	99b.p	475.5	484.9	501.9	514.5	530.7	534.1	537.5	517.4	496.4	506.1	523.8	....
GDP Volume (2000=100)................	99bvp	88.5	90.2	93.4	95.7	98.7	99.4	100.0	96.2	92.3	94.2	97.4	....
GDP Deflator (2000=100)................	99bip	89.2	90.2	93.3	94.4	96.9	99.4	100.0	102.0	102.0	102.6	108.1	....
						Millions: Midyear Estimates							
Population.................................	99z	.07	.08	.08	.08	.08	† .08	.08	.08	.08	.08	.08	.08

Dominican Republic   243

		1994	1995	1996	1997	1998	1999	2000	2001	2002	2003	2004	2005
Exchange Rates							*Pesos per SDR: End of Period*						
Market Rate...............aa=.........	wa	19.071	20.015	20.220	19.383	22.230	22.014	21.725	21.551	28.813	55.352	48.313	49.852
						Pesos per US Dollar: End of Period (we) Period Average (wf)							
Market Rate...............ae=.........	we	13.064	13.465	14.062	14.366	15.788	16.039	16.674	17.149	21.194	37.250	31.109	34.879
Market Rate...............rf=.........	wf	13.160	13.597	13.775	14.265	15.267	16.033	16.415	16.952	18.610	30.831	42.120	30.409
						Index Numbers (2000=100): Period Averages							
Market Rate.................................	ahx	124.7	120.7	119.2	115.0	107.3	102.4	100.0	96.8	88.6	55.2	40.3	54.2
Nominal Effective Exchange Rate.....	nec	117.4	112.4	112.3	110.4	105.8	99.7	100.0	98.6	90.6	55.8	39.3	51.3
Real Effective Exchange Rate...........	rec	91.3	93.9	95.4	98.8	97.1	95.4	100.0	104.6	99.3	74.6	79.5	105.2
Fund Position							*Millions of SDRs: End of Period*						
Quota...	2f.s	158.8	158.8	158.8	158.8	158.8	218.9	218.9	218.9	218.9	218.9	218.9	218.9
SDRs...	1b.s	2.5	.3	.3	.2	.2	.2	.3	.3	.2	.1	1.0	.4
Reserve Position in the Fund............	1c.s	—	—	—	—	—	—	—	—	—	—	—	—
Total Fund Cred.&Loans Outstg........	2tl	129.9	107.5	66.5	21.1	39.7	39.7	39.7	39.7	19.9	87.6	131.3	280.2
International Liquidity						*Millions of US Dollars Unless Otherwise Indicated: End of Period*							
Total Reserves minus Gold...............	1l.d	252.1	365.6	350.3	391.0	501.9	694.0	627.2	1,099.5	468.4	253.1	798.3	1,843.2
SDRs......................................	1b.d	3.7	.5	.4	.3	.3	.3	.4	.4	.3	.1	1.6	.6
Reserve Position in the Fund..........	1c.d	—	—	—	—	—	—	—	—	—	—	—	—
Foreign Exchange........................	1d.d	248.4	365.0	349.8	390.7	501.6	693.7	626.8	1,099.0	468.1	253.0	796.7	1,842.6
Gold (Million Fine Troy Ounces)........	1ad	.018	.018	.018	.018	.018	.018	.018	.018	.018	.018	.018	.018
Gold (National Valuation)...............	1and	6.8	6.8	6.7	5.5	5.3	5.2	5.0	5.1	5.2	7.6	8.0	9.4
Monetary Authorities: Other Liab.....	4..d	916.0	967.7	975.1	938.2	881.2	865.5	879.3	838.7	668.0	643.6	645.0	599.1
Deposit Money Banks: Assets...........	7a.d	189.4	183.8	174.5	236.7	307.0	322.5	416.4	527.0	515.5	648.8	993.7	1,084.4
Liabilities....................	7b.d	183.3	55.0	97.6	188.6	401.4	458.9	739.3	684.5	924.5	517.1	260.1	181.6
Other Banking Insts.: Liabilities........	7f.d	91.2	8.4	10.9	6.3	17.2	22.7	24.3	27.2	36.5	26.9	33.7	17.2
Monetary Authorities							*Millions of Pesos: End of Period*						
Foreign Assets..............................	11	4,804	6,577	6,962	7,696	10,071	13,599	13,128	22,364	13,208	15,926	30,584	75,078
Claims on Central Government........	12a	558	605	1,236	1,537	1,632	2,416	4,026	4,023	4,631	75	39,610	93,465
Claims on Nonfin.Pub.Enterprises.....	12c	2,959	1,609	1,632	1,665	1,987	2,520	2,631	2,676	2,638	3,105	4,916	5,280
Claims on Private Sector..................	12d	45	45	45	45	5	5	2	1				281
Claims on Deposit Money Banks......	12e	2,075	2,092	3,108	2,161	2,917	2,992	2,874	3,510	9,896	105,493	106,104	105,533
Claims on Other Banking Insts.........	12f	292	307	320	388	384	375	345	347	231	36	30	58
Reserve Money...............................	14	14,956	17,412	19,306	22,963	28,110	32,328	35,667	45,980	41,961	87,367	92,332	114,444
of which: Currency Outside DMBs..	14a	7,679	8,892	9,635	11,534	12,568	16,889	15,076	16,628	18,265	29,631	32,548	38,326
Liabs.of Centl.Bank: Securities.........	16ac	743	1,991	4,099	4,357	3,499	5,135	4,369	3,276	6,905	60,008	110,809	140,204
Foreign Liabilities..........................	16c	14,443	15,180	15,056	13,887	14,794	14,755	15,523	15,238	14,729	28,820	26,411	34,864
Central Government Deposits...........	16d	151	344	400	351	424	479	414	1,838	834	4,113	1,060	1,501
Counterpart Funds........................	16e	—	—	—	—	—	—	—	—	—			
Capital Accounts............................	17a	−16,906	−18,443	−20,241	−21,519	−23,395	−25,126	−26,960	−27,817	−28,456	−56,803	−52,482	−15,409
of which: Revaluation of Reserves..	17rv	−16,415	−16,961	−17,326	−17,376	−17,872	−18,169	−18,315	−18,315	−18,632	—	—	—
Other Items (Net)............................	17r	−2,653	−5,249	−5,318	−6,547	−6,435	−5,665	−6,008	−5,594	−5,369	1,130	3,114	4,089
Deposit Money Banks							*Millions of Pesos: End of Period*						
Reserves.......................................	20	9,214	10,654	10,761	12,964	16,947	17,331	26,692	30,404	28,653	58,047	56,548	74,854
Claims on Mon.Author.:Securities.....	20c	180	914	2,264	2,118	675	1,443	215	26	2,121	19,758	30,187	30,493
Foreign Assets..............................	21	2,474	2,475	2,453	3,400	4,846	5,172	6,943	9,037	10,925	24,167	30,914	37,824
Claims on Central Government........	22a	540	505	536	1,934	1,998	4,144	4,813	11,678	14,091	17,386	25,737	26,959
Claims on Local Government...........	22b	6	29	4	6	4	14	29	32	1	142	412	627
Claims on Nonfin.Pub.Enterprises.....	22c	1,290	1,453	2,221	2,308	3,263	3,271	2,521	2,540	2,943	4,539	3,487	1,895
Claims on Private Sector..................	22d	22,166	27,688	34,500	44,404	52,744	66,877	82,120	101,941	123,242	165,620	162,822	179,603
Claims on Other Banking Insts.........	22f	799	554	778	764	957	760	593	928	1,081	2,290	1,521	2,389
Demand Deposits..........................	24	8,470	10,064	13,540	16,081	16,782	18,884	20,290	24,529	25,341	41,736	43,241	54,344
Time, Savings,& Fgn.Currency Dep...	25	19,854	23,458	27,022	34,725	43,380	54,211	70,282	92,908	104,184	169,315	186,887	207,764
Bonds...	26ab	122	80	138	76	17	398	112	2	14	27	7	13
Foreign Liabilities..........................	26c	2,394	740	1,372	2,710	6,337	7,361	12,328	11,738	19,594	19,261	8,092	6,333
Central Government Deposits...........	26d	1,746	2,533	2,594	3,076	2,500	3,578	3,192	6,566	6,076	7,268	8,142	15,476
Credit from Monetary Authorities.....	26g	1,334	1,310	1,220	1,532	2,222	2,449	2,931	3,226	7,971	72,091	72,122	64,238
Capital Accounts............................	27a	4,050	4,581	5,203	6,524	8,220	10,224	12,667	16,707	19,901	−9,773	−7,730	−1,086
Other Items (Net)...........................	27r	−1,301	1,506	2,428	3,175	1,975	1,907	2,124	911	−26	−7,975	867	7,563
Monetary Survey							*Millions of Pesos: End of Period*						
Foreign Assets (Net)........................	31n	−9,559	−6,868	−7,013	−5,501	−6,213	−3,345	−7,780	4,424	−10,191	−7,988	26,995	71,705
Domestic Credit................................	32	26,759	29,919	38,278	49,624	60,051	76,324	93,474	115,762	141,948	181,813	229,333	293,578
Claims on Central Govt. (Net).......	32an	−798	−1,766	−1,221	43	706	2,503	5,233	7,296	11,812	6,080	56,146	103,447
Claims on Local Government..........	32b	6	29	4	6	4	14	29	32	1	142	412	627
Claims on Nonfin.Pub.Enterprises...	32c	4,249	3,062	3,853	3,973	5,250	5,791	5,152	5,216	5,582	7,644	8,403	7,175
Claims on Private Sector...............	32d	22,211	27,733	34,545	44,449	52,749	66,881	82,122	101,942	123,242	165,620	162,822	179,884
Claims on Other Banking Insts.......	32f	1,091	861	1,098	1,152	1,342	1,135	938	1,275	1,313	2,326	1,551	2,446
Money..	34	16,198	18,996	23,225	27,703	29,416	35,840	35,445	41,258	43,765	72,013	76,153	92,926
Quasi-Money................................	35	19,854	23,458	27,022	34,725	43,380	54,211	70,282	92,908	104,184	169,315	186,887	207,764
Bonds...	36ab	122	80	138	76	17	398	112	2	14	27	7	13
Liabs.of Centl.Bank: Securities.........	36ac	564	1,078	1,835	2,239	2,825	3,692	4,154	3,250	4,784	40,250	80,621	109,711
Capital Accounts............................	37a	−12,857	−13,863	−15,038	−14,996	−15,175	−14,902	−14,293	−11,111	−8,555	−66,576	−60,212	−16,495
Other Items (Net)...........................	37r	−6,682	−6,698	−5,917	−5,625	−6,625	−6,259	−10,008	−6,121	−12,434	−41,205	−27,128	−28,637
Money plus Quasi-Money.................	35l	36,052	42,454	50,247	62,428	72,795	90,051	105,727	134,166	147,948	241,328	263,040	300,690

		1994	1995	1996	1997	1998	1999	2000	2001	2002	2003	2004	2005
Other Banking Institutions						*Millions of Pesos: End of Period*							
Reserves	40	329	332	353	429	483	796	951	1,037	1,315	3,072	5,594	6,704
Claims on Mon.Author.:Securities	40c	—	—	—	1,080	1,153	1,483	1,596	1,772	3,781	4,532	5,207	5,175
Claims on Central Government	42a	522	774	569	452	837	971	971	699	872	893	742	643
Claims on Nonfin.Pub.Enterprises	42c	12	19	18	18	19	19	19	28	31	30	30	30
Claims on Private Sector	42d	12,263	12,513	13,797	16,324	19,797	24,375	30,407	34,552	36,922	43,819	56,390	65,439
Claims on Deposit Money Banks	42e	2,358	3,097	3,674	3,223	4,216	4,950	6,149	10,353	6,776	8,843	6,663	8,419
Time, Savings,& Fgn.Currency Dep	45	4,112	4,396	4,628	5,682	7,387	7,691	8,433	9,545	10,531	11,240	13,063	13,914
Bonds	46ab	7,290	8,474	9,418	11,295	13,120	17,634	22,433	27,956	27,359	32,854	41,462	47,447
Foreign Liabilities	46c	1,192	113	153	90	271	364	405	467	774	1,003	1,049	600
Credit from Monetary Authorities	46g	1,623	1,464	1,434	1,360	1,298	1,112	1,118	1,092	931	921	834	793
Credit from Deposit Money Banks	46h	424	460	478	457	539	458	513	495	569	584	553	472
Capital Accounts	47a	2,667	2,818	2,855	3,390	4,430	5,889	7,572	9,200	12,083	17,161	21,175	24,868
Other Items (Net)	47r	−1,824	−990	−558	−748	−542	−554	−380	−315	−2,550	−2,573	−3,509	−1,686
Banking Survey						*Millions of Pesos: End of Period*							
Foreign Assets (Net)	51n	−10,751	−6,981	−7,166	−5,592	−6,484	−3,709	−8,185	3,957	−10,965	−8,991	25,946	71,104
Domestic Credit	52	38,464	42,364	51,564	65,266	79,362	100,554	123,933	149,764	178,461	224,229	284,945	357,244
Claims on Central Govt. (Net)	52an	−276	−992	−652	496	1,543	3,474	6,205	7,995	12,684	6,973	56,888	104,089
Claims on Local Government	52b	6	29	4	6	4	14	29	32	1	142	412	627
Claims on Nonfin.Pub.Enterprises	52c	4,261	3,081	3,871	3,991	5,269	5,810	5,171	5,243	5,612	7,674	8,433	7,205
Claims on Private Sector	52d	34,474	40,246	48,342	60,772	72,545	91,256	112,529	136,494	160,164	209,439	219,212	245,322
Liquid Liabilities	55l	39,835	46,518	54,522	67,681	79,699	96,946	113,209	142,674	157,164	249,496	270,509	307,900
Bonds	56ab	7,412	8,554	9,556	11,371	13,137	18,032	22,545	27,958	27,373	32,881	41,468	47,460
Liabs.of Centl.Bank: Securities	56ac	564	1,078	1,835	1,158	1,672	2,208	2,558	1,478	1,003	35,718	75,414	104,537
Capital Accounts	57a	−10,190	−11,045	−12,182	−11,606	−10,745	−9,013	−6,720	−1,911	3,528	−49,415	−39,037	8,373
Other Items (Net)	57r	−9,907	−9,721	−9,333	−8,931	−10,886	−11,327	−15,843	−16,478	−21,573	−53,442	−37,463	−39,922
Interest Rates						*Percent Per Annum*							
Money Market Rate	60b	....	....	14.70	13.01	16.68	15.30	18.28	13.47	14.50	24.24	36.76	12.57
Savings Rate	60k	4.87	4.66	5.00	4.74	4.51	4.54	4.29	4.29	4.30	4.26	4.36	4.12
Savings Rate (Foreign Currency)	60k.f	....	....	4.67	4.29	3.62	3.58	4.16	4.00	3.81	3.83	2.88	2.05
Deposit Rate	60l	13.70	14.94	13.91	13.40	17.65	16.07	17.65	15.61	16.54	20.50	21.12	13.86
Deposit Rate (Foreign Currency)	60l.f	....	....	6.69	6.98	6.50	6.66	7.57	6.88	6.37	6.55	5.31	3.19
Lending Rate	60p	28.68	30.68	23.73	21.01	25.64	25.05	26.80	24.26	26.06	31.39	32.63	24.11
Lending Rate (Foreign Currency)	60p.f	....	....	13.87	12.75	11.95	11.73	11.56	11.17	10.27	10.58	10.79	9.41
Prices and Labor						*Index Numbers (2000=100): Period Averages*							
Consumer Prices	64	64.7	72.9	76.8	83.2	† 87.2	92.8	100.0	108.9	114.6	146.0	221.2	230.4
						Number in Thousands: Period Averages							
Labor Force	67d	....	3,132	2,965	3,594	3,594	....	....	....	3,684	....	3,934	....
Employment	67e	2,401	2,401	2,523	2,652	2,889	2,980	3,041	3,002	3,106	3,093	3,210	....
Unemployment	67c	457	452	† 506	504	....	....	....	....	....	....	....	....
Unemployment Rate (%)	67r	16.0	15.9	† 16.7	15.9	....	....	....	....	....	....	....	....
Intl. Transactions & Positions						*Millions of US Dollars*							
Exports	70..d	644.0	872.1	945.5	1,017.4	880.2	805.2	966.2	804.8	833.7	1,040.7	1,250.7	1,397.9
Imports, f.o.b.	71.vd	2,991.7	3,164.2	3,580.7	4,192.0	4,896.6	5,206.8	6,416.1	5,936.9	6,037.3	5,265.8	5,368.1	7,206.6
						1995=100							
Volume of Exports	72	96	100	106	109	103	....	....	....	....	....	....	....
						1995=100: Indices of Unit Values in US Dollars							
Unit Value of Exports/Export Prices	74..d	89	102	95	106	85	....	....	....	....	....	....	....

		1994	1995	1996	1997	1998	1999	2000	2001	2002	2003	2004	2005
Balance of Payments						*Millions of US Dollars: Minus Sign Indicates Debit*							
Current Account, n.i.e.	78ald	−283.0	−182.8	−212.7	−163.0	−338.4	−429.2	−1,026.5	−740.8	−797.9	1,036.2	1,142.2	−142.6
Goods: Exports f.o.b.	78aad	3,452.5	3,779.5	4,052.8	4,613.7	4,980.5	5,136.7	5,736.7	5,276.3	5,165.0	5,470.8	5,935.9	6,132.5
Goods: Imports f.o.b.	78abd	−4,903.2	−5,170.4	−5,727.0	−6,608.7	−7,597.3	−8,041.1	−9,478.5	−8,779.3	−8,837.7	−7,626.8	−7,888.0	−9,613.9
Trade Balance	78acd	−1,450.7	−1,390.9	−1,674.2	−1,995.0	−2,616.8	−2,904.4	−3,741.8	−3,503.0	−3,672.7	−2,156.0	−1,952.1	−3,481.4
Services: Credit	78add	1,787.9	1,951.3	2,140.0	2,446.6	2,501.5	2,850.3	3,227.6	3,110.3	3,070.8	3,468.8	3,503.9	3,884.7
Services: Debit	78aed	−921.1	−966.4	−1,121.4	−1,171.3	−1,319.5	−1,248.0	−1,373.3	−1,283.9	−1,313.5	−1,219.4	−1,213.2	−1,389.8
Balance on Goods & Services	78afd	−583.9	−406.0	−655.6	−719.7	−1,434.8	−1,302.1	−1,887.5	−1,676.6	−1,915.4	93.4	338.6	−986.5
Income: Credit	78agd	101.4	128.1	130.3	140.4	168.2	218.3	299.7	271.2	300.4	340.7	336.3	440.7
Income: Debit	78ahd	−783.3	−897.1	−855.1	−935.8	−1,058.3	−1,193.2	−1,341.0	−1,362.9	−1,452.2	−1,733.8	−2,060.2	−2,326.6
Balance on Gds, Serv. & Inc.	78aid	−1,265.8	−1,175.0	−1,380.4	−1,515.1	−2,324.9	−2,277.0	−2,928.8	−2,768.3	−3,067.2	−1,299.7	−1,385.3	−2,872.3
Current Transfers, n.i.e.: Credit	78ajd	996.8	1,007.7	1,187.6	1,373.1	2,016.9	1,997.1	2,095.6	2,232.0	2,451.9	2,512.2	2,701.4	2,923.3
Current Transfers: Debit	78akd	−14.0	−15.5	−19.9	−21.0	−30.4	−149.3	−193.3	−204.5	−182.6	−176.3	−173.9	−193.6
Capital Account, n.i.e.	78bcd	—	—	....	—	—	....	—	—	—	—	—	—
Capital Account, n.i.e.: Credit	78bad	—	—	....	—	—	....	—	—	—	—	—	—
Capital Account: Debit	78bbd	—	—	....	—	—	....	—	—	—	—	—	—
Financial Account, n.i.e.	78bjd	368.0	253.6	64.1	447.6	688.1	1,061.0	1,596.6	1,707.4	383.0	−15.9	249.1	752.8
Direct Investment Abroad	78bdd			....			....			—	—	—	—
Dir. Invest. in Rep. Econ., n.i.e.	78bed	206.8	414.3	96.5	420.6	699.8	1,337.8	952.9	1,079.1	916.8	613.0	758.4	898.8
Portfolio Investment Assets	78bfd	−38.9	−2.9	−7.3	−5.6	−17.5	−433.0	268.4	123.5	−14.0	−19.7	−7.6	−93.6
Equity Securities	78bkd	....	....	−4.0	−2.1	−13.7	−428.9	270.6	128.2	−2.5	−6.5	−2.2	−10.6
Debt Securities	78bld	−38.9	−2.9	−3.3	−3.5	−3.8	−4.1	−2.2	−4.7	−11.5	−13.2	−5.4	−83.0
Portfolio Investment Liab., n.i.e.	78bgd	—	....	....	−1.9	−3.8	−3.8	−3.9	480.2	−11.7	563.5	−19.8	46.0
Equity Securities	78bmd	....	....	....			....			—	—	—	—
Debt Securities	78bnd	—		....	−1.9	−3.8	−3.8	−3.9	480.2	−11.7	563.5	−19.8	46.0
Financial Derivatives Assets	78bwd	....	....	....	....	....	....			—	—	—	—
Financial Derivatives Liabilities	78bxd	....	....	....	....	....	....			—	—	—	—
Other Investment Assets	78bhd	176.8	−263.1	42.3	−220.1	−66.4	−53.4	−165.0	−155.5	−1,402.2	−1,159.1	−416.0	−140.8
Monetary Authorities	78bod	−15.2	−.6	−.9	−.9	−1.0	−1.0	−1.2	−.8	−3.9	1.8	−2.0	−1.6
General Government	78bpd						....			—	—	—	—
Banks	78bqd	18.0	−39.0	17.0	−40.7	−53.2	−18.8	−64.4	−94.9	11.0	−136.6	−408.0	16.4
Other Sectors	78brd	174.0	−223.5	26.2	−178.5	−12.2	−33.6	−99.4	−59.8	−1,409.3	−1,024.3	−6.0	−155.6
Other Investment Liab., n.i.e.	78bid	23.3	105.3	−67.4	254.6	76.0	213.4	544.2	180.1	894.1	−13.6	−65.9	42.4
Monetary Authorities	78bsd	31.1	27.1	−22.8	−17.3	−88.7	−24.7	72.0	−22.3	91.0	−223.3	−38.6	−37.9
General Government	78btd	−59.5	−18.8	−35.3	−64.2	−38.5	124.2	119.1	119.3	252.6	445.8	305.8	156.2
Banks	78bud	45.4	32.1	89.7	172.3	218.5	106.9	234.2	−37.0	115.6	−100.5	−94.4	−47.7
Other Sectors	78bvd	6.3	64.9	−99.0	163.8	−15.3	7.0	118.9	120.1	434.9	−135.6	−238.7	−28.2
Net Errors and Omissions	78cad	−596.0	75.3	108.8	−193.7	−338.6	−480.4	−618.5	−451.9	−139.3	−1,568.2	−846.5	61.7
Overall Balance	78cbd	−511.0	146.1	−39.8	90.9	11.1	151.4	−48.4	514.7	−554.2	−548.0	544.8	671.9
Reserves and Related Items	79dad	511.0	−146.1	39.8	−90.9	−11.1	−151.4	48.4	−514.7	554.2	548.0	−544.8	−671.9
Reserve Assets	79dbd	384.7	−131.2	15.2	−39.5	−98.2	−193.6	69.9	−518.2	526.0	357.8	−540.2	−1,104.8
Use of Fund Credit and Loans	79dcd	−8.1	−34.0	−59.4	−62.4	26.8	—	—	—	−25.7	94.5	65.5	219.0
Exceptional Financing	79ded	134.4	19.1	84.1	11.0	60.3	42.2	−21.5	3.5	53.9	95.7	−70.1	213.9
International Investment Position						*Millions of US Dollars*							
Assets	79aad	....	....	....	....	....	....	....	....	2,119.3	2,947.6	....	....
Direct Investment Abroad	79abd	....	....	....	....	....	....	....	....			....	....
Portfolio Investment	79acd	....	....	....	....	....	....	....	....	95.2	114.9	....	....
Equity Securities	79add	....	....	....	....	....	....	....	....	11.6	18.1	....	....
Debt Securities	79aed	....	....	....	....	....	....	....	....	83.6	96.8	....	....
Financial Derivatives	79ald	....	....	....	....	....	....	....	....			....	....
Other Investment	79afd	....	....	....	....	....	....	....	....	1,394.5	2,553.4	....	....
Monetary Authorities	79agd	....	....	....	....	....	....	....	....	56.6	54.9	....	....
General Government	79ahd	....	....	....	....	....	....	....	....			....	....
Banks	79aid	....	....	....	....	....	....	....	....	448.0	584.6	....	....
Other Sectors	79ajd	....	....	....	....	....	....	....	....	889.9	1,913.9	....	....
Reserve Assets	79akd	....	....	....	....	....	....	....	....	629.6	279.3	....	....
Liabilities	79lad	....	....	....	....	....	....	....	....	10,917.2	11,399.2	....	....
Dir. Invest. in Rep. Economy	79lbd	....	....	....	....	....	....	....	....	3,668.7	3,571.8	....	....
Portfolio Investment	79lcd	....	....	....	....	....	....	....	....	1,031.2	1,332.0	....	....
Equity Securities	79ldd	....	....	....	....	....	....	....	....			....	....
Debt Securities	79led	....	....	....	....	....	....	....	....	1,031.2	1,332.0	....	....
Financial Derivatives	79lld	....	....	....	....	....	....	....	....			....	....
Other Investment	79lfd	....	....	....	....	....	....	....	....	6,217.3	6,495.4	....	....
Monetary Authorities	79lgd	....	....	....	....	....	....	....	....	465.3	354.8	....	....
General Government	79lhd	....	....	....	....	....	....	....	....	3,177.9	3,791.6	....	....
Banks	79lid	....	....	....	....	....	....	....	....	528.7	428.1	....	....
Other Sectors	79ljd	....	....	....	....	....	....	....	....	2,045.4	1,920.9	....	....
Government Finance						*Millions of Pesos: Year Ending December 31*							
Deficit (-) or Surplus	80	−690.6	1,720.3	540.6	2,038.0	2,109.8	−1,267.2	3,449.5	....	216.0	....	20,158.4	−2,891.4
Total Revenue and Grants	81y	21,499.9	24,890.8	27,133.6	34,729.1	38,867.3	43,947.3	51,651.8	....	67,593.2	....	127,588.0	158,720.2
Revenue	81	21,482.3	24,890.8	26,921.3	34,729.1	38,564.8	43,483.6	51,271.3	....	67,077.5	....	126,281.9	157,585.0
Grants	81z	17.6	—	212.3	—	302.5	463.7	380.5	....	515.7	....	1,306.1	1,135.3
Exp. & Lending Minus Repay	82z	22,190.5	23,170.5	26,593.0	32,691.1	36,757.5	45,214.5	48,202.3	....	67,377.2	....	107,429.6	161,611.6
Expenditure	82	22,190.5	23,170.5	26,593.0	32,691.1	36,757.5	45,164.5	48,202.3	....	67,377.2	....	107,429.6	161,611.6
Lending Minus Repayments	83	—	—	—	—	—	50.0	—	....		....		
Total Financing	80h	690.6	−1,720.3	−540.6	−2,038.4	−2,110.0	1,217.1	−3,449.7	....	−216.0	....	−20,158.5	2,891.4
Domestic	84a	2,522.1	1.8	1,289.3	379.2	−8.4	1,862.4	6.4	....	3,569.5	....	−5,869.0	9,638.2
Foreign	85a	−1,831.5	−1,722.1	−1,829.9	−2,417.6	−2,101.6	−645.4	−3,456.1	....	−3,785.5	....	−14,289.5	−6,746.8

		1994	1995	1996	1997	1998	1999	2000	2001	2002	2003	2004	2005
National Accounts							*Millions of Pesos*						
Househ.Cons.Expend.,incl.NPISHs....	96f	147,136	169,346	186,101	211,003	236,316	260,448	297,652	328,698	361,812	465,432	701,840	864,886
Government Consumption Expend...	91f	8,737	9,766	11,489	18,316	21,422	25,038	30,496	35,420	40,908	44,649	53,268	69,882
Gross Fixed Capital Formation..........	93e	35,065	37,371	41,946	51,267	73,589	77,224	90,370	82,939	98,203	95,027	155,327	158,468
Changes in Inventories....................	93i	—	—	—	—	—	—	—	—	—	—	—	—
Exports of Goods and Services..........	90c	66,117	75,474	82,298	99,491	111,560	125,906	144,039	140,144	150,584	265,733	386,215	296,821
Imports of Goods and Services (-).....	98c	75,989	82,976	89,230	110,378	135,666	149,000	178,175	170,361	187,058	269,699	381,900	334,326
Gross Domestic Product (GDP)........	99b	181,066	208,980	232,604	269,699	307,220	339,615	384,382	416,840	464,447	601,142	914,751	1,055,731
Net Primary Income from Abroad.....	98.n	−8,767	−10,235	−9,735	−11,249	−13,374	−15,528	−16,961	−18,442	−21,344	−42,171	−71,827	−56,893
Gross National Income (GNI)............	99a	172,299	198,745	222,869	258,450	293,846	324,087	367,422	398,398	443,103	558,971	842,924	998,838
Consumption of Fixed Capital..........	99cf	8,254	9,737	11,002	12,892	14,519	16,718	19,474	21,974	24,146	30,198	46,631	....
GDP Volume 1970 Prices.................	99b.p	4,375	4,579	4,907	5,308	5,702	6,167	6,668	6,910	7,217	7,082	7,220	....
GDP Volume (2000=100)...............	99bvp	65.6	69.5	74.6	80.7	87.4	92.7	100.0	102.3	107.4	107.0	109.9	120.0
GDP Deflator (2000=100)...............	99bip	71.8	78.2	81.1	87.0	91.5	95.3	100.0	106.0	112.5	146.1	216.6	228.8
							Millions: Midyear Estimates						
Population.................................	99z	7.29	7.39	7.50	7.60	7.71	7.83	7.94	8.05	8.17	8.29	8.41	8.53

		1994	1995	1996	1997	1998	1999	2000	2001	2002	2003	2004	2005
Exchange Rates		*E. Caribbean Dollars per SDR: End of Period (aa) E. Caribbean Dollars per US Dollar: End of Period (ae)*											
Official Rate	aa	3.9416	4.0135	3.8825	3.6430	3.8017	3.7058	3.5179	3.3932	3.6707	4.0121	4.1931	3.8590
Official Rate	ae	2.7000	2.7000	2.7000	2.7000	2.7000	2.7000	2.7000	2.7000	2.7000	2.7000	2.7000	2.7000
Fund Position		*Millions of SDRs: End of Period*											
Quota	2f.s	46.50	46.50	46.50	46.50	46.50	63.60	65.90	65.90	65.90	65.90	65.90	65.90
SDRs	1b.s	3.36	3.47	3.60	3.67	3.80	3.89	3.91	4.02	4.07	4.11	1.56	1.55
Reserve Position in the Fund	1c.s	.53	.53	.53	.53	.53	.58	.59	.59	.59	.60	.60	.60
Total Fund Cred.&Loans Outstg	2tl	1.71	1.15	.59	.19	1.65	1.63	1.63	1.63	2.86	8.26	11.80	13.94
International Liquidity		*Millions of US Dollars: End of Period*											
Total Reserves minus Gold	1l.d	261.52	312.93	291.36	307.84	360.76	367.63	386.41	448.54	508.25	543.73	634.07	600.02
SDRs	1b.d	4.91	5.16	5.17	4.95	5.36	5.34	5.10	5.05	5.54	6.11	2.42	2.22
Reserve Position in the Fund	1c.d	.77	.78	.76	.71	.74	.80	.77	.75	.81	.90	.94	.86
Foreign Exchange	1d.d	255.84	306.99	285.43	302.19	354.66	361.49	380.55	442.74	501.91	536.72	630.72	596.93
Monetary Authorities: Other Liab	4..d	9.19	8.23	9.16	5.35	3.32	5.74	7.97	7.28	4.40	4.64	2.81	4.54
Deposit Money Banks: Assets	7a.d	270.67	304.74	312.47	321.14	402.51	495.69	478.78	618.11	746.99	956.87	1,176.25	1,276.04
Liabilities	7b.d	263.29	263.56	335.81	381.54	388.92	447.97	476.56	525.38	577.00	618.68	732.17	755.86
Monetary Authorities		*Millions of E. Caribbean Dollars: End of Period*											
Foreign Assets	11	706.09	844.91	786.67	831.17	974.05	992.59	1,043.32	1,211.06	1,370.68	1,466.13	1,716.83	1,630.79
Claims on Central Government	12a	116.46	105.54	109.13	95.34	89.32	94.20	96.60	91.07	72.75	89.36	59.31	58.25
Claims on Private Sector	12d	—	7.36	8.13	9.88	10.64	10.94	12.94	14.65	14.01	12.47	10.65	9.46
Claims on Deposit Money Banks	12e	7.22	1.33	1.10	1.08	1.09	.90	19.75	.61	.54	.52	10.44	8.53
Claims on Nonbank Financial Insts	12g	1.62	5.12	5.99	6.60	7.58	7.86	10.93	12.90	12.73	13.17	13.02	22.49
Reserve Money	14	730.35	808.81	760.96	812.36	954.70	1,016.00	1,060.05	1,207.38	1,308.01	1,448.23	1,649.17	1,561.44
of which: Currency Outside DMBs	14a	285.55	311.58	298.36	315.31	347.02	391.46	389.47	375.92	395.72	429.61	486.14	521.40
Foreign Liabilities	16c	31.55	26.82	27.01	15.11	15.24	21.51	27.25	25.16	22.40	45.66	57.06	66.05
Central Government Deposits	16d	47.37	47.83	65.80	60.70	74.93	68.26	66.64	56.79	71.34	57.96	104.90	95.36
Capital Accounts	17a	82.62	133.13	105.15	105.01	110.92	84.98	112.99	122.58	148.93	131.16	118.98	135.43
Other Items (Net)	17r	−60.51	−52.33	−47.90	−49.11	−73.10	−84.25	−83.38	−81.61	−79.97	−101.37	−119.87	−128.79
Deposit Money Banks		*Millions of E. Caribbean Dollars: End of Period*											
Reserves	20	448.45	475.41	454.93	503.49	625.33	652.56	670.63	845.93	919.40	981.19	1,185.64	1,040.36
Foreign Assets	21	730.82	822.79	843.68	867.07	1,086.77	1,338.36	1,292.71	1,668.90	2,016.87	2,583.54	3,175.87	3,445.31
Claims on Central Government	22a	410.53	519.58	567.50	625.09	749.90	853.94	1,063.19	1,086.18	1,195.31	1,198.57	1,318.61	1,554.73
Claims on Local Government	22b	9.83	11.59	9.57	9.73	16.16	21.85	46.65	57.92	69.20	84.52	122.07	74.25
Claims on Nonfin.Pub.Enterprises	22c	202.93	253.66	270.23	281.12	311.51	363.39	415.04	470.05	498.18	511.23	654.20	736.30
Claims on Private Sector	22d	3,187.72	3,511.33	3,940.59	4,471.39	4,839.12	5,333.95	5,892.02	6,017.45	6,251.22	6,292.30	6,740.63	7,546.17
Claims on Nonbank Financial Insts	22g	62.49	61.87	75.76	69.66	89.36	120.92	119.22	133.72	147.24	219.51	259.11	285.31
Demand Deposits	24	657.61	761.15	758.35	809.04	945.35	1,017.05	1,028.78	1,102.10	1,175.77	1,364.21	1,776.59	1,931.00
Time, Savings,& Fgn.Currency Dep	25	2,885.29	3,276.61	3,401.37	3,695.73	4,172.08	4,798.86	5,363.40	5,735.46	6,195.26	6,638.21	7,159.27	7,718.68
Foreign Liabilities	26c	710.90	711.61	906.69	1,030.16	1,050.09	1,209.51	1,286.72	1,418.52	1,557.91	1,670.45	1,976.85	2,040.84
Central Government Deposits	26d	593.72	678.28	763.19	849.00	1,007.02	1,078.17	1,167.22	1,231.14	1,335.81	1,402.96	1,622.98	1,736.94
Credit from Monetary Authorities	26g	16.66	8.12	12.88	11.71	34.07	23.63	48.95	105.35	64.78	30.80	20.88	11.17
Capital Accounts	27a	376.16	415.02	431.08	489.34	539.75	655.66	698.11	829.14	937.38	1,004.09	1,188.67	1,433.05
Other Items (Net)	27r	−187.57	−194.55	−111.30	−57.43	−30.21	−97.92	−93.72	−141.57	−169.51	−239.84	−289.12	−189.24
Monetary Survey		*Millions of E. Caribbean Dollars: End of Period*											
Foreign Assets (Net)	31n	694.47	929.27	696.64	652.97	995.49	1,099.92	1,022.07	1,436.27	1,807.24	2,333.56	2,858.78	2,969.22
Domestic Credit	32	3,350.71	3,749.95	4,157.91	4,659.12	5,031.65	5,660.85	6,422.73	6,596.01	6,853.48	6,960.21	7,449.71	8,454.64
Claims on Central Govt. (Net)	32an	−114.11	−100.99	−152.36	−189.27	−242.72	−198.29	−74.07	−110.68	−139.10	−172.98	−349.96	−219.32
Claims on Local Government	32b	9.83	11.59	9.57	9.73	16.16	21.85	46.65	57.92	69.20	84.52	122.07	74.25
Claims on Nonfin.Pub.Enterprises	32c	203.17	253.66	270.23	281.12	311.51	363.62	415.04	470.05	498.18	511.23	654.20	736.30
Claims on Private Sector	32d	3,187.72	3,518.69	3,948.71	4,481.27	4,849.75	5,344.89	5,904.96	6,032.10	6,265.23	6,304.77	6,751.28	7,555.62
Claims on Nonbank Financial Inst	32g	64.11	67.00	81.75	76.26	96.94	128.78	130.15	146.63	159.98	232.67	272.13	307.79
Money	34	944.20	1,081.70	1,058.81	1,126.64	1,294.45	1,411.55	1,421.16	1,482.41	1,572.42	1,805.33	2,263.94	2,454.33
Quasi-Money	35	2,885.29	3,277.43	3,402.19	3,696.55	4,173.90	4,800.68	5,365.22	5,737.33	6,197.10	6,639.04	7,160.10	7,719.52
Capital Accounts	37a	458.79	548.16	536.23	594.35	650.66	740.64	811.09	951.71	1,086.31	1,135.25	1,307.65	1,568.48
Other Items (Net)	37r	−243.10	−228.07	−142.67	−105.46	−91.87	−192.11	−152.68	−139.18	−195.11	−285.84	−423.19	−318.46
Money plus Quasi-Money	35l	3,829.49	4,359.13	4,460.99	4,823.20	5,468.34	6,212.24	6,786.38	7,219.74	7,769.51	8,444.37	9,424.04	10,173.84
Money (National Definitions)		*Millions of E. Caribbean Dollars: End of Period*											
M1	59ma	793.20	912.86	882.90	963.94	1,091.06	1,193.49	1,214.24	1,248.49	1,321.66	1,508.13	1,895.18	2,086.69
M2	59mb	3,395.26	3,874.39	3,948.43	4,325.35	4,881.69	5,399.32	5,971.19	6,322.12	6,736.98	7,379.69	8,362.55	9,055.64
Interest Rates		*Percent Per Annum*											
Discount Rate (End of Period)	60	9.00	9.00	9.00	8.00	8.00	8.00	8.00	7.00	7.00	6.50	6.50	6.50
Money Market Rate	60b	5.25	5.25	5.25	5.25	5.25	5.25	5.25	† 5.64	6.32	6.07	4.67	4.01
Savings Rate	60k	8.00	8.00	8.00	8.00	8.00	8.00	8.00	8.00	8.00	† 3.90	3.59	3.17
Deposit Rate	60l	3.87	4.06	4.16	4.20	4.30	4.35	4.46	4.37	4.04	4.43	3.76	4.08
Deposit Rate (Fgn. Currency)	60l.f	....	....	....	....	....	....	....	....	....	4.06	3.65	3.52
Lending Rate	60p	11.71	11.94	11.74	11.77	11.60	11.91	11.98	11.55	11.47	13.34	10.93	11.42

		1994	1995	1996	1997	1998	1999	2000	2001	2002	2003	2004	2005
Balance of Payments					*Millions of US Dollars: Minus Sign Indicates Debit*								
Current Account, n.i.e.	78ald	−212.3	−215.4	−329.3	−402.7	−365.8	−450.4	−438.3	−475.8	−570.6	....	....	....
Goods: Exports f.o.b.	78aad	300.9	350.3	337.8	298.2	316.1	327.4	359.2	303.1	310.4	....	....	....
Goods: Imports f.o.b.	78abd	−1,040.2	−1,106.7	−1,190.8	−1,245.8	−1,298.6	−1,383.2	−1,425.5	−1,309.9	−1,315.2	....	....	....
Trade Balance	78acd	−739.3	−756.4	−853.0	−947.6	−982.5	−1,055.8	−1,066.3	−1,006.8	−1,004.8	....	....	....
Services: Credit	78add	1,026.4	1,010.5	1,064.0	1,156.5	1,256.5	1,306.0	1,285.5	1,209.9	1,169.4	....	....	....
Services: Debit	78aed	−456.0	−508.8	−537.3	−580.4	−627.2	−663.6	−614.3	−615.2	−642.7	....	....	....
Balance on Goods & Services	78afd	−168.8	−254.6	−326.3	−371.5	−353.2	−413.4	−395.0	−412.1	−478.1	....	....	....
Income: Credit	78agd	24.6	32.7	26.7	25.1	35.3	37.5	43.3	38.8	33.9	....	....	....
Income: Debit	78ahd	−142.1	−157.7	−153.7	−156.8	−181.8	−207.5	−250.7	−215.9	−235.7	....	....	....
Balance on Gds, Serv. & Inc.	78aid	−286.3	−379.6	−453.3	−503.1	−499.7	−583.4	−602.4	−589.2	−679.9	....	....	....
Current Transfers, n.i.e.: Credit	78ajd	127.1	219.4	175.1	157.6	193.9	185.1	227.5	189.2	192.6	....	....	....
Current Transfers: Debit	78akd	−53.2	−55.2	−51.1	−57.2	−60.0	−52.1	−63.4	−75.7	−83.4	....	....	....
Capital Account, n.i.e.	78bcd	67.8	94.3	73.5	89.2	255.3	108.6	122.3	134.2	132.2	....	....	....
Capital Account, n.i.e.: Credit	78bad	77.0	100.2	91.8	98.0	264.4	118.0	133.9	142.2	140.4	....	....	....
Capital Account: Debit	78bbd	−9.1	−6.0	−18.3	−8.8	−9.1	−9.4	−11.6	−8.0	−8.1	....	....	....
Financial Account, n.i.e.	78bjd	152.6	137.3	260.5	362.1	194.2	406.9	378.6	345.9	434.8	....	....	....
Direct Investment Abroad	78bdd	—	—	—	—	—	—	—	−.1	—	....	....	....
Dir. Invest. in Rep. Econ., n.i.e.	78bed	179.8	210.0	183.3	261.3	312.9	335.2	306.8	281.1	316.3	....	....	....
Portfolio Investment Assets	78bfd	−2.0	−5.7	−.4	—	−.4	−10.5	−1.7	−5.7	−27.4	....	....	....
Equity Securities	78bkd	....	....	....	....	....	....	....	....	....	....	....	....
Debt Securities	78bld	....	....	....	....	....	....	....	....	....	....	....	....
Portfolio Investment Liab., n.i.e.	78bgd	1.1	−.4	6.1	20.2	6.0	58.9	69.7	54.4	195.1	....	....	....
Equity Securities	78bmd	....	....	....	....	....	....	....	....	....	....	....	....
Debt Securities	78bnd	....	....	....	....	....	....	....	....	....	....	....	....
Financial Derivatives Assets	78bwd	....	....	....	....	....	....	....	....	....	....	....	....
Financial Derivatives Liabilities	78bxd	....	....	....	....	....	....	....	....	....	....	....	....
Other Investment Assets	78bhd	−18.3	−51.0	−31.3	−16.2	−49.2	19.3	−61.7	−54.3	−52.2	....	....	....
Monetary Authorities	78bod	....	....	....	....	....	....	....	....	....	....	....	....
General Government	78bpd	....	....	....	....	....	....	....	....	....	....	....	....
Banks	78bqd	....	....	....	....	....	....	....	....	....	....	....	....
Other Sectors	78brd	....	....	....	....	....	....	....	....	....	....	....	....
Other Investment Liab., n.i.e.	78bid	−8.0	−15.7	102.7	96.8	−75.1	4.0	65.5	70.6	2.9	....	....	....
Monetary Authorities	78bsd	—	—	—	—	—	—	—	—	—	....	....	....
General Government	78btd	....	....	....	....	....	....	....	....	....	....	....	....
Banks	78bud	....	....	....	....	....	....	....	....	....	....	....	....
Other Sectors	78bvd	....	....	....	....	....	....	....	....	....	....	....	....
Net Errors and Omissions	78cad	−16.9	35.5	−23.7	−25.3	−32.3	−43.5	−50.3	61.6	61.4	....	....	....
Overall Balance	78cbd	−8.8	51.6	−19.0	23.3	51.5	21.6	12.3	66.0	57.8	....	....	....
Reserves and Related Items	79dad	8.8	−51.6	19.0	−23.3	−51.5	−21.6	−12.3	−66.0	−57.8	....	....	....
Reserve Assets	79dbd	9.6	−50.8	19.9	−22.8	−53.5	−21.6	−12.3	−66.0	−59.5	....	....	....
Use of Fund Credit and Loans	79dcd	−.8	−.9	−.8	−.6	2.1	—	—	—	1.7	....	....	....
Exceptional Financing	79ded	....	....	....	....	....	....	....	....	....	....	....	....
National Accounts						*Millions of E. Caribbean Dollars*							
Gross Domestic Product (GDP)	99b	4,795.5	4,963.1	5,199.6	5,490.4	5,854.0	6,204.5	6,461.6	6,493.1	6,569.9	....	....	....
GDP Volume 1990 Prices	99b.p	4,188.8	4,216.2	4,328.9	4,469.2	4,647.3	4,837.6	4,973.8	4,909.0	4,918.2	....	....	....
GDP Volume (2000=100)	99bvp	84.2	84.8	87.0	89.9	93.4	97.3	100.0	98.7	98.9	....	....	....
GDP Deflator (2000=100)	99bip	88.1	90.6	92.5	94.6	97.0	98.7	100.0	101.8	102.8	....	....	....
						Millions: Midyear Estimates							
Population	99z	.561	.566	.570	.573	.576	.579	.582	.585	.589	.593	.598	....

Ecuador 248

		1994	1995	1996	1997	1998	1999	2000	2001	2002	2003	2004	2005
Exchange Rates		*Sucres per SDR: End of Period*											
Principal Rate	aa	3,312.4	4,345.8	5,227.0	5,974.5	9,609.8	27,783.7	32,572.8	31,418.3	33,988.0	37,149.3	38,825.3	35,731.8
		Sucres per US Dollar: End of Period (ae) Period Average (rf)											
Principal Rate	ae	2,269.0	2,923.5	3,635.0	4,428.0	6,825.0	20,243.0	25,000.0	25,000.0	25,000.0	25,000.0	25,000.0	25,000.0
Principal Rate	rf	2,196.7	2,564.5	3,189.5	3,998.3	5,446.6	11,786.8	24,988.4	25,000.0	25,000.0	25,000.0	25,000.0	25,000.0
		Index Numbers (2000=100): Period Averages											
Principal Rate	ahx	1,139.3	977.7	796.5	624.6	468.0	228.7	100.0	100.0	100.0	100.0	100.0	100.0
Nominal Effective Exchange Rate	nec	822.3	712.4	609.6	520.5	416.7	214.9	100.0	105.3	111.2	110.2	106.1	103.1
Real Effective Exchange Rate	rec	146.7	144.4	142.1	147.5	149.8	110.7	100.0	139.3	159.2	162.4	154.6	148.3
Fund Position		*Millions of SDRs: End of Period*											
Quota	2f.s	219.2	219.2	219.2	219.2	219.2	302.3	302.3	302.3	302.3	302.3	302.3	302.3
SDRs	1b.s	3.0	2.1	1.9	.4	.2	1.7	.2	1.8	1.4	.7	36.1	15.2
Reserve Position in the Fund	1c.s	17.1	17.2	17.2	17.2	17.2	17.2	17.2	17.2	17.2	17.2	17.2	17.2
Total Fund Cred.&Loans Outstg	2tl	135.7	116.7	100.9	98.9	49.5	—	—	113.3	151.1	226.7	262.3	186.8	54.7
International Liquidity		*Millions of US Dollars Unless Otherwise Indicated: End of Period*											
Total Reserves minus Gold	1l.d	1,844.2	1,627.6	1,858.5	2,092.8	1,619.7	1,642.4	946.9	839.8	714.6	812.6	1,069.6	1,714.2
SDRs	1b.d	4.3	3.1	2.7	.5	.3	2.3	.3	2.3	1.9	1.0	56.1	21.8
Reserve Position in the Fund	1c.d	25.0	25.5	24.7	23.1	24.2	23.5	22.3	21.6	23.3	25.5	26.6	24.5
Foreign Exchange	1d.d	1,814.9	1,599.0	1,831.1	2,069.1	1,595.3	1,616.5	924.3	815.9	689.4	786.1	986.9	1,667.9
Gold (Million Fine Troy Ounces)	1ad	.414	.414	.414	.414	.414	†.845	.845	.845	.845	.845	.845	.845
Gold (National Valuation)	1and	165.6	166.6	166.6	166.7	166.7	245.4	232.7	233.8	293.3	348.0	368.0	433.4
Monetary Authorities: Other Liab	4..d	4,052.7	196.1	178.3	147.5	310.6	673.6	400.6	375.5	154.4	53.5	39.8	14.9
Banking Institutions: Assets	7a.d	355.4	398.4	561.1	938.3	972.3	748.9	819.4	1,013.1	1,367.1	1,985.6	2,453.0	2,875.5
Liabilities	7b.d	847.8	1,074.6	1,229.4	1,795.2	1,527.0	862.0	595.3	512.3	452.5	472.1	574.4	650.1
Nonbank Financial Insts.: Assets	7e.d	....	....	....	....	20.1	16.8	26.7	41.5	32.6	35.8	50.4	55.3
Liabilities	7f.d	....	....	....	....	523.3	383.2	231.4	274.5	.3	.1	3.3	2.7
Monetary Authorities		*Millions of US Dollars: End of Period*											
Foreign Assets	11	1,986.6	1,746.7	1,992.2	2,254.8	†1,663.1	†1,527.7	1,538.6	†1,563.0	†1,522.2	1,715.9	2,051.2	2,869.3
Claims on Central Government	12a	4,021.3	194.7	166.1	129.0	†303.0	†1,479.2	1,425.0	†1,278.8	†1,145.0	1,244.3	1,155.4	1,146.9
Claims on State & Local Govts	12b	—	.1	—	—	†—	†—	—	†—	†—	1.5	2.6	1.9
Claims on Nonfin.Pub.Enterprises	12c	.1		—	—	†—	†—	—	†—	†—			
Claims on Private Sector	12d	21.2	6.1	8.2	7.2	†18.4	†1.8	3.6	†2.9	†16.8	15.2	161.7	157.3
Claims on Banking Institutions	12e	15.7	185.8	267.4	44.8	†944.0	†424.4	314.4	†348.5	†272.7	100.1	92.8	91.8
Claims on Nonbank Financial Insts	12g	—	—	—	—	†—	†—	24.6	†25.3	†26.7	18.3	9.1	1.6
Reserve Money	14	1,237.8	1,120.3	1,198.6	1,285.0	†1,053.3	†828.6	474.6	†528.7	†432.0	503.8	552.1	779.9
of which: Currency Outside Banks	14a	493.6	469.6	516.6	537.5	†426.6	†576.3	31.7	†21.8	†39.6	49.7	58.1	62.8
Other Liabilities to Banking Insts	14n	—	—	—	—	†319.7	†223.8	4.0	†8.7	†3.0	8.6	13.6	5.9
Time, Savings,&Fgn.Currency Dep	15	175.6	130.9	121.1	111.9	†—	†86.1	115.0	†98.2	†97.3	125.3	170.9	291.3
Liabs. of Central Bank: Securities	16ac	36.0	19.8	9.4	.4	†.1	†117.9	2.1	†45.9	†—	—	—	—
Restricted Deposits	16b	.3	.2	.2	.1	†—	†—	—	†—	†—	—	—	—
Foreign Liabilities	16c	4,250.9	369.6	323.4	280.9	†380.2	†673.6	548.2	†565.4	†462.7	443.3	329.8	93.2
Central Government Deposits	16d	816.1	634.1	699.4	600.5	†391.2	†388.7	887.9	†818.0	†864.1	1,076.7	1,218.9	1,613.8
Liab. to Nonbank Financial Insts	16j	....	....	....	....	†—	†—	—	†—	†—	.1	—	—
Capital Accounts	17a	344.6	331.8	533.1	448.8	†1,169.7	†1,243.2	1,542.2	†1,571.6	†1,363.4	1,432.8	1,583.9	1,702.6
Other Items (Net)	17r	−816.3	−473.4	−451.2	−291.9	†−385.7	†−128.8	−268.0	†−418.1	†−239.0	−495.4	−396.5	−217.9
Banking Institutions		*Millions of US Dollars: End of Period*											
Reserves	20	413.4	444.9	539.0	566.6	†686.5	†180.8	243.5	†250.7	†326.3	258.0	340.2	450.2
Claims on Mon.Author.:Securities	20c	36.0	19.8	9.4	.4	†.1	†117.9	2.1	†8.7	†4.2	12.0	30.4	28.1
Other Claims on Monetary Author	20n	....	....	....	....	†—	†—	—	†—	†—	—	—	—
Foreign Assets	21	355.4	398.4	561.1	938.3	†972.3	†748.9	819.4	†1,013.1	†1,367.1	1,985.6	2,453.0	2,875.5
Claims on Central Government	22a	64.3	129.3	221.3	387.8	†892.9	†490.1	399.0	†568.0	†527.7	349.9	276.4	276.7
Claims on State & Local Govts	22b	—	—	—	—	†—	†—	—	†—	†—	11.1	7.8	6.2
Claims on Nonfin.Pub.Enterprises	22c	—	—	—	—	†—	†—	—	†—	†—	1.5	1.1	.7
Claims on Private Sector	22d	4,648.0	5,387.6	5,591.5	6,740.6	†6,126.3	†4,400.6	4,766.7	†5,861.5	†5,150.0	5,398.4	6,635.5	8,211.2
Claims on Nonbank Financial Insts	22g	.1	—	21.2	24.4	†45.5	†—	—	†—	†131.4	343.0	287.7	333.9
Demand Deposits	24	977.4	765.9	819.1	883.3	†951.3	†614.9	996.7	†1,552.7	†1,629.1	1,793.0	2,315.0	2,726.2
Time, Savings,& Fgn.Currency Dep	25	2,905.3	3,606.4	4,186.3	4,611.2	†3,701.0	†1,239.2	2,434.3	†3,087.3	†3,073.6	3,791.3	4,648.6	5,572.8
Money Market Instruments	26aa	61.7	161.5	508.2	687.8	†661.7	†347.0	233.6	†171.7	†—	—	—	—
Restricted Deposits	26b	84.5	121.4	162.7	174.9	†—	†1,057.5	364.8	†159.0	†25.8	1.0	1.6	1.3
Foreign Liabilities	26c	847.8	1,074.6	1,229.4	1,795.2	†1,527.0	†862.0	595.3	†512.3	†452.5	472.1	574.4	650.1
Central Government Deposits	26d	—	2.6	4.1	6.5	†131.2	†48.0	128.6	†1,007.0	†1,120.1	1,290.2	1,674.2	2,069.2
Credit from Monetary Authorities	26g	26.1	162.8	132.9	6.8	†652.5	†311.1	136.4	†169.1	†71.2	54.4	52.6	25.7
Liab. to Nonbank Financial Insts	26j	165.9	237.7	18.3	13.8	†34.3	†88.7	135.1	†139.4	†67.6	74.3	103.6	172.3
Capital Accounts	27a	1,306.8	1,614.0	1,685.5	1,937.0	†1,719.8	†−95.8	−365.0	†−875.2	†−985.9	−793.9	−713.7	−531.2
Other Items (Net)	27r	−858.1	−1,366.8	−1,803.0	−1,458.4	†−655.1	†1,465.7	1,570.9	†1,778.7	†2,052.8	1,677.0	1,375.7	1,496.4
Banking Survey		*Millions of US Dollars: End of Period*											
Foreign Assets (Net)	31n	−2,756.6	700.9	1,000.5	1,117.0	†728.3	†741.1	1,214.6	†1,498.4	†1,974.2	2,786.0	3,600.0	5,001.5
Domestic Credit	32	7,938.8	5,081.0	5,304.8	6,681.9	†6,863.7	†5,935.0	5,602.3	†5,911.4	†5,013.4	5,016.2	5,644.1	6,453.4
Claims on Central Govt. (Net)	32an	3,269.5	−312.7	−316.1	−90.3	†673.5	†1,532.6	807.5	†21.7	†−311.5	−772.6	−1,461.3	−2,259.4
Claims on State and Local Govts	32b	—	—	—	—	†—	†—	—	†—	†—	12.5	10.4	8.0
Claims on Nonfin.Pub.Enterprises	32c	.1	—	—	—	†—	†—	—	†—	†—	1.5	1.1	.7
Claims on Private Sector	32d	4,669.2	5,393.7	5,599.8	6,747.7	†6,144.8	†4,402.4	4,770.2	†5,864.4	†5,166.8	5,413.6	6,797.1	8,368.6
Claims on Nonbank Financial Insts	32g	.1	—	21.2	24.4	†45.5	†—	24.6	†25.3	†158.1	361.2	296.8	335.5
Money	34	1,711.2	1,379.3	1,445.1	1,551.8	†1,546.7	†1,255.9	1,245.2	†1,814.1	†1,794.8	1,985.3	2,510.0	3,000.3
Quasi-Money	35	3,080.8	3,737.2	4,307.4	4,723.1	†3,701.0	†1,325.4	2,549.3	†3,185.4	†3,170.9	3,916.6	4,819.5	5,864.0
Money Market Instruments	36aa	61.7	161.5	508.2	687.8	†661.7	†347.0	233.6	†171.7	†—	—	—	—
Liabs. of Central Bank: Securities	36ac	36.0	19.8	9.4	.4	†.1	†117.9	2.1	†45.9	†—	—	—	—
Restricted Deposits	36b	84.7	121.6	162.8	175.0	†—	†1,057.5	364.8	†159.0	†25.8	1.0	1.6	1.3
Liab. to Nonbank Financial Insts	36j	165.9	237.7	18.3	13.8	†34.3	†88.7	135.1	†139.4	†67.6	74.4	103.6	172.3
Capital Accounts	37a	1,651.3	1,945.8	2,218.7	2,385.8	†2,889.5	†1,147.4	1,177.3	†696.4	†377.5	638.9	870.2	1,171.4
Other Items (Net)	37r	−1,609.5	−1,821.0	−2,364.6	−1,738.8	†−1,241.3	†1,336.3	1,109.6	†1,197.8	†1,551.0	1,186.0	939.1	1,245.6
Money plus Quasi-Money	35l	4,792.0	5,116.6	5,752.5	6,274.9	†5,247.6	†2,581.2	3,794.5	†4,999.5	†4,965.7	5,901.9	7,329.5	8,864.3

Ecuador 248

		1994	1995	1996	1997	1998	1999	2000	2001	2002	2003	2004	2005
Nonbank Financial Institutions						*Millions of US Dollars: End of Period*							
Reserves	40	....	....	....	....	2.0	† 1.3	5.0	† 8.3	† 1.2	3.5	3.0	12.6
Claims on Mon.Author.:Securities	40c	....	....	....	....	—	† —	—	† —	† .7	—	—	—
Other Claims on Monetary Author	40n	....	....	....	....	....	....	....	—	† —	—	—	—
Foreign Assets	41	....	....	....	....	20.1	† 16.8	26.7	† 41.5	† 32.6	35.8	50.4	55.3
Claims on Central Government	42a	....	....	....	....	8.1	† 257.5	227.9	† 151.6	† 125.1	109.0	124.9	79.2
Claims on State & Local Govts	42b	....	....	....	....	—	† —	—	† —	† —	—	—	—
Claims on Nonfin.Pub.Enterprises	42c	....	....	....	....	—	† —	—	† —	† —	—	—	—
Claims on Private Sector	42d	....	....	....	....	994.1	† 738.6	420.2	† 383.8	† 21.6	10.5	28.2	39.9
Claims on Banking Institutions	42e	....	....	....	....	8.1	† 40.7	332.9	† 6.7	† 303.7	261.3	301.4	281.8
Restricted Deposits	46b	....	....	....	....	17.9	† 11.1	20.6	† 15.3	† —	—	35.8	42.1
Foreign Liabilities	46c	....	....	....	....	523.3	† 383.2	321.4	† 274.5	† .3	.1	3.3	2.7
Central Government Deposits	46d	....	....	....	....	92.6	† 80.0	104.1	† 106.8	† 98.6	98.3	135.9	101.4
Credit from Monetary Authorities	46g	....	....	....	....	232.0	† 176.8	125.0	† 75.9	† 32.1	20.1	10.5	3.2
Credit from Banking Institutions	46h	....	....	....	....	.7	† —	1.2	† 16.8	† 3.1	2.3	2.0	1.7
Capital Accounts	47a	....	....	....	....	149.0	† 134.8	133.3	† 80.2	† 160.9	167.9	244.0	268.0
Insurance Technical Reserves	47d	....	....	....	....	....	....	....	—	† —	—	—	—
Other Items (Net)	47r	....	....	....	....	17.0	† 269.0	307.0	† 22.5	† 190.1	131.4	76.5	49.7
Interest Rates							*Percent Per Annum*						
Discount Rate (End of Period)	60	44.88	59.41	46.38	37.46	61.84	64.40	† 13.16	16.44	14.55	11.19	9.86	9.61
Savings Rate	60k	16.71	21.64	19.90	16.62	16.25	† 4.91	4.47	3.49	2.45	2.24	1.99	1.67
Deposit Rate	60l	33.65	43.31	41.50	28.09	39.39	† 10.03	8.46	6.58	5.47	5.53	4.08	3.53
Lending Rate	60p	43.99	55.67	54.50	43.02	49.55	† 16.53	16.26	15.46	15.08	13.08	9.65	9.34
Prices, Production, Labor						*Index Numbers (2000=100): Period Averages*							
Producer Prices	63	....	....	....	....	18.7	37.8	100.0	99.8	106.5	114.3	124.7	142.9
Consumer Prices	64	12.3	† 15.1	18.8	24.6	33.5	51.0	100.0	137.7	154.9	167.1	† 171.7	175.9
Crude Petroleum Production	66aa	31.6	32.0	96.1	96.9	93.7	93.2	100.0	101.6	98.0	104.3	43.5	44.3
					Number in Thousands: Period Averages								
Labor Force	67d	2,905	3,104	3,169	3,326	3,560	3,770	3,709	4,124	3,801	3,992	4,221	....
Employment	67e	2,698	2,892	2,889	3,062	3,151	3,226	3,376	3,673	3,459	3,531	3,859	....
Unemployment	67c	207	213	335	312	409	543	333	451	354	461	362	....
Unemployment Rate (%)	67r	7.1	6.9	10.4	9.2	11.5	14.4	9.0	11.0	9.3	11.5	8.6	10.7
Intl. Transactions & Positions							*Millions of US Dollars*						
Exports	70..d	3,819.9	4,307.2	5,198.6	5,264.4	4,203.1	4,451.1	4,926.6	4,678.4	5,041.5	6,222.7	7,752.9	10,100.0
Imports, c.i.f.	71..d	3,622.0	4,152.6	4,283.7	4,954.8	5,575.7	3,017.3	3,721.1	5,362.9	6,431.1	6,702.7	8,226.3	10,286.9
Imports, f.o.b.	71.vd	3,252.5	3,774.8	3,906.1	4,520.1	5,109.9	2,736.9	3,401.0	4,936.0	5,953.4	6,228.3	7,554.6	9,549.4
							2000=100						
Volume of Exports	72	89.1	99.7	98.3	101.3	95.9	97.2	100.0	101.1	99.2	106.7	133.2	116.7
Volume of Imports	73	74.7	100.1	85.6	125.3	155.4	95.9	100.0	119.5	148.1	161.1	167.8	204.0
Unit Value of Exports/Export Prices	74..d	73.0	75.4	29.1	28.7	21.6	78.1	100.0	87.8	94.3	106.6	117.8	150.2
Balance of Payments						*Millions of US Dollars: Minus Sign Indicates Debit*							
Current Account, n.i.e	78ald	−898	−1,000	−55	−457	−2,099	918	921	−695	−1,399	−472	−157	....
Goods: Exports f.o.b	78aad	3,936	4,468	4,929	5,360	4,326	4,615	5,137	4,781	5,198	6,197	7,813	....
Goods: Imports f.o.b	78abd	−3,787	−4,535	−4,008	−4,869	−5,458	−3,028	−3,743	−5,179	−6,196	−6,268	−7,492	....
Trade Balance	78acd	149	−66	921	491	−1,132	1,588	1,395	−397	−998	−71	321	....
Services: Credit	78add	676	728	683	686	678	730	849	862	884	882	921	....
Services: Debit	78aed	−1,107	−1,173	−1,110	−1,230	−1,241	−1,181	−1,269	−1,434	−1,632	−1,590	−1,814	....
Balance on Goods & Services	78afd	−283	−512	494	−52	−1,695	1,136	975	−969	−1,745	−779	−572	....
Income: Credit	78agd	61	98	80	128	119	75	70	48	30	27	33	....
Income: Debit	78ahd	−999	−1,029	−1,121	−1,154	−1,290	−1,383	−1,476	−1,412	−1,335	−1,492	−1,512	....
Balance on Gds, Serv. & Inc	78aid	−1,221	−1,442	−547	−1,078	−2,865	−171	−431	−2,333	−3,051	−2,243	−2,051	....
Current Transfers, n.i.e.: Credit	78ajd	391	506	616	738	933	1,188	1,437	1,686	1,709	1,794	1,913	....
Current Transfers: Debit	78akd	−69	−64	−124	−117	−166	−99	−85	−47	−58	−22	−19	....
Capital Account, n.i.e	78bcd	18	17	14	11	14	2	−1	−63	16	17	18	....
Capital Account, n.i.e.: Credit	78bad	21	21	18	17	23	11	8	21	24	26	28	....
Capital Account: Debit	78bbd	−3	−4	−4	−6	−9	−9	−10	−84	−8	−9	−10	....
Financial Account, n.i.e	78bjd	332	−43	103	−14	1,448	−1,344	−6,602	1,032	1,069	232	320	....
Direct Investment Abroad	78bdd	....	....	....	....	....	....	....	....	....	....	....	....
Dir. Invest. in Rep. Econ., n.i.e	78bed	576	452	500	724	870	648	720	1,330	1,275	1,555	1,160	....
Portfolio Investment Assets	78bfd	....	....	....	....	....	....	....	....	....	....	....	....
Equity Securities	78bkd	....	....	....	....	....	....	....	....	....	....	....	....
Debt Securities	78bld	....	....	....	....	....	....	....	....	....	....	....	....
Portfolio Investment Liab., n.i.e	78bgd	6	3	−4	−242	−34	−46	−5,583	117	—	8	—	....
Equity Securities	78bmd	6	13	6	22	5	1	—	1	1	9	1	....
Debt Securities	78bnd	—	−10	−10	−264	−40	−47	−5,583	116	−1	−1	−1	....
Financial Derivatives Assets	78bwd	....	....	....	....	....	....	....	....	....	....	....	....
Financial Derivatives Liabilities	78bxd	....	....	....	....	....	....	....	....	....	....	....	....
Other Investment Assets	78bhd	−177	−668	−302	−560	−54	−725	−1,274	−1,284	−1,351	−880	−1,550	....
Monetary Authorities	78bod	....	....	....	....	....	....	....	—	—	—	—	....
General Government	78bpd	....	....	....	....	....	....	....	—	—	—	—	....
Banks	78bqd	....	....	....	....	....	....	....	—	—	—	—	....
Other Sectors	78brd	−177	−668	−302	−560	−54	−725	−1,274	−1,284	−1,351	−880	−1,550	....
Other Investment Liab., n.i.e	78bid	−75	170	−91	64	666	−1,221	−465	868	1,145	−451	710	....
Monetary Authorities	78bsd	83	−54	−48	−18	230	−76	−135	−144	−138	−47	−64	....
General Government	78btd	−727	−692	127	−190	−37	117	206	188	−117	−88	−377	....
Banks	78bud	26	31	95	26	−24	−72	−37	−108	−19	−22	−20	....
Other Sectors	78bvd	544	885	−265	245	497	−1,190	−499	932	1,418	−295	1,172	....
Net Errors and Omissions	78cad	−226	−433	−187	−62	−145	−521	−15	−532	94	293	154	....
Overall Balance	78cbd	−775	−1,459	−125	−521	−781	−944	−5,697	−258	−221	70	335	....
Reserves and Related Items	79dad	775	1,459	125	521	781	944	5,697	258	221	−70	−335	....
Reserve Assets	79dbd	−578	174	−247	−253	461	489	−307	105	68	−150	−275	....
Use of Fund Credit and Loans	79dcd	122	−29	−23	−3	−67	−68	151	48	95	48	−112	....
Exceptional Financing	79ded	1,231	1,314	395	777	388	523	5,853	105	58	32	52	....

Ecuador 248

		1994	1995	1996	1997	1998	1999	2000	2001	2002	2003	2004	2005
International Investment Position							*Millions of US Dollars*						
Assets	79aad	2,442	2,388	2,650	2,942	2,387	1,319	1,904	2,451	2,709	3,709	4,534	....
Direct Investment Abroad	79abd	—	—	—	—	—	—	—	—	—	—	—	....
Portfolio Investment	79acd	—	—	—	—	—	—	—	—	—	—	—	....
Equity Securities	79add	—	—	—	—	—	—	—	—	—	—	—	....
Debt Securities	79aed	—	—	—	—	—	—	—	—	—	—	—	....
Financial Derivatives	79ald	—	—	—	—	—	—	—	—	—	—	—	....
Other Investment	79afd	538	658	674	715	619	445	724	1,377	1,701	2,549	3,096	....
Monetary Authorities	79agd	—	—	—	—	—	—	—	—	—	—	—	....
General Government	79ahd	—	—	—	—	—	—	—	—	—	—	—	....
Banks	79aid	538	658	674	715	619	445	724	1,377	1,701	2,549	3,096	....
Other Sectors	79ajd	—	—	—	—	—	—	—	—	—	—	—	....
Reserve Assets	79akd	1,904	1,730	1,976	2,227	1,768	874	1,180	1,074	1,008	1,161	1,438	....
Liabilities	79lad	18,366	18,391	19,442	20,912	23,255	23,416	21,335	24,059	26,802	28,073	29,784	....
Dir. Invest. in Rep. Economy	79lbd	3,166	3,619	4,118	4,842	5,712	6,361	7,081	8,410	9,686	11,240	12,482	....
Portfolio Investment	79lcd	199	6,019	6,039	6,382	6,437	6,465	4,017	4,134	4,134	4,142	4,199	....
Equity Securities	79ldd	8	20	26	48	53	54	54	55	56	66	67	....
Debt Securities	79led	191	5,999	6,013	6,334	6,383	6,411	3,963	4,079	4,078	4,077	4,132	....
Financial Derivatives	79lld	—	—	—	—	—	—	—	—	—	—	—	....
Other Investment	79lfd	15,001	8,753	9,284	9,688	11,106	10,590	10,238	11,515	12,982	12,690	13,103	....
Monetary Authorities	79lgd	729	669	591	549	721	665	681	356	334	398	298	....
General Government	79lhd	11,526	4,408	4,578	4,274	4,670	5,109	5,204	6,162	6,573	6,678	6,378	....
Banks	79lid	856	1,142	1,137	1,364	1,674	1,298	1,158	1,626	897	706	708	....
Other Sectors	79ljd	1,891	2,534	2,979	3,501	4,041	3,517	3,194	3,370	5,178	4,908	5,719	....
Government Finance						*Millions of US Dollars: Year Ending December 31*							
Deficit (-) or Surplus	80	52.4	−163.8	−88.7	−291.4	68.7	−99.0	90.0	98.9	135.1	−321.2	−24.6	287.1
Revenue	81	2,570.9	3,131.4	3,334.1	3,380.3	3,280.3	2,705.1	3,056.6	3,873.7	4,205.3	4,761.6	5,460.0	5,694.6
Expenditure	82	2,518.5	3,295.2	3,422.7	3,671.7	3,211.6	2,804.1	2,966.6	3,774.8	4,070.2	5,082.8	5,484.6	5,407.5
Financing													
Domestic	84a	237.5	365.4	150.2	824.4	−68.8	32.3	−269.4	−22.3	17.4	87.6	463.3	278.0
Foreign	85a	−290.0	−201.6	−61.5	−533.0	.1	66.8	179.4	−76.9	−152.7	233.5	−438.7	−565.1
National Accounts							*Millions of US Dollars*						
Househ.Cons.Expend.,incl.NPISHs	96f.d	12,592	13,827	14,022	15,682	16,120	11,035	10,199	14,491	16,837	18,473	19,769	....
Government Consumption Expend	91f.d	2,237	2,525	2,567	2,902	2,857	2,088	1,564	2,134	2,550	2,583	2,740	....
Gross Fixed Capital Formation	93e.d	3,521	3,797	3,852	4,234	4,623	2,826	3,265	4,541	5,549	6,192	6,571	....
Changes in Inventories	93i.d	540	557	338	838	1,253	−371	−60	854	1,191	1,329	1,852	....
Exports of Goods and Services	90c.d	4,576	5,196	5,612	6,058	4,997	5,257	5,906	5,613	5,829	6,461	8,029	....
Imports of Goods and Services (-)	98c.d	4,894	5,707	5,124	6,078	6,595	4,161	4,939	6,608	7,644	7,837	8,679	....
Gross Domestic Product (GDP)	99b.d	18,573	20,196	21,268	23,636	23,255	16,675	15,934	21,024	24,311	27,201	30,282	....
Net Primary Income from Abroad	98.n	−1,279	−1,262	−1,304	−1,422	−1,625	−1,741	−2,229	−1,911	....	....	....	....
Gross National Income (GNI)	99a	15,327	16,677	17,736	18,347	18,098	11,948	11,698	15,208				
GDP Volume 2000 Prices	99bpd	14,941	15,203	15,568	16,199	16,541	15,499	15,934	16,749	17,321	17,781	19,016	20,285
GDP Volume (2000=100)	99bvp	93.8	95.4	97.7	101.7	103.8	† 97.3	100.0	105.1	108.7	111.6	119.3	127.3
GDP Deflator (2000=100)	99bip	124.3	132.8	136.6	145.9	140.6	107.6	100.0	125.5	140.4	153.0	159.2	....
							Millions: Midyear Estimates						
Population	99z	11.19	11.40	11.59	11.78	11.95	12.13	12.31	12.49	12.67	12.85	13.04	13.23

Egypt 469

		1994	1995	1996	1997	1998	1999	2000	2001	2002	2003	2004	2005
Exchange Rates						*Pounds per SDR: End of Period*							
Market Rate............aa=........	wa	4.9504	5.0392	4.8718	4.5713	4.7704	4.6734	4.8077	5.6427	6.1178	9.1435	9.5221	8.1929
Market Rate............ae=........	we	3.3910	3.3900	3.3880	3.3880	3.3880	3.4050	3.6900	4.4900	4.5000	6.1532	6.1314	5.7322
Fund Position						*Millions of SDRs: End of Period*							
Quota........................	2f.s	678	678	678	678	678	944	944	944	944	944	944	944
SDRs........................	1b.s	59	70	86	84	114	30	37	28	67	127	106	71
Reserve Position in the Fund............	1c.s	54	54	54	54	54	120	120	—	—	—	—	—
Total Fund Cred.&Loans Outstg.......	2tl	132	70	11	—	—	—	—	—	—	—	—	—
International Liquidity						*Millions of US Dollars Unless Otherwise Indicated: End of Period*							
Total Reserves minus Gold..............	1l.d	13,481	16,181	17,398	18,665	18,124	14,484	13,118	12,926	13,242	13,589	14,273	20,609
SDRs........................	1b.d	86	103	123	113	160	41	48	35	91	189	165	101
Reserve Position in the Fund.........	1c.d	78	80	77	73	76	165	156	—	—	—	—	—
Foreign Exchange.....................	1d.d	13,316	15,998	17,198	18,479	17,888	14,278	12,913	12,891	13,151	13,400	14,108	20,508
Gold (Million Fine Troy Ounces).......	1ad	2.432	2.432	2.432	2.432	2.432	2.432	2.432	2.432	2.432	2.432	2.432	2.432
Gold (National Valuation)........	1and	694	704	695	609	541	475	511	488	571	631	717	779
Monetary Authorities:Other Assets....	3..d	1,293	1,131	1,003	938	874	811	762	715	668	629	528	453
Other Liab....	4..d	12,551	13,298	12,324	11,384	11,873	11,296	11,091	10,569	11,866	13,061	13,481	12,026
Deposit Money Banks: Assets..........	7a.d	11,432.3	11,070.3	10,736.2	9,153.2	7,815.1	7,441.1	7,297.1	5,915.0	6,279.5	7,782.2	10,913.7	13,740.4
Liabilities.......	7b.d	1,465.3	1,500.2	1,844.2	3,555.7	4,995.3	4,318.3	4,232.6	4,268.9	4,264.0	3,553.2	3,225.3	3,382.4
Other Banking Insts.: Assets............	7e.d	29.5	29.8	22.0	16.9	14.8	7.3	7.0	10.3	7.7	24.8	46.6	25.0
Liabilities...............	7f.d	457.1	275.5	255.4	267.4	219.9	215.1	240.8	161.5	173.2	166.9	149.0	132.5
Monetary Authorities						*Millions of Pounds: End of Period*							
Foreign Assets.............................	11	60,529	61,901	65,189	68,799	66,782	52,923	52,478	61,332	63,203	88,391	92,422	123,569
Claims on Central Government.........	12a	50,978	51,615	47,015	44,368	61,209	75,447	95,715	116,392	131,068	177,255	248,614	194,894
Claims on Nonfin.Pub.Enterprises.....	12c	799	799	900	849	817	1,029	1,177	1,330	1,661	2,103	2,257	2,381
Claims on Deposit Money Banks......	12e	12,224	12,892	12,700	12,438	8,359	6,462	6,577	7,094	6,621	7,048	7,631	20,213
Claims on Other Banking Insts.........	12f	2,040	2,095	2,147	2,261	2,275	3,336	2,846	2,901	2,319	2,509	2,849	2,450
Reserve Money.........................	14	47,888	52,357	54,562	60,610	72,336	73,522	87,271	102,094	111,002	155,065	183,888	191,728
of which: Currency Outside DMBs..	14a	20,612	22,750	24,954	28,215	31,502	35,310	37,902	40,548	45,281	52,475	59,795	69,331
Foreign Liabilities.......................	16c	43,215	45,430	41,807	38,570	40,224	38,464	40,926	47,454	53,398	80,365	82,656	68,938
Central Government Deposits..........	16d	33,617	29,661	28,476	26,738	22,296	23,298	27,676	42,862	43,420	59,364	107,643	67,702
Other Items (Net).........................	17r	1,851	1,855	3,105	2,797	4,586	3,913	2,920	−3,359	−2,948	−17,487	−20,413	15,139
Deposit Money Banks						*Millions of Pounds: End of Period*							
Reserves............................	20	25,402	28,094	28,146	30,241	33,262	34,636	46,432	61,180	62,156	104,221	123,935	139,689
Foreign Assets.............................	21	38,767	37,528	36,374	31,011	26,477	25,337	26,926	26,559	28,258	47,886	66,916	78,763
Claims on Central Government........	22a	42,398	41,882	47,567	54,479	47,244	40,363	47,276	54,991	80,056	91,095	102,951	113,735
Claims on Nonfin.Pub.Enterprises.....	22c	29,998	33,180	37,481	38,643	38,801	42,109	38,141	42,062	42,655	45,896	52,549	60,105
Claims on Private Sector..............	22d	48,831	66,777	83,810	105,545	133,799	159,958	176,693	197,038	207,089	225,023	233,685	247,615
Claims on Other Banking Insts........	22f	1,284	1,630	2,424	2,988	4,251	2,958	3,429	4,918	6,186	5,459	4,695	5,100
Demand Deposits..........................	24	15,919	17,282	18,026	18,920	19,335	20,506	21,747	23,515	27,021	36,627	43,230	51,806
Time, Savings,& Fgn.Currency Dep....	25	109,810	121,175	135,764	150,966	162,512	174,713	198,421	228,053	256,045	308,286	352,164	387,828
Bonds..................................	26ab	—	—	800	1,675	1,675	2,238	2,238	2,238	1,563	1,263	1,113	813
Restricted Deposits......................	26b	9,182	10,858	12,513	14,081	15,771	18,113	17,502	19,658	20,161	22,750	22,912	19,794
Foreign Liabilities........................	26c	4,969	5,086	6,248	12,047	16,924	14,704	15,618	19,167	19,188	21,864	19,776	19,389
Central Government Deposits..........	26d	7,805	11,016	13,638	14,670	18,906	23,889	28,596	34,429	40,488	51,498	57,958	56,893
Credit from Monetary Authorities.....	26g	17,571	20,842	20,648	20,938	11,244	7,256	7,464	7,547	7,475	7,675	8,110	26,246
Other Items (Net)...........................	27r	21,423	22,832	28,165	29,609	37,468	43,943	47,310	52,141	54,461	69,616	79,469	82,239
Monetary Survey						*Millions of Pounds: End of Period*							
Foreign Assets (Net)......................	31n	51,111	48,914	53,508	49,194	36,111	25,092	22,860	21,270	18,875	34,049	56,907	114,006
Domestic Credit............................	32	134,906	157,300	179,230	207,724	247,195	278,013	309,006	342,342	387,126	438,479	481,998	501,685
Claims on Central Govt. (Net)........	32an	51,953	52,820	52,467	57,439	67,252	68,623	86,720	94,091	127,216	157,489	185,964	184,034
Claims on Nonfin.Pub.Enterprises...	32c	30,797	33,979	38,381	39,492	39,618	43,138	39,318	43,393	44,316	47,999	54,806	62,486
Claims on Private Sector..............	32d	48,831	66,777	83,810	105,545	133,799	159,958	176,693	197,038	207,089	225,023	233,685	247,615
Claims on Other Banking Insts.......	32f	3,324	3,724	4,571	5,248	6,526	6,294	6,275	7,820	8,505	7,968	7,544	7,550
Money.......................................	34	38,275	41,540	44,521	48,708	58,577	59,066	62,195	67,078	75,781	93,520	108,498	125,466
of which: Foreign Currency Deps....	34a	9,892	10,980	10,260	9,332	10,225	11,148	17,493	31,330	32,734	52,864	56,810	40,816
Quasi-Money...............................	35	109,834	121,227	135,882	151,129	162,795	174,844	198,804	228,413	257,031	310,114	353,389	388,757
of which: Fgn. Currency Deposits...	35a	30,851	33,335	32,015	31,792	33,271	37,435	47,102	60,149	65,939	95,788	107,031	101,442
Bonds....................................	36ab	—	—	800	1,675	1,675	2,238	2,238	2,238	1,563	1,263	1,113	813
Restricted Deposits......................	36b	9,182	10,858	12,513	14,081	15,771	18,113	17,502	19,658	20,161	22,750	22,912	19,794
Other Items (Net).........................	37r	28,727	32,590	39,021	41,325	44,489	48,845	51,125	46,226	51,466	44,880	52,994	80,861
Money plus Quasi-Money................	35l	148,109	162,766	180,404	199,837	221,372	233,909	260,999	295,491	332,813	403,634	461,887	514,223
Other Banking Institutions													
Specialized Banks						*Millions of Pounds: End of Period*							
Cash.................................	40	169	262	288	300	467	382	583	912	1,338	2,725	2,288	1,388
Foreign Assets.............................	41	100	101	74	57	50	25	26	46	35	153	286	144
Claims on Nonfin.Pub.Enterprises.....	42c	2,067	2,130	2,170	2,112	2,073	2,397	2,246	2,262	2,720	2,447	2,526	2,265
Claims on Private Sector................	42d	7,425	8,785	11,355	13,814	17,607	20,657	22,884	25,728	27,614	30,261	30,856	33,425
Demand Deposits.........................	44	912	1,195	1,434	2,010	2,366	652	660	774	753	1,058	826	1,129
Time and Savings Deposits.............	45	2,322	2,751	3,464	4,297	5,703	8,835	9,807	11,304	13,382	16,360	18,919	22,246
Restricted Deposits.......................	46b	20	32	36	42	59	53	43	14	13	36	76	22
Foreign Liabilities........................	46c	1,550	934	865	906	745	732	889	725	779	1,027	914	759
Central Government Deposits..........	46d	713	893	1,614	1,980	1,712	1,860	2,058	2,146	2,133	2,274	2,344	2,340
Credit from Monetary Authorities.....	46g	2,043	2,112	2,155	2,279	2,299	3,375	3,372	3,435	2,856	3,042	3,378	2,713
Credit from Deposit Money Banks....	46h	1,021	1,500	2,292	2,790	3,932	2,442	2,911	4,496	5,324	4,899	4,267	4,999
Other Items (Net).........................	47r	1,180	1,861	2,027	1,980	3,381	5,513	5,999	6,054	6,465	6,890	5,234	3,013
Post Office: Savings Deposits.........	45..i	1,866	2,591	3,524	4,877	6,680	8,783	11,322	14,584	18,902	24,037	30,067	37,428

		1994	1995	1996	1997	1998	1999	2000	2001	2002	2003	2004	2005
Banking Survey					*Millions of Pounds: End of Period*								
Foreign Assets (Net)	51n	49,661	48,081	52,717	48,346	35,416	24,384	21,997	20,591	18,130	33,175	56,280	113,390
Domestic Credit	52	142,295	166,797	190,938	222,041	266,064	301,818	337,171	374,998	425,773	486,385	537,292	565,969
Claims on Central Govt. (Net)	52an	53,175	55,127	55,223	61,079	72,968	75,668	96,030	106,577	144,035	180,655	215,419	220,178
Claims on Nonfin.Pub.Enterprises	52c	32,864	36,108	40,551	41,603	41,691	45,535	41,564	45,655	47,035	50,446	57,332	64,751
Claims on Private Sector	52d	56,256	75,562	95,164	119,359	151,406	180,615	199,577	222,766	234,703	255,283	264,541	281,040
Liquid Liabilities	55l	153,040	169,041	188,538	210,721	235,654	251,797	282,205	321,241	364,512	442,364	509,411	573,638
Bonds	56ab	—	—	800	1,675	1,675	2,238	2,238	2,238	1,563	1,263	1,113	813
Restricted Deposits	56b	9,202	10,890	12,550	14,123	15,830	18,166	17,546	19,672	20,174	22,786	22,988	19,816
Other Items (Net)	57r	29,714	34,948	41,768	43,868	48,322	54,003	57,178	52,439	57,657	53,146	60,061	85,093
Interest Rates						*Percent Per Annum*							
Discount Rate (End of Period)	60	14.00	13.50	13.00	12.25	12.00	12.00	12.00	11.00	10.00	10.00	10.00	10.00
Treasury Bill Rate	60c	....	....	....	8.8	8.8	9.0	9.1	7.2	5.5	6.9	9.9	8.6
Deposit Rate	60l	11.8	10.9	10.5	9.8	9.4	9.2	9.5	9.5	9.3	8.2	7.7	7.2
Lending Rate	60p	16.5	16.5	15.6	13.8	13.0	13.0	13.2	13.3	13.8	13.5	13.4	13.1
Prices and Labor					*Index Numbers (2000=100): Period Averages*								
Industrial Share Price	62	....	....	....	63.80	67.43	83.34	100.00	109.41	119.62	133.56	199.23	333.00
Wholesale Prices	63	80.0	85.1	92.2	96.0	97.4	98.2	100.0	101.0	107.5	122.9	† 143.9	151.5
Consumer Prices	64	70.1	81.1	86.9	91.0	† 94.5	97.4	100.0	102.3	105.1	† 109.8	122.2	128.1
					Number in Thousands: Period Averages								
Labor Force	67d	17,174	17,365	....	....	18,027	18,616	....	19,253	20,176	20,546	20,861	....
Employment	67e	15,241	15,344	....	15,830	16,183	16,750	17,203	17,557	17,856	18,406	18,620	....
Unemployment	67c	1,877	1,917	....	† 1,446	1,448	1,481	1,698	1,783	2,021	2,140	2,242	....
Unemployment Rate (%)	67r	11.0	11.3	....	† 8.4	8.2	8.1	9.0	9.2	10.2	10.4	10.8	....
Intl. Transactions & Positions						*Millions of Pounds*							
Exports	70	11,767.9	11,703.8	12,004.1	13,285.9	10,605.9	12,086.1	16,273.8	16,343.3	21,183.5	36,822.9	46,665.3	61,618.3
Suez Canal Dues	70.s	6,998.1	6,692.9	6,381.4	6,072.5	6,108.9	6,015.3	6,223.1	7,545.6	8,978.4	15,158.6	18,988.7	20,029.9
Imports, c.i.f.	71	34,598.9	39,892.0	44,218.0	44,769.0	54,771.0	54,399.0	48,645.0	50,660.0	56,480.0	65,082.0	79,708.0	114,687.1
Balance of Payments					*Millions of US Dollars: Minus Sign Indicates Debit*								
Current Account, n.i.e.	78ald	31	−254	−192	−711	−2,566	−1,635	−971	−388	622	3,743	3,922	....
Goods: Exports f.o.b.	78aad	4,044	4,670	4,779	5,525	4,403	5,237	7,061	7,025	7,118	8,987	12,320	....
Goods: Imports f.o.b.	78abd	−9,997	−12,267	−13,169	−14,157	−14,617	−15,165	−15,382	−13,960	−12,879	−13,189	−18,895	....
Trade Balance	78acd	−5,953	−7,597	−8,390	−8,632	−10,214	−9,928	−8,321	−6,935	−5,762	−4,201	−6,576	....
Services: Credit	78add	8,070	8,590	9,271	9,380	8,141	9,494	9,803	9,042	9,320	11,073	14,197	....
Services: Debit	78aed	−5,645	−4,873	−5,084	−6,770	−6,492	−6,452	−7,513	−7,037	−6,629	−6,474	−8,020	....
Balance on Goods & Services	78afd	−3,528	−3,880	−4,203	−6,021	−8,565	−6,886	−6,031	−4,929	−3,071	398	−399	....
Income: Credit	78agd	1,330	1,578	1,901	2,122	2,030	1,788	1,871	1,468	698	578	572	....
Income: Debit	78ahd	−2,114	−1,983	−1,556	−1,185	−1,075	−1,045	−983	−885	−965	−832	−818	....
Balance on Gds, Serv. & Inc.	78aid	−4,312	−4,285	−3,858	−5,085	−7,610	−6,143	−5,143	−4,346	−3,338	145	−645	....
Current Transfers, n.i.e.: Credit	78ajd	4,622	4,284	3,888	4,738	5,166	4,564	4,224	4,056	4,002	3,708	4,615	....
Current Transfers: Debit	78akd	−279	−253	−222	−363	−122	−55	−52	−98	−42	−109	−48	....
Capital Account, n.i.e.	78bcd	—	—	—	....	....	....	....	....	—	....	....	....
Capital Account, n.i.e.: Credit	78bad	—	—	—	....	....	....	....	....	—	....	....	....
Capital Account: Debit	78bbd	—	—	—	....	....	....	....	....	—	....	....	....
Financial Account, n.i.e.	78bjd	−1,450	−1,845	−1,459	1,958	1,901	−1,421	−1,646	190	−3,333	−5,725	−4,461	....
Direct Investment Abroad	78bdd	−43	−93	−5	−129	−45	−38	−51	−12	−28	−21	−159	....
Dir. Invest. in Rep. Econ., n.i.e.	78bed	1,256	598	636	891	1,076	1,065	1,235	510	647	237	1,253	....
Portfolio Investment Assets	78bfd	—	....	—	....	−63	−22	−3	−2	−6	−25	324	....
Equity Securities	78bkd	—	....	—	....	−63	−22	−3	−2	−6	−25	324	....
Debt Securities	78bld	—	....	—	....	....	....	....	....	....	....	....	....
Portfolio Investment Liab., n.i.e.	78bgd	3	20	545	816	−537	617	269	1,463	−672	−18	−85	....
Equity Securities	78bmd	—	....	—	515	−160	658	269	39	−217	37	26	....
Debt Securities	78bnd	3	20	545	301	−377	−41	....	1,424	−455	−55	−111	....
Financial Derivatives Assets	78bwd	—	....	—	....	....	....	....	....	....	....	....	....
Financial Derivatives Liabilities	78bxd	—	....	—	....	....	....	....	....	....	....	....	....
Other Investment Assets	78bhd	−905	−396	−565	−170	39	−1,805	−2,991	−1,261	−2,943	−4,651	−5,888	....
Monetary Authorities	78bod	−25	65	65	37	24	−14	−21	−73	29	−38	−4	....
General Government	78bpd	—	....	—	....	....	....	....	....	....	....	....	....
Banks	78bqd	−634	371	338	1,599	1,357	372	257	1,369	−331	−1,682	−3,215	....
Other Sectors	78brd	−246	−832	−968	−1,806	−1,342	−2,163	−3,227	−2,556	−2,641	−2,931	−2,669	....
Other Investment Liab., n.i.e.	78bid	−1,761	−1,974	−2,070	551	1,431	−1,240	−105	−509	−331	−1,248	94	....
Monetary Authorities	78bsd	−5	−21	−4	−19	−204	−3	−5	104	5	6	−16	....
General Government	78btd	−1,536	−1,783	−2,578	−1,506	−946	−989	−1,109	−1,157	−1,358	−1,673	−1,740	....
Banks	78bud	−256	−148	324	1,715	1,393	−692	−129	−56	−9	−601	−326	....
Other Sectors	78bvd	36	−22	188	361	1,188	444	1,138	601	1,031	1,020	2,175	....
Net Errors and Omissions	78cad	255	272	−74	−1,882	−722	−1,558	587	−1,146	1,906	1,575	−45	....
Overall Balance	78cbd	−1,164	−1,827	−1,725	−635	−1,387	−4,614	−2,030	−1,345	−804	−407	−584	....
Reserves and Related Items	79dad	1,164	1,827	1,725	635	1,387	4,614	2,030	1,345	804	407	584	....
Reserve Assets	79dbd	−1,193	−409	−1,010	−1,185	535	4,027	1,306	507	−57	−395	−684	....
Use of Fund Credit and Loans	79dcd	−22	−95	−85	−15	—	—	—	—	—	—	—	....
Exceptional Financing	79ded	2,379	2,331	2,820	1,836	852	587	724	838	861	801	1,269	....
Government Finance					*Millions of Pounds: Year Ending June 30*								
Deficit (-) or Surplus	80	589	1,828	† −4,411	−5,178	−2,591	−220	−4,161	−8,018	−9,623	−9,946	....	....
Revenue	81	67,828	73,654	† 69,233	72,782	69,091	90,163	95,900	99,480	100,329	112,597	....	....
Grants Received	81z	2,811	2,056	† 1,954	1,392	1,689	1,649	1,773	1,571	3,713	2,954	....	....
Expenditure	82	65,382	68,689	† 74,400	78,503	72,048	84,906	92,950	105,086	106,506	118,376	....	....
Lending Minus Repayments	83	4,668	5,193	† 1,198	849	1,323	7,126	8,884	3,983	7,159	7,121	....	....
Total Net Borrowing	84	−589	−1,828	† 4,411	5,178	2,591	....	....	....	....	....	....	....
Financing													
Domestic	84a	1,454	−60	† 5,844	6,785	4,397	....	....	....	....	....	....	....
Foreign	85a	−2,043	−1,768	† −1,433	−1,607	−1,806	....	....	....	....	....	....	....

Egypt 469

		1994	1995	1996	1997	1998	1999	2000	2001	2002	2003	2004	2005
National Accounts						*Millions of Pounds: Year Ending June 30*							
Househ.Cons.Expend.,incl.NPISHs....	**96f**	130,500	151,900	176,490	200,500	220,400	230,800	258,000	270,000	279,000	304,300	343,000	381,000
Government Consumption Expend...	**91f**	18,000	21,500	23,800	26,100	32,500	35,700	38,100	40,600	47,200	53,300	61,900	69,500
Gross Fixed Capital Formation..........	**93e**	29,000	33,100	36,760	47,700	61,300	64,000	64,400	63,600	67,500	68,100	79,600	92,500
Changes in Inventories....................	**93i**	—	2,000	1,340	−1,000	500	2,500	2,100	1,900	1,700	2,900	2,600	2,500
Exports of Goods and Services..........	**90c**	39,500	45,990	47,620	50,100	46,600	46,300	55,100	62,700	69,400	90,000	138,600	166,200
Imports of Goods and Services (-).....	**98c**	50,100	58,290	61,100	66,200	73,900	71,700	77,600	80,100	85,900	101,100	140,400	175,100
Gross Domestic Product (GDP)........	**99b**	175,000	204,000	229,400	257,200	287,400	307,600	340,100	358,700	378,900	417,500	485,300	536,600
GDP Volume 1991/92 Prices............	**99b.p**	148,820	155,730	163,500	172,480	....	....	....	....	....	....	....	....
GDP Volume 1996/97 Prices............	**99b.p**	....	....	....	257,200	276,600	293,500	309,300	320,200	330,400	....	....	....
GDP Volume 2001/02.....................	**99b.p**	....	....	....	....	....	....	....	....	378,900	390,700	407,000	427,100
GDP Volume (2000=100)...............	**99bvp**	71.7	75.1	78.8	† 83.2	89.4	94.9	100.0	103.5	† 106.8	110.1	114.7	120.4
GDP Deflator (2000=100)...............	**99bip**	71.7	79.9	85.6	90.9	94.5	95.3	100.0	101.9	104.3	111.4	124.4	131.0
						Millions: Midyear Estimates							
Population...............................	**99z**	60.10	61.22	62.38	63.56	64.77	66.02	67.29	68.58	69.91	71.27	72.64	74.03

		1994	1995	1996	1997	1998	1999	2000	2001	2002	2003	2004	2005
Exchange Rates						*Colones per SDR: End of Period (aa) Colones per US Dollar: End of Period (ae)*							
Market Rate	aa	12.774	13.014	12.589	11.813	12.327	12.016	11.407	10.996	11.896	13.002	13.589	12.506
Market Rate	ae	8.750	8.755	8.755	8.755	8.755	8.755	8.750	8.750	8.750	8.750	8.750	8.750
Fund Position						*Millions of SDRs: End of Period*							
Quota	2f.s	125.6	125.6	125.6	125.6	125.6	171.3	171.3	171.3	171.3	171.3	171.3	171.3
SDRs	1b.s	.1	25.0	25.0	25.0	25.0	25.0	25.0	25.0	25.0	25.0	25.0	25.0
Reserve Position in the Fund	1c.s	—	—	—	—	—	—	—	—	—	—	—	—
Total Fund Cred.&Loans Outstg	2tl	—	—	—	—	—	—	—	—	—	—	—	—
International Liquidity						*Millions of US Dollars Unless Otherwise Indicated: End of Period*							
Total Reserves minus Gold	1l.d	649.4	758.3	936.9	1,307.9	1,613.1	1,819.8	1,772.6	1,593.7	1,472.8	1,792.3	1,754.0	1,722.8
SDRs	1b.d	.1	37.1	35.9	33.7	35.2	34.3	32.6	31.4	34.0	37.1	38.8	35.7
Reserve Position in the Fund	1c.d	—	—	—	—	—	—	—	—	—	—	—	—
Foreign Exchange	1d.d	649.3	721.2	901.0	1,274.2	1,577.9	1,785.5	1,740.0	1,562.3	1,438.9	1,755.2	1,715.2	1,687.1
Gold (Million Fine Troy Ounces)	1ad	.469	.469	.469	.469	.469	.469	.469	.469	.469	.469	.419	.326
Gold (National Valuation)	1and	179.8	181.5	173.2	152.5	152.5	152.4	120.7	117.8	117.8	117.8	138.9	110.2
Monetary Authorities: Other Liab	4..d	158.6	175.6	217.9	244.4	169.5	166.5	190.9	159.5	130.8	299.0	226.4	221.0
Banking Institutions: Assets	7a.d	59.6	69.9	106.2	113.4	121.3	125.3	280.0	793.8	867.0	975.9	1,102.1	1,260.9
Liabilities	7b.d	142.3	361.7	404.6	534.9	514.4	549.7	671.2	949.9	1,085.1	1,573.5	1,784.4	1,786.7
Nonbank Financial Insts.:Assets	7e.d	....	....	....	....	....	....	2.1	27.3	43.7	86.2	170.1	144.9
Liabs	7f.d	....	....	....	....	....	....	60.0	73.1	91.1	153.7	201.0	223.3
Monetary Authorities						*Millions of US Dollars: End of Period*							
Foreign Assets	11	854.1	937.9	1,110.3	1,452.9	1,776.8	1,971.2	† 1,992.6	1,810.7	1,689.8	2,007.5	1,989.6	1,929.7
Claims on Central Government	12a	721.6	708.2	663.9	649.7	614.9	637.2	† 678.6	692.4	708.8	708.7	712.9	712.3
Claims on Local Government	12b	1.3	1.3	1.2	1.1	.9	.8	† .7	.6	.5	.3	.2	.1
Claims on Nonfin.Pub.Enterprises	12c	—	—	—	—	—	—	† —	—	—	—	—	—
Claims on Private Sector	12d	—	—	—	—	—	—	† 5.9	5.9	13.7	13.7	13.7	13.7
Claims on Banking Institutions	12e	262.0	340.3	401.0	421.1	476.0	518.7	† 119.8	105.5	88.0	87.1	1.9	1.4
Claims on Nonbank Financial Insts	12g	—	—	—	—	—	—	† 698.2	658.2	625.8	588.8	593.9	551.4
Reserve Money	14	1,229.9	1,382.2	1,520.6	1,722.9	1,866.3	2,056.4	† 1,318.3	932.9	723.9	1,105.4	887.4	922.1
of which: Currency Outside Banks	14a	339.4	357.6	355.0	369.7	403.0	538.4	† 451.5	220.2	60.6	36.4	35.4	34.2
Time, Savings,& Fgn.Currency Dep	15	96.1	101.3	37.4	8.4	6.4	2.9	† 5.2	20.1	25.5	31.7	38.7	45.7
Liabs. of Central Bank: Securities	16ac	324.1	210.7	294.8	427.3	478.9	596.2	† 1,155.4	1,327.6	1,287.9	1,223.2	1,314.5	1,257.7
Restricted Deposits	16b		.1					† .8	.8	.8	.8	3.2	3.0
Foreign Liabilities	16c	158.6	175.6	217.9	244.4	169.5	166.5	† 190.9	159.5	130.8	299.0	226.4	221.0
Central Government Deposits	16d	235.7	204.0	140.3	141.1	469.6	529.3	† 634.2	613.5	691.0	467.5	531.8	452.6
Capital Accounts	17a	255.5	227.2	226.0	230.8	249.4	266.3	† 249.7	172.7	185.3	188.0	222.0	215.8
Other Items (Net)	17r	−461.1	−313.5	−260.0	−250.2	−371.4	−489.6	† −58.8	46.2	81.4	90.4	88.4	90.6
Banking Institutions						*Millions of US Dollars: End of Period*							
Reserves	20	858.9	967.1	1,094.6	1,222.4	1,337.9	1,464.9	† 782.2	712.2	660.2	987.7	840.4	873.7
Claims on Mon.Author.:Securities	20c	182.8	137.8	106.3	138.4	61.7	357.3	† 627.9	984.4	1,063.2	936.0	974.9	822.7
Foreign Assets	21	59.6	69.9	106.2	113.4	121.3	125.3	† 280.0	793.8	867.0	975.9	1,102.1	1,260.9
Claims on Central Government	22a	157.3	157.0	170.4	144.0	90.3	128.3	† 364.8	590.4	409.2	454.6	572.6	520.9
Claims on Local Government	22b				1.9	2.8	8.0	† —					
Claims on Private Sector	22d	2,634.0	3,378.7	3,828.7	4,520.6	5,039.4	5,475.9	† 5,857.3	5,456.3	5,639.5	6,115.1	6,393.4	7,014.1
Claims on Nonbank Financial Insts	22g	—	—	—	—	—	—	† 151.6	350.0	380.5	341.6	307.3	291.7
Demand Deposits	24	404.4	449.3	570.6	562.1	601.7	618.7	† 630.2	977.7	1,027.1	1,085.6	1,218.8	1,319.0
Time, Savings,& Fgn.Currency Dep	25	2,723.2	3,078.6	3,577.8	4,080.8	4,459.0	4,791.7	† 4,976.7	5,082.5	4,990.4	5,013.8	5,052.0	5,114.5
Money Market Instruments	26aa	20.6	65.0	127.4	187.6	191.6	241.3	† 327.4	322.6	339.8	415.9	462.1	627.0
Foreign Liabilities	26c	142.3	361.7	404.6	534.9	514.4	549.7	† 671.2	949.9	1,085.1	1,573.5	1,784.4	1,786.7
Central Government Deposits	26d	138.0	205.9	215.3	242.7	324.0	303.3	† 335.5	416.5	457.8	479.2	494.4	452.0
Credit from Monetary Authorities	26g	2.0	—	—	26.9	81.2	148.1	† 92.5	106.1	87.6	86.9	1.2	1.3
Liab. to Nonbank Financial Insts	26j	77.1	79.3	88.7	138.0	129.2	80.8	† 473.0	414.3	353.8	313.0	318.9	315.5
Capital Accounts	27a	272.3	345.8	445.4	489.1	570.5	609.0	† 640.4	694.2	762.5	836.6	920.5	1,012.8
Other Items (Net)	27r	112.6	124.6	−123.6	−121.4	−218.1	217.2	† −83.0	−76.6	−84.7	6.3	−61.6	155.3
Banking Survey						*Millions of US Dollars: End of Period*							
Foreign Assets (Net)	31n	612.8	470.5	594.0	786.9	1,214.2	1,380.3	† 1,410.5	1,495.1	1,340.9	1,111.0	1,081.0	1,182.9
Domestic Credit	32	3,140.4	3,835.2	4,308.6	4,933.5	4,954.8	5,422.3	† 6,787.5	6,723.8	6,629.1	7,276.0	7,567.9	8,199.7
Claims on Central Govt. (Net)	32an	505.1	455.3	478.7	409.9	−88.4	−67.1	† 73.7	252.8	−30.9	216.5	259.4	328.7
Claims on Local Government	32b	1.3	1.3	1.2	3.0	3.8	8.8	† .7	.6	.5	.3	.2	.1
Claims on Nonfin.Pub.Enterprises	32c						4.7	† —					
Claims on Private Sector	32d	2,634.0	3,378.7	3,828.7	4,520.6	5,039.4	5,475.9	† 5,863.2	5,462.2	5,653.1	6,128.8	6,407.1	7,027.8
Claims on Nonbank Financial Insts	32g	—	—	—	—	—	—	† 849.8	1,008.2	1,006.4	930.3	901.2	843.1
Money	34	746.5	812.0	927.7	933.1	1,007.7	1,160.2	† 1,093.0	1,198.1	1,090.4	1,198.6	1,255.8	1,356.1
Quasi-Money	35	2,819.3	3,180.0	3,615.1	4,089.2	4,465.4	4,794.6	† 4,981.9	5,102.6	5,015.9	5,045.6	5,090.7	5,160.2
Money Market Instruments	36aa	20.6	65.0	127.4	187.6	191.6	241.3	† 327.4	322.6	339.8	415.9	462.1	627.0
Liabs. of Central Bank: Securities	36ac	141.4	72.9	188.5	288.9	417.2	238.8	† 527.6	343.2	224.7	287.3	339.6	435.0
Restricted Deposits	36b		.1	—	—	—	—	† .8	.8	.8	.8	3.2	3.0
Liab. to Nonbank Financial Insts	36j	77.1	79.3	88.7	138.0	129.2	80.8	† 473.0	414.3	353.8	313.0	318.9	315.5
Capital Accounts	37a	527.8	573.0	671.5	719.9	819.9	875.2	† 890.1	866.9	947.8	1,024.6	1,142.5	1,228.6
Other Items (Net)	37r	−579.6	−476.5	−716.3	−636.3	−862.0	−588.4	† −95.8	−29.6	−3.4	101.1	36.1	257.2
Money plus Quasi-Money	35l	3,565.8	3,991.9	4,542.9	5,022.3	5,473.1	5,954.9	† 6,074.9	6,300.6	6,106.4	6,244.2	6,346.5	6,516.3
Nonbank Financial Institutions						*Millions of US Dollars: End of Period*							
Reserves	40	....	....	....	....	....	....	8.3		2.6	68.5	1.3	.3
Claims on Mon.Author.:Securities	40c	....	....	....	....	....	....	148.9	133.0	158.8	133.0	157.6	164.4
Foreign Assets	41	....	....	....	....	....	....	2.1	27.3	43.7	86.2	170.1	144.9
Claims on Banking Institutions	42e	....	....	....	....	....	....	354.6	369.1	304.3	243.2	225.3	236.2
Bonds	46ab	....	....	....	....	....	....						1.4
Foreign Liabilities	46c	....	....	....	....	....	....	60.0	73.1	91.1	153.7	201.0	223.3
Central Government Deposits	46d	....	....	....	....	....	....						.2
Credit from Monetary Authorities	46g	....	....	....	....	....	....	451.5	419.4	388.3	357.5	326.2	298.0
Capital Accounts	47a	....	....	....	....	....	....	31.3	35.9	43.8	47.8	53.2	55.9
Other Items (Net)	47r	....	....	....	....	....	....	−29.0	1.1	−13.8	−28.0	−26.1	−33.1

El Salvador 253

		1994	1995	1996	1997	1998	1999	2000	2001	2002	2003	2004	2005
Interest Rates							*Percent Per Annum*						
Money Market Rate	60b	....	....	....	10.43	9.43	10.68	6.93	5.28	4.40	3.86	4.36	5.18
Deposit Rate	60l	13.57	14.37	13.98	11.77	10.32	10.75	9.31	....	....	....	....	....
Deposit Rate (Fgn. Currency)	60l.f	....	....	8.38	7.68	6.86	6.61	6.50	5.48	3.41	3.37	3.34	3.44
Lending Rate	60p	19.03	19.08	18.57	16.05	14.98	15.46	13.96	....	....	....	....	....
Lending Rate (Fgn. Currency)	60p.f	....	....	12.53	10.82	9.93	10.38	10.74	9.60	7.14	6.56	6.30	6.87
Prices and Labor						*Index Numbers (2000=100): Period Averages*							
Producer Prices	63	....	....	....	....	....	93.9	100.0	101.0	99.0	101.9	108.8	117.9
Wholesale Prices	63a	89.1	98.4	103.1	104.2	97.9	96.5	100.0	98.1	94.0	96.2	101.7	108.3
Consumer Prices	64	75.2	82.7	90.8	94.9	97.3	97.8	100.0	103.8	105.7	107.9	112.7	118.0
						Number in Thousands: Period Averages							
Labor Force	67d	2,010	2,136	2,227	2,256	2,403	2,445	....	....	2,573	2,707	2,710	....
Employment	67e	1,951	1,973	2,056	2,076	2,227	2,275	2,323	2,451	2,413	2,520	2,526	....
Unemployment	67c	162	163	171	180	176	170	174	183	160	187	184	....
Unemployment Rate (%)	67r	7.7	7.7	7.7	8.0	7.3	7.0	7.0	7.0	6.2	6.9	....	....
Intl. Transactions & Positions							*Millions of US Dollars*						
Exports	70..d	843.9	998.0	1,024.4	1,371.1	1,256.4	1,176.6	1,332.3	1,213.1	1,237.6	1,255.0	1,381.5	1,572.1
Imports, c.i.f.	71..d	2,248.7	2,853.3	2,670.9	2,980.5	3,121.4	3,140.0	3,794.9	3,866.2	3,901.9	4,375.0	4,870.8	5,362.5
Balance of Payments						*Millions of US Dollars: Minus Sign Indicates Debit*							
Current Account, n.i.e.	78ald	−18.0	−261.6	−169.0	−97.8	−90.7	−239.3	−430.5	−150.3	−405.2	−764.1	−611.5	....
Goods: Exports f.o.b.	78aad	1,252.3	1,651.1	1,787.4	2,437.1	2,459.5	2,534.3	2,963.2	2,891.6	3,019.7	3,152.6	3,329.6	....
Goods: Imports f.o.b.	78abd	−2,422.3	−3,113.5	−3,029.7	−3,580.3	−3,765.2	−3,890.4	−4,702.8	−4,824.1	−4,884.7	−5,428.0	−5,948.8	....
Trade Balance	78acd	−1,170.0	−1,462.3	−1,242.3	−1,143.2	−1,305.7	−1,356.1	−1,739.6	−1,932.5	−1,865.0	−2,275.4	−2,619.1	....
Services: Credit	78add	387.2	388.6	414.4	475.8	588.5	640.4	698.4	703.6	783.3	853.4	971.6	....
Services: Debit	78aed	−428.9	−509.8	−504.6	−628.0	−737.3	−822.9	−933.3	−954.0	−1,023.0	−1,033.4	−1,080.4	....
Balance on Goods & Services	78afd	−1,211.7	−1,583.5	−1,332.5	−1,295.4	−1,454.5	−1,538.6	−1,974.5	−2,182.9	−2,104.7	−2,455.4	−2,727.9	....
Income: Credit	78agd	35.5	54.0	44.1	75.1	111.4	112.9	141.3	168.9	159.1	140.4	144.1	....
Income: Debit	78ahd	−130.1	−120.7	−134.4	−238.3	−274.4	−395.1	−394.4	−434.6	−482.5	−563.3	−603.5	....
Balance on Gds, Serv. & Inc.	78aid	−1,306.4	−1,650.2	−1,422.8	−1,458.6	−1,617.5	−1,820.8	−2,227.6	−2,448.6	−2,428.1	−2,878.3	−3,187.3	....
Current Transfers, n.i.e.: Credit	78ajd	1,290.9	1,393.2	1,258.6	1,363.6	1,534.1	1,590.5	1,830.3	2,373.5	2,111.1	2,200.2	2,634.4	....
Current Transfers: Debit	78akd	−2.5	−4.6	−4.8	−2.7	−7.3	−9.0	−33.2	−75.2	−88.2	−85.9	−58.6	....
Capital Account, n.i.e.	78bcd	—	—	—	11.6	28.6	78.6	109.0	198.9	208.9	112.9	99.7	....
Capital Account, n.i.e.: Credit	78bad	—	—	—	11.6	28.9	78.8	109.4	199.3	209.4	113.4	100.5	....
Capital Account: Debit	78bbd	—	—	....	—	−.3	−.2	−.4	−.4	−.5	−.5	−.8	....
Financial Account, n.i.e.	78bjd	115.8	438.3	358.1	653.2	1,034.3	574.5	287.5	230.3	688.0	1,239.8	426.4	....
Direct Investment Abroad	78bdd	—	—	−2.4	—	−1.0	−53.8	5.0	9.7	25.7	−18.6	−7.4	....
Dir. Invest. in Rep. Econ., n.i.e.	78bed	—	38.0	−4.8	59.0	1,103.7	215.9	173.4	278.9	470.0	172.3	465.9	....
Portfolio Investment Assets	78bfd	—	—	.5	—	—	−1.7	−8.9	−126.5	−289.2	−263.7	−124.8	....
Equity Securities	78bkd	—	—	.5	—	—	—	—	—	—	—	—	....
Debt Securities	78bld	—	—	....	—	—	−1.7	−8.9	−126.5	−289.2	−263.7	−124.8	....
Portfolio Investment Liab., n.i.e.	78bgd	—	68.5	150.0	115.9	−226.4	75.2	−16.8	155.5	554.8	452.9	424.8	....
Equity Securities	78bmd	—	....	....	—	—	—	—	2.4	−2.4	—	—	....
Debt Securities	78bnd	—	68.5	150.0	115.9	−226.4	75.2	−16.8	153.1	557.2	452.9	424.8	....
Financial Derivatives Assets	78bwd	....	....	....	....	....	....	....	....	....	....	....	....
Financial Derivatives Liabilities	78bxd	....	....	....	....	....	....	....	....	....	....	....	....
Other Investment Assets	78bhd	−8.7	24.2	4.7	−19.9	12.2	−126.9	−245.2	−629.1	−223.7	8.0	−153.0	....
Monetary Authorities	78bod	—	35.0	—	—	—	—	—	—	—	—	—	....
General Government	78bpd	—	—	—	—	—	—	—	—	—	—	—	....
Banks	78bqd	−8.7	−10.2	—	2.1	−8.0	−4.6	−146.4	−391.3	−83.1	133.7	−19.7	....
Other Sectors	78brd	—	−.6	4.7	−21.9	20.2	−122.3	−98.8	−237.8	−140.6	−125.7	−133.3	....
Other Investment Liab., n.i.e.	78bid	124.5	307.5	210.2	498.2	145.7	465.8	380.0	541.8	150.4	888.9	−179.1	....
Monetary Authorities	78bsd	−147.2	38.2	51.2	27.9	−72.2	−2.1	−19.5	−30.8	−27.7	76.7	−40.8	....
General Government	78btd	177.0	46.4	162.8	154.6	162.9	51.4	83.3	201.0	217.6	33.2	−144.8	....
Banks	78bud	94.7	219.9	−3.2	130.8	−20.4	35.0	120.0	278.3	139.2	491.5	214.0	....
Other Sectors	78bvd	—	3.1	−.6	184.9	75.5	381.5	196.2	93.3	−178.7	287.5	−207.5	....
Net Errors and Omissions	78cad	15.4	−28.4	−24.2	−204.4	−668.9	−206.0	−11.5	−456.6	−615.2	−272.4	45.4	....
Overall Balance	78cbd	113.3	148.3	164.8	362.7	303.3	207.8	−45.5	−177.7	−123.5	316.2	−40.0	....
Reserves and Related Items	79dad	−113.3	−148.3	−164.8	−362.7	−303.3	−207.8	45.5	177.7	123.5	−316.2	40.0	....
Reserve Assets	79dbd	−113.3	−148.3	−164.8	−362.7	−303.3	−207.8	45.5	177.7	123.5	−316.2	40.0	....
Use of Fund Credit and Loans	79dcd	—	—	—	—	—	—	—	—	—	—	—	....
Exceptional Financing	79ded	—	—	—	—	—	—	—	—	—	—	—	....

2006, International Monetary Fund : *International Financial Statistics Yearbook*

		1994	1995	1996	1997	1998	1999	2000	2001	2002	2003	2004	2005
International Investment Position							*Millions of US Dollars*						
Assets	79aad	....	....	1,771.3	2,153.8	2,445.6	2,832.4	3,004.0	3,329.7	3,880.5	4,473.1	4,750.6	....
Direct Investment Abroad	79abd	—	—	55.7	55.7	56.7	110.5	103.9	64.3	34.0	146.4	97.0	....
Portfolio Investment	79acd	—	—	—	—	—	2.1	11.0	152.5	595.8	859.7	1,057.7	....
Equity Securities	79add	....	....	—	—	—	—	—	17.8	260.1	260.4	257.9	....
Debt Securities	79aed	....	....	—	—	—	2.1	11.0	134.7	335.7	599.3	799.8	....
Financial Derivatives	79ald	....	....	—	—	—	—	—	—	—	—	—	....
Other Investment	79afd	59.9	70.1	615.9	635.8	623.5	747.5	995.8	1,401.3	1,659.3	1,556.9	1,703.1	....
Monetary Authorities	79agd	....	....	—	—	—	—	—	—	—	—	—	....
General Government	79ahd	....	....	22.0	22.0	22.0	22.0	22.0	—	—	—	—	....
Banks	79aid	....	....	115.8	113.8	121.8	123.5	273.1	658.5	738.8	601.2	607.9	....
Other Sectors	79ajd	....	....	478.0	500.0	479.7	602.0	700.7	742.8	920.5	955.7	1,095.2	....
Reserve Assets	79akd	812.9	959.6	1,099.7	1,462.3	1,765.4	1,972.3	1,893.2	1,711.6	1,591.4	1,910.1	1,892.9	....
Liabilities	79lad	....	....	4,335.6	4,990.5	6,025.5	6,854.7	7,358.3	8,340.2	9,743.9	11,364.5	11,983.1	....
Dir. Invest. in Rep. Economy	79lbd	—	—	421.2	480.3	1,583.9	1,815.2	2,000.6	2,240.9	3,133.7	3,306.6	3,772.5	....
Portfolio Investment	79lcd	—	—	241.0	357.0	130.5	205.0	202.8	352.6	948.6	1,402.5	1,569.6	....
Equity Securities	79ldd	....	....	—	—	—	—	—	2.4	—	—	—	....
Debt Securities	79led	—	—	241.0	357.0	130.5	205.0	202.8	350.2	948.6	1,402.5	1,569.6	....
Financial Derivatives	79lld	....	....	—	—	—	—	—	—	—	—	—	....
Other Investment	79lfd	2,198.1	2,530.1	3,673.3	4,153.3	4,311.1	4,834.5	5,154.9	5,746.7	5,661.6	6,655.4	6,641.0	....
Monetary Authorities	79lgd	....	....	220.4	237.5	165.4	202.4	181.9	153.6	126.0	202.3	176.2	....
General Government	79lhd	....	....	2,075.8	2,194.9	2,350.1	2,423.2	2,448.3	2,678.0	2,510.7	2,629.0	2,626.4	....
Banks	79lid	....	....	406.2	531.0	516.5	548.3	673.8	950.0	1,104.0	1,596.3	1,810.7	....
Other Sectors	79ljd	....	....	970.9	1,189.9	1,279.1	1,660.6	1,850.9	1,965.1	1,921.0	2,227.8	2,027.7	....
Government Finance							*Millions of Colones: Year Ending December 31*						
Deficit (-) or Surplus	80	† −521.8	−455.2	−1,841.3	−1,102.1	−1,920.9	−2,456.0	−2,658.6	....	....	....	....	....
Total Revenue and Grants	81y	† 9,529.7	11,436.9	12,248.9	12,204.7	13,202.2	12,570.2	13,857.3	....	....	....	....	....
Revenue	81	....	....	....	....	13,104.2	12,471.4	13,030.6	....	....	....	....	....
Grants	81z	....	....	....	....	98.0	98.8	826.7	....	....	....	....	....
Exp. & Lending Minus Repay.	82z	† 10,051.5	11,892.1	14,090.2	13,306.8	15,123.1	15,026.2	16,515.9	....	....	....	....	....
Expenditure	82	† 9,970.9	11,755.7	14,070.3	13,533.6	15,227.1	15,094.3	16,628.1	....	....	....	....	....
Lending Minus Repayments	83	† 80.6	136.4	19.9	−226.8	−104.0	−68.1	−112.2	....	....	....	....	....
Total Financing	80h	† 521.9	455.2	1,841.3	1,102.1	1,920.1	2,456.0	2,658.7	....	....	....	....	....
Domestic	84a	† −844.2	−542.3	−86.2	−553.4	2,159.8	1,296.7	1,300.6	....	....	....	....	....
Foreign	85a	† 1,366.1	997.5	1,927.5	1,655.5	−239.7	1,159.3	1,358.1	....	....	....	....	....
Use of Cash Balances	87	−527.8	−313.6	....	....	....	....	....	....	....	....	....	....
Total Debt by Residence	88	† 21,305.8	22,066.6	23,968.0	24,759.7	24,663.7	27,714.1	30,634.4	....	....	....	....	....
Domestic	88a	† 8,463.0	8,226.3	7,883.7	7,460.9	7,119.9	8,015.2	10,687.0	....	....	....	....	....
Foreign	89a	† 12,842.8	13,840.3	16,084.3	17,298.8	17,543.8	19,698.9	19,947.4	....	....	....	....	....
National Accounts							*Millions of Colones*						
Househ.Cons.Expend.,incl.NPISHs	96f	61,658	72,725	79,765	85,266	89,356	93,740	101,117	107,136	110,374	116,198	125,801	....
Government Consumption Expend	91f	5,942	7,188	8,443	8,847	10,248	10,935	11,696	12,677	13,097	14,112	14,535	....
Gross Fixed Capital Formation	93e	13,067	15,566	14,275	15,672	17,527	17,532	19,471	19,857	20,596	21,794	21,538	....
Changes in Inventories	93i	865	1,107	−559	−936	927	394	−8	292	−324	—	—	....
Exports of Goods and Services	90c	14,126	17,997	19,034	25,243	26,062	27,213	31,508	31,220	33,014	34,882	37,715	....
Imports of Goods and Services (-)	98c	24,909	31,406	30,644	36,607	38,987	40,685	48,794	50,320	51,527	56,258	61,131	....
Gross Domestic Product (GDP)	99b	70,749	83,177	90,313	97,484	105,134	109,128	114,989	120,862	125,230	130,728	138,459	....
Net Primary Income from Abroad	98.n	−804	−839	−1,063	−1,430	−1,427	−2,470	−2,216	−2,325	−2,830	−3,567	−4,354	....
Gross National Income (GNI)	99a	69,936	82,328	89,241	96,045	103,698	106,649	112,765	118,528	122,391	127,151	134,096	....
GDP Volume 1990 Prices	99b.p	53,151	56,721	57,688	60,138	62,393	64,545	65,934	67,023	68,517	69,759	70,835	....
GDP Volume (2000=100)	99bvp	80.6	86.0	87.5	91.2	94.6	97.9	100.0	101.7	103.9	105.8	107.4	....
GDP Deflator (2000=100)	99bip	76.3	84.1	89.8	92.9	96.6	96.9	100.0	103.4	104.8	107.5	112.1	....
							Millions: Midyear Estimates						
Population	99z	5.55	5.67	5.79	5.91	6.04	6.16	6.28	6.40	6.52	6.64	6.76	6.88

Equatorial Guinea 642

		1994	1995	1996	1997	1998	1999	2000	2001	2002	2003	2004	2005
Exchange Rates					*Francs per SDR: End of Period*								
Official Rate	aa	† 780.44	728.38	753.06	807.94	791.61	† 896.19	918.49	935.39	850.37	771.76	747.90	794.73
					Francs per US Dollar: End of Period(ae)Period Average(rf)								
Official Rate	ae	† 534.60	490.00	523.70	598.81	562.21	† 652.95	704.95	744.31	625.50	519.36	481.58	556.04
Official Rate	rf	† 555.20	499.15	511.55	583.67	589.95	† 615.70	711.98	733.04	696.99	581.20	528.28	527.47
					Index Numbers (2000=100): Period Averages								
Nominal Effective Exchange Rate	nec	120.07	125.64	123.85	113.50	113.48	109.85	100.00	99.03	102.29	113.96	119.82	119.64
Real Effective Exchange Rate	rec	97.05	115.61	115.06	106.23	112.84	107.76	100.00	105.12	114.93	134.40	143.81	149.87
Fund Position					*Millions of SDRs: End of Period*								
Quota	2f.s	24.30	24.30	24.30	24.30	24.30	32.60	32.60	32.60	32.60	32.60	32.60	32.60
SDRs	1b.s	.01	.01	.01	—	.01	—	.09	.79	.44	.03	.44	.44
Reserve Position in the Fund	1c.s	—	—	—	—	—	—	—	—	—	—	—	—
Total Fund Cred.&Loans Outstg.	2tl	13.43	12.70	11.93	9.75	7.64	5.80	3.77	1.75	.83	.18	—	—
International Liquidity					*Millions of US Dollars Unless Otherwise Indicated: End of Period*								
Total Reserves minus Gold	1l.d	.39	.04	.52	4.93	.80	3.35	23.01	70.85	88.54	237.69	944.98	2,102.49
SDRs	1b.d	.02	.01	.01	—	.01	—	.12	.99	.60	.04	.68	.63
Reserve Position in the Fund	1c.d	—	—	—	—	—	—	—	—	—	—	—	—
Foreign Exchange	1d.d	.37	.03	.51	4.93	.79	3.35	22.89	69.86	87.94	237.65	944.30	2,101.49
Monetary Authorities: Other Liab.	4..d	9.16	2.97	.12	.11	4.80	7.46	7.52	6.94	7.53	10.19	10.01	8.71
Deposit Money Banks: Assets	7a.d	5.78	5.08	4.92	2.38	18.07	39.45	27.51	41.56	106.01	73.28	110.02	153.60
Liabilities	7b.d	2.67	3.56	1.96	6.18	5.22	19.31	21.88	18.71	4.73	7.65	15.54	
Monetary Authorities					*Billions of Francs: End of Period*								
Foreign Assets	11	.21	.02	.27	2.95	.45	2.19	16.22	52.74	55.38	123.45	455.08	1,169.07
Claims on Central Government	12a	17.84	17.42	17.33	15.86	14.03	20.90	14.24	3.90	2.50	1.44	.79	.27
Claims on Deposit Money Banks	12e	—	—	—	—	—	—	—	—	—	—	—	—
Claims on Other Banking Insts.	12f	—	—	—	—	—	—	—	—	—	—	—	—
Reserve Money	14	4.38	8.72	9.99	10.97	8.79	17.17	25.57	47.45	49.61	120.29	150.53	267.75
of which: Currency Outside DMBs..	14a	3.77	6.78	8.50	6.59	5.79	12.06	15.20	17.63	25.95	35.12	45.73	57.66
Foreign Liabilities	16c	15.38	10.70	9.05	7.94	8.74	10.07	8.77	6.80	5.42	5.43	4.82	4.84
Central Government Deposits	16d	.06	.07	.08	.48	1.08	1.19	1.92	7.44	6.61	4.03	303.16	899.44
Capital Accounts	17a	4.82	4.53	4.63	4.95	4.83	5.56	5.91	6.22	5.90	5.56	5.33	5.62
Other Items (Net)	17r	−6.58	−6.58	−6.15	−5.54	−8.96	−10.90	−11.71	−11.26	−9.66	−10.42	−7.97	−8.33
Deposit Money Banks					*Billions of Francs: End of Period*								
Reserves	20	.62	1.95	1.49	4.38	3.00	5.11	10.37	29.02	22.86	84.37	104.71	209.97
Foreign Assets	21	3.09	2.49	2.57	1.43	10.16	25.76	19.39	30.93	66.31	38.06	52.98	85.41
Claims on Central Government	22a	.23	.25	.51	1.63	.94	† .46	1.89	.30	4.14	2.09	5.79	3.53
Claims on Nonfin.Pub.Enterprises	22c	.72	.72	.96	.80	.72	.03	—	.40	1.45	.86	.76	1.44
Claims on Private Sector	22d	2.25	3.40	6.20	12.02	14.13	21.29	27.06	36.49	52.77	50.76	62.08	92.39
Claims on Other Banking Insts.	22f	—	—	—	—	—	—	—	—	—	—	—	—
Claims on Nonbank Financial Insts.	22g	—	—	—	—	—	—	—	—	—	—	—	—
Demand Deposits	24	2.24	2.73	5.78	7.07	9.19	16.39	23.14	29.88	46.52	78.53	124.71	176.45
Time and Savings Deposits	25	1.76	2.05	2.23	4.38	5.86	6.72	9.58	16.42	25.81	40.79	36.65	44.82
Foreign Liabilities	26c	1.24	1.60	.92	3.67	2.94	12.61	9.90	15.97	11.56	2.46	3.64	8.64
Long-Term Foreign Liabilities	26cl	.19	.14	.11	.03	—	—	.55	.31	.15	—	.05	—
Central Government Deposits	26d	.46	.88	1.86	3.10	6.12	† 10.76	6.49	24.82	50.83	33.85	35.42	131.80
Credit from Monetary Authorities	26g	—	—	—	—	—	—	—	—	—	—	—	—
Capital Accounts	27a	1.36	2.30	1.26	3.02	5.26	6.67	7.69	13.44	16.02	21.43	29.50	35.55
Other Items (Net)	27r	−.33	−.91	−.43	−1.03	−.42	−.50	1.37	−3.70	−3.36	−.92	−3.64	−4.52
Monetary Survey					*Billions of Francs: End of Period*								
Foreign Assets (Net)	31n	−13.51	−9.94	−7.23	−7.26	−1.07	5.27	16.40	60.58	104.57	153.62	499.56	1,240.99
Domestic Credit	32	20.52	20.83	23.05	26.72	22.66	30.73	34.78	8.84	3.41	17.27	−269.17	−933.62
Claims on Central Govt. (Net)	32an	17.55	16.72	15.90	13.90	7.78	9.41	7.72	−28.05	−50.81	−34.35	−332.01	−1,027.45
Claims on Nonfin.Pub.Enterprises	32c	.72	.72	.96	.80	.72	.03	—	.40	1.45	.86	.76	1.44
Claims on Private Sector	32d	2.25	3.40	6.20	12.02	14.13	21.29	27.06	36.49	52.77	50.76	62.08	92.39
Claims on Other Banking Insts.	32f	—	—	—	—	—	—	—	—	—	—	—	—
Claims on Nonbank Financial Inst..	32g	—	—	—	—	.03	—	—	—	—	—	—	—
Money	34	6.01	9.51	14.28	13.66	14.99	28.45	38.33	48.31	73.28	114.45	170.53	234.23
Quasi-Money	35	1.76	2.05	2.23	4.38	5.86	6.72	9.58	16.42	25.81	40.79	36.65	44.82
Other Items (Net)	37r	−.73	−.66	−.68	1.59	.75	.84	3.27	4.69	8.90	15.65	23.21	28.32
Money plus Quasi-Money	35l	7.76	11.56	16.51	18.04	20.85	35.16	47.91	64.73	99.08	155.24	207.18	279.05
Interest Rates					*Percent Per Annum*								
Discount Rate (End of Period)	60	† 7.75	8.60	7.75	7.50	7.00	7.60	7.00	6.50	6.30	6.00	6.00	5.50
Deposit Rate	60l	8.08	5.50	5.46	5.00	5.00	5.00	5.00	5.00	5.00	5.00	5.00	4.92
Lending Rate	60p	17.50	16.00	22.00	22.00	22.00	22.00	22.00	20.67	18.00	18.00	18.00	17.67
Prices					*Index Numbers (1990=100): Period Averages*								
Consumer Prices	64	68.2	81.8	85.5	88.1	95.1	95.4	100.0	108.8	117.1	125.7	131.0	....
Intl. Transactions & Positions					*Millions of Francs*								
Exports	70	34,420	42,683	89,682	289,204	258,989	436,531	781,038	1,344,393	1,475,524	1,627,942	2,480,297	3,665,904
Imports, c.i.f.	71	20,514	24,897	149,384	192,800	187,015	261,672	321,101	595,960	353,373	711,389	813,559	1,081,310

Equatorial Guinea   642

		1994	1995	1996	1997	1998	1999	2000	2001	2002	2003	2004	2005
Balance of Payments					*Millions of US Dollars: Minus Sign Indicates Debit*								
Current Account, n.i.e.	78ald	−.38	−123.40	−344.04	....	....	....	....	....	....	....	....	....
Goods: Exports f.o.b.	78aad	62.00	89.93	175.31	....	....	....	....	....	....	....	....	....
Goods: Imports f.o.b.	78abd	−36.95	−120.57	−292.04	....	....	....	....	....	....	....	....	....
Trade Balance	78acd	25.05	−30.64	−116.73	....	....	....	....	....	....	....	....	....
Services: Credit	78add	3.36	4.18	4.88	....	....	....	....	....	....	....	....	....
Services: Debit	78aed	−23.82	−75.54	−184.58	....	....	....	....	....	....	....	....	....
Balance on Goods & Services	78afd	4.59	−102.00	−296.43	....	....	....	....	....	....	....	....	....
Income: Credit	78agd	—	.10	.16	....	....	....	....	....	....	....	....	....
Income: Debit	78ahd	−8.75	−25.03	−45.18	....	....	....	....	....	....	....	....	....
Balance on Gds, Serv. & Inc	78aid	−4.16	−126.93	−341.44	....	....	....	....	....	....	....	....	....
Current Transfers, n.i.e.: Credit	78ajd	5.67	6.83	4.03	....	....	....	....	....	....	....	....	....
Current Transfers: Debit	78akd	−1.89	−3.30	−6.62	....	....	....	....	....	....	....	....	....
Capital Account, n.i.e.	78bcd	—	—	—	....	....	....	....	....	....	....	....	....
Capital Account, n.i.e.: Credit	78bad	—	—	—	....	....	....	....	....	....	....	....	....
Capital Account: Debit	78bbd	....	....	....	....	....	....	....	....	....	....	....	....
Financial Account, n.i.e.	78bjd	−15.04	101.56	313.75	....	....	....	....	....	....	....	....	....
Direct Investment Abroad	78bdd				....	....	....	....	....	....	....	....	....
Dir. Invest. in Rep. Econ., n.i.e.	78bed	17.00	126.92	376.18	....	....	....	....	....	....	....	....	....
Portfolio Investment Assets	78bfd	—	—	—	....	....	....	....	....	....	....	....	....
Equity Securities	78bkd	—	—	—	....	....	....	....	....	....	....	....	....
Debt Securities	78bld	—	—	—	....	....	....	....	....	....	....	....	....
Portfolio Investment Liab., n.i.e.	78bgd	—	—	—	....	....	....	....	....	....	....	....	....
Equity Securities	78bmd	—	—	—	....	....	....	....	....	....	....	....	....
Debt Securities	78bnd	—	—	—	....	....	....	....	....	....	....	....	....
Financial Derivatives Assets	78bwd	....	....	....	....	....	....	....	....	....	....	....	....
Financial Derivatives Liabilities	78bxd	....	....	....	....	....	....	....	....	....	....	....	....
Other Investment Assets	78bhd	....	....	....	....	....	....	....	....	....	....	....	....
Monetary Authorities	78bod	....	....	....	....	....	....	....	....	....	....	....	....
General Government	78bpd	—	—	—	....	....	....	....	....	....	....	....	....
Banks	78bqd	—	—	—	....	....	....	....	....	....	....	....	....
Other Sectors	78brd	—	—	—	....	....	....	....	....	....	....	....	....
Other Investment Liab., n.i.e.	78bid	−32.04	−25.36	−62.43	....	....	....	....	....	....	....	....	....
Monetary Authorities	78bsd	—	—	—	....	....	....	....	....	....	....	....	....
General Government	78btd	−7.32	−13.95	−3.84	....	....	....	....	....	....	....	....	....
Banks	78bud	−1.98	1.84	−1.57	....	....	....	....	....	....	....	....	....
Other Sectors	78bvd	−22.73	−13.25	−57.02	....	....	....	....	....	....	....	....	....
Net Errors and Omissions	78cad	−2.93	10.33	24.82	....	....	....	....	....	....	....	....	....
Overall Balance	78cbd	−18.36	−11.52	−5.46	....	....	....	....	....	....	....	....	....
Reserves and Related Items	79dad	18.36	11.52	5.46	....	....	....	....	....	....	....	....	....
Reserve Assets	79dbd	−.92	−8.98	−3.59	....	....	....	....	....	....	....	....	....
Use of Fund Credit and Loans	79dcd	2.08	−1.11	−1.11	....	....	....	....	....	....	....	....	....
Exceptional Financing	79ded	17.20	21.61	10.17	....	....	....	....	....	....	....	....	....
National Accounts						*Millions of Francs*							
Househ.Cons.Expend.,incl.NPISHs.	96f	41,563	46,101	66,778	86,774	118,085	234,477	373,054	484,524	457,900	531,624	827,331	1,184,414
Government Consumption Expend	91f	10,671	13,442	14,855	24,012	29,332	41,221	55,947	56,723	96,679	85,099	119,392	158,947
Gross Fixed Capital Formation	93e	51,745	62,438	157,860	259,558	331,753	448,481	313,569	363,917	1,147,772	842,177	647,920	320,711
Changes in Inventories	93i	−20	−9	−11	−13	....	....						
Exports of Goods and Services	90c	39,109	45,183	102,812	292,909	273,561	419,199	903,284	1,227,766	1,437,580	1,633,818	2,496,558	3,597,196
Imports of Goods and Services (-)	98c	73,276	85,319	212,555	358,426	466,522	721,335	760,576	952,620	1,867,984	1,573,797	1,727,402	1,877,227
Gross Domestic Product (GDP)	99b	69,811	81,850	129,750	304,827	286,209	422,043	885,278	1,180,317	1,271,955	1,518,921	2,363,800	3,384,040
GDP Volume 2000 Prices	99b.p	131,223	134,795	186,527	416,979	496,521	639,034	882,174	1,346,181	1,404,898	1,421,970	1,716,667	1,820,282
GDP Volume (2000=100)	99bvp	14.9	15.3	21.1	47.3	56.3	72.4	100.0	152.6	159.3	161.2	194.6	206.3
GDP Deflator (2000=100)	99bip	53.0	60.5	69.3	72.8	57.4	65.8	100.0	87.4	90.2	106.4	137.2	185.3
						Millions: Midyear Estimates							
Population	99z	.39	.40	.41	.42	.43	.44	.45	.46	.47	.48	.49	.50

Eritrea 643

		1994	1995	1996	1997	1998	1999	2000	2001	2002	2003	2004	2005
Exchange Rates						*Nakfa per SDR: End of Period*							
Official Rate	aa	8.6861	9.3946	9.2403	† 9.6134	10.6967	13.1761	13.2897	17.3397	19.2117	20.4878	21.4121	21.9750
						Nakfa per US Dollar: End of Period (ae) Period Average (rf)							
Official Rate	ae	5.9500	6.3200	6.4260	† 7.1250	7.5969	9.6000	10.2000	13.7975	14.1313	13.7875	13.7875	15.3750
Official Rate	rf	5.4702	6.1642	6.3577	† 6.8373	7.3619	8.1526	9.6250	11.3095	13.9582	13.8779	13.7875	15.3679
Fund Position						*Millions of SDRs: End of Period*							
Quota	2f.s	11.5	11.5	11.5	11.5	11.5	15.9	15.9	15.9	15.9	15.9	15.9	15.9
SDRs	1b.s	—	—	—	—	—	—	—	—	—	—	—	—
Reserve Position in the Fund	1c.s	—	—	—	—	—	—	—	—	—	—	—	—
Total Fund Cred.&Loans Outstg	2tl	—	—	—	—	—	—	—	—	—	—	—	—
International Liquidity						*Millions of US Dollars Unless Otherwise Indicated: End of Period*							
Total Reserves minus Gold	1l.d	....	40.5	81.3	199.4	23.1	34.2	25.5	39.8	30.3	24.7	34.7	27.9
SDRs	1b.d	—	—	—	—	—	—	—	—	—	—	—	—
Reserve Position in the Fund	1c.d	—	—	—	—	—	—	—	—	—	—	—	—
Foreign Exchange	1d.d	....	40.5	81.3	199.4	23.1	34.2	25.5	39.7	30.3	24.7	34.7	27.9
Gold (Million Fine Troy Ounces)	1ad	....	....	....	.104	.157	.085	.039	.039	—	—	—	—
Gold (National Valuation)	1and	....	20.9	27.2	42.6	44.7	19.7	10.4	10.5	—	—	—	—
Monetary Authorities:Other Assets	3..d	....	43.7	36.1	2.5	1.0	1.6	1.5	1.4	1.3	1.9	1.9	1.9
Other Liab	4..d	....	19.0	18.8	16.3	16.3	30.1	33.6	28.9	26.9	44.5	36.8	41.4
Banking Institutions: Assets	7a.d	....	317.9	309.3	50.0	72.6	88.9	89.5	153.3	187.2	227.8	237.3	166.0
Liabilities	7b.d	....	4.4	2.4	2.6	2.2	1.7	13.5	7.1	2.9	3.0	2.6	2.0
Monetary Authorities						*Millions of Nakfa: End of Period*							
Foreign Assets	11	....	664	930	1,742	522	534	383	713	452	366	505	455
Claims on Central Government	12a	....	1,013	1,820	2,009	1,788	3,794	4,155	4,043	5,450	7,232	7,676	8,782
Claims on Private Sector	12d	....	40	60	102	75	95	161	117	188	155	156	224
Claims on Banking Institutions	12e	....	—	100	235	381	371	448	653	887	236	249	194
Reserve Money	14	....	1,340	2,494	4,701	3,065	4,239	4,563	4,407	5,152	5,849	6,210	6,678
of which: Currency Outside Banks	14a	....	—	—	574	825	1,138	1,468	1,868	2,279	2,765	3,253	3,654
Foreign Currency Deposits	15	....	157	157	22	23	77	100	108	48	20	18	20
Foreign Liabilities	16c	....	13	15	13	11	113	139	194	193	310	189	201
Central Government Deposits	16d	....	131	203	401	369	926	604	806	912	991	1,030	1,441
Capital Accounts	17a	....	117	148	213	350	470	796	718	752	844	1,013	1,118
Other Items (Net)	17r	....	−41	−108	−1,261	−1,051	−1,030	−1,056	−707	−80	−23	127	199
Banking Institutions						*Millions of Nakfa: End of Period*							
Reserves	20	....	1,340	2,494	4,049	2,154	2,897	3,055	2,447	2,827	2,973	2,906	2,984
Foreign Assets	21	....	2,009	1,987	356	551	854	913	2,115	2,679	3,141	3,272	2,289
Claims on Central Government	22a	....	—	—	135	2,262	3,207	4,639	5,397	6,076	5,714	7,408	8,919
Claims on State and Local Govts	22b	....	—	—	—	—	—	—	—	—	—	—	—
Claims on Nonfin.Pub.Enterprises	22c	....	461	459	385	265	697	402	349	365	392	492	481
Claims on Private Sector	22d	....	592	1,468	1,639	2,475	1,775	1,823	2,367	2,726	3,372	4,024	4,640
Demand Deposits	24	....	1,135	1,474	1,355	1,456	2,133	2,425	3,081	3,667	4,036	4,491	5,414
Time, Savings,& Fgn.Currency Dep	25	....	1,927	2,264	2,961	3,624	4,641	5,566	7,579	9,316	10,708	11,890	12,691
Foreign Liabilities	26c	....	28	15	19	17	16	138	98	42	41	36	28
Central Government Deposits	26d	....	121	196	244	378	362	372	435	379	435	631	526
Credit from Monetary Authorities	26g	....	—	100	235	362	364	474	760	886	147	147	123
Capital Accounts	27a	....	159	245	169	253	297	353	413	441	844	1,361	2,078
Other Items (Net)	27r	....	1,032	2,114	1,581	1,619	1,614	1,504	308	−59	−618	−454	−1,544
Banking Survey						*Millions of Nakfa: End of Period*							
Foreign Assets (Net)	31n	....	2,632	2,886	2,067	1,046	1,258	1,018	2,536	2,896	3,157	3,552	2,516
Domestic Credit	32	....	1,853	3,407	3,625	6,120	8,304	10,230	11,042	13,514	15,441	18,094	21,227
Claims on Central Govt. (Net)	32an	....	760	1,421	1,499	3,304	5,713	7,818	8,200	10,235	11,521	13,422	15,735
Claims on State and Local Govts	32b	....	—	—	—	—	—	—	—	—	—	—	—
Claims on Nonfin.Pub.Enterprises	32c	....	461	459	385	265	697	402	349	365	392	492	481
Claims on Private Sector	32d	....	632	1,528	1,740	2,551	1,870	1,985	2,483	2,913	3,528	4,180	4,864
Money	34	....	1,135	1,474	2,007	2,367	3,465	3,930	5,035	5,982	6,932	7,806	9,113
Quasi-Money	35	....	2,084	2,422	2,983	3,646	4,718	5,666	7,686	9,364	10,728	11,907	12,711
Capital Accounts	37a	....	276	392	382	604	767	1,149	1,131	1,193	1,688	2,374	3,195
Other Items (Net)	37r	....	991	2,006	321	549	612	502	−275	−129	−750	−440	−1,275
Money plus Quasi-Money	35l	....	3,219	3,896	4,989	6,013	8,184	9,596	12,721	15,347	17,659	19,713	21,823
Money (National Definitions)						*Millions of Nakfa: End of Period*							
Reserve Money	19mb	....	1,340	2,494	4,701	3,065	4,239	4,563	4,407	5,152	5,844	6,210	6,678
M1	59ma	....	1,135	1,474	2,007	2,365	3,348	3,915	5,027	5,982	6,927	7,799	9,102
M2	59mb	....	3,013	3,622	4,693	5,636	7,437	8,712	10,941	13,146	14,841	16,535	18,503

Eritrea 643

2006, International Monetary Fund : *International Financial Statistics Yearbook*

		1994	1995	1996	1997	1998	1999	2000	2001	2002	2003	2004	2005
Balance of Payments						*Millions of US Dollars: Minus Sign Indicates Debit*							
Current Account, n.i.e.	78ald	123.7	−31.6	−59.8	5.1	−292.7	−208.8	−104.7	....	....	....	....	....
Goods: Exports f.o.b.	78aad	78.0	86.0	98.0	56.8	28.1	20.7	36.8					
Goods: Imports f.o.b.	78abd	−488.9	−453.5	−552.8	−525.3	−508.3	−510.2	−471.4					
Trade Balance	78acd	−410.9	−367.5	−454.8	−468.5	−480.2	−489.5	−434.6					
Services: Credit	78add	89.9	48.6	104.9	159.2	81.8	47.6	60.9					
Services: Debit	78aed	−7.7	−44.7	−53.7	−100.3	−187.1	−104.6	−28.4					
Balance on Goods & Services	78afd	−328.7	−363.7	−403.6	−409.6	−585.5	−546.5	−402.0					
Income: Credit	78agd	3.6	7.8	8.3	10.8	11.6	8.5	9.1					
Income: Debit	78ahd	....	....	−15.6	−14.4	−7.3	−2.1	−10.5					
Balance on Gds, Serv. & Inc.	78aid	−325.1	−355.9	−410.9	−413.2	−581.2	−540.2	−403.4					
Current Transfers, n.i.e.: Credit	78ajd	465.3	324.9	354.6	423.5	293.3	346.5	306.1					
Current Transfers: Debit	78akd	−16.5	−.6	−3.5	−5.3	−4.9	−15.1	−7.3					
Capital Account, n.i.e.	78bcd	....	....	....	....	2.7	.6	....					
Capital Account, n.i.e.: Credit	78bad	....	....	....	....	2.7	.6	....					
Capital Account: Debit	78bbd	....	....	....	....	....	....	....					
Financial Account, n.i.e.	78bjd	−7.9	69.2	181.4	255.4	197.0	196.3	63.2					
Direct Investment Abroad	78bdd	....	....	....	....	....	....	....					
Dir. Invest. in Rep. Econ., n.i.e.	78bed	....	....	36.7	41.1	148.5	83.2	27.9					
Portfolio Investment Assets	78bfd	....	....	....	....	....	....	....					
Equity Securities	78bkd	....	....	....	....	....	....	....					
Debt Securities	78bld	....	....	....	....	....	....	....					
Portfolio Investment Liab., n.i.e.	78bgd	....	....	....	....	....	....	....					
Equity Securities	78bmd	....	....	....	....	....	....	....					
Debt Securities	78bnd	....	....	....	....	....	....	....					
Financial Derivatives Assets	78bwd	....	....	....	....	....	....	....					
Financial Derivatives Liabilities	78bxd	....	....	....	....	....	....	....					
Other Investment Assets	78bhd	−39.8	60.8	137.3	184.5	−20.0	−26.2	−25.9					
Monetary Authorities	78bod	....	....	....	....	....	....	....					
General Government	78bpd	....	....	....	....	....	....	....					
Banks	78bqd	−39.8	60.8	137.3	184.5	−15.3	−23.9	−25.1					
Other Sectors	78brd	....	....	....	....	−4.7	−2.4	−.8					
Other Investment Liab., n.i.e.	78bid	31.9	8.4	7.4	29.9	68.5	139.3	61.2					
Monetary Authorities	78bsd	—	—	—	—	—	—	—					
General Government	78btd	32.9	8.4	7.4	29.9	59.3	128.9	52.3					
Banks	78bud	....	....	....	....	10.1	10.4	8.8					
Other Sectors	78bvd	−1.0	—	—	—	−.9	....	—					
Net Errors and Omissions	78cad	−61.5	−40.5	−64.5	−140.4	−66.5	12.8	−22.9					
Overall Balance	78cbd	54.3	−2.9	57.1	120.1	−159.5	.9	−64.3					
Reserves and Related Items	79dad	−54.3	2.9	−57.1	−120.1	159.5	−.9	64.3					
Reserve Assets	79dbd	−54.3	2.9	−57.1	−120.1	159.5	−.9	61.2					
Use of Fund Credit and Loans	79dcd	—	—	—	—	—	—	—					
Exceptional Financing	79ded	....	....	....	....	....	....	3.2					
						Millions: Midyear Estimates							
Population	99z	3.07	3.10	3.15	3.22	3.31	3.43	3.56	3.71	3.88	4.05	4.23	4.40

Estonia 939

		1994	1995	1996	1997	1998	1999	2000	2001	2002	2003	2004	2005
Exchange Rates						*Krooni per SDR: End of Period*							
Official Rate....................	aa	18.088	17.038	17.888	19.343	18.882	21.359	21.915	22.234	20.306	18.440	17.815	18.896
					Krooni per US Dollar: End of Period (ae) Period Average (rf)								
Official Rate....................	ae	12.390	11.462	12.440	14.336	13.410	15.562	16.820	17.692	14.936	12.410	11.471	13.221
Official Rate....................	rf	12.991	11.465	12.038	13.882	14.075	14.678	16.969	17.478	16.612	13.856	12.596	12.584
Fund Position						*Millions of SDRs: End of Period*							
Quota................................	2f.s	46.50	46.50	46.50	46.50	46.50	65.20	65.20	65.20	65.20	65.20	65.20	65.20
SDRs.................................	1b.s	1.09	.20	.12	.01	.05	.99	.01	.03	.05	.05	.05	.05
Reserve Position in the Fund...........	1c.s	.01	.01	.01	.01	.01	.01	.01	.01	.01	.01	.01	.01
Total Fund Cred.&Loans Outstg.......	2tl	41.85	61.81	54.15	40.01	21.31	18.41	14.53	10.66	—	—	—	—
International Liquidity					*Millions of US Dollars Unless Otherwise Indicated: End of Period*								
Total Reserves minus Gold..............	1l.d	443.35	579.91	636.82	757.72	810.60	853.49	920.64	820.24	1,000.42	1,373.36	1,788.23	1,943.21
SDRs...............................	1b.d	1.58	.29	.17	.01	.07	1.36	.02	.03	.07	.08	.08	.08
Reserve Position in the Fund.........	1c.d	.01	.01	.01	.01	.01	.01	.01	.01	.01	.01	.01	.01
Foreign Exchange.................	1d.d	441.76	579.61	636.64	757.70	810.53	852.12	920.62	820.20	1,000.34	1,373.27	1,788.13	1,943.12
Gold (Million Fine Troy Ounces)........	1ad	.0080	.0080	.0080	.0080	.0080	.0080	.0080	.0080	.0080	.0080	.0080	.0080
Gold (National Valuation)...............	1and	3.61	3.19	3.03	2.39	2.37	2.38	2.25	2.29	2.83	3.44	3.61	4.24
Monetary Authorities:Other Liab......	4..d	60.88	65.84	48.52	24.75	1.02	.63	3.29	1.04	7.03	39.11	44.25	3.66
Banks: Assets..............	7a.d	243.80	322.58	320.69	563.45	483.29	563.67	615.88	874.72	1,104.93	1,375.84	2,387.66	3,312.09
Liabilities...........	7b.d	55.98	140.83	337.97	913.11	884.58	879.19	976.66	989.70	1,582.58	2,808.67	5,137.62	6,048.64
Monetary Authorities						*Millions of Krooni: End of Period*							
Foreign Assets...................	11	5,540.6	6,688.0	7,954.2	10,900.8	10,908.7	13,334.3	15,539.2	14,573.2	14,995.0	17,194.7	20,625.9	25,798.7
Claims on Central Government........	12a	—	3.0	48.5	4.1	3.0	3.1	3.4	1.3	.2	.2	—	—
Claims on Nonfin.Pub.Enterprises...	12c	14.8	.8	—	—	—	—	—	—	—	—	—	—
Claims on Private Sector.................	12d	8.2	14.5	44.2	44.1	57.2	66.5	69.5	74.8	78.8	75.4	54.7	46.7
Claims on Banks..................	12e	480.9	194.0	168.0	82.4	280.3	267.3	9.8	8.0	9.0	—	—	31.3
Reserve Money..................	14	4,225.1	5,066.7	6,190.9	8,526.7	9,070.3	11,496.0	13,207.1	11,910.2	11,732.1	13,450.4	16,672.1	22,170.9
of which: Currency Outside Banks..	14a	3,071.3	3,803.6	4,268.5	4,588.5	4,538.6	5,711.3	6,201.3	6,951.9	6,994.9	7,139.7	7,714.2	8,747.1
Foreign Liabilities...................	16c	1,511.2	1,807.7	1,572.3	1,128.8	416.1	403.0	373.8	255.4	104.9	485.3	507.6	48.4
Central Government Deposits.........	16d	.2	.1	.3	355.5	6.4	27.1	7.2	7.8	5.6	5.1	4.9	5.2
Capital Accounts...................	17a	1,256.1	1,223.2	1,325.9	1,881.1	2,276.5	2,141.3	2,424.1	2,889.7	3,377.5	3,512.0	3,692.8	3,869.3
Other Items (Net)...................	17r	−948.0	−1,197.4	−874.7	−860.7	−520.1	−396.2	−390.3	−405.8	−137.1	−182.4	−196.7	−217.0
Banking Institutions						*Millions of Krooni: End of Period*							
Reserves..................	20	1,208.4	1,293.1	1,922.5	3,885.3	4,509.5	5,790.9	6,787.1	4,896.6	4,678.0	6,243.0	8,875.8	13,327.3
Foreign Assets..................	21	3,020.7	3,697.4	3,989.4	8,077.7	6,480.9	8,771.9	10,358.9	15,475.5	16,503.6	17,073.6	27,389.1	43,787.8
Claims on Central Government........	22a	297.0	345.4	614.0	561.1	303.6	404.5	445.4	445.5	480.2	538.1	475.4	482.9
Claims on Local Government...........	22b	108.3	303.9	159.9	547.2	651.5	767.6	822.9	1,296.9	1,959.1	2,311.9	2,380.8	2,408.3
Claims on Nonfin.Pub.Enterprises.....	22c	346.0	334.5	304.6	328.6	225.8	372.5	262.7	141.8	245.0	221.4	651.5	718.7
Claims on Private Sector.................	22d	4,176.0	6,041.3	10,088.3	16,908.5	18,532.4	19,810.4	22,134.0	26,246.5	31,433.7	41,693.3	59,943.0	98,905.1
Claims on Nonbank Financial Insts....	22g	12.2	628.9	2,036.4	5,127.7	6,336.8	6,489.2	12,370.2	16,106.6	22,644.3	27,104.3	30,004.5	21,235.4
Demand Deposits..................	24	3,248.6	4,399.6	7,019.6	9,357.2	8,577.3	11,600.5	14,456.8	17,967.9	20,225.5	23,603.3	28,388.2	39,841.7
Time, Savings,& Fgn.Currency Dep...	25	2,088.8	2,616.6	3,560.9	6,467.6	8,208.1	9,024.3	12,292.5	15,855.1	18,099.7	19,497.4	22,073.3	34,000.6
Money Market Instruments..............	26aa	220.2	11.5	—	44.8	85.9	266.3	296.5	508.9	999.2	280.7	276.4	1,074.2
Bonds...............................	26ab	40.0	82.5	67.5	70.0	65.6	113.0	41.5	14.1	310.2	612.9	1,055.7	766.7
Foreign Liabilities...................	26c	693.5	1,614.2	4,204.4	13,090.4	11,862.2	13,682.0	16,427.2	17,509.9	23,638.1	34,854.5	58,934.1	79,966.7
Central Government Deposits..........	26d	1,180.9	1,894.8	1,735.4	2,472.6	1,881.5	1,345.4	2,342.5	2,311.4	3,268.3	3,006.8	4,457.0	6,199.5
Counterpart Funds..................	26e	112.0	102.0	—	—	—	—	—	—	—	—	—	—
Government Lending Funds..............	26f	487.1	819.5	987.7	739.7	555.2	540.7	450.9	306.4	240.4	222.4	149.3	123.9
Credit from Monetary Authorities.....	26g	401.7	88.6	47.9	23.2	14.5	11.4	8.4	6.3	6.6	7.5	—	31.3
Capital Accounts..................	27a	994.4	1,834.9	2,519.4	5,372.5	7,845.3	8,459.5	8,340.0	10,432.5	11,239.7	12,195.2	13,738.4	17,488.2
Other Items (Net)...................	27r	−298.6	−819.7	−1,027.6	−2,202.0	−2,055.1	−2,636.0	−1,475.3	−303.2	−83.8	905.0	647.7	1,372.6
Banking Survey						*Millions of Krooni: End of Period*							
Foreign Assets (Net)......................	31n	6,356.5	6,963.5	6,166.8	4,759.3	5,111.3	8,021.2	9,097.1	12,283.4	7,755.6	−1,071.5	−11,426.7	−10,428.5
Domestic Credit..........................	32	3,781.4	5,777.4	11,663.5	20,796.6	24,222.7	26,541.6	33,758.5	41,994.3	53,567.5	68,933.1	89,048.2	117,592.6
Claims on Central Govt. (Net)........	32an	−884.1	−1,546.6	−1,073.3	−2,262.9	−1,581.4	−964.9	−1,901.0	−1,872.4	−2,793.4	−2,473.4	−3,986.4	−5,721.8
Claims on Local Government...........	32b	108.3	303.9	159.9	547.2	651.5	767.6	822.9	1,296.9	1,959.1	2,311.9	2,380.8	2,408.3
Claims on Nonfin.Pub.Enterprises...	32c	360.8	335.3	304.6	328.6	225.8	372.5	262.7	141.8	245.0	221.4	651.5	718.7
Claims on Private Sector...............	32d	4,184.3	6,055.8	10,132.5	16,952.7	18,589.7	19,876.9	22,203.5	26,321.2	31,512.5	41,768.7	59,997.6	98,951.8
Claims on Nonbank Financial Inst..	32g	12.2	628.9	2,139.7	5,231.0	6,337.1	6,489.5	12,370.5	16,106.7	22,644.3	27,104.5	30,004.7	21,235.6
Money..................................	34	6,319.9	8,203.2	11,289.7	13,998.0	13,119.8	17,335.5	20,884.1	24,948.2	27,274.5	30,806.6	36,177.5	48,673.4
Quasi-Money.........................	35	2,191.8	2,650.5	3,562.9	6,467.6	8,208.1	9,054.3	12,292.5	15,855.1	18,099.7	19,497.4	22,073.3	34,000.6
Money Market Instruments..............	36aa	220.2	11.5	—	44.8	85.9	266.3	296.5	508.9	999.2	280.7	276.4	1,074.2
Bonds...............................	36ab	40.0	82.5	67.5	70.0	65.6	113.0	41.5	14.1	310.2	612.9	1,055.7	766.7
Counterpart Funds..................	36e	112.0	102.0	—	—	—	—	—	—	—	—	—	—
Government Lending Funds..............	36f	487.1	819.5	987.7	739.7	555.2	540.7	450.9	306.4	240.4	222.4	149.3	123.9
Capital Accounts....................	37a	2,250.4	3,058.1	3,845.3	7,253.6	10,121.8	10,600.8	10,764.1	13,322.2	14,617.2	15,707.2	17,431.2	21,357.6
Other Items (Net)..................	37r	−1,483.5	−2,186.4	−1,922.7	−3,017.9	−2,822.4	−3,347.7	−1,873.9	−677.1	−218.2	734.3	458.1	1,167.7
Money plus Quasi-Money................	35l	8,511.7	10,853.7	14,852.6	20,465.6	21,327.9	26,389.9	33,176.6	40,803.2	45,374.2	50,304.0	58,250.8	82,674.0
Interest Rates						*Percent Per Annum*							
Money Market Rate......................	60b	5.67	4.94	3.53	6.45	11.66	5.39	† 5.68	5.31	3.88	2.92	2.50	2.38
Deposit Rate................................	60l	11.51	8.74	6.05	6.19	8.07	4.19	3.76	4.03	2.74	2.40	2.16	2.13
Lending Rate................................	60p	24.65	19.01	14.87	11.76	15.06	11.09	7.43	7.78	6.70	5.51	5.66	4.93
Prices and Labor						*Index Numbers (2000=100): Period Averages*							
Share Prices...............................	62	....	....	....	200.5	118.3	75.9	100.0	91.6	122.5	171.0	242.0	416.7
Producer Prices............................	63	59.3	74.5	85.5	† 92.6	96.6	95.4	100.0	104.4	104.8	105.1	108.1	110.3
Consumer Prices...........................	64	49.1	63.2	77.8	† 86.0	93.1	96.1	100.0	105.7	109.5	111.0	114.4	119.0
Harmonized CPI (2002=100)...........	64h	....	....	....	....	....	....	....	....	100.0	† 101.4	104.5	108.8
						Number in Thousands: Period Averages							
Labor Force.................................	67d	....	734	....	708	711	....	705	661	653	661	659	....
Employment.................................	67e	693	656	646	† 648	640	579	572	578	586	594	596	....
Unemployment.............................	67c	56	68	68	† 66	66	81	90	83	67	66	64	52
Unemployment Rate (%).................	67r	7.6	9.7	9.9	† 9.7	9.8	12.2	13.6	12.6	10.3	10.0	9.7	7.9

Estonia 939

		1994	1995	1996	1997	1998	1999	2000	2001	2002	2003	2004	2005
Intl. Transactions & Positions							*Millions of Krooni*							
Exports	70	† 16,941	19,043	21,283	29,586	35,232	35,025	53,900	57,858	56,991	62,628	74,637	96,900
Imports, c.i.f.	71	† 21,525	27,441	34,936	48,930	55,221	50,439	72,214	75,080	79,472	89,426	104,901	127,457
Imports, f.o.b.	71.v	† 19,883	26,881	35,920	56,909	59,945	55,651	66,792	69,428	....	....	....	....
Balance of Payments						*Millions of US Dollars: Minus Sign Indicates Debit*								
Current Account, n.i.e.	78ald	−166.3	−157.8	−398.2	−561.7	−478.4	−294.6	−299.0	−324.6	−779.3	−1,115.4	−1,457.6	−1,444.9
Goods: Exports f.o.b.	78aad	1,225.0	1,696.3	1,811.8	2,289.6	2,690.1	2,453.1	3,298.0	3,367.4	3,507.9	4,597.0	5,982.7	7,783.0
Goods: Imports f.o.b.	78abd	−1,581.4	−2,362.3	−2,830.6	−3,413.7	−3,805.4	−3,330.6	−4,079.5	−4,142.1	−4,625.9	−6,164.0	−8,002.1	−9,627.8
Trade Balance	78acd	−356.5	−666.0	−1,018.8	−1,124.1	−1,115.2	−877.5	−781.5	−774.7	−1,118.0	−1,567.0	−2,019.3	−1,844.8
Services: Credit	78add	515.3	876.8	1,107.9	1,318.0	1,479.6	1,489.7	1,485.6	1,607.4	1,705.8	2,223.7	2,830.1	3,155.9
Services: Debit	78aed	−410.2	−497.7	−589.6	−726.6	−910.1	−917.6	−885.9	−962.6	−1,106.3	−1,393.0	−1,755.8	−2,156.0
Balance on Goods & Services	78afd	−251.3	−286.9	−500.6	−532.7	−545.7	−305.4	−181.8	−129.9	−518.5	−736.3	−945.1	−844.8
Income: Credit	78agd	37.3	63.6	112.2	115.1	133.5	133.8	119.0	172.9	205.0	249.3	436.0	669.3
Income: Debit	78ahd	−66.9	−60.8	−110.3	−260.8	−214.5	−235.5	−321.7	−453.5	−530.2	−785.3	−1,072.9	−1,369.2
Balance on Gds, Serv. & Inc.	78aid	−280.9	−284.1	−498.7	−678.4	−626.7	−407.1	−384.5	−410.6	−843.7	−1,272.3	−1,582.0	−1,544.8
Current Transfers, n.i.e.: Credit	78ajd	120.3	134.5	116.7	135.3	172.9	153.7	114.6	115.3	125.7	266.5	424.3	497.4
Current Transfers: Debit	78akd	−5.7	−8.2	−16.3	−18.6	−24.6	−41.3	−29.1	−29.4	−61.3	−109.5	−299.9	−397.6
Capital Account, n.i.e.	78bcd	−.6	−.8	−.7	−.2	1.8	1.2	25.9	14.5	38.2	49.6	93.2	139.8
Capital Account, n.i.e.: Credit	78bad	.5	1.4	.2	.7	2.1	1.4	26.2	14.9	39.2	57.8	100.0	146.3
Capital Account: Debit	78bbd	−1.1	−2.2	−.8	−.9	−.3	−.2	−.2	−.4	−1.0	−8.2	−6.8	−6.5
Financial Account, n.i.e.	78bjd	167.2	233.4	540.8	802.8	508.1	418.2	392.9	269.4	751.5	1,274.6	1,621.8	1,702.0
Direct Investment Abroad	78bdd	−2.4	−2.5	−40.0	−136.6	−6.3	−82.9	−63.4	−200.1	−131.9	−156.1	−268.2	−608.9
Dir. Invest. in Rep. Econ., n.i.e.	78bed	214.4	201.5	150.2	266.2	580.5	305.2	387.3	542.5	284.5	919.0	971.8	2,996.8
Portfolio Investment Assets	78bfd	−22.5	−33.2	−52.7	−165.0	−10.9	−132.3	15.5	−118.8	−192.0	−394.3	−380.6	−871.6
Equity Securities	78bkd	−14.5	5.1	−15.0	−87.8	35.1	12.9	3.5	14.3	.3	−75.5	−232.4	−387.7
Debt Securities	78bld	−8.0	−38.2	−37.6	−77.2	−46.0	−145.2	12.1	−133.2	−192.3	−318.8	−148.2	−483.9
Portfolio Investment Liab., n.i.e.	78bgd	8.4	11.1	198.0	427.5	1.1	153.3	75.6	84.7	344.9	561.2	1,114.3	−1,360.3
Equity Securities	78bmd	8.4	9.9	172.2	127.8	25.7	235.4	−28.5	31.9	53.3	110.6	176.2	−1,349.3
Debt Securities	78bnd	—	1.2	25.7	299.7	−24.6	−82.1	104.1	52.8	291.6	450.5	938.1	−11.1
Financial Derivatives Assets	78bwd	....	....	....	....	....	....	−4.7	−.1	−2.6	−9.9	−2.9	1.3
Financial Derivatives Liabilities	78bxd	....	....	....	....	....	....	5.4	−2.1	−1.4	8.1	2.6	−8.8
Other Investment Assets	78bhd	−146.7	−98.9	−7.2	−334.2	−168.5	−110.3	−166.7	−220.3	50.5	−154.4	−901.2	−886.9
Monetary Authorities	78bod	.1	.1	.1				−18.3	−9.6	−11.3	−2.8	.1	−.8	−.1
General Government	78bpd	.4	−.4	−3.3	−24.7	−61.9	−60.8	43.1	35.9	−23.4	39.8	−12.6	−6.0
Banks	78bqd	−102.8	−41.1	20.9	−195.9	61.3	−53.8	−77.0	−219.3	−28.3	−87.0	−674.6	−1,004.2
Other Sectors	78brd	−44.4	−57.5	−24.9	−113.5	−167.9	22.5	−123.3	−25.6	105.1	−107.3	−213.2	123.3
Other Investment Liab., n.i.e.	78bid	115.9	155.4	292.5	744.8	112.1	285.2	143.8	183.6	399.4	501.1	1,086.0	2,440.6
Monetary Authorities	78bsd	6.2	−13.5	−6.7	−2.5	−1.1	7.3	1.7	−5.4	32.5	43.5	17.9	−54.7
General Government	78btd	19.8	61.0	31.2	−3.3	4.4	9.8	−17.2	−7.3	−53.1	29.2	−15.5	−13.6
Banks	78bud	37.5	82.2	173.6	492.4	−17.3	188.3	76.8	59.4	344.1	336.3	948.0	2,021.6
Other Sectors	78bvd	52.3	25.7	94.3	258.2	126.0	79.8	82.5	136.9	75.9	92.0	135.7	487.3
Net Errors and Omissions	78cad	17.2	8.7	−35.6	−25.1	5.9	−5.5	7.8	−1.2	58.9	−39.4	13.8	−11.4
Overall Balance	78cbd	17.5	83.5	106.3	215.9	37.3	119.3	127.6	−41.9	69.3	169.4	271.2	385.5
Reserves and Related Items	79dad	−17.5	−83.5	−106.3	−215.9	−37.3	−119.3	−127.6	41.9	−69.3	−169.4	−271.2	−385.5
Reserve Assets	79dbd	−17.5	−112.9	−95.2	−196.4	−11.7	−115.3	−122.4	46.9	−55.2	−169.4	−271.2	−385.5
Use of Fund Credit and Loans	79dcd	—	29.4	−11.1	−19.4	−25.6	−4.0	−5.2	−4.9	−14.0	....	....	....
Exceptional Financing	79ded	....	....	....	....	....	....	....	....	....	....	....	....
International Investment Position						*Millions of US Dollars*								
Assets	79aad	....	....	1,344.1	2,045.5	2,300.4	2,415.1	2,614.0	2,920.5	4,078.2	6,137.7	8,783.7	10,709.7
Direct Investment Abroad	79abd	....	....	107.7	215.3	198.4	281.2	259.1	441.8	676.0	1,028.3	1,418.8	1,975.6
Portfolio Investment	79acd	....	....	121.0	249.3	211.2	305.2	271.8	262.1	824.1	1,560.5	2,244.0	2,963.6
Equity Securities	79add	....	....	26.1	98.5	31.5	12.4	26.4	22.5	36.8	210.3	534.9	1,015.5
Debt Securities	79aed	....	....	94.9	150.9	179.7	292.9	245.4	239.6	787.3	1,350.2	1,709.1	1,948.1
Financial Derivatives	79ald	....	....					9.1	8.7	13.0	26.9	32.1	27.2
Other Investment	79afd	....	....	475.9	820.4	1,077.4	972.4	1,151.0	1,385.3	1,561.8	2,137.4	3,292.6	3,793.7
Monetary Authorities	79agd	....	....	—	—	—	—	1.0	6.9	.9	.9	1.9	1.7
General Government	79ahd	....	....	4.6	26.7	97.7	129.6	87.5	98.0	52.7	37.3	54.4	56.4
Banks	79aid	....	....	246.9	392.8	360.9	374.4	411.8	601.1	782.6	1,043.4	1,857.8	2,555.5
Other Sectors	79ajd	....	....	224.3	400.8	618.7	468.4	650.8	679.2	725.5	1,055.8	1,378.5	1,180.1
Reserve Assets	79akd	....	....	639.6	760.5	813.5	856.2	922.9	822.5	1,003.2	1,384.7	1,796.2	1,949.5
Liabilities	79lad	....	....	1,974.9	3,757.8	4,451.9	5,199.6	5,389.5	6,017.7	8,488.0	13,378.7	20,099.8	23,363.6
Dir. Invest. in Rep. Economy	79lbd	....	....	824.6	1,147.9	1,821.7	2,467.3	2,644.7	3,159.9	4,226.4	7,001.8	10,064.2	12,720.6
Portfolio Investment	79lcd	....	....	117.4	954.2	702.9	771.8	761.4	764.3	1,378.9	2,383.4	4,504.7	3,388.3
Equity Securities	79ldd	....	....	76.3	572.9	301.2	500.7	431.6	403.0	634.9	949.6	1,942.0	1,195.6
Debt Securities	79led	....	....	41.1	381.3	401.7	271.2	329.8	361.3	744.0	1,433.9	2,562.7	2,192.8
Financial Derivatives	79lld	....	....					10.2	6.3	5.9	16.8	20.7	10.0
Other Investment	79lfd	....	....	1,033.0	1,655.6	1,927.4	1,960.4	1,973.1	2,087.2	2,876.7	3,976.6	5,510.1	7,244.6
Monetary Authorities	79lgd	....	....	151.4	55.7	30.8	25.8	22.1	14.4	17.1	39.1	44.3	3.7
General Government	79lhd	....	....	175.3	161.4	173.6	178.6	153.6	155.6	113.9	174.2	171.5	135.3
Banks	79lid	....	....	299.1	747.1	692.7	778.2	809.0	827.8	1,362.5	1,971.1	3,174.2	4,701.4
Other Sectors	79ljd	....	....	407.1	691.5	1,030.3	977.8	988.6	1,089.5	1,383.3	1,792.2	2,120.2	2,404.2
Government Finance						*Millions of Krooni: Year Ending December 31*								
Deficit (-) or Surplus	80	416.8	−233.6	−433.7	1,632.4	−42.3	−120.9	137.4	2,492.0	....	....	....	....
Revenue	81	10,566.8	14,649.3	17,544.8	22,360.5	24,006.5	23,397.4	26,474.5	29,602.4	....	....	....	....
Grants Received	81z	—	132.0	—	25.0	124.0	302.5	258.5	624.0	....	....	....	....
Expenditure	82	9,590.3	14,523.5	17,713.7	20,551.8	24,103.3	26,815.5	27,373.3	29,236.5	....	....	....	....
Lending Minus Repayments	83	559.7	491.4	264.8	201.3	69.5	−2,994.7	−777.7	−1,502.1	....	....	....	....
Financing													
Domestic	84a	....	−150.2	49.3	−974.0	524.0	469.7	−87.4	−2,177.9	....	....	....	....
Foreign	85a	....	383.8	384.4	−658.4	−481.7	−348.8	−50.0	−314.1	....	....	....	....
Total Debt													
Domestic	88a	....	....	682.1	572.5	413.4	338.8	210.0	180.0	....	....	....	....
Foreign	89a	....	....	2,584.6	2,770.9	2,715.6	3,175.1	2,505.6	2,411.1	....	....	....	....

Estonia 939

National Accounts		1994	1995	1996	1997	1998	1999	2000	2001	2002	2003	2004	2005
							Millions of Krooni						
Househ.Cons.Expend.,incl.NPISHs....	96f	18,295	23,971	33,123	39,974	45,648	47,359	52,873	59,775	68,254	73,966	79,200	88,661
Government Consumption Expend...	91f	8,121	11,780	14,187	15,570	17,046	18,333	18,775	20,193	22,425	24,643	26,870	30,090
Gross Fixed Capital Formation..........	93e	8,299	11,168	14,535	18,984	23,366	20,239	23,769	28,134	33,555	36,761	40,180	48,066
Changes in Inventories......................	93i	181	305	564	1,882	311	132	2,060	2,336	3,610	3,991	3,985	4,436
Exports of Goods and Services..........	90c	22,500	29,476	35,220	50,297	58,707	59,062	82,112	87,725	86,830	94,667	110,965	138,875
Imports of Goods and Services (-).....	98c	25,755	32,754	41,382	57,779	66,381	62,853	85,511	91,304	95,152	104,250	121,815	148,939
Gross Domestic Product (GDP)........	99b	31,349	43,061	55,895	68,576	78,028	81,776	92,938	104,459	116,915	127,334	141,493	164,918
Net Primary Income from Abroad.....	98.n	−376	21	145	−1,949	−1,166	−1,470	−3,653	−4,971	−5,419	−7,389	−9,194	−8,627
Gross National Income (GNI)............	99a	30,974	43,082	56,041	66,627	76,862	80,306	89,285	99,488	111,496	119,945	132,299	156,291
Net Current Transf.from Abroad.......	98t	1,486	1,446	1,210	1,620	2,080	1,654	1,959	2,660	1,858	1,839	2,081	1,405
Gross Nat'l Disposable Inc.(GNDI)....	99i	32,482	44,553	57,203	67,937	79,258	81,787	91,193	102,072	113,304	119,370	131,983	158,138
Gross Saving..................................	99s	6,043	8,777	9,941	12,704	16,248	16,268	19,596	22,181	22,676	23,175	28,311	38,945
Consumption of Fixed Capital..........	99cf	5,257	7,015	8,655	10,718	13,366	14,817	11,896	18,290	18,691	17,981	18,096	22,739
GDP Volume 2000 Prices.................	99b.p	67,844	70,916	74,036	82,253	85,906	86,170	92,938	98,945	106,111	113,208	122,049	133,985
GDP Volume (2000=100)...............	99bvp	73.0	76.3	79.7	88.5	92.4	92.7	100.0	106.5	114.2	121.8	131.3	144.2
GDP Deflator (2000=100)...............	99bip	46.2	60.7	75.5	83.4	90.8	94.9	100.0	105.6	110.2	112.5	115.9	123.1
							Millions: Midyear Estimates						
Population...............................	99z	1.48	1.45	1.42	1.41	1.39	1.38	1.37	1.36	1.35	1.34	1.34	1.33

Ethiopia 644

		1994	1995	1996	1997	1998	1999	2000	2001	2002	2003	2004	2005
Exchange Rates						*Birr per SDR: End of Period*							
Official Rate	aa	8.6861	9.3946	9.2403	9.2613	10.5644	11.1640	10.8324	10.7555	11.6659	12.8100	13.4365	12.4078
						Birr per US Dollar: End of Period (ae) Period Average (rf)							
Official Rate	ae	5.9500	6.3200	6.4260	6.8640	7.5030	8.1340	8.3140	8.5583	8.5809	8.6206	8.6519	8.6812
Official Rate	rf	5.4650	6.1583	6.3517	6.7093	7.1159	7.9423	8.2173	8.4575	8.5678	8.5997	8.6356	8.6664
Fund Position						*Millions of SDRs: End of Period*							
Quota	2f.s	98.3	98.3	98.3	98.3	98.3	133.7	133.7	133.7	133.7	133.7	133.7	133.7
SDRs	1b.s	.3	.2	—	.1	.1	—	—	.1	.1	.1	.3	.1
Reserve Position in the Fund	1c.s	7.0	7.0	7.1	7.1	7.1	7.1	7.1	7.1	7.2	7.2	7.2	7.2
Total Fund Cred.&Loans Outstg.	2tl	49.4	49.4	64.2	64.2	76.1	69.0	59.1	84.0	105.4	105.8	118.0	112.1
International Liquidity						*Millions of US Dollars Unless Otherwise Indicated: End of Period*							
Total Reserves minus Gold	1l.d	544.2	771.5	732.2	501.1	511.1	458.5	306.3	433.2	881.7	955.6	1,496.8	1,121.5
SDRs	1b.d	.4	.3	—	.1	.1	.1	—	.2	.1	.1	.5	.2
Reserve Position in the Fund	1c.d	10.2	10.5	10.1	9.5	10.0	9.7	9.2	9.0	9.7	10.7	11.2	10.3
Foreign Exchange	1d.d	533.6	760.8	722.0	491.4	501.0	448.7	297.1	424.1	871.9	944.8	1,485.1	1,111.0
Gold (Million Fine Troy Ounces)	1ad	.113	.113	.301	.301	.303	.303	.205	.205	.246	—	—	—
Gold (National Valuation)	1and	11.4	11.4	.4	.4	.4	.3	.3	.3	.3	—	—	—
Monetary Authorities: Other Liab.	4..d	319.0	286.3	279.3	4.2	.3	.9	.4	.3	3.7	.1	.3	.4
Deposit Money Banks: Assets	7a.d	533.3	454.2	435.9	680.8	652.9	542.1	597.3	624.4	698.9	862.3	607.8	851.0
Liabilities	7b.d	108.3	192.3	221.5	225.4	218.4	250.2	227.0	180.8	187.5	210.6	190.6	189.9
Other Banking Insts.: Assets	7e.d	3.5	2.5	8.6	9.3	9.2	6.8	5.7	.6	1.3	2.6	6.5	6.6
Liabilities	7f.d	52.8	45.0	39.0	36.9	27.2	28.1	29.5	28.9	29.5	29.5	32.9	36.8
Monetary Authorities						*Millions of Birr: End of Period*							
Foreign Assets	11	3,413.5	4,891.8	4,722.6	3,456.1	3,893.3	3,666.4	2,535.9	3,614.8	7,682.8	9,134.2	13,184.7	10,583.4
Claims on Central Government	12a	8,443.5	8,182.1	7,694.6	8,549.3	9,218.4	10,301.1	13,896.5	12,524.9	15,100.4	15,665.4	22,726.2	28,151.1
Claims on Other Financial Insts.	12f	464.0	465.1	465.1	465.1	465.1	466.1	395.3	395.3	395.3	395.3	395.3	1.0
Reserve Money	14	7,084.4	7,976.6	6,664.0	7,249.7	6,362.5	6,050.6	8,394.9	7,639.8	10,301.8	11,858.5	22,472.8	24,494.5
of which: Currency Outside DMBs	14a	5,380.4	5,718.0	5,401.5	4,964.3	3,977.7	4,506.8	4,590.8	4,870.3	5,686.3	6,874.3	8,274.5	9,623.3
Foreign Liabilities	16c	2,327.4	2,273.5	2,388.0	622.9	806.4	777.6	643.6	906.1	1,261.7	1,357.0	1,587.5	1,394.3
Central Government Deposits	16d	2,082.8	2,229.8	2,294.8	2,544.4	2,630.9	3,296.7	3,133.0	5,344.7	8,155.2	7,928.8	7,440.9	8,989.8
Central Government Lending Funds	16f				792.3	1,041.6	1,650.7	1,381.3	460.4	584.8	436.8	736.9	855.3
Capital Accounts	17a	728.4	879.5	1,159.7	1,198.1	1,272.5	1,422.3	1,646.1	2,100.5	2,674.5	3,763.4	3,452.7	3,405.8
Other Items (Net)	17r	98.0	179.6	375.9	63.1	1,462.9	1,235.7	1,628.8	83.4	200.4	−149.5	615.4	−404.3
Deposit Money Banks						*Millions of Birr: End of Period*							
Reserves	20	1,665.7	2,197.1	1,227.7	2,173.1	2,312.2	1,314.6	3,197.1	2,213.0	3,833.2	4,913.9	14,239.6	14,491.5
Foreign Assets	21	3,173.0	2,870.6	2,801.3	4,673.0	4,899.0	4,409.5	4,965.7	5,344.1	5,997.4	7,433.3	5,258.3	7,387.9
Claims on Central Government	22a	2,617.2	2,773.0	2,612.7	2,361.0	2,629.4	5,233.7	5,556.2	7,499.5	9,242.8	10,992.2	6,060.0	7,847.0
Claims on Nonfin.Pub.Enterprises	22c	1,630.0	1,630.0	1,794.6	1,589.7	1,612.2	798.3	775.5	851.8	646.8	829.5	2,592.5	2,768.3
Claims on Private Sector	22d	1,988.1	3,706.0	6,448.6	8,007.1	8,693.6	11,216.2	11,836.2	12,187.0	12,057.4	12,946.0	14,432.6	20,234.5
Claims on Other Financial Insts.	22f			279.0	248.0	217.0	486.5	435.0	389.5	369.5	407.2	570.9	1,002.1
Demand Deposits	24	3,803.5	3,711.4	3,761.7	5,967.2	6,501.2	7,143.8	8,004.3	8,484.8	10,185.4	11,659.4	13,933.1	16,132.1
Time, Savings,& Fgn.Currency Dep.	25	3,637.4	4,549.7	6,069.6	7,241.7	7,554.9	8,474.9	10,001.9	11,609.8	12,976.3	14,612.6	17,292.9	20,987.5
Foreign Liabilities	26c	644.4	1,215.6	1,423.5	1,547.3	1,638.5	2,035.0	1,887.1	1,547.3	1,608.7	1,815.3	1,649.3	1,648.4
Central Government Deposits	26d	619.2	810.1	736.7	91.9	75.9	56.3	72.2	57.4	86.8	107.4	858.6	1,465.2
Central Government Lending Funds	26f	—	—	43.4	51.1	21.0	44.2	36.4	45.5	45.7	33.1	26.2	22.4
Capital Accounts	27a	439.2	567.4	1,270.0	1,351.4	1,808.8	1,939.5	2,235.6	2,553.6	2,528.8	2,801.7	3,087.6	3,645.1
Other Items (Net)	27r	1,930.2	2,322.4	1,859.0	2,801.2	2,763.1	3,765.1	4,528.3	4,186.3	4,715.5	6,492.7	6,306.2	9,830.5
Monetary Survey						*Millions of Birr: End of Period*							
Foreign Assets (Net)	31n	3,614.7	4,273.2	3,712.3	5,958.9	6,347.3	5,263.2	4,970.9	6,505.6	10,809.8	13,395.3	15,206.2	14,928.7
Domestic Credit	32	12,440.8	13,716.4	16,263.1	18,583.8	20,128.9	25,149.0	29,689.5	28,445.8	29,570.3	33,203.1	38,479.6	49,555.4
Claims on Central Govt. (Net)	32an	8,358.7	7,915.3	7,275.8	8,273.9	9,140.9	12,181.8	16,247.5	14,622.2	16,101.3	18,621.4	20,486.7	25,543.0
Claims on Nonfin.Pub.Enterprises	32c	1,630.0	1,630.0	1,794.6	1,589.7	1,612.2	798.3	775.5	851.8	646.8	829.5	2,592.5	2,768.3
Claims on Private Sector	32d	1,988.1	3,706.0	6,448.6	8,007.1	8,693.6	11,216.2	11,836.2	12,187.0	12,057.4	12,949.7	14,434.2	20,241.0
Claims on Other Financial Insts.	32f	464.0	465.1	744.1	713.1	682.1	952.6	830.3	784.8	764.8	802.5	966.2	1,003.1
Money	34	9,184.0	9,429.5	9,174.0	11,024.0	10,511.0	12,067.0	13,225.7	13,865.2	16,557.9	18,591.1	22,312.0	25,980.7
Quasi-Money	35	3,637.4	4,549.7	6,069.6	7,241.7	7,554.9	8,474.9	10,001.9	11,609.8	12,976.3	14,612.6	17,292.9	20,987.5
Central Government Lending Funds	36f	—	—	43.4	843.4	1,062.6	1,694.9	1,417.6	505.9	630.5	469.9	763.1	877.7
Capital Accounts	37a	1,167.6	1,447.0	2,429.6	2,549.5	3,081.3	3,361.7	3,881.7	4,654.3	5,203.3	6,565.1	6,540.3	7,051.0
Other Items (Net)	37r	2,066.5	2,563.5	2,258.8	2,884.2	4,266.5	4,813.6	6,133.5	4,316.2	5,012.0	6,355.8	6,777.5	9,587.2
Money plus Quasi-Money	35l	12,821.4	13,979.2	15,243.6	18,265.6	18,065.9	20,541.9	23,227.5	25,475.0	29,534.2	33,207.6	39,604.9	46,968.2
Other Banking Institutions						*Millions of Birr: End of Period*							
Reserves	40	233.7	9.7	8.1	22.7	8.1	57.6	28.4	17.4	18.0	31.4	72.6	10.7
Foreign Assets	41	20.7	15.9	55.4	63.5	69.1	55.3	47.1	4.9	11.2	22.0	54.7	57.2
Claims on Central Government	42a	123.2	—	—	—	—	—	42.5	42.5	34.0	34.0	104.6	96.6	88.7
Claims on Nonfin.Pub.Enterprises	42c	—	492.4	574.8	396.7	299.7	257.9	226.0	200.8	197.4	175.7	179.5	179.0
Claims on Private Sector	42d	1,205.7	701.4	1,173.4	1,773.5	2,475.8	3,222.0	3,540.1	2,401.7	2,036.3	1,966.4	2,330.5	4,235.8
Claims on Deposit Money Banks	42e	—	—	—	—	—	170.3	110.4	83.4	118.4	146.6	156.4	237.2
Demand Deposits	44	—	9.5	22.2	31.3	15.8	26.0	11.4	5.6	3.4	6.3	13.5	5.9
Time and Savings Deposits	45	538.1	48.6	2.1	234.4	681.4	734.6	717.4	678.3	742.3	711.7	685.1	674.7
Foreign Liabilities	46c	314.4	284.6	250.4	253.5	204.3	228.2	245.6	247.5	253.1	254.2	284.3	319.9
Central Govt. Lending Funds	46f	54.1	13.8	13.8	13.8	13.8	13.8	13.8	13.8	83.8	72.6	72.6	73.1
Credit from Monetary Authorities	46g	464.0	465.1	465.1	465.1	465.1	387.8	387.8	387.8	387.8	381.4	381.4	381.4
Credit from Deposit Money Banks	46h	116.1	414.6	685.5	958.1	894.5	1,410.1	1,646.7	456.3	369.5	408.2	565.3	901.0
Capital Accounts	47a	101.1	176.9	390.8	361.2	380.5	397.4	415.0	429.3	425.9	524.9	520.3	1,859.4
Other Items (Net)	47r	−4.5	−193.7	−18.2	−61.0	197.3	607.7	557.0	523.6	149.6	87.4	367.9	593.2

Ethiopia   644

		1994	1995	1996	1997	1998	1999	2000	2001	2002	2003	2004	2005
Banking Survey						*Millions of Birr: End of Period*							
Foreign Assets (Net)	51n	3,321.0	4,004.5	3,517.3	5,768.9	6,212.1	5,090.4	4,772.4	6,262.9	10,567.9	13,163.2	14,976.6	14,666.0
Domestic Credit	52	13,305.7	14,445.1	17,267.2	20,040.9	22,222.3	27,718.7	32,667.9	30,297.5	31,073.1	34,647.2	40,120.1	53,055.8
Claims on Central Government(Net	52an	8,481.9	7,915.3	7,275.8	8,273.9	9,140.9	12,224.3	16,290.0	14,656.2	16,135.3	18,726.0	20,583.3	25,631.7
Claims on Nonfin. Pub. Enterprises.	52c	1,630.0	2,122.4	2,369.4	1,986.4	1,911.9	1,056.2	1,001.6	1,052.6	844.2	1,005.2	2,772.1	2,947.3
Claims on Private Sector	52d	3,193.8	4,407.4	7,622.0	9,780.6	11,169.4	14,438.3	15,376.3	14,588.7	14,093.7	14,916.1	16,764.7	24,476.8
Liquid Liabilities	55l	13,125.8	14,027.6	15,259.8	18,508.6	18,755.0	21,245.0	23,927.9	26,141.4	30,261.9	33,894.2	40,230.9	47,638.2
Central Government Lending Funds..	56f	54.1	13.8	57.2	857.2	1,076.4	1,708.7	1,431.4	519.7	714.3	542.5	835.7	950.8
Capital Accounts	57a	1,268.7	1,623.9	2,820.4	2,910.7	3,461.8	3,759.2	4,296.7	5,083.6	5,629.2	7,090.0	7,060.6	8,910.4
Other Items (Net)	57r	2,178.1	2,784.4	2,647.1	3,533.3	5,141.3	6,096.2	7,784.3	4,815.6	5,035.7	6,283.7	6,969.5	10,222.4
Money (National Definitions)						*Millions of Birr: End of Period*							
Base Money	19ma	7,070.8	7,963.0	6,650.4	7,249.7	6,362.5	6,050.6	8,394.9	7,639.8	10,301.8	11,858.5	22,705.6	24,269.2
M1	59ma	9,230.2	10,050.3	10,031.2	11,017.7	10,581.8	12,157.9	13,322.7	14,000.4	16,811.9	18,858.4	18,662.9	21,205.8
M2	59mb	12,867.6	15,076.6	16,093.6	18,493.8	18,818.1	21,487.8	24,218.8	26,542.1	30,812.9	34,509.8	35,882.0	42,098.9
Interest Rates						*Percent Per Annum*							
Discount Rate	60	12.00	12.00	....	....	....	....	....	....	....	....	....	....
Treasury Bill Rate	60c	12.00	12.00	7.22	3.97	3.48	3.65	2.74	3.06	1.30	† 1.31	.56	.25
Savings Rate	60k	....	....	....	....	....	....	....	....	3.00	3.00	3.00	3.00
Deposit Rate	60l	11.50	11.46	9.42	7.00	6.00	6.32	6.00	6.00	3.79	3.35	3.38	3.46
Lending Rate	60p	14.33	15.08	13.92	10.50	10.50	10.58	10.89	10.87	8.66	† 7.00	7.00	7.00
Government Bond Yield	61	13.00	13.00	13.00						....	† 3.05	3.91	3.98
Prices and Labor						*Index Numbers (2000=100): Period Averages*							
Consumer Prices	64	83.9	92.3	† 87.6	89.7	† 92.0	99.3	100.0	91.8	93.3	109.8	113.4	126.6
						Number in Thousands: Period Averages							
Labor Force	67d	....	24,606	....	26,408	....	27,272	....	....	....	....	....	....
Unemployment	67c	65	23	28	35	29	26	....	....	....	....	....	....
Intl. Transactions & Positions						*Millions of Birr*							
Exports	70	2,062.4	2,602.9	2,650.6	3,941.3	3,967.0	3,711.0	3,990.7	3,850.0	4,114.5	4,268.6	5,857.3	7,650.4
Imports, c.i.f	71	5,658.0	7,052.5	8,899.2	....	10,792.0	12,274.0	10,368.6	15,297.1	13,899.7	18,222.5	26,662.7	35,770.2
Balance of Payments						*Millions of US Dollars: Minus Sign Indicates Debit*							
Current Account, n.i.e	78ald	125.4	39.4	79.6	−40.3	−332.6	−465.2	13.5	−373.4	−136.6	−136.4	−667.8	....
Goods: Exports f.o.b	78aad	372.0	423.0	417.5	588.3	560.3	467.4	486.1	455.6	480.2	496.4	678.3	....
Goods: Imports f.o.b	78abd	−925.7	−1,092.8	−1,002.8	−1,001.6	−1,359.8	−1,387.2	−1,131.4	−1,625.8	−1,455.0	−1,895.0	−2,768.5	....
Trade Balance	78acd	−553.7	−669.8	−585.3	−413.4	−799.4	−919.8	−645.3	−1,170.3	−974.8	−1,398.6	−2,090.2	....
Services: Credit	78add	294.6	344.5	377.2	390.7	391.5	473.6	506.2	523.1	585.4	761.7	1,005.5	....
Services: Debit	78aed	−310.4	−352.8	−349.8	−394.2	−455.6	−466.3	−489.6	−524.5	−580.4	−708.7	−958.3	....
Balance on Goods & Services	78afd	−569.5	−678.1	−557.9	−416.9	−863.5	−912.5	−628.7	−1,171.6	−969.8	−1,345.6	−2,043.0	....
Income: Credit	78agd	42.9	68.4	41.2	24.2	21.0	16.6	16.2	16.3	14.3	18.9	31.7	....
Income: Debit	78ahd	−74.6	−87.1	−75.2	−65.5	−64.2	−50.4	−52.0	−48.3	−36.9	−43.1	−60.3	....
Balance on Gds, Serv. & Inc	78aid	−601.1	−696.9	−591.8	−458.2	−906.7	−946.3	−664.5	−1,203.7	−992.3	−1,369.8	−2,071.6	....
Current Transfers, n.i.e.: Credit.	78ajd	728.5	737.3	679.0	425.5	589.8	500.7	697.9	854.3	876.4	1,266.5	1,420.6	....
Current Transfers: Debit	78akd	−2.0	−1.1	−7.5	−7.6	−15.7	−19.7	−19.9	−24.0	−20.7	−33.1	−16.8	....
Capital Account, n.i.e	78bcd	3.7	2.6	.9	—	1.4	1.8	....	....	....	—	—	....
Capital Account, n.i.e.: Credit.	78bad	3.7	2.6	.9	—	1.4	1.8	....	....	....	—	—	....
Capital Account: Debit	78bbd	—	....	....	....	....	....	....	....	....	—	—	....
Financial Account, n.i.e	78bjd	−199.0	−24.9	−499.6	241.2	−21.3	−180.1	28.4	−178.4	−82.7	246.9	73.2	....
Direct Investment Abroad	78bdd	—	....	....	....	....	....	....	....	....	....	....	....
Dir. Invest. in Rep. Econ., n.i.e.	78bed	—	....	....	....	....	....	....	....	....	....	....	....
Portfolio Investment Assets	78bfd	—	....	....	....	....	....	....	....	....	—	—	....
Equity Securities	78bkd	—	....	....	....	....	....	....	....	....	—	—	....
Debt Securities	78bld	—	....	....	....	....	....	....	....	....	—	—	....
Portfolio Investment Liab., n.i.e.	78bgd	—	....	....	....	....	....	....	....	....	—	—	....
Equity Securities	78bmd	—	....	....	....	....	....	....	....	....	—	—	....
Debt Securities	78bnd	—	....	....	....	....	....	....	....	....	—	—	....
Financial Derivatives Assets	78bwd	....	....	....	....	....	....	....	....	....	....	....	....
Financial Derivatives Liabilities	78bxd	....	....	....	....	....	....	....	....	....	....	....	....
Other Investment Assets	78bhd	−318.5	57.7	−306.8	318.5	59.8	−85.3	116.1	22.9	−4.1	68.8	−261.8	....
Monetary Authorities	78bod	....	....	....	....	....	....	....	....	....	....	....	....
General Government	78bpd	....	....	....	....	....	....	....	....	....	....	....	....
Banks	78bqd	−358.5	44.7	−283.0	350.7	26.3	−69.6	23.2	29.7	75.2	95.0	−251.0	....
Other Sectors	78brd	40.0	13.1	−23.8	−32.2	33.5	−15.8	92.8	−6.8	−79.4	−26.2	−10.7	....
Other Investment Liab., n.i.e.	78bid	119.5	−82.6	−192.8	−77.3	−81.0	−94.7	−87.7	−201.3	−78.6	178.1	335.0	....
Monetary Authorities	78bsd	25.4	.4	−7.8	−.1	−.4	.4	47.0	−54.6	5.7	11.0	9.2	....
General Government	78btd	82.4	−145.1	−131.5	−91.0	−79.9	−125.7	−171.9	−107.9	−78.8	147.7	386.2	....
Banks	78bud	55.3	91.2	205.6	15.0	2.4	62.2	4.1	−70.5	6.7	24.0	−18.6	....
Other Sectors	78bvd	−43.6	−29.1	−259.0	−1.2	−3.1	−31.6	33.0	31.7	−12.2	−4.5	−41.7	....
Net Errors and Omissions	78cad	69.5	−122.4	−45.8	−629.5	−7.9	407.2	−231.3	−229.0	−915.1	−390.1	−354.1	....
Overall Balance	78cbd	−.4	−105.2	−464.8	−428.6	−360.4	−236.3	−189.5	−780.8	−1,134.5	−279.6	−948.8	....
Reserves and Related Items	79dad	.4	105.2	464.8	428.6	360.4	236.3	189.5	780.8	1,134.5	279.6	948.8	....
Reserve Assets	79dbd	−124.7	−204.8	20.0	192.1	179.0	−49.7	−108.6	126.7	471.4	76.9	544.3	....
Use of Fund Credit and Loans	79dcd	20.8	—	21.2	—	16.9	−9.7	−13.0	31.8	27.1	.6	17.8	....
Exceptional Financing	79ded	104.3	310.0	423.6	236.5	164.5	295.7	311.0	622.2	635.9	202.1	386.8	....

Ethiopia 644

		1994	1995	1996	1997	1998	1999	2000	2001	2002	2003	2004	2005
Government Finance						*Millions of Birr: Year Ending July 7*							
Deficit (-) or Surplus........................	80	−2,814.8	−1,379.3	−749.2	−635.8	−1,786.5	−2,524.3	....	....	....	....	....	....
Total Revenue and Grants..............	81y	5,060.7	6,874.1	7,824.0	9,381.4	9,673.5	8,265.5	....	....	....	....	....	....
Revenue.....................................	81	3,842.6	5,839.2	6,817.3	7,877.4	8,400.2	7,847.0	....	....	....	....	....	....
Grants.......................................	81z	1,218.1	1,034.9	1,006.7	1,504.0	1,273.3	418.5	....	....	....	....	....	....
Exp. & Lending Minus Repay..........	82z	7,875.5	8,253.4	8,573.2	10,017.2	11,460.0	10,789.8	....	....	....	....	....	....
Total Financing...............................	80h	2,814.8	1,379.3	749.2	635.8	1,786.5	2,524.5	....	....	....	....	....	....
Domestic....................................	84a	709.6	60.0	−652.6	−92.1	1,007.0	1,175.8	....	....	....	....	....	....
Foreign......................................	85a	2,105.2	1,319.3	1,401.8	727.9	779.5	1,348.7	....	....	....	....	....	....
Use of Cash Balances...................	87	2,105.2	1,319.3	1,401.8	727.9	779.5	1,348.7	....	....	....	....	....	....
Total Debt by Residence..................	88	37,063.1	39,599.8	38,967.1	38,748.5	41,947.3	49,485.0	....	....	....	....	....	....
Domestic....................................	88a	11,778.3	11,654.8	11,950.8	12,359.0	13,339.0	14,700.3	....	....	....	....	....	....
Foreign......................................	89a	25,284.8	27,945.0	27,016.3	26,389.5	28,608.3	34,784.7	....	....	....	....	....	....
National Accounts						*Millions of Birr: Year Ending July 7*							
Househ.Cons.Expend.,incl.NPISHs....	96f	23,748	27,942	31,299	41,665	35,110	38,999	40,566	43,416	47,741	50,006	67,817	77,172
Government Consumption Expend...	91f	3,155	3,675	4,173	5,157	6,233	9,105	12,029	9,065	10,461	13,150	12,038	13,560
Gross Capital Formation..................	93	4,294	5,569	7,246	7,691	7,713	7,790	7,995	8,747	....	....	....	....
Exports of Goods and Services..........	90c	3,223	4,852	5,240	6,780	7,382	7,258	8,086	8,106	8,079	9,796	11,636	13,191
Imports of Goods and Services (-).....	98c	6,091	8,154	9,284	10,663	11,767	14,884	16,105	16,335	17,824	20,175	25,358	28,258
GDP at Factor Cost.........................	99ba	28,329	33,885	37,938	41,465	44,840	48,803	53,190	54,211	51,761	57,077	....	....
Net Primary Income from Abroad.....	98.n	−460	−378	−275	−224	−178	....	....	....	....	....	....	....
Gross National Income (GNI)............	99a	27,869	33,508	37,662	41,241	44,857	....	....	....	....	....	....	....
GDP Fact.Cost,Vol.'80/81 Prices.......	99bap	12,852	13,639	15,126	15,941	15,644	16,483	17,464	19,004	19,520	18,800	....	....
GDP Volume (2000=100)................	99bvp	73.6	78.1	86.6	91.3	89.6	94.4	100.0	108.8	111.8	107.7	....	....
GDP Deflator (2000=100)...............	99bip	72.4	81.6	82.3	85.4	94.1	97.2	100.0	93.7	87.1	99.7	....	....
						Millions: Midyear Estimates							
Population...............................	99z	58.22	60.01	61.75	63.45	65.13	66.82	68.53	70.26	72.01	73.79	75.60	77.43

		1994	1995	1996	1997	1998	1999	2000	2001	2002	2003	2004	2005
Exchange Rates						*Euros per SDR: End of Period*							
Market Rate	aa	....	....	....	....	....	1.36623	1.40023	1.42600	1.29639	1.17654	1.14016	1.21155
							Euros per US Dollar: End of Period (ae) Period Average (rf)						
Market Rate	ae	....	....	....	....	....	.99542	1.07469	1.13469	.95356	.79177	.73416	.84767
Market Rate	rf	....	....	....	....	....	.93863	1.08540	1.11751	1.06255	.88603	.80537	.80412
							Index Numbers (2000=100): Period Averages						
Nominal Effective Exchange Rate	neu	122.87	129.46	129.19	116.93	117.06	111.46	100.00	101.19	104.28	116.07	119.98	120.27
Real Effective Exchange Rate	reu	125.64	133.09	134.31	120.99	117.85	112.83	100.00	101.90	105.19	116.38	121.02	120.34
International Liquidity						*Millions of US Dollars Unless Otherwise Indicated: End of Period*							
Tot.Res.minus Gold (Eurosyst.Def)	1l.d	....	....	....	....	....	256,780	242,325	234,965	246,995	222,870	211,437	184,719
SDRs	1b.d	3,519	5,572	5,440	5,359	6,015	4,546	4,032	4,757	4,866	5,275	5,100	4,905
Reserve Position in the Fund	1c.d	12,941	16,100	16,572	18,637	27,364	24,245	19,662	22,294	26,317	29,431	25,452	12,457
Foreign Exchange	1d.d	....	....	....	....	....	227,989	218,631	207,914	215,811	188,165	180,885	167,357
of which: Fin.Deriv.rel.to Res	1ddd	....	....	....	....	....	−209	679	346	456	865	88	−50
Other Reserve Assets	1e.d	....	....	....	....	....	—	—	—	—	—	—	—
Gold (Million Fine Troy Ounces)	1ad	....	....	....	....	....	402.76	399.54	401.88	399.02	393.54	390.00	375.86
Gold (Eurosystem Valuation)	1and	....	....	....	....	....	116,901	109,653	111,119	136,765	164,206	170,819	192,816
Memo:Euro Cl. on Non-EA Res	1dgd	....	....	....	....	....	....	....	....	....	....	....	....
Non-Euro Cl. on EA Res	1dhd	....	....	....	....	....	14,691	14,685	21,797	23,451	25,674	25,950	30,201
Mon. Auth.: Other Foreign Assets	3..d	....	....	....	....	....	....	....	....	....	....	....	....
Foreign Liabilities	4..d	....	....	....	....	....	49,993	27,856	31,417	34,461	34,777	37,055	32,581
Banking Insts: Foreign Assets	7a.d	....	....	....	....	....	1,725,335	1,880,119	2,117,536	2,579,880	3,243,168	4,008,457	4,339,528
Foreign Liabs.	7b.d	....	....	....	....	....	1,884,341	2,139,832	2,368,395	2,719,020	3,291,925	3,834,283	4,148,767
Monetary Authorities (Eurosyst.)						*Billions of Euros: End of Period*							
Foreign Assets (on Non-EA Ctys)	11	....	....	....	323.7	322.4	400.6	380.7	399.0	374.2	317.9	294.1	337.0
Claims on General Government	12a.u	....	....	....	132.9	106.6	105.8	110.7	127.5	110.2	144.1	161.5	186.2
Claims on EA Banking Sector	12e.u	....	....	....	216.2	205.7	426.3	429.9	390.2	399.0	458.8	537.4	632.3
Claims on Other Resident Sectors	12d.u	....	....	....	4.5	4.3	11.5	12.7	11.1	9.9	10.3	12.1	13.0
Currency in Circulation	14a	....	....	....	355.0	359.1	393.3	390.2	285.9	392.9	450.5	517.3	582.7
Liabilities to EA Banking Sector	14c.u	....	....	....	92.4	94.2	279.3	270.4	342.4	283.3	285.8	306.8	346.5
Deposits of Other Resident Sect.	15..u	....	....	....	3.4	3.5	8.8	9.8	14.4	15.6	16.9	15.0	14.5
Bonds & Money Mkt. Instruments	16n.u	....	....	....	28.2	13.8	7.9	3.8	4.6	3.6	1.6	.5	.1
Foreign Liabs. (to Non-EA Ctys)	16c	....	....	....	32.8	18.6	49.8	29.9	35.6	32.9	27.5	27.2	27.6
Central Government Deposits	16d.u	....	....	....	51.7	54.4	53.4	47.1	35.1	29.5	21.3	24.7	24.4
Capital Accounts	17a	....	....	....	106.0	97.2	174.5	197.6	209.9	166.0	143.8	138.4	201.9
Other Items (Net)	17r	....	....	....	7.8	−1.7	−22.8	−14.7	−.1	−30.5	−16.2	−24.9	−29.1
Banking Institutions (Oth.MFIs)						*Billions of Euros: End of Period*							
Claims on EA Banking Sector	20..u	....	....	....	3,639.2	3,973.4	4,369.2	4,563.5	4,917.0	5,188.8	5,467.5	5,880.4	6,082.5
Foreign Assets (on Non-EA Ctys)	21	....	....	....	1,595.4	1,587.8	1,717.4	2,020.5	2,402.7	2,460.1	2,567.8	2,942.9	3,678.5
Claims on General Government	22a.u	....	....	....	1,874.9	1,934.0	1,952.4	1,813.9	1,899.4	1,948.0	2,060.1	2,111.7	2,261.1
Claims on Oth. Resident Sectors	22d.u	....	....	....	5,130.7	5,652.5	6,207.1	6,866.3	7,413.2	7,711.1	8,144.8	8,677.3	9,531.8
Demand (Overnight) Deposits	24..u	621.7	949.9	1,072.7	1,233.0	1,387.1	1,538.2	1,648.9	1,936.9	2,041.0	2,251.7	2,390.9	2,847.5
Deposits with Agreed Maturity	25a.u	....	....	....	1,901.9	1,929.1	2,043.3	2,159.6	2,257.5	2,264.7	2,295.3	2,404.9	2,644.0
Deposits Redeemable at Notice	25b.u	....	....	....	1,328.4	1,392.6	1,331.5	1,276.9	1,350.2	1,421.7	1,519.7	1,616.4	1,502.2
Repurchase Agreements	25f.u	....	....	....	205.4	176.5	144.1	174.9	218.5	226.9	208.7	228.8	221.9
Money Market Fund Shares	26m.u	....	....	....	252.2	241.4	293.4	323.3	436.5	533.4	648.8	677.4	698.9
Bonds & Money Mkt. Instruments	26n.u	....	....	....	2,063.5	2,261.5	2,531.1	2,712.9	2,882.8	2,993.4	3,161.4	3,496.9	3,858.3
Foreign Liabs. (to Non-EA Ctys)	26c	....	....	....	1,381.3	1,507.0	1,875.7	2,299.7	2,687.4	2,592.8	2,606.4	2,815.0	3,516.8
Central Government Deposits	26d.u	....	....	....	102.1	95.4	90.0	117.4	103.9	106.9	134.4	137.7	149.2
Credit fr. EA Banking Sector	26g.u	....	....	....	3,009.6	3,305.3	3,597.3	3,679.3	3,829.6	4,136.6	4,364.9	4,709.0	4,850.9
Capital Accounts	27a	....	....	....	687.1	753.7	846.4	936.5	1,038.2	1,105.1	1,145.0	1,199.5	1,307.7
Other Items (Net)	27r	....	....	....	75.6	98.1	−45.1	−65.1	−109.2	−114.6	−96.2	−63.9	−43.5
Banking Survey						*Billions of Euros: End of Period*							
Foreign Assets (Net)	31n.u	....	....	....	505.0	384.6	192.5	71.7	78.7	208.7	251.8	394.7	471.1
Domestic Credit	32..u	....	....	....	6,989.1	7,547.6	8,133.5	8,639.2	9,312.3	9,642.8	10,203.6	10,800.3	11,818.7
Claims on General Govt. (Net)	32anu	....	....	....	1,853.9	1,890.8	1,914.8	1,760.2	1,887.9	1,921.8	2,048.5	2,110.9	2,273.8
Claims on Oth. Resident Sectors	32d.u	....	....	....	5,135.2	5,656.8	6,218.6	6,879.1	7,424.4	7,721.0	8,155.1	8,689.4	9,544.9
Currency in Circulation	34a.u	292.2	303.8	313.3	320.6	323.4	350.8	348.4	239.7	341.2	397.9	468.4	532.8
Demand (Overnight) Deposits	34b.u	624.5	952.6	1,075.7	1,236.4	1,390.5	1,547.0	1,658.7	1,951.0	2,056.3	2,268.4	2,405.8	2,861.9
Deposits with Agreed Maturity	35a.u	....	....	....	1,901.9	1,929.1	2,043.3	2,159.6	2,257.9	2,265.0	2,295.5	2,405.0	2,644.2
of which: Over 2-Yr. Maturity	35abu	....	....	....	1,004.1	1,033.0	1,161.0	1,168.3	1,169.1	1,189.5	1,256.5	1,365.1	1,522.1
Deposits Redeemable at Notice	35b.u	....	....	....	1,328.4	1,392.6	1,331.5	1,276.9	1,350.2	1,421.7	1,519.7	1,616.4	1,502.2
of which: Over 3-Mos Notice	35bbu	....	....	....	219.5	214.4	112.2	125.4	115.8	105.6	92.2	91.1	87.7
Repurchase Agreements	35f.u	....	....	....	205.4	176.5	144.1	174.9	218.5	226.9	208.7	228.8	221.9
Money Market Fund Shares	36m.u	....	....	....	244.3	231.1	280.0	300.0	398.0	471.0	581.5	604.9	615.8
Bonds & Money Mkt. Instruments	36n.u	....	....	....	1,361.0	1,456.5	1,591.8	1,662.8	1,760.7	1,819.0	1,878.5	2,061.7	2,326.2
of which: Over 2-Yr. Maturity	36nau	....	....	....	1,230.5	1,312.3	1,446.1	1,525.3	1,613.6	1,689.3	1,785.4	1,958.0	2,195.9
Capital Accounts	37a	....	....	....	698.9	680.7	805.1	889.6	991.6	1,002.9	1,004.7	1,047.0	1,195.5
Other Items (Net)	37r.u	....	....	....	197.1	351.8	232.3	240.0	223.3	247.5	300.4	357.1	389.2
Money (Eurosystem Definition)						*Billions of Euros: End of Period*							
M1	59mau	1,343.1	1,423.1	1,528.5	1,626.9	1,785.4	1,972.0	2,084.6	2,279.0	2,499.4	2,727.1	2,948.9	3,479.6
M1 Growth Rate	59max	....	....	....	....	9.6	10.1	5.7	5.7	9.6	10.1	8.4	11.6
M2	59mbu	3,243.8	3,397.5	3,562.5	3,687.1	3,920.1	4,142.3	4,299.6	4,684.4	4,981.4	5,295.8	5,632.3	6,153.9
M3	59mcu	3,735.8	3,937.4	4,090.3	4,267.3	4,472.0	4,709.0	4,910.3	5,446.7	5,807.8	6,178.7	6,568.2	7,121.5
Nonmonetary Liabs. of MFIs	59mfu	2,124.9	2,471.8	2,774.3	3,153.1	3,240.3	3,524.4	3,708.6	3,890.1	3,987.3	4,138.7	4,461.2	5,001.1

		1994	1995	1996	1997	1998	1999	2000	2001	2002	2003	2004	2005
Interest Rates						*Percent Per Annum*							
Discount Rate (End of Period).........	60	....	....	....	....	....	4.00	5.75	4.25	3.75	3.00	3.00	3.25
Eurosyst. Refinancing Rate.............	60r	....	....	....	....	....	2.71	....	† 4.30	3.29	2.32	2.03	2.10
Eurosyst. Deposit Facility Rate.........	60x						1.71	3.06	3.23	2.21	1.25	1.00	1.02
Interbank Rate (Overnight)..............	60a	6.18	6.09	4.58	4.02	3.73	2.74	4.12	4.38	3.28	2.32	2.05	2.09
Money Market Rate.....................	60b	6.53	6.82	5.09	4.38	3.96	2.97	4.39	4.26	3.32	2.34	2.11	2.19
Deposit Rate...........................	60l	....	....	4.08	3.41	3.20	2.45	3.45	3.49	2.80	....	....	....
Households: Stocks, up to 2 years..	60lhs	....	....	....	....	....	....	....	....	....	2.22	1.91	1.93
New Business, up to 1 year.........	60lhn	....	....	....	....	....	....	....	....	....	2.11	1.91	1.98
Corporations: Stocks, up to 2 years	60lcs	....	....	....	....	....	....	....	....	....	2.37	2.10	2.13
New Business, up to 1 year.........	60lcn	....	....	....	....	....	....	....	....	....	2.24	2.00	2.05
REPOS, Stocks.........................	60lcr	....	....	....	....	....	....	....	....	....	2.28	1.97	2.02
Lending Rate...........................	60p	....	....	8.88	7.58	6.73	5.65	6.60	6.83	6.14	....	....	....
Households: Stocks, up to 1 year....	60phs	....	....	....	....	....	....	....	....	....	8.55	8.21	7.96
New Bus., Floating & up to 1 year	60pns	....	....	....	....	....	....	....	....	....	6.85	6.84	6.75
House Purch., Stocks,Over 5 years	60phm	....	....	....	....	....	....	....	....	....	5.38	4.96	4.66
House Purch., New Bus., 5-10 yrs	60phn	....	....	....	....	....	....	....	....	....	4.94	4.81	4.17
Corporations: Stocks, up to 1 year..	60pcs	....	....	....	....	....	....	....	....	....	4.71	4.43	4.32
New Bus., Over € 1 mil.,up to 1 yi	60pcn	....	....	....	....	....	....	....	....	....	3.28	2.99	3.02
Government Bond Yield..................	61	8.18	8.73	7.23	5.96	4.70	4.65	5.44	5.03	4.92	4.16	4.14	3.44
Prices, Production, Labor						*Index Numbers (2000=100): Period Averages*							
Producer Prices.........................	63	....	....	....	....	† 95.4	95.0	100.0	102.2	102.1	103.6	105.8	110.1
Harmonized CPI (hcpi)...................	64h	....	....	....	....	96.6	97.7	100.0	102.1	104.4	106.6	† 108.9	111.2
Wages/Labor Costs......................	65..c	....	....	....	....	95.2	97.3	100.0	103.2	107.1	....	....	....
Employment.............................	67..c						97.9	100.0	101.4	101.8	....	....	....
						Number in Thousands: Period Averages							
Unemployment..........................	67c.c	....	....	....	....	....	12,253	11,092	11,042	11,654	12,334	12,680	12,497
Unemployment Rate (%).................	67r.c	....	....	....	....	....	9	8	8	8	9	9	9
Intl. Transactions & Positions						*Billions of Euros*							
Exports.................................	70	....	....	....	....	791.5	† 895.5	1,048.7	1,080.6	1,082.0	1,109.4	1,190.4	1,237.9
Imports, c.i.f...........................	71	....	....	....	....	709.3	† 851.9	1,002.6	1,030.5	1,023.9	1,056.2	1,142.6	1,214.7
						2000=100							
Volume of Exports......................	72	....	....	....	....	† 87.0	88.9	100.0	105.1	108.1	104.2	109.1	99.4
Volume of Imports......................	73	....	....	....	....	† 89.0	94.5	100.0	99.0	98.4	102.8	108.3	104.7
Unit Value of Exports...................	74	....	....	....	....	† 90.5	92.4	100.0	101.0	100.1	101.5	104.0	124.4
Unit Value of Imports...................	75	....	....	....	....	† 79.4	82.0	100.0	100.2	97.9	102.4	105.2	113.5
Balance of Payments						*Billions of US Dollars Minus Sign Indicates Debit*							
Current Account, n.i.e....................	78ald	....	....	....	....	31.35	−25.31	−81.55	† −19.31	51.06	37.03	62.73	−28.06
Goods: Exports f.o.b....................	78aad	....	....	....	....	878.06	867.34	907.88	† 920.86	997.54	1,171.84	1,402.54	1,516.19
Goods: Imports f.o.b....................	78abd	....	....	....	....	−756.11	−787.36	−879.08	† −855.64	−875.37	−1,051.22	−1,272.11	−1,448.24
Trade Balance.......................	78acd	....	....	....	....	121.95	79.98	28.80	† 65.22	122.17	120.62	130.42	67.95
Services: Credit........................	78add	....	....	....	....	258.93	259.05	259.06	† 287.09	313.48	375.55	449.74	493.15
Services: Debit.........................	78aed	....	....	....	....	−265.56	−278.41	−278.42	† −290.51	−299.91	−353.25	−413.98	−450.31
Balance on Goods & Services.......	78afd	....	....	....	....	115.33	60.62	9.44	† 61.81	135.73	142.92	166.18	110.79
Income: Credit.........................	78agd	....	....	....	....	222.66	226.52	257.86	† 243.99	232.31	275.51	336.99	399.09
Income: Debit..........................	78ahd	....	....	....	....	−253.59	−263.81	−299.29	† −279.69	−270.65	−317.57	−370.70	−453.07
Balance on Gds, Serv. & Inc........	78aid	....	....	....	....	84.40	23.32	−31.99	† 26.11	97.39	100.86	132.46	56.82
Current Transfers, n.i.e.: Credit......	78ajd	....	....	....	....	70.06	69.75	62.45	† 71.21	80.04	92.08	102.14	104.70
Current Transfers: Debit...............	78akd	....	....	....	....	−123.10	−118.39	−112.01	† −116.63	−126.37	−155.91	−171.88	−189.58
Capital Account, n.i.e....................	78bcd	....	....	....	....	13.92	13.55	8.41	† 5.62	9.62	15.00	21.79	15.37
Capital Account, n.i.e.: Credit........	78bad	....	....	....	....	19.85	20.25	16.16	† 15.50	18.06	27.08	30.04	29.02
Capital Account: Debit.................	78bbd	....	....	....	....	−5.93	−6.70	−7.75	† −9.88	−8.44	−12.08	−8.25	−13.65
Financial Account, n.i.e.................	78bjd	....	....	....	....	−86.05	2.42	14.00	† −41.45	−15.31	−33.43	−29.77	77.80
Direct Investment Abroad.............	78bdd	....	....	....	....	−195.08	−348.80	−413.73	† −297.98	−163.40	−165.81	−178.69	−287.29
Dir. Invest. in Rep. Econ., n.i.e......	78bed	....	....	....	....	101.63	216.31	379.50	† 199.75	183.75	151.10	126.20	94.50
Portfolio Investment Assets...........	78bfd	....	....	....	....	−403.37	−341.75	−385.32	† −255.02	−163.20	−313.23	−420.80	−551.73
Equity Securities.....................	78bkd	....	....	....	....	−129.30	−175.70	−267.63	† −90.84	−34.01	−91.18	−128.78	−174.29
Debt Securities......................	78bld	....	....	....	....	−274.06	−166.04	−117.68	† −164.18	−129.19	−222.04	−292.02	−377.43
Portfolio Investment Liab., n.i.e......	78bgd	....	....	....	....	280.04	305.10	268.07	† 318.31	298.28	397.98	496.56	747.68
Equity Securities.....................	78bmd	....	....	....	....	117.31	91.18	37.96	† 207.33	78.45	126.85	163.14	343.76
Debt Securities......................	78bnd	....	....	....	....	162.73	213.92	230.11	† 110.98	219.83	271.12	333.43	403.92
Financial Derivatives Assets..........	78bwd	....	....	....	....		....	....	....	....	....	....	....
Financial Derivatives Liabilities.......	78bxd	....	....	....	....	−9.74	3.50	−9.00	† −.84	−11.08	−14.80	−6.31	−18.96
Other Investment Assets..............	78bhd	....	....	....	....	−86.08	−30.34	−165.78	† −243.80	−220.11	−284.39	−391.98	−708.11
Monetary Authorities................	78bod	....	....	....	....	−.84	−1.23	−.99	† .22	−.78	−.92	−.15	−1.38
General Government..................	78bpd	....	....	....	....	−.76	3.56	−2.43	† 2.69	−.05	−.17	−2.69	6.64
Banks...............................	78bqd	....	....	....	....	−21.81	17.75	−118.43	† −209.01	−164.43	−173.58	−326.68	−483.43
Other Sectors.......................	78brd	....	....	....	....	−63.19	−50.43	−43.94	† −37.70	−54.85	−109.71	−62.47	−229.94
Other Investment Liab., n.i.e.........	78bid	....	....	....	....	226.54	198.40	340.26	† 238.13	60.46	195.72	345.25	801.70
Monetary Authorities................	78bsd	....	....	....	....	4.02	7.23	.55	† 3.82	18.23	11.17	8.66	7.99
General Government..................	78btd	....	....	....	....	−6.82	−14.09	.01	† −.67	−7.29	−3.63	−4.77	−2.96
Banks...............................	78bud	....	....	....	....	211.64	174.04	273.42	† 216.66	23.59	151.81	310.01	598.60
Other Sectors.......................	78bvd	....	....	....	....	16.88	31.21	66.28	† 18.33	25.93	36.37	31.35	198.07
Net Errors and Omissions..............	78cad	....	....	....	....	31.15	−2.23	42.98	† 38.62	−42.50	−51.91	−70.39	−89.00
Overall Balance......................	78cbd	....	....	....	....	−9.64	−11.58	−16.15	† −16.51	2.88	−33.32	−15.64	−23.89
Reserves and Related Items............	79dad	....	....	....	....	9.64	11.58	16.15	† 16.51	−2.88	33.32	15.64	23.89
Reserve Assets.......................	79dbd	....	....	....	....	9.64	11.58	16.15	† 16.51	−2.88	33.32	15.64	23.89
Use of Fund Credit and Loans........	79dcd	....	....	....	....	—	....	....	....	....	....	....	....
Exceptional Financing..................	79ded	....	....	....	....	—	....	....	....	....	....	....	....

		1994	1995	1996	1997	1998	1999	2000	2001	2002	2003	2004	2005
International Investment Position							*Billions of US Dollars*						
Assets..............................	79aad	....	....	....	....	....	5,891.88	6,298.70	† 6,722.59	7,614.08	10,019.27	11,757.09	12,399.84
Direct Investment Abroad..............	79abd	....	....	....	....	....	1,237.50	1,516.39	† 1,719.72	1,968.83	2,716.06	3,083.74	3,025.78
Portfolio Investment......................	79acd	....	....	....	....	....	2,086.54	2,196.73	† 2,216.48	2,414.74	3,327.55	4,065.58	4,433.51
Equity Securities...........................	79add	....	....	....	....	....	1,010.30	1,075.95	† 984.14	894.78	1,357.64	1,687.52	1,949.99
Debt Securities...........................	79aed	....	....	....	....	....	1,076.24	1,120.78	† 1,232.34	1,519.96	1,969.91	2,378.07	2,483.52
Financial Derivatives....................	79ald	....	....	....	....	....	111.63	98.44	† 114.49	142.53	199.56	221.18	273.68
Other Investment........................	79afd	....	....	....	....	....	2,082.52	2,135.85	† 2,325.91	2,704.22	3,389.09	4,004.17	4,289.48
Monetary Authorities..................	79agd	....	....	....	....	....	2.91	3.29	† 2.71	3.64	6.33	6.25	6.54
General Government...................	79ahd	....	....	....	....	....	126.11	124.59	† 112.36	119.99	119.65	134.34	117.02
Banks...................................	79aid	....	....	....	....	....	1,318.79	1,354.84	† 1,511.70	1,768.72	2,245.80	2,724.91	2,953.48
Other Sectors...........................	79ajd	....	....	....	....	....	634.71	653.12	† 699.13	811.87	1,017.31	1,138.68	1,212.45
Reserve Assets...........................	79akd	....	....	....	....	....	373.68	351.29	† 345.99	383.76	387.01	382.41	377.39
Liabilities..............................	79lad	....	....	....	....	....	6,270.39	6,719.64	† 7,074.11	8,262.31	11,040.35	13,049.73	13,651.94
Dir. Invest. in Rep. Economy..........	79lbd	....	....	....	....	....	903.23	1,170.55	† 1,358.24	1,754.67	2,663.28	3,039.48	2,720.16
Portfolio Investment......................	79lcd	....	....	....	....	....	2,988.76	2,918.08	† 2,939.81	3,336.58	4,483.68	5,496.09	5,975.29
Equity Securities...........................	79ldd	....	....	....	....	....	1,735.05	1,500.54	† 1,445.76	1,432.63	1,963.97	2,428.62	2,876.13
Debt Securities...........................	79led	....	....	....	....	....	1,253.71	1,417.53	† 1,494.05	1,903.95	2,519.70	3,067.46	3,099.16
Financial Derivatives....................	79lld	....	....	....	....	....	95.54	96.55	† 112.25	155.14	209.99	241.41	293.46
Other Investment........................	79lfd	....	....	....	....	....	2,282.87	2,534.47	† 2,663.81	3,015.92	3,683.41	4,272.75	4,663.04
Monetary Authorities..................	79lgd	....	....	....	....	....	39.68	39.31	† 35.84	60.18	82.71	....	....
General Government...................	79lhd	....	....	....	....	....	51.44	48.29	† 50.51	59.14	55.85	....	....
Banks...................................	79lid	....	....	....	....	....	1,830.41	2,013.49	† 2,127.38	2,349.74	2,866.67	....	....
Other Sectors...........................	79ljd	....	....	....	....	....	361.35	433.38	† 450.08	546.87	678.18	....	....
National Accounts							*Billions of Euros:*						
Househ.Cons.Expend.,incl.NPISHs....	96f.c	....	....	....	....	3,309.5	† 3,482.2	3,763.2	3,923.2	4,144.9	4,270.2	4,414.7	4,560.2
Government Consumption Expend...	91f.c	....	....	....	....	1,168.0	† 1,229.8	1,307.2	1,371.4	1,465.5	1,523.1	1,576.9	1,632.0
Gross Fixed Capital Formation..........	93e.c	....	....	....	....	1,186.8	† 1,291.4	1,420.2	1,443.7	1,466.4	1,494.3	1,558.8	1,631.4
Changes in Inventories...................	93i.c	....	....	....	....	59.9	† 22.3	28.4	−8.8	−14.6	1.3	17.7	37.3
Exports of Goods and Services..........	90c.c	....	....	....	....	1,925.5	† 2,052.7	2,448.1	2,563.8	2,625.3	2,624.5	2,815.9	3,004.0
Imports of Goods and Services (-).....	98c.c	....	....	....	....	1,778.2	† 1,951.1	2,391.0	2,450.4	2,436.4	2,463.8	2,657.1	2,891.1
Gross Domestic Product (GDP).........	99b.c	....	....	....	....	5,871.4	† 6,132.8	6,425.6	6,842.9	7,251.1	7,449.5	7,726.9	7,973.8
Net Primary Income from Abroad.....	98.nc	....	....	....	....	−35.6	† −39.1	....	....	....	....	....	....
GDP Volume 1995 Prices.................	99b.r	....	....	....	....	5,647.3	† 5,819.7	6,008.7	6,227.3	6,279.4	6,317.5	6,427.7	6,529.3
GDP Volume (2000=100)...............	99bvr	....	....	....	....	94.5	† 96.9	100.0	103.6	104.5	105.1	107.0	108.7
GDP Deflator (2000=100)...............	99bir	....	....	....	....	94.8	† 98.5	100.0	102.8	108.0	110.3	112.4	114.2

Fiji   819

		1994	1995	1996	1997	1998	1999	2000	2001	2002	2003	2004	2005
Exchange Rates		*Fiji Dollars per SDR: End of Period*											
Official Rate.................................	aa	2.0570	2.1248	1.9900	2.0902	2.7965	2.6981	2.8479	2.9017	2.8072	2.5589	2.5547	2.4939
		Fiji Dollars per US Dollar: End of Period (ae) Period Average (rf)											
Official Rate.................................	ae	1.4090	1.4294	1.3839	1.5492	1.9861	1.9658	2.1858	2.3089	2.0648	1.7221	1.6450	1.7449
Official Rate.................................	rf	1.4641	1.4063	1.4033	1.4437	1.9868	1.9696	2.1286	2.2766	2.1869	1.8958	1.7330	1.6911
		Index Numbers (2000=100): Period Averages											
Official Rate.................................	ahx	145.2	151.1	151.4	147.3	107.0	107.9	100.0	93.3	97.3	112.3	122.7	125.7
Nominal Effective Exchange Rate.....	nec	119.2	118.3	118.5	121.1	100.3	100.4	100.0	99.4	101.1	106.0	107.8	107.7
Real Effective Exchange Rate...........	rec	118.7	116.5	116.5	120.1	102.3	102.5	100.0	100.5	100.8	107.6	109.8	109.2
Fund Position		*Millions of SDRs: End of Period*											
Quota...	2f.s	51.10	51.10	51.10	51.10	51.10	70.30	70.30	70.30	70.30	70.30	70.30	70.30
SDRs..	1b.s	7.39	7.67	7.99	8.29	8.62	4.10	4.47	4.81	5.02	5.18	5.35	5.59
Reserve Position in the Fund...........	1c.s	9.99	10.00	10.05	10.08	10.12	14.94	14.98	15.00	15.07	15.19	15.26	15.31
Total Fund Cred.&Loans Outstg........	2tl	—	—	—	—	—	—	—	—	—	—	—	—
International Liquidity		*Millions of US Dollars Unless Otherwise Indicated: End of Period*											
Total Reserves minus Gold..............	1l.d	273.14	349.03	427.24	360.29	385.67	428.69	411.79	366.39	358.82	423.62	478.10	314.72
SDRs..	1b.d	10.79	11.41	11.49	11.18	12.14	5.63	5.82	6.04	6.83	7.70	8.31	7.99
Reserve Position in the Fund.........	1c.d	14.58	14.87	14.45	13.60	14.25	20.50	19.52	18.85	20.49	22.57	23.70	21.89
Foreign Exchange.......................	1d.d	247.77	322.76	401.30	335.51	359.29	402.55	386.45	341.50	331.50	393.35	446.10	284.84
Gold (Million Fine Troy Ounces)........	1ad	.001	.001	.001	.001	.001	.001	.001	.001	.001	.001	.001	.008
Gold (National Valuation)................	1and	.32	.32	.31	.24	.24	.24	.23	.23	.29	.35	.38	.43
Monetary Authorities: Other Liab.....	4..d												
Deposit Money Banks: Assets...........	7a.d	62.91	50.13	78.07	89.31	136.34	200.07	81.06	84.21	93.30	147.74	115.42	124.22
Liabilities	7b.d	65.66	73.89	124.33	123.48	108.04	159.49	114.08	120.65	148.10	181.70	135.44	162.18
Monetary Authorities		*Millions of Fiji Dollars: End of Period*											
Foreign Assets...............................	11	384.9	498.9	591.2	558.1	765.5	842.7	900.1	846.0	741.2	729.5	786.5	549.2
Claims on Central Government........	12a	—	—	—	—	—	50.7	56.1	66.2	59.0	90.4	78.8	140.6
Claims on Official Entities................	12bx	.1	.1	—	—	—	—	—	—	—	—	—	—
Reserve Money..............................	14	223.6	243.4	247.9	260.4	276.8	434.2	352.2	420.0	460.1	606.8	519.8	531.4
of which: Currency Outside DMBs..	14a	115.6	117.8	125.4	134.0	159.8	189.9	163.3	181.7	202.6	226.2	252.3	280.1
Liabs.of Central Bank: Securities......	16ac	126.6	220.5	253.3	210.7	252.9	255.8	415.7	338.6	219.9	119.1	254.6	86.0
Foreign Liabilities..........................	16c	—	—	—	—	—	—	—	—	—	—	—	—
Central Government Deposits...........	16d	14.8	6.8	47.2	40.0	22.3	42.6	22.5	17.3	6.0	8.0	12.0	6.7
Capital Accounts............................	17a	45.8	49.3	42.3	50.5	197.1	169.0	136.5	115.3	103.1	90.6	88.9	80.8
Other Items (Net)...........................	17r	−25.8	−21.0	.4	−3.4	16.4	−8.3	29.2	21.0	11.1	−4.7	−10.1	−15.2
Deposit Money Banks		*Millions of Fiji Dollars: End of Period*											
Reserves.......................................	20	107.9	125.5	120.2	126.4	111.5	237.3	174.2	233.3	243.9	372.7	252.5	251.3
Claims on Mon.Author.:Securities.....	20c	44.0	104.1	106.0	60.4	44.4	54.5	43.7	17.1	29.8	54.2	97.0	35.3
Foreign Assets...............................	21	88.6	71.7	108.0	138.4	270.8	393.3	177.2	194.4	192.7	254.4	189.9	216.7
Claims on Central Government........	22a	80.7	65.4	78.8	87.0	107.0	117.8	95.3	129.9	164.2	222.8	185.3	216.8
Claims on Official Entities................	22bx	144.4	137.7	145.8	164.5	154.4	137.1	138.7	120.0	97.7	100.1	127.3	141.9
Claims on Private Sector..................	22d	1,080.9	1,112.2	1,165.0	1,013.9	963.8	997.0	1,145.9	1,081.8	1,136.1	1,326.4	1,565.8	1,949.3
Demand Deposits...........................	24	216.0	257.0	317.3	300.8	315.6	475.1	402.0	420.2	480.0	642.9	727.8	893.5
Time Deposits...............................	25	1,069.7	1,089.6	1,032.1	913.2	859.9	851.6	920.1	846.2	870.6	1,080.5	1,167.7	1,316.7
Money Market Instruments..............	26aa	13.0	11.4	11.4	10.5	13.1	22.4	13.7	14.1	15.9	23.1	22.9	23.4
Foreign Liabilities..........................	26c	92.5	105.6	172.1	191.3	214.6	313.5	249.3	278.6	305.8	312.9	222.8	283.0
Central Government Deposits...........	26d	40.5	40.1	21.0	37.8	78.6	122.5	54.6	56.1	59.2	68.9	74.0	73.2
Other Items (Net)...........................	27r	114.7	112.8	170.1	136.9	37.1	151.8	155.1	135.1	161.6	133.0	202.3	221.6
Monetary Survey		*Millions of Fiji Dollars: End of Period*											
Foreign Assets (Net).......................	31n	381.0	464.9	527.2	505.2	821.7	922.5	827.9	761.8	628.0	671.0	753.6	483.0
Domestic Credit.............................	32	1,250.7	1,268.3	1,321.3	1,187.6	1,124.3	1,137.5	1,358.8	1,324.6	1,391.7	1,662.9	1,871.2	2,368.7
Claims on Central Govt. (Net)........	32an	25.3	18.4	10.5	9.1	6.1	3.3	74.2	122.8	158.0	236.4	178.1	277.5
Claims on Official Entities.............	32bx	144.5	137.8	145.8	164.5	154.4	137.1	138.7	120.0	97.7	100.1	127.3	141.9
Claims on Private Sector...............	32d	1,080.9	1,112.2	1,165.0	1,013.9	963.8	997.0	1,145.9	1,081.8	1,136.1	1,326.4	1,565.8	1,949.3
Money..	34	331.6	374.8	444.9	434.8	480.9	672.0	580.0	606.9	696.1	877.5	995.1	1,173.7
Quasi-Money.................................	35	1,069.7	1,089.6	1,032.1	913.2	859.9	851.6	920.1	846.2	870.6	1,080.5	1,167.7	1,316.7
Money Market Instruments..............	36aa	13.0	11.4	11.4	10.5	13.1	22.4	13.7	14.1	15.9	23.1	22.9	23.4
Liabs.of Central Bank: Securities.......	36ac	82.5	116.4	147.3	150.3	208.4	201.3	372.0	321.4	190.1	64.9	157.6	50.7
Capital Accounts............................	37a	45.8	49.3	42.3	50.5	197.1	169.0	136.5	115.3	103.1	90.6	88.9	80.8
Other Items (Net)...........................	37r	89.0	91.8	170.5	133.4	186.6	143.5	164.3	182.5	144.1	197.2	192.5	206.4
Money plus Quasi-Money.................	35l	1,401.4	1,464.3	1,476.9	1,348.0	1,340.8	1,523.7	1,500.1	1,453.1	1,566.7	1,958.0	2,162.8	2,490.4
Nonbank Financial Institutions		*Millions of Fiji Dollars: End of Period*											
Claims on Central Government........	42a.l	58.1	58.2	77.4	127.7	127.0	134.8	146.8	164.2	186.2	201.0	222.2	206.5
Claims on Local Government...........	42b.l	20.6	26.8	26.9	—	—	—	—	—	—	—	—	—
Claims on Nonfin.Pub.Enterprises.....	42c.l	26.7	36.2	54.4	—	—	—	—	—	—	—	—	—
Claims on Private Sector.................	42d.l	59.0	68.3	73.8	93.5	100.5	119.8	126.7	134.5	139.2	153.4	168.6	180.8
Incr.in Total Assets(Within Per.)........	49z.l	23.2	27.6	15.1	−14.4	14.8	28.7	25.9	34.0	31.2	10.6	28.5	8.6
Money (National Definitions)		*Millions of Fiji Dollars: End of Period*											
M1..	59ma	367.5	412.5	456.3	445.3	493.9	694.5	593.7	620.9	712.0	900.0	1,018.0	1,197.1
M2..	59mb	1,455.5	1,524.4	1,488.4	1,358.5	1,353.8	1,546.1	1,513.9	1,467.1	1,582.5	1,980.5	2,185.7	2,513.8
Interest Rates		*Percent Per Annum*											
Bank Rate (End of Period)................	60	6.00	6.00	6.00	1.88	2.50	2.50	8.00	1.75	1.75	1.75	2.25	2.75
Money Market Rate........................	60b	4.10	3.95	2.43	1.91	1.27	1.27	2.58	.79	.92	.86	.90	1.28
Treasury Bill Rate...........................	60c	2.69	3.15	2.98	2.60	2.00	2.00	3.63	1.51	1.66	1.06	1.56	1.94
Deposit Rate..................................	60l	3.15	3.18	3.38	3.08	2.17	1.24	.90	.78	.62	.51	.38	.38
Lending Rate.................................	60p	11.28	11.06	11.33	11.03	9.66	8.77	8.40	8.34	8.05	7.60	7.17	6.78
Government Bond Yield...................	61	6.49	6.69	7.41	7.08	6.49	6.17	5.57	4.79	4.28	3.27	2.56	2.76

Fiji 819

Prices, Production, Labor		1994	1995	1996	1997	1998	1999	2000	2001	2002	2003	2004	2005
		Index Numbers (2000=100): Period Averages											
Consumer Prices	64	84.3	86.2	88.8	91.8	97.0	98.9	100.0	104.3	105.1	109.5	112.5	115.2
Wage Rates	65	93.7	94.9	106.6	98.8	94.6	99.0	100.0	104.3	105.2	109.5	....	....
Industrial Production	66	78.9	† 81.2	87.8	93.6	96.8	105.4	100.0	110.6	111.4	110.5	121.4	....
Tourist Arrivals	66.t	108.4	108.3	115.5	122.2	126.3	139.4	100.0	118.3	135.3	146.5	....	....
Industrial Employment	67	86.6	88.3	100.4	102.2	101.8	100.6	100.0	104.1	106.8	108.6	....	....
		Number in Thousands: Period Averages											
Labor Force	67d	....	....	298	....	320	331	342	....	....	....	....	....
Employment	67e	96	98	111	113	113	111	111	115	118	120	....	....
Unemployment	67c	16	15	....	....	....	25	42	....	....	....	....	....
Unemployment Rate (%)	67r	5.7	5.4	....	....	....	7.6	12.1	....	....	....	....	....
Intl. Transactions & Positions		*Millions of Fiji Dollars*											
Exports	70	657.04	764.48	821.07	758.13	905.64	947.64	1,025.53	1,007.81	1,192.08	1,273.07	1,175.18	1,220.61
Imports, c.i.f.	71	1,209.85	1,253.83	1,384.46	1,392.66	1,434.17	1,778.71	1,756.39	1,807.86	1,953.22	2,214.59	2,204.73	2,722.79
Imports, f.o.b.	71.v	1,053.70	1,070.80	1,178.70	1,182.20	1,221.00	....	1,756.40	1,808.00	1,953.32	1,953.31		
Balance of Payments		*Millions of US Dollars: Minus Sign Indicates Debit*											
Current Account, n.i.e.	78ald	−112.8	−112.7	13.5	−34.1	−59.9	12.7	....	....	....	....	....	....
Goods: Exports f.o.b.	78aad	490.2	519.6	672.2	535.6	428.9	537.7	....	....	....	....	....	....
Goods: Imports f.o.b.	78abd	−719.7	−761.4	−839.9	−818.9	−614.6	−653.3	....	....	....	....	....	....
Trade Balance	78acd	−229.5	−241.8	−167.7	−283.2	−185.6	−115.6	....	....	....	....	....	....
Services: Credit	78add	534.7	564.1	612.6	667.9	503.2	525.1	....	....	....	....	....	....
Services: Debit	78aed	−366.0	−398.6	−412.9	−405.6	−352.0	−389.8	....	....	....	....	....	....
Balance on Goods & Services	78afd	−60.8	−76.3	31.9	−20.9	−34.4	19.7	....	....	....	....	....	....
Income: Credit	78agd	49.2	55.4	63.6	61.7	54.6	47.3	....	....	....	....	....	....
Income: Debit	78ahd	−105.7	−94.6	−91.6	−99.2	−110.6	−82.8	....	....	....	....	....	....
Balance on Gds, Serv. & Inc.	78aid	−117.3	−115.5	4.0	−58.4	−90.4	−15.8	....	....	....	....	....	....
Current Transfers, n.i.e.: Credit	78ajd	38.1	36.0	44.1	54.6	45.3	42.7	....	....	....	....	....	....
Current Transfers: Debit	78akd	−33.5	−33.1	−34.6	−30.3	−14.7	−14.2	....	....	....	....	....	....
Capital Account, n.i.e.	78bcd	43.4	87.0	70.8	48.5	60.6	14.0	....	....	....	....	....	....
Capital Account, n.i.e.: Credit	78bad	76.0	120.1	114.5	88.9	100.6	59.3	....	....	....	....	....	....
Capital Account: Debit	78bbd	−32.6	−33.1	−43.8	−40.5	−40.0	−45.3	....	....	....	....	....	....
Financial Account, n.i.e.	78bjd	61.0	88.3	3.6	−15.1	28.7	−104.0	....	....	....	....	....	....
Direct Investment Abroad	78bdd	.3	2.8	−9.8	−30.0	−62.6	−53.0	....	....	....	....	....	....
Dir. Invest. in Rep. Econ., n.i.e.	78bed	67.5	69.5	2.4	15.6	107.0	−33.2	....	....	....	....	....	....
Portfolio Investment Assets	78bfd	—	—	—	—	—	....	....	....	....	....	....	....
Equity Securities	78bkd	—	—	—	—	—	....	....	....	....	....	....	....
Debt Securities	78bld	—	—	—	—	—	....	....	....	....	....	....	....
Portfolio Investment Liab., n.i.e.	78bgd	—	—	—	—	—	....	....	....	....	....	....	....
Equity Securities	78bmd	—	—	—	—	—	....	....	....	....	....	....	....
Debt Securities	78bnd	—	—	—	—	—	....	....	....	....	....	....	....
Financial Derivatives Assets	78bwd	—	—	—	—	—	....	....	....	....	....	....	....
Financial Derivatives Liabilities	78bxd	—	—	—	—	—	....	....	....	....	....	....	....
Other Investment Assets	78bhd	1.2	12.0	−25.9	−21.1	−66.6	−62.2	....	....	....	....	....	....
Monetary Authorities	78bod	—	—	—	—	—	....	....	....	....	....	....	....
General Government	78bpd	—	—	—	—	—	....	....	....	....	....	....	....
Banks	78bqd	1.2	12.0	−25.9	−21.1	−66.6	−62.2	....	....	....	....	....	....
Other Sectors	78brd	—	—	—	—	—	....	....	....	....	....	....	....
Other Investment Liab., n.i.e.	78bid	−8.1	3.9	36.8	20.4	51.0	44.4	....	....	....	....	....	....
Monetary Authorities	78bsd	—	—	—	—	—	....	....	....	....	....	....	....
General Government	78btd	—	—	—	—	—	....	....	....	....	....	....	....
Banks	78bud	−8.1	3.9	36.8	20.4	51.0	44.4	....	....	....	....	....	....
Other Sectors	78bvd	—	—	—	—	—	....	....	....	....	....	....	....
Net Errors and Omissions	78cad	30.9	30.4	−9.7	−24.3	−24.6	32.5	....	....	....	....	....	....
Overall Balance	78cbd	22.5	93.0	78.1	−25.1	4.9	−44.9	....	....	....	....	....	....
Reserves and Related Items	79dad	−22.5	−93.0	−78.1	25.1	−4.9	44.9	....	....	....	....	....	....
Reserve Assets	79dbd	10.7	−76.6	−71.1	29.7	−27.4	−30.5	....	....	....	....	....	....
Use of Fund Credit and Loans	79dcd	—	—	—	—	—	....	....	....	....	....	....	....
Exceptional Financing	79ded	−33.2	−16.4	−7.0	−4.6	22.5	75.3	....	....	....	....	....	....
Government Finance		*Millions of Fiji Dollars: Year Ending December 31*											
Deficit (-) or Surplus	80	−114.6	−92.7	−211.4	−281.9	−104.3	....	....	....	....	....	....	....
Total Revenue and Grants	81y	697.9	718.9	743.6	803.4	1,141.2	....	....	....	....	....	....	....
Revenue	81	693.4	712.6	736.3	798.5	1,138.6	....	....	....	....	....	....	....
Grants	81z	4.5	6.3	7.3	4.9	2.6	....	....	....	....	....	....	....
Exp. & Lending Minus Repay.	82z	812.5	811.6	955.0	1,085.3	1,245.5	....	....	....	....	....	....	....
Expenditure	82	794.4	803.6	945.2	1,081.8	1,231.5	....	....	....	....	....	....	....
Lending Minus Repayments	83	18.1	8.0	9.8	3.5	14.0	....	....	....	....	....	....	....
Total Financing	80h	114.6	92.7	211.4	281.9	104.3	....	....	....	....	....	....	....
Domestic	84a	83.6	71.5	193.9	273.2	93.5	....	....	....	....	....	....	....
Foreign	85a	31.0	21.2	17.5	8.7	10.8	....	....	....	....	....	....	....
Total Debt by Residence	88	981.8	1,001.8	1,133.5	1,356.3	1,454.9	....	....	....	....	....	....	....
Domestic	88a	792.2	807.3	942.8	1,156.1	1,060.6	....	....	....	....	....	....	....
Foreign	89a	189.6	194.5	190.7	200.2	394.3	....	....	....	....	....	....	....

Fiji 819

National Accounts		1994	1995	1996	1997	1998	1999	2000	2001	2002	2003	2004	2005
						Millions of Fiji Dollars							
Househ.Cons.Expend.,incl.NPISHs....	**96f**	1,666.0	1,764.7	1,858.2	1,868.8	1,934.3	1,976.2	2,069.0	2,188.0	....	....	....	....
Government Consumption Expend...	**91f**	437.2	446.4	474.1	507.5	572.6	607.7	633.7	655.4	....	....	....	....
Gross Fixed Capital Formation.........	**93e**	320.5	350.0	296.8	312.2	482.2	507.2	403.1	516.8	....	....	....	....
Changes in Inventories....................	**93i**	40.0	30.0	40.0	40.0	40.0	40.0	40.0	40.0				
Exports of Goods and Services.........	**90c**	1,507.8	1,532.2	1,771.4	1,765.1	1,837.5	2,210.3	2,092.2	2,136.0	....	....	....	....
Imports of Goods and Services (-).....	**98c**	1,588.8	1,630.6	1,758.3	1,766.7	1,918.3	2,349.5	2,355.0	2,327.0	....	....	....	....
Gross Domestic Product (GDP)........	**99b**	2,673.1	2,744.1	2,956.8	3,003.5	3,262.7	3,792.6	3,562.1	3,748.1	3,979.5	4,332.4	4,693.6	....
Net National Income......................	**99e**	....	2,553.0	2,719.3	2,803.0	2,857.5	3,179.8	3,196.3	3,339.1				
GDP at Factor Cost..........................	**99ba**	2,293.4	2,373.0	2,578.4	2,586.8	2,815.1	3,280.2	3,150.8	3,301.7	3,475.4	3,679.9	4,001.1	....
Net Primary Income from Abroad.....	**98.n**	54.1	81.6	70.2	67.6	152.0	100.9	76.1	202.4	....	....	....	....
Gross National Income (GNI)...........	**99a**	2,590.3	2,744.7	2,923.0	3,006.8	3,172.4	3,511.0	3,459.5	3,676.6	....	....	....	....
Consumption of Fixed Capital.........	**99cf**	183	192	204	204	315	331	263	337	....	....	....	....
GDP at Fact.Cost,Vol.'95 Prices.......	**99bap**	....	2,373.0	2,487.2	2,432.7	2,465.1	2,682.3	2,645.6	2,691.3	2,769.9	2,803.4	2,960.5	....
GDP Volume (2000=100)................	**99bvp**	87.5	† 89.7	94.0	92.0	93.2	101.4	100.0	101.7	104.7	106.0	111.9	....
GDP Deflator (2000=100)................	**99bip**	83.2	84.0	87.0	89.3	95.9	102.7	100.0	103.0	105.4	110.2	113.5	....
						Millions: Midyear Estimates							
Population................................	**99z**	.76	.77	.78	.79	.79	.80	.81	.82	.83	.83	.84	.85

Finland 172

		1994	1995	1996	1997	1998	1999	2000	2001	2002	2003	2004	2005
Exchange Rates						*Euros per SDR: End of Period*								
Official Rate..................................	aa	6.9244	6.4790	6.6777	7.3139	7.1753	1.3662	1.4002	1.4260	1.2964	1.1765	1.1402	1.2116
						Euros per US Dollar: End of Period (ae) Period Average (rf)								
Official Rate..................................	ae	4.7432	4.3586	4.6439	5.4207	5.0960	.9954	1.0747	1.1347	.9536	.7918	.7342	.8477
Official Rate..................................	rf	5.2235	4.3667	4.5936	5.1914	5.3441	.9386	1.0854	1.1175	1.0626	.8860	.8054	.8041
						Markkaa per ECU: End of Period (ea) Period Average (eb)								
ECU Rate..................................	ea	5.8343	5.7282	5.8188	5.9856	5.9458	....	....	....	....	....	....	....
ECU Rate..................................	eb	6.2084	5.7122	5.8245	5.8874	5.9855	....	....	....	....	....	....	....
						Index Numbers (2000=100): Period Averages								
Official Rate (1995=100)...............	ahx	83.9	100.0	95.0	84.1	81.7	....	....	....	....	....	....	....
Nominal Effective Exchange Rate.....	neu	103.6	114.8	111.3	107.9	107.2	104.9	100.0	101.3	102.4	106.9	108.4	108.4
Real Effective Exchange Rate...........	reu	112.4	125.5	117.4	110.8	106.5	100.0	100.0	103.3	103.6	107.2	110.6	110.7
Fund Position						*Millions of SDRs: End of Period*								
Quota..................................	2f.s	861.8	861.8	861.8	861.8	861.8	1,263.8	1,263.8	1,263.8	1,263.8	1,263.8	1,263.8	1,263.8
SDRs..................................	1b.s	222.7	241.6	201.6	241.7	247.5	211.3	106.5	186.3	147.0	131.0	106.7	113.3
Reserve Position in the Fund..........	1c.s	196.1	259.5	292.8	414.2	595.0	464.3	381.8	439.0	476.8	522.1	406.0	198.3
of which: Outstg.Fund Borrowing...	2c	—	—	—	—	31.3	—	—	—	—	—	—	—
Total Fund Cred.&Loans Outstg......	2tl	—	—	—	—	—	—	—	—	—	—	—	—
International Liquidity						*Millions of US Dollars Unless Otherwise Indicated: End of Period*								
Total Res.Min.Gold (Eurosys.Def).....	1l.d	10,662.0	10,038.3	6,916.3	8,416.6	9,694.5	† 8,219.7	7,976.9	7,983.3	9,285.0	10,514.9	12,318.2	10,588.3
SDRs..................................	1b.d	325.1	359.2	289.9	326.1	348.5	290.1	138.7	234.1	199.9	194.6	165.7	161.9
Reserve Position in the Fund..........	1c.d	286.3	385.8	421.1	558.8	837.8	637.3	497.5	551.7	648.3	775.8	630.5	283.4
Foreign Exchange..........................	1d.d	10,050.6	9,293.4	6,205.3	7,531.7	8,508.2	7,292.4	7,340.7	7,197.6	8,436.8	9,544.5	11,522.0	10,143.1
o/w:Fin.Deriv.Rel.to Reserves.......	1ddd	....	....	....	....	....	....	....	....	1.05	7.58	1.36	−1.18
Other Reserve Assets.................	1e.d	—	—	—	—	—	—	—	—	—	—	—	—
Gold (Million Fine Troy Ounces).....	1ad	2.003	1.600	1.600	1.600	2.002	1.577	1.577	1.577	1.577	1.577	1.580	1.580
Gold (Eurosystem Valuation)............	1and	459.6	399.7	375.1	321.4	427.8	457.7	432.8	436.0	540.5	658.0	692.0	810.5
Memo:Euro Cl. on Non-EA Res.......	1dgd	....	....	....	....	....	2,686	—	—	30	254	311	312
Non-Euro Cl. on EA Res........	1dhd	....	....	....	....	....	682	812	653	733	976	947	919
Mon. Auth.: Other Foreign Assets.....	3..d	....	....	....	....	....	† —	—	—	733.0	975.1	932.5	906.0
Foreign Liabilities.................	4..d	27.5	278.6	201.2	107.8	143.9	† 437.0	458.7	97.8	4.2	314.5	1,266.8	601.6
Banking Insts.: Foreign Assets..........	7a.d	22,295	24,169	26,986	21,364	21,845	† 15,715	19,914	35,258	41,884	51,763	66,705	61,329
Foreign Liab....................	7b.d	30,679	29,269	25,884	17,916	19,991	† 9,372	15,472	28,041	26,341	25,265	34,950	39,518
Monetary Authorities						*Millions of Markkaa through 1998; Millions of Euros Beginning 1999: End of Period*								
Fgn. Assets (Cl.on Non-EA Ctys).......	11	52,752	48,916	36,461	51,505	51,999	10,926	8,897	9,419	9,398	9,002	9,716	9,776
Claims on General Government........	12a.u	....	....	....	....	....	91	107	142	111	115	130	139
o/w: Claims on Gen.Govt.in Cty.....	12a	1,806	1,882	1,907	2,015	2,074	—	—	—	—	—	—	—
Claims on Banking Institutions........	12e.u	....	....	....	....	....	4,565	1,654	2,327	6,820	7,269	7,340	8,391
o/w: Claims on Bank.Inst.in Cty.....	12e	1,718	8,415	13,301	2,837	19	1,513	471	1,294	2,970	2,850	2,450	1,692
Claims on Other Resident Sectors.....	12d.u	....	....	....	....	....	535	429	361	385	349	346	395
o/w: Cl. on Oth.Res.Sect.in Cty......	12d	3,951	3,302	2,462	1,877	1,541	234	171	106	34	7	7	7
Currency Issued..........................	14a	14,315	15,611	16,891	17,817	17,689	3,350	3,336	2,687	6,258	7,215	8,643	9,738
Liabilities to Banking Insts...........	14c.u	....	....	....	....	....	8,238	2,646	5,007	5,923	4,918	3,677	3,536
o/w: Liabs to Bank.Inst.in Cty.......	14c	43,148	42,766	22,359	18,412	17,888	4,884	2,475	4,111	3,759	2,146	3,156	3,535
Demand Dep. of Other Res.Sect.......	14d.u	....	....	....	....	....	—	—	—	—	—	—	—
o/w:D.Dep.of Oth.Res.Sect.in Cty...	14d	—	—	—	—	—	—	—	—	—	—	—	—
Other Dep. of Other Res.Sect...........	15..u	....	....	....	....	....	1	—	—	—	—	—	—
o/w:O.Dep.of Oth.Res.Sect.in Cty...	15	1,549	994	574	32	6	1	—	—	—	—	—	—
Bonds & Money Mkt. Instruments.....	16n.u	....	....	....	....	....	—	—	—	—	—	—	—
Foreign Liab. (to Non-EA Ctys).........	16c	130	1,214	934	584	733	435	493	111	4	249	930	510
Central Government Deposits...........	16d.u	....	....	....	....	....	—	—	—	—	—	—	—
o/w: Cent.Govt.Dep. in Cty...........	16d	93	75	—	—	—	—	—	—	—	—	—	—
Capital Accounts..........................	17a	6,749	6,691	6,716	6,810	6,785	4,552	5,061	5,332	5,342	4,654	4,833	5,246
Other Items (Net).........................	17r	−5,756	−4,836	6,658	14,579	12,533	−459	−449	−890	−812	−302	−551	−330
Memo: Currency Put into Circ..........	14m	....	....	....	....	....	....	....	....	3,446	3,918	4,796	5,812
Banking Institutions						*Millions of Markkaa through 1998; Millions of Euros Beginning 1999: End of Period*								
Claims on Monetary Authorities.......	20	46,653	45,976	25,604	21,711	20,774	4,884	2,475	4,111	3,759	2,146	3,156	3,535
Claims on Bk.Inst.in Oth.EA Ctys.....	20b.u	....	....	....	....	....	5,775	7,515	3,951	2,866	3,622	5,306	7,085
Fgn. Assets (Cl.on Non-EA Ctys).......	21	105,751	105,344	125,320	115,806	111,320	15,643	21,401	40,007	39,939	40,984	48,972	51,987
Claims on General Government........	22a.u	....	....	....	....	....	8,690	9,017	11,543	10,356	8,464	7,203	7,441
o/w: Claims on Gen.Govt.in Cty.....	22a	15,630	37,442	30,796	37,738	41,067	7,792	7,738	9,842	8,005	6,742	6,001	6,557
Claims on Other Resident Sectors.....	22d.u	....	....	....	....	....	65,481	70,733	78,285	84,208	94,637	104,759	120,103
o/w: Cl. on Oth.Res.Sect.in Cty......	22d	360,408	350,038	347,768	337,266	358,798	64,975	70,091	77,784	83,773	93,389	102,930	118,145
Demand Deposits..........................	24..u	....	....	....	....	....	38,335	37,129	39,014	40,952	44,455	46,158	49,368
o/w:D.Dep.of Oth.Res.Sect.in Cty...	24	143,547	163,521	191,188	201,557	211,632	38,277	37,033	38,866	40,807	44,382	46,041	49,216
Other Deposits.............................	25..u	....	....	....	....	....	22,246	23,873	25,103	27,418	26,429	28,076	29,686
o/w:O.Dep.of Oth.Res.Sect.in Cty...	25	145,670	142,710	104,963	102,154	103,542	22,209	23,823	24,980	27,213	26,157	27,450	28,992
Money Market Fund Shares.............	26m.u	....	....	....	....	....	360	1,524	2,906	4,668	7,080	8,974	10,288
Bonds & Money Mkt. Instruments.....	26n.u	....	....	....	....	....	24,953	23,708	25,475	28,218	31,509	38,365	45,751
Foreign Liab. (to Non-EA Ctys).........	26c	145,519	127,572	120,204	97,118	101,876	9,329	16,628	31,818	25,118	20,004	25,659	33,498
Central Government Deposits...........	26d.u	....	....	....	....	....	2,553	4,368	1,697	1,424	2,824	3,091	3,634
o/w: Cent.Govt.Dep. in Cty...........	26d	11,250	19,057	19,881	27,569	17,951	2,552	4,368	1,696	1,423	2,823	3,090	2,733
Credit from Monetary Authorities.....	26g	1,718	8,415	13,301	2,837	19	1,514	455	1,293	2,970	2,850	2,450	1,692
Liab. to Bk.Inst.in Oth. EA Ctys........	26h.u	....	....	....	....	....	3,153	1,964	2,397	2,387	2,616	5,427	3,177
Capital Accounts..........................	27a	31,789	31,579	29,799	34,003	34,113	6,763	8,156	16,986	17,304	18,650	18,368	21,290
Other Items (Net).........................	27r	48,948	45,947	50,152	47,285	62,826	−8,733	−6,665	−8,790	−9,329	−6,562	−7,155	−8,225

Finland 172

		1994	1995	1996	1997	1998	1999	2000	2001	2002	2003	2004	2005
Banking Survey (Nat'l Residency)		*Millions of Markkaa through 1998; Millions of Euros Beginning 1999: End of Period*											
Foreign Assets (Net)	31n	12,854	25,474	40,643	69,609	60,710	20,912	21,967	21,602	29,347	35,537	39,177	40,058
Domestic Credit	32	370,451	373,532	363,052	351,327	385,529	70,449	73,632	86,036	90,389	97,315	105,848	121,976
Claims on General Govt. (Net)	32an	6,092	20,192	12,821	12,184	25,190	5,240	3,370	8,146	6,582	3,919	2,911	3,824
Claims on Other Resident Sectors	32d	364,359	353,340	350,231	339,143	360,339	65,209	70,262	77,890	83,807	93,396	102,937	118,152
Currency Issued	34a.n	14,315	15,611	16,891	17,817	17,689	3,350	3,336	2,687	6,258	7,215	8,643	9,738
Demand Deposits	34b.n	143,547	163,521	191,188	201,557	211,632	38,277	37,033	38,866	40,807	44,382	46,041	49,216
Other Deposits	35..n	147,218	143,704	105,537	102,186	103,548	22,210	23,823	24,980	27,213	26,157	27,450	28,992
Money Market Fund Shares	36m	....	....	....	....	....	360	1,524	2,906	4,668	7,080	8,974	10,288
Bonds & Money Mkt. Instruments	36n	....	....	....	....	....	24,953	23,708	25,475	28,218	31,509	38,365	45,751
o/w: Over Two Years	36na	....	....	....	....	....	4,985	8,682	9,419	10,048	10,600	14,128	18,797
Capital Accounts	37a	38,538	38,270	36,514	40,813	40,897	11,315	13,217	22,318	22,646	23,304	23,201	26,536
Other Items (Net)	37r	39,688	37,901	53,564	58,563	72,473	−9,104	−7,043	−9,594	−10,071	−6,794	−7,632	−8,480
Banking Survey (EA-Wide Residency)		*Millions of Euros: End of Period*											
Foreign Assets (Net)	31n.u	....	....	....	....	....	16,805	13,177	17,497	24,215	29,733	32,099	27,755
Domestic Credit	32..u	....	....	....	....	....	72,244	75,918	88,634	93,636	100,741	109,347	124,444
Claims on General Govt. (Net)	32anu	....	....	....	....	....	6,228	4,756	9,988	9,043	5,755	4,242	3,946
Claims on Other Resident Sect.	32d.u	....	....	....	....	....	66,016	71,162	78,646	84,593	94,986	105,105	120,498
Currency Issued	34a.u	....	....	....	....	....	3,350	3,336	2,687	6,258	7,215	8,643	9,738
Demand Deposits	34b.u	....	....	....	....	....	38,335	37,129	39,014	40,952	44,455	46,158	49,368
Other Deposits	35..u	....	....	....	....	....	22,247	23,873	25,103	27,418	26,429	28,076	29,686
o/w: Other Dep. Over Two Yrs.	35abu	....	....	....	....	....	2,088	2,631	2,230	3,094	2,423	2,601	2,405
Money Market Fund Shares	36m.u	....	....	....	....	....	360	1,524	2,906	4,668	7,080	8,974	10,288
Bonds & Money Mkt. Instruments	36n.u	....	....	....	....	....	24,953	23,708	25,475	28,218	31,509	38,365	45,751
o/w: Over Two Years	36nau	....	....	....	....	....	4,985	8,682	9,419	10,048	10,600	14,128	18,797
Capital Accounts	37a	....	....	....	....	....	11,315	13,217	22,318	22,646	23,304	23,201	26,536
Other Items (Net)	37r.u	....	....	....	....	....	−11,511	−13,693	−11,372	−12,306	−9,517	−11,954	−19,161
Interest Rates		*Percent Per Annum*											
Discount Rate (End of Period)	60	5.25	4.88	4.00	4.00	3.50	....	....	....	....	....	2.25	
Money Market Rate	60b	5.35	5.75	3.63	3.23	3.57	2.96	4.39	4.26	3.32	2.33	2.11	2.18
Deposit Rate	60l	3.27	3.19	2.35	2.00	....	1.22	1.63	1.94	1.49	....	1.03	....
Households: Stocks, up to 2 years	60lhs	....	....	....	....	....	....	....	....	....	2.36	2.06	2.10
New Business, up to 1 year	60lhn	....	....	....	....	....	....	....	....	....	2.17	1.96	2.06
Corporations: Stocks, up to 2 years	60lcs	....	....	....	....	....	....	....	....	....	2.21	1.93	1.99
New Business, up to 1 year	60lcn	....	....	....	....	....	....	....	....	....	2.20	1.92	1.99
Lending Rate	60p	7.91	7.75	6.16	5.29	5.35	4.71	5.61	5.79	4.82	....	3.69	....
Households: Stocks, up to 1 year	60phs	....	....	....	....	....	....	....	....	....	8.17	7.87	8.01
New Bus., Floating & up to 1 year	60pns	....	....	....	....	....	....	....	....	....	5.08	4.86	4.03
House Purch., Stocks,Over 5 years	60phm	....	....	....	....	....	....	....	....	....	3.96	3.42	3.27
House Purch., New Bus., 5-10 yrs	60phn	....	....	....	....	....	....	....	....	....	4.33	4.39	3.55
Corporations: Stocks, up to 1 year	60pcs	....	....	....	....	....	....	....	....	....	3.88	3.61	3.41
New Bus., Over € 1 mil.,up to 1 yr	60pcn	....	....	....	....	....	....	....	....	....	3.26	3.02	2.97
Prices, Production, Labor		*Index Numbers (2000=100): Period Averages*											
Industrial Share Prices	62	16.5	18.3	16.2	21.5	30.4	52.3	100.0	57.5	44.5	38.1	41.0	48.0
Prices: Domestic Supply	63	92.6	93.2	92.3	93.8	92.5	† 92.4	† 100.0	99.7	98.5	98.4	99.9	103.6
Producer, Manufacturing	63ey	91.7	94.8	† 94.9	96.1	94.7	93.7	100.0	97.8	94.8	92.8	93.1	95.0
Consumer Prices	64	91.7	† 92.6	93.2	94.3	95.6	96.7	† 100.0	102.6	104.2	105.1	105.3	† 106.2
Harmonized CPI	64h	....	92.5	93.5	94.6	95.9	97.1	100.0	102.7	104.7	† 106.1	106.2	107.1
Wages: Hourly Earnings	65ey	81.1	84.7	88.2	90.4	93.6	96.1	† 100.0	104.5	108.2	112.6	116.8	121.0
Industrial Production	66	64.0	69.1	71.3	77.3	84.3	89.0	100.0	99.8	100.9	103.2	108.4	105.8
Industrial Employment, Seas.Adj.	67eyc	86.4	92.5	93.0	93.8	96.2	98.8	100.0	100.7	99.4	95.2	92.9	93.3
		Number in Thousands: Period Averages											
Labor Force	67d	....	2,481	2,490	2,484	2,507	2,557	2,609	2,626	2,610	2,600	2,593	2,620
Employment	67e	2,080	2,128	2,158	† 2,194	2,247	2,317	2,355	2,388	2,372	2,365	2,365	2,401
Unemployment	67c	456	382	448	409	372	348	321	302	237	235	229	222
Unemployment Rate (%)	67r	18.4	17.2	17.9	† 16.4	14.7	13.9	12.6	11.7	9.1	9.0	8.8	8.4
Intl. Transactions & Positions		*Millions of Markkaa through 1998 Millions of Euros Beginning 1999*											
Exports	70	153,690	172,380	176,592	204,202	229,233	† 39,306	49,485	47,768	47,245	46,378	48,915	52,395
Newsprint	70ul	2,915	3,187	3,342	3,169	3,205	† 593	594	....	....	....	....	....
Imports, c.i.f.	71	119,897	122,428	134,422	154,681	172,315	† 29,691	36,837	35,845	35,611	36,775	40,729	46,769
		1995=100											
Volume of Exports	72	93.3	100.0	105.6	118.4	....	....	....	....	....	....	....	....
Newsprint	72ul	115.1	100.0	92.7	107.5	109.6	111.7	....	....	....	....	....	....
Volume of Imports	73	92.9	100.0	107.8	117.0	....	....	....	....	....	....	....	....
Unit Value of Exports	74	94.1	100.0	100.0	101.6	....	....	....	....	....	....	....	....
Newsprint	74ul	79.5	100.0	113.2	92.5	91.8	....	....	....	....	....	....	....
Unit Value of Imports	75	100.6	100.0	101.9	105.1	....	....	....	....	....	....	....	....
Export Prices (2000=100)	76	91.7	98.2	99.0	97.0	96.9	† 92.6	† 100.0	95.6	90.4	86.5	87.0	88.6
Import Prices (2000=100)	76.x	88.8	88.8	90.1	91.1	87.9	† 88.4	† 100.0	97.1	94.2	93.7	97.1	103.4

Finland 172

<table>
<thead>
<tr><th></th><th></th><th>1994</th><th>1995</th><th>1996</th><th>1997</th><th>1998</th><th>1999</th><th>2000</th><th>2001</th><th>2002</th><th>2003</th><th>2004</th><th>2005</th></tr>
</thead>
<tbody>
<tr><td>**Balance of Payments**</td><td></td><td colspan="12">*Millions of US Dollars: Minus Sign Indicates Debit*</td></tr>
<tr><td>Current Account, n.i.e.</td><td>78ald</td><td>1,110</td><td>5,231</td><td>5,003</td><td>6,633</td><td>7,340</td><td>8,045</td><td>8,975</td><td>8,704</td><td>10,148</td><td>7,119</td><td>9,698</td><td>4,983</td></tr>
<tr><td>Goods: Exports f.o.b.</td><td>78aad</td><td>29,881</td><td>40,558</td><td>40,725</td><td>41,148</td><td>43,393</td><td>41,983</td><td>45,703</td><td>42,980</td><td>44,856</td><td>52,736</td><td>61,203</td><td>65,272</td></tr>
<tr><td>Goods: Imports f.o.b.</td><td>78abd</td><td>−22,158</td><td>−28,121</td><td>−29,411</td><td>−29,604</td><td>−30,903</td><td>−29,815</td><td>−32,019</td><td>−30,321</td><td>−31,974</td><td>−39,790</td><td>−48,363</td><td>−55,127</td></tr>
<tr><td>Trade Balance</td><td>78acd</td><td>7,723</td><td>12,437</td><td>11,314</td><td>11,544</td><td>12,490</td><td>12,168</td><td>13,684</td><td>12,659</td><td>12,882</td><td>12,947</td><td>12,840</td><td>10,145</td></tr>
<tr><td>Services: Credit</td><td>78add</td><td>5,490</td><td>7,415</td><td>7,129</td><td>6,640</td><td>6,698</td><td>6,522</td><td>6,177</td><td>5,832</td><td>6,490</td><td>7,893</td><td>9,896</td><td>10,217</td></tr>
<tr><td>Services: Debit</td><td>78aed</td><td>−7,335</td><td>−9,584</td><td>−8,817</td><td>−8,235</td><td>−7,767</td><td>−7,615</td><td>−8,440</td><td>−8,105</td><td>−8,009</td><td>−10,056</td><td>−12,274</td><td>−12,941</td></tr>
<tr><td>Balance on Goods & Services</td><td>78afd</td><td>5,878</td><td>10,268</td><td>9,627</td><td>9,949</td><td>11,421</td><td>11,075</td><td>11,421</td><td>10,386</td><td>11,363</td><td>10,784</td><td>10,463</td><td>7,422</td></tr>
<tr><td>Income: Credit</td><td>78agd</td><td>1,789</td><td>2,879</td><td>2,868</td><td>4,136</td><td>4,237</td><td>5,664</td><td>7,265</td><td>8,568</td><td>8,657</td><td>9,079</td><td>12,797</td><td>13,404</td></tr>
<tr><td>Income: Debit</td><td>78ahd</td><td>−6,103</td><td>−7,318</td><td>−6,503</td><td>−6,600</td><td>−7,320</td><td>−7,712</td><td>−8,989</td><td>−9,573</td><td>−9,259</td><td>−11,754</td><td>−12,559</td><td>−14,281</td></tr>
<tr><td>Balance on Gds, Serv. & Inc.</td><td>78aid</td><td>1,564</td><td>5,828</td><td>5,992</td><td>7,485</td><td>8,338</td><td>9,026</td><td>9,698</td><td>9,381</td><td>10,761</td><td>8,109</td><td>10,701</td><td>6,544</td></tr>
<tr><td>Current Transfers, n.i.e.: Credit</td><td>78ajd</td><td>410</td><td>1,536</td><td>1,253</td><td>1,210</td><td>1,523</td><td>1,658</td><td>1,611</td><td>1,562</td><td>1,732</td><td>2,020</td><td>2,113</td><td>1,899</td></tr>
<tr><td>Current Transfers: Debit</td><td>78akd</td><td>−863</td><td>−2,133</td><td>−2,242</td><td>−2,062</td><td>−2,521</td><td>−2,640</td><td>−2,334</td><td>−2,239</td><td>−2,344</td><td>−3,010</td><td>−3,116</td><td>−3,460</td></tr>
<tr><td>Capital Account, n.i.e.</td><td>78bcd</td><td>—</td><td>66</td><td>56</td><td>247</td><td>91</td><td>49</td><td>103</td><td>83</td><td>89</td><td>104</td><td>124</td><td>42</td></tr>
<tr><td>Capital Account, n.i.e.: Credit</td><td>78bad</td><td>—</td><td>114</td><td>130</td><td>247</td><td>91</td><td>85</td><td>111</td><td>93</td><td>93</td><td>108</td><td>124</td><td>42</td></tr>
<tr><td>Capital Account: Debit</td><td>78bbd</td><td>—</td><td>−48</td><td>−74</td><td>—</td><td>—</td><td>−36</td><td>−7</td><td>−10</td><td>−4</td><td>−5</td><td>....</td><td>....</td></tr>
<tr><td>Financial Account, n.i.e.</td><td>78bjd</td><td>4,093</td><td>−4,284</td><td>−7,718</td><td>−2,976</td><td>−1,722</td><td>−6,414</td><td>−8,841</td><td>−10,942</td><td>−8,603</td><td>−12,194</td><td>−11,086</td><td>−1,739</td></tr>
<tr><td>Direct Investment Abroad</td><td>78bdd</td><td>−4,354</td><td>−1,494</td><td>−3,583</td><td>−5,260</td><td>−18,698</td><td>−6,739</td><td>−23,898</td><td>−8,458</td><td>−7,801</td><td>2,741</td><td>1,539</td><td>−3,071</td></tr>
<tr><td>Dir. Invest. in Rep. Econ., n.i.e.</td><td>78bed</td><td>1,496</td><td>1,044</td><td>1,118</td><td>2,129</td><td>12,029</td><td>4,649</td><td>9,125</td><td>3,739</td><td>8,156</td><td>3,534</td><td>3,075</td><td>4,522</td></tr>
<tr><td>Portfolio Investment Assets</td><td>78bfd</td><td>775</td><td>204</td><td>−4,186</td><td>−4,600</td><td>−3,906</td><td>−15,699</td><td>−18,920</td><td>−11,594</td><td>−13,432</td><td>−9,799</td><td>−24,074</td><td>−15,766</td></tr>
<tr><td>Equity Securities</td><td>78bkd</td><td>−78</td><td>−209</td><td>−736</td><td>−1,694</td><td>−2,099</td><td>−5,527</td><td>−7,164</td><td>−5,153</td><td>−5,387</td><td>−5,532</td><td>−9,799</td><td>−8,800</td></tr>
<tr><td>Debt Securities</td><td>78bld</td><td>853</td><td>414</td><td>−3,450</td><td>−2,906</td><td>−1,807</td><td>−10,173</td><td>−11,756</td><td>−6,441</td><td>−8,045</td><td>−4,267</td><td>−14,274</td><td>−6,966</td></tr>
<tr><td>Portfolio Investment Liab., n.i.e.</td><td>78bgd</td><td>6,180</td><td>−1,779</td><td>1,153</td><td>3,843</td><td>3,866</td><td>13,550</td><td>17,116</td><td>5,985</td><td>8,899</td><td>7,920</td><td>11,323</td><td>11,254</td></tr>
<tr><td>Equity Securities</td><td>78bmd</td><td>2,541</td><td>2,027</td><td>1,915</td><td>4,023</td><td>7,931</td><td>10,279</td><td>10,114</td><td>3,960</td><td>2,527</td><td>−597</td><td>101</td><td>4,988</td></tr>
<tr><td>Debt Securities</td><td>78bnd</td><td>3,640</td><td>−3,807</td><td>−761</td><td>−181</td><td>−4,065</td><td>3,271</td><td>7,002</td><td>2,025</td><td>6,372</td><td>8,517</td><td>11,222</td><td>6,265</td></tr>
<tr><td>Financial Derivatives Assets</td><td>78bwd</td><td>51</td><td>38</td><td>38</td><td>−72</td><td>89</td><td></td><td></td><td></td><td></td><td></td><td></td><td></td></tr>
<tr><td>Financial Derivatives Liabilities</td><td>78bxd</td><td>5</td><td>600</td><td>325</td><td>114</td><td>−725</td><td>−419</td><td>−630</td><td>38</td><td>−325</td><td>1,717</td><td>524</td><td>1,816</td></tr>
<tr><td>Other Investment Assets</td><td>78bhd</td><td>−668</td><td>−2,863</td><td>−4,683</td><td>−2,201</td><td>331</td><td>−3,324</td><td>−5,636</td><td>−10,117</td><td>−1,328</td><td>−16,081</td><td>−12,449</td><td>−1,567</td></tr>
<tr><td>Monetary Authorities</td><td>78bod</td><td>99</td><td>146</td><td>27</td><td>94</td><td>145</td><td>−343</td><td>−129</td><td>77</td><td>−53</td><td>−55</td><td>156</td><td>10</td></tr>
<tr><td>General Government</td><td>78bpd</td><td>−445</td><td>−366</td><td>−719</td><td>−609</td><td>−126</td><td>−224</td><td>−171</td><td>−966</td><td>−617</td><td>−3,048</td><td>−967</td><td>1,450</td></tr>
<tr><td>Banks</td><td>78bqd</td><td>−511</td><td>−1,926</td><td>−3,815</td><td>−1,725</td><td>41</td><td>−1,566</td><td>−4,107</td><td>−8,197</td><td>1,204</td><td>−10,282</td><td>−11,185</td><td>−1,780</td></tr>
<tr><td>Other Sectors</td><td>78brd</td><td>189</td><td>−717</td><td>−175</td><td>39</td><td>270</td><td>−1,191</td><td>−1,229</td><td>−1,032</td><td>−1,863</td><td>−2,696</td><td>−453</td><td>−1,247</td></tr>
<tr><td>Other Investment Liab., n.i.e.</td><td>78bid</td><td>607</td><td>−35</td><td>2,099</td><td>3,072</td><td>5,292</td><td>1,567</td><td>14,001</td><td>9,465</td><td>−2,773</td><td>−2,225</td><td>8,974</td><td>1,072</td></tr>
<tr><td>Monetary Authorities</td><td>78bsd</td><td>−107</td><td>92</td><td>−96</td><td>−173</td><td>−180</td><td>−872</td><td>1,433</td><td>282</td><td>1,127</td><td>695</td><td>−2,133</td><td>−3,391</td></tr>
<tr><td>General Government</td><td>78btd</td><td>965</td><td>−331</td><td>764</td><td>1,478</td><td>394</td><td>−420</td><td>−1,272</td><td>467</td><td>343</td><td>2,396</td><td>125</td><td>−846</td></tr>
<tr><td>Banks</td><td>78bud</td><td>−1,088</td><td>869</td><td>−626</td><td>1,876</td><td>3,607</td><td>−154</td><td>4,098</td><td>8,762</td><td>−4,665</td><td>−3,460</td><td>13,196</td><td>4,477</td></tr>
<tr><td>Other Sectors</td><td>78bvd</td><td>837</td><td>−666</td><td>2,056</td><td>−110</td><td>1,471</td><td>3,014</td><td>9,742</td><td>−47</td><td>422</td><td>−1,856</td><td>−2,214</td><td>833</td></tr>
<tr><td>Net Errors and Omissions</td><td>78cad</td><td>−489</td><td>−1,384</td><td>−375</td><td>−1,600</td><td>−5,412</td><td>−1,667</td><td>114</td><td>2,565</td><td>−1,747</td><td>4,462</td><td>2,170</td><td>−3,483</td></tr>
<tr><td>Overall Balance</td><td>78cbd</td><td>4,714</td><td>−372</td><td>−3,036</td><td>2,304</td><td>296</td><td>13</td><td>351</td><td>410</td><td>−113</td><td>−508</td><td>906</td><td>−197</td></tr>
<tr><td>Reserves and Related Items</td><td>79dad</td><td>−4,714</td><td>372</td><td>3,036</td><td>−2,304</td><td>−296</td><td>−13</td><td>−351</td><td>−410</td><td>113</td><td>508</td><td>−906</td><td>197</td></tr>
<tr><td>Reserve Assets</td><td>79dbd</td><td>−4,714</td><td>372</td><td>3,036</td><td>−2,304</td><td>−296</td><td>−13</td><td>−351</td><td>−410</td><td>113</td><td>508</td><td>−906</td><td>197</td></tr>
<tr><td>Use of Fund Credit and Loans</td><td>79dcd</td><td>—</td><td>—</td><td>—</td><td>—</td><td>—</td><td>—</td><td>—</td><td>—</td><td>—</td><td>—</td><td>—</td><td>—</td></tr>
<tr><td>Exceptional Financing</td><td>79ded</td><td>....</td><td>....</td><td>....</td><td>....</td><td>....</td><td>....</td><td>....</td><td>....</td><td>....</td><td>....</td><td>....</td><td>....</td></tr>
<tr><td>**International Investment Position**</td><td></td><td colspan="12">*Millions of US Dollars*</td></tr>
<tr><td>Assets</td><td>79aad</td><td>51,570</td><td>57,970</td><td>65,385</td><td>71,091</td><td>85,854</td><td>109,967</td><td>148,094</td><td>161,069</td><td>202,570</td><td>292,266</td><td>364,548</td><td>....</td></tr>
<tr><td>Direct Investment Abroad</td><td>79abd</td><td>12,534</td><td>14,993</td><td>17,666</td><td>20,297</td><td>29,407</td><td>33,850</td><td>52,109</td><td>52,226</td><td>63,924</td><td>76,154</td><td>80,470</td><td>....</td></tr>
<tr><td>Portfolio Investment</td><td>79acd</td><td>3,417</td><td>3,572</td><td>7,713</td><td>11,659</td><td>16,825</td><td>33,621</td><td>51,125</td><td>55,905</td><td>76,017</td><td>107,009</td><td>145,938</td><td>....</td></tr>
<tr><td>Equity Securities</td><td>79add</td><td>418</td><td>738</td><td>1,564</td><td>3,245</td><td>5,271</td><td>13,670</td><td>20,263</td><td>20,157</td><td>22,939</td><td>36,088</td><td>52,839</td><td>....</td></tr>
<tr><td>Debt Securities</td><td>79aed</td><td>2,999</td><td>2,835</td><td>6,149</td><td>8,414</td><td>11,554</td><td>19,951</td><td>30,862</td><td>35,748</td><td>53,078</td><td>70,921</td><td>93,100</td><td>....</td></tr>
<tr><td>Financial Derivatives</td><td>79ald</td><td>103</td><td>41</td><td>−5</td><td>259</td><td>151</td><td>3,469</td><td>2,816</td><td>2,110</td><td>4,069</td><td>26,131</td><td>38,806</td><td>....</td></tr>
<tr><td>Other Investment Abroad</td><td>79afd</td><td>24,395</td><td>28,153</td><td>32,173</td><td>29,385</td><td>29,684</td><td>30,348</td><td>33,637</td><td>42,407</td><td>48,736</td><td>71,799</td><td>86,324</td><td>....</td></tr>
<tr><td>Monetary Authorities</td><td>79agd</td><td>969</td><td>911</td><td>830</td><td>617</td><td>1,078</td><td>821</td><td>887</td><td>767</td><td>997</td><td>1,260</td><td>1,195</td><td>....</td></tr>
<tr><td>General Government</td><td>79ahd</td><td>2,481</td><td>2,966</td><td>3,636</td><td>3,497</td><td>3,611</td><td>3,670</td><td>3,460</td><td>4,352</td><td>5,740</td><td>9,197</td><td>11,184</td><td>....</td></tr>
<tr><td>Banks</td><td>79aid</td><td>12,021</td><td>14,203</td><td>17,872</td><td>18,430</td><td>18,004</td><td>18,169</td><td>20,957</td><td>31,303</td><td>33,145</td><td>47,794</td><td>63,065</td><td>....</td></tr>
<tr><td>Other Sectors</td><td>79ajd</td><td>8,924</td><td>10,073</td><td>9,835</td><td>6,842</td><td>6,992</td><td>7,688</td><td>8,334</td><td>5,986</td><td>8,854</td><td>13,547</td><td>10,880</td><td>....</td></tr>
<tr><td>Reserve Assets</td><td>79akd</td><td>11,122</td><td>11,210</td><td>7,839</td><td>9,490</td><td>9,787</td><td>8,679</td><td>8,408</td><td>8,420</td><td>9,824</td><td>11,173</td><td>13,009</td><td>....</td></tr>
<tr><td>Liabilities</td><td>79lad</td><td>107,281</td><td>111,245</td><td>118,245</td><td>119,705</td><td>186,126</td><td>325,521</td><td>329,900</td><td>261,959</td><td>256,656</td><td>335,481</td><td>386,407</td><td>....</td></tr>
<tr><td>Dir. Invest. in Rep. Economy</td><td>79lbd</td><td>6,714</td><td>8,465</td><td>8,797</td><td>9,530</td><td>16,455</td><td>18,320</td><td>24,272</td><td>24,071</td><td>34,007</td><td>50,325</td><td>54,630</td><td>....</td></tr>
<tr><td>Portfolio Investment</td><td>79lcd</td><td>69,508</td><td>69,408</td><td>75,311</td><td>76,436</td><td>131,124</td><td>266,119</td><td>253,376</td><td>178,121</td><td>158,592</td><td>196,743</td><td>218,157</td><td>....</td></tr>
<tr><td>Equity Securities</td><td>79ldd</td><td>12,767</td><td>14,625</td><td>23,457</td><td>28,870</td><td>79,722</td><td>219,531</td><td>204,361</td><td>128,039</td><td>89,176</td><td>103,315</td><td>101,244</td><td>....</td></tr>
<tr><td>Debt Securities</td><td>79led</td><td>56,741</td><td>54,782</td><td>51,855</td><td>47,566</td><td>51,403</td><td>46,587</td><td>49,015</td><td>50,083</td><td>69,416</td><td>93,428</td><td>116,913</td><td>....</td></tr>
<tr><td>Financial Derivatives</td><td>79lld</td><td>−1,092</td><td>354</td><td>723</td><td>1,153</td><td>229</td><td>2,965</td><td>1,925</td><td>1,678</td><td>3,102</td><td>26,020</td><td>37,545</td><td>....</td></tr>
<tr><td>Other Investment</td><td>79lfd</td><td>32,151</td><td>33,018</td><td>33,414</td><td>32,586</td><td>38,317</td><td>38,118</td><td>50,327</td><td>58,089</td><td>60,955</td><td>62,392</td><td>76,076</td><td>....</td></tr>
<tr><td>Monetary Authorities</td><td>79lgd</td><td>996</td><td>1,176</td><td>1,018</td><td>713</td><td>734</td><td>−690</td><td>614</td><td>887</td><td>2,274</td><td>3,816</td><td>1,976</td><td>....</td></tr>
<tr><td>General Government</td><td>79lhd</td><td>4,016</td><td>3,886</td><td>4,299</td><td>5,340</td><td>6,133</td><td>5,575</td><td>4,040</td><td>4,273</td><td>5,221</td><td>6,821</td><td>7,991</td><td>....</td></tr>
<tr><td>Banks</td><td>79lid</td><td>12,620</td><td>13,824</td><td>12,527</td><td>13,003</td><td>16,135</td><td>14,484</td><td>17,825</td><td>31,785</td><td>29,773</td><td>27,963</td><td>42,769</td><td>....</td></tr>
<tr><td>Other Sectors</td><td>79ljd</td><td>14,519</td><td>14,133</td><td>15,570</td><td>13,530</td><td>15,316</td><td>18,749</td><td>27,848</td><td>21,144</td><td>23,687</td><td>23,792</td><td>23,340</td><td>....</td></tr>
<tr><td>**Government Finance**</td><td></td><td colspan="12"></td></tr>
<tr><td>Central Government</td><td></td><td colspan="12">*Millions of Markkaa through 1998; Millions of Euros Beginning 1999: Year Ending December 31*</td></tr>
<tr><td>Deficit (-) or Surplus</td><td>80</td><td>−58,781</td><td>−53,599</td><td>−36,571</td><td>−15,523</td><td>−1,904</td><td>1,583</td><td>3,920</td><td>−291</td><td>2,362</td><td>31</td><td>1,647</td><td>1,975</td></tr>
<tr><td>Total Revenue and Grants</td><td>81y</td><td>173,827</td><td>187,954</td><td>199,273</td><td>205,870</td><td>226,344</td><td>32,853</td><td>37,936</td><td>37,345</td><td>37,301</td><td>36,996</td><td>38,359</td><td>41,343</td></tr>
<tr><td>Revenue</td><td>81</td><td>168,307</td><td>178,584</td><td>192,955</td><td>199,126</td><td>221,033</td><td>32,853</td><td>37,936</td><td>37,345</td><td>37,301</td><td>36,996</td><td>38,359</td><td>41,343</td></tr>
<tr><td>Grants</td><td>81z</td><td>5,520</td><td>9,370</td><td>6,318</td><td>6,744</td><td>5,311</td><td>—</td><td>—</td><td>—</td><td>—</td><td>—</td><td>—</td><td>—</td></tr>
<tr><td>Exp. & Lending Minus Repay</td><td>82z</td><td>232,608</td><td>241,553</td><td>235,844</td><td>221,394</td><td>228,250</td><td>31,270</td><td>34,016</td><td>37,637</td><td>34,939</td><td>36,965</td><td>36,712</td><td>39,368</td></tr>
<tr><td>Expenditure</td><td>82</td><td>223,119</td><td>232,883</td><td>231,425</td><td>219,527</td><td>230,509</td><td>36,353</td><td>36,646</td><td>35,574</td><td>34,352</td><td>34,613</td><td>37,324</td><td>38,385</td></tr>
<tr><td>Lending Minus Repayments</td><td>83</td><td>9,489</td><td>8,670</td><td>4,419</td><td>1,867</td><td>−2,259</td><td>−5,083</td><td>−2,630</td><td>2,063</td><td>588</td><td>2,352</td><td>−612</td><td>983</td></tr>
<tr><td>Total Financing</td><td>80h</td><td>58,751</td><td>53,599</td><td>36,571</td><td>15,524</td><td>1,906</td><td>−1,583</td><td>−3,920</td><td>292</td><td>−2,362</td><td>−30</td><td>−1,647</td><td>−1,974</td></tr>
<tr><td>Total Net Borrowing</td><td>84</td><td>58,781</td><td>53,599</td><td>36,571</td><td>15,524</td><td>1,906</td><td>....</td><td>−4,141</td><td>−1,701</td><td>−2,529</td><td>3,827</td><td>400</td><td>−3,565</td></tr>
<tr><td>Net Domestic</td><td>84a</td><td>26,024</td><td>53,823</td><td>36,203</td><td>34,420</td><td>9,721</td><td>....</td><td>−4,141</td><td>−1,701</td><td>−2,529</td><td>3,827</td><td>400</td><td>−3,565</td></tr>
<tr><td>Net Foreign</td><td>85a</td><td>32,727</td><td>−224</td><td>368</td><td>−18,896</td><td>−7,815</td><td>—</td><td>—</td><td>—</td><td>—</td><td>—</td><td>—</td><td>—</td></tr>
<tr><td>Use of Cash Balances</td><td>87</td><td>—</td><td>—</td><td>—</td><td>—</td><td>—</td><td>—</td><td>221</td><td>1,992</td><td>167</td><td>−3,857</td><td>−2,047</td><td>1,591</td></tr>
<tr><td>Total Debt by Currency</td><td>88</td><td>314,285</td><td>362,202</td><td>396,718</td><td>419,346</td><td>421,390</td><td>68,052</td><td>63,435</td><td>61,760</td><td>59,253</td><td>63,320</td><td>63,788</td><td>60,044</td></tr>
<tr><td>Domestic</td><td>88b</td><td>123,434</td><td>174,874</td><td>196,836</td><td>210,088</td><td>211,413</td><td>57,008</td><td>53,844</td><td>52,678</td><td>51,456</td><td>62,079</td><td>63,745</td><td>60,000</td></tr>
<tr><td>Foreign</td><td>89b</td><td>190,851</td><td>187,328</td><td>199,882</td><td>209,258</td><td>209,977</td><td>11,044</td><td>9,590</td><td>9,082</td><td>7,797</td><td>1,241</td><td>43</td><td>44</td></tr>
<tr><td>General Government</td><td></td><td colspan="12">*As Percent of Gross Domestic Product*</td></tr>
</tbody>
</table>

Finland   172

		1994	1995	1996	1997	1998	1999	2000	2001	2002	2003	2004	2005
National Accounts							*Billions of Markkaa through 1998; Billions of Euros Beginning in 1999*						
Househ.Cons.Expend.,incl.NPISHs....	**96f**	276.46	295.97	309.87	326.69	348.07	† 60.35	64.45	67.92	71.14	74.92	77.69	81.35
Government Consumption Expend...	**91f**	122.51	129.82	136.79	142.09	149.51	† 26.02	26.94	28.51	30.46	31.95	33.66	35.00
Gross Fixed Capital Formation.........	**93e**	82.73	95.33	101.96	118.67	133.15	† 23.49	25.75	27.73	26.58	26.32	28.20	29.76
Changes in Inventories....................	**93i**	7.18	7.38	−1.68	2.81	5.88	† −.02	1.04	.14	.55	.73	.80	1.63
Exports of Goods and Services.........	**90c**	182.58	207.31	219.19	247.35	267.33	† 45.43	55.88	54.21	54.00	53.10	56.63	60.15
Imports of Goods and Services (-).....	**98c**	152.19	164.16	175.36	196.18	206.13	† 35.18	44.16	43.12	42.76	44.17	48.50	54.61
Gross Domestic Product (GDP).........	**99b**	522.57	571.65	590.78	641.43	697.82	† 120.97	130.86	136.47	140.85	143.81	149.73	155.32
Net Primary Income from Abroad.....	**98.n**	−22.75	−20.45	−16.55	−12.36	−16.30	† −1.81	−1.32	−.66	.29	−2.05	−.53	−.18
Gross National Income (GNI)............	**99a**	499.82	552.57	574.73	629.06	681.26	† 119.16	129.54	135.82	141.15	141.76	149.20	155.14
Net Current Transf.from Abroad......	**98t**	−2.42	−.75	−3.78	−3.61	−5.43	† −1.98	−2.03	−2.27	−2.76	.02	....	....
Gross Nat'l Disposable Inc.(GNDI)....	**99i**	497.13	543.18	565.18	619.22	668.89	† 117.18	127.52	133.54	138.39	141.78	....	....
Gross Saving.................................	**99s**	96.29	122.15	121.05	152.93	171.82	† 30.90	36.20	37.23	36.95	35.21	....	....
Consumption of Fixed Capital..........	**99cf**	101.49	102.84	104.47	108.28	113.68	† 19.85	21.19	22.35	22.59	23.31	24.01	24.85
GDP Volume 2000 Ref., Chained.....	**99b.p**	593.91	619.75	643.25	683.07	716.94	† 124.65	130.86	132.21	135.12	138.41	143.42	146.41
GDP Volume (2000=100)................	**99bvp**	76.3	79.7	82.7	87.8	92.1	95.3	100.0	101.0	103.3	105.8	109.6	111.9
GDP Deflator (2000=100)................	**99bip**	88.0	92.2	91.8	93.9	97.3	† 97.0	100.0	103.2	104.2	103.9	104.4	106.1
							Millions: Midyear Estimates						
Population...............................	**99z**	5.09	5.11	5.13	5.14	5.15	5.16	5.18	5.19	5.21	5.22	5.24	5.25

France 132

		1994	1995	1996	1997	1998	1999	2000	2001	2002	2003	2004	2005
Exchange Rates													
						Euros per SDR: End of Period							
Market Rate	aa	7.8044	7.2838	7.5306	8.0794	7.9161	1.3662	1.4002	1.4260	1.2964	1.1765	1.1402	1.2116
						Euros per US Dollar: End of Period (ae) Period Average (rf)							
Market Rate	ae	5.3460	4.9000	5.2370	5.9881	5.6221	.9954	1.0747	1.1347	.9536	.7918	.7342	.8477
Market Rate	rf	5.5520	4.9915	5.1155	5.8367	5.8995	.9386	1.0854	1.1175	1.0626	.8860	.8054	.8041
						Francs per ECU: End of Period (ea) Period Average (eb)							
ECU Rate	ea	6.5758	6.4458	6.5619	6.6135	6.5596	....	....	....	....	....	....	....
ECU Rate	eb	6.5796	6.5250	6.4928	6.6122	6.6015	....	....	....	....	....	....	....
						Index Numbers (2000=100): Period Averages							
Market Rate (1995=100)	ahx	90.0	100.0	97.5	85.6	84.7	....	....	....	....	....	....	....
Nominal Effective Exchange Rate	neu	106.3	110.3	110.0	105.5	104.6	104.4	100.0	100.4	101.7	106.2	107.6	107.7
Real Effective Exchange Rate	reu	116.1	118.1	114.4	108.4	107.5	105.4	100.0	97.2	98.0	101.2	102.7	101.5
Fund Position							*Millions of SDRs: End of Period*						
Quota	2f.s	7,415	7,415	7,415	7,415	7,415	10,739	10,739	10,739	10,739	10,739	10,739	10,739
SDRs	1b.s	248	643	682	720	786	253	309	392	458	512	563	614
Reserve Position in the Fund	1c.s	1,627	1,854	1,875	2,119	3,162	3,950	3,471	3,894	4,250	4,242	3,453	2,014
of which: Outstg.Fund Borrowing	2c	—	—	—	—	382	—	—	—	—	—	—	—
International Liquidity						*Millions of US Dollars Unless Otherwise Indicated: End of Period*							
Total Res.Min.Gold (Eurosys.Def)	1l.d	26,257	26,853	26,796	30,927	44,312	† 39,701	37,039	31,749	28,365	30,186	35,314	27,753
SDRs	1b.d	362	955	981	971	1,107	347	402	492	622	761	875	878
Reserve Position in the Fund	1c.d	2,375	2,756	2,695	2,859	4,452	5,421	4,522	4,894	5,778	6,303	5,363	2,878
Foreign Exchange	1d.d	23,520	23,142	23,120	27,097	38,753	33,933	32,114	26,363	21,965	23,122	29,077	23,996
o/w:Fin.Deriv.Rel.to Reserves	1ddd	....	....	....	....	....	....	—	—	—	—	—	—
Other Reserve Assets	1e.d	....	....	....	....	....	....	—	—	—	—	—	—
Gold (Million Fine Troy Ounces)	1ad	81.85	81.85	81.85	81.89	102.37	97.25	97.25	97.25	97.25	97.25	95.98	90.85
Gold (Eurosystem Valuation)	1and	30,730	31,658	30,368	25,002	29,871	28,225	26,689	26,888	33,331	40,576	42,039	46,607
Memo:Euro Cl. on Non-EA Res.	1dgd	....	....	....	....	....	....						
Non-Euro Cl. on EA Res.	1dhd	....	....	....	....		3,330	3,870	3,562	3,861	3,035	4,171	8,043
Mon. Auth.: Other Foreign Assets	3..d	....	....	....	....	....	....	....	....	....	....	....	....
Foreign Liabilities	4..d	11,650	11,649	† 796	618	1,014	† 7,678	1,007	3,233	1,838	4,801	9,956	9,692
Banking Insts.: Foreign Assets	7a.d	599,906	705,082	684,056	736,795	....	† 430,976	435,489	447,009	538,479	635,130	828,745	1,025,106
Foreign Liab.	7b.d	592,630	662,469	671,759	694,578	....	† 337,028	384,578	399,215	464,826	547,132	701,857	899,664
Monetary Authorities					*Billions of Francs through 1998; Millions of Euros Beginning 1999: End of Period*								
Fgn. Assets (Cl.on Non-EA Ctys)	11	372	346	† 309	335	420	68,150	68,300	66,406	58,934	55,979	58,346	65,470
Claims on General Government	12a.u	....	....	....	....	....	4,051	4,044	3,691	3,314	5,029	5,680	6,896
o/w: Claims on Gen.Govt.in Cty	12a	72	59	58	52	51	4,051	4,044	3,691	3,314	5,029	5,680	6,896
Claims on Banking Institutions	12e.u	....	....	....	....	....	65,188	42,512	44,767	81,628	84,513	90,541	103,972
o/w: Claims on Bank.Inst.in Cty.	12e	200	147	143	125	167	48,448	29,013	16,413	16,107	11,084	17,315	27,054
Claims on Other Resident Sectors	12d.u	....	....	....	....	....	380	361	341	323	294	258	230
o/w: Cl. on Oth.Res.Sect.in Cty	12d	4	6	18	19	20	380	361	341	323	294	258	230
Currency Issued	14a	270	275	278	283	287	49,282	49,187	34,575	74,153	84,978	97,834	110,171
Liabilities to Banking Insts.	14c.u	....	....	....	....	....	51,345	28,083	29,467	34,591	27,774	28,675	28,553
o/w: Liabs to Bank.Inst.in Cty.	14c	10	30	33	36	129	24,371	28,083	29,467	34,591	27,774	28,675	28,553
Demand Dep. of Other Res.Sect.	14d.u	....	....	....	....	....	1,573	801	846	811	752	363	768
o/w:D.Dep.of Oth.Res.Sect.in Cty.	14d	3	4	4	4	4	1,573	801	846	811	752	363	768
Other Dep. of Other Res.Sect.	15..u	....	....	....	....	....	—	—	—	—	—	—	—
o/w:O.Dep.of Oth.Res.Sect.in Cty.	15	....	....	....	....	....	—	—	—	—	—	—	—
Bonds & Money Mkt. Instruments	16n.u	....	....	....	....	....	—	—	—	—	—	—	—
Foreign Liab. (to Non-EA Ctys)	16c	62	57	† 4	4	6	7,643	1,082	3,669	1,753	3,801	7,309	8,216
Central Government Deposits	16d.u	....	....	....	....	....	1,057	1,982	2,455	811	280	295	320
o/w: Cent.Govt.Dep. in Cty.	16d	123	58	20	43	89	1,057	1,982	2,455	811	280	295	320
Capital Accounts	17a	201	177	191	201	168	35,675	39,750	44,024	39,842	36,766	34,180	46,963
Other Items (Net)	17r	−23	−44	−3	−39	−25	−8,807	−5,668	169	−7,762	−8,535	−13,831	−18,423
Memo: Currency Put into Circ.	14m	....	....	....	....	....	....	....	....	41,636	43,250	47,679	52,844
Banking Institutions					*Billions of Francs through 1998; Millions of Euros Beginning 1999: End of Period*								
Claims on Monetary Authorities	20	26	47	51	48	....	24,371	28,083	29,467	34,591	27,774	26,384	25,692
Claims on Bk.Inst.in Oth.EA Ctys	20b.u	....	....	....	....	....	192,409	186,176	211,491	231,399	262,766	314,768	403,721
Fgn. Assets (Cl.on Non-EA Ctys)	21	3,207	3,455	3,582	4,412	....	429,003	468,016	507,215	513,473	502,874	608,432	868,955
Claims on General Government	22a.u	....	....	....	....	....	387,081	338,822	336,930	375,275	402,395	407,907	491,612
o/w: Claims on Gen.Govt.in Cty.	22a	1,074	1,275	1,566	1,729	....	312,765	268,206	269,527	279,124	299,509	295,268	319,380
Claims on Other Resident Sectors	22d.u	....	....	....	....	....	1,159,879	1,276,183	1,380,548	1,402,545	1,499,829	1,616,015	1,731,840
o/w: Cl. on Oth.Res.Sect.in Cty.	22d	6,589	6,745	6,653	6,785	....	1,115,273	1,225,195	1,314,276	1,325,885	1,403,834	1,496,580	1,589,818
Demand Deposits	24..u	....	....	....	....	....	247,576	269,174	305,546	295,536	350,139	364,054	404,132
o/w:D.Dep.of Oth.Res.Sect.in Cty.	24	1,415	1,557	1,554	1,670	....	243,048	264,944	300,271	290,917	344,061	357,103	395,266
Other Deposits	25..u	....	....	....	....	....	650,373	654,500	684,583	710,793	752,835	800,245	821,445
o/w:O.Dep.of Oth.Res.Sect.in Cty.	25	3,012	3,374	3,582	3,855	....	633,043	636,781	666,151	691,318	731,410	772,532	790,492
Money Market Fund Shares	26m.u	....	....	....	....	....	179,867	210,662	255,856	297,874	324,445	350,522	382,381
Bonds & Money Mkt. Instruments	26n.u	....	....	....	....	....	478,806	502,177	554,152	561,360	593,490	664,167	729,877
o/w: Held by Resid.of Cty	26n	2,538	2,548	2,266	2,151	....							
Foreign Liab. (to Non-EA Ctys)	26c	3,168	3,246	3,518	4,159	....	335,485	413,303	452,984	443,240	433,200	515,276	762,621
Central Government Deposits	26d.u	....	....	....	....	....	11,472	5,865	4,937	12,110	39,745	46,371	50,066
o/w: Cent.Govt.Dep. in Cty.	26d	55	124	156	152	....	11,205	5,637	4,403	11,666	38,999	43,937	45,185
Credit from Monetary Authorities	26g	200	147	143	125	167	48,448	29,013	16,413	16,107	11,084	14,571	24,071
Liab. to Bk.Inst.in Oth. EA Ctys	26h.u	....	....	....	....	....	150,040	139,026	149,425	170,842	173,576	201,540	226,396
Capital Accounts	27a	1,293	1,284	1,288	1,320	....	245,638	249,326	270,482	284,117	294,879	310,242	316,107
Other Items (Net)	27r	−785	−759	−654	−459	....	−154,962	−175,766	−228,727	−234,696	−277,755	−293,482	−195,276

		1994	1995	1996	1997	1998	1999	2000	2001	2002	2003	2004	2005
Banking Survey (Nat'l Residency)		Billions of Francs through 1998; Millions of Euros Beginning 1999: End of Period											
Foreign Assets (Net)	31n	349	497	† 369	584	....	291,224	292,786	326,850	412,752	467,022	539,909	702,670
Domestic Credit	32	7,560	7,903	8,118	8,390	....	1,420,207	1,490,187	1,580,977	1,596,169	1,669,387	1,753,554	1,870,819
Claims on General Govt. (Net)	32an	968	1,152	1,447	1,586	....	304,554	264,631	266,360	269,961	265,259	256,716	280,771
Claims on Other Resident Sectors	32d	6,593	6,751	6,671	6,804	....	1,115,653	1,225,556	1,314,617	1,326,208	1,404,128	1,496,838	1,590,048
Currency Issued	34a.n	270	275	278	283	287	49,282	49,187	34,575	74,153	84,978	97,834	110,171
Demand Deposits	34b.n	1,418	1,561	1,557	1,674	....	244,621	265,745	301,117	291,728	344,813	357,466	396,034
Other Deposits	35..n	3,012	3,374	3,582	3,855	....	633,043	636,781	666,151	691,318	731,410	772,532	790,492
Money Market Fund Shares	36m	....	....	....	....	....	179,867	210,662	255,856	297,874	324,445	350,522	382,381
Bonds & Money Mkt. Instruments	36n	2,538	2,548	2,266	2,151	....	478,806	502,177	554,152	561,360	593,490	664,167	729,877
o/w: Over Two Years	36na	....	....	....	....	....	322,255	338,332	357,016	354,893	375,237	404,784	458,608
Capital Accounts	37a	1,494	1,462	1,479	1,521	....	281,313	289,076	314,506	323,959	331,645	344,422	363,070
Other Items (Net)	37r	–824	–819	–675	–509	....	–155,502	–170,655	–218,530	–231,471	–274,371	–293,480	–198,536
Banking Survey (EA-Wide Residency)		Millions of Euros: End of Period											
Foreign Assets (Net)	31n.u	....	....	....	....	....	154,025	121,931	116,968	127,414	121,852	144,193	163,588
Domestic Credit	32..u	....	....	....	....	....	1,538,862	1,611,563	1,714,118	1,768,536	1,867,522	1,983,194	2,180,192
Claims on General Govt. (Net)	32anu	....	....	....	....	....	378,603	335,019	333,229	365,668	367,399	366,921	448,122
Claims on Other Resident Sect.	32d.u	....	....	....	....	....	1,160,259	1,276,544	1,380,889	1,402,868	1,500,123	1,616,273	1,732,070
Currency Issued	34a.u	....	....	....	....	....	49,282	49,187	34,575	74,153	84,978	97,834	110,171
Demand Deposits	34b.u	....	....	....	....	....	249,149	269,975	306,392	296,347	350,891	364,417	404,900
Other Deposits	35..u	....	....	....	....	....	650,373	654,500	684,583	710,793	752,835	800,245	821,445
o/w: Other Dep. Over Two Yrs	35abu	....	....	....	....	....	299,627	281,832	279,539	285,760	303,383	310,903	313,208
Money Market Fund Shares	36m.u	....	....	....	....	....	179,867	210,662	255,856	297,874	324,445	350,522	382,381
Bonds & Money Mkt. Instruments	36n.u	....	....	....	....	....	478,806	502,177	554,152	561,360	593,490	664,167	729,877
o/w: Over Two Years	36nau	....	....	....	....	....	322,255	338,332	357,016	354,893	375,237	404,784	458,608
Capital Accounts	37a	....	....	....	....	....	281,313	289,076	314,506	323,959	331,645	344,422	363,070
Other Items (Net)	37r.u	....	....	....	....	....	–195,904	–242,083	–318,978	–368,536	–448,909	–494,220	–468,064
Money (National Definitions)		Billions of Francs: End of Period											
M1	59ma	1,671	1,800	1,815	1,933	1,993	....	....	....	....	....	....	....
M1, Seasonally Adjusted	59mac	1,559	1,581	1,666	1,735	1,884	....	....	....	....	....	....	....
M2	59mb	3,003	3,246	3,363	3,624	3,781	....	....	....	....	....	....	....
M2, Seasonally Adjusted	59mbc	2,806	2,935	3,143	3,356	3,641	....	....	....	....	....	....	....
M3	59mc	5,225	5,463	5,281	5,385	5,532	....	....	....	....	....	....	....
M3, Seasonally Adjusted	59mcc	5,083	5,283	5,318	5,263	5,492	....	....	....	....	....	....	....
L	59mf	5,296	5,541	5,364	5,511	5,622	....	....	....	....	....	....	....
L, Seasonally Adjusted	59mfc	5,142	5,360	5,409	5,369	5,590	....	....	....	....	....	....	....
Interest Rates		Percent Per Annum											
Repurchase of Agreements	60a	5.44	4.96	3.60	3.15	3.28	....	....	....	....	....	....	....
Money Market Rate	60b	5.69	6.35	3.73	3.24	3.39	....	....	....	....	....	....	....
Treasury Bill Rate	60c	5.79	6.58	3.84	3.35	3.45	2.72	4.23	4.26	3.28	2.27	....	....
Deposit Rate	60l	4.50	4.50	3.67	3.50	3.21	2.69	2.63	3.00	3.00	2.69	2.25	2.15
Households: Stocks, up to 2 years	60lhs	....	....	....	....	....	....	....	....	....	2.81	2.52	2.49
New Business, up to 1 year	60lhn	....	....	....	....	....	....	....	....	....	2.32	2.06	2.15
Corporations: Stocks, up to 2 years	60lcs	....	....	....	....	....	....	....	....	....	2.73	2.46	2.47
New Business, up to 1 year	60lcn	....	....	....	....	....	....	....	....	....	2.24	2.01	2.06
REPOS, Stocks	60lcr	....	....	....	....	....	....	....	....	....	3.41	2.63	2.25
Lending Rate	60p	7.89	8.12	6.77	6.34	6.55	6.36	6.70	6.98	6.60	6.60	6.60	....
Households: Stocks, up to 1 year	60phs	....	....	....	....	....	....	....	....	....	8.61	8.25	8.29
New Bus., Floating & up to 1 year	60pns	....	....	....	....	....	....	....	....	....	5.66	5.29	4.84
House Purch., Stocks,Over 5 years	60phm	....	....	....	....	....	....	....	....	....	5.47	5.03	4.68
House Purch., New Bus., 5-10 yrs	60phn	....	....	....	....	....	....	....	....	....	4.34	4.04	3.58
Corporations: Stocks, up to 1 year	60pcs	....	....	....	....	....	....	....	....	....	3.77	3.69	3.89
New Bus., Over € 1 mil.,up to 1 yr	60pcn	....	....	....	....	....	....	....	....	....	2.96	2.78	2.75
Government Bond Yield	61	7.35	7.59	6.39	5.63	4.72	4.69	5.45	5.05	4.93	4.18	4.15	3.46
Prices, Production, Labor		Index Numbers (2000=100): Period Averages											
Share Prices	62	32.7	29.6	33.7	44.4	59.8	74.0	100.0	80.1	60.4	....	....	....
Producer Prices	63	....	....	....	....	....	† 95.8	100.0	101.2	101.0	101.9	104.0	107.2
Intermediate Indust. Goods	63a	95.5	† 101.3	98.6	98.0	97.1	95.8	100.0	101.2	100.7	101.1	103.7	106.7
Imported Raw Materials	63b	81.4	88.3	78.9	88.9	75.6	76.6	100.0	91.8	85.5	80.7	94.6	111.2
Consumer Prices	64	92.5	94.1	96.0	97.2	† 97.8	98.3	100.0	101.7	103.6	105.8	108.0	109.9
Harmonized CPI	64h	....	93.8	95.8	97.0	97.7	98.2	100.0	101.8	103.7	† 106.0	108.5	110.5
Labor Costs	65	86.3	87.0	† 88.5	91.0	93.6	95.7	100.0	104.5	108.4	112.8	116.1	119.2
Industrial Production	66	97.7	87.0	86.7	90.4	93.9	96.1	100.0	101.2	100.0	99.6	102.0	102.2
Industrial Employment,Seas. Adj.	67..c	100.8	100.9	99.7	98.9	99.0	98.6	100.0	100.9	99.1	96.9	94.4	92.4
		Number in Thousands: Period Averages											
Labor Force	67d	....	26,083	26,404	26,404	26,435	....	26,226	26,385	26,653	27,287	27,455	....
Employment	67e	21,875	20,233	22,311	20,413	22,479	20,864	23,262	23,759	23,942	24,485	24,720	....
Unemployment	67c	3,329	† 2,893	3,063	3,102	2,977	2,772	2,338	2,125	2,259	2,396	2,440	2,413
Unemployment Rate (%)	67r	12.4	11.6	12.1	12.3	11.8	11.7	10.0	8.8	8.9	9.7	9.9	....
Intl. Transactions & Positions		Billions of Francs through 1998; Billions of Euros Beginning 1999											
Exports	70	196.38	214.69	224.10	258.29	275.38	† 284.13	325.71	331.90	330.49	322.34	341.46	353.58
Imports, c.i.f.	71	1,298.43	1,403.80	1,441.62	1,585.34	1,708.92	† 277.03	337.67	337.20	330.80	327.39	355.91	387.99
Imports, f.o.b.	71.v	190.05	205.61	212.64	234.52	254.69	† 269.83	329.91	331.37	325.30	321.98	346.23	378.55
		2000=100											
Volume of Exports	72	53.8	59.5	64.6	75.0	82.7	88.6	100.0	63.4	66.5	65.3	70.5	74.4
Volume of Imports	73	55.1	59.0	62.8	70.6	79.4	87.4	100.0	64.2	66.5	66.1	74.1	80.2
Unit Value of Exports	74	112.1	111.2	107.8	105.3	102.1	98.6	100.0	110.9	106.7	106.7	104.9	104.0
Unit Value of Imports	75	104.3	104.5	102.5	102.0	97.8	93.9	100.0	102.4	96.9	96.9	94.7	94.1

France 132

		1994	1995	1996	1997	1998	1999	2000	2001	2002	2003	2004	2005
Balance of Payments						*Billions of US Dollars: Minus Sign Indicates Debit*							
Current Account, n.i.e.	78ald	7.42	10.84	20.56	37.80	37.70	41.51	18.58	28.76	11.00	11.80	−6.81	−33.29
Goods: Exports f.o.b.	78aad	230.81	278.63	281.85	286.07	303.02	299.95	298.20	294.62	307.20	361.91	421.27	439.22
Goods: Imports f.o.b.	78abd	−223.56	−267.63	−266.91	−259.17	−278.08	−283.01	−301.82	−291.78	−299.56	−358.49	−429.94	−471.36
Trade Balance	78acd	7.25	11.00	14.94	26.90	24.94	16.94	−3.62	2.84	7.64	3.43	−8.67	−32.14
Services: Credit	78add	75.52	84.09	83.53	80.79	84.96	82.09	80.92	82.30	86.13	98.76	109.52	115.99
Services: Debit	78aed	−57.67	−66.12	−67.28	−64.16	−67.73	−63.52	−61.04	−56.86	−68.91	−82.86	−98.46	−106.10
Balance on Goods & Services	78afd	25.10	28.97	31.19	43.52	42.17	35.50	16.25	28.27	24.86	19.32	2.39	−22.26
Income: Credit	78agd	41.56	45.18	47.55	57.13	66.66	71.24	72.39	74.11	58.04	88.73	116.43	135.45
Income: Debit	78ahd	−48.32	−54.15	−50.25	−50.04	−58.00	−52.21	−56.81	−59.04	−57.43	−76.80	−103.72	−119.13
Balance on Gds, Serv. & Inc.	78aid	18.34	20.01	28.48	50.62	50.83	54.53	31.84	43.34	25.46	31.25	15.09	−5.95
Current Transfers, n.i.e.: Credit	78ajd	18.22	22.01	22.76	19.61	19.65	18.77	17.87	17.28	19.77	24.05	26.03	26.04
Current Transfers: Debit	78akd	−29.15	−31.17	−30.68	−32.43	−32.79	−31.79	−31.13	−31.86	−34.23	−43.49	−47.93	−53.39
Capital Account, n.i.e.	78bcd	−4.18	.51	1.23	1.48	1.47	1.42	1.39	−.31	−.19	−8.23	1.81	.66
Capital Account, n.i.e.: Credit	78bad	.99	1.16	1.88	2.41	2.10	1.99	1.92	1.10	.91	1.93	3.35	2.57
Capital Account: Debit	78bbd	−5.16	−.66	−.65	−.93	−.63	−.57	−.53	−1.41	−1.10	−10.16	−1.54	−1.91
Financial Account, n.i.e.	78bjd	−4.78	−7.32	−22.34	−37.60	−29.29	−50.47	−32.55	−33.25	−20.34	13.54	−12.96	−38.49
Direct Investment Abroad	78bdd	−24.44	−15.82	−30.36	−35.49	−45.70	−133.92	−174.32	−86.98	−50.60	−53.36	−76.65	−133.60
Dir. Invest. in Rep. Econ., n.i.e.	78bed	15.80	23.74	21.97	23.05	29.52	45.98	42.37	50.36	49.54	43.07	38.71	70.69
Portfolio Investment Assets	78bfd	−21.96	−7.42	−46.63	−60.79	−105.22	−126.89	−97.44	−85.48	−84.65	−192.72	−224.64	−238.21
Equity Securities	78bkd	−1.02	1.78	−1.08	−9.67	−24.46	−20.78	−32.54	−19.15	−16.35	−48.08	−60.86	−54.09
Debt Securities	78bld	−20.94	−9.20	−45.55	−51.12	−80.76	−106.11	−64.90	−66.34	−68.30	−144.64	−163.78	−184.13
Portfolio Investment Liab., n.i.e.	78bgd	−27.90	13.08	−15.35	35.32	59.75	117.56	132.33	106.90	76.76	198.85	165.70	226.38
Equity Securities	78bmd	5.26	6.82	12.20	11.97	17.21	49.37	49.97	13.65	−4.37	20.72	31.78	64.20
Debt Securities	78bnd	−33.16	6.26	−27.56	23.36	42.54	68.19	82.36	93.25	81.13	178.13	133.91	162.18
Financial Derivatives Assets	78bwd	—	—	−6.47	—	—	—	—	—	—	—	—	—
Financial Derivatives Liabilities	78bxd	—	1.00	7.81	4.10	−.44	−1.53	4.78	2.29	5.31	−7.05	6.21	9.90
Other Investment Assets	78bhd	23.05	−40.16	26.31	−53.64	26.11	−27.15	.63	−59.15	−44.17	−14.88	−116.14	−278.17
Monetary Authorities	78bod	−.24	.50	.13	−.43	−.05	−10.25	−6.00	−12.50	−4.63	—	11.42	4.34
General Government	78bpd	3.08	−.64	1.11	1.18	.86	.16	−.08	.14	.52	−2.43	2.03	1.69
Banks	78bqd	22.72	−43.19	28.59	−46.82	41.70	−11.77	7.08	−46.96	−35.09	−3.92	−121.45	−287.82
Other Sectors	78brd	−2.50	3.18	−3.52	−7.57	−16.40	−5.29	−.37	.18	−4.98	−8.53	−8.14	3.61
Other Investment Liab., n.i.e.	78bid	30.67	18.26	20.38	49.85	6.70	75.47	59.09	38.82	27.47	39.62	193.86	304.53
Monetary Authorities	78bsd	−14.41	.45	−.47	.13	.31	28.80	−23.39	1.15	−1.28	2.11	1.82	−3.37
General Government	78btd	3.16	1.10	−.01	4.67	.15	2.82	2.69	1.32	.25	−.44	2.42	−6.20
Banks	78bud	32.11	13.13	15.83	39.05	2.26	43.91	55.65	42.81	29.22	39.27	169.34	285.21
Other Sectors	78bvd	9.81	3.59	5.04	6.00	3.98	−.06	24.14	−6.46	−.72	−1.32	20.28	28.90
Net Errors and Omissions	78cad	3.99	−3.31	.78	4.26	9.94	6.09	10.14	−.77	5.57	−15.84	22.07	62.07
Overall Balance	78cbd	2.45	.71	.24	5.94	19.82	−1.45	−2.43	−5.57	−3.97	1.27	4.11	−9.05
Reserves and Related Items	79dad	−2.45	−.71	−.24	−5.94	−19.82	1.45	2.43	5.57	3.97	−1.27	−4.11	9.05
Reserve Assets	79dbd	−2.45	−.71	−.24	−5.94	−19.82	1.45	2.43	5.57	3.97	−1.27	−4.11	9.05
Use of Fund Credit and Loans	79dcd	—	—	—	—	—	—	—	—	—	—	—	—
Exceptional Financing	79ded	....	....	....	—	—	—	—	—	—	—	—	—
International Investment Position						*Billions of US Dollars*							
Assets	79aad	1,202.25	1,383.08	1,482.34	1,698.37	2,052.67	2,212.67	2,369.05	2,443.06	2,771.30	3,681.32	4,473.01	4,886.04
Direct Investment Abroad	79abd	300.86	374.96	482.74	598.65	747.30	806.59	942.50	900.69	896.32	1,212.80	1,407.43	1,488.52
Portfolio Investment	79acd	184.92	203.62	248.12	340.21	489.01	590.20	663.73	728.48	931.87	1,369.57	1,747.91	1,857.00
Equity Securities	79add	53.74	58.36	73.52	99.13	143.05	190.67	210.01	201.73	200.09	340.24	446.50	529.28
Debt Securities	79aed	131.17	145.25	174.60	241.09	345.96	399.53	453.71	526.75	731.78	1,029.33	1,301.42	1,327.72
Financial Derivatives	79ald	24.78	31.33	34.71	42.62	76.07	110.00	95.00	109.81	108.12	136.35	168.71	226.17
Other Investment	79afd	633.73	714.57	659.48	661.24	670.19	637.82	604.27	645.38	773.21	891.83	1,071.62	1,239.99
Monetary Authorities	79agd	1.23	.92	.75	1.88	2.09	11.55	16.10	27.94	37.33	43.70	34.71	27.03
General Government	79ahd	31.28	34.80	33.33	29.79	31.63	28.73	27.17	26.26	29.47	36.50	36.55	32.24
Banks	79aid	469.32	530.27	484.61	498.42	487.70	457.70	429.70	453.08	541.55	621.43	788.51	991.77
Other Sectors	79ajd	131.89	148.59	140.79	131.15	148.77	139.84	131.29	138.10	164.86	190.20	211.86	188.95
Reserve Assets	79akd	57.96	58.61	57.30	55.65	70.09	68.05	63.55	58.70	61.77	70.77	77.34	74.35
Liabilities	79lad	1,227.25	1,418.35	1,438.55	1,543.08	1,919.90	2,202.79	2,250.41	2,245.20	2,607.28	3,525.65	4,312.03	4,692.61
Dir. Invest. in Rep. Economy	79lbd	301.83	341.10	359.21	399.73	548.62	597.23	536.81	463.39	564.72	776.03	928.16	957.04
Portfolio Investment	79lcd	366.66	456.61	460.09	518.04	671.45	865.56	949.20	985.38	1,105.85	1,626.50	1,991.54	2,084.31
Equity Securities	79ldd	102.21	120.76	155.32	208.58	300.44	482.21	502.10	415.97	345.13	490.90	595.65	694.14
Debt Securities	79led	264.45	335.86	304.77	309.46	371.01	383.36	447.11	569.41	760.73	1,135.60	1,395.89	1,390.17
Financial Derivatives	79lld	20.24	32.94	38.32	45.24	81.09	105.08	98.26	104.79	112.32	147.80	175.03	243.45
Other Investment	79lfd	538.52	587.69	580.93	580.07	618.74	634.91	666.14	691.64	824.38	975.33	1,217.30	1,407.81
Monetary Authorities	79lgd	1.72	2.00	2.26	2.30	2.68	28.03	2.33	3.35	2.20	4.40	6.17	2.87
General Government	79lhd	9.45	11.24	10.64	16.33	15.05	14.47	15.82	17.01	20.45	23.73	28.25	19.00
Banks	79lid	435.09	466.41	468.95	472.90	501.82	500.89	530.29	548.26	662.88	788.33	1,008.49	1,198.74
Other Sectors	79ljd	92.26	108.04	99.08	88.53	99.18	91.52	117.71	123.03	138.85	158.87	174.39	187.19
Government Finance													
Central Government						*Billions of Francs through 1998; Millions of Euros Beginning 1999: Year Ending December 31*							
Deficit (-) or Surplus	80	−412.0	−502.6	−413.3	−284.4	....	....	....	....	....	....	....	....
Revenue	81	2,983.5	3,116.5	3,271.2	3,438.7	....	....	....	....	....	....	....	....
Grants Received	81z	48.8	53.0	46.6	51.8	....	....	....	....	....	....	....	....
Exp. & Lending Minus Repay.	82z	3,429.8	3,662.0	3,740.9	3,797.3	....	....	....	....	....	....	....	....
Expenditure	82	3,458.2	3,564.7	3,687.2	3,789.2	....	....	....	....	....	....	....	....
Lending Minus Repayments	83	−28.4	97.3	53.7	8.1	....	....	....	....	....	....	....	....
Overall Adj. to Cash Basis	80x	−14.5	−10.1	9.8	22.4	....	....	....	....	....	....	....	....
Financing													
Net Borrowing	84	326.7	451.5	364.9	....	....	....	....	....	....	....	....	....
Domestic	84a	375.9	396.1	350.0	....	....	....	....	....	....	....	....	....
Foreign	85a	−49.2	55.4	14.9	....	....	....	....	....	....	....	....	....
Use of Cash Balances	87	85.3	51.1	48.4	....	....	....	....	....	....	....	....	....
Debt: Francs	88b	2,859.2	3,214.2	3,506.8	3,738.2	3,977.9	....	....	....	....	....	....	....
Foreign Currency	89b	62.6	58.6	57.1	56.4	49.8	....	....	....	....	....	....	....
General Government						*As Percent of Gross Domestic Product*							

France 132

		1994	1995	1996	1997	1998	1999	2000	2001	2002	2003	2004	2005
National Accounts						*Billions of Francs through 1998; Billions of Euros Beginning 1999:*								
Househ.Cons.Expend.,incl.NPISHs....	96f.c	4,321.5	† 4,436.1	4,583.1	4,642.7	4,831.5	† 758.1	803.3	838.2	866.1	900.0	938.3	976.0
Government Consumption Expend...	91f.c	1,797.6	† 1,850.9	1,922.1	1,984.7	2,004.5	† 316.7	330.1	341.2	362.2	378.4	393.6	405.6
Gross Fixed Capital Formation.........	93e.c	1,396.7	† 1,419.6	1,440.5	1,451.4	1,555.4	† 256.7	280.7	291.6	290.6	300.5	318.4	336.6
Changes in Inventories....................	93i.c	−1.9	† 41.4	−13.2	.7	75.5	† 6.2	14.3	8.9	3.2	−.2	4.6	8.1
Exports of Goods and Services..........	90c.c	1,655.0	† 1,784.7	1,866.9	2,136.8	2,278.5	† 357.6	411.7	421.0	419.9	407.7	427.1	446.3
Imports of Goods and Services (-).....	98c.c	1,589.4	† 1,695.4	1,745.8	1,895.6	2,056.7	† 329.0	398.7	403.8	393.4	391.6	423.0	462.6
Gross Domestic Product (GDP)........	99b.c	7,579.4	† 7,837.4	8,053.7	8,320.7	8,688.6	† 1,366.5	1,441.4	1,497.2	1,548.6	1,594.8	1,659.0	1,710.0
Net Primary Income from Abroad.....	98.nc	−28.7	−41.0	−4.6	19.0	39.9	† 20.9	19.8	17.7	4.2	9.9	10.0	8.8
Gross National Income (GNI)............	99a.c	7,610.3	7,852.2	8,095.6	8,375.2	8,753.9	† 1,387.4	1,461.2	1,514.9	1,552.8	1,604.7	1,669.0	1,718.8
Net Current Transf.from Abroad.......	98t.c	−28.9	−18.2	−31.9	−34.3	−40.1	† −46.5	−58.8	−56.5	−56.6	−82.6	....	....
Gross Nat'l Disposable Inc.(GNDI)....	99i.c	7,418.0	7,666.5	7,892.3	8,170.9	8,542.0	† 1,340.8	1,402.4	1,458.4	1,496.2	1,522.1	....	....
Gross Saving...............................	99s.c	1,440.5	1,512.2	1,528.7	1,673.8	1,837.3	† 282.8	299.3	308.1	299.9	285.8	314.3	....
Consumption of Fixed Capital.........	99cfc	1,037.9	1,064.9	1,110.1	1,141.3	1,172.2	† 166.0	178.4	189.0	197.2	203.3	212.6	220.5
GDP Vol. 1995 Ref., Chained..........	99b.r	7,657.2	7,837.4	7,921.9	8,097.3	8,268.1	† 1,318.7	1,371.7	1,397.2	1,411.5	1,426.9	1,460.0	1,477.3
GDP Volume (2000=100)...............	99bvr	85.1	87.1	88.0	90.0	91.9	† 96.1	100.0	101.9	102.9	104.0	106.4	107.7
GDP Deflator (2000=100)...............	99bir	94.2	† 95.2	96.8	97.8	100.0	† 98.6	100.0	102.0	104.4	106.4	108.1	110.2
						Millions: Midyear Estimates								
Population.................................	99z	57.94	58.20	58.44	58.66	58.86	59.06	59.28	59.51	59.76	60.01	60.26	60.50

Gabon 646

		1994	1995	1996	1997	1998	1999	2000	2001	2002	2003	2004	2005
Exchange Rates						*Francs per SDR: End of Period*							
Official Rate	aa	† 780.44	728.38	753.06	807.94	791.61	† 896.19	918.49	935.39	850.37	771.76	747.90	794.73
						Francs per US Dollar: End of Period (ae) Period Average (rf)							
Official Rate	ae	† 534.60	490.00	523.70	598.81	562.21	† 652.95	704.95	744.31	625.50	519.36	481.58	556.04
Official Rate	rf	† 555.20	499.15	511.55	583.67	589.95	† 615.70	711.98	733.04	696.99	581.20	528.28	527.47
						Index Numbers (2000=100): Period Averages							
Official Rate	ahx	128.1	142.3	138.8	121.8	120.5	115.5	100.0	96.9	102.2	122.4	134.6	134.8
Nominal Effective Exchange Rate	nec	105.6	110.0	110.3	106.1	106.4	104.5	100.0	100.0	101.6	106.3	108.5	108.1
Real Effective Exchange Rate	rec	103.4	114.2	112.6	110.6	111.3	106.2	100.0	100.1	100.0	104.8	105.1	102.6
Fund Position						*Millions of SDRs: End of Period*							
Quota	2f.s	110.30	110.30	110.30	110.30	110.30	154.30	154.30	154.30	154.30	154.30	154.30	154.30
SDRs	1b.s	.17	—	.02	—	.01	—	.05	.04	—	—	4.03	.08
Reserve Position in the Fund	1c.s	.05	.05	.07	.07	.07	.11	.15	.18	.18	.18	.18	.22
Total Fund Cred.&Loans Outstg	2tl	61.42	64.95	83.26	97.20	80.52	62.60	68.38	59.64	49.53	39.42	64.36	47.64
International Liquidity						*Millions of US Dollars Unless Otherwise Indicated: End of Period*							
Total Reserves minus Gold	1l.d	175.19	148.09	248.72	282.60	15.41	17.95	190.09	9.85	139.65	196.57	443.42	668.56
SDRs	1b.d	.25	—	.03	—	.01	.01	.07	.06	—	—	6.26	.12
Reserve Position in the Fund	1c.d	.08	.08	.09	.09	.09	.15	.19	.23	.24	.27	.28	.31
Foreign Exchange	1d.d	174.86	148.01	248.59	282.51	15.30	17.79	189.83	9.57	139.40	196.30	436.88	668.13
Gold (Million Fine Troy Ounces)	1ad	.013	.013	.013	.013	.013	.013	.013	.013	.013	.013	.013	.013
Gold (National Valuation)	1and	† 4.85	4.95	4.73	3.74	3.69	† 3.73	3.50	3.57	4.40	5.36	5.63	6.59
Monetary Authorities: Other Liab.	4..d	33.67	34.56	33.52	53.73	34.62	46.34	44.91	41.61	48.64	64.32	59.34	54.26
Deposit Money Banks: Assets	7a.d	82.23	75.69	159.03	64.55	71.56	74.88	239.68	132.33	115.94	166.73	402.16	477.11
Liabilities	7b.d	41.28	79.93	94.16	50.58	56.73	77.78	91.62	81.39	131.84	138.52	140.12	103.05
Monetary Authorities						*Billions of Francs: End of Period*							
Foreign Assets	11	96.30	74.99	132.74	171.45	10.74	14.15	136.47	9.99	90.10	104.88	216.26	375.41
Claims on Central Government	12a	95.83	101.92	123.60	87.49	211.13	200.78	157.33	248.21	231.47	196.78	197.18	174.08
Claims on Deposit Money Banks	12e	.16	3.74	.75	—	8.11	11.63	.22	3.00	8.00	—	—	—
Claims on Other Banking Insts	12f	—	—	—	—	—	—	—	—	—	—	—	—
Reserve Money	14	133.91	128.24	165.20	167.93	153.60	141.52	192.68	184.59	186.61	213.40	258.85	350.72
of which: Currency Outside DMBs	14a	76.93	100.69	110.88	121.03	124.72	105.26	116.18	128.19	132.02	124.22	138.69	198.03
Foreign Liabilities	16c	65.94	64.24	80.26	110.71	83.21	86.36	94.46	86.76	72.54	63.83	76.71	68.03
Central Government Deposits	16d	18.51	10.67	32.35	16.13	12.14	26.10	43.18	24.57	100.81	50.30	109.45	136.83
Capital Accounts	17a	12.49	11.53	11.89	12.32	11.87	13.76	14.46	15.24	14.52	13.35	14.22	15.40
Other Items (Net)	17r	−38.56	−34.03	−32.61	−48.15	−30.85	−41.17	−50.75	−49.97	−44.90	−39.23	−45.82	−21.48
Deposit Money Banks						*Billions of Francs: End of Period*							
Reserves	20	56.87	27.06	48.32	44.10	27.47	34.75	75.73	56.10	54.19	88.82	119.47	148.84
Foreign Assets	21	43.96	37.09	83.28	38.65	40.23	48.89	168.96	98.49	72.52	86.59	193.67	265.29
Claims on Central Government	22a	172.94	161.16	152.37	143.46	135.76	137.99	92.91	88.71	104.98	104.94	92.97	91.78
Claims on Nonfin.Pub.Enterprises	22c	10.17	9.49	13.60	26.91	23.20	22.32	17.11	21.39	13.53	8.92	16.08	7.51
Claims on Private Sector	22d	157.20	196.08	191.93	269.89	285.12	286.06	313.79	375.00	415.74	380.53	330.26	379.54
Claims on Other Banking Insts	22f	.88	.88	.91	1.39	.60	.74	.74	.60	.63	.59	.59	.59
Claims on Nonbank Financial Insts	22g	7.07	10.22	7.99	7.66	7.55	10.53	25.30	22.05	25.70	22.74	27.57	30.24
Demand Deposits	24	117.96	117.90	159.11	174.41	156.99	161.85	203.51	203.74	214.27	220.52	248.06	326.41
Time and Savings Deposits	25	130.98	139.87	144.78	169.98	176.47	177.21	206.85	234.47	252.33	246.66	271.50	312.13
Bonds	26ab	.30	.23	.15	.08	3.09	5.55	2.65	2.25	1.85	.41	—	—
Foreign Liabilities	26c	13.73	36.34	46.79	28.24	22.66	38.99	56.61	58.85	74.03	57.40	58.40	43.49
Long-Term Foreign Liabilities	26cl	8.34	2.83	2.52	2.05	9.24	11.80	7.98	1.72	8.44	14.54	9.07	13.81
Central Government Deposits	26d	32.21	15.35	20.93	20.62	21.82	29.67	112.30	71.32	41.42	47.38	69.84	104.85
Credit from Monetary Authorities	26g	.16	3.74	.75	—	8.11	11.63	.22	3.00	8.00	—	—	—
Capital Accounts	27a	133.44	128.50	123.58	115.89	122.47	120.48	85.73	107.75	120.20	136.94	150.79	152.18
Other Items (Net)	27r	11.97	−2.78	−.21	20.78	−.92	−15.89	18.68	−20.73	−33.25	−30.72	−27.06	−29.08
Monetary Survey						*Billions of Francs: End of Period*							
Foreign Assets (Net)	31n	52.25	8.68	86.45	69.10	−64.14	−74.10	146.38	−38.86	7.62	55.70	265.74	515.37
Domestic Credit	32	393.36	453.74	437.12	500.04	629.38	602.65	451.70	660.10	649.82	616.82	485.35	442.06
Claims on Central Govt. (Net)	32an	218.05	237.06	222.68	194.19	312.92	283.00	94.76	241.03	194.22	204.04	110.85	24.18
Claims on Nonfin.Pub.Enterprises	32c	10.17	9.49	13.60	26.91	23.20	22.32	17.11	21.39	13.53	8.92	16.08	7.51
Claims on Private Sector	32d	157.20	196.08	191.93	269.89	285.12	286.06	313.79	375.00	415.74	380.53	330.26	379.54
Claims on Other Banking Insts	32f	.88	.88	.91	1.39	.60	.74	.74	.60	.63	.59	.59	.59
Claims on Nonbank Financial Inst	32g	7.07	10.22	7.99	7.66	7.55	10.53	25.30	22.05	25.70	22.74	27.57	30.24
Money	34	195.01	219.09	276.00	298.25	283.12	268.61	320.46	332.22	346.69	345.10	387.45	528.29
Quasi-Money	35	130.98	139.87	144.78	169.98	176.47	177.21	206.85	234.47	252.33	246.66	271.50	312.13
Bonds	36ab	.30	.23	.15	.08	3.09	5.55	2.65	2.25	1.85	.41	—	—
Other Items (Net)	37r	119.33	103.23	102.64	100.84	102.57	77.17	68.12	52.30	56.56	80.34	92.13	117.02
Money plus Quasi-Money	35l	325.98	358.96	420.78	468.22	459.59	445.82	527.31	566.69	599.03	591.76	658.95	840.42
Interest Rates						*Percent Per Annum*							
Discount Rate (End of Period)	60	† 7.75	8.60	7.75	7.50	7.00	7.60	7.00	6.50	6.30	6.00	6.00	5.50
Deposit Rate	60l	8.08	5.50	5.46	5.00	5.00	5.00	5.00	5.00	5.00	5.00	5.00	4.92
Lending Rate	60p	17.50	16.00	22.00	22.00	22.00	22.00	22.00	20.67	18.00	18.00	18.00	17.67
Prices and Production						*Index Numbers (2000=100): Period Averages*							
Consumer Prices	64	87.1	95.5	96.2	100.0	101.5	99.5	100.0	102.1	102.2	104.5	104.9	104.9
Crude Petroleum	66aa	97.8	101.1	106.7	108.8	107.6	101.3	100.0	85.2	79.1	80.5	70.3	70.5
Intl. Transactions & Positions						*Billions of Francs*							
Exports	70	1,304.90	1,354.40	1,628.70	1,765.20	1,130.20	1,473.80	1,852.56	1,848.72	1,680.44	1,642.47	1,849.00	2,452.73
Imports, c.i.f.	71	420.00	440.20	489.30	644.30	650.80	518.00	708.00	629.50	664.93	602.12	676.20	738.46
Imports, c.i.f., from DOTS	71y	392.82	464.29	459.63	719.62	645.74	963.12	993.69	1,071.32	797.63	. . . .	. . . .	. . . .

Gabon 646

		1994	1995	1996	1997	1998	1999	2000	2001	2002	2003	2004	2005
Balance of Payments		*Millions of US Dollars: Minus Sign Indicates Debit*											
Current Account, n.i.e.	78ald	317.4	464.7	888.6	531.4	−595.5	390.4	1,001.0	517.4	336.3	574.5	....	....
Goods: Exports f.o.b.	78aad	2,365.3	2,727.8	3,334.2	3,032.7	1,907.6	2,498.8	3,320.6	2,613.8	2,555.9	3,178.5	....	....
Goods: Imports f.o.b.	78abd	−776.7	−880.9	−961.6	−1,030.6	−1,163.2	−910.5	−798.1	−847.5	−942.0	−1,042.7	....	....
Trade Balance	78acd	1,588.6	1,846.9	2,372.5	2,002.1	744.4	1,588.3	2,522.6	1,766.3	1,613.9	2,135.7	....	....
Services: Credit	78add	219.6	217.1	233.9	232.8	219.6	280.9	177.8	168.3	143.8	172.5	....	....
Services: Debit	78aed	−826.7	−891.6	−917.8	−952.7	−990.9	−867.0	−857.6	−709.8	−810.9	−839.6	....	....
Balance on Goods & Services	78afd	981.4	1,172.4	1,688.6	1,282.3	−27.0	1,002.2	1,842.8	1,224.9	946.8	1,468.6	....	....
Income: Credit	78agd	11.9	35.0	42.8	39.1	57.4	84.2	48.4	29.8	17.7	85.2	....	....
Income: Debit	78ahd	−509.9	−700.5	−805.8	−755.5	−572.6	−653.1	−827.1	−659.0	−497.1	−798.3	....	....
Balance on Gds, Serv. & Inc.	78aid	483.4	507.0	925.5	565.8	−542.1	433.3	1,064.1	595.7	467.5	755.5	....	....
Current Transfers, n.i.e.: Credit	78ajd	18.7	58.0	65.1	62.7	36.6	42.6	16.0	34.3	4.7	7.2	....	....
Current Transfers: Debit	78akd	−184.8	−100.3	−102.1	−97.1	−90.0	−85.6	−79.1	−112.6	−135.9	−188.2	....	....
Capital Account, n.i.e.	78bcd	—	4.8	5.1	5.8	1.8	5.4	−.3	2.9	2.6	43.1	....	....
Capital Account, n.i.e.: Credit	78bad	—	5.6	9.6	7.5	3.6	5.7	—	2.9	2.6	43.1	....	....
Capital Account: Debit	78bbd	....	−.8	−4.5	−1.7	−1.8	−.3	−.3	−.1			....	....
Financial Account, n.i.e.	78bjd	−745.0	−515.6	−852.9	−538.5	−224.1	−756.9	−567.8	−674.0	−451.4	−564.1	....	....
Direct Investment Abroad	78bdd	—	−35.0	−2.3	−21.0	−33.2	−73.9	−25.3	−3.8	23.0	−16.0	....	....
Dir. Invest. in Rep. Econ., n.i.e.	78bed	−99.6	−314.5	−489.1	−311.3	146.6	−156.6	−42.6	−89.1	45.8	279.2	....	....
Portfolio Investment Assets	78bfd	....	−29.8	−21.1	260.1	19.1	22.4	−9.2	−.8	.6	2.5	....	....
Equity Securities	78bkd	....	−45.0	−16.7	311.3	19.1	44.0	−9.6	−.9	—	−.1	....	....
Debt Securities	78bld	....	15.2	−4.4	−51.2	—	−21.5	.4	.1	.5	2.6	....	....
Portfolio Investment Liab., n.i.e.	78bgd	....	80.3	4.6	−20.7	−.2	−.7	−1.6	1.2	−2.1	3.7	....	....
Equity Securities	78bmd	....	—	—	—	—	—	—	—	—	—	....	....
Debt Securities	78bnd	....	80.3	4.6	−20.7	−.2	−.7	−1.6	1.2	−2.1	3.7	....	....
Financial Derivatives Assets	78bwd	....	....	....	....	....	....	....	....	....	....	....	....
Financial Derivatives Liabilities	78bxd	....	....	....	....	....	....	....	....	....	....	....	....
Other Investment Assets	78bhd	−258.6	−37.7	−216.3	−6.8	−199.1	−126.5	−729.2	−296.3	−181.2	−355.6	....	....
Monetary Authorities	78bod	....						....				....	....
General Government	78bpd	....	—	—	—	—	—	....	96.1	37.3	−24.2	....	....
Banks	78bqd	−22.9	13.8	−90.3	76.5	−2.7	−14.1	−168.6	96.1	37.3	−24.2	....	....
Other Sectors	78brd	−235.8	−51.5	−126.0	−83.3	−196.4	−112.5	−560.6	−392.5	−218.4	−331.4	....	....
Other Investment Liab., n.i.e.	78bid	−386.7	−178.7	−128.8	−438.8	−157.4	−421.6	240.2	−285.2	−337.5	−477.9	....	....
Monetary Authorities	78bsd	−203.9	−1.0	30.2	27.1	−23.7	−14.4	10.4	−10.5	−17.0	−10.5	....	....
General Government	78btd	−133.1	−57.5	−42.2	−99.0	−292.7	−286.7	76.7	−355.4	−331.3	−340.1	....	....
Banks	78bud	−54.9	20.9	19.8	−35.5	2.7	28.1	18.0	−5.5	18.3	−18.1	....	....
Other Sectors	78bvd	5.2	−141.1	−136.7	−331.4	156.3	−148.6	135.0	86.2	−7.4	−109.2	....	....
Net Errors and Omissions	78cad	254.6	−182.2	−126.4	−110.4	94.7	−74.8	−152.4	−104.0	−109.6	−154.4	....	....
Overall Balance	78cbd	−173.0	−228.3	−85.6	−111.8	−723.1	−435.9	280.5	−257.8	−222.1	100.9	....	....
Reserves and Related Items	79dad	173.0	228.3	85.6	111.8	723.1	435.9	−280.5	257.8	222.1	100.9	....	....
Reserve Assets	79dbd	−173.8	42.2	−112.8	−66.8	272.2	−4.9	−171.8	173.0	−115.0	−25.4	....	....
Use of Fund Credit and Loans	79dcd	40.9	5.0	26.4	19.4	−22.7	−24.5	7.2	−11.0	−13.3	−14.6	....	....
Exceptional Financing	79ded	306.0	181.0	172.0	159.2	473.7	465.4	−115.9	95.8	350.4	140.8	....	....
National Accounts		*Billions of Francs*											
Househ.Cons.Expend.,incl.NPISHs	96f	994.1	955.0	1,042.0	1,120.0	1,202.0	1,302.4	2,164.7	....	....	....	....	....
Government Consumption Expend	91f	278.9	348.8	398.3	433.0	461.0	444.4	352.0	....	....	....	....	....
Gross Fixed Capital Formation	93e	490	561	683	937	1,016	751	918	970	984	841	970	....
Changes in Inventories	93i	19	25	2	—	—	—	—	—	—	—	—	....
Exports of Goods and Services	90c	1,435.0	1,423.0	1,785.0	1,867.0	1,250.0	1,209.2	1,299.6	1,920.1	2,060.8	2,197.4	2,335.0	....
Imports of Goods and Services (-)	98c	890.0	838.0	974.0	1,189.0	1,204.0	1,027.6	1,222.8	1,291.2	1,367.3	1,443.6	1,533.1	....
Gross Domestic Product (GDP)	99b	2,326.8	2,474.6	2,936.6	3,168.4	2,725.0	2,679.7	3,511.3	3,176.7	3,464.6	3,520.5	3,818.7	....
Net Primary Income from Abroad	98.n	−308.2	−376.8	−400.7	−395.8	−416.7	....	....	....	....	....	....	....
Gross National Income (GNI)	99a	2,050.3	2,116.8	2,500.2	2,774.7	2,399.6	2,346.9	3,018.5	2,751.2	2,904.4	3,025.4	3,184.7	....
Consumption of Fixed Capital	99cf	243.7	274.2	308.5	347.1	390.5	....	....	....	....	....	....	....
		Millions: Midyear Estimates											
Population	99z	1.09	1.12	1.15	1.18	1.21	1.24	1.27	1.30	1.32	1.34	1.36	1.38

Gambia, The 648

		1994	1995	1996	1997	1998	1999	2000	2001	2002	2003	2004	2005
Exchange Rates							*Dalasis per SDR: End of Period*							
Market Rate	aa	13.983	14.330	14.225	14.207	15.476	15.849	19.397	21.279	31.802	46.005	46.083	40.212
						Dalasis per US Dollar: End of Period (ae) Period Average (rf)								
Market Rate	ae	9.579	9.640	9.892	10.530	10.991	11.547	14.888	16.932	23.392	30.960	29.674	28.135
Market Rate	rf	9.576	9.546	9.789	10.200	10.643	11.395	12.788	15.687	19.918	27.306	30.030	28.575
						Index Numbers (2000=100): Period Averages								
Market Rate	ahx	132.84	133.29	130.02	124.81	119.59	111.74	100.00	81.26	64.54	46.87	42.38	44.56
Nominal Effective Exchange Rate	nec	106.79	101.94	102.77	106.49	107.84	102.88	100.00	85.65	66.46	42.27	37.48	39.07
Real Effective Exchange Rate	rec	109.64	106.22	104.43	107.74	107.24	104.68	100.00	86.92	71.68	51.84	51.20	53.47
Fund Position							*Millions of SDRs: End of Period*							
Quota	2f.s	22.90	22.90	22.90	22.90	22.90	31.10	31.10	31.10	31.10	31.10	31.10	31.10
SDRs	1b.s	.18	.09	.20	.09	.30	.49	.17	.01	.01	.02	.48	.11
Reserve Position in the Fund	1c.s	1.48	1.48	1.48	1.48	1.48	1.48	1.48	1.48	1.48	1.48	1.48	1.48
Total Fund Cred.&Loans Outstg.	2tl	23.94	19.84	14.71	9.58	8.91	9.26	14.42	20.61	23.50	23.50	15.94	14.57
International Liquidity						*Millions of US Dollars Unless Otherwise Indicated: End of Period*								
Total Reserves minus Gold	1l.d	98.02	106.15	102.13	96.04	106.36	111.25	109.43	106.01	106.88	59.31	83.77	98.31
SDRs	1b.d	.26	.13	.29	.11	.42	.67	.23	.02	.02	.03	.75	.16
Reserve Position in the Fund	1c.d	2.17	2.21	2.14	2.00	2.09	2.04	1.93	1.87	2.02	2.21	2.31	2.12
Foreign Exchange	1d.d	95.59	103.81	99.71	93.92	103.85	108.54	107.27	104.13	104.84	57.07	80.72	96.03
Monetary Authorities: Other Liab.	4..d	2.17	.03	.03	.03	.03	.02	.02	.01	.01	.01	.01	.01
Deposit Money Banks: Assets	7a.d	3.59	5.64	3.43	10.68	6.54	10.92	9.23	.92	24.28	34.09	50.79	39.31
Liabilities	7b.d	3.03	2.52	6.28	14.52	12.93	17.01	10.38	8.88	18.20	1.35	2.71	1.33
Monetary Authorities							*Millions of Dalasis: End of Period*							
Foreign Assets	11	948.01	1,030.19	1,011.63	1,010.13	1,163.67	1,277.17	1,626.32	1,793.06	2,499.12	1,834.48	2,468.80	2,749.03
Claims on Central Government	12a	297.93	253.65	259.73	240.84	239.90	239.39	223.20	250.52	405.91	1,176.72	1,307.96	1,211.05
Claims on Official Entities	12bx	—	—	—	—	—	—	—	—	—	—	—	—
Claims on Private Sector	12d	17.02	20.45	21.54	21.08	20.86	21.91	22.71	24.13	23.72	24.39	28.82	30.77
Claims on Deposit Money Banks	12e	—	—	—	—	—	—	—	56.98	31.35	21.20	33.62	33.62
Reserve Money	14	307.08	385.02	386.85	490.42	525.60	601.65	702.68	850.40	1,140.53	1,855.88	2,060.73	2,306.59
of which: Currency Outside DMBs	14a	207.36	247.97	255.03	360.51	347.55	379.72	540.26	600.75	797.37	1,182.89	1,416.27	1,424.20
Restricted Deposits	16b	—	—	—	—	—	—	—	—	—	—	—	—
Foreign Liabilities	16c	355.53	284.55	209.48	136.34	138.14	147.09	280.06	438.74	747.51	1,081.38	735.05	586.19
Central Government Deposits	16d	597.69	559.54	669.41	718.02	782.05	808.47	984.40	767.72	750.76	404.54	1,563.16	1,684.59
Capital Accounts	17a	79.15	80.93	81.15	81.06	87.56	89.47	107.64	117.28	171.17	243.90	244.30	214.24
Other Items (Net)	17r	−76.49	−5.74	−53.99	−153.79	−108.92	−108.22	−202.54	−49.45	150.13	−528.91	−764.04	−767.13
of which: Valuation Adjustment	17rv	213.42	252.36	230.73	130.07	152.51	387.78	290.14	85.61	550.36	1,193.77	1,279.30	1,046.56
Deposit Money Banks							*Millions of Dalasis: End of Period*							
Reserves	20	97.09	117.71	128.16	129.91	178.05	221.93	162.43	249.65	367.65	586.28	670.93	942.73
Foreign Assets	21	34.41	54.36	33.94	112.47	71.90	126.06	137.47	15.51	568.05	1,055.55	1,507.23	1,105.84
Claims on Central Government	22a	100.50	228.00	355.70	447.25	516.62	587.86	819.73	1,078.99	913.64	653.96	1,195.55	1,762.19
Claims on Official Entities	22bx	.10	.18	.43	1.11	3.86	9.20	11.86	75.79	74.69	205.87	86.46	122.85
Claims on Private Sector	22d	385.44	342.35	341.89	425.26	489.76	591.41	652.18	873.21	1,203.05	1,609.04	1,425.27	1,688.22
Demand Deposits	24	200.17	223.50	198.46	268.90	279.02	336.32	443.27	524.66	959.40	1,690.14	1,691.34	1,896.41
Time and Savings Deposits	25	393.49	443.45	514.30	560.66	685.01	754.26	998.82	1,241.90	1,445.75	1,720.00	2,324.35	2,824.59
Restricted Deposits	26b	—	—	—	—	—	—	—	—	—	—	—	—
Foreign Liabilities	26c	28.98	24.25	62.10	152.86	142.17	196.46	132.14	175.83	425.63	41.68	80.52	37.49
Central Government Deposits	26d	3.96	3.96	3.96	3.96	3.96	3.96	3.96	3.96	3.96	—	—	—
Credit from Monetary Authorities	26g	—	—	—	—	—	—	—	—	—	—	—	—
Capital Accounts	27a	72.28	77.98	88.13	113.08	126.34	188.41	246.75	315.19	491.54	604.35	652.55	904.39
Other Items (Net)	27r	−81.34	−30.54	−6.83	16.54	23.69	57.05	−41.27	31.61	−199.20	54.53	136.68	−41.05
Monetary Survey							*Millions of Dalasis: End of Period*							
Foreign Assets (Net)	31n	597.91	775.76	773.99	833.41	955.26	1,059.68	1,351.60	1,194.00	1,894.03	1,766.97	3,160.47	3,231.19
Domestic Credit	32	199.34	281.13	305.92	413.56	484.99	637.34	741.32	1,530.96	1,866.29	3,265.44	2,480.90	3,130.49
Claims on Central Govt. (Net)	32an	−203.22	−81.85	−57.94	−33.89	−29.49	14.82	54.57	557.83	564.83	1,426.14	940.35	1,288.65
Claims on Official Entities	32bx	.10	.18	.43	1.11	3.86	9.20	11.86	75.79	74.69	205.87	86.46	122.85
Claims on Private Sector	32d	402.46	362.80	363.43	446.34	510.62	613.32	674.89	897.34	1,226.77	1,633.43	1,454.09	1,718.99
Money	34	407.53	471.47	453.49	629.41	626.57	716.04	983.53	1,125.41	1,756.77	2,873.03	3,107.61	3,320.61
Quasi-Money	35	393.49	443.45	514.30	560.66	685.01	754.26	998.82	1,241.90	1,445.75	1,720.00	2,324.35	2,824.59
Restricted Deposits	36b	—	—	—	—	—	—	—	—	—	—	—	—
Capital Accounts	37a	151.43	158.91	169.28	194.14	213.90	277.88	354.39	432.47	662.71	848.25	896.85	1,118.63
Other Items (Net)	37r	−155.20	−16.94	−57.16	−137.25	−85.23	−51.17	−243.82	−74.82	−104.91	−408.87	−687.45	−902.14
Money plus Quasi-Money	35l	801.02	914.92	967.79	1,190.07	1,311.58	1,470.30	1,982.35	2,367.31	3,202.52	4,593.03	5,431.96	6,145.20
Interest Rates							*Percent Per Annum*							
Discount Rate (End of Period)	60	13.50	14.00	14.00	14.00	12.00	10.50	10.00	13.00	18.00	29.00	28.00	14.00
Savings Rate	60k	9.50	9.50	9.50	9.50	9.50	9.33	8.17	8.00	8.00	9.29	9.67	8.33
Deposit Rate	60l	12.58	12.50	12.50	12.50	12.50	12.50	12.50	12.50	12.71	16.42	22.00	17.33
Lending Rate	60p	25.00	25.04	25.50	25.50	25.38	24.00	24.00	24.00	24.00	29.33	36.50	34.92
Prices							*Index Numbers (2000=100): Period Averages*							
Consumer Prices	64	84.9	90.9	91.8	94.4	97.7	99.8	100.0	104.4	113.4	132.7	151.6	156.4
Intl. Transactions & Positions							*Millions of Dalasis*							
Exports	70	337.80	155.23	209.15	149.82	223.51	136.74	191.81	156.87	239.02	218.45	300.30	257.18
Imports, c.i.f.	71	2,032.75	1,741.26	2,527.62	1,773.80	2,426.63	2,187.86	2,391.29	2,102.08	2,944.10	4,286.99	6,869.60	6,772.38
National Accounts							*Millions of Dalasis: Year Ending June 30*							
Gross Domestic Product (GDP)	99b	2,886.3	....	....	....	....	....	....	....	....	....	....	....
							Millions: Midyear Estimates							
Population	99z	1.08	1.12	1.15	1.19	1.23	1.28	1.32	1.36	1.40	1.44	1.48	1.52

Georgia 915

		1994	1995	1996	1997	1998	1999	2000	2001	2002	2003	2004	2005
Exchange Rates						*Lari per SDR: End of Period*							
Official Rate	aa	....	1.8284	1.8348	1.7594	2.5345	2.6489	2.5732	2.5889	2.8414	3.0834	2.8342	2.5620
					Lari per US Dollar: End of Period (ae) Period Average (rf)								
Official Rate	ae	....	1.2300	1.2760	1.3040	1.8000	1.9300	1.9750	2.0600	2.0900	2.0750	1.8250	1.7925
Official Rate	rf	....	....	1.2628	1.2975	1.3898	2.0245	1.9762	2.0730	2.1957	2.1457	1.9167	1.8127
					Index Numbers (2000=100): Period Averages								
Nominal Effective Exchange Rate	nec	158.36	100.00	117.88	138.71	159.99	....	....	....	....	....	....	....
Real Effective Exchange Rate	rec	44.73	100.00	129.37	136.48	135.73	....	....	....	....	....	....	....
Fund Position						*Millions of SDRs: End of Period*							
Quota	2f.s	111.00	111.00	111.00	111.00	111.00	150.30	150.30	150.30	150.30	150.30	150.30	150.30
SDRs	1b.s	1.61	1.12	.05	.10	3.69	6.13	2.51	3.15	2.13	3.31	7.22	.71
Reserve Position in the Fund	1c.s	.01	.01	.01	.01	.01	.01	.01	.01	.01	.01	.01	.01
Total Fund Cred.& Loans Outstg	2tl	27.75	77.70	133.20	188.70	215.76	233.33	213.68	228.65	228.03	194.26	171.26	162.54
International Liquidity					*Millions of US Dollars Unless Otherwise Indicated: End of Period*								
Total Reserves minus Gold	1l.d	....	194.01	188.91	199.80	122.99	132.39	109.41	159.37	197.55	190.72	382.90	473.24
SDRs	1b.d	2.35	1.66	.07	.13	5.20	8.42	3.27	3.96	2.89	4.91	11.22	1.02
Reserve Position in the Fund	1c.d	.01	.01	.01	.01	.01	.01	.01	.01	.01	.01	.02	.01
Foreign Exchange	1d.d	....	192.33	188.83	199.66	117.78	123.96	106.13	155.40	194.64	185.79	371.66	472.21
Gold(Millions Fine Troy Ounces)	1ad	....	—	—	—	—	—	—	—	—	—	—	—
Gold (National Valuation)	1and	....	—	—	—	—	—	—	1.74	—	—	—	.62
Monetary Authorities:Other Assets	3..d	....	.11	.06	27.75	36.68	41.18	38.79	40.27	46.60	55.98	62.81	55.06
Other Liab	4..d	....	.06	.06	.06	.06	.06	—	—	—	—	—	—
Banking Institutions: Assets	7a.d	....	26.88	33.88	39.10	46.41	48.57	54.11	84.53	94.32	114.47	158.80	155.97
Liabilities	7b.d	....	49.26	4.80	11.95	35.99	46.94	57.64	70.76	88.07	97.60	118.40	289.41
Monetary Authorities						*Millions of Lari: End of Period*							
Foreign Assets	11	....	238.75	241.15	260.50	221.53	255.50	216.12	†337.19	422.35	407.02	705.41	857.39
Claims on Central Government	12a	....	112.45	296.72	437.52	541.78	717.82	802.49	†767.62	776.87	816.53	841.41	832.85
Claims on State and Local Govts	12b	....							†—				
Claims on Nonfin. Pub. Enterprises	12c	....	—	—	—	—	—	—	†79.04	95.28	114.18	110.10	94.80
Claims on Private Sector	12d	....	—	—	36.67	66.67	80.86	77.88	†1.17	1.59	2.01	2.44	2.07
Claims on Banking Institutions	12e	....	3.66	14.30	5.26	6.56	1.86	4.49	†1.76	.25	6.81	.31	1.72
Claims on Nonbank Financial Insts	12g	....	....	....	....								
Reserve Money	14	....	153.28	208.96	277.07	259.72	308.47	391.66	†431.42	516.34	589.94	866.66	1,007.37
of which: Currency Outside Banks	14a	....	124.78	176.76	239.87	212.19	244.00	315.18	†348.85	390.79	441.54	615.99	736.28
Other Liabs. to Banking Insts	14n	....	....	....	....	....	—	—	.31	—	.35	17.04	—
Time, Savings,& Fgn. Currency Dep	15	....	—	—	—	—	—	—	†1.87	1.56	1.08	1.42	.55
Liabs. of Central Bank: Securities	16ac	....	....	....	....	....	....	—	.11	2.17	2.13	12.94	1.56
Restricted Deposits	16b	....	....	....	....	....	....	....	—	—	—	—	—
Foreign Liabilities	16c	....	142.14	244.47	368.19	612.84	697.55	626.45	†674.90	745.30	715.14	600.03	515.11
Central Government Deposits	16d	....	57.17	87.86	52.08	46.35	22.49	20.26	†28.50	18.78	31.49	106.75	185.45
Liab. to Nonbank Financial Insts	16j	....	—	—	—	—	—	—	†—	—	—	—	—
Capital Accounts	17a	....	14.88	18.53	94.02	−14.88	182.32	176.07	†74.20	54.89	49.03	98.09	117.24
Other Items (Net)	17r	....	−12.61	−7.65	−51.41	−67.49	−154.79	−113.47	†−24.51	−42.70	−42.61	−43.26	−38.46
Banking Institutions						*Millions of Lari: End of Period*							
Reserves	20	....	38.00	30.39	39.62	45.01	56.37	76.65	†82.45	126.13	148.91	220.40	268.93
Claims on Mon.Author.:Securities	20c	....	....	....									
Other Claims on Monetary Author	20n	....	....	....	....								
Foreign Assets	21	....	33.06	43.23	50.99	83.55	93.73	106.86	†174.12	197.13	237.52	289.82	279.58
Claims on Central Government	22a	....	.06	—	3.78	—	1.70	5.41	†21.34	47.91	53.48	53.13	26.46
Claims on State and Local Govts	22b	....	1.42	1.26	1.09	1.12	—	.30	†2.04	2.87	10.61	.24	.02
Claims on Nonfin. Pub. Enterprises	22c	....							†25.00	39.62	39.33	23.47	50.21
Claims on Private Sector	22d	....	148.71	127.80	175.06	239.95	339.74	446.96	†496.38	602.46	743.93	960.39	1,714.36
Claims on Nonbank Fin. Insts	22g	....	.31	.06	—	—	—	—	†—	—	—	—	—
Demand Deposits	24	....	34.93	40.51	42.17	43.07	35.38	57.73	†45.33	62.01	75.32	202.68	263.25
Time,Savings,& Fgn.Currency Dep	25	....	28.51	46.69	94.82	118.63	171.44	254.51	†341.94	415.86	550.92	701.48	924.83
Money Market Instruments	26aa	....							†—	—	—	—	—
Restricted Deposits	26b	....	....	....	....	....	....	....	6.45	59.50	54.53	17.27	15.24
Foreign Liabilities	26c	....	60.59	6.12	15.58	64.79	90.59	113.84	†145.76	184.06	202.52	216.07	518.77
Central Government Deposits	26d	....	9.35	23.84	15.95	19.02	11.68	13.14	†26.31	21.72	19.04	11.35	18.68
Credit from Monetary Authorities	26g	....	—	—	—	—	—	—	†1.21	.61	7.12	—	2.50
Liab. to Nonbank Financial Insts	26j	....	—	—	—	—	—	—	†.15	—	—	73.00	91.39
Capital Accounts	27a	....	61.09	90.82	145.14	200.17	280.27	376.61	†270.56	316.08	354.10	372.92	479.84
Other Items (Net)	27r	....	27.08	−5.22	−43.12	−76.05	−97.82	−179.64	†−36.36	−43.70	−29.76	−47.33	25.06
Banking Survey						*Millions of Lari: End of Period*							
Foreign Assets (Net)	31n	....	69.09	33.79	−72.29	−372.55	−438.90	−417.31	†−309.34	−309.88	−273.13	179.13	103.09
Domestic Credit	32	....	196.41	314.15	586.09	784.16	1,105.95	1,299.65	†1,337.79	1,526.11	1,729.56	1,873.08	2,516.64
Claims on Central Govt. (Net)	32an	....	45.98	185.03	373.26	476.42	685.35	774.51	†734.16	784.28	819.49	776.45	655.18
Claims on State and Local Govts	32b	....	1.42	1.26	1.09	1.12	—	.30	†2.04	2.87	10.61	.24	.02
Claims on Nonfin.Pub. Enterprises	32c	....							†104.04	134.90	153.51	133.57	145.01
Claims on Private Sector	32d	....	148.71	127.80	211.73	306.62	420.60	524.84	†497.55	604.06	745.95	962.82	1,716.43
Claims on Nonbank Fin. Insts	32g	....	.31	.06	—	—	—	—	†—	—	—	—	—
Money	34	....	159.71	217.26	282.04	255.27	279.38	372.91	†394.18	452.80	516.86	818.67	999.54
Quasi-Money	35	....	28.51	46.69	94.82	118.63	171.44	254.51	†343.81	417.42	551.99	702.91	925.38
Money Market Instruments	36aa	....							†—	—	—	—	—
Liabs. of Central Banks: Securities	36ac	....	....	....	....	....	....	....					
Restricted Deposits	36b	....	....	....	....	....	....	....	6.55	61.67	56.67	30.21	16.80
Liab. to Nonbank Financial Insts	36j	....	—	—	—	—	—	—	†.15	—	—	73.00	91.39
Capital Accounts	37a	....	75.97	109.35	239.16	185.30	462.58	552.68	†344.76	370.96	403.14	471.01	597.07
Other Items (Net)	37r	....	1.31	−25.36	−102.21	−147.58	−246.36	−297.77	†−61.00	−86.62	−72.22	−43.59	−10.45
Money plus Quasi-Money	35l	....	188.22	263.95	376.86	373.89	450.82	627.42	†737.99	870.22	1,068.85	1,521.57	1,924.92

Georgia 915

		1994	1995	1996	1997	1998	1999	2000	2001	2002	2003	2004	2005
Money (National Definitions)						*Millions of Lari: End of Period*							
Reserve Money	19mb	....	....	....	....	....	....	....	429.86	508.97	579.91	836.54	1,001.50
M2	59mb	....	....	....	....	....	....	....	403.84	462.27	527.40	846.10	1,069.90
M3	59mc	....	....	....	....	....	....	....	732.45	863.57	1,060.39	1,511.93	1,911.20
Interest Rates						*Percent Per Annum*							
Money Market Rate	60b	....	....	43.39	26.58	43.26	34.61	18.17	† 17.52	27.69	16.88	11.87	7.71
Treasury Bill Rate	60c	....	....	....	....	....	....	....	29.93	43.42	44.26	19.16	....
Deposit Rate	60l	....	....	31.05	13.73	17.00	14.58	10.17	7.75	9.82	9.28	7.24	7.55
Deposit Rate (Foreign Currency)	60l.f	....	....	24.55	19.11	15.75	14.58	12.00	10.42	10.23	9.19	7.66	5.94
Lending Rate	60p	....	....	58.24	50.64	46.00	33.42	32.75	27.25	31.83	32.27	31.23	21.63
Lending Rate (Foreign Currency)	60p.f	....	....	51.92	54.16	46.75	42.92	36.58	32.17	29.27	27.62	27.06	24.18
Prices and Labor						*Index Numbers (2000=100): Period Averages*							
Producer Prices	63	....	....	....	....	82.7	† 94.5	100.0	† 103.7	109.9	....	....	....
Consumer Prices	64	19.9	52.2	72.7	77.8	80.6	96.1	100.0	104.6	110.5	115.8	122.4	132.4
						Number in Thousands: Period Averages							
Labor Force	67d	....	....	....	1,999	2,026	2,010	2,052	2,113	2,104	2,050	2,041	2,023
Employment	67e	....	....	....	1,848	1,731	1,733	1,839	1,878	1,839	1,815	1,783	1,745
Unemployment	67c	....	....	....	152	295	277	212	236	265	236	258	278
Unemployment Rate (%)	67r	....	....	....	7.6	14.5	13.8	10.3	11.1	12.6	11.5	12.6	13.8
Intl. Transactions & Positions						*Millions of Lari*							
Exports	70	163	194	251	312	267	481	637	658	760	990	1,240	1,571
Imports, c.i.f.	71	288	507	868	1,224	1,229	1,184	1,402	1,561	1,747	2,449	3,542	4,515
Imports, f.o.b.	71.v	259	456	781	1,103	1,107	....	....	....	....	....	....	....
Balance of Payments						*Millions of US Dollars: Minus Sign Indicates Debit*							
Current Account, n.i.e.	78ald	....	....	....	−514.2	−275.7	−198.4	−269.0	−211.7	−221.3	−374.8	−425.6	−750.7
Goods: Exports f.o.b.	78aad	....	....	....	376.5	299.9	329.5	459.0	496.1	601.7	830.6	1,092.5	1,472.4
Goods: Imports f.o.b.	78abd	....	....	....	−1,162.9	−994.5	−863.4	−970.5	−1,045.6	−1,084.7	−1,466.6	−2,008.6	−2,686.3
Trade Balance	78acd	....	....	....	−786.4	−694.6	−533.9	−511.5	−549.5	−483.0	−636.0	−916.0	−1,213.9
Services: Credit	78add	....	....	....	198.0	365.3	216.9	206.4	314.1	392.2	442.7	538.5	695.6
Services: Debit	78aed	....	....	....	−249.7	−345.2	−224.0	−216.3	−236.9	−356.7	−388.7	−482.4	−624.0
Balance on Goods & Services	78afd	....	....	....	−838.1	−674.5	−541.0	−521.4	−472.3	−447.5	−582.0	−859.9	−1,142.3
Income: Credit	78agd	....	....	....	186.6	243.4	211.4	178.6	97.7	160.6	177.4	251.7	263.6
Income: Debit	78ahd	....	....	....	−59.2	−52.7	−64.5	−61.1	−65.4	−127.4	−145.0	−155.0	−169.2
Balance on Gds, Serv. & Inc.	78aid	....	....	....	−710.7	−483.8	−394.1	−403.9	−440.0	−414.3	−549.7	−763.2	−1,048.0
Current Transfers, n.i.e.: Credit	78ajd	....	....	....	205.5	219.9	228.7	163.2	246.4	222.0	211.1	389.1	351.6
Current Transfers: Debit	78akd	....	....	....	−9.0	−11.8	−33.0	−28.3	−18.1	−29.0	−36.2	−51.5	−54.3
Capital Account, n.i.e.	78bcd	....	....	....	−6.5	−6.1	−7.1	−4.8	−5.2	18.4	19.9	40.8	59.6
Capital Account, n.i.e.: Credit	78bad	....	....	....	—	—	—	—	....	27.1	27.9	44.2	62.6
Capital Account: Debit	78bbd	....	....	....	−6.5	−6.1	−7.1	−4.8	−5.2	−8.6	−8.0	−3.4	−3.0
Financial Account, n.i.e.	78bjd	....	....	....	322.7	348.8	135.5	92.8	209.7	19.2	322.7	479.0	663.3
Direct Investment Abroad	78bdd	....	....	....	—	—	−1.0	.5	.1	−4.1	−3.8	−9.6	89.5
Dir. Invest. in Rep. Econ., n.i.e.	78bed	....	....	....	242.5	265.3	82.3	131.1	109.8	167.4	339.4	499.1	447.8
Portfolio Investment Assets	78bfd	....	....	....	....	....	....	2.7	−.1	—	—	−13.1	13.1
Equity Securities	78bkd	....	....	....	....	....	....	2.7	....	—	—	−13.1	13.1
Debt Securities	78bld	....	....	....	....	....	....	—	....	—	—	—	—
Portfolio Investment Liab., n.i.e.	78bgd	....	....	....	2.4	—	6.2	—	—	—	—	—	2.5
Equity Securities	78bmd	....	....	....	2.4	—	6.2	—	—	—	—	—	2.5
Debt Securities	78bnd	....	....	....	....	....	....	—	—	—	—	—	—
Financial Derivatives Assets	78bwd	....	....	....	....	....	....	—	—	—	—	—	—
Financial Derivatives Liabilities	78bxd	....	....	....	....	....	....	—	—	—	—	—	—
Other Investment Assets	78bhd	....	....	....	−24.8	−86.9	9.3	−7.7	−24.6	−72.8	−15.3	−25.7	−16.4
Monetary Authorities	78bod	....	....	....	....	....	....	—	—	—	—	—	—
General Government	78bpd	....	....	....	—	−45.0	—	—	....	−5.0	−5.0	−4.7	−6.7
Banks	78bqd	....	....	....	−15.0	−23.2	9.3	−7.7	−24.6	−59.3	.5	−21.1	−3.2
Other Sectors	78brd	....	....	....	−9.8	−18.7	—	—	....	−8.5	−10.8	.1	−6.5
Other Investment Liab., n.i.e.	78bid	....	....	....	102.6	170.4	38.7	−33.8	124.5	−71.3	2.4	28.2	126.8
Monetary Authorities	78bsd	....	....	....	....	....	....	—	—	—	−.5	—	—
General Government	78btd	....	....	....	90.0	141.5	17.6	−41.1	99.1	−132.6	−56.7	−47.3	−73.2
Banks	78bud	....	....	....	7.4	37.4	26.3	7.3	25.4	16.3	4.1	27.6	165.0
Other Sectors	78bvd	....	....	....	5.2	−8.5	−5.2	—	—	45.1	55.4	48.0	35.1
Net Errors and Omissions	78cad	....	....	....	136.0	−170.5	55.7	187.4	34.9	−6.0	−17.0	1.6	11.5
Overall Balance	78cbd	....	....	....	−62.0	−103.5	−14.3	6.4	27.7	−189.7	−49.1	95.7	−16.3
Reserves and Related Items	79dad	....	....	....	62.0	103.5	14.3	−6.4	−27.7	189.7	49.1	−95.7	16.3
Reserve Assets	79dbd	....	....	....	−14.1	67.6	−9.6	19.8	−47.0	−37.7	6.2	−178.8	−111.5
Use of Fund Credit and Loans	79dcd	....	....	....	76.1	35.8	23.9	−26.2	19.4	−.1	−47.4	−34.2	−12.5
Exceptional Financing	79ded	....	....	....	....	....	....	....	....	227.4	90.4	117.3	140.3
Government Finance						*Millions of Lari: Year Ending December 31*							
Deficit (-) or Surplus	80	....	....	....	....	−175.39	−128.46	−193.61	−103.96	−185.15	−153.85	−150.61	−8.97
Total Revenue and Grants	81y	....	....	....	....	621.87	723.96	640.26	740.34	818.01	914.76	1,709.18	2,607.55
Revenue	81	....	....	....	....	591.43	674.62	625.93	692.26	795.41	866.35	1,585.23	2,503.38
Grants	81z	....	....	....	....	30.44	49.35	14.33	48.08	22.60	48.41	123.95	104.17
Exp.& Lending Minus Repayments	82z	....	....	....	....	797.25	852.42	833.87	844.30	1,003.16	1,068.60	1,859.78	2,616.52
Expenditure	82	....	....	....	....	761.51	849.12	737.78	726.57	834.12	927.88	1,692.46	2,421.53
Lending Minus Repayments	83	....	....	....	....	35.74	3.30	96.09	117.73	169.04	140.72	167.32	194.99
Total Financing	80h	....	....	....	....	175.39	128.46	193.61	103.96	185.13	153.85	150.61	8.97
Domestic	84a	....	....	....	....	145.47	109.77	149.18	2.21	53.05	63.15	16.55	−116.77
Foreign	85a	....	....	....	....	29.91	18.69	44.44	101.75	132.08	90.70	134.06	125.74
Total Debt by Residence	88	....	....	....	....	2,857.83	4,077.92	4,192.54	4,449.53	4,843.33	4,608.05	4,306.62	4,076.11
Domestic	88a	....	....	....	....	556.52	1,343.49	1,497.97	1,492.41	1,520.35	1,567.90	1,575.78	1,535.35
Foreign	89a	....	....	....	....	2,301.30	2,734.43	2,694.56	2,957.12	3,322.98	3,040.15	2,730.84	2,540.76

Georgia 915

		1994	1995	1996	1997	1998	1999	2000	2001	2002	2003	2004	2005
National Accounts							*Millions of Lari*						
Househ.Cons.Expend.,incl.NPISHs....	96f	....	3,368	4,074	4,648	4,225	4,600	5,470	5,265	5,802	6,181	7,208	....
Government Consumption Expend...	91f	....	295	298	463	557	603	516	644	730	787	1,379	....
Gross Fixed Capital Formation..........	93e	....	714	718	841	1,283	1,486	1,538	1,818	1,826	2,257	2,698	....
Changes in Inventories....................	93i	....	173	40	−28	81	14	69	72	75	89	80	....
Exports of Goods and Services..........	90c	....	516	516	711	827	1,080	1,390	1,633	2,179	2,727	3,100	....
Imports of Goods and Services (-).....	98c	....	1,053	1,252	1,920	1,864	2,160	2,397	2,594	3,161	3,975	4,734	....
Gross Domestic Product (GDP).........	99b	....	....	3,868	4,555	5,022	5,669	6,015	6,648	7,457	8,564	9,970	....
Statistical Discrepancy....................	99bs			−525	−160	−87	45	−569	−189	6	499	7	....
GDP Volume 1996 Prices.................	99b.p	....	....	3,869	4,275	4,408	4,535	4,618	4,839	5,106	5,670	6,026	....
GDP Volume (2000=100)...............	99bvp	....	....	83.8	92.6	95.5	98.2	100.0	104.8	110.6	122.8	130.5	....
GDP Deflator (2000=100)...............	99bip	....	....	76.8	81.8	87.5	96.0	100.0	105.5	112.1	116.0	127.0	....
							Millions: Midyear Estimates						
Population...............................	99z	5.13	5.03	4.95	4.89	4.83	4.77	4.72	4.67	4.61	4.56	4.52	4.47

		1994	1995	1996	1997	1998	1999	2000	2001	2002	2003	2004	2005
Exchange Rates						*Euros per SDR: End of Period*							
Market Rate	aa	2.2610	2.1309	2.2357	2.4180	2.3556	1.3662	1.4002	1.4260	1.2964	1.1765	1.1402	1.2116
							Euros per US Dollar: End of Period (ae) Period Average (rf)							
Market Rate	ae	1.5488	1.4335	1.5548	1.7921	1.6730	.9954	1.0747	1.1347	.9536	.7918	.7342	.8477
Market Rate	rf	1.6228	1.4331	1.5048	1.7341	1.7597	.9386	1.0854	1.1175	1.0626	.8860	.8054	.8041
						Deutsche Mark per ECU: End of Period (ea) Period Average (eb)								
ECU Rate	ea	1.9053	1.8840	1.9465	1.9763	1.9558	....	....	....	....	....	....	....
ECU Rate	eb	1.9248	1.8736	1.9096	1.9642	1.9692	....	....	....	....	....	....	....
						Index Numbers (2000=100): Period Averages								
Market Rate (1995=100)	ahx	88.4	100.0	95.2	82.7	81.5	....	....	....	....	....	....	....
Nominal Effective Exchange Rate	neu	110.2	116.7	113.4	107.2	107.7	105.2	100.0	100.5	102.0	107.2	109.0	109.1
Real Effective Exchange Rate	reu	110.5	119.9	118.7	111.2	108.8	106.4	100.0	100.1	99.3	102.0	100.8	98.4
Fund Position						*Millions of SDRs: End of Period*							
Quota	2f.s	8,242	8,242	8,242	8,242	8,242	13,008	13,008	13,008	13,008	13,008	13,008	13,008
SDRs	1b.s	763	1,346	1,326	1,325	1,327	1,427	1,353	1,426	1,456	1,307	1,327	1,324
Reserve Position in the Fund	1c.s	2,760	3,505	3,803	4,407	5,698	4,677	4,191	4,696	4,925	5,152	4,419	2,437
of which: Outstg.Fund Borrowing	2c	—	—	—	—	530	—	—	—	—	—	—	—
International Liquidity						*Millions of US Dollars Unless Otherwise Indicated: End of Period*							
Total Res.Min.Gold (Eurosys.Def)	1l.d	77,363	85,005	83,178	77,587	74,024	† 61,039	56,890	51,404	51,171	50,694	48,823	45,140
SDRs	1b.d	1,114	2,001	1,907	1,788	1,868	1,959	1,763	1,793	1,980	1,942	2,061	1,892
Reserve Position in the Fund	1c.d	4,030	5,210	5,468	5,946	8,023	6,419	5,460	5,901	6,695	7,656	6,863	3,483
Foreign Exchange	1d.d	72,219	77,794	75,803	69,853	64,133	† 52,661	49,667	43,710	42,495	41,095	39,899	39,765
o/w:Fin.Deriv.Rel.to Reserves	1ddd	....	....	....	....	....	—	—	—	—	—	—	—
Other Reserve Assets	1e.d	....	....	....	....	....	—	—	—	—	—	—	—
Gold (Million Fine Troy Ounces)	1ad	95.18	95.18	95.18	95.18	118.98	111.52	111.52	111.13	110.79	110.58	110.38	110.21
Gold (Eurosystem Valuation)	1and	8,838	9,549	8,804	7,638	10,227	32,368	30,606	30,728	37,972	46,141	48,347	56,536
Memo:Euro Cl. on Non-EA Res	1dgd	....	....	....	....	....	9,191	279	264	315	379	409	354
Non-Euro Cl. on EA Res	1dhd	....	....	....	....	....	—	—	—	—	—	—	—
Mon. Auth.: Other Foreign Assets	3..d	1,539	1,371	944	559	680	† 9,204	291	276	327	394	425	413
Foreign Liabilities	4..d	15,620	11,435	10,035	9,436	9,551	† 6,195	6,125	7,670	9,409	13,178	10,792	7,399
Banking Insts.: Foreign Assets	7a.d	484,892	578,196	606,018	650,287	828,893	† 513,967	579,527	641,339	774,425	1,018,880	1,223,062	1,172,695
Foreign Liab	7b.d	378,834	482,236	490,213	561,585	760,827	† 491,336	559,069	571,750	629,904	719,203	787,908	740,000
Monetary Authorities						*Billions of Deutsche Mark through 1998; Billions of Euros Beginning 1999: End of Period*							
Fgn. Assets (Cl.on Non-EA Ctys)	11	128.7	132.9	132.2	129.7	135.1	102.2	94.1	93.5	85.3	77.0	71.7	86.5
Claims on General Government	12a.u	....	....	....	....	....	4.4	4.4	4.4	4.4	4.4	4.4	4.4
o/w: Claims on Gen.Govt.in Cty	12a	26.6	24.7	24.0	24.2	24.3	4.4	4.4	4.4	4.4	4.4	4.4	4.4
Claims on Banking Institutions	12e.u	....	....	....	....	....	135.9	151.5	135.3	145.1	181.4	212.8	248.6
o/w: Claims on Bank.Inst.in Cty	12e	217.7	213.1	226.2	235.2	216.0	90.6	139.2	123.0	127.9	164.3	192.6	206.1
Claims on Other Resident Sectors	12d.u	....	....	....	....	....	—	—	—	—	—	—	—
o/w: Cl. on Oth.Res.Sect.in Cty	12d	....	....	....	....	....	—	—	—	—	—	—	—
Currency Issued	14a	250.9	263.5	275.7	276.2	271.0	148.2	142.2	82.8	112.2	125.9	141.3	159.1
Liabilities to Banking Insts	14c.u	....	....	....	....	....	48.8	53.9	88.4	74.0	89.4	104.9	121.6
o/w: Liabs to Bank.Inst.in Cty	14c	56.2	49.7	51.9	48.7	57.7	41.9	47.0	57.4	44.8	44.7	41.5	46.5
Demand Dep. of Other Res.Sect.	14d.u	....	....	....	....	....	.5	.4	1.0	.6	.6	.4	.4
o/w:D.Dep.of Oth.Res.Sect.in Cty	14d	.7	.7	1.3	1.1	1.0	.5	.4	1.0	.6	.5	.4	.4
Other Dep. of Other Res.Sect.	15..u	....	....	....	....	....	—	—	—	—	—	—	—
o/w:O.Dep.of Oth.Res.Sect.in Cty	15	....	....	....	....	....	—	—	—	—	—	—	—
Bonds & Money Mkt. Instruments	16n.u	....	....	....	....	....	—	—	—	—	—	—	—
Foreign Liab. (to Non-EA Ctys)	16c	19.6	16.4	15.6	16.9	16.0	6.2	6.6	8.7	9.0	10.4	7.9	6.3
Central Government Deposits	16d.u	....	....	....	....	....	—	—	—	—	—	—	—
o/w: Cent.Govt.Dep. in Cty	16d	.2	.1	.4	.3	.2	—	—	—	—	—	—	—
Capital Accounts	17a	23.1	22.4	23.1	24.6	21.5	41.7	46.0	48.4	40.8	35.5	34.2	50.7
Other Items (Net)	17r	22.2	17.9	14.4	21.3	8.0	−2.8	1.0	3.9	−1.6	1.1	.2	1.4
Memo: Net Claims on Eurosystem	12e.s	....	....	....	....	....	38.5	5.4	−18.6	−12.1	−27.9	−43.6	−33.3
Currency Put into Circ	14m	....	....	....	....	....	....	....	....	141.3	170.5	204.7	234.2
Banking Institutions						*Billions of Deutsche Mark through 1998; Billions of Euros Beginning 1999: End of Period*							
Claims on Monetary Authorities	20	86.5	87.0	88.6	89.5	92.1	45.6	51.0	56.4	45.6	46.9	41.2	47.9
Claims on Bk.Inst.in Oth.EA Ctys	20b.u	....	....	....	....	....	203.1	244.4	286.3	346.8	375.5	419.7	509.4
Fgn. Assets (Cl.on Non-EA Ctys)	21	751.0	828.8	942.2	1,165.4	1,386.7	511.6	622.8	727.7	738.5	806.7	897.9	994.1
Claims on General Government	22a.u	....	....	....	....	....	735.7	720.4	708.8	709.4	702.3	738.4	734.0
o/w: Claims on Gen.Govt.in Cty	22a	937.4	1,078.7	1,161.4	1,223.7	1,251.8	632.1	616.9	587.8	586.4	585.6	603.8	580.7
Claims on Other Resident Sectors	22d.u	....	....	....	....	....	2,391.7	2,529.4	2,608.3	2,630.8	2,630.9	2,620.3	2,673.6
o/w: Cl. on Oth.Res.Sect.in Cty	22d	3,451.4	3,630.7	3,900.1	4,137.6	4,471.9	2,326.4	2,445.7	2,497.1	2,505.8	2,497.4	2,479.7	2,504.6
Demand Deposits	24..u	....	....	....	....	....	426.0	448.2	532.7	582.9	631.4	655.0	725.4
o/w:D.Dep.of Oth.Res.Sect.in Cty	24	505.3	545.4	631.8	650.0	747.7	419.5	441.4	525.0	574.8	622.1	646.2	715.8
Other Deposits	25..u	....	....	....	....	....	1,541.7	1,533.6	1,557.2	1,542.8	1,551.3	1,580.2	1,581.7
o/w:O.Dep.of Oth.Res.Sect.in Cty	25	1,523.6	1,572.2	1,649.6	1,692.4	1,752.4	1,435.6	1,432.3	1,457.8	1,461.6	1,474.1	1,512.5	1,522.1
Money Market Fund Shares	26m.u	....	....	....	....	....	20.8	19.3	32.6	37.2	36.7	31.5	31.7
Bonds & Money Mkt. Instruments	26n.u	....	....	....	....	....	1,348.1	1,455.8	1,488.3	1,517.5	1,531.1	1,594.6	1,655.0
o/w: Held by Resid.of Cty	26n	1,612.5	1,786.9	1,948.0	2,075.8	2,196.0	....	....	....	....	....	....	....
Foreign Liab. (to Non-EA Ctys)	26c	586.7	691.3	762.2	1,006.4	1,272.9	489.1	600.8	648.8	600.7	569.4	578.5	627.3
Central Government Deposits	26d.u	....	....	....	....	....	46.6	69.9	49.1	47.7	45.9	43.8	41.6
o/w: Cent.Govt.Dep. in Cty	26d	249.5	245.4	248.1	248.4	251.3	45.9	67.6	46.9	45.6	44.2	41.4	38.8
Credit from Monetary Authorities	26g	217.7	213.1	226.2	235.2	216.0	92.1	139.3	125.0	125.4	162.8	190.9	204.6
Liab. to Bk.Inst.in Oth. EA Ctys	26h.u	....	....	....	....	....	166.3	190.5	215.9	242.4	241.6	257.6	268.8
Capital Accounts	27a	410.1	438.1	463.9	507.0	544.9	237.0	258.5	275.7	291.7	294.4	288.1	302.7
Other Items (Net)	27r	120.7	132.8	162.7	201.0	221.4	−480.0	−547.8	−537.5	−517.3	−502.2	−502.7	−479.7

Germany 134

		1994	1995	1996	1997	1998	1999	2000	2001	2002	2003	2004	2005
Banking Survey (Nat'l Residency)		\multicolumn{12}{c}{*Billions of Deutsche Mark through 1998; Billions of Euros Beginning 1999: End of Period*}											
Foreign Assets (Net)	31n	273.3	254.0	296.6	271.7	233.0	266.1	271.3	361.9	486.5	594.4	719.0	925.8
Domestic Credit	32	4,165.6	4,488.6	4,837.1	5,137.0	5,496.5	2,917.1	2,999.4	3,042.3	3,051.0	3,043.3	3,046.4	3,050.9
Claims on General Govt. (Net)	32an	714.2	857.8	937.0	999.4	1,024.6	590.6	553.8	545.3	545.2	545.9	566.7	546.3
Claims on Other Resident Sectors	32d	3,451.4	3,630.7	3,900.1	4,137.6	4,471.9	2,326.4	2,445.7	2,497.1	2,505.8	2,497.4	2,479.7	2,504.6
Currency Issued	34a.n	250.9	263.5	275.7	276.2	271.0	148.2	142.2	82.8	112.2	125.9	141.3	159.1
Demand Deposits	34b.n	506.1	546.2	633.0	651.1	748.7	420.0	441.8	526.0	575.4	622.6	646.5	716.2
Other Deposits	35.n	1,523.6	1,572.2	1,649.6	1,692.4	1,752.4	1,435.6	1,432.3	1,457.8	1,461.6	1,474.1	1,512.5	1,522.1
Money Market Fund Shares	36m	....	....	....	....	....	20.8	19.3	32.6	37.2	36.7	31.5	31.7
Bonds & Money Mkt. Instruments	36n	1,612.5	1,786.9	1,948.0	2,075.8	2,196.0	1,348.1	1,455.8	1,488.3	1,517.5	1,531.1	1,594.6	1,655.0
o/w: Over Two Years	36na	....	....	....	....	....	1,226.2	1,303.8	1,316.1	1,326.4	1,355.6	1,437.9	1,498.2
Capital Accounts	37a	433.2	460.5	487.0	531.6	566.4	278.7	304.5	324.1	332.5	329.9	322.3	353.4
Other Items (Net)	37r	112.7	113.3	140.3	181.5	194.9	−468.2	−525.1	−507.3	−498.8	−482.6	−483.2	−460.9
Banking Survey (EA-Wide Residency)		\multicolumn{12}{c}{*Billions of Euros: End of Period*}											
Foreign Assets (Net)	31n.u	....	....	....	....	....	118.6	109.5	163.8	214.2	303.8	383.2	447.0
Domestic Credit	32..u	....	....	....	....	....	3,085.2	3,184.4	3,272.4	3,296.9	3,291.8	3,319.3	3,370.4
Claims on General Govt. (Net)	32anu	....	....	....	....	....	693.5	655.0	664.1	666.1	660.8	699.1	696.8
Claims on Other Resident Sect.	32d.u	....	....	....	....	....	2,391.7	2,529.4	2,608.3	2,630.8	2,630.9	2,620.3	2,673.6
Currency Issued	34a.u	....	....	....	....	....	148.2	142.2	82.8	112.2	125.9	141.3	159.1
Demand Deposits	34b.u	....	....	....	....	....	426.5	448.7	533.7	583.5	631.9	655.4	725.8
Other Deposits	35..u	....	....	....	....	....	1,541.7	1,533.6	1,557.2	1,542.8	1,551.3	1,580.2	1,581.7
o/w: Other Dep. Over Two Yrs.	35abu	....	....	....	....	....	664.4	674.0	672.8	670.2	683.7	708.9	713.2
Money Market Fund Shares	36m.u	....	....	....	....	....	20.8	19.3	32.6	37.2	36.7	31.5	31.7
Bonds & Money Mkt. Instruments	36n.u	....	....	....	....	....	1,348.1	1,455.8	1,488.3	1,517.5	1,531.1	1,594.6	1,655.0
o/w: Over Two Years	36nau	....	....	....	....	....	1,226.2	1,303.8	1,316.1	1,326.4	1,355.6	1,437.9	1,498.2
Capital Accounts	37a	....	....	....	....	....	278.7	304.5	324.1	332.5	329.9	322.3	353.4
Other Items (Net)	37r.u	....	....	....	....	....	−560.3	−610.1	−582.4	−614.6	−611.3	−622.7	−689.2
Money (National Definitions)		\multicolumn{12}{c}{*Billions of Deutsche Mark: End of Period*}											
Central Bank Money,Seas. Adj.	19mbc	249.7	258.8	274.3	282.5	281.8	....	....	....	....	....	....	....
M1, Seasonally Adjusted	59mac	703.0	729.0	805.0	872.9	930.6	....	....	....	....	....	....	....
Money M2, Seasonally Adjusted	59mbc	1,279.2	1,206.5	1,224.6	1,265.7	1,322.1	....	....	....	....	....	....	....
Money M3, Seasonally Adjusted	59mcc	1,875.1	1,885.6	2,026.1	2,151.3	2,245.2	....	....	....	....	....	....	....
M3, Extended, Seasonally Adjusted	59mcd	2,179.7	2,215.8	2,341.6	2,460.5	2,569.4	....	....	....	....	....	....	....
Interest Rates		\multicolumn{12}{c}{*Percent Per Annum*}											
Discount Rate (End of Period)	60	4.50	3.00	2.50	2.50	2.50	....	....	....	....	....	....	....
Money Market Rate	60b	5.35	4.50	3.27	3.18	3.41	2.73	4.11	4.37	3.28	2.32	2.05	2.09
Treasury Bill Rate	60c	5.05	4.40	3.30	3.32	3.42	2.88	4.32	3.66	2.97	1.98	2.00	2.03
Deposit Rate	60l	4.47	3.85	2.83	2.69	2.88	2.43	3.40	3.56	2.65	....	....	....
Households: Stocks, up to 2 years	60lhs	....	....	....	....	....	....	....	....	....	2.22	1.92	1.98
New Business, up to 1 year	60lhn	....	....	....	....	....	....	....	....	....	2.15	1.93	1.91
Corporations: Stocks, up to 2 years	60lcs	....	....	....	....	....	....	....	....	....	2.26	2.00	2.06
New Business, up to 1 year	60lcn	....	....	....	....	....	....	....	....	....	2.20	1.94	2.01
Lending Rate	60p	11.48	10.94	10.02	9.13	9.02	8.81	9.63	10.01	9.70	....	....	....
Households: Stocks, up to 1 year	60phs	....	....	....	....	....	....	....	....	....	9.07	8.79	8.75
New Bus., Floating & up to 1 year	60pns	....	....	....	....	....	....	....	....	....	5.53	5.12	5.16
House Purch., Stocks,Over 5 years	60phm	....	....	....	....	....	....	....	....	....	5.89	5.71	5.50
House Purch., New Bus., 5-10 yrs	60phn	....	....	....	....	....	....	....	....	....	5.01	4.93	4.29
Corporations: Stocks, up to 1 year	60pcs	....	....	....	....	....	....	....	....	....	5.03	4.73	4.60
New Bus., Over € 1 mil.,up to 1 yr	60pcn	....	....	....	....	....	....	....	....	....	3.52	3.26	3.23
Government Bond Yield	61	6.67	6.50	5.63	5.08	4.39	4.26	5.24	4.70	4.61	3.81	3.75	3.18
Prices, Production, Labor		\multicolumn{12}{c}{*Index Numbers (2000=100): Period Averages*}											
Share Prices	62	39.7	38.7	44.1	60.4	77.3	80.1	100.0	76.2	57.6	45.5	55.8	64.9
Producer Prices	63	96.6	† 98.3	97.1	98.2	97.8	96.8	100.0	103.0	† 102.6	104.4	106.1	110.9
Consumer Prices	64	92.3	93.9	95.3	97.1	98.0	98.6	100.0	102.0	103.4	104.5	106.2	108.3
Harmonized CPI	64h	....	94.2	95.3	96.8	97.3	98.0	100.0	101.2	102.6	† 103.7	105.5	107.5
Industrial Production	66	86.7	† 87.4	87.6	90.3	93.6	94.8	100.0	100.2	99.2	99.6	102.6	106.1
Wages: Hrly Earn.,s.a.	65..c	83.3	87.0	91.1	92.7	94.6	97.2	100.0	103.3	106.5	108.0	110.0	111.3
		\multicolumn{12}{c}{*Number in Thousands: Period Averages*}											
Labor Force	67d	39	40,083	39,455	39,694	39,709	39,905	39,731	39,966	40,022	40,195	40,047	....
Employment	67e	† 36,075	36,048	35,982	35,805	35,860	36,402	36,604	36,816	36,536	36,172	38,780	38,669
Unemployment	67c	3,693	3,612	3,980	4,400	4,266	4,093	3,887	3,852	4,071	4,380	4,387	4,813
Unemployment Rate (%)	67r	10.6	10.4	11.5	12.7	12.3	11.7	10.7	10.4	10.9	11.7	11.7	12.9
Intl. Transactions & Positions		\multicolumn{12}{c}{*Billions of Deutsche Mark through 1998; Billions of Euros Beginning 1999*}											
Exports	70	694.69	749.54	788.94	888.64	954.67	† 510.01	597.44	638.27	651.32	664.46	733.46	786.23
Imports, c.i.f.	71	622.92	664.23	690.40	772.33	828.29	† 444.80	538.31	542.77	518.53	534.53	577.38	625.63
Imports, f.o.b.	71.v	605.96	646.14	671.59	751.29	805.72	† 432.68	523.65	527.99	504.41	519.30	....	....
		\multicolumn{12}{c}{*1995=100*}											
Volume of Exports	72	96.0	† 100.0	107.6	120.7	130.5	136.4	....	....	....	....	....	....
Volume of Imports	73	98.4	† 100.0	106.0	115.5	126.9	132.9	....	....	....	....	....	....
		\multicolumn{12}{c}{*2000=100*}											
Unit Value of Exports	74	98.0	† 100.2	98.1	98.4	97.9	96.4	† 100.0	101.9	99.3	96.6	95.7	96.1
Unit Value of Imports	75	90.8	† 93.3	91.5	93.9	91.7	90.1	† 100.0	100.0	95.1	90.1	89.3	91.3
Export Prices	76	94.5	95.8	95.8	97.2	97.2	96.6	100.0	101.0	100.9	† 100.9	101.5	102.7
Import Prices	76.x	89.5	89.7	90.1	93.3	90.4	89.9	100.0	100.6	98.1	† 96.3	97.4	101.6

		1994	1995	1996	1997	1998	1999	2000	2001	2002	2003	2004	2005
Balance of Payments						*Billions of US Dollars: Minus Sign Indicates Debit*							
Current Account, n.i.e.	78ald	−30.78	−29.75	−13.98	−9.35	−14.80	−26.79	−31.96	.48	41.05	45.80	101.79	115.52
Goods: Exports f.o.b.	78aad	430.55	523.58	522.58	510.02	541.38	537.37	543.28	563.67	609.78	744.79	901.31	972.37
Goods: Imports f.o.b.	78abd	−379.52	−459.67	−453.20	−439.90	−465.26	−468.59	−487.82	−476.26	−484.02	−600.05	−713.75	−783.13
Trade Balance	78acd	51.03	63.91	69.38	70.12	76.12	68.78	55.46	87.41	125.76	144.74	187.56	189.24
Services: Credit	78add	65.71	80.23	83.84	82.73	84.51	83.92	83.15	88.71	103.14	123.27	143.19	154.94
Services: Debit	78aed	−112.06	−132.38	−134.22	−129.46	−134.80	−141.00	−137.25	−141.92	−144.81	−172.24	−194.82	−203.34
Balance on Goods & Services	78afd	4.68	11.76	19.00	23.40	25.83	11.70	1.36	34.21	84.08	95.77	135.94	140.83
Income: Credit	78agd	70.92	81.87	83.43	82.31	84.71	92.40	106.64	91.21	97.98	117.77	149.33	172.69
Income: Debit	78ahd	−69.47	−84.60	−82.60	−84.68	−95.00	−104.55	−114.30	−100.96	−115.01	−135.76	−148.36	−162.01
Balance on Gds, Serv. & Inc.	78aid	6.13	9.02	19.84	21.03	15.53	−.45	−6.30	24.46	67.06	77.78	136.91	151.51
Current Transfers, n.i.e.: Credit	78ajd	13.63	16.44	17.50	15.95	15.96	17.29	15.35	15.34	15.92	18.95	19.84	22.06
Current Transfers: Debit	78akd	−50.54	−55.21	−51.32	−46.33	−46.30	−43.63	−41.00	−39.32	−41.93	−50.94	−54.96	−58.05
Capital Account, n.i.e.	78bcd	−1.67	−2.73	−2.18	—	.72	−.15	6.19	−.33	−.23	.35	.51	−1.69
Capital Account, n.i.e.: Credit	78bad	1.56	1.68	2.76	2.83	3.31	3.01	9.41	1.87	2.09	3.23	3.30	4.31
Capital Account: Debit	78bbd	−3.23	−4.41	−4.94	−2.82	−2.59	−3.16	−3.22	−2.20	−2.32	−2.87	−2.79	−6.00
Financial Account, n.i.e.	78bjd	32.33	39.21	14.13	.80	20.01	−26.89	28.99	−16.13	−40.75	−56.38	−142.97	−126.64
Direct Investment Abroad	78bdd	−18.94	−39.10	−50.75	−42.72	−89.93	−108.67	−59.74	−39.25	−19.63	−5.53	−1.08	−47.09
Dir. Invest. in Rep. Econ., n.i.e.	78bed	7.29	11.99	6.43	12.80	23.64	55.91	210.09	26.17	53.61	27.72	−15.10	32.03
Portfolio Investment Assets	78bfd	−41.48	−18.05	−30.89	−90.02	−145.49	−190.26	−191.55	−111.68	−57.85	−48.03	−136.85	−263.77
Equity Securities	78bkd	−20.97	.28	−17.52	−42.62	−78.33	−87.57	−127.50	−27.65	−10.41	.83	−9.32	−77.30
Debt Securities	78bld	−20.51	−18.33	−13.38	−47.39	−67.17	−102.69	−64.04	−84.03	−47.44	−48.86	−127.53	−186.47
Portfolio Investment Liab., n.i.e.	78bgd	10.64	53.15	93.91	91.03	150.91	177.85	40.88	138.36	121.37	127.08	149.24	248.71
Equity Securities	78bmd	3.92	−1.51	12.98	12.87	56.77	28.71	−27.96	76.89	13.82	25.54	−9.58	51.59
Debt Securities	78bnd	6.72	54.66	80.92	78.16	94.14	149.15	68.84	61.47	107.55	101.54	158.82	197.11
Financial Derivatives Assets	78bwd	—	—	—	—	—	—	—	—	—	—	—	—
Financial Derivatives Liabilities	78bxd	.81	−.56	−5.73	−8.70	−7.99	−2.10	−11.44	6.05	−1.14	−2.30	−6.98	−6.08
Other Investment Assets	78bhd	−.71	−61.28	−39.77	−83.53	−86.02	−80.18	−70.86	−102.46	−164.86	−170.72	−181.66	−153.12
Monetary Authorities	78bod	.17	.28	.35	.29	−.11	−51.70	39.37	20.70	−33.41	−.21	−4.03	−26.05
General Government	78bpd	1.45	−7.95	−1.48	−3.22	−2.66	7.73	−18.62	14.30	6.16	.83	2.67	4.81
Banks	78bqd	14.99	−55.16	−39.14	−80.52	−79.66	−46.01	−92.58	−118.51	−127.05	−135.16	−152.35	−113.12
Other Sectors	78brd	−17.33	1.57	.50	−.08	−3.59	19.13	−8.34	−18.96	−10.56	−36.19	−27.95	−18.75
Other Investment Liab., n.i.e.	78bid	74.72	93.06	40.95	121.95	174.89	111.24	120.92	66.67	27.76	15.39	49.46	62.68
Monetary Authorities	78bsd	−4.08	−5.30	−2.34	−.79	4.33	−2.21	.37	2.35	.53	2.13	−2.98	−2.72
General Government	78btd	2.15	1.60	2.64	−7.75	.10	−12.29	.29	.68	−1.37	4.05	−3.56	5.06
Banks	78bud	69.30	83.75	36.59	120.23	159.85	103.54	110.00	52.84	25.88	8.59	42.04	33.66
Other Sectors	78bvd	7.34	13.00	4.06	10.26	10.62	22.21	10.26	10.80	2.72	.63	13.95	26.67
Net Errors and Omissions	78cad	−1.93	.50	.83	4.79	−1.91	39.72	−8.44	10.51	−2.05	9.55	38.86	10.21
Overall Balance	78cbd	−2.04	7.23	−1.20	−3.76	4.02	−14.11	−5.22	−5.47	−1.98	−.68	−1.81	−2.60
Reserves and Related Items	79dad	2.04	−7.23	1.20	3.76	−4.02	14.11	5.22	5.47	1.98	.68	1.81	2.60
Reserve Assets	79dbd	2.04	−7.23	1.20	3.76	−4.02	14.11	5.22	5.47	1.98	.68	1.81	2.60
Use of Fund Credit and Loans	79dcd												
Exceptional Financing	79ded	....	....	....	....	....	....	....	....	....	....	....	....
International Investment Position						*Billions of US Dollars*							
Assets	79aad	1,431.95	1,663.83	1,699.68	1,749.43	2,208.94	2,390.41	2,591.04	2,693.16	3,150.18	4,014.06	4,634.43	....
Direct Investment Abroad	79abd	188.32	234.13	250.14	296.28	365.22	412.87	486.75	551.09	602.72	727.20	754.61	....
Portfolio Investment	79acd	320.00	385.42	413.69	502.70	724.01	893.30	995.95	975.78	1,079.68	1,384.50	1,661.22	....
Equity Securities	79add	145.79	165.97	187.49	241.39	370.57	507.08	573.06	490.74	437.76	577.21	673.37	....
Debt Securities	79aed	174.22	219.45	226.20	261.31	353.44	386.21	422.89	485.04	641.93	807.29	987.85	....
Financial Derivatives	79ald												....
Other Investment	79afd	850.27	959.66	958.95	879.65	1,039.60	990.77	1,021.04	1,084.14	1,378.64	1,805.52	2,121.43	....
Monetary Authorities	79agd	1.52	1.36	.93	.54	.64	49.14	6.46	−15.04	19.69	23.06	28.75	....
General Government	79ahd	52.34	62.62	59.52	55.32	61.63	44.38	61.07	44.79	45.76	53.02	60.48	....
Banks	79aid	426.96	504.96	516.49	545.60	662.82	625.10	679.87	768.93	997.42	1,292.08	1,533.76	....
Other Sectors	79ajd	369.45	390.72	382.01	278.19	314.50	272.15	273.63	285.46	315.76	437.36	498.44	....
Reserve Assets	79akd	73.35	84.62	76.90	70.79	80.11	93.48	87.30	82.16	89.14	96.84	97.17	....
Liabilities	79lad	1,236.60	1,534.68	1,610.14	1,663.59	2,200.26	2,300.10	2,534.42	2,530.26	3,033.51	3,832.66	4,365.23	....
Dir. Invest. in Rep. Economy	79lbd	85.72	101.48	101.73	190.74	252.41	290.45	462.53	416.83	529.34	655.59	675.63	....
Portfolio Investment	79lcd	493.72	636.90	705.19	756.01	1,023.21	1,083.63	1,043.22	1,063.75	1,297.36	1,744.43	2,116.17	....
Equity Securities	79ldd	99.51	110.78	140.29	186.98	289.98	375.41	300.75	294.69	212.67	364.86	411.76	....
Debt Securities	79led	394.21	526.13	564.90	569.04	733.23	708.22	742.47	769.06	1,084.69	1,379.57	1,704.41	....
Financial Derivatives	79lld	—											....
Other Investment	79lfd	657.16	796.29	803.22	716.84	924.65	926.02	1,028.67	1,049.68	1,206.80	1,432.65	1,573.43	....
Monetary Authorities	79lgd	22.13	20.88	18.88	6.91	9.55	6.21	6.13	7.71	9.44	13.19	10.81	....
General Government	79lhd	33.51	46.24	45.54	27.24	26.99	13.80	12.71	13.60	18.82	21.52	26.04	....
Banks	79lid	380.24	485.00	493.21	564.48	760.33	781.77	847.60	860.22	981.40	1,137.29	1,248.84	....
Other Sectors	79ljd	221.29	244.18	245.59	118.21	127.78	124.24	162.23	168.15	197.14	260.64	287.74	....
Government Finance													
Central Government						*Billions of Deutsche Mark through 1998; Millions of Euros Beginning 1999: Year Ending December 31*							
Deficit (-) or Surplus	80	−44.85	−61.83	−74.19	−48.97p	−35.12p	....	....	....	....	....	....	....
Revenue	81	1,099.41	1,124.66	1,133.06	1,160.25	1,188.14	....	....	....	....	....	....	....
Grants Received	81z	5.24	6.10	6.70	6.44	6.31	....	....	....	....	....	....	....
Expenditure	82	1,142.81	1,188.04	1,213.20	1,214.65	1,233.89	....	....	....	....	....	....	....
Lending Minus Repayments	83	15.84	3.60	3.02	−3.01	−17.98	....	....	....	....	....	....	....
Overall Cash Adjustment	80x	9.15	−.95	2.27	−4.02	−13.66	....	....	....	....	....	....	....
Financing													
Net Borrowing	84	34.23	46.86	70.19	50.41	35.73	25.10	....	....	....	....	....	....
Net borrowing: Domestic	84a	57.19	−11.61	15.91	−29.50	−44.59	2.16	....	....	....	....	....	....
Net borrowing: Foreign	85a	−22.96	58.47	54.28	79.91	80.32	22.94	....	....	....	....	....	....
Use of Cash Balances	87	10.62	14.97	4.00	−1.44	−.61	−6.30	....	....	....	....	....	....
Debt	88	1,004.15	1,289.81	1,373.07	1,423.68	1,461.87	772.44	....	....	....	....	....	....
Debt: Domestic	88a	610.53	762.27	791.26	758.67	716.52	368.41	....	....	....	....	....	....
Debt: Foreign	89a	393.62	527.54	581.81	665.01	745.35	404.03	....	....	....	....	....	....
General Government						*As Percent of Gross Domestic Product*							

Germany 134

		1994	1995	1996	1997	1998	1999	2000	2001	2002	2003	2004	2005
National Accounts		*Billions of Deutsche Mark: through 1998; Billions of Euros Beginning 1999*											
Househ.Cons.Expend.,incl.NPISHs....	**96f.c**	2,016.7	2,087.2	2,134.8	2,182.3	2,224.8	† 1,175.0	1,214.2	1,258.6	1,266.7	1,287.6	1,312.5	1,332.2
Government Consumption Expend...	**91f.c**	678.5	707.7	727.1	726.5	736.1	† 387.2	391.9	400.2	412.3	415.5	412.8	417.2
Gross Fixed Capital Formation.........	**93e.c**	785.9	792.0	782.0	787.0	810.7	† 428.4	442.4	422.9	392.9	384.4	384.9	384.7
Changes in Inventories....................	**93i.c**	−3.2	11.4	−7.4	4.0	19.9	† 3.9	6.8	−11.0	−24.0	−11.6	−4.0	1.3
Exports of Goods and Services..........	**90c.c**	804.3	866.0	913.5	1,029.3	1,101.6	† 591.5	688.4	735.6	765.6	772.7	842.8	901.7
Imports of Goods and Services (-).....	**98c.c**	799.3	849.1	880.6	982.5	1,049.1	† 574.1	681.1	693.1	668.5	685.1	733.4	789.6
Gross Domestic Product (GDP)........	**99b.c**	3,482.9	3,615.3	3,669.5	3,746.5	3,843.9	† 2,012.0	2,062.5	2,113.2	2,145.0	2,163.4	2,215.7	2,247.4
Net Primary Income from Abroad.....	**98.nc**	−18.7	−26.8	−19.3	−27.1	−39.8	† −21.5	−19.3	−21.0	−24.2	−16.1	.4	3.8
Gross National Income (GNI)............	**99a.c**	3,464.2	3,588.5	3,650.1	3,719.4	3,804.1	† 1,990.5	2,043.2	2,092.2	2,120.9	2,147.3	2,216.0	2,251.2
Net Current Transf.from Abroad.......	**98t.c**	−39.7	−32.7	−33.7	−36.3	−39.5	† −19.7	−21.5	−24.1	−23.3	−24.1	−47.0	....
Gross Nat'l Disposable Inc.(GNDI)....	**99i.c**	3,341.6	3,471.8	3,537.6	3,612.6	3,719.4	† 1,970.7	2,021.7	2,068.0	2,097.6	2,123.2	2,169.0	....
Gross Saving....................	**99s.c**	745.1	770.2	764.8	787.1	819.1	† 408.5	415.6	410.3	419.0	422.3	451.8	....
Consumption of Fixed Capital..........	**99cfc**	510.0	529.0	540.0	553.8	567.6	† 297.1	308.5	316.4	321.1	321.4	326.5	327.7
GDP Volume 1995 Ref., Chained.....	**99b.r**	3,548.2	3,615.3	3,651.2	3,717.1	3,792.5	† 1,978.1	2,041.6	2,066.9	2,068.1	2,064.2	2,097.9	2,116.5
GDP Volume (2000=100)................	**99bvr**	88.9	90.5	91.4	93.1	95.0	† 96.9	100.0	101.2	101.3	101.1	102.8	103.7
GDP Deflator (2000=100)................	**99bir**	97.2	99.0	99.5	99.8	100.3	† 100.7	100.0	101.2	102.7	103.7	104.5	105.1
		Millions: Midyear Estimates											
Population..............................	**99z**	81.31	81.66	81.92	82.09	82.19	82.27	82.34	82.43	82.51	82.58	82.65	82.69

Ghana 652

		1994	1995	1996	1997	1998	1999	2000	2001	2002	2003	2004	2005
Exchange Rates						*Cedis per SDR: End of Period*							
Market Rate	aa	1,536.68	2,154.33	2,522.74	3,066.48	3,274.49	4,852.02	9,182.45	9,201.70	11,472.74	13,154.28	14,061.36	13,050.41
						Cedis per US Dollar: End of Period (ae) Period Average (rf)							
Market Rate	ae	1,052.63	1,449.28	1,754.39	2,272.73	2,325.58	3,535.14	7,047.65	7,321.94	8,438.82	8,852.32	9,054.26	9,130.82
Market Rate	rf	956.71	1,200.43	1,637.23	2,050.17	2,314.15	2,669.30	5,455.06	7,170.76	7,932.70	8,677.37	9,004.63	9,072.54
						Index Numbers (2000=100): Period Averages							
Nominal Effective Exchange Rate	nec	434.73	332.54	251.45	215.74	205.08	184.96	100.00	76.33	67.58	55.00	49.43	48.52
Real Effective Exchange Rate	rec	108.84	125.29	136.41	143.48	154.52	153.95	100.00	100.63	99.81	100.48	99.41	109.51
Fund Position						*Millions of SDRs: End of Period*							
Quota	2f.s	274.0	274.0	274.0	274.0	274.0	369.0	369.0	369.0	369.0	369.0	369.0	369.0
SDRs	1b.s	2.9	1.6	1.6	2.5	42.4	13.3	.4	3.2	2.7	31.5	13.3	.8
Reserve Position in the Fund	1c.s	17.4	17.4	17.4	17.4	17.4	41.1	—	—	—	—	—	—
Total Fund Cred.&Loans Outstg	2tl	479.7	436.2	377.3	257.0	236.9	225.8	224.5	225.7	267.3	304.9	301.6	291.7
International Liquidity						*Millions of US Dollars Unless Otherwise Indicated: End of Period*							
Total Reserves minus Gold	1l.d	583.9	697.5	828.7	537.8	377.0	453.8	232.1	298.2	539.7	1,352.8	1,626.7	1,752.9
SDRs	1b.d	4.2	2.4	2.2	3.4	59.7	18.2	.5	4.0	3.7	46.8	20.7	1.1
Reserve Position in the Fund	1c.d	25.4	25.8	25.0	23.4	24.5	56.5	—	—	—	—	—	—
Foreign Exchange	1d.d	554.3	669.2	801.5	511.0	292.8	379.1	231.5	294.2	536.1	1,306.0	1,605.9	1,751.8
Gold (Million Fine Troy Ounces)	1ad	.275	.275	.275	.275	.277	.279	.280	.281	.281	.281	.281	.281
Gold (National Valuation)	1and	77.2	77.4	77.2	77.3	78.8	78.9	79.3	78.9	96.5	116.1	122.6	144.5
Monetary Authorities:Other Assets	3..d	36.6	52.4	55.4	47.0	47.8	48.7	48.9	37.5	37.8	38.1	38.3	4.2
Other Liab.	4..d	96.5	34.8	45.4	126.7	53.3	41.0	119.0	38.0	46.9	48.2	78.0	56.2
Banking Institutions: Assets	7a.d	405.4	327.9	396.7	392.3	242.9	194.4	168.6	181.4	207.5	331.1	411.9	382.5
Liabilities	7b.d	32.4	45.8	62.8	75.7	26.1	140.4	116.3	51.7	66.3	140.5	148.9	199.0
Monetary Authorities						*Billions of Cedis: End of Period*							
Foreign Assets	11	663.2	1,079.9	1,182.1	1,337.6	† 1,464.0	1,382.3	2,522.4	2,865.4	5,728.2	12,967.2	15,996.3	17,313.7
Claims on Central Government	12a	893.0	1,405.5	1,553.3	2,001.7	† 10,999.6	15,242.7	24,281.3	2,480.3	30,939.8	7,520.0	12,108.2	12,451.6
Claims on Nonfin.Pub.Enterprises	12c	148.8	151.9	135.8	71.9	† 37.5	54.6	23.8	4.4	283.4	3.4	471.8	3.4
Claims on Private Sector	12d	—	—	—	—	† 26.8	32.2	42.5	52.7	72.5	70.1	91.4	111.4
Claims on Banking Institutions	12e	6.7	8.3	9.4	33.0	† 50.3	465.9	842.8	1,398.4	1,136.1	597.1	16.2	82.3
Claims on Nonbank Financial Insts	12g	—	37.2	10.7	4.6	† .9	.9	.9	.3	.3	4.7	.3	.3
Reserve Money	14	461.3	623.1	902.2	1,203.1	† 1,518.0	2,101.6	3,247.1	4,580.0	6,696.0	8,578.1	10,116.6	10,803.8
of which: Currency Outside Banks	14a	368.8	546.3	724.0	981.8	† 1,164.6	1,585.9	2,637.6	3,089.0	4,671.6	6,337.8	7,306.5	8,032.3
Other Liabs. to Banking Insts	14n	—	—	—	—	† 56.6	124.6	328.9	87.5	598.5	2,273.2	2,584.4	1,364.0
Time, Savings,& Fgn.Ccy. Deposits	15	—	—	—	—	† 8.8	135.7	546.8	30.2	32.8	181.1	706.3	101.9
Liabs. of Central Bank: Securities	16ac	479.5	722.4	518.2	182.6	† —	—	—	—	—	1,817.3	3,545.3	5,559.9
Restricted Deposits	16b	.9	.9	.9	—	† —	—	—	—	—	—	—	—
Foreign Liabilities	16c	838.7	990.3	1,031.5	1,076.0	† 899.6	1,240.6	2,900.1	2,354.7	3,462.6	4,438.0	4,948.0	4,320.4
Central Government Deposits	16d	318.1	494.3	324.5	484.7	† 9,945.0	13,768.5	21,704.2	525.5	28,127.8	5,086.5	6,145.0	7,495.8
Capital Accounts	17a	127.1	296.7	351.1	626.1	† 419.8	500.3	815.7	797.5	1,163.1	1,044.7	797.2	718.1
Other Items (Net)	17r	−514.0	−444.9	−237.2	−123.7	† −268.6	−692.6	−1,829.8	−1,574.0	−1,920.6	−2,256.4	−158.6	−401.1
Banking Institutions						*Billions of Cedis: End of Period*							
Reserves	20	88.8	106.8	194.1	219.3	† 365.3	559.0	779.1	1,398.0	1,576.2	2,325.4	2,822.0	2,818.5
Claims on Mon.Author.:Securities	20c	410.5	614.8	512.1	182.6	† —	—	—	—	—	1,033.2	1,585.9	993.4
Other Claims on Monetary Author.	20n	—	—	—	—	† 56.6	124.6	259.8	65.6	598.5	584.1	191.3	80.0
Foreign Assets	21	426.8	475.3	695.9	891.7	† 564.9	687.2	1,188.3	1,328.4	1,751.3	2,930.9	3,729.4	3,492.3
Claims on Central Government	22a	.3	.3	74.1	752.3	† 1,444.5	2,413.5	2,913.6	4,481.3	5,603.6	6,214.0	7,665.3	8,999.6
Claims on Local Government	22b	—	—	—	—	† —	—	—	.2	—	—	—	—
Claims on Nonfin.Pub.Enterprises	22c	29.5	44.5	57.4	144.0	† 263.8	373.2	1,225.6	1,805.4	949.7	2,003.1	1,708.3	2,495.4
Claims on Private Sector	22d	273.3	393.3	680.9	1,156.6	† 1,591.9	2,553.0	3,751.1	4,460.5	5,813.2	7,759.7	10,357.7	15,006.9
Claims on Nonbank Financial Insts	22g	.2	1.7	—	—	† 26.7	77.7	392.5	343.6	801.1	74.6	44.0	87.9
Demand Deposits	24	320.9	371.1	485.0	788.5	† 981.8	892.1	791.7	1,930.3	3,339.5	4,342.8	6,358.0	6,614.3
Time, Savings,& Fgn.Ccy. Deposits	25	478.3	752.4	1,116.8	1,585.7	† 1,793.4	2,332.3	3,659.5	5,006.2	6,909.9	9,218.4	11,193.0	13,232.4
Money Market Instruments	26aa	—	—	—	—	† —	11.5	.1	93.6	137.6	—	—	284.9
Restricted Deposits	26b	—	—	—	—	† 120.9	141.2	727.7	1,186.3	603.6	588.1	528.6	644.6
Foreign Liabilities	26c	34.1	66.3	110.2	172.0	† 60.6	496.3	819.7	378.8	559.7	1,243.9	1,348.1	1,817.3
Central Government Deposits	26d	69.2	76.0	105.4	45.9	† 197.4	286.2	256.1	406.7	743.0	1,460.0	1,954.0	2,781.6
Credit from Monetary Authorities	26g	19.8	50.9	40.1	48.2	† 87.7	514.7	931.5	1,114.1	850.4	650.9	63.4	576.5
Liab. to Nonbank Financial Insts	26j	—	—	—	—	† 16.9	56.2	167.0	284.6	431.9	221.3	597.2	937.0
Capital Accounts	27a	257.2	276.2	363.7	534.2	† 608.5	879.2	1,419.3	1,923.2	2,359.0	3,077.7	4,016.0	4,922.0
Other Items (Net)	27r	49.9	43.7	−6.5	171.9	† 446.7	1,178.5	1,737.5	1,559.3	1,158.9	2,121.8	2,045.7	2,163.5
Banking Survey						*Billions of Cedis: End of Period*							
Foreign Assets (Net)	31n	217.1	498.6	736.3	981.3	† 1,068.7	332.5	−9.1	1,460.3	3,457.1	10,216.2	13,429.6	14,668.4
Domestic Credit	32	957.7	1,464.1	2,082.3	3,600.4	† 4,249.3	6,693.2	10,670.3	12,696.5	15,592.7	17,103.3	24,348.1	28,879.2
Claims on Central Govt. (Net)	32an	506.0	835.5	1,197.5	2,223.3	† 2,301.8	3,601.5	5,234.5	6,029.4	7,672.6	7,187.5	11,674.5	11,173.9
Claims on Local Government	32b	—	—	—	—	† —	—	—	.2	—	—	—	—
Claims on Nonfin.Pub.Enterprises	32c	178.3	196.4	193.2	215.9	† 301.3	427.8	1,249.3	1,809.8	1,233.1	2,006.5	2,180.2	2,498.9
Claims on Private Sector	32d	273.3	393.3	680.9	1,156.6	† 1,618.7	2,585.3	3,793.6	4,513.2	5,885.7	7,829.9	10,449.1	15,118.3
Claims on Nonbank Financial Insts.	32g	.2	38.9	10.7	4.6	† 27.6	78.6	392.8	343.9	801.4	79.3	44.3	88.1
Money	34	693.5	925.3	1,218.6	1,779.3	† 2,151.2	2,490.2	3,441.5	5,035.0	8,048.6	10,723.4	13,745.3	14,707.5
Quasi-Money	35	478.3	752.4	1,116.8	1,585.7	† 1,802.2	2,468.0	4,206.3	5,036.4	6,942.7	9,399.6	11,899.4	13,334.3
Money Market Instruments	36aa	—	—	—	—	† —	11.5	.1	93.6	137.6	—	—	284.9
Liabs. of Central Bank: Securities	36ac	69.0	107.6	6.1	—	† —	—	—	—	—	784.1	1,959.3	4,566.5
Restricted Deposits	36b	.9	.9	.9	—	† 120.9	141.2	727.7	1,186.3	603.6	588.1	528.6	644.6
Liab. to Nonbank Financial Insts	36j	—	—	—	—	† 16.9	56.2	167.0	284.6	431.9	221.3	597.2	937.0
Capital Accounts	37a	384.3	572.9	714.7	1,160.3	† 1,028.1	1,379.5	2,234.9	2,720.7	3,522.1	4,122.4	4,813.2	5,640.1
Other Items (Net)	37r	−451.2	−396.5	−238.5	56.5	† 198.8	479.1	−116.3	−199.8	−636.7	1,480.4	4,234.6	3,432.7
Money plus Quasi-Money	35l	1,171.8	1,677.7	2,335.3	3,364.9	† 3,953.4	4,958.3	7,647.8	10,071.4	14,991.3	20,123.0	25,644.7	28,041.8

Ghana 652

		1994	1995	1996	1997	1998	1999	2000	2001	2002	2003	2004	2005
Interest Rates						*Percent Per Annum*							
Discount Rate (End of Period)	60	33.00	45.00	45.00	45.00	37.00	27.00	27.00	27.00	24.50	21.50	18.50	15.50
Money Market Rate	60b	....	....	....	....	....	....	....	....	....	24.71	15.73	14.70
Treasury Bill Rate	60c	27.72	35.38	41.64	42.77	34.33	26.37	36.28	40.96	25.11	27.25	16.57	14.89
Savings Rate	60k	17.63	22.19	27.51	27.49	23.48	14.75	15.83	17.21	11.13	11.08	9.50	8.35
Deposit Rate	60l	23.15	28.73	34.50	35.76	32.05	23.56	28.60	30.85	16.21	14.32	13.63	10.16
Government Bond Yield	61	....	....	....	....	....	....	....	....	....	....	21.50	20.54
Prices and Labor						*Index Numbers (2000=100): Period Averages*							
Consumer Prices	64	20.7	33.1	48.5	† 62.0	71.1	79.9	100.0	132.9	152.6	193.3	217.7	250.6
						Number in Thousands: Period Averages							
Unemployment	67c	37	41	....	....	....	....	....	....	....	....	....	....
Intl. Transactions & Positions						*Billions of Cedis*							
Exports	70	1,359	2,070	2,733	3,353	4,151	5,293	7,322	....	....	....	....	....
Cocoa Beans	70r	266	457	791	826	1,437	1,422	2,170	....	....	....	....	....
Imports, c.i.f.	71	2,029	2,289	3,452	4,769	5,932	9,347	16,171	....	....	....	....	....
Volume of Exports							*1995=100*						
Cocoa Beans	72r	94.2	100.0	142.6	10.3	129.6	152.1	....	....	....	....	....	....
Export Prices													
Cocoa Beans (Unit Value)	74r	61.8	100.0	121.4	....	242.8	204.6	....	....	....	....	....	....
Balance of Payments						*Millions of US Dollars: Minus Sign Indicates Debit*							
Current Account, n.i.e.	78ald	−254.6	−143.7	−306.9	−403.5	−521.7	−964.3	−386.5	−324.6	−32.0	255.2	−235.7	....
Goods: Exports f.o.b.	78aad	1,237.7	1,431.2	1,570.0	1,489.9	2,090.8	2,005.5	1,936.3	1,867.1	2,015.2	2,562.4	2,784.6	....
Goods: Imports f.o.b.	78abd	−1,579.9	−1,687.8	−1,950.7	−2,143.7	−2,991.6	−3,279.9	−2,766.6	−2,968.5	−2,707.0	−3,276.1	−4,297.3	....
Trade Balance	78acd	−342.2	−256.6	−380.7	−653.9	−900.8	−1,274.4	−830.3	−1,101.4	−691.8	−713.7	−1,512.6	....
Services: Credit	78add	147.5	150.6	156.8	164.9	440.9	467.8	504.2	531.7	554.9	630.0	702.3	....
Services: Debit	78aed	−420.8	−431.7	−424.8	−468.7	−659.4	−646.0	−583.7	−606.1	−620.9	−903.7	−1,058.5	....
Balance on Goods & Services	78afd	−615.5	−537.7	−648.7	−957.7	−1,119.3	−1,452.6	−909.8	−1,175.8	−757.8	−987.4	−1,868.8	....
Income: Credit	78agd	−3.0	13.7	23.5	26.7	26.7	15.0	15.6	16.3	14.7	21.4	44.5	....
Income: Debit	78ahd	−107.9	−142.9	−163.4	−32.6	−163.0	−146.8	−123.2	−124.1	−188.9	−178.0	−242.3	....
Balance on Gds, Serv. & Inc.	78aid	−726.4	−666.9	−788.6	−963.6	−1,255.6	−1,584.4	−1,017.4	−1,283.6	−932.0	−1,144.0	−2,066.6	....
Current Transfers, n.i.e.: Credit	78ajd	487.3	538.9	497.9	576.5	751.0	637.9	649.3	978.4	912.2	1,408.4	1,831.0	....
Current Transfers: Debit	78akd	−15.5	−15.7	−16.2	−16.4	−17.1	−17.8	−18.4	−19.4	−12.2	−9.2	—	....
Capital Account, n.i.e.	78bcd	−.1	—	—	—	—	—	—	—	—	—	—	....
Capital Account, n.i.e.: Credit	78bad	—	—	—	—	—	—	—	—	—	—	—	....
Capital Account: Debit	78bbd	−.1	—	—	—	—	—	—	—	—	—	—	....
Financial Account, n.i.e.	78bjd	481.7	459.1	285.5	492.8	560.9	746.0	369.3	392.2	−38.7	347.3	201.6	....
Direct Investment Abroad	78bdd	—	—	—	—	—	—	—	—	—	—	—	....
Dir. Invest. in Rep. Econ., n.i.e.	78bed	233.0	106.5	120.0	81.8	167.4	243.7	165.9	89.3	58.9	136.7	139.3	....
Portfolio Investment Assets	78bfd	—	—	—	—	—	—	—	—	—	—	—	....
Equity Securities	78bkd	—	—	—	—	—	—	—	—	—	—	—	....
Debt Securities	78bld	—	—	—	—	—	—	—	—	—	—	—	....
Portfolio Investment Liab., n.i.e.	78bgd	—	—	—	—	—	—	—	—	—	—	—	....
Equity Securities	78bmd	—	—	—	—	—	—	—	—	—	—	—	....
Debt Securities	78bnd	—	—	—	—	—	—	—	—	—	—	—	....
Financial Derivatives Assets	78bwd	....	—	—	—	—	—	—	—	—	—	—	....
Financial Derivatives Liabilities	78bxd	....	—	—	—	—	—	—	—	—	—	—	....
Other Investment Assets	78bhd	−119.6	116.6	50.0	—	45.0	47.5	70.0	65.0	94.7	68.0	−175.0	....
Monetary Authorities	78bod	—	—	—	—	—	—	—	—	—	—	—	....
General Government	78bpd	—	41.6	—	—	—	47.5	70.0	—	14.7	—	—	....
Banks	78bqd	−93.3	—	—	—	—	—	—	—	—	—	—	....
Other Sectors	78brd	−26.3	75.0	50.0	—	45.0	—	—	65.0	80.0	68.0	−175.0	....
Other Investment Liab., n.i.e.	78bid	368.3	236.0	115.5	411.0	348.5	454.8	133.4	237.9	−192.3	142.6	237.3	....
Monetary Authorities	78bsd	−19.4	—	—	—	—	—	—	—	—	—	—	....
General Government	78btd	295.3	135.5	313.9	404.5	327.2	144.8	81.7	45.6	−115.2	62.7	139.2	....
Banks	78bud	64.8	−54.2	−148.4	32.9	88.0	186.4	40.8	144.3	−123.8	9.7	−94.6	....
Other Sectors	78bvd	27.6	154.7	−50.0	−26.4	−66.7	123.6	10.9	48.0	46.7	70.2	192.7	....
Net Errors and Omissions	78cad	26.1	−132.6	−3.7	−12.1	−11.5	81.9	−352.1	−189.1	57.1	−98.8	20.9	....
Overall Balance	78cbd	253.1	182.8	−25.0	77.2	27.6	−136.4	−369.3	−121.5	−13.6	503.6	−13.2	....
Reserves and Related Items	79dad	−253.1	−182.8	25.0	−77.2	−27.6	136.4	369.3	121.5	13.6	−503.6	13.2	....
Reserve Assets	79dbd	−170.2	−117.5	110.3	88.5	−1.5	89.4	344.5	−80.3	−155.8	−657.6	−177.5	....
Use of Fund Credit and Loans	79dcd	−82.9	−65.2	−85.3	−165.8	−26.1	−15.0	−2.3	.8	51.4	54.6	−5.3	....
Exceptional Financing	79ded	—	—	—	—	—	—	—	62.0	27.0	201.0	118.0	99.4	196.0	....
Government Finance						*Billions of Cedis: Year Ending December 31*							
Deficit (-) or Surplus	80	111.7	70.3	−335.5	−297.6	−1,048.8	....	....	....	....	....	....	....
Revenue	81	1,221.8	1,691.0	2,191.0	2,549.9	3,276.1	....	....	....	....	....	....	....
Grants Received	81z	39.5	93.8	77.5	66.6	161.9	....	....	....	....	....	....	....
Expenditure	82	1,141.3	1,698.7	2,515.2	2,908.9	4,513.2	....	....	....	....	....	....	....
Lending Minus Repayments	83	8.3	15.8	88.8	5.2	−26.4	....	....	....	....	....	....	....
Financing													
Domestic	84a	−26.7	−27.7	531.1	728.0	672.6	....	....	....	....	....	....	....
Foreign	85a	−85.0	−42.6	−195.7	−430.3	376.2	....	....	....	....	....	....	....

Ghana 652

National Accounts		1994	1995	1996	1997	1998	1999	2000	2001	2002	2003	2004	2005
						Billions of Cedis: End of Period							
Househ.Cons.Expend.,incl.NPISHs....	**96f**	3,834.9	5,909.9	8,629.0	11,267.0	....	....	....	....	....	....	....	....
Government Consumption Expend...	**91f**	714.3	935.9	1,365.6	1,743.8	....	....	....	....	....	....	....	....
Gross Fixed Capital Formation..........	**93e**	1,174.5	1,638.0	2,332.0	3,338.2	....	....	....	....	....	....	....	....
Changes in Inventories....................	**93i**	72.2	−85.9	102.2	127.3	....	....	....	....	....	....	....	....
Exports of Goods and Services..........	**90c**	1,171.5	1,898.9	2,827.3	2,794.6	....	....	....	....	....	....	....	....
Imports of Goods and Services (-).....	**98c**	1,762.2	2,544.2	3,916.9	5,157.5	....	....	....	....	....	....	....	....
Gross Domestic Product (GDP).........	**99b**	5,205.2	7,752.6	11,339.2	14,113.4	....	....	....	....	....	....	....	....
Net Primary Income from Abroad.....	**98.n**	106.1	155.1	220.0	273.9	....	....	....	....	....	....	....	....
Gross National Income (GNI)............	**99a**	5,099.1	7,597.5	11,119.2	13,839.5	....	....	....	....	....	....	....	....
Consumption of Fixed Capital..........	**99cf**	411.2	514.0	800.8	996.7	....	....	....	....	....	....	....	....
GDP Volume 1993 Prices.................	**99b.p**	3,999.1	4,160.0	4,351.2	4,533.0	....	....	....	....	....	....	....	....
GDP Volume (1995=100).................	**99bvp**	96.1	100.0	104.6	109.0	....	....	....	....	....	....	....	....
GDP Deflator (1995=100)................	**99bip**	69.8	100.0	139.8	167.1	....	....	....	....	....	....	....	....
						Millions: Midyear Estimates							
Population..............................	**99z**	17.28	17.73	18.16	18.59	19.01	19.43	19.87	20.31	20.76	21.21	21.66	22.11

Greece 174

		1994	1995	1996	1997	1998	1999	2000	2001	2002	2003	2004	2005
Exchange Rates		*Drachmas per SDR Through 2000, Euros per SDR Thereafter End of Period*											
Market Rate..................	aa	350.51	352.36	355.20	381.31	397.87	450.79	476.37	1.4260	1.2964	1.1765	1.1402	1.2116
		Drachmas per US Dollar through 2000, Euros per US Dollar Thereafter: End of Period (ae) Period Average (rf)											
Market Rate..................	ae	240.10	237.04	247.02	282.61	282.57	328.44	365.62	1.1347	.9536	.7918	.7342	.8477
Market Rate..................	rf	242.60	231.66	240.71	273.06	295.53	305.65	365.40	1.1175	1.0626	.8860	.8054	.8041
		Drachmas per ECU through 1998; Drachmas per Euro through 2000: End of Period (ea) Period Average (eb)											
Euro Rate..................	ea	294.78	303.76	306.83	312.12	330.01	† 330.35	340.75	....	....	....	....	....
Euro Rate..................	eb	287.21	299.54	301.48	308.51	331.50	† 325.76	336.66	....	....	....	....	....
		Index Numbers (2000=100): Period Averages											
Market Rate..................	ahx	150.0	157.3	151.3	133.5	123.4	119.0	100.0	....	....	....	....	....
Nominal Effective Exchange Rate.....	neu	123.0	119.8	117.5	114.3	107.6	106.9	100.0	99.4	100.3	103.5	104.3	104.4
Real Effective Exchange Rate...........	reu	94.3	100.9	104.0	107.4	104.3	106.3	100.0	101.0	104.1	109.2	112.9	115.8
Fund Position		*Millions of SDRs: End of Period*											
Quota..................	2f.s	587.6	587.6	587.6	587.6	587.6	823.0	823.0	823.0	823.0	823.0	823.0	823.0
SDRs..................	1b.s	.2	—	.4	.2	.3	3.8	9.2	7.7	11.1	14.4	17.4	20.3
Reserve Position in the Fund...........	1c.s	113.7	113.7	113.7	113.7	191.5	285.0	227.8	284.3	322.5	334.3	270.6	117.7
Total Fund Cred.&Loans Outstg.......	2tl	—	—	—	—	—	—	—					
International Liquidity		*Millions of US Dollars Unless Otherwise Indicated: End of Period*											
Total Res.Min.Gold(Eurosys.Def.)......	1l.d	14,487.9	14,780.0	17,501.4	12,594.8	17,458.4	18,122.3	13,424.3	† 5,154.2	8,082.8	4,361.4	1,191.0	506.4
SDRs..................	1b.d	.3	—	.6	.3	.5	5.2	12.0	9.7	15.1	21.4	27.0	29.1
Reserve Position in the Fund..........	1c.d	166.0	169.0	163.5	153.4	269.6	391.1	296.8	357.3	438.4	496.7	420.2	168.3
Foreign Exchange..................	1d.d	14,321.6	14,611.0	17,337.3	12,441.1	17,188.3	17,726.0	13,115.5	† 4,787.2	7,629.3	3,843.3	743.7	309.1
o/w:Fin.Deriv.Rel.to Reserves.......	1ddd	....	....	....	....	....	....	....	....	....	....	....	....
Other Reserve Assets..............	1e.d	....	....	....	....	....	....	....	....	....	....	....	....
Gold (Million Fine Troy Ounces).......	1ad	3.448	3.461	3.469	3.644	3.623	4.237	4.262	3.942	3.935	3.451	3.463	3.471
Gold (Eurosystem Valuation)...........	1and	850.9	871.7	833.2	684.5	685.3	781.8	753.2	1,090.0	1,348.7	1,439.9	1,516.8	1,780.6
Memo:Euro Cl. on Non-EA Res.........	1dgd	....	....	....	....	....	....	....	61.0	—	—	—	—
Non-Euro Cl. on EA Res..........	1dhd	....	....	....	....	....	....	....	5,566.3	4,014.4	2,979.4	1,834.7	1,129.0
Mon. Auth.: Other Foreign Assets....	3..d	....	....	....	....	....	....	....					
Foreign Liabilities..................	4..d	777.5	860.4	795.5	1,336.5	888.4	733.4	179.1	665.4	713.1	764.1	884.0	1,018.1
Banking Insts.: Foreign Assets..........	7a.d	6,051.3	8,962.9	12,656.1	15,994.8	15,550.7	13,848.5	12,627.4	† 16,386.0	21,765.8	32,368.2	39,507.7	41,059.5
Foreign Liab..........	7b.d	26,410.3	34,286.1	38,540.2	42,278.6	46,854.1	41,732.5	39,645.4	† 9,636.1	18,557.8	27,716.5	44,525.7	53,216.3
Monetary Authorities		*Billions of Drachmas through 2000; Billions of Euros Beginning 2001: End of Period*											
Fgn. Assets (Cl.on Non-EA Ctys).......	11	4,463.9	4,333.9	5,253.9	4,020.3	5,414.0	6,434.2	4,961.0	6.97	9.00	5.10	3.22	3.27
Claims on General Government........	12a.u	....	....	....	....	....	....	....	18.45	19.13	19.60	22.06	21.69
o/w: Claims on Gen.Govt.in Cty.....	12a	7,352.3	7,059.4	6,457.6	6,012.1	5,757.9	5,911.7	5,759.1	17.23	17.02	15.25	14.54	13.71
Claims on Banking Institutions.........	12e.u	....	....	....	....	....	....	....	5.16	5.19	6.49	2.21	4.77
o/w: Claims on Bank.Inst.in Cty.....	12e	377.8	461.4	332.8	791.9	447.2	54.4	299.3	.65	3.02	4.42	.27	2.43
Claims on Other Resident Sectors.....	12d.u	....	....	....	....	....	....	....	.17	.20	.23	.25	.27
o/w: Cl. on Oth.Res.Sect.in Cty.....	12d	4.8	14.1	19.9	21.9	24.6	27.3	37.5	.17	.20	.23	.25	.27
Currency Issued..................	14a	1,839.8	2,061.0	2,251.1	2,451.5	2,519.4	3,154.1	3,097.3	8.71	9.21	10.65	12.76	14.36
Liabilities to Banking Insts..............	14c.u	....	....	....	....	....	....	....	15.79	19.89	18.50	12.36	12.82
o/w: Liabs to Bank.Inst.in Cty.......	14c	5,364.8	5,084.2	5,406.7	5,189.2	6,634.0	7,033.2	5,955.8	7.70	1.71	2.41	5.39	4.35
Demand Dep. of Other Res.Sect.....	14d.u	....	....	....	....	....	....	....	.42	.34	.31	.60	.25
o/w:D.Dep.of Oth.Res.Sect.in Cty...	14d	27.3	47.3	29.7	5.2	4.5	165.8	60.8	.42	.34	.31	.60	.25
Other Dep. of Other Res.Sect...........	15..u	....	....	....	....	....	....	....	.36	.30	.19	.11	.14
o/w:O.Dep.of Oth.Res.Sect.in Cty...	15	....	....	....	....	....	....	....	.36	.30	.19	.11	.14
Bonds & Money Mkt. Instruments...	16n.u	....	....	....	....	....	....	....	1.68	1.56	.55	.54	.11
o/w:Bonds Held by Resid.of Cty.......	16n	3,342.7	2,742.2	2,102.0	1,533.9	1,065.9	1,015.0	606.0					
Foreign Liab. (to Non-EA Ctys)........	16c	186.7	203.9	196.5	377.7	251.0	240.9	65.5	.76	.68	.61	.65	.86
Central Government Deposits...........	16d.u	....	....	....	....	....	....	....	.44	.08	.07	.49	.84
o/w: Cent.Govt.Dep. in Cty...........	16d	237.6	621.2	672.5	443.4	345.5	128.9	194.6	.44	.08	.07	.49	.84
Capital Accounts..................	17a	69.5	71.8	74.1	166.2	196.1	290.0	293.1	2.53	2.51	1.68	.99	1.54
Other Items (Net)..........................	17r	1,130.5	1,037.1	1,331.6	679.1	627.4	399.7	783.8	.08	−1.04	−1.12	−.75	−.92
Memo: Net Claims on Eurosystem....	12e.s	....	....	....	....	....	....	....	−7.06	−17.16	−15.05	−5.92	−7.41
Currency Put into Circ..............	14m	....	....	....	....	....	....	....			9.98	11.38	13.19	15.61
Banking Institutions		*Billions of Drachmas through 2000; Billions of Euros Beginning 2001: End of Period*											
Claims on Monetary Authorities.......	20	2,905.2	5,000.4	5,080.2	5,583.7	7,464.1	8,196.2	7,034.8	11.52	4.84	2.48	5.39	4.35
Claims on Bk.Inst.in Oth.EA Ctys.......	20b.u	....	....	....	....	....	....	....	9.42	10.80	12.13	12.71	13.34
Fgn. Assets (Cl.on Non-EA Ctys).......	21	1,452.9	2,124.6	3,126.3	4,520.3	4,394.2	4,548.4	4,616.8	18.59	20.76	25.63	29.01	34.81
Claims on General Government.......	22a.u	....	....	....	....	....	....	....	45.94	46.13	40.00	35.82	45.58
o/w: Claims on Gen.Govt.in Cty.....	22a	9,522.7	10,448.8	11,082.1	11,565.5	11,354.2	12,447.7	14,506.2	45.87	45.24	36.96	34.47	42.96
Claims on Other Resident Sectors.....	22d.u	....	....	....	....	....	....	....	84.80	97.28	113.03	132.51	156.03
o/w: Cl. on Oth.Res.Sect.in Cty.....	22d	7,531.6	9,142.9	10,371.1	11,902.0	13,721.5	17,734.0	21,775.7	83.13	94.47	110.44	129.71	153.37
Demand Deposits..................	24..u	....	....	....	....	....	....	....	70.39	71.37	79.14	91.10	98.96
o/w:D.Dep.of Oth.Res.Sect.in Cty...	24	1,619.7	1,874.6	2,340.2	2,699.4	3,104.6	4,337.2	4,287.4	70.19	71.18	78.96	90.89	98.71
Other Deposits..................	25..u	....	....	....	....	....	....	....	59.04	55.49	49.47	48.96	63.33
o/w:O.Dep.of Oth.Res.Sect.in Cty...	25	11,925.5	13,684.8	15,339.1	16,704.7	16,564.0	17,975.3	19,164.2	57.93	54.53	48.96	48.46	63.13
Money Market Fund Shares...........	26m.u	....	....	....	....	....	....	....	9.66	10.72	15.73	15.35	4.92
Bonds & Money Mkt. Instruments...	26n.u	....	....	....	....	....	....	....	.29	.43	.73	.73	.48
o/w: Held by Resid.of Cty..............	26n	838.4	570.8	59.8	126.7	163.6	78.7	85.3	....	....	....	....	....
Foreign Liab. (to Non-EA Ctys)........	26c	6,341.1	8,127.2	9,520.2	11,948.4	13,239.6	13,706.6	14,495.2	10.93	17.70	21.95	32.69	45.11
Central Government Deposits...........	26d.u	....	....	....	....	....	....	....	1.38	2.32	2.48	3.33	3.66
o/w: Cent.Govt.Dep. in Cty...........	26d	....	....	....	....	....	....	....	1.38	2.32	2.48	3.33	3.66
Credit from Monetary Authorities.....	26g	486.3	551.0	409.4	826.6	1,771.1	3,342.1	3,930.6	.71	2.15	4.43	.27	2.43
Liab. to Bk.Inst.in Oth. EA Ctys........	26h.u	....	....	....	....	....	....	....	4.67	6.40	5.43	4.17	6.93
Capital Accounts..................	27a	1,481.2	1,740.7	1,881.7	2,217.3	2,860.2	5,157.3	5,876.1	19.49	19.88	17.49	19.53	23.31
Other Items (Net)..................	27r	−1,279.8	167.7	109.4	−951.6	−769.2	−1,670.9	94.8	−6.29	−6.63	−3.58	−.69	4.98

Greece 174

Greece 174

		1994	1995	1996	1997	1998	1999	2000	2001	2002	2003	2004	2005
Banking Survey (Nat'l Residency)		*Billions of Drachmas through 2000; Billions of Euros Beginning 2001: End of Period*											
Foreign Assets (Net)	31n	−611.0	−1,872.7	−1,336.5	−3,785.5	−3,682.5	−2,965.0	−4,982.8	17.17	4.90	10.62	13.82	5.71
Domestic Credit	32	24,173.8	26,044.0	27,258.3	29,058.1	30,512.8	35,991.7	41,884.0	144.58	154.54	160.33	175.15	205.81
Claims on General Govt. (Net)	32an	16,637.4	16,887.0	16,867.2	17,134.2	16,766.7	18,230.5	20,070.7	61.28	59.87	49.67	45.19	52.17
Claims on Other Resident Sectors	32d	7,536.5	9,157.0	10,391.0	11,924.0	13,746.1	17,761.3	21,813.3	83.30	94.67	110.67	129.96	153.64
Currency Issued	34a.n	1,839.8	2,061.0	2,251.1	2,451.5	2,519.4	3,154.1	3,097.3	8.71	9.21	10.65	12.76	14.36
Demand Deposits	34b.n	1,647.0	1,921.9	2,369.9	2,704.5	3,109.1	4,503.0	4,348.3	70.61	71.52	79.27	91.49	98.96
Other Deposits	35..n	11,925.5	13,684.8	15,339.1	16,704.7	16,564.0	17,975.3	19,164.2	58.29	54.83	49.15	48.56	63.27
Money Market Fund Shares	36m	....	....	....	....	....	....	....	9.66	10.72	15.73	15.35	4.92
Bonds & Money Mkt. Instruments	36n	4,181.1	3,313.0	2,161.9	1,660.6	1,229.5	1,093.7	691.4	1.96	1.98	1.28	1.26	.59
o/w: Over Two Years	36na	....	....	....	....	....	....	....	1.79	1.67	.80	.78	.15
Capital Accounts	37a	1,550.7	1,812.5	1,955.7	2,383.5	3,056.3	5,447.3	6,169.2	22.02	22.39	19.17	20.53	24.85
Other Items (Net)	37r	2,418.7	1,378.1	1,844.1	−632.1	352.0	853.5	3,431.0	−9.49	−11.21	−4.29	−.98	4.56
Banking Survey (EA-Wide Residency)		*Billions of Euros: End of Period*											
Foreign Assets (Net)	31n.u	....	....	....	....	....	....	....	13.87	11.38	8.18	−1.12	−7.89
Domestic Credit	32..u	....	....	....	....	....	....	....	147.54	160.35	170.31	186.83	219.07
Claims on General Govt. (Net)	32anu	....	....	....	....	....	....	....	62.57	62.87	57.05	54.07	62.77
Claims on Other Resident Sect.	32d.u	....	....	....	....	....	....	....	84.97	97.49	113.25	132.76	156.30
Currency Issued	34a.u	....	....	....	....	....	....	....	8.71	9.21	10.65	12.76	14.36
Demand Deposits	34b.u	....	....	....	....	....	....	....	70.81	71.71	79.45	91.70	99.21
Other Deposits	35..u	....	....	....	....	....	....	....	59.40	55.79	49.65	49.06	63.48
o/w: Other Dep. Over Two Yrs.	35abu	....	....	....	....	....	....	....	2.10	2.87	3.26	3.05	3.48
Money Market Fund Shares	36m.u	....	....	....	....	....	....	....	9.66	10.72	15.73	15.35	4.92
Bonds & Money Mkt. Instruments	36n.u	....	....	....	....	....	....	....	1.96	1.98	1.28	1.26	.59
o/w: Over Two Years	36nau	....	....	....	....	....	....	....	1.79	1.67	.80	.78	.15
Capital Accounts	37a	....	....	....	....	....	....	....	22.02	22.39	19.17	20.53	24.85
Other Items (Net)	37r.u	....	....	....	....	....	....	....	−11.14	−.06	2.56	−4.94	3.77
Interest Rates		*Percent Per Annum*											
Discount Rate (End of Period)	60	20.5	18.0	16.5	14.5	....	† 11.8	8.1	....	....	....	....	....
Money Market Rate	60b	24.60	16.40	13.80	12.80	13.99	....	....	....	....	....	....	....
Treasury Bill Rate	60c	17.5	14.2	11.2	11.4	10.3	8.3	† 6.2	4.1	3.5	2.3	2.3	2.3
Deposit Rate	60l	18.92	15.75	13.51	10.11	10.70	8.69	6.13	3.32	2.76	2.48	2.29	2.23
Households: Stocks, up to 2 years	60lhs	....	....	....	....	....	....	....	....	....	2.63	2.42	2.34
New Business, up to 1 year	60lhn	....	....	....	....	....	....	....	....	....	2.48	2.29	2.23
Corporations: Stocks, up to 2 years	60lcs	....	....	....	....	....	....	....	....	....	2.43	2.16	2.10
New Business, up to 1 year	60lcn	....	....	....	....	....	....	....	....	....	2.49	2.17	2.09
REPOS, Stocks	60lcr	....	....	....	....	....	....	....	....	....	2.26	2.01	2.03
Lending Rate	60p	27.44	23.05	20.96	18.92	18.56	15.00	12.32	8.59	7.41	6.79	....	....
Households: Stocks, up to 1 year	60phs	....	....	....	....	....	....	....	....	....	13.55	13.02	12.61
New Bus., Floating & up to 1 year	60pns	....	....	....	....	....	....	....	....	....	10.57	9.55	8.47
House Purch., Stocks,Over 5 years	60phm	....	....	....	....	....	....	....	....	....	5.33	5.07	4.84
House Purch., New Bus., 5-10 yrs	60phn	....	....	....	....	....	....	....	....	....	6.52	6.09	5.91
Corporations: Stocks, up to 1 year	60pcs	....	....	....	....	....	....	....	....	....	5.94	5.77	5.76
New Bus., Over € 1 mil.,up to 1 yr	60pcn	....	....	....	....	....	....	....	....	....	3.98	3.67	3.62
Government Bond Yield	61	....	....	....	....	8.48	6.30	6.10	5.30	5.12	4.27	4.26	3.59
Prices, Production, Labor		*Index Numbers (2000=100): Period Averages*											
Producer Prices	63	....	82.5	87.2	90.2	92.8	95.0	100.0	103.6	106.0	108.5	112.3	118.9
Consumer Prices	64	† 72.5	78.9	85.4	† 90.1	94.4	96.9	100.0	103.4	107.1	110.9	114.1	† 118.2
Harmonized CPI	64h	....	80.0	86.3	91.0	95.2	97.2	100.0	103.7	107.7	† 111.4	114.8	118.8
Wages: Monthly Earnings	65	....	....	....	....	....	96.9	100.0	101.5	105.9	124.3	130.4	132.5
Industrial Production	66	....	81.7	82.4	84.0	91.5	93.3	100.0	98.2	99.0	99.3	100.2	99.5
		Number in Thousands: Period Averages											
Labor Force	67d	4,188	4,249	4,314	4,294	4,526	4,586	4,612	4,580	4,656	4,734	4,819	4,846
Employment	67e	3,790	3,824	3,872	3,854	4,018	4,014	4,088	4,086	4,176	4,275	4,313	4,369
Unemployment	67c	404	425	446	440	508	555	523	494	480	460	506	478
Unemployment Rate (%)	67r	9.6	10.0	10.3	10.3	† 11.2	12.1	11.4	10.8	10.3	9.7	10.5	9.9
Intl. Transactions & Positions		*Millions of US Dollars*											
Exports	70..d	8,807.6	10,960.8	11,948.2	11,127.7	10,731.9	10,475.1	10,747.0	9,483.3	10,315.2	13,195.2	14,995.7	15,511.2
Imports, c.i.f.	71..d	21,381.3	26,795.2	29,672.4	27,898.7	29,388.1	28,719.5	29,221.4	29,927.7	31,164.4	44,375.2	51,559.4	49,817.4
		1995=100											
Volume of Exports	72	90.7	100.0	106.8	118.7	134.9	143.7	....	....	....	....	....	....
Volume of Imports	73	92.3	100.0	109.0	110.7	134.5	141.9	....	....	....	....	....	....
Unit Value of Exports	74	99.3	100.0	105.2	100.7	93.3	92.7	....	....	....	....	....	....
Unit Value of Imports	75	98.3	100.0	105.4	112.3	109.7	109.0	....	....	....	....	....	....
		2000=100											
Export Prices	76	70.2	† 77.4	83.5	84.8	86.8	88.1	100.0	100.7	101.8	101.5	106.6	110.6
Import Prices	76.x	80.7	† 86.3	88.1	89.9	95.2	95.4	100.0	103.1	103.4	104.1	107.4	116.9

Greece 174

		1994	1995	1996	1997	1998	1999	2000	2001	2002	2003	2004	2005
Balance of Payments						*Millions of US Dollars: Minus Sign Indicates Debit*							
Current Account, n.i.e.	78ald	−146	−2,864	−4,554	−4,860	....	−7,295	−9,820	−9,400	−9,582	−12,804	−13,476	−17,879
Goods: Exports f.o.b.	78aad	5,338	5,918	5,890	5,576	....	8,545	10,202	10,615	9,865	12,578	15,739	17,631
Goods: Imports f.o.b.	78abd	−16,611	−20,343	−21,395	−20,951	....	−26,496	−30,440	−29,702	−31,321	−38,184	−47,360	−51,884
Trade Balance	78acd	−11,273	−14,425	−15,505	−15,375	....	−17,951	−20,239	−19,087	−21,455	−25,606	−31,621	−34,253
Services: Credit	78add	9,213	9,605	9,348	9,287	....	16,506	19,239	19,456	20,142	24,283	33,085	34,159
Services: Debit	78aed	−3,774	−4,368	−4,238	−4,650	....	−9,251	−11,286	−11,589	−9,819	−11,250	−14,020	−14,742
Balance on Goods & Services	78afd	−5,834	−9,188	−10,395	−10,738	....	−10,696	−12,286	−11,220	−11,132	−12,573	−12,556	−14,836
Income: Credit	78agd	1,099	1,312	1,156	1,208	....	2,577	2,807	1,885	1,532	2,911	3,495	4,072
Income: Debit	78ahd	−2,347	−2,996	−3,337	−2,840	....	−3,248	−3,692	−3,652	−3,488	−7,413	−8,920	−11,102
Balance on Gds, Serv. & Inc.	78aid	−7,082	−10,872	−12,576	−12,370	....	−11,367	−13,171	−12,987	−13,088	−17,075	−17,980	−21,866
Current Transfers, n.i.e.: Credit	78ajd	6,964	8,039	8,053	7,538	....	4,957	4,116	4,592	5,536	7,202	7,901	8,615
Current Transfers: Debit	78akd	−28	−31	−31	−28	....	−884	−764	−1,005	−2,029	−2,930	−3,396	−4,628
Capital Account, n.i.e.	78bcd	—	—	—	—	....	2,211	2,112	2,153	1,530	1,411	2,990	2,563
Capital Account, n.i.e.: Credit	78bad	—	—	—	—	....	2,318	2,244	2,320	1,707	1,585	3,278	2,905
Capital Account: Debit	78bbd	—	—	—	—	....	−107	−131	−167	−177	−173	−288	−342
Financial Account, n.i.e.	78bjd	6,903	3,162	8,658	119	....	7,478	10,830	537	11,578	6,417	6,836	15,633
Direct Investment Abroad	78bdd	—	—	—	—	....	−542	−2,099	−611	−668	−375	−1,028	−1,458
Dir. Invest. in Rep. Econ., n.i.e.	78bed	981	1,053	1,058	984	....	567	1,083	1,585	53	1,332	2,105	640
Portfolio Investment Assets	78bfd	—	—	—	—	....	−858	−1,184	−474	−1,917	−9,805	−13,835	−23,194
Equity Securities	78bkd	—	—	—	—	....	−166	−846	−1,020	−316	−505	−830	−2,189
Debt Securities	78bld	—	—	—	—	....	−692	−338	546	−1,600	−9,300	−13,005	−21,004
Portfolio Investment Liab., n.i.e.	78bgd	—	—	—	—	....	6,754	9,262	9,012	12,340	23,456	31,301	32,308
Equity Securities	78bmd	—	—	—	—	....	−2,589	1,637	1,829	1,400	2,568	4,290	6,293
Debt Securities	78bnd	—	—	—	—	....	9,343	7,625	7,183	10,939	20,887	27,010	26,015
Financial Derivatives Assets	78bwd	....	....	....	....	....							
Financial Derivatives Liabilities	78bxd	....	....	....	....	....	419	348	74	−175	111	−429	13
Other Investment Assets	78bhd	—	—	—	980	....	−2,913	6,970	−1,539	−6,952	−4,413	−7,463	−8,740
Monetary Authorities	78bod	....	....	....	....	....	....	....	....	3,622	−1,043	−1,078	−295
General Government	78bpd	—	—	—	980	....	−2,913	6,970	−1,539	—	—	—	—
Banks	78bqd	—	—	—	—	....				−1,589	−2,602	−5,068	−8,577
Other Sectors	78brd					....				−8,984	−768	−1,317	133
Other Investment Liab., n.i.e.	78bid	5,922	2,109	7,600	−1,845	....	4,050	−3,551	−7,511	8,897	−3,888	−3,813	16,064
Monetary Authorities	78bsd	−1,791	−2,385	−2,194	−2,570	....	—	—		9,176	−2,311	−11,799	1,434
General Government	78btd	4,703	3,441	3,530	7,101	....	....	....	....	−4,326	−2,888	−1,271	−1,074
Banks	78bud	89	−2,110	−598	−3,348	....	1,644	−3,425	−6,989	8,249	2,773	10,661	17,646
Other Sectors	78bvd	2,921	3,163	6,862	−3,028	....	2,406	−126	−522	−4,202	−1,462	−1,403	−1,942
Net Errors and Omissions	78cad	−448	−321	111	226	....	42	−550	1,011	−1,663	253	373	−421
Overall Balance	78cbd	6,309	−23	4,215	−4,515	....	2,435	2,573	−5,699	1,863	−4,722	−3,277	−104
Reserves and Related Items	79dad	−6,309	23	−4,215	4,515	....	−2,435	−2,573	5,699	−1,863	4,722	3,277	104
Reserve Assets	79dbd	−6,309	23	−4,215	4,515	....	−2,435	−2,573	5,699	−1,863	4,722	3,277	104
Use of Fund Credit and Loans	79dcd					....	....	....	....	....	....	....	....
Exceptional Financing	79ded	—	—	—	—	....	....	....	....	....	....	....	....
International Investment Position						*Millions of US Dollars*							
Assets	79aad	....	....	....	....	55,491	59,106	57,194	59,753	83,972	112,652	139,964	153,083
Direct Investment Abroad	79abd	....	....	....	....	2,792	3,809	5,852	7,020	9,001	11,271	13,791	13,345
Portfolio Investment	79acd	....	....	....	....	4,503	4,778	3,848	9,376	17,974	34,966	52,666	69,979
Equity Securities	79add	....	....	....	....	1,177	1,147	1,346	2,559	3,020	4,893	6,200	8,326
Debt Securities	79aed	....	....	....	....	3,326	3,631	2,502	6,817	14,953	30,073	46,465	61,652
Financial Derivatives	79ald	....	....	....	....	12	13	12	88	315	326	821	659
Other Investment	79afd	....	....	....	....	38,726	40,361	35,227	37,099	47,250	60,288	69,978	66,813
Monetary Authorities	79agd	....	....	....	....	7,239	6,134	477	3,958	2,343	2,708	3,328	3,217
General Government	79ahd	....	....	....	....	—	—	—	—	—	—	—	—
Banks	79aid	....	....	....	....	18,712	20,881	20,908	19,510	26,440	36,782	41,988	41,338
Other Sectors	79ajd	....	....	....	....	12,775	13,346	13,841	13,631	18,468	20,798	24,662	22,259
Reserve Assets	79akd	....	....	....	....	9,458	10,145	12,255	6,169	9,432	5,801	2,708	2,287
Liabilities	79lad	....	....	....	....	91,539	102,665	106,690	116,557	164,027	229,229	309,039	327,829
Dir. Invest. in Rep. Economy	79lbd	....	....	....	....	13,084	15,386	12,480	13,941	15,561	21,576	28,482	29,312
Portfolio Investment	79lcd	....	....	....	....	45,330	52,758	57,294	59,610	78,524	122,191	188,456	202,113
Equity Securities	79ldd	....	....	....	....	12,001	15,211	9,584	7,711	8,425	16,140	28,386	37,963
Debt Securities	79led	....	....	....	....	33,329	37,547	47,710	51,899	70,098	106,052	160,070	164,151
Financial Derivatives	79lld	....	....	....	....	—	—	—	—	—	—	—	—
Other Investment	79lfd	....	....	....	....	33,125	34,521	36,917	43,006	69,943	85,462	92,101	96,404
Monetary Authorities	79lgd	....	....	....	....	—	—	—	7,132	18,259	19,391	8,916	8,514
General Government	79lhd	....	....	....	....	8,071	7,949	8,837	10,101	11,922	14,151	15,668	13,040
Banks	79lid	....	....	....	....	15,384	16,551	18,846	14,879	26,452	35,378	51,054	61,901
Other Sectors	79ljd	....	....	....	....	9,670	10,021	9,233	10,894	13,310	16,543	16,462	12,948
Government Finance						*Billions of Drachmas: Year Ending December 31*							
Budgetary Central Government													
Deficit (-) or Surplus	80	−5,050.3	−3,252.2	−2,904.2	−2,505.4	−2,125.5	−1,930.0	....	....	....	....	....	....
Total Revenue and Grants	81y	6,191.7	7,113.6	7,956.4	9,185.4	10,412.5	11,603.0	....	....	....	....	....	....
Revenue	81	5,883.4	6,753.5	7,306.9	....	....	....	....	....	....	....	....	....
Grants Received	81z	308.3	360.1	649.5	....	....	....	....	....	....	....	....	....
Expenditure	82	11,242.0	10,365.8	10,860.6	11,690.8	12,538.0	13,533.0	....	....	....	....	....	....
Financing													
Net Borrowing	84	5,050.3	3,252.2	2,904.2	2,505.4	2,125.5	1,930.0	....	....	....	....	....	....
Borrowing: Domestic	84c	6,439.2	5,111.7	5,180.4	....	....	....	....	....	....	....	....	....
Borrowing: Foreign	85c	1,138.0	914.0	1,362.0	....	....	....	....	....	....	....	....	....
Amortization	84y	−2,526.9	−2,773.5	−3,638.2	−3,589.4	−3,536.4	−3,362.3	....	....	....	....	....	....
General Government						*As Percent of Gross Domestic Product*							

Greece 174

		1994	1995	1996	1997	1998	1999	2000	2001	2002	2003	2004	2005
National Accounts						*Billions of Drachmas through 2000; Billions of Euros Beginning 2001*							
Househ.Cons.Expend.,incl.NPISHs....	**96f**	17,731.0	† 19,901.5	22,050.6	23,901.9	25,850.0	27,105.3	29,741.0	† 89.2	94.8	102.2	113.0	121.5
Government Consumption Expend...	**91f**	3,342.0	† 4,174.2	4,348.0	5,013.5	5,506.9	5,920.2	7,355.8	† 22.6	25.5	25.9	27.9	29.6
Gross Fixed Capital Formation..........	**93e**	4,529.2	† 5,065.9	5,828.2	6,558.8	7,615.1	8,699.0	9,785.0	† 31.3	33.8	39.3	42.4	42.9
Changes in Inventories....................	**93i**	25.8	† 85.9	96.4	93.0	79.7	−48.0	128.8	† −.1	—	—	—	.1
Exports of Goods and Services..........	**90c**	4,288.3	† 4,800.1	5,245.5	6,523.7	7,150.6	8,607.0	10,610.6	† 31.2	29.5	30.5	35.1	37.7
Imports of Goods and Services (-).....	**98c**	5,801.7	† 6,792.5	7,633.8	8,958.0	10,159.8	11,886.0	15,236.0	† 44.2	43.4	45.4	50.0	50.8
Gross Domestic Product (GDP).........	**99b**	24,296.0	27,235.1	29,935.2	33,132.8	36,042.1	38,397.8	42,385.0	† 133.1	143.5	155.5	168.4	181.1
Net Primary Income from Abroad.....	**98.n**	212.8	861.8	835.2	897.5	976.6	510.8	356.8	† −.9	−1.0	−1.7	−1.3	−3.3
Gross National Income (GNI)............	**99a**	24,195.7	† 28,096.9	30,770.4	34,061.0	37,018.7	38,908.5	42,713.9	† 132.2	142.5	153.9	167.1	177.7
Net Current Transf.from Abroad.......	**98t**	....	....	....	....	....	....	....	† 1.6	1.0	1.0	.2	−.1
Gross Nat'l Disposable Inc.(GNDI)....	**99i**	....	....	....	....	....	....	....	† 133.8	143.4	154.9	167.3	177.6
Gross Saving..................................	**99s**	....	....	....	....	....	....	....	† 19.0	19.9	23.7	26.4	26.4
Consumption of Fixed Capital..........	**99cf**	2,117.2	2,469.1	2,737.6	2,976.8	3,260.0	3,475.7	....	† 11.6	12.4	13.4	14.5	15.5
GDP Volume 1995 Ref., Chained.....	**99b.p**	26,674.9	27,235.2	27,877.5	28,891.4	29,863.2	30,939.7	32,217.2	† 99.5	103.3	108.2	113.3	117.4
GDP Volume (2000=100)...............	**99bvp**	82.8	84.5	86.5	89.7	92.7	96.0	100.0	105.2	109.3	114.5	119.8	124.2
GDP Deflator (2000=100)...............	**99bip**	69.2	† 76.0	81.6	87.2	91.7	94.3	100.0	101.7	105.6	109.2	113.0	117.2
						Millions: Midyear Estimates							
Population...............................	**99z**	10.56	10.66	10.74	10.81	10.87	10.93	10.98	11.02	11.05	11.07	11.10	11.12

2006, International Monetary Fund : *International Financial Statistics Yearbook*

Grenada 328

		1994	1995	1996	1997	1998	1999	2000	2001	2002	2003	2004	2005
Exchange Rates		*E.Caribbean Dollars per SDR: End of Period (aa) E.Caribbean Dollars per US Dollar: End of Period (ae)*											
Official Rate	aa	3.9416	4.0135	3.8825	3.6430	3.8017	3.7058	3.5179	3.3932	3.6707	4.0121	4.1931	3.8590
Official Rate	ae	2.7000	2.7000	2.7000	2.7000	2.7000	2.7000	2.7000	2.7000	2.7000	2.7000	2.7000	2.7000
		Index Numbers (2000=100): Period Averages											
Official Rate	ahx	100.0	100.0	100.0	100.0	100.0	100.0	100.0	100.0	100.0	100.0	100.0	100.0
Nominal Effective Exchange Rate	nec	92.3	91.4	92.6	94.6	95.8	97.1	100.0	101.9	101.1	97.3	94.5	94.4
Real Effective Exchange Rate	rec	100.2	96.8	97.0	97.5	98.0	97.9	100.0	100.6	98.9	95.0	91.7	91.0
Fund Position		*Millions of SDRs: End of Period*											
Quota	2f.s	8.50	8.50	8.50	8.50	8.50	11.70	11.70	11.70	11.70	11.70	11.70	11.70
SDRs	1b.s	.02	.02	.04	—	.03	—	—	—	—	—	.01	.01
Reserve Position in the Fund	1c.s	—	—	—	—	—	—	—	—	—	—	—	—
Total Fund Cred.&Loans Outstg	2tl	—	—	—	—	—	—	—	—	—	2.93	5.86	5.86
International Liquidity		*Millions of US Dollars Unless Otherwise Indicated: End of Period*											
Total Reserves minus Gold	1l.d	31.23	36.73	35.73	42.67	46.84	50.84	57.66	63.94	87.84	83.23	121.73	94.25
SDRs	1b.d	.03	.02	.06	.01	.04	—	—	—	—	—	.01	.02
Reserve Position in the Fund	1c.d	—	—	—	—	—	—	—	—	—	—	—	—
Foreign Exchange	1d.d	31.20	36.71	35.67	42.66	46.80	50.84	57.66	63.94	87.84	83.22	121.72	94.23
Monetary Authorities: Other Liab	4..d												
Deposit Money Banks: Assets	7a.d	51.88	59.06	61.88	57.07	54.97	72.71	69.81	113.23	137.94	171.00	270.10	205.02
Liabilities	7b.d	41.15	38.98	50.55	68.25	69.12	74.01	76.85	99.94	104.39	107.89	151.59	175.23
Monetary Authorities		*Millions of E. Caribbean Dollars: End of Period*											
Foreign Assets	11	84.27	99.27	96.50	115.30	126.52	137.20	155.57	173.02	237.88	225.95	330.08	256.14
Claims on Central Government	12a	24.38	21.77	20.97	18.71	18.74	16.33	13.84	11.17	5.64	26.78	26.58	24.63
Claims on Deposit Money Banks	12e	.27	.09	.01	.02	.03	.02	.04	.01	—	.02	.02	.01
Reserve Money	14	107.30	116.40	116.77	131.40	139.75	148.10	163.52	181.87	215.94	235.46	329.30	254.43
of which: Currency Outside DMBs	14a	52.96	53.83	53.18	58.35	64.08	64.75	71.14	70.20	75.15	84.68	102.10	105.26
Foreign Liabilities	16c	—	—	—	—	—	—	—	—	—	11.76	24.55	22.59
Central Government Deposits	16d	1.62	4.73	.71	2.63	5.54	5.66	5.92	2.33	27.58	5.53	2.83	3.76
Other Items (Net)	17r	—	—	—	—	—	-.22	—	—	—	—	—	—
Deposit Money Banks		*Millions of E. Caribbean Dollars: End of Period*											
Reserves	20	56.10	56.87	59.35	73.43	76.10	92.36	98.26	107.62	138.17	149.50	237.62	148.81
Foreign Assets	21	140.08	159.47	167.09	154.08	148.42	196.32	188.48	305.73	372.43	461.70	729.27	553.55
Claims on Central Government	22a	42.98	46.44	55.93	74.32	80.49	64.91	84.37	101.89	115.60	143.93	124.15	101.98
Claims on Local Government	22b	.06	—	—	—	—	—	.79	3.51	—	—	—	—
Claims on Nonfin.Pub.Enterprises	22c	6.71	6.12	16.07	20.92	25.88	26.13	46.43	65.79	75.83	31.42	22.87	32.17
Claims on Private Sector	22d	414.60	437.29	495.26	587.95	684.68	767.87	878.39	886.41	896.24	932.95	996.59	1,088.32
Claims on Nonbank Financial Insts	22g	4.24	6.06	10.31	10.09	15.59	23.33	31.50	39.30	55.85	29.87	17.46	17.99
Demand Deposits	24	91.48	99.39	102.26	104.29	121.61	137.81	141.20	152.68	185.25	211.56	332.51	253.13
Time, Savings,& Fgn.Currency Dep	25	409.15	455.19	504.59	564.27	627.50	722.76	846.61	949.71	1,013.31	1,059.95	1,190.91	1,198.23
Foreign Liabilities	26c	111.11	105.24	136.50	184.29	186.63	199.83	207.51	269.84	281.85	291.31	409.29	473.13
Central Government Deposits	26d	24.37	30.55	41.02	42.04	56.74	71.04	71.67	65.49	95.51	99.86	144.23	139.52
Credit from Monetary Authorities	26g	.25	.07	.02	.02	2.72	.02	.03	.01	—	1.86	.02	.58
Capital Accounts	27a	50.00	50.47	54.27	60.91	64.96	74.66	83.00	95.94	119.35	144.83	146.26	141.19
Other Items (Net)	27r	-21.59	-28.66	-34.64	-35.01	-29.00	-35.18	-21.78	-23.42	-41.15	-59.99	-95.27	-262.96
Monetary Survey		*Millions of E. Caribbean Dollars: End of Period*											
Foreign Assets (Net)	31n	113.24	153.50	127.09	85.10	88.31	133.70	136.54	208.91	328.45	384.58	625.50	313.96
Domestic Credit	32	466.97	482.40	556.82	667.32	763.09	822.09	977.73	1,040.25	1,026.07	1,059.57	1,040.60	1,121.81
Claims on Central Govt. (Net)	32an	41.36	32.93	35.18	48.36	36.96	4.54	20.62	45.24	-1.86	65.32	3.67	-16.67
Claims on Local Government	32b	.06	—	—	—	—	—	.79	3.51	—	—	—	—
Claims on Nonfin.Pub.Enterprises	32c	6.71	6.12	16.07	20.92	25.88	26.35	46.43	65.79	75.83	31.42	22.87	32.17
Claims on Private Sector	32d	414.60	437.29	495.26	587.95	684.68	767.87	878.39	886.41	896.24	932.95	996.59	1,088.32
Claims on Nonbank Financial Inst	32g	4.24	6.06	10.31	10.09	15.59	23.33	31.50	39.30	55.85	29.87	17.46	17.99
Money	34	144.57	153.47	155.46	162.65	185.69	202.56	212.44	222.94	260.84	296.29	434.89	358.40
Quasi-Money	35	409.15	455.19	504.59	564.27	627.50	722.76	846.61	949.71	1,013.31	1,059.95	1,190.91	1,198.23
Capital Accounts	37a	53.67	54.20	57.88	64.30	68.50	78.10	86.27	99.09	122.76	148.56	150.16	144.78
Other Items (Net)	37r	-27.18	-26.95	-34.02	-38.80	-30.27	-47.64	-31.05	-22.59	-42.39	-60.64	-109.86	-265.64
Money plus Quasi-Money	35l	553.73	608.65	660.05	726.92	813.18	925.32	1,059.05	1,172.65	1,274.15	1,356.23	1,625.80	1,556.62
Money (National Definitions)		*Millions of E. Caribbean Dollars: End of Period*											
M1	59ma	124.16	131.65	131.44	144.51	159.41	175.15	182.38	192.34	211.98	241.08	340.25	315.34
M2	59mb	504.52	550.69	600.74	671.52	750.44	854.56	985.84	1,090.37	1,167.38	1,260.37	1,483.35	1,469.02
Interest Rates		*Percent Per Annum*											
Discount Rate (End of Period)	60	9.00	9.00	9.00	8.00	8.00	8.00	8.00	7.00	7.00	6.50	6.50	6.50
Money Market Rate	60b	5.25	5.25	5.25	5.25	5.25	5.25	5.25	† 5.64	6.32	6.07	4.67	4.01
Treasury Bill Rate	60c	6.50	6.50	6.50	6.50	6.50	6.50	6.50	† 7.00	7.00	6.50	5.50	5.50
Savings Rate	60k	5.46	5.00	5.00	5.33	6.00	6.00	6.00	6.00	5.83	† 3.25	3.53	3.30
Deposit Rate	60l	3.61	3.67	3.74	3.93	4.16	4.30	4.24	4.23	3.59	3.39	3.32	2.88
Deposit Rate (Fgn. Currency)	60l.f	....	....	....	....	....	....	....	....	....	3.69	2.46	2.47
Lending Rate	60p	11.03	11.08	9.99	11.24	11.73	11.62	11.60	10.19	11.31	12.05	10.18	10.13
Prices		*Index Numbers (2000=100): Period Averages*											
Consumer Prices	64	91.2	92.9	94.8	† 96.0	97.3	97.9	100.0	101.7	102.8	....	....	....
Intl. Transactions & Positions		*Millions of E. Caribbean Dollars*											
Exports	70	64.30	58.70	54.00	61.50	72.50	127.20	191.26	160.72	157.31	112.51	81.98	....
Imports, c.i.f.	71	320.60	333.80	411.10	468.20	540.40	576.48	669.30	591.82	573.83	693.32	751.71	....

Grenada 328

		1994	1995	1996	1997	1998	1999	2000	2001	2002	2003	2004	2005
Balance of Payments		*Millions of US Dollars: Minus Sign Indicates Debit*											
Current Account, n.i.e.	78ald	−26.93	−40.84	−55.54	−67.87	−81.51	−53.04	−84.33	−98.54	−116.22	....	....	....
Goods: Exports f.o.b.	78aad	25.24	24.57	24.96	32.80	45.95	74.30	82.96	63.60	41.99	....	....	....
Goods: Imports f.o.b.	78abd	−119.45	−129.78	−147.44	−154.90	−183.01	−184.57	−220.94	−196.83	−181.42	....		
Trade Balance	78acd	−94.21	−105.21	−122.48	−122.10	−137.06	−110.28	−137.98	−133.23	−139.43			
Services: Credit	78add	101.53	99.19	106.70	106.14	119.77	143.72	152.76	133.34	133.04	....		
Services: Debit	78aed	−41.26	−38.46	−45.78	−56.48	−70.16	−79.86	−87.41	−82.22	−88.16			
Balance on Goods & Services	78afd	−33.94	−44.48	−61.56	−72.44	−87.45	−46.41	−72.63	−82.10	−94.56			
Income: Credit	78agd	3.61	4.91	4.71	4.70	4.13	4.33	5.08	3.73	4.13	....		
Income: Debit	78ahd	−12.43	−18.36	−20.10	−21.65	−27.38	−30.15	−36.89	−41.81	−48.92			
Balance on Gds, Serv. & Inc.	78aid	−42.76	−57.92	−76.94	−89.39	−110.70	−72.23	−104.43	−120.18	−139.35			
Current Transfers, n.i.e.: Credit	78ajd	19.75	21.58	25.47	25.53	34.19	26.76	30.35	31.00	31.83			
Current Transfers: Debit	78akd	−3.92	−4.50	−4.07	−4.01	−5.00	−7.57	−10.25	−9.36	−8.70			
Capital Account, n.i.e.	78bcd	21.67	25.84	31.42	31.78	28.58	31.18	32.13	42.36	31.83			
Capital Account, n.i.e.: Credit	78bad	23.04	27.28	31.42	33.42	30.36	33.10	34.21	44.39	33.87			
Capital Account: Debit	78bbd	−1.38	−1.44	—	−1.64	−1.78	−1.92	−2.08	−2.04	−2.04			
Financial Account, n.i.e.	78bjd	4.06	3.10	27.39	59.16	55.77	27.56	63.74	47.26	108.25	....		
Direct Investment Abroad	78bdd	—	—	—	—	—	—	—	—	—			
Dir. Invest. in Rep. Econ., n.i.e.	78bed	19.31	19.98	16.95	33.50	48.69	41.55	37.41	58.75	57.61			
Portfolio Investment Assets	78bfd	−.38	−.87	—	−.04	.04	−.36	−.07	−.42	−1.69			
Equity Securities	78bkd	....	....	....	....	....	....	....	....	....			
Debt Securities	78bld	....	....	....	....	....	....	....	....	....			
Portfolio Investment Liab., n.i.e.	78bgd	—	—	—	—	−.01	.75	19.52	.17	109.42			
Equity Securities	78bmd	....	....	....	....	....	....	....	....	....			
Debt Securities	78bnd	....	....	....	....	....	....	....	....	....			
Financial Derivatives Assets	78bwd	....	....	....	....	....	....	....	....				
Financial Derivatives Liabilities	78bxd	....	....	....	....	....	....	....					
Other Investment Assets	78bhd	−23.59	−11.02	−3.70	−5.89	−3.80	−12.39	−11.07	−5.31	−14.21			
Monetary Authorities	78bod	....	....	....	....	....	....	....	....	....			
General Government	78bpd	....	....	....	....	....	....	....	....	....			
Banks	78bqd	....	....	....	....	....	....	....	....	....			
Other Sectors	78brd	—	—	—	—	....	....	....	....	....			
Other Investment Liab., n.i.e.	78bid	8.72	−4.99	14.15	31.59	10.85	−2.00	17.96	−5.93	−42.89			
Monetary Authorities	78bsd	—	—	—	—	—	—	—	—	—			
General Government	78btd	....	....	....	....	....	....	....	....	....			
Banks	78bud	....	....	....	....	....	....	....	....	....			
Other Sectors	78bvd	....	....	....	....	....	....	....	....	....			
Net Errors and Omissions	78cad	5.88	17.94	−2.83	−16.14	1.26	−1.04	−4.95	14.77	7.36			
Overall Balance	78cbd	4.68	6.03	.45	6.93	4.09	4.66	6.60	5.84	31.22			
Reserves and Related Items	79dad	−4.68	−6.03	−.45	−6.93	−4.09	−4.66	−6.60	−5.84	−31.22			
Reserve Assets	79dbd	−4.68	−6.03	−.45	−6.93	−4.09	−4.66	−6.60	−5.84	−31.22			
Use of Fund Credit and Loans	79dcd	—	—	—	—	—	—	—	—	—			
Exceptional Financing	79ded	—	—	—	....	....	....	....	....	....			
Government Finance		*Millions of E. Caribbean Dollars: Year Ending December 31*											
Deficit (-) or Surplus	80	−7.86	16.79	....	....	....	....	....	....	....			
Revenue	81	194.26	205.00	....	....	....	....	....	....	....			
Grants Received	81z	26.50	21.48	....	....	....	....	....	....	....			
Expenditure	82	228.62	209.69	....	....	....	....	....	....	....			
Lending Minus Repayments	83	—	—	....	....	....	....	....	....	....			
National Accounts		*Millions of E. Caribbean Dollars*											
Househ.Cons.Expend.,incl.NPISHs.	96f	420.2	503.3	563.1	617.0	693.8	595.6	659.6	725.9	807.8	870.3	934.9	....
Government Consumption Expend.	91f	126.6	123.7	130.3	137.5	150.8	151.0	162.7	184.5	196.0	186.3	217.8	
Gross Fixed Capital Formation	93e	239.6	227.3	280.4	311.2	343.9	408.9	484.4	386.0	361.6	500.6	420.0	....
Exports of Goods and Services	90c	342.3	334.2	355.4	375.1	447.4	588.7	636.5	531.8	472.6	487.7	505.1	
Imports of Goods and Services (-)	98c	433.9	454.5	524.1	574.0	683.6	719.0	837.4	760.8	737.7	846.6	897.8	
Gross Domestic Product (GDP)	99b	708.9	746.0	805.1	866.8	952.4	1,025.1	1,105.8	1,067.5	1,100.3	1,198.2	1,180.1	
Net Primary Income from Abroad	98.n	−23.8	−36.3	−41.6	−45.8	−62.8	−71.0	−91.1	−111.9	−128.2	−116.8	−127.3	
Gross National Income (GNI)	99a	685.1	709.7	763.5	821.1	889.7	954.1	1,014.7	955.6	972.1	1,081.4	1,052.8	
Net Current Transf.from Abroad	98t	42.7	46.1	51.2	53.9	78.9	75.6	78.0	....	....	....		
Gross Nat'l Disposable Inc.(GNDI)	99i	727.9	755.8	805.2	857.3	961.4	1,016.5	1,095.6	....	....	....		
Gross Saving	99s	181.1	128.8	123.5	129.3	113.4	325.0	175.6	....	....	....		
		Millions: Midyear Estimates											
Population	99z	.10	.10	.10	.10	.10	.10	.10	.10	.10	.10	.10	.10

Guatemala 258

		1994	1995	1996	1997	1998	1999	2000	2001	2002	2003	2004	2005
Exchange Rates		*Quetzales per SDR: End of Period*											
Market Rate..............aa=.........	wa	8.2460	8.9810	8.5782	8.3342	9.6425	10.7342	10.0731	10.0544	10.6140	11.9482	12.0334	10.8772
		Quetzales per US Dollar: End of Period (we) Period Average (wf)											
Market Rate..............ae=.........	we	5.6485	6.0418	5.9656	6.1769	6.8482	7.8208	7.7312	8.0005	7.8072	8.0407	7.7484	7.6103
Market Rate..............rf=.........	wf	5.7512	5.8103	6.0495	6.0653	6.3947	7.3856	7.7632	7.8586	7.8216	7.9408	7.9465	7.6339
Secondary Rate...................	xe	1.00	1.00	1.00	1.00	1.00	1.00	1.00	....	....	....	....	....
Secondary Rate...................	xf	1.00	1.00	1.00	1.00	1.00	1.00	1.00	....	....	....	....	....
Fund Position		*Millions of SDRs: End of Period*											
Quota............................	2f.s	153.8	153.8	153.8	153.8	153.8	210.2	210.2	210.2	210.2	210.2	210.2	210.2
SDRs.............................	1b.s	11.4	10.6	10.2	9.4	8.7	8.4	7.5	6.7	6.1	5.5	5.1	4.6
Reserve Position in the Fund...........	1c.s	—	—	—	—	—	—	—	—	—	—	—	—
of which: Outstg.Fund Borrowing...	2c	—	—	—	—	—	—	—	—	—	—	—	—
Total Fund Cred.&Loans Outstg........	2tl	—	—	—	—	—	—	—	—	—	—	—	—
International Liquidity		*Millions of US Dollars Unless Otherwise Indicated: End of Period*											
Total Reserves minus Gold..............	1l.d	863.1	702.0	869.7	1,111.1	1,335.1	1,189.2	1,746.4	2,292.2	2,299.1	2,833.2	3,426.3	3,663.8
SDRs.............................	1b.d	16.6	15.8	14.6	12.7	12.2	11.5	9.8	8.5	8.2	8.2	8.0	6.5
Reserve Position in the Fund.........	1c.d	—	—	—	—	—	—	—	—	—	—	—	—
Foreign Exchange.................	1d.d	846.5	686.2	855.1	1,098.4	1,322.9	1,177.7	1,736.6	2,283.7	2,290.9	2,825.0	3,418.3	3,657.3
Gold (Million Fine Troy Ounces)........	1ad	.209	.210	.212	.213	.215	.215	.216	.217	.216	.220	.219	.221
Gold (National Valuation)...............	1and	8.8	8.9	8.9	9.0	9.1	9.1	9.1	9.2	9.1	9.3	9.3	9.3
Monetary Authorities: Other Liab.....	4..d	66.5	55.4	48.1	184.3	152.3	126.4	102.3	90.1	79.1	69.1	.9	.3
Deposit Money Banks: Assets...........	7a.d	17.7	66.3	81.2	72.6	65.6	84.1	123.6	203.4	245.2	293.5	314.2	295.3
Liabilities..................	7b.d	373.3	266.2	375.4	413.4	500.9	452.5	613.8	656.6	689.2	732.1	860.6	1,076.0
Other Banking Insts.: Assets............	7e.d	4.1	4.3	4.5	1.8	12.1	4.3	3.2	6.1	22.8	30.1	27.8	7.1
Liabilities..................	7f.d	100.2	515.8	554.3	592.0	615.8	633.7	654.1	526.0	534.3	552.4	567.8	571.2
Monetary Authorities		*Millions of Quetzales: End of Period*											
Foreign Assets........................	11	1,292.5	1,157.7	1,341.6	† 7,566.2	10,109.3	10,521.1	15,038.3	19,265.5	18,920.6	24,029.8	27,840.5	29,217.3
Claims on Central Government........	12a	357.6	187.4	698.0	† 78.7	.2	.2	.2	.2	.2	.2	—	—
Claims on Local Government............	12b	2.0	1.3	.6	† .3	—	—	—	—	—	—	—	—
Claims on Nonfin.Pub.Enterprises.....	12c	7.4	7.4	—	† —	—	—	—	—	—	—	—	—
Claims on Private Sector.............	12d	—	—	—	† 29.7	30.0	29.9	30.6	31.5	32.2	33.2	—	—
Claims on Deposit Money Banks......	12e	61.3	123.3	97.5	† 81.9	228.5	652.6	793.8	2,227.2	2,146.5	2,081.3	2,077.3	2,059.7
Claims on Other Banking Insts.........	12f	188.3	148.4	97.1	† 44.1	12.8	41.7	7.5	7.4	.4	.4	.4	.4
Reserve Money......................	14	5,494.3	5,689.3	6,418.2	† 10,746.6	10,324.2	10,608.5	12,653.6	14,702.7	17,403.2	19,340.6	22,824.7	24,540.8
of which: Currency Outside DMBs..	14a	3,714.6	4,018.9	4,179.1	† 4,890.2	5,632.5	7,752.8	7,298.2	8,360.7	8,729.4	10,608.8	11,194.8	12,517.1
Time and Foreign Currency Deposits.	15	3,845.6	4,600.0	6,582.4	† 665.2	1,103.4	1,995.1	6,872.7	8,083.6	8,997.9	9,925.3	9,478.8	10,303.5
Liabs. of Central Bank: Securities.....	16ac	372.9	76.0	50.3	† 212.7	67.5	60.9	58.4	57.1	53.8	53.9	52.2	—
Foreign Liabilities.....................	16c	615.9	588.8	561.6	† 1,138.6	1,043.2	988.6	790.8	721.2	617.7	556.0	6.8	2.4
Central Government Deposits...........	16d	1,566.3	1,439.6	1,872.3	† 5,293.5	7,586.1	6,405.8	5,527.8	9,162.1	6,446.5	8,700.0	11,805.1	11,530.2
Liabilities to Other Banking Insts......	16i	—	—	—	† 2.0	—	—	—	—	1.4	.5	.5	2.0
Capital Accounts.....................	17a	363.5	384.6	372.1	† 330.2	366.4	396.6	3,595.0	3,958.3	2,924.3	2,824.8	2,740.3	2,905.2
Other Items (Net).....................	17r	−10,349.5	−11,152.8	−13,622.1	† −10,587.9	−10,110.0	−9,210.0	−13,627.9	−15,153.2	−15,344.9	−15,256.2	−16,990.2	−18,006.7
Deposit Money Banks		*Millions of Quetzales: End of Period*											
Reserves.............................	20	2,175.5	4,019.2	4,794.7	† 5,731.3	4,823.0	3,121.7	5,132.4	6,120.3	9,051.8	7,879.7	9,474.8	10,196.0
Foreign Assets.......................	21	100.1	400.8	484.2	† 448.4	449.5	657.4	955.4	1,627.4	1,914.5	2,360.2	2,434.4	2,247.1
Claims on Central Government........	22a	2,869.7	1,292.5	1,676.9	† 2,870.0	2,389.0	2,277.1	3,361.2	4,654.9	4,799.2	5,104.9	6,866.7	10,335.4
Claims on Local Government............	22b	—	—	—	† 81.3	14.4	14.6	38.1	30.4	67.4	—	—	—
Claims on Nonfin.Pub.Enterprises.....	22c	—	—	—	† —	—	63.1	—	—	—	—	—	.2
Claims on Private Sector.............	22d	9,156.9	13,898.6	15,446.7	† 16,603.7	21,142.4	24,115.9	26,416.0	30,155.3	32,502.5	35,350.6	41,007.1	47,955.2
Claims on Other Banking Insts.........	22f	—	—	—	† 2,116.8	2,482.6	2,034.7	2,155.3	2,174.0	1,854.3	1,530.5	1,889.4	1,299.0
Demand Deposits....................	24	3,336.2	3,728.4	4,617.5	† 6,856.2	7,866.9	7,614.1	11,271.5	12,512.2	13,930.4	16,188.0	17,470.8	20,855.1
Time, Savings,& Fgn.Currency Dep...	25	7,450.0	8,900.3	8,802.5	† 10,535.8	12,976.8	13,682.8	16,506.1	20,722.1	23,935.5	27,270.2	31,924.2	36,217.5
Bonds............................	26ab	—	—	—	† 5,139.9	4,480.2	4,266.1	4,286.1	3,917.4	3,655.9	2,699.8	2,497.7	2,698.6
Foreign Liabilities.....................	26c	2,108.7	1,608.2	2,239.3	† 2,553.6	3,430.5	3,539.0	4,745.1	5,253.0	5,380.4	5,886.7	6,668.5	8,188.9
Central Government Deposits..........	26d	71.0	171.5	194.4	† 410.7	677.9	1,197.0	2,675.4	3,722.9	4,739.6	3,853.0	5,861.1	8,069.4
Credit from Monetary Authorities.....	26g	66.0	123.5	97.6	† 7.4	162.7	804.6	755.1	2,195.8	2,102.0	2,063.8	2,063.9	—
Liabilities to Other Banking Insts......	26i	—	—	—	† 478.9	575.9	578.0	658.0	1,277.6	1,013.7	900.1	1,149.3	1,210.5
Capital Accounts.....................	27a	1,586.7	1,821.9	2,019.8	† 2,315.5	2,775.7	3,810.3	4,464.9	2,834.7	3,077.5	3,315.1	4,002.3	7,427.8
Other Items (Net).....................	27r	−316.4	3,257.3	4,431.4	† −446.5	−1,645.7	−3,207.4	−7,303.8	−7,673.4	−7,645.3	−9,950.9	−9,965.3	−12,634.9
Monetary Survey		*Millions of Quetzales: End of Period*											
Foreign Assets (Net)........................	31n	−1,332.0	−638.5	−975.1	† 4,322.4	6,085.1	6,650.9	10,457.8	14,918.7	14,837.0	19,947.3	23,599.5	23,273.0
Domestic Credit.........................	32	10,944.6	13,924.5	15,852.6	† 16,120.4	17,807.4	20,974.4	23,805.7	24,168.7	28,070.2	29,466.8	32,097.4	39,990.6
Claims on Central Govt. (Net)........	32an	1,590.0	−131.2	308.2	† −2,755.5	−5,874.8	−5,325.5	−4,841.8	−8,229.9	−6,386.7	−7,447.8	−10,799.5	−9,264.2
Claims on Local Government........	32b	2.0	1.3	.6	† 81.6	14.4	14.6	38.1	30.4	67.4	—	—	—
Claims on Nonfin.Pub.Enterprises....	32c	7.4	7.4	—	† —	—	63.1	—	—	—	—	—	.2
Claims on Private Sector...............	32d	9,156.9	13,898.6	15,446.7	† 16,633.4	21,172.4	24,145.8	26,446.6	30,186.8	32,534.7	35,383.7	41,007.1	47,955.2
Claims on Other Banking Insts.......	32f	188.3	148.4	97.1	† 2,160.9	2,495.4	2,076.4	2,162.8	2,181.4	1,854.7	1,530.9	1,889.8	1,299.4
Money.................................	34	7,073.6	7,771.8	8,822.4	† 11,997.5	13,613.5	15,467.6	18,832.2	21,059.0	22,835.7	26,937.7	28,741.0	33,473.7
Quasi-Money..........................	35	11,295.6	13,500.3	15,384.9	† 11,201.0	14,080.2	15,677.9	23,378.8	28,805.7	32,933.4	37,195.5	41,403.0	46,521.0
Bonds............................	36ab	—	—	—	† 5,139.9	4,480.2	4,266.1	4,286.1	3,917.4	3,655.9	2,699.8	2,497.7	2,698.6
Liabs. of Central Bank: Securities.....	36ac	372.9	76.0	50.3	† 212.7	67.5	60.9	58.4	57.1	53.8	53.9	52.2	—
Liabilities to Other Banking Insts......	36i	—	—	—	† 480.9	575.9	578.0	658.0	1,277.6	1,015.1	900.6	1,149.8	1,212.5
Capital Accounts..........................	37a	1,950.2	2,206.5	2,391.9	† 2,645.7	3,142.1	4,206.9	8,059.9	6,793.0	6,001.8	6,139.9	6,742.7	10,333.0
Other Items (Net).....................	37r	−11,079.8	−10,268.6	−11,772.0	† −11,234.9	−12,066.9	−12,632.1	−21,009.9	−22,822.4	−23,588.5	−24,513.3	−24,889.3	−30,975.2
Money plus Quasi-Money................	35l	18,369.2	21,272.1	24,207.3	† 23,198.5	27,693.7	31,145.5	42,211.0	49,864.7	55,769.1	64,133.2	70,143.9	79,994.7

Guatemala 258

		1994	1995	1996	1997	1998	1999	2000	2001	2002	2003	2004	2005
Other Banking Institutions					*Millions of Quetzales: End of Period*								
Reserves	40	31.5	48.3	69.6	† 14.9	120.8	45.8	30.2	50.6	49.5	70.0	17.7	32.0
Foreign Assets	41	23.4	26.2	26.6	† 10.9	83.2	33.9	24.7	48.6	177.6	242.1	215.6	54.1
Claims on Central Government	42a	48.4	42.6	111.5	† 77.0	120.0	88.7	155.6	220.0	235.6	385.3	708.3	1,010.3
Claims on Nonfin.Pub.Enterprises	42c	—	—	—	† 13.2	.2	.2	.2	.2	.2	—	.2	.2
Claims on Private Sector	42d	2,055.3	2,512.4	2,655.5	† 3,388.5	4,310.1	3,859.8	3,181.8	2,813.0	2,185.7	2,209.3	2,120.0	1,861.2
Claims on Deposit Money Banks	42e	309.3	458.5	443.5	† 555.7	550.1	453.8	540.5	567.2	556.4	267.0	258.2	185.6
Time, Savings,& Fgn.Currency Dep	45	—	—	—	† 3.8	201.4	4.5	3.3	5.9	4.0	4.4	1.3	.8
Bonds	46ab	1,710.5	1,176.0	1,378.7	† 2,298.6	2,692.3	2,192.6	2,314.7	2,171.6	1,843.1	1,476.8	1,258.9	2,027.2
Foreign Liabilities	46c	566.1	3,116.1	3,306.8	† 3,656.5	4,216.9	4,956.2	5,057.0	4,208.6	4,171.5	4,441.6	4,399.2	4,347.1
Credit from Monetary Authorities	46g	195.4	144.2	102.3	† —	—	—	—	—	—	—	—	—
Credit from Deposit Money Banks	46h	877.6	1,637.1	1,689.4	† 1,584.0	1,925.9	2,110.8	1,629.1	1,436.3	1,264.7	1,473.1	1,803.2	1,121.6
Capital Accounts	47a	−107.4	−2,559.7	−2,667.4	† −2,849.0	−3,329.4	−4,019.0	−4,242.2	−3,414.7	−3,417.2	−3,641.6	−3,506.0	−3,503.7
Other Items (Net)	47r	−774.3	−425.7	−503.1	† −633.7	−522.7	−762.9	−828.9	−708.1	−661.1	−580.5	−636.4	−849.4
Banking Survey					*Millions of Quetzales: End of Period*								
Foreign Assets (Net)	51n	−1,874.7	−3,728.4	−4,255.3	† 676.8	1,951.4	1,728.6	5,425.5	10,758.7	10,843.2	15,747.8	19,415.9	18,980.1
Domestic Credit	52	12,860.0	16,331.1	18,522.5	† 17,438.2	19,743.0	22,853.3	24,980.5	25,020.5	28,640.8	30,530.6	33,036.2	41,562.8
Claims on Central Govt. (Net)	52an	1,638.4	−88.6	419.7	† −2,678.5	−5,754.8	−5,236.8	−4,686.2	−8,009.9	−6,151.0	−7,062.5	−10,091.1	−8,253.9
Claims on Local Government	52b	2.0	1.3	.6	† 81.6	15.1	21.2	38.1	30.4	71.2	—	—	—
Claims on Nonfin.Pub.Enterprises	52c	7.4	7.4	—	† 13.2	.2	63.3	.2	.2	.2	—	.2	.4
Claims on Private Sector	52d	11,212.2	16,411.0	18,102.2	† 20,021.9	25,482.5	28,005.6	29,628.4	32,999.8	34,720.5	37,593.1	43,127.2	49,816.4
Liquid Liabilities	55l	18,337.7	21,223.8	24,137.7	† 23,186.8	27,912.3	31,097.0	42,176.7	49,815.0	55,709.7	64,064.3	70,126.3	79,957.0
Bonds	56ab	1,710.5	1,176.0	1,378.7	† 7,438.5	7,172.5	6,458.7	6,600.8	6,089.0	5,499.0	4,176.6	3,756.5	4,725.8
Liabs. of Central Bank: Securities	56ac	372.9	76.0	50.3	† 212.7	67.5	60.9	58.4	57.1	53.8	53.9	52.2	—
Capital Accounts	57a	1,842.8	−353.2	−275.5	† −203.3	−187.3	187.9	3,817.7	3,378.3	2,584.6	2,498.2	3,236.6	6,829.3
Other Items (Net)	57r	−11,278.7	−9,519.9	−11,024.0	† −12,519.7	−13,270.6	−13,222.6	−22,247.6	−23,560.2	−24,363.1	−24,514.7	−24,719.4	−30,969.1
Money (National Definitions)					*Millions of Quetzales: End of Period*								
Base Money	19ma	....	....	....	10,509.9	10,243.6	11,089.1	12,302.5	13,953.2	16,280.5	17,038.4	19,074.2	21,142.5
M1	59ma	....	....	....	11,948.2	13,565.6	15,497.2	18,651.8	20,112.6	21,624.5	26,051.1	27,878.5	32,816.2
M2	59mb	....	....	....	27,564.1	30,999.7	33,456.2	39,497.4	47,228.2	51,474.0	58,281.6	58,013.9	66,043.6
Interest Rates					*Percent Per Annum*								
Money Market Rate	60b	....	....	....	7.77	6.62	9.23	9.33	10.58	9.11	6.65	6.16	6.54
Savings Rate	60k	....	....	....	5.13	4.50	5.19	5.41	4.51	3.31	2.09	1.77	1.71
Deposit Rate	60l	9.69	7.87	7.65	† 5.83	5.44	7.96	10.17	8.75	6.92	4.78	4.19	4.35
Lending Rate	60p	22.93	21.16	22.72	† 18.64	16.56	19.51	20.88	18.96	16.86	14.98	13.81	13.03
Prices and Labor					*Index Numbers (2000=100): Period Averages*								
Consumer Prices	64	64.0	69.3	77.0	84.1	90.0	94.4	† 100.0	107.6	116.3	122.6	131.7	142.8
					Number in Thousands: Period Averages								
Labor Force	67d	2,326	....	....	....	....	3,982	....	....	....	....	....	....
Employment	67e	830	856	852	844	887	893	908	928	953	958	....	....
Unemployment	67c	1	1	....	....	....	....	2	....	2	....	....	....
Intl. Transactions & Positions					*Millions of US Dollars*								
Exports	70..d	1,550.2	1,990.8	2,056.3	2,390.6	2,562.7	2,493.6	2,711.2	2,463.6	2,473.2	2,631.7	2,938.7	3,476.9
Imports, c.i.f.	71..d	2,781.4	3,292.5	3,146.2	3,851.9	4,650.9	4,560.0	5,171.4	5,606.4	6,304.1	6,721.5	7,811.6	8,809.8
Imports, f.o.b.	71.vd	2,595.9	3,061.7	2,925.7	3,581.7	4,319.7	4,240.4	4,808.5	5,210.0	5,866.0	6,253.1	7,279.0	8,174.2

Guatemala 258

		1994	1995	1996	1997	1998	1999	2000	2001	2002	2003	2004	2005
Balance of Payments		*Millions of US Dollars: Minus Sign Indicates Debit*											
Current Account, n.i.e.	78ald	−625.3	−572.0	−451.5	−633.5	−1,039.1	−1,025.9	−1,049.6	−1,252.9	−1,234.9	−1,039.2	−1,188.3	....
Goods: Exports f.o.b.	78aad	1,550.1	2,157.5	2,236.9	2,602.9	2,846.9	2,780.6	3,085.1	2,859.8	2,818.9	3,059.9	3,429.5	....
Goods: Imports f.o.b.	78abd	−2,546.6	−3,032.6	−2,880.3	−3,542.7	−4,255.7	−4,225.7	−4,742.0	−5,142.0	−5,791.0	−6,175.7	−7,189.1	....
Trade Balance	78acd	−996.5	−875.1	−643.4	−939.8	−1,408.8	−1,445.1	−1,656.9	−2,282.2	−2,972.1	−3,115.9	−3,759.6	....
Services: Credit	78add	697.5	665.9	559.0	588.8	639.9	699.5	777.0	1,044.8	1,145.4	1,058.8	1,178.2	....
Services: Debit	78aed	−644.9	−694.9	−659.7	−650.5	−791.8	−790.7	−825.4	−927.9	−1,066.1	−1,126.1	−1,293.8	....
Balance on Goods & Services	78afd	−943.9	−904.1	−744.1	−1,001.5	−1,560.7	−1,536.3	−1,705.3	−2,165.3	−2,892.8	−3,183.2	−3,875.2	....
Income: Credit	78agd	63.6	46.6	40.2	72.4	91.4	76.2	214.4	317.5	161.1	179.1	173.3	....
Income: Debit	78ahd	−193.6	−205.7	−270.1	−311.1	−275.1	−280.7	−424.0	−401.9	−479.5	−497.0	−492.1	....
Balance on Gds, Serv. & Inc.	78aid	−1,073.9	−1,063.2	−974.0	−1,240.2	−1,744.4	−1,740.8	−1,914.9	−2,249.7	−3,211.1	−3,501.0	−4,194.0	....
Current Transfers, n.i.e.: Credit	78ajd	456.4	508.2	537.1	628.8	742.9	754.4	908.2	1,024.3	2,077.7	2,558.9	3,048.6	....
Current Transfers: Debit	78akd	−7.8	−17.0	−14.6	−22.1	−37.6	−39.5	−42.9	−27.5	−101.5	−97.0	−42.9	....
Capital Account, n.i.e.	78bcd	—	61.6	65.0	85.0	71.0	68.4	85.5	93.4	124.2	133.8	135.3	....
Capital Account, n.i.e.: Credit	78bad	—	61.6	65.0	85.0	71.0	68.4	85.5	93.4	124.2	133.8	135.3	....
Capital Account: Debit	78bbd	—	—	—	—	—	—	—	—	—	—	—	....
Financial Account, n.i.e.	78bjd	655.2	494.8	672.3	737.4	1,136.7	637.5	1,520.7	1,546.7	1,196.5	1,516.3	1,597.8	....
Direct Investment Abroad	78bdd	—	....	....	....	....	....	....	—	—	—	—	....
Dir. Invest. in Rep. Econ., n.i.e.	78bed	65.2	75.2	76.9	84.4	672.8	154.6	229.9	455.5	110.6	131.0	154.7	....
Portfolio Investment Assets	78bfd	−9.8	−22.2	−11.5	−18.1	−11.6	−26.0	−36.3	−45.0	−38.3	18.1	111.1	....
Equity Securities	78bkd	—	....	....	....	....	....	....	—	—	—	—	....
Debt Securities	78bld	−9.8	−22.2	−11.5	−18.1	−11.6	−26.0	−36.3	−45.0	−38.3	18.1	111.1	....
Portfolio Investment Liab., n.i.e.	78bgd	7.1	5.9	−4.5	249.7	65.8	136.5	78.9	175.3	−107.8	−11.0	238.0	....
Equity Securities	78bmd	—	....	....	....	....	....	....	—	—	—	—	....
Debt Securities	78bnd	7.1	5.9	−4.5	249.7	65.8	136.5	78.9	175.3	−107.8	−11.0	238.0	....
Financial Derivatives Assets	78bwd	—	....	....	....	....	....	....	—	—	—	—	....
Financial Derivatives Liabilities	78bxd	—	....	....	....	....	....	....	—	—	—	—	....
Other Investment Assets	78bhd	116.8	125.1	199.2	221.2	241.7	199.9	213.2	156.7	196.4	173.5	252.0	....
Monetary Authorities	78bod	—	....	....	....	....	....	....	—	—	—	—	....
General Government	78bpd	−49.2	....	....	....	....	....	....	—	—	—	—	....
Banks	78bqd	—	....	....	....	....	....	....	—	—	—	—	....
Other Sectors	78brd	166.0	125.1	199.2	221.2	241.7	199.9	213.2	156.7	196.4	173.5	252.0	....
Other Investment Liab., n.i.e.	78bid	475.9	310.8	412.2	200.2	168.0	172.5	1,035.0	804.0	1,035.6	1,204.7	842.0	....
Monetary Authorities	78bsd	−63.9	−78.3	−56.3	−108.6	−54.2	−25.6	−24.0	−11.2	−11.3	−11.7	−68.3	....
General Government	78btd	132.7	11.8	91.1	89.5	252.4	295.9	92.7	42.6	172.7	307.9	79.4	....
Banks	78bud	—	7.3	19.4	−4.6	3.2	23.0	−17.4	21.8	—	—	—	....
Other Sectors	78bvd	407.1	370.0	358.0	223.9	−33.4	−120.8	983.7	750.9	874.3	908.5	831.0	....
Net Errors and Omissions	78cad	−23.6	−136.2	−71.7	40.7	66.8	195.0	86.1	87.2	−64.7	−60.8	63.5	....
Overall Balance	78cbd	6.3	−151.8	214.1	229.6	235.4	−125.0	642.7	474.4	21.1	550.1	608.3	....
Reserves and Related Items	79dad	−6.3	151.8	−214.1	−229.6	−235.4	125.0	−642.7	−474.4	−21.1	−550.1	−608.3	....
Reserve Assets	79dbd	−47.3	157.3	−199.0	−257.7	−263.0	125.0	−642.7	−474.4	−21.2	−550.1	−608.3	....
Use of Fund Credit and Loans	79dcd	—	—	—	—	—	—	—	—	—	—	—	....
Exceptional Financing	79ded	41.0	−5.5	−15.1	28.1	27.6	....	....	—	—	—	—	....
Government Finance		*Millions of Quetzales: Year Ending December 31*											
Deficit (-) or Surplus	80	† −938.7	−218.4	−268.0	−2,244.3	−2,708.9	−3,804.2	−2,709.8	−3,105.0	−1,351.8	−3,540.2	−2,386.1	−3,736.8
Revenue	81	† 5,712.3	7,227.7	8,605.1	9,730.3	12,714.0	14,735.7	16,050.5	17,656.4	20,503.5	21,811.6	22,338.1	24,404.7
Grants Received	81z	† 74.3	39.1	53.0	55.1	94.2	188.2	348.5	565.7	377.8	278.4	309.3	359.0
Exp. & Lending Minus Repay.	82z	† 6,725.3	7,485.2	8,926.1	12,029.7	15,517.1	18,728.1	19,108.8	21,327.1	22,233.1	25,630.2	25,033.5	28,500.5
Expenditure	82	† 6,592.2	7,512.4	8,378.5	11,408.0	15,517.1	18,728.1	19,108.8	21,327.1	22,233.1	25,630.2	25,033.5	28,500.5
Lending Minus Repayments	83	† 237.8	308.4	235.9	—	—	—	—	—	—	—	—	—
Adjustment to Cash Basis	82x	† −104.7	−335.6	311.7	621.7	—	—	—	—	—	—	—	—
Financing (by Residence of Lender)													
Domestic	84a	† −187.5	433.0	−54.7	92.9	1,306.7	1,541.9	2,058.4	−129.2	156.4	1,199.3	−1,050.2	4,093.1
Foreign	85a	† 1,126.2	−214.6	322.7	2,151.4	1,402.2	2,262.3	651.4	3,234.2	1,195.4	2,340.9	3,436.3	−356.3
Debt: Domestic	88a	4,854.7	4,485.2	5,093.0	5,862.2	6,259.8	7,807.1	8,629.7	9,281.1	8,169.9	11,192.5	12,840.8	16,425.7
Foreign	89a	887.8	1,203.5	1,308.2	1,491.3	1,693.8	2,034.4	2,058.0	2,350.1	2,956.4	3,385.8	3,841.6	3,722.9
National Accounts		*Millions of Quetzales*											
Househ.Cons.Expend.,incl.NPISHs.	96f	63,893	72,899	83,072	93,804	105,429	114,554	125,661	139,917	156,945	171,080	190,986	217,326
Government Consumption Expend.	91f	4,468	4,692	4,851	5,391	7,041	8,552	10,486	12,420	13,005	14,349	13,792	14,316
Gross Fixed Capital Formation	93e	10,622	12,360	12,727	16,302	20,645	24,205	24,147	25,486	28,164	28,345	31,499	36,619
Changes in Inventories	93i	1,087	460	−614	−1,540	929	−728	2,560	3,822	6,660	8,828	11,466	10,327
Exports of Goods and Services	90c	13,170	16,400	17,005	19,370	22,537	25,711	30,241	30,999	31,153	33,036	36,452	38,010
Imports of Goods and Services (-)	98c	18,571	21,656	21,562	25,454	32,559	37,008	43,351	47,774	53,652	58,039	67,446	72,900
Gross Domestic Product (GDP)	99b	74,669	85,157	95,479	107,873	124,022	135,287	149,743	164,870	182,275	197,599	216,749	243,699
Net Primary Income from Abroad	98.n	−856	−926	−1,400	−1,451	−979	−1,480	−1,751	−899	−2,603	−2,799	−2,828	−2,870
Gross National Income (GNI)	99a	73,813	84,231	94,079	106,422	123,043	133,807	147,992	163,971	179,672	194,800	213,921	240,829
Consumption of Fixed Capital	99cf	1,672	1,990	2,361	2,742	3,231	3,850	4,576	5,300	6,065	6,909	7,759	8,700
GDP Volume 1958 Prices	99b.p	3,983	4,180	4,303	4,491	4,716	4,897	5,074	5,192	5,309	5,422	5,571	5,747
GDP Volume (2000=100)	99bvp	78.5	82.4	84.8	88.5	93.0	96.5	100.0	102.3	104.6	106.9	109.8	113.3
GDP Deflator (2000=100)	99bip	63.5	69.0	75.2	81.4	89.1	93.6	100.0	107.6	116.3	123.5	131.8	143.7
		Millions: Midyear Estimates											
Population	99z	9.75	9.97	10.20	10.43	10.66	10.91	11.17	11.43	11.71	12.00	12.29	12.60

		1994	1995	1996	1997	1998	1999	2000	2001	2002	2003	2004	2005
Exchange Rates						*Francs per SDR: End of Period*							
Official Rate	aa	1,432.1	1,483.5	1,494.2	1,544.8	1,827.7	2,382.7	2,452.4	2,498.8	2,620.2	2,964.2	3,516.3	6,442.8
					Francs per US Dollar: End of Period (ae) Period Average (rf)								
Official Rate	ae	981.0	998.0	1,039.1	1,145.0	1,298.0	1,736.0	1,882.3	1,988.3	1,976.0	2,000.0	2,550.0	4,500.0
Official Rate	rf	976.6	991.4	1,004.0	1,095.3	1,236.8	1,387.4	1,746.9	1,950.6	1,975.8	1,984.9	2,225.0	3,644.3
Fund Position						*Millions of SDRs: End of Period*							
Quota	2f.s	78.70	78.70	78.70	78.70	78.70	107.10	107.10	107.10	107.10	107.10	107.10	107.10
SDRs	1b.s	3.79	5.01	.54	1.97	1.02	.94	.19	.63	1.22	.15	—	.01
Reserve Position in the Fund	1c.s	.07	.07	.08	.08	.08	.08	.08	.08	.08	.08	.08	.08
Total Fund Cred.&Loans Outstg	2tl	48.64	63.11	57.32	73.39	90.05	92.71	86.63	98.08	102.23	91.70	78.52	61.11
International Liquidity					*Millions of US Dollars Unless Otherwise Indicated: End of Period*								
Total Reserves minus Gold	1l.d	87.85	86.76	87.34	121.63	236.71	199.68	147.91	200.23	171.40	....	110.48	95.06
SDRs	1b.d	5.53	7.45	.77	2.66	1.43	1.29	.25	.80	1.66	.22	—	.02
Reserve Position in the Fund	1c.d	.10	.10	.11	.10	.11	.10	.10	.09	.10	.11	.12	.11
Foreign Exchange	1d.d	82.22	79.21	86.46	118.88	235.17	198.29	147.56	199.34	169.64	....	110.37	94.93
Gold (Million Fine Troy Ounces)	1ad	....	....	....	....	....	....	.072	.030	.268	....	.006	.004
Gold (National Valuation)	1and	70.16	98.70	106.20	100.26	12.02	8.81	10.22	6.17	90.85	....	1.29	1.27
Monetary Authorities: Other Liab	4..d	6.70	5.30	44.61	10.13	10.51		7.78	21.94	7.62	11.09	13.04	7.27
Deposit Money Banks: Assets	7a.d	86.27	90.89	81.05	73.08	85.27	77.53	80.32	68.46	73.85	68.11	110.60	88.61
Liabilities	7b.d	52.39	79.93	70.17	53.86	58.75	62.70	40.88	27.33	38.68	34.73	38.04	27.62
Monetary Authorities						*Millions of Francs: End of Period*							
Foreign Assets	11	155,011	185,089	201,116	254,054	319,566	....	303,361	407,345	332,610	268,660	285,007	433,471
Claims on Central Government	12a	225,807	332,922	429,007	532,766	662,569	....	802,821	1,421,713	842,762	1,130,869	1,304,367	2,513,388
Claims on Nonfin.Pub.Enterprises	12c	3,059	3,685	4,063	4,659	31,740	....	33,048	33,236	2,670	2,688	2,660	4,793
Claims on Private Sector	12d	129	108	159	3,362	5,763	....	5,313	12,924	26,619	33,503	31,941	131,308
Claims on Deposit Money Banks	12e	8,587	8,632	8,196	26,227	6,701	....	8,090	3,043	4,349	1,557	2,009	14,548
Claims on Other Banking Insts	12f	48	493	—	—	439	....	193	78	—	—	—	56
Reserve Money	14	176,724	198,442	195,681	248,968	† 262,015	....	385,183	442,501	538,658	634,343	861,418	986,111
of which: Currency Outside DMBs	14a	154,748	167,144	154,420	191,635	209,682	....	288,468	310,063	349,781	478,133	536,169	786,587
Foreign Liabilities	16c	76,223	98,912	132,011	124,978	178,215	....	227,096	288,707	282,906	293,998	309,344	426,458
Central Government Deposits	16d	151,170	249,942	313,926	444,141	590,113	....	576,045	1,170,909	407,441	574,870	613,880	1,640,583
Capital Accounts	17a	57,608	55,460	51,645	52,291	55,559	....	74,939	91,303	54,101	111,184	131,732	232,683
Other Items (Net)	17r	−69,088	−71,830	−50,726	−49,316	−59,124	....	−110,436	−115,080	−74,095	−177,118	−290,390	−188,271
Deposit Money Banks						*Millions of Francs: End of Period*							
Reserves	20	15,380	28,310	31,930	46,130	50,064	59,859	66,492	101,186	138,767	116,171	232,320	142,830
Foreign Assets	21	84,630	90,710	84,220	83,670	110,678	134,586	151,182	136,119	145,935	136,221	282,018	398,734
Claims on Central Government	22a	13,210	29,910	38,500	46,750	44,054	39,287	18,037	46,993	134,114	285,888	386,175	502,955
Claims on Nonfin.Pub.Enterprises	22c	10	270	430	260	273	54	185	60	9,964	3,891	1	65
Claims on Private Sector	22d	144,410	181,410	188,270	184,070	156,383	178,654	203,379	210,107	215,213	255,654	276,869	474,102
Demand Deposits	24	94,430	104,060	112,590	130,430	144,030	139,940	177,997	226,047	300,520	386,359	518,469	590,420
Time, Savings,& Fgn.Currency Dep	25	52,180	64,950	77,710	83,430	81,176	99,528	111,339	129,777	144,302	206,281	356,870	606,326
Foreign Liabilities	26c	51,400	79,770	72,920	61,670	76,257	108,851	76,944	54,341	76,439	69,457	97,008	124,307
Central Government Deposits	26d	17,100	16,490	15,800	19,960	23,575	25,296	23,108	27,527	30,135	40,470	60,652	88,526
Credit from Monetary Authorities	26g	10,360	11,580	10,360	10,660	7,239	7,822	8,995	4,775	15,456	6,407	2,903	2,176
Capital Accounts	27a	46,400	50,870	38,980	49,600	34,986	43,293	53,695	53,017	81,611	71,187	177,045	196,757
Other Items (Net)	27r	−14,230	2,920	14,960	5,120	−5,811	−12,290	−12,803	−1,019	−4,470	17,664	−35,565	−89,826
Monetary Survey						*Millions of Francs: End of Period*							
Foreign Assets (Net)	31n	112,018	97,118	80,405	151,077	175,772	....	150,503	200,416	119,201	41,426	160,672	281,440
Domestic Credit	32	218,403	282,366	330,703	307,766	287,534	....	466,370	526,693	794,387	1,098,650	1,331,455	1,899,268
Claims on Central Govt. (Net)	32an	70,747	96,400	137,781	115,415	92,935	....	221,705	270,270	539,300	801,417	1,016,010	1,287,234
Claims on Nonfin.Pub.Enterprises	32c	3,069	3,955	4,493	4,919	32,013	....	33,233	33,296	12,634	6,579	2,661	4,858
Claims on Private Sector	32d	144,539	181,518	188,429	187,432	162,146	....	208,692	223,031	241,832	289,157	308,810	605,410
Claims on Other Banking Insts	32f	48	493	—	—	439	....	193	78	—	—	—	56
Money	34	252,582	274,125	273,465	331,666	† 361,469	....	499,885	559,993	681,228	893,055	1,143,312	1,394,203
Quasi-Money	35	52,180	64,950	77,710	83,430	81,176	99,528	111,339	129,777	144,302	206,281	356,870	606,326
Capital Accounts	37a	104,008	106,330	90,625	101,891	90,545	....	128,634	144,320	135,712	182,371	308,777	429,440
Other Items (Net)	37r	−78,353	−65,895	−30,726	−58,161	−69,885	....	−122,984	−106,980	−47,654	−141,631	−316,832	−249,261
Money plus Quasi-Money	35l	304,762	339,075	351,175	415,096	† 442,645	....	611,224	689,770	825,530	1,099,336	1,500,182	2,000,529
Interest Rates						*Percent Per Annum*							
Refinancing Rate (End of Period)	60	17.00	18.00	18.00	15.00	....	....	11.50	16.25	16.25	16.25	16.25	22.25
Savings Rate	60k	16.00	15.50	....	....	....	....	....	....	....	....	....	....
Deposit Rate	60l	18.00	17.50	....	....	6.38	5.67	7.50	8.03	7.40	6.50	8.85	14.35
Lending Rate	60p	22.00	21.50	....	....	19.56	19.88	19.38	....	....	....	....	....

Guinea 656

		1994	1995	1996	1997	1998	1999	2000	2001	2002	2003	2004	2005
Balance of Payments		*Millions of US Dollars: Minus Sign Indicates Debit*											
Current Account, n.i.e.	78ald	−248.0	−216.5	−177.3	−91.1	−183.6	−214.4	−155.2	−102.2	−199.8	−187.5	−174.8	....
Goods: Exports f.o.b.	78aad	515.7	582.8	636.5	630.1	693.0	635.7	666.3	731.1	708.6	609.3	725.6	....
Goods: Imports f.o.b.	78abd	−685.4	−621.7	−525.3	−512.5	−572.0	−581.7	−587.1	−561.9	−668.5	−644.3	−688.4	....
Trade Balance	78acd	−169.7	−39.0	111.2	117.6	121.0	54.0	79.3	169.2	40.1	−35.0	37.2	....
Services: Credit	78add	152.9	117.5	124.1	110.7	110.8	113.2	68.0	102.8	90.5	133.7	85.4	....
Services: Debit	78aed	−366.0	−389.3	−422.2	−321.6	−382.7	−364.4	−284.9	−319.0	−330.6	−307.3	−275.2	....
Balance on Goods & Services	78afd	−382.9	−310.8	−186.8	−93.3	−150.9	−197.2	−137.7	−47.0	−200.1	−208.6	−152.7	....
Income: Credit	78agd	6.5	12.9	12.8	7.8	9.0	24.7	23.5	11.3	6.1	12.6	9.8	....
Income: Debit	78ahd	−79.8	−97.5	−105.7	−121.3	−133.5	−106.9	−101.1	−113.6	−51.6	−124.3	−37.1	....
Balance on Gds, Serv. & Inc.	78aid	−456.1	−395.5	−279.8	−206.9	−275.5	−279.4	−215.3	−149.3	−245.6	−320.3	−180.0	....
Current Transfers, n.i.e.: Credit	78ajd	280.6	258.3	137.8	131.4	116.2	80.0	88.6	91.6	70.5	194.6	55.1	....
Current Transfers: Debit	78akd	−72.5	−79.3	−35.3	−15.6	−24.3	−15.1	−28.5	−44.5	−24.8	−61.7	−49.9	....
Capital Account, n.i.e.	78bcd	—	—	—	—	—	—	—	—	91.9	57.6	−30.2	....
Capital Account, n.i.e.: Credit	78bad	—	—	—	—	—	—	—	—	91.9	57.6	—	....
Capital Account: Debit	78bbd	....	....	....	....	....	—	—	—	—	—	−30.2	....
Financial Account, n.i.e.	78bjd	84.2	109.2	47.5	−89.3	8.0	117.1	8.4	−12.1	−115.1	58.6	77.7	....
Direct Investment Abroad	78bdd	....	....	−.5	—	—	—	—	—	—	—	—	....
Dir. Invest. in Rep. Econ., n.i.e.	78bed	.2	.8	23.8	17.3	17.8	63.5	9.9	1.7	30.0	79.0	—	....
Portfolio Investment Assets	78bfd	....	....	....	....	−82.7	−20.0	8.7	4.6	5.1	−4.6	14.8	....
Equity Securities	78bkd	....	....	....	....	....	—	—	—	—	—	—	....
Debt Securities	78bld	....	....	....	....	−82.7	−20.0	8.7	4.6	5.1	−4.6	14.8	....
Portfolio Investment Liab., n.i.e.	78bgd	....	....	....	....	....	—	—	—	—	—	—	....
Equity Securities	78bmd	....	....	....	....	....	—	—	—	—	—	—	....
Debt Securities	78bnd	....	....	....	....	....	—	—	—	—	—	—	....
Financial Derivatives Assets	78bwd	....	....	....	....	....	....	....	....	....	....	....	....
Financial Derivatives Liabilities	78bxd	....	....	....	....	....	....	....	....	....	....	....	....
Other Investment Assets	78bhd	−14.5	−73.7	−19.8	−99.1	−14.6	.6	−17.0	11.7	−71.0	−4.4	49.5	....
Monetary Authorities	78bod	−6.5	9.0	6.0	2.4	1.2	−.9	−13.7	1.5	—	1.8	7.0	....
General Government	78bpd	....	....	....	....	....	—	—	—	—	—	—	....
Banks	78bqd	−2.2	−4.6	9.0	9.3	−12.5	7.6	−1.3	9.5	−69.1	−6.1	42.5	....
Other Sectors	78brd	−5.8	−78.2	−34.7	−110.8	−3.3	−6.0	−2.0	.6	−2.0	—	—	....
Other Investment Liab., n.i.e.	78bid	98.5	182.2	44.0	−7.5	87.5	73.0	6.8	−30.1	−79.2	−11.4	13.4	....
Monetary Authorities	78bsd	.1	−.5	39.1	−35.3	−3.0	.2	−.8	13.4	1.6	2.0	2.9	....
General Government	78btd	79.6	106.5	−14.4	48.2	37.6	84.2	61.6	26.5	−36.3	−8.9	7.2	....
Banks	78bud	8.3	26.0	−9.8	−18.1	6.7	3.7	−23.1	−12.4	—	−4.2	3.3	....
Other Sectors	78bvd	10.5	50.2	29.0	−2.3	46.2	−15.0	−30.8	−57.5	−44.5	−.4	—	....
Net Errors and Omissions	78cad	39.7	34.8	69.9	49.8	17.8	21.4	83.9	−2.2	143.1	−157.1	68.6	....
Overall Balance	78cbd	−124.1	−72.5	−59.9	−130.6	−157.8	−75.9	−62.9	−116.5	−79.8	−228.5	−58.6	....
Reserves and Related Items	79dad	124.1	72.5	59.9	130.6	157.8	75.9	62.9	116.5	79.8	228.5	58.6	....
Reserve Assets	79dbd	32.4	−43.8	−6.5	−20.3	60.7	60.6	50.5	−3.9	75.7	131.5	11.8	....
Use of Fund Credit and Loans	79dcd	7.0	22.1	−8.4	22.4	22.8	3.7	−7.9	14.8	5.7	−14.8	−19.5	....
Exceptional Financing	79ded	84.7	94.2	74.9	128.5	74.3	11.5	20.4	105.7	−1.6	111.8	66.3	....
Government Finance		*Millions of Francs: Year Ending December 31*											
Deficit (-) or Surplus	80	....	....	....	....	−192,650	−116,309f	....	....	....	....	....	....
Revenue	81	....	....	....	....	497,293	574,901f	....	....	....	....	....	....
Grants Received	81z	....	....	....	....	106,481	320,500f	....	....	....	....	....	....
Expenditure	82	....	....	....	....	792,554	1,010,060f	....	....	....	....	....	....
Lending Minus Repayments	83	....	....	....	....	3,870	1,650f	....	....	....	....	....	....
Financing													
Domestic	84a	....	....	....	....	−2,610	8,249f	....	....	....	....	....	....
Foreign	85a	....	....	....	....	195,260	108,060f	....	....	....	....	....	....
		Millions: Midyear Estimates											
Population	99z	7.28	7.52	7.74	7.93	8.09	8.26	8.43	8.62	8.81	9.00	9.20	9.40

Guinea-Bissau 654

		1994	1995	1996	1997	1998	1999	2000	2001	2002	2003	2004	2005
Exchange Rates							*Francs per SDR: End of Period*						
Official Rate	aa	345.18	501.49	772.88	807.94	791.61	896.19	918.49	935.39	850.37	771.76	747.90	794.73
						Francs per US Dollar: End of Period (ae) Period Average (rf)							
Official Rate	ae	236.45	337.37	537.48	598.81	562.21	652.95	704.95	744.31	625.50	519.36	481.58	556.04
Official Rate	rf	198.34	278.04	405.75	583.67	589.95	†615.70	711.98	733.04	696.99	581.20	528.28	527.47
Fund Position							*Millions of SDRs: End of Period*						
Quota	2f.s	10.50	10.50	10.50	10.50	10.50	14.20	14.20	14.20	14.20	14.20	14.20	14.20
SDRs	1b.s	—	.01	.01	.04	.02	.06	.03	.16	.30	.80	.44	.40
Reserve Position in the Fund	1c.s	—	—	—	—	—	—	—	—	—	—		
Total Fund Cred.&Loans Outstg	2tl	3.15	3.98	5.33	9.04	10.95	12.63	18.97	18.45	17.24	13.78	10.17	8.05
International Liquidity						*Millions of US Dollars Unless Otherwise Indicated: End of Period*							
Total Reserves minus Gold	1l.d	18.43	20.27	11.53	33.70	35.76	35.28	66.73	69.47	102.71	32.90	73.09	79.81
SDRs	1b.d	—	.01	.01	.06	.03	.08	.04	.20	.40	1.18	.68	.57
Reserve Position in the Fund	1c.d	—	—	—	—	—	—	—	—	—	—		
Foreign Exchange	1d.d	18.43	20.26	11.52	33.65	35.73	35.21	66.69	69.28	102.31	31.71	72.41	79.24
Monetary Authorities: Other Liab	4..d	42.6	38.6	18.2	1.8	.7	1.4	−.6	1.0	−.1	−.7	.6	1.7
Deposit Money Banks: Assets	7a.d	12.1	18.7	16.7	19.2	19.3	16.6	2.3	3.8	8.7	11.6	13.4	4.1
Liabilities	7b.d	7.2	6.9	7.5	11.7	12.9	11.1	13.7	11.5	13.5	—	1.1	5.7
Monetary Authorities							*Millions of Francs: End of Period*						
Foreign Assets	11	4,357	6,837	6,196	20,183	20,105	23,038	47,044	51,711	64,246	17,087	35,197	44,380
Claims on Central Government	12a	4,144	4,728	7,679	10,690	12,453	13,081	20,343	20,288	20,214	17,885	15,098	13,879
Claims on Other Financial Insts	12f												
Reserve Money	14	5,300	6,998	9,709	21,922	19,011	25,561	47,936	55,559	72,528	23,336	37,019	50,072
of which: Currency Outside DMBs	14a	3,015	4,278	6,370	20,137	17,642	24,186	44,245	53,054	70,223	21,282	32,570	40,661
Foreign Liabilities	16c	11,157	15,012	13,878	8,359	9,055	12,251	17,006	18,019	14,565	10,271	7,902	7,363
Central Government Deposits	16d	4,915	7,722	9,080	6,110	8,148	2,994	3,567	3,742	492	1,928	4,638	737
Other Items (Net)	17r	−8,542	−13,840	−18,793	−5,518	−3,655	−4,686	−1,122	−5,320	−3,049	−564	736	86
Deposit Money Banks							*Millions of Francs: End of Period*						
Reserves	20	2,420	3,362	2,614	4,392	2,728	2,728	6,256	2,397	1,667	2,027	4,467	7,409
Foreign Assets	21	2,856	6,295	8,989	11,479	10,827	10,827	1,621	2,850	5,470	6,032	6,464	2,270
Claims on Central Government	22a	576	567	77	21	21	21	—	—	—	456	1,008	1,282
Claims on Private Sector	22d	4,617	4,612	5,305	7,651	9,859	9,859	12,121	4,436	4,211	2,651	2,251	3,326
Claims on Other Financial Insts	22f	—	—	—	—	—	—	—	—	—	—	—	—
Demand Deposits	24	1,855	2,880	4,507	16,431	14,476	14,476	19,985	16,261	14,623	8,319	10,277	10,868
Time & Foreign Currency Deposits	25	3,207	4,395	6,320	1,132	1,355	1,355	1,037	794	1,282	564	577	1,138
Foreign Liabilities	26c	1,700	2,330	3,999	6,984	7,220	7,220	2,924	543	439	2	521	3,166
Long-Term Foreign Liabilities	26cl	6	8	13	14	14	14	6,744	8,001	8,001	—	—	—
Central Government Deposits	26d	47	14	561	820	1,014	1,014	1,066	1,144	1,156	1,286	1,742	3,231
Credit from Monetary Authorities	26g	4,328	4,328	97	—	—	—	—	—	—	—	—	—
Other Items (Net)	27r	−674	881	1,489	−1,838	−644	−644	−11,758	−17,061	−14,153	995	1,073	−4,116
Monetary Survey							*Millions of Francs: End of Period*						
Foreign Assets (Net)	31n	−5,644	−4,211	−2,692	16,318	14,657	14,394	28,735	35,999	54,712	12,845	33,238	36,121
Domestic Credit	32	4,374	2,171	3,420	11,432	13,172	18,954	27,831	19,838	22,777	17,777	11,977	14,519
Claims on Central Govt. (Net)	32an	−2,302	−3,959	−3,923	331	613	9,095	15,709	15,402	18,566	15,126	9,726	11,193
Claims on Private Sector	32d	6,677	6,129	7,343	11,101	12,559	9,859	12,121	4,436	4,211	2,651	2,251	3,326
Claims on Other Financial Insts	32f	—	—	—	—	—	—	—	—	—	—	—	—
Money	34	4,910	7,211	10,891	36,625	32,194	39,420	64,524	69,535	85,074	29,922	42,964	51,679
Quasi-Money	35	3,207	4,395	6,320	1,132	1,355	1,355	1,037	794	1,282	564	577	1,138
Long-Term Foriegn Liabilities	36cl	6	8	13	14	14	14	6,744	8,001	8,001	—	—	—
Other Items (Net)	37r	−11,538	−16,195	−19,639	−10,020	−5,733	−7,440	−15,739	−22,493	−16,868	137	1,673	−2,177
Money plus Quasi-Money	35l	8,116	11,606	17,212	37,757	33,548	40,774	65,561	70,329	86,356	30,486	43,541	52,817
Interest Rates							*Percent Per Annum*						
Bank Rate (End of Period)	60	6.00	6.00	6.00	6.00	6.00	6.00	6.00	6.00	6.00	4.50	4.00	4.00
Money Market Rate	60b	4.95	4.95	4.95	4.95	4.95	4.95	4.95	4.95	4.95	4.95	4.95	4.95
Deposit Rate	60l	3.50	3.50	3.50	3.50	3.50	3.50	3.50	3.50	3.50	3.50	3.50	3.50
Lending Rate	60p	36.33	32.92	51.75	....	....	....	....	....	....	....	....	....
Prices							*Index Numbers (2000=100): Period Averages*						
Consumer Prices	64	26.6	38.7	58.4	87.0	92.7	92.1	100.0	†103.3	106.8	103.0	103.9	107.4
Intl. Transactions & Positions							*Millions of Francs*						
Exports	70	16,580	12,310	11,030	28,300	15,800	31,500	44,300	46,100	37,600	37,900	46,500	42,200
Imports, c.i.f	71	32,530	36,990	35,240	51,700	37,200	31,100	42,400	45,400	40,400	37,800	50,700	63,300

Guinea-Bissau 654

		1994	1995	1996	1997	1998	1999	2000	2001	2002	2003	2004	2005
Balance of Payments						*Millions of US Dollars: Minus Sign Indicates Debit*							
Current Account, n.i.e......................	78ald	−47.63	−50.65	−60.43	−30.28	....	....	....	−26.89	−8.63	−6.47	....	....
Goods: Exports f.o.b......................	78aad	33.21	23.90	21.61	48.86	....	....	....	62.89	54.38	65.01	....	....
Goods: Imports f.o.b......................	78abd	−53.80	−59.34	−56.80	−62.49	....	....	....	−61.72	−58.50	−65.30	....	....
Trade Balance................................	78acd	−20.59	−35.44	−35.19	−13.63	....	....	....	1.17	−4.12	−.29	....	....
Services: Credit............................	78add	5.61	5.69	6.96	8.00	....	....	....	4.46	6.50	6.00	....	....
Services: Debit.............................	78aed	−27.11	−29.91	−29.25	−26.15	....	....	....	−30.27	−27.41	−36.21	....	....
Balance on Goods & Services.......	78afd	−42.09	−59.66	−57.48	−31.78	....	....	....	−24.63	−25.03	−30.50	....	....
Income: Credit............................	78agd	—	—	—	—	....	....	....	.57	1.29	2.08	....	....
Income: Debit..............................	78ahd	−26.27	−21.09	−18.65	−14.30	....	....	....	−12.58	−10.05	−10.91	....	....
Balance on Gds, Serv. & Inc.........	78aid	−68.36	−80.75	−76.13	−46.08	....	....	....	−36.64	−33.79	−39.34	....	....
Current Transfers, n.i.e.: Credit......	78ajd	21.79	31.42	15.70	15.80	....	....	....	9.76	30.22	39.69	....	....
Current Transfers: Debit..................	78akd	−1.06	−1.32	—	—	....	....	....	−.01	−5.05	−6.83	....	....
Capital Account, n.i.e......................	78bcd	44.42	49.20	40.70	32.20	....	....	....	25.33	38.86	42.82	....	....
Capital Account, n.i.e.: Credit........	78bad	44.42	49.20	40.70	32.20	....	....	....	25.05	40.36	42.82	....	....
Capital Account: Debit..................	78bbd	—	—	—	—	....	....	....	.28	−1.50	—	....	....
Financial Account, n.i.e.................	78bjd	−26.98	−28.25	−12.30	2.03	....	....	....	−17.34	−21.40	−13.06	....	....
Direct Investment Abroad..............	78bdd	....	....	....	....	....	....	....	.40	−1.02	−.52	....	....
Dir. Invest. in Rep. Econ., n.i.e........	78bed	....	....	....	....	....	....	....	.40	3.56	4.01	....	....
Portfolio Investment Assets..........	78bfd	....	....	....	....	....	....	....	—	1.15	.60	....	....
Equity Securities.....................	78bkd	....	....	....	....	....	....	....	—	1.15	—	....	....
Debt Securities........................	78bld	....	....	....	....	....	....	....	—	—	.60	....	....
Portfolio Investment Liab., n.i.e......	78bgd	....	....	....	....	....	....	....	—	.65	.34	....	....
Equity Securities.....................	78bmd	....	....	....	....	....	....	....	—	.65	.34	....	....
Debt Securities........................	78bnd	....	....	....	....	....	....	....	....	....	....	....	....
Financial Derivatives Assets..........	78bwd	....	....	....	....	....	....	....	....	....	....	....	....
Financial Derivatives Liabilities.......	78bxd	....	....	....	....	....	....	....	....	....	....	....	....
Other Investment Assets..............	78bhd	....	....	....	−5.80	....	....	....	4.21	−6.85	−18.99	....	....
Monetary Authorities..................	78bod	....	....	....	....	....	....	....	....	....	....	....	....
General Government...................	78bpd	....	....	....	....	....	....	....	....	....	....	....	....
Banks....................................	78bqd	....	....	....	−5.80	....	....	....	4.21	−3.73	−16.33	....	....
Other Sectors...........................	78brd	....	....	....	....	....	....	....	....	−3.12	−2.66	....	....
Other Investment Liab., n.i.e.........	78bid	−26.98	−28.25	−12.30	7.83	....	....	....	−22.34	−18.89	1.50	....	....
Monetary Authorities...................	78bsd	—	−6.88	—	.43	....	....	....	1.08	−1.27	−.45	....	....
General Government....................	78btd	−26.98	−21.37	−12.30	7.40	....	....	....	−20.08	−29.27	7.63	....	....
Banks....................................	78bud	....	....	....	....	....	....	....	−4.12	−.15	.46	....	....
Other Sectors...........................	78bvd	....	....	....	....	....	....	....	.78	11.80	−6.14	....	....
Net Errors and Omissions.................	78cad	−24.34	−10.90	−11.47	−19.19	....	....	....	5.86	−2.97	6.15	....	....
Overall Balance...........................	78cbd	−54.53	−40.60	−43.50	−15.24	....	....	....	−13.04	5.86	29.44	....	....
Reserves and Related Items.............	79dad	54.53	40.60	43.50	15.24	....	....	....	13.04	−5.86	−29.44	....	....
Reserve Assets............................	79dbd	6.24	−3.64	−8.90	−35.15	....	....	....	−6.34	−18.00	−38.22	....	....
Use of Fund Credit and Loans.......	79dcd	−.43	1.19	1.94	5.11	....	....	....	−.67	−1.60	−4.85	....	....
Exceptional Financing..................	79ded	48.72	43.05	50.46	45.28	....	....	....	20.05	13.73	13.64	....	....
International Investment Position							*Millions of US Dollars*						
Assets..	79aad	....	....	....	....	....	....	....	73.33	113.28	180.14	....	....
Direct Investment Abroad..............	79abd	....	....	....	....	....	....	....	—	1.12	.58	....	....
Portfolio Investment.....................	79acd	....	....	....	....	....	....	....	—	—	—	....	....
Equity Securities.....................	79add	....	....	....	....	....	....	....	—	—	—	....	....
Debt Securities........................	79aed	....	....	....	....	....	....	....	—	—	—	....	....
Financial Derivatives....................	79ald	....	....	....	....	....	....	....	—	—	—	....	....
Other Investment........................	79afd	....	....	....	....	....	....	....	3.85	9.45	13.21	....	....
Monetary Authorities..................	79agd	....	....	....	....	....	....	....	....	....	....	....	....
General Government...................	79ahd	....	....	....	....	....	....	....	....	....	....	....	....
Banks....................................	79aid	....	....	....	....	....	....	....	3.85	8.74	11.61	....	....
Other Sectors...........................	79ajd	....	....	....	....	....	....	....	....	.71	1.60	....	....
Reserve Assets............................	79akd	—	.01	....	....	....	....	....	69.47	102.71	166.35	....	....
Liabilities...................................	79lad	....	....	....	....	....	....	....	814.96	1,256.20	1,194.98	....	....
Dir. Invest. in Rep. Economy..........	79lbd	....	....	....	....	....	....	....	.39	3.02	1.55	....	....
Portfolio Investment.....................	79lcd	....	....	....	....	....	....	....	—	.72	1.26	....	....
Equity Securities.....................	79ldd	....	....	....	....	....	....	....	—	.72	1.26	....	....
Debt Securities........................	79led	....	....	....	....	....	....	....	—	—	—	....	....
Financial Derivatives....................	79lld	....	....	....	....	....	....	....	—	—	—	....	....
Other Investment........................	79lfd	4.60	5.91	....	....	....	....	....	814.57	1,252.45	1,192.17	....	....
Monetary Authorities..................	79lgd	....	....	....	....	....	....	....	24.25	23.29	19.80	....	....
General Government...................	79lhd	....	....	....	....	....	....	....	778.02	1,215.40	263.02	....	....
Banks....................................	79lid	....	....	....	....	....	....	....	11.53	13.74	1.06	....	....
Other Sectors...........................	79ljd	....	....	....	....	....	....	....	.77	.03	908.29	....	....
National Accounts							*Millions of Francs*						
Househ.Cons.Expend.,incl.NPISHs....	96f	119,594	117,485	128,800	134,300	115,900	105,800	162,786	141,975	143,447	143,969	153,620	164,501
Government Consumption Expend...	91f	15,645	10,033	10,891	23,700	22,900	28,400	16,133	14,331	11,793	9,352	9,979	10,687
Gross Fixed Capital Formation.........	93e	23,302	22,373	21,248	21,278	....	....	....	....	....	....	....	....
Changes in Inventories....................	93i	−7,021	154	5,624	27	....	....	....	....	....	....	....	....
Exports of Goods and Services.........	90c	23,222	16,051	17,304	33,700	18,100	34,300	34,887	30,340	23,976	23,928	25,532	27,339
Imports of Goods and Services (-).....	98c	48,871	42,122	47,932	62,500	42,600	45,100	73,042	56,906	54,567	51,901	55,385	59,303
Gross Domestic Product (GDP).........	99b	125,800	124,100	135,900	163,100	121,800	138,200	153,410	145,867	141,914	138,698	147,999	158,483
Gross National Income (GNI)..........	99a	....	....	....	....	....	....	....	....	....	....	....	....
GDP Volume 1986 Prices................	99b.p	103,500	104,500	109,500	116,672	83,800	90,200	96,900	97,000	90,200	90,700	....	....
GDP Volume (2000=100)...............	99bvp	106.8	107.8	113.0	120.4	86.5	93.1	100.0	100.1	93.1	93.6	....	....
GDP Deflator (2000=100)...............	99bip	76.8	75.0	78.4	88.3	91.8	96.8	100.0	95.0	99.4	96.6	....	....
							Millions: Midyear Estimates						
Population...............................	99z	1.15	1.19	1.22	1.26	1.29	1.33	1.37	1.41	1.45	1.49	1.54	1.59

Guyana   336

		1994	1995	1996	1997	1998	1999	2000	2001	2002	2003	2004	2005
Exchange Rates						*Guyana Dollars per SDR: End of Period*							
Market Rate.....................	aa	208.0	208.9	203.1	194.3	228.5	247.7	240.7	238.2	260.7	288.6	310.2	286.2
						Guyana Dollars per US Dollar: End of Period (ae) Period Average (rf)							
Market Rate.....................	ae	142.5	140.5	141.3	144.0	162.3	180.5	184.8	189.5	191.8	194.3	199.8	200.3
Market Rate.....................	rf	138.3	142.0	140.4	142.4	150.5	178.0	182.4	187.3	190.7	193.9	198.3	199.9
						Index Numbers (2000=100): Period Averages							
Market Rate.....................	ahx	132.1	128.6	129.9	127.9	121.5	102.6	100.0	97.4	95.7	94.1	92.0	91.3
Nominal Effective Exchange Rate.....	nec	115.5	110.1	111.8	117.8	114.8	98.4	100.0	100.5	98.8	92.7	87.4	86.0
Real Effective Exchange Rate...........	rec	95.9	97.7	101.9	107.1	106.2	95.7	100.0	100.2	101.3	97.7	93.5	95.0
Fund Position						*Millions of SDRs: End of Period*							
Quota.................	2f.s	67.20	67.20	67.20	67.20	67.20	90.90	90.90	90.90	90.90	90.90	90.90	90.90
SDRs........................	1b.s	.05	.09	.07	.14	.17	.92	7.02	1.96	3.43	3.26	4.60	.34
Reserve Position in the Fund...........	1c.s	—	—	—	—	—	—	—	—	—	—	—	—
Total Fund Cred.&Loans Outstg........	2tl	122.25	115.60	117.11	116.44	109.50	102.15	90.12	77.67	70.73	64.18	56.71	63.60
International Liquidity						*Millions of US Dollars Unless Otherwise Indicated: End of Period*							
Total Reserves minus Gold.............	1l.d	247.13	268.94	329.68	315.51	276.60	268.28	304.96	287.26	284.47	276.39	231.84	251.87
SDRs..........................	1b.d	.08	.14	.11	.20	.24	1.27	9.15	2.47	4.66	4.84	7.15	.49
Reserve Position in the Fund..........	1c.d	—	—	—	—	—	—	—	—	—	—	—	—
Foreign Exchange......................	1d.d	247.05	268.80	329.57	315.31	276.36	267.01	295.81	284.79	279.81	271.55	224.70	251.39
Monetary Authorities: Other Liab.....	4..d	656.62	725.00	448.57	286.86	222.56	187.68	186.51	179.00	69.17	61.43	53.22	55.09
Deposit Money Banks: Assets..........	7a.d	24.88	27.03	26.55	24.29	23.91	40.13	38.77	46.36	63.06	92.70	108.91	141.18
Liabilities..................	7b.d	20.57	20.52	25.62	34.47	31.93	22.23	20.66	17.55	25.94	25.43	36.01	53.25
Other Banking Insts.: Assets............	7e.d	1.21	1.28	1.38	2.38	1.98	2.59	7.32	7.67	11.73	8.39	10.49	12.45
Liabilities..................	7f.d	—	7.30	1.03	1.12	.69	.46	3.42	5.38	5.06	5.00	5.14	5.16
Monetary Authorities						*Millions of Guyana Dollars: End of Period*							
Foreign Assets........................	11	35,741	38,398	46,466	43,578	40,149	44,590	54,645	53,979	53,634	52,731	44,881	50,511
Claims on Central Government........	12a	118,849	125,918	96,232	76,959	67,904	71,686	72,208	70,613	50,267	50,956	50,523	50,725
Claims on Nonfin.Pub.Enterprises.....	12c	1,098	811	2,441	3,238	3,320	4,709	4,710	4,710	4,710	4,710	4,710	4,710
Reserve Money......................	14	16,453	19,603	20,760	24,314	27,179	26,128	29,794	33,043	36,359	40,112	43,760	48,689
of which: Currency Outside DMBs..	14a	8,167	8,967	9,959	11,210	11,334	13,394	14,495	15,138	15,410	17,888	19,546	21,527
Time, Savings,& Fgn.Currency Dep....	15	335	561	489	749	694	1,219	1,146	921	565	692	575	625
Restricted Deposits.....................	16b	—	—	—	—	—	—	—	—	—	—	—	—
Foreign Liabilities.....................	16c	119,000	126,005	87,146	63,931	61,126	59,184	56,151	52,417	31,701	30,457	28,222	29,234
Central Government Deposits..........	16d	22,623	21,335	30,256	27,147	22,066	34,594	39,130	37,965	37,399	36,750	27,247	26,232
Capital Accounts......................	17a	2,345	3,253	2,567	3,449	5,184	5,891	6,822	7,290	6,636	6,889	7,368	7,083
Other Items (Net).....................	17r	−5,068	−5,631	3,921	4,187	−4,875	−6,030	−1,482	−2,334	−4,049	−6,503	−7,056	−5,917
Deposit Money Banks						*Millions of Guyana Dollars: End of Period*							
Reserves...........................	20	8,171	10,326	10,781	13,315	16,070	12,419	15,510	18,340	21,031	21,883	23,318	26,565
Foreign Assets........................	21	3,546	3,798	3,750	3,497	3,880	7,243	7,163	8,786	12,091	18,006	21,755	28,271
Claims on Central Government........	22a	15,651	14,847	17,251	18,028	15,851	13,346	20,264	20,766	23,959	32,249	38,136	40,433
Claims on Local Government...........	22b	—	36	1	4	500	48	39	1	7	62	50	81
Claims on Nonfin.Pub.Enterprises.....	22c	188	410	254	216	410	683	420	852	807	822	1,265	1,486
Claims on Private Sector..............	22d	13,900	21,107	36,309	44,863	51,838	55,823	58,341	58,943	59,200	48,594	48,386	52,813
Claims on Other Banking Insts........	22f	13	73	183	118	195	569	660	464	724	855	490	532
Demand Deposits......................	24	4,941	6,336	7,565	8,064	7,639	9,949	11,286	10,945	12,700	14,223	17,052	17,873
Time, Savings,& Fgn.Currency Dep....	25	28,764	36,661	44,708	49,032	53,981	57,049	61,514	69,109	72,942	76,696	81,894	88,221
Restricted Deposits.....................	26b	334	330	330	318	307	70	66	56	56	58	58	58
Foreign Liabilities.....................	26c	2,931	2,883	3,619	4,964	5,181	4,012	3,816	3,325	4,975	4,940	7,193	10,664
Central Government Deposits..........	26d	3,246	2,071	2,920	5,662	5,782	3,857	7,284	5,488	7,375	8,361	8,648	16,314
Liabilities to Other Banking Insts......	26i	1,356	1,827	2,757	3,778	5,898	5,796	8,455	8,009	9,222	10,934	11,921	9,910
Capital Accounts......................	27a	3,968	5,392	13,712	15,054	19,385	21,477	22,277	22,722	22,308	14,667	15,005	16,102
Other Items (Net).....................	27r	−4,072	−4,903	−7,079	−6,828	−9,429	−12,081	−12,302	−11,501	−11,759	−7,407	−8,369	−8,961
Monetary Survey						*Millions of Guyana Dollars: End of Period*							
Foreign Assets (Net).......................	31n	−82,644	−86,692	−40,549	−21,819	−22,278	−11,363	1,840	7,023	29,049	35,341	31,221	38,883
Domestic Credit........................	32	123,830	139,796	119,495	110,619	112,172	108,412	110,227	112,896	94,900	93,137	107,666	108,234
Claims on Central Govt. (Net)........	32an	108,630	117,360	80,307	62,178	55,908	46,581	46,058	47,927	29,452	38,094	52,764	48,612
Claims on Local Government.........	32b	—	36	1	4	500	48	39	1	7	62	50	81
Claims on Nonfin.Pub.Enterprises...	32c	1,286	1,220	2,695	3,455	3,730	5,392	5,129	5,562	5,518	5,532	5,976	6,196
Claims on Private Sector.............	32d	13,900	21,107	36,309	44,863	51,838	55,823	58,341	58,943	59,200	48,594	48,386	52,813
Claims on Other Banking Insts.......	32f	13	73	183	118	195	569	660	464	724	855	490	532
Money..............................	34	13,115	15,310	17,531	19,281	18,980	23,350	25,788	26,089	28,116	32,117	36,604	39,406
Quasi-Money..........................	35	29,100	37,222	45,197	49,780	54,675	58,268	62,660	70,029	73,507	77,389	82,469	88,846
Restricted Deposits....................	36b	334	330	330	318	307	70	66	56	56	58	58	58
Liabilities to Other Banking Insts.....	36i	1,356	1,827	2,757	3,778	5,898	5,796	8,455	8,009	9,222	10,934	11,921	9,910
Capital Accounts......................	37a	6,313	8,645	16,278	18,503	24,569	27,368	29,099	30,013	28,944	21,556	22,372	23,185
Other Items (Net).....................	37r	−9,032	−10,231	−3,146	−2,860	−14,536	−17,803	−14,000	−14,277	−15,896	−13,575	−14,536	−14,287
Money plus Quasi-Money..............	35l	42,214	52,532	62,727	69,061	73,655	81,618	88,448	96,119	101,624	109,506	119,072	128,252
Other Banking Institutions						*Millions of Guyana Dollars: End of Period*							
Cash................................	40	9	21	50	29	44	184	331	464	623	666	791	746
Foreign Assets........................	41	172	180	195	342	321	467	1,353	1,454	2,248	1,630	2,096	2,493
Claims on Central Government........	42a	3,444	3,410	4,339	5,055	5,226	4,725	5,227	7,020	7,872	9,668	9,897	11,446
Claims on Local Government...........	42b	17	17	—	—	—	—	—	—	—	—	—	—
Claims on Private Sector..............	42d	2,446	3,615	5,335	6,609	8,718	14,759	15,939	18,034	19,185	21,667	21,505	22,427
Claims on Deposit Money Banks.....	42e	131	555	460	233	287	255	1,168	1,790	2,594	2,757	2,814	2,962
Time, Savings,& Fgn.Currency Dep....	45	5,254	6,360	8,450	10,477	12,065	13,352	15,641	19,648	23,099	25,098	26,364	28,525
Foreign Liabilities.....................	46c	—	1,025	145	162	111	83	632	1,020	970	971	1,026	1,032
Capital Accounts......................	47a	778	1,078	1,990	2,658	3,515	4,721	5,358	5,828	5,735	6,567	7,090	8,022
Other Items (Net).....................	47r	188	−665	−205	−1,027	−1,095	2,234	2,386	2,265	2,718	3,751	2,622	2,494

Guyana 336

		1994	1995	1996	1997	1998	1999	2000	2001	2002	2003	2004	2005
Banking Survey					*Millions of Guyana Dollars: End of Period*								
Foreign Assets (Net)	51n	−82,472	−87,537	−40,499	−21,639	−22,068	−10,978	2,561	7,456	30,328	36,000	32,291	40,344
Domestic Credit	52	129,724	146,764	128,986	122,165	125,921	127,328	130,733	137,487	121,232	123,615	138,577	141,575
Claims on Central Govt. (Net)	52an	112,074	120,769	84,646	67,234	61,134	51,306	51,285	54,947	37,323	47,761	62,661	60,058
Claims on Local Government	52b	17	53	1	4	500	48	39	1	7	62	50	81
Claims on Nonfin.Pub.Enterprises	52c	1,286	1,220	2,695	3,455	3,730	5,392	5,129	5,562	5,518	5,532	5,976	6,196
Claims on Private Sector	52d	16,346	24,722	41,644	51,472	60,556	70,583	74,280	76,977	78,385	70,260	69,891	75,240
Liquid Liabilities	55l	47,459	58,871	71,128	79,509	85,676	94,786	103,758	115,303	124,100	133,938	144,645	156,031
Restricted Deposits	56b	334	330	330	318	307	70	66	56	56	58	58	58
Capital Accounts	57a	7,091	9,723	18,268	21,161	28,084	32,089	34,457	35,841	34,679	28,122	29,463	31,207
Other Items (Net)	57r	−7,633	−9,697	−1,238	−461	−10,215	−10,596	−4,987	−6,257	−7,274	−2,503	−3,297	−5,378
Money (National Definitions)						*Millions of Guyana Dollars: End of Period*							
Base Money	19ma	....	....	....	....	11,334	13,394	14,495	15,138	15,410	17,888	19,546	21,527
Reserve Money	19mb	....	....	....	....	27,173	26,122	29,788	33,037	36,352	40,105	43,283	48,085
M1	59ma	....	....	....	....	17,821	21,548	24,827	24,807	26,365	30,793	34,606	37,839
M2	59mb	....	....	....	....	68,696	76,980	85,445	93,035	98,147	106,259	114,495	124,011
Interest Rates						*Percent Per Annum*							
Discount Rate (End of Period)	60	20.25	17.25	12.00	11.00	11.25	13.25	11.75	8.75	6.25	5.50	6.00	6.00
Treasury Bill Rate	60c	17.66	17.51	11.35	8.91	8.33	11.31	9.88	7.78	4.94	3.04	3.62	3.79
Savings Rate	60k	9.94	10.95	8.75	7.48	7.16	7.73	7.65	7.09	5.02	3.84	3.43	3.36
Deposit Rate	60l	11.42	12.90	10.49	8.56	8.10	9.08	8.71	7.63	4.53	3.18	2.67	2.60
Lending Rate	60p	18.36	19.22	17.79	17.04	16.77	17.11	17.30	17.01	16.33	14.99	14.54	14.54
Prices					*Index Numbers (2000=100): Period Averages*								
Consumer Prices	64	67.3	75.5	80.9	83.8	87.6	94.2	100.0	102.6	108.1	114.6	119.9	127.5
Intl. Transactions & Positions						*Millions of Guyana Dollars*							
Exports	70	61,031.4	66,370.3	81,636.6	84,468.0	82,747.6	93,085.4	91,520.5	91,831.2	94,479.2	99,592.4	117,705.8	110,535.9
Imports, c.i.f.	71	70,000.6	74,911.5	83,894.8	91,062.3	90,890.3	97,497.0	106,113.3	109,251.0	109,865.3	111,692.7	129,267.9	157,833.0
						2000=100							
Volume of Exports	72	86	115	75	132	96	103	100	89	89	98	96	....
Balance of Payments					*Millions of US Dollars: Minus Sign Indicates Debit*								
Current Account, n.i.e.	78ald	−124.9	−134.8	−32.7	−63.1	−55.6	−49.5	−82.2	−95.6	−66.2	−46.9	−30.2	....
Goods: Exports f.o.b.	78aad	463.4	495.7	572.3	590.6	545.1	522.3	502.9	485.4	490.1	508.0	584.0	....
Goods: Imports f.o.b.	78abd	−504.0	−536.5	−549.8	−590.7	−552.9	−518.7	−550.1	−541.0	−513.9	−525.3	−598.1	....
Trade Balance	78acd	−40.6	−40.8	22.5	−.1	−7.8	3.6	−47.2	−55.6	−23.8	−17.3	−14.1	....
Services: Credit	78add	120.7	133.5	140.1	148.1	141.8	147.0	169.3	172.0	172.3	156.8	164.0	....
Services: Debit	78aed	−160.9	−171.8	−153.8	−165.0	−173.9	−178.1	−193.2	−192.4	−195.8	−172.1	−184.3	....
Balance on Goods & Services	78afd	−80.8	−79.2	8.8	−17.0	−39.9	−27.5	−71.1	−76.0	−47.3	−32.6	−34.4	....
Income: Credit	78agd	8.7	12.2	11.6	12.5	11.9	11.2	11.7	10.1	7.8	4.7	4.0	....
Income: Debit	78ahd	−114.8	−129.9	−94.1	−98.6	−71.6	−72.2	−69.8	−73.7	−66.7	−62.2	−46.1	....
Balance on Gds, Serv. & Inc.	78aid	−186.9	−196.8	−73.7	−103.1	−99.6	−88.5	−129.2	−139.6	−106.2	−90.1	−76.5	....
Current Transfers, n.i.e.: Credit	78ajd	68.1	67.4	69.1	67.1	74.3	76.1	100.8	98.1	128.7	127.4	139.7	....
Current Transfers: Debit	78akd	−6.2	−5.3	−28.1	−27.1	−30.3	−37.1	−53.8	−54.1	−88.7	−84.2	−93.4	....
Capital Account, n.i.e.	78bcd	8.3	9.5	—	23.7	13.1	15.5	16.3	31.9	31.1	43.8	45.9	....
Capital Account, n.i.e.: Credit	78bad	11.0	12.5	—	23.7	13.1	15.5	16.3	31.9	31.1	43.8	45.9	....
Capital Account: Debit	78bbd	−2.7	−3.0	—	....	....	....	....	....	....	....	....	....
Financial Account, n.i.e.	78bjd	126.9	71.1	69.5	96.9	65.9	52.9	110.5	84.4	54.3	35.0	−7.0	....
Direct Investment Abroad	78bdd	....	....	....	....	....	....	....	....	....	....	....	....
Dir. Invest. in Rep. Econ., n.i.e.	78bed	106.7	74.4	59.0	52.0	44.0	46.0	67.1	56.0	43.6	26.1	30.0	....
Portfolio Investment Assets	78bfd	....	....	−.4	−2.3	1.0	−17.0	3.0	−8.0	−17.0	−26.8	−16.2	....
Equity Securities	78bkd	....	....	....	....	....	....	....	....	....	....	....	....
Debt Securities	78bld	....	....	−.4	−2.3	1.0	−17.0	3.0	−8.0	−17.0	−26.8	−16.2	....
Portfolio Investment Liab., n.i.e.	78bgd	15.8	3.2	4.8	9.2	−3.0	−10.0	−12.0	−3.0	8.0	−.5	10.6	....
Equity Securities	78bmd	....	....	....	....	....	....	....	....	....	....	....	....
Debt Securities	78bnd	15.8	3.2	4.8	9.2	−3.0	−10.0	−12.0	−3.0	8.0	−.5	10.6	....
Financial Derivatives Assets	78bwd	....	....	....	....	....	....	....	....	....	....	....	....
Financial Derivatives Liabilities	78bxd	....	....	....	....	....	....	....	....	....	....	....	....
Other Investment Assets	78bhd	−5.8	−8.9	40.2	67.0	59.7	47.4	66.1	65.8	45.3	68.0	15.9	....
Monetary Authorities	78bod	....	....	....	....	....	....	....	....	....	....	....	....
General Government	78bpd	1.3	−2.2	40.2	67.0	59.7	47.4	66.1	65.8	45.3	68.0	61.4	....
Banks	78bqd	4.2	−2.8	....	....	....	....	....	....	....	....	....	....
Other Sectors	78brd	−11.2	−3.9	....	....	....	....	....	....	....	....	−45.5	....
Other Investment Liab., n.i.e.	78bid	10.2	2.3	−34.1	−29.0	−35.8	−13.5	−13.7	−26.4	−25.6	−31.8	−47.3	....
Monetary Authorities	78bsd	1.3	18.6	—	—	—	—	—	—	—	—	—	....
General Government	78btd	−1.0	−5.4	−34.1	−29.0	−45.8	−23.5	−23.7	−26.4	−25.6	−31.8	−47.3	....
Banks	78bud	−2.9	−.4	....	....	....	....	....	....	....	....	....	....
Other Sectors	78bvd	12.9	−10.5	....	....	10.0	10.0	10.0	....	....	—	....	....
Net Errors and Omissions	78cad	−16.3	11.2	−24.9	−59.1	−36.4	2.7	−4.4	5.5	−4.5	−22.1	35.9	....
Overall Balance	78cbd	−6.0	−43.0	11.9	−1.6	−13.0	21.6	40.2	26.2	14.7	9.8	44.6	....
Reserves and Related Items	79dad	6.0	43.0	−11.9	1.6	13.0	−21.6	−40.2	−26.2	−14.7	−9.8	−44.6	....
Reserve Assets	79dbd	−21.8	.8	−13.9	2.9	22.6	−11.4	−24.0	−10.4	−5.9	−.5	−33.3	....
Use of Fund Credit and Loans	79dcd	−8.8	−9.7	2.0	−1.3	−9.6	−10.2	−16.2	−15.8	−8.9	−9.3	−11.2	....
Exceptional Financing	79ded	36.6	52.0	—	....	....	....	....	....	....	....	....	....

Guyana   336

		1994	1995	1996	1997	1998	1999	2000	2001	2002	2003	2004	2005
Government Finance		*Millions of Guyana Dollars: Year Ending December 31*											
Deficit (-) or Surplus.........................	80	−5,092	−2,886	−3,115	−6,611	....	....	....	....	....	....	....	....
Total Revenue and Grants..............	81y	29,133	32,428	37,180	39,071	....	....	....	....	....	....	....	....
Revenue......................................	81	28,138	30,823	34,666	36,006	....	....	....	....	....	....	....	....
Grants..	81z	995	1,605	2,515	3,065	....	....	....	....	....	....	....	....
Exp. & Lending Minus Repay..........	82z	34,226	35,314	40,295	45,682	....	....	....	....	....	....	....	....
Expenditure................................	82	34,226	35,314	40,295	45,682	....	....	....	....	....	....	....	....
Lending Minus Repayments..........	83	—	—	—	—	....	....	....	....	....	....	....	....
Total Financing...............................	80h	5,092	2,886	3,115	6,611	....	....	....	....	....	....	....	....
Total Net Borrowing.....................	84	−699	2,826	−931	4,310	....	....	....	....	....	....	....	....
Net Domestic...............................	84a	−4,394	1,627	−7,298	−162	....	....	....	....	....	....	....	....
Net Foreign.................................	85a	3,695	1,199	6,367	4,473	....	....	....	....	....	....	....	....
Use of Cash Balances...................	87	5,791	60	4,046	2,301	....	....	....	....	....	....	....	....
Total Debt..	88	316,419	322,444	249,167	258,325	....	....	....	....	....	....	....	....
Domestic......................................	88a	31,490	33,252	37,478	35,888	....	....	....	....	....	....	....	....
Foreign..	89a	284,929	289,191	211,688	222,436	....	....	....	....	....	....	....	....
National Accounts		*Millions of Guyana Dollars*											
Househ.Cons.Expend.,incl.NPISHs....	96f	36,131	40,897	44,224	47,147	....	....	....	74,008	70,287	71,615	85,100	....
Government Consumption Expend...	91f	11,817	14,092	17,330	21,747	....	....	....	30,505	32,976	37,928	37,732	....
Gross Fixed Capital Formation..........	93e	34,348	40,077	43,436	47,099	....	....	....	....	....	....	....	....
Exports of Goods and Services..........	90c	59,185	70,315	82,155	84,375	....	....	....	....	....	....	....	....
Imports of Goods and Services (-).....	98c	64,370	74,912	83,895	91,749	....	....	....	....	....	....	....	....
Gross Domestic Product (GDP).........	99b	75,412	88,271	99,038	106,678	108,002	120,668	130,013	133,404	138,448	144,064	156,358	....
Net Primary Income from Abroad.....	98.n	−11,473	−12,203	−7,319	−10,406	....	....	....	....	....	....	....	....
Gross National Income (GNI)............	99a	63,939	76,068	91,719	95,399	....	....	....	....	....	....	....	....
Net National Income.......................	99e	63,939	76,068	91,719	95,399	....	....	....	....	....	....	....	....
GDP Volume 1988 Prices.................	99b.p	4,452	4,677	5,048	5,360	5,270	5,426	5,352	5,474	5,536	5,501	5,639	....
GDP Volume (2000=100)...............	99bvp	83.2	87.4	94.3	100.1	98.5	101.4	100.0	102.3	103.4	102.8	105.4	....
GDP Deflator (2000=100)...............	99bip	69.7	77.7	80.8	81.9	84.4	91.5	100.0	100.3	102.9	107.8	114.1	....
		Millions: Midyear Estimates											
Population...............................	99z	.73	.73	.73	.74	.74	.74	.74	.75	.75	.75	.75	.75

Haiti 263

		1994	1995	1996	1997	1998	1999	2000	2001	2002	2003	2004	2005
Exchange Rates		*Gourdes per SDR: End of Period*											
Market Rate........................	aa	18.900	24.022	21.703	23.357	23.239	24.658	29.347	33.101	51.130	62.537	57.821	61.459
		Gourdes per US Dollar: End of Period (ae) Period Average (rf)											
Market Rate........................	ae	12.947	16.160	15.093	17.311	16.505	17.965	22.524	26.339	37.609	42.085	37.232	43.000
Market Rate........................	rf	15.040	15.110	15.701	16.655	16.766	16.938	21.171	24.429	29.250	42.367	38.352	40.449
Fund Position		*Millions of SDRs: End of Period*											
Quota..............................	2f.s	44.1	60.7	60.7	60.7	60.7	60.7	60.7	60.7	60.7	81.9	81.9	81.9
SDRs...............................	1b.s	—	.4	—	.1	.4	.6	.1	.4	.4	.2	.1	8.6
Reserve Position in the Fund............	1c.s	—	—	—	—	—	—	.1	.1	.1	.1	.1	.1
Total Fund Cred.&Loans Outstg........	2tl	3.8	18.2	31.6	31.6	40.8	32.6	30.4	30.4	19.7	9.1	6.1	23.5
International Liquidity		*Millions of US Dollars Unless Otherwise Indicated: End of Period*											
Total Reserves minus Gold..............	1l.d	51.1	191.6	216.1	207.1	258.2	264.0	182.1	141.4	81.7	62.0	114.4	133.1
SDRs...............................	1b.d	—	.5	.1	.1	.5	.9	.1	.5	.5	.3	.2	12.3
Reserve Position in the Fund.........	1c.d	.1	.1	.1	.1	.1	.1	.1	.1	.1	.1	.1	.1
Foreign Exchange....................	1d.d	51.0	191.0	216.0	206.9	257.6	263.1	182.0	140.8	81.1	61.6	114.1	120.7
Gold (Million Fine Troy Ounces)........	1ad	.019	.019	.019	.020	.020	.001	.001	.001	.001	.001	.001	.001
Monetary Authorities: Other Liab.....	4..d	48.3	20.6	82.1	59.6	60.4	60.7	61.4	62.2	61.1	63.8	65.9	68.3
Deposit Money Banks: Assets..........	7a.d	96.1	98.1	114.9	133.1	124.4	150.7	199.1	177.0	137.8	237.1	243.8	287.4
Liabilities................	7b.d	.8	4.9	6.9	17.9	8.3	16.7	21.8	18.7	20.8	26.7	38.5	31.7
Monetary Authorities		*Millions of Gourdes: End of Period*											
Foreign Assets.......................	11	273.4	3,073.7	3,988.0	† 4,757.2	5,308.4	5,916.0	5,549.2	6,988.4	7,274.7	8,684.2	10,720.0	13,139.9
Claims on Central Government........	12a	5,860.7	7,074.0	7,238.8	† 7,668.1	8,273.3	10,302.3	11,802.0	13,846.8	17,920.5	22,663.1	24,618.8	25,812.0
Claims on Local Government..........	12b			12.9	† 8.5	5.0	1.7	.6					
Claims on Nonfin.Pub.Enterprises.....	12c	328.1	152.1	80.8	† 50.9	85.5	84.5	1,820.3	1,996.3	2,155.5	2,162.9	2,116.8	2,108.6
Claims on Private Sector............	12d	—		141.2	† 163.5	233.1	304.2	358.8	452.9	543.7	721.9	1,000.8	1,120.0
Claims on Deposit Money Banks......	12e	415.6	65.0	70.2	† 129.2	106.2	264.6	228.5	93.1	423.7	813.5	91.2	292.5
Claims on Other Banking Insts.......	12f	—	28.6		† —								
Claims on Nonbank Financial Insts...	12g	—		4.7	† 22.4	19.8	13.9	12.0	9.8	7.7	5.2	2.6	—
Reserve Money.......................	14	6,954.9	7,975.8	7,645.1	† 7,653.3	7,672.5	9,894.3	12,452.2	14,556.2	18,038.3	23,702.1	28,011.4	29,037.3
of which: Currency Outside DMBs..	14a	3,029.5	3,536.7	3,435.7	† 3,935.4	3,905.4	4,927.1	5,807.2	6,584.3	8,687.5	9,843.2	10,218.3	12,218.3
Time, Savings,& Fgn.Currency Dep...	15	—	—	—	† 8.4	37.3	55.9	84.0	101.8	122.0	36.7	310.4	222.1
Liabs. of Central Bank: Securities.....	16ac	—	—	—	† 857.0	1,980.0	2,335.0	944.0	2,432.0	2,563.0	4,996.0	3,544.0	6,113.1
Foreign Liabilities....................	16c	136.0	768.7	1,595.1	† 1,768.4	1,944.1	1,893.6	2,273.8	2,643.1	3,306.9	3,253.0	2,805.4	4,379.7
Central Government Deposits..........	16d	892.7	1,983.0	1,617.2	† 1,514.2	1,647.6	1,895.3	1,125.1	1,093.7	1,440.9	2,005.7	3,813.6	3,290.2
Capital Accounts.....................	17a	564.0	1,139.1	857.2	† 1,266.5	1,313.1	1,566.8	3,974.8	4,143.9	4,504.9	3,656.1	2,692.1	2,306.1
Other Items (Net).....................	17r	−1,669.8	−1,473.3	−178.0	† −268.1	−563.6	−753.7	−1,082.6	−1,583.5	−1,650.2	−2,598.8	−2,626.8	−2,875.6
Deposit Money Banks		*Millions of Gourdes: End of Period*											
Reserves.............................	20	3,718.1	3,608.0	3,979.8	† 3,323.6	3,411.0	4,394.1	6,297.4	7,713.6	8,805.2	12,936.4	17,140.4	15,503.8
Claims on Mon.Author.:Securities.....	20c	—	—	—	† 857.0	1,980.0	2,335.0	944.0	2,432.0	2,563.0	4,996.0	3,544.0	6,113.1
Foreign Assets.......................	21	1,243.6	1,584.9	1,734.2	† 2,303.9	2,053.8	2,706.8	4,484.6	4,662.5	5,183.1	9,979.6	9,076.6	12,358.8
Claims on Central Government........	22a	114.1	11.3	6.5	† 6.5	6.5	169.3	164.3	99.3	59.3	—	—	222.0
Claims on Private Sector..................	22d	3,253.2	5,072.4	5,825.0	† 8,511.2	9,156.2	10,128.9	12,074.3	12,914.0	16,785.7	20,448.6	20,859.4	25,477.2
Claims on Other Banking Insts.........	22f	—	—	—	† —	—	—	170.0	—				
Demand Deposits....................	24	1,578.0	2,372.7	2,211.1	† 2,435.2	2,544.2	3,241.3	3,251.2	3,749.2	4,394.7	6,142.5	7,145.5	8,355.9
Time, Savings,& Fgn.Currency Dep...	25	6,486.8	8,018.7	9,064.7	† 11,499.7	13,209.8	15,997.4	20,102.3	22,847.1	27,582.9	41,036.9	41,942.6	49,440.1
Bonds.............................	26ab	—	—	—	† 46.1	44.9	21.9	113.6	148.2	385.2	481.9	685.4	948.5
Foreign Liabilities....................	26c	10.7	78.6	104.5	† 310.3	136.4	299.8	490.4	492.9	782.1	1,124.7	1,433.4	1,363.3
Central Government Deposits..........	26d	27.6	37.5	54.5	† 514.7	475.1	402.9	257.2	157.5	80.3	361.9	322.3	930.0
Credit from Monetary Authorities.....	26g	—	72.6	81.9	† 49.0	42.8	134.7	72.1	32.1	293.0	33.0	3.0	3.0
Capital Accounts.....................	27a	395.7	525.7	946.2	† 1,060.5	1,314.2	1,346.0	1,752.2	2,050.9	2,343.3	3,067.5	3,112.9	3,761.6
Other Items (Net).....................	27r	−169.8	−829.1	−917.4	† −913.2	−1,159.9	−1,709.9	−1,904.3	−1,656.4	−2,465.2	−3,887.7	−4,024.7	−5,127.5
Monetary Survey		*Millions of Gourdes: End of Period*											
Foreign Assets (Net)......................	31n	1,370.3	3,811.3	4,022.6	† 4,982.4	5,281.4	6,429.4	7,269.6	8,514.9	8,368.7	14,286.2	15,557.8	19,755.7
Domestic Credit.....................	32	8,440.9	10,317.9	11,638.2	† 14,402.1	15,656.7	18,706.6	25,020.0	28,067.9	35,951.2	43,634.2	44,462.5	50,519.6
Claims on Central Govt. (Net)........	32an	4,861.4	5,064.8	5,573.6	† 5,645.7	6,157.1	8,173.4	10,584.0	12,694.9	16,458.6	20,295.6	20,482.9	21,813.8
Claims on Local Government..........	32b			12.9	† 8.5	5.0	1.7	.6					
Claims on Nonfin.Pub.Enterprises...	32c	326.3	152.1	80.8	† 50.9	85.5	84.5	1,820.3	1,996.3	2,155.5	2,162.9	2,116.8	2,108.6
Claims on Private Sector............	32d	3,253.2	5,072.4	5,966.2	† 8,674.6	9,389.3	10,433.0	12,433.1	13,367.0	17,329.4	21,170.5	21,860.2	26,597.2
Claims on Other Banking Insts.......	32f	—	28.6	—	† —	—	—	170.0	—				
Claims on Nonbank Financial Inst..	32g	—		4.7	† 22.4	19.8	13.9	12.0	9.8	7.7	5.2	2.6	—
Money..............................	34	5,095.5	6,703.9	5,823.9	† 6,633.5	6,650.9	8,422.8	9,220.2	10,610.2	13,501.5	16,222.1	18,047.4	21,341.8
Quasi-Money.........................	35	6,486.8	8,018.7	9,064.7	† 11,508.1	13,247.1	16,053.3	20,186.3	22,948.9	27,704.8	41,073.6	42,253.0	49,662.2
Bonds..............................	36ab	—	—	—	† 46.1	44.9	21.9	113.6	148.2	385.2	481.9	685.4	948.5
Capital Accounts.....................	37a	959.7	1,664.7	1,803.4	† 2,327.0	2,627.3	2,912.7	5,727.0	6,194.8	6,848.1	6,723.6	5,805.0	6,067.8
Other Items (Net).....................	37r	−2,730.8	−2,258.1	−1,031.3	† −1,130.1	−1,632.1	−2,274.8	−2,957.5	−3,319.3	−4,119.7	−6,580.9	−6,770.6	−7,745.0
Money plus Quasi-Money............	35l	11,582.3	14,722.5	14,888.6	† 18,141.5	19,898.0	24,476.2	29,406.4	33,559.1	41,206.3	57,295.7	60,300.4	71,004.0
Money (National Definitions)		*Millions of Gourdes: End of Period*											
Reserve Money......................	19mb	....	....	....	8,518.6	9,689.8	12,285.2	13,480.1	17,090.0	20,723.2	28,734.8	31,865.8	35,372.5
M1..................................	59ma	....	....	....	6,357.8	6,445.4	8,153.1	9,052.1	10,313.2	13,065.8	15,959.2	17,361.2	20,488.4
M2..................................	59mb	....	....	....	13,783.7	14,783.8	17,666.3	20,069.5	21,921.6	26,191.6	33,215.7	36,445.6	40,489.3
M3..................................	59mc	....	....	....	17,903.6	19,563.8	24,152.9	29,140.7	33,174.1	40,922.5	57,217.6	59,702.6	70,754.7
Interest Rates		*Percent per Annum*											
Treasury Bill Rate...........................	60c	....	....	....	14.13	16.21	7.71	12.33	13.53	7.56	20.50	12.24	8.29
Savings Rate..............................	60k	....	....	....	5.36	5.50	3.51	3.57	3.35	2.52	3.01	2.22	1.15
Savings Rate (Foreign Currency)........	60k.f	....	....	....	....	....	....	....	1.73	1.47	1.38	1.25	.65
Deposit Rate..............................	60l	....	....	....	10.74	13.06	7.39	11.85	13.66	8.24	13.99	10.79	3.39
Deposit Rate (Foreign Currency).......	60l.f	....	....	....	....	....	....	....	4.66	2.83	3.39	2.77	2.87
Lending Rate..............................	60p	....	....	....	21.00	23.62	22.88	25.09	28.63	25.67	30.58	34.08	27.38
Lending Rate (Foreign Currency).......	60p.f	....	....	....	....	....	....	....	14.76	12.23	13.92	14.13	13.13
Prices		*Index Numbers (2000=100): Period Averages*											
Consumer Prices.........................	64	39.4	50.3	60.7	73.1	80.9	87.9	100.0	114.2	125.4	174.7	† 214.5	248.5

Haiti 263

		1994	1995	1996	1997	1998	1999	2000	2001	2002	2003	2004	2005
Intl. Transactions & Positions						*Millions of Gourdes*							
Exports...............................	70	1,236.7	1,666.5	1,413.9	3,537.1	5,365.0	5,661.3	6,725.3	6,700.7	8,203.0	14,682.2	15,006.8	19,016.9
Imports, c.i.f..........................	71	3,783.6	9,866.2	10,448.2	10,792.1	13,365.6	17,366.9	21,936.2	24,745.7	33,060.7	50,323.7	50,087.8	58,801.7
Balance of Payments						*Millions of US Dollars: F.Y. Ending Sept 30; Minus Sign Indicates Debit*							
Current Account, n.i.e..............	78ald	−23.4	−87.1	−137.7	−47.7	28.7	−59.8	−85.2	−94.6	−47.6	−13.1	....	....
Goods: Exports f.o.b...............	78aad	60.3	88.3	82.5	205.4	294.8	343.3	331.7	305.2	274.4	333.2	....	....
Goods: Imports f.o.b...............	78abd	−171.5	−517.2	−498.6	−559.6	−822.1	−1,017.5	−1,086.7	−1,055.4	−980.4	−1,115.8	....	....
Trade Balance......................	78acd	−111.2	−428.9	−416.1	−354.2	−527.3	−674.3	−755.0	−750.2	−706.0	−782.7	....	....
Services: Credit.....................	78add	6.7	104.1	109.1	173.7	179.0	188.0	172.0	139.0	148.0	136.0	....	....
Services: Debit......................	78aed	−63.9	−284.5	−283.3	−331.5	−218.5	−234.6	−264.0	−242.5	−251.6	−259.0	....	....
Balance on Goods & Services.......	78afd	−168.4	−609.3	−590.3	−512.0	−566.7	−720.9	−847.0	−853.7	−809.6	−905.7	....	....
Income: Credit......................	78agd				....							....	....
Income: Debit.......................	78ahd	−11.2	−30.6	−9.9	−13.6	−11.1	−12.6	−9.2	−9.5	−13.7	−14.3	....	....
Balance on Gds, Serv. & Inc......	78aid	−179.6	−639.9	−600.2	−525.6	−577.8	−733.5	−856.2	−863.1	−823.3	−919.9	....	....
Current Transfers, n.i.e.: Credit......	78ajd	156.2	552.9	462.5	477.9	606.5	673.7	771.0	768.6	775.7	906.8	....	....
Current Transfers: Debit...........	78akd	—	—	—	—	—	—	—	—	—	—	....	....
Capital Account, n.i.e..............	78bcd	—	—	....	....	—	—	—	—	—	—	....	....
Capital Account, n.i.e.: Credit.......	78bad	—	—	....	....	—	—	—	—	—	—	....	....
Capital Account: Debit.............	78bbd	—	....	....	....	—	—	—	—	—	—	....	....
Financial Account, n.i.e............	78bjd	−15.8	99.2	67.9	61.5	186.8	85.3	−16.0	82.5	−17.3	−76.5	....	....
Direct Investment Abroad..........	78bdd	—	....	....	....	—	—	—	—	—	—	....	....
Dir. Invest. in Rep. Econ., n.i.e.......	78bed	—	7.4	4.1	4.0	10.8	30.0	13.3	4.4	5.7	7.8	....	....
Portfolio Investment Assets..........	78bfd	—	....	....	....	—	—	—	—	—	—	....	....
Equity Securities..................	78bkd	—	....	....	....	—	—	—	—	—	—	....	....
Debt Securities....................	78bld	—	....	....	....	—	—	—	—	—	—	....	....
Portfolio Investment Liab., n.i.e....	78bgd	—	....	....	....	—	—	—	—	—	—	....	....
Equity Securities..................	78bmd	—	....	....	....	—	—	—	—	—	—	....	....
Debt Securities....................	78bnd	—	....	....	....	—	—	—	—	—	—	....	....
Financial Derivatives Assets........	78bwd	....	....	....	....	....	....	....	....	....	....	....	....
Financial Derivatives Liabilities.......	78bxd	....	....	....	....	....	....	....	....	....	....	....	....
Other Investment Assets............	78bhd	−5.5	−11.2	−4.6	21.6	86.8	−15.3	−43.3	−3.0	27.3	−98.0	....	....
Monetary Authorities..............	78bod	....	....	....	....	—	—	—	—	—	—	....	....
General Government...............	78bpd	—	—	—	—	—	2.0	−5.4	2.8	.1	−.6	....	....
Banks...............................	78bqd	−5.5	−11.2	−4.6	3.6	2.8	−3.4	−63.9	17.2	−.8	−50.3	....	....
Other Sectors.....................	78brd	—	—	—	18.0	84.0	−14.0	26.0	−23.0	28.0	−47.0	....	....
Other Investment Liab., n.i.e.......	78bid	−10.3	103.1	68.4	35.9	89.2	70.6	14.0	81.1	−50.3	13.7	....	....
Monetary Authorities..............	78bsd	2.1				—	—	—	—	—	—	....	....
General Government...............	78btd	−12.4	112.5	68.8	37.7	37.7	71.9	22.4	−3.0	−46.6	5.1	....	....
Banks...............................	78bud	—	.4	−.4	12.3	−4.6	−.5	8.8	−.9	4.2	1.3	....	....
Other Sectors.....................	78bvd	—	−9.8	.1	−14.1	56.0	−.7	−17.2	85.0	−7.8	7.3	....	....
Net Errors and Omissions............	78cad	−10.5	125.9	19.5	16.1	−181.3	1.0	44.3	6.9	−3.1	85.0	....	....
Overall Balance....................	78cbd	−49.7	138.1	−50.4	29.9	34.2	26.5	−56.9	−5.2	−67.9	−4.6	....	....
Reserves and Related Items.............	79dad	49.7	−138.1	50.4	−29.9	−34.2	−26.5	56.9	5.2	67.9	4.6	....	....
Reserve Assets......................	79dbd	12.8	−175.6	48.5	−50.6	−28.9	−36.5	57.3	−5.3	49.0	22.1	....	....
Use of Fund Credit and Loans........	79dcd	—	−6.6	−2.6	20.6	−5.3	10.0	−5.8	—	−9.2	−14.5	....	....
Exceptional Financing...............	79ded	36.9	44.1	4.4	....	—	—	5.5	10.5	28.2	−3.0	....	....
International Investment Position						*Millions of US Dollars*							
Assets...............................	79aad	....	....	....	....	493.3	545.1	531.1	539.3	463.7	539.6	....	....
Direct Investment Abroad...............	79abd	....	....	....	....	—	—	—	—	—	—	....	....
Portfolio Investment..................	79acd	....	....	....	....	—	—	—	—	—	—	....	....
Equity Securities..................	79add	....	....	....	....	—	—	—	—	—	—	....	....
Debt Securities....................	79aed	....	....	....	....	—	—	—	—	—	—	....	....
Financial Derivatives.................	79ald	....	....	....	....	—	—	—	—	—	—	....	....
Other Investment.....................	79afd	....	....	....	....	200.6	215.9	259.2	262.2	234.9	332.9	....	....
Monetary Authorities..............	79agd	....	....	....	....	—	—	—	—	—	—	....	....
General Government...............	79ahd	....	....	....	....	—	—	—	—	—	—	....	....
Banks...............................	79aid	....	....	....	....	121.5	124.9	188.8	171.6	172.4	222.7	....	....
Other Sectors.....................	79ajd	....	....	....	....	79.1	91.1	70.4	90.6	62.5	110.2	....	....
Reserve Assets......................	79akd	....	....	....	....	292.7	329.2	271.9	277.0	228.8	206.7	....	....
Liabilities............................	79lad	....	....	....	....	1,327.7	1,427.8	1,437.9	1,536.8	1,553.5	1,634.1	....	....
Dir. Invest. in Rep. Economy........	79lbd	....	....	....	....	51.5	81.5	94.7	99.1	104.8	112.6	....	....
Portfolio Investment..................	79lcd	....	....	....	....	—	—	—	—	—	—	....	....
Equity Securities..................	79ldd	....	....	....	....	—	—	—	—	—	—	....	....
Debt Securities....................	79led	....	....	....	....	—	—	—	—	—	—	....	....
Financial Derivatives.................	79lld	....	....	....	....	—	—	—	—	—	—	....	....
Other Investment.....................	79lfd	....	....	....	....	1,276.3	1,346.4	1,343.3	1,437.8	1,448.7	1,521.6	....	....
Monetary Authorities..............	79lgd	....	....	....	....	98.0	108.6	99.8	100.9	92.5	81.3	....	....
General Government...............	79lhd	....	....	....	....	1,104.2	1,165.6	1,179.6	1,188.9	1,211.9	1,287.4	....	....
Banks...............................	79lid	....	....	....	....	12.7	12.2	21.0	20.0	24.2	25.5	....	....
Other Sectors.....................	79ljd	....	....	....	....	61.4	60.1	42.9	127.9	120.1	127.4	....	....
Government Finance						*Millions of Gourdes: Year Ending September 30*							
Deficit (-) or Surplus...................	80	−947.1	−986.1	−329.5	−320.5	−776.5	−1,647.7	−1,774.1	−1,887.0	−2,542.3	−3,363.9	−4,674.9	....
Revenue..............................	81	874.8	2,456.0	3,436.1	4,781.8	5,330.0	6,211.2	6,169.4	6,332.2	7,721.7	10,502.5	12,469.0	....
Grants Received......................	81z	2.2	696.7	354.3	694.6	644.7	47.0	197.2	369.8	112.7	283.3	21.0	....
Expenditure..........................	82	1,824.1	4,138.8	4,119.9	5,796.9	6,751.2	7,905.9	8,140.7	8,589.0	10,376.7	14,149.7	17,164.9	....
Financing													
Net Domestic Borrowing..............	84a	1,109.6	885.7	650.4	223.7	431.5	1,900.1	1,529.9	2,143.8	2,874.7	3,478.4	4,565.1	....
Monetary Authorities.................	84aa	1,109.6	885.7	650.4	223.7	591.5	1,799.6	1,566.1	2,148.0	2,912.3	3,795.7	4,678.9	....
Other..............................	84ac	—	—	—	—	−160.0	100.5	−36.2	−4.2	−37.6	−317.3	−113.8	....
Net Foreign Borrowing..............	85a	—	1,031.3	−260.7	−272.0	−421.7	−577.5	−389.5	−309.6	−277.2	−743.3	−969.9	....
Use of Cash Balances...................	87	−88.1	−975.8	−28.4	−327.3	85.5	−544.4	371.5	233.3	−20.8	19.3	−1,784.0	....
Adjustment to Financing..............	84x	−74.4	44.9	−31.8	696.1	681.2	869.5	262.2	−180.5	−34.4	609.5	2,863.7	....

Haiti   263

		1994	1995	1996	1997	1998	1999	2000	2001	2002	2003	2004	2005
National Accounts					*Millions of Gourdes: Year Ending September 30*								
Househ.Cons.Expend.,incl.NPISHs....	**96f**	31,310	38,167	41,719	49,393	57,148	62,157	72,446	83,921	92,906	121,371	142,230	162,292
Gross Fixed Capital Formation..........	**93e**	1,857	4,867	13,122	13,247	16,382	19,182	21,208	22,158	23,570	36,758	38,386	46,072
Exports of Goods and Services..........	**90c**	1,942	3,845	5,284	5,646	6,237	8,482	9,849	10,594	11,403	18,946	21,555	24,222
Imports of Goods and Services (-).....	**98c**	4,173	11,634	13,479	14,280	16,770	20,568	25,923	30,973	33,851	57,317	61,784	64,552
Gross Domestic Product (GDP).........	**99b**	30,936	35,265	46,647	54,005	62,997	69,254	77,580	85,700	94,028	119,758	140,387	168,034
GDP Volume 1976 Prices.................	**99b.p**	4,150	4,334	4,451	....	....	....	....	....	....	....	....	....
GDP Volume 1987 Prices.................	**99b.p**	....	....	12,083	12,410	12,681	13,025	13,138	13,001	12,968	13,015	12,558	12,783
GDP Volume (2000=100).................	**99bvp**	85.8	89.6	† 92.0	94.5	96.5	99.1	100.0	99.0	98.7	99.1	95.6	97.3
GDP Deflator (2000=100)................	**99bip**	46.5	50.8	65.4	73.7	84.1	90.0	100.0	111.6	122.8	155.8	189.3	222.6
					Millions: Midyear Estimates								
Population.............................	**99z**	7.29	7.39	7.50	7.60	7.71	7.83	7.94	8.05	8.17	8.29	8.41	8.53

		1994	1995	1996	1997	1998	1999	2000	2001	2002	2003	2004	2005
Exchange Rates						*Lempiras per SDR: End of Period*							
Market Rate	aa	13.7227	15.3751	18.5057	17.6673	19.4415	19.9067	19.7270	20.0068	23.0076	26.3733	28.9369	27.0063
						Lempiras per US Dollar: End of Period (ae) Period Average (rf)							
Market Rate	ae	9.4001	10.3432	12.8694	13.0942	13.8076	14.5039	15.1407	15.9197	16.9233	17.7482	18.6328	18.8952
Market Rate	rf	8.4088	9.4710	11.7053	13.0035	13.3850	14.2132	14.8392	15.4737	16.4334	17.3453	18.2062	18.8323
Fund Position						*Millions of SDRs: End of Period*							
Quota	2f.s	95.00	95.00	95.00	95.00	95.00	129.50	129.50	129.50	129.50	129.50	129.50	129.50
SDRs	1b.s	.15	.10	.06	.06	.05	.68	.08	.25	.35	.08	.06	.20
Reserve Position in the Fund	1c.s	—	—	—	—	—	8.63	8.63	8.63	8.63	8.63	8.63	8.63
Total Fund Cred.&Loans Outstg	2tl	74.81	66.36	40.28	33.90	80.04	153.33	165.75	175.12	144.59	115.42	125.71	117.63
International Liquidity						*Millions of US Dollars Unless Otherwise Indicated: End of Period*							
Total Reserves minus Gold	1l.d	171.01	261.45	249.19	580.37	818.07	1,257.58	1,313.04	1,415.56	1,524.10	1,430.03	1,970.38	2,327.21
SDRs	1b.d	.21	.15	.09	.07	.07	.94	.10	.32	.47	.11	.09	.28
Reserve Position in the Fund	1c.d	—	—	—	—	—	11.84	11.24	10.84	11.73	12.82	13.40	12.33
Foreign Exchange	1d.d	170.80	261.30	249.10	580.30	818.00	1,244.80	1,301.70	1,404.40	1,511.90	1,417.10	1,956.90	2,314.60
Gold (Million Fine Troy Ounces)	1ad	.021	.021	.021	.021	.021	.021	.021	.021	.021	.021	.021	.021
Gold (National Valuation)	1and	8.30	8.41	8.03	6.43	6.25	6.28	5.99	6.05	7.11	9.26	9.93	11.34
Monetary Authorities: Other Liab	4..d	599.86	595.09	509.27	379.96	361.89	443.44	427.88	412.08	400.10	396.09	409.23	369.83
Deposit Money Banks: Assets	7a.d	84.32	123.47	209.97	228.00	275.70	379.81	451.94	487.77	565.46	551.08	657.10	668.32
Liabilities	7b.d	68.89	103.20	154.84	271.39	344.95	297.64	272.02	228.04	230.62	221.51	400.94	450.00
Other Banking Insts.: Assets	7e.d	10.20	9.29	12.39	8.06	6.80	7.67	11.77	11.42	10.01	8.25	6.62	8.99
Liabilities	7f.d	15.80	16.49	13.01	15.80	17.19	9.84	38.26	56.86	39.01	23.75	14.44	10.67
Monetary Authorities						*Millions of Lempiras: End of Period*							
Foreign Assets	11	1,930	3,058	3,641	† 10,437	14,282	21,375	23,151	25,978	29,586	29,402	40,945	48,291
Claims on Central Government	12a	1,512	1,284	1,220	† 1,462	1,534	1,014	1,109	935	919	2,296	1,182	901
Claims on Local Government	12b	60	53	92	† 48	45	42	39	36	33	29	26	22
Claims on Private Sector	12d	58	64	58	† 1	1	1	1	1	—	—	—	—
Claims on Deposit Money Banks	12e	678	616	721	† 136	99	60	33	215	5	269	—	100
Claims on Other Banking Insts	12f	569	572	555	† 157	108	108	97	74	61	49	38	22
Reserve Money	14	2,723	3,373	4,842	† 9,045	10,501	11,720	12,813	14,071	17,762	18,935	26,262	34,389
of which: Currency Outside DMBs	14a	1,995	2,111	2,630	† 3,315	3,744	4,714	4,727	5,166	5,549	6,448	7,639	8,962
Time, Savings,& Fgn.Currency Dep	15	86	318	219	† 791	503	1,582	3,599	5,979	6,662	7,501	9,121	11,155
Foreign Liabilities	16c	6,479	6,654	6,672	† 4,975	5,920	7,377	7,415	7,510	7,317	7,030	7,625	6,988
Central Government Deposits	16d	1,229	1,562	2,042	† 2,878	4,766	7,409	6,112	4,834	5,081	5,222	6,674	5,532
Capital Accounts	17a	1,422	1,762	1,930	† 1,623	908	945	973	1,080	1,136	1,457	3,015	2,855
Other Items (Net)	17r	−7,133	−8,022	−9,419	† −7,072	−6,528	−6,432	−6,483	−6,236	−7,353	−8,099	−10,508	−11,583
Deposit Money Banks						*Millions of Lempiras: End of Period*							
Reserves	20	668	1,118	1,968	† 5,021	6,018	6,374	7,134	8,091	11,269	11,042	16,312	22,633
Foreign Assets	21	793	1,277	2,702	† 2,985	3,807	5,509	6,843	7,765	9,570	9,781	12,244	12,628
Claims on Central Government	22a	1,287	1,205	867	† 275	77	41	370	732	935	1,260	1,745	2,069
Claims on Local Government	22b	1	10	15	† 54	147	125	136	79	255	354	500	645
Claims on Private Sector	22d	6,364	7,711	10,966	† 16,744	23,247	28,014	32,021	35,524	38,001	45,208	52,558	62,603
Claims on Other Banking Insts	22f	37	55	29	† 26	43	473	195	280	391	3,674	3,503	3,239
Demand Deposits	24	1,761	2,368	3,074	† 4,287	4,841	5,666	6,180	6,344	7,658	9,315	9,840	12,020
Time, Savings,& Fgn. Currency Dep	25	4,287	5,626	8,721	† 13,657	18,094	22,228	27,819	32,585	37,027	42,288	51,805	62,247
Bonds	26ab	14	29	33	† 61	90	58	50	42	33	66	41	35
Foreign Liabilities	26c	648	1,067	1,993	† 3,554	4,763	4,317	4,119	3,630	3,903	3,931	7,471	8,503
Central Government Deposits	26d	300	270	331	† 1,059	2,004	2,846	2,457	2,103	2,651	2,491	2,679	3,667
Credit from Monetary Authorities	26g	691	619	760	† 156	90	60	33	215	11	269	—	100
Liabilities to Other Banking Insts	26i	....	....	....	833	1,453	2,575	2,897	3,421	3,205	5,266	4,948	4,754
Capital Accounts	27a	1,670	2,224	2,846	† 3,885	4,876	5,958	7,168	8,343	8,888	9,860	12,264	14,384
Other Items (Net)	27r	−222	−829	−1,212	† −2,385	−2,872	−3,173	−4,024	−4,212	−2,956	−2,168	−2,185	−1,894
Monetary Survey						*Millions of Lempiras: End of Period*							
Foreign Assets (Net)	31n	−4,404	−3,386	−2,322	† 4,894	7,406	15,190	18,460	22,602	27,936	28,222	38,092	45,428
Domestic Credit	32	8,359	9,122	11,427	† 14,830	18,432	19,563	25,397	30,724	32,863	45,158	50,197	60,301
Claims on Central Govt. (Net)	32an	1,270	657	−287	† −2,200	−5,158	−9,200	−7,091	−5,271	−5,877	−4,157	−6,427	−6,229
Claims on Local Government	32b	61	63	107	† 102	192	168	175	116	288	383	526	666
Claims on Private Sector	32d	6,422	7,775	11,024	† 16,745	23,247	28,015	32,021	35,525	38,001	45,208	52,558	62,603
Claims on Other Banking Insts	32f	606	627	583	† 183	151	581	292	354	452	3,723	3,541	3,261
Money	34	3,845	4,678	6,053	† 8,294	9,349	11,050	11,954	12,388	14,224	17,251	20,019	24,093
Quasi-Money	35	4,374	5,945	8,941	† 14,448	18,597	23,810	31,418	38,564	43,689	49,789	60,926	73,402
Bonds	36ab	14	29	33	† 61	90	58	50	42	33	66	41	35
Liabilities to Other Banking Insts	36i	....	....	....	833	1,453	2,575	2,897	3,421	3,205	5,266	4,948	4,754
Capital Accounts	37a	3,093	3,986	4,775	† 5,509	5,784	6,903	8,141	9,423	10,024	11,317	15,279	17,239
Other Items (Net)	37r	−7,370	−8,902	−10,697	† −9,420	−9,436	−9,643	−10,602	−10,512	−10,375	−10,310	−12,923	−13,794
Money plus Quasi-Money	35l	8,219	10,623	14,994	† 22,742	27,946	34,860	43,371	50,952	57,913	67,040	80,945	97,495
Other Banking Institutions						*Millions of Lempiras: End of Period*							
Reserves	40	139	124	121	† 661	759	654	1,057	945	1,089	1,507	2,552	3,136
Foreign Assets	41	96	96	160	† 106	94	111	178	182	169	146	123	170
Claims on Central Government	42a	110	137	156	† 294	79	54	46	209	304	2,090	1,600	1,286
Claims on Local Government	42b	86	93	95	† 136	131	112	110	99	55	51	51	51
Claims on Private Sector	42d	1,261	1,529	1,507	† 3,044	3,337	3,969	4,363	5,282	5,904	4,085	4,388	4,737
Claims on Deposit Money Banks	42e	27	38	34	† 881	1,462	2,597	2,918	3,463	3,300	5,321	4,983	4,804
Demand Deposits	44	21	19	20	† 26	18	40	38	41	34	49	37	48
Time, Savings,& Fgn.Currency Dep	45	744	938	1,063	† 3,387	3,154	3,504	3,531	4,121	4,435	2,805	3,017	3,216
Bonds	46ab	1	1	—	† 17	7	—	—	—	—	105	361	592
Foreign Liabilities	46c	149	171	167	† 207	237	143	579	905	660	422	269	202
Central Government Deposits	46d	326	425	407	† 636	1,091	1,462	1,851	1,685	1,729	1,924	1,910	1,375
Credit from Monetary Authorities	46g	647	586	584	† 177	110	112	102	74	61	49	38	27
Credit from Deposit Money Banks	46h	36	54	28	† 70	92	527	186	213	315	3,655	3,470	3,232
Capital Accounts	47a	407	449	497	† 2,058	2,087	2,866	3,479	4,378	4,783	4,977	5,541	6,625
Other Items (Net)	47r	−611	−623	−693	† −1,456	−935	−1,157	−1,094	−1,237	−1,196	−787	−945	−1,134

Honduras 268

		1994	1995	1996	1997	1998	1999	2000	2001	2002	2003	2004	2005
Banking Survey						*Millions of Lempiras: End of Period*							
Foreign Assets (Net)	51n	−4,457	−3,461	−2,329	† 4,792	7,262	15,158	18,059	21,879	27,445	27,946	37,947	45,396
Domestic Credit	52	8,884	9,830	12,195	† 17,484	20,737	21,655	27,774	34,276	36,945	45,736	50,786	61,739
Claims on Central Govt. (Net)	52an	1,054	369	−537	† −2,542	−6,171	−10,609	−8,896	−6,746	−7,303	−3,991	−6,737	−6,318
Claims on Local Government	52b	146	156	202	† 238	323	280	285	215	344	434	577	717
Claims on Private Sector	52d	7,683	9,305	12,530	† 19,788	26,584	31,983	36,384	40,807	43,905	49,293	56,946	67,339
Liquid Liabilities	55l	8,845	11,455	15,956	† 25,494	30,359	37,749	45,883	54,170	61,293	68,388	81,446	97,623
Bonds	56ab	14	30	33	† 78	97	58	50	42	34	171	402	628
Capital Accounts	57a	3,500	4,434	5,272	† 7,566	7,870	9,769	11,620	13,802	14,806	16,294	20,820	23,864
Other Items (Net)	57r	−7,932	−9,550	−11,396	† −10,861	−10,328	−10,764	−11,721	−11,859	−11,742	−11,171	−13,936	−14,979
Money (National Definitions)						*Millions of Lempiras: End of Period*							
Base Money	19ma	....	....	4,627	8,102	9,281	10,079	10,353	9,790	10,992	11,945	14,666	16,443
M1	59ma	3,783	4,474	5,690	7,609	8,577	10,450	10,943	11,515	13,192	15,804	17,499	20,996
M2	59mb	8,537	10,224	12,560	20,344	23,706	28,723	33,482	36,253	40,336	45,865	54,347	67,336
M3	59mc	9,834	12,173	16,727	25,716	30,395	37,155	43,924	50,115	56,733	64,752	77,251	92,402
Interest Rates						*Percent Per Annum*							
Savings Rate	60k	9.44	10.02	9.93	12.56	12.27	12.05	10.88	9.96	8.26	6.60	6.04	6.00
Savings Rate (Fgn.Currency)	60k.f	....	....	....	4.66	4.53	3.99	3.67	3.18	1.95	1.29	1.16	1.23
Deposit Rate	60l	11.56	11.97	16.70	21.28	18.58	19.97	15.93	14.48	13.74	11.48	11.09	10.90
Deposit Rate (Fgn.Currency)	60l.f	....	....	....	9.89	9.53	9.09	7.53	6.36	4.05	2.80	2.59	2.61
Lending Rate	60p	24.68	26.95	29.74	32.07	30.69	30.15	26.82	23.76	22.69	20.80	19.88	18.83
Lending Rate (Fgn.Currency)	60p.f	....	....	....	12.88	12.53	12.60	12.91	12.68	11.48	10.00	8.77	8.63
Government Bond Yield	61	23.11	27.24	35.55	29.59	20.34	16.04	14.79	15.28	11.97	11.26	11.67	11.32
Prices and Labor						*Index Numbers (2000=100): Period Averages*							
Consumer Prices	64	36.8	47.7	59.0	† 70.9	80.6	90.0	100.0	109.7	118.1	127.2	137.5	149.6
						Number in Thousands: Period Averages							
Labor Force	67d	....	1,866	2,074	2,158	2,223	2,388	2,351	2,438	....	....	2,592	....
Employment	67e	....	1,806	1,985	2,088	2,135	2,299	....	2,335	2,289	2,351	2,439	....
Unemployment	67c	....	59	89	69	88	89	....	103	94	130	153	....
Unemployment Rate (%)	67r	....	3.2	4.3	3.2	3.9	3.7	....	4.2	3.8	5.1	5.9	....
Intl. Transactions & Positions						*Millions of US Dollars*							
Exports	70..d	842.0	1,220.2	1,316.0	1,445.7	1,532.8	1,164.4	1,380.0	1,324.4	1,321.2	1,321.2	1,537.4	1,679.3
Imports, c.i.f.	71..d	1,055.9	1,642.7	1,839.9	2,148.6	2,534.8	2,676.1	2,854.7	2,941.6	2,981.2	3,275.6	3,916.2	4,613.0
Imports, f.o.b.	71.vd	955.6	1,486.6	1,665.1	1,944.4	2,293.9	2,421.8	2,583.5	2,662.1	2,697.9	2,964.4	3,534.2	....
						2000=100							
Volume of Exports	72	77.0	84.5	99.5	82.6	92.6	60.4	100.0	102.0	102.9	93.5	109.0	101.5
Export Prices	74..d	98.4	132.4	118.6	135.6	138.2	102.9	100.0	101.0	95.2	82.4	102.2	135.3
Balance of Payments						*Millions of US Dollars: Minus Sign Indicates Debit*							
Current Account, n.i.e.	78ald	−343.3	−200.9	−335.4	−272.2	−394.8	−624.6	−262.2	−339.2	−260.5	−281.7	−426.3	−85.6
Goods: Exports f.o.b.	78aad	1,101.5	1,377.2	1,638.4	1,856.5	2,047.9	1,756.3	2,011.6	1,935.5	1,977.1	2,090.1	2,392.8	2,647.8
Goods: Imports f.o.b.	78abd	−1,351.1	−1,518.6	−1,925.8	−2,150.4	−2,370.5	−2,509.6	−2,669.6	−2,769.4	−2,806.1	−3,035.0	−3,676.7	−4,187.5
Trade Balance	78acd	−249.6	−141.4	−287.4	−293.9	−322.6	−753.3	−658.0	−833.9	−829.0	−944.9	−1,283.9	−1,539.7
Services: Credit	78add	242.4	257.6	283.3	334.9	377.1	474.1	478.9	487.3	530.3	598.4	719.3	779.1
Services: Debit	78aed	−311.0	−333.7	−327.8	−360.9	−446.8	−502.4	−597.4	−626.6	−616.7	−673.0	−756.8	−847.8
Balance on Goods & Services	78afd	−318.2	−217.5	−331.9	−319.9	−392.3	−781.6	−776.5	−973.2	−915.4	−1,019.4	−1,321.4	−1,608.4
Income: Credit	78agd	24.0	32.3	61.2	70.0	59.5	80.5	118.5	92.0	58.1	47.2	50.7	102.3
Income: Debit	78ahd	−238.1	−258.2	−292.0	−281.8	−263.6	−235.7	−251.2	−262.0	−251.1	−305.1	−410.0	−433.7
Balance on Gds, Serv. & Inc.	78aid	−532.3	−443.4	−562.7	−531.7	−596.4	−936.8	−909.7	−1,143.3	−1,108.4	−1,277.3	−1,680.7	−1,939.8
Current Transfers, n.i.e.: Credit	78ajd	190.2	243.7	271.7	306.8	241.7	354.6	717.9	894.0	946.7	1,085.0	1,368.8	1,984.5
Current Transfers: Debit	78akd	−1.2	−1.2	−44.4	−47.3	−40.1	−42.4	−70.4	−89.9	−98.7	−89.4	−114.4	−130.3
Capital Account, n.i.e.	78bcd	—	—	28.5	14.6	29.4	110.9	30.1	36.7	23.5	22.4	21.9	18.6
Capital Account, n.i.e.: Credit	78bad	—	—	29.2	15.3	29.4	110.9	30.1	36.7	23.5	22.4	21.9	18.6
Capital Account: Debit	78bbd	—	—	−.7	−.7	—	—	—	—	—	—	—	—
Financial Account, n.i.e.	78bjd	157.5	114.6	70.2	243.3	113.9	203.4	−28.8	123.6	160.9	135.5	731.7	−185.6
Direct Investment Abroad	78bdd	—	—	—	—	—	—	—	—	—	—	—	—
Dir. Invest. in Rep. Econ., n.i.e.	78bed	34.8	50.0	90.9	121.5	99.0	237.3	281.9	193.1	175.3	247.2	324.6	463.9
Portfolio Investment Assets	78bfd	—	—	16.0	—	—	−72.4	−59.4	−3.6	−3.8	−4.1	−4.3	−4.6
Equity Securities	78bkd	....	....	16.0	—	—	—	—	—	—	—	—	—
Debt Securities	78bld	....	....	....	....	—	−72.4	−59.4	−3.6	−3.8	−4.1	−4.3	−4.6
Portfolio Investment Liab., n.i.e.	78bgd	—	—	....	....	—	—	−1.2	—	—	—	—	—
Equity Securities	78bmd	—	—	....	....	—	—	—	—	—	—	—	—
Debt Securities	78bnd	—	—	....	....	—	—	−1.2	—	—	—	—	—
Financial Derivatives Assets	78bwd	....	....	....	....	—	—	—	—	—	—	—	—
Financial Derivatives Liabilities	78bxd	....	....	....	....	−25.8	−16.1	—	—	—	—	—	—
Other Investment Assets	78bhd	8.9	−12.8	−89.4	−53.4	−61.7	−132.2	−203.8	−99.1	21.9	−56.3	34.7	−31.2
Monetary Authorities	78bod	3.3	11.7	....	....	—	—	—	—	—	—	—	—
General Government	78bpd	14.4	14.4	....	....	—	—	—	—	—	—	—	—
Banks	78bqd	−8.8	−38.9	−89.4	−53.4	−61.7	−132.2	−97.9	−65.1	−83.5	12.4	−6.6	−18.0
Other Sectors	78brd	....	....	....	....	—	—	−105.9	−34.0	105.4	−68.7	41.3	−13.2
Other Investment Liab., n.i.e.	78bid	113.8	77.4	52.7	175.2	102.4	186.8	−46.3	33.2	−32.5	−51.2	376.7	−613.7
Monetary Authorities	78bsd	−60.7	−73.1	−180.1	−24.1	−27.2	−22.2	−32.5	−20.6	−23.1	−15.7	−15.8	−9.4
General Government	78btd	96.2	101.7	141.9	−48.4	−30.3	168.8	10.4	127.1	−6.2	21.9	163.4	−660.5
Banks	78bud	−2.2	6.3	34.5	113.8	51.1	−11.5	−39.5	−43.6	−5.5	−16.3	76.2	55.7
Other Sectors	78bvd	80.5	42.5	56.4	133.9	108.8	51.7	15.3	−29.7	2.3	−41.0	152.9	.5
Net Errors and Omissions	78cad	115.5	45.0	157.9	196.5	96.1	122.0	104.3	104.8	57.3	−73.7	46.0	−89.5
Overall Balance	78cbd	−70.3	−41.3	−78.8	182.2	−155.4	−188.3	−156.6	−74.1	−18.7	−197.5	373.3	−342.0
Reserves and Related Items	79dad	70.3	41.3	78.8	−182.2	155.4	188.3	156.6	74.1	18.7	197.5	−373.3	342.0
Reserve Assets	79dbd	−74.1	−90.3	12.7	−307.9	−229.8	−441.9	−32.3	−85.6	−92.0	99.8	−519.8	−349.8
Use of Fund Credit and Loans	79dcd	−16.1	−13.7	−38.0	−8.8	64.8	99.5	16.4	12.0	−39.7	−41.1	15.1	−11.5
Exceptional Financing	79ded	160.4	145.3	104.1	134.5	320.4	530.6	172.5	147.7	150.5	138.8	131.4	703.3

		1994	1995	1996	1997	1998	1999	2000	2001	2002	2003	2004	2005
Government Finance						*Millions of Lempiras: Year Ending December 31*							
Deficit (-) or Surplus........................	80	−1,458.6	−1,326.1	−1,516.1	−1,260.2	−277.5	−1,115.4	−3,847.6	−6,776.9	−5,143.6	−6,526.7	−4,199.3	....
Total Revenue and Grants.............	81y	4,952.1	7,296.6	8,512.4	11,091.2	14,012.5	16,395.1	17,128.1	20,092.8	31,590.3	23,562.1	27,821.1	....
Revenue....................................	81	4,809.8	7,139.5	8,256.8	10,773.8	13,641.8	15,136.2	15,872.0	17,626.3	29,158.6	22,233.9	26,526.1	....
Grants......................................	81z	142.3	157.1	255.6	317.4	370.7	1,258.9	1,256.1	2,466.5	2,431.7	1,328.2	1,295.0	....
Exp. & Lending Minus Repay.........	82z	6,410.7	8,622.7	10,028.5	12,351.4	14,290.0	17,510.5	20,975.7	26,869.7	36,733.9	30,088.8	32,020.4	....
Expenditure..............................	82	6,030.7	7,780.4	9,778.8	12,727.6	14,583.9	16,312.8	20,477.8	25,710.5	35,631.9	29,417.2	31,909.2	....
Lending Minus Repayments.........	83	380.0	842.3	249.7	−376.2	−293.9	1,197.7	497.9	1,159.2	1,102.0	671.6	111.2	....
Total Financing.............................	80h	1,458.6	1,326.1	1,516.1	1,260.2	277.5	1,115.4	3,847.6	6,776.9	5,143.6	6,526.7	4,199.3	....
Domestic...................................	84a	505.2	−134.8	337.4	129.0	−685.8	−3,282.5	1,722.4	1,082.5	2,742.6	3,980.3	−1,508.7	....
Foreign.....................................	85a	953.4	1,460.9	1,178.7	1,131.2	963.3	4,397.9	2,125.2	5,694.4	2,401.0	2,546.4	5,708.0	....
Total Debt by Residence.................	88	30,997.1	36,435.5	44,360.1	46,672.5	50,721.6	56,112.1	58,646.1	64,455.4	71,279.2	84,696.9	93,842.5	....
Domestic...................................	88a	3,570.3	3,711.7	3,875.5	4,424.1	3,970.4	3,280.2	3,825.0	4,526.6	5,009.4	9,006.2	7,445.9	....
Foreign.....................................	89a	27,426.8	32,723.8	40,484.6	42,248.4	46,751.2	52,831.9	54,821.1	59,928.8	66,269.8	75,690.7	86,396.6	....
Memorandum Item:													
Intragovernmental Debt...............	88s	−332.2	−347.8	−394.1	−304.4	−330.2	−163.4	−20.3	....	....	−8.2	....	....
National Accounts						*Millions of Lempiras*							
Househ.Cons.Expend.,incl.NPISHs....	96f	18,113	23,819	30,782	39,626	46,930	53,168	63,119	72,223	81,957	91,097	103,219	121,178
Government Consumption Expend...	91f	2,780	3,495	4,556	5,422	7,117	8,726	11,218	13,792	14,925	16,209	18,126	21,566
Gross Fixed Capital Formation..........	93e	8,110	8,994	11,468	15,732	19,874	23,045	23,372	23,525	23,992	27,826	36,388	36,739
Changes in Inventories...................	93i	2,751	2,842	3,400	3,994	1,910	3,687	4,095	5,756	3,710	4,261	5,304	10,328
Exports of Goods and Services.........	90c	11,498	16,390	22,378	28,322	32,699	31,627	36,960	37,480	41,194	46,644	56,672	64,462
Imports of Goods and Services (-).....	98c	14,391	18,033	24,821	31,775	38,092	43,157	49,363	53,744	57,655	65,572	82,466	96,745
Gross Domestic Product (GDP).........	99b	28,862	37,507	47,763	61,322	70,438	77,096	89,401	99,032	108,124	120,465	137,242	157,529
Net Primary Income from Abroad.....	98.n	−1,843	−2,532	−3,069	−2,812	−2,845	−2,335	−2,125	−2,791	−3,348	−4,768	−6,867	−6,642
Gross National Income (GNI)............	99a	27,019	34,975	44,694	58,510	67,593	74,761	87,276	96,241	104,776	115,697	130,375	150,887
Consumption of Fixed Capital..........	99cf	1,707	2,258	2,845	3,528	4,086	4,645	5,269	5,908	6,507	7,180	7,966	8,929
GDP Volume 1978 Prices.................	99b.p	5,907	6,148	6,368	6,686	6,880	6,750	7,138	7,324	7,523	7,785	8,176	8,507
GDP Volume (2000=100)...............	99bvp	82.8	86.1	89.2	93.7	96.4	94.6	100.0	102.6	105.4	109.1	114.5	119.2
GDP Deflator (2000=100)...............	99bip	39.0	48.7	59.9	73.2	81.7	91.2	100.0	108.0	114.8	123.5	134.0	147.8
						Millions: Midyear Estimates							
Population................................	99z	5.47	5.62	5.78	5.94	6.10	6.27	6.42	6.58	6.74	6.89	7.05	7.20

Hungary 944

		1994	1995	1996	1997	1998	1999	2000	2001	2002	2003	2004	2005
Exchange Rates		Forint per SDR: End of Period											
Official Rate	aa	161.591	207.321	237.163	274.572	308.401	346.586	370.978	350.665	306.110	308.963	279.992	305.263
		Forint per US Dollar: End of Period (ae) Period Average (rf)											
Official Rate	ae	110.690	139.470	164.930	203.500	219.030	252.520	284.730	279.030	225.160	207.920	180.290	213.580
Official Rate	rf	105.160	125.681	152.647	186.789	214.402	237.146	282.179	286.490	257.887	224.307	202.746	199.583
		Index Numbers (2000=100): Period Averages											
Official Rate	ahx	267.5	224.8	184.4	151.0	131.2	118.7	100.0	98.2	109.4	125.4	138.9	141.1
Nominal Effective Exchange Rate	nec	203.9	158.9	135.8	124.7	111.1	105.7	100.0	101.2	108.4	108.2	110.7	111.6
Real Effective Exchange Rate	rec	94.5	90.9	93.1	97.6	96.9	99.1	100.0	107.4	118.9	121.6	130.0	132.6
Fund Position		Millions of SDRs: End of Period											
Quota	2f.s	755	755	755	755	755	1,038	1,038	1,038	1,038	1,038	1,038	1,038
SDRs	1b.s	1	1	—	—	1	3	9	16	24	31	38	45
Reserve Position in the Fund	1c.s	56	56	56	56	56	177	202	322	437	455	346	135
Total Fund Cred.&Loans Outstg	2tl	782	259	119	119	—	—	—	—	—	—	—	—
International Liquidity		Millions of US Dollars Unless Otherwise Indicated: End of Period											
Total Reserves minus Gold	1l.d	6,735	11,974	9,720	8,408	9,319	10,954	11,190	10,727	10,348	12,737	15,908	18,539
SDRs	1b.d	2	1	—	—	1	4	12	21	33	46	58	64
Reserve Position in the Fund	1c.d	82	83	81	81	79	243	263	405	595	676	538	192
Foreign Exchange	1d.d	6,652	11,890	9,639	8,332	9,239	10,707	10,915	10,302	9,721	12,015	15,312	18,283
Gold (Million Fine Troy Ounces)	1ad	.110	.111	.101	.101	.101	.101	.101	.101	.101	.101	.099	.099
Gold (National Valuation)	1and	42	43	37	29	29	29	28	28	35	42	43	51
Monetary Authorities:Other Liabs	4..d	19,191	20,836	16,239	11,647	11,677	9,847	8,537	6,614	5,338	4,393	2,976	1,525
Deposit Money Banks: Assets	7a.d	1,030	921	1,679	2,495	3,306	3,594	2,745	4,439	4,359	5,939	7,200	6,990
Liabilities	7b.d	2,379	2,878	3,077	4,482	5,464	5,577	5,514	5,966	7,432	13,667	18,912	22,400
Monetary Authorities		Billions of Forint: End of Period											
Foreign Assets	11	784.0	1,680.7	1,614.9	1,723.3	2,054.3	2,992.4	3,463.4	3,336.2	2,469.2	2,834.2	2,887.1	3,967.2
Claims on Consolidated Cent.Govt.	12a	2,558.3	3,144.7	2,902.9	2,854.0	2,930.0	2,488.2	2,202.4	1,664.6	1,216.3	910.2	614.2	277.7
Other Claims on Residents	12d	4.4	3.8	.6	.7	.8	.7	.7	.7	.8	3.3	2.6	2.5
Claims on Banking Institutions	12e	405.8	302.6	231.4	185.3	178.4	126.6	93.8	46.9	22.8	12.5	11.0	4.0
Reserve Money	14	614.1	723.5	662.0	860.3	1,037.5	1,309.7	1,535.9	1,562.6	1,648.6	1,816.0	2,028.8	2,199.3
of which: Currency Outside DMBs	14a	410.7	443.9	497.7	562.6	669.0	855.3	883.9	1,037.6	1,181.9	1,346.8	1,341.6	1,600.2
Other Liabilities to Banks	14n	533.9	748.4	920.8	835.4	820.5	1,075.0	774.8	526.9	648.0	387.5	548.4	1,318.3
Time & Foreign Currency Deposits	15	7.0	8.6	6.9	7.8	21.4	15.3	12.9	6.4	6.7	7.2	4.9	5.1
Money Market Instruments	16aa	—	—	—	68.9	152.2	—	349.7	402.7	.1	.4	.3	.2
Bonds	16ab	6.4	5.2	3.5	2.3	—	—	—	—	—	—	—	—
Liabs. of Central Bank: Securities	16ac	21.0	44.2	76.2	272.5	340.7	242.7	305.8	248.6	142.4	105.5	47.5	41.8
Foreign Liabilities	16c	148.3	104.9	57.8	138.2	42.6	137.0	334.4	268.3	121.4	127.6	57.4	66.7
Long-Term Foreign Liabilities	16cl	2,102.3	2,854.7	2,648.7	2,264.7	2,515.1	2,349.6	2,096.3	1,577.2	1,080.5	785.7	479.1	259.0
Consolidated Centr.Govt.Deposits	16d	316.8	561.8	389.9	328.4	194.1	555.8	434.4	745.1	197.7	297.8	345.6	304.6
Capital Accounts	17a	31.6	55.2	59.3	72.7	128.2	74.0	65.0	65.0	40.9	12.7	91.1	48.4
Other Items (Net)	17r	−28.0	26.5	−74.1	−86.3	−87.2	−149.9	−147.5	−354.2	−177.3	219.7	−88.4	8.0
Banking Institutions		Billions of Forint: End of Period											
Reserves	20	194.1	273.7	154.0	291.1	365.6	447.5	646.9	520.1	464.1	406.8	677.3	599.2
Claims on Mon.Author.:Securities	20c	21.0	44.2	76.2	272.5	353.5	242.7	346.2	284.2	145.3	108.3	48.0	42.2
Other Claims on Monetary Author	20n	533.9	748.4	920.8	835.4	820.5	1,075.0	774.6	526.9	648.3	430.9	547.9	1,317.3
Foreign Assets	21	114.0	128.5	276.9	507.7	724.0	907.5	781.5	1,238.6	981.5	1,234.7	1,298.1	1,492.9
Claims on Consolidated Cent.Govt	22a	649.7	742.4	934.2	979.7	1,159.9	1,112.0	1,191.3	1,501.0	1,996.4	2,119.9	2,173.5	2,288.7
Claims on Local Government	22b	47.6	49.9	38.5	30.3	44.4	50.3	57.6	73.2	115.9	147.8	184.5	243.3
Other Claims on Residents	22d	1,152.9	1,263.1	1,520.7	† 2,076.9	2,440.4	2,968.0	4,247.6	5,025.8	5,989.2	7,985.9	9,479.5	11,269.3
Demand Deposits	24	553.9	561.4	730.6	960.9	1,120.8	1,275.7	1,491.8	1,738.3	2,113.3	2,287.1	2,308.0	3,033.3
Time, Savings,& Fgn.Currency Dep	25	1,266.0	1,696.7	2,074.9	2,437.2	2,781.1	3,161.6	3,592.2	4,166.4	4,626.6	5,272.7	6,052.6	6,365.9
Bonds	26ab	26.7	15.8	30.8	36.8	29.6	51.0	70.7	114.2	405.1	980.1	1,142.3	1,187.8
Foreign Liabilities	26c	134.3	196.0	307.9	593.3	689.2	746.7	725.8	610.4	562.7	1,036.5	1,070.5	1,667.1
Long-Term Foreign Liabilities	26cl	129.1	205.4	199.7	318.8	507.5	661.7	844.2	1,054.4	1,110.7	1,805.1	2,339.1	3,117.1
Consolidated Centr.Govt.Deposits	26d	31.1	13.0	10.0	7.6	5.0	4.7	23.3	28.6	27.8	54.2	60.2	69.3
Credit from Monetary Authorities	26g	405.8	302.6	231.4	185.3	178.4	126.6	91.5	44.6	21.1	11.6	10.7	4.0
Money Market Fund Shares	26m		9.7	23.9	35.1	47.6	71.2	81.5	121.6	186.3	174.5	299.2	498.4
Capital Accounts	27a	230.8	316.7	382.9	559.8	596.7	662.9	817.6	957.6	1,043.8	1,243.3	1,463.8	1,690.4
Other Items (Net)	27r	−64.5	−67.0	−70.6	−141.3	−47.6	40.9	307.3	333.7	243.1	−430.7	−337.6	−380.6
Banking Survey		Billions of Forint End of Period											
Foreign Assets (Net)	31n	615.4	1,508.3	1,526.2	1,499.5	2,046.6	3,016.2	3,184.6	3,696.2	2,766.6	2,904.8	3,057.2	3,726.2
Domestic Credit	32	4,064.9	4,629.1	4,997.2	† 5,605.5	6,376.3	6,058.8	7,242.0	7,491.7	9,093.1	10,815.2	12,048.5	13,707.5
Claims on Cons.Cent.Govt.(Net)	32an	2,860.1	3,312.3	3,437.3	3,497.7	3,890.8	3,039.7	2,936.0	2,392.0	2,987.2	2,678.2	2,381.8	2,192.5
Claims on Local Government	32b	47.6	49.9	38.5	30.3	44.4	50.3	57.6	73.2	115.9	147.8	184.5	243.3
Other Claims on Residents	32d	1,157.2	1,266.9	1,521.4	† 2,077.6	2,441.2	2,968.8	4,248.3	5,026.6	5,990.0	7,989.2	9,482.1	11,271.8
Money	34	973.9	1,011.2	1,238.6	1,530.1	1,792.7	2,137.9	2,379.7	2,779.0	3,298.0	3,638.8	3,654.2	4,633.6
Quasi-Money	35	1,273.0	1,705.3	2,081.8	2,445.1	2,802.5	3,176.9	3,605.1	4,172.8	4,633.3	5,280.0	6,057.5	6,371.0
Money Market Instruments	36aa	—	—	—	68.9	152.2	—	349.7	402.7	.1	.4	.3	.2
Bonds	36ab	33.1	21.0	34.4	39.0	29.6	51.0	70.7	114.2	405.1	980.1	1,142.3	1,187.8
Long-Term Foreign Liabilities	36cl	2,231.3	3,060.1	2,848.4	2,583.4	3,022.6	3,011.3	2,940.5	2,631.7	2,191.3	2,590.8	2,818.2	3,376.0
Money Market Fund Shares	36m	....	9.7	23.9	35.1	47.6	71.2	81.5	121.6	186.3	174.5	299.2	498.4
Capital Accounts	37a	262.4	371.8	442.2	632.5	724.9	736.9	882.6	1,022.6	1,084.7	1,255.9	1,555.0	1,738.8
Other Items (Net)	37r	−92.5	−40.5	−144.7	−227.6	−147.5	−109.0	118.4	−56.6	61.0	−200.5	−420.9	−372.0
Money plus Quasi-Money	35l	2,246.9	2,716.5	3,320.3	3,975.1	4,595.2	5,314.8	5,984.8	6,951.8	7,931.3	8,918.7	9,711.7	11,004.5
Money (National Definition)		Billions of Forint: End of Period											
Monetary Base	19ma	621.0	749.6	859.1	994.6	1,244.0	1,465.8	1,649.1	1,608.5	1,763.9	2,091.8	2,014.7	2,405.0
M1	59ma	1,038.1	1,166.4	1,374.8	1,703.3	1,987.4	2,358.4	2,653.8	3,113.3	3,648.0	4,027.6	4,169.3	5,188.5
M2	59mb	2,148.6	2,590.2	3,162.5	3,787.3	4,373.4	5,063.0	5,680.6	6,634.2	7,543.2	8,575.1	9,427.3	10,654.2
M3	59mc	2,157.2	2,605.4	3,196.7	3,923.1	4,585.2	5,187.3	6,129.5	7,177.7	7,846.9	8,788.8	9,804.5	11,232.1
M4	59md	2,628.1	3,285.5	4,170.2	5,293.9	6,352.9	7,557.1	8,690.1	10,058.9	11,387.4	13,084.1	14,504.6	16,542.4

		1994	1995	1996	1997	1998	1999	2000	2001	2002	2003	2004	2005
Interest Rates							*Percent Per Annum*						
Discount Rate (End of Period)	60	25.0	28.0	23.0	20.5	17.0	14.5	11.0	9.8	8.5	12.5	9.5	6.0
Treasury Bill Rate	60c	26.9	32.0	24.0	20.1	17.8	14.7	11.0	10.8	8.9	8.2	11.3	7.0
Deposit Rate	60l	20.3	† 24.4	18.6	16.9	14.4	11.9	9.5	8.4	7.4	11.0	9.1	5.2
Lending Rate	60p	27.4	32.6	27.3	21.8	19.3	16.3	12.6	12.1	10.2	9.6	12.8	8.5
Prices, Production, Labor							*Index Numbers (2000=100): Period Averages*						
Producer Prices	63	40.6	52.2	63.6	76.5	85.2	89.5	100.0	104.8	103.3	105.8	109.6	113.6
Consumer Prices	64	38.6	† 49.6	61.3	72.5	82.8	91.1	100.0	109.2	115.0	120.3	128.5	133.0
Harmonized CPI (2002=100)	64h	....	....	....	....	....	....	....	....	100.0	† 104.7	111.8	115.7
Wages: Avg. Earnings	65	40.0	46.4	54.6	67.7	79.1	88.7	100.0	113.2	130.2	146.7	159.1	173.2
Industrial Production	66	53.2	59.4	61.4	68.2	76.7	84.6	100.0	103.6	106.4	113.2	121.5	130.4
Industrial Employment	67	108.3	102.5	97.1	96.4	97.9	98.7	100.0	99.3	97.3	95.3	93.0	90.2
							Number in Thousands: Period Averages						
Labor Force	67d	4,201	4,095	4,048	3,995	4,010	4,095	4,120	4,102	4,109	4,167	4,153	4,205
Employment	67e	3,752	3,679	3,648	3,646	3,696	3,809	3,856	3,868	3,871	3,922	3,900	3,902
Unemployment	67c	449	417	400	349	314	285	264	234	239	245	253	304
Unemployment Rate (%)	67r	10.7	10.2	9.9	8.7	7.8	7.0	6.4	5.7	5.8	5.9	6.1	7.2
Intl. Transactions & Positions							*Billions of Forint*						
Exports	70	1,101.4	1,622.1	2,392.1	3,567.0	4,934.4	5,938.6	7,942.8	8,748.3	8,874.0	9,528.6	11,093.9	12,343.2
Imports, c.i.f.	71	1,505.7	1,936.1	2,764.0	3,961.0	5,511.4	6,645.6	9,064.0	9,665.0	9,704.1	10,662.8	12,063.7	13,047.1
Imports, f.o.b.	71.v	1,518.1	1,913.1	2,735.5	3,919.9	5,451.0	6,558.0	8,958.4	9,534.9	9,578.8	10,513.7	11,869.4	12,851.5
							2000=100						
Volume of Exports	72	39.3	42.6	44.5	† 57.8	70.9	82.2	100.0	107.8	114.1	124.6	147.4	163.2
Volume of Imports	73	45.3	43.5	45.9	† 58.0	72.4	82.8	100.0	104.0	109.3	120.4	138.8	146.4
Export Prices	76	42.8	57.3	67.6	77.7	87.7	91.0	100.0	102.2	97.1	96.7	95.2	94.5
Import Prices	76.x	41.8	55.0	66.4	75.3	83.9	88.6	100.0	102.5	96.9	97.0	96.2	97.5
Balance of Payments							*Millions of US Dollars: Minus Sign Indicates Debit*						
Current Account, n.i.e.	78ald	−4,054	−1,650	−1,766	−2,080	−3,391	−3,775	−4,004	−3,205	−4,693	−7,231	−8,639	−7,962
Goods: Exports f.o.b.	78aad	7,648	14,619	15,966	19,284	23,698	25,608	28,762	31,080	34,792	43,475	56,065	61,834
Goods: Imports f.o.b.	78abd	−11,364	−16,078	−17,640	−20,611	−25,583	−27,778	−31,675	−33,318	−36,911	−46,753	−59,071	−63,751
Trade Balance	78acd	−3,716	−1,459	−1,673	−1,328	−1,885	−2,170	−2,913	−2,237	−2,119	−3,279	−3,006	−1,917
Services: Credit	78add	3,117	5,146	5,866	5,793	5,401	5,213	5,901	7,029	7,417	8,701	10,751	12,328
Services: Debit	78aed	−2,958	−3,839	−3,979	−4,049	−4,198	−4,360	−4,775	−5,550	−6,849	−9,150	−10,604	−11,729
Balance on Goods & Services	78afd	−3,557	−152	213	416	−682	−1,317	−1,787	−759	−1,551	−3,728	−2,860	−1,318
Income: Credit	78agd	676	983	1,321	1,546	1,252	902	1,165	1,302	1,236	1,371	1,882	1,702
Income: Debit	78ahd	−2,082	−2,684	−3,297	−4,246	−4,205	−3,794	−3,740	−4,152	−4,870	−5,541	−7,978	−8,623
Balance on Gds, Serv. & Inc.	78aid	−4,963	−1,852	−1,764	−2,283	−3,635	−4,208	−4,361	−3,609	−5,184	−7,898	−8,956	−8,239
Current Transfers, n.i.e.: Credit	78ajd	2,871	482	270	463	510	711	674	781	1,070	1,283	1,633	2,489
Current Transfers: Debit	78akd	−1,961	−279	−272	−260	−266	−278	−316	−377	−579	−616	−1,315	−2,212
Capital Account, n.i.e.	78bcd	—	60	156	117	189	29	270	317	191	−27	328	884
Capital Account, n.i.e.: Credit	78bad	—	80	266	266	408	509	458	417	238	240	518	1,000
Capital Account: Debit	78bbd	—	−20	−110	−149	−219	−480	−188	−101	−48	−267	−190	−116
Financial Account, n.i.e.	78bjd	3,370	5,706	−429	2,095	4,439	6,469	4,960	2,775	2,565	7,368	12,025	14,775
Direct Investment Abroad	78bdd	−49	−59	4	−449	−278	−248	−589	−364	−282	−1,661	−1,118	−1,386
Dir. Invest. in Rep. Econ., n.i.e.	78bed	1,144	4,804	3,289	4,155	3,343	3,308	2,770	3,944	3,013	2,177	4,666	6,604
Portfolio Investment Assets	78bfd	6	−1	−35	−134	−93	−75	−309	−149	−43	15	−442	−869
Equity Securities	78bkd	−10	—	−15	−32	−45	16	−151	−55	−50	−42	−439	−314
Debt Securities	78bld	16	—	−20	−102	−48	−91	−158	−95	7	57	−3	−555
Portfolio Investment Liab., n.i.e.	78bgd	2,458	2,213	−396	−939	1,925	2,065	−141	1,523	1,844	2,902	7,353	5,654
Equity Securities	78bmd	224	−62	359	979	556	1,191	−369	134	−137	269	1,491	−16
Debt Securities	78bnd	2,234	2,275	−754	−1,918	1,369	874	229	1,389	1,982	2,633	5,862	5,671
Financial Derivatives Assets	78bwd	....	157	17	12	185	852	754	582	1,796	2,320	4,214	3,664
Financial Derivatives Liabilities	78bxd	....	102	−1	−4	−38	−899	−698	−471	−1,647	−2,069	−3,800	−3,881
Other Investment Assets	78bhd	362	−1,083	−2,013	−1,095	−591	−579	939	−2,754	−1,599	−2,317	−1,824	−1,324
Monetary Authorities	78bod	....	−17	14	1	4	—	−8	4	36	−1,049	1,100	−11
General Government	78bpd	156	27	44	189	75	30	38	−9	14	198	−66	−129
Banks	78bqd	191	125	−1,129	−789	−333	−430	755	−1,463	528	−951	−347	−146
Other Sectors	78brd	15	−1,218	−942	−496	−337	−178	154	−1,287	−2,176	−515	−2,511	−1,037
Other Investment Liab., n.i.e.	78bid	−551	−427	−1,294	549	−13	2,046	2,232	465	−517	6,000	2,977	6,313
Monetary Authorities	78bsd	17	−906	−1,875	−659	−15	286	613	−644	−622	588	−916	−36
General Government	78btd	−1,761	−438	−331	−106	−288	235	−225	−47	766	319	160	521
Banks	78bud	365	323	394	1,123	619	522	401	294	647	3,986	2,463	4,569
Other Sectors	78bvd	828	595	518	190	−329	1,002	1,442	862	−1,308	1,107	1,270	1,259
Net Errors and Omissions	78cad	209	1,267	802	−307	−285	−389	−174	29	145	226	−1,733	−2,792
Overall Balance	78cbd	−475	5,384	−1,237	−175	951	2,335	1,052	−84	−1,792	336	1,981	4,904
Reserves and Related Items	79dad	475	−5,384	1,237	175	−951	−2,335	−1,052	84	1,792	−336	−1,981	−4,904
Reserve Assets	79dbd	640	−4,599	1,441	175	−791	−2,335	−1,052	84	1,792	−336	−1,981	−4,904
Use of Fund Credit and Loans	79dcd	−165	−785	−203	—	−160	—	—	—	—	—	—	—
Exceptional Financing	79ded	....	—	—	—	—	—	—	—	—	—	—	—

Hungary 944

		1994	1995	1996	1997	1998	1999	2000	2001	2002	2003	2004	2005
International Investment Position					*Millions of US Dollars*								
Assets................................	79aad	....	....	....	14,952	16,989	19,845	19,629	22,743	24,288	31,978	42,521	46,699
Direct Investment Abroad...............	79abd	....	....	....	647	784	924	1,280	1,556	2,166	3,509	6,027	6,604
Portfolio Investment.....................	79acd	....	....	....	171	293	367	667	814	931	1,045	1,613	2,577
Equity Securities..........................	79add	....	....	....	32	87	73	221	271	355	425	940	1,425
Debt Securities.........................	79aed	....	....	....	139	206	294	447	543	576	620	673	1,152
Financial Derivatives.....................	79ald	....	....	....	—	9	880	859	1,165	909	1,604	2,481	2,627
Other Investment.........................	79afd	....	....	....	5,698	6,556	6,690	5,606	8,452	9,898	13,040	16,449	16,300
Monetary Authorities..................	79agd	....	....	....	32	23	20	75	63	30	1,107	23	31
General Government...................	79ahd	....	....	....	657	570	530	469	478	531	362	460	510
Banks....................................	79aid	....	....	....	2,323	3,083	3,387	2,559	4,040	3,862	5,313	6,421	6,198
Other Sectors...........................	79ajd	....	....	....	2,686	2,879	2,753	2,503	3,871	5,475	6,258	9,545	9,561
Reserve Assets............................	79akd	....	....	....	8,437	9,348	10,983	11,217	10,755	10,383	12,780	15,951	18,590
Liabilities...................................	79lad	....	....	....	42,987	47,827	53,873	53,010	58,653	73,854	102,881	138,560	142,409
Dir. Invest. in Rep. Economy..........	79lbd	....	....	....	17,968	20,733	23,260	22,870	27,407	36,224	48,340	62,687	61,221
Portfolio Investment.....................	79lcd	....	....	....	12,408	14,558	16,955	14,812	15,691	20,910	27,793	43,153	46,017
Equity Securities.........................	79ldd	....	....	....	2,494	2,341	4,356	2,986	2,906	3,784	5,604	11,359	13,246
Debt Securities..........................	79led	....	....	....	9,914	12,217	12,599	11,825	12,786	17,126	22,189	31,794	32,772
Financial Derivatives.....................	79lld	....	....	....	450	11	164	276	483	624	2,000	2,605	2,442
Other Investment.........................	79lfd	....	....	....	12,161	12,524	13,494	15,053	15,072	16,096	24,748	30,114	32,729
Monetary Authorities..................	79lgd	....	....	....	1,216	1,094	1,322	1,863	1,165	574	1,240	357	293
General Government...................	79lhd	....	....	....	1,635	1,380	1,532	1,246	1,167	2,118	2,806	3,215	3,325
Banks....................................	79lid	....	....	....	4,290	5,185	5,297	5,476	5,581	6,784	11,993	15,788	18,350
Other Sectors............................	79ljd	....	....	....	5,019	4,866	5,343	6,468	7,159	6,620	8,709	10,755	10,761
Government Finance					*Billions of Forint: Year Ending December 31*								
Deficit (-) or Surplus..................	80	−310.8	−355.5	−213.1	−383.6	−631.5	−420.0	−449.3	−444.8	−1,569.0	−1,062.9	−1,284.1	....
Total Revenue and Grants.............	81y	2,085.4	2,393.6	2,908.9	3,205.9	4,072.5	4,663.1	5,228.1	5,831.5	6,191.5	6,942.8	7,690.3	....
Revenue.....................................	81	2,085.2	2,393.4	2,908.5	3,205.3	4,065.5	4,649.9	5,193.7	5,801.1	6,152.8	6,902.4	7,375.7	....
Grants..	81z	.2	.2	.4	.6	7.0	13.2	34.4	30.4	38.7	40.4	314.6	....
Exp. & Lending Minus Repay..........	82z	2,396.2	2,749.1	3,122.0	3,589.5	4,704.0	5,083.1	5,677.4	6,276.3	7,760.5	8,005.7	8,974.4	....
Expenditure................................	82	2,390.9	2,734.4	3,122.1	3,644.0	4,671.6	5,070.0	5,682.5	6,273.3	7,672.0	8,040.6	8,998.2	....
Lending Minus Repayments..........	83	5.3	14.7	−.1	−54.5	32.4	13.1	−5.1	3.0	88.5	−34.9	−23.8	....
Total Financing.............................	80h	310.8	355.5	213.2	....	....	....	....	444.8	1,569.0	1,062.9	1,284.1	....
Total Net Borrowing.....................	84	203.9	204.4	380.6	....	....	....	....	635.9	1,279.1	1,062.8	1,420.6	....
Net Domestic............................	84a	202.4	198.5	373.7	....	....	....	....	408.0	1,028.2	476.2	770.7	....
Net Foreign...............................	85a	1.5	5.9	6.9	....	....	....	....	227.9	250.9	586.6	649.9	....
Use of Cash Balances...................	87	106.9	151.1	−167.4	....	....	....	....	−191.1	289.9	.1	−136.5	....
Total Debt by Residence.................	88	3,801.0	4,781.6	4,959.1	5,405.7	6,161.5	6,890.5	7,228.7	7,721.6	9,223.7	10,588.1	11,592.4	....
Domestic.....................................	88a	3,564.5	4,461.7	4,669.2	5,055.4	5,867.3	5,940.0	6,144.2	6,486.1	7,806.0	8,494.4	8,996.7	....
Foreign.......................................	89a	236.5	319.9	289.9	350.3	294.2	950.5	1,084.5	1,235.5	1,417.7	2,093.7	2,595.7	....
Memorandum Item:													
Privatization Receipts..................	83a	31.0	150.0	219.9	161.9	13.0	4.0	.9	....	....	....	....	....
National Accounts					*Billions of Forint*								
Househ.Cons.Expend.,incl.NPISHs....	96f	3,151.7	3,730.3	4,400.4	5,283.0	6,297.2	7,274.2	8,489.1	9,723.8	11,228.3	12,816.0	13,785.2	14,864.1
Government Consumption Expend...	91f	527.1	617.7	703.6	900.8	1,024.6	1,156.7	1,352.8	1,541.3	1,849.7	2,088.8	2,189.1	2,247.1
Gross Fixed Capital Formation.........	93e	878.5	1,125.4	1,475.5	1,898.9	2,384.6	2,724.5	3,099.1	3,499.7	3,941.5	4,156.0	4,631.2	5,057.0
Changes in Inventories..................	93i	90.1	143.4	282.5	370.6	526.0	548.0	868.0	462.7	292.7	401.6	549.8	104.4
Exports of Goods and Services..........	90c	1,262.5	2,505.2	3,341.8	4,709.2	6,247.0	7,329.0	9,820.3	10,913.0	10,848.5	11,515.3	13,142.5	14,469.7
Imports of Goods and Services (-).....	98c	1,545.1	2,507.9	3,310.0	4,621.8	6,392.0	7,639.0	10,357.7	11,150.7	11,245.4	12,327.0	13,868.4	14,940.0
Gross Domestic Product (GDP)........	99b	4,364.8	5,614.0	6,893.9	8,540.7	10,087.4	11,393.5	13,272.2	14,989.8	16,915.3	18,650.7	20,429.5	21,802.3
GDP Volume 1991 Prices.................	99b.p	2,478.8	2,515.7	....	....	....	....	....	....	....	....	....	....
GDP Volume 2000 Prices................	99b.p	....	10,820.8	10,963.6	11,464.2	12,021.4	12,520.7	13,272.2	13,846.9	14,375.4	14,861.6	15,637.1	16,280.7
GDP Volume (2000=100)...............	99bvp	80.3	† 81.5	82.6	86.4	90.6	94.3	100.0	104.3	108.3	112.0	117.8	122.7
GDP Deflator (2000=100)...............	99bip	40.9	51.9	62.9	74.5	83.9	91.0	100.0	108.3	117.7	125.5	130.6	133.9
					Millions: Midyear Estimates								
Population..............................	99z	10.34	10.33	10.32	10.30	10.27	10.25	10.23	10.20	10.18	10.15	10.12	10.10

Iceland 176

		1994	1995	1996	1997	1998	1999	2000	2001	2002	2003	2004	2005
Exchange Rates							*Kronur per SDR: End of Period*						
Official Rate	aa	99.708	96.964	96.185	97.389	97.605	99.576	110.356	129.380	109.550	105.489	94.796	90.015
						Kronur per US Dollar: End of Period (ae) Period Average (rf)							
Official Rate	ae	68.300	65.230	66.890	72.180	69.320	72.550	84.700	102.950	80.580	70.990	61.040	62.980
Official Rate	rf	69.944	64.692	66.500	70.904	70.958	72.335	78.616	97.425	91.662	76.709	70.192	62.982
						Index Numbers (2000=100): Period Averages							
Official Rate	ahx	112.0	121.1	117.7	110.4	110.4	108.3	100.0	80.8	85.8	102.1	111.8	124.4
Nominal Effective Exchange Rate	nec	93.9	94.9	95.1	97.2	100.6	100.0	100.0	84.3	86.4	91.7	93.4	103.1
Real Effective Exchange Rate	rec	92.0	91.7	91.8	93.2	96.3	97.4	100.0	87.5	93.0	98.9	101.6	114.6
Fund Position							*Millions of SDRs: End of Period*						
Quota	2f.s	85.3	85.3	85.3	85.3	85.3	117.6	117.6	117.6	117.6	117.6	117.6	117.6
SDRs	1b.s	.1	—	—	—	—	—	—	.1	.1	—	.1	—
Reserve Position in the Fund	1c.s	10.5	10.5	10.5	10.5	10.5	18.6	18.6	18.6	18.6	18.6	18.6	18.6
Total Fund Cred.&Loans Outstg.	2tl	—	—	—	—	—	—	—	—	—	—	—	—
International Liquidity						*Millions of US Dollars Unless Otherwise Indicated: End of Period*							
Total Reserves minus Gold	1l.d	292.9	308.1	453.7	383.7	426.4	478.4	388.9	338.2	440.1	792.3	1,046.2	1,035.7
SDRs	1b.d	.1	—	—	—	—	—	—	.1	.1	—	.1	—
Reserve Position in the Fund	1c.d	15.3	15.6	15.1	14.2	14.8	25.5	24.2	23.3	25.3	27.6	28.9	26.6
Foreign Exchange	1d.d	277.5	292.5	438.6	369.5	411.6	452.9	364.6	314.8	414.7	764.6	1,017.3	1,009.1
Gold (Million Fine Troy Ounces)	1ad	.049	.049	.049	.049	.056	.056	.059	.062	.063	.063	.064	.064
Gold (National Valuation)	1and	2.5	2.6	2.7	2.6	2.8	† 17.0	16.4	17.0	21.4	26.4	28.0	32.9
Monetary Authorities: Other Liab.	4..d	137.5	176.5	75.5	75.1	130.9	67.5	186.1	145.5	204.8	1.7	2.3	2.4
Deposit Money Banks: Assets	7a.d	152.6	87.0	108.6	133.0	119.0	218.1	266.0	324.0	567.3	1,592.5	2,856.6	8,496.2
Liabilities	7b.d	464.1	419.4	639.0	875.8	1,477.8	1,989.9	2,649.4	2,503.0	2,807.6	3,046.2	3,660.2	6,444.0
Monetary Authorities							*Millions of Kronur: End of Period*						
Foreign Assets	11	24,347	25,961	36,151	33,274	35,136	† 37,139	34,495	36,819	37,376	58,272	65,718	67,529
Claims on Central Government	12a	24,546	18,476	10,534	12,852	5,011	† 3,988	4,579	2,466	1,841	758	72	55
Claims on Private Sector	12d	408	413	487	142	113	† 86	52	28	41	44	45	38
Claims on Deposit Money Banks	12e	2,226	5,353	1,878	6,496	19,600	† 29,520	38,978	54,053	69,141	24,038	31,771	77,772
Claims on Other Financial Insts.	12f	4,490	3,380	3,443	3,472	7,770	† 9,672	13,074	22,774	8,227	4,193	8,993	11,902
Reserve Money	14	20,949	17,164	21,691	24,153	24,690	† 38,442	33,921	29,942	33,961	21,732	52,249	47,596
of which: Currency Outside DMBs	14a	4,641	5,169	5,475	5,751	6,322	† 7,125	7,151	7,406	7,666	8,390	9,153	10,500
Foreign Liabilities	16c	9,389	11,513	5,049	5,418	9,073	† 4,900	15,763	14,979	16,499	124	142	150
Central Government Deposits	16d	7,419	6,177	6,850	6,438	13,176	† 15,550	16,594	33,488	22,667	22,901	17,833	75,923
Capital Accounts	17a	16,656	16,849	17,613	19,217	19,652	† 20,320	23,422	36,456	40,629	41,952	35,775	32,863
Other Items (Net)	17r	1,602	1,879	1,290	1,009	1,039	† 1,192	1,477	1,275	2,869	595	601	764
Deposit Money Banks							*Millions of Kronur: End of Period*						
Reserves	20	11,540	10,325	13,418	14,100	13,990	29,026	25,731	20,701	† 25,294	13,294	29,413	36,906
Foreign Assets	21	8,105	5,213	7,285	11,076	11,276	13,689	20,641	29,939	† 45,715	113,053	174,366	535,094
Claims on Central Government	22a	19,168	11,432	13,241	10,578	6,287	7,271	4,126	13,077	9,037	17,168	4,594	7,191
Claims on Private Sector	22d	196,262	208,982	236,720	348,883	376,255	461,004	663,599	772,541	† 858,886	1,097,188	1,531,303	2,518,766
Claims on Other Financial Insts.	22f	4,485	1,750	1,167	1,680	375	934	2,486	2,167	† —			
Demand Deposits	24	30,313	33,146	36,081	42,600	51,852	63,346	65,117	63,413	† 80,089	106,362	132,517	164,393
Savings Deposits	25	132,482	133,341	140,725	150,977	171,434	198,763	225,879	271,691	† 306,132	367,306	405,590	535,578
Bonds	26a	22,337	24,095	32,166	40,731	53,419	62,938	169,070	196,279	† 274,353	564,111	999,662	1,931,451
Restricted Deposits	26b	—	6	2	5	2	1						
Foreign Liabilities	26c	31,697	27,356	42,741	63,215	102,438	144,370	224,406	257,682	† 226,236	216,253	223,418	405,845
Credit from Monetary Authorities	26g	4,833	4,860	1,954	6,480	21,000	30,797	39,016	54,194	† 69,311	24,062	33,256	79,059
Capital Accounts	27a	23,186	23,296	27,617	28,907	35,604	42,424	66,448	95,709	† 116,685	157,014	335,787	543,264
Other Items (Net)	27r	−7,623	−8,278	−9,330	53,400	−27,551	−30,706	−73,352	−100,540	† −133,875	−194,406	−390,553	−561,680
Monetary Survey							*Millions of Kronur: End of Period*						
Foreign Assets (Net)	31n	−8,635	−7,695	−4,354	−24,282	−65,099	† −98,432	−185,033	−205,903	† −159,644	−45,053	16,524	196,628
Domestic Credit	32	241,940	238,256	258,743	371,168	382,635	† 467,406	671,321	779,565	† 855,364	1,096,450	1,527,175	2,462,029
Claims on Central Govt. (Net)	32an	36,295	23,731	16,925	16,991	−1,878	† −4,291	−7,889	−17,946	† −11,789	−4,975	−13,167	−68,677
Claims on Private Sector	32d	196,670	209,395	237,207	349,025	376,368	† 461,090	663,651	772,569	† 858,927	1,097,232	1,531,348	2,518,804
Claims on Other Financial Inst.	32f	8,975	5,130	4,610	5,152	8,145	† 10,606	15,560	24,942	† 8,227	4,193	8,993	11,902
Money	34	34,954	38,315	41,556	48,351	58,174	† 70,471	72,268	70,819	† 87,755	114,751	141,669	174,893
Quasi-Money	35	132,482	133,341	140,725	150,977	171,434	198,763	225,879	271,691	† 306,132	367,306	405,590	535,578
Bonds	36a	22,337	24,095	32,166	40,731	53,419	62,938	169,070	196,279	† 274,353	564,111	999,662	1,931,451
Capital Accounts	37a	39,842	40,145	45,230	48,124	55,256	† 62,744	89,870	132,165	† 157,314	198,966	371,562	576,127
Other Items (Net)	37r	1,354	−5,215	−5,163	58,700	−20,732	† −25,944	−70,798	−97,289	† −129,834	−193,739	−374,784	−559,439
Money plus Quasi-Money	35l	167,436	171,656	182,281	199,328	229,608	† 269,234	298,147	342,510	† 393,888	482,058	547,260	710,470
Interest Rates							*Percent Per Annum*						
Discount Rate (End of Period)	60	4.70	5.93	5.70	6.55	† 8.50	10.00	12.40	12.00	8.20	7.70	10.25	....
Money Market Rate	60b	4.96	6.58	6.96	7.38	8.12	9.24	11.61	14.51	11.21	5.14	6.22	....
Treasury Bill Rate	60c	4.95	7.22	6.97	7.04	7.40	8.61	11.12	11.03	8.01	4.93	6.04	....
Deposit Rate	60l	3.03	3.69	4.25	4.72	4.50	4.82	7.11	6.94	4.69	4.81	4.85	....
Housing Bond Rate	60m	5.75	5.80	5.78	5.30	4.71	4.78	6.31	6.07	5.18	4.64	4.64	....
Lending Rate	60p	10.57	11.58	12.43	12.89	12.78	13.30	16.80	17.95	15.37	11.95	12.02	....
Government Bond Yield	61	5.02	7.18	5.61	5.49	4.73	4.28	5.35	5.33	5.23	4.41	3.88	....
Prices, Production, Labor							*Index Numbers (2000=100): Period Averages*						
Consumer Prices	64	85.6	87.0	89.0	90.6	92.1	95.1	100.0	106.4	111.9	† 114.2	117.4	122.3
Wages	65a	67.6	71.6	75.1	81.2	87.5	92.9	100.0	109.6	115.5	121.7	129.0	138.3
Total Fish Catch	66al	86.2	92.0	117.4	133.5	91.5	86.1	100.0	117.0	126.2	118.2	103.0	99.4
							Number in Thousands: Period Averages						
Labor Force	67d	145	149	148	148	152	157	160	163	162	162	161	....
Employment	67e	138	142	142	142	148	153	156	159	157	157	156	....
Unemployment	67c	6	7	6	5	4	3	2	2	4	5	5	....
Unemployment Rate (%)	67r	4.7	4.9	4.4	3.9	2.8	1.9	1.4	1.4	2.5	3.3	3.1	....

Iceland 176

		1994	1995	1996	1997	1998	1999	2000	2001	2002	2003	2004	2005
Intl. Transactions & Positions							*Millions of Kronur*						
Exports	70	113,279	116,613	108,977	131,228	145,008	145,132	148,516	196,803	204,078	182,960	202,824	185,286
Fish	70al	54,644	50,535	46,030	46,712	54,722	60,028	57,442	66,986	72,691	68,422	69,289	57,134
Fishmeal	70z	4,757	4,789	8,792	9,460	9,896	7,404	9,299	12,906	18,064	13,044	6,020	2,719
Imports, c.i.f.	71	102,499	113,388	135,165	141,355	176,521	181,321	203,847	218,296	207,632	213,590	249,063	287,257
							1995=100						
Volume of Exports	72	102.3	100.0	109.0	111.1	107.9	....	....	....	....	....	....	....
Volume of Imports	73	93.9	100.0	116.5	123.7	154.2	....	....	....	....	....	....	....
Unit Value of Exports	74	95.4	100.0	98.4	99.6	....	....	....	....	....	....	....	....
Unit Value of Imports	75	96.1	100.0	102.7	103.4	....	....	....	....	....	....	....	....
Balance of Payments							*Millions of US Dollars: Minus Sign Indicates Debit*						
Current Account, n.i.e.	78ald	116	52	−131	−128	−555	−589	−847	−336	146	−543	−1,330	−2,627
Goods: Exports f.o.b.	78aad	1,560	1,804	1,890	1,855	1,927	2,009	1,902	2,016	2,240	2,386	2,896	3,107
Goods: Imports f.o.b.	78abd	−1,288	−1,598	−1,871	−1,850	−2,279	−2,316	−2,376	−2,091	−2,090	−2,596	−3,415	−4,590
Trade Balance	78acd	272	206	19	5	−351	−307	−474	−75	150	−210	−519	−1,482
Services: Credit	78add	619	691	768	843	953	930	1,044	1,086	1,118	1,378	1,623	1,999
Services: Debit	78aed	−577	−642	−741	−802	−965	−1,027	−1,164	−1,074	−1,123	−1,501	−1,835	−2,550
Balance on Goods & Services	78afd	314	255	46	47	−363	−404	−595	−63	145	−333	−731	−2,033
Income: Credit	78agd	72	82	104	101	120	129	147	171	305	374	466	1,503
Income: Debit	78ahd	−262	−280	−274	−272	−298	−304	−390	−435	−318	−569	−1,048	−2,070
Balance on Gds, Serv. & Inc.	78aid	124	56	−124	−125	−541	−579	−837	−326	132	−528	−1,314	−2,600
Current Transfers, n.i.e.: Credit	78ajd	12	15	10	17	4	5	6	8	36	12	10	11
Current Transfers: Debit	78akd	−21	−20	−17	−20	−18	−15	−16	−17	−22	−28	−27	−38
Capital Account, n.i.e.	78bcd	−6	−4	—	—	−5	−1	−3	4	−1	−5	−3	−27
Capital Account, n.i.e.: Credit	78bad	6	12	10	11	9	17	17	15	14	15	32	14
Capital Account: Debit	78bbd	−12	−17	−10	−11	−14	−18	−21	−12	−15	−20	−35	−41
Financial Account, n.i.e.	78bjd	−291	2	318	203	683	864	846	172	−58	529	2,015	2,023
Direct Investment Abroad	78bdd	−23	−25	−64	−57	−75	−125	−375	−332	−340	−376	−2,567	−6,998
Dir. Invest. in Rep. Econ., n.i.e.	78bed	−1	−9	83	148	150	65	155	166	96	322	759	2,472
Portfolio Investment Assets	78bfd	−72	−64	−51	−202	−303	−448	−667	−64	−324	−593	−1,561	−4,528
Equity Securities	78bkd	−24	−44	−68	−180	−253	−369	−651	−67	−265	−531	−1,603	−3,091
Debt Securities	78bld	−48	−20	17	−22	−51	−79	−16	3	−59	−62	42	−1,437
Portfolio Investment Liab., n.i.e.	78bgd	242	215	175	−39	68	1,030	1,142	665	467	3,591	8,403	16,956
Equity Securities	78bmd	—	—	1	−1	14	56	−44	43	55	−72	289	72
Debt Securities	78bnd	242	214	174	−38	54	974	1,186	622	413	3,663	8,115	16,884
Financial Derivatives Assets	78bwd	−49	−17	—	—	—	59	15	—	—	—	—	—
Financial Derivatives Liabilities	78bxd	55	16	−1	−1	−1	−57	−16	—	—	—	—	—
Other Investment Assets	78bhd	−31	25	−30	−162	2	−173	−79	−475	−336	−2,076	−3,447	−10,936
Monetary Authorities	78bod	—	—	—	—	—	—	—	—	—	—	—	—
General Government	78bpd	—	—	—	—	—	—	—	—	—	—	—	—
Banks	78bqd	−17	49	−37	−86	28	−92	−71	−216	−380	−2,157	−3,187	−10,466
Other Sectors	78brd	−15	−24	7	−76	−26	−81	−8	−259	19	81	−260	−470
Other Investment Liab., n.i.e.	78bid	−412	−139	206	517	843	511	671	213	379	−339	427	5,057
Monetary Authorities	78bsd	41	21	−99	—	55	−3	142	−33	48	−206	—	1
General Government	78btd	−76	60	−17	34	81	43	27	79	41	−76	−51	−123
Banks	78bud	−158	−54	288	307	420	441	332	−104	296	−37	668	3,487
Other Sectors	78bvd	−219	−166	34	176	287	31	170	271	−5	−20	−190	1,692
Net Errors and Omissions	78cad	31	−45	−33	−119	−91	−189	−70	111	−26	326	−479	703
Overall Balance	78cbd	−150	4	153	−44	32	86	−74	−48	61	307	202	71
Reserves and Related Items	79dad	150	−4	−153	44	−32	−86	74	48	−61	−307	−202	−71
Reserve Assets	79dbd	150	−4	−153	44	−32	−86	74	48	−61	−307	−202	−71
Use of Fund Credit and Loans	79dcd	—	—	—	—	—	—	—	—	—	—	—	—
Exceptional Financing	79ded	—	—	—	—	—	—	—	—	—	....	....	....
International Investment Position							*Millions of US Dollars*						
Assets	79aad	872	1,009	1,306	1,599	2,199	3,374	3,738	4,040	5,079	9,976	18,920	38,412
Direct Investment Abroad	79abd	149	180	241	272	342	456	665	843	1,256	1,726	4,036	9,742
Portfolio Investment	79acd	118	198	264	488	967	1,902	2,205	1,916	1,982	3,695	6,130	10,200
Equity Securities	79add	48	103	183	398	830	1,718	2,128	1,795	1,853	3,369	5,838	8,576
Debt Securities	79aed	71	95	81	90	137	185	78	121	129	326	292	1,624
Financial Derivatives	79ald	59	81	80	76	78	16	—	—	—	—	—	—
Other Investment	79afd	248	235	259	376	384	506	463	925	1,380	3,736	7,679	17,410
Monetary Authorities	79agd	—	—	—	—	—	—	—	—	—	—	—	—
General Government	79ahd	—	—	—	—	—	—	—	—	—	—	—	—
Banks	79aid	119	80	115	164	142	184	229	442	1,101	3,510	7,165	16,507
Other Sectors	79ajd	129	155	144	211	243	321	233	483	279	226	515	904
Reserve Assets	79akd	298	315	461	386	427	495	405	355	462	819	1,074	1,060
Liabilities	79lad	4,245	4,478	4,720	5,024	6,371	7,553	9,050	9,833	12,276	17,835	29,894	51,070
Dir. Invest. in Rep. Economy	79lbd	127	129	200	336	466	482	492	688	798	1,192	2,087	3,966
Portfolio Investment	79lcd	1,882	2,128	2,213	2,039	2,200	3,127	4,105	4,578	6,084	10,932	21,335	36,249
Equity Securities	79ldd	—	—	1	—	14	66	15	118	445	599	1,419	2,230
Debt Securities	79led	1,882	2,128	2,212	2,039	2,186	3,061	4,090	4,460	5,640	10,333	19,916	34,019
Financial Derivatives	79lld	56	74	74	74	74	16	—	—	—	—	—	—
Other Investment	79lfd	2,180	2,146	2,233	2,575	3,631	3,928	4,454	4,567	5,394	5,711	6,472	10,855
Monetary Authorities	79lgd	81	103	2	1	57	51	187	145	205	2	2	2
General Government	79lhd	287	377	334	345	446	444	456	520	631	713	684	509
Banks	79lid	459	421	660	903	1,427	1,814	2,273	2,097	3,039	3,349	4,249	7,286
Other Sectors	79ljd	1,352	1,246	1,238	1,326	1,701	1,618	1,538	1,804	1,520	1,648	1,537	3,057

Iceland 176

		1994	1995	1996	1997	1998	1999	2000	2001	2002	2003	2004	2005
Government Finance						*Millions of Kronur: Year Ending December 31*							
Deficit (-) or Surplus	80	−21,972	−20,270	−4,389	1,863	† 16,284	20,435	9,548	−25,714	−4,133	11,843	22,408	81,889
Total Revenue and Grants	81y	130,008	135,715	150,816	155,200	† 167,388	194,993	207,561	219,748	230,510	249,606	280,696	399,289
Revenue	81	129,409	135,715	150,816	155,200	† 166,529	194,250	206,993	219,029	229,815	248,201	280,028	398,562
Grants	81z	599	—	—		† 859	743	568	719	695	1,405	668	727
Exp. & Lending Minus Repay	82z	151,980	155,985	155,205	153,337	† 151,104	174,558	198,013	245,462	234,643	237,763	258,288	317,400
Expenditure	82	142,756	146,826	156,454	152,990	† 159,651	177,964	195,411	221,305	246,810	268,714	280,382	308,383
Lending Minus Repayments	83	9,224	9,159	−1,248	347	† −8,547	−3,406	2,602	24,157	−12,167	−30,951	−22,094	9,017
Financing													
Total Financing	80h	....	....	....	....	† −16,284	−20,435	−9,548	25,714	4,134	−11,842	−22,408	−81,889
Total Net Borrowing	84	21,972	20,270	4,389	−1,863	† −10,498	−20,691	−9,246	26,539	−4,292	−13,452	−14,110	−57,555
Net Domestic	84a	10,493	5,185	−2,254	4,660	† 48	−19,586	−17,443	−4,840	−492	10,308	....	....
Net Foreign	85a	11,479	15,085	6,643	−6,523	† −10,546	−1,105	8,197	31,379	−3,800	−23,760	....	....
Use of Cash Balances	87	....	....	....	....	† −5,786	256	−302	−825	8,426	1,610	−8,298	−24,334
Total Debt by Residence	88	197,106	213,575	225,677	226,111	† 209,020	190,693	187,972	242,353	279,055	255,697	241,734	190,827
Domestic	88a	83,473	86,314	93,459	99,483	† 92,938	74,480	61,643	69,160	70,336	89,749	86,569	97,252
Foreign	89a	113,633	127,261	132,218	126,628	† 116,082	116,213	126,329	173,193	208,719	165,948	155,165	93,575
National Accounts						*Millions of Kronur*							
Househ.Cons.Expend.,incl.NPISHs	96f	247,821	258,215	278,656	305,395	340,908	378,130	413,488	432,161	445,619	476,879	525,808	599,222
Government Consumption Expend	91f	93,823	98,961	105,563	114,112	129,129	143,825	159,260	178,200	202,135	213,502	228,287	246,325
Gross Fixed Capital Formation	93e	74,398	75,386	97,867	103,501	139,220	136,263	152,825	164,746	139,295	164,698	215,647	285,933
Changes in Inventories	93i	260	3,052	25	102	906	120	2,494	−2,084	−182	−1,453	−918	−862
Exports of Goods and Services	90c	157,436	161,250	176,836	190,709	204,270	212,237	229,577	299,492	305,607	288,552	316,904	313,950
Imports of Goods and Services (-)	98c	134,631	144,725	173,755	187,946	230,382	242,045	279,345	307,642	292,915	314,314	368,962	448,578
Gross Domestic Product (GDP)	99b	431,795	445,106	477,691	525,873	584,051	628,530	678,299	764,873	799,560	827,863	916,765	995,990
Net Primary Income from Abroad	98.n	−13,659	−12,829	−11,317	−12,116	−12,647	−12,567	−19,409	−25,285	−6,245	−16,502	−17,717	....
Gross National Income (GNI)	99a	425,449	439,310	473,875	498,267	554,695	595,881	641,566	715,351	759,994	780,985	841,204	....
Consumption of Fixed Capital	99cf	63,427	64,960	67,526	60,216	62,837	69,729	77,346	91,328	97,219	98,638	106,046	....
GDP Volume 1990 Prices	99b.p	376,465	376,770	396,438	414,939	....	....	....	....	....	....	....	....
GDP Volume 2000 Prices	99b.p	....	....	....	590,384	624,461	651,294	678,299	704,270	696,902	717,868	776,712	820,136
GDP Volume (2000=100)	99bvp	79.0	79.0	83.2	† 87.0	92.1	96.0	100.0	103.8	102.7	105.8	114.5	120.9
GDP Deflator (2000=100)	99bip	80.6	83.0	84.7	89.1	93.5	96.5	100.0	108.6	114.7	115.3	118.0	121.4
						Millions: Midyear Estimates							
Population	99z	.26	.27	.27	.27	.28	.28	.28	.28	.29	.29	.29	.29

India 534

		1994	1995	1996	1997	1998	1999	2000	2001	2002	2003	2004	2005
Exchange Rates		*Rupees per SDR: End of Period*											
Market Rate	aa	45.810	52.295	51.666	52.999	59.813	59.690	60.911	60.549	65.298	67.768	67.688	64.410
		Rupees per US Dollar: End of Period (ae) Period Average (rf)											
Market Rate	ae	31.380	35.180	35.930	39.280	42.480	43.490	46.750	48.180	48.030	45.605	43.585	45.065
Market Rate	rf	31.374	32.427	35.433	36.313	41.259	43.055	44.942	47.186	48.610	46.583	45.316	44.100
Fund Position		*Millions of SDRs: End of Period*											
Quota	2f.s	3,056	3,056	3,056	3,056	3,056	4,158	4,158	4,158	4,158	4,158	4,158	4,158
SDRs	1b.s	1	93	85	57	59	3	1	4	5	2	3	3
Reserve Position in the Fund	1c.s	213	213	213	213	213	489	489	489	489	887	917	631
Total Fund Cred.&Loans Outstg.	2tl	2,763	1,967	1,085	590	285	39	—	—	—	—	—	—
International Liquidity		*Millions of US Dollars Unless Otherwise Indicated: End of Period*											
Total Reserves minus Gold	1l.d	19,698	17,922	20,170	24,688	27,341	32,667	37,902	45,870	67,665	98,938	126,593	131,924
SDRs	1b.d	2	139	122	77	83	4	2	5	7	3	5	4
Reserve Position in the Fund	1c.d	310	316	306	287	300	671	637	614	665	1,318	1,424	902
Foreign Exchange	1d.d	19,386	17,467	19,742	24,324	26,958	31,992	37,264	45,251	66,994	97,617	125,164	131,018
Gold (Million Fine Troy Ounces)	1ad	11.800	12.780	12.781	12.740	11.487	11.502	11.502	11.502	11.502	11.502	11.502	11.502
Gold (National Valuation)	1and	3,355	3,669	3,614	2,880	2,492	2,403	2,252	2,252	2,712	3,323	3,808	4,102
Monetary Authorities		*Billions of Rupees: Last Friday of Period*											
Foreign Assets	11	721.3	749.0	847.8	1,058.1	1,256.4	1,525.2	1,876.8	2,326.0	3,379.6	4,612.5	5,706.7	6,467.2
Claims on Central Government	12a	1,034.9	1,128.0	1,360.6	1,373.8	1,571.3	1,631.0	1,538.5	1,553.0	1,190.3	565.4	857.3	760.9
Claims on Deposit Money Banks	12e	25.2	60.1	7.9	12.7	31.9	26.8	68.0	70.8	.7	.1	6.7	4.8
Claims on Other Financial Insts.	12f	120.7	125.2	124.0	134.9	146.2	158.6	210.4	194.9	107.4	67.7	82.6	70.0
Reserve Money	14	1,543.8	1,737.8	1,903.2	2,116.1	2,378.7	2,649.3	2,854.2	3,145.1	3,438.3	3,911.5	4,549.6	5,228.2
of which: Currency Outside DMBs	14a	948.5	1,136.2	1,295.2	1,443.0	1,624.4	1,925.0	2,038.5	2,296.9	2,609.8	3,004.8	3,418.4	3,946.7
Foreign Liabilities	16c	126.6	102.8	56.1	31.3	17.0	2.3	—	—	—	—	752.0	812.6
Central Government Deposits	16d	.7	.7	.6	.6	.6	1.4	1.4	1.4	1.4	1.4	113.2	110.9
Capital Accounts	17a	154.8	159.2	158.8	166.8	167.4	164.3	161.7	157.5	111.5	113.2	113.2	110.9
Other Items (Net)	17r	76.4	61.7	221.5	264.7	442.0	524.2	676.2	840.7	1,126.8	1,219.5	1,238.6	1,151.1
Deposit Money Banks		*Billions of Rupees: Last Friday of Period*											
Reserves	20	628.8	646.9	568.7	604.3	783.7	661.7	747.4	769.8	733.6	799.5	1,182.7	1,298.0
Claims on Central Government	22a	1,223.3	1,291.1	1,545.9	1,896.4	2,237.7	2,768.1	3,333.8	4,082.5	5,097.4	6,358.9	6,950.0	6,983.7
Claims on Private Sector	22d	2,429.9	2,713.9	3,264.2	3,640.0	4,196.4	5,054.7	6,064.3	6,626.1	8,052.8	8,831.7	11,531.9	14,553.2
Demand Deposits	24	710.8	686.2	808.5	933.1	1,039.1	1,203.4	1,435.5	1,523.9	1,689.0	1,984.2	2,602.0	3,221.7
Time Deposits	25	3,034.0	3,366.2	4,084.4	4,914.7	5,963.3	6,991.9	8,197.5	9,522.0	11,283.7	12,617.0	14,527.4	16,595.0
Credit from Monetary Authorities	26g	77.6	138.4	18.1	7.7	63.1	25.5	66.9	69.9	.7	.3	1.5	.1
Other Items (Net)	27r	459.7	461.1	467.8	285.2	152.3	263.6	445.6	362.6	910.3	1,388.5	2,533.6	3,018.1
Monetary Survey		*Billions of Rupees: Last Friday of Period*											
Foreign Assets (Net)	31n	594.8	646.2	791.7	1,026.8	1,239.3	1,522.9	1,876.8	2,326.0	3,379.6	4,612.5	5,706.7	6,467.2
Domestic Credit	32	4,808.2	5,257.5	6,294.0	7,044.4	8,151.0	9,610.9	11,145.5	12,455.1	14,446.4	15,822.2	18,669.9	21,555.2
Claims on Central Govt. (Net)	32an	2,257.6	2,418.4	2,905.9	3,269.6	3,808.4	4,397.6	4,870.8	5,634.1	6,286.2	6,922.8	7,055.3	6,932.0
Claims on Private Sector	32d	2,429.9	2,713.9	3,264.2	3,640.0	4,196.4	5,054.7	6,064.3	6,626.1	8,052.8	8,831.7	11,531.9	14,553.2
Claims on Other Financial Insts.	32f	120.7	125.2	124.0	134.9	146.2	158.6	210.4	194.9	107.4	67.7	82.6	70.0
Money	34	1,695.0	1,883.5	2,148.9	2,419.3	2,703.5	3,161.2	3,495.9	3,846.0	4,324.9	5,026.0	6,067.7	7,213.2
Quasi-Money	35	3,034.0	3,366.2	4,084.4	4,914.7	5,963.3	6,991.9	8,197.5	9,522.0	11,283.7	12,617.0	14,527.4	16,595.0
Other Items (Net)	37r	673.9	653.9	852.4	737.3	723.6	980.7	1,328.9	1,413.1	2,217.4	2,791.7	3,781.5	4,214.2
Money plus Quasi-Money	35l	4,729.0	5,249.7	6,233.4	7,334.0	8,666.8	10,153.0	11,693.4	13,368.0	15,608.6	17,643.0	20,595.1	23,808.1
Interest Rates		*Percent Per Annum*											
Bank Rate (End of Period)	60	12.00	12.00	12.00	9.00	9.00	8.00	8.00	6.50	6.25	6.00	6.00	6.00
Money Market Rate	60b	7.14	15.57	11.04	5.29	....	....	....	....	....	....	....	....
Lending Rate	60p	14.75	15.46	15.96	13.83	13.54	12.54	12.29	12.08	11.92	11.46	10.92	10.75
Prices, Production, Labor		*Index Numbers (2000=100): Period Averages*											
Share Prices	62	88.2	72.8	73.3	82.4	72.4	89.9	100.0	75.5	70.7	117.6	138.6	198.5
Wholesale Prices	63	71.8	† 78.5	82.0	85.7	90.7	93.9	100.0	104.8	107.5	113.3	120.7	126.4
Consumer Prices	64	63.0	69.5	75.7	81.1	91.9	96.1	100.0	103.7	108.2	112.4	116.6	121.5
Industrial Production	66	64.9	† 73.1	79.4	83.7	86.5	93.1	100.0	102.1	107.3	114.2	123.7	133.5
		Number in Thousands: Period Averages											
Employment	67e	27,375	27,987	27,941	28,245	28,166	28,113	27,960	27,789	27,206	....	....	....
Unemployment	67c	36,692	36,742	37,430	39,140	40,090	40,371	41,344	41,996	41,171	41,389	40,458	....
Intl. Transactions & Positions		*Billions of Rupees*											
Exports	70	785	995	1,172	1,271	1,379	1,536	1,907	2,045	2,448	2,743	3,424	4,200
Imports, c.i.f.	71	842	1,127	1,344	1,505	1,772	2,024	2,317	2,378	2,747	3,375	4,413	5,936
		2000=100											
Unit Value of Exports	74	79	78	81	94	98	97	100	99	99	108	117	....
Unit Value of Imports	75	67	72	82	83	84	92	100	101	112	112	141	....

India 534

		1994	1995	1996	1997	1998	1999	2000	2001	2002	2003	2004	2005
Balance of Payments						*Millions of US Dollars: Minus Sign Indicates Debit*							
Current Account, n.i.e.	78ald	−1,676	−5,563	−5,956	−2,965	−6,903	−3,228	−4,601	1,410	7,059	6,853	....	....
Goods: Exports f.o.b.	78aad	25,523	31,239	33,737	35,702	34,076	36,877	43,247	44,793	51,141	59,338	....	....
Goods: Imports f.o.b.	78abd	−29,673	−37,957	−43,789	−45,730	−44,828	−45,556	−53,887	−51,211	−54,700	−68,208	....	....
Trade Balance	78acd	−4,150	−6,719	−10,052	−10,028	−10,752	−8,679	−10,640	−6,418	−3,559	−8,870	....	....
Services: Credit	78add	6,038	6,775	7,238	9,111	11,691	14,509	16,684	17,337	19,478	23,397	....	....
Services: Debit	78aed	−8,200	−10,268	−11,171	−12,443	−14,540	−17,221	−19,187	−20,099	−21,041	−25,710	....	....
Balance on Goods & Services	78afd	−6,312	−10,212	−13,984	−13,360	−13,601	−11,441	−13,143	−9,181	−5,122	−11,183	....	....
Income: Credit	78agd	821	1,486	1,411	1,484	1,806	1,919	2,521	3,524	3,188	3,779	....	....
Income: Debit	78ahd	−4,370	−5,219	−4,667	−5,002	−5,443	−5,629	−7,414	−7,666	−7,097	−8,230	....	....
Balance on Gds, Serv. & Inc.	78aid	−9,861	−13,945	−17,240	−16,878	−17,238	−15,151	−18,036	−13,323	−9,031	−15,635	....	....
Current Transfers, n.i.e.: Credit	78ajd	8,208	8,410	11,350	13,975	10,402	11,958	13,548	15,140	16,788	22,833	....	....
Current Transfers: Debit	78akd	−23	−27	−66	−62	−67	−35	−114	−407	−698	−345	....	....
Capital Account, n.i.e.	78bcd	....	....	....	—	—	....	716	743	102	3,839	....	....
Capital Account, n.i.e.: Credit	78bad	....	....	....	—	—	....	2,758	2,227	1,409	5,595	....	....
Capital Account: Debit	78bbd	....	....	....	—	—	....	−2,042	−1,484	−1,307	−1,756	....	....
Financial Account, n.i.e.	78bjd	10,576	3,861	11,848	9,635	8,584	9,579	9,623	7,252	11,882	14,791	....	....
Direct Investment Abroad	78bdd	−83	−117	−239	−113	−48	−79	−510	−1,398	−1,678	−1,324	....	....
Dir. Invest. in Rep. Econ., n.i.e.	78bed	973	2,144	2,426	3,577	2,635	2,169	3,584	5,472	5,626	4,585	....	....
Portfolio Investment Assets	78bfd	....	....	....	—	—	—	—	—	—	—	....	....
Equity Securities	78bkd	....	....	....	—	—	—	—	—	—	—	....	....
Debt Securities	78bld	....	....	....	—	—	—	—	—	—	—	....	....
Portfolio Investment Liab., n.i.e.	78bgd	5,491	1,590	3,958	2,556	−601	2,317	2,345	2,853	1,022	8,216	....	....
Equity Securities	78bmd	5,491	1,590	3,958	2,556	−601	2,317	2,345	2,853	1,022	8,216	....	....
Debt Securities	78bnd	....	....	....	—	—	....	....	....	....	....	....	....
Financial Derivatives Assets	78bwd	....	....	....	—	—	....	....	....	....	....	....	....
Financial Derivatives Liabilities	78bxd	....	....	....	—	—	....	....	....	....	....	....	....
Other Investment Assets	78bhd	1,170	−1,179	−4,710	−4,743	−3,239	−450	1,712	−2,834	3,699	−3,259	....	....
Monetary Authorities	78bod	1	....	....	—	—	−498	9,069	7,365	10,163	13,057	....	....
General Government	78bpd	9	−29	−5	67	11	33	−104	646	400	−4,341	....	....
Banks	78bqd	−1,029	−92	−1,642	−2,156	−1,355	1,140	−369	−3,012	−2,836	−4,608	....	....
Other Sectors	78brd	2,189	−1,058	−3,063	−2,653	−1,896	−1,126	−6,884	−7,833	−4,028	−7,366	....	....
Other Investment Liab., n.i.e.	78bid	3,024	1,423	10,413	8,357	9,837	5,623	2,492	3,160	3,213	6,574	....	....
Monetary Authorities	78bsd	142	−65	45	233	122	1,344	−127	211	320	−427	....	....
General Government	78btd	92	1,483	1,698	397	−72	237	1,467	2,949	2,893	7,001	....	....
Banks	78bud	1,307	266	2,989	1,098	1,739	2,458	562	—			....	....
Other Sectors	78bvd	1,483	−261	5,680	6,629	8,047	1,584	590	—			....	....
Net Errors and Omissions	78cad	1,492	970	−1,934	−1,348	1,390	313	331	−715	−191	183	....	....
Overall Balance	78cbd	10,391	−733	3,958	5,321	3,071	6,664	6,069	8,690	18,853	25,667	....	....
Reserves and Related Items	79dad	−10,391	733	−3,958	−5,321	−3,071	−6,664	−6,069	−8,690	−18,853	−25,667	....	....
Reserve Assets	79dbd	−9,238	1,956	−2,676	−4,637	−2,659	−6,327	−6,017	−8,690	−18,853	−25,667	....	....
Use of Fund Credit and Loans	79dcd	−1,153	−1,223	−1,282	−684	−412	−337	−52	—	—	—	....	....
Exceptional Financing	79ded	....	....	....	—	—	....	—	—	—	—	....	....
International Investment Position						*Millions of US Dollars*							
Assets	79aad	....	....	37,716	41,539	46,823	54,717	62,474	73,618	95,590	137,124	169,250	....
Direct Investment Abroad	79abd	....	....	617	706	1,707	1,859	2,616	4,006	5,825	7,079	9,568	....
Portfolio Investment	79acd	....	....	283	276	130	121	504	653	782	757	806	....
Equity Securities	79add	....	....	172	165	25	21	270	339	374	396	396	....
Debt Securities	79aed	....	....	111	111	105	100	234	314	408	361	410	....
Financial Derivatives	79ald	....	....	—	—	—	—	—	—	—	—	—	....
Other Investment	79afd	....	....	10,098	10,906	11,833	14,043	16,457	14,241	12,883	16,326	17,367	....
Monetary Authorities	79agd	....	....	—	—	—	—	—	—	—	—	—	....
General Government	79ahd	....	....	1,057	1,026	1,002	1,011	1,032	1,061	1,227	1,413	1,523	....
Banks	79aid	....	....	7,270	7,688	7,681	10,599	12,648	10,786	8,856	11,094	10,016	....
Other Sectors	79ajd	....	....	1,771	2,192	3,150	2,433	2,777	2,394	2,801	3,819	5,828	....
Reserve Assets	79akd	....	....	26,718	29,651	33,153	38,694	42,897	54,717	76,100	112,962	141,508	....
Liabilities	79lad	....	....	118,763	122,199	125,850	131,564	138,629	142,737	155,985	184,131	210,132	....
Dir. Invest. in Rep. Economy	79lbd	....	....	10,630	14,065	15,426	17,517	20,326	25,419	31,221	39,104	44,511	....
Portfolio Investment	79lcd	....	....	18,743	20,410	23,105	25,009	31,296	31,539	32,409	43,723	55,467	....
Equity Securities	79ldd	....	....	13,631	14,109	13,080	15,734	17,414	18,613	20,088	33,953	42,768	....
Debt Securities	79led	....	....	5,112	6,301	10,025	9,275	13,882	12,926	12,321	9,770	12,699	....
Financial Derivatives	79lld	....	....	—	—	—	—	—	—	—	—	—	....
Other Investment	79lfd	....	....	89,390	87,724	87,319	89,038	87,007	85,779	92,355	101,304	110,154	....
Monetary Authorities	79lgd	....	....	1,836	1,149	819	387	282	386	446	661	898	....
General Government	79lhd	....	....	47,828	45,408	45,244	45,991	43,331	43,860	43,844	43,657	45,641	....
Banks	79lid	....	....	17,155	16,169	16,111	17,294	19,595	20,197	27,165	33,575	34,700	....
Other Sectors	79ljd	....	....	22,571	24,998	25,145	25,366	23,799	21,335	20,900	23,410	28,915	....
Government Finance						*Billions of Rupees: Year Beginning April 1*							
Deficit (-) or Surplus	80	−567.5	−598.5	−668.8	−741.9	−917.2	−1,061.5	−1,087.1p	−1,079.2f	....	....	....	....
Revenue	81	1,283.2	1,488.8	1,717.1	1,864.5	2,015.3	2,349.7	2,696.9p	3,093.7f	....	....	....	....
Grants Received	81z	10.4	11.4	11.9	10.2	9.9	11.1	7.3p	7.0f	....	....	....	....
Expenditure	82	1,540.6	1,763.1	2,010.6	2,305.8	2,610.5	3,013.1	3,486.8p	3,953.1f	....	....	....	....
Lending Minus Repayments	83	320.5	335.6	387.2	310.7	331.9	409.1	304.5p	226.8f	....	....	....	....
Financing													
Net Borrowing: Domestic	84a	519.4	611.8	634.3	740.1	900.4	1,041.0	1,055.3p	1,060.6f	....	....	....	....
Foreign	85a	35.8	3.2	29.9	10.9	19.2	11.8	5.7p	18.7f	....	....	....	....
Use of Cash Balances	87	12.3	−16.6	4.6	−9.1	−2.4	8.6	26.1p	—f	....	....	....	....
Debt: Domestic	88a	4,586.9	5,213.0	5,835.2	7,229.6	8,345.5	9,625.9	11,052.1p	12,563.6f	....	....	....	....
Foreign	89a	509.3	512.5	542.4	553.3	572.5	584.4	584.3p	595.9f	....	....	....	....

		1994	1995	1996	1997	1998	1999	2000	2001	2002	2003	2004	2005
National Accounts						*Billions of Rupees: Year Beginning April 1*							
Househ.Cons.Expend.,incl.NPISHs....	96f	6,641.6	7,658.0	9,036.5	9,816.7	11,394.1	12,662.9	13,505.2	14,704.2	15,401.8	17,222.9	18,906.2	....
Government Consumption Expend...	91f	1,086.4	1,288.2	1,457.3	1,721.9	2,140.3	2,522.9	2,644.2	2,803.6	2,888.6	3,078.2	3,515.6	....
Gross Fixed Capital Formation.........	93e	2,222.4	2,894.1	3,118.5	3,304.2	3,743.4	4,572.4	4,786.0	5,272.6	5,896.1	6,820.0	8,069.0	....
Changes in Inventories.....................	93i	145.5	257.7	−139.9	132.9	−21.3	394.6	182.7	130.3	154.4	191.5	422.0	....
Exports of Goods and Services.........	90c	1,016.1	1,307.3	1,448.5	1,652.0	1,952.8	2,277.0	2,781.3	2,907.6	3,555.6	4,078.0	5,915.6	....
Imports of Goods and Services (-).....	98c	1,047.1	1,449.5	1,610.2	1,843.3	2,247.5	2,657.0	2,975.2	3,110.5	3,799.8	4,434.0	6,550.6	....
Gross Domestic Product (GDP).........	99b	10,127.7	11,880.1	13,682.1	15,225.5	17,409.9	19,588.1	21,076.6	22,813.1	24,497.4	27,602.2	31,214.1	35,292.4
Net Primary Income from Abroad.....	98.n	−130.8	−134.8	−130.8	−132.1	−149.7	−154.3	−227.3	−200.7	−166.9	−182.5	−179.2	....
Gross National Income (GNI)............	99a	9,996.9	11,745.3	13,551.3	15,093.4	17,260.2	19,433.8	20,849.3	22,612.4	24,330.5	27,419.7	31,035.0	....
Gross Nat'l Disposable Inc.(GNDI)....	99i	9,271.1	10,787.1	12,625.9	14,011.1	16,012.5	19,965.2	21,437.4	23,346.0	25,122.7	28,467.9	31,952.4	....
Gross Saving...................................	99s	2,514.6	2,987.5	3,172.6	3,521.8	3,749.3	4,873.0	4,962.7	5,379.7	6,489.9	7,975.1	9,074.2	....
Consumption of Fixed Capital..........	99cf	979.9	1,179.3	1,365.0	1,520.0	1,680.7	1,866.5	2,027.3	2,211.6	2,356.0	2,565.7	2,947.6	3,240.9
GDP at Factor Cost.........................	99ba	9,170.6	10,732.7	12,435.5	13,901.5	15,981.3	17,922.9	19,301.8	20,974.5	22,555.7	25,434.0	28,439.0	32,006.1
GDP at Fact.Cost,Vol.'93/94 Prices...	99bap	8,380.3	8,995.6	9,700.8	10,166.0	10,827.5	11,483.7	....	....	....	....	....	....
GDP at Fact.Cost,Vol.'99/00 Prices...	99bap	....	....	....	....	....	17,922.9	18,703.7	19,780.6	20,525.9	22,260.4	23,936.7	25,865.9
GDP Volume 1993/94 Prices.............	99b.p	9,244.6	9,939.5	10,674.5	11,152.5	11,820.2	12,662.8	13,162.0	13,840.1	14,476.0	15,674.0	....	....
GDP Volume (2000=100)..................	99bvp	69.9	75.1	80.9	84.8	90.3	95.8	100.0	105.8	109.7	119.0	128.0	138.3
GDP Deflator (2000=100)...............	99bip	67.9	74.1	79.6	84.9	91.6	96.9	100.0	102.8	106.5	110.7	115.1	119.9
						Millions: Midyear Estimates							
Population...............................	99z	918.29	935.57	952.83	970.04	987.18	1,004.20	1,021.08	1,037.81	1,054.37	1,070.80	1,087.12	1,103.37

Indonesia 536

		1994	1995	1996	1997	1998	1999	2000	2001	2002	2003	2004	2005
Exchange Rates						*Rupiah per SDR: End of Period*							
Market Rate	aa	3,211.7	3,430.8	3,426.7	6,274.0	11,299.4	9,724.2	12,501.4	13,070.0	12,154.1	12,578.7	14,427.5	14,049.7
					Rupiah per US Dollar: End of Period (ae) Period Average (rf)								
Market Rate	ae	2,200.0	2,308.0	2,383.0	4,650.0	8,025.0	7,085.0	9,595.0	10,400.0	8,940.0	8,465.0	9,290.0	9,830.0
Market Rate	rf	2,160.8	2,248.6	2,342.3	2,909.4	10,013.6	7,855.2	8,421.8	10,260.9	9,311.2	8,577.1	8,938.9	9,704.7
Fund Position						*Millions of SDRs: End of Period*							
Quota	2f.s	1,498	1,498	1,498	1,498	1,498	2,079	2,079	2,079	2,079	2,079	2,079	2,079
SDRs	1b.s	—	1	2	370	222	—	24	13	14	2	2	5
Reserve Position in the Fund	1c.s	214	270	298	—	—	145	145	145	145	145	145	145
Total Fund Cred.&Loans Outstg	2tl	—	—	—	2,201	6,456	7,467	8,318	7,252	6,518	6,915	6,237	5,462
International Liquidity						*Millions of US Dollars Unless Otherwise Indicated: End of Period*							
Total Reserves minus Gold	1l.d	12,133	13,708	18,251	16,587	22,713	26,445	28,502	27,246	30,971	34,962	34,952	32,989
SDRs	1b.d	—	1	2	499	312	—	32	16	19	4	2	7
Reserve Position in the Fund	1c.d	312	401	429	—	—	200	190	183	198	216	226	208
Foreign Exchange	1d.d	11,820	13,306	17,820	16,088	22,401	26,245	28,280	27,048	30,754	34,742	34,724	32,774
Gold (Million Fine Troy Ounces)	1ad	3.101	3.101	3.101	3.101	3.101	3.101	3.101	3.101	3.101	3.101	3.101	3.100
Gold (National Valuation)	1and	1,067	1,079	1,030	809	803	812	766	772	1,077	1,291	1,351	1,590
Monetary Authorities: Other Liab	4..d	20	21	21	419	3,374	3,586	2,260	2,151	2,136	2,146	1,918	1,370
Banking Institutions: Assets	7a.d	5,843	7,407	8,737	10,067	14,412	16,931	10,649	10,555	10,084	9,136	7,414	12,182
Liabilities	7b.d	10,766	11,678	12,482	15,147	12,192	14,137	9,659	6,577	5,805	3,716	6,480	6,927
Monetary Authorities						*Billions of Rupiah: End of Period*							
Foreign Assets	11	38,405	43,642	60,607	99,716	194,054	194,325	294,112	† 304,982	293,802	313,585	† 344,125	345,942
Claims on Central Government	12a	7,510	4,672	4,269	5,470	35,700	248,095	233,669	† 270,228	306,822	263,394	† 273,670	297,275
Claims on State and Local Govts	12b	—	—	—	—	—	—	—	† —	—	—	† —	—
Claims on Nonfin.Pub.Enterprises	12c	8	4	—	—	—	—	—	† —	—	—	† —	—
Claims on Private Sector	12d	196	218	197	205	265	1,230	6,382	† 35,146	35,248	35,448	† 38,351	24,649
Claims on Banking Institutions	12e	13,333	15,722	14,438	58,624	113,543	14,437	18,790	† 12,150	11,104	9,286	† 10,111	9,389
Claims on Nonbank Financial Insts	12g	274	734	744	8,535	53,356	28,984	29,571	† 1,132	1,482	1,701	† 1,494	1,473
Reserve Money	14	23,053	27,160	36,895	51,013	90,690	125,848	156,420	† 181,223	179,578	202,562	† 205,909	269,656
of which: Currency Outside Banks	14a	18,634	20,807	22,486	28,423	41,393	58,352	72,370	† 76,342	80,659	94,539	† 109,028	124,000
Other Liabs. to Banking Insts	14n	15,051	11,851	18,553	14,885	49,590	63,049	60,076	† 55,742	77,654	107,025	† 130,652	93,559
Time, Savings,&Fgn.Currency Dep	15							192	† 411	447	333	† 272	315
Liabs. of Central Bank: Securities	16ac	—	—	—	—	—	—	—	† —	—	—	† —	—
Restricted Deposits	16b	497	461	436	267	660	244	290	† —	—	—	† 12	10
Foreign Liabilities	16c	43	49	50	15,761	100,025	98,018	125,676	† 117,149	98,319	105,147	† 107,807	90,206
Central Government Deposits	16d	13,536	15,558	16,856	33,472	35,438	83,990	96,820	† 93,643	114,881	73,244	† 47,050	47,789
Liab. to Nonbank Financial Insts	16j	....	....	....	....	....	....					† —	
Capital Accounts	17a	7,399	8,807	7,421	56,851	122,284	84,687	118,814	† 127,678	123,943	97,017	† 120,397	119,084
Other Items (Net)	17r	147	1,106	45	301	−1,770	31,235	24,237	† 47,793	53,636	38,083	† 55,653	58,109
Banking Institutions						*Billions of Rupiah: End of Period*							
Reserves	20	5,051	7,371	14,896	24,172	50,229	68,479	66,537	† 93,357	94,633	105,650	† 137,379	181,111
Claims on Mon.Author.:Securities	20c	7,619	5,152	11,225	6,318	44,964	63,049	58,700	† 55,742	76,859	102,259	† 103,509	74,231
Other Claims on Monetary Author	20n	....	....	....	....	....	....	....	—	—	—	† —	—
Foreign Assets	21	12,874	17,096	20,820	46,810	115,657	120,209	102,179	† 109,774	90,147	77,340	† 68,874	119,752
Claims on Central Government	22a	2,843	4,165	5,727	8,571	10,230	274,551	439,177	† 423,735	393,338	361,397	† 324,674	321,018
Claims on State and Local Govts	22b	113	276	290	292	319	214	376	† 446	310	2,718	† 708	487
Claims on Nonfin.Pub.Enterprises	22c	6,866	8,423	9,248	11,036	15,128	11,854	10,343	† 10,748	15,946	11,107	† 13,908	17,220
Claims on Private Sector	22d	198,311	243,067	295,195	381,741	508,558	225,236	270,301	† 298,901	352,378	426,685	† 567,576	708,422
Claims on Nonbank Financial Insts	22g	2,329	2,785	4,897	6,353	5,763	1,998	2,554	† 4,025	5,602	7,214	† 16,909	23,291
Demand Deposits	24	24,135	28,639	31,766	43,879	49,185	57,646	82,241	† 92,971	101,515	118,766	† 136,422	146,768
Time, Savings,& Fgn. Currency Dep	25	130,280	171,257	226,097	279,073	481,350	525,227	587,730	† 667,278	694,504	733,245	† 785,260	928,945
Money Market Instruments	26aa	2,437	4,162	3,353	4,306	3,223	2,986	2,253	† 1,847	1,962	6,273	† 2,670	2,280
Restricted Deposits	26b	1,541	1,779	2,099	1,419	2,417	1,659	4,783	† 7,966	5,075	3,096	† 5,484	5,805
Foreign Liabilities	26c	24,885	26,952	29,744	70,434	97,842	100,375	92,675	† 68,406	51,895	31,458	† 60,195	68,088
Central Government Deposits	26d	12,720	13,278	16,004	14,935	21,117	25,525	52,285	† 54,013	41,727	45,608	† 50,975	64,295
Credit from Monetary Authorities	26g	11,432	10,394	11,622	23,008	112,947	33,360	16,547	† 15,225	12,694	10,971	† 10,111	9,389
Liab. to Nonbank Financial Insts	26j	1,326	1,564	2,533	7,536	39,332	14,725	14,690	† 2,845	4,652	4,860	† 4,415	4,401
Capital Accounts	27a	26,775	36,506	42,523	53,408	−94,556	−17,346	52,327	† 66,788	93,697	112,141	† 134,239	147,773
Other Items (Net)	27r	475	−6,196	−3,443	−12,705	37,991	21,433	44,638	† 19,388	21,493	27,954	† 43,765	67,789
Banking Survey						*Billions of Rupiah: End of Period*							
Foreign Assets (Net)	31n	26,351	33,737	51,633	60,331	111,844	116,141	177,941	† 229,202	233,736	254,321	† 244,997	307,401
Domestic Credit	32	192,194	235,508	287,707	373,796	572,764	682,647	843,268	† 896,706	954,519	990,812	† 1,139,263	1,281,751
Claims on Central Govt. (Net)	32an	−15,903	−19,999	−22,864	−34,366	−10,625	413,131	523,741	† 546,307	543,553	505,939	† 500,318	506,208
Claims on State and Local Govts	32b	113	276	290	292	319	214	376	† 446	310	2,718	† 708	487
Claims on Nonfin.Pub.Enterprises	32c	6,874	8,427	9,248	11,036	15,128	11,854	10,343	† 10,748	15,946	11,107	† 13,908	17,220
Claims on Private Sector	32d	198,507	243,285	295,392	381,946	508,823	226,466	276,683	† 334,047	387,626	462,133	† 605,927	733,072
Claims on Nonbank Financial Inst	32g	2,603	3,519	5,641	14,888	59,119	30,982	32,125	† 5,157	7,084	8,915	† 18,403	24,764
Money	34	42,887	49,572	54,534	72,431	90,768	116,880	160,923	† 170,050	182,647	213,681	† 245,675	270,834
Quasi-Money	35	130,280	171,257	226,097	279,073	481,350	525,227	587,922	† 667,689	694,951	733,579	† 785,552	929,260
Money Market Instruments	36aa	2,437	4,162	3,353	4,306	3,223	2,986	2,253	† 1,847	1,962	6,273	† 2,670	2,280
Liabs. of Central Bank: Securities	36ac	—	—	—	—	—	—	—	† —	—	—	† —	—
Restricted Deposits	36b	2,038	2,240	2,535	1,686	3,077	1,903	5,073	† 7,966	5,075	3,096	† 5,495	5,816
Liab. to Nonbank Financial Insts	36j	1,326	1,564	2,533	7,536	39,332	14,725	14,690	† 2,845	4,652	4,860	† 4,415	4,401
Capital Accounts	37a	34,174	45,313	49,944	110,259	27,728	67,341	171,141	† 194,466	217,640	209,158	† 254,637	266,857
Other Items (Net)	37r	5,403	−4,863	345	−41,164	39,129	69,726	79,208	† 81,044	81,328	74,485	† 85,837	109,705
Money plus Quasi-Money	35l	173,167	220,829	280,631	351,504	572,118	642,107	748,845	† 837,739	877,598	947,260	† 1,031,207	1,200,093
Money (National Definitions)						*Billions of Rupiah: End of Period*							
Base Money	19ma	....	25,852	34,405	46,086	75,120	101,790	125,615	127,796	138,250	166,474	206,180	269,971
M1	59ma	....	52,677	64,089	78,343	101,197	124,633	162,186	177,731	191,939	223,799	245,946	271,166
M2	59mb	....	222,638	288,632	355,643	577,381	646,205	747,028	844,053	883,908	955,692	1,033,877	1,202,100

Indonesia 536

		1994	1995	1996	1997	1998	1999	2000	2001	2002	2003	2004	2005
Interest Rates						*Percent Per Annum*							
Discount Rate (End of Period)..........	60	12.44	13.99	12.80	20.00	38.44	12.51	14.53	17.62	12.93	8.31	7.43	12.75
Money Market Rate........................	60b	9.74	13.64	13.96	27.82	62.79	23.58	10.32	15.03	13.54	7.76	5.38	6.78
Deposit Rate.................................	60l	12.53	16.72	17.26	20.01	39.07	25.74	12.50	15.48	15.50	10.59	6.44	8.08
Deposit Rate (Foreign Currency).......	60l.f	....	....	....	....	....	7.45	5.56	5.37	3.26	2.17	1.74	2.63
Lending Rate.................................	60p	17.76	18.85	19.22	21.82	32.15	27.66	18.46	18.55	18.95	16.94	14.12	14.05
Lending Rate (Foreign Currency).......	60p.f	....	....	....	....	....	....	....	8.95	7.38	6.52	5.70	6.36
Prices, Production, Labor						*Index Numbers (2000=100): Period Averages*							
Share Prices.................................	62	....	101.0	119.2	121.5	84.8	110.0	100.0	82.1	91.6	104.3	163.1	220.2
Wholesale Prices: Incl. Petroleum.....	63	30.5	33.9	36.6	39.9	80.5	† 88.9	† 100.0	113.0	118.0	122.0	131.0	151.0
Excl. Petroleum..............	63a	34.1	38.9	41.3	44.5	80.2	† 94.6	100.0	117.1	124.2	126.2	132.4	82.8
Consumer Prices............................	64	40.3	44.0	† 47.6	50.5	80.0	96.4	100.0	111.5	124.7	† 133.0	141.3	156.0
Crude Petroleum Production...........	66aa	113.7	113.4	112.8	83.6	103.9	95.8	100.0	94.7	88.6	80.0	....	....
Manufacturing Production...............	66ey	107.7	119.8	125.7	115.9	94.7	96.5	† 100.0	98.9	91.9	113.6	117.4	118.9
						Number in Thousands: Period Averages							
Employment.................................	67e	80,110	80,110	85,702	87,050	87,674	88,817	89,838	90,807	91,647	....	....	....
Unemployment.............................	67c	3,738	....	4,287	4,197	5,062	6,030	5,813	8,005	9,132	....	....	....
Unemployment Rate (%).................	67r	4.4	....	4.0	4.7	5.5	6.4	6.1	8.1	9.1	....	....	....
Intl. Transactions & Positions						*Millions of US Dollars*							
Exports.......................................	70..d	40,055	45,417	49,814	56,298	50,370	51,243	65,403	56,447	58,120	61,058	71,585	47,903
Crude Petroleum & Products...........	70a.d	6,006	6,441	7,243	6,822	4,264	3,855	7,761	6,916	6,544	7,167	8,053	5,584
Crude Petroleum......................	70aad	5,072	5,146	5,712	5,479	3,349	3,162	3,690	5,715	5,205	5,579	6,241	4,466
Imports, c.i.f................................	71..d	31,983	40,630	42,929	51,304	35,280	33,321	43,595	31,010	31,289	32,610	46,524	38,936
						2000=100							
Volume of Exports........................	72	78.0	81.5	85.6	110.0	102.3	84.0	100.0	121.0	99.7	97.0	101.2	64.2
Crude Petroleum......................	72aa	149.5	139.2	130.8	133.4	125.8	218.6	100.0	112.4	99.6	89.3	80.3	42.8
Export Prices						*2000=100: Indices of Unit Values in US Dollars*							
Exports (Unit Value).....................	74..d	90.3	103.1	109.0	103.6	80.8	64.9	100.0	89.9	95.5	102.7	120.4	81.4
Crude Petroleum (Unit Value)........	74aad	55.7	60.7	71.4	68.9	43.8	55.0	100.0	78.0	86.4	206.0	129.0	....
Crude Petroleum (Ofc.Price)..........	76aad	56.3	61.0	71.3	66.7	43.2	61.7	100.0	84.1	88.0	101.8	128.9	186.3
Balance of Payments						*Millions of US Dollars: Minus Sign Indicates Debit*							
Current Account, n.i.e....................	78ald	−2,792	−6,431	−7,663	−4,889	4,097	5,783	7,992	6,901	7,824	8,387	1,562	929
Goods: Exports f.o.b.....................	78aad	40,223	47,454	50,188	56,298	50,371	51,242	65,407	57,365	59,165	64,391	70,766	86,224
Goods: Imports f.o.b.....................	78abd	−32,322	−40,921	−44,240	−46,223	−31,942	−30,598	−40,365	−34,668	−35,652	−39,548	−50,615	−63,856
Trade Balance.............................	78acd	7,901	6,533	5,948	10,075	18,429	20,643	25,042	22,696	23,513	24,844	20,151	22,368
Services: Credit.............................	78add	4,797	5,469	6,599	6,941	4,479	4,599	5,214	5,500	6,663	5,293	12,045	13,155
Services: Debit..............................	78aed	−11,416	−13,540	−15,139	−16,607	−12,088	−12,376	−15,637	−15,880	−17,045	−17,400	−20,856	−25,015
Balance on Goods & Services.......	78afd	1,282	−1,538	−2,592	409	10,820	12,866	14,619	12,316	13,131	12,736	11,340	10,508
Income: Credit.............................	78agd	1,048	1,306	1,210	1,855	1,910	1,891	2,458	2,004	1,318	1,054	1,995	3,309
Income: Debit..............................	78ahd	−5,741	−7,180	−7,218	−8,187	−10,099	−10,887	−10,901	−8,940	−8,365	−7,272	−12,912	−14,077
Balance on Gds, Serv. & Inc.........	78aid	−3,411	−7,412	−8,600	−5,923	2,631	3,869	6,176	5,381	6,083	6,519	423	−260
Current Transfers, n.i.e.: Credit......	78ajd	619	981	937	1,034	1,466	1,914	1,816	1,520	2,210	2,053	2,433	2,413
Current Transfers: Debit................	78akd	—	—	—	—	—	—	—	—	−470	−184	−1,294	−1,223
Capital Account, n.i.e....................	78bcd	—	—	—	—	—	—	—	—	—	—	—	334
Capital Account, n.i.e.: Credit........	78bad	—	—	—	—	—	—	—	—	—	—	—	....
Capital Account: Debit..................	78bbd	—	—	—	—	—	—	—	—	—	—	—	....
Financial Account, n.i.e.................	78bjd	3,839	10,259	10,847	−603	−9,633	−5,944	−7,896	−7,617	−1,103	−949	1,852	−2,272
Direct Investment Abroad.............	78bdd	−609	−603	−600	−178						....	−3,408	−3,118
Dir. Invest. in Rep. Econ., n.i.e.......	78bed	2,109	4,346	6,194	4,677	−241	−1,866	−4,550	−2,977	145	−597	1,896	5,163
Portfolio Investment Assets...........	78bfd	—	....	—	—	—	—	—	—	—	....	353	768
Equity Securities.......................	78bkd	....	....	....	....	....	....	....	....	....	....	−106	38
Debt Securities.........................	78bld	—	....	....	....	....	....	....	....	....	....	459	730
Portfolio Investment Liab., n.i.e......	78bgd	3,877	4,100	5,005	−2,632	−1,878	−1,792	−1,911	−244	1,222	2,251	4,056	5,316
Equity Securities.......................	78bmd	1,900	1,493	1,819	−4,987	−4,371	−782	−1,021	442	877	1,130	2,043	−165
Debt Securities.........................	78bnd	1,977	2,607	3,186	2,355	2,493	−1,010	−890	−686	345	1,121	2,013	5,481
Financial Derivatives Assets...........	78bwd	....	....	....	....	....	....	....	....	....	....	....	....
Financial Derivatives Liabilities.......	78bxd	....	....	....	....	....	....	....	....	....	....	....	....
Other Investment Assets...............	78bhd	—	....	—	—	−44	−72	−150	−125	−500	−5	985	−9,158
Monetary Authorities..................	78bod	....	....	....	....	....	....	....	....	....	....	....	....
General Government...................	78bpd	....	....	....	....	....	....	....	....	....	....	....	....
Banks.......................................	78bqd	—	....	....	....	....	....	....	....	....	....	1,701	−4,662
Other Sectors............................	78brd	—	....	....	....	−44	−72	−150	−125	−500	−5	1,155	−1,337
Other Investment Liab., n.i.e..........	78bid	−1,538	2,416	248	−2,470	−7,470	−2,214	−1,285	−4,271	−1,970	−2,599	−2,030	−1,242
Monetary Authorities..................	78bsd	—	—	—	—	—	—	—	—	—	—	—	—
General Government...................	78btd	137	6	−663	−265	4,210	3,979	2,094	635	457	−398	−2,695	−848
Banks.......................................	78bud	527	1,953	−758	−276	−2,305	125	−1,420	−1,867	−1,217	−69	678	402
Other Sectors............................	78bvd	−2,202	457	1,669	−1,929	−9,375	−6,318	−1,959	−3,039	−1,210	−2,132	−14	−797
Net Errors and Omissions................	78cad	−263	−2,255	1,319	−2,645	2,099	2,077	3,829	701	−1,763	−3,791	−3,092	666
Overall Balance...........................	78cbd	784	1,573	4,503	−8,137	−3,437	1,916	3,926	−15	4,958	3,647	321	−343
Reserves and Related Items.............	79dad	−784	−1,573	−4,503	8,137	3,437	−1,916	−3,926	15	−4,958	−3,647	−321	343
Reserve Assets.............................	79dbd	−784	−1,573	−4,503	5,113	−2,345	−3,286	−5,051	1,371	−4,010	−4,236	686	1,487
Use of Fund Credit and Loans........	79dcd	—	—	—	3,025	5,782	1,371	1,125	−1,356	−948	588	−1,007	−1,144
Exceptional Financing...................	79ded	....	....	....	....	....	....	....	....	....	....	....	....

		1994	1995	1996	1997	1998	1999	2000	2001	2002	2003	2004	2005
International Investment Position						*Millions of US Dollars*							
Assets	79aad	....	....	....	....	....	....	....	41,880	47,912	53,875	53,003	....
Direct Investment Abroad	79abd	....	....	....	....	....	....	....	−1,413	−328	−208	−102	....
Portfolio Investment	79acd	....	....	....	....	....	....	....	2,894	2,473	2,888	2,802	....
Equity Securities	79add	....	....	....	....	....	....	....	17	23	31	51	....
Debt Securities	79aed	....	....	....	....	....	....	....	2,878	2,451	2,857	2,751	....
Financial Derivatives	79ald	....	....	....	....	....	....	....	40	84	33	32	....
Other Investment	79afd	....	....	....	....	....	....	....	12,344	13,641	14,864	13,950	....
Monetary Authorities	79agd	....	....	....	....	....	....	....	927	1,265	1,906	2,334	....
General Government	79ahd	....	....	....	....	....	....	....	—	44	42	850	....
Banks	79aid	....	....	....	....	....	....	....	8,022	8,260	7,025	5,094	....
Other Sectors	79ajd	....	....	....	....	....	....	....	3,394	4,072	5,891	5,672	....
Reserve Assets	79akd	....	....	....	....	....	....	....	28,014	32,042	36,297	36,321	....
Liabilities	79lad	....	....	....	....	....	....	....	155,091	148,581	162,447	171,853	....
Dir. Invest. in Rep. Economy	79lbd	....	....	....	....	....	....	....	15,203	7,103	10,328	15,858	....
Portfolio Investment	79lcd	....	....	....	....	....	....	....	13,315	14,332	23,297	25,692	....
Equity Securities	79ldd	....	....	....	....	....	....	....	4,475	6,452	14,808	15,554	....
Debt Securities	79led	....	....	....	....	....	....	....	8,840	7,881	8,489	10,138	....
Financial Derivatives	79lld	....	....	....	....	....	....	....	79	63	32	40	....
Other Investment	79lfd	....	....	....	....	....	....	....	126,494	127,082	128,790	130,264	....
Monetary Authorities	79lgd	....	....	....	....	....	....	....	12,386	10,769	12,191	11,601	....
General Government	79lhd	....	....	....	....	....	....	....	58,060	63,429	68,421	67,927	....
Banks	79lid	....	....	....	....	....	....	....	7,102	7,185	3,759	5,164	....
Other Sectors	79ljd	....	....	....	....	....	....	....	48,945	45,699	44,420	45,572	....
Government Finance						*Billions of Rupiah: Year Beginning April 1*							
Deficit (-) or Surplus	80	3,581	10,085	6,180	−4,211	−28,191	† −12,645	3,139	−40,485	−23,574	−33,669	−26,272	....
Revenue	81	69,402	80,427	90,298	113,882	157,412	† 198,673	210,443	300,600	298,528	340,658	522,226	....
Grants Received	81z	67	—	—	—	—	—	—	478	78	437	737	....
Expenditure	82	61,866	66,723	77,964	112,893	174,097	225,874	227,892	341,563	322,180	374,764	427,226	....
Lending Minus Repayments	83	4,022	3,619	6,154	5,200	11,506	−14,556	−20,588	—	—	—	....	
Financing													
Net Borrowing: Domestic	84a	−4,295	....	−3,058	5,210	9,593	−9,446	8,721	32,178	16,946	32,115	....	....
Net borrowing: Foreign	85a	−303	−1,677	−2,659	−4,674	49,705	15,942	16,196	10,267	6,628	1,554	−23,779	....
Use of Cash Balances	87	1,017	....	−463	3,676	−31,106	6,149	−28,056	−1,960	—	—		
Debt: Domestic	88a	939	3,229	83	4,097	13,481	6,481	1,940	1,018	....	....	....	
Debt: Foreign	89a	138,841	136,781	127,324	450,890	514,134	490,685	613,199	621,446	582,631	598,412	....	
National Accounts						*Billions of Rupiah*							
Househ.Cons.Expend.,incl.NPISHs	96f	228,119	279,876	332,094	387,171	647,824	813,183	856,798	1,039,655	1,231,965	1,372,078	1,532,888	1,785,596
Government Consumption Expend	91f	31,014	35,584	40,299	42,952	54,416	72,631	90,780	113,416	132,219	163,701	191,056	224,981
Gross Fixed Capital Formation	93e	105,381	129,218	157,653	177,686	243,043	221,472	275,881	323,875	353,967	392,789	492,850	599,795
Changes in Inventories	93i	13,327	15,900	5,800	21,615	−82,716	−96,461	33,283	47,194	35,980	122,682	34,515	7,172
Exports of Goods and Services	90c	101,332	119,593	137,533	174,871	506,245	390,560	569,490	642,595	595,514	613,721	729,321	915,610
Imports of Goods and Services (-)	98c	96,953	125,657	140,812	176,600	413,058	301,654	423,318	506,426	480,815	462,941	623,525	797,276
Gross Domestic Product (GDP)	99b	382,220	454,514	532,568	627,695	955,754	1,099,732	1,389,770	1,684,281	1,863,275	2,036,352	2,273,142	2,729,708
Net Primary Income from Abroad	98.n	−10,248	−13,366	−14,272	−18,355	−53,894	−83,764	−92,162	−61,051	−54,513	−77,414	−78,414	−85,355
Gross National Income (GNI)	99a	371,971	441,148	518,296	609,340	901,860	1,015,967	1,297,608	1,623,229	1,808,762	1,958,938	2,194,728	2,644,354
Consumption of Fixed Capital	99cf	19,111	22,726	26,629	31,385	47,788	54,987	69,489	84,214	93,164	101,818	113,086	136,485
GDP Volume 1993 Prices	99b.p	354,641	383,792	413,798	433,246	376,375	379,353	398,017	....	....	....	....	
GDP Volume 2000 Prices	99b.p	....	....	....	....	....	....	1,389,770	1,442,985	1,506,124	1,577,171	1,656,826	1,749,547
GDP Volume (2000=100)	99bvp	89.1	96.4	104.0	108.9	94.6	95.3	† 100.0	103.8	108.4	113.5	119.2	125.9
GDP Deflator (2000=100)	99bip	30.9	33.9	36.9	41.5	72.7	83.0	100.0	116.7	123.7	129.1	137.2	156.0
						Millions: Midyear Estimates							
Population	99z	192.88	195.65	198.39	201.09	† 203.78	206.47	209.17	211.89	214.62	217.35	220.08	222.78

		1994	1995	1996	1997	1998	1999	2000	2001	2002	2003	2004	2005
Exchange Rates						*Rials per SDR: End of Period*							
Official Rate	aa	2,534.26	2,597.64	2,515.19	2,366.94	2,465.36	2,405.04	2,948.39	2,200.47 †	10,810.87	12,292.11	13,655.62	12,993.49
						Rials per US Dollar: End of Period (ae) Period Average (rf)							
Official Rate	ae	1,735.97	1,747.50	1,749.14	1,754.26	1,750.93	1,752.29	2,262.93	1,750.95 †	7,951.98	8,272.11	8,793.00	9,091.00
Official Rate	rf	1,748.75	1,747.93	1,750.76	1,752.92	1,751.86	1,752.93	1,764.43	1,753.56 †	6,906.96	8,193.89	8,613.99	8,963.96
						Rials per US Dollar: End of Period							
Market Rate	aea	....	....	....	4,645	5,721	8,135	7,909	7,924	....	....	....	....
						Rials per US Dollar: Months Ending the 20th							
Weighted Average	yf	1,222	1,726	2,194	2,780	3,206	4,172	5,731	6,163	....	....	....	....
						Index Numbers (2000=100): Period Averages							
Nominal Effective Exchange Rate	nec	220.02	126.53	125.27	136.67	137.66	100.94	100.00	108.61	106.69	93.49	83.32	78.09
Real Effective Exchange Rate	rec	82.02	65.63	79.63	97.75	110.19	91.32	100.00	115.86	125.76	124.39	123.49	127.73
Fund Position						*Millions of SDRs: End of Period*							
Quota	2f.s	1,079	1,079	1,079	1,079	1,079	1,497	1,497	1,497	1,497	1,497	1,497	1,497
SDRs	1b.s	98	90	240	245	1	101	267	267	268	268	274	275
Reserve Position in the Fund	1c.s	—	—	—	—	—	—	—	—	—	—	—	—
Total Fund Cred.&Loans Outstg	2tl	—	—	—	—	—	—	—	—	—	—	—	—
International Liquidity						*Millions of US Dollars Unless Otherwise Indicated: End of Period*							
SDRs	1b.d	143	134	345	330	2	139	349	336	364	399	425	393
Reserve Position in the Fund	1c.d	—	—	—	—	—	—	—	—	—	—	—	—
Gold (Million Fine Troy Ounces)	1ad	4.740	4.842	....	....	....	....	....	....	....	....	....	....
Gold (National Valuation)	1and	242	252	....	....	....	....	....	....	....	....	....	....
Monetary Authorities:Other Assets	3..d	....	....	....	....	....	....	....	....	....	....	....	....
Deposit Money Banks: Assets	7a.d	3,321	3,354	4,319	4,403	4,648	2,258	3,112	6,298	7,244	8,903	27,670	30,378
Liabilities	7b.d	5,589	4,015	2,668	2,128	2,771	3,410	3,486	6,695	8,657	13,749	25,452	28,280
Other Banking Insts.: Liabilities	7f.d	53	118	110	66	136	250	266	403	409	522	2,151	2,023
Monetary Authorities						*Billions of Rials: Months Ending the 20th*							
Foreign Assets	11	9,681	14,413	19,454	15,669	9,827	11,413	24,478	28,151	154,928	188,442	263,305	396,520
Claims on Central Government	12a	28,169	32,648	42,461	42,624	55,710	61,731	60,207	64,673	101,692	111,341	107,594	103,416
Claims on Official Entities	12bx	5,549	10,704	18,826	15,618	18,842	19,794	23,189	16,287	19,200	21,897	23,417	27,501
Claims on Deposit Money Banks	12e	1,967	10,462	2,056	11,162	9,565	13,392	17,567	18,589	17,732	23,823	30,956	28,273
Reserve Money	14	22,165	32,805	41,708	51,298	60,533	70,911	82,726	88,015	111,487	127,554	145,986	178,490
of which: Currency Outside DMBs	14a	6,199	7,949	9,598	11,271	14,050	16,652	20,020	21,840	25,945	30,809	34,247	39,232
Nonfin.Pub.Ent. Deps	14e	1,604	2,020	2,639	2,642	4,662	5,304	7,859	4,552	5,401	6,800	8,611	10,915
Restricted Deposits	16b	4,004	7,085	8,764	6,789	3,810	4,066	3,351	4,133	1,182	1,415	1,216	879
Foreign Liabilities	16c	2,883	2,679	3,466	5,057	8,012	6,562	7,094	13,991	83,330	77,087	82,275	172,063
Central Government Deposits	16d	6,752	9,738	13,035	13,837	13,814	18,275	28,645	37,312	57,194	60,139	92,882	108,358
Capital Accounts	17a	903	989	1,004	1,003	1,012	1,097	1,064	1,235	3,225	3,991	4,790	6,449
Other Items (Net)	17r	8,658	14,929	14,820	7,089	6,763	5,420	2,561	−16,986	37,132	75,318	98,124	89,471
Deposit Money Banks						*Billions of Rials: Months Ending the 20th*							
Reserves	20	14,179	22,519	28,865	36,563	40,385	47,190	51,536	58,559	72,743	82,353	88,542	103,251
Foreign Assets	21	5,766	5,861	7,555	7,724	8,138	3,957	7,043	11,027	57,605	73,648	243,304	276,165
Claims on Central Government	22a	1,232	1,827	1,823	1,821	1,821	7,494	5,800	5,648	7,187	15,856	21,327	19,335
Claims on Private Sector	22d	27,535	32,938	41,043	52,579	63,716	85,701	112,986	155,268	206,970	291,624	407,108	515,715
Demand Deposits	24	18,120	24,373	33,628	41,064	48,732	59,996	74,291	99,275	123,963	147,018	169,348	210,510
Time and Savings Deposits	25	29,377	37,599	49,426	62,881	74,438	90,435	108,884	143,689	181,022	234,086	302,760	371,702
Foreign Liabilities	26c	9,703	7,016	4,667	3,734	4,851	5,975	7,890	11,723	68,837	113,736	223,804	257,091
Credit from Monetary Authorities	26g	1,967	10,462	2,056	11,162	9,565	13,392	17,567	18,589	17,732	23,823	30,956	28,273
Capital Accounts	27a	3,724	3,724	3,724	3,724	3,724	3,764	3,764	8,564	8,564	8,564	8,564	56,580
Other Items (Net)	27r	−14,180	−20,030	−14,215	−23,878	−27,250	−29,220	−35,031	−51,338	−55,612	−63,745	24,849	−9,689
Monetary Survey						*Billions of Rials: Months Ending the 20th*							
Foreign Assets (Net)	31n	2,860	10,578	18,876	14,603	5,102	2,833	16,538	13,465	60,366	71,268	200,530	243,531
Domestic Credit	32	59,484	74,426	101,566	115,511	151,740	187,227	211,234	246,942	319,626	416,605	514,036	601,340
Claims on Central Govt. (Net)	32an	22,556	24,674	31,026	30,370	43,463	48,057	34,512	30,557	39,216	45,566	18,121	−17,690
Claims on Official Entities	32bx	9,393	16,814	29,498	32,562	44,561	53,469	63,736	61,117	73,440	79,415	88,807	103,315
Claims on Private Sector	32d	27,535	32,938	41,043	52,579	63,716	85,701	112,986	155,268	206,970	291,624	407,108	515,715
Money	34	25,923	34,342	45,865	54,977	67,444	81,952	102,170	125,667	155,309	184,627	212,205	260,656
Quasi-Money	35	29,377	37,599	49,426	62,881	74,438	90,435	108,884	143,689	181,022	234,086	302,760	371,702
Restricted Deposits	36b	4,004	7,085	8,764	6,789	3,810	4,066	3,351	4,133	1,182	1,415	1,216	879
Other Items (Net)	37r	3,040	5,977	16,387	5,467	11,150	13,608	13,367	−13,082	42,479	67,746	198,385	211,633
Money plus Quasi-Money	35l	55,299	71,941	95,291	117,858	141,883	172,387	211,054	269,356	336,331	418,712	514,965	632,358
Other Banking Institutions						*Billions of Rials: Months Ending the 20th*							
Cash	40	218	361	671	912	1,549	1,901	3,417	3,094	7,449	7,667	8,724	10,772
Claims on Central Government	42a	2	2	2	2	2	941	1,249	1,755	1,846	3,522	4,470	4,295
Claims on Official Entities	42bx	141	90	591	1,002	195	208	222	909	885	1,340	1,183
Claims on Private Sector	42d	7,504	9,831	13,506	18,611	25,812	36,411	51,503	66,108	88,257	105,605	131,732	180,434
Demand Deposits	44	870	1,287	2,129	3,325	4,002	4,001	6,023	6,948	11,435	14,789	16,093	19,369
Private Sector	44x	870	1,287	2,129	3,325	4,002	4,001	6,023	6,948	11,435	14,784	16,093	19,359
Official Entities	44y	—	—	—	—	—	—	—	—	—	5		10
Time and Savings Deposits	45	1,409	2,367	3,327	5,591	9,157	12,584	15,831	24,110	35,582	46,604	67,137	102,529
Foreign Liabilities	46c	91	207	192	116	238	438	601	705	3,253	4,319	18,912	18,393
Central Government Deposits	46d	114	124	175	158	106	69	87	112	557	2,986	6,646	13,220
Credit from Monetary Authorities	46g	795	3,437	8,126	3,518	4,635	5,895	9,358	652	2,025	4,410	4,468	4,744
Capital Accounts	47a	1,928	1,928	1,940	1,940	1,940	1,940	2,960	6,385	6,409	6,409	11,484	21,946
Other Items (Net)	47r	2,658	935	−1,548	5,469	8,287	14,522	21,517	32,267	39,201	38,170	21,525	16,492
Liquid Liabilities	55l	57,360	75,232	100,077	125,862	153,493	187,070	229,491	297,320	375,899	472,437	589,471	743,484
Interest Rates						*Percent Per Annum*							
Deposit Rate (End of Period)	60l	....	....	....	....	....	....	....	....	....	11.68	11.70	11.78
Lending Rate (End of Period)	60p	....	....	....	....	....	....	....	....	....	....	16.65	16.00

Iran, Islamic Republic of 429

		1994	1995	1996	1997	1998	1999	2000	2001	2002	2003	2004	2005
Prices and Production		*Index Numbers (2000=100)*											
Share Prices	62	18.3	36.8	76.9	73.8	65.2	70.1	100.0	133.8	178.7	307.3	510.2	475.5
Wholesale Prices	63	26.7	42.9	57.0	63.1	70.6	† 84.1	† 100.0	105.9	114.6	126.7	142.6	160.4
Home Goods	63a	26.8	41.1	53.8	60.2	70.4	† 84.4	100.0	107.3	118.0	132.1	148.7	167.4
Consumer Prices	64	27.3	40.8	52.6	61.7	72.8	87.4	100.0	111.3	127.2	148.2	170.1	192.9
Crude Petroleum Production	66aa	95.6	95.7	97.6	96.4	95.4	93.2	100.0	96.8	90.9	99.3	103.3	103.3
Intl. Transactions & Positions		*Millions of US Dollars Year Ending March 20*											
Exports	70..d	19,434	18,360	22,391	18,381	13,118	21,030	28,345	23,904	28,237	33,991	44,403	58,400
Imports, c.i.f.	71..d	13,774	13,882	16,274	14,196	14,323	12,683	14,347	17,627	21,180	27,676	35,207	41,561
Volume of Exports								*2000=100*					
Petroleum	72a	107.5	110.2	110.5	107.4	102.2	95.4	100.0	....	....	....	....	....
Crude Petroleum	72aa	110.0	111.6	111.6	107.1	105.2	95.1	100.0	....	....	....	....	....
Export Prices	76	....	178.7	169.5	127.2	79.9	110.6	100.0	....	....	....	....	....
Import Prices	76.x	....	102.5	118.8	107.3	145.0	114.1	100.0	....	....	....	....	....
Balance of Payments		*Millions of US$: Year Beginning March 21: Minus Sign Indicates Debit*											
Current Account, n.i.e.	78ald	4,956	3,358	5,232	2,213	−2,139	6,555	12,481	....	....	....	....	....
Goods: Exports f.o.b.	78aad	19,434	18,360	22,391	18,381	13,118	21,030	28,345	....	....	....	....	....
Goods: Imports f.o.b.	78abd	−12,617	−12,774	−14,989	−14,123	−14,286	−13,433	−15,207	....	....	....	....	....
Trade Balance	78acd	6,817	5,586	7,402	4,258	−1,168	7,597	13,138	....	....	....	....	....
Services: Credit	78add	438	593	860	1,192	1,793	1,216	1,382	....	....	....	....	....
Services: Debit	78aed	−3,226	−2,339	−3,083	−3,371	−2,760	−2,457	−2,296	....	....	....	....	....
Balance on Goods & Services	78afd	4,029	3,840	5,179	2,079	−2,135	6,356	12,224	....	....	....	....	....
Income: Credit	78agd	142	316	488	466	230	181	404	....	....	....	....	....
Income: Debit	78ahd	−413	−794	−898	−725	−731	−473	−604	....	....	....	....	....
Balance on Gds, Serv. & Inc.	78aid	3,758	3,362	4,769	1,820	−2,636	6,064	12,024	....	....	....	....	....
Current Transfers, n.i.e.: Credit	78ajd	1,200	—	471	400	500	508	539	....	....	....	....	....
Current Transfers: Debit	78akd	−2	−4	−8	−7	−3	−17	−82	....	....	....	....	....
Capital Account, n.i.e.	78bcd	—	—	—	—	—	—	—	....	....	....	....	....
Capital Account, n.i.e.: Credit	78bad	—	—	—	—	—	—	—	....	....	....	....	....
Capital Account: Debit	78bbd	—	—	—	—	—	—	—	....	....	....	....	....
Financial Account, n.i.e.	78bjd	−346	−774	−5,508	−4,822	2,270	−5,894	−10,189	....	....	....	....	....
Direct Investment Abroad	78bdd	—	—	—	—	—	—	—	....	....	....	....	....
Dir. Invest. in Rep. Econ., n.i.e.	78bed	2	17	26	53	24	35	39	....	....	....	....	....
Portfolio Investment Assets	78bfd	—	—	—	—	—	—	—	....	....	....	....	....
Equity Securities	78bkd	—	—	—	—	—	—	—	....	....	....	....	....
Debt Securities	78bld	—	—	—	—	—	—	—	....	....	....	....	....
Portfolio Investment Liab., n.i.e.	78bgd	—	—	—	—	—	—	—	....	....	....	....	....
Equity Securities	78bmd	—	—	—	—	—	—	—	....	....	....	....	....
Debt Securities	78bnd	—	—	—	—	—	—	—	....	....	....	....	....
Financial Derivatives Assets	78bwd	....	....	....	....	—	—	—	....	....	....	....	....
Financial Derivatives Liabilities	78bxd	....	....	....	....	—	—	—	....	....	....	....	....
Other Investment Assets	78bhd	−1,258	−419	−1,305	2,293	963	−1,650	−8,257	....	....	....	....	....
Monetary Authorities	78bod	....	....	....	....	—	—	—	....	....	....	....	....
General Government	78bpd	−42	235	−48	−99	−21	−6	−5,932	....	....	....	....	....
Banks	78bqd	−1,216	−654	−1,257	2,392	984	−1,638	−1,783	....	....	....	....	....
Other Sectors	78brd	—	—	—	—	—	−6	−542	....	....	....	....	....
Other Investment Liab., n.i.e.	78bid	910	−372	−4,229	−7,168	1,283	−4,279	−1,971	....	....	....	....	....
Monetary Authorities	78bsd	−252	−64	−283	179	93	−5,517	−1,410	....	....	....	....	....
General Government	78btd	10,447	1,684	−4,523	−4,035	−489	104	−621	....	....	....	....	....
Banks	78bud	—	—	—	—	—	—	—	....	....	....	....	....
Other Sectors	78bvd	−9,285	−1,992	577	−3,312	1,679	1,134	60	....	....	....	....	....
Net Errors and Omissions	78cad	−3,702	202	2,717	−1,088	−1,122	−210	−1,209	....	....	....	....	....
Overall Balance	78cbd	908	2,786	2,441	−3,697	−991	451	1,083	....	....	....	....	....
Reserves and Related Items	79dad	−908	−2,786	−2,441	3,697	991	−451	−1,083	....	....	....	....	....
Reserve Assets	79dbd	−908	−2,786	−2,441	3,697	991	−451	−1,083	....	....	....	....	....
Use of Fund Credit and Loans	79dcd	—	—	—	—	—	—	—	....	....	....	....	....
Exceptional Financing	79ded	....	....	....	....	—	—	—	....	....	....	....	....
Government Finance		*Billions of Rials: Year Beginning March 21*											
Deficit (-) or Surplus	80	332	245	493	−3,060	−17,344	−927	−3,981	−2,571	−20,300	−31,371	−40,853	....
Revenue	81	29,245	41,575	57,276	62,378	53,626	92,316	104,641	125,480	165,210	325,153	403,081	....
Grants	81z	....	....	....	....	....	....	....	....	....	....	....	....
Exp. & Lending Minus Repay	82z	....	....	....	....	....	....	....	....	....	....	....	....
Expenditure	82	28,912	41,331	56,783	65,438	70,970	93,243	108,622	128,050	185,510	356,523	443,934	....
Lending Minus Repayments	83	....	....	....	....	....	....	....	....	....	....	....	....
Total Financing	80h	−332	−245	−493	3,060	17,344	927	3,981	2,571	20,300	31,371	40,853	....
National Accounts		*Billions of Rials: Year Beginning March 21*											
Househ.Cons.Expend.,incl.NPISHs	96f	60,138	87,496	113,240	140,807	181,172	225,770	276,612	323,314	417,081	505,739	640,266	....
Government Consumption Expend	91f	21,005	29,708	35,174	38,207	47,037	55,998	80,554	94,029	118,943	134,524	160,218	....
Gross Fixed Capital Formation	93e	28,819	38,954	65,626	83,765	96,051	124,202	153,462	187,999	262,588	318,820	401,765	....
Changes in Inventories	93i	866	15,329	23,485	20,855	12,044	5,670	37,958	32,734	62,585	83,785	104,666	....
Exports of Goods and Services	90c	39,632	40,362	51,746	51,007	44,857	93,509	131,811	137,732	245,868	302,169	408,414	....
Imports of Goods and Services (-)	98c	17,024	24,386	37,160	44,728	51,567	64,931	101,190	126,201	210,570	285,191	364,559	....
Gross Domestic Product (GDP)	99b	130,564	185,928	248,348	292,678	329,134	436,625	580,474	671,735	926,477	1,109,532	1,406,032	....
Net Primary Income from Abroad	98.n	−2,267	−1,346	−1,649	−491	380	−532	278	1,455	−15,932	−21,772	−24,936	....
Gross National Income (GNI)	99a	128,298	184,582	246,699	292,187	329,514	436,093	580,752	673,190	910,545	1,087,760	1,381,096	....
GDP Volume 1997 Prices	99b.p	257,496	264,327	283,097	292,677	300,701	306,514	322,278	334,105	359,216	384,773	404,335	....
GDP Volume (2000=100)	99bvp	79.9	82.0	87.8	90.8	93.3	95.1	100.0	103.7	111.5	119.4	125.5	....
GDP Deflator (2000=100)	99bip	28.2	39.1	48.7	55.5	60.8	79.1	100.0	111.6	143.2	160.1	193.1	....
		Millions: Midyear Estimates											
Population	99z	61.36	62.32	63.24	64.10	64.92	65.67	66.36	67.00	67.59	68.17	68.80	69.52

Iraq   433

		1994	1995	1996	1997	1998	1999	2000	2001	2002	2003	2004	2005
Exchange Rates						*SDRs per Dinar: End of Period*							
Principal Rate...............................	ac	2.2036	2.1641	2.2371	2.3842	2.2847	2.3438	2.4690	2.5597	2.3662	....	....	....
						US Dollars per Dinar: End of Period (ag) Period Average (rh)							
Principal Rate...............................	ag	3.2169	3.2169	3.2169	3.2169	3.2169	3.2169	3.2169	3.2169	3.2169	....	....	....
Principal Rate...............................	rh	3.2169	3.2169	3.2169	3.2169	3.2169	3.2169	3.2169	3.2169	3.2169	....	.0007	....
						Index Numbers (2000=100): Period Averages							
Principal Rate...............................	ahx	100.0	100.0	100.0	100.0	100.0	100.0	100.0	100.0	100.0	....	—	....
Nominal Effective Exchange Rate.....	nec	70.9	70.2	74.0	79.9	83.8	91.7	100.0	103.1	101.0	92.0	87.1	86.7
Fund Position						*Millions of SDRs: End of Period*							
Quota...	2f.s	504.0	504.0	504.0	504.0	504.0	504.0	504.0	504.0	504.0	504.0	1,188.4	1,188.4
SDRs...	1b.s	—	—	—	—	—	—	—	—	—	—	296.1	293.6
Reserve Position in the Fund............	1c.s	—	—	—	—	—	—	—	—	—	—	171.1	171.1
Total Fund Cred.&Loans Outstg........	2tl	—	—	—	—	—	—	—	—	—	—	297.1	297.1
International Liquidity						*Millions of US Dollars Unless Otherwise Indicated: End of Period*							
SDRs...	1b.d	—	—	—	—	—	—	—	—	—	—	459.9	419.6
Reserve Position in the Fund..........	1c.d	—	—	—	—	—	—	—	—	—	—	265.7	244.5
Production						*Index Numbers (2000=100): Period Averages*							
Crude Petroleum............................	66aa	23.2	23.2	24.4	47.0	76.6	93.6	100.0	93.0	73.4	49.6	81.1	70.2
Intl. Transactions & Positions						*Millions of Dinars*							
Imports, c.i.f., from DOTS................	71y	155.0	206.9	176.7	353.2	576.0	656.0	1,064.8	1,751.4	1,810.7	....	....	....
						Millions: Midyear Estimates							
Population..................................	99z	20.97	21.63	22.30	22.98	23.66	24.36	25.07	25.81	26.55	27.30	28.06	28.81

Ireland 178

2006, International Monetary Fund : International Financial Statistics Yearbook

		1994	1995	1996	1997	1998	1999	2000	2001	2002	2003	2004	2005
Exchange Rates							*SDRs per Euro: End of Period*						
Market Rate	ac	1.0598	1.0801	1.1691	1.0601	1.0563	.7319	.7142	.7013	.7714	.8499	.8771	.8254
							US Dollars per Euro: End of Period (ag) Period Average (rh)						
Market Rate	ag	1.5471	1.6055	1.6811	1.4304	1.4873	1.0046	.9305	.8813	1.0487	1.2630	1.3621	1.1797
Market Rate	rh	1.4978	1.6038	1.6006	1.5180	1.4257	1.0668	.9240	.8956	.9444	1.1308	1.2433	1.2458
							ECUs per Pound: End of Period (ec) Period Average (ed)						
ECU Rate	ec	1.2578	1.2218	1.3417	1.2960	1.2697	....	....	....	....	....	....	....
ECU Rate	ed	1.2604	1.2263	1.2611	1.3380	1.2717	....	....	....	....	....	....	....
							Index Numbers (2000=100): Period Averages						
Market Rate (1995=100)	ahx	93.4	100.0	99.8	94.7	88.9	....	....	....	....	....	....	....
Nominal Effective Exchange Rate	neu	112.50	113.64	116.15	116.76	111.12	107.11	100.00	100.54	102.59	110.25	112.52	112.72
Fund Position							*Millions of SDRs: End of Period*						
Quota	2f.s	525	525	525	525	525	838	838	838	838	838	838	838
SDRs	1b.s	101	107	115	123	137	29	37	43	49	53	57	62
Reserve Position in the Fund	1c.s	152	197	226	252	414	303	252	268	345	387	269	123
Total Fund Cred.&Loans Outstg	2tl	—	—	—	—	—	—	—	—	—	—	—	—
International Liquidity							*Millions of US Dollars Unless Otherwise Indicated: End of Period*						
Total Res.Min.Gold (Eurosys.Def)	1l.d	6,115	8,630	8,205	6,526	9,397	† 5,325	5,360	5,587	5,415	4,079	2,831	779
SDRs	1b.d	148	159	165	166	193	40	48	55	66	79	89	88
Reserve Position in the Fund	1c.d	222	294	325	340	582	416	329	336	469	575	418	176
Foreign Exchange	1d.d	5,745	8,178	7,715	6,020	8,622	4,869	4,983	5,196	4,879	3,425	2,324	514
o/w:Fin.Deriv.Rel.to Reserves	1ddd	....	....	....	....	....	—	—	—	—	—	—	—
Other Reserve Assets	1e.d	....	....	....	....	....	—	—	—	—	—	—	—
Gold (Million Fine Troy Ounces)	1ad	.360	.361	.361	.361	.451	.176	.176	.176	.176	.176	.176	.176
Gold (Eurosystem Valuation)	1and	141	137	143	116	132	51	48	49	60	73	77	90
Memo:Euro Cl. on Non-EA Res	1dgd	....	....	....	....	....	43.17	19.54	185.07	372.29	1,207.43	1,472.43	2,531.64
Non-Euro Cl. on EA Res	1dhd	....	....	....	....	....	94.34	275.49	357.68	292.01	318.05	111.69	50.62
Mon. Auth.: Other Foreign Assets	3..d	....	....	....	....	....	—	—	—	—	—	—	—
Foreign Liabilities	4..d	....	....	....	....	....	† 1,389	573	78	91	110	475	13
Banking Insts.: Foreign Assets	7a.d	30,088	46,679	70,324	101,447	142,089	† 78,106	135,339	173,199	236,529	324,806	433,634	518,137
Foreign Liab	7b.d	28,127	49,100	70,169	99,225	142,772	† 77,733	141,507	191,246	255,228	338,470	428,831	488,093
Monetary Authorities							*Millions of Pounds through 1998; Millions of Euros Beginning 1999: End of Period*						
Fgn. Assets (Cl.on Non-EA Ctys)	11	4,173	5,471	4,959	4,634	6,445	5,411	6,333	6,617	5,601	4,296	3,642	2,901
Claims on General Government	12a.u	....	....	....	....	....	2,109	2,183	2,029	1,650	2,958	3,495	4,093
o/w: Claims on Gen.Govt.in Cty	12a	254	183	132	132	132	279	229	29	—	21	—	22
Claims on Banking Institutions	12e.u	....	....	....	....	....	8,662	9,012	13,977	11,939	18,947	19,208	23,439
o/w: Claims on Bank.Inst.in Cty	12e	....	....	....	....	....	5,062	8,407	13,201	11,158	17,535	17,508	21,070
Claims on Other Resident Sectors	12d.u	....	....	....	....	....	—	—	—	—	7	6	4
o/w: Cl. on Oth.Res.Sect.in Cty	12d	—	....	....	....	....	—	—	—	—	7	6	4
Currency Issued	14a	1,907	2,092	2,287	2,619	3,040	4,848	5,368	4,704	4,278	4,650	6,437	7,247
Liabilities to Banking Insts	14c.u	....	....	....	....	....	4,228	6,426	8,619	10,405	17,702	16,077	19,694
o/w: Liabs to Bank.Inst.in Cty	14c	685	1,188	1,030	1,326	2,258	2,074	2,426	3,506	4,509	3,815	4,342	8,252
Demand Dep. of Other Res.Sect	14d.u	....	....	....	....	....	—	—	—	—	—	—	—
o/w:D.Dep.of Oth.Res.Sect.in Cty	14d	....	....	....	....	....	—	—	—	—	—	—	—
Other Dep. of Other Res.Sect	15..u	....	....	....	....	....	—	—	—	—	—	—	—
o/w:O.Dep.of Oth.Res.Sect.in Cty	15	....	....	....	....	....	—	—	—	—	—	—	—
Bonds & Money Mkt. Instruments	16n.u	....	....	....	....	....	—	—	—	—	—	—	—
Foreign Liab. (to Non-EA Ctys)	16c	—	—	—	—	—	1,383	616	89	87	87	349	11
Central Government Deposits	16d.u	....	....	....	....	....	3,546	2,139	5,151	3,826	3,529	3,877	4,240
o/w: Cent.Govt.Dep. in Cty	16d	836	1,082	1,178	1,191	1,674	3,546	2,139	5,151	3,826	3,529	3,877	4,240
Capital Accounts	17a	1,416	1,264	841	1,265	1,248	2,593	2,923	3,073	2,069	1,838	1,587	1,632
Other Items (Net)	17r	−417	28	−245	−1,635	−1,642	−416	58	985	−1,475	−1,596	−1,975	−2,386
Memo: Currency Put into Circ	14m	....	....	....	....	....	....	....	....	6,583	8,197	11,491	14,180
Banking Institutions							*Millions of Pounds through 1998; Millions of Euros Beginning 1999: End of Period*						
Claims on Monetary Authorities	20	675	1,436	1,348	1,686	2,706	2,486	....	4,324	4,909	4,303	4,760	8,720
Claims on Bk.Inst.in Oth.EA Ctys	20b.u	....	....	....	....	....	34,495	49,609	63,850	75,392	94,066	109,995	132,572
Fgn. Assets (Cl.on Non-EA Ctys)	21	19,448	29,074	41,832	70,922	95,535	77,748	145,448	196,527	225,545	257,170	318,357	439,211
Claims on General Government	22a.u	....	....	....	....	....	29,909	30,698	38,230	40,400	60,322	73,682	83,533
o/w: Claims on Gen.Govt.in Cty	22a	3,581	4,637	4,049	4,220	4,676	6,335	5,465	5,363	5,017	5,279	4,751	4,607
Claims on Other Resident Sectors	22d.u	....	....	....	....	....	109,999	136,032	161,126	175,193	199,215	247,207	315,742
o/w: Cl. on Oth.Res.Sect.in Cty	22d	16,571	29,106	33,978	44,058	54,020	91,795	110,652	129,079	142,382	160,220	200,306	260,299
Demand Deposits	24..u	....	....	....	....	....	12,711	15,117	18,871	19,671	49,721	55,371	65,794
o/w:D.Dep.of Oth.Res.Sect.in Cty	24	3,539	6,808	7,552	5,199	6,802	12,649	15,032	18,768	19,624	48,828	54,260	64,586
Other Deposits	25..u	....	....	....	....	....	67,614	76,097	81,626	93,246	75,417	85,604	101,134
o/w:O.Dep.of Oth.Res.Sect.in Cty	25	13,848	20,494	24,324	32,890	38,108	59,223	67,035	71,694	80,225	62,017	70,603	82,360
Money Market Fund Shares	26m.u	....	....	....	....	....	—	7,742	9,504	15,681	17,646	25,361	26,800
Bonds & Money Mkt. Instruments	26n.u	....	....	....	....	....	24,237	28,224	41,322	43,636	65,518	118,023	186,406
Foreign Liab. (to Non-EA Ctys)	26c	18,180	30,582	41,740	69,369	95,994	77,377	152,076	217,004	243,376	267,989	314,831	413,743
Central Government Deposits	26d.u	....	....	....	....	....	1,274	1,970	1,471	790	1,747	1,525	2,885
o/w: Cent.Govt.Dep. in Cty	26d	360	239	248	299	332	1,274	1,970	1,454	790	747	825	1,207
Credit from Monetary Authorities	26g	403	37	261	1,637	1,755	5,245	....	13,316	11,290	17,738	17,641	21,218
Liab. to Bk.Inst.in Oth. EA Ctys	26h.u	....	....	....	....	....	44,248	44,476	50,923	63,083	86,853	102,433	122,789
Capital Accounts	27a	4,854	6,486	7,249	10,280	12,881	22,091	26,993	31,133	33,664	37,769	44,257	53,732
Other Items (Net)	27r	−909	−394	−167	1,211	1,067	−158	....	−1,113	−2,996	−5,321	−11,015	−14,721

Ireland 178

		1994	1995	1996	1997	1998	1999	2000	2001	2002	2003	2004	2005
Banking Survey (Nat'l Residency)		*Millions of Pounds through 1998; Millions of Euros Beginning 1999: End of Period*											
Foreign Assets (Net)	31n	5,440	3,963	5,051	6,187	5,986	31,539	....	52,094	54,300	72,185	109,477	147,612
Domestic Credit	32	19,210	32,604	36,733	46,920	56,822	93,589	112,237	127,866	142,783	161,251	200,361	259,485
Claims on General Govt. (Net)	32an	2,639	3,498	2,755	2,862	2,802	1,794	1,585	−1,213	401	1,024	49	−818
Claims on Other Resident Sectors	32d	16,571	29,106	33,978	44,058	54,020	91,795	110,652	129,079	142,382	160,227	200,312	260,303
Currency Issued	34a.n	1,907	2,092	2,287	2,619	3,040	5,528	5,368	4,704	4,278	4,650	6,437	7,247
Demand Deposits	34b.n	3,539	6,808	7,552	5,199	6,802	12,649	15,032	18,768	19,624	48,828	54,260	64,586
Other Deposits	35..n	13,848	20,494	24,324	32,890	38,108	59,223	67,035	71,694	80,225	62,017	70,603	82,360
Money Market Fund Shares	36m	....	....	....	....	....	—	7,742	9,504	15,681	17,646	25,361	26,800
Bonds & Money Mkt. Instruments	36n	....	....	....	....	....	24,237	28,224	41,322	43,636	65,518	118,023	186,406
o/w: Over Two Years	36na	....	....	....	....	....	10,200	11,038	12,563	14,377	32,411	61,946	103,182
Capital Accounts	37a	6,271	7,750	8,090	11,545	14,129	24,684	29,916	34,206	35,733	39,607	45,844	55,364
Other Items (Net)	37r	−914	−577	−469	853	732	−1,191	....	−240	−2,092	−4,827	−10,659	−15,663
Banking Survey (EA-Wide Residency)		*Millions of Euros: End of Period*											
Foreign Assets (Net)	31n.u	....	....	....	....	....	4,399	−911	−13,949	−12,317	−6,610	6,819	28,358
Domestic Credit	32..u	....	....	....	....	....	137,197	164,804	194,763	212,627	257,226	318,988	396,247
Claims on General Govt. (Net)	32anu	....	....	....	....	....	27,198	28,772	33,637	37,434	58,004	71,775	80,501
Claims on Other Resident Sect.	32d.u	....	....	....	....	....	109,999	136,032	161,126	175,193	199,222	247,213	315,746
Currency Issued	34a.u	....	....	....	....	....	5,528	5,368	4,704	4,278	4,650	6,437	7,247
Demand Deposits	34b.u	....	....	....	....	....	12,711	15,117	18,871	19,671	49,721	55,371	65,794
Other Deposits	35..u	....	....	....	....	....	67,614	76,097	81,626	93,246	75,417	85,604	101,134
o/w: Other Dep. Over Two Yrs.	35abu	....	....	....	....	....	7,633	8,496	9,904	13,499	16,643	21,378	26,368
Money Market Fund Shares	36m.u	....	....	....	....	....	—	7,742	9,504	15,681	17,646	25,361	26,800
Bonds & Money Mkt. Instruments	36n.u	....	....	....	....	....	24,237	28,224	41,322	43,636	65,518	118,023	186,406
o/w: Over Two Years	36nau	....	....	....	....	....	10,200	11,038	12,563	14,377	32,411	61,946	103,182
Capital Accounts	37a	....	....	....	....	....	24,684	29,916	34,206	35,733	39,607	45,844	55,364
Other Items (Net)	37r.u	....	....	....	....	....	6,824	1,431	−9,421	−11,933	−1,940	−10,802	−18,137
Nonbank Financial Institutions		*Millions of Pounds: End of Period*											
Cash	40..k	1,676	† 18	6	5	5	....	....	....	....	....	....	....
Foreign Assets	41..k	704	† 2	5	8	11	....	....	....	....	....	....	....
Claims on Central Government	42a.k	1,777	† 717	762	786	819	....	....	....	....	....	....	....
Claims on Private Sector	42d.k	8,438	† 644	703	878	1,051	....	....	....	....	....	....	....
Quasi-Monetary Liabilities	45..k	9,274	† 917	1,039	1,154	1,237	....	....	....	....	....	....	....
Foreign Liabilities	46c.k	2,233	† 2	5	8	10	....	....	....	....	....	....	....
Cred.from Deposit Money Banks	46h.k	1,285	† 394	339	448	564	....	....	....	....	....	....	....
Capital Accounts	47a.k	928	† 35	78	53	56	....	....	....	....	....	....	....
Other Items (Net)	47r.k	−1,125	† 33	15	15	18	....	....	....	....	....	....	....
Interest Rates		*Percent Per Annum*											
Discount Rate (End of Period)	60	6.25	6.50	6.25	6.75	4.06	....	....	....	....	....	....	....
Money Market Rate	60b	† 5.75	5.45	5.74	6.43	3.23	3.14	4.84	3.31	2.88	2.08	2.13	2.40
Treasury Bill Rate	60c	5.87	6.19	5.36	6.03	5.37	....	....	....	....	....	....	....
Deposit Rate	60l	.33	.44	.29	.46	.43	.10	.10	.10	.10	.04	.01	.01
Households: Stocks, up to 2 years	60lhs	....	....	....	....	....	....	....	....	....	2.19	1.91	2.00
Corporations: Stocks, up to 2 years	60lcs	....	....	....	....	....	....	....	....	....	2.27	2.02	2.09
Lending Rate	60p	6.13	6.56	5.85	6.57	6.22	3.34	4.77	4.84	3.83	2.85	2.57	2.65
Households: Stocks, up to 1 year	60phs	....	....	....	....	....	....	....	....	....	9.47	9.38	8.39
New Bus., Floating & up to 1 year	60pns	....	....	....	....	....	....	....	....	....	5.79	5.17	4.98
House Purch., Stocks,Over 5 years	60phm	....	....	....	....	....	....	....	....	....	3.96	3.51	3.41
Corporations: Stocks, up to 1 year	60pcs	....	....	....	....	....	....	....	....	....	5.46	4.92	4.73
New Bus., Over € 1 mil.,up to 1 yr	60pcn	....	....	....	....	....	....	....	....	....	4.39	4.17	4.08
Government Bond Yield	61	8.19	8.30	7.48	6.49	4.99	....	....	....	....	....	....	....
Prices, Production, Labor		*Index Numbers (2000=100): Period Averages*											
Share Prices	62	34.8	38.1	47.6	64.6	90.9	93.6	100.0	108.2	87.2	81.9	102.9	122.7
Wholesale Prices	63	89.9	91.8	92.3	91.8	93.2	94.2	† 100.0	102.9	103.1	97.4	99.0	....
Output Manufacturing Industry	63a	90.5	92.8	93.4	92.9	93.7	94.6	† 100.0	101.7	100.5	92.4	90.2	90.1
Consumer Prices	64	86.0	88.2	89.7	91.0	93.2	94.7	100.0	† 104.9	109.8	113.6	116.1	118.9
Harmonized CPI	64h	....	87.8	89.7	90.8	92.7	95.0	100.0	104.0	108.9	† 113.2	115.9	118.4
Wages: Weekly Earnings	65ey	77.4	79.1	81.1	85.0	88.5	93.7	† 100.0	109.1	115.2	122.6	128.7	133.6
Industrial Production	66	41.2	† 49.6	53.6	63.0	75.5	86.6	100.0	110.0	117.9	123.5	123.8	127.6
Manufacturing Employment	67ey	80.2	85.1	89.2	94.4	97.1	96.2	100.0	101.0	96.3	92.5	89.8	88.5
		Number in Thousands: Period Averages											
Labor Force	67d	1,503	1,559	1,608	1,634	1,748	1,809	1,848	1,886	1,928	1,983	2,031	2,109
Employment	67e	1,221	† 1,282	1,329	1,380	1,521	1,616	1,692	1,741	1,765	1,811	1,865	1,952
Unemployment	67c	282	277	279	254	227	193	155	145	162	172	166	157
Unemployment Rate (%)	67r	15.1	14.1	11.8	10.1	7.1	5.3	4.1	4.0	4.4	4.7	4.5	4.3
Intl. Transactions & Positions		*Millions of Pounds through 1998; Millions of Euros Beginning 1999*											
Exports	70	22,753	27,825	30,407	35,336	45,145	† 66,956	83,889	92,730	92,893	81,639	83,807	88,091
Imports, c.i.f.	71	17,283	20,619	22,429	25,882	31,278	† 44,327	55,909	57,230	54,805	47,107	49,347	55,586
		2000=100											
Volume of Exports	72	38.2	45.8	50.4	57.9	72.0	83.8	100.0	105.0	104.3	99.2	110.5	112.8
Volume of Imports	73	46.5	53.2	58.5	67.2	79.3	85.9	100.0	99.4	97.3	90.0	97.9	112.2
Unit Value of Exports	74	85.9	87.4	86.9	87.9	90.2	95.1	100.0	101.2	101.0	93.7	85.7	88.2
Unit Value of Imports	75	85.1	88.4	87.1	87.5	89.5	92.2	100.0	103.0	99.0	90.7	88.7	89.5

		1994	1995	1996	1997	1998	1999	2000	2001	2002	2003	2004	2005
Balance of Payments		*Millions of US Dollars: Minus Sign Indicates Debit*											
Current Account, n.i.e.	78ald	1,577	1,721	2,049	1,866	1,016	245	−516	−690	−1,101	89	−1,423	−3,945
Goods: Exports f.o.b.	78aad	33,642	44,423	49,184	55,293	78,562	67,831	73,530	77,623	84,216	88,590	99,713	102,934
Goods: Imports f.o.b.	78abd	−24,275	−30,866	−33,430	−36,668	−53,172	−44,244	−48,520	−50,360	−50,769	−51,709	−60,206	−65,286
Trade Balance	78acd	9,366	13,557	15,754	18,625	25,390	23,587	25,010	27,263	33,447	36,882	39,506	37,649
Services: Credit	78add	4,319	5,017	5,749	6,186	16,735	15,688	18,538	23,465	29,900	42,061	52,459	53,780
Services: Debit	78aed	−8,452	−11,303	−13,448	−15,195	−29,626	−26,534	−31,272	−35,339	−42,829	−54,596	−64,517	−66,195
Balance on Goods & Services	78afd	5,233	7,270	8,055	9,616	12,499	12,741	12,276	15,389	20,519	24,346	27,448	25,233
Income: Credit	78agd	3,513	5,110	5,576	7,353	25,430	24,442	27,613	28,850	27,200	34,095	41,991	50,367
Income: Debit	78ahd	−8,919	−12,435	−13,772	−17,059	−38,800	−38,191	−41,160	−45,202	−49,515	−58,879	−71,259	−80,197
Balance on Gds, Serv. & Inc.	78aid	−173	−55	−141	−90	−870	−1,008	−1,271	−962	−1,796	−438	−1,820	−4,597
Current Transfers, n.i.e.: Credit	78ajd	2,850	3,009	3,538	3,083	7,428	5,308	4,143	7,400	7,538	7,027	6,685	7,260
Current Transfers: Debit	78akd	−1,100	−1,233	−1,349	−1,128	−5,543	−4,055	−3,388	−7,128	−6,842	−6,500	−6,288	−6,609
Capital Account, n.i.e.	78bcd	387	817	785	871	1,218	593	1,074	635	512	126	520	379
Capital Account, n.i.e.: Credit	78bad	477	914	881	962	1,327	674	1,167	719	656	617	682	541
Capital Account: Debit	78bbd	−90	−96	−96	−91	−108	−81	−93	−84	−144	−491	−163	−162
Financial Account, n.i.e.	78bjd	−3,963	−33	−2,780	−7,484	4,686	−4,185	7,912	16	468	−3,481	3,851	1,932
Direct Investment Abroad	78bdd	−438	−820	−727	−1,008	−4,955	−6,102	−4,641	−4,103	−11,065	−5,594	−15,816	−13,113
Dir. Invest. in Rep. Econ., n.i.e.	78bed	838	1,447	2,618	2,743	11,035	18,323	25,501	9,573	29,477	22,411	11,040	−21,355
Portfolio Investment Assets	78bfd	−1,019	−1,056	−183	−716	−66,738	−82,813	−83,075	−111,347	−105,469	−163,841	−167,776	−143,843
Equity Securities	78bkd	—	—	—	—	−27,624	−36,357	−28,849	−23,808	−27,200	−29,545	−46,185	−55,568
Debt Securities	78bld	−1,019	−1,056	−183	−716	−39,114	−46,457	−54,226	−87,539	−78,270	−134,296	−121,591	−88,275
Portfolio Investment Liab., n.i.e.	78bgd	−379	771	982	−2,505	54,735	67,377	77,906	89,085	69,368	119,397	158,710	197,246
Equity Securities	78bmd	—	—	—	—	47,948	52,061	69,606	79,352	69,104	76,776	82,765	90,343
Debt Securities	78bnd	−379	771	982	−2,505	6,787	15,316	8,300	9,733	265	42,621	75,945	106,903
Financial Derivatives Assets	78bwd	....	....	....	....	....	....	416	−576	1,606	−406	−420	−6,567
Financial Derivatives Liabilities	78bxd	....	....	—	....	....	....	−42	957	−26	−120	2,972	−2,322
Other Investment Assets	78bhd	−4,483	−16,572	−22,162	−48,337	−25,211	−38,545	−37,036	−21,431	−33,183	−65,871	−55,985	−125,559
Monetary Authorities	78bod	—	—	—	—	....	....	−16	−121	−583	−1,576	308	−981
General Government	78bpd	−76	76	—	—	....	....	−2,057	725	3,327	31	−381	−226
Banks	78bqd	−2,919	−14,083	−19,623	−43,421	....	....	−12,563	−5,348	−20,722	−35,458	−39,629	−85,384
Other Sectors	78brd	−1,489	−2,565	−2,539	−4,916	....	....	−22,400	−16,687	−15,205	−28,867	−16,284	−38,968
Other Investment Liab., n.i.e.	78bid	1,519	16,197	16,691	42,340	35,820	37,576	28,882	37,859	49,759	90,542	71,126	117,445
Monetary Authorities	78bsd	—	—	—	—	—	—	3,493	922	−1,583	7,461	−4,349	−9
General Government	78btd	−1,585	−808	−947	−812	....	....	−160	−2	−34	−286	−9	−149
Banks	78bud	3,103	17,005	17,639	43,152	....	....	19,637	18,656	32,823	62,487	63,749	51,903
Other Sectors	78bvd	....	....	....	....	....	....	5,913	18,283	18,554	20,881	11,735	24,392
Net Errors and Omissions	78cad	1,823	−167	−106	3,639	−3,708	1,373	−8,509	434	−171	1,375	−4,382	−272
Overall Balance	78cbd	−176	2,339	−52	−1,109	3,212	−1,973	−39	395	−292	−1,890	−1,435	−1,906
Reserves and Related Items	79dad	176	−2,339	52	1,109	−3,212	1,973	39	−395	292	1,890	1,435	1,906
Reserve Assets	79dbd	176	−2,339	52	1,109	−3,212	1,973	−121	−395	292	1,890	1,435	1,906
Use of Fund Credit and Loans	79dcd	—	—	—	—	—	—	—	—	—	—	—	—
Exceptional Financing	79ded	....	....	....	....	....	....	160	....	....	....	....	....
International Investment Position		*Millions of US Dollars*											
Assets	79aad	....	....	....	....	....	....	....	749,233	972,186	1,350,983	1,691,755	....
Direct Investment Abroad	79abd	....	....	....	....	....	....	....	40,819	58,881	74,489	104,969	....
Portfolio Investment	79acd	....	....	....	....	....	....	....	432,843	573,968	834,914	1,067,253	....
Equity Securities	79add	....	....	....	....	....	....	....	133,758	152,856	222,503	306,779	....
Debt Securities	79aed	....	....	....	....	....	....	....	299,084	421,112	612,411	760,474	....
Financial Derivatives	79ald	....	....	....	....	....	....	....	7,874	4,293	7,317	9,650	....
Other Investment	79afd	....	....	....	....	....	....	....	262,055	329,562	430,105	506,968	....
Monetary Authorities	79agd	....	....	....	....	....	....	....	669	1,489	3,589	3,577	....
General Government	79ahd	....	....	....	....	....	....	....	3,954	744	928	1,429	....
Banks	79aid	....	....	....	....	....	....	....	117,373	149,583	198,371	245,899	....
Other Sectors	79ajd	....	....	....	....	....	....	....	140,059	177,746	227,216	256,064	....
Reserve Assets	79akd	....	....	....	....	....	....	....	5,641	5,481	4,159	2,914	....
Liabilities	79lad	....	....	....	....	....	....	....	764,959	996,758	1,384,382	1,727,539	....
Dir. Invest. in Rep. Economy	79lbd	....	....	....	....	....	....	....	134,052	182,899	222,960	233,962	....
Portfolio Investment	79lcd	....	....	....	....	....	....	....	363,168	468,835	669,643	892,365	....
Equity Securities	79ldd	....	....	....	....	....	....	....	279,225	343,771	481,712	613,776	....
Debt Securities	79led	....	....	....	....	....	....	....	83,943	125,064	187,931	278,589	....
Financial Derivatives	79lld	....	....	....	....	....	....	....	2,944	—	—	—	....
Other Investment	79lfd	....	....	....	....	....	....	....	264,795	345,024	491,779	601,212	....
Monetary Authorities	79lgd	....	....	....	....	....	....	....	4,635	3,905	13,201	9,257	....
General Government	79lhd	....	....	....	....	....	....	....	501	541	318	385	....
Banks	79lid	....	....	....	....	....	....	....	153,426	204,554	301,414	389,099	....
Other Sectors	79ljd	....	....	....	....	....	....	....	106,234	129,691	166,319	185,839	....
Government Finance													
Central Government		*Millions of Pounds through 1998; Millions of Euros Beginning 1999: Year Ending December 31*											
Deficit (-) or Surplus	80	−322.6	−259.5	102.0	289.7	1,226.2	† 1,513.0	3,171.2	649.7	94.9	....	....	....
Revenue	81	11,676.6	12,423.4	13,422.3	15,108.6	17,175.6	† 29,441.7	29,865.1	30,204.1	32,610.5	....	....	....
Expenditure	82	11,999.2	12,682.9	13,320.3	14,818.9	15,949.4	† 27,928.7	26,693.9	29,554.4	32,515.6	....	....	....
Financing													
Net Borrowing	84	−18.6	535.0	164.5	−109.3	−881.8	† −1,686.3	−3,177.3	−80.9	−742.6	....	....	....
Use of Cash Balances	87	341.2	−275.5	−266.5	−180.4	−344.4	† 173.3	6.1	−569.0	647.7	....	....	....
General Government		*As Percent of Gross Domestic Product*											

Ireland 178

		1994	1995	1996	1997	1998	1999	2000	2001	2002	2003	2004	2005
National Accounts						*Millions of Pounds through 1998; Millions of Euros Beginning in 1999*							
Househ.Cons.Expend.,incl.NPISHs....	**96f**	21,621	23,192	25,311	27,900	31,219	† 43,721	49,488	54,349	59,019	62,935	66,439	73,875
Government Consumption Expend...	**91f**	5,838	6,177	6,514	7,274	7,978	† 11,383	13,050	15,474	17,692	19,232	21,017	22,779
Gross Fixed Capital Formation.........	**93e**	6,043	7,072	8,512	10,650	13,275	† 21,712	25,321	27,056	28,983	31,816	36,509	43,245
Changes in Inventories....................	**93i**	−135	428	427	683	886	† 391	819	377	114	498	80	125
Exports of Goods and Services.........	**90c**	25,923	31,679	35,453	42,121	52,585	† 79,096	100,719	113,642	119,701	112,759	117,363	127,218
Imports of Goods and Services (-).....	**98c**	22,301	26,936	30,142	35,442	45,678	† 66,816	87,110	96,301	98,508	91,981	94,616	106,159
Statistical Discrepancy.....................	**99bs**	−365	−202	−440	−426	318	† −31	777	835	990	−473	−514	−761
Gross Domestic Product (GDP)........	**99b**	36,624	41,409	45,634	52,760	60,582	† 90,612	104,379	117,114	130,515	139,097	148,556	160,322
Net Primary Income from Abroad.....	**98.n**	−3,716	−4,685	−5,147	−6,332	−7,389	† −14,253	−16,224	−20,009	−26,041	−27,426	−26,004	−24,699
Gross National Income (GNI)...........	**99a**	32,908	36,725	40,487	46,428	53,193	† 76,359	88,155	97,105	104,474	111,671	122,552	135,623
Net National Income......................	**99e**	29,170	32,366	35,618	40,392	46,109	† 69,242	79,024	86,497	94,112	103,032	109,965	....
GDP Volume 1995 Ref., Chained.....	**99b.p**	37,736	41,409	44,719	49,564	53,830	† 76,261	....	....	....	....	....	....
GDP Volume 2003 Ref., Chained.....	**99b.p**	....	....	....	....	....	† 108,223	118,198	125,504	133,178	139,097	145,318	152,091
GDP Volume (2000=100)................	**99bvp**	57.5	63.1	68.2	75.6	82.1	† 91.6	100.0	106.2	112.7	117.7	122.9	128.7
GDP Deflator (2000=100)...............	**99bip**	77.4	79.8	81.4	84.9	89.8	† 94.8	100.0	105.7	111.0	113.2	115.8	119.4
						Millions: Midyear Estimates							
Population................................	**99z**	3.58	3.61	3.64	3.67	3.71	3.75	3.80	3.86	3.93	4.01	4.08	4.15

Israel 436

		1994	1995	1996	1997	1998	1999	2000	2001	2002	2003	2004	2005
Exchange Rates					*New Sheqalim per SDR: End of Period*								
Market Rate	aa	4.4058	4.6601	4.6748	4.7709	5.8588	5.7000	5.2651	5.5497	6.4400	6.5071	6.6904	6.5789
					New Sheqalim per US Dollar: End of Period (ae) Period Average (rf)								
Market Rate	ae	3.0180	3.1350	3.2510	3.5360	4.1610	4.1530	4.0410	4.4160	4.7370	4.3790	4.3080	4.6030
Market Rate	rf	3.0111	3.0113	3.1917	3.4494	3.8001	4.1397	4.0773	4.2057	4.7378	4.5541	4.4820	4.4877
					Index Numbers (2000=100): Period Averages								
Nominal Effective Exchange Rate	nec	117.12	109.95	106.60	105.75	100.54	93.02	100.00	101.01	88.25	84.97	82.19	81.50
Real Effective Exchange Rate	rec	93.17	93.92	98.15	102.61	99.83	95.05	100.00	99.12	89.54	84.82	79.75	78.04
Fund Position					*Millions of SDRs: End of Period*								
Quota	2f.s	666.2	666.2	666.2	666.2	666.2	928.2	928.2	928.2	928.2	928.2	928.2	928.2
SDRs	1b.s	.2	.4	1.0	—	.2	.1	.8	1.4	3.4	6.4	9.8	13.0
Reserve Position in the Fund	1c.s	—	—	—	—	—	65.5	89.9	157.4	304.0	354.8	298.3	141.2
Total Fund Cred.&Loans Outstg	2tl	178.6	111.7	22.3	—	—	—	—	—	—	—	—	—
International Liquidity					*Millions of US Dollars Unless Otherwise Indicated: End of Period*								
Total Reserves minus Gold	1l.d	6,792.4	8,119.3	11,414.6	20,332.1	22,674.3	22,604.9	23,281.2	23,378.6	24,082.9	26,315.1	27,094.4	28,059.4
SDRs	1b.d	.4	.6	1.4	—	.3	.2	1.1	1.7	4.6	9.5	15.2	18.6
Reserve Position in the Fund	1c.d	—	—	—	—	—	89.9	117.1	197.8	413.3	527.2	463.2	201.8
Foreign Exchange	1d.d	6,792.0	8,118.7	11,413.2	† 20,332.0	22,674.0	22,514.8	23,163.0	23,179.1	23,665.0	25,778.4	26,616.0	27,839.0
Gold (Million Fine Troy Ounces)	1ad	.009	.009	.009	.009	—	—	—	—	—	—	—	—
Gold (National Valuation)	1and	.4	.5	.4	.4	—	—	—	—	—	—	—	—
Monetary Authorities: Other Liab	4..d	37.8	38.6	38.1	30.0	21.9	17.8	18.1	17.0	16.0	15.5	14.9	12.6
Deposit Money Banks: Assets	7a.d	11,330.0	12,055.9	12,945.4	10,823.5	12,746.6	14,146.6	16,095.4	15,644.9	14,475.2	17,936.1	21,753.2	25,395.4
Liabilities	7b.d	13,098.9	14,514.4	15,113.4	16,738.3	18,334.0	20,452.0	21,872.6	22,106.4	21,821.6	21,796.1	21,432.9	21,073.4
Monetary Authorities					*Millions of New Sheqalim: End of Period*								
Foreign Assets	11	20,508	25,578	37,130	70,970	94,326	93,878	94,084	103,248	114,102	115,275	116,789	129,244
Claims on Central Government	12a	9,976	10,818	12,304	12,199	12,288	12,416	12,530	12,204	11,056	10,048	8,758	6,832
Claims on Deposit Money Banks	12e	15,555	4,503	1,236	1,519	838	810	787	802	3,006	2,727	2,191	1,064
Reserve Money	14	26,166	19,157	25,838	56,659	64,802	80,218	80,706	81,237	68,440	63,312	48,964	43,404
of which: Currency Outside DMBs	14a	5,467	6,731	7,772	8,767	10,051	12,178	12,347	14,580	15,580	16,184	17,758	20,957
Foreign Cur.Deps	14cf	16,413	10,119	7,982	7,633	7,931	10,741	9,100	10,773	7,066	2,624	1,591	1,104
Foreign Liabilities	16c	901	641	228	106	91	74	73	75	76	68	64	58
Central Government Deposits	16d	17,456	19,325	23,013	26,509	39,407	32,242	37,369	39,290	51,914	62,643	78,418	90,659
Other Items (Net)	17r	1,516	1,775	1,591	1,414	3,152	−5,430	−10,747	−4,348	7,734	2,027	292	3,019
Deposit Money Banks					*Millions of New Sheqalim: End of Period*								
Reserves	20	20,743	12,425	18,085	48,103	54,578	68,029	67,882	65,788	52,630	46,825	30,872	22,346
Foreign Assets	21	34,194	37,795	42,086	38,272	53,038	58,751	65,041	69,088	68,569	78,542	93,713	116,895
Claims on Central Government	22a	66,289	69,960	77,542	66,136	63,806	61,984	44,464	43,883	45,563	49,349	55,939	61,985
Claims on Private Sector	22d	154,285	185,123	219,842	254,886	303,434	347,382	390,938	439,228	480,467	462,949	482,871	540,180
Demand Deposits	24	8,946	9,870	12,227	13,502	14,937	17,933	18,536	23,053	22,619	26,483	35,012	39,942
Time and Savings Deposits	25	139,899	171,485	217,117	251,747	306,960	352,568	381,425	412,502	451,051	439,538	450,464	494,679
Restricted Deposits	26b	28,730	22,979	21,481	19,368	17,063	13,593	11,002	6,489	8,147	6,366	5,930	5,816
Foreign Liabilities	26c	39,533	45,503	49,134	59,187	76,288	84,937	88,387	97,622	103,369	95,445	92,333	97,001
Central Government Deposits	26d	23,211	26,684	27,590	28,190	24,286	24,300	21,082	22,058	25,412	23,391	32,785	48,461
Credit from Monetary Authorities	26g	15,569	4,212	1,186	1,506	835	814	787	806	3,004	2,725	2,187	1,098
Other Items (Net)	27r	19,621	24,570	28,821	33,895	34,486	42,001	47,106	55,462	33,631	43,715	44,684	54,404
Monetary Survey					*Millions of New Sheqalim: End of Period*								
Foreign Assets (Net)	31n	14,268	17,229	29,854	49,949	70,986	67,618	70,665	74,639	79,226	98,304	118,105	149,080
Domestic Credit	32	189,882	219,891	259,086	278,521	315,834	365,240	389,482	433,967	459,760	436,312	436,365	469,877
Claims on Central Govt. (Net)	32an	35,598	34,768	39,244	23,635	12,401	17,858	−1,457	−5,261	−20,707	−26,637	−46,506	−70,303
Claims on Private Sector	32d	154,285	185,123	219,842	254,886	303,434	347,382	390,938	439,228	480,467	462,949	482,871	540,180
Money	34	14,523	16,716	20,131	22,401	25,145	30,263	31,030	37,796	38,364	42,838	52,931	61,077
Quasi-Money	35	153,587	187,829	235,519	271,480	326,491	376,013	407,831	442,567	475,268	470,048	478,441	529,649
Restricted Deposits	36b	28,730	22,979	21,481	19,368	17,063	13,593	11,002	6,489	8,147	6,366	5,930	5,816
Other Items (Net)	37r	7,310	9,596	11,809	15,221	18,120	12,990	10,283	21,759	17,211	15,362	17,168	22,410
Money plus Quasi-Money	35l	168,109	204,545	255,650	293,881	351,636	406,276	438,862	480,363	513,632	512,886	531,372	590,726
Interest Rates					*Percent Per Annum*								
Discount Rate	60	17.0	14.2	15.3	13.7	13.5	11.2	8.2	5.7	9.2	5.2	3.9	4.4
Treasury Bill Rate	60c	11.8	14.4	15.3	13.4	11.3	11.4	8.8	6.5	7.4	7.0	4.8	4.3
Deposit Rate	60l	12.2	14.1	14.5	13.1	11.0	11.3	8.6	6.2	6.0	6.6	3.6	3.2
Lending Rate	60p	17.4	20.2	20.7	18.7	16.2	16.4	12.9	10.0	9.9	10.7	7.4	6.4
Prices, Production, Labor					*Index Numbers (2000=100): Period Averages*								
Share Prices	62	37.3	42.6	42.9	58.4	60.0	99.5	100.0	93.1	74.3	115.7	135.8	180.8
Prices: Industrial Products	63	67.7	74.9	81.4	86.5	90.1	96.5	100.0	99.9	103.8	108.2	114.1	† 121.3
Consumer Prices	64	66.8	73.5	81.8	89.1	94.0	98.9	† 100.0	101.1	† 106.8	107.6	107.1	108.5
Wages: Daily Earnings	65	52.8	† 60.6	68.9	79.2	87.1	94.1	100.0	108.5	109.7	111.9	114.5	117.7
Industrial Employment	67	† 92.0	† 100.6	102.2	101.1	100.2	98.7	100.0	97.2	93.3	91.0	92.1	93.6
					Number in Thousands: Period Averages								
Labor Force	67d	2,030	† 2,110	2,157	2,210	† 2,266	2,345	2,435	2,499	2,547	2,610	2,679	2,740
Employment	67e	1,871	† 1,965	2,013	2,040	† 2,073	2,137	2,221	2,265	2,284	2,330	2,401	2,493
Unemployment	67c	158	† 145	144	170	† 193	209	214	234	262	280	278	246
Unemployment Rate (%)	67r	7.8	† 6.9	6.7	7.7	† 8.5	8.9	8.8	9.4	10.3	10.7	10.4	9.0
Intl. Transactions & Positions					*Millions of US Dollars*								
Exports	70..d	16,884	19,046	20,610	22,503	22,993	25,794	31,404	29,081	29,347	31,784	38,618	42,659
Imports, c.i.f	71..d	25,237	29,579	31,620	30,782	29,342	33,166	31,404	35,449	35,517	36,303	42,864	47,142
Imports,c.i.f.,excl. Military Gds	71.md	23,776	28,287	29,951	29,084	27,470	31,090	35,750	33,303	33,106	34,212	40,969	44,944
					2000=100								
Volume of Exports	72	54.6	58.6	† 63.0	69.4	73.6	79.7	100.0	† 95.9	96.9	100.4	116.0	119.0
Volume of Imports	73	64.5	70.9	† 75.6	76.6	76.8	88.0	100.0	† 92.6	93.4	91.9	102.6	105.2
Unit Value of Exports(US$)	74..d	98.0	102.7	† 102.7	101.8	98.8	99.9	100.0	† 96.4	96.4	100.6	105.8	114.3
Unit Value of Imports(US$)	75..d	102.8	111.5	† 110.7	105.7	99.9	97.0	100.0	† 98.6	98.5	104.4	112.0	120.2

Israel 436

		1994	1995	1996	1997	1998	1999	2000	2001	2002	2003	2004	2005
Balance of Payments		*Millions of US Dollars: Minus Sign Indicates Debit*											
Current Account, n.i.e.	78ald	−3,447	−4,790	−5,248	−3,458	−1,257	−1,689	−1,285	−1,648	−1,300	814	1,845	2,385
Goods: Exports f.o.b.	78aad	17,242	19,694	21,515	22,873	23,114	25,816	31,188	27,967	27,535	30,098	36,541	39,746
Goods: Imports f.o.b.	78abd	−22,728	−26,965	−28,654	−28,157	−26,619	−30,567	−34,728	−31,714	−31,971	−33,161	−39,488	−43,780
Trade Balance	78acd	−5,486	−7,271	−7,140	−5,284	−3,505	−4,751	−3,540	−3,747	−4,436	−3,063	−2,948	−4,034
Services: Credit	78add	6,579	7,788	8,063	8,772	9,545	11,699	14,703	11,992	11,271	12,660	15,040	16,877
Services: Debit	78aed	−7,590	−8,326	−8,902	−9,004	−9,258	−10,196	−11,838	−11,782	−10,837	−11,190	−12,825	−13,604
Balance on Goods & Services	78afd	−6,497	−7,808	−7,978	−5,516	−3,219	−3,248	−675	−3,536	−4,002	−1,593	−733	−761
Income: Credit	78agd	1,160	1,641	1,690	1,889	2,490	2,701	3,553	2,640	2,386	2,729	2,793	4,190
Income: Debit	78ahd	−3,711	−4,296	−5,095	−5,882	−6,605	−7,455	−10,645	−7,436	−6,483	−6,739	−6,502	−7,073
Balance on Gds., Serv. & Inc.	78aid	−9,048	−10,463	−11,384	−9,508	−7,333	−8,002	−7,767	−8,332	−8,099	−5,603	−4,441	−3,644
Current Transfers, n.i.e.: Credit	78ajd	5,850	5,941	6,440	6,377	6,683	7,122	7,467	7,791	8,162	7,543	7,349	7,022
Current Transfers: Debit	78akd	−250	−268	−304	−328	−606	−809	−985	−1,107	−1,362	−1,125	−1,063	−993
Capital Account, n.i.e.	78bcd	786	809	773	728	577	569	455	679	166	485	540	548
Capital Account, n.i.e.: Credit	78bad	786	809	773	728	577	569	455	679	166	485	540	548
Capital Account: Debit	78bbd	—											
Financial Account, n.i.e.	78bjd	−959	4,206	4,537	7,207	1,455	3,759	1,902	−296	−2,345	−2,747	−5,250	−5,231
Direct Investment Abroad	78bdd	−742	−820	−815	−923	−1,125	−831	−3,337	−688	−982	−2,065	−3,449	−2,291
Dir. Invest. in Rep. Econ., n.i.e.	78bed	442	1,351	1,398	1,635	1,738	3,130	5,067	3,628	1,767	3,867	1,734	6,066
Portfolio Investment Assets	78bfd	−1,772	154	276	126	−102	−683	−2,814	−1,623	−2,708	−2,621	−2,051	−7,797
Equity Securities	78bkd	303	16	160	166	154	382	−1,544	−421	−611	−757	−469	−2,559
Debt Securities	78bld	−2,075	138	116	−40	−255	−1,065	−1,270	−1,201	−2,097	−1,864	−1,582	−5,238
Portfolio Investment Liab., n.i.e.	78bgd	481	978	1,438	1,702	430	1,411	4,425	569	459	594	3,571	3,684
Equity Securities	78bmd	469	991	1,440	1,719	476	1,496	4,418	576	434	424	3,683	3,627
Debt Securities	78bnd	13	−13	−3	−16	−46	−84	7	−8	25	170	−113	58
Financial Derivatives Assets	78bwd	—	−56	92	89	208	....	....	8	−11	−4	−26	29
Financial Derivatives Liabilities	78bxd												
Other Investment Assets	78bhd	−1,063	−586	845	1,600	−1,595	−3,555	−3,618	−2,631	−1,593	−1,921	−5,626	−4,946
Monetary Authorities	78bod	....	....	....	....	....							
General Government	78bpd	−28	−1,230	864	−19	−13	−458	−1	−561	110	−13	13	1,306
Banks	78bqd	−1,736	−216	−1,165	1,686	−1,808	−758	−1,189	−392	340	−1,255	−3,658	−5,087
Other Sectors	78brd	701	860	1,146	−66	225	−2,340	−2,429	−1,678	−2,043	−653	−1,981	−1,164
Other Investment Liab., n.i.e.	78bid	1,695	3,185	1,303	2,978	1,901	4,288	2,180	440	722	−597	596	24
Monetary Authorities	78bsd	—											
General Government	78btd	−64	215	77	−263	−390	370	−67	187	15	−68	−243	−288
Banks	78bud	1,000	1,219	612	2,352	1,525	2,384	1,644	1,318	117	−558	−1,121	−116
Other Sectors	78bvd	760	1,751	615	889	766	1,533	603	−1,065	590	29	1,960	427
Net Errors and Omissions	78cad	1,510	154	1,015	2,466	−936	−2,765	−752	1,653	2,410	1,253	947	3,182
Overall Balance	78cbd	−2,111	379	1,078	6,943	−161	−127	321	388	−1,068	−195	−1,918	883
Reserves and Related Items	79dad	2,111	−379	−1,078	−6,943	161	127	−321	−388	1,068	195	1,918	−883
Reserve Assets	79dbd	−124	−1,022	−3,284	−9,337	−1,872	−1,006	−943	106	804	−1,022	−279	−1,894
Use of Fund Credit and Loans	79dcd	—	−101	−129	−31								
Exceptional Financing	79ded	2,235	745	2,336	2,426	2,033	1,133	622	−494	265	1,217	2,197	1,011
International Investment Position		*Millions of US Dollars*											
Assets	79aad	26,345	31,327	35,412	45,282	54,965	59,800	67,969	71,877	77,698	88,653	102,012	116,476
Direct Investment Abroad	79abd	—	2,867	3,283	5,223	5,376	6,283	9,091	9,249	10,319	13,064	16,742	18,690
Portfolio Investment	79acd	2,866	2,801	2,609	2,711	3,027	4,983	7,281	7,975	10,126	13,643	16,454	24,900
Equity Securities	79add	374	430	356	447	499	1,432	2,506	2,024	1,766	3,115	4,011	7,574
Debt Securities	79aed	2,492	2,371	2,253	2,264	2,528	3,551	4,775	5,951	8,360	10,528	12,443	17,326
Financial Derivatives	79ald	—											
Other Investment	79afd	16,315	17,271	17,873	16,943	23,812	25,850	28,234	31,192	33,086	35,484	41,572	44,668
Monetary Authorities	79agd	—											
General Government	79ahd	—	795	766	921	1,078	1,534	1,535	2,096	1,986	1,999	1,986	680
Banks	79aid	9,789	10,262	11,223	9,155	11,070	11,571	12,613	12,887	12,900	14,710	18,716	22,036
Other Sectors	79ajd	6,526	6,214	5,884	6,867	11,664	12,745	14,086	16,209	18,200	18,775	20,870	21,952
Reserve Assets	79akd	7,164	8,388	11,648	20,405	22,750	22,684	23,362	23,462	24,168	26,462	27,244	28,217
Liabilities	79lad	47,586	58,088	64,169	74,686	79,915	108,860	120,555	108,869	105,532	123,409	136,305	152,875
Dir. Invest. in Rep. Economy	79lbd	474	5,741	7,096	9,566	11,913	18,665	22,572	23,017	23,212	29,291	31,696	36,750
Portfolio Investment	79lcd	12,437	14,998	19,427	25,847	26,980	45,293	51,300	39,083	33,724	44,712	53,921	66,655
Equity Securities	79ldd	2,893	4,706	6,806	10,789	9,912	27,147	32,637	21,061	15,198	24,509	31,513	43,518
Debt Securities	79led	9,544	10,292	12,621	15,058	17,068	18,146	18,663	18,022	18,526	20,203	22,408	23,137
Financial Derivatives	79lld	—											
Other Investment	79lfd	34,676	37,350	37,647	39,273	41,022	44,902	46,683	46,770	48,596	49,406	50,688	49,470
Monetary Authorities	79lgd	317	235	98	30	21	17	17	16	16	16	15	14
General Government	79lhd	12,944	13,335	13,289	12,724	12,614	12,857	12,704	12,839	13,016	13,127	12,957	12,545
Banks	79lid	13,500	14,958	15,428	17,470	19,129	21,218	22,668	23,790	24,505	24,745	23,988	23,205
Other Sectors	79ljd	7,915	8,822	8,832	9,049	9,258	10,810	11,294	10,124	11,059	11,518	13,728	13,707
Government Finance		*Millions of New Sheqalim: Year Ending December 31*											
Deficit (-) or Surplus	80	−6,882	−11,971	−13,253	1,017	−5,519	−8,698	4,019	−17,270	....	....	....	....
Revenue	81	88,559	108,032	123,796	145,110	159,911	173,187	194,736	195,376	....	....	....	....
Grants Received	81z	7,927	6,340	12,953	11,437	12,158	12,327	11,957	11,534	....	....	....	....
Expenditure	82	102,350	125,369	149,571	165,250	183,046	197,954	208,603	224,287	....	....	....	....
Lending Minus Repayments	83	1,018	974	431	−9,720	−5,458	−3,742	−5,929	−107	....	....	....	....
Financing													
Domestic	84a	655	12,615	7,431	−5,091	538	11,602	−1,783	17,750	....	....	....	....
Foreign	85a	6,227	−644	5,822	4,074	4,981	−2,904	−2,236	−480	....	....	....	....
Debt: Domestic	88a	211,726	240,333	277,034	292,401	318,398	330,062	328,534	348,388	....	....	....	....
Foreign	89a	71,069	75,083	83,673	92,523	114,261	113,472	111,644	121,212	....	....	....	....

Israel 436

National Accounts		1994	1995	1996	1997	1998	1999	2000	2001	2002	2003	2004	2005
		Millions of New Sheqalim											
Househ.Cons.Expend.,incl.NPISHs....	96f	141,769	† 157,994	183,328	202,989	221,946	241,816	263,158	273,584	289,836	294,939	309,956	326,971
Government Consumption Expend...	91f	64,081	† 79,106	94,020	104,712	114,333	123,943	131,474	139,873	152,954	150,071	150,009	154,500
Gross Fixed Capital Formation..........	93e	55,333	† 68,438	79,203	83,872	85,711	91,935	92,707	91,029	91,950	89,949	92,536	96,985
Changes in Inventories.....................	93i	3,094	† 2,795	1,984	2,411	3,139	6,402	8,905	10,329	327	−4,353	−1,244	5,264
Exports of Goods and Services..........	90c	73,553	† 83,096	94,578	109,388	124,382	155,781	187,400	168,262	184,167	194,617	230,754	254,364
Imports of Goods and Services (-).....	98c	106,579	† 121,735	136,914	145,696	154,369	189,138	212,768	204,469	225,487	222,879	258,161	284,115
Gross Domestic Product (GDP).........	99b	231,251	† 269,693	316,200	357,676	395,142	430,739	470,876	478,607	493,747	502,343	523,851	553,970
Net Primary Income from Abroad.....	98.n	−3,722	† 4,444	6,971	10,110	12,578	16,064	25,663	16,911	15,404	13,298	13,033	8,450
Gross National Income (GNI)............	99a	227,529	† 265,249	309,229	347,566	382,564	414,675	445,213	461,696	478,343	489,045	510,818	545,520
Consumption of Fixed Capital..........	99cf	31,886	† 38,544	45,014	52,028	59,202	67,448	70,249	75,383	86,521	88,496	90,970	93,902
Net National Income......................	99e	195,643	† 226,706	264,215	295,538	323,362	347,227	374,963	386,313	391,822	400,548	419,848	451,618
GDP Volume 1990 Prices................	99b.p	131,280	140,540	....	....	....	....	....	....	....	....	....	....
GDP Volume 2000 Prices................	99b.p	....	† 377,507	397,746	412,132	427,348	437,327	470,878	469,669	464,043	472,057	493,011	518,500
GDP Volume (2000=100)...............	99bvp	74.9	† 80.2	84.5	87.5	90.8	92.9	100.0	99.7	98.5	100.3	104.7	110.1
GDP Deflator (2000=100)...............	99bip	65.6	† 71.4	79.5	86.8	92.5	98.5	100.0	101.9	106.4	106.4	106.3	106.8
		Millions: Midyear Estimates											
Population................................	99z	5.20	5.37	5.53	5.68	5.82	5.95	6.08	6.22	6.35	6.47	6.60	6.72

Italy 136

		1994	1995	1996	1997	1998	1999	2000	2001	2002	2003	2004	2005
Exchange Rates							*Euros per SDR: End of Period*							
Market Rate	aa	2,379.2	2,355.7	2,200.9	2,373.6	2,327.6	1.3662	1.4002	1.4260	1.2964	1.1765	1.1402	1.2116
						Euros per US Dollar: End Period (ae) Period Average (rf)								
Market Rate	ae	1,629.7	1,584.7	1,530.6	1,759.2	1,653.1	.9954	1.0747	1.1347	.9536	.7918	.7342	.8477
Market Rate	rf	1,612.4	1,628.9	1,542.9	1,703.1	1,736.2	.9386	1.0854	1.1175	1.0626	.8860	.8054	.8041
						Lire per ECU: End of Period (ea) Period Average (eb)								
ECU Rate	ea	1,997.5	2,082.7	1,913.7	1,940.7	1,936.3	....	....	....	....	....	....	....
ECU Rate	eb	1,913.9	2,131.3	1,958.6	1,929.7	1,943.7	....	....	....	....	....	....	....
						Index Numbers (2000=100): Period Averages								
Market Rate (1995=100)	ahx	101.1	100.0	105.5	95.7	93.9	....	....	....	....	....	....	....
Nominal Effective Exchange Rate	neu	107.6	97.8	106.6	106.6	106.5	104.2	100.0	100.4	101.6	105.8	107.2	107.3
Real Effective Exchange Rate	reu	95.9	89.3	102.7	104.7	103.5	103.6	100.0	103.6	106.6	113.8	120.3	123.9
Fund Position							*Millions of SDRs: End of Period*							
Quota	2f.s	4,591	4,591	4,591	4,591	4,591	7,056	7,056	7,056	7,056	7,056	7,056	7,056
SDRs	1b.s	86	—	20	50	79	122	182	236	79	105	93	160
Reserve Position in the Fund	1c.s	1,393	1,321	1,290	1,661	3,075	2,584	2,230	2,560	2,874	2,796	2,385	1,230
of which: Outstg.Fund Borrowing	2c	—	—	—	—	257	—	—	—	—	—	—	—
Total Fund Cred.&Loans Outstg	2tl	—	—	—	—	—	—	—	—	—	—	—	—
International Liquidity						*Millions of US Dollars Unless Otherwise Indicated: End of Period*								
Total Res.Min.Gold (Eurosys.Def)	1l.d	32,265	34,905	45,948	55,739	29,888	† 22,422	25,567	24,419	28,603	30,365	27,859	25,515
SDRs	1b.d	125	—	29	67	111	168	238	297	108	156	145	229
Reserve Position in the Fund	1c.d	2,033	1,963	1,855	2,241	4,330	3,546	2,906	3,217	3,907	4,154	3,703	1,758
Foreign Exchange	1d.d	30,107	32,942	44,064	53,431	25,447	† 18,708	22,423	20,905	24,588	26,054	24,011	23,528
o/w:Fin.Deriv.Rel.to Reserves	1ddd	....	....	....	....	....	—	—	—	—	—	—	—
Other Reserve Assets	1e.d	....	....	....	....	....	—	—	—	—	—	—	—
Gold (Million Fine Troy Ounces)	1ad	66.67	66.67	66.67	66.67	83.36	78.83	78.83	78.83	78.83	78.83	78.83	78.83
Gold (Eurosystem Valuation)	1and	26,342	25,570	25,369	21,806	24,711	22,880	21,635	21,796	27,019	32,891	34,527	40,439
Memo:Euro Cl. on Non-EA Res	1dgd	....	....	....	....	....	1	476	451	537	125	139	215
Non-Euro Cl. on EA Res	1dhd	....	....	....	....	....	3,620	2,812	4,814	5,556	8,145	7,621	8,175
Mon. Auth.: Other Foreign Assets	3..d	....	....	....	....	....	....	....	....	....	....	....	....
Foreign Liabilities	4..d	1,510	2,598	1,249	1,123	1,045	† 6,315	235	2,198	3,078	509	925	2,027
Banking Insts.: Foreign Assets	7a.d	123,919	145,842	193,215	177,149	193,743	† 90,837	85,886	75,040	94,258	117,858	122,626	110,304
Foreign Liab	7b.d	230,505	216,808	237,872	223,249	236,896	† 136,369	146,783	150,863	153,427	201,524	214,467	212,370
Monetary Authorities						*Trillions of Lire through 1998; Billions of Euros Beginning 1999: End of Period*								
Fgn. Assets (Cl.on Non-EA Ctys)	11	93.90	95.59	108.65	135.62	90.33	45.80	50.49	52.42	52.74	49.88	45.55	56.09
Claims on General Government	12a.u						60.12	63.25	65.06	44.49	53.72	60.52	67.35
o/w: Claims on Gen.Govt.in Cty	12a	195.88	196.42	168.95	174.17	156.37	60.12	63.25	65.06	44.49	53.72	60.52	67.35
Claims on Banking Institutions	12e.u	....	....	....	....	....	51.35	36.49	33.51	19.96	22.48	34.87	43.30
o/w: Claims on Bank.Inst.in Cty	12e	42.50	41.04	50.03	32.30	11.04	36.01	26.53	10.70	7.76	9.72	15.61	22.27
Claims on Other Resident Sectors	12d.u						7.36	8.29	6.75	5.28	5.75	6.94	7.33
o/w: Cl. on Oth.Res.Sect.in Cty	12d	.56	2.64	—	—	—	7.13	8.06	6.49	5.25	5.74	6.86	6.75
Currency Issued	14a	101.86	105.22	108.16	116.27	124.88	71.96	76.42	65.89	65.49	76.09	86.79	97.89
Liabilities to Banking Insts	14c.u						24.84	25.52	26.28	18.43	18.03	19.05	19.55
o/w: Liabs to Bank.Inst.in Cty	14c	87.54	72.30	73.69	79.08	13.78	9.23	7.75	26.28	10.45	10.30	12.97	11.45
Demand Dep. of Other Res.Sect	14d.u						.39	.08	.23	.01	.08	.11	.05
o/w:D.Dep.of Oth.Res.Sect.in Cty	14d	....	....	....	....	....	.39	.08	.23	.01	.08	.11	.05
Other Dep. of Other Res.Sect	15..u	....	....	....	....	....	—	—	—	—	—	—	—
o/w:O.Dep.of Oth.Res.Sect.in Cty	15	....	....	....	....	....	—	—	—	—	—	—	—
Bonds & Money Mkt. Instruments	16n.u	....	....	....	....	....	....	....	....	....	....	....	....
o/w: Held by Resid.of Cty	16n	1.47	1.99	1.66	1.20	.92	....	....	....	....	....	....	....
Foreign Liab. (to Non-EA Ctys)	16c	2.46	4.12	1.91	1.98	1.73	6.29	.25	2.49	2.94	.40	.68	1.72
Central Government Deposits	16d.u						29.08	19.37	23.46	21.32	13.30	15.86	14.66
o/w: Cent.Govt.Dep. in Cty	16d	63.94	72.13	54.76	57.78	42.21	29.08	19.37	23.46	21.32	13.30	15.86	14.66
Capital Accounts	17a	90.66	94.79	99.84	98.93	75.85	35.37	40.44	41.46	25.26	25.02	27.45	43.09
Other Items (Net)	17r	−15.09	−14.85	−12.39	−13.15	−1.61	−3.30	−3.56	−2.09	−10.98	−1.08	−2.05	−2.89
Memo: Net Claims on Eurosystem	12e.s						−3.85	−10.31	18.16	−6.15	−5.95	2.37	−1.39
Currency Put into Circ	14m	....	....	....	....	....	....	....	....	71.23	81.78	92.87	105.99
Banking Institutions						*Trillions of Lire through 1998; Billions of Euros Beginning 1999: End of Period*								
Claims on Monetary Authorities	20	93.29	79.31	81.70	87.81	23.65	9.90	8.16	25.73	10.34	10.38	13.13	11.62
Claims on Bk.Inst.in Oth.EA Ctys	20b.u						67.89	69.20	62.36	86.55	91.52	112.16	125.07
Fgn. Assets (Cl.on Non-EA Ctys)	21	201.96	231.12	295.73	311.64	320.28	90.42	92.30	85.15	89.88	93.32	90.03	93.50
Claims on General Government	22a.u						243.13	211.34	211.95	207.66	237.56	241.40	242.05
o/w: Claims on Gen.Govt.in Cty	22a	434.80	413.46	442.92	408.43	395.40	240.00	206.65	207.15	201.86	219.97	215.32	220.37
Claims on Other Resident Sectors	22d.u						811.05	926.19	997.04	1,063.70	1,148.35	1,213.49	1,311.88
o/w: Cl. on Oth.Res.Sect.in Cty	22d	983.66	1,027.70	1,060.42	1,123.53	1,224.36	788.23	896.82	966.60	1,030.75	1,110.79	1,178.90	1,271.53
Demand Deposits	24..u						386.95	410.65	449.75	492.52	519.59	549.46	593.89
o/w:D.Dep.of Oth.Res.Sect.in Cty	24	471.38	471.06	498.87	531.72	601.15	384.91	407.91	446.12	488.03	515.62	546.14	590.52
Other Deposits	25..u						194.71	194.55	192.43	205.83	181.59	188.52	196.26
o/w:O.Dep.of Oth.Res.Sect.in Cty	25	458.91	476.50	469.39	359.51	287.75	190.61	190.26	190.54	201.04	176.29	178.63	185.35
Money Market Fund Shares	26m.u	....	....	....	....	....	13.06	10.04	26.10	41.69	106.70	100.66	88.17
Bonds & Money Mkt. Instruments	26n.u	....	....	....	....	....	271.55	302.48	334.67	367.97	399.96	442.99	484.42
o/w: Held by Resid.of Cty	26n	303.38	341.95	399.97	510.23	544.00	....	....	....	....	....	....	....
Foreign Liab. (to Non-EA Ctys)	26c	375.66	343.58	364.08	392.74	391.61	135.75	157.75	171.18	146.30	159.56	157.45	180.02
Central Government Deposits	26d.u						7.96	7.00	7.51	7.12	7.75	7.23	9.14
o/w: Cent.Govt.Dep. in Cty	26d	13.23	9.29	11.15	12.73	13.40	7.92	6.96	7.21	7.11	7.73	7.22	8.21
Credit from Monetary Authorities	26g	42.50	41.04	50.03	32.30	11.04	33.29	26.46	10.81	7.62	9.16	15.63	22.12
Liab. to Bk.Inst.in Oth. EA Ctys	26h.u						98.65	107.61	109.57	111.65	118.93	126.29	146.23
Capital Accounts	27a	219.39	232.44	250.19	257.05	280.93	118.27	123.93	133.63	146.17	156.73	163.18	191.41
Other Items (Net)	27r	−170.74	−164.29	−162.91	−164.86	−166.20	−37.79	−33.28	−53.44	−68.74	−78.87	−81.30	−127.64
Post Office: Checking Deposits	24..i	8.16	8.49	7.28	6.67	1.66	....	....	....	....	....	....	....
Post Office: Savings Deposits	25..i	39.15	43.94	46.26	52.00	58.33	....	....	....	....	....	....	....
Savings Certif	26abi	87.05	97.77	110.61	117.35	121.65	....	....	....	....	....	....	....

		1994	1995	1996	1997	1998	1999	2000	2001	2002	2003	2004	2005
Banking Survey (Nat'l Residency)		\multicolumn{12}{c}{*Trillions of Lire through 1998; Billions of Euros Beginning 1999: End of Period*}										
Foreign Assets (Net)........................	31n	−82.27	−20.99	38.39	52.54	17.26	−11.03	−27.51	−23.60	9.43	12.70	30.19	29.18
Domestic Credit..............................	32	1,672.10	1,708.99	1,770.52	1,811.64	1,902.18	1,058.49	1,148.44	1,214.62	1,253.91	1,369.21	1,438.52	1,543.12
Claims on General Govt. (Net)........	32an	687.88	678.65	710.10	688.11	677.82	263.13	243.56	241.53	217.92	252.67	252.76	264.85
Claims on Other Resident Sectors.....	32d	984.22	1,030.34	1,060.42	1,123.53	1,224.36	795.36	904.89	973.09	1,036.00	1,116.53	1,185.76	1,278.28
Currency Issued.............................	34a.n	110.02	113.71	115.44	122.94	126.54	71.96	76.42	65.89	65.49	76.09	86.79	97.89
Demand Deposits............................	34b.n	471.38	471.06	498.87	531.72	601.15	385.30	407.99	446.35	488.03	515.70	546.25	590.56
Other Deposits..............................	35..n	498.06	520.44	515.65	411.52	346.08	190.61	190.26	190.54	201.04	176.29	178.63	185.35
Money Market Fund Shares.............	36m	....	....	....	....	....	13.06	10.04	26.10	41.69	106.70	100.66	88.17
Bonds & Money Mkt. Instruments....	36n	391.90	441.72	512.24	628.77	666.57	271.55	302.48	334.67	367.97	399.96	442.99	484.42
o/w: Over Two Years......	36na	....	....	....	....	....	259.05	289.12	322.13	353.93	388.79	433.97	473.59
Capital Accounts...........................	37a	310.05	327.22	350.03	355.99	356.78	153.63	164.37	175.10	171.43	181.75	190.63	234.50
Other Items (Net)...........................	37r	−191.58	−186.14	−183.31	−186.74	−177.68	−38.66	−30.63	−47.64	−72.32	−74.61	−77.32	−108.71
Banking Survey (EA-Wide Residency)		\multicolumn{12}{c}{*Billions of Euros: End of Period*}										
Foreign Assets (Net)........................	31n.u	....	....	....	....	....	−5.81	−15.21	−36.11	−6.62	−16.76	−22.55	−32.14
Domestic Credit..............................	32..u	....	....	....	....	....	1,084.62	1,182.69	1,249.82	1,292.69	1,424.35	1,499.27	1,604.81
Claims on General Govt. (Net)........	32anu	....	....	....	....	....	266.21	248.22	246.04	223.71	270.24	278.84	285.60
Claims on Other Resident Sect......	32d.u	....	....	....	....	....	818.41	934.47	1,003.78	1,068.98	1,154.11	1,220.43	1,319.21
Currency Issued.............................	34a.u	....	....	....	....	....	71.96	76.42	65.89	65.49	76.09	86.79	97.89
Demand Deposits............................	34b.u	....	....	....	....	....	387.33	410.74	449.98	492.53	519.67	549.57	593.93
Other Deposits..............................	35..u	....	....	....	....	....	194.71	194.55	192.43	205.83	181.59	188.52	196.26
o/w: Other Dep. Over Two Yrs....	35abu	....	....	....	....	....	17.00	11.49	6.41	4.07	4.32	3.71	4.60
Money Market Fund Shares.............	36m.u	....	....	....	....	....	13.06	10.04	26.10	41.69	106.70	100.66	88.17
Bonds & Money Mkt. Instruments....	36n.u	....	....	....	....	....	271.55	302.48	334.67	367.97	399.96	442.99	484.42
o/w: Over Two Years......	36nau	....	....	....	....	....	259.05	289.12	322.13	353.93	388.79	433.97	473.59
Capital Accounts...........................	37a	....	....	....	....	....	153.63	164.37	175.10	171.43	181.75	190.63	234.50
Other Items (Net)...........................	37r.u	....	....	....	....	....	−13.44	8.89	−30.46	−58.87	−58.21	−82.53	−122.62
Money (National Definitions)		\multicolumn{12}{c}{*Trillions of Lire: End of Period*}										
M2...	59mb	847.42	834.15	863.29	930.99	975.34	....	....	....	....	....	....	....
Interest Rates		\multicolumn{12}{c}{*Percent Per Annum*}										
Discount Rate (End of Period)..........	60	7.50	9.00	7.50	5.50	3.00	....	....	....	....	....	....	....
Money Market Rate........................	60b	8.51	10.46	8.82	6.88	4.99	2.95	4.39	4.26	3.32	2.33	2.10	2.18
Treasury Bill Rate...........................	60c	9.17	10.85	8.46	6.33	4.59	3.01	4.53	4.05	3.26	2.19	2.08	2.17
Deposit Rate.................................	60l	6.20	6.45	6.49	4.83	3.16	1.61	1.84	1.96	1.43	.95	....	....
Households: Stocks, up to 2 years..	60lhs	....	....	....	....	....	....	....	....	....	1.97	1.52	1.45
New Business, up to 1 year.........	60lhn	....	....	....	....	....	....	....	....	....	1.67	1.49	1.51
REPOS, Stocks.............................	60lcr	....	....	....	....	....	....	....	....	....	2.19	1.92	2.00
Lending Rate.................................	60p	11.22	12.47	12.06	9.75	7.88	5.58	6.26	6.53	5.78	5.03	....	5.31
Households: Stocks, up to 1 year....	60phs	....	....	....	....	....	....	....	....	....	8.35	8.16	7.94
New Bus., Floating & up to 1 year	60pns	....	....	....	....	....	....	....	....	....	10.58	10.91	10.55
House Purch., Stocks,Over 5 years	60phm	....	....	....	....	....	....	....	....	....	5.05	4.48	4.24
House Purch., New Bus., 5-10 yrs	60phn	....	....	....	....	....	....	....	....	....	5.13	4.96	4.19
Corporations: Stocks, up to 1 year..	60pcs	....	....	....	....	....	....	....	....	....	5.36	5.03	4.85
New Bus., Over € 1 mil.,up to 1 yr	60pcn	....	....	....	....	....	....	....	....	....	3.30	2.93	3.02
Government Bond Yield..................	61	10.56	12.21	9.40	6.86	4.90	4.73	5.58	5.19	5.03	4.25	4.26	3.56
Govt. Bond Yield (Medium-Term).....	61b	10.57	11.98	8.93	6.47	4.55	4.04	5.29	4.64	4.48	3.36	3.34	2.90
Prices, Production, Labor		\multicolumn{12}{c}{*Index Numbers (2000=100): Period Averages*}										
Share Prices.................................	62	34.2	31.4	31.5	43.2	69.1	77.0	100.0	81.1	64.3	58.1	66.8	79.5
Producer Prices..............................	63	84.9	91.5	93.3	94.5	94.6	94.3	100.0	101.9	† 101.8	103.4	106.2	110.4
Consumer Prices............................	64	84.3	† 88.7	92.2	94.1	95.9	97.5	100.0	102.8	105.3	108.1	110.5	112.7
Harmonized CPI..............................	64h	....	88.8	92.3	94.0	95.9	97.5	100.0	102.3	105.0	† 107.9	110.4	112.8
Wages: Contractual........................	65	84.6	87.2	90.0	93.2	95.8	98.0	100.0	101.8	104.5	107.2	110.5	113.9
Industrial Production......................	66	88.0	92.9	91.3	94.9	96.0	95.9	100.0	99.0	97.4	96.9	96.3	95.5
Industrial Employment....................	67	102.4	100.7	99.6	98.9	99.8	100.0	100.0	100.8	101.9	103.7	104.5	105.6
		\multicolumn{12}{c}{*Number in Thousands: Period Averages*}										
Labor Force.................................	67d	22,680	22,734	22,849	22,889	23,363	23,361	23,720	23,900	24,086	24,229	....	....
Employment.................................	67e	20,393	20,240	20,328	20,384	20,591	20,847	21,210	21,605	21,913	22,241	22,404	22,563
Unemployment..............................	67c	2,508	2,638	2,555	2,585	2,634	2,560	2,388	2,164	2,062	2,048	1,960	1,889
Unemployment Rate (%).................	67r	11.1	11.7	11.2	11.3	11.3	11.0	10.2	9.1	8.6	8.5	8.1	7.7
Intl. Transactions & Positions		\multicolumn{12}{c}{*Billions of Lire through 1998; Millions of Euros Beginning 1999*}										
Exports.......................................	70	308,045	381,175	388,885	409,128	426,182	† 221,040	260,414	272,990	269,064	264,615	284,412	300,247
Imports, c.i.f.................................	71	272,382	335,661	321,286	357,587	378,784	† 207,016	258,507	263,756	261,226	262,997	285,633	309,785
		\multicolumn{12}{c}{*2000=100*}										
Volume of Exports.........................	72	82.8	93.8	† 91.7	93.5	94.2	91.7	100.0	101.5	98.6	96.0	98.9	96.8
Volume of Imports.........................	73	72.7	79.8	† 76.0	83.2	89.6	93.0	100.0	99.5	98.8	99.5	103.1	101.7
Unit Value of Exports.....................	74	74.1	81.0	† 84.5	87.2	90.2	92.6	100.0	103.6	105.0	105.8	110.3	117.5
Unit Value of Imports.....................	75	75.2	84.4	† 84.5	85.9	84.6	86.0	100.0	102.7	102.2	101.9	106.7	116.3

Italy 136

		1994	1995	1996	1997	1998	1999	2000	2001	2002	2003	2004	2005
Balance of Payments		*Millions of US Dollars: Minus Sign Indicates Debit*											
Current Account, n.i.e.	78ald	13,209	25,076	39,999	32,403	19,998	8,111	−5,781	−652	−9,369	−19,406	−15,137	−26,814
Goods: Exports f.o.b.	78aad	191,421	233,998	252,039	240,404	242,572	235,856	240,473	244,931	252,618	298,118	352,166	371,635
Goods: Imports f.o.b.	78abd	−159,854	−195,269	−197,921	−200,527	−206,941	−212,420	−230,925	−229,392	−239,206	−286,641	−341,255	−371,230
Trade Balance	78acd	31,568	38,729	54,118	39,878	35,631	23,437	9,549	15,540	13,412	11,477	10,911	405
Services: Credit	78add	53,681	61,619	65,660	66,991	67,549	58,788	56,556	57,676	60,439	71,767	83,706	94,624
Services: Debit	78aed	−48,238	−55,050	−57,605	−59,227	−63,379	−57,707	−55,601	−57,753	−63,166	−74,332	−81,987	−94,135
Balance on Goods & Services	78afd	37,011	45,299	62,173	47,642	39,801	24,517	10,504	15,463	10,685	8,912	12,630	895
Income: Credit	78agd	28,599	34,168	40,142	45,734	51,319	46,361	38,671	38,574	43,303	48,780	53,219	60,767
Income: Debit	78ahd	−45,289	−49,812	−55,101	−56,936	−63,636	−57,411	−50,680	−48,911	−57,854	−69,003	−71,424	−78,420
Balance on Gds, Serv. & Inc.	78aid	20,321	29,655	47,213	36,440	27,483	13,467	−1,506	5,127	−3,865	−11,312	−5,574	−16,759
Current Transfers, n.i.e.: Credit	78ajd	12,254	14,287	14,320	15,552	14,402	16,776	15,797	16,136	20,871	20,650	21,854	24,395
Current Transfers: Debit	78akd	−19,366	−18,866	−21,535	−19,588	−21,887	−22,132	−20,073	−21,915	−26,375	−28,744	−31,417	−34,451
Capital Account, n.i.e.	78bcd	1,026	1,671	66	3,434	2,358	2,964	2,879	846	−80	2,941	2,645	2,195
Capital Account, n.i.e.: Credit	78bad	2,213	2,797	1,414	4,582	3,359	4,572	4,172	2,098	2,060	4,950	4,113	4,521
Capital Account: Debit	78bbd	−1,187	−1,125	−1,348	−1,148	−1,001	−1,608	−1,293	−1,252	−2,140	−2,009	−1,468	−2,325
Financial Account, n.i.e.	78bjd	−14,207	−2,889	−7,982	−6,878	−18,074	−17,415	7,504	−3,570	11,224	20,437	8,165	22,841
Direct Investment Abroad	78bdd	−5,239	−7,024	−8,697	−10,414	−12,407	−6,723	−12,077	−21,758	−17,247	−8,986	−19,144	−40,501
Dir. Invest. in Rep. Econ., n.i.e.	78bed	2,199	4,842	3,546	3,700	2,635	6,943	13,176	14,874	14,699	16,538	16,772	19,169
Portfolio Investment Assets	78bfd	−37,718	−4,938	−25,598	−61,857	−109,064	−129,624	−80,263	−36,167	−15,265	−57,408	−26,394	−108,365
Equity Securities	78bkd	−3,360	1,014	−1,036	−15,116	−26,570	−63,277	−77,036	−9,988	−5,198	−15,999	−16,178	−25,137
Debt Securities	78bld	−34,358	−5,952	−24,562	−46,741	−82,493	−66,347	−3,227	−26,179	−10,067	−41,409	−10,216	−83,228
Portfolio Investment Liab., n.i.e.	78bgd	29,895	45,583	74,655	73,375	111,987	104,607	57,020	29,329	32,924	60,150	58,551	165,471
Equity Securities	78bmd	−1,395	5,358	9,331	9,414	14,423	−4,537	−2,426	−245	−6,268	−2,010	17,183	2,637
Debt Securities	78bnd	31,290	40,225	65,324	63,962	97,563	109,144	59,446	29,573	39,193	62,160	41,368	162,834
Financial Derivatives Assets	78bwd	87	−852	−1,009	−1,118	−850	161	744	−2,277	−6,137	−10,284	−6,657	−10,227
Financial Derivatives Liabilities	78bxd	628	1,079	1,272	1,273	1,041	1,709	1,588	1,839	3,431	4,814	8,941	13,356
Other Investment Assets	78bhd	2,092	−28,947	−68,358	−25,541	−21,232	−33,573	242	2,032	6,229	−20,584	−47,563	−100,468
Monetary Authorities	78bod	....	....	....	....	....	5,396	3,034	−27,626	13,536	−65	−8,703	−4,350
General Government	78bpd	−2,023	−2,148	−1,112	−62	−1,101	−163	−649	−355	1,372	1,405	−537	−5,290
Banks	78bqd	22,599	−18,689	−45,046	−1,602	−7,052	−9,643	2,388	12,091	−34,000	429	−28,323	−24,830
Other Sectors	78brd	−18,483	−8,110	−22,199	−23,877	−13,078	−29,163	−4,532	17,921	25,320	−22,353	−9,999	−65,998
Other Investment Liab., n.i.e.	78bid	−6,152	−12,632	16,206	13,703	9,816	39,085	27,074	8,560	−7,412	36,199	23,659	84,407
Monetary Authorities	78bsd	−95	1,062	−1,269	−48	−128	916	−690	1,928	869	−2,548	388	1,104
General Government	78btd	−1,812	4,893	−2,583	−1,798	−5,739	−3,255	−3,549	−759	−537	−1,015	−655	1,304
Banks	78bud	−1,527	−22,716	26,613	6,861	12,780	1,109	24,875	12,783	−6,123	43,746	14,719	59,506
Other Sectors	78bvd	−2,719	4,129	−6,555	8,688	2,903	40,315	6,438	−5,392	−1,621	−3,984	9,207	22,493
Net Errors and Omissions	78cad	1,547	−21,054	−20,176	−15,810	−25,754	−1,711	−1,355	2,787	1,395	−2,858	1,484	749
Overall Balance	78cbd	1,575	2,804	11,907	13,150	−21,472	−8,051	3,247	−588	3,169	1,115	−2,844	−1,030
Reserves and Related Items	79dad	−1,575	−2,804	−11,907	−13,150	21,472	8,051	−3,247	588	−3,169	−1,115	2,844	1,030
Reserve Assets	79dbd	−1,575	−2,804	−11,907	−13,150	21,472	8,051	−3,247	588	−3,169	−1,115	2,844	1,030
Use of Fund Credit and Loans	79dcd	—	—	—	—	—	—	—	—	—	—	—	—
Exceptional Financing	79ded	....	....	....	—	....	....	....	....	....	....	....	....
International Investment Position		*Millions of US Dollars*											
Assets	79aad	516,329	597,810	727,498	809,597	1,002,865	1,081,092	1,119,403	1,078,294	1,201,351	1,565,536	1,808,319	....
Direct Investment Abroad	79abd	91,097	109,176	113,251	130,668	165,412	181,852	180,278	182,377	194,497	238,888	280,481	....
Portfolio Investment	79acd	150,426	171,793	192,351	257,494	394,501	546,903	590,758	552,026	595,925	796,330	914,109	....
Equity Securities	79add	14,015	13,982	16,915	26,600	37,690	210,929	285,555	239,474	247,464	331,049	380,208	....
Debt Securities	79aed	136,411	157,811	175,436	230,894	356,811	335,974	305,203	312,552	348,461	465,282	533,901	....
Financial Derivatives	79ald	—	—	—	—	—	2,951	3,533	4,326	11,051	22,705	28,490	....
Other Investment	79afd	217,192	256,520	350,907	344,344	388,310	304,085	297,776	293,350	344,256	444,351	522,853	....
Monetary Authorities	79agd	—	—	—	—	—	−4,190	−6,715	20,629	8,944	12,244	23,711	....
General Government	79ahd	16,459	19,542	21,777	20,180	22,567	20,417	23,316	23,057	25,403	28,930	31,463	....
Banks	79aid	121,726	146,945	214,524	198,520	225,089	138,717	140,448	119,069	181,177	226,349	276,619	....
Other Sectors	79ajd	79,006	90,034	114,606	125,644	140,653	149,141	140,727	130,595	128,732	176,829	191,059	....
Reserve Assets	79akd	57,615	60,321	70,989	77,091	54,642	45,302	47,058	46,215	55,622	63,262	62,386	....
Liabilities	79lad	587,612	650,102	761,656	807,436	1,022,771	1,027,672	1,079,981	1,055,436	1,273,301	1,652,965	1,932,012	....
Dir. Invest. in Rep. Economy	79lbd	60,955	65,980	74,640	83,158	105,397	108,638	121,169	113,435	130,820	180,891	220,716	....
Portfolio Investment	79lcd	188,595	237,861	333,422	385,388	544,602	549,251	576,343	565,874	708,817	925,482	1,081,347	....
Equity Securities	79ldd	11,118	16,434	27,245	35,500	65,833	53,380	59,289	40,659	33,899	43,241	74,743	....
Debt Securities	79led	177,477	221,427	306,177	349,888	478,769	495,871	517,055	525,215	674,918	882,241	1,006,604	....
Financial Derivatives	79lld	—	—	—	—	—	3,244	2,641	4,550	8,919	15,896	26,345	....
Other Investment	79lfd	338,063	346,261	353,593	338,891	372,772	366,538	379,828	371,577	424,744	530,696	603,604	....
Monetary Authorities	79lgd	485	1,554	239	175	56	950	235	2,196	3,078	633	1,046	....
General Government	79lhd	21,551	26,328	22,187	21,470	15,595	8,881	7,272	6,062	6,341	6,504	6,274	....
Banks	79lid	229,119	228,859	247,732	239,171	268,935	241,669	265,041	260,813	296,677	386,978	442,179	....
Other Sectors	79ljd	86,907	89,521	83,436	78,075	88,186	115,039	107,280	102,506	118,648	136,581	154,105	....
Government Finance													
Central Government		*Trillions of Lire through 1998; Billions of Euros Beginning 1999: Year Ending December 31*											
Deficit (-) or Surplus	80	−175.6	−128.2	−143.4	−30.6	−51.1	−5.2	−17.9	−52.2	−34.4	−17.4	−44.9	−58.9
Revenue	81	477.1	524.8	549.6	621.3	594.6	353.1	350.6	351.7	352.7	381.5	394.7	384.0
Expenditure	82	624.3	625.0	660.1	602.2	614.4	333.1	344.5	384.6	372.3	398.6	433.5	440.0
Lending Minus Repayments	83	28.3	28.0	32.9	49.7	31.3	25.2	24.0	19.4	14.9	.3	6.1	2.9
Financing	80h	175.6	128.2	143.4	30.6	51.1	5.2	17.9	52.2	34.4	17.4	44.9	58.9
Domestic	84a	132.1	67.1	41.7	−74.0	−88.8	−87.3	−31.2	40.2	13.7	−43.1	35.0	−31.8
Foreign	85a	43.5	61.1	101.6	104.6	140.0	92.6	49.1	12.0	20.7	60.5	9.8	90.7
Total Debt by Residence	88	2,036.3	2,192.2	2,314.1	2,360.9	2,388.0	1,250.9	1,260.8	1,313.4	1,320.0	1,322.4	1,368.5	1,424.7
Debt: Domestic	88a	1,729.9	1,846.3	1,887.4	1,835.2	1,734.0	820.5	789.7	833.7	825.7	775.4	811.7	781.0
Foreign	89a	306.4	345.9	426.7	525.7	654.0	430.4	471.2	479.7	494.3	547.0	556.8	643.7
Net Borrowing: Lire	84b	147.5	100.9	129.9	....	....	....	....	....	....	....	....	....
Net Borrowing: Foreign Currency	85b	9.2	25.8	12.9	....	....	....	....	....	....	....	....	....
Monetary Operations	86c	.1	.1	.1	....	....	....	....	....	....	....	....	....
General Government		*As Percent of Gross Domestic Product*											

Italy   136

2006, International Monetary Fund : *International Financial Statistics Yearbook*

		1994	1995	1996	1997	1998	1999	2000	2001	2002	2003	2004	2005
National Accounts							*Trillions of Lire through 1998; Billions of Euros Beginning 1999*						
Househ.Cons.Expend.,incl.NPISHs....	**96f.c**	996.0	1,071.3	1,125.5	1,187.4	1,250.8	† 674.6	713.7	737.7	760.3	789.0	814.4	834.1
Government Consumption Expend...	**91f.c**	327.2	329.5	354.8	371.9	382.7	† 205.5	219.7	236.9	248.8	262.9	275.5	287.6
Gross Fixed Capital Formation..........	**93e.c**	314.4	349.7	368.2	384.1	407.7	† 221.3	242.0	253.8	270.9	271.8	286.5	291.8
Changes in Inventories...................	**93i.c**	4.2	14.2	4.3	9.0	7.0	† 4.8	4.5	3.2	2.8	4.2	2.9	4.6
Exports of Goods and Services..........	**90c.c**	388.2	472.1	480.7	512.2	532.2	† 275.8	322.2	338.3	333.2	327.9	351.9	373.0
Imports of Goods and Services (-).....	**98c.c**	330.5	402.4	389.9	433.9	467.2	† 254.9	311.1	321.1	320.8	320.5	342.3	373.7
Gross Domestic Product (GDP).........	**99b.c**	1,699.5	1,834.3	1,943.6	2,030.7	2,113.2	† 1,127.1	1,191.1	1,248.6	1,295.2	1,335.4	1,388.9	1,417.2
Net Primary Income from Abroad.....	**98.nc**	−31.8	−28.3	−24.6	−13.1	−14.5	† −4.9	−8.9	−8.2	−10.1	−11.0	−7.9	−4.6
Gross National Income (GNI)............	**99a.c**	1,667.7	1,806.0	1,919.0	2,017.6	2,098.7	† 1,122.2	1,182.1	1,240.4	1,285.1	1,324.4	1,381.0	1,412.6
Net Current Transf.from Abroad.......	**98t.c**	....	....	....	....	....	† −4.4	−3.9	−5.3	−6.6	−8.4	....	....
Gross Nat'l Disposable Inc.(GNDI)....	**99i.c**	....	....	....	....	....	† 1,105.7	1,163.8	1,216.0	1,257.1	1,292.1	....	....
Gross Saving.................................	**99s.c**	325.7	403.2	432.0	451.3	455.7	† 237.7	244.8	260.6	269.4	264.0	282.1	281.2
Consumption of Fixed Capital..........	**99cfc**	219.5	244.0	258.4	272.0	284.5	† 153.5	163.0	172.0	181.8	189.6	199.9	207.8
GDP Volume 1995 Ref., Chained.....	**99b.r**	1,783.8	1,834.3	1,847.4	1,882.3	1,909.4	† 1,005.1	1,041.1	1,059.8	1,063.4	1,063.8	1,075.2	1,074.8
GDP Volume (2000=100)...............	**99bvr**	88.5	91.0	91.6	93.4	94.7	† 96.5	100.0	101.8	102.1	102.2	103.3	103.2
GDP Deflator (2000=100)...............	**99bir**	83.3	87.4	92.0	94.3	96.7	† 98.0	100.0	103.0	106.5	109.7	112.9	115.3
							Millions: Midyear Estimates						
Population..............................	**99z**	57.18	57.30	57.40	57.49	57.56	57.64	57.71	57.80	57.88	57.96	58.03	58.09

Jamaica 343

		1994	1995	1996	1997	1998	1999	2000	2001	2002	2003	2004	2005
Exchange Rates						*Jamaica Dollars per SDR: End of Period*							
Market Rate...........aa=........	wa	48.469	58.889	50.135	49.033	52.174	56.672	59.172	59.426	69.012	89.927	95.432	92.017
						Jamaica Dollars per US Dollar: End of Period (we) Period Average (wf)							
Market Rate...........ae=........	we	33.202	39.616	34.865	36.341	37.055	41.291	45.415	47.286	50.762	60.517	61.450	64.381
Market Rate...........rf=........	wf	33.086	35.142	37.120	35.404	36.550	39.044	42.986	45.996	48.416	57.741	61.197	62.281
Fund Position						*Millions of SDRs: End of Period*							
Quota............................	2f.s	200.9	200.9	200.9	200.9	200.9	273.5	273.5	273.5	273.5	273.5	273.5	273.5
SDRs............................	1b.s	—	.3	—	.2	.5	.5	.1	1.2	.7	—	.1	—
Reserve Position in the Fund...........	1c.s												
Total Fund Cred.&Loans Outstg.......	2tl	217.6	161.7	112.2	87.1	74.7	60.8	46.3	31.9	17.4	6.0	.6	—
International Liquidity					*Millions of US Dollars Unless Otherwise Indicated: End of Period*								
Total Reserves minus Gold..............	1l.d	735.9	681.3	880.0	682.1	709.5	554.5	1,053.7	1,900.5	1,645.1	1,194.9	1,846.5	2,169.8
SDRs............................	1b.d	—	.5	.1	.2	.7	.7	.1	1.5	.9	.1	.1	—
Reserve Position in the Fund.........	1c.d												
Foreign Exchange................	1d.d	735.9	680.8	879.9	681.9	708.8	553.8	1,053.6	1,899.0	1,644.2	1,194.8	1,846.4	2,169.8
Other Official Insts.: Assets.........	3b.d	8.3	7.7	8.0	1.0	1.0	3.2	3.1	6.6	2.9	4.3	5.2	6.9
Monetary Authorities: Other Liab.....	4..d	58.2	....	....	....	....	....	....	....	....	....	6.0	5.4
Deposit Money Banks: Assets........	7a.d	449.5	489.0	464.6	542.0	457.9	571.8	593.8	811.8	898.8	941.6	1,160.2	1,120.6
Liabilities.......	7b.d	393.2	336.2	370.2	371.6	328.0	267.2	219.7	368.7	360.2	432.9	591.8	722.8
Other Banking Insts.: Assets..............	7e.d	34.1	7.0	9.1	16.7	23.8	33.7	37.8	133.7	348.8	378.5	523.6	371.7
Liabilities..............	7f.d	53.8	47.0	43.5	11.7	6.4	5.4	12.9	53.5	215.9	270.9	390.5	41.3
Monetary Authorities						*Millions of Jamaica Dollars: End of Period*							
Foreign Assets.....................	11	24,486	27,084	30,663	24,739	26,280	22,850	47,664	89,818	83,151	72,171	113,769	139,725
Claims on Central Government........	12a	7,466	15,702	20,751	39,777	51,219	57,268	54,930	56,038	57,270	78,188	85,171	81,396
Claims on Deposit Money Banks.......	12e	—	—	—	—	—	—	—	—	—	—	—	—
Reserve Money.....................	14	24,969	32,381	33,668	38,770	47,324	45,343	48,887	45,735	44,292	55,127	61,625	61,909
of which: Currency Outside DMBs..	14a	7,118	9,516	10,760	12,449	13,504	17,821	17,607	18,783	20,399	23,186	26,683	29,668
Foreign Liabilities.................	16c	12,480	8,077	2,136	1,588	1,345	906	685	448	441	469	424	347
Central Government Deposits..........	16d	26,512	28,948	37,755	41,571	45,837	48,058	64,072	110,622	98,225	86,452	136,390	161,258
Capital Accounts....................	17a	1,972	2,396	2,060	2,015	2,143	2,326	2,427	2,437	2,827	3,656	3,900	3,761
Other Items (Net)....................	17r	−33,981	−29,015	−24,205	−19,427	−19,150	−16,515	−13,477	−13,386	−5,363	4,654	−3,399	−6,155
Deposit Money Banks						*Millions of Jamaica Dollars: End of Period*							
Reserves...........................	20	18,794	25,623	23,568	29,167	30,812	26,972	32,236	40,378	44,099	46,530	37,668	33,267
Foreign Assets.....................	21	14,924	19,373	16,197	19,697	16,966	23,608	26,967	38,388	45,624	56,983	71,293	72,143
Claims on Central Government........	22a	16,967	13,716	22,281	23,898	23,280	30,373	34,886	93,576	80,134	87,205	94,649	97,956
Claims on Local Government..........	22b	6	6	2	3	1	—	—	—	—	3	4	4
Claims on Nonfin.Pub.Enterprises.....	22c	1,016	2,081	1,902	3,326	3,462	3,236	4,269	6,094	15,869	17,967	19,761	24,567
Claims on Private Sector.............	22d	32,164	44,408	52,006	57,482	74,777	84,593	102,602	42,312	56,047	76,845	91,428	107,523
Claims on Other Banking Insts........	22f	686	803	380	512	342	579	1,059	42	284	132	72	961
Demand Deposits....................	24	14,134	19,804	22,788	22,022	23,160	27,211	30,289	35,359	39,020	39,871	48,010	54,396
Time and Savings Deposits..............	25	44,300	57,075	62,243	74,017	80,138	86,054	100,215	106,772	120,730	136,079	152,372	163,932
Foreign Liabilities.................	26c	13,055	13,319	12,905	13,504	12,153	11,031	9,978	17,436	18,284	26,201	36,365	46,534
Central Government Deposits..........	26d	6,529	6,945	6,690	8,086	5,736	8,075	15,816	11,261	12,286	10,863	14,306	9,428
Credit from Monetary Authorities.....	26g	283	3,721	8,120	5,239	101	1,527	3,044	83	135	168	230	234
Capital Accounts....................	27a	7,580	8,911	12,042	12,070	24,868	28,002	25,499	26,772	27,890	31,557	39,011	41,509
Other Items (Net).....................	27r	−1,322	−3,766	−8,454	−852	3,483	7,452	17,177	23,107	23,713	40,927	24,580	20,387
Monetary Survey						*Millions of Jamaica Dollars: End of Period*							
Foreign Assets (Net).....................	31n	13,876	25,061	31,818	29,345	29,748	34,521	63,967	110,322	110,051	102,484	148,273	164,987
Domestic Credit......................	32	25,492	41,074	53,129	75,593	101,760	120,167	118,003	76,315	99,211	163,137	140,472	141,800
Claims on Central Govt. (Net)........	32an	−8,608	−6,475	−1,413	14,019	22,926	31,508	9,928	27,732	26,893	68,078	29,124	8,666
Claims on Local Government..........	32b	6	6	2	3	1	—	—	—	—	3	4	4
Claims on Nonfin.Pub.Enterprises...	32c	1,016	2,081	1,902	3,326	3,462	3,236	4,269	6,094	15,869	17,967	19,761	24,567
Claims on Private Sector.............	32d	32,391	44,660	52,258	57,734	75,029	84,845	102,747	42,447	56,171	76,957	91,511	107,602
Claims on Other Banking Insts.......	32f	686	803	380	512	342	579	1,059	42	284	132	72	961
Money.............................	34	21,252	29,320	33,548	34,470	36,664	45,042	47,897	54,142	59,419	63,057	74,693	84,065
Quasi-Money.......................	35	44,300	57,075	62,243	74,017	80,138	86,054	100,215	106,772	120,730	136,079	152,372	163,932
Capital Accounts....................	37a	9,553	11,307	14,102	14,086	27,011	30,328	27,927	29,210	30,716	35,214	42,911	45,270
Other Items (Net)....................	37r	−35,736	−31,567	−24,946	−17,635	−12,305	−6,735	5,932	−3,487	−1,597	31,271	18,768	13,520
Money plus Quasi-Money..............	35l	65,552	86,396	95,791	108,487	116,803	131,095	148,112	160,914	180,149	199,136	227,065	247,996
Other Banking Institutions						*Millions of Jamaica Dollars: End of Period*							
Reserves...........................	40	1,276	1,287	1,390	1,233	1,279	765	454	828	744	495	820	704
Foreign Assets.....................	41	1,133	277	318	608	882	1,393	1,718	6,322	17,706	22,904	32,174	23,928
Claims on Central Government........	42a	1,681	2,818	4,404	4,281	1,894	1,500	2,004	4,167	2,612	9,333	6,858	7,733
Claims on Private Sector.............	42d	7,627	9,890	10,662	7,069	5,781	4,354	2,855	3,372	3,572	5,954	6,860	8,677
Claims on Deposit Money Banks......	42e	1,148	932	865	1,442	379	299	143	251	370	85	172	205
Demand Deposits....................	44	—	—	—	—	—	—	—	—	—	—	—	—
Time and Savings Deposits..............	45	6,998	7,077	6,996	6,862	5,759	4,938	3,966	7,290	8,368	9,330	11,436	12,140
Foreign Liabilities.................	46c	1,786	1,863	1,516	425	237	224	586	2,531	10,959	16,395	23,998	2,656
Credit from Deposit Money Banks....	46h	1,312	1,096	5,463	4,098	1,120	—	170	160	196	50	24	2
Capital Accounts....................	47a	2,521	2,924	3,013	1,688	2,946	2,820	4,117	4,760	4,943	6,141	7,126
Other Items (Net)....................	47r	249	2,244	649	1,559	153	−1,111	−367	844	720	8,052	5,284	19,324
Banking Survey						*Millions of Jamaica Dollars: End of Period*							
Foreign Assets (Net).....................	51n	13,223	23,476	30,620	29,527	30,393	35,690	65,100	114,113	116,798	108,993	156,449	186,259
Domestic Credit......................	52	34,114	52,979	67,815	86,431	109,094	125,442	121,804	83,813	105,117	178,292	154,117	157,249
Claims on Central Govt. (Net)........	52an	−6,927	−3,658	2,991	18,299	24,821	33,008	11,932	31,899	29,505	77,411	35,981	16,399
Claims on Local Government..........	52b	6	6	2	3	1	—	—	—	—	3	4	4
Claims on Nonfin.Pub.Enterprises...	52c	1,016	2,081	1,902	3,326	3,462	3,236	4,269	6,094	15,869	17,967	19,761	24,567
Claims on Private Sector..............	52d	40,018	54,550	62,920	64,803	80,810	89,198	105,603	45,819	59,743	82,912	98,371	116,280
Liquid Liabilities....................	55l	71,273	92,186	101,398	114,116	121,282	135,267	151,624	167,375	187,772	207,972	237,682	259,432
Capital Accounts....................	57a	12,074	14,231	17,116	15,773	29,957	34,587	30,747	33,327	35,476	40,157	49,052	52,397
Other Items (Net).....................	57r	−36,010	−29,961	−20,078	−13,931	−11,753	−8,723	4,533	−2,776	−1,334	39,157	23,833	31,680

Jamaica 343

		1994	1995	1996	1997	1998	1999	2000	2001	2002	2003	2004	2005
Interest Rates							*Percent Per Annum*						
Treasury Bill Rate	60c	42.98	27.65	37.95	21.14	25.65	20.75	18.24	16.71	15.54	25.94	15.47	13.39
Savings Rate	60k	15.00	15.00	15.00	10.96	9.69	8.75	8.50	7.75	7.50	5.21	1.25	1.00
Deposit Rate	60l	36.41	23.21	25.16	13.95	15.61	13.48	11.62	9.64	8.58	8.46	7.98	7.50
Lending Rate	60p	49.46	43.58	39.83	32.86	31.59	27.01	23.35	20.61	18.50	18.89	18.14	17.36
Government Bond Yield	61	26.82	26.85	26.87	26.85	....	....	....	....	....	....	....	....
Prices and Labor							*Index Numbers (2000=100): Period Averages*						
Industrial Share Prices	62	50.2	60.2	48.9	58.6	73.8	69.3	100.0	110.6	134.1	184.7	334.1	374.7
Consumer Prices	64	48.3	57.9	73.2	80.3	87.3	92.4	100.0	107.0	114.6	126.4	143.6	165.6
							Number in Thousands: Period Averages						
Labor Force	67d	1,140	1,150	1,143	1,134	1,129	1,119	1,105	1,105	1,125	1,098	1,196	....
Employment	67e	923	963	960	956	954	937	936	942	1,026	1,057	1,059	....
Unemployment	67c	167	187	183	187	175	175	172	165	172	129	137	....
Unemployment Rate (%)	67r	15.4	16.2	16.0	16.5	15.5	15.7	15.5	15.0	14.3	10.9	11.4	....
Intl. Transactions & Positions							*Millions of Jamaica Dollars*						
Exports	70	40,121	49,916	51,513	48,971	47,940	48,425	55,621	56,061	53,897	67,931	85,017	93,441
Imports, c.i.f.	71	73,631	99,418	109,687	110,932	110,926	113,472	141,987	154,526	171,201	209,852	230,964	277,869
							2000=100						
Volume of Exports	72	96.8	90.9	100.1	101.4	104.7	103.2	100.0	104.1	106.7	108.3	111.1	117.2
Balance of Payments							*Millions of US Dollars: Minus Sign Indicates Debit*						
Current Account, n.i.e.	78ald	81.6	−98.9	−142.6	−332.2	−333.8	−216.3	−367.4	−758.8	−1,074.0	−773.4	−509.2	....
Goods: Exports f.o.b.	78aad	1,548.0	1,796.0	1,721.0	1,700.3	1,613.4	1,499.1	1,562.8	1,454.4	1,309.1	1,385.6	1,601.6	....
Goods: Imports f.o.b.	78abd	−2,099.2	−2,625.3	−2,715.2	−2,832.6	−2,743.9	−2,685.6	−3,004.3	−3,072.6	−3,179.6	−3,328.2	−3,546.1	....
Trade Balance	78acd	−551.2	−829.3	−994.2	−1,132.3	−1,130.5	−1,186.5	−1,441.5	−1,618.2	−1,870.5	−1,942.6	−1,944.5	....
Services: Credit	78add	1,480.2	1,597.9	1,601.9	1,698.9	1,770.4	1,978.4	2,025.7	1,897.0	1,912.3	2,137.7	2,297.1	....
Services: Debit	78aed	−955.3	−1,103.8	−1,149.2	−1,231.7	−1,293.6	−1,323.0	−1,422.5	−1,513.9	−1,597.4	−1,586.1	−1,725.4	....
Balance on Goods & Services	78afd	−26.3	−335.2	−541.5	−665.1	−653.7	−531.1	−838.3	−1,235.1	−1,555.6	−1,391.1	−1,372.8	....
Income: Credit	78agd	104.6	146.6	141.8	147.3	156.3	165.8	193.1	218.2	221.0	217.6	269.6	....
Income: Debit	78ahd	−456.6	−517.3	−366.5	−439.2	−464.4	−498.3	−543.0	−656.0	−826.3	−789.0	−852.1	....
Balance on Gds, Serv. & Inc.	78aid	−378.3	−705.9	−766.2	−957.0	−961.8	−863.6	−1,188.2	−1,672.9	−2,160.9	−1,962.5	−1,955.3	....
Current Transfers, n.i.e.: Credit	78ajd	504.2	669.6	709.3	705.7	727.6	757.9	969.4	1,090.7	1,337.9	1,523.5	1,892.0	....
Current Transfers: Debit	78akd	−44.3	−62.6	−85.7	−80.9	−99.6	−110.6	−148.6	−176.6	−251.0	−334.4	−445.9	....
Capital Account, n.i.e.	78bcd	10.4	10.5	16.6	−11.6	−8.7	−10.9	2.2	−22.3	−16.9	.1	2.2	....
Capital Account, n.i.e.: Credit	78bad	33.2	34.5	42.5	21.7	20.3	19.1	29.6	15.2	18.9	19.3	35.8	....
Capital Account: Debit	78bbd	−22.8	−24.0	−25.9	−33.3	−29.0	−30.0	−27.4	−37.5	−35.8	−19.2	−33.6	....
Financial Account, n.i.e.	78bjd	256.1	108.3	388.6	163.5	337.3	94.8	853.9	1,660.5	909.9	313.3	1,214.7	....
Direct Investment Abroad	78bdd	−52.7	−66.3	−93.3	−56.6	−82.0	−94.9	−74.3	−89.0	−73.9	−116.3	−60.0	....
Dir. Invest. in Rep. Econ., n.i.e.	78bed	129.7	147.4	183.7	203.3	369.1	523.7	468.3	613.9	481.1	720.7	601.6	....
Portfolio Investment Assets	78bfd	—	—	—	—	−3.9	−3.7	−70.0	−39.3	−351.3	−1,105.2	−1,132.8	....
Equity Securities	78bkd	....	....	....	....	—	—	—	—	—	—	—	....
Debt Securities	78bld	—	—	—	—	−3.9	−3.7	−70.0	−39.3	−351.3	−1,105.2	−1,132.8	....
Portfolio Investment Liab., n.i.e.	78bgd	—	—	—	5.7	10.9	8.6	5.9	69.7	155.8	819.6	1,228.8	....
Equity Securities	78bmd	....	....	....	....	—	—	—	—	—	—	—	....
Debt Securities	78bnd	—	—	—	5.7	10.9	8.6	5.9	69.7	155.8	819.6	1,228.8	....
Financial Derivatives Assets	78bwd	....	....	....	....	—	—	—	—	—	—	—	....
Financial Derivatives Liabilities	78bxd	....	....	....	....	—	—	—	—	—	—	—	....
Other Investment Assets	78bhd	−141.3	−148.8	−13.8	−113.2	−59.1	−122.7	−95.5	−215.5	−161.4	−307.6	−127.4	....
Monetary Authorities	78bod	—	—	—	—	—	—	—	—	—	—	—	....
General Government	78bpd	—	—	—	—	—	—	—	—	3.5	1.2	−1.0	....
Banks	78bqd	−177.9	−199.2	−88.1	−186.9	−142.3	−215.1	−181.5	−282.9	−227.0	−362.8	−175.5	....
Other Sectors	78brd	36.6	50.4	74.3	73.7	83.2	92.4	86.0	67.4	62.1	54.0	49.1	....
Other Investment Liab., n.i.e.	78bid	320.4	176.0	312.0	124.3	102.3	−216.2	619.5	1,320.7	859.6	302.1	704.5	....
Monetary Authorities	78bsd	—	—	—	—	—	—	—	—	—	—	—	....
General Government	78btd	−127.4	−97.0	−144.7	43.1	−41.3	−331.4	383.6	653.4	77.1	−363.7	480.1	....
Banks	78bud	142.2	74.7	130.7	156.7	205.5	122.2	167.9	250.5	158.0	395.5	235.4	....
Other Sectors	78bvd	305.6	198.3	326.0	−75.5	−61.9	−7.0	68.0	416.8	624.5	270.3	−11.0	....
Net Errors and Omissions	78cad	9.6	7.1	8.8	9.9	49.1	−4.0	29.7	−14.4	−60.9	28.4	−14.1	....
Overall Balance	78cbd	357.7	27.0	271.4	−170.4	43.9	−136.4	518.4	865.0	−242.0	−431.6	693.6	....
Reserves and Related Items	79dad	−357.7	−27.0	−271.4	170.4	−43.9	136.4	−518.4	−865.0	242.0	431.6	−693.6	....
Reserve Assets	79dbd	−321.0	55.8	−201.7	205.0	−26.9	155.3	−499.4	−846.6	260.8	447.7	−685.6	....
Use of Fund Credit and Loans	79dcd	−38.2	−84.6	−71.9	−34.6	−17.0	−18.9	−19.0	−18.3	−18.9	−16.1	−8.0	....
Exceptional Financing	79ded	1.5	1.9	2.2	—	—	—	—	—	—	—	—	....
National Accounts							*Millions of Jamaica Dollars*						
Househ.Cons.Expend.,incl.NPISHs	96f	111,242	143,438	166,989	180,041	191,055	206,298	233,177	267,025	295,938	342,787	385,783	....
Government Consumption Expend	91f	16,469	22,635	32,476	40,235	47,156	46,926	53,647	57,976	65,792	73,422	78,126	....
Gross Fixed Capital Formation	93e	43,499	57,901	70,022	76,494	72,660	73,531	90,338	108,323	129,497	140,427	....	....
Changes in Inventories	93i	333	688	460	614	393	319	611	408	664	769	....	....
Exports of Goods and Services	90c	83,815	103,214	106,090	103,466	114,038	124,754	146,163	144,614	147,948	191,473	....	....
Imports of Goods and Services (-)	98c	93,908	124,175	133,943	137,264	142,266	149,721	184,815	205,484	229,947	278,656	....	....
Gross Domestic Product (GDP)	99b	161,450	203,701	242,094	263,586	283,036	302,102	339,115	373,285	410,133	472,906	540,086	....
Net Primary Income from Abroad	98.n	−7,952	−8,575	−4,852	−4,655	−9,847	−12,543	−14,058	−20,277	−28,872	−35,881	....	....
Gross National Income (GNI)	99a	153,498	195,126	237,242	258,931	273,189	289,264	325,471	352,816	379,893	434,559	....	....
GDP Volume 1996 Prices	99b.p	219,187	224,565	225,129	222,707	220,172	222,475	224,052	227,461	229,976	235,167	237,375	....
GDP Volume (2000=100)	99bvp	97.8	100.2	100.5	99.4	98.3	99.3	100.0	101.5	102.6	105.0	105.9	....
GDP Deflator (2000=100)	99bip	48.7	59.9	71.0	78.2	84.9	89.7	100.0	108.4	117.8	132.9	150.3	....
							Millions: Midyear Estimates						
Population	99z	2.46	2.48	2.51	2.53	2.55	2.57	2.58	2.60	2.61	2.63	2.64	2.65

		1994	1995	1996	1997	1998	1999	2000	2001	2002	2003	2004	2005
Exchange Rates						*Yen per SDR: End of Period*							
Market Rate	aa	145.61	152.86	166.80	175.34	162.77	140.27	149.70	165.64	163.01	159.15	161.70	168.61
					Yen per US Dollar: End of Period (ae) Period Average (rf)								
Market Rate	ae	99.74	102.83	116.00	129.95	115.60	102.20	114.90	131.80	119.90	107.10	104.12	117.97
Market Rate	rf	102.21	94.06	108.78	120.99	130.91	113.91	107.77	121.53	125.39	115.93	108.19	110.22
					Index Numbers (2000=100): Period Averages								
Market Rate	ahx	105.6	115.2	99.1	89.2	82.7	94.6	100.0	88.7	86.1	93.1	99.6	97.9
Nominal Effective Exchange Rate	neu	94.8	99.4	86.2	81.3	76.5	89.4	100.0	90.5	85.7	85.4	87.1	85.3
Real Effective Exchange Rate	reu	105.2	110.3	93.9	89.4	83.4	94.3	100.0	89.4	80.2	77.1	77.9	74.6
Fund Position						*Millions of SDRs: End of Period*							
Quota	2f.s	8,242	8,242	8,242	8,242	8,242	13,313	13,313	13,313	13,313	13,313	13,313	13,313
SDRs	1b.s	1,427	1,821	1,837	1,955	1,891	1,935	1,870	1,892	1,857	1,861	1,828	1,808
Reserve Position in the Fund	1c.s	5,912	5,449	4,639	6,777	6,813	4,774	4,032	4,019	5,298	5,204	4,371	2,013
of which: Outstg.Fund Borrowing	2c	2,913	1,137	—	—	508	—	—	—	—	—	—	—
International Liquidity					*Millions of US Dollars Unless Otherwise Indicated: End of Period*								
Total Reserves minus Gold	1l.d	125,860	183,250	216,648	219,648	215,471	286,916	354,902	395,155	461,186	663,289	833,891	834,275
SDRs	1b.d	2,083	2,707	2,642	2,638	2,663	2,656	2,437	2,377	2,524	2,766	2,839	2,584
Reserve Position in the Fund	1c.d	8,631	8,100	6,671	9,144	9,593	6,552	5,253	5,051	7,203	7,733	6,789	2,877
Foreign Exchange	1d.d	115,146	172,443	207,335	207,866	203,215	277,708	347,212	387,727	451,458	652,790	824,264	828,813
Gold (Million Fine Troy Ounces)	1ad	24.23	24.23	24.23	24.23	24.23	24.23	24.55	24.60	24.60	24.60	24.60	24.60
Gold (National Valuation)	1and	1,238	1,260	1,219	1,144	1,194	1,164	1,119	1,082	1,171	1,280	1,337	1,231
Deposit Money Banks: Assets	7a.d	991,478	1,069,795	900,940	990,635	943,546	760,709	738,876	708,522	757,364	746,081	826,331	897,941
Liabilities	7b.d	717,676	734,542	690,224	709,950	693,631	533,627	533,424	521,465	561,288	546,627	598,806	549,752
Monetary Authorities						*Trillions of Yen: End of Period*							
Foreign Assets	11	7.25	11.54	17.49	16.86	† 3.86	4.19	4.14	4.03	4.72	4.79	4.89	5.18
Claims on Central Government	12a	21.98	25.08	31.30	32.87	† 67.92	62.98	54.18	79.88	87.49	97.93	99.52	103.42
Claims on Private Sector	12d	—	—	—	—	† —	—	—	—	.15	1.95	2.10	2.07
Claims on Deposit Money Banks	12e	12.92	11.62	9.91	13.80	† 20.81	46.13	51.26	36.38	36.06	30.06	41.61	48.59
Reserve Money	14	49.44	53.32	57.84	62.09	64.36	92.98	74.45	88.91	99.40	111.36	115.63	116.64
of which: Currency Outside DMBs	14a	42.35	46.23	49.08	52.73	54.31	59.40	61.95	66.69	71.33	72.46	73.31	75.32
Foreign Liabilities	16c	—	—	—	—	† .06	.04	.02	.93	1.38	2.01	2.16	3.83
Central Government Deposits	16d	5.03	5.85	7.64	3.79	† 12.32	17.04	27.42	25.42	20.77	16.07	24.54	27.62
Other Items (Net)	17r	−12.31	−10.93	−6.77	−2.35	† 15.85	3.24	7.69	5.03	6.87	5.28	5.79	11.17
Deposit Money Banks						*Trillions of Yen: End of Period*							
Reserves	20	7.09	7.09	8.75	9.36	10.03	30.22	11.33	19.27	26.59	34.29	37.56	33.88
Foreign Assets	21	98.89	110.01	104.51	128.73	109.07	77.74	84.90	93.38	90.81	79.91	86.04	105.93
Claims on Central Government	22a	40.14	38.50	37.04	37.68	52.66	74.32	120.25	115.51	118.59	152.21	159.80	158.10
Claims on Local Government	22b	17.38	19.78	20.72	21.39	23.75	24.79	24.33	25.27	25.67	26.13	27.25	29.09
Claims on Nonfin.Pub.Enterprises	22c	12.55	11.57	10.06	9.01	8.34	8.06	8.99	10.58	11.56	13.81	15.38	16.53
Claims on Private Sector	22d	559.81	569.20	575.88	578.79	601.64	586.93	576.65	561.80	532.54	508.52	495.37	491.28
Demand Deposits	24	109.31	125.31	139.06	151.55	160.09	180.13	185.91	215.11	276.65	291.04	304.67	323.88
Time, Savings,& Fgn.Currency Dep	25	382.44	377.04	373.00	374.11	387.86	383.27	381.76	361.53	317.22	313.36	309.69	302.32
Certificates of Deposit	26aa	7.32	10.22	14.16	19.10	19.23	15.21	20.24	27.95	18.39	17.86	19.89	20.49
Bonds	26ab	63.90	62.22	62.10	53.56	57.13	57.12	50.12	44.94	37.20	30.99	27.59	25.82
Foreign Liabilities	26c	71.58	75.53	80.07	92.26	80.18	54.54	61.29	68.73	67.30	58.54	62.35	64.85
Credit from Monetary Authorities	26g	12.92	11.62	9.91	13.80	† 20.81	46.13	51.26	36.38	36.06	30.06	41.61	48.59
Other Items (Net)	27r	88.38	94.20	78.67	80.58	80.19	65.67	75.85	71.19	52.92	73.01	55.61	48.85
Monetary Survey						*Trillions of Yen: End of Period*							
Foreign Assets (Net)	31n	34.56	46.01	41.94	53.33	† 32.69	27.36	27.73	27.76	26.85	24.14	26.42	42.43
Domestic Credit	32	646.82	658.28	667.36	675.96	† 742.00	740.04	756.98	767.62	755.22	784.48	774.88	772.87
Claims on Central Govt. (Net)	32an	57.09	57.73	60.70	66.76	† 108.27	120.26	147.00	169.97	185.30	234.07	234.78	233.90
Claims on Local Government	32b	17.38	19.78	20.72	21.39	23.75	24.79	24.33	25.27	25.67	26.13	27.25	29.09
Claims on Nonfin.Pub.Enterprises	32c	12.55	11.57	10.06	9.01	8.34	8.06	8.99	10.58	11.56	13.81	15.38	16.53
Claims on Private Sector	32d	559.81	569.20	575.88	578.79	601.64	586.93	576.65	561.80	532.69	510.47	497.47	493.34
Money	34	151.67	171.54	188.15	204.28	214.40	239.54	247.86	281.80	347.98	363.49	377.98	399.20
Quasi-Money	35	382.44	377.04	373.00	374.11	387.86	383.27	381.76	361.53	317.22	313.36	309.69	302.32
Certificates of Deposit	36aa	7.32	10.22	14.16	19.10	19.23	15.21	20.24	27.95	18.39	17.86	19.89	20.49
Bonds	36ab	63.90	62.22	62.10	53.56	57.13	57.12	50.12	44.94	37.20	30.99	27.59	25.82
Other Items (Net)	37r	76.07	83.27	71.91	78.23	† 96.07	72.27	84.72	79.17	61.27	82.92	66.16	67.47
Money plus Quasi-Money	35l	534.10	548.59	561.14	578.39	602.26	622.80	629.62	643.33	665.20	676.85	687.67	701.52
Other Banking Institutions						*Trillions of Yen: End of Period*							
Cash	40	76.56	82.47	87.21	84.43	....	....	....	....	....	....	....	....
Claims on Central Government	42a	126.45	142.11	151.55	170.24	....	....	....	....	....	....	....	....
Claims on Local Government	42b	82.91	89.40	100.50	110.58	....	....	....	....	....	....	....	....
Claims on Nonfin.Pub.Enterprises	42c	47.27	50.76	54.46	57.78	....	....	....	....	....	....	....	....
Claims on Private Sector	42d	324.62	327.79	339.87	332.09	....	....	....	....	....	....	....	....
Demand and Time Deposits	45a	456.40	479.69	502.71	531.44	....	....	....	....	....	....	....	....
Deposits with Trust Fund Bureau	46b	153.18	150.65	155.69	153.94	....	....	....	....	....	....	....	....
Insurance Reserves	47d	79.86	88.88	88.16	95.68	....	....	....	....	....	....	....	....
Other Items (Net)	47r	−31.64	−26.70	−12.97	−25.95	....	....	....	....	....	....	....	....
Nonbank Financial Institutions						*Trillions of Yen: End of Period*							
Cash	40..s	30.88	33.05	27.86	33.77	....	....	....	....	....	....	....	....
Claims on Central Government	42a.s	20.86	29.58	29.72	31.36	....	....	....	....	....	....	....	....
Claims on Local Government	42b.s	4.44	6.78	7.90	8.79	....	....	....	....	....	....	....	....
Claims on Nonfin.Pub.Enterprises	42c.s	4.42	4.44	4.83	5.20	....	....	....	....	....	....	....	....
Claims on Private Sector	42d.s	114.86	112.66	120.58	108.74	....	....	....	....	....	....	....	....
Insurance and Pension Reserves	47d.s	199.49	210.48	226.01	230.02	....	....	....	....	....	....	....	....
Other Items (Net)	47r.s	−24.04	−23.98	−35.12	−42.17	....	....	....	....	....	....	....	....

Japan 158

		1994	1995	1996	1997	1998	1999	2000	2001	2002	2003	2004	2005
Financial Survey		*Trillions of Yen: End of Period*											
Foreign Assets (Net)........................	51n	34.56	46.01	41.94	† 90.22	109.48	103.15	110.55	123.25	116.68	....	....	....
Domestic Credit................................	52	1,372.64	1,421.79	1,476.78	† 1,524.71	1,551.73	1,632.01	1,622.45	1,604.30	1,564.85	....	....	....
Claims on Central Govt. (Net).......	52an	204.40	229.42	241.97	† 287.42	317.87	363.67	392.86	408.45	433.89	....		
Claims on Local Government..........	52b	104.72	115.95	129.13	† 127.42	135.38	144.48	150.40	154.06	159.81	....		
Claims on Nonfin.Pub.Enterprises...	52c	64.24	66.77	69.35	† 111.30	92.31	92.85	93.94	95.44	93.13	....		
Claims on Private Sector...............	52d	999.29	1,009.65	1,036.33	† 998.58	1,006.17	1,031.01	985.26	946.35	878.01	....		
Liquid Liabilities.............................	55l	945.09	976.19	1,019.37	† 920.87	955.29	983.02	989.24	1,002.50	1,009.00	....		
Bonds..	56ab	63.90	62.22	62.10	† 121.12	116.88	121.41	117.09	111.78	85.94	....		
Deposits with Fiscal Loan Fund.......	56b	153.18	150.65	155.69	† 147.35	152.85	156.60	159.19	147.35	129.52	....		
Insurance and Pension Reserves......	57d	279.35	299.37	314.17	† 360.26	373.34	384.24	396.87	400.74	401.63	....		
Other Items (Net)...........................	57r	−34.32	−20.63	−32.62	† 65.34	62.85	89.88	70.61	65.18	55.45	....	....	....
Money (National Definitions)		*Trillions of Yen: End of Period*											
M1..	59ma	151.67	171.54	188.15	204.28	† 214.40	239.54	247.86	281.80	347.98	363.49	377.98	399.20
M1, Seasonally Adjusted.................	59mac	141.13	157.38	177.39	192.93	† 203.87	229.51	234.52	274.71	342.02	357.51	372.21	390.83
M2 + CDs......................................	59mba	541.42	558.80	575.30	597.49	† 621.49	638.01	649.86	671.28	683.59	694.71	707.55	722.01
M2 + CDs, Seasonally Adjusted.......	59mbf	530.81	544.18	565.15	586.19	† 610.27	627.09	635.11	662.94	677.24	688.65	701.71	714.59
M3 + CDs......................................	59mca	936.28	969.73	1,000.09	1,032.36	† 1,085.25	1,115.15	1,126.44	1,135.28	1,141.14	1,128.42	1,145.86	1,154.73
Interest Rates		*Percent Per Annum*											
Discount Rate (End of Period)..........	60	1.750	.500	.500	.500	.500	.500	.500	.100	.100	.100	.100	.100
Money Market Rate........................	60b	2.196	1.213	.470	.484	.371	.059	.108	.058	.011	.001	.001	.001
Private Bill Rate.............................	60bs	2.242	1.218	.594	.620	.717	.155	.227	....	....	....	....	....
Deposit Rate...................................	60l	1.698	.902	.301	.301	.266	.117	.070	.057	.036	.043	.080	.271
Lending Rate..................................	60p	4.133	3.506	2.658	2.449	2.321	2.161	2.067	1.969	1.865	1.822	1.767	1.677
Government Bond Yield..................	61	3.714	2.532	2.225	1.688	1.097	† 1.771	1.748	1.330	1.252	1.013	1.501	1.361
Prices, Production, Labor		*Index Numbers (2000=100): Period Averages*											
Share Prices...................................	62	103.4	89.3	103.8	90.2	76.2	89.6	100.0	77.3	63.3	59.4	72.3	82.1
Wholesale Prices............................	63	104.9	104.1	102.4	103.0	101.5	100.0	100.0	97.7	95.7	95.0	96.1	97.7
Consumer Prices............................	64	98.6	98.5	98.6	100.4	101.0	100.7	100.0	99.3	98.4	98.1	98.1	97.8
Wages: Monthly Earnings...............	65	94.5	96.5	98.3	99.7	99.5	99.7	100.0	99.4	97.2	96.8	96.4	96.7
Industrial Production......................	66	92.0	95.5	97.7	101.2	94.5	94.8	100.0	93.7	92.6	95.4	100.5	101.7
Mfg. Employment, Seas. Adj............	67eyc	113.6	111.5	109.0	107.8	105.9	102.8	100.0	97.0	92.2	89.4	88.4	88.5
		Number in Thousands: Period Averages											
Labor Force....................................	67d	66,450	66,660	67,110	67,870	67,930	67,790	67,660	67,520	66,890	66,660	66,420	....
Employment...................................	67e	64,530	64,570	64,860	65,570	65,140	64,623	64,464	64,121	63,303	63,189	63,286	63,502
Unemployment...............................	67c	1,920	2,098	2,250	2,303	2,787	3,171	3,198	3,395	3,588	3,504	3,134	2,940
Unemployment Rate (%).................	67r	2.9	3.2	3.4	3.4	4.1	4.7	4.7	5.0	5.4	5.3	4.7	4.4
Intl. Transactions & Positions		*Billions of Yen*											
Exports...	70	40,470	41,532	44,729	50,938	50,644	47,549	51,649	49,010	52,109	54,549	61,170	65,662
Imports, c.i.f...................................	71	28,051	31,534	37,992	40,956	36,653	35,270	40,915	42,402	42,177	44,319	49,147	56,852
		2000=100											
Volume of Exports..........................	72	78.0	† 80.5	81.1	90.7	89.5	91.5	100.0	89.9	† 97.4	102.2	113.0	113.8
Volume of Imports..........................	73	72.4	† 81.4	85.4	86.9	82.3	90.2	100.0	98.7	† 100.2	107.4	114.9	117.9
Unit Value of Exports......................	74	100.6	† 100.0	106.8	108.8	109.6	100.9	100.0	105.6	† 103.7	103.5	104.8	111.6
Unit Value of Imports......................	75	95.0	† 94.8	108.7	115.3	109.0	95.7	† 100.0	98.2	100.0	98.2	101.7	114.3
Export Prices..................................	76	110.3	† 107.9	113.0	115.1	116.6	104.9	100.0	103.0	101.9	97.8	96.4	98.3
Import Prices..................................	76.x	94.0	† 93.9	103.0	110.7	105.3	95.5	100.0	102.5	101.0	100.1	104.3	118.0

Japan 158

2006, International Monetary Fund : *International Financial Statistics Yearbook*

		1994	1995	1996	1997	1998	1999	2000	2001	2002	2003	2004	2005
Balance of Payments						*Billions of US Dollars: Minus Sign Indicates Debit*							
Current Account, n.i.e.	78ald	130.26	111.04	65.79	96.81	118.75	114.60	119.66	87.80	112.45	136.22	172.06	165.78
Goods: Exports f.o.b.	78aad	385.70	428.72	400.29	409.24	374.04	403.69	459.51	383.59	395.58	449.12	539.00	567.57
Goods: Imports f.o.b.	78abd	−241.51	−296.93	−316.70	−307.64	−251.66	−280.37	−342.80	−313.38	−301.75	−342.72	−406.87	−473.61
Trade Balance	78acd	144.19	131.79	83.58	101.60	122.39	123.32	116.72	70.21	93.83	106.40	132.13	93.96
Services: Credit	78add	58.30	65.27	67.71	69.30	62.41	61.00	69.24	64.52	65.71	77.62	97.61	110.21
Services: Debit	78aed	−106.36	−122.63	−129.99	−123.45	−111.83	−115.16	−116.86	−108.25	−107.94	−111.53	−135.51	−134.26
Balance on Goods & Services	78afd	96.13	74.43	21.31	47.45	72.97	69.16	69.09	26.48	51.60	72.49	94.23	69.91
Income: Credit	78agd	155.19	192.45	112.44	111.83	100.33	92.05	97.20	103.09	91.48	95.21	113.33	141.06
Income: Debit	78ahd	−114.96	−148.16	−58.95	−53.63	−45.71	−34.47	−36.80	−33.87	−25.71	−23.97	−27.63	−37.62
Balance on Gds, Serv. & Inc.	78aid	136.36	118.72	74.80	105.65	127.59	126.74	129.49	95.70	117.37	143.73	179.93	173.36
Current Transfers, n.i.e.: Credit	78ajd	1.83	1.98	6.02	6.01	5.53	6.21	7.38	6.15	10.04	6.51	6.91	9.74
Current Transfers: Debit	78akd	−7.94	−9.66	−15.03	−14.84	−14.37	−18.35	−17.21	−14.06	−14.96	−14.02	−14.78	−17.31
Capital Account, n.i.e.	78bcd	−1.85	−2.23	−3.29	−4.05	−14.45	−16.47	−9.26	−2.87	−3.32	−4.00	−4.79	−4.88
Capital Account, n.i.e.: Credit	78bad	—	.01	1.22	1.52	1.57	.75	.78	.99	.91	.39	.44	.83
Capital Account: Debit	78bbd	−1.85	−2.24	−4.51	−5.57	−16.02	−17.21	−10.04	−3.86	−4.24	−4.39	−5.23	−5.71
Financial Account, n.i.e.	78bjd	−85.11	−63.98	−28.02	−120.51	−114.82	−38.85	−78.31	−48.16	−63.38	71.92	22.50	−122.68
Direct Investment Abroad	78bdd	−18.09	−22.51	−23.45	−26.06	−24.62	−22.27	−31.53	−38.50	−32.02	−28.77	−30.96	−45.44
Dir. Invest. in Rep. Econ., n.i.e.	78bed	.91	.04	.21	3.20	3.27	12.31	8.23	6.19	9.09	6.24	7.80	3.21
Portfolio Investment Assets	78bfd	−91.97	−86.05	−100.61	−47.06	−95.24	−154.41	−83.36	−106.79	−85.93	−176.29	−173.77	−196.40
Equity Securities	78bkd	−14.00	.07	−8.17	−13.73	−14.00	−32.40	−19.72	−11.28	−37.28	−4.47	−31.47	−22.97
Debt Securities	78bld	−77.97	−86.11	−92.43	−33.34	−81.24	−122.01	−63.64	−95.51	−48.65	−171.82	−142.30	−173.43
Portfolio Investment Liab., n.i.e.	78bgd	64.53	59.79	66.79	79.19	56.06	126.93	47.39	60.50	−20.04	81.18	196.72	183.13
Equity Securities	78bmd	48.95	50.60	49.45	27.00	16.11	103.89	−1.29	39.10	−16.69	87.78	98.28	131.32
Debt Securities	78bnd	15.58	9.19	17.34	52.19	39.95	23.04	48.67	21.40	−3.35	−6.59	98.44	51.81
Financial Derivatives Assets	78bwd	.43	−1.20	98.70	86.17	90.75	83.80	106.74	102.79	77.25	64.96	56.44	230.59
Financial Derivatives Liabilities	78bxd	−.20	−9.12	−105.95	−92.02	−89.65	−86.43	−111.41	−101.40	−74.77	−59.38	−54.04	−237.12
Other Investment Assets	78bhd	−35.12	−102.24	5.21	−191.96	37.94	266.34	−4.15	46.59	36.41	149.89	−48.01	−106.60
Monetary Authorities	78bod	....	....	....	....	....	....	....	....	....	....	....	....
General Government	78bpd	−8.76	−8.66	−5.28	−9.12	−15.50	−11.56	−1.89	−3.95	.92	4.49	3.87	14.29
Banks	78bqd	−10.67	−85.62	75.57	−140.18	54.14	239.40	36.51	15.59	1.59	140.78	3.24	−29.80
Other Sectors	78brd	−15.69	−7.96	−65.08	−42.66	−.70	38.50	−38.77	34.95	33.90	4.62	−55.12	−91.08
Other Investment Liab., n.i.e.	78bid	−5.60	97.30	31.08	68.03	−93.33	−265.12	−10.21	−17.55	26.63	34.10	68.31	45.94
Monetary Authorities	78bsd	—	—	—	—	—	—	—	—	.06	5.14	.99	12.24
General Government	78btd	−2.00	1.18	−2.12	−.11	−1.30	.55	−.93	7.01	.06	5.14	.99	12.24
Banks	78bud	4.87	17.27	−9.06	43.34	−23.75	−189.16	28.22	4.99	22.46	−26.22	42.73	−9.38
Other Sectors	78bvd	−8.47	78.86	42.27	24.80	−68.28	−76.50	−37.49	−29.54	4.11	55.17	24.59	43.07
Net Errors and Omissions	78cad	−18.03	13.78	.65	34.31	4.36	16.97	16.87	3.72	.39	−16.99	−28.92	−15.90
Overall Balance	78cbd	25.27	58.61	35.14	6.57	−6.16	76.26	48.95	40.49	46.13	187.15	160.85	22.33
Reserves and Related Items	79dad	−25.27	−58.61	−35.14	−6.57	6.16	−76.26	−48.95	−40.49	−46.13	−187.15	−160.85	−22.33
Reserve Assets	79dbd	−25.27	−58.61	−35.14	−6.57	6.16	−76.26	−48.95	−40.49	−46.13	−187.15	−160.85	−22.33
Use of Fund Credit and Loans	79dcd	—	—	—	—	—	—	—	—	—	—	—	—
Exceptional Financing	79ded	....	....	....	....	....	....	....	....	....	....	....	....
International Investment Position							*Billions of US Dollars*						
Assets	79aad	2,424.24	2,632.86	2,652.61	2,737.45	2,986.33	3,013.60	2,969.59	2,881.51	3,052.08	3,599.80	4,166.99	4,290.87
Direct Investment Abroad	79abd	275.57	238.45	258.61	271.90	270.04	248.78	278.44	300.11	304.23	335.50	370.54	386.59
Portfolio Investment	79acd	858.69	855.07	933.20	902.26	1,056.49	1,242.37	1,306.48	1,289.75	1,394.52	1,721.32	2,009.67	2,114.89
Equity Securities	79add	....	146.26	154.90	158.77	209.38	285.34	262.25	227.35	210.82	274.46	364.69	408.57
Debt Securities	79aed	....	708.81	778.30	743.49	847.11	957.04	1,044.23	1,062.40	1,183.70	1,446.86	1,644.98	1,706.31
Financial Derivatives	79ald	....	3.21	3.97	4.41	5.09	4.46	3.31	3.00	3.37	4.90	5.75	26.31
Other Investment	79afd	1,162.87	1,351.31	1,239.23	1,338.08	1,438.88	1,230.34	1,020.36	888.23	882.34	865.03	938.51	920.10
Monetary Authorities	79agd												
General Government	79ahd	165.01	184.05	170.47	162.32	196.16	230.91	210.17	191.93	206.97	228.79	233.11	198.81
Banks	79aid	752.12	911.23	773.14	861.44	876.07	630.02	529.23	467.46	486.66	447.35	462.07	463.01
Other Sectors	79ajd	245.74	256.02	295.63	314.32	366.65	369.41	280.96	228.84	188.71	188.88	243.33	258.28
Reserve Assets	79akd	127.10	184.82	217.61	220.81	215.83	287.66	360.99	400.41	467.62	673.06	842.52	842.98
Liabilities	79lad	1,733.92	1,815.26	1,761.59	1,778.72	1,832.69	2,184.48	1,811.65	1,521.42	1,589.92	1,986.18	2,382.51	2,759.11
Dir. Invest. in Rep. Economy	79lbd	19.17	33.51	29.94	27.08	26.07	46.12	50.32	50.32	78.14	89.73	96.99	100.90
Portfolio Investment	79lcd	630.67	545.42	556.25	582.48	632.76	1,165.44	884.32	665.79	610.42	867.17	1,153.39	1,542.42
Equity Securities	79ldd	250.88	306.28	315.65	279.53	304.33	833.43	550.23	376.05	339.93	561.02	743.30	1,126.07
Debt Securities	79led	379.79	239.14	240.60	302.95	328.43	332.01	334.09	289.75	270.49	306.14	410.09	416.35
Financial Derivatives	79lld	—	2.85	2.72	4.10	4.54	3.10	3.19	3.54	3.71	6.79	10.77	33.23
Other Investment	79lfd	1,084.08	1,233.48	1,172.69	1,165.06	1,169.32	969.83	873.82	801.77	897.65	1,022.50	1,121.36	1,082.55
Monetary Authorities	79lgd	99.85	—	—	—	—	—	—	—	—	—	—	—
General Government	79lhd	—	14.96	11.35	10.12	9.65	11.62	9.68	8.15	5.26	5.14	19.96	35.30
Banks	79lid	694.94	745.42	701.56	714.28	751.47	570.71	603.99	568.40	631.12	660.40	709.31	702.88
Other Sectors	79ljd	289.29	473.10	459.78	440.66	408.20	387.50	260.15	225.21	261.27	356.96	392.08	344.37

National Accounts		1994	1995	1996	1997	1998	1999	2000	2001	2002	2003	2004	2005
							Billions of Yen						
Househ.Cons.Expend.,incl.NPISHs....	96f.c	267,142	271,396	277,718	283,437	281,498	282,764	282,596	283,324	282,387	281,372	284,922	288,628
Government Consumption Expend...	91f.c	71,559	74,653	77,331	78,956	80,303	82,188	84,866	87,010	88,196	88,374	89,075	90,250
Gross Fixed Capital Formation..........	93e.c	138,670	138,090	142,813	141,459	130,184	126,415	126,511	122,649	114,047	112,489	113,377	116,700
Changes in Inventories...................	93i.c	−710	2,233	3,499	3,137	28	−1,717	−365	−22	−1,139	−258	484	....
Exports of Goods and Services.........	90c.c	44,270	45,230	49,561	56,074	55,051	51,144	55,256	52,567	55,829	58,882	66,286	71,913
Imports of Goods and Services (-).....	98c.c	34,387	38,272	47,022	50,316	45,607	43,251	47,940	49,393	49,417	50,907	56,660	64,957
Gross Domestic Product (GDP)........	99b.c	486,526	493,272	502,609	512,249	502,973	495,227	501,068	496,777	489,618	490,544	496,058	502,457
Net Primary Income from Abroad.....	98.nc	3,812	3,836	5,471	6,758	6,940	6,384	6,421	8,321	8,193	8,524	9,620	11,849
Gross National Income (GNI)............	99a.c	490,339	497,108	508,079	519,007	509,912	501,611	507,489	505,098	497,812	499,068	505,678	514,305
Net Current Transf.from Abroad.......	98t.c	−13,570	−14,672	−10,509	−15,397	−19,818	−19,913	−18,762	—	—	—	—	....
Gross Nat'l Disposable Inc.(GNDI)....	99i.c	482,076	486,901	505,762	513,220	502,955	499,001	499,494	....	....	....	....	....
Gross Saving...................................	99s.c	150,179	148,959	157,999	157,300	147,390	139,993	140,110	....	....	....	....	....
Consumption of Fixed Capital..........	99cf	86,732	89,117	92,215	94,237	96,271	95,429	97,995	99,380	98,554	101,301	....	....
GDP Volume 1995 Prices................	99b.r	476,294	483,008	493,348	498,775	489,141	487,974	501,575	503,523	504,244	514,956	528,936	545,501
GDP Volume (2000=100)................	99bvr	95.0	96.3	98.4	99.4	97.5	97.3	100.0	100.4	100.5	102.7	105.5	108.8
GDP Deflator (2000=100)................	99bir	102.3	102.2	102.0	102.8	102.9	101.6	100.0	98.8	97.2	95.4	93.9	92.2
							Millions: Midyear Estimates						
Population..............................	99z	125.12	125.47	125.81	126.14	126.46	126.76	127.03	127.29	127.52	127.74	127.92	128.08

Jordan 439

		1994	1995	1996	1997	1998	1999	2000	2001	2002	2003	2004	2005
Exchange Rates						*SDRs per Dinar: End of Period*							
Official Rate	ac	.9772	.9488	.9809	1.0454	1.0017	1.0276	1.0825	1.1223	1.0375	.9492	.9082	.9868
						US Dollars per Dinar: End of Period (ag) Period Average (rh)							
Official Rate	ag	1.4265	1.4104	1.4104	1.4104	1.4104	1.4104	1.4104	1.4104	1.4104	1.4104	1.4104	1.4104
Official Rate	rh	1.4312	1.4276	1.4104	1.4104	1.4104	1.4104	1.4104	1.4105	1.4104	1.4104	1.4104	1.4104
Fund Position						*Millions of SDRs: End of Period*							
Quota	2f.s	121.7	121.7	121.7	121.7	121.7	170.5	170.5	170.5	170.5	170.5	170.5	170.5
SDRs	1b.s	.5	.8	.6	.1	.6	.2	.5	.9	.6	.7	1.1	.4
Reserve Position in the Fund	1c.s	—	—	—	—	—	—	.1	.1	.1	.1	.1	.1
Total Fund Cred.&Loans Outstg	2tl	98.9	169.2	236.1	316.6	333.4	362.9	354.3	344.5	355.0	283.6	217.5	165.3
International Liquidity						*Millions of US Dollars Unless Otherwise Indicated: End of Period*							
Total Reserves minus Gold	1l.d	1,692.6	1,972.9	1,759.3	2,200.3	1,750.4	2,629.1	3,331.3	3,062.2	3,975.9	5,194.3	5,266.6	5,250.3
SDRs	1b.d	.7	1.2	.8	.2	.8	.3	.6	1.2	.9	1.1	1.7	.6
Reserve Position in the Fund	1c.d	—	—	—	—	—	—	.1	.1	.1	.1	.1	.2
Foreign Exchange	1d.d	1,691.9	1,971.7	1,758.5	2,200.1	1,749.6	2,628.8	3,330.6	3,061.0	3,975.0	5,193.1	5,264.8	5,249.5
Gold (Million Fine Troy Ounces)	1ad	.794	.793	.800	.812	.827	.486	.401	.405	.410	.411	.411	.411
Gold (National Valuation)	1and	198.5	195.9	197.7	200.7	204.3	120.0	99.1	112.2	141.2	171.3	179.6	212.3
Monetary Authorities: Other Liab	4..d	117.5	82.3	71.3	43.8	32.8	230.6	177.6	181.3	180.3	176.1	158.3	158.3
Deposit Money Banks: Assets	7a.d	2,399.3	2,655.3	2,845.0	3,077.5	3,607.1	4,101.5	5,235.3	6,104.4	6,336.8	6,180.4	7,055.0	7,562.5
Liabilities	7b.d	2,518.5	2,926.5	3,100.7	3,084.7	3,079.7	3,285.2	3,819.0	4,213.5	4,718.1	4,379.0	4,892.5	5,233.7
Other Banking Insts.: Liabilities	7f.d	120.6	130.3	117.0	126.0	124.7	120.9	114.9	....	....	....	....	....
Monetary Authorities						*Millions of Dinars: End of Period*							
Foreign Assets	11	1,904.3	2,185.2	2,253.9	2,557.1	2,297.7	2,889.6	3,267.4	3,064.2	3,694.0	4,571.1	4,628.2	4,639.9
Claims on Central Government	12a	905.3	867.1	930.9	989.4	1,033.4	1,015.8	1,125.7	1,097.0	1,007.1	938.8	891.0	1,065.0
Claims on Nonfin.Pub.Enterprises	12c	.1	.1	.7	.3	4.5	.1	—	—	—	—	—	—
Claims on Private Sector	12d	6.5	7.6	8.0	8.7	9.4	11.9	13.2	13.7	14.5	15.1	18.3	18.2
Claims on Deposit Money Banks	12e	367.6	369.0	399.0	361.1	347.8	326.1	317.9	332.5	317.7	351.7	370.8	492.2
Reserve Money	14	2,349.5	2,498.9	2,164.4	2,104.0	2,005.0	2,246.9	2,264.8	2,135.7	2,218.9	2,593.6	2,676.6	3,170.2
of which: Currency Outside DMBs	14a	1,072.6	1,050.9	952.1	987.6	952.8	1,106.6	1,239.9	1,202.4	1,252.7	1,443.7	1,414.4	1,657.3
Time,Savings,& Fgn.Currency Dep	15	6.2	10.5	3.5	13.3	84.4	294.3	82.4	240.7	222.3	329.8	148.2	366.1
Liabs. of Central Bank: Securities	16ac	280.1	320.0	617.5	1,055.6	971.5	970.0	1,422.0	1,233.5	1,643.5	2,176.0	2,534.0	2,279.5
Foreign Liabilities	16c	183.6	236.7	291.3	333.9	356.1	516.6	453.2	435.5	470.0	423.6	351.7	279.8
Central Government Deposits	16d	225.1	163.5	323.7	321.0	137.7	145.9	420.7	401.6	401.9	190.8	218.2	132.9
Capital Accounts	17a	45.6	49.3	53.0	52.8	53.5	53.0	66.3	92.3	102.3	160.8	179.4	60.2
Other Items (Net)	17r	93.8	150.1	139.2	36.0	84.7	16.6	−12.5	−32.0	−25.6	2.0	−199.8	−73.4
Deposit Money Banks						*Millions of Dinars: End of Period*							
Reserves	20	1,576.9	1,799.6	1,854.9	2,163.8	2,015.9	2,389.2	2,518.2	2,383.3	2,826.5	3,586.8	3,784.1	4,186.6
Foreign Assets	21	1,681.9	1,882.6	2,017.1	2,182.0	2,557.5	2,907.9	3,711.8	4,328.0	4,492.8	4,381.9	5,002.0	5,361.8
Claims on Central Government	22a	307.0	240.0	238.1	163.0	412.5	618.5	733.1	902.5	1,087.9	887.8	1,101.8	1,337.4
Claims on Nonfin.Pub.Enterprises	22c	341.8	362.1	408.2	425.0	376.7	307.8	316.9	284.3	261.3	278.0	472.6	528.1
Claims on Private Sector	22d	2,804.0	3,239.0	3,398.8	3,587.0	3,868.4	4,113.1	4,311.1	4,804.2	4,927.4	5,103.0	6,025.5	7,844.5
Claims on Nonbank Financial Insts	22g	12.3	17.8	24.2	26.2	30.5	31.9	34.8	48.4	39.3	23.1	45.5	62.8
Demand Deposits	24	666.0	664.7	578.1	636.1	648.5	658.0	774.2	888.3	1,019.2	1,385.0	1,721.1	2,362.8
Time,Savings,& Fgn.Currency Dep	25	2,782.4	3,040.5	3,209.8	3,469.3	3,734.4	4,212.9	4,651.8	4,963.3	5,430.2	6,082.8	6,922.7	8,007.0
Money Market Instruments	26aa	28.1	22.6	24.9	24.9	27.5	29.7	33.0	33.3	43.0	61.1	80.4	98.1
Foreign Liabilities	26c	1,765.5	2,074.9	2,198.4	2,187.1	2,183.5	2,329.2	2,707.7	2,987.4	3,345.1	3,104.7	3,468.8	3,710.7
Central Government Deposits	26d	499.8	550.9	634.6	736.3	848.3	1,011.0	1,062.8	1,071.4	914.8	692.5	757.3	754.0
Credit from Monetary Authorities	26g	362.4	404.4	390.5	370.3	357.8	333.6	323.5	336.1	318.2	355.5	388.2	432.0
Capital Accounts	27a	582.8	701.7	771.0	1,047.7	1,181.3	1,316.6	1,378.0	1,436.2	1,545.1	1,623.2	1,874.4	2,252.5
Other Items (Net)	27r	37.0	81.5	134.2	75.4	280.3	477.4	694.9	1,034.7	1,019.6	955.8	1,218.6	1,704.1
Monetary Survey						*Millions of Dinars: End of Period*							
Foreign Assets (Net)	31n	1,637.2	1,756.2	1,781.3	2,218.1	2,315.6	2,951.7	3,818.3	3,969.3	4,371.7	5,424.7	5,809.8	6,011.2
Domestic Credit	32	3,763.7	4,135.6	4,158.1	4,244.9	4,845.2	4,988.6	5,096.5	5,707.3	6,055.8	6,412.8	7,628.3	10,059.0
Claims on Central Govt. (Net)	32an	487.4	392.7	210.8	95.1	459.9	477.3	375.3	526.5	778.3	943.3	1,017.3	1,515.5
Claims on Nonfin.Pub.Enterprises	32c	341.9	362.2	408.9	425.0	381.2	307.9	316.9	284.3	261.3	278.0	472.6	528.1
Claims on Private Sector	32d	2,810.5	3,246.7	3,406.8	3,595.6	3,877.8	4,125.0	4,324.3	4,817.9	4,941.9	5,118.1	6,043.8	7,862.7
Claims on Nonbank Financial Insts	32g	12.3	17.8	24.2	26.2	30.5	31.9	34.8	48.4	39.3	23.1	45.5	62.8
Money	34	1,741.6	1,738.7	1,532.8	1,626.1	1,612.6	1,766.1	2,017.4	2,094.6	2,273.1	2,829.9	3,138.5	4,022.6
Quasi-Money	35	2,788.6	3,051.0	3,213.3	3,482.7	3,818.8	4,507.2	4,734.2	5,204.0	5,652.5	6,412.6	7,070.9	8,373.1
Money Market Instruments	36aa	28.1	22.6	24.9	24.9	27.5	29.7	33.0	33.3	43.0	61.1	80.4	98.1
Capital Accounts	37a	628.4	751.0	824.0	1,100.4	1,234.7	1,369.6	1,471.7	1,528.5	1,647.4	1,784.0	2,053.8	2,312.7
Other Items (Net)	37r	214.2	328.5	344.4	228.9	467.1	267.6	658.6	816.2	811.5	749.9	1,094.5	1,263.7
Money plus Quasi-Money	35l	4,530.2	4,789.7	4,746.1	5,108.8	5,431.4	6,273.3	6,751.6	7,298.6	7,925.6	9,242.5	10,209.4	12,395.6
Other Banking Institutions						*Millions of Dinars: End of Period*							
Cash	40	59.9	63.3	54.3	53.0	41.2	22.5	71.2	....	....	....	....	....
Claims on Private Sector	42d	284.8	306.2	315.0	334.9	349.3	362.2	343.0	....	....	....	....	....
Deposits	45	47.4	32.7	24.5	17.0	11.8	8.8	9.5	....	....	....	....	....
Foreign Liabilities	46c	84.6	92.4	83.0	89.3	88.4	85.7	81.5	....	....	....	....	....
Central Govt. Lending Funds	46f	16.2	16.2	15.0	14.3	13.7	13.1	50.3	....	....	....	....	....
Capital Accounts	47a	91.6	111.5	132.0	153.2	164.5	177.4	186.4	....	....	....	....	....
Other Items (Net)	47r	104.9	116.8	114.9	114.2	112.0	99.7	86.4	....	....	....	....	....
Liquid Liabilities	55l	4,517.8	4,759.1	4,716.3	5,072.7	5,402.0	6,259.6	6,689.9	....	....	....	....	....
Interest Rates						*Percent Per Annum*							
Discount Rate (End of Period)	60	8.50	8.50	8.50	7.75	9.00	8.00	6.50	5.00	4.50	2.50	3.75	6.50
Money Market Rate	60b	....	....	....	....	....	5.19	5.28	4.63	3.49	2.58	2.18	3.59
Savings Rate	60k	....	....	....	....	....		4.49	4.04	3.52	2.49	1.28	.76	.74
Deposit Rate (Period Average)	60l	7.09	7.68	8.50	9.10	8.21	8.30	6.97	5.81	4.43	3.14	2.49	2.91
Lending Rate (Period Average)	60p	10.45	10.66	11.25	12.25	12.61	12.33	11.80	10.94	10.18	9.30	8.26	7.61

		1994	1995	1996	1997	1998	1999	2000	2001	2002	2003	2004	2005
Prices and Production		Index Numbers (2000=100): Period Averages											
Producer Prices (2002=100)	63	....	....	....	....	....	....	....	....	100.0	102.6	108.7	119.0
Wholesale Prices	63a	104.4	101.9	103.9	105.6	† 106.3	103.7	100.0	98.5	96.9	98.1	106.3	113.7
Consumer Prices	64	85.3	87.3	93.0	† 95.8	98.7	99.3	† 100.0	101.8	103.6	105.3	108.9	112.7
Industrial Production	66	† 83.4	93.8	89.0	92.1	94.0	96.2	† 100.0	106.6	118.5	108.5	121.5	133.9
Intl. Transactions & Positions							*Millions of Dinars*						
Exports	70	995.1	1,241.2	1,288.0	1,301.0	1,271.8	1,298.8	1,346.5	1,626.5	1,963.9	2,184.9	2,780.5	3,050.0
Imports, c.i.f.	71	2,362.6	2,590.3	3,043.6	2,908.1	2,714.4	2,635.2	3,259.4	3,453.7	3,599.2	4,072.0	5,762.9	7,448.9
							2000=100						
Volume of Exports	72	† 77.7	84.5	82.2	87.8	90.3	92.9	100.0	123.3	141.8	152.4	189.7	181.9
Volume of Imports	73	† 86.9	84.2	90.7	88.6	83.8	82.8	100.0	103.2	104.1	108.6	135.5	154.7
Unit Value of Exports	74	† 94.5	110.0	117.0	113.6	107.3	104.6	100.0	101.4	101.7	101.9	113.7	131.0
Unit Value of Imports	75	† 83.5	94.6	103.2	100.9	100.1	97.7	100.0	102.3	105.1	115.3	130.2	148.0
Balance of Payments						*Millions of US Dollars: Minus Sign Indicates Debit*							
Current Account, n.i.e	78ald	−398.0	−258.6	−221.9	29.3	14.1	404.9	59.4	−4.1	537.2	1,178.6	−17.9	....
Goods: Exports f.o.b	78aad	1,424.5	1,769.6	1,816.9	1,835.5	1,802.4	1,831.9	1,899.3	2,294.4	2,770.0	3,081.6	3,882.9	....
Goods: Imports f.o.b	78abd	−3,003.8	−3,287.8	−3,818.1	−3,648.5	−3,403.9	−3,292.0	−4,073.7	−4,301.5	−4,500.9	−5,077.9	−7,261.1	....
Trade Balance	78acd	−1,579.4	−1,518.2	−2,001.1	−1,813.0	−1,601.6	−1,460.1	−2,174.4	−2,007.0	−1,730.9	−1,996.3	−3,378.1	....
Services: Credit	78add	1,562.0	1,709.2	1,846.3	1,736.8	1,825.1	1,701.7	1,637.0	1,482.5	1,775.0	1,739.9	2,100.1	....
Services: Debit	78aed	−1,392.7	−1,614.9	−1,597.7	−1,537.2	−1,783.8	−1,698.0	−1,722.1	−1,725.9	−1,882.9	−1,889.2	−2,145.8	....
Balance on Goods & Services	78afd	−1,410.1	−1,424.0	−1,752.6	−1,613.4	−1,560.2	−1,456.4	−2,259.5	−2,250.4	−1,838.8	−2,145.6	−3,423.8	....
Income: Credit	78agd	72.7	115.7	111.7	248.2	306.9	467.6	670.3	648.7	484.1	492.7	515.2	....
Income: Debit	78ahd	−387.5	−394.5	−412.7	−457.0	−445.0	−479.7	−535.4	−461.2	−372.3	−374.3	−325.5	....
Balance on Gds, Serv. & Inc	78aid	−1,724.9	−1,702.8	−2,053.6	−1,822.1	−1,698.3	−1,468.5	−2,124.5	−2,062.9	−1,727.0	−2,027.3	−3,234.1	....
Current Transfers, n.i.e.: Credit	78ajd	1,447.4	1,591.8	1,970.2	2,096.1	1,984.3	2,154.9	2,611.3	2,365.8	2,524.3	3,501.0	3,562.5	....
Current Transfers: Debit	78akd	−120.5	−147.6	−138.5	−244.6	−271.9	−281.4	−427.4	−306.9	−260.1	−295.1	−346.3	....
Capital Account, n.i.e	78bcd	—	197.2	157.7	163.8	81.1	87.6	64.9	21.6	68.8	93.5	2.0	....
Capital Account, n.i.e.: Credit	78bad	—	197.2	157.7	163.8	81.1	87.6	64.9	21.6	68.8	93.5	2.0	....
Capital Account: Debit	78bbd	—	—	—	—	—	—	—	—	—	—	—	....
Financial Account, n.i.e	78bjd	188.9	230.0	233.9	242.3	−177.3	230.9	270.9	−319.0	474.8	−199.4	−307.2	....
Direct Investment Abroad	78bdd	23.1	27.3	43.3	—	—	−4.5	−1.8	−5.6	—	—	....	....
Dir. Invest. in Rep. Econ., n.i.e	78bed	2.9	13.3	15.5	360.9	310.0	158.0	800.8	120.2	64.0	424.1	620.3	....
Portfolio Investment Assets	78bfd	—	....	....	....	....	37.8	−45.1	−227.1	−191.8	−118.9	−217.2	....
Equity Securities	78bkd	—	....	....	....	....	37.8	−45.1	−227.1	−191.8	−118.9	−217.2	....
Debt Securities	78bld	—	....	....	....	....	....	....	....	....	....	....	....
Portfolio Investment Liab., n.i.e	78bgd	—	....	—	....	....	−28.1	−140.9	−171.7	−52.2	−349.1	−119.9	....
Equity Securities	78bmd	—	....	—	....	....	21.9	−16.8	−145.1	−52.2	−57.8	−119.9	....
Debt Securities	78bnd	—	....	....	....	....	−49.9	−124.1	−26.5	—	−291.3	—	....
Financial Derivatives Assets	78bwd	....	....	....	....	....	....	....	....	....	....	....	....
Financial Derivatives Liabilities	78bxd	....	....	....	....	....	....	....	....	....	....	....	....
Other Investment Assets	78bhd	62.5	−313.4	−5.9	16.4	−80.3	−541.7	−942.2	−615.1	11.4	283.1	−659.9	....
Monetary Authorities	78bod	−163.5	−313.4	−5.9	16.4	−80.3	−41.9	148.5	30.6	54.7	11.3	—	....
General Government	78bpd	—	....	....	....	....	—	—	—	—	—	—	....
Banks	78bqd	—	....	....	....	....	−499.9	−1,090.7	−645.7	−43.3	271.8	−659.9	....
Other Sectors	78brd	225.9	....	....	....	....	....	....	....	....	....	....	....
Other Investment Liab., n.i.e	78bid	100.4	502.8	181.0	−135.0	−407.1	609.4	600.1	580.3	643.3	−438.6	69.5	....
Monetary Authorities	78bsd	−8.7	−34.4	−11.0	−27.6	−11.0	183.5	−69.8	4.7	−15.0	−13.4	−29.3	....
General Government	78btd	−235.4	96.8	17.8	−91.4	−391.0	285.8	154.3	231.7	106.5	−327.2	−195.1	....
Banks	78bud	344.5	440.5	174.2	−15.9	−5.1	197.0	395.2	309.6	466.0	−99.4	329.3	....
Other Sectors	78bvd	—	—	—	—	—	−56.8	120.5	34.3	85.8	1.4	−35.4	....
Net Errors and Omissions	78cad	−55.8	−339.9	−357.9	−160.8	−454.0	28.7	297.7	57.7	−150.5	275.5	501.7	....
Overall Balance	78cbd	−264.9	−171.3	−188.2	274.6	−536.1	752.1	692.9	−243.9	930.3	1,348.2	178.6	....
Reserves and Related Items	79dad	264.9	171.3	188.2	−274.6	536.1	−752.1	−692.9	243.9	−930.3	−1,348.2	−178.6	....
Reserve Assets	79dbd	−216.8	−371.5	−280.7	−677.1	−83.4	−794.5	−681.7	256.0	−942.8	−1,248.2	−80.5	....
Use of Fund Credit and Loans	79dcd	57.6	106.5	97.6	110.3	22.4	39.7	−11.2	−12.1	12.5	−100.0	−98.1	....
Exceptional Financing	79ded	424.1	436.3	371.4	292.2	597.0	2.7	—	—	—	—	—	....
International Investment Position						*Millions of US Dollars*							
Assets	79aad	....	....	....	....	....	....	....	....	....	....	....	....
Direct Investment Abroad	79abd	....	....	—	—	—	....	....	....	....	....	....	....
Portfolio Investment	79acd	....	....	74.3	143.9	145.1	139.5	184.6	411.7	603.7	722.6	939.9	....
Equity Securities	79add	....	....	44.6	65.9	64.9	48.0	56.7	89.8	107.6	103.0	126.4	....
Debt Securities	79aed	....	....	29.8	78.0	80.3	91.5	127.9	321.9	496.1	619.6	813.5	....
Financial Derivatives	79ald	....	....	....	....	....	....	....	....	....	....	....	....
Other Investment	79afd	....	....	4,037.2	4,184.1	4,793.0	5,333.6	6,274.1	6,886.3	6,882.9	6,596.2	7,253.9	....
Monetary Authorities	79agd	....	....	1,266.6	1,250.4	1,330.9	1,371.7	1,223.4	1,193.7	1,149.8	1,138.5	1,138.6	....
General Government	79ahd	....	....	....	....	....	....	....	....	....	....	....	....
Banks	79aid	....	....	2,770.7	2,933.7	3,462.1	3,961.9	5,050.6	5,692.7	5,733.2	5,457.7	6,115.2	....
Other Sectors	79ajd	....	....	—	—	—	—	—	—	—	—	—	....
Reserve Assets	79akd	....	....	1,957.0	2,401.0	1,954.7	2,749.1	3,430.5	3,174.3	4,117.1	5,365.7	5,446.3	....
Liabilities	79lad	....	....	....	....	....	....	....	....	....	....	....	....
Dir. Invest. in Rep. Economy	79lbd	....	....	....	....	....	....	....	....	....	....	....	....
Portfolio Investment	79lcd	....	....	622.6	588.9	456.8	456.8	350.9	320.2	320.2	—	—	....
Equity Securities	79ldd	....	....	—	—	—	—	—	—	—	—	—	....
Debt Securities	79led	....	....	622.6	588.9	456.8	456.8	350.9	320.2	320.2	—	—	....
Financial Derivatives	79lld	....	....	....	....	....	....	....	....	....	....	....	....
Other Investment	79lfd	....	....	10,017.2	9,867.8	10,474.0	11,092.4	11,056.0	11,400.0	12,518.5	12,554.4	12,953.4	....
Monetary Authorities	79lgd	....	....	450.9	535.6	579.0	789.3	680.1	654.8	690.8	618.3	505.9	....
General Government	79lhd	....	....	6,282.2	5,991.4	6,520.2	6,755.7	6,259.0	6,215.7	6,718.1	7,161.9	7,197.2	....
Banks	79lid	....	....	3,100.8	3,084.8	3,079.6	3,285.2	3,819.0	4,213.5	4,718.1	4,379.0	4,892.5	....
Other Sectors	79ljd	....	....	183.2	256.0	295.2	262.2	297.9	315.9	391.5	395.2	357.8	....

Jordan   439

		1994	1995	1996	1997	1998	1999	2000	2001	2002	2003	2004	2005
Government Finance								*Millions of Dinars: Year Ending December 31*					
Deficit (-) or Surplus.........................	80	45.2	49.3	−66.3	−163.4	−327.1	−140.4	−119.8	−155.5	....	....	....	....
Revenue..............................	81	1,162.4	1,332.6	1,366.9	1,312.6	1,422.4	1,530.5	1,506.6	1,578.7	....	....	....	....
Grants Received.........................	81z	175.6	182.8	219.9	205.0	172.2	198.5	240.2	249.4	....	....	....	....
Expenditure...............................	82	1,312.8	1,471.5	1,666.9	1,681.9	1,876.8	1,804.1	1,868.6	2,027.7	....	....	....	....
Lending Minus Repayments...........	83	−20.0	−5.4	−13.8	−.9	44.9	65.3	−2.0	−44.1	....	....		
Financing													
Net Borrowing: Dinars..................	84b	−15.5	−18.3	−15.2	−11.6	−7.3	−2.8	−33.2	−110.7	....	....	....	....
Foreign Currency...............	85b	75.4	287.8	302.1	84.3	−12.3	55.7	−103.3	−5.8	....	....		
Use of Cash Balances....................	87	−105.1	−318.8	−220.6	90.7	346.7	87.5	....	....	....	....		
Debt: Domestic..............................	88a	1,098.70	838.60	831.50	822.70	1,006.90	889.00	1,119.80	1,260.30	....	....		
Foreign..............................	89a	3,975.20	4,114.80	4,386.30	4,334.40	4,668.70	4,883.90	4,501.60	4,491.10	....			
National Accounts								*Millions of Dinars*					
Househ.Cons.Expend.,incl.NPISHs....	96f	2,824.5	3,046.0	3,451.5	3,647.3	4,111.9	4,177.8	4,838.0	5,160.9	5,300.6	5,642.3	....	....
Government Consumption Expend...	91f	985.6	1,111.0	1,204.1	1,312.5	1,367.0	1,386.7	1,421.6	1,458.4	1,541.6	1,670.8	....	....
Gross Fixed Capital Formation..........	93e	1,391.0	1,394.9	1,444.8	1,325.0	1,187.5	1,352.7	1,266.6	1,235.8	1,286.9	1,481.7	....	....
Changes in Inventories....................	93i	60.0	159.2	54.5	−3.2	36.5	−106.4	74.8	104.2	78.0	15.7	....	....
Exports of Goods and Services..........	90c	2,093.4	2,438.5	2,597.2	2,532.5	2,515.7	2,505.4	2,507.2	2,677.8	3,036.5	3,243.5	....	....
Imports of Goods and Services (-).....	98c	3,107.6	3,435.2	3,839.9	3,676.7	3,608.7	3,537.9	4,109.5	4,273.3	4,464.8	4,850.3	....	....
Gross Domestic Product (GDP)........	99b	4,246.9	4,715.0	4,912.2	5,137.4	5,609.9	5,778.2	5,998.6	6,363.7	6,778.8	7,203.6	....	....
Net Primary Income from Abroad.....	98.n	−151.4	−116.8	−112.3	−47.4	−5.8	−8.7	95.5	132.7	79.1	....		
Gross National Income (GNI)...........	99a	4,095.5	4,598.2	4,799.7	5,090.6	5,604.2	5,758.6	6,084.4	6,471.7	6,778.1	....		
Net National Income.......................	99e	3,816.6	4,164.5	4,305.5	4,525.5	4,987.9	5,083.4	5,413.6	5,780.6	5,930.6	6,123.5		
GDP Volume 1994 Prices.................	99b.p	4,358.2	4,627.6	4,723.5	4,880.5	5,027.5	5,181.4	5,393.7	5,658.1	....	....		
GDP Volume (2000=100)................	99bvp	80.8	85.8	87.6	90.5	93.2	96.1	100.0	104.9	110.0	113.5	....	....
GDP Deflator (2000=100)...............	99bip	87.6	91.6	93.5	94.7	100.3	100.3	100.0	101.1	102.8	105.8	....	....
							Millions: Midyear Estimates						
Population..............................	99z	4.09	4.29	4.45	4.59	4.72	4.84	4.97	5.11	5.26	5.41	5.56	5.70

Kazakhstan 916

		1994	1995	1996	1997	1998	1999	2000	2001	2002	2003	2004	2005
Exchange Rates						*Tenge per SDR: End of Period*							
Official Rate	aa	79.21	95.06	105.40	101.94	117.99	189.68	188.27	188.76	210.18	214.31	201.89	191.49
						Tenge per US Dollar: End of Period (ae) Period Average (rf)							
Official Rate	ae	54.26	63.95	73.30	75.55	83.80	138.20	144.50	150.20	154.60	144.22	130.00	133.98
Official Rate	rf	35.54	60.95	67.30	75.44	78.30	119.52	142.13	146.74	153.28	149.58	136.04	132.88
Fund Position						*Millions of SDRs: End of Period*							
Quota	2f.s	247.50	247.50	247.50	247.50	247.50	365.70	365.70	365.70	365.70	365.70	365.70	365.70
SDRs	1b.s	69.54	154.87	240.19	327.15	275.08	164.24	.01	—	.76	.78	.79	.81
Reserve Position in the Fund	1c.s	.01	.01	.01	.01	.01	.01	.01	.01	.01	.01	.01	.01
Total Fund Cred.&Loans Outstg	2tl	198.00	290.82	383.60	378.96	463.66	335.15	—	—	—	—	—	—
International Liquidity						*Millions of US Dollars Unless Otherwise Indicated: End of Period*							
Total Reserves minus Gold	1l.d	837.5	1,135.5	1,294.1	1,697.1	1,461.2	1,479.2	1,594.1	1,997.2	2,555.3	4,236.2	8,473.1	6,084.2
SDRs	1b.d	101.5	230.2	345.4	441.4	387.3	225.4	—	—	1.0	1.2	1.2	1.2
Reserve Position in the Fund	1c.d	.01	.01	.01	.01	.01	.01	.01	.01	.01	.01	.01	.01
Foreign Exchange	1d.d	736.0	905.3	948.7	1,255.7	1,073.9	1,253.8	1,594.1	1,997.2	2,554.2	4,235.0	8,471.9	6,083.0
Gold (Million Fine Troy Ounces)	1ad	.99	1.36	1.80	1.81	1.75	1.80	1.84	1.84	1.71	1.74	1.83	1.92
Gold (National Valuation)	1and	378.0	524.3	666.6	523.9	503.6	522.8	501.5	510.7	585.6	725.9	803.6	985.5
Monetary Authorities:Other Assets	3..d	1,117.5	1,432.0	1,425.4	†1,848.1	1,577.6	1,776.8	2,096.5	3,767.1	5,096.5	8,607.4	14,407.5	15,156.7
Other liab.	4..d	15.9	59.4	76.0	†50.0	19.6	18.3	2.0	2.3	2.5	45.4	3.3	75.6
Deposit Money Banks: Assets	7a.d	271.9	440.9	330.1	273.8	344.6	570.6	383.5	556.0	1,331.9	2,049.8	3,861.5	8,888.8
Liabilities	7b.d	1,195.8	414.2	138.1	207.5	390.5	232.2	379.6	982.2	1,802.5	3,952.5	7,485.0	15,065.3
Monetary Authorities						*Millions of Tenge: End of Period*							
Foreign Assets	11	66,143	106,300	129,801	†172,971	164,663	276,713	302,950	565,816	788,081	1,241,532	1,873,130	2,030,845
Claims on Central Government	12a	20,236	39,467	39,265	†77,078	87,931	109,304	41,568	19,134	19,230	2,946	4,997	5,223
Claims on Rest of the Economy	12d	760	332	16,906	†620	7,277	12,657	2,146	3,587	4,060	6,349	8,443	15,459
Claims on Deposit Money Banks	12e	13,355	10,487	9,059	†8,248	2,084	4,634	2,774	1,810	3,758	3,150	26,126	95
Reserve Money	14	31,171	66,550	84,354	†115,389	81,427	126,749	134,416	175,551	208,171	316,872	577,847	663,363
of which: Currency Outside Banks	14a	20,255	47,998	62,811	†92,796	68,728	103,486	106,428	131,175	161,701	238,545	379,273	411,813
Other Deposits	15	738	445	3,068	†18	47	1,107	702	750	138	82	112,465	10,083
Liabs. of Central Bank:Securities	16ac	....	....	....	6,855	12,046	6,206	49,180	17,796	65,166	205,681	407,667	161,275
Foreign Liabilities	16c	16,548	31,444	46,001	†42,409	56,354	66,097	286	345	390	6,543	429	10,135
Central Government Deposits	16d	8,337	14,641	13,908	†53,647	59,766	93,898	57,507	256,768	356,425	570,924	744,222	1,122,211
Capital Accounts	17a	47,653	62,822	64,993	†52,611	63,480	121,957	118,963	134,375	179,834	167,299	84,257	92,081
Other Items (Net)	17r	−3,953	−19,317	−17,293	†−12,012	−11,167	−12,707	−11,615	4,762	5,005	−13,424	−14,191	−7,526
Deposit Money Banks						*Millions of Tenge: End of Period*							
Reserves	20	8,638	14,771	16,891	†22,361	12,144	21,793	24,359	42,343	45,362	76,222	195,805	225,166
Claims on Central Bank: Securities	20c	....	....	....	....	2,018	4,235	41,591	7,182	25,119	85,282	192,162	83,554
Other Claims on Central Bank	20n	....	....	....	....	—	6,390	3,700	16,748	1	3,608	4,332	2,373
Foreign Assets	21	14,755	28,197	24,196	†20,685	28,874	78,863	55,410	83,512	205,913	295,626	501,993	1,190,918
Claims on Central Government	22a	426	5,104	8,691	†25,303	21,184	34,752	59,512	†75,847	107,424	106,226	125,696	129,700
Claims on Local Government	22b	....	....	....	....	....	....	....	5,205	1,792	2,993	3,360	2,676
Claims on Nonfin.Pub.Enterprises	22c	....	....	....	....	....	....	....	14,564	12,795	30,158	18,502	29,847
Claims on Rest of the Economy	22d	111,747	71,988	72,448	†85,866	102,887	153,534	288,856	†515,735	699,030	1,010,888	1,560,721	2,708,285
Claims on Nonbank Financial Insts.	22g	....	....	....	....	2,195	2,904	3,703	16,079	22,795	31,886	59,633	114,007
Demand Deposits	24	32,894	63,930	71,938	†57,998	49,511	101,050	126,124	137,014	219,423	238,890	373,288	523,838
Other Deposits	25	....	....	....	†22,073	29,767	66,844	160,150	†285,867	341,811	458,713	720,295	1,028,291
Bonds	26ab	92	1,902	119	†30	—	32	1,173	1,613	6,675	12,729	31,097	149,280
Restricted Deposits	26b	....	....	....	....	....	....	....	....	19,397	41,011	33,841	62,059	84,157
Foreign Liabilities	26c	64,883	26,485	10,120	†15,674	32,727	32,087	54,857	147,524	278,665	570,024	973,055	2,018,446
Central Government Deposits	26d	1,494	5,416	11,494	†26,484	10,986	15,178	17,242	†14,699	17,708	5,887	3,954	2,544
Liabilities to Local Government	26db	....	....	....	....	....	....	....	....	2,627	3,457	3,116	2,681	1,753
Credit from Central Bank	26g	14,204	5,883	11,482	†8,208	5,092	4,699	2,915	1,888	5,347	9,139	39,592	15,068
Capital Accounts	27a	14,662	29,259	39,289	†40,183	59,735	89,539	107,159	159,897	179,516	258,048	405,326	642,169
Other Items (Net)	27r	7,338	−12,815	−22,216	†−16,436	−18,517	−6,957	7,509	6,690	26,616	52,501	50,855	20,981
Monetary Survey						*Millions of Tenge: End of Period*							
Foreign Assets (Net)	31n	−533	76,568	97,876	†135,572	104,455	257,392	303,217	501,460	714,938	960,591	1,401,638	1,193,182
Domestic Credit	32	123,338	96,834	111,908	†108,737	150,721	204,074	321,036	376,057	489,536	611,520	1,030,495	1,878,690
Claims on Central Govt. (Net)	32an	10,831	24,514	22,554	†22,250	38,363	34,979	26,331	†−176,487	−247,478	−467,639	−617,482	−989,831
Claims on Local Government	32b	....	....	....	....	....	....	....	2,578	−1,666	−123	678	923
Claims on Nonfin.Pub.Enterprises	32c	....	....	....	....	....	....	....	14,564	12,795	30,158	18,502	29,847
Claims on Rest of the Economy	32d	112,507	72,320	89,354	†86,487	110,163	166,191	291,002	†519,321	703,090	1,017,237	1,569,164	2,723,744
Claims on Nonbank Fin. Insts.	32g	....	....	....	....	2,195	2,904	3,703	16,079	22,795	31,886	59,633	114,007
Money	34	55,417	115,384	139,452	†150,908	118,735	205,929	236,163	270,009	381,975	479,023	755,296	942,783
Quasi-Money	35	....	....	....	†22,091	29,815	67,951	160,852	†286,617	341,949	458,795	832,760	1,038,374
Bonds	36ab	92	1,902	119	†30	—	32	1,173	1,613	6,675	12,729	31,097	149,280
Liabs. of Central Bank: Securities	36ac	92	1,902	119	6,855	†10,028	1,971	7,589	10,614	40,047	120,399	215,505	77,721
Restricted Deposits	36b	....	....	....	....	....	....	....	....	19,397	41,011	33,841	62,059	84,157
Capital Accounts	37a	62,315	92,081	104,282	†92,794	123,215	211,495	226,122	294,271	359,350	425,347	489,583	734,249
Other Items (Net)	37r	4,982	−35,966	−34,069	†−28,369	−26,617	−25,912	−7,647	−5,006	33,466	41,975	45,833	45,307
Money plus Quasi-Money	35l	55,417	115,384	139,452	†172,999	148,549	273,880	397,015	†556,626	723,925	937,819	1,588,056	1,981,157
Interest Rates						*Percent Per Annum*							
Refinancing Rate (End of Per.)	60	230.00	†52.50	35.00	18.50	25.00	18.00	14.00	9.00	7.50	7.00	7.00	8.00
Treasury Bill Rate	60c	214.34	48.98	28.91	15.15	23.59	15.63	6.59	5.28	5.20	5.86	3.28	3.28
Prices and Labor						*Index Numbers (2000=100): Period Averages*							
Producer Prices	63	....	42.2	†52.3	60.4	61.0	72.5	100.0	100.3	100.5	109.9	128.3	158.7
Consumer Prices	64	16.9	46.6	†64.9	76.1	81.6	88.4	100.0	108.4	114.7	122.1	130.5	140.4
Wages: Monthly Earnings	65	12.0	33.3	47.6	59.4	67.4	82.5	100.0	120.4	141.4	160.9	197.1	236.4
Total Employment	67	212.6	185.4	178.7	148.3	128.2	108.5	100.0	103.7	106.9	110.4	114.5	118.8
						Number in Thousands: Period Averages							
Employment	67e	6,582	6,552	6,519	6,472	6,128	6,105	6,201	6,699	6,709	6,985	7,166	7,244
Unemployment	67c	536	808	971	967	925	950	906	780	691	672	657	639
Unemployment Rate (%)	67r	7.5	11.0	13.0	13.0	13.1	13.5	12.8	10.4	9.3	8.8	8.4	8.1

2006, International Monetary Fund : *International Financial Statistics Yearbook*

Kazakhstan 916

		1994	1995	1996	1997	1998	1999	2000	2001	2002	2003	2004	2005
Intl. Transactions & Positions					*Millions of US Dollars*								
Exports	70..d	3,230.8	5,250.2	5,911.0	6,497.0	5,334.1	5,871.6	8,812.2	8,639.1	9,670.3	12,926.7	20,093.1	27,849.0
Imports, c.i.f.	71..d	3,561.2	3,806.7	4,241.1	4,300.8	4,313.9	3,655.1	5,040.0	6,446.0	6,584.0	8,408.7	12,781.2	17,352.5
Balance of Payments				*Millions of US Dollars: Minus Sign Indicates Debit*									
Current Account, n.i.e.	78ald	....	-213.1	-751.0	-799.3	-1,224.9	-171.0	366.3	-1,389.5	-1,024.3	-272.6	454.9	-485.7
Goods: Exports f.o.b.	78aad	....	5,440.0	6,291.6	6,899.3	5,870.5	5,988.7	9,288.1	8,927.8	10,026.9	13,232.6	20,603.1	28,300.6
Goods: Imports f.o.b.	78abd	....	-5,325.9	-6,626.7	-7,175.7	-6,671.7	-5,645.0	-7,119.7	-7,944.4	-8,039.8	-9,553.6	-13,817.7	-17,978.8
Trade Balance	78acd	....	114.1	-335.1	-276.4	-801.2	343.7	2,168.4	983.4	1,987.1	3,679.0	6,785.4	10,321.8
Services: Credit	78add	....	535.1	674.4	841.9	904.3	932.5	1,053.0	1,260.2	1,540.4	1,712.3	1,999.1	2,251.0
Services: Debit	78aed	....	-775.8	-928.3	-1,124.4	-1,154.1	-1,104.2	-1,850.0	-2,634.6	-3,538.3	-3,752.7	-5,026.2	-7,466.4
Balance on Goods & Services	78afd	....	-126.6	-589.0	-558.9	-1,051.0	172.0	1,371.4	-391.0	-10.7	1,638.6	3,758.4	5,106.4
Income: Credit	78agd	....	44.6	56.7	73.8	95.5	108.6	138.6	224.8	233.8	255.3	422.5	680.8
Income: Debit	78ahd	....	-190.1	-277.1	-388.8	-391.8	-608.3	-1,392.7	-1,461.7	-1,361.1	-2,001.9	-3,237.8	-5,860.4
Balance on Gds, Serv. & Inc.	78aid	....	-272.1	-809.4	-873.9	-1,347.3	-327.7	117.3	-1,628.0	-1,138.1	-108.0	943.1	-73.2
Current Transfers, n.i.e.: Credit	78ajd	....	79.9	83.4	104.7	141.4	174.7	352.2	394.4	425.9	278.6	352.9	809.1
Current Transfers: Debit	78akd	....	-20.9	-25.0	-30.1	-19.0	-18.0	-103.2	-156.0	-312.1	-443.3	-841.1	-1,221.5
Capital Account, n.i.e.	78bcd	....	-380.6	-315.5	-439.8	-369.1	-234.0	-290.5	-185.0	-119.8	-27.8	-20.3	13.9
Capital Account, n.i.e.: Credit	78bad	....	116.1	87.9	58.3	65.9	61.1	66.4	99.2	109.8	123.1	114.4	120.9
Capital Account: Debit	78bbd	....	-496.7	-403.4	-498.1	-435.0	-295.1	-356.9	-284.2	-229.7	-150.9	-134.6	-106.9
Financial Account, n.i.e.	78bjd	....	1,162.5	2,005.1	2,901.6	2,229.1	1,299.2	1,307.0	2,613.7	1,359.1	2,765.8	4,509.2	517.9
Direct Investment Abroad	78bdd	....	-.3	....	-1.4	-8.1	-3.6	-4.4	25.6	-426.4	121.3	1,279.0	-17.3
Dir. Invest. in Rep. Econ., n.i.e.	78bed	....	964.2	1,137.0	1,321.4	1,151.4	1,587.0	1,282.5	2,835.0	2,590.2	2,092.0	4,112.6	1,738.4
Portfolio Investment Assets	78bfd	....	....	....	-1.2	-5.3	-5.6	-85.5	-1,348.9	-1,063.9	-2,073.1	-1,092.1	-5,151.7
Equity Securities	78bkd	....	....	....	-1.2	-.4	-1.8	.7	-10.4	-374.4	-311.8	-362.8	-420.7
Debt Securities	78bld	....	....	....	....	-4.9	-3.8	-86.2	-1,338.5	-689.5	-1,761.2	-729.3	-4,731.1
Portfolio Investment Liab., n.i.e.	78bgd		7.2	223.5	405.4	66.2	-39.9	30.4	31.4	-182.9	182.1	674.3	1,107.8
Equity Securities	78bmd							19.3	55.4	39.3	63.8	-13.7	152.3
Debt Securities	78bnd		7.2	223.5	405.4	66.2	-39.9	11.1	-23.9	-222.1	118.3	688.0	955.5
Financial Derivatives Assets	78bwd		....	....	....	....	....					-44.6	-119.7
Financial Derivatives Liabilities	78bxd		....	....	....	....	....	—	—	—	15.9	-1.8	7.0
Other Investment Assets	78bhd	....	-657.4	243.8	-139.5	-220.5	-778.4	42.9	464.8	-1,116.8	-977.5	-4,461.4	-4,249.1
Monetary Authorities	78bod	....	21.3	2.1	....	....	-.3	-.4	.3	-14.8	-128.9	-9.3	-73.5
General Government	78bpd	....	—	27.8	.3	-41.1	16.3	-.4	209.7	321.2	275.0	—	—
Banks	78bqd	....	-152.3	174.4	-66.0	-67.9	-205.8	154.4	-63.6	-624.7	-314.3	-1,755.1	-3,153.8
Other Sectors	78brd	....	-526.4	39.5	-73.8	-111.5	-588.6	-110.7	318.5	-798.6	-809.3	-2,697.0	-1,021.8
Other Investment Liab., n.i.e.	78bid	....	848.8	400.8	1,316.9	1,245.4	539.7	41.0	605.7	1,558.8	3,405.0	4,043.3	7,202.5
Monetary Authorities	78bsd	....	-4.9	12.1	-5.0	-37.7	....	-2.6	.4	.2	85.5	-67.4	-17.3
General Government	78btd	....	331.3	323.4	317.2	673.3	291.5	88.1	51.3	1.7	57.4	-65.7	-848.0
Banks	78bud	....	-251.5	-125.7	161.4	60.2	-20.2	165.0	432.8	937.0	2,147.5	2,956.4	6,546.3
Other Sectors	78bvd	....	773.9	191.0	843.3	549.6	268.4	-209.5	121.2	619.9	1,114.7	1,219.9	1,521.5
Net Errors and Omissions	78cad	....	-270.1	-780.0	-1,114.1	-1,078.4	-641.6	-812.7	-654.5	320.2	-931.9	-944.9	-1,990.9
Overall Balance	78cbd	....	298.7	158.6	548.4	-443.3	252.6	570.1	384.7	535.1	1,533.5	3,999.0	-1,944.7
Reserves and Related Items	79dad	....	-298.7	-158.6	-548.4	443.3	-252.6	-570.1	-384.7	-535.1	-1,533.5	-3,999.0	1,944.7
Reserve Assets	79dbd	....	-440.1	-293.7	-542.0	321.7	-77.1	-129.1	-384.7	-535.1	-1,533.5	-3,999.0	1,944.7
Use of Fund Credit and Loans	79dcd	....	141.4	135.1	-6.4	121.6	-175.5	-441.0	—	—	—	—	—
Exceptional Financing	79ded	....	....	....									
International Investment Position					*Millions of US Dollars*								
Assets	79aad	....	....	....	2,629.1	2,391.8	2,598.4	4,612.9	6,117.0	9,321.5	14,283.7	23,167.9	30,367.7
Direct Investment Abroad	79abd	....	....	....	2.6	3.1	3.1	15.5	-9.7	417.2	300.4	-971.8	-983.9
Portfolio Investment	79acd	....	....	....	2.0	4.2	1.0	69.7	1,430.8	2,396.1	4,563.6	5,903.3	10,956.8
Equity Securities	79add	....	....	....	—	—	—	3.4	15.2	308.9	641.5	1,075.2	1,509.5
Debt Securities	79aed	....	....	....	2.0	4.2	1.0	66.3	1,415.6	2,087.2	3,922.0	4,828.1	9,447.3
Financial Derivatives	79ald	....	....	....			2.0					48.4	164.3
Other Investment	79afd	....	....	....	335.3	417.7	592.2	2,432.1	2,187.8	3,367.4	4,457.6	8,907.4	13,160.8
Monetary Authorities	79agd	....	....	....	.3	.1	.3	.7	.3	54.3	183.3	192.6	266.1
General Government	79ahd	....	....	....	46.8	46.8	46.8	852.3	636.1	314.9	39.9	39.9	39.9
Banks	79aid	....	....	....	288.2	370.8	545.1	359.8	423.0	1,048.3	1,340.0	3,060.2	6,176.7
Other Sectors	79ajd	....	....	....				1,219.3	1,128.4	1,949.9	2,894.4	5,614.7	6,678.1
Reserve Assets	79akd	....	....	....	2,289.2	1,964.8	2,002.1	2,095.7	2,508.2	3,140.8	4,962.1	9,280.5	7,069.7
Liabilities	79lad	....	....	....	2,595.3	3,594.3	3,678.4	15,726.9	19,192.4	23,056.5	29,041.5	38,654.3	49,842.7
Dir. Invest. in Rep. Economy	79lbd	....	....	....	50.1	122.3	115.9	10,077.7	12,916.6	15,464.3	17,587.1	22,327.0	25,152.2
Portfolio Investment	79lcd	....	....	....	623.9	663.4	617.2	695.9	725.0	337.8	581.0	1,306.2	2,570.8
Equity Securities	79ldd	....	....	....	53.9	49.9	37.7	101.6	146.9	142.0	221.6	287.5	541.0
Debt Securities	79led	....	....	....	570.0	613.5	579.5	594.3	578.1	195.7	359.4	1,018.8	2,029.8
Financial Derivatives	79lld	....	....	....						25.0	40.9	38.8	44.3
Other Investment	79lfd	....	....	....	1,921.3	2,808.6	2,945.3	4,953.3	5,550.8	7,229.4	10,832.5	14,982.3	22,075.4
Monetary Authorities	79lgd	....	....	....	553.0	655.4	462.6	1.9	2.3	2.5	88.0	20.7	3.1
General Government	79lhd	....	....	....	1,175.3	1,896.4	2,231.3	2,277.0	2,249.0	2,294.1	2,423.2	2,382.7	1,426.6
Banks	79lid	....	....	....	193.0	256.8	251.4	392.2	859.3	1,791.8	3,999.1	6,972.1	13,508.4
Other Sectors	79ljd	....	....	....				2,282.3	2,440.2	3,141.0	4,322.2	5,606.8	7,137.3
Government Finance				*Millions of Tenge: Year Ending December 31*									
Deficit (-) or Surplus	80	-30,382	-25,181	-59,564	-63,998	-72,073	-69,830	-3,279	-12,998	-13,004	-46,182	-18,697	46,662
Total Revenue and Grants	81y	79,474	178,347	306,943	405,624	379,521	395,580	590,236	733,893	807,853	1,004,565	1,286,734	2,111,006
Revenue	81	79,413	178,347	306,943	405,342	379,311	392,951	587,039	733,659	807,853	1,004,565	1,286,734	2,111,006
Grants Received	81z	61	—	—	282	210	2,629	3,197	234				
Exp. & Lending Minus Repay.	82z	109,856	203,528	366,507	469,622	451,594	465,410	593,515	746,891	820,857	1,050,747	1,305,431	2,064,344
Expenditure	82	109,672	210,603	381,602	439,476	426,142	447,426	576,182	726,015	801,071	1,026,991	1,287,938	2,057,105
Lending Minus Repayments	83	184	-7,075	-15,095	30,146	25,452	17,984	17,333	20,876	19,786	23,756	17,492	7,239
Total Financing													
Domestic	84a	....	....	....	17,170	20,504	20,671	-28,515	2,591	64,929	38,908	68,064	66,676
Foreign	85a	....	....	....	46,828	51,569	49,159	31,794	10,407	-51,925	7,274	-49,368	-113,337

Kazakhstan 916

National Accounts		1994	1995	1996	1997	1998	1999	2000	2001	2002	2003	2004	2005
							Billions of Tenge						
Househ.Cons.Expend.,incl.NPISHs....	96f	328.85	721.13	952.79	1,179.14	1,270.02	1,460.12	1,608.99	1,882.49	2,061.81	2,512.84	3,142.46	3,812.07
Government Consumption Expend...	91f	45.23	137.75	182.79	207.02	186.87	232.71	313.98	436.04	438.41	519.20	681.79	851.90
Gross Fixed Capital Formation.........	93e	110.65	233.81	243.88	271.77	272.44	326.26	450.26	771.38	907.13	1,062.66	1,472.42	1,853.02
Changes in Inventories....................	93i	10.90	2.69	−15.28	−10.94	1.49	32.19	21.34	102.26	123.33	122.80	72.07	197.35
Exports of Goods and Services..........	90c	156.96	395.27	499.32	583.86	525.95	856.23	1,471.61	1,491.86	1,774.50	2,232.98	3,065.81	4,064.64
Imports of Goods and Services (-)......	98c	199.53	441.67	509.74	626.10	604.22	808.94	1,276.48	1,526.29	1,776.40	1,985.29	2,552.97	3,387.32
Gross Domestic Product (GDP).........	99b	453.07	1,048.99	1,353.75	1,604.76	1,652.55	2,098.57	2,589.70	3,157.75	3,528.77	4,465.19	5,881.58	7,391.67
Net Primary Income from Abroad.....	98.n	−2.17	−9.11	−12.28	−23.38	−23.33	−62.78	−162.36	−167.26	−173.11	−261.02	−377.36	−688.28
Gross National Income (GNI)...........	99a	421.30	1,005.08	1,403.47	1,648.76	1,709.93	1,953.68	2,437.54	3,083.33	3,603.17	4,350.96	5,492.77	6,768.79
Net Current Transf.from Abroad.......	98t	7.36	7.88	9.81	5.63	6.11	18.38	35.45	33.96	17.37	−24.22	−65.95	−54.80
Gross Nat'l Disposable Inc.(GNDI)....	99i	428.66	1,012.96	1,413.29	1,654.40	1,716.05	1,972.06	2,472.99	3,117.29	3,620.55	4,326.74	5,426.82	6,713.98
Gross Saving....................................	99s	54.58	154.09	277.71	268.23	259.16	279.23	550.01	798.76	1,120.33	1,294.70	1,602.58	2,050.01
Consumption of Fixed Capital..........	99cf	84.31	154.42	228.04	253.96	238.76	286.95	420.52	498.16	576.88	666.02	822.51	....
GDP, Production Based...................	99bp	423.47	1,014.19	1,415.75	1,672.14	1,733.26	2,016.46	2,599.90	3,250.59	3,776.28	4,611.98	5,870.13	7,457.06
Statistical Discrepancy....................	99bs	−29.60	−34.80	61.99	67.39	80.71	−82.11	10.20	92.85	247.51	146.79	−11.45	65.40
GDP Volume (2000=100)................	99bvp	† 96.3	88.4	88.9	90.4	88.7	91.1	100.0	113.5	124.7	136.3	149.3	163.5
GDP Deflator (2000=100)...............	99bip	† 18.2	45.8	58.8	68.6	72.0	89.0	100.0	107.4	109.3	126.5	152.1	174.6
							Millions: Midyear Estimates						
Population.............................	99z	16.05	15.87	15.68	15.50	15.32	15.16	15.03	14.94	14.89	14.86	14.84	14.83

Kenya   664

		1994	1995	1996	1997	1998	1999	2000	2001	2002	2003	2004	2005
Exchange Rates						*Shillings per SDR: End of Period*							
Principal Rate	aa	65.458	83.153	79.118	84.568	87.165	100.098	101.674	98.779	104.781	113.140	120.117	103.432
						Shillings per US Dollar: End of Period (ae) Period Average (rf)							
Principal Rate	ae	44.839	55.939	55.021	62.678	61.906	72.931	78.036	78.600	77.072	76.139	77.344	72.367
Principal Rate	rf	56.051	51.430	57.115	58.732	60.367	70.326	76.176	78.563	78.749	75.936	79.174	75.554
Fund Position						*Millions of SDRs: End of Period*							
Quota	2f.s	199.4	199.4	199.4	199.4	199.4	271.4	271.4	271.4	271.4	271.4	271.4	271.4
SDRs	1b.s	.5	.2	.5	.5	.4	1.7	.2	.8	.6	1.4	.4	
Reserve Position in the Fund	1c.s	12.3	12.3	12.3	12.4	12.4	12.4	12.5	12.5	12.6	12.7	12.7	12.7
Total Fund Cred.&Loans Outstg	2tl	277.3	251.5	234.5	185.6	139.5	95.8	97.2	78.6	64.6	75.6	66.1	111.1
International Liquidity						*Millions of US Dollars Unless Otherwise Indicated: End of Period*							
Total Reserves minus Gold	1l.d	557.6	353.4	746.5	787.9	783.1	791.6	897.7	1,064.9	1,068.0	1,481.9	1,519.3	1,798.8
SDRs	1b.d	.7	.3			.6	2.4	.3	1.0	.8	2.0	.6	
Reserve Position in the Fund	1c.d	18.0	18.3	17.7	16.7	17.5	17.1	16.2	15.8	17.1	18.8	19.7	18.2
Foreign Exchange	1d.d	538.9	334.8	728.0	770.6	765.0	772.2	881.2	1,048.1	1,050.0	1,461.0	1,499.0	1,780.6
Gold (Million Fine Troy Ounces)	1ad	.080	.080	.080	.080	—	—	—	—	.001	.001	.001	.001
Gold (National Valuation)	1and	15.2	15.4	14.8	23.1	—	.1	.1	.1	.2	.2	.2	.2
Monetary Authorities: Other Liab.	4..d	278.1	265.7	261.6	205.8	174.8	126.5	127.9	99.2	88.1	125.4	123.2	216.0
Deposit Money Banks: Assets	7a.d	425.4	439.6	444.2	594.2	501.6	313.6	500.7	395.0	546.6	408.6	616.8	732.8
Liabilities	7b.d	293.1	103.8	103.3	165.2	195.8	218.2	173.0	162.3	142.1	107.4	151.9	110.9
Other Banking Insts.: Assets	7e.d	—	.1	.2	.1	.9		1.8	.1	.1	.8	.8	.2
Liabilities	7f.d	11.0	8.7	7.0	18.9	1.2	.8	.5	.4	.2			
Monetary Authorities						*Millions of Shillings: End of Period*							
Foreign Assets	11	28,227	25,683	47,266	44,499	47,103	57,816	71,245	83,499	82,304	112,771	117,710	130,583
Claims on Central Government	12a	53,857	98,401	57,287	47,905	43,585	39,028	36,742	37,421	40,947	40,836	47,657	58,462
Claims on Private Sector	12d	—	839	1,151	1,053	1,291	1,380	1,386	1,496	1,670	1,820	1,984	2,060
Claims on Deposit Money Banks	12e	10,072	9,766	9,056	9,124	1,140	904	4,884	1,362	7,484	674	67	8,259
Reserve Money	14	58,472	76,610	82,903	84,621	84,269	89,341	88,758	87,859	98,311	97,205	111,433	114,379
of which: Currency Outside DMBs	14a	24,817	28,887	30,390	36,178	38,713	42,963	43,466	45,349	53,895	55,550	62,728	66,327
Foreign Liabilities	16c	18,277	20,944	18,604	15,720	12,246	9,655	9,982	7,796	6,790	9,549	9,528	15,628
Central Government Deposits	16d	32,920	55,239	27,349	11,698	17,172	18,922	26,526	28,537	25,886	42,237	28,868	43,281
Counterpart Funds	16e	127	6	—	—	—	—	—	—	—	—	—	—
Capital Accounts	17a	3,235	4,155	4,819	5,612	7,281	8,800	9,322	9,622	13,548	14,805	15,696	14,641
Other Items (Net)	17r	−20,875	−22,265	−18,915	−15,070	−27,850	−27,589	−20,331	−10,036	−12,129	−7,696	1,893	11,434
Deposit Money Banks						*Millions of Shillings: End of Period*							
Reserves	20	31,790	35,316	42,460	39,736	34,970	36,081	31,762	37,062	34,165	31,588	39,959	42,262
Foreign Assets	21	19,073	24,594	24,440	37,240	31,051	22,871	39,072	31,049	42,126	31,113	47,704	53,033
Claims on Central Government	22a	38,088	26,417	42,576	46,121	70,550	68,415	71,206	89,091	98,549	137,614	109,869	129,475
Claims on Local Government	22b	249	304	358	582	595	895	1,143	659	687	658	338	630
Claims on Nonfin.Pub.Enterprises	22c	5,174	4,987	5,290	7,572	6,922	6,479	7,013	6,839	7,846	6,403	11,291	11,116
Claims on Private Sector	22d	79,467	119,261	148,018	186,558	202,592	239,586	247,913	239,340	248,536	261,261	324,604	351,647
Claims on Other Banking Insts	22f	2,671	4,897	5,852	3,176	2,283	1,294	752	561	982	513	569	786
Claims on Nonbank Financial Insts	22g	3,506	4,539	6,676	8,774	10,608	12,095	14,720	15,533	21,090	24,536	27,505	32,089
Demand Deposits	24	34,909	36,186	40,337	44,708	46,670	56,411	64,911	75,559	86,070	128,297	136,729	157,460
Time & Foreign Currency Deposits	25	89,908	129,961	170,009	206,488	211,161	215,348	221,665	224,238	241,727	244,327	288,010	316,276
Money Market Instruments	26aa	4,458	3,932	2,965	5,651	5,899	3,963	4,817	3,851	6,142	4,881	7,658	5,393
Foreign Liabilities	26c	13,144	5,807	5,681	10,356	12,122	15,914	13,501	12,756	10,954	8,176	11,747	8,025
Central Government Deposits	26d	4,950	5,531	3,822	4,226	9,592	8,754	8,385	5,310	4,333	7,922	10,341	15,307
Credit from Monetary Authorities	26g	—	—	—	448	4,335	1,614	3,635	2,974	2,673	740	57	—
Credit from Other Banking Insts	26i	10,697	6,403	8,165	6,005	5,082	3,879	2,683	1,676	1,827	2,026	3,098	1,483
Liab. to Nonbank Financial Insts	26j	12	2		49	3	4	2	3	2	230	196	281
Capital Accounts	27a	23,024	33,200	42,210	53,168	54,349	46,063	53,097	54,343	53,905	60,959	66,934	79,459
Other Items (Net)	27r	−1,083	−707	2,482	−1,340	10,355	35,766	40,885	39,424	46,350	36,129	37,067	37,355
Monetary Survey						*Millions of Shillings: End of Period*							
Foreign Assets (Net)	31n	15,878	23,525	47,420	55,664	53,785	55,119	86,833	93,996	106,687	126,160	144,138	159,963
Domestic Credit	32	145,142	198,876	236,037	285,817	311,661	341,495	345,964	357,093	390,088	423,482	484,608	527,677
Claims on Central Govt. (Net)	32an	54,075	64,048	68,693	78,101	87,370	79,767	73,037	92,665	109,277	128,290	118,317	129,349
Claims on Local Government	32b	249	304	358	582	595	895	1,143	659	687	658	338	630
Claims on Nonfin.Pub.Enterprises	32c	5,174	4,987	5,290	7,572	6,922	6,479	7,013	6,839	7,846	6,403	11,291	11,116
Claims on Private Sector	32d	79,467	120,100	149,169	187,611	203,883	240,966	249,299	240,836	250,206	263,081	326,587	353,707
Claims on Other Banking Insts	32f	2,671	4,897	5,852	3,176	2,283	1,294	752	561	982	513	569	786
Claims on Nonbank Financial Insts	32g	3,506	4,539	6,676	8,774	10,608	12,095	14,720	15,533	21,090	24,536	27,505	32,089
Money	34	62,407	66,525	76,238	89,487	93,489	109,067	118,672	125,670	149,130	193,130	209,368	230,845
Quasi-Money	35	89,908	129,961	170,009	206,488	211,161	215,348	221,665	224,238	241,727	244,327	288,010	316,276
Money Market Instruments	36aa	4,458	3,932	2,965	5,651	5,899	3,963	4,817	3,851	6,142	4,881	7,658	5,393
Counterpart Funds	36e	127	6	—	—	—	—	—	—	—	—	—	—
Liab. to Other Banking Insts	36i	10,697	6,403	8,165	6,005	5,082	3,879	2,683	1,676	1,827	2,026	3,098	1,483
Liab. to Nonbank Financial Insts	36j	12	2		49	3	4	2	3	2	230	196	281
Capital Accounts	37a	26,258	37,355	47,029	58,780	61,630	54,863	62,419	63,965	67,453	75,764	82,630	94,100
Other Items (Net)	37r	−32,845	−21,783	−20,947	−24,980	−11,819	9,490	22,539	31,686	30,495	29,284	37,785	39,263
Money plus Quasi-Money	35l	152,314	196,486	246,246	295,975	304,650	324,415	340,337	349,909	390,857	437,457	497,379	547,121

Kenya 664

		1994	1995	1996	1997	1998	1999	2000	2001	2002	2003	2004	2005
Other Banking Institutions						*Millions of Shillings: End of Period*							
Reserves.....	40	92	7,478	4,708	1,413	1,097	822	572	225	231	181	184	176
Foreign Assets.....	41	1	8	10	9	58	1	138	11	11	63	63	13
Claims on Central Government........	42a	24,065	10,748	7,193	8,826	7,163	8,122	9,323	10,454	11,268	12,292	13,734	13,357
Claims on Local Government...........	42b	35	35	16	7	8	8	—	—	—	—	—	—
Claims on Nonfin.Pub.Enterprises.....	42c	1,031	48	34	10	6	6	6	—	—	—	—	1,184
Claims on Private Sector.................	42d	37,808	40,629	36,398	27,632	28,723	24,378	25,860	16,460	17,575	15,340	14,825	13,417
Claims on Deposit Money Banks......	42e	9,115	5,537	7,653	3,735	5,802	4,103	4,129	2,107	1,509	2,427	1,416	2,609
Claims on Nonbank Financial Insts....	42g	591	503	146	119	103	96	114	97	24	58	57	127
Demand Deposits.....................	44	12,718	5,506	2,844	2,126	2,241	1,898	1,594	1,605	1,499	1,694	1,847	1,909
Time and Savings Deposits..............	45	42,832	42,335	36,397	22,364	24,752	23,335	23,586	20,349	20,450	21,711	21,345	22,122
Money Market Instruments..............	46aa	—	90	—	—	—	—	—	—	—	—	—	—
Foreign Liabilities.....................	46c	494	487	384	1,185	75	58	41	33	17	—	—	—
Central Government Deposits..........	46d	908	572	459	667	661	775	775	486	308	51	63	51
Credit from Monetary Authorities.....	46g	—	9	—	—	—	—	—	—	—	—	—	—
Credit from Deposit Money Banks.....	46h	674	2,843	2,847	1,630	1,442	232	581	160	—	—	105	650
Liab. to Nonbank Financial Insts.......	46j	2	1	—	—	—	550	—	—	—	—	—	—
Capital Accounts.....................	47a	7,773	7,148	6,366	4,257	4,279	4,410	3,545	2,343	2,339	2,318	2,364	2,335
Other Items (Net).....................	47r	7,337	5,994	6,859	9,522	9,511	6,278	10,019	4,378	6,005	4,588	4,553	3,815
Banking Survey						*Millions of Shillings: End of Period*							
Foreign Assets (Net).................	51n	15,386	23,046	47,046	54,488	53,769	55,062	86,929	93,973	106,682	126,222	144,201	159,975
Domestic Credit.....................	52	205,092	245,370	273,513	318,568	344,721	372,036	379,740	383,058	417,665	450,609	512,592	554,926
Claims on Central Govt. (Net).......	52an	77,232	74,224	75,427	86,260	93,872	87,114	81,585	102,633	120,237	140,532	131,988	142,655
Claims on Local Government.......	52b	284	339	374	589	603	903	1,143	659	687	658	338	630
Claims on Nonfin.Pub.Enterprises...	52c	6,204	5,035	5,324	7,582	6,928	6,485	7,019	6,839	7,846	6,403	11,291	12,300
Claims on Private Sector...............	52d	117,275	160,729	185,567	215,243	232,606	265,344	275,159	257,296	267,781	278,421	341,412	367,123
Claims on Nonbank Financial Insts.	52g	4,096	5,043	6,821	8,893	10,711	12,191	14,834	15,631	21,113	24,594	27,563	32,216
Liquid Liabilities.....................	55l	207,772	236,849	280,780	319,052	330,547	348,826	364,945	371,638	412,575	460,681	520,387	570,976
Money Market Instruments..............	56aa	4,458	4,023	2,965	5,651	5,899	3,963	4,817	3,851	6,142	4,881	7,658	5,393
Counterpart Funds.....................	56e	127	6										
Liab. to Nonbank Financial Insts.......	56j	14	3	—	49	3	554	2	3	2	230	196	281
Capital Accounts.....................	57a	34,031	44,503	53,395	63,037	65,909	59,273	65,964	66,308	69,792	78,082	84,994	96,435
Other Items (Net).....................	57r	−25,924	−16,968	−16,580	−14,733	−3,869	14,482	30,942	35,232	35,835	32,958	43,557	41,816
Interest Rates						*Percent Per Annum*							
Discount Rate (End of Period)..........	60	21.50	24.50	26.88	32.27	17.07	26.46	....	....	....	....		
Treasury Bill Rate....................	60c	23.32	18.29	22.25	22.87	22.83	13.87	12.05	12.60	8.95	3.51	3.17	8.43
Savings Rate.......................	60k	20.80	12.77	13.45	11.87	10.29	5.45	4.95	4.52	3.84	2.41	1.17	1.19
Savings Rate (Fgn. Currency)...........	60k.f	....	....	....	....	....	....	....	....	....	....	.91	1.23
Deposit Rate.......................	60l	....	13.60	17.59	16.72	18.40	9.55	8.10	6.64	5.49	4.13	† 2.43	5.08
Deposit Rate (Fgn. Currency)..........	60l.f	....	....	....	....	....	....	....	....	....	....	1.62	2.29
Lending Rate.......................	60p	36.24	28.80	33.79	30.25	29.49	22.38	22.34	19.67	18.45	16.57	† 12.53	12.88
Lending Rate (Fgn. Currency)..........	60p.f	....	....	....	....	....	....	....	....	....	....	5.83	6.36
Prices, Production, Labor						*Index Numbers (2000=100): Period Averages*							
Consumer Prices.....................	64	65.4	66.5	72.4	† 80.6	86.0	90.9	100.0	105.7	107.8	118.4	132.2	145.8
Industrial Production (1995=100)....	66	83.2	100.0	90.7	....	....	....	....	....	....	....	....	....
						Number in Thousands: Period Averages							
Employment.........................	67e	1,506	1,557	1,607	1,647	1,665	1,673	1,677	....	....	....	....	....
Intl. Transactions & Positions						*Millions of Shillings*							
Exports.............................	70	87,142	97,284	118,226	119,960	121,252	122,067	132,183	152,712	166,635	183,121	212,602	248,929
Imports, c.i.f.........................	71	115,080	155,168	168,486	190,674	193,032	198,313	236,613	250,782	255,569	282,616	360,812	464,495
						2000=100							
Volume of Exports (1995=100)........	72	83	100	....	....	....	....	....	....	....	....	....	....
Volume of Imports....................	73	77	90	89	95	96	87	100	....	....	....	....	....
Export Prices........................	74	73	79	84	98	99	93	100	....	....	....	....	....
Unit Value of Imports.................	75	60	69	76	81	83	90	100	....	....	....	....	....

		1994	1995	1996	1997	1998	1999	2000	2001	2002	2003	2004	2005
Balance of Payments		*Millions of US Dollars: Minus Sign Indicates Debit*											
Current Account, n.i.e.	78ald	97.9	−400.4	−73.5	−456.8	−475.3	−89.6	−199.4	−341.4	−136.9	67.7	−378.5	....
Goods: Exports f.o.b.	78aad	1,537.0	1,923.7	2,083.3	2,062.6	2,017.0	1,756.7	1,782.2	1,891.4	2,162.5	2,412.2	2,722.7	....
Goods: Imports f.o.b.	78abd	−1,775.3	−2,673.9	−2,598.2	−2,948.4	−3,028.7	−2,731.8	−3,043.9	−3,238.2	−3,159.0	−3,554.8	−4,320.2	....
Trade Balance	78acd	−238.4	−750.1	−514.8	−885.9	−1,011.7	−975.1	−1,261.7	−1,346.9	−996.5	−1,142.6	−1,597.5	....
Services: Credit	78add	1,117.3	1,024.5	936.2	914.5	830.4	934.5	993.4	1,089.4	1,018.1	1,153.2	1,479.1	....
Services: Debit	78aed	−686.8	−868.1	−854.0	−826.0	−694.7	−570.4	−718.7	−765.8	−645.9	−670.9	−794.4	....
Balance on Goods & Services	78afd	192.2	−593.7	−432.6	−797.4	−876.0	−611.0	−987.0	−1,023.3	−624.2	−660.4	−912.8	....
Income: Credit	78agd	20.9	25.6	21.4	23.0	41.2	31.7	45.0	46.1	35.4	59.6	45.0	....
Income: Debit	78ahd	−385.7	−350.5	−242.2	−254.9	−214.7	−190.9	−178.1	−167.3	−178.2	−147.8	−159.4	....
Balance on Gds, Serv. & Inc.	78aid	−172.6	−918.6	−653.4	−1,029.4	−1,049.4	−770.2	−1,120.2	−1,144.5	−767.1	−748.5	−1,027.2	....
Current Transfers, n.i.e.: Credit	78ajd	333.7	563.6	585.4	572.5	578.6	685.3	926.6	804.8	632.1	818.6	649.7	....
Current Transfers: Debit	78akd	−63.2	−45.5	−5.4		−4.5	−4.7	−5.8	−1.6	−1.9	−2.3	−.9	....
Capital Account, n.i.e.	78bcd	−.4	−.4	−.4	76.8	84.3	55.4	49.6	51.5	81.2	163.0	145.2	....
Capital Account, n.i.e.: Credit	78bad	—	....	....	76.8	84.3	55.4	49.6	51.5	82.1	163.0	145.2	....
Capital Account: Debit	78bbd	−.4	....	−.4						−.9			....
Financial Account, n.i.e.	78bjd	−41.7	247.9	589.1	362.6	562.1	165.7	269.8	148.1	−173.9	406.3	39.6	....
Direct Investment Abroad	78bdd	—	....	.5	−2.1	....	....	—	—	−7.4	−2.1	−4.4	....
Dir. Invest. in Rep. Econ., n.i.e.	78bed	3.7	32.5	12.7	19.7	11.4	13.8	110.9	5.3	27.6	81.7	46.1	....
Portfolio Investment Assets	78bfd	—	....	....	....	....	....	−10.9	−6.9	−10.0	−38.6	−71.7	....
Equity Securities	78bkd	—	....	....	....	....	....	−.5	−.9	−2.0	−12.2	−25.8	....
Debt Securities	78bld	—	....	....	....	....	....	−10.4	−6.0	−8.1	−26.4	−45.9	....
Portfolio Investment Liab., n.i.e.	78bgd	—	6.0	7.5	34.2	1.3	−8.0	−3.5	5.5	5.3	.9	5.4	....
Equity Securities	78bmd	—	6.0	7.5	26.9	1.3	−8.0	−6.0	2.4	3.0	.6	3.2	....
Debt Securities	78bnd	—	....	....	7.3			2.5	3.1	2.3	.3	2.1	....
Financial Derivatives Assets	78bwd	....	....	....	....	....	....	....	....	....	....	....	....
Financial Derivatives Liabilities	78bxd	....	....	....	....	....	....	....	....	....	....	....	....
Other Investment Assets	78bhd	171.1	277.1	628.2	−53.6	−58.6	−89.8	−55.7	−86.4	−132.6	−67.4	−308.4	....
Monetary Authorities	78bod	....	....	....	....	....	....	....	....	....	....	....	....
General Government	78bpd	—	....	....	−4.7	....	....	−5.3	−6.6	−7.8	−11.0	−212.6	....
Banks	78bqd	−61.2	....	....	−44.2	−44.4	−74.3						....
Other Sectors	78brd	232.3	277.1	628.2	−4.7	−14.3	−15.5	−50.4	−79.8	−124.9	−56.4	−95.8	....
Other Investment Liab., n.i.e.	78bid	−216.5	−67.7	−59.9	364.6	608.0	249.7	228.9	230.6	−56.7	431.7	372.6	....
Monetary Authorities	78bsd	—	—	—	—	—	—	—	—	—	—	—	....
General Government	78btd	−113.3	−5.7	5.0	−110.9	−109.4	−257.4	243.8	−158.4	−133.7	−81.3	−171.4	....
Banks	78bud	32.1					22.6	31.0					....
Other Sectors	78bvd	−135.3	−61.9	−64.9	475.5	694.8	476.1	−14.9	389.0	77.0	513.0	544.0	....
Net Errors and Omissions	78cad	5.8	11.4	−128.2	32.8	−88.6	−165.5	−127.1	151.7	213.2	−211.9	202.7	....
Overall Balance	78cbd	61.6	−141.6	387.0	15.5	82.6	−34.0	−7.2	10.0	−16.4	425.2	9.0	....
Reserves and Related Items	79dad	−61.6	141.6	−387.0	−15.5	−82.6	34.0	7.2	−10.0	16.4	−425.2	−9.0	....
Reserve Assets	79dbd	−95.3	174.2	−378.1	70.8	5.4	−9.2	−107.1	−167.8	−1.7	−412.6	−58.7	....
Use of Fund Credit and Loans	79dcd	19.3	−39.1	−24.6	−67.3	−62.8	−59.5	1.3	−23.6	−18.4	16.7	−14.1	....
Exceptional Financing	79ded	14.4	6.5	15.8	−19.0	−25.2	102.7	113.0	181.4	36.5	−29.3	63.8	....
Government Finance		*Millions of Shillings: Year Ending June 30*											
Deficit (-) or Surplus	80	−23,415	−6,172	6,228	† −13,605	−5,304	−2,271	7,461	−13,105	−26,990	−35,769	−4,830	1,387
Total Revenue and Grants	81y	112,413	138,181	156,804	† 156,167	179,055	201,177	188,350	216,393	205,546	225,692	270,905	304,707
Revenue	81	103,250	125,312	145,558	† 150,384	173,783	196,257	184,103	192,313	198,723	210,750	254,681	289,802
Grants	81z	9,163	12,869	11,246	5,783	5,272	4,920	4,247	24,080	6,823	14,942	16,224	14,905
Expenditure	82	135,828	144,353	150,576	† 169,772	184,359	203,448	180,889	229,498	232,536	261,461	275,735	303,320
Statistical Discrepancy	80xx	....	....	....	† −1,048	64	−178	1	—	535	989	4,882	5,910
Total Financing	80h	23,415	6,172	−6,228	† 14,653	5,240	2,449	−7,462	13,105	26,455	34,780	−51	−7,297
Domestic	84a	21,962	16,977	−5,437	† 21,287	12,441	11,194	11,876	616	39,766	46,923	8,809	−6,672
Foreign	85a	1,453	−10,805	−791	−6,634	−7,201	−8,745	−19,338	12,489	−13,311	−12,143	−8,860	−625
Total Debt	88	....	....	....	463,507	441,561	455,050	550,185	† 605,791	613,739	689,013	747,416	749,548
Domestic	88a	....	....	....	145,810	145,541	150,499	163,405	† 211,813	235,991	289,377	306,235	315,573
Foreign	89a	....	....	....	317,697	296,020	304,551	386,780	393,978	377,748	399,636	441,182	433,976
National Accounts		*Millions of Shillings*											
Househ.Cons.Expend.,incl.NPISHs.	96f	250,098	322,622	359,442	453,173	513,249	540,400	757,727	812,269	814,919	868,547	954,649	....
Government Consumption Expend.	91f	60,719	69,057	84,523	100,712	113,568	125,943	145,701	159,536	173,297	202,927	216,563	....
Gross Fixed Capital Formation	93e	75,616	99,497	104,470	109,873	113,879	112,961	161,714	185,186	177,781	179,248	208,248	....
Changes in Inventories	93i	1,683	2,020	3,000	5,400	6,210	7,142	6,826	11,596	−8,404	19,519	24,596	....
Exports of Goods and Services	90c	148,225	152,596	172,459	174,846	171,895	189,265	214,831	228,054	252,207	281,394	357,243	....
Imports of Goods and Services (-)	98c	135,641	180,139	195,155	220,769	224,772	232,233	292,493	345,899	326,340	360,960	473,982	....
Gross Domestic Product (GDP)	99b	400,700	465,654	528,740	623,235	694,029	743,479	967,838	1,025,918	1,038,764	1,141,780	1,273,716	1,438,592
Net Primary Income from Abroad	98.n	−23,074	−19,832	−15,837	−13,623	−10,468	−11,196	−10,140	−9,523	−11,249	−6,696	−7,342	....
Gross National Income (GNI)	99a	377,626	445,821	512,130	609,730	681,652	732,283	957,698	1,016,395	1,027,515	1,135,084	1,266,374	....
GDP Volume 1982 Prices	99b.p	103,054	107,595	112,058	115,418	115,736	111,573	119,454	....	....	....	....	....
GDP Volume 2001 Prices	99b.p	....	....	....	....	....	....	982,855	1,025,918	1,029,978	1,058,470	1,104,356	....
GDP Volume (2000=100)	99bvp	86.3	90.1	93.8	96.6	96.9	93.4	† 100.0	104.4	104.8	107.7	112.4	....
GDP Deflator (2000=100)	99bip	48.0	53.4	58.2	66.6	74.0	82.2	100.0	101.6	102.4	109.5	117.1	....
		Millions: Midyear Estimates											
Population	99z	26.49	27.23	27.94	† 28.64	29.33	30.01	30.69	31.36	32.04	32.73	33.47	34.26

Korea, Republic of 542

		1994	1995	1996	1997	1998	1999	2000	2001	2002	2003	2004	2005
Exchange Rates					*Won per SDR: End of Period*								
Market Rate	aa	1,151.38	1,151.58	1,213.93	2,286.98	1,695.27	1,561.92	1,647.53	1,650.71	1,612.66	1,772.17	1,607.52	1,445.85
					Won per US Dollar: End of Period (ae) Period Average (rf)								
Market Rate	ae	788.70	774.70	844.20	1,695.00	1,204.00	1,138.00	1,264.50	1,313.50	1,186.20	1,192.60	1,035.10	1,011.60
Market Rate	rf	803.45	771.27	804.45	951.29	1,401.44	1,188.82	1,130.96	1,290.99	1,251.09	1,191.61	1,145.32	1,024.12
Fund Position					*Millions of SDRs: End of Period*								
Quota	2f.s	799.6	799.6	799.6	799.6	799.6	1,633.6	1,633.6	1,633.6	1,633.6	1,633.6	1,633.6	1,633.6
SDRs	1b.s	52.3	65.7	82.3	43.6	8.1	.5	2.7	2.7	8.7	14.2	21.1	30.5
Reserve Position in the Fund	1c.s	363.6	438.5	474.3	443.7	.1	208.6	208.6	208.8	384.0	507.7	507.7	214.0
Total Fund Cred.&Loans Outstg	2tl	—	—	—	8,200.0	12,000.0	4,462.5	4,462.5	—	—	—	—	—
International Liquidity					*Millions of US Dollars Unless Otherwise Indicated: End of Period*								
Total Reserves minus Gold	1l.d	25,639.3	32,677.7	34,037.1	20,367.9	51,974.5	73,987.3	96,130.5	102,753.3	121,345.2	155,284.2	198,996.6	210,317.2
SDRs	1b.d	76.3	97.7	118.4	58.8	11.4	.7	3.5	3.3	11.8	21.1	32.8	43.7
Reserve Position in the Fund	1c.d	530.8	651.8	682.0	598.7	.1	286.3	271.8	262.4	522.0	754.4	788.4	305.8
Foreign Exchange	1d.d	25,032.1	31,928.2	33,236.7	19,710.4	51,963.0	73,700.3	95,855.1	102,487.5	120,811.4	154,508.8	198,175.3	209,967.7
Gold (Million Fine Troy Ounces)	1ad	.325	.327	.327	.335	.435	.437	.439	.442	.444	.449	.454	.458
Gold (National Valuation)	1and	33.6	34.4	36.0	36.9	66.3	67.1	67.6	68.3	69.2	70.9	72.3	73.6
Monetary Authorities: Other Liab.	4..d	442.4	158.6	381.1	140.1	160.9	307.6	286.1	4,877.1	8,371.9	6,952.5	19,906.1	16,107.3
Deposit Money Banks: Assets	7a.d	20,937.9	27,806.5	33,909.6	32,748.7	34,309.6	34,748.2	34,562.3	28,086.2	25,851.3	30,923.2	39,510.6	37,865.4
Liabilities	7b.d	21,170.3	31,446.0	43,181.5	27,975.3	29,455.3	27,546.5	24,804.8	21,289.5	36,680.7	43,689.0	50,731.1	55,190.8
Other Banking Insts.: Assets	7e.d	7,897.0	4,136.0	7,144.0	10,761.0	10,027.0	8,975.0	11,926.0	13,058.0	17,371.0	....	....	....
Liabilities	7f.d	21,692.0	21,816.0	26,857.0	29,661.0	22,466.0	18,033.0	15,222.0	13,387.0	16,521.0	....	....	....
Monetary Authorities					*Billions of Won: End of Period*								
Foreign Assets	11	20,880	25,390	28,173	29,227	64,832	85,342	121,558	142,589	155,362	194,033	228,060	228,998
Claims on Central Government	12a	2,628	1,951	2,235	5,562	5,961	6,382	4,958	5,570	5,091	6,110	4,514	7,100
Claims on Official Entities	12bx	570	570	370	2,370	8,640	2,370	2,370	2,370	2,370	1,370	—	143
Claims on Deposit Money Banks	12e	28,971	28,076	24,378	62,442	37,830	26,003	15,563	11,637	6,849	8,117	8,298	8,641
Reserve Money	14	25,204	29,306	25,723	22,519	20,703	28,487	28,238	32,827	37,987	40,749	38,792	43,249
of which: Currency Outside DMBs	14a	13,127	15,061	15,453	15,448	13,670	19,475	17,636	18,702	19,863	20,111	20,772	21,959
Liabs.of the Central Bank:Securities	16ac	29,114	29,598	29,068	26,701	53,580	61,389	79,142	93,120	104,929	133,938	170,192	176,605
Foreign Liabilities	16c	349	123	322	18,991	20,537	7,320	7,714	6,406	9,931	8,292	20,605	16,294
Central Government Deposits	16d	6,477	6,917	6,684	5,410	5,917	9,126	10,608	7,347	11,178	5,482	1,196	1,481
Other Items (Net)	17r	−8,095	−9,956	−6,640	25,980	16,526	13,775	18,747	22,466	5,647	21,170	10,087	7,253
Deposit Money Banks					*Billions of Won: End of Period*								
Reserves	20	11,947	14,092	10,181	6,798	6,610	8,958	10,434	14,063	17,904	20,427	17,793	21,020
Claims on Mon.Author.:Securities	20c	12,700	15,775	18,419	20,996	29,559	27,375	33,073	36,238	43,515	51,019	53,923	68,897
Foreign Assets	21	16,514	21,542	28,627	55,509	41,309	39,543	43,704	36,891	30,665	36,879	40,897	38,305
Claims on Central Government	22a	5,196	5,373	4,897	6,341	13,564	21,372	23,677	22,959	24,369	29,538	37,369	51,754
Claims on Private Sector	22d	173,903	200,769	240,936	293,812	318,667	383,884	457,258	520,733	628,230	684,192	693,139	744,121
Demand Deposits	24	19,593	23,672	24,221	19,331	21,569	25,139	29,193	34,918	43,265	45,226	47,424	55,045
Time, Savings,& Fgn.Currency Dep	25	100,668	115,072	138,769	168,482	222,926	284,916	366,041	414,031	455,741	488,084	481,575	489,560
Bonds	26ab	2,923	4,782	6,167	5,954	17,072	11,287	14,699	19,920	45,236	54,005	66,560	76,735
Restricted Deposits	26b	792	904	988	1,214	772	803	1,030	908	974	1,159	1,068	873
Foreign Liabilities	26c	16,697	24,361	36,454	47,418	35,464	31,348	31,366	27,964	43,511	52,104	52,512	55,831
Central Government Deposits	26d	286	948	1,632	3,290	4,499	5,493	9,442	10,446	12,743	18,968	20,133	20,762
Central Govt. Lending Funds	26f	11,032	13,493	14,828	23,193	26,703	29,946	29,182	29,340	25,461	25,323	22,947	26,401
Credit from Monetary Authorities	26g	29,256	28,429	24,460	63,076	38,738	26,242	17,191	13,515	10,591	12,682	9,060	9,168
Capital Accounts	27a	20,406	22,523	24,877	22,673	21,891	28,152	29,883	34,792	38,696	41,158	46,056	61,103
Other Items (Net)	27r	18,605	23,366	30,663	28,825	20,075	37,807	40,120	45,051	68,465	83,347	95,787	128,618
Monetary Survey					*Billions of Won: End of Period*								
Foreign Assets (Net)	31n	20,347	22,448	20,024	18,327	50,140	86,217	126,182	145,110	132,585	170,517	195,841	195,177
Domestic Credit	32	186,520	213,688	255,240	314,581	351,179	412,126	479,780	546,056	645,391	705,594	722,700	790,777
Claims on Central Govt. (Net)	32an	1,061	−541	−1,183	3,204	9,108	13,135	8,585	10,736	5,539	11,198	20,555	36,610
Claims on Official Entities	32bx	570	570	370	2,370	8,640	2,370	2,370	2,370	2,370	1,370	—	143
Claims on Private Sector	32d	184,888	213,658	256,054	309,008	333,431	396,621	468,825	532,951	637,482	693,025	702,145	754,024
Money	34	32,511	38,873	39,542	35,036	35,583	44,375	46,997	53,506	63,151	65,481	68,423	77,274
Quasi-Money	35	100,668	115,073	138,770	168,495	222,956	284,943	366,052	414,072	455,754	488,102	481,604	489,560
Bonds	36ab	19,338	18,606	16,817	11,659	41,092	45,301	60,767	76,802	106,650	136,924	182,829	184,443
Restricted Deposits	36b	792	904	988	1,214	772	803	1,030	908	974	1,159	1,068	873
Central Govt. Lending Funds	36f	11,032	13,493	14,828	23,193	26,703	29,946	29,182	29,340	25,461	25,323	22,947	26,401
Other Items (Net)	37r	42,526	49,187	64,320	93,311	74,214	92,975	101,934	116,539	125,986	159,121	161,670	207,379
Money plus Quasi-Money	35l	133,179	153,946	178,312	203,532	258,538	329,317	413,049	467,577	518,904	553,583	550,027	566,859
Other Banking Institutions													
Development Institutions					*Billions of Won: End of Period*								
Claims on Private Sector	42d	26,771	30,616	35,600	48,097	55,361	55,283	58,351	55,843	51,933	56,062	62,354	69,174
Bonds	46ab	16,617	19,639	23,764	34,782	36,096	34,666	35,251	34,317	32,620	35,584	39,032	41,420
Counterpart Funds	46e	1	1	1	1	1	1	—	—	—	—	—	—
Central Govt. Lending Funds	46f	2,967	3,018	3,336	3,822	14,549	15,380	16,889	14,533	13,644	10,199	9,518	8,202
Credit from Deposit Money Banks	46h	5,450	5,710	5,564	2,130	2,397	1,358	704	1,594	560	662	688	826
Capital Accounts	47a	1,615	1,614	1,814	2,909	4,486	6,247	3,773	6,931	6,926	7,688	10,129	15,291
Other Items (Net)	47r	121	634	1,122	4,454	−2,168	−2,367	1,734	−1,532	−1,817	1,929	2,988	3,434
Trust Accounts of Coml. Banks					*Billions of Won: End of Period*								
Claims on Private Sector	42d.g	143,539	182,319	216,569	253,305	307,920	273,872	178,537	181,683	197,589	152,187	146,529	150,381
Claims on Deposit Money Banks	42e.g	1,118	1,475	1,982	2,797	8,570	9,366	6,787	10,967	5,972	10,671	6,522	4,155
Quasi-Monetary Liabilities	45..g	93,415	124,891	151,093	171,456	138,941	115,360	77,594	81,330	73,713	58,135	47,899	48,514
Other Items (Net)	47r.g	51,242	58,903	67,458	84,646	177,549	167,878	107,730	111,319	129,848	104,723	105,152	106,022
Postal Savings Deposits	45..h	5,948	5,321	6,421	7,280	11,491	14,980	22,150	26,111	29,400	35,985	32,808	35,855

Korea, Republic of 542

		1994	1995	1996	1997	1998	1999	2000	2001	2002	2003	2004	2005
Nonbank Financial Institutions						*Billions of Won: End of Period*							
Cash	40..s	3,633	5,984	8,310	12,071	7,906	5,836	6,638	6,602	3,686	3,511	3,797	4,921
Claims on Central Government	42a.s	269	107	123	163	510	1,677	2,571	4,536	12,202	18,850	27,894	35,063
Claims on Private Sector	42d.s	38,931	43,207	51,210	55,510	43,442	42,937	53,578	58,010	65,418	70,299	71,893	75,878
Real Estate	42h.s	4,504	5,124	6,173	7,333	8,703	9,752	10,113	9,757	9,435	9,313	9,774	9,942
Incr.in Total Assets(Within Per.)	49z.s	7,230	10,951	13,101	12,461	357	15,997	13,896	16,280	25,095	20,435	26,662	25,083
Liquid Liabilities	55l	228,909	278,174	327,515	370,197	401,064	453,822	506,155	568,417	618,332	644,192	626,937	646,306
Interest Rates							*Percent Per Annum*						
Discount Rate (End of Period)	60	5.0	5.0	5.0	5.0	3.0	3.0	3.0	2.5	2.5	2.5	2.0	2.0
Money Market Rate	60b	12.5	12.6	12.4	13.2	15.0	5.0	5.2	4.7	4.2	4.0	3.6	3.3
Corporate Bond Rate	60bc	12.9	13.8	11.8	13.4	15.1	8.9	9.4	7.1	6.6	5.4	4.7	4.7
Deposit Rate	60l	8.5	8.8	7.5	† 10.8	13.3	7.9	7.9	5.8	4.9	4.3	3.9	3.7
Lending Rate	60p	8.5	9.0	8.8	† 11.9	15.3	9.4	8.5	7.7	6.8	6.2	5.9	5.6
Government Bond Yield	61	12.3	12.4	10.9	11.7	12.8	8.7	8.5	6.7	6.5	4.9	4.5	4.7
Prices, Production, Labor						*Index Numbers (2000=100): Period Averages*							
Share Prices	62	132.2	125.8	113.6	89.2	55.8	109.5	100.0	78.3	103.5	92.9	113.9	146.3
Producer Prices	63	79.5	83.2	85.9	89.2	100.1	98.0	100.0	99.5	99.2	101.4	107.6	109.9
Consumer Prices	64	78.8	82.3	86.4	90.2	97.0	97.8	100.0	104.1	106.9	110.7	114.7	117.8
Wages: Monthly Earnings	65ey	70.1	78.0	87.2	93.4	91.0	92.1	100.0	105.8	118.5	128.7	140.9	152.3
Industrial Production	66	58.0	64.9	70.4	73.7	69.0	85.6	100.0	100.7	108.8	114.6	126.3	134.1
Manufacturing Employment	67ey	110.8	112.2	110.1	105.7	91.2	93.8	100.0	99.4	98.8	97.9	99.9	98.6
						Number in Thousands: Period Averages							
Labor Force	67d	20,353	20,797	21,188	21,604	21,390	21,634	21,951	22,181	22,877	22,916	23,417	....
Employment	67e	19,837	20,432	20,817	21,106	19,994	20,281	21,156	21,572	22,169	22,139	22,557	....
Unemployment	67c	489	419	425	557	1,463	1,353	974	899	752	818	868	887
Unemployment Rate (%)	67r	2.4	2.0	2.0	2.6	6.8	6.3	4.4	4.0	3.3	3.6	3.7	3.7
Intl. Transactions & Positions							*Millions of US Dollars*						
Exports	70..d	96,013	125,058	129,715	136,164	132,313	143,685	172,268	150,439	162,471	193,817	253,845	284,419
Imports, c.i.f.	71..d	102,348	135,119	150,339	144,616	93,282	119,752	160,481	141,098	152,126	178,827	224,463	261,238
							2000=100						
Volume of Exports	72	37.7	46.1	54.1	62.1	74.0	82.9	100.0	100.7	114.1	133.4	163.4	178.3
Volume of Imports	73	59.4	73.7	85.2	86.9	65.1	84.0	100.0	97.7	109.7	117.7	131.8	140.1
Unit Value of Exports	74	107.0	110.3	99.9	107.6	126.4	104.7	100.0	99.2	91.9	89.7	92.7	83.9
Unit Value of Imports	75	78.2	79.7	79.7	88.1	108.3	91.8	100.0	103.9	96.8	100.7	108.7	106.2
Export Prices	76	91.6	92.9	89.0	94.8	124.5	101.0	100.0	96.2	89.5	87.5	92.9	86.7
Import Prices	76.x	70.7	74.8	75.3	82.4	105.7	92.9	100.0	103.5	97.1	98.9	108.9	112.0
Balance of Payments						*Millions of US Dollars: Minus Sign Indicates Debit*							
Current Account, n.i.e.	78ald	−4,024	−8,665	−23,210	−8,384	40,371	24,522	12,251	8,033	5,394	11,950	28,174	16,559
Goods: Exports f.o.b.	78aad	94,983	124,934	130,038	138,731	132,251	145,375	176,221	151,478	163,414	197,289	257,710	288,996
Goods: Imports f.o.b.	78abd	−98,000	−129,298	−145,115	−141,986	−90,586	−116,912	−159,267	−137,990	−148,637	−175,337	−220,141	−255,523
Trade Balance	78acd	−3,017	−4,365	−15,077	−3,256	41,665	28,463	16,954	13,488	14,777	21,952	37,569	33,473
Services: Credit	78add	16,805	22,827	23,412	26,301	25,565	26,529	30,534	29,055	28,388	32,957	41,882	45,375
Services: Debit	78aed	−18,606	−25,806	−29,592	−29,502	−24,541	−27,180	−33,381	−32,927	−36,585	−40,381	−49,928	−58,467
Balance on Goods & Services	78afd	−4,818	−7,343	−21,257	−6,456	42,689	27,812	14,106	9,616	6,580	14,528	29,523	20,381
Income: Credit	78agd	2,835	3,486	3,576	3,788	2,675	3,245	6,375	6,650	6,900	7,176	9,410	10,244
Income: Debit	78ahd	−3,322	−4,788	−5,480	−6,338	−8,313	−8,404	−8,797	−7,848	−6,467	−6,850	−8,328	−11,564
Balance on Gds, Serv. & Inc.	78aid	−5,305	−8,646	−23,161	−9,007	37,051	22,653	11,685	8,418	7,012	14,854	30,606	19,061
Current Transfers, n.i.e.: Credit	78ajd	3,672	4,104	4,279	5,288	6,737	6,421	6,500	6,687	7,314	7,859	9,151	10,124
Current Transfers: Debit	78akd	−2,392	−4,123	−4,328	−4,665	−3,416	−4,552	−5,934	−7,072	−8,932	−10,764	−11,583	−12,626
Capital Account, n.i.e.	78bcd	−437	−488	−598	−608	171	−389	−615	−731	−1,087	−1,398	−1,753	−2,313
Capital Account, n.i.e.: Credit	78bad	8	15	19	17	464	95	98	42	47	59	72	176
Capital Account: Debit	78bbd	−445	−502	−617	−624	−293	−484	−713	−773	−1,133	−1,457	−1,825	−2,489
Financial Account, n.i.e.	78bjd	10,732	17,273	24,009	−9,150	−8,381	12,709	12,725	3,025	7,338	15,308	9,352	2,804
Direct Investment Abroad	78bdd	−2,461	−3,552	−4,585	−4,404	−4,740	−4,198	−4,999	−2,420	−2,617	−3,426	−4,658	−4,312
Dir. Invest. in Rep. Econ., n.i.e.	78bed	809	1,776	2,325	2,844	5,412	9,333	9,283	3,528	2,392	3,526	9,246	4,339
Portfolio Investment Assets	78bfd	−2,481	−2,907	−6,413	1,076	−1,999	1,282	−520	−5,521	−5,032	−4,390	−9,918	−13,554
Equity Securities	78bkd	−382	−238	−653	−320	42	−271	−480	−492	−1,460	−1,993	−3,622	−3,471
Debt Securities	78bld	−2,098	−2,669	−5,760	1,395	−2,041	1,553	−40	−5,029	−3,571	−2,397	−6,297	−10,083
Portfolio Investment Liab., n.i.e.	78bgd	8,713	14,619	21,514	13,308	775	7,908	12,697	12,227	5,378	22,690	18,375	13,899
Equity Securities	78bmd	3,614	4,219	5,954	2,525	3,856	12,072	13,094	10,266	395	14,419	9,469	3,110
Debt Securities	78bnd	5,099	10,400	15,561	10,783	−3,081	−4,164	−397	1,962	4,983	8,272	8,906	10,789
Financial Derivatives Assets	78bwd	452	623	414	932	412	401	532	463	1,288	800	2,523	3,538
Financial Derivatives Liabilities	78bxd	−565	−744	−331	−1,021	−1,066	−915	−711	−586	−926	−1,194	−2,360	−5,202
Other Investment Assets	78bhd	−7,369	−13,991	−13,487	−13,568	6,693	−2,606	−2,289	7,085	1,591	−5,132	−8,138	−3,975
Monetary Authorities	78bod	−72	−36	—	−86	−36	−164	−44	−38	−40	−48	−55	−8
General Government	78bpd	−296	−156	−543	−149	−46	−169	−155	−509	−311	−27	−1,577	−253
Banks	78bqd	−5,061	−9,199	−8,173	−8,336	6,970	−203	−1,219	8,755	3,087	−3,174	−4,906	−585
Other Sectors	78brd	−1,940	−4,600	−4,770	−4,996	−194	−2,071	−871	−1,124	−1,145	−1,885	−1,601	−3,129
Other Investment Liab., n.i.e.	78bid	13,632	21,450	24,571	−8,317	−13,868	1,502	−1,268	−11,751	5,263	2,434	4,282	8,071
Monetary Authorities	78bsd	−2	−10	−29	23	25	148	28	63	−52	−35	−10	379
General Government	78btd	−335	−593	−493	4,671	4,628	3,309	110	−397	−1,436	−5,255	−2,549	−2,679
Banks	78bud	7,368	11,389	9,952	−9,785	−6,233	1,418	−4,538	−4,147	6,257	198	2,059	4,292
Other Sectors	78bvd	6,600	10,664	15,142	−3,226	−12,288	−3,372	3,132	−7,271	493	7,526	4,782	6,078
Net Errors and Omissions	78cad	−1,657	−1,081	1,214	−4,839	−6,231	−3,581	−571	2,951	124	−68	2,903	2,815
Overall Balance	78cbd	4,614	7,039	1,416	−22,979	25,930	33,260	23,790	13,278	11,769	25,791	38,675	19,864
Reserves and Related Items	79dad	−4,614	−7,039	−1,416	22,979	−25,930	−33,260	−23,790	−13,278	−11,769	−25,791	−38,675	−19,864
Reserve Assets	79dbd	−4,614	−7,039	−1,416	11,875	−30,968	−22,989	−23,790	−7,586	−11,769	−25,791	−38,675	−19,864
Use of Fund Credit and Loans	79dcd	—	—	—	11,104	5,038	−10,271	—	−5,692	—	—	—	—
Exceptional Financing	79ded	....	....	....	....	....	....	....	....	....	....	....	....

		1994	1995	1996	1997	1998	1999	2000	2001	2002	2003	2004	2005
International Investment Position							*Millions of US Dollars*						
Assets..................................	79aad	....	....	....	....	....	....	....	186,577	208,527	260,035	328,103	....
Direct Investment Abroad.............	79abd	....	....	....	....	....	....	....	19,967	20,735	24,986	32,166	....
Portfolio Investment.....................	79acd	....	....	....	....	....	....	....	7,813	11,492	17,343	28,368	....
Equity Securities.....................	79add	....	....	....	....	....	....	....	1,301	1,794	3,416	9,009	....
Debt Securities........................	79aed	....	....	....	....	....	....	....	6,513	9,698	13,927	19,359	....
Financial Derivatives..................	79ald	....	....	....	....	....	....	....	414	917	777	1,078	....
Other Investment.......................	79afd	....	....	....	....	....	....	....	55,561	53,970	61,574	67,422	....
Monetary Authorities...............	79agd	....	....	....	....	....	....	....	2,446	2,878	2,942	3,319	....
General Government..................	79ahd	....	....	....	....	....	....	....	973	1,111	1,210	2,723	....
Banks...................................	79aid	....	....	....	....	....	....	....	40,059	40,084	45,325	51,922	....
Other Sectors.........................	79ajd	....	....	....	....	....	....	....	12,083	9,898	12,097	9,458	....
Reserve Assets...........................	79akd	....	....	....	....	....	....	....	102,822	121,414	155,355	199,069	....
Liabilities..................................	79lad	....	....	....	....	....	....	....	249,964	279,463	344,175	418,360	....
Dir. Invest. in Rep. Economy..........	79lbd	....	....	....	....	....	....	....	53,208	62,658	66,070	87,766	....
Portfolio Investment.....................	79lcd	....	....	....	....	....	....	....	105,593	116,636	167,808	212,966	....
Equity Securities.....................	79ldd	....	....	....	....	....	....	....	69,968	77,017	120,071	156,463	....
Debt Securities........................	79led	....	....	....	....	....	....	....	35,624	39,619	47,738	56,503	....
Financial Derivatives..................	79lld	....	....	....	....	....	....	....	417	936	899	904	....
Other Investment.......................	79lfd	....	....	....	....	....	....	....	90,747	99,233	109,398	116,724	....
Monetary Authorities...............	79lgd	....	....	....	....	....	....	....	1,515	1,458	1,885	2,161	....
General Government..................	79lhd	....	....	....	....	....	....	....	17,891	16,662	10,300	8,152	....
Banks...................................	79lid	....	....	....	....	....	....	....	38,661	47,035	53,438	54,850	....
Other Sectors.........................	79ljd	....	....	....	....	....	....	....	32,680	34,078	43,775	51,560	....
Government Finance						*Billions of Won: Year Ending December 31*							
Deficit (-) or Surplus....................	80	984	1,035	431	−5,747	....	....	....	....	....	....	....	
Revenue.....................................	81	61,109	72,087	84,272	91,979	....	....	....	....	....	....	....	
Grants Received...........................	81z	—	—	—	—	....	....	....	....	....	....	....	
Expenditure................................	82	53,887	62,320	72,600	79,004	....	....	....	....	....	....	....	
Lending Minus Repayments...........	83	6,238	8,732	11,241	18,722	....	....	....	....	....	....	....	
Financing													
Domestic..................................	84a	−589	−678	−136	−1,214	....	....	....	....	....	....	....	
Foreign.....................................	85a	−395	−357	−295	6,961	....	....	....	....	....	....	....	
Debt...	88	30,466	31,537	33,687	47,045	....	....	....	....	....	....	....	
Domestic..................................	88a	24,800	26,296	28,636	31,724	....	....	....	....	....	....	....	
Foreign.....................................	89a	5,666	5,241	5,051	15,321	....	....	....	....	....	....	....	
National Accounts							*Billions of Won*						
Househ.Cons.Expend.,incl.NPISHs....	96f	177,904	208,462	236,194	258,636	238,811	274,934	312,301	343,417	381,063	389,177	401,469	424,630
Government Consumption Expend...	91f	38,942	44,687	52,138	56,749	61,981	65,174	70,098	80,298	88,512	96,203	105,517	113,773
Gross Fixed Capital Formation.........	93e	123,899	148,820	168,157	174,961	146,914	157,407	179,908	183,792	199,047	216,807	230,217	236,444
Changes in Inventories....................	93i	1,825	1,410	6,225	1,706	−25,903	−3,199	−494	−1,315	−41	292	6,430	6,212
Exports of Goods and Services..........	90c	90,624	114,978	124,988	159,091	223,481	206,842	236,210	235,187	241,209	274,995	342,866	342,800
Imports of Goods and Services (-).....	98c	93,149	119,336	140,574	162,056	161,180	171,437	217,979	220,914	231,765	257,728	309,647	322,567
Statistical Discrepancy....................	99bs	164	−183	1,468	2,049	−1	−221	−1,377	1,657	6,238	4,928	2,530	5,331
Gross Domestic Product (GDP)........	99b	340,208	398,838	448,596	491,135	484,103	529,500	578,665	622,123	684,263	724,675	779,381	806,622
Net Primary Income from Abroad.....	98.n	−865	−1,379	−1,740	−2,677	−7,857	−6,144	−2,505	−1,095	806	745	1,794	−736
Gross National Income (GNI)..........	99a	339,343	397,459	446,856	488,457	476,245	523,355	576,160	621,028	685,069	725,420	781,174	805,886
Consumption of Fixed Capital.........	99cf	36,221	48,131	56,784	66,147	74,349	79,006	83,416	88,113	91,113	98,851	105,618	110,729
GDP Volume 2000 Prices................	99b.p	427,868	467,099	499,790	523,035	487,184	533,399	578,665	600,866	642,748	662,655	693,996	721,491
GDP Volume (2000=100)................	99bvp	73.9	80.7	86.4	90.4	84.2	92.2	100.0	103.8	111.1	114.5	119.9	124.7
GDP Deflator (2000=100)...............	99bip	79.5	85.4	89.8	93.9	99.4	99.3	100.0	103.5	106.5	109.4	112.3	111.8
						Millions: Midyear Estimates							
Population...............................	99z	44.59	45.01	45.41	45.79	46.15	46.48	46.78	47.04	47.27	47.46	47.64	47.82

Kuwait   443

		1994	1995	1996	1997	1998	1999	2000	2001	2002	2003	2004	2005
Exchange Rates						*SDRs per Dinar: End of Period*							
Official Rate...............	ac	2.2824	2.2504	2.3190	2.4308	2.3551	2.3953	2.5130	2.5846	2.4554	2.2835	2.1850	2.3961
					US Dollars per Dinar: End of Period (ag) Period Average (rh)								
Official Rate...............	ag	3.3320	3.3453	3.3346	3.2798	3.3161	3.2875	3.2742	3.2481	3.3382	3.3933	3.3933	3.4247
Official Rate...............	rh	3.3600	3.3509	3.3399	3.2966	3.2814	3.2850	3.2600	3.2607	3.2906	3.3557	3.3933	3.4247
Fund Position						*Millions of SDRs: End of Period*							
Quota............................	2f.s	995.2	995.2	995.2	995.2	995.2	1,381.1	1,381.1	1,381.1	1,381.1	1,381.1	1,381.1	1,381.1
SDRs..............................	1b.s	55.0	61.3	68.2	74.1	82.5	53.7	69.8	85.9	97.7	107.5	117.1	128.7
Reserve Position in the Fund...........	1c.s	142.6	139.0	136.5	167.5	244.8	368.3	373.8	476.1	528.3	522.7	458.9	208.8
of which: Outstg.Fund Borrowing...	2c	—	—	—	—	31.8	—	—	—	—	—	—	—
International Liquidity					*Millions of US Dollars Unless Otherwise Indicated: End of Period*								
Total Reserves minus Gold...............	1l.d	3,500.7	3,560.8	3,515.1	3,451.8	3,947.1	4,823.7	7,082.4	9,897.3	9,208.1	7,577.0	8,241.9	8,862.8
SDRs..............................	1b.d	80.3	91.1	98.0	100.0	116.2	73.8	90.9	108.0	132.9	159.8	181.8	183.9
Reserve Position in the Fund..........	1c.d	208.2	206.6	196.3	226.1	344.6	505.5	487.0	598.3	718.2	776.8	712.7	298.5
Foreign Exchange..................	1d.d	3,212.2	3,263.2	3,220.8	3,125.7	3,486.3	4,244.4	6,504.4	9,191.1	8,357.0	6,640.5	7,347.4	8,380.4
Gold (Million Fine Troy Ounces)........	1ad	2.539	2.539	2.539	2.539	2.539	2.539	2.539	2.539	2.539	2.539	2.539	2.539
Gold (National Valuation)...............	1and	105.6	106.0	105.7	104.0	105.1	104.2	103.9	103.1	105.9	107.7	107.7	108.7
Deposit Money Banks: Assets...........	7a.d	6,419.1	7,127.7	7,230.3	6,945.2	5,928.5	5,873.8	6,444.9	6,582.6	8,148.5	8,229.9	10,831.5	12,993.4
Liabilities...............	7b.d	2,377.0	2,239.0	2,536.6	4,009.2	3,595.3	3,971.0	3,913.3	5,101.3	6,782.3	6,531.6	6,183.4	7,741.2
Other Financial Insts.: Assets...........	7e.d	3,706.5	3,666.7	3,556.0	4,339.1	5,498.4	6,013.2	7,184.2	6,795.5	7,001.5	8,235.1	8,901.0	9,845.0
Liab.....................	7f.d	1,533.7	1,584.6	1,592.9	2,330.6	3,504.4	3,693.2	4,582.2	4,628.6	4,637.1	5,182.7	5,354.1	5,331.6
Monetary Authorities						*Millions of Dinars: End of Period*							
Foreign Assets.......................	11	1,168.2	1,124.1	1,112.0	1,108.7	1,186.3	1,476.1	2,157.3	3,037.7	2,748.0	2,216.5	2,405.8	2,564.8
Claims on Central Government........	12a	59.2	2.3	41.2	39.3	.1	45.1	—	—	—	—	—	14.5
Claims on Deposit Money Banks......	12e	90.8	—	—	6.0	—	—	14.0	—	—	—	—	—
Reserve Money.......................	14	504.0	470.9	474.7	426.9	448.4	582.9	534.6	521.4	590.2	690.1	782.3	800.0
of which: Currency Outside DMBs..	14a	351.3	311.5	350.1	345.3	348.7	442.9	416.6	401.2	442.2	494.1	531.0	578.7
Other Liabilities to DMBs............	14n	—	68.0	20.0	40.0	75.0	21.5	654.5	1,399.3	1,193.0	348.0	125.0	440.4
Liabs. of Central Bank: Securities.....	16ac	—	—	—	—	—	—	—	—	—	—	—	124.0
Central Government Deposits..........	16d	368.8	163.9	265.7	298.7	229.0	450.8	547.8	602.3	381.9	440.7	681.2	557.9
Capital Accounts......................	17a	209.7	193.7	188.5	189.6	186.1	186.5	188.0	187.5	195.9	218.5	234.9	325.6
Other Items (Net).....................	17r	236.1	230.0	204.2	198.9	247.9	279.5	246.4	327.2	387.0	519.2	582.4	331.4
Deposit Money Banks						*Millions of Dinars: End of Period*							
Reserves........................	20	151.8	158.1	123.0	79.0	98.0	141.2	119.3	119.5	143.7	199.4	251.2	217.6
Claims on Mon.Auth.:Securities.......	20c	—	—	—	—	—	—	—	—	—	—	—	124.0
Other Claims on Monetary Author....	20n	—	68.0	20.0	40.0	75.0	21.5	654.5	1,399.3	1,193.0	348.0	125.0	440.4
Foreign Assets.......................	21	1,926.5	2,130.7	2,168.3	2,117.6	1,787.8	1,786.7	1,968.4	2,026.6	2,441.0	2,425.3	3,192.0	3,794.1
Claims on Central Government........	22a	5,881.7	5,760.3	4,901.3	4,782.8	4,641.5	4,619.6	4,246.8	4,127.4	4,118.2	4,009.7	3,768.7	3,572.5
Claims on Private Sector...............	22d	1,703.2	2,436.3	3,173.1	4,324.2	4,801.6	5,015.1	5,251.7	6,125.3	6,953.4	8,419.4	9,867.0	11,827.3
Demand Deposits....................	24	774.7	873.5	892.5	902.2	794.7	928.5	1,051.1	1,240.2	1,624.6	2,117.4	2,643.3	3,148.7
Time and Savings Deposits............	25	5,616.9	6,189.8	6,088.3	6,368.5	6,413.1	6,306.6	6,695.5	7,567.1	7,579.6	7,789.7	8,481.0	9,358.8
Foreign Liabilities.....................	26c	713.4	669.3	760.7	1,222.4	1,084.2	1,207.9	1,195.2	1,570.5	2,031.7	1,924.9	1,822.2	2,260.4
Central Government Deposits..........	26d	421.3	459.4	374.1	343.6	256.8	195.0	185.1	230.9	299.4	315.2	842.0	995.8
Credit from Monetary Authorities.....	26g	112.0	6.0	—	6.0	.7	—	14.0	—	—	—	—	—
Capital Accounts......................	27a	1,090.1	1,201.5	1,259.0	1,407.8	1,469.9	1,511.9	1,776.3	1,681.9	1,763.4	2,008.7	2,311.3	2,741.8
Other Items (Net).....................	27r	935.0	1,154.1	1,011.2	1,093.1	1,384.5	1,433.9	1,323.5	1,507.4	1,550.5	1,246.0	1,104.2	1,470.4
Monetary Survey						*Millions of Dinars: End of Period*							
Foreign Assets (Net)...................	31n	2,381.3	2,585.5	2,519.6	2,003.9	1,889.9	2,054.9	2,930.5	3,493.8	3,157.2	2,717.0	3,775.6	4,098.4
Domestic Credit.......................	32	6,854.0	7,575.6	7,475.8	8,504.0	8,957.4	9,034.0	8,765.6	9,419.5	10,390.3	11,673.3	12,112.5	13,860.6
Claims on Central Govt. (Net)........	32an	5,150.8	5,139.3	4,302.7	4,179.8	4,155.8	4,018.9	3,513.9	3,294.2	3,437.0	3,253.9	2,245.5	2,033.3
Claims on Private Sector...............	32d	1,703.2	2,436.3	3,173.1	4,324.2	4,801.6	5,015.1	5,251.7	6,125.3	6,953.4	8,419.4	9,867.0	11,827.3
Money..............................	34	1,126.0	1,185.0	1,242.6	1,247.5	1,143.4	1,371.4	1,467.7	1,641.4	2,066.7	2,611.5	3,174.2	3,727.4
Quasi-Money.........................	35	5,616.9	6,189.8	6,088.3	6,368.5	6,413.1	6,306.6	6,695.5	7,567.1	7,579.6	7,789.7	8,481.0	9,358.8
Other Items (Net).....................	37r	2,493.0	2,786.6	2,664.5	2,892.0	3,290.8	3,410.6	3,532.9	3,704.8	3,901.2	3,989.0	4,232.9	4,996.9
Money plus Quasi-Money..................	35l	6,742.9	7,374.8	7,330.9	7,616.0	7,556.5	7,678.0	8,163.2	9,208.5	9,646.3	10,401.2	11,655.2	13,086.2
Other Financial Institutions						*Millions of Dinars: End of Period*							
Cash..................................	40	120.5	95.7	125.8	153.9	258.7	207.8	154.1	167.7	133.6	135.9	172.5	269.5
Foreign Assets.......................	41	1,112.4	1,096.1	1,066.4	1,323.0	1,658.1	1,829.1	2,194.2	2,092.1	2,097.4	2,426.9	2,623.1	2,874.7
Claims on Private Sector...............	42d	596.6	632.9	707.6	904.0	1,244.9	931.7	766.0	852.1	970.3	1,514.4	1,892.1	3,057.0
Foreign Liabilities.....................	46c	460.3	473.7	477.7	710.6	1,056.8	1,123.4	1,399.5	1,425.0	1,389.1	1,527.3	1,577.8	1,556.8
Central Government Deposits..........	46d	119.9	101.1	142.7	94.5	84.8	7.5	7.0	7.5	.3	63.8	73.1	74.0
Credit from Deposit Money Banks.....	46h	134.7	185.5	158.5	206.9	296.1	207.7	239.8	392.6	416.9	572.0	556.8	634.3
Capital Accounts......................	47a	686.0	769.1	861.6	1,018.3	1,325.5	1,255.0	1,294.7	1,005.4	1,029.5	1,285.1	1,476.1	2,240.8
Other Items (Net).....................	47r	428.5	295.3	259.4	350.8	398.6	374.9	173.8	281.4	365.5	629.0	1,003.9	1,695.3
Interest Rates						*Percent Per Annum*							
Discount Rate (End of Period)........	60	7.00	7.25	7.25	7.50	7.00	6.75	7.25	4.25	3.25	3.25	4.75	6.00
Money Market Rate......................	60b	6.31	7.43	6.98	7.05	7.24	6.32	6.82	4.62	2.99	2.47	2.14	2.83
Treasury Bill Rate.....................	60c	6.32	7.35	6.93	6.98	....	....	....	....	....	....	....	....
Deposit Rate.........................	60l	5.70	6.53	6.05	5.93	6.32	5.76	5.89	4.47	3.15	2.42	2.65	3.47
Lending Rate.........................	60p	7.61	8.37	8.77	8.80	8.21	8.93	8.56	8.87	7.88	6.48	5.42	7.50
Prices, Production, Labor						*Index Numbers (2000=100): Period Averages*							
Wholesale Prices......................	63	97.4	98.7	103.8	102.5	100.8	99.6	100.0	102.0	105.3	107.4	107.8	112.6
Consumer Prices......................	64	88.4	90.7	94.0	94.6	94.7	97.5	† 100.0	101.3	102.2	103.2	104.5	108.8
Crude Petroleum Production............	66aa	112.3	112.7	114.2	115.2	115.3	104.5	100.0	93.4	88.3	88.5	111.4	126.0
						Number in Thousands: Period Averages							
Labor Force...........................	67d	....	748	1,140	1,217	....	....	....	....	....	....	....	....
Intl. Transactions & Positions						*Millions of Dinars*							
Exports...............................	70	3,342.3	3,814.5	4,458.0	4,314.3	2,911.6	3,702.8	5,962.7	4,969.7	4,666.2	6,162.1	8,428.1	13,101.6
Oil Exports..........................	70a	3,112.7	3,597.1	4,231.3	4,085.4	2,581.8	3,356.4	5,578.3	4,590.8	4,272.8	5,663.5	7,861.1	12,392.6
Imports, c.i.f.........................	71	1,988.2	2,323.1	2,507.2	2,501.6	2,626.2	2,318.3	2,195.4	2,413.3	2,735.8	3,274.1	3,722.2	5,106.4

Kuwait 443

		1994	1995	1996	1997	1998	1999	2000	2001	2002	2003	2004	2005
Balance of Payments		*Millions of US Dollars: Minus Sign Indicates Debit*											
Current Account, n.i.e.	78ald	3,243	5,016	7,107	7,935	2,215	5,010	14,672	8,324	4,251	9,416	18,884	....
Goods: Exports f.o.b.	78aad	11,284	12,833	14,946	14,281	9,618	12,223	19,478	16,238	15,366	21,794	30,221	....
Goods: Imports f.o.b.	78abd	−6,600	−7,254	−7,949	−7,747	−7,714	−6,708	−6,451	−7,046	−8,124	−9,882	−10,920	....
Trade Balance	78acd	4,685	5,579	6,997	6,534	1,903	5,516	13,027	9,192	7,242	11,912	19,301	....
Services: Credit	78add	1,415	1,401	1,520	1,760	1,762	1,560	1,822	1,663	1,648	3,144	3,322	....
Services: Debit	78aed	−4,531	−5,381	−5,100	−5,129	−5,542	−5,171	−4,920	−5,354	−5,837	−6,617	−7,591	....
Balance on Goods & Services	78afd	1,569	1,598	3,417	3,165	−1,877	1,905	9,929	5,500	3,053	8,439	15,032	....
Income: Credit	78agd	4,174	6,125	6,409	7,744	7,163	6,094	7,315	5,426	3,708	3,725	6,844	....
Income: Debit	78ahd	−1,004	−1,243	−1,229	−1,467	−1,296	−985	−616	−525	−365	−369	−445	....
Balance on Gds, Serv. & Inc.	78aid	4,739	6,480	8,597	9,441	3,990	7,013	16,628	10,401	6,397	11,795	21,432	....
Current Transfers, n.i.e.: Credit	78ajd	94	54	53	79	98	99	85	52	49	67	88	....
Current Transfers: Debit	78akd	−1,590	−1,518	−1,543	−1,586	−1,874	−2,102	−2,041	−2,129	−2,195	−2,446	−2,637	....
Capital Account, n.i.e.	78bcd	−205	−194	−204	−96	79	703	2,217	2,931	1,672	1,429	434	....
Capital Account, n.i.e.: Credit	78bad	—	—	3	115	289	716	2,236	2,951	1,708	1,463	475	....
Capital Account: Debit	78bbd	−205	−194	−207	−211	−210	−13	−20	−20	−36	−34	−41	....
Financial Account, n.i.e.	78bjd	3,304	157	−7,632	−6,211	−2,920	−5,706	−13,773	−6,313	−5,163	−11,942	−19,820	....
Direct Investment Abroad	78bdd	1,519	1,022	−1,740	969	1,867	−23	303	−365	155	4,983	−1,873	....
Dir. Invest. in Rep. Econ., n.i.e.	78bed	—	7	347	20	59	72	16	−147	7	−67	−20	....
Portfolio Investment Assets	78bfd	394	−2,064	−788	−6,926	−4,768	−2,638	−12,923	−7,366	−3,425	−13,580	−14,001	....
Equity Securities	78bkd	—	—	—	—	—	—	—	—	—	—	—	....
Debt Securities	78bld	394	−2,064	−788	−6,926	−4,768	−2,638	−12,923	−7,366	−3,425	−13,580	−14,001	....
Portfolio Investment Liab., n.i.e.	78bgd	—	−50	27	—	—	79	254	−78	161	336	288	....
Equity Securities	78bmd	—	—	—	—	—	—	—	—	—	—	—	....
Debt Securities	78bnd	—	−50	27	—	—	79	254	−78	161	336	288	....
Financial Derivatives Assets	78bwd	—	—	—	—	—	—	—	—	—	—	—	....
Financial Derivatives Liabilities	78bxd	—	—	—	—	—	—	—	—	—	—	—	....
Other Investment Assets	78bhd	529	−221	−745	3,356	646	−3,512	−1,108	505	−3,754	−3,329	−3,936	....
Monetary Authorities	78bod	—	—	—	—	—	—	—	—	—	—	—	....
General Government	78bpd	825	724	−1,122	2,993	−10	−3,288	−284	900	−3,879	−3,319	−1,863	....
Banks	78bqd	−401	−734	−23	260	929	−161	−1,004	241	−599	81	−2,148	....
Other Sectors	78brd	104	−211	401	102	−272	−62	179	−636	724	−91	75	....
Other Investment Liab., n.i.e.	78bid	862	1,464	−4,733	−3,629	−725	315	−316	1,138	1,695	−285	−278	....
Monetary Authorities	78bsd	−3	−54	−17	3	−10	—	7	—	26	30	31	....
General Government	78btd	525	1,541	−5,371	−6,290	−1,316	−115	−838	−33	401	−181	−27	....
Banks	78bud	589	−97	304	1,523	−456	302	−297	1,301	1,356	−550	−387	....
Other Sectors	78bvd	−249	74	351	1,134	1,057	128	812	−130	−89	416	105	....
Net Errors and Omissions	78cad	−6,292	−5,120	704	−1,623	885	912	−847	−2,038	−1,733	−727	1,128	....
Overall Balance	78cbd	50	−141	−25	6	258	918	2,268	2,905	−973	−1,824	626	....
Reserves and Related Items	79dad	−50	141	25	−6	−258	−918	−2,268	−2,905	973	1,824	−626	....
Reserve Assets	79dbd	−50	141	25	−6	−258	−918	−2,268	−2,905	973	1,824	−626	....
Use of Fund Credit and Loans	79dcd	—	—	—	—	—	—	—	—	—	—	—	....
Exceptional Financing	79ded	—	—	—	—	—	—	—	—	—	—	—	....
Government Finance		*Millions of Dinars: Year Ending December 31*											
Deficit (-) or Surplus	80	−984	−623	1,020	1,050	−1,336	296	3,055	1,854	1,534	2,522	3,542	8,052
Total Revenue and Grants	81y	2,787	3,076	4,198	4,179	2,858	3,710	6,434	5,632	5,632	6,801	8,402	12,858
Revenue	81	2,787	3,076	4,198	4,179	2,858	3,710	6,434	5,632	5,632	6,801	8,402	12,347
Grants	81z	—	—	—	—	—	—	—	—	—	—	—	511
Exp. & Lending Minus Repay.	82z	3,770	3,699	3,178	3,129	4,195	3,414	3,378	3,778	4,098	4,279	4,860	4,806
Expenditure	82	3,770	3,699	3,178	3,129	4,195	3,414	3,378	3,778	4,098	4,279	4,860	4,806
Lending Minus Repayments	83	—	—	—	—	—	—	—	—	—	—	—	—
National Accounts		*Millions of Dinars*											
Househ.Cons.Expend.,incl.NPISHs.	96f	3,029	3,461	4,199	4,279	4,608	4,776	4,913	5,320	5,747	5,960	6,205	....
Government Consumption Expend.	91f	2,503	2,612	2,570	2,451	2,412	2,463	2,485	2,529	2,929	3,281	3,455	....
Gross Capital Formation	93	1,192	1,197	1,424	1,256	1,459	1,335	868	910	1,980	2,012	2,331	....
Gross Fixed Capital Formation	93e	982	1,100	1,318	1,240	1,448	1,300	846	910	1,980	2,012	2,331	....
Changes in Inventories	93i	210	97	106	15	11	35	21	....	....	....	....	....
Exports of Goods and Services	90c	3,753	4,248	4,930	4,866	3,468	4,212	6,534	5,490	5,171	7,432	9,885	....
Imports of Goods and Services (-)	98c	3,098	3,405	3,695	3,645	4,040	3,616	3,488	3,803	4,243	4,917	5,455	....
Gross Domestic Product (GDP)	99b	7,380	8,114	9,429	9,207	7,906	9,170	11,312	10,446	11,585	13,768	16,420	....
Net Primary Income from Abroad	98.n	941	1,457	1,551	1,904	1,788	1,555	2,055	1,503	1,016	1,000	1,886	....
Gross National Income (GNI)	99a	8,321	9,571	10,980	11,111	9,694	10,725	13,367	11,949	12,601	14,768	18,306	....
Consumption of Fixed Capital	99cf	639	711	671	701	768	614	399	419	1,051	1,069	1,238	....
GDP Volume 1984 Prices	99b.p	9,453	9,583	....	....	....	....	....	....	....	....	....	....
GDP Volume 1995 Prices	99b.p	....	8,114	8,162	8,366	8,672	8,517	8,916	8,981	9,440	10,704	11,367	....
GDP Volume (2000=100)	99bvp	89.8	† 91.0	91.5	93.8	97.3	95.5	100.0	100.7	105.9	120.1	127.5	....
GDP Deflator (2000=100)	99bip	72.7	78.8	91.0	86.7	71.9	84.9	100.0	91.7	96.7	101.4	113.9	....
		Millions: Midyear Estimates											
Population	99z	1.74	1.70	1.73	1.82	1.95	2.10	2.23	† 2.34	2.44	2.52	2.61	2.69

Kyrgyz Republic   917

		1994	1995	1996	1997	1998	1999	2000	2001	2002	2003	2004	2005
Exchange Rates						*Soms per SDR: End of Period*								
Official Rate....................	aa	15.547	16.649	24.014	23.443	41.362	62.352	62.936	59.969	62.667	65.665	64.643	59.030
						Soms per US Dollar: End of Period (ae) Period Average (rf)								
Official Rate....................	ae	10.650	11.200	16.700	17.375	29.376	45.429	48.304	47.719	46.095	44.190	41.625	41.301
Official Rate....................	rf	10.842	10.822	12.810	17.362	20.838	39.008	47.704	48.378	46.937	43.648	42.650	41.012
Fund Position						*Millions of SDRs: End of Period*								
Quota..........................	2f.s	64.5	64.5	64.5	64.5	64.5	88.8	88.8	88.8	88.8	88.8	88.8	88.8
SDRs...........................	1b.s	.7	9.6	5.1	.7	.2	3.7	.5	1.1	.5	6.9	12.8	3.7
Reserve Position in the Fund..........	1c.s	—	—	—	—	—	—	—	—	—	—	—	—
Total Fund Cred.&Loans Outstg.......	2tl	53.3	83.6	97.1	122.2	124.4	138.7	144.3	142.7	136.3	135.9	133.2	124.5
International Liquidity						*Millions of US Dollars Unless Otherwise Indicated: End of Period*								
Total Reserves minus Gold..............	1l.d	26.2	81.0	94.6	170.2	163.8	229.7	239.0	263.5	288.8	364.6	528.2	569.7
SDRs.........................	1b.d	1.0	14.3	7.4	.9	.3	5.1	.7	1.3	.6	10.3	19.9	5.3
Reserve Position in the Fund........	1c.d	—	—	—	—	—	—	—	—	—	—	—	—
Foreign Exchange...............	1d.d	25.2	66.7	87.2	169.3	163.4	224.6	238.3	262.2	288.2	354.3	508.3	564.5
Gold (Million Fine Troy Ounces)........	1ad	....	.1362	.1235	.0830	.0831	.0831	.0831	.0831	.0831	.0831	.0831	.0831
Gold (National Valuation)...............	1and	....	43.22	28.13	29.08	23.88	24.17	22.80	22.97	28.48	34.67	36.39	42.63
Monetary Authorities: Other Liab.....	4..d	....	73.5	65.8	59.2	39.7	44.1	55.5	57.4	58.1	57.5	58.1	58.8
Banking Institutions: Assets.............	7a.d	....	19.6	13.1	34.3	17.1	15.8	18.0	32.8	72.6	124.0	193.5	223.0
Liabilities........	7b.d	....	2.8	1.8	13.1	8.3	1.8	3.0	3.4	36.4	71.9	101.4	176.2
Monetary Authorities						*Millions of Soms: End of Period*								
Foreign Assets....................	11	....	1,393	2,035	3,368	5,517	11,338	12,687	13,632	14,620	17,197	23,540	25,305
Claims on General Government........	12a	....	2,049	3,911	4,473	4,940	5,787	6,144	6,186	7,090	6,752	6,672	6,554
Claims on Banking Institutions.........	12e	....	1,153	124	92	333	543	609	506	490	421	412	348
Reserve Money....................	14	....	2,044	2,533	3,069	3,303	4,317	4,821	5,375	7,670	10,171	12,392	15,482
of which: Currency Outside Banks..	14a	....	1,938	2,416	2,678	2,829	3,578	4,102	5,016	6,866	9,302	11,109	13,065
Other Liabilities to DMBs................	14n	....	—	—	200	36	243	189	—	—	147	—	50
Foreign Liabilities..................	16c	....	2,216	3,430	3,893	6,314	10,652	11,763	11,296	11,218	11,461	11,034	9,776
General Government Deposits.........	16d	....	15	147	253	250	1,152	1,059	2,035	1,980	1,585	6,150	5,359
Capital Accounts....................	17a	....	136	243	506	949	1,118	989	1,096	1,518	1,105	1,227	1,463
Other Items (Net)....................	17r	....	171	−311	−40	−133	98	493	323	−378	−350	−439	−267
Banking Institutions						*Millions of Soms: End of Period*								
Reserves..........................	20	....	113	110	381	449	739	700	343	792	773	1,270	2,400
Other Claims on Monetary Author.....	20n	....	—	—	162	107	172	172	3	8	180	49	50
Foreign Assets....................	21	....	219	219	596	503	719	870	1,563	3,344	5,478	8,055	9,212
Claims on General Government........	22a	....	83	93	323	378	150	202	487	597	746	938	1,141
Claims on Rest of the Economy........	22d	....	2,024	2,026	1,047	1,804	2,448	2,679	2,780	3,098	3,963	6,633	8,007
Demand Deposits....................	24	....	545	478	442	379	624	504	542	811	1,314	1,935	2,123
Time & Foreign Currency Deposits.....	25	....	295	295	1,095	1,745	2,418	2,791	2,676	3,346	4,085	6,372	6,170
Foreign Liabilities..................	26c	....	31	31	228	245	84	143	164	1,680	3,179	4,222	7,276
General Government Deposits.........	26d	....	—	—	30	45	64	49	71	107	188	225	920
Credit from Monetary Authorities.....	26g	....	1,188	1,188	118	318	605	619	597	575	543	572	461
Capital Accounts....................	27a	....	120	149	735	980	1,125	1,229	1,802	2,134	2,365	2,963	3,905
Other Items (Net)....................	27r	....	261	307	−138	−471	−694	−712	−676	−813	−535	656	−45
Banking Survey						*Millions of Soms: End of Period*								
Foreign Assets (Net)................	31n	....	−635	−1,207	−157	−539	1,321	1,651	3,736	5,067	8,034	16,340	17,465
Domestic Credit....................	32	....	4,142	5,882	5,579	6,852	7,208	7,957	7,396	8,750	9,738	7,910	9,464
Claims on General Govt. (Net).......	32an	....	2,117	3,856	4,513	5,023	4,721	5,238	4,567	5,601	5,726	1,234	1,417
Claims on Rest of the Economy.....	32d	....	2,024	2,026	1,066	1,828	2,487	2,720	2,829	3,149	4,012	6,677	8,047
Money............................	34	....	2,482	2,893	3,119	3,208	4,203	4,606	5,558	7,677	10,616	13,045	15,188
Quasi-Money........................	35	....	295	295	1,095	1,745	2,418	2,791	2,676	3,346	4,085	6,372	6,170
Capital Accounts....................	37a	....	256	392	1,242	1,929	2,243	2,218	2,898	3,651	3,470	4,190	5,368
Other Items (Net)....................	37r	....	461	1,069	−85	−641	−423	−131	−200	−1,051	−650	384	−142
Money plus Quasi-Money................	35l	....	2,777	3,188	4,214	4,953	6,621	7,397	8,234	11,024	14,701	19,416	21,359
Interest Rates						*Percent per Annum*								
Lombard Rate........................	60.a	94.1	64.1	43.1	43.2	54.0	51.6	32.8	10.7	6.8	4.0	4.6	4.3
Money Market Rate....................	60b	....	....	....	....	44.0	43.7	24.3	11.9	....	....	....	3.2
Treasury Bill Rate....................	60c	143.1	34.9	40.1	35.8	43.7	47.2	32.3	19.1	10.2	7.2	4.9	4.4
Deposit Rate........................	60l	....	....	36.7	39.6	35.8	35.6	18.4	12.5	5.9	5.0	6.7	5.8
Lending Rate........................	60p	....	....	65.0	49.4	73.4	60.9	51.9	37.3	24.8	19.1	29.3	26.6
Prices and Labor						*Index Numbers (2000=100): Period Averages*								
Producer Prices.....................	63	24.1	29.4	36.2	45.7	49.3	† 77.1	100.0	109.1	114.9	121.4	132.1	136.2
Consumer Prices.....................	64	....	34.2	45.1	55.7	61.5	† 84.2	100.0	106.9	109.2	112.4	117.1	122.2
Wages: Average Earnings...............	65	19.8	31.2	41.7	57.6	71.2	82.1	100.0	118.2	136.9	161.6	186.6	217.4
Employment						*Number in Thousands: Period Averages*								
Employment.........................	67e	....	....	671	626	595	576	557	537	518	506	499	....
Unemployment.......................	67c	....	50	75	62	63	56	59	61	60	59	58	62
Unemployment Rate...................	67r	.8	3.0	4.5	3.1	3.2	3.0	3.1	3.2	....	....	....	....
Intl. Transactions & Positions						*Millions of US Dollars*								
Exports...........................	70..d	340.0	408.9	505.4	603.8	513.6	453.8	504.5	476.1	485.5	581.7	718.8	672.0
Imports, c.i.f......................	71..d	315.9	522.3	837.7	709.3	841.5	599.7	554.1	467.2	586.7	717.0	941.0	1,102.2

Kyrgyz Republic 917

		1994	1995	1996	1997	1998	1999	2000	2001	2002	2003	2004	2005
Balance of Payments		*Millions of US Dollars: Minus Sign Indicates Debit*											
Current Account, n.i.e.	78ald	−84.0	−234.7	−424.8	−138.5	−412.5	−252.2	−124.3	−56.7	−80.0	−99.0	−100.7	....
Goods: Exports f.o.b.	78aad	340.0	408.9	531.2	630.8	535.1	462.6	510.9	480.3	498.1	590.3	733.2	....
Goods: Imports f.o.b.	78abd	−426.1	−531.0	−782.9	−646.1	−755.7	−551.1	−506.9	−449.5	−572.1	−723.8	−904.5	....
Trade Balance	78acd	−86.1	−122.0	−251.7	−15.3	−220.7	−88.6	4.0	30.8	−74.0	−133.5	−171.3	....
Services: Credit	78add	32.7	39.2	31.5	45.0	62.8	64.9	61.8	80.3	142.0	154.7	208.9	....
Services: Debit	78aed	−71.1	−195.1	−249.0	−171.2	−175.7	−154.6	−148.8	−126.1	−148.4	−151.2	−231.0	....
Balance on Goods & Services	78afd	−124.6	−278.0	−469.2	−141.4	−333.5	−178.2	−82.9	−15.0	−80.5	−130.0	−193.4	....
Income: Credit	78agd	....	3.7	4.4	6.8	12.6	10.9	17.0	11.8	6.3	5.2	11.2	....
Income: Debit	78ahd	−22.0	−39.2	−43.9	−71.4	−91.7	−84.9	−98.9	−71.8	−63.7	−67.6	−101.4	....
Balance on Gds, Serv. & Inc.	78aid	−146.6	−313.4	−508.7	−206.1	−412.6	−252.2	−164.9	−75.0	−137.8	−192.3	−283.6	....
Current Transfers, n.i.e.: Credit.	78ajd	63.4	80.4	85.9	69.8	2.2	1.1	42.9	22.8	60.7	100.4	200.6	....
Current Transfers: Debit	78akd	−.8	−1.7	−1.9	−2.2	−2.0	−1.2	−2.4	−4.5	−2.9	−7.0	−17.6	....
Capital Account, n.i.e.	78bcd	−62.4	−29.0	−15.9	−8.4	−8.1	−15.2	−11.4	−32.0	−7.9	−.9	−19.9	....
Capital Account, n.i.e.: Credit	78bad	.3	2.2	9.0	6.2	26.4	24.0	22.8	9.2	35.1	36.0	33.7	....
Capital Account: Debit	78bbd	−62.7	−31.3	−25.0	−14.6	−34.5	−39.2	−34.2	−41.2	−43.0	−36.9	−53.6	....
Financial Account, n.i.e.	78bjd	85.7	260.1	362.5	250.4	299.8	244.2	99.8	54.5	108.7	24.9	185.7	....
Direct Investment Abroad	78bdd	....	....	....	....	−22.6	−6.1	−4.5	−6.1	—	—	−43.9	....
Dir. Invest. in Rep. Econ., n.i.e.	78bed	38.2	96.1	47.2	83.8	109.2	44.4	−2.4	5.0	4.7	45.5	175.4	....
Portfolio Investment Assets	78bfd	....	−.1	.1	.6	−.2	—	−1.6	1.2	−2.5	1.1	−2.5	....
Equity Securities	78bkd	....	....	....	....	—	—	—	—	—	—	—	....
Debt Securities	78bld	....	−.1	.1	.6	−.2	—	−1.6	1.2	−2.5	1.1	−2.5	....
Portfolio Investment Liab., n.i.e.	78bgd	....	1.8	−1.8	5.0	−4.1	−.1	.3	—	−9.5	5.0	—	....
Equity Securities	78bmd	....	....	....	....	—	—	—	—	—	—	—	....
Debt Securities	78bnd	....	1.8	−1.8	5.0	−4.1	−.1	.3	—	−9.5	5.0	—	....
Financial Derivatives Assets	78bwd	....	....	....	19.0	30.6	26.4	25.8	17.6	−5.1	−20.0	−20.5	....
Financial Derivatives Liabilities	78bxd	....	....	....	....	....	....	....	....	....	....		....
Other Investment Assets	78bhd	−43.2	11.9	1.9	−43.1	−84.1	−.7	−27.3	−4.0	21.5	−78.7	−29.6	....
Monetary Authorities	78bod	....	−1.0	....	−3.0	−2.0	—	8.6	—	23.9	−2.1	—	....
General Government	78bpd	−1.7	−2.1	13.3	—	−.3	−.3	−.1	−.1	—	−.2	—	....
Banks	78bqd	1.3	−1.2	1.6	−18.7	9.6	−1.4	−1.6	−16.5	−42.3	−50.2	−49.4	....
Other Sectors	78brd	−42.9	16.2	−13.0	−21.5	−91.4	.9	−34.3	12.6	39.9	−26.3	19.8	....
Other Investment Liab., n.i.e.	78bid	90.8	150.4	315.1	185.1	271.1	180.3	109.5	40.8	99.6	72.1	106.8	....
Monetary Authorities	78bsd	−35.4	.5	.2	—	−.1	—	—	—	—	—	—	....
General Government	78btd	110.9	102.0	104.7	137.2	137.8	199.2	121.4	82.4	66.9	73.4	93.6	....
Banks	78bud	3.6	−3.3	−2.1	14.0	1.0	−2.8	−.3	3.9	32.7	36.6	25.8	....
Other Sectors	78bvd	11.7	51.2	212.2	33.9	132.4	−16.1	−11.5	−45.6	—	−38.0	−12.5	....
Net Errors and Omissions	78cad	65.7	−77.1	58.4	−57.4	63.5	−2.9	3.1	21.3	−.3	121.7	79.5	....
Overall Balance	78cbd	5.0	−80.7	−19.8	46.2	−57.2	−26.1	−32.9	−12.9	20.4	46.8	144.5	....
Reserves and Related Items	79dad	−5.0	80.7	19.8	−46.2	57.2	26.1	32.9	12.9	−20.4	−46.8	−144.5	....
Reserve Assets	79dbd	−31.9	.1	−18.6	−82.8	5.9	−61.3	−21.3	−17.7	−43.0	−64.2	−166.2	....
Use of Fund Credit and Loans	79dcd	13.8	46.3	19.6	34.1	2.8	19.4	7.4	−2.1	−8.0	−.9	−3.9	....
Exceptional Financing	79ded	13.1	34.4	18.8	2.6	48.6	68.0	46.8	32.7	30.6	18.3	25.6	....
International Investment Position		*Millions of US Dollars*											
Assets	79aad	190.1	202.4	203.9	341.3	366.2	394.2	489.3	488.8	551.3	711.6	1,048.1	....
Direct Investment Abroad	79abd	—	—	—	—	22.6	28.7	33.2	39.3	39.3	39.3	83.2	....
Portfolio Investment	79acd	—	.1	.6	—	.2	.2	3.1	3.7	6.2	7.6	10.7	....
Equity Securities	79add	—	—	—	—	—	—	—	—	—	—	—	....
Debt Securities	79aed	—	.1	.6	—	.2	.2	3.1	3.7	6.2	7.6	10.7	....
Financial Derivatives	79ald	—	—	—	31.7	7.8	7.3	19.5	17.2	—	—	—	....
Other Investment	79afd	92.2	88.6	75.8	113.7	146.9	174.9	229.5	192.8	216.1	305.5	410.2	....
Monetary Authorities	79agd	—	—	—	—	—	—	2.4	2.3	1.5	1.2	.9	....
General Government	79ahd	72.4	67.7	56.3	42.7	69.1	65.6	57.1	49.3	27.0	29.8	21.4	....
Banks	79aid	19.9	20.9	19.5	38.1	29.2	30.8	70.7	35.8	94.1	156.8	311.0	....
Other Sectors	79ajd	—	—	—	32.9	48.7	78.5	99.3	105.4	93.6	117.8	76.9	....
Reserve Assets	79akd	97.9	113.7	127.5	195.9	188.6	183.2	204.0	235.9	289.7	359.3	543.9	....
Liabilities	79lad	528.4	913.8	1,301.5	1,711.7	1,962.5	2,128.9	2,195.2	2,241.2	2,350.6	2,584.2	2,822.4	....
Dir. Invest. in Rep. Economy	79lbd	48.2	144.3	191.0	274.1	383.3	431.6	446.6	440.8	479.1	491.5	677.0	....
Portfolio Investment	79lcd	—	1.8	—	5.0	.9	—	9.6	112.6	103.4	102.6	97.3	....
Equity Securities	79ldd	—	—	—	—	—	—	—	—	—	—	—	....
Debt Securities	79led	—	1.8	—	5.0	.9	—	9.6	112.6	103.4	102.6	97.3	....
Financial Derivatives	79lld	—	—	—	—	—	—	—	—	29.7	24.6	—	....
Other Investment	79lfd	480.2	767.8	1,110.3	1,432.6	1,578.3	1,697.3	1,739.0	1,687.8	1,738.3	1,965.6	2,048.1	....
Monetary Authorities	79lgd	77.8	124.3	139.6	164.9	175.2	190.3	188.0	179.3	185.2	201.9	206.9	....
General Government	79lhd	393.1	547.8	673.7	839.9	979.4	1,122.2	1,207.5	1,158.1	1,298.0	1,477.9	1,656.9	....
Banks	79lid	9.3	6.0	4.0	17.9	18.9	16.1	3.7	5.6	38.5	79.8	115.9	....
Other Sectors	79ljd	—	89.7	293.0	409.9	404.8	368.7	339.8	344.7	216.5	206.0	68.4	....
Government Finance		*Millions of Soms: Year Ending December 31*											
Deficit (-) or Surplus	80	−921.6	−1,864.6	−1,269.3	−1,605.4	−1,035.8	−1,213.5	−1,244.8	286.8	−798.1	−681.0	−505.8	224.4
Total Revenue and Grants	81y	1,891.2	2,745.9	3,933.1	5,090.3	6,262.6	7,828.7	10,039.6	12,543.7	14,392.1	16,214.9	18,335.9	20,368.0
Exp. & Lending Minus Repay.	82z	2,812.8	4,610.5	5,202.4	6,695.7	7,298.4	9,042.2	11,284.4	12,256.9	15,190.2	16,895.9	18,841.7	20,143.7
Financing													
Domestic	84a	406.5	995.5	604.8	287.9	68.7	−379.6	−334.1	−101.8	−52.5	−96.7	209.8	−460.5
Foreign	85a	515.1	851.1	664.5	1,317.5	966.8	1,593.1	1,579.0	−185.1	850.6	777.8	296.0	236.1

Kyrgyz Republic 917

		1994	1995	1996	1997	1998	1999	2000	2001	2002	2003	2004	2005
National Accounts							*Millions of Soms*						
Househ.Cons.Expend.,incl.NPISHs....	96f	9,422	12,111	19,212	21,151	30,163	37,848	42,930	47,893	50,897	65,344	71,747	85,251
Government Consumption Expend....	91f	2,272	3,155	4,333	5,307	6,103	9,320	13,099	12,912	14,033	14,116	17,146	18,873
Gross Fixed Capital Formation.........	93e	1,493	3,338	5,296	3,802	4,404	7,663	11,782	10,721	12,418	11,600	13,925	14,548
Changes in Inventories.....................	93i	−409	−377	600	2,781	780	993	1,136	724	852	−1,678	−256	−147
Exports of Goods and Services.........	90c	4,058	4,758	7,193	11,749	12,471	20,571	27,351	27,133	29,831	32,442	40,152	39,080
Imports of Goods and Services (-).....	98c	4,816	6,839	13,234	14,174	19,834	27,782	31,099	27,353	32,664	37,953	48,364	58,228
Statistical Discrepancy.....................	99bs	....	....	....	....	....	....	—	—	−504	−273	3,588	−615
Gross Domestic Product (GDP).........	99b	12,019	16,145	23,399	30,686	34,181	48,744	65,358	73,883	75,367	83,872	94,351	100,116
Net Primary Income from Abroad.....	98.n	−190	−200	−485	−1,004	−1,748	−2,940	−3,848	−3,139	−2,825	−2,617	−4,210	....
Gross National Income (GNI)...........	99a	11,830	15,945	22,914	29,682	32,433	45,804	61,510	70,744	72,542	81,255	90,141	....
Net Current Transf.from Abroad.......	98t	665	820	1,438	1,161	1,043	1,969	3,911	2,507	5,487	4,598	8,551	....
Gross Nat'l Disposable Inc.(GNDI)....	99i	12,495	16,765	24,352	30,843	33,476	47,773	65,421	73,251	78,028	85,853	98,691	....
Gross Saving.................................	99s	801	1,500	807	4,385	−2,790	605	9,393	12,446	13,099	6,392	9,798	....
Consumption of Fixed Capital..........	99cf	1,220	1,644	2,963	3,731	4,902	6,332	8,623	8,920	9,259	9,145	9,983	....
GDP Volume 1995 Prices.................	99b.p	17,067	16,145	17,289	19,003	19,406	20,101	21,215	....	....	....	....	....
GDP Volume 2000 Prices.................	99b.p	....	....	....	....	....	....	65,358	68,836	68,836	73,651	78,841	78,363
GDP Volume (2000=100).................	99bvp	80.4	76.1	81.5	89.6	91.5	94.7	† 100.0	105.3	105.3	112.7	120.6	119.9
GDP Deflator (2000=100)................	99bip	22.9	32.5	43.9	52.4	57.2	78.7	100.0	107.3	109.5	113.9	119.7	127.8
							Millions: Midyear Estimates						
Population...................................	99z	4.54	4.59	4.65	4.72	4.80	4.88	4.95	5.02	5.08	5.14	5.20	5.26

Lao People's Democratic Republic   544

		1994	1995	1996	1997	1998	1999	2000	2001	2002	2003	2004	2005
Exchange Rates						*Kip per SDR: End of Period*							
Official Rate	aa	1,049.63	† 1,372.03	1,344.49	3,554.60	6,017.92	10,431.08	10,707.31	11,926.37	14,519.67	15,553.65	16,114.81	15,354.65
						Kip per US Dollar: End of Period (ae) Period Average (rf)							
Official Rate	ae	719.00	† 923.00	935.00	2,634.50	4,274.00	7,600.00	8,218.00	9,490.00	10,680.00	10,467.00	10,376.50	10,743.00
Official Rate	rf	717.67	† 804.69	921.02	1,259.98	3,298.33	7,102.03	7,887.64	8,954.58	10,056.33	10,569.04	10,585.54	10,655.17
Fund Position						*Millions of SDRs: End of Period*							
Quota	2f.s	39.10	39.10	39.10	39.10	39.10	39.10	39.10	52.90	52.90	52.90	52.90	52.90
SDRs	1b.s	7.46	9.49	7.17	9.31	4.32	.05	.07	2.72	4.47	12.87	9.90	9.86
Reserve Position in the Fund	1c.s	—	—	—	—	—	—	—	—	—	—	—	—
Total Fund Cred.&Loans Outstg	2tl	32.24	42.80	46.61	48.96	44.27	38.41	32.55	29.75	31.77	29.85	24.57	20.47
International Liquidity						*Millions of US Dollars Unless Otherwise Indicated: End of Period*							
Total Reserves minus Gold	1l.d	60.93e	92.11	169.50	112.18	112.21	101.19	138.97	130.93	191.59	208.59	223.25	234.29
SDRs	1b.d	10.89	14.10	10.31	12.56	6.09	.07	.10	3.42	6.07	19.13	15.37	14.09
Reserve Position in the Fund	1c.d	—	—	—	—	—	—	—	—	—	—	—	—
Foreign Exchange	1d.d	50.03e	78.01	159.19	99.62	106.13	101.12	138.87	127.51	185.51	189.46	207.87	220.21
Gold (Million Fine Troy Ounces)	1ad	.0171	.0171	.0171	.0171	.0171	.1171	.0169	.0723	.0723	.1171	.1171	.1457
Gold (National Valuation)	1and	.60	.60	.60	.60	.60	4.10	.59	2.53	2.53	4.10	4.10	5.10
Deposit Money Banks: Assets	7a.d	.10	.10	.11	.07	.11	.15	.13	.09	.15	.16	.22	.22
Liabilities	7b.d	.03	.04	.05	.03	.04	.04	.04	.04	.08	.07	.10	.11
Monetary Authorities						*Billions of Kip: End of Period*							
Foreign Assets	11	43.96	85.18	158.64	295.70	479.76	799.78	1,146.86	1,265.54	2,069.17	2,226.69	2,359.91	2,573.17
Claims on Central Government	12a	12.16	4.25	4.25	4.70	91.27	198.83	158.51	184.98	239.27	234.17	185.86	260.85
Claims on Nonfin.Pub.Enterprises	12c	1.86	6.98	10.87	59.54	112.80	223.71	346.10	488.49	566.64	523.51	575.14	228.40
Claims on Private Sector	12d	6.83	10.40	13.90	38.22	72.05	143.25	143.23	150.82	175.88	153.24	153.59	126.52
Claims on Deposit Money Banks	12e	37.05	46.59	52.37	57.94	80.35	301.90	445.60	347.66	218.07	137.63	131.04	221.94
Reserve Money	14	74.23	84.17	104.37	150.09	281.75	481.75	766.65	822.49	1,079.11	1,329.94	1,545.29	1,823.23
of which: Currency Outside DMBs	14a	38.61	41.95	42.97	53.31	63.16	77.79	67.83	113.08	228.81	399.10	666.42	804.55
Foreign Liabilities	16c	33.84	58.72	62.67	174.04	266.43	400.67	348.51	354.80	461.31	464.28	395.97	314.25
Central Government Deposits	16d	13.52	7.45	64.82	52.74	77.51	235.23	505.77	281.32	650.15	608.53	636.86	693.50
Government Lending Funds	16f	12.07	16.17	18.04	31.09	54.37	87.33	211.05	346.68	428.12	323.82	303.63	340.05
Capital Accounts	17a	15.23	26.44	25.21	91.25	172.61	456.94	463.05	706.21	838.10	896.94	954.06	423.90
Other Items (Net)	17r	−47.02	−39.56	−35.08	−43.10	−16.43	5.86	−54.42	−73.99	−187.77	−348.27	−430.27	−183.96
Deposit Money Banks						*Billions of Kip: End of Period*							
Reserves	20	36.45	44.16	59.24	77.70	212.42	402.96	688.77	714.46	939.28	1,109.01	982.05	962.67
Foreign Assets	21	69.79	91.20	107.47	180.35	452.00	1,142.98	1,075.88	865.78	1,577.12	1,713.16	2,271.14	2,382.04
Claims on Central Government	22a	26.81	19.38	39.18	40.78	37.86	11.35	7.64	29.74	69.16	324.36	355.84	464.04
Claims on Nonfin.Pub.Enterprises	22c	15.57	20.69	26.06	60.88	110.75	221.69	296.54	528.24	566.40	402.59	423.46	508.08
Claims on Private Sector	22d	92.02	118.46	141.79	247.35	460.77	728.69	1,074.91	1,354.49	1,329.22	1,318.96	1,528.05	2,017.24
Demand Deposits	24	22.73	25.22	32.59	26.62	105.82	141.19	272.23	256.88	358.15	437.29	537.54	610.26
Time, Savings,& Fgn.Currency Dep	25	104.69	126.09	169.37	326.07	696.95	1,325.52	1,911.25	2,193.15	2,942.40	3,401.38	3,947.56	4,001.43
Foreign Liabilities	26c	21.51	39.76	46.87	77.24	169.34	281.96	349.38	376.08	863.70	752.28	988.65	1,166.92
Central Government Deposits	26d	12.69	15.41	21.60	36.34	103.46	247.16	79.93	51.42	37.20	80.71	114.94	222.75
Credit from Monetary Authorities	26g	35.04	41.93	49.12	51.46	81.67	314.49	489.84	383.78	252.38	165.62	98.39	150.10
Capital Accounts	27a	47.45	56.55	66.51	126.78	215.97	457.31	519.89	574.10	487.44	201.02	60.18	191.97
Other Items (Net)	27r	−3.47	−11.05	−12.31	−37.46	−99.42	−259.97	−478.79	−342.73	−460.11	−170.23	−186.74	−8.97
Monetary Survey						*Billions of Kip: End of Period*							
Foreign Assets (Net)	31n	58.40	77.90	156.57	224.77	496.00	1,260.13	1,524.85	1,400.44	2,321.28	2,723.29	3,246.44	3,474.04
Domestic Credit	32	129.04	157.30	149.62	362.39	704.53	1,045.12	1,441.22	2,404.02	2,259.22	2,267.59	2,470.14	2,688.88
Claims on Central Govt. (Net)	32an	12.77	.78	−43.00	−43.61	−51.84	−272.21	−419.56	−118.02	−378.92	−130.71	−210.10	−191.36
Claims on Nonfin.Pub.Enterprises	32c	17.43	27.67	36.93	120.42	223.55	445.39	642.63	1,016.73	1,133.04	926.10	998.60	736.48
Claims on Private Sector	32d	98.85	128.86	155.69	285.58	532.82	871.94	1,218.14	1,505.31	1,505.10	1,472.20	1,681.64	2,143.76
Money	34	61.34	67.18	75.56	79.94	168.98	218.98	344.35	371.84	587.00	836.54	1,207.29	1,414.91
Quasi-Money	35	104.69	126.09	169.37	326.07	696.95	1,325.52	1,911.25	2,193.15	2,942.40	3,401.38	3,947.56	4,001.43
Other Items (Net)	37r	21.41	41.93	61.27	181.15	334.60	761.06	710.77	1,239.46	1,051.07	752.95	561.71	747.06
Money plus Quasi-Money	35l	166.03	193.27	244.93	406.00	865.93	1,544.50	2,255.60	2,564.99	3,529.40	4,237.92	5,154.85	5,416.34
Interest Rates						*Percent Per Annum*							
Bank Rate (End of Period)	60	30.00	32.08	35.00	....	35.00	34.89	35.17	35.00	20.00	20.00	20.00	20.00
Treasury Bill Rate	60c	....	20.46	....	....	23.66	30.00	29.94	22.70	21.41	24.87	20.37	18.61
Deposit Rate	60l	12.00	14.00	16.00	....	17.79	13.42	12.00	6.50	6.00	6.58	7.85	4.75
Lending Rate	60p	24.00	† 25.67	27.00	....	29.28	32.00	32.00	26.17	29.33	30.50	29.25	26.83
Prices						*Index Numbers (2000=100): Period Averages*							
Consumer Prices	64	10.6	12.7	† 14.4	18.3	35.0	† 79.9	100.0	107.8	119.3	137.7	152.2	163.1
Intl. Transactions & Positions						*Millions of US Dollars*							
Exports	70..d	300.5	311.0	322.8	359.0	369.5	310.8	330.3	331.3	297.7	378.1	361.1	505.7
Imports, c.i.f	71..d	564.1	588.8	689.6	706.0	552.8	524.8	535.3	527.9	431.1	524.2	505.8	808.5

Lao People's Democratic Republic 544

		1994	1995	1996	1997	1998	1999	2000	2001	2002	2003	2004	2005
Balance of Payments					*Millions of US Dollars: Minus Sign Indicates Debit*								
Current Account, n.i.e....................	78ald	−284.0	−346.2	−346.8	−305.5	−150.1	−121.1	−8.5	−82.4	....	....	....	....
Goods: Exports f.o.b....................	78aad	305.5	310.9	322.8	318.3	342.1	338.2	330.3	311.1	....	....	....	....
Goods: Imports f.o.b....................	78abd	−519.2	−626.8	−643.7	−601.3	−506.8	−527.7	−535.3	−527.9	....	....	....	....
Trade Balance............................	78acd	−213.7	−315.9	−320.9	−283.0	−164.7	−189.5	−205.0	−216.8	....	....	....	....
Services: Credit...........................	78add	87.0	96.8	104.4	105.8	145.0	130.0	175.7	166.1	....	....	....	....
Services: Debit............................	78aed	−152.1	−121.6	−126.0	−110.5	−95.5	−51.8	−43.1	−31.6	....	....	....	....
Balance on Goods & Services.......	78afd	−278.8	−340.7	−342.5	−287.7	−115.2	−111.3	−72.4	−82.3	....	....	....	....
Income: Credit............................	78agd	7.2	7.4	9.2	11.1	6.9	10.5	7.3	5.8	....	....	....	....
Income: Debit.............................	78ahd	−9.2	−12.9	−13.5	−28.9	−41.8	−49.9	−59.7	−39.6	....	....	....	....
Balance on Gds, Serv. & Inc.........	78aid	−280.8	−346.2	−346.8	−305.5	−150.1	−150.7	−124.7	−116.1	....	....	....	....
Current Transfers, n.i.e.: Credit......	78ajd	—	—	—	—	—	80.2	116.3	33.7	....	....	....	....
Current Transfers: Debit................	78akd	−3.2	—	—	—	—	−50.6	....	....	....	....	....	....
Capital Account, n.i.e....................	78bcd	9.5	13.2	35.0	33.4	43.1	—	....	....	....	....	....	....
Capital Account, n.i.e.: Credit........	78bad	9.5	21.7	44.9	40.3	49.4	—	....	....	....	....	....	....
Capital Account: Debit..................	78bjd	—	−8.5	−9.9	−6.9	−6.3	—	....	....	....	....	....	....
Financial Account, n.i.e.................	78bjd	24.3	90.0	135.7	3.5	−43.4	−46.9	126.1	135.7	....	....	....	....
Direct Investment Abroad..............	78bdd	—	—	....	—	—	—	....	....	....	....	....	....
Dir. Invest. in Rep. Econ., n.i.e.......	78bed	59.2	95.1	159.8	—	—	—	33.9	23.9	....	....	....	....
Portfolio Investment Assets...........	78bfd	—	—	....	—	—	—	....	....	....	....	....	....
Equity Securities...........................	78bld	—	—	....	—	—	—	....	....	....	....	....	....
Debt Securities............................	78bld	—	—	....	—	—	—	....	....	....	....	....	....
Portfolio Investment Liab., n.i.e......	78bgd	—	—	—	—	—	—	....	....	....	....	....	....
Equity Securities...........................	78bmd	—	—	—	—	—	—	....	....	....	....	....	....
Debt Securities............................	78bnd	—	—	....	—	—	—	....	....	....	....	....	....
Financial Derivatives Assets...........	78bwd	....	....	....	—	....	—	....	....	....	....	....	....
Financial Derivatives Liabilities.......	78bxd	....	....	....	....	....	—	....	....	....	....	....	....
Other Investment Assets...............	78bhd	−9.6	−1.5	−14.1	39.5	−22.8	−43.2	18.8	25.2	....	....	....	....
Monetary Authorities..................	78bod	....	....	....	....	....	....	....	....	....	....	....	....
General Government....................	78bpd	—	—	....	....	....	....	....	....	....	....	....	....
Banks.......................................	78bqd	−9.6	−1.5	−14.1	39.5	−22.8	−43.2	18.8	25.2	....	....	....	....
Other Sectors............................	78brd	—	—	—	—	—	—	....	....	....	....	....	....
Other Investment Liab., n.i.e.........	78bid	−25.3	−3.6	−10.0	−36.0	−20.6	−3.7	73.3	86.6	....	....	....	....
Monetary Authorities..................	78bsd	—	−15.4	−17.5	−18.2	−25.3	—	....	....	....	....	....	....
General Government....................	78btd	−8.3	—	—	—	—	—	67.2	79.0	....	....	....	....
Banks.......................................	78bud	−17.0	11.8	7.5	−17.8	4.7	−3.7	6.2	7.6	....	....	....	....
Other Sectors............................	78bvd	—	—	—	—	—	—	....	....	....	....	....	....
Net Errors and Omissions..............	78cad	71.8	92.4	17.7	−100.5	−103.8	−165.1	−74.2	−57.2	....	....	....	....
Overall Balance...........................	78cbd	−178.4	−150.6	−158.4	−369.1	−254.2	−333.1	43.4	−3.9	....	....	....	....
Reserves and Related Items.............	79dad	178.4	150.6	158.4	369.1	254.2	333.1	−43.4	3.9	....	....	....	....
Reserve Assets.............................	79dbd	−5.6	−73.0	−70.7	25.4	28.1	12.4	−35.7	7.4	....	....	....	....
Use of Fund Credit and Loans.......	79dcd	8.1	15.6	5.5	3.3	−6.4	−8.0	−7.7	−3.6	....	....	....	....
Exceptional Financing..................	79ded	175.9	208.0	223.6	340.4	232.5	328.7	....	....	....	....	....	....
National Accounts							*Billions of Kip*							
Gross Domestic Product (GDP)........	99b	1,107.8	1,430.4	1,725.7	2,201.0	4,240.0	10,329.0	13,669.5	15,701.8	18,390.0	20,307.1	26,590.1	30,599.9
GDP Volume 1990 Prices................	99b.p	780.7	835.7	893.3	955.0	993.1	1,065.4	1,127.1	1,192.1	1,262.7	1,335.9	1,428.0	1,532.0
GDP Volume (2000=100)................	99bvp	69.3	74.1	79.3	84.7	88.1	94.5	100.0	105.8	112.0	118.5	126.7	135.9
GDP Deflator (2000=100)...............	99bip	11.7	14.1	15.9	19.0	35.2	79.9	100.0	108.6	120.1	125.3	153.5	164.7
						Millions: Midyear Estimates								
Population............................	99z	4.57	4.69	4.80	4.92	5.04	5.16	5.28	5.40	5.53	5.66	5.79	5.92

Latvia 941

		1994	1995	1996	1997	1998	1999	2000	2001	2002	2003	2004	2005
Exchange Rates						*Lats per SDR: End of Period*							
Official Rate	aa	.800	.798	.800	.796	.801	.800	.799	.802	.808	.804	.801	.848
						Lats per US Dollar: End of Period (ae) Period Average (rf)							
Official Rate	ae	.548	.537	.556	.590	.569	.583	.613	.638	.594	.541	.516	.593
Official Rate	rf	.560	.528	.551	.581	.590	.585	.607	.628	.618	.571	.540	.565
Fund Position						*Millions of SDRs: End of Period*							
Quota	2f.s	91.50	91.50	91.50	91.50	91.50	126.80	126.80	126.80	126.80	126.80	126.80	126.80
SDRs	1b.s	.21	1.49	1.56	1.50	.21	2.24	—	.07	.05	.09	.10	.10
Reserve Position in the Fund	1c.s	.01	.01	.01	.01	.01	.01	.06	.06	.06	.06	.06	.06
Total Fund Cred.&Loans Outstg	2tl	109.80	107.89	90.36	63.67	45.37	34.31	26.69	19.06	11.44	3.81	—	—
International Liquidity						*Millions of US Dollars Unless Otherwise Indicated: End of Period*							
Total Reserves minus Gold	1l.d	545.18	505.70	654.07	760.20	801.23	872.00	850.91	1,148.74	1,241.42	1,432.44	1,911.98	2,232.13
SDRs	1b.d	.31	2.22	2.25	2.03	.29	3.07	.01	.09	.07	.14	.15	.14
Reserve Position in the Fund	1c.d	.01	.01	.01	.01	.01	.01	.07	.08	.08	.08	.09	.08
Foreign Exchange	1d.d	544.86	503.47	651.81	758.17	800.93	868.92	850.83	1,148.59	1,241.27	1,432.22	1,911.74	2,231.91
Gold (Million Fine Troy Ounces)	1ad	.2492	.2492	.2493	.2491	.2493	.2493	.2487	.2486	.2486	.2486	.2486	.2487
Gold (National Valuation)	1and	74.80	74.77	74.78	73.13	71.44	72.41	68.38	69.66	85.90	102.67	110.27	128.45
Monetary Authorities:Other Assets	3..d	—	—	—	—	.01	.01	.01	—	.01	.01	.05	.01
Other Liab	4..d	—	—	—	—	—	.01	.01	.01	.01	.02	.01	.02
Deposit Money Banks: Assets	7a.d	664.25	599.56	1,021.16	1,546.56	1,258.96	1,489.19	2,112.97	2,271.57	3,019.08	4,071.00	5,816.06	5,677.16
Liabilities	7b.d	448.07	452.38	852.57	1,297.97	1,342.03	1,767.48	2,141.32	2,649.83	3,735.76	5,454.74	8,277.84	10,258.60
Monetary Authorities						*Millions of Lats: End of Period*							
Foreign Assets	11	341.98	313.52	407.63	461.47	461.23	535.64	568.45	780.39	793.51	836.43	1,067.63	1,405.84
Claims on Central Government	12a	6.59	39.38	22.33	72.88	81.00	57.70	73.47	43.33	76.13	65.29	93.21	98.82
Claims on Banks	12e	21.40	22.04	20.22	7.55	52.04	63.32	42.53	18.83	30.69	59.32	12.88	23.30
Reserve Money	14	269.43	273.62	336.66	441.74	471.45	526.28	566.72	641.88	759.87	807.63	957.53	1,381.95
of which: Currency Outside Banks	14a	213.06	209.54	264.00	332.65	340.19	377.41	427.66	485.19	543.13	601.05	645.41	786.39
Foreign Liabilities	16c	88.46	86.56	72.55	51.17	36.66	31.54	28.35	21.58	15.63	12.19	29.42	15.32
Central Government Deposits	16d	10.78	3.62	35.40	24.91	42.03	79.03	45.93	119.59	62.08	80.25	105.67	68.39
Capital Accounts	17a	8.02	11.00	20.89	36.60	47.22	47.23	52.02	61.64	82.76	83.17	92.23	86.96
Other Items (Net)	17r	−6.71	.15	−15.32	−12.52	−3.09	−27.40	−8.56	−2.13	−19.99	−22.20	−11.13	−24.66
Banking Institutions						*Millions of Lats: End of Period*							
Reserves	20	57.29	64.15	71.69	107.23	129.93	144.46	135.11	153.25	213.73	204.90	310.82	593.55
Foreign Assets	21	364.01	321.96	567.77	912.47	716.35	868.20	1,295.25	1,449.26	1,793.33	2,202.41	3,001.09	3,366.56
Claims on Central Government	22a	† 97.14	120.81	140.09	113.01	71.41	114.01	138.36	170.10	180.33	273.65	246.07	227.37
Claims on Local Government	22b	6.66	11.51	15.52	2.66	4.41	15.77	36.22	51.71	42.70	67.84	67.74	89.77
Claims on Nonfin.Pub.Enterprises	22c	39.59	24.99	17.71	28.15	23.82	30.61	52.53	81.21	112.50	87.42	87.69	107.50
Claims on Private Sector	22d	335.67	184.13	202.99	344.28	533.10	612.18	804.74	1,100.54	1,506.83	2,189.49	3,283.84	5,349.36
Claims on Nonbank Financial Insts	22g				19.24	25.34	25.90	56.69	190.68	254.59	294.93	403.16	718.17
Demand Deposits	24	138.08	144.24	156.36	232.76	259.75	257.52	332.97	374.97	501.36	630.02	860.97	1,264.02
Time, Savings,& Fgn.Currency Dep	25	346.82	195.06	230.50	331.56	357.60	398.73	554.19	716.43	847.19	1,081.23	1,423.30	2,002.16
Money Market Instruments	26aa	—	—	—	—	—	—	—	—	.61			
Foreign Liabilities	26c	245.54	242.93	474.03	765.80	763.61	1,030.44	1,312.63	1,690.59	2,219.04	2,951.02	4,271.37	6,083.35
Central Government Deposits	26d	† 13.92	36.98	6.31	50.33	32.83	18.10	10.14	31.37	55.07	22.80	64.61	13.30
Government Lending Funds	26f	61.43	39.68	22.00	19.66	16.73	22.48	22.55	21.26	9.94	6.80	5.39	4.89
Credit from Central Bank	26g	1.44	3.52	4.32	6.94	54.94	63.18	42.53	18.83	30.69	59.32	12.88	23.30
Capital Accounts	27a	96.79	77.58	118.67	117.56	62.05	40.07	230.18	314.26	389.68	493.07	647.10	867.91
Other Items (Net)	27r	−3.64	−12.44	3.58	2.43	−43.16	−19.39	13.70	29.04	50.45	76.39	114.80	193.35
Banking Survey						*Millions of Lats: End of Period*							
Foreign Assets (Net)	31n	371.98	306.00	428.82	556.97	377.31	341.86	522.72	517.48	352.18	75.64	−232.07	−1,326.28
Domestic Credit	32	† 460.96	340.22	356.93	504.98	664.22	759.05	1,105.94	1,486.61	2,055.94	2,875.56	4,011.45	6,509.30
Claims on Central Govt. (Net)	32an	† 79.04	119.59	120.71	110.66	77.55	74.60	155.77	62.46	139.31	235.88	169.01	244.50
Claims on Local Government	32b	6.66	11.51	15.52	2.66	4.41	15.77	36.22	51.71	42.70	67.84	67.74	89.77
Claims on Nonfin.Pub.Enterprises	32c	39.59	24.99	17.71	28.15	23.82	30.61	52.53	81.21	112.50	87.42	87.69	107.50
Claims on Private Sector	32d	335.67	184.13	202.99	344.28	533.10	612.18	804.74	1,100.54	1,506.83	2,189.49	3,283.84	5,349.36
Claims on Nonbank Fin. Insts	32g				19.24	25.34	25.90	56.69	190.68	254.59	294.93	403.16	718.17
Money	34	351.13	353.78	425.65	567.27	601.27	639.34	764.57	863.59	1,047.50	1,232.74	1,507.68	2,052.42
Quasi-Money	35	346.82	195.06	230.50	331.56	357.60	398.73	554.19	716.43	847.19	1,081.23	1,423.30	2,002.16
Money Market Instruments	36aa	—	—	—	—	—	—	—	—	.61			
Government Lending Funds	36f	61.43	39.68	22.00	19.66	16.73	22.48	22.55	21.26	9.94	6.80	5.39	4.89
Capital Accounts	37a	104.81	88.58	139.56	154.16	109.27	87.30	282.19	375.89	472.43	576.24	739.33	954.86
Other Items (Net)	37r	−31.24	−30.88	−31.97	−10.69	−43.34	−46.94	5.14	26.91	30.46	54.19	103.68	168.69
Money plus Quasi-Money	35l	697.95	548.84	656.15	898.83	958.87	1,038.07	1,318.77	1,580.02	1,894.69	2,313.97	2,930.98	4,054.58
Interest Rates						*Percent Per Annum*							
Discount Rate (End of Period)	60	25.00	24.00	9.50	4.00	4.00	4.00	3.50	3.50	3.00	3.00	4.00	4.00
Money Market Rate	60b	37.18	22.39	13.08	3.76	4.42	4.72	2.97	5.23	3.01	2.86	3.25	2.49
Treasury Bill Rate	60c	....	28.24	16.27	4.73	5.27	6.23	† 4.85	5.63	3.52	3.24	....	....
Deposit Rate	60l	31.68	14.79	11.71	5.90	5.33	5.04	4.38	5.24	3.23	3.02	3.27	2.78
Lending Rate	60p	55.86	34.56	25.78	15.25	14.29	14.20	11.87	11.17	7.97	5.38	7.45	6.11
Prices and Labor						*Index Numbers (2000=100): Period Averages*							
Share Prices	62	....	....	....	345.8	181.4	72.4	100.0	136.1	149.1	172.2	....	....
Producer Prices	63	76.7	85.9	97.6	101.6	103.5	99.4	† 100.0	101.7	102.7	105.9	115.0	124.0
Consumer Prices	64	57.1	71.3	83.9	90.9	95.2	97.4	100.0	† 102.5	104.5	107.5	114.2	121.9
Harmonized CPI (2002=100)	64h	....	....	....	....	....	....	....	....	100.0	† 102.9	109.3	116.9
Wages: Average Earnings	65	50.5	62.9	72.5	87.5	93.3	97.0	100.0	104.9	111.5	121.6	133.1	154.8
Industrial Employment	67	110.6	104.9	104.7	102.0	107.5	99.9	100.0	97.2	96.5	99.3	99.6	97.9
						Number in Thousands: Period Averages							
Labor Force	67d	1,300	....	1,182	1,186	1,168	1,157	1,132	1,106	1,124	1,126	1,136	....
Employment	67e	1,083	1,046	1,018	1,037	1,043	1,038	1,038	1,037	989	1,007	1,018	....
Unemployment	67c	84	83	91	85	111	109	93	92	90	91	91	85
Unemployment Rate (%)	67r	6.5	6.6	7.2	7.0	9.2	9.1	7.8	7.7	8.5	8.6	8.5	....

Latvia 941

		1994	1995	1996	1997	1998	1999	2000	2001	2002	2003	2004	2005
Intl. Transactions & Positions						*Millions of Lats*							
Exports............................	70	553	688	795	972	1,069	1,008	1,131	1,256	1,409	1,651	2,150	2,871
Imports, c.i.f............................	71	....	960	1,278	1,582	1,881	1,724	1,934	2,202	2,497	2,989	3,805	4,835
Imports, f.o.b............................	71.v	695	923	1,223	1,513	1,796	1,652	....	....	....	....	....	....
						(2000=100) Period Averages							
Volume of Exports...................	72	52.0	59.1	63.9	84.7	85.7	87.3	100.0	102.5	112.2	121.5	....	....
Unit Value of Exports.................	74	84.0	97.5	103.6	105.2	105.1	101.2	† 100.0	102.6	105.4	113.8	129.1	142.3
Balance of Payments						*Millions of US Dollars: Minus Sign Indicates Debit*							
Current Account, n.i.e...................	78ald	201	−16	−280	−345	−650	−654	−371	−626	−624	−910	−1,766	−1,959
Goods: Exports f.o.b.................	78aad	1,022	1,368	1,488	1,838	2,011	1,889	2,080	2,243	2,545	3,171	4,221	5,306
Goods: Imports f.o.b.................	78abd	−1,322	−1,947	−2,286	−2,686	−3,141	−2,916	−3,123	−3,578	−4,024	−5,174	−7,002	−8,272
Trade Balance........................	78acd	−301	−580	−798	−848	−1,130	−1,027	−1,044	−1,335	−1,479	−2,003	−2,781	−2,966
Services: Credit.......................	78add	657	720	1,126	1,033	1,108	1,024	1,150	1,179	1,239	1,506	1,780	2,159
Services: Debit........................	78aed	−297	−246	−742	−662	−806	−689	−690	−672	−701	−930	−1,178	−1,556
Balance on Goods & Services.......	78afd	60	−106	−414	−477	−827	−691	−584	−828	−942	−1,427	−2,179	−2,363
Income: Credit........................	78agd	51	71	140	177	207	158	215	278	289	369	500	765
Income: Debit.........................	78ahd	−42	−53	−99	−122	−154	−214	−198	−221	−235	−382	−772	−943
Balance on Gds, Serv. & Inc.......	78aid	68	−87	−373	−422	−774	−747	−566	−770	−888	−1,440	−2,451	−2,541
Current Transfers, n.i.e.: Credit........	78ajd	136	75	98	91	137	114	406	373	538	924	1,289	1,358
Current Transfers: Debit.................	78akd	−3	−5	−5	−14	−13	−21	−211	−229	−275	−394	−604	−776
Capital Account, n.i.e...................	78bcd	....	....	....	14	14	13	35	41	21	76	144	193
Capital Account, n.i.e.: Credit........	78bad	....	....	....	14	14	13	40	50	26	80	150	201
Capital Account: Debit.................	78bbd	....	....	....	—	—	—	−5	−9	−6	−4	−7	−8
Financial Account, n.i.e.................	78bjd	363	636	537	347	601	768	413	900	687	889	1,957	2,526
Direct Investment Abroad.............	78bdd	65	65	−3	−6	−54	−17	−12	−18	−3	−36	−103	−135
Dir. Invest. in Rep. Econ., n.i.e........	78bed	214	180	382	521	357	348	413	132	254	292	699	632
Portfolio Investment Assets...........	78bfd	−22	−37	−165	−539	−33	58	−351	−57	−220	−286	−13	−270
Equity Securities.....................	78bkd	−12	−7	12	−113	7	77	−34	6	−2	6	−22	−58
Debt Securities.......................	78bld	−10	−30	−177	−426	−40	−19	−317	−64	−218	−292	9	−212
Portfolio Investment Liab., n.i.e......	78bgd	....	—	24	−32	27	215	27	187	20	70	260	137
Equity Securities.....................	78bmd	....	—	−2	6	30	7	−7	1	23	39	23	13
Debt Securities.......................	78bnd	....	....	26	−39	−3	209	34	186	−3	31	237	124
Financial Derivatives Assets..........	78bwd	....	....	....	....	....	....	2	3	−7	−5	−35	59
Financial Derivatives Liabilities.......	78bxd	....	....	....	....	....	....	—	−3	20	11	−13	−134
Other Investment Assets.............	78bhd	−387	−31	−214	−326	75	−214	−389	−79	−472	−685	−1,767	−339
Monetary Authorities..................	78bod	5	1	−1	—	—	36	—	—	—	1	−2	−1
General Government...................	78bpd	....	....	....	—	—	—	—	−5	6	—	−31	−23
Banks................................	78bqd	−400	99	−261	−253	67	−275	−370	−107	−469	−635	−1,601	172
Other Sectors........................	78brd	8	−130	48	−73	9	25	−18	32	−8	−51	−134	−487
Other Investment Liab., n.i.e..........	78bid	493	458	513	730	229	379	724	734	1,095	1,528	2,929	2,577
Monetary Authorities..................	78bsd	−5	—	—	—	—	—	—	1	−1	—	44	−36
General Government...................	78btd	54	55	45	20	45	14	−8	7	−3	−65	20	−59
Banks................................	78bud	272	88	385	558	69	354	719	529	984	1,480	2,533	2,482
Other Sectors........................	78bvd	172	315	84	152	115	4	12	197	115	113	331	190
Net Errors and Omissions..............	78cad	−508	−653	−46	87	97	38	−74	—	−71	24	69	−235
Overall Balance.....................	78cbd	57	−33	211	102	63	165	3	314	12	79	403	524
Reserves and Related Items............	79dad	−57	33	−211	−102	−63	−165	−3	−314	−12	−79	−403	−524
Reserve Assets........................	79dbd	−103	36	−186	−65	−38	−150	7	−305	−2	−69	−397	−524
Use of Fund Credit and Loans........	79dcd	47	−3	−25	−37	−25	−15	−10	−10	−10	−11	−6	—
Exceptional Financing.................	79ded	....	....	....	....	....	....	....	....	....	....	....	....
International Investment Position						*Millions of US Dollars*							
Assets.................................	79aad	....	1,851	2,366	3,262	3,051	3,278	3,840	4,128	5,136	6,658	9,339	9,972
Direct Investment Abroad.............	79abd	....	231	209	222	281	244	24	39	59	100	220	294
Portfolio Investment.................	79acd	....	62	227	755	590	518	858	671	912	1,255	1,327	1,520
Equity Securities.....................	79add	....	21	9	123	113	22	57	50	53	49	75	119
Debt Securities.......................	79aed	....	41	218	633	477	495	801	621	859	1,207	1,252	1,400
Financial Derivatives.................	79ald	....	—	—	4	6	4	1	4	12	18	55	30
Other Investment....................	79afd	....	972	1,158	1,447	1,301	1,568	2,038	2,196	2,825	3,749	5,715	5,768
Monetary Authorities..................	79agd	....	2	3	7	4	2	2	2	3	2	4	5
General Government...................	79ahd	....	—	—	—	—	—	18	23	18	19	55	70
Banks................................	79aid	....	542	800	1,047	872	1,135	1,516	1,615	2,120	2,843	4,546	4,220
Other Sectors........................	79ajd	....	429	356	393	425	431	501	555	685	885	1,109	1,473
Reserve Assets........................	79akd	....	586	772	833	873	944	919	1,218	1,327	1,535	2,022	2,361
Liabilities.............................	79lad	....	1,932	2,717	3,710	4,252	5,110	6,164	7,167	9,105	11,787	16,738	18,853
Dir. Invest. in Rep. Economy..........	79lbd	....	616	936	1,272	1,558	1,794	2,084	2,328	2,751	3,283	4,575	4,783
Portfolio Investment.................	79lcd	....	23	46	13	42	248	255	428	511	687	1,029	1,045
Equity Securities.....................	79ldd	....	7	5	9	41	51	40	42	70	121	144	156
Debt Securities.......................	79led	....	16	41	4	1	197	215	386	442	566	885	889
Financial Derivatives.................	79lld	....	—	—	4	2	9	—	7	29	43	32	35
Other Investment....................	79lfd	....	1,294	1,735	2,422	2,650	3,059	3,826	4,404	5,813	7,773	11,102	12,990
Monetary Authorities..................	79lgd	....	161	130	87	65	49	36	27	17	8	49	9
General Government...................	79lhd	....	242	279	284	343	345	327	324	337	297	338	284
Banks................................	79lid	....	399	782	1,332	1,278	1,619	2,328	2,615	3,688	5,380	8,159	10,093
Other Sectors........................	79ljd	....	492	544	719	965	1,047	1,135	1,438	1,771	2,088	2,557	2,605
Government Finance						*Millions of Lats: Year Ending December 31*							
Deficit (-) or Surplus.................	80	....	....	† −44.13	† 23.34	† 5.32	−140.15	−118.96	−67.96	−98.27	−90.79	−81.63	−99.43
Total Revenue and Grants.............	81y	....	357.10	† 874.92	1,174.54	† 1,289.69	1,291.17	1,305.64	1,383.04	1,545.13	1,726.54	2,062.77	2,640.98
Exp. & Lending Minus Repay..........	82z	....	....	† 919.05	† 1,151.20	† 1,284.37	1,431.32	1,424.60	1,451.00	1,643.40	1,817.33	2,144.40	2,740.41
Expenditure........................	82	....	445.60	† 907.14	† 1,116.81	† 1,283.65	1,419.29	1,412.14	1,442.07	1,648.65	1,830.97	2,164.47	2,738.58
Lending Minus Repayments..........	83	....	....	† 11.91	34.39	† .72	12.03	12.46	8.93	−5.25	−13.64	−20.07	1.83
Total Financing........................	80h	....	....	† 44.13	−23.34	† −5.32	140.15	118.96	67.96	98.27	90.79	81.63	99.34
Domestic...........................	84a	....	....	† 31.81	−41.06	† −18.38	13.28	130.97	−37.57	86.96	135.84	−45.73	114.51
Foreign.............................	85a	....	....	† 12.32	17.72	† 13.06	126.87	−12.01	105.53	11.31	−45.05	127.36	−15.17

		1994	1995	1996	1997	1998	1999	2000	2001	2002	2003	2004	2005
National Accounts							*Millions of Lats*						
Househ.Cons.Expend.,incl.NPISHs....	96f	1,206.1	1,637.3	2,106.1	2,402.5	2,531.3	2,693.2	2,970.5	3,260.2	3,575.9	3,987.6	4,623.9	5,690.1
Government Consumption Expend...	91f	410.6	630.4	664.8	742.7	917.3	966.1	988.0	1,068.3	1,207.6	1,371.2	1,479.3	1,585.6
Gross Fixed Capital Formation..........	93e	303.9	354.9	512.8	613.7	979.5	980.0	1,151.5	1,297.5	1,370.6	1,560.1	2,041.8	2,664.3
Changes in Inventories....................	93i	86.9	14.2	21.1	82.3	−39.7	19.4	−25.1	91.4	165.4	278.1	429.2	240.1
Exports of Goods and Services..........	90c	948.8	1,101.0	1,440.1	1,669.1	1,841.4	1,708.1	1,978.3	2,170.3	2,353.7	2,689.3	3,268.3	4,300.3
Imports of Goods and Services (-).....	98c	906.8	1,157.8	1,668.8	1,947.3	2,326.8	2,109.8	2,312.4	2,667.8	2,914.9	3,493.4	4,428.9	5,576.6
Gross Domestic Product (GDP)........	99b	2,262.4	2,580.1	3,076.2	3,562.9	3,902.9	4,265.0	4,750.8	5,219.9	5,758.3	6,392.8	7,413.6	8,903.8
Net Primary Income from Abroad.....	98.n	−4.0	11.5	23.0	32.1	31.9	−40.2	−11.5	12.7	16.8	−15.1	−158.1	−123.6
Gross National Income (GNI)............	99a	2,258.3	2,591.6	3,099.1	3,594.9	3,934.8	4,224.8	4,739.3	5,232.6	5,775.1	6,377.7	7,255.5	8,780.2
Net Current Transf.from Abroad.......	98t	74.3	−214.9	−217.3	−248.4	−237.6	−280.3	−278.0	−306.4	....	....	....	....
Gross Nat'l Disposable Inc.(GNDI)....	99i	2,112.9	2,376.7	2,881.8	3,346.5	3,697.2	3,911.9	4,423.5	4,889.7	....	....	....	....
Gross Saving.................................	99s	716.0	359.6	379.7	494.8	559.4	619.9	899.1	994.7	1,153.6	1,321.0	1,513.8	1,786.8
Consumption of Fixed Capital..........	99cf	254.7	676.1	713.5	799.6	971.0	1,016.2	1,034.1	1,070.0	1,114.2	1,201.3	1,372.0	1,365.2
GDP Volume 2000 Prices.................	99b.p	3,638.7	3,606.0	3,742.7	4,052.7	4,244.1	4,443.5	4,750.8	5,132.9	5,465.1	5,858.4	6,358.7	7,006.5
GDP Volume (2000=100).................	99bvp	76.6	75.9	78.8	85.3	89.3	93.5	100.0	108.0	115.0	123.3	133.8	147.5
GDP Deflator (2000=100)...............	99bip	62.2	71.6	82.2	87.9	92.0	96.0	100.0	101.7	105.4	109.1	116.6	127.1
							Millions: Midyear Estimates						
Population...............................	99z	2.54	2.50	2.46	2.43	2.41	2.39	2.37	2.36	2.34	2.33	2.32	2.31

Lebanon 446

		1994	1995	1996	1997	1998	1999	2000	2001	2002	2003	2004	2005
Exchange Rates						*Pounds per SDR: End of Period*							
Market Rate	aa	2,404.4	2,372.4	2,231.7	2,060.3	2,123.3	2,069.1	1,964.1	1,894.5	2,049.5	2,240.1	2,341.2	2,154.6
				Pounds per US Dollar: End of Period (ae) Period Average (rf)									
Market Rate	ae	1,647.0	1,596.0	1,552.0	1,527.0	1,508.0	1,507.5	1,507.5	1,507.5	1,507.5	1,507.5	1,507.5	1,507.5
Market Rate	rf	1,680.1	1,621.4	1,571.4	1,539.5	1,516.1	1,507.8	1,507.5	1,507.5	1,507.5	1,507.5	1,507.5	1,507.5
				Index Numbers (2000=100): Period Averages									
Market Rate	ahx	89.76	92.98	95.94	97.95	99.42	99.97	100.00	100.07	100.13	100.13	100.13	100.13
Nominal Effective Exchange Rate	nec	69.10	68.50	72.89	81.80	88.49	91.38	100.00	105.43	103.18	93.22	87.74	86.98
Fund Position						*Millions of SDRs: End of Period*							
Quota	2f.s	146.0	146.0	146.0	146.0	146.0	203.0	203.0	203.0	203.0	203.0	203.0	203.0
SDRs	1b.s	11.4	12.3	13.3	14.3	15.4	16.4	18.2	19.4	20.1	20.6	21.2	22.0
Reserve Position in the Fund	1c.s	18.8	18.8	18.8	18.8	18.8	18.8	18.8	18.8	18.8	18.8	18.8	18.8
Total Fund Cred.&Loans Outstg	2tl	—	—	—	—	—	—	—	—	—	—	—	—
International Liquidity					*Millions of US Dollars Unless Otherwise Indicated: End of Period*								
Total Reserves minus Gold	1l.d	3,884.2	4,533.3	5,931.9	5,976.4	6,556.3	7,775.6	5,943.7	5,013.8	7,243.8	12,519.4	11,734.6	11,887.1
SDRs	1b.d	16.6	18.3	19.2	19.3	21.7	22.5	23.7	24.3	27.3	30.7	32.9	31.4
Reserve Position in the Fund	1c.d	27.5	28.0	27.1	25.4	26.5	25.8	24.5	23.7	25.6	28.0	29.2	26.9
Foreign Exchange	1d.d	3,840.1	4,487.0	5,885.6	5,931.6	6,508.0	7,727.3	5,895.4	4,965.8	7,190.9	12,460.8	11,672.4	11,828.7
Gold (Million Fine Troy Ounces)	1ad	9.222	9.222	9.222	9.222	9.222	9.222	9.222	9.222	9.222	9.222	9.222	9.222
Gold (National Valuation)	1and	3,534.5	3,571.8	3,410.0	2,670.3	2,651.0	2,678.0	2,524.6	2,561.1	3,216.3	3,833.5	4,006.0	4,736.4
Monetary Authorities: Other Liab	4..d	29.5	71.3	54.4	72.9	174.0	156.3	138.4	152.0	158.0	134.7	128.4	106.4
Deposit Money Banks: Assets	7a.d	3,806.5	3,970.7	4,329.2	6,014.4	6,620.8	5,910.8	8,159.3	8,615.7	9,503.8	9,908.3	13,552.9	13,278.6
Liabilities	7b.d	1,579.7	2,063.4	2,989.5	4,189.3	5,908.2	6,392.5	7,190.2	7,347.2	7,360.2	9,327.6	12,096.3	11,633.4
Monetary Authorities						*Billions of Pounds: End of Period*							
Foreign Assets	11	12,208.7	12,923.9	14,486.2	13,191.4	13,851.8	15,725.0	12,730.1	10,531.7	12,566.0	21,216.7	20,423.6	22,033.3
Claims on Central Government	12a	31.6	57.2	63.6	354.8	113.0	147.5	2,060.8	6,835.9	3,829.0	12,064.4	13,641.6	14,518.0
Claims on Private Sector	12d	73.1	120.0	338.7	587.7	640.3	578.7	628.8	696.1	914.4	973.4	900.4	779.2
Claims on Deposit Money Banks	12e	166.8	289.9	105.1	96.8	346.1	405.9	734.8	781.0	1,719.6	1,826.8	1,859.2	1,795.7
Reserve Money	14	3,816.7	4,624.5	5,604.4	8,404.0	7,944.3	8,378.2	8,927.4	12,246.5	13,487.7	29,908.7	30,906.2	30,268.4
of which: Currency Outside DMBs	14a	938.8	1,046.2	1,160.7	1,210.1	1,241.3	1,369.3	1,423.4	1,381.7	1,375.3	1,530.6	1,586.5	1,534.7
Foreign Liabilities	16c	48.6	113.8	84.4	111.3	262.3	235.6	208.7	229.1	238.3	203.1	193.6	160.4
Long-Term Foreign Liabilities	16cl	....	....	....	—	1,068.1	1,068.1	1,068.1	1,386.2	1,418.9	1,342.6	961.0	489.9
Central Government Deposits	16d	8,477.5	8,352.6	8,808.2	4,805.6	4,842.1	6,222.7	4,431.8	4,144.1	2,475.7	2,339.2	2,879.5	3,885.2
Capital Accounts	17a	88.5	134.1	312.7	328.1	796.7	883.1	911.9	1,049.2	1,255.5	1,913.9	1,899.8	1,615.8
Other Items (Net)	17r	6,142.7	6,078.2	5,406.6	581.5	37.8	69.5	606.6	−210.5	152.9	373.9	−387.8	1,314.4
of which: Valuation Adjustment	17rv	6,094.0	5,912.1	5,222.7	3,616.3	3,046.4	2,918.3	2,521.6	2,742.2	102.5	645.9	372.4	1,392.0
Deposit Money Banks						*Billions of Pounds: End of Period*							
Reserves	20	2,786.4	3,541.5	4,377.9	6,224.6	6,513.4	6,826.7	7,330.8	10,655.9	11,959.8	28,332.5	29,878.7	30,917.3
Foreign Assets	21	6,269.3	6,337.3	6,718.9	9,184.0	9,984.2	8,910.5	12,300.2	12,988.2	14,327.0	14,936.8	20,430.9	20,017.4
Claims on Central Government	22a	6,908.6	7,948.9	12,060.3	13,234.2	17,942.1	21,840.8	23,271.3	23,066.8	26,577.4	21,005.8	24,155.4	26,696.5
Claims on Private Sector	22d	7,799.8	10,320.0	12,687.0	15,451.3	18,681.5	20,994.3	22,243.2	22,192.0	22,926.5	22,835.7	24,020.4	24,466.8
Demand Deposits	24	492.7	508.0	568.7	685.5	758.3	845.8	862.2	889.6	1,094.3	1,277.3	1,389.3	1,358.5
Time & Foreign Currency Deposits	25	18,193.7	21,297.8	26,935.9	32,621.4	38,067.1	42,458.0	46,720.0	50,344.6	54,356.3	60,514.1	66,879.0	70,273.7
Foreign Liabilities	26c	2,601.7	3,293.1	4,639.8	6,397.1	8,909.6	9,636.7	10,839.2	11,075.9	11,095.5	14,061.4	18,235.2	17,537.4
Central Government Deposits	26d	255.4	261.0	285.1	216.6	346.1	701.7	720.9	525.5	591.0	1,325.3	1,480.0	1,704.9
Credit from Monetary Authorities	26g	166.8	289.9	105.1	96.8	346.1	405.9	734.8	781.0	1,719.6	1,826.8	1,859.2	1,795.7
Capital Accounts	27a	675.8	1,145.9	1,943.5	2,990.1	3,619.9	4,019.3	4,376.3	4,463.2	5,023.5	5,498.6	5,808.5	6,410.7
Other Items (Net)	27r	1,378.0	1,351.9	1,366.1	1,086.5	1,074.0	504.8	892.1	823.1	1,910.6	2,607.3	2,834.3	3,017.1
Monetary Survey						*Billions of Pounds: End of Period*							
Foreign Assets (Net)	31n	15,827.6	15,854.3	16,481.0	15,866.9	13,596.1	13,695.1	12,914.3	10,828.7	14,140.4	20,546.4	21,464.6	23,863.0
Domestic Credit	32	6,080.2	9,832.4	16,056.3	24,605.7	32,188.6	36,636.9	43,051.4	48,121.2	51,180.6	53,214.8	58,358.4	60,870.4
Claims on Central Govt. (Net)	32an	−1,792.7	−607.5	3,030.6	8,566.8	12,866.8	15,063.9	20,179.4	25,233.1	27,339.7	29,405.7	33,437.5	35,624.3
Claims on Private Sector	32d	7,872.9	10,440.0	13,025.7	16,039.0	19,321.8	21,573.0	22,872.0	22,888.1	23,840.9	23,809.1	24,920.9	25,246.0
Money	34	1,436.8	1,560.6	1,753.4	1,929.4	2,051.5	2,260.8	2,389.3	2,365.3	2,566.4	2,847.0	3,030.6	2,952.1
Quasi-Money	35	18,214.5	21,322.7	27,161.6	32,640.2	38,087.2	42,564.3	46,845.5	50,545.1	54,611.1	61,788.7	68,129.2	71,405.6
Other Items (Net)	37r	14,444.4	14,627.6	14,067.7	9,519.2	8,692.3	8,425.2	9,252.5	8,781.6	8,246.1	9,771.5	8,663.2	10,375.6
Money plus Quasi-Money	35l	19,651.3	22,883.3	28,915.1	34,569.6	40,138.8	44,825.1	49,234.8	52,910.4	57,177.5	64,635.7	71,159.8	74,357.7
Interest Rates						*Percent Per Annum*							
Discount Rate (End of Period)	60	16.49	19.01	25.00	30.00	30.00	25.00	20.00	20.00	20.00	20.00	20.00	12.00
Treasury Bill Rate	60c	15.09	19.40	15.19	13.42	12.70	11.57	11.18	11.18	10.90	....	5.25	5.22
Deposit Rate	60l	14.80	16.30	15.54	13.37	13.61	12.50	11.21	10.85	11.03	8.69	7.37	8.15
Lending Rate	60p	23.88	24.69	25.21	20.29	....	19.48	18.15	17.19	16.58	13.43	10.81	10.64
Intl. Transactions & Positions						*Millions of US Dollars*							
Exports	70..d	470	656	736	643	662	677	715	890	1,046	1,524	1,748	1,837
Imports, c.i.f.	71..d	2,598	5,480	7,540	7,467	7,070	6,207	6,230	7,293	6,447	7,171	9,400	9,359

Lebanon 446

		1994	1995	1996	1997	1998	1999	2000	2001	2002	2003	2004	2005
Balance of Payments					*Millions of US Dollars: Minus Sign Indicates Debit*								
Current Account, n.i.e.	78ald	....	....	....	....	....	....	....	....	−4,385	−5,463	−4,805	....
Goods: Exports f.o.b.	78aad	....	....	....	....	....	....	....	....	1,018	1,444	1,598	....
Goods: Imports f.o.b.	78abd	....	....	....	....	....	....	....	....	−5,979	−6,667	−8,704	....
Trade Balance	78acd	....	....	....	....	....	....	....	....	−4,962	−5,223	−7,105	....
Services: Credit	78add	....	....	....	....	....	....	....	....	4,429	9,462	9,700	....
Services: Debit	78aed	....	....	....	....	....	....	....	....	−3,367	−6,500	−8,263	....
Balance on Goods & Services	78afd	....	....	....	....	....	....	....	....	−3,899	−2,261	−5,669	....
Income: Credit	78agd	....	....	....	....	....	....	....	....	567	1,511	1,316	....
Income: Debit	78ahd	....	....	....	....	....	....	....	....	−1,131	−5,040	−2,168	....
Balance on Gds, Serv. & Inc	78aid	....	....	....	....	....	....	....	....	−4,463	−5,791	−6,521	....
Current Transfers, n.i.e.: Credit	78ajd	....	....	....	....	....	....	....	....	2,591	4,079	5,325	....
Current Transfers: Debit	78akd	....	....	....	....	....	....	....	....	−2,513	−3,751	−3,609	....
Capital Account, n.i.e.	78bcd	....	....	....	....	....	....	....	....	13	29	50	....
Capital Account, n.i.e.: Credit	78bad	....	....	....	....	....	....	....	....	13	30	54	....
Capital Account: Debit	78bbd	....	....	....	....	....	....	....	....	—	−1	−3	....
Financial Account, n.i.e.	78bjd	....	....	....	....	....	....	....	....	3,350	4,003	4,817	....
Direct Investment Abroad	78bdd	....	....	....	....	....	....	....	....	—	457	−385	....
Dir. Invest. in Rep. Econ., n.i.e.	78bed	....	....	....	....	....	....	....	....	1,336	2,523	1,311	....
Portfolio Investment Assets	78bfd	....	....	....	....	....	....	....	....	101	−773	−614	....
Equity Securities	78bkd	....	....	....	....	....	....	....	....	157	−254	−349	....
Debt Securities	78bld	....	....	....	....	....	....	....	....	−57	−519	−265	....
Portfolio Investment Liab., n.i.e.	78bgd	....	....	....	....	....	....	....	....	2,881	2,475	2,843	....
Equity Securities	78bmd	....	....	....	....	....	....	....	....	—	207	148	....
Debt Securities	78bnd	....	....	....	....	....	....	....	....	2,881	2,267	2,696	....
Financial Derivatives Assets	78bwd	....	....	....	....	....	....	....	....	....	....	....	....
Financial Derivatives Liabilities	78bxd	....	....	....	....	....	....	....	....	....	....	....	....
Other Investment Assets	78bhd	....	....	....	....	....	....	....	....	−843	−3,562	−1,140	....
Monetary Authorities	78bod	....	....	....	....	....	....	....	....	—	—	—	....
General Government	78bpd	....	....	....	....	....	....	....	....	—	−25	45	....
Banks	78bqd	....	....	....	....	....	....	....	....	—	−4,834	−1,375	....
Other Sectors	78brd	....	....	....	....	....	....	....	....	−843	1,297	191	....
Other Investment Liab., n.i.e.	78bid	....	....	....	....	....	....	....	....	−125	2,885	2,802	....
Monetary Authorities	78bsd	....	....	....	....	....	....	....	....	—	—	—	....
General Government	78btd	....	....	....	....	....	....	....	....	−48	619	−18	....
Banks	78bud	....	....	....	....	....	....	....	....	1	1,100	1,240	....
Other Sectors	78bvd	....	....	....	....	....	....	....	....	−78	1,166	1,580	....
Net Errors and Omissions	78cad	....	....	....	....	....	....	....	....	−1,196	−2,572	−403	....
Overall Balance	78cbd	....	....	....	....	....	....	....	....	−2,219	−4,002	−340	....
Reserves and Related Items	79dad	....	....	....	....	....	....	....	....	2,219	4,002	340	....
Reserve Assets	79dbd	....	....	....	....	....	....	....	....	2,219	4,002	340	....
Use of Fund Credit and Loans	79dcd	....	....	....	....	....	....	....	....	—	—	—	....
Exceptional Financing	79ded	....	....	....	....	....	....	....	....	—	—	—	....
Government Finance						*Billions of Pounds: Year Ending December 31*							
Deficit (-) or Surplus	80	−2,631.0	−3,309.3	−4,198.3	−5,902.8	−3,936.1	−4,029.8	−4,788.1	−4,003.3	−3,670.4	−4,011.6	−2,734.5	....
Revenue	81	2,241.0	3,032.7	3,533.7	3,753.2	4,449.4	4,868.2	4,171.7	4,259.6	5,385.3	6,180.8	7,000.3	....
Grants Received	81z	507.0	—	—	72.0	—	12.0	—	.2	.1	.1	.2	....
Expenditure	82	5,379.0	6,342.0	7,732.0	9,728.0	8,385.5	8,910.0	8,959.8	8,263.1	9,055.8	10,192.5	9,735.0	....
Lending Minus Repayments	83	—	—	—	—	—	—	—	—	—	—	—	....
Financing													
Domestic	84a	1,946.0	2,452.3	3,334.3	5,158.3	1,468.8	2,008.3	2,361.2	435.0	−3,785.8	1,559.1	−673.7	....
Foreign	85a	685.0	857.0	864.0	744.5	2,467.3	2,021.5	2,426.9	3,568.3	7,456.2	2,452.5	3,408.3	....
Debt: Domestic	88a	9,347.5	11,997.2	17,228.8	19,797.1	21,685.7	25,382.8	27,161.2	28,213.8	26,302.3	26,843.0	26,371.1	....
Debt: Foreign	89a	1,286.0	2,157.8	2,958.5	3,713.3	6,282.5	8,350.8	10,494.7	14,423.5	21,972.4	23,453.4	27,688.9	....
						Millions: Midyear Estimates							
Population	99z	3.09	3.18	3.24	3.29	3.33	3.36	3.40	3.43	3.47	3.50	3.54	3.58

		1994	1995	1996	1997	1998	1999	2000	2001	2002	2003	2004	2005
Exchange Rates						*Loti per SDR: End of Period*							
Principal Rate...................	aa	5.17298	5.42197	6.73325	6.56747	8.25106	8.44711	9.86107	15.23974	11.74625	9.86684	8.74345	9.04013
					Loti per US Dollar: End of Period (ae) Period Average (rf)								
Principal Rate...................	ae	3.54350	3.64750	4.68250	4.86750	5.86000	6.15450	7.56850	12.12650	8.64000	6.64000	5.63000	6.32500
Principal Rate...................	rf	3.55080	3.62709	4.29935	4.60796	5.52828	6.10948	6.93983	8.60918	10.54075	7.56475	6.45969	6.35933
					Index Numbers (2000=100): Period Averages								
Principal Rate...................	ahx	194.6	190.4	161.7	150.0	126.0	113.0	100.0	81.3	66.7	91.6	107.2	108.8
Nominal Effective Exchange Rate.....	nec	190.0	179.6	154.0	145.7	126.7	112.8	100.0	82.7	67.2	92.0	105.8	106.4
Real Effective Exchange Rate...........	rec	138.6	138.7	125.2	125.4	115.2	109.5	100.0	86.2	78.0	112.2	132.2	132.7
Fund Position						*Millions of SDRs: End of Period*							
Quota...................	2f.s	23.90	23.90	23.90	23.90	23.90	34.90	34.90	34.90	34.90	34.90	34.90	34.90
SDRs...................	1b.s	.33	.24	.92	.89	.86	.85	.51	.46	.44	.42	.40	.31
Reserve Position in the Fund...........	1c.s	3.51	3.51	3.51	3.52	3.53	3.53	3.54	3.54	3.54	3.54	3.56	3.60
Total Fund Cred.&Loans Outstg.......	2tl	27.63	25.82	23.48	20.39	16.76	12.46	8.53	12.13	16.19	17.88	24.50	24.50
International Liquidity				*Millions of US Dollars Unless Otherwise Indicated: End of Period*									
Total Reserves minus Gold..............	1l.d	372.62	456.74	460.51	571.74	575.08	499.56	417.89	386.49	406.37	460.33	501.50	520.42
SDRs...................	1b.d	.47	.35	1.33	1.20	1.22	1.17	.66	.58	.60	.63	.62	.44
Reserve Position in the Fund..........	1c.d	5.13	5.22	5.05	4.75	4.98	4.85	4.61	4.45	4.82	5.26	5.53	5.15
Foreign Exchange...................	1d.d	367.02	451.17	454.13	565.78	568.89	493.54	412.62	381.46	400.95	454.44	495.35	514.83
Monetary Authorities: Other Liab.....	4..d	1.85	33.39	28.73	26.79	24.79	42.72	37.78	27.16	52.98	47.33	55.69	51.75
Deposit Money Banks: Assets...........	7a.d	48.52	65.04	58.36	41.80	72.97	80.37	80.48	65.11	76.28	126.11	222.70	196.33
Liabilities...................	7b.d	10.29	16.51	12.83	11.69	8.05	6.48	8.48	8.48	11.53	34.58	24.14	16.89
Monetary Authorities						*Millions of Maloti: End of Period*							
Foreign Assets...................	11	1,337.58	1,802.01	2,310.26	2,929.82	3,549.85	3,349.33	3,486.14	5,138.38	3,858.43	3,341.55	3,351.46	3,645.16
Claims on Central Government........	12a	381.63	287.92	318.78	166.39	145.88	110.39	105.04	250.96	192.44	176.44	214.25	221.62
Claims on Private Sector................	12d	—	8.91	8.69	10.52	11.54	12.20	13.90	13.56	13.53	14.99	16.30	19.48
Claims on Deposit Money Banks......	12e	.44	—	—	—	—	—	—	—	—	—	—	—
Reserve Money...................	14	249.15	329.83	346.37	388.95	540.13	717.32	669.79	499.36	500.91	533.95	566.78	754.40
of which: Currency Outside DMBs..	14a	52.57	74.11	84.09	92.51	134.50	122.66	139.34	147.14	179.68	183.52	204.54	212.78
Foreign Liabilities...................	16c	149.49	261.78	292.62	264.26	283.56	368.13	370.06	514.22	647.88	490.68	527.75	548.79
Central Government Deposits........	16d	1,134.25	1,350.19	1,659.50	2,062.82	2,125.51	1,602.59	1,356.38	1,502.35	1,257.31	1,263.91	1,411.84	1,422.01
Capital Accounts...................	17a	82.34	185.68	368.79	409.22	735.54	805.41	1,208.99	2,858.28	1,772.05	1,393.32	1,204.24	1,338.33
Other Items (Net)...................	17r	104.42	−28.64	−29.55	−18.54	22.52	−21.54	−.14	28.69	−113.75	−148.87	−128.60	−177.27
Deposit Money Banks						*Millions of Maloti: End of Period*							
Reserves...................	20	180.45	165.68	245.58	245.22	490.59	573.72	506.81	127.06	159.15	181.10	172.46	275.41
Foreign Assets...................	21	171.94	237.24	273.27	203.46	427.54	494.65	609.09	789.61	659.10	837.34	1,253.79	1,241.81
Claims on Central Government........	22a	103.95	74.91	74.35	74.23	51.53	586.38	586.20	691.32	812.38	991.45	543.43	461.65
Claims on Nonfin.Pub.Enterprises.....	22c	30.92	80.53	141.33	127.62	225.53	105.28	79.22	46.39	42.75	38.94	52.16	33.37
Claims on Private Sector................	22d	686.72	654.32	656.14	972.25	822.12	810.29	834.11	873.00	1,008.39	453.58	496.79	754.36
Claims on Other Banking Insts...	22f	10.39	—	—	—	—	—	—	—	—	—	—	—
Claims on Nonbank Financial Insts...	22g	—	—	—	—	—	—	—	—	—	—	—	2.37
Demand Deposits...................	24	434.02	445.91	548.00	686.57	836.92	821.27	873.73	939.04	1,099.15	1,185.21	1,197.50	1,427.86
Time and Savings Deposits...............	25	550.42	601.05	692.40	743.97	785.67	720.52	664.94	700.44	727.24	760.10	783.63	760.54
Money Market Instruments.............	26aa	12.22	7.48	2.68	9.10	1.97	4.82	10.12	34.05	8.25	17.43	16.90	—
Foreign Liabilities...................	26c	36.47	60.23	60.06	56.89	47.20	39.89	140.01	102.82	99.63	229.64	135.90	106.86
Central Government Deposits..........	26d	39.59	37.53	43.66	46.04	76.77	77.12	68.38	63.31	63.89	68.35	57.76	171.88
Capital Accounts...................	27a	233.51	119.12	56.11	−74.15	−38.31	209.92	318.90	279.18	286.81	303.43	345.75	403.50
Other Items (Net)...................	27r	−121.85	−58.63	−12.26	154.37	307.15	696.78	539.35	408.55	396.80	−61.74	−18.80	−101.66
Monetary Survey						*Millions of Maloti: End of Period*							
Foreign Assets (Net)...................	31n	1,323.56	1,717.24	2,230.85	2,812.12	3,646.68	3,435.95	3,585.17	5,310.96	3,770.03	3,458.57	3,941.61	4,231.32
Domestic Credit...................	32	39.77	−281.13	−503.89	−757.85	−945.69	−55.17	193.70	309.56	748.28	343.15	−146.67	−101.03
Claims on Central Govt. (Net)........	32an	−688.26	−1,024.89	−1,310.03	−1,868.24	−2,004.88	−982.95	−733.52	−623.38	−316.38	−164.36	−711.92	−910.62
Claims on Nonfin.Pub.Enterprises.....	32c	30.92	80.53	141.33	127.62	225.53	105.28	79.22	46.39	42.75	38.94	52.16	33.37
Claims on Private Sector................	32d	686.72	663.24	664.82	982.77	833.66	822.49	848.00	886.56	1,021.91	468.57	513.09	773.84
Claims on Other Banking Insts.......	32f	10.39	—	—	—	—	—	—	—	—	—	—	—
Claims on Nonbank Financial Insts.	32g	—	—	—	—	—	—	—	—	—	—	—	2.37
Money...................	34	486.59	537.70	641.62	787.03	983.17	957.32	1,035.96	1,292.27	1,440.94	1,537.75	1,589.42	1,829.48
Quasi-Money...................	35	550.42	601.05	692.40	743.97	785.67	720.52	664.94	700.44	727.24	760.10	783.63	760.54
Money Market Instruments.............	36aa	12.22	7.48	2.68	9.10	1.97	4.82	10.12	34.05	8.25	17.43	16.90	—
Capital Accounts...................	37a	315.85	304.80	424.89	335.07	697.22	1,015.34	1,527.89	3,137.46	2,058.86	1,696.74	1,549.99	1,741.83
Other Items (Net)...................	37r	−1.74	−14.91	−34.64	179.09	232.96	682.78	539.95	456.30	283.02	−210.31	−145.00	−201.54
Money plus Quasi-Money.............	35l	1,037.01	1,138.74	1,334.02	1,531.00	1,768.83	1,677.84	1,700.90	1,992.71	2,168.18	2,297.85	2,373.05	2,590.01
Interest Rates						*Percent Per Annum*							
Discount Rate (End of Period)..........	60	13.50	15.50	17.00	15.60	19.50	19.00	15.00	13.00	16.19	15.00	13.00	13.00
Treasury Bill Rate...................	60c	9.44	12.40	13.89	14.83	15.47	12.45	9.06	9.49	11.34	11.96	8.52	7.23
Savings Rate...................	60k	6.75	9.53	10.67	10.08	9.47	5.95	3.50	4.00	4.00	3.39	1.89	1.75
Deposit Rate...................	60l	8.43	13.34	12.73	11.81	10.73	7.45	4.92	4.83	5.19	5.16	4.24	3.95
Lending Rate...................	60p	14.25	16.38	17.71	18.03	20.06	19.06	17.11	16.55	17.11	16.02	12.38	11.72
Prices						*Index Numbers (2000=100): Period Averages*							
Consumer Prices...................	64	63.8	69.7	76.2	. . . .	. . . .	94.2	100.0	90.4	120.9	129.0	135.5	140.2
Intl. Transactions & Positions						*Millions of Maloti*							
Exports...................	70	509.0	581.0	812.0	904.0	1,071.0	1,050.8	1,526.8	2,410.6	3,931.7	3,631.1	4,567.0	4,292.5
Imports, c.i.f...................	71	3,000.0	3,576.0	4,303.0	4,722.0	5,202.1	5,290.8	5,614.3	6,396.6	8,516.9	8,419.6	9,237.4	8,966.7

		1994	1995	1996	1997	1998	1999	2000	2001	2002	2003	2004	2005
Balance of Payments					*Millions of US Dollars: Minus Sign Indicates Debit*								
Current Account, n.i.e.	78ald	108.1	−323.0	−302.5	−269.2	−280.2	−220.8	−151.4	−95.1	−126.7	−134.7	−76.0	....
Goods: Exports f.o.b.	78aad	143.5	160.0	186.9	196.1	193.4	172.5	211.1	278.6	357.3	475.0	707.3	....
Goods: Imports f.o.b.	78abd	−810.2	−985.2	−998.6	−1,024.4	−866.0	−779.2	−727.6	−678.6	−762.7	−994.4	−1,302.0	....
Trade Balance	78acd	−666.7	−825.2	−811.8	−828.3	−672.5	−606.7	−516.5	−400.0	−405.5	−519.4	−594.7	....
Services: Credit	78add	37.8	39.0	42.6	86.9	53.6	43.7	42.7	40.5	34.9	50.0	63.9	....
Services: Debit	78aed	−64.2	−61.1	−55.9	−67.6	−52.2	−50.1	−42.5	−49.0	−56.0	−85.0	−96.1	....
Balance on Goods & Services	78afd	−693.2	−847.3	−825.1	−809.0	−671.2	−613.1	−516.4	−408.5	−426.5	−554.4	−626.9	....
Income: Credit	78agd	369.6	471.6	453.0	447.4	357.7	325.0	288.8	235.3	206.8	304.1	379.1	....
Income: Debit	78ahd	−39.4	−157.4	−119.5	−110.0	−123.6	−80.6	−62.6	−56.7	−28.6	−54.3	−76.3	....
Balance on Gds, Serv. & Inc.	78aid	−363.0	−533.2	−491.6	−471.6	−437.1	−368.6	−290.2	−229.9	−248.3	−304.7	−324.1	....
Current Transfers, n.i.e.: Credit	78ajd	472.1	211.3	190.2	202.9	158.0	149.4	139.8	137.2	123.3	171.8	250.7	....
Current Transfers: Debit	78akd	−.9	−1.2	−1.1	−.5	−1.2	−1.6	−1.0	−2.5	−1.7	−1.9	−2.5	....
Capital Account, n.i.e.	78bcd	—	43.7	45.5	44.5	22.9	15.2	22.0	16.8	23.5	27.5	33.4	....
Capital Account, n.i.e.: Credit	78bad	—	43.7	45.5	44.5	22.9	15.2	22.0	16.8	23.5	27.5	33.4	....
Capital Account: Debit	78bbd	—	—	—	—	—	—	—	....	—	....	—	....
Financial Account, n.i.e.	78bjd	33.0	349.1	350.6	323.7	316.1	135.8	85.2	88.6	92.0	98.2	63.3	....
Direct Investment Abroad	78bdd		....	....	....	....	....	....	....	—	—	−.1	....
Dir. Invest. in Rep. Econ., n.i.e.	78bed	18.7	275.3	287.5	268.1	264.8	163.3	117.8	117.0	84.1	115.7	123.5	....
Portfolio Investment Assets	78bfd	—	....	....	....	....	....	....	....	—	....	....	....
Equity Securities	78bkd	—	....	....	....	....	....	....	....	—	....	....	....
Debt Securities	78bld	—	....	....	....	....	....	....	....	—	....	....	....
Portfolio Investment Liab., n.i.e.	78bgd	—	....	....	....	....	....	....	....	....	....	....	....
Equity Securities	78bmd	—	....	....	....	....	....	....	....	....	....	....	....
Debt Securities	78bnd	—	....	....	....	....	....	....	....	....	....	....	....
Financial Derivatives Assets	78bwd	....											
Financial Derivatives Liabilities	78bxd	....											
Other Investment Assets	78bhd	−13.4	18.8	−7.0	−5.0	−1.7	−11.0	−19.1	−20.2	1.5	−8.8	−48.9	....
Monetary Authorities	78bod		....	....	....	....	....	....	....	....	....	....	....
General Government	78bpd	—	....	....	....	....	....	....	....	....	....	....	....
Banks	78bqd	−13.4	18.8	−7.0	−5.0	−1.7	−11.0	−19.1	−20.2	1.5	−8.8	−48.9	....
Other Sectors	78brd	—	....	....	....	....	....	....	....	....	....	....	....
Other Investment Liab., n.i.e.	78bid	27.6	55.0	70.1	60.5	53.0	−16.6	−13.5	−8.2	6.4	−8.7	−11.2	....
Monetary Authorities	78bsd	.3	6.3	−.2	—	.1	−5.4	−3.5	16.0	3.9	−17.8	.9	....
General Government	78btd	26.0	49.2	71.8	68.6	59.8	−9.3	−15.1	−19.0	2.9	−10.0	1.6	....
Banks	78bud	1.9	....	....	−7.2	−6.7	−1.2	5.2	−4.8	—	19.2	−13.7	....
Other Sectors	78bvd	−.5	−.5	−1.4	−.9	−.1	−.6	−.1	−.5	−.4	−.1	—	....
Net Errors and Omissions	78cad	−20.3	28.1	23.3	42.1	56.8	29.0	62.1	155.4	−166.4	−56.6	−15.8	....
Overall Balance	78cbd	120.9	97.8	116.9	141.0	115.6	−40.8	17.8	165.7	−177.6	−65.7	4.9	....
Reserves and Related Items	79dad	−120.9	−97.8	−116.9	−141.0	−115.6	40.8	−17.8	−165.7	177.6	65.7	−4.9	....
Reserve Assets	79dbd	−124.6	−95.1	−113.5	−136.8	−110.7	46.7	−12.6	−170.2	172.4	63.2	−14.7	....
Use of Fund Credit and Loans	79dcd	3.8	−2.7	−3.4	−4.3	−4.9	−5.9	−5.2	4.5	5.2	2.5	9.8	....
Exceptional Financing	79ded	....	....	....	....	....	....	....					
International Investment Position						*Millions of US Dollars*								
Assets	79aad	....	....	....	....	....	....	....	....	....	....	....	....
Direct Investment Abroad	79abd	....	—	—	—	....	....	....	....	....	....	....	....
Portfolio Investment	79acd	....	—	—	—	—	—	—	—	—	—	—	....
Equity Securities	79add	....	—	—	—	—	—	—	—	—	—	—	....
Debt Securities	79aed	....	—	—	—	—	—	—	—	—	—	—	....
Financial Derivatives	79ald	....									—		
Other Investment	79afd	....	71.8	61.9	114.5	83.8	79.6	80.5	65.1	89.4	126.6	222.7	....
Monetary Authorities	79agd	....	—	—	—	—	—	—	—	—	—	—	....
General Government	79ahd	....	—	—	—	—	—	—	—	—	—	—	....
Banks	79aid	....	71.8	61.9	114.5	83.8	79.6	80.5	65.1	89.4	126.6	222.7	....
Other Sectors	79ajd	....	—	—	—	—	—	—	—	—	—	—	....
Reserve Assets	79akd	....	456.7	460.5	571.7	575.1	499.8	419.8	423.7	446.6	503.2	593.9	....
Liabilities	79lad	....	....	....	....	....	....	....	....	....	....	....	....
Dir. Invest. in Rep. Economy	79lbd	....	—	—	—	—	—	—	—	—	—	—	....
Portfolio Investment	79lcd	....	—	—	—	—	—	—	—	—	—	—	....
Equity Securities	79ldd	....	—	—	—	—	—	—	—	—	—	—	....
Debt Securities	79led	....	—	—	—	—	—	—	—	—	—	—	....
Financial Derivatives	79lld	....									—		
Other Investment	79lfd	....	566.8	535.6	512.6	590.7	559.5	600.9	580.9	702.2	802.1	886.4	....
Monetary Authorities	79lgd	....	39.9	35.1	28.8	24.7	18.2	11.7	57.3	96.9	100.1	131.8	....
General Government	79lhd	....	510.3	487.7	475.3	543.5	534.8	570.7	515.1	593.8	667.5	730.5	....
Banks	79lid	....	16.5	12.8	8.5	22.4	6.5	18.5	8.5	11.5	34.6	24.1	....
Other Sectors	79ljd	....	—	—	—	—	—	—	—	—	—	—	....
Government Finance					*Millions of Maloti: Year Beginning April 1*								
Deficit (-) or Surplus	80	149.3	108.6	137.4	88.8	−188.8	−286.8	−204.8	−42.6	−342.9	−247.3	....	....
Revenue	81	1,438.5	1,681.6	2,034.6	2,353.4	2,158.7	2,275.7	2,626.6	2,787.5	3,035.0	3,368.1	....	....
Grants Received	81z	143.6	163.2	203.4	178.7	120.0	130.0	125.6	188.8	286.7	276.8		
Exp. & Lending Minus Repay	82z	1,432.8	1,736.2	2,100.6	2,443.3	2,467.5	2,692.5	2,957.0	3,018.9	3,664.6	3,892.2	....	....
Expenditure	82	994.1	1,118.1	1,179.0	1,537.6	1,971.7	2,311.5	2,457.9	2,393.3	2,935.0	3,151.3	....	....
Lending Minus Repayments	83	438.7	618.1	921.6	905.7	495.8	381.0	499.1	625.6	729.6	740.9	....	....
Financing													
Domestic	84a	−252.5	−319.5	−537.3	−559.8	155.1	386.3	426.5	10.7	328.5	273.2	....	....
Foreign	85a	103.2	210.9	399.9	471.0	33.7	−99.8	−221.7	31.9	14.4	−25.9	....	....
Debt: Domestic	88a	....	....	....	190.2	160.1	730.1	788.5	763.3	929.0	1,159.7	....	....
Debt: Foreign	89a	1,704.4	1,861.5	2,255.1	2,313.4	3,185.1	3,121.9	4,319.6	6,246.2	6,059.5	4,432.0	....	....

Lesotho 666

National Accounts		1994	1995	1996	1997	1998	1999	2000	2001	2002	2003	2004	2005
		Millions of Maloti: Year Beginning April 1											
Househ.Cons.Expend.,incl.NPISHs....	96f	3,544.8	4,075.2	4,863.4	5,398.3	5,543.7	5,777.6	6,041.6	6,469.9	7,550.6	7,801.0	8,260.7	9,271.0
Government Consumption Expend...	91f	486.5	607.2	658.6	801.2	1,023.4	1,033.2	1,139.5	1,167.4	1,148.5	1,238.2	1,250.5	1,400.1
Gross Fixed Capital Formation.........	93e	1,693.1	2,071.2	2,360.2	2,593.5	2,411.0	2,651.0	2,657.1	2,810.0	3,254.6	3,558.0	3,620.1	3,743.2
Changes in Inventories....................	93i	−44.6	−24.3	7.8	−47.1	−93.4	−56.2	−138.1	−171.1	−135.4	49.9	8.7	—
Exports of Goods and Services..........	90c	642.8	720.4	965.6	1,261.3	1,320.7	1,322.4	1,775.6	2,747.0	4,111.9	3,932.7	4,928.1	4,614.6
Imports of Goods and Services (-).....	98c	3,357.4	4,066.1	4,801.8	5,287.6	5,284.6	5,275.6	5,511.9	6,458.3	8,560.1	8,526.1	9,235.3	9,665.2
Gross Domestic Product (GDP).........	99b	2,965.3	3,383.7	4,053.6	4,719.6	4,920.7	5,564.9	5,963.5	6,564.8	7,370.2	8,053.8	8,833.0	9,326.2
Net Primary Income from Abroad.....	98.n	1,345.5	1,410.9	1,421.5	1,538.9	1,384.7	1,492.5	1,522.3	1,509.0	1,698.1	1,874.4	2,050.7	2,066.2
Gross National Income (GNI)............	99a	4,310.8	4,794.6	5,475.1	6,258.5	6,305.4	7,057.4	7,486.0	8,073.8	9,068.3	9,928.2	10,883.7	11,289.0
Net National Income.....................	99e	5,103.1	5,713.2	6,473.4	7,396.3	7,272.9	8,055.5	8,529.7	9,154.8	10,584.6	11,397.7	12,670.5	13,109.5
GDP Volume 1995 Prices................	99b.p	3,241.5	3,383.7	3,721.0	4,024.0	3,837.0	3,846.0	3,897.0	4,022.0	4,162.7	4,291.4	4,426.5	4,479.9
GDP Volume (2000=100)...............	99bvp	83.2	86.8	95.5	103.3	98.5	98.7	100.0	103.2	106.8	110.1	113.6	115.0
GDP Deflator (2000=100)...............	99bip	59.8	65.3	71.2	76.6	83.8	94.6	100.0	106.7	115.7	122.6	130.4	136.0
		Millions: Midyear Estimates											
Population...............................	99z	1.67	1.69	1.71	1.74	1.76	1.77	1.79	1.80	1.80	1.80	1.80	1.79

Liberia 668

		1994	1995	1996	1997	1998	1999	2000	2001	2002	2003	2004	2005
Exchange Rates						*Liberian Dollars per SDR: End of Period*							
Market Rate	aa	1.4599	1.4865	1.4380	1.3493	† 60.8973	54.2141	55.6994	62.2081	88.3688	75.0415	84.6390	80.7538
						Liberian Dollars per US Dollar: End of Period (ae) Period Average (rf)							
Market Rate	ae	1.0000	1.0000	1.0000	1.0000	† 43.2500	39.5000	42.7500	49.5000	65.0000	50.5000	54.5000	56.5000
Market Rate	rf	1.0000	1.0000	1.0000	1.0000	† 41.5075	41.9025	40.9525	48.5833	61.7542	59.3788	54.9058	57.0958
Fund Position						*Millions of SDRs: End of Period*							
Quota	2f.s	71.30	71.30	71.30	71.30	71.30	71.30	71.30	71.30	71.30	71.30	71.30	71.30
SDRs	1b.s	—	—	—	—	—	—	—	—	—	—	—	—
Reserve Position in the Fund	1c.s	.03	.03	.03	.03	.03	.03	.03	.03	.03	.03	.03	.03
Total Fund Cred.&Loans Outstg	2tl	225.83	225.74	225.74	225.70	225.26	224.82	224.36	223.91	223.67	223.67	223.67	223.63
International Liquidity						*Millions of US Dollars: End of Period*							
Total Reserves minus Gold	1l.d	5.07	28.09	.38	.42	.62	.43	.27	.48	3.30	7.38	18.74	25.40
SDRs	1b.d	—	—	—	—	—	—	—	—	—	—	—	—
Reserve Position in the Fund	1c.d	.04	.04	.04	.04	.04	.04	.04	.04	.04	.04	.05	.04
Foreign Exchange	1d.d	5.03	28.05	.34	.38	.58	.39	.23	.44	3.26	7.33	18.69	25.35
Monetary Authorities: Other Liab	4..d	9.08	9.68	12.40	12.56	10.87	10.48	9.78	6.38	7.16	7.16	7.09	7.40
Banking Institutions: Assets	7a.d	9.46	12.04	9.49	15.59	10.36	16.80	12.39	11.04	10.36	15.21	35.73	47.38
Liabilities	7b.d	46.33	15.35	5.12	8.44	2.47	3.01	10.01	11.87	9.65	10.55	22.54	25.56
Monetary Authorities						*Millions of Liberian Dollars: End of Period*							
Foreign Assets	11	5.1	28.1	.4	.4	26.7	17.0	† 11.4	23.8	214.4	372.5	1,021.7	1,434.8
Claims on Central Government	12a	1,284.9	1,513.0	1,803.1	1,916.2	35,687.0	32,605.1	† 36,643.0	41,690.6	59,640.5	50,482.3	56,911.6	56,360.4
Claims on Nonfin.Pub.Enterprises	12c	4.8	4.8	5.6	5.6	5.8	5.5	† —	—	.8	.6	.5	.6
Claims on Private Sector	12d	15.5	15.4	20.5	20.2	25.5	24.6	† 48.9	16.5	50.5	64.5	100.0	119.8
Claims on Banking Institutions	12e	51.4	61.5	2.5	2.3	4.3	1.7	† 77.3	134.9	163.0	65.7	81.1	75.8
Claims on Nonbank Financial Insts	12g	.7	—	.2	.2	1.5	1.5	† —					
Reserve Money	14	551.1	723.4	852.6	920.5	938.4	979.9	† 1,384.7	1,548.2	1,645.9	1,793.0	2,910.3	3,696.0
of which: Currency Outside Banks	14a	302.9	485.8	568.4	576.6	565.5	556.9	† 698.3	845.1	1,045.0	1,303.7	1,754.9	2,168.9
Other Liabs. to Banking Insts	14n	—	—	—	—	—	—	† 6.3	5.5	865.5	715.6	710.1	2.0
Time Deposits	15	2.1	2.7	3.9	4.8	3.0	1.7	† 533.2	716.9	83.8	65.8	70.2	15.7
Restricted Deposits	16b	—	—	—	—	—	—	† 14.0	14.0	18.8	138.4	18.8	18.8
Foreign Liabilities	16c	622.4	651.1	646.9	622.4	28,629.2	25,893.0	† 27,242.9	30,922.3	44,487.4	38,133.7	43,466.2	42,141.8
Central Government Deposits	16d	74.2	15.1	18.6	20.0	137.4	71.0	† 8.9	42.2	70.8	193.4	63.2	86.2
Capital Accounts	17a	60.8	12.7	42.3	61.8	9,259.2	7,735.2	† 7,619.1	8,815.5	14,414.3	11,330.8	12,176.6	12,383.3
Other Items (Net)	17r	51.8	217.7	267.8	315.3	−3,216.4	−2,025.2	† −14.4	−184.8	−1,498.7	−1,246.7	−1,281.6	−333.7
Banking Institutions						*Millions of Liberian Dollars: End of Period*							
Reserves	20	215.4	201.8	188.4	240.0	768.5	815.2	† 1,168.2	1,397.3	782.4	692.5	1,531.5	1,763.7
Other Claims on Monetary Author	20n	—	—	—	—	—	—	† 6.3	5.5	865.5	715.6	710.1	2.0
Foreign Assets	21	9.5	12.0	9.5	15.6	447.9	660.2	† 529.8	546.7	673.2	768.2	1,947.2	2,676.8
Claims on Central Government	22a	5.4	5.1	3.5	—	306.2	358.1	† 425.3	580.9	921.3	661.4	738.7	787.6
Claims on Nonfin.Pub.Enterprises	22c	63.1	21.0	5.7	7.9	12.2	44.5	† 39.5	64.6	85.1	58.4	105.8	82.8
Claims on Private Sector	22d	222.7	176.0	55.4	82.7	1,148.1	900.9	† 663.2	877.0	1,125.9	1,071.7	1,550.9	1,944.4
Claims on Nonbank Financial Insts	22g	—	2.1	5.3	—	—	—	† 123.6	181.2	104.7	85.9	186.7	109.7
Demand Deposits	24	155.3	167.0	127.4	110.0	1,005.5	1,247.9	† 898.8	851.6	1,318.2	1,391.3	1,971.9	2,701.9
Time and Savings Deposits	25	324.4	360.9	195.5	235.5	335.8	324.7	† 391.5	422.4	535.2	443.8	960.3	1,491.0
Restricted Deposits	26b	—	—	—	—	—	—	† 152.1	152.1	201.4	419.8	432.6	445.8
Foreign Liabilities	26c	46.3	15.3	5.1	8.4	106.9	119.0	† 427.9	587.4	627.2	532.6	1,228.3	1,444.2
Central Government Deposits	26d	35.3	30.3	10.6	51.1	112.0	165.4	† 134.1	122.8	202.1	160.2	161.9	166.0
Credit from Monetary Authorities	26g	23.7	16.9	—	—	1.9	2.0	† 104.3	115.8	37.0	34.2	29.9	67.0
Capital Accounts	27a	33.5	3.8	3.4	−5.5	36.3	685.6	† 785.0	1,097.0	1,057.3	661.1	1,039.7	1,487.6
Other Items (Net)	27r	−102.4	−176.3	−74.1	−53.4	1,084.5	234.3	† 62.1	304.1	579.6	410.8	946.3	−436.5
Banking Survey						*Millions of Liberian Dollars: End of Period*							
Foreign Assets (Net)	31n	−654.2	−626.3	−642.2	−614.9	−28,261.6	−25,334.9	† −27,129.6	−30,939.3	−44,227.0	−37,525.6	−41,725.6	−39,474.4
Domestic Credit	32	1,487.6	1,692.0	1,870.1	1,961.7	36,936.9	33,703.9	† 37,800.5	43,245.7	61,655.8	52,071.1	59,369.1	59,153.1
Claims on Central Govt. (Net)	32an	1,180.7	1,472.6	1,777.4	1,845.0	35,743.8	32,726.8	† 36,925.4	42,106.4	60,288.8	50,790.0	57,425.2	56,895.8
Claims on Nonfin.Pub.Enterprises	32c	68.0	25.8	11.3	13.5	18.0	50.1	† 39.5	64.6	85.9	59.0	106.3	83.3
Claims on Private Sector	32d	238.2	191.5	75.8	102.9	1,173.6	925.5	† 712.1	893.5	1,176.4	1,136.2	1,650.9	2,064.2
Claims on Nonbank Fin. Insts	32g	.7	2.1	5.5	.2	1.5	1.5	† 123.6	181.2	104.7	85.9	186.7	109.7
Money	34	458.3	652.8	696.2	686.8	1,571.0	1,804.8	† 1,597.0	1,703.4	2,363.5	2,755.6	3,727.5	4,871.6
Quasi-Money	35	326.5	363.6	199.4	240.3	338.8	326.4	† 924.7	1,139.3	619.1	509.6	1,030.4	1,506.8
Restricted Deposits	36b	—	—	—	—	—	—	† 166.1	166.1	220.2	558.2	451.4	464.6
Capital Accounts	37a	94.3	16.6	45.7	56.3	9,295.6	8,420.7	† 8,404.1	9,912.5	15,471.6	11,991.9	13,216.3	13,871.0
Other Items (Net)	37r	−45.7	32.7	286.6	363.5	−2,530.0	−2,182.9	† −421.1	−614.8	−1,245.5	−1,269.7	−782.1	−1,035.2
Money plus Quasi-Money	35l	784.8	1,016.4	895.6	927.0	1,909.8	2,131.2	† 2,521.8	2,842.7	2,982.6	3,265.3	4,757.9	6,378.4
Money (National Definitions)						*Millions of Liberian Dollars: End of Period*							
M1	59ma	....	....	....	....	....	....	1,597.0	1,696.7	2,363.1	2,695.0	3,726.8	4,870.9
M2	59mb	....	....	....	....	....	....	1,988.6	2,119.2	2,898.4	3,138.8	4,687.1	6,361.9
Interest Rates						*Percent Per Annum*							
Savings Rate	60k	6.16	6.12	....	6.08	6.00	6.02	5.83	5.63	5.43	4.50	4.60	3.69
Deposit Rate	60l	6.34	6.37	....	6.43	6.22	6.25	6.18	5.94	6.25	5.29	3.84	3.43
Lending Rate	60p	14.53	15.57	....	16.83	† 21.74	16.72	20.53	22.14	20.21	17.06	18.10	17.03
						Millions: Midyear Estimates							
Population	99z	2.07	2.14	2.28	2.48	† 2.70	2.91	3.07	3.16	3.21	3.22	3.24	3.28

Libya 672

		1994	1995	1996	1997	1998	1999	2000	2001	2002	2003	2004	2005
Exchange Rates		*SDRs per Dinar: End of Period (ac) US Dollars per Dinar: End of Period (ag)*											
Official Rate	ac	1.5770	1.5770	1.5770	1.5770	1.5770	1.5770	1.4204	1.2240	.6080	.5175	.5175	.5175
Official Rate	ag	2.3022	2.3442	2.2677	2.1278	2.2205	2.1645	1.8507	1.5382	.8266	.7690	.8037	.7396
Fund Position		*Millions of SDRs: End of Period*											
Quota	2f.s	818	818	818	818	818	1,124	1,124	1,124	1,124	1,124	1,124	1,124
SDRs	1b.s	325	350	374	398	426	373	413	441	449	462	475	495
Reserve Position in the Fund	1c.s	319	319	319	319	319	396	396	396	396	396	396	396
Total Fund Cred.&Loans Outstg.	2tl	—	—	—	—	—	—	—	—	—	—	—	—
International Liquidity		*Millions of US Dollars Unless Otherwise Indicated: End of Period*											
Total Reserves minus Gold	1l.d	....	....	....	....	7,270	7,280	12,461	14,800	14,307	19,584	25,689	39,508
SDRs	1b.d	474	520	538	538	600	511	538	554	610	686	738	707
Reserve Position in the Fund	1c.d	466	474	459	430	449	543	515	497	538	588	614	565
Foreign Exchange	1d.d	....	....	....	....	6,221	6,226	11,408	13,749	13,159	18,310	24,336	38,235
Gold (Million Fine Troy Ounces)	1ad	....	....	....	....	4.616	4.624	4.624	4.624	4.624	4.624	4.624	4.624
Gold (National Valuation)	1and	....	....	....	....	194	194	194	194	194	194	194	194
Deposit Money Banks: Assets	7a.d	319	380	483	979	619	735	937	928	646	608	1,053	1,512
Liabilities	7b.d	169	109	207	2,965	2,165	1,834	1,461	2,484	† 78	187	113	53
Monetary Authorities		*Millions of Dinars: End of Period*											
Foreign Assets	11	1,745.0	2,487.4	2,815.9	3,658.5	3,658.5	3,813.4	7,295.9	9,489.2	18,443.2	26,580.4	33,072.7	54,459.7
Claims on Central Government	12a	4,815.0	5,064.6	5,107.4	5,406.7	5,927.2	5,320.1	6,832.6	6,789.0	7,010.0	7,012.3	828.2	828.2
Claims on Nonfin.Pub.Enterprises	12c	1,890.1	2,208.3	2,336.3	1,671.4	1,559.2	1,704.0	2,567.9	2,694.2	† 1,232.9	1,644.9	1,842.1	3,075.0
Claims on Private Sector	12d	6.7	6.6	6.4	6.4	6.4	7.1	8.0	9.5	11.1	12.8	14.7	16.4
Claims on Deposit Money Banks	12e	283.5	283.5	200.0	144.4	144.4	144.4	115.5	86.6	57.8	28.9	1.0	1.8
Reserve Money	14	4,627.4	4,985.7	5,434.8	† 5,821.2	5,760.4	5,455.4	5,404.8	5,946.9	6,101.3	6,782.3	9,920.7	14,388.0
of which: Currency Outside DMBs	14a	1,989.8	2,035.4	2,419.8	2,534.2	2,698.6	2,657.5	2,711.0	2,577.4	2,613.3	2,763.5	2,612.7	3,310.6
Nonfin.Pub.Enterp.Dep.	14e	478.8	603.9	414.5	536.2	176.3	133.7	200.8	297.8	349.9	240.8	246.3	529.8
Time & Foreign Currency Deposits	15	615.0	701.4	522.8	† 62.6	65.3	19.4	38.9	245.2	† 139.1	108.3	44.9	34.5
Restricted Deposits	16b	988.1	344.8	414.2	414.2	332.0	428.1	561.9	738.2	1,468.2	1,702.2	1,351.6	1,548.9
Foreign Liabilities	16c	—	—	—	618.3	476.9	† 623.8	1,501.5	1,673.2	† 3.8	4.5	6.9	11.8
Central Government Deposits	16d	678.2	708.3	741.2	† 3,368.6	3,696.4	4,450.6	6,941.0	7,439.1	7,935.9	12,199.9	18,755.0	35,128.5
Capital Accounts	17a	367.3	367.3	367.3	† 1,214.3	1,250.0	1,076.6	1,520.0	2,634.6	9,919.5	13,991.0	4,314.5	5,634.4
Other Items (Net)	17r	1,464.3	2,942.9	2,985.8	−611.4	−285.3	−1,064.9	851.9	391.3	† 1,187.2	491.2	1,365.2	1,635.0
Deposit Money Banks		*Millions of Dinars: End of Period*											
Reserves	20	2,204.6	2,336.6	2,606.1	2,705.8	2,776.1	2,428.4	2,357.2	2,346.1	2,541.1	3,257.8	6,341.6	9,154.4
Foreign Assets	21	138.6	162.2	212.8	460.3	278.6	339.7	506.4	603.1	781.1	791.2	1,309.9	2,044.8
Claims on Central Government	22a	1,451.1	1,451.1	1,436.5	1,387.5	1,387.5	1,387.5	1,392.5	1,810.5	1,810.5	1,810.5	373.0	373.0
Claims on Nonfin. Pub. Enterprises	22c	146.2	153.2	328.8	† 1,440.7	1,491.9	1,866.4	1,776.5	3,163.7	† 1,906.1	2,499.1	1,995.1	1,775.1
Claims on Private Sector	22d	3,223.6	3,468.1	2,878.4	3,109.1	3,123.4	3,989.1	4,004.0	4,039.0	4,464.7	4,285.2	4,437.6	4,556.9
Claims on Other Banking Insts	22f	....	....	....	....	....	40.3	49.7	27.3	29.1	27.6	27.9	.6
Claims on Nonbank Financial Insts.	22g						124.2	506.7	75.6	69.8	145.9	214.7	6.9
Demand Deposits	24	3,417.3	3,612.1	3,489.4	3,556.5	3,753.4	4,162.8	4,363.1	4,370.1	5,286.7	5,566.1	6,801.6	8,666.2
Time & Foreign Currency Deposits	25	1,260.5	1,550.4	1,744.0	1,555.2	1,838.0	† 2,202.1	2,156.7	2,271.6	2,026.2	2,420.6	2,554.0	3,033.6
Restricted Deposits	26b	173.9	271.7	277.3	368.1	331.0	266.5	341.0	709.1	667.3	791.5	856.5	1,154.4
Foreign Liabilities	26c	60.8	38.5	75.7	† 1,393.3	975.0	847.4	789.5	1,614.8	† 94.4	243.5	141.1	71.5
Central Government Deposits	26d	171.5	114.3	340.0	385.0	354.9	284.6	267.9	259.0	609.3	678.2	1,146.7	1,210.0
Credit from Monetary Authorities	26g	283.5	283.5	203.6	147.9	147.9	147.9	119.1	90.2	61.3	32.4	1.0	1.3
Capital Accounts	27a	405.2	411.8	491.5	601.3	659.7	728.5	793.9	962.4	1,234.9	1,469.5	1,566.4	1,842.4
Other Items (Net)	27r	1,391.7	1,289.9	841.1	1,096.3	997.9	1,535.8	1,761.8	1,787.8	† 1,622.3	1,615.3	1,632.5	1,932.3
Monetary Survey		*Millions of Dinars: End of Period*											
Foreign Assets (Net)	31n	1,822.8	2,611.1	2,953.0	2,107.2	2,485.2	2,681.9	5,511.3	6,804.3	† 19,126.1	27,123.6	34,234.6	56,421.2
Domestic Credit	32	10,683.0	11,529.3	11,012.6	† 9,268.2	9,444.3	9,703.5	9,929.0	10,910.7	† 7,989.0	4,560.2	−10,168.4	−25,706.4
Claims on Central Govt. (Net)	32an	5,416.4	5,693.1	5,462.7	† 3,040.6	3,263.4	1,972.4	1,016.2	901.4	275.3	−4,055.3	−18,700.5	−35,137.3
Claims on Nonfin.Pub.Enterprises	32c	2,036.3	2,361.5	2,665.1	† 3,112.1	3,051.1	3,570.4	4,344.4	5,857.9	† 3,139.0	4,144.0	3,837.2	4,850.1
Claims on Private Sector	32d	3,230.3	3,474.7	2,884.8	3,115.5	3,129.8	3,996.2	4,012.0	4,048.5	4,475.8	4,298.0	4,452.3	4,573.3
Claims on Other Banking Insts	32f	....	....	....	—	—	40.3	49.7	27.3	29.1	27.6	27.9	.6
Claims on Nonbank Fin. Insts.	32g						124.2	506.7	75.6	69.8	145.9	214.7	6.9
Money	34	5,885.9	6,251.4	6,323.7	6,654.5	6,683.8	7,001.2	7,313.5	7,402.7	8,359.9	8,680.5	10,154.0	13,383.9
Quasi-Money	35	1,875.5	2,251.8	2,266.8	1,617.8	1,903.3	2,221.5	2,195.6	2,516.8	† 2,165.3	2,528.9	2,598.9	3,068.1
Restricted Deposits	36b	1,162.0	616.5	691.5	782.3	663.0	694.6	902.9	1,447.3	2,135.5	2,493.7	2,208.1	2,703.3
Capital Accounts	37a	766.1	772.7	852.4	1,815.6	1,909.7	1,805.1	2,313.9	3,597.0	11,154.4	15,460.5	5,880.9	7,476.8
Other Items (Net)	37r	2,810.1	4,242.6	3,824.9	505.8	770.0	663.0	2,714.5	2,750.9	† 3,300.0	2,520.1	3,224.4	4,082.7
Money plus Quasi-Money	35l	7,761.4	8,503.2	8,590.5	8,272.3	8,587.1	9,222.7	9,509.1	9,919.5	† 10,525.2	11,209.4	12,752.9	16,452.0
Other Banking Institutions		*Millions of Dinars: End of Period*											
Cash	40	.3	.3	.6	.3	.7	.9	.9	.6	.9	.7	.8	....
Claims on Private Sector	42d	533.4	549.5	564.6	603.4	618.4	672.9	720.6	905.1	1,419.5	1,722.1	1,955.8	....
Claims on Deposit Money Banks	42e	116.2	118.9	121.4	136.3	113.6	170.8	228.5	918.9	549.2	818.1	918.2	....
Deposits	45	65.9	71.7	82.5	101.3	96.9	131.2	120.3	92.7	103.3	76.5	103.7	....
Government Lending Funds	46f	7.8	7.0	33.9	33.9	29.6	17.5	50.3	260.0	302.8	32.0	32.0	....
Capital Accounts	47a	493.8	497.0	499.1	502.6	505.3	500.5	505.5	506.2	510.5	2,203.2	2,206.9	....
Other Items (Net)	47r	82.0	93.0	71.1	102.2	100.9	195.4	273.9	965.7	1,053.0	229.2	532.2	....
Interest Rates		*Percent Per Annum*											
Discount Rate (End of Period)	60	....	....	....	....	3.0	5.0	5.0	5.0	5.0	5.0	4.0	4.0
Money Market Rate	60b	....	....	....	....	4.0	4.0	4.0	4.0	4.0	4.0	4.0	....
Deposit Rate	60l	....	....	....	....	....	3.2	3.0	3.0	3.0	3.0	2.1	....
Lending Rate	60p	....	....	....	....	....	7.0	7.0	7.0	7.0	7.0	6.1	6.1
Prices		*Index Numbers (2000=100): Period Averages*											
Consumer Prices	64	83.7	89.8	93.4	96.7	100.3	† 103.0	100.0	91.2	82.2	80.5	78.7	....

		1994	1995	1996	1997	1998	1999	2000	2001	2002	2003	2004	2005
Intl. Transactions & Positions							*Millions of Dinars*							
Exports............................	70	3,177.2	3,222.1	3,578.7	3,455.6	3,113.6	3,685.9	6,503.3	6,646.6	12,511.1	18,917.1	27,200.7	39,774.9
Imports, c.i.f........................	71	1,487.9	1,728.5	1,914.8	2,138.6	2,555.8	1,928.5	1,911.5	2,660.5	5,585.9	5,598.5	8,255.2	9,420.4
							2000=100							
Volume of Exports.................	72	133.3	† 132.5	122.6	129.0	94.2	107.9	100.0	110.5	94.6	....	....	....
Volume of Imports.................	73	162.9	† 170.9	184.8	208.4	156.1	146.8	100.0	173.2	213.8	....	....	....
Unit Value of Exports.............	74	49.4	† 52.1	63.6	57.4	48.3	65.3	100.0	102.6	216.9	....	....	....
Unit Value of Imports.............	75	71.5	† 79.7	82.1	83.3	87.5	103.1	100.0	98.1	116.7	....	....	....
Balance of Payments						*Millions of US Dollars: Minus Sign Indicates Debit*								
Current Account, n.i.e.............	78ald	26	1,672	1,238	1,567	−209	2,136	7,740	3,417	117	3,642	3,705	....
Goods: Exports f.o.b...............	78aad	7,704	7,483	7,930	8,177	5,326	7,276	13,508	10,985	9,851	14,664	17,425	....
Goods: Imports f.o.b...............	78abd	−6,760	−5,181	−5,845	−5,928	−4,930	−4,302	−4,129	−4,825	−7,408	−7,200	−8,768	....
Trade Balance.................	78acd	945	2,302	2,085	2,249	396	2,974	9,379	6,160	2,443	7,464	8,657	....
Services: Credit....................	78add	37	31	26	28	40	59	172	184	401	442	437	....
Services: Debit....................	78aed	−718	−575	−772	−748	−735	−989	−895	−1,034	−1,544	−1,597	−1,764	....
Balance on Goods & Services.......	78afd	263	1,758	1,339	1,529	−299	2,044	8,656	5,310	1,300	6,309	7,330	....
Income: Credit....................	78agd	448	435	474	530	533	546	723	684	1,249	1,587	1,339	....
Income: Debit....................	78ahd	−403	−302	−295	−293	−218	−235	−1,152	−1,849	−1,653	−2,581	−2,640	....
Balance on Gds, Serv. & Inc.......	78aid	308	1,892	1,518	1,765	15	2,355	8,227	4,145	896	5,315	6,029	....
Current Transfers, n.i.e.: Credit...	78ajd	5	4	3	3	4	7	16	20	13	255	254	....
Current Transfers: Debit.............	78akd	−286	−224	−283	−202	−229	−226	−503	−748	−792	−1,928	−2,578	....
Capital Account, n.i.e.............	78bcd	—	....	....	....	....	....	—	—	—	—	—	....
Capital Account, n.i.e.: Credit........	78bad	—	....	....	....	....	....	—	—	—	—	—	....
Capital Account: Debit.............	78bbd	—	....	....	....	....	....	—	—	—	—	—	....
Financial Account, n.i.e...........	78bjd	147	−207	186	−732	−467	−1,045	−149	−711	89	−167	1,047	....
Direct Investment Abroad.............	78bdd	−26	−69	−52	−233	−256	−226	−98	−175	136	−63	210	....
Dir. Invest. in Rep. Econ., n.i.e....	78bed	−73	−88	−112	−68	−128	−128	141	133	145	142	1,146	....
Portfolio Investment Assets...........	78bfd	−126	−106	—	−641	−178	−3	−706	−1,359	72	−607	−187	....
Equity Securities....................	78bkd	−126	−106	—	−641	−178	−3	−13	−985	21	−18	27	....
Debt Securities....................	78bld	—	....	....	....	....	....	−693	−374	51	−589	−214	....
Portfolio Investment Liab., n.i.e.....	78bgd	—	....	....	....	....	....	—	—	—	—	—	....
Equity Securities....................	78bmd	—	....	....	....	....	....	—	—	—	—	—	....
Debt Securities....................	78bnd	—	....	....	....	....	....	—	—	—	—	—	....
Financial Derivatives Assets...........	78bwd	....	....	....	....	....	....	....	....	....	....	....	....
Financial Derivatives Liabilities.......	78bxd	....	....	....	....	....	....	....	....	....	....	....	....
Other Investment Assets.............	78bhd	−1,754	−1,363	−1,435	−861	−138	−315	−333	−97	62	−163	−1,767	....
Monetary Authorities.................	78bod	−9	38	−27	38	−6	−650	—	—	—	—	—	....
General Government.............	78bpd	−1,728	−1,372	−1,275	−561	−497	496	—	—	—	6	—	....
Banks............................	78bqd	−17	−29	−133	−338	365	−161	−294	−121	102	−152	−2,077	....
Other Sectors....................	78brd	....	....	....	....	....	....	−39	24	−40	−17	310	....
Other Investment Liab., n.i.e.........	78bid	2,126	1,419	1,785	1,071	233	−373	847	787	−326	524	1,645	....
Monetary Authorities.............	78bsd	169	171	367	−181	−5	−78	—	309	−197	−7	—	....
General Government.............	78btd	1,942	1,301	1,392	1,305	221	−230	—	—	—	—	—	....
Banks............................	78bud	14	−53	27	−52	17	−65	847	488	−149	548	1,855	....
Other Sectors....................	78bvd	....	....	....	....	....	....	—	−10	20	−17	−210	....
Net Errors and Omissions.............	78cad	100	236	−203	718	250	−403	−1,133	−1,413	72	−459	980	....
Overall Balance....................	78cbd	274	1,701	1,221	1,553	−426	688	6,458	1,293	278	3,016	5,732	....
Reserves and Related Items...........	79dad	−274	−1,701	−1,221	−1,553	426	−688	−6,458	−1,293	−278	−3,016	−5,732	....
Reserve Assets....................	79dbd	−274	−1,701	−1,221	−1,553	426	−688	−6,458	−1,293	−278	−3,016	−5,661	....
Use of Fund Credit and Loans.......	79dcd	—	—	—	—	—	—	—	—	—	—	—	....
Exceptional Financing.................	79ded	....	....	....	....	....	....	—	—	—	—	−71	....
National Accounts							*Millions of Dinars*							
Househ.Cons.Expend.,incl.NPISHs....	96f	5,993	6,276	6,809	8,368	8,072	8,514	8,268	9,945	14,021	12,335	10,473	10,183
Government Consumption Expend...	91f	2,254	2,383	2,903	3,333	3,339	3,102	3,616	3,925	4,077	6,405	6,336	5,664
Gross Fixed Capital Formation.........	93e	1,622	1,245	1,640	1,685	1,397	1,536	2,288	2,232	3,516	3,251	6,507	9,903
Changes in Inventories....................	93i	6	54	248	64	127	46	74	74	150	....	....	....
Exports of Goods and Services.........	90c	2,695	3,116	3,490	3,790	2,468	3,374	6,186	5,478	11,645	19,393	26,737	39,019
Imports of Goods and Services (-).....	98c	2,603	2,394	2,910	3,091	2,661	2,433	2,690	3,433	8,868	11,294	13,481	16,025
Gross Domestic Product (GDP)........	99b	9,967	10,680	12,180	14,149	12,742	14,139	17,668	18,147	24,391	30,090	36,572	48,745
Net Primary Income from Abroad.....	98.n	−114	−146	−202	−201	−248	−243	−341	−445	−672	....	....	....
Gross National Income (GNI)...........	99a	9,853	10,534	11,978	13,948	12,494	13,896	17,209	16,751	23,637	....	....	....
							Millions: Midyear Estimates							
Population..............................	99z	4.71	† 4.81	4.90	5.00	5.10	5.20	5.31	5.41	5.52	5.63	5.74	5.85

Lithuania   946

		1994	1995	1996	1997	1998	1999	2000	2001	2002	2003	2004	2005
Exchange Rates						*Litai per SDR: End of Period*							
Official Rate	aa	5.839	5.946	5.752	5.397	5.632	5.490	5.212	5.027	4.502	4.104	3.936	4.159
					Litai per US Dollar: End of Period (ae) Period Average (rf)								
Official Rate	ae	4.000	4.000	4.000	4.000	4.000	4.000	4.000	4.000	3.311	2.762	2.535	2.910
Official Rate	rf	3.978	4.000	4.000	4.000	4.000	4.000	4.000	4.000	3.677	3.061	2.781	2.774
Fund Position						*Millions of SDRs: End of Period*							
Quota	2f.s	103.50	103.50	103.50	103.50	103.50	144.20	144.20	144.20	144.20	144.20	144.20	144.20
SDRs	1b.s	10.38	12.22	7.09	7.95	11.50	3.19	1.01	14.67	39.31	.04	.06	.05
Reserve Position in the Fund	1c.s	.01	.01	.01	.01	.02	.02	.02	.02	.02	.02	.02	.02
Total Fund Cred.&Loans Outstg.	2tl	134.55	175.95	190.11	200.46	179.83	167.76	147.06	120.32	89.27	30.19	16.82	—
International Liquidity						*Millions of US Dollars Unless Otherwise Indicated: End of Period*							
Total Reserves minus Gold	1l.d	525.48	757.05	772.25	1,009.95	1,409.13	1,195.01	1,311.55	1,617.72	2,349.32	3,371.98	3,512.58	3,720.17
SDRs	1b.d	15.15	18.16	10.20	10.73	16.19	4.38	1.32	18.43	53.44	.06	.09	.08
Reserve Position in the Fund	1c.d	.01	.01	.01	.01	.02	.02	.02	.02	.02	.02	.02	.02
Foreign Exchange	1d.d	510.33	738.88	762.04	999.21	1,392.92	1,190.61	1,310.21	1,599.27	2,295.86	3,371.89	3,512.47	3,720.07
Gold (Million Fine Troy Ounces)	1ad	.1858	.1860	.1863	.1864	.1861	.1863	.1863	.1861	.1862	.1862	.1858	.1858
Gold (National Valuation)	1and	61.86	61.95	62.04	52.74	50.87	47.10	47.10	51.47	63.82	77.69	81.40	95.34
Monetary Authorities: Other Liab.	4..d	26.38	.28	1.30	.35	.33	.25	.18	51.85	58.65	67.27	4.02	8.90
Banking Institutions: Assets	7a.d	96.68	123.35	293.60	370.63	302.15	423.30	693.30	751.85	723.77	926.83	1,848.92	2,527.76
Liabilities	7b.d	82.70	88.45	195.83	292.48	438.15	522.70	503.05	599.83	827.32	1,816.55	2,725.23	4,947.60
Monetary Authorities						*Millions of Litai: End of Period*							
Foreign Assets	11	2,618.1	3,284.7	3,345.3	4,258.6	5,847.7	4,976.2	5,375.7	6,629.3	7,933.5	9,448.3	9,028.5	11,047.6
Claims on Central Government	12a	—	19.2	—	—	—	6.8	6.8	6.8	6.8	5.4	4.1	2.7
Claims on Private Sector	12d	5.9	12.1	9.9	7.6	6.9	6.1	5.5	6.4	7.8	9.6	10.8	9.6
Claims on Banking Institutions	12e	157.0	168.1	142.4	70.4	52.3	30.1	23.7	15.3	15.9	10.0	10.0	—
Claims on Nonbank Financial Insts.	12g	—	.3	3.1	19.4	9.0	20.0						
Reserve Money	14	1,812.4	2,446.2	2,499.3	3,308.8	4,260.4	4,088.3	3,952.4	4,279.6	5,168.0	6,540.2	7,001.6	8,933.9
of which: Currency Outside Banks	14a	1,334.3	1,907.0	1,899.3	2,535.5	2,800.4	2,738.7	2,658.3	2,919.9	3,756.4	4,632.0	5,121.2	6,118.4
Foreign Currency Deposits	15	1.9	43.8	19.8	8.2	6.5	1.5	.1	.1	.1	.1	.1	—
Foreign Liabilities	16c	891.2	1,047.3	1,098.7	1,083.3	1,014.1	922.0	767.1	812.2	596.1	309.7	76.4	25.9
Central Government Deposits	16d	45.0	111.0	66.0	268.7	904.4	302.1	781.8	1,488.2	1,950.3	2,213.7	1,470.9	1,401.6
Counterpart Funds	16e	14.7	37.5	41.9	38.1	40.8	30.8	29.2	28.2	28.5	29.0	29.4	1.5
Central Government Lending Funds	16f	.6	.7	—	.6	1.5							
Capital Accounts	17a	54.8	−77.8	−48.4	−247.3	−111.8	−90.4	117.2	270.4	453.2	612.6	730.2	925.9
Other Items (Net)	17r	−39.6	−124.3	−176.6	−104.3	−202.1	−215.1	−236.1	−220.9	−232.2	−232.0	−255.3	−228.6
Banking Institutions						*Millions of Litai: End of Period*							
Reserves	20	464.1	522.7	583.6	742.1	1,447.5	1,342.3	1,282.4	1,343.1	1,391.8	1,897.1	1,864.1	2,802.4
Foreign Assets	21	386.7	493.4	1,174.4	1,482.5	1,208.6	1,693.2	2,773.2	3,007.4	2,396.7	2,560.0	4,686.1	7,356.3
Claims on Central Government	22a	240.8	505.2	860.7	1,890.0	1,965.5	1,665.9	2,151.1	2,637.3	2,950.8	2,691.3	2,787.4	3,216.9
Claims on State and Local Govts.	22b	2.0	7.7	37.1	51.9	123.8	212.3	273.5	279.6	302.5	397.1	411.8	450.1
Claims on Nonfin.Pub.Enterprises	22c	398.6	237.5	134.4	109.4	272.7	276.9	304.5	253.1	197.8	148.0	88.5	167.0
Claims on Private Sector	22d	† 2,974.6	3,654.8	3,496.2	4,161.9	4,866.7	5,538.7	5,203.2	5,531.7	7,213.5	11,460.2	16,019.3	24,804.4
Claims on Nonbank Financial Insts.	22g	20.6	49.5	44.7	150.2	462.8	448.3	513.5	791.3	980.5	1,358.0	1,895.6	4,243.4
Demand Deposits	24	1,134.8	1,566.5	1,694.3	2,543.1	2,757.9	2,528.9	3,002.6	3,808.0	4,553.0	5,891.9	7,334.5	10,590.0
Time, Savings,& Fgn.Currency Dep.	25	1,879.5	2,086.2	1,793.3	2,153.8	2,750.0	3,695.6	4,782.8	5,946.2	6,505.4	7,001.5	9,293.4	12,213.7
Foreign Liabilities	26c	330.8	353.8	783.3	1,169.9	1,752.6	2,090.8	2,012.2	2,399.3	2,739.6	5,017.5	6,907.1	14,398.5
Central Government Deposits	26d	357.6	683.7	779.3	1,008.1	792.0	778.4	740.7	438.9	439.4	652.4	1,143.4	1,416.8
Counterpart Funds	26e	28.2	52.6	59.3	50.7	22.8	19.5	23.3	2.0	10.0	1.4	2.0	1.7
Central Government Lending Funds	26f	337.7	480.3	473.3	615.4	754.1	555.5	287.3	19.6	23.8	37.9	39.1	71.4
Credit from Monetary Authorities	26g	157.0	168.1	142.0	70.3	52.3	30.2	23.8	15.4	15.8	9.9	9.9	—
Capital Accounts	27a	936.1	996.7	1,448.1	2,021.4	2,690.4	2,849.7	2,928.6	1,992.6	2,226.6	2,484.5	2,979.0	3,636.3
Other Items (Net)	27r	† −674.3	−917.1	−841.8	−1,044.7	−1,224.5	−1,370.9	−1,299.9	−778.5	−1,080.0	−585.3	44.5	712.2
Banking Survey						*Millions of Litai: End of Period*							
Foreign Assets (Net)	31n	1,782.8	2,377.0	2,637.7	3,488.0	4,289.6	3,656.6	5,369.6	6,425.2	6,994.5	6,681.1	6,731.1	3,979.5
Domestic Credit	32	† 3,239.9	3,691.6	3,740.8	5,113.6	6,008.9	7,094.5	6,935.6	7,579.1	9,270.0	13,203.5	18,603.2	30,075.7
Claims on Central Govt. (Net)	32an	−161.8	−270.3	15.4	613.2	269.1	592.2	635.4	717.0	567.9	−169.4	177.2	401.2
Claims on State and Local Govts.	32b	2.0	7.7	37.1	51.9	123.8	212.3	273.5	279.6	302.5	397.1	411.8	450.1
Claims on Nonfin.Pub.Enterprises	32c	398.6	237.5	134.4	109.4	272.7	276.9	304.5	253.1	197.8	148.0	88.5	167.0
Claims on Private Sector	32d	† 2,980.5	3,666.9	3,506.1	4,169.5	4,873.6	5,544.8	5,208.7	5,538.1	7,221.3	11,469.8	16,030.1	24,814.0
Claims on Nonbank Fin. Insts.	32g	20.6	49.8	47.8	169.6	469.7	468.3	513.5	791.3	980.5	1,358.0	1,895.6	4,243.4
Money	34	2,475.7	3,488.4	3,610.9	5,109.9	5,570.8	5,275.0	5,672.6	6,744.5	8,329.2	10,535.1	12,472.0	16,721.5
Quasi-Money	35	1,881.4	2,130.0	1,813.1	2,162.0	2,756.5	3,697.0	4,782.9	5,946.3	6,505.5	7,001.6	9,293.5	12,213.7
of which: Fgn. Currency Deposits	35b	1,169.6	1,462.9	1,325.4	1,539.0	2,006.8	2,724.6	3,554.5	4,181.5	3,613.8	3,427.0	4,319.7	6,200.3
Counterpart Funds	36e	42.9	90.1	101.2	88.8	63.6	50.3	52.5	30.2	38.5	30.4	31.4	3.2
Central Government Lending Funds	36f	338.3	481.0	473.3	616.0	755.6	555.5	287.3	19.6	23.8	37.9	39.1	71.4
Capital Accounts	37a	990.9	918.9	1,399.7	1,774.1	2,578.6	2,759.3	3,045.8	2,263.0	2,679.8	3,097.1	3,709.2	4,562.2
Other Items (Net)	37r	† −706.5	−1,039.8	−1,019.7	−1,149.2	−1,426.6	−1,586.0	−1,535.9	−999.3	−1,312.3	−817.5	−210.9	483.6
Money plus Quasi-Money	35l	4,357.1	5,618.4	5,424.0	7,271.9	8,327.3	8,972.0	10,455.4	12,690.8	14,834.7	17,536.7	21,765.5	28,935.2
Money (National Definitions)						*Millions of Litai: End of Period*							
Monetary Base	19ma	....	....	2,482.0	3,277.5	4,247.9	3,852.0	3,940.8	4,263.0	5,148.2	6,521.5	6,978.9	8,919.3
M1	59ma	....	....	3,610.9	5,109.9	5,570.7	5,274.9	5,672.6	6,744.3	8,329.2	10,535.2	12,472.0	16,721.4
M2	59mb	....	....	5,424.1	7,271.8	8,327.1	8,971.9	10,455.4	12,690.6	14,834.6	17,536.8	21,765.5	28,935.2
Interest Rates						*Percent Per Annum*							
Money Market Rate	60b	69.48	26.73	20.26	9.55	† 6.12	6.26	3.60	3.37	2.21	1.79	1.53	1.97
Money Market Rate (Fgn. Currency)	60b.f	....	....	....	....	5.52	5.05	6.10	4.03	1.92	1.72	1.73	2.59
Treasury Bill Rate	60c	....	26.82	20.95	8.64	10.69	11.14	† 9.27	5.68	3.72	2.61	....	....
Savings Rate	60k	....	....	....	....	....	6.46	6.43	6.32	3.36	2.14	2.03	....
Savings Rate (Fgn. Currency)	60k.f	....	....	....	....	....	4.06	4.18	3.61	1.81	1.43	1.45	....
Deposit Rate	60l	48.43	20.05	13.95	7.89	5.98	4.94	3.86	3.00	1.70	1.27	1.22	....
Deposit Rate (Fgn. Currency)	60l.f	24.91	15.97	9.36	5.49	4.24	4.38	4.39	3.11	1.80	1.52	1.44	....
Lending Rate	60p	62.30	27.08	21.56	14.39	12.21	13.09	12.14	9.63	6.84	5.84	5.74	....
Lending Rate (Fgn. Currency)	60p.f	51.98	26.93	21.63	12.39	10.28	11.46	10.62	8.01	5.74	4.29	3.95	....

Lithuania 946

		1994	1995	1996	1997	1998	1999	2000	2001	2002	2003	2004	2005
Prices, Production, Labor		*Index Numbers (2000=100): Period Averages*											
Producer Prices	63	57.8	74.1	† 86.9	90.6	83.9	85.1	100.0	96.3	92.8	92.5	99.6	112.7
Consumer Prices	64	49.4	68.9	85.9	93.5	98.3	† 99.0	100.0	101.3	101.6	100.4	101.6	104.3
Harmonized CPI (2002=100)	64h	....	....	....	....	....	....	....	....	100.0	† 101.7	102.9	105.7
Wages: Average Earnings	65	35.4	50.7	68.5	84.5	95.2	100.7	100.0	100.9	102.9	106.5	113.9	126.3
Industrial Production	66	....	84.2	87.1	† 94.1	107.3	94.9	100.0	116.1	119.3	135.9	151.5	164.2
Manufacturing Employment	67	† 94.1	107.3	94.9	94.1	107.3	94.9	100.0	† 116.1	121.1	122.8	119.2	122.4
		Number in Thousands: Period Averages											
Labor Force	67d	1,741	1,753	2,037	1,820	1,843	1,862	1,794	1,760	1,630	1,642	1,621	....
Employment	67e	1,656	1,632	1,620	1,571	1,489	1,457	1,398	1,352	1,406	1,438	1,463	....
Unemployment	67c	78	128	109	120	123	177	226	224	191	159	126	101
Unemployment Rate (%)	67r	4.5	7.3	6.2	6.7	6.5	10.0	12.6	12.5	11.3	11.3	6.8	8.3
Intl. Transactions & Positions		*Millions of Litai*											
Exports	70	8,077	8,157	10,622	12,801	12,941	11,015	14,193	17,117	19,117	21,263	25,819	32,807
Imports, c.i.f	71	9,355	12,052	15,532	20,098	21,456	18,508	20,877	24,241	27,479	29,438	34,384	42,975
Balance of Payments		*Millions of US Dollars: Minus Sign Indicates Debit*											
Current Account, n.i.e	78ald	−94.0	−614.4	−722.6	−981.3	−1,298.2	−1,194.0	−674.9	−573.6	−720.7	−1,278.4	−1,724.6	−1,771.3
Goods: Exports f.o.b	78aad	2,029.2	2,706.1	3,413.2	4,192.4	3,961.6	3,146.7	4,050.4	4,889.0	6,028.4	7,657.8	9,306.3	11,789.3
Goods: Imports f.o.b	78abd	−2,234.1	−3,404.0	−4,309.3	−5,339.9	−5,479.9	−4,551.2	−5,154.1	−5,997.0	−7,343.3	−9,362.0	−11,688.9	−14,632.3
Trade Balance	78acd	−204.9	−697.9	−896.2	−1,147.5	−1,518.3	−1,404.6	−1,103.8	−1,108.0	−1,314.9	−1,704.2	−2,382.6	−2,843.0
Services: Credit	78add	321.9	485.2	797.5	1,031.8	1,109.0	1,091.5	1,058.8	1,157.0	1,463.7	1,878.0	2,444.4	3,104.3
Services: Debit	78aed	−376.5	−498.1	−676.7	−897.4	−868.5	−786.1	−678.7	−700.3	−915.0	−1,263.6	−1,632.1	−2,051.8
Balance on Goods & Services	78afd	−259.4	−710.8	−775.4	−1,013.0	−1,277.8	−1,099.1	−723.7	−651.4	−766.1	−1,089.8	−1,570.2	−1,790.5
Income: Credit	78agd	21.4	50.9	52.0	80.4	124.6	114.8	185.5	205.7	191.6	235.2	354.9	449.7
Income: Debit	78ahd	−12.8	−63.7	−143.0	−278.8	−380.0	−372.6	−379.3	−385.7	−375.0	−717.4	−967.3	−1,074.5
Balance on Gds, Serv. & Inc	78aid	−250.8	−723.7	−866.4	−1,211.4	−1,533.2	−1,356.8	−917.5	−831.1	−949.5	−1,572.0	−2,182.5	−2,415.3
Current Transfers, n.i.e.: Credit	78ajd	161.6	112.3	149.4	237.0	240.4	167.4	246.8	262.0	231.7	301.5	612.1	933.2
Current Transfers: Debit	78akd	−4.8	−3.0	−5.6	−7.0	−5.4	−4.6	−4.3	−4.5	−2.9	−7.8	−154.2	−289.1
Capital Account, n.i.e	78bcd	12.9	−39.0	5.5	4.1	−1.7	−3.3	2.1	1.4	56.5	67.5	287.2	355.4
Capital Account, n.i.e.: Credit	78bad	12.9	3.3	5.5	4.5	.9	2.7	2.6	1.5	56.8	68.3	288.1	355.5
Capital Account: Debit	78bbd	—	−42.3	—	−.4	−2.6	−6.0	−.4	−.1	−.4	−.8	−1.0	−.1
Financial Account, n.i.e	78bjd	240.9	534.5	645.6	1,005.6	1,443.9	1,060.7	702.4	777.6	1,048.4	1,642.3	1,141.2	2,047.8
Direct Investment Abroad	78bdd	....	−1.0	−.1	−26.9	−4.2	−8.6	−3.7	−7.1	−17.7	−37.2	−262.6	−328.9
Dir. Invest. in Rep. Econ., n.i.e	78bed	31.3	72.6	152.4	354.5	925.5	486.5	378.9	445.8	712.5	179.2	773.2	1,009.1
Portfolio Investment Assets	78bfd	−.2	−10.5	−26.9	7.7	−10.1	−1.9	−141.4	26.2	−124.5	29.8	−219.9	−778.5
Equity Securities	78bkd	−.2	−3.0	.8	.1	−.3	−3.0	−1.4	1.1	−3.7	−1.8	−18.8	−185.1
Debt Securities	78bld	....	−7.5	−27.7	7.6	−9.8	1.1	−140.0	25.1	−120.9	31.6	−201.0	−593.4
Portfolio Investment Liab., n.i.e	78bgd	4.6	26.6	89.6	180.5	−42.7	507.5	405.9	238.0	148.8	222.3	431.1	423.7
Equity Securities	78bmd	4.6	6.2	15.9	30.5	11.4	8.9	121.5	−16.3	5.6	4.2	7.9	30.3
Debt Securities	78bnd	—	20.4	73.7	150.1	−54.1	498.6	284.4	254.3	143.2	218.0	423.1	393.4
Financial Derivatives Assets	78bwd	....	....	....	....	—	—	—	18.3	19.6	28.1	60.0	27.4
Financial Derivatives Liabilities	78bxd	....	....	....	....	—	—	—	−19.6	−22.7	−56.2	−57.4	−14.5
Other Investment Assets	78bhd	−26.4	−36.1	−170.4	−219.3	−24.0	−182.5	39.9	−225.0	154.7	−100.9	−683.8	−763.1
Monetary Authorities	78bod	....	67.0	.2	.1	—	—	—	—	—	—	—	—
General Government	78bpd	....	....	....	....	—	—	—	—	−2.6	—	−7.3	—
Banks	78bqd	−17.3	−18.0	−139.5	−88.1	57.2	−125.7	−142.2	−158.2	212.7	−161.0	−671.1	−394.7
Other Sectors	78brd	−9.2	−85.0	−31.1	−131.3	−81.2	−56.7	182.1	−64.2	−58.0	60.1	−5.4	−368.4
Other Investment Liab., n.i.e	78bid	231.6	482.8	601.0	709.1	599.3	259.7	22.8	300.9	177.7	1,377.2	1,100.7	2,472.7
Monetary Authorities	78bsd	−.9	−25.1	1.0	−1.0	—	−.1	−102.0	51.7	−3.6	−8.0	−66.7	5.5
General Government	78btd	85.5	178.5	228.5	42.9	129.3	212.0	—	−53.7	−70.6	−9.4	−308.2	−191.0
Banks	78bud	75.8	10.8	108.5	104.3	177.9	99.9	53.1	169.4	111.8	737.6	870.3	2,571.0
Other Sectors	78bvd	71.2	318.5	263.1	562.8	292.1	−52.1	71.7	133.5	140.0	657.0	605.3	87.1
Net Errors and Omissions	78cad	−46.9	287.2	66.7	195.8	282.9	−42.2	128.3	153.6	78.5	181.2	191.8	86.3
Overall Balance	78cbd	112.8	168.3	−4.8	224.2	426.8	−178.7	158.0	359.0	462.7	612.7	−104.4	718.2
Reserves and Related Items	79dad	−112.8	−168.3	4.8	−224.2	−426.8	178.7	−158.0	−359.0	−462.7	−612.7	104.4	−718.2
Reserve Assets	79dbd	−179.7	−231.3	−15.9	−238.2	−398.8	195.3	−130.7	−325.0	−422.5	−531.2	124.2	−692.7
Use of Fund Credit and Loans	79dcd	66.9	63.0	20.7	14.1	−28.0	−16.6	−27.3	−34.0	−40.2	−81.4	−19.8	−25.5
Exceptional Financing	79ded	—	—	—	—	—	—	—	—	—	—	—	—
International Investment Position		*Millions of US Dollars*											
Assets	79aad	997.6	1,274.6	1,692.7	2,148.6	2,472.2	2,452.7	2,677.7	3,126.3	4,225.5	5,717.0	7,413.0	9,051.0
Direct Investment Abroad	79abd	.2	1.2	2.8	26.0	16.5	25.9	29.3	47.9	59.5	119.7	422.8	708.3
Portfolio Investment	79acd	.6	11.1	38.1	29.7	38.0	32.5	172.3	138.2	286.3	268.8	516.7	1,255.2
Equity Securities	79add	.2	3.1	2.6	2.9	2.9	5.9	6.0	4.9	10.5	11.8	36.2	220.5
Debt Securities	79aed	.5	7.9	35.5	26.8	35.1	26.7	166.4	133.2	275.8	257.0	480.5	1,034.8
Financial Derivatives	79ald	—	—	—	—	—	—	—	—	—	.2	—	9.6
Other Investment	79afd	409.4	443.4	817.5	1,030.2	957.7	1,152.1	1,117.4	1,271.1	1,459.7	1,878.7	2,879.5	3,262.4
Monetary Authorities	79agd	67.2	.2	.1	—	—	—	—	—	—	—	—	—
General Government	79ahd	—	—	—	—	—	—	—	—	—	—	—	—
Banks	79aid	103.3	119.2	243.3	331.3	273.7	390.5	539.7	636.5	504.0	736.3	1,479.1	1,670.5
Other Sectors	79ajd	238.9	323.9	574.1	699.0	684.0	761.7	577.7	634.5	955.6	1,142.4	1,400.4	1,591.8
Reserve Assets	79akd	587.4	819.0	834.3	1,062.7	1,460.0	1,242.1	1,358.7	1,669.2	2,420.0	3,449.7	3,594.0	3,815.5
Liabilities	79lad	1,115.8	1,795.8	2,813.2	3,964.8	4,928.8	6,114.1	6,693.3	7,331.4	9,373.3	12,575.8	15,956.7	17,697.7
Dir. Invest. in Rep. Economy	79lbd	262.2	353.9	700.3	1,040.6	1,625.3	2,063.0	2,334.3	2,665.5	3,981.3	4,959.8	6,388.9	6,460.9
Portfolio Investment	79lcd	12.9	40.5	306.8	416.1	368.2	833.6	1,140.4	1,312.6	1,511.2	2,077.3	2,812.0	2,826.8
Equity Securities	79ldd	5.8	12.4	31.5	61.3	67.1	62.0	128.1	95.6	111.0	144.0	172.5	176.7
Debt Securities	79led	7.2	28.1	275.3	354.7	301.1	771.6	1,012.3	1,217.1	1,400.3	1,933.3	2,639.5	2,650.2
Financial Derivatives	79lld	—	—	—	—	—	—	—	—	10.1	10.2	2.9	4.0
Other Investment	79lfd	840.7	1,401.4	1,806.1	2,508.1	2,935.3	3,217.5	3,218.6	3,353.3	3,870.5	5,528.6	6,752.9	8,406.0
Monetary Authorities	79lgd	221.6	261.6	275.1	270.8	253.5	230.5	191.8	203.1	180.0	112.1	30.1	8.9
General Government	79lhd	235.2	424.0	447.4	549.2	694.2	881.3	767.0	694.1	669.2	717.7	478.0	254.7
Banks	79lid	86.1	99.2	182.3	282.8	463.3	539.8	568.2	691.1	933.4	1,910.2	2,839.2	5,075.2
Other Sectors	79ljd	297.8	616.7	901.3	1,405.4	1,524.3	1,566.0	1,691.6	1,765.0	2,087.9	2,788.5	3,405.6	3,067.2

Lithuania 946

		1994	1995	1996	1997	1998	1999	2000	2001	2002	2003	2004	2005
Government Finance						*Millions of Litai: Year Ending December 31*							
Deficit (-) or Surplus	80	−797.0	−1,151.5	−1,145.1	† −735.8	−183.6	−3,006.6	−584.7	−171.8	−593.3	....	....	....
Total Revenue and Grants	81y	4,034.1	5,661.1	7,157.3	† 10,198.6	11,474.9	11,051.0	11,135.3	11,999.1	14,180.0	....	....	....
Revenue	81	4,031.9	5,661.1	7,128.8	† 10,198.3	11,474.9	11,051.0	11,135.3	11,759.2	13,846.8	....	....	....
Grants	81z	2.2	—	28.5	.3	—	—	—	239.9	333.2	....	....	....
Exp.& Lending Minus Repayments	82z	4,831.1	6,812.6	8,302.4	† 10,934.4	11,658.5	14,057.6	11,720.0	12,170.9	14,773.3	....	....	....
Expenditure	82	4,292.1	6,079.1	7,894.1	† 10,515.0	13,037.6	13,260.8	12,447.3	12,616.8	15,098.8	....	....	....
Lending Minus Repayments	83	539.0	733.5	408.3	419.4	−1,379.1	796.8	−727.3	−445.9	−325.5	....	....	....
Total Financing													
Domestic	84a	518.2	417.9	138.7	† 451.6	−574.1	129.1	−334.2	−307.2	178.8	....	....	....
Foreign	85a	278.8	733.6	1,006.4	† 284.2	757.7	2,877.5	918.9	479.0	414.5	....	....	....
Total Debt by Currency	88z	2,639.1	4,470.6	4,749.9	8,077.4	9,613.6	12,069.3	12,729.9	12,903.6	13,161.5	13,137.3	....	....
National	88b	654.3	1,111.4	2,024.0	2,470.1	2,876.1	2,354.1	2,827.4	3,047.4	3,983.7	4,267.0	....	....
Foreign	89b	1,984.8	3,359.2	2,725.9	5,607.3	6,737.5	9,715.2	9,902.5	9,856.2	9,177.8	8,870.3	....	....
National Accounts							*Millions of Litai*						
Househ.Cons.Expend.,incl.NPISHs	96f	11,489	17,076	21,499	24,789	27,380	28,387	† 29,772	31,610	33,464	36,659	40,633	46,381
Government Consumption Expend	91f	3,319	5,602	7,201	8,967	10,767	9,634	† 9,913	9,692	10,056	10,428	11,163	11,908
Gross Fixed Capital Formation	93e	3,905	5,460	6,902	9,049	10,723	9,614	† 8,565	9,785	10,549	12,024	13,585	15,858
Changes in Inventories	93i	−792	273	−210	625	618	121	† 497	203	856	979	1,497	1,933
Exports of Goods and Services	90c	9,361	12,765	16,843	20,897	20,282	16,953	† 20,466	24,214	27,444	29,137	32,636	41,496
Imports of Goods and Services (-)	98c	10,378	15,609	19,944	24,949	25,393	21,350	† 23,336	26,898	30,420	32,456	37,074	46,492
Gross Domestic Product (GDP)	99b	16,904	25,568	32,290	39,378	44,377	43,359	† 45,848	48,563	51,948	56,772	62,440	71,084
Net Primary Income from Abroad	98.n	34	−51	−364	−794	−1,022	−1,031	† −800	−641	−546	−1,425	−1,632	−1,139
Gross National Income (GNI)	99a	16,938	25,516	31,926	38,584	43,356	42,328	† 45,049	47,922	51,402	55,347	60,808	69,945
Net Current Transf.from Abroad	98t	624	437	575	920	940	651	† 970	1,030	852	890	1,131	1,219
Gross Nat'l Disposable Inc.(GNDI)	99i	17,562	25,954	32,501	39,504	44,296	42,980	† 46,019	48,952	52,254	56,237	61,939	71,164
Gross Saving	99s	2,754	3,276	3,801	5,748	6,148	4,959	† 6,362	7,692	8,734	9,149	10,143	12,875
Consumption of Fixed Capital	99cf	1,496	2,861	4,219	5,067	5,649	6,020	6,300	6,667	6,849	7,078	7,550	8,458
GDP Volume 2000 Ref., Chained	99b.p	35,905	37,086	38,821	41,541	44,565	43,810	† 45,848	48,802	52,097	57,568	61,586	66,188
GDP Volume (2000=100)	99bvp	78.3	80.9	84.7	90.6	97.2	95.6	100.0	106.4	113.6	125.6	134.3	144.4
GDP Deflator (2000=100)	99bip	47.1	68.9	83.2	94.8	99.6	99.0	100.0	99.5	99.7	98.6	101.4	107.4
							Millions: Midyear Estimates						
Population	99z	3.65	3.63	3.60	3.57	3.55	3.52	3.50	3.48	3.47	3.45	3.44	3.43

		1994	1995	1996	1997	1998	1999	2000	2001	2002	2003	2004	2005
Exchange Rates		*Euros per SDR: End of Period*											
Market Rate..............................	aa	46.478	43.725	46.022	49.814	48.682	1.3662	1.4002	1.4260	1.2964	1.1765	1.1402	1.2116
					Euros per US Dollar: End of Period (ae) Period Average (rf)								
Market Rate..............................	ae	31.838	29.415	32.005	36.920	34.575	.9954	1.0747	1.1347	.9536	.7918	.7342	.8477
Market Rate..............................	rf	33.456	29.480	30.962	35.774	36.299	.9386	1.0854	1.1175	1.0626	.8860	.8054	.8041
					Francs per ECU: End of Period (ea) Period Average (eb)								
ECU Rate..............................	ea	39.161	38.697	40.102	40.781	40.340	....	....	....	....	....	....	....
ECU Rate..............................	eb	39.661	38.548	39.295	40.529	40.621	....	....	....	....	....	....	....
					Index Numbers (2000=100): Period Averages								
Market Rate (1995=100)...............	ahx	88.2	100.0	95.1	82.4	81.2	....	....	....	....	....	....	....
Nominal Effective Exchange Rate.....	nec	109.0	111.1	108.5	104.2	104.2	103.1	100.0	100.1	101.0	104.4	105.4	105.5
Real Effective Exchange Rate...........	rec	110.1	112.2	108.8	103.8	103.3	102.1	100.0	100.5	101.8	105.4	106.6	107.1
Fund Position					*Millions of SDRs: End of Period*								
Quota..............................	2f.s	135.50	135.50	135.50	135.50	135.50	279.10	279.10	279.10	279.10	279.10	279.10	279.10
SDRs..............................	1b.s	7.22	7.46	7.75	8.04	8.72	1.78	3.22	5.00	6.72	8.29	9.83	11.43
Reserve Position in the Fund...........	1c.s	23.61	22.94	23.56	21.75	59.37	54.37	55.47	78.95	104.75	120.26	89.66	40.65
of which: Outstg.Fund Borrowing...	2c	—	—	—	—	31.34	—	—	—	—	—	—	—
International Liquidity					*Millions of US Dollars Unless Otherwise Indicated: End of Period*								
Total Res.Min.Gold (Eurosys.Def).....	1l.d	75.73	74.98	73.68	64.07	....	† 77.40	76.61	105.62	151.72	279.91	298.37	241.10
SDRs..............................	1b.d	10.54	11.09	11.14	10.85	12.28	2.45	4.19	6.28	9.14	12.32	15.26	16.33
Reserve Position in the Fund.........	1c.d	34.46	34.10	33.87	29.35	83.60	74.62	72.27	99.21	142.41	178.70	139.25	58.10
Foreign Exchange.................	1d.d	30.73	29.79	28.67	23.87	....	.33	.15	.13	.18	88.89	143.87	166.68
o/w:Fin.Deriv.Rel.to Reserves......	1ddd	....	....	....	....								
Other Reserve Assets...............	1e.d	....	....	....	....								
Gold (Million Fine Troy Ounces).....	1ad	.305	.305	.305	.305		.076	.076	.076	.076	.075	.074	.074
Gold (Eurosystem Valuation)............	1and	16.90	18.28	16.81	14.44		22.16	20.96	21.11	26.05	31.29	32.41	37.96
Memo:Euro Cl. on Non-EA Res......	1dgd	....	....	....	....								
Non-Euro Cl. on EA Res.........	1dhd	....	....	....	....		—	—	—	—	—	—	—
Mon. Auth.: Other Foreign Assets....	3..d	....	....	....	....		—	—	—	—	—	—	—
Foreign Liabilities.................	4..d	30.78	29.58	28.43	24.11	....	† 2,171.54	47.73	56.03	56.59	90.59	150.08	426.64
Banking Insts.: Foreign Assets..........	7a.d	451,135	504,838	496,510	471,904	....	† 178,653	174,954	207,513	237,001	301,437	332,047	355,164
Foreign Liab..........	7b.d	386,770	434,105	415,569	389,816	....	† 164,243	159,292	163,497	173,268	198,972	221,673	235,525
Monetary Authorities					*Billions of Francs through 1998; Millions of Euros Beginning 1999: End of Period*								
Fgn. Assets (Cl.on Non-EA Ctys)......	11	8.5	8.3	7.5	6.2	....	952	156	333	436	762	957	1,529
Claims on General Government........	12a.u	....	....	....	....		97	45	20	46	113	83	62
o/w: Claims on Gen.Govt.in Cty....	12a	5.5	4.9	4.8	4.7		—	—	—	—	—	—	—
Claims on Banking Institutions......	12e.u	....	....	....	....		13,038	19,495	16,751	23,568	26,306	32,695	41,130
o/w: Claims on Bank.Inst.in Cty....	12e	.1	.2	1.0	2.6		9,000	19,282	16,511	23,371	23,423	28,406	31,869
Claims on Other Resident Sectors.....	12d.u	....	....	....	....		163	242	217	342	502	853	895
o/w: Cl. on Oth.Res.Sect.in Cty...	12d	....	....	....	....		—	—	—	—	93	23	—
Currency Issued..............................	14a	5.5	4.9	5.7	5.7		585	661	647	677	821	1,117	1,266
Liabilities to Banking Insts................	14c.u	....	....	....	....		11,509	19,272	16,555	23,197	25,845	32,405	41,013
o/w: Liabs to Bank.Inst.in Cty........	14c	....	....	....	....		4,183	4,912	5,981	4,638	6,766	5,063	6,810
Demand Dep. of Other Res.Sect......	14d.u	....	....	....	....		18	16	15	—	—	—	—
o/w:D.Dep.of Oth.Res.Sect.in Cty...	14d	....	....	....	....		3	—	—	—	—	—	—
Other Dep. of Other Res.Sect.......	15..u	....	....	....	....		—	—	—	—	—	—	—
o/w:O.Dep.of Oth.Res.Sect.in Cty...	15	....	....	....	....		—	—	—	—	—	—	—
Bonds & Money Mkt. Instruments.....	16n.u	....	....	....	....		—	—	—	—	—	—	—
o/w: Held by Resid.of Cty...........	16n	....	....	....	....		—	—	—	—	—	—	—
Foreign Liab. (to Non-EA Ctys).......	16c	1.0	.9	.9	.9		2,162	51	64	54	72	110	362
Central Government Deposits...........	16d.u	....	....	....	....		485	569	581	526	592	555	515
o/w: Cent.Govt.Dep. in Cty........	16d	3.4	3.4	3.3	3.4	....	485	569	581	526	592	555	515
Capital Accounts..............................	17a	4.2	4.2	4.3	4.5	....	199	203	188	205	192	546	622
Other Items (Net)..............................	17r	.1	—	−.9	−1.1	....	−709	−833	−730	−268	−145	−161	−161
Memo: Net Claims on Eurosystem.....	12e.s	....	....	....	....		−3,376	−14,211	−10,425	−18,408	−16,583	−23,766	−26,239
Currency Put into Circ..............	14m	....	....	....	....		....	....	....	9,932	19,900	28,459	35,469
Banking Institutions					*Billions of Francs through 1998; Millions of Euros Beginning 1999: End of Period*								
Claims on Monetary Authorities.......	20	3.0	3.7	19.1	13.6	....	4,183	4,912	5,981	4,638	6,766	5,063	6,810
Claims on Bk.Inst.in Oth.EA Ctys....	20b.u	....	....	....	....		228,490	254,464	283,512	291,098	307,198	322,883	326,752
Fgn. Assets (Cl.on Non-EA Ctys).......	21	14,363.0	14,849.8	15,890.8	17,422.7	....	177,835	188,021	235,462	225,995	238,667	243,776	301,063
Claims on General Government.......	22a.u	....	....	....	....		53,469	46,551	49,303	48,921	60,573	66,277	73,719
o/w: Claims on Gen.Govt.in Cty....	22a	12.2	54.3	22.1	19.9	....	733	1,078	1,050	1,027	1,291	1,189	1,253
Claims on Other Resident Sectors.....	22d.u	....	....	....	....		82,554	98,232	107,910	105,621	108,296	109,911	147,151
o/w: Cl. on Oth.Res.Sect.in Cty....	22d	489.7	525.4	552.9	616.0		19,778	22,495	29,128	24,879	26,536	29,115	39,071
Demand Deposits..............................	24..u	....	....	....	....		42,610	50,376	50,708	48,161	50,277	56,020	70,520
o/w:D.Dep.of Oth.Res.Sect.in Cty...	24	78.5	72.7	79.5	81.5		26,687	34,188	31,842	31,519	33,777	40,613	51,196
Other Deposits..............................	25..u	....	....	....	....		89,947	99,507	104,401	102,256	104,507	113,466	112,363
o/w:O.Dep.of Oth.Res.Sect.in Cty...	25	1,674.0	1,677.1	1,933.2	2,155.8		32,027	34,711	38,855	39,367	41,854	46,048	58,606
Money Market Fund Shares............	26m.u	....	....	....	....		65,940	76,337	119,162	138,406	161,713	157,449	176,884
Bonds & Money Mkt. Instruments.....	26n.u	....	....	....	....		38,771	44,774	52,322	54,359	74,347	76,923	89,004
o/w: Held by Resid.of Cty.............	26n	293.8	453.3	599.1	797.7	....							
Foreign Liab. (to Non-EA Ctys).........	26c	12,313.8	12,769.2	13,300.3	14,392.0	....	163,491	171,190	185,518	165,222	157,539	162,744	199,648
Central Government Deposits...........	26d.u	....	....	....	....		4,595	12,745	8,819	3,178	5,686	4,443	3,401
o/w: Cent.Govt.Dep. in Cty........	26d	53.8	59.8	72.1	79.6	....	3,377	3,213	2,118	1,915	2,965	2,841	1,219
Credit from Monetary Authorities.....	26g	3.8	35.5	3.8	4.6	....	9,000	19,282	16,511	23,371	23,423	28,406	31,869
Liab. to Bk.Inst.in Oth. EA Ctys........	26h.u	....	....	....	....		105,620	93,339	119,350	116,015	116,903	119,246	138,185
Capital Accounts..............................	27a	486.3	526.5	549.0	562.0	....	16,551	34,090	37,432	39,962	39,712	41,124	43,037
Other Items (Net)..............................	27r	† −36.2	−161.0	−51.9	−1.0	....	10,005	−9,459	−12,056	−14,657	−12,605	−11,911	−9,415
Central Govt. Monetary Liabilities....	25.iu	....	....	....	12,008	12,778	327	344	438	502	694	608	665

Luxembourg 137

		1994	1995	1996	1997	1998	1999	2000	2001	2002	2003	2004	2005
Banking Survey (Nat'l Residency)		*Billions of Francs through 1998; Millions of Euros Beginning 1999: End of Period*											
Foreign Assets (Net)	31n	2,056.7	2,088.0	2,597.1	3,036.0	....	164,333	185,959	209,704	237,495	256,087	282,175	329,634
Domestic Credit	32	†450.2	521.4	504.4	557.6	....	16,649	19,791	27,479	23,465	24,363	26,931	38,590
Claims on General Govt. (Net)	32an	†−39.5	−4.0	−48.5	−58.4	....	−3,129	−2,704	−1,649	−1,414	−2,266	−2,207	−481
Claims on Other Resident Sectors	32d	489.7	525.4	552.9	616.0	....	19,778	22,495	29,128	24,879	26,629	29,138	39,071
Currency Issued	34a.n	5.5	4.9	5.7	5.7	....	585	661	647	677	821	1,117	1,266
Demand Deposits	34b.n	78.5	72.7	79.5	81.5	....	26,690	34,188	31,842	31,519	33,777	40,613	51,196
Other Deposits	35..n	1,674.0	1,677.1	1,933.2	2,155.8	....	32,027	34,711	38,855	39,367	41,854	46,048	58,606
Money Market Fund Shares	36m	....	....	....	....	....	35,981	40,002	55,128	70,340	79,973	84,270	97,012
Bonds & Money Mkt. Instruments	36n	293.8	453.3	599.1	797.7	....	55,678	66,598	79,848	78,841	74,399	76,901	89,537
o/w: Over Two Years	36na	....	....	....	....	....	31,161	34,014	37,960	40,999	45,217	54,463	68,588
Capital Accounts	37a	490.5	530.7	553.3	566.5	....	16,750	34,292	37,620	40,168	39,904	41,670	43,659
Other Items (Net)	37r	†−35.4	−129.4	−69.0	−13.7	....	13,271	−4,703	−6,707	90	9,720	18,445	26,856
Banking Survey (EA-Wide Residency)													
Foreign Assets (Net)	31n.u	....	....	....	....	....	13,134	16,937	50,213	61,155	81,819	81,878	102,582
Domestic Credit	32..u	....	....	....	....	....	131,203	131,756	148,048	151,226	163,206	172,126	217,912
Claims on General Govt. (Net)	32anu	....	....	....	....	....	48,486	33,281	39,922	45,264	54,408	61,361	69,866
Claims on Other Resident Sect.	32d.u	....	....	....	....	....	82,717	98,474	108,127	105,962	108,798	110,765	148,046
Currency Issued	34a.u	....	....	....	....	....	585	661	647	677	821	1,117	1,266
Demand Deposits	34b.u	....	....	....	....	....	42,628	50,391	50,723	48,161	50,277	56,020	70,520
Other Deposits	35..u	....	....	....	....	....	89,947	99,507	104,401	102,256	104,507	113,466	112,363
o/w: Other Dep. Over Two Yrs.	35abu	....	....	....	....	....	6,926	3,823	5,371	5,038	7,839	12,504	18,214
Money Market Fund Shares	36m.u	....	....	....	....	....	65,940	76,337	119,162	138,406	161,713	157,449	176,884
Bonds & Money Mkt. Instruments	36n.u	....	....	....	....	....	38,771	44,774	52,322	54,359	74,347	76,923	89,004
o/w: Over Two Years	36nau	....	....	....	....	....	31,161	34,014	38,011	41,048	45,127	54,479	68,406
Capital Accounts	37a	....	....	....	....	....	16,750	34,292	37,620	40,168	39,904	41,670	43,659
Other Items (Net)	37r.u	....	....	....	....	....	−110,285	−157,271	−166,615	−171,646	−186,544	−192,640	−173,201
Money (National Definitions)		*Billions of Francs: End of Period*											
Money	59ma	104.5	....	111.4	115.0	....	....	....	....	....	....	....	....
Quasi-Money	59maa	399.6	....	423.5	396.0	....	....	....	....	....	....	....	....
Broad Money	59mb	504.1	....	534.9	511.0	....	....	....	....	....	....	....	....
Interest Rates		*Percent Per Annum*											
Money Market Rate	60b	5.16	4.26	3.29	3.36	3.48	....	....	....	....	....	....	....
Deposit Rate	60l	5.00	5.00	3.54	3.46	3.31	....	....	....	....	....	....	....
Households: Stocks, up to 2 years	60lhs	....	....	....	....	....	....	....	....	....	2.02	1.73	....
New Business, up to 1 year	60lhn	....	....	....	....	....	....	....	....	....	2.05	1.78	1.94
Corporations: Stocks, up to 2 years	60lcs	....	....	....	....	....	....	....	....	....	2.29	2.03	....
New Business, up to 1 year	60lcn	....	....	....	....	....	....	....	....	....	2.29	2.05	2.09
Lending Rate	60p	6.58	6.50	5.50	5.50	5.27	....	....	....	....	....	....	....
House Purch.,Stocks, Over 5yrs.	60phm	....	....	....	....	....	....	....	....	....	3.89	3.56	....
Corporations: Stocks, up to 1 year	60pcs	....	....	....	....	....	....	....	....	....	3.53	3.20	....
New Bus., Over €1 mil.,up to 1 yr	6Cpcn	....	....	....	....	....	....	....	....	....	3.34	3.15	....
Government Bond Yield	61	6.38	6.05	5.21	5.39	5.29	....	....	....	....	....	....	....
Prices, Production, Labor		*Index Numbers (2000=100): Period Averages*											
Share Prices (1995=100)	62	110.4	100.0	117.5	152.5	194.2	....	....	99.8	99.0	100.2	109.3	118.1
Producer Prices in Industry	63a	†94.1	97.8	94.7	96.1	98.5	†95.4	100.0	102.7	†104.8	106.9	109.3	112.0
Consumer Prices	64	90.8	92.5	†93.8	95.1	96.0	96.9	100.0	102.4	104.5	†107.2	110.6	114.8
Harmonized CPI	64h	....	92.1	93.2	94.5	95.4	96.4	100.0	103.1	105.2	110.7	117.8	125.2
Industrial Production	66	79.7	†81.3	81.4	86.1	86.0	95.9	100.0	†105.6	109.0	111.0	113.9	117.4
Employment	67	....	....	....	....	....							
		Number in Thousands: Period Averages											
Employment	67e	....	214	220	227	237	248	265	280	289	294	302	311
Unemployment	67c	5	5	6	6	6	5	5	5	6	8	9	9
Unemployment Rate (%)	67r	2.8	3.0	3.3	3.6	3.1	2.9	2.7	2.6	2.9	3.8	4.2	4.2
Intl. Transactions & Positions		*Billions of Francs through 1998; Millions of Euros Beginning 1999*											
Exports	70	219.10	228.40	223.20	250.10	287.30	†7.42	8.62	9.21	9.01	8.83	9.79	10.11
Imports, c.i.f.	71	280.00	287.30	299.20	335.70	370.60	†10.38	11.65	12.47	12.28	12.11	13.53	14.03

Balance of Payments		1994	1995	1996	1997	1998	1999	2000	2001	2002	2003	2004	2005
						Millions of US Dollars: Minus Sign Indicates Debit							
Current Account, n.i.e.	78ald	....	2,426	2,219	1,834	1,626	1,650	2,562	1,674	2,410	1,867	3,562	3,756
Goods: Exports f.o.b.	78aad	....	8,578	7,944	7,745	8,557	8,565	8,635	8,996	9,535	11,040	13,670	14,400
Goods: Imports f.o.b.	78abd	....	−10,269	−9,872	−9,770	−10,881	−11,151	−11,056	−11,395	−11,599	−13,977	−17,111	−18,605
Trade Balance	78acd	....	−1,690	−1,928	−2,025	−2,324	−2,586	−2,420	−2,399	−2,064	−2,936	−3,441	−4,205
Services: Credit	78add	....	10,619	11,930	12,583	14,084	17,134	20,301	19,945	20,350	25,396	33,183	40,254
Services: Debit	78aed	....	−7,519	−8,483	−8,683	−9,947	−11,840	−13,581	−13,708	−12,266	−15,397	−20,748	−24,801
Balance on Goods & Services	78afd	....	1,410	1,519	1,874	1,813	2,708	4,300	3,838	6,020	7,063	8,994	11,247
Income: Credit	78agd	....	48,798	40,476	38,439	46,814	47,931	50,400	52,302	49,151	51,159	61,499	70,594
Income: Debit	78ahd	....	−47,209	−39,220	−37,971	−46,578	−48,413	−51,678	−53,941	−52,458	−55,745	−65,632	−76,869
Balance on Gds, Serv. & Inc.	78aid	....	2,999	2,774	2,342	2,049	2,227	3,022	2,199	2,713	2,477	4,862	4,972
Current Transfers, n.i.e.: Credit	78ajd	....	1,791	2,186	1,985	2,185	2,282	2,750	2,269	3,582	3,725	4,435	4,919
Current Transfers: Debit	78akd	....	−2,364	−2,741	−2,493	−2,608	−2,859	−3,211	−2,793	−3,885	−4,334	−5,735	−6,135
Capital Account, n.i.e.	78bcd	....	....	....	....	....	....	....	....	−117	−151	−242	−160
Capital Account, n.i.e.: Credit	78bad	....	....	....	....	....	....	....	....	64	54	33	38
Capital Account: Debit	78bbd	....	....	....	....	....	....	....	....	−181	−204	−274	−198
Financial Account, n.i.e.	78bjd	....	....	....	....	....	....	....	....	−2,743	−1,650	−3,579	−3,631
Direct Investment Abroad	78bdd	....	....	....	....	....	....	....	....	−128,843	−100,446	−82,943	−78,335
Dir. Invest. in Rep. Econ., n.i.e.	78bed	....	....	....	....	....	....	....	....	118,445	90,817	78,678	68,622
Portfolio Investment Assets	78bfd	....	....	....	....	....	....	....	....	6,254	−78,422	−87,546	−263,153
Equity Securities	78bkd	....	....	....	....	....	....	....	....	4,301	−35,857	−45,835	−123,620
Debt Securities	78bld	....	....	....	....	....	....	....	....	1,953	−42,565	−41,711	−139,533
Portfolio Investment Liab., n.i.e.	78bgd	....	....	....	....	....	....	....	....	64,215	99,487	139,607	316,580
Equity Securities	78bmd	....	....	....	....	....	....	....	....	36,085	70,444	121,544	275,791
Debt Securities	78bnd	....	....	....	....	....	....	....	....	28,130	29,043	18,063	40,789
Financial Derivatives Assets	78bwd	....	....	....	....	....	....	....	....	....	....		
Financial Derivatives Liabilities	78bxd	....	....	....	....	....	....	....	....	−38	6,844	−2,847	−3,038
Other Investment Assets	78bhd	....	....	....	....	....	....	....	....	−42,433	−35,042	−116,640	−214,393
Monetary Authorities	78bod	....	....	....	....	....	....	....	....	—	−7,641	−7,210	−5,755
General Government	78bpd	....	....	....	....	....	....	....	....	—	−1	—	−1
Banks	78bqd	....	....	....	....	....	....	....	....	19,337	−3,623	−43,871	−36,573
Other Sectors	78brd	....	....	....	....	....	....	....	....	−61,771	−23,777	−65,559	−172,064
Other Investment Liab., n.i.e.	78bid	....	....	....	....	....	....	....	....	−20,342	15,114	68,113	170,087
Monetary Authorities	78bsd	....	....	....	....	....	....	....	....	−887	−5,824	6,208	322
General Government	78btd	....	....	....	....	....	....	....	....	3	−1	−16	—
Banks	78bud	....	....	....	....	....	....	....	....	−27,719	17,866	31,295	41,383
Other Sectors	78bvd	....	....	....	....	....	....	....	....	8,261	3,073	30,626	128,382
Net Errors and Omissions	78cad	....	....	....	....	....	....	....	....	485	41	267	−13
Overall Balance	78cbd	....	....	....	....	....	....	....	....	35	108	8	−48
Reserves and Related Items	79dad	....	....	....	....	....	....	....	....	−35	−108	−8	48
Reserve Assets	79dbd	....	—	....	—	....	....	....	....	−35	−108	−8	48
Use of Fund Credit and Loans	79dcd	....	....	....	....	....	....	....	....	—	—	—	—
Exceptional Financing	79ded	....	....	....	....	....	....	....	....	—	....	....	....

International Investment Position													
						Millions of US Dollars							
Assets	79aad	....	....	....	....	....	....	....	....	1,967,151	2,719,566	3,299,509	....
Direct Investment Abroad	79abd	....	....	....	....	....	....	....	....	502,441	741,181	881,148	....
Portfolio Investment	79acd	....	....	....	....	....	....	....	....	923,391	1,333,237	1,615,581	....
Equity Securities	79add	....	....	....	....	....	....	....	....	304,988	488,272	637,048	....
Debt Securities	79aed	....	....	....	....	....	....	....	....	618,403	844,965	978,533	....
Financial Derivatives	79ald	....	....	....	....	....	....	....	....	7,767	8,780	12,201	....
Other Investment	79afd	....	....	....	....	....	....	....	....	533,374	636,057	790,248	....
Monetary Authorities	79agd	....	....	....	....	....	....	....	....	....	....	....	....
General Government	79ahd	....	....	....	....	....	....	....	....	....	....	....	....
Banks	79aid	....	....	....	....	....	....	....	....	....	....	....	....
Other Sectors	79ajd	....	....	....	....	....	....	....	....	....	....	....	....
Reserve Assets	79akd	....	....	....	....	....	....	....	....	178	311	331	....
Liabilities	79lad	....	....	....	....	....	....	....	....	1,949,229	2,689,172	3,261,696	....
Dir. Invest. in Rep. Economy	79lbd	....	....	....	....	....	....	....	....	514,550	775,856	948,987	....
Portfolio Investment	79lcd	....	....	....	....	....	....	....	....	982,982	1,334,618	1,668,605	....
Equity Securities	79ldd	....	....	....	....	....	....	....	....	849,537	1,143,406	1,443,749	....
Debt Securities	79led	....	....	....	....	....	....	....	....	133,445	191,212	224,856	....
Financial Derivatives	79lld	....	....	....	....	....	....	....	....	1,166	14,353	15,492	....
Other Investment	79lfd	....	....	....	....	....	....	....	....	450,531	564,344	628,612	....
Monetary Authorities	79lgd	....	....	....	....	....	....	....	....	....	....	....	....
General Government	79lhd	....	....	....	....	....	....	....	....	....	....	....	....
Banks	79lid	....	....	....	....	....	....	....	....	....	....	....	....
Other Sectors	79ljd	....	....	....	....	....	....	....	....	....	....	....	....

Government Finance													
Central Government													
						Millions of Francs through 1998; Millions of Euros Beginning 1999: Year Ending December 31							
Deficit (-) or Surplus	80	2,656	12,573	25,846	12,609	....	....	....	....	....	....	....	....
Revenue	81	217,830	220,074	239,082	261,696	....	....	....	....	....	....	....	....
Grants Received	81z	596	797	507	7,037	....	....	....	....	....	....	....	....
Expenditure	82	205,656	211,557	222,710	240,847	....	....	....	....	....	....	....	....
Lending Minus Repayments	83	700	613	641	−5,563	....	....	....	....	....	....	....	....
Adjustment for Complem. Period	80x	−9,414	3,872	9,608	−20,840	....	....	....	....	....	....	....	....
Financing													
Total Financing	84	−2,656	−11,810	−25,846	−12,609	....	....	....	....	....	....	....	....
Domestic	84a	−2,300	−11,776	−25,598	−12,455	....	....	....	....	....	....	....	....
Foreign	85a	−356	−34	−248	−154	....	....	....	....	....	....	....	....
Debt: Domestic	88a	....	....	....	24,616	....	....	....	....	....	....	....	....
Foreign	89a	....	....	....	6,311	....	....	....	....	....	....	....	....
General Government													
						As Percent of Gross Domestic Product							

Luxembourg 137

		1994	1995	1996	1997	1998	1999	2000	2001	2002	2003	2004	2005
National Accounts						*Billions of Francs through 1998; Billions of Euros Beginning 1999*							
Househ.Cons.Expend.,incl.NPISHs....	96f	245.7	† 263.9	275.3	290.0	311.9	† 7.9	8.5	9.2	9.6	10.5	11.1	11.6
Government Consumption Expend...	91f	91.3	† 97.0	104.3	110.4	111.1	† 3.1	3.3	3.6	3.9	4.2	4.6	4.9
Gross Fixed Capital Formation.........	93e	115.1	† 121.2	128.3	143.8	153.1	† 4.7	4.6	5.1	5.3	5.4	5.5	6.0
Changes in Inventories....................	93i	2.8	† −1.7	.4	3.5	10.8	† .1	.5	.4	−.1	—	—	.3
Exports of Goods and Services.........	90c	547.6	† 648.5	708.2	800.9	895.8	† 26.7	33.0	33.1	33.8	34.6	40.2	46.4
Imports of Goods and Services (-).....	98c	489.0	† 519.3	579.2	686.2	780.1	† 22.9	28.4	29.1	29.0	29.1	34.3	39.8
Gross Domestic Product (GDP).........	99b	513.6	† 609.6	637.2	662.4	702.5	† 19.9	22.0	22.6	24.0	25.7	27.1	29.3
Net Primary Income from Abroad.....	98.n	48.2	† 32.2	30.1	14.0	−11.5	† −.6	−2.0	....	....	....	....	....
Gross National Income (GNI)............	99a	529.4	† 564.5	593.2	637.5	646.3	† 17.9	19.2	20.1	20.8	20.8	23.3	24.4
Net Current Transf.from Abroad.......	98t						† .1	−.5	−1.8	....	....	....	....
Gross Nat'l Disposable Inc.(GNDI)....	99i	....	....	....	....	....	† 18.0	18.7	18.3	....	....	....	....
Consumption of Fixed Capital..........	99cf	79.2	82.7	86.9	87.9	92.6	† 2.6	2.9	3.1	3.2	3.2	3.4	....
GDP Volume 1995 Ref., Chained.....	99b.p	525.6	609.6	618.8	655.6	698.1	† 18.8	20.3	20.9	21.6	22.1	23.0	23.9
GDP Volume (2000=100)................	99bvp	64.0	74.3	75.4	79.9	85.1	† 92.2	100.0	102.5	106.2	108.4	113.0	117.6
GDP Deflator (2000=100)................	99bip	90.4	† 92.5	95.2	93.4	93.1	† 98.0	100.0	100.1	102.8	107.7	108.8	113.4
						Millions: Midyear Estimates							
Population................................	99z	.40	.41	.41	.42	.42	.43	.44	.44	.45	.45	.46	.46

Macedonia, FYR 962

		1994	1995	1996	1997	1998	1999	2000	2001	2002	2003	2004	2005
Exchange Rates						*Denar per SDR: End of Period*							
Market Rate	aa	59.264	56.456	59.547	74.776	72.987	82.816	86.420	86.930	79.665	72.887	69.990	74.120
						Denar per US Dollar: End of Period (ae) Period Average (rf)							
Market Rate	ae	40.596	37.980	41.411	55.421	51.836	60.339	66.328	69.172	58.598	49.050	45.068	51.859
Market Rate	rf	43.263	37.882	39.981	50.004	54.462	56.902	65.904	68.037	64.350	54.322	49.410	49.284
						Index Numbers (2000=100): Period Averages							
Nominal Effective Exchange Rate	nec	72.88	89.22	92.16	88.89	87.79	94.75	100.00	105.66	107.98	112.84	116.01	117.18
Real Effective Exchange Rate	rec	123.81	134.68	123.13	107.31	98.94	97.30	100.00	100.06	99.66	101.52	102.30	99.76
Fund Position						*Millions of SDRs: End of Period*							
Quota	2f.s	49.6	49.6	49.6	49.6	49.6	68.9	68.9	68.9	68.9	68.9	68.9	68.9
SDRs	1b.s	—	.2	—	.3	.8	.9	.5	1.8	4.5	.2	.5	.5
Reserve Position in the Fund	1c.s	—	—	—	—	—	—	—	—	—	—	—	—
Total Fund Cred.&Loans Outstg	2tl	14.0	38.1	47.4	65.3	72.7	74.1	62.3	56.3	49.6	46.0	40.3	43.5
International Liquidity						*Millions of US Dollars Unless Otherwise Indicated: End of Period*							
Total Reserves minus Gold	1l.d	149.05	257.49	239.55	257.00	306.11	429.92	429.38	745.17	722.03	897.67	904.97	1,228.51
SDRs	1b.d	—	.2	—	.4	1.1	1.2	.7	2.2	6.1	.3	.8	.8
Reserve Position in the Fund	1c.d	—	—	—	—	—	—	—	—	—	—	—	—
Foreign Exchange	1d.d	149.04	257.26	239.51	256.61	305.04	428.73	428.73	742.94	715.91	897.39	904.21	1,227.73
Gold (Million Fine Troy Ounces)	1ad	.045	.046	.076	.081	.100	.102	.112	.194	.198	.089	.197	.218
Gold (National Valuation)	1and	16.36	17.61	27.98	23.45	28.50	29.69	30.66	53.68	67.81	37.08	86.47	111.98
Other Liab	4..d	—	—	—	—	—	—	14.01	—	—	—	—	—
Deposit Money Banks: Assets	7a.d	232.98	254.61	229.70	286.84	337.78	404.22	430.92	643.02	560.34	674.80	823.90	728.63
Liabilities	7b.d	528.30	84.62	138.39	185.76	250.00	262.28	233.08	195.31	205.59	199.65	223.31	276.33
Monetary Authorities						*Millions of Denar: End of Period*							
Foreign Assets	11	6,715	10,732	11,453	15,894	18,977	30,072	47,910	70,945	45,560	45,835	44,412	69,245
Claims on Central Government	12a	2,400	2,395	3,049	8,706	8,675	8,116	5,869	8,796	8,275	3,878	3,467	3,911
Claims on Deposit Money Banks	12e	2,333	4,673	5,642	3,672	3,538	1,918	1,259	394	410	240	199	1,203
Reserve Money	14	6,360	† 8,306	8,044	9,872	10,421	13,508	19,804	21,402	22,209	23,944	23,865	30,934
of which: Currency Outside DMBs	14a	4,786	5,965	6,401	6,846	6,964	8,271	9,522	14,134	14,136	14,177	14,162	14,439
Restricted Deposits	16b	—	114	136	9	56	271	135	588	560	648	223	411
Foreign Liabilities	16c	831	2,150	2,822	4,882	5,308	6,137	6,314	4,897	3,949	3,353	2,819	3,224
Central Government Deposits	16d	31	2,633	3,695	5,070	6,152	9,465	16,759	24,926	17,318	11,667	12,554	24,419
Capital Accounts	17a	4,682	5,059	5,771	8,398	8,130	9,547	11,076	12,348	9,984	7,729	7,154	11,024
Other Items (Net)	17r	−360	−462	−325	41	1,123	1,178	950	15,974	225	2,612	1,463	4,347
Deposit Money Banks						*Millions of Denar: End of Period*							
Reserves	20	1,470	1,836	1,125	2,158	2,379	3,861	6,192	6,195	6,364	8,098	8,110	14,972
Foreign Assets	21	9,458	9,670	9,512	15,897	17,509	24,390	28,582	44,479	32,835	33,099	37,131	37,786
Claims on Central Government	22a	48,954	5,624	6,311	1,782	1,288	1,289	7,337	7,744	8,257	6,745	7,164	7,260
Claims on Local Government	22b	—	2	12	27	20	14	44	7	11	2	20	13
Claims on Nonfin.Pub.Enterprises	22c	—	528	121	208	293	237	515	755	814	458	677	517
Claims on Private Sector	22d	66,392	39,181	46,826	50,711	34,531	43,611	42,157	41,151	43,104	49,937	61,470	73,582
Demand Deposits	24	5,080	5,567	4,854	6,281	7,336	10,458	11,896	11,168	12,255	12,800	13,154	15,206
Time, Savings,& Fgn.Currency Dep	25	9,726	8,417	8,652	11,537	13,573	17,846	23,294	49,200	42,096	52,584	65,009	76,990
Restricted Deposits	26b	38,938	1,039	1,111	1,006	1,099	1,185	1,373	1,708	692	567	680	650
Foreign Liabilities	26c	21,447	3,214	5,731	10,295	12,959	15,826	15,460	13,510	12,047	9,793	10,064	14,330
Central Government Deposits	26d	2,411	1,481	1,345	1,678	2,181	2,904	5,214	4,150	2,692	2,034	1,660	1,593
Credit from Monetary Authorities	26g	1,961	4,016	4,395	2,388	2,303	1,287	805	427	398	374	779	937
Capital Accounts	27a	15,567	17,483	23,799	23,157	23,651	29,046	33,120	30,105	30,102	31,723	34,664	37,211
Other Items (Net)	27r	31,132	15,624	14,021	14,441	−7,082	−5,150	−6,335	−9,937	−8,897	−11,536	−11,438	−12,787
Monetary Survey						*Millions of Denar: End of Period*							
Foreign Assets (Net)	31n	−6,106	15,038	12,412	16,614	18,219	32,499	54,718	30,969	66,617	65,789	68,660	89,477
Domestic Credit	32	115,304	43,635	51,406	54,797	36,637	41,075	34,027	45,516	38,805	47,321	58,584	59,271
Claims on Central Govt. (Net)	32an	48,912	3,905	4,320	3,740	1,630	−2,964	−8,767	3,594	−5,124	−3,078	−3,583	−14,841
Claims on Local Government	32b	—	2	12	27	20	14	44	7	11	2	20	13
Claims on Nonfin.Pub.Enterprises	32c	—	528	121	208	293	237	515	755	814	458	677	517
Claims on Private Sector	32d	66,392	39,181	46,826	50,711	34,531	43,611	42,157	41,151	43,104	49,937	61,470	73,582
Money	34	9,965	† 12,223	11,788	13,702	14,952	19,795	22,392	11,168	27,722	28,291	28,884	31,219
Quasi-Money	35	8,507	† 8,417	8,652	11,537	13,573	17,846	23,294	49,200	42,096	52,584	65,009	76,990
Restricted Deposits	36b	38,938	1,153	1,247	1,015	1,155	1,456	1,508	1,708	1,381	1,215	903	1,061
Capital Accounts	37a	20,249	22,542	29,570	31,555	31,781	38,593	44,196	30,105	40,994	39,452	41,818	48,235
Other Items (Net)	37r	31,624	14,338	12,561	13,602	−6,605	−4,116	−2,645	−15,696	−6,771	−8,433	−9,370	−8,757
Money plus Quasi-Money	35l	18,472	† 20,640	20,440	25,239	28,525	37,641	45,686	60,368	69,818	80,875	93,893	108,209
Interest Rates						*Percent Per Annum*							
Bank Rate (End of Period)	60	33.00	15.00	9.20	8.90	8.90	8.90	7.90	10.70	10.70	6.50	6.50	6.50
Deposit Rate	60l	117.56	24.07	12.75	11.64	11.68	11.40	11.18	9.97	9.56	7.97	6.54	6.60
Lending Rate	60p	159.82	45.95	21.58	21.42	21.03	20.45	18.93	19.35	18.36	16.00	12.44	12.17
Prices, Production, Labor						*Index Numbers (2000=100): Period Averages*							
Producer Prices	63	81.3	85.1	84.8	88.4	91.9	91.9	100.0	102.0	101.1	100.9	101.8	105.0
Consumer Prices	64	78.0	90.8	92.9	95.3	95.2	94.5	100.0	105.5	107.4	108.7	109.6	109.7
Wages: Average Monthly	65	76.2	84.2	86.5	88.9	92.1	94.7	100.0	103.6	110.7	116.0	120.5	123.6
Industrial Production	66	114.0	102.5	105.8	107.5	112.3	109.4	100.0	89.9	86.0	90.9	88.8	95.1
						Number in Thousands: Period Averages							
Employment	67e	396	357	538	512	540	545	550	599	561	545	523	545
Unemployment	67c	186	216	251	288	284	261	262	263	263	316	309	324
Intl. Transactions & Positions						*Millions of US Dollars*							
Exports	70..d	1,086.3	1,204.1	1,147.4	1,236.8	1,310.7	1,191.3	1,322.6	1,157.5	1,115.5	1,367.0	1,675.9	2,041.3
Imports, c.i.f	71..d	1,484.1	1,718.9	1,626.9	1,778.5	1,914.7	1,776.2	2,093.9	1,693.6	1,995.2	2,306.4	2,931.6	3,228.0

		1994	1995	1996	1997	1998	1999	2000	2001	2002	2003	2004	2005
Balance of Payments						*Millions of US Dollars: Minus Sign Indicates Debit*							
Current Account, n.i.e.	78ald	....	....	−288.1	−275.5	−269.7	−32.4	−72.4	−243.6	−357.9	−149.0	−414.8	....
Goods: Exports f.o.b.	78aad	....	....	1,147.4	1,201.4	1,291.5	1,190.0	1,320.7	1,155.4	1,112.1	1,362.7	1,672.4	....
Goods: Imports f.o.b.	78abd	....	....	−1,464.0	−1,589.1	−1,806.6	−1,685.8	−2,011.1	−1,681.8	−1,916.5	−2,210.6	−2,784.5	....
Trade Balance	78acd	....	....	−316.5	−387.6	−515.1	−495.8	−690.4	−526.4	−804.3	−847.9	−1,112.1	....
Services: Credit	78add	....	....	154.3	128.3	149.3	272.8	316.7	244.6	253.0	326.9	407.9	....
Services: Debit	78aed	....	....	−309.3	−272.9	−209.1	−230.9	−268.0	−263.8	−275.3	−337.0	−462.3	....
Balance on Goods & Services	78afd	....	....	−471.5	−532.2	−574.9	−453.8	−641.7	−545.6	−826.6	−858.1	−1,166.4	....
Income: Credit	78agd	....	....	45.3	39.0	23.5	24.2	41.6	52.6	51.0	60.4	84.6	....
Income: Debit	78ahd	....	....	−75.0	−72.6	−68.5	−66.5	−87.3	−93.3	−80.8	−91.9	−123.8	....
Balance on Gds, Serv. & Inc.	78aid	....	....	−501.2	−565.8	−619.9	−496.1	−687.3	−586.3	−856.4	−889.6	−1,205.7	....
Current Transfers, n.i.e.: Credit	78ajd	....	....	475.4	535.0	542.7	618.5	788.2	725.7	535.7	778.9	836.9	....
Current Transfers: Debit	78akd	....	....	−262.3	−244.8	−192.5	−154.8	−173.3	−383.0	−37.2	−38.2	−46.0	....
Capital Account, n.i.e.	78bcd	....	....	....	....	−1.8	—	.3	1.3	8.3	−6.7	−4.6	....
Capital Account, n.i.e.: Credit	78bad	....	....	....	....	—	—	.3	3.6	9.9	—	—	....
Capital Account: Debit	78bbd	....	....	....	....	−1.8	—	—	−2.3	−1.7	−6.7	−4.6	....
Financial Account, n.i.e.	78bjd	....	....	174.3	186.8	329.9	14.2	290.3	325.7	257.2	237.0	439.6	....
Direct Investment Abroad	78bdd	....	....	....	....	—	−.3	.6	−.9	−.1	−.3	−1.2	....
Dir. Invest. in Rep. Econ., n.i.e.	78bed	....	....	11.2	15.7	127.7	32.7	174.5	441.5	77.8	96.3	157.0	....
Portfolio Investment Assets	78bfd	....	....	−.5	−2.5	.2	.1	−.8	3.2	1.2	.3	−.9	....
Equity Securities	78bkd	....	....	−.5	−2.5	—	—	—	—	.3	.1	.2	....
Debt Securities	78bld	....	....	....	....	.2	.1	−.8	3.2	.9	.3	−1.1	....
Portfolio Investment Liab., n.i.e.	78bgd	....	....	.8	4.6	.1	—	−.1	.4	.1	3.3	14.7	....
Equity Securities	78bmd	....	....	.8	4.6	—	—	—	—	—	.7	15.3	....
Debt Securities	78bnd	....	....	....	....	.1	—	−.1	.4	—	2.6	−.7	....
Financial Derivatives Assets	78bwd	....	....	....	....	....	....	....	....	....	....	....	....
Financial Derivatives Liabilities	78bxd	....	....	....	....	....	....	....	....	....	....	....	....
Other Investment Assets	78bhd	....	....	−133.2	−73.0	−58.9	−184.1	−77.7	−98.1	246.2	−3.8	6.6	....
Monetary Authorities	78bod	....	....	....	....	−15.2	−6.2	14.1	−236.8	223.0	17.8	26.4	....
General Government	78bpd	....	....	....	....	....	....	....	....	....	....	....	....
Banks	78bqd	....	....	25.3	−57.5	−31.3	−114.9	−62.1	−237.6	159.4	−43.4	−94.8	....
Other Sectors	78brd	....	....	−158.5	−15.6	−12.3	−62.9	−29.6	376.2	−136.3	21.8	75.0	....
Other Investment Liab., n.i.e.	78bid	....	....	295.9	242.0	260.9	165.8	193.7	−20.4	−67.9	141.2	263.4	....
Monetary Authorities	78bsd	....	....	—	—	—	—	14.7	140.1	−154.2	—	—	....
General Government	78btd	....	....	59.9	−71.6	109.2	89.4	77.3	−65.4	11.0	28.3	38.4	....
Banks	78bud	....	....	−1.2	29.8	105.1	68.1	−44.0	−38.3	−4.6	−34.2	−23.9	....
Other Sectors	78bvd	....	....	237.3	283.8	46.5	8.2	145.7	−56.8	79.9	147.1	248.9	....
Net Errors and Omissions	78cad	....	....	18.8	−29.9	−15.1	159.9	61.0	2.3	−29.7	−26.0	7.8	....
Overall Balance	78cbd	....	....	−95.1	−118.6	43.3	141.7	279.2	85.6	−122.1	55.4	28.0	....
Reserves and Related Items	79dad	....	....	95.1	118.6	−43.3	−141.7	−279.2	−85.6	122.1	−55.4	−28.0	....
Reserve Assets	79dbd	....	....	7.6	−35.1	−53.2	−143.5	−263.6	−78.0	130.9	−50.7	−19.4	....
Use of Fund Credit and Loans	79dcd	....	....	13.5	24.6	9.9	1.8	−15.6	−7.6	−8.8	−4.7	−8.6	....
Exceptional Financing	79ded	....	....	73.9	129.2	—	—	—	—	—	—	—	....
International Investment Position					*Millions of US Dollars*								
Assets	79aad	....	....	....	....	....	....	....	....	....	....	....	....
Direct Investment Abroad	79abd	....	....	—	—	—	—	—	—	—	—	—	....
Portfolio Investment	79acd	....	....	—	—	—	—	—	—	3.5	4.0	5.6	....
Equity Securities	79add	....	....	—	—	—	—	—	—	—	—	—	....
Debt Securities	79aed	....	....	—	—	—	—	—	—	3.5	4.0	5.6	....
Financial Derivatives	79ald	....	....	....	....	....	....	....	....	....	....	....	....
Other Investment	79afd	....	....	229.3	286.8	337.8	425.4	458.8	895.7	601.4	711.0	833.8	....
Monetary Authorities	79agd	....	....	—	—	—	21.2	21.4	252.7	49.2	41.4	16.2	....
General Government	79ahd	....	....	....	....	....	....	....	....	....	....	....	....
Banks	79aid	....	....	229.3	286.8	337.8	404.2	437.4	643.0	552.2	669.6	817.6	....
Other Sectors	79ajd	....	....	....	....	....	....	....	....	....	....	....	....
Reserve Assets	79akd	....	....	267.5	280.4	367.2	478.3	712.6	775.2	734.4	893.3	975.2	....
Liabilities	79lad	....	....	....	....	....	....	....	....	....	....	....	....
Dir. Invest. in Rep. Economy	79lbd	....	....	—	—	—	—	—	—	—	—	—	....
Portfolio Investment	79lcd	....	....	—	—	—	—	—	—	—	—	—	....
Equity Securities	79ldd	....	....	—	—	—	—	—	—	—	—	—	....
Debt Securities	79led	....	....	—	—	—	—	—	—	—	—	—	....
Financial Derivatives	79lld	....	....	....	....	....	....	....	....	....	....	....	....
Other Investment	79lfd	....	....	1,243.1	1,259.7	1,545.0	1,603.7	1,603.0	1,654.3	1,642.8	1,859.2	2,022.5	....
Monetary Authorities	79lgd	....	....	68.2	88.1	102.4	101.7	95.4	225.0	67.4	68.4	62.5	....
General Government	79lhd	....	....	1,041.2	999.3	1,126.2	1,156.3	1,216.3	1,147.8	1,131.6	1,256.5	1,350.4	....
Banks	79lid	....	....	121.3	156.3	289.7	321.2	217.4	177.3	188.4	174.4	162.3	....
Other Sectors	79ljd	....	....	12.4	16.0	26.8	24.5	73.9	104.2	255.4	360.0	447.2	....
Government Finance					*Millions of Denar: Year Ending December 31*								
Deficit (-) or Surplus	80	....	2,267.6	175.3	....	....	....	....	....	....	....	....	....
Total Revenue and Grants	81y	....	40,437.0	39,865.2	....	....	....	....	....	....	....	....	....
Revenue	81	....	39,775.8	39,766.1	....	....	....	....	....	....	....	....	....
Grants	81z	....	661.2	99.1	....	....	....	....	....	....	....	....	....
Exp. & Lending Minus Repay.	82z	....	38,169.4	39,689.9	....	....	....	....	....	....	....	....	....
Expenditure	82	....	36,511.0	37,423.3	....	....	....	....	....	....	....	....	....
Lending Minus Repayments	83	....	1,658.4	2,266.6	....	....	....	....	....	....	....	....	....
Total Financing	80h	....	−2,267.6	−175.3	....	....	....	....	....	....	....	....	....
Total Net Borrowing	84	....	−3,445.2	−175.5	....	....	....	....	....	....	....	....	....
Net Domestic	84a	....	−3,334.1	−1,200.0	....	....	....	....	....	....	....	....	....
Net Foreign	85a	....	−111.1	1,024.5	....	....	....	....	....	....	....	....	....
Use of Cash Balances	87	....	1,177.6	.2	....	....	....	....	....	....	....	....	....

Macedonia, FYR   962

National Accounts		1994	1995	1996	1997	1998	1999	2000	2001	2002	2003	2004	2005
							Millions of Denar						
Househ.Cons.Expend.,incl.NPISHs....	96f	110,847	119,381	127,253	135,487	141,078	145,693	175,965	163,788	188,179	191,873	206,610	....
Government Consumption Expend...	91f	27,875	31,491	31,985	36,700	39,504	43,009	43,021	57,983	54,616	51,980	55,112	....
Gross Fixed Capital Formation..........	93e	22,461	28,027	30,654	32,236	33,982	34,710	38,332	34,716	40,448	42,110	47,286	....
Changes in Inventories....................	93i	182	7,162	4,790	6,778	9,426	6,461	14,274	9,902	9,828	8,151	9,916	....
Exports of Goods and Services..........	90c	55,920	55,961	49,722	69,408	80,343	88,143	114,958	99,833	92,781	95,254	106,758	....
Imports of Goods and Services (-).....	98c	70,876	72,501	67,961	94,590	109,355	109,007	150,161	132,381	141,882	137,882	160,425	....
GDP, Production Based...................	99bp	146,409	169,521	176,444	186,019	194,979	209,010	236,389	233,841	243,970	251,486	265,257	....
Statistical Discrepancy....................	99bs	—	—	—	—	—	—	—	—	—	—	—	....
GDP Volume 1995 Prices..............	99b.p	171,432	169,521	171,530	174,000	179,879	187,684	196,222	187,342	188,941	194,263	202,189	....
GDP Deflator (2000=100)...............	99bip	70.9	83.0	85.4	88.7	90.0	92.4	100.0	103.6	107.2	107.5	108.9	....
GDP Volume (2000=100)................	99bvp	87.4	86.4	87.4	88.7	91.7	95.6	100.0	95.5	96.3	99.0	103.0	....
							Millions: Midyear Estimates						
Population................................	99z	2	2	2	2	2	2	2	2	2	2	2	2

Madagascar 674

		1994	1995	1996	1997	1998	1999	2000	2001	2002	2003	2004	2005
Exchange Rates						*Ariary per SDR: End of Period*							
Official Rate	aa	1,130.2	1,017.6	1,244.8	1,426.1	1,521.3	1,796.1	1,706.9	1,666.7	1,749.6	1,812.3	2,903.2	† 3,087.0
					Ariary per US Dollar: End of Period (ae) Period Average (rf)								
Official Rate	ae	774.2	684.6	865.7	1,056.9	1,080.4	1,308.6	1,310.1	1,326.2	1,287.0	1,219.6	1,869.4	† 2,159.8
Official Rate	rf	613.5	853.1	812.3	1,018.2	1,088.3	1,256.8	1,353.5	1,317.7	1,366.4	1,238.3	1,868.9	2,003.0
Fund Position						*Millions of SDRs: End of Period*							
Quota	2f.s	90.4	90.4	90.4	90.4	90.4	122.2	122.2	122.2	122.2	122.2	122.2	122.2
SDRs	1b.s	—	—	—	—	—	.1	—	.1	—	—	.1	—
Reserve Position in the Fund	1c.s	—	—	—	—	—	—	—	—	—	—	—	—
Total Fund Cred.&Loans Outstg	2tl	58.6	48.9	50.8	51.5	41.2	45.8	80.0	101.4	110.0	115.9	145.4	148.6
International Liquidity					*Millions of US Dollars Unless Otherwise Indicated: End of Period*								
Total Reserves minus Gold	1l.d	71.6	109.0	240.9	281.6	171.4	227.2	285.2	398.3	363.3	414.3	503.5	481.3
SDRs	1b.d	—	—	.1	.1	—	.1	—	.1	—	—	.2	—
Reserve Position in the Fund	1c.d	—	—	—	—	—	—	—	—	—	—	—	—
Foreign Exchange	1d.d	71.6	108.9	240.8	281.5	171.3	227.0	285.1	398.2	363.2	414.2	503.3	481.2
Deposit Money Banks: Assets	7a.d	157.7	176.6	137.9	151.7	142.0	140.5	180.4	158.4	188.5	230.4	260.8	229.3
Liabilities	7b.d	38.6	33.5	37.3	32.0	40.0	40.0	50.9	62.2	57.7	57.3	61.4	40.9
Monetary Authorities						*Billions of Ariary: End of Period*							
Foreign Assets	11	47.61	74.91	208.72	298.58	185.35	297.44	390.76	526.46	458.61	508.08	932.06	1,013.86
Claims on Central Government	12a	282.47	289.16	287.40	272.03	350.45	376.20	405.68	419.26	427.42	474.41	379.45	396.92
Claims on Nonfin.Pub.Enterprises	12c	1.39	2.52	2.83	3.01	3.17	3.16	22.21	55.28	72.82	3.54	3.86	4.46
Claims on Deposit Money Banks	12e	26.93	35.01	25.49	21.45	20.54	15.03	11.90	8.07	5.44	3.45	−7.67	1.07
Reserve Money	14	178.78	231.79	344.62	348.36	370.99	467.79	522.84	677.01	707.13	705.46	839.79	937.54
of which: Currency Outside DMBs	14a	122.91	151.74	165.87	204.05	233.97	286.97	357.82	431.92	466.02	514.00	591.38	599.12
Time, Savings,& Fgn. Currency Dep	15	....	1.5	.3	.6	.7	1.0	—	—	.1	.1	.2	.3
Foreign Liabilities	16c	143.91	113.60	128.49	133.87	116.42	129.56	174.21	202.06	209.78	224.24	438.01	515.71
Central Government Deposits	16d	56.68	110.56	121.88	174.29	131.64	127.34	172.05	177.74	110.42	134.98	114.72	71.73
Counterpart Funds	16e	—	—	—	—	—	—	—	—	—	—	—	—
Capital Accounts	17a	8.76	24.52	6.70	18.78	18.83	21.45	18.59	24.30	48.00	48.95	19.98	18.79
Other Items (Net)	17r	−29.73	−80.25	−77.55	−80.81	−79.00	−55.36	−57.16	−72.08	−111.10	−124.25	−105.04	−127.75
Deposit Money Banks						*Billions of Ariary: End of Period*							
Reserves	20	55.87	80.05	178.74	144.31	135.74	177.42	164.68	245.05	240.99	190.92	248.35	338.37
Foreign Assets	21	122.07	120.88	119.40	160.31	153.39	183.83	236.36	210.10	242.57	280.98	487.58	495.29
Claims on Central Government	22a	50.12	34.81	41.25	71.30	87.29	96.19	121.30	236.48	305.32	359.75	271.10	192.84
Claims on Private Sector	22d	267.71	310.08	314.73	359.53	362.35	387.50	460.65	500.15	486.90	594.89	814.70	997.07
Demand Deposits	24	197.79	217.86	267.66	328.73	356.62	423.09	445.77	614.82	659.56	658.46	808.05	815.57
Time Deposits	25	131.23	154.11	175.16	202.41	190.04	220.12	287.34	304.12	332.75	414.38	587.55	616.89
Bonds	26ab	8.53	11.69	19.10	14.07	25.96	30.36	33.86	34.55	35.47	35.44	28.35	29.07
Foreign Liabilities	26c	25.62	18.98	27.34	27.15	38.19	52.58	69.19	53.41	52.62	52.62	94.85	72.71
Long-Term Foreign Liabilities	26cl	4.24	3.98	4.98	6.66	5.02	14.04	12.35	23.05	12.73	17.29	19.91	15.66
Central Government Deposits	26d	28.27	24.78	32.08	31.51	28.24	26.97	40.10	67.03	78.82	80.64	127.33	221.65
Central Govt. Lending Funds	26f	.28	.17	.58	.48	.71	1.22	1.07	1.45	2.18	2.90	2.82	2.33
Credit from Monetary Authorities	26g	26.93	34.88	25.49	21.45	20.54	15.03	11.90	8.07	5.44	3.45	−7.67	1.07
Capital Accounts	27a	19.51	41.40	107.13	129.18	79.90	89.15	103.58	124.13	145.25	158.29	173.68	209.45
Other Items (Net)	27r	53.37	37.96	−5.41	−26.19	−5.92	−27.61	−22.17	−38.84	−49.05	3.08	−13.13	39.17
Treasury Claims: Private Sector	22d.i	2.05	2.80	2.65	.27	.11	.42	.11	.23	.61	.25	.11	—
Post Office: Checking Deposits	24..i	.90	1.15	2.31	2.99	2.38	2.45	15.21	39.28	26.94	4.36	3.09	2.73
Treasury: Checking Deposits	24..r	1.95	1.95	1.95	1.95	1.95	1.95	1.95	1.95	1.95	1.95	1.95	1.95
Monetary Survey						*Billions of Ariary: End of Period*							
Foreign Assets (Net)	31n	.15	63.22	172.29	297.87	184.12	299.12	383.72	481.09	438.77	512.20	886.79	920.73
Domestic Credit	32	516.74	501.24	492.26	500.09	643.38	708.73	797.69	966.41	1,103.22	1,216.97	1,227.07	1,297.90
Claims on Central Govt. (Net)	32an	247.64	188.63	174.71	137.55	277.85	318.08	314.82	410.97	543.50	618.54	408.50	296.37
Claims on Private Sector	32d	269.10	312.60	317.55	362.54	365.53	390.66	482.87	555.44	559.73	598.43	818.56	1,001.53
Money	34	320.70	369.60	433.54	532.79	590.63	710.06	803.59	1,046.74	1,125.58	1,172.46	1,399.43	1,414.69
Quasi-Money	35	131.23	155.61	175.47	203.00	190.72	221.15	287.36	304.16	332.81	414.48	587.79	617.17
Bonds	36ab	8.53	11.69	19.10	14.07	25.96	30.36	33.86	34.55	35.47	35.44	28.35	29.07
Long-Term Foreign Liabilities	36cl	4.24	3.98	4.98	6.66	5.02	14.04	12.35	23.05	12.73	17.29	19.91	15.66
Other Items (Net)	37r	52.20	23.67	31.46	41.44	15.22	32.24	44.25	39.00	35.40	89.51	78.37	142.03
Money plus Quasi-Money	35l	451.93	525.21	609.01	735.79	781.35	931.22	1,090.95	1,350.90	1,458.39	1,586.94	1,987.22	2,031.87
Liquid Liabilities	55l	494.63	580.28	721.59	900.23	1,014.17	1,217.93	1,405.47	....	....	....	....	....
Interest Rates						*Percent Per Annum*							
Discount Rate (End of Period)	60	....	....	....	....	....	15.00	....	....	....	....	....	....
Base Rate (End of Period)	60a	15.6	31.3	26.4	12.8	9.3	....	....	11.0	9.0	7.0	11.7	16.0
Money Market Rate	60b	....	29.0	10.0	....	12.0	17.3	16.0	9.0	9.0	10.5	16.5	16.5
Treasury Bill Rate	60c	....	....	....	....	....	....	....	10.3	....	11.9	12.9	18.8
Deposit Rate	60l	19.5	18.5	19.0	14.4	8.0	15.3	15.0	12.0	12.0	11.5	15.2	18.8
Lending Rate	60p	30.5	37.5	32.8	30.0	27.0	28.0	26.5	25.3	25.3	24.3	25.5	27.0
Prices and Labor						*Index Numbers (2000=100): Period Averages*							
Consumer Prices	64	41.0	61.1	73.2	76.5	81.2	89.3	† 100.0	106.9	124.0	122.5	139.4	165.2
						Number in Thousands: Period Averages							
Employment	67e	322	337	....	....	....	....	....	....	....	....	....	....
Unemployment	67c	4	3	....	....	....	....	....	....	....	....	....	....
Intl. Transactions & Positions						*Billions of Ariary*							
Exports	70	249.34	313.88	370.02	421.93	585.49	733.94	1,115.28	1,222.82	664.07	1,060.09	1,831.48	1,502.27
Imports, c.i.f	71	281.72	466.78	422.96	506.95	754.18	932.51	1,349.44	1,258.40	823.93	1,373.31	2,741.61	3,104.69

Madagascar 674

2006, International Monetary Fund : *International Financial Statistics Yearbook*

		1994	1995	1996	1997	1998	1999	2000	2001	2002	2003	2004	2005
Balance of Payments		*Millions of US Dollars: Minus Sign Indicates Debit*											
Current Account, n.i.e.	78ald	−277	−276	−291	−266	−301	−252	−283	−170	−298	−439	....	....
Goods: Exports f.o.b.	78aad	450	507	509	516	538	584	824	928	486	856	....	....
Goods: Imports f.o.b.	78abd	−546	−628	−629	−694	−693	−742	−997	−955	−603	−1,109	....	....
Trade Balance	78acd	−96	−122	−120	−178	−154	−158	−174	−27	−117	−254	....	....
Services: Credit	78add	206	242	293	272	291	326	364	351	224	270	....	....
Services: Debit	78aed	−328	−359	−373	−386	−436	−456	−522	−511	−398	−545	....	....
Balance on Goods & Services	78afd	−218	−238	−200	−292	−299	−289	−332	−187	−291	−529	....	....
Income: Credit	78agd	2	7	6	20	25	21	22	24	26	16	....	....
Income: Debit	78ahd	−158	−174	−169	−115	−103	−63	−64	−106	−101	−95	....	....
Balance on Gds, Serv. & Inc.	78aid	−374	−405	−363	−387	−377	−331	−373	−270	−366	−607	....	....
Current Transfers, n.i.e.: Credit	78ajd	114	141	94	156	109	111	122	114	88	349	....	....
Current Transfers: Debit	78akd	−17	−12	−23	−35	−33	−32	−31	−15	−21	−180	....	....
Capital Account, n.i.e.	78bcd	62	45	5	115	103	129	115	113	58	140	....	....
Capital Account, n.i.e.: Credit	78bad	62	45	5	115	103	129	115	113	58	140	....	....
Capital Account: Debit	78bbd	—	—	....	....	....	....	....	—	—	—	....	....
Financial Account, n.i.e.	78bjd	−122	−198	133	110	−76	−14	−31	−139	−54	−118	....	....
Direct Investment Abroad	78bdd	—	—	....	....	....	....	....	—	—	—	....	....
Dir. Invest. in Rep. Econ., n.i.e.	78bed	6	10	10	14	17	58	83	93	8	13	....	....
Portfolio Investment Assets	78bfd	....	....	....	....	....	....	....	—	—	—	....	....
Equity Securities	78bkd	....	....	....	....	....	....	....	—	—	—	....	....
Debt Securities	78bld	....	....	....	....	....	....	....	—	—	—	....	....
Portfolio Investment Liab., n.i.e.	78bgd	....	....	....	....	....	....	....	—	—	—	....	....
Equity Securities	78bmd	....	....	....	....	....	....	....	—	—	—	....	....
Debt Securities	78bnd	....	....	....	....	....	....	....	—	—	—	....	....
Financial Derivatives Assets	78bwd	....	....	....	....	....	....	....	....	....	....	....	....
Financial Derivatives Liabilities	78bxd	....	....	....	....	....	....	....	....	....	....	....	....
Other Investment Assets	78bhd	19	−62	37	135	−68	−73	−87	−128	42	−27	....	....
Monetary Authorities	78bod	38	−45	....	157	−84	−71	−40	−144	58	5	....	....
General Government	78bpd	....	....	....	....	....	....	....	....	....	....	....	....
Banks	78bqd	−18	−12	37	−22	16	−2	−48	15	−16	−32	....	....
Other Sectors	78brd	−1	−5	....	....	....	....	....	....	....	....	....	....
Other Investment Liab., n.i.e.	78bid	−147	−145	86	−39	−25	1	−26	−103	−104	−104	....	....
Monetary Authorities	78bsd	−235	−230	—	—	—	—	−1	—	2	−1	....	....
General Government	78btd	79	91	−167	−28	−26	−3	−28	−84	−93	−95	....	....
Banks	78bud	6	−8	....	−4	9	6	15	−11	−3	3	....	....
Other Sectors	78bvd	3	3	253	−8	−7	−2	−12	−8	−10	−11	....	....
Net Errors and Omissions	78cad	61	98	59	25	−25	32	39	−57	11	52	....	....
Overall Balance	78cbd	−276	−330	−94	−16	−299	−104	−160	−253	−283	−365	....	....
Reserves and Related Items	79dad	276	330	94	16	299	104	160	253	283	365	....	....
Reserve Assets	79dbd	−14	−2	−137	−214	205	11	−30	18	8	−28	....	....
Use of Fund Credit and Loans	79dcd	−12	−15	3	1	−14	6	45	27	12	8	....	....
Exceptional Financing	79ded	303	347	228	229	108	88	145	208	264	384	....	....
Government Finance		*Billions of Ariary: Year Ending December 31*											
Deficit (-) or Surplus	80	−73.5	−42.6	−43.5	−85.7	−129.4	−124.9	−125.1	−240.6	....	....	....	....
Revenue	81	152.4	229.9	281.4	349.4	415.4	533.4	613.6	605.8	....	....	....	....
Grants Received	81z	54.8	78.4	136.7	147.1	141.6	154.0	189.3	200.7	....	....	....	....
Expenditure	82	346.9	468.8	563.4	575.9	695.5	813.8	910.2	1,036.4	....	....	....	....
Lending Minus Repayments	83	8.9	5.9	13.2	1.8	−7.8	10.2	5.3	5.4	....	....	....	....
Adjustment to Cash Basis	80x	75.0	123.9	115.1	−4.5	1.4	11.7	−12.6	−5.4	....	....	....	....
Financing													
Domestic	84a	42.7	−7.6	−3.0	−29.1	152.2	25.2	24.3	116.2	....	....	....	....
Foreign	85a	30.9	50.2	46.5	114.8	−22.8	89.4	91.5	103.6	....	....	....	....
Adjustment to Total Financing	84x	....	....	—	—	—	10.4	9.3	20.8	....	....	....	....
Debt: Domestic	88a	224.8	215.3	179.1	....	....	....	....	....	....	....	....	....
Debt: Foreign	89a	3,129.3	3,014.5	....	....	....	....	....	....	....	....	....	....
National Accounts		*Billions of Ariary*											
Househ.Cons.Expend.,incl.NPISHs.	96f	1,620.6	2,424.2	2,892.6	3,258.9	3,545.2	4,006.4	4,496.6	4,800.2	5,244.2	5,873.6	6,830.4	8,563.8
Government Consumption Expend.	91f	144.8	180.8	146.4	219.5	324.2	348.2	412.8	527.8	502.0	710.2	745.2	809.6
Gross Fixed Capital Formation	93e	199.1	295.0	377.6	427.9	535.6	674.8	850.0	1,068.0	803.8	1,097.8	2,038.6	2,556.8
Exports of Goods and Services	90c	402.4	683.6	665.2	787.7	871.6	1,173.4	1,596.8	1,725.4	958.6	1,351.6	2,479.0	3,057.9
Imports of Goods and Services (-)	98c	540.6	854.9	836.9	1,083.9	1,206.9	1,525.9	2,107.8	2,149.2	1,500.4	2,254.6	3,937.6	4,742.7
Gross Domestic Product (GDP)	99b	1,826.3	2,695.7	3,244.9	3,610.2	4,069.9	4,676.8	5,248.4	5,968.6	6,008.4	6,778.6	8,155.6	10,245.4
GDP Volume 1984 Prices	99b.p	379.8	386.3	394.5	409.1	425.2	445.1	466.2	494.2	431.6	473.8	498.8	522.0
GDP Volume (2000=100)	99bvp	81.5	82.9	84.6	87.8	91.2	95.5	100.0	106.0	92.6	101.6	107.0	112.0
GDP Deflator (2000=100)	99bip	42.7	62.0	73.1	78.4	85.0	93.3	100.0	107.3	123.7	127.1	145.2	174.3
		Millions: Midyear Estimates											
Population	99z	13.54	13.95	14.37	14.81	15.27	15.73	16.20	16.67	17.14	17.63	18.11	18.61

Malawi   676

		1994	1995	1996	1997	1998	1999	2000	2001	2002	2003	2004	2005
Exchange Rates						*Kwacha per SDR: End of Period*							
Official Rate	aa	22.3337	22.7479	22.0340	28.6416	61.7894	63.7362	104.3318	84.5705	118.4665	161.3258	169.1899	176.9159
					Kwacha per US Dollar: End of Period (ae) Period Average (rf)								
Official Rate	ae	15.2986	15.3031	15.3231	21.2278	43.8836	46.4377	80.0760	67.2941	87.1385	108.5660	108.9432	123.7806
Official Rate	rf	8.7364	15.2837	15.3085	16.4442	31.0727	44.0881	59.5438	72.1973	76.6866	97.4325	108.8975	118.4197
					Index Numbers (2000=100): Period Averages								
Official Rate	ahx	743.2	373.0	372.3	348.8	195.9	129.3	100.0	79.7	74.7	58.9	52.3	48.3
Nominal Effective Exchange Rate	nec	496.0	239.5	261.2	263.0	165.3	119.5	100.0	89.8	89.7	68.0	61.9	60.5
Real Effective Exchange Rate	rec	98.8	86.2	123.1	128.2	97.1	98.8	100.0	104.7	109.3	80.3	73.3	75.2
Fund Position						*Millions of SDRs: End of Period*							
Quota	2f.s	50.90	50.90	50.90	50.90	50.90	69.40	69.40	69.40	69.40	69.40	69.40	69.40
SDRs	1b.s	4.25	.59	.94	.07	4.84	.29	.36	.67	.07	.32	.77	.74
Reserve Position in the Fund	1c.s	2.22	2.22	2.22	2.22	2.24	2.24	2.24	2.27	2.28	2.29	2.29	2.29
Total Fund Cred.&Loans Outstg	2tl	76.90	78.02	83.06	78.42	72.57	63.79	63.35	57.90	69.55	68.77	59.55	52.60
International Liquidity					*Millions of US Dollars Unless Otherwise Indicated: End of Period*								
Total Reserves minus Gold	1l.d	42.80	110.01	220.54	142.18	255.44	246.43	242.98	202.51	161.47	122.04	128.05	158.65
SDRs	1b.d	6.20	.88	1.36	.09	6.82	.39	.47	.84	.09	.47	1.20	1.05
Reserve Position in the Fund	1c.d	3.25	3.31	3.20	3.00	3.15	3.07	2.91	2.85	3.11	3.40	3.56	3.27
Foreign Exchange	1d.d	33.35	105.82	215.98	139.09	245.48	242.96	239.59	198.82	158.28	118.16	123.30	154.32
Gold (Million Fine Troy Ounces)	1ad	.013	.013	.013	.013	.013	.013	.013	.013	.013	.013	.013	.013
Gold (National Valuation)	1and	.55	.54	.54	.54	.54	.54	.54	.54	.51	.54	.54	.54
Monetary Authorities: Other Liab.	4..d	21.92	.02	.02	.09	.06	.59	19.86	.06	50.00	7.55	.02	.09
Deposit Money Banks: Assets	7a.d	25.61	29.39	36.17	41.63	61.64	49.74	58.27	76.10	49.31	51.71	52.61	38.89
Liabilities	7b.d	27.22	9.80	10.37	10.67	13.75	16.03	16.86	15.09	12.83	14.76	15.60	14.80
Other Banking Institutions: Assets	7e.d	—	—	—	—	—	9.84	4.06	5.59	7.09	11.05	14.67	11.68
Liabilities	7f.d	—	—	—	.06	—	8.87	10.64	10.87	18.38	12.88	8.43	.08
Monetary Authorities						*Millions of Kwacha: End of Period*							
Foreign Assets	11	613.6	1,670.0	3,387.7	3,342.4	11,327.9	11,468.6	19,500.3	13,663.9	14,115.5	14,127.8	14,009.0	19,704.0
Claims on Central Government	12a	1,309.5	1,266.2	710.8	877.0	3,727.9	2,559.3	445.8	5,846.3	13,407.4	14,707.0	18,990.0	22,761.3
Claims on Nonfin.Pub.Enterprises	12c	115.5	127.0	159.3	187.5	191.4	274.6	313.7	313.7				
Claims on Deposit Money Banks	12e	—	—	140.0									
Claims on Other Banking Insts	12f	28.2	13.4	10.5	9.8	9.4	8.2	112.2	3.5	3.3	2.9	1.7	1.9
Reserve Money	14	1,244.8	2,360.6	3,269.7	3,277.0	4,542.6	6,001.4	6,349.2	8,497.7	10,767.2	13,742.9	17,967.5	20,609.6
of which: Currency Outside DMBs	14a	624.7	987.5	1,223.8	1,375.3	1,986.5	2,959.3	4,023.7	4,066.3	5,964.0	7,838.1	10,992.8	11,946.0
Liabs. of Central Bank: Securities	16ac							1,713.3	8,519.2	6,425.0	2,914.0	4,555.9	5,041.1
Restricted Deposits	16b	—											
Foreign Liabilities	16c	2,052.7	1,775.2	1,830.5	2,247.9	4,486.2	4,093.5	8,200.3	4,900.3	12,596.9	11,914.2	10,076.8	9,317.4
Central Government Deposits	16d	349.5	591.8	883.3	291.3	4,564.6	3,035.3	1,513.5	2,182.9	3,655.9	6,461.6	6,944.4	11,368.0
Capital Accounts	17a	330.3	280.7	476.8	653.9	1,072.0	1,101.6	1,547.2	1,269.9	1,641.9	2,076.6	2,162.9	2,247.7
Other Items (Net)	17r	−1,910.6	−1,931.6	−2,052.0	−2,053.3	591.2	78.9	1,048.6	−5,542.5	−7,560.8	−8,271.6	−8,706.7	−6,116.5
Deposit Money Banks						*Millions of Kwacha: End of Period*							
Reserves	20	591.4	1,311.7	1,814.5	1,803.6	2,273.6	2,877.1	2,290.1	4,158.7	4,837.7	5,350.5	7,033.9	7,860.9
Claims on Mon.Author.:Securities	20c							250.0	1,419.6	1,342.1	340.0	210.0	418.0
Foreign Assets	21	391.7	449.8	554.2	883.7	2,705.0	2,310.0	4,666.1	5,121.3	4,296.4	5,613.5	5,731.3	4,813.8
Claims on Central Government	22a	387.9	867.3	1,746.3	1,206.7	1,388.0	1,412.7	2,418.9	2,731.4	6,748.3	10,967.5	10,711.0	12,363.5
Claims on Nonfin.Pub.Enterprises	22c	47.6	183.0	398.0	413.6	185.8	1,442.9	1,218.2	575.1	676.5	277.4	299.5	307.2
Claims on Private Sector	22d	1,178.1	1,252.6	1,406.8	1,603.3	3,478.8	3,717.1	5,817.5	6,454.0	7,363.5	9,808.7	13,926.3	17,500.3
Demand Deposits	24	895.9	1,218.1	1,518.0	1,824.4	2,996.3	3,976.2	5,594.0	6,649.4	7,929.3	9,925.2	14,730.2	19,356.1
Time, Savings,& Fgn. Currency Dep.	25	1,119.5	1,936.4	3,048.1	2,712.4	4,692.1	5,715.7	8,779.5	11,860.7	14,114.1	18,048.4	20,725.3	22,691.4
Foreign Liabilities	26c	416.5	150.0	158.8	226.4	603.5	744.4	1,349.7	1,015.7	1,118.0	1,602.9	1,699.2	1,832.2
Central Government Deposits	26d	2.7	471.8	469.7	557.2	1,016.1	1,349.9	783.9	565.8	788.6	518.9	434.5	422.2
Credit from Monetary Authorities	26g	6.8	9.5	7.7	3.9	3.0	—	—	—	—	—	—	—
Capital Accounts	27a	410.5	598.2	845.2	1,113.4	1,497.8	2,284.9	3,238.9	3,730.4	4,902.6	6,563.9	7,317.1	8,722.7
Other Items (Net)	27r	−255.2	−319.6	−127.7	−526.9	−777.6	−2,311.4	−3,085.2	−3,361.9	−3,588.1	−4,301.8	−6,994.4	−9,761.1
Monetary Survey						*Millions of Kwacha: End of Period*							
Foreign Assets (Net)	31n	−1,463.8	194.6	1,952.6	1,751.8	8,943.1	8,940.7	14,616.5	12,869.2	4,697.0	6,224.2	7,964.3	13,368.2
Domestic Credit	32	2,714.5	2,645.9	3,078.7	3,449.4	3,400.7	5,029.5	8,029.0	13,175.5	23,754.5	28,782.9	36,549.6	41,143.9
Claims on Central Govt. (Net)	32an	1,345.1	1,069.8	1,104.1	1,235.2	−464.8	−413.2	567.3	5,829.0	15,711.2	18,693.9	22,322.1	23,334.6
Claims on Nonfin.Pub.Enterprises	32c	163.1	310.0	557.3	601.0	377.2	1,717.5	1,532.0	888.9	676.5	277.4	299.5	307.2
Claims on Private Sector	32d	1,178.1	1,252.6	1,406.8	1,603.3	3,478.8	3,717.1	5,817.5	6,454.0	7,363.5	9,808.7	13,926.3	17,500.3
Claims on Other Banking Insts	32f	28.2	13.4	10.5	9.8	9.4	8.2	112.2	3.5	3.3	2.9	1.7	1.9
Money	34	1,535.4	2,211.2	2,756.8	3,213.0	5,248.4	7,007.3	9,736.5	11,048.7	13,979.0	17,763.4	25,723.0	31,302.1
Quasi-Money	35	1,119.5	1,936.4	3,048.1	2,712.4	4,692.1	5,715.7	8,779.5	11,860.7	14,114.1	18,048.4	20,725.3	22,691.4
Liabs. of Central Bank: Securities	36ac							1,463.3	7,099.6	5,082.9	2,574.0	4,345.9	4,623.1
Restricted Deposits	36b	—											
Capital Accounts	37a	740.8	878.9	1,322.0	1,767.2	2,569.9	3,386.6	4,786.1	5,000.4	6,544.5	8,640.5	9,480.0	10,970.4
Other Items (Net)	37r	−2,145.0	−2,186.0	−2,095.7	−2,491.4	−166.6	−2,139.2	−2,119.9	−8,964.7	−11,269.1	−12,019.1	−15,760.4	−15,074.9
Money plus Quasi-Money	35l	2,654.9	4,147.6	5,805.0	5,925.4	9,940.6	12,722.9	18,516.0	22,909.4	28,093.1	35,811.8	46,448.4	53,993.5
Other Banking Institutions						*Millions of Kwacha: End of Period*							
Reserves	40	7.9	45.3	3.1	23.4	19.6	45.1	152.7	278.6	334.9	746.2	939.7	1,391.9
Claims on Mon.Author.:Securities	40c	—	—	—	—	—	—	—	706.6	457.7	654.2	386.3	651.5
Foreign Assets	41						457.1	324.9	376.4	617.4	1,199.2	1,598.3	1,446.0
Claims on Central Government	42a	284.7	351.3	414.3	648.9	1,086.5	752.7	1,415.2	2,369.2	3,225.0	5,910.5	5,964.7	4,742.8
Claims on Nonfin.Pub.Enterprises	42c	5.7	9.8	11.2	—	—	75.2	29.9	48.2	31.8	40.0	5.7	—
Claims on Private Sector	42d	118.8	134.8	167.9	275.3	388.1	2,515.8	3,604.6	3,981.4	4,494.9	3,091.7	3,346.1	8,312.4
Claims on Deposit Money Banks	42e	8.4	4.8	18.8	19.8	31.4	563.6	887.1	648.6	482.4	536.7	817.8	703.4
Demand Deposits	44	19.5	22.0	29.8	39.5	504.7	—	157.1	822.6	364.4	1,196.7	1,336.7	2,198.5
Time, Savings,& Fgn. Currency Dep.	45	319.8	404.3	580.1	612.5	663.9	3,271.6	4,083.3	5,329.6	5,580.7	7,015.6	9,400.8	13,303.4
Foreign Liabilities	46c	—	—	—	1.3	—	412.1	852.3	731.4	1,602.0	1,398.1	918.0	10.3
Credit from Monetary Authorities	46g	—	—	—	—	—	10.7	102.0	.9				
Credit from Deposit Money Banks	46h	—	—	—	—	—	84.0	250.5	195.0	281.5	834.6	174.5	512.4
Capital Accounts	47a	124.0	152.3	216.6	308.2	429.9	569.5	905.7	1,121.3	1,607.5	2,074.4	2,127.8	2,414.3
Other Items (Net)	47r	−37.9	−32.6	−211.3	6.0	−73.0	61.6	63.5	208.2	208.1	−340.8	−899.2	−1,191.1

		1994	1995	1996	1997	1998	1999	2000	2001	2002	2003	2004	2005
Banking Survey						*Millions of Kwacha: End of Period*								
Foreign Assets (Net)	51n	−1,463.8	194.6	1,952.6	1,750.5	8,943.1	8,985.7	14,089.1	12,514.2	3,712.4	6,025.3	8,644.6	14,803.8
Domestic Credit	52	3,095.4	3,128.4	3,661.6	4,363.7	4,865.8	8,365.1	12,966.5	19,570.8	31,502.9	37,822.2	45,864.4	54,197.2
Claims on Central Govt. (Net)	52an	1,629.8	1,421.1	1,518.4	1,884.1	621.7	339.5	1,982.5	8,198.3	18,936.2	24,604.4	28,286.8	28,077.3
Claims on Nonfin.Pub.Enterprises	52c	168.8	319.8	568.5	601.0	377.2	1,792.6	1,561.9	937.1	708.3	317.4	305.2	307.2
Claims on Private Sector	52d	1,296.8	1,387.5	1,574.7	1,878.6	3,866.9	6,232.9	9,422.1	10,435.4	11,858.4	12,900.4	17,272.4	25,812.7
Liquid Liabilities	55l	2,986.3	4,528.6	6,411.8	6,554.0	11,089.6	15,949.4	22,603.6	28,783.0	33,703.3	43,277.8	56,246.1	68,103.6
Liabs.of Central Bank: Securities	56ac	—	—	—	—	—	—	1,463.3	6,393.0	4,625.1	1,919.8	3,959.5	3,971.6
Restricted Deposits	56b	—	—	—	—	—	—						
Capital Accounts	57a	864.8	1,031.2	1,538.7	2,075.4	2,999.8	3,956.1	5,691.9	6,121.6	8,152.0	10,714.9	11,607.8	13,384.7
Other Items (Net)	57r	−2,219.5	−2,236.8	−2,336.3	−2,515.1	−280.5	−2,554.8	−2,703.2	−9,212.7	−11,265.2	−12,064.9	−17,304.5	−16,458.9
Nonbank Financial Institutions						*Millions of Kwacha: End of Period*								
Claims on Central Government	42a.s	93.51	172.57	216.19	232.89	437.70	575.90	202.47	393.05	463.81	547.24	826.83	....
Claims on Private Sector	42d.s	269.01	377.83	584.02	230.34	332.00	352.89	176.86	301.35	125.74	430.28	2,301.06	....
of which: Policy Loans	42dxs	12.48	15.25	16.38	22.30	33.31	23.59	31.50	133.28	24.26	24.65	61.77	....
Incr.in Total Assets(Within Per.)	49z.s	103.28	242.14	296.06	−247.43	416.41	168.14	−120.83	876.12	−56.81	136.69	8,589.81	....
Interest Rates						*Percent Per Annum*								
Discount Rate (End of Period)	60	40.00	50.00	27.00	23.00	43.00	47.00	50.23	46.80	40.00	35.00	25.00	25.00
Treasury Bill Rate	60c	27.68	46.30	30.83	18.31	32.98	42.85	39.52	42.41	41.75	39.32	28.58	24.36
Deposit Rate	60l	25.00	37.27	26.33	10.21	19.06	33.21	33.25	34.96	28.08	25.13	13.73	10.92
Lending Rate	60p	31.00	47.33	45.33	28.25	37.67	53.58	53.13	56.17	50.54	48.92	36.83	33.08
Government Bond Yield	61	23.50	38.58	42.67	39.25	....	....	....	....	....	....	....	....
Prices, Production, Labor						*Index Numbers (2000=100): Period Averages*								
Consumer Prices	64	14.9	27.4	37.6	41.1	53.3	77.2	† 100.0	122.7	140.8	154.3	171.9	198.4
Industrial Production	66	109.8	111.2	115.2	113.5	110.3	98.0	100.0	91.0	91.3	88.6	....	....
						Number in Thousands: Period Averages								
Employment	67e	653	701	....	....	....	....	....	....	....	....	....	....
Intl. Transactions & Positions						*Millions of Kwacha*								
Exports	70	2,954	6,193	7,359	8,827	13,861	19,907	23,625	31,817	31,417	51,672	52,628	58,810
Imports, c.i.f.	71	4,214	7,255	9,545	12,848	16,431	29,696	32,283	39,480	53,658	76,650	101,554	129,856
Imports, f.o.b.	71.v	2,793	4,353	5,727	7,709	10,799	18,455	28,389	....	....	....	....	....
Balance of Payments						*Millions of US Dollars: Minus Sign Indicates Debit*								
Current Account, n.i.e.	78ald	−180.7	−78.0	−147.4	−276.2	−4.4	−157.5	−73.5	−60.0	−200.7	....	....	....
Goods: Exports f.o.b.	78aad	323.1	445.5	509.6	540.2	539.6	448.4	403.1	427.9	422.4	....	....	....
Goods: Imports f.o.b.	78abd	−483.1	−508.8	−587.5	−698.7	−500.6	−575.0	−462.0	−472.2	−573.2	....	....	....
Trade Balance	78acd	−160.1	−63.3	−77.9	−158.4	39.0	−126.6	−58.8	−44.3	−150.8	....	....	....
Services: Credit	78add	26.1	24.2	36.6	38.8	31.5	49.2	34.3	43.6	49.4	....	....	....
Services: Debit	78aed	−147.7	−151.4	−185.7	−219.2	−161.5	−184.7	−167.1	−171.4	−221.9	....	....	....
Balance on Goods & Services	78afd	−281.7	−190.6	−227.0	−338.8	−91.1	−262.1	−191.7	−172.1	−323.3	....	....	....
Income: Credit	78agd	4.9	3.7	9.5	12.2	11.5	25.5	33.3	12.2	6.0	....	....	....
Income: Debit	78ahd	−47.2	−48.0	−44.8	−40.9	−48.1	−50.5	−50.5	−42.6	−44.5	....	....	....
Balance on Gds, Serv. & Inc.	78aid	−324.1	−234.9	−262.3	−367.6	−127.7	−287.0	−209.0	−202.5	−361.8	....	....	....
Current Transfers, n.i.e.: Credit	78ajd	154.0	171.0	138.0	116.2	134.1	137.7	143.1	148.8	170.0	....	....	....
Current Transfers: Debit	78akd	−10.6	−14.2	−23.0	−24.9	−10.8	−8.2	−7.6	−6.2	−8.9	....	....	....
Capital Account, n.i.e.	78bcd	....	....	....	....	....	....	....	....	....	....	....	....
Capital Account, n.i.e.: Credit	78bad	....	....	....	....	....	....	....	....	....	....	....	....
Capital Account: Debit	78bbd	....	....	....	....	....	....	....	....	....	....	....	....
Financial Account, n.i.e.	78bjd	200.5	87.6	170.5	146.5	237.8	219.6	188.8	213.4	134.0	....	....	....
Direct Investment Abroad	78bdd	....	....	....	....	....	....	....	....	....	....	....	....
Dir. Invest. in Rep. Econ., n.i.e.	78bed	25.0	5.6	15.8	14.9	12.1	58.5	26.0	19.3	5.9	....	....	....
Portfolio Investment Assets	78bfd	....	....	....	....	....	....	....	....	....	....	....	....
Equity Securities	78bkd	....	....	....	....	....	....	....	....	....	....	....	....
Debt Securities	78bld	....	....	....	....	....	....	....	....	....	....	....	....
Portfolio Investment Liab., n.i.e.	78bgd	....	....	....	....	....	....	....	....	....	....	....	....
Equity Securities	78bmd	....	....	....	....	....	....	....	....	....	....	....	....
Debt Securities	78bnd	....	....	....	....	....	....	....	....	....	....	....	....
Financial Derivatives Assets	78bwd	....	....	....	....	....	....	....	....	....	....	....	....
Financial Derivatives Liabilities	78bxd	....	....	....	....	....	....	....	....	....	....	....	....
Other Investment Assets	78bhd	....	....	....	....	....	....	....	....	....	....	....	....
Monetary Authorities	78bod	....	....	....	....	....	....	....	....	....	....	....	....
General Government	78bpd	....	....	....	....	....	....	....	....	....	....	....	....
Banks	78bqd	....	....	....	....	....	....	....	....	....	....	....	....
Other Sectors	78brd	....	....	....	....	....	....	....	....	....	....	....	....
Other Investment Liab., n.i.e.	78bid	175.6	81.9	154.7	131.7	225.7	161.1	162.8	194.1	128.1	....	....	....
Monetary Authorities	78bsd	—	—	—	—	—	—	—	—	—	....	....	....
General Government	78btd	130.1	49.9	131.5	128.1	169.4	106.2	107.9	139.2	73.3	....	....	....
Banks	78bud	....	....	....	....	....	....	....	....	....	....	....	....
Other Sectors	78bvd	45.4	32.0	23.2	3.6	56.3	54.8	54.8	54.8	54.8	....	....	....
Net Errors and Omissions	78cad	−6.0	−84.3	−144.6	145.2	−407.6	−28.8	−23.9	−221.5	156.7	....	....	....
Overall Balance	78cbd	13.9	−74.8	−121.6	15.5	−174.1	33.3	91.4	−68.0	90.0	....	....	....
Reserves and Related Items	79dad	−13.9	74.8	121.6	−15.5	174.1	−33.3	−91.4	68.0	−90.0	....	....	....
Reserve Assets	79dbd	−34.7	73.1	114.5	−9.1	181.4	−21.4	−90.6	75.0	−105.5	....	....	....
Use of Fund Credit and Loans	79dcd	20.8	1.6	7.1	−6.5	−7.3	−11.9	−.8	−7.0	15.5	....	....	....
Exceptional Financing	79ded	....	....	....	....	....	....	....	....	....	....	....	....

Malawi 676

		1994	1995	1996	1997	1998	1999	2000	2001	2002	2003	2004	2005
National Accounts							*Millions of Kwacha*						
Househ.Cons.Expend.,incl.NPISHs....	96f	5,869.4	16,204.8	29,391.0	36,539.0	43,058.4	68,121.1	84,230.3	97,136.5	135,724.6	161,408.1	201,324.7	282,789.2
Government Consumption Expend...	91f	4,073.1	4,474.6	4,882.0	7,673.0	7,987.2	10,527.8	15,134.0	19,591.4	21,858.1	28,025.3	34,990.1	41,344.5
Gross Fixed Capital Formation.........	93e	2,764.3	3,164.7	3,404.5	4,079.7	6,035.8	9,870.5	12,792.2	15,740.8	14,110.2	17,742.3	18,984.3	21,945.9
Changes in Inventories....................	93i	240.0	500.8	757.9	881.7	1,179.2	1,734.9	2,261.1	2,768.8	3,238.1	3,687.4	4,320.4	5,094.0
Exports of Goods and Services..........	90c	3,050.1	7,177.7	8,362.7	9,522.1	17,744.4	21,940.9	26,045.6	33,980.6	35,528.2	46,151.0	58,914.3	61,785.8
Imports of Goods and Services (-).....	98c	5,514.3	10,164.3	11,879.0	14,900.7	20,728.6	33,898.3	36,647.9	45,291.2	62,103.3	85,096.4	111,324.7	161,237.5
Gross Domestic Product (GDP)........	99b	10,482.6	21,358.3	34,919.2	43,794.8	55,276.3	78,297.0	103,815.0	123,926.9	148,356.0	171,917.8	207,209.0	245,749.9
Net Primary Income from Abroad.....	98.n	−375.3	−725.1	−596.7	−589.7	−1,230.4	−1,185.5	−1,110.3	−2,302.7	−2,794.1	−3,267.8	−4,992.8	−5,162.4
Gross National Income (GNI)...........	99a	10,107.3	20,633.2	34,322.5	43,205.1	54,045.9	77,111.5	102,704.7	121,624.2	145,561.9	168,650.0	202,216.2	240,587.6
GDP Volume 1994 Prices.................	99b.p	10,483.0	12,056.5	13,039.7	13,868.0	14,193.6	14,371.4	13,165.9	12,620.0	12,882.8	13,385.5	14,065.7	14,358.6
GDP Volume (2000=100)...............	99bvp	† 79.6	91.6	99.0	105.3	107.8	109.2	100.0	95.9	97.8	101.7	106.8	109.1
GDP Deflator (2000=100)...............	99bip	12.7	22.5	34.0	40.0	49.4	69.1	100.0	124.5	146.0	162.9	186.8	217.1
							Millions: Midyear Estimates						
Population................................	99z	9.97	10.11	10.32	10.59	10.90	11.21	11.51	11.80	12.07	12.34	12.61	12.88

Malaysia 548

		1994	1995	1996	1997	1998	1999	2000	2001	2002	2003	2004	2005
Exchange Rates							*Ringgit per SDR: End of Period*						
Official Rate	aa	3.7372	3.7787	3.6366	5.2511	5.3505	5.2155	4.9511	4.7756	5.1662	5.6467	5.9014	5.4026
						Ringgit per US Dollar: End of Period (ae) Period Average (rf)							
Official Rate	ae	2.5600	2.5420	2.5290	3.8919	3.8000	3.8000	3.8000	3.8000	3.8000	3.8000	3.8000	3.7800
Official Rate	rf	2.6243	2.5044	2.5159	2.8132	3.9244	3.8000	3.8000	3.8000	3.8000	3.8000	3.8000	3.7871
						Index Numbers (2000=100): Period Averages							
Official Rate	ahx	144.9	151.5	151.0	137.8	97.1	100.0	100.0	100.0	100.0	100.0	100.0	100.3
Nominal Effective Exchange Rate	nec	127.5	127.4	131.2	126.8	98.7	98.4	100.0	105.4	104.8	99.6	95.9	95.5
Real Effective Exchange Rate	rec	122.5	122.4	126.9	122.6	97.9	98.7	100.0	104.9	105.0	99.2	94.9	95.3
Fund Position							*Millions of SDRs: End of Period*						
Quota	2f.s	833	833	833	833	833	1,487	1,487	1,487	1,487	1,487	1,487	1,487
SDRs	1b.s	93	102	115	130	146	61	81	100	111	120	128	137
Reserve Position in the Fund	1c.s	274	456	478	445	445	608	608	608	581	586	500	199
of which: Outstg.Fund Borrowing	2c	—	—	—	—	—	—	—	—	—	—	—	—
Total Fund Cred.&Loans Outstg.	2tl	—	—	—	—	—	—	—	—	—	—	—	—
International Liquidity						*Millions of US Dollars Unless Otherwise Indicated: End of Period*							
Total Reserves minus Gold	1l.d	25,423	23,774	27,009	20,788	25,559	30,588	28,330	29,522	33,361	43,822	65,881	69,858
SDRs	1b.d	135	151	166	175	205	83	105	125	151	178	199	196
Reserve Position in the Fund	1c.d	400	678	688	600	626	835	792	764	790	871	776	285
Foreign Exchange	1d.d	24,888	22,945	26,156	20,013	24,728	29,670	27,432	28,633	32,419	42,772	64,906	69,377
Gold (Million Fine Troy Ounces)	1ad	2.390	2.390	2.390	2.350	2.350	1.180	1.170	1.170	1.170	1.170	1.170	1.170
Gold (National Valuation)	1and	122	124	120	111	116	57	53	51	56	61	64	59
Monetary Authorities: Other Liab.	4..d	11.7	10.5	6.3	.7	.8	.5	1.3	.7	514.3	816.4	2,988.2	2,435.3
Banking Institutions: Assets	7a.d	4,168.0	4,178.0	4,166.0	6,277.9	5,784.2	6,764.5	7,853.0	7,519.9	7,039.9	5,701.8	10,686.6	8,653.6
Liabilities	7b.d	8,161.0	8,242.0	11,637.0	12,785.1	9,509.1	7,540.9	6,973.2	6,287.8	9,296.1	10,923.4	16,843.6	18,370.8
Monetary Authorities							*Millions of Ringgit: End of Period*						
Foreign Assets	11	68,200	63,790	†70,737	60,369	99,427	117,255	113,247	†116,922	†131,411	170,474	253,504	266,294
Claims on Central Government	12a	980	2,155	†7,113	7,153	3,926	2,377	1,838	†1,422	†601	99	221	961
Claims on State and Local Govts	12b	—	—	†—					†—	†—			
Claims on Nonfin.Pub.Enterprises	12c	—	—	†—					†20,812	†6,164	6,164	6,164	4,551
Claims on Private Sector	12d	601	566	†8,270	9,843	16,018	22,517	29,476	†6,590	†1,822	1,602	1,464	1,258
Claims on Banking Institutions	12e	3,443	3,250	†3,676	27,451	2,512	2,135	1,616	†3,412	†6,297	7,233	9,189	10,096
Claims on Nonbank Financial Insts	12g	2,718	3,505	†634	508	2,114	2,282	2,157	†—	†15,863	14,384	13,595	11,133
Reserve Money	14	38,482	47,970	†64,559	82,896	36,178	45,675	41,372	†40,022	†42,581	45,534	50,085	52,623
of which: Currency Outside Banks	14a	15,884	17,433	†18,820	21,169	17,982	23,978	22,052	†21,960	†23,711	25,944	28,537	30,166
Other Liabs. to Banking Insts	14n	—	—	†6,036	7,030	19,014	46,152	43,509	†46,165	†64,287	92,316	133,456	154,558
Time, Savings,&Fgn.Currency Dep.	15	16	5	†5,790	2,320	9,079	2,043	9,171	†10,637	†12,632	7,455	12,406	13,262
Liabs. of Central Bank: Securities	16ac	—	—	†4,968	909	4	379	7,085	†—	†—	—	—	—
Restricted Deposits	16b	....	....	....	....	....	....	....	†—	†—			
Foreign Liabilities	16c	30	27	†16	3	3	2	5	†3	†1,954	3,102	11,355	9,206
Central Government Deposits	16d	8,469	8,379	†11,401	10,545	25,281	18,514	17,845	†25,237	†7,455	4,443	20,405	22,034
Liab. to Nonbank Financial Insts	16j	....	....	....	....	....	....	....		†3	1	2	3
Capital Accounts	17a	3,507	3,513	†3,633	4,085	4,099	31,413	27,384	†25,505	†30,961	43,192	53,843	40,106
Other Items (Net)	17r	25,438	13,374	†−5,974	−2,466	30,339	2,389	1,962	†1,591	†2,285	3,914	2,585	2,504
Banking Institutions							*Millions of Ringgit: End of Period*						
Reserves	20	46,063	44,680	†45,594	61,977	18,195	21,713	19,018	†18,114	†19,000	19,751	21,606	22,558
Claims on Mon.Author.:Securities	20c	—	—	†3,634				9	6,325	†7,198	9,827	3,586	7,691
Other Claims on Monetary Author.	20n	—	—	†2,295	2,933	19,022	46,152	43,459	†38,720	†53,611	81,312	119,591	143,616
Foreign Assets	21	10,709	10,528	†11,391	24,433	21,980	25,705	29,841	†28,575	†26,752	21,667	40,609	32,710
Claims on Central Government	22a	14,137	13,179	†15,451	17,106	24,782	22,492	25,638	†28,809	†28,754	32,751	36,899	34,556
Claims on State & Local Govts	22b	—	—	†593	799	763	569	649	†841	†525	553	785	322
Claims on Nonfin.Pub.Enterprises	22c	—	—	†—	3,104	3,928	4,736	4,570	†3,013	†3,446	4,177	5,352	3,706
Claims on Private Sector	22d	212,876	276,222	†351,101	436,478	432,937	426,082	451,665	†448,594	†465,036	496,624	529,174	577,785
Claims on Nonbank Financial Insts	22g	—	—	†12,740	19,750	26,774	23,251	24,167	†47,215	†60,838	60,116	54,721	53,385
Demand Deposits	24	31,724	36,191	†39,439	40,976	35,115	45,739	53,455	†56,414	†63,877	75,684	84,443	92,695
Time, Savings,& Fgn.Currency Dep.	25	160,848	193,647	†225,952	269,698	287,979	321,610	348,748	†388,050	†395,539	426,919	473,510	500,741
Money Market Instruments	26aa	46,614	64,432	†42,425	58,569	58,515	31,315	32,868	†11,122	†14,315	18,077	25,479	42,414
Restricted Deposits	26b	....	....	....	....	....	....	....	—	†—			
Foreign Liabilities	26c	17,030	15,935	†29,303	49,758	36,134	28,655	26,498	†23,894	†35,325	41,509	64,006	69,442
Central Government Deposits	26d	3,502	5,362	†23,124	23,870	26,748	34,328	29,154	†15,421	†25,143	26,388	23,637	26,074
Credit from Monetary Authorities	26g	1,781	1,772	†2,220	29,842	1,001	556	82	†6,100	†4,948	5,427	7,928	7,676
Liab. to Nonbank Financial Insts	26j	....	....	....	....	....	....	....	25,136	†24,306	26,194	25,358	22,604
Capital Accounts	27a	32,401	40,224	†50,654	72,502	83,507	84,851	86,810	†59,634	†65,485	72,168	75,117	77,583
Other Items (Net)	27r	−10,115	−12,954	†29,683	21,364	19,382	23,655	27,717	†35,308	†38,891	34,411	32,846	37,103
Banking Survey							*Millions of Ringgit: End of Period*						
Foreign Assets (Net)	31n	61,849	58,357	†52,809	35,040	85,269	114,303	116,585	†121,601	†120,884	147,530	218,752	220,358
Domestic Credit	32	219,341	281,887	†361,375	460,325	459,214	451,464	493,160	†516,639	†550,452	585,640	604,333	639,550
Claims on Central Govt. (Net)	32an	3,146	1,594	†−11,962	−10,156	−23,321	−27,972	−19,523	†−10,427	†−3,243	2,018	−6,922	−12,591
Claims on State & Local Govts	32b	—	—	†593	799	763	569	649	†841	†525	553	785	322
Claims on Nonfin.Pub.Enterprises	32c	—	—	†—	3,104	3,928	4,736	4,570	†23,826	†9,611	10,341	11,516	8,257
Claims on Private Sector	32d	213,477	276,788	†359,370	446,321	448,955	448,598	481,141	†455,184	†466,858	498,227	530,638	579,043
Claims on Nonbank Financial Inst.	32g	2,718	3,505	†13,375	20,257	28,889	25,533	26,323	†47,215	†76,701	74,501	68,316	64,518
Money	34	56,175	63,594	†73,055	81,655	57,425	73,720	79,381	†78,374	†87,588	101,627	112,980	122,861
Quasi-Money	35	160,863	193,651	†231,741	272,018	297,059	323,652	357,919	†398,687	†408,171	434,374	485,917	514,002
Money Market Instruments	36aa	46,614	64,432	†42,425	58,569	58,515	31,315	32,868	†11,122	†14,315	18,077	25,479	42,414
Liabs. of Central Bank: Securities	36ac	—	—	†1,334	909	4	370	760	†—	†—	—	—	—
Restricted Deposits	36b	....	....	....	....	....	....	....					
Liab. to Nonbank Financial Insts	36j	....	....	....	....	....	....	....	25,136	†24,309	26,195	25,360	22,606
Capital Accounts	37a	35,908	43,737	†54,287	76,587	87,607	116,264	114,194	†85,139	†96,446	115,360	128,959	117,689
Other Items (Net)	37r	−18,370	−25,170	†11,343	5,628	43,874	20,446	24,623	†39,781	†40,506	37,536	44,391	40,335
Money plus Quasi-Money	35l	217,038	257,245	†304,796	353,672	354,484	397,373	437,300	†477,061	†495,759	536,001	598,897	636,864

Malaysia 548

		1994	1995	1996	1997	1998	1999	2000	2001	2002	2003	2004	2005
Money (National Definitions)		*Millions of Ringgit: End of Period*											
Reserve Money	19mb	39,445	47,331	64,559	82,896	36,178	45,675	41,372	40,023	42,582	45,534	50,087	52,623
M1	59ma	46,471	51,924	60,585	63,365	54,135	73,447	78,216	80,728	89,072	102,104	114,269	124,023
M2	59mb	160,366	198,873	238,209	292,217	296,472	337,138	354,702	362,512	383,542	426,061	534,163	616,178
M3	59mc	222,330	271,948	329,708	390,809	401,459	434,590	456,496	469,519	501,125	549,649	617,639	667,327
Nonbank Financial Institutions		*Millions of Ringgit: End of Period*											
Claims on Central Government	42a.s	6,050.1	....	....	....	....	....	....	....	....	....	....	....
Claims on Private Sector	42d.s	6,555.5	....	....	....	....	....	....	....	....	....	....	....
Real Estate	42h.s	834.7	....	....	....	....	....	....	....	....	....	....	....
Interest Rates		*Percent Per Annum*											
Discount Rate (End of Period)	60	4.51	6.47	7.28	....	....	....	....	....	....	....	....	....
Money Market Rate	60b	4.20	5.60	6.92	7.61	8.46	3.38	2.66	2.79	2.73	2.74	2.70	2.72
Treasury Bill Rate	60c	3.68	5.50	6.41	6.41	6.86	3.53	2.86	2.79	2.73	2.79	2.40	2.48
Savings Rate	60k	3.67	3.61	3.87	4.18	4.26	3.10	2.73	2.55	2.25	1.95	1.71	1.47
Deposit Rate	60l	4.89	5.93	7.09	7.78	8.51	4.12	3.36	3.37	3.21	3.07	3.00	3.00
Lending Rate	60p	8.76	8.73	9.94	10.63	12.13	8.56	7.67	7.13	6.53	6.30	6.05	5.95
Government Bond Yield	61	5.11	6.51	6.39	6.87	7.66	5.63	5.11	3.54	3.47	3.60	4.09	3.57
Prices, Production, Labor		*Index Numbers (2000=100): Period Averages*											
Share Prices	62	125.7	117.1	134.9	116.3	61.6	82.4	100.0	76.0	84.5	83.8	101.2	107.6
Producer Prices	63	81.7	† 86.2	88.2	90.5	100.3	97.0	100.0	95.0	99.2	104.8	114.4	122.0
Consumer Prices	64	† 82.8	85.7	88.7	91.1	95.9	98.5	† 100.0	101.4	103.3	104.3	† 105.9	109.0
Industrial Production	66	† 59.7	67.5	74.9	82.9	77.0	83.9	† 100.0	96.7	101.2	110.5	122.5	127.5
Total Employment	67	82.0	82.3	90.4	92.2	92.6	95.0	100.0	100.7	102.7	106.2	107.5	108.1
		Number in Thousands: Period Averages											
Labor Force	67d	7,846	7,893	8,616	8,784	8,890	9,145	9,591	9,699	9,887	10,240	10,354	10,437
Employment	67e	7,618	7,645	8,400	8,569	8,603	8,831	9,291	9,357	9,543	9,870	9,987	10,065
Unemployment	67c	228	248	217	215	287	314	299	342	344	370	367	372
Unemployment Rate (%)	67r	2.9	2.8	2.5	2.5	3.2	3.5	3.1	3.5	3.5	3.6	3.5	3.5
Intl. Transactions & Positions		*Millions of Ringgit*											
Exports	70	153,921	184,987	197,026	220,890	286,563	321,560	373,270	334,420	354,407	377,602	477,829	533,372
Rubber	70l	2,927	4,038	3,510	2,971	2,829	2,344	2,571	1,886	2,492	3,583	5,197	5,785
Palm Oil	70dg	8,365	10,395	9,435	10,817	17,779	14,475	9,948	9,876	14,861	20,286	20,029	19,035
Tin	70q	507	545	533	477	485	491	435	461	426	284	947	934
Imports, c.i.f.	71	155,921	194,345	197,280	220,936	228,124	248,478	311,459	280,691	303,502	311,402	400,133	433,196
Volume of Exports		*2000=100*											
Rubber	72l	104.0	103.6	100.2	104.1	101.1	98.5	100.0	84.0	93.0	96.7	117.1	115.3
Palm Oil	72dg	74.3	75.1	83.1	85.6	84.8	101.1	100.0	118.1	122.7	141.5	134.8	147.5
Tin	72q	176.2	170.8	166.6	154.2	108.6	116.5	100.0	132.3	131.3	73.5	145.4	163.0
Export Prices													
Rubber (Wholesale Price)	76l	109.5	151.6	136.2	111.0	108.8	90.6	100.0	87.3	103.8	143.9	179.3	194.9
Palm Oil (Unit Value)	74dg	113.2	139.2	114.2	127.0	210.8	143.9	100.0	84.1	121.7	144.2	149.4	129.7
Tin (Unit Value)	76q	65.3	73.4	73.6	71.5	102.7	96.9	100.0	80.1	74.9	87.0	147.1	133.5

Malaysia 548

Balance of Payments		1994	1995	1996	1997	1998	1999	2000	2001	2002	2003	2004	2005
		Millions of US Dollars: Minus Sign Indicates Debit											
Current Account, n.i.e.	78ald	−4,520	−8,644	−4,462	−5,935	9,529	12,604	8,488	7,287	7,190	13,381	14,871	....
Goods: Exports f.o.b.	78aad	56,897	71,767	76,985	77,538	71,883	84,097	98,429	87,981	93,383	104,999	126,642	....
Goods: Imports f.o.b.	78abd	−55,320	−71,871	−73,137	−74,029	−54,378	−61,453	−77,602	−69,597	−75,248	−79,289	−99,149	....
Trade Balance	78acd	1,577	−103	3,848	3,510	17,505	22,644	20,827	18,383	18,135	25,711	27,493	....
Services: Credit	78add	9,320	11,602	15,135	15,727	11,517	11,919	13,941	14,455	14,878	13,577	16,768	....
Services: Debit	78aed	−12,052	−14,981	−17,573	−18,297	−13,127	−14,735	−16,747	−16,657	−16,448	−17,532	−19,078	....
Balance on Goods & Services	78afd	−1,155	−3,483	1,411	940	15,895	19,828	18,020	16,182	16,565	21,757	25,183	
Income: Credit	78agd	2,308	2,623	2,693	2,485	1,542	2,003	1,986	1,847	2,139	3,448	4,216	
Income: Debit	78ahd	−5,903	−6,767	−7,383	−7,851	−5,446	−7,499	−9,594	−8,590	−8,734	−9,376	−10,677	
Balance on Gds, Serv. & Inc.	78aid	−4,750	−7,626	−3,279	−4,426	11,991	14,332	10,412	9,439	9,970	15,829	18,722	
Current Transfers, n.i.e.: Credit	78ajd	411	700	766	944	728	801	756	537	661	508	447	
Current Transfers: Debit	78akd	−182	−1,717	−1,948	−2,453	−3,190	−2,529	−2,680	−2,689	−3,442	−2,955	−4,298	
Capital Account, n.i.e.	78bcd	−82	—	—	—	....	....	....	—	—	—	—	
Capital Account, n.i.e.: Credit	78bad	—	—	—	—	....	....	....	—	—	—	—	
Capital Account: Debit	78bbd	−82	—	—	—	....	....	....	—	—	—	—	
Financial Account, n.i.e.	78bjd	1,288	7,643	9,477	2,198	−2,550	−6,619	−6,276	−3,892	−3,142	−3,196	3,969	
Direct Investment Abroad	78bdd	—	—	—	—	—	−1,422	−2,026	−267	−1,905	−1,369	−2,061	
Dir. Invest. in Rep. Econ., n.i.e.	78bed	4,342	4,178	5,078	5,137	2,163	3,895	3,788	554	3,203	2,473	4,624	
Portfolio Investment Assets	78bfd	—	—	—	—	—	−133	−387	254	−563	−196	−287	
Equity Securities	78bkd	—	—	—	—	—	....	....	....	−43	−18	23	
Debt Securities	78bld	—	—	—	—	—	....	....	....	−520	−178	−309	
Portfolio Investment Liab., n.i.e.	78bgd	−1,649	−436	−268	−248	283	−892	−2,145	−666	−836	1,174	8,895	
Equity Securities	78bmd	—	—	—	—	—	....	....	....	−55	1,339	4,239	
Debt Securities	78bnd	−1,649	−436	−268	−248	283	....	....	....	−781	−165	4,656	
Financial Derivatives Assets	78bwd	....	....	....	....	....	160	279	−234	−174	−24	−1,520	
Financial Derivatives Liabilities	78bxd	....	....	....	....	....	−291	−220	−3	−139	142	1,814	
Other Investment Assets	78bhd	504	1,015	4,134	−4,604	−5,269	−7,936	−5,565	−2,702	−4,597	−4,502	−11,166	
Monetary Authorities	78bod	....	....	....	....	....	....	....	....	....	....	....	
General Government	78bpd	−52	5	33	−14	−11	....	....	....	−3	5	6	
Banks	78bqd	−1,281	28	3,339	−979	−2,677	....	....	....	−96	904	−4,698	
Other Sectors	78brd	1,837	982	762	−3,611	−2,581	....	....	....	−4,497	−5,411	−6,473	
Other Investment Liab., n.i.e.	78bid	−1,909	2,885	533	1,912	272	....	....	−829	1,868	−895	3,670	
Monetary Authorities	78bsd	−3	—	—	—	—	....	....	....	....	−62	—	
General Government	78btd	−163	−216	−597	−350	180	....	....	....	1,245	−2,891	−307	
Banks	78bud	−3,789	—	—	—	—	....	....	....	862	1,715	1,684	
Other Sectors	78bvd	2,047	3,102	1,130	2,263	92	....	....	....	−239	343	2,292	
Net Errors and Omissions	78cad	154	−762	−2,502	−137	3,039	−1,273	−3,221	−2,394	−391	−4	3,034	
Overall Balance	78cbd	−3,160	−1,763	2,513	−3,875	10,018	4,712	−1,009	1,000	3,657	10,181	21,875	
Reserves and Related Items	79dad	3,160	1,763	−2,513	3,875	−10,018	−4,712	1,009	−1,000	−3,657	−10,181	−21,875	
Reserve Assets	79dbd	3,160	1,763	−2,513	3,875	−10,018	−4,712	1,009	−1,000	−3,657	−10,181	−21,875	
Use of Fund Credit and Loans	79dcd	—	—	—	—	—	—	—	—	—	—	—	
Exceptional Financing	79ded	....	....	....	....	....	....	....	....	....	....	....	

International Investment Position													
		Millions of US Dollars											
Assets	79aad	34,122	....	....	....	....	....	....	60,515	66,950	80,287	110,695	
Direct Investment Abroad	79abd	2,635	....	....	....	....	....	....	8,354	10,225	12,019	12,807	
Portfolio Investment	79acd	650	....	....	....	....	....	....	1,632	2,207	2,490	2,519	
Equity Securities	79add	650	....	....	....	....	....	....	961	1,010	1,083	928	
Debt Securities	79aed	—	....	....	....	....	....	....	671	1,198	1,407	1,592	
Financial Derivatives	79ald	—	....	....	....	....	....	....	11	400	319	167	
Other Investment	79afd	4,164	....	....	....	....	....	....	19,748	19,619	20,689	28,514	
Monetary Authorities	79agd	—	....	....	....	....	....	....	....	....	....	....	
General Government	79ahd	—	....	....	....	....	....	....	....	....	....	....	
Banks	79aid	4,164	....	....	....	....	....	....	....	....	....	....	
Other Sectors	79ajd	—	....	....	....	....	....	....	....	....	....	....	
Reserve Assets	79akd	26,673	....	....	....	....	....	....	30,769	34,498	44,770	66,687	
Liabilities	79lad	39,757	....	....	....	....	....	....	95,854	102,969	115,084	138,288	
Dir. Invest. in Rep. Economy	79lbd	22,916	....	....	....	....	....	....	33,972	37,542	41,188	43,573	
Portfolio Investment	79lcd	7,238	....	....	....	....	....	....	15,369	15,844	22,822	38,402	
Equity Securities	79ldd	4,300	....	....	....	....	....	....	12,631	13,882	20,818	27,924	
Debt Securities	79led	2,938	....	....	....	....	....	....	2,739	1,963	2,003	10,478	
Financial Derivatives	79lld	—	....	....	....	....	....	....	311	283	208	223	
Other Investment	79lfd	9,604	....	....	....	....	....	....	46,202	49,300	50,866	56,089	
Monetary Authorities	79lgd	—	....	....	....	....	....	....	....	....	....	....	
General Government	79lhd	2,956	....	....	....	....	....	....	....	....	....	....	
Banks	79lid	6,647	....	....	....	....	....	....	....	....	....	....	
Other Sectors	79ljd	—	....	....	....	....	....	....	....	....	....	....	

Government Finance													
		Millions of Ringgit: Year Ending December 31											
Deficit (-) or Surplus	80	4,408	1,861	1,815	6,627	−5,002	−9,488	....	....	....	....	....	....
Revenue	81	49,446	50,954	58,279	65,736	56,710	58,675	....	....	....	....	....	....
Expenditure	82	45,038	49,093	56,464	59,109	60,371	68,210	....	....	....	....	....	....
Lending Minus Repayments	83	....	....	....	....	1,341	−47	....	....	....	....	....	....
Financing													
Net Borrowing: Domestic	84a	1,751	—	1,291	−2,048	11,040	5,423	....	....	....	....	....	....
Net borrowing: Foreign	85a	−4,757	−1,635	−2,177	−1,682	1,819	2,923	....	....	....	....	....	....
Special Receipts	86	519	166	475	....	....	....	....	....	....	....	....	....
Use of Cash Balances	87	−1,921	−392	−1,404	† −2,897	−7,857	1,142	....	....	....	....	....	....
Debt: Domestic	88b	78,260	78,038	79,211	76,968	88,197	93,750	....	....	....	....	....	....
Debt: Foreign	89b	14,818	13,331	10,471	12,951	14,924	18,369	....	....	....	....	....	....

Malaysia 548

		1994	1995	1996	1997	1998	1999	2000	2001	2002	2003	2004	2005
National Accounts							*Millions of Ringgit*						
Househ.Cons.Expend.,incl.NPISHs....	96f	94,088	106,613	116,794	127,783	117,718	125,056	145,355	150,644	159,506	172,366	192,771	215,876
Government Consumption Expend...	91f	23,973	27,527	28,178	30,341	27,670	33,044	35,676	42,265	49,516	54,911	59,317	64,081
Gross Fixed Capital Formation.........	93e	78,664	96,967	107,825	121,494	75,982	65,841	87,729	83,345	83,764	87,089	91,818	98,930
Changes in Inventories....................	93i	1,870	120	−2,579	−398	−427	1,476	5,982	−3,339	3,105	−1,812	10,552	−200
Exports of Goods and Services..........	90c	174,255	209,323	232,358	262,885	327,836	364,861	427,004	389,255	415,040	447,846	544,956	611,082
Imports of Goods and Services (-).....	98c	177,389	218,077	228,843	260,310	265,536	289,514	358,530	327,767	348,919	365,383	449,262	494,529
Gross Domestic Product (GDP)........	99b	195,461	222,473	253,732	281,795	283,243	300,764	343,215	334,404	362,012	395,017	450,152	495,239
Net Primary Income from Abroad.....	98.n	−9,412	−10,377	−11,801	−15,095	−15,321	−20,886	−28,909	−25,623	−25,061	−22,537	−23,908	−23,909
Gross National Income (GNI)............	99a	186,049	212,095	241,931	266,699	267,923	279,878	314,306	308,781	336,951	372,633	425,603	471,332
GDP Volume 1987 Prices.................	99b.p	151,713	166,625	183,292	196,714	182,237	193,422	210,557	211,227	220,422	232,496	249,314	262,175
GDP Volume (2000=100)................	99bvp	72.1	79.1	87.1	93.4	86.5	91.9	100.0	100.3	104.7	110.4	118.4	124.5
GDP Deflator (2000=100)...............	99bip	79.0	81.9	84.9	87.9	95.4	95.4	100.0	97.1	100.8	104.2	110.8	115.9
							Millions: Midyear Estimates						
Population...............................	99z	19.84	20.36	20.89	21.43	21.96	22.49	23.00	23.49	23.97	24.44	24.89	25.35

Maldives 556

		1994	1995	1996	1997	1998	1999	2000	2001	2002	2003	2004	2005
Exchange Rates						*Rufiyaa per SDR: End of Period*							
Market Rate	aa	17.182	17.496	16.925	15.881	16.573	16.154	15.335	16.086	17.402	19.020	19.879	18.295
						Rufiyaa per US Dollar: End of Period (ae) Period Average (rf)							
Market Rate	ae	11.770	11.770	11.770	11.770	11.770	11.770	11.770	12.800	12.800	12.800	12.800	12.800
Market Rate	rf	11.586	11.770	11.770	11.770	11.770	11.770	11.770	12.242	12.800	12.800	12.800	12.800
Fund Position						*Millions of SDRs: End of Period*							
Quota	2f.s	5.5	5.5	5.5	5.5	5.5	8.2	8.2	8.2	8.2	8.2	8.2	8.2
SDRs	1b.s	—	—	.1	.1	.1	.1	.2	.2	.3	.3	.3	.3
Reserve Position in the Fund	1c.s	.9	.9	.9	.9	.9	1.6	1.6	1.6	1.6	1.6	1.6	1.6
Total Fund Cred.&Loans Outstg	2tl	—	—	—	—	—	—	—	—	—	—	—	4.1
International Liquidity						*Millions of US Dollars Unless Otherwise Indicated: End of Period*							
Total Reserves minus Gold	1l.d	31.22	47.95	76.17	98.31	118.54	127.12	122.80	93.07	133.14	159.49	203.58	186.26
SDRs	1b.d	.05	.07	.09	.11	.14	.19	.26	.31	.38	.45	.50	.46
Reserve Position in the Fund	1c.d	1.28	1.31	1.26	1.19	1.24	2.13	2.02	1.95	2.11	2.31	2.41	2.22
Foreign Exchange	1d.d	29.89	46.57	74.81	97.01	117.15	124.80	120.52	90.80	130.65	156.73	200.66	183.59
Gold (Million Fine Troy Ounces)	1ad	—	—	—	—	—	—	—	—	—	—	—	—
Gold (National Valuation)	1and	—	—	—	—	—	—	—	—	—	—	—	—
Monetary Authorities: Other Liab	4..d	16.13	16.21	16.20	.86	.86	.86	.86	.79	.79	.79	.86	.92
Deposit Money Banks: Assets	7a.d	10.23	14.02	22.35	13.40	23.65	19.09	22.12	26.88	33.73	63.90	80.35	47.13
Liabilities	7b.d	13.61	19.03	12.83	12.20	15.06	26.90	32.42	27.58	35.02	16.61	20.20	87.43
Monetary Authorities						*Millions of Rufiyaa: End of Period*							
Foreign Assets	11	371.46	574.22	906.33	1,166.94	1,405.06	1,506.08	1,455.28	1,201.21	1,715.08	2,051.37	2,616.48	2,394.89
Claims on Central Government	12a	999.33	1,076.06	987.57	920.12	1,024.38	1,156.15	1,409.01	1,584.47	1,704.26	1,517.24	1,291.42	1,770.16
Claims on Nonfin.Pub.Enterprises	12c	6.16	8.42	7.86	—	3.20	2.48	1.57	1.48	1.48	1.48	1.48	—
Claims on Deposit Money Banks	12e	6.57	5.62	1.37	1.41	1.42	1.43						
Reserve Money	14	975.53	986.34	1,162.06	1,343.99	1,491.29	1,593.63	1,665.84	1,829.82	2,178.71	2,135.39	2,695.91	2,858.74
of which: Currency Outside DMBs	14a	382.27	405.83	425.85	489.68	524.92	593.34	618.14	566.52	569.88	624.90	762.54	883.25
Foreign Currency Deposits	15	5.50	17.00	26.64	32.70	20.69	26.51	37.35	10.16	14.88	10.00	47.41	24.18
Liabs. of Central Bank: Securities	16ac	—	121.00	199.00	330.00	480.00	568.99	666.91	323.02	554.40	684.11	376.38	313.51
Foreign Liabilities	16c	189.90	190.76	190.65	10.10	10.13	10.15	10.16	10.15	10.15	10.16	10.96	86.83
Central Government Deposits	16d	84.03	202.75	174.37	190.26	253.97	266.18	262.12	315.30	340.96	375.00	431.55	326.81
Capital Accounts	17a	90.55	62.72	105.60	130.39	105.39	118.28	179.30	185.61	89.11	183.52	194.24	349.40
Other Items (Net)	17r	38.01	83.75	44.81	51.02	72.58	82.40	44.18	113.09	232.61	171.90	152.93	205.58
Deposit Money Banks						*Millions of Rufiyaa: End of Period*							
Reserves	20	498.55	491.78	660.80	821.61	870.72	984.48	1,025.38	1,237.95	1,587.94	1,528.52	1,895.39	1,944.77
Claims on Mon.Author.:Securities	20c	—	121.00	199.00	330.00	473.44	568.99	666.91	299.87	479.47	484.83	171.71	218.56
Foreign Assets	21	120.46	165.04	263.03	157.70	278.39	224.66	260.40	344.09	431.71	817.91	1,028.49	603.30
Claims on Central Government	22a	—	—	—	—	—	—	—	—	25.60	21.33	12.80
Claims on Nonfin.Pub.Enterprises	22c	137.24	160.98	147.32	103.78	161.89	193.80	183.15	182.55	209.55	88.88	248.51	487.92
Claims on Private Sector	22d	507.38	655.09	717.40	996.79	1,253.18	1,302.81	1,407.08	1,827.24	2,107.21	2,250.84	3,547.77	5,480.48
Demand Deposits	24	356.06	393.70	552.92	619.23	725.45	935.95	1,074.43	1,022.15	1,252.96	1,398.76	1,662.46	2,105.75
Time, Savings,& Fgn. Currency Dep	25	429.26	569.91	785.77	1,075.30	1,423.72	1,318.10	1,252.06	1,658.63	2,064.84	2,428.39	3,459.38	3,627.48
Foreign Liabilities	26c	160.22	224.00	150.98	143.65	177.25	316.60	381.62	353.07	448.23	212.59	258.56	1,119.05
Central Government Deposits	26d	31.52	58.43	90.24	93.48	126.08	160.95	182.16	222.09	259.80	292.26	424.93	503.20
Credit from Monetary Authorities	26g	6.63	5.15	1.34	.89	.89	.14						
Capital Accounts	27a	143.77	157.69	281.00	358.92	486.96	496.18	610.86	572.11	646.51	685.56	875.49	1,098.49
Other Items (Net)	27r	136.17	185.01	125.30	118.41	97.27	46.82	41.80	63.65	143.55	179.01	232.36	293.86
Monetary Survey						*Millions of Rufiyaa: End of Period*							
Foreign Assets (Net)	31n	141.80	324.50	827.73	1,170.89	1,496.07	1,403.99	1,323.90	1,182.08	1,688.41	2,646.53	3,375.45	1,792.31
Domestic Credit	32	1,534.56	1,639.37	1,595.54	1,736.95	2,062.60	2,228.11	2,556.53	3,058.35	3,421.73	3,216.78	4,254.03	6,921.36
Claims on Central Govt. (Net)	32an	883.78	814.88	722.96	636.38	644.33	729.02	964.73	1,047.08	1,103.50	875.57	456.26	952.95
Claims on Nonfin.Pub.Enterprises	32c	143.40	169.40	155.18	103.78	165.09	196.28	184.72	184.03	211.03	90.37	250.00	487.92
Claims on Private Sector	32d	507.38	655.09	717.40	996.79	1,253.18	1,302.81	1,407.08	1,827.24	2,107.21	2,250.84	3,547.77	5,480.48
Money	34	833.31	876.53	1,033.48	1,168.34	1,355.45	1,554.02	1,730.15	1,624.42	1,856.33	2,069.07	2,476.91	3,033.30
Quasi-Money	35	434.76	586.91	812.41	1,108.00	1,444.41	1,344.61	1,289.41	1,668.79	2,079.71	2,438.39	3,506.79	3,651.66
Liabs. of Central Bank: Securities	36ac	—	—	—	—	6.56	.01	—	23.15	74.93	199.28	204.67	94.95
Capital Accounts	37a	234.32	220.41	386.60	489.31	592.35	614.46	790.16	757.72	735.62	869.08	1,069.74	1,447.89
Other Items (Net)	37r	173.97	280.02	190.78	142.18	159.89	119.00	70.71	166.34	363.56	287.47	371.37	485.87
Money plus Quasi-Money	35l	1,268.07	1,463.44	1,845.89	2,276.34	2,799.86	2,898.63	3,019.56	3,293.21	3,936.04	4,507.47	5,983.70	6,684.96
Money (National Definitions)						*Millions of Rufiyaa: End of Period*							
Reserve Money	19mb	981.03	1,003.34	1,188.70	1,376.52	1,511.97	1,620.15	1,703.19	1,839.99	2,193.59	2,145.40	2,743.32	2,882.93
Narrow Money	59maa	833.31	876.53	1,033.48	1,168.34	1,355.45	1,554.02	1,730.14	1,624.42	1,856.33	2,069.07	2,476.91	3,033.30
Quasi Money	59mab	434.76	586.90	812.41	1,108.01	1,444.42	1,344.61	1,289.40	1,668.79	2,079.71	2,438.39	3,506.79	3,651.66
Broad Money	59mba	1,268.07	1,463.43	1,845.89	2,276.19	2,799.87	2,898.63	3,019.54	3,293.21	3,936.04	4,507.47	5,983.70	6,684.96
Interest Rates						*Percent Per Annum*							
Discount Rate (End of Period)	60	....	....	....	....	....	....	....	18.00	18.54	19.00	18.25	18.00
Money Market Rate	60b	5.00	6.80	6.80	6.80	6.80	6.80	6.80	....	....	....	....	....
Savings Rate	60k	....	....	6.00	6.00	6.00	6.00	6.00	6.00	5.50	5.25	† 3.00	3.00
Savings Rate (Foreign Currency)	60k.f	....	....	....	....	....	....	....	....	....	....	3.00	3.00
Deposit Rate	60l	....	....	6.80	6.80	6.80	6.93	6.88	6.97	7.50	7.50	† 6.50	6.50
Deposit Rate (Foreign Currency)	60l.f	....	....	....	....	....	....	....	....	....	....	6.50	6.50
Lending Rate	60p	....	....	15.00	15.00	15.00	12.50	13.00	13.00	13.54	14.00	† 13.00	13.00
Lending Rate (Foreign Currency)	60p.f	....	....	....	....	15.00	14.50	15.00	15.00	15.00	14.33	13.25	13.00
Prices, Production, Labor						*Index Numbers (2000=100): Period Averages*							
Consumer Prices	64	82.7	87.2	92.7	99.7	98.3	101.2	100.0	100.7	101.6	98.7	105.0	108.5
Total Fish Catch	66al	90.1	90.5	91.3	88.2	99.7	106.8	100.0	108.3	138.8	131.9	135.2	158.5
Tourist Bed Night Index	66.t	59.7	69.2	77.2	83.1	88.1	94.4	100.0	99.9	103.3	119.5	129.8	83.8
						Number in Thousands: Period Averages							
Labor Force	67d	....	67	....	....	....	....	86	....	....	....	....	....

Maldives 556

		1994	1995	1996	1997	1998	1999	2000	2001	2002	2003	2004	2005
Intl. Transactions & Positions								*Millions of US Dollars*					
Exports	70..d	47.9	49.6	59.2	69.9	74.3	63.7	75.9	76.2	90.4	112.5	122.4	103.5
Imports, c.i.f.	71..d	221.7	267.9	301.7	348.8	354.0	402.2	388.6	393.5	391.7	470.8	641.8	744.9
Imports, f.o.b.	71.vd	195.1	235.8	265.5	307.0	311.5	353.9	342.0	346.3	344.7	414.3	564.8	655.5
Balance of Payments						*Millions of US Dollars: Minus Sign Indicates Debit*							
Current Account, n.i.e.	78ald	−11.1	−18.2	−7.4	−34.7	−21.9	−78.9	−51.5	−58.7	−35.7	−31.8	−133.9	....
Goods: Exports f.o.b.	78aad	75.4	85.0	79.9	89.7	95.6	91.5	108.7	110.2	132.3	152.0	181.0	....
Goods: Imports f.o.b.	78abd	−195.1	−235.8	−265.5	−307.0	−311.5	−353.9	−342.0	−346.3	−344.7	−414.3	−567.3	....
Trade Balance	78acd	−119.6	−150.8	−185.6	−217.3	−215.9	−262.4	−233.3	−236.0	−212.4	−262.3	−386.4	....
Services: Credit	78add	197.4	232.8	289.0	312.2	331.3	342.8	348.5	354.1	362.9	432.1	507.2	....
Services: Debit	78aed	−62.8	−76.7	−87.9	−94.2	−98.9	−108.1	−109.7	−109.8	−111.1	−121.0	−157.8	....
Balance on Goods & Services	78afd	15.0	5.4	15.5	.6	16.6	−27.8	5.5	8.2	39.3	48.8	−36.9	....
Income: Credit	78agd	3.8	4.5	6.0	7.5	8.6	9.0	10.3	8.2	5.6	6.2	8.3	....
Income: Debit	78ahd	−24.0	−24.5	−27.8	−34.9	−36.8	−40.1	−40.3	−45.4	−41.1	−44.6	−51.1	....
Balance on Gds, Serv. & Inc.	78aid	−5.2	−14.6	−6.4	−26.8	−11.6	−58.8	−24.5	−29.1	3.9	10.4	−79.7	....
Current Transfers, n.i.e.: Credit	78ajd	16.3	23.0	26.2	20.0	20.3	20.4	19.3	19.9	10.6	12.7	6.9	....
Current Transfers: Debit	78akd	−22.2	−26.6	−27.3	−27.9	−30.6	−40.5	−46.2	−49.6	−50.2	−54.9	−61.1	....
Capital Account, n.i.e.	78bcd	—	—	—	—	—	—	—	—	—	—	—	....
Capital Account, n.i.e.: Credit	78bad	—	—	—	—	—	—	—	—	—	—	—	....
Capital Account: Debit	78bbd	—	—	—	—	—	—	—	—	—	—	—	....
Financial Account, n.i.e.	78bjd	27.5	67.6	52.2	71.0	60.2	76.2	40.2	35.5	73.5	56.3	152.5	....
Direct Investment Abroad	78bdd	—	—	—	—	—	—	—	—	—	—	—	....
Dir. Invest. in Rep. Econ., n.i.e.	78bed	8.7	7.2	9.3	11.4	11.5	12.3	13.0	11.7	12.4	13.5	14.7	....
Portfolio Investment Assets	78bfd	—	—	—	—	—	—	—	—	—	—	—	....
Equity Securities	78bkd	—	—	—	—	—	—	—	—	—	—	—	....
Debt Securities	78bld	—	—	—	—	—	—	—	—	—	—	—	....
Portfolio Investment Liab., n.i.e.	78bgd	—	—	—	—	—	—	—	—	—	—	—	....
Equity Securities	78bmd	—	—	—	—	—	—	—	—	—	—	—	....
Debt Securities	78bnd	....	....	....	....	....	....	....	....	....	....	....	....
Financial Derivatives Assets	78bwd	....	....	....	....	....	....	....	....	....	....	....	....
Financial Derivatives Liabilities	78bxd	....	....	....	....	....	....	....	....	....	....	....	....
Other Investment Assets	78bhd	13.2	29.8	32.6	53.8	30.8	47.5	22.8	21.3	26.7	28.3	107.0	....
Monetary Authorities	78bod	....	....	....	....	....	....	....	....	....	....	....	....
General Government	78bpd	—	—	—	—	—	—	—	—	—	—	—	....
Banks	78bqd	.1	−3.8	−8.3	10.8	−12.2	4.6	−2.8	−3.0	−7.2	−28.5	−18.4	....
Other Sectors	78brd	13.1	33.6	41.0	42.9	42.9	42.9	25.6	24.3	33.9	56.8	125.3	....
Other Investment Liab., n.i.e.	78bid	5.5	30.5	10.2	5.8	17.9	16.4	4.4	2.4	34.4	14.4	30.8	....
Monetary Authorities	78bsd	.7	.1	—	−15.3	—	—	—	−.1	—	—	.1	....
General Government	78btd	8.2	24.8	17.3	21.9	14.6	5.2	−1.9	7.8	26.8	33.8	27.2	....
Banks	78bud	−3.4	5.7	−7.1	−.8	3.3	11.2	6.3	−5.3	7.6	−19.3	3.6	....
Other Sectors	78bvd	—	—	—	—	—	—	—	—	....	....	....	....
Net Errors and Omissions	78cad	−10.9	−32.2	−16.4	−14.0	−18.2	11.4	6.9	−6.5	2.3	1.7	25.4	....
Overall Balance	78cbd	5.5	17.2	28.3	22.2	20.2	8.6	−4.3	−29.7	40.1	26.2	44.1	....
Reserves and Related Items	79dad	−5.5	−17.2	−28.3	−22.2	−20.2	−8.6	4.3	29.7	−40.1	−26.2	−44.1	....
Reserve Assets	79dbd	−5.5	−17.2	−28.3	−22.2	−20.2	−8.6	4.3	29.7	−40.1	−26.2	−44.1	....
Use of Fund Credit and Loans	79dcd	—	—	—	—	—	—	—	—	—	—	—	....
Exceptional Financing	79ded	—	—	—	—	—	—	—	—	—	—	—	....
International Investment Position							*Millions of US Dollars*						
Assets	79aad	....	....	....	....	....	....	....	....	....	....	....	....
Direct Investment Abroad	79abd	—	—	—	—	—	—	—	—	—	—	—	....
Portfolio Investment	79acd	—	—	—	—	—	—	—	—	—	—	—	....
Equity Securities	79add	—	—	—	—	—	—	—	—	—	—	—	....
Debt Securities	79aed	—	—	—	—	—	—	—	—	—	—	—	....
Financial Derivatives	79ald	....	....	....	....	....	....	....	....	....	....	....	....
Other Investment	79afd	10.2	14.0	22.3	11.5	23.7	19.1	21.9	24.9	32.1	60.6	79.0	....
Monetary Authorities	79agd	—	—	—	—	—	—	—	—	—	—	—	....
General Government	79ahd	—	—	—	—	—	—	—	—	—	—	—	....
Banks	79aid	10.2	14.0	22.3	11.5	23.7	19.1	21.9	24.9	32.1	60.6	79.0	....
Other Sectors	79ajd	—	—	—	—	—	—	—	—	—	—	—	....
Reserve Assets	79akd	32.0	49.3	77.6	99.7	119.9	128.5	124.1	94.3	134.6	161.0	205.2	....
Liabilities	79lad	....	....	....	....	....	....	....	....	....	....	....	....
Dir. Invest. in Rep. Economy	79lbd	—	—	—	—	—	—	—	—	—	—	—	....
Portfolio Investment	79lcd	—	—	—	—	—	—	—	—	—	—	—	....
Equity Securities	79ldd	—	—	—	—	—	—	—	—	—	—	—	....
Debt Securities	79led	—	—	—	—	—	—	—	—	—	—	—	....
Financial Derivatives	79lld	....	....	....	....	....	....	....	....	....	....	....	....
Other Investment	79lfd	141.9	173.1	178.1	178.9	201.6	213.8	212.4	210.6	259.8	281.6	350.3	....
Monetary Authorities	79lgd	16.1	16.2	16.2	.9	.9	.9	.9	.8	.8	.8	.9	....
General Government	79lhd	110.8	136.2	148.4	165.3	184.7	185.6	178.0	181.5	223.1	264.2	329.3	....
Banks	79lid	15.0	20.6	13.5	12.8	16.1	27.3	33.6	28.3	35.9	16.6	20.2	....
Other Sectors	79ljd	—	—	—	—	—	—	—	—	—	—	—	....
Government Finance						*Millions of Rufiyaa: Year Ending December 31*							
Deficit (-) or Surplus	80	−206.6	−300.1	−133.8	−81.3	−123.1	−281.1	−321.5	−363.3	−402.4	−300.3	−157.9	−1,197.3p
Revenue	81	981.7	1,209.5	1,324.9	1,656.5	1,765.7	2,062.6	2,206.8	2,310.9	2,582.4	2,964.3	3,351.8	3,660.9p
Grants Received	81z	162.6	199.2	242.9	168.2	164.5	162.7	165.9	211.7	132.5	123.6	72.9	881.7p
Expenditure	82	1,357.5	1,717.8	1,692.6	1,936.9	2,113.9	2,494.9	2,739.9	2,912.1	3,135.5	3,551.9	3,779.1	5,830.9p
Lending Minus Repayments	83	−6.6	−9.0	9.0	−30.9	−60.6	11.5	−45.7	−26.2	−18.2	−163.7	−196.5	−91.0p
Financing													
Domestic	84a	106.4	2.1	−29.2	−90.9	−6.2	224.4	317.9	217.5	30.0	−118.9	−245.8	881.1p
Foreign	85a	100.2	298.0	163.0	172.2	129.3	56.7	3.6	145.8	372.4	419.2	403.7	316.2p
Debt: Domestic	88a	960.9	1,063.0	957.6	877.1	980.3	1,101.0	1,317.4	1,495.1	1,653.2	1,464.7	1,256.2	1,723.7p
Debt: Foreign	89a	862.7	1,160.7	1,323.7	1,495.9	1,625.2	1,681.9	1,685.5	1,831.3	2,203.7	2,622.9	3,026.6	3,342.8p

Maldives 556

		1994	1995	1996	1997	1998	1999	2000	2001	2002	2003	2004	2005
National Accounts							*Millions of Rufiyaa*						
Government Consumption Expend...	**91f**	....	788	859	1,060	1,184	1,386	1,599	1,619	....	....	....	....
Gross Fixed Capital Formation..........	**93e**	....	1,479	1,053	2,087	2,042	2,400	1,727	2,079	....	....	....	....
Exports of Goods and Services..........	**90c**	555	4,961	4,954	5,476	5,859	6,107	6,796	6,817	....	....	....	....
Imports of Goods and Services (-).....	**98c**	2,571	3,153	3,361	4,774	4,961	5,604	5,809	6,022	....	....	....	....
Gross Domestic Product (GDP).........	**99b**	4,125	4,696	5,301	5,982	6,357	6,935	7,348	7,651	8,201	8,863	9,939	9,799
GDP Volume 1995 Prices.................	**99b.p**	3,978	4,272	4,660	5,145	5,648	6,057	6,345	6,564	6,993	7,590	8,312	7,881
GDP Volume (2000=100)................	**99bvp**	62.7	67.3	73.4	81.1	89.0	95.4	100.0	103.5	110.2	119.6	131.0	124.2
GDP Deflator (2000=100)................	**99bip**	90	95	98	100	97	99	100	101	101	101	103	107
							Millions: Midyear Estimates						
Population................................	**99z**	.24	.25	.26	.27	.27	.28	.29	.30	.31	.31	.32	.33

Mali 678

		1994	1995	1996	1997	1998	1999	2000	2001	2002	2003	2004	2005
Exchange Rates							*Francs per SDR: End of Period*						
Official Rate	aa	† 780.44	728.38	753.06	807.94	791.61	† 896.19	918.49	935.39	850.37	771.76	747.90	794.73
					Francs per US Dollar: End of Period (ae) Period Average (rf)								
Official Rate	ae	† 534.60	490.00	523.70	598.81	562.21	† 652.95	704.95	744.31	625.50	519.36	481.58	556.04
Official Rate	rf	† 555.20	499.15	511.55	583.67	589.95	† 615.70	711.98	733.04	696.99	581.20	528.28	527.47
Fund Position							*Millions of SDRs: End of Period*						
Quota	2f.s	68.9	68.9	68.9	68.9	68.9	93.3	93.3	93.3	93.3	93.3	93.3	93.3
SDRs	1b.s	.1	.3	.2	—	.1	.4	.1	.3	—	.6	.4	.2
Reserve Position in the Fund	1c.s	8.7	8.7	8.8	8.8	8.8	8.8	8.8	8.8	8.8	8.9	9.0	9.1
Total Fund Cred.&Loans Outstg	2tl	74.1	99.0	114.6	130.2	132.4	140.9	134.7	136.0	121.8	113.6	93.2	76.4
International Liquidity					*Millions of US Dollars Unless Otherwise Indicated: End of Period*								
Total Reserves minus Gold	1l.d	† 221.4	323.0	431.5	414.9	402.9	349.7	381.3	348.9	594.5	952.5	860.7	854.6
SDRs	1b.d	.2	.5	.3	.1	.1	.6	.1	.4	—	.9	.6	.3
Reserve Position in the Fund	1c.d	12.7	13.0	12.6	11.8	12.4	12.1	11.4	11.1	12.0	13.2	13.9	13.1
Foreign Exchange	1d.d	† 208.5	309.5	418.6	403.0	390.4	337.1	369.7	337.4	582.4	938.4	846.2	841.2
Gold (Million Fine Troy Ounces)	1ad	.019	—	—	—	—	—	—	—	—	—	—	—
Gold (National Valuation)	1and	7.0	—	—	—	—	—	—	—	—	—	—	—
Monetary Authorities: Other Liab	4..d	9.7	1.9	−6.9	3.7	1.8	3.1	2.0	2.7	5.7	6.9	8.6	7.4
Deposit Money Banks: Assets	7a.d	118.7	163.6	136.7	117.6	125.2	116.6	140.1	195.0	189.9	218.8	278.9	246.2
Liabilities	7b.d	34.3	102.1	70.0	28.2	49.1	87.9	79.6	83.9	115.2	146.8	178.8	201.6
Monetary Authorities							*Billions of Francs: End of Period*						
Foreign Assets	11	118.4	158.2	226.0	248.4	226.5	228.3	268.8	259.7	371.8	494.7	414.5	475.2
Claims on Central Government	12a	58.7	65.1	77.0	99.8	105.9	112.9	108.9	135.9	125.3	117.6	99.1	83.6
Claims on Deposit Money Banks	12e												
Claims on Other Financial Insts	12f	—	—	—	—	—	—	—	—	—	—	—	—
Reserve Money	14	115.9	127.7	151.1	162.8	153.7	173.1	219.0	245.2	359.3	474.2	402.7	462.3
of which: Currency Outside DMBs	14a	91.1	107.5	120.3	129.5	135.3	123.4	146.9	179.0	247.5	340.9	275.4	344.9
Foreign Liabilities	16c	63.0	73.1	82.7	107.5	105.9	128.4	125.2	129.2	107.1	91.3	73.9	64.8
Central Government Deposits	16d	12.8	27.1	63.0	70.6	63.7	41.5	34.7	17.2	17.8	25.8	15.7	21.2
Other Items (Net)	17r	−14.6	−4.6	6.2	7.4	9.2	−1.8	−1.2	4.1	12.9	21.0	21.3	10.4
Deposit Money Banks							*Billions of Francs: End of Period*						
Reserves	20	25.3	17.1	29.5	32.1	16.5	47.7	70.7	59.2	99.7	132.4	125.0	115.9
Foreign Assets	21	63.4	80.2	71.6	70.4	70.4	76.2	98.8	145.2	118.8	113.6	134.3	136.9
Claims on Central Government	22a	28.0	19.4	24.0	21.1	13.6	14.0	17.8	27.7	23.3	14.3	15.7	43.9
Claims on Private Sector	22d	84.9	130.3	171.2	195.9	251.0	286.5	283.6	342.2	412.2	482.3	515.4	515.2
Claims on Other Financial Insts	22f	—	—	—	—	—	—	—	—	—	—	—	—
Demand Deposits	24	83.0	90.5	119.5	126.2	131.8	142.3	143.6	197.8	238.2	272.8	294.1	297.1
Time Deposits	25	63.1	56.4	76.4	89.0	91.9	97.0	116.1	110.0	137.0	173.4	197.1	199.5
Foreign Liabilities	26c	11.5	45.3	30.5	5.9	19.5	50.3	45.2	52.4	59.7	60.2	69.1	94.8
Long-Term Foreign Liabilities	26cl	6.9	4.7	6.1	10.9	8.1	7.1	10.9	10.1	12.4	16.0	17.0	17.2
Central Government Deposits	26d	39.3	50.8	71.5	68.2	78.0	102.3	129.8	159.2	158.5	178.7	158.6	131.9
Credit from Monetary Authorities	26g	—	—	.1	—	—	—	—	—	—	—	—	—
Other Items (Net)	27r	−2.1	−.7	−8.0	19.3	22.2	25.3	25.3	44.8	48.3	41.6	54.6	71.2
Treasury Claims: Private Sector	22d.i	2.1	1.5	2.0	4.5	3.9	5.2	2.7	1.3	—	.6	.1	.8
Post Office: Checking Deposits	24..i	—	—	—	—	—	—	—	—	—	—	—	—
Monetary Survey							*Billions of Francs: End of Period*						
Foreign Assets (Net)	31n	107.3	120.0	184.3	205.5	171.5	125.9	197.2	223.2	323.8	456.8	405.8	452.4
Domestic Credit	32	119.5	136.9	137.6	178.0	228.8	269.5	245.8	329.4	384.4	409.8	455.8	489.6
Claims on Central Govt. (Net)	32an	32.6	5.1	−35.6	−22.4	−26.1	−22.2	−40.5	−14.0	−27.8	−73.1	−59.7	−26.4
Claims on Private Sector	32d	86.9	131.8	173.2	200.4	254.9	291.7	286.3	343.5	412.2	482.9	515.5	516.0
Claims on Other Financial Insts	32f	—	—	—	—	—	—	—	—	—	—	—	—
Money	34	174.2	198.2	240.4	256.0	267.6	266.0	291.2	377.2	486.1	614.2	569.7	642.4
Quasi-Money	35	63.1	56.4	76.4	89.0	91.9	97.0	116.1	110.0	137.0	173.4	197.1	199.5
Long-Term Foreign Liabilities	36cl	6.9	4.7	6.1	10.9	8.1	7.1	10.9	10.1	12.4	16.0	17.0	17.2
Other Items (Net)	37r	−17.3	−2.4	−1.0	27.5	32.8	25.2	24.9	55.4	72.8	63.1	77.9	82.8
Money plus Quasi-Money	35l	237.2	254.6	316.8	345.0	359.5	363.1	407.2	487.2	623.1	787.5	766.8	841.9
Interest Rates							*Percent Per Annum*						
Bank Rate (End of Period)	60	6.00	6.00	6.00	6.00	6.00	6.00	6.00	6.00	6.00	4.50	4.00	4.00
Money Market Rate	60b	4.95	4.95	4.95	4.95	4.95	4.95	4.95	4.95	4.95	4.95	4.95	4.95
Deposit Rate	60l	3.50	3.50	3.50	3.50	3.50	3.50	3.50	3.50	3.50	3.50	3.50	3.50
Prices							*Index Numbers (2000=100): Period Averages*						
Consumer Prices	64	81.1	92.0	98.3	† 98.0	101.9	100.7	100.0	105.2	110.5	109.0	105.6	112.4
Intl. Transactions & Positions							*Billions of Francs*						
Exports	70	185.95	220.50	221.41	327.70	331.10	351.57	392.30	531.60	609.00	539.40	542.50	606.60
Imports, c.i.f	71	327.22	385.40	395.17	431.20	448.80	507.30	573.90	725.70	646.80	725.30	702.60	817.60

Mali 678

		1994	1995	1996	1997	1998	1999	2000	2001	2002	2003	2004	2005
Balance of Payments					*Millions of US Dollars: Minus Sign Indicates Debit*								
Current Account, n.i.e.	78ald	−162.6	−283.8	−260.8	−178.4	−208.2	−253.0	−254.5	−310.0	−148.8	−271.0	....	....
Goods: Exports f.o.b.	78aad	334.9	441.8	432.8	561.5	556.2	571.0	545.1	725.2	875.1	927.8	....	....
Goods: Imports f.o.b.	78abd	−449.2	−556.8	−551.5	−545.7	−558.2	−605.5	−592.1	−734.7	−712.5	−988.3	....	....
Trade Balance	78acd	−114.3	−115.0	−118.6	15.7	−2.0	−34.5	−46.9	−9.6	162.7	−60.5	....	....
Services: Credit	78add	69.0	87.6	91.9	81.2	83.4	110.0	99.0	151.2	169.4	224.3	....	....
Services: Debit	78aed	−317.0	−434.5	−383.4	−350.0	−353.3	−372.0	−334.9	−421.4	−387.0	−482.2	....	....
Balance on Goods & Services	78afd	−362.3	−461.9	−410.2	−253.1	−272.0	−296.5	−282.8	−279.7	−54.9	−318.5	....	....
Income: Credit	78agd	9.3	8.3	26.5	19.0	29.3	31.3	20.6	22.1	36.1	21.3	....	....
Income: Debit	78ahd	−49.7	−48.9	−69.5	−70.7	−80.1	−101.4	−118.7	−188.2	−276.3	−181.2	....	....
Balance on Gds, Serv. & Inc.	78aid	−402.7	−502.6	−453.2	−304.8	−322.8	−366.6	−380.9	−445.8	−295.1	−478.4	....	....
Current Transfers, n.i.e.: Credit	78ajd	281.3	266.8	218.3	151.9	151.6	145.8	157.2	160.7	182.1	265.5	....	....
Current Transfers: Debit	78akd	−41.2	−48.0	−25.9	−25.5	−37.1	−32.2	−30.8	−25.0	−35.7	−58.1	....	....
Capital Account, n.i.e.	78bcd	99.1	126.2	138.0	111.4	124.0	113.3	101.6	107.4	104.2	113.7	....	....
Capital Account, n.i.e.: Credit	78bad	99.1	126.2	138.1	112.5	124.0	113.4	101.6	107.5	104.4	113.7	....	....
Capital Account: Debit	78bbd	....	....	—	−1.1	—	−.1	—	−.1	−.2	—	....	....
Financial Account, n.i.e.	78bjd	−7.0	118.6	138.0	53.1	48.0	116.9	220.4	146.2	188.6	290.1	....	....
Direct Investment Abroad	78bdd	—	—	−1.6	6.8	—	−.8	−4.0	−17.3	−1.6	−1.4	....	....
Dir. Invest. in Rep. Econ., n.i.e.	78bed	17.4	111.4	44.8	63.0	8.9	2.2	82.4	121.7	243.8	132.3	....	....
Portfolio Investment Assets	78bfd	—	—	−1.1	−4.2	−4.5	−21.1	15.5	−.8	−.5	−27.1	....	....
Equity Securities	78bkd	—	....	−.1	−.1	3.9	—	−.1	−.1	−.6	.2	....	....
Debt Securities	78bld	—	....	−1.0	−4.1	−8.4	−21.1	15.6	−.7	.1	−27.2	....	....
Portfolio Investment Liab., n.i.e.	78bgd	—	....	1.6	−3.6	−.4	22.0	1.0	12.4	54.1	27.6	....	....
Equity Securities	78bmd	—	....	—	.2	−.1	22.9	.4	13.5	−2.1	.9	....	....
Debt Securities	78bnd	—	....	1.6	−3.8	−.3	−1.0	.6	−1.1	56.2	26.7	....	....
Financial Derivatives Assets	78bwd	....	....	—	—	—	—	—	—	—	—	....	....
Financial Derivatives Liabilities	78bxd	....	....	.1	.1	—	—	—	—	—	—	....	....
Other Investment Assets	78bhd	−104.0	−52.3	22.3	−85.4	−33.8	−45.4	−87.0	−87.7	−248.4	3.7	....	....
Monetary Authorities	78bod	....	....	—	—	—	—	—	—	—	—	....	....
General Government	78bpd	—	....	—	—	—	—	−1.4	—	—	—	....	....
Banks	78bqd	−100.3	−33.2	32.3	1.8	1.4	3.9	−42.5	−64.2	30.4	15.6	....	....
Other Sectors	78brd	−3.7	−19.2	−10.0	−87.2	−35.2	−49.3	−43.1	−23.5	−278.7	−11.9	....	....
Other Investment Liab., n.i.e.	78bid	79.6	59.6	71.9	76.4	77.9	160.1	212.5	117.8	141.1	155.1	....	....
Monetary Authorities	78bsd	—	—	−9.3	10.2	−2.2	1.7	−.6	.7	2.6	1.7	....	....
General Government	78btd	33.1	89.8	80.5	57.7	98.3	97.9	88.3	111.5	87.5	104.4	....	....
Banks	78bud	11.9	−1.4	−40.5	7.0	18.9	48.1	−1.9	8.4	25.9	11.1	....	....
Other Sectors	78bvd	34.5	−28.7	41.2	1.5	−37.2	12.5	126.6	−2.7	25.1	37.9	....	....
Net Errors and Omissions	78cad	5.6	−13.0	14.2	4.0	−9.7	9.5	−4.8	9.4	−6.1	4.6	....	....
Overall Balance	78cbd	−65.0	−52.0	29.4	−9.9	−45.9	−13.4	62.6	−47.0	137.8	137.4	....	....
Reserves and Related Items	79dad	65.0	52.0	−29.4	9.9	45.9	13.4	−62.6	47.0	−137.8	−137.4	....	....
Reserve Assets	79dbd	−37.6	−80.2	−132.0	−37.6	33.7	1.6	−57.9	14.0	−159.0	−177.4	....	....
Use of Fund Credit and Loans	79dcd	32.7	38.4	22.4	21.3	2.7	11.7	−8.3	1.5	−18.3	−11.8	....	....
Exceptional Financing	79ded	69.9	93.8	80.1	26.2	9.4	—	3.7	31.5	39.5	51.9	....	....
International Investment Position					*Millions of US Dollars*								
Assets	79aad	....	....	673.4	598.1	628.6	673.9	596.7	671.1	1,223.5	1,314.4	....	....
Direct Investment Abroad	79abd	....	....	1.8	−6.9	−.1	.7	.6	15.9	2.1	6.6	....	....
Portfolio Investment	79acd	....	....	60.1	4.5	7.4	49.3	28.4	35.0	41.1	98.3	....	....
Equity Securities	79add	....	....	.9	.5	.3	.2	1.7	.4	1.5	1.1	....	....
Debt Securities	79aed	....	....	59.2	4.0	7.1	49.1	26.6	34.6	39.7	97.2	....	....
Financial Derivatives	79ald	....	....	—	—	.1	—	—	.1	.1	.1	....	....
Other Investment	79afd	....	....	179.9	185.5	214.9	274.2	185.0	271.5	589.5	300.8	....	....
Monetary Authorities	79agd	....	....	—	—	—	—	—	—	—	—	....	....
General Government	79ahd	....	....	—	—	—	—	1.4	—	—	—	....	....
Banks	79aid	....	....	136.7	117.6	123.9	103.0	100.7	187.3	182.7	193.3	....	....
Other Sectors	79ajd	....	....	43.2	67.9	91.0	171.3	82.9	84.2	406.8	107.5	....	....
Reserve Assets	79akd	....	....	431.5	414.9	406.2	349.7	382.7	348.7	590.8	908.7	....	....
Liabilities	79lad	....	....	2,717.7	3,299.8	3,411.3	3,265.5	3,053.3	3,021.8	3,766.9	4,460.6	....	....
Dir. Invest. in Rep. Economy	79lbd	....	....	64.1	454.8	309.9	228.1	132.4	210.4	524.2	682.6	....	....
Portfolio Investment	79lcd	....	....	5.3	4.5	10.4	41.0	4.7	16.7	76.4	46.9	....	....
Equity Securities	79ldd	....	....	.9	.9	.5	37.0	.8	14.0	13.8	17.1	....	....
Debt Securities	79led	....	....	4.4	3.7	9.9	4.0	4.0	2.7	62.6	29.8	....	....
Financial Derivatives	79lld	....	....	.1	.2	—	—	—	—	—	—	....	....
Other Investment	79lfd	....	....	2,648.2	2,840.1	3,091.1	2,996.4	2,916.2	2,794.6	3,166.3	3,731.1	....	....
Monetary Authorities	79lgd	....	....	158.5	179.6	188.3	196.6	177.8	173.6	171.6	178.0	....	....
General Government	79lhd	....	....	2,391.6	2,569.2	2,804.9	2,509.2	2,295.1	2,238.5	2,576.0	3,170.3	....	....
Banks	79lid	....	....	25.6	28.2	49.9	88.2	79.9	89.5	154.3	207.3	....	....
Other Sectors	79ljd	....	....	72.5	63.2	48.0	202.3	363.4	293.1	264.3	175.5	....	....
Government Finance					*Billions of Francs; Year Ending December 31*								
Deficit (-) or Surplus	80	−43.4	−36.7	−11.1	−29.9	† −38.6	−61.4	−69.1	−112.2	−84.8	−89.6p	....	....
Total Revenue and Grants	81y	236.7	269.7	314.0	320.5	† 344.8	356.1	371.1	420.4	474.2	542.7	....	....
Revenue	81	138.9	177.3	217.5	236.3	† 254.9	272.7	269.9	320.1	388.4	434.4p	....	....
Grants	81z	97.8	92.4	96.5	84.2	† 89.9	83.4	101.2	100.3	85.8	108.3p	....	....
Exp.& Lending Minus Repay	82z	....	....	....	....	† 383.4	417.5	440.2	532.6	559.0	632.3p	....	....
Expenditure	82	280.1	306.4	325.1	350.4	† 387.0	419.7	442.7	543.2	563.9	634.6p	....	....
Lending Minus Repay	83	....	....	....	....	† −3.6	−2.2	−2.5	−10.6	−4.9	−2.3p	....	....
Statistical Discrepancy	80xx	−29.7	−14.0	−18.9	−8.5	−10.0	2.4	1.6	—	—	−p	....	....
Total Financing	80h	73.1	50.7	30.0	38.4	48.5	59.1	67.4	112.2	85.1	89.5p	....	....
Domestic	84a	−3.6	−40.1	−52.1	−10.6	−9.5	−1.2	3.0	6.1	−3.4	−36.4p	....	....
Foreign	85a	76.7	90.8	82.1	49.0	58.0	60.3	64.4	106.1	88.5	125.9p	....	....
Debt													
Total Debt	88	....	....	....	....	....	....	....	....	....	....	....	....
Domestic	88a	....	....	....	....	....	....	....	....	....	....	....	....
Foreign	89a	1,576.6	1,395.2	1,498.4	1,614.8	1,684.3	1,618.0	1,701.6	1,731.7	1,776.1	1,825.7p	....	....

Mali 678

		1994	1995	1996	1997	1998	1999	2000	2001	2002	2003	2004	2005
National Accounts							*Billions of Francs*						
Househ.Cons.Expend.,incl.NPISHs....	96f	749.0	983.3	1,100.9	1,083.5	1,228.3	1,355.7	1,417.6	1,541.5	1,548.1	1,654.9	1,735.1	1,731.4
Government Consumption Expend...	91f	187.9	262.0	271.9	290.6	322.9	308.5	310.8	346.3	368.1	383.9	472.6	495.0
Gross Fixed Capital Formation..........	93e	249.3	300.2	317.1	348.1	305.4	313.0	356.4	420.6	439.5	446.8	....	....
Changes in Inventories....................	93i	−10.8	43.2	−49.6	8.7	35.8	24.2	17.4	119.6	−14.5	167.3	....	....
Exports of Goods and Services..........	90c	224.7	264.2	268.4	375.7	377.3	419.4	458.6	642.3	727.9	674.8	640.5	718.1
Imports of Goods and Services (-)....	98c	421.2	494.8	478.2	523.8	537.8	601.9	659.9	847.4	766.2	833.6	794.0	828.9
Gross Domestic Product (GDP)........	99b	978.7	1,358.1	1,430.5	1,582.8	1,731.9	1,818.9	1,900.9	2,222.9	2,302.9	2,494.1	2,517.1	2,699.3
GDP Volume 1987 Prices................	99b.p	708.9	755.9	783.0	....	....	....	....	....	....	....	....	....
GDP Volume (1995=100)...............	99bvp	93.8	100.0	103.6	....	....	....	....	....	....	....	....	....
GDP Deflator (1995=100)...............	99bip	76.8	100.0	101.7	....	....	....	....	....	....	....	....	....
						Millions: Midyear Estimates							
Population..............................	99z	9.88	10.15	10.42	10.71	11.01	11.32	11.65	11.99	12.36	12.74	13.12	13.52

		1994	1995	1996	1997	1998	1999	2000	2001	2002	2003	2004	2005

Exchange Rates

		1994	1995	1996	1997	1998	1999	2000	2001	2002	2003	2004	2005
						SDRs per Lira: End of Period							
Official Rate	ac	1.8609	1.9090	1.9338	1.8969	1.8818	1.7681	1.7532	1.7602	1.8443	1.9648	2.0214	1.9290
						US Dollars per Lira: End of Period (ag) Period Average (rh)							
Official Rate	ag	2.7166	2.8377	2.7807	2.5594	2.6496	2.4268	2.2843	2.2121	2.5074	2.9197	3.1393	2.7570
Official Rate	rh	2.6486	2.8333	2.7745	2.5924	2.5743	2.5039	2.2855	2.2226	2.3100	2.6543	2.9036	2.8959
						Index Numbers (2000=100): Period Averages							
Official Rate	ahx	115.9	124.0	121.4	113.4	112.6	109.6	100.0	97.2	101.1	116.1	127.0	126.7
Nominal Effective Exchange Rate	nec	100.2	101.4	100.9	101.2	105.5	103.1	100.0	100.6	102.0	107.2	110.9	109.8
Real Effective Exchange Rate	rec	97.5	99.1	98.6	99.7	104.4	102.9	100.0	101.5	104.6	108.5	112.9	112.7

Fund Position

		1994	1995	1996	1997	1998	1999	2000	2001	2002	2003	2004	2005
						Millions of SDRs: End of Period							
Quota	2f.s	67.5	67.5	67.5	67.5	67.5	102.0	102.0	102.0	102.0	102.0	102.0	102.0
SDRs	1b.s	35.6	37.6	39.7	41.9	44.4	22.5	24.5	26.4	28.9	29.8	30.8	32.1
Reserve Position in the Fund	1c.s	25.4	27.3	30.7	31.6	31.6	40.3	40.3	40.3	40.3	40.3	40.3	40.3

International Liquidity

		1994	1995	1996	1997	1998	1999	2000	2001	2002	2003	2004	2005
					Millions of US Dollars Unless Otherwise Indicated: End of Period								
Total Reserves minus Gold	1l.d	1,849.6	1,604.5	1,619.8	1,487.6	1,662.7	1,788.0	1,470.2	1,666.2	2,209.3	2,728.7	2,732.0	2,576.4
SDRs	1b.d	52.0	56.0	57.2	56.6	62.5	30.9	31.9	33.2	39.3	44.3	47.8	45.9
Reserve Position in the Fund	1c.d	37.1	40.5	44.1	42.7	44.5	55.3	52.5	50.6	54.7	59.8	62.5	57.5
Foreign Exchange	1d.d	1,760.5	1,508.0	1,518.6	1,388.3	1,555.7	1,701.9	1,385.8	1,582.4	2,115.2	2,624.5	2,621.7	2,473.0
Gold (Million Fine Troy Ounces)	1ad	.105	.041	.044	.011	.006	.006	.004	.005	.004	.004	.004	.004
Gold (National Valuation)	1and	40.0	15.9	7.2	3.3	1.8	1.8	1.0	1.4	1.2	1.5	1.9	2.3
Monetary Authorities:Other Assets	3..d	27.2	.1	.1	....	.1	....	....	....	....	....	....	....
Banking Institutions: Assets	7a.d	1,129.8	† 2,235.5	2,875.5	3,415.0	5,850.0	6,815.0	8,595.6	6,890.9	9,416.4	† 12,415.1	16,981.9	22,070.1
Liabilities	7b.d	621.5	† 1,576.0	2,333.9	2,972.8	5,242.4	6,339.0	7,905.0	6,164.1	8,361.4	† 10,922.0	15,108.7	20,198.8
Other Banking Insts.: Assets	7e.d	13.7	11.0	9.1	18.0	18.6	15.9	15.6	....	....	....	....	....
Liabilities	7f.d	366.3	—	—	—	—	.5	....	....	....	....	....	....

Monetary Authorities

		1994	1995	1996	1997	1998	1999	2000	2001	2002	2003	2004	2005
						Millions of Liri: End of Period							
Foreign Assets	11	698.01	593.74	568.12	575.53	639.77	740.30	644.17	753.93	880.86	† 936.19	861.02	922.24
Claims on Central Government	12a	39.22	67.73	74.28	59.16	24.32	6.15	9.18	5.80	4.29	† 7.77	21.34	9.12
Claims on Private Sector	12d	....	....	....	....	....	....	....	....	....	2.03	2.24	2.34
Claims on Banking Institutions	12e	....	....	....	....	....	....	....	....	....	.71	.68	.57
Reserve Money	14	584.20	512.98	491.66	498.99	514.05	549.32	568.41	589.40	657.24	† 623.26	651.70	655.58
of which: Currency Outside DMBs	14a	365.91	352.47	362.97	364.42	368.97	385.57	397.36	419.14	436.83	† 460.43	485.99	498.92
Other Liabs. to Banking Insts	14n	....	....	....	....	....	....	....	....	....	108.24	22.37	46.86
Time, Savings,&Fgn.Currency Dep	15	....	....	....	....	....	....	....	....	....	2.47	4.12	.82
Foreign Liabilities	16c	—	—	—	—	—	—	—	—	6.99	† 25.68	1.22	.87
Central Government Deposits	16d	22.25	42.01	33.53	35.70	47.61	96.21	56.18	69.08	104.00	† 83.29	115.73	147.95
Capital Accounts	17a	18.07	46.92	46.84	46.97	47.01	99.44	95.49	95.46	101.46	† 112.21	105.60	100.33
Other Items (Net)	17r	112.70	59.56	70.38	53.03	55.43	1.48	−66.73	5.79	15.46	† −8.45	−15.21	−17.79

Banking Institutions

		1994	1995	1996	1997	1998	1999	2000	2001	2002	2003	2004	2005
						Millions of Liri: End of Period							
Reserves	20	194.50	† 101.31	97.78	126.14	141.73	172.17	153.63	173.57	295.92	† 260.87	192.58	209.27
Foreign Assets	21	415.89	† 787.78	1,034.11	1,334.30	2,207.90	2,808.27	3,762.92	3,115.08	3,755.44	† 4,252.17	5,409.44	8,005.11
Claims on Central Government	22a	135.88	† 149.80	196.50	297.01	391.72	463.02	466.15	550.96	550.82	† 663.22	660.93	624.53
Claims on Nonfin.Pub.Enterprises	22c	....	....	....	....	....	....	....	....	....	159.65	182.01	149.85
Claims on Private Sector	22d	985.51	† 1,097.10	1,261.33	1,350.46	1,492.26	1,658.93	1,822.57	1,976.37	2,015.43	† 1,911.38	2,034.52	2,183.14
Claims on Nonbank Financial Insts	22g	....	....	....	....	....	....	....	....	....	14.40	27.47	31.08
Demand Deposits	24	72.15	† 80.93	87.31	111.39	146.77	190.52	194.40	215.70	241.81	† 829.42	894.61	951.18
Time and Savings Deposits	25	1,105.35	† 1,254.60	1,414.07	1,567.09	1,698.96	1,860.65	1,944.22	2,117.15	2,357.95	† 1,556.94	1,533.60	1,590.69
Restricted Deposits	26b	....	....	....	....	....	....	....	....	....	268.44	279.02	292.49
Foreign Liabilities	26c	228.78	† 555.36	839.34	1,161.54	1,978.55	2,612.12	3,460.58	2,786.53	3,334.70	† 3,740.81	4,812.77	7,326.36
Central Government Deposits	26d	....	....	....	....	....	....	....	....	....	19.21	21.37	42.94
Credit from Monetary Authorities	26g	....	....	....	....	....	....	....	....	....	.20	.22	.24
Liabilities to Nonfin. Institutions	26j	....	....	....	....	....	....	....	....	....	3.32	1.95	2.46
Capital Accounts	27a	40.98	† 128.61	147.62	198.02	299.97	336.14	372.76	447.91	430.77	† 782.35	895.69	1,012.91
Other Items (Net)	27r	284.51	† 116.48	101.40	69.86	109.36	102.95	233.31	248.67	252.37	† 63.15	70.50	−16.30

Banking Survey

		1994	1995	1996	1997	1998	1999	2000	2001	2002	2003	2004	2005
						Millions of Liri: End of Period							
Foreign Assets (Net)	31n	885.12	† 826.16	762.89	748.29	869.13	936.44	946.51	1,082.47	1,294.62	† 1,421.87	1,456.47	1,600.12
Domestic Credit	32	1,136.14	† 1,265.87	1,489.64	1,660.93	1,848.85	2,017.02	2,228.28	2,451.52	2,452.34	† 2,656.52	2,792.12	2,809.82
Claims on Central Govt. (Net)	32an	150.63	† 168.77	228.31	310.47	356.59	358.09	405.71	475.16	436.92	† 568.49	545.17	442.75
Claims on Nonfin.Pub.Enterprises	32c	....	....	....	....	....	....	....	....	....	159.65	182.01	149.85
Claims on Private Sector	32d	985.51	† 1,097.10	1,261.33	1,350.46	1,492.26	1,658.93	1,822.57	1,976.37	2,015.43	† 1,913.40	2,036.77	2,185.48
Claims on Nonbank Financial Insts	32g	....	....	....	....	....	....	....	....	....	14.40	27.47	31.08
Money	34	463.55	† 498.91	489.66	489.63	525.09	580.70	595.72	635.61	680.12	† 1,289.85	1,380.60	1,450.10
Quasi-Money	35	1,105.35	† 1,254.60	1,414.07	1,567.09	1,698.96	1,860.65	1,944.22	2,117.15	2,357.95	† 1,559.40	1,537.72	1,591.51
Restricted Deposits	36b	....	....	....	....	....	....	....	....	....	268.44	279.02	292.49
Liabs. to Nonbank Financial Insts	36j	....	....	....	....	....	....	....	....	....	3.32	1.95	2.46
Capital Accounts	37a	....	....	....	....	....	....	....	....	....	894.56	1,001.29	1,113.24
Other Items (Net)	37r	452.35	† 338.52	348.80	352.50	493.93	512.11	634.85	781.24	708.89	† 62.98	49.17	−40.17
Money plus Quasi-Money	35l	1,568.90	† 1,753.51	1,903.73	2,056.72	2,224.05	2,441.35	2,539.94	2,752.76	3,038.07	† 2,849.25	2,918.33	3,041.61

Interest Rates

		1994	1995	1996	1997	1998	1999	2000	2001	2002	2003	2004	2005
						Percent Per Annum							
Discount Rate (End of Period)	60	5.50	5.50	5.50	5.50	5.50	4.75	4.75	4.25	3.75	† 3.00	3.00	3.25
Treasury Bill Rate	60c	4.29	4.65	4.99	5.08	5.41	5.15	4.89	4.93	4.03	3.29	2.94	3.18
Deposit Rate	60l	4.50	4.50	4.50	4.56	4.64	4.66	4.86	4.84	4.30	3.44	2.63	2.71
Lending Rate	60p	8.50	† 7.38	7.77	7.99	8.09	7.70	7.28	6.90	6.04	5.85	5.32	5.51

Prices, Production, Labor

		1994	1995	1996	1997	1998	1999	2000	2001	2002	2003	2004	2005
						Index Numbers (2000=100): Period Averages							
Consumer Prices	64	85.0	88.8	90.6	93.4	95.6	97.7	100.0	102.9	† 105.2	106.6	109.5	112.8
Harmonized CPI	64h	....	....	88.0	91.5	94.9	97.1	100.0	102.5	105.2	† 107.2	110.1	112.9
Industrial Production	66	† 64.1	64.5	65.1	64.8	71.2	76.6	100.0	85.2	85.3	88.5	87.4	....
						Number in Thousands: Period Averages							
Labor Force	67d	135	138	141	142	143	146	152	156	† 159	160	159	....
Employment	67e	134	149	140	137	137	138	145	146	† 148	147	148	....
Unemployment	67c	6	5	6	7	7	8	7	7	† 7	8	8	7
Unemployment Rate (%)	67r	4.1	3.7	4.4	5.0	5.1	5.3	4.5	4.7	† 4.7	5.0	5.7	....

Malta 181

2006, International Monetary Fund : *International Financial Statistics Yearbook*

		1994	1995	1996	1997	1998	1999	2000	2001	2002	2003	2004	2005
Intl. Transactions & Positions							*Millions of Liri*						
Exports	70	592.42	674.94	624.15	628.93	711.99	791.14	1,072.44	880.68	961.15	928.49	909.32	804.94
Imports, c.i.f.	71	918.77	1,037.65	1,007.80	984.23	1,034.92	1,136.23	1,492.37	1,226.42	1,227.53	1,279.83	1,316.93	1,290.21
Balance of Payments							*Millions of US Dollars: Minus Sign Indicates Debit*						
Current Account, n.i.e.	78ald	−131.5	−407.8	−438.7	−228.1	−219.1	−124.2	−498.4	−168.8	56.4	−224.5	−415.9	−612.8
Goods: Exports f.o.b.	78aad	1,618.5	1,949.4	1,772.8	1,663.4	1,824.5	2,017.3	2,479.0	2,002.3	2,311.4	2,503.2	2,672.4	2,458.1
Goods: Imports f.o.b.	78abd	−2,221.0	−2,759.3	−2,611.1	−2,384.6	−2,497.5	−2,680.2	−3,232.6	−2,568.4	−2,667.9	−3,189.3	−3,624.3	−3,662.3
Trade Balance	78acd	−602.5	−810.0	−838.4	−721.2	−673.0	−662.9	−753.6	−566.1	−356.5	−686.1	−951.9	−1,204.2
Services: Credit	78add	994.6	1,045.1	1,069.2	1,104.1	1,182.8	1,217.6	1,092.1	1,097.5	1,199.1	1,376.3	1,389.6	1,428.1
Services: Debit	78aed	−686.5	−707.4	−710.3	−675.1	−719.7	−761.5	−757.6	−745.4	−776.3	−860.7	−818.3	−859.1
Balance on Goods & Services	78afd	−294.5	−472.3	−479.5	−292.2	−209.9	−206.9	−419.2	−213.9	66.3	−170.5	−380.6	−635.2
Income: Credit	78agd	219.4	286.3	308.2	360.4	511.1	1,241.3	901.6	836.1	853.0	897.4	964.7	1,201.6
Income: Debit	78ahd	−150.6	−247.6	−298.0	−351.6	−578.1	−1,201.2	−1,008.8	−799.1	−832.1	−914.0	−940.9	−1,206.1
Balance on Gds, Serv. & Inc.	78aid	−225.7	−433.6	−469.3	−283.3	−276.9	−166.7	−526.4	−176.9	87.2	−187.1	−356.8	−639.6
Current Transfers, n.i.e.: Credit	78ajd	101.2	80.3	86.7	122.4	115.0	120.5	104.4	190.4	256.4	218.1	237.8	364.4
Current Transfers: Debit	78akd	−7.1	−54.6	−56.0	−67.2	−57.2	−77.9	−76.4	−182.3	−287.2	−255.5	−296.9	−337.6
Capital Account, n.i.e.	78bcd	—	12.9	58.4	8.4	28.6	25.7	18.6	1.5	6.6	17.2	84.1	179.9
Capital Account, n.i.e.: Credit	78bad	—	16.8	64.4	32.9	33.3	31.1	24.1	4.4	8.5	18.6	87.4	191.2
Capital Account: Debit	78bbd	—	−3.9	−6.0	−24.4	−4.7	−5.4	−5.5	−2.9	−1.9	−1.4	−3.3	−11.3
Financial Account, n.i.e.	78bjd	480.9	39.4	220.8	128.0	301.5	435.1	232.0	143.1	231.7	260.6	4.3	495.6
Direct Investment Abroad	78bdd	1.0	−1.2	−72.9	−34.0	−20.8	−59.1	−21.0	−9.5	29.0	−575.2	−.4	28.0
Dir. Invest. in Rep. Econ., n.i.e.	78bed	151.7	129.2	293.2	82.3	283.2	857.4	600.1	235.9	−436.5	996.4	309.8	551.6
Portfolio Investment Assets	78bfd	304.4	−459.9	−120.2	107.6	−141.5	−470.7	−781.7	−282.7	−385.2	−1,571.0	−1,659.1	−2,896.5
Equity Securities	78bkd	247.2	−.1	−1.1	−10.1	6.2	−11.8	2.8	46.7	48.4	−11.6	−28.9	−85.4
Debt Securities	78bld	57.2	−459.8	−119.1	117.7	−147.7	−458.9	−784.6	−329.4	−433.6	−1,559.5	−1,630.2	−2,811.2
Portfolio Investment Liab., n.i.e.	78bgd	—	1.9	3.0	.4	115.3	−33.6	70.7	−215.2	2.3	−20.2	−2.4	7.3
Equity Securities	78bmd	—	−4.1	2.8	.5	42.3	−34.7	67.8	−212.5	13.0	−13.5	2.4	9.1
Debt Securities	78bnd	—	6.0	.2	—	73.0	1.1	2.9	−2.7	−10.7	−6.7	−4.8	−1.8
Financial Derivatives Assets	78bwd	—	—	—	—	—	—	—	—	—	−5.0	−761.6	−1,125.6
Financial Derivatives Liabilities	78bxd	—	—	—	—	—	—	—	—	—	30.0	764.3	1,080.0
Other Investment Assets	78bhd	103.4	−279.4	−561.6	−976.3	−2,059.1	−1,599.6	−220.7	1,102.3	−581.1	−51.1	−1,050.1	−3,146.7
Monetary Authorities	78bod	—	—	—	—	—	—	—	—	—	—	—	—
General Government	78bpd	−.5	−5.2	5.7	−1.1	—	−.1	.4	−1.1	−.5	—	—	—
Banks	78bqd	79.6	−280.5	−581.2	−934.5	−2,077.1	−1,605.1	−264.6	1,104.8	−635.1	−92.8	−981.1	−3,184.6
Other Sectors	78brd	24.4	6.3	14.0	−40.7	18.0	5.6	43.6	−1.4	54.6	41.7	−69.0	37.9
Other Investment Liab., n.i.e.	78bid	−79.7	648.7	679.3	948.0	2,124.4	1,740.6	584.6	−687.6	1,603.2	1,456.5	2,403.9	5,997.5
Monetary Authorities	78bsd	—	—	—	—	—	—	—	8.0	−8.3	16.6	51.3	5.3
General Government	78btd	6.0	−7.7	−8.5	.6	−8.3	−7.0	−16.1	5.4	13.4	43.0	−30.8	−25.0
Banks	78bud	−274.6	681.2	597.7	903.5	2,183.7	1,807.8	573.3	−726.8	1,597.3	1,278.0	2,445.6	5,920.4
Other Sectors	78bvd	188.8	−24.8	90.1	43.9	−50.9	−60.2	19.4	42.1	−24.1	84.2	60.0	96.7
Net Errors and Omissions	78cad	33.4	48.8	74.1	98.4	79.9	−98.4	25.9	279.3	−6.9	90.7	120.8	155.0
Overall Balance	78cbd	382.8	−306.8	−85.4	6.7	190.9	238.3	−221.9	255.0	287.9	144.0	−206.6	217.7
Reserves and Related Items	79dad	−382.8	306.8	85.4	−6.7	−190.9	−238.3	221.9	−255.0	−287.9	−144.0	206.6	−217.7
Reserve Assets	79dbd	−382.8	306.8	85.4	−6.7	−190.9	−238.3	221.9	−255.0	−287.9	−144.0	206.6	−217.7
Use of Fund Credit and Loans	79dcd	—	—	—	—	—	—	—	—	—	—	—	—
Exceptional Financing	79ded	—	—	—	—	—	—	—	—	—	—	—	—
International Investment Position							*Millions of US Dollars*						
Assets	79aad	3,479.5	4,101.6	4,754.1	5,297.3	8,018.0	9,924.6	10,224.7	9,478.4	12,886.6	17,918.7	22,907.3	....
Direct Investment Abroad	79abd	28.3	32.3	107.8	139.9	170.4	185.2	203.1	258.8	271.9	851.2	1,000.6	....
Portfolio Investment	79acd	886.4	1,394.0	1,505.3	1,286.5	1,495.8	2,113.7	2,820.5	3,025.6	4,352.4	7,027.2	9,358.2	....
Equity Securities	79add	2.4	3.8	4.8	15.3	6.5	184.9	170.9	119.7	297.7	471.6	520.5	....
Debt Securities	79aed	884.0	1,390.2	1,500.4	1,271.2	1,489.3	1,928.8	2,649.6	2,905.9	4,054.7	6,555.7	8,837.7	....
Financial Derivatives	79ald	—	—	—	—	—	—	—	—	—	5.2	802.1	....
Other Investment	79afd	689.2	1,027.4	1,600.3	2,433.7	4,656.2	5,829.2	5,729.7	4,511.9	6,053.6	7,277.3	9,012.5	....
Monetary Authorities	79agd	—	—	—	—	—	—	—	—	—	—	7.2	....
General Government	79ahd	2.7	7.9	2.7	3.8	3.8	3.8	3.1	2.9	4.0	4.6	5.0	....
Banks	79aid	396.1	693.8	1,261.3	2,073.0	4,299.2	5,474.7	5,446.9	4,221.3	5,483.1	6,512.9	8,077.4	....
Other Sectors	79ajd	290.4	325.8	336.2	356.9	353.1	350.7	279.6	287.6	566.6	759.9	923.0	....
Reserve Assets	79akd	1,875.6	1,647.8	1,540.8	1,437.2	1,695.6	1,796.5	1,471.4	1,682.2	2,208.7	2,757.7	2,733.9	....
Liabilities	79lad	2,126.0	2,949.6	3,879.4	4,507.0	7,228.1	9,242.8	9,991.1	8,949.4	11,269.9	15,672.9	20,703.6	....
Dir. Invest. in Rep. Economy	79lbd	415.9	561.9	844.0	857.8	1,174.0	1,872.3	2,385.2	2,551.4	2,413.4	3,208.7	3,999.8	....
Portfolio Investment	79lcd	17.4	229.1	228.9	282.1	390.3	516.5	569.4	342.4	369.3	413.0	434.5	....
Equity Securities	79ldd	—	—	—	—	7.1	194.0	262.4	39.3	52.7	47.5	47.6	....
Debt Securities	79led	17.4	229.1	228.9	282.1	383.2	322.5	307.0	303.1	316.6	365.5	387.0	....
Financial Derivatives	79lld	—	—	—	—	—	—	—	—	—	31.6	833.4	....
Other Investment	79lfd	1,692.7	2,158.6	2,806.6	3,367.1	5,663.9	6,854.0	7,036.5	6,055.5	8,487.3	12,019.6	15,435.9	....
Monetary Authorities	79lgd	—	—	—	—	—	—	—	8.3	—	17.5	75.0	5.5	....
General Government	79lhd	152.9	151.7	144.7	135.2	163.3	155.7	162.4	150.6	179.9	262.8	251.9	....
Banks	79lid	702.0	1,378.8	1,950.0	2,559.4	4,921.9	6,223.8	6,446.9	5,470.3	7,864.0	11,107.5	14,566.2	....
Other Sectors	79ljd	837.8	628.1	711.9	672.5	578.6	474.6	418.8	434.6	425.8	574.3	612.4	....

Malta 181

		1994	1995	1996	1997	1998	1999	2000	2001	2002	2003	2004	2005
Government Finance						*Millions of Liri: Year Ending December 31*							
Deficit (-) or Surplus.........................	80	−37.57	−30.87	−92.92	−126.04	−76.48	† −89.24	−89.41	−98.73	....	....	....	....
Total Revenue and Grants..............	81y	358.31	406.84	407.43	450.75	460.31	492.56	534.97	577.99	....	....	....	....
Revenue.......................................	81	345.46	402.32	386.63	440.94	450.27	482.88	525.42	576.60	....	....	....	....
Grants..	81z	12.85	4.52	20.80	9.81	10.04	9.68	9.55	1.39	....	....	....	....
Exp. & Lending Minus Repay.........	82z	395.88	437.71	500.35	576.79	536.79	581.80	624.38	676.72	....	....	....	....
Expenditure................................	82	402.47	447.46	500.00	535.42	576.32	† 581.80	624.38	676.72	....	....	....	....
Lending Minus Repayments.........	83	−6.59	−9.75	.35	41.37	−39.53	† —	—	—	....	....	....	....
Total Financing.............................	80h	37.57	30.87	92.92	126.04	76.48	† 89.25	89.39	98.74	....	....	....	....
Total Net Borrowing....................	84	35.61	32.89	104.04	145.21	† —	77.77	87.29	87.23	....	....	....	....
Net Domestic.............................	84b	28.70	35.44	105.44	146.60	100.00	† 79.93	92.39	86.10	....	....	....	....
Net Foreign................................	85b	6.91	−2.55	−1.40	−1.39	−4.14	† −2.16	−5.10	1.13	....	....	....	....
Use of Cash Balances...................	87	1.96	−2.02	−11.12	−19.17	−19.38	† 11.48	2.10	11.51	....	....	....	....
Total Debt by Residence.................	88	339.59	410.79	514.47	661.35	761.59	839.85	924.97	1,012.69	....	....	....	....
Domestic.......................................	88a	283.33	357.36	462.68	610.90	715.08	795.50	885.72	972.31	....	....	....	....
Foreign...	89a	56.26	53.43	51.79	50.45	46.51	44.35	39.25	40.38	....	....	....	....
National Accounts							*Millions of Liri*						
Househ.Cons.Expend.,incl.NPISHs....	96f	608.3	700.4	764.9	946.0	981.6	1,054.5	1,116.7	1,148.2	1,146.1	1,190.0	1,228.0	1,287.5
Government Consumption Expend...	91f	209.5	235.2	259.8	281.7	297.6	303.8	326.1	358.6	378.1	398.3	416.0	425.4
Gross Fixed Capital Formation..........	93e	305.4	365.2	345.3	318.1	357.9	341.3	373.5	332.8	280.4	363.1	363.1	400.5
Changes in Inventories.....................	93i	10.0	1.2	−1.4	−13.5	−57.7	−36.1	80.4	6.3	−9.7	−41.4	−31.3	40.1
Exports of Goods and Services..........	90c	994.4	1,074.7	1,045.6	1,069.7	1,167.2	1,292.1	1,567.4	1,395.4	1,515.7	1,461.3	1,401.1	1,345.8
Imports of Goods and Services (-).....	98c	1,099.0	1,231.2	1,212.8	1,180.7	1,248.1	1,374.5	1,750.6	1,490.8	1,489.3	1,526.0	1,529.4	1,566.0
Gross Domestic Product (GDP).........	99b	1,028.5	1,145.5	1,201.3	1,421.5	1,498.5	1,581.1	1,713.5	1,750.5	1,821.2	1,845.1	1,847.4	1,933.2
Net Primary Income from Abroad.....	98.n	19.3	12.0	3.2	3.3	−25.4	15.5	−50.4	16.5	10.7	−4.9	3.7	−10.7
Gross National Income (GNI)............	99a	1,047.9	1,157.5	1,204.5	1,424.7	1,473.2	1,596.5	1,663.1	1,767.0	1,831.9	1,840.3	1,851.1	1,922.6
Consumption of Fixed Capital..........	99cf	60.0	77.2	86.9	188.9	204.7	216.7	232.8	248.2	253.6	263.8	291.1	277.5
GDP Volume 1995 Prices...............	99b.p	1,047.8	1,145.5	1,191.2	1,249.0	1,291.8	1,344.2	1,428.9	....	....	....	....	....
GDP Volume 2000 Prices...............	99b.p	....	....	....	....	....	....	1,713.5	1,706.3	1,735.7	1,691.1	1,681.8	1,721.4
GDP Volume (2000=100)...............	99bvp	73.3	80.2	83.4	87.4	90.4	94.1	† 100.0	99.6	101.3	98.7	98.1	100.5
GDP Deflator (2000=100)...............	99bip	81.9	83.4	84.1	94.9	96.7	98.1	100.0	102.6	104.9	109.1	109.8	112.3
						Millions: Midyear Estimates							
Population...............................	99z	.37	.38	.38	.38	.39	.39	.39	.39	.40	.40	.40	.40

Mauritania 682

		1994	1995	1996	1997	1998	1999	2000	2001	2002	2003	2004	2005
Exchange Rates						*Ouguiyas per SDR: End of Period*							
Official Rate	aa	187.401	203.813	204.837	227.146	289.744	308.815	328.724	331.928	365.317	394.674	....	....
						Ouguiyas per US Dollar End of Period (ae) Period Average (rf)							
Official Rate	ae	128.370	137.110	142.450	168.350	205.780	225.000	252.300	264.120	268.710	265.600	....	....
Official Rate	rf	123.575	129.768	137.222	151.853	188.476	209.514	238.923	255.629	271.739	263.030		
Fund Position						*Millions of SDRs: End of Period*							
Quota	2f.s	47.5	47.5	47.5	47.5	47.5	64.4	64.4	64.4	64.4	64.4	64.4	64.4
SDRs	1b.s	—	—	1.0	.3	—	—	.3	.2	.2	.1	—	.1
Reserve Position in the Fund	1c.s												
Total Fund Cred.&Loans Outstg	2tl	58.8	67.1	74.6	83.4	78.3	77.6	75.4	83.2	82.9	70.2	58.2	48.5
International Liquidity						*Millions of US Dollars Unless Otherwise Indicated: End of Period*							
Total Reserves minus Gold	1l.d	39.7	85.5	141.2	200.8	202.9	224.3	279.9	284.5	396.2	415.3	....	....
SDRs	1b.d	—	.1	1.4	.4	—	—	.4	.2	.2	.1	—	.1
Reserve Position in the Fund	1c.d	—	—	—	—	—	—	—	—	—	—	—	—
Foreign Exchange	1d.d	39.7	85.4	139.8	200.4	202.8	224.3	279.5	284.3	396.0	415.2	....	....
Gold (Million Fine Troy Ounces)	1ad	.012	.012	.012	.012	.012	.012	.012	.012	.012	.012	....	....
Gold (National Valuation)	1and	4.3	4.4	4.2	3.3	3.3	3.3	3.1	3.1	3.1	4.0	....	....
Monetary Authorities: Other Liab	4..d	199.2	212.0	205.3	209.7	209.6	202.0	195.0	195.2	197.2	184.1	....	....
Deposit Money Banks: Assets	7a.d	27.7	25.9	27.0	24.7	24.1	22.1	21.6	19.0	19.4	18.5	....	....
Liabilities	7b.d	105.8	67.4	35.5	26.4	15.0	13.6	12.5	12.1	12.1	17.5	....	....
Monetary Authorities						*Millions of Ouguiyas: End of Period*							
Foreign Assets	11	5,746	12,425	21,030	34,425	42,546	51,335	71,429	76,028	107,383	111,024	....	....
Claims on Central Government	12a	17,949	17,109	17,109	17,102	17,012	16,912	16,912	16,912	16,912	22,130		
Claims on Nonfin.Pub.Enterprises	12c	60	60	60	60	60	60	60	60	60	60		
Claims on Private Sector	12d	581	695	755	1,023	1,003	1,065	1,185	869	889	1,090	....	
Claims on Deposit Money Banks	12e	2,571	1,872	2,334	2,793	2,789	2,232	1,539	1,539	1,539	21,400		
Claims on Nonbank Financial Insts	12g	49	49	49	49	49	49	49	49	49	49		
Reserve Money	14	21,966	20,724	10,462	9,089	8,406	8,788	9,222	9,723	10,038	10,009		
of which: Currency Outside DMBs	14a	8,598	7,383	5,093	5,854	5,801	5,963	6,402	6,688	6,282	6,412		
Restricted Deposits	16b	91	147	91	82	55	154	225	49	49	49		
Foreign Liabilities	16c	12,093	14,649	15,543	19,232	23,096	23,968	24,848	27,905	30,301	27,845		
Long-Term Foreign Liabilities	16cl	16,342	16,702	15,160	17,069	20,923	22,108	24,794	23,873	22,684	21,041		
Central Government Deposits	16d	8,024	13,342	30,844	42,765	51,300	55,512	68,516	68,413	96,974	128,029		
Capital Accounts	17a	4,888	4,415	4,059	4,821	5,161	5,594	6,339	6,912	7,181	7,126		
Other Items (Net)	17r	−36,448	−37,769	−34,822	−37,606	−46,075	−44,471	−42,770	−41,418	−40,395	−38,353		
Deposit Money Banks						*Millions of Ouguiyas: End of Period*							
Reserves	20	12,775	12,486	5,355	3,083	2,390	2,984	2,887	3,105	3,884	3,521	....	
Foreign Assets	21	3,561	3,556	3,853	4,165	4,962	4,964	5,450	5,022	5,224	4,901	....	
Claims on Central Government	22a	916	782	2,742	4,302	4,202	4,637	3,882	6,152	8,602	5,479	....	
Claims on Nonfin.Pub.Enterprises	22c	—	—	—	—	—	—	—	—	—	—	....	
Claims on Private Sector	22d	42,500	30,722	34,634	37,279	39,835	46,942	58,486	68,939	82,534	90,197	....	
Claims on Nonbank Financial Insts	22g	—	—	—	—	—	—	—	—	—	—		
Demand Deposits	24	11,145	10,674	11,015	11,629	12,467	13,697	17,749	21,033	22,628	25,790		
Time Deposits	25	7,612	7,817	8,476	9,101	9,282	8,708	8,800	10,929	13,192	14,313		
Foreign Liabilities	26c	13,583	9,246	5,054	4,451	3,078	3,058	3,164	3,195	3,255	4,646		
Long-Term Foreign Liabilities	26cl	—	—	—	—	—	—	—	—	—	—		
Central Government Deposits	26d	1,552	3,198	3,428	4,058	6,487	13,596	18,085	23,365	34,050	11,757		
Central Govt. Lending Funds	26f	1,208	—	—	—	—	—	—	—	—	—		
Credit from Monetary Authorities	26g	3,358	7	7	7	7	7	7	7	7	20,477		
Capital Accounts	27a	21,972	20,709	22,359	23,260	24,203	25,169	28,636	29,923	32,358	33,243		
Other Items (Net)	27r	−678	−4,105	−3,755	−3,677	−4,135	−4,708	−5,736	−5,233	−5,246	−6,126		
Monetary Survey						*Millions of Ouguiyas: End of Period*							
Foreign Assets (Net)	31n	−32,711	−24,616	−10,874	−2,162	411	7,165	24,073	26,077	56,367	62,393	....	
Domestic Credit	32	52,479	32,877	21,077	12,992	4,374	557	−6,027	1,203	−21,978	−20,781	....	
Claims on Central Govt. (Net)	32an	9,289	1,351	−14,421	−25,419	−36,573	−47,559	−65,807	−68,714	−105,510	−112,177		
Claims on Nonfin.Pub.Enterprises	32c	60	60	60	60	60	60	60	60	60	60		
Claims on Private Sector	32d	43,081	31,417	35,389	38,302	40,838	48,007	59,671	69,808	83,423	91,287		
Claims on Nonbank Financial Inst	32g	49	49	49	49	49	49	49	49	49	49		
Money	34	19,816	18,202	16,227	17,579	18,504	19,675	24,151	27,721	28,910	32,202		
Quasi-Money	35	7,612	7,817	8,476	9,101	9,282	8,708	8,800	10,929	13,192	14,313		
Restricted Deposits	36b	91	147	91	82	55	154	225	49	49	49		
Central Govt. Lending Funds	36f	1,208	—	—	—	—	—	—	—	—	—		
Other Items (Net)	37r	−8,959	−17,905	−14,591	−15,932	−23,649	−20,815	−15,130	−11,418	−7,762	−4,957		...;
Money plus Quasi-Money	35l	27,428	26,019	24,703	26,680	27,786	28,383	32,951	38,650	42,102	46,515		
Interest Rates						*Percent Per Annum*							
Discount Rate (End of Period)	60	....	....	....	....	....	....	....	....	....	11.00	....	....
Deposit Rate	60l	....	....	....	....	....	....	....	....	....	8.00		
Lending Rate	60p	....	....	....	....	....	....	....	....	....	21.00	....	....
Prices						*Index Numbers (2000=100): Period Averages*							
Consumer Prices	64	73.8	78.6	82.3	86.1	93.1	96.8	100.0	104.7	108.8	114.4	126.3	141.6

Mauritania 682

		1994	1995	1996	1997	1998	1999	2000	2001	2002	2003	2004	2005
Intl. Transactions & Positions													
Balance of Payments		*Millions of US Dollars: Minus Sign Indicates Debit*											
Current Account, n.i.e.	78ald	−69.9	22.1	91.3	47.8	77.2	....	....	....	....	....	....	....
Goods: Exports f.o.b.	78aad	399.7	476.4	480.0	423.6	358.6	....	....	....	....	....	....	....
Goods: Imports f.o.b.	78abd	−352.3	−292.6	−346.1	−316.5	−318.7	....	....	....	....	....	....	....
Trade Balance	78acd	47.4	183.8	133.9	107.2	40.0	....	....	....	....	....	....	....
Services: Credit	78add	26.0	27.9	31.6	34.9	34.0	....	....	....	....	....	....	....
Services: Debit	78aed	−181.1	−217.0	−231.3	−200.0	−152.5	....	....	....	....	....	....	....
Balance on Goods & Services	78afd	−107.7	−5.3	−65.8	−57.9	−78.6	....	....	....	....	....	....	....
Income: Credit	78agd	1.1	1.3	.9	1.4	2.5	....	....	....	....	....	....	....
Income: Debit	78ahd	−47.7	−49.5	−45.9	−40.3	−34.0	....	....	....	....	....	....	....
Balance on Gds, Serv. & Inc.	78aid	−154.3	−53.5	−110.8	−96.8	−110.2	....	....	....	....	....	....	....
Current Transfers, n.i.e.: Credit	78ajd	113.3	94.7	217.5	157.9	198.3	....	....	....	....	....	....	....
Current Transfers: Debit	78akd	−28.9	−19.2	−15.5	−13.3	−10.8	....	....	....	....	....	....	....
Capital Account, n.i.e.	78bcd	—	—	—	—	—	....	....	....	....	....	....	....
Capital Account, n.i.e.: Credit	78bad	—	—	—	—	—	....	....	....	....	....	....	....
Capital Account: Debit	78bbd	—	—	—	—	—	....	....	....	....	....	....	....
Financial Account, n.i.e.	78bjd	−11.4	−10.2	−86.1	−17.3	−25.9	....	....	....	....	....	....	....
Direct Investment Abroad	78bdd						....	....	....	....	....	....	....
Dir. Invest. in Rep. Econ., n.i.e.	78bed	2.1	7.0	—	—	.1	....	....	....	....	....	....	....
Portfolio Investment Assets	78bfd						....	....	....	....	....	....	....
Equity Securities	78bkd	—	—	—	—	—	....	....	....	....	....	....	....
Debt Securities	78bld	—	—	—	—	—	....	....	....	....	....	....	....
Portfolio Investment Liab., n.i.e.	78bgd	−.2	−.5	−.4	—	−.4	....	....	....	....	....	....	....
Equity Securities	78bmd	—	—	—	—	—	....	....	....	....	....	....	....
Debt Securities	78bnd	−.2	−.5	−.4	—	−.4	....	....	....	....	....	....	....
Financial Derivatives Assets	78bwd	....	....	....	....	....	....	....	....	....	....	....	....
Financial Derivatives Liabilities	78bxd	....	....	....	....	....	....	....	....	....	....	....	....
Other Investment Assets	78bhd	169.3	211.5	236.0	191.1	190.1	....	....	....	....	....	....	....
Monetary Authorities	78bod	....	....	....	....	....	....	....	....	....	....	....	....
General Government	78bpd	−2.2	−.4	−.2	—	—	....	....	....	....	....	....	....
Banks	78bqd	—	—	—	—	—	....	....	....	....	....	....	....
Other Sectors	78brd	171.5	211.9	236.2	191.1	190.1	....	....	....	....	....	....	....
Other Investment Liab., n.i.e.	78bid	−182.6	−228.2	−321.6	−208.4	−215.7	....	....	....	....	....	....	....
Monetary Authorities	78bsd	—	—	—	—	—	....	....	....	....	....	....	....
General Government	78btd	−7.0	.2	−.2	5.3	.7	....	....	....	....	....	....	....
Banks	78bud	—	—	—	—	—	....	....	....	....	....	....	....
Other Sectors	78bvd	−175.5	−228.4	−321.4	−213.7	−216.4	....	....	....	....	....	....	....
Net Errors and Omissions	78cad	−23.5	−18.1	−1.0	−3.0	−8.1	....	....	....	....	....	....	....
Overall Balance	78cbd	−104.7	−6.2	4.2	27.6	43.2	....	....	....	....	....	....	....
Reserves and Related Items	79dad	104.7	6.2	−4.2	−27.6	−43.2	....	....	....	....	....	....	....
Reserve Assets	79dbd	46.9	−42.9	−58.3	−58.8	−46.3	....	....	....	....	....	....	....
Use of Fund Credit and Loans	79dcd	17.9	12.2	10.9	12.0	−6.9	....	....	....	....	....	....	....
Exceptional Financing	79ded	40.0	36.9	43.3	19.3	10.0	....	....	....	....	....	....	....
Government Finance		*Billions of Ouguiyas: Year Ending December 31*											
Deficit (-) or Surplus	80	−3.19	1.58	11.26	....	....	....	....	....	....	....	....	....
Revenue	81	29.46	33.21	44.72	....	....	....	....	....	....	....	....	....
Grants Received	81z	2.55	2.75	3.28	....	....	....	....	....	....	....	....	....
Exp. & Lending Minus Repay	82z	35.20	34.38	36.74	....	....	....	....	....	....	....	....	....
Financing													
Domestic	84a	−1.47	−7.52	−15.81	....	....	....	....	....	....	....	....	....
Foreign	85a	4.66	5.94	4.55	....	....	....	....	....	....	....	....	....
National Accounts		*Millions of Ouguiyas*											
Househ.Cons.Expend.,incl.NPISHs	96f	87,863	79,984	99,913	111,300	139,600	145,070	161,920	161,970	....	....	....	....
Government Consumption Expend	91f	25,883	30,072	31,111	32,460	34,900	41,270	46,950	50,760	....	....	....	....
Gross Fixed Capital Formation	93e	20,147	23,684	17,326	25,090	25,500	25,960	29,610	32,730	....	....	....	....
Changes in Inventories	93i	3,590	4,308	9,015	2,630	60	6,420	5,150	8,100	....	....	....	....
Exports of Goods and Services	90c	52,479	65,306	70,066	69,480	73,800	90,310	94,220	100,680	....	....	....	....
Imports of Goods and Services (-)	98c	65,800	66,015	79,113	78,330	94,500	107,010	116,100	137,100	....	....	....	....
Gross Domestic Product (GDP)	99b	124,162	137,339	148,318	162,620	185,300	202,000	221,700	247,100	267,155	352,518	....	....
		Millions: Midyear Estimates											
Population	99z	2.24	2.30	2.36	2.43	2.50	2.57	2.64	2.72	2.81	2.89	2.98	3.07

Mauritius 684

		1994	1995	1996	1997	1998	1999	2000	2001	2002	2003	2004	2005
Exchange Rates						*Rupees per SDR: End of Period*							
Market Rate..........................	aa	26.077	26.258	25.842	30.041	34.896	34.955	36.327	38.197	39.694	38.766	43.802	43.831
						Rupees per US Dollar: End of Period (ae) Period Average (rf)							
Market Rate..........................	ae	17.863	17.664	17.972	22.265	24.784	25.468	27.882	30.394	29.197	26.088	28.204	30.667
Market Rate..........................	rf	17.960	17.386	17.948	21.057	23.993	25.186	26.250	29.129	29.962	27.901	27.499	29.496
Fund Position						*Millions of SDRs: End of Period*							
Quota............................	2f.s	73.3	73.3	73.3	73.3	73.3	101.6	101.6	101.6	101.6	101.6	101.6	101.6
SDRs.............................	1b.s	21.3	21.7	22.2	22.5	22.8	16.1	16.5	16.8	17.0	17.2	17.5	18.0
Reserve Position in the Fund...........	1c.s	7.3	7.3	7.4	7.4	7.4	14.5	14.5	14.5	14.5	21.9	21.9	17.5
Total Fund Cred.&Loans Outstg.......	2tl	—	—	—	—	—	—	—	—	—	—	—	—
International Liquidity						*Millions of US Dollars Unless Otherwise Indicated: End of Period*							
Total Reserves minus Gold..............	1l.d	747.6	863.3	896.1	693.3	559.0	731.0	897.4	835.6	1,227.4	1,577.3	1,605.9	1,339.9
SDRs.............................	1b.d	31.2	32.2	31.9	30.3	32.2	22.1	21.4	21.1	23.2	25.6	27.2	25.7
Reserve Position in the Fund.........	1c.d	10.7	10.9	10.6	9.9	10.4	19.9	18.9	18.2	19.7	32.5	34.0	25.0
Foreign Exchange.....................	1d.d	705.7	820.2	853.7	653.0	516.5	689.1	857.1	796.3	1,184.5	1,519.2	1,544.7	1,289.2
Gold (Million Fine Troy Ounces)........	1ad	.062	.062	.062	.062	.062	.062	.062	.062	.062	.062	.062	.062
Gold (National Valuation)................	1and	4.0	4.1	4.0	6.1	11.9	12.3	12.3	12.3	12.3	21.1	23.9	25.9
Government Assets......................	3bad	.1	....	....	....	....	....	....	....	....	....	....	....
Monetary Authorities: Other Liab.....	4..d	1.9	.7	1.1	.9	.6	.2	.7	.3	.6	6.3	7.0	4.5
Banking Institutions: Assets...........	7a.d	178.3	264.2	263.6	327.4	361.0	383.8	400.2	427.0	486.4	5,965.7	7,403.8	8,620.5
Liabilities..................	7b.d	39.8	67.5	59.5	38.4	127.9	104.3	106.6	98.3	205.5	3,998.7	4,878.0	5,202.4
Monetary Authorities						*Millions of Rupees: End of Period*							
Foreign Assets.........................	11	13,425.7	15,322.0	16,176.8	15,571.8	14,150.3	18,930.9	25,366.1	† 25,782.0	36,151.5	† 41,698.4	45,968.9	41,883.9
Claims on Central Government..........	12a	1,527.2	439.0	703.1	1,416.1	4,709.2	2,188.2	2,159.1	† 2,171.6	1,703.4	† 810.8	1,881.5	3,714.4
Claims on State and Local Govts......	12b	....	....	....	....	....	....	—	—	—	† —	—	—
Claims on Nonfin.Pub.Enterprises.....	12c	....	....	....	....	....	....	—	—	—	† 85.2	116.5	182.8
Claims on Private Sector................	12d	....	....	....	....	....	....	—	—	—	—	—	—
Claims on Banking Institutions..........	12e	291.0	672.8	446.2	410.8	707.8	375.1	328.3	† 660.3	2,171.0	† 2,172.7	1,937.0	2,032.1
Claims on Nonbank Financial Insts...	12g	—	24.8	162.6	378.9	570.0	506.4	356.4	† 215.7	55.4	† 51.9	309.4	277.2
Reserve Money.........................	14	8,403.1	9,628.3	9,123.0	8,923.4	9,759.6	10,522.3	11,763.5	† 12,989.7	14,920.7	† 16,149.0	18,805.1	22,015.8
of which: Currency Outside Banks..	14a	4,412.2	4,847.2	5,050.7	5,410.4	5,832.9	6,126.7	6,647.6	† 7,329.0	8,286.0	† 9,267.0	10,651.5	11,664.1
Other Liabs. to Banking Insts........	14n	434.0	490.9	2,237.4	190.2	—	—	—	† —	—	† 6,155.9	6,956.2	3,492.9
Time, Savings,&Fgn.Currency Dep....	15					—	—	—	† —	—	† 236.9	265.2	303.2
Liabs. of Central Bank: Securities.....	16ac	—	159.0	717.7	240.0	—	—	—	† —	—	† 2,577.0	3,364.7	1,195.2
Restricted Deposits......................	16b					—	—	—	† —	—	† 67.5	63.3	61.8
Foreign Liabilities......................	16c	33.2	12.1	19.9	20.7	14.8	5.7	19.2	† 10.4	17.9	† 165.6	196.4	139.1
Central Government Deposits...........	16d	6.2	452.7	251.2	3.1	13.6	3.4	3,421.0	† 757.7	9,394.2	† 6,093.9	1,944.6	1,973.5
Liab. to Nonbank Financial Insts.......	16j	....	....	....	....	....	....	....	† —	—	—	—	—
Capital Accounts.......................	17a	443.6	446.4	439.9	506.0	582.4	583.3	604.9	† 634.3	631.1	† 13,389.7	18,545.1	19,520.6
Other Items (Net).....................	17r	5,923.9	5,269.2	4,699.6	7,894.3	9,766.9	10,885.8	12,401.3	† 14,437.5	15,117.4	† −16.6	72.8	−611.7
Banking Institutions						*Millions of Rupees: End of Period*							
Reserves...............................	20	3,982.4	4,740.9	4,067.2	3,506.9	3,899.8	4,365.3	5,030.0	† 5,512.9	6,523.1	† 6,855.8	8,064.9	10,022.0
Claims on Mon.Author.: Securities...	20c	434.0	490.9	2,237.4	190.2	—	—	—	† —	—	† 6,132.8	6,669.2	3,469.4
Other Claims on Monetary Author....	20n	....	....	....	....	....	....	—	—	—	† —	—	—
Foreign Assets.........................	21	3,185.7	4,667.7	4,736.9	7,289.0	8,947.3	9,775.5	11,159.4	† 12,978.1	13,591.6	† 155,630.5	208,818.4	264,362.8
Claims on Central Government........	22a	10,344.5	14,623.7	14,219.6	17,025.7	13,318.5	15,759.0	15,001.3	† 18,157.4	28,648.0	† 36,707.9	43,202.4	44,754.3
Claims on State and Local Govts......	22b	....	....	....	....	....	....	—	—	—	† 59.6	65.5	59.1
Claims on Nonfin.Pub.Enterprises....	22c	109.6	272.1	468.2	562.8	778.1	1,389.6	2,076.7	† 2,377.8	1,391.8	† 6,050.0	5,808.8	9,728.5
Claims on Private Sector................	22d	29,001.8	33,026.9	34,447.6	43,292.3	56,432.2	61,742.1	69,163.8	† 76,405.4	83,690.4	† 114,564.0	128,161.7	139,492.4
Claims on Nonbank Financial Insts...	22g	....	....	....	....	....	....	—	—	—	† 2,122.4	2,405.4	3,869.2
Demand Deposits......................	24	4,442.7	4,683.1	4,771.2	5,193.1	5,726.6	5,840.7	6,560.7	† 7,969.6	9,751.9	† 19,283.2	22,588.5	24,711.2
Time, Savings,& Fgn.Currency Dep...	25	37,151.5	44,994.8	48,855.0	57,696.1	64,377.2	75,462.6	82,244.8	† 90,551.8	101,305.9	† 157,879.8	192,227.9	232,911.8
Money Market Instruments..............	26aa	93.9	90.9	196.3	167.9	197.3	104.0	126.4	† 185.2	148.0	† 92.4	166.1	924.2
Restricted Deposits....................	26b	30.4	27.7	24.9	15.7	17.4	43.1	14.3	† 26.5	25.9	† —	—	—
Foreign Liabilities......................	26c	710.7	1,192.9	1,068.8	855.5	3,169.0	2,655.5	2,971.7	† 2,986.4	5,741.7	† 104,318.2	137,580.7	159,541.3
Central Government Deposits..........	26d	84.2	1,468.0	319.6	277.0	132.0	264.4	190.9	† 225.0	234.1	† 1,614.9	1,867.3	1,946.1
Credit from Monetary Authorities.....	26g	156.2	550.0	—	250.0	475.0	250.0	250.0	† 660.3	2,171.0	† 2,203.0	1,961.5	2,029.2
Liab. to Nonbank Financial Insts.......	26j	....	....	....	....	....	....	....	† —	—	† 2,231.4	557.3	500.8
Capital Accounts.......................	27a	5,144.4	5,447.8	6,620.4	7,842.4	9,092.1	10,848.6	11,953.6	† 12,037.2	14,477.0	† 31,281.8	37,991.8	42,617.3
Other Items (Net).....................	27r	−756.0	−633.0	−1,679.3	−430.8	189.3	−2,437.4	−1,881.2	† 789.6	−10.6	† 9,218.1	8,255.2	10,575.6
Banking Survey						*Millions of Rupees: End of Period*							
Foreign Assets (Net)...................	31n	15,867.5	18,784.7	19,825.0	21,984.6	19,913.8	26,045.2	33,534.6	† 35,763.3	43,983.5	† 92,845.0	117,010.3	146,566.3
Domestic Credit.......................	32	40,892.7	46,465.8	49,430.3	62,395.7	75,662.4	81,317.5	85,145.4	† 98,345.2	105,860.7	† 152,742.9	178,139.2	198,158.2
Claims on Central Govt. (Net)........	32an	11,781.3	13,142.0	14,351.9	18,161.7	17,882.1	17,679.4	13,548.5	† 19,346.3	20,723.1	† 29,809.8	41,272.0	44,549.2
Claims on State and Local Govts....	32b	....	....	....	....	....	....	—	—	—	† 59.6	65.5	59.1
Claims on Nonfin.Pub.Enterprises...	32c	109.6	272.1	468.2	562.8	778.1	1,389.6	2,076.7	† 2,377.8	1,391.8	† 6,050.0	5,808.8	9,728.5
Claims on Private Sector................	32d	29,001.8	33,026.9	34,447.6	43,292.3	56,432.2	61,742.1	69,163.8	† 76,405.4	83,690.4	† 114,649.2	128,278.2	139,675.1
Claims on Nonbank Financial Insts.	32g	—	24.8	162.6	378.9	570.0	506.4	356.4	† 215.7	55.4	† 2,174.2	2,714.7	4,146.4
Money................................	34	8,863.4	9,570.5	9,827.0	10,609.6	11,586.4	11,997.7	13,294.2	† 15,446.4	18,149.5	† 28,577.5	33,330.3	36,702.8
Quasi-Money.........................	35	37,151.5	44,994.8	48,855.0	57,696.1	64,377.2	75,462.6	82,244.8	† 90,551.8	101,305.9	† 158,116.7	192,493.1	233,215.0
Money Market Instruments..............	36aa	93.9	90.9	196.3	167.9	197.3	104.0	126.4	† 185.2	148.0	† 92.4	166.1	924.2
Liabs. of Central Bank: Securities......	36ac	—	159.0	717.7	240.0	—	—	—	† —	—	† 2,577.0	3,364.7	1,195.2
Restricted Deposits....................	36b	30.4	27.7	24.9	15.7	17.4	43.1	14.3	† 26.5	25.9	† —	—	—
Liab. to Nonbank Financial Insts.......	36j	....	....	....	....	....	....	....	† —	—	† 2,231.4	557.3	500.8
Capital Accounts.......................	37a	5,588.0	5,894.2	7,060.3	8,348.4	9,674.5	11,431.9	12,558.5	† 12,671.5	15,108.1	† 44,671.5	56,536.9	62,138.0
Other Items (Net).....................	37r	5,033.1	4,513.4	2,574.1	7,302.7	9,723.4	8,323.3	10,441.8	† 15,227.1	15,106.8	† 9,253.8	8,637.7	9,986.9
Money plus Quasi-Money..............	35l	46,014.9	54,565.3	58,682.0	68,305.7	75,963.6	87,460.3	95,539.0	† 105,998.2	119,455.4	† 186,694.3	225,823.5	269,917.7
Interest Rates						*Percent Per Annum*							
Discount Rate (End of Period)..........	60	13.80	11.40	11.82	10.46	17.19	....	....	....	....	....	....	....
Money Market Rate....................	60b	10.23	10.35	9.96	9.43	8.99	10.01	7.66	7.25	6.20	3.22	1.33	2.45
Savings Rate...........................	60k	8.50	8.08	8.00	8.00	8.08	9.00	7.46	7.08	6.44	5.25	3.88	4.73
Deposit Rate..........................	60l	11.04	12.23	10.77	9.08	9.28	10.92	9.61	9.78	9.88	9.53	8.15	7.25
Lending Rate..........................	60p	18.92	20.81	20.81	18.92	19.92	21.63	20.77	21.10	21.00	21.00	21.00	21.04

		1994	1995	1996	1997	1998	1999	2000	2001	2002	2003	2004	2005
Prices and Labor						*Index Numbers (2000=100): Period Averages*							
Share Prices	62	96.2	92.5	81.6	92.6	110.4	101.5	100.0	91.3	90.0	115.6	156.1	184.0
Consumer Prices	64	69.6	73.8	78.7	† 84.0	89.8	96.0	100.0	† 105.4	112.1	116.5	122.0	128.0
						Number in Thousands: Period Averages							
Labor Force	67d	499	484	482	491	499	507	514	512	514	523	533	543
Employment	67e	292	290	287	288	295	297	298	477	477	482	488	491
Unemployment	67c	....	24	28	32	34	39	45	35	37	41	45	52
Unemployment Rate	67r	....	5.1	5.8	6.6	6.9	7.7	8.8	6.9	7.3	7.7	8.5	9.5
Intl. Transactions & Positions							*Millions of Rupees*						
Exports	70	24,097	26,756	32,312	33,694	39,634	40,025	40,882	47,511	53,893	53,022	54,905	63,370
Imports, c.i.f.	71	34,548	34,363	41,082	46,093	49,811	56,629	54,928	57,940	64,608	65,942	76,387	93,371
Imports, f.o.b.	71.v	31,601	31,508	38,073	42,570	46,015	....	....	....	....	....	....	....
							2000=100						
Volume of Exports	72	80.2	83.9	88.4	† 91.7	95.4	97.7	100.0	115.6	120.7	112.3	106.1	113.8
Volume of Imports	73	80.3	75.5	84.1	96.2	99.3	106.5	100.0	97.7	103.4	100.6	96.9	97.2
Export Prices	76	73.2	77.7	86.4	† 89.3	101.8	101.1	100.0	101.8	110.7	116.7	128.6	139.3
Import Prices	76.x	73.7	78.0	83.5	† 85.5	90.6	96.2	100.0	107.7	112.8	120.3	144.9	180.8
Balance of Payments					*Millions of US Dollars: Minus Sign Indicates Debit*								
Current Account, n.i.e.	78ald	−232.1	−21.9	34.0	−88.9	3.3	−124.2	−36.9	276.1	249.4	93.2	−107.5	....
Goods: Exports f.o.b.	78aad	1,376.9	1,571.7	1,810.6	1,600.1	1,669.3	1,589.2	1,552.2	1,628.2	1,801.3	1,898.1	2,004.3	....
Goods: Imports f.o.b.	78abd	−1,773.9	−1,812.2	−2,136.3	−2,036.1	−1,933.3	−2,107.9	−1,944.4	−1,846.0	−2,012.6	−2,201.1	−2,579.4	....
Trade Balance	78acd	−397.0	−240.5	−325.7	−436.0	−264.0	−518.7	−392.1	−217.7	−211.3	−303.0	−575.0	....
Services: Credit	78add	632.7	777.7	960.8	893.7	916.9	1,035.6	1,070.2	1,222.0	1,148.7	1,280.1	1,455.6	....
Services: Debit	78aed	−546.4	−641.3	−672.9	−656.3	−718.0	−728.2	−762.5	−810.1	−792.7	−906.3	−1,023.5	....
Balance on Goods & Services	78afd	−310.6	−104.2	−37.9	−198.6	−65.1	−211.3	−84.5	194.1	144.7	70.8	−142.9	....
Income: Credit	78agd	31.7	52.2	31.1	47.0	47.8	43.0	48.7	75.2	79.9	47.0	51.8	....
Income: Debit	78ahd	−56.4	−71.3	−75.1	−64.6	−74.4	−59.5	−64.9	−60.9	−66.7	−77.1	−65.7	....
Balance on Gds, Serv. & Inc.	78aid	−335.3	−123.3	−81.8	−216.3	−91.7	−227.8	−100.7	208.4	157.9	40.8	−156.8	....
Current Transfers, n.i.e.: Credit	78ajd	129.6	146.8	182.8	206.4	186.8	196.4	167.6	193.1	195.3	163.0	168.1	....
Current Transfers: Debit	78akd	−26.3	−45.4	−67.0	−79.0	−91.8	−92.8	−103.8	−125.4	−103.8	−110.6	−118.7	....
Capital Account, n.i.e.	78bcd	−1.3	−1.1	−.8	−.5	−.8	−.5	−.6	−1.4	−1.9	−.9	−1.6	....
Capital Account, n.i.e.: Credit	78bad	—	—	—	—	—	—	—	.4	—	—	—	....
Capital Account: Debit	78bbd	−1.3	−1.1	−.8	−.5	−.8	−.5	−.6	−1.8	−1.9	−.9	−1.6	....
Financial Account, n.i.e.	78bjd	41.4	25.1	91.9	−18.6	−26.0	180.5	258.0	−240.2	84.2	89.7	8.9	....
Direct Investment Abroad	78bdd	−1.1	−3.6	−2.7	−3.2	−13.7	−6.4	−13.0	−2.9	−8.7	6.0	−31.8	....
Dir. Invest. in Rep. Econ., n.i.e.	78bed	20.0	18.7	36.7	55.3	12.2	49.4	265.6	−27.7	32.1	62.6	13.9	....
Portfolio Investment Assets	78bfd	−.3	—	−2.0	−96.8	43.6	59.5	−18.8	−17.7	−18.3	−27.1	−52.4	....
Equity Securities	78bkd	—	—	—	—	−3.3	59.5	−18.8	−17.7	−18.3	−27.1	−52.4	....
Debt Securities	78bld	−.3	—	−2.0	−96.8	46.9	—	—	—	—	—	—	....
Portfolio Investment Liab., n.i.e.	78bgd	2.1	175.9	36.8	30.6	−28.7	−15.3	−120.4	−1.6	.9	8.9	15.3	....
Equity Securities	78bmd	2.1	22.0	36.8	30.6	5.0	−15.3	−3.5	−8.7	−.7	8.1	19.3	....
Debt Securities	78bnd	—	154.0	—	—	−33.7	—	−116.8	7.1	1.6	.8	−3.9	....
Financial Derivatives Assets	78bwd	....	—	—	—	—	—	—	....	....	....	....	....
Financial Derivatives Liabilities	78bxd	....	—	—	—	—	—	—	—	....	....	....	....
Other Investment Assets	78bhd	−64.6	−136.4	17.9	−115.7	−66.7	−245.9	−307.6	−253.0	−106.7	−22.8	−49.4	....
Monetary Authorities	78bod	....	....	....	....	—	—	—	—	—	—	—	....
General Government	78bpd	—	—	—	—	—	—	—	—	—	—	—	....
Banks	78bqd	−11.5	−85.2	−3.9	−121.2	−69.1	−32.9	−51.5	−61.7	−20.4	14.1	−44.2	....
Other Sectors	78brd	−53.1	−51.2	21.8	5.5	2.4	−213.0	−256.1	−191.3	−86.2	−36.9	−5.2	....
Other Investment Liab., n.i.e.	78bid	85.2	−29.5	5.1	111.2	27.3	339.4	452.1	62.7	184.9	62.0	113.2	....
Monetary Authorities	78bsd	—	—	—	—	—	—	—	—	—	—	—	....
General Government	78btd	−14.1	−18.8	−20.4	9.0	−14.2	−11.4	91.6	−118.7	34.5	−8.2	−7.3	....
Banks	78bud	9.2	27.7	−6.9	−10.1	96.4	−20.4	13.7	.4	93.1	6.1	56.7	....
Other Sectors	78bvd	90.1	−38.5	32.5	112.3	−54.9	371.2	346.8	181.0	57.3	64.1	63.8	....
Net Errors and Omissions	78cad	148.5	106.7	−76.8	73.4	−41.9	133.9	10.1	−86.3	9.4	40.4	72.7	....
Overall Balance	78cbd	−43.5	108.8	48.3	−34.6	−65.4	189.7	230.6	−51.8	341.1	222.4	−27.5	....
Reserves and Related Items	79dad	43.5	−108.8	−48.3	34.6	65.4	−189.7	−230.6	51.8	−341.1	−222.4	27.5	....
Reserve Assets	79dbd	43.5	−108.8	−48.3	34.6	65.4	−189.7	−230.6	51.8	−341.1	−222.4	27.5	....
Use of Fund Credit and Loans	79dcd	—	—	—	—	—	—	—	—	—	—	—	....
Exceptional Financing	79ded	—	—	—	—	—	—	—	—	—	—	—	....
International Investment Position							*Millions of US Dollars*						
Assets	79aad	....	....	....	....	....	....	....	....	....	....	....	....
Direct Investment Abroad	79abd	—	—	—	—	—	—	—	—	—	—	—	....
Portfolio Investment	79acd	—	—	—	—	—	—	—	—	—	—	—	....
Equity Securities	79add	....	—	—	—	—	—	—	—	—	—	—	....
Debt Securities	79aed	....	—	—	—	—	—	—	—	—	—	—	....
Financial Derivatives	79ald	....	—	—	—	—	—	—	—	—	—	—	....
Other Investment	79afd	167.6	275.9	288.1	342.9	396.3	405.3	420.1	445.9	497.1	560.7	554.4	....
Monetary Authorities	79agd	—	—	—	—	—	—	—	—	—	—	—	....
General Government	79ahd	—	—	—	—	—	—	—	—	—	—	—	....
Banks	79aid	142.5	227.9	228.4	298.8	361.0	383.8	400.2	427.0	465.5	503.1	512.5	....
Other Sectors	79ajd	25.1	48.0	59.7	44.1	35.3	21.4	19.9	19.0	31.6	57.6	41.9	....
Reserve Assets	79akd	751.8	867.5	900.2	699.5	571.0	743.3	909.8	848.0	1,239.8	1,598.4	1,629.9	....
Liabilities	79lad	....	....	....	....	....	....	....	....	....	....	....	....
Dir. Invest. in Rep. Economy	79lbd	—	—	—	—	—	—	—	—	—	—	—	....
Portfolio Investment	79lcd	—	156.3	167.2	150.9	117.7	178.2	46.6	47.9	52.2	51.6	62.5	....
Equity Securities	79ldd	....	—	—	—	—	40.2	33.4	22.2	22.5	33.8	49.9	....
Debt Securities	79led	....	156.3	167.2	150.9	117.7	138.0	13.1	25.7	29.7	17.8	12.7	....
Financial Derivatives	79lld	....	—	—	—	—	—	—	—	—	—	—	....
Other Investment	79lfd	1,128.3	1,189.2	1,259.9	1,167.2	1,202.3	1,157.1	1,225.0	1,034.8	1,160.4	1,229.9	1,199.8	....
Monetary Authorities	79lgd	—	—	—	—	—	—	—	—	—	—	—	....
General Government	79lhd	324.8	328.3	352.6	300.1	294.1	273.4	358.3	230.2	285.6	300.4	294.4	....
Banks	79lid	39.8	67.5	59.5	38.4	127.9	104.3	106.6	98.3	196.7	225.3	267.3	....
Other Sectors	79ljd	763.7	793.4	847.9	828.7	780.3	779.4	760.1	706.3	678.2	704.2	638.2	....

Mauritius 684

		1994	1995	1996	1997	1998	1999	2000	2001	2002	2003	2004	2005
Government Finance						*Millions of Rupees: Year Ending June 30*							
Deficit (-) or Surplus........................	80	† −167	−814	−3,084	−3,427	858	† −1,558	−1,458	† 1,171	−5,608	−6,036	−5,648	−4,432
Revenue..	81	14,076	14,396	14,469	18,276	20,327	† 23,082	25,587	† 25,374	27,418	32,447	36,075	38,876
Grants Received........................	81z	130	262	221	63	216	† 135	161	† 199	317	363	618	444
Expenditure................................	82	14,271	15,502	17,280	20,260	21,446	† 25,479	27,032	† 30,592	32,843	37,887	41,902	43,104
Lending Minus Repayments...........	83	102	−31	493	1,506	−1,761	† −703	174	† −6,189	500	959	439	648
Financing													
Net Borrowing: Domestic..............	84a	† 1,738	2,059	1,543	3,228	3,010	† 1,191	3,561	† 2,241	9,419	12,846	−2,704	5,264
Net borrowing: Foreign.................	85a	† −113	−371	2,374	198	−275	† −1,170	−510	† −3,584	1,030	87	−468	524
Use of Cash Balances...................	87	† −1,458	−874	−834	1	−3,594	† 1,538	−1,593	† 172	−4,841	−6,897	8,820	−1,356
Debt: Domestic...........................	88a	14,149	17,311	19,215	21,921	22,857	† 24,326	29,424	† 33,764	48,973	63,531	62,224	70,507
Debt: Foreign..............................	89a	5,766	5,778	9,159	9,666	10,752	† 10,037	9,891	† 6,816	8,785	9,074	8,445	9,290
National Accounts						*Millions of Rupees*							
Househ.Cons.Expend.,incl.NPISHs....	96f	39,845	44,023	48,937	54,149	† 61,331	67,418	72,536	78,773	86,736	96,153	111,819	128,968
Government Consumption Expend...	91f	9,337	9,957	11,387	12,415	† 13,753	15,485	16,986	18,196	19,855	22,272	25,043	27,017
Gross Fixed Capital Formation.........	93e	11,576	11,119	12,741	14,530	† 16,826	19,590	20,340	20,463	21,456	20,450	38,003	39,744
Changes in Inventories....................	93i	908	1,470	−123	3,180	† 2,920	−521	3,846	−2,631	482	1,384	5,110	2,883
Exports of Goods and Services..........	90c	36,249	41,205	50,465	54,194	† 65,711	69,099	73,841	90,463	88,301	88,714	94,859	111,097
Imports of Goods and Services (-)....	98c	41,833	42,908	51,010	58,498	† 66,543	72,861	74,513	82,636	83,964	86,694	99,024	122,673
Gross Domestic Product (GDP).........	99b	63,906	70,247	79,365	88,175	† 100,042	108,077	120,290	132,146	142,484	157,383	175,810	187,037
Net Primary Income from Abroad.....	98.n	−443	−332	−789	−372	† −637	−594	−783	393	396	−833	−390	−272
Gross National Income (GNI)............	99a	63,463	69,915	78,576	87,803	† 99,405	107,483	119,507	132,539	142,880	156,550	175,420	186,765
GDP Volume 1992 Prices..............	99b.p	54,924	57,263	60,395	63,845	† 67,750	69,601	....	....	....	....	....	....
GDP Volume 1999 Prices.................	99b.p	....	....	....	....	....		108,077	117,831	120,850	123,173	128,435	135,411	138,912
GDP Volume (2000=100)...............	99bvp	72.4	75.5	79.6	84.1	89.3	† 91.7	100.0	102.6	104.5	109.0	114.9	117.9
GDP Deflator (2000=100)...............	99bip	73.4	77.4	82.9	87.1	93.2	98.0	100.0	107.1	113.3	120.0	127.2	131.9
						Millions: Midyear Estimates							
Population.................................	99z	1.11	1.12	1.14	1.15	1.16	1.17	1.19	1.20	1.21	1.22	1.23	1.24

		1994	1995	1996	1997	1998	1999	2000	2001	2002	2003	2004	2005
Exchange Rates						*Pesos per SDR: End of Period*							
Market Rate..............aa=........	wa	7.7737	11.3605	11.2893	10.9064	13.8902	13.0585	12.4717	11.4894	14.0201	16.6964	17.4943	15.4042
					Pesos per US Dollar: End of Period (we) Period Average (wf)								
Market Rate..............ae=........	we	5.3250	7.6425	7.8509	8.0833	9.8650	9.5143	9.5722	9.1423	10.3125	11.2360	11.2648	10.7777
Market Rate..............rf=........	wf	3.3751	6.4194	7.5994	7.9185	9.1360	9.5604	9.4556	9.3423	9.6560	10.7890	11.2860	10.8979
Fund Position						*Millions of SDRs: End of Period*							
Quota.................................	2f.s	1,753	1,753	1,753	1,753	1,753	2,586	2,586	2,586	2,586	2,586	2,586	2,586
SDRs...................................	1b.s	121	1,074	179	490	240	575	281	283	288	292	299	312
Reserve Position in the Fund..........	1c.s	—	—	—	—	—	—	—	—	226	527	578	416
Total Fund Cred.&Loans Outstg........	2tl	2,644	10,648	9,234	6,735	5,952	3,259	—	—	—	—	—	—
International Liquidity						*Millions of US Dollars Unless Otherwise Indicated: End of Period*							
Total Reserves minus Gold..............	1l.d	6,278	16,847	19,433	28,797	31,799	31,782	35,509	44,741	50,594	58,956	64,141	74,054
SDRs..........................	1b.d	177	1,597	257	661	337	790	366	356	392	433	465	445
Reserve Position in the Fund..........	1c.d	—	—	—	—	—	—	—	—	308	782	898	594
Foreign Exchange.........................	1d.d	6,101	15,250	19,176	28,136	31,461	30,992	35,142	44,384	49,895	57,740	62,778	73,015
Gold (Million Fine Troy Ounces).......	1ad	.426	.514	.255	.190	.223	.159	.249	.231	.225	.170	.139	.108
Monetary Authorities: Other Liab....	4..d	66	91	84	560	552	377	226	321	196	174	156	313
Banking Institutions: Assets...........	7a.d	2,829	4,089	4,825	12,612	14,954	20,292	35,890	51,851	60,841	87,435	95,997	120,059
Liabilities...................	7b.d	43,800	44,355	38,029	41,380	39,852	40,010	50,627	47,626	54,715	98,689	116,129	140,790
Nonbank Financial Insts.: Assets......	7e.d	....	....	....									
Liabilities...................	7f.d	....	....	....									
Monetary Authorities						*Millions of Pesos: End of Period*							
Foreign Assets........................	11	34,490	122,814	140,217	† 239,470	323,604	310,238	349,523	† 418,141	537,205	672,129	724,435	796,331
Claims on Central Government........	12a	2,000	13,211	10,488	† —	—	—	—	† —	—	—	—	—
Claims on State and Local Govts......	12b	....	....	....	....	....	....	....					
Claims on Nonfin.Pub.Enterprises....	12c	—	—	—	† —	—	—	—	† —	—	—	—	—
Claims on Private Sector...............	12d	—	—	—	† —	—	—	—	† —	—	—	—	—
Claims on Banking Institutions........	12e	102,100	45,021	11,883	† 2,430	699	96,326	95,120	† 83,533	110,132	89,564	105,243	124,445
Claims on Nonbank Financial Insts...	12g	38,043	78,001	70,327	† 81,067	93,796	99,926	102,755	† 103,817	97,200	92,059	81,901	81,106
Reserve Money........................	14	60,923	81,274	100,069	† 109,136	145,959	198,731	219,225	† 225,730	263,937	303,614	340,178	380,034
of which: Currency Outside Banks..	14a	52,035	60,839	74,338	† 94,185	115,917	164,158	181,938	† 198,849	232,082	263,387	300,982	335,905
Other Liabs. to Banking Insts...........	14n	—	—	—	† 41,771	60,983	87,549	49,125	† 129,308	246,549	288,884	307,877	350,382
Time, Savings,&Fgn.Currency Dep....	15	10	6	12	† 4,795	3,736	7,756	13,151	† —	—	—	—	—
Liabs. of Central Bank: Securities.....	16ac				† —	—	—	20,989	† 125,583	130,703	112,603	154,880	168,555
Restricted Deposits....................	16b	....	....	....	....	....	....	....	8,955	14,040	16,707	19,455	6,149
Foreign Liabilities........................	16c	20,906	121,665	104,910	† 77,835	88,390	46,072	2,169	† 2,940	2,045	1,955	1,736	3,324
Central Government Deposits.........	16d	71,270	26,195	16,124	† 82,330	95,005	185,941	274,351	† 180,545	103,270	126,084	124,958	195,724
Liab. to Nonbank Financial Insts........	16j	8,884	23,420	18,732	† 21,159	12,936	5,387	5	† —	—	—	—	—
Capital Accounts.......................	17a	2,327	3,367	3,346	† 30,030	49,767	35,949	30,163	† −4,447	24,470	24,712	−14,609	−86,280
Other Items (Net).........................	17r	12,313	3,120	−10,279	† −44,090	−38,676	−60,893	−61,781	† −63,123	−40,475	−20,806	−22,897	−16,004
Banking Institutions						*Millions of Pesos: End of Period*							
Reserves..............................	20	10,879	117,373	241,398	† 42,922	71,803	114,991	72,272	† 116,266	183,557	223,979	271,134	325,428
Claims on Mon.Author.:Securities.....	20c	—	—	—	† —	—	—	845	† 108,791	165,523	172,226	135,413	176,263
Other Claims on Monetary Author....	20n	—	—	—	† 12,851	235	264	271	† —	4	3	14	—
Foreign Assets.........................	21	15,065	31,250	37,877	† 102,614	147,522	193,066	344,894	† 475,450	635,134	982,527	1,070,318	1,276,752
Claims on Central Government........	22a	106,267	185,036	176,293	† 545,296	601,093	759,777	901,439	† 869,043	879,997	911,969	919,479	934,928
Claims on State and Local Govts......	22b	23,773	16,574	13,032	† 20,902	24,641	25,908	31,249	† 36,075	42,485	55,455	100,315	111,311
Claims on Nonfin.Pub.Enterprises....	22c	8,083	8,868	7,629	† 12,454	15,137	12,860	19,645	† 18,461	20,772	33,089	48,024	39,914
Claims on Private Sector.................	22d	550,204	537,611	474,757	† 801,971	866,844	883,086	943,328	† 820,433	982,635	1,055,007	1,128,629	1,323,449
Claims on Nonbank Financial Insts...	22g	48,480	117,201	235,663	† 328,585	463,576	642,663	606,910	† 796,740	808,889	813,302	749,029	748,394
Demand Deposits.......................	24	93,080	87,695	131,732	† 173,026	193,564	233,478	273,265	† 327,497	368,757	421,303	442,239	529,120
Time, Savings,& Fgn.Currency Dep...	25	283,140	416,152	511,140	† 852,953	993,605	1,153,602	1,019,917	† 1,111,996	1,115,009	1,221,283	1,382,333	1,438,922
Money Market Instruments..............	26aa	30,693	50,762	52,031	† 241,844	255,835	324,367	320,638	† 17,018	24,715	27,520	32,598	37,131
Restricted Deposits.....................	26b	....	....	....	....	....	....	....					
Foreign Liabilities.......................	26c	233,235	338,986	298,561	† 336,668	393,141	380,662	486,519	† 436,707	571,189	1,108,987	1,294,776	1,497,216
Central Government Deposits.........	26d	8,510	18,349	27,075	† 22,031	29,454	21,358	19,915	† 36,726	55,125	52,765	53,834	89,765
Credit from Monetary Authorities.....	26g	46,223	48,184	16,769	† 7,021	6,361	101,918	102,149	† 85,208	110,949	91,178	106,709	124,618
Liab. to Nonbank Financial Insts.......	26j	39,508	76,040	119,675	† 243,813	349,299	366,103	329,631	† 622,486	377,446	399,398	149,784	204,117
Capital Accounts.......................	27a	44,014	21,911	20,970	† 26,784	41,678	42,913	38,862	† 9,843	43,571	41,899	299,770	362,554
Other Items (Net).......................	27r	−15,652	−44,166	8,696	† −36,546	−72,087	8,213	329,958	† 593,778	1,052,236	883,224	660,312	652,996
Banking Survey						*Millions of Pesos: End of Period*							
Foreign Assets (Net).......................	31n	−204,586	−306,587	−225,377	† −72,419	−10,405	76,571	205,729	† 453,945	599,105	543,714	498,241	572,543
Domestic Credit........................	32	697,070	911,958	944,990	† 1,685,913	1,940,628	2,216,921	2,311,061	† 2,427,299	2,673,584	2,782,032	2,848,585	2,953,613
Claims on Central Govt. (Net).......	32an	28,487	153,703	143,582	† 440,935	476,633	552,478	607,113	† 651,772	721,602	733,120	740,687	649,439
Claims on State and Local Govts....	32b	23,773	16,574	13,032	† 20,902	24,641	25,908	31,249	† 36,075	42,485	55,455	100,315	111,311
Claims on Nonfin.Pub.Enterprises...	32c	8,083	8,868	7,629	† 12,454	15,137	12,860	19,645	† 18,461	20,772	33,089	48,024	39,914
Claims on Private Sector...............	32d	550,204	537,611	474,757	† 801,971	866,844	883,086	943,328	† 820,433	982,635	1,055,007	1,128,629	1,323,449
Claims on Nonbank Financial Inst..	32g	86,523	195,202	305,990	† 409,652	557,373	742,589	709,665	† 900,558	906,090	905,361	830,930	829,500
Money.................................	34	145,115	148,534	206,070	† 267,211	323,912	407,601	465,485	† 526,346	600,839	684,690	743,221	865,024
Quasi-Money............................	35	283,150	416,158	511,152	† 857,749	997,340	1,161,358	1,033,068	† 1,111,996	1,115,009	1,221,283	1,382,333	1,438,922
Money Market Instruments..............	36aa	30,693	50,762	52,031	† 241,844	255,835	324,367	320,638	† 17,018	24,715	27,520	32,598	37,131
Liabs. of Central Bank: Securities.....	36ac	—	—	—	† —	—	—	20,989	† 125,583	130,703	112,603	154,880	168,555
Restricted Deposits.....................	36b	....	....	....	....	....	....	....	8,955	14,040	16,707	19,455	6,149
Liab. to Nonbank Financial Insts.......	36j	48,392	99,460	138,407	† 264,973	362,235	371,490	329,636	† 622,486	377,446	399,398	149,784	204,117
Capital Accounts.........................	37a	46,341	25,278	24,316	† 56,813	91,445	78,862	69,025	† 5,396	68,041	66,611	285,161	276,274
Other Items (Net).........................	37r	−61,207	−134,821	−212,364	† −75,095	−100,544	−50,188	277,947	† 463,462	941,897	796,935	579,394	529,984
Money plus Quasi-Money.................	35l	428,265	564,692	717,222	† 1,124,959	1,321,252	1,568,960	1,498,554	† 1,638,343	1,715,848	1,905,973	2,125,554	2,303,946

Mexico 273

		1994	1995	1996	1997	1998	1999	2000	2001	2002	2003	2004	2005
Nonbank Financial Institutions					*Millions of Pesos End of Period*								
Reserves	40	....	....	....	86	14,568	10,418	10,648	†4,773	72	220	522	52
Claims on Mon.Author.:Securities	40c	....	....	....	—	—	—	680	†4,546	10,721	14,843	46,697	44,344
Other Claims on Monetary Author.	40n	....	....	....	....	....	....	....	†—	—	—	—	—
Foreign Assets	41	....	....	....	—	—	—	—	†—	—	—	—	—
Claims on Central Government	42a	....	....	....	25,866	77,863	145,919	209,235	†309,187	390,111	476,465	530,790	634,310
Claims on State and Local Govts	42b	....	....	....	793	901	979	1,002	†992	972	405	340	288
Claims on Nonfin.Pub.Enterprises	42c	....	....	....					†—				
Claims on Private Sector	42d	....	....	....	39,982	46,419	54,664	63,399	†89,489	126,641	153,630	175,017	200,523
Claims on Banking Institutions	42e	....	....	....	149,809	159,688	183,637	150,659	†136,945	128,082	126,856	123,712	121,734
Restricted Deposits	46b	....	....	....	....	....	....	....					
Foreign Liabilities	46c	....	....	....	—	—	—	—	†—	—	—	—	—
Central Government Deposits	46d	....	....	....	4,139	7,072	7,324	361	†308	193	162	119	89
Credit from Monetary Authorities	46g	....	....	....	86,892	104,060	116,901	118,479	†119,054	113,485	106,962	100,637	94,603
Credit from Banking Institutions	46h	....	....	....	6,662	6,912	5,779	6,577	†9,109	7,142	7,485	7,012	6,512
Capital Accounts	47a	....	....	....	70,189	133,345	207,111	249,549	†336,953	416,398	512,246	606,907	712,475
Insurance Technical Reserves	47d	....	....	....	47,642	67,485	92,471	112,448	†138,604	169,110	189,282	215,869	257,613
Other Items (Net)	47r	....	....	....	1,012	−19,435	−33,969	−51,791	†−58,096	−49,729	−43,718	−53,466	−70,041
Financial Survey					*Millions of Pesos: End of Period*								
Foreign Assets (Net)	51n	....	....	....	−72,419	−10,405	76,571	205,729	†453,945	599,105	543,714	498,241	572,543
Domestic Credit	52	....	....	....	1,338,763	1,501,367	1,668,570	1,874,670	†1,926,101	2,285,026	2,507,009	2,723,683	2,959,145
Claims on Central Govt. (Net)	52an	....	....	....	462,662	547,424	691,073	816,047	†960,651	1,111,520	1,209,423	1,271,358	1,283,660
Claims on State and Local Govts	52b	....	....	....	21,695	25,542	26,887	32,251	†37,067	43,457	55,860	100,655	111,599
Claims on Nonfin.Pub.Enterprises	52c	....	....	....	12,454	15,137	12,860	19,645	†18,461	20,772	33,089	48,024	39,914
Claims on Private Sector	52d	....	....	....	841,953	913,263	937,750	1,006,727	†909,922	1,109,276	1,208,637	1,303,646	1,523,972
Liquid Liabilities	55l	....	....	....	1,124,873	1,306,684	1,558,542	1,487,906	†1,573,496	1,671,172	1,875,975	2,095,093	2,301,752
Money Market Instruments	56aa	....	....	....	241,844	255,835	324,367	320,638	†15,787	23,622	26,419	31,687	35,791
Liabs. of Central Bank: Securities	56ac	....	....	....	....	....	....	20,309	†121,037	119,982	97,759	108,183	124,210
Restricted Deposits	56b	....	....	....	....	....	....	....	4,563	14,028	16,701	19,449	6,149
Capital Accounts	57a	....	....	....	127,002	224,790	285,973	318,574	†342,349	484,439	578,857	892,068	988,749
Insurance Technical Reserves	57d	....	....	....	47,642	67,485	92,471	112,448	†138,604	169,110	189,282	215,869	257,613
Other Items (Net)	57r	....	....	....	−275,018	−363,833	−516,213	−179,475	†184,210	401,778	265,729	−140,426	−182,577
Money (National Definitions)					*Millions of Pesos End of Period*								
Base Money	19ma	56,935	66,809	83,991	108,891	131,528	188,718	208,943	225,580	263,937	303,614	340,178	380,034
M1	59ma	163,828	171,638	245,260	325,760	388,240	489,943	565,014	680,706	766,486	857,692	946,567	1,069,012
M2	59mb	554,930	754,407	995,166	1,290,063	1,663,220	2,030,685	2,331,055	2,731,762	3,027,890	3,420,526	3,777,229	4,349,047
M3	59mc	657,102	784,495	1,025,835	1,320,540	1,689,755	2,047,566	2,359,433	2,760,176	3,053,144	3,454,361	3,866,384	4,488,225
M4	59md	724,203	869,209	1,116,079	1,400,372	1,775,644	2,121,261	2,415,814	2,809,004	3,096,919	3,487,026	3,905,356	4,528,087
M4a	59mda	737,608	898,115	1,183,256	1,521,907	1,903,797	2,278,628	2,571,000	2,982,719	3,304,619	3,750,715	4,222,003	4,862,096
M4 National Currency	59mdb	530,328	754,710	985,566	1,278,477	1,633,640	1,977,057	2,279,009	2,653,662	2,949,614	3,361,912	3,746,011	4,339,470
M4 Foreign Currency	59mdd	193,876	114,498	130,512	121,895	142,004	144,204	136,805	155,342	147,305	125,114	159,345	188,617
Interest Rates					*Percent Per Annum*								
Money Market Rate	60b	16.47	†60.92	33.61	21.91	26.89	24.10	16.96	12.89	8.17	6.83	7.15	9.59
Treasury Bill Rate	60c	14.10	48.44	31.39	19.80	24.76	21.41	15.24	11.31	7.09	6.23	6.82	9.20
Savings Rate	60k	5.38	6.67	6.58	7.57	6.38	5.85	4.86	3.26	2.00	1.72	1.42	.93
Deposit Rate	60l	15.03	39.82	26.40	16.36	15.45	11.60	8.26	6.23	3.76	3.09	2.70	3.46
Average Cost of Funds	60n	15.50	45.12	†31.57	20.04	22.39	20.89	14.59	10.95	6.17	5.15	5.41	7.64
Lending Rate	60p	19.30	59.43	36.39	22.14	26.36	23.74	16.93	12.80	8.20	6.91	7.22	9.90
Government Bond Yield	61	....	51.74	32.81	21.44	....	20.11	†15.81	†10.28	10.13	8.98	9.54	9.42
Prices, Production, Labor					*Index Numbers (2000=100): Period Averages*								
Share Prices	62	38.7	34.1	48.5	68.2	65.1	81.8	100.0	93.9	100.0	110.3	163.9	221.9
Wholesale Prices	63	32.1	44.5	59.5	70.0	81.2	92.7	100.0	105.0	110.4	†118.6	129.7	135.1
Consumer Prices	64	30.9	41.7	56.0	67.6	78.3	91.3	100.0	†106.4	111.7	116.8	122.3	127.1
Wages, Monthly	65	115.4	100.9	90.9	90.4	93.0	94.4	100.0	106.7	108.7	110.2	110.5	110.3
Industrial Production	66	76.4	70.4	77.5	84.7	90.0	94.2	100.0	96.5	96.4	96.3	100.3	101.9
Manufacturing Production	66ey	72.2	68.7	76.2	83.6	89.8	93.5	100.0	96.2	95.6	94.3	98.1	99.3
Mining Production	66zx	87.1	84.8	91.8	95.8	98.4	96.3	100.0	101.5	101.9	105.6	109.2	110.6
Crude Petroleum	66aa	87.3	85.9	94.2	99.3	101.6	97.1	100.0	102.4	103.3	108.8	109.6	108.9
					Number in Thousands: Period Averages								
Labor Force	67d	....	35,558	36,581	38,345	39,507	39,751	39,634	39,683	41,086	41,516	43,399	....
Employment	67e	....	33,881	35,226	37,360	38,659	38,953	39,502	39,386	40,302	40,633	42,306	....
Unemployment	67c	....	1,677	1,355	985	904	695	659	687	784	883	1,093	....
Unemployment Rate (%)	67r	....	4.7	3.7	2.6	2.3	1.8	1.6	1.7	1.9	2.1	2.5	....
Intl. Transactions & Positions					*Millions of US Dollars*								
Excluding Maquiladoras													
Exports	70n.d	34,318	46,864	59,084	65,266	64,376	72,954	86,987	81,562	82,641	87,561	101,252	125,217
Imports, f.o.b	71nvd	58,362	44,893	58,961	73,475	82,816	91,655	112,749	110,798	109,383	111,933	128,723	146,285
Including Maquiladoras													
Exports	70..d	60,882	79,542	96,000	110,431	117,460	136,391	166,368	158,547	160,682	165,396	189,084	213,891
Imports, f.o.b	71.vd	79,346	72,453	89,469	109,808	125,373	141,975	174,501	168,276	168,679	170,490	197,347	221,415

Mexico 273

Balance of Payments		1994	1995	1996	1997	1998	1999	2000	2001	2002	2003	2004	2005
						Millions of US Dollars: Minus Sign Indicates Debit							
Current Account, n.i.e.	78ald	−29,662	−1,576	−2,537	−7,695	−16,017	−13,956	−18,707	−17,675	−13,544	−8,641	−6,631	−4,804
Goods: Exports f.o.b.	78aad	60,882	79,542	96,000	110,431	117,539	136,362	166,121	158,780	161,046	164,766	187,999	214,233
Goods: Imports f.o.b.	78abd	−79,346	−72,453	−89,469	−109,808	−125,373	−141,975	−174,458	−168,397	−168,679	−170,546	−196,810	−221,820
Trade Balance	78acd	−18,464	7,089	6,531	623	−7,834	−5,613	−8,337	−9,617	−7,633	−5,780	−8,811	−7,587
Services: Credit	78add	10,321	9,780	10,723	11,183	11,661	11,734	13,756	12,701	12,740	12,617	14,004	16,089
Services: Debit	78aed	−13,043	−9,715	−10,818	−12,614	−13,008	−14,471	−17,360	−17,194	−17,660	−18,141	−19,779	−21,447
Balance on Goods & Services	78afd	−21,185	7,153	6,436	−807	−9,181	−8,350	−11,942	−14,110	−12,553	−11,304	−14,586	−12,944
Income: Credit	78agd	3,347	3,713	4,032	4,431	4,909	4,475	5,977	5,326	4,051	3,858	5,617	5,323
Income: Debit	78ahd	−15,605	−16,402	−17,507	−16,536	−17,733	−16,366	−19,712	−18,205	−15,294	−15,037	−14,691	−17,652
Balance on Gds, Serv. & Inc.	78aid	−33,444	−5,536	−7,039	−12,913	−22,005	−20,242	−25,677	−26,989	−23,796	−22,483	−23,660	−25,273
Current Transfers, n.i.e.: Credit	78ajd	3,822	3,995	4,533	5,243	6,015	6,313	6,999	9,336	10,287	13,880	17,108	20,526
Current Transfers: Debit	78akd	−40	−35	−30	−25	−27	−27	−30	−22	−35	−37	−80	−57
Capital Account, n.i.e.	78bcd	....	....	—	—	—	—	—	—	—	—	—	—
Capital Account, n.i.e.: Credit	78bad	....	....	—	—	—	—	—	—	—	—	—	—
Capital Account: Debit	78bbd	....	....	—	—	—	—	—	—	—	—	—	—
Financial Account, n.i.e.	78bjd	15,787	−10,487	13,298	24,445	19,871	18,052	23,659	25,664	25,951	21,093	10,847	12,758
Direct Investment Abroad	78bdd	....	....	—	—	—	—	—	−4,404	−891	−1,253	−4,432	−6,171
Dir. Invest. in Rep. Econ., n.i.e.	78bed	10,973	9,526	9,186	12,830	12,409	13,631	17,588	27,151	18,275	14,184	18,674	18,055
Portfolio Investment Assets	78bfd	−767	−662	544	−708	−769	−836	1,290	3,857	1,134	91	1,718	—
Equity Securities	78bkd	—	—	—	—	—	—	—	—	—	—	—	—
Debt Securities	78bld	−767	−662	544	−708	−769	−836	1,290	3,857	1,134	91	1,718	—
Portfolio Investment Liab., n.i.e.	78bgd	8,182	−9,715	12,585	4,704	1,027	12,005	−1,134	3,882	−632	3,864	5,942	10,189
Equity Securities	78bmd	4,084	519	2,801	3,215	−666	3,769	447	151	−104	−123	−2,522	3,353
Debt Securities	78bnd	4,099	−10,234	9,785	1,488	1,693	8,236	−1,581	3,731	−528	3,987	8,465	6,836
Financial Derivatives Assets	78bwd	....	....	....	....	....	....	....	....	....	....	....	....
Financial Derivatives Liabilities	78bxd	....	....	....	....	....	....	....	....	....	....	....	....
Other Investment Assets	78bhd	−4,903	−6,694	−6,885	7,423	1,200	−3,169	5,809	−3,287	11,601	8,627	−6,413	−6,368
Monetary Authorities	78bod												
General Government	78bpd	−1,400	−3,619	−22	56	25	—	—	—	—	—	—	—
Banks	78bqd	−885	−1,510	−1,017	5,111	−1,208	−1,894	45	−5,423	7,401	4,456	−2,724	−5,256
Other Sectors	78brd	−2,618	−1,565	−5,846	2,256	2,384	−1,275	5,764	2,136	4,199	4,171	−3,689	−1,112
Other Investment Liab., n.i.e.	78bid	2,302	−2,942	−2,132	196	6,004	−3,580	107	−1,534	−3,535	−4,419	−4,643	−2,947
Monetary Authorities	78bsd		−788	−1,459	—	—	—	—	—	—	—	—	—
General Government	78btd	−986	210	−659	206	1,355	−4,294	−2,896	−603	316	832	752	1,494
Banks	78bud	2,799	−5,297	—	—	97	−2,312	−883	−4,222	−2,861	−1,145	−2,686	−5,401
Other Sectors	78bvd	488	2,933	−14	−10	4,552	3,026	3,886	3,291	−990	−4,106	−2,709	960
Net Errors and Omissions	78cad	−3,323	−4,248	236	2,412	−684	153	2,174	−675	−5,048	−2,635	−111	−989
Overall Balance	78cbd	−17,199	−16,312	10,997	19,162	3,170	4,250	7,126	7,314	7,359	9,817	4,104	6,965
Reserves and Related Items	79dad	17,199	16,312	−10,997	−19,162	−3,170	−4,250	−7,126	−7,314	−7,359	−9,817	−4,104	−6,965
Reserve Assets	79dbd	18,398	−9,648	−1,805	−10,512	−2,120	−596	−2,862	−7,338	−7,376	−9,833	−4,120	−6,980
Use of Fund Credit and Loans	79dcd	−1,199	11,950	−2,057	−3,485	−1,075	−3,681	−4,288	—	—	—	—	—
Exceptional Financing	79ded	—	14,010	−7,135	−5,165	24	27	24	24	16	16	16	15

International Investment Position													
							Millions of US Dollars						
Assets	79aad	....	....	....	....	....	....	....	111,278	105,770	108,476	118,379	....
Direct Investment Abroad	79abd	....	....	....	....	....	....	....	11,944	12,067	14,039	17,529	....
Portfolio Investment	79acd	....	....	....	....	....	....	....	5,747	3,806	3,321	1,545	....
Equity Securities	79add	....	....	....	....	....	....	....	—	—	—	—	....
Debt Securities	79aed	....	....	....	....	....	....	....	5,747	3,806	3,321	1,545	....
Financial Derivatives	79ald	....	....	....	....	....	....	....					....
Other Investment	79afd	....	....	....	....	....	....	....	52,707	41,914	33,681	37,805	....
Monetary Authorities	79agd	....	....	....	....	....	....	....	....	....	....	....	....
General Government	79ahd	....	....	....	....	....	....	....	....	....	....	....	....
Banks	79aid	....	....	....	....	....	....	....	....	....	....	....	....
Other Sectors	79ajd	....	....	....	....	....	....	....	....	....	....	....	....
Reserve Assets	79akd	....	....	....	....	....	....	....	40,880	47,984	57,435	61,501	....
Liabilities	79lad	....	....	....	....	....	....	....	359,553	361,570	386,208	428,685	....
Dir. Invest. in Rep. Economy	79lbd	....	....	....	....	....	....	....	140,376	155,701	167,365	183,967	....
Portfolio Investment	79lcd	....	....	....	....	....	....	....	132,643	122,709	139,431	166,200	....
Equity Securities	79ldd	....	....	....	....	....	....	....	54,940	44,564	56,516	73,967	....
Debt Securities	79led	....	....	....	....	....	....	....	77,703	78,145	82,915	92,233	....
Financial Derivatives	79lld	....	....	....	....	....	....	....					....
Other Investment	79lfd	....	....	....	....	....	....	....	86,534	83,160	79,412	78,519	....
Monetary Authorities	79lgd	....	....	....	....	....	....	....	....	....	....	....	....
General Government	79lhd	....	....	....	....	....	....	....	....	....	....	....	....
Banks	79lid	....	....	....	....	....	....	....	....	....	....	....	....
Other Sectors	79ljd	....	....	....	....	....	....	....	....	....	....	....	....

Government Finance													
						Millions of Pesos: Year Ending December 31							
Deficit (-) or Surplus	80	−386	−9,784	−5,546	−34,161	−55,591	−71,289	−69,256	−42,377	−111,592	−75,772	−78,008	−63,821
Total Revenue and Grants	81y	211,434	278,626	379,573	459,047	488,959	620,135	791,040	859,998	875,710	1,049,198	1,170,956	1,299,711
Revenue	81	211,434	278,626	379,573	459,047	488,959	620,135	791,040	859,998	875,710	1,049,198	1,170,956	1,299,711
Grants	81z	—	—	—	—	—	—	—	—	—	—	—	—
Exp.& Lending Minus Repayments	82z	211,820	288,410	385,119	493,208	544,550	691,424	860,296	902,375	987,302	1,124,970	1,248,964	1,363,532
Expenditure	82	217,249	285,147	382,499	505,902	556,079	689,921	848,502	897,049	1,009,733	1,118,033	1,248,109	1,357,867
Lending Minus Repayments	83	−5,429	3,263	2,620	−12,694	−11,529	1,503	11,794	5,326	−22,431	6,937	855	5,665
Total Financing	80h	386	9,784	5,546	34,161	55,591	71,289	69,256	42,377	111,592	75,772	78,008	63,821
Domestic	84a	4,934	−90,101	24,233	56,387	35,073	64,994	117,589	46,922	125,971	80,538	65,763	81,744
Foreign	85a	−4,548	99,885	−18,687	−22,226	20,518	6,295	−48,333	−4,545	−14,379	−4,766	12,246	−17,923
Total Debt by Residence	88	417,115	751,601	787,822	821,777	1,073,220	1,175,528	1,276,451	1,306,415	1,504,286	1,667,603	1,776,043	1,871,287
Domestic	88a	178,960	155,360	192,162	273,656	378,256	506,389	675,107	763,559	907,408	1,011,889	1,099,206	1,242,154
Foreign	89a	238,155	596,241	595,660	548,121	694,964	669,139	601,344	542,856	596,878	655,714	676,836	629,133

Mexico 273

		1994	1995	1996	1997	1998	1999	2000	2001	2002	2003	2004	2005
National Accounts							*Billions of Pesos*						
Househ.Cons.Expend.,incl.NPISHs....	96f.c	1,016.13	1,232.00	1,646.26	2,042.08	2,593.35	3,084.14	3,682.55	4,044.88	4,326.51	4,731.20	5,253.41	5,717.04
Government Consumption Expend...	91f.c	164.16	191.98	243.71	314.62	399.96	506.46	612.62	683.38	759.87	855.75	913.97	966.82
Gross Fixed Capital Formation..........	93e.c	274.86	296.71	451.08	619.49	804.00	973.80	1,174.30	1,161.95	1,205.94	1,304.89	1,514.57	1,616.40
Changes in Inventories....................	93i.c	33.54	67.39	132.48	201.46	131.41	104.55	128.74	51.35	87.39	111.39	189.37	208.49
Exports of Goods and Services........	90c.c	238.96	558.80	811.51	962.22	1,180.39	1,414.34	1,704.08	1,598.52	1,678.38	1,919.36	2,280.51	2,505.12
Imports of Goods and Services (-).....	98c.c	307.49	509.86	759.45	965.61	1,262.76	1,488.56	1,810.58	1,730.39	1,794.95	2,031.15	2,438.04	2,639.53
Gross Domestic Product (GDP).........	99b.c	1,420.16	1,837.02	2,525.58	3,174.28	3,846.35	4,594.72	5,491.71	5,809.69	6,263.14	6,891.43	7,713.80	8,374.35
Net Primary Income from Abroad.....	98.nc	−42.27	−84.09	−104.38	−98.79	−120.79	−119.90	−131.71	−126.13	−117.25	−133.30	....	....
Gross National Income (GNI)..........	99a.c	1,377.89	1,752.93	2,421.19	3,075.49	3,725.56	4,474.82	5,360.00	5,683.56	6,145.89	6,758.13	....	....
GDP Volume 1993 Prices................	99b.r	1,311.66	1,230.77	1,294.20	1,381.84	1,451.35	1,505.88	1,605.13	1,604.60	1,616.99	1,640.26	1,705.80	1,756.21
GDP Volume (2000=100)...............	99bvr	81.7	76.7	80.6	86.1	90.4	93.8	100.0	100.0	100.7	102.2	106.3	109.4
GDP Deflator (2000=100)...............	99bir	31.6	43.6	57.0	67.1	77.5	89.2	100.0	105.8	113.2	122.8	132.2	139.4
							Millions: Midyear Estimates						
Population.................................	99z	90.92	92.52	94.10	95.64	97.14	98.63	100.09	101.53	102.95	104.34	105.70	107.03

2006, International Monetary Fund : *International Financial Statistics Yearbook*

Micronesia, Federated States of 868

		1994	1995	1996	1997	1998	1999	2000	2001	2002	2003	2004	2005
Exchange Rates						*US Dollars per SDR: End of Period*							
Market Rate.............................	aa	1.4599	1.4865	1.4380	1.3493	1.4080	1.3725	1.3029	1.2567	1.3595	1.4860	1.5530	1.4293
Fund Position						*Millions of SDRs: End of Period*							
Quota...................................	2f.s	3.5	3.5	3.5	3.5	3.5	5.1	5.1	5.1	5.1	5.1	5.1	5.1
SDRs.....................................	1b.s	.9	.9	.9	1.0	1.0	1.1	1.1	1.1	1.2	1.2	1.2	1.2
Reserve Position in the Fund...........	1c.s	—	—	—	—	—	—	—	—	—	—	—	—
Total Fund Cred.&Loans Outstg.......	2tl	—	—	—	—	—	—	—	—	—	—	—	—
International Liquidity						*Millions of US Dollars Unless Otherwise Indicated: End of Period*							
Total Reserves minus Gold...............	1l.d	....	69.500	89.600	85.801	101.602	92.669	113.047	98.330	117.391	89.607	54.839	49.953
SDRs...................................	1b.d	1.264	1.349	1.357	1.325	1.442	1.455	1.442	1.445	1.598	1.777	1.890	1.783
Reserve Position in the Fund.........	1c.d	.001	.001	.001	.001	.001	.001	.001	.001	.001	.001	.001	.001
Foreign Exchange......................	1d.d	....	68.150	88.242	84.475	100.159	91.213	111.605	96.885	115.792	87.829	52.948	48.170
Gold (Million Fine Troy Ounces).......	1ad	....	—	—	—	—	—	—	—	—	—	—	—
Gold (National Valuation)...............	1and	....	—	—	—	—	—	—	—	—	—	—	—
Monetary Authorities:Other Assets...	3..d	....	60.749	54.035	51.537	55.579	55.283	47.408	36.989	33.503	41.792	43.751	49.020
Other Liab..............	4..d	....	—	—	—	—	—	—	—	—	—	—	—
Banking Institutions: Assets.............	7a.d	....	82.200	97.210	96.273	93.042	93.472	91.259	97.967	112.961	117.521	115.506	106.676
Liabilities..................	7b.d	....	1.962	1.332	.948	.131	.107			5.226	1.604	1.663	2.076
Monetary Authorities						*Millions of US Dollars: End of Period*							
Foreign Assets.........................	11	....	130.249	143.635	137.338	157.181	147.952	160.455	135.319	150.894	131.399	98.590	98.973
Foreign Liabilities......................	16c	....	—	—	—	—	—	—	—	—	—	—	—
Central Government Deposits...........	16d	....	130.249	143.635	137.338	157.181	147.952	160.456	135.319	150.893	131.399	98.589	98.973
Other Items (Net)......................	17r	....	—	—	—	—	—	−.001	—	.001	—	.001	—
Banking Institutions						*Millions of US Dollars: End of Period*							
Foreign Assets.........................	21	....	82.200	97.210	96.273	93.042	93.472	91.259	97.967	112.961	117.521	115.506	106.676
Claims on Central Government.........	22a	....	—	—	—	—	—	—	.173	—	—	—	—
Claims on State & Local Govts.........	22b	....	—	—	—	—	.787	.442	—	.117	—	—	—
Claims on Nonfin.Pub.Enterprises.....	22c	....	.699	.106	—	—	.001	—	—	—	—	—	—
Claims on Private Sector................	22d	....	65.572	60.141	58.129	65.618	70.749	71.595	69.907	50.558	40.048	43.176	49.466
Demand Deposits.......................	24	....	19.863	19.528	21.514	21.284	19.891	18.802	21.245	19.697	22.476	23.578	25.007
Time, Savings,& Fgn. Currency Dep..	25	....	87.971	82.067	83.947	84.933	89.926	89.965	94.015	81.766	75.187	74.030	74.175
Foreign Liabilities......................	26c	....	1.962	1.332	.948	.131	.107	—	—	5.226	1.604	1.663	2.076
Central Government Deposits..........	26d	....	4.949	14.976	11.745	11.736	11.351	10.336	7.727	12.754	12.659	16.660	11.837
Liab. to Nonbank Financial Insts.......	26j	....	.365	2.836	1.446	.587	2.007	.958	1.827	3.268	3.643	2.353	3.479
Capital Accounts.......................	27a	....	39.137	43.175	44.506	46.739	46.152	47.017	49.433	48.543	50.472	52.805	51.393
Other Items (Net)......................	27r	....	−5.776	−6.457	−9.704	−6.750	−4.425	−3.782	−6.200	−7.618	−8.472	−12.407	−11.825
Banking Survey						*Millions of US Dollars: End of Period*							
Foreign Assets (Net).....................	31n	....	210.487	239.513	232.663	250.092	241.317	251.714	233.286	258.629	247.316	212.433	203.573
Domestic Credit........................	32	....	−68.927	−98.364	−90.954	−103.299	−87.766	−98.755	−72.966	−112.972	−104.010	−72.073	−61.344
Claims on Central Govt. (Net).........	32an	....	−135.198	−158.611	−149.083	−168.917	−159.303	−170.792	−142.873	−163.647	−144.058	−115.249	−110.810
Claims on Local Government..........	32b	....	—	—	—	—	—	—	—	—	—	—	—
Claims on Nonfin.Pub.Enterprises...	32c	....	.699	.106	—	—	.787	.442	—	.117	—	—	—
Claims on Private Sector...............	32d	....	65.572	60.141	58.129	65.618	70.749	71.595	69.907	50.558	40.048	43.176	49.466
Money..................................	34	....	19.863	19.528	21.514	21.284	19.891	18.802	21.245	19.697	22.476	23.578	25.007
Quasi-Money...........................	35	....	87.971	82.067	83.947	84.933	89.926	89.965	94.015	81.766	75.187	74.030	74.175
Liab. to Nonbank Financial Insts.......	36j	....	.365	2.836	1.446	.587	2.007	.958	1.827	3.268	3.643	2.353	3.479
Capital Accounts........................	37a	....	39.137	43.175	44.506	46.739	46.152	47.017	49.433	48.543	50.472	52.805	51.393
Other Items (Net)......................	37r	....	−5.776	−6.457	−9.704	−6.750	−4.425	−3.783	−6.200	−7.617	−8.472	−12.406	−11.825
Money plus Quasi-Money................	35l	....	107.834	101.595	105.461	106.217	109.817	108.767	115.260	101.463	97.663	97.608	99.182
Interest Rates						*Percent Per Annum*							
Savings Rate.............................	60k	....	3.17	3.01	3.00	2.90	2.72	2.67	2.47	1.33	.95	.88	.95
Deposit Rate.............................	60l	....	5.33	4.58	4.21	3.98	3.72	4.59	3.17	1.47	1.02	1.02	1.62
Lending Rate.............................	60p	....	15.00	15.00	15.00	15.00	15.17	15.33	15.33	15.28	15.00	15.38	16.38
						Millions: Midyear Estimates							
Population.............................	99z	† .11	.11	.11	.11	.11	.11	.11	.11	.11	.11	.11	.11

Moldova 921

		1994	1995	1996	1997	1998	1999	2000	2001	2002	2003	2004	2005
Exchange Rates					*Lei per SDR: End of Period*								
Official Rate	aa	6.2336	6.6877	6.7215	6.2882	11.7185	15.9077	16.1343	16.4517	18.7913	19.6445	19.3522	18.3404
						Lei per US Dollar: End of Period (ae) Period Average (rf)							
Official Rate	ae	4.2700	4.4990	4.6743	4.6605	8.3226	11.5902	12.3833	13.0909	13.8220	13.2200	12.4611	12.8320
Official Rate	rf	....	4.4958	4.6045	4.6236	5.3707	10.5158	12.4342	12.8651	13.5705	13.9449	12.3297	12.5996
						Index Numbers (2000=100): Period Averages							
Nominal Effective Exchange Rate	nec	71.34	126.25	139.31	160.83	159.48	102.92	100.00	103.11	97.99	87.17	92.96	89.29
Real Effective Exchange Rate	rec	116.29	100.59	101.42	116.76	113.36	86.49	100.00	104.12	98.54	93.08	106.78	109.12
Fund Position						*Millions of SDRs: End of Period*							
Quota	2f.s	90.00	90.00	90.00	90.00	90.00	123.20	123.20	123.20	123.20	123.20	123.20	123.20
SDRs	1b.s	14.62	8.81	5.45	.89	.50	.23	.26	.59	.20	.03	.05	.01
Reserve Position in the Fund	1c.s	.01	.01	.01	.01	.01	.01	.01	.01		.01	.01	.01
Total Fund Cred.&Loans Outstg	2tl	112.45	154.85	172.29	172.73	125.56	127.69	118.30	116.29	111.78	95.95	81.37	66.78
International Liquidity					*Millions of US Dollars Unless Otherwise Indicated: End of Period*								
Total Reserves minus Gold	1l.d	179.92	257.01	311.96	365.99	143.56	185.70	222.49	228.53	268.86	302.27	470.26	597.45
SDRs	1b.d	21.34	13.10	7.84	1.21	.70	.32	.34	.74	.27	.04	.07	.01
Reserve Position in the Fund	1c.d	.01	.01	.01	.01	.01	.01	.01	.01	.01	.01	.01	.01
Foreign Exchange	1d.d	158.57	243.90	304.11	364.77	142.85	185.37	222.15	227.78	268.58	302.22	470.18	597.43
Gold (Million Fine Troy Ounces)	1ad	—	—	—	—	—	—	—	—	—	—	—	
Gold (National Valuation)	1and	—	—	—	—	—	—	—	—	—	—	—	
Monetary Authorities: Other Liab	4..d	10.10	7.42	4.94	4.00	2.77	10.06	9.66	1.30	.83	1.53	1.54	....
Dep.Money Banks: Assets Conv	7axd	18.86	32.77	37.41	23.78	32.33	53.42	67.22	59.77	70.05	103.79	95.72	....
Assets Nonconv	7ayd	7.79	5.24	5.55	9.25	3.44	2.23	5.16	4.92	7.15	8.06	3.27	....
Dep.Money Banks: Liab. Conv	7bxd	1.42	10.60	50.70	58.10	67.27	41.78	44.42	41.70	44.51	54.58	60.05	....
Liab. Nonconv	7byd	.41	3.10	1.55	4.91	7.62	3.33	5.45	5.80	9.00	5.20	8.93	....
Monetary Authorities						*Millions of Lei: End of Period*							
Foreign Assets	11	825.14	1,198.42	† 1,486.91	1,716.60	1,199.82	2,207.49	2,876.49	3,008.38	3,727.14	4,010.31	6,111.68	....
Claims on Central Government	12a	284.01	452.92	† 496.12	524.83	1,409.21	1,737.46	1,730.79	1,899.28	2,158.18	2,175.41	2,740.99	....
Claims on Private Sector	12d	—	1.79	† 2.88	3.92	5.10	6.03	7.28	7.10	6.37	6.11	5.78	....
Claims on Deposit Money Banks	12e	274.67	366.55	† 362.63	286.02	233.02	130.27	105.44	91.15	81.40	72.29	62.28	....
Reserve Money	14	551.94	779.85	† 854.28	1,135.64	1,059.95	1,486.63	1,945.86	2,488.94	3,262.81	3,804.18	5,319.06	....
of which: Currency Outside DMB	14a	345.55	640.15	† 731.06	972.10	† 855.45	1,122.07	1,469.26	1,834.20	2,288.56	2,740.52	3,699.91	....
Other Liabilities to DMBs	14n			† —	3.00	3.50	20.00	43.00	15.50	23.00	92.59	1,227.86	....
Restricted Deposits	16b			† —							14.99	3.97	....
Foreign Liabilities	16c	744.09	1,068.96	† 1,181.13	1,104.75	1,494.36	2,147.89	2,028.31	1,930.21	2,112.02	1,905.15	1,593.65	....
Central Government Deposits	16d	17.45	21.38	† 126.37	9.99	60.00	85.72	277.93	100.52	71.91	3.81	44.85	....
Capital Accounts	17a	24.72	79.11	† 95.26	91.92	93.42	146.03	231.02	357.04	334.38	439.69	555.83	....
Other Items (Net)	17r	45.63	70.37	† 91.49	186.07	135.91	194.99	193.90	113.70	168.96	3.72	175.52	....
Deposit Money Banks						*Millions of Lei: End of Period*							
Reserves	20	52.44	54.38	36.54	52.05	† 200.66	360.92	465.22	652.38	979.20	1,063.38	1,614.23	....
											92.59	1,227.86	
Other Claims on Monetary Author	20n	—	—	—	—	† —							....
Foreign Assets	21	113.76	171.03	200.79	153.90	† 297.69	644.99	896.23	846.80	1,067.07	1,478.66	1,233.37	....
Claims on Central Government	22a	31.56	10.31	13.68	67.58	† 184.46	267.81	335.33	571.44	668.42	598.05	788.23	....
Claims on Local Government	22b	22.82	2.59	13.19	23.68	† 33.01	14.98	17.24	25.45	105.86	70.48	79.33	....
Claims on Nonfin.Pub.Enterprises	22c	493.91	692.37	852.27	1,120.82	† 144.17	146.32	230.71	293.61	315.16	449.14	552.56	....
Claims on Private Sector	22d	174.79	433.62	600.88	617.05	† 1,265.65	1,453.15	2,025.31	2,804.49	3,867.39	5,605.06	6,794.87	....
Claims on Nonbank Financial Insts	22g					† 23.06	37.30	28.36	5.65	9.47	1.01	51.24	....
Demand Deposits	24	173.69	244.57	263.13	326.49	† 210.00	357.76	553.75	665.76	1,271.14	1,674.28	2,401.62	....
Time, Savings,& Fgn.Currency Dep	25	228.68	358.18	435.57	624.02	† 698.48	1,040.18	1,548.25	2,350.96	3,165.91	4,357.36	6,155.22	....
Money Market Instruments	26aa	—	—	—	—	† 1.21	2.10	.20	.29	.28	.86	.46	....
Restricted Deposits	26b	—	—	—	—	† —					32.41	29.90	....
Foreign Liabilities	26c	7.80	61.64	244.21	293.67	† 623.24	522.87	621.93	617.29	739.57	790.40	859.55	....
Central Government Deposits	26d	56.54	35.81	27.84	33.55	† 13.51	44.72	57.11	270.93	502.38	753.60	716.78	....
Credit from Monetary Authorities	26g	292.23	389.12	368.12	285.91	† 229.83	130.27	106.44	93.15	85.31	72.31	63.29	....
Liabs. to Nonbank Financial Insts	26j					† .77	1.55	2.22	2.45	26.48	13.71	49.92	....
Capital Accounts	27a	333.05	569.03	731.41	839.27	† 756.20	1,242.83	1,692.04	1,896.54	2,099.43	2,506.26	3,020.63	....
Other Items (Net)	27r	−202.72	−294.04	−352.93	−367.84	† −384.56	−416.81	−583.56	−697.56	−877.92	−842.81	−955.69	....
Monetary Survey						*Millions of Lei: End of Period*							
Foreign Assets (Net)	31n	187.01	238.85	† 262.37	472.08	† −620.10	181.71	1,122.48	1,307.68	1,942.62	2,793.42	4,891.85	....
Domestic Credit	32	933.10	1,536.40	† 1,824.80	2,314.34	† 2,991.14	3,532.62	4,039.97	5,235.57	6,556.57	8,147.84	10,251.37	....
Claims on Central Govt. (Net)	32an	241.58	406.04	† 355.59	548.88	† 1,520.16	1,874.84	1,731.07	2,099.27	2,252.32	2,016.06	2,767.60	....
Claims on Local Government	32b	22.82	2.59	† 13.19	23.68	† 33.01	14.98	17.24	25.45	105.86	70.48	79.33	....
Claims on Nonfin.Pub.Enterprises	32c	493.91	692.37	† 852.27	1,120.82	† 144.17	146.32	230.71	293.61	315.16	449.14	552.56	....
Claims on Private Sector	32d	174.79	435.41	† 603.76	620.97	† 1,270.75	1,459.19	2,032.59	2,811.59	3,873.76	5,611.17	6,800.65	....
Claims on Nonbank Financial Inst	32g			† —		† 23.06	37.30	28.36	5.65	9.47	1.01	51.24	....
Money	34	524.20	885.04	† 994.51	1,298.83	† 1,065.46	1,479.84	2,023.22	2,500.00	3,559.80	4,415.07	6,106.45	....
Quasi-Money	35	229.01	360.18	† 435.57	624.02	† 698.48	1,040.18	1,548.25	2,350.96	3,165.91	.86	.46	....
Money Market Instruments	36aa	—	—	† —	—	† 1.21	2.10	.20	.29	.28	47.40	33.86	....
Restricted Deposits	36b	—	—	† —	—	† —					13.71	49.92	....
Liabs. to Nonbank Financial Insts	36j	—	—	† —	—	† .77	1.55	2.22	2.45	26.48	2,945.95	3,576.46	....
Capital Accounts	37a	357.77	648.15	† 826.67	931.20	† 849.62	1,388.86	1,923.05	2,253.58	2,433.81			....
Other Items (Net)	37r	9.13	−118.10	† −169.58	−67.63	† −244.50	−198.19	−334.50	−564.03	−687.09	−839.07	−779.15	....
Money plus Quasi-Money	35l	753.21	1,245.22	† 1,430.08	1,922.86	† 1,763.94	2,520.02	3,571.47	4,850.95	6,725.71	8,772.43	12,261.67	....
Money (National Definitions)						*Millions of Lei: End of Period*							
Reserve Money	19mb	552.10	781.50	854.00	1,122.60	1,059.90	1,498.60	1,945.70	2,488.90	3,262.70	3,804.00	5,313.10	7,002.90
M1	59ma	524.40	885.70	998.50	1,298.50	1,057.70	1,462.00	1,963.10	2,573.50	3,345.40	4,151.50	5,564.20	7,333.20
M2	59mb	675.80	1,107.20	1,292.10	1,739.50	1,357.90	1,811.10	2,514.50	3,464.70	4,517.80	5,622.00	8,137.00	11,125.60
M2, Seasonally Adjusted	59mbc	....	....	....	....	....	....	2,303.20	3,253.80	4,306.90	5,410.90	7,926.00	10,914.60
M3	59mc	753.10	1,243.80	1,434.00	1,922.60	1,755.70	2,504.30	3,509.70	4,787.20	6,511.40	8,509.20	11,719.70	15,826.80
M3, Seasonally Adjusted	59mcc	....	....	....	....	....	....	3,281.10	4,558.90	6,283.10	8,280.70	11,491.20	15,468.40

Moldova 921

		1994	1995	1996	1997	1998	1999	2000	2001	2002	2003	2004	2005
Interest Rates						*Percent Per Annum*							
Refinancing Rate	60a	143.94	28.25	20.15	19.03	....	....	....	....	....	....	....	....
Money Market Rate	60b	....	....	....	28.10	30.91	32.60	20.77	11.04	5.13	11.51	13.19	5.87
Money Market Rate (Fgn. Cur.)	60b.f	....	....	....	....	....	11.88	6.86	9.06	4.80	2.51	.78	2.49
Treasury Bill Rate	60c	....	52.90	39.01	23.63	30.54	28.49	22.20	14.24	5.89	15.08	11.89	3.70
Deposit Rate	60l	....	....	25.43	23.47	21.68	27.54	24.87	20.93	14.20	12.55	15.12	13.22
Deposit Rate (Foreign Currency)	60l.f	....	....	....	....	9.86	5.27	5.12	4.09	3.22	3.13	4.97	5.16
Lending Rate	60p	....	....	36.67	33.33	30.83	35.54	33.78	28.69	23.52	19.29	20.94	19.26
Lending Rate (Foreign Currency)	60p.f	....	....	....	....	22.03	20.37	17.12	14.22	12.32	10.98	11.40	11.10
Prices and Labor						*Index Numbers (2000=100): Period Averages*							
Consumer Prices	64	33.5	36.8	45.4	50.8	54.7	76.2	100.0	109.8	115.6	129.2	145.3	164.4
						Number in Thousands: Period Averages							
Labor Force	67d	....	....	1,686	....	1,659	1,682	1,655	1,617	1,615	1,474	1,433	....
Employment	67e	1,681	1,673	1,660	1,646	1,642	1,494	1,515	1,499	1,505	1,357	1,316	....
Unemployment	67c	21	25	23	28	32	187	140	118	110	117	116	104
Unemployment Rate (%)	67r	1.1	1.0	1.5	1.5	1.9	2.1	2.3	2.2	2.1	2.0	2.0	....
Intl. Transactions & Positions						*Millions of US Dollars*							
Exports	70..d	558	739	823	890	644	474	472	568	644	789	980	1,091
Imports, c.i.f.	71..d	703	841	1,072	1,171	1,024	586	776	893	1,039	1,403	1,773	2,293
Imports, f.o.b.	71.vd	672	809	1,083	1,238	1,032	611	770	880	1,038	1,429	....	....
Balance of Payments						*Millions of US Dollars: Minus Sign Indicates Debit*							
Current Account, n.i.e.	78ald	−82.0	−87.8	−194.8	−274.9	−334.7	−78.6	−108.2	−36.5	−74.9	−140.0	−52.9	−307.5
Goods: Exports f.o.b.	78aad	618.5	739.0	822.9	889.6	643.6	474.3	476.8	564.6	659.7	805.1	994.1	1,104.4
Goods: Imports f.o.b.	78abd	−672.4	−809.2	−1,082.5	−1,237.6	−1,031.7	−611.5	−770.3	−879.7	−1,037.5	−1,428.1	−1,748.2	−2,295.2
Trade Balance	78acd	−53.9	−70.2	−259.7	−348.0	−388.1	−137.2	−293.6	−315.1	−377.8	−623.0	−754.2	−1,190.8
Services: Credit	78add	32.8	144.5	106.0	167.7	152.0	135.7	164.9	171.4	217.5	254.4	355.1	424.0
Services: Debit	78aed	−79.0	−196.3	−166.4	−196.1	−198.6	−177.9	−201.6	−208.8	−257.0	−299.8	−373.8	−444.9
Balance on Goods & Services	78afd	−100.0	−122.0	−320.0	−376.4	−434.6	−179.4	−330.3	−352.4	−417.3	−668.4	−772.9	−1,211.7
Income: Credit	78agd	10.8	14.2	99.3	132.7	136.8	120.5	139.1	173.9	229.4	340.8	490.0	539.3
Income: Debit	78ahd	−26.1	−32.4	−44.2	−85.3	−102.3	−95.8	−117.5	−78.1	−123.3	−116.6	−133.9	−180.5
Balance on Gds, Serv. & Inc.	78aid	−115.4	−140.2	−264.9	−329.0	−400.1	−154.7	−308.7	−256.6	−311.2	−444.2	−416.7	−852.9
Current Transfers, n.i.e.: Credit	78ajd	36.9	66.6	72.9	104.1	110.9	111.5	213.6	236.0	255.6	331.7	399.0	587.4
Current Transfers, n.i.e.: Debit	78akd	−3.6	−14.1	−2.8	−50.0	−45.5	−35.4	−13.1	−15.9	−19.3	−27.5	−35.2	−42.1
Capital Account, n.i.e.	78bcd	−1.0	−.4	−.1	−.2	−.4	1.1	−14.3	−20.7	−19.3	−19.0	−18.3	−16.9
Capital Account, n.i.e.: Credit	78bad	—	—	.1	.1	2.1	1.5	2.8	1.1	1.2	4.6	7.2	5.2
Capital Account: Debit	78bbd	−1.0	−.4	−.1	−.3	−2.5	−.4	−17.1	−21.8	−20.4	−23.6	−25.5	−22.2
Financial Account, n.i.e.	78bjd	211.1	−68.8	76.6	95.2	5.2	−34.6	126.4	17.0	67.0	67.7	96.5	227.8
Direct Investment Abroad	78bdd	....	−.5	−.6	−.5	.7	−.1	−.1	−.1	−.5	−.1	−3.2	.2
Dir. Invest. in Rep. Econ., n.i.e.	78bed	11.6	25.9	23.7	78.7	75.5	37.9	126.6	53.0	132.7	78.3	90.6	225.3
Portfolio Investment Assets	78bfd	−.4	—	—	—	—	—	—	−3.2	−1.5	.4	−1.5	−1.2
Equity Securities	78bkd	−.4	....	....	....	....	—	—	—	—	−.1	−.2	—
Debt Securities	78bld	....	....	....	....	....	—	—	−3.2	−1.5	.5	−1.3	−1.2
Portfolio Investment Liab., n.i.e.	78bgd	.6	−.5	30.8	18.6	−59.1	−7.3	−4.0	−3.9	−25.9	−24.2	−8.3	−5.8
Equity Securities	78bmd	.6	−.5	.8	3.7	6.5	5.2	2.9	2.8	2.3	.7	−.8	.6
Debt Securities	78bnd	....	—	30.0	14.9	−65.6	−12.5	−6.9	−6.8	−28.2	−24.9	−7.5	−6.4
Financial Derivatives Assets	78bwd	....	....	....	....	....	....	....	....	....	—	−.5	−1.7
Financial Derivatives Liabilities	78bxd	....	....	....	....	....	....	....	....	....	.1	1.0	1
Other Investment Assets	78bhd	−81.7	−116.4	−51.4	1.8	−86.8	−107.4	−35.9	−22.2	−40.0	−11.3	−46.4	−103.1
Monetary Authorities	78bod	−1.3	2.9	.3	3.7	2.9	—	.1	—	—	—	−18.8	−14.1
General Government	78bpd	−4.1	11.9	12.2	1.6	−.6	−4.3	—	8.3	.5	−.2	.3	−.2
Banks	78bqd	−10.1	−13.5	−6.5	10.6	−10.9	−15.4	−16.5	1.2	−15.7	−19.6	5.8	−50.7
Other Sectors	78brd	−66.2	−117.7	−57.4	−14.2	−78.2	−87.8	−19.6	−31.7	−24.8	8.6	−33.7	−38.1
Other Investment Liab., n.i.e.	78bid	281.0	22.7	74.0	−3.4	74.8	42.3	39.8	−6.6	2.1	24.6	64.8	114.0
Monetary Authorities	78bsd	3.1	1.8	−1.9	−2.7	5.2	−2.4	—	—	—	—	—	—
General Government	78btd	147.0	−19.7	43.2	−59.2	9.7	−22.4	−11.1	−14.3	−12.6	−25.1	−19.1	−14.8
Banks	78bud	−.8	11.4	21.9	11.8	6.9	−21.2	4.2	−2.3	11.0	14.0	16.5	12.1
Other Sectors	78bvd	131.6	29.2	10.7	46.6	53.1	88.3	46.7	9.9	3.8	35.6	67.5	116.7
Net Errors and Omissions	78cad	−115.2	−18.4	15.5	−7.9	−22.8	−3.8	−9.1	15.5	−19.9	75.5	124.5	193.1
Overall Balance	78cbd	12.9	−175.4	−102.7	−187.8	−352.8	−115.9	−5.2	−24.7	−47.1	15.7	149.8	96.4
Reserves and Related Items	79dad	−12.9	175.4	102.7	187.8	352.8	115.9	5.2	24.7	47.1	−15.7	−149.8	−96.4
Reserve Assets	79dbd	−103.1	−76.7	−56.9	−50.2	225.7	−48.8	−47.4	−9.5	−27.0	−14.1	−148.0	−128.5
Use of Fund Credit and Loans	79dcd	71.5	64.8	25.2	.8	−64.4	4.0	−12.7	−2.3	−5.6	−22.2	−21.6	−21.7
Exceptional Financing	79ded	18.7	187.3	134.4	237.2	191.4	160.6	65.3	36.5	79.6	52.0	19.7	53.8

Moldova 921

		1994	1995	1996	1997	1998	1999	2000	2001	2002	2003	2004	2005
International Investment Position						*Millions of US Dollars*							
Assets	79aad	303.2	499.7	616.8	661.9	474.1	585.8	656.5	679.3	764.8	832.8	1,050.6	1,240.4
Direct Investment Abroad	79abd	17.8	18.3	23.1	23.5	22.8	22.9	23.0	23.1	23.5	23.6	26.9	28.1
Portfolio Investment	79acd	.4	.4	.4	.4	.4	.4	.4	3.6	5.1	4.7	6.1	7.3
Equity Securities	79add	.4	.4	.4	.4	.4	.4	.4	.4	.4	.5	.7	.7
Debt Securities	79aed	—	—	—	—	—	—	—	3.2	4.7	4.2	5.5	6.7
Financial Derivatives	79ald											.4	2.1
Other Investment	79afd	105.3	224.0	279.8	275.8	314.1	382.1	410.5	424.2	467.3	502.3	546.9	605.5
Monetary Authorities	79agd	9.9	7.1	6.8	3.1	.1	.1	.1	—	—	—	19.4	—
General Government	79ahd	31.7	19.9	7.9	6.2	6.8	10.1	9.9	1.3	.8	1.1	.8	1.0
Banks	79aid	27.4	40.8	47.3	36.7	44.9	58.1	74.4	72.7	89.6	115.2	112.5	156.5
Other Sectors	79ajd	36.3	156.3	217.9	229.9	262.4	313.9	326.1	350.2	376.9	386.0	414.3	448.0
Reserve Assets	79akd	179.8	257.0	313.5	362.2	136.9	180.4	222.6	228.5	268.9	302.3	470.3	597.4
Liabilities	79lad	723.1	1,029.8	1,282.9	1,588.5	1,814.7	1,928.3	2,104.7	2,130.5	2,355.2	2,528.6	2,636.4	2,906.1
Dir. Invest. in Rep. Economy	79lbd	28.6	94.2	116.9	186.4	244.3	310.3	438.6	536.1	674.9	755.6	911.9	1,128.7
Portfolio Investment	79lcd	.7	.4	60.7	296.3	232.3	86.6	201.3	161.5	133.7	110.9	51.1	45.0
Equity Securities	79ldd	.7	.4	.8	6.0	10.4	11.5	11.9	14.1	14.5	16.5	19.3	19.6
Debt Securities	79led	—	.1	59.9	290.3	221.9	75.1	189.5	147.4	119.2	94.3	31.8	25.4
Financial Derivatives	79lld	—	—	—	—	—	—	—	—	—	—	1.1	1.2
Other Investment	79lfd	693.9	935.2	1,105.3	1,105.8	1,338.1	1,531.4	1,464.8	1,432.9	1,546.6	1,662.1	1,672.3	1,731.2
Monetary Authorities	79lgd	170.6	238.5	254.1	236.7	181.2	175.5	154.1	146.1	152.0	142.6	126.4	95.5
General Government	79lhd	345.5	425.8	479.0	463.4	573.1	631.1	625.8	603.1	655.7	714.2	667.4	632.2
Banks	79lid	1.1	12.4	32.7	42.1	51.4	31.0	34.8	32.3	43.2	57.6	74.3	85.1
Other Sectors	79ljd	176.6	258.5	339.5	363.6	532.4	693.8	650.1	651.4	695.9	747.8	804.3	918.5
Government Finance						*Millions of Lei: Year Ending December 31*							
Deficit(-) or Surplus	80	....	−412	−443	−679	−288	−420	−206	208	−320	....	....	....
Total Revenue and Grants	81y	....	1,903	2,022	3,150	2,946	3,300	4,500	4,519	5,422	....	....	....
Revenue	81	....	1,858	1,976	2,844	2,809	3,064	4,034	4,078	4,978	....	....	....
Grants	81z	....	45	46	306	137	236	466	441	445	....	....	....
Exp. & Lending Minus Repayments.	82z	....	2,315	2,465	3,828	3,234	3,721	4,706	4,311	5,742	....	....	....
Expenditure	82	....	2,315	2,217	3,710	3,272	3,660	4,739	4,336	5,757	....	....	....
Lending Minus Repayments	83	....	—	248	119	−38	60	−33	−25	−14	....	....	....
Financing: Domestic	84a	....	....	236	302	591	224	238	313	884	....	....	....
Financing: Foreign	85a	....	....	208	376	−302	196	−32	−520	−564	....	....	....
National Accounts						*Millions of Lei*							
Househ.Cons.Expend.,incl.NPISHs	96f	2,487	3,616	5,243	6,017	6,876	9,137	14,031	16,385	18,493	24,711	28,125	33,650
Government Consumption Expend	91f	1,086	1,755	2,113	2,663	2,327	1,954	2,472	2,878	4,796	5,739	5,173	6,196
Gross Fixed Capital Formation	93e	914	1,034	1,540	1,774	2,012	2,272	2,472	3,190	3,682	4,624	6,787	8,954
Changes in Inventories	93i	451	578	351	349	349	548	1,364	1,246	1,204	1,274	1,657	1,997
Exports (Net)	90n	−202	−503	−1,449	−1,887	−2,441	−1,588	−4,319	−4,647	−5,619	−9,233	−9,709	−14,042
Gross Domestic Product (GDP)	99b	4,737	6,480	7,798	8,917	9,122	12,322	16,020	19,052	22,556	27,619	32,032	36,755
Net Primary Income from Abroad	98.n	−24	....	−114	−209	−365	....	....	....	....	....	....	....
Gross National Income (GNI)	99a	4,713	6,480	8,070	9,207	9,279	12,678	16,814	20,484	24,805	30,838	....	....
Net Current Transf.from Abroad	98t	125	97	317	403	438	798	1,795	2,003	2,101	4,237	....	....
Gross Nat'l Disposable Inc.(GNDI)	99i	4,838	6,577	8,386	9,610	9,717	13,476	18,609	22,486	26,906	35,075	....	....
Gross Saving	99s	1,265	1,206	1,031	930	513	2,385	2,106	3,224	3,617	4,624	....	....
						Millions: Midyear Estimates							
Population	99z	4.35	4.34	4.33	† 4.31	4.30	4.29	4.27	4.26	4.25	4.23	4.22	4.21

Mongolia 948

		1994	1995	1996	1997	1998	1999	2000	2001	2002	2003	2004	2005
Exchange Rates						*Togrogs per SDR: End of Period*							
Market Rate	aa	604.51	704.03	997.24	1,097.16	1,270.04	1,471.84	1,429.29	1,384.92	1,529.46	1,735.61	1,877.59	1,745.14
					Togrogs per US Dollar: End of Period (ae) Period Average (rf)								
Market Rate	ae	414.09	473.62	693.51	813.16	902.00	1,072.37	1,097.00	1,102.00	1,125.00	1,168.00	1,209.00	1,221.00
Market Rate	rf	412.72	448.61	548.40	789.99	840.83	1,021.87	1,076.67	1,097.70	1,110.31	1,146.54	1,185.28	1,205.25
Fund Position						*Millions of SDRs: End of Period*							
Quota	2f.s	37.10	37.10	37.10	37.10	37.10	51.10	51.10	51.10	51.10	51.10	51.10	51.10
SDRs	1b.s	1.98	1.70	.30	.52	.34	.12	.01	.01	.03	.03	.03	.01
Reserve Position in the Fund	1c.s	—	—	—	—	—	.02	.04	.06	.08	.10	.12	.14
Total Fund Cred.&Loans Outstg	2tl	37.87	31.62	30.31	35.25	34.32	37.47	38.58	37.27	31.34	33.36	28.50	24.49
International Liquidity				*Millions of US Dollars Unless Otherwise Indicated: End of Period*									
Total Reserves Minus Gold	1l.d	81.39	117.03	107.44	175.71	94.09	136.49	178.77	205.70	349.65	236.08	236.34	430.31
SDRs	1b.d	2.89	2.52	.43	.70	.48	.16	.01	.02	.04	.04	.04	.02
Reserve Position in the Fund	1c.d	.01	.01	.01	.01	.01	.03	.05	.08	.12	.14	.19	.19
Foreign Exchange	1d.d	78.49	114.50	107.00	175.00	93.60	136.30	178.70	205.60	349.50	235.90	236.10	430.10
Gold (Million Fine Troy Ounces)	1ad	.03	.10	.15	.08	.03	—	.08	.18	.14	.02	.03	—
Gold (National Valuation)	1and	11.00	34.50	53.60	24.60	9.10	.40	23.31	50.91	49.79	6.65	14.06	—
Monetary Authorities: Other Liab.	4..d	28.77	30.17	16.04	4.50	—	5.30	—	—	—	25.03	18.52	16.75
Deposit Money Banks: Assets	7a.d	41.71	53.66	60.86	81.68	28.95	38.90	48.85	47.50	62.87	113.27	169.48	261.34
Liabilities	7b.d	11.90	14.06	12.38	15.06	22.14	9.13	10.20	11.58	14.65	44.03	76.83	96.99
Monetary Authorities						*Millions of Togrogs: End of Period*							
Foreign Assets	11	40,380	60,836	67,814	113,878	114,319	174,385	210,591	227,812	302,920	252,482	252,328	414,804
Claims on Central Government	12a	13,661	4,520	38,953	23,980	26,111	24,136	21,443	13,570	—	164,482	105,300	99,373
Claims on Deposit Money Banks	12e	10,375	7,740	1,712	3,093	5,631	6,651	4,777	7,348	8,038	12,689	22,332	17,744
Reserve Money	14	29,081	37,508	51,167	62,967	74,491	112,062	134,689	143,780	175,292	200,789	234,858	281,188
of which: Currency Outside DMBs	14a	18,946	25,591	40,136	49,768	56,446	87,281	100,910	109,131	120,755	131,482	143,513	152,369
Liabs. of Central Bank: Securities	16ac	2,106	830	—	19,296	11,715	21,200	21,080	50,000	61,000	76,000	68,551	125,161
Foreign Liabilities	16c	34,804	36,548	41,343	42,328	43,585	60,832	55,148	51,622	47,931	87,126	75,899	63,192
Central Government Deposits	16d	2,465	9,500	8,388	14,417	3,673	4,833	19,289	16,930	33,517	91,714	53,026	90,298
Capital Accounts	17a	4,998	7,998	24,004	37,082	41,049	37,921	44,431	41,992	33,160	41,084	31,985	46,092
Other Items (Net)	17r	−9,039	−19,289	−16,422	−35,140	−28,452	−31,676	−37,826	−55,594	−39,941	−67,060	−84,359	−74,010
Deposit Money Banks						*Millions of Togrogs: End of Period*							
Reserves	20	10,319	12,531	17,848	13,457	17,921	24,171	33,858	34,637	54,530	73,480	88,487	126,033
Claims on Mon.Author.:Securities	20c	2,106	830	—	19,055	11,697	21,200	21,080	49,651	60,768	75,487	68,551	125,161
Foreign Assets	21	17,272	25,412	42,207	66,416	26,116	41,711	53,591	52,341	70,730	132,295	204,906	319,094
Claims on Central Government	22a	737	643	10,472	35,451	38,328	39,269	43,371	32,458	30,743	46,905	31,226	3,167
Claims on Nonfin.Pub.Enterprises	22c	12,193	10,883	8,660	7,963	10,151	4,661	5,929	9,823	11,492	16,022	12,769	34,158
Claims on Private Sector	22d	40,763	51,838	59,763	44,256	77,293	75,821	83,959	139,989	232,768	441,515	612,025	849,647
Demand Deposits	24	14,104	17,045	20,702	26,341	26,136	27,544	29,842	46,995	66,944	81,337	78,572	116,755
Time, Savings,& Fgn.Currency Dep.	25	43,906	59,408	58,757	93,957	84,668	105,341	128,068	174,909	282,398	490,463	625,120	892,666
Money Market Instruments	26aa	—	—	287	29	26	24	—	—	173	4,036	645	10,550
Restricted Deposits	26b	—	—	15,821	6,430	6,938	3,604	5,814	7,699	11,580	13,193	11,034	22,860
Foreign Liabilities	26c	4,926	6,660	8,585	12,246	19,973	9,794	11,193	12,758	16,477	51,429	92,887	118,428
Central Government Deposits	26d	8,451	16,655	21,768	33,258	20,081	24,126	26,732	35,927	29,665	22,720	42,994	56,089
Credit from Monetary Authorities	26g	10,152	7,402	18,574	763	4,459	1,900	1,647	4,094	4,327	12,839	23,838	18,150
Capital Accounts	27a	15,892	18,725	4,789	28,518	34,167	41,568	50,527	62,730	79,596	131,959	196,808	244,318
Other Items (Net)	27r	−14,041	−23,758	−10,334	−14,944	−14,943	−7,070	−12,034	−26,214	−30,131	−22,270	−53,935	−22,555
Monetary Survey						*Millions of Togrogs: End of Period*							
Foreign Assets (Net)	31n	17,920	43,040	60,093	125,718	76,876	145,470	197,841	215,773	309,242	246,222	288,448	552,278
Domestic Credit	32	56,446	41,730	93,206	67,882	137,089	119,493	109,584	144,015	212,851	555,047	665,301	839,958
Claims on Central Govt. (Net)	32an	3,483	−20,992	19,270	11,755	40,685	34,446	18,793	−6,829	−32,439	96,953	40,506	−43,847
Claims on Nonfin.Pub.Enterprises	32c	12,193	10,883	8,660	7,963	10,151	4,661	5,929	9,823	11,492	16,022	12,769	34,158
Claims on Private Sector	32d	40,770	51,839	65,277	48,164	86,253	80,386	84,862	141,021	233,799	442,072	612,025	849,647
Money	34	33,050	42,637	60,838	76,109	82,582	114,826	130,751	156,126	187,699	212,819	222,085	269,124
Quasi-Money	35	43,906	59,408	58,757	93,957	84,668	105,341	128,068	174,909	282,398	490,463	625,120	892,666
Money Market Instruments	36aa	—	—	287	29	26	24	—	—	173	4,036	645	10,550
Liabs. of Central Bank: Securities	36ac	—	—	—	241	18	—	—	349	232	513	—	—
Restricted Deposits	36b	—	—	15,821	6,430	6,938	3,604	5,814	7,699	11,580	13,193	11,034	22,860
Capital Accounts	37a	20,891	26,723	28,794	65,599	75,216	79,489	94,958	104,722	112,756	173,043	228,793	290,410
Other Items (Net)	37r	−23,480	−43,998	−11,198	−48,764	−35,483	−38,322	−52,165	−84,017	−72,745	−92,796	−133,928	−93,373
Money plus Quasi-Money	35l	76,956	102,045	119,595	170,066	167,250	220,167	258,819	331,035	470,097	703,282	847,205	1,161,790
Interest Rates						*Percent per Annum*							
Bank Rate (End of Period)	60	180.00	150.00	109.00	45.50	23.30	11.40	8.65	8.60	9.90	11.50	15.75	4.40
Deposit Rate (End of Period)	60l	115.71	74.62	44.75	36.37	27.51	23.42	16.80	14.30	13.22	14.00	14.15	13.00
Lending Rate (End of Period)	60p	279.22	134.37	87.91	82.05	46.77	39.29	32.75	30.24	28.38	26.31	25.38	23.56
Prices and Production					*Index Numbers (2000=100): Period Averages*								
Consumer Prices	64	† 38.0	38.0	55.8	76.2	83.3	89.6	100.0	106.3	107.3	112.8	122.0	137.6
Industrial Production ('90=100)	66	65.3	....	....	....	....	....	....	....	....	....	....	....
Intl. Transactions & Positions						*Millions of US Dollars*							
Exports	70..d	353.2	473.3	423.0	568.5	345.2	454.2	535.8	521.4	524.0	615.9	869.7	1,064.9
Imports, c.i.f.	71..d	229.1	415.3	438.5	468.3	503.3	512.8	614.5	637.7	690.7	801.0	1,021.1	1,184.3

Mongolia 948

		1994	1995	1996	1997	1998	1999	2000	2001	2002	2003	2004	2005
Balance of Payments		*Millions of US Dollars: Minus Sign Indicates Debit*											
Current Account, n.i.e.	78ald	46.4	38.9	−100.5	55.2	−128.5	−112.2	−156.1	−154.2	−158.0	−148.1	−24.6	....
Goods: Exports f.o.b.	78aad	367.0	451.0	423.4	568.5	462.4	454.3	535.8	523.2	524.0	627.3	872.1	....
Goods: Imports f.o.b.	78abd	−333.3	−425.7	−459.7	−453.1	−524.2	−510.7	−608.4	−623.8	−680.2	−826.9	−901.0	....
Trade Balance	78acd	33.7	25.3	−36.3	115.4	−61.8	−56.4	−72.6	−100.6	−156.2	−199.6	−28.9	....
Services: Credit	78add	45.4	57.3	55.7	52.7	77.8	75.8	77.7	113.5	183.9	207.9	338.4	....
Services: Debit	78aed	−91.2	−95.4	−112.8	−105.1	−146.8	−145.7	−162.8	−205.4	−265.8	−257.1	−503.7	....
Balance on Goods & Services	78afd	−12.1	−12.8	−93.4	63.0	−130.8	−126.3	−157.7	−192.5	−238.1	−248.8	−194.2	....
Income: Credit	78agd	3.2	3.0	13.4	6.1	10.1	6.7	13.0	14.8	14.1	13.9	16.5	....
Income: Debit	78ahd	−22.5	−28.4	−26.7	−18.1	−9.7	−6.6	−19.5	−16.8	−18.6	−25.4	−27.7	....
Balance on Gds, Serv. & Inc.	78aid	−31.4	−38.2	−106.7	51.0	−130.4	−126.2	−164.2	−194.5	−242.6	−260.3	−205.3	....
Current Transfers, n.i.e.: Credit	78ajd	77.8	77.1	6.2	4.2	5.5	17.6	25.0	40.3	126.9	167.1	230.9	....
Current Transfers: Debit	78akd	—	—	—	—	−3.6	−3.6	−16.9	—	−42.3	−54.9	−50.2	....
Capital Account, n.i.e.	78bcd	—	—	—	—	—	—	—	—	—	—	—	....
Capital Account, n.i.e.: Credit	78bad	—	—	—	—	—	....	—	—	—	—	—	....
Capital Account: Debit	78bbd	—	—	—	—	—	—	—	—	—	—	—	....
Financial Account, n.i.e.	78bjd	−39.0	−15.9	41.3	27.0	126.2	69.6	89.9	107.0	157.4	5.0	−23.2	....
Direct Investment Abroad	78bdd	—	—	—	—	—	....	—	—	—	—	—	....
Dir. Invest. in Rep. Econ., n.i.e.	78bed	6.9	9.8	15.9	25.0	18.9	30.4	53.7	43.0	77.8	131.5	92.9	....
Portfolio Investment Assets	78bfd	—	—	—	—	—	....	—	—	—	50.0	−2.5	....
Equity Securities	78bkd	—	—	—	—	—	....	—	—	—	....	−2.5	....
Debt Securities	78bld	—	—	—	—	—	....	....	—	—	50.0	—	....
Portfolio Investment Liab., n.i.e.	78bgd	—	1.0	—	—	—	....	....	....	....	....	−50.0	....
Equity Securities	78bmd	—	—	—	—	—	....	....	....	....	....	—	....
Debt Securities	78bnd	—	1.0	—	—	—	....	....	....	....	....	−50.0	....
Financial Derivatives Assets	78bwd	....	....	....	....	....	....	....	....	....	....	....	....
Financial Derivatives Liabilities	78bxd	—	....	....	....	....	....	....	....	....	....	....	....
Other Investment Assets	78bhd	−51.0	−49.2	−76.4	−108.1	−54.8	−51.8	−44.3	−5.2	−32.1	9.6	−132.2	....
Monetary Authorities	78bod	—	—	—	—	—	....	....	....	....	....	....	....
General Government	78bpd	—	—	—	—	—	....	....	—	—	....	....	....
Banks	78bqd	−15.3	−15.3	−9.3	−18.1	—	−14.8	−10.7	1.1	−24.4	46.8	15.0	....
Other Sectors	78brd	−35.7	−33.9	−67.1	−90.0	−54.8	−37.0	−33.6	−6.3	−7.8	−37.2	−147.2	....
Other Investment Liab., n.i.e.	78bid	5.1	22.5	101.8	110.1	162.1	91.0	80.5	69.2	111.7	−186.1	68.6	....
Monetary Authorities	78bsd	—	—	—	—	−5.2	—	—	—	—	—	—	....
General Government	78btd	7.9	22.5	56.1	79.3	80.8	91.4	60.5	66.2	72.5	−144.5	112.9	....
Banks	78bud	—	—	—	—	40.0	−4.8	−2.3	.6	6.9	2.4	27.3	....
Other Sectors	78bvd	−2.8	—	45.7	30.8	46.5	4.4	22.3	2.4	32.3	−44.0	−71.6	....
Net Errors and Omissions	78cad	−1.0	9.1	−28.1	−75.6	−50.2	23.6	−19.3	−32.2	14.1	−5.9	1.4	....
Overall Balance	78cbd	6.4	32.1	−87.3	6.6	−52.5	−19.0	−85.5	−79.4	13.4	−149.0	−46.3	....
Reserves and Related Items	79dad	−6.4	−32.1	87.3	−6.6	52.5	19.0	85.5	79.4	−13.4	149.0	46.3	....
Reserve Assets	79dbd	−27.4	−22.6	19.6	−61.2	−6.3	−40.6	−2.5	−15.8	−58.1	96.8	−34.4	....
Use of Fund Credit and Loans	79dcd	21.1	−9.5	−1.8	6.7	−1.3	4.2	1.8	−1.6	−7.7	2.8	−7.2	....
Exceptional Financing	79ded	—	—	69.5	47.9	60.2	55.5	86.2	96.9	52.3	49.4	88.0	....
Government Finance		*Millions of Togrogs: Year Ending December 31*											
Deficit (-) or Surplus	80	−23,647	−29,185	−49,679	† −65,909	−94,913	−99,816	−63,227	−45,824	−71,590	−61,882	−39,373	73,261
Total Revenue and Grants	81y	65,267	113,568	126,725	† 176,152	192,103	203,452	308,283	367,420	477,049	553,889	713,114	837,858
Revenue	81	62,002	108,483	122,316	† 171,744	183,552	196,561	303,215	358,244	470,207	545,227	707,062	833,568
Grants	81z	3,265	5,085	4,409	† 4,408	8,551	6,891	5,068	9,176	6,842	8,662	6,052	4,291
Exp. & Lending Minus Repay	82z	88,914	142,753	176,404	† 242,061	287,016	303,268	371,510	413,244	548,639	615,771	752,486	764,597
Expenditure	82	63,824	97,656	121,233	† 176,436	201,279	232,795	306,037	353,580	481,567	525,297	643,586	690,107
Lending Minus Repayments	83	25,090	45,097	55,171	† 65,625	85,737	70,473	65,473	59,664	67,072	90,475	108,900	74,490
Total Financing	80h	23,648	29,185	49,679	† 65,909	94,913	99,816	63,227	45,824	....	61,882	39,373	−73,261
Domestic	84a	5,010	5,271	14,804	† −24,989	26,319	−6,020	−3,346	−26,166	....	228,922	−38,004	−156,138
Foreign	85a	18,638	23,914	34,875	† 90,898	68,594	105,836	66,573	71,990	....	−167,040	77,417	82,877
Total Debt by Residence	88	196,533	241,503	365,158	† 509,635	676,717	906,723	959,889	961,785	....	....	....	....
Domestic	88a	5,281	233	41,206	† 69,151	82,158	90,039	104,192	82,865	....	....	....	....
Foreign	89a	191,252	241,270	323,952	† 440,484	594,559	816,684	855,697	878,920	....	....	....	....
National Accounts		*Millions of Togrogs*											
Househ.Cons.Expend.,incl.NPISHs.	96f	243,443	348,964	431,658	503,782	553,304	631,916	730,007	834,662	957,790	1,024,971	1,187,277	1,338,061
Government Consumption Expend.	91f	80,139	72,331	92,963	113,956	147,493	158,126	183,213	217,491	236,659	253,391	321,976	342,286
Gross Fixed Capital Formation	93e	82,432	149,150	181,082	214,947	274,335	323,448	321,971	351,594	360,918	498,480	616,571	718,799
Changes in Inventories	93i	7,962	25,343	12,281	18,608	13,705	18,952	46,614	50,615	38,690	57,478	81,433	85,227
Exports of Goods and Services	90c	168,857	264,109	262,168	491,338	452,342	541,978	660,953	700,370	786,572	957,557	1,435,295	1,724,887
Imports of Goods and Services (-)	98c	173,853	270,760	313,278	441,508	562,622	670,826	831,014	911,680	1,051,168	1,242,806	1,665,597	1,892,897
Gross Domestic Product (GDP)	99b	408,981	589,137	666,874	901,123	878,556	1,003,594	1,111,744	1,243,052	1,329,460	1,549,069	1,976,954	2,316,362
Net Primary Income from Abroad.	98.n	−11,030	−11,353	−7,278	−9,491	−79	−4,001	−5,604	31,722	66,511	72,001	160,238	190,000
Gross National Income (GNI)	99a	313,371	538,901	639,281	823,144	817,315	921,344	1,013,282	1,147,363	1,307,297	1,533,170	2,071,119	2,456,505
GDP Volume 2000 Prices	99b.p	833,629	886,366	907,222	943,496	976,824	1,008,236	1,018,886	1,029,542	1,070,681	1,130,285	1,251,426	1,329,455
GDP Volume (2000=100)	99bvp	81.8	87.0	89.0	92.6	95.9	99.0	100.0	101.0	105.1	110.9	122.8	130.5
GDP Deflator (2000=100)	99bip	45.0	60.9	67.4	87.5	82.4	91.2	100.0	110.7	113.8	125.6	144.8	159.7
		Millions: Midyear Estimates											
Population	99z	2.36	2.39	2.41	2.43	2.45	2.47	2.50	2.52	2.55	2.58	2.61	2.65

		1994	1995	1996	1997	1998	1999	2000	2001	2002	2003	2004	2005
Exchange Rates		*E. Caribbean Dollars per SDR: End of Period (aa) E. Caribbean Dollars per US Dollar: End of Period (ae)*											
Official Rate.................................	aa	3.9416	4.0135	3.8825	3.6430	3.8017	3.7058	3.5179	3.3932	3.6707	4.0121	4.1931	3.8590
Official Rate.................................	ae	2.7000	2.7000	2.7000	2.7000	2.7000	2.7000	2.7000	2.7000	2.7000	2.7000	2.7000	2.7000
International Liquidity		*Millions of US Dollars: End of Period*											
Total Reserves minus Gold...............	1l.d	7.62	8.81	8.66	11.30	24.78	14.02	10.40	12.50	14.40	15.23	14.10	13.95
Foreign Exchange..........................	1d.d	7.62	8.81	8.66	11.30	24.78	14.02	10.40	12.50	14.40	15.23	14.10	13.95
Monetary Authorities: Other Liab.....	4..d	—	—	—	—	—	—	—	—	—	—	—	—
Deposit Money Banks: Assets...........	7a.d	15.45	19.09	23.50	32.75	33.01	44.27	44.99	44.94	45.93	55.71	61.75	58.42
Liabilities..................	7b.d	6.80	10.06	9.04	7.29	9.20	8.86	11.29	9.23	9.85	10.35	11.73	13.48
Monetary Authorities		*Millions of E. Caribbean Dollars: End of Period*											
Foreign Assets................................	11	20.18	23.87	23.52	30.69	67.35	38.39	28.63	33.99	38.89	41.11	38.07	37.66
Claims on Central Government........	12a	1.83	1.83	1.83	1.89	1.83	1.93	1.71	.88	.86	.87	.93	.83
Claims on Deposit Money Banks......	12e	.02	.01	.01	.02	.02	.03	.02	.01	.01	.01	.02	.01
Reserve Money...............................	14	21.95	23.92	24.65	31.08	66.90	37.47	28.15	32.33	36.65	38.89	35.66	35.01
of which: Currency Outside DMBs..	14a	7.44	7.72	9.03	17.55	13.27	13.36	9.66	11.83	10.81	12.55	12.96	12.29
Foreign Liabilities..........................	16c	—	—	—	—	—	—	—	—	—	—	—	—
Central Government Deposits...........	16d	.08	1.79	.71	1.52	2.29	2.87	2.21	2.55	3.10	3.10	3.35	3.49
Other Items (Net)...........................	17r	—	—	—	—	—	—	—	—	—	—	—	—
Deposit Money Banks		*Millions of E. Caribbean Dollars: End of Period*											
Reserves.......................................	20	13.28	17.85	13.73	20.03	67.15	23.99	18.61	21.60	26.33	29.24	34.87	32.20
Foreign Assets................................	21	41.71	51.55	63.45	88.42	89.14	119.52	121.47	121.34	124.02	150.41	166.73	157.74
Claims on Central Government........	22a	.50	.25	.50	.50	.25	2.17	2.33	.87	2.27	1.18	.97	.77
Claims on Local Government...........	22b	—	.52	—	—	—	—	—	.10	—	—	—	—
Claims on Nonfin.Pub.Enterprises.....	22c	.09	2.80	3.12	2.68	—	—	—	—	—	—	—	.28
Claims on Private Sector.................	22d	74.97	70.24	65.39	57.41	32.78	22.72	23.12	23.88	22.24	22.94	23.71	28.07
Claims on Nonbank Financial Insts...	22g	.31	.62	.50	.40	.36	.33	.25	1.79	.12	.39	.81	—
Demand Deposits...........................	24	22.14	20.54	18.06	24.17	34.61	23.79	20.82	20.96	22.90	30.57	32.03	27.13
Time, Savings,& Fgn.Currency Dep...	25	79.27	78.58	71.48	71.51	82.33	83.05	79.19	81.02	79.57	83.36	92.18	102.61
Foreign Liabilities..........................	26c	18.36	27.17	24.41	19.68	24.84	23.92	30.49	24.93	26.60	27.96	31.67	36.40
Central Government Deposits...........	26d	1.97	5.17	11.72	28.97	22.12	18.08	14.94	19.15	29.04	39.44	45.97	36.56
Credit from Monetary Authorities.....	26g	.01	—	.01	—	.01	1.03	—	.01	.01	.12	.37	—
Capital Accounts...........................	27a	5.07	4.69	2.14	4.59	5.44	6.89	8.20	9.80	11.32	13.75	18.44	20.85
Other Items (Net)...........................	27r	4.04	7.68	18.88	20.50	20.32	11.97	12.15	13.72	5.54	8.96	6.42	−4.50
Monetary Survey		*Millions of E. Caribbean Dollars: End of Period*											
Foreign Assets (Net).......................	31n	43.53	48.26	62.56	99.43	131.65	133.99	119.62	130.41	136.31	163.57	173.13	159.00
Domestic Credit.............................	32	75.64	69.29	58.91	32.38	10.80	6.18	10.26	5.81	−6.65	−17.17	−22.91	−10.10
Claims on Central Govt. (Net)........	32an	.28	−4.88	−10.10	−28.10	−22.34	−16.86	−13.11	−19.96	−29.02	−40.50	−47.42	−38.45
Claims on Local Government..........	32b	—	.52	—	—	—	—	—	.10	—	—	—	—
Claims on Nonfin.Pub.Enterprises...	32c	.09	2.80	3.12	2.68	—	—	—	—	—	—	—	.28
Claims on Private Sector...............	32d	74.97	70.24	65.39	57.41	32.78	22.72	23.12	23.88	22.24	22.94	23.71	28.07
Claims on Nonbank Financial Inst...	32g	.31	.62	.50	.40	.36	.33	.25	1.79	.12	.39	.81	—
Money..	34	29.57	28.26	27.10	41.72	47.88	37.15	31.48	32.80	33.71	43.12	44.99	39.42
Quasi-Money.................................	35	79.27	78.58	71.48	71.51	82.33	83.05	79.19	81.02	79.57	83.36	92.18	102.61
Capital Accounts...........................	37a	5.07	4.69	2.14	4.59	5.44	6.89	8.20	9.80	11.32	13.75	18.44	20.85
Other Items (Net)..........................	37r	5.25	6.02	20.76	13.98	6.80	13.09	11.01	12.61	5.06	6.17	−5.39	−13.98
Money plus Quasi-Money...............	35l	108.84	106.84	98.57	113.23	130.21	120.20	110.67	113.82	113.28	126.47	137.17	142.03
Money (National Definitions)		*Millions of E. Caribbean Dollars: End of Period*											
M1...	59ma	20.34	20.88	22.94	34.29	37.41	31.44	26.11	25.45	26.33	32.73	36.05	31.96
M2...	59mb	85.49	81.42	84.08	98.84	117.44	111.30	101.05	102.03	99.80	108.26	119.51	123.65
Interest Rates		*Percent Per Annum*											
Discount Rate (End of Period)..........	60	9.00	9.00	9.00	8.00	8.00	8.00	8.00	7.00	7.00	6.50	6.50	6.50
Money Market Rate.......................	60b	5.25	5.25	5.25	5.25	5.25	5.25	5.25	† 5.64	6.32	6.07	4.67	4.01
Savings Rate................................	60k	4.00	4.00	4.00	4.00	4.00	4.21	4.50	4.50	4.50	† 4.20	3.38	3.42
Deposit Rate................................	60l	3.25	3.24	3.29	3.02	2.74	3.14	3.35	3.35	3.08	3.06	2.29	2.52
Deposit Rate (Fgn. Currency)...........	60l.f	....	....	....	....	....	....	....	....	....	5.70	4.34	4.31
Lending Rate................................	60p	13.06	12.63	12.37	12.37	12.15	11.52	11.52	11.52	11.34	12.10	10.95	10.56

		1994	1995	1996	1997	1998	1999	2000	2001	2002	2003	2004	2005
Balance of Payments						*Millions of US Dollars: Minus Sign Indicates Debit*							
Current Account, n.i.e.	**78ald**	−12.24	−1.96	15.71	−1.97	3.41	−1.41	−6.51	−5.62	−8.16	....	....	....
Goods: Exports f.o.b.	**78aad**	2.92	12.14	41.34	8.20	1.20	1.26	1.12	.73	1.47	....	....	....
Goods: Imports f.o.b.	**78abd**	−30.04	−33.90	−35.97	−28.11	−19.35	−19.27	−19.02	−17.05	−22.38	....	....	....
Trade Balance	**78acd**	−27.12	−21.76	5.38	−19.91	−18.15	−18.00	−17.90	−16.33	−20.91	....	....	....
Services: Credit	**78add**	27.16	24.61	15.54	13.88	13.00	20.26	15.83	14.21	14.13	....	....	....
Services: Debit	**78aed**	−14.32	−14.77	−17.39	−12.92	−20.71	−21.53	−18.73	−24.03	−23.22	....	....	....
Balance on Goods & Services	**78afd**	−14.28	−11.92	3.53	−18.95	−25.87	−19.28	−20.81	−26.15	−30.01	....	....	....
Income: Credit	**78agd**	−.01	.66	.54	.97	.77	1.19	1.48	1.28	1.45	....	....	....
Income: Debit	**78ahd**	−4.44	−2.93	−2.00	−3.29	−2.55	−7.13	−4.17	−1.94	−4.54	....	....	....
Balance on Gds, Serv. & Inc.	**78aid**	−18.73	−14.19	2.08	−21.27	−27.64	−25.22	−23.50	−26.81	−33.10	....	....	....
Current Transfers, n.i.e.: Credit	**78ajd**	10.61	13.55	14.90	20.38	33.24	26.49	18.90	23.66	28.13	....	....	....
Current Transfers: Debit	**78akd**	−4.12	−1.33	−1.26	−1.08	−2.19	−2.69	−1.91	−2.47	−3.19	....	....	....
Capital Account, n.i.e.	**78bcd**	10.10	5.16	−12.50	3.56	3.59	1.33	4.43	7.70	12.55	....	....	....
Capital Account, n.i.e.: Credit	**78bad**	10.10	6.67	2.32	7.19	7.22	4.96	7.32	9.66	14.64	....	....	....
Capital Account: Debit	**78bbd**	—	−1.51	−14.81	−3.63	−3.63	−3.63	−2.89	−1.96	−2.09	....	....	....
Financial Account, n.i.e.	**78bjd**	.73	1.93	−6.00	−9.07	3.92	−5.90	3.59	−3.16	−.14	....	....	....
Direct Investment Abroad	**78bdd**	—	—	—	—	—	—	—	—	—	....	....	....
Dir. Invest. in Rep. Econ., n.i.e.	**78bed**	7.16	3.03	−.32	2.57	2.57	8.21	3.46	.96	2.09	....	....	....
Portfolio Investment Assets	**78bfd**	−.03	−.03	—	—	—	—	—	—	—	....	....	....
Equity Securities	**78bkd**	....	....	....	....	....	....	....	....	....	....	....	....
Debt Securities	**78bld**	....	....	....	....	....	....	....	....	....	....	....	....
Portfolio Investment Liab., n.i.e.	**78bgd**	—	.06	—	.06	.09	−.03	.55	−.60	−.22	....	....	....
Equity Securities	**78bmd**	....	....	....	....	....	....	....	....	....	....	....	....
Debt Securities	**78bnd**	....	....	....	....	....	....	....	....	....	....	....	....
Financial Derivatives Assets	**78bwd**	....	....	....	....	....	....	....	....	....	....	....	....
Financial Derivatives Liabilities	**78bxd**	....	....	....	....	....	....	....	....	....	....	....	....
Other Investment Assets	**78bhd**	−3.60	−4.20	−.84	−1.23	−1.09	−.93	−4.61	−.83	−.25	....	....	....
Monetary Authorities	**78bod**	....	....	....	....	....	....	....	....	....	....	....	....
General Government	**78bpd**	....	....	....	....	....	....	....	....	....	....	....	....
Banks	**78bqd**	....	....	....	....	....	....	....	....	....	....	....	....
Other Sectors	**78brd**	....	....	....	....	....	....	....	....	....	....	....	....
Other Investment Liab., n.i.e.	**78bid**	−2.81	3.06	−4.84	−10.47	2.35	−13.16	4.19	−2.69	−1.77	....	....	....
Monetary Authorities	**78bsd**	....	....	....	....	....	....	....	....	....	....	....	....
General Government	**78btd**	....	....	....	....	....	....	....	....	....	....	....	....
Banks	**78bud**	....	....	....	....	....	....	....	....	....	....	....	....
Other Sectors	**78bvd**	....	....	....	....	....	....	....	....	....	....	....	....
Net Errors and Omissions	**78cad**	2.97	−3.94	2.63	10.11	2.61	−4.71	−5.06	3.20	−2.57	....	....	....
Overall Balance	**78cbd**	1.57	1.19	−.15	2.63	13.53	−10.69	−3.55	2.12	1.67	....	....	....
Reserves and Related Items	**79dad**	−1.57	−1.19	.15	−2.63	−13.53	10.69	3.55	−2.12	−1.67	....	....	....
Reserve Assets	**79dbd**	−1.57	−1.19	.15	−2.63	−13.53	10.69	3.55	−2.12	−1.67	....	....	....
Use of Fund Credit and Loans	**79dcd**	....	....	....	....	....	....	....	....	....	....	....	....
Exceptional Financing	**79ded**	....	....	....	....	....	....	....	....	....	....	....	....
National Accounts						*Millions of E. Caribbean Dollars*							
Gross Domestic Product (GDP)	**99b**	171.8	162.5	174.2	110.5	101.4	95.6	93.9	93.7	102.6	102.5	111.0	114.0
GDP Volume 1990 Prices	**99b.p**	132.1	121.9	95.9	76.7	69.0	60.2	58.4	56.9	58.8	68.9	60.9	59.1
GDP Volume (2000=100)	**99bvp**	226.2	208.7	164.2	131.3	118.2	103.1	100.0	97.4	100.7	118.0	104.3	101.2
GDP Deflator (2000=100)	**99bip**	80.9	82.9	113.0	89.6	91.4	98.8	100.0	102.4	108.5	92.5	113.4	120.0
						Millions: Midyear Estimates							
Population	**99z**	.0108	.0102	.0092	.0078	.0062	.0048	.0039	.0035	.0035	.0038	.0042	.0045

Morocco 686

		1994	1995	1996	1997	1998	1999	2000	2001	2002	2003	2004	2005
Exchange Rates						*Dirhams per SDR: End of Period*							
Official Rate	aa	13.080	12.589	12.653	13.107	13.031	13.845	13.836	14.528	13.822	13.002	12.762	13.220
						Dirhams per US Dollar: End of Period (ae) Period Average (rf)							
Official Rate	ae	8.960	8.469	8.800	9.714	9.255	10.087	10.619	11.560	10.167	8.750	8.218	9.249
Official Rate	rf	9.203	8.540	8.716	9.527	9.604	9.804	10.626	11.303	11.021	9.574	8.868	8.865
						Index Numbers (2000=100): Period Averages							
Official Rate	ahx	115.5	124.4	121.8	111.5	110.6	108.3	100.0	94.0	96.5	111.0	119.8	119.9
Nominal Effective Exchange Rate	nec	93.5	94.9	95.1	95.7	97.1	97.6	100.0	97.4	96.2	96.2	95.9	95.4
Real Effective Exchange Rate	rec	92.2	95.2	95.6	95.3	97.9	98.0	100.0	95.9	95.6	94.6	93.5	91.9
Fund Position						*Millions of SDRs: End of Period*							
Quota	2f.s	428	428	428	428	428	588	588	588	588	588	588	588
SDRs	1b.s	18	17	5	1	2	62	92	98	90	76	77	55
Reserve Position in the Fund	1c.s	30	30	30	30	30	70	70	70	70	70	70	70
Total Fund Cred.&Loans Outstg	2tl	101	35	2	—	—	—	—	—	—	—	—	—
International Liquidity						*Millions of US Dollars Unless Otherwise Indicated: End of Period*							
Total Reserves minus Gold	1l.d	4,352	3,601	3,794	3,993	4,435	5,689	4,823	8,474	10,133	13,851	16,337	16,187
SDRs	1b.d	26	26	7	1	3	85	119	123	122	112	120	79
Reserve Position in the Fund	1c.d	44	45	44	41	43	97	92	89	96	105	109	101
Foreign Exchange	1d.d	4,281	3,530	3,743	3,951	4,389	5,507	4,612	8,262	9,915	13,634	16,107	16,008
Gold (Million Fine Troy Ounces)	1ad	.704	.704	.704	.704	.704	.704	.706	.707	.708	.708	.708	.708
Gold (National Valuation)	1and	218	230	222	201	211	193	184	169	193	224	239	280
Monetary Authorities: Other Liab.	4..d	47	41	62	84	78	82	84	80	80	135	217	261
Deposit Money Banks: Assets	7a.d	755	653	665	† 381	496	477	599	568	888	996	1,508	2,185
Liabilities	7b.d	672	442	520	† 351	462	457	407	336	269	412	408	491
Other Banking Insts.: Liabilities	7f.d	1,534	1,589	1,452	....	....	....	....	....	....	....	....	....
Monetary Authorities						*Millions of Dirhams: End of Period*							
Foreign Assets	11	41,001	32,509	35,402	40,808	43,070	59,392	53,224	99,920	104,979	123,156	136,793	152,252
Claims on Central Government	12a	8,305	18,389	19,179	† 27,860	27,459	21,129	24,310	15,993	16,485	18,093	18,532	13,999
Claims on Private Sector	12d	8,416	9,129	9,075	† 40	114	47	82	64	65	73	86	95
Claims on Deposit Money Banks	12e	512	500	1,250	† 1,210	3,381	1,346	7,161	7	1	—	3	
Reserve Money	14	50,746	53,384	57,467	† 62,557	66,999	75,912	78,356	95,151	98,581	114,594	129,054	141,345
of which: Currency Outside DMBs	14a	41,107	43,261	46,581	48,662	50,644	56,713	58,169	66,025	69,565	74,893	79,715	89,304
Foreign Liabilities	16c	1,745	787	577	† 817	725	826	893	927	809	1,183	1,787	2,414
Central Government Deposits	16d	605	633	816	† 786	826	532	806	10,806	11,322	13,801	15,207	13,591
Capital Accounts	17a	....	....	....	4,799	4,877	4,977	5,107	5,252	5,410	5,455	5,411	5,502
Other Items (Net)	17r	5,139	5,722	6,046	† 959	597	−332	−384	3,848	5,408	6,289	3,955	3,494
Deposit Money Banks						*Millions of Dirhams: End of Period*							
Reserves	20	8,293	9,018	9,419	† 11,936	13,380	17,100	18,980	27,466	27,535	39,446	48,618	50,279
Foreign Assets	21	6,765	5,533	5,855	† 3,703	4,592	4,812	6,356	6,566	9,030	8,713	12,392	20,213
Claims on Central Government	22a	50,746	49,633	50,048	58,616	58,614	54,917	61,729	73,161	76,923	77,123	72,033	75,391
Claims on Private Sector	22d	70,408	81,777	90,545	† 151,203	167,602	183,531	199,576	208,026	214,949	232,159	248,420	281,329
Claims on Other Financial Insts	22f	1,409	1,637	627	† 25,580	29,834	32,884	34,309	35,883	39,075	40,004	42,677	45,476
Demand Deposits	24	79,099	84,606	87,323	† 116,054	124,767	140,895	156,545	181,099	199,374	222,896	247,310	283,997
Time Deposits	25	45,958	50,552	54,962	† 64,121	65,114	69,389	76,281	84,294	83,337	87,360	87,741	99,094
Foreign Liabilities	26c	6,020	3,745	4,579	† 3,409	4,276	4,605	4,322	3,881	2,740	3,603	3,352	4,541
Credit from Monetary Authorities	26g	1,108	1,232	2,508	† 1,209	3,381	1,346	7,161	7	1	—	3	—
Capital Accounts	27a	....	....	....	38,743	44,973	47,759	48,890	57,568	59,850	66,685	75,024	76,225
Other Items (Net)	27r	5,436	7,463	7,122	† 27,502	29,511	29,383	27,751	24,253	22,210	16,901	10,710	8,831
Post Office: Checking Deposits	24..i	1,833	1,701	1,721	1,871	....	....	....	....	....	....	....	....
Treasury: Checking Deposits	24..r	4,950	5,088	6,311	6,202	....	....	....	....	....	....	....	....
Monetary Survey						*Millions of Dirhams: End of Period*							
Foreign Assets (Net)	31n	40,002	33,509	36,101	† 40,285	42,661	58,773	54,365	101,678	110,460	127,083	144,046	165,510
Domestic Credit	32	145,462	166,721	176,690	† 262,513	282,797	291,976	319,200	322,321	336,175	353,651	366,541	402,699
Claims on Central Govt. (Net)	32an	65,229	74,178	76,443	† 85,690	85,247	75,514	85,233	78,348	82,086	81,415	75,358	75,799
Claims on Private Sector	32d	78,824	90,906	99,620	† 152,069	168,609	185,819	200,635	208,711	216,539	234,604	251,527	284,428
Claims on Other Financial Insts	32f	1,409	1,637	627	† 24,754	28,941	30,643	33,332	35,262	37,550	37,632	39,656	42,472
Money	34	128,284	135,964	143,818	† 166,843	179,795	200,597	216,503	249,693	272,184	298,983	328,689	375,663
Quasi-Money	35	45,958	50,552	54,962	† 64,121	65,114	69,389	76,281	84,294	83,337	87,360	87,741	99,094
Other Items (Net)	37r	11,222	13,714	14,011	† 71,834	80,549	80,896	80,781	90,012	91,114	94,391	94,157	93,452
Money plus Quasi-Money	35l	174,242	186,516	198,780	† 230,964	244,909	269,986	292,784	333,987	355,521	386,343	416,430	474,757
Other Banking Institutions						*Millions of Dirhams: End of Period*							
Reserves	40	1,383	1,301	1,469	....	....	....	....	....	....	....	....	....
Claims on Central Government	42a	10,966	13,063	16,164	....	....	....	....	....	....	....	....	....
Claims on Official Entities	42bx	—	—	—	....	....	....	....	....	....	....	....	....
Claims on Private Sector	42d	41,311	44,167	47,249	....	....	....	....	....	....	....	....	....
Time Deposits	45	24,606	28,574	32,745	....	....	....	....	....	....	....	....	....
Bonds	46ab	10,628	10,987	11,848	....	....	....	....	....	....	....	....	....
Long-Term Foreign Liabilities	46cl	13,744	13,461	12,776	....	....	....	....	....	....	....	....	....
Central Govt. Lending Funds	46f	393	277	271	....	....	....	....	....	....	....	....	....
Credit from Monetary Authorities	46g	8	—	—	....	....	....	....	....	....	....	....	....
Credit from Deposit Money Banks	46h	604	623	683	....	....	....	....	....	....	....	....	....
Capital Accounts	47a	8,093	9,122	10,068	....	....	....	....	....	....	....	....	....
Other Items (Net)	47r	−4,416	−4,513	−3,509	....	....	....	....	....	....	....	....	....
Liquid Liabilities	55l	198,848	215,090	231,525	....	....	....	....	....	....	....	....	....
Interest Rates						*Percent Per Annum*							
Discount Rate (End of Period)	60	7.17	....	....	....	6.04	5.42	5.00	4.71	3.79	3.25	3.25	3.25
Money Market Rate	60b	12.29	10.06	8.42	7.89	6.30	5.64	5.41	4.44	2.99	3.22	2.39	2.78
Treasury Bill Rate	60c	....	....	....	....	....	....	....	....	....	....	....	....
Deposit Rate	60l	....	....	....	....	7.3	6.4	5.2	5.0	4.5	3.8	3.6	3.5
Lending Rate	60p	10.0	....	....	....	13.5	13.5	13.3	13.3	13.1	12.6	11.5	....
Govt.Bond Yield: Long-Term	61	....	....	....	....	....	....	....	....	....	....	5.7	5.4
Med.-Term	61a	....	....	....	....	....	....	....	....	....	5.6	4.3	....

Morocco 686

		1994	1995	1996	1997	1998	1999	2000	2001	2002	2003	2004	2005
Prices, Production, Labor													

		1994	1995	1996	1997	1998	1999	2000	2001	2002	2003	2004	2005
Prices, Production, Labor		*Index Numbers (2000=100): Period Averages*											
Wholesale Prices	63	86.8	92.5	96.5	† 95.0	97.6	96.0	100.0	99.6	101.8	97.2	....	....
Producer Prices: Manufacturing	63ey	....	....	....	93.4	90.9	91.5	100.0	98.2	97.0	98.2	103.2	112.6
Consumer Prices	64	85.9	91.2	93.9	94.9	97.5	98.1	100.0	100.6	103.4	104.6	106.2	107.2
Manufacturing Production	66ey	86.2	85.8	89.3	92.2	94.5	96.7	100.0	103.3	106.3	110.0	113.4	116.3
Mining Production	66zx	95.6	96.4	98.7	107.5	107.1	103.6	100.0	102.4	105.0	100.5	108.6	115.7
Energy Production	66ze	92.8	91.8	91.8	97.7	97.1	103.4	100.0	107.3	106.9	97.8	113.9	130.3
		Number in Thousands: Period Averages											
Labor Force	67d	....	4,863	4,875	5,068	5,138	† 10,278	10,285	10,230	10,379	10,902	11,015	11,140
Employment	67e	....	3,870	4,034	4,224	4,168	† 8,846	8,891	8,955	9,176	9,603	9,822	9,913
Unemployment	67c	....	1,112	871	845	969	† 1,433	1,394	1,275	1,203	1,299	1,193	1,227
Unemployment Rate (%)	67r	....	22.9	18.1	16.9	19.1	† 13.9	13.6	12.5	11.6	11.9	10.8	11.0
Intl. Transactions & Positions		*Millions of Dirhams*											
Exports	70	50,965	58,673	60,013	67,057	68,608	72,283	78,827	80,667	86,389	83,887	87,895	93,625
Imports, c.i.f.	71	76,059	85,493	84,612	90,712	98,676	97,454	122,527	124,718	130,409	136,070	157,921	180,268
Imports, f.o.b.	71.v	60,168	78,654	77,843	83,455	90,782	97,457	122,527	114,744	....	....	....	....
		2000=100											
Volume of Exports	72	† 79.5	78.9	76.7	82.0	† 84.0	91.8	100.0	101.9	106.6	102.3	103.4	....
Volume of Imports	73	† 58.4	65.7	61.3	66.1	† 81.7	89.2	100.0	98.3	104.7	113.7	125.9	....
Unit Value of Exports	74	† 89.9	99.7	105.4	106.2	† 103.5	101.7	100.0	100.4	102.8	104.6	105.9	....
Unit Value of Imports	75	† 112.6	110.4	116.9	112.9	† 98.6	98.5	100.0	103.6	101.8	98.1	101.4	....
Balance of Payments		*Millions of US Dollars: Minus Sign Indicates Debit*											
Current Account, n.i.e.	78ald	−723	−1,296	−58	−169	−146	−171	−501	1,606	1,472	1,552	922	....
Goods: Exports f.o.b.	78aad	5,541	6,871	6,886	7,039	7,144	7,509	7,419	7,142	7,839	8,771	9,922	....
Goods: Imports f.o.b.	78abd	−7,648	−9,353	−9,080	−8,903	−9,463	−9,957	−10,654	−10,164	−10,900	−13,117	−16,408	....
Trade Balance	78acd	−2,107	−2,482	−2,193	−1,864	−2,319	−2,448	−3,235	−3,022	−3,061	−4,345	−6,487	....
Services: Credit	78add	2,014	2,173	2,743	2,471	2,827	3,115	3,034	4,029	4,360	5,478	6,710	....
Services: Debit	78aed	−1,730	−1,890	−1,782	−1,724	−1,963	−2,003	−1,892	−2,118	−2,413	−2,861	−3,451	....
Balance on Goods & Services	78afd	−1,822	−2,199	−1,233	−1,117	−1,455	−1,335	−2,093	−1,111	−1,115	−1,728	−3,228	....
Income: Credit	78agd	224	251	189	172	194	187	276	326	377	370	505	....
Income: Debit	78ahd	−1,394	−1,569	−1,498	−1,348	−1,227	−1,172	−1,140	−1,159	−1,115	−1,162	−1,176	....
Balance on Gds, Serv. & Inc.	78aid	−2,992	−3,516	−2,541	−2,292	−2,489	−2,321	−2,958	−1,944	−1,853	−2,520	−3,898	....
Current Transfers, n.i.e.: Credit	78ajd	2,355	2,298	2,565	2,204	2,438	2,246	2,574	3,670	3,441	4,214	4,974	....
Current Transfers, n.i.e.: Debit	78akd	−86	−78	−82	−81	−95	−96	−118	−120	−115	−141	−154	....
Capital Account, n.i.e.	78bcd	−3	−6	73	−5	−10	−9	−6	−9	−6	−10	−8	....
Capital Account, n.i.e.: Credit	78bad	—	—	78	1	—	—	—	—	—	—	—	....
Capital Account: Debit	78bbd	−4	−6	−5	−5	−10	−9	−6	−9	−6	−10	−8	....
Financial Account, n.i.e.	78bjd	1,248	−984	−897	−990	−644	−13	−774	−966	−1,336	−1,091	69	....
Direct Investment Abroad	78bdd	−24	−15	−30	−9	−20	−18	−59	−97	−28	−13	−20	....
Dir. Invest. in Rep. Econ., n.i.e.	78bed	551	92	76	4	12	3	221	144	79	2,313	769	....
Portfolio Investment Assets	78bfd	—	—	—	—	—	—	—	—	—	—	—	....
Equity Securities	78bkd	—	—	—	—	—	—	—	—	—	—	—	....
Debt Securities	78bld	—	—	—	—	—	—	—	—	—	—	—	....
Portfolio Investment Liab., n.i.e.	78bgd	238	20	142	38	24	6	18	−7	−8	8	572	....
Equity Securities	78bmd	238	20	142	38	24	6	18	−7	−8	8	572	....
Debt Securities	78bnd	—	—	—	—	—	—	—	—	—	—	—	....
Financial Derivatives Assets	78bwd	....	....	....	....	....	....	....	....	....	....	....	....
Financial Derivatives Liabilities	78bxd	....	....	....	....	....	....	....	....	....	....	....	....
Other Investment Assets	78bhd	344	—	—	—	—	—	....	—	—	−869	−454	....
Monetary Authorities	78bod	....	....	....	....	....	....	....	—	—	—	—	....
General Government	78bpd	—	—	—	—	—	....	—	—	—	—	—	....
Banks	78bqd	—	—	—	....	....	....	—	—	—	−529	—	....
Other Sectors	78brd	344	—	—	....	....	....	—	—	—	−340	−454	....
Other Investment Liab., n.i.e.	78bid	139	−1,083	−1,085	−1,022	−660	−4	−953	−1,006	−1,380	−2,529	−797	....
Monetary Authorities	78bsd	19	—	—	—	—	—	—	—	—	—	—	....
General Government	78btd	−421	−967	−867	−1,232	−954	−1,293	−1,208	−1,215	−1,465	−1,830	−1,321	....
Banks	78bud	−48	−132	−167	−123	−197	−152	−80	−93	−128	−214	−213	....
Other Sectors	78bvd	588	16	−50	333	492	1,441	335	302	214	−486	737	....
Net Errors and Omissions	78cad	−39	391	209	175	160	123	114	230	−182	−297	−247	....
Overall Balance	78cbd	483	−1,895	−673	−988	−640	−69	−1,166	861	−52	154	736	....
Reserves and Related Items	79dad	−483	1,895	673	988	640	69	1,166	−861	52	−154	−736	....
Reserve Assets	79dbd	−362	984	−274	−553	−248	−1,636	416	−3,842	−644	−1,649	−1,901	....
Use of Fund Credit and Loans	79dcd	−152	−101	−47	−3	—	—	—	—	—	—	—	....
Exceptional Financing	79ded	31	1,013	995	1,544	887	1,705	751	2,982	696	1,495	1,166	....

Morocco 686

		1994	1995	1996	1997	1998	1999	2000	2001	2002	2003	2004	2005
International Investment Position							*Millions of US Dollars*						
Assets........................	79aad	....	....	....	....	....	....	....	....	12,192	17,022	20,207	....
Direct Investment Abroad.............	79abd	....	....	....	....	....	....	....	....	453	560	676	....
Portfolio Investment......................	79acd	....	....	....	....	....	....	....	....	85	116	156	....
Equity Securities.........................	79add	....	....	....	....	....	....	....	....	82	116	156	....
Debt Securities..........................	79aed	....	....	....	....	....	....	....	....	3	—	—	....
Financial Derivatives....................	79ald	....	....	....	....	....	....	....	....	—	—	—	....
Other Investment........................	79afd	....	....	....	....	....	....	....	....	468	1,305	1,221	....
Monetary Authorities..................	79agd	....	....	....	....	....	....	....	....	—	—	—	....
General Government...................	79ahd	....	....	....	....	....	....	....	....	64	77	84	....
Banks.....................................	79aid	....	....	....	....	....	....	....	....	25	629	643	....
Other Sectors...........................	79ajd	....	....	....	....	....	....	....	....	378	600	495	....
Reserve Assets...........................	79akd	....	....	....	....	....	....	....	....	11,186	15,040	18,154	....
Liabilities....................................	79lad	....	....	....	....	....	....	....	....	28,641	34,727	38,589	....
Dir. Invest. in Rep. Economy..........	79lbd	....	....	....	....	....	....	....	....	12,130	17,106	19,883	....
Portfolio Investment......................	79lcd	....	....	....	....	....	....	....	....	636	840	1,720	....
Equity Securities.........................	79ldd	....	....	....	....	....	....	....	....	613	799	1,679	....
Debt Securities..........................	79led	....	....	....	....	....	....	....	....	22	41	41	....
Financial Derivatives....................	79lld	....	....	....	....	....	....	....	....	—	—	—	....
Other Investment........................	79lfd	....	....	....	....	....	....	....	....	15,875	16,780	16,986	....
Monetary Authorities..................	79lgd	....	....	....	....	....	....	....	....	80	135	217	....
General Government...................	79lhd	....	....	....	....	....	....	....	....	9,104	9,020	8,562	....
Banks.....................................	79lid	....	....	....	....	....	....	....	....	1,280	1,302	1,131	....
Other Sectors...........................	79ljd	....	....	....	....	....	....	....	....	5,412	6,324	7,076	....
Government Finance						*Millions of Dirhams: Year Ending December 31*							
Deficit (-) or Surplus......................	80	−8,915	† −12,365	−9,485	−4,778	−13,197	3,046	−20,778	−10,042	−17,251	−15,469	−15,432	−19,557
Revenue.....................................	81	81,442	† 82,018	79,180	88,845	91,189	111,406	100,902	127,444	104,723	116,446	125,060	140,206
Expenditure................................	82	90,072	† 93,889	88,667	96,461	105,539	109,424	122,019	137,887	122,242	131,670	140,810	160,052
Lending Minus Repayments...........	83	285	† 494	−2	−2,838	−1,153	−1,064	−339	−401	−268	245	−318	−289
Financing													
Net Borrowing: Domestic..............	84a	13,949	† 14,843	12,914	18,069	10,722	12,973	15,038	28,699	28,680	26,312	19,796	30,088
Net borrowing: Foreign.................	85a	−4,428	† −2,111	−2,666	−8,398	−4,738	−4,394	−6,320	−9,861	−11,199	−8,746	−6,451	−1,428
Use of Cash Balances...................	87	−606	† −367	−763	−4,893	7,213	−11,625	12,062	−8,796	−231	−2,098	2,087	−9,103
Debt: Domestic..........................	88a	93,843	† 93,843	110,461	121,526	131,034	136,668	149,388	175,899	191,554	211,485	223,963	258,529
Debt: Foreign.............................	89a	134,952	† 129,766	131,038	130,377	125,864	123,955	118,646	110,597	92,800	78,924	70,400	68,972
National Accounts							*Billions of Dirhams*						
Househ.Cons.Expend.,incl.NPISHs....	96f	196.76	201.42	227.44	218.61	234.26	229.09	242.97	257.97	264.87	273.35	298.81	307.80
Government Consumption Expend...	91f	48.53	50.06	53.82	56.61	62.00	66.15	67.69	75.82	79.96	88.11	93.05	101.26
Gross Fixed Capital Formation.........	93e	57.90	60.39	61.94	65.79	75.74	81.90	85.42	85.37	91.14	100.50	109.08	115.92
Changes in Inventories...................	93i	1.72	−1.99	.60	.11	.48	−1.98	−1.48	2.35	−.83	.58	2.01	2.90
Exports of Goods and Services.........	90c	59.43	64.48	69.60	73.56	77.72	84.66	92.96	106.95	115.15	117.02	127.50	145.81
Imports of Goods and Services (-).....	98c	76.20	83.39	82.02	85.55	93.50	99.54	116.20	120.48	128.25	134.45	157.06	180.60
Gross Domestic Product (GDP)........	99b	279.58	282.47	319.39	318.34	344.01	345.59	354.21	383.18	397.78	419.49	443.67	457.62
Net Primary Income from Abroad.....	98.n	10.12	8.79	12.73	11.17	14.40	13.24	18.20	31.74	29.38	32.66	38.11	45.92
Gross National Income (GNI)...........	99a	289.44	290.44	332.02	329.51	358.41	358.84	372.41	414.93	427.16	452.15	481.78	503.54
GDP Volume 1980 Prices...............	99b.p	121.60	113.62	127.03	124.20	133.73	133.62	134.90	143.39	147.97	156.14	162.77	165.56
GDP Volume (2000=100)..............	99bvp	90.1	84.2	94.2	92.1	99.1	99.1	100.0	106.3	109.7	115.7	120.7	122.7
GDP Deflator (2000=100)..............	99bip	87.6	94.7	95.8	97.6	98.0	98.5	100.0	101.8	102.4	102.3	103.8	105.3
							Millions: Midyear Estimates						
Population................................	99z	26.55	27.00	27.45	27.90	28.34	28.79	29.23	29.67	30.12	30.57	31.02	31.48

Mozambique 688

		1994	1995	1996	1997	1998	1999	2000	2001	2002	2003	2004	2005
Exchange Rates						*Meticais per SDR: End of Period*							
Market Rate	aa	9,709.5	16,187.9	16,359.7	15,574.4	17,411.7	18,254.4 † 22,332.5		29,307.5	32,430.4	35,450.3	29,350.8	34,564.0
						Meticais per US Dollar: End of Period (ae) Period Average (rf)							
Market Rate	ae	6,651.0	10,890.0	11,377.0	11,543.0	12,366.0	13,300.0 † 17,140.5		23,320.4	23,854.3	23,856.7	18,899.3	24,183.0
Market Rate	rf	6,038.6	9,024.3	11,293.7	11,543.6	11,874.6	12,775.1	15,227.2	20,703.6	23,678.0	23,782.3	22,581.3	23,061.0
Fund Position						*Millions of SDRs: End of Period*							
Quota	2f.s	84.00	84.00	84.00	84.00	84.00	113.60	113.60	113.60	113.60	113.60	113.60	113.60
SDRs	1b.s	.03	.03	.04	.04	.04	.05	.05	.05	.05	.05	.05	.16
Reserve Position in the Fund	1c.s	.01	.01	.01	.01	.01	.01	.01	.01	.01	.01	.01	.01
Total Fund Cred.&Loans Outstg	2tl	145.24	135.79	125.89	140.11	147.24	145.42	168.47	155.89	147.16	140.75	127.04	109.80
International Liquidity						*Millions of US Dollars Unless Otherwise Indicated: End of Period*							
Total Reserves minus Gold	1l.d	177.51	195.32	344.06	517.35	608.50	654.01	723.18	713.22	802.50	937.50	1,130.96	1,053.82
SDRs	1b.d	.05	.05	.05	.05	.06	.06	.06	.06	.07	.08	.08	.23
Reserve Position in the Fund	1c.d	.01	.01	.01	.01	.01	.01	.01	.01	.01	.01	.01	.01
Foreign Exchange	1d.d	177.45	195.26	344.00	517.29	608.43	653.93	723.11	713.15	802.42	937.41	1,130.86	1,053.58
Monetary Authorities: Other Liab	4..d	645.60	551.40	537.91	591.66	593.36	587.88	545.92	470.15	480.28	494.89	5.18	2.40
Banking Institutions: Assets	7a.d	220.79	274.47	250.19	242.10	204.66	192.08	315.88	341.14	382.98	364.05	331.63	415.76
Liabilities	7b.d	56.24	76.77	60.68	95.78	80.14	41.92	72.64	83.70	42.03	57.71	72.36	75.16
Monetary Authorities						*Billions of Meticais: End of Period*							
Foreign Assets	11	1,367.2	2,424.4	4,359.3	6,359.0	7,928.0	9,089.9	13,018.5	17,297.2	20,164.1	23,900.1	25,328.9	29,977.3
Claims on Central Government	12a	578.4	663.2	496.9	369.8	82.7	6.9	6.8	6.8	10.0	.7	.4	1,500.4
Claims on Local Government	12b	.3	.2	1.5	.2	.2	.2	.2	.2	.2	.2	.2	.2
Claims on Nonfin.Pub.Enterprises	12c	.5	50.5	34.0	.5	.5	.5	.5	.5	.5	.5	.5	.5
Claims on Private Sector	12d	2.2	.9	14.3	54.7	74.7	73.9						
Claims on Banking Institutions	12e	781.5	734.9	768.6	566.7	589.5	552.8	682.8	491.3	598.8	399.6	266.3	707.6
Reserve Money	14	1,481.4	1,951.1	2,469.5	2,866.6	2,760.2	3,244.5	4,078.8	6,239.4	7,317.3	8,917.4	10,732.9	12,621.0
of which: Currency Outside Banks	14a	762.4	1,130.2	1,394.4	1,544.1	1,649.7	2,174.2	2,425.3	2,970.4	3,485.8	4,258.8	5,224.7	6,110.2
Time & Foreign Currency Deposits	15	27.9	84.3	14.8	52.0	72.2	66.0	31.5	46.2				
Liabs. of Central Bank: Securities	16ac	—	—	—	—	135.0	145.0	200.0	5.0	2,821.3	3,607.1	4,125.1	300.0
Foreign Liabilities	16c	5,704.1	8,202.9	8,179.2	9,011.7	9,901.3	10,473.4	13,119.6	15,532.9	16,229.1	16,796.0	3,826.7	3,853.1
Central Government Deposits	16d	1,295.4	1,711.8	3,006.9	4,145.1	4,909.8	5,051.4	5,301.0	4,405.0	4,314.3	5,726.3	10,946.6	16,232.0
o/w: Cent.Govt.Earmarked Funds	16df	960.6	1,125.3	2,151.5	2,900.6	3,735.6	4,118.1	3,319.7	1,807.9	1,937.2	1,280.5	1,769.9	891.6
Capital Accounts	17a	896.8	969.7	1,201.4	1,294.0	1,363.9	1,581.6	1,679.9	4,741.0	4,685.2	5,002.4	542.1	2,968.3
Other Items (Net)	17r	−6,675.5	−9,045.6	−9,197.3	−10,018.5	−10,466.7	−10,837.7	−10,702.0	−13,173.6	−14,593.5	−15,748.1	−4,577.1	−3,788.4
of which: Valuation Adjustment	17rv	−5,663.9	−8,339.7	−8,683.2	−8,762.3	−9,192.1	−9,675.9	−10,916.7	−13,841.8	−15,036.7	−15,616.8	−4,333.5	−2,745.7
Banking Institutions						*Billions of Meticais: End of Period*							
Reserves	20	744.6	838.6	1,111.4	1,389.9	1,310.0	1,013.1	1,545.2	3,306.8	3,773.6	4,862.1	5,295.3	6,055.6
Claims on Mon.Author.:Securities	20c	—	—	—	—	135.0	145.0			2,684.0	3,607.1	4,125.1	300.0
Foreign Assets	21	1,468.5	2,989.0	2,846.4	2,794.5	2,530.8	2,554.7	5,414.3	7,955.6	9,135.8	8,685.1	6,267.5	10,054.3
Claims on Central Government	22a		.1	65.2	.1	8.3	232.7	1,610.6	2,274.1	2,834.7	4,880.0	8,747.9	13,102.4
Claims on Local Government	22b	.6	1.1	1.2	103.9	1.9	149.7	1.5					
Claims on Nonfin.Pub.Enterprises	22c	170.4	111.0	65.0	223.0	181.1	46.2	85.9	12,050.1	12,756.5	12,012.8	10,665.0	16,732.4
Claims on Private Sector	22d	1,538.2	2,373.3	3,440.3	5,114.8	6,467.0	8,552.7	10,987.7	1,893.1	1,768.9	2,306.8	2,847.1	4,482.3
Claims on Nonbank Financial Insts	22g		.7	11.4	12.5	1.3	46.4	269.7					
Demand Deposits	24	1,653.2	2,130.4	2,486.7	3,283.0	3,894.7	4,693.0	5,992.9	6,912.7	7,850.1	9,768.8	11,054.9	14,919.3
Time & Foreign Currency Deposits	25	1,380.7	2,303.3	2,800.9	3,388.4	4,144.1	5,893.5	9,328.8	12,860.0	16,287.4	18,631.0	18,210.8	22,833.4
Foreign Liabilities	26c	374.1	836.1	690.4	1,105.6	991.1	557.5	1,245.1	1,952.0	1,002.6	1,376.9	1,367.5	1,817.5
Central Government Deposits	26d	228.7	375.0	430.9	350.0	313.1	356.4	588.0	1,780.4	1,638.9	2,137.1	3,945.5	5,166.4
o/w: Cent.Govt.Earmarked Funds	26df	22.5	141.3	204.1	95.9	92.7	91.4	37.8	513.3	273.2	434.5	1,220.8	1,964.1
Credit from Central Bank	26g	581.2	671.0	691.1	560.6	477.4	458.3	965.5	637.5	560.8	134.8	116.0	535.1
Capital Accounts	27a	770.4	1,415.7	1,934.5	2,723.9	3,146.1	3,809.9	5,367.1	7,175.9	8,914.3	7,888.6	7,025.7	7,764.8
Other Items (Net)	27r	−1,066.0	−1,417.7	−1,493.5	−1,772.7	−2,331.2	−3,028.0	−3,573.2	−3,838.8	−3,300.6	−3,583.3	−3,772.8	−2,309.3
Banking Survey						*Billions of Meticais: End of Period*							
Foreign Assets (Net)	31n	−3,242.5	−3,625.5	−1,663.9	−963.8	−433.4	613.7	4,068.1	7,767.9	12,068.2	14,412.3	26,402.2	34,361.1
Domestic Credit	32	766.5	1,114.2	691.9	1,384.6	1,594.7	3,701.5	7,073.8	10,039.4	11,417.6	11,337.7	7,368.8	14,419.9
Claims on Central Govt.(Net)	32an	−945.7	−1,423.5	−2,875.8	−4,125.2	−5,132.0	−5,168.1	−4,271.6	−3,904.6	−3,108.5	−2,982.7	−6,144.0	−6,795.5
Claims on Local Government	32b	.9	1.3	2.7	104.1	2.1	149.9	1.7	.2	.2	.2	.2	.2
Claims on Nonfin.Pub.Enterprises	32c	170.9	161.5	99.0	223.6	181.6	46.8	86.4	12,050.6	12,757.0	12,013.3	10,665.5	16,732.9
Claims on Private Sector	32d	1,540.4	2,374.2	3,454.6	5,169.5	6,541.6	8,626.6	10,987.7	1,893.1	1,768.9	2,306.8	2,847.1	4,482.3
Claims on Nonbank Financial Inst	32g	—	.7	11.4	12.5	1.3	46.4	269.7	—	—	—	—	—
Money	34	2,417.9	3,264.0	3,917.2	4,901.7	5,613.0	6,994.4	8,557.2	10,066.0	11,520.8	14,263.4	16,579.1	21,465.8
Quasi-Money	35	1,408.6	2,387.6	2,815.6	3,440.4	4,216.3	5,959.5	9,360.3	12,906.2	16,287.4	18,631.0	18,210.8	22,833.4
Liabs. of Central Bank: Securities	36ac	—	—	—	—	—	—	200.0	5.0	137.3			
Capital Accounts	37a	1,667.2	2,385.4	3,135.9	4,017.9	4,510.0	5,391.4	7,047.1	11,916.9	13,599.5	12,891.0	7,567.8	10,733.0
Other Items (Net)	37r	−7,969.7	−10,548.3	−10,840.7	−11,939.2	−13,178.0	−14,030.1	−14,023.2	−17,086.8	−18,059.1	−20,035.5	−8,586.7	−6,251.2
Money plus Quasi-Money	35l	3,826.5	5,651.6	6,732.9	8,342.0	9,829.2	12,953.9	17,917.5	22,972.2	27,808.2	32,894.4	34,789.9	44,299.2
Money (National Definitions)						*Billions of Meticais: End of Period*							
Base Money	19ma	....	....	....	2,792.1	2,691.7	3,117.3	3,939.8	6,056.5	7,133.7	8,681.5	10,433.4	12,184.8
M1	59ma	....	....	....	6,123.1	7,019.2	9,410.7	13,199.8	17,002.7	19,852.7	23,155.8	24,479.8	32,287.3
M2	59mb	....	....	....	7,413.5	8,720.0	11,721.6	16,778.7	21,814.1	26,145.0	32,256.9	34,236.8	43,440.9
Interest Rates						*Percent Per Annum*							
Discount Rate (End of Period)	60	69.70	57.75	32.00	12.95	9.95	9.95	9.95	9.95	9.95	9.95	9.95	9.95
Money Market Rate	60b	....	....	....	....		9.92	16.12	† 25.00	20.40	13.34	9.87	6.35
Treasury Bill Rate	60c	....	....	....	....	....	....	16.97	24.77	29.55	15.31	12.37	9.10
Deposit Rate	60l	33.38	38.84	18.14	25.43	8.22	7.86	9.70	† 15.01	17.99	12.15	9.91	7.80
Lending Rate	60p	....	....	....	....		24.35	19.63	19.04	† 22.73	26.71	24.69	22.08	19.47
Prices						*Index Numbers (2000=100): Period Averages*							
Consumer Prices	64	34.5	† 53.3	79.2	85.0	86.2	88.7	100.0	109.0	127.4	144.4	162.7	† 174.4
Intl. Transactions & Positions						*Millions of US Dollars*							
Exports	70..d	157	168	217	222	230	263	364	703	810	1,045	1,504	1,790
Imports, c.i.f	71..d	1,019	704	759	739	790	1,139	1,158	1,063	1,640	1,753	1,970	2,420

Mozambique 688

Balance of Payments		1994	1995	1996	1997	1998	1999	2000	2001	2002	2003	2004	2005
		Millions of US Dollars: Minus Sign Indicates Debit											
Current Account, n.i.e.	78ald	−467.2	−444.7	−420.5	−295.6	−429.3	−912.0	−763.6	−657.2	−869.1	−816.5	−607.4	−760.6
Goods: Exports f.o.b.	78aad	149.5	168.9	226.1	230.0	244.6	283.8	364.0	726.0	809.8	1,043.9	1,503.9	1,745.3
Goods: Imports f.o.b.	78abd	−916.7	−705.2	−704.4	−684.0	−735.6	−1,090.0	−1,046.0	−997.3	−1,476.5	−1,648.1	−1,849.7	−2,242.3
Trade Balance	78acd	−767.2	−536.3	−478.3	−454.0	−491.0	−806.2	−682.0	−271.3	−666.6	−604.2	−345.8	−497.1
Services: Credit	78add	191.1	242.4	253.2	278.7	286.2	295.2	325.4	249.7	339.4	303.9	255.6	341.8
Services: Debit	78aed	−323.3	−350.0	−319.0	−328.6	−396.2	−405.7	−445.8	−618.4	−577.0	−573.9	−531.4	−648.4
Balance on Goods & Services	78afd	−899.4	−643.9	−544.1	−503.9	−601.0	−916.7	−802.4	−640.0	−904.2	−874.1	−621.7	−803.7
Income: Credit	78agd	54.8	59.1	61.0	63.6	46.3	57.8	79.3	56.0	52.1	55.9	74.5	98.8
Income: Debit	78ahd	−187.2	−199.1	−162.1	−168.2	−187.8	−214.8	−271.4	−290.7	−655.3	−221.4	−374.0	−458.8
Balance on Gds, Serv. & Inc.	78aid	−1,031.8	−783.9	−645.2	−608.5	−742.5	−1,073.7	−994.5	−874.7	−1,507.4	−1,039.6	−921.2	−1,163.6
Current Transfers, n.i.e.: Credit	78ajd	564.6	339.2	224.7	312.9	313.2	256.3	337.3	254.6	827.0	293.2	370.5	479.0
Current Transfers: Debit	78akd	—	—	—	—	—	−94.6	−106.4	−37.1	−188.7	−70.0	−56.7	−76.0
Capital Account, n.i.e.	78bcd	—	—	—	—	—	180.3	226.8	256.7	222.0	270.7	578.1	187.9
Capital Account, n.i.e.: Credit	78bad	—	—	—	—	—	180.3	226.8	256.7	222.5	271.2	581.2	191.8
Capital Account: Debit	78bbd	—	—	—	—	—	—	—	—	−.4	−.5	−3.1	−3.9
Financial Account, n.i.e.	78bjd	344.4	366.7	235.0	182.2	300.4	403.9	83.2	−24.8	−731.7	372.8	−46.5	94.8
Direct Investment Abroad	78bdd	—	—	—	—	—	—	—	—	—	—	—	—
Dir. Invest. in Rep. Econ., n.i.e.	78bed	35.0	45.0	72.5	64.4	212.7	381.7	139.2	255.4	347.6	336.7	244.7	107.9
Portfolio Investment Assets	78bfd	—	—	—	—	—	—	—	—	32.2	5.0	−25.4	−88.8
Equity Securities	78bkd	—	—	—	—	—	—	—	—	32.2	5.0	−25.4	−88.8
Debt Securities	78bld	—	—	—	—	—	—	—	—	—	—	—	....
Portfolio Investment Liab., n.i.e.	78bgd	—	—	—	—	—	—	—	—	—	—	—	....
Equity Securities	78bmd	—	—	—	—	—	—	—	—	—	—	—	....
Debt Securities	78bnd	—	—	—	—	—	—	—	—	—	—	—	....
Financial Derivatives Assets	78bwd	....	....	....	....	....	....	....	....	....	....	....	....
Financial Derivatives Liabilities	78bxd	....	....	....	....	....	....	....	....	....	....	....	....
Other Investment Assets	78bhd	—	—	—	—	19.0	2.6	−145.0	−33.8	−207.7	−77.1	−88.7	−78.5
Monetary Authorities	78bod	—	—	—	—	1.3	1.7	—	−.8	−5.6	6.9	−186.4	40.9
General Government	78bpd	—	—	—	—	—	—	—	—	—	—	—	—
Banks	78bqd	—	—	—	—	17.7	13.9	−124.0	−23.9	−74.6	13.1	57.8	−76.3
Other Sectors	78brd	—	—	—	—	—	−13.0	−21.0	−9.1	−127.5	−97.1	39.9	−43.1
Other Investment Liab., n.i.e.	78bid	309.4	321.7	162.5	117.8	68.7	19.6	89.0	−246.4	−903.8	108.2	−177.1	154.2
Monetary Authorities	78bsd	—	—	—	—	—	—	−5.8	−40.8	10.1	22.3	−48.4	−.4
General Government	78btd	309.4	321.7	86.2	48.8	−.8	−261.7	−171.4	−263.1	−1,302.9	53.0	−47.6	95.8
Banks	78bud	—	—	—	—	20.3	−33.6	16.6	35.1	−43.0	15.7	9.6	6.4
Other Sectors	78bvd	—	—	76.3	69.0	49.2	320.7	284.6	−18.4	432.0	17.3	−90.8	52.4
Net Errors and Omissions	78cad	−443.2	−308.6	−238.3	−364.8	−263.8	1.5	37.5	−59.6	−60.0	208.2	216.4	281.0
Overall Balance	78cbd	−566.0	−386.6	−423.8	−478.2	−392.7	−326.3	−416.1	−484.9	−1,438.8	35.3	140.7	−196.9
Reserves and Related Items	79dad	566.0	386.6	423.8	478.2	392.7	326.3	416.1	484.9	1,438.8	−35.3	−140.7	196.6
Reserve Assets	79dbd	−12.0	16.4	161.0	162.3	91.5	−44.0	−76.8	18.8	−97.8	−181.5	−169.1	129.9
Use of Fund Credit and Loans	79dcd	10.4	−14.4	−14.4	19.9	9.6	−2.9	31.1	−15.8	−11.5	−9.1	−20.4	−25.3
Exceptional Financing	79ded	567.6	384.6	277.1	296.0	291.6	373.2	461.8	481.9	1,548.2	155.3	48.8	92.1
International Investment Position		*Millions of US Dollars*											
Assets	79aad	....	....	....	....	....	....	....	....	....	....	....	....
Direct Investment Abroad	79abd	....	....	....	....	....	....	....	....	....	....	....	....
Portfolio Investment	79acd	....	....	....	....	....	....	....	....	....	....	68.5	157.3
Equity Securities	79add	....	....	....	....	....	....	....	....	....	....	68.5	157.3
Debt Securities	79aed	....	....	....	....	....	....	....	....	....	....	—	—
Financial Derivatives	79ald	....	....	....	....	....	....	....	....	....	....	....	....
Other Investment	79afd	....	....	....	....	....	....	....	....	....	....	884.3	923.8
Monetary Authorities	79agd	....	....	....	....	....	....	....	....	....	....	197.5	156.5
General Government	79ahd	....	....	....	....	....	....	....	....	....	....	—	—
Banks	79aid	....	....	....	....	....	....	....	....	....	....	263.1	328.4
Other Sectors	79ajd	....	....	....	....	....	....	....	....	....	....	423.8	438.9
Reserve Assets	79akd	....	....	....	....	....	....	....	....	....	....	1,159.3	1,029.4
Liabilities	79lad	....	....	....	....	....	....	....	....	....	....	10,464.0	10,898.9
Dir. Invest. in Rep. Economy	79lbd	....	....	....	....	....	....	....	....	....	....	4,360.6	4,468.4
Portfolio Investment	79lcd	....	....	....	....	....	....	....	....	....	....	—	—
Equity Securities	79ldd	....	....	....	....	....	....	....	....	....	....	—	—
Debt Securities	79led	....	....	....	....	....	....	....	....	....	....	—	—
Financial Derivatives	79lld	....	....	....	....	....	....	....	....	....	....	....	....
Other Investment	79lfd	....	....	....	....	....	....	....	....	....	....	6,103.4	6,430.4
Monetary Authorities	79lgd	....	....	....	....	....	....	....	....	....	....	200.3	159.6
General Government	79lhd	....	....	....	....	....	....	....	....	....	....	4,475.5	4,784.3
Banks	79lid	....	....	....	....	....	....	....	....	....	....	67.4	73.8
Other Sectors	79ljd	....	....	....	....	....	....	....	....	....	....	1,360.3	1,412.7
National Accounts		*Billions of Meticais*											
Househ.Cons.Expend.,incl.NPISHs	96f	12,295	20,564	30,692	35,729	38,902	41,133	45,345	55,406	60,299	77,338	87,726	102,710
Government Consumption Expend	91f	2,588	2,009	2,625	3,655	4,902	6,410	6,485	10,324	10,847	14,236	16,738	19,869
Gross Fixed Capital Formation	93e	2,976	5,578	6,617	8,195	8,625	10,507	17,484	15,284	20,398	17,858	....	....
Changes in Inventories	93i	330	755	524	−3	2,758	8,663	1,514	4,531	8,506	13,392	....	....
Exports of Goods and Services	90c	1,547	2,601	3,982	4,509	4,933	5,291	7,216	16,200	23,175	28,928	45,173	52,578
Imports of Goods and Services (-)	98c	6,416	10,830	11,722	12,273	13,112	19,739	21,410	25,213	26,341	37,849	46,295	55,413
Gross Domestic Product (GDP)	99b	13,319	20,678	32,718	39,813	47,008	52,264	56,635	76,532	96,884	113,902	133,510	157,542
Gross National Income (GNI)	99a	11,665	16,128	....	....	....	....	....	....	....	....	....	....
GDP Volume 1996 Prices	99b.p	29,665	30,646	32,719	36,341	40,932	44,018	44,873	50,751	55,170	59,549	63,891	68,810
GDP Volume (2000=100)	99bvp	66.1	68.3	72.9	81.0	91.2	98.1	100.0	113.1	122.9	132.7	142.4	153.3
GDP Deflator (2000=100)	99bip	35.6	53.5	79.2	86.8	91.0	94.1	100.0	119.5	139.1	151.5	165.6	181.4
		Millions: Midyear Estimates											
Population	99z	15.33	15.85	16.32	16.75	17.14	17.53	17.91	18.30	18.68	19.05	19.42	19.79

Myanmar 518

		1994	1995	1996	1997	1998	1999	2000	2001	2002	2003	2004	2005
Exchange Rates						*Kyats per SDR: End of Period*							
Official Rate..............................	aa	8.5085	8.5085	8.5085	8.5085	8.5085	8.5085	8.5085	8.5085	8.5085	8.5085	8.5085	8.5085
						Kyats per US Dollar: End of Period (ae) Period Average (rf)							
Official Rate..............................	ae	5.8283	5.7239	5.9171	6.3061	6.0428	6.1992	6.5303	6.7704	6.2584	5.7259	5.4787	5.9530
Official Rate..............................	rf	5.9446	5.6106	5.8609	6.1838	6.2738	6.2233	6.4257	6.6841	6.5734	6.0764	5.7459	5.7610
Fund Position						*Millions of SDRs: End of Period*							
Quota.......................................	2f.s	184.9	184.9	184.9	184.9	184.9	258.4	258.4	258.4	258.4	258.4	258.4	258.4
SDRs..	1b.s	.1	.1	.1	.1	.2	.1	.1	.4	.1	.1	—	.2
Reserve Position in the Fund..........	1c.s	—	—	—	—	—	—	—	—	—	—	—	—
Total Fund Cred.&Loans Outstg........	2tl	—	—	—	—	—	—	—	—	—	—	—	—
International Liquidity						*Millions of US Dollars Unless Otherwise Indicated: End of Period*							
Total Reserves minus Gold..............	1l.d	422.0	561.1	229.2	249.8	314.9	265.5	223.0	400.5	470.0	550.2	672.1	770.7
SDRs..	1b.d	.1	.1	.1	.1	.3	.2	.1	.6	.1	.1	—	.2
Reserve Position in the Fund.........	1c.d	—	—	—	—	—	—	—	—	—	—	—	—
Foreign Exchange.....................	1d.d	421.9	561.1	229.1	249.7	314.6	265.3	222.8	399.9	469.9	550.1	672.1	770.5
Gold (Million Fine Troy Ounces)........	1ad	.251	.231	.231	.231	.231	.231	.231	.231	.231	.231	.231	.231
Gold (National Valuation)..............	1and	12.8	12.0	11.6	10.9	11.4	11.1	10.6	10.2	11.0	12.0	12.6	11.6
Monetary Authorities: Other Liab.....	4..d	346.0	328.6	335.3	343.0	337.5	338.8	336.3	531.3	542.1	555.3	569.4	595.4
Deposit Money Banks: Assets..........	7a.d	161.7	195.4	122.0	144.6	232.3	223.5	184.8	173.3	236.0	285.3	305.3	393.4
Liabilities..................	7b.d	1,972.9	2,119.6	1,961.2	1,706.0	1,640.0	1,705.2	1,698.9	1,645.1	1,606.6	1,858.0	1,992.6	2,153.9
Monetary Authorities						*Millions of Kyats: End of Period*							
Foreign Assets............................	11	2,656	3,587	2,119	1,690	3,663	2,494	2,933	4,149	5,136	4,410	3,798	6,253
Claims on Central Government........	12a	116,131	142,023	182,431	214,392	281,383	331,425	447,581	675,040	892,581	1,262,588	1,686,341	2,165,154
Claims on Deposit Money Banks......	12e	3,639	5,191	5,923	23,785	15,553	19,602	15,918	21,576	38,732	93,952	55,280	11,169
Reserve Money...........................	14	97,584	124,675	164,513	213,025	270,104	320,579	431,085	653,723	882,043	1,289,016	1,666,058	2,074,452
of which: Currency Outside DMBs..	14a	89,084	114,524	152,789	194,129	237,098	272,769	344,728	494,521	718,633	1,102,937	1,347,598	1,743,654
Other Liabilities to DMBs................	14n	23,320	24,284	22,904	22,624	24,435	23,402	23,847	23,850	24,916	24,285	23,902	26,223
Foreign Liabilities........................	16c	2,056	1,843	1,965	2,121	2,117	2,108	2,170	3,551	3,562	3,379	3,270	3,431
Capital Accounts.........................	17a	788	1,086	1,082	1,681	2,882	4,874	5,282	8,952	10,083	18,911	19,683	35,933
Other Items (Net).........................	17r	−1,317	−1,086	9	414	1,061	2,558	4,047	10,689	15,845	25,359	32,506	42,537
Deposit Money Banks						*Millions of Kyats: End of Period*							
Reserves...................................	20	−11,374	−17,511	−12,258	14,570	44,356	57,339	70,591	99,973	113,696	104,837	175,028	167,776
Other Claims on Monetary Author.....	20n	23,320	24,284	22,904	22,624	24,435	23,402	23,847	23,850	24,916	24,285	23,902	26,223
Foreign Assets............................	21	1	3	8	20	1	369	3	13	9	—	—	—
Claims on Central Govt. (Net).........	22an	−727	−305	−2,402	2,312	−30,179	12,460	36,159	40,985	43,248	35,546	89,217	100,358
Claims on Local Government.........	22b	511	310	184	61	61	—	—	—	—	—	—	—
Claims on Nonfin.Pub.Enterprises.....	22c	11,343	8,351	10,631	11,419	46,688	53,960	69,158	72,338	69,162	68,107	50,959	34,415
Claims on Private Sector................	22d	28,262	45,956	75,346	115,505	155,761	188,149	266,466	416,176	608,401	341,547	428,931	570,924
Demand Deposits.........................	24	9,183	11,241	14,961	25,600	44,782	72,707	119,746	206,349	290,520	82,948	139,880	209,324
Time, Savings,& Fgn.Currency Dep.....	25	33,942	54,572	82,786	102,944	151,363	216,459	335,574	450,560	541,307	386,298	594,169	697,736
Restricted Deposits......................	26b	1,179	1,814	2,349	1,739	1,549	1,635	1,703	1,760	2,661	2,812	2,298	1,919
Foreign Liabilities........................	26c	11,725	11,889	11,494	10,549	10,287	10,611	10,961	10,995	10,557	11,306	11,443	12,412
Credit from Monetary Authorities.....	26g	1,777	5,038	3,835	10,119	5,762	5,030	7,439	15,601	44,251	96,692	48,210	7,739
Capital Accounts.........................	27a	3,228	4,128	7,790	10,733	12,546	17,908	24,094	32,285	47,881	62,272	74,061	64,791
Other Items (Net).........................	27r	−9,696	−27,593	−28,802	4,827	14,829	11,329	−33,294	−64,216	−77,742	−67,995	−102,024	−94,225
Monetary Survey						*Millions of Kyats: End of Period*							
Foreign Assets (Net)......................	31n	−11,124	−10,143	−11,332	−10,960	−8,740	−9,856	−10,195	−10,384	−8,974	−10,275	−10,915	−9,590
Domestic Credit...........................	32	155,520	196,335	266,191	343,689	453,714	585,994	819,364	1,204,539	1,613,392	1,707,788	2,255,448	2,870,851
Claims on Central Govt. (Net)........	32an	115,404	141,718	180,029	216,704	251,204	343,885	483,740	716,025	935,829	1,298,134	1,775,558	2,265,512
Claims on Local Government.........	32b	511	310	184	61	61	—	—	—	—	—	—	—
Claims on Nonfin.Pub.Enterprises...	32c	11,343	8,351	10,631	11,419	46,688	53,960	69,158	72,338	69,162	68,107	50,959	34,415
Claims on Private Sector..............	32d	28,262	45,956	75,346	115,505	155,761	188,149	266,466	416,176	608,401	341,547	428,931	570,924
Money......................................	34	98,289	125,956	167,971	219,983	282,087	345,765	464,968	701,153	1,009,471	1,186,104	1,487,655	1,953,375
Quasi-Money..............................	35	33,942	54,572	82,786	102,944	151,363	216,459	335,574	450,560	541,307	386,298	594,169	697,736
Restricted Deposits......................	36b	1,179	1,814	2,349	1,739	1,549	1,635	1,703	1,760	2,661	2,812	2,298	1,919
Capital Accounts.........................	37a	4,016	5,213	8,871	12,413	15,428	22,782	29,376	41,237	57,964	81,183	93,744	100,724
Other Items (Net).........................	37r	6,977	−1,361	−7,120	−4,354	−5,458	−10,503	−22,454	−556	−6,982	41,127	66,667	107,507
Money plus Quasi-Money...............	35l	132,231	180,528	250,758	322,927	433,451	562,224	800,542	1,151,713	1,550,778	1,572,402	2,081,824	2,651,111
Interest Rates						*Percent Per Annum*							
Central Bank Rate (End of Per.)........	60	11.00	12.50	15.00	15.00	15.00	12.00	10.00	10.00	10.00	10.00	10.00	10.00
Deposit Rate...............................	60l	9.00	9.75	12.50	12.50	12.50	11.00	9.75	9.50	9.50	9.50	9.50	9.50
Lending Rate...............................	60p	16.50	16.50	16.50	16.50	16.50	16.13	15.25	15.00	15.00	15.00	15.00	15.00
Government Bond Yield..................	61	10.50	10.50	13.13	14.00	14.00	† 11.00	9.00	9.00	9.00	9.00	9.00	9.00
Prices and Labor						*Index Numbers (2000=100): Period Averages*							
Consumer Prices...........................	64	29.6	37.0	43.0	55.8	84.6	† 100.1	100.0	121.1	190.2	259.8	271.6	297.0
						Number in Thousands: Period Averages							
Employment...............................	67e	16,817	....	....	17,964	18,359	....	....	....	....	....	....	....
Unemployment............................	67c	541	....	....	535	452	425	382	398	436	327	291	....
Intl. Transactions & Positions						*Millions of Kyats*							
Exports.......................................	70	4,776.7	4,825.8	4,419.5	5,415.8	6,737.2	7,073.5	10,600.5	15,929.4	19,980.3	15,123.0	13,687.0	21,887.4
Imports, c.i.f.................................	71	5,285.9	7,564.2	8,032.0	12,735.9	16,920.7	14,463.9	15,426.3	19,248.3	15,373.2	12,720.7	12,636.8	11,104.3

		1994	1995	1996	1997	1998	1999	2000	2001	2002	2003	2004	2005
Balance of Payments						*Millions of US Dollars: Minus Sign Indicates Debit*							
Current Account, n.i.e.	78ald	−130.3	−261.0	−282.6	−415.9	−499.1	−284.7	−211.7	−153.5	96.6	−19.3	111.5	....
Goods: Exports f.o.b.	78aad	861.6	942.6	946.9	983.7	1,077.3	1,293.9	1,661.6	2,521.8	2,421.1	2,709.7	2,926.6	....
Goods: Imports f.o.b.	78abd	−1,474.2	−1,773.9	−1,887.2	−2,126.4	−2,478.2	−2,181.3	−2,165.4	−2,443.7	−2,022.1	−1,911.6	−1,998.7	....
Trade Balance	78acd	−612.6	−831.3	−940.2	−1,142.7	−1,400.9	−887.3	−503.8	78.1	399.0	798.1	927.9	....
Services: Credit	78add	272.2	364.6	431.9	526.6	633.2	512.2	477.9	407.7	426.0	249.1	254.7	....
Services: Debit	78aed	−129.5	−246.2	−304.9	−447.5	−368.8	−291.1	−328.1	−361.2	−309.5	−420.0	−459.6	....
Balance on Goods & Services	78afd	−470.0	−712.9	−813.2	−1,063.6	−1,136.5	−666.3	−354.0	124.6	515.5	627.3	723.0	....
Income: Credit	78agd	7.2	15.5	9.1	6.6	11.0	51.6	35.5	36.6	36.6	29.4	40.4	....
Income: Debit	78ahd	−74.5	−125.4	−53.6	−20.4	−11.4	−54.6	−168.8	−549.4	−619.7	−771.0	−785.8	....
Balance on Gds, Serv. & Inc.	78aid	−537.3	−822.8	−857.7	−1,077.5	−1,137.0	−669.2	−487.3	−388.2	−67.6	−114.2	−22.4	....
Current Transfers, n.i.e.: Credit	78ajd	407.6	569.9	604.1	691.6	638.1	384.8	289.7	248.9	187.6	118.0	160.6	....
Current Transfers: Debit	78akd	−.6	−8.1	−29.1	−30.0	−.3	−.3	−14.1	−14.3	−23.4	−23.0	−26.7	....
Capital Account, n.i.e.	78bcd				....	....	....	....	....	....	....	....	....
Capital Account, n.i.e.: Credit	78bad	—	—	—	....	....	....	....	....	....	....	....	....
Capital Account: Debit	78bbd	—	—	—	....	....	....	....	....	....	....	....	....
Financial Account, n.i.e.	78bjd	186.4	245.2	269.4	473.5	540.9	251.2	212.8	347.7	−32.0	137.1	125.2	....
Direct Investment Abroad	78bdd	....	....	....	....	....	....	....	....	....	....	....	....
Dir. Invest. in Rep. Econ., n.i.e.	78bed	126.9	279.9	313.4	390.8	317.8	255.6	258.3	210.3	152.1	251.5	213.5	....
Portfolio Investment Assets	78bfd	....	....	....	....	....	....	....	....	....	....	....	....
Equity Securities	78bkd	....	....	....	....	....	....	....	....	....	....	....	....
Debt Securities	78bld	....	....	....	....	....	....	....	....	....	....	....	....
Portfolio Investment Liab., n.i.e.	78bgd	....	....	....	....	....	....	....	....	....	....	....	....
Equity Securities	78bmd	....	....	....	....	....	....	....	....	....	....	....	....
Debt Securities	78bnd	....	....	....	....	....	....	....	....	....	....	....	....
Financial Derivatives Assets	78bwd	....	....	....	....	....	....	....	....	....	....	....	....
Financial Derivatives Liabilities	78bxd	....	....	....	....	....	....	....	....	....	....	....	....
Other Investment Assets	78bhd	....	....	....	....	....	....	....	....	....	....	....	....
Monetary Authorities	78bod	....	....	....	....	....	....	....	....	....	....	....	....
General Government	78bpd	....	....	....	....	....	....	....	....	....	....	....	....
Banks	78bqd	....	....	....	....	....	....	....	....	....	....	....	....
Other Sectors	78brd	....	....	....	....	....	....	....	....	....	....	....	....
Other Investment Liab., n.i.e.	78bid	59.5	−34.7	−44.0	82.7	223.0	−4.4	−45.4	137.4	−184.1	−114.3	−88.3	....
Monetary Authorities	78bsd	2.6	2.4	−3.1	−5.6	−2.7	1.1	7.2	200.8	−11.6	−21.2	−13.4	....
General Government	78btd	56.8	−37.1	−40.9	88.3	229.3	−4.1	−56.8	−62.7	−171.2	−91.2	−85.2	....
Banks	78bud	....	....	....	....	−3.6	−1.3	4.1	−.8	−1.3	5.3	12.4	....
Other Sectors	78bvd	....	....	....	....	....	....	....	—	—	−7.2	−2.2	....
Net Errors and Omissions	78cad	−10.4	−16.3	−11.8	−26.3	18.7	−12.4	−24.5	−14.3	−19.1	−78.9	−142.7	....
Overall Balance	78cbd	45.8	−32.2	−25.0	31.3	60.4	−45.9	−23.4	179.8	45.4	38.9	94.0	....
Reserves and Related Items	79dad	−45.8	32.2	25.0	−31.3	−60.4	45.9	23.4	−179.8	−45.4	−38.9	−94.0	....
Reserve Assets	79dbd	−45.8	32.2	25.0	−31.3	−60.4	45.9	23.4	−179.8	−45.4	−38.9	−94.0	....
Use of Fund Credit and Loans	79dcd	—	—	—	—	—	—	—	—	—	—	—	....
Exceptional Financing	79ded	....	....	....	—	—	....	....	—	—	—	—	....
International Investment Position						*Millions of US Dollars*							
Assets	79aad	....	....	....	....	....	....	....	....	....	....	....	....
Direct Investment Abroad	79abd	....	....	....	....	....	—	—	....	....	....	....	....
Portfolio Investment	79acd	....	....	....	....	....	—	—	....	....	....	....	....
Equity Securities	79add	....	....	....	....	....	—	—	....	....	....	....	....
Debt Securities	79aed	....	....	....	....	....	—	—	....	....	....	....	....
Financial Derivatives	79ald	....	....	....	....	....	....	....	....	....	....	....	....
Other Investment	79afd	....	....	....	....	....	....	....	....	....	....	....	....
Monetary Authorities	79agd	....	....	....	....	....	....	....	....	....	....	....	....
General Government	79ahd	....	....	....	....	....	....	....	....	....	....	....	....
Banks	79aid	....	....	....	....	....	....	....	....	....	....	....	....
Other Sectors	79ajd	....	....	....	....	....	....	....	....	....	....	....	....
Reserve Assets	79akd	....	....	....	....	....	331.7	290.4	460.4	560.5	665.5	792.5	....
Liabilities	79lad	....	....	....	....	....	....	....	....	....	....	....	....
Dir. Invest. in Rep. Economy	79lbd	....	....	....	....	....	3,130.7	3,211.0	3,304.8	3,735.0	4,392.6	4,814.6	....
Portfolio Investment	79lcd	....	....	....	....	....	....	....	....	....	....	....	....
Equity Securities	79ldd	....	....	....	....	....	—	—	....	....	....	....	....
Debt Securities	79led	....	....	....	....	....	—	—	....	....	....	....	....
Financial Derivatives	79lld	....	....	....	....	....	....	....	....	....	....	....	....
Other Investment	79lfd	....	....	....	....	....	5,430.3	5,109.9	5,064.9	5,287.6	5,708.7	5,873.6	....
Monetary Authorities	79lgd	....	....	....	....	....	....	....	....	....	....	....	....
General Government	79lhd	....	....	....	....	....	—	—	....	....	—	—	....
Banks	79lid	....	....	....	....	....	....	....	....	....	....	....	....
Other Sectors	79ljd	....	....	....	....	....	....	....	....	....	....	....	....
Government Finance						*Millions of Kyats: Year Beginning April 1*							
Deficit (-) or Surplus	80	−15,757	−24,924	−25,052	−10,343	−6,946	−30,444	−86,578	−105,899	−72,676	....	....	....
Revenue	81	32,029	39,429	54,726	86,690	116,066	122,895	134,308	164,488	279,651	....	....	....
Grants Received	81z	429	744	421	1,548	524	221	242	288	358	....	....	....
Expenditure	82	48,021	64,884	80,120	98,426	124,064	153,497	221,255	271,371	353,389	....	....	....
Lending Minus Repayments	83	194	213	79	155	−528	63	−127	−696	−704	....	....	....
Financing													
Domestic	84a	15,749	25,201	25,230	9,833	5,680	30,311	86,661	106,029	72,764	....	....	....
Foreign	85a	8	−277	−178	510	1,266	133	−83	−130	−88	....	....	....

Myanmar 518

		1994	1995	1996	1997	1998	1999	2000	2001	2002	2003	2004	2005
National Accounts							*Millions of Kyats: Year Beginning April 1*						
Househ.Cons.Expend.,incl.NPISHs....	96f	417,230	523,876	701,220	987,513	1,420,612	1,903,431	2,237,477	3,139,927	5,049,366	6,865,352	7,979,598	....
Gross Fixed Capital Formation.........	93e	54,596	82,582	118,313	150,240	206,912	255,408	300,981	413,182	551,749	850,124	1,060,038	....
Changes in Inventories...................	93i	3,875	3,540	−21,262	−10,276	−7,604	38,859	16,709	−2,610	19,095	418	33,934	....
Exports of Goods and Services..........	90c	5,405	5,033	5,488	6,290	6,728	8,887	12,639	16,350	19,955	14,119	16,697	....
Imports of Goods and Services (-).....	98c	8,332	10,302	11,779	14,258	16,872	16,265	15,073	18,377	14,910	13,398	11,339	....
Gross Domestic Product (GDP)........	99b	472,774	604,729	791,980	1,119,509	1,609,776	2,190,320	2,552,733	3,548,472	5,625,255	7,716,616	9,078,929	....
Net Primary Income from Abroad.....	98.n	−396	−689	−116	−69	34	−36	−118	−204	−20	−16	−97	....
Gross National Income (GNI)............	99a	472,378	604,040	791,864	1,119,440	1,609,810	2,190,284	2,552,615	3,548,268	5,625,235	7,716,600	9,078,831	....
GDP Volume 1985/86 Prices............	99b.p	62,406	66,742	71,042	75,123	79,460	88,134	93,629	....	....	....	....	....
GDP Volume 2000/01 Prices............	99b.p	....	....	....	....	....	....	2,552,733	2,842,314	3,184,117	3,624,816	....	....
GDP Volume (2000=100)................	99bvp	66.7	71.3	75.9	80.2	84.9	94.1	† 100.0	111.3	124.7	142.0	....	....
GDP Deflator (2000=100)...............	99bip	27.8	33.2	40.9	54.7	74.3	91.2	100.0	124.8	176.7	212.9	....	....
							Millions: Midyear Estimates						
Population..............................	99z	43.78	44.50	45.19	45.86	46.50	47.12	47.72	48.32	48.90	49.46	50.00	50.52

Namibia 728

		1994	1995	1996	1997	1998	1999	2000	2001	2002	2003	2004	2005
Exchange Rates						*Namibia Dollars per SDR: End of Period*							
Market Rate	aa	5.17298	5.42197	6.73325	6.56747	8.25106	8.44711	9.86107	15.23974	11.74625	9.86684	8.74345	9.04013
						Namibia Dollars per US Dollar: End of Period (ae) Period Average (rf)							
Market Rate	ae	3.54350	3.64750	4.68250	4.86750	5.86000	6.15450	7.56850	12.12650	8.64000	6.64000	5.63000	6.32500
Market Rate	rf	3.55080	3.62709	4.29935	4.60796	5.52828	6.10948	6.93983	8.60918	10.54075	7.56475	6.45969	6.35933
Fund Position						*Millions of SDRs: End of Period*							
Quota	2f.s	100	100	100	100	100	137	137	137	137	137	137	137
SDRs	1b.s	—	—	—	—	—	—	—	—	—	—	—	—
Reserve Position in the Fund	1c.s	—	—	—	—	—	—	—	—	—	—	—	—
Total Fund Cred.&Loans Outstg.	2tl	—	—	—	—	—	—	—	—	—	—	—	—
International Liquidity						*Millions of US Dollars Unless Otherwise Indicated: End of Period*							
Total Reserves minus Gold	1l.d	202.62	220.99	193.87	250.53	260.25	305.49	259.84	234.25	323.13	325.22	345.06	312.10
SDRs	1b.d	.02	.02	.02	.02	.02	.02	.02	.02	.02	.03	.03	.03
Reserve Position in the Fund	1c.d	.01	.03	.04	.04	.05	.05	.05	.05	.06	.08	.09	.10
Foreign Exchange	1d.d	202.59	220.94	193.81	250.47	260.18	305.42	259.77	234.18	323.05	325.11	344.94	311.98
Gold (Million Fine Troy Ounces)	1ad	—	—	—	—	—	—	—	—	—	—	—	—
Gold (National Valuation)	1and	—	—	—	—	—	—	—	—	—	—	—	—
Monetary Authorities: Other Liab.	4..d	200.87	212.20	181.89	4.96	6.63	7.70	8.48	5.86	.83	1.04	1.50	2.23
Banking Institutions: Assets	7a.d	55.02	38.72	74.70	110.33	93.58	142.63	231.65	21.48	203.13	142.47	147.61	45.16
Liabilities	7b.d	115.64	140.06	65.11	175.39	120.21	72.16	140.67	141.55	295.99	357.34	411.32	383.54
Monetary Authorities						*Millions of Namibia Dollars: End of Period*							
Foreign Assets	11	725.8	818.1	918.0	1,236.0	1,550.1	1,885.6	2,032.0	† 2,703.5	2,893.8	2,117.8	1,986.2	1,998.7
Claims on Central Government	12a	720.0	783.7	856.9	—	—	—	—	† —	† —	—	—	—
Claims on State and Local Govts.	12b	—	—	—	—	—	—	—	† —	† —	—	—	—
Claims on Nonfin.Pub.Enterprises	12c	—	—	—	—	—	—	—	† —	† —	—	—	—
Claims on Private Sector	12d	—	—	—	—	—	—	—	† —	† 16.6	19.0	13.6	13.4
Claims on Banking Institutions	12e	.5	.7	.7	.7	.5	.7	.7	† —	† 117.5	95.3	238.7	515.2
Claims on Nonbank Financial Insts.	12g	....	....	....	....	....	....	....	1.1	† —			
Reserve Money	14	373.6	415.6	508.3	609.3	631.4	906.7	849.6	† 907.3	† 973.2	1,087.2	1,238.6	1,372.6
of which: Currency Outside Banks	14a	216.9	233.3	281.7	334.5	363.6	420.8	479.2	† 505.3	† 543.7	584.6	632.7	680.0
Other Liabs. to Banking Insts.	14n	—	—	—	—	—	—	—	† —	† 7.6	85.7	—	—
Time, Savings,&Fgn.Currency Dep.	15	....	....	....	....	....	....	....	—	† .1	—	—	—
Liabs. of Central Bank: Securities	16ac	....	....	....	....	....	....	....	.1	† —	—	—	—
Restricted Deposits	16b	....	....	....	....	....	....	....	—	† .1	—	—	—
Foreign Liabilities	16c	711.8	774.0	851.7	24.1	38.8	47.4	64.2	† 71.1	† 7.2	6.9	8.4	14.1
Central Government Deposits	16d	291.2	280.8	162.4	374.4	416.1	471.8	446.3	† 360.5	† 1,114.8	430.1	889.7	608.1
Liab. to Nonbank Financial Insts.	16j	....	....	....	....	....	....	....	—	† —	—	—	—
Capital Accounts	17a	71.2	119.5	303.8	316.5	513.4	562.9	783.9	† 1,587.9	† 1,103.8	743.4	611.2	667.1
Other Items (Net)	17r	−1.5	12.6	−50.6	−87.7	−49.3	−102.5	−111.3	† −222.2	† −178.9	−121.2	−509.4	−134.6
Banking Institutions						*Millions of Namibia Dollars: End of Period*							
Reserves	20	156.8	182.3	227.5	276.9	267.1	512.4	370.5	† 402.0	† 417.0	588.9	585.1	672.4
Claims on Mon.Author.:Securities	20c	....	....	....	....	....	....	....	—	† —	—	—	—
Other Claims on Monetary Author.	20n	....	....	....	....	....	....	....	—	† —	—	—	—
Foreign Assets	21	195.0	141.2	349.8	537.0	548.4	877.8	1,753.3	† 260.4	† 1,755.0	946.0	831.0	285.6
Claims on Central Government	22a	269.8	261.3	600.9	826.2	853.6	1,229.5	983.4	† 1,042.7	† 1,347.0	1,702.1	2,180.3	2,586.1
Claims on State and Local Govts.	22b	22.6	24.5	23.9	22.6	23.9	21.3	17.2	† 37.4	† 10.3	19.3	20.3	22.4
Claims on Nonfin.Pub.Enterprises	22c	58.8	79.9	76.7	153.6	150.2	145.2	445.7	† 182.4	† 225.0	144.3	347.6	289.5
Claims on Private Sector	22d	4,917.0	6,262.4	7,016.1	7,956.1	8,752.8	9,233.7	10,791.7	† 12,614.2	† 14,817.7	16,657.2	19,905.1	23,908.9
Claims on Nonbank Financial Insts.	22g	8.7	9.7	18.1	17.7	18.1	24.7	58.4	† 15.2	† 14.0	—	11.7	30.1
Demand Deposits	24	1,411.7	1,527.7	2,479.9	2,536.6	3,305.5	4,056.5	5,273.1	† 5,786.3	† 6,343.4	7,265.4	8,898.0	8,728.8
Time, Savings,& Fgn.Currency Dep.	25	2,782.7	3,646.7	3,948.0	4,381.3	4,348.4	5,103.3	5,092.9	† 5,222.5	† 5,546.7	5,776.6	6,291.0	7,961.4
Money Market Instruments	26aa	195.0	184.4	243.5	204.8	188.0	45.8	45.4	† —	† —	—	—	—
Restricted Deposits	26b	....	....	....	....	....	....	....	—	† —	153.1	190.6	314.6
Foreign Liabilities	26c	409.8	510.9	304.9	853.7	704.4	444.1	1,064.7	† 1,716.6	† 2,557.3	2,372.8	2,315.7	2,425.9
Central Government Deposits	26d	99.5	91.5	85.0	221.0	176.9	92.8	255.0	† 262.0	† 383.1	765.3	418.9	572.2
Credit from Monetary Authorities	26g	.5	.7	.5	.5	15.6	120.7	18.9	† 124.8	† 20.1	14.4	302.7	408.8
Liab. to Nonbank Financial Insts.	26j	....	....	....	....	....	....	....	—	† 415.3	804.8	1,599.6	2,839.1
Capital Accounts	27a	1,056.8	1,253.7	1,436.2	1,677.4	1,879.2	2,180.6	2,528.3	† 2,862.2	† 2,803.1	3,655.0	3,976.5	4,174.4
Other Items (Net)	27r	−327.4	−254.3	−185.0	−85.2	−4.0	1.0	141.9	† −1,419.9	† 517.1	−749.7	−111.8	369.9
Banking Survey						*Millions of Namibia Dollars: End of Period*							
Foreign Assets (Net)	31n	−200.7	−325.5	111.2	895.2	1,355.2	2,272.0	2,656.4	† 1,176.2	† 2,084.3	684.1	493.1	−155.7
Domestic Credit	32	5,606.2	7,049.1	8,345.1	8,380.8	9,205.5	10,089.8	11,595.1	† 13,270.6	† 14,932.7	17,346.6	21,170.0	25,670.1
Claims on Central Govt. (Net)	32an	599.1	672.7	1,210.3	230.8	260.5	664.8	282.1	† 420.2	† −150.9	506.7	871.7	1,405.7
Claims on State and Local Govts.	32b	22.7	24.5	23.9	22.6	23.9	21.3	17.2	† 37.4	† 10.3	19.3	20.3	22.4
Claims on Nonfin.Pub.Enterprises	32c	58.8	79.9	76.7	153.6	150.2	145.2	445.7	† 182.4	† 225.0	144.3	347.6	289.5
Claims on Private Sector	32d	4,917.0	6,262.4	7,016.1	7,956.1	8,752.8	9,233.8	10,791.7	† 12,614.2	† 14,834.3	16,676.3	19,918.7	23,922.4
Claims on Nonbank Financial Inst.	32g	8.7	9.7	18.1	17.7	18.1	24.7	58.4	† 16.4	† 14.0	—	11.7	30.1
Money	34	1,628.5	1,761.0	2,761.6	2,871.1	3,669.1	4,477.2	5,752.3	† 6,291.6	† 6,887.0	7,850.0	9,530.7	9,408.8
Quasi-Money	35	2,782.7	3,646.7	3,948.0	4,381.3	4,348.4	5,103.3	5,092.9	† 5,222.5	† 5,546.7	5,776.6	6,291.0	7,961.4
Money Market Instruments	36aa	195.0	184.4	243.5	204.8	188.0	45.8	45.4	† —	† —	—	—	—
Liabs. of Central Bank: Securities	36ac	....	....	....	....	....	....	....	.1	† —	—	—	—
Restricted Deposits	36b	—	—	—	—	—	—	—	—	† .1	153.1	190.6	314.6
Liab. to Nonbank Financial Insts.	36j	....	....	....	....	....	....	....	—	† 415.3	804.8	1,599.6	2,839.1
Capital Accounts	37a	1,128.1	1,373.2	1,740.0	1,994.0	2,392.6	2,743.5	3,312.2	† 4,450.1	† 3,906.9	4,398.5	4,587.7	4,841.4
Other Items (Net)	37r	−328.9	−241.7	−236.7	−175.1	−37.3	−8.0	48.7	† −1,517.4	† 261.0	−952.4	−536.4	149.1
Money plus Quasi-Money	35l	4,411.2	5,407.7	6,709.6	7,252.4	8,017.5	9,580.5	10,845.2	† 11,514.1	† 12,433.7	13,626.7	15,821.6	17,370.2
Money (National Definitions)						*Millions of Namibia Dollars: End of Period*							
M1	59ma	....	....	....	....	....	....	....	....	6,887.0	8,080.8	9,569.8	9,408.9
M2	59mb	....	....	....	....	....	....	....	....	12,433.7	13,626.7	15,828.9	17,370.2

Namibia 728

		1994	1995	1996	1997	1998	1999	2000	2001	2002	2003	2004	2005
Interest Rates							*Percent Per Annum*						
BoN Overdraft Rate	60	15.50	17.50	17.75	16.00	18.75	11.50	11.25	9.25	12.75	7.75	7.50	7.00
Money Market Rate	60b	10.25	13.08	15.00	15.41	17.14	13.17	9.19	9.53	10.46	10.03	6.93	6.87
Treasury Bill Rate	60c	11.35	13.91	15.25	15.69	17.24	13.28	10.26	9.29	11.00	10.51	7.78	7.09
Deposit Rate	60l	9.18	10.84	12.56	12.70	12.94	10.82	7.39	6.79	7.81	8.76	6.35	6.24
Lending Rate	60p	17.05	18.51	19.16	20.18	20.72	18.48	15.28	14.53	13.84	14.70	11.39	10.61
Government Bond Yield	61	14.63	16.11	15.48	14.70	15.10	14.90	13.81	11.39	12.86	12.72	† 11.88	10.68
Prices						*Index Numbers (2002=100): Period Averages*							
Consumer Prices	64	....	....	....	....	....	....	....	....	100.0	107.2	111.6	114.1
Intl. Transactions & Positions							*Millions of Namibia Dollars*						
Exports	70	4,646	5,112	6,095	6,167	6,812	7,539	9,164	10,148	11,295	9,533	11,815	12,655
Imports, c.i.f.	71	5,015	5,860	7,182	8,077	9,112	9,834	10,755	13,319	15,495	14,978	15,633	15,580
Imports, f.o.b.	71.v	4,555	5,311	6,589	7,399	8,374	8,992	9,851	12,281	....	....	....	....
Balance of Payments						*Millions of US Dollars: Minus Sign Indicates Debit*							
Current Account, n.i.e.	78ald	85.3	175.9	115.8	90.4	161.8	157.9	292.7	57.9	127.7	335.7	572.6	....
Goods: Exports f.o.b.	78aad	1,320.4	1,418.4	1,403.7	1,343.3	1,278.3	1,196.8	1,309.5	1,147.0	1,071.6	1,262.0	1,827.5	....
Goods: Imports f.o.b.	78abd	−1,406.3	−1,548.2	−1,530.9	−1,615.0	−1,450.9	−1,401.3	−1,310.0	−1,349.0	−1,282.5	−1,726.0	−2,110.3	....
Trade Balance	78acd	−85.8	−129.7	−127.1	−271.7	−172.6	−204.5	−.5	−202.0	−210.9	−464.0	−282.8	....
Services: Credit	78add	259.0	315.3	337.4	380.1	327.0	323.5	221.9	293.9	283.2	420.2	482.4	....
Services: Debit	78aed	−468.3	−551.5	−580.9	−533.7	−456.9	−445.7	−332.6	−275.6	−223.8	−249.4	−385.1	....
Balance on Goods & Services	78afd	−295.1	−365.9	−370.7	−425.2	−302.4	−326.7	−111.2	−183.7	−151.5	−293.2	−185.4	....
Income: Credit	78agd	213.8	374.0	319.2	252.0	226.7	270.9	247.9	199.7	172.6	283.9	368.5	....
Income: Debit	78ahd	−159.8	−235.1	−249.0	−180.6	−165.9	−108.4	−226.3	−269.2	−133.9	−54.0	−217.6	....
Balance on Gds, Serv. & Inc.	78aid	−241.1	−227.1	−300.5	−353.8	−241.6	−164.2	−89.5	−253.2	−112.8	−63.4	−34.6	....
Current Transfers, n.i.e.: Credit	78ajd	349.2	426.9	437.3	462.2	418.2	380.4	419.2	346.7	270.4	426.2	642.1	....
Current Transfers: Debit	78akd	−22.7	−23.9	−21.0	−18.0	−14.7	−58.4	−37.0	−35.6	−29.9	−27.2	−34.9	....
Capital Account, n.i.e.	78bcd	43.2	40.1	42.1	33.5	23.8	22.9	112.6	95.8	40.7	68.3	77.2	....
Capital Account, n.i.e.: Credit	78bad	43.8	40.7	42.5	33.9	24.2	23.2	112.9	96.0	40.9	68.6	77.6	....
Capital Account: Debit	78bbd	−.6	−.6	−.5	−.4	−.4	−.3	−.3	−.2	−.2	−.4	−.5	....
Financial Account, n.i.e.	78bjd	−102.1	−205.3	−174.0	−71.4	−145.6	−288.9	−488.6	−500.0	−346.8	−663.7	−717.0	....
Direct Investment Abroad	78bdd	6.1	3.5	21.7	−.7	2.2	.7	−1.7	12.5	4.7	10.8	21.6	....
Dir. Invest. in Rep. Econ., n.i.e.	78bed	98.0	153.0	128.7	91.0	96.2	1.6	118.9	36.1	51.2	33.3	88.2	....
Portfolio Investment Assets	78bfd	−17.0	−5.1	−8.1	−14.6	−11.1	−26.8	−118.4	−180.2	−144.1	−217.4	−249.9	....
Equity Securities	78bkd	−5.0	−3.8	−7.9	−14.6	−7.4	−18.6	−104.7	−173.2	−138.1	−208.9	−238.0	....
Debt Securities	78bld	−12.0	−1.3	−.3	—	−3.6	−8.2	−13.7	−7.0	−6.0	−8.4	−11.8	....
Portfolio Investment Liab., n.i.e.	78bgd	64.2	82.2	31.2	26.0	−4.4	40.7	34.7	25.9	8.2	3.9	4.5	....
Equity Securities	78bmd	37.5	45.7	51.2	28.8	18.1	40.7	34.7	25.9	8.2	3.9	4.5	....
Debt Securities	78bnd	26.7	36.5	−20.0	−2.8	−22.4	—	—	—	—	—	—	....
Financial Derivatives Assets	78bwd	....	....	....	....	....	....	....	....	....	....	....	....
Financial Derivatives Liabilities	78bxd	....	....	....	....	....	....	....	....	....	....	....	....
Other Investment Assets	78bhd	−301.0	−428.0	−411.2	−289.9	−175.5	−304.7	−502.3	−378.4	−247.2	−452.8	−467.8	....
Monetary Authorities	78bod	....	....	....	....	....	....	....	....	....	....	....	....
General Government	78bpd	9.5	−1.4	−1.2	−1.1	−.9	−.8	−3.4	−2.8	−2.3	−4.3	−6.2	....
Banks	78bqd	.1	14.8	−48.6	−40.6	−2.1	−54.2	−118.7	34.4	47.7	28.1	59.6	....
Other Sectors	78brd	−310.7	−441.5	−361.4	−248.2	−172.6	−249.7	−380.2	−410.0	−292.6	−476.6	−521.2	....
Other Investment Liab., n.i.e.	78bid	47.6	−10.9	63.8	116.7	−53.1	−.4	−19.2	−15.9	−19.7	−41.5	−113.6	....
Monetary Authorities	78bsd	....	....	....	....	....	....	....	....	....	....	....	....
General Government	78btd	4.9	21.8	27.7	17.4	16.9	−.4	−2.1	−2.0	−2.4	−7.3	−4.5	....
Banks	78bud	66.8	4.9	−49.0	116.5	−28.5	—	—	—	—	—	—	....
Other Sectors	78bvd	−24.1	−37.7	85.0	−17.1	−41.4	—	−17.7	−13.9	−17.3	−34.2	−109.1	....
Net Errors and Omissions	78cad	48.5	13.4	39.1	15.3	15.7	−41.2	−100.7	−12.6	−31.8	−69.3	−69.7	....
Overall Balance	78cbd	75.0	24.2	22.9	67.8	55.8	−149.3	−184.1	−358.8	−210.3	−329.1	−136.9	....
Reserves and Related Items	79dad	−75.0	−24.2	−22.9	−67.8	−55.8	149.3	184.1	358.8	210.3	329.1	136.9	....
Reserve Assets	79dbd	−75.0	−24.2	−22.9	−67.8	−55.8	−57.1	−10.6	−70.7	−17.9	96.6	16.5	....
Use of Fund Credit and Loans	79dcd	—	—	—	—	—	—	—	—	—	—	—	....
Exceptional Financing	79ded	....	....	....	....	....	206.4	194.7	429.5	228.2	232.5	120.4	....
International Investment Position							*Millions of US Dollars*						
Assets	79aad	2,788.0	2,692.6	2,095.9	....	....	....	1,213.5	996.9	1,427.3	2,937.1	....	....
Direct Investment Abroad	79abd	15.8	14.8	13.0	....	....	....	44.9	10.1	19.6	33.2	....	....
Portfolio Investment	79acd	165.1	164.8	128.8	....	....	....	610.5	624.5	675.3	2,354.4	....	....
Equity Securities	79add	85.2	90.2	72.8	....	....	....	603.7	....	....	....	....	....
Debt Securities	79aed	79.9	74.6	56.0	....	....	....	6.8	....	....	....	....	....
Financial Derivatives	79ald	—	—	—	....	....	....	—	....	....	....	....	....
Other Investment	79afd	2,404.1	2,291.4	1,760.6	....	....	....	295.1	139.3	408.2	230.5	....	....
Monetary Authorities	79agd	—	—	—	....	....	....	—	—	—	—	....	....
General Government	79ahd	7.3	8.5	7.7	....	....	....	—	—	—	—	....	....
Banks	79aid	38.1	29.9	67.5	....	....	....	51.7	63.1	259.3	110.6	....	....
Other Sectors	79ajd	2,358.7	2,253.1	1,685.4	....	....	....	243.4	76.3	148.9	119.9	....	....
Reserve Assets	79akd	202.9	221.6	193.5	....	....	....	262.9	222.9	324.1	319.1	....	....
Liabilities	79lad	2,420.2	2,685.1	2,355.2	....	....	....	1,807.3	1,310.8	2,556.6	4,019.3	....	....
Dir. Invest. in Rep. Economy	79lbd	1,601.2	1,707.7	1,492.2	....	....	....	1,276.3	715.0	1,822.5	2,951.9	....	....
Portfolio Investment	79lcd	289.8	390.4	334.9	....	....	....	75.0	27.2	41.7	57.7	....	....
Equity Securities	79ldd	69.1	119.0	141.8	....	....	....	1.7	4.6	6.8	5.8	....	....
Debt Securities	79led	220.7	271.4	193.1	....	....	....	73.3	22.6	34.9	51.8	....	....
Financial Derivatives	79lld	—	—	—	....	....	....	—	—	—	—	....	....
Other Investment	79lfd	529.1	587.0	528.1	....	....	....	455.9	568.6	692.4	1,009.7	....	....
Monetary Authorities	79lgd	203.2	214.9	183.0	....	....	....	—	—	—	—	....	....
General Government	79lhd	29.9	51.5	46.8	....	....	....	129.2	155.8	218.0	302.0	....	....
Banks	79lid	143.9	134.1	136.0	....	....	....	70.1	79.3	187.8	358.7	....	....
Other Sectors	79ljd	152.1	186.4	162.3	....	....	....	256.6	333.5	286.6	348.9	....	....

Namibia 728

		1994	1995	1996	1997	1998	1999	2000	2001	2002	2003	2004	2005
Government Finance						*Millions of Namibia Dollars: Year Beginning April 1*							
Deficit (-) or Surplus........................	80	−195.3	−476.1	−891.1	−439.4	−749.2	−679.3	−849.7p	....	....	....	....	....
Revenue..	81	3,610.8	4,028.7	4,611.5	5,591.7	6,094.7	7,184.9	7,765.3p	....	....	....	....	....
Grants Received...........................	81z	38.4	44.9	50.3	54.0	37.4	68.4	128.7p	....	....	....	....	....
Expenditure.................................	82	3,812.7	4,502.3	5,461.6	6,041.5	6,839.7	7,831.3	8,610.0p	....	....	....	....	....
Lending Minus Repayments...........	83	31.8	47.4	91.3	43.6	41.6	101.3	133.7p	....	....	....	....	....
National Accounts						*Millions of Namibia Dollars*							
Househ.Cons.Expend.,incl.NPISHs....	96f	6,355	7,189	8,653	10,160	11,185	12,239	14,120	15,829	....	....	....	....
Government Consumption Expend...	91f	3,267	3,839	4,551	5,064	5,556	6,265	6,819	7,562	....	....	....	....
Gross Fixed Capital Formation..........	93e	2,255	2,817	3,535	3,288	4,321	4,760	4,464	5,932	....	....	....	....
Changes in Inventories....................	93i	252	−60	−65	92	518	57	171	418	....	....	....	....
Exports of Goods and Services..........	90c	5,599	6,288	7,593	7,961	8,637	9,548	10,680	11,462	....	....	....	....
Imports of Goods and Services (-).....	98c	5,926	7,073	8,796	9,638	10,900	11,773	12,354	14,243	....	....	....	....
Gross Domestic Product (GDP)........	99b	11,549	12,706	15,011	16,754	18,790	20,693	23,264	26,689	....	....	....	....
Statistical Discrepancy.....................	99bs	−253	−294	−459	−174	−528	−402	−634	−271	....	....	....	....
Net Primary Income from Abroad.....	98.n	182	569	310	305	484	−105	−356	2	....	....	....	....
Gross National Income (GNI)............	99a	11,731	13,275	15,321	17,059	19,274	20,588	22,908	26,691	....	....	....	....
Net Current Transf.from Abroad.......	98t	1,099	1,393	1,750	1,929	2,243	2,543	3,006	3,026	....	....	....	....
Gross Nat'l Disposable Inc.(GNDI)....	99i	12,830	14,669	17,071	18,988	21,516	23,130	25,914	29,718	....	....	....	....
Gross Saving..................................	99s	3,208	3,641	3,867	3,764	4,775	4,626	4,975	6,327	....	....	....	....
Consumption of Fixed Capital..........	99cf	....	1,721	1,945	2,191	2,482	2,851	3,104	3,558	....	....	....	....
GDP Volume 1995 Prices.................	99b.p	12,204	12,706	13,111	13,665	14,114	14,597	15,074	....	....	....	....	....
GDP Volume (2000=100)...............	99bvp	81.0	84.3	87.0	90.7	93.6	96.8	100.0	....	....	....	....	....
GDP Deflator (2000=100)...............	99bip	61.3	64.8	74.2	79.4	86.3	91.9	100.0	....	....	....	....	....
						Millions: Midyear Estimates							
Population...............................	99z	1.60	1.65	1.70	1.76	1.81	1.85	1.89	1.93	1.96	1.99	2.01	2.03

Nepal 558

		1994	1995	1996	1997	1998	1999	2000	2001	2002	2003	2004	2005
Exchange Rates						*Rupees per SDR: End of Period*							
Market Rate	aa	72.817	83.243	82.007	85.408	95.288	94.326	96.806	96.108	106.450	110.021	111.506	105.837
						Rupees per US Dollar: End of Period (ae) Period Average (rf)							
Market Rate	ae	49.880	56.000	57.030	63.300	67.675	68.725	74.300	76.475	78.300	74.040	71.800	74.050
Market Rate	rf	49.398	51.890	56.692	58.010	65.976	68.239	71.094	74.949	77.877	76.141	73.674	71.368
Fund Position						*Millions of SDRs: End of Period*							
Quota	2f.s	52.0	52.0	52.0	52.0	52.0	71.3	71.3	71.3	71.3	71.3	71.3	71.3
SDRs	1b.s	.1	—	—	.1	—	.2	—	.1	—	.5	6.2	6.1
Reserve Position in the Fund	1c.s	5.7	5.7	5.7	5.7	5.7	5.7	5.7	5.7	5.7	5.8		
Total Fund Cred.&Loans Outstg	2tl	37.7	32.5	27.2	22.0	17.2	12.9	9.5	6.2	2.8	7.7	14.3	14.3
International Liquidity						*Millions of US Dollars Unless Otherwise Indicated: Data as of Middle of Month*							
Total Reserves minus Gold	1l.d	693.6	586.4	571.4	626.2	756.3	845.1	945.4	1,037.7	1,017.6	1,222.5	1,462.2	1,499.0
SDRs	1b.d	.1	—	—	.1	—	.3	—	.1	—	.8	9.7	8.8
Reserve Position in the Fund	1c.d	8.4	8.5	8.2	7.7	8.1	7.9	7.5	7.2	7.8	8.6	—	—
Foreign Exchange	1d.d	685.1	577.9	563.1	618.4	748.2	836.9	937.9	1,030.4	1,009.8	1,213.1	1,452.5	1,490.2
Gold (Million Fine Troy Ounces)	1ad	.153	.153	.153	.153	.153	.153	.153	.153	.153	.153	.153	.129
Gold (National Valuation)	1and	6.5	6.5	6.5	6.5	6.5	6.5	6.5	6.5	6.5	6.5	6.5	5.4
Monetary Authorities: Other Liab	4..d	62.1	54.0	45.0	20.1	27.8	18.5	16.8	8.8	7.4	14.8	26.5	21.8
Deposit Money Banks: Assets	7a.d	161.6	208.9	218.1	246.1	299.0	345.3	459.9	335.8	324.8	284.5	332.5	397.7
Liabilities	7b.d	66.1	67.4	87.7	111.3	149.7	174.9	206.8	224.9	242.8	248.5	296.4	287.5
Monetary Authorities						*Millions of Rupees: Data as of Middle of Month*							
Foreign Assets	11	35,627	33,960	33,883	59,104	52,331	59,155	71,427	80,535	80,842	91,702	106,180	112,013
Claims on Central Government	12a	19,439	24,001	24,714	30,590	29,805	30,539	34,366	32,612	37,834	30,028	40,508	42,054
Claims on Private Sector	12d	503	547	895	1,460	1,356	1,460	1,478	1,856	2,569	1,751	1,769	2,612
Claims on Deposit Money Banks	12e	21	12	646	5	6	5	5	6	928	25	250	59
Claims on Other Financial Insts	12f	484	844	1,122	1,613	1,631	1,613	1,560	1,666	1,512	1,488	1,387	1,238
Reserve Money	14	28,792	31,266	34,368	55,371	50,203	55,371	66,062	74,012	73,924	76,063	87,723	95,835
of which: Currency Outside DMBs	14a	21,005	23,230	25,428	37,829	32,244	36,929	44,526	51,699	56,022	58,076	65,767	71,525
Private Sector Deposits	14d	1,097	1,396	1,358	4,346	2,287	4,346	3,160	3,570	2,350	2,557	3,315	3,603
Foreign Liabilities	16c	5,840	5,725	4,798	3,154	3,516	2,488	2,167	1,267	879	1,944	3,492	3,121
Central Government Deposits	16d	7,782	7,459	7,447	11,473	10,474	11,473	13,081	13,247	15,646	18,595	28,757	26,150
Capital Accounts	17a	12,077	15,982	16,128	22,881	21,545	22,953	25,752	27,982	31,650	31,331	28,990	31,453
Other Items (Net)	17r	1,584	−1,069	−1,481	−122	−610	472	1,759	167	1,587	−2,939	1,131	1,417
Deposit Money Banks						*Millions of Rupees: Data as of Middle of Month*							
Reserves	20	7,321	8,488	7,583	9,972	15,673	14,096	18,376	18,742	15,552	15,430	18,640	20,707
Foreign Assets	21	8,060	11,698	12,438	15,577	20,238	23,729	34,174	25,679	25,429	21,063	23,873	29,446
Claims on Central Government	22a	8,776	6,497	7,610	8,621	8,957	13,330	15,471	28,318	36,045	44,678	47,147	48,020
Claims on Nonfin.Pub.Enterprises	22c	1,621	1,721	1,713	1,459	993	1,438	1,909	1,911	3,573	2,704	4,050	6,107
Claims on Private Sector	22d	36,462	49,494	56,848	65,541	84,875	97,306	114,913	....	....	....	....	....
Claims on Other Financial Insts	22f	29	211	4,023	4,668	530	5,915	7,419	8,144	8,673	9,667	11,396	11,377
Demand Deposits	24	8,422	8,927	8,758	9,090	10,979	13,832	15,343	....	....	....		
Time and Savings Deposits	25	42,172	50,490	58,744	70,555	89,850	109,521	132,550	145,946	152,019	171,641	193,304	212,275
Foreign Liabilities	26c	3,297	3,776	5,003	7,048	10,134	12,020	15,367	17,202	19,015	18,398	21,280	21,287
Credit from Monetary Authorities	26g	21	12	646	6	6	6	45	6	928	25	250	59
Other Items (Net)	27r	8,356	14,906	17,063	19,138	20,297	20,435	28,958	....	....			
Monetary Survey						*Millions of Rupees: Data as of Middle of Month*							
Foreign Assets (Net)	31n	34,550	36,158	36,519	64,479	58,918	68,376	88,067	87,745	86,377	92,423	105,281	117,050
Domestic Credit	32	59,539	75,863	89,486	102,486	117,680	140,135	164,043	....	....	....	....	....
Claims on Central Govt. (Net)	32an	20,433	23,039	24,877	27,738	28,287	32,396	36,757	47,682	58,234	56,111	58,898	63,924
Claims on Nonfin.Pub.Enterprises	32c	1,628	1,729	1,720	1,466	1,000	1,446	1,917	1,918	3,581	2,712	4,058	6,115
Claims on Private Sector	32d	36,965	50,041	57,742	67,001	86,231	98,766	116,391	....	....	....	....	....
Claims on Other Financial Insts	32f	513	1,054	5,145	6,281	2,161	7,528	8,978	9,810	10,185	11,155	12,783	12,615
Money	34	30,524	33,553	35,544	51,265	45,509	55,107	63,028	....	....	....	....	....
Quasi-Money	35	42,172	50,490	58,744	70,555	89,850	109,521	132,550	145,946	152,019	171,641	193,304	212,275
Other Items (Net)	37r	21,393	27,979	31,717	45,130	41,239	43,868	56,517	....	....	....	....	....
Money plus Quasi-Money	35l	72,696	84,043	94,288	121,820	135,359	164,628	195,578	....	....	....	....	....
Interest Rates						*Percent Per Annum: Data as of Middle of Month*							
Discount Rate	60	11.00	11.00	11.00	9.00	9.00	9.00	7.50	6.50	5.50	5.50	5.50	6.00
Treasury Bill Rate	60c	6.50	9.90	11.51	2.52	3.70	4.30	5.30	5.00	3.80	3.85	2.40	2.20
Deposit Rate	60l	8.75	....	9.63	9.79	8.92	7.31	5.96	4.75	....	....	2.65	2.25
Lending Rate	60p	....	....	12.88	14.54	14.00	11.33	9.46	7.67	....	....	8.50	8.13
Government Bond Yield	61	9.00	3.00	9.00	9.00	9.00	9.00	8.75	8.50	8.50	8.25	7.50	6.50
Prices						*Index Numbers (2000=100): Period Averages*							
Consumer Prices	64	66.8	71.9	78.5	† 81.6	90.8	97.6	100.0	102.7	105.8	111.8	115.0	122.9
Intl. Transactions & Positions						*Millions of Rupees*							
Exports	70	17,896	17,895	21,830	23,555	31,288	41,088	57,231	55,221	44,184	50,450	55,669	59,235
Imports, c.i.f	71	57,072	69,028	79,247	97,974	81,901	97,057	111,800	110,362	110,552	133,539	137,670	132,744

Nepal 558

Balance of Payments						*Millions of US Dollars: Minus Sign Indicates Debit*							
Current Account, n.i.e.	78ald	−351.9	−356.4	−326.6	−388.1	−67.2	−256.5	−298.7	−339.3	55.6	119.9	51.7	....
Goods: Exports f.o.b.	78aad	368.7	349.9	388.7	413.8	482.0	612.3	776.1	720.5	632.0	703.2	763.6	....
Goods: Imports f.o.b.	78abd	−1,158.9	−1,310.8	−1,494.7	−1,691.9	−1,239.1	−1,494.2	−1,590.1	−1,485.7	−1,425.4	−1,665.9	−1,812.5	....
Trade Balance	78acd	−790.3	−961.0	−1,105.9	−1,278.1	−757.1	−881.9	−814.0	−765.2	−793.4	−962.7	−1,048.9	....
Services: Credit	78add	579.2	679.0	757.5	865.7	565.1	655.1	505.9	413.3	305.2	372.1	460.9	....
Services: Debit	78aed	−296.6	−313.3	−242.8	−224.5	−196.2	−212.5	−199.9	−214.7	−236.8	−266.2	−373.1	....
Balance on Goods & Services	78afd	−507.6	−595.2	−591.3	−637.0	−388.1	−439.2	−508.0	−566.6	−724.9	−856.8	−961.2	....
Income: Credit	78agd	34.6	43.6	33.1	31.9	45.4	55.8	72.2	70.3	56.9	48.7	63.0	....
Income: Debit	78ahd	−30.8	−34.9	−32.0	−28.6	−26.5	−28.4	−35.2	−58.8	−71.2	−69.0	−78.0	....
Balance on Gds, Serv. & Inc.	78aid	−503.9	−586.5	−590.2	−633.7	−369.2	−411.9	−471.0	−555.2	−739.2	−877.1	−976.2	....
Current Transfers, n.i.e.: Credit	78ajd	160.7	239.2	281.6	267.4	326.0	182.3	189.0	240.2	828.1	1,022.5	1,090.6	....
Current Transfers: Debit	78akd	−8.7	−9.1	−18.0	−21.8	−24.1	−26.9	−16.7	−24.3	−33.2	−25.4	−62.8	....
Capital Account, n.i.e.	78bcd	—	—	—	—	—	—	—	—	102.4	24.8	15.7	....
Capital Account, n.i.e.: Credit	78bad	—	—	—	—	—	—	—	—	102.4	24.8	15.7	....
Capital Account: Debit	78bbd	—	—	—	—	—	—	—	—	....	....	....	....
Financial Account, n.i.e.	78bjd	407.3	368.5	275.2	340.3	212.9	−24.5	76.1	−216.9	−404.8	−354.1	−508.9	....
Direct Investment Abroad	78bdd	—	—	—	—	—	—	—	—	....	....	....	....
Dir. Invest. in Rep. Econ., n.i.e.	78bed	—	—	19.2	23.1	12.0	—	—	—	−6.0	14.8	−.4	....
Portfolio Investment Assets	78bfd	—	—	—	—	—	—	—	—	....	....	....	....
Equity Securities	78bkd	—	—	—	—	—	—	—	—	....	....	....	....
Debt Securities	78bld	—	—	—	—	—	—	—	....	....	....	....	....
Portfolio Investment Liab., n.i.e.	78bgd	—	—	—	—	—	—	—	—	....	....	....	....
Equity Securities	78bmd	—	—	—	—	—	—	—	—	....	....	....	....
Debt Securities	78bnd	—	—	—	—	—	—	—	—	....	....	....	....
Financial Derivatives Assets	78bwd	....	....	....	....	....	....	....	....	....	....	....	....
Financial Derivatives Liabilities	78bxd	....	....	....	....	....	....	....	....	....	....	....	....
Other Investment Assets	78bhd	159.2	264.4	91.6	89.4	90.8	48.2	128.6	11.2	−470.4	−436.7	−350.8	....
Monetary Authorities	78bod	....	....	....	....	....	—	—	—	....	....	....	....
General Government	78bpd	—	—	—	—	—	—	—	—	....	....	....	....
Banks	78bqd	—	—	—	—	—	—	—	—	....	....	....	....
Other Sectors	78brd	159.2	264.4	91.6	89.4	90.8	48.2	128.6	11.2	−470.4	−436.7	−350.8	....
Other Investment Liab., n.i.e.	78bid	248.0	104.1	164.5	227.8	110.0	−72.8	−52.6	−228.0	71.5	67.8	−157.7	....
Monetary Authorities	78bsd	4.3	.1	−3.3	1.0	.4	−2.0	4.5	−3.5	1.8	.2	−1.6	....
General Government	78btd	237.5	106.8	128.4	165.9	151.8	−56.2	−61.0	−63.5	−71.3	−67.6	−90.7	....
Banks	78bud	5.4	−4.5	38.2	68.8	17.0	13.2	67.4	3.2	33.3	19.2	4.7	....
Other Sectors	78bvd	.8	1.7	1.2	−7.8	−59.1	−27.8	−63.5	−164.3	107.8	116.0	−70.1	....
Net Errors and Omissions	78cad	7.1	2.8	82.3	216.6	134.0	58.3	145.7	256.5	−66.6	309.9	339.9	....
Overall Balance	78cbd	62.5	15.0	30.9	168.8	279.7	−222.7	−77.0	−299.6	−313.4	100.6	−101.7	....
Reserves and Related Items	79dad	−62.5	−15.0	−30.9	−168.8	−279.7	222.7	77.0	299.6	313.4	−100.6	101.7	....
Reserve Assets	79dbd	−65.0	−7.0	−23.4	−161.7	−273.0	−144.4	−291.0	−5.2	65.5	−218.1	−178.2	....
Use of Fund Credit and Loans	79dcd	2.5	−8.0	−7.5	−7.2	−6.6	−5.9	−4.4	−4.3	−4.3	7.1	10.0	....
Exceptional Financing	79ded	—	....	....	....	....	373.0	372.4	309.1	252.3	110.4	270.0	....

Government Finance						*Millions of Rupees: Year Ending July 15*							
Deficit (-) or Surplus	80	−7,463	−7,894	−10,976	−10,908	−13,846	−13,349	−12,454	−18,498	−16,506	−11,391	....	
Revenue	81	18,862	23,206	26,643	29,346	31,494	34,814	40,491	46,607	48,326	53,657	....	
Grants Received	81z	2,394	3,937	4,825	5,988	5,403	4,337	5,712	6,753	6,686	8,372	....	
Expenditure	82	29,309	36,242	43,520	47,073	51,963	54,720	60,794	73,905	73,394	74,715	....	
Lending Minus Repayments	83	−590	−1,205	−1,076	−831	−1,220	−2,220	−2,137	−2,047	−1,876	−1,295	....	
Financing													
Net Borrowing: Domestic	84a	−233	2,410	3,500	3,967	5,572	4,693	4,323	10,954	10,558	7,937	....	
Foreign	85a	7,696	5,484	7,476	6,941	8,274	8,656	8,131	7,544	2,948	3,454	....	
Use of Cash Balances	87	—	—	—	—	—	—	—	—	—	—	....	
Debt: Domestic	88a	30,631	32,058	34,242	35,891	38,407	49,670	54,357	60,044	73,621	81,703	....	
Foreign	89a	101,967	113,000	128,044	132,087	161,208	173,861	190,691	201,551	220,126	221,992	....	

National Accounts						*Millions of Rupees: Year Ending July 15*							
Househ.Cons.Expend.,incl.NPISHs.	96f	154,009	166,443	191,469	216,364	231,392	264,944	287,947	309,107	329,199	355,535	383,978	
Government Consumption Expend.	91f	15,987	20,267	23,018	24,987	28,015	30,529	33,964	40,150	42,327	46,653	50,412	
Gross Fixed Capital Formation	93e	42,032	48,370	56,081	60,794	65,375	65,269	73,324	78,013	81,613	86,963	92,619	
Changes in Inventories	93i	2,612	6,861	11,936	10,290	9,353	4,792	18,948	20,784	20,056	30,542	39,488	
Exports of Goods and Services	90c	47,548	53,084	55,405	73,853	68,659	78,150	88,360	91,821	77,068	75,764	85,409	
Imports of Goods and Services (-)	98c	62,972	75,850	88,996	105,775	101,949	101,648	123,055	129,104	127,961	140,522	157,023	
Gross Domestic Product (GDP)	99b	199,216	219,175	248,913	280,513	300,845	342,036	379,488	410,789	422,301	454,934	494,882	
GDP Volume 1994/95 Prices	99b.p	204,397	209,976	221,930	233,040	240,816	251,758	267,096	279,750	278,848	286,480	296,459	
GDP Volume (2000=100)	99bvp	76.5	78.6	83.1	87.2	90.2	94.3	100.0	104.7	104.4	107.3	111.0	....
GDP Deflator (2000=100)	99bip	68.6	73.5	78.9	84.7	87.9	95.6	100.0	103.4	106.6	111.8	117.5	....

						Millions: Midyear Estimates							
Population	99z	21.14	21.68	22.23	22.78	23.33	23.88	24.43	24.98	25.52	26.05	26.59	27.13

		1994	1995	1996	1997	1998	1999	2000	2001	2002	2003	2004	2005
Exchange Rates						*Guilders per SDR through 1998, Euros per SDR Thereafter: End of Period*							
Market Rate	aa	2.5330	2.3849	2.5072	2.7217	2.6595	1.3662	1.4002	1.4260	1.2964	1.1765	1.1402	1.2116
				Guilders per US Dollar through 1998, Euros per US Dollar Thereafter: End of Period (ae) Period Average (rf)									
Market Rate	ae	1.7351	1.6044	1.7436	2.0172	1.8888	.9954	1.0747	1.1347	.9536	.7918	.7342	.8477
Market Rate	rf	1.8200	1.6057	1.6859	1.9513	1.9837	.9386	1.0854	1.1175	1.0626	.8860	.8054	.8041
				Guilders per ECU: End of Period (ea) Period Average (eb)									
ECU Rate	ea	2.1280	2.0554	2.1665	2.2280	2.2037	....	....	....	....	....	....	....
ECU Rate	eb	2.1528	2.0774	2.1113	2.2048	2.2227	....	....	....	....	....	....	....
				Index Numbers (2000=100): Period Averages									
Market Rate (1995=100)	ahx	88.3	100.0	95.2	82.3	81.0	....	....	....	....	....	....	....
Nominal Effective Exchange Rate	neu	109.7	115.3	112.5	106.2	106.4	104.5	100.0	100.7	101.9	106.3	107.6	107.7
Real Effective Exchange Rate	reu	107.4	111.4	108.0	102.3	104.1	103.2	100.0	102.8	105.9	111.3	113.6	112.9
Fund Position						*Millions of SDRs: End of Period*							
Quota	2f.s	3,444	3,444	3,444	3,444	3,444	5,162	5,162	5,162	5,162	5,162	5,162	5,162
SDRs	1b.s	442	616	566	586	644	742	501	598	513	523	501	501
Reserve Position in the Fund	1c.s	802	1,169	1,275	1,625	2,113	1,880	1,524	1,872	2,095	2,055	1,718	834
of which: Outstg.Fund Borrowing	2c	—	—	—	—	193	—	—	—	—	—	—	—
International Liquidity					*Millions of US Dollars Unless Otherwise Indicated: End of Period*								
Total Res.Min.Gold (Eurosys.Def)	1l.d	34,532	33,714	26,767	24,865	21,418	† 9,886	9,643	9,034	9,563	11,167	10,246	9,124
SDRs	1b.d	645	916	814	791	907	1,019	653	752	697	778	778	716
Reserve Position in the Fund	1c.d	1,171	1,738	1,834	2,193	2,975	2,580	1,986	2,352	2,849	3,054	2,667	1,192
Foreign Exchange	1d.d	32,716	31,060	24,119	21,881	17,536	6,287	7,004	5,930	6,017	7,336	6,801	7,216
o/w:Fin.Deriv.Rel.to Reserves	1ddd	....	....	....	....	....	−319.46	10.24	79.32	−45.09	−174.29	−84.45	16.52
Other Reserve Assets	1e.d	....	....	....	....	....	—	—	—	—	—	—	—
Gold (Million Fine Troy Ounces)	1ad	34.77	34.77	34.77	27.07	33.83	31.57	29.32	28.44	27.38	25.00	25.00	22.34
Gold (Eurosystem Valuation)	1and	8,477	9,168	8,622	5,801	7,299	9,164	8,046	7,863	9,385	10,430	10,948	11,462
Memo:Euro Cl. on Non-EA Res.	1dgd	....	....	....	....	....	817	135	170	500	346	392	225
Non-Euro Cl. on EA Res.	1dhd	....	....	....	....	....	1,195	491	1,355	1,516	1,465	1,855	1,365
Mon. Auth.: Other Foreign Assets	3..d	....	....	....	....	....	—	—	—	—	—	—	—
Foreign Liabilities	4..d	263	141	79	64	725	† 542	115	45	737	1,221	133	533
Banking Insts.: Foreign Assets	7a.d	200,374	234,141	238,726	263,592	....	† 155,624	163,895	211,400	256,244	308,245	376,874	409,044
Foreign Liab.	7b.d	186,977	220,964	245,746	290,784	....	† 194,072	206,125	250,057	305,752	328,222	392,490	416,355
Monetary Authorities				*Billions of Guilders through 1998; Billions of Euros Beginning 1999: End of Period*									
Fgn. Assets (Cl.on Non-EA Ctys)	11	75.69	69.77	62.72	62.96	55.75	20.63	19.64	20.18	19.46	17.94	16.26	17.65
Claims on General Government	12a.u	....	....	....	....	....	7.58	8.63	7.71	7.41	7.97	6.61	7.49
o/w: Claims on Gen.Govt.in Cty.	12a	4.12	4.20	4.47	4.74	4.90	1.73	1.53	1.90	.72	.41	.83	.46
Claims on Banking Institutions	12e.u	....	....	....	....	....	22.76	11.98	7.96	16.18	20.71	28.76	35.20
o/w: Claims on Bank.Inst.in Cty.	12e	8.26	9.97	16.05	11.37	18.68	9.88	9.20	3.71	10.07	15.80	20.30	25.07
Claims on Other Resident Sectors	12d.u	....	....	....	....	....	.31	.40	.49	.52	.46	.48	.35
o/w: Cl. on Oth.Res.Sect.in Cty.	12d	.35	.35	.28	.22	.22	.12	.09	.10	.07	.04	.04	—
Currency Issued	14a	40.93	41.30	41.67	42.10	40.90	18.98	18.73	11.39	19.36	21.90	26.45	29.70
Liabilities to Banking Insts.	14c.u	....	....	....	....	....	20.70	9.40	12.05	12.43	13.69	15.18	17.29
o/w: Liabs to Bank.Inst.in Cty.	14c	18.74	11.09	8.39	13.06	17.16	7.52	9.38	10.21	8.47	12.67	11.57	16.30
Demand Dep. of Other Res.Sect.	14d.u	....	....	....	....	....	—	—	.01	.01	—	—	—
o/w:D.Dep.of Oth.Res.Sect.in Cty.	14d	.10	.02	.06	.06	.14	—	—	.01	.01	—	—	—
Other Dep. of Other Res.Sect.	15..u	....	....	....	....	....	—	—	—	—	—	—	—
o/w:O.Dep.of Oth.Res.Sect.in Cty.	15	....	....	....	....	....	—	—	—	—	—	—	—
Bonds & Money Mkt. Instruments	16n.u	....	....	....	....	....	—	—	—	—	—	—	—
Foreign Liab. (to Non-EA Ctys)	16c	.46	.23	.14	.13	1.37	.54	.12	.05	.70	.97	.10	.45
Central Government Deposits	16d.u	....	....	....	....	....	.01	.04	.02	—	.04	.04	.02
o/w: Cent.Govt.Dep. in Cty.	16d	9.61	14.84	14.44	.09	5.10	.01	.04	.02	—	.04	.04	.02
Capital Accounts	17a	20.06	17.21	19.65	24.96	17.09	12.99	14.53	15.02	13.22	12.48	13.03	16.18
Other Items (Net)	17r	−1.47	−.39	−.83	−1.10	−2.21	−1.95	−2.18	−2.20	−2.14	−1.28	−1.97	−1.64
Memo: Net Claims on Eurosystem	12e.s	....	....	....	....	....	−1.25	2.16	.32	—	2.03	1.94	7.05
Currency Put into Circ.	14m	....	....	....	....	....	—	—	—	17.47	21.04	23.14	23.90
Banking Institutions				*Billions of Guilders through 1998; Billions of Euros Beginning 1999: End of Period*									
Claims on Monetary Authorities	20	2.80	3.09	3.38	3.36	....	7.14	9.24	9.68	8.37	12.54	11.22	15.42
Claims on Bk.Inst.in Oth.EA Ctys	20b.u	....	....	....	....	....	64.46	65.38	76.53	75.42	96.04	102.85	100.50
Fgn. Assets (Cl.on Non-EA Ctys)	21	347.67	375.66	416.24	531.72	....	154.91	176.14	239.87	244.34	244.06	276.69	346.74
Claims on General Government	22a.u	....	....	....	....	....	110.03	106.62	105.40	119.55	127.46	135.17	144.06
o/w: Claims on Gen.Govt.in Cty.	22a	129.20	133.64	136.46	140.36	....	65.24	56.43	53.75	55.91	58.90	58.85	58.62
Claims on Other Resident Sectors	22d.u	....	....	....	....	....	496.17	577.35	627.59	679.84	737.66	816.00	913.74
o/w: Cl. on Oth.Res.Sect.in Cty.	22d	559.34	626.83	698.86	788.56	....	484.02	560.82	605.67	656.64	705.80	775.21	868.69
Demand Deposits	24..u	....	....	....	....	....	118.42	131.89	150.97	152.52	156.07	162.25	182.92
o/w:D.Dep.of Oth.Res.Sect.in Cty.	24	114.04	134.71	155.58	170.49	....	115.67	128.40	147.78	148.89	151.96	158.48	178.75
Other Deposits	25..u	....	....	....	....	....	242.68	270.83	295.28	307.65	342.31	363.00	409.10
o/w:O.Dep.of Oth.Res.Sect.in Cty.	25	353.92	363.23	372.14	395.16	....	228.50	257.67	278.65	292.82	327.29	341.62	392.58
Money Market Fund Shares	26m.u	....	....	....	....	....	—	—	—	—	—	—	—
Bonds & Money Mkt. Instruments	26n.u	....	....	....	....	....	154.93	172.70	207.03	225.67	250.25	293.02	351.15
o/w: Held by Resid.of Cty.	26n	169.53	187.19	193.55	196.41	....	....	....	....	....	....	....	....
Foreign Liab. (to Non-EA Ctys)	26c	324.42	354.51	428.48	586.57	....	193.18	221.52	283.74	291.55	259.88	288.15	352.93
Central Government Deposits	26d.u	....	....	....	....	....	1.93	.96	1.30	1.18	2.06	1.36	1.81
o/w: Cent.Govt.Dep. in Cty.	26d	.79	1.02	1.51	1.82	....	1.92	.94	1.23	1.18	1.04	1.16	1.65
Credit from Monetary Authorities	26g	7.92	10.15	13.10	14.69	....	10.21	9.97	4.19	10.60	16.66	21.95	26.14
Liab. to Bk.Inst.in Oth. EA Ctys.	26h.u	....	....	....	....	....	54.32	50.71	55.98	74.46	112.08	127.75	124.44
Capital Accounts	27a	57.52	61.65	78.17	86.89	....	47.70	58.33	60.75	63.73	63.28	64.75	70.63
Other Items (Net)	27r	10.88	26.74	12.40	11.97	....	9.34	17.81	−.16	.17	15.17	19.69	1.34

Netherlands 138

		1994	1995	1996	1997	1998	1999	2000	2001	2002	2003	2004	2005
Banking Survey (Nat'l Residency)						*Billions of Guilders through 1998; Billions of Euros Beginning 1999: End of Period*							
Foreign Assets (Net)	31n	98.48	90.68	50.34	7.98	....	43.19	54.60	64.91	57.26	85.42	90.38	124.62
Domestic Credit	32	682.62	749.16	824.11	931.97	....	549.19	617.88	660.17	712.16	764.08	833.73	926.10
Claims on General Govt. (Net)	32an	122.92	121.98	124.98	143.19	....	65.05	56.97	54.40	55.45	58.23	58.49	57.41
Claims on Other Resident Sectors	32d	559.69	627.18	699.13	788.78	....	484.14	560.91	605.77	656.71	705.84	775.24	868.69
Currency Issued	34a.n	40.93	41.30	41.67	42.10	40.90	18.98	18.73	11.39	19.36	21.90	26.45	29.70
Demand Deposits	34b.n	114.14	134.74	155.65	170.55	....	115.67	128.40	147.78	148.90	151.96	158.48	178.75
Other Deposits	35..n	353.92	363.23	372.14	395.16	....	228.50	257.67	278.65	292.82	327.29	341.62	392.58
Money Market Fund Shares	36m	....	....	....	....	....							
Bonds & Money Mkt. Instruments	36n	169.53	187.19	193.55	196.41	....	154.93	172.70	207.03	225.67	250.25	293.02	351.15
o/w: Over Two Years	36na	....	....	....	....	....	134.74	152.76	175.59	188.59	216.71	254.82	319.05
Capital Accounts	37a	77.58	78.86	97.82	111.85	17.09	60.69	72.86	75.77	76.94	75.75	77.79	86.81
Other Items (Net)	37r	25.01	34.52	13.62	23.88		13.59	22.10	4.45	5.74	23.04	27.48	13.04
Banking Survey (EA-Wide Residency)						*Billions of Euros: End of Period*							
Foreign Assets (Net)	31n.u	....	....	....	....	....	−18.19	−25.87	−23.74	−28.45	1.15	4.70	11.00
Domestic Credit	32..u	....	....	....	....	....	612.15	692.00	739.87	806.14	871.45	956.86	1,063.81
Claims on General Govt. (Net)	32anu	....	....	....	....	....	115.67	114.25	111.79	125.78	133.33	140.39	149.72
Claims on Other Resident Sect.	32d.u	....	....	....	....	....	496.48	577.75	628.09	680.36	738.12	816.47	914.09
Currency Issued	34a.u	....	....	....	....	....	18.98	18.73	11.39	19.36	21.90	26.45	29.70
Demand Deposits	34b.u	....	....	....	....	....	118.42	131.89	150.98	152.53	156.08	162.25	182.92
Other Deposits	35..u	....	....	....	....	....	242.68	270.83	295.28	307.65	342.31	363.00	409.10
o/w: Other Dep. Over Two Yrs.	35abu	....	....	....	....	....	57.62	66.15	62.84	62.99	63.58	70.89	78.49
Money Market Fund Shares	36m.u												
Bonds & Money Mkt. Instruments	36n.u	....	....	....	....	....	154.93	172.70	207.03	225.67	250.25	293.02	351.15
o/w: Over Two Years	36nau	....	....	....	....	....	134.74	152.76	175.59	188.59	216.71	254.82	319.05
Capital Accounts	37a	....	....	....	....	....	60.69	72.86	75.77	76.94	75.75	77.79	86.81
Other Items (Net)	37r.u	....	....	....	....	....	−1.74	−.89	−24.31	−4.45	27.01	39.78	16.44
Money (National Definitions)						*Billions of Guilders: End of Period*							
M2: National Definition	59mb	466.02	486.57	514.99	553.24	....	....	....	....	....	....	....	....
M2: Seasonally Adjusted	59mbc	469.75	489.45	515.51	553.72	....	....	....	....	....	....	....	....
Nonbank Financial Institutions						*Billions of Guilders: End of Period*							
Cash	40..l	10.87	10.99	11.58	11.90	11.81	....	....					
Foreign Assets	41..l	115.34	145.81	188.36	271.83	380.97	....	....					
Claims on Central Government	42a.l	161.40	175.66	190.88	192.82	181.40	....	....					
Claims on Local Government	42b.l	31.81	31.55	30.19	27.52	25.53	....	....					
Claims on Private Sector	42d.l	346.67	369.32	411.29	457.37	501.60	....	....					
Real Estate	42h.l	59.78	60.40	63.96	64.18	66.41	....	....					
Capital Accounts	47a.l	702.32	767.87	871.78	994.43	1,138.09	....	....					
Other Items (Net)	47r.l	23.56	25.85	24.49	31.19	29.64	....	....					
Interest Rates						*Percent Per Annum*							
Rate on Advances	60a	4.50	2.98	2.00	2.75	2.75	....	....	....	....	....	....	....
Money Market Rate	60b	5.14	4.22	2.89	3.07	3.21	....	....	....	....	....	....	....
Deposit Rate	60l	† 4.70	4.40	3.54	3.18	3.10	2.74	2.89	3.10	2.77	2.49	2.31	2.34
Households: Stocks, up to 2 years	60lhs	....	....	....	....	....	....	....	....	....	2.95	2.81	3.18
New Business, up to 1 year	60lhn	....	....	....	....	....	....	....	....	....	2.55	2.31	2.34
Corporations: Stocks, up to 2 years	60lcs	....	....	....	....	....	....	....	....	....	2.64	2.28	2.20
New Business, up to 1 year	60lcn	....	....	....	....	....	....	....	....	....	2.30	2.07	2.11
Lending Rate	60p	8.29	7.21	5.90	6.13	6.50	† 3.46	4.79	5.00	3.96	3.00	2.75	2.77
Households: Stocks, up to 1 year	60phs	....	....	....	....	....	....	....	....	....	6.80	6.46	6.26
New Bus., Floating & up to 1 year	60pns	....	....	....	....	....	....	....	....	....	7.98	7.80	7.30
House Purch., Stocks,Over 5 years	60phm	....	....	....	....	....	....	....	....	....	5.47	5.12	4.83
House Purch., New Bus., 5-10 yrs	60phn	....	....	....	....	....	....	....	....	....	4.92	4.80	4.11
Corporations: Stocks, up to 1 year	60pcs	....	....	....	....	....	....	....	....	....	4.30	4.27	4.16
New Bus., Over € 1 mil.,up to 1 yr	60pcn	....	....	....	....	....	....	....	....	....	3.07	2.78	2.94
Government Bond Yield	61	7.20	7.20	6.49	5.81	4.87	4.92	5.51	5.17	5.00	4.18	4.10	3.37
Prices, Production, Labor						*Index Numbers (2000=100): Period Averages*							
Share Prices	62	28.1	29.9	38.0	56.7	74.5	84.7	100.0	81.9	63.1	45.7	51.0	57.9
Manufacturing	62a	29.4	31.3	39.4	60.1	75.9	82.7	100.0	82.3	63.2	....	....	....
Prices: Final Products	63	† 89.7	91.1	92.9	94.6	94.4	† 95.4	100.0	103.0	103.8	105.3	109.5	112.5
Consumer Prices	64	87.5	† 89.3	91.1	93.1	95.0	97.1	† 100.0	104.2	107.6	109.9	111.2	113.1
Harmonized CPI	64h	....	91.1	92.4	94.1	95.8	97.8	100.0	105.2	109.2	† 111.7	113.2	114.9
Wages: Hourly Rates	65	† 85.7	86.6	88.1	90.8	93.7	96.4	† 100.0	103.9	107.7	110.6	112.3	113.3
Industrial Production	66	90.5	90.9	93.0	93.3	95.6	96.8	100.0	100.6	101.5	100.1	102.6	101.4
						Number in Thousands: Period Averages							
Labor Force	67d	6,466	6,596	6,686	6,832	6,941	7,069	7,187	7,314	7,427	7,401	7,398	7,401
Employment	67e	5,591	6,288	6,441	6,638	6,881	7,113	7,286	7,559	7,607	7,560	7,461	7,441
Unemployment	67c	486	464	440	375	286	221	188	146	174	251	320	....
Unemployment Rate (%)	67r	7.6	† 7.0	6.6	5.5	4.1	3.1	3.8	3.4	4.1	5.4	6.5	6.5
Intl. Transactions & Positions						*Millions of Guilders through 1998; Millions of Euros Beginning 1999*							
Exports	70	282,209	314,693	332,920	380,018	398,686	† 188,046	231,855	241,342	234,284	228,745	255,530	278,061
Imports, c.i.f.	71	256,442	283,538	304,559	347,286	371,760	† 176,115	216,058	218,332	205,019	206,025	228,009	248,849
						2000=100							
Volume of Exports	72	† 66.2	71.9	† 75.1	81.8	87.8	91.8	100.0	101.7	102.6	105.6	116.3	123.1
Volume of Imports	73	† 64.1	71.7	† 75.2	80.1	87.7	94.2	100.0	97.2	94.9	97.9	106.1	114.5
Unit Value of Exports	74	† 87.0	88.6	† 88.8	94.3	91.3	88.9	100.0	102.6	97.3	94.6	93.7	97.6
Unit Value of Imports	75	† 85.6	85.8	† 86.6	91.8	89.5	89.4	100.0	104.2	99.0	95.9	97.2	98.3

Netherlands 138

		1994	1995	1996	1997	1998	1999	2000	2001	2002	2003	2004	2005
Balance of Payments						*Millions of US Dollars: Minus Sign Indicates Debit*							
Current Account, n.i.e.	78ald	17,294	25,773	21,502	25,077	13,031	15,684	7,264	9,810	11,017	29,690	54,414	40,187
Goods: Exports f.o.b.	78aad	141,810	195,600	195,079	188,988	196,041	195,694	205,271	203,201	209,516	262,340	315,124	341,228
Goods: Imports f.o.b.	78abd	−123,124	−171,788	−172,312	−168,051	−175,611	−179,747	−187,471	−184,015	−190,950	−226,591	−272,179	−296,904
Trade Balance	78acd	18,686	23,812	22,767	20,937	20,430	15,947	17,800	19,187	18,565	35,749	42,946	44,324
Services: Credit	78add	41,523	45,917	47,237	48,975	49,760	52,023	49,319	51,248	56,138	63,612	73,774	78,576
Services: Debit	78aed	−41,303	−44,770	−45,278	−45,699	−47,285	−49,458	−51,339	−53,713	−57,204	−63,607	−69,443	−71,827
Balance on Goods & Services	78afd	18,905	24,959	24,726	24,213	22,906	18,511	15,779	16,722	17,499	35,754	47,277	51,074
Income: Credit	78agd	29,466	35,755	36,297	39,176	35,287	43,567	45,506	43,458	40,304	58,233	80,103	84,798
Income: Debit	78ahd	−25,799	−28,508	−32,750	−32,193	−37,980	−40,040	−47,803	−43,631	−40,245	−57,232	−65,015	−85,339
Balance on Gds, Serv. & Inc	78aid	22,571	32,206	28,272	31,196	20,213	22,038	13,482	16,549	17,558	36,755	62,365	50,532
Current Transfers, n.i.e.: Credit	78ajd	4,197	4,725	4,319	4,346	3,799	4,564	4,399	4,475	4,961	7,506	8,817	7,558
Current Transfers: Debit	78akd	−9,474	−11,159	−11,089	−10,465	−10,981	−10,918	−10,618	−11,214	−11,501	−14,572	−16,769	−17,903
Capital Account, n.i.e.	78bcd	−1,006	−1,099	−2,024	−1,297	−420	−214	−97	−3,200	−545	−2,654	−1,143	−1,464
Capital Account, n.i.e.: Credit	78bad	564	856	1,267	1,099	1,037	1,685	2,216	1,118	857	1,427	1,668	1,717
Capital Account: Debit	78bbd	−1,569	−1,955	−3,291	−2,396	−1,457	−1,899	−2,314	−4,317	−1,402	−4,080	−2,812	−3,181
Financial Account, n.i.e.	78bjd	−9,969	−18,839	−5,474	−14,304	−14,398	−9,857	−7,604	−3,852	−4,527	−24,212	−53,457	−31,852
Direct Investment Abroad	78bdd	−17,581	−20,188	−31,937	−24,499	−36,938	−57,151	−74,510	−50,764	−31,758	−44,752	−17,293	−116,874
Dir. Invest. in Rep. Econ., n.i.e.	78bed	7,127	12,206	16,604	11,033	37,619	41,168	63,119	51,980	25,457	21,019	377	42,881
Portfolio Investment Assets	78bfd	−9,570	−16,498	−25,013	−38,942	−69,294	−94,489	−65,635	−60,994	−64,293	−58,115	−97,753	−75,971
Equity Securities	78bkd	−6,595	−8,730	−2,895	−12,140	−19,890	−52,668	−23,448	−29,565	−7,917	−14,020	−31,042	−12,950
Debt Securities	78bld	−2,975	−7,768	−22,119	−26,802	−49,404	−41,821	−42,187	−31,429	−56,375	−44,095	−66,711	−63,021
Portfolio Investment Liab., n.i.e.	78bgd	−834	6,123	13,432	17,752	30,074	100,100	55,242	74,193	49,777	80,991	66,017	155,706
Equity Securities	78bmd	−1,385	−743	3,280	774	3,825	30,490	16,970	12,947	−149	898	1,747	87,350
Debt Securities	78bnd	551	6,865	10,152	16,979	26,248	69,609	38,272	61,246	49,926	80,093	64,270	68,355
Financial Derivatives Assets	78bwd	11,888	18,454	23,385	31,899	53,364	63,426	82,999	87,517	70,419	126,911	165,590	156,278
Financial Derivatives Liabilities	78bxd	−12,256	−20,198	−24,134	−32,346	−52,388	−59,241	−86,979	−93,354	−77,263	−127,141	−167,108	−160,597
Other Investment Assets	78bhd	7,270	−8,127	1,582	−37,217	−56,475	−6,247	−28,347	−69,657	−28,292	−66,297	−66,869	−53,573
Monetary Authorities	78bod	—	—	—	—	−235	−6,493	675	−1,175	360	277	−335	196
General Government	78bpd	−44	7	−270	146	181	−1,441	534	−837	−1,621	−1,730	84	−73
Banks	78bqd	9,437	−3,474	2,926	−31,241	−49,373	9,484	−18,044	−60,704	−20,587	−56,184	−57,572	−43,715
Other Sectors	78brd	−2,124	−4,660	−1,075	−6,122	−7,047	−7,798	−11,513	−6,940	−6,444	−8,660	−9,045	−9,981
Other Investment Liab., n.i.e.	78bid	3,988	9,389	20,607	58,015	79,641	2,578	46,507	57,227	51,425	43,172	63,582	20,299
Monetary Authorities	78bsd	91	−137	−42	41	930	6,191	−3,542	1,977	2,279	−3,544	2,085	−2,638
General Government	78btd	1,151	24	−131	−536	284	640	329	2,828	4	−133	−1,845	259
Banks	78bud	−493	4,174	15,697	52,519	60,697	−1,540	18,370	57,763	52,158	41,211	77,337	35,142
Other Sectors	78bvd	3,239	5,327	5,083	5,990	17,730	−2,712	31,351	−5,340	−3,016	5,638	−13,995	−12,465
Net Errors and Omissions	78cad	−5,819	−7,745	−19,700	−12,185	−553	−10,224	657	−3,110	−6,077	−3,641	−827	−9,319
Overall Balance	78cbd	500	−1,911	−5,695	−2,709	−2,339	−4,611	219	−351	−132	−817	−1,013	−2,448
Reserves and Related Items	79dad	−500	1,911	5,695	2,709	2,339	4,611	−219	351	132	817	1,013	2,448
Reserve Assets	79dbd	−500	1,911	5,695	2,709	2,339	4,611	−219	351	132	817	1,013	2,448
Use of Fund Credit and Loans	79dcd	—	—	—	—	—	—	—	—	—	—	—	—
Exceptional Financing	79ded	....	....	....	....	....	....	....	....	....	....	....	....
International Investment Position						*Millions of US Dollars*							
Assets	79aad	458,187	651,022	696,815	746,983	957,865	1,067,094	1,135,472	1,238,991	1,489,744	1,964,301	2,337,765	....
Direct Investment Abroad	79abd	142,953	172,672	194,026	198,554	229,000	260,875	305,461	332,156	396,530	531,151	595,360	....
Portfolio Investment	79acd	119,467	164,011	204,757	242,157	363,140	453,076	478,298	485,696	570,003	788,343	996,207	....
Equity Securities	79add	67,258	91,747	107,709	124,066	173,149	249,426	253,589	235,023	217,387	326,472	405,573	....
Debt Securities	79aed	52,209	72,264	97,049	118,091	189,990	203,649	224,709	250,673	352,616	461,872	590,634	....
Financial Derivatives	79ald	—	—	—	—	—	39,730	29,247	44,606	71,812	86,711	85,887	....
Other Investment	79afd	147,863	267,157	258,384	273,551	336,185	294,344	304,831	359,604	432,450	536,574	638,961	....
Monetary Authorities	79agd	—	—	—	—	252	3,230	2,528	3,245	3,545	4,054	4,662	....
General Government	79ahd	21,945	23,983	23,124	21,255	22,597	22,292	20,918	19,908	23,438	6,259	7,003	....
Banks	79aid	84,664	179,830	174,050	190,892	241,262	197,327	203,777	255,845	302,647	403,484	485,574	....
Other Sectors	79ajd	41,254	63,344	61,211	61,404	72,073	71,495	77,608	80,606	102,820	122,776	141,722	....
Reserve Assets	79akd	47,903	47,181	39,648	32,720	29,540	19,070	17,636	16,929	18,948	21,521	21,349	....
Liabilities	79lad	484,362	586,113	658,741	721,135	973,527	1,098,954	1,194,727	1,291,908	1,608,297	2,024,228	2,360,175	....
Dir. Invest. in Rep. Economy	79lbd	93,409	116,049	126,543	122,193	164,473	192,228	243,732	282,882	349,969	457,984	501,070	....
Portfolio Investment	79lcd	176,410	225,266	276,532	318,336	445,573	536,599	567,014	547,592	647,363	843,681	1,008,710	....
Equity Securities	79ldd	105,239	129,955	179,628	224,692	308,671	363,796	350,571	283,978	262,251	288,664	336,704	....
Debt Securities	79led	71,171	95,311	96,904	93,645	136,902	172,803	216,443	263,614	385,112	555,018	672,006	....
Financial Derivatives	79lld	—	—	—	—	—	30,542	24,442	49,469	86,573	94,850	98,660	....
Other Investment	79lfd	214,543	244,798	255,666	280,606	363,006	339,585	359,538	411,965	524,392	627,712	751,735	....
Monetary Authorities	79lgd	263	141	80	64	725	3,271	115	1,666	4,889	2,595	5,094	....
General Government	79lhd	10,864	11,537	10,971	9,891	10,232	13,090	12,785	14,629	17,838	4,366	2,736	....
Banks	79lid	158,290	184,237	195,974	223,450	297,011	265,713	268,848	316,907	403,206	508,729	618,294	....
Other Sectors	79ljd	45,126	48,882	48,641	47,200	55,038	57,511	77,789	78,764	98,458	112,022	125,610	....
Government Finance													
Central Government						*Millions of Guilders through 1998; Millions of Euros Beginning 1999: Year Ending December 31*							
Deficit (-) or Surplus	80	2,763	−23,018	−9,626	−10,921	−3,177	† −5,815	−372	−3,500	−6,902	−10,718	−7,147	....
Total Revenue and Grants	81y	199,517	204,769	189,159	197,347	210,688	† 105,280	108,309	115,142	120,325	122,592	135,725	....
Revenue	81	199,508	204,611	188,965	196,930	210,397	† 105,177	108,111	115,044	120,315	122,440	135,455	....
Grants	81z	9	158	194	417	291	† 103	198	98	10	152	270	....
Exp. & Lending Minus Repay.	82z	196,754	227,787	198,785	208,268	213,865	† 111,095	108,681	118,642	127,227	133,310	142,872	....
Total Financing	80h	−2,763	23,018	9,626	10,921	3,177	† 5,815	372	3,500	6,902	10,718	7,365	....
Total Net Borrowing	84	−1,685	28,816	9,885	−4,072	13,348	† 2,254	−1,032	3,521	9,183	12,289	4,665	....
Net Domestic	84a	−1,685	28,816	9,885	−4,072	13,348	† 2,254	−1,032	3,521	9,183	12,289	4,665	....
Net Foreign	85a	—	—	—	—	—	† —						....
Use of Cash Balances	87	−1,078	−5,798	−259	14,993	−10,171	† 3,561	1,404	−21	−2,281	−1,571	2,700	....
Total Debt by Currency	88z	374,645	399,825	410,989	417,467	431,383	† 200,984	204,476	211,675	226,756	256,388	231,027	....
National	88b	374,645	399,825	410,989	417,467	431,383	† 200,984	204,476	211,675	226,756	256,388	231,027	....
Foreign	89b	—	—	—	—	—	† —						....
General Government						*As Percent of Gross Domestic Product*							

		1994	1995	1996	1997	1998	1999	2000	2001	2002	2003	2004	2005
National Accounts		*Billions of Guilders through 1998; Billions of Euros Beginning 1999:*											
Househ.Cons.Expend.,incl.NPISHs....	**96f.c**	313.0	332.9	354.0	375.0	402.3	† 195.8	210.8	224.2	233.0	236.5	239.2	244.0
Government Consumption Expend...	**91f.c**	153.3	160.2	160.5	168.5	177.4	† 85.9	91.9	101.4	110.2	116.0	118.5	120.5
Gross Fixed Capital Formation..........	**93e.c**	128.4	139.9	152.4	165.5	177.3	† 88.4	91.7	94.7	92.9	90.7	94.6	97.6
Changes in Inventories....................	**93i.c**	.1	1.5	.5	2.3	4.4	† −.1	.4	1.5	−1.3	−.1	.8	−1.4
Exports of Goods and Services..........	**90c.c**	348.4	399.4	420.2	477.5	499.7	† 243.5	292.9	301.2	298.5	301.4	328.1	357.5
Imports of Goods and Services (-).....	**98c.c**	309.7	361.1	383.0	434.8	462.3	† 227.2	269.7	275.3	268.1	268.3	292.6	316.3
Gross Domestic Product (GDP).........	**99b.c**	633.6	672.7	704.6	754.2	798.8	† 386.2	418.0	447.7	465.2	476.3	488.6	501.9
Net Primary Income from Abroad.....	**98.n**	1.7	8.0	3.5	13.1	8.6	† 4.2	9.0	3.4	4.3	.8	1.1	3.9
Gross National Income (GNI)...........	**99a**	616.0	674.0	697.8	748.0	784.8	† 390.4	427.0	451.1	469.5	482.4	503.8	510.2
Net Current Transf.from Abroad......	**98t.c**	....	....	....	....	....	† −2.2	−3.3	−3.7	−4.3	....	....	....
Gross Nat'l Disposable Inc.(GNDI)....	**99i.c**	....	....	....	....	....	† 373.6	400.8	422.6	434.5	443.3	....	....
Gross Saving..................................	**99s.c**	....	....	....	....	....	† 43.1	47.8	42.5	31.1	26.2	....	....
Consumption of Fixed Capital..........	**99cfc**	98.1	100.7	104.9	109.8	116.7	† 56.5	61.2	65.5	69.0	71.4	....	....
GDP Volume 1995 Ref., Chained.....	**99b.r**	646.4	755.4	781.1	814.5	846.5	† 402.1	418.0	426.0	426.3	427.8	436.1	442.8
GDP Volume (2000=100)................	**99bvr**	70.2	82.0	84.8	88.4	91.9	† 96.2	100.0	101.9	102.0	102.3	104.3	105.9
GDP Deflator (2000=100)...............	**99bir**	98.0	100.0	101.2	103.2	105.0	106.6	110.8	100.0	103.8	106.1	106.9	108.7
		Millions: Midyear Estimates											
Population................................	**99z**	15.36	15.46	15.55	15.64	15.73	15.81	15.90	15.98	16.07	16.15	16.23	16.30

Netherlands Antilles 353

		1994	1995	1996	1997	1998	1999	2000	2001	2002	2003	2004	2005
Exchange Rates				*Guilders per SDR: End of Period (aa) Guilders per US Dollar: End of Period (ae)*									
Official Rate	aa	2.613	2.661	2.574	2.415	2.520	2.457	2.332	2.250	2.434	2.660	2.780	2.558
Official Rate	ae	1.790	1.790	1.790	1.790	1.790	1.790	1.790	1.790	1.790	1.790	1.790	1.790
				Index Numbers (2000=100): Period Averages									
Official Rate	ahx	100.0	100.0	100.0	100.0	100.0	100.0	100.0	100.0	100.0	100.0	100.0	100.0
Nominal Effective Exchange Rate	nec	59.2	58.4	74.1	81.7	87.2	93.1	100.0	104.1	126.8	144.6	153.0	158.7
Real Effective Exchange Rate	rec	151.2	144.8	116.4	108.0	100.2	96.0	100.0	98.6	108.8	110.6	106.9	105.3
International Liquidity				*Millions of US Dollars Unless Otherwise Indicated: End of Period*									
Total Reserves minus Gold	1l.d	179	203	189	214	248	265	261	301	406	373	415	462
Foreign Exchange	1d.d	179	203	189	214	248	265	261	301	406	373	415	462
Gold (Million Fine Troy Ounces)	1ad	.548	.548	.548	.548	.421	.421	.421	.421	.421	.421	.421	.421
Gold (National Valuation)	1and	38	117	106	106	100	100	78	78	78	132	152	152
Monetary Authorities: Other Liab.	4..d	26	32	10	8	1	1	2	—	1	—	—	2
Deposit Money Banks: Assets	7a.d	748	442	400	396	471	473	552	862	653	710	760	1,096
Liabilities	7b.d	720	391	402	392	421	455	568	664	496	477	510	746
OBU: Assets	7k.d	29,152	26,085	28,106	31,393	36,430	32,792	34,466	38,254	42,584	39,961	42,134	34,174
Liabilities	7m.d	28,315	15,256	26,263	29,437	33,772	30,029	31,423	34,567	38,954	36,472	38,275	30,902
Monetary Authorities				*Millions of Guilders End of Period*									
Foreign Assets	11	435.2	683.3	546.5	591.5	625.9	655.1	608.7	678.7	867.9	905.3	1,015.7	1,121.1
Claims on Central Government	12a	59.9	69.2	68.6	82.0	79.1	117.5	94.8	150.5	124.4	119.9	185.6	183.6
Reserve Money	14	375.0	449.6	385.2	445.2	489.1	460.0	497.9	678.6	847.8	796.8	954.2	1,028.0
of which: Currency Outside DMBs	14a	198.2	209.6	195.6	188.0	186.6	197.0	188.9	218.2	235.2	232.9	231.3	239.9
Time Deposits	15	13.2	30.3	—	—	—	—	—	—	—	—	—	50.0
Foreign Liabilities	16c	47.0	58.0	18.7	15.1	2.5	.9	3.1	.8	1.7	.8	.4	3.2
Central Government Deposits	16d	13.0	46.0	38.7	45.1	55.5	164.7	170.7	168.1	123.0	94.9	107.3	40.3
Capital Accounts	17a	65.8	201.6	185.4	185.4	182.4	182.4	141.5	141.6	141.4	240.2	274.7	308.4
Other Items (Net)	17r	−18.9	−33.0	−12.9	−17.3	−24.5	−35.4	−109.7	−159.9	−121.6	−107.5	−135.3	−125.2
Deposit Money Banks				*Millions of Guilders: End of Period*									
Reserves	20	128.5	209.7	164.4	232.1	263.0	251.3	304.7	432.1	596.3	557.7	644.5	628.4
Foreign Assets	21	1,339.5	791.7	715.9	709.7	843.6	846.0	987.5	1,542.1	1,168.3	1,270.1	1,359.6	1,961.9
Claims on Local Government	22b	126.5	103.1	158.5	142.8	121.5	126.9	101.1	122.7	181.8	207.2	288.7	297.2
Claims on Private Sector	22d	2,034.4	2,130.2	2,275.8	2,262.8	2,299.8	2,529.3	2,677.4	2,686.9	2,782.5	2,834.4	3,059.7	3,450.3
Demand Deposits	24	560.7	653.6	702.9	710.7	721.7	770.3	806.8	896.4	1,064.9	1,007.7	1,096.8	1,174.7
Time and Savings Deposits	25a	1,201.7	1,231.4	1,266.4	1,325.7	1,417.1	1,484.6	1,552.9	1,743.7	1,921.2	2,195.4	2,434.6	2,583.9
Foreign Currency Deposits	25b	399.7	470.4	413.5	409.4	399.5	456.7	449.2	558.4	603.4	677.9	753.1	848.8
Foreign Liabilities	26c	1,289.6	699.0	719.1	701.5	752.9	813.6	1,017.5	1,188.7	888.2	854.2	913.3	1,335.8
Central Government Deposits	26d	36.0	22.6	36.5	45.7	46.2	30.0	34.5	41.8	39.3	34.9	45.8	51.6
Capital Accounts	27a	274.4	245.7	301.5	301.0	318.4	332.5	332.2	390.1	421.7	394.3	481.8	663.5
Other Items (Net)	27r	−133.2	−88.0	−125.3	−146.6	−127.9	−134.2	−122.4	−35.3	−209.8	−295.0	−372.9	−320.5
Girosystem Curacao													
Private Sector Deposits	24..i	87.1	71.4	—	....	....	....	....	....	....	....	....	....
Central Government Deposits	26d.i	34.9	1.5	—	....	....	....	....	....	....	....	....	....
Monetary Survey				*Millions of Guilders End of Period*									
Foreign Assets (Net)	31n	438.1	718.0	524.6	584.6	714.1	686.6	575.6	1,031.3	1,146.3	1,320.4	1,461.6	1,744.0
Domestic Credit	32	2,377.5	2,423.3	2,510.7	2,485.9	2,503.4	2,664.6	2,812.9	2,906.7	3,198.3	3,331.7	3,765.3	4,195.8
Claims on Central Govt. (Net)	32an	86.1	87.0	76.4	80.1	67.1	−6.6	−36.4	8.1	189.5	272.4	363.9	397.9
Claims on Local Government	32b	256.5	206.0	158.5	142.8	136.5	141.9	171.9	211.7	226.3	224.9	341.7	347.6
Claims on Private Sector	32d	2,034.9	2,130.3	2,275.8	2,263.0	2,299.8	2,529.3	2,677.4	2,686.9	2,782.5	2,834.4	3,059.7	3,450.3
Money	34	894.3	964.9	923.7	923.8	947.8	979.0	1,000.0	1,142.9	1,316.4	1,246.8	1,406.5	1,574.3
Quasi-Money	35	1,614.6	1,732.1	1,679.9	1,735.1	1,816.6	1,941.3	2,002.1	2,302.1	2,524.6	2,873.3	3,187.7	3,482.7
Other Items (Net)	37r	306.7	444.3	431.7	411.6	453.1	430.9	386.4	493.0	503.6	532.0	632.7	882.8
Money plus Quasi-Money	35l	2,508.9	2,697.0	2,603.6	2,658.9	2,764.4	2,920.3	3,002.1	3,445.0	3,841.0	4,120.1	4,594.2	5,057.0
Interest Rates				*Percent Per Annum*									
Discount Rate (End of Period)	60	5.00	6.00	6.00	6.00	6.00	6.00	6.00	6.00	6.00	....	....	....
Treasury Bill Rate	60c	4.48	5.46	5.66	5.77	5.82	6.15	6.15	6.15	4.96	2.80	3.86	3.52
Deposit Rate	60l	4.05	3.75	3.67	3.66	3.58	3.59	3.63	3.65	3.62	3.48	2.92	2.78
Lending Rate	60p	12.73	12.93	13.21	13.29	13.58	13.60	9.98	10.44	10.14	11.26	10.56	9.60
Government Bond Yield	61	7.48	8.02	8.25	8.67	8.60	8.75	8.77	9.00	8.20	6.72	7.09	6.46
Prices and Labor				*Index Numbers (2000=100): Period Averages*									
Consumer Prices	64	84.7	87.0	† 90.2	93.1	94.2	94.5	100.0	101.8	102.2	104.3	105.7	109.3
				Number in Thousands: Period Averages									
Labor Force	67d	....	62	66	66	62	61	58	56	58	61	61	63
Employment	67e	55	54	57	55	51	....	50	48	49	52	51	51
Unemployment	67c	8	8	9	10	10	....	8	9	9	9	10	11
Unemployment Rate (%)	67r	12.8	13.1	14.2	15.5	16.8	14.1	14.2	15.8	15.6	15.1	16.1	18.2
Intl. Transactions & Positions				*Millions of Guilders*									
Exports	70	2,462	....	....	....	2,093	2,597	3,596	4,292	2,880	2,078	2,452	2,819
Imports, c.i.f.	71	3,146	....	....	....	3,691	3,124	5,123	5,059	4,060	4,665	5,519	6,176
Imports, f.o.b.	71.v	2,809	....	....	....	....	....	....	....	....	....	....	....

Netherlands Antilles   353

Balance of Payments		1994	1995	1996	1997	1998	1999	2000	2001	2002	2003	2004	2005
		Millions of US Dollars: Minus Sign Indicates Debit											
Current Account, n.i.e.....................	78ald	−97.9	127.6	−253.8	−65.1	−136.9	−277.1	−50.7	−210.9	−58.7	6.8	−92.1	....
Goods: Exports f.o.b....................	78aad	351.1	586.5	614.6	501.4	465.6	467.0	676.1	638.2	575.5	681.5	799.8	....
Goods: Imports f.o.b....................	78abd	−1,271.6	−1,621.5	−1,743.7	−1,476.6	−1,513.2	−1,584.2	−1,661.7	−1,752.4	−1,602.4	−1,684.4	−1,967.6	....
Trade Balance......................	78acd	−920.5	−1,034.9	−1,129.1	−975.3	−1,047.7	−1,117.2	−985.6	−1,114.3	−1,026.9	−1,002.9	−1,167.9	....
Services: Credit..........................	78add	1,414.2	1,491.6	1,405.9	1,425.0	1,508.9	1,518.7	1,613.4	1,649.5	1,628.2	1,705.7	1,855.7	....
Services: Debit...........................	78aed	−670.5	−563.3	−624.0	−574.7	−611.3	−661.9	−733.5	−766.9	−769.6	−811.6	−835.0	....
Balance on Goods & Services......	78afd	−176.8	−106.6	−347.3	−125.0	−150.0	−260.4	−105.8	−231.7	−168.4	−108.8	−147.3	....
Income: Credit..........................	78agd	133.7	117.4	135.4	100.8	146.2	101.0	126.0	103.7	90.9	89.8	94.7	....
Income: Debit..........................	78ahd	−99.4	−99.4	−71.7	−54.1	−109.3	−121.4	−103.2	−83.8	−90.1	−97.1	−105.0	....
Balance on Gds, Serv. & Inc........	78aid	−142.5	−88.5	−283.5	−78.3	−113.1	−280.8	−83.0	−211.7	−167.6	−116.0	−157.6	....
Current Transfers, n.i.e.: Credit......	78ajd	217.9	365.8	174.7	165.3	137.2	179.6	246.6	217.0	365.5	399.1	319.6	....
Current Transfers: Debit...............	78akd	−173.3	−149.6	−145.0	−152.1	−160.9	−175.8	−214.3	−216.2	−256.6	−276.3	−254.0	....
Capital Account, n.i.e.................	78bcd	−.7	61.9	71.3	75.1	86.9	108.4	29.8	37.2	27.7	26.2	79.3	....
Capital Account, n.i.e.: Credit.......	78bad	1.0	66.8	71.9	76.9	91.3	109.8	31.3	37.9	29.3	32.8	80.2	....
Capital Account: Debit.................	78bbd	−1.7	−4.9	−.6	−1.7	−4.4	−1.5	−1.4	−.6	−1.6	−6.6	−.8	....
Financial Account, n.i.e................	78bjd	−2.3	−142.5	95.8	−31.2	58.0	69.5	−122.2	351.6	32.3	−52.1	−52.7	....
Direct Investment Abroad...............	78bdd	−1.0	−1.3	.8	6.5	2.0	1.2	2.3	−.5	−1.1	.9	−25.2	....
Dir. Invest. in Rep. Econ., n.i.e........	78bed	21.5	−150.0	−59.8	−88.5	−52.6	−21.8	−62.6	−4.7	7.8	−80.6	−25.5	....
Portfolio Investment Assets...........	78bfd	−69.1	−18.0	−22.3	9.2	−21.2	−7.1	−38.0	−31.6	−38.4	−.8	−93.9	....
Equity Securities........................	78bkd	—	−15.7	−19.2	−5.4	−3.9	−3.0	−33.9	−7.2	−8.5	−42.6	−16.4	....
Debt Securities........................	78bld	−69.1	−2.3	−3.1	14.6	−17.3	−4.1	−4.1	−24.4	−29.9	41.8	−77.4	....
Portfolio Investment Liab., n.i.e.....	78bgd	10.9	1.1	−8.2	−.2	−.2	−3.1	.1	−.2	.9	5.0	−1.7	....
Equity Securities........................	78bmd	—	—	....	....	....			—	—	—	—	....
Debt Securities........................	78bnd	10.9	1.1	−8.2	−.2	−.2	−3.1	.1	−.2	.9	5.0	−1.7	....
Financial Derivatives Assets...........	78bwd	....	....	....	....	....	....	—	.1	—	—	—	....
Financial Derivatives Liabilities.......	78bxd	....	....	....	....	....	....	—	—	—	—	—	....
Other Investment Assets...............	78bhd	15.3	67.1	84.6	46.1	111.7	34.1	−40.8	75.9	23.9	−119.5	−84.0	....
Monetary Authorities..................	78bod	....	−.8	5.1	2.8	3.9	2.6	−.1	−1.2	.4	.1	—	....
General Government..................	78bpd	—	2.2	7.2	2.0	4.4		−.9	−.8	—	−5.7	—	....
Banks...................................	78bqd	−55.8	−3.4	42.8	19.3	21.7	57.2	5.2	1.5	30.9	1.2	12.2	....
Other Sectors.........................	78brd	71.1	69.1	29.4	21.9	81.7	−25.7	−45.0	76.5	−7.5	−115.1	−96.2	....
Other Investment Liab., n.i.e.........	78bid	20.1	−41.3	100.7	−4.4	18.4	66.2	16.8	312.6	39.2	143.0	177.5	....
Monetary Authorities..................	78bsd	—	—	....	....	....	....	1.3	—	—	—	—	....
General Government..................	78btd	−38.3	−19.9	−19.9	−38.2	−51.2	−67.8	−33.3	−12.9	−20.7	−37.1	−26.8	....
Banks...................................	78bud	59.7	−5.8	45.8	−5.7	−.1	3.0	40.0	91.8	−2.7	−6.1	−25.0	....
Other Sectors.........................	78bvd	−1.3	−15.6	74.8	39.5	69.7	131.1	8.8	233.7	62.5	186.2	229.4	....
Net Errors and Omissions...............	78cad	24.9	13.4	14.8	14.9	17.4	24.5	13.4	39.8	51.0	46.3	71.3	....
Overall Balance........................	78cbd	−75.9	60.4	−71.9	−6.3	25.5	−74.7	−129.6	217.7	52.3	27.1	5.8	....
Reserves and Related Items............	79dad	75.9	−60.4	71.9	6.3	−25.5	74.7	129.6	−217.7	−52.3	−27.1	−5.8	....
Reserve Assets........................	79dbd	75.9	−60.4	53.8	−27.8	−75.6	8.3	47.8	−231.9	−68.2	−49.7	−35.4	....
Use of Fund Credit and Loans........	79dcd	—	....	....	....	....	....						
Exceptional Financing...................	79ded	—	....	18.1	34.1	50.2	66.5	81.8	14.2	15.9	22.6	29.5	....
Government Finance		*Millions of Guilders: Year Ending December 31*											
Deficit (-) or Surplus......................	80	−40.6p	† −100.2	....	....	....	....	....	....	....	....	....	
Revenue...............................	81	663.3p	† 462.2	....	....	....	....	....	....	....	....	....	
Grants Received......................	81z	91.9p	† 92.8	....	....	....	....	....	....	....	....	....	
Expenditure............................	82	795.4p	† 655.1	....	....	....	....	....	....	....	....	....	
Lending Minus Repayments...........	83	.4p	† .1	....	....	....	....	....	....	....	....	....	
Financing													
Domestic.................................	84a	40.6p	† 100.2	....	....	....	....	....	....	....	....	....	
Foreign..................................	85a	—p	† —	....	....	....	....	....	....	....	....	....	
Debt: Domestic..........................	88a	618.5p	† 704.6	....	....	....	....	....	....	....	....	....	
Foreign..............................	89a	—p	† —	....	....	....	....	....	....	....	....	....	
		Millions: Midyear Estimates											
Population..............................	99z	.19	.19	.18	.18	.18	.18	.18	.18	.18	.18	.18	.18

New Zealand 196

		1994	1995	1996	1997	1998	1999	2000	2001	2002	2003	2004	2005
Exchange Rates					*SDRs per New Zealand Dollar: End of Period*								
Market Rate	ac	.4401	.4395	.4910	.4311	.3742	.3793	.3379	.3306	.3873	.4374	.4626	.4767
					US Dollars per New Zealand Dollar: End of Period (ag) Period Average (rh)								
Market Rate	ag	.6425	.6533	.7060	.5817	.5269	.5206	.4402	.4155	.5265	.6500	.7184	.6814
Market Rate	rh	.5937	.6564	.6876	.6630	.5367	.5295	.4574	.4206	.4642	.5823	.6640	.7044
					Index Numbers (2000=100): Period Averages								
Market Rate	ahx	129.8	143.5	150.3	145.0	117.3	115.8	100.0	92.0	101.5	127.3	145.2	154.0
Nominal Effective Exchange Rate	nec	113.5	119.2	126.9	130.2	114.0	110.4	100.0	97.8	105.6	120.0	128.1	134.2
Real Effective Exchange Rate	rec	114.7	121.5	129.1	131.8	115.2	110.2	100.0	98.1	107.2	121.6	130.1	137.5
Fund Position					*Millions of SDRs: End of Period*								
Quota	2f.s	650	650	650	650	650	895	895	895	895	895	895	895
SDRs	1b.s	—	1	—	—	1	5	10	13	16	19	22	24
Reserve Position in the Fund	1c.s	101	110	127	132	253	309	246	308	338	433	305	115
Total Fund Cred.&Loans Outstg.	2tl	—	—	—	—	—	—	—	—	—	—	—	—
International Liquidity					*Millions of US Dollars Unless Otherwise Indicated: End of Period*								
Total Reserves minus Gold	1l.d	3,709	4,410	5,953	4,451	4,204	4,455	3,952	3,565	4,963	6,085	6,947	8,893
SDRs	1b.d	—	1	—	—	2	7	13	16	22	28	34	34
Reserve Position in the Fund	1c.d	147	164	182	178	356	424	320	387	459	644	474	165
Foreign Exchange	1d.d	3,561	4,245	5,771	4,273	3,846	4,025	3,619	3,161	4,482	5,414	6,439	8,694
Monetary Authorities	1dad	2,351	2,575	2,714	2,751	2,461	2,804	2,328	2,078	2,940	3,515	3,395	4,627
Government	1dbd	1,210	1,670	3,057	1,522	1,385	1,221	1,291	1,084	1,542	1,899	3,044	4,067
Gold (Million Fine Troy Ounces)	1ad	—	—	—	—	—	—	—	—	—	—	—	—
Gold (National Valuation)	1and	—	—	—	—	—	—	—	—	—	—	—	—
Monetary Authorities: Other Liab.	4..d	—	178	299	461	383	379	605	302	501	473	679	790
Banking Institutions: Assets	7a.d	1,559	1,955	3,552	1,915	2,829	4,786	6,953	9,788	12,991	14,664	16,101	8,260
Liabilities	7b.d	12,319	14,439	17,197	17,024	20,031	25,261	25,554	27,632	33,990	41,785	53,906	53,886
Monetary Authorities					*Millions of New Zealand Dollars: End of Period*								
Foreign Assets	11	5,772	7,024	8,856	8,544	8,799	9,077	10,330	9,310	10,410	10,155	10,864	14,328
Claims on Central Government	12a	2,918	3,065	3,118	3,097	3,119	1,892	2,489	2,373	2,676	2,677	3,983	4,682
Claims on Banking Institutions	12e	301	476	1,305	1,079	451	2,178	1,802	2,247	2,931	2,829	1,079	517
Reserve Money	14	1,891	2,026	1,972	2,068	2,198	3,870	2,925	3,196	3,472	3,546	3,141	5,235
of which: Currency Outside DMBs	14a	1,367	1,489	1,497	1,633	1,724	2,077	2,069	2,241	2,451	2,597	2,188	3,020
Liabs.of Central Bank: Securities	16ac	1,185	1,218	1,242	1,250	1,076	—	—	—	—	—	—	—
Foreign Liabilities	16c	—	273	424	793	726	728	1,374	727	952	728	945	1,159
Central Government Deposits	16d	5,219	6,319	8,959	7,871	7,574	7,751	9,463	9,129	10,756	10,578	10,038	11,152
Capital Accounts	17a	748	769	745	801	853	843	893	914	868	838	1,836	2,006
Other Items (Net)	17r	−53	−39	−62	−63	−58	−45	−34	−36	−31	−30	−33	−26
Banking Institutions					*Millions of New Zealand Dollars: End of Period*								
Reserves	20	467	606	532	409	448	1,592	818	908	944	909	933	1,220
Claims on Mon.Author.:Securities	20c	1,185	1,218	1,242	1,250	1,076	—	—	—	—	—	—	—
Foreign Assets	21	2,427	2,993	5,031	3,292	5,369	9,194	15,794	23,558	24,675	22,560	22,413	12,123
Claims on Central Government	22a	5,932	4,249	3,302	3,572	4,384	6,921	7,149	5,818	8,183	7,920	5,601	5,034
Claims on Private Sector	22d	74,588	85,150	94,647	105,190	112,124	121,884	129,301	137,818	147,781	162,631	180,764	206,715
Demand Deposits	24	8,155	8,865	9,094	9,728	10,633	12,528	13,593	16,506	17,487	19,068	19,578	18,957
Time, Savings,Fgn.Currency Dep.	25	57,423	62,850	74,458	78,117	78,762	81,043	82,164	85,727	92,559	102,782	109,088	124,370
of which: Fgn Currency Deposits	25b	1,849	2,030	3,764	2,806	4,198	2,521	3,296	3,194	2,638	4,667	5,620	7,769
Foreign Liabilities	26c	19,174	22,101	24,359	29,267	38,016	48,523	58,051	66,504	64,559	64,285	75,037	79,081
Central Government Deposits	26d	9	19	25	33	29	61	52	53	48	57	68	67
Capital Accounts	27a	5,158	5,798	5,547	7,262	8,224	9,348	9,685	11,790	14,022	17,803	18,396	19,063
Other Items (Net)	27r	−5,320	−5,418	−8,727	−10,693	−12,263	−11,911	−10,483	−12,477	−7,093	−9,973	−12,455	−16,446
Banking Survey					*Millions of New Zealand Dollars: End of Period*								
Foreign Assets (Net)	31n	−10,976	−12,357	−10,896	−18,224	−24,575	−30,980	−33,300	−34,363	−30,427	−32,298	−42,704	−53,790
Domestic Credit	32	78,210	86,126	92,084	103,955	112,023	122,884	129,423	136,826	147,836	162,593	180,242	205,212
Claims on Central Govt. (Net)	32an	3,622	976	−2,564	−1,234	−101	1,001	122	−992	55	−38	−522	−1,503
Claims on Private Sector	32d	74,588	85,150	94,647	105,190	112,124	121,884	129,301	137,818	147,781	162,631	180,764	206,715
Money	34	9,594	10,398	10,619	11,386	12,378	14,649	15,700	18,795	20,018	21,705	21,789	22,471
Quasi-Money	35	57,423	62,850	74,458	78,117	78,762	81,043	82,164	85,727	92,559	102,782	109,088	124,370
Capital Accounts	37a	5,906	6,567	6,292	8,062	9,077	10,190	10,578	12,704	14,890	18,641	20,232	21,069
Other Items (Net)	37r	−5,688	−6,045	−10,180	−11,834	−12,767	−13,977	−12,319	−14,762	−10,058	−12,833	−13,570	−16,488
Money plus Quasi-Money	35l	67,017	73,247	85,076	89,503	91,140	95,692	97,865	104,522	112,577	124,487	130,877	146,840
Money (National Definitions)					*Millions of New Zealand Dollars: End of Period*								
M1	59ma	10,948	10,334	10,565	11,327	12,888	14,880	15,932	19,094	20,312	22,135	22,834	22,427
M2	59mb	27,840	31,990	32,836	33,336	37,873	40,964	41,319	47,412	51,193	53,293	54,708	61,101
M3R	59mca	58,385	65,515	73,469	78,652	78,786	84,669	86,644	92,732	103,352	113,171	117,055	128,158
M3 Broad Money	59mcb	67,948	77,854	87,719	91,411	92,383	98,748	105,179	117,213	131,820	139,575	148,283	158,323
Nonbank Financial Institutions					*Millions of New Zealand Dollars: End of Period*								
Claims on Central Government	42a.s	2,435.4	....	....	....	....	....	....	....	....	....	....	....
Claims on Local Government	42b.s	546.4	526.9	624.7	551.3	....	....	....	....	....	....	....	....
Claims on Private Sector	42d.s	4,507.9	986.8	934.2	636.5	....	....	....	....	....	....	....	....
Real Estate	42h.s	1,590.9	....	....	....	....	....	....	....	....	....	....	....
Incr.in Total Assets(Within Per.)	49z.s	−618.4	....	....	....	....	....	....	....	....	....	....	....
Interest Rates					*Percent Per Annum*								
Discount Rate (End of Period)	60	9.75	9.80	8.80	9.70	5.60	5.00	6.50	4.75	5.75	5.00	6.50	7.25
Money Market Rate	60b	6.13	8.91	9.38	7.38	6.86	4.33	6.12	5.76	5.40	5.33	5.77	6.76
Treasury Bill Rate	60c	6.69	8.82	9.09	7.53	7.10	4.58	6.39	5.56	5.52	5.21	5.85	6.53
Deposit Rate	60l	6.38	8.49	8.49	7.26	6.78	4.56	6.36	5.35	5.33	5.10	5.77	6.68
Lending Rate	60p	9.69	12.09	12.27	11.35	11.22	8.49	10.22	9.88	9.83	9.81	10.38	11.53
Government Bond Yield	61	7.48	7.94	8.04	7.21	6.47	6.13	6.85	6.12	6.28	5.51	5.98	5.98

New Zealand 196

		1994	1995	1996	1997	1998	1999	2000	2001	2002	2003	2004	2005
Prices, Production, Labor							*Index Numbers (2000=100): Period Averages*						
Share Prices	62	68.0	71.7	80.5	93.7	109.9	97.7	100.0	105.3	115.8	128.6	163.9	197.0
Input Prices: All Industry	63	89.8	90.5	91.1	91.4	92.0	93.0	100.0	106.0	106.2	105.3	107.1	112.9
Consumer Prices	64	† 89.7	93.1	95.2	96.3	97.6	97.4	100.0	102.6	105.4	107.2	109.7	113.0
Labor Cost Index	65a	90.0	91.3	93.1	95.2	97.0	98.5	100.0	101.9	104.1	106.5	108.9	112.0
Manufacturing Prod	66ey	75.4	95.0	97.2	97.5	94.4	96.3	100.0	100.3	105.4	106.5	110.4	107.7
Manufacturing Employment	67ey	100.8	104.7	103.6	100.6	102.8	99.2	100.0	103.1	103.2	99.1	102.5	99.1
							Number in Thousands: Period Averages						
Labor Force	67d	1,766	1,809	1,866	† 1,886	1,891	1,907	1,923	1,958	2,012	2,046	2,099	2,152
Employment	67e	1,623	1,696	1,753	† 1,761	1,751	1,778	1,809	1,854	1,908	1,951	2,017	2,073
Unemployment	67c	185	158	154	† 165	191	217	230	194	171	142	106	85
Unemployment Rate (%)	67r	8.1	6.3	6.1	† 6.6	7.4	6.8	6.0	5.3	5.2	4.6	3.9	3.7
Intl. Transactions & Positions							*Millions of New Zealand Dollars*						
Exports	70	20,518.6	20,786.7	20,875.9	21,457.7	22,415.5	23,582.9	29,257.1	32,670.0	31,033.7	28,397.2	30,711.9	30,817.3
Butter	70fl	790.5	777.9	907.7	919.3	985.9	885.7	1,052.3	1,039.8	1,052.3	944.7	959.5	937.3
Imports, c.i.f.	71	19,980.6	21,250.5	21,398.8	21,963.9	23,347.7	27,113.6	30,735.7	31,682.2	32,337.4	31,781.7	34,915.5	37,278.8
Imports, f.o.b.	71.v	18,490.9	19,714.7	19,847.4	20,440.4	21,681.9	25,435.7	28,851.1	29,612.3	30,328.6	29,817.0	32,707.9	34,860.7
							2000=100						
Volume of Exports	72	† 81.3	83.7	87.8	92.9	92.4	94.8	100.0	103.2	108.9	111.8	119.4	117.7
Butter	72fl	74.3	68.8	80.9	97.2	87.8	91.0	100.0	86.4	114.1	107.5	97.3	94.3
Volume of Imports	73	† 77.5	82.6	85.4	88.5	90.7	102.8	100.0	101.9	111.3	123.8	142.4	151.3
Butter (Unit Value)	74fl	104.6	107.2	106.1	91.3	104.6	91.9	100.0	112.9	88.5	82.7	89.0	92.6
Export Price Index	76	86.8	85.4	82.4	80.0	83.7	84.9	100.0	109.0	97.6	87.1	88.1	89.2
Import Price Index	76.x	83.8	83.8	81.5	80.8	83.8	85.9	100.0	101.2	94.7	83.6	79.8	80.0
Butter (Wholesale Price)	76fl	101.8	107.7	....	95.9	116.0	116.0	100.0	....	....	....	....	....
Balance of Payments							*Millions of US Dollars: Minus Sign Indicates Debit*						
Current Account, n.i.e.	78ald	−2,384	−3,003	−3,891	−4,304	−2,157	−3,515	−2,661	−1,435	−2,467	−3,569	−6,456	....
Goods: Exports f.o.b.	78aad	12,176	13,554	14,338	14,282	12,246	12,657	13,530	13,920	14,517	16,834	20,463	....
Goods: Imports f.o.b.	78abd	−10,769	−12,584	−13,815	−13,380	−11,333	−13,028	−12,850	−12,448	−14,351	−17,291	−21,890	....
Trade Balance	78acd	1,408	971	523	903	912	−371	680	1,471	166	−457	−1,427	....
Services: Credit	78add	3,667	4,481	4,653	4,254	3,763	4,386	4,415	4,378	5,218	6,524	7,801	....
Services: Debit	78aed	−4,101	−4,694	−4,897	−4,903	−4,499	−4,581	−4,544	−4,316	−4,718	−5,653	−6,976	....
Balance on Goods & Services	78afd	973	757	279	254	176	−567	551	1,534	666	414	−602	....
Income: Credit	78agd	358	940	372	393	880	919	693	611	1,138	1,417	1,530	....
Income: Debit	78ahd	−4,045	−4,895	−5,085	−5,249	−3,493	−4,036	−4,141	−3,733	−4,346	−5,622	−7,586	....
Balance on Gds, Serv. & Inc	78aid	−2,713	−3,198	−4,434	−4,601	−2,437	−3,684	−2,897	−1,588	−2,542	−3,791	−6,657	....
Current Transfers, n.i.e.: Credit	78ajd	638	558	897	680	681	609	634	585	642	856	901	....
Current Transfers: Debit	78akd	−309	−363	−354	−383	−401	−440	−398	−433	−567	−635	−699	....
Capital Account, n.i.e.	78bcd	617	1,224	1,336	242	−181	−217	−180	482	814	502	157	....
Capital Account, n.i.e.: Credit	78bad	995	1,652	1,838	783	263	260	238	844	1,171	1,065	963	....
Capital Account: Debit	78bbd	−379	−427	−502	−541	−444	−477	−418	−362	−357	−563	−807	....
Financial Account, n.i.e.	78bjd	2,220	4,665	3,571	4,045	1,580	1,974	1,966	1,075	2,386	3,869	8,871	....
Direct Investment Abroad	78bdd	−1,725	337	1,533	45	−928	−803	−752	1,078	−404	−519	886	....
Dir. Invest. in Rep. Econ., n.i.e.	78bed	2,543	3,659	2,231	2,624	1,191	1,412	3,994	820	1,764	3,706	2,506	....
Portfolio Investment Assets	78bfd	−72	−284	−430	−1,612	−467	−666	−2,318	−1,243	−951	−865	−2,001	....
Equity Securities	78bkd	−152	−216	−339	−925	114	−893	−1,763	−941	....	−920	−1,786	....
Debt Securities	78bld	81	−68	−90	−687	−581	227	−555	−303	55	−214	....
Portfolio Investment Liab., n.i.e.	78bgd	614	96	−104	403	425	−2,285	102	2,028	2,634	1,885	8,320	....
Equity Securities	78bmd	23	−100	175	88	22	172	−551	24	752	719	99	....
Debt Securities	78bnd	591	197	−279	315	402	−2,458	652	2,004	1,882	1,166	8,222	....
Financial Derivatives Assets	78bwd	....	....	....	....	....	....	....	....	....	....	....	....
Financial Derivatives Liabilities	78bxd	....	....	....	....	....	....	....	....	....	....	....	....
Other Investment Assets	78bhd	−78	−392	−920	991	−305	−1,282	−22	−4,664	−659	−113	54	....
Monetary Authorities	78bod	—	—	—	....	....	....	....	....	....	....	....	....
General Government	78bpd	−82	−57	−94	238	55	212	....	....	....	....	....	....
Banks	78bqd	66	−346	−932	819	−285	−1,591	....	....	....	....	....	....
Other Sectors	78brd	−61	11	106	−65	−75	97	....	....	....	....	....	....
Other Investment Liab., n.i.e.	78bid	937	1,249	1,262	1,595	1,665	5,597	961	3,057	2	−225	−894	....
Monetary Authorities	78bsd	—	—	—	—	—	—	....	....	....	....	....	....
General Government	78btd	−290	−144	−135	−73	68	13	....	....	....	....	....	....
Banks	78bud	767	1,096	964	1,131	1,559	5,446	....	....	....	....	....	....
Other Sectors	78bvd	460	297	432	537	38	138	....	....	....	....	....	....
Net Errors and Omissions	78cad	281	−2,502	756	−1,426	271	1,947	731	−308	354	−20	−1,943	....
Overall Balance	78cbd	733	384	1,772	−1,442	−486	188	−143	−187	1,086	783	629	....
Reserves and Related Items	79dad	−733	−384	−1,772	1,442	486	−188	143	187	−1,086	−783	−629	....
Reserve Assets	79dbd	−733	−384	−1,772	1,442	486	−188	143	187	−1,086	−783	−629	....
Use of Fund Credit and Loans	79dcd	—	—	—	—	—	—	....	....	....	....	....	....
Exceptional Financing	79ded	....	....	....	....	....	....	....	....	....	....	....	....

New Zealand   196

		1994	1995	1996	1997	1998	1999	2000	2001	2002	2003	2004	2005
IIP:End-March Stocks Through 1999							*Millions of US Dollars*						
Assets	79aad	13,206	16,201	23,573	23,023	19,348	21,320	32,453	33,116	42,539	55,848	66,583	....
Direct Investment Abroad	79abd	5,163	7,630	8,928	6,749	5,775	7,155	8,491	7,175	9,268	11,346	12,895	....
Portfolio Investment	79acd	1,362	1,707	5,815	6,434	6,476	6,760	11,264	11,783	13,612	19,888	24,874	....
Equity Securities	79add	834	1,226	4,407	4,895	4,620	4,447	6,721	7,114	7,652	13,432	17,512	....
Debt Securities	79aed	529	481	1,408	1,539	1,855	2,313	4,543	4,669	5,960	6,456	7,361	....
Financial Derivatives	79ald	—	—	—	—	—	—	4,289	2,462	3,484	4,678	5,968	....
Other Investment	79afd	2,793	2,898	4,245	5,313	2,804	3,555	4,456	8,130	11,212	13,888	15,900	....
Monetary Authorities	79agd	....	....	....	....	....	—	....	....	....	....	....	....
General Government	79ahd	....	....	....	....	....	198	....	....	....	....	....	....
Banks	79aid	....	....	....	....	....	2,100	....	....	....	....	....	....
Other Sectors	79ajd	....	....	....	....	....	1,257	....	....	....	....	....	....
Reserve Assets	79akd	3,888	3,967	4,584	4,528	4,293	3,850	3,952	3,566	4,963	6,048	6,946	....
Liabilities	79lad	51,100	62,339	71,631	78,547	68,752	67,651	73,165	71,913	96,438	125,812	157,128	....
Dir. Invest. in Rep. Economy	79lbd	19,315	25,574	33,381	37,491	34,889	33,555	24,815	21,729	31,195	46,311	54,703	....
Portfolio Investment	79lcd	17,595	19,809	19,361	20,166	17,581	17,710	24,715	25,578	33,799	43,095	58,196	....
Equity Securities	79ldd	816	1,483	288	1,045	208	241	4,582	4,170	5,652	8,965	12,078	....
Debt Securities	79led	16,779	18,327	19,072	19,121	17,373	17,469	20,133	21,408	28,147	34,130	46,118	....
Financial Derivatives	79lld	—	—	—	—	—	—	3,256	2,640	4,139	5,475	8,236	....
Other Investment	79lfd	14,189	16,955	18,889	20,890	16,282	16,387	20,379	21,966	27,305	30,931	35,994	....
Monetary Authorities	79lgd	....	....	....	....	....	—	....	....	....	....	....	....
General Government	79lhd	....	....	....	....	....	428	....	....	....	....	....	....
Banks	79lid	....	....	....	....	....	10,924	....	....	....	....	....	....
Other Sectors	79ljd	....	....	....	....	....	5,034	....	....	....	....	....	....
Government Finance							*Millions of New Zealand Dollars: Fiscal Year (see note)*						
Deficit (-) or Surplus	80	679	396	4,932	3,913	484	2,049	−385	....	....	....	....	....
Revenue	81	30,236	32,861	33,975	33,285	33,827	33,359	34,440	....	....	....	....	....
Expenditure	82	29,662	29,954	30,593	31,465	33,005	33,869	34,386	....	....	....	....	....
Lending Minus Repayments	83	−105	2,511	−1,550	−2,093	338	−2,559	439	....	....	....	....	....
Financing													
Debt: Domestic	88a	20,194	21,060	19,866	15,688	18,307	19,440	20,041	....	....	....	....	....
Foreign	89a	26,289	23,418	21,896	20,649	19,969	17,384	16,368	....	....	....	....	....
National Accounts							*Millions of New Zealand Dollars; Year Beginning April 1*						
Househ.Cons.Expend.,incl.NPISHs	96f.c	51,192	54,546	58,079	60,565	63,461	65,985	68,692	72,436	76,710	81,728	87,531	92,651
Government Consumption Expend	91f.c	15,267	16,303	16,933	18,364	18,653	20,131	20,297	21,789	22,864	24,307	26,482	28,827
Gross Fixed Capital Formation	93e.c	18,355	20,600	21,539	21,408	20,742	22,889	23,595	25,846	27,749	31,527	34,923	37,227
Changes in Inventories	93i.c	1,166	1,182	809	817	270	1,537	1,419	1,888	779	1,140	1,566	892
Exports of Goods and Services	90c.c	26,951	27,125	27,528	28,531	30,394	33,526	41,159	43,694	42,339	40,455	43,142	43,585
Imports of Goods and Services (-)	98c.c	25,296	26,373	26,943	28,100	30,091	34,371	39,219	40,778	40,095	40,159	44,733	47,511
Gross Domestic Product (GDP)	99b.c	87,639	93,386	97,952	101,589	103,429	109,696	115,941	124,875	130,344	139,002	148,912	155,672
Net Primary Income from Abroad	98.nc	−5,686	−5,998	−7,264	−6,399	−4,978	−6,605	−7,580	−7,091	−6,531	−7,183	−10,319	1,967
Gross National Income (GNI)	99a.c	81,953	87,388	90,688	95,190	98,451	103,091	108,361	117,784	123,813	131,819	138,593	157,639
Consumption of Fixed Capital	99cfc	12,536	13,099	13,679	14,048	14,771	15,440	16,558	17,393	18,388	19,056	20,074	....
GDP Volume 1995/96 Prices	99b.r	89,882	93,385	96,367	99,240	100,381	105,593	108,209	112,300	117,318	121,853	126,030	128,608
GDP Volume (2000=100)	99bvr	83.1	86.3	89.1	91.7	92.8	97.6	100.0	103.8	108.4	112.6	116.5	118.9
GDP Deflator (2000=100)	99bir	91.0	93.3	94.9	95.5	96.2	97.0	100.0	103.8	103.7	106.5	110.3	113.0
							Millions: Midyear Estimates						
Population	99z	3.61	3.66	3.70	3.73	3.75	3.78	3.82	3.86	3.90	3.95	3.99	4.03

Nicaragua 278

		1994	1995	1996	1997	1998	1999	2000	2001	2002	2003	2004	2005
Exchange Rates						*Córdobas per SDR: End of Period*							
Principal Rate....................	aa	10.38	11.84	12.83	13.49	15.76	16.91	17.01	17.39	19.95	23.11	25.36	24.51
						Córdobas per US Dollar: End of Period (ae) Period Average (rf)							
Principal Rate....................	ae	7.11	7.97	8.92	10.00	11.19	12.32	13.06	13.84	14.67	15.55	16.33	17.15
Principal Rate....................	rf	6.72	7.55	8.44	9.45	10.58	11.81	12.68	13.37	14.25	15.10	15.94	16.73
						Index Numbers (2000=100): Period Averages							
Principal Rate....................	ahx	188.78	169.05	150.47	133.96	120.10	107.34	100.00	94.85	88.99	83.99	79.57	75.78
Nominal Effective Exchange Rate.....	nec	2.73	2.44	2.24	2.09	1.95	1.77	1.70	1.65	1.57	1.45	1.35	1.28
Real Effective Exchange Rate..........	rec	111.25	102.17	99.42	96.74	98.88	96.88	100.00	100.87	96.89	91.21	89.05	88.70
Fund Position						*Millions of SDRs: End of Period*							
Quota...............	2f.s	96.10	96.10	96.10	96.10	96.10	130.00	130.00	130.00	130.00	130.00	130.00	130.00
SDRs...............	1b.s	.01	—	.02	.03	.15	.16	.05	.26	.02	.04	.32	.22
Reserve Position in the Fund...........	1c.s												
Total Fund Cred.&Loans Outstg.......	2tl	34.92	26.41	20.02	20.02	36.84	113.15	129.33	125.33	128.29	143.50	159.51	140.48
International Liquidity						*Millions of US Dollars Unless Otherwise Indicated: End of Period*							
Total Reserves minus Gold..............	1l.d	141.01	136.20	197.32	377.94	350.41	509.71	488.46	379.93	448.13	502.06	668.20	727.81
SDRs...............	1b.d	.01	—	.02	.04	.21	.21	.06	.33	.03	.06	.50	.31
Reserve Position in the Fund.........	1c.d												
Foreign Exchange........................	1d.d	141.00	136.20	197.30	377.90	350.20	509.50	488.40	379.60	448.10	502.00	667.70	727.50
Gold (Million Fine Troy Ounces)....	1ad	.013	.015	.015	.015	.015	.015	.015	.015	.015	.015	—	—
Gold (National Valuation)......	1and	.55	.63	.63	.63	.63	.63	.62	.62	.62	.62	—	—
Monetary Authorities: Other Liab.....	4..d	3,470.70	2,936.22	2,113.12	2,086.84	2,046.56	1,993.95	2,134.78	1,949.79	1,979.26	2,014.99	1,905.83	1,924.35
Deposit Money Banks: Assets...........	7a.d	53.56	45.00	146.65	211.27	162.15	143.98	65.66	88.39	92.50	97.14	117.73	141.28
Liabilities.....................	7b.d	31.62	31.34	44.61	54.65	55.09	109.86	90.42	102.58	107.00	108.99	110.47	202.56
Nonbank Financial Insts.: Assets...	7e.d	5.64	1.90	.18	.16	—	—	—	—	—	—	—	—
Liabilities.....................	7f.d	—	—	33.90	36.76	.06	8.97	9.32	21.56	3.31	8.51	10.60	19.75
Monetary Authorities						*Millions of Córdobas: End of Period*							
Foreign Assets.......................	11	1,226.6	1,283.5	† 2,197.5	4,034.7	4,199.5	6,466.0	6,620.8	† 5,470.2	6,854.8	8,069.0	11,097.9	12,705.2
Claims on Central Government........	12a	23,256.5	22,469.2	† 18,132.0	21,451.1	23,769.1	26,884.0	28,400.1	† 43,286.6	44,767.5	46,585.0	46,366.5	47,971.7
Claims on Nonfin.Pub.Enterprises.....	12c	380.9	468.4	† 98.3	101.0	113.1	124.4	77.4	† 124.6	134.7	50.4	260.0	260.0
Claims on Private Sector..................	12d	—	12.7	† 206.0	260.4	314.7	303.4	307.3	† 42.7	45.1	39.1	68.3	85.5
Claims on Deposit Money Banks......	12e	824.4	743.4	† 152.3	806.5	99.1	326.8	2,012.8	† 434.5	10.6	1.2	.3	.6
Claims on Nonbank Financial Insts...	12g	1,206.1	1,151.2	† 3,168.2	3,003.9	4,028.3	4,203.4	4,453.3	† .9	.9	1.0	.9	.9
Reserve Money..........................	14	1,533.3	1,894.5	† 2,545.9	3,372.6	4,038.1	4,267.6	4,468.1	† 6,071.7	6,724.5	8,015.9	9,271.8	10,709.1
of which: Currency Outside DMBs..	14a	688.3	771.0	† 864.1	1,096.1	1,339.6	1,734.8	1,760.5	† 1,949.4	2,085.8	2,506.6	3,103.3	3,808.0
Time, Savings,& Fgn.Currency Dep...	15	17.6	11.6	† 46.2	48.3	60.1	66.6	468.6	† .4	.4	.4	—	—
Liabs. of Central Bank: Securities....	16ac	—	—	† 436.4	3,643.5	2,250.3	2,302.9	3,658.1	† 8,732.8	9,640.6	7,953.3	6,419.7	5,527.8
Foreign Liabilities.........................	16c	25,045.1	23,699.6	† 19,114.4	21,128.0	23,489.4	26,475.1	30,074.8	† 29,166.7	31,597.0	34,652.3	35,165.6	36,436.4
Central Government Deposits...........	16d	329.6	198.5	† 276.3	190.0	745.4	1,695.4	1,997.8	† 742.4	2,087.3	3,468.1	6,254.6	7,398.0
Liab. to Nonbank Financial Insts.......	16j	184.3	122.0	† 118.6	13.4	.1	—	—	† —	—	—	—	—
Capital Accounts.......................	17a	212.8	299.3	† 1,494.2	1,838.3	2,498.0	4,303.8	3,315.9	† 370.6	420.3	481.9	525.8	509.2
Other Items (Net)........................	17r	−428.2	−97.1	† −77.6	−576.4	−557.5	−803.3	−2,111.5	† 4,274.8	1,343.4	173.6	156.4	443.3
of which: Valuation Adjustment.....	17rv	—	—	† —	—	—	—	−1,280.3	—	—	—	—	—
Deposit Money Banks						*Millions of Córdobas: End of Period*							
Reserves.................................	20	773.6	1,112.0	† 1,680.9	2,324.5	2,752.8	2,627.3	2,728.5	† 4,114.0	4,643.9	5,502.9	6,162.9	6,894.1
Claims on Mon.Author.:Securities....	20c	—	—	† 158.2	1,365.2	1,367.0	1,506.2	2,885.4	† 7,407.8	8,690.9	7,486.0	6,412.9	5,467.0
Foreign Assets.........................	21	380.9	358.4	† 1,308.7	2,111.7	1,815.1	1,773.5	857.3	† 1,223.4	1,357.0	1,510.7	1,922.4	2,422.3
Claims on Central Government........	22a	—	—	† 513.7	372.5	356.8	1,107.1	1,400.3	† 1,659.4	2,326.0	3,194.5	4,654.6	5,274.9
Claims on Local Government............	22b	5.2	—	† 34.5	6.7	6.7	210.3	243.0	† 6.0	23.1	57.5	—	7.7
Claims on Nonfin.Pub.Enterprises.....	22c	41.4	10.0	† 24.0	5.5	5.5	26.1	23.7	† 111.0	110.5	439.3	599.2	576.0
Claims on Private Sector..................	22d	4,075.5	5,159.0	† 4,675.7	6,707.4	9,715.5	13,270.5	15,240.8	† 9,783.2	11,228.2	14,173.9	18,075.7	23,853.0
Claims on Nonbank Financial Insts...	22g	—	—	† —	—	—	—	—	† 115.7	67.3	149.6	198.7	177.3
Demand Deposits........................	24	407.6	471.4	† 787.4	958.7	1,195.6	1,406.0	1,565.5	† 1,316.2	1,280.5	1,696.0	1,702.3	1,973.8
Time, Savings,& Fgn.Currency Dep...	25	2,500.7	3,629.5	† 5,747.6	9,249.8	12,404.3	14,622.3	15,632.1	† 17,046.0	19,647.4	21,717.0	25,581.6	27,575.5
Money Market Instruments..............	26aa	—	—	† 365.1	508.9	360.3	320.1	270.2	† —	—	—	—	—
Foreign Liabilities.........................	26c	224.9	249.6	† 398.1	546.2	616.7	1,353.1	1,180.7	† 1,419.8	1,569.9	1,695.0	1,803.9	3,472.9
Central Government Deposits...........	26d	539.9	654.9	† 755.7	1,098.1	798.2	1,662.2	1,381.8	† 2,270.9	2,363.1	3,193.7	3,526.2	5,117.4
Credit from Monetary Authorities.....	26g	779.0	752.1	† 35.5	743.4	34.7	27.5	2,340.9	† 476.2	8.0	214.1	290.3	332.8
Liab. to Nonbank Financial Insts.......	26j	1,198.1	1,389.6	† 273.8	483.6	676.2	879.2	970.6	† 1,175.6	1,311.7	1,274.8	1,812.6	2,083.4
Capital Accounts.......................	27a	648.8	406.0	† 825.0	222.4	1,201.4	1,998.5	2,696.9	† 1,654.6	2,135.1	2,593.8	3,555.0	4,191.0
Other Items (Net)............................	27r	−1,022.4	−913.7	† −792.5	−918.4	−1,267.9	−1,748.2	−2,659.7	† −939.0	131.3	130.1	−245.4	−74.5
Monetary Survey						*Millions of Córdobas: End of Period*							
Foreign Assets (Net)......................	31n	−23,662.5	−22,307.3	† −16,006.2	−15,527.8	−18,091.5	−19,588.9	−23,777.3	† −23,892.9	−24,955.1	−26,767.6	−23,949.2	−24,782.0
Domestic Credit.............................	32	28,096.1	28,417.1	† 25,820.5	30,619.7	36,766.2	42,771.5	46,766.3	† 52,116.7	54,253.0	58,028.5	60,443.2	65,691.6
Claims on Central Govt. (Net)....	32an	22,387.0	21,615.8	† 17,613.8	20,534.7	22,582.4	24,633.4	26,420.8	† 41,932.7	42,643.1	43,117.7	41,240.3	40,731.1
Claims on Local Government..........	32b	5.2	—	† 34.5	6.7	6.7	210.3	243.0	† 6.0	23.1	57.5	—	7.7
Claims on Nonfin.Pub.Enterprises.....	32c	422.3	478.4	† 122.3	106.5	118.5	150.5	101.1	† 235.6	245.2	489.6	859.2	836.1
Claims on Private Sector.................	32d	4,075.5	5,171.7	† 4,881.7	6,967.9	10,030.2	13,573.9	15,548.1	† 9,825.9	11,273.3	14,213.0	18,144.0	23,938.5
Claims on Nonbank Financial Inst..	32g	1,206.1	1,151.2	† 3,168.2	3,003.9	4,028.3	4,203.4	4,453.3	† 116.6	68.2	150.6	199.6	178.2
Money...	34	1,097.2	1,242.4	† 1,654.9	2,064.4	2,551.2	3,151.0	3,411.7	† 3,267.1	3,368.1	4,208.3	4,806.7	5,784.7
Quasi-Money...............................	35	2,518.3	3,641.1	† 5,793.8	9,298.1	12,464.3	14,688.9	16,100.7	† 17,046.0	19,647.6	21,717.4	25,581.6	27,575.5
Money Market Instruments.............	36aa	—	—	† 365.1	508.9	360.3	320.1	270.2	† —	—	—	—	—
Liabs. of Central Bank: Securities....	36ac	—	—	† 278.2	2,278.3	883.3	796.6	772.7	† 1,325.0	949.8	467.2	6.8	60.8
Liab. to Nonbank Financial Insts.......	36j	1,382.4	1,511.6	† 392.4	497.1	676.3	879.3	970.6	† 1,175.7	1,311.8	1,274.9	1,812.7	2,083.4
Capital Accounts............................	37a	861.6	705.3	† 2,319.2	2,060.7	3,699.4	6,302.3	6,012.8	† 2,025.2	2,555.4	3,075.8	4,080.8	4,700.1
Other Items (Net)...........................	37r	−1,425.9	−990.6	† −989.4	−1,615.5	−1,960.1	−2,955.6	−4,549.7	† 3,384.3	1,465.1	517.4	205.5	705.1
Money plus Quasi-Money................	35l	3,615.5	4,883.5	† 7,448.6	11,362.5	15,015.5	17,839.9	19,512.4	† 20,313.5	23,015.9	25,925.7	30,388.3	33,360.2

Nicaragua 278

		1994	1995	1996	1997	1998	1999	2000	2001	2002	2003	2004	2005
Nonbank Financial Institutions		*Millions of Córdobas: End of Period*											
Reserves..............................	40	181.5	122.0	† 122.4	4.5	.2	.1	—	.1	.7	.9	.1	.1
Foreign Assets........................	41	40.1	15.1	† 1.6	1.6	—	—	—	—	—	—	—	—
Claims on Central Government........	42a	—	—	† 319.3	367.0	—	—	—	—	—	—	—	—
Claims on Private Sector..............	42d	—	—	† 441.6	503.7	689.8	906.2	1,028.3	1,290.6	1,046.2	1,174.8	1,332.2	1,556.2
Claims on Deposit Money Banks......	42e	1,198.8	1,391.2	† 3.6	113.3	13.5	31.7	14.0	75.3	176.1	159.1	57.2	79.5
Foreign Liabilities......................	46c	—	—	† 302.5	367.4	.6	110.5	121.7	298.4	48.6	132.3	173.1	338.6
Central Government Deposits..........	46d	—	—	† —	—	19.1	125.0	226.1	315.5	333.6	285.1	245.6	258.5
Credit from Monetary Authorities.....	46g	1,206.1	1,151.2	† 89.7	99.8	79.8	47.6	26.2	—	—	—	—	—
Capital Accounts......................	47a	133.8	159.8	† 517.3	563.1	578.7	667.7	753.6	800.0	857.2	937.5	992.6	1,062.2
Other Items (Net)......................	47r	80.5	217.3	† −21.1	−40.2	25.3	−12.8	−85.3	−48.0	−16.4	−20.0	−21.7	−23.5
Financial Survey		*Millions of Córdobas: End of Period*											
Foreign Assets (Net)...................	51n	−23,622.4	−22,292.2	† −16,307.1	−15,893.6	−18,092.1	−19,699.4	−23,899.0	† −24,191.4	−25,003.7	−26,899.8	−24,122.3	−25,120.5
Domestic Credit.......................	52	26,890.0	27,265.9	† 23,413.1	28,486.5	33,408.6	39,349.3	43,115.2	† 52,975.2	54,897.3	58,767.6	61,330.3	66,811.1
Claims on Central Govt. (Net).......	52an	22,387.0	21,615.8	† 17,933.1	20,901.7	22,563.3	24,508.4	26,194.7	† 41,617.1	42,309.5	42,832.6	40,994.8	40,472.6
Claims on Local Government.........	52b	5.2	—	† 34.5	6.7	6.7	210.3	243.0	† 6.0	23.1	57.5	—	7.7
Claims on Nonfin.Pub.Enterprises...	52c	422.3	478.4	† 122.3	106.5	118.5	150.5	101.1	† 235.6	245.2	489.6	859.2	836.1
Claims on Private Sector..............	52d	4,075.5	5,171.7	† 5,323.2	7,471.6	10,720.1	14,480.1	16,576.4	† 11,116.5	12,319.5	15,387.9	19,476.2	25,494.7
Liquid Liabilities......................	55l	3,434.0	4,761.5	† 7,326.3	11,358.0	15,015.3	17,839.8	19,512.4	† 20,313.4	23,015.1	25,924.7	30,388.3	33,360.1
Money Market Instruments..............	56aa	—	—	† 365.1	508.9	360.3	320.1	270.2	† —	—	—	—	—
Liabs. of Central Bank: Securities.....	56ac	—	—	† 278.2	2,278.3	883.3	796.6	772.7	† 1,325.0	949.8	467.2	6.8	60.8
Capital Accounts......................	57a	995.4	865.1	† 2,836.6	2,623.8	4,278.1	6,970.0	6,766.4	† 2,825.2	3,412.5	4,013.2	5,073.4	5,762.3
Other Items (Net)......................	57r	−1,161.8	−652.9	† −3,700.1	−4,176.0	−5,220.5	−6,276.6	−8,105.4	† 4,320.1	2,516.1	1,462.6	1,739.5	2,507.4
Interest Rates		*Percent Per Annum*											
Discount Rate (End of period)..........	60	10.50	....	....	....	....	....	....	....	....	....		
Savings Rate...........................	60k	8.81	8.87	9.04	8.87	8.59	† 8.39	8.71	8.55	6.23	4.23	3.43	3.34
Savings Rate (Foreign Currency).......	60k.f	4.64	5.07	5.51	5.28	5.19	† 5.81	5.37	5.49	4.11	3.19	2.65	2.53
Deposit Rate...........................	60l	11.70	11.15	12.35	12.41	10.77	† 11.83	10.80	11.56	7.79	5.55	4.72	4.03
Deposit Rate (Foreign Currency).......	60l.f	5.67	6.03	7.25	7.55	7.22	† 7.95	8.86	9.01	6.94	5.08	3.91	3.39
Lending Rate...........................	60p	20.14	19.89	20.72	21.02	21.63	† 17.57	18.14	18.55	18.30	15.55	13.49	12.10
Lending Rate (Foreign Currency).......	60p.f	....	15.50	16.89	17.63	17.90	† 15.50	15.39	15.87	14.28	12.05	10.94	10.32
Prices and Labor		*Index Numbers (2000=100): Period Averages*											
Consumer Prices.......................	64.c	52.7	58.5	65.3	71.3	80.6	89.6	100.0	107.4	111.6	117.4	127.3	139.3
		Number in Thousands: Period Averages											
Labor Force............................	67d	1,419	1,478	1,537	1,598	1,661	1,729	1,815	1,900	1,926	1,999	....	....
Employment...........................	67e	1,177	1,228	1,292	1,370	1,442	1,544	1,637	1,697	1,720	1,766	....	....
Unemployment........................	67c	243	250	245	228	220	185	178	203	206	234	....	....
Unemployment Rate (%)................	67r	17.1	16.9	16.0	14.3	13.2	10.7	9.8	10.7	10.7	11.7	....	....
Intl. Transactions & Positions		*Millions of US Dollars*											
Exports................................	70..d	334.6	466.0	466.4	576.7	573.2	546.1	642.8	589.4	561.0	604.5	755.6	857.9
Imports, c.i.f...........................	71..d	866.6	975.2	1,153.8	1,449.8	1,491.7	1,861.1	1,805.5	1,775.3	1,753.7	1,879.4	2,212.3	2,595.1
Imports, f.o.b..........................	71.vd	780.5	881.4	1,043.4	1,370.6	1,397.0	1,698.1	1,653.2	1,617.3	1,598.8	1,720.2	2,022.0	2,378.1

		1994	1995	1996	1997	1998	1999	2000	2001	2002	2003	2004	2005
Balance of Payments					*Millions of US Dollars: Minus Sign Indicates Debit*								
Current Account, n.i.e.	78ald	−910.9	−722.5	−824.8	−840.8	−686.6	−928.4	−838.6	−799.5	−698.6	−651.1	−695.6	−799.8
Goods: Exports f.o.b.	78aad	375.9	545.0	595.2	744.8	761.0	748.6	880.6	894.7	916.8	1,049.6	1,364.8	1,551.5
Goods: Imports f.o.b.	78abd	−804.4	−929.5	−1,121.7	−1,473.1	−1,509.6	−1,819.8	−1,801.5	−1,804.3	−1,834.4	−2,021.3	−2,439.6	−2,865.2
Trade Balance	78acd	−428.5	−384.5	−526.5	−728.3	−748.6	−1,071.2	−920.9	−909.6	−917.6	−971.7	−1,074.8	−1,313.7
Services: Credit	78add	112.7	116.6	128.8	156.8	183.7	214.2	221.3	223.1	225.5	257.6	285.8	309.1
Services: Debit	78aed	−172.9	−220.5	−252.8	−239.4	−267.8	−334.7	−343.4	−352.1	−337.2	−363.4	−387.5	−426.4
Balance on Goods & Services	78afd	−488.7	−488.4	−650.5	−810.9	−832.7	−1,191.7	−1,043.0	−1,038.6	−1,029.3	−1,077.5	−1,176.5	−1,431.0
Income: Credit	78agd	6.7	7.1	10.5	14.7	26.0	30.7	30.7	14.7	9.2	6.7	9.3	22.3
Income: Debit	78ahd	−478.9	−379.2	−334.8	−279.4	−211.2	−227.5	−232.5	−255.0	−209.6	−197.4	−201.6	−141.5
Balance on Gds, Serv. & Inc.	78aid	−960.9	−860.5	−974.8	−1,075.6	−1,017.9	−1,388.5	−1,244.8	−1,278.9	−1,229.7	−1,268.2	−1,368.8	−1,550.2
Current Transfers, n.i.e.: Credit	78ajd	50.0	138.0	150.0	234.8	331.3	460.1	406.2	479.4	531.1	617.1	673.2	750.4
Current Transfers: Debit	78akd	—	—	—	—	—	—	—	—	—	—	—	—
Capital Account, n.i.e.	78bcd	244.6	227.0	262.1	194.1	194.4	307.2	296.3	297.7	312.2	284.0	306.9	289.2
Capital Account, n.i.e.: Credit	78bad	244.6	227.0	262.1	194.1	194.4	307.2	296.3	297.7	312.2	284.0	306.9	289.2
Capital Account: Debit	78bbd	—	—	—	—	—	—	—	—	—	—	—	—
Financial Account, n.i.e.	78bjd	−895.2	−611.5	−332.0	33.5	231.6	525.5	49.1	12.9	188.8	104.6	57.6	222.5
Direct Investment Abroad	78bdd	—	—	—	—	—	—	—	—	—	—	—	—
Dir. Invest. in Rep. Econ., n.i.e.	78bed	46.7	88.9	120.0	203.4	218.2	337.3	266.9	150.2	203.9	201.3	250.0	241.4
Portfolio Investment Assets	78bfd	—	—	—	—	—	—	—	—	—	—	—	—
Equity Securities	78bkd	—	—	—	—	—	—	—	—	—	—	—	—
Debt Securities	78bld	—	—	—	—	—	—	—	—	—	—	—	—
Portfolio Investment Liab., n.i.e.	78bgd	—	—	—	—	—	—	—	—	—	—	—	—
Equity Securities	78bmd	—	—	—	—	—	—	—	—	—	—	—	—
Debt Securities	78bnd	—	—	—	—	—	—	—	—	—	—	—	—
Financial Derivatives Assets	78bwd	—	—	—	—	—	—	—	—	—	—	—	....
Financial Derivatives Liabilities	78bxd	—	—	—	—	—	—	—	—	—	—	—	....
Other Investment Assets	78bhd	−1.3	−32.0	−54.3	−70.8	55.2	22.2	79.9	−22.6	2.9	−16.0	−8.2	−20.8
Monetary Authorities	78bod	—	—	—	—	—	—	—	—	—	—	—	—
General Government	78bpd	—	—	—	—	—	—	—	—	—	—	—	—
Banks	78bqd	−1.3	−32.0	−54.3	−70.8	55.2	22.2	79.9	−22.6	2.9	−16.0	−8.2	−20.8
Other Sectors	78brd	—	—	—	—	—	—	—	—	—	—	—	—
Other Investment Liab., n.i.e.	78bid	−940.6	−668.4	−397.7	−99.1	−41.8	166.0	−297.7	−114.7	−18.0	−80.7	−184.2	1.9
Monetary Authorities	78bsd	−544.3	−221.7	−126.1	−106.0	−18.1	62.4	−61.2	−14.1	−28.7	1.7	−6.6	−25.8
General Government	78btd	−418.7	−381.2	−295.4	−103.1	−154.8	−63.9	−73.6	−81.9	−184.4	−186.1	−154.9	−65.2
Banks	78bud	14.3	5.8	6.0	25.1	.3	63.6	−19.2	38.4	−35.9	−10.7	−4.0	92.9
Other Sectors	78bvd	8.1	−71.3	17.8	84.9	130.8	103.9	−143.7	−57.1	231.0	114.4	−18.7	—
Net Errors and Omissions	78cad	42.7	142.7	146.5	320.1	−141.3	−299.5	37.4	−3.6	−203.4	−207.0	−70.0	26.2
Overall Balance	78cbd	−1,518.8	−964.3	−748.2	−293.1	−401.9	−395.2	−455.8	−492.5	−401.0	−469.5	−401.1	−261.9
Reserves and Related Items	79dad	1,518.8	964.3	748.2	293.1	401.9	395.2	455.8	492.5	401.0	469.5	401.1	261.9
Reserve Assets	79dbd	−84.6	11.5	−53.1	−173.2	30.3	−156.5	16.8	113.9	−84.9	−68.7	−168.7	−46.0
Use of Fund Credit and Loans	79dcd	26.1	−12.9	−9.3	—	22.6	105.3	20.9	−5.0	4.0	21.6	23.9	−28.4
Exceptional Financing	79ded	1,577.3	965.7	810.6	466.3	349.0	446.4	418.1	383.6	481.8	516.7	546.0	336.4
Government Finance					*Millions of Córdobas: Year Ending December 31*								
Deficit (-) or Surplus	80	−637	−69	−254	−244	−415	−1,282	−2,357	−4,255	−1,416	−1,741	−1,575	....
Revenue	81	2,530	3,136	3,654	4,660	5,906	6,739	7,541	7,654	8,589	10,157	12,251	....
Grants Received	81z	601	1,191	1,149	822	675	1,935	1,874	1,284	1,522	2,079	2,374	....
Expenditure	82	3,689	4,246	5,055	5,719	6,995	9,774	11,755	13,063	11,527	14,000	16,199	....
Lending Minus Repayments	83	79	150	2	6	—	182	17	130	—	−23		....
Financing													
Domestic	84a	−153	101	−598	−22	−1,266	−1,305	619	2,692	−378	−1,372	−2,518	....
Foreign	85a	790	−32	852	265	1,680	2,586	1,738	1,563	1,794	3,112	4,093	....
National Accounts					*Millions of Córdobas*								
Househ.Cons.Expend.,incl.NPISHs	96f	16,162.8	18,707.7	21,844.0	25,135.6	29,202.8	34,422.2	39,460.9	43,920.5	47,535.7	55,535.1	63,276.9	73,234.6
Government Consumption Expend	91f	3,085.6	3,772.3	4,333.9	4,798.5	5,859.0	7,226.6	8,613.1	9,823.6	9,973.1	7,041.0	8,026.4	9,137.5
Gross Fixed Capital Formation	93e	4,062.4	4,855.2	6,093.1	7,762.5	9,574.4	14,698.9	14,349.1	14,757.6	14,261.8	15,402.1	18,978.1	22,916.8
Changes in Inventories	93i	14.0	430.8	1,125.4	2,199.4	2,158.1	2,252.5	1,124.1	822.6	695.8	619.1	454.5	1,203.7
Exports of Goods and Services	90c	3,123.2	4,594.5	5,605.7	7,374.7	8,683.2	9,729.4	11,932.4	12,476.7	12,846.4	15,239.8	19,457.2	22,982.9
Imports of Goods and Services (-)	98c	6,439.7	8,331.1	10,993.4	15,303.7	17,673.0	24,131.8	25,527.7	26,645.7	27,936.4	31,878.6	38,532.4	47,313.7
Gross Domestic Product (GDP)	99b	20,008.4	24,029.3	28,008.7	31,967.1	37,804.5	44,197.8	49,952.0	55,155.3	57,376.3	61,958.5	71,660.8	82,161.8
Net Primary Income from Abroad	98.n	−3,174.5	−2,801.0	−2,735.6	−2,500.9	−1,960.8	−2,324.0	−2,559.7	−3,230.8	−2,856.0	−4,514.5	−4,802.6	−6,102.5
Gross National Income (GNI)	99a	16,833.8	21,228.3	25,273.1	29,466.1	35,843.7	41,873.7	47,392.2	51,924.6	54,520.4	57,444.0	66,858.2	76,059.3
GDP Volume 1994 Prices	99b.p	20,008.4	21,191.3	22,535.7	23,429.6	24,299.2	26,008.9	27,075.7	27,877.4	28,087.5	28,795.5	30,276.5	31,482.5
GDP Volume (2000=100)	99bvp	† 73.9	78.3	83.2	86.5	89.7	96.1	100.0	103.0	103.7	106.4	111.8	116.3
GDP Deflator (2000=100)	99bip	54.2	61.5	67.4	74.0	84.3	92.1	100.0	107.2	110.7	116.6	128.3	141.5
					Millions: Midyear Estimates								
Population	99z	4.37	4.48	4.58	4.67	4.77	4.86	4.96	5.06	5.16	5.27	5.38	5.49

Niger 692

		1994	1995	1996	1997	1998	1999	2000	2001	2002	2003	2004	2005
Exchange Rates						*Francs per SDR: End of Period*							
Official Rate................................	aa	† 780.44	728.38	753.06	807.94	791.61	† 896.19	918.49	935.39	850.37	771.76	747.90	794.73
						Francs per US Dollar: End of Period (ae) Period Average (rf)							
Official Rate................................	ae	† 534.60	490.00	523.70	598.81	562.21	† 652.95	704.95	744.31	625.50	519.36	481.58	556.04
Official Rate................................	rf	† 555.20	499.15	511.55	583.67	589.95	† 615.70	711.98	733.04	696.99	581.20	528.28	527.47
Fund Position						*Millions of SDRs: End of Period*							
Quota................................	2f.s	48.3	48.3	48.3	48.3	48.3	65.8	65.8	65.8	65.8	65.8	65.8	65.8
SDRs................................	1b.s	.3	.2	1.3	.1	.1	1.0	—	.3	.5	1.8	.6	.2
Reserve Position in the Fund............	1c.s	8.6	8.6	8.6	8.6	8.6	8.6	8.6	8.6	8.6	8.6	8.6	8.6
Total Fund Cred.&Loans Outstg........	2tl	41.8	35.0	36.6	45.0	54.1	49.6	56.8	64.3	78.3	88.4	87.2	89.3
International Liquidity						*Millions of US Dollars Unless Otherwise Indicated: End of Period*							
Total Reserves minus Gold..............	1l.d	110.3	94.7	78.5	53.3	53.1	39.2	80.4	107.0	133.9	260.1	258.0	249.5
SDRs................................	1b.d	.4	.3	1.9	.2	.2	1.3	—	.3	.7	2.7	.9	.3
Reserve Position in the Fund.........	1c.d	12.5	12.7	12.3	11.6	12.1	11.7	11.2	10.8	11.6	12.7	13.3	12.3
Foreign Exchange.....................	1d.d	97.4	81.7	64.3	41.5	40.8	26.1	69.2	95.9	121.6	244.7	243.7	236.9
Gold (Million Fine Troy Ounces)........	1ad	.011	—	—	—	—	—	—	—	—	—	—	—
Gold (National Valuation)...............	1and	4.1	—	—	—	—	—	—	—	—	—	—	—
Monetary Authorities: Other Liab.....	4..d	2.9	1.5	2.2	.4	1.1	2.2	1.6	1.3	3.2	−3.4	4.7	5.1
Deposit Money Banks: Assets..........	7a.d	40.6	41.5	35.1	40.9	37.9	44.2	41.3	53.7	48.4	65.4	80.9	86.3
Liabilities...................	7b.d	49.9	44.9	41.7	32.9	30.5	39.5	42.0	35.7	26.2	50.5	41.6	64.7
Monetary Authorities						*Billions of Francs: End of Period*							
Foreign Assets.........................	11	58.9	46.4	41.1	31.9	29.8	25.6	56.7	79.6	83.8	135.1	124.2	138.8
Claims on Central Government........	12a	47.3	52.5	57.2	67.7	74.3	69.5	79.9	85.6	99.7	109.2	107.6	107.8
Claims on Deposit Money Banks......	12e	1.1	4.9	4.6	3.2	3.9	1.2	1.2	1.2	1.2	1.2	1.2	1.1
Claims on Other Financial Insts.......	12f	—	—	—	—	—	—	—	—	—	—	—	—
Reserve Money.........................	14	60.5	68.4	64.4	50.7	32.5	43.0	44.6	66.3	63.2	116.1	128.9	138.1
of which: Currency Outside DMBs..	14a	48.7	59.6	57.7	41.7	24.5	34.1	32.2	49.3	39.3	84.9	96.8	108.1
Foreign Liabilities.....................	16c	34.2	26.3	28.7	36.6	43.4	45.9	53.3	61.0	68.6	66.5	67.5	73.8
Central Government Deposits..........	16d	15.6	8.3	8.1	8.5	16.4	4.1	30.4	38.0	45.2	46.4	22.9	32.6
Other Items (Net)......................	17r	−3.0	.9	1.7	7.1	15.7	3.3	9.5	1.1	7.7	16.5	13.7	3.0
Deposit Money Banks						*Billions of Francs: End of Period*							
Reserves................................	20	9.7	8.3	5.9	8.1	7.7	8.8	10.5	15.2	22.1	30.1	31.0	28.3
Foreign Assets.........................	21	21.7	20.3	18.4	24.5	21.3	28.9	29.1	39.9	30.3	34.0	39.0	48.0
Claims on Central Government........	22a	13.4	12.4	14.1	16.7	12.9	12.1	15.3	10.7	10.4	10.9	10.3	12.1
Claims on Private Sector..............	22d	71.4	42.0	43.3	35.5	49.4	47.7	61.4	66.0	75.8	83.0	101.1	121.3
Claims on Other Financial Insts.......	22f	—	—	—	—	—	—	—	—	—	—	—	—
Demand Deposits......................	24	40.3	38.4	30.2	28.8	32.0	33.9	43.3	52.4	54.2	61.6	81.8	81.4
Time Deposits.........................	25	37.2	33.6	34.3	25.3	20.6	23.8	27.2	32.7	40.5	44.4	50.3	56.2
Foreign Liabilities.....................	26c	23.3	18.4	18.5	19.7	17.2	25.8	29.6	26.6	16.1	26.0	17.4	30.3
Long-Term Foreign Liabilities.........	26cl	3.3	3.6	3.3	—	—	—	—	—	.3	.3	2.6	5.6
Central Government Deposits..........	26d	21.0	19.3	19.8	3.9	9.8	8.8	10.2	12.0	13.5	12.8	13.8	19.2
Credit from Monetary Authorities.....	26g	27.8	4.9	4.6	2.0	3.9	1.2	1.2	1.2	1.2	1.2	1.2	1.1
Other Items (Net)......................	27r	−36.8	−35.1	−29.0	5.2	7.7	4.0	4.9	7.0	12.7	11.6	14.2	15.8
Treasury Claims: Private Sector.......	22d.i											.4	
Post Office: Checking Deposits.......	24..i	2.1	1.8	2.6	2.5	2.7	.3	1.2	1.9	1.7	2.4	3.2	2.5
Monetary Survey						*Billions of Francs: End of Period*							
Foreign Assets (Net).....................	31n	23.2	22.1	12.2	—	−9.4	−17.2	2.9	31.9	29.4	76.6	78.3	82.6
Domestic Credit........................	32	97.6	81.2	89.3	110.1	113.1	116.6	117.3	114.3	128.9	146.3	185.5	191.8
Claims on Central Govt. (Net).......	32an	26.1	39.2	46.0	74.5	63.7	68.9	55.8	48.3	53.1	63.3	84.0	70.5
Claims on Private Sector..............	32d	71.4	42.0	43.3	35.6	49.4	47.7	61.4	66.0	75.8	83.0	101.4	121.3
Claims on Other Financial Insts......	32f	—	—	—	—	—	—	—	—	—	—	—	—
Money................................	34	91.8	100.2	90.7	73.1	59.6	68.8	76.9	104.0	95.6	149.5	181.9	192.2
Quasi-Money...........................	35	37.2	33.6	34.3	25.3	20.6	23.8	27.2	32.7	40.5	44.4	50.3	56.2
Long-Term Foreign Liabilities...........	36cl	3.3	3.6	3.3	—	—	—	—	—	.3	.3	2.6	5.6
Other Items (Net)......................	37r	−11.6	−34.1	−26.8	11.7	23.4	6.9	16.1	9.5	21.8	28.8	29.0	20.4
Money plus Quasi-Money................	35l	129.0	133.8	125.0	98.4	80.2	92.6	104.1	136.8	136.1	193.9	232.2	248.4
Interest Rates						*Percent Per Annum*							
Bank Rate (End of Period)..............	60	6.00	6.00	6.00	6.00	6.00	6.00	6.00	6.00	6.00	4.50	4.00	4.00
Money Market Rate......................	60b	4.95	4.95	4.95	4.95	4.95	4.95	4.95	4.95	4.95	4.95	4.95	4.95
Deposit Rate............................	60l	3.50	3.50	3.50	3.50	3.50	3.50	3.50	3.50	3.50	3.50	3.50	3.50
Prices						*Index Numbers (2000=100): Period Averages*							
Consumer Prices......................	64	79.4	87.8	92.4	† 95.1	99.5	97.2	100.0	104.0	106.7	105.0	105.3	113.5
Intl. Transactions & Positions						*Millions of Francs*							
Exports...............................	70	125,100	143,800	166,300	158,500	197,000	176,600	201,500	199,700	194,800	204,600	201,300	216,300
Imports, c.i.f...........................	71	182,097	186,501	229,271	218,067	277,886	252,700	281,400	302,100	326,400	361,500	417,300	485,300

Niger 692

		1994	1995	1996	1997	1998	1999	2000	2001	2002	2003	2004	2005
Balance of Payments		*Millions of US Dollars: Minus Sign Indicates Debit*											
Current Account, n.i.e.	78ald	−126.1	−151.7	−108.8	−132.9	−152.4	−137.2	−104.1	−92.3	−164.8	−218.7	....	....
Goods: Exports f.o.b.	78aad	226.8	288.1	325.0	271.5	334.0	286.8	283.1	272.5	279.4	351.8	....	....
Goods: Imports f.o.b.	78abd	−271.3	−305.6	−351.3	−299.8	−403.9	−335.4	−323.7	−331.3	−371.2	−488.5	....	....
Trade Balance	78acd	−44.5	−17.6	−26.3	−28.3	−69.9	−48.6	−40.6	−58.8	−91.7	−136.7		
Services: Credit	78add	30.4	33.3	43.4	39.0	35.3	34.1	37.5	56.7	50.6	63.3		
Services: Debit	78aed	−149.1	−151.8	−162.0	−153.3	−152.4	−139.6	−131.9	−147.2	−152.3	−192.5		
Balance on Goods & Services	78afd	−163.2	−136.0	−144.9	−142.5	−187.0	−154.1	−134.9	−149.2	−193.4	−265.9		
Income: Credit	78agd	15.6	5.8	15.5	7.7	13.0	14.0	13.1	12.3	13.2	17.3		
Income: Debit	78ahd	−45.2	−52.9	−43.3	−36.2	−36.4	−32.9	−29.5	−27.2	−37.4	−43.4		
Balance on Gds, Serv. & Inc.	78aid	−192.8	−183.2	−172.7	−171.0	−210.4	−173.0	−151.4	−164.1	−217.6	−292.0		
Current Transfers, n.i.e.: Credit	78ajd	115.1	60.6	100.4	59.3	76.1	57.4	63.8	87.9	65.1	82.9		
Current Transfers: Debit	78akd	−48.5	−29.1	−36.5	−21.3	−18.1	−21.5	−16.5	−16.0	−12.3	−9.5		
Capital Account, n.i.e.	78bcd	88.2	65.3	92.9	63.8	69.6	62.0	55.4	40.2	91.8	92.3		
Capital Account, n.i.e.: Credit	78bad	88.2	65.3	92.9	63.9	69.6	62.0	55.4	40.2	91.9	92.4		
Capital Account: Debit	78bbd	....	....	....	....	....	—	....	....	−.1	−.1		
Financial Account, n.i.e.	78bjd	29.9	−46.1	31.6	56.0	48.9	47.6	97.5	60.5	69.1	97.1		
Direct Investment Abroad	78bdd	1.8	−7.1	−7.5	−1.6	−.2	.2	.6	3.6	1.7	—		
Dir. Invest. in Rep. Econ., n.i.e.	78bed	−11.3	7.2	9.9	18.2	−1.0	.3	8.4	22.9	2.4	14.9		
Portfolio Investment Assets	78bfd	....	....	−.6	−1.3	−.9	−.4	−.2	−1.9	−.8	−4.4		
Equity Securities	78bkd	....	....	−.1	—	−.5	−.4		−1.9	−.5	−4.3		
Debt Securities	78bld	....	....	−.5	−1.3	−.4		−.2		−.3	−.2		
Portfolio Investment Liab., n.i.e.	78bgd	....	....	.5	.5	—	.7	8.7	5.7	1.2	6.9		
Equity Securities	78bmd	....	....	.1	.5	—	.3	.5	.5	—	—		
Debt Securities	78bnd	....	....	.5	....	....	.4	8.3	5.2	1.2	6.9		
Financial Derivatives Assets	78bwd	....	....	....	....	....	−.5	....	....	....	....		
Financial Derivatives Liabilities	78bxd	....	....	....	....	....		....	....	....	....		
Other Investment Assets	78bhd	22.3	−18.4	4.3	.1	2.2	−11.5	−14.8	−27.1	15.6	−42.4		
Monetary Authorities	78bod	....	....	....	....	....	....	....	....	....	....		
General Government	78bpd	.3	—	....	....	....	....	....	....	−.6	.7		
Banks	78bqd	....	....	4.9	−14.0	4.9	−9.1	−.1	−19.4	16.4	−5.0		
Other Sectors	78brd	22.0	−18.4	−.6	14.1	−2.7	−2.5	−14.7	−7.7	−.2	−38.1		
Other Investment Liab., n.i.e.	78bid	17.1	−27.8	24.9	40.2	48.8	58.8	94.8	57.4	49.1	122.1		
Monetary Authorities	78bsd	−22.3	−2.3	.1	−1.7	.6	1.4	−.4	−.3	1.5	.4		
General Government	78btd	6.7	−14.8	8.4	56.8	50.3	8.9	87.8	42.5	48.3	93.7		
Banks	78bud	19.4	−10.8	−.9	2.8	−6.9	14.4	4.7	−3.0	−12.0	17.0		
Other Sectors	78bvd	13.3	.1	17.3	−17.7	4.8	34.1	2.7	18.1	11.2	11.0		
Net Errors and Omissions	78cad	−67.8	114.4	−28.7	−15.0	17.5	25.6	−13.6	13.8	−8.6	−14.6		
Overall Balance	78cbd	−75.8	−18.1	−13.0	−28.1	−16.3	−2.0	35.1	22.2	−12.5	−43.8		
Reserves and Related Items	79dad	75.8	18.1	13.0	28.1	16.3	2.0	−35.1	−22.2	12.5	43.8		
Reserve Assets	79dbd	28.7	−25.8	10.8	16.1	4.1	8.0	−44.3	−31.8	−5.4	29.2		
Use of Fund Credit and Loans	79dcd	5.4	−10.2	2.2	12.0	12.2	−6.1	9.2	9.6	17.9	14.6		
Exceptional Financing	79ded	41.7	54.1	—	—	....	....	....	....	....	....		
International Investment Position		*Millions of US Dollars*											
Assets	79aad	....	....	146.3	104.5	110.9	91.4	141.1	182.8	192.5	192.2		
Direct Investment Abroad	79abd	....	....	8.5	7.1	8.1	1.9	1.0	−1.7	−3.9	−4.6		
Portfolio Investment	79acd	....	....	—	—	9.7	7.3	6.0	6.4	8.9	—		
Equity Securities	79add	....	....	—	—	.5	.4	.5	.4	.5	—		
Debt Securities	79aed	....	....	—	—	9.3	6.9	5.6	6.0	8.3	—		
Financial Derivatives	79ald	....	....	—	—	—	—	—	—	—	—		
Other Investment	79afd	....	....	59.4	43.8	40.0	43.8	52.2	69.5	52.4	68.7		
Monetary Authorities	79agd	....	....	—	—	—	—	—	—	—	—		
General Government	79ahd	....	....	—	—	—	—	—	—	.7	—		
Banks	79aid	....	....	22.5	33.3	30.4	34.7	32.2	49.6	40.8	54.8		
Other Sectors	79ajd	....	....	7.1	4.0	3.7	1.6	3.5	8.2	4.2	3.4		
Reserve Assets	79akd	....	....	78.4	53.6	53.1	38.4	81.8	108.6	135.1	128.2		
Liabilities	79lad	....	....	1,635.5	1,561.3	1,700.1	1,532.5	1,720.6	1,539.0	1,978.9	2,030.6		
Dir. Invest. in Rep. Economy	79lbd	....	....	95.1	39.9	40.9	38.5	45.4	61.5	70.0	78.8		
Portfolio Investment	79lcd	....	....	6.6	4.8	4.4	3.7	12.2	8.9	6.2	14.4		
Equity Securities	79ldd	....	....	6.2	4.8	4.4	3.7	3.9	3.8	4.8	5.2		
Debt Securities	79led	....	....	.4	—	—	—	8.3	5.1	1.4	9.2		
Financial Derivatives	79lld	....	....	—	—	—	—	—	—	—	—		
Other Investment	79lfd	....	....	1,533.8	1,516.6	1,654.8	1,490.4	1,663.0	1,468.6	1,902.7	1,937.3		
Monetary Authorities	79lgd	....	....	55.1	61.2	77.2	70.4	75.6	82.1	109.6	135.7		
General Government	79lhd	....	....	....	....	....	....	....	....	....	....		
Banks	79lid	....	....	28.7	28.4	22.7	33.2	35.4	30.9	23.7	47.1		
Other Sectors	79ljd	....	....	77.7	39.8	1.0	2.6	2.1	2.4	6.5	1.5		
National Accounts		*Billions of Francs*											
Househ.Cons.Expend.,incl.NPISHs.	96f	604.5	761.8	808.1	853.7	997.1	1,011.1	874.0	1,080.1	1,029.1	1,137.3	1,152.8	1,277.0
Government Consumption Expend.	91f	127.4	131.9	137.5	138.8	139.8	199.3	172.3	159.2	254.2	326.3	271.0	260.4
Gross Fixed Capital Formation	93e	102.3	98.4	122.3	129.3	181.2	124.0	146.4	153.1	170.5	167.3	....	....
Changes in Inventories	93i	32.0	20.9	38.6	42.7	17.2	3.0	78.2	2.8	99.6	94.1	....	....
Exports of Goods and Services	90c	141.4	167.1	188.2	181.0	217.9	197.6	228.2	241.2	230.0	241.3	248.2	285.7
Imports of Goods and Services (-)	98c	220.6	232.6	261.5	262.5	328.2	292.4	324.3	350.6	364.8	395.8	413.6	455.0
Gross Domestic Product (GDP)	99b	787.1	947.5	1,033.2	1,083.0	1,225.0	1,242.6	1,176.4	1,295.2	1,418.7	1,466.3	1,474.9	1,595.4
GDP Volume 1987 Prices	99b.p	722.7	741.5	766.9	788.0	870.1	865.2	853.0	913.6	941.0	991.1	1,000.0	
GDP Volume (2000=100)	99bvp	84.7	86.9	89.9	92.4	102.0	101.4	100.0	107.1	110.3	116.2	117.2	....
GDP Deflator (2000=100)	99bip	79.0	92.6	97.7	99.7	102.1	104.1	100.0	102.8	109.3	107.3	106.9	....
		Millions: Midyear Estimates											
Population	99z	9.61	9.93	10.27	10.62	11.00	11.38	11.78	12.19	12.62	13.05	13.50	13.96

Nigeria 694

		1994	1995	1996	1997	1998	1999	2000	2001	2002	2003	2004	2005
Exchange Rates						*Naira per SDR: End of Period*							
Principal Rate	aa	32.113	32.534	31.471	29.530	† 30.816	134.437	142.734	141.948	171.843	202.835	205.541	184.376
						Naira per US Dollar: End of Period (ae) Period Average (rf)							
Principal Rate	ae	21.997	21.887	21.886	21.886	† 21.886	97.950	109.550	112.950	126.400	136.500	132.350	129.000
Principal Rate	rf	21.996	21.895	21.884	21.886	† 21.886	92.338	101.697	111.231	120.578	129.222	132.888	131.274
						Index Numbers (2000=100): Period Averages							
Principal Rate	ahx	462.5	464.3	464.5	464.5	464.5	112.0	100.0	91.4	84.5	78.7	76.5	77.5
Nominal Effective Exchange Rate	nec	364.9	189.1	182.8	197.6	212.0	102.8	100.0	96.2	87.0	74.2	67.9	68.0
Real Effective Exchange Rate	rec	145.0	122.9	151.2	172.4	196.1	98.8	100.0	111.1	111.0	105.0	107.8	123.8
Fund Position						*Millions of SDRs: End of Period*							
Quota	2f.s	1,282	1,282	1,282	1,282	1,282	1,753	1,753	1,753	1,753	1,753	1,753	1,753
SDRs	1b.s	—	—	—	—	1	—	—	1	—	—	—	—
Reserve Position in the Fund	1c.s	—	—	—	—	—	—	—	—	—	—	—	—
of which: Outstg.Fund Borrowing	2c	—	—	—	—	—	—	—	—	—	—	—	—
Total Fund Cred.&Loans Outstg	2tl	—	—	—	—	—	—	—	—	—	—	—	—
International Liquidity						*Millions of US Dollars Unless Otherwise Indicated: End of Period*							
Total Reserves minus Gold	1l.d	1,386	1,443	4,076	7,582	7,101	5,450	9,911	10,457	7,331	7,128	16,956	28,280
SDRs	1b.d	—	1	1	1	1	—	—	1	—	—	—	—
Reserve Position in the Fund	1c.d	—	—	—	—	—	—	—	—	—	—	—	—
Foreign Exchange	1d.d	1,386	1,443	4,075	7,581	7,100	5,450	9,910	10,456	7,331	7,128	16,955	28,279
Gold (Million Fine Troy Ounces)	1ad	.687	.687	.687	.687	.687	.687	.687	.687	.687	.687	.687	.687
Gold (National Valuation)	1and	.86	.87	.87	.87	.87	.19	.17	.17	.15	.14	.14	.15
Monetary Authorities: Other Liab.	4..d	2,747	2,450	2,162	2,313	1,630	172	1,224	1,080	875	685	2,239	1,422
Deposit Money Banks: Assets	7a.d	1,157	3,490	2,899	3,180	4,395	1,651	2,035	2,701	3,150	3,206	3,637	3,591
Liabilities	7b.d	130	137	148	137	299	56	138	152	150	154	143	180
Monetary Authorities						*Millions of Naira: End of Period*							
Foreign Assets	11	33,467	41,426	180,799	173,665	149,268	506,794	1,091,108	1,156,578	1,013,516	1,065,099	2,478,626	3,637,880
Claims on Central Government	12a	308,858	438,481	313,849	406,053	456,985	532,292	513,003	716,769	532,453	552,859	441,590	337,042
Claims on State & Local Govts	12b	124	25	2	7	7	7	7	—	—	—	—	—
Claims on Nonfin.Pub.Enterprises	12c	3,655	3,480	1,525	1,453	926	692	951	1,080	164	212	1,931	2,449
Claims on Private Sector	12d	763	604	967	778	517	884	2,163	3,103	1,646	1,705	1,931	2,265
Claims on Deposit Money Banks	12e	12,987	24,222	27,697	21,282	21,818	22,070	36,176	20,604	5,554	15,572	91,982	92,743
Claims on Nonbank Financial Insts	12g	2,941	3,160	3,267	5,916	4,580	4,568	4,881	6,330	5,488	6,878	11,344	11,331
Reserve Money	14	151,737	182,795	193,953	202,667	236,470	287,893	426,610	571,924	646,876	924,393	875,830	790,694
of which: Currency Outside DMBs	14a	90,601	106,843	116,121	130,668	156,716	186,457	274,011	338,671	386,942	412,155	458,587	563,220
Foreign Liabilities	16c	60,418	53,618	47,322	50,632	35,685	16,871	134,065	121,940	110,557	93,437	296,349	183,474
Central Government Deposits	16d	66,740	194,599	253,754	394,740	362,429	516,967	856,007	896,015	574,918	362,083	1,205,811	1,686,172
Capital Accounts	17a	47,539	39,647	35,062	37,055	43,683	219,944	307,976	276,033	97,559	314,657	544,588	779,126
Other Items (Net)	17r	36,362	40,738	−1,987	−75,940	−44,167	25,633	−76,369	38,548	128,911	−52,246	104,826	644,243
Deposit Money Banks						*Millions of Naira: End of Period*							
Reserves	20	53,441	60,281	64,343	64,903	65,895	120,585	170,099	318,986	321,495	362,400	364,193	515,207
Foreign Assets	21	25,449	76,390	63,440	69,590	96,184	161,754	222,988	305,029	398,210	437,659	481,296	463,239
Claims on Central Government	22a	47,829	22,894	56,469	46,187	58,881	202,253	292,975	182,116	467,522	378,205	609,075	630,848
Claims on State & Local Govts	22b	2,117	2,909	3,528	1,475	935	2,095	7,558	26,796	17,327	20,235	24,632	54,527
Claims on Private Sector	22d	141,400	201,181	251,325	309,883	365,609	446,959	580,442	817,690	931,138	1,182,964	1,494,611	1,936,620
Demand Deposits	24	74,398	85,564	104,017	131,887	150,977	209,899	356,954	448,021	503,870	577,664	728,552	946,640
Time, Savings,& Fgn.Currency Dep	25	88,505	111,255	134,756	154,633	198,337	298,908	386,396	499,162	653,241	759,633	932,930	1,089,450
Money Market Instruments	26aa	329	283	692	130	285	74	572	627	877	1,138	1,044	3,279
Bonds	26ab	3,030	9,002	9,899	14,488	10,929	18,100	18,212	25,610	24,533	30,657	38,396	62,155
Foreign Liabilities	26c	2,860	2,988	3,229	3,009	6,540	5,474	15,099	17,185	18,951	21,081	18,894	23,278
Central Government Deposits	26d	1,834	3,773	6,098	11,143	13,521	40,773	73,961	28,342	52,636	79,764	117,231	119,070
Credit from Monetary Authorities	26g	10,526	15,172	17,377	8,434	7,762	6,554	5,360	14,547	22,159	44,303	62,080	42,688
Capital Accounts	27a	38,284	45,000	60,985	89,814	108,733	139,748	146,330	226,060	294,921	291,500	348,388	591,739
Other Items (Net)	27r	50,472	90,619	102,051	78,501	90,422	214,116	271,178	391,063	564,502	575,723	726,293	722,142
Monetary Survey						*Millions of Naira: End of Period*							
Foreign Assets (Net)	31n	−4,362	61,210	193,687	189,613	203,226	646,203	1,164,931	1,322,480	1,282,217	1,388,239	2,644,679	3,894,366
Domestic Credit	32	439,114	474,361	371,079	365,871	512,490	632,010	472,012	829,528	1,328,183	1,701,210	1,262,071	1,169,839
Claims on Central Govt. (Net)	32an	288,114	263,003	110,466	46,358	139,916	176,805	−123,990	−25,472	372,421	489,217	−272,377	−837,353
Claims on State & Local Govts	32b	2,241	2,934	3,530	1,482	941	2,102	7,564	26,796	17,327	20,235	24,632	54,527
Claims on Nonfin.Pub.Enterprises	32c	3,655	3,480	1,525	1,453	926	692	951	1,080	164	212	1,931	2,449
Claims on Private Sector	32d	142,163	201,785	252,292	310,661	366,127	447,843	582,606	820,793	932,783	1,184,669	1,496,542	1,938,885
Claims on Nonbank Fin. Insts	32g	2,941	3,160	3,267	5,916	4,580	4,568	4,881	6,330	5,488	6,878	11,344	11,331
Money	34	178,440	207,509	235,577	275,098	327,300	400,826	649,684	816,708	946,253	1,225,559	1,330,658	1,541,650
Quasi-Money	35	88,505	111,255	134,756	154,633	198,337	298,908	386,396	499,162	653,241	759,633	932,930	1,089,450
Money Market Instruments	36aa	329	283	692	130	285	74	572	627	877	1,138	1,044	3,279
Bonds	36ab	3,030	9,002	9,899	14,488	10,929	18,100	18,212	25,610	24,533	30,657	38,396	62,155
Capital Accounts	37a	85,823	84,647	96,047	126,868	152,416	359,692	454,306	502,093	392,480	606,157	892,975	1,370,865
Other Items (Net)	37r	78,625	122,876	87,794	−15,734	26,450	200,612	127,774	307,809	593,015	466,305	710,747	996,805
Money plus Quasi-Money	35l	266,945	318,763	370,334	429,731	525,638	699,735	1,036,080	1,315,869	1,599,495	1,985,192	2,263,588	2,631,100
Interest Rates						*Percent Per Annum*							
Discount Rate (End of Period)	60	13.50	13.50	13.50	13.50	13.50	18.00	14.00	20.50	16.50	15.00	15.00	13.00
Treasury Bill Rate	60c	12.87	12.50	12.25	12.00	12.26	17.82	15.50	17.50	19.03	14.79	14.34	7.63
Deposit Rate	60l	13.09	13.53	13.06	7.17	10.11	12.81	11.69	15.26	16.67	14.22	13.70	10.53
Lending Rate	60p	20.48	20.23	19.84	17.80	18.18	20.29	21.27	23.44	24.77	20.71	19.18	17.95
Prices and Production						*Index Numbers (2000=100): Period Averages*							
Consumer Prices	64	32.9	56.8	73.5	79.5	87.7	91.9	† 100.0	118.8	134.2	153.1	182.8	207.5
Industrial Production	66	90.9	90.6	93.2	93.9	94.0	91.3	100.0	101.4	102.7	102.6	106.4	110.5
Crude Petroleum Production	66aa	83.9	86.2	89.2	91.6	93.5	93.9	100.0	102.9	105.9	105.6	105.4	105.4
Manufacturing Production	66ey	104.3	98.6	100.4	100.1	96.3	99.6	100.0	100.0	85.1	96.7	109.1	105.4

		1994	1995	1996	1997	1998	1999	2000	2001	2002	2003	2004	2005
Intl. Transactions & Positions							*Millions of US Dollars*							
Exports.....................	70..d	9,415	† 12,342	16,154	15,207	9,855	13,856	20,975	17,261	15,107	19,887	31,148	42,277
Crude Petroleum (Naira)................	70aa	9,171	† 11,449	15,866	14,850	8,565	12,665	18,897	17,769	14,855	19,596	28,428	36,194
Imports, c.i.f...................	71..d	6,613	† 8,222	6,438	9,501	9,211	8,588	8,721	11,586	7,547	10,853	14,164	15,200
Volume of Exports							*2000=100*							
Crude Petroleum...................	72aa	92	91	103	106	122	101	100	106	85	98	118	115
Balance of Payments							*Millions of US Dollars: Minus Sign Indicates Debit*							
Current Account, n.i.e............	78ald	−2,128	−2,578	3,507	552	−4,244	506	7,429	2,478	1,083	9,504	12,264	....
Goods: Exports f.o.b...............	78aad	9,459	11,734	16,117	15,207	8,971	12,876	19,132	17,992	15,613	22,629	23,657	....
Goods: Imports f.o.b...............	78abd	−6,511	−8,222	−6,438	−9,501	−9,211	−8,588	−8,717	−11,097	−10,876	−10,499	−11,096	....
Trade Balance..................	78acd	2,948	3,513	9,679	5,706	−240	4,288	10,415	6,895	4,738	12,130	12,561	....
Services: Credit.................	78add	371	608	733	786	884	980	1,853	1,653	2,524	3,473	3,336	....
Services: Debit...................	78aed	−3,007	−4,619	−4,827	−4,712	−4,166	−3,476	−3,300	−4,640	−4,922	−5,715	−4,969	....
Balance on Goods & Services.......	78afd	312	−499	5,584	1,781	−3,522	1,792	8,948	3,909	2,340	9,889	10,929	....
Income: Credit..................	78agd	49	101	115	258	333	240	218	199	184	82	157	....
Income: Debit...................	78ahd	−2,986	−2,979	−3,137	−3,404	−2,624	−2,818	−3,365	−2,997	−2,854	−1,518	−1,074	....
Balance on Gds, Serv. & Inc........	78aid	−2,626	−3,377	2,562	−1,365	−5,813	−786	5,800	1,111	−330	8,453	10,012	....
Current Transfers, n.i.e.: Credit.....	78ajd	550	804	947	1,920	1,574	1,301	1,637	1,373	1,422	1,063	2,273	....
Current Transfers: Debit.............	78akd	−52	−5	−2	−4	−5	−9	−8	−6	−9	−12	−21	....
Capital Account, n.i.e............	78bcd	—	—	—	—	—	....	....	....	....	....	....	....
Capital Account, n.i.e.: Credit.......	78bad	—	—	—	—	—	....	....	....	....	....	....	....
Capital Account: Debit...........	78bbd	—	—	—	—	—	....	....	....	....	....	....	....
Financial Account, n.i.e............	78bjd	329	−46	−4,155	−425	1,502	−4,002	−6,219	−3,035	−8,554	−11,799	−4,487	....
Direct Investment Abroad............	78bdd	....	....	....	....	....	....	....	....	....	....	....	....
Dir. Invest. in Rep. Econ., n.i.e.......	78bed	1,959	1,079	1,593	1,539	1,051	1,005	1,140	1,191	1,874	2,006	1,875	....
Portfolio Investment Assets...........	78bfd	—	—	—	9	51	50	502	832	134	147	352	....
Equity Securities.................	78bkd	—	—	—	—	—	—	—	—	—	—	—	....
Debt Securities..................	78bld	—	—	—	9	51	50	502	832	134	147	352	....
Portfolio Investment Liab., n.i.e......	78bgd	−27	−82	−173	−76	−59	−39	—	—	—	—	—	....
Equity Securities.................	78bmd	—	—	—	....	....	....	....	....	....	....	....	....
Debt Securities..................	78bnd	−27	−82	−173	−76	−59	−39	—	—	—	—	—	....
Financial Derivatives Assets...........	78bwd	....	....	....	....	....	....	....	....	....	....	....	....
Financial Derivatives Liabilities.......	78bxd	....	....	....	....	....	....	....	....	....	....	....	....
Other Investment Assets..............	78bhd	−1,286	−3,295	−4,320	−2,183	−332	−3,319	−4,534	−3,071	−5,890	−10,115	−2,288	....
Monetary Authorities.............	78bod	....	....	....	....	....	....	....	....	....	....	....	....
General Government.................	78bpd	−969	−1,030	—	—	—	—	—	—	—	—	—	....
Banks.........................	78bqd	320	−560	138	−80	−284	−651	602	738	773	305	328	....
Other Sectors..................	78brd	−637	−1,705	−4,458	−2,103	−48	−2,668	−5,136	−3,809	−6,662	−10,420	−2,616	....
Other Investment Liab., n.i.e........	78bid	−317	2,251	−1,256	286	792	−1,699	−3,327	−1,985	−4,673	−3,838	−4,426	....
Monetary Authorities.............	78bsd	—	—	—	—	—	—	—	—	—	—	—	....
General Government.................	78btd	−1,885	−1,535	−3,039	−2,883	−1,637	−1,659	−979	−850	−1,364	−1,395	−1,693	....
Banks.........................	78bud	−1	—	−4	1	21	34	—	—	—	—	—	....
Other Sectors..................	78bvd	1,570	3,787	1,787	3,167	2,407	−74	−2,348	−1,136	−3,309	−2,442	−2,733	....
Net Errors and Omissions............	78cad	−139	−149	−113	−111	−132	−41	1,880	779	2,782	1,035	714	....
Overall Balance..................	78cbd	−1,938	−2,774	−761	15	−2,873	−3,538	3,089	223	−4,689	−1,260	8,491	....
Reserves and Related Items.............	79dad	1,938	2,774	761	−15	2,873	3,538	−3,089	−223	4,689	1,260	−8,491	....
Reserve Assets.................	79dbd	−327	217	−2,634	−3,507	481	1,650	−4,459	−509	2,744	214	−9,531	....
Use of Fund Credit and Loans.......	79dcd	—	—	—	—	—	—	—	—	—	—	—	....
Exceptional Financing.................	79ded	2,265	2,557	3,395	3,491	2,392	1,887	1,369	286	1,945	1,047	1,040	....
Government Finance							*Millions of Naira: Year Ending December 31*							
Deficit (-) or Surplus.................	80	−70,270	1,000	37,049	−5,000	−133,389	−285,105	−103,777	−221,049	−301,402	−202,800	−142,700	−161,417
Revenue............................	81	90,623	249,768	325,144	351,262	310,174	662,585	597,282	796,977	716,754	1,023,200	1,234,600	1,660,601
Grants Received............................	81z	—	—	—	—	—	—	—	—	—	—	—	—
Expenditure........................	82	160,893	248,768	288,095	356,262	443,563	947,690	701,059	1,018,026	1,018,156	1,226,000	1,377,300	1,822,018
Lending Minus Repayments............	83	—	—	—	—	—	—	—	—	—	—	—	—
Financing														
Net Borrowing: Domestic............	84a	60,248	7,102	−143,190	−60,637	103,886	264,064	103,777	194,053	149,027	163,700	40,600	108,000
Foreign........	85a	8,391	22,455	7,825	13,383	16,605	21,041		26,996	52,798	67	700	38,417
Use of Cash Balances....................	87	1,632	−30,558	98,315	52,254	12,898	—	....	—	99,577	39,033	101,400	15,000
Debt: Domestic........................	88a	299,361	248,774	343,674	359,028	537,489	....	....	1,016,974	1,166,001	1,329,680	1,370,325	1,525,907
Central Bank........................	88aa	199,662	187,509	247,461	264,229	435,131	....	....	719,944	519,771	613,790	403,462	408,421
Commercial Banks....................	88ab	47,829	20,113	45,107	41,450	54,114	....	....	199,262	460,230	500,430	669,070	726,227
Other............................	88ac	51,870	41,152	51,106	53,349	48,244	−18,561	103,777	97,768	186,000	215,460	297,793	391,259
Debt: Foreign............................	89a	648,813	716,775	617,320	595,932	633,017	28,040	28,279	3,176,291	3,932,885	447,829	4,890,270	2,695,072
National Accounts							*Billions of Naira*							
Househ.Cons.Expend.,incl.NPISHs.....	96f	694	† 1,543	2,368	2,435	2,757	1,969	2,447	3,643	4,015	5,493	6,470	....
Government Consumption Expend....	91f	89	† 123	143	171	204	253	260	403	478	450	493	....
Gross Fixed Capital Formation..........	93e	85	† 114	172	206	193	176	269	372	500	866	1,382	....
Changes in Inventories.................	93i	—	† —	—	—	1	1	1	1	1	1	1	....
Exports of Goods and Services..........	90c	217	† 679	853	1,148	754	1,650	2,932	2,231	2,564	3,479	4,358	....
Imports of Goods and Services (-).......	98c	170	† 482	712	1,020	1,027	728	927	1,785	1,954	3,098	4,150	....
Gross Domestic Product (GDP)........	99b	915	† 1,978	2,824	2,940	2,881	3,321	4,981	4,864	5,603	7,191	8,553	12,440
Net Primary Income from Abroad.....	98.n	−66	† −204	−211	−226	−176	−238	−362	−347	−386	−427	−461	....
Gross National Income (GNI)............	99a	849	† 1,774	2,613	2,714	2,705	3,082	4,619	4,517	5,217	6,764	8,092	....
Consumption of Fixed Capital..........	99cf	19	† 20	22	24	26	29	32	36	39	43	47	....
GDP at Fact.Cost,Vol.'84 Prices........	99bap	101	† 104	108	111	114	117	121	126	131	136	....	....
GDP Volume (2000=100)...............	99bvp	83.7	85.5	88.8	91.7	93.8	96.4	100.0	104.2	108.5	112.6	....	....
GDP Deflator (2000=100)...............	99bip	22.0	† 46.4	63.9	64.4	61.7	69.1	100.0	93.7	103.7	128.2	....	....
							Millions: Midyear Estimates							
Population..............................	99z	101.20	103.91	106.64	109.37	112.11	114.85	117.61	120.37	123.13	125.91	128.71	131.53

Norway 142

		1994	1995	1996	1997	1998	1999	2000	2001	2002	2003	2004	2005
Exchange Rates						*Kroner per SDR: End of Period*							
Official Rate	aa	9.8715	9.3931	9.2641	9.8707	10.7010	11.0343	11.5288	11.3251	9.4700	9.9263	9.3802	9.6762
						Kroner per US Dollar: End of Period (ae) Period Average (rf)							
Official Rate	ae	6.7620	6.3190	6.4425	7.3157	7.6000	8.0395	8.8485	9.0116	6.9657	6.6800	6.0400	6.7700
Official Rate	rf	7.0576	6.3352	6.4498	7.0734	7.5451	7.7992	8.8018	8.9917	7.9838	7.0802	6.7408	6.4425
		Kroner per ECU through 1998; Kroner per Euro Beginning 1999; End of Period (ea) Period Average (eb)											
Euro Rate	ea	8.3175	8.3067	8.0615	8.0867	8.8708	† 8.0765	8.2335	7.9735	7.2900	8.4200	8.2400	7.9900
Euro Rate	ag	....	....	....	....	....	1.0046	.9305	.8813	1.0487	1.2630	1.3621	1.1797
Euro Rate	eb	8.3760	8.2859	8.1971	8.0131	8.4541	† 8.3140	8.1133	8.0493	7.5099	7.9992	8.3708	8.0125
Euro Rate	rh	....	....	....	....	....	1.0668	.9240	.8956	.9444	1.1308	1.2433	1.2458
						Index Numbers (2000=100): Period Averages							
Official Rate	ahx	124.6	138.7	136.2	124.4	116.4	112.6	100.0	97.7	110.7	123.5	130.4	136.4
Nominal Effective Exchange Rate	neu	105.0	108.1	108.0	108.1	103.6	102.4	100.0	102.8	111.6	108.9	105.2	110.2
Real Effective Exchange Rate	reu	83.3	88.5	90.9	94.3	95.4	99.2	100.0	107.2	120.9	120.4	118.3	126.2
Fund Position						*Millions of SDRs: End of Period*							
Quota	2f.s	1,104.6	1,104.6	1,104.6	1,104.6	1,104.6	1,671.7	1,671.7	1,671.7	1,671.7	1,671.7	1,671.7	1,671.7
SDRs	1b.s	266.7	311.5	247.2	257.9	294.1	298.0	235.4	282.1	232.1	225.4	232.3	214.9
Reserve Position in the Fund	1c.s	440.9	636.2	643.8	725.5	899.1	621.2	448.1	577.3	729.8	669.5	559.2	210.9
of which: Outstg.Fund Borrowing	2c	—	—	—	—	35.3	—	—	—	—	—	—	—
International Liquidity					*Millions of US Dollars Unless Otherwise Indicated: End of Period*								
Total Reserves minus Gold	1l.d	19,025.5	22,517.8	26,516.7	23,400.3	19,048.1	23,807.3	27,597.4	23,277.5	31,999.8	37,220.0	44,307.5	46,985.9
SDRs	1b.d	389.4	463.0	355.5	347.9	414.1	409.0	306.6	354.5	315.5	335.0	360.8	307.1
Reserve Position in the Fund	1c.d	643.7	945.6	925.8	978.9	1,266.0	852.6	583.8	725.6	992.2	994.9	868.5	301.5
Foreign Exchange	1d.d	17,992.4	21,109.2	25,235.5	22,073.5	17,368.0	22,545.7	26,706.9	22,197.5	30,692.1	35,890.2	43,078.2	46,377.4
Gold (Million Fine Troy Ounces)	1ad	1.184	1.184	1.184	1.184	1.184	1.184	1.183	1.183	1.182	1.180	—	—
Gold (National Valuation)	1and	42.1	45.1	44.2	38.8	37.5	35.3	256.5	260.3	402.8	490.6	—	—
Deposit Money Banks: Assets	7a.d	7,267.4	7,473.0	9,087.8	9,781.4	12,324.9	12,418.4	15,280.1	15,092.7	17,642.0	28,587.7	25,182.4	35,398.8
Liabilities	7b.d	9,241.3	9,617.3	19,885.4	25,617.0	29,849.7	31,818.9	37,022.4	39,759.2	52,761.4	69,457.7	76,042.3	94,581.3
Other Banking Insts.: Liabilities	7f.d	6,040.1	6,434.6	6,198.7	7,081.2	8,179.1	8,774.8	10,659.0	13,445.0	19,430.1	25,815.8	33,134.5	34,014.5
Monetary Authorities						*Billions of Kroner: End of Period*							
Foreign Assets	11	143.58	142.78	225.37	284.17	312.96	† 187.33	241.34	207.72	221.55	249.16	....	....
Claims on Central Government	12a	13.69	18.06	12.41	10.65	9.43	10.79	12.73	11.53	12.84	22.91	....	....
Claims on Deposit Money Banks	12e	5.86	10.09	.23	7.50	16.47	25.63	22.14	15.21	1.07	12.92	....	....
Reserve Money	14	44.09	46.39	70.96	62.79	55.89	83.95	70.29	69.75	104.09	74.40	....	....
of which: Currency Outside DMBs	14a	37.95	39.08	39.87	42.22	42.14	43.51	42.43	42.10	40.41	41.69	....	....
Central Government Deposits	16d	87.24	98.39	131.24	201.16	222.73	† 57.22	85.68	83.55	52.76	108.59	....	....
Other Items (Net)	17r	31.80	26.15	35.81	38.37	60.24	82.58	120.25	81.16	78.61	102.00	....	....
Deposit Money Banks						*Billions of Kroner: End of Period*							
Reserves	20	4.32	5.15	28.06	17.28	14.07	38.36	27.82	29.75	65.87	39.49	47.70	53.38
Foreign Assets	21	49.14	47.22	58.55	71.56	93.67	99.84	135.21	136.01	122.89	190.97	152.10	239.65
Claims on Central Government	22a	73.87	70.56	78.49	60.79	87.04	45.42	38.58	9.60	8.11	13.02	13.94	21.37
Claims on Local Government	22b	11.31	12.78	15.16	15.71	26.89	17.38	11.93	10.39	6.53	6.28	6.45	5.62
Claims on Nonfin.Pub.Enterprises	22c	9.24	5.80	8.04	9.19	12.03	11.21	14.05	13.96	17.07	16.02	24.40	25.16
Claims on Private Sector	22d	479.68	527.46	599.82	708.01	801.58	849.70	969.64	1,075.45	1,144.61	1,232.53	1,354.10	1,582.28
Claims on Other Financial Insts	22f	37.11	34.04	40.46	50.13	75.74	72.54	82.55	92.65	108.23	119.24	103.59	113.85
Demand Deposits	24	314.80	316.29	349.70	371.96	453.20	479.34	521.01	616.02	671.85	706.25	700.07	791.18
Time, Savings,& Fgn.Currency Dep	25	149.24	164.57	166.71	150.52	157.80	141.03	159.08	128.06	133.64	127.91	198.55	210.10
Foreign Liabilities	26c	62.49	60.77	128.11	187.41	226.86	255.81	327.59	358.29	367.52	463.98	459.30	640.32
Central Government Deposits	26d	33.02	34.00	37.62	32.09	57.40	25.90	24.64	6.71	7.63	11.29	7.36	10.92
Credit from Bank of Norway	26g	5.30	10.47	.45	7.88	18.79	25.94	24.70	16.72	8.81	19.99	5.27	27.21
Other Items (Net)	27r	99.57	115.92	145.98	182.80	196.97	206.44	222.75	242.00	283.86	288.13	331.73	361.60
Monetary Survey						*Billions of Kroner: End of Period*							
Foreign Assets (Net)	31n	123.81	125.01	142.13	159.34	169.03	† 3.79	−12.31	−58.28	−77.03	−75.41	....	....
Domestic Credit	32	505.25	536.90	586.05	621.74	735.92	† 924.49	1,019.76	1,123.97	1,237.79	1,290.67	....	....
Claims on Central Govt. (Net)	32an	−32.71	−43.77	−77.96	−161.81	−183.66	† −26.91	−59.01	−69.13	−39.44	−83.95	....	....
Claims on Local Government	32b	11.31	12.78	15.16	15.71	26.89	17.38	11.93	10.39	6.53	6.28	....	....
Claims on Nonfin.Pub.Enterprises	32c	9.24	5.80	8.04	9.19	12.03	11.21	14.05	13.96	17.16	16.02	....	....
Claims on Private Sector	32d	480.30	528.05	600.35	708.52	802.11	850.26	970.24	1,076.09	1,145.30	1,233.09	....	....
Claims on Other Financial Insts	32f	37.11	34.04	40.46	50.13	78.55	72.54	82.55	92.65	108.23	119.24	....	....
Money	34	354.96	358.71	392.72	416.99	497.51	525.43	565.12	659.62	713.76	747.99	....	....
Quasi-Money	35	149.27	164.59	166.73	150.53	157.81	141.04	159.08	128.06	133.64	128.08	....	....
Other Items (Net)	37r	124.58	137.62	168.72	213.56	249.62	261.81	283.25	278.00	313.35	339.19	....	....
Money plus Quasi-Money	35l	504.23	523.30	559.45	567.52	655.32	666.47	724.20	787.68	847.41	876.07	....	....
Money (National Definitions)						*Billions of Kroner: End of Period*							
Broad Money (M2), Unadjusted	59mb	501.3	† 542.4	575.6	590.2	616.9	683.9	753.3	818.9	882.0	902.9	976.0	1,091.8
Broad Money (M2), Seasonally Adj	59mbc	500.2	† 542.0	575.5	590.2	616.9	683.9	752.9	818.0	880.8	901.8	975.2	1,091.7

		1994	1995	1996	1997	1998	1999	2000	2001	2002	2003	2004	2005
Other Banking Institutions													
State Lending Institutions						*Billions of Kroner: End of Period*							
Claims on State and Local Govts......	42b	35.40	36.68	37.90	41.84	42.36	46.17	18.28	18.74	20.82	20.95	19.65	19.55
Claims on Private Sector.................	42d	139.53	138.56	135.69	131.73	140.96	146.46	152.02	161.47	166.59	167.91	167.20	171.56
Bonds (Net)..................................	46ab	16.68	10.39	11.81	16.01	20.16	28.65	.06	.05	.03	.02	.02	.01
Foreign Liabilities.........................	46c	1.81	1.14	1.17	.33	1.39	—	—	—	—	—	—	—
Central Govt. Lending Funds............	46f	155.32	154.28	153.78	152.38	158.75	162.43	168.96	177.87	187.59	189.79	187.92	191.79
Capital Accounts..........................	47a	10.30	10.39	8.61	8.45	8.25	6.74	5.46	6.88	4.50	3.52	3.70	4.28
Other Items (Net)..........................	47r	−9.18	−.95	−1.79	−3.61	−5.23	−5.19	−4.17	−4.57	−4.72	−4.47	−4.79	−4.96
Mortgage Institutions						*Billions of Kroner: End of Period*							
Foreign Assets.............................	41..l	23.95	24.02	22.11	19.36	29.99	33.39	30.32	39.59	56.61	60.68	59.86	88.67
Claims on Central Government........	42a.l	1.48	1.94	1.55	1.22	1.53	1.09	1.16	1.26	.68	.91	.46	.38
Claims on State and Local Govt.......	42b.l	1.91	2.64	4.33	5.60	5.55	8.08	49.83	60.37	65.25	79.40	99.72	113.76
Claims on Nonfin.Pub.Enterprises.....	42c.l	1.32	1.34	1.70	1.37	1.90	4.68	2.78	5.69	5.98	7.70	9.60	10.50
Claims on Private Sector...............	42d.l	62.34	60.05	55.55	66.33	88.87	82.04	93.61	103.07	112.08	124.20	129.75	115.65
Credit Market Instruments..............	46aal	6.97	7.40	5.49	3.70	3.13	8.21	4.81	5.57	1.75	5.81	3.25	3.75
Bonds (net).................................	46abl	35.01	36.46	37.21	33.14	36.46	36.63	58.57	58.89	62.41	51.39	50.83	51.25
Foreign Liabilities.........................	46c.l	39.04	39.52	38.76	51.47	60.77	70.55	94.32	121.16	135.34	172.45	200.13	230.28
Capital Accounts..........................	47a.l	7.76	7.59	6.64	6.51	8.31	8.73	11.04	11.23	11.57	12.23	12.14	12.27
Other Items (Net)..........................	47r.l	2.23	−.99	−2.87	−.93	19.17	5.16	8.97	13.13	29.52	30.99	33.04	31.42
Nonbank Financial Institutions						*Billions of Kroner: End of Period*							
Claims on Central Government........	42a.s	40.47	42.34	42.83	49.16	35.95	34.07	31.34	43.74	46.25	67.33	62.43	60.13
Claims on Local Government...........	42b.s	32.27	30.85	29.55	27.42	28.61	35.07	38.14	43.52	39.08	48.29	44.32	46.40
Claims on Private Sector................	42d.s	65.71	73.90	77.07	71.55	75.08	80.43	92.75	103.63	105.19	132.10	149.64	160.74
Claims on Other Financial Insts.......	42f.s	28.05	32.58	38.85	42.54	48.10	46.36	36.98	50.38	58.03	59.07	66.11	77.06
Incr.in Total Assets(Within Per.)........	49z.s	7.94	10.92	6.91	3.02	−.86	5.77	5.74	45.69	−28.21	100.19	23.47	19.44
Interest Rates						*Percent Per Annum*							
Discount Rate (End of Period)...........	60	6.75	6.75	6.00	5.50	10.00	7.50	9.00	8.50	8.50	4.25	3.75	4.25
Avg.Cost for Centr.Bank Funding.....	60.a	6.46	5.40	4.96	4.80	6.18	6.86	7.31	7.45	8.22	5.60	2.22	3.16
Deposit Rate................................	60l	5.21	4.95	4.15	3.63	7.24	5.38	6.73	† 6.43	6.46	2.12	1.48	1.83
Lending Rate................................	60p	8.38	7.60	6.68	6.00	9.80	7.61	8.93	8.69	8.71	4.73	4.04	4.04
Three Month Interbank Rate............	60zb	5.85	5.48	4.90	3.73	5.79	6.54	6.75	7.23	6.91	4.10	2.01	2.21
Government Bond Yield..................	61	7.13	6.82	5.94	5.13	5.35	5.38	6.38	6.31	6.33	4.50	3.60	3.28
Prices, Production, Labor						*Index Numbers (2000=100): Period Averages*							
Industrial Share Prices....................	62	44.1	47.0	56.4	79.9	78.7	80.3	100.0	....	....	....	....	....
Producer Prices............................	63	84.9	87.1	89.0	90.2	90.7	93.5	† 100.0	95.3	90.0	93.2	104.2	121.5
Consumer Prices...........................	64	87.1	89.2	90.4	92.7	† 94.8	97.0	100.0	103.0	104.3	106.9	107.4	109.1
Wages: Monthly Earnings................	65	....	....	....	....	91.3	96.1	100.0	104.5	110.0	115.2	120.0	124.1
Industrial Production......................	66	85.2	90.4	95.0	98.4	97.4	97.1	100.0	98.7	99.6	95.5	97.4	96.9
Crude Petroleum Production..........	66aa	81.0	87.3	98.7	100.2	95.7	96.1	100.0	101.4	96.9	92.7	90.0	....
						Number in Thousands: Period Averages							
Labor Force.................................	67d	2,151	2,186	2,240	2,287	2,323	2,333	2,350	2,362	2,379	2,375	2,382	2,400
Employment................................	67e	2,035	2,079	2,132	2,195	2,248	2,258	2,269	2,278	2,286	2,269	2,276	2,289
Unemployment.............................	67c	117	107	108	93	74	75	81	84	75	92	92	83
Unemployment Rate (%)................	67r	5.4	4.9	4.8	4.1	3.2	3.2	3.3	2.7	3.2	3.9	3.9	3.5
Intl. Transactions & Positions						*Millions of Kroner*							
Exports......................................	70	243,809	265,883	320,130	342,421	304,653	355,172	529,814	532,042	473,265	476,981	549,672	657,070
Imports, c.i.f...............................	71	192,073	208,627	229,720	252,232	282,638	266,677	302,852	296,135	276,563	279,240	323,081	353,220
						2000=100							
Volume of Exports........................	72	73.8	78.0	88.0	92.8	93.0	95.1	100.0	104.6	107.1	107.4	† 108.4	107.5
Volume of Imports........................	73	63.5	69.0	75.9	82.8	93.5	93.9	100.0	101.3	102.6	105.7	† 117.7	128.9
Unit Value of Exports.....................	74	61.0	62.9	67.9	68.8	61.0	69.1	100.0	95.2	84.6	83.9	† 97.1	117.8
Unit Value of Imports.....................	75	103.7	104.3	103.5	101.7	100.8	96.6	100.0	100.3	93.3	93.4	† 96.8	96.9

Norway 142

		1994	1995	1996	1997	1998	1999	2000	2001	2002	2003	2004	2005
Balance of Payments		*Millions of US Dollars: Minus Sign Indicates Debit*											
Current Account, n.i.e.	78ald	3,760	5,233	10,969	10,036	6	8,378	25,851	26,171	24,473	28,876	34,711	49,488
Goods: Exports f.o.b.	78aad	35,016	42,385	50,081	49,375	40,888	46,224	60,463	59,527	59,616	68,666	82,877	104,362
Goods: Imports f.o.b.	78abd	−27,520	−33,701	−37,109	−37,727	−38,827	−35,501	−34,488	−33,055	−35,277	−40,503	−49,258	−54,224
Trade Balance	78acd	7,496	8,685	12,972	11,648	2,061	10,723	25,975	26,472	24,340	28,162	33,619	50,138
Services: Credit	78add	12,247	13,672	14,819	15,708	15,542	15,878	17,263	17,603	18,689	20,982	25,572	28,670
Services: Debit	78aed	−12,065	−13,147	−13,435	−14,233	−14,820	−14,882	−14,465	−15,104	−16,910	−19,179	−23,069	−27,320
Balance on Goods & Services	78afd	7,678	9,210	14,356	13,123	2,783	11,719	28,773	28,971	26,119	29,966	36,121	51,488
Income: Credit	78agd	3,415	4,590	5,164	5,590	6,809	6,100	6,641	7,556	9,322	12,606	14,060	17,738
Income: Debit	78ahd	−5,589	−6,509	−7,046	−7,284	−8,053	−7,998	−8,278	−8,737	−8,690	−10,723	−12,884	−16,693
Balance on Gds, Serv. & Inc.	78aid	5,504	7,291	12,475	11,429	1,539	9,821	27,136	27,790	26,752	31,850	37,297	52,532
Current Transfers, n.i.e.: Credit	78ajd	1,291	1,280	1,329	1,468	1,500	1,681	1,605	1,760	1,810	1,972	2,451	2,670
Current Transfers: Debit	78akd	−3,035	−3,339	−2,835	−2,861	−3,034	−3,124	−2,890	−3,379	−4,089	−4,946	−5,037	−5,715
Capital Account, n.i.e.	78bcd	−157	−170	−127	−184	−116	−116	−91	−4	−191	678	−154	−199
Capital Account, n.i.e.: Credit	78bad	93	86	65	30	44	40	135	113	44	964	105	552
Capital Account: Debit	78bbd	−250	−255	−192	−214	−160	−156	−225	−118	−235	−286	−260	−751
Financial Account, n.i.e.	78bjd	−1,363	−542	−1,462	−6,607	61	431	−13,395	−27,393	−9,238	−19,860	−20,387	−42,961
Direct Investment Abroad	78bdd	−2,166	−2,859	−5,886	−5,003	−3,200	−6,018	−8,511	859	−3,850	−4,369	−3,607	−14,245
Dir. Invest. in Rep. Econ., n.i.e.	78bed	2,736	2,393	3,179	3,886	4,354	8,056	5,806	2,109	502	3,563	2,474	3,285
Portfolio Investment Assets	78bfd	992	−3,531	−9,833	−12,618	−9,348	−7,228	−25,143	−29,674	−22,987	−19,283	−38,031	−40,564
Equity Securities	78bkd	213	−379	−1,177	−2,644	−9,066	−2,378	−11,034	−12,342	−6,829	−8,498	−7,270	−20,290
Debt Securities	78bld	780	−3,151	−8,657	−9,974	−282	−4,850	−14,109	−17,333	−16,158	−10,785	−30,761	−20,274
Portfolio Investment Liab., n.i.e.	78bgd	−518	655	100	2,500	7,289	4,238	9,843	2,590	4,675	13,123	9,353	25,495
Equity Securities	78bmd	654	636	−237	−1,190	—	−1,033	1,630	2,698	352	2,040	4,493	5,147
Debt Securities	78bnd	−1,172	19	337	3,691	7,289	5,271	8,213	−108	4,322	11,083	4,860	20,348
Financial Derivatives Assets	78bwd	....	....	−43	17	−162	152	−329	−1,228	−4,270	35	−636	61
Financial Derivatives Liabilities	78bxd	....	....	101	125	74	92	−131	91	−556	−161	780	—
Other Investment Assets	78bhd	154	961	−67	−1,403	−3,632	−7,663	−14,100	−3,931	−12,474	−25,024	−16,177	−38,174
General Government	78bpd	−13	−156	71	91	−1,167	−1,099	−2,072	1,379	457	−14,642	−17,858	−20,488
Banks	78bqd	−638	435	−1,216	−1,465	−1,062	−969	−1,806	505	674	−4,291	963	−11,042
Other Sectors	78brd	804	682	1,077	−29	−1,403	−5,595	−10,223	−5,816	−13,605	−5,963	475	−6,865
Other Investment Liab., n.i.e.	78bid	−2,562	1,840	10,987	5,888	4,685	8,802	19,171	1,791	29,723	12,256	25,458	21,180
Monetary Authorities	78bsd	139	−624	1,505	−803	19	−19	3	44	410	−1,721	382	1,292
General Government	78btd	−164	3	—	94	1,346	3,460	9,657	−96	15,678	9,992	22,306	−437
Banks	78bud	−604	247	8,677	4,126	−856	1,789	1,321	2,320	8,549	377	4,266	19,352
Other Sectors	78bwd	−1,933	2,214	806	2,472	4,176	3,573	8,190	−477	5,086	3,608	−1,496	973
Net Errors and Omissions	78cad	−1,987	−3,947	−2,910	−4,443	−6,335	−2,710	−8,680	−1,120	−9,320	−9,366	−8,943	−1,761
Overall Balance	78cbd	253	575	6,470	−1,198	−6,384	5,984	3,686	−2,346	5,723	328	5,227	4,567
Reserves and Related Items	79dad	−253	−575	−6,470	1,198	6,384	−5,984	−3,686	2,346	−5,723	−328	−5,227	−4,567
Reserve Assets	79dbd	−253	−575	−6,470	1,198	6,384	−5,984	−3,686	2,346	−5,723	−328	−5,227	−4,567
Use of Fund Credit and Loans	79dcd	—	—	—	—	—	—	—	—	—	—	—	—
Exceptional Financing	79ded	....	....	....	....	....	....	....	....	....	....	....	....
Government Finance		*Millions of Kroner: Year Ending December 31*											
Deficit (-) or Surplus	80	−14,774	14,487	6,519	8,816	−32,427	−47,230	101,351	96,615	38,244	43,518	....	....
Revenue	81	348,841	383,106	425,506	469,040	464,460	495,055	642,546	710,627	698,626	721,551	....	....
Grants Received	81z	1,423	1,345	1,299	1,322	1,087	938	1,273	1,329	1,243	1,532	....	....
Expenditure	82	357,877	361,579	375,265	387,218	412,173	436,850	465,218	490,627	569,873	583,758	....	....
Lending Minus Repayments	83	7,161	8,385	45,021	74,328	85,801	106,373	77,250	124,714	91,752	95,807	....	....
Financing													
Domestic	84a	20,459	−18,296	11,276	14,516	38,579	1,692	−198,292	−82,176	−124,112	−132,148	....	....
Foreign	85a	−5,684	3,809	−17,795	−23,332	−6,152	45,538	105,500	−13,750	86,900	89,500	....	....
Debt: Domestic	88a	201,763	198,384	186,071	195,983	184,220	149,470	149,553	142,977	171,500	208,761	....	....
Foreign	89a	74,157	77,901	62,527	42,400	37,180	92,881	197,401	182,483	264,630	356,808	....	....
National Accounts		*Billions of Kroner*											
Househ.Cons.Expend.,incl.NPISHs.	96f	435.35	462.26	498.97	527.14	554.54	584.27	625.50	651.34	680.68	720.03	760.92	795.70
Government Consumption Expend.	91f	193.83	202.14	214.68	227.49	247.44	263.73	281.12	314.80	338.47	354.22	370.79	387.52
Gross Fixed Capital Formation	93e	174.38	186.55	208.60	245.70	284.91	271.83	272.77	278.94	274.68	276.61	309.84	356.33
Changes in Inventories	93i	15.84	28.04	12.08	18.87	23.79	20.73	35.04	20.68	17.77	14.28	32.55	36.29
Exports of Goods and Services	90c	333.20	355.95	419.40	460.86	427.08	486.23	685.95	697.30	624.39	637.37	732.44	862.22
Imports of Goods and Services (-)	98c	279.18	297.50	326.80	368.70	405.62	393.76	431.30	436.81	416.85	425.76	489.61	534.22
Gross Domestic Product (GDP)	99b	873.41	937.45	1,026.92	1,111.35	1,132.13	1,233.04	1,469.08	1,526.23	1,519.13	1,576.75	1,716.93	1,903.84
Net Primary Income from Abroad	98.n	−15.42	−12.18	−12.18	−11.83	−9.37	−14.82	−14.42	−10.77	4.13	13.59	7.46	−8.93
Gross National Income (GNI)	99a	857.99	925.27	1,014.74	1,099.52	1,122.77	1,218.22	1,454.66	1,515.46	1,523.27	1,590.34	1,724.40	1,912.78
Net Current Transf.from Abroad	98t	−12.23	−13.03	−9.71	−9.87	−11.56	−11.28	−11.36	−14.55	−17.78	−20.95	−17.29	−20.40
Gross Nat'l Disposable Inc.(GNDI)	99i	845.76	912.25	1,005.03	1,089.65	1,111.21	1,206.94	1,443.30	1,500.91	1,505.49	1,569.39	1,707.11	1,892.38
Gross Saving	99s	216.58	247.84	291.39	335.03	309.24	358.94	536.68	534.78	486.34	495.15	575.40	686.53
Consumption of Fixed Capital	99cf	143.16	149.05	154.78	164.11	175.57	188.47	204.86	215.86	219.57	224.31	235.04	247.22
GDP Volume 2003 Ref., Chained	99b.p	1,205.34	1,257.86	1,323.95	1,392.64	1,429.26	1,459.75	1,501.17	1,542.09	1,559.15	1,576.74	1,625.28	1,661.99
GDP Volume (2000=100)	99bvp	80.3	83.8	88.2	92.8	95.2	97.2	100.0	102.7	103.9	105.0	108.3	110.7
GDP Deflator (2000=100)	99bip	74.0	76.2	79.3	81.5	80.9	86.3	100.0	101.1	99.6	102.2	107.9	117.1
		Millions: Midyear Estimates											
Population	99z	4.33	4.36	4.39	4.42	4.45	4.47	4.50	4.53	4.55	4.58	4.60	4.62

		1994	1995	1996	1997	1998	1999	2000	2001	2002	2003	2004	2005
Exchange Rates													
		Rials Omani per SDR: End of Period (aa) Rials Omani per US Dollar: End of Period (ae)											
Official Rate	aa	.5613	.5716	.5529	.5188	.5414	.5277	.5010	.4832	.5227	.5714	.5971	.5496
Official Rate	ae	.3845	.3845	.3845	.3845	.3845	.3845	.3845	.3845	.3845	.3845	.3845	.3845
		Index Numbers (2000=100): Period Averages											
Official Rate	ahx	100.0	100.0	100.0	100.0	100.0	100.0	100.0	100.0	100.0	100.0	100.0	100.0
Nominal Effective Exchange Rate	nec	89.9	84.9	88.8	93.7	97.6	96.7	100.0	103.7	102.6	96.1	91.9	91.6
Fund Position		*Millions of SDRs: End of Period*											
Quota	2f.s	119.4	119.4	119.4	119.4	119.4	194.0	194.0	194.0	194.0	194.0	194.0	194.0
SDRs	1b.s	6.2	7.5	8.8	10.1	11.5	1.3	3.1	5.0	6.5	7.8	9.0	10.3
Reserve Position in the Fund	1c.s	36.0	34.5	34.0	31.1	31.1	49.8	49.8	65.0	73.4	77.6	63.7	24.2
of which: Outstg.Fund Borrowing	2c	—	—	—	—	—	—	—	—	—	—	—	—
International Liquidity		*Millions of US Dollars Unless Otherwise Indicated: End of Period*											
Total Reserves minus Gold	1l.d	1,646.2	1,830.7	1,961.6	2,069.6	1,937.7	2,767.5	2,379.9	2,364.9	3,173.5	3,593.5	3,597.3	4,358.1
SDRs	1b.d	9.0	11.1	12.7	13.6	16.2	1.8	4.1	6.3	8.9	11.6	13.9	14.8
Reserve Position in the Fund	1c.d	52.5	51.2	48.8	42.0	43.9	68.3	64.9	81.6	99.8	115.3	98.9	34.6
Foreign Exchange	1d.d	1,584.7	1,768.3	1,900.1	2,014.0	1,877.7	2,697.3	2,310.9	2,277.0	3,064.8	3,466.6	3,484.5	4,308.7
Gold (Million Fine Troy Ounces)	1ad	.289	.291	.291	.291	.291	.291	.291	.291	.001	.001	.001	.001
Gold (National Valuation)	1and	68.3	68.3	68.3	68.3	68.3	68.3	68.3	80.5	.2	.3	.3	.3
Monetary Authorities:Other Assets	3..d	38.4	....	80.6	120.3	147.8	555.9	39.7	50.4	41.7	42.1	50.0	30.7
Other Liab	4..d	1.2	1.7	1.0	1.7	1.2	1.1	1.0	1.0	1.1	1.1	2.4	2.5
Deposit Money Banks: Assets	7a.d	863.5	999.1	944.1	1,776.8	1,222.7	992.3	1,215.5	997.9	1,241.9	1,290.3	1,877.0	2,449.6
Liabilities	7b.d	239.5	441.4	652.4	1,326.5	1,522.2	1,662.4	1,641.8	1,532.5	1,401.8	1,176.1	953.6	685.1
Monetary Authorities		*Millions of Rials Omani: End of Period*											
Foreign Assets	11	635.0	730.4	780.8	822.4	771.6	1,090.4	941.4	940.3	1,220.3	1,382.2	1,383.7	1,675.9
Claims on Central Government	12a	97.0	89.4	47.0	32.7	159.6	4.1	5.0	79.5	25.7	4.3	3.6	.8
Reserve Money	14	296.3	306.9	326.5	354.3	379.5	375.3	408.3	444.3	578.7	612.5	562.1	799.4
of which: Currency Outside DMBs	14a	245.5	235.9	231.2	242.2	244.2	273.5	276.8	275.9	289.6	303.8	329.0	383.2
Foreign Liabilities	16c	.5	.6	.4	.6	.5	.4	.4	.4	.4	.4	.9	1.0
Central Government Deposits	16d	14.8	41.0	31.1	46.6	57.0	242.6	26.0	19.4	16.1	68.5	85.9	168.3
Capital Accounts	17a	235.2	251.9	268.3	283.1	297.9	312.4	342.8	373.5	406.8	403.4	412.3	453.7
Other Items (Net)	17r	185.3	219.5	201.5	170.4	196.3	163.8	168.8	182.2	243.9	301.7	326.0	254.2
Deposit Money Banks		*Millions of Rials Omani: End of Period*											
Reserves	20	51.6	67.8	86.9	116.0	132.2	99.2	129.7	136.2	164.2	129.0	165.1	137.2
Foreign Assets	21	332.0	384.2	363.0	683.2	470.1	381.5	467.4	383.7	477.5	496.1	721.7	941.9
Claims on Central Government	22a	97.9	91.9	175.8	157.4	198.0	334.7	323.0	427.0	357.2	417.7	439.9	254.1
Claims on Nonfin.Pub.Enterprises	22c	3.0	3.1	4.8	.6	—	4.1	16.3	28.1	46.0	69.0	87.3	111.8
Claims on Private Sector	22d	1,227.3	1,357.5	1,564.9	2,170.9	2,563.1	2,783.9	2,809.7	3,001.4	3,012.7	3,060.1	3,258.8	3,663.0
Demand Deposits	24	227.4	235.4	272.1	307.5	261.6	237.7	272.5	425.7	482.0	504.2	582.7	750.4
Quasi-Monetary Deposits	25	931.1	1,040.5	1,130.5	1,484.5	1,625.4	1,756.2	1,854.7	1,924.0	1,991.3	2,024.3	2,032.6	2,436.6
Foreign Liabilities	26c	92.1	169.7	250.9	510.0	585.3	639.2	631.3	589.3	539.0	452.2	366.7	263.4
Central Government Deposits	26d	148.9	140.7	211.3	289.8	292.4	316.1	306.0	285.5	276.4	300.0	441.4	543.5
Capital Accounts	27a	167.6	174.9	193.8	304.2	425.6	454.2	433.3	425.8	432.8	509.3	587.3	659.6
Other Items (Net)	27r	144.7	143.3	136.9	232.0	173.1	200.0	248.3	326.2	336.2	381.9	662.2	454.4
Monetary Survey		*Millions of Rials Omani: End of Period*											
Foreign Assets (Net)	31n	874.5	944.2	892.6	994.9	656.0	832.3	777.1	734.4	1,158.4	1,425.7	1,737.9	2,353.4
Domestic Credit	32	1,261.5	1,360.3	1,550.2	2,025.2	2,571.2	2,568.1	2,822.0	3,231.1	3,149.1	3,182.6	3,262.2	3,317.8
Claims on Central Govt. (Net)	32an	31.2	−.4	−19.6	−146.3	8.1	−219.9	−4.1	201.6	90.4	53.5	−83.9	−457.0
Claims on Nonfin.Pub.Enterprises	32c	3.0	3.1	4.8	.6	—	4.1	16.3	28.1	46.0	69.0	87.3	111.8
Claims on Private Sector	32d	1,227.3	1,357.5	1,564.9	2,170.9	2,563.1	2,783.9	2,809.7	3,001.4	3,012.7	3,060.1	3,258.8	3,663.0
Money	34	472.9	471.3	503.4	549.7	505.8	511.2	549.3	701.6	771.7	808.0	911.7	1,133.6
Quasi-Money	35	931.1	1,040.5	1,130.5	1,484.5	1,625.4	1,756.2	1,854.7	1,924.0	1,991.3	2,024.3	2,032.6	2,436.6
Other Items (Net)	37r	731.9	792.7	808.9	985.9	1,096.0	1,132.9	1,195.0	1,339.9	1,544.6	1,776.0	2,055.9	2,101.0
Money plus Quasi-Money	35l	1,404.1	1,511.8	1,633.9	2,034.2	2,131.2	2,267.5	2,404.1	2,625.6	2,762.9	2,832.3	2,944.3	3,570.2
Interest Rates		*Percent Per Annum*											
Deposit Rate	60l	4.34	6.53	6.85	7.30	8.46	8.12	7.63	4.50	2.89	2.37	2.32	3.30
Lending Rate	60p	8.57	9.38	9.23	9.30	10.09	10.32	10.06	9.23	8.55	8.23	7.57	7.01
Prices and Production		*Index Numbers (2000=100): Period Averages*											
Consumer Prices	64	98.8	101.2	102.1	101.6	100.7	101.2	100.0	98.9	98.3	†97.9	98.2	99.4
Crude Petroleum	66aa	84.6	89.3	93.1	93.9	92.8	93.9	100.0	99.7	93.7	85.6	81.9	80.9
Intl. Transactions & Positions		*Millions of Rials Omani*											
Exports	70	2,132.0	2,333.2	2,824.5	2,933.8	2,118.0	2,783.0	4,352.0	4,258.0	4,295.5	4,486.6	5,129.8	7,187.0
Crude Petroleum	70aa	1,577.8	1,796.1	2,211.0	2,171.3	1,374.3	2,059.8	3,356.7	2,934.4	2,859.3	3,014.8	3,489.5	5,070.9
Imports, c.i.f.	71	1,505.3	1,633.2	1,760.1	1,932.5	2,184.6	1,797.1	1,937.7	2,229.3	2,309.1	2,527.0	3,408.7	3,394.0
Volume of Exports								*2000=100*					
Crude Petroleum	72aa	82.8	87.1	90.1	93.6	91.9	94.4	100.0	101.4	93.7	85.2	80.7	80.2
Unit Value of Imports	75	108.7	119.0	102.2	101.9	121.8	106.0	100.0	99.8	93.4	88.8	115.0	120.9
Export Prices								*2000=100: Index of Prices in US Dollars*					
Crude Petroleum	76aad	56.9	61.3	72.7	69.7	44.6	64.9	100.0	86.1	90.9	104.2	128.8	188.1

Oman 449

		1994	1995	1996	1997	1998	1999	2000	2001	2002	2003	2004	2005
Balance of Payments						*Millions of US Dollars: Minus Sign Indicates Debit*							
Current Account, n.i.e.	78ald	−805	−801	243	−166	−3,164	−460	3,129	1,885	1,367	880	443	....
Goods: Exports f.o.b.	78aad	5,542	6,065	7,373	7,657	5,520	7,237	11,318	11,073	11,172	11,670	13,345	....
Goods: Imports f.o.b.	78abd	−3,693	−4,050	−4,231	−4,645	−5,213	−4,299	−4,593	−5,310	−5,636	−6,086	−7,873	....
Trade Balance	78acd	1,849	2,015	3,142	3,012	307	2,938	6,725	5,763	5,536	5,584	5,472	....
Services: Credit	78add	13	13	237	269	388	413	452	486	515	646	830	....
Services: Debit	78aed	−900	−985	−1,328	−1,556	−1,891	−1,714	−1,758	−1,898	−1,872	−2,174	−2,740	....
Balance on Goods & Services	78afd	962	1,043	2,051	1,725	−1,196	1,638	5,418	4,352	4,179	4,056	3,562	....
Income: Credit	78agd	257	325	255	385	339	187	291	323	250	247	261	....
Income: Debit	78ahd	−724	−699	−693	−776	−840	−846	−1,129	−1,258	−1,460	−1,751	−1,554	....
Balance on Gds, Serv. & Inc.	78aid	495	669	1,613	1,335	−1,697	979	4,581	3,417	2,969	2,552	2,269	....
Current Transfers, n.i.e.: Credit	78ajd	65	68	—	—	—	—	—	—	—	—	—	....
Current Transfers: Debit	78akd	−1,365	−1,537	−1,371	−1,501	−1,467	−1,438	−1,451	−1,532	−1,602	−1,672	−1,826	....
Capital Account, n.i.e.	78bcd	—	—	10	31	−6	−3	8	−10	6	10	21	....
Capital Account, n.i.e.: Credit	78bad	—	—	29	55	20	16	34	8	37	26	26	....
Capital Account: Debit	78bbd	—	—	−18	−23	−27	−18	−26	−18	−31	−16	−5	....
Financial Account, n.i.e.	78bjd	230	−19	261	51	1,489	128	−370	−220	−1,081	−279	990	....
Direct Investment Abroad	78bdd	—	—	—	—	—	—	—	—	—	—	—	....
Dir. Invest. in Rep. Econ., n.i.e.	78bed	76	46	61	65	102	40	82	389	25	528	−17	....
Portfolio Investment Assets	78bfd	—	—	—	—	—	—	—	—	—	—	—	....
Equity Securities	78bkd	....	....	....	....	....	....	....	....	....	....	....	....
Debt Securities	78bld	....	....	....	....	....	....	....	....	....	....	....	....
Portfolio Investment Liab., n.i.e.	78bgd	....	....	8	18	185	25	−36	13	−18	55	277	....
Equity Securities	78bmd	....	....	10	85	240	12	−10	−3	34	94	147	....
Debt Securities	78bnd	....	....	−3	−68	−55	13	−26	16	−52	−39	130	....
Financial Derivatives Assets	78bwd	....	....	....	....	....	....	....	....	....	....	....	....
Financial Derivatives Liabilities	78bxd	....	....	....	....	....	....	....	....	....	....	....	....
Other Investment Assets	78bhd	−174	−52	−237	−715	642	−307	−497	85	−443	−153	−670	....
Monetary Authorities	78bod	....	....	....	....	....	....	....	....	....	....	....	....
General Government	78bpd	−104	−88	−291	117	88	−538	−273	−133	−198	−109	−77	....
Banks	78bqd	−10	62	55	−832	554	232	−224	219	−245	−44	−593	....
Other Sectors	78brd	−60	−26	—	—	—	—	—	—	—	—	—	....
Other Investment Liab., n.i.e.	78bid	328	−13	429	684	559	369	81	−707	−645	−709	1,400	....
Monetary Authorities	78bsd	—	—	—	—	—	—	—	—	—	—	—	....
General Government	78btd	325	−18	140	−112	−26	101	−114	−448	−599	−421	195	....
Banks	78bud	3	5	289	676	315	138	−21	−117	−164	−247	50	....
Other Sectors	78bvd	....	....	—	120	271	130	216	−142	118	−41	1,155	....
Net Errors and Omissions	78cad	−86	388	−327	617	910	539	−504	−641	16	45	−972	....
Overall Balance	78cbd	−661	−432	187	533	−771	205	2,263	1,015	309	656	482	....
Reserves and Related Items	79dad	661	432	−187	−533	771	−205	−2,263	−1,015	−309	−656	−482	....
Reserve Assets	79dbd	661	432	−187	−533	771	−205	−2,263	−1,015	−309	−656	−482	....
Use of Fund Credit and Loans	79dcd	—	—	—	—	—	—	—	—	—	—	—	....
Exceptional Financing	79ded	....	....	....	....	....	....	—	—	—	—	—	....
Government Finance						*Millions of Rials Omani: Year Ending December 31*							
Deficit (-) or Surplus	80	−485.9	−468.1	−259.7	−28.3	−376.9	−474.1	−363.2	−324.1	....	....	....	....
Revenue	81	1,386.7	1,487.9	1,602.8	1,867.4	1,426.6	1,401.8	1,831.2	2,077.2	....	....	....	....
Grants Received	81z	29.9	13.2	10.8	20.7	8.8	5.6	13.2	2.9	....	....	....	....
Expenditure	82	1,912.7	1,971.2	1,879.4	1,848.0	1,820.1	1,859.4	2,179.5	2,295.1	....	....	....	....
Lending Minus Repayments	83	−10.2	−2.0	−6.1	68.4	−7.8	22.1	28.1	109.1	....	....	....	....
Financing													
Domestic	84a	141.8	46.4	−250.6	35.5	9.1	105.7	76.6	86.4	....	....	....	....
Foreign	85a	344.1	421.7	510.3	−7.2	367.8	368.4	286.6	237.7	....	....	....	....
Debt: Domestic	88a	313.9	306.7	325.2	314.1	471.0	493.1	392.1	623.4	....	....	....	....
Foreign	89a	1,148.8	1,148.0	1,201.1	1,132.5	1,086.1	1,118.4	1,064.8	900.5	....	....	....	....
National Accounts						*Millions of Rials Omani*							
Househ.Cons.Expend.,incl.NPISHs	96f	2,349	2,600	2,799	2,901	3,120	3,001	3,021	3,367	3,430	3,656	4,341	....
Government Consumption Expend	91f	1,429	1,462	1,446	1,415	1,402	1,440	1,580	1,712	1,800	1,853	2,032	....
Gross Capital Formation	93	782	795	805	1,075	1,299	897	912	970	977	1,307	1,785	....
Exports of Goods and Services	90c	2,136	2,337	2,926	3,047	2,229	2,937	4,521	4,393	4,494	4,735	5,450	....
Imports of Goods and Services (-)	98c	1,728	1,887	2,101	2,348	2,633	2,234	2,395	2,771	2,887	3,175	4,080	....
Gross Domestic Product (GDP)	99b	4,967	5,307	5,874	6,090	5,416	6,041	7,639	7,670	7,815	8,376	9,527	11,817
Net Primary Income from Abroad	98.n	−683	−713	−695	−727	−747	−815	−282	−275	−481	−593	−513	....
Gross National Income (GNI)	99a	4,121	4,594	5,179	5,363	4,669	5,226	7,357	7,395	7,334	7,783	9,014	....
GDP Volume 1988 Prices	99b.p	4,564	4,784	4,923	5,227	5,368	5,356	5,650	6,074	6,230	6,355	6,713	....
GDP Volume (2000=100)	99bvp	80.8	84.7	87.1	92.5	95.0	94.8	100.0	107.5	110.3	112.5	118.8	....
GDP Deflator (2000=100)	99bip	80.5	82.0	88.2	86.2	74.6	83.4	100.0	93.4	92.8	97.5	105.0	....
						Millions: Midyear Estimates							
Population	99z	2.11	2.18	2.24	2.30	2.35	2.40	2.44	2.47	2.49	2.51	2.53	2.57

Pakistan 564

		1994	1995	1996	1997	1998	1999	2000	2001	2002	2003	2004	2005
Exchange Rates					*Rupees per SDR: End of Period (aa)*								
Market Rate	aa	44.963	50.912	57.691	59.434	64.608	† 71.075	75.607	76.489	79.578	85.020	91.820	85.513
					Rupees per US Dollar: End of Period (ae) Period Average (rf)								
Market Rate	ae	30.800	34.250	40.120	44.050	45.885	† 51.785	58.029	60.864	58.534	57.215	59.124	59.830
Market Rate	rf	30.567	31.643	36.079	41.112	45.047	† 49.501	53.648	61.927	59.724	57.752	58.258	59.514
					Index Numbers (2000=100): Period Averages								
Nominal Effective Exchange Rate	nec	152.51	140.17	126.80	118.21	111.98	101.64	100.00	90.59	92.22	88.46	83.70	81.08
Real Effective Exchange Rate	rec	111.44	110.72	107.28	108.79	106.75	99.49	100.00	91.48	94.78	91.78	91.11	94.04
Fund Position					*Millions of SDRs: End of Period*								
Quota	2f.s	758	758	758	758	758	1,034	1,034	1,034	1,034	1,034	1,034	1,034
SDRs	1b.s	—	10	9	8	1	—	11	3	2	167	158	151
Reserve Position in the Fund	1c.s	—	—	—	—	—	—	—	—	—	—	—	—
Total Fund Cred.&Loans Outstg	2tl	1,097	1,115	1,001	980	996	1,271	1,198	1,456	1,506	1,425	1,208	1,044
International Liquidity					*Millions of US Dollars Unless Otherwise Indicated: Last Thursday of Period*								
Total Reserves minus Gold	1l.d	2,929	1,733	548	1,195	1,028	1,511	1,513	3,640	8,078	10,941	9,799	10,033
SDRs	1b.d	—	15	13	11	1	—	14	4	2	248	245	216
Reserve Position in the Fund	1c.d	—	—	—	—	—	—	—	—	—	—	—	—
Foreign Exchange	1d.d	2,929	1,718	535	1,184	1,027	1,511	1,499	3,636	8,076	10,693	9,554	9,817
Gold (Million Fine Troy Ounces)	1ad	2.052	2.055	2.056	2.066	2.077	2.088	2.091	2.091	2.093	2.096	2.099	2.099
Gold (National Valuation)	1and	792	721	689	635	618	543	543	595	684	733	817	915
Monetary Authorities: Other Liab	4..d	271	226	689	615	856	890	973	950	705	713	708	703
Deposit Money Banks: Assets	7a.d	1,582	1,605	1,546	1,406	1,281	1,365	1,440	1,771	1,574	1,582	3,175	2,167
Liabilities	7b.d	2,380	3,007	3,373	2,330	2,091	1,614	1,331	898	585	478	646	525
Monetary Authorities					*Millions of Rupees: Last Thursday of Period*								
Foreign Assets	11	115,577	86,701	61,805	93,159	77,768	104,870	115,554	249,986	511,539	676,336	632,633	654,600
Claims on General Government	12a	211,343	264,623	314,989	293,523	375,659	534,632	583,026	438,828	247,746	113,371	379,146	548,884
of which: Provincial Government	12ax	2,258	5,184	15,931	12,700	12,657	8,050	3,388	874	874	37,067	7,242	14,503
Claims on Private Sector	12d												
Claims on Deposit Money Banks	12e	89,110	98,220	67,864	119,962	171,286	192,862	195,646	184,842	160,603	194,671	207,726	214,573
Claims on Nonbank Financial Insts	12g	37,113	41,589	42,217	40,401	50,137	60,351	68,395	40,992	32,844	25,976	18,774	15,415
Reserve Money	14	282,541	333,207	321,058	367,082	414,627	468,491	458,843	588,677	640,534	746,510	895,970	985,352
of which: Currency Outside DMBs	14a	195,827	234,011	252,069	272,052	301,146	341,024	410,469	429,360	487,745	567,519	655,287	732,011
Restricted Deposits	16b	—	—	—	—	—	8,115	11,124	13,187	18,049	19,315	22,862	23,028
Foreign Liabilities	16c	57,671	64,514	85,382	85,329	103,651	136,435	147,011	169,163	161,125	161,894	152,768	131,314
General Government Deposits	16d	37,682	34,365	28,502	30,603	63,742	138,006	199,021	43,203	96,550	71,757	70,976	166,700
Counterpart Funds	16e	614	644	686	644	585	660	532	589	562	607	648	525
Capital Accounts	17a	32,364	34,618	39,009	39,567	40,644	46,408	55,522	54,763	56,060	58,849	66,329	81,697
Other Items (Net)	17r	5,157	−17,803	−29,979	−16,581	1,464	34,249	22,172	4,074	−52,992	−74,554	9,952	29,440
Deposit Money Banks					*Millions of Rupees: Last Thursday of Period*								
Reserves	20	93,268	109,689	80,122	100,518	119,696	145,480	145,480	81,205	169,195	150,861	172,747	233,785	247,298
Foreign Assets	21	48,721	54,958	62,022	61,940	58,800	70,682	83,534	107,789	92,157	90,535	187,711	129,635
Claims on General Government	22a	251,172	263,013	333,162	396,083	395,218	321,548	355,499	325,670	601,005	689,873	548,460	622,208
of which: Provincial Government	22ax	11,488	13,387	11,657	13,081	16,355	19,846	44,262	43,617	35,485	22,854	21,707	34,983
Claims on Nonfin.Pub.Enterprises	22c	10,704	13,227	14,815	15,457	14,467	13,261	13,465	12,343	13,426	15,904	15,780	124,893
Claims on Private Sector	22d	374,759	451,686	523,555	598,487	672,465	748,532	854,604	916,721	965,066	1,199,277	1,620,884	1,861,899
Claims on Nonbank Financial Insts	22g	—	—	—	—	—	—	—	—	—	—	—	78,271
Demand Deposits	24	235,265	253,189	269,947	420,823	423,091	447,919	457,773	524,429	628,531	816,587	1,026,569	1,571,500
Time Deposits	25	278,960	322,037	448,144	470,719	530,230	521,619	600,662	685,205	809,592	878,563	1,043,698	875,677
Foreign Liabilities	26c	73,295	102,995	135,309	102,617	95,936	83,579	77,248	54,662	34,230	27,330	38,223	31,422
General Government Deposits	26d	41,168	47,719	47,800	47,799	66,536	96,763	84,259	102,692	131,705	165,510	196,745	231,438
Counterpart Funds	26e												
Central Government Lending Funds	26f	12,235	11,853	11,788	11,634	11,676	11,493	11,244	11,148	11,071	16,154	7	9,314
Credit from Monetary Authorities	26g	77,758	86,766	57,795	108,583	126,448	148,604	144,839	120,372	136,900	155,270	176,354	192,709
Liab. to Nonbank Financial Insts	26j												1,540
Capital Accounts	27a												521,812
Other Items (Net)	27r	59,943	68,014	42,893	10,310	6,729	−10,474	12,282	33,210	70,486	108,923	125,024	−371,208
Monetary Survey					*Millions of Rupees: Last Thursday of Period*								
Foreign Assets (Net)	31n	33,332	−25,850	−96,864	−32,847	−63,019	−44,462	−25,171	133,950	408,341	577,648	629,354	621,499
Domestic Credit	32	806,241	952,054	1,152,436	1,265,549	1,377,668	1,443,555	1,591,709	1,588,659	1,631,832	1,807,134	2,315,323	2,853,432
Claims on General Govt. (Net)	32an	383,665	445,552	571,849	611,204	640,599	621,411	655,245	618,603	620,496	565,977	659,885	772,954
Claims on Nonfin.Pub.Enterprises	32c	10,704	13,227	14,815	15,457	14,467	13,261	13,465	12,343	13,426	15,904	15,780	124,893
Claims on Private Sector	32d	374,759	451,686	523,555	598,487	672,465	748,532	854,604	916,721	965,066	1,199,277	1,620,884	1,861,899
Claims on Nonbank Financial Insts	32g	37,113	41,589	42,217	40,401	50,137	60,351	68,395	40,992	32,844	25,976	18,774	93,686
Money	34	435,388	490,961	528,011	699,806	732,291	795,370	876,014	964,921	1,118,403	1,387,601	1,687,355	2,306,838
Quasi-Money	35	278,960	322,037	448,144	470,719	530,230	521,619	600,662	685,205	809,592	878,563	1,043,698	875,677
Restricted Deposits	36b	—	—	—	—	—	8,115	11,124	13,187	18,049	19,315	22,862	23,028
Counterpart Funds	36e	614	644	686	644	585	660	532	589	562	607	648	525
Central Government Lending Funds	36f	12,235	11,853	11,788	11,634	11,676	11,493	11,244	11,148	11,071	16,154	7	9,314
Liab. to Nonbank Financial Insts	36j												1,540
Capital Accounts	37a	32,364	34,618	39,009	39,567	40,644	46,408	55,522	54,763	56,060	58,849	66,329	603,509
Other Items (Net)	37r	80,011	66,092	27,934	10,332	−777	15,428	11,439	−7,204	26,436	23,692	123,777	−345,501
Money plus Quasi-Money	35l	714,348	812,998	976,155	1,170,525	1,262,521	1,316,989	1,476,676	1,650,126	1,927,995	2,266,163	2,731,053	3,182,515
Other Banking Institutions					*Millions of Rupees: Last Thursday of Period*								
Post Office: Savings Deposits	45..i	9,891	12,370	14,189	18,622	22,473	27,603	36,022	39,638	59,445	76,193	53,901	40,229
Liquid Liabilities	55l	724,239	825,368	990,344	1,189,147	1,284,994	1,344,592	1,512,698	1,689,764	1,987,440	2,342,356	2,784,954	3,222,744
Interest Rates					*Percent Per Annum*								
Discount Rate (End of Period)	60	† 15.00	17.00	20.00	18.00	16.50	13.00	13.00	10.00	7.50	7.50	7.50	9.00
Money Market Rate	60b	8.36	11.52	11.40	12.10	10.76	9.04	8.57	8.49	5.53	2.14	2.70	6.83
Treasury Bill Rate	60c	11.26	12.49	13.61	† 15.74	....	....	8.38	10.71	6.08	1.93	2.48	7.18
Government Bond Yield	61	7.07	6.63	6.06	5.43	4.79	4.16	....	....	....	....	....	....

Pakistan 564

		1994	1995	1996	1997	1998	1999	2000	2001	2002	2003	2004	2005
Prices, Production, Labor						*Index Numbers (2000=100): Period Averages*							
Share Prices	62	204.1	145.2	119.2	111.2	80.2	79.2	100.0	75.6	82.2	141.7	218.9	283.0
Wholesale Prices	63	62.9	70.9	78.7	87.6	89.6	96.2	100.0	104.6	† 107.7	114.6	124.3	135.2
Consumer Prices	64	62.7	70.5	77.8	86.6	92.0	95.8	100.0	† 103.1	106.5	109.6	117.8	128.5
Manufacturing Production	66ey	87.0	90.5	89.9	89.5	95.8	102.9	100.0	† 110.3	114.3	130.3	153.4	....
						Number in Thousands: Period Averages							
Labor Force	67d	33,324	33,191	34,342	36,407	38,174	39,400	38,005	40,662	42,388	45,230	....	....
Employment	67e	31,288	31,407	32,491	34,597	36,419	37,296	36,847	37,481	38,882	41,750	....	....
Unemployment	67c	1,591	1,783	1,845	2,254	2,279	2,334	3,127	3,181	3,506	3,480	....	....
Unemployment Rate (%)	67r	4.8	5.4	5.4	6.1	5.9	5.9	7.8	7.8	8.3	7.7	....	....
Intl. Transactions & Positions							*Millions of Rupees*						
Exports	70	225,200	252,714	335,313	359,046	382,477	417,322	484,476	572,471	591,714	688,882	779,286	955,464
Imports, c.i.f	71	271,744	362,686	437,769	476,346	419,311	505,451	582,681	631,005	670,575	752,788	1,045,981	1,509,814
							2000=100						
Volume of Exports	72	92.6	73.4	87.0	† 81.9	79.5	89.3	100.0	102.1	109.3	109.9	103.1	126.5
Volume of Imports	73	86.4	93.6	91.6	† 94.3	89.5	101.3	100.0	112.1	123.0	122.7	141.6	165.0
Unit Value of Exports	74	55.1	69.4	76.8	† 88.1	98.4	101.0	100.0	108.4	100.0	103.6	111.9	114.8
Unit Value of Imports	75	51.4	58.1	64.2	† 74.2	72.1	85.5	100.0	108.5	105.5	116.8	132.3	152.7
Balance of Payments					*Millions of US Dollars: Minus Sign Indicates Debit*								
Current Account, n.i.e	78ald	−1,812	−3,349	−4,436	−1,712	−2,248	−920	−85	1,878	3,854	3,573	−817	−3,463
Goods: Exports f.o.b	78aad	7,117	8,356	8,507	8,351	7,850	7,673	8,739	9,131	9,832	11,869	13,297	15,382
Goods: Imports f.o.b	78abd	−9,355	−11,248	−12,164	−10,750	−9,834	−9,520	−9,896	−9,741	−10,428	−11,978	−16,693	−21,560
Trade Balance	78acd	−2,239	−2,891	−3,656	−2,399	−1,984	−1,847	−1,157	−610	−596	−109	−3,396	−6,178
Services: Credit	78add	1,753	1,857	2,016	1,625	1,404	1,373	1,380	1,459	2,429	2,968	2,749	3,677
Services: Debit	78aed	−2,529	−2,938	−3,459	−2,658	−2,261	−2,146	−2,252	−2,330	−2,241	−3,294	−5,333	−7,482
Balance on Goods & Services	78afd	−3,015	−3,972	−5,099	−3,433	−2,841	−2,620	−2,029	−1,481	−408	−435	−5,980	−9,983
Income: Credit	78agd	149	187	175	147	83	119	118	113	128	180	221	657
Income: Debit	78ahd	−1,830	−2,125	−2,198	−2,366	−2,263	−1,959	−2,336	−2,189	−2,414	−2,404	−2,584	−3,173
Balance on Gds, Serv. & Inc	78aid	−4,695	−5,910	−7,121	−5,652	−5,021	−4,460	−4,247	−3,557	−2,694	−2,659	−8,343	−12,499
Current Transfers, n.i.e.: Credit	78ajd	2,919	2,611	2,739	3,981	2,801	3,582	4,200	5,496	6,593	6,300	7,666	9,126
Current Transfers: Debit	78akd	−35	−49	−54	−40	−28	−42	−38	−61	−45	−68	−140	−90
Capital Account, n.i.e	78bcd	—	—	—	—	....	....	....	....	40	1,138	591	202
Capital Account, n.i.e.: Credit	78bad	—	—	—	—	....	....	....	....	40	1,140	596	214
Capital Account: Debit	78bbd	—	—	—	—	....	....	....	....	—	−2	−5	−12
Financial Account, n.i.e	78bjd	2,977	2,449	3,496	2,321	−1,873	−2,364	−3,099	−389	−784	−1,751	−1,810	4,116
Direct Investment Abroad	78bdd	−1	—	−7	24	−50	−21	−11	−31	−28	−19	−56	−44
Dir. Invest. in Rep. Econ., n.i.e	78bed	421	723	922	716	506	532	308	383	823	534	1,118	2,183
Portfolio Investment Assets	78bfd	—	—	—	—	....	....	....	....	....	−2	9	18
Equity Securities	78bkd	—	—	—	—	....	....	....	....	....	−2	9	18
Debt Securities	78bld	—	—	—	—	....	....	....	....	....	....	—	....
Portfolio Investment Liab., n.i.e	78bgd	1,471	4	261	279	−57	46	−451	−192	−567	−119	392	906
Equity Securities	78bmd	1,254	10	285	330	−22	66	35	−130	79	−26	49	451
Debt Securities	78bnd	217	−6	−24	−51	−35	−20	−486	−62	−646	−93	343	455
Financial Derivatives Assets	78bwd	....	....	....	....	....	....	....	....	....	....		
Financial Derivatives Liabilities	78bxd	....	....	....	....	....	....	....	....	....	....		
Other Investment Assets	78bhd	−283	−196	−164	−21	44	−523	−437	53	−64	−542	−1,339	146
Monetary Authorities	78bod	....	....	....	....	....	....	....	....	....	—	—	—
General Government	78bpd	−19	6	116	96	247	−358	−15	44	−5	19	−1	2
Banks	78bqd	−108	−116	8	−40	172	−25	−18	−17	−6	−247	−984	471
Other Sectors	78brd	−157	−85	−288	−77	−375	−140	−404	26	−53	−314	−354	−327
Other Investment Liab., n.i.e	78bid	1,369	1,919	2,484	1,323	−2,316	−2,398	−2,508	−602	−948	−1,603	−1,934	907
Monetary Authorities	78bsd	−282	−50	474	−71	91	−262	−168	−13	−254		−15	8
General Government	78btd	1,132	1,034	700	1,878	−795	2	−729	−37	−162	−1,571	−1,335	662
Banks	78bud	313	613	310	−1,044	−663	−1,292	−1,160	−14	−81	29	22	76
Other Sectors	78bvd	205	321	1,000	559	−949	−846	−451	−538	−451	−61	−606	161
Net Errors and Omissions	78cad	178	−304	160	−72	1,011	768	557	708	974	−52	685	−380
Overall Balance	78cbd	1,343	−1,204	−780	538	−3,110	−2,516	−2,627	2,197	4,084	2,908	−1,351	475
Reserves and Related Items	79dad	−1,343	1,204	780	−538	3,110	2,516	2,627	−2,197	−4,084	−2,908	1,351	−475
Reserve Assets	79dbd	−1,744	1,180	946	−511	222	−842	7	−2,716	−4,525	−3,003	1,728	−176
Use of Fund Credit and Loans	79dcd	401	23	−166	−27	20	391	−101	328	68	−112	−323	−244
Exceptional Financing	79ded	—	—	—	—	2,868	2,966	2,721	192	373	207	−55	−55
International Investment Position							*Millions of US Dollars*						
Assets	79aad	....	....	....	....	....	....	....	....	....	16,048p	16,997p	....
Direct Investment Abroad	79abd	....	....	....	....	....	....	....	....	....	638p	731p	....
Portfolio Investment	79acd	....	....	....	....	....	....	....	....	....	72p	117p	....
Equity Securities	79add	....	....	....	....	....	....	....	....	....	61p	106p	....
Debt Securities	79aed	....	....	....	....	....	....	....	....	....	11p	11p	....
Financial Derivatives	79ald	....	....	....	....	....	....	....	....	....	—p	—p	....
Other Investment	79afd	....	....	....	....	....	....	....	....	....	3,676p	5,324p	....
Monetary Authorities	79agd	....	....	....	....	....	....	....	....	....	....	....	
General Government	79ahd	....	....	....	....	....	....	....	....	....	....	....	
Banks	79aid	....	....	....	....	....	....	....	....	....	....	....	
Other Sectors	79ajd	....	....	....	....	....	....	....	....	....	....	....	
Reserve Assets	79akd	....	....	....	....	....	....	....	....	....	11,662p	10,825p	....
Liabilities	79lad	....	....	....	....	....	....	....	....	....	44,304p	46,026p	....
Dir. Invest. in Rep. Economy	79lbd	....	....	....	....	....	....	....	....	....	7,083p	8,218p	....
Portfolio Investment	79lcd	....	....	....	....	....	....	....	....	....	1,400p	1,805p	....
Equity Securities	79ldd	....	....	....	....	....	....	....	....	....	435p	638p	....
Debt Securities	79led	....	....	....	....	....	....	....	....	....	965p	1,167p	....
Financial Derivatives	79lld	....	....	....	....	....	....	....	....	....	—p	—p	....
Other Investment	79lfd	....	....	....	....	....	....	....	....	....	35,821p	36,003p	....
Monetary Authorities	79lgd	....	....	....	....	....	....	....	....	....	....	....	
General Government	79lhd	....	....	....	....	....	....	....	....	....	....	....	
Banks	79lid	....	....	....	....	....	....	....	....	....	....	....	
Other Sectors	79ljd	....	....	....	....	....	....	....	....	....	....	....	

Pakistan 564

		1994	1995	1996	1997	1998	1999	2000	2001	2002	2003	2004	2005
Government Finance						*Millions of Rupees: Year Ending June 30*							
Deficit (-) or Surplus.........................	80	−113,462	−123,742	−169,477	−189,788	−171,925	−202,024	−172,117	−160,994	−176,274p	−132,156	−97,906	−248,865
Revenue............................	81	273,238	321,323	370,510	384,263	433,636	464,372	531,300	535,091	619,069p	768,662	815,452	844,873
Grants Received............................	81z	5,665	5,513	4,804	—	—	—	37,991	46,779	91,136p	35,841	17,058	18,563
Expenditure............................	82	362,891	425,418	515,219	547,768	584,624	627,147	725,642	739,662	837,396p	882,969	901,244	1,071,616
Lending Minus Repayments...........	83	29,474	25,160	29,572	26,283	20,937	39,249	15,766	3,202	49,083p	53,690	29,172	40,685
Financing													
Domestic............................	84a	78,040	82,235	128,717	142,159	129,295	91,750	143,408	85,878	142,272p	86,167	138,577	206,296
Foreign............................	85a	35,422	41,507	40,760	47,629	42,630	110,274	28,709	75,116	34,002p	45,989	−40,671	42,569
Debt............................	88	....	....	....	....	2,117,616	....	2,832,571	....	....	2,887,134	....	....
Domestic............................	88a	....	....	....	....	1,183,232	....	1,659,121	....	....	1,858,406	....	....
Foreign............................	89a	....	....	....	....	934,384	....	1,173,450	....	....	1,028,728	....	....
National Accounts						*Billions of Rupees: Year Ending June 30*							
Househ.Cons.Expend.,incl.NPISHs....	96f	1,109.90	1,351.40	1,545.20	1,818.20	1,929.70	2,224.00	2,851.35	3,163.87	3,278.91	3,548.16	4,052.90	5,235.38
Government Consumption Expend...	91f	189.10	219.12	268.10	288.81	301.61	304.40	330.69	327.56	388.45	428.69	462.46	512.93
Gross Fixed Capital Formation.........	93e	280.50	317.80	368.10	396.90	402.80	409.40	607.41	659.33	680.37	736.43	864.70	999.31
Changes in Inventories....................	93i	24.60	28.20	34.34	38.28	71.40	48.00	51.70	56.20	58.00	80.63	94.29	103.30
Exports of Goods and Services.........	90c	254.18	311.80	358.37	390.52	441.41	451.10	514.28	617.15	677.86	815.16	883.70	1,001.01
Imports of Goods and Services (-).....	98c	297.30	362.41	454.29	504.37	469.31	498.50	561.99	661.46	681.88	786.22	825.40	1,304.33
Gross Domestic Product (GDP)........	99b	1,561.10	1,865.90	2,120.20	2,428.30	2,677.70	2,938.40	3,793.44	4,162.65	4,401.70	4,822.84	5,532.66	6,547.59
Net Primary Income from Abroad.....	98.n	4.00	14.04	−7.14	−19.35	−24.36	−25.55	−47.96	−54.48	23.67	151.81	124.48	125.22
Gross National Income (GNI)...........	99a	1,565.10	1,880.00	2,113.00	2,409.00	2,653.30	2,912.80	3,745.48	4,108.17	4,425.36	4,974.65	5,657.14	6,672.81
Consumption of Fixed Capital.........	99cf	100.10	119.40	136.20	159.20	180.70	188.50	317.25	342.91	366.76	391.02	489.17	557.44
GDP Volume 1981 Prices................	99b.p	570.86	600.19	630.15	629.55	645.61	669.24	697.75	....	....	....	....	....
GDP Volume 2000 Prices..............	99b.p	....	....	....	....	....	....	3,793.44	3,863.99	3,988.38	4,185.82	4,453.09	4,799.72
GDP Volume (2000=100)..............	99bvp	81.8	86.0	90.3	90.2	92.5	95.9	† 100.0	101.9	105.1	110.3	117.4	126.5
GDP Deflator (2000=100)...............	99bip	50.3	57.2	61.9	70.9	76.3	80.8	100.0	107.7	110.4	115.2	124.2	136.4
						Millions: Midyear Estimates							
Population............................	99z	123.10	126.08	129.25	132.58	† 136.00	139.38	142.65	145.77	148.79	151.77	154.79	157.94

		1994	1995	1996	1997	1998	1999	2000	2001	2002	2003	2004	2005
Exchange Rates						*Balboas per SDR: End of Period*							
Official Rate	aa	1.4599	1.4865	1.4380	1.3493	1.4080	1.3725	1.3029	1.2567	1.3595	1.4860	1.5530	1.4293
						Balboas per US Dollar: End of Period							
Official Rate	ae	1.0000	1.0000	1.0000	1.0000	1.0000	1.0000	1.0000	1.0000	1.0000	1.0000	1.0000	1.0000
Fund Position						*Millions of SDRs: End of Period*							
Quota	2f.s	149.6	149.6	149.6	149.6	149.6	206.6	206.6	206.6	206.6	206.6	206.6	206.6
SDRs	1b.s	—	.6	—	.4	.1	1.2	.3	1.1	.8	.6	.6	.8
Reserve Position in the Fund	1c.s	11.9	11.9	11.9	11.9	11.9	11.9	11.9	11.9	11.9	11.9	11.9	11.9
Total Fund Cred.&Loans Outstg	2tl	91.3	74.4	91.0	105.4	125.5	108.3	69.1	42.9	36.7	30.0	23.3	16.7
International Liquidity					*Millions of US Dollars Unless Otherwise Indicated: End of Period*								
Total Reserves minus Gold	1l.d	704.3	781.4	866.5	1,147.8	954.5	822.9	722.6	1,091.8	1,182.8	1,011.0	630.6	1,210.5
SDRs	1b.d	—	.8	—	.5	.1	1.6	.3	1.4	1.1	.8	.9	1.1
Reserve Position in the Fund	1c.d	17.3	17.6	17.1	16.0	16.7	16.3	15.5	14.9	16.1	17.6	18.4	17.0
Foreign Exchange	1d.d	686.9	762.9	849.4	1,131.3	937.7	805.0	706.8	1,075.5	1,165.6	992.5	611.4	1,192.5
Gold (National Valuation)	1and	—	—	—	—	—	—	—	—	—	—	—	—
Monetary Authorities: Other Liab	4..d	292	343	158	149	123	118	108	104	90	74	70	59
Deposit Money Banks: Assets	7a.d	16,617	15,664	15,484	16,595	13,209	12,362	12,620	12,521	10,061	9,870	11,805	12,050
Liabilities	7b.d	14,846	13,930	13,954	14,825	11,745	11,845	11,776	12,081	9,568	8,415	9,761	10,513
Monetary Authorities						*Millions of Balboas: End of Period*							
Foreign Assets	11	704.3	781.4	866.5	1,147.8	954.5	822.9	722.6	1,091.8	1,182.8	1,011.0	630.6	1,210.5
Claims on Central Government	12a	1,014.0	945.6	1,280.9	1,080.7	1,099.7	1,047.3	839.2	791.9	806.6	759.3	1,087.0	1,057.1
Claims on Official Entities	12bx												
Claims on Private Sector	12d	300.6	318.8	301.0	292.7	403.2	583.8	747.8	976.0	1,118.9	1,228.3	1,304.7	1,220.8
Claims on Deposit Money Banks	12e	732.8	948.8	615.4	765.2	949.4	999.8	908.6	607.1	264.2	103.6	72.2	120.1
Bankers Deposits	14c	167.4	172.7	266.0	252.7	272.6	284.1	301.8	280.0	276.6	278.2	285.4	322.0
Demand Deposits	14d	75.4	77.0	83.0	105.8	97.8	80.6	80.7	104.0	99.5	96.7	106.0	119.7
Time, Savings,& Fgn.Currency Dep	15	192.5	205.0	227.2	240.8	283.4	296.5	367.4	474.0	594.0	619.1	612.9	626.7
Foreign Liabilities	16c	425.0	453.7	289.0	291.7	299.6	266.5	198.4	157.5	140.3	118.2	106.4	82.6
Central Government Deposits	16d	1,716.2	1,857.8	1,871.5	2,025.2	2,039.7	2,094.5	1,883.8	2,061.0	1,918.7	1,664.0	1,512.6	1,943.1
Capital Accounts	17a	228.3	297.7	424.9	471.5	534.3	536.1	534.3	533.1	535.8	539.1	540.9	555.3
Other Items (Net)	17r	−53.2	−69.4	−97.8	−101.4	−130.1	−104.5	−148.2	−142.8	−192.3	−213.1	−69.7	−41.0
Deposit Money Banks						*Millions of Balboas: End of Period*							
Foreign Assets	21	16,616.6	15,663.9	15,483.8	16,595.2	13,208.7	12,362.1	12,620.5	12,521.1	10,061.4	9,870.6	11,804.7	12,050.0
Claims on Central Government	22a	74.3	62.3	79.4	73.2	86.2	143.0	160.9	135.9	269.1	371.0	367.0	338.0
Claims on Private Sector	22d	5,118.6	5,852.4	6,347.6	7,294.0	9,010.2	10,507.1	11,092.3	11,842.8	10,881.9	10,645.0	11,220.0	12,968.0
Demand Deposits	24	728.6	737.7	758.3	889.7	1,027.5	1,062.2	1,095.0	1,193.0	1,224.0	1,360.0	1,508.0	1,792.0
Time and Savings Deposits	25	3,845.5	4,204.2	4,476.5	5,138.6	5,795.3	6,376.7	7,054.9	7,653.6	7,478.0	7,769.0	8,448.9	9,022.0
Foreign Liabilities	26c	14,845.9	13,929.8	13,954.3	14,825.0	11,744.7	11,844.5	11,775.8	12,081.2	9,568.0	8,415.0	9,760.6	10,513.0
Capital Accounts	27a	1,321.3	1,431.8	1,660.8	1,945.1	2,171.5	2,257.8	2,551.9	2,561.3	2,356.0	2,745.0	3,319.0	3,537.0
Other Items (Net)	27r	1,068.2	1,275.1	1,060.9	1,164.1	1,566.1	1,471.0	1,396.1	1,010.7	586.4	597.0	355.2	492.0
Monetary Survey						*Millions of Balboas: End of Period*							
Foreign Assets (Net)	31n	2,050.0	2,061.7	2,107.0	2,626.3	2,118.9	1,074.0	1,368.9	1,374.1	1,535.9	2,347.8	2,568.3	2,664.9
Domestic Credit	32	4,791.3	5,321.3	6,137.3	6,715.5	8,559.6	10,186.7	10,956.4	11,685.6	11,157.9	11,339.6	12,466.1	13,640.7
Claims on Central Govt. (Net)	32an	−627.9	−849.9	−511.3	−871.2	−853.8	−904.2	−883.6	−1,133.2	−842.9	−533.7	−58.6	−548.0
Claims on Private Sector	32d	5,419.2	6,171.2	6,648.6	7,586.7	9,413.4	11,090.9	11,840.1	12,818.8	12,000.8	11,873.3	12,524.7	14,188.8
Deposit Money	34	804.1	814.7	841.3	995.5	1,125.2	1,142.7	1,175.8	1,296.9	1,323.5	1,456.7	1,614.0	1,911.7
Quasi-Money	35	4,038.0	4,409.2	4,703.7	5,379.4	6,078.7	6,673.2	7,422.3	8,127.6	8,072.0	8,388.1	9,061.8	9,648.7
Capital Accounts	37a	1,549.6	1,729.6	2,085.7	2,416.6	2,715.4	2,794.0	3,086.2	3,094.4	2,891.8	3,284.1	3,859.9	4,092.3
Other Items (Net)	37r	449.6	429.6	613.7	550.3	759.1	650.8	641.1	540.7	406.5	558.4	498.7	652.9
Money plus Quasi-Money	35l	4,842.1	5,223.9	5,544.9	6,374.9	7,203.9	7,815.9	8,598.0	9,424.6	9,395.6	9,844.9	10,675.8	11,560.4
Interest Rates						*Percent Per Annum*							
Money Market Rate	60b	....	....	....	....	....	....	....	....	2.22	1.50	1.90	3.13
Savings Rate	60k	....	....	....	....	....	....	....	2.83	2.23	1.55	1.36	1.66
Deposit Rate	60l	6.11	7.18	7.20	7.03	6.76	6.92	7.07	6.83	4.97	3.98	2.23	2.70
Lending Rate	60p	10.15	11.10	10.62	10.63	10.82	10.05	† 10.48	10.97	10.58	9.93	8.82	8.67
Prices, Production and Labor						*Index Numbers (2000=100): Period Averages*							
Wholesale Prices	63	90.7	93.4	95.3	93.2	89.6	92.0	100.0	96.8	93.9	95.5	99.7	105.3
Consumer Prices	64	93.4	94.3	95.5	96.8	97.3	98.5	100.0	100.3	† 101.3	101.4	101.8	105.1
Manufacturing Production (1995)	66ey	99.3	100.0	99.9	105.6	109.8	105.3	....	....	....	....	....	....
						Number in Thousands: Period Averages							
Labor Force	67d	967	1,008	....	1,049	1,049	1,089	....	....	1,222	1,251	1,285	....
Employment	67e	832	867	867	909	936	961	940	984	1,050	1,081	1,127	....
Unemployment	67c	135	141	145	140	147	128	147	170	172	170	158	....
Unemployment Rate (%)	67r	14.0	14.0	14.3	13.4	13.6	11.8	13.5	14.7	14.1	13.6	12.3	....
Intl. Transactions & Positions						*Millions of Balboas*							
Exports	70	583.3	625.2	....	722.8	784.1	822.1	859.5	910.5	846.4	864.2	943.7	1,080.0
Imports, c.i.f.	71	2,404.1	2,510.7	2,779.9	3,002.0	3,398.3	3,515.8	3,378.7	2,963.5	2,982.0	3,086.1	3,594.2	4,180.0
Imports, f.o.b.	71.v	2,177.5	2,280.2	2,548.1	2,738.5	2,806.4	3,214.7	3,097.7	2,714.5	....	....	....	....
						2000=100							
Volume of Exports	72	....	....	....	....	133.6	107.1	100.0	....	81.0	84.5	83.3	....

		1994	1995	1996	1997	1998	1999	2000	2001	2002	2003	2004	2005
Balance of Payments						*Millions of US Dollars: Minus Sign Indicates Debit*							
Current Account, n.i.e.	78ald	15.9	−470.6	−200.6	−506.7	−1,016.0	−1,158.8	−672.5	−170.3	−95.5	−502.7	−1,127.3	−817.7
Goods: Exports f.o.b.	78aad	6,044.8	6,090.9	5,822.9	6,669.7	6,331.8	5,288.1	5,838.5	5,992.4	5,314.7	5,071.9	6,133.4	7,187.8
Goods: Imports f.o.b.	78abd	−6,294.9	−6,679.8	−6,467.0	−7,354.9	−7,627.3	−6,628.1	−6,981.4	−6,688.6	−6,349.8	−6,274.2	−7,721.7	−8,545.8
Trade Balance	78acd	−250.1	−588.9	−644.1	−685.2	−1,295.5	−1,340.0	−1,142.9	−696.2	−1,035.1	−1,202.3	−1,588.3	−1,358.0
Services: Credit	78add	1,403.7	1,519.4	1,592.0	1,720.7	1,891.5	1,847.5	1,994.4	1,992.8	2,277.9	2,500.8	2,725.8	3,126.5
Services: Debit	78aed	−1,064.3	−1,087.8	−1,034.0	−1,293.2	−1,253.3	−1,146.3	−1,140.8	−1,102.9	−1,309.8	−1,305.7	−1,450.4	−1,693.5
Balance on Goods & Services	78afd	89.3	−157.3	−86.1	−257.7	−657.3	−638.8	−289.3	193.7	−67.0	−7.2	−312.9	75.0
Income: Credit	78agd	1,202.9	1,644.1	1,422.1	1,436.0	1,679.3	1,500.5	1,575.3	1,384.0	953.2	783.1	786.0	1,048.3
Income: Debit	78ahd	−1,425.2	−2,110.0	−1,671.3	−1,835.6	−2,196.6	−2,191.6	−2,135.5	−1,974.1	−1,225.5	−1,525.0	−1,828.4	−2,184.4
Balance on Gds, Serv. & Inc.	78aid	−133.0	−623.2	−335.3	−657.3	−1,174.6	−1,329.9	−849.5	−396.4	−339.3	−749.1	−1,355.3	−1,061.1
Current Transfers, n.i.e.: Credit	78ajd	185.5	184.1	167.7	185.2	195.2	202.7	208.7	277.9	298.8	310.6	323.3	343.3
Current Transfers: Debit	78akd	−36.6	−31.5	−33.0	−34.6	−36.6	−31.6	−31.7	−51.8	−55.0	−64.2	−95.3	−99.9
Capital Account, n.i.e.	78bcd	....	8.5	2.5	72.7	50.9	3.0	1.7	1.6	—	—	—	—
Capital Account, n.i.e.: Credit	78bad	....	8.5	2.5	72.7	50.9	3.0	1.7	1.6	—	—	—	—
Capital Account: Debit	78bbd	....	....	....	....	—	—	—	—	—	—	—	—
Financial Account, n.i.e.	78bjd	−288.2	115.6	561.2	972.3	1,249.2	1,836.9	331.8	1,301.0	194.3	−13.5	407.5	1,862.7
Direct Investment Abroad	78bdd	....	....	....	....	—	—	—	—	—	—	—	—
Dir. Invest. in Rep. Econ., n.i.e.	78bed	401.5	223.0	415.5	1,299.3	1,203.1	755.6	623.9	467.1	98.6	770.8	1,012.3	1,027.0
Portfolio Investment Assets	78bfd	−48.4	318.5	487.8	−1,036.5	431.7	−550.2	−93.0	−752.7	−11.9	−30.6	−605.2	−1,050.1
Equity Securities	78bkd	....	.2	−10.2	−.8	−5.1	−28.7	2.0	−1.2	3.0	3.0	−1.7	32.4
Debt Securities	78bld	−48.4	318.3	498.0	−1,035.7	436.8	−521.5	−95.0	−751.5	−14.9	−33.6	−603.5	−1,082.5
Portfolio Investment Liab., n.i.e.	78bgd	−.4	−.3	−67.1	−80.3	209.2	239.5	163.7	727.1	102.2	139.6	775.9	402.0
Equity Securities	78bmd	.4	.2	−.1	−.1	—	—	—	—	—	—	—	—
Debt Securities	78bnd	−.8	−.5	−67.0	−80.2	209.2	239.5	163.7	727.1	102.2	139.6	775.9	402.0
Financial Derivatives Assets	78bwd	....	....	....	....	—	—	—	—	—	—	—	—
Financial Derivatives Liabilities	78bxd	....	....	....	....	—	—	—	—	—	—	—	—
Other Investment Assets	78bhd	−5,277.7	−371.3	406.2	−478.7	772.8	1,991.8	489.3	818.4	3,270.4	441.5	−1,489.3	−485.7
Monetary Authorities	78bod	....	....	....	....	—	—	−5.2	5.2	—	—	—	—
General Government	78bpd	....	−1.0	−38.2	−2.3	−263.3	266.6	−4.0	−2.1	−.9	32.1	−598.5	496.7
Banks	78bqd	−5,254.4	−176.3	533.1	−276.1	1,284.6	1,968.7	185.4	1,016.2	3,294.5	529.2	−652.7	−315.3
Other Sectors	78brd	−23.3	−194.0	−88.7	−200.3	−248.5	−238.3	302.7	−195.7	−23.2	−119.8	−238.1	−667.1
Other Investment Liab., n.i.e.	78bid	4,636.8	−54.3	−681.2	1,268.5	−1,367.6	−599.8	−852.1	41.1	−3,265.0	−1,334.8	713.8	1,969.5
Monetary Authorities	78bsd	−1.3	54.6	−1.7	6.8	−1.0	−.7	−6.4	3.7	−.9	1.6	—	—
General Government	78btd	−198.8	−36.1	−50.5	130.4	85.6	33.7	−2.6	3.5	46.1	10.2	−37.0	−54.2
Banks	78bud	4,915.5	−122.8	−793.7	1,033.2	−1,446.8	−550.8	−425.5	−3.3	−3,311.7	−1,349.3	701.9	1,893.9
Other Sectors	78bvd	−78.6	50.0	164.7	98.1	−5.4	−82.0	−417.6	37.2	1.5	2.7	48.9	129.8
Net Errors and Omissions	78cad	−89.5	15.2	−96.3	−195.0	−389.1	−490.1	262.5	−498.6	45.2	247.6	323.6	−370.2
Overall Balance	78cbd	−361.8	−331.3	266.8	343.3	−105.0	191.0	−76.5	633.7	144.0	−268.6	−396.1	674.8
Reserves and Related Items	79dad	361.8	331.3	−266.8	−343.3	105.0	−191.0	76.5	−633.7	−144.0	268.6	396.1	−674.8
Reserve Assets	79dbd	−105.7	−77.7	−297.7	−611.1	19.8	−184.5	108.1	−623.3	−135.9	268.2	397.0	−521.4
Use of Fund Credit and Loans	79dcd	12.5	−25.9	24.2	19.6	27.3	−23.5	−51.7	−33.3	−8.1	−9.5	−10.0	−9.7
Exceptional Financing	79ded	454.9	434.9	6.8	248.2	57.9	17.0	20.1	22.9	—	10.0	9.1	−143.7
International Investment Position						*Millions of US Dollars*							
Assets	79aad	....	25,275.7	24,677.0	26,871.0	25,636.9	24,379.8	23,880.9	24,395.3	21,273.9	20,593.5	22,289.1	24,346.2
Direct Investment Abroad	79abd	....	—	—	—	—	—	—	—	—	—	—	—
Portfolio Investment	79acd	....	1,889.4	1,401.6	2,438.1	2,006.4	2,556.6	2,649.6	3,373.0	3,384.8	3,413.6	4,018.8	5,068.9
Equity Securities	79add	....	7.6	17.8	18.6	23.7	52.4	50.4	51.6	48.6	45.6	47.3	14.9
Debt Securities	79aed	....	1,881.8	1,383.8	2,419.5	1,982.7	2,504.2	2,599.2	3,321.4	3,336.2	3,368.0	3,971.5	5,054.0
Financial Derivatives	79ald	....	—	—	—	—	—	—	—	—	—	—	—
Other Investment	79afd	....	22,605.0	22,196.8	22,675.5	21,892.3	19,901.0	19,418.2	18,586.4	15,316.0	14,873.4	16,360.0	16,845.7
Monetary Authorities	79agd	....	—	—	—	—	—	5.2	—	—	—	—	—
General Government	79ahd	....	27.7	63.9	66.2	329.5	62.9	66.9	69.0	69.9	36.7	635.2	138.5
Banks	79aid	....	20,768.8	20,235.7	20,511.8	19,227.2	17,258.5	17,073.1	16,043.5	12,749.0	12,219.8	12,869.8	13,185.1
Other Sectors	79ajd	....	1,808.5	1,897.2	2,097.5	2,335.6	2,574.4	2,278.2	2,473.9	2,497.1	2,616.9	2,855.0	3,522.1
Reserve Assets	79akd	....	781.3	1,078.6	1,757.4	1,738.2	1,922.2	1,813.1	2,435.9	2,573.2	2,306.5	1,910.3	2,431.6
Liabilities	79lad	....	31,056.1	30,081.7	32,548.8	32,658.1	33,000.0	32,300.8	33,502.2	30,382.1	29,759.7	32,277.1	35,480.8
Dir. Invest. in Rep. Economy	79lbd	....	3,244.6	3,660.1	4,959.4	6,260.1	7,015.6	6,774.9	7,314.3	7,412.9	8,183.7	9,196.0	10,223.0
Portfolio Investement	79lcd	....	432.7	3,593.9	3,528.5	3,733.8	3,948.2	4,097.6	4,821.4	4,833.7	4,956.8	5,702.8	5,961.1
Equity Securities	79ldd	....	.1	—	—	—	—	—	—	—	—	—	—
Debt Securities	79led	....	432.6	3,593.9	3,528.5	3,733.8	3,948.2	4,097.6	4,821.4	4,833.7	4,956.8	5,702.8	5,961.1
Financial Derivatives	79lld	....	....	....	....	—	—	—	—	—	—	—	—
Other Investment	79lfd	....	27,378.8	22,827.7	24,060.9	22,664.2	22,036.8	21,428.3	21,366.5	18,135.5	16,619.2	17,378.3	19,296.7
Monetary Authorities	79lgd	....	271.5	290.1	309.9	343.5	314.7	246.3	213.9	208.9	205.3	196.9	184.5
General Government	79lhd	....	4,637.4	1,086.8	1,178.0	1,339.3	1,398.1	1,353.6	1,335.1	1,417.2	1,435.3	1,442.9	1,351.6
Banks	79lid	....	20,710.4	19,916.7	20,949.9	19,456.3	18,939.8	18,520.3	18,470.0	15,158.3	13,624.0	14,332.0	16,225.9
Other Sectors	79ljd	....	1,759.5	1,534.1	1,623.1	1,525.1	1,384.2	1,308.1	1,347.5	1,351.0	1,354.7	1,406.5	1,534.7
Government Finance						*Millions of Balboas: Year Ending December 31*							
Deficit (-) or Surplus	80	146.0	230.5	−60.9	17.9	−64.2	34.4	30.2	....	....	....	....	....
Revenue	81	2,010.5	2,065.1	2,140.3	2,202.8	2,331.2	2,664.5	2,688.4	....	....	....	....	....
Grants Received	81z	15.5	8.5	4.6	63.5	72.3	6.8	17.8	....	....	....	....	....
Expenditure	82	1,958.7	1,953.3	2,255.3	2,341.3	2,606.8	2,650.9	2,803.9	....	....	....	....	....
Lending Minus Repayments	83	−78.7	−110.2	−49.5	−92.9	−139.1	−14.0	−127.9	....	....	....	....	....
Financing													
Total Financing	84	−146.0	−230.5	60.9	−17.9	64.2	−34.4	−30.2	....	....	....	....	....
Domestic	84a	−135.2	−253.2	3.7	−133.6	−297.9	−237.2	−200.7	....	....	....	....	....
Foreign	85a	−10.8	22.7	57.2	115.7	362.1	202.8	170.5	....	....	....	....	....
Debt: Domestic	88a	1,805.6	1,681.4	1,794.2	1,737.5	1,737.6	2,108.8	2,090.4	2,089.0	2,122.1	2,094.3	2,683.9	....
Debt: Foreign	89a	2,812.9	3,001.5	4,542.2	4,659.6	5,042.5	5,457.6	5,552.3	6,243.3	6,298.0	6,420.8	7,127.9	....

Panama 283

		1994	1995	1996	1997	1998	1999	2000	2001	2002	2003	2004	2005
National Accounts							*Millions of Balboas*						
Househ.Cons.Expend.,incl.NPISHs....	96f	4,150.7	4,090.0	5,456.1	5,790.3	6,781.3	7,146.0	6,962.2	7,276.3	7,885.2	8,015.7	9,061.0	....
Government Consumption Expend...	91f	1,144.8	1,194.1	1,256.8	1,260.8	1,386.9	1,492.4	1,532.9	1,646.1	1,819.3	1,807.0	1,929.7	....
Gross Fixed Capital Formation..........	93e	1,828.8	2,057.9	1,878.4	2,021.3	2,441.4	2,556.5	2,461.9	1,794.2	1,664.8	2,207.3	2,443.1	....
Changes in Inventories...................	93i	244.8	336.3	613.9	567.9	533.7	398.6	343.2	288.3	268.1	249.4	301.8	....
Exports of Goods and Services..........	90c	7,711.6	7,979.4	7,777.6	9,086.2	8,656.1	7,623.0	8,433.6	8,586.5	8,278.9	8,225.2	9,627.8	....
Imports of Goods and Services (-).....	98c	7,346.8	7,751.6	7,660.7	8,642.5	8,866.9	7,760.2	8,113.3	7,783.9	7,643.9	7,571.4	9,159.1	....
Gross Domestic Product (GDP).........	99b	8,469.2	8,657.8	9,322.1	10,084.0	10,932.5	11,456.3	11,620.5	11,807.5	12,272.4	12,933.2	14,204.2	....
Net Primary Income from Abroad.....	98.n	−272.3	−421.5	−578.1	−729.5	−818.9	−990.7	−838.6	−910.1	−565.7	−969.7	−1,286.0	....
Gross National Income (GNI)............	99a	7,461.6	7,484.6	8,744.0	9,354.5	10,113.6	10,465.6	10,781.9	10,897.4	11,706.7	11,963.5	12,918.2	....
Consumption of Fixed Capital..........	99cf	533.3	558.9	639.3	790.4	814.4	915.4	928.4	958.2	981.7	992.6	1,039.6	....
GDP Volume 1996 Prices................	99b.p	8,911.2	9,067.3	9,322.1	9,924.4	10,653.0	11,070.3	11,370.9	11,436.2	11,691.1	12,182.8	13,103.8	13,939.5
GDP Volume (2000=100)...............	99bvp	78.4	79.7	82.0	87.3	93.7	97.4	100.0	100.6	102.8	107.1	115.2	122.6
GDP Deflator (2000=100)...............	99bip	93.0	93.4	97.9	99.4	100.4	101.3	100.0	101.0	102.7	103.9	106.1	....
							Millions: Midyear Estimates						
Population..............................	99z	2.62	2.67	2.73	2.78	2.84	2.89	2.95	3.01	3.06	3.12	3.18	3.23

Papua New Guinea 853

		1994	1995	1996	1997	1998	1999	2000	2001	2002	2003	2004	2005
Exchange Rates						*SDRs per Kina: End of Period*							
Market Rate.............................	ac	.5812	.5039	.5164	.4232	.3388	.2703	.2498	.2115	.1830	.2019	.2061	.2260
					US Dollars per Kina: End of Period (ag) Period Average (rh)								
Market Rate.............................	ag	.8485	.7490	.7425	.5710	.4770	.3710	.3255	.2658	.2488	.3000	.3200	.3230
Market Rate.............................	rh	.9950	.7835	.7588	.6975	.4859	.3939	.3617	.2964	.2573	.2814	.3104	.3224
					Index Numbers (2000=100): Period Averages								
Market Rate.............................	ahx	275.1	216.6	209.8	192.8	134.3	108.9	100.0	81.9	71.2	77.8	85.8	89.1
Nominal Effective Exchange Rate.....	nec	212.4	161.7	159.4	157.1	127.0	103.2	100.0	88.3	75.6	75.2	77.3	78.8
Real Effective Exchange Rate...........	rec	125.3	106.5	113.9	114.1	100.6	91.4	100.0	93.5	87.4	97.2	99.5	100.6
Fund Position						*Millions of SDRs: End of Period*							
Quota.................................	2f.s	95.30	95.30	95.30	95.30	95.30	131.60	131.60	131.60	131.60	131.60	131.60	131.60
SDRs.................................	1b.s	.07	.47	.04	.06	.04	.53	9.34	6.93	4.46	2.48	.47	.02
Reserve Position in the Fund............	1c.s	.05	.05	.05	.05	.05	.05	.18	.30	.36	.40	.43	.44
Total Fund Cred.&Loans Outstg........	2tl	10.71	33.34	35.34	35.34	32.35	15.68	29.89	85.54	85.54	81.79	41.38	—
International Liquidity				*Millions of US Dollars Unless Otherwise Indicated: Approximately End of Period*									
Total Reserves minus Gold..............	1l.d	96.06	261.35	583.89	362.68	192.88	205.14	286.87	422.65	321.51	494.18	632.56	718.10
SDRs.................................	1b.d	.11	.69	.06	.08	.05	.72	12.17	8.71	6.06	3.68	.73	.03
Reserve Position in the Fund.........	1c.d	.08	.08	.08	.07	.07	.07	.23	.38	.49	.59	.66	.63
Foreign Exchange........................	1d.d	95.88	260.58	583.75	362.53	192.76	204.35	274.46	413.56	314.96	489.90	631.17	717.45
Gold (Million Fine Troy Ounces)........	1ad	.063	.014	.063	.063	.063	.063	.063	.063	.063	.063	.063	.063
Gold (National Valuation)................	1and	2.39	2.11	21.02	16.17	13.31	10.35	9.08	7.42	21.89	25.83	27.55	30.65
Monetary Authorities: Other Liab.....	4..d	84.39	62.28	3.39	2.79	.66	.73	.76	3.73	.11	4.72	.79	.36
Banking Institutions: Assets.............	7a.d	175.61	100.11	119.12	117.38	136.34	103.23	95.83	112.09	153.53	106.67	116.61	212.41
Liabilities....................	7b.d	120.46	41.39	23.07	7.99	54.53	37.44	18.13	13.88	25.99	16.88	21.93	30.98
Monetary Authorities						*Millions of Kina: Last Wednesday of Period*							
Foreign Assets............................	11	112.51	357.55	789.20	666.07	391.06	552.92	909.24	† 1,671.95	1,376.51	1,742.65	2,072.30	2,368.05
Claims on Central Government........	12a	776.65	592.62	587.28	880.81	1,284.96	599.66	163.60	† 128.15	663.39	349.57	104.76	134.51
Claims on State and Local Govts......	12b	....	....	....	....	....	....	....					
Claims on Nonfin.Pub.Enterprises....	12c	—	—	—	—	—	—	—	† —	—	—	—	—
Claims on Private Sector.................	12d	.55	.64	.67	.67	.75	.64	3.35	5.75	† 49.83	50.04	7.10	7.49	9.60
Claims on Banking Institutions.........	12e	282.50	233.80	228.94	216.27	121.10	53.63	53.27	† 187.20	74.99	50.49	24.15	23.85
Claims on Nonbank Financial Insts....	12g	—	—	—	—	—	—	—	† .94	.94	6.45	1.05	1.26
Reserve Money...........................	14	221.65	255.66	488.98	321.12	387.47	671.55	561.51	† 589.98	669.33	668.71	870.76	935.39
of which: Currency Outside Banks..	14a	179.00	194.21	216.40	234.85	278.09	357.49	306.93	† 267.11	362.61	387.90	399.54	445.47
Other Liabs. to Banking Insts.........	14n	—	—	—	—	—	—	—	† 100.96	29.20	128.81	270.28	344.23
Time, Savings,&Fgn.Currency Dep....	15	.50	.50	.50	.50	.50	.50	.50	† 1.05	1.54	1.73	2.57	2.21
Restricted Deposits.......................	16b	....	....	....	....	....	....	....	.07	.09	.10	.10	.11
Liabs. of Central Bank:Securities.......	16ac								† —				
Foreign Liabilities........................	16c	117.88	149.33	73.01	88.39	96.88	59.97	121.95	† 418.46	467.88	420.85	203.31	1.12
Central Government Deposits...........	16d	663.01	623.10	840.32	977.77	916.71	100.24	30.76	† 240.84	113.56	106.10	104.87	646.47
Liab. to Nonbank Financial Insts.......	16j	....	....	....	....	....	....	....	—	—	—	—	—
Capital Accounts...........................	17a	140.20	122.57	122.13	245.05	254.78	261.74	329.89	† 682.65	844.40	792.37	733.88	625.78
Other Items (Net).........................	17r	28.95	33.45	81.15	131.08	141.41	115.55	87.23	† 4.06	39.87	37.60	24.00	−18.04
Banking Institutions						*Millions of Kina: Last Wednesday of Period*							
Reserves.................................	20	40.67	56.20	116.43	67.21	106.03	310.37	250.67	† 315.02	302.21	277.24	463.83	483.80
Claims on Mon.Author.:Securities....	20c	—	—	—	—	—	—	—	† 95.04	—	—	265.53	289.70
Other Claims on Monetary Author....	20n	—	—	—	—	—	—	—	† —	25.58	119.82	—	49.95
Foreign Assets............................	21	206.97	133.66	160.44	205.57	285.83	278.26	294.40	† 421.69	617.09	355.55	364.40	617.63
Claims on Central Government........	22a	446.27	727.57	1,105.13	1,107.80	888.60	791.57	1,065.24	† 1,059.02	1,038.71	1,249.86	1,594.45	2,013.66
Claims on State and Local Govts......	22b	5.95	1.58	1.91	1.29	5.05	5.46	1.05	† .94	2.38	6.04	3.67	1.84
Claims on Nonfin.Pub.Enterprises.....	22c	374.70	329.25	315.00	297.71	202.94	153.06	123.02	† 113.64	127.88	72.85	44.32	79.00
Claims on Private Sector.................	22d	897.99	900.78	908.93	1,223.08	1,577.98	1,554.88	1,668.15	† 1,705.71	1,730.15	1,699.91	1,715.01	2,122.09
Claims on Nonbank Financial Insts....	22g	—	—	—	—	—	—	—	† —				
Demand Deposits.........................	24	433.46	501.18	692.31	752.74	829.35	982.38	1,061.86	† 1,017.10	1,187.28	1,293.13	1,780.95	2,514.15
Time, Savings,& Fgn. Currency Dep..	25	1,049.85	1,192.55	1,410.43	1,659.12	1,620.62	1,638.32	1,758.57	† 2,040.53	2,012.33	1,724.00	1,724.05	2,100.92
Money Market Instruments..............	26aa	....	....	....	....	....	....	....	—	—	—	—	—
Restricted Deposits.......................	26b	....	....	....	....	....	....	....	—	—	—	—	—
Foreign Liabilities........................	26c	141.97	55.26	31.07	14.00	114.33	100.91	55.70	† 52.20	104.45	56.25	68.54	95.91
Central Government Deposits...........	26d	73.13	122.48	167.22	170.65	287.49	211.71	255.06	† 249.19	222.60	240.36	274.67	361.39
Credit from Monetary Authorities.....	26g	282.50	233.80	228.94	216.28	121.10	53.63	53.39	† 46.72	46.63	50.06	23.68	23.42
Liab. to Nonbank Financial Insts.......	26j	....	....	....	....	....	....	....	—	—	—	—	—
Capital Accounts...........................	27a	78.36	92.65	114.78	139.25	212.80	332.05	284.09	† 442.32	488.38	700.21	784.83	942.42
Other Items (Net).........................	27r	−86.72	−48.88	−36.92	−49.39	−119.26	−225.40	−66.14	† −137.02	−217.66	−282.74	−205.50	−340.53
Banking Survey						*Millions of Kina: Last Wednesday of Period*							
Foreign Assets (Net)......................	31n	59.63	286.63	845.56	769.26	465.68	670.29	1,025.98	† 1,622.98	1,421.27	1,621.11	2,164.85	2,928.65
Domestic Credit............................	32	1,765.96	1,806.86	1,911.38	2,363.02	2,755.96	2,796.02	2,740.98	† 2,568.18	3,277.34	3,045.33	3,091.22	3,354.11
Claims on Central Govt. (Net)........	32an	486.77	574.60	684.87	840.19	969.35	1,079.27	943.01	† 697.13	1,365.95	1,252.98	1,319.67	1,140.31
Claims on State and Local Govts....	32b	5.95	1.58	1.91	1.29	5.05	5.46	1.05	† .94	2.38	6.04	3.67	1.84
Claims on Nonfin.Pub.Enterprises...	32c	374.70	329.25	315.00	297.71	202.94	153.06	123.02	† 113.64	127.88	72.85	44.32	79.00
Claims on Private Sector.................	32d	898.54	901.42	909.60	1,223.83	1,578.62	1,558.23	1,673.90	† 1,755.53	1,780.19	1,707.01	1,722.50	2,131.69
Claims on Nonbank Financial Insts.	32g	—	—	—	—	—	—	—	† .94	.94	6.45	1.05	1.26
Money.................................	34	614.48	700.64	1,064.87	1,006.66	1,110.79	1,343.56	1,372.69	† 1,285.91	1,555.33	1,684.77	2,188.19	2,967.59
Quasi-Money...............................	35	1,050.35	1,193.05	1,410.93	1,659.62	1,621.12	1,638.82	1,759.07	† 2,041.57	2,013.87	1,725.73	1,726.62	2,103.13
Money Market Instruments..............	36aa	....	....	....	....	....	....	....	—	—	—	—	—
Liabs. of Central Bank: Securities.....	36ac	—	—	—	—	—	—	—	† —	—	—	—	—
Restricted Deposits.......................	36b	....	....	....	....	....	....	....	—	.07	.09	.10	.10	.11
Liab. to Nonbank Financial Insts.......	36j	....	....	....	....	....	....	....	—	—	—	—	—
Capital Accounts...........................	37a	218.56	215.22	236.91	384.30	467.58	593.78	613.99	† 1,124.97	1,332.78	1,492.58	1,518.71	1,568.19
Other Items (Net).........................	37r	−57.81	−15.42	44.23	81.69	22.15	−109.85	21.22	† −261.36	−203.46	−236.75	−177.53	−356.27
Money plus Quasi-Money...............	35l	1,664.83	1,893.69	2,475.80	2,666.29	2,731.91	2,982.37	3,131.76	† 3,327.48	3,569.19	3,410.50	3,914.80	5,070.72

Papua New Guinea 853

		1994	1995	1996	1997	1998	1999	2000	2001	2002	2003	2004	2005
Money (National Definitions)						*Millions of Kina: Last Wednesday of Period*							
Reserve Money	19mb	219.62	250.40	332.83	302.10	384.20	667.86	557.61	588.40	690.40	785.20	863.30	889.33
M1*	59maa	571.31	645.86	864.89	919.50	1,021.30	1,233.70	1,271.71	1,321.20	1,535.30	1,708.30	2,214.70	2,968.44
M3*	59mca	1,664.71	1,842.24	2,431.56	2,598.20	2,645.80	2,880.00	3,034.68	3,091.30	3,226.00	3,109.80	3,597.80	4,702.92
Interest Rates							*Percent Per Annum*						
Discount Rate (End of Period)	60	6.55	† 18.00	14.86	9.49	17.07	16.66	9.79	11.73	11.71	† 15.50	12.67	9.67
Money Market Rate	60b	....	....	....	....	....	....	9.54	11.05	9.11	13.58	7.79	4.36
Treasury Bill Rate	60c	† 7.82	17.40	14.44	9.94	21.18	22.70	17.00	12.36	10.93	18.69	8.85	3.81
Savings Rate	60k	....	4.00	4.00	3.83	3.94	4.13	4.06	3.88	2.44	2.40	1.63	1.64
Deposit Rate	60l	5.09	† 7.30	7.13	4.13	8.36	8.13	8.46	5.46	3.18	4.38	1.73	.85
Lending Rate	60p	9.16	13.14	13.30	10.45	17.70	18.90	17.54	16.21	13.89	13.36	13.25	11.47
Government Bond Yield	61	....	....	....	....	....	....	....	....	....	....	....	8.00
Prices and Labor						*Index Numbers (2000=100): Period Averages*							
Share Prices (2001=100)	62	....	....	....	....	....	....	100.00	161.90	193.42	227.85	347.48	
Consumer Prices	64	48.7	57.1	63.7	66.3	75.3	86.5	100.0	109.3	122.2	140.2	143.2	145.6
Total Employment	67	96.2	91.7	98.5	98.3	96.1	98.5	† 100.0	98.2	99.7	105.9	105.4	107.5
Intl. Transactions & Positions							*Millions of Kina*						
Exports	70	2,670.4	3,388.3	3,313.6	3,048.8	3,707.7	4,879.4	5,812.7	6,076.6	6,386.7	7,842.3	8,233.0	9,922.0
Imports, c.i.f.	71	1,530.8	1,862.4	2,296.6	2,429.0	2,549.6	3,059.0	3,195.7	3,633.0	4,826.3	4,865.7	5,408.5	5,364.9
Imports, f.o.b.	71.v	1,333.1	1,619.6	1,996.5	2,112.1	2,217.0	2,660.0	2,778.9	3,160.0	4,196.8	4,231.0	4,703.0	4,665.1
							2000=100						
Volume of Exports	72	† 108.3	101.1	95.8	85.4	94.9	102.7	100.0	† 94.4	88.1	104.8	99.1	....
Unit Value of Exports	74	† 31.7	45.5	47.1	50.3	60.5	74.2	100.0	† 108.9	119.7	129.4	146.0	....
Balance of Payments						*Millions of US Dollars: Minus Sign Indicates Debit*							
Current Account, n.i.e.	78ald	402.1	491.9	188.9	−192.2	−28.9	94.7	345.4	282.1	....	....	....	....
Goods: Exports f.o.b.	78aad	2,651.0	2,670.4	2,529.8	2,160.1	1,773.3	1,927.4	2,094.1	1,812.9	....	....	....	....
Goods: Imports f.o.b.	78abd	−1,324.9	−1,262.4	−1,513.3	−1,483.3	−1,078.3	−1,071.4	−998.8	−932.4	....	....	....	....
Trade Balance	78acd	1,326.1	1,408.0	1,016.6	676.8	695.0	856.0	1,095.3	880.5	....	....	....	....
Services: Credit	78add	235.4	321.3	432.2	396.9	318.0	247.5	242.7	285.1	....	....	....	....
Services: Debit	78aed	−608.0	−642.1	−778.5	−923.6	−793.8	−727.9	−772.3	−662.0	....	....	....	....
Balance on Goods & Services	78afd	953.5	1,087.2	670.2	150.1	219.2	375.6	565.7	503.7	....	....	....	....
Income: Credit	78agd	22.4	22.5	32.1	35.1	20.9	18.6	32.0	20.0	....	....	....	....
Income: Debit	78ahd	−423.4	−510.7	−461.2	−344.8	−279.7	−291.1	−242.1	−250.2	....	....	....	....
Balance on Gds, Serv. & Inc.	78aid	552.5	599.1	241.1	−159.5	−39.6	103.1	355.6	273.4	....	....	....	....
Current Transfers, n.i.e.: Credit	78ajd	58.8	66.7	252.1	69.9	82.4	60.3	62.4	75.9	....	....	....	....
Current Transfers: Debit	78akd	−209.3	−173.9	−304.2	−102.6	−71.6	−68.7	−72.7	−67.3	....	....	....	....
Capital Account, n.i.e.	78bcd	—	—	—	—	—	—	—	—	....	....	....	....
Capital Account, n.i.e.: Credit	78bad	19.9	15.7	15.2	13.9	9.7	7.8	7.2	5.9	....	....	....	....
Capital Account: Debit	78bbd	−19.9	−15.7	−15.2	−13.9	−9.7	−7.8	−7.2	−5.9	....	....	....	....
Financial Account, n.i.e.	78bjd	−609.2	−444.7	46.6	8.0	−179.7	16.0	−254.1	−151.9	....	....	....	....
Direct Investment Abroad	78bdd	—	—	—	—	—	—	....	....	....	....	....	....
Dir. Invest. in Rep. Econ., n.i.e.	78bed	57.0	454.6	111.3	28.6	109.6	296.5	95.9	62.5	....	....	....	....
Portfolio Investment Assets	78bfd	−2.1	−48.7	69.9	−25.5	87.0	89.0	−123.8	−72.7	....	....	....	....
Equity Securities	78bkd	—	....	....	....	....	....	....	....	....	....	....	....
Debt Securities	78bld	−2.1	−48.7	69.9	−25.5	87.0	89.0	−123.8	−72.7	....	....	....	....
Portfolio Investment Liab., n.i.e.	78bgd	....	—	—	—	—	—	—	—	....	....	....	....
Equity Securities	78bmd	....	....	....	....	....	....	....	....	....	....	....	....
Debt Securities	78bnd	....	—	—	—	—	—	—	—	....	....	....	....
Financial Derivatives Assets	78bwd	....	....	....	....	....	....	....	....	....	....	....	....
Financial Derivatives Liabilities	78bxd	....	....	....	....	....	....	....	....	....	....	....	....
Other Investment Assets	78bhd	58.8	−283.8	180.0	29.6	−55.0	10.7	−41.0	−66.9	....	....	....	....
Monetary Authorities	78bod	....	....	....	....	....	....	....	....	....	....	....	....
General Government	78bpd	—	....	....	....	....	....	....	....	....	....	....	....
Banks	78bqd	—	....	....	....	....	−2.1	−21.2	−26.7	....	....	....	....
Other Sectors	78brd	58.8	−283.8	180.0	29.6	−55.0	12.8	−19.8	−40.2	....	....	....	....
Other Investment Liab., n.i.e.	78bid	−722.9	−566.8	−314.6	−24.7	−321.2	−380.2	−185.2	−74.7	....	....	....	....
Monetary Authorities	78bsd	....	....	−68.2	—	—	—	—	—	....	....	....	....
General Government	78btd	−102.1	−23.5	10.0	−62.7	−44.2	39.4	.2	49.0	....	....	....	....
Banks	78bud	−26.9	27.4	−34.0	−42.3	16.4	—	—	—	....	....	....	....
Other Sectors	78bvd	−593.9	−570.7	−222.4	80.3	−293.4	−419.6	−185.4	−123.7	....	....	....	....
Net Errors and Omissions	78cad	37.1	−86.6	−33.1	7.3	−12.5	14.3	13.1	−1.6	....	....	....	....
Overall Balance	78cbd	−170.1	−39.5	202.5	−177.0	−221.0	125.0	104.5	128.6	....	....	....	....
Reserves and Related Items	79dad	170.1	39.5	−202.5	177.0	221.0	−125.0	−104.5	−128.6	....	....	....	....
Reserve Assets	79dbd	33.8	−177.4	−329.7	83.7	149.1	−49.7	−127.9	−203.6	....	....	....	....
Use of Fund Credit and Loans	79dcd	−30.6	35.0	2.9	—	−4.2	−22.8	18.1	70.9	....	....	....	....
Exceptional Financing	79ded	166.8	181.9	124.4	93.2	76.1	−52.5	5.3	4.1	....	....	....	....
Government Finance						*Millions of Kina: Year Ending December 31*							
Deficit (-) or Surplus	80	† −136.78	−31.77	35.39	15.41	−137.40	−241.79	−181.40	−132.51	−263.81	....	....	....
Total Revenue and Grants	81y	† 1,443.43	1,692.95	1,896.12	2,024.01	1,991.20	2,216.11	2,865.41	2,836.06	2,666.47	....	....	....
Revenue	81	† 1,278.62	1,499.84	1,730.67	1,711.98	1,686.46	1,750.59	2,459.72	2,724.83	2,618.91	....	....	....
Grants	81z	† 164.81	193.11	165.45	312.03	304.74	465.52	405.69	111.23	47.56	....	....	....
Exp. & Lending Minus Repay.	82z	† 1,580.21	1,724.72	1,860.73	2,008.60	2,128.60	2,457.90	3,046.81	2,968.57	2,930.28	....	....	....
Expenditure	82	1,580.99	1,721.93	1,857.29	2,003.70	2,127.26	2,457.83	3,048.41	2,968.57	2,930.28	....	....	....
Lending Minus Repayments	83	† −.78	2.79	3.44	4.90	1.34	.07	−1.60			....	....	....
Total Financing	80h	† 136.78	31.77	−35.39	−15.40	137.40	241.80	181.40	132.51	263.81	....	....	....
Domestic	84a	† 255.22	75.30	−45.49	57.90	253.72	304.29	1.50	−177.05	519.16	....	....	....
Foreign	85a	† −118.44	−43.53	10.10	−73.30	−116.32	−62.49	179.90	309.56	−255.35	....	....	....
Total Debt by Residence	88	† 2,961.20	3,324.20	3,780.80	4,418.00	5,177.70	5,609.20	5,621.60	7,097.30	8,127.90	....	....	....
Domestic	88a	† 1,424.30	1,605.70	1,969.50	2,251.70	2,473.00	2,021.40	1,783.30	2,115.10	2,530.50	....	....	....
Foreign	89a	† 1,536.90	1,718.50	1,811.30	2,166.30	2,704.70	3,587.80	3,838.30	4,982.20	5,597.40	....	....	....

		1994	1995	1996	1997	1998	1999	2000	2001	2002	2003	2004	2005
National Accounts						*Millions of Kina*							
Househ.Cons.Expend.,incl.NPISHs....	96f	2,558	2,704	3,149	4,288	4,589	4,984	4,343	4,962	7,060	6,515	6,891	....
Government Consumption Expend...	91f	1,029	1,058	1,353	1,364	1,409	1,496	1,613	1,688	1,788	1,917	1,938	....
Gross Fixed Capital Formation..........	93e	1,040	1,210	1,171	1,082	1,091	1,068	1,988	2,200	2,264	2,281	2,294	....
Changes in Inventories....................	93i	142	149	375	409	307	377	144	186	206	222	236	
Exports of Goods and Services..........	90c	2,961	3,781	4,036	3,480	4,217	5,572	6,443	6,792	7,100	8,724	9,130	....
Imports of Goods and Services (-).....	98c	2,199	2,707	3,289	3,543	3,810	4,669	4,794	5,432	6,761	6,790	7,455	....
Gross Domestic Product (GDP).........	99b	5,530	6,195	6,795	7,080	7,804	8,828	9,736	10,396	11,657	12,949	13,861	....
Net Primary Income from Abroad.....	98.n	−247	−208	−308	−310	−343	−360	−391	−408	−415	−424	−435	....
Gross National Income (GNI)............	99a	5,284	5,986	6,487	6,769	7,460	8,468	9,344	9,988	11,242	12,445	12,600	....
Consumption of Fixed Capital..........	99cf	492	566	562	521	536	507	549	642	690	777	827	....
GDP Volume 1998 Prices.................	99b.p	7,733	7,467	7,960	7,455	7,804	7,948	7,750	7,741	7,728	7,953	8,183	....
GDP Volume (2000=100)...............	99bvp	† 99.8	96.3	102.7	96.2	100.7	102.6	100.0	99.9	99.7	102.6	105.6	....
GDP Deflator (2000=100)..............	99bip	56.9	66.0	68.0	75.6	79.6	88.4	100.0	106.9	120.1	129.6	134.8	....
						Millions: Midyear Estimates							
Population..............................	99z	4.57	4.69	4.81	† 4.93	5.05	5.18	5.30	5.42	5.54	5.66	5.77	5.89

Paraguay 288

		1994	1995	1996	1997	1998	1999	2000	2001	2002	2003	2004	2005
Exchange Rates						*Guaranies per SDR: End of Period*							
Market Rate....................aa=.........	wa	2,809.8	2,942.7	3,033.6	3,184.2	3,999.1	4,568.9	4,595.2	5,884.0	9,657.5	9,086.6	9,706.3	8,747.1
					Guaranies per US Dollar: End of Period (we) Period Average (wf)								
Market Rate....................ae=.........	we	1,924.7	1,979.7	2,109.7	2,360.0	2,840.2	3,328.9	3,526.9	4,682.0	7,103.6	6,115.0	6,250.0	6,120.0
Market Rate....................rf=..........	wf	1,904.8	1,963.0	2,056.8	2,177.9	2,726.5	3,119.1	3,486.4	4,105.9	5,716.3	6,424.3	5,974.6	6,178.0
					Index Numbers (2000=100): Period Averages								
Market Rate..................................	ahx	183.0	177.6	169.5	160.1	128.1	112.2	100.0	85.6	62.1	54.5	58.4	56.4
Nominal Effective Exchange Rate.....	nec	131.4	133.6	133.0	132.6	111.0	108.8	100.0	93.3	79.4	69.0	71.4	65.0
Real Effective Exchange Rate...........	rec	102.4	103.5	106.9	109.8	100.2	102.9	100.0	97.1	86.3	80.5	83.7	78.0
Fund Position						*Millions of SDRs: End of Period*							
Quota...	2f.s	72.10	72.10	72.10	72.10	72.10	99.90	99.90	99.90	99.90	99.90	99.90	99.90
SDRs...	1b.s	67.63	70.58	73.30	76.08	79.14	74.81	78.49	81.33	83.25	84.63	86.04	88.21
Reserve Position in the Fund...........	1c.s	14.53	14.53	14.53	14.53	14.53	21.48	21.48	21.48	21.48	21.48	21.48	21.48
Total Fund Cred.&Loans Outstg........	2tl	—	—	—	—	—	—	—	—	—	—	—	—
International Liquidity					*Millions of US Dollars Unless Otherwise Indicated: End of Period*								
Total Reserves minus Gold...............	1l.d	1,030.73	1,092.91	1,049.29	835.68	864.74	978.05	762.83	713.51	629.19	968.86	1,168.05	1,297.09
SDRs..	1b.d	98.73	104.92	105.40	102.65	111.44	102.68	102.26	102.21	113.18	125.75	133.62	126.08
Reserve Position in the Fund..........	1c.d	21.20	21.59	20.89	19.60	20.45	29.48	27.98	26.99	29.20	31.91	33.35	30.69
Foreign Exchange..........................	1d.d	910.80	966.40	923.00	713.42	732.85	845.89	632.58	584.32	486.82	811.19	1,001.07	1,140.32
of which: US Dollars....................	1dxd	583.80	602.40	415.53	521.25	561.87	736.13	525.20	467.98	353.95	674.97	749.50	905.76
Gold (Million Fine Troy Ounces).......	1ad	.035	.035	.035	.035	.035	.035	.035	.035	.035	.035	—	—
Gold (National Valuation)...............	1and	13.40	13.50	12.90	10.10	10.03	10.15	9.60	9.66	12.14	14.51	—	—
Monetary Authorities:Other Assets...	3..d	3.98	3.44	3.44	3.44	7.07	9.84	14.06	12.41	3.25	9.03	7.43	8.80
Other Liab.................	4..d	86.57	85.11	76.47	67.87	60.76	53.37	44.88	93.88	115.11	63.96	80.16	69.30
Deposit Money Banks: Assets...........	7a.d	298.21	502.97	474.74	378.52	416.19	402.43	498.84	447.92	288.26	389.83	383.75	346.86
Liabilities.................	7b.d	124.57	453.01	256.93	304.67	232.03	119.86	105.33	96.63	69.12	46.44	50.41	55.10
Other Banking Insts.: Assets............	7e.d	—	.34	.67	12.91	11.01	9.63	15.76	18.88	4.30	3.64	2.09	3.38
Liabilities...................	7f.d	32.78	—	—	8.54	2.12	.60	2.01	1.79	.72	4.32	3.92	4.89
Monetary Authorities						*Billions of Guaranies: End of Period*							
Foreign Assets...............................	11	2,016.58	† 2,239.16	2,263.63	1,993.00	2,521.04	3,341.31	2,804.01	3,420.08	4,528.71	6,038.97	7,362.96	8,025.11
Claims on Central Government........	12a	1,047.15	† 1,038.99	1,088.06	695.48	928.81	1,113.16	1,063.78	1,477.66	2,240.39	2,159.88	2,256.35	2,260.81
Claims on Local Government...........	12b	.82	† .67	.62	1.06	1.11	1.16	1.21	1.26	1.31	1.36	1.41	1.46
Claims on Nonfin.Pub.Enterprises.....	12c	222.35	† 239.15	268.00	303.76	329.42	358.39	381.19	216.23	283.50	291.82	364.87	485.86
Claims on Private Sector.................	12d	6.58	† 7.24	11.90	14.73	18.41	22.28	25.61	28.05	32.57	34.23	34.07	33.16
Claims on Deposit Money Banks.....	12e	98.07	† 580.74	840.71	528.45	45.40	4.57	7.19	6.64	4.26	1.66	1.60	1.60
Claims on Other Banking Insts.........	12f	15.65	† 21.31	104.20	20.03	33.85	26.94	35.98	44.16	58.07	27.04	—	—
Claims on Nonbank Financial Insts...	12g	—	† 23.14	21.34	8.26	96.05	103.46	113.11	123.08	133.01	142.87	152.21	160.94
Reserve Money...............................	14	1,378.91	† 1,738.50	1,704.98	1,829.88	1,949.68	2,127.14	2,105.35	2,234.23	2,293.74	3,461.11	4,063.10	4,245.30
of which: Currency Outside DMBs..	14a	800.46	† 956.00	961.77	1,122.90	1,264.08	1,398.68	1,327.19	1,377.21	1,451.20	1,814.57	2,116.69	2,528.73
Time & Foreign Currency Deposits....	15	455.51	† 448.56	648.47	635.95	833.43	1,040.74	1,090.23	1,366.33	1,577.06	1,599.30	1,777.26	1,832.88
Liabs. of Central Bank: Securities.....	16ac	35.50	† 201.90	250.79	319.05	381.75	75.88	45.93	284.47	578.50	1,070.96	1,551.75	2,293.25
Restricted Deposits........................	16b	26.47	† 26.01	51.75	54.55	58.21	72.21	80.31	87.29	124.18	131.52	110.90	63.75
Foreign Liabilities..........................	16c	166.62	† 168.94	161.28	158.14	172.57	176.91	159.11	435.14	805.79	388.26	500.19	422.71
Central Government Deposits...........	16d	414.23	† 580.16	572.39	469.51	553.16	1,327.51	813.38	723.61	730.01	1,120.48	1,188.92	1,098.80
Capital Accounts............................	17a	332.20	† 519.10	611.14	2,381.56	1,619.77	2,138.81	2,151.12	2,589.63	4,076.37	2,708.77	2,935.68	2,727.97
Other Items (Net)...........................	17r	597.76	† 467.22	597.65	−2,205.47	−1,594.49	−1,987.93	−2,013.36	−2,403.53	−2,903.84	−1,782.57	−1,954.33	−1,715.72
Deposit Money Banks						*Billions of Guaranies: End of Period*							
Reserves...	20	913.28	† 1,032.56	1,173.75	1,189.09	1,421.92	1,636.09	1,740.62	2,106.19	2,250.36	3,085.37	3,508.21	3,288.00
Claims on Mon.Author.:Securities.....	20c	35.50	† 173.67	238.76	287.18	209.91	60.79	39.94	172.61	324.57	642.36	1,210.28	2,064.79
Foreign Assets...............................	21	573.75	† 998.40	1,001.22	881.95	1,181.98	1,334.07	1,768.39	2,076.09	2,017.85	2,366.29	2,394.57	2,115.83
Claims on Central Government.........	22a	—	† 46.59	98.35	187.73	286.85	454.60	356.87	294.61	534.58	656.78	562.24	435.16
Claims on Local Government...........	22b	.01	† 22.00	1.57	7.07	36.64	5.55	8.98	4.35	.95	1.78	5.85	11.81
Claims on Nonfin.Pub.Enterprises...	22c	1.46	† —	—	—	.79	1.27	—	.02	—	—	—	—
Claims on Private Sector.................	22d	3,164.92	† 3,795.04	4,660.78	5,217.41	5,093.49	5,654.33	5,937.32	6,757.09	6,777.93	5,054.30	5,832.53	6,579.66
Claims on Other Banking Insts.........	22f	11.58	† 15.57	8.99	29.18	20.03	16.63	37.90	29.44	26.52	28.72	44.93	29.76
Claims on Nonbank Financial Insts...	22g	—	† 39.39	25.98	33.45	25.52	40.35	45.80	63.21	3.21	.09	1.23	.32
Demand Deposits...........................	24	499.43	† 594.44	681.90	698.08	678.97	730.19	1,192.53	1,326.51	1,273.39	1,918.52	2,610.19	3,190.63
Time, Savings,& Fgn.Currency Dep...	25	2,663.58	† 3,286.94	3,844.68	4,156.49	4,522.84	5,470.17	5,444.15	6,477.35	6,582.20	6,362.06	6,851.85	6,830.76
Money Market Instruments..............	26aa	—	† 50.16	36.98	49.11	13.11	9.42	39.32	12.13	17.09	9.17	124.55	83.09
Bonds...	26ab	3.76	† 1.94	4.13	5.85	15.72	12.97	14.17	37.05	144.60	30.35	—	—
Restricted Deposits........................	26b	—	† 3.29	15.01	3.03	18.71	23.10	60.16	51.18	92.43	98.49	101.38	73.89
Foreign Liabilities..........................	26c	239.68	† 899.23	541.86	709.87	658.96	397.35	373.41	447.87	483.82	281.87	314.55	336.08
Central Government Deposits...........	26d	432.74	† 324.39	886.07	758.05	721.32	728.42	777.54	895.15	919.28	901.47	1,080.59	1,251.51
Credit from Monetary Authorities.....	26g	94.01	† 156.36	346.59	321.61	33.27	68.68	86.49	89.30	131.15	78.52	37.98	35.83
Liabilities to Other Banking Insts......	26i	.01	† 19.24	31.45	31.02	50.11	68.47	102.10	235.49	215.34	396.44	414.78	422.45
Capital Accounts............................	27a	719.50	† 1,020.67	1,347.22	1,627.11	1,609.57	1,715.53	1,890.09	2,132.39	2,372.02	2,147.99	2,270.17	2,392.89
Other Items (Net)...........................	27r	47.82	† −233.45	−526.49	−527.15	−45.45	−20.59	−44.14	−200.81	−295.34	−389.19	−246.19	−91.80

		1994	1995	1996	1997	1998	1999	2000	2001	2002	2003	2004	2005
Monetary Survey						*Billions of Guaranies: End of Period*							
Foreign Assets (Net)........................	31n	2,184.04	† 2,169.39	2,561.72	2,006.94	2,871.50	4,101.12	4,039.88	4,613.16	5,256.96	7,735.13	8,942.79	9,382.15
Domestic Credit.............................	32	3,623.54	† 4,344.52	4,831.32	5,369.00	5,596.47	5,742.22	6,416.82	7,420.40	8,442.74	6,376.91	6,986.19	7,648.62
Claims on Central Govt. (Net).......	32an	200.17	† 181.02	−272.06	−344.34	−58.82	−488.16	−170.27	153.51	1,125.66	794.70	549.08	345.65
Claims on Local Government..........	32b	.83	† 22.67	2.18	8.13	37.75	6.71	10.19	5.61	2.26	3.14	7.26	13.27
Claims on Nonfin.Pub.Enterprises...	32c	223.81	† 239.15	268.00	303.76	330.20	359.66	381.19	216.25	283.50	291.82	364.87	485.86
Claims on Private Sector..............	32d	3,171.50	† 3,802.28	4,672.68	5,232.14	5,111.89	5,676.61	5,962.93	6,785.14	6,810.51	5,088.53	5,866.61	6,612.82
Claims on Other Banking Insts.......	32f	27.23	† 36.87	113.19	49.21	53.88	43.58	73.88	73.60	84.59	55.76	44.93	29.76
Claims on Nonbank Fin. Insts.........	32g	—	† 62.53	47.32	120.10	121.57	143.81	158.91	186.29	136.22	142.95	153.44	161.26
Money..	34	1,370.31	† 1,699.93	1,708.85	1,886.18	1,984.45	2,166.89	2,562.25	2,743.15	2,759.53	3,788.14	4,784.12	5,784.67
Quasi-Money................................	35	3,119.08	† 3,735.50	4,493.15	4,792.44	5,356.27	6,510.91	6,534.39	7,843.68	8,159.26	7,961.37	8,629.11	8,663.63
Money Market Instruments............	36aa	—	† 50.16	36.98	49.11	13.11	9.42	39.32	12.13	17.09	9.17	124.55	83.09
Bonds..	36ab	3.76	† 1.94	4.13	5.85	15.72	12.97	14.17	37.05	144.60	30.35	—	—
Liabs. of Central Bank: Securities...	36ac	—	† 28.23	12.03	31.87	171.84	15.09	5.99	111.85	253.93	428.59	341.47	228.46
Restricted Deposits......................	36b	26.47	† 29.30	66.76	57.58	76.92	95.31	140.47	138.48	216.61	230.01	212.28	137.64
Liabilities to Other Banking Insts......	36i	.01	† 19.24	31.45	31.02	50.11	68.47	102.10	235.49	215.34	396.44	414.78	422.45
Capital Accounts..........................	37a	1,051.70	† 1,539.78	1,958.36	4,008.68	3,229.34	3,854.34	4,041.20	4,722.02	6,448.39	4,856.76	5,205.85	5,120.86
Other Items (Net).........................	37r	236.25	† −590.17	−918.67	−3,486.79	−2,429.78	−2,890.06	−2,983.19	−3,810.29	−4,515.04	−3,588.79	−3,783.18	−3,410.03
Money plus Quasi-Money..............	35l	4,489.40	† 5,435.43	6,202.01	6,678.62	7,340.72	8,677.80	9,096.64	10,586.83	10,918.78	11,749.51	13,413.23	14,448.30
Other Banking Institutions						*Billions of Guaranies: End of Period*							
Reserves.....................................	40	51.64	† 47.07	52.55	69.01	73.66	72.99	92.44	105.47	100.84	117.62	101.53	131.04
Claims on Mon.Author.: Securities...	40c	—	† 1.29	.46	.02	3.36	5.08	5.99	2.17	6.26	—	.22	4.13
Foreign Assets.............................	41	—	† .68	1.41	30.08	31.26	31.92	55.87	87.53	30.13	22.07	13.05	20.59
Claims on Central Government........	42a	—	† 2.11	3.65	4.30	3.58	5.79	6.52	5.28	36.86	34.92	37.55	38.82
Claims on Local Government..........	42b	—	† —	—	.01	.03	.04	.12	.03	.09	—	—	2.50
Claims on Nonfin.Pub.Enterprises.....	42c	—	† —	—	—	—	.08	—	—	—	—	—	.02
Claims on Private Sector..............	42d	858.31	† 447.38	505.38	655.57	662.12	626.43	773.75	888.45	820.28	932.02	916.41	1,267.00
Claims on Deposit Money Banks.....	42e	122.40	† 30.14	38.50	39.56	57.90	87.07	74.99	92.86	95.22	148.65	100.26	82.15
Claims on Nonbank Financial Insts....	42g	—	† 4.24	6.59	7.46	.12	1.80	4.17	18.63	4.74	2.21	1.50	1.81
Time, Savings,& Fgn.Currency Dep...	45	270.97	† 352.02	401.87	501.74	491.48	475.48	615.14	766.92	747.24	931.67	905.64	1,206.18
Bonds..	46ab	222.27	† 6.76	6.76	8.36	7.25	6.42	7.81	7.77	5.02	4.62	1.30	.03
Foreign Liabilities.........................	46c	63.06	† —	—	19.91	6.03	1.98	7.14	8.28	5.03	26.21	24.45	29.81
Central Government Deposits..........	46d	—	† 2.28	—	—	—	—	—	—	—	—	—	.11
Credit from Monetary Authorities.....	46g	11.89	† 12.15	11.84	19.81	32.52	26.77	36.27	52.80	64.76	32.96	3.57	4.00
Credit from Deposit Money Banks....	46h	1.77	† 15.86	17.52	36.28	41.58	42.75	69.07	43.87	13.96	18.78	4.66	4.67
Capital Accounts..........................	47a	422.30	† 193.46	227.94	274.99	307.21	324.11	349.50	382.56	337.58	311.64	270.80	356.19
Other Items (Net).........................	47r	40.09	† −49.62	−57.40	−55.07	−54.05	−46.33	−71.07	−61.78	−79.17	−68.38	−39.88	−52.93
Banking Survey						*Billions of Guaranies: End of Period*							
Foreign Assets (Net).....................	51n	2,120.97	† 2,170.07	2,563.13	2,017.11	2,896.73	4,131.06	4,088.61	4,692.41	5,282.06	7,730.99	8,931.40	9,372.94
Domestic Credit............................	52	4,454.62	† 4,759.09	5,233.74	5,987.13	6,208.44	6,332.78	7,127.51	8,259.19	9,220.12	7,290.30	7,896.73	8,928.90
Claims on Central Govt. (Net)........	52an	200.17	† 180.85	−268.41	−340.05	−55.25	−482.37	−163.75	158.80	1,162.52	829.62	586.64	384.36
Claims on Local Government.........	52b	.83	† 22.67	2.18	8.14	37.78	6.75	10.31	5.64	2.35	3.14	7.26	15.77
Claims on Nonfin.Pub.Enterprises...	52c	223.81	† 239.15	268.00	303.76	330.20	359.74	381.19	216.25	283.50	291.82	364.87	485.88
Claims on Private Sector..............	52d	4,029.80	† 4,249.65	5,178.06	5,887.71	5,774.01	6,303.04	6,736.68	7,673.59	7,630.78	6,020.56	6,783.02	7,879.81
Claims on Nonbank Fin. Insts.........	52g	—	† 66.77	53.91	127.56	121.69	145.62	163.08	204.92	140.96	145.16	154.94	163.07
Liquid Liabilities..........................	55l	4,708.73	† 5,740.38	6,551.33	7,111.35	7,758.54	9,080.29	9,619.33	11,248.29	11,565.22	12,563.58	14,217.34	15,523.74
Money Market Instruments..............	56aa	—	† 50.16	36.98	49.11	13.11	9.42	39.32	12.13	17.09	9.17	124.55	83.09
Bonds..	56ab	226.03	† 8.70	10.89	14.21	22.97	19.39	21.97	44.82	149.62	34.97	1.30	.03
Liabs. of Central Bank: Securities.....	56ac	—	† 26.94	11.56	31.84	168.48	10.01	—	109.69	247.68	428.59	341.25	224.33
Restricted Deposits......................	56b	26.47	† 29.40	66.76	57.58	76.92	95.31	140.47	138.48	216.61	230.01	212.28	137.64
Capital Accounts..........................	57a	1,474.00	† 1,733.23	2,186.30	4,283.67	3,536.55	4,178.45	4,390.71	5,104.58	6,785.96	5,168.40	5,476.65	5,477.05
Other Items (Net).........................	57r	140.37	† −659.65	−1,066.95	−3,543.53	−2,471.40	−2,929.04	−2,995.69	−3,706.39	−4,480.00	−3,413.44	−3,545.25	−3,144.00
Money (National Definitions)						*Billions of Guaranies: End of Period*							
Base Money................................	19ma	1,342.25	1,650.91	1,703.49	1,831.80	1,987.33	2,138.55	2,106.94	2,227.57	2,193.18	3,461.74	4,060.38	4,240.52
M1..	59ma	1,272.60	1,539.36	1,570.67	1,789.14	1,922.27	2,103.85	2,478.22	2,700.36	2,728.70	3,788.88	4,705.78	5,674.71
M2..	59mb	2,166.15	2,827.35	3,204.72	3,437.43	3,341.82	3,706.11	3,824.42	4,068.44	3,914.07	5,079.18	6,299.83	7,328.80
M3..	59mc	3,499.99	4,201.08	5,121.65	5,848.77	6,383.03	7,532.20	7,833.10	9,332.98	9,275.38	10,362.82	11,733.89	12,708.50
M4..	59md	3,503.75	4,204.77	5,122.88	5,848.77	6,385.00	7,541.01	7,850.33	9,363.84	9,411.11	10,402.64	11,742.09	12,711.05
M5..	59me	3,693.60	4,381.96	5,262.52	5,849.76	6,385.00	7,541.01	7,850.33	9,363.84	9,411.11	10,402.64	11,742.09	12,711.05
Interest Rates						*Percent Per Annum*							
Discount Rate (End of Period)..........	60	19.15	20.50	15.00	20.00	20.00	20.00	20.00	20.00	20.00	20.00	20.00	20.00
Money Market Rate......................	60b	18.64	20.18	16.35	12.48	20.74	17.26	10.70	13.45	13.19	13.02	1.33	2.29
Savings Rate...............................	60k	† 12.00	11.53	9.92	6.93	5.12	6.06	6.43	5.67	9.42	6.90	1.33	.20
Savings Rate (Fgn.Currency)...........	60k.f	4.27	4.68	4.08	3.22	2.74	2.40	2.35	2.07	1.40	.59	.15	.11
Deposit Rate...............................	60l	23.12	21.16	17.16	13.00	† 16.21	19.75	15.72	16.22	22.86	15.83	5.11	1.66
Deposit Rate (Fgn.Currency)...........	60l.f	....	....	....	....	5.44	5.02	4.56	3.46	1.66	1.27	.68	1.18
Lending Rate...............................	60p	† 35.47	33.94	31.88	27.79	30.49	30.21	26.78	28.25	38.66	49.99	33.54	29.91
Lending Rate (Fgn.Currency)...........	60p.f	12.68	14.03	14.35	13.53	13.03	12.17	11.87	11.16	9.31	10.35	8.08	9.13
Prices and Labor						*Index Numbers (2000=100): Period Averages*							
Producer Prices............................	63	....	....	71.2	72.1	82.8	87.2	100.0	105.8	126.9	160.4	169.7	185.0
Consumer Prices..........................	64	57.8	65.6	72.0	77.1	86.0	91.8	100.0	107.3	118.5	135.4	141.3	150.9
						Number in Thousands: Period Averages							
Labor Force................................	67d	† 1,053	....	....	....	....	....	....	....	....	....	....	....
Employment................................	67e	† 1,050	† 1,160	1,190	1,771	2,151	2,196	2,558	2,373	2,260	2,351	....	....
Unemployment.............................	67c	† 48	....	106	....	....	....	....	....	215	164	....	....
Unemployment Rate (%).................	67r	† 4.4	....	8.2	....	....	9.4	10.3	....	14.7	11.2	....	....
Intl. Transactions & Positions						*Millions of U.S. Dollars*							
Exports......................................	70..d	816.8	919.2	1,043.5	1,088.6	1,014.0	740.9	869.4	990.2	950.6	1,241.5	1,625.7	1,687.8
Imports, c.i.f................................	71..d	2,421.8	3,143.8	3,203.9	3,099.2	2,897.0	1,906.0	2,193.0	2,182.0	1,672.0	2,065.0	3,097.0	2,880.0
Imports, f.o.b...............................	71.vd	2,140.4	2,782.2	2,850.5	3,403.0	2,470.8	1,725.1	2,050.4	1,988.8	1,510.3	1,865.3	2,651.7	3,207.2
						1990=100							
Volume of Exports........................	72	66.6	....	....	....	....	....	....	....	....	....	....	....

Paraguay 288

		1994	1995	1996	1997	1998	1999	2000	2001	2002	2003	2004	2005
Balance of Payments		*Millions of US Dollars: Minus Sign Indicates Debit*											
Current Account, n.i.e.	78ald	−274.1	−92.3	−352.9	−650.4	−160.0	−165.4	−162.8	−266.4	92.6	132.5	20.4	....
Goods: Exports f.o.b.	78aad	3,360.1	4,218.6	3,796.9	3,327.5	3,548.6	2,312.4	2,329.0	1,889.7	1,858.0	2,175.3	2,811.7	....
Goods: Imports f.o.b.	78abd	−3,603.5	−4,489.0	−4,383.4	−4,192.4	−3,941.5	−2,752.9	−2,866.1	−2,503.6	−2,137.9	−2,450.5	−3,203.0	....
Trade Balance	78acd	−243.4	−270.4	−586.5	−864.9	−392.9	−440.5	−537.2	−613.9	−279.9	−275.2	−391.3	....
Services: Credit	78add	426.2	583.8	600.5	655.0	625.5	575.4	595.3	555.2	568.4	582.7	585.8	....
Services: Debit	78aed	−593.4	−710.7	−658.8	−654.6	−575.9	−493.0	−420.2	−390.0	−354.6	−333.1	−336.9	....
Balance on Goods & Services	78afd	−410.6	−397.3	−644.8	−864.5	−343.3	−358.1	−362.0	−448.7	−66.1	−25.5	−142.4	....
Income: Credit	78agd	247.9	272.6	280.9	278.1	266.3	212.5	260.5	255.9	195.7	166.3	185.9	....
Income: Debit	78ahd	−134.1	−162.9	−171.2	−244.9	−260.3	−195.0	−238.1	−240.1	−152.9	−172.8	−217.2	....
Balance on Gds, Serv. & Inc.	78aid	−296.8	−287.6	−535.1	−831.3	−337.3	−340.6	−339.6	−432.9	−23.3	−32.0	−173.8	....
Current Transfers, n.i.e.: Credit	78ajd	25.6	199.7	183.0	182.2	178.3	176.7	178.3	168.0	117.5	166.0	195.7	....
Current Transfers: Debit	78akd	−2.9	−4.4	−.8	−1.3	−1.0	−1.5	−1.5	−1.5	−1.6	−1.5	−1.5	....
Capital Account, n.i.e.	78bcd	8.8	10.6	14.2	7.5	5.4	19.6	3.0	15.0	4.0	15.0	16.0	....
Capital Account, n.i.e.: Credit	78bad	8.8	10.6	14.2	7.5	5.4	19.6	3.0	15.0	4.0	15.0	16.0	....
Capital Account: Debit	78bbd	....	—	—	—	—	—	—	—	—	—	—	....
Financial Account, n.i.e.	78bjd	212.9	232.5	152.4	421.3	312.9	89.2	63.9	148.2	40.5	173.2	113.0	....
Direct Investment Abroad	78bdd	....	−5.1	−5.2	−5.7	−5.6	−5.6	−5.7	−5.8	−5.5	−5.5	−6.0	....
Dir. Invest. in Rep. Econ., n.i.e.	78bed	137.1	103.2	149.4	235.8	341.9	94.5	104.1	84.2	10.0	32.8	92.5	....
Portfolio Investment Assets	78bfd	....	−.8	−3.6	−4.3	—	−.7	−6.8	1.4	.2	—	—	....
Equity Securities	78bkd	....	—	—	—	—	—	—	—	—	—	—	....
Debt Securities	78bld	....	−.8	−3.6	−4.3	9.7	−2.2	.6	.5	—	—	—	....
Portfolio Investment Liab., n.i.e.	78bgd	....	—	−.1	—	—	—	—	.5	−.1	−.1	−.4	−.1	....
Equity Securities	78bmd	....	—	—	—	—	—	—	....	—	—	—	—	....
Debt Securities	78bnd	....	—	−.1	—	—	—	—	.5	−.1	−.1	−.4	−.1	....
Financial Derivatives Assets	78bwd	....	—	—	—	—	—	—	—	—	—	—	....
Financial Derivatives Liabilities	78bxd	....	—	—	—	—	—	—	—	—	—	—	....
Other Investment Assets	78bhd	−89.8	−58.5	−31.9	72.9	−5.0	−117.7	−212.4	64.4	−16.1	212.5	−8.5	....
Monetary Authorities	78bod	.1	—	—	—	—	—	—	—	—	—	—	....
General Government	78bpd	23.1	−43.1	−59.0	−45.8	60.7	−63.6	−81.2	78.8	−77.7	−38.0	−20.1	....
Banks	78bqd	−1.5	−169.7	3.5	100.5	−42.7	−1.9	−69.3	68.2	122.5	−108.7	7.4	....
Other Sectors	78brd	−111.5	154.3	23.6	18.2	−23.0	−52.2	−61.9	−82.6	−60.9	359.2	4.2	....
Other Investment Liab., n.i.e.	78bid	165.6	193.7	43.8	122.6	−27.4	127.0	175.4	4.8	52.2	−66.3	35.2	....
Monetary Authorities	78bsd	−1.6	−8.7	−3.5	−5.0	−4.3	−3.8	−3.3	−3.2	−4.4	−4.4	−4.3	....
General Government	78btd	29.8	101.6	122.5	137.1	112.3	97.6	90.4	41.9	23.0	53.1	5.4	....
Banks	78bud	97.3	118.6	−188.4	71.6	−50.7	−101.5	−8.9	−30.5	6.3	−23.9	18.9	....
Other Sectors	78bvd	40.1	−17.8	113.2	−81.1	−84.7	134.7	97.2	−3.4	27.3	−91.1	15.2	....
Net Errors and Omissions	78cad	353.0	−106.0	139.8	5.8	−141.6	−244.3	−243.4	52.9	−262.8	−87.8	120.5	....
Overall Balance	78cbd	300.6	44.8	−46.5	−215.8	16.7	−300.9	−339.3	−50.2	−125.7	232.8	270.0	....
Reserves and Related Items	79dad	−300.6	−44.8	46.5	215.8	−16.7	300.9	339.3	50.2	125.7	−232.8	−270.0	....
Reserve Assets	79dbd	−339.3	−60.2	39.4	205.8	−23.4	−116.7	210.1	45.4	85.6	−303.2	−181.2	....
Use of Fund Credit and Loans	79dcd	—	—	—	—	—	—	—	—	—	—	—	....
Exceptional Financing	79ded	38.7	15.4	7.1	10.0	6.7	417.6	129.2	4.8	40.1	70.4	−88.8	....
International Investment Position		*Millions of US Dollars*											
Assets	79aad	....	2,569.4	2,566.7	2,284.6	2,311.9	2,576.7	2,602.6	3,216.3	3,125.7	2,455.2	2,659.2	....
Direct Investment Abroad	79abd	....	178.6	186.0	194.1	201.3	208.2	213.9	139.7	137.7	143.2	149.2	....
Portfolio Investment	79acd	....	6.3	9.9	14.2	8.9	20.1	11.9	15.0	13.3	4.7	4.7	....
Equity Securities	79add	....	3.4	3.4	3.4	7.8	16.8	10.3	14.3	12.6	4.0	4.0	....
Debt Securities	79aed	....	2.9	6.5	10.8	1.1	3.3	1.6	.7	.7	.7	.7	....
Financial Derivatives	79ald	....	—	—	—	—	—	—	—	—	—	—	....
Other Investment	79afd	....	1,278.1	1,308.5	1,230.5	1,226.9	1,360.2	1,605.0	2,338.5	2,324.5	1,314.2	1,317.3	....
Monetary Authorities	79agd	....	—	—	—	—	—	—	—	—	—	—	....
General Government	79ahd	....	188.3	247.3	293.1	232.6	296.2	377.4	332.7	410.4	448.4	468.6	....
Banks	79aid	....	511.6	507.6	404.2	442.5	443.4	512.8	444.6	280.5	389.2	381.8	....
Other Sectors	79ajd	....	578.2	553.6	533.2	551.8	620.6	714.8	1,561.2	1,633.6	476.6	466.9	....
Reserve Assets	79akd	....	1,106.4	1,062.3	845.8	874.8	988.2	771.9	723.1	650.2	993.1	1,187.9	....
Liabilities	79lad	....	2,877.1	2,954.2	3,132.1	3,385.5	3,982.3	4,377.8	4,057.4	3,939.8	4,226.0	4,343.4	....
Dir. Invest. in Rep. Economy	79lbd	....	705.2	829.3	977.7	1,196.1	1,215.7	1,324.5	1,135.4	901.5	1,084.5	1,244.1	....
Portfolio Investment	79lcd	....	.1	—	—	—	—	.5	.4	.3	—	—	....
Equity Securities	79ldd	....	—	—	—	—	—	—	—	—	—	—	....
Debt Securities	79led	....	.1	—	—	—	—	.5	.4	.3	—	—	....
Financial Derivatives	79lld	....	—	—	—	—	—	—	—	—	—	—	....
Other Investment	79lfd	....	2,171.8	2,124.9	2,154.4	2,189.4	2,766.6	3,052.8	2,921.6	3,038.0	3,141.5	3,099.3	....
Monetary Authorities	79lgd	....	50.8	47.3	42.3	38.0	34.3	32.7	31.2	28.6	22.3	17.9	....
General Government	79lhd	....	1,004.6	1,054.8	1,146.0	1,318.1	1,854.3	2,001.7	1,963.6	2,090.4	2,302.8	2,250.8	....
Banks	79lid	....	406.5	218.1	289.5	238.4	136.6	127.6	97.0	66.4	42.7	63.2	....
Other Sectors	79ljd	....	709.9	804.7	676.6	594.9	741.4	890.8	829.8	852.7	773.8	767.5	....
Government Finance		*Billions of Guaranies: Year Ending December 31*											
Deficit (-) or Surplus	80	294.8	−10.2	−183.3	−251.6	−81.3	−806.2	−1,080.5	−229.7	....	....	....	
Revenue	81	2,196.7	2,724.1	2,919.5	3,192.9	3,715.7	4,004.0	4,201.7	4,838.7	....	....	....	
Grants	81z	25.8	28.8	35.4	68.4	44.7	49.7	46.1	135.9	....	....	....	
Expenditure	82	1,953.7	2,726.9	3,116.6	3,469.6	3,811.7	4,687.3	5,216.3	5,201.4	....	....	....	
Lending Minus Repayments	83	−25.9	36.1	21.5	43.2	30.0	172.6	112.0	2.8	....	....	....	
Total Financing	80h	−294.8	10.2	183.3	251.6	81.3	806.2	1,080.5	229.7	....	....	....	

Paraguay 288

National Accounts		1994	1995	1996	1997	1998	1999	2000	2001	2002	2003	2004	2005
						Billions of Guaranies							
Househ.Cons.Expend.,incl.NPISHs....	96f	13,231.8	15,089.2	16,853.3	17,704.3	20,101.4	19,762.5	22,406.8	24,604.3	27,526.7	34,044.8	....	....
Government Consumption Expend...	91f	1,012.5	1,275.9	1,528.5	1,693.0	1,928.3	2,135.4	2,601.6	2,479.9	2,470.2	2,679.3	....	....
Gross Fixed Capital Formation..........	93e	3,366.5	4,082.8	4,478.4	4,749.1	5,168.2	5,342.1	5,638.6	5,295.0	5,812.5	7,373.6	....	....
Changes in Inventories....................	93i	127.7	151.8	156.7	181.0	205.6	221.7	242.5	265.5	292.3	315.7	....	....
Exports of Goods and Services..........	90c	5,120.9	6,163.8	5,707.7	5,696.2	6,613.4	5,548.6	5,260.1	6,170.1	9,822.8	12,524.1	....	....
Imports of Goods and Services (-).....	98c	7,899.3	9,064.9	8,919.8	9,089.3	10,580.0	8,866.1	9,228.7	10,696.0	13,947.6	18,131.9	....	....
Gross Domestic Product (GDP)........	99b	14,960.1	17,698.6	19,804.8	20,934.3	23,436.9	24,144.3	26,921.0	28,118.8	31,976.9	38,805.5	....	....
Net Primary Income from Abroad.....	98.n	78.8	158.8	145.1	221.7	304.5	132.2	380.7	164.2	629.4	725.4	....	....
Gross National Income (GNI)............	99a	15,039.0	17,857.4	19,949.9	21,156.0	23,741.4	24,276.5	27,301.7	28,283.0	32,606.3	39,530.9	....	....
Consumption of Fixed Capital..........	99cf	1,161.0	1,378.1	1,549.9	1,639.2	1,835.0	1,889.6	2,051.6	2,142.8	2,407.0	3,104.4	....	....
GDP Volume 1982 Prices................	99b.p	1,038.5	1,087.4	1,101.2	1,129.7	1,125.0	1,130.4	1,126.4	1,157.0	1,130.2	1,159.0	....	....
GDP Volume (2000=100)...............	99bvp	92.2	96.5	97.8	100.3	99.9	100.4	100.0	102.7	100.3	102.9	....	....
GDP Deflator (2000=100)...............	99bip	60.3	68.1	75.3	77.5	87.2	89.4	100.0	101.7	118.4	140.1	....	....
						Millions: Midyear Estimates							
Population.................................	99z	4.71	4.83	4.95	5.08	5.21	5.34	5.47	5.60	5.74	5.88	6.02	6.16

Peru 293

		1994	1995	1996	1997	1998	1999	2000	2001	2002	2003	2004	2005
Exchange Rates						*Nuevos Soles per SDRs: End of Period*							
Market Rate	aa	3.1825	3.4338	3.7387	3.6835	4.4494	4.8175	4.5954	4.3282	4.7774	5.1459	5.0962	4.9024
						Nuevos Soles per US$: End of Period(ae) Period Avg.(rf)							
Market Rate	ae	2.1800	2.3100	2.6000	2.7300	3.1600	3.5100	3.5270	3.4440	3.5140	3.4630	3.2815	3.4300
Market Rate	rf	2.1950	2.2533	2.4533	2.6642	2.9300	3.3833	3.4900	3.5068	3.5165	3.4785	3.4132	3.2958
Fund Position						*Millions of SDRs: End of Period*							
Quota	2f.s	466.1	466.1	466.1	466.1	466.1	638.4	638.4	638.4	638.4	638.4	638.4	638.4
SDRs	1b.s	.3	.5	.2	.2	1.5	.3	1.1	1.4	.5	.3	.2	.3
Reserve Position in the Fund	1c.s	—	—	—	—	—	—	—	—	—	—	—	—
Total Fund Cred.&Loans Outstg	2tl	642.7	642.7	642.7	749.6	642.5	535.4	428.3	307.8	173.9	93.6	66.9	40.1
International Liquidity						*Millions of US Dollars Unless Otherwise Indicated: End of Period*							
Total Reserves minus Gold	1l.d	6,992.4	8,221.7	10,578.3	10,982.2	9,565.5	8,730.5	8,374.0	8,671.8	9,339.0	9,776.8	12,176.4	13,599.4
SDRs	1b.d	.4	.7	.3	.2	2.1	.4	1.5	1.7	.7	.4	.4	.5
Reserve Position in the Fund	1c.d	—	—	—	—	—	—	—	—	—	—	—	—
Foreign Exchange	1d.d	6,992.0	8,221.0	10,578.0	10,982.0	9,563.4	8,730.1	8,372.5	8,670.1	9,338.3	9,776.4	12,176.1	13,598.9
Gold (Million Fine Troy Ounces)	1ad	1.116	1.116	1.115	1.115	1.100	1.100	1.100	1.115	1.115	1.115	1.115	1.115
Gold (National Valuation)	1and	362.9	366.6	349.7	272.0	268.8	270.9	254.1	261.6	386.7	462.7	488.7	575.9
Monetary Authorities: Other Liab.	4..d	540.6	573.4	494.2	497.8	446.6	693.8	832.8	842.0	791.0	884.1	984.2	919.3
Deposit Money Banks: Assets	7a.d	1,183.8	1,544.9	2,047.2	1,215.7	1,245.8	1,388.6	1,299.8	1,365.7	1,218.1	1,290.6	1,094.6	1,350.6
Liabilities	7b.d	765.8	1,566.1	1,812.4	3,473.6	3,291.0	2,286.3	2,031.7	1,562.9	1,002.1	913.7	970.4	1,302.3
Other Banking Insts.: Assets	7e.d	12.7	12.7	12.7	12.7	1.0	—	—	—	—	—	—	—
Liabilities	7f.d	71.0	71.0	71.1	71.0	10.3	—	—	—	—	—	—	—
Monetary Authorities						*Millions of Nuevos Soles: End of Period*							
Foreign Assets	11	16,001	19,093	25,933	31,208	32,399	33,548	33,200	33,344	36,836	38,410	44,751	51,617
Claims on Central Government	12a	614	614	614	614	614	538	425	396	350	237	39	—
Claims on Deposit Money Banks	12e	64	4	107	—	203	263	97	—	170	—	—	2,850
Claims on Other Banking Insts	12f	—	—	—	—	—	—	—	—	—	—	—	—
Reserve Money	14	7,487	9,823	13,536	18,773	19,847	22,952	23,405	24,474	26,510	24,865	26,166	34,098
of which: Currency Outside DMBs	14a	2,385	3,043	3,245	3,827	3,950	4,609	4,537	4,945	5,615	6,370	8,036	10,116
Time, Savings,& Fgn.Currency Dep	15	202	78	118	77	83	75	78	114	148	179	192	195
Restricted Deposits	16b	1	1	1	1	—	1	—	—	—	—	—	1
Foreign Liabilities	16c	3,224	3,531	3,688	4,105	4,257	5,015	4,905	4,232	3,611	3,540	3,569	3,350
Central Government Deposits	16d	3,684	5,384	8,498	7,989	7,558	4,057	2,454	1,447	2,430	3,188	4,835	5,295
Capital Accounts	17a	377	457	592	735	867	871	854	962	1,146	1,272	1,058	1,046
Other Items (Net)	17r	1,705	437	221	141	604	1,379	2,025	2,511	3,511	5,603	8,970	10,484
Deposit Money Banks						*Millions of Nuevos Soles: End of Period*							
Reserves	20	5,326	6,846	10,240	12,135	11,126	11,897	12,382	13,252	14,353	14,573	17,533	26,268
Foreign Assets	21	2,581	3,569	5,323	3,307	3,924	4,874	4,584	4,704	4,280	4,466	3,590	4,632
Claims on Central Government	22a	1,607	1,028	924	2,437	3,764	4,954	4,778	6,506	6,908	6,631	5,988	6,487
Claims on Local Government	22b	50	31	170	244	94	380	433	337	205	340	313	182
Claims on Official Entities	22bx	270	204	264	376	968	398	464	419	493	294	332	406
Claims on Private Sector	22d	13,095	19,090	28,512	37,812	45,835	49,221	47,569	45,464	45,229	43,123	42,974	49,946
Claims on Other Banking Insts	22f	3	3	3	—	—	—	—	—	—	—	—	—
Demand Deposits	24	3,193	4,357	5,633	7,950	10,174	11,018	9,110	8,977	8,359	8,193	9,942	11,606
Time, Savings,& Fgn.Currency Dep	25	13,501	17,362	25,136	29,510	33,269	37,779	38,737	39,589	42,065	41,187	40,717	48,985
Bonds	26ab	102	251	539	806	933	969	871	783	952	457	468	513
Foreign Liabilities	26c	1,670	3,618	4,712	9,448	10,367	8,025	7,166	5,382	3,521	3,161	3,183	4,467
Central Government Deposits	26d	2,367	1,561	4,808	3,710	3,849	3,718	3,635	3,510	4,065	4,350	4,873	6,581
Credit from Monetary Authorities	26g	64	4	107	—	203	263	97	—	170	—	—	2,850
Capital Accounts	27a	4,792	6,261	8,514	11,045	14,309	18,857	20,518	22,616	23,701	21,540	21,422	22,070
Other Items (Net)	27r	−2,757	−2,643	−4,013	−6,157	−7,392	−8,904	−9,925	−10,177	−11,366	−9,462	−9,877	−9,150
Monetary Survey						*Millions of Nuevos Soles: End of Period*							
Foreign Assets (Net)	31n	13,688	15,513	22,856	20,962	21,700	25,382	25,713	28,433	33,984	36,174	41,590	48,433
Domestic Credit	32	9,588	14,025	17,181	29,784	39,869	47,717	47,579	48,165	46,690	43,088	39,937	45,146
Claims on Central Govt. (Net)	32an	−3,830	−5,303	−11,768	−8,648	−7,028	−2,282	−887	1,945	763	−669	−3,682	−5,389
Claims on Local Government	32b	50	31	170	244	94	380	433	337	205	340	313	182
Claims on Official Entities	32bx	270	204	264	376	968	398	464	419	493	294	332	406
Claims on Private Sector	32d	13,095	19,090	28,512	37,812	45,835	49,221	47,569	45,464	45,229	43,123	42,974	49,946
Claims on Other Banking Insts	32f	3	3	3	—	—	—	—	—	—	—	—	—
Money	34	5,589	7,498	8,972	15,175	19,165	22,273	21,072	21,445	22,049	21,351	23,728	26,339
Quasi-Money	35	13,703	17,440	25,254	29,587	33,352	37,854	38,815	39,703	42,213	41,366	40,909	49,180
Bonds	36ab	102	251	539	806	933	969	871	783	952	457	468	513
Restricted Deposits	36b	1	1	1	1	—	1	—	—	—	—	—	1
Capital Accounts	37a	5,169	6,718	9,106	11,780	15,176	19,728	21,373	23,578	24,846	22,812	22,480	23,116
Other Items (Net)	37r	−1,288	−2,370	−3,835	−6,603	−7,058	−7,726	−8,839	−8,913	−9,387	−6,724	−6,059	−5,569
Money plus Quasi-Money	35l	19,292	24,938	34,226	44,762	52,518	60,127	59,887	61,148	64,262	62,717	64,637	75,518
Other Banking Institutions						*Millions of Nuevos Soles: End of Period*							
Reserves	40	—	—	—	—	—	—	—	—	—	—	—	—
Foreign Assets	41	28	29	33	35	3	—	—	—	—	—	—	—
Claims on Central Government	42a	55	58	65	69	—	—	—	—	—	8	—	—
Claims on Official Entities	42bx	20	21	24	25	—	—	—	—	—	—	—	—
Claims on Private Sector	42d	718	744	803	828	910	809	761	644	657	686	709	752
Claims on Deposit Money Banks	42e	2	2	2	2	—	—	—	—	90	35	18	2
Demand Deposits	44	9	9	9	9	21	21	20	20	20	—	—	—
Time, Savings,& Fgn.Currency Dep	45	42	43	46	47	37	10	9	8	8	28	27	28
Bonds	46ab	6	6	6	6	—	—	—	—	—	—	—	—
Foreign Liabilities	46c	155	164	185	193	33	—	—	—	—	—	—	—
Central Government Deposits	46d	5	6	6	6	—	—	—	—	—	—	—	—
Credit from Monetary Authorities	46g	—	—	—	—	—	—	—	—	—	—	—	—
Credit from Deposit Money Banks	46h	4	4	5	5	—	—	—	—	—	—	—	—
Capital Accounts	47a	671	698	757	782	865	939	975	1,023	1,132	1,111	1,101	1,139
Other Items (Net)	47r	−70	−76	−87	−92	−42	−160	−244	−406	−413	−410	−401	−413

		1994	1995	1996	1997	1998	1999	2000	2001	2002	2003	2004	2005
Banking Survey		\multicolumn{12}{c}{*Millions of Nuevos Soles: End of Period*}											
Foreign Assets (Net)	51n	13,561	15,378	22,704	20,803	21,671	25,382	25,713	28,433	33,984	36,174	41,590	48,433
Domestic Credit	52	10,373	14,840	18,063	30,698	40,778	48,526	48,340	48,809	47,346	43,782	40,646	45,898
Claims on Central Govt. (Net)	52an	−3,780	−5,250	−11,708	−8,586	−7,028	−2,282	−887	1,945	763	−661	−3,682	−5,389
Claims on Local Government	52b	50	31	170	244	94	380	433	337	205	340	313	182
Claims on Official Entities	52bx	290	225	287	400	968	398	464	419	493	294	332	406
Claims on Private Sector	52d	13,812	19,834	29,314	38,640	46,745	50,030	48,330	46,108	45,886	43,810	43,683	50,699
Liquid Liabilities	55l	19,343	24,990	34,281	44,818	52,575	60,158	59,917	61,176	64,290	62,745	64,665	75,546
Bonds	56ab	108	257	545	812	933	969	871	783	952	457	468	513
Restricted Deposits	56b	1	1	1	1	—	1	—	—	—	—	—	1
Capital Accounts	57a	5,840	7,416	9,863	12,562	16,041	20,667	22,348	24,601	25,978	23,923	23,580	24,256
Other Items (Net)	57r	−1,358	−2,446	−3,922	−6,691	−7,100	−7,886	−9,082	−9,319	−9,890	−7,169	−6,479	−5,984
Money (National Definitions)		\multicolumn{12}{c}{*Millions of Nuevos Soles: End of Period*}											
Monetary Base	19ma	2,672	3,658	3,996	4,761	5,023	5,876	5,642	6,087	6,759	7,441	9,327	11,724
Money	59na	3,723	4,595	5,409	6,464	6,482	7,311	7,087	7,509	8,197	9,312	12,420	13,879
Quasi-Money in National Currency	59maa	2,412	3,299	4,200	5,552	5,217	5,342	5,732	6,643	7,102	7,477	9,657	14,035
Quasi-Money in Foreign Currency	59mab	11,518	14,410	21,200	24,471	28,162	31,674	32,508	32,121	33,626	34,018	33,762	39,064
Interest Rates		\multicolumn{12}{c}{*Percent Per Annum*}											
Discount Rate (End of Period)	60	16.08	18.44	18.16	15.94	18.72	17.80	14.00	5.00	4.50	3.25	3.75	4.00
Savings Rate	60k	17.99	11.80	10.99	10.70	10.12	9.54	7.75	5.88	1.78	1.48	1.28	1.20
Deposit Rate	60l	22.35	15.70	14.90	15.01	15.11	16.27	13.29	9.92	4.19	3.83	2.98	3.43
Lending Rate	60p	53.56	27.16	26.07	29.96	30.80	30.79	27.91	20.43	14.73	14.21	14.49	14.97
Prices, Production, Labor		\multicolumn{12}{c}{*Index Numbers (2000=100): Period Averages*}											
Share Prices	62	83.6	87.9	92.8	126.3	105.3	111.9	100.0	85.2	84.8	126.9	209.0	297.1
Wholesale Prices	63	65.6	72.5	79.3	85.2	91.4	† 95.8	100.0	101.4	100.3	102.0	107.4	109.8
Consumer Prices	64	64.5	71.7	80.0	86.9	93.1	96.4	100.0	† 102.0	102.2	104.5	108.3	110.1
Manufacturing Production	66ey	87.5	92.3	93.7	98.6	95.2	94.5	100.0	100.5	104.7	107.1	114.5	122.3
Industrial Employment	67	112.2	109.4	† 106.9	108.7	106.2	100.5	100.0	100.5	100.6	102.5	107.3	112.9
		\multicolumn{12}{c}{*Number in Thousands: Period Averages*}											
Labor Force	67d	2,930	3,103	6,501	7,220	7,440	7,736	7,616	8,182	12,892	† 3,738	3,761	....
Employment	67e	2,682	2,901	6,130	6,745	6,929	7,211	7,128	7,620	† 3,334	3,361	3,367	....
Unemployment	67c	263	221	† 462	565	582	625	566	651	† 359	386	394	....
Unemployment Rate (%)	67r	8.9	7.1	† 7.0	7.7	7.8	8.0	7.4	7.9	† 9.7	10.3	10.5	....
Intl. Transactions & Positions		\multicolumn{12}{c}{*Millions of US Dollars*}											
Exports	70..d	4,424.1	5,491.4	5,877.6	6,824.6	5,756.8	6,087.5	6,954.9	7,025.7	7,713.9	9,090.7	12,616.9	17,206.1
Imports, c.i.f.	71..d	6,701.1	9,299.8	9,442.2	10,280.6	9,914.7	8,152.0	8,887.9	....	....	....	....	....
Imports, f.o.b.	71.vd	5,584.2	7,749.8	7,868.5	8,567.2	8,262.2	6,793.3	7,406.6	7,273.4	7,439.9	8,244.4	9,812.4	12,084.0
		\multicolumn{12}{c}{*2000=100*}											
Volume of Exports	72	82.0	82.1	85.9	94.1	81.7	88.8	100.0	113.6	125.9	122.0	135.6	149.3
		\multicolumn{12}{c}{*2000=100: Indexes of Unit Values in US Dollars*}											
Unit Value of Exports/Export Prices	74..d	88.5	107.2	106.8	103.6	83.9	82.7	100.0	84.8	88.0	98.5	125.6	173.5
Balance of Payments		\multicolumn{12}{c}{*Millions of US Dollars: Minus Sign Indicates Debit*}											
Current Account, n.i.e.	78ald	−2,701	−4,625	−3,646	−3,367	−3,321	−1,464	−1,526	−1,144	−1,063	−935	−11	1,030
Goods: Exports f.o.b.	78aad	4,424	5,491	5,878	6,825	5,757	6,088	6,955	7,026	7,714	9,091	12,616	17,247
Goods: Imports f.o.b.	78abd	−5,499	−7,733	−7,869	−8,503	−8,194	−6,743	−7,366	−7,221	−7,422	−8,255	−9,824	−12,084
Trade Balance	78acd	−1,075	−2,241	−1,991	−1,678	−2,437	−655	−411	−195	292	836	2,792	5,163
Services: Credit	78add	1,064	1,131	1,414	1,553	1,775	1,594	1,529	1,455	1,530	1,695	1,914	2,179
Services: Debit	78aed	−1,534	−1,864	−2,085	−2,339	−2,432	−2,256	−2,234	−2,345	−2,471	−2,549	−2,756	−3,092
Balance on Goods & Services	78afd	−1,545	−2,975	−2,662	−2,465	−3,094	−1,318	−1,115	−1,085	−649	−18	1,949	4,250
Income: Credit	78agd	338	574	610	720	786	655	737	670	370	322	332	618
Income: Debit	78ahd	−2,282	−3,056	−2,508	−2,542	−1,990	−1,767	−2,146	−1,771	−1,827	−2,466	−3,753	−5,629
Balance on Gds, Serv. & Inc.	78aid	−3,489	−5,457	−4,560	−4,287	−4,298	−2,430	−2,525	−2,186	−2,106	−2,162	−1,472	−761
Current Transfers, n.i.e.: Credit	78ajd	795	837	922	928	989	992	1,008	1,050	1,052	1,234	1,467	1,797
Current Transfers: Debit	78akd	−7	−5	−8	−8	−12	−27	−9	−8	−8	−6	−6	−6
Capital Account, n.i.e.	78bcd	−58	32	22	−50	−57	−54	−251	−143	−107	−107	−86	−152
Capital Account, n.i.e.: Credit	78bad	31	65	51	24	21	25	24	32	14	14	37	13
Capital Account: Debit	78bbd	−89	−34	−29	−74	−78	−79	−275	−175	−121	−121	−123	−164
Financial Account, n.i.e.	78bjd	3,870	3,718	3,797	5,696	1,773	545	1,015	1,534	1,983	820	2,375	82
Direct Investment Abroad	78bdd	—	−8	17	−85	−62	−128	—	−74	—	−60	—	—
Dir. Invest. in Rep. Econ., n.i.e.	78bed	3,289	2,557	3,471	2,139	1,644	1,940	810	1,144	2,156	1,335	1,816	2,519
Portfolio Investment Assets	78bfd	−56	−9	−119	−257	−194	−227	−481	−318	−316	−1,287	−425	−817
Equity Securities	78bkd	−32	−4	−113	−119	−188	−223	−478	−341	−388	−1,287	−426	−818
Debt Securities	78bld	−24	−5	−6	−138	−6	−4	−3	23	72	—	1	1
Portfolio Investment Liab., n.i.e.	78bgd	548	163	286	406	−224	−125	75	−54	1,724	1,211	1,244	2,585
Equity Securities	78bmd	465	171	294	156	−346	−107	123	43	−9	1	−47	766
Debt Securities	78bnd	83	−8	−8	250	122	−18	−48	−97	1,733	1,210	1,291	1,819
Financial Derivatives Assets	78bwd	....	....	....	....	....	....	....	....	....	....	....	....
Financial Derivatives Liabilities	78bxd	....	....	....	....	....	....	....	....	....	....	....	....
Other Investment Assets	78bhd	−564	−270	−499	391	64	126	191	664	—	127	13	−1,037
Monetary Authorities	78bod	−2	−2	−33	−104	20	−5	−31	−16	152	119	85	−162
General Government	78bpd	—	—	—	—	—	—	−60	−5	−4	−203	−64	−214
Banks	78bqd	−272	−425	−464	869	25	−102	233	48	35	186	71	−308
Other Sectors	78brd	−290	157	−2	−374	19	233	49	638	−183	25	−79	−352
Other Investment Liab., n.i.e.	78bid	653	1,285	640	3,102	545	−1,041	421	171	−1,581	−506	−273	−3,167
Monetary Authorities	78bsd	37	−23	−87	−8	−38	−33	24	−11	−4	−8	6	5
General Government	78btd	98	−213	−438	713	−22	−69	666	599	−781	−294	−130	−2,692
Banks	78bud	−247	704	224	1,667	−225	−1,001	−168	−499	−513	−84	53	298
Other Sectors	78bvd	765	817	941	730	830	62	−101	82	−284	−119	−202	−778
Net Errors and Omissions	78cad	443	285	708	−225	365	112	631	185	197	783	178	450
Overall Balance	78cbd	1,553	−590	880	2,055	−1,241	−862	−130	432	1,010	561	2,456	1,411
Reserves and Related Items	79dad	−1,553	590	−880	−2,055	1,241	862	130	−432	−1,010	−561	−2,456	−1,411
Reserve Assets	79dbd	−3,059	−921	−1,784	−1,493	1,142	985	329	−276	−851	−515	−2,442	−1,472
Use of Fund Credit and Loans	79dcd	—	—	—	149	−145	−147	−141	−154	−172	−110	−40	−40
Exceptional Financing	79ded	1,506	1,512	904	−711	244	24	−58	−1	14	64	26	100

		1994	1995	1996	1997	1998	1999	2000	2001	2002	2003	2004	2005
International Investment Position						*Millions of US Dollars*							
Assets....................................	79aad	10,712	12,400	14,771	16,140	15,105	14,434	14,369	14,405	15,706	18,029	21,204	24,915
Direct Investment Abroad..............	79abd	109	567	543	602	438	651	505	649	666	814	874	1,047
Portfolio Investment.....................	79acd	313	356	501	828	1,142	1,373	2,070	2,372	2,702	4,573	5,238	6,643
Equity Securities........................	79add	313	294	416	582	867	1,070	1,661	1,948	2,293	3,896	4,346	5,576
Debt Securities..........................	79aed	—	62	85	246	275	303	409	424	409	677	892	1,068
Financial Derivatives...................	79ald	—	—	—	—	—	—	—	—	—	—	—	—
Other Investment.......................	79afd	3,477	3,742	4,208	3,699	3,656	3,526	3,240	2,555	2,656	2,445	2,453	3,114
Monetary Authorities..................	79agd	64	62	62	48	49	50	46	47	—	—	—	—
General Government....................	79ahd	—	—	—	—	—	—	—	—	—	—	—	—
Banks....................................	79aid	1,062	1,487	1,951	1,082	1,057	1,159	926	878	843	657	586	894
Other Sectors..........................	79ajd	2,350	2,193	2,195	2,569	2,550	2,317	2,268	1,630	1,813	1,788	1,867	2,219
Reserve Assets............................	79akd	6,813	7,735	9,518	11,011	9,869	8,883	8,553	8,829	9,682	10,197	12,639	14,111
Liabilities...................................	79lad	36,200	40,390	43,533	40,228	41,099	41,162	41,321	41,456	43,411	45,461	47,379	48,151
Dir. Invest. in Rep. Economy..........	79lbd	4,451	5,510	6,720	7,753	8,297	9,791	11,062	11,835	12,549	12,876	13,310	15,829
Portfolio Investment.....................	79lcd	1,636	1,681	3,185	8,138	7,312	7,013	6,384	6,436	7,544	8,723	9,987	12,338
Equity Securities........................	79ldd	1,547	1,599	3,111	3,685	2,737	2,859	2,278	2,427	2,990	2,999	2,952	3,717
Debt Securities..........................	79led	89	81	73	4,453	4,575	4,154	4,106	4,010	4,554	5,724	7,035	8,621
Financial Derivatives...................	79lld	—	—	—	—	—	—	—	—	—	—	—	—
Other Investment.......................	79lfd	30,113	33,199	33,629	24,336	25,490	24,357	23,874	23,185	23,318	23,863	24,082	19,984
Monetary Authorities..................	79lgd	1,137	1,131	1,013	1,092	947	745	592	410	256	151	122	80
General Government....................	79lhd	24,978	26,612	25,661	13,969	14,663	14,743	14,758	14,681	15,754	16,593	16,977	13,415
Banks....................................	79lid	797	1,501	1,728	3,398	3,174	2,173	2,005	1,506	993	909	961	1,260
Other Sectors..........................	79ljd	3,200	3,954	5,226	5,876	6,705	6,696	6,520	6,589	6,315	6,210	6,022	5,229
Government Finance						*Millions of Nuevos Soles: Year Ending December 31*							
Deficit (-) or Surplus......................	80	−3,123	−4,099	−1,980	−1,260	−1,877	−5,485	−5,197	−5,290	−4,263	−3,713	−2,977	−1,900
Revenue..................................	81	14,808	18,729	22,260	25,325	26,726	26,020	28,240	27,350	28,930	31,929	35,570	41,531
Grants Received..........................	81z	201	111	325	325	405	445	635	702	....	....	....	....
Expenditure.............................	82	16,985	21,903	23,183	25,406	28,056	31,415	33,202	32,413	33,062	35,510	38,415	43,298
Lending Minus Repayments...........	83	946	925	1,058	1,179	547	90	235	227	132	132	132	132
Financing													
Domestic...................................	84a	664	1,222	891	1,248	1,316	5,815	3,093	3,225	267	327	−862	5,020
Foreign...................................	85a	2,460	2,877	1,090	12	561	−330	2,104	2,065	3,997	3,386	3,838	−3,120
National Accounts						*Millions of Nuevos Soles*							
Househ.Cons.Expend.,incl.NPISHs....	96f	71,306	85,933	98,598	110,782	118,279	122,286	131,745	135,876	143,027	149,824	161,041	170,849
Government Consumption Expend...	91f	8,672	11,786	13,827	15,487	17,296	18,854	19,717	20,214	20,234	21,892	23,728	26,441
Gross Fixed Capital Formation.........	93e	20,901	29,095	30,747	37,472	39,163	37,867	37,610	35,132	35,128	37,748	42,230	48,908
Changes in Inventories..................	93i	1,030	918	537	479	93	−1,074	−79	275	2,232	2,037	1,101	−1,137
Exports of Goods and Services.........	90c	12,590	15,118	17,975	22,272	22,076	25,855	29,867	30,128	32,780	37,378	48,968	63,403
Imports of Goods and Services (-).....	98c	15,922	21,991	24,754	29,219	31,014	29,907	33,434	33,312	34,530	37,387	42,809	49,949
Gross Domestic Product (GDP)........	99b	98,577	120,858	136,929	157,274	165,893	173,881	185,426	188,313	198,871	211,492	234,261	258,516
GDP Volume 1994 Prices................	99b.p	98,577	107,039	109,709	117,214	116,413	117,446	120,881	121,104	127,086	132,119	138,474	147,709
GDP Volume (2000=100)................	99bvp	81.5	88.5	90.8	97.0	96.3	97.2	100.0	100.2	105.1	109.3	114.6	122.2
GDP Deflator (2000=100)...............	99bip	65.2	73.6	81.4	87.5	92.9	96.5	100.0	101.4	102.0	104.4	110.3	114.1
						Millions: Midyear Estimates							
Population...............................	99z	23.42	23.84	24.26	24.68	25.11	25.54	25.95	26.36	26.76	27.16	27.56	27.97

Philippines 566

		1994	1995	1996	1997	1998	1999	2000	2001	2002	2003	2004	2005
Exchange Rates		*Pesos per SDR: End of Period*											
Market Rate	aa	35.647	38.967	37.801	53.936	54.996	55.330	65.143	64.601	72.185	82.574	87.383	75.847
		Pesos per US Dollar: End of Period (ae) Period Average (rf)											
Market Rate	ae	24.418	26.214	26.288	39.975	39.059	40.313	49.998	51.404	53.096	55.569	56.267	53.067
Market Rate	rf	26.417	25.714	26.216	29.471	40.893	39.089	44.192	50.993	51.604	54.203	56.040	55.085
		Index Numbers (2000=100): Period Averages											
Market Rate	ahx	166.7	170.8	167.6	151.6	107.7	112.5	100.0	86.2	85.2	81.1	78.4	79.8
Nominal Effective Exchange Rate	nec	147.5	145.8	148.6	142.5	111.5	112.0	100.0	90.9	89.7	81.3	75.7	76.9
Real Effective Exchange Rate	rec	117.2	120.4	130.2	128.7	107.8	114.1	100.0	95.6	96.2	89.1	86.2	92.3
Fund Position		*Millions of SDRs: End of Period*											
Quota	2f.s	633	633	633	633	633	880	880	880	880	880	880	880
SDRs	1b.s	17	5	2	1	1	5	1	11	7	1	1	1
Reserve Position in the Fund	1c.s	87	87	87	87	87	87	87	87	87	87	87	87
Total Fund Cred.&Loans Outstg	2tl	729	489	282	634	1,114	1,328	1,559	1,553	1,240	806	487	272
International Liquidity		*Millions of US Dollars Unless Otherwise Indicated: End of Period*											
Total Reserves minus Gold	1l.d	6,038	6,396	10,058	7,297	9,274	13,270	13,090	13,476	13,329	13,655	13,116	15,926
SDRs	1b.d	24	8	2	2	2	7	2	14	10	2	1	1
Reserve Position in the Fund	1c.d	127	129	125	118	123	120	113	110	119	130	136	125
Foreign Exchange	1d.d	5,887	6,259	9,931	7,178	9,150	13,143	12,975	13,353	13,200	13,523	12,980	15,800
Gold (Million Fine Troy Ounces)	1ad	2.892	3.580	4.651	4.988	5.432	6.199	7.228	7.980	8.729	8.217	7.119	4.968
Gold (National Valuation)	1and	1,104	1,403	1,715	1,472	1,555	1,782	1,973	2,216	3,036	3,408	3,112	2,568
Monetary Authorities: Other Liab	4..d	2,295	2,523	2,489	2,578	3,272	4,423	4,826	6,029	5,555	6,011	4,725	3,678
Deposit Money Banks: Assets	7a.d	6,036	6,402	8,185	8,878	9,153	10,114	8,181	7,468	8,074	8,239	9,637	12,963
Liabilities	7b.d	4,640	6,420	14,364	15,406	12,751	11,978	10,302	8,730	8,009	7,582	8,987	10,791
Other Banking Insts.: Liabilities	7f.d	963	1,080	49	62	64	46	45	47	312	44	48	57
OBU: Foreign Assets	7k.d	485	283	174	203	123	121	137	304	313	291	294	1,108
Foreign Liabilities	7m.d	1,674	1,545	1,647	1,826	1,296	1,167	928	987	807	819	820	2,258
Monetary Authorities		*Billions of Pesos: End of Period*											
Foreign Assets	11	173.78	203.60	308.76	349.29	422.13	605.18	751.29	804.92	861.63	937.49	903.08	981.35
Claims on Central Government	12a	233.87	227.85	240.26	226.57	194.18	237.91	165.80	132.96	149.43	125.10	76.71	48.00
Claims on Local Government	12b	—	—	—	—	—	—	—	—	—	—	—	—
Claims on Nonfin.Pub.Enterprises	12c	1.97	1.93	1.82	2.98	4.26	17.76	38.33	30.12	56.04	83.45	80.73	73.11
Claims on Deposit Money Banks	12e	6.17	7.31	7.68	26.43	18.20	12.69	48.98	40.94	17.46	27.83	18.09	12.24
Claims on Other Financial Insts	12f	4.60	6.26	6.48	8.02	13.51	14.18	15.10	10.87	9.85	9.14	10.56	10.32
Claims on Nonbank Financial Insts	12g	—	—	—	—	—	—	—	—	—	—	—	—
Reserve Money	14	226.93	255.17	338.17	317.63	323.83	442.74	395.88	351.91	409.34	447.56	466.39	576.42
of which: Currency Outside DMBs	14a	95.68	110.89	122.95	143.64	146.06	218.47	192.30	194.67	220.04	238.61	259.57	273.71
Time Deposits	15	24.69	28.37	39.89	13.61	15.47	31.12	52.36	26.65	49.80	33.30	24.06	26.62
Liabs. of Central Bank: Securities	16ac	4.57	.63	.25	.03	.03	.03	.03	—	—	—	—	—
Restricted Deposits	16b	4.92	2.12	1.68	1.68	1.69	.39	.04	.04	.32	.22	.68	.90
Foreign Liabilities	16c	82.01	85.22	76.10	137.26	189.08	251.76	342.86	410.25	384.47	400.54	308.42	215.83
Central Government Deposits	16d	84.54	73.43	106.54	78.35	59.49	90.74	95.42	86.52	78.89	104.23	60.29	85.33
Capital Accounts	17a	26.49	30.15	30.08	71.98	88.15	100.23	159.45	188.96	197.81	222.77	240.90	264.68
Other Items (Net)	17r	−33.76	−28.15	−27.71	−7.24	−25.44	−29.28	−26.54	−44.50	−26.23	−25.61	−11.55	−44.77
Deposit Money Banks		*Billions of Pesos: End of Period*											
Reserves	20	123.30	123.93	142.84	161.06	168.17	190.99	178.09	181.18	216.57	206.93	202.31	294.93
Claims on Mon.Author.:Securities	20c	.94	.08	.08	.03	.03	.03	.03	—	—	—	—	—
Foreign Assets	21	147.38	167.83	215.16	354.90	357.52	407.73	409.03	383.90	428.72	457.81	542.22	687.91
Claims on Central Government	22a	147.56	177.21	237.53	304.31	300.34	332.42	432.55	534.56	563.11	635.41	797.43	756.01
Claims on Local Government	22b	2.37	4.68	6.95	9.07	10.34	12.20	15.52	17.15	18.41	20.27	24.42	26.23
Claims on Nonfin.Pub.Enterprises	22c	17.07	14.87	16.37	25.65	40.56	47.68	59.18	82.78	99.18	168.77	170.41	202.34
Claims on Private Sector	22d	491.98	715.32	1,063.80	1,370.07	1,279.19	1,249.58	1,316.59	1,293.29	1,303.35	1,317.66	1,439.68	1,407.87
Claims on Other Financial Insts	22f	24.61	27.09	60.26	76.61	117.98	130.68	175.13	157.71	166.94	179.86	126.43	135.03
Demand Deposits	24	55.08	72.04	96.41	111.92	134.09	172.87	192.98	191.94	252.77	274.92	300.96	336.41
Time, Savings,& Fgn.Currency Dep	25	613.16	765.20	949.71	1,225.32	1,332.79	1,483.42	1,622.30	1,720.15	1,833.30	1,893.55	2,097.57	2,215.36
Money Market Instruments	26aa	4.61	6.24	6.64	12.07	6.11	7.19	4.21	3.98	3.37	3.46	1.08	1.04
Restricted Deposits	26b	3.42	3.55	2.99	3.28	7.05	4.03	5.16	4.76	3.86	3.68	5.46	1.33
Foreign Liabilities	26c	113.29	168.29	377.59	615.86	498.05	482.86	515.10	448.75	425.22	421.30	505.66	572.67
Central Government Deposits	26d	26.62	39.41	51.73	38.90	32.43	39.86	33.97	42.39	39.87	33.91	51.28	69.02
Credit from Monetary Authorities	26g	17.06	16.67	15.26	15.02	10.38	8.47	38.09	26.73	16.31	19.63	10.32	9.98
Capital Accounts	27a	132.36	184.71	243.17	327.28	376.53	440.89	467.48	479.22	511.74	539.22	557.16	533.05
Other Items (Net)	27r	−10.40	−25.10	−.51	−47.95	−123.31	−268.28	−293.17	−267.36	−290.14	−202.97	−226.60	−228.55
Monetary Survey		*Billions of Pesos: End of Period*											
Foreign Assets (Net)	31n	125.86	117.92	70.23	−48.93	92.51	278.29	302.37	329.81	480.66	573.46	631.23	880.76
Domestic Credit	32	813.42	1,062.38	1,475.20	1,906.05	1,868.45	1,911.82	2,088.82	2,130.52	2,247.55	2,401.52	2,614.80	2,504.55
Claims on Central Govt. (Net)	32an	270.27	292.21	319.53	413.64	402.61	439.74	468.97	538.61	593.77	622.37	762.57	649.65
Claims on Local Government	32b	2.37	4.68	6.95	9.07	10.34	12.20	15.52	17.15	18.41	20.27	24.42	26.23
Claims on Nonfin.Pub.Enterprises	32c	19.04	16.80	18.19	28.63	44.82	65.44	97.51	112.90	155.23	252.22	251.14	275.45
Claims on Private Sector	32d	492.53	715.34	1,063.80	1,370.08	1,279.19	1,249.59	1,316.59	1,293.29	1,303.35	1,317.66	1,439.68	1,407.87
Claims on Other Financial Insts	32f	29.21	33.35	66.73	84.63	131.49	144.86	190.22	168.58	176.79	188.99	136.99	145.35
Claims on Nonbank Financial Insts	32g	—	—	—	—	—	—	—	—	—	—	—	—
Money	34	159.90	194.63	233.12	266.33	285.95	395.56	390.55	392.25	478.48	519.84	567.74	620.22
Quasi-Money	35	637.85	793.58	989.60	1,238.93	1,348.25	1,514.53	1,674.66	1,746.80	1,883.10	1,926.86	2,121.63	2,241.98
Money Market Instruments	36aa	4.61	6.24	6.64	12.07	6.11	7.19	4.21	3.98	3.37	3.46	1.08	1.04
Liabs. of Central Bank: Securities	36ac	3.63	.55	.17	—	—	—	—	—	—	—	—	—
Restricted Deposits	36b	8.34	5.67	4.67	4.96	8.73	4.42	5.20	4.80	4.17	3.90	6.14	2.23
Capital Accounts	37a	158.84	214.86	273.25	399.26	464.68	541.12	626.94	668.17	709.55	761.99	798.05	797.73
Other Items (Net)	37r	−33.90	−35.22	37.98	−64.42	−152.77	−272.71	−310.36	−355.66	−350.46	−241.08	−248.61	−277.90
Money plus Quasi-Money	35l	797.75	988.20	1,222.72	1,505.26	1,634.20	1,910.09	2,065.21	2,139.05	2,361.58	2,446.70	2,689.36	2,862.20

Philippines 566

		1994	1995	1996	1997	1998	1999	2000	2001	2002	2003	2004	2005
Other Banking Institutions						*Billions of Pesos: End of Period*							
Reserves..................................	40	15.51	18.57	18.50	19.78	15.34	14.92	23.56	18.68	20.87	21.65	24.81	28.96
Claims on Central Government........	42a	12.93	19.09	3.38	3.95	2.35	1.74	3.46	1.91	24.35	4.60	6.22	8.83
Claims on Private Sector.................	42d	115.93	143.41	127.55	139.92	144.74	145.55	152.43	166.17	161.22	189.60	211.22	242.85
Time and Savings Deposits..............	45	69.09	93.73	106.89	120.70	119.08	120.58	131.77	151.64	171.99	187.29	213.87	250.31
Bonds.......................................	46ab	2.28	3.65	4.22	5.39	6.38	6.29	6.38	5.49	5.14	2.76	3.38	3.54
Foreign Liabilities............................	46c	23.51	28.31	1.29	2.49	2.49	1.87	2.23	2.44	16.56	2.44	2.67	3.00
Credit from Monetary Authorities.....	46g	3.56	3.65	3.67	5.08	10.59	10.74	11.95	8.40	7.34	7.54	9.05	8.72
Capital Accounts............................	47a	27.08	32.99	27.33	35.93	40.73	48.63	49.27	48.26	49.40	46.22	44.26	49.57
Other Items (Net)............................	47r	18.85	18.74	6.04	−5.95	−16.84	−25.89	−22.15	−29.48	−43.98	−30.41	−30.99	−34.49
Money (National Definitions)						*Billions of Pesos: End of Period*							
Reserve Money...............................	19mb	182.41	212.74	243.26	266.46	239.83	321.73	308.21	312.87	356.08	374.56	410.54	446.81
Narrow Money...............................	59maa	151.95	184.93	221.96	258.32	281.51	394.13	386.98	387.99	470.06	510.27	556.42	605.35
Quasi-Money.................................	59mab	451.05	570.26	652.81	795.63	856.92	963.78	1,036.21	1,133.07	1,196.24	1,211.24	1,326.26	1,446.16
M3..	59mc	607.61	761.43	881.40	1,066.02	1,144.55	1,365.10	1,427.40	1,525.03	1,669.66	1,724.97	1,883.76	2,052.55
M4..	59md	766.40	968.12	1,198.97	1,499.45	1,622.49	1,886.76	2,013.38	2,111.12	2,298.11	2,401.45	2,649.30	2,814.33
Interest Rates						*Percent Per Annum*							
Discount Rate (End of Period)...........	60	8.300	10.830	11.700	14.640	12.400	7.894	13.806	8.298	4.193	5.532	8.357	5.699
Money Market Rate........................	60b	13.989	11.925	12.770	16.155	13.900	10.165	10.835	9.751	7.149	6.969	7.047	7.314
Treasury Bill Rate...........................	60c	12.714	11.761	12.338	12.893	15.004	9.996	9.913	9.734	5.494	5.872	7.320	6.132
Savings Rate.................................	60k	8.068	8.044	7.945	8.951	10.952	7.640	7.308	7.655	4.240	4.214	4.265	3.760
Savings Rate (Foreign Currency).......	60k.f	2.268	2.275	2.200	2.200	2.200	2.200	2.200	2.004	1.288	.885	.837	.940
Deposit Rate.................................	60l	10.539	8.392	9.683	10.194	12.106	8.167	8.305	8.744	4.608	5.221	6.178	5.556
Deposit Rate (Foreign Currency).......	60l.f	4.203	5.295	5.097	5.322	5.441	5.037	5.207	3.804	2.322	1.908	1.916	2.407
Lending Rate.................................	60p	15.057	14.682	14.840	16.276	16.777	11.776	10.907	12.402	9.139	9.472	10.079	10.185
Government Bond Yield..................	61	13.250	14.250	13.990	13.008	† 17.985	12.332	11.767	13.399	8.688	8.715	10.270	8.660
Prices, Production, Labor						*Index Numbers (2000=100): Period Averages*							
Share Prices..................................	62	137.3	122.4	119.3	103.9	69.1	106.7	100.0	64.4	48.4	40.8	57.9	145.6
Producer Prices..............................	63	66.7	69.6	72.4	74.9	† 83.1	88.9	100.0	117.0	120.4	130.2	140.0	154.0
Consumer Prices............................	64	† 68.6	73.2	78.7	83.1	90.8	96.2	100.0	106.8	110.0	113.8	120.6	129.8
Manufacturing Production..............	66ey	58.6	69.1	75.2	81.7	† 80.1	86.7	100.0	108.3	106.5	115.1	125.1	141.3
Manufacturing Empl. (1990=100)....	67ey	85.8	....	....	....	....	....	....	....	....	....	....	....
						Number in Thousands: Period Averages							
Labor Force..................................	67d	27,654	28,380	29,732	30,355	29,674	30,759	30,912	32,809	33,936	34,571	35,862	36,458
Employment.................................	67e	25,032	25,676	27,186	27,715	26,631	27,742	27,453	29,156	30,062	30,635	31,613	32,313
Unemployment.............................	67c	2,622	2,704	2,546	2,640	3,043	3,017	3,459	3,653	3,874	3,936	4,249	4,145
Unemployment Rate (%).................	67r	9.5	9.5	8.6	8.7	10.1	9.8	11.2	11.1	11.4	11.4	11.8	11.4
Intl. Transactions & Positions						*Millions of Pesos*							
Exports...	70	350,078	450,487	535,054	738,415	1,206,197	1,432,594	1,773,137	1,665,023	1,884,323	1,965,589	2,224,271	2,196,760
Sugar...	70i	1,629	1,713	3,544	2,864	3,200	2,597	2,227	1,124	1,830	3,112	3,733	3,598
Coconut Oil.................................	70ai	12,552	21,242	14,960	19,846	28,857	13,379	20,450	21,292	18,196	27,365	32,379	36,258
Imports, c.i.f.................................	71	596,611	729,960	894,665	1,139,830	1,290,274	1,273,001	1,636,810	1,780,531	1,919,156	2,141,226	2,373,188	2,587,381
Imports, f.o.b...............................	71.v	562,163	679,701	835,863	1,060,815	1,213,859	1,201,519	1,526,636	1,684,742	1,827,806	2,030,102	2,258,633	2,474,759
						2000=100							
Volume of Exports.........................	72	86.2	56.1	62.2	73.6	79.7	86.9	100.0	88.6	104.9	97.9	107.1	....
Sugar...	72i	128.6	108.2	224.4	139.7	130.5	100.7	100.0	40.0	62.6	97.2	162.7	157.3
Coconut Oil.................................	72ai	81.8	129.2	76.4	104.1	113.6	46.1	100.0	136.6	91.0	114.3	92.4	111.2
Volume of Imports.........................	73	143.3	83.4	97.9	106.4	84.9	94.8	100.0	113.6	115.6	115.8	137.4	....
Export Prices.................................	76	80.7	81.3	86.2	89.4	96.7	106.3	100.0	95.5	88.6	96.7	96.7	....
Sugar (Wholesale Price).................	76i	53.3	65.3	65.1	67.0	98.0	118.6	100.0	116.2	120.9	132.5	94.6	94.3
Coconut Oil (W'sale price).............	76ai	68.7	76.1	92.1	89.5	111.2	138.2	100.0	73.0	95.6	110.4	161.5	146.4
Import Prices.................................	76.x	104.0	101.0	106.1	108.1	111.1	103.8	100.0	92.2	97.3	101.3	102.0	....

		1994	1995	1996	1997	1998	1999	2000	2001	2002	2003	2004	2005
Balance of Payments					*Millions of US Dollars: Minus Sign Indicates Debit*								
Current Account, n.i.e.	78ald	−2,950	−1,980	−3,953	−4,351	1,546	−2,874	−2,225	−1,744	−279	288	1,629	2,338
Goods: Exports f.o.b.	78aad	13,483	17,447	20,543	25,228	29,496	34,243	37,347	31,313	34,403	35,339	38,794	40,231
Goods: Imports f.o.b.	78abd	−21,333	−26,391	−31,885	−36,355	−29,524	−40,220	−43,318	−37,578	−39,933	−41,190	−44,478	−47,777
Trade Balance	78acd	−7,850	−8,944	−11,342	−11,127	−28	−5,977	−5,971	−6,265	−5,530	−5,851	−5,684	−7,546
Services: Credit	78add	6,768	9,348	12,947	15,137	7,477	3,468	3,377	3,072	3,428	3,389	4,043	4,462
Services: Debit	78aed	−4,654	−6,926	−9,429	−14,122	−10,107	−5,088	−5,247	−5,360	−5,430	−5,352	−5,819	−5,858
Balance on Goods & Services	78afd	−5,736	−6,522	−7,824	−10,112	−2,658	−7,597	−7,841	−8,553	−7,532	−7,814	−7,460	−8,942
Income: Credit	78agd	3,782	6,067	6,059	7,698	6,440	2,723	3,336	3,553	3,306	3,330	3,725	3,937
Income: Debit	78ahd	−1,932	−2,405	−2,777	−3,017	−2,671	−3,784	−3,363	−3,604	−3,733	−3,614	−3,796	−4,060
Balance on Gds, Serv. & Inc	78aid	−3,886	−2,860	−4,542	−5,431	1,111	−8,658	−7,868	−8,604	−7,959	−8,098	−7,531	−9,065
Current Transfers, n.i.e.: Credit	78ajd	1,041	1,147	1,185	1,670	758	5,969	5,909	7,119	7,948	8,626	9,420	11,706
Current Transfers: Debit	78akd	−105	−267	−596	−590	−323	−185	−266	−259	−268	−240	−260	−303
Capital Account, n.i.e.	78bcd	—	—	—	—	—	163	138	62	27	54	17	40
Capital Account, n.i.e.: Credit	78bad	—	—	—	—	—	270	168	86	50	82	46	58
Capital Account: Debit	78bbd	—	—	—	—	—	−107	−30	−24	−23	−28	−29	−18
Financial Account, n.i.e.	78bjd	5,120	5,309	11,277	6,498	483	4,209	3,234	366	394	480	−1,669	97
Direct Investment Abroad	78bdd	−302	−399	−182	−136	−160	−133	−125	140	−65	−303	−579	−162
Dir. Invest. in Rep. Econ., n.i.e.	78bed	1,591	1,478	1,517	1,222	2,287	1,247	2,240	195	1,542	491	688	1,132
Portfolio Investment Assets	78bfd	−632	−1,429	191	−9	−603	−603	−812	−57	−628	−818	−862	−1,153
Equity Securities	78bkd	....	....	21	30	−184	−55	−42	30	−8	−48	−15	−24
Debt Securities	78bld	−632	−1,429	170	−39	−419	−548	−770	−87	−620	−770	−847	−1,129
Portfolio Investment Liab., n.i.e.	78bgd	901	2,619	5,126	600	−325	4,265	259	97	1,361	1,381	288	3,813
Equity Securities	78bmd	....	....	2,101	−406	264	489	−202	125	227	501	518	1,461
Debt Securities	78bnd	901	2,619	3,025	1,006	−589	3,776	461	−28	1,134	880	−230	2,352
Financial Derivatives Assets	78bwd	....	....	....	....	....	51	166	83	85	54	58	98
Financial Derivatives Liabilities	78bxd	....	....	....	....	....	−43	−122	−98	−106	−118	−85	−141
Other Investment Assets	78bhd	—	—	−1,745	425	809	−1,051	2,454	761	−256	743	−907	−3,532
Monetary Authorities	78bod	....	....	....	....	—	—	....	....	....	....	....	....
General Government	78bpd	....	....	....	....	—	—	....	....	....	....	....	....
Banks	78bqd	....	....	−1,745	425	809	−938	2,270	908	−241	370	−588	−2,288
Other Sectors	78brd	....	....	—	—	—	−113	184	−147	−15	373	−319	−1,244
Other Investment Liab., n.i.e.	78bid	3,562	3,040	6,370	4,396	−1,525	476	−826	−755	−1,539	−950	−270	42
Monetary Authorities	78bsd	—	—	199	−98	5	−175	60	620	−662	2	−1,118	−488
General Government	78btd	−1,121	−408	−808	−218	−207	269	−184	−65	90	−64	−362	−521
Banks	78bud	1,694	1,648	5,036	1,668	−1,118	−184	−325	−752	49	−453	1,234	964
Other Sectors	78bvd	2,989	1,800	1,943	3,044	−205	566	−377	−558	−1,016	−435	−24	87
Net Errors and Omissions	78cad	157	−2,094	−2,986	−5,241	−750	2,269	−1,624	629	33	−901	−280	−789
Overall Balance	78cbd	2,327	1,235	4,338	−3,094	1,279	3,767	−477	−687	175	−79	−303	1,686
Reserves and Related Items	79dad	−2,327	−1,235	−4,338	3,094	−1,279	−3,767	477	687	−175	79	303	−1,686
Reserve Assets	79dbd	−2,107	−873	−4,037	2,610	−1,938	−3,943	69	−469	252	356	1,637	−1,600
Use of Fund Credit and Loans	79dcd	−220	−362	−301	485	659	288	303	−8	−407	−607	−472	−321
Exceptional Financing	79ded	—	—	—	—	—	−112	105	1,164	−21	330	−862	235
International Investment Position						*Millions of US Dollars*							
Assets	79aad	....	....	....	....	....	....	....	29,179	31,033	31,768	33,325	....
Direct Investment Abroad	79abd	....	....	....	....	....	....	....	1,033	1,099	1,298	1,877	....
Portfolio Investment	79acd	....	....	....	....	....	....	....	2,605	3,199	3,912	4,774	....
Equity Securities	79add	....	....	....	....	....	....	....	110	118	166	182	....
Debt Securities	79aed	....	....	....	....	....	....	....	2,495	3,081	3,746	4,592	....
Financial Derivatives	79ald	....	....	....	....	....	....	....	—	—	—	—	....
Other Investment	79afd	....	....	....	....	....	....	....	9,848	10,369	9,495	10,445	....
Monetary Authorities	79agd	....	....	....	....	....	....	....	—	—	—	—	....
General Government	79ahd	....	....	....	....	....	....	....	33	35	35	35	....
Banks	79aid	....	....	....	....	....	....	....	5,662	5,753	5,352	5,929	....
Other Sectors	79ajd	....	....	....	....	....	....	....	4,153	4,581	4,108	4,481	....
Reserve Assets	79akd	....	....	....	....	....	....	....	15,693	16,366	17,063	16,229	....
Liabilities	79lad	....	....	....	....	....	....	....	65,712	69,411	73,259	72,735	....
Dir. Invest. in Rep. Economy	79lbd	....	....	....	....	....	....	....	10,684	12,029	11,794	12,896	....
Portfolio Investment	79lcd	....	....	....	....	....	....	....	16,136	18,190	20,783	20,035	....
Equity Securities	79ldd	....	....	....	....	....	....	....	1,897	2,291	2,750	3,131	....
Debt Securities	79led	....	....	....	....	....	....	....	14,239	15,899	18,033	16,904	....
Financial Derivatives	79lld	....	....	....	....	....	....	....	—	—	—	—	....
Other Investment	79lfd	....	....	....	....	....	....	....	38,892	39,192	40,682	39,804	....
Monetary Authorities	79lgd	....	....	....	....	....	....	....	4,663	3,738	3,648	2,329	....
General Government	79lhd	....	....	....	....	....	....	....	13,120	14,054	15,619	15,759	....
Banks	79lid	....	....	....	....	....	....	....	5,236	5,886	6,077	6,341	....
Other Sectors	79ljd	....	....	....	....	....	....	....	15,873	15,514	15,338	15,375	....
Government Finance						*Millions of Pesos: Year Ending December 31*							
Deficit (-) or Surplus	80	18,114	11,074	6,256	1,564	−49,981	−111,658	−136,110	−147,023	−210,741	−199,868	−187,057	−146,778
Revenue	81	334,488	360,232	409,880	470,087	462,119	478,210	504,349	561,857	566,089	625,432	699,699	795,621
Grants Received	81z	739	988	569	1,756	396	292	1,376	1,991	1,052	1,198	74	88
Expenditure	82	309,942	341,726	401,017	466,690	511,078	585,425	638,665	706,443	775,256	818,422	881,110	940,590
Lending Minus Repayments	83	7,171	8,420	3,176	3,589	1,418	4,735	3,170	4,428	2,626	8,076	5,720	1,897
Financing													
Domestic	84a	−4,408	2,272	−348	5,254	37,635	28,858	90,927	124,108	101,628	56,006	105,890	54,113
Foreign	85a	−13,706	−13,346	−5,908	−6,818	12,346	82,800	45,183	22,915	109,113	143,862	81,167	92,665
Debt: Domestic	88a	638,025	....	....	....	....	....	....	....	....	....	....	....
Foreign	89a	317,068	....	....	....	....	....	....	....	....	....	....	....

Philippines 566

National Accounts		1994	1995	1996	1997	1998	1999	2000	2001	2002	2003	2004	2005
							Billions of Pesos						
Househ.Cons.Expend.,incl.NPISHs....	96f	1,258.8	1,411.9	1,595.3	1,762.0	1,980.1	2,161.6	2,335.5	2,565.0	2,751.0	2,988.2	3,344.2	3,773.1
Government Consumption Expend...	91f	182.8	217.0	259.5	319.9	354.4	389.2	438.9	444.8	456.9	477.4	492.1	525.7
Gross Fixed Capital Formation.........	93e	400.1	423.2	508.7	592.6	563.6	568.2	710.5	651.3	698.1	726.9	784.0	808.0
Changes in Inventories....................	93i	7.2	4.7	12.9	8.7	−21.5	−10.0	−.4	37.8	2.1	−.3	31.9	12.5
Exports of Goods and Services..........	90c	572.6	693.0	879.8	1,188.0	1,389.9	1,532.2	1,858.6	1,785.2	1,991.3	2,142.0	2,470.7	2,564.4
Imports of Goods and Services (-).....	98c	679.4	842.1	1,070.6	1,438.9	1,566.6	1,527.4	1,794.7	1,899.4	2,010.5	2,398.4	2,659.0	2,816.1
Gross Domestic Product (GDP).........	99b	1,692.9	1,906.0	2,171.9	2,426.7	2,665.1	2,976.9	3,354.7	3,631.5	3,963.9	4,316.4	4,858.8	5,418.3
Net Primary Income from Abroad.....	98.n	43.5	52.6	89.4	101.6	137.1	159.3	211.3	245.1	255.0	315.1	376.4	457.5
Gross National Income (GNI)............	99a	1,736.4	1,958.6	2,261.3	2,528.3	2,802.1	3,136.2	3,566.1	3,876.6	4,218.9	4,631.5	5,235.2	5,876.3
Consumption of Fixed Capital..........	99cf	151.5	172.0	190.5	....	....	....	....	....	....	....	....	....
GDP Volume 1985 Prices.................	99b.p	766.4	802.2	849.1	893.2	888.0	918.2	955.0	987.4	1,042.1	1,093.3	1,148.0	1,203.5
GDP Volume (2000=100)................	99bvp	80.3	84.0	88.9	93.5	93.0	96.1	100.0	103.4	109.1	114.5	120.2	126.0
GDP Deflator (2000=100)................	99bip	62.9	67.6	72.8	77.3	85.4	92.3	100.0	104.7	108.3	112.4	120.5	128.2
							Millions: Midyear Estimates						
Population...............................	99z	66.92	68.40	69.87	71.35	72.82	74.29	75.77	77.24	78.71	80.17	81.62	83.05

		1994	1995	1996	1997	1998	1999	2000	2001	2002	2003	2004	2005
Exchange Rates													
						Zlotys per SDR: End of Period							
Market Rate	aa	3.5579	3.6687	4.1349	4.7467	4.9337	5.6936	5.3982	5.0097	5.2189	5.5587	4.6441	4.6613
						Zlotys per US Dollar: End of Period (ae) Period Average (rf)							
Market Rate	ae	2.4372	2.4680	2.8755	3.5180	3.5040	4.1483	4.1432	3.9863	3.8388	3.7408	2.9904	3.2613
Market Rate	rf	2.2723	2.4250	2.6961	3.2793	3.4754	3.9671	4.3461	4.0939	4.0800	3.8891	3.6576	3.2355
						Index Numbers (2000=100): Period Averages							
Market Rate	ahx	191.2	179.0	161.2	132.8	125.0	109.6	100.0	106.0	106.4	111.6	119.3	134.3
Nominal Effective Exchange Rate	nec	143.7	125.5	117.5	108.3	104.6	97.6	100.0	109.9	105.4	95.0	93.7	104.8
Real Effective Exchange Rate	rec	73.0	78.9	85.6	88.4	93.4	91.1	100.0	112.7	108.1	96.3	96.2	107.4
Fund Position													
						Millions of SDRs: End of Period							
Quota	2f.s	989	989	989	989	989	1,369	1,369	1,369	1,369	1,369	1,369	1,369
SDRs	1b.s	1	2	3	4	5	8	14	21	29	37	45	54
Reserve Position in the Fund	1c.s	77	77	77	77	77	172	172	367	479	538	451	209
Total Fund Cred.&Loans Outstg	2tl	919	—	—	—	—	—	—	—	—	—	—	—
International Liquidity													
						Millions of US Dollars Unless Otherwise Indicated: End of Period							
Total Reserves minus Gold	1l.d	5,841.8	14,774.1	17,844.0	20,407.2	27,325.2	26,354.7	26,562.0	25,648.4	28,649.7	32,579.1	35,323.9	40,863.7
SDRs	1b.d	1.5	2.2	4.4	5.4	7.1	11.2	17.7	25.8	39.5	54.8	70.1	77.8
Reserve Position in the Fund	1c.d	112.6	114.6	110.9	104.1	108.6	236.4	224.4	461.0	651.0	799.4	700.9	299.0
Foreign Exchange	1d.d	5,727.7	14,657.2	17,728.7	20,297.7	27,209.5	26,107.1	26,319.9	25,161.6	27,959.2	31,724.9	34,552.8	40,486.9
Gold (Million Fine Troy Ounces)	1ad	.473	.473	.473	.904	3.305	3.306	3.306	3.308	3.309	3.307	3.308	3.308
Gold (National Valuation)	1and	189.0	189.0	189.0	262.4	950.0	959.4	901.5	914.7	1,134.0	1,380.5	1,448.8	1,697.2
Monetary Authorities: Other Liab.	4..d	355.6	363.5	246.4	914.3	1,028.2	1,939.3	498.6	588.2	145.6	233.4	142.1	2,010.0
Deposit Money Banks: Assets	7a.d	7,742.2	7,154.4	6,132.1	7,275.5	5,405.3	7,874.1	11,323.1	15,307.2	13,707.8	14,920.9	28,111.2	28,376.2
Liabilities	7b.d	1,543.2	2,070.1	2,746.5	4,284.0	5,213.8	6,745.7	6,608.9	7,766.1	9,069.2	12,638.8	17,008.2	16,744.5
Monetary Authorities													
						Millions of Zlotys: End of Period							
Foreign Assets	11	15,475	37,532	52,498	75,500	99,213	113,910	114,258	106,183	114,772	128,207	110,456	139,428
Claims on General Government	12a	19,530	11,534	12,761	16,792	17,765	18,803	16,745	18,426	6,579	384	—	—
Claims on Other Resident Sectors	12d	23	22	59	66	60	71	68	23	23	24	108	107
Claims on Deposit Money Banks	12e	7,450	8,244	11,246	9,710	8,044	7,394	7,121	6,033	5,421	4,833	4,348	3,129
Reserve Money	14	19,615	28,441	34,262	45,919	53,656	52,957	48,818	63,704	62,066	66,337	69,583	73,429
of which: Currency Outside DMBs	14a	12,274	19,530	23,563	27,256	30,225	38,083	34,113	38,213	42,193	49,417	50,776	57,155
Nonreserve Liabilities to Banks	16b	3,462	9,465	14,660	15,662	28,576	24,694	33,738	24,167	20,953	14,202	13,940	31,221
Foreign Liabilities	16c	4,135	897	708	3,216	3,603	8,045	2,066	2,345	559	873	425	6,555
General Government Deposits	16d	2,773	3,440	6,127	4,285	4,010	7,040	9,774	7,689	7,414	11,429	14,595	17,515
Capital Accounts	17a	300	400	400	400	1,548	1,548	1,594	1,694	1,748	1,845	2,059	2,278
Other Items (Net)	17r	12,193	14,689	20,406	32,586	33,688	45,894	42,202	31,064	34,055	38,761	14,311	11,666
Deposit Money Banks													
						Millions of Zlotys: End of Period							
Reserves	20	7,343	8,806	10,633	15,049	23,336	14,867	14,661	21,485	19,857	16,903	18,396	13,538
Claims on Mon.Author.:Securities	20c	1,879	4,585	11,018	13,927	28,321	24,539	33,507	24,133	20,735	14,225	13,912	31,156
Other Claims on Monetary Author.	20n	998	3,528	2,739	1,288	—	—	4,000	8	12	54	2,621	
Foreign Assets	21	18,869	17,657	17,633	25,595	18,940	32,666	46,914	61,019	52,622	55,816	84,064	92,543
Claims on General Government	22a	27,204	38,920	48,638	50,980	57,431	63,792	54,591	65,668	78,040	96,008	100,193	97,785
Claims on Other Resident Sectors	22d	41,908	56,946	81,194	107,294	135,498	169,828	197,759	212,575	221,809	236,650	245,176	268,875
Demand Deposits	24	15,175	17,817	28,702	34,425	41,438	49,970	48,420	51,941	70,683	84,142	95,278	117,575
Time, Savings,& Fgn.Currency Dep	25	49,844	66,913	84,186	111,084	149,104	175,302	211,926	244,644	216,524	214,605	219,938	232,988
Foreign Liabilities	26c	3,761	5,109	7,898	15,071	18,269	27,983	27,382	30,958	34,815	47,279	50,861	54,609
General Government Deposits	26d	3,688	5,506	7,942	9,857	12,515	14,113	16,152	16,966	19,991	20,125	24,993	29,647
of which: Local Govt. Dep.	26db	1,503	2,523	3,401	4,395	5,551	7,146	7,472	7,313	8,434	8,818	11,335	13,722
Credit from Monetary Authorities	26g	7,020	7,788	10,685	9,180	7,565	7,010	6,800	5,763	4,023	3,636	3,407	3,769
Capital Accounts	27a	9,990	12,999	18,534	24,715	30,049	34,294	39,562	46,441	45,695	47,181	55,776	59,795
Other Items (Net)	27r	8,724	14,310	13,907	9,801	4,586	−2,980	−2,809	−7,832	1,339	2,648	11,542	8,135
Monetary Survey													
						Millions of Zlotys: End of Period							
Foreign Assets (Net)	31n	26,448	49,183	61,524	82,808	96,281	110,548	131,725	133,899	132,020	135,871	143,234	170,808
Domestic Credit	32	82,205	98,476	128,583	160,990	194,228	231,341	243,237	272,037	279,045	301,512	305,889	319,604
Claims on General Govt. (Net)	32an	40,274	41,508	47,330	53,630	58,671	61,442	45,409	59,439	57,214	64,838	60,605	50,622
Claims on Other Resident Sectors	32d	41,932	56,968	81,253	107,360	135,558	169,899	197,827	212,598	221,831	236,674	245,284	268,982
Money	34	27,450	37,439	52,331	61,686	71,670	88,201	82,574	94,158	112,889	133,576	146,098	174,834
Quasi-Money	35	49,852	66,913	84,331	114,705	149,110	175,307	211,930	244,647	216,527	214,608	226,134	242,862
Capital Accounts	37a	10,290	13,399	18,934	25,115	31,598	35,842	41,156	48,135	47,443	49,026	57,834	62,073
Other Items (Net)	37r	21,062	29,908	34,511	42,291	38,132	42,539	39,301	18,996	34,206	40,174	19,056	10,642
Money plus Quasi-Money	35l	77,302	104,352	136,662	176,392	220,780	263,508	294,505	338,805	329,416	348,183	372,232	417,697
Interest Rates													
						Percent Per Annum							
Discount Rate (End of Period)	60	28.0	25.0	22.0	24.5	18.3	19.0	21.5	14.0	7.8	5.8	7.0	4.5
Money Market Rate	60b	23.3	25.8	20.6	22.4	20.6	13.6	18.2	16.2	9.4	5.8	6.0	5.3
Treasury Bill Rate	60c	28.8	25.6	20.3	21.6	19.1	13.1	16.6	....	....	....	....	....
Deposit Rate	60l	† 33.4	26.8	20.0	19.4	18.2	11.2	14.2	11.8	6.2	3.7	3.8	2.8
Lending Rate	60p	32.8	† 33.5	26.1	25.0	24.5	16.9	20.0	18.4	12.0	7.3	7.6	6.8
Prices, Production, Labor													
						Index Numbers (2000=100): Period Averages							
Share Prices (1995=100)	62	....	100.0	168.9	....	....	....	....	....	....	....	....	....
Producer Prices: Industry	63	51.4	64.6	† 73.1	82.0	88.0	92.8	100.0	101.7	102.8	105.6	113.0	114.0
Consumer Prices	64	42.9	55.0	65.9	75.8	† 84.7	90.9	100.0	105.5	107.5	108.3	112.2	114.6
Harmonized CPI (2002=100)	64h	....	....	....	....	....	....	....	....	100.0	† 100.7	104.3	106.6
Wages: Average Earnings	65	33.7	47.7	60.3	72.3	83.1	90.6	100.0	106.9	111.0	114.2	119.8	123.2
Industrial Production	66	63.3	† 69.7	76.2	84.8	88.8	93.0	100.0	100.4	101.8	110.7	124.8	129.9
Industrial Employment	67	113.5	114.5	113.0	112.4	111.2	106.2	100.0	94.9	89.6	87.1	86.7	88.0
						Number in Thousands: Period Averages							
Labor Force	67d	17,122	17,004	17,076	17,100	17,162	....	17,311	17,376	17,213	16,945	17,025	....
Employment	67e	14,658	14,791	14,969	15,177	15,354	14,747	14,526	14,207	13,782	13,617	13,795	14,116
Unemployment	67c	2,838	2,629	2,360	1,826	1,831	2,350	2,703	2,912	3,162	3,238	3,200	3,045
Unemployment Rate (%)	67r	16.0	15.2	13.2	10.5	10.4	13.0	13.9	16.2	17.8	19.9	19.4	17.8

Poland 964

		1994	1995	1996	1997	1998	1999	2000	2001	2002	2003	2004	2005
Intl. Transactions & Positions							*Millions of Zlotys*							
Exports	70	39,246	55,515	65,819	84,480	95,015	108,706	137,909	148,115	167,338	208,944	272,106	288,682
Imports, c.i.f.	71	49,072	70,502	100,231	138,898	162,458	182,362	213,072	206,253	224,816	265,134	324,663	326,120
Imports, f.o.b.	71.v	42,287	61,306	87,157	120,781	141,268	....	....	....	....	....	....	....
							2000=100							
Volume of Exports	72	48.9	57.4	63.7	71.8	79.5	79.8	100.0	113.9	122.2	143.2	170.1	188.6
Volume of Imports	73	39.7	47.9	61.6	75.1	86.7	89.8	100.0	103.6	110.6	119.1	140.2	147.8
Export Prices	76	57.4	70.0	75.7	85.2	91.4	98.3	100.0	96.1	99.9	105.4	116.5	111.8
Import Prices	76.x	56.8	68.4	75.5	85.8	88.5	94.2	100.0	94.4	94.9	103.7	109.4	104.7
Balance of Payments							*Millions of US Dollars: Minus Sign Indicates Debit*							
Current Account, n.i.e.	78ald	954	854	–3,264	–5,744	–6,901	–12,487	–9,981	–5,375	–5,009	–4,599	–10,522	–4,364
Goods: Exports f.o.b.	78aad	18,355	25,041	27,557	30,731	32,467	30,060	35,902	41,663	46,742	61,007	81,862	95,846
Goods: Imports f.o.b.	78abd	–18,930	–26,687	–34,844	–40,553	–45,303	–45,132	–48,209	–49,324	–53,991	–66,732	–87,484	–98,540
Trade Balance	78acd	–575	–1,646	–7,287	–9,822	–12,836	–15,072	–12,307	–7,661	–7,249	–5,725	–5,622	–2,694
Services: Credit	78add	6,699	10,675	9,747	8,915	10,840	8,363	10,398	9,753	10,037	11,174	13,465	16,157
Services: Debit	78aed	–3,859	–7,138	–6,343	–5,743	–6,624	–6,982	–8,993	–8,966	–9,186	–10,647	–12,460	–14,227
Balance on Goods & Services	78afd	2,265	1,891	–3,883	–6,650	–8,620	–13,691	–10,902	–6,874	–6,398	–5,198	–4,617	–764
Income: Credit	78agd	546	1,089	1,527	1,467	2,226	1,837	2,250	2,625	1,948	2,108	1,995	2,701
Income: Debit	78ahd	–3,109	–3,084	–2,602	–2,596	–3,404	–2,847	–3,709	–4,015	–3,837	–5,745	–13,534	–13,244
Balance on Gds, Serv. & Inc.	78aid	–298	–104	–4,958	–7,779	–9,798	–14,701	–12,361	–8,264	–8,287	–8,835	–16,156	–11,307
Current Transfers, n.i.e.: Credit	78ajd	2,174	2,459	2,825	2,700	3,520	2,898	3,008	3,737	4,181	5,316	8,283	11,030
Current Transfers: Debit	78akd	–922	–1,501	–1,131	–665	–623	–684	–628	–848	–903	–1,080	–2,649	–4,087
Capital Account, n.i.e.	78bcd	9,215	285	94	66	63	55	34	76	–7	–46	998	995
Capital Account, n.i.e.: Credit	78bad	9,215	285	5,833	91	117	95	110	113	46	60	1,144	1,183
Capital Account: Debit	78bbd	—	—	–5,739	–25	–54	–40	–76	–37	–53	–106	–146	–188
Financial Account, n.i.e.	78bjd	–9,065	9,260	6,673	7,410	13,282	10,462	10,221	3,173	7,180	8,686	8,315	14,242
Direct Investment Abroad	78bdd	–29	–42	–53	–45	–316	–31	–16	90	–230	–305	–794	–1,455
Dir. Invest. in Rep. Econ., n.i.e.	78bed	1,875	3,659	4,498	4,908	6,365	7,270	9,343	5,714	4,131	4,589	12,873	7,724
Portfolio Investment Assets	78bfd	–624	1	1	282	815	–130	–548	–84	48	–1,157	–1,296	–1,330	–2,443
Equity Securities	78bkd	—	127	–17	56	1	–172	–20	–67	–268	183	–57	–572
Debt Securities	78bld	–624	–126	299	759	–131	–376	–64	115	–889	–1,479	–1,273	–1,871
Portfolio Investment Liab., n.i.e.	78bgd	—	1,176	22	1,295	1,827	691	3,423	1,067	3,051	3,740	10,612	15,156
Equity Securities	78bmd	—	219	749	599	1,734	14	447	–307	–545	–837	1,660	1,342
Debt Securities	78bnd	—	957	–727	696	93	677	2,976	1,374	3,596	4,577	8,952	13,814
Financial Derivatives Assets	78bwd	—	—	—	—	—	579	—	—	—	—	....	....
Financial Derivatives Liabilities	78bxd	—	—	–3	–12	—	–10	269	–336	–898	–870	209	289
Other Investment Assets	78bhd	–1,841	3,356	6,191	–754	2,107	–3,339	–3,870	–4,072	1,887	–493	–11,897	–2,565
Monetary Authorities	78bod	194	65	37	—	1	1	2	3	—	—	–29	81
General Government	78bpd	34	46	5,767	41	53	–6	–48	–38	–37	–47	–39	–160
Banks	78bqd	–1,718	1,057	453	–1,076	2,207	–2,694	–3,015	–3,398	3,107	351	–10,367	–805
Other Sectors	78brd	–351	2,188	–66	281	–154	–640	–809	–639	–1,183	–797	–1,462	–1,681
Other Investment Liab., n.i.e.	78bid	–8,446	1,110	–4,264	1,203	3,429	5,850	1,156	662	396	3,321	–1,358	–2,464
Monetary Authorities	78bsd	15	14	102	–561	199	380	–1,393	118	–473	–68	–106	1,910
General Government	78btd	–8,709	–3	–6,033	–52	–370	–224	–290	–3,047	–503	–1,236	–2,287	–6,443
Banks	78bud	170	575	314	719	1,483	2,013	–474	283	–550	2,063	1,093	536
Other Sectors	78bvd	78	524	1,353	1,097	2,117	3,681	3,313	3,308	1,922	2,562	–58	1,533
Net Errors and Omissions	78cad	–98	–564	321	1,309	–520	2,126	350	1,699	–1,516	–2,835	2,010	–2,727
Overall Balance	78cbd	1,006	9,835	3,824	3,041	5,924	156	624	–427	648	1,206	801	8,146
Reserves and Related Items	79dad	–1,006	–9,835	–3,824	–3,041	–5,924	–156	–624	427	–648	–1,206	–801	–8,146
Reserve Assets	79dbd	–1,514	–8,431	–3,828	–3,044	–5,926	–156	–624	427	–648	–1,206	–801	–8,146
Use of Fund Credit and Loans	79dcd	603	–1,408	—	—	—	—	—	—	—	—	—	—
Exceptional Financing	79ded	–96	4	4	3	2	—	—	—	—	—	—	—
International Investment Position							*Millions of US Dollars*							
Assets	79aad	23,506	31,966	28,746	31,908	38,399	40,101	44,833	49,387	51,694	58,540	78,374	....
Direct Investment Abroad	79abd	461	539	735	678	1,165	1,024	1,018	1,156	1,457	2,146	3,216	....
Portfolio Investment	79acd	1,287	1,937	1,338	839	1,093	1,143	1,575	1,311	2,729	4,143	6,214	....
Equity Securities	79add	—	—	—	2	9	28	47	108	189	229	739	....
Debt Securities	79aed	—	—	—	837	1,084	1,115	1,528	1,203	2,540	3,914	5,475	....
Financial Derivatives	79afd	—	—	—	—	—	—	—	—	—	—	—	....
Other Investment	79afd	15,727	14,527	8,454	8,988	7,866	10,619	14,776	20,366	17,724	18,097	32,171	....
Monetary Authorities	79agd	252	187	150	5	4	2	1	—	—	15	43	....
General Government	79ahd	6,970	6,720	881	829	801	1,031	1,237	1,264	1,228	1,406	1,586	....
Banks	79aid	6,672	5,678	4,997	6,161	4,419	6,697	9,758	14,507	10,588	11,433	23,247	....
Other Sectors	79ajd	1,833	1,942	2,426	1,993	2,642	2,889	3,780	4,595	5,908	5,243	7,295	....
Reserve Assets	79akd	6,031	14,963	18,219	21,403	28,275	27,315	27,464	26,554	29,784	34,154	36,773	....
Liabilities	79lad	53,075	59,304	58,515	62,439	80,187	89,258	99,999	107,128	125,128	152,215	205,863	....
Dir. Invest. in Rep. Economy	79lbd	3,789	7,843	11,463	14,587	22,461	26,075	34,227	41,247	48,320	57,877	85,605	....
Portfolio Investment	79lcd	8,431	9,375	10,148	11,325	13,658	14,618	18,057	18,895	24,042	34,080	55,677	....
Equity Securities	79ldd	443	663	2,279	2,672	4,969	4,981	5,350	4,301	4,399	6,705	13,080	....
Debt Securities	79led	7,988	8,712	7,869	8,653	8,689	9,637	12,707	14,594	19,643	27,375	42,597	....
Financial Derivatives	79lld	—	—	—	—	—	—	—	—	—	—	—	....
Other Investment	79lfd	40,855	42,086	36,904	36,527	44,068	48,565	47,715	46,986	52,766	60,258	64,401	....
Monetary Authorities	79lgd	1,493	174	265	791	925	1,844	436	428	110	199	103	....
General Government	79lhd	34,507	35,955	28,709	26,584	27,061	25,199	23,749	19,006	20,775	22,814	21,476	....
Banks	79lid	1,394	1,834	2,231	3,054	4,735	6,404	5,812	6,437	6,882	10,321	13,105	....
Other Sectors	79ljd	3,461	4,123	5,699	6,098	11,347	15,118	17,718	21,115	24,999	26,924	29,717	....

Poland 964

		1994	1995	1996	1997	1998	1999	2000	2001	2002	2003	2004	2005
Government Finance							*Millions of Zlotys: Year Ending December 31*						
Deficit (-) or Surplus........................	80	−4,812	−5,762	−7,826	−8,304	−5,382	−5,021	1,935	−32,025	....	....	....	....
Total Revenue and Grants.............	81y	88,153	117,946	144,462	172,519	196,964	201,250	214,345	224,184	....	....	....	....
Revenue....................................	81	88,153	117,946	144,454	172,507	196,952	201,131	213,865	223,758	....	....	....	....
Grants.......................................	81z	—	—	8	12	12	119	480	426	....	....	....	....
Exp. & Lending Minus Repay..........	82z	92,965	123,708	152,288	180,823	202,346	206,271	212,410	256,209	....	....	....	....
Expenditure..............................	82	93,039	124,322	153,047	185,431	207,370	216,912	236,865	263,580	....	....	....	....
Lending Minus Repayments..........	83	−74	−614	−759	−4,608	−5,024	−10,641	−24,455	−7,371	....	....	....	....
Total Financing.............................	80h	4,812	5,762	7,826	8,304	5,382	5,021	−1,935	32,025	....	....	....	....
Domestic..................................	84a	5,855	2,604	8,695	8,393	4,379	4,445	−2,200	42,976	....	....	....	....
Foreign....................................	85a	−1,043	3,158	−869	−89	1,003	576	265	−10,951	....	....	....	....
Total Debt by Residence..................	88	152,238	167,267	185,603	221,650	237,400	266,750	270,980	291,524	....	....	....	....
Domestic..................................	88a	55,611	63,083	76,919	97,635	109,647	123,519	134,477	174,705	....	....	....	....
Foreign....................................	89a	96,627	104,184	108,684	124,015	127,753	143,231	136,503	116,819	....	....	....	....
National Accounts							*Millions of Zlotys*						
Househ.Cons.Expend.,incl.NPISHs....	96f	142,746	203,821	263,060	323,267	375,344	420,839	476,888	505,581	539,516	551,951	591,133	615,566
Government Consumption Expend...	91f	37,853	63,027	77,236	91,578	103,996	116,676	130,552	140,268	145,447	153,723	165,120	181,346
Gross Fixed Capital Formation..........	93e	40,385	59,736	83,671	115,479	144,671	162,458	176,739	161,277	151,472	153,758	165,848	176,923
Changes in Inventories...................	93i	−715	3,378	4,513	5,265	5,924	5,691	8,237	646	−884	4,270	18,384	8,403
Exports of Goods and Services..........	90c	53,218	78,234	94,239	120,634	156,122	161,040	201,908	210,919	231,535	280,888	346,631	362,630
Imports of Goods and Services (-).....	98c	48,389	70,975	100,284	140,870	185,155	200,396	249,702	239,486	259,227	302,470	364,959	365,677
Gross Domestic Product (GDP).........	99b	225,098	337,222	422,436	515,353	600,902	666,308	744,622	779,205	807,859	842,120	922,157	979,191
GDP Volume 1995 Ref., Chained.....	99b.p	287,883	337,222	358,261	383,648	402,760	420,982	438,631	443,548	449,757	467,033	491,630	507,574
GDP Volume (2000=100)...............	99bvp	65.6	76.9	81.7	87.5	91.8	96.0	100.0	101.1	102.5	106.5	112.1	115.7
GDP Deflator (2000=100)...............	99bip	46.1	58.9	69.5	79.1	87.9	93.2	100.0	103.5	105.8	106.2	110.5	113.6
							Millions: Midyear Estimates						
Population................................	99z	38.53	38.59	38.63	38.66	38.66	38.66	38.65	38.63	38.61	38.59	38.56	38.53

Portugal   182

		1994	1995	1996	1997	1998	1999	2000	2001	2002	2003	2004	2005
Exchange Rates						*Euros per SDR: End of Period*							
Market Rate	aa	232.2519	222.1009	224.8754	247.3526	241.9404	1.3662	1.4002	1.4260	1.2964	1.1765	1.1402	1.2116
						Euros per US Dollar: End of Period (ae) Period Average (rf)							
Market Rate	ae	159.0930	149.4130	156.3850	183.3260	171.8290	.9954	1.0747	1.1347	.9536	.7918	.7342	.8477
Market Rate	rf	165.9928	151.1055	154.2437	175.3124	180.1045	.9386	1.0854	1.1175	1.0626	.8860	.8054	.8041
						Escudos per ECU: End of Period (ea) Period Average (eb)							
ECU Rate	ea	195.17	191.58	194.27	202.13	201.22	....	....	....	....	....	....	....
ECU Rate	eb	196.37	194.12	193.18	197.96	201.99	....	....	....	....	....	....	....
						Index Numbers (2000=100): Period Averages							
Market Rate (1995=100)	ahx	91.2	100.0	97.9	86.3	84.0	....	....	....	....	....	....	....
Nominal Effective Exchange Rate	nec	106.0	107.8	108.0	105.7	104.8	103.2	100.0	100.5	101.3	104.6	105.4	105.6
Real Effective Exchange Rate	rec	101.0	104.0	104.8	102.8	103.2	102.6	100.0	102.4	104.9	109.6	110.6	110.7
Fund Position						*Millions of SDRs: End of Period*							
Quota	2f.s	558	558	558	558	558	867	867	867	867	867	867	867
SDRs	1b.s	48	57	68	79	96	32	41	49	56	61	66	72
Reserve Position in the Fund	1c.s	231	303	320	313	442	275	242	299	329	361	283	142
Total Fund Cred.&Loans Outstg.	2tl	—	—	—	—	—	—	—	—	—	—	—	—
International Liquidity						*Millions of US Dollars Unless Otherwise Indicated: End of Period*							
Total Res.Min.Gold (Eurosys.Def)	1l.d	15,513	15,850	15,918	15,660	15,825	† 8,427	8,909	9,667	11,179	5,876	5,174	3,479
SDRs	1b.d	71	85	98	107	135	44	54	62	76	91	103	103
Reserve Position in the Fund	1c.d	337	450	461	423	623	377	316	376	447	536	440	202
Foreign Exchange	1d.d	15,106	15,315	15,359	15,130	15,067	† 8,006	8,539	9,228	10,656	5,249	4,631	3,173
o/w:Fin.Deriv.Rel.to Reserves	1ddd	....	....	....	....	....	111.51	271.71	322.42	99.63	29.77	31.15	14.53
Other Reserve Assets	1e.d	....	....	....	....	....	—	—	—	—	—	—	—
Gold (Million Fine Troy Ounces)	1ad	16.07	16.07	16.07	16.07	20.09	19.51	19.51	19.51	19.03	16.63	14.86	13.42
Gold (Eurosystem Valuation)	1and	5,185	5,189	4,993	3,265	3,389	5,661	5,353	5,394	6,522	6,938	6,510	6,885
Memo:Euro Cl. on Non-EA Res.	1dgd	....	....	....	....	....	2,795	....	....	....	....	....	....
Non-Euro Cl. on EA Res	1dhd	....	....	....	....	....	871	978	594	380	424	1,021	615
Mon. Auth.: Other Foreign Assets	3..d	....	....	....	....	....	3,666	....	....	....	....	....	....
Foreign Liabilities	4..d	122	48	44	144	6	† 3,737	3,035	2,885	2,959	2,237	962	764
Banking Insts.: Foreign Assets	7a.d	28,500	35,922	37,500	47,451	54,669	† 25,167	29,902	26,870	28,929	34,875	37,669	36,831
Foreign Liab.	7b.d	21,527	32,432	36,975	48,282	60,976	† 31,352	47,625	50,006	62,149	84,365	93,120	86,532
Monetary Authorities						*Billions of Escudos through 1998; Billions of Euros Beginning 1999: End of Period*							
Fgn. Assets (Cl.on Non-EA Ctys)	11	3,294.8	3,142.8	3,250.5	3,469.8	3,324.6	16.72	15.73	19.79	17.87	11.29	9.30	10.19
Claims on General Government	12a.u						3.48	5.22	2.96	4.83	9.62	9.71	10.52
o/w: Claims on Gen.Govt.in Cty.	12a	289.9	267.6	248.2	217.6	94.6	.39						
Claims on Banking Institutions	12e.u	....	....	....	....	....	11.92	4.98	3.58	4.93	7.99	10.99	14.95
o/w: Claims on Bank.Inst.in Cty.	12e	560.1	631.9	261.8	112.5	246.4	2.58	3.30	2.24	1.03	2.54	3.14	5.57
Claims on Other Resident Sectors	12d.u	....	....	....	....	....	.30	.58	.43	.23	.24	.24	.17
o/w: Cl. on Oth.Res.Sect.in Cty.	12d	45.7	38.2	39.8	41.0	42.6	.22	.22	.23	.23	.24	.24	.17
Currency Issued	14a	795.8	841.0	880.9	776.1	923.6	7.25	6.53	5.92	8.46	9.87	11.80	13.27
Liabilities to Banking Insts.	14c.u						10.92	8.65	9.80	10.41	12.54	14.10	16.75
o/w: Liabs to Bank.Inst.in Cty.	14c	432.3	376.8	473.5	558.8	421.1	4.02	3.88	4.81	4.62	11.71	6.25	4.67
Demand Dep. of Other Res.Sect.	14d.u	....	....	....	....	....	—	.02	—	—	—	—	—
o/w:D.Dep.of Oth.Res.Sect.in Cty.	14d	21.6	.6	.2	1.9	.4	—	.02	—	—	—	—	—
Other Dep. of Other Res.Sect.	15..u	....	....	....	....	....	—	—	—	—	—	—	—
o/w:O.Dep.of Oth.Res.Sect.in Cty.	15	....	....	....	....	....	—	—	—	—	—	—	—
Bonds & Money Mkt. Instruments.	16n.u	....	....	....	....	....	4.57	3.78	2.94	2.03	1.05	—	—
Foreign Liab. (to Non-EA Ctys)	16c	19.4	7.2	6.9	26.4	1.1	3.72	3.26	3.27	2.82	1.77	.71	.65
Central Government Deposits	16d.u	....	....	....	....	....	2.24	.01	.01	—	—	—	—
o/w: Cent.Govt.Dep. in Cty.	16d	510.6	693.0	524.0	486.7	465.1	2.24	.01	.01	—	—	—	—
Capital Accounts	17a	446.7	303.7	310.3	693.0	588.3	3.98	4.70	5.37	4.87	4.33	4.17	5.78
Other Items (Net)	17r	1,964.1	1,858.4	1,604.5	1,299.0	1,308.6	−.27	−.44	−.55	−.74	−.43	−.54	−.61
Memo: Net Claims on Eurosystem	12e.s	....	....	....	....	....	2.45	−3.35	−3.44	−1.65	4.68	−.34	−3.13
Currency Put into Circ	14m	....	....	....	....	....				5.97	5.71	5.42	5.45
Banking Institutions						*Billions of Escudos through 1998; Billions of Euros Beginning 1999: End of Period*							
Claims on Monetary Authorities	20	2,158.1	2,090.4	1,891.3	1,648.1	1,617.9	4.25	3.45	2.76	1.88	.96	—	—
Claims on Bk.Inst.in Oth.EA Ctys	20b.u	....	....	....	....	....	18.39	17.30	24.44	25.33	32.03	31.00	30.40
Fgn. Assets (Cl.on Non-EA Ctys)	21	4,534.1	5,367.2	5,864.5	8,698.9	9,393.7	25.05	32.14	30.49	27.59	27.61	27.66	31.22
Claims on General Government	22a.u						9.53	8.90	10.13	9.54	9.65	10.53	10.99
o/w: Claims on Gen.Govt.in Cty.	22a	4,126.9	4,194.3	3,983.1	3,139.5	2,383.9	8.37	8.50	9.08	8.07	7.92	8.49	9.29
Claims on Other Resident Sectors	22d.u	....	....	....	....	....	133.65	168.23	184.22	195.85	202.82	216.33	233.89
o/w: Cl. on Oth.Res.Sect.in Cty.	22d	9,369.0	11,137.5	13,084.8	15,771.6	19,705.1	129.33	160.55	179.17	190.80	193.99	202.73	216.91
Demand Deposits	24..u	....	....	....	....	....	40.03	42.50	46.93	46.12	49.00	49.74	56.14
o/w:D.Dep.of Oth.Res.Sect.in Cty.	24	3,038.7	3,435.0	3,914.6	4,637.9	5,411.6	39.68	42.12	46.59	45.70	48.44	49.14	55.12
Other Deposits	25..u	....	....	....	....	....	71.25	75.32	78.58	77.80	79.03	86.37	94.43
o/w:O.Dep.of Oth.Res.Sect.in Cty.	25	10,360.4	11,116.5	11,465.1	11,956.0	12,064.7	67.51	71.56	72.37	71.57	71.40	75.19	83.23
Money Market Fund Shares	26m.u	....	....	....	....	....	—	.12	.17	.66	1.06	1.07	1.09
Bonds & Money Mkt. Instruments	26n.u						16.90	21.97	25.72	26.46	29.43	28.81	18.47
o/w: Held by Resid.of Cty	26n	169.0	125.7	257.7	331.5	599.5	....	....	....	....	....	....	....
Foreign Liab. (to Non-EA Ctys)	26c	3,424.8	4,845.8	5,782.4	8,851.3	10,477.5	31.21	51.18	56.74	59.26	66.80	68.37	73.35
Central Government Deposits	26d.u						5.08	6.42	4.29	5.41	4.07	3.59	4.62
o/w: Cent.Govt.Dep. in Cty.	26d	541.2	701.2	800.3	906.7	1,017.4	5.07	6.42	4.27	5.39	4.05	3.57	4.28
Credit from Monetary Authorities	26g	560.3	631.9	261.8	112.5	246.4	2.59	3.30	2.25	1.03	2.54	3.10	5.57
Liab. to Bk.Inst.in Oth. EA Ctys.	26h.u	....	....	....	....	....	22.51	23.30	32.35	36.07	41.17	37.90	42.36
Capital Accounts	27a	2,430.8	2,500.8	2,782.6	2,978.4	4,117.9	20.90	23.12	25.27	26.90	30.78	29.46	30.08
Other Items (Net)	27r	−338.0	−573.1	−443.1	−515.9	−834.3	−19.59	−17.21	−20.27	−19.52	−30.82	−22.90	−19.60

Portugal 182

		1994	1995	1996	1997	1998	1999	2000	2001	2002	2003	2004	2005
Banking Survey (Nat'l Residency)						*Billions of Escudos through 1998; Billions of Euros Beginning 1999: End of Period*							
Foreign Assets (Net).........................	31n	4,384.7	3,657.0	3,325.6	3,291.0	2,239.7	10.69	−5.57	−17.72	−23.46	−21.03	−24.25	−29.05
Domestic Credit.............................	32	12,779.7	14,243.5	16,031.6	17,776.3	20,743.7	131.00	162.84	184.20	193.71	198.11	207.89	222.09
Claims on General Govt. (Net)........	32an	3,365.0	3,067.8	2,907.0	1,963.7	996.0	1.45	2.07	4.80	2.68	3.88	4.92	5.01
Claims on Other Resident Sectors.....	32d	9,414.7	11,175.7	13,124.6	15,812.6	19,747.7	129.55	160.77	179.39	191.03	194.23	202.97	217.08
Currency Issued.............................	34a.n	795.8	841.0	880.9	776.1	923.6	7.25	6.53	5.92	8.46	9.87	11.80	13.27
Demand Deposits............................	34b.n	3,060.2	3,435.5	3,914.7	4,639.7	5,412.0	39.69	42.14	46.59	45.70	48.44	49.14	55.12
Other Deposits..............................	35..n	10,360.4	11,116.5	11,465.1	11,956.0	12,064.7	67.51	71.56	72.37	71.57	71.40	75.19	83.23
Money Market Fund Shares..............	36m						—	.12	.17	.66	1.06	1.07	1.09
Bonds & Money Mkt. Instruments....	36n	169.0	125.7	257.7	331.5	599.5	21.48	25.75	28.66	28.49	30.49	28.81	18.47
o/w: Over Two Years....................	36na	....	....	....	....	....	19.87	23.24	25.79	27.06	28.92	27.21	17.67
Capital Accounts............................	37a	2,877.5	2,804.5	3,093.0	3,671.4	4,706.2	24.88	27.81	30.64	31.77	35.12	33.63	35.86
Other Items (Net)...........................	37r	−99.4	−428.4	−256.4	−306.3	−722.4	−19.11	−16.65	−17.87	−16.40	−19.30	−16.01	−14.00
Banking Survey (EA-Wide Residency)						*Billions of Euros: End of Period*							
Foreign Assets (Net).........................	31n.u	....	....	....	....	....	6.84	−6.58	−9.74	−16.63	−29.67	−32.11	−32.59
Domestic Credit.............................	32..u	....	....	....	....	....	139.64	176.50	193.44	205.05	218.26	233.22	250.96
Claims on General Govt. (Net)........	32anu	....	....	....	....	....	5.70	7.69	8.78	8.96	15.20	16.65	16.90
Claims on Other Resident Sect.......	32d.u	....	....	....	....	....	133.94	168.80	184.65	196.08	203.05	216.57	234.06
Currency Issued.............................	34a.u	....	....	....	....	....	7.25	6.53	5.92	8.46	9.87	11.80	13.27
Demand Deposits............................	34b.u	....	....	....	....	....	40.03	42.52	46.93	46.13	49.00	49.74	56.14
Other Deposits..............................	35..u	....	....	....	....	....	71.25	75.32	78.58	77.80	79.03	86.37	94.43
o/w: Other Dep. Over Two Yrs........	35abu	....	....	....	....	....	4.03	3.84	3.57	4.43	4.44	6.68	12.68
Money Market Fund Shares..............	36m.u	....	....	....	....	....	—	.12	.17	.66	1.06	1.07	1.09
Bonds & Money Mkt. Instruments....	36n.u	....	....	....	....	....	21.48	25.75	28.66	28.49	30.49	28.81	18.47
o/w: Over Two Years....................	36nau	....	....	....	....	....	19.87	23.24	25.79	27.06	28.92	27.21	17.67
Capital Accounts............................	37a	....	....	....	....	....	24.88	27.81	30.64	31.77	35.12	33.63	35.86
Other Items (Net)...........................	37r.u	....	....	....	....	....	−18.40	−8.13	−7.20	−4.90	−15.98	−10.32	−.88
Money (National Definitions)						*Billions of Escudos: End of Period*							
M1...	59ma	3,589.4	3,901.2	4,302.2	4,882.1	5,757.4	....	....	....	....	....	....	....
M2...	59mb	10,586.2	11,434.5	12,468.2	13,316.2	14,401.3	....	....	....	....	....	....	....
Broad Money................................	59mc	10,020.3	11,102.1	11,907.3	12,825.5	13,667.5	....	....	....	....	....	....	....
Interest Rates						*Percent Per Annum*							
Discount Rate (End of Period)..........	60	8.88	8.50	6.70	5.31	3.00	....	....	....	....	....	....	....
Money Market Rate........................	60b	10.62	8.91	7.38	5.78	4.34	2.71	....	....	....	....	....	....
Treasury Bill Rate..........................	60c	....	7.75	5.75	4.43	....	....	....	....	....	....	....	....
Deposit Rate.................................	60l	8.37	8.38	6.32	4.56	3.37	2.40	....	....	....	....	....	....
Households: Stocks, up to 2 years..	60lhs	....	....	....	....	....	....	....	....	....	2.15	1.97	1.94
New Business, up to 1 year.......	60lhn	....	....	....	....	....	....	....	....	....	1.99	1.82	1.87
Corporations: Stocks, up to 2 years	60lcs	....	....	....	....	....	....	....	....	....	2.38	2.16	2.18
New Business, up to 1 year.........	60lcn	....	....	....	....	....	....	....	....	....	2.27	2.06	2.13
Lending Rate.................................	60p	15.01	13.80	11.73	9.15	7.24	5.19	....	....	....	....	....	....
Households: Stocks, up to 1 year....	60phs	....	....	....	....	....	....	....	....	....	8.83	9.15	9.05
New Bus., Floating & up to 1 year	60pns	....	....	....	....	....	....	....	....	....	9.18	7.65	7.57
House Purch., Stocks,Over 5 years	60phm	....	....	....	....	....	....	....	....	....	4.29	3.76	3.68
Corporations: Stocks, up to 1 year..	60pcs	....	....	....	....	....	....	....	....	....	4.82	4.58	4.57
New Bus., Over € 1 mil.,up to 1 yr	60pcn	....	....	....	....	....	....	....	....	....	3.86	3.51	3.73
Government Bond Yield..................	61	10.83	10.34	7.25	5.48	4.09	....	....	....	....	....	....	....
Prices, Production, Labor						*Index Numbers (2000=100): Period Averages*							
Share Prices (1995=100).................	62	104.1	100.0	117.3	183.4	287.7							
Producer Prices..............................	63	....	....	....	....	....	....	100.0	102.8	103.2	104.0	106.8	111.2
Consumer Prices............................	64	84.4	87.8	90.6	†92.5	95.0	97.2	100.0	104.4	†108.1	111.6	114.3	116.9
Harmonized CPI.............................	64h					95.2	97.3	100.0	104.4	108.3	†111.8	114.6	117.0
Industrial Production.......................	66	77.7	84.7	89.1	91.4	96.6	99.5	100.0	103.1	102.7	102.6	100.0	100.3
Labor Force						*Number in Thousands: Period Averages*							
Labor Force..................................	67d	4,799	4,777	4,809	4,645	5,117	5,155	5,235	5,314	5,379	5,460	5,488	5,545
Employment..................................	67e	4,482	4,442	4,467	4,307	†4,863	4,929	5,024	5,098	5,107	5,079	5,123	5,123
Unemployment..............................	67c	396	430	468	443	254	227	206	216	272	342	365	477
Unemployment Rate (%)................	67r	6.9	7.2	7.3	6.8	5.0	4.4	3.9	4.1	5.1	6.3	6.7	7.6
Intl. Transactions & Positions						*Billions of Escudos through 1998; Millions of Euros Beginning 1999*							
Exports..	70	2,975.6	3,501.8	3,795.9	4,195.1	4,461.0	†23,715.6	25,241.2	27,322.8	27,089.8	27,101.9	26,586.3	25,873.7
Imports, c.i.f.................................	71	4,514.3	5,028.7	5,427.1	6,139.7	6,914.8	†37,505.6	41,425.2	44,054.0	40,655.9	36,146.2	39,597.0	42,939.2
Imports, f.o.b.................................	71.v	4,092.7	4,559.1	4,920.3	....	....	....	....	....	....	....	....	....
Volume of Exports.........................	72	101.2	97.9	101.6	100.5	94.4	92.8	100.0	94.6	95.3	97.1	....	....
Volume of Imports.........................	73	101.6	97.6	101.5	100.7	103.9	100.5	100.0	96.5	93.6	94.5	....	....
Export Prices................................	76	101.3	100.1	93.3	96.0	96.2	94.6	100.0	95.7	94.3	91.5	....	....
Import Prices................................	76.x	95.1	95.6	92.2	92.7	90.5	91.7	100.0	91.5	89.1	90.0	....	....

(Volume of Exports etc. under header: 2000=100)

Portugal 182

		1994	1995	1996	1997	1998	1999	2000	2001	2002	2003	2004	2005
Balance of Payments							*Millions of US Dollars: Minus Sign Indicates Debit*						
Current Account, n.i.e.	78ald	−2,196	−132	−5,023	−6,756	−8,507	−10,414	−11,748	−11,355	−9,947	−9,207	−12,962	−17,007
Goods: Exports f.o.b.	78aad	18,645	24,024	24,914	24,211	25,160	24,899	24,663	24,456	25,975	32,055	37,128	38,167
Goods: Imports f.o.b.	78abd	−26,966	−32,934	−34,763	−34,710	−38,037	−39,326	−39,195	−38,362	−39,286	−46,233	−55,771	−59,022
Trade Balance	78acd	−8,321	−8,910	−9,849	−10,499	−12,876	−14,427	−14,532	−13,906	−13,311	−14,178	−18,644	−20,855
Services: Credit	78add	6,755	8,236	7,943	7,664	8,829	9,259	9,016	9,379	10,357	12,354	14,840	15,105
Services: Debit	78aed	−5,486	−6,611	−6,535	−6,235	−6,912	−7,323	−7,053	−6,826	−7,146	−8,293	−9,688	−10,056
Balance on Goods & Services	78afd	−7,052	−7,285	−8,441	−9,070	−10,960	−12,490	−12,569	−11,352	−10,101	−10,117	−13,492	−15,806
Income: Credit	78agd	2,232	4,095	4,403	4,015	4,496	4,261	4,570	5,435	4,722	6,399	7,915	7,703
Income: Debit	78ahd	−2,797	−4,074	−5,409	−5,486	−6,133	−6,029	−7,101	−8,787	−7,373	−8,740	−10,856	−11,635
Balance on Gds, Serv. & Inc	78aid	−7,616	−7,264	−9,447	−10,542	−12,597	−14,259	−15,100	−14,704	−12,752	−12,459	−16,433	−19,738
Current Transfers, n.i.e.: Credit	78ajd	7,410	9,046	6,627	5,671	6,170	6,079	5,415	5,582	5,445	6,443	7,151	7,038
Current Transfers: Debit	78akd	−1,989	−1,914	−2,203	−1,885	−2,080	−2,234	−2,063	−2,233	−2,641	−3,191	−3,680	−4,307
Capital Account, n.i.e.	78bcd	—	—	2,238	2,817	2,544	2,458	1,512	1,069	1,906	3,010	2,808	2,139
Capital Account, n.i.e.: Credit	78bad	—	—	2,370	3,006	2,725	2,642	1,681	1,278	2,111	3,246	3,130	2,485
Capital Account: Debit	78bbd	—	—	−132	−189	−181	−183	−169	−209	−205	−236	−322	−347
Financial Account, n.i.e.	78bjd	1,052	3,025	4,680	5,747	5,783	9,172	10,872	10,757	8,265	558	9,470	14,448
Direct Investment Abroad	78bdd	−287	−688	−727	−2,074	−4,039	−3,042	−8,183	−6,228	210	−8,096	−7,892	−1,195
Dir. Invest. in Rep. Econ., n.i.e.	78bed	1,270	685	1,347	2,357	3,004	1,168	6,682	6,174	1,755	8,776	2,103	3,200
Portfolio Investment Assets	78bfd	−3,456	−3,148	−5,754	−7,506	−5,996	−6,737	−4,582	−7,851	−7,034	−21,471	−13,598	−19,031
Equity Securities	78bkd	−66	−159	−964	−739	−974	−2,110	−1,044	−959	−813	−622	−1,708	−1,391
Debt Securities	78bld	−3,390	−2,989	−4,790	−6,767	−5,022	−4,626	−3,538	−6,892	−6,221	−20,849	−11,890	−17,639
Portfolio Investment Liab., n.i.e.	78bgd	3,934	2,066	4,198	8,072	5,383	9,945	2,792	10,661	10,249	16,002	14,706	17,004
Equity Securities	78bmd	562	−179	1,902	2,548	2,165	691	415	2,371	3,287	9,863	7,233	5,662
Debt Securities	78bnd	3,372	2,244	2,296	5,525	3,219	9,254	2,376	8,290	6,962	6,140	7,473	11,342
Financial Derivatives Assets	78bwd	—	—	44	215	1,117	2,682	3,673	3,226	3,796	4,590	4,135	4,845
Financial Derivatives Liabilities	78bxd	—	—	−74	−239	−985	−2,485	−3,351	−2,875	−3,802	−4,518	−4,226	−5,065
Other Investment Assets	78bhd	−7,098	−7,568	−2,002	−7,276	−7,100	183	−10,823	−7,252	−6,758	−8,799	147	−94
Monetary Authorities	78bod	—	−26	−5	1	−94	−1,005	10	22	−304	345	−954	−717
General Government	78bpd	....	....	−10	11	—	−12	−12	−49	3	−6	230	27
Banks	78bqd	−4,741	−6,679	−1,155	−5,882	−3,813	995	−7,201	−1,033	−29	−8,713	−1,453	−1,342
Other Sectors	78brd	−2,358	−863	−831	−1,406	−3,192	204	−3,619	−6,192	−6,428	−424	2,324	1,937
Other Investment Liab., n.i.e.	78bid	6,689	11,678	7,647	12,198	14,398	7,458	24,664	14,903	9,848	14,074	14,095	14,783
Monetary Authorities	78bsd	299	−99	169	1,645	837	−3	4,861	87	699	−6,725	7,229	5,595
General Government	78btd	−139	144	−376	106	−73	−43	−179	−190	179	−20	407	−877
Banks	78bud	7,069	11,189	7,035	9,508	12,352	6,999	18,231	14,480	8,456	19,391	3,468	9,489
Other Sectors	78bvd	−540	444	818	939	1,281	506	1,751	526	513	1,428	2,992	577
Net Errors and Omissions	78cad	−287	−3,193	−1,173	−563	689	−1,001	−265	381	794	−816	−1,180	−1,320
Overall Balance	78cbd	−1,430	−300	723	1,245	508	216	371	852	1,017	−6,455	−1,863	−1,741
Reserves and Related Items	79dad	1,430	300	−723	−1,245	−508	−216	−371	−852	−1,017	6,455	1,863	1,741
Reserve Assets	79dbd	1,430	300	−723	−1,245	−508	−216	−371	−852	−1,017	6,455	1,863	1,741
Use of Fund Credit and Loans	79dcd	—	—	—	—	—	—	—	—	—	—	—	—
Exceptional Financing	79ded	....	....	—	—	—	—	—	—	—	—	—	—
International Investment Position							*Millions of US Dollars*						
Assets	79aad	....	....	86,425	99,344	128,461	122,687	142,204	156,383	192,104	261,235	304,922	291,271
Direct Investment Abroad	79abd	—	—	4,726	5,932	9,622	10,685	19,552	22,086	21,148	35,883	48,336	44,457
Portfolio Investment	79acd	—	—	17,502	20,368	28,489	36,459	40,662	45,915	62,245	97,727	122,973	127,979
Equity Securities	79add	....	....	4,997	4,765	6,008	7,226	7,624	7,556	8,397	11,018	14,534	15,762
Debt Securities	79aed	....	....	12,505	15,602	22,480	29,233	33,038	38,359	53,848	86,709	108,439	112,217
Financial Derivatives	79ald	—	—	422	381	355	2,055	535	745	503	−35	−836	−75
Other Investment	79afd	32,543	37,810	42,030	52,341	68,409	59,388	67,229	72,555	90,508	114,847	122,765	108,546
Monetary Authorities	79agd	—	—	47	28	127	1,479	1,367	1,280	1,806	1,717	2,996	3,282
General Government	79ahd	15	28	80	78	47	66	74	1,481	1,497	1,556	1,347	1,278
Banks	79aid	25,149	30,288	29,900	38,718	44,389	39,680	45,076	44,488	51,019	68,231	73,456	66,890
Other Sectors	79ajd	7,379	7,494	12,003	13,516	23,846	18,163	20,711	25,306	36,186	43,343	44,966	37,096
Reserve Assets	79akd	21,669	21,954	21,745	20,321	21,586	14,100	14,227	15,082	17,701	12,813	11,684	10,364
Liabilities	79lad	....	....	93,951	113,075	154,894	158,443	186,340	205,703	261,547	354,742	419,905	402,815
Dir. Invest. in Rep. Economy	79lbd	—	—	18,947	18,605	24,465	23,922	32,043	36,023	44,637	62,201	70,567	64,517
Portfolio Investment	79lcd	13,656	16,430	21,327	36,207	46,933	51,718	52,413	57,446	76,005	111,280	139,397	139,972
Equity Securities	79ldd	3,597	3,651	6,573	12,663	18,806	19,487	18,873	15,605	17,492	34,661	47,722	49,726
Debt Securities	79led	10,059	12,779	14,755	23,544	28,127	32,230	33,541	41,841	58,513	76,619	91,675	90,246
Financial Derivatives	79lld	—	—	—	—	63	1,412	—	—	—	—	—	—
Other Investment	79lfd	37,266	49,532	53,677	58,263	83,432	81,391	101,884	112,234	140,905	181,262	209,941	198,326
Monetary Authorities	79lgd	362	278	440	2,084	3,049	2,732	7,470	7,282	9,025	3,286	11,650	15,018
General Government	79lhd	1,973	2,229	1,676	1,614	2,057	2,114	1,926	1,650	1,908	2,375	3,052	1,585
Banks	79lid	21,527	32,432	36,320	42,261	56,578	57,923	73,009	84,163	106,818	146,497	160,735	151,321
Other Sectors	79ljd	13,403	14,592	15,241	12,305	21,748	18,622	19,478	19,140	23,154	29,104	34,505	30,401
Government Finance													
Central Government					*Billions of Escudos through 1998; Millions of Euros Beginning 1999: Year Ending December 31*								
Deficit (-) or Surplus	80	−708.1	−795.8	−379.9	−372.2	−247.6	....	....	....	....	....	....	....
Revenue	81	5,016.5	5,456.7	5,759.9	6,391.8	6,984.7	....	....	....	....	....	....	....
Grants Received	81z	411.6	525.6	662.2	649.9	649.1	....	....	....	....	....	....	....
Expenditure	82	6,137.9	6,613.6	6,974.5	7,242.2	7,795.1	....	....	....	....	....	....	....
Lending Minus Repayments	83	−1.7	164.5	−172.5	171.7	86.3	....	....	....	....	....	....	....
Financing													
Domestic	84a	659.0	218.2	2.7	−12.1	669.1	....	....	....	....	....	....	....
Foreign	85a	49.1	577.6	377.2	384.3	−421.5	....	....	....	....	....	....	....
General Government					*As Percent of Gross Domestic Product*								

Portugal   182

National Accounts		1994	1995	1996	1997	1998	1999	2000	2001	2002	2003	2004	2005
		Billions of Escudos through 1998; Millions of Euros Beginning 1999											
Househ.Cons.Expend.,incl.NPISHs....	96f	9,870	10,456	11,052	11,639	12,646	† 72,820	78,101	81,800	85,385	87,854	92,280	96,534
Government Consumption Expend...	91f	2,781	3,019	3,298	3,546	3,896	† 21,257	23,623	25,436	27,144	27,628	29,372	31,034
Gross Fixed Capital Formation..........	93e	3,439	3,743	4,005	4,498	4,992	† 30,617	33,103	34,218	33,841	30,951	31,932	31,797
Changes in Inventories....................	93i	56	115	95	101	108	† 989	595	659	170	276	699	948
Exports of Goods and Services..........	90c	3,583	4,168	4,482	4,891	5,301	† 31,873	36,387	37,360	37,879	38,564	40,787	42,072
Imports of Goods and Services (-).....	98c	5,111	5,698	6,123	6,798	7,698	† 43,500	49,701	50,319	49,135	47,886	52,177	55,119
Gross Domestic Product (GDP).........	99b	14,617	15,802	16,809	17,876	19,246	† 114,193	122,270	129,308	135,434	137,523	143,029	147,395
Net Primary Income from Abroad.....	98.n	178	412	568	624	....	....	....	....	....	....	....	....
Gross National Income (GNI)............	99a	14,541	15,660	16,513	17,558	....	....	....	....	....	....	....	....
GDP Volume 1995 Prices................	99b.p	15,353	15,802	16,306	16,871	17,460	† 94,450	....	....	....	....	....	....
GDP Volume 2000 Ref., Chained.....	99b.p	....	....	....	....	....	117,653	122,270	124,735	125,687	124,279	125,748	126,218
GDP Volume (2000=100)................	99bvp	78.0	80.3	82.9	85.7	88.7	† 96.2	100.0	102.0	102.8	101.6	102.8	103.2
GDP Deflator (2000=100)................	99bip	76.4	80.3	82.8	85.1	88.5	† 97.1	100.0	103.7	107.8	110.7	113.7	116.8
		Millions: Midyear Estimates											
Population................................	99z	10.01	10.03	10.06	10.09	10.13	10.18	10.23	10.28	10.33	10.39	10.44	10.49

		1994	1995	1996	1997	1998	1999	2000	2001	2002	2003	2004	2005
Exchange Rates						*Riyals per SDR: End of Period*							
Official Rate	aa	5.3139	5.4108	5.2342	4.9113	5.1252	4.9959	4.7426	4.5745	4.9487	5.4089	5.6530	5.2025
						Riyals per US Dollar: End of Period (ae) Period Average (rf)							
Official Rate	ae	3.6400	3.6400	3.6400	3.6400	3.6400	3.6400	3.6400	3.6400	3.6400	3.6400	3.6400	3.6400
Official Rate	rf	3.6400	3.6400	3.6400	3.6400	3.6400	3.6400	3.6400	3.6400	3.6400	3.6400	3.6400	3.6400
						Index Numbers (2000=100): Period Averages							
Official Rate	ahx	100.0	100.0	100.0	100.0	100.0	100.0	100.0	100.0	100.0	100.0	100.0	100.0
Nominal Effective Exchange Rate	nec	87.1	83.1	85.8	91.6	96.7	95.6	100.0	104.3	102.4	94.3	89.3	88.5
Fund Position						*Millions of SDRs: End of Period*							
Quota	2f.s	190.5	190.5	190.5	190.5	190.5	263.8	263.8	263.8	263.8	263.8	263.8	263.8
SDRs	1b.s	19.9	21.2	22.5	23.8	25.1	10.7	15.8	17.9	20.0	21.7	23.4	25.4
Reserve Position in the Fund	1c.s	30.7	29.7	29.2	26.4	26.4	44.7	44.7	79.1	99.6	103.5	86.4	34.7
International Liquidity						*Millions of US Dollars Unless Otherwise Indicated: End of Period*							
Total Reserves minus Gold	1l.d	657.7	743.8	686.2	820.6	1,043.3	1,304.2	1,158.0	1,312.7	1,566.8	2,944.2	3,395.9	4,542.4
SDRs	1b.d	29.0	31.5	32.4	32.1	35.3	14.6	20.6	22.5	27.2	32.3	36.4	36.3
Reserve Position in the Fund	1c.d	44.7	44.2	42.0	35.6	37.2	61.4	58.3	99.4	135.4	153.7	134.1	49.5
Foreign Exchange	1d.d	584.0	668.1	611.8	752.9	970.8	1,228.2	1,079.1	1,190.8	1,404.2	2,758.1	3,225.4	4,456.5
Gold (Million Fine Troy Ounces)	1ad	.814	.268	.268	.054	.054	.019	.019	.019	.019	.019	.042	.019
Gold (National Valuation)	1and	41.6	41.6	41.6	15.7	15.5	5.5	5.2	5.3	6.7	7.9	18.3	9.9
Deposit Money Banks: Assets	7a.d	2,648.0	3,093.7	2,396.3	2,643.4	2,324.3	2,455.5	3,193.1	3,163.5	4,102.9	5,347.5	7,625.4	11,441.6
Liabilities	7b.d	1,381.3	1,768.2	1,026.6	1,274.4	1,497.6	1,605.5	611.3	586.9	655.0	1,050.9	2,097.2	2,647.8
Monetary Authorities						*Millions of Riyals: End of Period*							
Foreign Assets	11	2,546	2,859	2,649	3,044	3,854	4,767	4,234	4,798	5,727	10,746	12,428	16,570
Claims on Central Government	12a	....	437	546	437	—	1,467	—	124	135	16	—	—
Claims on Deposit Money Banks	12e	260	205	212	194	1,589	82	124	97	28	3	287	204
Reserve Money	14	2,030	2,131	2,261	2,481	2,557	2,868	3,061	3,416	3,995	4,590	6,019	8,251
of which: Currency Outside DMBs	14a	1,350	1,407	1,404	1,555	1,499	1,714	1,673	1,741	1,921	2,148	2,594	2,866
Central Government Deposits	16d	42	381	116	120	145	30	41	26	38	51	232	328
Capital Accounts	17a	705	1,178	1,242	1,339	1,466	1,536	1,456	1,402	1,848	6,112	6,428	8,042
Other Items (Net)	17r	30	−188	−212	−265	1,275	1,881	−202	174	8	11	35	153
Deposit Money Banks						*Millions of Riyals: End of Period*							
Reserves	20	680	739	852	919	1,064	1,169	1,368	1,678	2,068	2,435	3,397	5,182
Foreign Assets	21	9,639	11,261	8,723	9,622	8,460	8,938	11,623	11,515	14,934	19,465	27,756	41,648
Claims on Central Government	22a	10,050	10,028	11,873	12,863	16,151	19,064	17,225	23,882	22,319	23,518	21,316	18,897
Claims on Nonfin.Pub.Enterprises	22c	228	384	728	878	609	537	621	790	1,789	3,343	5,826	10,213
Claims on Private Sector	22d	9,544	10,267	10,251	12,548	14,451	15,664	17,338	17,614	19,374	23,865	29,995	49,090
Demand Deposits	24	2,561	2,313	2,481	2,575	2,717	2,465	2,776	3,479	4,368	9,130	12,004	19,497
Time, Savings,& Fgn.Currency Dep	25	14,509	14,901	15,772	17,466	19,117	21,804	24,307	23,535	25,858	25,945	30,267	41,909
Foreign Liabilities	26c	5,028	6,436	3,737	4,639	5,451	5,844	2,225	2,136	2,384	3,825	7,634	9,638
Central Government Deposits	26d	1,903	2,671	3,795	4,601	5,248	6,540	9,262	15,504	15,544	17,610	17,993	23,226
Credit from Monetary Authorities	26g	91	69	60	140	72	94	140	115	22	98	339	423
Capital Accounts	27a	5,049	5,473	5,702	6,249	6,821	7,467	8,070	8,925	10,189	10,618	13,476	16,816
Other Items (Net)	27r	1,001	815	880	1,160	1,309	1,157	1,394	1,785	2,120	5,399	6,578	13,522
Monetary Survey						*Millions of Riyals: End of Period*							
Foreign Assets (Net)	31n	7,156	7,682	7,635	8,026	6,862	7,861	13,631	14,174	18,274	26,378	32,546	48,574
Domestic Credit	32	17,879	18,064	19,488	22,007	25,819	30,162	25,881	26,883	28,038	33,083	38,915	54,649
Claims on Central Govt. (Net)	32an	8,105	7,413	8,508	8,579	10,757	13,960	7,922	8,475	6,872	5,872	3,091	−4,656
Claims on Nonfin.Pub.Enterprises	32c	228	384	728	878	609	537	621	790	1,789	3,343	5,826	10,213
Claims on Private Sector	32d	9,545	10,268	10,252	12,550	14,453	15,665	17,338	17,617	19,377	23,868	29,998	49,092
Money	34	3,910	3,720	3,885	4,131	4,216	4,179	4,449	5,219	6,289	11,278	14,599	22,362
Quasi-Money	35	14,509	14,901	15,772	17,466	19,117	21,804	24,307	23,535	25,858	25,945	30,267	41,909
Other Items (Net)	37r	6,616	7,125	7,467	8,437	9,348	12,041	10,755	12,303	14,165	22,238	26,595	38,951
Money plus Quasi-Money	35l	18,419	18,622	19,657	21,596	23,333	25,982	28,756	28,755	32,147	37,223	44,865	64,271
Interest Rates						*Percent Per Annum*							
Deposit Rate	60l	4.8	6.2	6.5	6.6	6.6	6.5	....	....	....	....	....	....
Lending Rate	60p	8.9	....	....	....	....	....	....	....	....	....	....	....
Prices and Production						*Index Numbers (2000=100): Period Averages*							
Consumer Prices	64	82.6	85.0	91.2	93.5	96.3	98.3	100.0	† 101.4	101.7	104.0	111.1	120.8
Crude Petroleum	66aa	57.6	63.6	67.6	87.4	94.9	93.3	100.0	95.4	90.9	108.2	109.9	113.2
Intl. Transactions & Positions						*Millions of Riyals*							
Exports	70	11,695	13,290	16,187	20,275	18,309	26,259	42,202	39,570	39,960	48,710	68,010	96,453
Imports, c.i.f	71	7,014	12,369	10,440	12,092	12,409	9,100	11,837	13,679	14,749	17,827	21,857	29,261
National Accounts						*Millions of Riyals*							
Househ.Cons.Expend.,incl.NPISHs	96f	8,030	9,497	8,996	9,335	9,450	9,525	9,843	10,030	12,651	14,723	17,781	....
Government Consumption Expend	91f	9,250	9,436	10,886	12,236	11,789	11,573	12,715	12,766	12,952	14,580	15,852	....
Gross Fixed Capital Formation	93e	6,575	8,895	11,532	14,226	11,540	8,273	12,584	14,558	21,940	29,800	30,154	....
Changes in Inventories	93i	8	1,495	262	345	395	245	443	500	618	900	946	....
Exports of Goods and Services	90c	12,046	13,134	14,419	19,855	19,074	27,085	43,496	42,034	42,698	52,852	66,940	....
Imports of Goods and Services (-)	98c	9,066	12,835	13,119	14,873	14,918	11,590	14,435	15,309	19,126	26,582	28,110	....
Gross Domestic Product (GDP)	99b	26,843	29,622	32,976	41,124	37,330	45,111	64,646	64,579	71,733	86,273	103,563	....
GDP Volume 1988 Prices	99b.p	26,303	27,075	28,379	33,561	37,574	39,381	....	....	....	....	....	....
GDP Volume 2001 Prices	99b.p	....	....	....	....	....	56,644	61,784	64,579	69,322	73,378	....	....
GDP Deflator (2000=100)	99bip	67.8	72.7	77.2	81.4	66.0	76.1	100.0	95.6	98.9	112.4	....	....
GDP Volume (2000=100)	99bvp	61.2	63.0	66.1	78.1	87.5	† 91.7	100.0	104.5	112.2	118.8	....	....
						Millions: Midyear Estimates							
Population	99z	.52	† .53	.54	.55	.56	.58	.61	.64	.69	.73	.78	.81

Romania 968

		1994	1995	1996	1997	1998	1999	2000	2001	2002	2003	2004	2005
Exchange Rates						*Lei per SDR: End of Period*							
Market Rate	aa	.258	.383	.580	1.083	1.542	2.506	3.378	3.971	4.554	4.844	4.514	† 4.442
						Lei per US Dollar: End of Period (ae) Period Average (rf)							
Market Rate	ae	.177	.258	.404	.802	1.095	1.826	2.593	3.160	3.350	3.260	2.907	† 3.108
Market Rate	rf	.166	.203	.308	.717	.888	1.533	2.171	2.906	3.306	3.320	3.264	2.914
						Index Numbers (2000=100): Period Averages							
Nominal Effective Exchange Rate	nec	945.16	743.03	508.05	247.40	206.86	125.89	100.00	78.01	65.98	56.81	53.28	59.03
Real Effective Exchange Rate	rec	77.40	75.52	67.76	80.09	103.82	89.04	100.00	101.53	102.32	99.07	101.64	119.94
Fund Position						*Millions of SDRs: End of Period*							
Quota	2f.s	754	754	754	754	754	1,030	1,030	1,030	1,030	1,030	1,030	1,030
SDRs	1b.s	38	38	3	77	1	7	1	5	2	—	—	—
Reserve Position in the Fund	1c.s	—	—	—	—	—	—	—	—	—	—	—	—
Total Fund Cred.&Loans Outstg	2tl	906	698	453	475	383	334	348	308	315	401	285	183
International Liquidity						*Millions of US Dollars Unless Otherwise Indicated: End of Period*							
Total Reserves minus Gold	1l.d	2,086	1,579	2,103	3,803	2,867	1,526	2,470	3,923	6,125	8,040	14,616	19,872
SDRs	1b.d	56	56	4	104	1	10	1	7	2	—	1	1
Reserve Position in the Fund	1c.d	—	—	—	—	—	—	—	—	—	—	—	—
Foreign Exchange	1d.d	2,031	1,523	2,099	3,700	2,866	1,516	2,469	3,916	6,123	8,040	14,616	19,872
Gold (Million Fine Troy Ounces)	1ad	2.625	2.703	2.818	3.019	3.224	3.323	3.374	3.382	3.386	3.378	3.377	3.371
Gold (National Valuation)	1and	965	780	520	458	358	967	920	939	1,180	1,410	1,480	1,728
Deposit Money Banks: Assets	7a.d	129	73	72	79	87	91	95	94	105	126	152	94
Liabilities	7b.d	687	823	1,238	1,148	933	611	508	661	1,004	2,214	4,981	8,763
Monetary Authorities						*Billions of Lei: End of Period*							
Foreign Assets	11	.28	.29	.64	2.48	2.52	4.56	8.81	15.37	24.48	30.80	46.79	66.59
Claims on Government	12a	.18	.36	—	.33	.91	2.14	1.62	.84	.25	—	—	—
Claims on Deposit Money Banks	12e	.24	.47	.88	.34	.36	.24	.23	.11	—	—	—	—
Reserve Money	14	.38	.60	.90	2.13	2.57	4.95	7.66	12.25	18.95	22.73	39.23	61.95
of which: Currency Outside DMBs	14a	.22	.38	.54	.92	1.15	1.74	2.57	3.56	4.56	5.80	7.46	11.39
Transit Accounts	14x	—	—	—	—	—	.03	.03	—	—	—	—	—
Foreign Liabilities	16c	.24	.35	.78	1.52	1.76	1.59	2.20	1.22	1.43	1.94	1.29	.81
Central Government Deposits	16d	.14	.27	−.03	.07	.02	.59	.34	.89	1.07	1.27	5.21	4.02
Other Items (Net)	17r	−.07	−.09	−.13	−.57	−.56	−.22	.43	1.96	3.28	4.86	1.06	−.19
Deposit Money Banks						*Billions of Lei: End of Period*							
Reserves	20	.24	.33	.36	.53	1.30	3.50	5.10	8.71	14.40	16.91	31.55	50.33
Foreign Assets	21	.27	.37	.66	1.36	1.73	2.29	4.01	5.10	3.99	3.54	5.25	4.52
Claims on Central Government	22a	.06	.18	.55	1.11	1.88	2.99	3.17	3.80	4.29	2.62	2.22	2.55
Claims on Nonfin.Pub.Enterprises	22c	.95	1.61	1.32	1.27	1.17	.92	1.09	1.66	2.42	3.09	3.07	3.07
Claims on Private Sector	22d	—	—	1.25	2.11	4.32	4.40	5.76	9.02	12.62	18.00	23.90	32.55
Claims on Nonbank Financial Insts	22g	—	—	.11	.20	.42	.45	.65	1.14	2.92	9.46	14.79	25.05
Demand Deposits	24	.25	.35	.59	.96	1.06	1.23	2.06	2.87	4.27	5.53	7.82	13.16
Transit Accounts	24x	.02	.04	.06	.01	.03	.04	.07	.14	.07	.11	.06	.10
Time and Savings Deposits	25	.36	.69	1.19	2.56	4.02	5.40	6.39	9.04	13.86	17.63	25.71	35.90
Foreign Currency Deposits	25b	.24	.40	.71	1.77	3.02	5.05	7.49	11.58	14.68	17.12	23.46	25.88
Foreign Liabilities	26c	.12	.21	.50	.92	1.02	1.12	1.32	2.09	3.36	7.22	14.48	27.23
Government Deposits	26d	.16	.18	.12	.22	.59	.58	.71	1.31	1.47	1.88	2.34	4.61
Credit from Monetary Authorities	26g	.23	.32	.80	.06	.06	.19	.23	.11	—	—	—	—
Capital Accounts	27a	.09	.25	.51	.97	1.09	1.75	2.47	4.95	6.45	8.06	10.94	15.86
Other Items (Net)	27r	.08	.06	−.23	−.89	−.05	−.78	−.93	−2.65	−3.53	−3.92	−4.02	−4.69
Monetary Survey						*Billions of Lei: End of Period*							
Foreign Assets (Net)	31n	.19	.10	.02	1.40	1.46	4.14	9.30	17.15	23.67	25.18	36.27	43.06
Domestic Credit	32	.89	1.70	3.14	4.73	8.10	9.73	11.24	14.27	19.96	30.02	36.44	54.59
Claims on Central Govt. (Net)	32an	−.06	.09	.46	1.14	2.20	3.95	3.74	2.45	2.00	−.52	−5.32	−6.09
Claims on Nonfin.Pub.Enterprises	32c	.95	1.61	1.32	1.27	1.17	.92	1.09	1.66	2.42	3.09	3.07	3.07
Claims on Private Sector	32d	—	—	1.25	2.11	4.32	4.40	5.76	9.02	12.62	18.00	23.90	32.55
Claims on Nonbank Financial Inst	32g	—	—	.11	.20	.42	.45	.65	1.14	2.92	9.46	14.79	25.05
Money	34	.47	.72	1.13	1.88	2.21	2.97	4.63	6.43	8.83	11.33	15.29	24.55
Transit Accounts	34x	.02	.04	.06	.01	.04	.06	.10	.14	.07	.11	.06	.10
Quasi-Money	35	.60	1.09	1.90	4.33	7.04	10.44	13.87	20.62	28.54	34.75	49.17	61.78
Other Items (Net)	37r	.02	−.04	.07	−.09	.29	.41	1.95	4.23	6.19	9.02	8.19	11.22
Money plus Quasi-Money	35l	1.06	1.81	3.03	6.21	9.25	13.41	18.51	27.05	37.37	46.08	64.46	86.33
Interest Rates						*Percent Per Annum*							
Bank Rate (End of Period)	60a	66.9	41.3	35.1	45.0	37.9	35.0	35.0	35.0	29.0	18.8	20.3	9.6
Treasury Bill Rate	60c	....	....	51.1	85.7	64.0	74.2	51.9	42.2	27.0	....	....	....
Prices, Production, Labor						*Index Numbers (2000=100): Period Averages*							
Producer Prices	63	6.5	8.8	13.2	† 33.9	† 45.1	65.2	† 100.0	138.1	169.9	203.1	241.8	267.2
Consumer Prices	64	6.3	8.4	11.6	29.6	47.1	68.6	100.0	134.5	164.8	189.9	† 212.5	231.6
Wages: Avg. Earnings	65	6.4	9.9	14.8	29.1	48.0	71.5	100.0	138.9	178.6	224.0	274.5	339.5
Industrial Production	66	105.6	115.6	† 127.0	118.7	† 98.4	93.3	100.0	108.5	† 115.0	118.8	124.0	126.7
						Number in Thousands: Period Averages							
Employment	67e	† 10,914	11,152	10,936	11,050	10,845	10,776	10,764	10,697	9,234	9,223	9,158	9,147
Unemployment	67c	† 1,230	1,111	814	749	917	1,119	1,067	867	955	704	800	514
Unemployment Rate (%)	67r	† 11.0	10.0	7.8	7.5	9.3	11.3	11.2	9.0	10.0	7.6	8.0	5.8
Intl. Transactions & Positions						*Millions of US Dollars*							
Exports	70..d	6,151.3	7,910.0	8,084.5	8,431.1	8,299.6	8,504.7	10,366.5	11,390.7	13,875.7	17,618.5	23,485.2	27,729.6
Imports, c.i.f	71..d	7,109.0	10,277.9	11,435.3	11,279.7	11,821.0	10,392.1	13,054.5	15,560.9	17,861.7	24,002.7	32,663.7	40,462.9
Imports, f.o.b	71.vd	6,562.4	9,486.7	10,555.0	10,411.4	10,911.0	9,592.1	12,049.6	14,362.9	16,486.7	22,155.1	30,149.3	37,348.1

Romania 968

		1994	1995	1996	1997	1998	1999	2000	2001	2002	2003	2004	2005
Balance of Payments		*Millions of US Dollars: Minus Sign Indicates Debit*											
Current Account, n.i.e.	78ald	−455	−1,780	−2,579	−2,104	−2,917	−1,297	−1,355	−2,229	−1,525	−3,311	−6,382	−8,312
Goods: Exports f.o.b.	78aad	6,151	7,910	8,085	8,431	8,302	8,503	10,366	11,385	13,876	17,618	23,485	27,730
Goods: Imports f.o.b.	78abd	−6,562	−9,487	−10,555	−10,411	−10,927	−9,595	−12,050	−14,354	−16,487	−22,155	−30,150	−37,348
Trade Balance	78acd	−411	−1,577	−2,470	−1,980	−2,625	−1,092	−1,684	−2,969	−2,611	−4,537	−6,665	−9,618
Services: Credit	78aed	1,044	1,494	1,563	1,523	1,226	1,365	1,747	2,032	2,347	3,028	3,614	4,950
Services: Debit	78aed	−1,215	−1,819	−1,948	−1,904	−1,829	−1,785	−1,993	−2,153	−2,338	−2,958	−3,879	−5,440
Balance on Goods & Services	78afd	−582	−1,902	−2,855	−2,361	−3,228	−1,512	−1,930	−3,090	−2,602	−4,467	−6,930	−10,109
Income: Credit	78agd	116	81	78	204	263	152	325	455	413	372	433	1,616
Income: Debit	78ahd	−245	−322	−387	−526	−705	−563	−610	−737	−872	−1,077	−3,582	−4,279
Balance on Gds, Serv. & Inc.	78aid	−711	−2,143	−3,164	−2,683	−3,670	−1,923	−2,215	−3,372	−3,061	−5,172	−10,079	−12,773
Current Transfers, n.i.e.: Credit	78ajd	317	473	667	731	886	804	1,079	1,417	1,808	2,200	4,188	5,065
Current Transfers: Debit	78akd	−61	−110	−82	−152	−133	−178	−219	−274	−272	−339	−491	−604
Capital Account, n.i.e.	78bcd	—	32	152	43	39	45	36	95	93	213	643	701
Capital Account, n.i.e.: Credit	78bad	—	32	152	43	39	46	37	108	100	223	669	795
Capital Account: Debit	78bbd	—	—	—	—	—	−1	−1	−13	−7	−10	−26	−94
Financial Account, n.i.e.	78bjd	535	812	1,486	2,458	2,042	697	2,102	2,938	4,079	4,400	10,761	12,690
Direct Investment Abroad	78bdd	—	−2	—	9	9	−16	11	17	−16	−39	−70	9
Dir. Invest. in Rep. Econ., n.i.e.	78bed	341	419	263	1,215	2,031	1,041	1,037	1,157	1,144	1,844	6,443	6,630
Portfolio Investment Assets	78bfd	75	−22	—	−6	1	9	28	−8	—	9	−559	−89
Equity Securities	78bkd	—	−4	—	−6	1	9	31	−7	—	14	−559	−237
Debt Securities	78bld	75	−18	—	—	—	—	−3	−1	—	−5	—	149
Portfolio Investment Liab., n.i.e.	78bgd	—	54	193	540	129	−724	73	583	382	569	28	1,093
Equity Securities	78bmd	—	—	—	195	95	68	58	8	21	69	111	233
Debt Securities	78bnd	—	54	193	345	34	−792	15	575	361	500	−83	860
Financial Derivatives Assets	78bwd	....	—	—	—	—	....	....	....	....	....	....	30
Financial Derivatives Liabilities	78bxd	....	—	—	—	—	—	....	—	....	....	....	−60
Other Investment Assets	78bhd	−671	186	−271	−6	208	246	−407	−44	692	72	−212	−1,066
Monetary Authorities	78bod	—	—	—	—	—	—	....	—	—	−1	—	−11
General Government	78bpd	−24	−62	−9	10	−10	9	−82	−44	−41	−36	−22	−17
Banks	78bqd	−621	254	−315	−140	179	236	−354	−102	536	229	−43	−204
Other Sectors	78brd	−26	−6	53	124	39	1	29	102	197	−120	−147	−834
Other Investment Liab., n.i.e.	78bid	790	177	1,301	706	−336	141	1,360	1,233	1,877	1,945	5,131	6,143
Monetary Authorities	78bsd	—	—	−150	—	—	73	−14	—	−100	—	99	—
General Government	78btd	75	−27	209	547	−7	40	681	320	465	889	1,015	593
Banks	78bud	190	−57	536	−132	−260	−54	−107	159	309	918	2,329	3,671
Other Sectors	78bvd	525	261	706	291	−69	82	800	754	1,203	138	1,688	1,879
Net Errors and Omissions	78cad	91	456	359	1,062	193	794	125	731	−856	−289	1,167	1,740
Overall Balance	78cbd	171	−480	−582	1,459	−643	239	908	1,535	1,791	1,013	6,189	6,819
Reserves and Related Items	79dad	−171	480	582	−1,459	643	−239	−908	−1,535	−1,791	−1,013	−6,189	−6,819
Reserve Assets	79dbd	−616	259	−218	−1,664	844	−173	−928	−1,484	−1,802	−1,134	−6,018	−6,784
Use of Fund Credit and Loans	79dcd	217	−316	−356	29	−126	−66	20	−51	11	120	−171	−152
Exceptional Financing	79ded	228	536	1,157	176	−75	—	....	....	....	....	....	117
International Investment Position		*Millions of US Dollars*											
Assets	79aad	8,847	8,492	7,871	9,156	8,559	8,410	9,631	11,550	13,447	15,755	24,160	30,475
Direct Investment Abroad	79abd	107	121	120	126	135	144	136	116	144	208	295	243
Portfolio Investment	79acd	1,179	1,224	13	50	51	34	6	11	22	13	606	596
Equity Securities	79add	1,176	1,211	—	—	—	—	—	—	18	10	29	253
Debt Securities	79aed	3	13	13	50	51	34	6	11	4	4	576	343
Financial Derivatives	79ald	—	—	—	—	—	—	—	—	—	—	—	−30
Other Investment	79afd	5,964	5,768	6,146	5,919	6,073	5,740	6,099	6,561	5,975	6,083	6,976	8,066
Monetary Authorities	79agd	—	—	10	10	10	10	10	10	10	15	16	24
General Government	79ahd	3,004	3,006	3,093	2,926	3,058	3,727	3,807	3,873	3,921	3,970	4,414	4,440
Banks	79aid	1,491	1,244	1,556	1,637	1,556	1,263	1,572	1,642	1,204	1,104	1,211	1,281
Other Sectors	79ajd	1,468	1,517	1,487	1,347	1,450	740	711	1,037	840	993	1,336	2,321
Reserve Assets	79akd	1,598	1,380	1,592	3,061	2,299	2,493	3,390	4,861	7,306	9,450	16,283	21,600
Liabilities	79lad	7,500	7,976	10,318	12,843	15,165	15,342	18,022	20,883	23,093	32,168	46,863	55,337
Dir. Invest. in Rep. Economy	79lbd	402	421	1,097	2,417	4,527	5,671	6,951	8,350	7,799	12,187	20,522	23,785
Portfolio Investment	79lcd	719	785	1,229	2,103	2,333	1,585	1,635	2,188	3,245	4,503	4,832	5,151
Equity Securities	79ldd	719	732	—	266	361	429	487	495	516	700	877	984
Debt Securities	79led	—	54	1,229	1,837	1,972	1,156	1,148	1,693	2,729	3,803	3,954	4,167
Financial Derivatives	79lld	—	—	—	—	—	—	—	—	—	—	—	−59
Other Investment	79lfd	6,379	6,770	7,991	8,323	8,305	8,085	9,436	10,345	12,049	15,478	21,509	26,459
Monetary Authorities	79lgd	1,383	1,358	969	886	617	609	590	523	465	633	581	298
General Government	79lhd	2,298	2,335	2,484	3,283	3,525	3,563	4,486	4,766	5,552	6,989	8,373	8,383
Banks	79lid	682	743	1,268	975	700	550	497	650	1,001	2,141	4,579	8,025
Other Sectors	79ljd	2,016	2,334	3,270	3,179	3,463	3,363	3,864	4,405	5,031	5,715	7,976	9,752
Government Finance		*Millions of Lei: Year Ending December 31*											
Deficit (-) or Surplus	80	−125	−213	−438	−976	−1,103	−923	−3,177	−3,541	....	....	....	....
Revenue	81	1,488	2,133	3,019	6,839	10,705	17,113	23,716	31,132	....	....	....	....
Grants	81z	—	—	—	—	70	424	88	134	....	....	....	....
Expenditure	82	1,591	2,293	3,403	7,973	12,459	19,134	27,399	35,484	....	....	....	....
Lending Minus Repayments	83	22	53	54	−158	−582	−674	−418	−676	....	....	....	....
Financing													
Domestic	84a	125	....	....	752	....	....	2,398	2,567	....	....	....	....
Foreign	85a	—	....	....	223	....	....	779	974	....	....	....	....

Romania 968

		1994	1995	1996	1997	1998	1999	2000	2001	2002	2003	2004	2005
National Accounts						*Millions of Lei*							
Househ.Cons.Expend.,incl.NPISHs....	96f	3,160	4,879	7,567	18,762	28,314	40,532	56,318	81,781	104,472	130,453	167,162	212,901
Government Consumption Expend...	91f	685	988	1,427	3,100	5,433	7,904	12,935	17,693	22,798	38,781	46,540	34,758
Gross Fixed Capital Formation..........	93e	1,010	1,542	2,500	5,354	6,792	9,663	15,195	24,115	32,284	42,293	53,292	66,248
Changes in Inventories...................	93i	225	209	316	−137	−159	−889	454	2,229	556	874	1,708	−1,170
Exports of Goods and Services..........	90c	1,239	1,992	3,065	7,380	8,456	15,290	26,419	38,915	53,677	68,584	88,555	94,847
Imports of Goods and Services (-).....	98c	1,342	2,396	3,983	9,166	11,456	17,927	30,944	47,965	62,311	83,419	110,884	124,599
Gross Domestic Product (GDP)........	99b	4,977	7,214	10,892	25,293	37,380	54,573	80,377	116,769	151,475	197,565	246,372	282,986
GDP Volume 1995 Prices................	99b.p	6,733	7,214	7,498	7,044	6,705	6,628	6,770	7,159	7,526	7,919	8,588	. . . .
GDP Volume (2000=100)...............	99bvp	99.4	106.5	110.8	104.0	99.0	97.9	100.0	105.7	111.2	117.0	126.8	. . . .
GDP Deflator (2000=100)...............	99bip	6.2	8.4	12.2	30.2	47.0	69.4	100.0	137.4	169.5	210.1	241.6	. . . .
						Millions: Midyear Estimates							
Population...............................	99z	22.82	22.68	22.55	22.44	22.32	22.22	22.12	22.03	21.94	21.87	21.79	21.71

2006, International Monetary Fund : *International Financial Statistics Yearbook*

Russian Federation 922

		1994	1995	1996	1997	1998	1999	2000	2001	2002	2003	2004	2005
Exchange Rates						*Rubles per SDR: End of Period*							
Official Rate	aa	5.1825	6.8973	7.9951	8.0415	† 29.0758	37.0578	36.6899	37.8778	43.2115	43.7685	43.0940	41.1380
						Rubles per US Dollar: End of Period (ae) Period Average (rf)							
Official Rate	ae	3.5500	4.6400	5.5600	5.9600	† 20.6500	27.0000	28.1600	30.1400	31.7844	29.4545	27.7487	28.7825
Official Rate	rf	2.1908	4.5592	5.1208	5.7848	† 9.7051	24.6199	28.1292	29.1685	31.3485	30.6920	28.8137	28.2844
						Index Numbers (2000=100): Period Averages							
Nominal Effective Exchange Rate	nec	508.14	311.87	300.49	304.06	245.65	96.71	100.00	106.39	99.64	94.49	95.85	96.11
Real Effective Exchange Rate	rec	103.29	113.24	140.02	149.45	132.07	90.61	100.00	120.25	123.57	127.31	137.33	149.24
Fund Position						*Millions of SDRs: End of Period*							
Quota	2f.s	4,313.1	4,313.1	4,313.1	4,313.1	4,313.1	5,945.4	5,945.4	5,945.4	5,945.4	5,945.4	5,945.4	5,945.4
SDRs	1b.s	2.1	78.5	3.1	90.7	.1	.4	.4	2.3	.9	.5	.6	3.9
Reserve Position in the Fund	1c.s	.8	.8	.9	.9	.9	.9	.9	1.1	1.2	1.4	1.8	137.0
Total Fund Cred.&Loans Outstg	2tl	2,875.6	6,469.8	8,698.2	9,805.9	13,732.0	11,102.3	8,912.8	5,914.8	4,767.3	3,411.2	2,293.8	—
International Liquidity						*Millions of US Dollars Unless Otherwise Indicated: End of Period*							
Total Reserves minus Gold	1l.d	3,980.4	14,382.8	11,276.4	12,894.7	7,801.4	8,457.2	24,264.3	32,542.4	44,053.6	73,174.9	120,808.8	175,891.4
SDRs	1b.d	3.1	116.7	4.5	122.4	.1	.6	.5	2.9	1.2	.7	.9	5.6
Reserve Position in the Fund	1c.d	1.2	1.1	1.3	1.2	1.3	1.3	1.2	1.4	1.6	2.1	2.8	195.9
Foreign Exchange	1d.d	3,976.1	14,264.9	11,270.6	12,771.1	7,800.0	8,455.4	24,262.6	32,538.1	44,050.8	73,172.1	120,805.1	175,689.9
Gold (Million Fine Troy Ounces)	1ad	8.417	9.414	13.490	16.297	14.738	13.326	12.359	13.599	12.464	12.545	12.441	12.438
Gold (National Valuation)	1and	2,525.1	2,824.1	4,047.1	4,889.2	4,421.6	3,998.3	3,707.8	4,079.8	3,739.3	3,763.4	3,732.4	† 6,349.0
Monetary Authorities:Other Assets	3..d	5,768.2	3,458.8	3,176.8	2,911.2	1,937.8	2,010.8	2,177.2	2,385.5	3,039.5	4,241.0	5,572.3	10,752.4
Other Liab	4..d	477.3	303.0	311.2	149.2	110.5	473.1	143.7	2,102.6	850.4	2,421.9	4,183.2	10,381.8
Deposit Money Banks: Assets	7a.d	13,891.6	9,946.1	13,107.0	12,513.8	11,251.1	14,281.9	17,435.3	18,146.2	19,033.0	20,660.0	25,480.5	37,967.0
Liabilities	7b.d	4,076.8	6,459.1	10,592.3	18,030.0	10,727.0	9,408.3	10,113.9	11,355.2	12,892.6	23,158.9	32,168.9	49,963.7
Monetary Authorities						*Millions of Rubles: End of Period*							
Foreign Assets	11	41,082	95,890	102,861	123,344	292,420	390,590	849,009	1,175,689	1,615,677	2,391,096	3,610,481	5,554,814
Claims on General Government	12a	84,498	138,578	187,365	226,049	525,374	572,030	504,702	488,102	551,547	477,640	426,555	276,042
Claims on Nonfin.Pub.Enterprises	12c	251	85	67	46	150	114	103	80	58	55	39	28
Claims on Private Sector	12d	72	237	813	281	412	316	264	168	2,181	2,264	2,282	2,439
Claims on Deposit Money Banks	12e	16,177	17,450	11,377	11,119	76,438	202,944	206,501	250,187	223,991	198,742	178,230	27,892
Reserve Money	14	62,357	129,601	164,929	210,450	269,665	446,432	746,252	963,137	1,263,728	1,947,711	2,417,881	2,959,306
of which: Currency Outside DMBs	14a	34,493	80,815	103,795	130,474	187,679	266,146	418,871	583,839	763,245	1,147,039	1,534,755	2,009,240
Time & Foreign Currency Deposits	15	4	17	23	240	1,828	1,575	7	2	29	5	17	35
Foreign Liabilities	16c	16,538	46,030	71,272	79,744	401,551	424,201	331,056	287,413	233,030	220,638	214,927	298,813
General Government Deposits	16d	17,096	24,898	15,062	21,313	41,863	75,871	240,488	294,914	357,878	446,001	1,047,912	2,146,031
of which: Local Govt. Deposits	16db	3,273	2,117	2,068	3,564	2,863	10,515	29,511	27,729	33,993	43,804	85,580	126,694
Capital Accounts	17a	17,014	27,530	54,179	69,552	118,113	151,844	166,048	242,312	364,731	298,234	188,043	210,373
Other Items (Net)	17r	29,071	24,164	−2,982	−20,460	61,775	66,072	76,728	126,448	174,058	157,208	348,807	246,657
Deposit Money Banks						*Millions of Rubles: End of Period*							
Reserves	20	24,151	36,712	48,301	74,981	77,728	168,180	310,781	356,771	471,563	768,914	847,419	906,548
Foreign Assets	21	49,316	46,150	72,875	74,582	232,336	385,611	490,977	546,926	604,953	608,529	707,052	1,092,784
Claims on General Government	22a	10,639	62,639	150,945	194,899	263,695	445,321	532,569	588,703	696,007	742,776	757,190	666,499
of which: Claims on Local Govts	22ab	—	722	2,796	18,699	26,174	22,080	20,538	27,612	52,314	98,844	133,748	153,467
Claims on Nonfin.Pub.Enterprises	22c	48,173	62,460	80,211	51,687	38,099	52,131	78,963	83,238	122,938	142,968	166,550	193,785
Claims on Private Sector	22d	74,017	133,786	166,517	250,134	410,691	631,137	969,413	1,473,097	1,915,108	2,772,461	4,108,955	5,557,570
Claims on Other Financial Insts	22f	—	525	242	8,077	7,526	13,738	15,378	23,232	32,948	55,561	73,747	99,562
Demand Deposits	24	32,589	69,332	87,303	163,658	150,931	250,927	444,625	586,721	706,693	1,003,198	1,277,488	1,805,708
Time, Savings,& Fgn.Currency Dep	25	61,183	124,497	164,899	160,771	287,686	463,999	688,453	944,814	1,361,495	1,780,146	2,450,337	3,362,568
of which: Fgn. Currency Deposits	25b	37,309	55,256	69,448	80,822	191,412	292,023	422,874	523,929	726,443	748,240	935,077	1,178,157
Money Market Instruments	26aa	3,516	11,858	26,653	31,485	42,062	113,089	199,080	263,885	399,866	545,464	533,652	579,953
Restricted Deposits	26b	—	—	9,929	17,423	65,596	100,849	90,509	77,582	43,759	30,360	36,112	32,068
Foreign Liabilities	26c	14,473	29,970	58,893	107,459	221,512	254,025	284,808	342,246	409,783	682,134	892,645	1,438,081
General Government Deposits	26d	6,914	9,741	12,142	19,105	22,723	31,272	58,923	73,538	67,892	85,484	141,762	189,128
of which: Local Govt. Deposits	26db	2,246	4,252	4,493	9,598	10,638	16,440	37,277	44,875	36,787	56,057	112,465	163,833
Credit from Monetary Authorities	26g	17,181	8,006	12,769	15,430	79,872	206,887	208,109	250,918	226,103	200,868	179,826	28,945
Capital Accounts	27a	26,211	56,810	106,684	124,005	102,678	166,259	234,223	352,141	491,277	686,650	898,313	1,244,995
Other Items (Net)	27r	44,229	32,058	39,819	15,024	57,015	108,811	189,351	180,122	136,649	76,905	250,778	−164,698
Monetary Survey						*Millions of Rubles: End of Period*							
Foreign Assets (Net)	31n	59,387	66,040	45,571	10,723	−98,306	97,976	724,122	1,092,956	1,577,817	2,096,853	3,209,961	4,910,704
Domestic Credit	32	193,640	363,671	558,956	690,755	1,181,361	1,607,644	1,801,981	2,288,168	2,895,017	3,662,240	4,345,644	4,460,766
Claims on General Govt. (Net)	32an	71,127	166,578	311,106	380,530	724,483	910,208	737,860	708,353	821,784	688,931	−5,929	−1,392,618
Claims on Nonfin.Pub.Enterprises	32c	48,424	62,545	80,278	51,733	38,249	52,245	79,066	83,318	122,996	143,023	166,589	193,813
Claims on Private Sector	32d	74,089	134,023	167,330	250,415	411,103	631,453	969,677	1,473,265	1,917,289	2,774,725	4,111,237	5,560,009
Claims on Other Financial Insts	32f	—	525	242	8,077	7,526	13,738	15,378	23,232	32,948	55,561	73,747	99,562
Money	34	68,544	151,267	192,373	299,349	344,113	527,627	880,524	1,193,395	1,498,463	2,181,933	2,848,345	3,858,515
Quasi-Money	35	61,187	124,514	164,922	161,011	289,514	465,574	688,460	944,816	1,361,524	1,780,151	2,450,354	3,362,603
Money Market Instruments	36aa	3,516	11,858	26,653	31,485	42,062	113,089	199,080	263,885	399,866	545,464	533,652	579,953
Restricted Deposits	36b	—	—	9,929	17,423	65,596	100,849	90,509	77,582	43,759	30,360	36,112	32,068
Capital Accounts	37a	43,225	84,340	160,863	193,557	220,791	318,103	400,271	594,453	856,008	984,884	1,086,356	1,455,368
Other Items (Net)	37r	76,555	57,732	49,787	−1,347	120,979	180,378	267,259	306,993	313,214	236,301	600,786	82,963
Money plus Quasi-Money	35l	129,731	275,781	357,295	460,360	633,627	993,201	1,568,984	2,138,211	2,859,987	3,962,084	5,298,699	7,221,118
Interest Rates						*Percent Per Annum*							
Refinancing Rate (End of Period)	60	....	160.00	48.00	28.00	60.00	55.00	25.00	25.00	21.00	16.00	13.00	12.00
Money Market Rate	60b	....	190.43	47.65	20.97	50.56	14.79	7.14	10.10	8.19	3.77	3.33	2.68
Treasury Bill Rate	60c	....	168.04	86.07	23.43	....	....	12.12	12.45	12.72	5.35	....	....
Deposit Rate	60l	....	101.96	55.05	† 16.77	17.05	13.68	6.51	4.85	4.96	4.48	3.79	3.99
Lending Rate	60p	....	320.31	146.81	† 32.04	41.79	39.72	24.43	17.91	15.71	12.98	11.40	10.68

		1994	1995	1996	1997	1998	1999	2000	2001	2002	2003	2004	2005
Prices and Labor		*Percent Change over Previous Period Unless Otherwise indicated*											
Producer Prices	63.xx	337.00	236.46	50.81	15.00	7.03	58.95	46.53	18.17	10.44	16.38	23.36	20.57
Consumer Prices (2000=100)	64	6.9	† 20.6	30.4	34.9	44.6	82.8	100.0	† 121.5	140.6	159.9	177.2	199.7
Wages	65.xx	255.9	142.2	64.8	23.7	15.3	55.4	51.9	43.1	27.2	26.1	13.4	22.0
		Index Numbers (2000=100): Period Averages											
Industrial Employment	67	134.4	125.6	115.3	105.4	101.4	98.2	100.0	99.3	95.7	89.9	99.3	103.0
		Number in Thousands: Period Averages											
Labor Force	67d	....	69,469	68,264	....	66,736	69,731	....	....	71,919	72,212	72,909	....
Employment	67e	64,785	64,149	62,928	60,021	63,575	64,400	62,675	64,412	66,071	65,766	66,496	....
Unemployment	67c	1,637	2,327	2,506	1,999	1,929	1,263	1,037	1,123	1,309	1,600	....	....
Unemployment Rate (%)	67r	† 7.5	8.9	9.9	11.3	13.3	12.7	10.6	9.0	....	....	....	....
Intl. Transactions & Positions		*Millions of US Dollars*											
Exports	70..d	† 67,826	82,913	90,563	89,008	74,884	75,665	105,565	101,884	107,301	135,929	183,207	243,569
Imports, c.i.f	71..d	† 55,497	68,863	74,879	79,076	63,817	43,588	49,125	59,140	67,063	83,677	107,120	137,833
Imports, f.o.b	71.vd	....	....	....	....	....	....	....	53,764	60,966	76,070	97,382	125,303
Balance of Payments		*Millions of US Dollars: Minus Sign Indicates Debit*											
Current Account, n.i.e	78ald	7,844	6,965	10,847	−80	219	24,616	46,839	33,935	29,116	35,410	58,592	84,249
Goods: Exports f.o.b	78aad	67,379	82,419	89,684	86,895	74,444	75,551	105,033	101,884	107,301	135,929	183,207	243,569
Goods: Imports f.o.b	78abd	−50,451	−62,603	−68,093	−71,983	−58,015	−39,537	−44,862	−53,764	−60,966	−76,070	−97,382	−125,303
Trade Balance	78acd	16,928	19,816	21,591	14,913	16,429	36,014	60,172	48,121	46,335	59,860	85,825	118,266
Services: Credit	78add	8,425	10,568	13,283	14,080	12,372	9,067	9,565	11,441	13,611	16,229	20,290	24,566
Services: Debit	78aed	−15,435	−20,206	−18,665	−20,025	−16,456	−13,351	−16,230	−20,572	−23,497	−27,122	−33,732	−39,261
Balance on Goods & Services	78afd	9,918	10,178	16,209	8,967	12,346	31,730	53,506	38,990	36,449	48,966	72,383	103,571
Income: Credit	78agd	3,499	4,281	4,336	4,366	4,301	3,881	4,753	6,800	5,677	11,057	11,998	18,165
Income: Debit	78ahd	−5,342	−7,650	−9,768	−13,058	−16,091	−11,597	−11,489	−11,038	−12,260	−24,228	−25,112	−36,324
Balance on Gds, Serv. & Inc	78aid	8,075	6,809	10,777	276	556	24,015	46,770	34,752	29,866	35,795	59,268	85,412
Current Transfers, n.i.e.: Credit	78ajd	311	894	771	410	308	1,183	807	744	1,352	2,537	3,640	4,686
Current Transfers: Debit	78akd	−542	−738	−701	−766	−644	−582	−738	−1,561	−2,103	−2,922	−4,317	−5,849
Capital Account, n.i.e	78bcd	2,408	−348	−463	−797	−382	−328	10,676	−9,378	−12,396	−993	−1,624	−12,137
Capital Account, n.i.e.: Credit	78bad	5,882	3,122	3,066	2,137	1,704	885	11,543	2,125	7,528	616	862	678
Capital Account: Debit	78bbd	−3,474	−3,470	−3,529	−2,934	−2,086	−1,213	−867	−11,503	−19,924	−1,609	−2,486	−12,815
Financial Account, n.i.e	78bjd	−29,340	−5,828	−19,890	3,596	−11,409	−17,008	−33,855	−3,308	1,345	3,558	−3,810	4,715
Direct Investment Abroad	78bdd	−281	−605	−922	−3,185	−1,270	−2,208	−3,177	−2,533	−3,533	−9,727	−13,782	−13,126
Dir. Invest. in Rep. Econ., n.i.e	78bed	690	2,065	2,579	4,865	2,761	3,309	2,714	2,748	3,461	7,958	15,444	14,600
Portfolio Investment Assets	78bfd	114	−1,704	−173	−156	−257	254	−411	77	−796	−2,180	−4,257	−10,666
Equity Securities	78bkd	−19	−42	−117	32	−10	5	−40	−60	85	−47	−25	−733
Debt Securities	78bld	133	−1,662	−56	−189	−247	249	−371	137	−880	−2,133	−4,231	−9,933
Portfolio Investment Liab., n.i.e	78bgd	−93	−739	4,584	17,795	6,293	−1,882	−12,808	−730	3,756	−2,329	4,406	−854
Equity Securities	78bmd	44	46	2,154	1,265	714	−287	150	542	2,626	422	233	−215
Debt Securities	78bnd	−137	−785	2,430	16,530	5,579	−1,595	−12,959	−1,272	1,130	−2,750	4,173	−639
Financial Derivatives Assets	78bwd	....	....	....	....	....	....	....	—	80	1,017	758	858
Financial Derivatives Liabilities	78bxd	....	....	....	....	....	....	....	—	−67	−377	−857	−1,091
Other Investment Assets	78bhd	−19,557	−150	−27,666	−20,206	−14,463	−12,791	−17,086	573	2,120	−15,352	−24,853	−30,839
Monetary Authorities	78bod	—	—	—	—	—	—	—	−266	971	467	306	205
General Government	78bpd	−3,119	−1,040	−319	7,158	−1,150	−1,348	−1,617	10,099	16,990	−299	200	11,073
Banks	78bqd	−3,117	4,318	−1,972	−1,082	501	−3,625	−3,332	−1,652	−675	−837	−1,964	−9,905
Other Sectors	78brd	−13,321	−3,428	−25,375	−26,281	−13,814	−7,818	−12,137	−7,609	−15,167	−14,683	−23,394	−32,213
Other Investment Liab., n.i.e	78bid	−10,213	−4,695	1,708	4,483	−4,474	−3,690	−3,087	−3,444	−3,676	24,547	19,331	45,834
Monetary Authorities	78bsd	−325	391	−230	−38	65	3	155	1,908	−1,273	1,636	1,909	6,309
General Government	78btd	−11,744	−8,716	−6,034	−10,764	−3,176	−1,975	−2,875	−7,480	−13,341	−3,705	−5,485	−19,256
Banks	78bud	1,305	2,448	4,258	8,649	−6,360	−1,270	568	1,839	2,584	11,546	6,709	18,087
Other Sectors	78bvd	551	1,182	3,714	6,636	4,997	−448	−935	289	8,354	15,070	16,197	40,693
Net Errors and Omissions	78cad	−25	−9,115	−7,712	−9,237	−9,806	−8,984	−9,737	−9,982	−6,502	−9,713	−6,268	−11,860
Overall Balance	78cbd	−19,113	−8,326	−17,218	−6,518	−21,378	−1,704	13,923	11,266	11,563	28,262	46,890	64,968
Reserves and Related Items	79dad	19,113	8,326	17,218	6,518	21,378	1,704	−13,923	−11,266	−11,563	−28,262	−46,890	−64,968
Reserve Assets	79dbd	1,935	−10,382	2,840	−1,930	5,306	−1,772	−16,009	−8,211	−11,375	−26,365	−45,236	−61,461
Use of Fund Credit and Loans	79dcd	1,514	5,473	3,237	1,526	5,206	−3,603	−2,899	−3,829	−1,493	−1,897	−1,655	−3,506
Exceptional Financing	79ded	15,663	13,235	11,141	6,923	10,866	7,078	4,985	773	1,305	—	—	—
International Investment Position		*Millions of US Dollars*											
Assets	79aad	22,245	28,645	29,041	33,440	25,557	28,392	237,659	251,083	280,191	328,738	392,965	....
Direct Investment Abroad	79abd	2,272	2,420	2,685	2,789	2,703	1,076	20,141	44,219	62,348	90,873	103,855	....
Portfolio Investment	79acd	486	764	1,230	1,383	1,308	861	1,268	1,342	2,537	4,410	8,389	....
Equity Securities	79add	7	27	43	12	18	6	46	132	81	126	158	....
Debt Securities	79aed	479	737	1,187	1,371	1,290	855	1,222	1,210	2,455	4,285	8,230	....
Financial Derivatives	79ald	—	—	—	—	—	—	—	—	—	55	153	....
Other Investment	79afd	12,982	8,254	9,802	11,484	9,323	14,000	188,278	168,900	167,514	156,461	156,027	....
Monetary Authorities	79agd	—	—	—	—	—	—	1,436	1,677	1,518	1,095	792	....
General Government	79ahd	—	—	—	—	—	—	122,526	100,425	95,170	85,028	85,295	....
Banks	79aid	12,982	8,254	9,802	11,484	9,323	14,000	15,585	16,947	17,796	18,961	21,304	....
Other Sectors	79ajd	—	—	—	—	—	—	48,731	49,851	53,030	51,378	48,636	....
Reserve Assets	79akd	6,505	17,207	15,324	17,784	12,223	12,455	27,972	36,622	47,793	76,938	124,541	....
Liabilities	79lad	7,380	15,492	22,162	32,829	29,925	24,087	185,226	216,164	251,281	332,901	389,033	....
Dir. Invest. in Rep. Economy	79lbd	332	345	426	970	373	731	32,204	52,919	70,884	96,729	114,926	....
Portfolio Investment	79lcd	369	437	567	1,032	495	346	32,132	52,317	66,911	93,358	109,738	....
Equity Securities	79ldd	79	132	122	241	36	40	11,109	27,353	35,762	57,982	68,134	....
Debt Securities	79led	290	305	445	791	459	306	21,023	24,964	31,149	35,376	41,605	....
Financial Derivatives	79lld	—	—	—	—	—	—	—	—	—	31	189	....
Other Investment	79lfd	6,679	14,710	21,169	30,827	29,057	23,010	120,890	110,929	113,486	142,783	164,180	....
Monetary Authorities	79lgd	4,198	9,617	12,508	13,231	19,335	15,238	11,939	9,741	7,531	7,807	8,244	....
General Government	79lhd	—	—	—	—	—	—	83,410	73,974	67,363	69,636	65,950	....
Banks	79lid	2,481	5,093	8,661	17,596	9,722	7,772	7,990	9,700	12,326	23,525	30,372	....
Other Sectors	79ljd	—	—	—	—	—	—	17,552	17,515	26,267	41,815	59,615	....

Russian Federation   922

		1994	1995	1996	1997	1998	1999	2000	2001	2002	2003	2004	2005
Government Finance							*Millions of Rubles: Year Ending December 31*						
Deficit (-) or Surplus	80	....	−69,508	−147,607	−150,415	−126,958	−56,641	173,468	275,321	179,220	314,251	825,937	1,623,317
Total Revenue and Grants	81y	....	226,071	281,770	322,690	299,403	608,033	1,127,571	1,598,482	2,219,266	2,577,933	3,456,733	5,138,843
Revenue	81	....	....	....	....	....	....	....	....	2,218,389	2,577,031	3,420,810	5,052,244
Grants	81z	....	....	....	....	....	....	....	....	877	902	35,923	86,599
Exp. & Lending Minus Repay	82z	....	295,579	429,377	473,105	426,361	664,674	954,103	1,323,161	2,040,046	2,263,682	2,630,796	3,515,526
Expenditure	82	....	277,744	409,792	454,768	416,872	655,391	1,004,265	1,376,552	2,042,943	2,351,111	2,692,245	3,515,526
Lending Minus Repayments	83	....	17,835	19,585	18,337	9,489	9,283	−50,162	−53,391	−2,897	−87,429	−61,449	—
Total Financing	80h	....	69,508	147,607	150,415	126,958	56,641	−173,468	−275,321	−179,220	−314,251	−825,937	−1,623,317
Total Net Borrowing	84	....	72,248	137,224	159,722	154,733	101,063	−173,468	−275,321	−179,220	−314,251	−825,937	−1,623,317
Net Domestic	84a	....	48,814	103,968	106,253	64,545	53,644	−40,331	−50,068	−9,210	−81,435	−652,106	−815,012
Net Foreign	85a	....	23,434	33,256	53,469	90,188	47,419	−133,137	−225,253	−170,010	−232,816	−173,831	−808,306
Use of Cash Balances	87	....	−2,740	10,383	−9,307	−27,775	−44,422	—	—	—	—	—	—
Total Debt by Currency	88z	....	787,689	1,122,323	1,302,052	3,786,106	....	....	....	4,550,774	4,004,304	....	3,075,479
Debt: Domestic	88b	....	226,505	427,323	565,992	750,556	....	801,530	755,896	886,249	830,798	98,848	875,434
Debt: Foreign	89b	....	561,184	695,000	736,060	3,035,550	....	....	....	3,664,525	3,173,506	....	2,200,045
National Accounts							*Billions of Rubles*						
Househ.Cons.Expend.,incl.NPISHs	96f	285	744	1,044	1,283	1,511	2,582	3,374	4,417	5,532	6,694	8,313	10,383
Government Consumption Expend	91f	137	273	391	494	493	703	1,102	1,470	1,911	2,331	2,802	3,559
Gross Fixed Capital Formation	93e	133	301	402	429	425	694	1,232	1,689	1,939	2,432	3,106	3,926
Changes in Inventories	93i	23	62	74	86	−31	21	134	274	230	323	426	586
Exports of Goods and Services	90c	170	418	523	579	821	2,085	3,219	3,300	3,814	4,656	5,858	7,588
Imports of Goods and Services (-)	98c	142	370	439	528	646	1,262	1,756	2,166	2,646	3,154	3,774	4,655
GDP, Production Based	99bp	611	1,429	2,008	2,343	2,630	4,823	7,306	8,944	10,831	13,243	16,966	21,598
Statistical Discrepancy	99bs	5	—	12	—	57	—	−40	51	−39	235	212	
							Millions: Midyear Estimates						
Population	99z	148.44	148.19	147.95	147.69	147.40	147.03	146.56	145.99	145.33	144.62	143.90	143.20

Rwanda 714

		1994	1995	1996	1997	1998	1999	2000	2001	2002	2003	2004	2005
Exchange Rates							*Francs per SDR: End of Period*						
Official Rate	aa	201.39	445.67	437.37	411.31	450.75	479.24	560.67	572.84	695.88	849.07	878.35	791.41
							Francs per US Dollar: End of Period (ae) Period Average (rf)						
Official Rate	ae	137.95	299.81	304.16	304.84	320.13	349.17	430.32	455.82	511.85	571.39	565.58	553.72
Official Rate	rf	140.70	262.18	306.10	301.32	313.72	337.83	393.43	442.80	476.33	537.66	574.62	555.94
Fund Position							*Millions of SDRs: End of Period*						
Quota	2f.s	59.50	59.50	59.50	59.50	59.50	80.10	80.10	80.10	80.10	80.10	80.10	80.10
SDRs	1b.s	1.75	13.65	12.71	19.64	17.36	10.54	.87	9.82	7.48	20.03	19.45	18.13
Reserve Position in the Fund	1c.s	9.79	—	—	—	—	—	—	—	—	—	—	—
Total Fund Cred.&Loans Outstg.	2tl	8.76	17.69	16.81	29.93	40.08	55.29	65.88	67.09	62.45	61.84	59.41	53.89
International Liquidity						*Millions of US Dollars Unless Otherwise Indicated: End of Period*							
Total Reserves minus Gold	1l.d	51.25	99.10	106.74	153.34	168.75	174.18	190.64	212.11	243.73	214.70	314.64	405.76
SDRs	1b.d	2.55	20.29	18.28	26.50	24.44	14.46	1.14	12.34	10.17	29.77	30.20	25.91
Reserve Position in the Fund	1c.d	14.29	—	—	—	—	—	—	—	—	—	—	—
Foreign Exchange	1d.d	34.40	78.80	88.47	126.84	144.31	159.72	189.50	199.77	233.55	184.93	284.44	379.85
Monetary Authorities: Other Liab.	4..d	40.45	28.36	20.62	21.89	50.05	21.13	17.89	15.69	17.82	8.29	2.56	1.29
Deposit Money Banks: Assets	7a.d	26.63	51.92	66.27	73.17	75.22	56.23	76.54	74.87	76.17	85.77	107.18	94.97
Liabilities	7b.d	5.61	4.09	4.53	12.63	11.91	5.31	8.24	10.37	15.41	22.26	22.45	21.32
Other Banking Insts.: Liabilities	7f.d	8.67	7.96	7.41	4.70	2.99	2.92	2.39	8.09	8.09	13.39	....	....
Monetary Authorities							*Millions of Francs: End of Period*						
Foreign Assets	11	7,089	29,710	32,469	46,720	54,058	60,882	82,068	97,124	124,753	124,585	178,311	224,675
Claims on Central Government	12a	32,834	34,359	35,125	42,125	44,447	50,716	43,469	43,469	43,050	43,917	42,126	42,126
Claims on Official Entities	12bx	680	762	730	729	729	219	149	129	129	128	116	61
Claims on Private Sector	12d	151	157	253	220	342	561	1,112	1,682	2,091	2,306	2,756	3,024
Claims on Deposit Money Banks	12e	846	1,725	153	301	908	1,793	2,646	1,522	2,236	1,369	1,578	1,380
Claims on Other Financial Insts.	12f	11	9	9	9	426	431	314	207	121	72	551	424
Reserve Money	14	19,708	27,340	33,507	37,314	34,016	39,051	35,803	43,767	43,358	48,331	63,973	101,976
of which: Currency Outside DMBs	14a	11,924	17,257	19,908	20,635	22,865	21,510	24,609	24,380	23,953	29,246	36,512	46,277
Time Deposits	15	291	207	201	181	142	855	434	1,630	1,648	1,374	1,595	1,688
Foreign Liabilities	16c	7,365	16,383	13,624	18,974	34,112	33,907	44,654	45,789	52,580	58,128	53,747	43,360
Central Government Deposits	16d	4,430	19,156	15,753	15,032	16,276	20,929	24,681	29,115	49,599	32,257	76,596	103,290
Counterpart Funds	16e	4,596	2,304	3,231	4,174	3,408	1,620	1,311	770	569	658	864	1,033
Capital Accounts	17a	13,981	20,238	13,149	11,680	12,589	15,613	15,373	18,080	23,169	29,061	27,917	26,182
Other Items (Net)	17r	−8,758	−18,904	−10,726	2,749	367	2,627	7,500	4,984	1,458	2,568	748	−5,839
Deposit Money Banks							*Millions of Francs: End of Period*						
Reserves	20	6,618	8,590	13,816	16,035	11,835	15,845	10,823	15,496	13,511	13,055	28,907	36,753
Foreign Assets	21	3,683	15,566	20,157	22,293	24,095	19,652	32,949	34,281	38,990	49,769	60,759	52,584
Claims on Central Government	22a	4,311	4,528	4,968	5,573	6,995	7,747	7,265	7,345	14,408	14,862	21,015	22,475
Claims on Official Entities	22bx	581	354	205	15	421	587	678	1,010	3,533	4,952	4,941	2,381
Claims on Private Sector	22d	16,234	28,381	28,615	44,948	54,079	59,686	69,289	75,264	82,906	94,658	127,568	158,328
Demand Deposits	24	16,165	22,586	24,979	34,523	31,509	36,936	37,575	38,522	45,346	52,220	62,604	82,524
Time and Savings Deposits	25	8,084	22,181	22,851	32,445	36,051	38,680	50,588	61,622	70,974	81,352	113,026	122,063
Foreign Liabilities	26c	776	1,226	1,378	3,847	3,816	1,856	3,546	4,749	7,887	12,919	12,724	11,805
Central Government Deposits	26d	3,370	5,482	10,944	9,072	12,322	9,705	9,442	5,401	5,235	6,298	9,341	11,157
Credit from Monetary Authorities	26g	287	1,624	63	63	61	1,550	2,358	1,352	2,080	1,216	1,624	2,059
Capital Accounts	27a	3,745	6,908	7,683	11,832	16,749	20,059	23,749	26,097	23,427	27,937	60,937	65,203
Other Items (Net)	27r	−998	−2,589	−136	−2,919	−3,083	−5,269	−6,252	−4,542	−1,599	−4,648	−17,064	−22,290
Monetary Survey							*Millions of Francs: End of Period*						
Foreign Assets (Net)	31n	2,632	27,666	37,624	46,191	40,225	44,771	66,817	80,867	103,276	103,307	172,599	222,093
Domestic Credit	32	47,175	44,016	43,307	69,621	78,951	89,482	88,263	94,857	91,816	122,615	113,785	115,815
Claims on Central Govt. (Net)	32an	29,346	14,249	13,396	23,594	22,844	27,829	16,611	16,298	2,623	20,224	−22,796	−49,847
Claims on Official Entities	32bx	1,261	1,116	935	744	1,150	806	827	1,139	3,662	5,080	5,058	2,442
Claims on Private Sector	32d	16,385	28,538	28,868	45,168	54,421	60,248	70,401	76,946	84,997	96,963	130,323	161,352
Claims on Other Financial Insts.	32f	184	113	108	115	536	599	424	474	534	348	1,200	1,868
Money	34	28,810	40,658	45,423	55,746	55,291	59,172	63,110	63,718	70,373	82,305	99,941	129,326
Quasi-Money	35	8,375	22,388	23,052	32,626	36,193	39,535	51,022	63,252	72,621	82,726	114,621	123,751
Other Items (Net)	37r	12,625	8,637	12,457	27,440	27,692	35,547	40,948	48,562	52,102	60,891	71,825	84,831
Money plus Quasi-Money	35l	37,185	63,046	68,475	88,372	91,484	98,707	114,132	126,970	142,994	165,032	214,562	253,077
Other Banking Institutions							*Millions of Francs: End of Period*						
Cash	40..k	1,340	1,363	1,559	1,495	862	1,445	1,090	1,638	1,261	427	....	....
Claims on Official Entities	42bxk	—	52	491	21	316	298	—	—	—	—	....	....
Claims on Private Sector	42d.k	3,024	3,835	3,126	4,152	5,161	5,807	6,224	6,371	7,078	9,748	....	....
Long Term Foreign Liabilities	46clk	1,199	2,386	2,253	1,433	957	1,021	1,027	3,706	4,140	7,772	....	....
Credit from Monetary Authorities	46g.k	9	9	9	9	9	431	314	207	121	—	....	....
Cred.from Deposit Money Banks	46h.k	—	—	—	—	—	—	—	—	—	768	....	....
Capital Accounts	47a.k	3,996	3,736	4,228	4,067	4,986	6,074	6,319	6,380	6,135	6,779	....	....
Other Items (Net)	47r.k	−763	−881	−1,314	159	386	24	−345	−2,367	−2,378	−5,144	....	....
Interest Rates							*Percent Per Annum*						
Discount Rate (End of Period)	60	11.00	16.00	16.00	10.75	11.38	11.19	11.69	13.00	13.00	14.50	14.50	12.50
Deposit Rate	60l	....	....	10.92	9.46	8.50	7.95	8.94	9.22	8.00	8.14	....	7.95
Prices							*Index Numbers (2000=100): Period Averages*						
Consumer Prices	64	....	76.9	82.6	92.5	98.2	95.9	100.0	103.0	105.3	† 112.8	126.4	137.9
Intl. Transactions & Positions							*Millions of Francs*						
Exports	70	4,056	14,731	18,569	26,190	18,696	20,388	20,521	37,314	26,339	30,916	56,457	69,588
Imports, c.i.f	71	17,270	62,193	78,837	89,694	89,218	84,508	82,586	110,488	96,460	132,134	163,373	239,932
							1995=100						
Volume of Exports	72	160	100	144	200	215	....	....	....	....	....	....	....
Export Prices	74	32	100	106	118	61	....	....	....	....	....	....	....

Rwanda 714

		1994	1995	1996	1997	1998	1999	2000	2001	2002	2003	2004	2005
Balance of Payments						*Millions of US Dollars: Minus Sign Indicates Debit*							
Current Account, n.i.e.	78ald	99	40	−35	−62	−83	−141	−94	−102	−126	−121	−198	−90
Goods: Exports f.o.b.	78aad	50	57	62	93	64	62	68	93	67	63	98	125
Goods: Imports f.o.b.	78abd	−575	−219	−219	−278	−233	−247	−223	−245	−233	−229	−276	−354
Trade Balance	78acd	−524	−162	−157	−185	−169	−185	−155	−152	−166	−166	−178	−229
Services: Credit	78add	—	18	22	51	48	51	59	66	65	76	103	120
Services: Debit	78aed	—	−155	−150	−198	−190	−193	−200	−189	−202	−204	−240	−286
Balance on Goods & Services	78afd	−524	−299	−286	−332	−310	−328	−296	−275	−302	−293	−315	−396
Income: Credit	78agd	—	24	5	8	9	8	14	14	8	6	6	15
Income: Debit	78ahd	—	−18	−19	−25	−16	−18	−28	−34	−27	−37	−39	−43
Balance on Gds, Serv. & Inc.	78aid	−524	−293	−299	−349	−317	−339	−310	−295	−321	−324	−349	−423
Current Transfers, n.i.e.: Credit	78ajd	623	338	266	312	251	210	233	210	215	223	169	350
Current Transfers: Debit	78akd	—	−5	−2	−25	−17	−13	−17	−18	−20	−20	−18	−18
Capital Account, n.i.e.	78bcd	—	—	—	—	—	70	62	50	66	41	61	93
Capital Account, n.i.e.: Credit	78bad	—	—	—	—	—	70	62	50	66	41	61	93
Capital Account: Debit	78bbd	—	—	—	—	—	—	—	—	—	—	—	—
Financial Account, n.i.e.	78bjd	−20	−11	25	47	−17	−33	11	−44	81	−24	−26	−68
Direct Investment Abroad	78bdd	—	—	—	—	—	—	—	—	—	—	—	—
Dir. Invest. in Rep. Econ., n.i.e.	78bed	—	2	2	3	7	2	8	5	3	5	8	8
Portfolio Investment Assets	78bfd	—	—	—	—	—	1	—	—	—	—	—	—
Equity Securities	78bkd	—	—	—	—	—	1	—	—	—	—	—	—
Debt Securities	78bld	—	—	—	—	—	—	—	—	—	—	—	—
Portfolio Investment Liab., n.i.e.	78bgd	—	—	—	—	—	—	—	—	—	—	—	—
Equity Securities	78bmd	—	—	—	—	—	—	—	—	—	—	—	—
Debt Securities	78bnd	—	—	—	—	—	—	—	—	—	—	—	—
Financial Derivatives Assets	78bwd	....	....	....	....	....	....	....	....	....	....	....	....
Financial Derivatives Liabilities	78bxd	....	....	....	....	....	....	....	....	....	....	....	....
Other Investment Assets	78bhd	—	−52	−14	1	−1	−10	23	—	8	−6	8	−14
Monetary Authorities	78bod	....	....	....	....	—	—	—	—	—	—	—	—
General Government	78bpd	—	—	—	—	—	—	—	—	—	—	—	—
Banks	78bqd	—	−39	−14	1	−1	−10	17	−5	−1	−6	8	−14
Other Sectors	78brd	—	−13	—	—	—	—	6	4	9	—	—	—
Other Investment Liab., n.i.e.	78bid	−20	39	36	43	−23	−25	−21	−48	70	−22	−41	−61
Monetary Authorities	78bsd	—	—	—	—	—	—	—	—	—	−1	−3	−20
General Government	78btd	−20	39	37	43	−22	−24	−23	−50	58	−30	−36	−36
Banks	78bud	—	—	—	—	—	—	—	—	—	—	—	—
Other Sectors	78bvd	—	—	−1	—	−1	−2	2	2	13	9	−2	−5
Net Errors and Omissions	78cad	−74	23	31	46	92	32	−110	26	−41	83	−205	−146
Overall Balance	78cbd	6	53	20	31	−7	−72	−131	−70	−21	−20	−368	−210
Reserves and Related Items	79dad	−6	−53	−20	−31	7	72	131	70	21	20	368	210
Reserve Assets	79dbd	−6	−66	−19	−48	−21	38	78	11	20	−46	101	95
Use of Fund Credit and Loans	79dcd	—	13	−1	18	13	21	14	2	−6	−1	−4	−8
Exceptional Financing	79ded	—	—	—	—	15	14	39	58	7	67	271	123
International Investment Position						*Millions of US Dollars*							
Assets	79aad	....	....	....	....	244	232	268	288	335	319	428	502
Direct Investment Abroad	79abd	....	....	....	....	—	—	—	—	—	—	—	—
Portfolio Investment	79acd	....	....	....	....	—	1	1	1	—	—	—	—
Equity Securities	79add	....	....	....	....	—	1	1	1	—	—	—	—
Debt Securities	79aed	....	....	....	....	—	—	—	—	—	—	—	—
Financial Derivatives	79ald	....	....	....	....	—	—	—	—	—	—	—	—
Other Investment	79afd	....	....	....	....	75	56	77	74	82	76	84	69
Monetary Authorities	79agd	....	....	....	....	—	—	—	—	—	—	—	—
General Government	79ahd	....	....	....	....	—	—	—	—	—	—	—	—
Banks	79aid	....	....	....	....	75	56	77	74	82	76	84	69
Other Sectors	79ajd	....	....	....	....	—	—	—	—	—	—	—	—
Reserve Assets	79akd	....	....	....	....	169	174	191	213	253	243	344	433
Liabilities	79lad	....	....	....	....	1,372	1,374	1,355	1,353	1,506	1,631	1,787	1,647
Dir. Invest. in Rep. Economy	79lbd	....	....	....	....	63	59	55	57	57	62	69	77
Portfolio Investment	79lcd	....	....	....	....	—	—	—	—	—	—	—	—
Equity Securities	79lsd	....	....	....	....	—	—	—	—	—	—	—	—
Debt Securities	79led	....	....	....	....	—	—	—	—	—	—	—	—
Financial Derivatives	79lld	....	....	....	....	—	—	—	—	—	—	—	—
Other Investment	79lfd	....	....	....	....	1,309	1,315	1,300	1,296	1,449	1,569	1,718	1,570
Monetary Authorities	79lgd	....	....	....	....	81	97	104	100	104	117	113	79
General Government	79lhd	....	....	....	....	1,201	1,198	1,175	1,174	1,316	1,432	1,587	1,477
Banks	79lid	....	....	....	....	12	5	8	10	17	—	—	—
Other Sectors	79ljd	....	....	....	....	16	15	13	11	12	21	19	14
Government Finance						*Millions of Francs: Year Ending December 31*							
Deficit (-) or Surplus	80	−3,194	5,300	−15,101	−12,275	−41,473	−41,161	−10,285	−41,307	−17,741	−30,660	....	....
Total Revenue and Grants	81y	7,547	61,528	70,828	95,768	99,019	103,803	132,809	150,370	172,000	175,653	....	....
Revenue	81	6,032	23,128	39,428	58,037	66,019	65,996	68,664	86,206	101,200	122,342	....	....
Grants	81z	1,515	38,400	31,400	37,731	33,000	37,807	64,145	64,164	70,800	53,311	....	....
Exp. & Lending Minus Repay.	82z	26,550	69,528	95,335	109,608	117,471	140,458	136,772	160,978	191,573	188,434	....	....
Expenditure	82	26,550	69,528	95,335	110,157	117,632	138,858	136,298	160,350	191,000	186,181	....	....
Lending Minus Repayments	83	—	—	—	−549	−161	1,600	474	628	573	2,253	....	....
Statistical Discrepancy	80xx	15,809	13,300	9,406	1,565	−23,021	−4,506	−6,322	−30,699	1,832	−17,879	....	....
Total Financing	80h	3,194	−5,300	15,101	12,275	41,473	41,161	10,285	41,307	17,741	30,660	....	....
Total Net Borrowing	84	3,194	−5,300	15,101	12,275	41,473	41,161	10,285	41,307	17,741	30,660	....	....
Net Domestic	84a	5,636	−12,742	4,464	645	−173	7,461	−8,650	−4,602	−17,937	15,300	....	....
Net Foreign	85a	−2,442	7,442	10,637	11,630	41,646	33,700	18,935	45,909	35,678	15,360	....	....
Total Debt by Residence	88	171,065	353,894	370,697	403,971	469,522	537,278	630,670	607,500	756,100	964,399	....	....
Domestic	88a	56,138	55,296	58,360	81,533	85,338	87,294	82,477	80,200	87,300	81,665	....	....
Foreign	89a	114,927	298,598	312,337	322,438	384,184	449,984	548,193	527,300	668,800	882,734	....	....

Rwanda 714

National Accounts		1994	1995	1996	1997	1998	1999	2000	2001	2002	2003	2004	2005
						Billions of Francs							
Househ.Cons.Expend.,incl.NPISHs....	96f	192.6	328.8	400.0	527.5	576.9	574.0	622.4	646.9	727.1	775.7	893.0	1,026.8
Government Consumption Expend...	91f	18.6	35.0	48.7	53.5	62.4	71.2	74.3	87.9	97.7	137.1	136.1	152.6
Gross Fixed Capital Formation..........	93e	16.6	45.5	61.0	77.0	92.0	111.1	123.7	138.9	139.6	166.8	215.8	245.5
Changes in Inventories....................	93i	—	—	—	—	—	—	—	—	—	—	....	....
Exports of Goods and Services..........	90c	6.7	17.5	25.6	43.5	34.8	38.2	58.9	69.6	63.2	75.0	108.6	112.9
Imports of Goods and Services (-).....	98c	68.7	87.6	111.1	143.3	144.8	149.6	173.5	189.0	202.5	249.4	299.2	374.9
Gross Domestic Product (GDP)........	99b	165.8	339.1	424.1	558.3	621.3	644.9	705.7	754.3	825.0	905.3	1,054.3	1,162.9
Net Primary Income from Abroad.....	98.n	−.9	1.6	−4.5	−4.3	−2.1	−3.8	−6.7	—	—	—	....	....
Gross National Income (GNI)............	99a	164.9	338.1	421.7	559.1	625.2	629.5	702.1	756.5	828.3	936.9	....	....
Net Current Transf.from Abroad.......	98t	391.7	223.0	200.1	171.7	163.0	200.3	204.6	....	....	....	....	....
Gross Saving...............................	99s	−68.7	−26.9	−22.7	−19.3	−1.2	1.8	18.3	....	....	....	....	....
GDP Volume 1995 Prices................	99b.p	252.0	336.5	386.6	442.0	482.7	513.9	548.9	580.8	633.7	639.1	667.0	....
GDP Volume (2000=100)...............	99bvp	17.4	34.6	44.8	65.5	81.8	98.7	100.0	106.4	108.8	116.3	146.3	178.8
GDP Deflator (2000=100)...............	99bip	135.3	138.8	134.1	120.8	107.7	92.6	100.0	100.4	107.5	110.3	102.1	92.2
						Millions: Midyear Estimates							
Population................................	99z	5.53	5.44	5.67	6.18	6.84	7.50	8.02	8.38	8.61	8.76	8.88	9.04

		1994	1995	1996	1997	1998	1999	2000	2001	2002	2003	2004	2005
Exchange Rates		*E. Caribbean Dollars per SDR: End of Period (aa) E. Caribbean Dollars per US Dollar: End of Period (ae)*											
Official Rate	aa	3.9416	4.0135	3.8825	3.6430	3.8017	3.7058	3.5179	3.3932	3.6707	4.0121	4.1931	3.8590
Official Rate	ae	2.7000	2.7000	2.7000	2.7000	2.7000	2.7000	2.7000	2.7000	2.7000	2.7000	2.7000	2.7000
		Index Numbers (2000=100): Period Averages											
Nominal Effective Exchange Rate	nec	94.51	92.31	93.19	95.26	96.92	97.27	100.00	101.76	101.08	97.27	94.66	94.23
Real Effective Exchange Rate	rec	90.12	88.13	88.02	95.07	97.92	99.95	100.00	101.68	101.19	95.74	89.33	84.84
Fund Position		*Millions of SDRs: End of Period*											
Quota	2f.s	6.50	6.50	6.50	6.50	6.50	8.90	8.90	8.90	8.90	8.90	8.90	8.90
SDRs	1b.s	—	—	—	—	—	—	—	.01	—	—	—	—
Reserve Position in the Fund	1c.s	.01	.01	.01	.01	.01	.07	.08	.08	.08	.08	.08	.08
Total Fund Cred.&Loans Outstg.	2tl	—	—	—	—	1.63	1.63	1.63	1.63	.81	—	—	—
International Liquidity		*Millions of US Dollars Unless Otherwise Indicated: End of Period*											
Total Reserves minus Gold	1l.d	31.82	33.47	32.73	36.07	46.80	49.58	45.20	56.43	65.75	64.80	78.47	71.61
SDRs	1b.d	—	—	—	—	—	—	—	.02	—	—	—	—
Reserve Position in the Fund	1c.d	.02	.02	.02	.02	.02	.10	.11	.10	.11	.12	.13	.12
Foreign Exchange	1d.d	31.80	33.45	32.71	36.05	46.78	49.48	45.09	56.31	65.64	64.68	78.34	71.49
Monetary Authorities: Other Liab.	4..d												
Deposit Money Banks: Assets	7a.d	73.44	76.69	88.78	121.88	123.28	112.59	148.52	165.58	222.11	288.85	279.05	261.02
Liabilities	7b.d	73.35	77.53	90.28	106.08	105.06	125.20	137.15	133.73	171.05	204.53	256.31	241.94
Monetary Authorities		*Millions of E. Caribbean Dollars: End of Period*											
Foreign Assets	11	85.89	90.55	88.42	97.45	126.44	134.09	122.18	153.84	178.15	175.93	205.47	186.36
Claims on Central Government	12a	5.01	4.48	4.07	3.25	8.78	8.83	10.95	11.62	10.05	4.22	7.25	7.25
Claims on Deposit Money Banks	12e	3.52	.01	—	.01	—	—	15.09	—	.02	.07	7.73	8.36
Reserve Money	14	94.35	92.97	89.90	95.82	114.73	129.56	139.86	154.44	179.84	174.91	213.22	194.80
of which: Currency Outside DMBs	14a	28.28	30.29	32.38	31.85	35.84	41.45	40.59	36.10	37.69	39.93	44.61	49.88
Foreign Liabilities	16c	—	—	—	—	6.18	6.02	5.72	5.51	2.98	—	—	—
Central Government Deposits	16d	.06	2.06	2.58	4.89	13.31	6.34	1.64	4.49	4.39	5.31	7.23	7.17
Other Items (Net)	17r	—	—	—	—	1.00	.99	1.00	1.02	1.00	—	—	—
Deposit Money Banks		*Millions of E. Caribbean Dollars: End of Period*											
Reserves	20	65.79	65.14	58.01	65.65	78.64	89.69	98.90	113.29	139.89	123.00	164.92	144.23
Foreign Assets	21	198.28	207.07	239.71	329.07	332.85	303.98	401.01	447.05	599.70	779.88	753.44	704.76
Claims on Central Government	22a	52.69	84.07	118.44	89.62	128.11	154.16	249.73	257.75	234.84	176.46	269.09	350.42
Claims on Local Government	22b	6.97	8.50	7.34	6.41	12.29	18.18	30.90	37.40	44.67	56.95	52.22	56.53
Claims on Nonfin.Pub.Enterprises	22c	52.51	87.13	105.75	117.67	135.32	160.45	158.26	191.67	225.42	252.13	367.88	418.35
Claims on Private Sector	22d	416.36	440.86	464.92	521.06	563.67	610.17	680.54	675.62	659.25	687.40	747.99	804.61
Claims on Nonbank Financial Insts	22g	.03	.50	1.10	1.69	3.34	5.77	5.95	6.39	6.44	41.99	74.42	86.93
Demand Deposits	24	48.73	60.14	61.20	60.80	76.13	76.24	85.96	82.48	95.09	113.94	168.33	160.73
Time, Savings,& Fgn.Currency Dep.	25	339.43	390.56	395.15	465.57	506.96	524.01	694.68	711.30	758.65	857.75	979.69	1,033.83
Foreign Liabilities	26c	198.05	209.32	243.75	286.42	283.67	338.05	370.30	361.07	461.84	552.24	692.02	653.23
Central Government Deposits	26d	141.79	169.22	194.81	202.28	225.67	256.83	292.30	338.94	345.50	339.58	419.78	476.40
Credit from Monetary Authorities	26g	3.50	4.87	11.71	4.65	10.60	7.67	20.53	7.43	9.61	15.96	6.72	.40
Capital Accounts	27a	49.79	60.03	70.40	81.09	84.98	96.50	103.25	123.29	175.76	206.65	224.59	290.18
Other Items (Net)	27r	11.35	−.87	18.26	30.36	66.21	43.12	58.26	104.70	63.76	31.70	−61.17	−48.94
Monetary Survey		*Millions of E. Caribbean Dollars: End of Period*											
Foreign Assets (Net)	31n	86.12	88.29	84.38	140.11	169.44	94.00	147.17	234.32	313.03	403.57	266.88	237.89
Domestic Credit	32	391.72	454.26	504.23	532.52	612.53	694.41	842.37	837.03	830.77	874.26	1,091.83	1,240.51
Claims on Central Govt. (Net)	32an	−84.15	−82.74	−74.88	−114.30	−102.09	−100.17	−33.26	−74.06	−105.00	−164.21	−150.67	−125.91
Claims on Local Government	32b	6.97	8.50	7.34	6.41	12.29	18.18	30.90	37.40	44.67	56.95	52.22	56.53
Claims on Nonfin.Pub.Enterprises	32c	52.51	87.13	105.75	117.67	135.32	160.46	158.26	191.67	225.42	252.13	367.88	418.35
Claims on Private Sector	32d	416.36	440.86	464.92	521.06	563.67	610.17	680.54	675.62	659.25	687.40	747.99	804.61
Claims on Nonbank Financial Inst.	32g	.03	.50	1.10	1.69	3.34	5.77	5.95	6.39	6.44	41.99	74.42	86.93
Money	34	77.02	90.44	93.61	92.88	111.98	117.79	126.64	119.11	132.81	164.87	213.13	210.62
Quasi-Money	35	339.43	390.56	395.15	465.57	507.96	525.01	695.68	712.31	759.65	857.75	979.69	1,033.83
Capital Accounts	37a	49.79	60.03	70.40	81.09	84.98	96.50	103.25	123.29	175.76	206.65	224.59	290.18
Other Items (Net)	37r	11.60	1.51	29.45	33.09	77.05	49.10	63.98	116.64	75.58	48.56	−58.69	−56.23
Money plus Quasi-Money	35l	416.44	481.00	488.76	558.46	619.94	642.81	822.32	831.42	892.46	1,022.62	1,192.82	1,244.45
Money (National Definitions)		*Millions of E. Caribbean Dollars: End of Period*											
M1	59ma	68.47	75.30	83.93	82.17	91.40	106.09	110.10	106.17	119.91	133.13	166.38	163.69
M2	59mb	390.12	438.38	462.66	525.05	545.92	607.38	776.67	794.23	844.80	903.05	1,098.69	1,150.84
Interest Rates		*Percent Per Annum*											
Discount Rate (End of Period)	60	9.00	9.00	9.00	8.00	8.00	8.00	8.00	7.00	7.00	6.50	6.50	6.50
Money Market Rate	60b	5.25	5.25	5.25	5.25	5.25	5.25	5.25	† 5.64	6.32	6.07	4.67	4.01
Treasury Bill Rate	60c	6.50	6.50	6.50	6.50	6.50	6.50	6.50	7.50	7.50	7.17	7.00	7.00
Savings Rate	60k	5.00	5.00	5.00	5.00	6.00	6.00	6.00	6.00	5.83	† 3.59	3.58	3.58
Deposit Rate	60l	3.99	4.52	4.27	4.27	4.22	4.31	4.32	4.23	4.01	4.49	4.54	4.53
Deposit Rate (Fgn. Currency)	60l.f	....	....	....	....	....	....	....	....	....	3.05	1.25	2.22
Lending Rate	60p	10.94	10.89	10.92	11.16	11.42	11.21	11.10	11.08	10.89	12.22	10.25	10.09
Prices		*Index Numbers (2000=100): Period Averages*											
Consumer Prices	64	80.1	† 82.4	84.1	91.6	94.8	98.1	100.0	102.1	104.2	106.6	109.0	111.0
Intl. Transactions & Positions		*Millions of E. Caribbean Dollars*											
Exports	70	59	51	59	111	76	76	89	84	73	130	127	135
Imports, c.i.f.	71	346	359	402	397	402	413	529	510	543	554	547	729

		1994	1995	1996	1997	1998	1999	2000	2001	2002	2003	2004	2005
Balance of Payments						*Millions of US Dollars: Minus Sign Indicates Debit*							
Current Account, n.i.e.	78ald	−24.30	−45.46	−65.07	−61.66	−46.31	−82.47	−66.16	−105.94	−124.02	....	....	....
Goods: Exports f.o.b.	78aad	28.57	36.56	39.08	45.49	44.40	44.96	51.46	55.02	64.42			
Goods: Imports f.o.b.	78abd	−98.27	−117.12	−131.93	−130.96	−130.99	−135.19	−172.67	−166.58	−177.59			
Trade Balance	78acd	−69.70	−80.56	−92.84	−85.47	−86.59	−90.23	−121.21	−111.56	−113.17	....		
Services: Credit	78add	92.38	81.95	88.54	94.75	100.58	101.06	98.53	99.00	90.56			
Services: Debit	78aed	−44.86	−55.07	−61.31	−65.20	−62.03	−85.34	−76.01	−74.91	−79.65			
Balance on Goods & Services	78afd	−22.18	−53.68	−65.61	−55.92	−48.03	−74.51	−98.70	−87.47	−102.26			
Income: Credit	78agd	2.91	6.77	3.14	2.89	4.84	6.45	5.53	4.67	5.51	....		
Income: Debit	78ahd	−15.91	−17.73	−18.76	−23.71	−30.19	−34.90	−35.64	−39.19	−43.68			
Balance on Gds, Serv. & Inc.	78aid	−35.19	−64.64	−81.24	−76.74	−73.39	−102.97	−128.81	−122.00	−140.43			
Current Transfers, n.i.e.: Credit	78ajd	16.56	23.26	20.80	21.76	33.66	24.05	69.90	26.61	28.30			
Current Transfers: Debit	78akd	−5.67	−4.08	−4.63	−6.67	−6.58	−3.56	−7.25	−10.55	−11.89			
Capital Account, n.i.e.	78bcd	1.73	7.26	5.45	4.17	8.25	5.81	5.99	10.31	14.59			
Capital Account, n.i.e.: Credit	78bad	2.61	7.41	5.63	4.36	8.43	5.99	6.17	10.50	14.77			
Capital Account: Debit	78bbd	−.88	−.16	−.19	−.19	−.19	−.19	−.19	−.19	−.19			
Financial Account, n.i.e.	78bjd	23.74	24.79	49.10	48.19	45.67	95.48	70.20	103.95	106.92			
Direct Investment Abroad	78bdd	—	—	—	—	—	—	—	−.13	—			
Dir. Invest. in Rep. Econ., n.i.e.	78bed	15.35	20.47	35.17	19.67	31.93	57.74	96.21	88.23	80.41			
Portfolio Investment Assets	78bfd	—	2.59	.88	.01	.01	.02	−.03	−1.09	—			
Equity Securities	78bkd	....	....	....	....	....	....	....	....	....			
Debt Securities	78bld	....	....	....	....	....	....	....	....	....			
Portfolio Investment Liab., n.i.e.	78bgd	.23	.15	7.09	15.44	2.22	14.14	5.06	35.64	31.47			
Equity Securities	78bmd	....	....	....	....	....	....	....	....	....			
Debt Securities	78bnd	....	....	....	....	....	....	....	....	....			
Financial Derivatives Assets	78bwd	....	....	....	....	....	....	....	....	....			
Financial Derivatives Liabilities	78bxd	....	....	....	....	....	....	....	....	....			
Other Investment Assets	78bhd	−10.04	−3.70	−1.01	−3.30	−3.59	−9.22	−10.74	−7.71	.64			
Monetary Authorities	78bod	....	....	....	....	....	....	....	....	....			
General Government	78bpd	....	....	....	....	....	....	....	....	....			
Banks	78bqd	....	....	....	....	....	....	....	....	....			
Other Sectors	78brd	....	....	....	....	....	....	....	....	....			
Other Investment Liab., n.i.e.	78bid	18.20	5.28	6.97	16.37	15.10	32.80	−20.30	−11.00	−5.60			
Monetary Authorities	78bsd	—	....	....	....	....	....	....	....	....			
General Government	78btd	....	....	....	....	....	....	....	....	....			
Banks	78bud	....	....	....	....	....	....	....	....	....			
Other Sectors	78bvd	....	....	....	....	....	....	....	....	....			
Net Errors and Omissions	78cad	−1.77	15.71	9.63	12.96	3.38	−16.02	−14.40	3.28	12.19	....		
Overall Balance	78cbd	−.61	2.29	−.89	3.66	10.99	2.79	−4.37	11.61	9.68			
Reserves and Related Items	79dad	.61	−2.29	.89	−3.66	−10.99	−2.79	4.37	−11.61	−9.68			
Reserve Assets	79dbd	.61	−2.29	.89	−3.66	−13.27	−2.79	4.37	−11.61	−8.62			
Use of Fund Credit and Loans	79dcd	—	—	—	—	2.28	—	—	—	−1.06			
Exceptional Financing	79ded	....	....	....	....	....	....	....	....	....			
Government Finance						*Millions of E. Caribbean Dollars: Year Ending December 31*							
Deficit (-) or Surplus	80	6.77p	....	....	....	....	....	....	....	....	....		
Revenue	81	181.84p	....	....	....	....	....	....	....	....			
Grants Received	81z	1.64p	....	....	....	....	....	....	....	....			
Expenditure	82	176.49p	....	....	....	....	....	....	....	....			
Lending Minus Repayments	83	.22p	....	....	....	....	....	....	....	....			
Financing													
Domestic	84a	−10.88p	....	....	....	....	....	....	....	....			
Foreign	85a	4.11p	....	....	....	....	....	....	....	....			
National Accounts						*Millions of E. Caribbean Dollars*							
Housch.Cons.Expend.,incl.NPISHs.	96f	295.3	351.7	402.1	425.0	423.7	556.5	526.7	468.2	570.7	497.6	537.9	....
Government Consumption Expend.	91f	111.1	126.5	132.1	143.2	148.3	174.6	187.8	191.5	187.2	176.2	217.4	....
Gross Fixed Capital Formation	93e	227.9	288.4	304.1	326.7	333.0	293.3	440.9	500.5	457.3	469.7	472.3	....
Exports of Goods and Services	90c	327.2	317.9	344.6	378.7	391.5	394.3	405.0	415.9	425.8	428.3	534.6	....
Imports of Goods and Services (-)	98c	386.4	464.9	521.7	529.6	521.1	595.4	671.5	652.0	694.5	587.5	670.1	....
Gross Domestic Product (GDP)	99b	575.1	619.5	661.0	743.9	775.4	823.2	888.9	924.0	946.4	984.4	1,092.2	....
Net Primary Income from Abroad	98.n	−35.3	−29.6	−42.1	−56.2	−68.5	−76.8	−80.3	−93.2	−102.5	−118.1	−125.5	....
Gross National Income (GNI)	99a	563.5	590.0	618.9	687.7	707.0	746.4	807.6	831.3	845.1	867.7	966.7	....
Net Current Transf.from Abroad	98t	29.4	53.9	43.7	40.7	73.1	55.3	169.2	43.4	44.4	48.9	49.6	....
Gross Nat'l Disposable Inc.(GNDI)	99i	592.9	643.9	662.6	728.4	780.1	801.7	976.7	874.7	889.5	916.6	1,016.4	....
Gross Saving	99s	162.8	165.7	128.4	160.2	208.0	70.7	262.2	211.5	121.4	133.2	261.1	....
GDP Volume 1990 Prices	99b.p	499.8	515.5	549.9	590.7	596.2	617.9	644.6	657.5	663.7	678.3	721.9	....
GDP Volume (2000=100)	99bvp	77.5	80.0	85.3	91.6	92.5	95.9	100.0	102.0	103.0	105.2	112.0	....
GDP Deflator (2000=100)	99bip	83.4	87.2	87.2	91.3	94.3	96.6	100.0	101.9	103.4	105.2	109.7	....
						Millions: Midyear Estimates							
Population	99z	.04	.04	.04	.04	.04	.04	.04	.04	.04	.04	.04	.04

St. Lucia 362

		1994	1995	1996	1997	1998	1999	2000	2001	2002	2003	2004	2005
Exchange Rates					*E.Caribbean Dollars per SDR: End of Period (aa) E.Caribbean Dollars per US Dollar: End of Period (ae)*								
Official Rate	aa	3.9416	4.0135	3.8825	3.6430	3.8017	3.7058	3.5179	3.3932	3.6707	4.0121	4.1931	3.8590
Official Rate	ae	2.7000	2.7000	2.7000	2.7000	2.7000	2.7000	2.7000	2.7000	2.7000	2.7000	2.7000	2.7000
					Index Numbers (2000=100): Period Averages								
Official Rate	ahx	100.0	100.0	100.0	100.0	100.0	100.0	100.0	100.0	100.0	100.0	100.0	100.0
Nominal Effective Exchange Rate	nec	94.8	91.8	93.0	95.2	96.4	96.9	100.0	102.2	101.4	98.4	96.0	95.2
Real Effective Exchange Rate	rec	94.9	93.7	92.9	92.1	94.3	96.1	100.0	99.5	98.5	93.6	92.1	92.2
Fund Position					*Millions of SDRs: End of Period*								
Quota	2f.s	11.00	11.00	11.00	11.00	11.00	15.30	15.30	15.30	15.30	15.30	15.30	15.30
SDRs	1b.s	1.36	1.39	1.42	1.45	1.48	1.50	1.43	1.46	1.48	1.49	1.50	1.52
Reserve Position in the Fund	1c.s	—	—	—	—	—	—	—	—	—	.01	.01	.01
Total Fund Cred.&Loans Outstg	2tl	—	—	—	—	—	—	—	—	—	—	—	—
International Liquidity				*Millions of US Dollars Unless Otherwise Indicated: End of Period*									
Total Reserves minus Gold	1l.d	57.79	63.09	56.14	60.98	70.61	74.52	78.83	88.94	93.89	106.90	132.54	116.39
SDRs	1b.d	1.99	2.07	2.04	1.95	2.08	2.06	1.87	1.84	2.01	2.22	2.34	2.18
Reserve Position in the Fund	1c.d	—	—	—	—	—	—	—	—	—	.01	.01	.01
Foreign Exchange	1d.d	55.80	61.02	54.10	59.03	68.54	72.45	76.96	87.10	91.88	104.68	130.19	114.20
Monetary Authorities: Other Liab	4..d	—	—	—	—	—	—	—	—	—	—	—	—
Deposit Money Banks: Assets	7a.d	25.22	30.03	30.28	32.55	53.05	54.27	50.37	65.21	86.16	158.84	164.58	175.70
Liabilities	7b.d	53.33	56.32	80.02	95.28	88.39	97.68	85.24	109.92	138.48	138.41	176.80	256.47
Monetary Authorities					*Millions of E. Caribbean Dollars: End of Period*								
Foreign Assets	11	156.60	170.50	151.87	165.08	191.27	201.81	213.57	241.07	254.50	289.76	359.29	315.81
Claims on Central Government	12a	15.08	18.54	29.25	19.05	18.38	18.39	16.87	11.04	10.87	9.36	9.30	9.31
Claims on Deposit Money Banks	12e	.02	.02	.02	.03	.09	.08	.02	.06	.05	.04	.05	.04
Reserve Money	14	160.39	178.76	170.95	173.81	197.97	204.43	212.27	247.18	252.34	283.31	339.37	300.02
of which: Currency Outside DMBs	14a	66.85	75.13	70.30	69.61	77.52	84.06	84.60	82.09	83.59	91.30	99.16	106.38
Foreign Liabilities	16c	—	—	—	—	—	—	—	—	—	—	—	—
Central Government Deposits	16d	11.44	10.29	10.18	10.35	11.77	15.86	18.19	5.00	13.08	15.84	29.27	25.15
Other Items (Net)	17r	−.13	—	—	—	—	—	—	—	—	—	—	—
Deposit Money Banks					*Millions of E. Caribbean Dollars: End of Period*								
Reserves	20	103.66	97.02	101.94	105.33	108.52	129.00	121.03	152.42	173.87	194.13	240.56	198.63
Foreign Assets	21	68.09	81.07	81.77	87.89	143.24	146.52	135.99	176.07	232.64	428.87	444.37	474.38
Claims on Central Government	22a	47.49	43.65	48.13	63.06	109.65	119.95	128.28	129.64	142.29	129.75	177.86	269.87
Claims on Local Government	22b	2.09	1.57	1.47	2.31	2.19	1.76	2.39	.25	.38	1.27	.25	.02
Claims on Nonfin.Pub.Enterprises	22c	57.48	72.67	67.82	64.61	46.72	47.09	65.51	64.56	65.30	96.04	99.88	119.96
Claims on Private Sector	22d	860.41	946.42	1,071.26	1,171.82	1,258.19	1,394.19	1,481.69	1,541.82	1,553.47	1,498.20	1,650.07	1,917.27
Claims on Nonbank Financial Insts	22g	8.72	8.28	13.60	14.50	14.11	30.47	30.66	25.91	28.27	31.60	30.83	36.76
Demand Deposits	24	177.90	197.88	187.87	203.35	213.17	241.09	240.25	243.09	247.76	310.71	424.93	503.87
Time, Savings,& Fgn.Currency Dep	25	618.95	673.13	731.81	756.03	848.10	912.16	978.34	1,046.25	1,070.30	1,113.29	1,119.30	1,260.53
Foreign Liabilities	26c	143.99	152.07	216.05	257.26	238.64	263.73	230.14	296.78	373.90	373.71	477.35	692.47
Central Government Deposits	26d	170.92	195.35	213.77	235.09	318.57	354.53	400.96	432.67	413.57	460.62	533.00	586.73
Credit from Monetary Authorities	26g	9.60	2.00	.09	2.10	—	.45	.93	63.23	48.53	4.07	—	10.16
Capital Accounts	27a	62.76	74.05	67.37	66.25	76.86	119.14	132.32	167.30	159.56	159.62	225.71	244.48
Other Items (Net)	27r	−36.19	−43.80	−30.97	−10.57	−12.71	−22.13	−17.40	−158.66	−117.40	−42.16	−136.47	−281.35
Monetary Survey					*Millions of E. Caribbean Dollars: End of Period*								
Foreign Assets (Net)	31n	80.70	99.51	17.58	−4.29	95.87	84.61	119.42	120.35	113.24	344.92	326.31	97.72
Domestic Credit	32	809.04	885.49	1,007.58	1,089.91	1,118.90	1,241.45	1,306.24	1,335.56	1,373.93	1,289.75	1,405.92	1,741.31
Claims on Central Govt. (Net)	32an	−119.78	−143.45	−146.57	−163.33	−202.30	−232.05	−274.00	−296.98	−273.49	−337.36	−375.10	−332.69
Claims on Local Government	32b	2.09	1.57	1.47	2.31	2.19	1.76	2.39	.25	.38	1.27	.25	.02
Claims on Nonfin.Pub.Enterprises	32c	57.61	72.67	67.82	64.61	46.72	47.09	65.51	64.56	65.30	96.04	99.88	119.96
Claims on Private Sector	32d	860.41	946.42	1,071.26	1,171.82	1,258.19	1,394.19	1,481.69	1,541.82	1,553.47	1,498.20	1,650.07	1,917.27
Claims on Nonbank Financial Inst	32g	8.72	8.28	13.60	14.50	14.11	30.47	30.66	25.91	28.27	31.60	30.83	36.76
Money	34	245.37	273.93	258.69	273.34	292.00	327.16	326.09	325.18	331.35	402.01	524.10	610.25
Quasi-Money	35	618.95	673.13	731.81	756.03	848.10	912.16	978.34	1,046.25	1,070.30	1,113.29	1,119.30	1,260.53
Capital Accounts	37a	65.69	77.02	70.24	68.95	79.68	121.89	134.93	169.82	162.28	162.59	228.82	247.34
Other Items (Net)	37r	−40.27	−39.09	−35.58	−12.71	−5.00	−35.15	−13.70	−85.33	−76.77	−43.22	−139.98	−279.09
Money plus Quasi-Money	35l	864.33	947.07	990.50	1,029.37	1,140.10	1,239.32	1,304.42	1,371.43	1,401.65	1,515.30	1,643.39	1,870.78
Money (National Definitions)					*Millions of E. Caribbean Dollars: End of Period*								
M1	59ma	211.86	239.75	225.68	239.26	247.90	267.62	286.05	283.83	287.62	343.13	481.19	547.32
M2	59mb	748.78	818.41	832.50	888.56	996.44	1,093.27	1,179.39	1,234.33	1,273.32	1,370.41	1,509.04	1,711.78
Interest Rates					*Percent Per Annum*								
Discount Rate (End of Period)	60	9.00	9.00	9.00	8.00	8.00	8.00	8.00	7.00	7.00	6.50	6.50	6.50
Money Market Rate	60b	5.25	5.25	5.25	5.25	5.25	5.25	5.25	† 5.64	6.32	6.07	4.67	4.01
Treasury Bill Rate	60c	7.00	7.00	7.00	7.00	7.00	7.00	7.00	6.80	6.80	6.33	6.40	4.73
Savings Rate	60k	6.00	6.00	6.00	6.00	6.00	6.00	6.00	5.96	5.83	† 4.09	3.51	3.37
Deposit Rate	60l	3.83	4.43	4.50	4.65	4.80	4.76	4.80	4.88	4.27	5.47	3.05	2.85
Deposit Rate (Fgn. Currency)	60l.f	....	....	....	....	....	....	....	....	....	4.74	1.81	4.23
Lending Rate	60p	11.06	12.68	12.82	12.68	11.40	12.79	13.06	12.97	12.59	15.00	11.07	10.27
Prices and Labor					*Index Numbers (2000=100): Period Averages*								
Consumer Prices	64	84.8	89.5	90.4	90.3	93.2	96.5	100.0	105.4	105.1	106.2	107.8	112.0
					Number in Thousands: Period Averages								
Labor Force	67d	....	....	....	70.3	71.9	73.1	76.0	75.1	75.6	82.1	....	....
Employment	67e	....	57.4	56.7	55.9	56.4	59.9	63.5	62.1	62.8	63.9	....	....
Unemployment	67c	....	10.8	11.1	14.4	15.5	13.2	12.5	13.0	12.8	18.2	....	....
Unemployment Rate (%)	67r	....	16.3	16.3	20.5	21.6	18.1	16.4	17.3	16.9	22.3	....	....
Intl. Transactions & Positions					*Millions of E. Caribbean Dollars*								
Exports	70	317.20	335.40	227.70	190.65	172.84	160.41	126.92	138.13	132.69	230.23	....	....
Imports, c.i.f.	71	818.10	828.90	845.10	896.40	885.60	958.50	958.50	958.50	834.30	1,088.10	1,239.98	1,485.00
					2002=100								
Export Prices	76	....	....	....	....	....	....	....	....	100.0	103.0	....	....
Import Prices	76.x	....	....	....	....	....	....	....	....	100.0	102.0	....	....

St. Lucia 362

		1994	1995	1996	1997	1998	1999	2000	2001	2002	2003	2004	2005
Balance of Payments						*Millions of US Dollars: Minus Sign Indicates Debit*							
Current Account, n.i.e.	78ald	−48.38	−33.09	−57.84	−78.32	−60.16	−96.85	−78.80	−74.99	−103.89	....	....	....
Goods: Exports f.o.b.	78aad	99.92	114.65	86.33	70.25	70.37	60.93	63.06	54.37	69.97	....	....	....
Goods: Imports f.o.b.	78abd	−265.62	−269.38	−267.40	−292.37	−295.06	−312.01	−312.46	−272.07	−277.00	....	....	....
Trade Balance	78acd	−165.70	−154.73	−181.08	−222.12	−224.69	−251.08	−249.40	−217.71	−207.03	....	....	....
Services: Credit	78add	237.69	265.03	266.79	288.42	319.50	306.26	321.11	283.41	258.12	....	....	....
Services: Debit	78aed	−104.16	−123.55	−122.44	−121.92	−132.18	−136.33	−124.20	−113.36	−124.51	....	....	....
Balance on Goods & Services	78afd	−32.18	−13.24	−36.72	−55.62	−37.36	−81.15	−52.48	−47.66	−73.42	....	....	....
Income: Credit	78agd	4.97	5.75	3.36	3.29	3.39	2.38	3.90	2.62	2.56	....	....	....
Income: Debit	78ahd	−38.33	−44.53	−37.66	−38.97	−45.68	−40.50	−47.77	−44.02	−46.06	....	....	....
Balance on Gds, Serv. & Inc.	78aid	−65.54	−52.02	−71.02	−91.30	−79.66	−119.27	−96.35	−89.06	−116.91	....	....	....
Current Transfers, n.i.e.: Credit	78ajd	25.46	28.42	28.53	24.60	29.56	32.06	28.93	27.51	28.58	....	....	....
Current Transfers: Debit	78akd	−8.30	−9.50	−15.35	−11.61	−10.06	−9.63	−11.38	−13.44	−15.56	....	....	....
Capital Account, n.i.e.	78bcd	10.71	13.21	10.40	9.59	24.65	25.11	14.18	26.40	21.44	....	....	....
Capital Account, n.i.e.: Credit	78bad	11.83	13.58	11.14	10.34	25.43	25.85	16.51	27.51	22.55	....	....	....
Capital Account: Debit	78bbd	−1.12	−.37	−.74	−.76	−.78	−.74	−2.33	−1.11	−1.11	....	....	....
Financial Account, n.i.e.	78bjd	41.71	27.62	49.21	85.12	58.51	66.25	70.88	43.73	68.40	....	....	....
Direct Investment Abroad	78bdd	—	—	—	—	—	—	—	—	—	....	....	....
Dir. Invest. in Rep. Econ., n.i.e.	78bed	32.52	32.75	18.41	47.83	83.40	82.81	54.90	23.57	48.05	....	....	....
Portfolio Investment Assets	78bfd	−.47	−.47	−.06	−.06	−.11	—	−.64	−4.29	−16.54	....	....	....
Equity Securities	78bkd	....	....	....	....	....	....	....	....	....	....	....	....
Debt Securities	78bld	....	....	....	....	....	....	....	....	....	....	....	....
Portfolio Investment Liab., n.i.e.	78bgd	.77	.71	1.74	3.00	3.44	1.66	29.03	17.40	35.19	....	....	....
Equity Securities	78bmd	....	....	....	....	....	....	....	....	....	....	....	....
Debt Securities	78bnd	....	....	....	....	....	....	....	....	....	....	....	....
Financial Derivatives Assets	78bwd	....	....	....	....	....	....	....	....	....	....	....	....
Financial Derivatives Liabilities	78bxd	....	....	....	....	....	....	....	....	....	....	....	....
Other Investment Assets	78bhd	1.47	−15.34	−9.06	3.26	−11.46	−19.33	−15.00	−17.46	−16.43	....	....	....
Monetary Authorities	78bod	....	....	....	....	....	....	....	....	....	....	....	....
General Government	78bpd	....	....	....	....	....	....	....	....	....	....	....	....
Banks	78bqd	....	....	....	....	....	....	....	....	....	....	....	....
Other Sectors	78brd	....	....	....	....	....	....	....	....	....	....	....	....
Other Investment Liab., n.i.e.	78bid	7.41	9.97	38.17	31.09	−16.75	1.11	2.60	24.51	18.13	....	....	....
Monetary Authorities	78bsd	—	—	—	—	—	—	—	—	—	....	....	....
General Government	78btd	....	....	....	....	....	....	....	....	....	....	....	....
Banks	78bud	....	....	....	....	....	....	....	....	....	....	....	....
Other Sectors	78bvd	....	....	....	....	....	....	....	....	....	....	....	....
Net Errors and Omissions	78cad	−7.49	−2.01	−8.04	−11.42	−13.16	9.47	−1.45	16.92	19.22	....	....	....
Overall Balance	78cbd	−3.45	5.72	−6.28	4.97	9.84	3.97	4.81	12.06	5.17	....	....	....
Reserves and Related Items	79dad	3.45	−5.72	6.28	−4.97	−9.84	−3.97	−4.81	−12.06	−5.17	....	....	....
Reserve Assets	79dbd	3.45	−5.72	6.28	−4.97	−9.84	−3.97	−4.81	−12.06	−5.17	....	....	....
Use of Fund Credit and Loans	79dcd	—	—	—	—	—	—	—	—	—	....	....	....
Exceptional Financing	79ded	....	....	....	....	....	....	....	....	....	....	....	....
National Accounts						*Millions of E. Caribbean Dollars*							
Houseb.Cons.Expend.,incl.NPISHs.	96f	872.1	925.6	1,039.7	1,078.1	1,059.8	1,130.8	1,178.6	1,106.0	1,209.1	1,426.0	1,502.1	1,539.3
Government Consumption Expend.	91f	217.1	259.7	261.2	284.1	390.8	408.7	430.1	489.5	492.1	458.0	481.9	436.9
Gross Fixed Capital Formation	93e	389.9	367.2	381.5	417.7	433.1	500.5	490.7	459.4	415.9	408.4	434.3	552.2
Exports of Goods and Services	90c	918.2	1,038.7	953.3	968.3	1,037.3	1,031.4	1,012.4	883.0	860.2	1,049.8	1,158.0	1,119.5
Imports of Goods and Services (-)	98c	997.4	1,049.1	1,047.6	1,130.8	1,145.7	1,201.9	1,204.1	1,087.2	1,078.2	1,348.2	1,451.9	1,291.0
Gross Domestic Product (GDP)	99b	1,399.9	1,542.2	1,588.2	1,617.5	1,775.3	1,869.4	1,907.8	1,850.7	1,899.2	1,994.1	2,124.4	2,355.8
Net Primary Income from Abroad	98.n	−90.1	−104.7	−92.6	−119.7	−124.4	−102.9	−118.9	−121.8	−93.6	−127.9	−140.2	....
Gross National Income (GNI)	99a	1,310.1	1,038.7	953.3	1,497.8	1,650.9	1,766.5	1,788.9	1,728.9	1,805.6	1,866.2	1,984.2	....
Net Current Transf.from Abroad	98t	48.2	51.1	35.6	56.3	52.7	59.4	51.0	38.6	44.0	35.6	32.5	....
Gross Nat'l Disposable Inc.(GNDI)	99i	1,358.3	1,089.8	988.9	1,554.1	1,703.6	1,826.0	1,839.8	1,767.5	1,849.6	1,901.9	2,016.7	....
Gross Saving	99s	258.8	277.8	225.4	191.9	252.9	286.5	231.1	172.0	148.4	17.9	32.8	....
GDP Volume 1990 Prices	99b.p	1,236.7	1,257.2	1,293.3	1,337.7	1,416.7	1,452.2	1,431.7	1,358.1	1,380.4	1,424.2	1,514.5	....
GDP Volume (2000=100)	99bvp	86.4	87.8	90.3	93.4	99.0	101.4	100.0	94.9	96.4	99.5	105.8	....
GDP Deflator (2000=100)	99bip	84.9	92.1	92.2	90.7	94.0	96.6	100.0	102.3	103.2	105.1	105.3	....
						Millions: Midyear Estimates							
Population	99z	.15	.15	.15	.15	.15	.15	.15	.16	.16	.16	.16	.16

St. Vincent and the Grenadines   364

		1994	1995	1996	1997	1998	1999	2000	2001	2002	2003	2004	2005
Exchange Rates		*E. Caribbean Dollars per SDR: End of Period (aa) E.Caribbean Dollars per US Dollar: End of Period (ae)*											
Official Rate	aa	3.9416	4.0135	3.8825	3.6430	3.8017	3.7058	3.5179	3.3932	3.6707	4.0121	4.1931	3.8590
Official Rate	ae	2.7000	2.7000	2.7000	2.7000	2.7000	2.7000	2.7000	2.7000	2.7000	2.7000	2.7000	2.7000
		Index Numbers (2000=100): Period Averages											
Official Rate	ahx	100.0	100.0	100.0	100.0	100.0	100.0	100.0	100.0	100.0	100.0	100.0	100.0
Nominal Effective Exchange Rate	nec	93.0	90.0	91.4	94.4	95.9	96.7	100.0	102.6	101.5	96.2	92.3	91.9
Real Effective Exchange Rate	rec	99.6	94.2	97.0	97.8	99.4	99.3	100.0	100.6	98.6	91.4	88.1	88.2
Fund Position		*Millions of SDRs: End of Period*											
Quota	2f.s	6.00	6.00	6.00	6.00	6.00	6.00	8.30	8.30	8.30	8.30	8.30	8.30
SDRs	1b.s	.09	.08	.07	.07	.07	.06	.06	.03	.02	—	—	—
Reserve Position in the Fund	1c.s	.50	.50	.50	.50	.50	.50	.50	.50	.50	.50	.50	.50
Total Fund Cred.&Loans Outstg	2tl	—	—	—	—	—	—	—	—	—			
International Liquidity		*Millions of US Dollars Unless Otherwise Indicated: End of Period*											
Total Reserves minus Gold	1l.d	31.25	29.83	30.19	31.19	38.77	42.58	55.18	61.44	53.20	51.19	74.98	69.51
SDRs	1b.d	.12	.12	.11	.09	.09	.09	.08	.04	.02	.01	—	—
Reserve Position in the Fund	1c.d	.73	.74	.72	.67	.70	.69	.65	.63	.68	.74	.78	.71
Foreign Exchange	1d.d	30.40	28.97	29.36	30.42	37.97	41.81	54.45	60.77	52.49	50.44	74.20	68.80
Monetary Authorities: Other Liab.	4..d												
Deposit Money Banks: Assets	7a.d	49.54	45.76	45.09	47.82	53.50	89.92	106.04	105.22	116.15	144.24	162.39	169.54
Liabilities	7b.d	26.77	32.13	35.35	29.73	24.98	51.95	56.70	71.93	67.59	78.61	78.50	94.30
Monetary Authorities		*Millions of E. Caribbean Dollars: End of Period*											
Foreign Assets	11	84.41	80.64	81.54	84.27	104.78	114.95	148.93	165.79	143.65	138.25	202.49	187.76
Claims on Central Government	12a	11.55	11.00	11.17	11.13	9.76	18.32	11.02	11.19	11.88	24.10	10.38	9.48
Claims on Deposit Money Banks	12e	.01	.01	—	.01	.01	.01	.03	.01	.02	—	.01	—
Reserve Money	14	91.59	86.68	84.45	92.10	111.29	129.99	156.75	171.71	153.57	160.21	169.89	173.19
of which: Currency Outside DMBs	14a	32.02	28.59	27.01	33.49	36.43	57.49	52.11	51.51	54.02	56.65	64.39	74.44
Foreign Liabilities	16c												
Central Government Deposits	16d	4.50	4.97	8.26	3.31	3.27	3.29	3.23	5.29	1.98	2.15	42.98	24.05
Other Items (Net)	17r	−.11											
Deposit Money Banks		*Millions of E. Caribbean Dollars: End of Period*											
Reserves	20	60.14	54.30	50.67	60.73	87.28	73.08	111.03	140.46	107.60	102.41	106.08	98.50
Foreign Assets	21	133.75	123.56	121.75	129.13	144.44	242.78	286.30	284.10	313.60	389.45	438.45	457.77
Claims on Central Government	22a	44.25	75.60	74.22	79.23	84.23	95.93	115.31	119.82	162.99	140.60	126.54	211.80
Claims on Local Government	22b	.26	.11	.06	.18	.16			.05	1.89	2.41	15.82	—
Claims on Nonfin.Pub.Enterprises	22c	47.55	22.03	24.94	21.04	18.71	19.98	22.06	34.10	24.50	28.73	49.87	46.87
Claims on Private Sector	22d	285.12	347.02	398.83	447.16	486.42	545.63	592.09	605.45	633.38	637.47	643.16	678.23
Claims on Nonbank Financial Insts	22g	5.85	6.12	13.50	14.45	14.80	14.69	10.71	9.41	8.14	10.28	33.84	14.21
Demand Deposits	24	84.23	84.01	92.62	116.52	134.18	154.24	186.82	211.61	215.82	229.41	261.27	288.12
Time, Savings,& Fgn.Currency Dep	25	282.14	303.39	321.29	344.21	397.65	453.14	459.71	491.56	523.17	531.71	574.17	595.94
Foreign Liabilities	26c	72.28	86.75	95.43	80.28	67.44	140.26	153.10	194.22	182.50	212.26	211.96	254.62
Central Government Deposits	26d	110.64	124.38	141.22	165.25	196.62	203.79	214.38	212.01	230.42	246.26	202.55	206.24
Credit from Monetary Authorities	26g	—	.01		.63	.50	.01	7.68	3.15	3.47	1.86	1.71	
Capital Accounts	27a	41.56	43.25	41.29	57.16	61.07	76.41	83.90	91.81	95.85	94.02	120.09	195.86
Other Items (Net)	27r	−13.95	−13.06	−7.89	−12.14	−21.43	−35.75	31.92	−10.97	.86	−4.18	42.01	−33.43
Monetary Survey		*Millions of E. Caribbean Dollars: End of Period*											
Foreign Assets (Net)	31n	145.87	117.45	107.85	133.11	181.78	217.46	282.13	255.67	274.75	315.44	428.98	390.90
Domestic Credit	32	279.55	332.52	373.23	404.63	414.18	487.47	533.57	562.73	610.37	595.18	634.06	730.28
Claims on Central Govt. (Net)	32an	−59.34	−42.75	−64.09	−78.20	−105.90	−92.83	−91.28	−86.29	−57.53	−83.71	−108.62	−9.02
Claims on Local Government	32b	.26	.11	.06	.18	.16			.05	1.89	2.41	15.82	—
Claims on Nonfin.Pub.Enterprises	32c	47.66	22.03	24.94	21.04	18.71	19.98	22.06	34.10	24.50	28.73	49.87	46.87
Claims on Private Sector	32d	285.12	347.02	398.83	447.16	486.42	545.63	592.09	605.45	633.38	637.47	643.16	678.23
Claims on Nonbank Financial Inst	32g	5.85	6.12	13.50	14.45	14.80	14.69	10.71	9.41	8.14	10.28	33.84	14.21
Money	34	116.26	112.87	120.22	150.52	170.68	211.76	239.06	263.12	269.85	286.07	325.66	362.57
Quasi-Money	35	282.14	303.39	321.29	344.21	397.65	453.14	459.71	491.56	523.17	531.71	574.17	595.94
Capital Accounts	37a	42.95	44.07	42.66	58.45	62.42	77.72	85.14	93.01	97.15	95.44	121.57	197.23
Other Items (Net)	37r	−15.93	−10.96	−3.09	−15.43	−34.78	−37.68	31.80	−29.31	−5.04	−2.61	41.64	−34.55
Money plus Quasi-Money	35l	398.40	416.26	441.51	494.73	568.33	664.90	698.77	754.69	793.01	817.78	899.82	958.50
Money (National Definitions)		*Millions of E. Caribbean Dollars: End of Period*											
M1	59ma	96.19	95.21	96.25	129.25	150.75	182.73	212.25	219.16	239.16	253.70	287.04	327.71
M2	59mb	346.28	373.68	390.05	444.59	516.06	580.48	635.54	654.87	709.26	722.43	821.49	874.08
Interest Rates		*Percent Per Annum*											
Discount Rate (End of Period)	60	9.00	9.00	9.00	8.00	8.00	8.00	8.00	7.00	7.00	6.50	6.50	6.50
Money Market Rate	60b	5.25	5.25	5.25	5.25	5.25	5.25	5.25	† 5.64	6.32	6.07	4.67	4.01
Treasury Bill Rate	60c	6.50	6.50	6.50	6.50	6.50	6.50	6.50	7.00	7.00	5.73	4.60	4.85
Savings Rate	60k	6.00	6.00	5.50	5.08	5.00	5.00	5.00	4.96	5.00	† 4.24	3.40	3.26
Deposit Rate	60l	3.89	4.34	4.14	4.21	4.27	4.46	4.54	4.56	4.35	4.56	3.30	2.88
Deposit Rate (Fgn. Currency)	60l.f	....	....	....	....	....	....	....	....	....	3.72	2.99	5.28
Lending Rate	60p	11.73	11.07	11.23	11.29	11.31	11.55	11.46	11.63	11.56	11.83	9.69	9.38
Prices		*Index Numbers (2000=100): Period Averages*											
Consumer Prices	64	90.6	92.2	96.3	96.7	98.8	99.8	100.0	† 100.8	101.6	101.9	104.9	108.8
Intl. Transactions & Positions		*Millions of E. Caribbean Dollars*											
Exports	70	136.1	115.2	125.2	125.0	134.0	131.4	128.0	112.0	106.0	103.0	90.0	108.0
Imports, c.i.f.	71	351.0	367.0	356.0	491.0	520.0	543.0	440.0	464.0	482.0	543.0	609.0	649.0

St. Vincent and the Grenadines   364

		1994	1995	1996	1997	1998	1999	2000	2001	2002	2003	2004	2005
Balance of Payments		*Millions of US Dollars: Minus Sign Indicates Debit*											
Current Account, n.i.e.	78ald	−57.43	−40.68	−35.52	−84.18	−92.29	−72.52	−29.38	−41.29	−42.27	....	....	....
Goods: Exports f.o.b.	78aad	48.86	61.94	52.59	47.30	50.10	49.61	51.75	42.76	40.45	....	....	
Goods: Imports f.o.b.	78abd	−115.43	−119.37	−128.07	−152.63	−169.96	−177.05	−144.36	−151.97	−157.22	....	....	
Trade Balance	78acd	−66.57	−57.43	−75.48	−105.33	−119.86	−127.44	−92.60	−109.21	−116.77	....		
Services: Credit	78add	63.40	74.37	96.67	99.44	107.32	125.92	126.23	131.38	136.52	....	....	
Services: Debit	78aed	−54.64	−55.14	−58.19	−76.37	−79.06	−65.96	−60.04	−59.58	−60.14	....	....	
Balance on Goods & Services	78afd	−57.81	−38.20	−37.00	−82.26	−91.60	−67.47	−26.41	−37.41	−40.39	....		
Income: Credit	78agd	3.46	4.01	4.04	2.67	3.04	3.16	3.14	2.37	3.37	....	....	
Income: Debit	78ahd	−15.27	−15.67	−13.04	−15.33	−16.76	−22.62	−22.43	−18.85	−17.40	....	....	
Balance on Gds, Serv. & Inc.	78aid	−69.63	−49.86	−46.00	−94.92	−105.31	−86.93	−45.70	−53.90	−54.41	....	....	
Current Transfers, n.i.e.: Credit	78ajd	19.42	16.81	19.74	20.81	21.60	23.40	24.70	23.24	23.74	....	....	
Current Transfers: Debit	78akd	−7.23	−7.63	−9.26	−10.07	−8.57	−8.99	−8.38	−10.63	−11.60	....		
Capital Account, n.i.e.	78bcd	4.01	5.87	3.83	5.91	13.56	7.86	5.60	8.76	10.61	....		
Capital Account, n.i.e.: Credit	78bad	5.37	6.92	4.94	7.02	14.82	9.13	6.86	10.03	11.87	....		
Capital Account: Debit	78bbd	−1.36	−1.05	−1.11	−1.11	−1.27	−1.27	−1.27	−1.27	−1.27	....		
Financial Account, n.i.e.	78bjd	39.90	35.11	41.82	81.46	92.08	54.38	24.57	49.74	12.74	....		
Direct Investment Abroad	78bdd	....	....	....	....	....	....	....	....	....	....		
Dir. Invest. in Rep. Econ., n.i.e.	78bed	46.91	30.64	42.67	92.48	88.95	56.80	37.75	21.04	32.49	....		
Portfolio Investment Assets	78bfd	.24	—	−.37	.07	−.37	−.22	−.52	.17	−5.40	....		
Equity Securities	78bkd	....	....										
Debt Securities	78bld	....	....										
Portfolio Investment Liab., n.i.e.	78bgd	.06	—	−2.37	1.61	.26	.11	1.96	3.32	6.41	....		
Equity Securities	78bmd	....	....										
Debt Securities	78bnd	....	....										
Financial Derivatives Assets	78bwd	....	....										
Financial Derivatives Liabilities	78bxd	....	....										
Other Investment Assets	78bhd	−8.92	2.06	−3.00	−3.04	−2.87	−8.42	−8.84	−10.71	−7.74	....		
Monetary Authorities	78bod	....	....										
General Government	78bpd	....	....										
Banks	78bqd	....	....										
Other Sectors	78brd	....	....										
Other Investment Liab., n.i.e.	78bid	1.60	2.41	4.89	−9.67	6.11	6.11	−5.78	35.93	−13.02	....		
Monetary Authorities	78bsd	—	—	—	—	—	—	—	—	—			
General Government	78btd	....	....										
Banks	78bud	....	....										
Other Sectors	78bvd	....	....										
Net Errors and Omissions	78cad	13.71	−1.68	−9.76	−2.12	−5.34	14.69	13.24	−8.14	12.98	....		
Overall Balance	78cbd	.18	−1.38	.36	1.07	8.00	4.40	14.02	9.07	−5.96	....		
Reserves and Related Items	79dad	−.18	1.38	−.36	−1.07	−8.00	−4.40	−14.02	−9.07	5.96	....		
Reserve Assets	79dbd	−.18	1.38	−.36	−1.07	−8.00	−4.40	−14.02	−9.07	5.96			
Use of Fund Credit and Loans	79dcd	—	—	—	—	—	—	—	—	—			
Exceptional Financing	79ded	....	....										
Government Finance		*Millions of E. Caribbean Dollars: Year Ending December 31*											
Deficit (-) or Surplus	80	−6.7	−2.2	−15.4	−83.7	−28.0	−26.4	−20.4	−8.7		....	....	
Revenue	81	195.6	204.1	220.1	240.5	260.3	276.1	278.9	294.0		....		
Grants Received	81z	2.1	1.5	1.4	12.8	32.6	12.6	9.7	50.5		....		
Expenditure	82	204.4	207.8	236.9	337.0	320.9	315.1	309.0	353.2		....		
Lending Minus Repayments	83	—	—	—	—	—	—	—	—		....	....	
Debt: Domestic	88a	124.5	133.7	139.4	144.0	147.1	167.4	195.0	212.6		....		
Debt: Foreign	89a	213.6	236.2	233.0	225.8	256.8	380.6	378.6	376.1		....		
National Accounts		*Millions of E. Caribbean Dollars*											
Househ.Cons.Expend.,incl.NPISHs	96f	484.1	460.5	490.6	619.3	639.8	601.7	557.5	571.3	590.1	647.4	749.6	....
Government Consumption Expend	91f	138.8	144.2	152.4	150.2	156.8	166.6	175.8	184.6	201.9	199.3	216.6	....
Gross Fixed Capital Formation	93e	185.4	215.4	212.8	243.8	306.2	308.4	247.1	277.8	292.8	343.9	384.3	....
Exports of Goods and Services	90c	303.9	368.0	402.9	396.1	424.7	473.5	480.6	470.2	476.6	475.6	472.5	....
Imports of Goods and Services (-)	98c	461.8	471.2	503.0	618.2	672.3	656.0	552.0	571.2	586.9	650.6	721.7	....
Gross Domestic Product (GDP)	99b	650.4	716.9	755.7	791.3	855.1	892.6	905.7	932.8	974.5	1,015.5	1,101.2	....
Net Primary Income from Abroad	98.n	−31.3	−31.5	−24.3	−34.1	−37.1	−52.5	−52.1	−44.5	−47.5	−63.7	−55.9	....
Gross National Income (GNI)	99a	627.0	682.0	738.0	759.0	820.0	839.0	852.0	887.5	938.6	961.2	1,045.3	....
Net Current Transf.from Abroad	98t	32.9	25.4	38.4	34.1	35.2	38.9	44.1	34.1	32.8	34.8	34.1	....
Gross Nat'l Disposable Inc.(GNDI)	99i	660.2	707.2	762.9	783.2	854.8	877.5	896.5	921.6	971.3	996.1	1,079.4	....
Gross Saving	99s	31.9	106.9	122.9	21.9	57.1	112.6	166.9	180.8	180.8	137.1	113.2	....
GDP Volume 1990 Prices	99b.p	576.8	620.5	629.5	652.5	686.0	714.5	727.7	735.4	755.4	785.7	812.4	....
GDP Volume (2000=100)	99bvp	79.3	85.3	86.5	89.7	94.3	98.2	100.0	101.1	103.8	108.0	111.6	....
GDP Deflator (2000=100)	99bip	90.6	92.8	96.5	97.4	100.2	100.4	100.0	101.9	103.7	103.8	108.9	....
		Millions: Midyear Estimates											
Population	99z	.11	.11	.11	.11	.11	.12	.12	.12	.12	.12	.12	.12

Samoa 862

		1994	1995	1996	1997	1998	1999	2000	2001	2002	2003	2004	2005
Exchange Rates						*SDRs per Tala: End of Period*							
Official Rate..................	ac	.2794	.2662	.2857	.2679	.2359	.2414	.2297	.2241	.2287	.2423	.2409	.2531
					US Dollars per Tala: End of Period (ag) Period Average (rh)								
Official Rate..................	ag	.4079	.3957	.4108	.3615	.3322	.3313	.2993	.2816	.3109	.3600	.3741	.3618
Official Rate..................	rh	.3945	.4045	.4062	.3912	.3398	.3320	.3057	.2880	.2963	.3336	.3598	.3690
					Index Numbers (2000=100): Period Averages								
Official Rate..................	ahx	129.1	132.3	132.9	128.0	111.2	108.6	100.0	94.2	96.9	109.1	117.7	120.7
Nominal Effective Exchange Rate.....	nec	110.2	107.6	108.1	108.8	107.9	102.4	100.0	101.9	101.7	101.6	101.1	101.7
Real Effective Exchange Rate...........	rec	112.1	102.0	105.5	111.9	111.2	104.4	100.0	102.7	108.6	106.3	120.4	120.2
Fund Position						*Millions of SDRs: End of Period*							
Quota..................	2f.s	8.50	8.50	8.50	8.50	8.50	11.60	11.60	11.60	11.60	11.60	11.60	11.60
SDRs..................	1b.s	1.99	2.04	2.10	2.14	2.19	2.24	2.29	2.34	2.38	2.40	2.43	2.46
Reserve Position in the Fund............	1c.s	.66	.67	.67	.68	.68	.68	.68	.68	.69	.69	.69	.69
Total Fund Cred.&Loans Outstg........	2tl												
International Liquidity				*Millions of US Dollars Unless Otherwise Indicated: End of Period*									
Total Reserves minus Gold..............	1l.d	50.80	55.31	60.80	64.21	61.42	68.20	63.66	56.64	62.49	83.91	95.51	92.23
SDRs..................	1b.d	2.91	3.03	3.02	2.89	3.09	3.07	2.99	2.95	3.23	3.57	3.77	3.52
Reserve Position in the Fund..........	1c.d	.97	1.00	.97	.92	.96	.94	.89	.86	.94	1.03	1.08	.99
Foreign Exchange..................	1d.d	46.92	51.28	56.82	60.39	57.37	64.19	59.78	52.83	58.32	79.31	90.67	87.72
Monetary Authorities: Other Liab.....	4..d	—	—	—	.01	.05	.03	.50	.05	.23	.09	.09	1.08
Deposit Money Banks: Assets........	7a.d	6.26	4.66	5.38	6.98	8.00	11.41	14.61	12.29	7.45	13.74	14.55	14.86
Liabilities..................	7b.d	2.86	.30	.94	2.36	1.40	6.80	6.62	6.77	5.04	9.30	12.13	9.91
Monetary Authorities						*Millions of Tala: End of Period*							
Foreign Assets..................	11	109.39	119.13	134.91	158.30	166.00	171.41	163.89	157.48	174.81	194.92	217.29	213.53
Claims on Central Government........	12a	.07	.07	—	—	—	—	—	—	—	—	—	—
Claims on Private Sector..............	12d	—	—	1.39	1.68	1.67	1.69	1.80	2.16	2.34	2.38	2.52	1.11
Claims on Deposit Money Banks......	12e	6.23	.06	.03	.06	.09	.06	.83	.33	.38	.72	.88	2.99
Reserve Money..................	14	60.11	62.73	75.57	90.03	48.86	59.31	64.52	61.40	73.85	81.76	94.71	97.96
of which: Currency Outside DMBs..	14a	16.82	21.60	20.96	30.39	24.82	29.09	28.87	29.97	32.57	35.73	38.94	48.50
Liabs. of Central Bank: Securities.....	16ac	—	—	—	—	25.51	27.39	15.66	7.74	15.96	33.54	41.19	21.86
Foreign Liabilities..................	16c	—	—	—	.03	.14	.10	1.66	.18	.73	.24	.23	2.98
Central Government Deposits..........	16d	49.07	48.36	56.78	69.60	90.21	83.37	78.12	85.59	79.89	74.92	73.63	86.29
Capital Accounts..................	17a	28.30	27.61	27.52	28.47	30.30	30.30	30.26	31.29	31.33	32.59	33.85	30.91
Other Items (Net)..................	17r	−21.78	−19.44	−23.54	−28.10	−27.26	−27.31	−23.70	−26.22	−24.23	−25.04	−22.92	−22.37
Deposit Money Banks						*Millions of Tala: End of Period*							
Reserves..................	20	43.29	41.13	54.41	59.64	24.04	30.22	35.65	31.43	41.28	46.03	55.77	49.46
Claims on Mon.Author.:Securities.....	20c	—	—	—	—	25.51	27.39	15.66	7.74	15.96	33.54	41.19	21.86
Foreign Assets..................	21	15.34	11.78	13.09	19.30	24.09	34.45	48.83	43.66	23.96	38.17	38.90	41.06
Claims on Central Government........	22a	3.67	1.30	.66	—	—	9.41	1.59	9.68	—	8.52	3.25	10.33
Claims on Nonfin.Pub.Enterprises.....	22c	3.16	3.70	4.08	3.24	3.26	13.61	18.79	16.77	18.59	15.05	10.61	15.86
Claims on Private Sector..............	22d	75.49	97.38	115.15	137.69	163.84	192.91	231.17	264.43	292.36	316.09	356.22	438.95
Demand Deposits..................	24	30.38	39.34	39.86	44.14	41.71	51.23	64.41	56.87	63.04	82.48	85.99	112.24
Time, Savings,& Fgn.Currency Dep...	25	90.88	110.77	121.68	135.62	148.84	168.92	196.65	220.78	243.43	268.16	293.59	323.27
Foreign Liabilities..................	26c	7.00	.76	2.30	6.52	4.20	20.53	22.13	24.05	16.22	25.82	32.42	27.40
Central Government Deposits..........	26d	2.32	3.36	8.31	16.56	14.09	23.79	19.10	17.76	12.35	11.14	17.34	19.68
Credit from Monetary Authorities.....	26g	6.23	.06	.03	.10	.09	.05	.77	.30	.53	2.74	2.99	3.18
Capital Accounts..................	27a	20.56	21.23	33.18	29.87	33.31	50.56	45.98	50.29	50.72	45.00	50.29	43.23
Other Items (Net)..................	27r	−16.42	−20.23	−17.97	−12.94	−1.50	−7.09	2.65	3.66	5.86	22.06	23.32	48.52
Monetary Survey						*Millions of Tala: End of Period*							
Foreign Assets (Net).....................	31n	117.73	130.15	145.70	171.05	185.75	185.23	188.93	176.91	181.82	207.03	223.54	224.21
Domestic Credit..................	32	31.00	50.73	56.19	56.45	64.47	110.46	156.13	189.69	221.05	255.98	281.63	360.28
Claims on Central Govt. (Net)........	32an	−47.65	−50.35	−64.43	−86.16	−104.30	−97.75	−95.63	−93.67	−92.24	−77.54	−87.72	−95.64
Claims on Nonfin.Pub.Enterprises...	32c	3.16	3.70	4.08	3.24	3.26	13.61	18.79	16.77	18.59	15.05	10.61	15.86
Claims on Private Sector..............	32d	75.49	97.38	116.54	139.37	165.51	194.60	232.97	266.59	294.70	318.47	358.74	440.06
Money..................	34	47.20	60.94	60.82	74.53	66.53	80.32	93.28	86.84	95.61	118.21	124.93	160.74
Quasi-Money..................	35	90.88	110.77	121.68	135.62	148.84	168.92	196.65	220.78	243.43	268.16	293.59	323.27
Capital Accounts..................	37a	48.86	48.84	60.70	58.34	63.61	80.86	76.24	81.58	82.05	77.59	84.14	74.14
Other Items (Net)..................	37r	−38.20	−39.67	−41.31	−41.00	−28.76	−34.41	−21.11	−22.59	−18.22	−.96	2.51	26.34
Money plus Quasi-Money..............	35l	138.08	171.71	182.50	210.15	215.37	249.24	289.93	307.62	339.04	386.37	418.52	484.01
Other Banking Institutions						*Millions of Tala: End of Period*							
Deposits..................	45	2.63	....	....	....	....	....	....	....	....	....	....	....
Liquid Liabilities..................	55l	140.71	....	....	....	....	....	....	....	....	....	....	....
Interest Rates						*Percent Per Annum*							
Deposit Rate..................	60l	5.50	5.50	5.50	5.50	6.50	6.50	6.46	5.53	5.10	5.10	5.10	5.10
Lending Rate..................	60p	12.00	12.00	12.00	12.00	11.50	11.50	11.00	9.93	9.75	9.75	9.75	9.75
Government Bond Yield..................	61	13.50	13.50	13.50	13.50	13.50	13.50	13.50	13.50	13.50	13.50	13.50	13.50
Prices and Production						*Index Numbers (2000=100): Period Averages*							
Consumer Prices..................	64	88.4	85.8	90.4	† 96.6	98.8	99.0	100.0	† 103.8	112.2	112.3	130.7	133.1
Manufacturing Prod.(1995=100).....	66ey	80.4	100.0	111.5	101.8	98.1	....	....	....	....	....	....	....
Intl. Transactions & Positions						*Thousands of Tala*							
Exports..................	70	9,121	21,859	24,868	38,531	43,243	61,695	46,833	54,049	46,201	44,261	29,870	32,303
Imports, c.i.f..................	71	206,347	235,353	247,126	247,377	285,652	346,765	† 297,504	416,167	430,375	381,754	431,628	507,710

Samoa 862

		1994	1995	1996	1997	1998	1999	2000	2001	2002	2003	2004	2005
Balance of Payments		*Millions of US Dollars: Minus Sign Indicates Debit*											
Current Account, n.i.e.	78ald	5.76	9.33	12.28	9.13	20.09	−18.79	....	....	....	....	−17.04	−28.63
Goods: Exports f.o.b.	78aad	3.52	8.76	10.08	14.63	20.40	18.15	....	....	....	....	11.90	11.97
Goods: Imports f.o.b.	78abd	−68.81	−80.29	−90.76	−100.11	−96.91	−115.66	....	....	....	....	−155.38	−187.16
Trade Balance	78acd	−65.29	−71.53	−80.67	−85.48	−76.51	−97.51	....	....	....	....	−143.48	−175.19
Services: Credit	78add	43.00	55.70	65.15	65.24	62.56	61.31	....	....	....	....	94.85	108.09
Services: Debit	78aed	−28.17	−35.19	−34.33	−40.08	−29.09	−24.55	....	....	....	....	−41.96	−49.30
Balance on Goods & Services	78afd	−50.46	−51.02	−49.85	−60.32	−43.04	−60.74	....	....	....	....	−90.59	−116.41
Income: Credit	78agd	4.03	4.66	5.45	5.52	5.97	2.75	....	....	....	....	4.39	5.98
Income: Debit	78ahd	−4.45	−4.42	−2.43	−4.14	−2.39	−2.36	....	....	....	....	−20.90	−19.88
Balance on Gds, Serv. & Inc.	78aid	−50.88	−50.79	−46.84	−58.94	−39.47	−60.34	....	....	....	....	−107.11	−130.31
Current Transfers, n.i.e.: Credit	78ajd	62.75	66.74	66.89	73.71	64.12	44.67	....	....	....	....	105.39	109.89
Current Transfers: Debit	78akd	−6.11	−6.62	−7.77	−5.65	−4.56	−3.12	....	....	....	....	−15.32	−8.21
Capital Account, n.i.e.	78bcd	—	—	—	—	—	24.46	....	....	....	....	43.88	41.28
Capital Account, n.i.e.: Credit	78bad	—	—	—	—	—	27.11	....	....	....	....	46.34	42.00
Capital Account: Debit	78bbd	—	—	—	—	—	−2.66	....	....	....	....	−2.46	−.72
Financial Account, n.i.e.	78bjd	−5.46	−5.60	−3.60	−5.93	−4.99	−.73	....	....	....	....	−7.36	−7.79
Direct Investment Abroad	78bdd	—	—	—	—	—	—	....	....	....	....	−.43	−2.05
Dir. Invest. in Rep. Econ., n.i.e.	78bed	—	—	—	—	—	—	....	....	....	....	2.24	−4.66
Portfolio Investment Assets	78bfd	—	—	—	—	—	—	....	....	....	....	.02	−.22
Equity Securities	78bkd	—	—	—	—	—	—	....	....	....	....	....	....
Debt Securities	78bld	—	—	—	—	—	—	....	....	....	....	....	....
Portfolio Investment Liab., n.i.e.	78bgd	....	....	....	....	....	....	....	....	....	....	.39	.12
Equity Securities	78bmd	....	....	....	....	....	....	....	....	....	....	....	....
Debt Securities	78bnd	....	....	....	....	....	....	....	....	....	....	....	....
Financial Derivatives Assets	78bwd	....	....	....	....	....	....	....	....	....	....	....	....
Financial Derivatives Liabilities	78bxd	....	....	....	....	....	....	....	....	....	....	....	....
Other Investment Assets	78bhd	—	—	—	—	—	—	....	....	....	....	−9.37	−.87
Monetary Authorities	78bod	....	....	....	....	....	....	....	....	....	....	....	....
General Government	78bpd	—	—	—	—	—	—	....	....	....	....	....	....
Banks	78bqd	—	—	—	—	—	—	....	....	....	....	−9.04	−.77
Other Sectors	78brd	—	—	—	—	—	—	....	....	....	....	−.33	−.10
Other Investment Liab., n.i.e.	78bid	−5.46	−5.60	−3.60	−5.93	−4.99	−.73	....	....	....	....	−.21	−.11
Monetary Authorities	78bsd	−.13	.01	−.01	−.01	.16	—	....	....	....	....	−.01	1.00
General Government	78btd	6.82	3.80	.20	−1.48	−1.04	−2.79	....	....	....	....	.37	−.04
Banks	78bud	.03	−1.12	1.65	1.05	−.54	5.42	....	....	....	....	2.35	−1.85
Other Sectors	78bvd	−12.18	−8.29	−5.44	−5.49	−3.57	−3.36	....	....	....	....	−2.92	.78
Net Errors and Omissions	78cad	−4.17	−1.70	−1.30	7.89	−9.59	2.10	....	....	....	....	−11.67	−5.82
Overall Balance	78cbd	−3.86	2.04	7.38	11.09	5.51	7.04	....	....	....	....	7.81	−.96
Reserves and Related Items	79dad	3.86	−2.04	−7.38	−11.09	−5.51	−7.04	....	....	....	....	−7.81	.96
Reserve Assets	79dbd	3.86	−2.04	−7.38	−11.09	−5.51	−7.04	....	....	....	....	−7.81	.96
Use of Fund Credit and Loans	79dcd	—	—	—	—	—	—	....	....	....	....	—	—
Exceptional Financing	79ded	—	—	—	....	—	....	....	....	....	....	....	....
National Accounts		*Millions of Tala*											
Gross Domestic Product (GDP)	99b	499.4	495.6	555.5	625.3	660.8	691.7	758.8	834.5	885.3	944.6	1,010.5	....
GDP Volume 1994 Prices	99b.p	499.4	532.1	570.8	575.4	589.2	602.7	645.0	685.2	693.4	686.4	708.4	....
GDP Volume (2000=100)	99bvp	77.4	82.5	88.5	89.2	91.4	93.4	100.0	106.2	107.5	106.4	109.8	....
GDP Deflator (2000=100)	99bip	85.0	79.2	82.7	92.4	95.3	97.6	100.0	103.5	108.5	117.0	121.3	....
		Millions: Midyear Estimates											
Population	99z	.17	.17	.17	.17	.17	.18	.18	.18	.18	.18	.18	.18

San Marino 135

		1994	1995	1996	1997	1998	1999	2000	2001	2002	2003	2004	2005
Exchange Rates		*Lire per SDR through 1998, Euros per SDR Thereafter: End of Period*											
Market Rate	aa	2,379.2	2,355.7	2,200.9	2,373.6	2,327.6	1.3662	1.4002	1.4260	1.2964	1.1765	1.1402	1.2116
		Lire per US Dollar through 1998, Euros per US Dollar Thereafter: End of Period (ae) Period Average (rf)											
Market Rate	ae	1,629.7	1,584.7	1,530.6	1,759.2	1,653.1	.9954	1.0747	1.1347	.9536	.7918	.7342	.8477
Market Rate	rf	1,612.4	1,628.9	1,542.9	1,703.1	1,736.2	.9386	1.0854	1.1175	1.0626	.8860	.8054	.8041
Fund Position		*Millions of SDRs: End of Period*											
Quota	2f.s	10.00	10.00	10.00	10.00	10.00	17.00	17.00	17.00	17.00	17.00	17.00	17.00
SDRs	1b.s	.11	.18	.25	.33	.42	.08	.20	.34	.43	.49	.56	.66
Reserve Position in the Fund	1c.s	2.35	2.35	2.35	2.35	2.35	4.10	4.10	4.10	4.10	4.10	4.10	4.10
Total Fund Cred.&Loans Outstg	2tl	—	—	—	—	—	—	—	—	—	—	—	—
International Liquidity		*Millions of US Dollars Unless Otherwise Indicated: End of Period*											
Total Reserves Minus Gold	1l.d	176.31	198.55	215.02	182.94	170.67	144.13	135.16	133.51	183.41	252.69	355.58	354.02
SDRs	1b.d	.16	.27	.36	.45	.59	.11	.26	.42	.58	.73	.87	.94
Reserve Position in the Fund	1c.d	3.43	3.50	3.38	3.17	3.31	5.63	5.34	5.15	5.58	6.09	6.37	5.86
Foreign Exchange	1d.d	172.72	194.78	211.27	179.32	166.77	138.39	129.56	127.93	177.25	245.87	348.34	347.22
Deposit Money Banks: Assets	7a.d	3,013.69	4,001.98	4,703.92	4,408.36	4,382.88	4,465.55	4,289.46	4,452.91	4,793.09	5,530.87	6,037.44	5,937.54
Liabilities	7b.d	2,248.21	3,156.34	4,048.64	3,793.34	3,817.43	3,870.92	3,839.12	3,968.26	3,428.61	4,259.72	5,153.35	4,996.87
Monetary Authorities		*Millions of Lire through 1998; Thousands of Euros Beginning 1999: End of Period*											
Foreign Assets	11	287,334	314,640	329,096	321,834	282,139	143,466	145,257	151,490	174,889	200,071	261,051	300,095
Claims on General Government	12a	4,242	1,233	1,855	16,966	28,514	14,559	14,851	14,259	15,310	15,427	13,958	13,673
Claims on Other Resident Sectors	12d	3,300	—	—	—	—	1,222	336	417	633	298	2,807	600
Claims on Deposit Money Banks	12e	30,273	34,373	40,896	18,542	1,855	745	4,012	9,845	3,093	7,343	—	—
Bankers Deposits	14c	—	—	—	—	3,255	294	2,288	12,867	1,911	6,764	22,556	19,291
Demand Deposits	14d	14,363	20,123	21,274	21,458	23,144	11,877	26,735	26,770	21,717	19,676	56,223	29,344
Time, Savings,& Fgn.Currency Dep	15	18,496	25,382	26,593	16,889	16,255	9,872	271	171	18,144	29,184	65	33,907
Foreign Liabilities	16c	—	—	—	2	191	1	1	12,867	14,732	800	554	58
General Government Deposits	16d	256,504	263,412	269,709	267,432	215,854	108,059	100,494	88,707	99,587	122,925	145,000	182,063
Capital Accounts	17a	36,014	41,630	54,185	62,912	67,261	36,544	38,912	40,624	41,169	46,829	49,667	51,754
Other Items (Net)	17r	−230	−301	85	−11,352	−13,452	−6,655	−4,247	−5,995	−3,335	−3,040	3,750	−2,049
Deposit Money Banks		*Millions of Lire through 1998; Thousands of Euros Beginning 1999: End of Period*											
Claims on Monetary Authorities	20	—	—	—	—	3,255	294	2,288	12,867	1,911	6,681	22,534	19,193
Foreign Assets	21	4,911,532	6,342,022	7,199,683	7,755,149	7,245,343	4,445,099	4,609,849	5,052,656	4,570,506	4,379,154	4,432,450	5,033,096
Claims on Other Resident Sectors	22d	1,118,058	1,225,826	1,303,523	1,593,667	1,865,082	1,038,224	1,289,841	1,450,709	1,641,906	1,961,168	2,596,875	2,915,530
Claims on Nonbank Fin. Insts	22g	143,263	167,394	172,262	189,366	236,356	131,490	165,072	199,835	327,016	380,835	522,739	583,555
Demand Deposits	24	795,744	565,206	415,528	420,685	464,148	274,054	272,388	317,164	618,910	634,108	693,647	830,778
Time, Savings,& Fgn.Currency Dep	25	1,092,784	1,473,536	1,264,306	1,537,896	1,486,230	884,782	984,725	1,222,172	1,845,299	1,891,256	2,157,768	2,382,061
Foreign Liabilities	26c	3,663,998	5,001,919	6,196,728	6,673,202	6,310,594	3,853,200	4,125,871	4,502,736	3,269,389	3,372,699	3,783,388	4,235,715
Credit from Monetary Authorities	26g	30,273	34,373	40,896	18,325	1,854	743	4,012	9,845	3,093	7,343	—	—
Capital Accounts	27a	575,336	701,667	814,326	857,474	1,033,915	583,206	670,996	790,635	807,930	878,385	909,090	989,445
Other Items (Net)	27r	14,718	−41,459	−56,316	30,600	53,294	19,121	9,057	−126,485	−3,282	−55,954	30,705	113,375
Monetary Survey		*Millions of Lire through 1998; Thousands of Euros Beginning 1999: End of Period*											
Foreign Assets (Net)	31n	1,534,868	1,654,743	1,332,051	1,403,779	1,216,697	735,364	629,234	688,543	1,461,274	1,205,725	909,559	1,097,419
Domestic Credit	32	1,012,359	1,131,041	1,207,931	1,532,567	1,914,098	1,077,436	1,369,605	1,576,513	1,885,278	2,234,802	2,991,379	3,331,294
Claims on General Govt. (Net)	32an	−252,262	−262,179	−267,854	−250,466	−187,340	−93,500	−85,643	−74,448	−84,277	−107,498	−131,042	−168,390
Claims on Other Resident Sectors	32d	1,121,358	1,225,826	1,303,523	1,593,667	1,865,082	1,039,446	1,290,176	1,451,126	1,642,539	1,961,466	2,599,682	2,916,130
Claims on Nonbank Fin. Insts	32g	143,263	167,394	172,262	189,366	236,356	131,490	165,072	199,835	327,016	380,835	522,739	583,555
Deposit Money	34	810,107	585,329	436,802	442,143	487,292	285,930	299,124	343,934	640,627	653,785	749,870	860,122
Quasi-Money	35	1,111,280	1,498,918	1,290,899	1,554,785	1,502,485	894,653	984,996	1,222,343	1,863,443	1,920,440	2,157,833	2,415,968
Capital Accounts	37a	611,350	743,297	868,511	920,386	1,101,176	619,751	709,908	831,260	849,099	925,213	958,757	1,041,199
Other Items (Net)	37r	14,488	−41,760	−56,231	19,031	39,841	12,464	4,810	−132,480	−6,616	−58,912	34,477	111,424
Interest Rates		*Percent Per Annum*											
Deposit Rate	60l	7.50	7.35	6.18	4.65	3.70	2.45	2.63	2.88	2.68	1.64	1.44	1.35
Lending Rate	60p	15.00	15.23	14.45	11.43	9.53	7.93	9.20	8.80	7.95	7.49	7.14	....
Prices and Tourism		*Index Numbers (2000=100): Period Averages*											
Consumer Prices (2003=100)	64	....	....	....	....	....	....	....	....	....	100.0	....	....
Tourist Arrivals	66ta	101.1	109.7	108.9	107.7	106.3	102.5	100.0	98.8	101.0	93.9	....	....
National Accounts		*Billions of Lire through 1998; Millions of Euros Beginning 1999*											
Househ.Cons.Expend.,incl.NPISHs	96f	....	....	....	795.41	834.22	† 447.82	465.30	475.09	479.96	....	....	....
Government Consumption Expend	91f	....	....	....	219.79	227.51	† 132.99	135.44	124.50	127.75	....	....	....
Changes in Inventories	93i	....	....	....	40.74	69.00	† 42.64	62.59	22.56	−11.56	....	....	....
Exports of Goods and Services	90c	....	....	....	3,002.40	2,834.65	† 1,581.15	1,627.05	1,682.77	1,660.20	....	....	....
Imports of Goods and Services (-)	98c	....	....	....	3,049.92	2,854.78	† 1,602.18	1,675.01	1,744.28	1,756.40	....	....	....
Gross Domestic Product (GDP)	99b	....	....	....	1,279.9	1,400.8	† 801.03	839.65	929.02	934.94	....	....	....
Net Primary Income from Abroad	98.n	....	....	....	−234.38	−267.59	† −158.52	−178.31	−229.13	−206.28	....	....	....
Gross National Income (GNI)	99a	....	....	....	1,045.48	1,133.25	† 642.51	661.34	699.89	728.66	....	....	....
Net Current Transf.from Abroad	98t	....	....	....	9.37	7.51	† 3.20	3.47	3.65	3.76	....	....	....
Gross Nat'l Disposable Inc.(GNDI)	99i	....	....	....	964.99	1,026.75	† 584.02	613.16	649.79	697.73	....	....	....
Gross Saving	99s	....	....	....	183.68	209.00	† 133.09	141.97	189.82	215.24	....	....	....
GDP Volume 1995 Prices	99b.p	....	....	....	1,210.84	1,301.90	† 732.87	749.01	806.44	793.00	....	....	....
GDP Volume (2000=100)	99bvp	....	....	....	83.5	89.8	† 97.8	100.0	107.7	105.9	....	....	....
GDP Deflator (2000=100)	99bip	....	....	....	94.3	96.0	† 97.5	100.0	102.8	105.2	....	....	....
		Millions: Midyear Estimates											
Population	99z	.025	.026	.026	.026	.026	.027	.027	.027	.027	.028	.028	.028

São Tomé and Príncipe   716

		1994	1995	1996	1997	1998	1999	2000	2001	2002	2003	2004	2005
Exchange Rates						*Dobras per SDR: End of Period*							
Market Rate	aa	1,730.4	2,611.6	4,074.0	9,403.9	9,694.3	10,019.3	11,218.9	11,335.3	12,496.5	14,051.2	15,691.6	17,050.8
					Dobras per US Dollar: End of Period (ae) Period Average (rf)								
Market Rate	ae	1,185.3	1,756.9	2,833.2	6,969.7	6,885.0	7,300.0	8,610.7	9,019.7	9,191.8	9,455.9	10,104.0	11,929.7
Market Rate	rf	732.6	1,420.3	2,203.2	4,552.5	6,883.2	7,119.0	7,978.2	8,842.1	9,088.3	9,347.6	9,902.3	10,558.0
Fund Position						*Millions of SDRs: End of Period*							
Quota	2f.s	5.50	5.50	5.50	5.50	5.50	7.40	7.40	7.40	7.40	7.40	7.40	7.40
SDRs	1b.s	.01	.03	.01	—	—	—	—	—	.01	.02	—	.03
Reserve Position in the Fund	1c.s	—	—	—	—	—	—	—	—	—	—	—	—
Total Fund Cred.&Loans Outstg.	2tl	.72	.56	.40	.24	.08	—	1.90	1.90	1.90	1.90	1.90	2.23
International Liquidity					*Millions of US Dollars Unless Otherwise Indicated: End of Period*								
Total Reserves minus Gold	1l.d	....	5.14	5.03	12.43	9.68	10.88	11.64	15.48	17.35	25.47	19.50	26.70
SDRs	1b.d	.01	.04	.02	—	—	—	—	—	.01	.02	—	.04
Reserve Position in the Fund	1c.d	—	—	—	—	—	—	—	—	—	—	—	—
Foreign Exchange	1d.d	....	5.09	5.01	12.43	9.68	10.88	11.64	15.48	17.34	25.45	19.50	26.66
Monetary Authorities: Other Liab.	4..d	....	4.22	4.36	4.98	—	—	—	—	—	—	.99	.98
Banking Institutions: Assets	7a.d	....	7.11	8.08	8.03	6.85	6.14	5.45	6.09	7.98	8.04	9.15	20.68
Liabilities	7b.d	....	1.49	.77	.37	1.34	.34	.43	.30	.32	.37	.28	1.65
Monetary Authorities						*Millions of Dobras: End of Period*							
Foreign Assets	11	....	9,026	14,252	86,611	101,965	114,071	147,576	192,855	217,780	287,299	246,516	652,922
Claims on Central Government	12a	....	10,290	28,743	28,939	28,831	34,535	32,653	56,425	57,432	61,309	81,777	78,824
Claims on Nonfin.Pub.Enterprises	12c	....	7,837	—	—	—	—	—	—	—	—	—	—
Claims on Private Sector	12d	....	80	204	50	44	38	36	—	—	4,571	7,043	8,061
Claims on Banking Institutions	12e	....	2,375	1,757	1,839	1,839	—	—	762	1,672	1,137	5,152	5,181
Reserve Money	14	....	10,462	18,945	46,401	51,085	43,332	56,046	97,885	111,903	184,470	137,325	217,349
of which: Currency Outside Banks	14a	....	4,794	6,845	14,818	18,652	20,945	25,048	35,763	39,424	55,854	60,003	72,516
Foreign Liabilities	16c	....	8,869	13,985	37,001	795	—	21,338	21,560	23,768	26,725	39,817	49,769
Central Government Deposits	16d	....	—	6,868	41,985	30,994	41,716	47,805	44,046	53,905	27,716	24,765	313,073
Counterpart Funds	16e	....	10,333	9,091	11,197	24,271	26,178	21,338	22,335	12,387	11,504	16,218	22,631
Capital Accounts	17a	....	1,887	−2,356	−13,966	46,025	54,327	57,154	64,493	76,544	100,236	119,817	150,579
of which: Valuation Adjustment	17rv	....	−2,018	−5,432	−21,841	29,394	34,783				28,465	46,504	−61,078
Other Items (Net)	17r	....	−1,942	−1,577	−5,179	−20,491	−16,909	−23,415	−277	−1,623	3,666	2,546	−8,413
Banking Institutions						*Millions of Dobras: End of Period*							
Reserves	20	....	5,488	12,730	30,646	30,485	26,620	35,474	62,633	75,299	129,769	62,968	157,110
Foreign Assets	21	....	12,491	22,880	55,935	47,139	44,819	46,923	54,919	73,357	76,016	92,458	246,763
Claims on Private Sector	22d	....	6,614	8,599	11,897	22,429	24,969	26,569	29,346	45,155	109,543	201,907	325,246
Demand Deposits	24	....	9,431	16,837	34,384	27,731	29,178	36,756	57,388	69,112	106,821	112,687	259,288
Time, Savings,& Fgn.Currency Dep.	25	....	6,110	13,830	31,992	35,892	39,793	50,401	61,815	88,046	138,138	136,869	252,222
of which: Fgn. Currency Deposits	25b	....	6,011	13,086	30,803	32,763	35,266	43,260	52,932	75,839	122,818	120,363	233,977
Foreign Liabilities	26c	....	2,626	2,173	2,562	9,205	2,485	3,679	2,721	2,901	3,510	2,802	19,663
Central Government Deposits	26d	....	2,462	3,313	1,516	2,447	1,251	2,295	529	1,295	999	4,713	6,464
Counterpart Funds	26e	....	609	105	105	105	2,134	2,134	2,134	2,134	2,134	2,134	—
Credit from Monetary Authorities	26g	....	250	1,150	3,700	1,200	—	—	—	—	—	3,991	—
Capital Accounts	27a	....	3,687	11,828	30,722	36,555	36,038	33,934	34,964	41,841	72,895	127,061	197,428
Other Items (Net)	27r	....	−582	−5,028	−6,503	−13,082	−14,470	−20,233	−12,651	−11,517	−9,168	−32,923	−5,947
Banking Survey						*Millions of Dobras: End of Period*							
Foreign Assets (Net)	31n	....	10,021	20,974	102,983	139,104	156,406	169,482	223,494	264,468	333,080	296,355	830,252
Domestic Credit	32	....	22,359	27,365	−2,615	17,863	16,574	9,159	41,196	47,387	146,707	261,250	92,594
Claims on Central Govt.(Net)	32an	....	7,829	18,562	−14,561	−4,610	−8,432	−17,446	11,850	2,232	32,594	52,300	−240,713
Claims on Nonfin.Pub.Enterprises	32c	....	7,837	—	—	—	—	—	—	—	—	—	—
Claims on Private Sector	32d	....	6,694	8,803	11,947	22,473	25,007	26,605	29,346	45,155	114,113	208,950	333,307
Money	34	....	14,225	23,683	49,202	47,584	50,123	61,885	95,483	108,597	162,775	172,817	338,518
Quasi-Money	35	....	6,110	13,830	31,992	35,892	39,793	50,401	61,815	88,046	138,138	136,869	252,222
Counterpart Funds	36e	....	10,942	9,196	11,302	24,375	28,311	23,472	24,469	14,521	13,637	18,352	22,631
Capital Accounts	37a	....	5,574	9,473	16,757	82,580	90,365	91,089	99,456	118,385	173,130	246,878	348,000
Other Items (Net)	37r	....	−4,470	−7,843	−8,885	−33,464	−35,613	−48,204	−16,534	−17,694	−7,892	−17,310	−38,531
Money plus Quasi-Money	35l	....	20,335	37,513	81,195	83,476	89,916	112,286	157,298	196,643	300,913	309,686	590,739
Interest Rates						*Percent Per Annum*							
Discount Rate (End of Period)	60	32.00	50.00	35.00	55.00	29.50	17.00	17.00	15.50	15.50	14.50	14.50	18.20
Deposit Rate	60l	35.00	35.00	31.00	36.75	38.29	27.00	† 21.00	15.00	15.00	11.79	11.49	....
Lending Rate	60p	30.00	52.00	38.00	51.50	55.58	40.33	† 39.67	37.00	37.08	32.68	29.77	....

São Tomé and Príncipe   716

		1994	1995	1996	1997	1998	1999	2000	2001	2002	2003	2004	2005
Balance of Payments		*Millions of US Dollars: Minus Sign Indicates Debit*											
Current Account, n.i.e......................	78ald	....	....	....	....	−10.47	−16.28	−19.13	−21.01	−22.77	....	....	....
Goods: Exports f.o.b......................	78aad	....	....	....	....	4.74	3.90	2.69	3.28	5.12	....	....	....
Goods: Imports f.o.b......................	78abd	....	....	....	....	−16.88	−21.94	−25.13	−24.43	−28.00	....	....	....
Trade Balance........................	78acd	....	....	....	....	−12.14	−18.04	−22.44	−21.14	−22.88	....	....	....
Services: Credit...........................	78add	....	....	....	....	6.56	12.48	13.56	12.78	13.41	....	....	....
Services: Debit...........................	78aed	....	....	....	....	−10.35	−11.83	−10.99	−12.07	−13.44	....	....	....
Balance on Goods & Services.......	78afd	....	....	....	....	−15.92	−17.40	−19.87	−20.43	−22.91	....	....	....
Income: Credit.............................	78agd	....	....	....	....	....	....	....	—	....	....	....	....
Income: Debit.............................	78ahd	....	....	....	....	−5.21	−5.32	−3.62	−4.62	−4.71	....	....	....
Balance on Gds, Serv. & Inc........	78aid	....	....	....	....	−21.13	−22.71	−23.49	−25.05	−27.62	....	....	....
Current Transfers, n.i.e.: Credit.....	78ajd	....	....	....	....	10.66	6.44	4.36	4.05	4.85	....	....	....
Current Transfers: Debit...............	78akd	....	....	....	....	....	....	....	—	....	....	....	....
Capital Account, n.i.e.....................	78bcd	....	....	....	....	3.90	9.27	12.00	15.20	12.14	....	....	....
Capital Account, n.i.e.: Credit......	78bad	....	....	....	....	3.90	9.27	12.00	15.20	12.14	....	....	....
Capital Account: Debit.................	78bbd	....	....	....	....	....	....	....	—	....	....	....	....
Financial Account, n.i.e..................	78bjd	....	....	....	....	.27	4.36	3.32	1.67	3.69	....	....	....
Direct Investment Abroad.............	78bdd	....	....	....	....	....	....	....	—	....	....	....	....
Dir. Invest. in Rep. Econ., n.i.e......	78bed	....	....	....	....	4.20	3.04	3.80	3.47	3.04	....	....	....
Portfolio Investment Assets...........	78bfd	....	....	....	....	....	....	....	....	....	....	....	....
Equity Securities........................	78bkd	....	....	....	....	....	....	....	—	....	....	....	....
Debt Securities...........................	78bld	....	....	....	....	....	....	....	—	....	....	....	....
Portfolio Investment Liab., n.i.e.....	78bgd	....	....	....	....	....	....	....	—	....	....	....	....
Equity Securities........................	78bmd	....	....	....	....	....	....	....	—	....	....	....	....
Debt Securities...........................	78bnd	....	....	....	....	....	....	....	—	....	....	....	....
Financial Derivatives Assets..........	78bwd	....	....	....	....	....	....	....	....	....	....	....	....
Financial Derivatives Liabilities.......	78bxd	....	....	....	....	....	....	....	....	....	....	....	....
Other Investment Assets...............	78bhd	....	....	....	....	−5.23	−5.18	−4.81	−4.82	−.25	....	....	....
Monetary Authorities..................	78bod	....	....	....	....	....	....	....	....	....	....	....	....
General Government....................	78bpd	....	....	....	....	....	....	....	....	....	....	....	....
Banks..	78bqd	....	....	....	....	−5.23	−5.18	−4.81	−4.82	−.25	....	....	....
Other Sectors............................	78brd	....	....	....	....	....	....	....	....	....	....	....	....
Other Investment Liab., n.i.e.........	78bid	....	....	....	....	1.30	6.50	4.33	3.01	.90	....	....	....
Monetary Authorities..................	78bsd	....	....	....	....	—	....	....	....	....	....	....	....
General Government....................	78btd	....	....	....	....	1.30	6.50	4.33	3.01	.90	....	....	....
Banks..	78bud	....	....	....	....	....	....	....	—	....	....	....	....
Other Sectors............................	78bvd	....	....	....	....	....	....	....	—	....	....	....	....
Net Errors and Omissions................	78cad	....	....	....	....	.26	.09	−1.66	2.66	−.04	....	....	....
Overall Balance........................	78cbd	....	....	....	....	−6.04	−2.56	−5.46	−1.48	−6.97	....	....	....
Reserves and Related Items...............	79dad	....	....	....	....	6.04	2.56	5.46	1.48	6.97	....	....	....
Reserve Assets............................	79dbd	....	....	....	....	2.70	−1.19	−1.50	−4.33	−2.37	....	....	....
Use of Fund Credit and Loans........	79dcd	....	....	....	....	−.22	−.11	2.48	—	—	....	....	....
Exceptional Financing...................	79ded	....	....	....	....	3.56	3.86	4.49	5.80	9.34	....	....	....
		Millions: Midyear Estimates											
Population.............................	99z	.13	.13	.13	.13	.13	.14	.14	.14	.15	.15	.15	.16

Saudi Arabia   456

		1994	1995	1996	1997	1998	1999	2000	2001	2002	2003	2004	2005
Exchange Rates						*Riyals per SDR: End of Period*							
Official Rate	aa	5.4744	5.5743	5.3924	5.0597	5.2801	5.1469	4.8859	4.7127	5.0982	5.5724	5.8238	5.3526
					Riyals per US Dollar: End of Period (ae) Period Average (rf)								
Official Rate	ae	3.7500	3.7500	3.7500	3.7500	3.7500	3.7500	3.7500	3.7500	3.7500	3.7500	3.7500	3.7450
Official Rate	rf	3.7500	3.7500	3.7500	3.7500	3.7500	3.7500	3.7500	3.7500	3.7500	3.7500	3.7500	3.7471
					Index Numbers (2000=100): Period Averages								
Official Rate	ahx	100.0	100.0	100.0	100.0	100.0	100.0	100.0	100.0	100.0	100.0	100.0	100.1
Nominal Effective Exchange Rate	nec	86.3	81.9	84.5	90.4	97.7	95.9	100.0	105.2	103.5	95.9	91.2	90.6
Real Effective Exchange Rate	rec	96.1	93.1	94.7	98.9	103.8	99.1	100.0	101.8	99.0	90.5	84.4	82.3
Fund Position						*Millions of SDRs: End of Period*							
Quota	2f.s	5,131	5,131	5,131	5,131	5,131	6,986	6,986	6,986	6,986	6,986	6,986	6,986
SDRs	1b.s	416	448	481	512	546	110	147	192	244	290	334	385
Reserve Position in the Fund	1c.s	604	575	561	532	524	987	1,043	2,036	2,621	3,047	2,253	1,334
of which: Outstg.Fund Borrowing	2c	—	—	—	—	—	—	—	—	—	—	—	—
International Liquidity				*Millions of US Dollars Unless Otherwise Indicated: Approximately End of Period*									
Total Reserves minus Gold	1l.d	7,378	8,622	† 14,321	14,876	14,220	16,997	19,585	17,596	20,610	22,620	27,291	26,530
SDRs	1b.d	607	666	692	691	769	152	191	242	332	431	519	550
Reserve Position in the Fund	1c.d	882	854	807	718	737	1,355	1,359	2,558	3,564	4,527	3,499	1,906
Foreign Exchange	1d.d	5,888	7,101	† 12,822	13,467	12,714	15,490	18,036	14,796	16,715	17,662	23,273	24,074
Gold (Million Fine Troy Ounces)	1ad	4.596	4.596	4.596	4.596	4.596	4.596	4.596	4.596	4.596	4.596	4.596	4.596
Gold (National Valuation)	1and	235	239	231	217	226	221	210	202	219	239	250	230
Deposit Money Banks: Assets	7a.d	26,173	26,126	28,312	26,537	22,918	24,397	26,988	26,491	25,464	21,622	24,746	24,392
Liabilities	7b.d	10,440	10,581	10,308	12,278	11,495	13,641	17,185	15,897	11,466	10,684	12,199	17,367
Other Banking Insts.: Assets	7e.d	1,149	1,015	1,023	1,041	1,041	1,041	997	1,001	1,005	1,015	1,045	....
Monetary Authorities						*Billions of Riyals: Approximately End of Period*							
Foreign Assets	11	185.56	174.04	196.07	219.03	175.60	147.39	183.54	181.80	157.46	223.77	329.14	573.68
Reserve Money	14	56.23	54.93	54.15	58.24	57.53	71.04	68.20	65.42	71.50	75.17	83.71	92.76
of which: Currency Outside DMBs	14a	44.97	43.89	43.04	45.82	45.02	55.06	51.02	49.25	52.33	55.44	60.13	64.29
Central Government Deposits	16d	35.53	34.63	45.52	48.51	48.74	30.99	51.47	51.60	51.72	56.55	98.20	240.65
Other Items (Net)	17r	93.80	84.48	96.40	112.28	69.33	45.35	63.87	64.79	34.23	92.05	147.24	240.27
Deposit Money Banks						*Billions of Riyals: Approximately End of Period*							
Reserves	20	11.65	11.18	11.21	12.55	12.57	16.55	18.88	19.15	43.86	26.66	32.04	32.65
Foreign Assets	21	98.15	97.97	106.17	99.52	85.94	91.49	101.20	99.34	95.49	81.08	92.80	91.35
Claims on Central Government	22a	50.03	52.28	65.27	83.21	89.37	102.27	112.27	123.83	123.43	150.72	146.66	127.81
Claims on Public Enterprises	22c	26.93	24.45	16.70	20.86	23.60	14.35	12.44	10.82	11.96	25.84	29.14	31.67
Claims on Private Sector	22d	113.19	121.15	123.55	133.68	160.66	162.19	172.24	187.06	205.83	228.49	313.93	435.93
Demand Deposits	24	80.73	81.52	90.08	95.47	95.39	101.76	114.69	130.45	150.24	167.78	203.81	220.28
Quasi-Monetary Deposits	25a	60.60	69.70	81.73	86.27	91.31	95.09	100.09	100.85	118.49	125.06	153.73	185.08
Foreign Currency Deposits	25b	47.29	46.32	44.10	44.88	50.61	49.72	49.29	50.57	60.39	65.56	67.57	79.84
Foreign Liabilities	26c	39.15	39.68	38.65	46.04	43.11	51.15	64.44	59.61	43.00	40.06	45.75	65.04
Credit from Monetary Authorities	26g	21.42	18.63	13.57	18.33	29.44	20.58	10.95	7.46	6.44	8.69	7.41	5.47
Capital Accounts	27a	36.96	39.25	42.65	44.87	47.60	48.69	52.38	53.85	57.85	59.18	68.81	92.22
Other Items (Net)	27r	13.80	11.94	12.11	13.96	14.68	19.84	25.20	37.41	44.16	46.46	67.48	71.46
Monetary Survey						*Billions of Riyals: Approximately End of Period*							
Foreign Assets (Net)	31n	244.55	232.33	263.59	272.50	218.44	187.72	220.30	221.53	209.95	264.79	376.20	599.98
Domestic Credit	32	154.62	163.26	160.00	189.24	224.88	247.81	245.48	270.12	289.50	348.50	391.52	354.76
Claims on Central Govt. (Net)	32an	14.50	17.66	19.75	34.69	40.63	71.27	60.80	72.24	71.71	94.17	48.46	−112.84
Claims on Public Enterprises	32c	26.93	24.45	16.70	20.86	23.60	14.35	12.44	10.82	11.96	25.84	29.14	31.67
Claims on Private Sector	32d	113.19	121.15	123.55	133.68	160.66	162.19	172.24	187.06	205.83	228.49	313.93	435.93
Money	34	125.69	125.41	133.11	141.29	140.41	156.82	165.71	179.70	202.57	223.22	263.94	284.57
Quasi-Money	35	107.89	116.02	125.83	131.15	141.92	144.81	149.38	151.42	178.88	190.62	221.30	264.92
Other Items (Net)	37r	165.59	154.17	164.64	189.30	160.99	133.90	150.69	160.52	118.00	199.45	282.48	405.25
Money plus Quasi-Money	35l	233.58	241.43	258.95	272.44	282.33	301.62	315.09	331.12	381.45	413.84	485.24	549.49
Other Banking Institutions						*Billions of Riyals: Approximately End of Period*							
Cash	40	17.21	14.34	21.92	28.20	21.62	13.00	15.42	20.95	15.07	18.49	23.15	....
Foreign Assets	41	4.31	3.81	3.84	3.90	3.90	3.90	3.74	3.75	3.77	3.81	3.92	....
Claims on Private Sector	42d	172.90	178.07	181.43	178.96	188.18	199.56	198.54	196.77	204.98	216.71	211.45	....
Capital Accounts	47a	190.46	190.46	190.46	190.46	190.46	191.33	191.19	191.19	191.19	201.89	202.45	....
Other Items (Net)	47r	3.95	5.76	16.73	20.61	23.25	25.13	26.50	30.28	32.64	37.12	36.07	....
Interest Rates						*Percent per Annum*							
Deposit Rate	60l	5.100	6.178	5.469	5.790	6.211	6.137	6.667	3.922	2.234	1.631	1.734	3.754
Prices, Production, Labor						*Index Numbers (2000=100): Period Averages*							
Share Prices	62	56.8	60.6	67.8	86.7	62.6	89.8	100.0	107.6	111.5	196.5	363.4	740.1
Wholesale Prices	63	94.5	101.4	101.1	101.1	99.2	99.6	100.0	99.9	99.9	100.7	103.8	106.8
Consumer Prices	64	96.9	101.6	102.8	102.9	102.5	† 101.1	100.0	98.9	99.1	99.7	100.0	100.7
Crude Petroleum	66aa	99.2	98.9	100.1	98.7	101.1	93.7	100.0	95.3	89.9	103.1	108.5	113.7
						Number in Thousands: Period Averages							
Employment	67e	2,496	2,495	....	....	....	† 5,593	† 5,713	† 5,809	† 5,913	....	....	....
Intl. Transactions & Positions						*Billions of Riyals*							
Exports	70	159.59	187.40	227.43	227.44	145.39	190.10	290.55	254.90	271.70	349.67	472.49	....
Petroleum	70a	143.02	163.30	203.52	200.04	122.14	168.52	266.10	219.42	239.30	308.52	415.86	....
Crude Petroleum	70aa	117.36	133.17	163.50	163.23	98.97	138.53	232.52	190.81	206.49	264.90	348.67	....
Refined Petroleum	70ab	25.66	30.13	40.02	36.81	23.16	30.00	33.58	28.61	32.81	43.61	67.19	....
Imports, c.i.f.	71	87.40	105.20	103.90	107.60	112.40	104.90	113.24	116.93	121.10	138.43	167.79	209.12
Volume of Exports						*2000=100*							
Petroleum	72a	101.8	101.9	102.4	101.6	103.9	93.8	100.0	95.0	83.8	102.0	108.9	....
Crude Petroleum	72aa	99.7	100.6	98.0	98.9	102.2	91.5	100.0	96.5	84.5	104.3	109.0	....
Refined Petroleum	72ab	111.2	107.6	121.8	113.4	111.5	104.2	100.0	88.2	80.9	91.9	108.7	....
Export Prices						*2000=100: Index of Prices in US Dollars*							
Crude Petroleum	76aad	63.6	70.2	83.0	78.5	50.7	73.4	100.0	104.3	103.0	117.4	143.1	205.8

Saudi Arabia   456

		1994	1995	1996	1997	1998	1999	2000	2001	2002	2003	2004	2005
Balance of Payments						*Millions of US Dollars: Minus Sign Indicates Debit*							
Current Account, n.i.e.	78ald	−10,473	−5,318	679	305	−13,132	411	14,317	9,353	11,873	28,048	51,926	87,131
Goods: Exports f.o.b.	78aad	42,557	49,974	60,648	60,651	38,770	50,689	77,481	67,973	72,464	93,244	125,998	174,635
Goods: Imports f.o.b.	78abd	−21,297	−25,616	−25,325	−26,335	−27,498	−25,683	−27,704	−28,607	−29,624	−33,868	−41,050	−51,327
Trade Balance	78acd	21,261	24,358	35,323	34,317	11,272	25,006	49,777	39,366	42,840	59,376	84,947	123,308
Services: Credit	78add	3,342	3,475	2,769	4,251	4,723	5,373	4,779	5,008	5,177	5,713	5,852	5,916
Services: Debit	78aed	−17,869	−19,257	−24,263	−25,929	−16,858	−18,830	−25,228	−19,281	−19,980	−20,857	−25,696	−27,947
Balance on Goods & Services	78afd	6,734	8,576	13,829	12,639	−863	11,549	29,327	25,093	28,037	44,232	65,103	101,277
Income: Credit	78agd	4,027	4,981	5,120	5,748	5,802	5,804	3,345	4,125	3,714	2,977	4,278	4,943
Income: Debit	78ahd	−2,557	−2,181	−2,677	−2,967	−3,037	−2,883	−2,865	−4,644	−3,925	−4,277	−3,800	−4,671
Balance on Gds, Serv. & Inc.	78aid	8,204	11,376	16,272	15,419	1,902	14,469	29,807	24,573	27,827	42,931	65,581	101,549
Current Transfers, n.i.e.: Credit	78ajd	—	—	—	—	—	—	—	—	—	—	—	—
Current Transfers: Debit	78akd	−18,677	−16,694	−15,592	−15,114	−15,034	−14,058	−15,490	−15,220	−15,954	−14,883	−13,655	−14,418
Capital Account, n.i.e.	78bcd	—	—	—	—	—	—	—	—	—	—	—	—
Capital Account, n.i.e.: Credit	78bad	—	—	—	—	—	—	—	—	—	—	—	—
Capital Account: Debit	78bbd	—	—	—	—	—	—	—	—	—	—	—	—
Financial Account, n.i.e.	78bjd	10,327	6,533	5,062	342	12,414	2,404	−11,652	−11,262	−9,137	−26,440	−47,428	−87,596
Direct Investment Abroad	78bdd	—	—	—	—	—	—	—	—	—	—	—	—
Dir. Invest. in Rep. Econ., n.i.e.	78bed	349	−1,875	−1,127	3,039	4,283	−779	−1,881	20	−614	−587	−334	−2,351
Portfolio Investment Assets	78bfd	−2,524	4,051	−2,638	−7,352	6,932	11,700	−9,378	−2,797	7,552	−18,738	−26,654	−48,013
Equity Securities	78bkd	—	—	—	—	—	—	—	—	—	—	—	—
Debt Securities	78bld	−2,524	4,051	−2,638	−7,352	6,932	11,700	−9,378	−2,797	7,552	−18,738	−26,654	−48,013
Portfolio Investment Liab., n.i.e.	78bgd	—	—	—	—	—	—	—	—	—	—	—	—
Equity Securities	78bmd	—	—	—	—	—	—	—	—	—	—	—	—
Debt Securities	78bnd	—	—	—	—	—	—	—	—	—	—	—	—
Financial Derivatives Assets	78bwd	....	....	....	....	....	....	....	....	....	....	....	....
Financial Derivatives Liabilities	78bxd	....	....	....	....	....	....	....	....	....	....	....	....
Other Investment Assets	78bhd	12,006	4,216	9,101	2,684	1,982	−10,663	−3,937	−7,197	−11,644	−6,333	−21,955	−42,380
Monetary Authorities	78bod	—	—	—	—	—	—	—	—	—	—	—	—
General Government	78bpd	—	—	—	—	—	—	—	—	—	—	—	—
Banks	78bqd	3,583	47	−2,187	1,775	3,619	−1,478	−2,591	490	1,033	3,842	−3,124	−1,933
Other Sectors	78brd	8,422	4,169	11,288	909	−1,637	−9,185	−1,346	−7,687	−12,677	−10,175	−18,831	−40,447
Other Investment Liab., n.i.e.	78bid	496	141	−273	1,971	−784	2,146	3,544	−1,288	−4,431	−783	1,516	5,149
Monetary Authorities	78bsd	—	—	—	—	—	—	—	—	—	—	—	—
General Government	78btd	—	—	—	—	—	—	—	—	—	—	—	—
Banks	78bud	496	141	−273	1,971	−784	2,146	3,544	−1,288	−4,431	−783	1,516	5,149
Other Sectors	78bvd	—	—	—	—	—	—	—	—	—	—	—	—
Net Errors and Omissions	78cad	—	—	—	—	—	—	—	—	—	—	—	—
Overall Balance	78cbd	−146	1,215	5,741	647	−718	2,815	2,665	−1,909	2,736	1,608	4,498	−464
Reserves and Related Items	79dad	146	−1,215	−5,741	−647	718	−2,815	−2,665	1,909	−2,736	−1,608	−4,498	464
Reserve Assets	79dbd	146	−1,215	−5,741	−647	718	−2,815	−2,665	1,909	−2,736	−1,608	−4,498	464
Use of Fund Credit and Loans	79dcd	—	—	—	—	—	—	—	—	—	—	—	—
Exceptional Financing	79ded	....	....	....	....	....	....	....	....	....	....	....	....
Government Finance							*Billions of Riyals*							
Deficit (-) or Surplus	80	....	....	−18.5	−17.0	−18.0	−44.0	−28.0	....	....	....	....	....
Total Revenue and Grants	81y	....	....	131.5	164.0	178.0	121.0	157.0	....	....	....	....	....
Revenue	81	....	....	131.5	164.0	178.0	121.0	157.0	....	....	....	....	....
Grants	81z	....	....	—	—	—	—	—	....	....	....	....	....
Exp. & Lending Minus Repay	82z	....	....	150.0	181.0	196.0	165.0	185.0	....	....	....	....	....
Expenditure	82	....	....	150.0	181.0	196.0	165.0	185.0	....	....	....	....	....
Lending Minus Repayments	83	....	....	—	—	—	—	—	....	....	....	....	....
National Accounts							*Billions of Riyals*							
Househ.Cons.Expend.,incl.NPISHs.	96f	240.48	250.28	259.49	261.43	251.42	252.22	258.13	259.55	260.40	269.98	285.71	305.64
Government Consumption Expend.	91f	122.55	125.92	144.78	161.80	155.19	154.09	183.80	188.70	184.52	198.15	221.80	268.51
Gross Fixed Capital Formation	93e	93.00	103.32	102.85	109.24	112.96	118.20	123.32	126.10	128.07	148.10	156.35	174.32
Changes in Inventories	93i	6.88	2.27	4.06	3.84	9.60	9.42	8.90	3.50	11.04	11.37	13.94	14.23
Exports of Goods and Services	90c	172.12	200.44	237.81	243.38	163.10	210.23	308.47	273.68	291.16	371.09	494.43	704.35
Imports of Goods and Services (-)	98c	131.98	148.72	158.24	161.78	145.62	140.57	175.97	165.22	168.11	194.04	233.46	306.31
Gross Domestic Product (GDP)	99b	503.05	533.50	590.75	617.90	546.65	603.59	706.66	686.30	707.07	804.65	938.77	1,160.74
Net Primary Income from Abroad.	98.n	2.82	8.21	.11	−.23	4.87	7.97	3.35	6.65	4.88	2.78	....	....
Gross National Income (GNI)	99a	505.87	541.71	590.86	617.67	551.52	611.56	710.00	692.95	711.95	804.65	938.77	1,160.74
GDP Volume 1999 Prices	99b.p	556.45	557.57	576.43	591.38	608.14	603.59	632.95	636.42	637.23	686.04	722.17	769.51
GDP Volume (2000=100)	99bvp	87.9	88.1	91.1	93.4	96.1	95.4	100.0	100.5	100.7	108.4	114.1	121.6
GDP Deflator (2000=100)	99bip	81.0	85.7	91.8	93.6	96.0	89.6	100.0	96.6	99.4	105.1	116.4	135.1
							Millions: Midyear Estimates							
Population	99z	18.22	18.68	19.19	19.73	20.30	20.89	21.48	22.09	22.70	23.33	23.95	24.57

Senegal 722

		1994	1995	1996	1997	1998	1999	2000	2001	2002	2003	2004	2005
Exchange Rates						*Francs per SDR: End of Period*							
Official Rate	aa	† 780.44	728.38	753.06	807.94	791.61	† 896.19	918.49	935.39	850.37	771.76	747.90	794.73
						Francs per US Dollar: End of Period (ae) Period Average (rf)							
Official Rate	ae	† 534.60	490.00	523.70	598.81	562.21	† 652.95	704.95	744.31	625.50	519.36	481.58	556.04
Official Rate	rf	† 555.20	499.15	511.55	583.67	589.95	† 615.70	711.98	733.04	696.99	581.20	528.28	527.47
Fund Position						*Millions of SDRs: End of Period*							
Quota	2f.s	118.9	118.9	118.9	118.9	118.9	161.8	161.8	161.8	161.8	161.8	161.8	161.8
SDRs	1b.s	.7	2.6	1.2	.3	.4	1.8	.7	6.0	6.7	7.1	4.7	1.0
Reserve Position in the Fund	1c.s	1.1	1.2	1.3	1.3	1.4	1.4	1.4	1.4	1.5	1.5	1.5	1.6
Total Fund Cred.&Loans Outstg	2tl	205.4	233.3	226.5	216.5	207.8	198.2	195.4	197.6	185.8	161.3	131.5	103.8
International Liquidity						*Millions of US Dollars Unless Otherwise Indicated: End of Period*							
Total Reserves minus Gold	1l.d	179.6	271.8	288.3	386.2	430.8	403.0	384.0	447.3	637.4	1,110.9	1,386.4	1,191.0
SDRs	1b.d	1.1	3.8	1.7	.5	.5	2.5	.9	7.5	9.1	10.6	7.3	1.4
Reserve Position in the Fund	1c.d	1.7	1.8	1.8	1.8	1.9	1.9	1.8	1.8	2.0	2.2	2.4	2.2
Foreign Exchange	1d.d	176.9	266.2	284.8	383.9	428.4	398.6	381.2	438.0	626.3	1,098.2	1,376.7	1,187.4
Gold (Million Fine Troy Ounces)	1ad	.029	—	—	—	—	—	—	—	—	—	—	—
Gold (National Valuation)	1and	10.8	—	—	—	—	—	—	—	—	—	—	—
Monetary Authorities: Other Liab	4..d	144.4	122.8	116.9	101.6	109.2	96.6	97.2	86.3	107.4	143.0	138.2	137.3
Deposit Money Banks: Assets	7a.d	131.4	159.9	146.7	151.3	220.4	258.2	220.8	239.9	361.6	490.6	595.4	510.8
Liabilities	7b.d	134.0	131.7	105.0	94.0	117.5	119.9	86.9	101.6	107.2	107.0	184.1	183.8
Monetary Authorities						*Billions of Francs: End of Period*							
Foreign Assets	11	96.0	133.2	151.0	231.3	242.2	263.1	270.7	332.9	398.7	577.0	667.7	662.2
Claims on Central Government	12a	265.5	271.4	229.7	293.7	296.4	279.1	256.6	301.0	292.0	262.2	226.0	203.8
Claims on Deposit Money Banks	12e	11.5	—	2.6	31.7	26.9	12.6	2.0	—	—	—	—	—
Claims on Other Financial Insts	12f	.6	.7	.5	.5	.4	—	—	—	—	—	—	—
Reserve Money	14	188.9	196.6	168.7	174.2	186.0	215.7	228.1	306.4	343.9	524.5	578.5	567.6
of which: Currency Outside DMBs	14a	145.6	152.1	141.9	142.3	158.5	179.4	171.5	211.7	191.9	337.5	342.3	378.6
Foreign Liabilities	16c	237.5	230.1	231.7	235.7	225.9	240.6	248.0	249.1	225.2	198.7	164.9	158.9
Central Government Deposits	16d	13.8	19.2	26.8	142.1	137.4	105.0	55.9	80.2	104.1	86.6	118.1	120.7
Other Items (Net)	17r	−66.5	−40.7	−43.5	5.0	16.6	−6.6	−2.7	−1.8	17.5	29.3	32.3	18.8
Deposit Money Banks						*Billions of Francs: End of Period*							
Reserves	20	31.8	31.1	24.9	32.4	27.1	35.7	55.9	93.4	153.8	185.5	235.8	188.5
Foreign Assets	21	70.2	78.4	76.8	90.6	123.9	168.6	155.6	178.5	226.2	254.8	286.7	284.0
Claims on Central Government	22a	57.9	61.5	120.0	109.6	122.4	110.6	94.0	101.8	60.6	69.1	71.7	70.4
Claims on Private Sector	22d	349.9	355.6	411.0	428.3	437.1	483.0	619.5	651.8	682.0	782.1	851.7	1,033.3
Claims on Other Financial Insts	22f	1.3	.2	—	—	—	—	—	—	—	—	—	—
Demand Deposits	24	155.3	160.2	198.5	196.3	234.0	255.9	287.7	315.3	366.1	484.7	532.5	576.0
Time Deposits	25	161.4	184.6	216.4	237.7	233.2	273.2	325.3	363.8	406.4	444.1	544.4	586.6
Foreign Liabilities	26c	58.3	51.4	42.4	50.0	62.5	72.5	56.4	65.2	54.3	36.1	64.2	75.2
Long-Term Foreign Liabilities	26cl	13.4	13.2	12.6	6.3	3.5	5.8	4.9	10.4	12.8	19.5	24.5	27.0
Central Government Deposits	26d	136.4	136.3	161.7	109.5	101.5	97.6	136.5	143.8	143.5	186.3	164.4	192.3
Credit from Monetary Authorities	26g	11.5	—	3.6	31.7	26.9	12.6	2.0	—	—	—	—	—
Other Items (Net)	27r	−25.1	−18.9	−2.5	29.4	48.9	80.5	112.3	127.0	139.5	120.8	116.0	119.1
Treasury Claims: Private Sector	22d.i	2.3	2.2	3.0	2.8	2.9	3.2	2.6	4.5	5.6	2.5	3.0	3.0
Post Office: Checking Deposits	24..i	3.9	4.3	2.8	4.0	4.1	3.9	4.1	4.7	5.3	8.5	12.8	7.6
Monetary Survey						*Billions of Francs: End of Period*							
Foreign Assets (Net)	31n	−129.5	−69.9	−46.3	36.1	77.7	118.7	121.9	197.1	345.4	597.0	725.3	712.2
Domestic Credit	32	529.0	538.1	575.5	584.5	621.5	674.1	781.9	835.3	792.2	848.8	879.7	1,002.0
Claims on Central Govt. (Net)	32an	174.9	179.5	161.0	152.9	181.1	187.8	159.7	179.0	104.7	64.2	25.1	−34.3
Claims on Private Sector	32d	352.2	357.8	414.1	431.1	439.9	486.2	622.2	656.3	687.6	784.6	854.7	1,036.3
Claims on Other Financial Insts	32f	1.9	.8	.5	.5	.4	—	—	—	—	—	—	—
Money	34	305.3	316.8	343.6	343.2	397.0	439.8	464.0	533.0	563.9	832.2	887.9	962.7
Quasi-Money	35	161.4	184.6	216.4	237.7	233.2	273.2	325.3	363.8	406.4	444.1	544.4	586.6
Long-Term Foreign Liabilities	36cl	13.4	13.2	12.6	6.3	3.5	5.8	4.9	10.4	12.8	19.5	24.5	27.0
Other Items (Net)	37r	−80.7	−46.4	−43.4	33.4	65.5	73.9	109.6	125.3	154.5	150.0	148.2	137.9
Money plus Quasi-Money	35l	466.7	501.4	560.0	580.9	630.2	713.0	789.3	896.8	970.3	1,276.2	1,432.3	1,549.3
Interest Rates						*Percent Per Annum*							
Bank Rate (End of Period)	60	6.00	6.00	6.00	6.00	6.00	6.00	6.00	6.00	6.00	4.50	4.00	4.00
Money Market Rate	60b	4.95	4.95	4.95	4.95	4.95	4.95	4.95	4.95	4.95	4.95	4.95	4.95
Deposit Rate	60l	3.50	3.50	3.50	3.50	3.50	3.50	3.50	3.50	3.50	3.50	3.50	3.50
Prices and Production						*Index Numbers (2000=100): Period Averages*							
Consumer Prices	64	86.5	93.3	† 95.8	97.3	98.5	99.3	100.0	103.1	105.4	105.3	105.9	107.7
Industrial Production	66	91.7	98.3	94.9	96.5	116.2	103.6	100.0	100.3	105.8	† 106.7	119.0	121.2
Intl. Transactions & Positions						*Billions of Francs*							
Exports	70	439.10	495.80	505.40	528.00	570.90	632.40	655.00	735.30	743.40	730.60	775.00	843.90
Imports, c.i.f	71	567.40	704.90	734.60	779.00	858.50	963.00	1,081.50	1,268.20	1,415.60	1,389.60	1,505.00	1,756.50

Senegal 722

		1994	1995	1996	1997	1998	1999	2000	2001	2002	2003	2004	2005
Balance of Payments													
		\multicolumn{12}{Millions of US Dollars: Minus Sign Indicates Debit}											
Current Account, n.i.e.	78ald	−187.5	−244.5	−200.7	−184.8	−247.5	−320.2	−332.4	−245.5	−316.8	−436.6	....	....
Goods: Exports f.o.b.	78aad	818.8	993.3	988.0	904.6	967.7	1,027.1	919.8	1,003.1	1,066.5	1,257.0	....	....
Goods: Imports f.o.b.	78abd	−1,022.0	−1,242.9	−1,264.0	−1,176.0	−1,280.6	−1,372.8	−1,336.6	−1,428.4	−1,603.9	−2,065.5	....	....
Trade Balance	78acd	−203.2	−249.6	−275.9	−271.5	−312.9	−345.8	−416.7	−425.3	−537.4	−808.5	....	....
Services: Credit	78add	412.3	512.5	378.7	371.7	425.1	416.1	386.9	398.1	456.2	569.0	....	....
Services: Debit	78aed	−492.7	−578.2	−395.8	−391.7	−442.9	−430.4	−405.0	−413.6	−474.3	−591.3	....	....
Balance on Goods & Services	78afd	−283.6	−315.3	−293.0	−291.5	−330.7	−360.0	−434.8	−440.8	−555.5	−830.8	....	....
Income: Credit	78agd	63.3	87.2	80.3	67.5	76.4	79.9	76.3	61.6	65.1	86.4	....	....
Income: Debit	78ahd	−164.5	−211.5	−154.5	−139.4	−164.4	−199.1	−187.7	−166.4	−195.1	−222.6	....	....
Balance on Gds, Serv. & Inc.	78aid	−384.7	−439.6	−367.2	−363.4	−418.6	−479.2	−546.3	−545.6	−685.5	−967.0	....	....
Current Transfers, n.i.e.: Credit	78ajd	267.0	284.7	244.3	258.8	254.7	225.4	274.9	353.6	414.4	595.6	....	....
Current Transfers: Debit	78akd	−69.7	−89.6	−77.8	−80.3	−83.6	−66.3	−61.0	−53.4	−45.8	−65.2	....	....
Capital Account, n.i.e.	78bcd	190.6	187.0	169.2	96.0	98.3	98.6	83.4	146.1	126.8	150.4	....	....
Capital Account, n.i.e.: Credit	78bad	200.5	201.2	169.3	96.3	98.8	99.0	83.6	146.1	127.1	150.9	....	....
Capital Account: Debit	78bbd	−9.9	−14.2	−.1	−.3	−.4	−.5	−.3	−.1	−.2	−.6	....	....
Financial Account, n.i.e.	78bjd	48.5	44.2	−177.6	3.5	−109.7	−54.8	27.1	−102.6	−88.2	2.5	....	....
Direct Investment Abroad	78bdd	−17.4	3.3	−2.0	.9	−10.3	−11.1	−.6	7.0	−34.0	−2.7	....	....
Dir. Invest. in Rep. Econ., n.i.e.	78bed	66.9	31.7	8.7	176.0	70.6	153.2	62.9	31.9	78.1	52.5	....	....
Portfolio Investment Assets	78bfd	−1.5	−.4	−25.8	−18.9	−21.9	−31.3	11.0	15.9	−25.0	−56.3	....	....
Equity Securities	78bkd	−1.5	−.4	−2.4	.9	−9.8	−6.2	−.2	7.0	.5	−7.9	....	....
Debt Securities	78bld	—	—	−23.4	−19.9	−12.1	−25.1	11.3	8.9	−25.5	−48.4	....	....
Portfolio Investment Liab., n.i.e.	78bgd	.5	4.0	−4.8	−8.1	−3.9	—	11.9	−8.3	−13.1	10.6	....	....
Equity Securities	78bmd	.5	4.1	—	8.4	2.6	3.4	−2.2	−5.2	3.2	3.6	....	....
Debt Securities	78bnd	—	−.1	−4.8	−16.4	−6.5	−3.4	14.1	−3.2	−16.4	6.9	....	....
Financial Derivatives Assets	78bwd	—	—	—	−.7	—	−.7	—	—	−.4	1.6	....	....
Financial Derivatives Liabilities	78bxd	—	—	—	—	.1	—	—	.4	−.4	.7	....	....
Other Investment Assets	78bhd	−92.5	−6.2	−70.7	−22.1	−58.8	−62.3	−4.4	−3.9	11.9	58.0	....	....
Monetary Authorities	78bod	....	....	—	—	—	—	—	—	—	—	....	....
General Government	78bpd	—	—	−3.1	−.9	−.4	—	—	—	−1.5	−1.8	....	....
Banks	78bqd	−108.8	10.9	31.0	−24.5	−42.4	−54.8	17.2	−33.0	−16.4	−8.3	....	....
Other Sectors	78brd	16.3	−17.1	−98.5	3.3	−15.9	−7.6	−21.6	29.2	29.8	68.1	....	....
Other Investment Liab., n.i.e.	78bid	92.6	11.8	−83.1	−123.7	−85.5	−102.6	−53.8	−145.3	−103.8	−61.9	....	....
Monetary Authorities	78bsd	−76.2	−35.7	1.6	.3	.7	2.5	8.9	−6.7	10.7	4.3	....	....
General Government	78btd	90.7	83.9	−140.0	−132.6	−112.9	−114.8	−132.7	−136.1	−161.6	−194.8	....	....
Banks	78bud	9.8	−27.1	−4.6	23.6	23.5	5.9	−6.1	7.8	−6.5	21.4	....	....
Other Sectors	78bvd	68.3	−9.3	60.0	−14.9	3.3	3.7	76.0	−10.4	53.7	107.1	....	....
Net Errors and Omissions	78cad	−28.9	−19.6	7.7	−9.3	10.7	8.2	−9.0	7.9	30.8	10.8	....	....
Overall Balance	78cbd	22.8	−32.9	−201.4	−94.7	−248.1	−268.2	−231.0	−194.1	−247.3	−272.8	....	....
Reserves and Related Items	79dad	−22.8	32.9	201.4	94.7	248.1	268.2	231.0	194.1	247.3	272.8	....	....
Reserve Assets	79dbd	−170.1	−74.8	−34.8	−137.4	−20.7	−31.6	−14.1	−90.3	−92.5	−18.1	....	....
Use of Fund Credit and Loans	79dcd	38.9	42.9	−9.8	−12.8	−11.6	−13.4	−3.3	3.4	−15.9	−34.5	....	....
Exceptional Financing	79ded	108.4	64.9	246.0	244.8	280.4	313.2	248.4	281.0	355.8	325.4	....	....
International Investment Position		\multicolumn{12}{Millions of US Dollars}											
Assets	79aad	....	561.4	640.7	711.7	860.1	889.8	830.1	906.2	1,360.0	1,667.8	....	....
Direct Investment Abroad	79abd	—	9.9	10.2	2.6	8.9	18.3	21.9	−5.2	55.1	75.5	....	....
Portfolio Investment	79acd	—	8.6	33.2	52.2	78.2	93.7	95.0	90.2	133.5	226.7	....	....
Equity Securities	79add	....	.9	3.2	.7	20.8	14.2	18.9	13.3	14.9	32.9	....	....
Debt Securities	79aed	....	7.6	30.0	51.5	57.4	79.5	76.1	76.8	118.6	193.8	....	....
Financial Derivatives	79ald	....	.1	.1	.8	—	.7	.7	1.1	—	.8	....	....
Other Investment	79afd	197.0	271.0	308.9	269.8	339.9	374.1	324.9	364.2	527.0	570.1	....	....
Monetary Authorities	79agd	—	—	—	—	—	—	—	—	—	—	....	....
General Government	79ahd	....	....	3.4	3.9	3.5	3.0	2.8	3.1	5.4	8.5	....	....
Banks	79aid	197.0	144.4	104.9	115.6	167.5	195.9	164.0	187.9	241.9	300.6	....	....
Other Sectors	79ajd	....	....	200.6	150.3	168.8	175.2	158.1	173.2	279.8	261.1	....	....
Reserve Assets	79akd	179.6	271.8	288.3	386.2	433.1	403.0	387.6	455.9	644.4	794.6	....	....
Liabilities	79lad	....	4,261.8	4,100.6	4,072.1	4,721.1	4,223.1	4,617.4	4,523.8	5,287.8	5,973.0	....	....
Dir. Invest. in Rep. Economy	79lbd	—	78.6	76.4	256.2	372.1	329.4	294.6	194.3	241.6	346.6	....	....
Portfolio Investment	79lcd	—	83.3	73.0	56.8	96.2	92.9	127.9	113.8	140.3	180.7	....	....
Equity Securities	79ldd	....	10.3	9.4	17.2	66.8	63.5	93.7	83.2	107.8	133.7	....	....
Debt Securities	79led	....	73.0	63.6	39.6	29.4	29.4	34.2	30.6	32.6	47.0	....	....
Financial Derivatives	79lfd	....	—	—	—	.1	—	—	.4	.1	.9	....	....
Other Investment	79lfd	3,443.6	4,099.9	3,951.2	3,759.1	4,252.7	3,800.8	4,194.9	4,215.3	4,905.8	5,444.9	....	....
Monetary Authorities	79lgd	446.1	470.1	442.5	394.6	402.4	369.0	353.6	341.8	368.4	383.9	....	....
General Government	79lhd	2,882.7	3,323.6	3,035.5	2,864.5	3,232.7	2,852.3	3,150.0	3,189.8	3,691.5	3,906.5	....	....
Banks	79lid	114.8	184.9	171.3	176.4	210.1	218.3	197.8	242.4	256.8	364.6	....	....
Other Sectors	79ljd	—	121.3	302.0	323.7	407.4	361.2	493.4	441.2	589.1	789.9	....	....
National Accounts		\multicolumn{12}{Billions of Francs}											
Househ.Cons.Expend.,incl.NPISHs.	96f	1,759.0	1,936.0	2,078.0	2,128.0	2,323.0	2,400.0	2,533.0	2,790.0	2,973.0	3,080.0	3,280.0	3,576.2
Government Consumption Expend.	91f	258.4	276.1	286.0	303.0	324.2	308.6	365.7	493.7	....	....	....	....
Gross Fixed Capital Formation	93e	459.0	461.0	525.0	532.0	686.0	709.0	746.0	813.0	923.0	843.0	962.0	....
Changes in Inventories	93i	−32.0	52.0	15.0	18.0	36.0	66.0	−14.0	−20.0	−122.0	49.0	−22.0	....
Exports of Goods and Services	90c	652.0	718.2	728.0	868.4	924.4	888.6	949.5	1,011.3	....	....	....	....
Imports of Goods and Services (-)	98c	841.0	909.0	849.0	915.0	1,017.0	1,110.3	1,240.0	1,350.3	1,449.0	1,544.0	1,670.0	2,073.1
Gross Domestic Product (GDP)	99b	2,153.0	2,435.0	2,591.0	2,727.0	2,968.0	3,167.0	3,332.0	3,571.0	3,720.0	4,008.0	4,023.7	4,407.5
Net Primary Income from Abroad	98.n	179.2	86.2	217.0	209.0	192.0	164.0	161.0	338.0	....	....	....	....
Gross National Income (GNI)	99a	2,393.0	2,652.0	2,875.0	2,936.0	3,279.0	3,400.0	3,455.0	3,853.0	4,046.0	4,225.0	4,457.0	....
GDP Volume 1987 Prices	99b.p	1,523.5	1,602.2	1,684.7	....	....	....	....	....	....	....	....	....
GDP Volume 1999 Prices	99b.p	....	....	2,727.0	2,812.0	2,978.0	3,167.0	3,268.0	3,418.0	3,440.0	3,669.0	3,874.0	....
GDP Volume (2000=100)	99bvp	75.5	79.4	† 83.4	86.0	91.1	96.9	100.0	104.6	105.3	112.3	118.5	....
GDP Deflator (2000=100)	99bip	85.6	92.1	93.2	95.1	97.7	98.1	100.0	102.5	106.1	107.1	101.9	....
		\multicolumn{12}{Millions: Midyear Estimates}											
Population	99z	8.89	9.12	9.36	9.60	9.84	10.09	10.34	10.60	10.86	11.12	11.39	11.66

		1994	1995	1996	1997	1998	1999	2000	2001	2002	2003	2004	2005
Exchange Rates						*Rupees per SDR: End of Period*							
Official Rate	aa	7.2345	7.2345	7.2345	6.9218	7.6699	7.3671	8.1642	7.2226	6.8474	8.1434	8.5131	7.8601
						Rupees per US Dollar: End of Period (ae) Period Average (rf)							
Official Rate	ae	4.9695	4.8639	4.9946	5.1249	5.4521	5.3676	6.2689	5.7522	5.0550	5.5000	5.5000	5.5000
Official Rate	rf	5.0559	4.7620	4.9700	5.0263	5.2622	5.3426	5.7138	5.8575	5.4800	5.4007	5.5000	5.5000
Fund Position						*Millions of SDRs: End of Period*							
Quota	2f.s	6.00	6.00	6.00	6.00	6.00	8.80	8.80	8.80	8.80	8.80	8.80	8.80
SDRs	1b.s	.02	.02	.02	.03	.03	.03	.01	.02	.01			
Reserve Position in the Fund	1c.s	.80	.80	.80	.80	—	—	—	—	—			
Total Fund Cred.&Loans Outstg	2tl												
International Liquidity						*Millions of US Dollars Unless Otherwise Indicated: End of Period*							
Total Reserves minus Gold	1l.d	30.15	27.10	21.76	26.32	21.59	30.35	43.75	37.13	69.79	67.39	34.59	56.24
SDRs	1b.d	.02	.03	.03	.04	.04	.04	.01	.02	.01			
Reserve Position in the Fund	1c.d	1.17	1.20	1.16	1.09	—	—	—	—	—		.01	
Foreign Exchange	1d.d	28.96	25.87	20.57	25.20	21.55	30.31	43.74	37.11	69.78	67.38	34.58	56.24
Monetary Authorities: Other Liab	4..d	—	—	2.50	12.64	31.75	39.35	64.35	64.88	158.77	126.06	89.82	71.71
Banking Institutions: Assets	7a.d	5.03	9.91	19.87	31.36	29.86	44.03	49.03	49.46	53.79	46.11	58.19	72.27
Liabilities	7b.d	6.42	10.36	17.97	33.40	34.71	47.05	100.74	91.90	106.54	80.17	77.05	106.44
Nonbank Financial Insts: Assets	7e.d	—	—	—	—	—	—	—	—	—	—	—	—
Liabilities	7f.d	19.17	19.72	18.55	17.49	18.45	17.96	16.59	19.64	23.92	23.04	24.61	25.31
Monetary Authorities						*Millions of Rupees: End of Period*							
Foreign Assets	11	142.8	126.8	99.2	127.1	115.2	160.2	271.1	210.6	352.3	369.2	187.8	308.7
Claims on Central Government	12a	529.2	663.3	790.5	926.8	575.0	640.1	698.8	774.0	1,293.2	1,011.7	1,400.6	1,340.8
Claims on Banking Institutions	12e	7.0	1.8	—	—	10.0	—	22.0	—	—	19.0	120.0	—
Reserve Money	14	566.7	684.8	778.6	924.0	468.7	512.8	528.7	566.8	717.9	578.7	1,056.1	1,092.3
of which: Currency Outside Banks	14a	139.4	146.8	163.9	192.2	206.4	247.9	264.4	279.9	301.0	305.9	295.8	325.7
Foreign Liabilities	16c	—	—	12.5	64.8	173.1	211.2	403.4	373.2	802.6	693.3	494.0	394.4
Central Government Deposits	16d	30.9	21.4	79.5	57.1	55.5	70.1	33.1	42.0	75.4	32.8	122.1	111.9
Capital Accounts	17a	13.9	13.9	13.9	13.8	14.1	25.9	43.2	51.4	56.7	109.7	56.1	24.2
Other Items (Net)	17r	67.4	71.7	5.1	−5.7	−11.2	−19.7	−16.6	−48.8	−7.0	−14.7	−19.9	26.7
Banking Institutions						*Millions of Rupees: End of Period*							
Reserves	20	426.9	539.6	614.2	731.1	261.6	264.1	263.6	286.1	416.0	271.9	759.3	765.7
Foreign Assets	21	25.0	48.2	99.3	160.7	162.8	236.4	307.4	284.5	271.9	253.6	320.1	397.5
Claims on Central Government	22a	813.6	841.0	958.9	1,086.9	2,106.7	2,526.6	2,805.7	3,101.6	3,182.4	3,335.5	2,746.6	2,638.5
Claims on Nonfin.Pub.Enterprises	22c	143.9	99.6	75.9	71.8	56.0	42.6	20.2	10.8	5.4	102.8	183.3	296.8
Claims on Private Sector	22d	227.7	275.1	314.6	387.6	459.9	503.4	581.6	655.5	773.9	993.8	1,164.1	1,247.3
Claims on Nonbank Financial Insts	22g	1.0	1.0	1.0	1.0	1.0	1.0	1.0	1.0	1.0	1.0	1.0	1.0
Demand Deposits	24	184.4	186.2	284.0	456.5	567.4	823.3	794.9	913.0	1,105.5	1,265.0	931.1	1,071.4
Time, Savings, Fgn. Ccy. Deposits	25	1,149.7	1,352.6	1,478.9	1,590.8	1,819.5	2,009.7	2,164.8	2,416.4	2,604.0	2,677.5	3,060.3	3,060.3
Money Market Instruments	26aa	—	—	3.2	4.6	6.8	2.4	6.6	3.4	4.4	8.1	14.3	12.7
Foreign Liabilities	26c	31.9	50.4	89.7	171.2	189.2	252.6	631.6	528.6	538.5	440.9	423.8	585.4
Central Government Deposits	26d	118.8	112.8	88.6	163.2	187.4	203.5	207.6	228.8	247.1	244.4	234.2	192.4
Credit from Monetary Authorities	26g	7.0	1.8	—	—	10.0	—	22.0	—	—	19.0	120.0	—
Capital Accounts	27a	85.4	80.2	174.6	207.2	241.1	270.8	300.8	329.4	343.1	376.3	364.8	389.7
Other Items (Net)	27r	60.9	20.6	−55.1	−154.5	26.6	11.9	−148.9	−80.2	−192.0	−72.8	26.0	35.0
Banking Survey						*Millions of Rupees: End of Period*							
Foreign Assets (Net)	31n	135.9	124.6	96.2	51.9	−84.4	−67.2	−456.5	−406.8	−716.9	−511.5	−409.9	−273.7
Domestic Credit	32	1,565.7	1,745.8	1,972.8	2,253.8	2,955.7	3,440.2	3,866.6	4,272.1	4,933.4	5,167.5	5,139.4	5,220.2
Claims on Central Govt. (Net)	32an	1,193.1	1,370.1	1,581.3	1,793.4	2,438.9	2,893.2	3,263.8	3,604.9	4,153.2	4,070.0	3,791.0	3,675.0
Claims on Nonfin.Pub.Enterprises	32c	143.9	99.6	75.9	71.8	56.0	42.6	20.2	10.8	5.4	102.8	183.3	296.8
Claims on Private Sector	32d	227.7	275.1	314.6	387.6	459.9	503.4	581.6	655.5	773.9	993.8	1,164.1	1,247.3
Claims on Nonbank Financial Insts	32g	1.0	1.0	1.0	1.0	1.0	1.0	1.0	1.0	1.0	1.0	1.0	1.0
Money	34	324.4	333.7	448.6	649.4	774.5	1,072.0	1,060.1	1,193.7	1,407.4	1,571.8	1,227.8	1,398.0
Quasi-Money	35	1,149.7	1,352.6	1,478.9	1,590.8	1,819.5	2,009.7	2,164.8	2,416.4	2,604.0	2,677.5	3,060.3	3,060.3
Money Market Instruments	36aa	—	—	3.2	4.6	6.8	2.4	6.6	3.4	4.4	8.1	14.3	12.7
Capital Accounts	37a	99.3	94.2	188.6	221.0	255.2	296.7	344.1	380.8	399.8	486.0	421.0	413.9
Other Items (Net)	37r	128.1	89.9	−50.2	−160.1	15.3	−7.8	−165.4	−128.9	−199.0	−87.5	6.1	61.7
Money plus Quasi-Money	35l	1,474.1	1,686.3	1,927.4	2,240.2	2,594.0	3,081.7	3,224.9	3,610.1	4,011.4	4,249.3	4,288.2	4,458.3
Nonbank Financial Institutions						*Millions of Rupees: End of Period*							
Reserves	40	—	—	.2	—	—	—	.2	.2	—	—	—	—
Foreign Assets	41	—	—	—	—	—	—	—	—	—	—	—	—
Claims on Central Government	42a	—	7.5	8.1	6.4	14.0	8.5	5.8	7.9	1.2	1.7	2.4	.5
Claims on Nonfin.Pub.Enterprises	42c	53.1	51.4	45.4	36.5	30.0	22.7	15.6	9.9	6.1	2.8	2.0	2.6
Claims on Private Sector	42d	106.2	122.4	141.6	163.8	176.2	184.7	202.1	217.9	252.3	267.4	286.4	301.4
Claims on Banking Institutions	42e	4.1	12.1	10.0	9.9	17.8	24.5	31.3	30.6	25.2	36.6	17.4	21.4
Money Market Instruments	46aa	—	3.1	2.3	6.7	4.0	.8	3.6	2.6	2.4	2.2	2.8	3.5
Foreign Liabilities	46c	95.2	95.9	92.6	89.7	100.6	96.4	104.0	113.0	120.9	126.7	135.3	139.2
Capital Accounts	47a	83.5	76.0	78.6	96.1	112.0	132.6	135.9	143.6	158.8	170.2	156.0	163.2
Other Items (Net)	47r	−15.3	18.5	31.7	24.2	21.5	10.6	11.4	7.4	2.8	9.4	14.1	20.0
Money (National Definitions)						*Millions of Rupees: End of Period*							
M1	59ma	326.0	334.3	449.6	648.7	773.8	1,071.2	1,137.5	1,290.6	1,576.9	1,570.9	1,226.9	1,397.0
M2	59mb	1,094.7	1,209.3	1,388.6	1,987.8	2,383.5	2,908.9	3,174.2	3,554.8	4,062.1	4,128.0	3,679.1	3,942.7
M2(p)	59mba	1,292.8	1,510.8	1,705.7	2,205.9	2,561.8	3,056.9	3,306.5	3,682.5	4,165.4	4,230.2	4,268.5	4,441.1
Interest Rates						*Percent Per Annum*							
Discount Rate (End of Period)	60	12.50	12.83	11.00	11.00	5.50	5.50	5.50	5.50	5.50	4.67	3.51	3.87
Treasury Bill Rate	60c	12.50	12.28	11.55	10.50	8.13	5.00	5.00	5.00	5.00	4.61	3.17	3.34
Savings Rate	60k	8.00	8.00	8.00	8.00	5.75	3.00	3.02	3.03	3.03	2.85	2.88	2.98
Deposit Rate	60l	8.85	9.22	9.90	9.20	7.53	5.13	4.77	4.92	4.93	3.99	3.55	3.72
Lending Rate	60p	15.72	15.76	16.22	14.88	14.39	12.01	11.45	11.14	11.09	11.08	10.13	9.98
Government Bond Yield	61	14.38	13.25	13.25	11.63	8.96	8.58	8.22	8.13	8.25	5.96	6.58	6.00

Seychelles 718

		1994	1995	1996	1997	1998	1999	2000	2001	2002	2003	2004	2005
Prices and Labor						*Index Numbers (2000=100): Period Averages*							
Consumer Prices........................	64	86.9	86.7	85.7	86.3	88.5	94.1	100.0	106.0	106.2	109.7	113.9	114.9
Employment.............................	67	78.7	79.9	81.5	87.8	91.2	96.5	100.0	103.1	105.6	102.7	101.7	107.2
						Number in Thousands: Period Averages							
Employment.............................	67e	25	26	26	28	29	31	32	33	34	33	33	35
Intl. Transactions & Positions						*Millions of Rupees*							
Exports..................................	70	262.15	253.50	693.43	569.23	643.67	775.12	1,106.05	1,265.77	1,248.90	1,478.50	1,599.30	2,172.50
Imports, c.i.f............................	71	1,042.38	1,109.20	1,881.88	1,711.22	2,018.90	2,318.20	1,954.70	2,788.80	2,304.00	2,228.80	2,738.96	3,025.00
Balance of Payments						*Millions of US Dollars: Minus Sign Indicates Debit*							
Current Account, n.i.e.................	78ald	23.83	−2.95	−59.25	−72.78	−118.03	−127.33	−51.33	−123.24	−130.64	−16.17	−28.15	....
Goods: Exports f.o.b..............	78aad	52.99	53.51	96.66	113.56	122.84	145.66	194.77	216.44	236.70	286.42	300.46	....
Goods: Imports f.o.b..............	78abd	−188.06	−214.26	−266.98	−303.50	−334.63	−369.75	−311.60	−421.93	−376.26	−377.58	−416.94	....
Trade Balance..................	78acd	−135.07	−160.75	−170.32	−189.94	−211.79	−224.09	−116.82	−205.50	−139.57	−91.16	−116.47	....
Services: Credit.................	78add	250.34	278.69	237.06	255.86	247.48	277.30	294.23	296.38	306.52	330.40	324.66	....
Services: Debit.................	78aed	−80.19	−103.48	−114.07	−127.61	−132.17	−155.98	−174.66	−169.20	−201.28	−218.38	−212.31	....
Balance on Goods & Services......	78afd	35.08	14.46	−47.33	−61.70	−96.49	−102.78	2.75	−78.31	−34.33	20.87	−4.12	....
Income: Credit..................	78agd	8.09	12.56	10.48	9.65	5.43	8.46	9.24	8.25	7.44	11.98	10.30	....
Income: Debit..................	78ahd	−19.84	−32.21	−25.52	−21.92	−25.31	−32.29	−57.66	−52.19	−99.98	−55.18	−43.62	....
Balance on Gds, Serv. & Inc.....	78aid	23.34	−5.20	−62.37	−73.97	−116.36	−126.61	−45.67	−122.25	−126.87	−22.33	−37.43	....
Current Transfers, n.i.e.: Credit......	78ajd	13.85	13.52	15.20	14.24	9.77	10.09	4.34	7.90	7.82	8.97	11.17	....
Current Transfers: Debit.............	78akd	−13.35	−11.28	−12.07	−13.05	−11.44	−10.81	−9.99	−8.90	−11.59	−2.81	−1.89	....
Capital Account, n.i.e................	78bcd	4.27	1.05	5.65	6.76	21.66	16.47	.89	9.44	5.03	7.42	.99	....
Capital Account, n.i.e.: Credit.......	78bad	4.27	1.05	5.65	6.76	21.66	16.47	.89	9.44	5.03	7.42	.99	....
Capital Account: Debit..............	78bbd	—	—	—	—	—	—	—	—	—	—	—	....
Financial Account, n.i.e.............	78bjd	−.20	−1.18	−15.95	9.52	27.08	13.91	−32.07	52.33	−63.97	−152.59	−190.65	....
Direct Investment Abroad...........	78bdd	−13.33	−16.97	−12.47	−9.89	−3.00	−8.98	−6.86	−8.54	−8.90	−8.15	−7.60	....
Dir. Invest. in Rep. Econ., n.i.e....	78bed	30.74	45.88	28.81	53.40	53.21	55.22	24.33	59.43	61.43	58.43	37.45	....
Portfolio Investment Assets...........	78bfd	−.93	−5.76	6.65	.09	−.78	−.02	−.09	.07	.07	−.01	−.04	....
Equity Securities................	78bkd	....	....	....	....	....	....	....	....	....	....	....	....
Debt Securities.................	78bld	−.93	−5.76	6.65	.09	−.78	−.02	−.09	.07	.07	−.01	−.04	....
Portfolio Investment Liab., n.i.e......	78bgd	.16	−.17	—	2.94	2.83	.56	1.05	1.09	1.11	1.14	1.11	....
Equity Securities................	78bmd	....	....	....	....	....	....	....	....	....	....	....	....
Debt Securities.................	78bnd	.16	−.17	—	2.94	2.83	.56	1.05	1.09	1.11	1.14	1.11	....
Financial Derivatives Assets........	78bwd	....	....	....	....	....	....	....	....	....	....	....	....
Financial Derivatives Liabilities.......	78bxd	....	....	....	....	....	....	....	....	....	....	....	....
Other Investment Assets...............	78bhd	1.60	−2.56	−11.79	−12.73	−5.66	−12.97	−14.86	−8.76	−9.84	−14.82	−12.27	....
Monetary Authorities..................	78bod	....	....	....	....	....	....	....	....	....	....	....	....
General Government.................	78bpd	....	....	....	....	....	....	....	....	....	....	....	....
Banks...............................	78bqd	....	....	....	....	....	....	....	....	....	....	....	....
Other Sectors.....................	78brd	1.60	−2.56	−11.79	−12.73	−5.66	−12.97	−14.86	−8.76	−9.84	−14.82	−12.27	....
Other Investment Liab., n.i.e.........	78bid	−18.44	−21.61	−27.14	−24.29	−19.52	−19.90	−35.64	9.03	−107.84	−189.18	−209.30	....
Monetary Authorities.................	78bsd	−2.06	−2.86	−3.14	−10.19	—	—	−3.39	−15.94	−68.09	−189.18	−209.30	....
General Government.................	78btd	−14.22	−16.23	−21.33	−12.83	−16.02	−18.27	−13.56	−31.94	−7.03	....	....	....
Banks...............................	78bud	—	—	—	—	—	—	—	−4.30	−5.70	....	....	....
Other Sectors.....................	78bvd	−2.16	−2.52	−2.68	−1.27	−3.50	−1.63	−18.68	61.21	−27.03	....	....	....
Net Errors and Omissions...........	78cad	−55.41	−28.70	7.04	11.65	−4.35	−2.14	−20.79	14.42	.51	39.76	32.54	....
Overall Balance.................	78cbd	−27.51	−31.78	−62.50	−44.84	−73.64	−99.09	−103.30	−47.06	−189.07	−121.58	−185.27	....
Reserves and Related Items...........	79dad	27.51	31.78	62.50	44.84	73.64	99.09	103.30	47.06	189.07	121.58	185.27	....
Reserve Assets.....................	79dbd	7.43	3.42	4.86	−5.12	3.26	−8.42	−19.39	10.32	−25.84	−3.12	32.97	....
Use of Fund Credit and Loans........	79dcd	—	—	—	—	—	—	—	—	—	—	—	....
Exceptional Financing...................	79ded	20.09	28.36	57.63	49.96	70.38	107.51	122.69	36.74	214.92	124.70	152.30	....
Government Finance						*Millions of Rupees: Year Ending December 31*							
Deficit (-) or Surplus........................	80	−54.0	−200.5	−365.4	107.6	38.6	−385.5	−496.5	....	....	270.4	142.3	351.7
Total Revenue and Grants..............	81y	1,288.9	1,172.2	1,164.1	1,288.8	1,400.7	1,533.6	1,426.7	....	....	1,867.6	1,885.0	2,167.3
Revenue...............................	81	1,271.1	1,158.4	1,151.1	1,273.5	1,372.9	1,491.9	1,377.1	....	....	1,856.8	1,881.5	2,117.8
Grants..................................	81z	17.8	13.8	13.0	15.3	27.8	41.7	49.6	....	....	10.8	3.5	49.5
Exp. & Lending Minus Repay..........	82z	1,342.9	1,372.7	1,529.5	1,181.2	1,362.1	1,919.1	1,923.2	....	....	1,597.2	1,742.7	1,815.6
Expenditure........................	82	1,325.9	1,276.5	1,495.2	1,680.9	1,879.7	1,905.0	1,969.8	....	....	1,596.1	1,741.6	1,808.8
Lending Minus Repayments..........	83	17.0	96.2	34.3	−499.7	−517.6	14.1	−46.6	....	....	1.2	1.0	6.8
Total Financing..........................	80h	54.0	200.5	365.4	−107.6	−38.6	385.5	496.5	....	....	−270.4	−142.7	−352.0
Domestic.............................	84a	63.8	246.0	324.1	−128.6	−4.3	433.6	−19.3	....	....	−283.0	−131.0	−485.8
Foreign................................	85a	−9.8	−45.5	41.3	21.0	−34.3	−48.1	515.8	....	....	12.6	−11.6	133.7
National Accounts						*Millions of Rupees*							
Househ.Cons.Expend.,incl.NPISHs....	96f	1,129.8	1,179.4	1,191.0	1,465.8	1,739.2	2,141.6	1,819.7	2,779.7	2,167.4	2,371.1	2,414.2	2,521.9
Government Consumption Expend...	91f	722.2	669.1	736.0	733.0	862.3	759.2	786.8	819.1	933.4	933.4	1,018.5	883.1
Gross Fixed Capital Formation..........	93e	648.5	733.9	822.6	863.1	1,100.0	....	....	....	....	....	....	....
Changes in Inventories....................	93i	17.4	.2	−19.0	109.1	56.0	....	....	....	....	....	....	....
Exports of Goods and Services........	90c	1,250.5	1,292.0	1,592.9	1,896.9	1,928.0	2,221.7	2,745.8	2,973.3	3,000.4	3,351.1	3,456.9	3,718.3
Imports of Goods and Services (-).....	98c	1,326.0	1,454.8	1,841.4	2,159.7	2,435.7	2,812.1	2,812.1	3,686.6	3,198.3	3,201.2	4,558.6	3,730.4
Gross Domestic Product (GDP).........	99b	2,459.4	2,419.8	2,500.3	2,829.5	3,201.3	3,323.2	3,531.7	3,617.8	3,829.9	3,796.1	3,868.6	3,840.9
Net Primary Income from Abroad.....	98.n	9.6	−91.9	−73.6	−62.1	−110.1	−128.2	−151.5	....	....	....	....	....
Gross National Income (GNI)............	99a	2,469.0	2,328.0	2,426.7	2,767.5	3,091.2	3,195.1	3,380.2	3,617.8	3,829.9	....	....	....
Consumption of Fixed Capital..........	99cf	211.5	210.2	240.5	276.9	291.3	318.5	....	....	....	....	....	....
GDP Volume 1986 Prices.................	99b.p	1,950.0	1,933.9	2,029.0	2,122.1	2,238.8	2,303.7	2,336.0	2,358.2	....	....	....	....
GDP Volume (2000=100).................	99bvp	83.5	82.8	86.9	90.8	95.8	98.6	100.0	101.0	....	....	....	....
GDP Deflator (2000=100).................	99bip	83.4	82.8	81.5	88.2	94.6	95.4	100.0	101.5	....	....	....	....
						Millions: Midyear Estimates							
Population..............................	99z	.07	.08	.08	.08	.08	.08	.08	.08	.08	.08	.08	.08

		1994	1995	1996	1997	1998	1999	2000	2001	2002	2003	2004	2005
Exchange Rates					*Leones per SDR: End of Period*								
Market Rate	aa	894.90	1,402.35	1,307.24	1,799.00	2,239.84	3,123.90	2,171.52	2,716.13	2,979.70	3,807.32	4,321.94	4,191.36
					Leones per US Dollar: End of Period (ae) Period Average (rf)								
Market Rate	ae	613.01	943.40	909.09	1,333.33	1,590.76	2,276.05	1,666.67	2,161.27	2,191.73	2,562.18	2,860.49	2,932.52
Market Rate	rf	586.74	755.22	920.73	981.48	1,563.62	1,804.20	2,092.13	1,986.15	2,099.03	2,347.94	2,701.30	2,889.59
					Index Numbers (2000=100): Period Averages								
Market Rate	ahx	354.3	282.8	226.2	217.8	132.9	116.5	100.0	105.4	99.0	88.7	77.0	71.9
Nominal Effective Exchange Rate	nec	286.7	218.3	180.2	187.2	118.1	104.7	100.0	109.9	100.1	78.4	62.7	58.3
Real Effective Exchange Rate	rec	104.9	94.7	95.2	108.4	92.3	108.4	100.0	109.4	94.5	77.7	69.4	70.9
Fund Position					*Millions of SDRs: End of Period*								
Quota	2f.s	77.2	77.2	77.2	77.2	77.2	103.7	103.7	103.7	103.7	103.7	103.7	103.7
SDRs	1b.s	6.2	11.5	5.3	8.3	7.4	15.2	4.0	.3	17.7	23.2	32.8	22.9
Reserve Position in the Fund	1c.s	—	—	—	—	—	—	—	—	—	—	—	—
Total Fund Cred.&Loans Outstg.	2tl	100.2	110.9	118.8	123.9	135.4	142.0	133.2	120.8	124.5	113.8	126.0	134.4
International Liquidity					*Millions of US Dollars Unless Otherwise Indicated: End of Period*								
Total Reserves minus Gold	1l.d	40.6	34.6	26.6	38.5	43.9	39.5	49.2	51.3	84.7	66.6	125.1	170.5
SDRs	1b.d	9.0	17.1	7.6	11.2	10.4	20.8	5.2	.4	24.0	34.5	51.0	32.8
Reserve Position in the Fund	1c.d	—	—	—	—	—	—	—	—	—	—	—	—
Foreign Exchange	1d.d	31.6	17.5	18.9	27.3	33.5	18.6	43.9	50.9	60.6	32.1	74.1	137.7
Monetary Authorities: Other Liab.	4..d	470.2	326.2	74.9	31.4	38.8	27.4	30.2	37.2	28.3	24.0	11.7	10.5
Deposit Money Banks: Assets	7a.d	16.9	22.5	19.9	15.6	19.2	17.9	24.4	21.9	26.6	30.8	35.0	51.1
Liabilities	7b.d	2.9	3.1										
Monetary Authorities					*Millions of Leones: End of Period*								
Foreign Assets	11	30,443	48,695	† 27,262	53,008	83,128	98,035	86,385	115,454	191,477	168,696	365,530	505,489
Claims on Central Government	12a	462,872	408,928	† 415,564	470,930	475,265	524,834	633,405	650,358	655,133	685,472	626,112	591,489
Claims on Nonfin.Pub.Enterprises	12c	....	....	203	203	13	66	13	13	13	13	13	13
Claims on Private Sector	12d	160	324	† 1,031	2,577	1,749	788	1,008	1,969	6,161	1,911	2,125	5,595
Claims on Deposit Money Banks	12e	—	—	† 1,173	495	1,049	1,736	606	969	278	59	3,163	3,356
Claims on Other Banking Insts.	12f	....	....	33	34	—	4	—	—	—	—	—	4,875
Claims on Nonbank Financial Insts.	12g	....	....	302	85	6	26	853	520	102	334	263	261
Reserve Money	14	31,352	35,148	† 43,548	91,008	72,415	100,627	109,843	142,103	177,441	217,217	244,622	303,961
of which: Currency Outside DMBs.	14a	23,604	30,023	† 36,186	57,260	61,492	82,815	88,854	116,153	148,015	188,448	204,733	231,274
Time, Savings,& Fgn.Currency Dep.	15	....	....	812	5,397	259	1,394	4,975	3,363	4,526	4,628	2,909	4,305
Restricted Deposits	16b			3	213	24	34	54	31	103	94	182	248
Foreign Liabilities	16c	377,912	463,327	† 223,385	264,752	365,182	505,898	339,520	408,560	433,041	494,654	593,480	594,123
Central Government Deposits	16d	5,936	10,955	† 2,042	4,528	4,615	5,472	8,415	13,195	42,510	14,849	36,920	73,049
Capital Accounts	17a	24,151	24,156	† 190,151	227,926	153,376	156,239	222,527	261,467	261,538	226,182	198,223	136,570
of which: Valuation Adjustment	17rv	−108,690	−111,158	† 832	−40,714	−57,997	−135,494	8,177	−9,614	−54,187	−116,625	−177,722	−216,852
Other Items (Net)	17r	54,124	−75,639	† −14,373	−66,491	−34,661	−144,178	36,937	−59,436	−65,996	−101,140	−79,131	−1,177
Deposit Money Banks					*Millions of Leones: End of Period*								
Reserves	20	7,523	4,701	† 5,926	26,240	8,088	23,229	20,543	17,047	21,696	20,099	27,999	56,276
Foreign Assets	21	10,378	21,232	† 18,079	20,852	30,555	40,852	40,611	47,295	58,383	78,839	100,055	149,884
Claims on Central Government	22a	9,921	12,763	† 18,470	10,311	41,161	72,209	71,752	100,748	130,035	121,829	151,374	205,695
Claims on Nonfin.Pub.Enterprises	22c	81	21	† 30	335	63	68	622	486	950	3,647	3,440	4,338
Claims on Private Sector	22d	16,576	17,276	† 20,705	24,506	26,895	24,234	27,035	32,974	50,559	91,406	133,362	154,052
Claims on Nonbank Financial Insts.	22g	....	....	598	594	2,094	2,165	10,803	11,649	16,732	14,397	15,547	16,649
Demand Deposits	24	14,719	19,462	† 15,616	24,494	25,875	47,800	48,447	67,452	90,808	94,415	127,416	176,649
Time, Savings,& Fgn.Currency Dep.	25	16,955	16,481	† 32,044	37,625	50,896	58,686	72,674	98,064	124,834	161,754	204,148	295,700
Foreign Liabilities	26c	1,761	2,896	† —									
Central Government Deposits	26d	1,916	2,172	† 2,102	3,190	5,059	14,107	13,266	10,894	21,244	23,196	19,547	34,485
Credit from Monetary Authorities	26g			† 74	74	42	21	—	—	—	—	—	—
Capital Accounts	27a	5,483	8,961	† 20,564	18,607	22,994	34,664	48,899	60,975	76,176	84,301	112,428	139,668
Other Items (Net)	27r	3,645	6,021	† −6,591	−1,153	3,990	7,480	−11,920	−27,186	−34,706	−33,450	−31,760	−59,609
Monetary Survey					*Millions of Leones: End of Period*								
Foreign Assets (Net)	31n	−338,852	−396,296	† −178,045	−190,891	−251,499	−367,011	−212,524	−245,811	−183,182	−247,119	−127,895	61,250
Domestic Credit	32	481,758	426,184	† 452,793	501,856	537,572	604,813	723,811	774,627	795,931	880,963	875,770	875,433
Claims on Central Govt. (Net)	32an	464,940	408,563	† 429,891	473,523	506,752	577,463	683,477	727,016	721,414	769,255	721,021	689,650
Claims on Nonfin.Pub.Enterprises	32c	81	21	† 233	538	76	134	635	499	963	3,661	3,453	4,351
Claims on Private Sector	32d	16,736	17,600	† 21,736	27,083	28,644	25,022	28,043	34,943	56,719	93,317	135,486	159,647
Claims on Other Banking Insts.	32f	....	....	33	34	—	4	—	—	—	—	—	4,875
Claims on Nonbank Financial Inst.	32g	....	....	900	679	2,100	2,190	11,656	12,169	16,834	14,730	15,810	16,910
Money	34	38,542	49,902	† 53,208	83,611	89,744	134,078	139,957	189,437	247,478	292,950	344,524	424,173
Quasi-Money	35	16,955	16,481	† 32,856	43,022	51,155	60,080	77,649	101,427	129,360	166,383	207,057	300,005
Restricted Deposits	36b			3	213	24	34	54	31	103	94	182	248
Capital Accounts	37a	29,633	33,116	† 210,715	246,533	176,370	190,903	271,426	322,443	337,714	310,483	310,651	276,238
Other Items (Net)	37r	57,775	−69,611	† −22,033	−62,414	−31,221	−147,294	22,201	−84,521	−101,905	−136,066	−114,538	−63,982
Money plus Quasi-Money	35l	55,497	66,383	† 86,064	126,633	140,899	194,159	217,605	290,864	376,838	459,333	551,581	724,178
Interest Rates					*Percent Per Annum*								
Treasury Bill Rate	60c	12.19	14.73	29.25	12.71	22.10	32.42	26.22	13.74	15.15	15.68	26.14	22.98
Deposit Rate	60l	11.63	7.03	13.96	9.91	7.12	9.50	9.25	7.67	8.23	8.42	10.14	11.07
Lending Rate	60p	27.33	28.83	32.12	23.87	23.83	26.83	26.25	24.27	22.17	20.00	22.08	24.58
Prices					*Index Numbers (2000=100): Period Averages*								
Consumer Prices	64	31.1	39.2	48.3	55.5	75.2	100.8	100.0	102.1	98.7	106.2	121.3	135.9
Intl. Transactions & Positions					*Millions of Leones*								
Exports	70	68,010	30,148	43,004	15,412	10,482	11,347	26,771	57,897	102,010	217,742	374,086	457,676
Imports, c.i.f.	71	88,492	102,488	193,628	80,010	148,226	153,856	314,639	368,323	554,838	707,909	775,045	995,950

		1994	1995	1996	1997	1998	1999	2000	2001	2002	2003	2004	2005
Balance of Payments		*Millions of US Dollars: Minus Sign Indicates Debit*											
Current Account, n.i.e.	78ald	−89.1	−118.1	−150.5	−54.9	−33.2	−99.3	−112.3	−97.9	−73.2	−80.0	−74.3	....
Goods: Exports f.o.b.	78aad	116.0	41.5	46.8	15.7	31.6	6.3	12.8	29.2	59.8	110.8	154.1	....
Goods: Imports f.o.b.	78abd	−188.7	−168.1	−226.5	−71.9	−88.8	−86.8	−136.9	−165.1	−254.9	−310.7	−252.5	....
Trade Balance	78acd	−72.7	−126.7	−179.7	−56.2	−57.2	−80.5	−124.1	−136.0	−195.1	−199.9	−98.4	....
Services: Credit	78add	100.2	86.8	62.9	31.9	19.1	22.3	42.2	52.0	38.3	66.1	61.4	....
Services: Debit	78aed	−107.6	−91.8	−107.7	−47.8	−39.2	−100.9	−112.8	−110.9	−80.8	−93.8	−89.4	....
Balance on Goods & Services	78afd	−80.1	−131.7	−224.5	−72.1	−77.4	−159.1	−194.7	−194.9	−237.5	−227.6	−126.5	....
Income: Credit	78agd	1.5	.7	.8	1.5	6.8	6.2	7.4	4.3	18.3	1.7	4.1	....
Income: Debit	78ahd	−57.0	−30.3	−12.4	−9.4	−27.3	−14.1	−12.6	−14.8	−21.1	−16.7	−71.1	....
Balance on Gds, Serv. & Inc	78aid	−135.7	−161.3	−236.1	−80.0	−97.8	−167.0	−199.9	−205.4	−240.4	−242.6	−193.5	....
Current Transfers, n.i.e.: Credit	78ajd	47.5	44.0	87.2	25.9	65.2	68.6	92.3	120.7	170.8	167.6	122.0	....
Current Transfers: Debit	78akd	−.9	−.8	−1.6	−.8	−.6	−1.0	−4.7	−13.2	−3.6	−5.0	−2.8	....
Capital Account, n.i.e.	78bcd	.1	—	.1	.1	—	—	—	.2	50.6	71.0	81.3	....
Capital Account, n.i.e.: Credit	78bad	.1	—	.1	.1	—	—	—	.4	50.6	71.0	81.3	....
Capital Account: Debit	78bbd	—	—	—	—	—	—	—	−.1				....
Financial Account, n.i.e.	78bjd	−25.5	97.9	31.2	15.4	10.6	−27.3	124.6	30.1	10.0	28.1	57.4	....
Direct Investment Abroad	78bdd	—	—	....	....	....	....	....	....	—	—	....	....
Dir. Invest. in Rep. Econ., n.i.e.	78bed	−2.9	7.3	.7	1.8	.1	.5	39.0	9.8	1.6	3.1	26.1	....
Portfolio Investment Assets	78bfd	—	—	....	....	....	....	....	....	.1	—	....	....
Equity Securities	78bkd	—	—	....	....	....	....	....	....	.1	—	....	....
Debt Securities	78bld	—	—	....	....	....	....	....	....			....	....
Portfolio Investment Liab., n.i.e.	78bgd	—	—	....	....	....	....	....	....			....	....
Equity Securities	78bmd	—	—	....	....	....	....	....	....			....	....
Debt Securities	78bnd	—	—	....	....	....	....	....	....			....	....
Financial Derivatives Assets	78bwd	....	....	....	....	....	....	....	....	....	....	....	....
Financial Derivatives Liabilities	78bxd	....	....	....	....	....	....	....	....	....	....	....	....
Other Investment Assets	78bhd	−.8	15.6	1.8	−.9	−50.8	−31.3	44.2	−3.5	8.1	.5	10.1	....
Monetary Authorities	78bod	....	....	....	....	....	....	....	....	.8	.5	—	....
General Government	78bpd	—	—	....	....	....	....	....	....	—	—	....	....
Banks	78bqd	4.4	15.9	3.5	−.9	−6.3	−5.7	.1	−3.4	1.9	—	5.7	....
Other Sectors	78brd	−5.2	−.4	−1.6	—	−44.4	−25.6	44.1	−.1	5.4	—	4.3	....
Other Investment Liab., n.i.e.	78bid	−21.8	75.1	28.7	14.5	61.3	3.4	41.3	23.7	.2	24.4	21.2	....
												4.2	....
Monetary Authorities	78bsd	—	—	—	—	—	—	—	—	—	—	−16.6	....
General Government	78btd	−15.2	69.2	30.7	14.6	62.4	30.3	43.4	45.7	.2	24.4		
Banks	78bud	2.8	−1.5	—	—	—	—	—	—	—	—	33.6	....
Other Sectors	78bvd	−9.5	7.4	−1.9	−.1	−1.1	−26.9	−2.1	−22.1	—	—	−59.5	....
Net Errors and Omissions	78cad	55.1	21.5	97.1	59.1	24.7	110.5	−2.5	97.2	−7.4	−47.6	4.9	....
Overall Balance	78cbd	−59.5	1.3	−22.2	19.7	2.1	−16.1	9.8	29.6	−20.1	−28.6	−4.9	....
Reserves and Related Items	79dad	59.5	−1.3	22.2	−19.7	−2.1	16.1	−9.8	−29.6	20.1	28.6	4.9	....
Reserve Assets	79dbd	−18.6	−17.2	10.9	−26.7	−18.2	7.2	2.0	−13.9	−32.3	24.3	−45.2	....
Use of Fund Credit and Loans	79dcd	55.1	15.9	11.3	7.0	16.1	8.9	−11.8	−15.8	5.0	−14.8	18.5	....
Exceptional Financing	79ded	22.9	—	....	....	....	....	....	....	47.4	19.2	21.7	....
International Investment Position		*Millions of US Dollars*											
Assets	79aad	....	....	....	....	....	....	....	50.9	84.9	65.1	131.2	....
Direct Investment Abroad	79abd	....	....	....	....	....	....	....	—	—	—	—	....
Portfolio Investment	79acd	....	....	....	....	....	....	....	.2	—	—	—	....
Equity Securities	79add	....	....	....	....	....	....	....		—	—	—	....
Debt Securities	79aed	....	....	....	....	....	....	....	.2	—	—	—	....
Financial Derivatives	79ald	....	....	....	....	....	....	....		—	—	—	....
Other Investment	79afd	....	....	....	....	....	....	....	9.4	8.6	8.1	25.0	....
Monetary Authorities	79agd	....	....	....	....	....	....	....	9.4	8.6	8.1	8.1	....
General Government	79ahd	....	....	....	....	....	....	....	—	—	—	—	....
Banks	79aid	....	....	....	....	....	....	....	—	—	—	16.9	....
Other Sectors	79ajd	....	....	....	....	....	....	....	—	—	—	—	....
Reserve Assets	79akd	....	....	....	....	....	....	....	41.2	76.3	57.0	106.2	....
Liabilities	79lad	....	....	....	....	....	....	....	1,265.9	1,516.6	1,624.5	1,770.4	....
Dir. Invest. in Rep. Economy	79lbd	....	....	....	....	....	....	....	—	18.5	15.8	27.9	....
Portfolio Investment	79lcd	....	....	....	....	....	....	....	—	—	—	—	....
Equity Securities	79ldd	....	....	....	....	....	....	....	—	—	—	—	....
Debt Securities	79led	....	....	....	....	....	....	....	—	—	—	—	....
Financial Derivatives	79lld	....	....	....	....	....	....	....	—	—	—	—	....
Other Investment	79lfd	....	....	....	....	....	....	....	1,265.9	1,498.2	1,608.7	1,742.5	....
Monetary Authorities	79lgd	....	....	....	....	....	....	....	151.8	283.6	266.8	283.3	....
General Government	79lhd	....	....	....	....	....	....	....	1,114.1	1,214.6	1,341.9	1,427.1	....
Banks	79lid	....	....	....	....	....	....	....	—	—	—	32.1	....
Other Sectors	79ljd	....	....	....	....	....	....	....	—	—	—	—	....
Government Finance		*Millions of Leones: Year Ending December 31*											
Deficit (-) or Surplus	80	−26,123	−39,835	−49,925	−48,300	† −47,724	−102,373	−124,064	−165,349	−163,447	−130,816	−70,273	....
Revenue	81	67,414	61,743	69,713	85,498	† 77,199	85,819	152,174	207,879	238,689	287,657	356,966	....
Grants Received	81z	11,117	5,734	8,529	9,495	† 22,456	65,391	106,107	86,143	161,355	179,343	259,376	....
Expenditure	82	104,654	107,312	128,167	143,293	† 147,052	252,884	370,697	455,922	562,267	597,999	688,092	....
Lending Minus Repayments	83	—	—	—	—	† 327	699	11,648	3,449	1,224	−183	−1,477	....
Financing													
Domestic	84a	−1,681	2,431	25,270	7,488	† 47,784	88,807	11,679	53,135	22,095	88,405	−1,949	....
Foreign	85a	27,804	37,404	24,655	40,812	† −60	13,566	112,385	106,204	157,768	56,133	122,171	....
Other Financing	84d	....	....	....	....	....	....	....	6,010	−16,416	−13,722	−49,949	....
Debt: Domestic	88a	24,311	26,007	41,613	52,368	† 133,201	231,666	232,663	288,477	347,178	413,683	435,935	....
Debt: Foreign	89a	444,894	656,205	966,326	941,853	† 1,840,991	2,755,965	2,153,630	3,120,009	3,268,965	4,196,338	4,900,305	....

Sierra Leone 724

National Accounts		1994	1995	1996	1997	1998	1999	2000	2001	2002	2003	2004	2005
		Millions of Leones: Year Ending December 31											
Househ.Cons.Expend.,incl.NPISHs....	96f	436,876	566,824	709,799	734,139	887,613	1,040,868	1,142,681	1,398,461	1,528,299	1,713,929	....	....
Government Consumption Expend...	91f	54,247	57,869	84,873	85,954	107,236	119,746	134,374	255,265	325,223	353,541	....	....
Gross Fixed Capital Formation..........	93e	43,901	37,011	78,163	41,765	59,204	52,885	84,761	90,091	114,690	322,945	....	....
Changes in Inventories....................	93i	2,507	−914	8,689	−5,460	−1,427	−10,856	1,143				....	....
Exports of Goods and Services..........	90c	106,848	129,878	171,391	165,415	203,345	225,868	230,179	228,694	293,879	323,534	....	....
Imports of Goods and Services (-).....	98c	109,853	133,973	177,254	192,770	206,062	229,815	261,561	484,986	618,709	850,982	....	....
Gross Domestic Product (GDP).........	99b	535,019	657,604	867,072	834,502	1,051,335	1,207,721	1,330,319	1,600,169	1,964,627	2,323,668	2,894,326	3,356,686
Net Primary Income from Abroad.....	98.n	−70,868	−78,196	−81,853	−92,289	−110,746	−144,985	−165,955	−129,157	−187,167	−194,998	....	....
Gross National Income (GNI)............	99a	473,474	626,173	773,754	725,680	817,068	1,128,867	....	....	....	....	....	....
Consumption of Fixed Capital..........	99cf	34,212	37,470	39,424	71,392	59,226	69,422	49,047	....	....	....	....	....
GDP Volume 1989/90 Prices...........	99b.p	81,066	74,583	79,128	65,205	64,658	59,407	61,669	72,874	92,886	101,513	108,986	117,193
GDP Volume (2000=100)...............	99bvp	131.5	120.9	128.3	105.7	104.8	96.3	100.0	118.2	150.6	164.6	176.7	190.0
GDP Deflator (2000=100)...............	99bip	30.6	40.9	50.8	59.3	75.4	94.2	100.0	101.8	98.0	106.1	123.1	132.8
		Millions: Midyear Estimates											
Population...............................	99z	4.12	4.14	4.17	4.21	4.28	4.38	4.51	4.68	4.89	5.12	5.34	5.53

Singapore 576

		1994	1995	1996	1997	1998	1999	2000	2001	2002	2003	2004	2005
Exchange Rates		\multicolumn{12}{c}{*Singapore Dollars per SDR: End of Period*}											
Market Rate	aa	2.1324	2.1023	2.0129	2.2607	2.3380	2.2866	2.2560	2.3262	2.3608	2.5273	2.5373	2.3786
		\multicolumn{12}{c}{*Singapore Dollars per US Dollar: End of Period (ae) Period Average (rf)*}											
Market Rate	ae	1.4607	1.4143	1.3998	1.6755	1.6605	1.6660	1.7315	1.8510	1.7365	1.7008	1.6338	1.6642
Market Rate	rf	1.5274	1.4174	1.4100	1.4848	1.6736	1.6950	1.7240	1.7917	1.7906	1.7422	1.6902	1.6644
		\multicolumn{12}{c}{*Index Numbers (2000=100): Period Averages*}											
Market Rate	ahx	113.0	121.6	122.2	116.4	103.1	101.7	100.0	96.2	96.3	98.9	102.0	103.6
Nominal Effective Exchange Rate	nec	94.3	97.1	101.3	103.3	105.0	99.7	100.0	101.6	100.8	98.4	97.9	98.7
Real Effective Exchange Rate	rec	104.4	106.2	108.9	110.2	107.5	100.2	100.0	100.5	97.9	94.3	93.3	92.1
Fund Position		\multicolumn{12}{c}{*Millions of SDRs: End of Period*}											
Quota	2f.s	357.6	357.6	357.6	357.6	357.6	862.5	862.5	862.5	862.5	862.5	862.5	862.5
SDRs	1b.s	24.1	33.1	42.5	52.2	64.9	89.2	105.3	119.6	130.2	139.6	188.9	199.6
Reserve Position in the Fund	1c.s	172.8	199.8	204.7	248.4	297.6	303.4	237.7	297.5	351.3	379.3	283.4	121.8
of which: Outstg.Fund Borrowing	2c	—	—	—	—	31.3	—	—	—	—	—	—	—
Total Fund Cred.&Loans Outstg.	2tl	—	—	—	—	—	—	—	—	—	—	—	—
International Liquidity		\multicolumn{12}{c}{*Millions of US Dollars Unless Otherwise Indicated: End of Period*}											
Total Reserves (see notes)	1l.d	58,177	68,695	76,847	71,289	74,928	76,843	80,132	75,375	82,021	95,746	112,232	115,794
SDRs	1b.d	35	49	61	70	91	122	137	150	177	207	293	285
Reserve Position in the Fund	1c.d	252	297	294	335	419	416	310	374	478	564	440	174
Foreign Exchange	1d.d	57,890	68,349	76,491	70,883	74,418	76,304	79,685	74,851	81,367	94,975	111,498	115,334
Monetary Authorities: Other Liab.	4..d	298	262	247	164	150	792	834	731	714	741	917	1,088
Deposit Money Banks: Assets	7a.d	38,992	39,115	43,079	46,963	44,434	52,703	47,567	52,976	53,501	52,827	61,848	70,716
Liabilities	7b.d	40,976	46,753	55,327	62,784	49,747	50,414	54,193	56,062	58,287	59,840	67,696	69,563
Other Banking Insts.: Assets	7e.d	163	168	154	124	107	80	75	51	43	16	17	31
Liabilities	7f.d	27	19	12	11	5	8	4	2	2	1	1	5
ACU: Foreign Assets	7k.d	326,698	373,774	396,655	425,242	394,550	364,733	360,440	339,255	346,865	359,009	403,436	440,481
Foreign Liabilities	7m.d	340,295	391,907	419,343	447,032	417,127	384,962	386,812	375,951	387,285	404,383	464,025	490,509
Monetary Authorities		\multicolumn{12}{c}{*Millions of Singapore Dollars: End of Period*}											
Foreign Assets	11	85,166	97,337	107,751	119,617	124,584	128,457	139,260	139,942	142,721	163,190	183,844	193,601
Claims on Central Government	12a	—	—	—	—	—	—	5,250	6,251	5,808	6,395	7,039	7,010
Reserve Money	14	15,577	17,040	18,189	19,200	16,641	21,395	18,471	20,032	19,964	20,653	21,835	23,396
of which: Currency Outside DMBs	14a	9,420	9,907	10,293	10,704	10,146	11,315	11,289	11,868	12,360	12,838	13,694	14,585
Foreign Liabilities	16c	435	371	346	274	249	1,319	1,444	1,353	1,240	1,261	1,498	1,811
Central Government Deposits	16d	35,669	44,471	51,554	57,520	57,484	58,994	69,958	85,106	94,404	94,391	98,497	107,772
Other Items (Net)	17r	33,485	35,455	37,662	42,623	50,210	46,749	54,637	39,702	32,921	53,280	69,053	67,632
Deposit Money Banks		\multicolumn{12}{c}{*Millions of Singapore Dollars: End of Period*}											
Reserves	20	6,150	7,152	7,900	8,498	6,423	10,076	7,174	8,199	7,633	7,798	8,173	8,813
Foreign Assets	21	56,956	55,321	60,302	78,687	73,782	87,803	82,363	98,058	92,905	89,848	101,048	117,686
Claims on Central Government	22a	13,568	15,754	17,538	18,883	26,477	30,949	33,719	40,512	42,621	45,556	45,058	43,750
Claims on Private Sector	22d	91,375	109,885	127,272	143,409	154,844	150,199	159,083	185,048	169,048	178,253	186,128	189,793
Demand Deposits	24	13,991	15,443	16,747	16,807	17,093	19,794	21,973	24,215	23,468	25,884	30,468	31,501
Time and Savings Deposits	25	70,569	76,618	84,911	95,933	133,545	143,365	137,636	144,826	144,480	156,106	162,816	173,712
Foreign Liabilities	26c	59,854	66,123	77,447	105,194	82,605	83,990	93,836	103,771	101,215	101,776	110,602	115,766
Central Government Deposits	26d	6,584	7,538	6,896	1,529	1,766	1,632	1,465	2,089	1,768	1,813	1,847	3,080
Other Items (Net)	27r	17,051	22,390	27,011	30,014	26,517	30,246	27,429	56,916	41,276	35,876	34,674	35,983
Monetary Survey		\multicolumn{12}{c}{*Millions of Singapore Dollars: End of Period*}											
Foreign Assets (Net)	31n	81,833	86,164	90,260	92,836	115,512	130,951	126,343	132,876	133,172	150,001	172,792	193,710
Domestic Credit	32	62,699	73,638	86,368	103,251	122,081	120,535	126,640	144,625	121,310	134,001	137,881	129,702
Claims on Central Govt. (Net)	32an	−28,685	−36,255	−40,912	−40,166	−32,773	−29,677	−32,454	−40,432	−47,743	−44,253	−48,247	−60,092
Claims on Private Sector	32d	91,384	109,893	127,280	143,417	154,854	150,212	159,094	185,057	169,052	178,254	186,129	189,794
Money	34	23,411	25,350	27,040	27,511	27,239	31,109	33,262	36,083	35,828	38,722	44,162	46,086
Quasi-Money	35	70,569	76,618	84,911	95,933	133,545	143,365	137,636	144,826	144,480	156,106	162,816	173,712
Other Items (Net)	37r	50,552	57,834	64,677	72,643	76,809	77,012	82,085	96,592	74,173	89,173	103,696	103,614
Money plus Quasi-Money	35l	93,980	101,968	111,951	123,444	160,784	174,474	170,898	180,909	180,308	194,828	206,978	219,798
Other Banking Institutions		\multicolumn{12}{c}{*Millions of Singapore Dollars: End of Period*}											
Finance Companies													
Cash	40	2,574	2,848	2,561	2,513	2,822	3,046	2,017	1,514	1,608	475	622	651
Foreign Assets	41	238	237	215	208	179	133	130	95	75	27	28	51
Claims on Private Sector	42d	15,110	16,717	17,073	18,034	16,891	15,751	15,880	11,919	10,752	6,632	6,854	7,825
Time and Savings Deposits	45	13,753	15,435	15,058	15,734	15,421	14,387	13,653	10,638	9,853	5,528	5,666	6,356
Foreign Liabilities	46c	39	26	16	18	9	14	6	4	3	2	2	9
Capital Accounts	47a	2,203	2,621	3,015	3,269	3,371	3,408	3,165	2,426	2,111	1,406	1,444	1,658
Other Items (Net)	47r	1,927	1,721	1,761	1,734	1,091	1,121	1,203	461	468	198	392	502
Post Office: Savings Deposits	45..i	20,127	22,188	24,734	25,130	....	....	....	....	....	....	....	....
Nonbank Financial Institutions		\multicolumn{12}{c}{*Millions of Singapore Dollars: End of Period*}											
Cash	40..s	1,772	2,269	2,657	3,041	3,809	4,036	3,796	4,057	4,081	4,049	4,375	4,533
Foreign Assets	41..s	1,090	1,546	2,082	2,055	2,696	3,574	7,254	10,926	12,880	16,809	17,779	....
Claims on Central Government	42a.s	918	901	746	815	933	2,417	3,169	6,100	8,280	10,247	13,068	....
Claims on Private Sector	42d.s	5,488	6,715	8,261	10,095	10,392	16,333	18,555	24,525	25,592	29,354	33,888	....
Fixed Assets	42h.s	335	657	1,173	1,377	1,861	1,874	1,868	1,891	2,342	2,344	2,172	2,081
Incr.in Total Assets(Within Per.)	49z.s	1,682	2,481	2,996	2,379	2,564	8,170	6,244	13,148	6,098	9,595	8,217	....
Money (National Definitions)		\multicolumn{12}{c}{*Millions of Singapore Dollars: End of Period*}											
M1	59ma	23,412	25,349	27,040	27,511	27,239	31,109	33,262	36,083	35,828	38,723	44,162	46,086
M2	59mb	93,981	101,967	111,951	123,443	160,784	174,474	170,898	180,909	180,308	194,829	206,978	219,798
M3	59mc	125,835	136,737	148,495	160,766	173,581	186,184	182,913	190,317	188,815	200,044	212,183	225,700
Interest Rates		\multicolumn{12}{c}{*Percent Per Annum*}											
Money Market Rate	60b	3.68	2.56	2.93	4.35	5.00	2.04	2.57	1.99	.96	.74	1.04	2.28
Treasury Bill Rate	60c	1.94	1.05	1.38	2.32	2.12	1.12	2.18	1.69	.81	.64	.96	2.04
Eurodollar Rate in Singapore	60d	4.86	6.04	5.52	5.75	5.53	5.42	6.55	3.66	1.80	1.22	1.67	3.63
Savings Rate	60k	2.31	2.81	2.72	2.75	3.11	1.37	1.33	1.16	.61	.28	.23	.24
Deposit Rate	60l	3.00	3.50	3.41	3.47	4.60	1.68	1.71	1.54	.91	.51	.41	.44
Lending Rate	60p	5.88	6.37	6.26	6.32	7.44	5.80	5.83	5.66	5.37	5.31	5.30	5.30

Singapore 576

		1994	1995	1996	1997	1998	1999	2000	2001	2002	2003	2004	2005
Prices, Production, Labor					*Index Numbers (2000=100): Period Averages*								
Share Prices	62	92.3	87.2	96.5	89.1	59.6	95.2	100.0	80.7	76.6	73.0	93.5	108.7
Wholesale Prices	63	92.7	92.7	92.8	91.8	† 89.0	90.8	100.0	98.4	† 97.0	98.9	104.0	114.0
Consumer Prices	64	94.0	95.6	97.0	98.9	98.6	98.7	100.0	101.0	100.6	101.1	† 102.8	103.3
Manufacturing Production	66ey	64.1	† 70.7	73.0	76.4	† 76.1	86.7	100.0	88.4	95.9	† 98.6	112.3	122.9
						Number in Thousands: Period Averages								
Labor Force	67d	1,693	1,748	1,801	1,876	1,932	1,976	2,192	2,120	2,129	2,150	....	....
Employment	67e	1,649	1,702	1,748	1,831	1,870	1,886	2,095	2,047	2,017	2,034	....	....
Unemployment	67c	1	1	2	3	4	6	4	6	12	16	10	....
Unemployment Rate (%)	67r	2.6	2.7	3.0	2.4	3.2	4.6	4.4	3.4	5.2	5.4		
Intl. Transactions & Positions						*Millions of Singapore Dollars*								
Exports	70	147,327	167,515	176,271	185,613	183,763	194,290	237,826	218,029	223,901	251,096	335,615	382,532
Imports, c.i.f	71	156,397	176,317	185,183	196,606	174,867	188,143	232,176	207,694	208,312	222,811	293,338	333,191
						2000=100								
Volume of Exports	72	61.7	71.4	75.9	81.1	† 81.9	86.4	100.0	95.3	† 100.1	116.5	155.4	173.5
Volume of Imports	73	71.2	80.4	85.4	92.0	† 83.5	88.3	100.0	89.2	....	....	....	....
Export Prices (Survey)	76	100.3	98.6	97.7	96.2	† 94.4	94.6	100.0	96.2	† 94.0	90.6	90.8	92.7
Import Prices (Survey)	76.x	94.5	94.5	93.4	92.0	† 90.3	91.8	100.0	100.3	† 99.6	100.0	101.6	106.9
Balance of Payments					*Millions of US Dollars: Minus Sign Indicates Debit*									
Current Account, n.i.e.	78ald	11,400	14,708	13,853	14,913	18,270	14,773	11,936	14,383	15,727	26,951	27,897	....
Goods: Exports f.o.b.	78aad	97,919	129,557	137,495	138,716	117,717	124,468	149,228	133,744	137,747	158,440	197,343	....
Goods: Imports f.o.b.	78abd	−96,565	−123,105	−130,310	−132,207	−104,306	−112,026	−136,505	−118,036	−120,166	−130,310	−166,104	....
Trade Balance	78acd	1,354	6,452	7,186	6,509	13,411	12,442	12,723	15,709	17,581	28,130	31,239	....
Services: Credit	78add	23,044	27,832	29,195	28,080	23,569	26,373	29,570	29,026	30,833	34,573	41,179	....
Services: Debit	78aed	−13,898	−20,819	−22,333	−22,321	−19,964	−24,772	−28,463	−29,186	−29,424	−33,174	−40,691	....
Balance on Goods & Services	78afd	10,500	13,465	14,047	12,268	17,016	14,042	13,830	15,549	18,990	29,529	31,726	....
Income: Credit	78agd	9,783	12,512	11,993	13,252	12,243	16,227	15,623	13,864	13,285	14,566	15,408	....
Income: Debit	78ahd	−8,222	−10,380	−11,116	−9,430	−9,869	−14,470	−16,357	−13,856	−15,408	−16,007	−18,094	....
Balance on Gds, Serv. & Inc.	78aid	12,061	15,598	14,925	16,089	19,390	15,799	13,096	15,556	16,867	28,088	29,041	....
Current Transfers, n.i.e.: Credit	78ajd	145	160	161	153	131	135	128	122	126	130	134	....
Current Transfers: Debit	78akd	−806	−1,050	−1,232	−1,330	−1,251	−1,161	−1,288	−1,296	−1,266	−1,267	−1,278	....
Capital Account, n.i.e.	78bcd	−84	−73	−139	−190	−226	−191	−163	−161	−160	−168	−182	....
Capital Account, n.i.e.: Credit	78bad	—	—	—	—	—	—	—	—	—	—	—	....
Capital Account: Debit	78bbd	−84	−73	−139	−190	−226	−191	−163	−161	−160	−168	−182	....
Financial Account, n.i.e.	78bjd	−8,841	−1,071	−7,848	−11,699	−17,985	−13,696	−5,526	−18,525	−10,296	−19,633	−12,874	....
Direct Investment Abroad	78bdd	−4,577	−4,463	−7,879	−12,444	−2,337	−7,779	−5,074	−22,799	−4,118	−3,710	−10,601	....
Dir. Invest. in Rep. Econ., n.i.e.	78bed	8,550	11,619	9,499	13,497	7,408	16,602	16,479	14,088	5,725	9,348	16,032	....
Portfolio Investment Assets	78bfd	−7,840	−6,927	−13,312	−14,968	−9,913	−12,486	−13,343	−11,468	−13,114	−13,473	−13,683	....
Equity Securities	78bkd	−7,414	−7,546	−10,337	−12,387	−5,631	−12,889	−8,415	−7,525	−7,253	−6,498	−8,375	....
Debt Securities	78bld	−426	620	−2,975	−2,580	−4,282	403	−4,928	−3,943	−5,862	−6,976	−5,308	....
Portfolio Investment Liab., n.i.e.	78bgd	114	−239	830	−226	1,255	3,398	−1,389	276	−346	3,004	2,338	....
Equity Securities	78bmd	169	−187	677	−444	1,002	3,118	−1,169	−213	−399	1,480	2,910	....
Debt Securities	78bnd	−55	−52	153	219	253	280	−220	488	54	1,524	−572	....
Financial Derivatives Assets	78bwd	....	....	....	....	....	....	....	....	....	....	....	....
Financial Derivatives Liabilities	78bxd	....	....	....	....	....	....	....	....	....	....	....	....
Other Investment Assets	78bhd	−10,999	−11,266	−11,750	−38,445	−3,785	−19,622	−15,493	−3,603	−6,973	−19,396	−36,626	....
Monetary Authorities	78bod	—	—	—	—	—	—	—	—	—	—	—	....
General Government	78bpd	—	—	—	—	—	—	—	—	—	—	—	....
Banks	78bqd	−4,291	1,163	−3,359	−12,289	2,200	−9,873	1,969	−5,876	1,155	10,747	−5,294	....
Other Sectors	78brd	−6,708	−12,428	−8,392	−26,156	−5,984	−9,749	−17,462	2,272	−8,129	−30,143	−31,333	....
Other Investment Liab., n.i.e.	78bid	5,911	10,204	14,765	40,887	−10,613	6,190	13,294	4,981	8,530	4,594	29,667	....
Monetary Authorities	78bsd	—	—	—	—	—	—	—	—	—		....	....
General Government	78btd	−4											
Banks	78bud	5,409	3,970	8,102	18,878	−11,082	3,155	7,702	8,219	−340	−9,091	3,984	....
Other Sectors	78bvd	506	6,235	6,663	22,009	469	3,036	5,592	−3,238	8,870	13,686	25,683	....
Net Errors and Omissions	78cad	2,261	−4,923	1,532	5,091	2,931	3,302	504	3,437	−3,943	−475	−2,753	....
Overall Balance	78cbd	4,736	8,641	7,399	8,114	2,989	4,188	6,751	−867	1,327	6,675	12,087	....
Reserves and Related Items	79dad	−4,736	−8,641	−7,399	−8,114	−2,989	−4,188	−6,751	867	−1,327	−6,675	−12,087	....
Reserve Assets	79dbd	−4,736	−8,641	−7,399	−8,114	−2,989	−4,188	−6,751	867	−1,327	−6,675	−12,087	....
Use of Fund Credit and Loans	79dcd	—	—	—	—	—	—	—	—	—	—	—	....
Exceptional Financing	79ded	....	—	—	—	—	—	—	—	—	—		....
International Investment Position						*Millions of US Dollars*								
Assets	79aad	....	....	....	....	....	....	....	377,362	422,283	465,736	541,339	....
Direct Investment Abroad	79abd	....	....	....	....	....	....	....	81,060	91,609	96,556	111,490	....
Portfolio Investment	79acd	....	....	....	....	....	....	....	58,968	69,559	85,669	102,554	....
Equity Securities	79add	....	....	....	....	....	....	....	30,820	32,932	41,225	49,878	....
Debt Securities	79aed	....	....	....	....	....	....	....	28,148	36,627	44,444	52,676	....
Financial Derivatives	79ald	....	....	....	....	....	....	....	....	....	....	....	....
Other Investment	79afd	....	....	....	....	....	....	....	161,730	178,925	187,563	214,769	....
Monetary Authorities	79agd	....	....	....	....	....	....	....	....	....	....	....	....
General Government	79ahd	....	....	....	....	....	....	....	....	....	....	....	....
Banks	79aid	....	....	....	....	....	....	....	....	....	....	....	....
Other Sectors	79ajd	....	....	....	....	....	....	....	....	....	....	....	....
Reserve Assets	79akd	....	....	....	....	....	....	....	75,604	82,189	95,949	112,525	....
Liabilities	79lad	....	....	....	....	....	....	....	305,518	334,037	377,186	453,123	....
Dir. Invest. in Rep. Economy	79lbd	....	....	....	....	....	....	....	125,200	135,889	151,148	176,927	....
Portfolio Investment	79lcd	....	....	....	....	....	....	....	45,963	45,734	61,799	78,154	....
Equity Securities	79ldd	....	....	....	....	....	....	....	36,250	33,880	47,070	59,195	....
Debt Securities	79led	....	....	....	....	....	....	....	9,713	11,854	14,729	18,959	....
Financial Derivatives	79lld	....	....	....	....	....	....	....	....	....	....	....	....
Other Investment	79lfd	....	....	....	....	....	....	....	134,355	152,413	164,239	198,042	....
Monetary Authorities	79lgd	....	....	....	....	....	....	....	....	....	....	....	....
General Government	79lhd	....	....	....	....	....	....	....	....	....	....	....	....
Banks	79lid	....	....	....	....	....	....	....	....	....	....	....	....
Other Sectors	79ljd	....	....	....	....	....	....	....	....	....	....	....	....

Singapore 576

		1994	1995	1996	1997	1998	1999	2000	2001	2002	2003	2004	2005
Government Finance		*Millions of Singapore Dollars: Year Ending December 31*											
Deficit (-) or Surplus	80	13,086	15,870	18,868	13,612	23,163	14,577	18,094	−467	−2,595	10,422	10,128	13,398
Total Revenue and Grants	81y	33,094	40,026	47,617	57,048	59,724	49,950	52,255	35,393	27,703	33,108	35,269	38,989
Revenue	81	33,094	40,026	47,617	57,048	59,724	49,950	52,255	35,393	27,703	33,108	35,269	38,989
Grants	81z	—	—	—	—	—	—	—	—	—	—	—	—
Exp. & Lending Minus Repay.	82z	20,008	24,156	28,749	43,436	36,561	35,373	34,161	35,860	30,298	22,686	25,141	25,592
Expenditure	82	15,670	17,419	20,681	29,222	25,586	26,665	30,068	34,957	30,985	28,635	30,479	30,337
Lending Minus Repayments	83	4,338	6,737	8,068	14,214	10,975	8,708	4,093	903	−687	−5,948	−5,337	−4,745
Total Financing	80h	−13,086	−15,870	−18,868	−13,612	−23,163	−14,577	−18,093	467	2,595	−10,422	−10,128	−13,398
Total Net Borrowing	84	12,552	16,402	10,159	12,215	22,540	17,148	16,487	8,084	137	13,170	16,119	14,035
Use of Cash Balances	87	−25,638	−32,272	−29,027	−25,827	−45,703	−31,725	−34,580	−7,617	2,458	−23,592	−26,246	−27,433
Total Debt by Currency	88z	75,467	86,630	94,831	102,372	115,183	125,777	134,370	146,996	156,751	169,332	186,598	200,006
National	88b	....	....	94,831	102,372	115,183	125,777	134,370	146,996	156,751	169,332	186,598	200,006
Foreign	89b	....	....	—	—	—	—	—	—	—	—	—	—
National Accounts		*Millions of Singapore Dollars*											
Househ.Cons.Expend.,incl.NPISHs.	96f	47,183	49,085	52,377	56,119	52,906	57,215	65,214	67,478	73,820	74,312	79,166	81,526
Government Consumption Expend.	91f	9,008	10,124	12,207	13,179	13,882	14,007	17,414	18,577	19,454	19,108	19,364	20,687
Gross Fixed Capital Formation	93e	36,202	39,782	49,378	54,826	51,535	47,092	47,538	45,943	40,333	38,901	43,203	42,384
Changes in Inventories	93i	−500	865	−2,850	760	−7,219	−2,352	4,261	−5,369	−2,739	−13,705	−7,909	−6,276
Exports (Net)	90n	16,039	19,107	19,808	18,149	28,490	23,788	23,837	23,182	26,739	45,467	50,154	58,262
Gross Domestic Product (GDP)	99b	107,851	118,963	129,932	141,626	137,329	139,897	159,840	153,393	158,410	161,547	181,704	194,360
Net Primary Income from Abroad	98.n	2,384	3,027	1,238	5,674	3,971	2,978	−1,280	27	−3,778	−2,500	−4,528	....
Gross National Income (GNI)	99a	110,235	121,990	131,170	147,300	141,299	142,875	158,316	153,798	154,610	158,423	176,026	....
GDP Volume 1995 Prices	99b.p	110,109	118,963	128,679	139,696	138,637	148,108	162,379	....	....	....	....	....
GDP Volume 2000 Prices	99b.p	....	....	....	....	....	....	159,840	156,190	162,505	167,271	181,851	193,453
GDP Volume (2000=100)	99bvp	67.8	73.3	79.2	86.0	85.4	91.2	† 100.0	97.7	101.7	104.6	113.8	121.0
GDP Deflator (2000=100)	99bip	99.5	101.6	102.6	103.0	100.6	96.0	100.0	98.2	97.5	96.6	99.9	100.5
		Millions: Midyear Estimates											
Population	99z	3.37	3.48	3.59	3.70	3.82	3.92	4.02	4.10	4.16	4.22	4.27	4.33

Slovak Republic   936

		1994	1995	1996	1997	1998	1999	2000	2001	2002	2003	2004	2005
Exchange Rates						*Koruny per SDR: End of Period*							
Official Rate	aa	45.660	43.954	45.864	46.930	51.975	58.011	61.744	60.910	54.430	49.000	44.255	45.662
					Koruny per US Dollar: End of Period (ae) Period Average (rf)								
Official Rate	ae	31.277	29.569	31.895	34.782	36.913	42.266	47.389	48.467	40.036	32.975	28.496	31.948
Official Rate	rf	32.045	29.713	30.654	33.616	35.233	41.363	46.035	48.355	45.327	36.773	32.257	31.018
					Index Numbers (2000=100): Period Averages								
Nominal Effective Exchange Rate	nec	106.69	107.41	108.39	111.58	109.35	98.69	100.00	97.34	98.61	92.85	106.03	112.65
Real Effective Exchange Rate	rec	83.35	85.71	86.99	91.91	93.31	90.85	100.00	101.80	104.54	104.90	125.59	133.94
Fund Position						*Millions of SDRs: End of Period*							
Quota	2f.s	257.4	257.4	257.4	257.4	257.4	357.5	357.5	357.5	357.5	357.5	357.5	357.5
SDRs	1b.s	58.9	39.0	11.2	19.6	1.2	.6	.4	.5	.8	.9	.9	.9
Reserve Position in the Fund	1c.s	—	—	—	—	—	—	—	—	—	—	—	—
Total Fund Cred.&Loans Outstg.	2tl	439.8	307.5	222.0	184.4	134.6	96.5	—	—	—	—	—	—
International Liquidity					*Millions of US Dollars Unless Otherwise Indicated: End of Period*								
Total Reserves minus Gold	1l.d	1,691	3,364	3,419	3,230	2,869	3,371	4,022	4,141	8,809	11,678	14,417	14,901
SDRs	1b.d	86	58	16	26	2	1	—	1	1	1	1	1
Reserve Position in the Fund	1c.d	—	—	—	—	—	—	—	—	—	—	—	—
Foreign Exchange	1d.d	1,605	3,306	3,403	3,204	2,867	3,370	4,022	4,140	8,808	11,677	14,416	14,899
Gold (Million Fine Troy Ounces)	1ad	1.290	1.290	1.290	1.290	1.290	1.290	1.290	1.129	1.129	1.129	1.129	1.129
Gold (National Valuation)	1and	80	85	79	72	68	59	53	45	55	67	77	69
Monetary Authorities:Other Assets	3..d	153	171	129	202	609	564	203	762	657	367	3,397	5,365
Other Liab.	4..d	1,355	1,428	1,351	659	1,578	760	355	463	299	† 1,100	3,102	5,170
Deposit Money Banks: Assets	7a.d	1,427	1,823	2,514	3,618	3,794	1,618	2,346	2,390	2,053	† 2,324	2,871	3,026
Liabilities	7b.d	499	979	2,160	2,851	2,628	643	644	845	1,498	† 3,141	5,822	10,003
Monetary Authorities						*Millions of Koruny: End of Period*							
Foreign Assets	11	60,184	107,032	115,665	121,904	130,881	168,820	202,763	239,806	381,180	† 399,377	509,823	649,630
Claims on Central Government	12a	46,456	25,743	30,068	5,495	9,067	1,778	—	—	—	† 7,700		
Claims on Other Resident Sectors	12d	305	189	327	416	509	481	382	346	286	† 10,617	7,673	318
Claims on Banking Institutions	12e	36,143	36,485	36,585	41,340	55,242	40,225	36,236	37,802	15,073	† 8,067	4,768	3,873
Reserve Money	14	48,319	63,208	81,339	96,134	90,768	108,925	113,310	138,902	141,201	† 130,898	131,960	160,722
of which: Currency Outside BIs	14a	28,101	34,536	43,505	48,740	49,759	57,472	67,048	80,963	84,211	† 91,826	100,450	119,836
Other Liabilities to Banking Insts	14n	225	13,324	1,833	2,682	3,369	15,191	118,534	56,572	126,826	† 105,683	218,895	363,548
Other Deposits	15	25	60	131	117	86	364	545	739	1,636	† 1,465	1,016	533
Foreign Liabilities	16c	62,454	55,736	53,259	31,559	65,244	37,727	16,813	22,427	11,979	† 36,277	88,388	165,185
Central Government Deposits	16d	11,726	16,152	18,060	16,558	11,650	25,526	27,725	31,162	115,434	† 116,378	83,783	3,156
Bonds	16n	....	....	....	....	....	....	....	....	....	55,760	59,725	20,004
Capital Accounts	17a	7,977	8,239	9,244	9,316	10,322	10,580	10,573	14,787	10,802	† −16,105	−53,828	−50,093
Other Items (Net)	17r	12,362	12,730	18,779	12,791	14,261	12,991	−48,119	13,365	−11,340	† −4,596	−7,674	−9,234
Banking Institutions						*Millions of Koruny: End of Period*							
Reserves	20	3,445	7,607	10,830	12,541	10,335	12,222	51,141	45,042	48,677	† 37,378	30,295	40,622
Other Claims on Monetary Author.	20n	16,211	21,433	28,798	37,564	32,406	41,428	† 26,320	51,366	84,719	† 161,470	274,495	383,499
Foreign Assets	21	44,634	53,916	80,189	125,842	140,045	68,402	111,169	115,818	82,200	† 76,619	81,812	96,686
Claims on Central Government	22a	50,693	74,653	89,709	112,716	93,002	76,936	113,360	301,964	289,192	† 258,052	283,139	258,410
Claims on Other General Govt	22b	....	....	....	....	....	....	....	....	....	† 7,577	12,043	15,051
Claims on Other Resident Sectors	22d	201,643	211,839	280,307	† 399,242	420,986	460,428	479,203	379,653	435,123	† 379,002	406,270	521,423
Demand Deposits	24	94,931	113,179	129,528	116,651	96,863	95,586	118,916	144,603	160,560	† 261,072	303,057	347,940
Other Deposits	25	174,427	203,328	236,632	† 279,996	320,891	368,800	414,933	446,841	454,399	† 413,032	414,839	381,281
Bonds	26n	—	5,228	5,906	5,217	3,968	7,045	8,196	6,172	11,212	† 12,239	12,178	19,127
Foreign Liabilities	26c	14,909	28,342	68,212	98,410	95,367	25,815	28,616	39,167	54,736	† 103,566	165,916	319,587
Central Government Deposits	26d	12,151	25,436	33,197	31,917	28,018	23,248	34,230	41,446	42,246	† 12,117	41,610	77,576
Credit from Monetary Authorities	26g	37,705	38,406	40,224	51,606	61,528	40,741	37,402	30,661	13,016	† 7,913	4,737	3,842
Money Market Fund Shares	26m	....	....	....	....	....	....	....	....	....	....	32,872	45,979
Capital Accounts	27a	63,813	66,953	76,526	82,642	95,243	93,704	103,940	115,301	100,459	† 136,024	137,284	138,994
Other Items (Net)	27r	−82,948	−116,453	−113,127	† 7,453	−18,724	−5,567	25,943	62,414	98,066	† −25,865	−24,441	−18,635
Banking Survey						*Millions of Koruny: End of Period*							
Foreign Assets (Net)	31n	27,455	76,870	74,383	117,778	110,315	173,679	268,503	294,030	396,665	† 336,153	337,330	261,545
Domestic Credit	32	275,220	270,836	349,154	† 469,394	483,896	490,849	530,990	609,355	566,921	† 534,452	583,732	714,470
Claims on Central Govt. (Net)	32an	73,272	58,808	68,520	69,736	62,401	29,940	51,405	229,356	131,512	† 137,256	157,747	177,677
Claims on Other General Govt	32b	....	....	....	....	....	....	....	....	....	† 7,577	12,043	15,051
Claims on Other Resident Sectors	32d	201,948	212,028	280,634	† 399,658	421,495	460,909	479,585	379,999	435,409	† 389,619	413,942	521,741
Money	34	123,820	149,657	173,350	165,658	146,833	153,058	185,964	225,566	244,771	† 353,971	404,722	468,039
Quasi-Money	35	174,452	203,388	236,763	† 280,113	320,977	369,164	415,478	447,580	456,035	† 414,497	415,855	381,814
Money Market Fund Shares	36m	....	....	....	....	....	....	....	....	....	—	32,872	45,979
Bonds	36n	952	9,642	17,952	18,474	15,939	15,709	15,319	11,645	11,212	† 67,999	71,902	39,131
Capital Accounts	37a	71,790	75,192	85,770	91,958	105,565	104,284	114,513	130,088	111,261	† 119,919	83,457	88,901
Other Items (Net)	37r	−69,025	−90,788	−90,987	† 30,214	3,249	20,934	66,325	86,741	135,089	† −85,780	−87,745	−47,850
Money plus Quasi-Money	35l	298,272	353,045	410,113	† 445,771	467,810	522,222	601,442	673,146	700,806	† 768,468	820,577	849,853
Interest Rates						*Percent Per Annum*							
Bank Rate (End of Period)	60	12.00	9.75	8.80	8.80	8.80	8.80	8.80	† 7.75	6.50	6.00	4.00	3.00
Money Market Rate	60b	....	....	....	....	....	....	8.08	7.76	6.33	6.08	3.82	3.02
Deposit Rate	60l	9.32	9.01	9.30	13.44	16.25	14.37	8.45	6.46	6.65	5.33	4.14	† 2.44
Lending Rate	60p	14.56	16.85	13.92	18.65	21.17	21.07	14.89	11.24	10.25	8.46	9.07	† 6.68
Government Bond Yield	61	....	....	....	....	....	....	8.34	8.06	6.91	4.99	5.02	3.52

Slovak Republic 936

		1994	1995	1996	1997	1998	1999	2000	2001	2002	2003	2004	2005
Prices, Production, Labor		\multicolumn{12}{c}{*Index Numbers (2000=100): Period Averages*}											
Producer Prices	63	71.6	78.1	† 81.3	85.0	87.7	91.1	100.0	† 106.6	108.8	117.9	121.9	127.7
Consumer Prices	64	61.3	67.4	† 71.3	75.7	80.7	89.3	100.0	† 107.3	110.9	120.4	129.5	133.0
Harmonized CPI (2002=100)	64h	....	....	....	....	....	....	....	....	100.0	† 108.4	116.5	119.8
Wages	65	55.1	62.9	71.3	80.7	87.5	93.9	100.0	108.2	118.2	125.7	138.5	151.1
Industrial Production	66	78.0	86.1	88.3	89.4	94.2	92.2	100.0	106.9	113.7	119.5	124.2	129.0
Employment	67	100.0	102.2	103.0	102.6	102.8	100.6	100.0	107.4	107.6	109.5	109.8	112.1
		\multicolumn{12}{c}{*Number in Thousands: Period Averages*}											
Labor Force	67d	2,511	2,481	....	2,473	....	2,558	2,594	2,634	2,623	2,629	2,659	....
Employment	67e	2,110	2,147	2,225	2,206	2,199	2,132	2,102	2,124	2,127	2,165	2,170	2,216
Unemployment	67c	334	325	278	297	317	417	485	508	487	459	481	428
Unemployment Rate (%)	67r	13.7	13.1	11.3	11.8	12.5	16.2	18.6	19.2	18.5	17.5	18.1	16.2
Intl. Transactions & Positions		\multicolumn{12}{c}{*Millions of Koruny*}											
Exports	70	214,375	255,096	270,643	277,434	377,807	423,648	548,527	611,325	652,018	803,238	889,705	994,571
Imports, c.i.f	71	218,638	273,831	350,847	361,833	483,773	492,337	619,789	749,775	785,374	868,982	981,075	1,124,439
Imports, f.o.b	71.v	211,811	260,791	340,903	345,006	460,736	468,892	590,275	714,071	747,975	827,602	934,357	1,070,894
Balance of Payments		\multicolumn{12}{c}{*Millions of US Dollars: Minus Sign Indicates Debit*}											
Current Account, n.i.e	78ald	671	390	−2,090	−1,961	−2,126	−1,155	−694	....	−1,955	−282	....	....
Goods: Exports f.o.b	78aad	6,706	8,591	8,824	9,641	10,720	10,201	11,896	....	14,460	21,944	....	....
Goods: Imports f.o.b	78abd	−6,645	−8,820	−11,106	−11,725	−13,071	−11,310	−12,791	....	−16,626	−22,593	....	....
Trade Balance	78acd	61	−229	−2,283	−2,084	−2,351	−1,109	−895	....	−2,166	−649	....	....
Services: Credit	78add	2,261	2,378	2,066	2,167	2,292	1,899	2,241	....	2,812	3,297	....	....
Services: Debit	78aed	−1,600	−1,838	−2,028	−2,094	−2,276	−1,844	−1,805	....	−2,351	−3,056	....	....
Balance on Goods & Services	78afd	722	311	−2,245	−2,011	−2,334	−1,054	−459	....	−1,705	−408	....	....
Income: Credit	78agd	155	250	224	315	437	268	268	....	342	907	....	....
Income: Debit	78ahd	−275	−263	−270	−438	−595	−568	−623	....	−791	−1,026	....	....
Balance on Gds, Serv. & Inc	78aid	602	297	−2,291	−2,135	−2,492	−1,353	−814	....	−2,154	−527	....	....
Current Transfers, n.i.e.: Credit	78ajd	166	243	483	540	645	466	344	....	480	537	....	....
Current Transfers: Debit	78akd	−98	−150	−282	−367	−279	−268	−224	....	−282	−292	....	....
Capital Account, n.i.e	78bcd	84	46	30	—	70	158	91	....	110	102	....	....
Capital Account, n.i.e.: Credit	78bad	84	46	30	—	83	171	106	....	130	195	....	....
Capital Account: Debit	78bbd	—	—	—	—	−12	−13	−15	....	−20	−93	....	....
Financial Account, n.i.e	78bjd	71	1,211	2,268	1,780	1,912	1,789	1,472	....	5,230	1,661	....	....
Direct Investment Abroad	78bdd	−14	−10	−48	−95	−145	376	−22	....	−3	−24	....	....
Dir. Invest. in Rep. Econ., n.i.e	78bed	270	236	351	174	562	354	2,052	....	4,104	559	....	....
Portfolio Investment Assets	78bfd	−26	157	−12	−81	−57	247	−195	....	265	−742	....	....
Equity Securities	78bkd	−26	174	69	86	33	2	11	....	1	−347	....	....
Debt Securities	78bld	—	−17	−81	−167	−91	246	−206	....	263	−395	....	....
Portfolio Investment Liab., n.i.e	78bgd	304	53	29	93	841	405	1,016	....	289	168	....	....
Equity Securities	78bmd	111	−16	28	102	−35	47	−53	....	10	59	....	....
Debt Securities	78bnd	193	69	1	−10	876	358	1,069	....	279	109	....	....
Financial Derivatives Assets	78bwd	—	—	—	—	—	....	....	....	—	−43	....	....
Financial Derivatives Liabilities	78bxd	—	—	—	—	—	....	1	....	3	60	....	....
Other Investment Assets	78bhd	−548	−116	−334	−1,028	190	1,713	−973	....	738	−20	....	....
Monetary Authorities	78bod	....	....	....	....	—	—	—	....	....	—	....	....
General Government	78bpd	−211	140	337	61	117	9	1	....	299	58	....	....
Banks	78bqd	−344	−248	−662	−1,122	110	1,878	−748	....	569	114	....	....
Other Sectors	78brd	7	−8	−10	33	−37	−174	−226	....	−130	−192	....	....
Other Investment Liab., n.i.e	78bid	84	891	2,282	2,718	520	−1,307	−407	....	−165	1,703	....	....
Monetary Authorities	78bsd	38	42	52	153	55	14	−26	....	−198	618	....	....
General Government	78btd	−52	−173	−124	184	−321	55	149	....	−333	−30	....	....
Banks	78bud	38	463	1,440	1,084	−138	−1,882	30	....	390	1,260	....	....
Other Sectors	78bvd	60	559	914	1,298	924	506	−561	....	−23	−146	....	....
Net Errors and Omissions	78cad	380	144	162	280	−333	−14	51	....	298	27	....	....
Overall Balance	78cbd	1,205	1,791	370	99	−478	777	920	....	3,684	1,508	....	....
Reserves and Related Items	79dad	−1,205	−1,791	−370	−99	478	−777	−920	....	−3,684	−1,508	....	....
Reserve Assets	79dbd	−1,256	−1,590	−245	−47	545	−725	−794	....	−3,684	−1,508	....	....
Use of Fund Credit and Loans	79dcd	˙51	−201	−125	−52	−67	−52	−125	....	—	—	....	....
Exceptional Financing	79ded	....	....	....	....	....	....	....	....	....	....	....	....
International Investment Position		\multicolumn{12}{c}{*Millions of US Dollars*}											
Assets	79aad	8,421	10,156	10,311	10,648	10,322	8,652	10,089	10,535	14,680	19,479	....	....
Direct Investment Abroad	79abd	166	139	182	234	404	342	364	448	486	627	....	....
Portfolio Investment	79acd	429	259	282	330	406	146	336	858	686	1,786	....	....
Equity Securities	79add	424	234	171	71	35	28	15	19	42	447	....	....
Debt Securities	79aed	5	25	111	259	371	118	321	838	644	1,340	....	....
Financial Derivatives	79ald	—	—	—	—	—	—	—	—	—	59	....	....
Other Investment	79afd	5,633	5,896	5,948	6,461	6,267	4,419	5,006	4,769	4,313	4,878	....	....
Monetary Authorities	79agd	—	—	—	—	—	—	—	—	—	—	....	....
General Government	79ahd	2,947	2,928	2,393	2,136	1,897	1,657	1,484	1,465	1,101	1,248	....	....
Banks	79aid	1,451	1,676	2,276	3,141	3,203	1,526	2,186	2,002	1,660	1,538	....	....
Other Sectors	79ajd	1,234	1,291	1,280	1,185	1,167	1,236	1,335	1,301	1,552	2,092	....	....
Reserve Assets	79akd	2,192	3,862	3,898	3,623	3,244	3,745	4,384	4,461	9,196	12,129	....	....
Liabilities	79lad	6,137	7,316	9,769	11,848	14,656	13,200	14,368	15,956	20,513	28,183	....	....
Dir. Invest. in Rep. Economy	79lbd	897	1,297	2,046	2,083	2,890	3,188	4,504	5,582	8,530	11,864	....	....
Portfolio Investment	79lcd	583	608	563	595	1,549	2,039	2,830	2,878	3,323	4,166	....	....
Equity Securities	79ldd	56	43	62	157	102	341	260	401	509	493	....	....
Debt Securities	79led	527	565	500	438	1,447	1,698	2,570	2,477	2,814	3,673	....	....
Financial Derivatives	79lld	—	—	—	—	—	—	—	3	17	108	....	....
Other Investment	79lfd	4,657	5,411	7,161	9,170	10,217	7,974	7,034	7,493	8,644	12,046	....	....
Monetary Authorities	79lgd	682	537	442	507	536	522	324	266	435	1,049	....	....
General Government	79lhd	1,101	958	786	912	621	671	788	1,059	944	1,049	....	....
Banks	79lid	537	901	2,290	3,109	2,950	680	687	876	1,534	3,152	....	....
Other Sectors	79ljd	2,338	3,015	3,642	4,642	6,109	6,100	5,235	5,291	5,732	6,700	....	....

Slovak Republic   936

		1994	1995	1996	1997	1998	1999	2000	2001	2002	2003	2004	2005
Government Finance						*Millions of Koruny: Year Ending December 31*							
Deficit (-) or Surplus	80	....	....	−8,540	−28,430	−28,663	−26,637	−27,464	−32,012	110,172	−33,537	....	....
Total Revenue and Grants	81y	....	....	254,769	265,402	274,888	315,683	325,614	331,821	366,636	387,288	....	....
Revenue	81	....	....	254,510	265,146	274,677	315,436	325,402	331,649	366,552	387,242	....	....
Grants	81z	....	....	259	256	211	247	212	172	84	46	....	....
Exp. & Lending Minus Repay	82z	....	....	263,309	293,832	303,551	342,320	353,078	363,833	256,464	420,825	....	....
Expenditure	82	....	....	266,814	290,026	303,952	317,447	368,407	366,901	434,127	438,960	....	....
Lending Minus Repayments	83	....	....	−3,505	3,806	−401	24,873	−15,329	−3,068	−177,663	−18,135	....	....
Total Financing	80h	....	....	8,540	28,430	28,663	26,637	27,464	32,012	−110,172	33,537	....	....
Domestic	84a	....	....	12,761	21,518	−6,057	−2,112	−681	24,080	−104,078	36,489	....	....
Foreign	85a	....	....	−4,221	6,912	34,720	28,749	28,145	7,932	....	−2,952	....	....
Total Debt by Residence	88	....	....	153,910	194,125	215,605	238,061	274,870	417,450	399,947	439,097	....	....
Domestic	88a	....	....	120,741	144,581	141,813	133,625	137,849	293,003	289,132	335,130	....	....
Foreign	89a	....	....	33,169	49,544	73,792	104,436	137,021	124,447	110,815	103,967	....	....
National Accounts							*Millions of Koruny*						
Househ.Cons.Expend.,incl.NPISHs	96f	260,998	300,474	340,434	380,938	429,283	480,795	532,853	592,057	643,471	687,560	768,857	844,183
Government Consumption Expend	91f	102,846	118,427	143,290	153,250	169,808	167,358	187,763	209,199	225,347	249,136	270,730	275,139
Gross Fixed Capital Formation	93e	131,819	144,248	205,846	243,539	281,774	249,792	242,277	291,027	303,481	302,782	327,087	382,632
Changes in Inventories	93i	−27,884	−1,064	15,989	2,628	−16,120	−17,094	1,757	10,814	19,001	−4,275	25,481	35,693
Exports of Goods and Services	90c	296,372	336,007	345,557	405,319	466,740	518,078	661,682	741,313	788,589	927,747	1,018,835	1,133,998
Imports of Goods and Services (-)	98c	268,502	321,590	412,667	472,995	550,048	554,821	685,018	823,815	868,405	950,285	1,055,728	1,199,542
Gross Domestic Product (GDP)	99b	495,649	576,502	638,449	712,679	781,437	844,108	941,314	1,020,595	1,111,484	1,212,665	1,355,262	1,472,103
GDP Volume 1995 Prices	99b.p	544,674	576,502	611,935	640,151	667,107	676,919	696,049	718,504	748,082	779,198	821,399	871,658
GDP Volume (2000=100)	99bvp	78.3	82.8	87.9	92.0	95.8	97.3	100.0	103.2	107.5	111.9	118.0	125.2
GDP Deflator (2000=100)	99bip	67.3	73.9	77.1	82.3	86.6	92.2	100.0	105.0	109.9	115.1	122.0	124.9
							Millions: Midyear Estimates						
Population	99z	5.35	5.36	5.38	5.39	5.39	5.40	5.40	5.40	5.40	5.40	5.40	5.40

Slovenia 961

		1994	1995	1996	1997	1998	1999	2000	2001	2002	2003	2004	2005
Exchange Rates							*Tolars per SDR: End of Period*							
Official Rate	aa	184.61	187.28	203.44	228.27	226.97	270.07	296.25	315.37	300.55	281.39	273.71	289.33
					Tolars per US Dollar: End of Period (ae) Period Average (rf)									
Official Rate	ae	126.46	125.99	141.48	169.18	161.20	196.77	227.38	250.95	221.07	189.37	176.24	202.43
Official Rate	rf	128.81	118.52	135.36	159.69	166.13	181.77	222.66	242.75	240.25	207.11	192.38	192.71
Fund Position							*Millions of SDRs: End of Period*							
Quota	2f.s	150.50	150.50	150.50	150.50	150.50	231.70	231.70	231.70	231.70	231.70	231.70	231.70
SDRs	1b.s	.04	.04	.09	.05	.17	1.17	2.83	4.00	5.13	6.18	7.18	8.13
Reserve Position in the Fund	1c.s	12.87	12.88	12.88	12.88	46.46	78.40	63.19	64.16	88.77	97.34	77.26	36.12
Total Fund Cred.&Loans Outstg.	2tl	4.94	2.69	.90	—	—	—	—	—	—	—	—	—
International Liquidity					*Millions of US Dollars Unless Otherwise Indicated: End of Period*									
Total Reserves minus Gold	1l.d	1,498.98	1,820.79	2,297.36	3,314.67	3,638.52	3,168.00	3,196.01	4,329.99	6,980.23	8,496.91	8,793.39	8,076.37
SDRs	1b.d	.06	.06	.13	.07	.24	1.60	3.69	5.03	6.98	9.18	11.15	11.63
Reserve Position in the Fund	1c.d	18.80	19.14	18.51	17.37	65.41	107.61	82.33	80.63	120.69	144.65	119.98	51.62
Foreign Exchange	1d.d	1,480.12	1,801.59	2,278.71	3,297.22	3,572.87	3,058.79	3,110.00	4,244.33	6,852.57	8,343.09	8,662.27	8,013.12
Gold (Million Fine Troy Ounces)	1ad	.0003	.0003	.0003	.0003	.0003	.0003	.0003	.2431	.2429	.2429	.2428	.1625
Gold (National Valuation)	1and	.12	.13	.12	.09	.09	.09	.09	67.22	83.25	101.09	105.80	83.35
Monetary Authorities:Other Assets	3..d	103.28	170.14	33.70	41.27	46.83	51.95	58.05	76.11	84.72	87.22	100.90	98.68
Other Liab.	4..d	.09	.14	.42	.34	1.05	.63	.48	1.11	.19	.13	9.51	10.56
Deposit Money Banks: Assets	7a.d	2,301.70	2,395.17	2,581.52	1,869.71	2,003.17	1,807.96	2,006.24	3,266.75	2,258.44	2,578.94	3,074.14	4,357.24
Liabilities	7b.d	1,258.55	1,483.20	1,458.57	1,219.38	1,333.58	1,440.06	1,570.22	1,760.66	2,794.88	4,586.06	6,740.61	10,247.46
Monetary Authorities							*Billions of Tolars: End of Period*							
Foreign Assets	11	190.06	250.85	329.81	559.71	594.10	629.76	739.91	1,122.54	1,580.26	1,644.70	1,586.20	1,671.75
Claims on Central Government	12a	15.65	15.28	15.52	15.67	16.01	16.61	17.75	9.81	9.22	26.98	29.72	21.78
Claims on Private Sector	12d	.10	.11	.15	.19	.21	.22	.25	.26	.28	.27	.28	.26
Claims on Deposit Money Banks	12e	29.90	43.06	15.72	18.08	3.91	25.82	6.78	.47	1.29	.09	.08	.11
Reserve Money	14	80.49	100.79	116.55	143.36	171.63	208.23	212.18	287.44	282.27	297.48	309.02	326.05
of which: Currency Outside DMBs	14a	47.28	59.96	66.84	78.12	93.65	125.01	119.82	142.11	143.05	156.04	167.92	187.23
Liabs.of Central Bank: Securities	16ac	99.77	126.67	178.45	364.97	362.48	337.76	365.27	584.69	926.77	1,027.59	924.08	1,052.61
Restricted Deposits	16b	1.82	1.91	.86	2.29	4.30	4.30	4.58	4.91	4.76	8.22	.15	1.63
Foreign Liabilities	16c	.92	.52	.24	.06	.17	.12	.11	.28	.04	.02	1.68	2.14
Central Government Deposits	16d	27.41	47.51	22.30	23.12	18.50	26.25	39.08	60.01	164.77	146.72	188.72	81.34
Capital Accounts	17a	27.17	31.82	43.31	58.65	55.45	96.59	134.96	182.31	191.38	153.70	166.72	204.38
Other Items (Net)	17r	−1.88	.08	−.51	.77	1.69	−.83	8.52	13.45	21.06	38.30	25.92	25.75
Deposit Money Banks							*Billions of Tolars: End of Period*							
Reserves	20	31.07	38.13	48.11	63.09	74.44	79.37	87.42	138.59	130.57	130.65	128.83	129.93
Claims on Mon.Author.:Securities	20c	† 82.42	106.96	160.92	345.08	344.49	327.91	365.32	584.16	919.96	1,027.18	923.08	1,041.96
Foreign Assets	21	291.07	301.77	365.23	316.32	322.91	355.75	456.17	819.78	499.28	488.37	541.79	882.03
Claims on General Government	22a	257.88	315.96	319.59	372.50	407.79	428.33	479.56	548.89	606.08	638.58	745.12	813.23
Claims on Private Sector	22d	427.04	609.72	736.01	829.98	1,066.35	1,313.36	1,538.76	1,828.26	2,067.20	2,385.56	2,865.95	3,525.00
Claims on Other Financial Insts.	22f	5.53	12.75	9.38	12.36	20.36	37.82	51.56	59.05	81.10	106.70	128.00	210.64
Demand Deposits	24	84.15	104.10	127.42	151.36	191.99	237.01	263.47	317.30	533.30	608.48	808.11	917.31
Time, Savings,& Fgn.Currency Dep	25	494.13	647.77	807.04	1,005.28	1,188.44	1,334.29	1,618.56	2,152.14	2,255.13	2,348.74	2,369.98	2,497.48
Money Market Instruments	26aa	12.51	26.97	13.24	18.47	21.37	13.56	24.64	52.56	92.46	115.59	72.94	57.71
Bonds	26ab	8.27	18.09	23.84	33.95	36.28	40.80	53.96	66.30	92.64	114.68	168.15	199.77
Restricted Deposits	26b	10.28	10.98	17.04	17.63	14.93	10.80	15.09	23.08	19.80	18.78	20.26	19.63
Foreign Liabilities	26c	159.15	186.87	206.36	206.29	214.97	283.36	357.03	441.83	617.87	868.45	1,187.98	2,074.39
General Government Deposits	26d	87.22	94.87	140.69	167.98	191.06	190.17	147.10	124.77	173.63	144.60	128.78	198.25
of which: Local Govt. Deposits	26db	8.04	11.43	6.53	6.53	6.91	10.88	11.21	5.46	9.13	10.55	13.53	16.36
Central Govt. Lending Funds	26f	4.87	8.29	12.34	14.04	24.35	27.88	34.35	36.75	46.03	22.93	18.77	18.83
Credit from Monetary Authorities	26g	29.64	41.66	15.28	17.83	3.53	25.47	22.08	260.98	1.17	.01	—	—
Liabilities to Other Financ. Insts.	26i	5.53	10.39	15.43	23.33	33.20	41.84	57.15	71.15	87.67	120.80	142.50	150.69
Capital Accounts	27a	209.53	248.29	273.20	303.74	335.79	372.56	418.82	452.19	499.86	539.31	594.94	684.04
Other Items (Net)	27r	−10.29	−13.00	−12.64	−20.58	−19.57	−35.19	−33.47	−20.34	−115.38	−125.33	−179.64	−215.29
Monetary Survey							*Billions of Tolars: End of Period*							
Foreign Assets (Net)	31n	321.05	365.23	488.45	669.24	701.86	702.03	838.94	1,500.21	1,461.62	1,264.59	938.34	477.26
Domestic Credit	32	591.57	811.45	917.66	1,039.61	1,301.17	1,579.92	1,901.71	2,261.48	2,425.47	2,866.77	3,451.57	4,291.33
Claims on General Govt. (Net)	32an	158.89	188.87	172.13	197.08	214.24	228.52	311.14	373.91	276.89	374.23	457.34	555.42
Claims on Private Sector	32d	427.14	609.83	736.16	830.17	1,066.56	1,313.58	1,539.01	1,828.52	2,067.48	2,385.84	2,866.23	3,525.27
Claims on Other Financial Insts.	32f	5.53	12.75	9.38	12.36	20.36	37.82	51.56	59.05	81.10	106.70	128.00	210.64
Money	34	131.44	164.06	194.29	229.48	287.26	363.70	385.88	462.53	680.49	767.70	982.24	1,107.39
Quasi-Money	35	494.13	647.77	807.04	1,005.28	1,188.44	1,334.29	1,618.56	2,152.15	2,255.17	2,348.75	2,370.34	2,497.91
Money Market Instruments	36aa	12.51	26.97	13.24	18.47	21.37	13.56	24.64	52.56	92.46	115.59	72.94	57.71
Bonds	36ab	8.27	18.09	23.84	33.95	36.28	40.80	53.96	66.30	92.64	114.68	168.15	199.77
Liabs.of Central Bank: Securities	36ac	† 17.35	19.71	17.53	19.89	18.00	9.85	−.05	.52	6.81	.41	.99	10.65
Restricted Deposits	36b	12.10	12.90	17.90	19.92	19.23	15.10	19.68	27.99	24.56	27.00	20.41	21.26
Central Govt. Lending Funds	36f	4.87	8.29	12.34	14.04	24.35	27.88	34.35	36.75	46.03	22.93	18.77	18.83
Liabilities to Other Financ. Insts.	36i	5.53	10.39	15.43	23.33	33.20	41.84	57.15	71.15	87.67	120.80	142.50	150.69
Capital Accounts	37a	236.70	280.11	316.51	362.39	391.24	469.15	553.78	634.50	691.24	693.00	761.65	888.42
Other Items (Net)	37r	−10.29	−11.62	−12.02	−17.90	−16.34	−34.21	−7.30	257.23	−89.96	−79.51	−148.10	−184.03
Money plus Quasi-Money	35l	625.56	811.83	1,001.33	1,234.76	1,475.70	1,697.99	2,004.44	2,614.68	2,935.66	3,116.46	3,352.59	3,605.30
Money (National Definitions)							*Billions of Tolars: End of Period*							
M1	59ma	323.56	416.84	495.84	546.92	634.88	748.82	818.13	1,055.19	1,122.58	1,249.69	1,360.63	† 1,710.71
M2	59mb	679.47	876.50	1,067.95	1,286.38	1,535.69	1,692.88	1,982.93	2,576.75	2,861.19	3,038.05	3,280.90	† 3,521.44
M3	59mc	698.09	909.97	1,089.47	1,307.55	1,557.90	1,717.46	2,013.40	2,605.30	2,881.95	3,068.74	3,302.43	† 3,529.21
Interest Rates							*Percent Per Annum*							
Central Bank Rate (End of Per.)	60	17.00	11.00	11.00	11.00	11.00	9.00	11.00	12.00	10.50	7.25	5.00	5.00
Money Market Rate	60b	29.08	12.18	13.98	9.71	7.45	6.87	6.95	6.90	4.93	5.59	4.40	3.73
Treasury Bill Rate	60c	....	....	....	....	....	8.63	10.94	10.88	8.73	6.53	4.17	3.66
Deposit Rate	60l	28.10	15.38	15.08	13.19	10.54	7.24	10.05	9.81	8.24	5.95	3.82	3.18
Lending Rate	60p	38.87	23.36	22.60	20.02	16.09	12.38	15.77	15.05	13.17	10.75	8.65	7.80
Government Bond Yield	61	15.93	....	....	....	....	....	....	....	....	6.40	4.68	3.81

Slovenia 961

		1994	1995	1996	1997	1998	1999	2000	2001	2002	2003	2004	2005
Prices and Labor					*Index Numbers (2000=100): Period Averages*								
Producer Prices	63	67.2	75.8	80.9	85.8	91.0	92.9	100.0	109.0	114.6	117.5	122.5	125.9
Consumer Prices	64	59.4	† 67.4	† 74.0	80.2	86.5	91.8	100.0	108.4	116.5	123.0	127.4	130.6
Harmonized CPI	64h	....	....	74.0	80.2	86.5	91.8	100.0	108.6	116.7	123.3	127.8	131.0
Wages	65	49.4	58.4	67.4	75.3	82.5	90.4	100.0	111.9	122.9	132.1	139.2	144.7
Employment	67	93.2	93.1	92.7	92.9	91.5	94.7	100.0	100.7	101.0	100.1	100.9	101.6
					Number in Thousands: Period Averages								
Labor Force	67d	873	867	862	869	871	877	907	908	911	899	900	905
Employment	67e	746	745	742	743	733	758	801	806	809	801	807	813
Unemployment	67c	127	121	120	125	126	119	107	102	103	98	93	92
Unemployment Rate (%)	67r	14.5	14.0	13.9	14.4	14.5	13.6	11.8	11.2	11.3	10.9	10.3	10.2
Intl. Transactions & Positions						*Millions of US Dollars*							
Exports	70..d	6,828	8,316	8,312	8,372	9,048	8,546	8,732	9,252	10,357	12,767	15,879	17,793
Imports, c.i.f.	71..d	7,304	9,492	9,423	9,357	10,110	10,083	10,116	10,148	10,932	13,853	17,571	19,532
Balance of Payments					*Millions of US Dollars: Minus Sign Indicates Debit*								
Current Account, n.i.e.	78ald	574.8	−74.8	55.4	50.4	−118.0	−698.3	−547.7	30.9	334.9	−85.3	−669.7	−361.7
Goods: Exports f.o.b.	78aad	6,831.7	8,350.2	8,352.6	8,405.9	9,090.9	8,623.2	8,807.9	9,342.8	10,471.1	12,916.3	16,064.6	18,043.0
Goods: Imports f.o.b.	78abd	−7,168.2	−9,304.2	−9,178.7	−9,180.7	−9,882.9	−9,858.3	−9,946.9	−9,962.3	−10,718.9	−13,538.5	−17,322.1	−19,312.9
Trade Balance	78acd	−336.5	−953.9	−826.1	−774.8	−792.0	−1,235.1	−1,138.9	−619.5	−247.7	−622.1	−1,257.5	−1,269.9
Services: Credit	78add	1,808.1	2,026.9	2,134.7	2,040.5	2,024.6	1,875.3	1,887.6	1,959.6	2,315.8	2,791.2	3,454.5	3,992.4
Services: Debit	78aed	−1,164.7	−1,444.2	−1,494.2	−1,404.8	−1,523.8	−1,521.8	−1,437.9	−1,457.5	−1,732.0	−2,181.7	−2,604.4	−2,880.1
Balance on Goods & Services	78afd	306.9	−371.3	−185.6	−139.2	−291.2	−881.6	−689.2	−117.4	336.1	−12.5	−407.4	−157.6
Income: Credit	78agd	324.7	405.6	413.1	391.8	412.9	426.9	434.0	462.6	469.6	625.7	734.1	836.5
Income: Debit	78ahd	−153.3	−204.3	−259.9	−316.4	−357.0	−363.2	−407.8	−443.4	−605.0	−805.6	−1,034.2	−1,109.9
Balance on Gds, Serv. & Inc.	78aid	478.2	−170.0	−32.4	−63.8	−235.4	−817.9	−663.0	−98.2	200.8	−192.4	−707.5	−430.9
Current Transfers, n.i.e.: Credit	78ajd	237.2	247.7	250.9	259.5	299.8	334.9	340.8	390.0	452.1	508.0	677.7	910.1
Current Transfers: Debit	78akd	−140.6	−152.4	−163.1	−145.3	−182.4	−215.3	−225.4	−260.8	−317.9	−400.8	−640.0	−840.9
Capital Account, n.i.e.	78bcd	−3.2	−7.0	−1.9	1.1	−1.5	−.7	3.5	−3.6	−158.3	−190.9	−134.2	−155.5
Capital Account, n.i.e.: Credit	78bad	2.7	3.1	5.5	5.0	3.5	3.3	6.8	3.3	72.0	92.8	179.4	191.9
Capital Account: Debit	78bbd	−5.8	−10.1	−7.4	−3.9	−5.0	−4.0	−3.3	−6.9	−230.3	−283.7	−313.6	−347.4
Financial Account, n.i.e.	78bjd	138.6	516.3	534.5	1,162.9	215.8	576.1	680.4	1,204.3	1,847.5	499.9	643.3	1,203.3
Direct Investment Abroad	78bdd	12.7	10.0	−7.0	−31.0	5.5	−47.6	−65.3	−132.8	−147.7	−471.9	−550.5	−568.0
Dir. Invest. in Rep. Econ., n.i.e.	78bed	116.7	150.5	173.5	334.3	215.5	106.5	135.9	503.3	1,636.4	333.2	827.2	495.7
Portfolio Investment Assets	78bfd	−32.5	−28.9	6.4	−.2	−30.2	−7.8	−58.4	−107.5	−93.9	−220.0	−753.3	−1,513.8
Equity Securities	78bkd	....	....	....	....	....	−.5	−14.5	−23.3	−72.9	−101.3	−349.5	−748.0
Debt Securities	78bld	−32.5	−28.9	6.4	−.2	−30.2	−7.3	−43.9	−84.2	−21.0	−118.7	−403.8	−765.8
Portfolio Investment Liab., n.i.e.	78bgd	....	15.5	630.5	236.1	119.8	361.6	246.0	188.9	26.7	−37.0	60.5	9.6
Equity Securities	78bmd	....	....	....	52.2	7.2	−3.2	25.4	−2.3	10.7	16.1	45.5	154.6
Debt Securities	78bnd	....	15.5	630.5	184.0	112.6	364.8	220.6	191.2	16.0	−53.1	15.0	−145.0
Financial Derivatives Assets	78bwd	....	....	....	....	....	....	....	....	—	—	−2.7	−1.8
Financial Derivatives Liabilities	78bxd	....	....	....	....	....	....	....	....	—	—	—	−2.1
Other Investment Assets	78bhd	−211.5	−242.8	−442.0	262.3	−464.6	−568.5	−519.2	206.6	−623.7	−904.3	−1,731.6	−2,046.4
Monetary Authorities	78bod	−98.3	−66.8	131.4	−7.6	−5.4	−5.6	−5.9	−6.2	−5.4	−.2	−11.0	−2.2
General Government	78bpd	−.4	−2.2	−1.4	−1.3	−1.8	−1.6	−1.1	−.5	−.7	−.9	−13.1	−10.6
Banks	78bqd	−353.1	−302.3	−321.8	479.2	−51.8	−7.8	−253.7	−303.1	137.5	1.1	−327.1	−913.4
Other Sectors	78brd	240.3	128.4	−250.2	−208.0	−405.6	−553.5	−258.5	516.4	−755.1	−904.4	−1,380.4	−1,120.2
Other Investment Liab., n.i.e.	78bid	253.1	612.1	173.1	361.4	369.8	732.0	941.3	545.7	1,049.6	1,800.0	2,793.8	4,830.1
Monetary Authorities	78bsd	.1	.1	.2	..	.1	−.4	.1	..	..	..	124.9	3.7
General Government	78btd	92.2	137.6	−67.6	−25.7	−18.3	−3.2	79.6	−27.8	−88.4	−75.3	9.3	−35.3
Banks	78bud	40.6	267.3	−19.8	4.7	90.6	260.5	290.8	230.6	482.3	1,204.9	1,518.2	4,218.4
Other Sectors	78bvd	120.3	207.1	260.4	382.5	297.3	474.9	570.9	343.0	655.6	670.4	1,141.4	643.3
Net Errors and Omissions	78cad	−63.7	−194.6	2.0	74.0	61.4	41.5	42.1	53.0	−207.4	86.5	−135.9	−479.6
Overall Balance	78cbd	646.5	240.0	590.0	1,288.4	157.8	−81.4	178.3	1,284.6	1,816.7	310.2	−296.5	206.5
Reserves and Related Items	79dad	−646.5	−240.0	−590.0	−1,288.4	−157.8	81.4	−178.3	−1,284.6	−1,816.7	−310.2	296.5	−206.5
Reserve Assets	79dbd	−641.3	−236.5	−587.4	−1,287.2	−157.8	81.4	−178.3	−1,284.6	−1,816.7	−310.2	296.5	−206.5
Use of Fund Credit and Loans	79dcd	−5.2	−3.4	−2.6	−1.2								
Exceptional Financing	79ded	....	....	....	....	....	....	....	....	....	—	—	—
International Investment Position						*Millions of US Dollars*							
Assets	79aad	5,925.6	6,841.5	7,155.4	7,668.1	8,450.3	7,856.1	8,300.2	9,939.0	13,627.9	....	....	....
Direct Investment Abroad	79abd	354.0	489.9	459.5	459.4	636.2	626.5	767.6	1,005.1	1,475.9	....	....	....
Portfolio Investment	79acd	62.1	106.4	93.9	55.9	39.7	130.4	175.4	251.4	323.5	....	....	....
Equity Securities	79add	15.0	17.1	15.8	15.4	16.7	32.4	36.8	21.8	35.9	....	....	....
Debt Securities	79aed	47.0	89.3	78.1	40.4	22.9	98.0	138.6	229.6	287.6	....	....	....
Financial Derivatives	79ald	—	—	—	—	—	—	—	—	—	....	....	....
Other Investment	79afd	4,010.4	4,424.3	4,304.6	3,838.1	4,135.9	3,931.1	4,161.1	4,285.3	4,765.0	....	....	....
Monetary Authorities	79agd	103.3	170.1	33.3	40.7	46.3	51.8	57.9	76.0	84.7	....	....	....
General Government	79ahd	—	—	—	—	—	—	—	—	—	....	....	....
Banks	79aid	1,709.2	1,909.3	2,066.3	1,397.6	1,510.8	1,342.3	1,516.7	1,770.1	1,778.4	....	....	....
Other Sectors	79ajd	2,197.9	2,344.9	2,205.0	2,399.7	2,578.8	2,537.0	2,586.5	2,439.2	2,901.9	....	....	....
Reserve Assets	79akd	1,499.1	1,820.9	2,297.5	3,314.8	3,638.6	3,168.1	3,196.1	4,397.2	7,063.5	....	....	....
Liabilities	79lad	5,189.2	6,379.7	7,674.7	8,067.0	9,437.4	9,832.1	10,668.0	11,223.1	15,098.3	....	....	....
Dir. Invest. in Rep. Economy	79lbd	1,325.9	1,763.4	1,998.1	2,207.4	2,777.0	2,682.4	2,892.7	2,604.9	4,081.1	....	....	....
Portfolio Investment	79lcd	88.9	104.1	1,138.2	1,276.6	1,421.5	1,661.0	1,793.4	1,893.3	2,197.1	....	....	....
Equity Securities	79ldd	45.9	62.7	133.8	156.7	139.4	163.0	167.8	170.5	108.6	....	....	....
Debt Securities	79led	43.0	41.4	1,004.4	1,119.9	1,282.1	1,497.9	1,625.6	1,722.8	2,088.5	....	....	....
Financial Derivatives	79lld	—	—	—	—	—	—	—	—	—	....	....	....
Other Investment	79lfd	3,774.4	4,512.2	4,538.5	4,583.0	5,238.9	5,488.7	5,981.9	6,724.9	8,820.2	....	....	....
Monetary Authorities	79lgd	7.3	4.2	1.6	.2	.4	.3	—	—	—	....	....	....
General Government	79lhd	577.5	786.9	734.0	686.8	823.4	702.1	752.9	528.6	493.7	....	....	....
Banks	79lid	561.4	686.1	1,045.9	980.7	1,017.8	1,178.4	1,298.3	1,762.8	2,549.4	....	....	....
Other Sectors	79ljd	2,628.3	3,035.1	2,757.0	2,915.3	3,397.4	3,608.0	3,930.7	4,433.5	5,777.0	....	....	....

Slovenia   961

		1994	1995	1996	1997	1998	1999	2000	2001	2002	2003	2004	2005
Government Finance						*Billions of Tolars: Year Ending December 31*							
Deficit (-) or Surplus.........................	80	−5.06	−6.45	1.62	−43.20	−25.04	−29.63	−50.74	−49.74	−44.72	−77.33	−93.25	−79.64
Revenue....................................	81	768.50	926.42	1,041.64	1,163.38	1,332.10	1,445.54	1,559.91	1,848.64	1,950.33	2,234.66	2,432.29	2,603.00
Grants Received.........................	81z	—	.49	.96	1.76	2.45	3.18	6.44	10.06	13.23	12.16	.99	1.05
Expenditure...............................	82	773.56	933.36	1,040.98	1,208.34	1,366.47	1,477.07	1,621.84	1,920.38	2,110.64	2,322.60	2,517.03	2,686.46
Lending Minus Repayments...........	83	—	—	—	—	−6.88	1.28	−4.75	−11.94	−102.35	1.56	9.50	−2.78
Financing													
Net Borrowing: Domestic..............	84a	−5.41	−10.53	−11.65	12.32	22.95	−19.80	−18.82	52.61	163.81	46.35	134.93	124.70
Foreign..................................	85a	3.82	6.27	23.08	20.10	13.30	61.04	69.87	19.82	−21.30	−11.69	−50.63	−129.19
Use of Cash Balances...................	87	6.65	10.70	−13.05	10.78	−11.21	−11.61	−.32	−22.68	−97.79	42.67	8.95	84.13
National Accounts							*Billions of Tolars*							
Househ.Cons.Expend.,incl.NPISHs....	96f	1,050.2	1,438.9	1,641.8	1,828.5	2,013.5	2,271.9	2,467.7	2,718.3	2,973.2	3,242.2	3,461.5	3,632.9
Government Consumption Expend...	91f	374.3	458.7	525.3	592.1	654.9	735.4	829.8	958.0	1,057.5	1,139.1	1,219.1	1,287.4
Gross Fixed Capital Formation..........	93e	372.7	503.1	604.2	727.4	842.9	1,033.2	1,098.9	1,158.7	1,211.5	1,353.1	1,506.0	1,625.8
Changes in Inventories....................	93i	15.3	47.3	25.6	24.1	33.5	43.0	53.3	−.2	39.4	83.5	140.2	34.8
Exports of Goods and Services.........	90c	1,111.3	1,231.1	1,429.0	1,673.0	1,844.9	1,914.4	2,390.3	2,745.7	3,060.0	3,246.7	3,761.5	4,249.4
Imports of Goods and Services (-).....	98c	1,070.8	1,274.6	1,455.3	1,696.1	1,895.2	2,078.9	2,539.6	2,780.8	2,986.2	3,251.1	3,837.0	4,272.6
Gross Domestic Product (GDP)........	99b	1,853.0	2,404.6	2,770.6	3,149.0	3,494.6	3,919.0	4,300.3	4,799.6	5,355.4	5,813.5	6,251.2	6,557.7
Net Primary Income from Abroad.....	98.n	13.9	22.6	21.1	12.3	10.6	14.2	4.5	12.5	−27.6	−36.1	−57.7	−40.1
Gross National Income (GNI)...........	99a	1,866.9	2,427.2	2,791.7	3,161.2	3,505.2	3,933.2	4,304.8	4,812.0	5,327.8	5,777.4	6,193.5	6,517.6
Net Current Transf.from Abroad.......	98t	17.1	11.2	11.2	18.9	20.1	22.2	25.7	31.2	32.2	22.0	10.2	10.4
Gross Nat'l Disposable Inc.(GNDI)....	99i	1,884.0	2,438.4	2,802.9	3,180.1	3,525.3	3,955.4	4,330.6	4,843.2	5,360.0	5,799.4	6,203.8	6,528.0
Gross Saving..............................	99s	459.6	540.8	635.8	759.5	856.8	948.2	1,033.1	1,166.9	1,329.3	1,418.1	1,523.2	1,607.7
GDP Volume 1995 Prices................	99b.p	2,309.7	2,404.6	2,494.3	2,615.1	2,716.4	2,863.6	2,981.0	3,060.2	3,165.9	3,249.8	3,385.2	3,516.2
GDP Volume (2000=100)................	99bvp	77.5	80.7	83.7	87.7	91.1	96.1	100.0	102.7	106.2	109.0	113.6	118.0
GDP Deflator (2000=100)................	99bip	55.6	69.3	77.0	83.5	89.2	94.9	100.0	108.7	117.3	124.0	128.0	129.3
							Millions: Midyear Estimates							
Population...............................	99z	1.96	1.96	1.97	1.97	1.97	1.97	1.97	1.97	1.97	1.97	1.97	1.97

Solomon Islands   813

		1994	1995	1996	1997	1998	1999	2000	2001	2002	2003	2004	2005
Exchange Rates		*Solomon Islands Dollars per SDR: End of Period*											
Official Rate	aa	4.8597	5.1668	5.2081	6.4067	6.8417	6.9671	6.6441	6.9935	10.1381	11.1309	11.6592	10.8278
		Solomon Islands Dollars per US Dollar: End of Period (ae) Period Average (rf)											
Official Rate	ae	3.3289	3.4758	3.6219	4.7483	4.8591	5.0761	5.0994	5.5648	7.4571	7.4906	7.5075	7.5758
Official Rate	rf	3.2914	3.4059	3.5664	3.7169	4.8156	4.8381	5.0889	5.2780	6.7488	7.5059	7.4847	7.5299
		Index Numbers (2000=100): Period Averages											
Official Rate	ahx	154.6	149.5	142.8	136.3	105.7	103.2	100.0	93.9	76.1	67.8	68.0	67.6
Nominal Effective Exchange Rate	nec	126.6	116.9	113.8	116.2	103.2	98.3	100.0	103.4	80.1	64.4	60.3	59.1
Real Effective Exchange Rate	rec	84.9	83.1	88.1	95.4	92.8	94.1	100.0	108.7	90.1	78.5	77.1	79.5
Fund Position		*Millions of SDRs: End of Period*											
Quota	2f.s	7.50	7.50	7.50	7.50	7.50	10.40	10.40	10.40	10.40	10.40	10.40	10.40
SDRs	1b.s	.01	—	.01	—	—	.01	—	.01	—	—	—	—
Reserve Position in the Fund	1c.s	.54	.54	.54	.54	.54	.54	.54	.54	.55	.55	.55	.55
Total Fund Cred.&Loans Outstg.	2tl	—	—	—	—	—	—	—	—	—	—	—	—
International Liquidity		*Millions of US Dollars Unless Otherwise Indicated: End of Period*											
Total Reserves minus Gold	1l.d	17.42	15.91	32.58	36.34	49.03	51.14	32.04	19.34	18.25	37.20	80.58	95.42
SDRs	1b.d	.01	.01	.01	—	—	.01	—	.01	.01	—	—	—
Reserve Position in the Fund	1c.d	.79	.80	.77	.73	.76	.74	.71	.68	.75	.82	.85	.79
Foreign Exchange	1d.d	16.62	15.10	31.80	35.61	48.27	50.39	31.34	18.66	17.49	36.39	79.72	94.63
Monetary Authorities: Other Liab.	4..d	.42	.36	.63	.12	.44	.32	.25	—	—	1.05	1.10	.50
Deposit Money Banks: Assets	7a.d	3.57	1.30	3.27	3.94	1.29	6.06	2.43	5.51	5.36	7.37	9.57	9.98
Liabilities	7b.d	4.82	1.82	4.00	2.56	2.58	5.56	3.13	4.35	3.97	5.16	8.82	8.29
Monetary Authorities		*Millions of Solomon Islands Dollars: End of Period*											
Foreign Assets	11	58.21	55.39	117.71	153.90	237.13	261.57	163.40	106.81	136.03	277.21	604.31	718.03
Claims on Central Government	12a	64.47	77.98	73.06	76.36	76.15	46.56	44.47	174.96	173.47	173.01	172.84	173.23
Claims on Nonfin.Pub.Enterprises	12c	4.20	4.20	4.20	4.20	4.20	4.01	4.20	3.28	2.02	1.35	.67	.67
Claims on Deposit Money Banks	12e	—	—	—	—	—	—	—	—	—	—	—	—
Reserve Money	14	61.48	75.63	98.60	92.47	134.96	134.61	154.30	149.22	173.85	221.28	382.57	462.55
of which: Currency Outside DMBs	14a	50.23	54.93	59.67	70.79	81.28	100.07	88.15	84.57	91.39	101.43	123.24	152.90
Restricted Deposits	16b	.83	1.10	1.71	1.28	3.51	1.46	.66	5.70	6.01	.23	1.19	.86
Foreign Liabilities	16c	1.39	1.24	2.28	.59	2.13	1.64	1.29	—	.01	7.86	8.23	3.79
Central Government Deposits	16d	11.11	4.28	3.84	6.55	59.75	56.00	3.61	6.82	6.99	61.13	178.25	279.45
Capital Accounts	17a	57.39	59.41	68.82	103.81	108.23	109.93	104.45	108.91	−45.85	−20.36	28.91	−15.99
Other Items (Net)	17r	−5.32	−4.10	19.71	29.77	8.89	8.51	−52.24	14.39	170.50	181.42	178.68	161.27
Deposit Money Banks		*Millions of Solomon Islands Dollars: End of Period*											
Reserves	20	12.50	22.04	39.90	21.64	51.50	52.34	60.95	64.59	81.33	115.34	260.39	309.55
Foreign Assets	21	11.88	4.51	11.85	18.69	6.29	30.78	12.41	30.65	39.95	55.17	71.86	75.60
Claims on Central Government	22a	152.14	159.00	160.33	162.70	165.53	180.30	185.25	149.84	149.84	164.21	145.88	141.79
Claims on Local Government	22b	1.24	.22	.60	.31	.21	.22	.16	.16	.78	.72	.24	—
Claims on Nonfin.Pub.Enterprises	22c	.91	1.22	2.71	.75	.78	2.58	3.59	2.00	1.97	1.36	—	—
Claims on Private Sector	22d	107.06	121.96	128.20	141.27	176.99	191.74	195.22	152.73	171.32	215.99	238.59	389.12
Claims on Other Banking Insts	22f	—	—	—	—	—	—	—	—	—	—	—	—
Demand Deposits	24	112.65	116.02	138.08	141.66	130.82	166.48	162.85	162.63	164.51	230.09	251.11	387.77
Time and Savings Deposits	25	149.70	170.41	195.89	207.49	218.50	194.08	212.21	152.95	168.09	200.15	250.28	326.02
Money Market Instruments	26aa	.54	—	—	.31	—	.61	.56	.48	3.78	3.17	3.64	4.94
Foreign Liabilities	26c	16.05	6.33	14.49	12.16	12.54	28.21	15.94	24.23	29.59	38.69	66.18	62.79
Central Government Deposits	26d	5.24	9.32	7.83	8.22	4.35	12.88	2.35	1.10	2.89	3.93	43.52	18.61
Credit from Monetary Authorities	26g	—	—	—	—	—	—	—	—	—	—	—	—
Capital Accounts	27a	30.87	28.80	32.54	38.35	62.39	72.19	76.35	87.88	95.84	99.57	121.05	159.16
Other Items (Net)	27r	−29.31	−21.93	−45.25	−62.82	−27.31	−16.49	−12.68	−29.29	−19.53	−22.83	−18.81	−43.24
Monetary Survey		*Millions of Solomon Islands Dollars: End of Period*											
Foreign Assets (Net)	31n	52.64	52.33	112.79	159.84	228.74	262.49	158.58	113.23	146.36	285.83	601.76	727.06
Domestic Credit	32	313.68	350.97	357.41	370.82	359.75	356.53	426.93	475.05	489.51	491.56	336.46	406.74
Claims on Central Govt. (Net)	32an	200.27	223.37	221.72	224.29	177.57	157.98	223.76	316.88	313.44	272.16	96.96	16.95
Claims on Local Government	32b	1.24	.22	.60	.31	.21	.22	.16	.16	.78	.72	.24	—
Claims on Nonfin.Pub.Enterprises	32c	5.11	5.42	6.90	4.95	4.98	6.60	7.78	5.28	3.98	2.70	.67	.67
Claims on Private Sector	32d	107.06	121.96	128.20	141.27	176.99	191.74	195.22	152.73	171.32	215.99	238.59	389.12
Claims on Other Banking Insts.	32f	—	—	—	—	—	—	—	—	—	—	—	—
Money	34	162.88	170.96	197.75	212.45	212.10	266.54	251.00	247.20	255.90	331.52	374.35	540.67
Quasi-Money	35	149.70	170.41	195.89	207.49	218.50	194.08	212.21	152.95	168.09	200.15	250.28	326.02
Money Market Instruments	36aa	.54	—	—	.31	—	.61	.56	.48	3.78	3.17	3.64	4.94
Restricted Deposits	36b	.83	1.10	1.71	1.28	3.51	1.46	.66	5.70	6.01	.23	1.19	.86
Capital Accounts	37a	88.26	88.21	101.36	142.16	170.63	182.11	180.79	196.79	49.99	79.21	149.96	143.17
Other Items (Net)	37r	−35.88	−27.37	−26.51	−33.02	−16.25	−25.78	−59.72	−14.83	152.09	163.11	158.80	118.13
Money plus Quasi-Money	35l	312.58	341.37	393.64	419.93	430.60	460.62	463.21	400.15	424.00	531.67	624.64	866.70
Other Banking Institutions		*Millions of Solomon Islands Dollars: End of Period*											
Reserves	40	....	....	68.17	71.50	18.56	14.56	12.56	12.16	15.28	15.25	24.38	16.25
Claims on Private Sector	42d	....	....	113.32	125.99	139.13	140.53	142.24	143.89	144.60	141.01	204.87	123.14
Quasi-Monetary Liabilities	45	10.00	11.76	13.90	16.48	17.18	19.31	19.32	25.64	25.92	25.92	26.42	28.65
Central Govt. Lending Funds	46f	7.44	2.43	1.88	1.35	1.32	1.32	7.15	7.15	7.15	7.15	—	—
Credit from Monetary Authorities	46g	—	—	11.77	11.35	6.13	6.44	6.13	6.13	6.13	6.32	6.13	6.13
Credit from Deposit Money Banks	46h	....	....	—	—	—	—	—	—	—	—	—	—
Liabs. to Nonbank Financial Insts	46j	....	....	3.47	1.67	7.40	7.33	7.27	7.24	7.24	7.24	8.48	8.30
Capital Accounts	47a	....	....	15.02	22.33	30.71	24.65	−4.27	−10.71	−9.87	4.82	−16.11	−16.56
Other Items (Net)	47r	....	....	135.45	144.32	94.96	96.03	119.20	120.60	123.30	104.81	204.33	112.88

Solomon Islands   813

		1994	1995	1996	1997	1998	1999	2000	2001	2002	2003	2004	2005
Banking Survey		*Millions of Solomon Islands Dollars: End of Period*											
Foreign Assets (Net)	51n	52.64	52.33	112.79	159.84	228.74	262.49	158.58	113.23	146.36	285.83	601.76	727.06
Domestic Credit	52	....	....	470.73	496.81	498.88	497.06	569.17	618.94	634.11	632.57	541.33	529.88
Claims on Central Govt. (Net)	52an	200.27	223.37	221.72	224.29	177.57	157.98	223.76	316.88	313.44	272.16	96.96	16.95
Claims on Local Government	52b	1.24	.22	.60	.31	.21	.22	.16	.16	.78	.72	.24	—
Claims on Nonfin.Pub.Enterprises	52c	5.11	5.42	6.90	4.95	4.98	6.60	7.78	5.28	3.98	2.70	.67	.67
Claims on Private Sector	52d	....	....	241.52	267.26	316.12	332.26	337.46	296.61	315.91	356.99	443.46	512.26
Liquid Liabilities	55l	....	....	339.37	364.91	429.22	465.37	469.97	413.63	434.64	542.35	626.68	879.09
Money Market Instruments	56aa	.54	—	—	.31	—	.61	.56	.48	3.78	3.17	3.64	4.94
Restricted Deposits	56b	.83	1.10	1.71	1.28	3.51	1.46	.66	5.70	6.01	.23	1.19	.86
Central Govt. Lending Funds	56f	7.44	2.43	1.88	1.35	1.32	1.32	7.15	7.15	7.15	7.15	—	—
Liabs. to Nonbank Financial Insts.	56j	....	....	3.47	1.67	7.40	7.33	7.27	7.24	7.24	7.24	8.48	8.30
Capital Accounts	57a	....	....	116.38	164.49	201.34	206.77	176.53	186.08	40.13	84.03	133.85	126.61
Other Items (Net)	57r	....	....	120.71	122.65	84.84	76.69	65.61	111.90	281.52	274.24	369.26	237.14
Nonbank Financial Institutions		*Millions of Solomon Islands Dollars: End of Period*											
Reserves	40..m	26.98	....	....	38.85	47.24	45.73	59.08	13.99	31.99	48.40	75.40	140.43
Claims on Central Government	42a.m	73.98	....	....	83.78	125.30	118.73	104.86	112.67	94.27	94.27	126.09	121.32
Claims on Nonfin.Pub.Enterprises	42c.m	39.95	....	....	44.44	49.24	44.70	46.68	53.02	58.31	62.96	24.59	21.32
Claims on Private Sector	42d.m	31.83	....	....	53.47	59.76	61.66	59.01	55.56	54.89	51.52	78.15	50.21
Claims on Other Banking Insts.	42f.m	7.37	....	....	25.10	7.62	3.09	3.17	3.64	4.11	4.48	4.11	4.01
Capital Accounts	47a.m	223.57	....	....	317.28	359.00	384.31	380.05	356.73	369.87	402.34	474.66	524.98
Other Items (Net)	47r.m	−43.46	....	....	−71.64	−69.84	−110.39	−107.26	−117.85	−126.30	−140.70	−166.31	−187.69
Interest Rates		*Percent Per Annum*											
Treasury Bill Rate	60c	11.25	12.50	12.75	12.88	6.00	6.00	7.05	8.23	6.87	5.85	6.00	4.53
Deposit Rate	60l	9.00	8.38	6.46	2.42	2.33	2.88	2.54	1.35	.75	.75	.92	.98
Lending Rate	60p	15.72	16.59	17.78	15.71	14.84	14.50	15.49	15.72	16.42	16.33	16.07	16.08
Government Bond Yield	61	13.00	13.00	11.50	11.75	12.50	12.88	13.00	13.00	13.00	13.00	13.00	13.00
Prices, Production, Labor		*Index Numbers (2000=100): Period Averages*											
Consumer Prices	64	58.1	63.7	71.2	76.9	86.5	93.4	100.0	106.9	117.7	129.5	138.2	148.1
Copra Production	66ag	110.5	136.8	142.1	152.6	142.1	121.1	100.0	10.5	9.1	78.1	114.9	137.8
Fish Catch	66al	223.3	295.2	242.9	304.8	291.9	278.1	100.0	85.7	90.5	133.7	129.8	113.6
		Number in Thousands: Period Averages											
Labor Force	67d	....	....	....	....	....	85	....	....	....	....	....	....
Employment	67e	33	33	34	33	34	57	55	53	51	52	52	57
Unemployment	67c	....	....	....	....	....	28	....	....	....	....	....	....
Unemployment Rate	67r	....	....	....	....	....	21.6	....	....	....	....	....	....
Intl. Transactions & Positions		*Millions of Solomon Islands Dollars*											
Exports	70	467.87	573.15	576.60	581.53	568.75	607.37	331.30	248.69	390.01	557.01	727.70	771.64
Imports, c.i.f.	71	468.11	525.66	421.00	548.70	722.18	538.41	498.97	431.94	436.34	507.00	637.69	1,083.43
Balance of Payments		*Millions of US Dollars: Minus Sign Indicates Debit*											
Current Account, n.i.e.	78ald	−3.43	8.34	14.58	−37.91	8.12	21.48	....	....	....	....	....	....
Goods: Exports f.o.b.	78aad	142.16	168.30	161.51	156.45	141.83	164.57	....	....	....	....	....	....
Goods: Imports f.o.b.	78abd	−142.22	−154.53	−150.55	−184.53	−159.90	−110.04	....	....	....	....	....	....
Trade Balance	78acd	−.06	13.77	10.96	−28.09	−18.07	54.53	....	....	....	....	....	....
Services: Credit	78add	49.95	41.81	53.14	70.35	55.07	56.30	....	....	....	....	....	....
Services: Debit	78aed	−105.94	−76.93	−85.47	−107.18	−54.53	−87.49	....	....	....	....	....	....
Balance on Goods & Services	78afd	−56.06	−21.35	−21.37	−64.92	−17.53	23.34	....	....	....	....	....	....
Income: Credit	78agd	1.52	1.20	2.36	2.69	2.12	5.46	....	....	....	....	....	....
Income: Debit	78ahd	−4.44	−7.96	−9.42	−11.17	−10.01	−22.38	....	....	....	....	....	....
Balance on Gds, Serv. & Inc.	78aid	−58.97	−28.10	−28.43	−73.39	−25.42	6.41	....	....	....	....	....	....
Current Transfers, n.i.e.: Credit	78ajd	66.60	53.17	57.48	52.57	55.64	41.54	....	....	....	....	....	....
Current Transfers: Debit	78akd	−11.06	−16.74	−14.47	−17.08	−22.90	−26.48	....	....	....	....	....	....
Capital Account, n.i.e.	78bcd	2.70	.65	−2.19	−1.00	6.65	9.16	....	....	....	....	....	....
Capital Account, n.i.e.: Credit	78bad	2.86	1.50	.50	.30	6.91	9.16	....	....	....	....	....	....
Capital Account: Debit	78bbd	−.15	−.85	−2.69	−1.29	−.27	—	....	....	....	....	....	....
Financial Account, n.i.e.	78bjd	1.49	−8.31	−1.37	45.68	16.88	−33.77	....	....	....	....	....	....
Direct Investment Abroad	78bdd	—	—	—	—	—	—	....	....	....	....	....	....
Dir. Invest. in Rep. Econ., n.i.e.	78bed	2.10	2.03	5.94	33.85	8.80	9.90	....	....	....	....	....	....
Portfolio Investment Assets	78bfd	—	—	—	—	—	—	....	....	....	....	....	....
Equity Securities	78bkd	—	—	—	—	—	—	....	....	....	....	....	....
Debt Securities	78bld	—	—	—	—	—	—	....	....	....	....	....	....
Portfolio Investment Liab., n.i.e.	78bgd	—	—	—	—	—	—	....	....	....	....	....	....
Equity Securities	78bmd	—	—	—	—	—	—	....	....	....	....	....	....
Debt Securities	78bnd	—	—	—	—	—	—	....	....	....	....	....	....
Financial Derivatives Assets	78bwd	—	—	—	—	—	....	....	....	....	....	....	....
Financial Derivatives Liabilities	78bxd	—	—	—	—	—	....	....	....	....	....	....	....
Other Investment Assets	78bhd	—	—	—	—	—	.04	....	....	....	....	....	....
Monetary Authorities	78bod	—	—	—	—	—	—	....	....	....	....	....	....
General Government	78bpd	—	—	—	—	—	—	....	....	....	....	....	....
Banks	78bqd	—	—	—	—	—	—	....	....	....	....	....	....
Other Sectors	78brd	—	—	—	—	—	.04	....	....	....	....	....	....
Other Investment Liab., n.i.e.	78bid	−.61	−10.34	−7.32	11.84	8.08	−43.72	....	....	....	....	....	....
Monetary Authorities	78bsd	−1.25	.03	.08	−.62	−.37	—	....	....	....	....	....	....
General Government	78btd	−1.34	6.20	5.72	5.17	8.60	−11.02	....	....	....	....	....	....
Banks	78bud	3.31	−2.85	2.30	−.62	−1.23	−.27	....	....	....	....	....	....
Other Sectors	78bvd	−1.34	−13.71	−15.42	7.91	1.08	−32.43	....	....	....	....	....	....
Net Errors and Omissions	78cad	−2.80	−1.45	6.96	2.31	−14.41	−1.58	....	....	....	....	....	....
Overall Balance	78cbd	−2.04	−.77	17.98	9.09	17.24	−4.72	....	....	....	....	....	....
Reserves and Related Items	79dad	2.04	.77	−17.98	−9.09	−17.24	4.72	....	....	....	....	....	....
Reserve Assets	79dbd	2.04	.77	−17.98	−9.09	−17.24	4.72	....	....	....	....	....	....
Use of Fund Credit and Loans	79dcd	—	—	—	—	—	—	....	....	....	....	....	....
Exceptional Financing	79ded	—	—	—	—	—	....	....	....	....	....	....	....

Solomon Islands 813

		1994	1995	1996	1997	1998	1999	2000	2001	2002	2003	2004	2005
Government Finance					*Millions of Solomon Islands Dollars: Year Ending December 31*								
Deficit (-) or Surplus........................	80	−30.91	−4.56	−2.32	−54.71	−171.55	−66.02	....	....	....	....	....	....
Revenue......................................	81	272.89	309.54	336.58	314.69	347.35	397.58	277.77	....	....	....	....	....
Grants Received.............................	81z	35.20	45.90	52.10	—	38.30	60.00	1.00	....	....	....	....	....
Expenditure..................................	82	339.00	360.00	391.00	365.00	490.00	479.00	....	....	....	....	....	....
Lending Minus Repayments............	83	—	—	—	4.40	67.20	44.60	....	....	....	....	....	....
Net Borrowing: Domestic...............	84a	....	....	....	55.30	15.60	....	....	....	....	....	....	....
Foreign............................	85a	....	....	....	11.40	62.00	....	....	....	....	....	....	....
Total Debt....................................	88	....	....	....	....	....	913.00	978.70	....	....	....	....	....
Domestic.....................................	88a	....	....	....	....	....	316.10	385.00	....	....	....	....	....
Foreign.......................................	89a	....	....	358.30	463.70	622.00	596.90	593.70	....	....	....	....	....
National Accounts						*Millions of Solomon Islands Dollars*							
Househ.Cons.Expend.,incl.NPISHs....	96f	501.0	607.0	697.0	734.0	838.0	892.0	834.0	857.0	896.0	....	....	....
Government Consumption Expend...	91f	292.0	409.0	467.0	475.0	556.0	589.0	548.0	565.0	589.0	....	....	....
Gross Fixed Capital Formation..........	93e	212.0	219.0	261.0	282.0	313.0	336.0	315.0	322.0	363.0	....	....	....
Changes in Inventories....................	93i	12.0	19.0	18.0	20.0	24.0	24.0	23.0	24.0	—	....	....	....
Exports of Goods and Services.........	90c	639.0	717.0	855.0	900.0	1,016.0	1,089.0	1,017.0	1,043.0	1,092.0	....	....	....
Imports of Goods and Services.........	98c	604.0	730.0	861.0	893.0	1,021.0	1,090.0	1,017.0	1,045.0	1,092.0	....	....	....
Gross Domestic Product (GDP).........	99b	1,052.0	1,242.0	1,438.0	1,518.0	1,726.0	1,839.0	1,721.0	1,766.0	1,848.0	....	....	....
GDP Volume 1990 Prices.................	99b.p	714.0	762.0	788.0	770.0	779.0	769.0	661.0	628.0	603.0	....	....	....
GDP Volume (2000=100)...............	99bvp	108.0	115.3	119.2	116.5	117.9	116.3	100.0	95.0	91.2	....	....	....
						Millions: Midyear Estimates							
Population.................................	99z	.35	.36	.37	.38	.40	.41	.42	.43	.44	.45	.47	.48

South Africa 199

		1994	1995	1996	1997	1998	1999	2000	2001	2002	2003	2004	2005
Exchange Rates		*Rand per SDR: End of Period*											
Principal Rate.................aa=.........	wa	5.17298	5.42197	6.73325	6.56747	8.25106	8.44711	9.86107	15.23974	11.74625	9.86684	8.74345	9.04013
		Rand per US Dollar: End of Period (we) Period Average (wf)											
Principal Rate.................ae=.........	we	3.54350	3.64750	4.68250	4.86750	5.86000	6.15450	7.56850	12.12650	8.64000	6.64000	5.63000	6.32500
Principal Rate.................rf=.........	wf	3.55080	3.62709	4.29935	4.60796	5.52828	6.10948	6.93983	8.60918	10.54075	7.56475	6.45969	6.35933
		Index Numbers (2000=100): Period Averages											
Principal Rate........................	ahx	194.6	190.4	161.7	150.0	126.0	113.0	100.0	81.3	65.9	91.9	107.2	108.8
Nominal Effective Exchange Rate.....	nec	160.2	148.3	130.5	129.9	115.3	105.9	100.0	85.7	68.4	89.8	103.1	105.3
Real Effective Exchange Rate...........	rec	126.1	122.5	112.5	118.7	109.8	104.0	100.0	87.7	73.9	97.3	107.6	108.5
Fund Position		*Millions of SDRs: End of Period*											
Quota..	2f.s	1,365	1,365	1,365	1,365	1,365	1,869	1,869	1,869	1,869	1,869	1,869	1,869
SDRs..	1b.s	1	3	1	7	132	210	222	223	223	223	223	223
Reserve Position in the Fund...........	1c.s	—	—	—	—	—	—	—	—	—	1	1	1
Total Fund Cred.&Loans Outstg.......	2tl	614	614	614	307	—	—	—	—	—	—	—	—
International Liquidity		*Millions of US Dollars Unless Otherwise Indicated: End of Period*											
Total Reserves minus Gold..............	1l.d	1,685	2,820	942	4,799	4,357	6,353	6,083	6,045	5,904	6,496	13,141	18,579
SDRs...	1b.d	1	5	1	9	185	288	290	280	303	331	346	319
Reserve Position in the Fund..........	1c.d	—	—	—	—	—	—	—	—	1	1	1	1
Foreign Exchange.........................	1d.d	1,684	2,815	940	4,790	4,171	6,065	5,793	5,765	5,601	6,164	12,794	18,260
Gold (Million Fine Troy Ounces).......	1ad	4.20	4.25	3.79	3.99	4.00	3.94	5.90	5.72	5.58	3.98	3.98	3.99
Gold (National Valuation)...............	1and	1,445	1,481	1,261	1,048	1,034	1,020	1,451	1,427	1,735	1,476	1,578	2,051
Monetary Authorities:Other Assets....	3..d	392	306	227	24	19	12	10	6	8	15	14	19
Other Liab....	4..d	1,637	229	96	2,164	3,181	3,261	2,688	4,028	2,648	3,136	3,819	3,883
Banking Institutions: Assets.............	7a.d	1,042	799	1,412	1,603	2,874	5,122	5,432	7,341	11,685	24,336	26,085	26,421
Liabilities...................	7b.d	7,854	9,184	9,489	9,676	10,483	8,878	8,885	8,148	6,691	10,082	11,833	12,316
Monetary Authorities		*Millions of Rand: End of Period*											
Foreign Assets..................................	11	12,475	16,795	11,369	28,570	31,693	45,442	57,083	† 90,674	† 66,061	53,020	82,941	130,595
Claims on Central Government........	12a	10,367	6,957	12,132	11,064	12,603	10,983	10,422	† 9,065	† 54,750	40,524	33,675	15,756
Claims on State and Local Govts......	12b	—	—	—	—	—	—	—	† —	† —			
Claims on Nonfin.Pub.Enterprises...	12c	....	....	....	....	....	....	....	963	† 431	281	281	281
Claims on Private Sector..................	12d	4,296	3,003	2,055	2,502	704	603	598	† —	† 37	24	23	27
Claims on Banking Institutions........	12e	5,995	6,513	11,975	10,939	6,362	6,572	10,356	† 13,347	† 14,241	14,129	16,174	15,570
Claims on Nonbank Financial Insts...	12g	....	....	....	....	....	....	....		† 13	14	14	13
Reserve Money................................	14	19,331	25,083	28,497	31,766	33,499	41,306	43,254	† 49,254	† 55,431	61,995	71,179	79,554
of which: Currency Outside Banks..	14a	12,237	14,332	15,954	17,327	18,510	22,663	23,724	† 25,283	† 29,216	33,715	39,080	43,419
Other Liabs. to Banking Insts............	14n	16	8	20	5	1,875	7,040	21,629	† 28,165	† 53,423	8,604	19,803	5,327
Time, Savings,&Fgn.Currency Dep....	15	....	....	....	....	....	....	......	302	† 204	335	1,300	2,516
Liabs. of Central Bank: Securities......	16ac	—	—	—	—	—	—	—	† —	† —			
Restricted Deposits..........................	16b								—	† 1,244	164	269	8,247
Foreign Liabilities............................	16c	8,980	4,165	4,586	12,549	18,640	20,067	20,348	† 48,840	† 22,875	20,824	21,503	24,581
Central Government Deposits...........	16d	10,958	10,957	9,764	8,325	6,615	5,076	3,998	† 2,600	† 3,271	9,665	12,051	33,742
Liab. to Nonbank Financial Insts.......	16j	....	....	....	....	....	....	....	† —	† —			
Capital Accounts.............................	17a	1,272	1,338	1,641	1,644	2,057	2,132	2,478	† 3,776	† 7,956	7,861	8,153	8,892
Other Items (Net).............................	17r	−7,425	−8,283	−6,977	−1,213	−11,324	−12,021	−13,248	† −18,889	† −8,871	−1,456	−1,150	−618
Banking Institutions		*Millions of Rand: End of Period*											
Reserves..	20	6,586	10,356	11,702	13,514	14,726	17,969	19,761	† 23,757	† 26,304	28,507	32,018	37,912
Claims on Mon.Author.: Securities...	20c	....	....	....	....	....	....	....	10,085	† 11,125	7,131	6,944	6,047
Other Claims on Monetary Author...	20n	....	....	....	....	....	....	....		† 43,381	3,275	2,496	
Foreign Assets..................................	21	3,693	2,913	6,610	7,805	16,844	31,522	41,115	† 89,018	† 100,958	161,591	146,861	167,243
Claims on Central Government........	22a	21,501	24,813	27,437	37,011	46,206	50,100	53,546	† 58,386	† 69,099	86,393	99,695	93,529
Claims on State and Local Govts......	22b	—	—	—	—	—	—	—	† —	† 3,061	4,442	1,568	4,223
Claims on Nonfin.Pub.Enterprises...	22c	—	—	—	—	—	—	—	† 1,331	† 4,390	3,635	2,512	11,634
Claims on Private Sector..................	22d	278,079	324,111	380,493	434,884	506,140	553,159	637,212	† 778,673	† 682,038	805,695	922,960	1,087,627
Claims on Nonbank Financial Insts...	22g	....	....	....	....	....	....	....	26,359	† 46,661	65,059	56,243	71,167
Demand Deposits..............................	24	81,736	97,050	130,858	155,065	194,873	237,083	242,244	† 150,042	† 167,597	184,888	204,947	248,103
Time, Savings,&Fgn.Currency Dep....	25	141,757	162,301	165,626	195,762	205,958	205,309	232,628	† 405,878	† 428,462	499,348	536,280	643,089
Money Market Instruments..............	26aa	3,922	4,920	5,531	3,374	2,657	7,576	5,869	† 18,016	† 83,673	85,542	127,948	160,681
Restricted Deposits..........................	26b	....	....	....	....	....	....	....	—	† —			
Foreign Liabilities............................	26c	27,829	33,497	44,431	47,097	61,431	54,642	67,243	† 98,810	† 57,812	66,947	66,620	77,961
Central Government Deposits...........	26d	8,173	17,748	22,387	21,137	21,158	27,027	30,158	† 42,993	† 22,810	49,190	62,019	66,312
Credit from Monetary Authorities....	26g	296	49	43	108	64	411	1,686	† 21,285	† 24,226	13,565	14,031	12,534
Liab. to Nonbank Financial Insts.......	26j	....	....	....	....	....	....	....	32,744	† 47,993	50,497	39,690	54,926
Capital Accounts.............................	27a	23,998	29,302	34,470	41,664	51,920	63,470	75,581	† 96,032	† 104,367	111,695	125,699	134,709
Other Items (Net).............................	27r	22,148	17,326	22,896	29,007	45,855	57,232	96,225	† 121,808	† 50,078	104,057	94,062	81,066
Banking Survey		*Millions of Rand: End of Period*											
Foreign Assets (Net)......................	31n	−20,642	−17,954	−31,038	−23,270	−31,533	2,255	10,607	† 32,043	† 86,333	126,840	141,679	195,296
Domestic Credit.............................	32	295,112	330,179	389,966	455,999	537,880	582,741	667,622	† 829,183	† 834,398	947,212	1,042,901	1,184,202
Claims on Central Govt. (Net)........	32an	12,737	3,065	7,418	18,613	31,036	28,979	29,812	† 21,857	† 97,767	68,062	59,300	9,230
Claims on State and Local Govts....	32b	—	—	—	—	—	—	—	† —	† 3,061	4,442	1,568	4,223
Claims on Nonfin.Pub.Enterprises.	32c	—	—	—	—	—	—	—	† 2,295	† 4,821	3,916	2,792	11,915
Claims on Private Sector................	32d	282,375	327,114	382,548	437,386	506,844	553,762	637,810	† 778,673	† 682,075	805,719	922,983	1,087,654
Claims on Nonbank Financial Insts.	32g	....	....	....	....	....	....	....	26,359	† 46,673	65,073	56,257	71,179
Money...	34	94,511	111,844	147,664	173,335	213,532	259,935	266,184	† 175,325	† 196,813	218,602	244,027	291,522
Quasi-Money....................................	35	141,757	162,301	165,626	195,762	205,958	205,309	232,628	† 406,180	† 428,666	499,683	537,580	645,606
Money Market Instruments..............	36aa	3,922	4,920	5,531	3,374	2,657	7,576	5,869	† 18,016	† 83,673	85,542	127,948	160,681
Liabs. of Central Bank: Securities.....	36ac	—	—	—	—	—	—	—	† —	† —			
Restricted Deposits..........................	36b								—	† 1,244	164	269	8,247
Liab. to Nonbank Financial Insts.......	36j	....	....	....	....	....	....	....	32,744	† 47,993	50,497	39,690	54,926
Capital Accounts.............................	37a	25,270	30,640	36,111	43,308	53,977	65,602	78,059	† 99,808	† 112,323	119,556	133,852	143,601
Other Items (Net).............................	37r	9,010	2,520	3,996	16,950	30,222	46,574	95,488	† 129,152	† 50,020	100,008	101,214	74,915
Money plus Quasi-Money.................	35l	236,268	274,145	313,290	369,097	419,490	465,244	498,812	† 581,505	† 625,479	718,285	781,607	937,128

		1994	1995	1996	1997	1998	1999	2000	2001	2002	2003	2004	2005
Nonbank Financial Institutions							*Millions of Rand: End of Period*							
Reserves	40	....	....	....	....	....	....	....	—	† 6,063	6,788	7,565	10,825
Claims on Mon.Author.: Securities	40c	....	....	....	....	....	....	....	—	† —	—	—	147
Other Claims on Monetary Author.	40n	....	....	....	....	....	....	....	—	† —	—	—	83
Foreign Assets	41	....	....	....	....	....	....	....	—	† 176,361	160,648	166,862	213,964
Claims on Central Government	42a	66,880	84,992	93,588	106,149	103,428	103,059	122,381	† 133,932	† 324,829	352,478	391,816	409,986
Claims on State and Local Govts	42b	4,940	4,787	4,484	4,474	3,913	3,728	2,767	† 2,503	† 4,720	4,878	4,608	4,777
Claims on Nonfin.Pub.Enterprises	42c	17,949	17,978	16,485	19,656	17,291	17,825	17,774	† 21,228	† 107,430	151,292	150,076	218,619
Claims on Private Sector	42d	268,488	326,976	358,163	359,677	370,342	540,167	595,366	† 667,385	† 664,202	706,899	897,027	1,105,222
Claims on Banking Institutions	42e	43,655	60,144	58,805	68,998	80,453	98,868	92,396	† 106,932	† 230,228	265,406	320,647	359,960
Restricted Deposits	46b	....	....	....	....	....	....	....	—	† 1,796	2,282	2,738	4,378
Foreign Liabilities	46c	....	....	....	....	....	....	....	—	† 8,647	12,306	11,291	15,561
Central Government Deposits	46d	....	....	....	....	....	....	....	—	† 17,248	21,962	29,570	38,041
Credit from Monetary Authorities	46g	....	....	....	....	....	....	....	—	† 1,414	1,944	2,247	4,106
Credit from Banking Institutions	46h	....	....	....	....	....	....	....	—	† 37,309	35,161	46,945	54,701
Capital Accounts	47a	....	....	....	....	....	....	....	—	† 376,605	436,208	558,050	728,328
Insurance Technical Reserves	47d	466,957	562,515	623,177	678,437	712,927	945,610	1,013,594	† 1,148,858	† 1,229,522	1,313,249	1,476,580	1,754,353
Other Items (Net)	47r	−65,045	−67,638	−91,652	−119,483	−137,500	−181,963	−182,910	† −216,878	† −158,708	−174,723	−188,820	−275,885
Financial Survey							*Millions of Rand: End of Period*							
Foreign Assets (Net)	51n	−20,642	−17,954	−31,038	−23,270	−31,533	2,255	10,607	† 32,043	† 254,046	275,182	297,249	393,699
Domestic Credit	52	653,369	764,912	862,686	945,955	1,032,854	1,247,520	1,405,910	† 1,627,872	† 1,871,658	2,075,724	2,400,601	2,813,585
Claims on Central Govt. (Net)	52an	79,617	88,057	101,006	124,762	134,464	132,038	152,193	† 155,789	† 405,348	398,578	421,546	381,175
Claims on State and Local Govts.	52b	4,940	4,787	4,484	4,474	3,913	3,728	2,767	† 2,503	† 7,782	9,320	6,177	9,000
Claims on Nonfin.Pub.Enterprises.	52c	17,949	17,978	16,485	19,656	17,291	17,825	17,774	† 23,523	† 112,252	155,208	152,869	230,534
Claims on Private Sector	52d	550,863	654,090	740,711	797,063	877,186	1,093,929	1,233,176	† 1,446,058	† 1,346,276	1,512,618	1,820,010	2,192,876
Liquid Liabilities	55l	236,268	274,145	313,290	369,097	419,490	465,244	498,812	† 483,301	† 499,146	545,762	575,936	693,463
Money Market Instruments	56aa	3,922	4,920	5,531	3,374	2,657	7,576	5,869	† 18,016	† 24,812	16,541	23,820	30,282
Liabs. of Central Banks: Securities	56ac	—	—	—	—	—	—	—	† —	† —	....	....	....
Restricted Deposits	56b	....	....	....	....	....	....	....	—	† 1,992	2,446	3,007	12,625
Capital Accounts	57a	25,270	30,640	36,111	43,308	53,977	65,602	78,059	† 99,808	† 488,928	555,764	691,902	871,929
Insurance Technical Reserves	57d	466,957	562,515	623,177	678,437	712,927	945,610	1,013,594	† 1,148,858	† 1,229,522	1,313,249	1,476,580	1,754,353
Other Items (Net)	57r	−99,690	−125,262	−146,461	−171,531	−187,731	−234,257	−179,818	† −90,069	† −118,695	−82,855	−73,395	−155,368
Money (National Definitions)							*Millions of Rand: End of Period*							
M0	19mc	18,810	24,629	27,665	30,828	33,210	40,784	43,036	48,904	55,952	62,053	71,437	80,044
M1	59ma	94,538	112,745	147,580	173,092	213,921	258,282	266,924	313,211	358,251	387,788	421,494	503,053
M1A	59maa	57,810	67,503	82,270	101,174	114,813	145,146	147,583	175,326	196,980	218,955	244,458	291,952
M2	59mb	215,823	245,722	284,423	337,547	383,366	435,526	462,509	535,085	632,621	733,453	818,740	960,977
M3	59mc	244,150	281,156	319,428	374,218	428,672	472,177	507,591	595,473	715,817	808,047	914,150	1,096,240
M3 Seasonally Adjusted	59mcc	243,770	280,377	317,097	370,584	428,663	472,508	502,804	583,354	701,635	800,032	910,584	1,098,654
Interest Rates							*Percent Per Annum*							
Discount Rate (End of Period)	60	13.00	15.00	17.00	16.00	† 19.32	12.00	12.00	9.50	13.50	8.00	7.50	7.00
Money Market Rate	60b	10.24	13.07	15.54	15.59	17.11	13.06	9.54	† 8.49	11.11	10.93	7.15	6.62
Treasury Bill Rate	60c	10.93	13.53	15.04	15.26	16.53	12.85	10.11	9.68	11.16	10.67	7.53	6.91
Savings Rate	60k	....	....	....	....	....	....	1.27	3.44	4.76	4.30	3.32	3.26
Deposit Rate	60l	11.11	13.54	14.91	15.38	16.50	12.24	9.20	† 9.37	10.77	9.76	6.55	6.04
Lending Rate	60p	15.58	17.90	19.52	20.00	21.79	18.00	14.50	13.77	15.75	14.96	11.29	10.63
Government Bond Yield	61	14.83	16.11	15.48	14.70	15.12	14.90	13.79	11.41	11.50	9.62	9.53	8.07
Prices, Production, Labor							*Index Numbers (2000=100): Period Averages*							
Share Prices: All Shares	62	67.7	69.5	83.9	86.8	82.1	86.7	100.0	108.4	123.9	108.2	132.2	175.2
Industrial	62a	73.0	80.1	95.4	99.4	89.9	87.6	100.0	85.4	85.5	79.3	111.7	153.9
Gold Mining	62b	187.7	136.9	164.1	117.3	95.5	99.5	100.0	118.3	277.0	253.2	216.2	198.7
Producer Prices	63	66.7	73.1	78.1	83.7	86.6	91.6	100.0	108.5	123.9	125.9	126.8	130.7
Consumer Prices	64	66.6	72.4	77.8	84.4	90.3	94.9	100.0	105.7	115.4	122.1	123.8	128.1
Manufacturing Prod, Seas Adj	66eyc	87.2	94.3	97.7	100.2	96.9	96.4	100.0	102.8	107.4	105.4	110.0	113.8
Mining Production, Seas Adj	66zxc	105.2	104.3	102.6	104.7	103.5	101.5	100.0	101.4	102.2	106.6	110.3	111.8
Gold Production, Seas Adj	66krc	134.4	121.6	115.6	114.9	108.0	104.8	100.0	91.7	92.4	86.7	78.5	68.4
Mfg. Employment, Seas. Adj	67eyc	116.0	116.7	112.4	107.7	104.2	101.5	100.0	97.4	96.8	96.5	96.3	91.5
Mining Employment, Seas Adj	67zxc	146.0	142.8	136.1	131.5	110.4	103.9	100.0	97.7	99.0	102.2	109.6	106.4
						Number in Thousands: Period Averages								
Labor Force	67d	....	....	....	5,455	....	8,025	8,942	9,041	10,364	11,307	11,032	....
Employment	67e	5,328	5,271	5,236	5,145	4,966	4,867	4,734	4,658	5,576	6,397	6,659	7,091
Unemployment	67c	271	273	296	310	....	† 3,158	4,208	4,383	4,788	4,910	4,373	....
Unemployment Rate (%)	67r	4.4	4.5	5.1	5.4	....	† 23.3	25.8	29.7	30.7	29.7	27.0	....
Intl. Transactions & Positions							*Millions of Rand*							
Exports	70	89,907	101,051	126,101	142,937	† 145,518	163,182	208,476	249,348	311,679	274,505	296,080	329,078
Gold Output (Net)	70kr	23,671	22,537	26,300	25,818	25,907	23,289	27,159	30,909	42,344	34,749	32,830	27,023
Imports, c.i.f.	71	83,042	110,826	129,522	151,779	† 161,802	163,092	206,620	241,311	307,312	307,611	344,225	396,777
Imports, f.o.b.	71.v	76,154	98,039	115,524	129,735	143,326	147,091	186,382	213,763	272,682	256,833	304,432	349,210
						2000=100								
Volume of Exports	72	70.5	78.2	83.9	87.1	91.2	85.7	100.0	101.8	102.3	102.6	105.1	112.1
Volume of Imports	73	75.8	88.5	95.9	101.5	103.6	94.9	100.0	100.2	105.3	114.6	130.7	143.9
Unit Value of Exports	74	61.6	62.2	70.8	75.3	81.4	86.9	100.0	117.0	145.5	133.1	136.4	143.1
Unit Value of Imports	75	54.9	59.6	65.0	68.9	76.5	84.8	100.0	115.6	140.4	124.2	125.9	131.5

		1994	1995	1996	1997	1998	1999	2000	2001	2002	2003	2004	2005
Balance of Payments		*Millions of US Dollars: Minus Sign Indicates Debit*											
Current Account, n.i.e.	78ald	30	−2,493	−1,678	−2,227	−2,199	−675	−191	153	684	−2,323	−7,442	−10,079
Goods: Exports f.o.b.	78aad	26,251	29,783	30,426	31,167	29,199	28,534	31,950	31,064	31,772	38,700	48,237	54,581
Goods: Imports f.o.b.	78abd	−21,852	−27,404	−27,568	−28,848	−27,208	−24,526	−27,252	−25,809	−27,016	−35,270	−48,518	−56,459
Trade Balance	78acd	4,398	2,379	2,859	2,319	1,991	4,008	4,698	5,255	4,756	3,431	−281	−1,878
Services: Credit	78add	3,751	4,619	5,069	5,394	5,396	5,210	5,046	4,650	4,673	7,910	9,010	10,239
Services: Debit	78aed	−5,088	−5,971	−5,735	−6,003	−5,657	−5,759	−5,823	−5,227	−5,393	−8,230	−10,340	−11,836
Balance on Goods & Services	78afd	3,061	1,027	2,192	1,710	1,730	3,460	3,920	4,678	4,037	3,110	−1,611	−3,475
Income: Credit	78agd	972	1,136	1,077	1,399	1,474	1,791	2,511	2,480	2,179	2,857	3,259	4,603
Income: Debit	78ahd	−3,394	−4,011	−4,194	−4,612	−4,659	−5,000	−5,696	−6,267	−4,975	−7,447	−7,617	−9,470
Balance on Gds, Serv. & Inc.	78aid	639	−1,848	−925	−1,503	−1,455	251	736	891	1,240	−1,481	−5,970	−8,342
Current Transfers, n.i.e.: Credit	78ajd	143	196	54	138	60	66	106	126	139	252	257	240
Current Transfers: Debit	78akd	−752	−841	−807	−862	−804	−993	−1,033	−865	−695	−1,094	−1,730	−1,977
Capital Account, n.i.e.	78bcd	−67	−40	−47	−193	−56	−62	−52	−31	−15	44	52	30
Capital Account, n.i.e.: Credit	78bad	20	23	27	30	24	20	19	16	20	44	55	44
Capital Account: Debit	78bbd	−87	−63	−74	−223	−80	−82	−71	−47	−35	—	−2	−14
Financial Account, n.i.e.	78bjd	858	4,295	2,366	7,906	4,041	3,154	73	−1,188	−1,452	−1,961	7,394	11,572
Direct Investment Abroad	78bdd	−1,261	−2,494	−1,048	−2,324	−1,634	−1,584	−277	3,515	402	−553	−1,305	−68
Dir. Invest. in Rep. Econ., n.i.e.	78bed	374	1,248	816	3,811	550	1,503	969	7,270	735	783	701	6,257
Portfolio Investment Assets	78bfd	−82	−447	−2,000	−4,587	−5,575	−5,113	−3,672	−5,331	−875	−138	−950	−872
Equity Securities	78bkd	−29	−387	−1,698	−3,891	−4,768	−4,050	−3,019	−4,864	−572	−49	−795	−976
Debt Securities	78bld	−53	−61	−302	−696	−807	−1,064	−652	−467	−303	−89	−156	105
Portfolio Investment Liab., n.i.e.	78bgd	2,918	2,937	4,446	11,274	9,869	13,799	1,807	−2,971	457	862	7,100	5,733
Equity Securities	78bmd	88	2,914	2,318	5,473	8,632	9,001	4,169	−962	−388	685	6,661	6,915
Debt Securities	78bnd	2,830	23	2,127	5,802	1,237	4,798	−2,361	−2,009	845	176	439	−1,182
Financial Derivatives Assets	78bwd	....	....	....				−46	−144	—	—	—	....
Financial Derivatives Liabilities	78bxd	....	....	....	53	97	−76	2	—	—	—	—	....
Other Investment Assets	78bhd	−527	−234	−1,251	−2,208	−1,504	−3,795	34	−3,921	−288	−5,212	−216	−3,596
Monetary Authorities	78bod	44	75	12	206	—	6	—	—	—	1	4	−7
General Government	78bpd	−1	1	—	2	1	—	—	−407	−424	−376	−103	−415
Banks	78bqd	−314	354	−779	−347	−945	−2,212	−269	−2,695	−2,455	−7,976	−2,297	−3,206
Other Sectors	78brd	−255	−663	−484	−2,069	−560	−1,589	303	−819	2,591	3,139	2,180	32
Other Investment Liab., n.i.e.	78bid	−565	3,285	1,403	1,887	2,237	−1,535	1,354	249	−1,884	2,297	2,065	4,117
Monetary Authorities	78bsd	−104	−1,407	−89	2,186	1,172	106	−410	1,582	−1,688	169	510	527
General Government	78btd	−467	118	469	−120	−73	−270	6	134	1,944	−277	−285	319
Banks	78bud	360	2,945	1,044	−283	784	−945	1,196	−787	−1,568	−89	1,128	2,799
Other Sectors	78bvd	−354	1,629	−21	104	355	−426	563	−680	−572	2,494	712	472
Net Errors and Omissions	78cad	−449	−851	−2,401	−1,120	−1,742	−500	649	1,045	461	3,887	6,320	4,243
Overall Balance	78cbd	372	911	−1,761	4,366	45	1,916	480	−22	−322	−354	6,324	5,766
Reserves and Related Items	79dad	−372	−911	1,761	−4,366	−45	−1,916	−480	22	322	354	−6,324	−5,766
Reserve Assets	79dbd	−372	−911	1,761	−3,945	374	−1,916	−480	22	322	354	−6,324	−5,766
Use of Fund Credit and Loans	79dcd	—	—	—	−421	−418	—	—	—	—	—	—	—
Exceptional Financing	79ded	—	—	—	—	—	—	—	—	—	—	—	—
International Investment Position		*Millions of US Dollars*											
Assets	79aad	27,559	33,893	35,056	46,048	55,274	90,035	93,162	64,281	74,038	100,743	129,626	....
Direct Investment Abroad	79abd	19,105	23,301	24,349	23,250	26,858	32,990	32,325	17,580	21,980	27,185	38,483	....
Portfolio Investment	79acd	98	632	2,605	12,067	18,238	42,007	45,433	30,341	30,068	40,752	47,304	....
Equity Securities	79add	61	569	2,237	10,895	15,833	38,349	41,675	28,500	27,470	38,621	43,984	....
Debt Securities	79aed	38	63	368	1,171	2,405	3,657	3,758	1,841	2,598	2,131	3,320	....
Financial Derivatives	79ald	—											....
Other Investment	79afd	4,349	4,985	4,657	4,886	4,788	7,667	7,871	8,889	14,352	24,836	29,121	....
Monetary Authorities	79agd	392	306	227	24	19	12	10	6	8	9	6	....
General Government	79ahd	2,040	2,371	2,148	19	15	14	269	703	1,186	1,712	2,086	....
Banks	79aid	104	39	150	1,667	2,104	4,193	4,081	5,554	9,263	17,976	20,045	....
Other Sectors	79ajd	1,813	2,269	2,132	3,176	2,650	3,447	3,511	2,626	3,895	5,139	6,984	....
Reserve Assets	79akd	4,008	4,975	3,445	5,846	5,389	7,372	7,512	7,471	7,638	7,970	14,718	....
Liabilities	79lad	52,197	62,610	60,449	66,749	68,715	114,763	99,951	75,342	82,938	111,683	149,502	....
Dir. Invest. in Rep. Economy	79lbd	12,615	15,014	13,236	16,736	15,676	51,772	43,451	30,569	29,611	45,715	63,071	....
Portfolio Investment	79lcd	18,998	23,446	23,804	28,209	30,666	42,292	36,564	26,402	35,677	46,257	62,551	....
Equity Securities	79ldd	9,246	12,492	13,366	13,144	17,519	26,461	22,599	16,577	23,308	32,795	47,448	....
Debt Securities	79led	9,752	10,953	10,439	15,065	13,148	15,832	13,965	9,825	12,369	13,462	15,103	....
Financial Derivatives	79lld	4	10	14	—	—	—	—	—	—	—	—	....
Other Investment	79lfd	20,580	24,140	23,395	21,804	22,373	20,699	19,936	18,370	17,650	19,711	23,880	....
Monetary Authorities	79lgd	2,534	1,142	979	2,578	3,181	3,261	2,681	4,026	2,646	3,145	3,833	....
General Government	79lhd	3,108	3,072	3,244	955	956	627	589	717	2,805	2,747	2,672	....
Banks	79lid	5,944	9,038	9,310	8,885	9,616	8,296	8,781	7,148	5,960	6,243	8,077	....
Other Sectors	79ljd	8,993	10,889	9,861	9,386	8,620	8,515	7,885	6,480	6,240	7,576	9,298	....
Government Finance		*Millions of Rand: Year Ending December 31*											
Deficit (-) or Surplus	80	−38,690	−23,465	−28,563	−28,129	−19,464	−14,775	−16,428	−9,975	−6,031	−26,071	−35,018	−8,992
Total Revenue and Grants	81y	111,916	125,470	147,738	162,983	181,749	199,367	211,984	245,952	279,922	295,661	328,250	398,715
Expenditure	82	150,606	148,935	176,301	191,112	201,213	217,100	228,412	255,927	285,953	321,732	363,268	407,707
Total Financing	80h	38,690	23,465	28,563	28,129	19,465	14,775	16,428	9,975	6,031	26,071	35,024	8,996
Total Net Borrowing	84	37,928	25,504	24,224	26,507	21,647	13,269	17,790	19,348	7,777	45,916	43,705	32,033
Net Domestic	84a	35,317	24,323	21,596	23,553	21,591	7,651	10,299	6,489	−26,476	42,987	44,094	29,954
Net Foreign	85a	2,611	1,181	2,628	2,954	56	5,618	7,491	12,859	34,253	2,929	−389	2,079
Use of Cash Balances	87	762	−2,039	4,339	1,622	−2,182	1,509	−1,362	−9,373	−1,746	−19,845	−8,681	−23,037
Total Debt by Currency	88z	† 239,714	275,489	302,608	† 336,133	361,401	391,420	409,363	462,446	454,365	499,813	519,344	545,128
National	88b	† 231,656	265,879	288,349	† 320,981	345,559	371,395	378,245	395,827	374,488	427,196	455,137	476,341
Foreign	89b	8,058	9,610	14,259	15,152	15,842	20,025	31,118	66,619	79,877	72,617	64,207	68,787

National Accounts		1994	1995	1996	1997	1998	1999	2000	2001	2002	2003	2004	2005
							Millions of Rand						
Househ.Cons.Expend.,incl.NPISHs....	96f.c	298,173	343,037	385,921	434,307	470,165	514,271	580,802	639,800	722,091	785,632	870,411	967,940
Government Consumption Expend...	91f.c	96,503	100,424	118,013	131,903	139,371	149,952	167,348	186,280	215,301	242,913	273,361	307,395
Gross Fixed Capital Formation..........	93e.c	73,045	87,042	100,632	113,221	126,913	125,754	139,647	153,525	175,594	198,904	225,316	261,429
Changes in Inventories....................	93i.c	8,293	12,571	6,240	875	−686	7,534	7,096	2,455	12,050	14,091	19,289	16,310
Exports of Goods and Services.........	90c.c	106,562	124,816	152,816	168,659	190,453	206,144	257,011	305,584	382,290	350,793	368,412	412,727
Imports of Goods and Services (-).....	98c.c	95,747	121,093	143,340	160,718	181,972	185,037	229,757	265,927	339,532	326,334	378,283	435,032
Gross Domestic Product (GDP)........	99b.c	482,120	548,100	617,954	685,730	742,424	813,683	922,148	1,020,007	1,168,778	1,257,026	1,386,658	1,523,255
Net Primary Income from Abroad.....	98.nc	−8,599	−10,427	−13,380	−14,844	−17,488	−19,601	−22,024	−32,176	−29,400	−34,871	−28,108	−31,034
Gross National Income (GNI)............	99a.c	473,521	537,673	604,574	670,886	724,936	794,082	900,124	987,831	1,139,378	1,222,155	1,358,550	1,492,221
Consumption of Fixed Capital..........	99cf	64,500	71,827	78,817	87,188	96,615	107,966	119,237	130,848	149,329	161,653	172,721	190,719
GDP Volume 2000 Prices.................	99b.r	779,429	803,713	838,327	860,516	864,968	885,365	922,148	947,373	982,327	1,011,556	1,056,771	1,108,255
GDP Volume (2000=100)...............	99bvr	84.5	87.2	90.9	93.3	93.8	96.0	100.0	102.7	106.5	109.7	114.6	120.2
GDP Deflator (2000=100)...............	99bir	61.9	68.2	73.7	79.7	85.8	91.9	100.0	107.7	119.0	124.3	131.2	137.4
							Millions: Midyear Estimates						
Population...............................	99z	40.92	41.89	42.79	43.61	44.35	45.02	45.61	46.13	46.56	46.92	47.21	47.43

Spain 184

		1994	1995	1996	1997	1998	1999	2000	2001	2002	2003	2004	2005
Exchange Rates						*Euros per SDR: End of Period*							
Market Rate	aa	192.32	180.47	188.77	204.68	200.79	1.3662	1.4002	1.4260	1.2964	1.1765	1.1402	1.2116
						Euros per US Dollar: End of Period (ae) Period Average (rf)							
Market Rate	ae	131.74	121.41	131.28	151.70	142.61	.9954	1.0747	1.1347	.9536	.7918	.7342	.8477
Market Rate	rf	133.96	124.69	126.66	146.41	149.40	.9386	1.0854	1.1175	1.0626	.8860	.8054	.8041
						Pesetas per ECU: End of Period (ea) Period Average (eb)							
ECU Rate	ea	161.5520	155.5610	162.6500	167.3270	166.3860	....	....	....	....	....	....	....
ECU Rate	eb	158.4871	161.1758	158.6182	165.3915	167.4876	....	....	....	....	....	....	....
						Index Numbers (2000=100): Period Averages							
Market Rate (1995=100)	ahx	93.1	100.0	98.4	85.2	83.5	....	....	....	....	....	....	....
Nominal Effective Exchange Rate	neu	110.1	109.4	110.0	105.1	104.8	103.2	100.0	100.5	101.4	104.5	105.3	105.4
Real Effective Exchange Rate	reu	102.1	101.4	104.2	101.2	103.0	102.5	100.0	102.8	106.6	112.5	116.0	117.3
Fund Position						*Millions of SDRs: End of Period*							
Quota	2f.s	1,935	1,935	1,935	1,935	1,935	3,049	3,049	3,049	3,049	3,049	3,049	3,049
SDRs	1b.s	174	277	314	351	408	190	223	279	260	278	214	232
Reserve Position in the Fund	1c.s	760	1,065	1,110	1,409	1,558	1,111	908	1,055	1,171	1,253	1,014	526
of which: Outstg.Fund Borrowing...	2c	—	—	—	—	62	—	—	—	—	—	—	—
Total Fund Cred.&Loans Outstg.	2tl												
International Liquidity						*Millions of US Dollars Unless Otherwise Indicated: End of Period*							
Total Res.Min.Gold (Eurosys.Def)	1l.d	41,546	34,485	57,927	68,398	55,258	† 33,115	30,989	29,582	34,536	19,788	12,389	9,678
SDRs	1b.d	255	411	451	474	575	260	290	351	354	413	332	332
Reserve Position in the Fund	1c.d	1,109	1,583	1,597	1,902	2,193	1,525	1,182	1,326	1,592	1,862	1,575	752
Foreign Exchange	1d.d	40,182	32,491	55,879	66,023	52,490	31,329	29,516	27,905	32,590	17,513	10,481	8,594
o/w:Fin.Deriv.Rel.to Reserves	1ddd	....	....	....	....	....	−1.01	162.84	−55.52	400.60	1,001.56	20.43	−24.77
Other Reserve Assets	1e.d	....	....	....	....	....							
Gold (Million Fine Troy Ounces)	1ad	15.62	15.63	15.63	15.63	19.54	16.83	16.83	16.83	16.83	16.83	16.83	14.72
Gold (Eurosystem Valuation)	1and	4,217	4,221	4,221	4,139	5,617	4,885	4,619	4,653	5,768	7,021	7,370	7,550
Memo:Euro Cl. on Non-EA Res.	1dgd	....	....	....	....	....	4,134	36	—	—	—	—	—
Non-Euro Cl. on EA Res.	1dhd	....	....	....	....	....		—	—	—	—	601	2,750
Mon. Auth.: Other Foreign Assets	3..d	....	....	....	....	....						....	....
Foreign Liabilities	4..d	515	551	983	454	480	† 1,004	445	317	1,488	143	63	182
Banking Insts.: Foreign Assets	7a.d	110,693	146,061	129,727	111,176	126,792	† 61,250	77,370	81,999	95,103	101,125	153,239	167,654
Foreign Liab.	7b.d	100,658	109,245	123,359	135,020	179,175	† 125,663	147,328	157,560	176,270	231,737	244,313	241,053
Monetary Authorities						*Billions of Pesetas through 1998; Billions of Euros Beginning 1999: End of Period*							
Fgn. Assets (Cl.on Non-EA Ctys).	11	5,796	4,566	7,960	10,708	8,751	41.49	37.54	38.60	38.26	21.84	15.59	16.39
Claims on General Government	12a.u	....	....	....	....	....	15.17	14.45	13.95	14.17	30.28	36.59	51.87
o/w: Claims on Gen.Govt.in Cty.	12a	2,981	3,074	3,056	2,984	3,023	15.17	14.45	13.95	14.17	16.32	17.49	18.23
Claims on Banking Institutions	12e.u	....	....	....	....	....	60.01	61.42	39.71	40.86	51.46	55.76	53.83
o/w: Claims on Bank.Inst.in Cty.	12e	5,949	6,641	4,439	2,267	4,471	24.18	16.14	10.55	18.20	33.19	23.45	33.29
Claims on Other Resident Sectors	12d.u	....	....	....	....	....					.06	.05	.04
o/w: Cl. on Oth.Res.Sect.in Cty.	12d	21	20	21	21	22	—	—	—	—	.06	.05	.04
Currency Issued	14a	7,165	7,535	7,942	8,378	8,437	61.35	59.79	48.75	40.50	46.38	52.70	59.36
Liabilities to Banking Insts.	14c.u	....	....	....	....	....	15.94	8.39	14.73	27.88	33.76	34.59	40.20
o/w: Liabs to Bank.Inst.in Cty.	14c	1,430	1,394	1,310	1,484	1,788	12.49	8.39	14.73	9.29	14.41	13.09	16.53
Demand Dep. of Other Res.Sect.	14d.u	....	....	....	....	....	5.22	7.34	10.52	12.43	13.92	12.43	11.88
o/w:D.Dep.of Oth.Res.Sect.in Cty.	14d	132	193	175	207	190	5.22	7.34	10.52	12.43	13.92	12.43	11.88
Other Dep. of Other Res.Sect.	15..u	....	....	....	....	....	—	—	—	—	—	—	—
o/w:O.Dep.of Oth.Res.Sect.in Cty.	15	....	....	....	....	....	—	—	—	—	—	—	—
Bonds & Money Mkt. Instruments	16n.u	....	....	....	....	....	3.30	—	—	—	—	—	—
o/w: Held by Resid.of Cty	16n	2,860	2,334	1,947	1,613	1,219	....	....	....	....	....	....	....
Foreign Liab. (to Non-EA Ctys)	16c	68	67	129	69	69	1.00	.48	.36	1.42	.11	.05	.15
Central Government Deposits	16d.u	....	....	....	....	....	16.87	22.91	2.79	2.80	3.32	3.48	3.76
o/w: Cent.Govt.Dep. in Cty	16d	2,058	1,752	2,742	1,890	2,120	16.87	22.91	2.79	2.80	3.32	3.48	3.76
Capital Accounts	17a	1,166	1,267	1,594	2,752	2,870	16.01	17.25	17.51	12.26	8.67	7.42	9.84
Other Items (Net)	17r	−132	−243	−363	−412	−426	−3.01	−2.73	−2.39	−3.99	−2.53	−2.68	−3.05
Memo: Net Claims on Eurosystem	12e.s	....	....	....	....	....	32.38	45.28	29.16	4.06	−1.08	10.41	−6.62
Currency Put into Circ.	14m	....	....	....	....	....				59.09	65.73	74.20	83.02
Banking Institutions						*Billions of Pesetas through 1998; Billions of Euros Beginning 1999: End of Period*							
Claims on Monetary Authorities	20	4,328	3,725	3,262	3,093	2,992	15.79	8.39	14.73	9.29	14.41	13.09	16.53
Claims on Bk.Inst.in Oth.EA Ctys	20b.u	....	....	....	....	....	50.08	53.56	53.52	67.72	78.66	82.51	100.47
Fgn. Assets (Cl.on Non-EA Ctys)	21	14,565	17,737	17,057	16,909	18,155	60.97	83.15	93.04	90.69	80.07	112.50	142.12
Claims on General Government	22a.u	....	....	....	....	....	146.00	129.59	151.68	164.17	189.34	161.83	189.42
o/w: Claims on Gen.Govt.in Cty.	22a	20,853	22,358	24,083	22,400	21,258	136.21	124.10	133.84	138.22	147.75	130.64	129.72
Claims on Other Resident Sectors	22d.u	....	....	....	....	....	529.64	631.12	712.26	794.56	915.35	1,082.22	1,357.78
o/w: Cl. on Oth.Res.Sect.in Cty.	22d	50,345	53,764	57,682	65,592	76,417	519.57	615.88	688.45	770.91	886.18	1,050.39	1,320.98
Demand Deposits	24..u	....	....	....	....	....	127.47	140.23	159.67	175.19	191.06	214.72	433.70
o/w:D.Dep.of Oth.Res.Sect.in Cty.	24	10,159	10,291	11,144	13,391	16,768	125.54	137.52	157.23	173.08	187.93	211.56	428.80
Other Deposits	25..u	....	....	....	....	....	319.89	368.97	408.74	440.18	490.00	561.03	542.48
o/w:O.Dep.of Oth.Res.Sect.in Cty.	25	34,492	37,397	37,579	35,679	36,346	310.68	359.38	396.10	424.87	460.72	533.04	520.46
Money Market Fund Shares	26m.u	....	....	....	....	....	42.34	33.11	43.44	52.92	57.65	57.71	54.55
Bonds & Money Mkt. Instruments	26n.u	....	....	....	....	....	53.63	51.91	65.19	77.65	118.49	178.40	257.90
o/w: Held by Resid.of Cty.	26n	2,214	2,316	2,394	2,693	3,025	....	....	....	....	....	....	....
Foreign Liab. (to Non-EA Ctys)	26c	13,303	13,316	16,436	20,741	25,889	125.09	158.33	178.78	168.08	183.48	179.37	204.33
Central Government Deposits	26d.u	....	....	....	....	....	5.65	5.54	19.06	21.41	16.40	17.36	21.18
o/w: Cent.Govt.Dep. in Cty	26d	2,706	2,954	3,063	3,352	3,882	5.62	5.52	19.06	21.40	16.27	17.24	20.92
Credit from Monetary Authorities	26g	6,063	6,643	4,447	2,265	4,450	24.18	16.14	10.55	18.20	33.19	23.45	32.40
Liab. to Bk.Inst.in Oth. EA Ctys.	26h.u	....	....	....	....	....	54.22	64.81	63.22	86.99	101.55	115.69	152.25
Capital Accounts	27a	10,709	10,807	11,261	12,026	12,668	76.53	94.41	104.07	114.42	121.89	146.63	166.60
Other Items (Net)	27r	10,445	13,860	15,761	17,847	15,794	−26.52	−27.62	−27.49	−28.62	−35.87	−42.19	−59.06

Spain 184

		1994	1995	1996	1997	1998	1999	2000	2001	2002	2003	2004	2005
Banking Survey (Nat'l Residency)		*Billions of Pesetas through 1998; Billions of Euros Beginning 1999: End of Period*											
Foreign Assets (Net)	31n	6,990	8,921	8,452	6,808	949	16.83	8.88	3.12	−17.55	−48.39	−20.03	4.84
Domestic Credit	32	69,435	74,510	79,037	85,755	94,718	648.46	726.00	814.39	899.10	1,030.71	1,177.85	1,444.28
Claims on General Govt. (Net)	32an	19,069	20,726	21,334	20,142	18,279	128.89	110.12	125.94	128.19	144.48	127.41	123.26
Claims on Other Resident Sectors	32d	50,366	53,784	57,703	65,613	76,439	519.57	615.88	688.45	770.91	886.24	1,050.44	1,321.02
Currency Issued	34a.n	7,165	7,535	7,942	8,378	8,437	61.35	59.79	48.75	40.50	46.38	52.70	59.36
Demand Deposits	34b.n	10,291	10,484	11,319	13,598	16,959	130.76	144.86	167.74	185.51	201.85	223.99	440.68
Other Deposits	35..n	34,492	37,397	37,579	35,679	36,346	310.68	359.38	396.10	424.87	460.72	533.04	520.46
Money Market Fund Shares	36m	....	....	....	....	....	42.34	33.11	43.44	52.92	57.65	57.71	54.55
Bonds & Money Mkt. Instruments	36n	5,075	4,651	4,341	4,306	4,244	56.93	51.91	65.19	77.65	118.49	178.40	257.90
o/w: Over Two Years	36na	....	....	....	....	....	40.79	39.77	49.28	61.63	87.40	123.14	189.93
Capital Accounts	37a	11,875	12,074	12,855	14,778	15,538	92.54	111.65	121.58	126.68	130.56	154.05	176.45
Other Items (Net)	37r	7,529	11,289	13,454	15,824	14,143	−29.30	−25.82	−25.29	−26.57	−33.31	−42.07	−60.25
Banking Survey (EA-Wide Residency)		*Billions of Euros: End of Period*											
Foreign Assets (Net)	31n.u	....	....	....	....	....	−23.63	−38.12	−47.49	−40.56	−81.69	−51.31	−45.98
Domestic Credit	32..u	....	....	....	....	....	668.28	746.72	856.03	948.69	1,115.31	1,259.85	1,574.19
Claims on General Govt. (Net)	32anu	....	....	....	....	....	138.64	115.60	143.78	154.13	199.90	177.58	216.36
Claims on Other Resident Sect.	32d.u	....	....	....	....	....	529.64	631.12	712.26	794.56	915.41	1,082.27	1,357.83
Currency Issued	34a.u	....	....	....	....	....	61.35	59.79	48.75	40.50	46.38	52.70	59.36
Demand Deposits	34b.u	....	....	....	....	....	132.68	147.56	170.19	187.61	204.98	227.15	445.58
Other Deposits	35..u	....	....	....	....	....	319.89	368.97	408.74	440.18	490.00	561.03	542.48
o/w: Other Dep. Over Two Yrs.	35abu	....	....	....	....	....	32.17	44.32	49.80	64.14	88.74	142.43	262.28
Money Market Fund Shares	36m.u	....	....	....	....	....	42.34	33.11	43.44	52.92	57.65	57.71	54.55
Bonds & Money Mkt. Instruments	36n.u	....	....	....	....	....	56.93	51.91	65.19	77.65	118.49	178.40	257.90
o/w: Over Two Years	36nau	....	....	....	....	....	40.79	39.77	49.28	61.63	87.40	123.14	189.93
Capital Accounts	37a	....	....	....	....	....	92.54	111.65	121.58	126.68	130.56	154.05	176.45
Other Items (Net)	37r.u	....	....	....	....	....	−61.07	−64.39	−49.35	−17.40	−14.44	−22.51	−8.08
Money (National Definitions)		*Billions of Pesetas: End of Period*											
M1	59ma	17,337.6	17,887.8	19,116.1	21,834.9	25,270.6	....	....	....	....	....	....	....
M2	59mb	28,753.4	29,637.5	31,717.5	35,483.7	40,616.5	....	....	....	....	....	....	....
M3	59mc	63,675.8	70,439.4	73,819.5	77,136.6	78,665.1	....	....	....	....	....	....	....
ALP (Broad Money)	59md	70,045.8	76,479.0	82,118.8	85,674.3	86,588.1	....	....	....	....	....	....	....
Interest Rates		*Percent Per Annum*											
Discount Rate (End of Period)	60	7.38	9.00	6.25	4.75	3.00	....	....	....	....	....	....	....
Money Market Rate	60b	7.81	8.98	7.65	5.49	4.34	2.72	4.11	4.36	3.28	2.31	2.04	2.09
Treasury Bill Rate	60c	8.11	9.79	7.23	5.02	3.79	3.01	4.61	3.92	3.34	2.21	2.17	2.19
Deposit Rate	60l	6.70	7.68	6.12	3.96	2.92	1.85	2.95	3.08	2.50	....	....	....
Households: Stocks, up to 2 years	60lhs	....	....	....	....	....	....	....	....	....	2.25	1.84	1.86
New Business, up to 1 year	60lhn	....	....	....	....	....	....	....	....	....	2.08	1.96	2.07
Corporations: Stocks, up to 2 years	60lcs	....	....	....	....	....	....	....	....	....	2.25	2.00	2.05
New Business, up to 1 year	60lcn	....	....	....	....	....	....	....	....	....	2.17	2.02	2.05
REPOS, Stocks	60lcr	....	....	....	....	....	....	....	....	....	2.34	2.00	2.06
Lending Rate	60p	8.95	10.05	8.50	6.08	5.01	3.95	5.18	5.16	4.31	....	....	....
Households: Stocks, up to 1 year	60phs	....	....	....	....	....	....	....	....	....	7.48	6.57	5.79
New Bus., Floating & up to 1 year	60pns	....	....	....	....	....	....	....	....	....	8.18	8.06	7.97
House Purch., Stocks, Over 5 years	60phm	....	....	....	....	....	....	....	....	....	4.28	3.56	3.35
House Purch., New Bus., 5-10 yrs	60phn	....	....	....	....	....	....	....	....	....	5.95	6.75	6.56
Corporations: Stocks, up to 1 year	60pcs	....	....	....	....	....	....	....	....	....	3.99	3.54	3.50
New Bus., Over € 1 mil.,up to 1 yr	60pcn	....	....	....	....	....	....	....	....	....	3.09	2.84	2.87
Government Bond Yield	61	9.69	11.04	8.18	5.84	4.55	4.30	5.36	4.87	4.62	3.52	3.59	3.05
Prices, Production, Labor		*Index Numbers (2000=100): Period Averages*											
Share Prices	62	31.6	29.8	36.9	55.9	82.2	89.9	100.0	85.8	72.7	71.0	86.8	107.2
Industrial Prices	63	86.8	92.3	93.9	94.8	94.2	94.8	100.0	101.7	102.4	103.9	107.4	112.7
Consumer Prices	64	84.0	87.9	91.0	92.8	94.5	96.7	100.0	103.6	106.8	110.0	113.3	117.2
Harmonized CPI	64h	....	88.0	91.2	92.9	94.5	96.6	100.0	102.8	106.5	† 109.8	113.2	117.0
Wages	65	80.7	84.6	89.1	92.7	95.3	97.7	100.0	103.8	108.1	112.7	118.8	122.1
Industrial Production	66	80.0	83.9	82.7	88.5	93.4	95.8	100.0	98.5	98.7	100.0	101.6	102.3
Employment	67	81.0	83.2	85.6	88.2	91.2	95.5	100.0	102.0	112.3	115.3	118.3	126.1
		Number in Thousands: Period Averages											
Labor Force	67d	....	16,227.6	16,517.8	16,809.7	17,081.0	17,412.0	18,002.3	18,050.7	18,785.6	19,538.1	20,184.5	....
Employment	67e	12,207.0	12,512.0	12,835.0	13,259.5	13,807.6	14,568.0	15,369.7	15,945.6	16,257.5	16,694.6	17,116.6	18,973.0
Unemployment	67c	3,738	3,584	3,540	3,356	3,060	2,606	2,370	2,213	1,621	1,658	1,671	2,070
Unemployment Rate (%)	67r	24.2	22.9	22.2	20.8	18.8	15.9	14.1	13.1	11.4	8.8	10.3	9.2
Intl. Transactions & Positions		*Billions of Pesetas through 1998; Millions of Euros Beginning 1999*											
Exports	70	9,746.6	11,339.6	12,931.2	15,266.9	16,290.8	† 103,343.2	123,099.5	128,671.8	130,814.1	137,814.8	146,452.1	153,576.0
Imports, c.i.f.	71	12,306.3	14,106.7	15,435.7	17,966.0	19,837.9	† 135,866.3	166,138.4	171,690.8	172,788.6	184,094.8	207,125.5	231,345.1
		2000=100											
Volume of Exports	72	55.7	61.4	68.2	77.6	83.2	88.6	100.0	104.2	107.1	114.0	120.2	120.6
Volume of Imports	73	53.9	60.1	64.2	71.5	81.5	92.0	100.0	104.5	108.7	117.1	128.6	136.9
Unit Value of Exports	74	85.5	91.1	92.0	95.0	95.1	94.2	100.0	100.5	99.5	98.0	99.0	103.6
Unit Value of Imports	75	83.6	87.3	87.6	90.7	88.7	88.6	100.0	99.0	95.9	94.6	96.9	101.8

Spain 184

		1994	1995	1996	1997	1998	1999	2000	2001	2002	2003	2004	2005
Balance of Payments						*Millions of US Dollars: Minus Sign Indicates Debit*							
Current Account, n.i.e.	78ald	−6,389	−1,967	−2,234	−830	−7,251	−17,860	−23,076	−23,579	−22,592	−31,737	−54,865	−83,136
Goods: Exports f.o.b.	78aad	73,925	93,442	102,843	107,198	112,310	112,919	115,769	117,522	127,162	158,049	185,209	194,502
Goods: Imports f.o.b.	78abd	−88,817	−112,107	−118,909	−121,414	−133,949	−144,732	−152,856	−152,039	−161,794	−203,205	−251,939	−280,094
Trade Balance	78acd	−14,892	−18,665	−16,066	−14,216	−21,639	−31,813	−37,087	−34,518	−34,632	−45,155	−66,730	−85,592
Services: Credit	78add	33,859	40,468	44,477	43,667	48,455	52,331	52,453	55,651	60,247	74,308	86,078	93,540
Services: Debit	78aed	−18,865	−22,893	−25,526	−25,621	−28,626	−31,975	−33,171	−35,182	−38,712	−47,951	−59,188	−65,548
Balance on Goods & Services	78afd	102	−1,090	2,885	3,829	−1,809	−11,457	−17,805	−14,049	−13,097	−18,798	−39,841	−57,599
Income: Credit	78agd	8,687	14,205	15,582	15,041	15,925	14,935	18,562	19,870	21,132	25,524	33,948	38,766
Income: Debit	78ahd	−16,457	−19,607	−23,038	−22,466	−24,512	−24,442	−25,325	−31,085	−32,768	−38,589	−48,986	−60,218
Balance on Gds, Serv. & Inc.	78aid	−7,668	−6,492	−4,571	−3,596	−10,396	−20,964	−24,569	−25,264	−24,734	−31,862	−54,879	−79,051
Current Transfers, n.i.e.: Credit	78ajd	9,171	11,962	10,999	11,623	12,556	13,130	11,122	12,088	13,420	16,495	20,366	20,185
Current Transfers: Debit	78akd	−7,893	−7,437	−8,662	−8,856	−9,411	−10,026	−9,630	−10,403	−11,278	−16,370	−20,353	−24,270
Capital Account, n.i.e.	78bcd	2,305	6,112	6,637	6,485	6,418	6,924	4,797	4,811	7,236	9,274	10,450	9,862
Capital Account, n.i.e.: Credit	78bad	3,571	7,348	7,692	7,243	7,081	7,987	5,787	5,782	8,118	10,984	11,646	10,993
Capital Account: Debit	78bbd	−1,266	−1,236	−1,055	−758	−662	−1,063	−989	−971	−882	−1,710	−1,197	−1,131
Financial Account, n.i.e.	78bjd	4,491	−6,675	21,486	9,220	−13,075	−10,895	15,250	17,888	18,656	5,904	36,964	72,508
Direct Investment Abroad	78bdd	−4,051	−4,718	−7,063	−14,307	−20,371	−44,053	−57,411	−32,889	−33,653	−27,570	−61,504	−38,953
Dir. Invest. in Rep. Econ., n.i.e.	78bed	9,216	8,086	9,623	8,937	14,282	18,523	38,835	28,097	39,983	25,716	24,792	22,789
Portfolio Investment Assets	78bfd	−1,492	−490	−3,655	−16,450	−44,195	−47,396	−59,318	−44,992	−29,089	−90,833	−39,651	−118,259
Equity Securities	78bkd	−1,039	−533	−777	−5,271	−10,122	−17,279	−36,136	−247	123	−13,180	−15,063	−18,851
Debt Securities	78bld	−453	43	−2,878	−11,179	−34,074	−30,117	−23,183	−44,745	−29,212	−77,653	−24,588	−99,408
Portfolio Investment Liab., n.i.e.	78bgd	−20,856	21,656	3,127	11,775	16,740	44,921	58,146	27,971	34,105	44,763	141,686	170,429
Equity Securities	78bmd	1,154	4,216	147	−292	10,073	9,347	19,692	7,958	2,810	−3,649	10,918	−9,434
Debt Securities	78bnd	−22,010	17,440	2,980	12,067	6,667	35,574	38,455	20,013	31,294	48,412	130,768	179,863
Financial Derivatives Assets	78bwd	—	—	—	—	—	....	....	....	....	....	....	....
Financial Derivatives Liabilities	78bxd	158	−557	−875	41	−2,776	261	1,818	−269	−4,720	−3,785	74	−150
Other Investment Assets	78bhd	9,152	−36,818	2,477	−1,416	−21,596	−24,566	−18,486	10,476	−22,970	−13,304	−52,659	−40,989
Monetary Authorities	78bod	3	−71	−4	7	−422	−39,311	−7,837	14,992	6,115	5,211	−18,079	17,121
General Government	78bpd	−620	−402	−502	−377	−426	−209	−253	−283	−456	−89	−2,182	−195
Banks	78bqd	14,437	−26,898	9,967	13,176	−1,960	5,357	−7,511	−3,742	−17,953	−10,523	−20,402	−47,690
Other Sectors	78brd	−4,668	−9,446	−6,984	−14,222	−18,788	9,596	−2,884	−492	−10,676	−7,903	−11,995	−10,225
Other Investment Liab., n.i.e.	78bid	12,363	6,167	17,852	20,640	44,841	41,414	51,665	29,494	35,000	70,916	24,226	77,640
Monetary Authorities	78bsd	27	22	462	−465	−2	−11	−141	−185	1,119	−1,331	−89	131
General Government	78btd	3,007	1,493	−226	5	1,044	−296	902	575	1,573	−1,026	6,362	−498
Banks	78bud	10,572	4,050	18,648	20,488	38,944	25,719	36,676	15,281	26,982	61,853	17,691	60,990
Other Sectors	78bvd	−1,242	601	−1,032	612	4,856	16,002	14,229	13,824	5,326	11,420	262	17,016
Net Errors and Omissions	78cad	−371	−3,884	−1,608	−3,120	−446	−964	149	−461	390	1,070	1,039	−1,153
Overall Balance	78cbd	36	−6,414	24,280	11,755	−14,354	−22,795	−2,880	−1,341	3,690	−15,489	−6,412	−1,919
Reserves and Related Items	79dad	−36	6,414	−24,280	−11,755	14,354	22,795	2,880	1,341	−3,690	15,489	6,412	1,919
Reserve Assets	79dbd	−36	6,414	−24,280	−11,755	14,354	22,795	2,880	1,341	−3,690	15,489	6,412	1,919
Use of Fund Credit and Loans	79dcd	—	—	—	—	—							
Exceptional Financing	79ded	—	—	—	—	—	....	....	....	....	....	....	....
International Investment Position						*Millions of US Dollars*							
Assets	79aad	221,860	268,762	289,787	311,244	397,987	464,207	566,745	594,340	755,440	997,725	....	....
Direct Investment Abroad	79abd	30,052	36,225	40,548	50,322	70,130	112,802	159,959	184,462	224,364	279,818	....	....
Portfolio Investment	79acd	17,284	18,244	21,108	34,858	81,237	127,994	180,256	205,136	272,397	432,696	....	....
Equity Securities	79add	3,454	3,764	4,441	9,235	19,978	42,482	78,094	65,765	53,180	83,402	....	....
Debt Securities	79aed	13,830	14,480	16,667	25,623	61,259	85,513	102,161	139,371	219,217	349,294	....	....
Financial Derivatives	79afd											....	....
Other Investment	79afd	130,690	176,931	167,717	155,680	185,832	185,401	190,953	170,488	218,376	258,402	....	....
Monetary Authorities	79agd	159	247	229	198	582	36,652	42,557	26,059	24,206	23,648	....	....
General Government	79ahd	5,465	6,029	6,323	6,328	6,872	6,706	6,781	6,882	7,723	8,720	....	....
Banks	79aid	97,086	130,872	116,763	94,956	100,738	84,840	87,836	86,771	117,944	143,128	....	....
Other Sectors	79ajd	27,980	39,783	44,403	54,198	77,640	57,203	53,779	50,776	68,503	82,906	....	....
Reserve Assets	79akd	43,834	37,362	60,414	70,384	60,788	38,010	35,576	34,254	40,304	26,809	....	....
Liabilities	79lad	322,228	383,415	400,206	410,687	528,172	630,123	718,800	762,749	997,006	1,360,919	....	....
Dir. Invest. in Rep. Economy	79lbd	96,312	109,185	107,880	100,025	118,115	116,230	144,850	165,291	236,606	313,267	....	....
Portfolio Investment	79lcd	83,764	118,426	126,696	137,322	183,995	269,359	288,813	293,324	375,309	520,592	....	....
Equity Securities	79ldd	24,146	32,461	39,162	46,974	75,775	146,619	137,268	127,040	122,687	186,788	....	....
Debt Securities	79led	59,618	85,966	87,534	90,348	108,221	122,740	151,545	166,284	252,621	333,805	....	....
Financial Derivatives	79lld											....	....
Other Investment	79lfd	142,152	155,804	165,629	173,340	226,062	244,534	285,137	304,134	385,092	527,060	....	....
Monetary Authorities	79lgd	76	107	556	53	63	34	422	263	1,438	116	....	....
General Government	79lhd	9,989	12,355	11,503	10,158	11,725	9,939	10,343	10,125	11,972	12,888	....	....
Banks	79lid	104,912	114,506	127,770	138,350	183,084	191,090	219,207	225,809	286,551	400,933	....	....
Other Sectors	79ljd	27,175	28,836	25,801	24,779	31,191	43,471	55,165	67,937	85,131	113,123	....	....
Government Finance													
Central Government						*Billions of Pesetas through 1998; Millions of Euros Beginning 1999: Year Ending December 31*							
Deficit (-) or Surplus	80	−4,147.6	−3,606.3	−4,003.5	−1,909.4	−800.0	† −5,939	−840	−2,257	−3,568	−6,659	−2,310	2,181
Total Revenue and Grants	81y	12,960.3	14,077.2	14,629.7	16,636.5	17,519.0	† 110,370	118,693	125,193	108,456	109,655	114,793	128,777
Revenue	81	12,960.3	14,077.2	14,629.7	16,636.5	17,519.0	† 110,370	118,693	125,193	108,456	109,655	114,793	128,777
Grants	81z	—	—	—	—	—	†						
Exp. & Lending Minus Repay.	82z	17,107.9	17,683.5	18,633.2	18,545.9	18,319.0	† 116,309	119,534	127,451	112,024	116,314	117,103	126,596
Expenditure	82	16,438.3	17,241.5	18,322.2	18,694.0	18,633.4	† 116,724	121,124	128,077	111,082	113,787	114,734	122,755
Lending Minus Repayments	83	669.6	442.0	311.0	−148.1	−314.4	† −414	−1,591	−627	942	2,527	2,370	3,841
Total Financing	80h	4,147.2	3,605.7	4,003.0	1,908.8	800.2	† 5,939	840	2,257	3,568	6,659	2,310	−2,181
Total Net Borrowing	84	2,317.7	3,324.5	5,039.2	973.4	910.7	† 11,031	6,841	−2,644	5,994	116	3,524	68
Use of Cash Balances	87	−1,829.5	−281.2	1,036.2	−935.4	110.5	† 5,091	6,001	−4,901	2,426	−6,543	1,214	2,249
Total Debt by Residence	88	34,266.0	38,678.1	43,922.0	45,616.6	47,243.4	† 298,384	307,726	306,895	307,610	301,476	303,540	299,730
Domestic	88a	27,389.8	29,951.8	34,934.4	35,121.6	35,756.1	† 207,315	187,301	177,105	170,730	181,447	163,840	155,740
Foreign	89a	6,876.2	8,726.3	8,987.6	10,495.0	11,487.3	† 91,070	120,424	129,791	136,880	120,029	139,700	143,990
General Government						*As Percent of Gross Domestic Product*							

Spain 184

Billions of Pesetas: through 1998; Billions of Euros Beginning 1999

National Accounts		1994	1995	1996	1997	1998	1999	2000	2001	2002	2003	2004	2005
Househ.Cons.Expend.,incl.NPISHs....	96f.c	40,848	44,645	47,116	49,963	52,012	† 345	376	401	425	448	483	522
Government Consumption Expend...	91f.c	12,307	13,455	14,183	14,650	15,332	† 100	108	116	125	136	149	161
Gross Fixed Capital Formation..........	93e.c	14,259	16,015	16,882	18,301	20,086	† 142	163	177	191	211	234	266
Changes in Inventories....................	93i.c	244	279	249	210	359	† 3	3	3	3	3	3	3
Exports of Goods and Services..........	90c.c	14,209	16,656	18,636	22,055	23,935	† 155	183	194	199	206	217	230
Imports of Goods and Services (-)....	98c.c	14,313	16,641	18,227	21,342	23,876	† 165	203	211	214	223	248	277
Gross Domestic Product (GDP)........	99b.c	67,554	74,409	78,838	83,838	87,848	† 580	630	680	729	781	837	904
Net Primary Income from Abroad.....	98.n	−1,182	−607	−890	−1,135	−1,013	† −20	−27	−36	−41	−45	....	....
Gross National Income (GNI)............	99a	63,630	72,660	76,766	81,409	86,780	† 560	603	644	688	735	....	....
Net Current Transf.from Abroad......	98t	....	295	197	209	192	† 1	—	—	—	....	....	....
Gross Nat'l Disposable Inc.(GNDI)....	99i	....	72,954	76,963	81,618	86,972	† 561	604	644	688	625	....	....
Gross Saving....................................	99s	....	16,241	17,036	18,576	19,816	† 127	137	148	159	62	....	....
Consumption of Fixed Capital..........	99cf	7,428	7,951	8,363	8,851	11,430	† 74	83	90	98	—	....	....
GDP Volume 1995 Ref., Chained.....	99b.r	70,887	74,409	76,202	79,148	80,468	† 520.6	546.9	566.2	581.4	598.9	617.4	638.5
GDP Volume (2000=100)................	99bvr	77.9	81.8	83.7	87.0	88.4	† 95.2	100.0	103.5	106.3	109.5	112.9	116.8
GDP Deflator (2000=100)...............	99bir	82.7	86.8	89.8	91.9	94.7	† 96.7	100.0	104.2	108.8	113.1	117.7	122.9
						Millions: Midyear Estimates								
Population...............................	99z	39.81	39.92	40.02	40.12	40.24	40.43	40.72	41.12	41.61	42.14	42.65	43.06

Sri Lanka 524

		1994	1995	1996	1997	1998	1999	2000	2001	2002	2003	2004	2005
Exchange Rates						*Rupees per SDR: End of Period*							
Market Rate	aa	72.963	80.341	81.540	82.689	96.164	99.054	107.594	117.075	131.500	143.750	162.453	145.953
						Rupees per US Dollar: End of Period (ae) Period Average (rf)							
Market Rate	ae	49.980	54.048	56.705	61.285	68.297	72.170	82.580	93.159	96.725	96.738	104.605	102.117
Market Rate	rf	49.415	51.252	55.271	58.995	64.450	70.635	77.005	89.383	95.662	96.521	101.194	100.498
Fund Position						*Millions of SDRs: End of Period*							
Quota	2f.s	304	304	304	304	304	413	413	413	413	413	413	413
SDRs	1b.s	—	1	1	—	1	1	—	1	2	—	—	1
Reserve Position in the Fund	1c.s	20	20	20	20	20	48	48	48	48	48	48	48
Total Fund Cred.&Loans Outstg	2tl	423	400	369	321	261	188	123	171	228	265	189	267
International Liquidity						*Millions of US Dollars Unless Otherwise Indicated: End of Period*							
Total Reserves minus Gold	1l.d	2,046	2,088	1,962	2,024	1,980	1,636	1,039	1,287	1,631	2,265	2,132	2,651
SDRs	1b.d	—	1	2	—	1	1	—	1	2	—	—	2
Reserve Position in the Fund	1c.d	30	30	29	27	29	65	62	60	65	71	74	68
Foreign Exchange	1d.d	2,016	2,057	1,931	1,996	1,950	1,569	976	1,226	1,564	2,193	2,058	2,581
Gold (Million Fine Troy Ounces)	1ad	.063	.063	.063	.063	.063	.063	† .336	.255	.216	.165	.167	.167
Gold (National Valuation)	1and	6	6	5	5	4	4	† 108	71	75	69	73	86
Monetary Authorities: Other Liab.	4..d	505	575	859	820	728	833	707	636	671	....	....	....
Deposit Money Banks: Assets	7a.d	639	839	780	1,103	916	941	1,050	900	795	889	1,243	1,466
Liabilities	7b.d	615	1,004	964	1,094	859	764	909	1,009	865	863	1,066	1,388
FCBU: Assets	7k.d	540	574	504	682	479	439	429	422	330	424	520	834
Liabilities	7m.d	665	682	615	702	438	306	429	519	330	276	382	655
Monetary Authorities						*Millions of Rupees: End of Period*							
Foreign Assets	11	95,672	105,898	† 104,899	120,675	133,128	116,796	82,334	117,507	160,499	225,879	225,225	....
Claims on Central Government	12a	29,335	37,224	37,799	26,776	29,018	49,179	94,708	88,969	83,893	64,387	117,630	....
Claims on Deposit Money Banks	12e	3,376	2,812	2,259	1,692	1,122	748	520	150	2,657	2,627	2,547	....
Reserve Money	14	68,055	78,587	85,509	83,736	92,866	100,444	105,163	112,522	126,410	141,446	170,967	....
of which: Currency Outside DMBs	14a	38,907	42,199	42,565	45,680	51,767	58,481	62,647	65,536	75,292	85,601	99,669	....
Other Liabilities to DMBs	14n	....	....	—	—	—	—	—	—	11,156	20,974	7,213	....
Foreign Liabilities	16c	35,658	40,748	† 34,787	33,170	31,355	27,710	24,716	30,190	43,316	61,302	73,535	....
Central Government Deposits	16d	2,813	3,040	3,510	6,476	3,108	2,463	3,152	4,301	201	569	523	....
Capital Accounts	17a	25,358	30,829	28,343	35,547	47,532	49,043	59,866	71,449	72,920	74,331	100,409	....
Other Items (Net)	17r	−3,500	−7,269	† −7,191	−9,786	−11,594	−12,939	−15,335	−11,838	−6,953	−5,730	−7,245	....
Deposit Money Banks						*Millions of Rupees: End of Period*							
Reserves	20	25,389	35,449	41,188	36,500	39,667	40,110	39,542	49,760	53,234	51,083	70,904	87,481
Other Claims on Monetary Author.	20n	....	....	—	—	—	—	—	—	11,156	20,974	7,213	
Foreign Assets	21	31,918	† 45,338	44,212	67,596	62,560	67,946	86,682	83,814	76,921	86,011	129,987	149,654
Claims on Central Government	22a	21,039	† 23,808	29,579	42,469	53,514	60,618	69,336	119,616	125,439	129,523	124,877	....
Claims on Nonfin.Pub.Enterprises	22ca	3,118	13,305	15,491	14,658	10,836	13,715	38,254	40,811	43,031	36,192	41,171	16,672
Claims on Cooperatives	22cb	2,541	3,939	1,465	1,661	1,812	1,608	1,668	1,577	1,349	1,365	1,148	1,256
Claims on Private Sector	22d	62,676	206,783	228,992	261,359	291,969	323,374	362,435	395,216	452,054	527,079	640,162	776,733
Demand Deposits	24	31,415	32,970	35,516	40,108	44,470	50,059	55,788	56,665	64,052	76,014	88,777	116,620
Time and Savings Deposits	25	121,210	† 184,224	210,454	247,817	281,473	319,765	364,944	426,927	483,135	556,220	670,191	791,576
Foreign Liabilities	26c	30,746	54,256	54,678	67,030	58,656	55,141	75,101	94,030	83,655	83,513	111,464	141,753
Central Government Deposits	26d	9,290	† 9,483	12,947	13,765	11,646	13,122	13,292	26,333	14,535	16,436	19,802	27,063
Credit from Monetary Authorities	26g	4,054	3,625	4,050	4,775	4,813	5,171	5,886	4,811	4,858	6,577	6,502	9,174
Capital Accounts	27a	28,278	33,460	39,238	44,368	50,220	51,571	51,808	44,520	51,770	75,197	77,220	103,088
Other Items (Net)	27r	1,877	10,603	4,045	6,380	9,081	12,543	31,098	61,001	61,180	38,269	41,506	41,885
Monetary Survey						*Millions of Rupees: End of Period*							
Foreign Assets (Net)	31n	61,186	56,232	† 59,646	88,070	105,677	101,890	69,198	77,100	110,450	167,074	170,213	....
Domestic Credit	32	188,564	273,209	297,517	327,437	372,817	433,115	550,156	615,922	691,082	741,577	904,722	....
Claims on Central Govt. (Net)	32an	38,271	† 48,509	50,922	49,005	67,778	94,212	147,600	177,951	194,596	176,905	222,183	....
Claims on Nonfin.Pub.Enterprises	32ca	5,163	13,305	15,491	14,658	10,836	13,715	38,254	40,811	43,031	36,192	41,171	16,672
Claims on Cooperatives	32cb	2,541	3,939	1,465	1,661	1,812	1,608	1,668	1,577	1,349	1,365	1,148	1,256
Claims on Private Sector	32d	63,453	207,456	229,640	262,113	292,392	323,580	362,634	395,583	452,106	527,116	640,220	....
Money	34	70,463	75,218	78,202	85,851	96,269	108,554	118,478	122,211	139,361	161,635	188,454	....
Quasi-Money	35	120,539	† 184,224	210,454	247,817	281,473	319,765	364,944	426,927	483,135	556,220	670,191	791,576
Other Items (Net)	37r	56,278	68,364	† 68,507	81,838	100,753	106,685	135,933	167,378	179,037	190,796	216,291	....
Money plus Quasi-Money	35l	191,002	259,442	288,656	333,668	377,741	428,319	483,421	549,138	622,496	717,855	858,644	....
Interest Rates						*Percent Per Annum*							
Bank Rate (End of Period)	60	17.00	17.00	17.00	17.00	17.00	16.00	25.00	....	18.00	15.00	15.00	15.00
Money Market Rate	60b	18.54	41.87	24.33	18.42	15.74	16.69	17.30	21.24	12.33	9.68	8.87	10.15
Treasury Bill Rate	60c	12.68	16.81	† 17.40	....	12.59	12.51	14.02	17.57	12.47	8.09	7.71	9.03
Deposit Rate	60l	13.10	12.13	12.36	11.25	9.56	9.12	9.17	11.01	9.22	6.00	5.07	10.23
Lending Rate	60p	18.13	18.04	18.26	14.69	15.03	14.72	16.16	19.39	13.17	10.34	9.47	7.00
Prices and Labor						*Index Numbers (2000=100): Period Averages*							
Share Prices	62	....	148.8	124.4	135.9	123.7	111.4	100.0	91.6	143.2	203.1	275.5	404.6
Wholesale Prices	63	66.3	72.1	86.9	92.9	98.7	98.3	100.0	111.7	123.7	127.4	143.4	159.9
Consumer Prices	64	60.1	64.8	75.1	82.3	90.0	94.2	100.0	114.2	125.1	133.0	143.0	159.7
Wages: Agr. Minimum Rates	65	41.7	42.1	46.1	49.3	55.7	56.6	100.0	59.7	64.4	70.1	70.9	77.5
						Number in Thousands: Period Averages							
Labor Force	67d	6,079	6,106	6,242	6,266	6,661	6,673	6,827	6,773	7,145	7,654	8,061	....
Employment	67e	5,281	5,357	5,537	5,608	6,049	6,083	6,310	6,236	6,519	7,013	7,394	....
Unemployment	67c	798	749	705	658	611	591	517	537	626	641	667	....
Unemployment Rate (%)	67r	13.1	12.3	11.3	10.5	9.2	8.9	7.6	7.9	8.8	8.4	8.3	....

Sri Lanka   524

		1994	1995	1996	1997	1998	1999	2000	2001	2002	2003	2004	2005
Intl. Transactions & Positions							*Millions of Rupees*						
Exports........................	70	158,554	195,117	226,801	274,193	310,398	325,171	420,114	430,372	449,850	494,648	583,968	638,275
Tea............................	70s	20,964	24,638	34,068	42,533	50,280	43,727	53,133	61,602	63,105	68,063	74,898	81,483
Imports, c.i.f.................	71	236,030	265,996	299,663	344,533	381,943	415,487	485,084	532,963	584,491	643,749	808,364	888,358
							2000=100						
Volume of Exports.............	72	66.2	† 70.9	73.9	81.7	80.5	83.7	100.0	91.9	92.7	98.3	105.8	112.7
Tea............................	72s	79.7	83.6	84.7	93.2	94.4	93.4	100.0	102.3	101.2	102.8	104.2	107.2
Volume of Imports.............	73	71.1	† 73.1	73.4	82.5	89.5	89.8	100.0	90.8	100.6	111.3	122.4	125.9
Unit Value of Exports.........	74	57.2	† 65.7	73.3	80.1	92.0	92.3	100.0	111.7	112.7	120.8	131.9	134.9
Tea............................	74s	49.5	55.5	75.7	85.9	100.3	88.1	100.0	113.3	117.4	124.6	135.2	143.0
Unit Value of Imports.........	75	60.9	70.4	77.0	† 80.8	81.8	85.9	100.0	113.5	111.6	....	....	....
Balance of Payments							*Millions of US Dollars: Minus Sign Indicates Debit*						
Current Account, n.i.e.........	78ald	−757	−770	−683	−395	−228	−561	−1,044	−237	−268	−106	−677	....
Goods: Exports f.o.b..........	78aad	3,208	3,798	4,095	4,639	4,808	4,596	5,440	4,817	4,699	5,133	5,757	....
Goods: Imports f.o.b..........	78abd	−4,293	−4,783	−4,895	−5,278	−5,313	−5,365	−6,484	−5,377	−5,495	−6,005	−7,200	....
Trade Balance.................	78acd	−1,085	−985	−800	−640	−505	−769	−1,044	−560	−796	−872	−1,443	....
Services: Credit..............	78add	754	819	765	875	917	964	939	1,355	1,268	1,411	1,527	....
Services: Debit...............	78aed	−1,052	−1,199	−1,204	−1,303	−1,362	−1,414	−1,621	−1,749	−1,584	−1,679	−1,908	....
Balance on Goods & Services...	78afd	−1,383	−1,365	−1,239	−1,067	−950	−1,219	−1,727	−954	−1,112	−1,140	−1,824	....
Income: Credit................	78agd	144	223	175	233	214	167	149	108	75	170	157	....
Income: Debit.................	78ahd	−312	−361	−378	−393	−395	−419	−449	−375	−328	−341	−360	....
Balance on Gds, Serv. & Inc...	78aid	−1,552	−1,502	−1,442	−1,227	−1,131	−1,471	−2,027	−1,221	−1,364	−1,312	−2,027	....
Current Transfers, n.i.e.: Credit......	78ajd	882	847	881	967	1,054	1,078	1,166	1,155	1,287	1,414	1,564	....
Current Transfers: Debit......	78akd	−88	−115	−122	−135	−151	−168	−183	−172	−190	−209	−214	....
Capital Account, n.i.e........	78bcd	—	121	96	87	80	80	49	50	65	74	64	....
Capital Account, n.i.e.: Credit.......	78bad	—	124	100	91	85	85	55	55	71	81	71	....
Capital Account: Debit........	78bbd	—	−4	−4	−4	−5	−5	−6	−5	−6	−6	−7	....
Financial Account, n.i.e......	78bjd	959	730	452	467	345	413	447	−136	−196	−219	−133	....
Direct Investment Abroad......	78bdd	−8	—	—	—	—	—	—	—	−11	−27	−6	....
Dir. Invest. in Rep. Econ., n.i.e...	78bed	166	56	120	430	193	176	173	172	197	229	233	....
Portfolio Investment Assets...	78bfd	293	105	77	140	89	72	19	24	78	145	111	....
Equity Securities...........	78bkd	....	....	—	—	—	....	....	24	78	145	111	....
Debt Securities............	78bld	293	105	77	140	89	72	19	—	—	....	....	....
Portfolio Investment Liab., n.i.e...	78bgd	−266	−107	−70	−127	−113	−85	−63	−35	−53	−143	−100	....
Equity Securities...........	78bmd	....	....	....	....	....	....	....	−35	−53	−143	−100	....
Debt Securities............	78bnd	−266	−107	−70	−127	−113	−85	−63	—	—	....	....	....
Financial Derivatives Assets...	78bwd	....	....	—	....	....	....	....	....	....	....	....	....
Financial Derivatives Liabilities...	78bxd	....	....	—	....	....	....	....	....	....	....	....	....
Other Investment Assets.......	78bhd	−134	42	−28	−393	76	23	−244	183	104	−94	−354	....
Monetary Authorities.........	78bod	—	—	....	....	....	....	....	....	....	—	....	....
General Government...........	78bpd	9	4	−6	2	−3	−1	−4	—	—	—	....	....
Banks.......................	78bqd	−143	38	−22	−395	79	24	−239	183	104	−94	−354	....
Other Sectors...............	78brd	—	—	....	....	....	....	....	....	....	....	....	....
Other Investment Liab., n.i.e...	78bid	908	634	354	416	100	227	562	−480	−511	−328	−17	....
Monetary Authorities.........	78bsd	10	14	12	30	18	66	76	−33	27	40	179	....
General Government...........	78btd	247	448	218	144	204	62	47	−174	−324	−251	−275	....
Banks.......................	78bud	73	87	96	209	−131	−88	258	71	−145	−2	202	....
Other Sectors...............	78bvd	578	85	28	32	9	187	182	−343	−69	−115	−123	....
Net Errors and Omissions......	78cad	106	158	144	148	26	−27	186	15	136	−114	−189	....
Overall Balance..............	78cbd	308	239	9	307	224	−95	−361	−308	−262	−365	−935	....
Reserves and Related Items....	79dad	−308	−239	−9	−307	−224	95	361	308	262	365	935	....
Reserve Assets................	79dbd	−374	−205	36	−241	−141	195	447	−241	−444	−627	133	....
Use of Fund Credit and Loans...	79dcd	66	−34	−45	−66	−83	−100	−86	60	74	50	−112	....
Exceptional Financing.........	79ded	—	—	....	—	—	....	....	....	489	633	942	913
Government Finance							*Millions of Rupees: Year Ending December 31*						
Deficit (-) or Surplus........	80	−49,474	−55,196	−59,913	−40,234	−81,559	−76,359	−118,995	−138,133	−128,330	−122,726	−154,314	−171,377p
Revenue.......................	81	110,038	136,257	146,280	165,036	175,032	195,905	211,282	231,463	261,887	276,516	311,473	379,746p
Grants Received...............	81z	8,257	9,028	7,739	7,329	7,200	6,761	5,145	5,500	7,079	7,956	8,681	32,640p
Expenditure...................	82	157,476	195,880	212,787	228,732	253,808	267,611	322,048	367,966	389,442	409,782	473,485	583,504p
Lending Minus Repayments......	83	10,293	4,601	1,145	−16,133	9,983	11,414	13,374	7,130	7,854	−2,584	983	259p
Financing (by Residence of Lender)													
Domestic......................	84a	37,696	33,972	49,753	30,276	71,363	74,875	118,500	123,595	126,352	79,660	117,243	123,604p
Foreign.......................	85a	11,778	21,224	10,160	9,958	10,196	1,484	495	14,538	1,978	43,066	37,071	47,773p
Debt: Domestic................	88a	249,118	285,759	349,007	387,740	463,426	543,465	676,660	815,965	948,386	1,019,970	1,143,389	1,265,721p
Foreign.......................	89a	300,174	346,286	360,313	376,331	461,273	507,866	542,040	636,741	721,956	843,882	996,138	956,620p
Debt (by Currency)													
Debt: Rupees..................	88b	249,118	285,759	349,007	382,962	446,547	543,465	676,660	815,965	....	....	....	....
Intragovernmental Debt........	88s	—	—	—	—	—	—	—	—	....	....	....	....
Debt: Foreign Currency........	89b	300,174	346,286	360,313	383,615	461,454	508,396	542,207	634,622	....	....	....	....

Sri Lanka 524

National Accounts		1994	1995	1996	1997	1998	1999	2000	2001	2002	2003	2004	2005
							Millions of Rupees						
Househ.Cons.Expend.,incl.NPISHs....	**96f**	434,933	489,057	569,416	643,839	696,236	790,379	906,188	1,041,041	1,214,117	1,341,896	1,542,107	1,763,794
Government Consumption Expend...	**91f**	56,002	76,604	81,021	92,196	143,298	99,851	132,189	144,441	139,311	139,268	164,887	195,093
Gross Fixed Capital Formation.........	**93e**	154,260	170,875	183,509	216,873	261,726	301,728	352,644	309,644	330,543	386,621	506,675	625,649
Changes in Inventories....................	**93i**	2,250	950	2,755	230	4,844	95	40	40	4,261	2,135	268	334
Exports of Goods and Services.........	**90c**	195,805	237,711	268,640	325,289	369,485	392,437	490,676	525,398	570,833	632,907	736,967	792,415
Imports of Goods and Services (-).....	**98c**	264,166	307,425	337,213	388,154	429,925	478,526	624,048	613,167	677,180	741,667	921,537	1,011,583
Gross Domestic Product (GDP)........	**99b**	579,084	667,772	768,133	890,272	1,045,664	1,105,985	1,257,636	1,407,398	1,581,885	1,761,161	2,029,365	2,365,702
Net Primary Income from Abroad.....	**98.n**	−8,310	−6,958	−11,258	−9,409	−11,555	−17,831	−23,083	−23,830	−24,174	−16,535	−20,688	−30,049
GDP at Factor Cost........................	**99ba**	523,300	598,327	695,934	803,698	912,839	994,730	1,125,259	1,245,598	1,403,286	1,562,737	1,800,750	2,098,323
Gross National Income (GNI)...........	**99a**	570,774	660,814	756,875	880,828	1,034,109	1,088,154	1,234,599	1,383,568	1,557,479	1,744,154	2,008,723	2,335,814
GDP at Fact.Cost,Vol.'82 Prices.......	**99bap**	159,269	167,953	174,261	....	....	....	....	....	....	....	....	....
GDP at Fact.Cost,Vol.'96 Prices.......	**99bap**	....	....	695,934	739,763	774,796	808,340	857,035	843,794	877,248	930,057	980,720	1,039,735
GDP Volume (2000=100)...............	**99bvp**	74.2	78.3	† 81.2	86.3	90.4	94.3	100.0	98.5	102.4	108.5	114.4	121.3
GDP Deflator (2000=100)...............	**99bip**	62.7	67.9	76.2	82.7	89.7	93.7	100.0	112.4	121.8	128.0	139.8	153.7
							Millions: Midyear Estimates						
Population...............................	**99z**	18.67	18.87	19.07	19.27	19.47	19.66	19.85	20.03	20.21	20.39	20.57	20.74

Sudan 732

		1994	1995	1996	1997	1998	1999	2000	2001	2002	2003	2004	2005
Exchange Rates		*Dinars per SDR: End of Period*											
Market Rate	aa	58.39	78.24	208.40	232.35	334.83	353.70	335.30	328.55	355.76	386.59	389.23	329.50
		Dinars per US Dollar: End of Period (ae) Period Average (rf)											
Market Rate	ae	40.00	52.63	144.93	172.21	237.80	257.70	257.35	261.43	261.68	260.16	250.63	230.54
Market Rate	rf	28.96	58.09	125.08	157.57	200.80	252.55	257.12	258.70	263.31	260.98	257.91	243.61
Fund Position		*Millions of SDRs: End of Period*											
Quota	2f.s	169.7	169.7	169.7	169.7	169.7	169.7	169.7	169.7	169.7	169.7	169.7	169.7
SDRs	1b.s	—	—	—	—	—	—	—	—	.1	.2	—	—
Reserve Position in the Fund	1c.s	—	—	—	—	—	—	—	—	—	—	—	—
Total Fund Cred.&Loans Outstg	2tl	671.6	645.7	621.2	590.5	548.4	520.8	479.7	438.6	421.6	402.9	381.7	362.6
International Liquidity		*Millions of US Dollars Unless Otherwise Indicated: End of Period*											
Total Reserves minus Gold	1l.d	78.2	163.4	106.8	81.6	90.6	188.7	† 247.3	117.8	440.9	847.5	1,626.1	2,449.8
SDRs	1b.d	—	—	—	—	—	—	—	—	.2	.3	—	.1
Reserve Position in the Fund	1c.d	—	—	—	—	—	—	—	—	—	—	—	—
Foreign Exchange	1d.d	78.1	163.3	106.8	81.6	90.6	188.7	† 247.3	117.8	440.7	847.2	1,626.1	2,449.7
Monetary Authorities: Other Liab	4..d	2,471.8	3,407.1	2,549.9	2,464.4	2,538.9	2,618.8	2,640.2	2,654.1	2,793.2	3,005.8	3,068.9	3,034.0
Deposit Money Banks: Assets	7a.d	27.0	32.1	20.7	25.8	26.9	266.1	286.2	343.2	488.8	500.7	563.3	762.1
Liabilities	7b.d	3.8	5.3	3.0	2.6	2.0	13.4	14.8	34.8	52.4	56.9	72.3	120.1
Monetary Authorities		*Billions of Dinars: End of Period*											
Foreign Assets	11	3.13	8.61	15.50	14.07	21.58	48.64	† 73.11	41.25	119.85	229.81	420.36	580.45
Claims on Central Government	12a	22.03	32.90	76.03	84.76	101.77	134.79	† 168.95	195.46	230.35	277.93	288.26	239.98
of which:Accum. Interest Arrears	12ag	....	....	....	....	....	....	52.69	64.09	76.09	88.68	100.01	112.85
Claims on Nonfin.Pub.Enterprises	12c	.22	.22	.22	.22	.22	3.45	† 17.14	14.81	5.74	17.34	15.48	19.77
Claims on Deposit Money Banks	12e	.36	.36	.35	2.39	6.14	7.21	† 8.82	12.58	17.15	33.49	29.98	34.97
Reserve Money	14	20.21	35.72	64.94	87.18	112.81	152.42	† 223.58	233.59	283.30	360.59	462.17	641.00
of which: Currency Outside DMBs	14a	14.79	24.86	44.44	58.49	82.14	108.11	† 142.08	153.84	193.58	240.21	304.90	376.13
Quasi-Monetary Deposits	15	2.08	3.21	3.24	3.06	3.34	3.21	—	—	—	—	—	—
Cent. Bk. Liab.: Musharaka Certif	16ac	....	....	....	....	4.85	4.20	† 1.11	.64	.76	2.75	—	13.50
Foreign Liabilities	16c	134.16	224.80	485.58	547.81	767.53	838.10	† 820.43	818.50	859.84	914.84	894.68	799.42
Central Government Deposits	16d	.86	1.24	10.77	9.18	3.74	5.11	† 8.44	9.62	27.27	64.78	151.55	175.12
Capital Accounts	17a	.24	.43	1.24	1.16	2.05	2.61	† 4.24	4.32	9.11	13.16	22.34	44.44
Valuation Adjustment	17rv	−124.94	−206.55	−444.81	−514.97	−724.21	−772.02	† −776.69	−781.52	−783.05	−774.95	−758.65	−783.48
Other Items (Net)	17r	−6.88	−16.78	−28.85	−31.99	−40.39	−39.53	† −13.09	−21.04	−24.15	−22.62	−18.01	−14.84
Deposit Money Banks		*Billions of Dinars: End of Period*											
Reserves	20	5.58	8.01	14.27	28.07	30.62	37.91	57.15	57.41	67.68	91.01	118.43	170.11
Claims on Mon.Author.:Securities	20c	....	....	....	....	4.85	4.20	1.11	.64	.76	2.75	—	13.50
Foreign Assets	21	10.80	16.87	29.98	44.50	63.92	68.57	73.66	89.73	127.92	130.27	141.19	175.69
Claims on Central Government	22a	.21	.16	.12	.03	.13	.16	4.22	7.33	20.88	35.04	46.64	88.04
Claims on State and Local Govt	22b	.03	.13	.16	.17	.05	.07	.01	.53	1.33	1.28	1.28	.63
Claims on Nonfin.Pub.Enterprises	22c	1.22	1.19	1.67	1.68	2.57	4.72	5.65	9.06	11.56	11.30	13.37	20.18
Claims on Private Sector	22d	8.82	13.07	31.90	39.35	44.34	43.58	71.48	101.14	178.43	279.63	421.16	669.68
Claims on Nonbank Financial Insts	22f	.09	.12	.22	.36	.43	.35	2.09	.62	1.89	2.46	.58	9.52
Demand Deposits	24	9.49	15.60	30.92	41.35	46.94	56.90	84.13	109.14	147.46	194.63	279.46	393.72
Time and Savings Deposits	25	13.65	25.41	35.82	55.13	73.62	85.35	107.26	158.54	210.53	271.88	355.91	559.54
Foreign Liabilities	26c	1.51	2.81	4.30	4.41	4.72	3.44	3.81	9.11	13.72	14.79	18.13	27.68
Central Government Deposits	26d	.23	.31	.77	.40	.42	3.53	6.35	7.08	5.09	6.44	11.29	23.62
Credit from Monetary Authorities	26g	.10	.75	.08	.11	.32	3.01	2.51	2.51	7.26	14.91	10.65	6.65
Capital Accounts	27a	3.86	5.47	11.14	14.77	20.34	24.47	32.20	47.64	73.69	110.31	143.71	183.86
Valuation Adjustment	27rv	.70	1.08	1.39	2.81	2.36	−.39	−.78	−.17	−.69	−.40	−3.02	−6.41
Other Items (Net)	27r	−4.07	−13.51	−8.21	−6.53	−.93	−16.47	−19.62	−66.83	−46.63	−58.72	−73.47	−41.31
Monetary Survey		*Billions of Dinars: End of Period*											
Foreign Assets (Net)	31n	−121.73	−202.14	−444.40	−493.66	−686.75	−724.34	† −677.49	−696.62	−625.80	−569.55	−351.25	−70.96
Domestic Credit	32	31.52	46.24	98.78	116.99	145.34	178.50	† 254.74	312.25	417.81	553.76	623.93	849.06
Claims on Central Govt. (Net)	32an	21.14	31.51	64.61	75.22	97.74	126.32	† 158.38	186.10	218.87	241.74	172.06	129.27
Claims on State and Local Govt	32b	.03	.13	.16	.17	.05	.07	.01	.53	1.33	1.28	1.28	.63
Claims on Nonfin.Pub.Enterprises	32c	1.44	1.41	1.88	1.89	2.78	8.18	† 22.79	23.87	17.30	28.64	28.85	39.95
Claims on Private Sector	32d	8.82	13.07	31.90	39.35	44.34	43.58	71.48	101.14	178.43	279.63	421.16	669.68
Claims on Nonbank Financial Inst	32f	.09	.12	.22	.36	.43	.35	2.09	.62	1.89	2.46	.58	9.52
Money	34	24.28	40.46	75.36	99.85	129.08	165.01	† 234.59	271.39	352.26	458.48	604.37	813.01
Quasi-Money	35	15.73	28.62	39.06	58.20	76.95	88.56	† 112.60	161.39	211.00	275.61	356.08	565.18
Valuation Adjustment	37rv	−124.24	−205.47	−443.42	−512.15	−721.85	−772.41	† −777.47	−781.68	−783.73	−775.35	−761.66	−789.89
Other Items (Net)	37r	−6.00	−19.82	−16.90	−22.41	−24.72	−26.73	† 8.06	−34.90	12.48	25.56	73.90	189.80
Money plus Quasi-Money	35l	40.04	69.39	114.70	157.90	205.16	253.31	347.19	432.77	563.27	734.09	960.45	1,378.19
Prices and Labor		*Index Numbers (2000=100): Period Averages*											
Consumer Prices	64	12.1	20.4	47.5	69.7	81.6	† 94.6	100.0	105.8	114.6	123.5	133.8	145.2
		Number in Thousands: Period Averages											
Labor Force	67d	....	....	7,983	....	....	....	....	....	....	....	....	....
Intl. Transactions & Positions		*Millions of US Dollars: Year Ending June 30 through 1994, Year Ending December 31 Thereafter*											
Exports	70..d	502.6	555.6	620.3	594.2	595.8	780.0	1,806.7	1,698.7	1,949.1	2,542.2	3,777.8	4,824.3
Imports, c.i.f	71..d	1,227.4	† 1,218.8	1,547.5	1,579.6	1,914.7	1,415.0	1,552.7	2,300.9	2,446.4	2,881.9	4,075.2	6,756.8

Sudan 732

2006, International Monetary Fund : *International Financial Statistics Yearbook*

		1994	1995	1996	1997	1998	1999	2000	2001	2002	2003	2004	2005
Balance of Payments		*Millions of US Dollars: Minus Sign Indicates Debit*											
Current Account, n.i.e.	78ald	−601.7	−499.9	−826.8	−828.1	−956.5	−464.8	−556.8	−618.3	−1,008.1	−955.4	−870.9	−3,013.1
Goods: Exports f.o.b.	78aad	523.9	555.7	620.3	594.2	595.7	780.1	1,806.7	1,698.7	1,949.1	2,542.2	3,777.8	4,824.3
Goods: Imports f.o.b.	78abd	−1,045.4	−1,066.0	−1,339.5	−1,421.9	−1,732.2	−1,256.0	−1,366.3	−1,395.1	−2,293.8	−2,536.1	−3,586.2	−5,946.0
Trade Balance	78acd	−521.5	−510.3	−719.2	−827.7	−1,136.5	−475.9	440.4	303.6	−344.7	6.1	191.6	−1,121.7
Services: Credit	78aed	76.2	125.3	50.7	31.5	15.8	81.6	27.4	14.6	132.2	36.5	44.1	113.9
Services: Debit	78aed	−223.7	−172.3	−200.8	−172.8	−204.0	−274.9	−647.6	−660.3	−818.2	−830.3	−1,064.5	−1,844.4
Balance on Goods & Services	78afd	−669.0	−557.3	−869.3	−969.0	−1,324.7	−669.2	−179.8	−342.1	−1,030.7	−787.7	−828.8	−2,852.2
Income: Credit	78agd	1.6	1.9	6.3	16.9	13.7	19.1	4.6	17.8	29.2	10.0	21.8	44.1
Income: Debit	78ahd	−15.9	−4.9	−.7	−5.3	−10.6	−123.2	−579.6	−571.9	−638.0	−879.2	−1,134.5	−1,405.9
Balance on Gds, Serv. & Inc.	78aid	−683.3	−560.3	−863.7	−957.4	−1,321.6	−773.3	−754.8	−896.2	−1,639.5	−1,657.0	−1,941.5	−4,214.0
Current Transfers, n.i.e.: Credit	78ajd	120.1	346.2	236.3	439.1	731.8	702.2	651.3	730.4	1,085.9	1,218.4	1,580.2	1,680.5
Current Transfers, n.i.e.: Debit	78akd	−38.5	−285.8	−199.4	−309.8	−366.7	−393.7	−453.3	−452.5	−454.5	−516.8	−509.6	−479.6
Capital Account, n.i.e.	78bcd	....	....	....	....	−54.2	−22.9	−119.3	−93.3	† —	—	—	—
Capital Account, n.i.e.: Credit	78bad	....	....	....	....	13.0	45.8	16.5	11.9	† —	—	—	—
Capital Account: Debit	78bbd	....	....	....	....	−67.2	−68.7	−135.8	−105.2	† —	—	—	—
Financial Account, n.i.e.	78bjd	276.0	473.7	136.8	195.0	333.4	435.3	431.6	561.2	761.2	1,284.4	1,427.8	2,884.6
Direct Investment Abroad	78bdd	....	....	....	....	....	—	—	....	....	....	....	....
Dir. Invest. in Rep. Econ., n.i.e.	78bed	....	....	.4	97.9	370.7	370.8	392.2	574.0	713.2	1,349.2	1,511.1	2,304.6
Portfolio Investment Assets	78bfd	—	—	....	....	—	—	.7	14.8	35.3	19.9	50.6
Equity Securities	78bkd	....	....	....	....	—	—	....	....	—	—	—
Debt Securities	78bld	—	—	....	....	—	—	.7	14.8	35.3	19.9	50.6
Portfolio Investment Liab., n.i.e.	78bgd	—	—	....	....	—	—	—	—	—	—	—
Equity Securities	78bmd	—	—	....	....	—	—	—	—	—	—	—
Debt Securities	78bnd	—	—	....	....	—	—	—	....	—	—	—
Financial Derivatives Assets	78bwd	....	....	....	....	....	....	....	....	....	....	....	....
Financial Derivatives Liabilities	78bxd	....	....	....	....	....	....	....	....	....	....	....	....
Other Investment Assets	78bhd	....	....	....	....	−78.5	−38.4	−53.4	−55.1	−148.0	381.4	598.8	1,134.7
Monetary Authorities	78bod	....	....	....	....	....	—	—	....	—	−.2	−10.2	−13.0
General Government	78bpd	....	....	....	....	....	—	—	....	—	141.7	373.8	358.2
Banks	78bqd	....	....	....	....	−78.5	−38.4	−53.4	−55.1	−145.6	−9.0	−42.0	−198.7
Other Sectors	78brd	....	....	....	....	....	....	....	....	−2.4	248.9	277.2	988.3
Other Investment Liab., n.i.e.	78bid	276.0	473.7	136.4	97.1	41.2	102.9	92.8	41.6	181.2	−481.5	−702.0	−605.3
Monetary Authorities	78bsd	28.3	73.6	62.4	20.1	8.0	−3.7	14.0	40.6	64.2	....	....	44.7
General Government	78btd	−3.1	9.8	−22.5	−45.1	−1.0	—	—	—	† −87.8	−262.2	−384.5	−275.7
Banks	78bud	250.8	390.3	96.2	119.3	34.2	106.6	78.8	1.0	204.8	4.1	13.0	47.7
Other Sectors	78bvd	....	....	.3	2.8	....	....	....	....	....	−223.4	−330.6	−422.0
Net Errors and Omissions	78cad	344.8	89.3	727.5	651.2	750.5	167.2	368.4	−.5	492.2	−2.4	225.5	743.0
Overall Balance	78cbd	19.1	63.1	37.5	18.1	73.2	114.8	123.9	−150.9	245.3	326.6	782.4	614.5
Reserves and Related Items	79dad	−19.1	−63.1	−37.5	−18.1	−73.2	−114.8	−123.9	150.9	−245.3	−326.6	−782.4	−614.5
Reserve Assets	79dbd	−19.1	−23.6	−2.0	24.0	−16.0	−110.0	−108.0	127.6	−300.2	−422.7	−729.8	−827.6
Use of Fund Credit and Loans	79dcd	—	−39.5	−35.5	−42.1	−57.2	−37.8	−54.0	−52.3	−22.3	−26.3	−31.3	−28.3
Exceptional Financing	79ded	—	....	....	....	....	33.0	38.1	75.6	77.2	122.4	−21.2	241.4
Government Finance		*Millions of Dinars: Year Ending December 31*											
Deficit (-) or Surplus	80	−9	† −13,500	−34,600	−13,400	....	....	....	....	....	....	....	....
Revenue	81	13	† 36,500	62,900	107,300	....	....	....	....	....	....	....	....
Grants Received	81z	—	† —	—	—	....	....	....	....	....	....	....	....
Expenditure	82	22	† 50,000	97,500	120,700	....	....	....	....	....	....	....	....
Lending Minus Repayments	83	—	† —	—	—	....	....	....	....	....	....	....	....
Financing													
Domestic	84a	7	† 9,300	32,400	10,800	....	....	....	....	....	....	....	....
Foreign	85a	2	† 4,200	2,200	2,600	....	....	....	....	....	....	....	....
National Accounts		*Billions of Dinars: Yr.End.June 30 through '94, December 31 Thereafter*											
Gross Domestic Product (GDP)	99b	168	† 483	1,022	1,601	2,193	2,671	3,143	3,441	3,964	4,580	5,540	6,848
		Millions: Midyear Estimates											
Population	99z	28.66	† 29.35	30.06	30.78	31.50	32.21	32.90	33.57	34.21	34.86	35.52	36.23

Suriname 366

		1994	1995	1996	1997	1998	1999	2000	2001	2002	2003	2004	2005
Exchange Rates						*Surinamese Dollars per SDR: End of Period*							
Official Rate	aa	† .5978	.6050	.5766	.5410	.5646	1.3554	2.8384	2.7378	3.4192	† 3.9007	† 4.2164	3.9162
						Surinamese Dollars per US Dollar: End of Period (ae) Period Average (rf)							
Official Rate	ae	† .4095	.4070	.4010	.4010	.4010	.9875	2.1785	2.1785	2.5150	† 2.6250	† 2.7150	2.7400
Official Rate	rf	† .1341	.4422	.4013	.4010	.4010	.8594	1.3225	2.1785	2.3468	† 2.6013	† 2.7336	2.7317
Fund Position						*Millions of SDRs: End of Period*							
Quota	2f.s	67.60	67.60	67.60	67.60	67.60	92.10	92.10	92.10	92.10	92.10	92.10	92.10
SDRs	1b.s	—	7.75	8.22	8.23	8.25	2.00	1.77	1.56	1.42	1.32	1.21	1.06
Reserve Position in the Fund	1c.s	—	—	—	—	—	6.13	6.13	6.13	6.13	6.12	6.12	6.12
Total Fund Cred.&Loans Outstg	2tl	—	—	—	—	—	—	—	—	—	—		
International Liquidity						*Millions of US Dollars Unless Otherwise Indicated: End of Period*							
Total Reserves minus Gold	1l.d	39.70	132.92	96.32	109.11	106.14	38.46	62.99	119.25	106.16	105.76	129.40	125.78
SDRs	1b.d	—	11.52	11.82	11.11	11.62	2.75	2.31	1.95	1.93	1.96	1.89	1.52
Reserve Position in the Fund	1c.d	—	—	—	—	—	8.41	7.98	7.70	8.33	9.10	9.51	8.75
Foreign Exchange	1d.d	39.70	121.40	84.50	98.00	94.52	27.30	52.70	109.60	95.90	94.70	118.00	115.50
Gold (Million Fine Troy Ounces)	1ad	.054	.093	.134	.193	.128	.246	.256	.265	.021	.021	.021	.031
Gold (National Valuation)	1and	14.32	41.34	58.18	54.53	177.34	70.29	64.39	68.48	6.13	7.20	† 7.52	14.33
Monetary Authorities: Other Liab	4..d	18.08	3.25	3.03	74.81	229.66	111.10	103.74	77.92	1.05	.84	3.20	3.65
Deposit Money Banks: Assets	7a.d	49.67	68.84	116.40	128.94	122.43	180.59	131.02	188.33	142.10	194.35	243.67	242.53
Liabilities	7b.d	28.62	45.71	75.09	86.00	96.29	160.52	128.08	181.12	5.36	8.62	8.07	10.99
Monetary Authorities						*Thousands of Surinamese Dollars: End of Period*							
Foreign Assets	11	23,546	65,538	56,984	60,615	† 127,893	123,498	253,498	386,507	257,282	266,374	368,258	441,760
Claims on Central Government	12a	5,307	4,909	6,768	6,376	† 38,602	101,982	287,462	57,158	263,098	281,471	353,069	429,841
Claims on Nonfin.Pub.Enterprises	12c					† 4,052	3,783	6,564	1,293	1,523	1,450	1,426	—
Claims on Private Sector	12d	9	31	69	246	† 1,669	4,018	5,677	12,886	8,573	7,318	5,511	5,050
Claims on Deposit Money Banks	12e	13	—	26	13,414	† 19,077	38,249	43,064	44,884	21,721	22,838	22,838	22,838
Claims on Other Banking Insts	12f	—	—	—	—	† 218	511	623	719	783	671	671	671
Reserve Money	14	17,361	56,775	50,953	50,740	† 83,301	122,806	313,164	358,470	471,690	432,727	522,249	573,356
of which: Currency Outside DMBs	14a	10,486	25,199	27,404	32,256	† 50,478	81,686	150,657	182,476	† 203,804	209,008	246,826	278,903
Time & Fgn. Currency Deposits	15	—	—	—	—	† 192	232	1,442	1,082	1,380	1,436	1,556	1,624
Foreign Liabilities	16c	7,403	1,321	1,214	29,997	† 92,093	109,711	225,998	169,753	2,647	2,193	8,701	10,001
Central Government Deposits	16d	844	9,900	9,076	3,021	† 8,317	22,493	60,746	45,963	55,730	83,121	125,518	186,476
Capital Accounts	17a	4,668	4,723	4,589	4,420	† 11,398	28,757	20,218	−45,757	40,594	87,149	123,839	152,107
Other Items (Net)	17r	−1,401	−2,240	−1,985	−7,529	† −3,789	−11,958	−24,680	−26,063	−19,061	−26,503	−30,089	−23,404
Deposit Money Banks						*Thousands of Surinamese Dollars: End of Period*							
Reserves	20	6,242	29,584	19,142	18,531	31,462	32,392	122,759	124,630	† 220,338	228,082	246,917	244,828
Foreign Assets	21	20,341	28,016	46,675	51,705	49,095	178,333	285,419	410,276	† 357,389	510,166	661,553	664,519
Claims on Central Government	22a	392	567	913	8,639	20,814	23,594	64,030	95,884	† 98,779	99,032	162,650	199,526
Claims on Nonfin.Pub.Enterprises	22c	—	—	—	—	—	—	—	—	† 1,944	10,821	8,628	14,630
Claims on Private Sector	22d	6,645	20,120	45,486	63,383	79,103	106,703	93,296	147,134	† 401,942	566,365	755,405	939,751
Claims on Nonbank Financial Insts	22g	—	—	—	—	—	—	—	—	† 794	5,952	11,395	10,287
Demand Deposits	24	9,763	30,912	25,156	35,476	39,929	51,367	111,010	175,972	† 279,407	324,681	414,364	443,115
Quasi-Monetary Liabilities	25	7,218	20,995	52,609	61,973	87,578	108,151	160,966	178,435	† 696,805	921,143	1,250,933	1,384,062
Bonds	26ab	153	357	256	226	28	21	13	5	† —	—	—	—
Foreign Liabilities	26c	11,721	18,603	30,113	34,486	38,612	158,517	279,029	394,561	† 13,475	22,635	21,905	30,124
Central Government Deposits	26d	956	1,273	371	885	167	542	525	840	† 720	1,230	1,441	45,965
Credit from Monetary Authorities	26g	13	—	26	14,197	15,726	34,170	38,124	39,510	† 16,508	54,110	19,388	25,041
Capital Accounts	27a	2,852	5,263	8,732	11,681	12,516	20,933	29,669	73,054	† 75,037	82,159	139,898	168,866
Other Items (Net)	27r	945	885	−5,048	−16,666	−14,082	−32,678	−53,833	−84,453	† −766	14,459	−1,381	−23,632
Monetary Survey						*Thousands of Surinamese Dollars: End of Period*							
Foreign Assets (Net)	31n	24,763	73,630	72,332	47,837	† 46,283	33,603	33,889	232,469	† 598,549	751,712	999,205	1,066,154
Domestic Credit	32	10,554	14,456	43,789	74,737	† 135,975	217,555	396,382	268,272	† 720,987	888,729	1,171,796	1,367,315
Claims on Central Govt. (Net)	32an	3,900	−5,696	−1,767	11,109	† 50,932	102,541	290,222	106,240	† 305,427	296,151	388,759	396,925
Claims on Nonfin.Pub.Enterprises	32c	—	—	—	—	† 4,052	3,783	6,564	1,293	† 3,467	12,271	10,054	14,630
Claims on Private Sector	32d	6,654	20,152	45,556	63,628	† 80,773	110,720	98,973	160,020	† 410,515	573,683	760,916	944,801
Claims on Other Banking Insts	32f	—	—	—	—	† 218	511	623	719	† 783	671	671	671
Claims on Nonbank Financial Insts	32g	—	—	—	—	† —	—	—	—	† 794	5,952	11,395	10,287
Money	34	20,883	58,103	56,967	68,468	† 92,249	139,779	285,596	394,617	† 546,199	569,069	701,316	781,760
Quasi-Money	35	7,218	20,995	52,609	61,973	† 87,770	108,383	162,409	179,517	† 698,185	922,580	1,252,489	1,385,686
Bonds	36ab	153	357	256	226	† 28	21	13	5	† —	—	—	—
Capital Accounts	37a	7,520	9,986	13,321	16,101	† 13,914	49,690	49,887	27,297	† 115,631	169,308	263,737	320,973
Other Items (Net)	37r	−456	−1,355	−7,033	−24,194	† −21,704	−46,714	−67,634	−100,694	† −40,479	−20,516	−46,540	−54,950
Money plus Quasi-Money	35l	28,101	79,098	109,576	130,442	† 180,019	248,162	448,004	574,134	† 1,244,384	1,491,648	1,953,805	2,167,446
Money (National Definitions)						*Thousands of Surinamese Dollars: End of Period*							
M1	59ma	....	....	....	....	....	135,548	267,357	384,688	538,388	547,094	699,500	772,600
M2	59mb	....	....	....	....	....	159,755	306,019	426,711	596,375	621,610	795,700	890,300
M3	59mc	....	....	....	....	....	246,765	439,331	572,391	768,440	795,829	1,011,900	1,153,400
Interest Rates						*Percent per Annum*							
Deposit Rate	60l	7.45	21.00	17.83	17.25	16.00	15.60	15.48	11.86	9.00	8.28	8.34	7.97
Lending Rate	60p	15.38	40.18	35.78	33.13	27.50	27.33	28.95	25.73	22.18	21.04	20.44	18.06
Prices and Labor						*Index Numbers (2000=100): Period Averages*							
Consumer Prices	64	7.4	24.9	24.7	26.5	31.5	† 62.7	100.0	138.6	160.1	196.9	....	238.0
						Number in Thousands: Period Averages							
Labor Force	67d	90	90	....	....	....	86	....	....	....	....	....	....
Employment	67e	78	82	87	83	88	73	....	....	....	....	....	....
Unemployment	67c	11	8	11	10	10	12	....	....	....	....	....	....
Unemployment Rate (%)	67r	12.7	8.4	10.9	10.5	10.6	14.0	....	....	....	....	....	....
Intl. Transactions & Positions						*Millions of Surinamese Dollars*							
Exports	70	60.2	211.0	215.2	226.4	204.0	398.7	668.2	437.0	369.3	487.3	633.3	726.9
Imports, c.i.f	71	56.7	258.9	200.8	227.2	221.4	485.1	685.1	297.2	321.9	458.0	592.8	768.9

Suriname 366

		1994	1995	1996	1997	1998	1999	2000	2001	2002	2003	2004	2005
Balance of Payments		*Millions of US Dollars: Minus Sign Indicates Debit*											
Current Account, n.i.e.	78ald	58.6	73.4	−63.5	−67.7	−154.9	−29.1	32.3	−83.6	−131.0	−159.0	−137.7	−143.6
Goods: Exports f.o.b.	78aad	293.6	415.6	397.2	401.6	349.7	342.0	399.1	437.0	369.3	487.8	782.2	1,211.5
Goods: Imports f.o.b.	78abd	−194.3	−292.6	−398.8	−365.5	−376.9	−297.9	−246.1	−297.2	−321.9	−458.0	−740.1	−1,189.1
Trade Balance	78acd	99.3	123.0	−1.6	36.1	−27.2	44.1	153.0	139.8	47.4	29.8	42.1	22.4
Services: Credit	78add	72.6	104.1	103.8	91.6	72.0	79.1	90.9	59.4	38.5	59.0	141.3	204.1
Services: Debit	78aed	−113.5	−161.4	−169.5	−193.8	−196.9	−151.1	−215.5	−174.3	−166.1	−194.6	−271.0	−351.8
Balance on Goods & Services	78afd	58.4	65.7	−67.3	−66.1	−152.1	−27.9	28.4	24.9	−80.2	−105.8	−87.6	−125.3
Income: Credit	78agd	.9	2.7	7.0	7.4	6.5	7.9	13.2	5.4	8.4	11.7	15.6	24.0
Income: Debit	78ahd	−4.7	−5.3	−4.3	−10.0	−7.0	−7.6	−7.2	−113.0	−50.7	−60.2	−78.5	−64.4
Balance on Gds, Serv. & Inc.	78aid	54.6	63.1	−64.6	−68.7	−152.6	−27.6	34.4	−82.7	−122.5	−154.3	−150.5	−165.7
Current Transfers, n.i.e.: Credit	78ajd	6.2	12.6	3.6	4.0	1.3	1.8	1.2	2.1	12.9	24.8	75.8	52.3
Current Transfers: Debit	78akd	−2.2	−2.3	−2.5	−3.0	−3.6	−3.3	−3.3	−3.0	−21.4	−29.5	−63.0	−30.2
Capital Account, n.i.e.	78bcd	−.2	22.1	41.6	14.6	6.6	3.5	2.3	1.5	5.9	9.0	18.9	14.5
Capital Account, n.i.e.: Credit	78bad	.2	22.1	41.6	14.6	6.6	3.5	2.3	1.5	5.9	9.2	18.9	14.5
Capital Account: Debit	78bbd	−.4	—	—	—	—	—	—	—	—	−.2	....	....
Financial Account, n.i.e.	78bjd	−84.1	−29.5	27.7	26.9	30.5	−21.6	−139.1	104.1	−38.1	−36.5	−23.5	−20.6
Direct Investment Abroad	78bdd	—	—	—	—	—	....	....	....	—	—	—	....
Dir. Invest. in Rep. Econ., n.i.e.	78bed	−30.2	−20.6	19.1	−9.2	9.1	−61.5	−148.0	−26.8	−73.6	−76.1	−37.3	27.9
Portfolio Investment Assets	78bfd	—	—	—	—	—	....	....	....	—	—	—	....
Equity Securities	78bkd	—	—	—	—	—	....	....	....	—	—	—	....
Debt Securities	78bld	—	—	—	—	—	....	....	....	—	—	—	....
Portfolio Investment Liab., n.i.e.	78bgd	—	—	—	—	—	....	....	....	—	—	—	−2.0
Equity Securities	78bmd	—	—	—	—	—	....	....	....	—	—	—	....
Debt Securities	78bnd	—	—	—	—	—	....	....	....	—	—	—	−2.0
Financial Derivatives Assets	78bwd	....	....	....	....	....	....	....	....	....	....	....	....
Financial Derivatives Liabilities	78bxd	....	....	....	....	....	....	....	....	....	....	....	....
Other Investment Assets	78bhd	−19.1	3.2	25.5	15.2	18.6	27.1	24.6	40.7	23.9	46.9	−2.3	−31.9
Monetary Authorities	78bod	....	....	....	....	....	....	....	....	—	—	—	—
General Government	78bpd	—	—	—	—	—	....	....	....	—	—	—	—
Banks	78bqd	−31.3	−10.0	—	—	—	....	....	....	—	—	—	—
Other Sectors	78brd	12.2	13.2	25.5	15.2	18.6	27.1	24.6	40.7	23.9	46.9	−2.3	−31.9
Other Investment Liab., n.i.e.	78bid	−34.8	−12.1	−16.9	20.9	2.8	12.8	−15.7	90.2	11.6	−7.3	16.1	−14.6
Monetary Authorities	78bsd	—	—	—	—	—	—	—	1.6	−.9	4.3	—	—
General Government	78btd	2.1	4.2	−15.0	1.3	19.3	16.1	−21.4	50.7	−30.8	−23.0	−18.5	−14.4
Banks	78bud	−29.6	−10.1	—	—	—	—	—	−.8	6.4	−9.1	9.0	.1
Other Sectors	78bvd	−7.3	−6.2	−1.9	19.6	−16.5	−3.3	5.7	38.7	36.9	20.5	25.6	−.3
Net Errors and Omissions	78cad	60.0	56.6	−7.5	45.3	125.9	42.8	114.3	56.1	144.1	193.7	218.4	169.4
Overall Balance	78cbd	34.3	122.6	−1.7	19.1	8.1	−4.4	9.8	78.1	−19.1	7.2	76.1	19.7
Reserves and Related Items	79dad	−34.3	−122.6	1.7	−19.1	−8.1	4.4	−9.8	−78.1	19.1	−7.2	−76.1	−19.7
Reserve Assets	79dbd	−34.3	−122.6	1.7	−19.1	−8.1	4.4	−9.8	−78.1	19.1	−7.2	−76.1	−19.7
Use of Fund Credit and Loans	79dcd	—	—	—	—	—	—	—	—	—	—	—	—
Exceptional Financing	79ded	....	....	....	....	....	....	....	....	—	—	—	—
National Accounts		*Millions of Surinamese Dollars*											
Househ.Cons.Expend.,incl.NPISHs	96f	18	37	162	213	....	....	....	....	....	....	....	....
Government Consumption Expend	91f	7	45	45	60	86	201	257	413	606	929	....	....
Gross Capital Formation	93	28	91	232	224	318	435	609	963	1,443	1,778	....	....
Exports of Goods and Services	90c	76	229	193	195	167	364	641	1,074	941	1,437	....	....
Imports of Goods and Services (-)	98c	64	201	226	222	227	413	578	1,033	1,138	1,715	....	....
Gross Domestic Product (GDP)	99b	81	307	347	372	378	761	1,177	1,664	2,234	2,653	3,028	....
Net Primary Income from Abroad	98.n	—	−1	−3	−11	−12	−32	−63	−232	−102	−128	....	....
Gross National Income (GNI)	99a	64	252	287	301	366	619	954	1,243	1,845	2,443	....	....
Net National Income	99e	57	206	272	328	....	....	....	....	....	....	....	....
GDP Volume 1990 Prices	99b.p	4	4	4	4	4	4	4	4	4	5	5	....
GDP Volume	99bvp	91.8	92.8	93.4	99.4	101.7	100.1	100.0	104.5	107.7	113.4	118.7	....
GDP Deflator	99bip	7.5	28.1	31.6	31.8	31.6	64.7	100.0	135.3	176.2	198.8	216.8	....
		Millions: Midyear Estimates											
Population	99z	.41	.41	.42	.42	.43	.43	.43	.44	.44	.44	.45	.45

Swaziland 734

		1994	1995	1996	1997	1998	1999	2000	2001	2002	2003	2004	2005
Exchange Rates						*Lilangeni per SDR: End of Period*							
Official Rate	aa	5.17298	5.42197	6.73325	6.56747	8.25106	8.44711	9.86107	15.23974	11.74625	9.86684	8.74345	9.04013
						Lilangeni per US Dollar: End of Period (ae) Period Average (rf)							
Official Rate	ae	3.54350	3.64750	4.68250	4.86750	5.86000	6.15450	7.56850	12.12650	8.64000	6.64000	5.63000	6.32500
Official Rate	rf	3.55080	3.62709	4.29935	4.60796	5.52828	6.10948	6.93983	8.60918	10.54075	7.56475	6.45969	6.35933
Fund Position						*Millions of SDRs: End of Period*							
Quota	2f.s	36.50	36.50	36.50	36.50	36.50	50.70	50.70	50.70	50.70	50.70	50.70	50.70
SDRs	1b.s	5.89	5.90	5.93	5.94	5.96	2.42	2.44	2.45	2.46	2.47	2.47	2.48
Reserve Position in the Fund	1c.s	3.00	3.00	3.00	3.00	3.00	6.55	6.55	6.55	6.55	6.55	6.56	6.56
Total Fund Cred.&Loans Outstg.	2tl	—	—	—	—	—	—	—	—	—	—	—	—
International Liquidity					*Millions of US Dollars Unless Otherwise Indicated: End of Period*								
Total Reserves minus Gold	1l.d	296.97	298.20	254.00	294.84	358.61	375.93	351.79	271.78	275.84	277.51	323.56	243.90
SDRs	1b.d	8.60	8.77	8.52	8.02	8.39	3.33	3.18	3.08	3.35	3.67	3.84	3.55
Reserve Position in the Fund	1c.d	4.38	4.46	4.32	4.05	4.23	8.99	8.54	8.23	8.91	9.74	10.19	9.38
Foreign Exchange	1d.d	283.99	284.96	241.16	282.77	345.99	363.61	340.08	260.46	263.59	264.11	309.53	230.97
Monetary Authorities: Other Liab.	4..d	32.02	21.34	20.14	1.24	21.98	49.16	45.66	38.90	42.70	53.26	4.32	2.57
Banking Institutions: Assets	7a.d	43.59	47.52	107.45	91.79	99.16	135.46	84.13	71.92	89.30	76.51	97.50	70.10
Liabilities	7b.d	17.83	17.61	50.70	20.92	6.13	9.43	13.84	2.18	8.85	7.81	7.30	10.90
Monetary Authorities						*Millions of Emalangeni: End of Period*							
Foreign Assets	11	536.84	662.33	679.81	603.05	911.73	973.31	1,086.23	† 1,423.05	1,089.51	1,083.56	† 753.52	1,595.29
Claims on Central Government	12a	40.00	20.63	.06	—	—	—	—	—	57.32	82.64	† 100.23	100.57
Claims on State and Local Govts.	12b											† —	
Claims on Nonfin.Pub.Enterprises	12c	....	....	....	....	....	....	....	—	—	—	† —	
Claims on Private Sector	12d	10.63	12.52	14.02	13.06	12.30	15.23	16.34	† 15.50	12.98	12.02	† 12.37	8.88
Claims on Banking Institutions	12e	5.65	30.00	36.76	43.19	42.55	44.31	41.95	† 41.95	—	—	† 1.86	2.31
Claims on Nonbank Financial Insts.	12g	....	....	....	....	....	....	....	—	—	—	† —	
Reserve Money	14	300.24	307.81	284.95	300.47	275.33	307.27	293.36	† 254.08	329.38	430.32	† 482.39	496.52
of which: Currency Outside Banks	14a	69.59	80.33	90.85	109.00	107.23	136.95	148.06	† 114.48	135.46	199.88	† 235.85	242.08
Other Liabs. to Banking Insts.	14n	....	....	....	....	....	....	....	—	—	—	† —	
Time, Savings,&Fgn.Currency Dep.	15	36.90	52.57	53.45	77.68	48.33	50.14	68.30	† 79.54	90.05	91.81	† —	
Liabs. of Central Bank: Securities	16ac	....	....	....	....	....	....	....	—	—	—	† —	
Restricted Deposits	16b	....	....	....	....	....	....	....	—	—	—	† —	
Foreign Liabilities	16c	113.47	77.82	94.32	6.04	128.81	302.53	345.57	† 471.70	368.96	353.67	† 24.34	16.23
Central Government Deposits	16d	50.31	194.12	115.64	170.21	298.98	220.59	207.35	† 193.33	127.11	373.99	† 402.01	1,183.04
Liab. to Nonbank Financial Insts.	16j	....	....	....	....	....	....	....	—	—	—	† —	
Capital Accounts	17a	40.14	41.95	50.52	50.80	62.46	86.23	96.66	† 134.10	114.41	102.44	† −44.57	−15.25
Other Items (Net)	17r	52.05	51.21	131.77	54.09	152.68	66.10	133.28	† 347.74	129.90	−174.02	† 3.82	26.51
Banking Institutions						*Millions of Emalangeni: End of Period*							
Reserves	20	227.46	232.42	199.22	193.84	151.48	176.57	145.07	† 130.86	196.02	207.23	† 211.71	210.55
Claims on Mon.Author.: Securities	20c	....	....	....	....	....	....	....	—	—	—	† —	
Other Claims on Monetary Author.	20n	....	....	....	....	....	....	....	—	—	—	† —	
Foreign Assets	21	154.45	173.32	503.13	446.80	581.07	833.68	636.74	† 872.11	771.53	508.05	† 548.95	443.37
Claims on Central Government	22a	38.00	49.79	68.35	52.17	52.73	50.21	59.49	† 60.00	215.43	286.68	† 332.49	309.37
Claims on State and Local Govts.	22b	....	....	....	....	....	....	....	54.40	70.19	91.24	† 4.36	5.58
Claims on Nonfin.Pub.Enterprises	22c	....	....	....	....	....	....	....	34.24	50.49	38.26	† 69.74	70.01
Claims on Private Sector	22d	902.68	915.60	971.81	1,095.03	1,159.43	1,223.39	1,308.23	† 1,153.87	1,532.55	2,107.42	† 2,732.73	3,460.60
Claims on Nonbank Financial Insts.	22g	....	....	....	....	....	....	....	140.77	116.84	90.43	† 188.89	74.31
Demand Deposits	24	241.75	282.57	331.99	382.76	393.64	525.72	512.53	† 615.82	670.09	834.39	† 843.08	1,046.03
Time, Savings,&Fgn.Currency Dep.	25	833.28	811.70	951.43	1,135.61	1,375.32	1,512.47	1,349.40	† 1,470.65	1,686.86	1,829.35	† 2,081.96	2,175.15
Money Market Instruments	26aa	....	....	....	....	....	....	....	—	—	—	† —	
Restricted Deposits	26b	....	....	....	....	....	....	....	—	—	—	† —	
Foreign Liabilities	26c	63.17	64.22	237.41	101.82	35.92	58.04	104.72	† 26.45	76.42	51.84	† 41.08	68.91
Central Government Deposits	26d	90.88	114.57	101.22	10.17	14.25	14.70	.22	† .23	.23	.28	† 21.12	13.28
Credit from Monetary Authorities	26g	6.00	—	—	—	—	—	—	† —	—	—	† 34.05	—
Liab. to Nonbank Financial Insts.	26j	3.74	3.44	3.68	6.68	5.28	12.19	10.27	† 15.97	15.57	14.50	† 30.84	15.26
Capital Accounts	27a	92.33	97.61	75.09	127.53	114.39	139.44	157.73	† 292.70	378.31	487.94	† 1,007.35	1,106.22
Other Items (Net)	27r	−8.57	−2.96	41.69	23.28	5.91	21.29	14.67	† 24.44	125.55	111.00	† 29.39	148.94
Banking Survey						*Millions of Emalangeni: End of Period*							
Foreign Assets (Net)	31n	514.65	693.61	851.21	941.99	1,328.07	1,446.43	1,272.68	† 1,797.01	1,415.66	1,186.09	† 1,237.04	1,953.52
Domestic Credit	32	850.11	689.85	837.38	979.88	911.24	1,053.53	1,176.50	† 1,265.22	1,928.45	2,334.42	† 3,017.68	2,833.00
Claims on Central Govt. (Net)	32an	−63.19	−238.27	−148.45	−128.21	−260.49	−185.08	−148.08	† −133.57	145.40	−4.95	† 9.59	−786.38
Claims on State and Local Govts.	32b	....	....	....	....	....	....	....	54.40	70.19	91.24	† 4.36	5.58
Claims on Nonfin.Pub.Enterprises.	32c	....	....	....	....	....	....	....	34.24	50.49	38.26	† 69.74	70.01
Claims on Private Sector	32d	913.30	928.12	985.83	1,108.09	1,171.74	1,238.62	1,324.58	† 1,169.37	1,545.53	2,119.43	† 2,745.10	3,469.47
Claims on Nonbank Financial Insts.	32g	....	....	....	....	....	....	....	140.77	116.84	90.43	† 188.89	74.31
Money	34	311.59	363.16	423.03	491.75	500.87	662.69	660.58	† 730.30	805.55	1,034.27	† 1,080.64	1,294.76
Quasi-Money	35	870.18	864.27	1,004.88	1,213.29	1,423.66	1,562.61	1,417.69	† 1,550.19	1,776.91	1,921.16	† 2,081.96	2,175.15
Money Market Instruments	36aa	....	....	....	....	....	....	....	—	—	—	† —	
Restricted Deposits	36b	....	....	....	....	....	....	....	—	—	—	† —	
Liab. to Nonbank Financial Insts.	36j	3.74	3.44	3.68	6.68	5.28	12.19	10.27	† 15.97	15.57	14.50	† 30.84	15.26
Capital Accounts	37a	132.47	139.56	125.61	178.33	176.85	225.67	254.40	† 426.80	492.72	590.38	† 962.77	1,090.97
Other Items (Net)	37r	46.79	13.04	131.38	31.82	132.66	36.80	106.24	† 338.96	253.36	−39.80	† 98.51	210.37
Money plus Quasi-Money	35l	1,181.76	1,227.43	1,427.91	1,705.04	1,924.52	2,225.30	2,078.28	† 2,280.49	2,582.46	2,955.42	† 3,162.59	3,469.91
Money (National Definitions)						*Millions of Emalangeni: End of Period*							
M1	59ma	311.59	363.16	422.96	491.75	500.87	662.69	660.58	754.08	825.53	1,047.84	1,078.93	1,288.10
M2	59mb	1,181.76	1,227.43	1,427.91	1,705.04	1,924.52	2,225.30	2,078.27	2,300.95	2,602.44	2,969.00	3,276.73	3,562.52
Interest Rates						*Percent Per Annum*							
Discount Rate (End of Period)	60	12.00	15.00	16.75	15.75	18.00	12.00	11.00	9.50	13.50	8.00	7.50	7.00
Money Market Rate	60b	7.01	8.52	9.77	10.35	10.63	8.86	5.54	5.06	7.31	6.98	4.12	3.47
Treasury Bill Rate	60c	8.35	10.87	13.68	14.37	13.09	11.19	8.30	7.16	8.59	10.61	7.94	7.08
Savings Rate	60k	8.04	8.99	10.21	10.72	10.25	7.73	4.00	4.43	6.20	6.68	3.71	3.08
Deposit Rate	60l	7.54	9.44	11.08	12.00	11.92	9.86	6.53	6.15	8.02	7.59	4.63	4.01
Lending Rate	60p	14.25	17.05	18.67	19.50	19.50	17.42	14.00	13.25	15.25	14.63	11.29	10.63

Swaziland 734

		1994	1995	1996	1997	1998	1999	2000	2001	2002	2003	2004	2005
Prices and Labor						Index Numbers (2000=100): Period Averages							
Consumer Prices	64	60.7	68.2	72.5	77.7	84.0	89.1	100.0	105.9	118.7	127.3	131.7	138.0
						Number in Thousands: Period Averages							
Employment	67e	87	87	90	....	....	....	....	....	....	....	....	....
Intl. Transactions & Positions						Millions of Emalangeni							
Exports	70	2,808.5	3,147.6	3,656.7	4,429.7	5,376.9	5,723.5	6,312.0	9,072.9	10,846.4	12,300.3	12,518.9	12,763.2
Imports, c.i.f.	71	2,986.3	3,660.7	4,533.4	4,908.8	5,988.0	6,526.8	7,261.2	9,717.5	9,897.8	11,407.6	12,363.9	13,329.2
Balance of Payments						Millions of US Dollars: Minus Sign Indicates Debit							
Current Account, n.i.e.	78ald	1.8	−29.7	−52.0	−2.7	−93.3	−35.1	−74.9	−56.7	57.5	116.2	114.2	....
Goods: Exports f.o.b.	78aad	790.9	867.8	850.5	961.3	967.8	936.7	905.0	1,042.5	1,029.2	1,625.6	1,938.3	....
Goods: Imports f.o.b.	78abd	−841.0	−1,064.4	−1,054.4	−1,065.5	−1,073.8	−1,068.1	−1,041.1	−1,124.2	−938.7	−1,508.1	−1,913.9	....
Trade Balance	78acd	−50.1	−196.6	−203.9	−104.2	−106.0	−131.5	−136.1	−81.7	90.5	117.5	24.3	....
Services: Credit	78add	112.9	151.8	100.8	91.9	91.4	69.4	228.1	113.7	102.0	255.4	499.5	....
Services: Debit	78aed	−201.9	−209.5	−240.7	−244.8	−267.7	−192.0	−308.1	−225.4	−195.6	−299.5	−533.8	....
Balance on Goods & Services	78afd	−139.1	−254.2	−343.9	−257.1	−282.2	−254.0	−216.1	−193.4	−3.1	73.4	−10.0	....
Income: Credit	78agd	138.5	162.6	200.8	182.7	167.8	164.0	153.5	156.6	143.9	143.5	160.6	....
Income: Debit	78ahd	−155.0	−82.0	−68.7	−44.6	−111.4	−76.3	−119.4	−54.4	−145.8	−147.1	−128.7	....
Balance on Gds, Serv. & Inc.	78aid	−155.7	−173.7	−211.8	−119.0	−225.8	−166.3	−182.0	−91.1	−5.0	69.8	21.9	....
Current Transfers, n.i.e.: Credit	78ajd	252.6	257.2	268.7	226.8	242.7	241.4	234.1	229.7	198.5	333.3	424.4	....
Current Transfers: Debit	78akd	−95.1	−113.3	−108.9	−110.5	−110.3	−110.2	−127.0	−195.3	−135.9	−287.0	−332.2	....
Capital Account, n.i.e.	78bcd	−.2	—	.1	.1	—	—	.1	−.2	.5	....	−.6	....
Capital Account, n.i.e.: Credit	78bad	.1	.3	.1	.1	—	—	.1	.2	.5	....	—	....
Capital Account: Debit	78bbd	−.3	−.3	—	—	—	—	—	−.4	−.1	....	−.6	....
Financial Account, n.i.e.	78bjd	−54.1	−25.4	6.8	47.0	139.7	48.0	16.7	−67.3	−54.4	−27.3	−110.2	....
Direct Investment Abroad	78bdd	−64.7	−20.6	6.4	12.0	−23.9	−13.2	−17.2	17.6	−.2	−10.5	−3.6	....
Dir. Invest. in Rep. Econ., n.i.e.	78bed	63.3	51.8	21.7	−15.3	152.7	100.4	91.4	28.4	88.8	−60.9	68.4	....
Portfolio Investment Assets	78bfd	−3.9	−9.6	−2.0	−2.0	−2.8	3.2	−2.0	−5.4	3.9	−.3	−10.7	....
Equity Securities	78bkd	—	−1.9	−.2	−1.9	−1.3	1.5	−.1	−.1	—	—	.2	....
Debt Securities	78bld	−3.9	−7.6	−1.7	—	−1.5	1.7	−1.9	−5.3	3.9	−.3	−10.9	....
Portfolio Investment Liab., n.i.e.	78bgd	.1	.8	.4	−.1	3.4	2.7	1.4	−2.5	−2.0	−.1	−.3	....
Equity Securities	78bmd	.1	.8	.4	−.1	3.4	2.7	1.4	−2.5	−2.0	−.1	−.3	....
Debt Securities	78bnd	....	....	....	....	....	....	....	....	....	....	....	....
Financial Derivatives Assets	78bwd	....	....	....	....	....	....	....	....	....	....	....	....
Financial Derivatives Liabilities	78bxd	....	....	....	....	....	....	....	....	....	....	....	....
Other Investment Assets	78bhd	−80.5	−31.0	−120.0	−12.3	1.6	−122.4	−97.8	−89.8	−99.0	64.4	−117.5	....
Monetary Authorities	78bod	....	....	....	....	....	....	....	....	....	....	....	....
General Government	78bpd	−18.0	−6.7	−2.7	13.4	−4.8	16.3	8.1	.8	−23.9	−48.8	−53.3	....
Banks	78bqd	5.7	−5.3	−77.0	11.1	−22.9	−41.7	27.7	−27.7	9.6	35.7	−1.6	....
Other Sectors	78brd	−68.3	−19.0	−40.3	−36.8	29.2	−97.0	−133.7	−62.9	−84.6	77.5	−62.6	....
Other Investment Liab., n.i.e.	78bid	31.6	−16.7	100.2	64.7	8.8	77.4	41.0	−15.6	−45.9	−20.0	−46.6	....
Monetary Authorities	78bsd	30.5	−9.8	3.8	−19.2	22.2	28.5	6.2	14.7	−12.1	−2.7	−50.2	....
General Government	78btd	—	—	—	—	−.7	−4.6	−1.2	4.3	6.3	−2.2	6.8	....
Banks	78bud	.7	.4	41.5	−25.9	−13.8	.3	6.4	−9.5	4.7	−3.2	−1.7	....
Other Sectors	78bvd	.4	−7.3	54.9	109.8	1.0	53.1	29.5	−25.1	−44.9	−11.8	−1.6	....
Net Errors and Omissions	78cad	48.9	78.9	37.0	−16.8	4.1	13.4	51.7	67.7	−29.3	−133.0	−21.9	....
Overall Balance	78cbd	−3.6	23.8	−8.1	27.5	50.5	26.3	−6.5	−56.5	−25.8	−44.1	−18.5	....
Reserves and Related Items	79dad	3.6	−23.8	8.1	−27.5	−50.5	−26.3	6.5	56.5	25.8	44.1	18.5	....
Reserve Assets	79dbd	12.6	−29.8	−15.4	−25.3	−50.5	−26.3	6.5	56.5	25.8	44.1	18.5	....
Use of Fund Credit and Loans	79dcd	—	—	—	—	—	—	—	—	—	—	—	....
Exceptional Financing	79ded	−8.9	6.0	23.4	−2.2	−.7	−4.6	−1.2	4.3	6.3	....	—	....
International Investment Position						Millions of US Dollars							
Assets	79aad	838.2	982.9	965.1	977.2	958.5	1,152.2	1,150.0	951.5	1,504.1	1,652.3	2,388.1	....
Direct Investment Abroad	79abd	108.8	135.5	95.4	82.3	90.1	98.1	94.9	46.3	64.2	94.7	115.8	....
Portfolio Investment	79acd	7.3	16.6	14.8	16.1	16.0	11.8	11.5	11.0	10.7	14.2	17.8	....
Equity Securities	79add	.8	2.7	2.3	4.0	4.6	2.8	2.4	1.6	2.2	2.9	3.1	....
Debt Securities	79aed	6.6	14.0	12.5	12.0	11.4	9.0	9.1	9.4	8.5	11.4	14.7	....
Financial Derivatives	79ald	—	—	—	—	—	—	—	—	—	—	—	....
Other Investment	79afd	479.2	553.4	572.5	589.3	497.2	669.7	696.5	618.6	1,134.1	1,268.8	1,982.6	....
Monetary Authorities	79agd	....	....	....	....	....	....	....	....	....	....	....	....
General Government	79ahd	144.6	124.6	98.8	86.5	77.0	56.2	34.3	10.7	154.6	63.0	410.4	....
Banks	79aid	46.9	50.8	110.3	116.1	101.0	137.5	86.4	73.6	91.6	78.5	94.4	....
Other Sectors	79ajd	287.7	377.9	363.5	386.6	319.2	476.0	575.8	534.3	887.9	1,127.3	1,477.8	....
Reserve Assets	79akd	242.9	277.4	282.4	289.5	355.3	372.6	347.1	275.6	295.1	274.5	272.0	....
Liabilities	79lad	848.7	981.3	894.5	846.3	929.3	1,050.4	1,036.9	718.2	1,025.6	845.9	1,522.5	....
Dir. Invest. in Rep. Economy	79lbd	506.8	535.6	437.2	406.4	481.6	556.2	536.1	354.8	607.4	720.9	928.8	....
Portfolio Investment	79lcd	.7	1.4	1.5	1.4	4.3	6.8	6.8	2.4	1.0	1.2	1.1	....
Equity Securities	79ldd	.7	1.4	1.5	1.4	4.3	6.8	6.8	2.4	1.0	1.2	1.1	....
Debt Securities	79led	—	—	—	—	—	—	—	—	—	—	—	....
Financial Derivatives	79lld	—	—	—	—	—	—	—	—	—	—	—	....
Other Investment	79lfd	341.2	444.2	455.7	438.5	443.4	487.4	494.0	361.0	417.2	123.8	592.6	....
Monetary Authorities	79lgd	−.3	77.3	19.9	1.0	21.8	48.9	45.5	38.8	39.7	48.6	.3	....
General Government	79lhd	175.3	194.5	194.4	177.4	243.3	262.5	272.4	236.9	303.2	−4.3	508.9	....
Banks	79lid	21.7	21.5	54.9	28.2	10.4	10.3	14.3	2.2	8.8	7.8	7.3	....
Other Sectors	79ljd	144.5	150.9	186.5	231.8	167.9	165.7	161.8	83.2	65.5	71.7	76.1	....

Swaziland 734

		1994	1995	1996	1997	1998	1999	2000	2001	2002	2003	2004	2005
Government Finance		for title			*Millions of Emalangeni: Year Beginning April 1*								
Deficit (-) or Surplus	80	−197.5	68.3	−56.2	184.1	−7.1	−138.7	−141.4	−255.3	−593.1	−444.9	....	....
Revenue	81	1,168.7	1,447.7	1,684.0	2,020.5	2,230.3	2,536.1	2,713.2	2,922.7	3,262.8	3,681.6	....	....
Grants Received	81z	31.4	7.5	20.2	18.3	44.7	31.8	112.1	157.4	162.3	265.1	....	....
Expenditure	82	1,398.7	1,382.1	1,758.4	1,826.6	2,214.8	2,676.0	2,967.9	3,332.5	4,018.2	4,391.6	....	....
Lending Minus Repayments	83	−1.1	4.8	2.0	28.1	67.3	30.6	−1.2	2.9	—	—	....	....
Financing													
Domestic	84a	235.5	−80.6	41.4	−226.1	−191.2	133.1	122.5	−52.2	480.5	318.5	....	....
Foreign	85a	−38.0	12.3	14.8	42.0	198.3	5.6	18.9	307.5	112.6	126.4	....	....
Debt: Domestic	88a	53.7	62.9	102.9	97.6	85.6	78.0	78.0	78.0	300.0	300.0	....	....
Foreign	89a	791.9	914.5	1,150.5	820.0	1,060.6	1,467.9	2,069.8	2,690.0	3,351.0	2,755.8	....	....
National Accounts					*Millions of Emalangeni: Year Ending June 30*								
Househ.Cons.Expend.,incl.NPISHs	96f	3,052.1	3,932.6	4,801.5	4,752.6	5,392.8	6,522.3	7,263.4	7,410.9	9,059.1	10,971.2	9,996.6	11,026.1
Government Consumption Expend	91f	874.0	951.0	1,185.8	1,639.2	1,800.9	1,864.3	1,929.1	1,996.1	2,065.6	2,137.3	3,905.0	4,550.5
Gross Fixed Capital Formation	93e	840.7	950.0	1,125.4	1,308.1	1,665.4	1,577.1	1,916.7	1,984.5	2,225.0	1,793.0	....	....
Changes in Inventories	93i	33.9	37.4	51.2	53.9	—	—	—	—	61.6	66.0	....	....
Exports of Goods and Services	90c	2,970.6	3,698.4	4,090.0	5,003.2	5,917.4	6,146.9	7,763.3	9,990.6	10,841.8	11,210.1	13,047.5	14,435.7
Imports of Goods and Services (-)	98c	3,703.2	4,620.5	5,568.4	6,144.5	7,337.5	7,698.6	9,242.5	11,219.5	11,897.1	12,508.0	14,197.2	15,977.8
Gross Domestic Product (GDP)	99b	4,068.1	4,948.9	5,685.5	6,612.5	7,439.1	8,412.0	9,630.0	10,846.0	12,560.0	14,400.9	15,581.8	17,074.9
Net Primary Income from Abroad	98.n	−58.9	292.2	567.9	636.3	311.8	535.9	574.7	291.5	47.9	−83.9	....	....
Gross National Income (GNI)	99a	4,009.2	5,244.1	6,253.4	7,248.8	7,761.2	8,943.6	10,213.6	11,262.5	12,484.7	14,681.9	....	....
Consumption of Fixed Capital	99cf	214.2	235.8	258.4	297.2	334.6	377.4	434.0	499.1	935.5	1,232.5	....	....
Net National Income	99e	3,795.0	5,005.3	5,995.0	6,951.6	7,426.6	8,566.3	9,779.6	10,763.4	11,549.2	13,449.4	....	....
GDP Volume 1985 Prices	99b.p	1,450.3	1,505.2	1,563.7	1,623.6	1,676.5	1,735.6	1,770.9	1,802.3	....	....	....	....
GDP Volume (2000=100)	99bvp	81.9	85.0	88.3	91.7	94.7	98.0	100.0	101.8	....	....	....	....
GDP Deflator (2000=100)	99bip	51.6	60.5	66.9	74.9	81.6	89.1	100.0	110.7	....	....	....	....
					Millions: Midyear Estimates								
Population	99z	.94	.95	.97	† .99	1.00	1.01	1.02	1.03	1.03	1.03	1.03	1.03

		1994	1995	1996	1997	1998	1999	2000	2001	2002	2003	2004	2005

Exchange Rates

Kronor per SDR: End of Period

		1994	1995	1996	1997	1998	1999	2000	2001	2002	2003	2004	2005
Official Rate	aa	10.8927	9.8973	9.8802	10.6280	11.3501	11.7006	12.4232	13.4062	11.9978	10.6829	10.2725	11.3747

Kronor per US Dollar: End of Period (ae) Period Average (rf)

Official Rate	ae	7.4615	6.6582	6.8710	7.8770	8.0610	8.5250	9.5350	10.6675	8.8250	7.1892	6.6146	7.9584
Official Rate	rf	7.7160	7.1333	6.7060	7.6349	7.9499	8.2624	9.1622	10.3291	9.7371	8.0863	7.3489	7.4731

Kronor per ECU through 1998; Kronor per Euro Beginning 1999: End of Period (ea) Period Average (eb)

Euro Rate	ea	9.1779	8.6973	8.6280	8.7323	9.4880	†8.5625	8.8313	9.4200	9.1925	9.0800	9.0206	9.3885
Euro Rate	ag	....	....	....	....	....	1.0046	.9305	.8813	1.0487	1.2630	1.3621	1.1797
Euro Rate	eb	9.1579	9.3337	8.5156	8.6551	8.9085	†8.8102	8.4459	9.2553	9.1603	9.1243	9.1250	9.2806
Euro Rate	rh	....	....	....	....	....	1.0668	.9240	.8956	.9444	1.1308	1.2433	1.2458

Index Numbers (2000=100): Period Averages

Official Rate	ahx	118.5	128.2	136.2	119.7	114.9	110.5	100.0	88.6	94.1	113.2	124.4	122.6
Nominal Effective Exchange Rate	neu	99.1	98.9	108.2	103.8	101.9	100.2	100.0	91.7	93.4	98.2	99.7	98.0
Real Effective Exchange Rate	reu	96.9	98.2	110.7	107.5	105.8	101.8	100.0	92.0	91.1	94.0	96.4	94.3

Fund Position

Millions of SDRs: End of Period

Quota	2f.s	1,614	1,614	1,614	1,614	1,614	2,396	2,396	2,396	2,396	2,396	2,396	2,396
SDRs	1b.s	46	297	199	277	292	228	165	157	132	133	135	123
Reserve Position in the Fund	1c.s	451	451	451	589	900	863	683	827	1,050	988	842	372
of which: Outstg.Fund Borrowing	2c	—	—	—	—	112	—	—	—	—	—	—	—

International Liquidity

Millions of US Dollars Unless Otherwise Indicated: End of Period

Total Reserves minus Gold	1l.d	23,254	24,051	19,107	10,825	14,098	15,019	14,863	13,977	17,127	19,681	22,129	22,063
SDRs	1b.d	68	441	286	373	412	313	215	197	179	198	209	176
Reserve Position in the Fund	1c.d	659	671	649	795	1,267	1,184	890	1,039	1,428	1,468	1,308	532
Foreign Exchange	1d.d	22,527	22,939	18,172	9,657	12,420	13,522	13,757	12,740	15,520	18,015	20,611	21,355
Gold (Million Fine Troy Ounces)	1ad	6.069	4.702	4.702	4.722	4.722	5.961	5.961	5.961	5.961	5.961	5.961	5.414
Gold (National Valuation)	1and	310	245	237	223	233	286	272	262	284	310	324	271
Deposit Money Banks: Assets	7a.d	24,727	36,158	44,707	44,943	50,853	53,087	67,355	†61,174	72,534	101,906	156,605	160,899
Liabilities	7b.d	50,925	55,100	56,670	60,376	86,846	76,769	102,345	†78,869	91,640	108,859	157,117	139,927
Other Banking Insts.: Assets	7e.d	4,661	5,734	8,834	11,116	12,171	13,226	....	....	....	....	....	....
Liabilities	7f.d	22,196	16,597	14,535	13,686	29,960	34,387	....	....	....	....	....	....

Monetary Authorities

Billions of Kronor: End of Period

Foreign Assets	11	177.95	171.96	140.21	93.41	136.22	152.55	167.92	†176.08	176.77	165.88	168.13	197.90
Claims on Central Government	12a	87.52	71.03	59.05	53.09	32.84	†27.69	20.23	†	—	—	—	—
Claims on Banking Institutions	12e	.01	2.61	9.64	40.33	43.85	†45.63	43.20	†58.24	22.90	18.99	13.60	9.60
Reserve Money	14	200.59	170.74	114.30	84.76	87.95	102.91	97.77	†108.32	107.53	108.09	109.51	111.33
of which: Currency Outside Bls	14a	68.81	68.55	70.71	72.97	74.63	78.64	89.16	†97.89	96.28	97.13	98.19	100.37
Foreign Liabilities	16c	.22	3.48	4.14	3.98	4.10	†5.26	4.11	†2.86	.21	1.12	5.22	10.25
Central Government Deposits	16d	—	—	—	—	—	†2.17	1.59	†2.20	—	—	—	—
Capital Accounts	17a	76.62	74.46	75.71	82.25	100.07	114.42	108.24	†119.92	92.40	75.85	66.03	59.62
Other Items (Net)	17r	−11.95	−3.10	14.75	15.83	20.79	2.43	20.14	†1.01	−.46	−.19	.97	26.31

Banking Institutions

Billions of Kronor: End of Period

Reserves	20	8.75	9.42	11.13	10.17	13.52	30.67	9.80	†16.01	12.09	20.52	15.82	11.10
Other Claims on Monetary Author	20n								—	—	—	—	—
Foreign Assets	21	281.57	408.71	†572.15	682.15	698.05	741.63	961.14	†652.57	640.11	732.62	1,035.88	1,280.50
Claims on Central Government	22a	162.35	143.46	122.00	109.15	167.93	86.99	115.77	†117.82	89.28	7.49	7.62	15.51
Claims on Other General Govt	22b	17.54	24.99	31.05	36.85	37.58	42.74	39.61	†94.05	94.80	170.17	182.05	242.05
Claims on Other Resident Sectors	22d	605.08	596.72	†623.21	711.06	771.67	848.41	958.69	†2,298.02	2,421.69	2,537.93	2,697.16	2,986.90
Demand Deposits	24	....	....	....	....	....	....	....	619.27	635.68	677.45	839.32	973.11
Other Deposits	25	....	....	....	....	....	....	....	383.72	409.48	414.01	279.40	292.24
Demand,Time,Savings,Fgn.Cur.Dep.	25l	644.16	664.37	746.37	753.29	748.02	814.05	820.67	1,002.98	1,045.16	1,091.46	1,118.72	1,265.35
Bonds	26n	27.00	22.83	11.25	25.12	30.81	31.96	25.81	†1,023.27	1,055.54	1,181.10	1,336.35	1,654.10
Foreign Liabilities	26c	504.20	568.22	†639.64	788.10	985.94	924.94	1,256.78	†841.34	808.72	782.61	1,039.27	1,113.59
Central Government Deposits	26d	.43	1.61	2.38	.86	12.24	31.02	31.51	†11.72	9.58	14.97	7.46	18.66
Credit from Monetary Authorities	26g	.02	.01	10.53	31.65	29.26	34.44	45.78	†60.26	23.43	21.42	14.07	12.51
Capital Accounts	27a	83.63	100.76	61.74	74.37	82.99	88.53	95.95	†281.68	274.40	294.09	338.08	357.53
Other Items (Net)	27r	−184.16	−174.49	†−112.36	−124.00	−200.16	−174.50	−191.49	†−33.27	41.13	83.73	84.60	114.32

Banking Survey

Billions of Kronor: End of Period

Foreign Assets (Net)	31n	−44.90	8.97	†68.58	−16.52	−155.42	†−36.02	−131.83	†−15.54	7.95	114.77	159.53	354.56
Domestic Credit	32	872.05	834.59	†832.93	909.29	997.79	†972.64	1,101.21	†2,496.31	2,596.46	2,700.68	2,879.37	3,225.86
Claims on Central Govt. (Net)	32an	249.43	212.88	178.67	161.37	188.54	†81.49	102.91	†103.91	79.71	−7.48	.15	−3.16
Claims on Other General Govt.	32b	17.54	24.99	31.05	36.85	37.58	42.74	39.61	....	....	....	182.05	242.05
Claims on Other Resident Sectors	32d	605.08	596.72	†623.21	711.06	771.67	848.41	958.69	†2,298.36	2,421.96	2,537.99	2,697.16	2,986.97
Money	34	....	....	....	....	....	....	....	717.16	731.96	774.58	937.51	1,073.48
Quasi-Money	35	....	....	....	....	....	....	....	383.72	409.49	414.01	279.40	292.24
Money plus Quasi-Money	35l	728.05	750.56	817.08	826.26	822.65	892.69	909.84	1,100.88	1,141.45	1,188.59	1,216.91	1,365.72
Bonds	36n	27.00	22.83	11.25	25.12	30.81	31.96	25.81	†1,023.27	1,055.54	1,181.10	1,336.35	1,654.10
Capital Accounts	37a	160.25	175.22	137.45	156.62	183.06	202.95	204.20	†401.60	366.81	369.94	404.11	417.14
Other Items (Net)	37r	−88.15	−105.05	†−64.27	−115.23	−194.15	†−190.97	−170.46	†−35.48	40.62	76.46	81.53	143.46
Money + Quasi-Money,Seas.Adj.	35l.b	709.30	734.24	802.65	815.14	814.82	887.17	905.89	†1,090.42	1,130.61	1,177.30	1,205.35	1,352.75

Money (National Definitions)

Billions of Kronor: End of Period

M0	19mc	....	68.30	71.94	74.11	†78.09	87.33	88.92	96.73	95.83	98.43	98.20	100.37
M1	59ma	....	....	....	....	641.07	744.57	772.44	826.03	857.64	903.94	949.56	1,086.67
M2	59mb	....	....	....	....	876.40	961.67	996.94	1,057.10	1,090.11	1,141.28	1,167.22	1,296.92
M3	59mc	712.33	749.25	833.60	843.27	†976.06	1,101.01	1,168.49	1,164.60	1,261.32	1,304.47	1,356.73	1,531.35

Sweden 144

		1994	1995	1996	1997	1998	1999	2000	2001	2002	2003	2004	2005
Other Banking Institutions						*Billions of Kronor: End of Period*							
Cash...	40	.64	.02	—	—	—	—	....	....	....	....	....	....
Foreign Assets.............................	41	46.15	38.26	† 60.70	87.56	98.11	112.75	....	....	....	....	....	....
Claims on Central Government........	42a	28.84	23.98	16.02	16.26	18.53	18.67	....	....	....	....	....	....
Claims on Local Government...........	42b	.02	.01	† 35.70	39.04	40.72	42.16	....	....	....	....	....	....
Claims on Private Sector.................	42d	1,133.60	1,162.92	† 1,154.15	1,161.62	1,200.06	1,249.53	....	....	....	....	....	....
Claims on Deposit Money Banks......	42e	25.92	† 28.69	39.90	46.18	59.23	54.60	....	....	....	....	....	....
Time, Savings,& Fgn. Currency Dep..	45	92.34	134.44	167.26	173.49	2.43	.52	....	....	....	....	....	....
Bonds..	46ab	915.53	856.98	804.90	736.65	720.90	648.43	....	....	....	....	....	....
Foreign Liabilities.........................	46c	41.49	24.08	† 99.87	107.80	241.51	293.15	....	....	....	....	....	....
Central Govt. Lending Funds............	46f	247.18	230.97	† 189.15	184.74	211.22	155.66	....	....	....	....	....	....
Credit from Deposit Money Banks....	46h	66.74	81.61	96.58	170.02	222.74	250.19	....	....	....	....	....	....
Capital Accounts..........................	47a	73.35	82.26	60.74	65.24	68.36	73.71	....	....	....	....	....	....
Other Items (Net)...........................	47r	−201.50	−156.47	−112.04	−87.29	−50.51	56.06	....	....	....	....	....	....
Nonbank Financial Institutions						*Billions of Kronor: End of Period*							
Claims on Central Bank..................	40..l	8.63	7.21	† 6.76	—	—	—	—	—	—	—	—	....
Foreign Assets.............................	41..l	102.79	131.88	† 51.82	77.41	119.68	154.47	264.15	259.66	250.17	259.73	267.87	....
Claims on Central Government........	42a.l	161.20	254.55	† 247.21	259.93	290.98	341.92	285.64	306.40	370.19	393.98	441.45	....
Claims on State & Local Govts.........	42b.l	....	....	† 1.69	5.09	.96	1.98	1.56	1.51	1.96	1.96	3.09	....
Claims on Nonfin.Pub.Enterprises....	42c.l	....	....	† 35.83	47.13	43.35	49.91	61.12	91.90	94.13	90.21	89.86	....
Claims on Other Resident Sectors.....	42d.l	215.18	239.53	† 6.14	4.91	1.43	1.24	.90	3.24	2.49	1.10	.56	....
Claims on Banking Institutions.........	42e.l	....	....	211.54	230.24	239.02	217.46	226.92	236.42	306.97	338.79	325.72	....
Foreign Liabilities.........................	46c.l	....	....	† .40	.77	.71	.02	.10	.52	.25	.65	.34	....
Credit from Banking Institutions.......	46h.l	....	....	† 12.86	19.26	24.36	3.98	28.73	19.68	37.75	37.61	29.66	....
Capital.......................................	47a.l	....	....	† 420.22	493.56	548.85	714.36	711.17	648.28	603.32	695.83	796.93	....
Insurance and Technical Reserves.....	47d.l	....	....	546.92	643.96	767.76	933.16	1,018.14	1,135.96	1,019.94	1,105.15	1,148.81	....
Other Items (Net)..........................	47r.l	....	....	† −419.42	−532.85	−646.26	−884.56	−917.85	−905.32	−635.36	−753.46	−847.18	....
Interest Rates						*Percent Per Annum*							
Bank Rate (End of Period)..............	60	7.00	7.00	3.50	2.50	2.00	1.50	2.00	2.00	† 4.50	3.00	2.00	1.50
Repurchase Rate (End of Period)......	60a	† 7.51	8.91	4.27	4.19	3.50	3.25	3.89	3.75	3.75	2.75	2.00	1.50
Money Market Rate.......................	60b	7.36	8.54	6.28	4.21	4.24	3.14	3.81	4.09	4.19	3.29	....	....
Treasury Bill Rate.........................	60c	7.40	8.75	5.79	4.11	4.19	3.12	3.95	4.00	4.07	3.03	2.11	1.72
Deposit Rate (End of Period)...........	60l	4.91	6.16	2.47	2.50	1.91	1.65	2.15	2.10	2.26	1.51	1.00	.79
Lending Rate (End of Period)..........	60p	10.64	11.11	7.38	7.01	5.94	5.53	5.83	5.55	5.64	4.79	4.00	3.31
Government Bond Yield..................	61	9.52	10.24	8.06	6.61	4.99	4.98	5.37	5.11	5.30	4.64	4.42	3.38
Prices, Production, Labor						*Index Numbers (2000=100): Period Averages*							
Share Prices................................	62	26	29	....	50	59	69	100	71	54	....	....	....
Forest Industries...........................	62a	72	76	....	97	94	101	100	127	154	....	....	....
Industrials..................................	62b	48	† 55	63	87	86	93	100	93	87	....	....	....
Prices: Domestic Supply.................	63	87.8	94.6	92.9	94.0	93.5	94.5	100.0	103.2	103.8	102.9	105.3	110.6
Consumer Prices..........................	64	95.4	97.7	98.3	98.9	98.7	99.1	100.0	102.4	104.6	106.6	107.0	107.5
Harmonized CPI...........................	64h	....	94.7	95.4	97.2	98.2	98.7	100.0	102.7	104.7	† 107.1	108.2	109.0
Wages: Hourly Earnings.................	65	78.2	82.4	87.8	91.7	95.0	96.7	100.0	102.9	106.4	109.4	112.3	115.7
Industrial Production......................	66	91.3	82.3	83.5	88.0	91.8	94.0	100.0	99.5	100.7	103.3	106.5	108.3
Industrial Employment...................	67	95.6	100.8	101.6	100.5	100.9	100.1	100.0	97.6	93.8	90.9	89.4	86.1
						Number in Thousands: Period Averages							
Labor Force................................	67d	4,268	4,319	4,310	4,264	4,256	4,308	4,362	4,414	4,421	4,451	4,459	4,533
Employment................................	67e	3,928	3,986	3,963	3,922	3,979	4,068	4,159	4,239	4,244	4,234	4,213	4,263
Unemployment.............................	67c	340	333	347	342	277	241	203	175	176	217	246	270
Unemployment Rate (%).................	67r	8.0	7.7	8.0	8.0	6.5	5.6	4.7	4.0	4.0	4.9	5.5	6.0
Intl. Transactions & Positions						*Millions of Kronor*							
Exports......................................	70	471,600	567,700	569,200	632,800	675,300	700,800	804,200	806,500	805,800	825,800	904,500	971,900
Imports, c.i.f...............................	71	399,130	460,500	448,700	501,100	545,300	568,100	672,400	662,700	656,700	679,300	738,900	831,100
						2000=100							
Volume of Exports........................	72	58.9	65.9	69.6	77.0	84.0	89.1	100.0	98.5	101.2	106.1	116.8	....
Volume of Imports........................	73	64.0	69.3	71.1	78.7	86.3	89.3	100.0	94.9	94.4	100.4	108.1	....
Export Prices...............................	76	91.2	101.6	96.6	97.5	97.0	96.1	100.0	101.6	99.7	97.4	97.2	101.2
Import Prices...............................	76.x	87.1	92.8	89.5	91.3	90.4	92.6	100.0	104.5	104.8	102.6	105.2	112.9

Sweden 144

		1994	1995	1996	1997	1998	1999	2000	2001	2002	2003	2004	2005
Balance of Payments		\multicolumn{12}{c}{*Millions of US Dollars: Minus Sign Indicates Debit*}											
Current Account, n.i.e.	78ald	743	4,940	5,892	7,406	4,639	5,982	6,617	6,696	12,784	22,844	27,485	23,643
Goods: Exports f.o.b.	78aad	60,199	79,903	84,690	83,194	85,179	87,568	87,431	76,200	84,172	102,080	125,214	134,904
Goods: Imports f.o.b.	78abd	−50,641	−63,926	−66,053	−65,195	−67,547	−71,854	−72,216	−62,368	−67,541	−83,147	−101,799	−115,203
Trade Balance	78acd	9,558	15,978	18,636	17,999	17,632	15,714	15,215	13,832	16,631	18,933	23,415	19,701
Services: Credit	78add	13,674	15,622	16,930	17,769	17,952	19,904	20,252	21,997	24,009	30,654	38,719	43,167
Services: Debit	78aed	−14,690	−17,216	−18,755	−19,524	−21,721	−22,617	−23,440	−23,020	−23,958	−28,771	−33,056	−35,155
Balance on Goods & Services	78afd	8,542	14,384	16,811	16,245	13,862	13,001	12,027	12,809	16,682	20,816	29,079	27,713
Income: Credit	78agd	9,611	14,906	14,338	14,404	16,564	19,871	20,074	17,934	18,018	22,934	28,816	35,016
Income: Debit	78ahd	−15,530	−21,379	−22,641	−20,513	−22,349	−23,291	−22,137	−20,786	−19,044	−22,637	−25,592	−34,471
Balance on Gds, Serv. & Inc.	78aid	2,623	7,910	8,508	10,135	8,077	9,581	9,964	9,957	15,657	21,113	32,303	28,259
Current Transfers, n.i.e.: Credit	78ajd	544	1,555	2,524	2,319	2,266	2,341	2,602	2,578	3,345	3,577	3,680	4,922
Current Transfers: Debit	78akd	−2,424	−4,525	−5,140	−5,048	−5,704	−5,940	−5,950	−5,839	−6,218	−1,845	−8,498	−9,537
Capital Account, n.i.e.	78bcd	23	14	9	−228	868	−2,143	384	509	−79	−46	94	309
Capital Account, n.i.e.: Credit	78bad	37	32	31	211	1,502	1,289	1,226	1,111	529	552	591	564
Capital Account: Debit	78bbd	−14	−18	−22	−439	−634	−3,432	−841	−601	−609	−599	−497	−255
Financial Account, n.i.e.	78bjd	6,078	−5,052	−10,046	−10,121	5,961	−1,413	−3,297	1,824	−10,704	−20,163	−34,769	−22,226
Direct Investment Abroad	78bdd	−6,685	−11,399	−5,112	−12,119	−22,671	−19,554	−39,962	−6,959	−10,673	−17,341	−15,369	−27,560
Dir. Invest. in Rep. Econ., n.i.e.	78bed	6,269	14,939	5,492	10,271	19,413	59,386	22,125	13,085	11,709	3,268	−588	10,679
Portfolio Investment Assets	78bfd	−2,459	−10,765	−13,136	−13,818	−17,615	−36,749	−12,772	−23,041	−4,038	−13,701	−24,796	−13,019
Equity Securities	78bkd	−2,509	−9,378	−7,518	−10,179	−7,427	−29,766	758	−22,642	−124	−4,618	−6,210	261
Debt Securities	78bld	51	−1,386	−5,618	−3,640	−10,188	−6,983	−13,530	−400	−3,914	−9,083	−18,585	−13,281
Portfolio Investment Liab., n.i.e.	78bgd	721	8,201	1,661	−2,384	2,023	1,882	9,017	10,338	−6,691	4,134	−265	17,099
Equity Securities	78bmd	6,795	1,853	4,047	−1,687	−328	−3,895	17,997	−2,336	2,536	452	300	2,030
Debt Securities	78bnd	−6,074	6,348	−2,386	−697	2,351	5,777	−8,980	12,674	−9,227	3,682	−565	15,069
Financial Derivatives Assets	78bwd	....	20,264	24,800	31,244	30,125	22,982	31,481	33,678	37,720	40,045	27,730	30,463
Financial Derivatives Liabilities	78bxd	....	−21,096	−23,243	−29,280	−31,428	−22,923	−31,795	−38,894	−37,888	−38,964	−27,969	−31,268
Other Investment Assets	78bhd	−3,400	−12,197	−10,828	−9,670	−5,901	−10,333	−16,000	929	−998	−8,349	−16,930	−18,297
Monetary Authorities	78bod	....	....	....	....	....	....	....	....	....	....	....	227
General Government	78bpd	−290	−483	−303	−322	−244	−642	−150	37	−1,589	442	−557	227
Banks	78bqd	2,902	−8,037	−10,239	−4,971	−1,135	−5,296	−13,279	1,672	697	−8,688	−14,006	−18,137
Other Sectors	78brd	−6,012	−3,677	−287	−4,377	−4,522	−4,396	−2,571	−779	−106	−103	−2,367	−387
Other Investment Liab., n.i.e.	78bid	11,633	6,999	10,320	15,635	32,015	3,897	34,609	12,689	155	10,744	23,417	9,678
Monetary Authorities	78bsd	—	—	—	−39	88	−243	−556	−812	993	2,605	2,445	2,210
General Government	78btd	5,075	8,842	1,817	−1,583	578	1,047	129	−32	683	−392	−392	−81
Banks	78bud	−1,957	−1,055	2,935	9,269	20,205	−3,846	29,682	10,077	−1,299	1,905	21,175	10,090
Other Sectors	78bvd	8,515	−788	5,569	7,988	11,144	6,938	5,354	3,455	−222	7,175	189	−2,541
Net Errors and Omissions	78cad	−4,462	−1,566	−2,241	−3,769	−8,214	−545	−3,534	−10,078	−1,336	−558	6,091	−1,477
Overall Balance	78cbd	2,381	−1,664	−6,386	−6,712	3,254	1,881	170	−1,048	665	2,076	−1,100	249
Reserves and Related Items	79dad	−2,381	1,664	6,386	6,712	−3,254	−1,881	−170	1,048	−665	−2,076	1,100	−249
Reserve Assets	79dbd	−2,381	1,664	6,386	6,712	−3,254	−1,881	−170	1,048	−665	−2,076	1,100	−249
Use of Fund Credit and Loans	79dcd	—	—	—	—	—	—	—	—	—	—	—	—
Exceptional Financing	79ded	—	—	—	—	—	—	—	....	....	....	....	—
International Investment Position		\multicolumn{12}{c}{*Millions of US Dollars*}											
Assets	79aad	165,515	227,989	248,580	241,838	295,255	353,559	365,450	368,231	412,424	556,611	692,646	....
Direct Investment Abroad	79abd	59,237	69,088	71,751	79,099	94,674	104,948	115,582	123,275	144,127	181,307	216,311	....
Portfolio Investment	79acd	22,114	36,947	50,357	69,478	100,589	142,802	133,506	144,072	139,935	210,128	272,841	....
Equity Securities	79add	18,227	29,738	38,859	51,248	71,207	108,387	89,546	103,990	92,376	141,731	179,243	....
Debt Securities	79aed	3,887	7,209	11,498	18,230	29,382	34,415	43,960	40,082	47,559	68,397	93,597	....
Financial Derivatives	79ald	—	15,920	16,446	16,450	15,579	14,990	18,679	15,663	24,563	29,938	33,971	....
Other Investment	79afd	60,310	80,352	89,652	65,265	67,529	72,855	81,368	70,405	84,687	112,868	144,666	....
Monetary Authorities	79agd	....	....	....	....	....	....	....	....	....	....	....	....
General Government	79ahd	5,227	6,158	6,258	6,174	6,517	6,508	5,984	5,856	8,124	9,314	10,778	....
Banks	79aid	24,660	36,346	44,681	46,599	46,143	48,128	56,018	47,948	57,671	78,700	104,864	....
Other Sectors	79ajd	30,423	37,848	38,713	12,492	14,869	18,219	19,365	16,601	18,892	24,854	29,024	....
Reserve Assets	79akd	23,855	25,682	20,375	11,546	16,884	17,964	16,316	14,816	19,112	22,369	24,858	....
Liabilities	79lad	261,074	324,863	352,787	339,476	389,867	430,625	424,279	421,706	476,006	629,115	788,074	....
Dir. Invest. in Rep. Economy	79lbd	23,454	33,042	34,056	42,399	53,792	68,053	77,009	91,567	117,781	151,915	197,846	....
Portfolio Investment	79lcd	57,897	77,348	99,549	207,565	225,711	259,959	225,025	207,798	207,123	286,014	350,813	....
Equity Securities	79ldd	35,918	48,061	70,295	79,472	94,033	129,384	106,660	76,522	54,043	89,738	124,104	....
Debt Securities	79led	21,979	29,287	29,253	128,093	131,678	130,575	118,365	131,276	153,080	196,277	226,708	....
Financial Derivatives	79lld	—	16,821	17,610	16,420	15,936	14,095	15,276	14,225	25,453	30,545	36,136	....
Other Investment	79lfd	179,723	197,651	201,572	73,091	94,427	88,518	106,969	108,116	125,649	160,640	203,279	....
Monetary Authorities	79lgd	—	—	146	—	—	—	—	—	—	—	—	....
General Government	79lhd	57,227	65,934	64,328	1,836	2,238	2,857	1,922	1,579	2,739	2,814	2,562	....
Banks	79lid	50,928	55,270	56,615	51,247	68,238	59,978	80,756	81,747	97,609	116,128	162,861	....
Other Sectors	79ljd	71,567	76,447	80,483	20,009	23,951	25,683	24,291	24,790	25,301	41,699	37,855	....
Government Finance		\multicolumn{12}{c}{*Billions of Kronor: Year Ending December 31*}											
Deficit (-) or Surplus	80	† −133.63	−153.18	−58.02	† −16.66	6.84	64.01	125.82	....	† 1.11	−46.35	−53.35	16.49
Revenue	81	† 419.06	459.93	590.08	640.06	696.46	715.81	790.96	....	† 730.45	661.74	694.66	745.84
Grants Received	81z	—	5.66	10.40	8.88	9.87	9.28	9.02	....	....	....	....	....
Expenditure	82	† 552.69	618.77	658.50	† 665.60	699.49	661.08	674.16	....	† 729.34	708.09	748.01	729.35
Lending Minus Repayments	83	....	....	....	....	....	....	....	....	....	....	....	....
Financing													
Domestic	84a	† 129.85	135.42	27.07	−11.34	−20.25	47.13	8.78	....	† 28.99	98.65	58.03	49.65
Foreign	85a	† 3.78	17.76	30.95	28.01	13.43	−111.15	−135.30	....	−25.50	−42.42	−29.42	1.63
Total Debt	88	† 1,098.92	1,169.48	1,189.53	1,208.36	1,217.64	1,142.23	1,008.30	† 1,156.83	1,160.32	† 1,228.74	1,257.70	1,309.47
Debt: Domestic	88a	† 585.96	638.76	627.85	618.69	614.53	650.28	598.86	† 933.50	962.48	† 898.31	956.70	1,005.98
Debt: Foreign	89a	† 512.96	530.72	561.68	589.67	603.11	491.95	409.44	223.33	197.84	330.43	301.00	303.49

Sweden 144

National Accounts		1994	1995	1996	1997	1998	1999	2000	2001	2002	2003	2004	2005
							Billions of Kronor						
Househ.Cons.Expend.,incl.NPISHs....	96f	† 851.70	885.18	908.85	946.97	980.83	1,031.86	1,096.42	1,124.24	1,160.70	1,202.67	1,240.97	1,282.91
Government Consumption Expend...	91f	† 467.92	482.57	505.78	515.72	542.89	571.81	584.83	614.62	658.15	691.69	704.85	727.69
Gross Fixed Capital Formation..........	93e	† 255.00	282.85	293.47	296.63	324.50	358.33	389.01	395.62	392.07	392.84	413.76	454.63
Changes in Inventories....................	93i	† 17.31	21.48	7.14	9.37	15.31	5.35	16.47	5.90	1.66	9.88	3.65	1.64
Exports of Goods and Services..........	90c	† 589.38	700.87	694.15	789.38	842.47	890.69	1,018.54	1,048.44	1,042.95	1,070.18	1,182.57	1,298.76
Imports of Goods and Services (-).....	98c	519.57	† 585.07	579.96	653.42	718.76	761.67	887.98	900.47	883.92	907.85	972.61	1,092.63
Gross Domestic Product (GDP)........	99b	† 1,661.59	1,787.89	1,829.43	1,904.66	1,987.24	2,096.36	2,217.29	2,288.35	2,371.61	2,459.41	2,573.18	2,673.00
Net Primary Income from Abroad.....	98.n	−41.09	−42.38	−41.29	−42.05	−28.49	−20.97	−19.33	−22.67	−8.23	22.77	−5.20	−6.77
Gross National Income (GNI)............	99a	1,620.50	1,745.51	1,788.14	1,862.60	1,958.76	2,075.39	2,197.96	2,265.68	2,363.37	2,482.18	2,567.98	2,666.23
Net Current Transf.from Abroad.......	98t	−9.54	−10.79	−6.70	−12.06	−15.95	−20.27	−20.10	−21.06	−24.18	−21.65	−35.54	−40.41
Gross Nat'l Disposable Inc.(GNDI)....	99i	1,610.96	1,734.71	1,781.44	1,850.54	1,942.81	2,055.12	2,177.86	2,244.62	2,339.20	2,460.53	2,532.45	2,625.82
Gross Saving....................................	99s	291.33	366.96	366.81	387.85	419.09	451.45	496.62	505.76	520.35	566.16	586.63	615.22
Consumption of Fixed Capital..........	99cf	192.9	199.5	207.8	218.4	232.3	251.5	274.1	292.4	302.3	301.6	310.9	327.6
Net National Income......................	99e	1,427.64	1,545.99	1,580.31	1,644.16	1,726.49	1,823.94	1,923.87	1,973.26	2,061.10	2,180.56	2,257.06	2,338.64
GDP Volume 2000 Ref., Chained.....	99b.p	1,820.17	1,891.26	1,916.61	1,961.34	2,033.19	2,125.20	2,217.29	2,240.99	2,285.73	2,324.43	2,411.47	2,476.62
GDP Volume (2000=100)...............	99bvp	82.1	85.3	86.4	88.5	91.7	95.8	100.0	101.1	103.1	104.8	108.8	111.7
GDP Deflator (2000=100)...............	99bip	† 91.3	94.5	95.5	97.1	97.7	98.6	100.0	102.1	103.8	105.8	106.7	107.9
							Millions: Midyear Estimates						
Population...............................	99z	8.79	8.83	8.85	8.86	8.86	8.86	8.88	8.90	8.93	8.97	9.01	9.04

Switzerland 146

		1994	1995	1996	1997	1998	1999	2000	2001	2002	2003	2004	2005
Exchange Rates					*Francs per SDR: End of Period*								
Market Rate..................................	aa	1.9146	1.7102	1.9361	1.9636	1.9382	2.1955	2.1322	2.1079	1.8854	1.8380	1.7574	1.8785
				Francs per US Dollar: End of Period (ae) Period Average (rf)									
Market Rate..................................	ae	1.3115	1.1505	1.3464	1.4553	1.3765	1.5996	1.6365	1.6773	1.3868	1.2369	1.1316	1.3143
Market Rate..................................	rf	1.3677	1.1825	1.2360	1.4513	1.4498	1.5022	1.6888	1.6876	1.5586	1.3467	1.2435	1.2452
				Index Numbers (2000=100): Period Averages									
Market Rate..................................	ahx	123.7	142.9	136.6	116.3	116.6	112.4	100.0	100.1	108.6	125.4	135.8	135.7
Nominal Effective Exchange Rate.....	neu	102.1	109.5	107.5	100.6	102.7	101.4	100.0	103.7	108.2	108.6	108.4	108.2
Real Effective Exchange Rate...........	reu	93.5	100.1	100.4	96.7	102.2	101.5	100.0	105.8	111.6	112.8	114.5	115.3
Fund Position					*Millions of SDRs: End of Period*								
Quota..	2f.s	2,470	2,470	2,470	2,470	2,470	3,459	3,459	3,459	3,459	3,459	3,459	3,459
SDRs...	1b.s	162	181	88	170	192	345	125	225	54	25	46	42
Reserve Position in the Fund............	1c.s	643	981	1,065	1,407	1,828	1,218	964	1,259	1,410	1,383	1,154	571
of which: Outstg.Fund Borrowing...	2c	—	—	—	—	230							
International Liquidity					*Millions of US Dollars Unless Otherwise Indicated: End of Period*								
Total Reserves minus Gold..............	1l.d	34,729	36,413	38,433	39,028	41,191	36,321	32,272	32,006	40,155	47,652	55,497	36,297
SDRs.....................................	1b.d	236	269	126	230	271	473	162	283	74	37	71	60
Reserve Position in the Fund..........	1c.d	939	1,459	1,531	1,899	2,574	1,672	1,256	1,582	1,917	2,056	1,792	816
Foreign Exchange.....................	1d.d	33,554	34,685	36,775	36,899	38,346	34,176	30,854	30,141	38,164	45,560	53,634	35,421
Gold (Million Fine Troy Ounces)........	1ad	83.28	83.28	83.28	83.28	83.28	83.28	77.79	70.68	61.62	52.51	43.54	41.48
Gold (National Valuation)...............	1and	9,077	10,347	8,841	8,182	8,667	7,464	21,219	19,664	21,156	21,932	19,123	21,342
Monetary Authorities: Other Liab.....	4..d				33	119	134	124	375	401	393	291	368
Deposit Money Banks: Assets..........	7a.d	187,875	212,374	† 263,362	314,438	369,712	463,670	465,833	446,488	557,850	616,287	680,718	709,244
Liabilities...................	7b.d	171,093	184,869	† 223,836	268,969	300,777	395,023	440,005	415,253	498,607	546,820	608,308	634,711
Trustee Accounts: Assets.................	7k.d	271,584	288,831	† 294,323	293,492	311,232	292,460	325,518	323,209	328,419	327,835	363,438	387,912
Liabilities......................	7m.d	213,280	232,765	† 239,280	241,593	255,032	243,663	264,004	265,599	273,602	276,692	306,107	324,491
Monetary Authorities					*Billions of Francs: End of Period*								
Foreign Assets..............................	11	59.98	56.30	63.13	69.04	69.34	71.05	88.14	87.52	85.45	86.42	84.83	76.14
Claims on Central Government........	12a	5.13	5.19	5.26	7.12	7.22	7.14	7.71	8.32	9.36	10.04	9.81	8.20
Claims on Deposit Money Banks......	12e	1.30	1.87	2.86	1.09	17.73	28.53	24.46	25.99	28.01	27.14	24.52	26.20
Reserve Money..............................	14	39.33	38.40	40.35	39.43	42.47	49.67	44.41	49.96	46.56	50.24	48.68	49.92
of which: Currency Outside DMBs..	14a	32.64	33.02	34.61	34.33	35.43	39.44	37.78	42.17	41.94	42.93	42.14	43.83
Central Government Deposits...........	16d	.75	1.12	1.08	† 2.69	15.36	17.16	10.21	2.59	7.29	3.01	2.32	3.32
Other Items (Net)............................	17r	26.33	23.84	29.83	35.15	36.46	39.87	65.68	69.29	68.96	70.35	68.17	57.31
Deposit Money Banks					*Billions of Francs: End of Period*								
Reserves......................................	20	7.64	8.27	† 9.61	9.83	10.95	17.17	12.51	12.74	13.62	14.33	13.17	13.60
Foreign Assets..............................	21	246.40	244.34	† 354.59	457.60	508.91	741.69	762.34	748.90	773.63	762.29	770.30	932.16
Claims on Central Government........	22a	49.57	† 50.70	† 52.66	52.44	51.68	53.46	59.29	56.88	61.84	59.05	58.71	55.14
Claims on Private Sector.................	22d	594.37	611.70	† 608.17	625.65	635.67	676.49	668.94	660.94	662.90	686.97	716.75	762.34
Demand Deposits............................	24	62.22	67.63	† 93.57	105.45	113.88	124.00	122.25	131.40	149.32	194.49	181.92	194.73
Time and Savings Deposits...............	25	343.60	358.01	† 374.36	396.05	413.84	474.49	369.90	377.10	390.97	393.48	424.82	454.16
Bonds.......................................	26ab	164.72	161.13	† 149.66	137.25	127.55	123.04	128.19	129.07	129.91	120.29	116.22	115.50
Foreign Liabilities...........................	26c	224.39	212.69	† 301.37	391.43	414.02	631.88	720.07	696.50	691.47	676.36	688.36	834.20
Other Items (Net)............................	27r	103.04	115.54	† 106.06	115.34	137.93	135.39	162.68	145.39	150.31	138.02	147.61	164.64
Monetary Survey					*Billions of Francs: End of Period*								
Foreign Assets (Net).......................	31n	81.99	87.94	† 116.35	135.17	164.06	180.64	130.21	139.28	167.05	171.86	166.44	173.62
Domestic Credit.............................	32	648.31	† 666.47	† 665.01	† 682.53	679.22	719.93	725.73	723.56	726.80	753.06	782.96	822.35
Claims on Central Govt. (Net)........	32an	53.94	† 54.77	† 56.84	† 56.88	43.54	43.44	56.78	62.61	63.91	66.09	66.20	60.02
Claims on Private Sector................	32d	594.37	611.70	† 608.17	625.65	635.67	676.49	668.94	660.94	662.90	686.97	716.75	762.34
Money..	34	94.86	100.65	† 128.18	139.78	149.31	163.44	160.03	173.57	191.26	237.41	224.06	238.56
Quasi-Money................................	35	343.60	358.01	† 374.36	396.05	413.84	474.49	369.90	377.10	390.97	393.48	424.82	454.16
Bonds.......................................	36ab	164.72	161.13	† 149.66	137.25	127.55	123.04	128.19	129.07	129.91	120.29	116.22	115.50
Other Items (Net)...........................	37r	127.11	134.62	† 129.16	144.62	152.58	139.59	197.82	183.11	181.71	173.73	184.30	187.74
Money plus Quasi-Money...............	35l	438.46	458.66	† 502.54	535.83	563.15	637.93	529.93	550.66	582.23	630.90	648.88	692.72
Other Banking Institutions					*Billions of Francs: End of Period*								
Foreign Assets..............................	41..x	356.18	332.30	† 396.28	427.12	428.41	467.82	532.71	542.12	455.45	405.50	411.27	509.83
Domestic Liabilities........................	45..x	76.47	64.50	† 74.11	75.53	77.36	78.06	100.67	96.63	76.02	63.26	64.88	83.36
Foreign Liabilities...........................	46c.x	279.72	267.80	† 322.17	351.59	351.05	389.76	432.04	445.49	379.43	342.24	346.39	426.48
Nonbank Financial Institutions					*Billions of Francs: End of Period*								
Claims on Central Government........	42a.s	....	....	....	....	....	....	....	....	....	....	....	....
Claims on Priv.Sec.& Local Govt.....	42d.s	152.91	163.99	180.80	200.00	227.30	250.10	254.80	264.20	263.50	269.10	263.10	....
Real Estate.................................	42h.s	21.79	22.50	23.40	24.30	25.00	25.60	25.80	27.00	28.70	28.50	28.70	....
Incr.in Total Assets(Within Per.)........	49z.s	14.64	11.79	24.11	20.50	28.10	24.60	7.30	8.50	1.50	10.00	−8.30	....
Liquid Liabilities..........................	55l	514.93	523.16	† 576.65	611.36	640.51	715.99	630.59	647.29	658.25	694.16	713.75	776.08
Interest Rates					*Percent Per Annum*								
Bank Rate (End of Period)..............	60	3.50	1.50	1.00	1.00	1.00	.50	† 3.20	1.59	.50	.11	.54	.73
Money Market Rate.......................	60b	3.85	2.89	1.78	1.35	1.22	.93	† 3.50	1.65	.44	.09	.55	.63
Treasury Bill Rate...........................	60c	3.97	2.78	1.72	1.45	1.32	1.17	2.93	2.68	.94	.16	.37	.71
Deposit Rate................................	60l	3.63	1.28	1.34	1.00	.69	1.24	† 3.00	1.68	.43	.17	.39	.76
Lending Rate................................	60p	5.51	5.48	4.97	4.47	4.07	3.90	4.29	4.30	3.93	3.27	3.20	3.12
Government Bond Yield...................	61	5.23	3.73	3.63	3.08	† 2.71	3.62	3.55	3.56	2.40	2.78	2.38	1.96

		1994	1995	1996	1997	1998	1999	2000	2001	2002	2003	2004	2005
Prices, Production, Labor		*Index Numbers (2000=100): Period Averages*											
Share Prices	62	35.7	37.3	46.6	66.1	88.0	89.6	100.0	88.7	72.2	61.7	72.6	84.7
Producer Prices	63	104.0	103.9	102.0	101.3	100.1	99.1	100.0	100.5	100.0	100.0	101.2	102.0
Prices: Home & Imported Goods	63s	102.6	102.6	100.2	100.3	98.7	97.4	100.0	99.9	98.7	98.4	99.4	100.5
Consumer Prices	64	94.7	96.4	97.2	97.7	97.7	98.5	† 100.0	101.0	101.6	102.3	103.1	104.3
Wages: Hourly Earn	65	94.9	96.2	97.4	97.8	98.5	98.8	100.0	102.5	104.3	105.8	106.7	107.8
Industrial Production	66	80.6	82.2	82.2	86.0	89.1	92.2	100.0	99.3	94.2	94.5	98.4	100.9
Manufacturing Employment	67ey	107.1	105.7	103.0	100.4	99.9	99.0	100.0	101.4	98.7	95.5	93.8	94.0
		Number in Thousands: Period Averages											
Labor Force	67d	....	3,871	3,925	3,928	3,975	3,984	3,985	4,039	4,079	4,120	4,137	....
Employment	67e	3,719	3,747	3,781	3,766	3,833	3,862	3,870	3,938	3,959	3,951	3,959	....
Unemployment	67c	171	153	169	188	140	99	72	67	101	144	153	149
Unemployment Rate (%)	67r	4.7	4.2	4.7	5.2	3.9	2.7	2.0	1.9	2.8	3.8	4.3	3.8
Intl. Transactions & Positions		*Millions of Francs*											
Exports	70	90,213	92,012	94,174	105,133	109,113	114,446	126,549	131,717	135,741	135,472	146,312	156,977
Imports, c.i.f.	71	87,279	90,775	91,967	103,088	106,866	113,416	128,615	130,052	128,207	128,595	136,987	149,094
		2000=100											
Volume of Exports	72.a	76.5	79.8	80.8	† 87.0	90.1	93.0	100.0	102.8	108.5	108.7	114.4	120.7
Volume of Imports	73.a	70.1	74.6	75.7	† 80.5	85.7	93.1	100.0	101.1	103.1	103.2	106.9	110.7
Unit Value of Exports	74.a	93.1	91.2	92.1	† 95.4	95.7	97.3	100.0	101.2	98.9	98.5	101.0	102.8
Unit Value of Imports	75.a	96.8	94.5	94.5	† 99.6	96.9	94.8	100.0	100.0	96.7	96.9	99.6	104.8
Import Prices	76.x	99.5	99.7	96.0	97.9	95.8	93.7	100.0	98.4	95.6	94.7	95.5	97.1
Balance of Payments		*Millions of US Dollars: Minus Sign Indicates Debit*											
Current Account, n.i.e	78ald	16,729	20,703	19,916	25,317	25,194	28,578	33,562	22,483	24,930	44,925	58,294	49,710
Goods: Exports f.o.b.	78aad	82,625	97,139	95,544	95,039	93,782	91,787	94,810	95,897	100,786	115,443	138,225	146,109
Goods: Imports f.o.b.	78abd	−79,279	−93,880	−93,675	−92,302	−92,849	−90,937	−92,739	−94,258	−94,139	−108,484	−122,487	−141,259
Trade Balance	78acd	3,346	3,260	1,869	2,738	933	850	2,071	1,640	6,647	6,958	15,737	4,850
Services: Credit	78add	22,752	26,180	26,407	25,424	26,850	29,277	29,884	28,469	30,304	35,236	43,019	45,825
Services: Debit	78aed	−12,768	−15,037	−15,691	−14,100	−15,085	−15,861	−15,561	−16,460	−17,218	−19,038	−23,804	−25,307
Balance on Goods & Services	78afd	13,329	14,403	12,584	14,061	12,698	14,266	16,394	13,648	19,734	23,156	34,953	25,368
Income: Credit	78agd	26,747	31,575	32,997	35,066	45,926	50,081	61,843	53,074	42,150	63,757	72,854	87,957
Income: Debit	78ahd	−19,886	−20,867	−21,395	−19,761	−28,855	−30,620	−40,466	−39,001	−31,167	−36,598	−43,507	−56,639
Balance on Gds, Serv. & Inc.	78aid	20,190	25,111	24,186	29,366	29,769	33,727	37,771	27,721	30,717	50,316	64,299	56,686
Current Transfers, n.i.e.: Credit	78ajd	2,831	3,339	3,253	2,717	2,647	7,539	6,540	9,699	10,599	13,162	14,169	14,168
Current Transfers: Debit	78akd	−6,292	−7,748	−7,523	−6,767	−7,222	−12,688	−10,749	−14,937	−16,385	−18,552	−20,175	−21,144
Capital Account, n.i.e	78bcd	−350	−462	−214	−167	139	−515	−3,541	1,523	−1,159	−667	−1,409	−1,327
Capital Account, n.i.e.: Credit	78bad	31	10	19	36	755	53	490	2,314	274	492	336	350
Capital Account: Debit	78bbd	−380	−472	−233	−203	−616	−568	−4,031	−791	−1,433	−1,159	−1,745	−1,677
Financial Account, n.i.e	78bjd	−16,756	−11,231	−27,314	−24,712	−31,162	−33,040	−30,128	−36,926	−23,177	−24,999	−64,570	−101,372
Direct Investment Abroad	78bdd	−10,749	−11,289	−16,152	−17,732	−18,767	−33,256	−43,989	−18,376	−8,585	−15,673	−26,639	−42,556
Dir. Invest. in Rep. Econ., n.i.e.	78bed	3,683	4,158	4,373	7,306	9,649	12,426	19,788	9,473	6,783	17,487	1,627	6,456
Portfolio Investment Assets	78bfd	−19,112	−8,884	−22,731	−19,739	−14,882	−47,042	−23,169	−43,088	−29,159	−32,902	−42,412	−67,438
Equity Securities	78bkd	−8,073	−4,064	−14,686	−9,159	−2,529	−17,490	−20,424	−15,134	−7,454	−2,086	−11,303	−17,729
Debt Securities	78bld	−11,040	−4,820	−8,045	−10,580	−12,353	−29,552	−2,744	−27,954	−21,705	−30,816	−31,109	−49,709
Portfolio Investment Liab., n.i.e.	78bgd	911	4,960	12,895	9,033	10,247	5,916	10,247	1,894	7,482	−1,662	2,858	5,291
Equity Securities	78bmd	−1,573	5,851	11,677	6,945	8,632	5,562	8,777	1,840	5,678	−4,428	−2,788	3,951
Debt Securities	78bnd	2,484	−891	1,218	2,088	1,615	354	1,470	54	1,804	2,765	5,646	1,339
Financial Derivatives Assets	78bwd	....	....	....	....	....	....	....	....	....	....	....	....
Financial Derivatives Liabilities	78bxd	....	....	....	....	....	....	....	....	....	....	....	....
Other Investment Assets	78bhd	−30,778	−368	−70,353	−55,265	−60,089	−80,244	−101,376	21,392	−38,290	−4,631	−29,349	−83,363
Monetary Authorities	78bod	—	—	—	—	—	—	—	—	—	....	....	....
General Government	78bpd	−51	−15	42	197	204	197	31	46	62	113	98	−23
Banks	78bqd	−19,166	−9,423	−59,915	−52,384	−45,489	−76,859	−83,538	25,742	−53,922	−11,657	−14,589	−61,669
Other Sectors	78brd	−11,562	9,070	−10,480	−3,078	−14,804	−3,582	−17,869	−4,396	15,571	6,913	−14,858	−21,672
Other Investment Liab., n.i.e.	78bid	39,290	191	64,654	51,683	42,681	109,160	108,372	−8,220	38,591	12,383	29,344	80,240
Monetary Authorities	78bsd	−104	−3	−9	11	80	32	33	840	−860	−24	222	−117
General Government	78btd	40	267	31	121	−4	−53	−59	−26	154	−208	184	41
Banks	78bud	30,261	1,608	49,121	51,563	34,000	95,815	90,490	−14,861	35,979	6,296	27,627	62,583
Other Sectors	78bvd	9,093	−1,680	15,511	−11	8,606	13,365	17,908	5,827	3,319	6,319	1,311	17,733
Net Errors and Omissions	78cad	1,386	−8,980	10,134	1,717	7,008	2,292	−4,107	13,542	1,955	−15,855	9,303	35,297
Overall Balance	78cbd	1,009	29	2,521	2,154	1,179	−2,685	−4,214	622	2,549	3,405	1,618	−17,691
Reserves and Related Items	79dad	−1,009	−29	−2,521	−2,154	−1,179	2,685	4,214	−622	−2,549	−3,405	−1,618	17,691
Reserve Assets	79dbd	−1,009	−29	−2,521	−2,154	−1,179	2,685	4,214	−622	−2,549	−3,405	−1,618	17,691
Use of Fund Credit and Loans	79dcd	—	—	—	—	—	—	—	—	—	....	....	....
Exceptional Financing	79ded	—	—	—	—	—	—	—	—	—	....	....	....

Switzerland 146

		1994	1995	1996	1997	1998	1999	2000	2001	2002	2003	2004	2005
International Investment Position							*Millions of US Dollars*						
Assets..	79aad	745,816	860,214	924,274	1,009,487	1,196,819	1,237,507	1,360,092	1,311,756	1,505,682	1,760,219	1,982,532	1,967,767
Direct Investment Abroad..............	79abd	112,586	142,479	141,591	165,364	184,232	194,585	229,742	249,264	288,943	338,397	396,442	394,754
Portfolio Investment......................	79acd	293,846	347,040	359,820	382,782	469,522	502,909	501,704	485,312	520,617	657,540	758,086	726,966
Equity Securities.......................	79add	100,797	120,543	138,922	165,438	209,617	259,995	267,274	243,703	218,272	293,656	339,470	357,270
Debt Securities.........................	79aed	193,049	226,497	220,898	217,344	259,905	242,914	234,430	241,610	302,345	363,884	418,616	369,696
Financial Derivatives....................	79ald	—	—	—	—	—	—	—	—	—	—	—	—
Other Investment.........................	79afd	293,976	322,125	375,575	414,208	492,632	496,075	575,166	525,483	634,784	694,712	753,351	788,367
Monetary Authorities.................	79agd	—	—	—	—	—	—	—	—	—	—	—	—
General Government..................	79ahd	1,037	1,250	1,051	946	943	759	755	584	696	776	843	458
Banks......................................	79aid	163,590	183,006	231,511	276,736	332,647	342,082	413,332	375,251	465,885	508,314	542,192	566,365
Other Sectors...........................	79ajd	129,349	137,870	143,012	136,526	159,043	153,234	161,079	149,648	168,203	185,622	210,315	221,544
Reserve Assets..............................	79akd	45,409	48,569	47,288	47,132	50,432	43,939	53,480	51,697	61,337	69,569	74,653	57,681
Liabilities.....................................	79lad	472,874	556,487	587,559	700,953	838,861	917,806	1,077,283	997,577	1,126,304	1,335,707	1,513,348	1,604,383
Dir. Invest. in Rep. Economy..........	79lbd	61,691	73,324	69,001	74,142	88,201	90,510	101,706	103,922	143,911	184,295	221,296	195,176
Portfolio Investment......................	79lcd	162,400	208,583	203,380	272,805	353,572	344,178	410,239	349,706	350,201	450,150	520,924	600,877
Equity Securities.......................	79ldd	134,721	179,290	176,566	246,515	323,809	314,257	382,038	321,678	314,770	402,623	456,669	532,090
Debt Securities.........................	79led	27,679	29,293	26,814	26,289	29,763	29,921	28,201	28,028	35,431	47,526	64,255	68,787
Financial Derivatives....................	79lld	—	—	—	—	—	—	—	—	—	—	—	—
Other Investment.........................	79lfd	248,783	274,580	315,178	354,006	397,088	483,119	565,339	543,949	632,192	701,262	771,128	808,330
Monetary Authorities.................	79lgd	36	37	24	33	119	355	393	1,252	507	518	291	544
General Government..................	79lhd	258	568	514	596	626	484	413	380	616	465	705	645
Banks......................................	79lid	170,567	180,873	218,606	258,708	290,465	342,709	422,205	397,644	467,174	516,834	567,264	590,076
Other Sectors...........................	79ljd	77,923	93,102	96,034	94,669	105,879	139,570	142,328	144,674	163,895	183,444	202,867	217,065
Government Finance							*Millions of Francs: Year Ending December 31*						
Deficit (-) or Surplus......................	80	−4,443	−5,141	−4,404	−4,917	363	−2,399	3,820	1,367	−3,989	−2,950	−2,724	−395
Revenue......................................	81	33,752	32,202	35,279	34,695	39,359	37,742	44,031	43,018	35,537	40,259	42,290	44,156
Expenditure................................	82	36,759	37,474	39,417	38,151	41,634	40,839	40,832	42,147	39,526	43,645	44,992	44,391
Lending Minus Repayments............	83	1,436	−131	266	1,461	−2,638	−698	−621	−496	—	−436	22	160
Financing													
Net Domestic Borrowing...............	84a	7,399	6,472	5,706	8,486	13,860	−6,817	3,244	−2,419	14,277	1,886	3,466	3,537
Other Financing..........................	86c	−1,598	−1,050	1,202	−596	−4,245	−10,960	−9,000	−5,401	−3,223	−2,204	1,995	7,441
Use of Cash Balances...................	87	−1,358	−281	−2,504	−2,973	−9,978	20,176	1,936	6,453	−7,065	3,268	−2,737	−10,583
Total Debt....................................	88	75,714	82,152	88,418	97,050	109,620	102,254	108,108	106,813	122,366	123,711	126,685	....
National Accounts							*Billions of Francs*						
Househ.Cons.Expend.,incl.NPISHs....	96f.c	217.7	222.6	226.3	231.3	235.8	242.0	249.2	255.2	259.3	263.1	269.5	278.3
Government Consumption Expend...	91f.c	43.0	43.5	44.3	44.0	44.0	44.3	46.2	49.0	50.4	51.9	52.9	54.3
Gross Fixed Capital Formation..........	93e.c	86.9	86.8	82.9	82.5	87.2	88.9	94.9	93.8	92.8	89.9	93.4	97.5
Changes in Inventories...................	93i.c	−.4	.2	1.3	1.7	4.1	.3	1.5	6.1	.5	1.2	−2.6	−2.8
Exports of Goods and Services..........	90c.c	131.3	131.9	135.5	151.6	156.9	165.8	189.8	190.8	188.0	188.6	206.1	218.7
Imports of Goods and Services (-).....	98c.c	110.8	112.8	116.4	130.5	137.8	143.4	166.1	172.3	160.5	160.1	173.4	189.0
Gross Domestic Product (GDP).........	99b.c	367.7	372.3	374.0	380.6	390.2	397.9	415.5	422.5	430.5	434.6	445.9	456.9
Net Primary Income from Abroad.....	98.n	12.7	15.6	....	....	....	....	....	....	....	....	....	....
Gross National Income (GNI)............	99a	365.6	377.6	....	....	....	....	....	....	....	....	....	....
Net National Income......................	99e	328.8	339.8	....	....	....	....	....	....	....	....	....	....
GDP Volume 2000 Ref., Chained.....	99b.r	374.5	375.9	377.9	385.1	395.8	401.0	415.5	419.9	421.1	420.0	428.7	436.7
GDP Volume (2000=100)..............	99bvr	90.1	90.5	90.9	92.7	95.3	96.5	100.0	101.0	101.4	101.1	103.2	105.1
GDP Deflator (2000=100).............	99bir	98.2	99.0	99.0	98.8	98.6	99.2	100.0	100.6	102.2	103.5	104.0	104.6
							Millions: Midyear Estimates						
Population.................................	99z	6.97	7.00	7.04	7.07	7.11	7.14	7.17	7.19	7.21	7.23	7.24	7.25

Syrian Arab Republic   463

		1994	1995	1996	1997	1998	1999	2000	2001	2002	2003	2004	2005
Exchange Rates		*Pounds per SDR: End of Period (aa) Pounds per US Dollar: End of Period (ae)*											
Principal Rate	aa	16.387	16.686	16.141	15.145	15.805	15.406	14.625	14.107	15.261	16.680	17.433	16.044
Principal Rate	ae	11.225	11.225	11.225	11.225	11.225	11.225	11.225	11.225	11.225	11.225	11.225	11.225
Fund Position		*Millions of SDRs: End of Period*											
Quota	2f.s	210	210	210	210	210	294	294	294	294	294	294	294
SDRs	1b.s	—	—	—	—	—	—	—	—	—	—	37	37
Reserve Position in the Fund	1c.s	—	—	—	—	—	—	—	—	—	—	—	—
Total Fund Cred.&Loans Outstg	2tl	—	—	—	—	—	—	—	—	—	—	—	—
International Liquidity		*Millions of US Dollars Unless Otherwise Indicated: End of Period*											
SDRs	1b.d	—	—	—	—	—	—	—	—	—	—	57	52
Reserve Position in the Fund	1c.d	—	—	—	—	—	—	—	—	—	—		
Gold (Million Fine Troy Ounces)	1ad	.833	.833	.833	.833	.833	.833	.833	.833	.833	.833	.833	.833
Gold (National Valuation)	1and	29	29	29	29	29	29	29	29	29	29	29	29
Other Liab.	4..d	1,041	1,124	1,041	1,084	1,137	1,150	805	730	692	581	450	....
Monetary Authorities		*Millions of Pounds: End of Period*											
Foreign Assets	11	28,568	37,206	49,156	52,376	55,216	67,512	88,391	101,503	115,018	130,666	145,906	....
Claims on Central Government	12a	178,802	203,998	241,730	265,783	270,370	270,369	274,877	301,278	321,202	304,929	309,129	....
Claims on Official Entities	12bx	106	106	106	106	106	106	106	106	106	106	106	....
Claims on Deposit Money Banks	12e	90,674	104,602	112,460	126,599	135,455	164,991	161,558	157,174	156,554	174,811	144,469	....
Reserve Money	14	164,996	172,711	185,864	194,799	204,513	219,475	252,814	295,442	342,625	377,685	472,826	....
of which: Currency Outside DMBs	14a	135,021	143,800	153,715	159,808	178,191	182,184	203,863	229,266	258,359	285,015	333,055	....
Foreign Liabilities	16c	11,683	12,614	11,686	12,168	12,768	12,911	9,040	8,196	7,773	6,520	5,048	....
Central Government Deposits	16d	126,027	156,479	213,995	256,253	272,085	314,414	355,693	374,313	391,594	391,924	325,034	....
Capital Accounts	17a	18,755	23,902	23,902	33,839	38,195	43,909	51,426	55,814	55,815	59,195	80,383	....
Other Items (Net)	17r	−23,311	−19,794	−31,995	−52,193	−66,415	−87,732	−144,041	−173,704	−204,927	−224,813	−283,682	....
Deposit Money Banks		*Millions of Pounds: End of Period*											
Reserves	20	31,556	29,366	38,771	25,946	21,403	23,716	31,419	42,242	71,788	85,910	117,276	....
Foreign Assets	21	126,639	150,020	180,547	222,465	255,655	285,762	398,681	502,229	581,672	591,826	619,663	....
Claims on Central Government	22a	26,252	30,931	35,560	41,573	48,639	58,275	69,385	100,656	127,428	154,462	112,869	....
Claims on Official Entities	22bx	120,667	140,439	147,202	164,580	160,381	179,711	187,356	191,020	157,802	173,976	182,331	....
Claims on Private Sector	22d	52,343	63,667	66,633	73,351	72,617	75,345	76,611	78,737	83,676	108,658	147,769	....
Demand Deposits	24	68,885	78,028	84,685	93,665	97,683	121,471	151,753	176,845	222,391	329,809	280,878	....
Time and Savings Deposits	25	83,113	91,775	104,624	116,939	135,636	160,346	194,800	276,181	330,155	261,080	388,783	....
Restricted Deposits	26b	24,411	26,708	27,182	33,235	22,776	20,327	28,394	40,542	50,451	73,208	99,370	....
Foreign Liabilities	26c	10,347	5,574	5,551	2,782	3,653	4,915	4,583	3,891	11,116	13,576	5,270	....
Central Government Deposits	26d	6,327	7,780	8,643	12,863	13,686	14,960	18,078	19,310	20,154	26,536	35,042	....
Credit from Monetary Authorities	26g	90,741	104,712	119,897	136,811	135,199	149,810	160,744	150,193	168,217	178,531	145,867	....
Capital Accounts	27a	17,546	23,065	29,908	34,666	40,576	48,878	47,799	50,598	52,098	44,622	53,848	....
Other Items (Net)	27r	56,087	76,780	88,224	96,955	109,485	102,102	157,300	197,322	167,784	187,469	205,892	....
Monetary Survey		*Millions of Pounds: End of Period*											
Foreign Assets (Net)	31n	133,177	169,038	212,466	259,891	294,450	335,448	473,449	591,645	677,801	702,396	755,251	....
Domestic Credit	32	245,816	274,882	268,593	276,278	266,342	254,432	234,564	278,174	278,466	323,671	392,127	....
Claims on Central Govt. (Net)	32an	72,700	70,670	54,652	38,241	33,238	−730	−29,509	8,311	36,882	40,931	61,921	....
Claims on Official Entities	32bx	120,773	140,545	147,308	164,686	160,487	179,817	187,462	191,126	157,908	174,082	182,437	....
Claims on Private Sector	32d	52,343	63,667	66,633	73,351	72,617	75,345	76,611	78,737	83,676	108,658	147,769	....
Money	34	207,106	225,038	244,495	260,927	281,926	313,318	368,670	419,911	494,681	628,279	636,749	....
Quasi-Money	35	83,113	91,775	104,624	116,939	135,636	160,346	194,800	276,181	330,155	261,080	388,783	....
Restricted Deposits	36b	24,411	26,708	27,182	33,235	22,776	20,327	28,394	40,542	50,451	73,208	99,370	....
Other Items (Net)	37r	64,364	100,397	104,759	125,069	120,452	95,889	116,148	133,183	80,980	63,498	57,519	....
Money plus Quasi-Money	35l	290,219	316,813	349,119	377,866	417,562	473,663	563,470	696,092	824,836	889,359	1,025,532	....
Interest Rates		*Percent Per Annum*											
Discount Rate (End of Period)	60	5.00	5.00	5.00	5.00	5.00	5.00	5.00	5.00	5.00	....	....	....
Deposit Rate	60l	4.0	4.0	4.0	4.0	4.0	4.0	4.0	4.0	4.0	3.3	1.9	1.0
Lending Rate	60p	9.0	9.0	9.0	9.0	9.0	9.0	9.0	9.0	9.0	8.0	7.5	8.0
Prices, Production, Labor		*Index Numbers (2000=100): Period Averages*											
Wholesale Prices	63	96.1	102.7	106.0	108.7	108.0	† 106.0	100.0	95.0	102.0	....	....	....
Consumer Prices	64	91.4	98.7	106.9	108.9	† 108.0	104.0	100.0	103.0	104.0	....	....	....
Industrial Production	66	87.2	89.9	90.8	96.2	† 98.0	104.0	100.0	103.0	109.0	....	....	....
		Number in Thousands: Period Averages											
Labor Force	67d	....	....	....	....	4,411	4,527	4,937	5,457	5,460	5,032	....	....
Employment	67e	....	....	....	....	....	....	....	4,844	4,822	....	....	....
Unemployment	67c	....	....	....	....	....	....	....	613	638	....	....	....
Unemployment Rate (%)	67r	....	....	....	....	....	....	....	11.2	11.7	....	....	....
Intl. Transactions & Positions		*Millions of Pounds*											
Exports	70	34,200	40,000	44,890	43,960	32,440	38,880	† 216,190	243,000	315,920	265,038	249,014	....
Imports, c.i.f.	71	61,370	52,860	60,390	45,210	43,720	43,010	† 187,530	220,000	235,720	236,800	327,000	....
		1995=100											
Volume of Exports	72	102.4	100.0	98.2	109.6	....	....	....	....	....	....	....	....
Volume of Imports	73	111.3	100.0	100.8	87.9	....	....	....	....	....	....	....	....
Unit Value of Exports	74	80.0	100.0	105.6	83.3	....	....	....	....	....	....	....	....
Unit Value of Imports	75	89.0	100.0	105.9	90.7	....	....	....	....	....	....	....	....

Syrian Arab Republic   463

		1994	1995	1996	1997	1998	1999	2000	2001	2002	2003	2004	2005
Balance of Payments		*Millions of US Dollars: Minus Sign Indicates Debit*											
Current Account, n.i.e.	78ald	−791	263	40	461	58	201	1,061	1,221	1,440	728	205	....
Goods: Exports f.o.b.	78aad	3,329	3,858	4,178	4,057	3,142	3,806	5,146	5,706	6,668	5,762	5,561	....
Goods: Imports f.o.b.	78abd	−4,604	−4,004	−4,516	−3,603	−3,320	−3,590	−3,723	−4,282	−4,458	−4,430	−5,935	....
Trade Balance	78acd	−1,275	−146	−338	454	−178	216	1,423	1,424	2,210	1,332	−374	....
Services: Credit	78add	1,863	1,899	1,792	1,582	1,666	1,651	1,699	1,781	1,559	1,331	2,614	....
Services: Debit	78aed	−1,611	−1,537	−1,555	−1,489	−1,491	−1,612	−1,667	−1,694	−1,883	−1,806	−1,980	....
Balance on Goods & Services	78afd	−1,023	216	−101	547	−3	255	1,455	1,511	1,886	857	260	....
Income: Credit	78agd	638	444	534	421	369	356	345	379	250	282	385	....
Income: Debit	78ahd	−997	−1,004	−1,017	−1,006	−839	−899	−1,224	−1,162	−1,175	−1,139	−1,114	....
Balance on Gds, Serv. & Inc.	78aid	−1,382	−344	−584	−38	−473	−288	576	728	961	—	−469	....
Current Transfers, n.i.e.: Credit	78ajd	597	610	630	504	533	491	495	512	499	743	690	....
Current Transfers: Debit	78akd	−6	−3	−6	−5	−2	−2	−10	−19	−20	−15	−16	....
Capital Account, n.i.e.	78bcd	102	20	26	18	27	80	63	17	20	20	18	....
Capital Account, n.i.e.: Credit	78bad	102	20	26	18	27	80	63	17	20	20	20	....
Capital Account: Debit	78bbd	—	—	—	—	—	....	....	....	....	—	−2	....
Financial Account, n.i.e.	78bjd	1,159	521	782	65	196	173	−139	−244	−250	−138	−60	....
Direct Investment Abroad	78bdd	—	—	—	—	—	—	—	—	—	—	—	....
Dir. Invest. in Rep. Econ., n.i.e.	78bed	251	100	89	80	82	263	270	110	115	160	275	....
Portfolio Investment Assets	78bfd	—	—	—	—	—	—	—	—	—	—	—	....
Equity Securities	78bkd	—	—	—	—	—	—	—	—	—	—	—	....
Debt Securities	78bld	—	—	—	—	—	—	—	—	—	—	—	....
Portfolio Investment Liab., n.i.e.	78bgd	—	—	—	—	—	—	—	—	—	—	—	....
Equity Securities	78bmd	—	—	—	—	—	—	—	—	—	—	—	....
Debt Securities	78bnd	—	—	—	—	—	—	—	—	—	—	—	....
Financial Derivatives Assets	78bwd	....	....	....	....	....	....	....	....	....	....	....	....
Financial Derivatives Liabilities	78bxd	....	....	....	....	....	....	....	....	....	....	....	....
Other Investment Assets	78bhd	−718	1,510	1,660	1,496	1,422	1,332	1,206	1,136	1,180	—	—	....
Monetary Authorities	78bod	—	—	—	—	—	—	—	—	—	—	—	....
General Government	78bpd	—	—	—	—	—	—	—	—	—	—	—	....
Banks	78bqd	—	1,510	1,660	1,496	1,422	1,332	1,206	1,136	1,180	—	—	....
Other Sectors	78brd	−718	—	—	—	—	—	—	—	—	—	—	....
Other Investment Liab., n.i.e.	78bid	1,626	−1,089	−967	−1,511	−1,308	−1,422	−1,615	−1,490	−1,545	−298	−335	....
Monetary Authorities	78bsd	20	—	—	—	—	—	—	—	—	—	—	....
General Government	78btd	339	—	—	—	—	—	—	—	—	2	−235	....
Banks	78bud	−147	−1,089	−967	−1,511	−1,308	−1,422	−1,615	−1,490	−1,545	—	—	....
Other Sectors	78bvd	1,414	—	—	—	—	—	—	—	—	−300	−100	....
Net Errors and Omissions	78cad	96	35	139	−95	153	−195	−171	26	−160	85	254	....
Overall Balance	78cbd	566	839	987	449	434	259	814	1,020	1,050	695	417	....
Reserves and Related Items	79dad	−566	−839	−987	−449	−434	−259	−814	−1,020	−1,050	−695	−417	....
Reserve Assets	79dbd	−566	−839	−987	−449	−434	−259	−814	−1,020	−1,050	−719	−422	....
Use of Fund Credit and Loans	79dcd	—	—	—	—	—	—	—	—	—	—	—	....
Exceptional Financing	79ded	—	—	—	—	....	....	....	....	....	24	5	....
Government Finance		*Millions of Pounds: Year Ending December 31*											
Deficit (-) or Surplus	80	−18,860	−10,059	−1,577	−1,723	−5,534	5,827	....	....	....	....	....	....
Revenue	81	111,892	131,002	152,231	179,202	180,437	196,127	....	....	....	....	....	....
Grants Received	81z	1,264	896	1,788	798	2	—	....	....	....	....	....	....
Expenditure	82	132,016	141,957	155,596	181,723	185,973	190,300	....	....	....	....	....	....
National Accounts		*Millions of Pounds*											
Househ.Cons.Expend.,incl.NPISHs.	96f	348,865	378,143	489,728	515,411	542,374	575,866	572,761	571,863	603,241	634,922	....	....
Government Consumption Expend.	91f	68,019	76,709	81,316	84,994	88,521	86,857	112,244	121,723	124,770	143,549	....	....
Exports of Goods and Services	90c	167,327	177,229	219,872	241,719	241,316	264,704	326,715	359,278	404,099	345,954	....	....
Gross Capital Formation	93	151,622	155,504	163,076	155,464	162,446	153,706	156,092	198,166	206,607	243,644	....	....
Imports of Goods and Services (-)	98c	229,732	216,610	263,135	252,019	244,213	262,041	263,868	296,893	324,176	315,148	....	....
Gross Domestic Product (GDP)	99b	506,101	570,975	690,857	745,569	790,444	819,092	903,944	954,137	1,014,541	1,052,921	....	....
Consumption of Fixed Capital	99cf	17,674	20,344	26,257	30,151	31,668	34,282	38,551	38,499	40,313	....	....	....
GDP Volume 1995 Prices	99b.p	539,929	570,975	612,896	628,148	675,888	662,396	666,567	....	....	....	....	....
GDP Volume 2000 Prices	99b.p	....	....	....	....	....	....	903,944	934,409	964,574	....	....	....
GDP Volume (2000=100)	99bvp	81.0	85.7	91.9	94.2	101.4	99.4	† 100.0	103.4	106.7	....	....	....
GDP Deflator (2000=100)	99bip	69.1	73.7	83.1	87.5	86.2	91.2	100.0	102.1	105.2	....	....	....
		Millions: Midyear Estimates											
Population	99z	14.37	14.75	15.15	15.56	15.97	16.39	16.81	17.24	17.68	18.13	18.58	19.04

Tajikistan 923

		1994	1995	1996	1997	1998	1999	2000	2001	2002	2003	2004	2005
Exchange Rates		\multicolumn{12}{c}{*Somoni per SDR: End of Period*}											
Official Rate	aa	.058	.436	.472	1.008	1.377	1.971	† 2.866	3.205	4.079	4.393	4.716	4.573
		\multicolumn{12}{c}{*Somoni per US Dollar: End of Period (ae) Period Average (rf)*}											
Official Rate	ae	.039	.294	.328	.747	.978	1.436	† 2.200	2.550	3.000	2.957	3.037	3.199
Official Rate	rf	.024	.123	.296	.562	.777	1.238	† 2.076	2.372	2.764	3.061	2.971	3.117
Fund Position		\multicolumn{12}{c}{*Millions of SDRs: End of Period*}											
Quota	2f.s	60.00	60.00	60.00	60.00	60.00	87.00	87.00	87.00	87.00	87.00	87.00	87.00
SDRs	1b.s	—	—	2.21	9.06	2.05	.04	6.02	3.86	1.34	.57	.85	3.80
Reserve Position in the Fund	1c.s	—	—	—	—	—	—	—	—	—	—	—	—
Total Fund Cred.&Loans Outstg	2tl	—	—	15.00	22.50	70.30	73.21	85.03	87.66	69.17	67.16	78.70	88.91
International Liquidity		\multicolumn{12}{c}{*Millions of US Dollars Unless Otherwise Indicated: End of Period*}											
Total Reserves minus Gold	1l.d	....	....	....	36.5	53.6	55.2	92.9	92.6	89.5	111.9	157.5	168.2
SDRs	1b.d	—	—	3.2	12.2	2.9	—	7.8	4.9	1.8	.9	1.3	5.4
Reserve Position in the Fund	1c.d	—	—	—	—	—	—	—	—	—	—	—	—
Foreign Exchange	1d.d	....	....	....	24.3	50.7	55.1	85.0	87.7	87.7	111.0	156.2	162.8
Gold (Million Fine Troy Ounces)	1ad	....	....	....	.01	.01	.01	.01	.01	—	.01	.03	.04
Gold (National Valuation)	1and	....	....	....	2.4	2.3	2.3	1.4	1.7	—	5.7	14.6	20.7
Monetary Authorities:Other Liab	4..d	....	....	....	....	2.22	.14	.09	.24	.31	.39	.56	1.11
Deposit Money Banks: Assets	7a.d	....	....	....	....	1.04	1.10	1.44	2.44	2.82	9.67	13.65	48.95
Liabilities	7b.d	....	....	....	....	74.64	42.62	65.06	86.22	92.15	106.34	222.79	199.37
Monetary Authorities		\multicolumn{12}{c}{*Millions of Somoni: End of Period*}											
Foreign Assets	11	....	....	....	....	67.2	83.6	209.1	256.4	294.0	402.9	578.8	734.7
Claims on General Government	12a	....	....	....	....	102.4	64.9	131.9	92.8	156.8	153.8	153.8	153.8
Claims on Nonfin.Pub.Enterprises	12c	....	....	....	....	—	—	—	203.3	86.0	—	—	—
Claims on Private Sector	12d	....	....	....	....	16.7	96.5	1.1	215.9	171.4	142.1	128.7	127.3
Claims on Deposit Money Banks	12e	....	....	....	....	26.3	49.0	150.0	37.6	34.1	42.1	88.8	81.6
Reserve Money	14	....	....	....	....	62.2	78.5	126.5	153.4	184.8	252.1	276.9	305.3
of which: Currency Outside Banks	14a	....	....	....	....	46.6	62.0	86.8	103.6	135.8	158.1	175.4	155.3
Foreign Liabilities	16c	....	....	....	....	99.0	144.5	243.9	281.5	283.0	296.2	372.9	410.1
General Government Deposits	16d	....	....	....	....	9.4	21.2	48.2	38.1	65.3	137.0	182.5	209.0
Counterpart Funds	16e	....	....	....	....	3.0	15.0	38.8	85.8	101.0	94.6	166.0	164.8
Capital Accounts	17a	....	....	....	....	36.3	41.5	11.5	64.8	47.4	18.4	4.8	27.6
Other Items (Net)	17r	....	....	....	....	2.5	−7.1	22.2	−22.7	−29.4	−68.2	−66.0	−19.6
Deposit Money Banks		\multicolumn{12}{c}{*Millions of Somoni: End of Period*}											
Reserves	20	....	....	....	....	12.0	13.5	34.6	49.8	51.4	86.7	106.6	173.1
Foreign Assets	21	....	....	....	....	1.0	1.6	3.2	6.2	8.5	28.6	41.5	156.6
Claims on General Government	22a	....	....	....	....	1.1	1.1	1.3	3.1	.7	.3	.3	.3
Claims on Nonfin.Pub.Enterprises	22c	....	....	....	....	....	....	....	....	....	....	....	30.2
Claims on Private Sector	22d	....	....	....	....	115.7	142.1	245.0	359.5	456.1	523.7	942.5	1,113.3
Claims on Nonbank Financial Insts	22g	....	....	....	....	....	....	....	....	....	....	....	2.9
Demand Deposits	24	....	....	....	....	12.7	7.8	15.7	23.8	36.3	61.8	64.4	84.8
Other Deposits	25	....	....	....	....	10.2	18.9	42.7	61.9	99.7	158.3	191.7	301.9
Foreign Liabilities	26c	....	....	....	....	73.0	61.2	143.1	219.9	276.5	314.4	676.6	637.9
General Government Deposits	26d	....	....	....	....	—	3.8	10.9	9.0	7.9	17.1	26.0	38.4
Credit from Monetary Authorities	26g	....	....	....	....	16.8	44.2	44.2	34.1	29.2	43.8	51.6	47.0
Capital Accounts	27a	....	....	....	....	22.0	29.4	39.9	50.4	85.5	133.5	166.2	266.3
Other Items (Net)	27r	....	....	....	....	−4.9	−7.1	−12.4	19.7	−18.4	−89.5	−85.5	99.1
Monetary Survey		\multicolumn{12}{c}{*Millions of Somoni: End of Period*}											
Foreign Assets (Net)	31n	....	....	....	....	−103.8	−120.5	−174.8	−238.8	−257.0	−179.1	−429.3	−156.6
Domestic Credit	32	....	....	....	....	226.5	279.6	320.2	624.2	711.8	665.9	1,016.8	† 1,180.4
Claims on General Govt. (Net)	32an	....	....	....	....	94.1	41.0	74.1	48.8	84.3	.1	−54.4	−93.3
Claims on Nonfin.Pub.Enterprises	32c	....	....	....	....	....	....	....	....	....	....	....	30.2
Claims on Private Sector	32d	....	....	....	....	132.4	238.6	246.0	575.4	627.5	665.8	1,071.2	† 1,240.6
Claims on Nonbank Financial Insts.	32g	....	....	....	....	....	....	....	....	....	....	....	2.9
Money	34	....	....	....	....	59.4	69.9	102.7	128.8	173.2	222.2	241.1	241.0
Quasi-Money	35	....	....	....	....	13.2	20.5	44.9	70.5	106.8	172.3	192.2	304.5
Counterpart Funds	36e	....	....	....	....	3.0	15.0	38.8	85.8	101.0	94.6	166.0	164.8
Capital Accounts	37a	....	....	....	....	58.2	70.9	51.4	115.2	132.9	151.9	171.0	294.0
Other Items (Net)	37r	....	....	....	....	−13.0	−19.7	−102.8	−23.8	−68.3	−179.4	−225.0	† −28.3
Money plus Quasi-Money	35l	....	....	....	....	72.6	90.4	147.6	199.4	280.0	394.5	433.3	545.5
Interest Rates		\multicolumn{12}{c}{*Percent Per Annum*}											
Refinancing Rate	60	....	....	....	76.00	36.40	20.10	20.60	20.00	† 24.75	† 15.00	10.00	9.00
Deposit Rate	60l	....	....	....	23.93	9.82	5.24	1.26	5.19	† 9.21	9.67	9.75	9.75
Lending Rate	60p	....	....	....	75.52	50.89	26.24	25.59	21.05	† 14.20	16.57	20.32	23.27

		1994	1995	1996	1997	1998	1999	2000	2001	2002	2003	2004	2005
Balance of Payments						*Millions of US Dollars: Minus Sign Indicates Debit*							
Current Account, n.i.e.	78ald	....	....	....	....	....	....	....	....	−15.13	−4.76	−57.04	−18.86
Goods: Exports f.o.b.	78aad	....	....	....	....	....	....	....	....	699.15	906.20	1,096.93	1,108.09
Goods: Imports f.o.b.	78abd	....	....	....	....	....	....	....	....	−822.90	−1,025.73	−1,232.43	−1,430.93
Trade Balance	78acd	....	....	....	....	....	....	....	....	−123.75	−119.53	−135.50	−322.83
Services: Credit	78add	....	....	....	....	....	....	....	....	68.99	88.53	122.91	146.34
Services: Debit	78aed	....	....	....	....	....	....	....	....	−104.88	−121.53	−212.53	−251.52
Balance on Goods & Services	78afd	....	....	....	....	....	....	....	....	−159.64	−152.54	−225.12	−428.01
Income: Credit	78agd	....	....	....	....	....	....	....	....	1.23	.93	1.70	9.59
Income: Debit	78ahd	....	....	....	....	....	....	....	....	−42.36	−71.23	−59.24	−50.36
Balance on Gds, Serv. & Inc.	78aid	....	....	....	....	....	....	....	....	−200.77	−222.84	−282.66	−468.79
Current Transfers, n.i.e.: Credit	78ajd	....	....	....	....	....	....	....	....	201.72	285.11	348.41	599.91
Current Transfers: Debit	78akd	....	....	....	....	....	....	....	....	−16.08	−67.03	−122.80	−149.98
Capital Account, n.i.e.	78bcd	....	....	....	....	....	....	....	....	—	—	—	—
Capital Account, n.i.e.: Credit	78bad	....	....	....	....	....	....	....	....	—	—	—	—
Capital Account: Debit	78bbd	....	....	....	....	....	....	....	....	—	—	—	—
Financial Account, n.i.e.	78bjd	....	....	....	....	....	....	....	....	72.39	62.69	93.41	101.49
Direct Investment Abroad	78bdd	....	....	....	....	....	....	....	....	—	—	—	—
Dir. Invest. in Rep. Econ., n.i.e.	78bed	....	....	....	....	....	....	....	....	36.07	31.65	272.03	54.48
Portfolio Investment Assets	78bfd	....	....	....	....	....	....	....	....	—	—	—	....
Equity Securities	78bkd	....	....	....	....	....	....	....	....	—	—	—	....
Debt Securities	78bld	....	....	....	....	....	....	....	....	—	—	—	....
Portfolio Investment Liab., n.i.e.	78bgd	....	....	....	....	....	....	....	....	1.51	.34	5.30	—
Equity Securities	78bmd	....	....	....	....	....	....	....	....	1.51	.34	—	—
Debt Securities	78bnd	....	....	....	....	....	....	....	....	—	—	5.30	—
Financial Derivatives Assets	78bwd	....	....	....	....	....	....	....	....	....	....	....	....
Financial Derivatives Liabilities	78bxd	....	....	....	....	....	....	....	....	....	....	....	....
Other Investment Assets	78bhd	....	....	....	....	....	....	....	....	−23.44	−15.63	−28.44	−71.26
Monetary Authorities	78bod	....	....	....	....	....	....	....	....	—	—	—	....
General Government	78bpd	....	....	....	....	....	....	....	....	.17	−.41	−.45	−.49
Banks	78bqd	....	....	....	....	....	....	....	....	−6.59	−14.39	−7.35	−33.67
Other Sectors	78brd	....	....	....	....	....	....	....	....	−17.03	−.83	−20.64	−37.11
Other Investment Liab., n.i.e.	78bid	....	....	....	....	....	....	....	....	58.25	46.33	−155.47	118.27
Monetary Authorities	78bsd	....	....	....	....	....	....	....	....	—	—	—	—
General Government	78btd	....	....	....	....	....	....	....	....	−9.28	−2.12	−151.41	57.14
Banks	78bud	....	....	....	....	....	....	....	....	1.19	3.72	1.01	45.04
Other Sectors	78bvd	....	....	....	....	....	....	....	....	66.34	44.74	−5.07	16.09
Net Errors and Omissions	78cad	....	....	....	....	....	....	....	....	−55.60	−29.98	−32.51	−76.31
Overall Balance	78cbd	....	....	....	....	....	....	....	....	1.65	27.95	3.86	6.32
Reserves and Related Items	79dad	....	....	....	....	....	....	....	....	−1.65	−27.95	−3.86	−6.32
Reserve Assets	79dbd	....	....	....	....	....	....	....	....	.11	−40.46	−46.36	−25.63
Use of Fund Credit and Loans	79dcd	....	....	....	....	....	....	....	....	−23.95	−2.72	16.99	15.45
Exceptional Financing	79ded	....	....	....	....	....	....	....	....	22.19	15.24	25.50	3.86
Government Finance						*Millions of Somoni Year Ending December 31*							
Deficit (-) or Surplus	80	....	....	....	....	−25.78	−10.42	−3.75	1.42	....	....	....	....
Total Revenue and Grants	81y	....	....	....	....	97.20	140.57	189.88	288.66	....	....	....	....
Revenue	81	....	....	....	....	95.04	136.99	189.88	288.66	....	....	....	....
Grants Received	81z	....	....	....	....	2.16	3.58	—	—	....	....	....	....
Exp. & Lending Minus Repay.	82z	....	....	....	....	122.98	150.99	193.63	287.24	....	....	....	....
Expenditure	82	....	....	....	....	130.56	166.97	204.30	292.54	....	....	....	....
Lending Minus Repayments	83	....	....	....	....	−7.58	−15.98	−10.67	−5.30	....	....	....	....
Total Financing	80h	....	....	....	....	25.78	10.42	3.75	−1.42	....	....	....	....
Domestic	84a	....	....	....	....	23.10	32.68	8.81	4.26	....	....	....	....
Foreign	85a	....	....	....	....	2.68	−22.26	−5.06	−5.68	....	....	....	....
Total Debt by Residence	88	....	....	....	....	1,014.60	....	2,038.20	2,046.02	....	....	....	....
Domestic	88a	....	....	....	....	44.67	....	131.92	155.32	....	....	....	....
Foreign	89a	....	....	....	....	969.93	....	1,906.28	1,890.70	....	....	....	....
Population	99z	5.69	5.77	5.85	5.93	6.01	6.09	6.16	6.23	6.29	6.36	6.43	6.51

		1994	1995	1996	1997	1998	1999	2000	2001	2002	2003	2004	2005
Exchange Rates					*Shillings per SDR: End of Period*								
Official Rate	aa	764.16	818.10	856.51	842.70	958.87	1,094.34	1,046.58	1,151.54	1,327.30	1,580.51	1,619.73	1,665.83
				Shillings per US Dollar: End of Period (ae) Period Average (rf)									
Official Rate	ae	523.45	550.36	595.64	624.57	681.00	797.33	803.26	916.30	976.30	1,063.62	1,042.96	1,165.51
Official Rate	rf	509.63	574.76	579.98	612.12	664.67	744.76	800.41	876.41	966.58	1,038.42	1,089.33	1,128.93
Fund Position					*Millions of SDRs: End of Period*								
Quota	2f.s	146.9	146.9	146.9	146.9	146.9	198.9	198.9	198.9	198.9	198.9	198.9	198.9
SDRs	1b.s	—	.1	.1	.1	.3	.2	.1	.4	.1	.3	—	.5
Reserve Position in the Fund	1c.s	10.0	10.0	10.0	10.0	10.0	10.0	10.0	10.0	10.0	10.0	10.0	10.0
Total Fund Cred.&Loans Outstg	2tl	145.5	132.7	143.4	182.4	190.2	227.6	248.3	271.2	293.9	294.3	272.3	239.6
International Liquidity					*Millions of US Dollars Unless Otherwise Indicated: End of Period*								
Total Reserves minus Gold	1l.d	332.1	270.2	440.1	622.1	599.2	775.5	974.2	1,156.6	1,528.8	2,038.4	2,295.7	2,048.8
SDRs	1b.d	—	.1	.1	.1	.4	.3	.1	.5	.1	.5	.1	.7
Reserve Position in the Fund	1c.d	14.6	14.8	14.3	13.5	14.0	13.7	13.0	12.5	13.6	14.9	15.5	14.3
Foreign Exchange	1d.d	317.5	255.3	425.6	608.5	584.8	761.5	961.1	1,143.6	1,515.2	2,023.0	2,280.1	2,033.8
Monetary Authorities: Other Liab	4..d	900.7	836.9	808.7	574.9	574.5	678.5	755.2	747.7	881.5	1,061.5	1,074.4	995.0
Deposit Money Banks: Assets	7a.d	146.6	309.2	304.8	373.9	392.4	377.6	511.7	588.3	585.4	644.5	655.5	717.0
Liabilities	7b.d	20.9	51.4	8.1	7.8	3.6	2.2	5.2	17.6	36.0	6.5	18.3	47.4
Monetary Authorities					*Billions of Shillings: End of Period*								
Foreign Assets	11	173.82	150.65	264.72	390.09	407.27	618.47	782.42	1,059.85	1,492.78	2,167.75	2,394.81	2,387.40
Claims on Central Government	12a	270.60	326.37	299.38	269.69	234.08	302.79	296.67	296.67	201.46	202.20	199.21	389.68
Claims on Deposit Money Banks	12e	—	5.46	5.46	4.61	5.36	4.16	—	—	—	—	—	—
Reserve Money	14	226.44	314.89	335.77	364.94	418.73	508.67	556.43	584.37	695.70	783.31	967.78	1,236.08
of which: Currency Outside DMBs	14a	176.31	244.31	257.66	287.88	307.80	384.86	392.40	411.64	495.45	553.05	664.15	843.16
Foreign Liabilities	16c	517.26	499.09	509.17	373.50	397.37	543.32	606.65	685.16	860.56	1,129.02	1,120.60	1,159.67
Central Government Deposits	16d	29.56	39.67	82.66	87.32	83.03	84.01	137.32	161.98	198.65	357.82	377.99	429.73
Capital Accounts	17a	−242.89	−266.81	−238.07	−16.35	−2.23	45.81	25.67	102.44	99.71	149.85	141.33	178.40
Other Items (Net)	17r	−85.94	−104.36	−119.97	−145.02	−250.20	−256.39	−246.98	−177.42	−160.39	−50.05	−13.68	−226.81
Deposit Money Banks					*Billions of Shillings: End of Period*								
Reserves	20	49.91	66.03	72.80	59.71	113.20	123.20	172.10	177.33	195.15	226.87	310.42	395.43
Foreign Assets	21	76.74	170.16	181.55	233.56	267.26	301.08	410.99	539.06	571.57	685.49	683.67	835.64
Claims on Central Government	22a	124.41	181.09	261.94	247.39	312.75	331.26	403.76	295.70	364.64	322.41	338.54	713.05
Claims on Official Entities	22bx	57.18	46.83	17.34	16.22	3.06	4.72	2.98	1.02	—	—	—	—
Claims on Private Sector	22d	222.98	201.02	116.56	166.75	239.86	302.17	333.26	403.49	570.67	817.13	1,059.69	1,425.06
Demand Deposits	24	153.32	183.97	191.55	205.99	237.72	247.72	302.60	354.38	463.34	560.33	651.45	915.65
Time, Savings,& Fgn.Currency Dep	25	240.12	329.52	372.28	433.20	481.47	584.95	702.68	870.71	1,088.90	1,274.94	1,532.39	2,176.18
Foreign Liabilities	26c	10.92	28.26	4.83	4.88	2.46	1.77	4.16	16.17	35.19	6.88	19.04	55.23
Central Government Deposits	26d	22.52	21.75	20.96	28.43	25.33	21.56	26.09	29.32	30.82	81.83	135.46	187.20
Credit from Monetary Authorities	26g	1.34	7.59	.16	12.76	—	5.43	—	—	.08	.05	—	—
Capital Accounts	27a	139.91	−29.91	75.62	43.11	61.64	27.26	113.33	133.74	142.09	207.97	243.14	314.16
Other Items (Net)	27r	−36.90	123.95	−15.21	−4.74	127.52	173.73	174.23	12.28	−58.39	−80.11	−189.17	−279.25
Monetary Survey					*Billions of Shillings: End of Period*								
Foreign Assets (Net)	31n	−277.62	−206.54	−67.72	245.27	274.70	374.46	582.60	897.58	1,168.60	1,717.35	1,938.83	2,008.13
Domestic Credit	32	623.10	693.88	591.60	584.31	681.39	835.36	873.27	805.59	907.29	902.08	1,083.98	1,910.86
Claims on Central Govt. (Net)	32an	342.94	446.03	457.70	401.34	438.47	528.48	537.03	401.08	336.62	84.95	24.30	485.80
Claims on Official Entities	32bx	57.18	46.83	17.34	16.22	3.06	4.72	2.98	1.02	—	—	—	—
Claims on Private Sector	32d	222.98	201.02	116.56	166.75	239.86	302.17	333.26	403.49	570.67	817.13	1,059.69	1,425.06
Money	34	329.63	428.28	449.21	493.87	545.52	632.58	695.01	766.02	958.79	1,113.38	1,315.61	1,758.81
Quasi-Money	35	240.12	329.52	372.28	433.20	481.47	584.95	702.68	870.71	1,088.90	1,274.94	1,532.39	2,176.18
Capital Accounts	37a	−102.98	−296.72	−162.45	26.76	59.41	73.07	139.00	236.18	241.80	357.83	384.47	492.56
Other Items (Net)	37r	−121.29	26.26	−135.17	−124.25	−130.30	−80.78	−80.82	−169.74	−213.59	−126.72	−209.65	−508.56
Money plus Quasi-Money	35l	569.74	757.81	821.50	927.07	1,026.98	1,217.53	1,397.69	1,636.73	2,047.68	2,388.32	2,848.00	3,934.99
Other Banking Institutions					*Billions of Shillings: End of Period*								
Deposits	45	1.67	16.82	16.60	17.56	17.88	24.38	28.44	34.15	37.42	34.73	35.00	43.44
Liquid Liabilities	55l	571.42	774.63	838.09	944.63	1,044.87	1,241.91	1,426.13	1,670.88	2,085.11	2,423.05	2,882.99	3,978.43
Money (National Definitions)					*Billions of Shillings: End of Period*								
M0	19mc	226.44	314.89	335.77	364.94	418.73	508.67	556.43	584.37	695.70	783.31	967.78	1,236.08
M1	59ma	329.62	428.29	449.21	493.87	545.52	632.57	695.01	766.02	958.86	1,113.56	1,315.61	1,758.81
M2	59mb	486.49	613.70	684.99	760.35	844.93	972.09	1,093.61	1,233.67	1,507.58	1,721.30	2,050.76	2,808.25
M3	59mc	569.74	752.91	818.06	927.07	1,026.98	1,217.63	1,397.69	1,636.73	2,047.88	2,388.51	2,848.00	3,934.99
Interest Rates					*Percent Per Annum*								
Discount Rate (End of Period)	60	67.50	47.90	19.00	16.20	17.60	20.20	10.70	8.70	9.18	12.34	14.42	19.33
Treasury Bill Rate	60c	35.09	40.33	15.30	9.59	11.83	10.05	9.78	4.14	3.55	6.26	8.35	10.67
Savings Rate	60k	23.98	22.70	14.25	8.79	8.29	8.27	† 6.55	4.15	3.36	2.58	2.45	2.61
Deposit Rate	60l	....	24.63	13.59	7.83	7.75	7.75	† 7.39	4.81	3.29	3.05	4.20	4.70
Lending Rate	60p	39.00	42.83	† 33.97	26.27	22.89	21.89	† 21.58	20.26	16.43	14.48	13.92	15.12
Prices and Production					*Index Numbers (2000=100): Period Averages*								
Consumer Prices	64	43.0	55.2	66.8	77.6	87.5	94.4	100.0	† 105.1	106.2	109.9	110.0	119.4
Manufacturing Production	66ey	70.4	73.2	73.9	78.2	84.5	87.3	100.0	† 104.2	119.3	143.9	225.3	....
Intl. Transactions & Positions					*Millions of Shillings*								
Exports	70	265,177	390,378	455,519	459,549	391,805	412,204	531,058	681,186	873,819	1,174,785	1,448,589	1,676,087
Imports, c.i.f	71	765,757	968,910	804,949	818,703	967,080	1,161,841	1,219,385	1,504,415	1,604,945	2,210,265	2,732,323	3,011,910

Tanzania 738

		1994	1995	1996	1997	1998	1999	2000	2001	2002	2003	2004	2005
Balance of Payments		*Millions of US Dollars: Minus Sign Indicates Debit*											
Current Account, n.i.e.	78ald	−710.9	−646.3	−510.9	−629.8	−919.7	−835.3	−498.6	−456.5	−217.0	−393.4	−437.1	....
Goods: Exports f.o.b.	78aad	519.4	682.5	764.1	715.3	589.5	543.3	663.3	811.7	911.6	1,156.6	1,278.1	....
Goods: Imports f.o.b.	78abd	−1,309.3	−1,340.0	−1,213.1	−1,164.4	−1,365.3	−1,415.4	−1,367.6	−1,631.4	−1,526.5	−1,980.4	−2,184.1	....
Trade Balance	78acd	−789.9	−657.5	−449.0	−449.1	−775.9	−872.1	−704.3	−819.6	−614.9	−823.7	−906.0	....
Services: Credit	78add	418.2	582.6	608.1	494.1	555.0	600.3	627.4	710.2	675.3	707.6	901.4	....
Services: Debit	78aed	−503.3	−799.4	−953.4	−797.3	−988.1	−795.0	−682.4	−671.3	−675.3	−792.6	−1,012.3	....
Balance on Goods & Services	78afd	−875.0	−874.2	−794.3	−752.4	−1,209.0	−1,066.8	−759.3	−780.8	−614.9	−908.8	−1,016.9	....
Income: Credit	78agd	30.9	31.8	50.3	44.9	35.0	43.1	50.3	57.8	68.6	89.2	78.2	....
Income: Debit	78ahd	−153.4	−142.0	−105.4	−168.2	−136.8	−148.2	−180.4	−146.9	−91.5	−134.0	−116.9	....
Balance on Gds, Serv. & Inc.	78aid	−997.5	−984.5	−849.4	−875.7	−1,310.8	−1,171.9	−889.4	−869.8	−637.8	−953.6	−1,055.6	....
Current Transfers, n.i.e.: Credit	78ajd	311.5	370.5	370.9	313.6	426.6	445.6	463.7	496.4	482.8	624.7	680.8	....
Current Transfers: Debit	78akd	−25.0	−32.3	−32.3	−67.7	−35.5	−109.0	−72.9	−83.1	−61.9	−64.5	−62.3	....
Capital Account, n.i.e.	78bcd	262.6	190.9	191.0	360.6	422.9	347.8	420.4	1,049.3	793.6	709.5	385.4	....
Capital Account, n.i.e.: Credit	78bad	262.6	190.9	191.0	360.6	422.9	347.8	420.4	1,049.3	793.6	709.5	385.4	....
Capital Account: Debit	78bbd	—	—	—	—	—	—	—	—	—	....	....	....
Financial Account, n.i.e.	78bjd	−91.7	66.7	−92.8	3.6	77.6	565.2	492.6	−1,365.2	−917.7	−25.1	218.5	....
Direct Investment Abroad	78bdd	—	—	—	—	—	—	—	—	—	....	....	....
Dir. Invest. in Rep. Econ., n.i.e.	78bed	50.0	119.9	150.1	157.9	172.3	516.7	463.4	342.1	242.8	253.8	249.1	....
Portfolio Investment Assets	78bfd	—	—	—	—	—	—	—	—	—	....	....	....
Equity Securities	78bkd	—	—	—	—	—	—	—	—	—	....	....	....
Debt Securities	78bld	—	—	—	—	—	—	—	—	—	....	....	....
Portfolio Investment Liab., n.i.e.	78bgd	—	—	—	—	—	—	—	—	—	....	....	....
Equity Securities	78bmd	—	—	—	—	—	—	—	—	—	....	....	....
Debt Securities	78bnd	—	—	—	—	—	—	—	—	—	....	....	....
Financial Derivatives Assets	78bwd	—	—	—	—	....	....	....	....	....	....	....	....
Financial Derivatives Liabilities	78bxd	—	—	—	—	....	....	....	....	....	....	....	....
Other Investment Assets	78bhd	11.9	−75.1	20.1	−85.0	−50.7	14.8	−134.0	−80.1	2.9	−60.5	−10.5	....
Monetary Authorities	78bod	—	—	—	—	—	—	—	—	—	....	....	....
General Government	78bpd	—	—	—	—	—	—	—	—	—	....	....	....
Banks	78bqd	−75.6	−162.5	−19.6	−85.0	−50.7	14.8	−134.0	−80.1	2.9	−60.5	−10.5	....
Other Sectors	78brd	87.5	87.4	39.7	—	—	—	—	—	—	....	....	....
Other Investment Liab., n.i.e.	78bid	−153.6	21.8	−262.9	−69.3	−44.0	33.7	163.2	−1,627.2	−1,163.4	−218.5	−20.1	....
Monetary Authorities	78bsd	11.9	5.9	14.9	24.6	−48.7	9.8	49.7	−55.3	14.4	7.0	11.3	....
General Government	78btd	−202.0	−71.2	−225.9	−32.4	—	52.0	145.4	−1,717.6	−1,163.6	−117.2	40.6	....
Banks	78bud	6.7	22.9	−23.5	−67.6	−17.6	−1.4	3.0	13.0	18.6	−30.3	11.3	....
Other Sectors	78bvd	29.8	64.2	−28.5	6.2	22.4	−26.7	−34.9	132.7	−32.8	−78.0	−83.3	....
Net Errors and Omissions	78cad	121.4	30.0	158.6	−31.9	−90.3	−156.7	−415.7	721.5	668.1	103.7	33.4	....
Overall Balance	78cbd	−418.6	−358.7	−254.0	−297.5	−509.4	−79.0	−1.3	−50.9	327.0	394.7	200.2	....
Reserves and Related Items	79dad	418.6	358.7	254.0	297.5	509.4	79.0	1.3	50.9	−327.0	−394.7	−200.2	....
Reserve Assets	79dbd	−122.8	43.3	−195.4	−206.9	22.3	−176.4	−199.2	−191.3	−375.1	−520.1	−246.5	....
Use of Fund Credit and Loans	79dcd	−15.4	−19.6	15.7	53.2	9.6	51.5	27.6	29.5	29.1	−.3	−32.6	....
Exceptional Financing	79ded	556.8	335.1	433.8	451.2	477.5	204.0	172.9	212.7	19.0	125.6	78.9	....
International Investment Position		*Millions of US Dollars*											
Assets	79aad	....	....	....	....	....	....	....	....	....	....	....	....
Direct Investment Abroad	79abd	—	—	—	—	—	—	—	—	—	—	—	....
Portfolio Investment	79acd	—	—	—	—	—	—	—	—	—	—	—	....
Equity Securities	79add	—	—	—	—	—	—	—	—	—	—	—	....
Debt Securities	79aed	—	—	—	—	—	—	—	—	—	—	—	....
Financial Derivatives	79ald	....	....	....	....	....	....	....	....	....	....	....	....
Other Investment	79afd	146.6	309.2	304.8	373.9	392.4	377.6	511.6	562.7	579.6	629.2	684.6	....
Monetary Authorities	79agd	....	....	....	....	....	....	—	—	—	—	—	....
General Government	79ahd	....	....	....	....	....	....	....	....	....	....	....	....
Banks	79aid	....	....	304.8	373.9	392.4	377.6	511.6	562.7	579.6	629.2	684.6	....
Other Sectors	79ajd	....	....	....	....	....	....	....	....	....	....	....	....
Reserve Assets	79akd	330.4	269.6	439.6	621.7	599.0	775.4	974.0	1,106.8	1,514.0	1,990.2	2,397.0	....
Liabilities	79lad	9,037.5	9,645.7	9,965.9	7,271.3	7,229.0	7,648.1	9,540.3	11,056.3	10,901.3	11,745.3	14,626.3	....
Dir. Invest. in Rep. Economy	79lbd	71.0	224.2	351.7	490.2	619.0	700.0	1,310.1	3,612.6	2,327.6	2,537.2	2,986.1	....
Portfolio Investment	79lcd	—	—	—	—	—	—	—	—	—	—	—	....
Equity Securities	79ldd	—	—	—	—	—	—	—	—	—	—	—	....
Debt Securities	79led	—	—	—	—	—	—	—	—	—	—	—	....
Financial Derivatives	79lld	—	—	—	—	—	—	—	—	—	—	—	....
Other Investment	79lfd	8,966.5	9,421.5	9,614.2	6,781.1	6,610.0	6,948.1	8,230.2	7,443.7	8,573.7	9,208.1	11,640.2	....
Monetary Authorities	79lgd	212.4	197.2	206.2	246.0	315.9	370.3	431.3	393.3	467.8	511.4	514.5	....
General Government	79lhd	8,129.9	8,510.0	8,614.9	6,337.2	6,200.6	6,050.4	6,723.1	5,832.1	6,639.4	7,250.0	8,899.9	....
Banks	79lid	—	—	—	—	19.4	5.2	15.0	34.6	5.8	19.1	....	
Other Sectors	79ljd	624.2	714.3	793.0	197.8	74.1	526.4	1,070.6	1,203.3	1,431.8	1,441.0	2,206.8	....
Government Finance		*Millions of Shillings: Year Ending June 30*											
Deficit (-) or Surplus	80	−104,515	−64,559	−21,269	77,143	−68,138	24,422	−114,472	−87,860	−38,195	−205,663	−358,818	−710,405
Total Revenue and Grants	81y	349,234	389,743	495,255	653,446	738,443	859,268	1,057,952	1,215,930	1,401,774	1,695,299	2,150,823	2,735,985
Revenue	81	242,444	331,238	448,373	572,030	619,084	689,324	777,645	929,624	1,042,956	1,217,517	1,459,303	1,773,512
Grants	81z	106,790	58,505	46,882	81,416	119,359	169,944	280,307	286,306	358,818	477,782	691,519	962,473
Exp. & Lending Minus Repay	82z	374,962	398,024	420,522	515,390	730,338	816,706	1,168,779	1,311,928	1,441,669	1,843,204	2,521,881	3,275,561
Expenditure	82	374,962	398,024	420,522	515,390	730,338	816,706	1,168,779	1,305,035	1,441,669	1,842,953	2,521,881	3,275,561
Lending Minus Repayments	83	—	—	—	—	—	—	—	6,893	—	251	—	—
Financing													
Overall Adjustment	80x	−78,787	−56,278	−96,002	−60,913	−76,243	−18,140	−3,644	8,139	1,701	−57,758	12,240	−170,829
Total Financing	80h	104,515	64,559	21,269	−77,142	68,139	−24,424	114,472	87,860	38,191	205,663	358,818	710,405
Domestic	84a	40,557	61,603	56,169	−28,074	3,670	−5,740	9,055	−2,494	−83,087	−7,891	−39,343	144,945
Foreign	85a	63,958	2,956	−34,900	−49,068	64,468	−18,684	105,417	90,354	121,278	213,554	398,161	565,460

Tanzania   738

National Accounts		1994	1995	1996	1997	1998	1999	2000	2001	2002	2003	2004	2005
						Billions of Shillings							
Househ.Cons.Expend.,incl.NPISHs....	96f	1,931.98	2,532.84	3,130.07	3,968.07	4,909.25	5,667.44	6,069.58	6,917.58	7,499.65	8,549.07	9,980.16	11,407.32
Government Consumption Expend...	91f	393.50	462.32	435.33	413.56	433.79	451.14	482.72	516.33	598.94	712.74	855.28	1,037.67
Gross Fixed Capital Formation..........	93e	561.82	591.94	620.60	692.40	892.70	989.34	1,266.68	1,390.64	1,789.90	2,239.28	2,570.70	3,118.27
Changes in Inventories....................	93i	4.84	5.86	6.64	8.40	9.91	10.31	14.37	15.66	17.85	19.74	28.27	31.14
Exports of Goods and Services..........	90c	473.89	727.18	751.16	762.81	748.97	885.94	1,064.77	1,284.71	1,520.52	1,887.67	2,847.58	3,259.66
Imports of Goods and Services (-).....	98c	1,002.88	1,253.74	1,203.52	1,208.30	1,565.32	1,703.75	1,676.34	1,962.79	2,106.90	2,811.15	3,646.39	4,319.24
GDP, Production Based...................	99bp	2,298.87	3,020.50	3,767.64	4,703.46	5,571.26	6,432.91	7,268.38	8,274.61	9,431.96	10,677.87	12,365.50	14,209.09
Statistical Discrepancy....................	99bs	−64.28	−45.89	27.36	66.51	141.96	132.50	46.61	112.47	112.01	80.52	−270.11	−325.72
Net Primary Income from Abroad.....	98.n	−62.43	−63.38	−36.92	−75.78	−52.39	−55.19	−66.70	−74.93	−21.79	−45.34	−193.96	−268.64
Gross National Income (GNI)...........	99a	2,236.44	2,957.12	3,730.72	4,627.68	5,518.86	6,377.72	7,201.68	8,199.68	9,410.18	10,632.53	12,171.55	13,940.45
Net National Income......................	99e	2,175.83	2,876.16	3,640.05	4,515.24	5,385.60	6,216.13	7,007.78	7,963.11	9,119.20	10,289.18	11,780.13	13,487.97
GDP, Prod. Based, 1992 Prices........	99bpp	1,298.94	1,345.25	1,401.71	1,448.09	1,505.83	1,577.29	1,654.32	1,749.36	1,857.17	1,962.43	2,094.52	2,237.08
GDP Volume (2000=100)...............	99bvp	78.5	81.3	84.7	87.5	91.0	95.3	100.0	105.7	112.3	118.6	126.6	135.2
GDP Deflator (2000=100)...............	99bip	40.3	51.1	61.2	73.9	84.2	92.8	100.0	107.7	115.6	123.8	134.4	144.6
						Millions: Midyear Estimates							
Population...............................	99z	30.03	30.93	31.77	32.56	† 33.31	34.04	34.76	35.49	36.20	36.92	37.63	38.33

Thailand 578

2006, International Monetary Fund : *International Financial Statistics Yearbook*

		1994	1995	1996	1997	1998	1999	2000	2001	2002	2003	2004	2005
Exchange Rates					*Baht per SDR: End of Period*								
Official Rate	aa	36.628	37.445	36.826	†63.748	51.662	51.428	56.374	55.575	58.665	58.831	60.662	58.643
					Baht per US Dollar: End of Period (ae) Period Average (rf)								
Official Rate	ae	25.090	25.190	25.610	†47.247	36.691	37.470	43.268	44.222	43.152	39.591	39.061	41.030
Official Rate	rf	25.150	24.915	25.343	†31.364	41.359	37.814	40.112	44.432	42.960	41.485	40.222	40.220
Fund Position					*Millions of SDRs: End of Period*								
Quota	2f.s	574	574	574	574	574	1,082	1,082	1,082	1,082	1,082	1,082	1,082
SDRs	1b.s	22	30	41	358	278	188	63	4	3	—	1	—
Reserve Position in the Fund	1c.s	285	319	333	—	—	—	—	—	—	75	107	132
of which: Outstg.Fund Borrowing	2c	—	—	—	—	—	—	—	—	—	—	—	—
Total Fund Cred.&Loans Outstg	2tl	—	—	—	1,800	2,300	2,500	2,350	1,338	288	—	—	—
International Liquidity					*Millions of US Dollars Unless Otherwise Indicated: End of Period*								
Total Reserves minus Gold	1l.d	29,332	35,982	37,731	26,179	28,825	34,063	32,016	32,355	38,046	41,077	48,664	50,691
SDRs	1b.d	32	45	60	482	391	258	83	5	4	—	1	1
Reserve Position in the Fund	1c.d	416	474	480	—	—	—	—	—	—	111	165	188
Foreign Exchange	1d.d	28,884	35,463	37,192	25,697	28,434	33,805	31,933	32,350	38,042	40,965	48,498	50,502
Gold (Million Fine Troy Ounces)	1ad	2.474	2.474	2.474	2.474	2.474	2.474	2.367	2.480	2.500	2.600	2.700	2.700
Gold (National Valuation)	1and	947	963	914	713	711	718	645	686	869	1,071	1,167	1,374
Monetary Authorities: Other Liab	4..d	6	5	4	4,733	7,967	9,390	9,363	8,260	4,892	804	1,044	8,103
Banking Institutions: Assets	7a.d	6,766	9,399	7,100	8,765	13,012	15,561	17,045	17,255	15,096	14,394	14,509	16,308
Liabilities	7b.d	35,122	52,153	57,529	47,281	34,608	23,602	16,753	13,244	11,257	9,831	10,438	9,708
Monetary Authorities					*Billions of Baht: End of Period*								
Foreign Assets	11	759.0	929.7	988.8	1,270.7	1,083.4	1,303.3	1,413.2	†1,478.9	1,695.5	†1,707.8	1,986.6	2,455.8
Claims on Central Government	12a	19.9	15.4	17.2	14.6	152.9	120.7	88.3	†124.4	107.8	†116.2	113.3	111.6
Claims on State and Local Govts	12b	....	....	....	....	....	....			—	† —	—	—
Claims on Nonfin.Pub.Enterprises	12c	—	8.4	17.9	71.5	75.0	64.0	48.3	†33.4	23.0	†16.1	5.7	1.7
Claims on Private Sector	12d	—	—	—	—	—	—		† —		† —	.2	.1
Claims on Banking Institutions	12e	26.4	37.8	55.9	309.4	158.6	85.9	59.2	†45.2	83.4	†36.7	75.7	122.6
Claims on Nonbank Financial Insts	12g	....	....	....	....	....	....		338.9	414.6	†338.1	254.3	257.5
Reserve Money	14	325.2	398.5	448.9	525.9	491.9	632.0	514.5	†543.7	617.8	†691.1	776.7	816.0
of which: Currency Outside Banks	14a	235.9	276.6	292.2	327.6	309.3	476.3	389.1	†423.7	474.8	†530.1	571.1	603.4
Other Liabilities to Banks	14n	5.5	5.4	17.4	254.2	356.4	94.8	155.0	†220.5	194.0	†486.0	553.4	547.3
Time, Savings,&Fgn.Currency Dep	15	....	....	....	....	....	....				† —	—	—
Liabs. of Central Bank: Securities	16ac	....	....	....	....	....	....				† —	—	—
Restricted Deposits	16b	....	....	....	....	....	....			—	† —	—	—
Foreign Liabilities	16c	.1	.1	.1	338.4	411.1	480.4	537.6	†439.6	227.9	†31.8	40.8	332.4
Central Government Deposits	16d	228.0	319.9	335.4	270.1	85.2	52.3	37.7	†28.8	67.0	†51.0	56.3	27.2
Liab. to Nonbank Financial Insts	16j								170.9	112.0	†42.9	43.3	253.2
Capital Accounts	17a	306.8	337.8	377.8	803.2	814.0	1,013.2	1,159.7	†1,097.1	1,632.4	†902.2	960.1	911.0
Other Items (Net)	17r	−33.0	−34.4	−34.4	−164.6	−371.9	−547.1	−576.0	†−480.0	−526.9	†9.8	5.2	62.1
Banking Institutions					*Billions of Baht: End of Period*								
Reserves	20	87.9	121.8	148.7	182.1	164.9	311.8	278.3	†116.2	138.8	†156.3	195.4	209.1
Claims on Mon.Author.: Securities	20c	....	....	....	....	....	....		79.0	75.8	†123.1	210.2	254.7
Other Claims on Monetary Author	20n	17.7	17.3	27.2	346.1	536.4	169.9	224.5	†283.4	193.4	†372.6	346.3	296.5
Foreign Assets	21	169.8	236.8	181.8	414.1	477.4	583.1	737.5	†763.1	651.4	†569.4	566.7	669.1
Claims on Central Government	22a	92.2	76.8	50.5	35.1	258.8	433.9	484.7	†534.2	637.2	†649.3	633.7	628.8
Claims on State and Local Govts	22b								† —		†.3	.8	1.8
Claims on Nonfin.Pub.Enterprises	22c	157.3	170.8	205.4	193.9	204.6	259.3	296.1	†335.4	322.1	†339.3	347.7	321.4
Claims on Private Sector	22d	4,636.4	5,853.5	6,786.8	7,842.8	7,212.5	6,117.4	5,329.5	†4,975.1	5,589.0	†5,516.1	6,139.3	6,610.9
Claims on Nonbank Financial Insts	22g	....	....	....	....	....	....		673.1	375.2	†775.6	578.9	491.9
Demand Deposits	24	85.2	86.6	88.5	74.1	84.8	88.6	104.9	†127.2	152.7	†208.9	225.8	256.2
Time, Savings,& Fgn.Currency Dep	25	2,699.0	3,192.7	3,551.3	4,299.5	4,782.7	4,807.8	5,142.6	†5,392.5	5,540.0	†6,108.2	6,419.0	6,783.9
Money Market Instruments	26aa	....	....	....	....	....	....				†27.2	32.3	62.6
Restricted Deposits	26b	....	....	....	....	....	....				†5.0	2.4	2.0
Foreign Liabilities	26c	881.2	1,313.7	1,473.3	2,233.9	1,269.8	884.4	724.9	†585.7	485.8	†388.9	407.7	398.3
Central Government Deposits	26d	125.5	140.8	280.2	250.5	322.7	346.7	354.2	†385.5	437.0	†426.0	454.2	504.7
Credit from Monetary Authorities	26g	42.4	53.8	116.2	794.5	736.3	506.4	410.2	†403.6	31.5	†38.1	79.2	124.9
Liab. to Nonbank Financial Insts	26j	....	....	....	....	....	....		194.5	204.8	†210.2	184.8	155.4
Capital Accounts	27a	490.1	635.4	761.8	569.8	216.4	−24.6	−108.4	†−25.7	595.1	†721.7	834.9	995.2
Other Items (Net)	27r	130.3	191.3	141.1	444.8	946.7	925.4	698.0	†696.1	536.1	†367.8	378.6	201.1
Banking Survey					*Billions of Baht: End of Period*								
Foreign Assets (Net)	31n	47.4	−147.4	−302.8	−887.4	−120.1	521.6	888.2	†1,216.6	1,633.2	†1,856.6	2,104.8	2,394.1
Domestic Credit	32	4,742.7	5,916.2	6,748.8	8,404.0	8,177.1	7,223.9	6,806.8	†6,600.1	6,964.9	†7,274.0	7,563.4	7,893.8
Claims on Central Govt. (Net)	32an	−241.3	−368.6	−547.9	−470.9	3.7	155.6	181.1	†244.3	241.0	†288.4	236.5	208.6
Claims on State and Local Govts	32b	—	—	—	—	—	—		† —		†.3	.8	1.8
Claims on Nonfin.Pub.Enterprises	32c	157.3	179.2	223.4	265.4	279.6	323.3	344.3	†368.7	345.1	†355.3	353.3	323.1
Claims on Private Sector	32d	4,636.4	5,853.5	6,786.8	7,842.8	7,212.5	6,117.4	5,329.5	†4,975.1	5,589.0	†5,516.1	6,139.5	6,611.0
Claims on Nonbank Financial Insts	32g	....	....	....	....	....	....		1,012.0	789.8	†1,113.8	833.2	749.4
Money	34	321.9	364.2	383.4	404.5	394.9	566.5	495.5	†553.2	630.8	†741.4	803.8	863.0
Quasi-Money	35	2,699.0	3,192.7	3,551.3	4,299.5	4,782.7	4,807.8	5,142.6	†5,392.5	5,540.0	†6,108.2	6,419.0	6,783.9
Money Market Instruments	36aa	870.4	1,087.9	1,243.5	793.1	868.7	654.8	596.0	† —	—	†27.2	32.3	62.6
Liabs. of Central Bank: Securities	36ac	....	....	....	....	....	....				† —	—	—
Restricted Deposits	36b	....	....	....	....	....	....		—	—	†5.0	2.4	2.0
Liab. to Nonbank Financial Insts	36j	....	....	....	....	....	....		365.4	316.8	†253.1	228.1	408.6
Capital Accounts	37a	796.9	973.3	1,139.6	1,372.9	1,030.5	988.6	1,051.2	†1,071.4	2,227.4	†1,624.0	1,795.0	1,906.2
Other Items (Net)	37r	101.7	150.6	128.1	645.3	967.2	557.4	247.4	†434.2	−116.9	†371.7	387.6	261.7
Money plus Quasi-Money	35l	3,021.0	3,557.0	3,934.7	4,704.0	5,177.6	5,374.3	5,638.1	†5,945.7	6,170.7	†6,849.6	7,222.8	7,646.9
Money (National Definitions)					*Billions of Baht: End of Period*								
M0	19mc	329.9	404.3	452.9	474.1	475.2	621.8	527.2	556.3	632.7	699.7	800.5	842.5
M1	59ma	346.4	388.3	423.7	428.8	441.7	575.0	525.7	579.4	663.5	766.8	859.0	910.9
M2	59mb	2,829.4	3,310.6	3,726.7	4,339.3	4,753.4	4,854.7	5,032.7	5,243.7	5,378.9	5,641.8	5,948.4	6,438.9
M2a	59mba	3,557.5	4,193.4	4,725.2	4,779.2	5,118.1	5,182.5	5,296.9	5,538.4	5,530.2	5,813.2	6,180.4	6,510.0
M3	59mc	3,761.6	4,496.2	5,052.3	5,224.6	5,706.9	5,801.6	6,037.9	6,311.2	6,395.5	6,848.7	7,143.1	7,725.2

Thailand 578

		1994	1995	1996	1997	1998	1999	2000	2001	2002	2003	2004	2005
Interest Rates					*Percent Per Annum*								
Discount Rate (End of Period)	60	9.50	10.50	10.50	12.50	12.50	4.00	4.00	3.75	3.25	2.75	3.50	5.50
Money Market Rate	60b	7.25	10.96	9.23	14.59	13.02	1.77	1.95	2.00	1.76	1.31	1.23	2.62
Deposit Rate	60l	8.46	11.58	10.33	10.52	10.65	4.73	3.29	2.54	1.98	1.33	1.00	1.88
Lending Rate	60p	10.90	13.25	13.40	13.65	14.42	8.98	7.83	7.25	6.88	5.94	5.50	5.79
Government Bond Yield	61	10.75	10.75	10.75	10.75	10.25	6.69	6.95	5.82	5.07	3.76	5.09	5.13
Prices and Labor					*Index Numbers (2000=100): Period Averages*								
Share Prices	62	....	....	....	173.4	103.3	123.0	100.0	88.6	107.0	140.9	193.8	201.9
Producer Prices	63	77.8	† 84.1	85.7	90.0	101.0	96.2	100.0	102.5	104.2	108.4	115.7	126.2
Consumer Prices	64	76.8	81.3	86.0	90.8	98.2	98.5	100.0	101.6	102.3	104.1	107.0	111.8
					Number in Thousands: Period Averages								
Labor Force	67d	32,515	32,887	32,543	33,339	33,352	33,209	33,799	33,815	34,228	34,881	35,716	36,050
Employment	67e	32,093	32,512	32,232	33,162	32,138	32,087	33,001	32,110	33,026	33,818	34,717	35,170
Unemployment	67c	423	375	354	293	1,138	986	813	1,119	826	761	741	666
Unemployment Rate (%)	67r	1.3	1.1	1.1	.9	3.4	3.0	2.4	3.3	2.4	2.2	2.1	1.9
Intl. Transactions & Positions					*Billions of Baht*								
Exports	70	1,137.6	1,406.3	1,412.1	1,806.7	2,248.3	2,215.2	2,773.8	2,884.7	2,923.9	3,325.6	3,874.8	4,436.7
Rice	70n	59.3	48.6	50.7	65.1	86.8	73.6	65.6	70.1	70.0	75.8	108.4	93.5
Rubber	70l	41.8	61.3	63.4	57.4	55.4	43.9	60.7	58.7	74.6	115.8	137.5	148.9
Maize	70j	.6	.6	.4	.5	.9	.5	.4	2.5	1.2	1.6	6.0	1.6
Tin	70q	.4	.4	.8	1.4	2.5	2.5	.8	3.7	2.2	2.0	4.7	7.7
Imports, c.i.f.	71	1,369.0	1,763.6	1,832.8	1,924.3	1,774.1	1,907.4	2,494.1	2,752.3	2,774.8	3,138.8	3,801.2	4,756.0
					2000=100								
Volume of Exports	72	54.4	† 74.5	67.3	71.0	75.2	83.4	100.0	91.8	101.0	109.4	118.5	123.9
Rice	72n	79.0	100.8	88.8	90.6	106.4	111.2	100.0	124.7	119.2	119.4	162.3	122.6
Rubber	72l	67.4	68.8	75.7	75.6	78.7	80.0	100.0	100.4	109.6	122.4	119.0	116.2
Maize	72j	445.0	335.2	176.6	192.4	428.5	249.5	100.0	1,557.9	492.6	647.2	3,143.0	464.4
Tin	72q	21.0	20.4	37.6	61.7	86.5	95.6	100.0	146.0	98.1	76.2	105.2	192.9
Volume of Imports	73	105.8	† 118.9	105.7	93.3	67.9	82.2	100.0	89.1	99.9	111.9	124.2	134.9
Unit Value of Exports	74	62.8	† 68.0	75.2	91.5	106.9	94.7	100.0	112.2	103.1	108.5	118.2	130.1
Rice (Unit Value)	74n	114.4	73.6	87.1	109.6	124.5	101.2	100.0	85.8	89.6	96.8	101.8	116.4
Rice (Wholesale Price)	76n	82.9	97.8	104.9	116.1	154.6	115.2	100.0	93.9	100.9	101.3	121.0	141.7
Rubber (Unit Value)	74l	102.3	146.7	137.9	125.2	116.0	90.5	100.0	96.3	112.1	155.9	190.3	211.0
Rubber (Wholesale Price)	76l	105.7	147.0	132.6	119.1	111.4	89.7	100.0	95.4	122.7	167.7	195.8	225.4
Maize (Unit Value)	74j	33.4	41.6	62.6	71.9	52.0	53.5	100.0	40.6	63.8	62.6	48.0	85.1
Tin (Unit Value)	74q	64.4	71.1	72.7	82.4	104.7	93.1	100.0	89.2	81.6	93.2	158.9	141.5
Unit Value of Imports	75	52.6	† 58.8	67.7	81.4	98.7	86.9	100.0	120.3	108.6	109.6	120.6	140.0
Balance of Payments					*Millions of US Dollars: Minus Sign Indicates Debit*								
Current Account, n.i.e.	78ald	−8,085	−13,582	−14,691	−3,021	14,242	12,428	9,313	6,192	7,014	7,953	6,857	−3,719
Goods: Exports f.o.b.	78aad	44,478	55,447	54,408	56,656	52,753	56,775	67,894	63,082	66,089	78,083	94,979	109,216
Goods: Imports f.o.b.	78abd	−48,204	−63,415	−63,897	−55,084	−36,515	−42,762	−56,193	−54,539	−57,008	−66,909	−84,193	−106,054
Trade Balance	78acd	−3,726	−7,968	−9,488	1,572	16,238	14,013	11,701	8,543	9,081	11,175	10,785	3,162
Services: Credit	78add	11,640	14,845	17,007	15,763	13,156	14,635	13,868	13,024	15,391	15,798	19,040	20,647
Services: Debit	78aed	−15,396	−18,832	−19,585	−17,355	−11,998	−13,583	−15,460	−14,610	−16,720	−18,169	−23,077	−27,611
Balance on Goods & Services	78afd	−7,482	−11,955	−12,066	−20	17,395	15,066	10,109	6,957	7,751	8,804	6,748	−3,802
Income: Credit	78agd	2,562	3,801	3,969	3,742	3,324	3,092	4,235	3,833	3,356	3,015	3,119	3,391
Income: Debit	78ahd	−4,292	−5,915	−7,354	−7,223	−6,891	−6,083	−5,616	−5,200	−4,696	−4,807	−5,142	−6,312
Balance on Gds, Serv. & Inc.	78aid	−9,213	−14,068	−15,451	−3,500	13,828	12,075	8,727	5,591	6,411	7,012	4,726	−6,723
Current Transfers, n.i.e.: Credit	78ajd	1,901	1,190	1,651	1,392	820	806	952	990	978	1,326	2,479	3,351
Current Transfers: Debit	78akd	−774	−704	−891	−913	−405	−452	−366	−389	−375	−385	−348	−348
Capital Account, n.i.e.	78bcd	—	....	....	....	....	....	....	....	....	....	....	....
Capital Account, n.i.e.: Credit	78bad	—	....	....	....	....	....	....	....	....	....	....	....
Capital Account: Debit	78bbd		....	....	....	....	....	....	....	....	....	....	....
Financial Account, n.i.e.	78bjd	12,167	22,040	19,486	−12,056	−14,110	−11,073	−10,434	−3,658	−2,887	−7,626	−562	7,956
Direct Investment Abroad	78bdd	−493	−886	−931	−580	−130	−346	23	−344	−106	−488	−126	−283
Dir. Invest. in Rep. Econ., n.i.e.	78bed	1,366	2,068	2,336	3,895	7,315	6,103	3,366	3,892	953	1,949	1,412	4,014
Portfolio Investment Assets	78bfd	−5	−2	−41	−70	18	−2	−160	−360	−913	−939	1,214	−1,560
Equity Securities	78bkd	−5	−2	−41	—	—	—	—	—	−9	−149	−261	−314
Debt Securities	78bld	....	....	....	−70	18	−2	−160	−360	−905	−790	1,476	−1,246
Portfolio Investment Liab., n.i.e.	78bgd	2,486	4,215	3,585	4,598	338	−109	−546	−525	−694	851	892	7,247
Equity Securities	78bmd	−389	2,255	1,164	3,868	289	945	900	352	539	1,786	356	5,298
Debt Securities	78bnd	2,875	1,960	2,421	730	48	−1,054	−1,446	−877	−1,233	−935	536	1,948
Financial Derivatives Assets	78bwd	....	....	....	....	....	....	—	—	—	—	10	....
Financial Derivatives Liabilities	78bxd	....	....	....	....	....	....	—	—	—	—	6	....
Other Investment Assets	78bhd	−1,027	−2,738	2,661	−2,555	−3,407	−1,755	−2,203	577	4,135	−410	−1,984	−997
Monetary Authorities	78bod	—	....	....	....	....	....	....	....	....	....	....	....
General Government	78bpd	—	....	....	....	....	....	—	−31	−5	−3	162	−10
Banks	78bqd	−1,027	−2,737	2,741	−2,608	−3,460	−1,708	−2,189	743	4,235	−405	−425	−1,701
Other Sectors	78brd	—	−1	−80	53	53	−47	−14	−135	−94	−2	−1,721	714
Other Investment Liab., n.i.e.	78bid	9,839	19,383	11,876	−17,343	−18,243	−14,964	−10,914	−6,897	−6,263	−8,590	−1,986	−465
Monetary Authorities	78bsd	—	—	—	−5,262	658	2,731	43	894	5,352	3,031	3,022	....
General Government	78btd	−705	46	−58	737	100	−70	93	80	−1,361	−609	−1,882	−1,186
Banks	78bud	14,295	13,218	2,909	−3,045	−11,783	−11,566	−4,799	−2,534	−1,761	−1,636	−598	−1,052
Other Sectors	78bvd	−3,751	6,118	9,025	−9,774	−7,218	−6,060	−6,251	−5,338	−8,493	−9,375	−2,527	1,773
Net Errors and Omissions	78cad	87	−1,300	−2,627	−3,173	−2,828	33	−685	−258	1,410	191	−585	1,180
Overall Balance	78cbd	4,169	7,159	2,167	−18,250	−2,696	1,388	−1,806	2,276	5,537	518	5,710	5,417
Reserves and Related Items	79dad	−4,169	−7,159	−2,167	18,250	2,696	−1,388	1,806	−2,276	−5,537	−518	−5,710	−5,417
Reserve Assets	79dbd	−4,169	−7,159	−2,167	9,900	−1,433	−4,556	1,608	−1,307	−4,197	−122	−5,713	−5,417
Use of Fund Credit and Loans	79dcd	—	—	—	2,437	679	269	−192	−1,288	−1,360	−398	—	—
Exceptional Financing	79ded	....	....	....	5,913	3,450	2,898	391	320	19	3	4	....

Thailand 578

		1994	1995	1996	1997	1998	1999	2000	2001	2002	2003	2004	2005
International Investment Position					*Millions of US Dollars*								
Assets	79aad	....	46,982	46,005	35,007	41,368	48,360	53,797	54,317	58,458	63,940	73,063	....
Direct Investment Abroad	79abd	....	365	481	401	410	418	2,203	2,626	2,594	3,146	3,701	....
Portfolio Investment	79acd	....	—	—	43	28	29	488	825	1,689	2,834	1,644	....
Equity Securities	79add	....	....	....	....	....	....	53	82	84	434	713	....
Debt Securities	79aed	....	....	....	....	....	....	435	743	1,605	2,400	931	....
Financial Derivatives	79ald	....	—	—	—	—	—	517	141	282	614	643	....
Other Investment	79afd	....	9,672	6,879	7,671	11,394	13,132	17,928	17,684	14,968	15,197	17,244	....
Monetary Authorities	79agd	....											
General Government	79ahd	....	—	—	—	—	—	127	158	166	164	—	....
Banks	79aid	....	9,672	6,879	7,671	11,394	13,132	16,342	15,612	11,450	12,020	12,544	....
Other Sectors	79ajd	....						1,459	1,914	3,352	3,013	4,700	....
Reserve Assets	79akd	....	36,945	38,645	26,892	29,536	34,781	32,661	33,041	38,925	42,149	49,831	....
Liabilities	79lad	....	100,832	108,742	109,276	105,061	95,051	114,241	106,170	104,199	119,706	126,317	....
Dir. Invest. in Rep. Economy	79lbd	....	4,919	4,745	4,738	6,481	6,837	29,915	33,268	38,180	48,603	52,855	....
Portfolio Investment	79lcd	....	6,684	9,472	9,774	10,552	9,921	16,360	17,123	17,811	29,249	32,206	....
Equity Securities	79ldd	....	—	—	—	—	—	8,153	10,240	12,260	24,481	26,715	....
Debt Securities	79led	....	6,684	9,472	9,774	10,552	9,921	8,207	6,883	5,551	4,768	5,491	....
Financial Derivatives	79lld	....	—	—	—	—	—	684	507	541	768	843	....
Other Investment	79lfd	....	89,229	94,525	94,764	88,028	78,293	67,281	55,271	47,666	41,085	40,414	....
Monetary Authorities	79lgd	....	—	—	7,157	11,203	12,817	12,019	8,327	4,904	—	—	....
General Government	79lhd	....	3,126	2,994	3,672	4,768	7,102	7,347	7,296	6,315	6,036	4,292	....
Banks	79lid	....	41,346	41,410	38,898	28,083	17,450	13,656	10,434	9,297	8,282	8,166	....
Other Sectors	79ljd	....	44,757	50,121	45,037	43,974	40,924	34,259	29,214	27,150	26,767	27,956	....
Government Finance					*Millions of Baht: Year Ending December 31*								
Deficit (-) or Surplus	80	101,239	134,965	† 43,303	−15,061	−128,951	−154,193	−108,065	−122,993	−76,815	23,998	....	....
Total Revenue and Grants	81y	....	....	....	....	....	....	....	....	....	....	....	
Revenue	81	680,455	777,286	853,201	847,689	717,779	713,066	746,817	776,362	876,901	1,012,588	....	
Grants	81z	....	....	....	....	....	....	....	....	....	....	....	
Exp. & Lending Minus Repay	82z	....	....	....	....	....	....	....	....	....	....		
Expenditure	82	579,216	642,321	819,083	875,714	842,581	833,042	853,067	908,613	955,492	996,198		
Lending Minus Repayments	83	....	....	....	....	....	....	....	....	....	....		
Extrabudgetary Deficits/Surpluses	80xz			† 9,185	12,964	−4,149	−34,217	−1,815	9,258	1,776	7,608		
Total Financing	80h	−101,239	−134,965	† −43,303	15,061	128,951	154,192	108,065	122,993	76,815	−23,998	....	....
Total Net Borrowing	84	−80,051	−44,147	† −28,788	−76,109	−7,764	135,204	65,101	113,520	113,439	−35,268		
Net Domestic	84a	....	....	−25,123	−72,348	−3,361	84,566	48,967	112,595	145,487	3,579		
Net Foreign	85a	....	....	−3,665	−3,761	−4,403	50,638	16,134	925	−32,048	−38,847		
Use of Cash Balances	87	−21,188	−90,818	−14,515	91,170	136,715	18,988	42,964	9,473	−36,624	11,270	....	....
Total Debt by Currency	88z	219,829	193,630	175,594	299,547	674,032	991,104	1,104,586	1,263,856	1,691,215	1,631,125	1,810,439	1,857,247
National	88b	103,200	72,696	44,254	31,755	426,928	642,371	688,937	836,689	1,293,881	1,279,282	1,508,576	1,614,649
Foreign	89b	116,629	120,934	131,340	267,792	247,104	348,733	415,649	427,167	397,334	351,843	301,863	242,598
National Accounts					*Billions of Baht*								
Househ.Cons.Expend.,incl.NPISHs	96f	1,958.7	2,225.7	2,479.8	2,587.0	2,505.3	2,595.1	2,762.9	2,941.0	3,120.0	3,388.5	3,687.6	4,043.7
Government Consumption Expend	91f	354.4	414.4	469.5	476.7	511.7	533.0	557.8	581.1	603.9	635.3	721.3	838.8
Gross Fixed Capital Formation	93e	1,450.2	1,719.1	1,892.9	1,598.6	1,035.4	965.9	1,081.4	1,181.3	1,243.2	1,423.9	1,686.8	2,057.0
Changes in Inventories	93i	10.7	43.0	35.2	−5.5	−89.5	−15.3	42.7	55.8	54.1	53.6	75.0	188.0
Exports of Goods and Services	90c	1,410.8	1,751.7	1,809.9	2,272.1	2,724.0	2,703.3	3,287.3	3,380.8	3,499.0	3,886.6	4,587.9	5,232.9
Imports of Goods and Services (-)	98c	1,586.6	2,033.9	2,099.2	2,205.1	1,988.9	2,120.3	2,862.3	3,047.6	3,134.3	3,485.3	4,281.9	5,338.6
Statistical Discrepancy	99bs	31.1	66.1	22.9	8.8	−71.6	−24.6	52.9	41.1	64.7	26.5	26.8	81.0
Gross Domestic Product (GDP)	99b	3,629.3	4,186.2	4,611.0	4,732.6	4,626.4	4,637.1	4,922.7	5,133.5	5,450.6	5,929.0	6,503.5	7,103.0
Net Primary Income from Abroad	98.n	−55.8	−68.2	−102.1	−123.4	−160.0	−126.4	−76.9	−85.1	−88.6	−111.0	−126.2	−173.3
Gross National Income (GNI)	99a	3,573.6	4,118.0	4,509.0	4,609.2	4,466.4	4,510.6	4,845.9	5,048.4	5,362.0	5,817.9	6,377.3	6,929.7
Consumption of Fixed Capital	99cf	397.0	471.6	556.7	599.1	....	....	....	....	....	....	....	....
GDP Volume 1988 Prices	99b.p	2,693.0	2,941.7	3,115.3	3,072.6	2,749.7	2,872.0	3,008.4	3,073.6	3,237.0	3,464.7	3,678.5	3,842.5
GDP Volume (2000=100)	99bvp	89.5	97.8	103.6	102.1	91.4	95.5	100.0	102.2	107.6	115.2	122.3	127.7
GDP Deflator (2000=100)	99bip	82.4	87.0	90.5	94.1	102.8	98.7	100.0	102.1	102.9	104.6	108.0	113.0
					Millions: Midyear Estimates								
Population	99z	57.64	58.34	59.00	59.64	60.25	60.85	61.44	62.02	62.59	63.14	63.69	64.23

Togo 742

		1994	1995	1996	1997	1998	1999	2000	2001	2002	2003	2004	2005
Exchange Rates						*Francs per SDR: End of Period*							
Official Rate	aa	780.44	728.38	753.06	807.94	791.61	† 896.19	918.49	935.39	850.37	771.76	747.90	794.73
						Francs per US Dollar: End of Period (ae) Period Average (rf)							
Official Rate	ae	534.60	490.00	523.70	598.81	562.21	† 652.95	704.95	744.31	625.50	519.36	481.58	556.04
Official Rate	rf	† 555.20	499.15	511.55	583.67	589.95	† 615.70	711.98	733.04	696.99	581.20	528.28	527.47
						Index Numbers (2000=100): Period Averages							
Official Rate	ahx	128.1	142.3	138.8	121.8	120.5	115.5	100.0	96.9	102.2	122.4	134.6	134.8
Nominal Effective Exchange Rate	nec	93.1	97.5	98.9	96.2	104.1	102.2	100.0	103.2	106.5	115.8	120.5	120.0
Real Effective Exchange Rate	rec	87.2	101.1	103.5	104.2	109.3	104.0	100.0	102.3	105.8	109.5	110.9	113.6
Fund Position						*Millions of SDRs: End of Period*							
Quota	2f.s	54.3	54.3	54.3	54.3	54.3	73.4	73.4	73.4	73.4	73.4	73.4	73.4
SDRs	1b.s	—	.3	.2	—	.1	.2	—	.2	.2	.1	—	—
Reserve Position in the Fund	1c.s	.3	.3	.3	.3	.3	.3	.3	.3	.3	.3	.3	.3
Total Fund Cred.&Loans Outstg	2tl	56.0	70.4	62.5	64.9	67.4	60.4	53.3	45.3	38.0	28.2	17.4	9.8
International Liquidity						*Millions of US Dollars Unless Otherwise Indicated: End of Period*							
Total Reserves minus Gold	1l.d	94.4	130.4	88.5	118.6	117.7	122.1	152.3	126.4	205.1	204.9	359.7	194.6
SDRs	1b.d	.1	.4	.4	—	.1	.2	—	.2	.3	.2	—	—
Reserve Position in the Fund	1c.d	.4	.4	.4	.3	.4	.3	.4	.4	.4	.5	.5	.5
Foreign Exchange	1d.d	94.0	129.6	87.8	118.3	117.3	121.5	151.9	125.8	204.4	204.2	359.2	194.1
Gold (Million Fine Troy Ounces)	1ad	.013	—	—	—	—	—	—	—	—	—	—	—
Gold (National Valuation)	1and	4.7	—	—	—	—	—	—	—	—	—	—	—
Monetary Authorities: Other Liab	4..d	5.5	1.1	2.8	2.7	8.9	3.1	6.5	6.8	40.5	31.5	91.7	15.7
Deposit Money Banks: Assets	7a.d	109.7	111.1	100.6	66.3	69.1	60.0	81.4	87.2	103.6	118.7	172.2	165.6
Liabilities	7b.d	40.6	76.1	77.8	71.8	71.5	64.1	64.9	62.1	73.3	91.9	92.6	71.0
Monetary Authorities						*Billions of Francs: End of Period*							
Foreign Assets	11	50.5	63.9	46.3	71.0	66.2	79.7	107.4	94.1	128.3	106.4	173.2	108.2
Claims on Central Government	12a	49.8	71.1	70.2	66.0	76.5	67.8	66.9	65.9	53.6	46.2	35.4	26.7
Claims on Deposit Money Banks	12e	7.2	2.0	7.5	4.2	8.5	5.0	2.6	1.8	—	—	—	—
Claims on Other Financial Insts	12f	1.3	.3	.2	.3	.3	.3	.3	.3	.3	—	—	—
Reserve Money	14	62.8	80.9	70.7	71.2	79.0	90.3	109.4	102.3	108.4	85.7	112.3	90.4
of which: Currency Outside DMBs	14a	44.8	73.5	59.7	60.3	65.3	79.5	95.7	85.7	64.0	48.6	73.3	63.3
Foreign Liabilities	16c	46.7	51.8	48.6	54.1	58.3	56.2	53.6	47.5	57.6	38.1	57.1	16.5
Central Government Deposits	16d	9.6	8.1	8.4	9.9	5.8	3.8	3.7	8.6	7.6	18.1	28.3	19.5
Other Items (Net)	17r	−10.3	−3.6	−3.4	6.3	8.3	2.6	10.5	3.7	8.6	10.7	10.8	8.6
Deposit Money Banks						*Billions of Francs: End of Period*							
Reserves	20	15.1	12.5	14.9	17.7	7.9	9.0	13.4	12.8	33.7	38.0	33.9	24.7
Foreign Assets	21	58.6	54.4	52.7	39.7	38.8	39.2	57.4	64.9	64.8	61.6	82.9	92.1
Claims on Central Government	22a	12.4	12.3	16.5	17.4	16.7	14.1	10.8	7.9	6.6	6.4	22.9	17.1
Claims on Private Sector	22d	101.8	130.4	140.2	154.8	161.9	146.6	147.6	137.3	127.7	166.7	173.9	195.1
Claims on Other Financial Insts	22f	.5	—	—	—	—	—	—	—	—	—	—	—
Demand Deposits	24	49.3	56.4	59.9	60.6	63.5	61.1	78.4	73.0	82.4	103.3	116.9	121.5
Time Deposits	25	68.2	68.7	66.2	73.8	65.4	68.9	69.4	78.2	86.1	105.3	114.1	127.2
Foreign Liabilities	26c	19.9	33.7	37.3	42.5	39.1	40.1	44.4	45.2	45.2	47.3	44.4	38.9
Long-Term Foreign Liabilities	26cl	1.7	3.5	3.4	.5	1.2	1.7	1.4	1.0	.7	.5	.2	.6
Central Government Deposits	26d	39.1	37.4	32.8	29.8	28.9	20.6	17.2	15.1	18.1	18.7	23.5	20.3
Credit from Monetary Authorities	26g	7.4	2.0	7.6	4.7	8.5	5.0	2.6	2.1	—	—	2.3	1.4
Other Items (Net)	27r	2.7	7.9	16.9	17.7	18.8	11.4	16.0	8.3	.3	−2.3	12.2	19.0
Treasury Claims: Private Sector	22d.i	.6	.9	.7	.7	.5	.3	.3	.3	.3	.3	.3	.3
Post Office: Checking Deposits	24..i	1.0	1.3	1.2	1.7	1.2	1.9	1.5	1.2	1.5	1.3	1.1	1.1
Monetary Survey						*Billions of Francs: End of Period*							
Foreign Assets (Net)	31n	42.5	32.7	13.2	14.0	7.7	22.6	66.8	66.3	90.3	82.6	154.6	144.9
Domestic Credit	32	118.1	169.8	187.1	200.4	221.8	206.2	206.3	189.0	164.0	183.9	181.4	200.2
Claims on Central Govt. (Net)	32an	13.8	38.3	46.0	44.7	59.1	59.1	58.1	51.1	35.7	16.8	7.2	4.9
Claims on Private Sector	32d	102.5	131.2	140.9	155.5	162.4	146.8	147.8	137.6	127.9	167.0	174.2	195.4
Claims on Other Financial Insts	32f	1.8	.3	.2	.3	.3	.3	.3	.3	.3	—	—	—
Money	34	95.3	131.2	121.0	123.3	131.8	144.8	176.9	161.5	148.4	154.7	192.9	186.7
Quasi-Money	35	68.2	68.7	66.2	73.8	65.4	68.9	69.4	78.2	86.1	105.3	114.1	127.2
Long-Term Foreign Liabilities	36cl	1.7	3.5	3.4	.5	1.2	1.7	1.4	1.0	.7	.5	.2	.6
Other Items (Net)	37r	−4.6	−.9	9.6	16.9	31.1	13.4	25.5	14.5	19.0	6.0	28.7	30.6
Money plus Quasi-Money	35l	163.5	199.9	187.2	197.0	197.2	213.7	246.3	239.7	234.6	260.0	307.1	314.0
Interest Rates						*Percent Per Annum*							
Bank Rate (End of Period)	60	6.00	6.00	6.00	6.00	6.00	6.00	6.00	6.00	6.00	4.50	4.00	4.00
Money Market Rate	60b	4.95	4.95	4.95	4.95	4.95	4.95	4.95	4.95	4.95	4.95	4.95	4.95
Deposit Rate	60l	3.50	3.50	3.50	3.50	3.50	3.50	3.50	3.50	3.50	3.50	3.50	3.50
Prices and Labor						*Index Numbers (2000=100): Period Averages*							
Consumer Prices	64	73.7	85.8	89.9	† 97.3	98.2	98.1	100.0	103.9	107.1	106.1	106.5	113.7
						Number in Thousands: Period Averages							
Employment	67e	56	54	50	49	....	....	....	....	....	....	....	....
Intl. Transactions & Positions						*Millions of Francs*							
Exports	70	182,300	188,400	225,400	246,600	247,900	241,000	257,400	261,900	295,700	357,000	193,957	189,700
Imports, c.i.f.	71	123,265	295,700	339,900	376,400	346,700	301,300	345,100	378,300	401,200	490,200	293,823	314,352
						2000=100							
Export Prices	74	....	....	122.5	128.9	120.0	100.5	100.0	59.7	57.1	51.7	61.6	52.3
Unit Value of Imports	75	....	....	62.2	77.5	83.6	104.0	100.0	158.4	187.5	212.4	208.8	244.3

Togo 742

		1994	1995	1996	1997	1998	1999	2000	2001	2002	2003	2004	2005
Balance of Payments							*Millions of US Dollars: Minus Sign Indicates Debit*						
Current Account, n.i.e.	78ald	−56.3	−122.0	−153.9	−116.9	−140.1	−127.1	−139.6	−169.1	−139.9	−161.9	....	....
Goods: Exports f.o.b.	78aad	328.4	377.4	440.6	422.5	420.3	391.5	361.8	357.2	424.2	597.7		
Goods: Imports f.o.b.	78abd	−365.5	−506.5	−567.8	−530.6	−553.5	−489.4	−484.6	−516.1	−575.6	−754.5		
Trade Balance	78acd	−37.1	−129.1	−127.2	−108.1	−133.2	−98.0	−122.8	−158.9	−151.4	−156.8		
Services: Credit	78add	70.9	87.3	116.2	88.5	76.0	68.4	61.8	71.8	90.0	94.8		
Services: Debit	78aed	−125.3	−164.3	−201.4	−167.8	−149.2	−130.6	−117.5	−129.9	−148.1	−204.2		
Balance on Goods & Services	78afd	−91.6	−206.0	−212.3	−187.4	−206.4	−160.1	−178.5	−217.0	−209.5	−266.3		
Income: Credit	78agd	9.1	8.8	45.6	35.0	44.4	40.2	32.9	25.9	26.2	26.8		
Income: Debit	78ahd	−54.0	−42.4	−72.0	−63.9	−67.7	−78.6	−62.0	−55.2	−47.8	−50.2		
Balance on Gds, Serv. & Inc.	78aid	−136.5	−239.6	−238.8	−216.3	−229.7	−198.5	−207.6	−246.3	−231.1	−289.6		
Current Transfers, n.i.e.: Credit	78ajd	91.3	129.7	106.8	120.2	101.8	73.6	73.3	88.3	113.0	161.4		
Current Transfers: Debit	78akd	−11.2	−12.1	−21.9	−20.8	−12.2	−2.2	−5.4	−11.1	−21.8	−33.8		
Capital Account, n.i.e.	78bcd	—	—	5.6	5.8	6.1	6.9	8.7	21.4	13.6	20.6		
Capital Account, n.i.e.: Credit	78bad	—	—	5.6	5.8	6.1	6.9	8.7	21.4	13.6	20.6		
Capital Account: Debit	78bbd	—	....	—	—	—	—	—	—	—	—		
Financial Account, n.i.e.	78bjd	−40.5	−52.8	151.3	126.9	114.1	155.5	162.8	151.2	150.8	142.9		
Direct Investment Abroad	78bdd	—	5.8	−2.8	−2.5	−10.6	−2.9	−.4	7.3	−2.7	6.3		
Dir. Invest. in Rep. Econ., n.i.e.	78bed	15.4	26.2	17.3	21.0	30.2	42.6	41.9	63.6	53.7	33.7		
Portfolio Investment Assets	78bfd	.7	5.0	−16.1	6.7	−5.2	−1.3	.8	5.3	−1.1	−4.7		
Equity Securities	78bkd	1.1	5.0	−.3	7.0	−4.4	−2.8	.6	—	−2.0	−.2		
Debt Securities	78bld	−.4	—	−15.8	−.3	−.7	1.6	.2	5.3	.9	−4.5		
Portfolio Investment Liab., n.i.e.	78bgd	—	....	20.1	9.4	11.4	8.6	6.1	5.8	13.0	18.6		
Equity Securities	78bmd	—	....	18.8	10.6	11.6	8.5	6.1	1.5	6.1	9.8		
Debt Securities	78bnd	—	....	1.3	−1.2	−.2	.1	—	4.3	6.8	8.8		
Financial Derivatives Assets	78bwd	....	20.6	.3	2.1	−.1	—	—	—	—	—		
Financial Derivatives Liabilities	78bxd	....	....	1.6	−7.0	−.2	−.3	−.1	—	—	—		
Other Investment Assets	78bhd	−1.5	12.1	−19.2	−1.6	16.2	13.0	8.8	8.2	−3.8	−28.7		
Monetary Authorities	78bod	....	....	....			—	—	—	—	—		
General Government	78bpd	—	....	−3.7	12.2	5.3	7.8	7.5	4.8	−.3	3.1		
Banks	78bqd	—	....	4.6	....	−.7	.5	−16.8	−8.8	5.5	6.9		
Other Sectors	78brd	−1.5	12.1	−20.1	−13.8	11.6	4.7	18.1	12.3	−9.0	−38.6		
Other Investment Liab., n.i.e.	78bid	−55.2	−122.4	150.1	98.9	72.3	95.8	105.7	61.0	91.7	117.7		
Monetary Authorities	78bsd	—	—	3.8	4.8	5.8	−5.0	2.5	1.7	10.4	6.7		
General Government	78btd	−19.3	−133.5	67.8	62.0	45.0	33.2	41.6	28.6	19.6	25.8		
Banks	78bud	−66.2	....	13.1	....	−6.4	1.6	1.4	.4	−5.7	2.6		
Other Sectors	78bvd	30.3	11.0	65.4	32.0	28.0	65.9	60.1	30.3	67.5	82.6		
Net Errors and Omissions	78cad	−.2	−19.3	−27.9	−2.7	2.7	−3.7	5.0	−5.4	5.0	−10.2		
Overall Balance	78cbd	−97.1	−194.0	−24.9	13.1	−17.2	31.6	36.8	−2.0	29.6	−8.6		
Reserves and Related Items	79dad	97.1	194.0	24.9	−13.1	17.2	−31.6	−36.8	2.0	−29.6	8.6		
Reserve Assets	79dbd	−7.7	−26.9	34.3	−26.2	8.8	−22.2	−27.5	7.4	−20.1	22.4		
Use of Fund Credit and Loans	79dcd	9.3	22.0	−11.4	3.4	3.0	−9.4	−9.3	−10.2	−9.5	−13.8		
Exceptional Financing	79ded	95.5	199.0	2.0	9.7	5.4	—	—	4.8	—	—		
International Investment Position							*Millions of US Dollars*						
Assets	79aad	....	....	....	....	....	394.9	367.7	306.2	399.9	510.5	....	
Direct Investment Abroad	79abd	....	....	....	....	....	20.8	17.4	−12.7	−12.1	2.8		
Portfolio Investment	79acd	....	....	....	....	....	14.3	13.8	48.4	59.5	61.5		
Equity Securities	79add	....	....	....	....	....	6.6	7.3	6.6	8.7	5.1		
Debt Securities	79aed	....	....	....	....	....	7.7	6.5	41.8	50.8	56.5		
Financial Derivatives	79ald	....	....	....	....	....	.1	.1	—	—	.6		
Other Investment	79afd	....	....	....	....	....	237.7	195.5	144.3	180.2	263.1		
Monetary Authorities	79agd	....	....	....	....	....	—	—	—	—	—		
General Government	79ahd	....	....	....	....	....	35.8	21.3	—	5.8	3.5		
Banks	79aid	....	....	....	....	....	67.1	83.2	87.5	98.0	107.4		
Other Sectors	79ajd	....	....	....	....	....	134.8	91.0	56.8	76.4	152.2		
Reserve Assets	79akd	....	....	....	....	....	122.1	140.9	126.2	172.4	182.5		
Liabilities	79lad	....	....	....	....	....	1,728.8	1,745.3	1,735.4	2,149.4	2,546.2		
Dir. Invest. in Rep. Economy	79lbd	....	....	....	....	....	47.5	86.8	141.1	223.6	132.4		
Portfolio Investment	79lcd	....	....	....	....	....	24.2	30.1	33.2	53.7	29.1		
Equity Securities	79ldd	....	....	....	....	....	24.2	30.1	29.0	41.2	16.7		
Debt Securities	79led	....	....	....	....	....	.1	—	4.2	12.6	12.4		
Financial Derivatives	79lld	....	....	....	....	....	.7						
Other Investment	79lfd	....	....	....	....	....	1,656.5	1,628.4	1,561.2	1,872.1	2,384.7		
Monetary Authorities	79lgd	....	....	....	....	....	86.9	81.6	70.9	83.4	74.3		
General Government	79lhd	....	....	....	....	....	1,322.3	1,274.6	1,232.5	1,423.4	1,993.3		
Banks	79lid	....	....	....	....	....	56.0	76.7	51.2	49.2	70.7		
Other Sectors	79ljd	....	....	....	....	....	191.3	195.6	206.5	316.1	246.4		
Government Finance							*Billions of Francs: Year Ending December 31*						
Deficit (-) or Surplus	80	−59	−35	−24	−17	−48	−27	−43	....	....	....		
Total Revenue and Grants	81y	77	109	127	140	141	142	121	....	....	....		
Revenue	81	67	97	110	129	127	127	117	....	....	....		
Grants	81z	10	12	16	12	14	15	4	....	....	....		
Exp. & Lending Minus Repay	82z	136	144	151	157	188	169	164	....	....	....		
Expenditure	82	136	144	151	157	188	168	168	....	....	....		
Lending Minus Repayments	83	—	—	—	—	1	1	−3	....	....	....		
Statistical Discrepancy	80xx	21	−4	−5	−30	−1	4	28	....	....	....		
Total Financing													
Domestic	84a	19	19	7	13	10	1	−4	....	....	....		
Foreign	85a	19	20	22	34	39	23	20	....	....	....		

Togo 742

National Accounts		1994	1995	1996	1997	1998	1999	2000	2001	2002	2003	2004	2005
							Billions of Francs						
Househ.Cons.Expend.,incl.NPISHs....	96f	438.1	502.4	576.2	690.0	597.7	681.1	667.1	849.2	884.8	909.3	870.1	936.8
Government Consumption Expend...	91f	77.1	256.9	266.7	297.5	308.2	273.3	260.2	106.4	102.4	109.1	95.8	98.6
Gross Fixed Capital Formation..........	93e	63.1	97.2	96.7	98.9	152.6	115.4	139.1	147.9	158.1	198.7	....	....
Changes in Inventories.....................	93i	18.2	15.0	10.6	9.3	−.6	−.8	6.6	10.7	6.8	4.5	....	....
Exports of Goods and Services..........	90c	221.7	232.0	284.9	298.2	292.7	283.1	301.7	314.5	358.4	441.7	512.1	551.8
Imports of Goods and Services (-).....	98c	272.5	334.8	393.5	407.6	414.4	381.7	428.8	473.5	504.4	618.9	695.7	763.2
Gross Domestic Product (GDP)........	99b	545.6	768.6	841.6	986.2	936.3	970.3	946.0	955.3	1,006.0	1,044.5	1,071.6	1,146.7
Net National Income.......................	99e	468.3	574.8	664.3	775.3	742.2	764.2	829.7	....	....	....	....	....
GDP Volume 1978 Prices................	99b.p	208.9	225.3	245.2	280.5	274.0	280.8	278.6	278.1	289.6	297.4	306.3	....
GDP Volume (2000=100)...............	99bvp	75.0	80.9	88.0	100.7	98.3	100.8	100.0	99.8	103.9	106.8	110.0	....
GDP Deflator (2000=100)...............	99bip	76.9	100.5	101.1	103.6	100.6	101.8	100.0	101.2	102.3	103.4	103.0	....
							Millions: Midyear Estimates						
Population.................................	99z	4.38	4.51	4.66	4.83	5.01	5.19	5.36	5.53	5.68	5.84	5.99	6.15

Tonga   866

		1994	1995	1996	1997	1998	1999	2000	2001	2002	2003	2004	2005
Exchange Rates						*Pa'anga per SDR: End of Period*							
Official Rate....................	aa	1.8371	1.8883	1.7438	1.8377	2.2749	2.2066	2.5754	2.7736	3.0299	3.0020	2.9689	2.9439
					Pa'anga per US Dollar: End of Period (ae) Period Average (rf)								
Official Rate....................	ae	1.2584	1.2703	1.2127	1.3620	1.6156	1.6077	1.9767	2.2070	2.2287	2.0202	1.9117	2.0597
Official Rate....................	rf	1.3202	1.2709	1.2320	1.2635	1.4921	1.5991	1.7585	2.1236	2.1952	2.1459	1.9716	1.9430
Fund Position						*Millions of SDRs: End of Period*							
Quota........................	2f.s	5.00	5.00	5.00	5.00	5.00	6.90	6.90	6.90	6.90	6.90	6.90	6.90
SDRs........................	1b.s	.49	.04	.08	.11	.15	.03	.10	.15	.19	.22	.24	.28
Reserve Position in the Fund......	1c.s	1.20	1.21	1.21	1.21	1.22	1.70	1.71	1.71	1.71	1.71	1.71	1.71
Total Fund Cred.&Loans Outstg........	2tl	—	—	—	—	—	—	—	—	—	—	—	—
International Liquidity						*Millions of US Dollars Unless Otherwise Indicated: End of Period*							
Total Reserves minus Gold..............	1l.d	35.54	28.71	30.62	27.49	28.66	24.49	24.64	23.76	25.12	39.77	55.26	46.86
SDRs........................	1b.d	.71	.06	.11	.14	.21	.05	.12	.19	.26	.32	.38	.40
Reserve Position in the Fund..........	1c.d	1.76	1.80	1.74	1.63	1.72	2.33	2.23	2.15	2.33	2.54	2.66	2.45
Foreign Exchange..................	1d.d	33.07	26.85	28.77	25.72	26.72	22.11	22.29	21.42	22.54	36.91	52.23	44.01
Monetary Authorities: Other Liab.....	4..d	.36	.24	.10	.11	.39	.18	.26	.16	.18	.34	1.11	2.75
Deposit Money Banks: Assets..........	7a.d	1.84	1.96	1.39	1.61	4.27	2.89	11.50	10.30	5.07	11.68	6.42	3.69
Liabilities........	7b.d	.94	1.22	.63	4.34	4.86	4.36	6.92	5.06	5.76	10.55	5.12	6.10
Other Banking Insts.: Liabilities........	7f.d	4.33	3.83	3.51	2.94	2.46	2.32	1.49	1.34	1.19	.90	.55	.15
Monetary Authorities						*Thousands of Pa'anga: End of Period*							
Foreign Assets....................	11	41,812	31,493	33,157	32,798	36,311	34,569	25,977	29,709	44,696	56,743	93,377	86,745
Claims on Central Government........	12a	9,516	5,493	5,439	5,439	5,456	5,404	6,380	14,095	17,446	18,162	9,924	16,242
Claims on Deposit Money Banks.....	12e	—	—	—	—	—	—	9,078	5,447	1,816	—	—	—
Claims on Other Banking Insts.........	12f	—	—	—	—	—	—	—	—	—	—	—	—
Reserve Money....................	14	18,368	15,125	21,629	24,300	26,805	28,804	32,437	42,087	50,818	46,047	73,509	62,579
of which: Currency Outside DMBs..	14a	7,346	7,321	6,850	6,471	8,076	9,443	9,966	11,355	12,168	14,322	17,292	20,869
Liabs. of Central Bank: Securities.....	16ac	39,200	29,367	24,893	21,818	15,963	13,471	100	—	—	—	—	—
Foreign Liabilities..................	16c	455	306	122	155	623	295	517	356	412	687	2,129	5,660
Central Government Deposits..........	16d	2,142	1,814	1,577	1,366	6,358	7,126	5,777	6,715	15,149	31,168	29,654	32,663
Capital Accounts..................	17a	2,922	3,000	2,459	1,676	1,146	1,039	1,331	2,147	4,071	5,995	5,628	10,169
Other Items (Net)..................	17r	−11,759	−12,626	−12,084	−11,078	−9,118	−10,764	1,273	−2,054	−6,492	−8,992	−7,619	−8,083
Deposit Money Banks						*Thousands of Pa'anga: End of Period*							
Reserves........................	20	7,488	5,633	14,359	17,127	17,894	20,101	22,383	29,814	38,137	31,025	54,925	38,642
Foreign Assets....................	21	2,314	2,491	1,682	2,189	6,893	4,644	22,733	22,729	11,289	23,602	12,267	7,606
Claims on Central Government........	22a	6,262	9,057	8,970	10,616	10,039	9,632	9,094	9,361	8,215	8,949	9,203	2,008
Claims on Nonfin.Pub.Enterprises..	22c	152	103	497	164	1,551	1,392	3,068	6,111	8,571	12,071	6,899	6,055
Claims on Private Sector..........	22d	47,273	57,191	59,114	68,094	79,720	87,420	102,774	112,835	137,506	154,151	154,902	216,531
Claims on Other Banking Insts.........	22f	3,850	2,450	1,550	2,375	2,000	3,000	3,000	2,000	2,000	—	—	—
Demand Deposits..................	24	16,637	14,674	15,701	16,941	16,429	20,472	23,106	30,389	42,935	47,764	54,554	51,839
Time, Savings,& Fgn.Currency Dep...	25	44,553	48,567	51,483	56,684	67,350	72,854	89,042	98,505	96,094	110,814	123,870	148,869
Foreign Liabilities..................	26c	1,181	1,545	760	5,909	7,850	7,007	13,679	11,171	12,841	21,306	9,796	12,566
Central Government Deposits..........	26d	12,394	11,534	10,037	8,009	6,929	6,974	7,086	4,530	7,927	10,276	10,106	10,613
Credit from Monetary Authorities.....	26g	—	—	—	—	—	—	9,078	5,447	1,816	—	—	—
Liabilities to Other Banking Insts.......	26i	5,225	2,764	4,741	4,399	4,216	5,003	2,604	1,378	4,591	875	1,192	1,257
Capital Accounts..................	27a	30,646	30,746	31,565	30,274	31,312	27,336	29,254	31,194	32,290	36,441	30,799	33,944
Other Items (Net)....................	27r	−43,297	−32,905	−28,115	−21,651	−15,989	−13,457	−10,797	236	7,224	2,322	7,879	11,754
Monetary Survey						*Thousands of Pa'anga: End of Period*							
Foreign Assets (Net)...................	31n	42,490	32,133	33,957	28,923	34,731	31,910	34,514	40,912	42,732	58,352	93,719	76,125
Domestic Credit...................	32	52,517	60,946	63,956	77,313	85,479	92,748	111,453	133,157	150,662	151,889	141,168	197,560
Claims on Central Govt. (Net).......	32an	1,242	1,202	2,795	6,680	2,208	936	2,611	12,211	2,585	−14,333	−20,633	−25,026
Claims on Nonfin.Pub.Enterprises...	32c	152	103	497	164	1,551	1,392	3,068	6,111	8,571	12,071	6,899	6,055
Claims on Private Sector..............	32d	47,273	57,191	59,114	68,094	79,720	87,420	102,774	112,835	137,506	154,151	154,902	216,531
Claims on Other Banking Insts.......	32f	3,850	2,450	1,550	2,375	2,000	3,000	3,000	2,000	2,000	—	—	—
Money............................	34	25,535	21,995	22,826	23,412	24,505	29,915	33,072	41,744	55,103	62,086	71,846	72,708
Quasi-Money.....................	35	44,553	48,567	51,483	56,684	67,350	72,854	89,042	98,505	96,094	110,814	123,870	148,869
Liabs.of Central Bank: Securities......	36ac				939								
Liabilities to Other Banking Insts.......	36i	5,225	2,764	4,741	4,399	4,216	5,003	2,604	1,378	4,591	875	1,192	1,257
Capital Accounts..................	37a	33,568	33,746	34,024	31,950	32,458	28,375	30,585	33,341	36,361	42,436	36,427	44,113
Other Items (Net)....................	37r	−13,874	−13,993	−15,161	−11,148	−8,319	−11,489	−9,336	−900	1,245	−5,970	1,552	6,738
Money plus Quasi-Money..............	35l	70,088	70,562	74,309	80,096	91,855	102,769	122,114	140,249	151,197	172,900	195,716	221,577
Other Banking Institutions						*Thousands of Pa'anga: End of Period*							
Reserves........................	40	6,695	4,290	834	475	1,247	1,734	1,698	1,984	2,068	2,072	1,723	2,063
Claims on Central Government........	42a	2,000	2,000	1,700	1,700	1,700	2,000	1,500	200	200	1,200	8,434	4,730
Claims on Nonfin.Pub.Enterprises.....	42c	3,647	2,937	2,940	1,452	987	834	1,045	885	388	2,383	2,395	1,986
Claims on Private Sector..............	42d	31,176	37,063	38,270	41,669	41,055	31,939	33,247	35,412	40,175	43,870	36,488	39,460
Claims on Deposit Money Banks.....	42e	3,200	100	3,578	3,600	2,800	4,100	1,500	250	3,600	200	6,900	4,533
Savings Deposits..................	45	—	8	70	273	430	630	601	744	1,042	1,342	2,583	3,200
Bonds........................	46ab	9,189	1,823	2,005	3,908	4,604	5,022	5,696	9,133	13,915	17,516	19,730	15,900
Foreign Liabilities..................	46c	5,444	4,863	4,256	4,008	3,976	3,728	2,950	2,950	2,654	1,824	1,047	318
Central Government Deposits..........	46d	—	3,600	3,600	3,600	3,600	2,000	2,400	1,800	3,573	2,944	6,781	6,553
Central Govt. Lending Funds............	46f	15,761	16,155	17,411	16,743	15,950	14,552	13,036	11,395	9,347	8,469	7,549	6,630
Credit from Monetary Authorities.....	46g	—	—	—	—	—	—	—	—	—	—	—	—
Credit from Deposit Money Banks....	46h	—	2,100	1,200	2,200	2,000	2,000	3,000	2,000	2,000	—	—	—
Capital Accounts..................	47a	12,622	13,813	14,806	14,738	10,259	10,525	10,546	11,598	14,170	16,445	18,862	20,344
Other Items (Net)..................	47r	3,702	4,028	3,974	3,426	6,970	2,150	761	−889	−270	1,185	−612	−173

Tonga 866

		1994	1995	1996	1997	1998	1999	2000	2001	2002	2003	2004	2005
Banking Survey						*Thousands of Pa'anga: End of Period*							
Foreign Assets (Net).........................	51n	37,046	27,270	29,701	24,915	30,755	28,182	31,564	37,962	40,078	56,528	92,672	75,807
Domestic Credit...............................	52	85,490	96,896	101,716	116,159	123,621	122,521	141,845	165,854	185,852	196,398	181,704	237,183
Claims on Central Govt. (Net)........	52an	3,242	−398	895	4,780	308	936	1,711	10,611	−788	−16,077	−18,980	−26,849
Claims on Nonfin.Pub.Enterprises...	52c	3,799	3,040	3,437	1,616	2,538	2,226	4,113	6,996	8,959	14,454	9,294	8,041
Claims on Private Sector................	52d	78,449	94,254	97,384	109,763	120,775	119,359	136,021	148,247	177,681	198,021	191,390	255,991
Liquid Liabilities..........................	55l	63,393	66,280	73,545	79,894	91,038	101,665	121,017	139,009	150,171	172,170	196,576	222,714
Bonds..	56ab	9,189	1,823	2,005	3,908	4,604	5,022	5,696	9,133	13,915	17,516	19,730	15,900
Liabs.of Central Bank: Securities......	56ac	—	—	—	939	—	—	—	—	—	—	—	—
Central Govt. Lending Funds............	56f	15,761	16,155	17,411	16,743	15,950	14,552	13,036	11,395	9,347	8,469	7,549	6,630
Capital Accounts............................	57a	46,190	47,559	48,830	46,688	42,717	38,900	41,131	44,939	50,531	58,881	55,289	64,457
Other Items (Net)...........................	57r	−11,997	−7,651	−10,374	−7,098	67	−9,436	−7,471	−661	1,966	−4,110	−4,768	3,289
Money (National Definitions)						*Thousands of Pa'anga: End of Period*							
Reserve Money.............................	19mb	18,368	15,125	21,629	24,300	26,805	28,804	32,437	42,087	50,818	46,047	73,509	62,879
M1..	59ma	23,983	21,995	22,551	23,412	24,505	29,915	32,981	41,575	54,853	61,838	71,694	72,511
Quasi-Money................................	59mab	41,612	46,510	50,419	55,751	66,574	75,364	88,449	98,742	97,136	112,152	122,250	152,069
M2..	59mb	65,595	68,505	72,970	79,163	91,079	105,279	121,430	140,317	151,989	173,990	193,944	224,580
Interest Rates						*Percent Per Annum*							
Deposit Rate.................................	60l	4.64	4.72	5.53	5.57	5.63	5.42	5.36	5.47	5.47	5.47	5.85	5.90
Lending Rate.................................	60p	† 10.36	10.47	10.92	11.15	11.25	11.37	11.34	11.34	11.40	11.34	11.59	11.38
Prices and Labor						*Index Numbers (2000=100): Period Averages*							
Consumer Prices...........................	64	81.7	82.9	85.4	87.2	90.0	94.1	100.0	108.3	119.5	133.4	148.1	160.4
						Number in Thousands: Period Averages							
Labor Force.................................	67d	35	....	34	....	....	....	....	....	....	....	....	....
Intl. Transactions & Positions						*Thousands of Pa'anga Thousands of Pa'anga*							
Exports...	70	18,367	18,443	16,263	13,197	11,711	20,528	15,933	14,545	31,928	37,850	29,859	25,260
Imports, c.i.f.................................	71	91,210	98,034	91,807	92,100	102,490	116,274	122,113	154,304	195,264	200,293	206,520	213,734
Balance of Payments						*Thousands of US Dollars: Minus Sign Indicates Debit*							
Current Account, n.i.e....................	78ald	....	....	....	....	....	....	....	−10,803	−3,319	....	....	....
Goods: Exports f.o.b......................	78aad	....	....	....	....	....	....	....	6,657	18,126	....	....	....
Goods: Imports f.o.b......................	78abd	....	....	....	....	....	....	....	−63,688	−73,373	....	....	....
Trade Balance.............................	78acd	....	....	....	....	....	....	....	−57,031	−55,247	....	....	....
Services: Credit.............................	78add	....	....	....	....	....	....	....	19,584	22,628	....	....	....
Services: Debit..............................	78aed	....	....	....	....	....	....	....	−27,556	−31,937	....	....	....
Balance on Goods & Services.......	78afd	....	....	....	....	....	....	....	−65,004	−64,555	....	....	....
Income: Credit..............................	78agd	....	....	....	....	....	....	....	5,675	6,611	....	....	....
Income: Debit...............................	78ahd	....	....	....	....	....	....	....	−2,266	−3,791	....	....	....
Balance on Gds, Serv. & Inc.........	78aid	....	....	....	....	....	....	....	−61,595	−61,735	....	....	....
Current Transfers, n.i.e.: Credit......	78ajd	....	....	....	....	....	....	....	62,507	74,536	....	....	....
Current Transfers: Debit.................	78akd	....	....	....	....	....	....	....	−11,716	−16,120	....	....	....
Capital Account, n.i.e....................	78bcd	....	....	....	....	....	....	....	9,606	13,412	....	....	....
Capital Account, n.i.e.: Credit........	78bad	....	....	....	....	....	....	....	11,727	14,075	....	....	....
Capital Account: Debit...................	78bbd	....	....	....	....	....	....	....	−2,120	−663	....	....	....
Financial Account, n.i.e.................	78bjd	....	....	....	....	....	....	....	822	−3,174	....	....	....
Direct Investment Abroad..............	78bdd	....	....	....	....	....	....	....	....	....	....	....	....
Dir. Invest. in Rep. Econ., n.i.e......	78bed	....	....	....	....	....	....	....	....	....	....	....	....
Portfolio Investment Assets...........	78bfd	....	....	....	....	....	....	....	....	....	....	....	....
Equity Securities........................	78bkd	....	....	....	....	....	....	....	....	....	....	....	....
Debt Securities..........................	78bld	....	....	....	....	....	....	....	....	....	....	....	....
Portfolio Investment Liab., n.i.e......	78bgd	....	....	....	....	....	....	....	....	....	....	....	....
Equity Securities........................	78bmd	....	....	....	....	....	....	....	....	....	....	....	....
Debt Securities..........................	78bnd	....	....	....	....	....	....	....	....	....	....	....	....
Financial Derivatives Assets...........	78bwd	....	....	....	....	....	....	....	....	....	....	....	....
Financial Derivatives Liabilities.......	78bxd	....	....	....	....	....	....	....	....	....	....	....	....
Other Investment Assets................	78bhd	....	....	....	....	....	....	....	....	....	....	....	....
Monetary Authorities..................	78bod	....	....	....	....	....	....	....	....	....	....	....	....
General Government..................	78bpd	....	....	....	....	....	....	....	....	....	....	....	....
Banks..	78bqd	....	....	....	....	....	....	....	....	....	....	....	....
Other Sectors............................	78brd	....	....	....	....	....	....	....	....	....	....	....	....
Other Investment Liab., n.i.e.........	78bid	....	....	....	....	....	....	....	822	−3,174	....	....	....
Monetary Authorities..................	78bsd	....	....	....	....	....	....	....	—	—	....	....	....
General Government..................	78btd	....	....	....	....	....	....	....	....	....	....	....	....
Banks..	78bud	....	....	....	....	....	....	....	....	....	....	....	....
Other Sectors............................	78bvd	....	....	....	....	....	....	....	....	....	....	....	....
Net Errors and Omissions..............	78cad	....	....	....	....	....	....	....	2,093	−47	....	....	....
Overall Balance............................	78cbd	....	....	....	....	....	....	....	1,718	6,872	....	....	....
Reserves and Related Items............	79dad	....	....	....	....	....	....	....	−1,718	−6,872	....	....	....
Reserve Assets.............................	79dbd	....	....	....	....	....	....	....	−1,718	−6,872	....	....	....
Use of Fund Credit and Loans........	79dcd	....	....	....	....	....	....	....	—	—	....	....	....
Exceptional Financing....................	79ded	....	....	....	....	....	....	....	....	....	....	....	....
National Accounts						*Millions of Pa'anga: Year Ending June 30*							
Gross Domestic Product (GDP)........	99b	204.0	206.0	219.0	212.0	225.0	245.0	259.0	276.0	311.0	349.0	372.0	....
GDP Volume (1990=100)................	99bvp	106.7	....	....	....	....	....	....	....	....	....	....	....
GDP Deflator (1990=100)...............	99bip	120.7	....	....	....	....	....	....	....	....	....	....	....
						Millions: Midyear Estimates							
Population...............................	99z	.10	.10	.10	.10	.10	.10	.10	.10	.10	.10	.10	.10

Trinidad and Tobago 369

		1994	1995	1996	1997	1998	1999	2000	2001	2002	2003	2004	2005
Exchange Rates						*TT Dollars per SDR: End of Period*							
Market Rate	aa	8.6616	8.9146	8.9074	8.5001	9.2881	8.6467	8.2078	7.9051	8.5648	9.3615	9.7838	9.0191
					TT Dollars per US Dollar: End of Period (ae) Period Average (rf)								
Market Rate	ae	5.9332	5.9971	6.1945	6.2999	6.5965	6.2999	6.2996	6.2902	6.2999	6.2999	6.2999	6.3103
Market Rate	rf	5.9249	5.9478	6.0051	6.2517	6.2983	6.2989	6.2998	6.2332	6.2487	6.2951	6.2990	6.2996
					Index Numbers (2000=100): Period Averages								
Nominal Effective Exchange Rate	nec	95.20	93.67	96.43	95.11	96.39	97.72	100.00	103.08	103.87	101.47	99.75	99.19
Real Effective Exchange Rate	rec	96.61	94.24	94.74	92.65	96.20	97.81	100.00	105.56	108.24	106.36	105.05	107.83
Fund Position						*Millions of SDRs: End of Period*							
Quota	2f.s	246.8	246.8	246.8	246.8	246.8	335.6	335.6	335.6	335.6	335.6	335.6	335.6
SDRs	1b.s	.1	.1	—	.1	.1	—	.1	.2	.3	.7	1.7	2.6
Reserve Position in the Fund	1c.s	—	—	—	—	—	—	—	24.6	76.4	129.3	111.1	49.9
of which: Outstg.Fund Borrowing	2c	—	—	—	—	—	—	—	—	—	—	—	—
Total Fund Cred.&Loans Outstg	2tl	62.4	33.8	16.5	3.1	—	—	—	—	—	—	—	—
International Liquidity					*Millions of US Dollars Unless Otherwise Indicated: End of Period*								
Total Reserves minus Gold	1l.d	352.4	358.2	543.9	706.4	783.1	945.4	1,386.3	1,907.1	2,027.7	2,451.1	3,168.2	4,856.4
SDRs	1b.d	.1	.2	—	.1	.1	—	.1	.2	.4	1.1	2.7	3.7
Reserve Position in the Fund	1c.d	—	—	—	—	—	—	—	30.9	103.8	192.2	172.5	71.3
Foreign Exchange	1d.d	352.3	358.0	543.8	706.2	783.0	945.4	1,386.2	1,876.0	1,923.5	2,257.8	2,993.0	4,781.4
Gold (Million Fine Troy Ounces)	1ad	.054	.054	.054	.058	.059	.060	.060	.061	.061	.061	.061	.061
Gold (National Valuation)	1and	1.4	1.4	1.3	16.8	16.1	17.4	16.4	16.8	20.9	25.5	26.8	31.4
Monetary Authorities: Other Liab	4..d	55.0	33.7	32.2	29.3	31.8	37.7	32.3	38.5	37.9	38.2	43.5	38.4
Deposit Money Banks: Assets	7a.d	294.1	216.4	287.3	265.2	298.4	381.7	456.2	538.3	602.5	753.6	838.9	993.6
Liabilities	7b.d	50.5	98.7	137.6	154.1	182.2	239.8	256.0	549.9	596.3	962.9	673.8	843.9
Other Banking Insts.: Assets	7e.d	8.5	11.7	29.2	76.7	73.4	79.8	133.9	243.6	382.6	525.8	460.0	713.9
Liabilities	7f.d	62.4	62.2	58.2	30.2	41.2	37.6	58.2	115.5	221.8	268.8	135.0	242.5
Monetary Authorities						*Millions of TT Dollars: End of Period*							
Foreign Assets	11	4,602.3	4,577.1	† 4,764.4	5,641.3	6,210.7	7,457.7	10,196.3	13,303.6	14,025.3	16,523.0	20,917.3	34,165.3
Claims on Central Government	12a	1,514.0	724.1	† 93.6	752.4	709.4	899.8	765.4	961.3	1,104.7	1,129.9	925.7	2,145.1
Claims on Nonfin.Pub.Enterprises	12c	28.5	361.3	† 346.6	345.0	336.0	334.0	328.7	310.3	300.1	280.0	245.4	234.8
Claims on Private Sector	12d	—	—	† 52.7	48.4	44.9	41.0	36.5	27.8	23.9	21.0	18.0	15.2
Claims on Deposit Money Banks	12e	507.2	384.7	† 807.2	802.6	807.2	803.4	789.0	775.7	759.3	731.8	723.6	716.0
Claims on Other Banking Insts	12f	18.7	18.7	† .5	.5	2.7	.6	.6	.6	.6	.1	—	—
Claims on Nonbank Financial Insts	12g	—	—	† 56.9	48.1	36.7	31.8	23.4	15.1	6.4	6.1	6.6	7.3
Reserve Money	14	3,269.7	3,247.8	† 3,538.0	4,106.4	4,963.7	5,146.5	5,305.4	5,872.7	5,788.6	6,156.4	5,959.5	9,172.5
of which: Currency Outside DMBs	14a	744.6	832.8	† 909.8	1,063.0	1,046.8	1,292.4	1,271.0	1,373.5	1,501.8	1,708.6	1,957.4	2,425.4
Foreign Liabilities	16c	867.3	503.1	† 346.3	211.2	209.9	237.6	203.8	242.1	238.5	240.6	274.2	242.3
Central Government Deposits	16d	780.1	579.3	† 1,377.1	2,516.0	1,484.6	2,491.6	4,885.9	7,190.2	7,669.8	9,359.8	13,873.2	22,836.0
Capital Accounts	17a	433.4	469.7	† 548.2	638.9	754.2	752.5	832.9	838.7	734.1	699.7	690.9	735.6
Other Items (Net)	17r	1,320.3	1,266.0	† 312.3	165.8	735.6	940.0	912.0	1,250.7	1,789.4	2,235.3	2,039.0	4,297.3
Deposit Money Banks						*Millions of TT Dollars: End of Period*							
Reserves	20	2,320.3	2,245.4	† 2,370.0	2,772.7	3,058.6	3,021.7	3,214.3	3,935.6	3,534.6	3,541.4	3,352.9	4,757.5
Foreign Assets	21	1,745.0	1,297.7	† 1,779.4	1,671.0	1,968.2	2,404.5	2,874.0	3,386.3	3,795.9	4,747.9	5,285.2	6,270.2
Claims on Central Government	22a	899.4	1,729.1	† 2,084.6	3,823.1	2,293.1	2,728.1	2,411.9	3,411.6	3,566.4	3,616.4	4,067.8	4,996.3
Claims on Local Government	22b	1.9	1.9	† —	54.4	2.1	16.4	83.0	65.7	19.2	1.4	5.8	4.5
Claims on Nonfin.Pub.Enterprises	22c	377.9	801.3	† 779.5	773.8	904.0	562.1	265.7	802.7	1,149.5	1,030.7	797.5	2,060.9
Claims on Private Sector	22d	7,625.6	8,739.4	† 9,741.0	11,835.3	13,433.3	14,498.6	16,353.1	16,922.7	17,645.6	18,073.5	21,920.0	27,821.5
Claims on Other Banking Insts	22f	—	—	† 252.1	238.0	231.0	207.7	273.0	571.7	202.8	841.0	771.5	1,416.8
Claims on Nonbank Financial Insts	22g	—	—	† 1,711.1	616.6	111.2	128.0	220.7	565.0	1,255.1	1,427.2	1,275.4	632.4
Demand Deposits	24	2,798.8	2,921.0	† 2,524.6	3,130.4	2,819.7	3,182.0	3,722.4	4,829.4	5,620.0	5,108.0	5,795.3	9,358.6
Time, Savings,& Fgn.Currency Dep	25	8,651.1	8,966.8	† 12,194.9	13,215.0	15,516.0	15,790.9	17,905.9	18,432.8	18,792.7	18,712.4	21,785.1	25,746.9
Foreign Liabilities	26c	299.8	591.7	† 852.3	970.5	1,201.9	1,510.5	1,612.4	3,459.1	3,756.8	6,066.1	4,244.9	5,325.1
Central Government Deposits	26d	102.1	267.8	† 364.6	204.9	203.2	281.9	231.4	1,011.3	452.6	568.7	1,268.3	977.5
Credit from Monetary Authorities	26g	507.1	384.9	† 395.3	388.4	386.9	385.1	383.3	381.6	379.8	382.2	380.7	379.7
Liabilities to Other Banking Insts	26i	—	—	† 455.7	312.8	681.7	410.6	333.5	431.8	447.3	520.8	1,113.5	1,221.4
Capital Accounts	27a	1,291.0	1,389.4	† 1,754.6	2,278.3	2,529.1	2,990.9	3,813.4	4,293.2	4,775.2	5,454.2	6,680.3	6,873.3
Other Items (Net)	27r	−679.8	293.2	† 175.7	1,284.5	−1,337.0	−984.8	−2,306.6	−3,177.9	−3,055.4	−3,532.9	−3,792.1	−1,922.3
Monetary Survey						*Millions of TT Dollars: End of Period*							
Foreign Assets (Net)	31n	5,180.3	4,780.0	† 5,345.2	6,130.6	6,767.1	8,114.0	11,254.1	12,988.7	13,825.9	14,964.2	21,683.5	34,868.1
Domestic Credit	32	9,583.8	11,528.7	† 13,376.9	15,814.6	16,417.0	16,674.6	15,644.8	15,452.9	17,151.8	16,498.6	14,892.2	15,521.4
Claims on Central Govt. (Net)	32an	1,531.2	1,606.1	† 436.5	1,854.5	1,315.1	854.3	−1,940.0	−3,828.6	−3,451.3	−5,182.3	−10,148.1	−16,672.0
Claims on Local Government	32b	1.9	1.9	† —	54.4	2.1	16.4	83.0	65.7	19.2	1.4	5.8	4.5
Claims on Nonfin.Pub.Enterprises	32c	406.4	1,162.6	† 1,126.1	1,118.9	1,240.0	896.1	594.5	1,113.0	1,449.6	1,310.6	1,043.0	2,295.7
Claims on Private Sector	32d	7,625.6	8,739.4	† 9,793.7	11,883.6	13,478.2	14,539.6	16,389.6	16,950.5	17,669.5	18,094.5	21,938.0	27,836.7
Claims on Other Banking Insts	32f	18.7	18.7	† 252.6	238.5	233.7	208.4	273.6	572.3	203.4	841.1	771.5	1,416.8
Claims on Nonbank Financial Inst	32g	—	—	† 1,768.0	664.8	147.9	159.8	244.2	580.0	1,261.5	1,433.3	1,282.0	639.7
Money	34	3,748.2	3,923.4	† 3,685.0	4,464.1	4,724.8	5,306.8	5,658.0	6,766.6	7,834.2	7,723.0	8,375.4	13,292.6
Quasi-Money	35	8,651.1	8,966.8	† 12,194.9	13,215.0	15,516.0	15,790.9	17,905.9	18,432.8	18,792.7	18,712.4	21,785.1	25,746.9
Liabilities to Other Banking Insts	36i	—	—	† 455.7	312.8	681.7	410.6	333.5	431.8	447.3	520.8	1,113.5	1,221.4
Capital Accounts	37a	1,724.4	1,859.1	† 2,302.8	2,917.2	3,283.3	3,743.4	4,646.3	5,131.9	5,509.3	6,153.9	7,371.2	7,608.9
Other Items (Net)	37r	640.4	1,559.4	† 83.7	1,036.1	−1,021.8	−463.1	−1,644.8	−2,321.4	−1,605.8	−1,647.2	−2,069.6	2,519.7
Money plus Quasi-Money	35l	12,399.3	12,890.2	† 15,880.0	17,679.0	20,240.8	21,097.8	23,563.9	25,199.3	26,626.9	26,435.3	30,160.5	39,039.5

		1994	1995	1996	1997	1998	1999	2000	2001	2002	2003	2004	2005
Other Banking Institutions													
Other Banklike Institutions					*Millions of TT Dollars: End of Period*								
Reserves.............................	40	148.0	171.5	† 241.5	272.7	409.8	485.3	534.1	513.2	510.2	661.5	570.7	521.0
Foreign Assets......................	41	50.3	70.4	† 181.1	483.1	484.4	502.6	843.5	1,532.1	2,410.4	3,312.5	2,897.8	4,505.1
Claims on Central Government........	42a	588.7	965.4	† 1,190.0	1,437.1	1,075.4	1,098.9	1,471.6	672.5	925.5	1,513.7	1,650.4	1,379.3
Claims on Local Government...........	42b	—	—	† —	4.1	4.7	5.1	—	—	—	15.0	1.0	22.5
Claims on Nonfin.Pub.Enterprises.....	42c	65.5	33.0	† 147.5	137.0	80.3	196.2	291.2	562.1	419.0	550.6	452.1	398.1
Claims on Private Sector..............	42d	3,341.6	3,982.3	† 2,770.0	3,141.9	3,358.5	3,903.7	4,697.1	4,878.9	5,524.5	6,174.4	5,252.7	4,824.5
Claims on Deposit Money Banks......	42e	325.2	335.6	† 786.2	645.4	1,195.5	1,418.4	1,824.6	1,787.6	2,046.0	2,150.2	3,327.7	3,928.3
Claims on Nonbank Financial Insts....	42g	—	—	† 47.4	37.8	201.3	526.1	627.8	571.1	479.4	469.6	681.1	1,207.0
Time, Savings,& Fgn.Currency Dep...	45	2,894.1	3,138.9	† 2,993.9	3,180.3	4,017.2	4,792.5	4,746.6	5,704.3	4,858.3	5,177.1	6,208.4	5,340.4
Foreign Liabilities....................	46c	1.4	.3	† 169.5	152.5	238.0	207.3	341.5	705.6	1,380.4	1,681.0	842.2	1,524.0
Central Government Deposits...........	46d	—	—	† 47.8	100.7	33.6	34.8	87.8	20.3	79.0	131.1	8.8	1.8
Credit from Monetary Authorities.....	46g	—	—	† 25.3	44.6	52.7	49.9	42.6	34.7	23.6	17.0	9.7	3.8
Credit from Deposit Money Banks....	46h	30.3	48.5	† 92.1	249.0	70.0	670.3	530.1	840.8	633.8	453.0	433.9	208.5
Capital Accounts.....................	47a	512.2	690.3	† 666.3	764.7	1,049.3	1,294.1	1,658.2	2,015.6	2,482.6	3,145.1	4,179.6	4,440.3
Other Items (Net)....................	47r	1,081.3	1,680.2	† 1,368.9	1,667.1	1,349.1	1,087.5	2,883.1	1,196.2	2,857.2	4,243.3	3,151.0	5,267.0
Development Banks					*Millions of TT Dollars: End of Period*								
Reserves.............................	40..n	—	—	—	—	—	—	—	7.9	18.7	—	—	—
Claims on Central Government........	42a.n	27.8	33.7	—	—	—	—	—	—	—	—	—	—
Claims on Private Sector..............	42d.n	1,011.9	1,031.3	845.5	852.8	927.5	1,027.8	1,252.1	1,221.9	1,282.6	1,786.9	2,028.0	2,132.7
Claims on Deposit Money Banks......	42e.n	110.6	88.6	48.0	78.2	101.3	8.5	9.6	4.9	2.4	10.4	28.7	2.5
Foreign Liabilities....................	46c.n	368.9	373.0	190.9	37.9	33.6	29.4	25.3	21.0	16.8	12.6	8.4	6.3
Central Government Deposits...........	46d.n	517.4	500.8	446.8	440.3	430.7	426.9	405.2	519.3	505.4	500.7	476.1	855.7
Credit from Dep. Money Banks........	46h.n	28.0	40.2	16.0	30.0	17.3	18.4	19.7	21.4	23.1	44.9	39.7	43.8
Capital Accounts.....................	47a.n	282.4	275.0	204.4	356.0	377.7	404.0	443.1	299.4	341.6	402.6	444.7	464.1
Other Items (Net).....................	47r.n	−46.4	−35.4	35.4	66.8	169.5	157.6	368.3	373.7	416.8	836.6	1,087.7	765.4
Banking Survey					*Millions of TT Dollars: End of Period*								
Foreign Assets (Net)...................	51n	4,860.3	4,477.1	† 5,165.9	6,423.3	6,979.8	8,380.0	11,730.9	13,794.2	14,839.1	16,583.1	23,730.6	37,843.0
Domestic Credit.......................	52	14,083.2	17,054.9	† 17,630.1	20,645.8	21,366.6	22,762.3	23,217.9	22,247.5	24,995.0	25,536.0	23,701.1	23,211.2
Claims on Central Govt. (Net)........	52an	1,630.3	2,104.4	† 1,131.9	2,750.6	1,926.2	1,491.5	−961.4	−3,695.7	−3,110.2	−4,300.3	−8,982.5	−16,150.2
Claims on Local Government........	52b	1.9	1.9	† —	58.6	6.8	21.5	83.0	65.7	19.2	16.4	6.8	26.9
Claims on Nonfin.Pub.Enterprises...	52c	471.9	1,195.6	† 1,273.7	1,255.8	1,320.3	1,092.3	885.7	1,675.1	1,868.6	1,861.2	1,495.1	2,693.8
Claims on Private Sector............	52d	11,979.1	13,753.0	† 13,409.1	15,878.3	17,764.2	19,471.1	22,338.8	23,051.3	24,476.6	26,055.8	29,218.6	34,793.9
Claims on Nonbank Financial Inst...	52g	—	—	† 1,815.4	702.6	349.2	685.9	871.9	1,151.1	1,740.9	1,902.9	1,963.1	1,846.7
Liquid Liabilities......................	55l	15,145.4	15,857.6	† 18,632.3	20,586.7	23,848.2	25,404.9	27,776.4	30,382.5	30,956.4	30,950.9	35,798.2	43,858.9
Capital Accounts.....................	57a	2,519.0	2,824.4	† 3,173.5	4,038.0	4,710.3	5,441.5	6,747.7	7,446.9	8,333.5	9,701.6	11,995.5	12,513.3
Other Items (Net).....................	57r	1,279.1	2,850.0	† 990.2	2,444.5	−212.0	295.8	424.8	−1,787.7	544.3	1,466.6	−361.9	4,681.9
Interest Rates					*Percent Per Annum*								
Bank Rate (End of Period)...............	60	13.00	13.00	13.00	13.00	13.00	13.00	13.00	13.00	7.25	7.00	7.00	8.00
Treasury Bill Rate.............................	60c	10.00	8.41	10.44	9.83	11.93	10.40	10.56	8.55	4.83	4.71	4.77	4.86
Savings Rate...................................	60k	2.69	2.50	2.52	2.50	2.83	2.81	2.96	3.40	2.30	1.97	1.67	1.38
Deposit Rate.................................	60l	6.91	....	....	6.91	7.95	8.51	8.15	7.66	4.76	2.91	2.79	2.20
Deposit Rate (Foreign Currency)......	60l.f	....	....	....	6.35	6.69	6.41	6.74	7.07	4.13	2.62	2.15	2.77
Lending Rate.................................	60p	15.98	15.17	15.79	15.33	17.33	17.04	16.50	15.67	12.48	11.17	9.31	9.10
Prices, Production, Labor					*Index Numbers (2000=100): Period Averages*								
Share Prices.................................	62	18.8	26.2	35.0	53.0	91.7	87.4	100.0	93.2	105.0	128.8	198.6	242.9
Producer Prices.............................	63	88.1	91.2	93.9	95.7	97.1	98.7	100.0	100.9	101.5	102.4	106.0	108.4
Consumer Prices............................	64	78.4	82.5	85.3	88.4	93.4	96.6	100.0	† 105.5	109.9	114.1	118.3	126.5
Wages: Avg Weekly Earn.('90=100).	65	109.9	....	....	....	....	....	....	....	....	....	....	....
Industrial Production........................	66	† 63.6	68.3	72.2	76.9	85.6	94.9	100.0	111.5	128.3	140.4	148.9	164.3
Crude Petroleum Production............	66aa	109.5	109.2	108.0	103.5	102.8	104.6	100.0	94.9	109.5	112.4	103.0	120.7
Total Employment...........................	67	91.8	† 85.7	88.3	91.4	95.2	97.2	100.0	102.1	104.3	106.1	111.7	114.0
					Number in Thousands: Period Averages								
Labor Force...................................	67d	510	521	530	541	559	563	573	576	586	597	613	624
Employment..................................	67e	416	432	444	460	479	489	503	514	525	534	562	574
Unemployment..............................	67c	94	89	86	81	79	74	70	62	61	62	51	50
Unemployment Rate (%).................	67r	18.4	17.2	16.3	15.0	14.2	13.2	12.2	10.8	10.4	10.5	8.4	8.0
Intl. Transactions & Positions					*Millions of TT Dollars*								
Exports.......................................	70	11,061.8	14,601.8	15,012.7	15,891.8	14,221.6	17,662.1	26,925.3	26,678.2	24,244.9	32,596.0	40,146.9	53,395.1
Imports, c.i.f.................................	71	6,718.9	10,194.5	12,874.9	18,692.5	18,888.6	17,265.3	20,839.7	22,246.4	22,764.0	24,500.5	30,600.6	31,812.8

Trinidad and Tobago   369

		1994	1995	1996	1997	1998	1999	2000	2001	2002	2003	2004	2005
Balance of Payments		*Millions of US Dollars: Minus Sign Indicates Debit*											
Current Account, n.i.e.	78ald	217.8	293.8	105.1	−613.6	−643.5	30.6	544.3	416.0	76.4	984.7	....	....
Goods: Exports f.o.b.	78aad	1,777.6	2,456.1	2,354.1	2,448.0	2,258.0	2,815.8	4,290.3	4,304.2	3,920.0	5,204.9	....	....
Goods: Imports f.o.b.	78abd	−1,036.6	−1,868.5	−1,971.6	−2,976.6	−2,998.9	−2,752.2	−3,321.5	−3,586.1	−3,682.3	−3,911.7	....	....
Trade Balance	78acd	741.1	587.7	382.4	−528.6	−740.8	63.6	968.8	718.1	237.7	1,293.2		
Services: Credit	78add	326.6	342.6	461.2	546.5	671.7	603.2	553.8	573.8	637.0	685.2		
Services: Debit	78aed	−438.1	−241.9	−217.5	−254.1	−255.4	−274.0	−387.7	−370.0	−373.0	−371.4		
Balance on Goods & Services	78afd	629.5	688.4	626.2	−236.2	−324.5	392.8	1,134.9	921.9	501.7	1,607.0		
Income: Credit	78agd	56.7	76.6	39.1	63.8	64.0	68.3	80.9	108.7	63.7	78.2		
Income: Debit	78ahd	−468.7	−466.7	−553.1	−445.0	−405.3	−468.2	−709.4	−648.0	−543.5	−759.1		
Balance on Gds, Serv. & Inc.	78aid	217.5	298.3	112.2	−617.4	−665.8	−7.1	506.4	382.6	21.9	926.1		
Current Transfers, n.i.e.: Credit	78ajd	28.3	34.0	34.2	37.0	58.4	68.9	63.9	64.0	96.2	100.8		
Current Transfers: Debit	78akd	−27.9	−38.5	−41.3	−33.2	−36.2	−31.2	−26.0	−30.6	−41.7	−42.2		
Capital Account, n.i.e.	78bcd	−6.4	−11.9	....	....	....	....	....	....	....	....		
Capital Account, n.i.e.: Credit	78bad	1.1	1.1	....	....	....	....	....	....	....	....		
Capital Account: Debit	78bbd	−7.5	−13.0	....	....	....	....	....	....	....	....		
Financial Account, n.i.e.	78bjd	−32.2	−214.7	43.0	697.2	471.5	38.3	173.7	321.5	397.3	34.4		
Direct Investment Abroad	78bdd	—	—	....	....	....	−264.1	−25.2	−150.0	−106.4	225.2		
Dir. Invest. in Rep. Econ., n.i.e.	78bed	516.2	298.9	355.4	999.3	729.8	643.3	679.5	834.9	790.7	808.3		
Portfolio Investment Assets	78bfd	—	−7.9	—	—	−.4	−177.5	−30.0	−206.2	−70.1	−509.2		
Equity Securities	78bkd	—	−7.9	—	—	−.4	....	....	....	....	....		
Debt Securities	78bld	—					−177.5	−30.0	−206.2	−70.1	−509.2		
Portfolio Investment Liab., n.i.e.	78bgd	—	16.7	....	....	....	....	....	....	....	....		
Equity Securities	78bmd	—	16.7	....	....	....	....	....	....	....	....		
Debt Securities	78bnd	—	....	....	....	....	....	....	....	....	....		
Financial Derivatives Assets	78bwd	....	....	....	....	....	....						
Financial Derivatives Liabilities	78bxd	....	....	....	....	....	....						
Other Investment Assets	78bhd	−233.5	−57.3	3.0	32.6	1.0	512.3	397.7	285.0	−316.3	−256.6		
Monetary Authorities	78bod	—	—	....	....	....	295.2	383.6	26.5	17.8	26.2		
General Government	78bpd	−56.1	32.4	3.0	32.6	1.0	—	2.8	—	1.3	49.0		
Banks	78bqd	−109.3	−23.7	....	....	....	73.7	—	257.1	−335.4	−331.8		
Other Sectors	78brd	−68.2	−66.0	....	....	....	143.4	11.3	1.4	—	—		
Other Investment Liab., n.i.e.	78bid	−314.9	−465.1	−315.4	−334.7	−258.8	−675.7	−848.3	−442.2	99.4	−233.3		
Monetary Authorities	78bsd	—	—	—	—	−1.4	−170.8	−268.7	−61.2	—	—		
General Government	78btd	−7.2	−116.8	47.3	−245.4	−104.7	−4.9	−63.8	−14.7	—	—		
Banks	78bud	−10.2	−51.3	−27.3	−21.9	−49.6	—	−86.1	—	256.1	425.7		
Other Sectors	78bvd	−297.4	−297.0	−335.4	−67.4	−103.2	−500.0	−429.7	−366.3	−156.7	−659.0		
Net Errors and Omissions	78cad	6.3	16.5	90.0	110.0	252.2	93.2	−276.9	−235.3	−358.0	−610.3		
Overall Balance	78cbd	185.5	83.7	238.1	193.6	80.2	162.1	441.1	502.2	115.7	408.8		
Reserves and Related Items	79dad	−185.5	−83.7	−238.1	−193.6	−80.2	−162.1	−441.1	−502.2	−115.7	−408.8		
Reserve Assets	79dbd	−113.6	−40.1	−213.0	−175.3	−76.0	−162.1	−441.1	−502.2	−115.7	−408.8		
Use of Fund Credit and Loans	79dcd	−71.9	−43.6	−25.1	−18.4	−4.2	—	—	—	—	—		
Exceptional Financing	79ded	—	....	....	....	....	....	....	....	....	....		
Government Finance		*Millions of TT Dollars: Year Ending December 31*											
Deficit (-) or Surplus	80	117.5	62.5	....	....	....	....	....	....	....	....		
Revenue	81	7,905.1	8,847.3	....	....	....	....	....	....	....	....		
Grants Received	81z	36.0	51.6	....	....	....	....	....	....	....	....		
Expenditure	82	7,826.9	8,917.9	....	....	....	....	....	....	....	....		
Lending Minus Repayments	83	−3.3	−81.5	....	....	....	....	....	....	....	....		
Financing													
Domestic	84a	218.1	−878.7	....	....	....	....	....	....	....	....		
Foreign	85a	−335.6	816.2	....	....	....	....	....	....	....	....		
National Accounts		*Millions of TT Dollars*											
Househ.Cons.Expend.,incl.NPISHs	96f	15,196	15,479	17,131	20,702	21,911	25,106	29,357	30,856	33,403	34,592	37,160	....
Government Consumption Expend	91f	4,432	5,029	5,473	5,519	5,472	6,301	6,141	7,548	8,020	9,574	9,683	....
Gross Fixed Capital Formation	93e	5,799	5,932	7,984	10,494	11,945	8,833	8,575	10,525	....	....	....	
Changes in Inventories	93i	123	655	412	308	762	178	171	171	....	....	....	
Exports of Goods and Services	90c	13,504	17,042	17,778	19,306	18,453	21,437	30,397	30,427	28,303	36,892	44,484	....
Imports of Goods and Services (-)	98c	9,742	12,440	14,191	20,457	20,478	18,966	23,269	24,520	25,186	26,797	32,399	....
Gross Domestic Product (GDP)	99b	29,312	31,697	34,587	35,871	38,065	42,889	51,371	55,007	55,366	66,168	71,878	90,455
Net Primary Income from Abroad	98.n	−2,595	−2,916	−3,136	−2,490	−2,527	−2,516	−3,950	−3,350	−3,030	−4,294	−3,073	....
Gross National Income (GNI)	99a	26,717	28,781	31,451	33,381	35,898	40,373	47,421	51,657	52,384	61,874	68,805	....
Consumption of Fixed Capital	99cf	3,046	2,839	3,761	3,885	4,310	5,237	5,511	5,823	....	....	....	
GDP Volume 1985 Prices	99b.p	16,630	17,288	....	....	....	....	....	....	....	....		
GDP Volume 2000 Prices	99b.p	....	35,694	38,208	41,145	44,486	48,055	51,371	53,512	57,178	64,394	68,505	73,300
GDP Volume (2000=100)	99bvp	66.8	† 69.5	74.4	80.1	86.6	93.5	100.0	104.2	111.3	125.4	133.4	142.7
GDP Deflator (2000=100)	99bip	85.4	88.8	90.5	87.2	85.6	89.2	100.0	102.8	96.8	102.8	104.9	123.4
		Millions: Midyear Estimates											
Population	99z	1.25	1.26	1.27	1.27	1.28	1.28	1.28	1.29	1.29	1.30	1.30	1.31

		1994	1995	1996	1997	1998	1999	2000	2001	2002	2003	2004	2005
Exchange Rates						*Dinars per SDR: End of Period*							
Market Rate	aa	1.4470	1.4134	1.4358	1.5483	1.5502	1.7191	1.8049	1.8453	1.8137	1.7955	1.8627	1.9487
						Dinars per US Dollar: End of Period (ae) Period Average (rf)							
Market Rate	ae	.9912	.9508	.9985	1.1475	1.1010	1.2525	1.3853	1.4683	1.3341	1.2083	1.1994	1.3634
Market Rate	rf	1.0116	.9458	.9734	1.1059	1.1387	1.1862	1.3707	1.4387	1.4217	1.2885	1.2455	1.2974
						Index Numbers (2000=100): Period Averages							
Nominal Effective Exchange Rate	nec	103.22	103.59	103.43	102.20	101.56	101.74	100.00	98.31	97.62	92.37	88.00	84.10
Real Effective Exchange Rate	rec	98.38	100.40	100.54	100.22	100.42	101.46	100.00	97.65	97.44	92.53	89.35	85.31
Fund Position						*Millions of SDRs: End of Period*							
Quota	2f.s	206.0	206.0	206.0	206.0	206.0	286.5	286.5	286.5	286.5	286.5	286.5	286.5
SDRs	1b.s	1.8	4.7	11.1	12.1	2.1	19.3	3.0	1.3	2.0	1.7	6.0	1.5
Reserve Position in the Fund	1c.s	—	—	—	—	—	20.2	20.2	20.2	20.2	20.2	20.2	20.2
Total Fund Cred.&Loans Outstg.	2tl	207.3	197.1	165.0	128.4	91.8	55.2	24.7					
International Liquidity						*Millions of US Dollars Unless Otherwise Indicated: End of Period*							
Total Reserves minus Gold	1l.d	1,461.5	1,605.3	1,897.6	1,978.1	1,850.1	2,261.5	1,811.0	1,989.2	2,290.3	2,945.4	3,935.7	4,372.2
SDRs	1b.d	2.7	7.0	15.9	16.3	2.9	26.5	3.9	1.7	2.7	2.5	9.3	2.2
Reserve Position in the Fund	1c.d	.1	.1	.1	.1	.1	27.7	26.3	25.3	27.4	30.0	31.4	28.9
Foreign Exchange	1d.d	1,458.8	1,598.2	1,881.7	1,961.7	1,847.1	2,207.3	1,780.9	1,962.2	2,260.2	2,912.9	3,895.0	4,341.1
Gold (Million Fine Troy Ounces)	1ad	.216	.217	.217	.217	.217	.217	.220	.218	.218	.218	.218	.218
Gold (National Valuation)	1and	4.4	4.8	4.4	3.8	4.0	3.5	3.2	3.0	3.3	3.6	3.7	3.2
Deposit Money Banks: Assets	7a.d	536.9	451.6	569.5	607.8	643.6	621.1	669.9	550.0	641.0	706.2	755.3	939.4
Liabilities	7b.d	1,729.3	1,740.8	1,938.4	1,845.2	1,979.9	2,091.4	2,618.5	2,608.8	3,198.6	3,453.9	3,942.0	3,887.0
Other Banking Insts.: Liabilities	7f.d	—	—	—	—	—	—	—	—	—	—	—	—
Monetary Authorities						*Millions of Dinars: End of Period*							
Foreign Assets	11	1,462	1,536	1,913	2,277	2,053	2,868	2,527	2,899	3,097	3,594	4,814	6,030
Claims on Central Government	12a	93	85	103	58	78	79	132	147	129	51	71	57
Claims on Private Sector	12d	....	....	....	....	21	23	25	26	25	25	25	27
Claims on Deposit Money Banks	12e	835	829	178	115	† 93	93	449	854	503	435	91	—
Reserve Money	14	1,523	1,667	2,264	2,448	2,159	2,818	2,497	2,943	2,851	3,064	3,577	3,979
of which: Currency Outside DMBs	14a	1,196	1,315	1,473	1,594	1,695	1,994	2,229	2,378	2,518	2,664	2,968	3,478
Foreign Liabilities	16c	326	304	251	244	173	166	249	186	72	75	55	142
Central Government Deposits	16d	198	137	254	231	241	244	206	390	418	555	668	693
Capital Accounts	17a	119	128	134	143	151	103	116	125	150	146	161	164
Other Items (Net)	17r	224	214	−709	−616	−478	−268	66	281	263	265	551	1,136
Deposit Money Banks						*Millions of Dinars: End of Period*							
Reserves	20	294	275	760	816	356	853	468	749	700	697	902	1,195
Foreign Assets	21	532	429	569	697	709	778	928	808	855	853	906	1,281
Claims on Central Government	22a	544	341	291	682	556	942	1,561	1,487	1,543	1,664	2,145	2,271
Claims on Private Sector	22d	8,510	9,274	9,373	10,540	11,542	12,652	15,717	17,423	18,306	19,493	21,467	23,248
Demand Deposits	24	1,957	2,092	2,371	2,847	3,091	3,435	3,779	4,169	3,918	4,178	4,589	5,088
Quasi-Monetary Liabilities	25	4,003	4,166	4,736	5,660	5,871	7,122	8,372	9,304	10,149	10,868	12,151	13,275
Foreign Liabilities	26c	780	817	1,076	1,214	1,260	1,684	1,839	1,827	1,913	2,054	2,471	3,027
Long-Term Foreign Liabilities	26cl	934	839	859	904	919	936	1,788	2,004	2,355	2,119	2,257	2,273
Counterpart Funds	26e	—	—	—	—	—	—	—	—	—	—	—	—
Central Govt. Lending Funds	26f	—	—	—	—	—	—	—	—	—	—	—	—
Credit from Monetary Authorities	26g	1,175	1,119	206	153	127	113	470	870	514	444	93	4
Capital Accounts	27a	1,246	1,672	1,914	2,150	2,361	2,577	2,935	2,881	3,077	3,431	3,937	4,409
Other Items (Net)	27r	−214	−384	−171	−192	−467	−641	−510	−587	−522	−387	−78	−81
Post Office: Checking Deposits	24..i	122	184	230	162	164	321	328	430	416	402	438	557
Monetary Survey						*Millions of Dinars: End of Period*							
Foreign Assets (Net)	31n	888	846	1,154	1,516	1,328	1,796	1,367	1,694	1,968	2,318	3,194	4,143
Domestic Credit	32	9,072	9,746	9,743	11,212	† 12,121	13,774	17,558	19,122	20,001	21,079	23,478	25,467
Claims on Central Govt. (Net)	32an	562	473	371	672	557	1,099	1,816	1,673	1,670	1,562	1,985	2,192
Claims on Private Sector	32d	8,510	9,274	9,373	10,540	† 11,564	12,675	15,742	17,449	18,332	19,517	21,493	23,275
Money	34	3,319	3,637	4,109	4,645	4,994	5,794	6,369	7,014	6,892	7,265	8,036	9,140
Quasi-Money	35	4,003	4,166	4,736	5,660	5,871	7,122	8,372	9,304	10,149	10,868	12,151	13,275
Long-Term Foreign Liabilities	36cl	934	839	859	904	919	936	1,788	2,004	2,355	2,119	2,257	2,273
Counterpart Funds	36e	49	39	47	67	80	81	174	201	176	226	270	256
Central Govt. Lending Funds	36f	—	—	—	—	—	—	—	—	—	—	—	—
Other Items (Net)	37r	1,655	1,912	1,146	1,453	† 1,584	1,637	2,221	2,293	2,396	2,920	3,970	4,666
Money plus Quasi-Money	35l	7,322	7,803	8,845	10,304	10,865	12,916	14,742	16,318	17,042	18,133	20,186	22,414
Other Banking Institutions						*Millions of Dinars: End of Period*							
Foreign Assets (Net)	41n	29	18	7	37	28	41	36	−38	−29	−28	−44	−21
Claims on Central Govt. (Net)	42an	1	—	9	7	7	37	62	59	83	82	35	4
Claims on Private Sector	42d	2,171	2,395	2,684	2,984	3,311	3,510	1,915	2,079	2,167	1,971	1,403	1,133
Monetary Deposits	44	7	11	8	7	11	11	14	31	33	39	35	9
Time and Savings Deposits	45	418	443	489	507	674	791	657	763	874	898	636	589
Long-Term Foreign Liabilities	46cl	—	—	—	—	—	—	—	—	—	—	—	—
Central Govt. Lending Funds	46f	843	918	985	1,061	1,012	1,005	215	172	181	256	202	211
Capital Accounts	47a	952	1,049	1,115	1,192	1,246	1,296	1,086	1,039	1,078	827	526	302
Other Items (Net)	47r	−18	−7	104	260	402	486	41	95	55	6	−4	4
Banking Survey						*Millions of Dinars: End of Period*							
Foreign Assets (Net)	51n	917	864	1,161	1,553	1,356	1,837	1,403	1,655	1,938	2,290	3,150	4,121
Domestic Credit	52	11,244	12,142	12,437	14,203	† 15,439	17,321	19,535	21,260	22,251	23,133	24,916	26,603
Claims on Government (Net)	52an	563	473	380	679	564	1,136	1,878	1,732	1,753	1,644	2,020	2,196
Claims on Private Sector	52d	10,681	11,669	12,057	13,524	† 14,875	16,185	17,657	19,528	20,499	21,489	22,896	24,407
Liquid Liabilities	55l	7,746	8,256	9,341	10,819	11,551	13,717	15,412	17,111	17,949	19,070	20,857	23,012
Long Term Foreign Liabilities	56cl	934	839	859	904	919	936	1,788	2,004	2,355	2,119	2,257	2,273
Other Items (Net)	57r	3,482	3,911	3,397	4,033	† 4,325	4,505	3,737	3,800	3,886	4,235	4,963	5,439
Interest Rates						*Percent Per Annum*							
Discount Rate (End of Period)	60	8.88	8.88	7.88	....	....	....	....	....	....	....	....	....
Money Market Rate	60b	8.81	8.81	8.64	6.88	6.89	5.99	5.88	6.04	5.93	5.14	5.00	5.00

Tunisia 744

		1994	1995	1996	1997	1998	1999	2000	2001	2002	2003	2004	2005
Prices, Production, Labor		*Index Numbers (2000=100): Period Averages*											
Producer Prices	63	83.2	88.0	91.2	93.4	96.4	96.8	100.0	† 101.8	104.8	108.2	111.0	115.8
Consumer Prices	64	80.3	85.3	88.5	91.7	94.6	97.2	† 100.0	102.0	104.8	107.6	111.5	113.8
Industrial Production	66	75.6	78.0	80.1	83.5	89.3	94.1	100.0	105.9	105.9	105.7	110.8	111.8
Mining Production	66zx	64.7	81.9	86.3	76.7	93.2	99.6	100.0	98.8	93.5	98.2	97.6	96.1
Crude Petroleum Production	66aa	119.6	115.7	114.5	104.1	106.5	107.6	100.0	91.4	95.0	86.6	91.4	....
		Number in Thousands: Period Averages											
Labor Force	67d	2,772	....	....	2,978	....	3,144	3,216	3,293	3,376	3,461	3,329	....
Employment	67e	2,321	....	....	2,504	....	2,635	2,705	2,789	2,852	2,951	2,855	....
Unemployment	67c	160	190	181	225	278	278	305	288	294	311	474	....
Unemployment Rate	67r	15.6	....	....	15.7	....	15.8	15.6	15.0	14.9	14.3	13.9	....
Intl. Transactions & Positions		*Millions of Dinars*											
Exports	70	4,696.6	5,172.9	5,372.0	6,148.1	6,518.3	6,966.9	8,004.8	9,521.7	9,748.6	10,342.7	12,055.0	13,607.7
Imports, c.i.f	71	6,647.3	7,464.1	7,498.8	8,793.5	9,489.5	10,070.7	11,738.0	13,697.3	13,510.8	14,038.9	15,960.4	17,101.6
		1990=100											
Volume of Exports	72	137.1	....	....	....	....	....	....	....	....	....	....	....
Volume of Imports	73	119.8	....	....	....	....	....	....	....	....	....	....	....
Unit Value of Exports	74	100.8	....	....	....	....	....	....	....	....	....	....	....
Balance of Payments		*Millions of US Dollars: Minus Sign Indicates Debit*											
Current Account, n.i.e	78ald	−537	−774	−478	−595	−675	−442	−821	−840	−746	−730	−555	....
Goods: Exports f.o.b	78aad	4,643	5,470	5,519	5,559	5,724	5,873	5,840	6,628	6,857	8,027	9,679	....
Goods: Imports f.o.b	78abd	−6,210	−7,459	−7,280	−7,514	−7,875	−8,014	−8,093	−8,997	−8,981	−10,297	−12,114	....
Trade Balance	78acd	−1,567	−1,989	−1,761	−1,955	−2,152	−2,141	−2,253	−2,369	−2,123	−2,269	−2,434	....
Services: Credit	78add	2,267	2,509	2,632	2,613	2,757	2,920	2,767	2,912	2,681	2,937	3,629	....
Services: Debit	78aed	−1,361	−1,352	−1,244	−1,182	−1,257	−1,234	−1,218	−1,425	−1,450	−1,612	−1,986	....
Balance on Goods & Services	78afd	−661	−832	−373	−524	−651	−455	−705	−882	−893	−945	−791	....
Income: Credit	78agd	71	119	66	77	90	89	94	95	72	81	114	....
Income: Debit	78ahd	−745	−835	−1,030	−939	−947	−978	−1,036	−1,036	−1,056	−1,173	−1,412	....
Balance on Gds, Serv. & Inc	78aid	−1,336	−1,548	−1,338	−1,386	−1,507	−1,344	−1,647	−1,822	−1,877	−2,037	−2,088	....
Current Transfers, n.i.e.: Credit	78ajd	816	805	879	821	852	920	854	1,016	1,156	1,343	1,564	....
Current Transfers: Debit	78akd	−17	−31	−20	−30	−20	−18	−29	−34	−25	−36	−31	....
Capital Account, n.i.e	78bcd	−3	32	37	77	61	59	3	53	75	59	108	....
Capital Account, n.i.e.: Credit	78bad	5	47	46	95	83	72	9	56	83	66	113	....
Capital Account: Debit	78bbd	−8	−15	−9	−18	−22	−13	−6	−3	−8	−7	−6	....
Financial Account, n.i.e	78bjd	1,144	958	816	699	489	1,083	646	1,063	857	1,110	1,456	....
Direct Investment Abroad	78bdd	−6	5	−1	−6	1	−3	−1	−1	−4	−2	−2	....
Dir. Invest. in Rep. Econ., n.i.e	78bed	432	264	238	339	650	350	752	457	795	541	593	....
Portfolio Investment Assets	78bfd	−1	2	−5	−1	—	—	—	—	—	—	—	....
Equity Securities	78bkd	1	—	—	−1	—	—	—	—	—	—	—	....
Debt Securities	78bld	−2	2	−5	—	—	—	—	—	—	—	—	....
Portfolio Investment Liab., n.i.e	78bgd	16	23	67	109	33	10	−20	−15	6	14	24	....
Equity Securities	78bmd	6	12	29	55	58	−3	−18	−15	6	14	24	....
Debt Securities	78bnd	10	12	38	54	−25	13	−3	—	—	....	....	....
Financial Derivatives Assets	78bwd	—	—	—	—	—	—	—	—	—	—	—	....
Financial Derivatives Liabilities	78bxd	—	—	—	—	—	—	—	—	—	—	—	....
Other Investment Assets	78bhd	−326	−327	−705	−729	−508	−228	−624	−439	−882	−428	−283	....
Monetary Authorities	78bod	86	88	95	14	—	—	—	—	—	....	....	....
General Government	78bpd	—	—	—	—	—	—	—	—	—	....	....	....
Banks	78bqd	67	150	−305	−250	10	8	—	—	—	....	....	....
Other Sectors	78brd	−479	−565	−494	−493	−517	−236	−624	−439	−882	−428	−283	....
Other Investment Liab., n.i.e	78bid	1,029	990	1,221	987	313	954	540	1,059	942	985	1,123	....
Monetary Authorities	78bsd	—	−1	−11	28	—	—	—	—	—	....	....	....
General Government	78btd	411	546	517	324	−49	314	128	752	392	649	176	....
Banks	78bud	168	44	189	90	—	—	—	—	—	....	....	....
Other Sectors	78bvd	450	401	527	544	362	640	412	307	549	336	947	....
Net Errors and Omissions	78cad	−78	−119	67	206	−12	38	−33	13	−46	−56	−32	....
Overall Balance	78cbd	527	97	442	386	−138	738	−205	288	140	383	977	....
Reserves and Related Items	79dad	−527	−97	−442	−386	138	−738	205	−288	−140	−383	−977	....
Reserve Assets	79dbd	−527	−82	−395	−336	187	−688	245	−257	−140	−383	−977	....
Use of Fund Credit and Loans	79dcd	—	−15	−47	−51	−50	−50	−40	−31	—	....	....	....
Exceptional Financing	79ded	....	....	....	....	....	....	....	....	....	....	....	....
International Investment Position		*Millions of US Dollars*											
Assets	79aad	....	2,953	3,112	3,175	3,313	3,359	3,276	2,975	4,357	5,671	7,029	....
Direct Investment Abroad	79abd	....	28	29	32	35	34	32	32	37	43	47	....
Portfolio Investment	79acd	....	48	53	50	54	49	45	44	50	56	59	....
Equity Securities	79add	....	48	53	50	54	49	45	44	50	56	59	....
Debt Securities	79aed	....	—	—	—	—	—	—	—	—	—	—	....
Financial Derivatives	79ald	....	—	—	—	—	—	—	—	—	—	—	....
Other Investment	79afd	....	1,195	1,043	1,039	1,278	911	1,300	924	1,949	2,598	2,911	....
Monetary Authorities	79agd	....	—	—	—	—	—	—	—	—	—	—	....
General Government	79ahd	....	—	—	—	—	—	—	—	—	—	—	....
Banks	79aid	....	447	562	621	665	646	696	547	711	701	719	....
Other Sectors	79ajd	....	748	481	417	613	265	604	377	1,238	1,897	2,192	....
Reserve Assets	79akd	....	1,681	1,987	2,054	1,947	2,366	1,898	1,974	2,322	2,974	4,013	....
Liabilities	79lbd	....	23,341	23,399	21,212	23,731	21,983	24,043	24,876	29,520	34,763	38,108	....
Dir. Invest. in Rep. Economy	79lbd	....	11,534	11,218	9,263	11,114	9,152	11,545	11,519	13,861	16,229	17,625	....
Portfolio Investment	79lcd	....	947	1,012	1,035	1,161	1,065	993	475	498	618	659	....
Equity Securities	79ldd	....	947	1,012	1,035	1,161	1,065	993	475	498	618	659	....
Debt Securities	79led	....	—	—	—	—	—	—	—	—	—	—	....
Financial Derivatives	79lld	....	—	—	—	—	—	—	—	—	—	—	....
Other Investment	79lfd	....	10,860	11,170	10,914	11,456	11,766	11,506	12,881	15,161	17,916	19,824	....
Monetary Authorities	79lgd	....	—	—	—	—	—	32	—	—	—	—	....
General Government	79lhd	....	6,896	6,979	7,014	7,381	7,646	7,334	7,671	8,761	10,369	11,003	....
Banks	79lid	....	934	1,157	1,157	1,240	1,457	1,452	1,374	1,633	1,846	2,171	....
Other Sectors	79ljd	....	3,030	3,034	2,742	2,835	2,663	2,687	3,835	4,767	5,701	6,650	....

Tunisia   744

		1994	1995	1996	1997	1998	1999	2000	2001	2002	2003	2004	2005
Government Finance						*Millions of Dinars: Year Ending December 31*							
Deficit (-) or Surplus.........................	80	−219.2	−543.6	−599.0	−855.2	−200.2	−646.2	....	....	....	....	....	....
Revenue..	81	4,958.7	5,121.9	5,670.1	6,012.8	7,058.2	7,180.2	....	....	....	....	....	....
Grants Received.............................	81z	63.4	44.6	42.3	—	—	—	....	....	....	....	....	....
Expenditure..................................	82	5,101.2	5,584.2	6,208.3	6,677.4	7,160.2	7,864.8	....	....	....	....	....	....
Lending Minus Repayments...........	83	140.1	125.9	103.1	190.6	98.2	−38.4	....	....	....	....	....	....
Financing													
Domestic.....................................	84a	1.2	53.8	72.6	216.8	81.5	213.5	....	....	....	....	....	....
Foreign......................................	85a	218.0	489.8	526.4	542.4	10.0	349.6	....	....	....	....	....	....
Debt: Domestic..............................	88a	3,165.7	3,251.4	3,574.0	4,946.4	5,240.4	5,570.3	....	....	....	....	....	....
Foreign.................................	89a	6,169.9	6,556.5	6,969.0	8,116.5	8,236.4	9,572.2	....	....	....	....	....	....
National Accounts						*Millions of Dinars*							
Househ.Cons.Expend.,incl.NPISHs....	96f	9,799	10,728	11,618	12,591	13,717	14,900	16,187	17,561	18,772	20,309	22,195	23,718
Government Consumption Expend...	91f	2,582	2,778	2,965	3,296	3,530	3,836	4,147	4,486	4,748	5,057	5,405	5,773
Gross Fixed Capital Formation..........	93e	4,279	4,121	4,422	5,153	5,610	6,278	6,923	7,542	7,607	7,536	7,987	8,410
Changes in Inventories....................	93i	−382	91	347	372	459	216	365	487	77	548	591	286
Exports of Goods and Services..........	90c	7,106	7,657	8,029	9,147	9,712	10,489	11,872	13,711	15,535	14,109	16,440	17,854
Imports of Goods and Services (-).....	98c	7,570	8,323	8,315	9,660	10,467	11,047	12,842	15,029	14,816	15,356	17,469	18,838
Gross Domestic Product (GDP).........	99b	15,814	17,052	19,066	20,898	22,561	24,672	26,651	28,757	29,924	32,202	35,202	37,202
Net Primary Income from Abroad.....	98.n	−893	−794	−1,010	−1,002	−944	−1,018	−1,257	−1,312	−1,352	−1,334	−1,540	....
Gross National Income (GNI)............	99a	14,921	16,257	18,056	19,896	21,617	23,653	25,394	27,446	28,572	30,868	33,662	....
Net Current Transf.from Abroad.......	98t	700	687	806	859	931	1,041	1,102	1,388	1,549	1,641	1,965	....
Gross Nat'l Disposable Inc.(GNDI)....	99i	15,621	16,944	18,862	20,755	22,547	24,695	26,496	28,834	30,121	32,509	35,627	....
GDP Volume 1990 Prices................	99b.p	12,774	13,074	14,009	14,771	15,477	16,415	17,185	18,031	18,330	19,349	20,517	21,384
GDP Volume (2000=100)................	99bvp	74.3	76.1	81.5	86.0	90.1	95.5	100.0	104.9	106.7	112.6	119.4	124.4
GDP Deflator (2000=100)................	99bip	79.8	84.1	87.8	91.2	94.0	96.9	100.0	102.8	105.3	107.3	110.6	112.2
						Millions: Midyear Estimates							
Population.............................	99z	8.84	8.98	9.11	9.23	9.34	9.45	9.56	9.67	9.78	9.89	10.00	10.10

Turkey 186

		1994	1995	1996	1997	1998	1999	2000	2001	2002	2003	2004	2005
Exchange Rates						*New Liras per SDR: End of Period*							
Market Rate	aa	.0565	.0887	.1550	.2774	.4428	.7431	.8774	1.8224	2.2346	2.0754	2.0803	† 1.9224
						New Liras per US Dollar: End of Period (ae) Period Average (rf)							
Market Rate	ae	.0387	.0597	.1078	.2056	.3145	.5414	.6734	1.4501	1.6437	1.3966	1.3395	† 1.3451
Market Rate	rf	.0296	.0458	.0814	.1519	.2607	.4188	.6252	1.2256	1.5072	1.5009	1.4255	1.3436
Fund Position						*Millions of SDRs: End of Period*							
Quota	2f.s	642	642	642	642	642	964	964	964	964	964	964	964
SDRs	1b.s	1	2	1	1	1	—	22	4	23	20	9	11
Reserve Position in the Fund	1c.s	32	32	32	32	32	113	113	113	113	113	113	113
Total Fund Cred.&Loans Outstg.	2tl	236	461	461	440	276	649	3,205	11,233	16,246	16,213	13,848	10,247
International Liquidity						*Millions of US Dollars Unless Otherwise Indicated: End of Period*							
Total Reserves minus Gold	1l.d	7,169	12,442	16,436	18,658	19,489	23,346	22,488	18,879	27,069	33,991	35,669	50,579
SDRs	1b.d	1	3	1	1	1	—	29	4	31	30	14	16
Reserve Position in the Fund	1c.d	47	48	46	44	45	155	147	142	153	168	175	161
Foreign Exchange	1d.d	7,121	12,391	16,388	18,614	19,442	23,191	22,313	18,733	26,884	33,793	35,480	50,402
Gold (Million Fine Troy Ounces)	1ad	3.820	3.747	3.747	3.748	3.748	3.744	3.739	3.733	3.733	3.733	3.733	3.733
Gold (National Valuation)	1and	1,410	1,383	1,383	1,384	1,125	1,011	1,010	992	1,032	1,558	1,583	1,912
Monetary Authorities: Other Liab.	4..d	9,650	11,797	12,054	11,502	12,809	10,816	10,634	10,940	14,271	17,495	18,824	15,596
Deposit Money Banks: Assets	7a.d	8,655	9,951	9,400	10,474	11,616	14,896	17,072	12,218	12,559	13,554	20,189	22,377
Liabilities	7b.d	3,245	5,293	8,089	11,394	14,647	18,078	22,968	9,919	9,602	13,642	19,523	33,208
Other Banking Insts.: Assets	7e.d	478	1,015	942	1,062	1,084	1,146	1,082	1,090	901	868	666	448
Liabilities	7f.d	799	816	839	765	864	† 2,026	2,202	1,821	1,707	2,028	2,138	2,183
Monetary Authorities						*Millions of New Liras: End of Period*							
Foreign Assets	11	373	889	2,029	4,260	6,896	13,864	16,627	30,790	48,273	51,101	52,402	72,216
Claims on Central Government	12a	216	532	846	983	878	1,135	1,727	34,692	53,910	51,620	48,282	40,705
Claims on Nonfin.Pub.Enterprises	12c	26	1	2	2	2	3	2	4	5	3	1	
Claims on Deposit Money Banks	12e	21	29	73	823	2,072	3,088	6,543	9,665	2,703	1,765	1,152	1,026
Claims on Other Banking Insts	12f	—	—	—	—	9							
Claims on Nonbank Financial Insts.	12g	—	—	—	—	—	—	500	750	250	—	302	—
Reserve Money	14	283	508	972	1,943	3,506	6,923	10,118	18,064	21,250	25,193	33,625	47,696
of which: Currency Outside DMBs.	14a	101	189	316	599	1,031	1,887	3,197	4,463	6,899	9,775	12,444	18,272
Other Liabilities to DMBs	14n	9	21	47	—	—	—	—	7,200	9,574	8,259	3,622	6,009
Time and Savings Deposits	15	7	12	33	56	112	232	286	419	653	837	1,094	1,537
Foreign Currency Deposits	15.a	3	12	39	111	135	23	142	530	33	28	77	82
Restricted Deposits	16b	—	—	—	—	—	—	1	1				
Foreign Liabilities	16c	387	745	1,370	2,487	4,150	6,338	9,973	36,335	59,760	58,082	54,023	40,678
Central Government Deposits	16d	22	103	225	875	833	1,812	1,478	3,473	5,800	7,425	6,901	14,881
Capital Accounts	17a	14	19	114	204	436	1,327	2,233	9,410	5,017	3,192	2,874	2,790
Other Items (Net)	17r	−102	30	149	391	685	1,435	1,168	470	3,054	1,472	−76	−751
Deposit Money Banks						*Millions of New Liras: End of Period*							
Reserves	20	172	314	641	1,298	2,433	4,544	5,766	10,713	12,679	13,971	19,629	28,269
Other Claims on Monetary Auth.	20n	9	20	47	—	—	5	59	1,126	2,079	439	134	6
Foreign Assets	21	335	594	† 1,016	2,161	3,662	8,078	11,514	17,746	20,667	19,042	27,178	30,109
Claims on Central Government	22a	225	412	1,423	3,593	9,849	23,148	35,251	62,070	80,303	99,960	114,060	131,779
Claims on Local Government	22b	3	5	6	8	20	22	48	112	83	172	298	347
Claims on Nonfin.Pub.Enterprises	22c	45	40	49	217	290	625	541	390	51	193	353	831
Claims on Private Sector	22d	572	1,357	3,203	7,252	11,493	16,565	28,515	34,995	38,548	55,736	85,145	123,990
Claims on Other Banking Insts	22f	18	28	58	129	204	585	719	1,054	1,070	869	828	653
Claims on Nonbank Financial Insts.	22g	2	5	13	58	119	499	1,338	944	1,948	2,654	3,359	4,119
Demand Deposits	24	126	193	562	887	1,387	2,802	4,187	6,339	7,860	11,357	14,168	22,079
Time and Savings Deposits	25	435	959	2,098	4,237	9,138	17,651	24,519	35,910	50,706	67,863	89,558	123,664
Foreign Currency Deposits	25.a	562	1,146	2,410	4,894	8,654	18,398	25,278	59,597	72,287	68,817	76,330	76,709
Money Market Instruments	26aa	5	7	11	—	—	—	—	—	—	—	—	—
Bonds	26ab	16	37	6	81	123	† —						
Foreign Liabilities	26c	126	316	872	2,343	4,606	9,787	15,466	14,383	15,783	19,053	26,151	44,667
Central Government Deposits	26d	92	144	393	838	1,495	2,961	5,053	6,163	9,478	14,094	16,199	19,207
Credit from Monetary Authorities	26g	13	11	33	764	1,725	2,335	5,600	5,823	191	85	76	1,116
Capital Accounts	27a	182	384	869	1,864	3,944	6,645	9,628	21,348	31,953	42,099	50,049	61,264
Other Items (Net)	27r	−175	−423	† −796	−1,192	−3,003	−6,509	−5,980	−20,415	−30,832	−30,331	−21,547	−28,603
Monetary Survey						*Millions of New Liras: End of Period*							
Foreign Assets (Net)	31n	195	422	† 803	1,591	1,802	5,816	2,702	−2,182	−6,603	−6,991	−593	16,981
Domestic Credit	32	992	2,132	4,984	10,529	20,534	37,807	62,110	125,375	160,889	189,688	229,528	268,335
Claims on Central Govt. (Net)	32an	327	696	1,652	2,863	8,398	19,509	30,447	87,126	118,935	130,061	139,243	138,396
Claims on Local Government	32b	3	5	6	8	20	22	48	112	83	172	298	347
Claims on Nonfin.Pub.Enterprises	32c	71	41	51	219	291	627	543	394	56	196	354	831
Claims on Private Sector	32d	572	1,357	3,203	7,252	11,493	16,565	28,515	34,995	38,548	55,736	85,145	123,990
Claims on Other Banking Insts	32f	18	28	58	129	214	585	719	1,054	1,070	869	828	653
Claims on Nonbank Financial Inst.	32g	2	5	13	58	119	499	1,838	1,694	2,198	2,654	3,661	4,119
Money	34	228	384	882	1,492	2,433	4,710	7,407	10,840	14,814	21,194	26,782	40,751
Quasi-Money	35	1,006	2,130	4,580	9,298	18,040	36,303	50,226	96,457	123,680	137,545	167,059	201,993
Money Market Instruments	36aa	5	7	11	—	—	—	—	—	—	—	—	—
Bonds	36ab	16	37	6	81	123	† —						
Restricted Deposits	36b	—	—	—	—	—	—	1	1	—	—	—	—
Other Items (Net)	37r	−81	−4	† 307	1,248	1,740	2,610	7,179	15,896	15,792	23,959	35,095	41,547
Money plus Quasi-Money	35l	1,235	2,514	5,462	10,790	20,473	41,013	57,633	107,296	138,494	158,738	193,841	242,744

Turkey   186

		1994	1995	1996	1997	1998	1999	2000	2001	2002	2003	2004	2005
Other Banking Institutions						*Millions of New Liras: End of Period*							
Reserves	40	52	84	147	257	457	894	1,124	1,543	1,472	1,786	2,951	2,940
Foreign Assets	41	19	61	†101	218	341	620	728	1,580	1,480	1,212	893	603
Claims on Central Government	42a	5	8	17	43	86	334	395	434	848	1,099	1,273	1,880
Claims on Local Government	42b	6	10	24	45	93	387	715	920	1,205	1,644	2,140	2,717
Claims on Nonfin.Pub.Enterprises	42c	1	9	7	17	11	42	25	29	44	68	97	125
Claims on Private Sector	42d	45	78	170	332	573	825	1,070	1,883	2,516	2,749	3,056	3,410
Claims on Nonbank Financial Insts...	42g	—	—	1	5	7	35	36	56	86	116	186	268
Time and Savings Deposits	45	2	3	2	3	3	—	—	—	750	653	1,100	1,269
Bonds	46ab	39	51	70	130	104	—	—	—	—	—	—	—
Foreign Liabilities	46c	31	49	90	157	272	†1,097	1,483	2,640	2,805	2,832	2,864	2,936
Central Government Deposits	46d	24	44	67	142	214	181	245	519	590	580	518	593
Credit from Monetary Authorities	46g	—	—	15	30	47	82	100	225	197	119	72	2
Credit from Deposit Money Banks	46h	43	88	160	284	502	690	878	891	1,145	937	902	733
Capital Accounts	47a	13	33	86	194	384	763	1,298	2,204	3,397	4,807	5,509	6,620
Other Items (Net)	47r	−24	−18	†−23	−23	42	−6	−269	−1,103	−1,233	−1,254	−370	−210
Banking Survey						*Millions of New Liras: End of Period*							
Foreign Assets (Net)	51n	183	434	†814	1,652	1,871	†5,340	1,947	−3,242	−7,928	−8,612	−2,564	14,647
Domestic Credit	52	1,008	2,166	5,077	10,700	20,877	38,664	63,388	127,124	163,928	193,915	234,935	275,489
Claims on Central Govt. (Net)	52an	308	660	1,602	2,764	8,270	19,662	30,597	87,042	119,193	130,580	139,998	139,683
Claims on Local Government	52b	9	15	30	54	113	409	763	1,032	1,287	1,817	2,438	3,064
Claims on Nonfin.Pub.Enterprises...	52c	72	51	58	236	303	670	567	423	100	264	451	955
Claims on Private Sector	52d	617	1,435	3,372	7,584	12,066	17,389	29,585	36,878	41,063	58,485	88,200	127,400
Claims on Nonbank Financial Inst..	52g	2	5	14	62	126	534	1,875	1,750	2,284	2,770	3,848	4,386
Liquid Liabilities	55l	1,190	2,440	5,330	10,541	20,026	40,130	56,531	105,904	137,799	157,645	192,022	241,149
Bonds	56ab	55	87	76	212	227	† —	—	—	—	—	—	—
Other Items (Net)	57r	−67	71	†485	1,600	2,495	3,544	8,445	16,908	18,201	27,659	40,348	47,962
Interest Rates						*Percent Per Annum*							
Discount Rate (End of Period)	60	55.00	50.00	50.00	67.00	67.00	60.00	60.00	60.00	55.00	43.00	38.00	23.00
Interbank Money Market Rate	60b	136.47	72.30	76.24	70.32	74.60	73.53	56.72	91.95	49.51	36.16	21.42	14.73
Treasury Bill Rate	60c	....	....	....	....	....	....	25.18	85.33	59.50	34.90	22.08	....
Deposit Rate	60l	87.79	76.02	80.74	79.49	80.11	78.43	47.16	74.70	50.49	37.68	24.26	20.40
Prices, Production, Labor						*Index Numbers (2000=100): Period Averages*							
Producer Prices (2003=100)	63	....	....	....	....	....	....	....	....	....	100.0	114.6	121.4
Wholesale Prices	63a	†4.2	7.8	13.8	25.1	43.1	66.0	100.0	161.6	242.6	304.6	338.4	....
Consumer Prices	64	†3.4	6.3	11.4	21.2	39.2	64.6	100.0	154.4	223.8	†280.4	304.6	329.5
Industrial Production	66	76.0	82.5	87.3	96.7	97.9	94.3	100.0	91.3	99.9	108.7	119.3	125.7
						Number in Thousands: Period Averages							
Labor Force	67d	22,136	22,078	22,259	21,818	23,415	23,779	20,579	23,491	23,818	23,787	24,188	24,559
Employment	67e	20,396	21,378	21,698	20,815	21,958	22,049	22,031	21,524	21,354	21,291	21,709	22,059
Unemployment	67c	1,740	1,522	1,332	1,545	1,547	1,730	1,452	1,958	2,464	2,497	2,479	2,520
Unemployment Rate (%)	67r	7.6	6.6	5.8	6.9	6.2	7.3	6.6	8.4	10.3	10.5	10.3	10.3
Intl. Transactions & Positions						*Millions of US Dollars*							
Exports	70..d	18,106	21,637	23,225	26,261	26,974	26,587	27,775	31,334	34,561	46,576	61,682	71,928
Imports, c.i.f.	71..d	23,270	35,709	43,627	48,559	45,921	40,671	54,503	41,399	49,663	65,637	96,368	98,998
						2000=100							
Volume of Exports	72..d	†60.0	63.8	70.0	79.4	87.1	89.9	100.0	122.2	141.5	172.5	†198.6	219.1
Volume of Imports	73..d	†37.8	48.9	63.3	78.2	76.3	75.4	100.0	75.2	90.8	121.0	†153.2	171.9
Unit Value of Exports/Export Prices...	74..d	†113.9	128.3	122.6	116.8	112.1	104.5	100.0	97.4	95.7	105.3	†122.0	129.3
Unit Value of Imports/Import Prices..	75..d	†105.3	123.0	115.6	105.6	101.2	95.7	100.0	99.7	98.5	106.3	†119.6	127.9

Turkey 186

		1994	1995	1996	1997	1998	1999	2000	2001	2002	2003	2004	2005
Balance of Payments						*Millions of US Dollars: Minus Sign Indicates Debit*							
Current Account, n.i.e.	78ald	2,631	−2,338	−2,437	−2,638	1,985	−1,340	−9,821	3,392	−1,523	−8,036	−15,604	−23,082
Goods: Exports f.o.b.	78aad	18,390	21,975	32,067	32,110	30,662	28,842	30,721	34,373	40,124	51,206	67,047	76,887
Goods: Imports f.o.b.	78abd	−22,524	−35,089	−42,331	−47,158	−44,714	−39,027	−52,680	−38,106	−47,407	−65,216	−90,925	−109,658
Trade Balance	78acd	−4,134	−13,114	−10,264	−15,048	−14,052	−10,185	−21,959	−3,733	−7,283	−14,010	−23,878	−32,771
Services: Credit	78add	10,801	14,606	13,083	19,418	23,364	16,440	19,519	15,230	14,042	18,006	22,947	25,855
Services: Debit	78aed	−3,782	−5,024	−6,426	−8,506	−9,858	−8,949	−8,153	−6,098	−6,162	−7,502	−10,163	−11,890
Balance on Goods & Services	78afd	2,885	−3,532	−3,607	−4,136	−546	−2,694	−10,593	5,399	597	−3,506	−11,094	−18,806
Income: Credit	78agd	890	1,489	1,577	1,900	2,481	2,350	2,836	2,753	2,486	2,246	2,651	3,684
Income: Debit	78ahd	−4,154	−4,693	−4,504	−4,913	−5,465	−5,887	−6,838	−7,753	−7,042	−7,803	−8,288	−9,428
Balance on Gds, Serv. & Inc.	78aid	−379	−6,736	−6,534	−7,149	−3,530	−6,231	−14,595	399	−3,959	−9,063	−16,731	−24,550
Current Transfers, n.i.e.: Credit	78ajd	3,031	4,414	4,116	4,554	5,649	5,011	4,866	3,051	2,481	1,088	1,165	1,489
Current Transfers: Debit	78akd	−21	−16	−19	−43	−134	−120	−92	−58	−45	−61	−38	−21
Capital Account, n.i.e.	78bcd	—	—	—	—	—	—	....	....	—	—	—	....
Capital Account, n.i.e.: Credit	78bad	—	—	—	—	—	—	....	....	—	—	—	....
Capital Account: Debit	78bbd	—	—	—	—	—	—	....	....	—	—	—	....
Financial Account, n.i.e.	78bjd	−4,194	4,643	5,483	6,969	−840	4,979	8,584	−14,557	1,193	7,192	17,678	43,837
Direct Investment Abroad	78bdd	−49	−113	−110	−251	−367	−645	−870	−497	−176	−499	−859	−1,048
Dir. Invest. in Rep. Econ., n.i.e.	78bed	608	885	722	805	940	783	982	3,352	1,137	1,752	2,837	9,681
Portfolio Investment Assets	78bfd	35	−466	−1,380	−710	−1,622	−759	−593	−788	−2,096	−1,386	−1,388	−1,233
Equity Securities	78bkd	5	−75	7	−50	−21	−46	−33	−36	−42	−33	−25	−20
Debt Securities	78bld	30	−391	−1,387	−660	−1,601	−713	−560	−752	−2,054	−1,353	−1,363	−1,213
Portfolio Investment Liab., n.i.e.	78bgd	1,123	703	1,950	2,344	−5,089	4,188	1,615	−3,727	1,503	3,851	9,411	14,670
Equity Securities	78bmd	989	195	191	8	−518	428	489	−79	−16	905	1,427	5,669
Debt Securities	78bnd	134	508	1,759	2,336	−4,571	3,760	1,126	−3,648	1,519	2,946	7,984	9,001
Financial Derivatives Assets	78bwd	....	....	....	....	....	....	—	—	—	—	—	....
Financial Derivatives Liabilities	78bxd	....	....	....	....	....	....	—	—	—	—	—	....
Other Investment Assets	78bhd	2,423	−383	331	−1,750	−1,464	−2,304	−1,939	−601	−777	−986	−6,955	231
Monetary Authorities	78bod	−18	−102	−117	−98	−95	−98	1	−39	−30	−28	−24	−16
General Government	78bpd	....	....	....	....	....	....	....	....	....	....	....	....
Banks	78bqd	2,441	−281	1,448	−976	−942	−1,839	−1,574	233	643	348	−5,324	−204
Other Sectors	78brd	....	....	−1,000	−676	−427	−367	−366	−795	−1,390	−1,306	−1,607	451
Other Investment Liab., n.i.e.	78bid	−8,334	4,017	3,970	6,531	6,762	3,716	9,389	−12,296	1,602	4,460	14,632	21,536
Monetary Authorities	78bsd	1,415	1,734	1,380	1,245	760	−160	706	817	1,433	605	−51	−474
General Government	78btd	−2,516	−1,991	−2,108	−1,456	−1,655	−1,932	−883	−1,977	−669	−2,194	−1,163	−2,165
Banks	78bud	−7,053	1,973	3,046	2,232	3,195	2,655	3,736	−9,644	−2,016	2,846	6,564	10,393
Other Sectors	78bvd	−180	2,301	1,652	4,510	4,462	3,153	5,830	−1,492	2,854	3,203	9,282	13,782
Net Errors and Omissions	78cad	1,766	2,355	1,498	−988	−704	1,715	−2,697	−1,723	116	4,931	2,233	2,424
Overall Balance	78cbd	203	4,660	4,544	3,343	441	5,354	−3,934	−12,888	−214	4,087	4,307	23,179
Reserves and Related Items	79dad	−203	−4,660	−4,544	−3,343	−441	−5,354	3,934	12,888	214	−4,087	−4,307	−23,179
Reserve Assets	79dbd	−547	−5,007	−4,544	−3,316	−217	−5,724	−383	2,718	−6,177	−4,030	−787	−17,857
Use of Fund Credit and Loans	79dcd	344	347	—	−27	−224	519	3,316	10,169	6,390	−57	−3,520	−5,322
Exceptional Financing	79ded	—	—	—	—	—	−150	1,000	—	—	—	—	....
International Investment Position							*Millions of US Dollars*							
Assets	79aad	....	....	....	....	....	....	53,192	52,778	62,772	74,492	87,000	....
Direct Investment Abroad	79abd	—	—	—	—	—	—	3,668	4,581	5,847	6,138	7,060	....
Portfolio Investment	79acd	—	—	5	5	5	4	4	550	809	1,963	935	....
Equity Securities	79add	....	....	5	5	5	4	4	53	45	68	123	....
Debt Securities	79aed	....	....	—	—	—	—	—	497	764	1,895	812	....
Financial Derivatives	79ald	....	....	....	....	....	....	—	—	—	—	—	....
Other Investment	79afd	11,624	13,571	9,909	10,448	13,708	25,039	26,196	27,687	28,030	31,217	41,362	....
Monetary Authorities	79agd	1,061	1,103	1,160	1,211	1,265	1,320	1,392	1,418	1,411	1,391	1,372	....
General Government	79ahd	—	—	—	—	—	—	598	584	643	762	737	....
Banks	79aid	10,563	12,468	8,749	9,237	10,446	11,564	12,862	13,159	12,196	12,492	18,248	....
Other Sectors	79ajd	—	—	—	—	1,997	12,155	11,344	12,526	13,780	16,572	21,005	....
Reserve Assets	79akd	8,570	13,825	17,703	19,586	20,779	24,343	23,324	19,960	28,086	35,174	37,643	....
Liabilities	79lad	....	....	....	....	....	....	152,222	137,449	162,402	197,320	227,566	....
Dir. Invest. in Rep. Economy	79lbd	—	—	—	—	—	—	19,209	19,677	18,791	33,533	32,489	....
Portfolio Investment	79lcd	13,788	14,186	16,273	19,844	17,804	38,586	35,862	24,735	23,903	30,037	45,765	....
Equity Securities	79ldd	—	—	3,085	6,018	3,700	15,358	7,404	5,635	3,450	8,954	16,141	....
Debt Securities	79led	13,788	14,186	13,188	13,826	14,104	23,228	28,458	19,100	20,453	21,083	29,624	....
Financial Derivatives	79lld	....	....	....	....	....	....	—	—	—	—	—	....
Other Investment	79lfd	52,239	59,829	66,191	70,402	82,157	86,705	97,151	93,037	119,708	133,750	149,312	....
Monetary Authorities	79lgd	9,658	12,216	12,366	11,750	12,974	11,493	14,553	24,817	36,013	41,184	39,913	....
General Government	79lhd	21,660	21,428	23,700	21,915	22,146	21,480	22,307	20,856	35,781	38,402	40,371	....
Banks	79lid	5,814	8,025	11,160	12,518	15,976	18,714	22,210	11,777	9,833	13,248	20,585	....
Other Sectors	79ljd	15,107	18,160	18,965	24,219	31,061	35,018	38,081	35,587	38,081	40,916	48,443	....
Government Finance						*Millions of New Liras: Year Ending December 31*							
Revenue	81	751	1,402	2,726	6,327	12,657	19,798	35,426	54,433	....	....	....	....
Grants Received	81z	1	7	2	2	—	8	—	—	....	....	....	....
Expenditure	82	902	1,726	3,966	8,617	16,762	29,467	49,134	88,403	....	....	....	....
Lending Minus Repayments	83	—	—	—	156	282	414	554	993	....	....	....	....
Financing													
Domestic	84a	219	396	1,373	2,828	5,158	9,180	10,769	38,295	....	....	....	....
Foreign	85a	−69	−80	−134	−384	−771	896	3,494	−3,332	....	....	....	....
Total Debt	88	1,703	2,782	5,602	12,656	21,629	41,452	63,416	178,193	....	....	....	....
Domestic	88a	799	1,361	3,149	6,283	11,613	22,920	36,421	122,157	....	....	....	....
Foreign	89a	903	1,421	2,453	6,373	10,016	18,532	26,996	56,036	....	....	....	....

Turkey   186

National Accounts		1994	1995	1996	1997	1998	1999	2000	2001	2002	2003	2004	2005
							Millions of New Liras						
Househ.Cons.Expend.,incl.NPISHs....	96f	2,706	5,458	9,938	19,619	36,123	55,928	89,098	128,513	184,036	239,087	284,039	337,670
Government Consumption Expend...	91f	451	837	1,709	3,535	6,633	11,748	17,539	25,405	38,722	49,005	56,775	63,653
Gross Fixed Capital Formation..........	93e	952	1,850	3,706	7,618	12,839	16,931	27,848	32,409	46,043	55,618	76,722	95,307
Changes in Inventories....................	93i	−121	127	−80	−377	−212	1,149	2,685	−2,475	13,134	26,329	33,974	25,394
Exports of Goods and Services..........	90c	826	1,544	3,182	7,088	12,713	17,972	29,959	60,151	81,134	98,496	124,348	133,575
Imports of Goods and Services (-).....	98c	789	1,890	4,111	8,763	14,573	20,801	39,285	55,862	85,232	110,334	149,299	165,568
Gross Domestic Product (GDP).........	99b	3,868	7,762	14,772	28,836	52,225	77,415	124,583	178,412	277,574	359,763	430,511	487,202
Statistical Discrepancy.....................	99bs	−157	−164	427	115	−1,090	−5,510	−2,442	−9,729	−969	1,063	3,360	6,280
GDP Vol. 1995 Prices.....................	99b.p	7,242	7,762	8,306	8,932	9,208	8,774	9,420	8,714	9,406	9,951	10,840	11,640
GDP Volume (2000=100)................	99bvp	77.0	82.6	88.3	95.0	97.9	93.3	100.0	92.7	99.9	105.8	115.3	123.8
GDP Deflator (2000=100)................	99bip	4.0	7.5	13.4	24.4	42.8	66.6	100.0	154.5	223.0	272.8	299.7	315.9
							Millions: Midyear Estimates						
Population.................................	99z	61.52	62.62	63.74	64.88	66.03	67.15	68.23	69.28	70.28	71.25	72.22	73.19

Uganda 746

		1994	1995	1996	1997	1998	1999	2000	2001	2002	2003	2004	2005
Exchange Rates						*Shillings per SDR: End of Period*							
Principal Rate	aa	1,352.9	1,500.5	1,480.5	1,538.3	1,918.7	2,067.1	2,301.8	2,170.9	2,518.6	2,875.8	2,700.0	2,596.8
					Shillings per US Dollar: End of Period (ae) Period Average (rf)								
Principal Rate	ae	926.8	1,009.5	1,029.6	1,140.1	1,362.7	1,506.0	1,766.7	1,727.4	1,852.6	1,935.3	1,738.6	1,816.9
Principal Rate	rf	979.4	968.9	1,046.1	1,083.0	1,240.3	1,454.8	1,644.5	1,755.7	1,797.6	1,963.7	1,810.3	1,780.7
					Index Numbers (2000=100): Period Averages								
Principal Rate	ahx	167.65	169.08	156.31	151.25	132.31	112.55	100.00	93.17	91.00	83.32	90.52	91.91
Nominal Effective Exchange Rate	nec	134.58	130.83	128.03	130.55	119.45	105.40	100.00	98.46	96.64	80.71	83.72	84.10
Real Effective Exchange Rate	rec	126.03	123.27	123.72	130.39	115.73	105.81	100.00	97.46	93.49	81.84	84.60	88.77
Fund Position						*Millions of SDRs: End of Period*							
Quota	2f.s	133.9	133.9	133.9	133.9	133.9	180.5	180.5	180.5	180.5	180.5	180.5	180.5
SDRs	1b.s	2.1	.3	.7	4.0	3.5	1.7	2.7	1.5	2.2	3.2	.4	.8
Reserve Position in the Fund	1c.s	—	—	—	—	—	—	—	—	—	—	—	—
Total Fund Cred.&Loans Outstg	2tl	262.6	280.6	290.1	291.7	282.7	270.8	242.6	219.1	188.9	158.8	123.3	91.7
International Liquidity					*Millions of US Dollars Unless Otherwise Indicated: End of Period*								
Total Reserves minus Gold	1l.d	321.4	458.9	528.4	633.5	725.4	763.1	808.0	983.4	934.0	1,080.3	1,308.1	1,344.2
SDRs	1b.d	3.1	.5	1.1	5.4	5.0	2.3	3.5	1.9	3.0	4.8	.7	1.1
Reserve Position in the Fund	1c.d	—	—	—	—	—	—	—	—	—	—	—	—
Foreign Exchange	1d.d	318.3	458.4	527.3	628.1	720.4	760.8	804.5	981.5	931.1	1,075.5	1,307.4	1,343.1
Monetary Authorities: Other Liab	4..d	7.7	2.7	3.0	1.4	7.5	2.0	2.3	2.4	2.8	2.6	2.4	1.7
Deposit Money Banks: Assets	7a.d	145.2	132.5	142.6	160.8	190.2	199.8	265.6	248.6	240.1	362.2	411.2	349.5
Liabilities	7b.d	8.0	.1	—	2.0	2.1	25.5	41.7	32.1	38.7	25.8	28.2	10.8
Monetary Authorities						*Billions of Shillings: End of Period*							
Foreign Assets	11	299.21	466.80	538.08	660.96	951.07	1,090.38	1,363.64	1,624.55	1,660.49	2,141.52	2,289.79	2,460.07
Claims on Central Government	12a	963.06	1,152.68	1,227.76	1,348.13	1,591.13	1,801.56	1,911.39	1,678.33	2,022.48	1,900.14	1,969.96	1,798.70
Claims on Nonfin.Pub.Enterprises	12c	23.19	24.18	24.47	25.13	25.56	3.50	4.15	4.17	3.86	4.24	1.54	1.11
Claims on Private Sector	12d	1.47	.54	.54	.54	.45	27.35	52.43	85.64	82.98	60.03	66.45	98.19
Claims on Deposit Money Banks	12e	3.86	1.88	7.72	13.06	31.82	61.84	61.76	58.04	77.50	104.71	84.51	76.86
Reserve Money	14	253.14	287.89	321.37	350.61	420.77	484.14	589.68	668.44	739.76	820.95	989.18	1,119.63
of which: Currency Outside DMBs	14a	176.52	204.52	221.09	240.46	285.88	330.76	362.25	393.43	466.61	546.23	588.61	710.22
Liabs. of Central Bank: Securities	16ac	—	—	—	7.00	6.70	52.42	.02	20.02	38.71	38.21	16.00	—
Restricted Deposits	16b	9.33	10.45	9.96	13.43	26.58	123.49	125.60	133.22	151.19	169.04	155.92	184.76
Foreign Liabilities	16c	362.37	423.84	432.55	450.43	552.70	562.73	562.54	479.82	480.94	461.66	337.09	241.27
Central Government Deposits	16d	830.12	1,247.93	1,319.14	1,457.69	1,688.73	1,925.47	1,727.99	1,824.37	2,022.31	2,102.12	2,446.19	2,538.36
Capital Accounts	17a	20.49	56.71	140.81	215.89	408.85	492.39	433.31	305.79	494.48	556.95	477.28	401.34
Other Items (Net)	17r	−184.65	−380.74	−425.26	−447.22	−504.29	−656.00	−45.76	19.05	−80.09	61.71	−9.43	−50.45
Deposit Money Banks						*Billions of Shillings: End of Period*							
Reserves	20	75.12	79.60	109.62	104.22	129.41	121.02	188.93	233.79	205.80	207.26	375.63	448.28
Claims on Mon.Author.:Securities	20c	—	—	—	7.00	6.70	52.42	—	20.00	26.50	38.20	16.00	—
Foreign Assets	21	134.55	133.77	146.80	183.34	259.23	300.95	469.23	429.43	444.76	701.05	714.91	635.04
Claims on Central Government	22a	34.74	41.75	65.67	182.64	199.24	286.12	404.25	586.78	868.01	890.35	938.52	962.99
Claims on State and Local Govts	22b	—	—	—	—	—	1.41	1.04	.78	.88	.87	.58	.39
Claims on Nonfin.Pub.Enterprises	22c	51.21	56.63	65.85	65.83	63.59	70.66	115.36	141.41	192.47	212.51	264.86	365.14
Claims on Private Sector	22d	190.69	245.82	323.18	319.96	424.82	491.90	531.35	503.51	596.50	757.27	836.45	923.75
Demand Deposits	24	177.50	204.18	229.74	272.08	326.56	358.60	443.24	515.36	632.83	688.68	752.63	894.22
Time, Savings,& Fgn. Currency Dep	25	209.41	233.30	315.37	402.46	512.42	588.01	703.62	739.40	961.11	1,193.75	1,356.47	1,537.89
Foreign Liabilities	26c	7.44	.08	—	2.23	2.92	38.43	73.69	55.46	71.68	49.90	48.99	19.67
Central Government Deposits	26d	28.00	38.68	73.01	49.03	46.29	99.81	149.24	159.62	175.29	245.08	179.41	104.63
Central Government Lending Funds	26f	18.81	15.39	7.99	11.17	10.98	17.03	54.62	52.97	40.23	101.77	128.91	31.71
Credit from Monetary Authorities	26g	6.71	8.45	.15	7.24	23.40	27.22	22.22	20.30	21.48	20.30	60.12	35.76
Capital Accounts	27a	36.00	50.07	73.33	145.90	169.82	172.64	264.46	308.30	338.59	416.99	455.82	446.46
Other Items (Net)	27r	2.44	7.42	11.52	−27.12	−9.40	22.74	−.94	64.29	93.72	91.05	164.60	265.26
Monetary Survey						*Billions of Shillings: End of Period*							
Foreign Assets (Net)	31n	63.95	176.66	252.33	391.64	654.68	790.18	1,196.64	1,518.70	1,552.64	2,331.02	2,618.62	2,834.17
Domestic Credit	32	406.25	234.99	315.32	435.51	569.77	657.22	1,142.75	1,016.62	1,569.57	1,478.20	1,452.76	1,507.29
Claims on Central Govt. (Net)	32an	139.69	−92.18	−98.72	24.05	55.35	62.40	438.41	281.12	692.89	443.29	282.88	118.70
Claims on State and Local Govts	32b	—	—	—	—	—	1.41	1.04	.78	.88	.87	.58	.39
Claims on Nonfin.Pub. Enterprises	32c	74.40	80.81	90.32	90.96	89.15	74.16	119.52	145.57	196.32	216.75	266.40	366.25
Claims on Private Sector	32d	192.16	246.36	323.72	320.51	425.28	519.25	583.79	589.15	679.48	817.30	902.91	1,021.94
Money	34	354.02	408.70	450.84	512.53	612.44	689.36	805.49	908.80	1,099.44	1,234.91	1,341.24	1,604.45
Quasi-Money	35	209.41	233.30	315.37	402.46	512.42	588.01	703.62	739.40	961.11	1,193.75	1,356.47	1,537.89
Liabs. of Central Bank: Securities	36ac	—	—	—	—	—	—	.02	.02	12.21	.01	—	—
Restricted Deposits	36b	9.33	10.45	9.96	13.43	26.58	123.49	125.60	133.22	151.19	169.04	155.92	184.76
Central Government Lending Funds	36f	18.81	15.39	7.99	11.17	10.98	17.03	54.62	52.97	40.23	101.77	128.91	31.71
Capital Accounts	37a	56.48	106.77	214.14	361.79	578.66	665.03	697.77	614.10	833.07	973.94	933.11	847.81
Other Items (Net)	37r	−177.86	−362.97	−430.65	−474.22	−516.63	−635.52	−47.73	86.82	24.96	135.80	155.73	134.83
Money plus Quasi-Money	35l	563.43	642.00	766.21	914.99	1,124.86	1,277.37	1,509.11	1,648.20	2,060.55	2,428.66	2,697.71	3,142.34
Interest Rates						*Percent Per Annum*							
Bank Rate (End of Period)	60	15.00	13.30	15.85	14.08	9.10	15.75	18.86	8.88	13.08	25.62	16.15	14.36
Treasury Bill Rate	60c	12.52	8.75	11.71	10.59	7.77	7.43	13.19	11.00	5.85	16.87	9.02	8.51
Savings Rate	60k	5.95	2.76	3.18	3.76	4.14	3.95	3.99	3.72	1.81	2.38	2.03	1.83
Deposit Rate	60l	9.99	7.61	10.62	11.84	11.36	8.73	9.84	8.47	5.56	9.85	7.74	8.79
Lending Rate	60p	....	20.16	20.29	21.37	20.86	21.55	22.92	22.66	19.10	18.94	20.60	19.80
Prices						*Index Numbers (2000=100): Period Averages*							
Consumer Prices	64	73.3	79.6	85.3	91.3	† 91.2	97.3	100.0	102.0	101.7	109.6	113.3	122.5
Intl. Transactions & Positions						*Millions of Shillings*							
Exports	70	393,960	446,086	613,598	594,804	624,509	748,862	759,273	802,296	795,511	1,102,401	1,604,597	1,461,805
Imports, c.i.f. (Cash Basis)	71	850,411	1,024,317	1,247,379	1,425,904	1,753,335	1,955,849	2,486,275	2,798,212	1,998,152	2,456,629	3,646,108	3,382,926

Balance of Payments		1994	1995	1996	1997	1998	1999	2000	2001	2002	2003	2004	2005
		Millions of US Dollars: Minus Sign Indicates Debit											
Current Account, n.i.e.	78ald	−207.5	−338.9	−252.3	−366.8	−502.6	−710.7	−825.4	−367.6	−360.0	−352.2	−188.5	−266.7
Goods: Exports f.o.b.	78aad	463.0	560.3	639.3	592.6	510.2	483.5	449.9	475.6	480.7	563.0	708.9	862.5
Goods: Imports f.o.b.	78abd	−714.2	−926.8	−986.9	−1,042.6	−1,166.3	−989.1	−949.7	−975.4	−1,052.0	−1,244.9	−1,466.2	−1,783.6
Trade Balance	78acd	−251.2	−366.5	−347.6	−449.9	−656.1	−505.6	−499.8	−499.9	−571.3	−681.9	−757.3	−921.1
Services: Credit	78add	64.1	104.0	144.7	164.6	176.3	196.0	213.2	222.6	231.1	296.7	413.9	401.4
Services: Debit	78aed	−436.3	−562.7	−674.6	−668.9	−728.1	−419.2	−458.8	−503.7	−555.8	−503.5	−667.6	−803.3
Balance on Goods & Services	78afd	−623.4	−825.2	−877.5	−954.2	−1,208.0	−728.8	−745.4	−781.0	−896.0	−888.7	−1,011.0	−1,323.0
Income: Credit	78agd	13.8	17.7	29.7	40.5	50.7	35.1	53.1	37.5	24.2	27.6	35.7	49.7
Income: Debit	78ahd	−71.0	−113.3	−79.2	−55.7	−59.9	−162.5	−165.5	−202.7	−148.1	−170.7	−205.5	−206.7
Balance on Gds, Serv. & Inc.	78aid	−680.6	−920.8	−927.0	−969.4	−1,217.2	−856.2	−857.8	−946.2	−1,020.0	−1,031.9	−1,180.8	−1,479.9
Current Transfers, n.i.e.: Credit	78ajd	473.1	581.9	674.7	602.6	714.6	329.7	340.0	882.8	1,017.0	891.6	1,197.8	1,529.6
Current Transfers: Debit	78akd	—	—	—	—	—	−184.2	−307.6	−304.2	−357.1	−211.9	−205.4	−316.4
Capital Account, n.i.e.	78bcd	36.1	48.3	61.4	31.9	49.5	—	—	—	—	—	—	—
Capital Account, n.i.e.: Credit	78bad	36.1	48.3	61.4	31.9	49.5	—	—	—	—	—	—	—
Capital Account: Debit	78bbd	—	—	—	—	—	—	—	—	—	—	—	—
Financial Account, n.i.e.	78bjd	76.8	210.7	140.5	298.8	372.8	253.3	320.5	441.7	177.8	359.2	318.1	351.5
Direct Investment Abroad	78bdd	—	—	—	—	—	—	—	—	—	—	—	—
Dir. Invest. in Rep. Econ., n.i.e.	78bed	88.2	121.2	121.0	175.0	210.0	140.2	160.7	151.5	184.6	202.2	222.0	256.4
Portfolio Investment Assets	78bfd	—	—	—	—	—	—	—	—	1.5	−4.3	—	....
Equity Securities	78bkd	—	—	—	—	—	—	—	—	1.5	−4.3	—	....
Debt Securities	78bld	—	—	—	—	—	—	—	—	—	—	—	....
Portfolio Investment Liab., n.i.e.	78bgd	—	—	—	—	—	—	—	.4	.7	21.0	−17.2	−11.7
Equity Securities	78bmd	—	—	—	—	—	—	—	.4	.7	.6	.6	1.7
Debt Securities	78bnd	—	—	—	—	—	—	—	—	—	20.3	−17.8	−13.4
Financial Derivatives Assets	78bwd	....	....	....	....	....	....	....	....	....	....	....	....
Financial Derivatives Liabilities	78bxd	....	....	....	....	....	....	....	....	....	....	....	....
Other Investment Assets	78bhd	−40.3	−9.9	−37.2	−14.0	5.3	−8.2	−.9	29.4	−59.1	−124.9	.1	−2.4
Monetary Authorities	78bod	....	....	....	....	....	....	....	....	—	22.9	11.8	—
General Government	78bpd	—	—	—	—	—	—	—	—	5.3	−12.0	−12.3	6.6
Banks	78bqd	−53.0	12.7	−10.1	−18.2	−29.4	−9.6	−65.8	17.0	8.5	−109.7	−3.8	43.1
Other Sectors	78brd	12.7	−22.6	−27.1	4.2	34.7	1.4	64.9	12.4	−73.0	−26.1	4.4	−52.2
Other Investment Liab., n.i.e.	78bid	28.9	99.4	56.7	137.9	157.5	121.3	160.7	260.4	50.1	265.3	113.1	109.1
Monetary Authorities	78bsd	.9	1.7	1.1	.2	—	—	—	—	—	—	—	—
General Government	78btd	50.8	111.7	114.4	158.2	178.2	131.1	154.9	284.0	55.7	268.5	126.0	98.4
Banks	78bud	—	—	—	—	—	—	—	−6.7	9.0	2.2	−4.6	7.0
Other Sectors	78bvd	−22.8	−14.0	−58.8	−20.5	−20.7	−9.8	5.8	−16.9	−14.6	−5.4	−8.2	3.8
Net Errors and Omissions	78cad	32.5	28.8	41.3	−4.8	39.7	2.0	40.6	17.0	7.1	−9.8	−7.1	−3.1
Overall Balance	78cbd	−62.1	−51.2	−9.1	−40.9	−40.6	−455.4	−464.3	91.0	−175.1	−2.8	122.5	81.7
Reserves and Related Items	79dad	62.1	51.2	9.1	40.9	40.6	455.4	464.3	−91.0	175.1	2.8	−122.5	−81.7
Reserve Assets	79dbd	−166.9	−140.7	−68.9	−105.2	−91.7	−37.8	−45.1	−160.0	100.4	−77.1	−162.0	−92.5
Use of Fund Credit and Loans	79dcd	27.1	27.5	13.3	2.5	−12.2	−16.0	−37.4	−29.6	−39.4	−42.6	−52.7	−46.2
Exceptional Financing	79ded	201.9	164.3	64.8	143.6	144.4	509.2	546.8	98.7	114.2	122.5	92.2	56.9
International Investment Position		*Millions of US Dollars*											
Assets	79aad	....	....	....	....	....	963.0	1,073.7	1,231.9	1,174.1	1,469.0	1,729.4	1,751.8
Direct Investment Abroad	79abd	....	....	....	....	....	—	—	—	—	—	—	—
Portfolio Investment	79acd	....	....	....	....	....	—	—	—	—	—	—	—
Equity Securities	79add	....	....	....	....	....	—	—	—	—	—	—	—
Debt Securities	79aed	....	....	....	....	....	—	—	—	—	—	—	—
Financial Derivatives	79ald	....	....	....	....	....	—	—	—	—	—	—	—
Other Investment	79afd	....	....	....	....	....	199.8	265.6	248.6	240.1	388.7	421.3	407.6
Monetary Authorities	79agd	....	....	....	....	....	—	—	—	—	26.0	14.1	10.5
General Government	79ahd	....	....	....	....	....	—	—	—	—	—	.4	−.2
Banks	79aid	....	....	....	....	....	199.8	265.6	248.6	240.1	362.7	411.2	349.5
Other Sectors	79ajd	....	....	....	....	....	—	—	—	—	—	−4.4	47.7
Reserve Assets	79akd	....	....	....	....	....	763.1	808.1	983.3	934.0	1,080.3	1,308.1	1,344.2
Liabilities	79lad	....	....	....	....	....	4,773.5	4,394.6	4,783.5	5,295.4	6,124.3	6,781.0	6,587.6
Dir. Invest. in Rep. Economy	79lbd	....	....	....	....	....	666.9	807.1	962.3	1,146.9	1,349.1	1,571.1	1,827.6
Portfolio Investment	79lcd	....	....	....	....	....	—	—	—	—	22.4	11.1	16.7
Equity Securities	79ldd	....	....	....	....	....	—	—	—	—	—	.6	2.2
Debt Securities	79led	....	....	....	....	....	—	—	—	—	22.4	10.5	14.5
Financial Derivatives	79lld	....	....	....	....	....	—	—	—	—	—	—	—
Other Investment	79lfd	....	....	....	....	....	4,106.6	3,587.5	3,821.2	4,148.4	4,752.7	5,198.8	4,743.3
Monetary Authorities	79lgd	....	....	....	....	....	371.7	316.1	275.4	256.8	236.0	193.9	132.8
General Government	79lhd	....	....	....	....	....	3,580.0	3,088.7	3,378.9	3,686.5	4,250.5	4,753.8	4,347.1
Banks	79lid	....	....	....	....	....	37.3	58.5	51.7	60.7	79.0	67.0	71.5
Other Sectors	79ljd	....	....	....	....	....	117.7	124.2	115.2	144.4	187.3	184.1	191.9
Government Finance		*Millions of Shillings: Year Ending June 30*											
Deficit (-) or Surplus	80	−169,806	−131,554	−112,872	−120,191f	−49,043	−109,033	−640,250	−218,703	−473,266	−462,636	....	....
Revenue	81	399,152	531,194	622,790	744,344f	794,052	961,993	1,074,065	1,083,486	1,253,748	1,433,928	....	....
Grants Received	81z	282,487	253,876	325,023	351,091f	397,552	406,936	586,045	798,917	761,046	819,145	....	....
Expenditure	82	848,645	905,277	1,057,885	1,213,626f	1,237,646	1,475,643	1,817,223	2,127,236	2,483,210	2,728,226	....	....
Lending Minus Repayments	83	2,800	11,347	2,800	2,000f	3,000	2,319	483,137	−26,131	4,850	−12,518	....	....
Financing													
Total Financing	84	169,806	131,554	112,872	120,191f	49,043	109,034	640,250	218,703	473,266	462,636	....	....
Net Borrowing: Domestic	84a	−26,962	−86,701	−60,262	−51,990f	−87,500	−16,749	539,885	65,920	24,946	8,658	....	....
Net borrowing: Foreign	85a	243,227	211,719	209,432	231,400f	254,936	218,739	193,407	323,437	484,721	545,978	....	....
Use of Cash Balances	87	−51,017	−22,182	−34,200	−30,001f	−67,117	−146,123	−67,593	−186,878	−164,915	−90,848	....	....
Adj. to Total Financing	84x	4,558	28,718	−2,098	−29,218f	−51,276	53,167	−25,449	16,225	128,514	−1,153	....	....
Debt													
Domestic	88a	....	....	....	....	143,248	214,480	325,442	503,462	857,474	1,148,222	....	....
Debt: Foreign	89a	2,908,300	3,271,300	3,721,500	3,907,200	4,469,957	3,494,400	3,592,340	5,994,951	6,803,726	8,415,346	....	....

2006, International Monetary Fund : *International Financial Statistics Yearbook*

Uganda 746

		1994	1995	1996	1997	1998	1999	2000	2001	2002	2003	2004	2005
National Accounts							*Billions of Shillings*						
Househ.Cons.Expend.,incl.NPISHs....	96f	4,416.9	5,204.6	5,881.5	5,724.2	6,169.0	6,932.9	7,603.2	8,172.2	8,644.5	10,040.3	9,732.2	11,544.0
Government Consumption Expend...	91f	476.6	577.2	742.3	935.0	1,033.2	1,164.3	1,289.2	1,447.9	1,614.1	1,716.5	1,838.3	2,141.3
Gross Fixed Capital Formation..........	93e	762.4	1,008.8	1,101.3	1,177.4	1,434.0	1,728.7	1,745.2	1,960.4	2,183.0	2,734.7	2,850.0	3,422.2
Changes in Inventories....................	93i	−27.1	−5.2	−7.5	21.3	30.9	15.8	40.9	38.1	40.9	51.6	....	....
Exports of Goods and Services..........	90c	554.6	659.8	893.4	804.0	875.6	1,005.1	1,009.8	1,210.4	1,259.5	1,645.9	1,729.8	1,844.0
Imports of Goods and Services (-).....	98c	1,143.8	1,349.6	1,808.4	1,379.1	1,783.8	2,004.5	2,224.7	2,596.7	2,863.6	3,464.8	3,486.6	3,861.2
Gross Domestic Product (GDP).........	99b	5,059.5	5,855.5	6,406.1	7,146.3	7,861.2	8,754.2	9,448.7	10,173.5	10,852.3	12,739.6	12,663.8	15,090.3
GDP Volume 1997/1998 Prices........	99b.p	5,922.9	6,475.7	6,875.7	7,246.7	7,951.1	8,470.5	8,840.5	9,410.5	9,851.0	10,471.9	11,067.1	....
GDP Volume (2000=100)..............	99bvp	40.1	43.6	51.0	55.3	66.2	83.7	100.0	112.2	122.2	139.6	135.8	141.2
GDP Deflator (2000=100)................	99bip	133.7	142.2	133.0	136.7	125.7	110.8	100.0	96.0	94.0	96.6	98.7	113.1
							Millions: Midyear Estimates						
Population..............................	99z	20.26	20.89	21.53	22.18	22.85	23.56	24.31	25.11	25.96	26.87	27.82	28.82

		1994	1995	1996	1997	1998	1999	2000	2001	2002	2003	2004	2005
Exchange Rates					*Hryvnias per SDR: End of Period*								
Official Rate	aa	1.5212	2.6668	† 2.7163	2.5622	4.8253	7.1594	7.0807	6.6588	7.2495	7.9224	8.2393	7.2178
					Hryvnias per US Dollar: End of Period (ae) Period Average (rf)								
Official Rate	ae	1.0420	1.7940	† 1.8890	1.8990	3.4270	5.2163	5.4345	5.2985	5.3324	5.3315	5.3054	5.0500
Official Rate	rf	.3275	1.4731	† 1.8295	1.8617	2.4495	4.1304	5.4402	5.3722	5.3266	5.3327	5.3192	5.1247
					Index Numbers (2000=100): Period Averages								
Nominal Effective Exchange Rate	nec	304.39	161.83	138.41	160.04	147.01	117.15	100.00	109.04	111.56	103.21	97.34	99.22
Real Effective Exchange Rate	rec	83.13	99.42	119.08	140.94	128.65	101.47	100.00	111.20	107.09	98.26	96.18	105.98
Fund Position					*Millions of SDRs: End of Period*								
Quota	2f.s	997.30	997.30	997.30	997.30	997.30	1,372.00	1,372.00	1,372.00	1,372.00	1,372.00	1,372.00	1,372.00
SDRs	1b.s	123.73	97.06	46.72	52.70	129.53	47.86	191.19	199.80	20.81	14.27	.75	.70
Reserve Position in the Fund	1c.s	.01	—	—	.01	.01	—	—	—	—	—	—	—
Total Fund Cred.&Loans Outstg.	2tl	249.33	1,037.30	1,573.30	1,780.56	1,985.05	2,044.62	1,591.19	1,520.74	1,379.99	1,235.48	1,033.68	830.85
International Liquidity					*Millions of US Dollars Unless Otherwise Indicated: End of Period*								
Total Reserves minus Gold	1l.d	650.7	1,050.6	1,960.0	2,341.1	761.3	1,046.4	1,352.7	2,955.3	4,241.4	6,730.7	9,302.4	19,114.5
SDRs	1b.d	180.6	144.3	67.2	71.1	182.4	65.7	249.1	251.1	28.3	21.2	1.2	1.0
Reserve Position in the Fund	1c.d	—	—	—	—	—	—	—	—	—	—	—	—
Foreign Exchange	1d.d	470.1	906.3	1,892.8	2,270.0	578.9	980.7	1,103.6	2,704.3	4,213.1	6,709.5	9,301.3	19,113.5
Gold (Million Fine Troy Ounces)	1ad	.0360	.0470	.0316	.0613	.1100	.1624	.4536	.4831	.5037	.4969	.5109	.5336
Gold (National Valuation)	1and	13.7	18.3	11.6	17.7	31.6	47.2	123.7	134.1	175.4	206.5	222.3	275.9
Monetary Authorities:Other Assets	3..d	4.3	2.5	2.3	—	87.8	33.8	26.3	117.3	148.7	240.2	411.7	365.0
Other Liab.	4..d	7.3	22.1	36.6	67.6	175.6	172.4	122.4	83.2	70.6	86.3	2,323.8	....
Banking Institutions: Assets	7a.d	1,406.3	1,044.3	942.1	963.1	906.8	849.2	921.5	774.7	851.6	1,357.9	2,304.2	2,832.8
Liabilities	7b.d	724.8	302.0	334.4	949.9	507.2	338.7	462.6	650.9	807.8	1,718.8	2,247.1	5,243.6
Monetary Authorities					*Millions of Hryvnias: End of Period*								
Foreign Assets	11	696.8	2,027.1	3,729.0	4,479.4	† 3,525.4	6,251.8	8,987.5	† 17,237.5	24,662.6	38,584.2	† 53,828.2	100,393.3
Claims on Central Government	12a	1,410.7	4,393.1	6,211.3	7,430.1	† 15,075.2	19,712.8	20,854.0	† 20,494.9	19,717.5	19,078.9	† 18,000.8	10,315.1
Claims on State and Local Govts	12b	....	....	....	....	....	....	....	....	....	....	—	—
Claims on Nonfin.Pub.Enterprises	12c	4.8	—	—	—	† —	—	—	† 153.8	155.0	153.7	† 113.7	108.4
Claims on Private Sector	12d	.3	.1	1.2	35.0	† 104.8	154.0	178.7	† 26.4	32.7	37.2	† 144.2	147.2
Claims on Banking Institutions	12e	336.3	665.2	859.6	1,555.0	† 1,365.1	1,687.8	1,600.7	† 1,552.7	1,755.7	2,497.3	† 4,210.4	895.1
Claims on Nonbank Financial Insts	12g	—	—	—	—	† —	—	—	† 23.6	23.6	23.8	† 23.6	23.9
Reserve Money	14	1,528.2	3,557.1	4,974.9	7,410.5	† 8,639.6	12,209.2	17,564.3	† 23,055.0	30,808.0	40,089.4	† 53,763.2	82,759.7
of which: Currency Outside Banks	14a	793.1	2,623.3	4,040.6	6,132.3	† 7,157.3	9,583.3	12,799.0	† 19,464.8	26,433.8	33,119.3	† 42,344.9	60,231.4
Other Liabs. to Banking Insts	14n	....	....	....	....	....	....	....	2,079.8	205.4	354.0	† 1,755.6	2,957.6
Time, Savings,& Fgn.Currency Dep	15	2.1	3.1	158.4	21.8	† 31.1	23.1	57.1	† 110.3	205.6	76.9	† 102.9	71.2
Liabs. of Central Bank: Securities	16ac	....	....	....	....	....	....	....	....	....	....	† —	—
Restricted Deposits	16b	....	....	....	....	....	....	....	3.8	7.6	.1	† .2	—
Foreign Liabilities	16c	386.9	2,805.9	4,342.8	4,690.6	† 10,180.1	15,537.6	11,932.1	† 10,567.4	10,380.8	10,248.1	† 20,845.7	5,419.9
Central Government Deposits	16d	166.7	97.7	216.0	334.0	† 455.1	592.1	915.0	† 1,376.4	2,178.0	4,973.0	† 5,261.5	18,463.8
Liab. to Nonbank Financial Insts	16j	....	....	....	....	....	....	....	....	....	—	† .1	.4
Capital Accounts	17a	75.8	231.3	420.8	914.5	† 2,230.7	1,185.4	2,691.9	† 2,433.0	2,823.4	5,244.2	† 7,653.0	3,363.8
Other Items (Net)	17r	289.2	390.3	688.1	128.0	† −1,466.1	−1,741.0	−1,539.5	† −136.9	−261.5	−610.7	† −13,061.3	−1,153.8
Banking Institutions					*Millions of Hryvnias: End of Period*								
Reserves	20	762.9	960.3	848.6	925.5	† 1,454.6	2,613.3	4,749.6	† 3,687.9	4,515.7	7,125.8	† 11,629.3	22,559.5
Claims on Mon.Author.: Securities	20c	....	....	....	....	....	....	....	1,851.0	.1	—	† 141.8	2,426.6
Other Claims on Monetary Author	20n	....	....	....	....	....	....	....	....	....	—	† 37.2	2.0
Foreign Assets	21	1,465.3	1,873.4	1,779.7	1,829.0	† 3,107.6	4,429.7	5,007.8	† 4,104.5	4,540.9	7,239.4	† 12,224.9	14,305.4
Claims on Central Government	22a	—	207.6	774.5	1,815.4	† 1,530.5	1,133.3	804.5	† 1,214.7	2,381.4	2,459.6	† 2,710.3	3,530.2
Claims on State and Local Govts	22b	....	....	....	....	....	....	....	198.0	195.7	160.6	† 187.5	316.7
Claims on Nonfin.Pub.Enterprises	22c	1,426.7	3,662.8	4,932.0	5,549.0	† 1,440.9	1,782.4	1,916.1	† 2,876.7	3,688.9	5,654.7	† 6,329.0	7,123.6
Claims on Private Sector	22d	556.5	804.2	1,128.2	2,259.1	† 7,922.1	11,046.0	18,816.3	† 26,578.9	39,745.8	65,060.1	† 86,711.4	141,986.8
Claims on Nonbank Financial Insts	22g	—	4.1	5.5	—	† 129.4	153.5	219.0	† 198.4	222.0	686.2	† 1,229.6	2,814.9
Demand Deposits	24	1,061.9	2,041.9	2,253.9	2,887.3	† 3,205.0	4,568.9	8,013.5	† 10,301.5	13,806.8	19,968.3	† 24,669.1	38,243.0
Time, Savings,& Fgn.Currency Dep	25	1,353.7	2,244.9	2,890.6	3,468.6	† 5,139.1	7,683.9	10,725.0	† 15,279.8	23,834.8	41,256.5	† 58,290.2	94,501.5
Money Market Instruments	26aa	—	—	—	—	† 220.2	305.0	642.0	† 569.4	548.4	580.4	† 221.6	925.3
Restricted Deposits	26b	....	....	....	....	....	....	....	542.3	1,028.5	438.3	† 1,192.6	1,725.9
Foreign Liabilities	26c	755.2	541.8	631.6	1,803.8	† 1,738.2	1,766.6	2,514.0	† 3,448.9	4,307.6	9,163.6	† 11,921.5	26,480.1
Central Government Deposits	26d	323.7	514.4	795.5	805.0	† 544.2	487.7	1,358.8	† 984.0	725.7	763.2	† 930.9	1,150.6
Credit from Monetary Authorities	26g	169.4	632.0	699.7	979.8	† 1,237.2	1,569.4	1,604.9	† 1,125.8	1,305.5	2,377.3	† 4,067.2	764.5
Liab. to Nonbank Financial Insts	26j	—	16.6	3.4	5.8	† 227.3	211.4	334.6	† —	—	—	† 299.0	218.5
Capital Accounts	27a	396.9	1,406.2	3,018.1	4,261.4	† 5,462.2	7,497.7	9,182.9	† 7,856.4	9,983.1	12,883.7	† 19,832.9	28,040.5
Other Items (Net)	27r	150.7	131.1	−820.9	−1,827.9	† −1,961.1	−2,721.1	−2,527.8	† 602.1	−250.0	955.3	† −224.1	3,015.9
Banking Survey					*Millions of Hryvnias: End of Period*								
Foreign Assets (Net)	31n	1,020.0	552.8	534.3	−186.0	† −5,285.3	−6,622.6	−450.7	† 7,325.9	14,514.9	26,411.9	† 33,285.9	82,798.8
Domestic Credit	32	2,908.6	8,459.8	12,041.1	15,949.6	† 25,203.5	32,902.1	40,514.8	† 49,405.0	63,258.9	87,578.7	† 109,257.8	146,752.4
Claims on Central Govt. (Net)	32an	920.3	3,988.6	5,974.2	8,106.5	† 15,606.3	19,766.2	19,384.7	† 19,349.2	19,195.2	15,802.4	† 14,518.7	−5,769.1
Claims on State and Local Govts	32b	....	....	....	....	....	....	....	198.0	195.7	160.6	† 187.5	316.7
Claims on Nonfin.Pub.Enterprises	32c	1,431.5	3,662.8	4,932.0	5,549.0	† 1,440.9	1,782.4	1,916.1	† 3,030.5	3,843.9	5,808.4	† 6,442.7	7,232.0
Claims on Private Sector	32d	556.7	804.3	1,129.4	2,294.1	† 8,026.8	11,200.0	18,995.0	† 26,605.3	39,778.5	65,097.3	† 86,855.6	142,134.0
Claims on Nonbank Financial Inst.	32g	—	4.1	5.5	—	† 129.4	153.5	219.0	† 222.0	245.6	710.0	† 1,253.2	2,838.8
Money	34	1,860.0	4,681.9	6,315.5	9,050.4	† 10,386.0	14,161.8	20,828.1	† 29,795.6	40,281.1	53,129.4	† 67,090.3	98,572.6
Quasi-Money	35	1,355.7	2,248.1	3,048.9	3,490.4	† 5,170.2	7,707.0	10,782.1	† 15,390.2	24,040.4	41,333.4	† 58,393.0	94,572.7
Money Market Instruments	36aa	....	....	....	....	220.2	305.0	642.0	† 569.4	548.4	580.4	† 221.6	925.3
Liabs. of Central Bank: Securities	36ac	....	....	....	....	....	....	....	....	....	....	† —	—
Restricted Deposits	36b	....	....	....	....	....	....	....	546.1	1,036.1	438.4	† 1,192.8	1,726.3
Liab. to Nonbank Financial Insts	36j	—	16.6	3.4	5.8	† 227.3	211.4	334.6	† —	—	—	† 299.2	219.0
Capital Accounts	37a	472.7	1,637.5	3,438.9	5,176.0	† 7,692.8	8,683.1	11,874.8	† 10,289.4	12,806.4	18,127.9	† 27,485.9	31,404.3
Other Items (Net)	37r	240.1	445.1	−228.0	−1,953.1	† −3,551.1	−4,577.4	−4,063.0	† 140.1	−938.6	381.0	† −12,139.2	2,131.2
Money plus Quasi-Money	35l	3,215.7	6,930.0	9,364.4	12,540.8	† 15,556.2	21,868.8	31,610.3	† 45,185.8	64,321.5	94,462.9	† 125,483.3	193,145.3

Ukraine 926

		1994	1995	1996	1997	1998	1999	2000	2001	2002	2003	2004	2005
Money (National Definitions)						*Millions of Hryvnias: End of Period*							
Reserve Money	19mb	....	....	....	....	8,625.0	11,987.8	16,780.2	23,055.0	30,808.0	40,089.4	53,763.2	82,759.7
M0	19mc	793.0	2,623.0	4,041.0	6,132.0	7,158.0	9,583.0	12,799.0	19,465.0	26,434.0	33,119.0	42,344.9	60,231.4
M1	59ma	1,860.0	4,682.0	6,315.0	9,050.0	10,331.0	14,094.0	20,762.0	29,796.0	40,281.0	51,540.0	67,090.3	98,572.6
M2	59mb	3,216.0	6,846.0	9,024.0	12,448.0	15,432.0	21,714.0	31,544.0	45,186.0	64,321.0	94,855.0	125,483.3	193,145.3
M3	59mc	....	6,930.0	9,364.0	12,541.0	15,718.0	22,070.0	32,252.0	45,755.0	64,870.0	95,043.0	125,800.5	194,070.5
Interest Rates							*Percent Per Annum*						
Refinancing Rate (End of Period)	60	252.00	110.00	40.00	35.00	60.00	45.00	27.00	12.50	7.00	7.00	9.00	9.50
Money Market Rate	60b	....	....	....	22.05	40.41	44.98	18.34	16.57	5.50	7.90	6.34	4.16
Money Market Rate (Fgn. Cur.)	60b.f	....	....	....	....	10.61	5.44	6.27	5.87	3.14	3.61	2.15	2.85
Deposit Rate	60l	208.63	70.29	33.63	18.21	22.25	20.70	13.72	10.99	7.93	6.98	7.80	8.57
Deposit Rate (Foreign Currency)	60l.f	....	....	....	....	10.70	9.68	6.10	5.60	6.09	5.94	6.27	6.82
Lending Rate	60p	250.28	122.70	79.88	49.12	54.50	54.95	41.53	32.28	25.35	17.89	17.40	16.17
Lending Rate (Foreign Currency)	60p.f	....	....	....	....	19.98	20.62	17.42	13.51	11.98	11.95	12.29	11.60
Prices and Labor						*Percent Change over Previous Period*							
Wholesale Prices	63.xx	1,143.8	487.9	51.9	7.7	13.2	31.1	20.9	8.6	3.1	7.8	20.4	16.8
Consumer Prices	64.xx	891.2	376.7	80.3	15.9	10.6	22.7	28.2	12.0	.8	5.2	9.0	13.5
						Index Numbers (2000=100): Period Averages							
Industrial Employment	67	146.4	134.6	124.1	114.2	110.7	105.1	100.0	86.7	95.7	91.3	91.1	91.3
						Number in Thousands: Period Averages							
Labor Force	67d	....	25,562	....	....	25,936	22,747	23,127	22,755	22,702	22,614	....	....
Employment	67e	....	24,125	24,114	23,756	22,998	19,948	20,175	19,972	20,091	20,163	20,296	....
Unemployment	67c	....	1,437	1,998	2,330	2,937	2,614	2,656	2,455	2,141	2,008	1,907	....
Unemployment Rate (%)	67r	....	5.6	7.6	8.9	11.3	11.6	11.6	10.9	9.6	9.1	8.6	....
Intl. Transactions & Positions						*Millions of US Dollars*							
Exports	70..d	10,305	13,128	14,401	14,232	12,637	11,582	14,573	16,265	17,957	23,067	32,666	34,228
Imports, c.i.f.	71..d	10,748	15,484	17,603	17,128	14,676	11,846	13,956	15,775	16,977	23,020	28,997	36,136
Imports, f.o.b.	71.vd	10,589	....	....	....	....	....	....	....	....	....	....	....
Balance of Payments						*Millions of US Dollars: Minus Sign Indicates Debit*							
Current Account, n.i.e.	78ald	−1,163	−1,152	−1,184	−1,335	−1,296	1,658	1,481	1,402	3,174	2,891	6,909	2,531
Goods: Exports f.o.b.	78aad	13,894	14,244	15,547	15,418	13,699	13,189	15,722	17,091	18,669	23,739	33,432	35,024
Goods: Imports f.o.b.	78abd	−16,469	−16,946	−19,843	−19,623	−16,283	−12,945	−14,943	−16,893	−17,959	−23,221	−29,691	−36,159
Trade Balance	78acd	−2,575	−2,702	−4,296	−4,205	−2,584	244	779	198	710	518	3,741	−1,135
Services: Credit	78add	2,747	2,846	4,799	4,937	3,922	3,869	3,800	3,995	4,682	5,214	7,859	9,354
Services: Debit	78aed	−1,538	−1,334	−1,625	−2,268	−2,545	−2,292	−3,004	−3,580	−3,535	−4,444	−6,622	−7,548
Balance on Goods & Services	78afd	−1,366	−1,190	−1,122	−1,536	−1,207	1,821	1,575	613	1,857	1,288	4,978	671
Income: Credit	78agd	56	247	102	158	122	98	143	167	165	254	389	758
Income: Debit	78ahd	−400	−681	−673	−802	−993	−967	−1,085	−834	−769	−835	−1,034	−1,743
Balance on Gds, Serv. & Inc.	78aid	−1,710	−1,624	−1,693	−2,180	−2,078	952	633	−54	1,253	707	4,333	−314
Current Transfers, n.i.e.: Credit	78ajd	583	557	619	942	868	754	967	1,516	1,967	2,270	2,671	3,111
Current Transfers: Debit	78akd	−36	−85	−110	−97	−86	−48	−119	−60	−46	−86	−95	−266
Capital Account, n.i.e.	78bcd	97	6	5	—	−3	−10	−8	3	17	−17	7	−65
Capital Account, n.i.e.: Credit	78bad	106	6	5	—	—	—	—	8	28	11	21	14
Capital Account: Debit	78bbd	−9	—	—	—	−3	−10	−8	−5	−11	−28	−14	−79
Financial Account, n.i.e.	78bjd	−557	−726	317	1,413	−1,340	−879	−752	−191	−1,065	264	−4,339	8,103
Direct Investment Abroad	78bdd	−8	−10	5	−42	4	−7	−1	−23	5	−13	−4	−275
Dir. Invest. in Rep. Econ., n.i.e.	78bed	159	267	521	623	743	496	595	792	693	1,424	1,715	7,808
Portfolio Investment Assets	78bfd	—	−12	−1	−2	−2	−11	−4	1	2	1	−6	....
Equity Securities	78bkd	....	....	−11	−14	−3	−5	−2	−1	....	−4	−6	4
Debt Securities	78bld	....	−12	10	12	1	−6	−2	2	2	5	—	−4
Portfolio Investment Liab., n.i.e.	78bgd	—	16	199	1,605	−1,379	−75	−197	−867	−1,718	−923	2,073	2,757
Equity Securities	78bmd	....	....	46	248	227	129	−193	−734	−1,958	−1,705	−61	82
Debt Securities	78bnd	—	16	153	1,357	−1,606	−204	−4	−133	240	782	2,134	2,675
Financial Derivatives Assets	78bwd	....	....	....	....	....	....	....	....	....	....	....	....
Financial Derivatives Liabilities	78bxd	....	....	....	....	....	....	....	....	....	....	....	....
Other Investment Assets	78bhd	−3,026	−1,574	−821	−1,583	−1,321	−2,264	−449	−1,015	−781	−940	−12,313	−7,936
Monetary Authorities	78bod	....	....	....	....	....	....	−15	1	−23	−30	−266	267
General Government	78bpd	....	....	....	....	....	....	1,002	—	....	—	—	−5
Banks	78bqd	−779	−328	83	−536	−46	51	−64	137	−86	−455	−906	−601
Other Sectors	78brd	−2,247	−1,246	−904	−1,047	−1,275	−2,315	−1,372	−1,153	−672	−455	−11,141	−7,597
Other Investment Liab., n.i.e.	78bid	2,318	587	414	812	615	982	−696	921	734	715	4,196	5,749
Monetary Authorities	78bsd	—	—	—	—	—	—	—	—	−4	16	7	−18
General Government	78btd	−1,097	−783	−477	−267	−857	−231	−1,457	−537	−384	−379	922	93
Banks	78bud	577	724	565	−51	−264	−16	113	180	76	779	579	2,663
Other Sectors	78bvd	2,838	646	326	1,130	1,736	1,229	648	1,278	1,046	299	2,688	3,011
Net Errors and Omissions	78cad	423	248	259	−781	−818	−953	−148	−221	−895	−965	−54	156
Overall Balance	78cbd	−1,200	−1,624	−603	−703	−3,457	−184	573	993	1,231	2,173	2,523	10,725
Reserves and Related Items	79dad	1,200	1,624	603	703	3,457	184	−573	−993	−1,231	−2,173	−2,523	−10,725
Reserve Assets	79dbd	−549	−469	−894	−385	1,328	−281	−401	−1,609	−1,047	−2,045	−2,226	−10,425
Use of Fund Credit and Loans	79dcd	368	1,221	776	283	279	75	−603	−86	−181	−203	−298	−299
Exceptional Financing	79ded	1,380	871	721	805	1,850	390	431	702	−2	75	—	—

Ukraine 926

		1994	1995	1996	1997	1998	1999	2000	2001	2002	2003	2004	2005
International Investment Position							*Millions of US Dollars*						
Assets	79aad	....	....	....	....	....	....	....	6,220	7,676	11,037	15,919	27,290
Direct Investment Abroad	79abd	....	....	....	....	....	....	....	156	144	166	198	467
Portfolio Investment	79acd	....	....	....	....	....	....	....	30	28	26	43	48
Equity Securities	79add	....	....	....	....	....	....	....	20	19	23	40	36
Debt Securities	79aed	....	....	....	....	....	....	....	10	9	3	3	12
Financial Derivatives	79ald	....	....	....	....	....	....	....	—	—	—	—	—
Other Investment	79afd	....	....	....	....	....	....	....	2,945	3,087	3,908	6,153	7,384
Monetary Authorities	79agd	....	....	....	....	....	....	....	157	197	261	575	334
General Government	79ahd	....	....	....	....	....	....	....	—	—	—	90	99
Banks	79aid	....	....	....	....	....	....	....	731	840	1,355	2,303	2,823
Other Sectors	79ajd	....	....	....	....	....	....	....	2,057	2,050	2,292	3,185	4,128
Reserve Assets	79akd	....	....	....	....	....	....	....	3,089	4,417	6,937	9,525	19,391
Liabilities	79lad	....	....	....	....	....	....	....	25,968	28,003	31,427	40,283	56,091
Dir. Invest. in Rep. Economy	79lbd	....	....	....	....	....	....	....	4,801	5,924	7,566	9,606	17,311
Portfolio Investment	79lcd	....	....	....	....	....	....	....	2,980	3,293	4,065	6,391	9,191
Equity Securities	79ldd	....	....	....	....	....	....	....	763	668	464	589	796
Debt Securities	79led	....	....	....	....	....	....	....	2,217	2,625	3,601	5,802	8,395
Financial Derivatives	79lld	....	....	....	....	....	....	....	—	—	—	—	—
Other Investment	79lfd	....	....	....	....	....	....	....	18,187	18,786	19,796	24,286	29,589
Monetary Authorities	79lgd	....	....	....	....	....	....	....	1,972	1,933	1,909	1,685	1,254
General Government	79lhd	....	....	....	....	....	....	....	5,986	5,762	5,649	6,656	6,610
Banks	79lid	....	....	....	....	....	....	....	539	859	1,632	2,295	4,961
Other Sectors	79ljd	....	....	....	....	....	....	....	9,690	10,232	10,606	13,650	16,764
Government Finance						*Millions of Hryvnias: Year Ending December 31*							
Deficit (-) or Surplus	80	....	....	....	....	....	-2,747	-1,061	-1,800	....	....	....	....
Total Revenue and Grants	81y	....	....	....	....	....	31,172	47,062	57,354	....	....	....	....
Revenue	81	....	....	....	....	....	30,858	45,591	54,569	....	....	....	....
Grants	81z	....	....	....	....	....	314	1,470	2,785	....	....	....	....
Exp. & Lending Minus Repayments.	82z	....	....	....	....	....	33,919	48,123	59,154	....	....	....	....
Expenditure	82	....	....	....	....	....	33,900	48,074	58,974	....	....	....	....
Lending Minus Repayments	83	....	....	....	....	....	19	49	181	....	....	....	....
Financing: Domestic	84a	....	....	....	....	....	2,829	1,645	1,333	....	....	....	....
Financing: Foreign	85a	....	....	....	....	....	-82	-584	467	....	....	....	....
National Accounts							*Billions of Hryvnias*						
Househ.Cons.Expend.,incl.NPISHs	96f	5.8	30.1	58.0	67.1	74.8	91.1	115.9	140.0	153.6	180.7	222.3	294.5
Government Consumption Expend	91f	2.3	11.6	7.1	9.1	8.8	9.4	12.1	16.4	16.7	20.9	23.8	32.4
Gross Fixed Capital Formation	93e	2.9	12.8	17.0	18.7	20.2	25.3	33.6	40.3	43.4	55.2	78.0	93.5
Changes in Inventories	93i	1.4	1.8	1.5	1.3	1.1	-2.5	—	4.2	2.2	3.7	-4.9	.6
Exports of Goods and Services	90c	4.3	25.7	37.2	37.9	43.0	70.9	106.2	113.2	124.4	154.4	211.2	227.3
Imports of Goods and Services (-)	98c	4.6	27.3	39.3	40.8	45.3	63.7	97.6	109.9	114.5	147.5	185.3	223.6
Gross Domestic Product (GDP)	99b	12.0	54.5	81.5	93.4	102.6	130.4	170.1	204.2	225.8	267.3	345.1	424.7
Net Primary Income from Abroad	98.n	-.1	-.9	-1.0	-1.2	-2.1	-3.5	-5.1	-3.6	-3.2	....	....	....
Gross National Income (GNI)	99a	12.0	53.6	80.5	92.2	100.5	126.9	164.9	200.6	222.6	....	....	....
Net Current Transf.from Abroad	98t	.1	.7	.9	1.5	2.7	2.9	4.9	8.0	10.4	....	....	....
Gross Nat'l Disposable Inc.(GNDI)	99i	12.0	54.3	81.4	93.7	103.2	129.8	169.9	208.6	233.0	....	....	....
Gross Saving	99s	3.9	12.7	16.3	17.5	19.6	29.4	41.9	52.2	62.6	....	....	....
							Millions: Midyear Estimates						
Population	99z	51.78	51.53	51.18	50.73	50.22	49.67	49.12	48.57	48.04	47.51	46.99	46.48

United Arab Emirates   466

		1994	1995	1996	1997	1998	1999	2000	2001	2002	2003	2004	2005
Exchange Rates						*Dirhams per SDR: End of Period*							
Official Rate	aa	5.3591	5.4569	5.2788	4.9551	5.1710	5.0405	4.7849	4.6153	4.9928	5.4572	5.7034	5.2490
					Dirhams per US Dollar: End of Period (ae) Period Average (rf)								
Official Rate	ae	3.6710	3.6710	3.6710	3.6725	3.6725	3.6725	3.6725	3.6725	3.6725	3.6725	3.6725	3.6725
Official Rate	rf	3.6710	3.6710	3.6710	3.6711	3.6725	3.6725	3.6725	3.6725	3.6725	3.6725	3.6725	3.6725
					Index Numbers (2000=100): Period Averages								
Official Rate	ahx	100.0	100.0	100.0	100.0	100.0	100.0	100.0	100.0	100.0	100.0	100.0	100.0
Nominal Effective Exchange Rate	nec	81.4	77.2	80.0	85.4	93.2	95.0	100.0	104.2	102.3	95.3	91.3	91.1
Fund Position						*Millions of SDRs: End of Period*							
Quota	2f.s	392.1	392.1	392.1	392.1	392.1	611.7	611.7	611.7	611.7	611.7	611.7	611.7
SDRs	1b.s	55.0	55.9	57.6	58.4	59.2	4.5	3.1	1.8	1.1	.5	3.5	6.7
Reserve Position in the Fund	1c.s	149.1	185.8	204.4	197.4	233.9	212.6	164.8	179.8	235.8	239.3	203.2	93.0
of which: Outstg.Fund Borrowing	2c	—	—	—	—	—	—	—	—	—	—	—	—
International Liquidity					*Millions of US Dollars Unless Otherwise Indicated: End of Period*								
Total Reserves minus Gold	1l.d	6,658.8	7,470.9	8,055.5	8,372.3	9,077.1	10,675.1	13,522.7	14,146.4	15,219.4	15,087.8	18,529.9	21,010.3
SDRs	1b.d	80.3	83.1	82.8	78.7	83.3	6.2	4.0	2.2	1.5	.7	5.4	9.6
Reserve Position in the Fund	1c.d	217.7	276.2	293.9	266.3	329.3	291.7	214.7	225.9	320.6	355.6	315.5	133.0
Foreign Exchange	1d.d	6,360.8	7,111.6	7,678.8	8,027.3	8,664.4	10,377.1	13,303.9	13,918.2	14,897.2	14,731.5	18,209.0	20,867.7
Gold (Million Fine Troy Ounces)	1ad	.795	.795	.798	.795	.795	.397	.397	.397	.397	—	—	—
Gold (National Valuation)	1and	181.7	181.7	182.8	181.3	181.3	90.7	90.7	90.7	90.7	—	—	—
Deposit Money Banks: Assets	7a.d	17,737.4	17,377.8	19,086.9	20,735.7	22,108.9	22,010.3	24,454.7	26,822.6	30,595.0	30,422.6	34,412.8	47,659.1
Liabilities	7b.d	8,997.8	7,653.5	10,053.4	12,351.5	14,446.6	14,577.8	14,133.4	8,137.0	8,136.7	8,248.9	11,542.8	23,203.5
RLB: Foreign Assets	7k.d	106.0	134.0	134.6	154.7	200.7	265.5	147.9	245.6	15.2	—	—	—
Foreign Liabilities	7m.d	35.4	59.1	112.8	101.3	75.4	281.0	138.6	216.5	13.6	—	—	—
Monetary Authorities						*Millions of Dirhams: End of Period*							
Foreign Assets	11	25,812	28,408	30,567	31,692	34,512	40,185	50,781	52,479	56,259	55,530	68,568	78,181
Claims on Central Government	12a	—	—	—	—	—	—	—	—	—	—	—	2,425
Claims on Official Entities	12bx	—	—	—	—	—	—	—	—	—	—	—	—
Claims on Deposit Money Banks	12e	50	50	50	50	50	50	50	50	50	50	—	—
Claims on Other Financial Insts.	12f	—	—	—	—	—	—	—	—	—	—	—	—
Reserve Money	14	16,501	18,667	20,188	20,294	20,326	26,530	36,201	38,387	37,652	42,301	54,766	65,347
of which: Currency Outside DMBs	14a	6,031	6,404	6,767	7,366	8,195	10,272	10,017	10,537	11,938	13,785	15,778	17,522
Quasi-Monetary Deposits	15	—	—	—	—	—	—	—	—	—	—	—	—
Foreign Liabilities	16c	380	175	75	52	11	403	587	516	284	349	548	1,142
Central Government Deposits	16d	7,178	7,930	8,591	9,692	10,692	11,518	12,164	11,722	11,101	11,283	11,578	12,444
Capital Accounts	17a	1,708	1,711	1,704	1,692	1,700	1,755	1,745	1,739	1,753	1,771	1,781	1,763
Other Items (Net)	17r	96	−25	54	12	1,832	29	134	165	5,519	−125	−104	−91
Deposit Money Banks						*Millions of Dirhams: End of Period*							
Reserves	20	10,465	12,258	13,416	12,923	12,127	16,256	25,893	27,849	25,711	28,515	38,988	47,824
Foreign Assets	21	65,114	63,794	70,068	76,152	81,195	80,833	89,810	98,506	112,360	111,727	126,381	175,028
Claims on Central Government	22a	12,558	12,787	10,394	9,105	12,719	15,725	12,581	11,035	15,650	21,407	31,776	42,055
Claims on Official Entities	22bx	5,869	5,840	5,064	5,511	5,236	5,581	5,780	5,258	7,122	12,990	13,884	24,797
Claims on Private Sector	22d	63,836	71,759	78,927	89,925	102,416	110,276	119,828	130,549	145,592	165,143	204,727	290,239
Claims on Other Financial Insts.	22f	2,656	2,526	2,330	2,689	3,443	3,075	3,317	3,415	3,692	4,251	6,612	15,243
Demand Deposits	24	13,152	14,420	15,499	18,002	19,589	19,980	24,050	28,927	35,116	44,477	65,040	86,927
Time and Savings Deposits	25	54,635	60,537	64,676	69,437	71,000	79,847	92,902	116,981	126,592	142,338	167,588	219,615
Foreign Liabilities	26c	33,031	28,096	36,906	45,361	53,055	53,537	51,905	29,883	29,882	30,294	42,391	85,215
Central Government Deposits	26d	12,550	15,156	9,962	6,948	10,920	11,671	18,441	27,382	36,972	40,133	51,786	79,179
Central Govt. Lending Funds	26f	184	113	95	92	77	62	41	37	28	23	18	17
Credit from Monetary Authorities	26g	51	54	55	50	51	54	52	55	61	101	25	26
Capital Accounts	27a	19,563	21,616	23,273	25,435	29,883	31,910	34,226	36,769	40,975	44,455	52,463	78,132
Other Items (Net)	27r	27,331	28,971	29,733	30,980	32,560	34,685	35,592	36,578	40,501	42,212	43,057	46,075
Monetary Survey						*Millions of Dirhams: End of Period*							
Foreign Assets (Net)	31n	57,515	63,931	63,654	62,431	62,641	67,078	88,099	120,586	138,453	136,614	152,010	166,852
Domestic Credit	32	65,207	69,841	78,178	90,607	102,221	111,489	110,925	111,182	124,045	152,450	193,703	283,200
Claims on Central Govt. (Net)	32an	−7,170	−10,299	−8,159	−7,535	−8,893	−7,464	−18,024	−28,069	−32,423	−30,009	−31,588	−47,143
Claims on Official Entities	32bx	5,869	5,840	5,064	5,511	5,236	5,581	5,780	5,258	7,122	12,990	13,884	24,797
Claims on Private Sector	32d	63,852	71,774	78,943	89,942	102,435	110,297	119,852	130,578	145,654	165,218	204,795	290,303
Claims on Other Financial Insts.	32f	2,656	2,526	2,330	2,689	3,443	3,075	3,317	3,415	3,692	4,251	6,612	15,243
Money	34	19,183	20,824	22,266	25,368	27,784	30,252	34,067	39,464	47,054	58,262	80,818	104,449
Quasi-Money	35	54,635	60,537	64,676	69,437	71,000	79,847	92,902	116,981	126,592	142,338	167,588	219,615
Other Items (Net)	37r	48,904	52,410	54,885	58,233	66,076	68,468	72,055	75,323	88,852	88,463	97,308	125,987
Money plus Quasi-Money	35l	73,818	81,361	86,942	94,805	98,784	110,099	126,969	156,445	173,646	200,600	248,406	324,064
Production						*Index Numbers (2000=100): Period Averages*							
Crude Petroleum	66aa	94.8	95.5	95.8	97.8	96.3	98.9	100.0	94.4	86.9	87.5	101.9	105.4
Intl. Transactions & Positions						*Millions of US Dollars*							
Imports, c.i.f.	71..d	21,024	20,984	22,638	29,952	24,728	33,231	35,009	37,293	42,652	52,074	61,587	76,984
Government Finance						*Millions of Dirhams: Year Ending December 31*							
Deficit (-) or Surplus	80	74	−1,249	620	897	−532	57	....	....	....	....	....	....
Revenue	81	3,316	3,876	5,017	5,609	5,938	6,863	....	....	....	....	....	....
Grants Received	81z	12,731	12,708	12,555	13,403	13,318	13,371	....	....	....	....	....	....
Expenditure	82	15,973	17,833	16,952	18,050	19,170	20,050	....	....	....	....	....	....
Lending Minus Repayments	83	—	—	—	65	618	127	....	....	....	....	....	....
Financing													
Domestic	84a	−73	1,249	−620	−897	532	−57	....	....	....	....	....	....
Foreign	85a	—	—	—	—	—	—	....	....	....	....	....	....

United Arab Emirates 466

		1994	1995	1996	1997	1998	1999	2000	2001	2002	2003	2004	2005
National Accounts							*Billions of Dirhams*						
Househ.Cons.Expend.,incl.NPISHs....	**96f**	60.7	69.3	74.4	86.2	90.7	....	....	....	....	....	....	....
Government Consumption Expend...	**91f**	24.2	25.4	26.2	28.1	28.6	....	....	....	....	....	....	....
Gross Fixed Capital Formation..........	**93e**	37.5	39.8	40.9	48.8	49.2	....	....	....	....	....	....	....
Changes in Inventories....................	**93i**	2.0	2.1	2.3	2.2	2.2	....	....	....	....	....	....	....
Exports of Goods and Services..........	**90c**	104.8	109.4	125.8	128.6	115.0	....	....	....	....	....	....	....
Imports of Goods and Services (-).....	**98c**	94.6	99.0	105.9	112.7	115.0	....	....	....	....	....	....	....
Gross Domestic Product (GDP).........	**99b**	134.6	147.0	163.8	181.2	170.7	202.7	259.2	255.4	275.3	325.1	382.7	....
							Millions: Midyear Estimates						
Population................................	**99z**	2.31	2.43	2.57	2.71	2.86	3.04	3.25	3.49	3.76	4.03	4.28	4.50

United Kingdom   112

		1994	1995	1996	1997	1998	1999	2000	2001	2002	2003	2004	2005
Exchange Rates							*SDRs per Pound: End of Period*						
Market Rate......................	ac	1.0703	1.0427	1.1808	1.2257	1.1814	1.1777	1.1453	1.1541	1.1856	1.2010	1.2436	1.2047
						US Dollars per Pound: End of Period (ag) Period Average (rh)							
Market Rate......................	ag	1.5625	1.5500	1.6980	1.6538	1.6635	1.6164	1.4922	1.4504	1.6118	1.7847	1.9314	1.7219
Market Rate......................	rh	1.5316	1.5785	1.5617	1.6377	1.6564	1.6182	1.5161	1.4400	1.5013	1.6344	1.8318	1.8204
					ECUs per Pound through 1998; Euros per Pound Beginning 1999: End of Period (ec) Period Average (ed)								
Euro Rate......................	ec	1.2705	1.1832	1.3564	1.5011	1.4175	† 1.6090	1.6037	1.6458	1.5370	1.4131	1.4180	1.4596
Euro Rate......................	ed	1.2897	1.2070	1.2304	1.4452	1.4796	1.5189	1.6456	1.6092	1.5952	1.4481	1.4753	1.4638
						Index Numbers (2000=100): Period Averages							
Market Rate......................	ahx	101.0	104.1	103.0	108.0	109.3	106.7	100.0	95.0	99.0	107.8	120.8	120.1
Nominal Effective Exchange Rate.....	neu	83.5	79.9	81.0	93.7	97.1	96.9	100.0	98.3	98.7	93.8	97.6	96.8
Real Effective Exchange Rate...........	reu	74.4	72.5	75.1	89.0	94.7	95.9	100.0	99.5	99.5	94.0	98.7	97.6
Fund Position							*Millions of SDRs: End of Period*						
Quota..........................	2f.s	7,415	7,415	7,415	7,415	7,415	10,739	10,739	10,739	10,739	10,739	10,739	10,739
SDRs..........................	1b.s	335	279	239	350	332	374	250	234	267	255	211	201
Reserve Position in the Fund...........	1c.s	1,366	1,630	1,689	2,198	3,111	3,847	3,288	4,020	4,565	4,256	3,562	1,628
of which: Outstg.Fund Borrowing..	2c	—	—	—	—	382	—	—	—	—	—	—	—
Total Fund Cred.& Loans Outstg.......	2tl	—	—	—	—	—	—	—	—	—	—	—	—
International Liquidity						*Billions of US Dollars Unless Otherwise Indicated: End of Period*							
Total Reserves minus Gold..............	1l.d	41.01	42.02	39.90	32.32	32.21	† 33.30	38.77	34.19	37.55	38.48	40.69	38.48
SDRs..............................	1b.d	.49	.41	.34	.47	.47	.51	.33	.29	.36	.38	.33	.29
Reserve Position in the Fund..........	1c.d	1.99	2.42	2.43	2.97	4.38	5.28	4.28	5.05	6.21	6.32	5.53	2.33
Foreign Exchange....................	1d.d	38.53	39.18	37.12	28.88	27.36	† 27.50	34.16	28.84	30.98	31.78	34.83	35.87
Other Liquid Foreign Assets..............	1e.d	....	....	....	....	....	6.93	7.86	10.07	13.95	16.80	17.80	15.54
Gold (Million Fine Troy Ounces).......	1ad	18.44	18.43	18.43	18.42	23.00	20.55	15.67	11.42	10.09	10.07	10.04	9.99
Gold (National Valuation)................	1and	5.31	5.24	5.48	4.81	5.08	† 5.96	4.27	3.16	3.46	4.20	4.40	5.13
Banking Insts: Foreign Assets...........	7a.d	1,200.67	1,350.86	1,460.35	1,685.14	1,868.89	1,802.43	2,059.96	2,168.52	2,477.29	3,023.60	3,643.33	3,937.75
Foreign Liabs...................	7b.d	1,274.82	1,429.20	1,533.44	1,748.76	1,893.68	1,871.71	2,160.04	2,305.83	2,684.13	3,276.43	4,033.35	4,250.79
Monetary Authorities							*Billions of Pounds: End of Period*						
Foreign Assets......................	11	28.33	31.89	27.40	22.92	† 6.78	7.98	4.34	6.24	7.92	9.15	9.83	8.71
Claims on Central Govt. (Net)..........	12an	28.53	25.07	29.86	27.63	† 14.45	20.56	14.30	16.07	16.27	15.87	17.30	15.77
Claims on Private Sector.................	12d	—	—	—	—	6.91	5.86	8.41	5.48	8.20	6.40	5.97	6.98
Reserve Money............................	14	26.53	28.37	29.36	31.45	† 27.37	32.46	32.37	32.58	34.00	36.68	41.80	42.70
of which: Currency Outside DMBs..	14a	19.94	21.21	22.10	23.44	† 19.20	21.20	23.59	25.42	26.72	28.54	31.18	32.65
Foreign Liabilities............................	16c	31.86	31.16	28.36	23.60	† 2.28	9.62	6.28	4.75	7.92	7.49	9.00	12.55
Other Items (Net)........................	17r	−1.52	−2.57	−.46	−4.49	† −1.77	−7.68	−11.60	−9.54	−9.53	−12.75	−17.71	−23.79
Banking Institutions							*Billions of Pounds: End of Period*						
Reserves...............................	20	7.04	7.56	7.71	8.26	8.39	11.54	9.75	8.56	8.92	9.73	13.00	13.38
Foreign Assets........................	21	741.28	845.36	835.98	1,033.98	1,143.88	1,133.48	1,417.73	1,528.34	1,563.45	1,725.43	1,969.16	2,400.57
Claims on Central Govt. (Net).........	22an	11.80	19.72	14.92	10.59	10.74	† 8.17	−8.05	−1.94	8.52	1.18	8.43	7.34
Claims on Official Entities............	22bx	6.11	5.74	4.81	4.34	3.75	2.70	2.52	2.38	3.61	4.77	6.31	7.18
Claims on Private Sector.................	22d	745.43	829.14	911.89	973.04	1,016.77	† 1,094.38	1,254.26	1,367.68	1,479.34	1,624.56	1,807.60	1,995.54
Demand,Time,Savings,Fgn.Cur.Dep..	25l	407.82	493.35	567.10	716.04	764.79	912.34	1,013.77	1,101.61	1,157.07	1,271.23	1,399.55	1,595.08
Foreign Liabilities........................	26c	763.74	866.18	843.63	1,050.36	1,120.64	1,128.80	1,411.67	1,547.73	1,621.05	1,783.79	2,050.27	2,421.26
Other Items (Net)........................	27r	123.87	133.50	146.52	172.05	188.04	209.12	250.78	255.67	285.71	310.65	354.68	407.66
Banking Survey							*Billions of Pounds: End of Period*						
Foreign Assets (Net)........................	31n	−25.98	−20.09	−8.62	−17.05	† 27.48	3.04	4.12	−17.90	−57.60	−56.70	−80.28	−24.53
Domestic Credit........................	32	791.87	879.67	961.48	1,015.59	† 1,052.61	† 1,131.67	1,271.45	1,389.66	1,515.93	1,652.78	1,845.60	2,032.80
Claims on Central Govt. (Net)........	32an	40.34	44.79	44.78	38.22	† 25.19	† 28.73	6.26	14.13	24.79	17.05	25.73	23.11
Claims on Official Entities............	32bx	6.11	5.74	4.81	4.34	3.75	2.70	2.52	2.38	3.61	4.77	6.31	7.18
Claims on Private Sector...............	32d	745.43	829.14	911.89	973.04	1,023.68	† 1,100.24	1,262.68	1,373.15	1,487.53	1,630.96	1,813.56	2,002.51
Money Plus Quasi-Money.............	35l	427.76	514.56	589.20	739.48	† 783.99	933.54	1,037.36	1,127.03	1,183.79	1,299.77	1,430.73	1,627.72
Other Items (Net)........................	37r	121.90	130.53	145.60	167.31	† 296.10	† 201.17	238.21	244.73	274.54	296.32	334.59	380.55
Money (National Definitions)							*Billions of Pounds: End of Period*						
M0......................	19mc	23.32	24.54	26.15	27.80	29.35	32.77	34.57	37.32	39.54	42.32	44.47	47.09
M4......................	59md	567.16	623.39	682.79	722.13	783.35	816.60	884.87	942.59	1,008.75	1,081.30	1,179.21	1,328.33
							Millions of Pounds: Period Change						
MO, Seasonally Adjusted..............	19mcc	1,238	1,281	1,530	1,604	1,632	3,195	1,421	2,485	2,237	2,763	2,283	1,990
M4, Seasonally Adjusted..............	59mdc	25,609	55,586	59,851	80,304	59,497	31,957	67,239	60,220	68,342	72,997	96,756	150,521
Interest Rates							*Percent Per Annum*						
Money Market Rate......................	60b	4.88	6.08	5.96	6.61	7.21	5.20	5.77	5.08	3.89	3.59	4.29	4.70
Treasury Bill Rate......................	60c	5.15	6.33	5.78	6.48	6.82	5.04	5.80	4.77	3.86	3.55	4.43	4.55
Treas. Bill Rate(Bond Equivalent)......	60cs	5.18	6.40	5.89	6.62	7.23	5.14	5.83	4.79	3.96	3.55	4.44	4.59
Eurodollar Rate in London...............	60d	4.68	5.97	5.44	5.66	5.50	5.36	6.48	3.73	1.76	1.17	1.58	3.53
Deposit Rate........................	60l	3.66	4.11	3.05	3.63	4.48	....	....	....	....	....	....	....
Lending Rate........................	60p	5.48	6.69	5.96	6.58	7.21	5.33	5.98	5.08	4.00	3.69	4.40	4.65
Govt. Bond Yield: Short-Term..........	61a	7.83	7.93	7.28	6.98	5.77	5.38	5.79	5.03	4.82	4.24	4.81	4.38
Long-Term....................	61	8.05	8.26	8.10	7.09	5.45	4.70	4.68	4.78	4.83	4.64	4.77	4.39
Prices, Production, Labor							*Index Numbers (2000=100): Period Averages*						
Industrial Share Prices (1995=100)..	62	96.1	100.0	113.3	128.3	150.5	....	....	....	....	....	....	....
Prices: Manufacturing Output..........	63	91.1	94.8	97.2	98.1	98.1	98.5	100.0	99.7	99.8	101.3	103.8	106.7
Consumer Prices....................	64	84.7	87.6	89.7	92.5	95.7	97.2	100.0	101.8	103.5	106.5	109.7	112.8
Harmonized CPI..........................	64h	90.0	92.4	94.7	96.4	97.9	99.2	100.0	101.2	102.5	† 103.9	105.3	107.5
Wages: Avg. Monthly Earnings........	65..c	77.9	80.4	83.2	86.8	91.3	95.7	100.0	104.5	108.2	111.9	116.7	121.5
Industrial Production..................	66	91.6	† 93.2	94.5	95.8	96.0	98.1	100.0	98.5	96.6	96.3	97.0	95.3
Employment, Seas. Adj...................	67..c	90.1	91.3	92.6	94.9	96.5	98.2	100.0	101.2	101.6	101.8	102.7	103.6
							Number in Thousands: Period Averages						
Labor Force..........................	67d	....	....	28,552	28,716	28,713	29,194	29,412	29,638	29,934	29,235	29,369	....
Employment..........................	67e	25,717	26,026	26,323	26,814	27,116	27,442	27,793	28,225	28,415	27,821	28,438	....
Unemployment..........................	67c	2,637	2,442	2,300	1,986	1,786	1,724	1,584	1,486	1,520	1,479	1,414	874
Unemployment Rate (%)...............	67r	9.0	7.7	7.2	5.4	4.6	4.2	3.6	3.2	3.1	3.1	2.8	2.8

United Kingdom   112

		1994	1995	1996	1997	1998	1999	2000	2001	2002	2003	2004	2005
Intl. Transactions & Positions							*Millions of Pounds*						
Exports	70	133,030	153,353	167,764	171,595	164,066	165,739	186,171	185,673	184,161	186,175	186,418	204,402
Imports, c.i.f.	71	147,564	168,055	184,113	187,135	189,532	196,504	221,027	222,944	223,433	232,868	246,625	265,696
Imports, f.o.b. (on a BOP basis)	71.v	145,793	164,659	179,578	183,124	....	....	....	....	....	....	....	....
							2000=100						
Volume of Exports	72..c	66.7	73.3	78.9	† 85.5	86.4	89.2	100.0	102.1	100.9	100.7	102.2	111.2
Volume of Imports	73..c	61.9	65.7	71.9	† 79.0	85.7	91.4	100.0	105.3	110.2	112.2	119.9	128.1
Export Prices	76	107.6	111.3	112.0	† 106.2	101.0	98.9	100.0	98.3	98.3	100.1	100.4	104.4
Import Prices	76.x	104.5	111.2	111.0	† 103.6	98.3	96.8	100.0	99.2	96.7	96.0	95.5	99.5
Balance of Payments						*Billions of US Dollars: Minus Sign Indicates Debit*							
Current Account, n.i.e.	78ald	−10.23	−14.29	−11.28	−2.95	−6.63	−39.29	−36.68	−31.85	−24.57	−26.19	−42.97	−57.62
Goods: Exports f.o.b.	78aad	207.19	242.32	261.25	281.54	271.72	268.88	284.38	273.66	279.85	308.27	349.66	381.79
Goods: Imports f.o.b.	78abd	−224.14	−261.32	−282.48	−301.74	−307.85	−315.90	−334.23	−332.14	−350.69	−386.51	−460.36	−501.16
Trade Balance	78acd	−16.95	−19.01	−21.23	−20.20	−36.13	−47.01	−49.85	−58.48	−70.84	−78.24	−110.70	−119.37
Services: Credit	78add	69.54	78.78	89.04	99.79	110.94	118.61	120.06	119.56	132.99	152.91	188.61	192.32
Services: Debit	78aed	−59.77	−65.41	−72.77	−78.17	−87.97	−96.53	−99.19	−99.81	−109.67	−125.31	−149.33	−158.12
Balance on Goods & Services	78afd	−7.18	−5.64	−4.96	1.41	−13.16	−24.93	−28.98	−38.73	−47.52	−50.64	−71.43	−85.17
Income: Credit	78agd	113.97	138.87	144.06	157.40	172.05	162.16	203.75	202.41	187.50	206.25	260.13	335.19
Income: Debit	78ahd	−108.86	−135.59	−142.94	−152.09	−151.64	−164.57	−196.74	−186.02	−151.68	−165.58	−211.64	−284.98
Balance on Gds, Serv. & Inc.	78aid	−2.08	−2.35	−3.85	6.72	7.25	−27.34	−21.97	−22.33	−11.70	−9.97	−22.94	−34.96
Current Transfers, n.i.e.: Credit	78ajd	17.71	19.70	31.20	21.40	20.47	21.66	16.42	21.01	19.12	20.22	23.01	28.83
Current Transfers: Debit	78akd	−25.86	−31.64	−38.63	−31.08	−34.35	−33.61	−31.14	−30.52	−31.99	−36.44	−43.05	−51.49
Capital Account, n.i.e.	78bcd	.05	.84	1.97	1.61	.86	1.25	2.31	1.73	1.32	2.15	3.55	4.19
Capital Account, n.i.e.: Credit	78bad	1.93	1.84	3.01	3.06	2.51	2.63	3.94	4.79	3.51	4.59	6.60	7.66
Capital Account: Debit	78bbd	−1.88	−.99	−1.04	−1.45	−1.65	−1.38	−1.63	−3.06	−2.18	−2.45	−3.05	−3.48
Financial Account, n.i.e.	78bjd	4.71	7.47	5.85	−20.10	16.93	34.86	26.05	23.23	13.29	46.08	28.29	45.22
Direct Investment Abroad	78bdd	−34.90	−45.31	−34.82	−62.44	−122.06	−201.57	−245.38	−59.66	−49.46	−59.80	−95.86	−101.72
Dir. Invest. in Rep. Econ., n.i.e.	78bed	10.73	21.73	27.39	37.51	74.65	89.34	122.16	53.84	25.53	27.61	77.95	163.99
Portfolio Investment Assets	78bfd	31.47	−61.69	−93.37	−85.00	−53.23	−34.32	−97.19	−124.73	1.22	−58.42	−259.16	−293.19
Equity Securities	78bkd	−1.47	−13.15	−16.42	7.01	−4.95	−23.87	−28.46	−63.63	7.41	−29.79	−102.96	−114.19
Debt Securities	78bld	32.95	−48.55	−76.95	−92.01	−48.28	−10.45	−68.73	−61.10	−6.19	−28.63	−156.20	−179.01
Portfolio Investment Liab., n.i.e.	78bgd	47.01	58.79	67.99	43.66	35.14	183.82	255.78	69.56	76.24	156.82	158.44	240.63
Equity Securities	78bmd	7.35	8.07	9.40	7.85	63.17	116.04	179.17	33.11	4.22	15.56	−15.30	5.52
Debt Securities	78bnd	39.66	50.72	58.60	35.81	−28.03	67.78	76.61	36.45	72.02	141.26	173.74	235.11
Financial Derivatives Assets	78bwd	....	....	....	....	....	....	....	....	....	....	....	....
Financial Derivatives Liabilities	78bxd	3.67	2.63	1.52	1.90	−5.07	4.41	2.26	12.18	1.35	−8.49	−14.27	−4.43
Other Investment Assets	78bhd	−42.45	−74.90	−214.68	−277.94	−22.99	−96.81	−426.19	−255.00	−150.65	−421.25	−597.23	−922.81
Monetary Authorities	78bod	....	....	....	....	....	....	....	....	....	....	....	....
General Government	78bpd	−.69	−.74	−2.97	−.20	.12	−.51	−.40	.01	−1.05	−.58	−.58	−.25
Banks	78bqd	−72.66	−34.91	−102.10	−241.01	−31.23	19.86	−289.04	−124.85	−111.14	−258.62	−400.47	−549.63
Other Sectors	78brd	30.90	−39.25	−109.61	−36.73	8.12	−116.16	−136.75	−130.16	−38.46	−162.06	−196.17	−372.93
Other Investment Liab., n.i.e.	78bid	−10.81	106.22	251.82	322.22	110.48	89.99	414.60	327.05	109.07	409.62	758.42	962.74
Monetary Authorities	78bsd	—	—	—	—	—	—	—	—	—	—	—	—
General Government	78btd	.86	.59	−1.06	−1.74	.42	.54	—	.40	−1.01	.83	−.80	.38
Banks	78bud	76.62	41.95	111.45	243.12	84.79	20.33	308.95	182.41	141.42	279.18	566.50	522.44
Other Sectors	78bvd	−88.29	63.68	141.43	80.83	25.28	69.13	105.65	144.24	−31.35	129.62	192.72	439.93
Net Errors and Omissions	78cad	6.98	5.13	2.80	17.54	−11.42	2.15	13.62	2.43	9.32	−24.63	11.54	9.95
Overall Balance	78cbd	1.50	−.85	−.65	−3.90	−.26	−1.04	5.30	−4.46	−.63	−2.59	.41	1.73
Reserves and Related Items	79dad	−1.50	.85	.65	3.90	.26	1.04	−5.30	4.46	.63	2.59	−.41	−1.73
Reserve Assets	79dbd	−1.48	.90	.65	3.90	.26	1.04	−5.30	4.46	.63	2.59	−.41	−1.73
Use of Fund Credit and Loans	79dcd	—	—	—	—	—	—	—	—	—	—	—	—
Exceptional Financing	79ded	−.02	−.04	—	—	—	—	—	—	—	—	—	—
International Investment Position						*Billions of US Dollars*							
Assets	79aad	2,101.90	2,391.34	2,765.83	3,249.81	3,546.86	3,908.79	4,431.72	4,553.50	5,044.32	6,280.87	7,595.94	8,281.91
Direct Investment Abroad	79abd	275.23	315.74	342.31	369.24	498.36	691.91	906.40	875.03	1,001.64	1,193.58	1,276.88	1,238.00
Portfolio Investment	79acd	671.53	773.94	930.99	1,076.56	1,170.85	1,355.01	1,352.04	1,359.63	1,360.51	1,670.39	2,109.70	2,303.97
Equity Securities	79add	291.92	336.30	404.67	466.94	505.15	678.65	640.63	586.88	493.17	664.06	879.34	1,006.40
Debt Securities	79aed	379.62	437.63	526.32	609.62	665.70	676.35	711.41	772.75	867.35	1,006.33	1,230.36	1,297.57
Financial Derivatives	79ald	—	—	—	—	—	—	—	—	—	—	—	—
Other Investment	79afd	1,107.20	1,252.52	1,446.14	1,766.22	1,838.80	1,826.01	2,130.30	2,281.60	2,641.07	3,374.42	4,164.49	4,696.79
Monetary Authorities	79agd												
General Government	79ahd	14.09	14.71	19.33	19.02	19.00	5.74	5.80	5.66	7.26	8.64	9.93	9.22
Banks	79aid	877.15	979.78	1,063.88	1,367.32	1,457.48	1,364.00	1,579.68	1,641.21	1,891.53	2,359.23	2,907.49	3,180.46
Other Sectors	79ajd	215.96	258.04	362.92	379.88	362.33	456.27	544.82	634.72	742.28	1,006.56	1,247.08	1,507.12
Reserve Assets	79akd	47.93	49.15	46.39	37.79	38.84	35.86	42.97	37.24	41.10	42.48	44.87	43.15
Liabilities	79lad	2,073.93	2,426.47	2,876.76	3,359.17	3,761.70	4,012.73	4,483.80	4,658.06	5,122.14	6,397.51	7,878.57	8,652.91
Dir. Invest. in Rep. Economy	79lbd	203.05	226.63	259.17	287.31	355.40	404.51	463.13	527.39	547.63	633.78	741.48	816.72
Portfolio Investment	79lcd	499.95	629.75	814.74	964.37	1,152.22	1,338.96	1,489.27	1,390.04	1,438.28	1,867.23	2,261.71	2,454.71
Equity Securities	79ldd	197.10	267.66	383.89	499.23	668.90	824.10	901.93	767.90	660.48	874.08	1,007.33	1,056.87
Debt Securities	79led	302.85	362.09	430.85	465.14	483.32	514.87	587.34	622.14	777.80	993.15	1,254.38	1,397.84
Financial Derivatives	79lld	—	—	—	—	—	—	—	—	—	—	—	—
Other Investment	79lfd	1,370.94	1,570.09	1,802.85	2,107.49	2,254.08	2,269.26	2,531.40	2,740.63	3,136.23	3,896.50	4,875.38	5,381.48
Monetary Authorities	79lgd	—	—	—	—	—	—	—	—	—	—	—	—
General Government	79lhd	6.70	7.31	6.68	4.78	5.39	5.81	5.90	6.13	5.57	7.00	6.69	6.25
Banks	79lid	1,114.40	1,242.42	1,327.38	1,577.98	1,729.58	1,669.18	1,888.52	1,992.89	2,321.90	2,866.57	3,585.84	3,792.14
Other Sectors	79ljd	249.84	320.36	468.79	524.73	519.11	594.27	636.99	741.62	808.76	1,022.92	1,282.86	1,583.10

United Kingdom 112

		1994	1995	1996	1997	1998	1999	2000	2001	2002	2003	2004	2005
Government Finance						*Millions of Pounds: Year Ending December 31*							
Deficit (-) or Surplus........................	80	−39,868	−38,922	−27,440	−16,136	4,853	295	....	....	....	....	....	....
Revenue...........................	81	236,083	253,918	270,360	288,223	317,543	325,102	....	....	....	....	....	....
Grants Received........................	81z	1,752	1,233	2,424	1,739	1,384	3,176	....	....	....	....	....	....
Expenditure.................................	82	284,051	295,172	307,310	306,579	313,836	324,393	....	....	....	....	....	....
Lending Minus Repayments...........	83	−6,348	−1,099	−7,086	−481	238	3,590	....	....	....	....	....	....
Financing													
Domestic Borrowing.....................	84a	34,931	38,275	20,446	18,064	−2,908	2,984	....	....	....	....	....	....
Foreign Borrowing........................	85a	4,937	647	6,994	−1,928	−1,945	−3,279	....	....	....	....	....	....
						Millions of Pounds Year Beginning April 1							
Debt: Domestic..............................	88a	243,394	277,476	314,021	341,171	....	....	....	....	....	....	....	....
Foreign.....................................	89a	58,262	56,234	58,691	60,213	....	....	....	....	....	....	....	....
National Accounts						*Billions of Pounds*							
Househ.Cons.Expend.,incl.NPISHs....	96f.c	435.13	457.49	490.84	520.66	554.99	589.87	624.00	657.22	690.53	724.35	761.48	791.30
Government Consumption Expend...	91f.c	138.11	140.24	146.56	148.54	154.25	166.51	179.05	191.02	210.97	231.78	246.81	267.53
Gross Fixed Capital Formation..........	93e.c	108.65	117.91	126.43	133.59	151.51	156.57	161.47	165.87	173.74	178.71	194.45	205.47
Changes in Inventories...................	93i.c	3.71	4.51	1.77	4.62	5.03	6.06	5.27	6.19	2.91	3.98	4.86	3.72
Exports of Goods and Services..........	90c.c	180.76	204.15	225.16	234.02	232.03	239.78	267.60	273.14	276.51	285.40	298.69	322.30
Imports of Goods and Services (-).....	98c.c	185.38	207.22	227.68	232.26	239.18	255.24	286.96	299.93	307.39	314.84	333.67	366.54
Gross Domestic Product (GDP).........	99b.c	680.98	719.75	765.15	811.19	860.80	906.57	953.23	996.99	1,048.77	1,110.30	1,176.53	1,224.72
Net Primary Income from Abroad.....	98.nc	.29	−2.76	−2.30	.60	8.91	−1.83	.78	8.33	21.07	22.64	25.55	28.85
Gross National Income (GNI)...........	99a.c	681.26	716.99	762.85	811.80	869.71	904.74	954.00	1,005.31	1,069.84	1,132.94	1,202.08	1,253.56
Net Current Transf.from Abroad.......	98t.c	−2.31	−2.65	−1.90	−3.21	−4.97	−4.44	−6.25	−3.43	−6.71	−8.13	−9.92	−11.22
Gross Nat'l Disposable Inc.(GNDI)....	99i.c	678.42	714.34	760.95	808.59	864.74	900.30	947.75	1,001.89	1,063.13	1,124.81	1,192.16	1,242.34
Gross Saving.................................	99s.c	105.37	111.37	123.70	140.38	156.86	141.33	147.16	154.40	164.58	167.82	179.98	183.58
Consumption of Fixed Capital..........	99cfc	85.44	86.16	90.15	91.94	95.05	101.06	106.37	110.43	116.01	119.24	128.43	131.09
GDP Volume 2003 Ref., Chained.....	99b.r	859.57	884.75	909.10	936.72	968.04	997.30	1,035.30	1,059.65	1,081.47	1,110.30	1,146.52	1,167.79
GDP Volume (2000=100)................	99bvr	83.0	85.5	87.8	90.5	93.5	96.3	100.0	102.4	104.5	107.2	110.7	112.8
GDP Deflator (2000=100)................	99bir	86.0	88.4	91.4	94.1	96.6	98.7	100.0	102.2	105.3	108.6	111.5	113.9
						Millions: Midyear Estimates							
Population...............................	99z	57.48	57.67	57.87	58.06	58.26	58.47	58.67	58.87	59.08	59.28	59.48	59.67

		1994	1995	1996	1997	1998	1999	2000	2001	2002	2003	2004	2005
Exchange Rates					*End of Period (sa and sc) Period Averages (sb and sd)*								
US Dollar/SDR Rate.............aa=....	sa	1.4599	1.4865	1.4380	1.3493	1.4080	1.3725	1.3029	1.2567	1.3595	1.4860	1.5530	1.4293
US Dollar/SDR Rate........................	sb	1.4317	1.5170	1.4518	1.3760	1.3565	1.3673	1.3188	1.2730	1.2948	1.3988	1.4820	1.4773
SDR/US Dollar Rate.............ac=....	sc	.6850	.6727	.6954	.7412	.7102	.7286	.7675	.7957	.7356	.6730	.6439	.6997
SDR/US Dollar Rate........................	sd	.6985	.6592	.6888	.7267	.7372	.7314	.7583	.7855	.7723	.7152	.6749	.6773
				Dollars per ECU through 1998; Dollars per Euro Beginning 1999: End of Period (ea) Period Average (eb)									
Euro Rate..	ag	1.2300	1.3142	1.2530	1.1042	1.1668	1.0046	.9305	.8813	1.0487	1.2630	1.3621	1.1797
Euro Rate..	rh	1.1886	1.3081	1.2680	1.1341	1.1200	1.0668	.9240	.8956	.9444	1.1308	1.2433	1.2458
					Index Numbers (2000=100): Period Averages								
Nominal Effective Exchange Rate.....	neu	86.6	81.5	84.9	91.7	96.1	94.9	100.0	105.9	104.3	91.5	84.0	82.7
Real Effective Exchange Rate............	reu	87.4	80.5	82.2	86.5	91.6	90.6	100.0	103.8	105.8	96.7	88.6	90.0
Fund Position					*Billions of SDRs: End of Period*								
Quota..	2f.s	26.53	26.53	26.53	26.53	26.53	37.15	37.15	37.15	37.15	37.15	37.15	37.15
SDRs...	1b.s	6.88	7.42	7.17	7.43	7.53	7.54	8.09	8.58	8.95	8.50	8.77	5.74
Reserve Position in the Fund.............	1c.s	8.24	9.85	10.73	13.39	17.12	13.09	11.38	14.22	16.17	15.16	12.58	5.62
of which: Outstg.Fund Borrowing...	2c	—	—	—	—	.98	—	—	—	—	—	—	—
International Liquidity				*Billions of US Dollars Unless Otherwise Indicated: End of Period*									
Total Reserves minus Gold..............	1l.d	63.28	74.78	64.04	58.91	70.71	60.50	56.60	57.63	67.96	74.89	75.89	54.08
SDRs..	1b.d	10.04	11.04	10.31	10.03	10.60	10.35	10.54	10.78	12.17	12.64	13.63	8.21
Reserve Position in the Fund.........	1c.d	12.03	14.65	15.43	18.07	24.11	17.97	14.82	17.87	21.98	22.53	19.54	8.04
Foreign Exchange..........................	1d.d	41.22	49.10	38.29	30.81	36.00	32.18	31.24	28.98	33.82	39.72	42.72	37.84
Gold (Million Fine Troy Ounces)........	1ad	261.73	261.70	261.66	261.64	261.61	261.67	261.61	262.00	262.00	261.55	261.59	261.55
Gold (National Valuation)..................	1and	11.05	11.05	11.05	11.05	11.05	11.05	11.05	11.05	11.04	11.04	11.04	11.04
Monetary Authorities: Other Liab.....	4..d	.25	.39	.17	.46	.17	.07	.22	.06	21.23	25.81	30.86	30.59
Deposit Money Banks: Assets...........	7a.d	546.14	606.46	665.94	791.26	813.16	860.50	961.55	1,126.71	1,257.17	1,404.03	1,793.77	1,947.49
Liabilities...........	7b.d	941.32	1,011.91	1,028.68	1,207.31	1,265.47	1,311.60	1,411.34	1,523.67	1,829.34	2,123.67	2,699.09	2,913.36
Nonbank Financial Insts.: Assets......	7e.d												
Liabilities..................	7f.d	125.08	146.22	175.13	209.37	227.82	300.17	441.43	534.69	648.03	658.08	761.61	923.05
Monetary Authorities					*Billions of US Dollars: End of Period*								
Foreign Assets..................................	11	74.3	85.8	75.1	70.0	81.8	71.5	67.6	68.7	79.0	85.9	86.9	65.1
Claims on Central Government.........	12a	383.5	397.7	410.2	447.5	463.5	494.2	530.7	569.0	648.3	681.8	736.9	774.9
Claims on Banking Institutions.........	12e	.2	.1	.1	2.0	—	.2	.1	—	—	.1	—	.1
Claims on Nonbank Financial Insts....	12g	3.6	2.6	2.2	.7	.3	140.8	43.5	50.3	39.5	43.8	33.0	46.8
Federal Reserve Float.......................	13a	−.7	.1	4.3	.7	1.6	−.2	.9	—	.4	−.3	.9	.9
Reserve Money.................................	14	435.5	454.7	476.1	514.1	545.4	653.6	614.1	661.6	711.2	748.0	780.2	815.2
of which: Currency Outside Banks..	14a	363.5	381.9	406.1	437.6	473.2	567.7	578.5	599.4	644.2	680.1	707.6	742.7
Other Liabs. to Banking Insts...........	14n	3.9	4.5	7.5	7.2	5.9	6.1	6.3	2.5	9.5	7.6	5.3	5.0
Foreign Liabilities.............................	16c	.3	.4	.2	.5	.2	.1	.2	.1	21.2	25.8	30.9	30.6
Central Government Deposits...........	16d	36.4	45.0	37.1	29.2	32.9	54.8	31.3	31.9	33.5	38.2	40.9	31.7
Capital Accounts..............................	17a	14.5	15.2	16.1	17.3	18.8	19.6	20.2	20.8	23.4	25.0	31.2	33.5
Other Items (Net).............................	17r	−29.6	−33.5	−45.1	−47.5	−56.0	−27.6	−29.2	−28.9	−31.5	−33.3	−30.6	−28.2
Banking Institutions													
Commercial Banks					*Billions of US Dollars: End of Period*								
Reserves...	20	67.3	67.6	67.5	74.1	66.5	89.2	61.8	62.6	67.5	68.2	62.3	66.3
Foreign Assets..................................	21	38.9	34.1	102.0	151.0	237.1	295.9	374.2	481.9	497.5	592.7	722.6	801.1
Claims on Central Government.........	22a	290.4	278.7	261.8	270.1	214.1	228.9	184.5	162.7	205.8	132.9	110.1	97.1
Claims on State and Local Govts......	22b	97.6	93.4	94.2	96.7	104.8	110.8	114.1	120.2	121.7	132.5	140.8	157.7
Claims on Private Sector...................	22d	2,512.2	2,755.6	2,926.9	3,179.2	3,462.4	3,704.3	4,127.4	4,297.7	4,506.9	4,884.2	5,372.5	6,050.3
Claims on Nonbank Financial Insts....	22g	428.7	467.5	495.7	571.2	663.2	699.6	721.8	777.4	917.9	999.5	1,096.4	1,089.6
Demand Deposits.............................	24	756.7	710.8	676.3	656.4	622.9	626.4	540.9	628.8	571.5	602.4	647.0	610.5
Time and Savings Deposits...............	25	1,376.2	1,490.1	1,613.2	1,761.5	1,945.2	2,017.1	2,228.7	2,478.1	2,747.6	2,977.9	3,259.7	3,527.9
Money Market Instruments...............	26aa	331.7	390.9	488.2	585.8	601.0	729.8	840.3	852.8	816.0	841.1	963.6	1,154.8
Bonds...	26ab	142.6	161.1	168.9	192.6	220.2	240.6	273.2	310.2	332.2	379.1	437.4	494.1
Foreign Liabilities.............................	26c	311.3	305.3	327.5	381.2	490.3	537.6	614.3	685.9	731.0	821.9	1,037.7	1,212.4
Central Government Deposits...........	26d	23.8	19.0	28.7	27.8	13.2	49.6	16.4	47.5	31.1	30.2	26.9	33.9
Credit from Monetary Authorities....	26g	—	.3	8.7	3.5	3.3	—	1.9	—	.9	—	1.9	1.8
Liab. to Nonbank Financial Insts......	26j	30.5	36.7	39.0	58.1	104.9	145.6	172.4	196.6	226.8	235.3	244.1	268.5
Other Items (Net).............................	27r	462.3	582.5	597.6	675.2	747.2	782.2	895.8	702.5	860.4	922.0	886.4	958.1
Credit Unions and Savings Insts					*Billions of US Dollars: End of Period*								
Reserves...	20..t	41.2	43.8	41.7	43.0	54.2	66.5	64.4	85.2	93.1	98.7	94.3	89.1
Claims on Central Government.........	22a.t	49.2	36.7	34.8	30.2	23.3	19.8	17.0	18.8	17.0	21.2	17.4	20.1
Claims on State and Local Govts......	22b.t	2.0	2.0	2.1	2.1	2.5	3.0	3.2	4.5	5.5	6.3	7.1	8.6
Claims on Private Sector...................	22d.t	926.0	941.6	995.8	1,018.4	1,086.3	1,177.0	1,271.2	1,317.0	1,363.7	1,496.0	1,723.6	1,905.0
Claims on Nonbank Financial Insts....	22g.t	200.8	210.3	206.7	206.3	202.0	208.4	201.4	242.0	273.5	314.2	322.1	301.8
Demand Deposits.............................	24..t	109.2	109.4	109.7	108.5	114.1	114.4	121.5	128.2	135.0	148.0	156.0	164.3
Time and Savings Deposits...............	25..t	809.5	808.3	809.0	790.3	795.9	807.8	827.2	892.4	946.3	1,022.8	1,024.1	1,072.5
Money Market Instruments...............	26aat	122.8	133.6	141.5	154.2	183.5	216.5	233.8	275.4	313.1	376.2	466.6	504.5
Bonds...	26abt	3.1	3.1	2.7	2.8	2.6	2.7	6.3	3.6	3.4	5.1	7.6	8.7
Central Government Deposits..........	26d.t	100.0	97.4	121.9	138.0	180.1	243.7	260.0	259.1	231.7	249.3	309.3	325.5
Other Items (Net).............................	27r.t	74.5	82.6	96.4	106.3	92.1	89.6	108.4	108.9	123.1	134.9	200.8	249.2
Money Market Funds					*Billions of US Dollars: End of Period*								
Foreign Assets..................................	21..m	15.7	19.7	23.1	23.2	30.1	41.1	87.2	115.0	108.1	71.5	78.5	94.7
Claims on Central Government.........	22a.m	66.1	70.0	90.2	86.2	107.9	103.8	91.6	137.5	142.2	132.1	98.2	88.6
Claims on State and Local Govts......	22b.m	113.4	127.7	144.5	167.0	192.8	210.4	242.5	276.7	278.5	292.1	313.8	337.1
Claims on Private Sector...................	22d.m	202.3	257.0	297.8	372.4	497.3	650.1	800.6	846.2	813.3	718.6	666.8	750.5
Claims on Banking Institutions.........	22e.m	28.9	48.9	81.6	112.8	122.9	152.1	156.3	249.4	218.8	164.7	167.8	182.9
Claims on Nonbank Financial Insts....	22g.m	77.2	90.8	101.8	96.3	172.4	191.1	182.9	324.4	333.1	328.6	267.5	160.1
Time Deposits..................................	25..m	600.1	741.3	886.7	1,042.5	1,327.9	1,579.6	1,812.1	2,240.6	2,223.9	2,016.4	1,879.8	2,006.9
Other Items (Net).............................	27r.m	−96.6	−127.2	−147.6	−184.7	−204.5	−231.1	−251.1	−291.3	−329.9	−308.8	−287.2	−393.0

United States 111

		1994	1995	1996	1997	1998	1999	2000	2001	2002	2003	2004	2005
Banking Survey		*Billions of US Dollars: End of Period*											
Foreign Assets (Net)	31n	−182.6	−166.1	−127.5	−137.6	−141.5	−129.1	−85.4	−20.4	−67.6	−97.6	−180.4	−282.0
Domestic Credit	32	5,192.9	5,570.1	5,877.1	6,349.1	6,966.7	7,594.1	8,224.8	8,806.0	9,370.6	9,865.8	10,529.0	11,397.0
Claims on Central Govt. (Net)	32an	629.1	621.6	609.4	638.9	582.5	498.7	516.2	549.6	717.1	650.2	585.5	589.6
Claims on State and Local Govts	32b	213.0	223.1	240.8	265.7	300.2	324.1	359.8	401.3	405.7	430.8	461.7	503.4
Claims on Private Sector	32d	3,640.5	3,954.2	4,220.5	4,570.0	5,046.1	5,531.4	6,199.2	6,461.0	6,683.8	7,098.8	7,762.9	8,705.8
Claims on Nonbank Financial Insts.	32g	710.3	771.2	806.4	874.5	1,038.0	1,239.8	1,149.6	1,394.1	1,564.0	1,686.0	1,718.9	1,598.2
Money	34	1,230.3	1,203.0	1,193.0	1,203.5	1,211.8	1,309.8	1,242.3	1,357.3	1,351.8	1,431.2	1,511.8	1,519.7
Quasi-Money	35	2,785.9	3,039.7	3,308.9	3,594.3	4,069.0	4,404.5	4,868.0	5,611.1	5,917.8	6,017.1	6,163.7	6,607.2
Money Market Instruments	36aa	454.5	524.5	629.7	740.1	784.5	946.2	1,074.1	1,128.2	1,129.1	1,217.3	1,430.2	1,659.3
Bonds	36ab	145.7	164.2	171.6	195.5	222.8	243.3	279.4	313.8	335.6	384.2	445.1	502.8
Liab. to Nonbank Financial Insts.	36j	30.5	36.7	39.0	58.1	104.9	145.6	172.4	196.6	226.8	235.3	244.1	268.5
Other Items (Net)	37r	363.3	435.8	407.5	420.1	432.2	415.5	503.1	178.6	341.9	483.0	553.6	557.5
Money plus Quasi-Money	35l	4,016.2	4,242.7	4,501.9	4,797.8	5,280.8	5,714.2	6,110.3	6,968.3	7,269.6	7,448.3	7,675.6	8,126.9
Nonbank Financial Institutions													
Other Financial Institutions		*Billions of US Dollars: End of Period*											
Foreign Assets	41	—	—	—	—	—	—	—	—	—	—	—	—
Claims on Central Government	42a	152.5	231.2	142.9	166.7	190.7	113.2	144.1	147.7	160.6	200.7	125.0	125.6
Claims on State and Local Govts	42b	281.0	288.9	295.4	305.1	335.6	343.8	338.6	382.0	423.7	448.7	460.0	488.5
Claims on Private Sector	42d	3,778.7	4,400.9	5,200.2	6,135.9	7,329.1	8,877.7	9,370.9	9,776.0	9,708.7	11,840.4	13,777.9	15,675.1
Claims on Banking Institutions	42e	135.2	135.5	165.0	186.7	282.3	364.7	396.8	550.3	554.1	525.8	483.9	494.5
Credit Market Instruments	46aa	1,865.9	2,105.7	2,595.2	3,188.4	3,866.1	4,698.9	4,665.4	4,465.9	4,000.8	4,849.5	5,467.3	6,449.3
Bonds	46ab	831.2	994.0	1,128.2	1,212.3	1,430.0	1,555.2	1,684.4	2,045.2	2,372.7	2,774.6	3,298.5	3,865.7
Foreign Liabilities	46c	125.1	146.2	175.1	209.4	227.8	300.2	441.4	534.7	648.0	658.1	761.6	923.0
Credit from Monetary Authorities	46g	3.6	2.6	2.2	.7	.3	.2	.1					
Credit from Banking Institutions	46h	750.9	810.6	857.5	942.2	1,126.6	1,187.2	1,192.9	1,450.1	1,626.0	1,750.3	1,804.6	1,676.4
Liabs. to Insur. Cos. & Pen. Funds	46j	762.0	958.3	1,081.4	1,310.6	1,447.7	1,815.4	1,925.4	1,784.8	1,712.9	2,048.2	2,330.9	2,443.5
Other Items (Net)	47r	8.6	39.1	−36.1	−69.2	39.2	142.3	340.7	575.3	486.7	934.9	1,183.9	1,425.8
Insurance Companies & Pension Funds		*Billions of US Dollars: End of Period*											
Claims on Central Government	42a.s	595.7	592.7	567.3	539.7	487.5	475.2	434.3	404.2	447.8	452.1	449.1	478.5
Claims on State and Local Govts	42b.s	167.7	174.8	189.3	209.8	229.7	222.1	204.9	194.2	203.7	251.3	299.5	332.8
Claims on Private Sector	42d.s	3,666.6	4,335.1	4,872.7	5,666.9	6,423.8	7,144.9	6,994.1	6,853.1	6,115.2	7,329.0	8,107.2	8,550.9
Claims on Banking Institutions	42e.s	178.7	200.4	261.3	322.1	372.5	369.1	365.3	398.2	407.2	425.6	386.0	384.3
Claims on Nonbank Financial Insts.	42g.s	806.8	1,021.2	1,154.6	1,403.9	1,563.6	1,956.2	2,103.7	1,969.1	1,880.2	2,256.2	2,561.4	2,681.7
Insurance and Pension Reserves	47a.s	5,377.4	6,249.2	6,955.2	7,985.1	8,946.8	10,011.7	9,946.4	9,603.5	8,798.8	10,313.3	11,321.6	11,895.5
Other Items (Net)	47r.s	38.2	75.0	89.9	157.3	130.4	155.9	156.0	215.2	255.4	400.7	481.6	532.7
Financial Survey		*Billions of US Dollars: End of Period*											
Foreign Assets (Net)	51n	−307.7	−312.3	−302.6	−347.0	−369.4	−429.3	−526.8	−555.1	−715.7	−755.7	−942.0	−1,205.1
Domestic Credit	52	13,124.9	14,822.4	16,338.5	18,498.6	20,925.2	23,531.0	24,562.2	25,169.1	24,866.4	28,701.9	32,028.8	35,450.2
Claims on Central Govt. (Net)	52an	1,377.3	1,445.5	1,319.5	1,345.2	1,260.7	1,087.0	1,094.5	1,101.6	1,325.5	1,303.0	1,159.6	1,193.8
Claims on State and Local Govts.	52b	661.7	686.7	725.5	780.6	865.4	890.0	903.4	977.5	1,033.1	1,130.8	1,221.2	1,324.7
Claims on Private Sector	52d	11,085.8	12,690.2	14,293.5	16,372.8	18,799.0	21,554.0	22,564.2	23,090.0	22,507.7	26,268.1	29,648.0	32,931.8
Liquid Liabilities	55l	4,016.2	4,242.7	4,501.9	4,797.8	5,280.8	5,714.2	6,110.3	6,968.3	7,269.6	7,448.3	7,675.6	8,126.9
Credit Market Instruments	56aa	2,320.4	2,630.2	3,224.8	3,928.5	4,650.5	5,645.1	5,739.5	5,594.1	5,129.9	6,066.8	6,897.6	8,108.6
Bonds	56ab	976.9	1,158.1	1,299.8	1,407.8	1,652.8	1,798.6	1,963.9	2,359.0	2,708.3	3,158.8	3,743.6	4,368.4
Other Items (Net)	57r	5,503.5	6,479.0	7,009.3	8,017.6	8,971.8	9,943.8	10,221.7	9,692.5	9,043.0	11,272.3	12,770.0	13,641.2
Money (National Definitions)		*Billions of US Dollars: End of Period*											
Monetary Base	19ma	422.5	439.0	456.6	485.0	518.3	600.7	590.1	639.9	686.2	725.2	764.7	792.9
Monetary Base, Season. Adjusted	19mac	418.3	434.6	452.1	479.9	513.9	593.9	584.9	635.5	681.5	720.1	759.0	786.6
M1	59ma	1,174.2	1,152.1	1,104.5	1,096.9	1,120.2	1,148.0	1,111.6	1,208.3	1,245.0	1,332.1	1,401.3	1,396.8
M1, Seasonally Adjusted	59mac	1,150.3	1,126.8	1,080.0	1,072.2	1,094.9	1,123.1	1,087.6	1,182.1	1,219.0	1,304.2	1,372.1	1,368.8
M2	59mb	3,518.6	3,663.3	3,835.6	4,052.8	4,406.3	4,675.1	4,962.7	5,486.0	5,832.3	6,112.0	6,456.7	6,713.3
M2, Seasonally Adjusted	59mbc	3,497.6	3,640.6	3,815.3	4,031.7	4,383.7	4,648.7	4,931.3	5,451.4	5,800.6	6,079.6	6,421.9	6,675.7
M3	59mc	4,389.0	4,658.8	5,008.0	5,489.2	6,087.9	6,597.1	7,173.8	8,105.8	8,633.5	8,927.8	9,482.2	10,201.4
M3, Seasonally Adjusted	59mcc	4,369.8	4,636.3	4,985.5	5,460.9	6,051.9	6,551.5	7,117.6	8,035.4	8,568.0	8,872.3	9,433.0	10,154.0
L	59mf	5,344.6	5,732.8	6,111.6	6,636.7	....	....	....	....	....	....	....	....
L, Seasonally Adjusted	59mfc	5,315.8	5,702.3	6,083.6	6,611.3								
Debt	59mg	12,990.0	13,694.5	14,430.5	15,221.5	16,264.9	17,352.9	18,270.1	19,363.8	....	....	....	....
Debt, Seasonally Adjusted	59mgc	12,988.5	13,694.9	14,433.5	15,227.3	16,277.3	17,360.8	18,278.3	19,375.5	....	....	....	....
Treasury Securities by Holders		*Billions of US Dollars: End of Period*											
Total	59t	3,465.6	3,608.5	3,755.1	3,778.3	3,723.7	3,652.7	3,357.8	3,352.7	3,609.8	4,008.2	4,370.7	4,678.0
Nonresidents	59ta	632.6	816.9	1,040.3	1,153.2	1,166.2	1,058.4	1,021.4	1,095.2	1,285.5	1,533.6	1,900.2	2,196.8
Residents	59tb	2,833.0	2,791.6	2,714.7	2,625.1	2,557.4	2,594.3	2,336.3	2,257.5	2,324.3	2,474.6	2,470.5	2,481.3
Monetary Authorities	59tba	364.5	378.2	390.9	430.7	452.1	478.0	511.7	551.7	629.4	666.7	717.8	744.2
Commercial Banks	59tbb	290.4	278.7	261.8	270.1	214.1	228.9	184.5	162.7	205.8	132.9	110.1	97.1
Govt. Sponsored Enterprises	59tbc	51.9	58.0	18.8	25.9	25.2	30.9	13.3	13.6	25.7	13.5	12.9	13.1
Other Financial Institutions	59tbd	862.4	929.6	863.5	823.7	807.8	700.4	691.7	711.5	775.2	827.4	713.7	743.2
Nonfinancial Sectors	59tbe	1,263.7	1,147.1	1,179.7	1,074.7	1,058.2	1,156.1	935.1	818.0	688.1	834.2	916.1	883.6
Interest Rates		*Percent Per Annum*											
Discount Rate (End of Period)	60	4.75	5.25	5.00	5.00	4.50	5.00	6.00	1.25	.75	† 2.00	3.15	5.15
Federal Funds Rate	60b	4.20	5.84	5.30	5.46	5.35	4.97	6.24	3.89	1.67	1.13	1.35	3.21
Commercial Paper Rate	60bc	4.66	5.93	5.41	5.57	5.34	5.18	6.31	3.61	1.69	1.11	1.49	3.38
Treasury Bill Rate	60c	4.27	5.51	5.02	5.07	4.82	4.66	5.84	3.45	1.61	1.01	1.38	3.17
Treas. Bill Rate(Bond Equivalent)	60cs	4.35	5.65	5.14	5.20	4.90	4.77	6.03	3.48	1.63	1.02	1.39	3.21
Certificates of Deposit Rate	60lc	4.63	5.92	5.39	5.62	5.47	5.33	6.46	3.69	1.73	1.15	1.56	3.51
Lending Rate (Prime Rate)	60p	7.14	8.83	8.27	8.44	8.35	7.99	9.23	6.92	4.68	4.12	4.34	6.19
Govt. Bond Yield: Med.-Term	61a	6.26	6.26	5.99	6.10	5.14	5.49	6.22	4.08	3.10	2.11	2.78	3.93
Long-Term	61	7.08	6.58	6.44	6.35	5.26	5.64	6.03	5.02	4.61	4.02	4.27	4.29

		1994	1995	1996	1997	1998	1999	2000	2001	2002	2003	2004	2005
Prices, Production, Labor													
		Index Numbers (2000=100): Period Averages											
Industrial Share Prices....................	62	30.8	36.7	45.3	58.4	72.8	92.1	100.0	78.9	65.3	62.9	73.7	78.9
Producer Prices.............................	63	90.8	94.0	96.2	96.1	93.8	94.5	100.0	101.1	98.8	104.1	110.5	118.6
Industrial Goods........................	63a	89.5	93.1	94.5	94.8	92.6	93.9	100.0	100.7	98.3	103.2	109.5	118.9
Finished Goods..........................	63b	91.0	92.7	95.1	95.5	94.7	96.4	100.0	102.0	100.6	103.8	107.6	112.8
Consumer Goods....................	63ba	89.2	90.9	93.7	94.2	93.3	95.5	100.0	102.4	100.8	105.1	109.7	116.1
Capital Equipment.................	63bb	96.6	98.5	99.6	99.6	99.1	99.1	100.0	100.6	100.2	100.5	101.9	104.2
Consumer Prices...........................	64	86.1	88.5	91.1	93.2	94.7	96.7	100.0	102.8	104.5	106.8	109.7	113.4
Wages: Hourly Earnings(Mfg)..........	65ey	84.0	86.2	89.0	91.7	93.9	96.7	100.0	103.1	106.8	109.9	112.7	115.7
Industrial Production.....................	66	73.8	† 77.4	80.7	86.6	91.7	95.8	100.0	96.5	96.6	97.2	101.1	104.5
Crude Petroleum Production...........	66aa	114.4	112.7	111.1	110.8	107.4	101.0	100.0	99.6	98.7	97.9	93.1	88.0
Nonagr.Employment, Seas.Adj........	67..c	86.7	89.0	90.8	93.2	95.5	97.9	100.0	100.0	98.9	98.6	99.7	101.3
		Number in Thousands: Period Averages											
Labor Force.................................	67d	† 131,057	132,304	133,945	† 136,297	137,674	139,368	142,583	143,734	144,863	146,510	147,401	149,321
Employment...............................	67e	† 123,060	124,900	126,709	† 129,558	131,464	133,488	136,891	136,933	136,485	137,736	139,252	141,730
Unemployment............................	67c	† 7,997	7,404	7,236	† 6,739	6,210	5,880	5,692	6,801	8,378	8,774	8,149	7,591
Unemployment Rate (%).................	67r	† 6.1	5.6	5.4	† 4.9	4.5	4.2	4.0	4.7	5.8	6.0	5.5	5.1
Intl. Transactions & Positions		*Billions of US Dollars*											
Exports, f.a.s.................................	70	512.63	584.74	625.07	689.18	682.14	695.80	781.92	729.10	693.10	724.77	818.52	907.16
Imports, c.i.f.................................	71	689.22	770.85	822.02	899.02	944.35	1,059.44	1,259.30	1,179.18	1,200.23	1,303.05	1,525.68	1,732.35
Imports, f.o.b...............................	71.v	663.83	743.54	795.29	870.57	911.90	1,024.62	1,218.02	1,141.00	1,163.56	1,257.12	1,469.86	1,670.75
		2000=100											
Volume of Exports.........................	72	66.3	72.0	76.5	85.5	87.5	90.4	100.0	94.0	90.3	92.9	101.1	108.6
Volume of Imports........................	73	56.9	60.9	64.3	72.1	80.5	89.6	100.0	97.1	101.3	106.8	118.4	125.1
Export Prices................................	76	98.9	103.9	104.5	103.1	99.7	98.4	100.0	99.2	98.2	99.7	103.6	106.9
Import Prices................................	76.x	96.2	100.6	101.6	99.1	93.1	93.9	100.0	96.5	94.1	96.9	102.3	110.0
Balance of Payments		*Billions of US Dollars: Minus Sign Indicates Debit*											
Current Account, n.i.e....................	78ald	−121.64	−113.56	−124.73	−140.40	−213.50	−299.85	−415.15	−388.96	−472.44	−527.51	−665.29	−791.51
Goods: Exports f.o.b....................	78aad	504.91	577.04	614.01	680.33	672.38	686.27	774.63	721.84	685.93	716.70	811.01	898.46
Goods: Imports f.o.b....................	78abd	−668.69	−749.37	−803.11	−876.49	−917.11	−1,029.99	−1,224.42	−1,145.93	−1,164.74	−1,260.75	−1,472.96	−1,677.40
Trade Balance.........................	78acd	−163.78	−172.33	−189.10	−196.16	−244.74	−343.72	−449.78	−424.08	−478.81	−544.05	−661.95	−778.94
Services: Credit...........................	78add	198.35	217.35	237.62	254.13	260.81	279.61	295.97	283.05	288.79	299.39	340.93	376.79
Services: Debit............................	78aed	−133.08	−141.41	−152.55	−165.93	−180.67	−199.20	−223.74	−221.76	−231.05	−250.24	−290.28	−314.58
Balance on Goods & Services.......	78afd	−98.51	−96.39	−104.04	−107.96	−164.60	−263.31	−377.56	−362.80	−421.07	−494.90	−611.30	−716.73
Income: Credit............................	78agd	166.52	210.26	226.13	256.82	261.83	293.93	350.92	288.25	270.65	303.06	374.91	474.65
Income: Debit.............................	78ahd	−149.38	−189.36	−203.81	−244.20	−257.55	−280.04	−329.86	−263.12	−258.44	−266.47	−347.32	−463.35
Balance on Gds, Serv. & Inc........	78aid	−81.38	−75.49	−81.71	−95.34	−160.32	−249.42	−356.50	−337.66	−408.86	−458.30	−583.71	−705.44
Current Transfers, n.i.e.: Credit......	78ajd	7.99	8.63	10.40	9.89	9.64	8.88	10.83	9.01	12.32	14.92	19.37	15.77
Current Transfers: Debit...............	78akd	−48.25	−46.70	−53.42	−54.95	−62.82	−59.31	−69.47	−60.31	−75.91	−84.13	−100.95	−101.85
Capital Account, n.i.e....................	78bcd	−1.72	−.93	−.74	−1.03	−.77	−4.94	−1.01	−1.27	−1.47	−3.32	−2.26	−4.35
Capital Account, n.i.e.: Credit.......	78bad	.82	1.03	.79	.81	.87	1.04	1.00	.99	.97	1.00	1.02	1.06
Capital Account: Debit.................	78bbd	−2.55	−1.96	−1.52	−1.84	−1.64	−5.97	−2.01	−2.27	−2.44	−4.32	−3.28	−5.42
Financial Account, n.i.e..................	78bjd	121.72	96.02	131.05	222.30	76.51	227.40	486.66	405.15	506.85	536.82	579.62	771.35
Direct Investment Abroad.............	78bdd	−80.18	−98.78	−91.88	−104.82	−142.64	−224.93	−159.21	−142.35	−154.46	−149.90	−244.13	−9.07
Dir. Invest. in Rep. Econ., n.i.e.......	78bed	46.13	57.80	86.52	105.59	179.03	289.44	321.27	167.02	84.37	63.96	133.16	109.75
Portfolio Investment Assets...........	78bfd	−63.19	−122.39	−149.32	−116.85	−130.20	−122.24	−127.91	−90.64	−48.57	−146.72	−146.55	−180.13
Equity Securities.......................	78bkd	−48.29	−65.51	−82.71	−57.29	−101.36	−114.31	−106.71	−109.12	−16.95	−118.00	−84.76	−142.13
Debt Securities........................	78bld	−14.90	−56.89	−66.61	−59.57	−28.84	−7.93	−21.19	18.48	−31.61	−28.72	−61.79	−37.99
Portfolio Investment Liab., n.i.e.....	78bgd	139.41	210.35	332.78	333.11	187.56	285.60	436.57	428.34	427.61	520.31	766.18	908.55
Equity Securities.......................	78bmd	.89	16.52	11.06	67.03	41.96	112.29	193.60	121.46	54.07	33.98	61.79	86.60
Debt Securities........................	78bnd	138.52	193.83	321.72	266.08	145.61	173.31	242.97	306.88	373.54	486.33	704.39	821.95
Financial Derivatives Assets...........	78bwd	....	....	....	....	....	....	....	....	....	....	....	....
Financial Derivatives Liabilities.......	78bxd	....	....	....	....	....	—	—	....	....	....	....	....
Other Investment Assets...............	78bhd	−40.92	−121.38	−178.87	−262.82	−74.20	−165.64	−273.11	−144.71	−87.94	−31.33	−479.93	−251.70
Monetary Authorities..................	78bod	—	—	—	—	—	—	—	—	—	—	—	—
General Government..................	78bpd	−.39	−.98	−.99	.07	−.42	2.75	−.94	−.49	.35	.54	1.71	5.54
Banks......................................	78bqd	−4.20	−75.11	−91.56	−141.12	−35.57	−70.69	−133.38	−135.71	−38.26	−13.01	−361.62	−213.02
Other Sectors...........................	78brd	−36.33	−45.29	−86.33	−121.77	−38.20	−97.70	−138.79	−8.52	−50.02	−18.85	−120.02	−44.22
Other Investment Liab., n.i.e.........	78bid	120.47	170.43	131.82	268.09	56.96	165.17	289.05	187.50	285.83	280.50	550.88	193.95
Monetary Authorities..................	78bsd	9.59	46.72	56.88	−18.85	6.88	24.59	−2.52	35.29	72.19	38.64	51.78	−39.79
General Government..................	78btd	2.77	.90	.73	−2.70	−3.25	−.98	−.39	−4.78	2.66	1.99	.78	4.52
Banks......................................	78bud	108.00	64.18	22.18	171.31	30.27	67.20	122.72	88.40	117.63	145.85	405.99	204.12
Other Sectors...........................	78bvd	.10	58.63	52.03	118.33	23.07	74.37	169.24	68.58	93.35	94.02	92.33	25.09
Net Errors and Omissions................	78cad	−3.70	28.21	−12.26	−79.87	144.49	68.66	−70.21	−10.00	−29.24	−7.52	85.13	10.41
Overall Balance........................	78cbd	−5.35	9.75	−6.67	1.01	6.73	−8.73	.29	4.93	3.69	−1.53	−2.80	−14.10
Reserves and Related Items............	79dad	5.35	−9.75	6.67	−1.01	−6.73	8.73	−.29	−4.93	−3.69	1.53	2.80	14.10
Reserve Assets............................	79dbd	5.35	−9.75	6.67	−1.01	−6.73	8.73	−.29	−4.93	−3.69	1.53	2.80	14.10
Use of Fund Credit and Loans........	79dcd	—	—	—	—	—	—	—	—	—	—	—	—
Exceptional Financing...................	79ded	—	—	—	—	—	—	—	—	—	—	—	—

		1994	1995	1996	1997	1998	1999	2000	2001	2002	2003	2004	2005
International Investment Position						*Billions of US Dollars*							
Assets...........................	79aad	3,315.13	3,964.56	4,650.84	5,379.13	6,179.13	7,399.71	7,401.19	6,930.48	6,807.79	8,318.16	10,075.34	11,079.20
Direct Investment Abroad..............	79abd	1,114.58	1,363.79	1,608.34	1,879.29	2,279.60	2,839.64	2,694.01	2,314.93	2,022.59	2,729.13	3,287.90	3,524.46
Portfolio Investment.....................	79acd	937.15	1,203.93	1,487.55	1,751.18	2,069.38	2,551.95	2,425.53	2,169.74	2,079.89	2,953.78	3,553.39	4,074.00
Equity Securities.........................	79add	626.76	790.62	1,006.14	1,207.79	1,474.98	2,003.72	1,852.84	1,612.67	1,374.67	2,079.42	2,560.42	3,086.45
Debt Securities........................	79aed	310.39	413.31	481.41	543.40	594.40	548.23	572.69	557.06	705.23	874.36	992.97	987.54
Financial Derivatives....................	79ald	—	—	—	—	—	—	—	—	—	—	—	—
Other Investment......................	79afd	1,100.01	1,220.78	1,394.21	1,613.82	1,684.14	1,871.67	2,153.24	2,315.85	2,546.71	2,451.68	3,044.46	3,292.70
Monetary Authorities.................	79agd	—	—	—	—	—	—	—	—	—	—	—	—
General Government..................	79ahd	83.91	85.06	86.12	86.20	86.77	84.23	85.17	85.65	85.31	84.77	83.06	77.52
Banks..................................	79aid	693.12	768.15	857.51	982.10	1,009.05	1,082.93	1,231.52	1,390.90	1,559.46	1,772.90	2,227.86	2,430.66
Other Sectors........................	79ajd	322.98	367.57	450.58	545.52	588.32	704.52	836.56	839.30	901.95	594.00	733.54	784.52
Reserve Assets..........................	79akd	163.39	176.06	160.74	134.84	146.01	136.45	128.40	129.96	158.60	183.58	189.59	188.04
Liabilities.................................	79lad	3,450.39	4,270.39	5,010.86	6,201.86	7,249.90	8,437.12	8,982.20	9,269.93	9,262.12	10,657.94	12,524.08	13,625.38
Dir. Invest. in Rep. Economy..........	79lbd	757.85	1,005.73	1,229.12	1,637.41	2,179.04	2,798.19	2,783.24	2,560.29	2,021.82	2,454.88	2,703.70	2,797.17
Portfolio Investment....................	79lcd	1,413.54	1,848.75	2,284.15	2,767.48	3,198.67	3,583.08	3,862.63	4,153.84	4,330.53	5,295.17	6,272.33	7,001.02
Equity Securities.........................	79ldd	397.72	549.51	672.40	952.89	1,250.34	1,611.53	1,643.21	1,572.68	1,335.79	1,839.51	2,123.26	2,302.65
Debt Securities........................	79led	1,015.82	1,299.24	1,611.75	1,814.59	1,948.33	1,971.54	2,219.43	2,581.16	2,994.74	3,455.66	4,149.07	4,698.37
Financial Derivatives....................	79lld	—	—	—	—	—	—	—	—	—	—	—	—
Other Investment......................	79lfd	1,278.99	1,415.92	1,497.59	1,796.97	1,872.19	2,055.85	2,336.33	2,555.80	2,909.78	2,907.90	3,548.06	3,827.19
Monetary Authorities.................	79lgd	157.19	169.48	186.85	211.63	228.25	250.66	255.97	279.76	301.27	317.91	332.74	352.15
General Government..................	79lhd	23.68	23.57	22.59	21.71	18.39	21.14	19.32	17.01	17.14	16.63	16.49	16.00
Banks..................................	79lid	858.31	922.44	941.35	1,104.22	1,139.88	1,206.00	1,322.14	1,460.72	1,694.03	2,122.48	2,691.17	2,895.29
Other Sectors........................	79ljd	239.82	300.42	346.81	459.41	485.68	578.05	738.90	798.31	897.34	450.88	507.67	563.75
Government Finance						*Billions of US Dollars: Year Ending December 31*							
Deficit (-) or Surplus................	80	−184.6	−146.2	−110.8	−2.4	54.4	156.7	254.6	92.4	−230.5	−396.3	−400.2	−318.1
Total Revenue and Grants..............	81y	1,277.5	1,367.2	1,474.7	1,619.3	1,747.7	1,858.3	2,042.7	1,995.3	1,814.4	1,795.7	1,926.2	2,197.3
Revenue..	81	1,277.5	1,367.2	1,474.7	1,619.3	1,747.7	1,858.3	2,042.7	1,995.3	1,814.4	1,795.7	1,926.2	2,197.3
Grants.......................................	81z												
Exp. & Lending Minus Repay..........	82z	1,462.1	1,513.4	1,585.4	1,621.8	1,693.3	1,701.6	1,788.1	1,902.8	2,044.9	2,191.9	2,326.4	2,515.4
Expenditure.................................	82	....	....	....	....	....	....	....	....	....	....	....	....
Lending Minus Repayments..........	83	....	....	....	....	....	....	....	....	....	....	....	....
Total Financing.............................	80h	184.6	146.2	110.8	2.4	−54.4	−156.7	−254.6	−92.4	230.5	396.3	400.2	318.0
Total Net Borrowing.....................	84	161.3	151.1	119.9	4.3	−62.2	−92.2	−316.7	−43.1	235.8	381.2	368.0	313.0
Net Domestic...............................	84a	....	....	....	....	....	....	....	....	....	....	....	....
Net Foreign..................................	85a	....	....	....	....	....	....	....	....	....	....	....	....
Use of Cash Balances...................	87	23.3	−4.9	−9.1	−1.9	7.9	−64.4	62.1	−49.3	−5.2	15.0	32.2	5.0
Total Debt by Residence..................	88	3,551.7	3,698.7	3,842.1	3,866.5	3,805.7	3,711.6	3,413.2	3,394.4	3,647.9	4,042.9	4,382.6	4,703.5
Domestic......................................	88a	2,884.4	2,863.5	2,740.0	2,624.9	2,527.0	2,442.9	2,379.0	2,343.2	2,401.1	2,505.3	2,438.4	2,662.4
Foreign..	89a	667.3	835.2	1,102.1	1,241.6	1,278.7	1,268.7	1,034.2	1,051.2	1,246.8	1,537.6	1,944.2	2,041.1
National Accounts						*Billions of US Dollars*							
Househ.Cons.Expend.,incl.NPISHs....	96f.c	4,743.3	4,975.8	5,256.8	5,547.4	5,879.5	6,282.5	6,739.4	7,055.1	7,350.8	7,709.9	8,214.3	8,745.8
Government Consumption Expend...	91f.c	1,104.1	1,136.5	1,171.1	1,216.6	1,256.0	1,334.0	1,417.1	1,501.7	1,616.9	1,736.7	1,843.4	1,962.7
Gross Fixed Capital Formation..........	93e.c	1,254.6	1,345.6	1,454.4	1,570.0	1,700.7	1,845.6	1,983.5	1,970.1	1,914.5	2,010.2	2,245.2	2,486.5
Changes in Inventories....................	93i.c	63.8	31.1	30.8	72.0	70.8	66.9	56.5	−31.7	11.9	15.5	55.5	18.9
Exports of Goods and Services........	90c.c	720.9	812.2	868.6	955.4	955.9	991.3	1,096.3	1,032.8	1,005.9	1,045.7	1,173.8	1,301.2
Imports of Goods and Services (-).....	98c.c	814.5	903.6	964.8	1,056.9	1,115.9	1,251.8	1,475.8	1,399.9	1,430.3	1,546.5	1,797.8	2,027.7
Gross Domestic Product (GDP).........	99b.c	7,072.2	7,397.7	7,816.8	8,304.3	8,747.0	9,268.4	9,817.0	10,128.0	10,469.6	10,971.3	11,734.3	12,487.2
Net Primary Income from Abroad.....	98.nc	26.2	35.8	35.0	33.0	21.4	33.8	39.0	43.7	30.6	68.1	53.8	33.6
Gross National Income (GNI)...........	99a.c	6,955.9	7,332.3	7,758.2	8,266.6	8,783.0	9,337.9	9,983.1	10,261.3	10,521.2	10,992.3	11,711.2	12,465.8
Net Current Transf. from Abroad......	98t.c	37.8	35.4	39.1	41.6	48.8	47.2	56.1	47.0	64.5	71.7	81.5	89.4
Gross Saving.................................	99s.c	1,070.7	1,184.6	1,291.2	1,461.1	1,598.7	1,674.3	1,770.5	1,657.6	1,489.1	1,474.1	1,572.1	1,668.0
Consumption of Fixed Capital..........	99cfc	833.7	878.4	918.1	974.5	1,030.2	1,101.3	1,187.8	1,281.5	1,292.0	1,331.3	1,435.3	1,574.1
GDP Volume 2000 Ref., Chained.....	99b.r	7,835.5	8,031.7	8,328.9	8,703.5	9,066.9	9,470.4	9,817.0	9,890.7	10,048.9	10,320.6	10,755.7	11,134.8
GDP Volume (2000=100)...............	99bvr	79.8	81.8	84.8	88.7	92.4	96.5	100.0	100.8	102.4	105.1	109.6	113.4
GDP Deflator (2000=100)...............	99bir	90.3	92.1	93.9	95.4	96.5	97.9	100.0	102.4	104.2	106.3	109.1	112.1
						Millions: Midyear Estimates							
Population..............................	99z	266.71	269.60	272.51	275.43	278.36	281.27	284.15	287.00	289.82	292.62	295.41	298.21

Uruguay 298

		1994	1995	1996	1997	1998	1999	2000	2001	2002	2003	2004	2005
Exchange Rates						*Pesos per SDR: End of Period*							
Market Rate	aa	8.1766	10.5704	12.5289	13.5465	15.2307	15.9417	16.3059	18.5594	36.9789	43.5389	40.9218	34.4454
						Pesos per US Dollar: End of Period (ae) Period Average (rf)							
Market Rate	ae	5.6010	7.1110	8.7130	10.0400	10.8170	11.6150	12.5150	14.7680	27.2000	29.3000	26.3500	24.1000
Market Rate	rf	5.0439	6.3490	7.9718	9.4418	10.4719	11.3393	12.0996	13.3191	21.2570	28.2087	28.7037	24.4786
						Index Numbers (2000=100): Period Averages							
Market Rate	ahx	241.3	191.3	152.2	128.3	115.5	106.7	100.0	90.9	61.1	42.9	42.2	49.4
Nominal Effective Exchange Rate	nec	177.9	148.7	122.4	108.9	102.0	103.1	100.0	97.4	82.6	56.8	53.8	60.2
Real Effective Exchange Rate	rec	87.8	90.7	91.4	94.6	96.2	101.0	100.0	99.2	88.1	68.6	68.5	76.6
Fund Position						*Millions of SDRs: End of Period*							
Quota	2f.s	225	225	225	225	225	307	307	307	307	307	307	307
SDRs	1b.s	—	2	3	—	1	1	—	1	4	3	1	4
Reserve Position in the Fund	1c.s	15	15	15	15	15	36	36	36				
Total Fund Cred.&Loans Outstg	2tl	20	14	6	—	114	114	114	114	1,319	1,626	1,728	1,612
International Liquidity						*Millions of US Dollars Unless Otherwise Indicated: End of Period*							
Total Reserves minus Gold	1l.d	969	1,150	1,251	1,556	2,073	2,081	2,479	3,097	769	2,083	2,508	3,074
SDRs	1b.d	—	4	4	—	1	1	—	2	6	4	1	6
Reserve Position in the Fund	1c.d	22	23	22	21	22	49	46	45				
Foreign Exchange	1d.d	946	1,124	1,225	1,536	2,051	2,031	2,432	3,050	763	2,079	2,507	3,068
Gold (Million Fine Troy Ounces)	1ad	1.704	1.715	1.736	1.760	1.783	1.800	1.081	.008	.008	.008	.008	.008
Gold (National Valuation)	1and	497	525	672	651	517	518	295	2	3	3	4	4
Monetary Authorities: Other Assets	3..d	234	238	255	266	270	251	253	257	780	463	320	611
Other Liab.	4..d	1,030	976	941	911	884	730	673	489	476	217	220	89
Banking Institutions: Assets	7a.d	3,499	3,479	4,179	4,758	5,015	5,803	6,252	7,271	4,138	3,725	3,813	3,998
Liabilities	7b.d	3,335	3,364	3,966	4,697	5,315	6,076	6,815	7,969	3,586	2,512	1,926	1,968
Nonbank Financial Insts.:Assets	7e.d	91	207	242	200	191	86	1,160	1,294	461	773	1,322	1,108
Liabilities	7f.d	77	185	219	180	162	63	868	993	304	706	1,239	884
Monetary Authorities						*Millions of Pesos: End of Period*							
Foreign Assets	11	9,847.2	14,662.8	18,854.9	23,437.0	† 30,926.9	33,135.3	37,944.3	49,565.5	42,221.0	74,714.4	74,621.6	88,904.5
Claims on Central Government	12a	8,305.9	11,543.8	13,985.3	16,586.3	† 22,043.9	25,926.4	33,860.7	8,160.5	72,765.2	75,217.1	93,483.7	76,181.3
Claims on Local Government	12b	.2	.2	.3	.3	† .3	.3	.3	.3	.7	.8	.8	.6
Claims on Nonfin.Pub.Enterprises	12c	3,226.9	3,984.7	4,694.5	5,334.5	† 5,253.2	4,998.1	4,701.6	4,677.3	7,439.7	5,656.2	4,117.4	3,251.1
Claims on Private Sector	12d	130.2	150.5	114.9	163.0	† 433.6	458.2	484.3	284.3	2,163.3	2,066.7	1,642.5	1,572.4
Claims on Banking Institutions	12e	4,070.7	5,385.7	6,769.6	8,927.5	† 10,258.1	10,803.3	10,447.5	11,928.4	33,030.2	6,187.5	3,954.9	5,999.6
Reserve Money	14	11,314.0	14,760.9	19,563.8	24,455.0	† 27,602.3	33,455.0	36,591.5	46,166.3	46,478.7	74,668.0	61,211.1	68,839.8
of which: Currency Outside Banks	14a	3,313.8	4,327.1	5,269.3	6,498.2	† 7,084.0	7,639.0	7,284.0	7,095.1	7,673.4	9,440.5	10,803.7	13,315.1
Time, Savings,& Fgn.Currency Dep	15	997.0	2,083.1	3,926.9	4,872.6	† 6,298.9	7,247.2	5,131.6	5,844.2	7,727.1	7,866.5	9,074.7	9,478.8
Liabs. of Central Bank: Securities	16ac	—	1,341.9	533.3	803.2	† 1,367.8	1,882.5	519.8	531.9	914.0	7,116.4	14,830.3	21,784.5
Foreign Liabilities	16c	5,936.0	7,089.4	8,275.1	9,147.0	† 11,305.1	10,303.5	10,289.0	9,342.1	61,702.3	77,141.3	76,530.7	57,678.9
Central Government Deposits	16d	8,342.1	11,089.0	14,208.1	18,471.3	† 26,237.6	26,300.6	38,629.3	16,040.6	38,167.3	8,263.0	28,100.9	31,844.7
Capital Accounts	17a	−2,490.5	682.8	363.4	−779.7	† 508.4	596.1	−865.1	−334.2	2,100.1	−8,176.5	−11,361.3	−11,681.6
Other Items (Net)	17r	1,482.5	−1,319.3	−2,451.2	−2,520.7	† −4,404.1	−4,463.3	−2,857.4	−2,974.6	530.4	−3,036.2	−565.7	−2,035.6
Banking Institutions						*Millions of Pesos: End of Period*							
Reserves	20	7,651.2	9,419.5	12,931.7	15,780.5	† 17,771.7	21,389.5	23,776.6	37,789.7	39,548.8	63,422.8	47,853.9	55,299.6
Claims on Mon.Author.:Securities	20c	—	593.2	524.5	397.3	† 911.4	1,735.1	477.7	531.9	806.4	172.3	1,328.6	8,211.9
Foreign Assets	21	19,599.6	24,741.8	36,409.7	47,774.0	† 54,248.8	67,402.9	78,243.2	107,379.3	112,543.6	109,142.7	100,472.6	96,345.8
Claims on Central Government	22a	3,917.9	3,944.5	4,980.3	7,368.4	† 9,239.7	6,207.5	7,677.1	11,414.2	29,319.8	27,677.1	26,975.5	23,819.9
Claims on Local Government	22b	115.9	194.0	248.9	302.6	† 3,706.8	3,994.3	1,871.6	2,088.1	2,097.4	2,495.7	2,725.1	2,216.5
Claims on Nonfin.Pub.Enterprises	22c	284.7	535.1	712.6	820.2	† 949.2	1,238.3	1,548.5	2,275.2	5,250.4	4,413.8	3,736.6	4,148.9
Claims on Private Sector	22d	20,896.4	32,241.8	43,728.0	58,466.5	† 107,287.7	118,105.4	124,044.4	133,635.6	171,868.8	138,471.2	113,489.5	109,251.3
Demand Deposits	24	2,012.5	2,658.7	3,474.1	3,738.0	† 7,314.2	7,216.6	7,053.7	6,641.0	6,556.6	9,706.8	10,928.0	15,440.9
Time, Savings,& Fgn.Currency Dep	25	26,920.9	37,093.6	50,401.5	65,891.6	† 82,057.8	94,100.1	105,053.1	128,569.9	167,909.3	186,530.5	178,603.7	171,282.0
Money Market Instruments	26aa	—				† 3,531.2	4,640.4	4,905.9	5,890.4	10,211.1	11,540.9	2,084.4	1,618.1
Foreign Liabilities	26c	18,677.1	23,918.8	34,553.9	47,156.4	† 57,489.0	70,576.9	85,293.2	117,692.2	97,548.7	73,595.2	50,760.8	47,433.7
Central Government Deposits	26d	1,570.0	1,844.5	2,655.0	4,522.6	† 7,537.6	4,803.5	3,860.6	4,600.4	9,249.9	23,660.5	16,237.0	22,447.9
Credit from Monetary Authorities	26g	818.2	1,042.4	1,475.9	2,072.7	† 10,135.3	10,162.5	10,602.5	11,941.2	35,542.2	5,669.6	2,397.5	5,045.4
Liab. to Nonbank Financial Insts	26j	—			85.7	† 215.4	183.1	227.6	144.9				
Capital Accounts	27a	3,249.6	5,630.9	8,053.5	10,033.8	† 32,788.5	36,132.5	31,353.1	26,216.6	−7,089.4	10,176.7	26,424.3	25,531.1
Other Items (Net)	27r	−782.6	−518.9	−1,078.1	−2,591.3	† −6,953.9	−7,742.6	−10,710.5	−6,582.7	41,506.7	24,915.3	9,145.9	10,494.8
Banking Survey						*Millions of Pesos: End of Period*							
Foreign Assets (Net)	31n	4,833.6	8,396.3	12,435.6	14,907.5	† 16,381.6	19,657.8	20,605.4	29,910.5	−4,486.4	33,120.6	47,802.7	80,137.7
Domestic Credit	32	26,966.0	39,661.2	51,601.6	66,048.1	† 115,139.1	129,824.4	131,698.5	141,896.5	243,488.0	224,074.9	201,833.0	166,149.4
Claims on Central Govt. (Net)	32an	2,311.7	2,554.8	2,102.4	960.9	† −2,491.7	1,029.9	−952.2	−1,066.3	54,667.8	70,970.6	76,121.3	45,708.5
Claims on Local Government	32b	116.1	194.2	249.2	302.9	† 3,707.1	3,994.6	1,871.9	2,088.4	2,098.1	2,496.5	2,725.9	2,217.2
Claims on Nonfin.Pub.Enterprises	32c	3,511.7	4,519.8	5,407.1	6,154.8	† 6,202.4	6,236.4	6,250.1	6,952.4	12,690.1	10,069.9	7,853.9	7,400.0
Claims on Private Sector	32d	21,026.6	32,392.3	43,842.9	58,629.5	† 107,721.3	118,563.5	124,528.7	133,919.9	174,032.0	140,537.9	115,132.0	110,823.7
Money	34	5,341.1	7,066.3	8,819.1	10,294.6	† 14,420.3	14,873.9	14,355.8	13,755.2	14,278.4	19,177.4	22,225.4	29,680.3
Quasi-Money	35	27,918.0	39,176.7	54,328.4	70,764.3	† 88,356.7	101,347.2	110,184.6	134,414.2	175,636.4	194,397.0	187,678.4	180,760.7
Money Market Instruments	36aa	—			—	† 3,531.2	4,640.4	4,905.9	5,890.4	10,211.1	11,540.9	2,084.4	1,618.1
Liabs. of Central Bank: Securities	36ac	—	748.7	8.8	405.9	† 456.4	147.4	42.0	—	107.7	6,944.2	13,501.7	13,572.7
Liabs. to Nonbank Financial Insts	36j	—			85.7	† 215.4	183.1	227.6	144.9				
Capital Accounts	37a	759.1	6,313.7	8,416.9	9,254.1	† 33,296.9	36,728.6	30,488.0	25,882.5	−4,989.3	2,000.3	15,063.0	13,849.5
Other Items (Net)	37r	−2,218.5	−5,247.7	−7,535.9	−9,848.9	† −8,756.2	−8,438.4	−7,900.1	−8,280.1	43,757.3	23,135.8	9,082.7	6,805.8
Money plus Quasi-Money	35l	33,259.1	46,243.0	63,147.4	81,058.8	† 102,777.1	116,221.1	124,540.4	148,169.3	189,914.8	213,574.4	209,903.8	210,441.1

Uruguay 298

		1994	1995	1996	1997	1998	1999	2000	2001	2002	2003	2004	2005
Nonbank Financial Institutions		*Millions of Pesos: End of Period*											
Reserves	40	3.1	5.6	7.0	4.5	5.2	9.3	72.7	101.4	99.7	80.6	66.8	61.9
Claims on Mon.Author.:Securities	40c	2.5	2.1	2.7	2.7	2.4	2.1	22.6	22.7	4.4	3.6	—	—
Foreign Assets	41	510.0	1,469.4	2,109.7	2,011.3	2,066.0	994.3	14,513.2	19,110.9	12,531.9	22,635.1	34,834.8	26,708.9
Claims on Central Government	42a	2.6	3.7	4.3	4.3	4.2	2.1	20.4	15.8	13.7	23.1	151.4	139.2
Claims on Private Sector	42d	.2	1.3	1.8	2.0	.4	.1	3.4	7.0	25.8	18.0	15.9	17.1
Claims on Banking Institutions	42e	2.5	5.2	3.0	3.4	2.8	2.4	17.1	34.8	9.9	25.4	54.9	25.6
Foreign Currency Deposits	45	.1	.2	.4	.2	.2	.1	1.7	1.6	1.1	.8	1.0	.9
Foreign Liabilities	46c	431.8	1,315.2	1,910.2	1,807.3	1,753.5	736.6	10,864.5	14,657.8	8,264.9	20,674.0	32,654.3	21,316.0
Central Government Deposits	46d	.5	.6	.8	.4	.5	.3	3.8	5.1	14.1	9.6	6.4	12.3
Capital Accounts	47a	101.3	189.2	272.2	336.0	389.9	288.1	4,296.5	5,090.3	4,973.8	3,331.2	3,287.5	4,613.6
Other Items (Net)	47r	−12.9	−17.8	−55.1	−115.7	−63.0	−14.7	−517.1	−462.2	−568.3	−1,229.7	−825.3	1,010.0
Money (National Definitions)		*Millions of Pesos: End of Period*											
Base Money	19ma	4,593.9	5,927.9	7,649.8	9,570.5	12,910.0	9,879.3	9,503.6	8,288.0	11,969.4	14,308.1	15,827.5	24,590.1
M1	59ma	6,226.1	8,273.3	10,712.5	12,577.3	14,500.8	15,000.7	14,237.2	13,729.4	14,206.0	19,444.6	22,281.4	29,693.0
M2	59mb	10,031.1	14,351.6	17,990.9	21,392.5	24,763.1	26,094.9	26,832.6	27,217.0	24,410.2	30,294.5	34,699.9	44,124.0
Interest Rates		*Percent Per Annum*											
Discount Rate (End of Period)	60	182.30	178.70	160.30	95.50	73.70	66.39	57.26	71.66	316.01	46.27	10.00	10.00
Discount Rate (Fgn.Cur.)(End Per)	60..f	17.40	17.60	17.50	17.30	15.30	15.68	16.73	14.06	16.96	14.44	12.37	....
Money Market Rate	60b	39.82	36.81	28.47	23.43	20.48	13.96	14.82	22.10	86.10	20.76	3.57	1.25
Treasury Bill Rate	60c	44.60	39.40	29.20	23.18	....	....	....	....	....	32.53	14.75	4.14
Treasury Bill Rate (Fgn.Currency)	60c.f	4.91	6.11	5.36	5.18	....	....	....	....	....	....	....	....
Savings Rate	60k	23.77	23.57	22.12	16.96	10.55	7.96	6.27	5.90	† 4.81	3.72	2.55	1.33
Savings Rate (Fgn.Currency)	60k.f	2.41	2.81	2.70	2.67	2.35	1.76	1.74	1.19	† .88	.64	.45	.51
Deposit Rate	60l	55.78	57.68	42.43	29.57	22.76	21.49	18.26	21.60	† 62.58	29.69	6.20	2.84
Deposit Rate (Fgn.Currency)	60l.f	3.86	5.10	5.42	5.42	5.50	5.58	5.80	4.78	† 3.61	2.41	1.03	1.28
Lending Rate	60p	89.28	93.05	85.93	67.19	54.39	50.03	46.06	48.56	† 118.38	58.94	23.68	13.61
Lending Rate (Fgn.Currency)	60p.f	10.41	12.33	11.72	11.30	11.08	11.26	12.04	11.12	† 11.20	10.35	7.35	6.77
Prices, Production, Labor		*Index Numbers (2000=100): Period Averages*											
Wholesale Prices	63	43.1	59.4	74.3	86.4	94.4	93.6	100.0	† 106.6	140.6	195.3	224.0	218.3
Consumer Prices	64	37.3	53.0	68.0	81.5	90.3	95.5	100.0	104.4	118.9	142.0	155.0	162.3
Manufacturing Production	66ey	102.1	99.3	103.3	109.3	111.9	104.5	100.0	94.1	....	....	....	....
		Number in Thousands: Period Averages											
Labor Force	67d	1,307	1,343	....	....	1,239	....	1,235	1,270	....	1,241	....	....
Employment	67e	1,188	1,206	1,175	1,172	1,104	1,082	1,068	1,076	1,038	1,032	1,092	....
Unemployment	67c	120	138	159	152	124	138	168	193	211	209	164	....
Unemployment Rate (%)	67r	9.2	10.3	11.9	11.4	10.1	11.3	13.6	15.3	17.0	16.9	13.1	....
Intl. Transactions & Positions		*Millions of US Dollars*											
Exports	70..d	1,913.4	2,106.0	2,397.2	2,725.7	2,770.7	2,237.1	2,294.7	2,060.4	1,861.0	2,206.0	2,930.8	3,404.5
Imports, c.i.f.	71..d	2,786.1	2,866.9	3,322.8	3,726.8	3,810.5	3,356.8	3,465.8	3,060.8	1,964.3	2,190.4	3,113.6	3,878.9
Balance of Payments		*Millions of US Dollars: Minus Sign Indicates Debit*											
Current Account, n.i.e	78ald	−438.3	−212.5	−233.4	−287.4	−475.5	−507.6	−566.2	−487.7	322.2	−55.5	42.5	−2.3
Goods: Exports f.o.b	78aad	1,917.6	2,147.6	2,448.5	2,793.1	2,829.3	2,290.6	2,383.8	2,139.4	1,922.1	2,281.1	3,145.0	3,758.0
Goods: Imports f.o.b	78abd	−2,623.6	−2,710.6	−3,135.4	−3,497.5	−3,601.4	−3,187.2	−3,311.1	−2,914.7	−1,873.8	−2,097.8	−2,992.2	−3,729.9
Trade Balance	78acd	−706.0	−563.0	−686.9	−704.4	−772.1	−896.6	−927.3	−775.3	48.3	183.3	152.8	28.2
Services: Credit	78add	1,330.7	1,359.2	1,398.7	1,424.1	1,319.1	1,261.6	1,275.7	1,122.5	753.7	802.8	1,150.8	1,329.4
Services: Debit	78aed	−861.6	−857.7	−839.0	−888.6	−883.6	−802.3	−881.8	−801.4	−600.3	−635.8	−786.1	−895.9
Balance on Goods & Services	78afd	−236.9	−61.5	−127.2	−168.9	−336.6	−437.3	−533.4	−454.2	201.7	350.3	517.5	461.7
Income: Credit	78agd	282.5	404.3	460.5	547.3	608.0	735.5	781.5	832.0	453.4	241.7	372.6	567.0
Income: Debit	78ahd	−525.1	−631.3	−649.2	−740.0	−805.9	−879.3	−841.8	−895.2	−405.1	−730.1	−960.4	−1,152.3
Balance on Gds, Serv. & Inc	78aid	−479.5	−288.5	−315.9	−361.6	−534.5	−581.1	−593.7	−517.4	250.0	−138.1	−70.3	−123.5
Current Transfers, n.i.e.: Credit	78ajd	49.2	84.0	90.7	83.0	75.0	78.4	48.0	48.0	83.7	94.9	127.2	138.5
Current Transfers: Debit	78akd	−8.0	−8.0	−8.2	−8.8	−16.0	−4.9	−20.5	−18.3	−11.5	−12.3	−14.3	−17.2
Capital Account, n.i.e	78bcd	—	—	—	—	—	—	—	—	—	—	—	—
Capital Account, n.i.e.: Credit	78bad	—	—	—	—	—	—	—	—	—	—	—	—
Capital Account: Debit	78bbd	—	—	—	—	—	—	—	—	—	—	—	—
Financial Account, n.i.e	78bjd	537.2	421.7	233.6	608.7	545.1	147.1	779.3	457.3	−1,927.5	4.2	−82.9	870.1
Direct Investment Abroad	78bdd	—	—	—	−13.2	−9.3	—	.6	−6.2	−53.8	−15.0	−17.7	4.5
Dir. Invest. in Rep. Econ., n.i.e.	78bed	154.5	156.6	136.8	126.4	164.1	235.3	273.5	271.0	174.6	416.5	332.6	710.6
Portfolio Investment Assets	78bfd	—	—	—	—	—	−44.3	−98.1	236.7	95.2	−512.6	−695.7	266.3
Equity Securities	78bkd	—	—	—	—	—	—	—	10.2	—	—	.9	1.0
Debt Securities	78bld	—	—	—	—	—	−44.3	−98.1	226.5	95.2	−512.6	−696.6	265.3
Portfolio Investment Liab., n.i.e.	78bgd	158.1	288.8	179.9	209.6	419.4	128.2	289.5	264.4	204.5	201.6	273.4	530.0
Equity Securities	78bmd	—	—	—	—	—	—	—	—	28.1	—	20.1	20.1
Debt Securities	78bnd	158.1	288.8	179.9	209.6	419.4	128.2	289.5	236.3	204.5	201.6	253.3	509.9
Financial Derivatives Assets	78bwd	....	....	....	....	....	....	....	....	....	....	....	....
Financial Derivatives Liabilities	78bxd	....	....	....	....	....	....	....	....	....	....	....	....
Other Investment Assets	78bhd	−71.8	−961.9	−1,238.5	−626.6	−428.0	−119.3	−690.4	−2,275.2	1,825.5	−1,254.8	−259.7	−1,086.5
Monetary Authorities	78bod	−10.1	—	—	—	—	—	.9	−5.3	−522.6	270.4	218.0	−324.8
General Government	78bpd	—	—	—	—	—	—	—	10.0	2.0	−14.8	−1.0	—
Banks	78bqd	−44.0	−961.3	−1,232.4	−636.4	−428.0	65.4	−549.3	−2,210.5	3,014.5	−1,399.6	−397.6	−843.6
Other Sectors	78brd	−17.7	−.6	−6.1	9.8	—	−184.7	−142.0	−69.4	−668.4	−110.8	−79.1	81.8
Other Investment Liab., n.i.e	78bid	296.4	938.2	1,155.4	912.5	398.9	−52.8	1,004.2	1,966.6	−4,173.5	1,168.5	284.2	445.2
Monetary Authorities	78bsd	5.7	−62.5	−10.3	−31.3	−37.2	−135.7	−38.8	−52.4	−13.1	−66.8	−27.0	−31.4
General Government	78btd	134.0	18.6	20.3	96.8	169.1	260.5	200.7	144.4	666.6	328.9	39.5	51.1
Banks	78bud	99.8	1,017.9	1,112.9	778.9	272.9	−161.3	862.5	1,780.5	−4,693.7	963.9	366.8	405.2
Other Sectors	78bvd	56.9	−35.8	32.5	68.1	−5.9	−16.3	−20.2	94.1	−133.3	−57.5	−95.1	20.3
Net Errors and Omissions	78cad	10.2	18.6	152.2	78.8	285.5	250.9	−46.6	334.4	−2,291.8	1,009.2	344.7	−71.5
Overall Balance	78cbd	109.1	227.8	152.4	400.1	355.1	−109.6	166.5	304.0	−3,897.1	957.9	304.4	796.4
Reserves and Related Items	79dad	−109.1	−227.8	−152.4	−400.1	−355.1	109.6	−166.5	−304.0	3,897.1	−957.9	−304.4	−796.4
Reserve Assets	79dbd	−98.5	−218.0	−140.8	−391.7	−515.2	109.6	−166.5	−304.0	2,331.2	−1,380.4	−454.2	−620.9
Use of Fund Credit and Loans	79dcd	−10.6	−9.8	−11.6	−8.3	160.1	—	—	—	—	1,565.9	422.5	−175.5
Exceptional Financing	79ded	—	—	—	....	—	—	—	—	—	—	149.8	—

Uruguay 298

		1994	1995	1996	1997	1998	1999	2000	2001	2002	2003	2004	2005
International Investment Position							*Millions of US Dollars*						
Assets	79aad	....	....	....	....	....	12,747.3	13,789.1	16,986.1	10,271.7	14,223.5	15,381.7	17,391.4
Direct Investment Abroad	79abd	—	—	—	—	—	47.2	54.0	132.0	108.0	111.6	122.8	119.2
Portfolio Investment	79acd	50.4	52.4	56.9	61.7	66.9	842.3	799.0	1,203.4	999.3	1,753.6	2,448.7	2,182.3
Equity Securities	79add	—	—	—	—	—	—	—	—	—	—	—	—
Debt Securities	79aed	50.4	52.4	56.9	61.7	66.9	842.3	799.0	1,203.4	999.3	1,753.6	2,448.7	2,182.3
Financial Derivatives	79ald	....	....	....	....	....							
Other Investment	79afd	3,892.6	4,805.5	6,060.9	6,718.3	7,276.9	8,691.9	10,158.3	12,550.7	8,392.1	10,324.4	10,298.3	12,018.5
Monetary Authorities	79agd	80.2	83.3	49.1	111.8	113.1	—	103.4	177.0	600.4	390.9	172.8	487.5
General Government	79ahd	—	—	—	—	—	—	—	—	—	—	—	5.1
Banks	79aid	3,758.3	4,667.5	5,951.0	6,555.5	7,108.0	5,457.5	6,607.2	8,804.8	3,197.6	5,215.0	5,140.0	5,977.4
Other Sectors	79ajd	54.1	54.7	60.8	51.0	55.8	3,234.4	3,447.7	3,568.8	4,594.1	4,718.5	4,985.5	5,548.5
Reserve Assets	79akd	2,292.9	2,490.6	2,600.2	2,776.8	3,320.6	3,165.9	2,777.8	3,100.0	772.3	2,033.9	2,511.9	3,071.5
Liabilities	79lad	....	....	....	....	....	14,511.7	15,583.1	18,800.6	11,970.9	15,479.8	17,042.7	18,471.9
Dir. Invest. in Rep. Economy	79lbd	—	—	—	—	—	1,790.3	2,088.0	2,406.2	1,402.5	1,799.6	2,110.3	2,991.4
Portfolio Investment	79lcd	1,668.6	1,954.9	2,136.7	2,187.3	2,606.7	2,340.2	2,721.1	3,053.0	2,433.9	2,738.9	3,830.7	4,398.8
Equity Securities	79ldd	—	—	—	—	—	—	—	—	—	—	—	—
Debt Securities	79led	1,668.6	1,954.9	2,136.7	2,187.3	2,606.7	2,340.2	2,721.1	3,053.0	2,433.9	2,738.9	3,830.7	4,398.8
Financial Derivatives	79lld	....	....	....	....	....							
Other Investment	79lfd	7,501.7	8,436.9	9,467.3	10,297.2	11,055.7	10,381.2	10,774.0	13,341.4	8,134.5	10,941.3	11,101.7	11,081.7
Monetary Authorities	79lgd	150.2	68.0	50.3	77.4	232.0	218.9	518.5	550.8	2,192.2	2,811.4	3,058.9	2,456.4
General Government	79lhd	1,416.9	1,537.6	1,507.2	1,594.8	1,738.3	1,976.2	1,904.1	2,077.6	2,493.8	2,836.0	2,892.9	2,978.7
Banks	79lid	4,150.3	5,182.4	6,275.2	7,152.8	7,628.9	6,911.5	7,753.9	9,679.6	2,999.5	4,572.7	4,518.4	4,926.5
Other Sectors	79ljd	1,784.3	1,648.9	1,634.6	1,472.2	1,456.5	1,274.6	597.5	1,033.4	449.0	721.2	631.5	720.1
Government Finance						*Millions of Pesos: Year Ending December 31*							
Deficit (-) or Surplus	80	−2,308	−1,467	−2,379	−2,435	−1,817	† −8,882	−8,322	−11,554	....	....	....	....
Revenue	81	26,409	33,923	45,535	60,165	70,664	† 67,197	68,167	65,933	....	....	....	....
Expenditure	82	28,717	35,390	47,914	62,363	72,673	† 76,079	76,489	77,487	....	....	....	....
Lending Minus Repayments	83	—	—	—	237	−192	† —	—	—	....	....	....	....
Financing													
Net Borrowing	84	2,308	....	....	....	....	....	....	....	....	....	....	....
Domestic	84a	1,378	....	....	....	....	....	....	....	....	....	....	....
Foreign	85a	930	....	....	....	....	....	....	....	....	....	....	....
Use of Cash Balances	87	—	....	....	....	....	....	....	....	....	....	....	....
Debt: Domestic	88a	7,728	....	....	....	....	....	....	....	....	....	....	....
Foreign	89a	13,893	....	....	....	....	....	....	....	....	....	....	....
National Accounts						*Millions of Pesos*							
Househ.Cons.Expend.,incl.NPISHs.	96f	64,230	89,265	117,978	148,387	169,442	173,360	181,114	183,519	192,167	235,345	279,641	301,998
Government Consumption Expend.	91f	10,464	14,505	20,952	25,324	29,357	30,871	32,070	33,837	33,622	35,833	41,137	45,903
Gross Fixed Capital Formation	93e	12,820	16,573	22,835	29,609	35,522	34,377	32,029	30,943	26,360	29,785	42,798	53,000
Changes in Inventories	93i	1,169	2,304	2,089	1,585	1,657	1,536	1,891	3,106	3,707	9,947	6,816	1,099
Exports of Goods and Services	90c	17,423	23,275	32,169	42,109	46,511	42,758	46,915	45,353	57,325	82,301	117,188	122,368
Imports of Goods and Services (-)	98c	17,965	23,403	32,478	42,088	48,222	45,758	50,993	49,546	52,214	77,535	108,227	113,326
Gross Domestic Product (GDP)	99b	88,140	122,521	163,546	204,926	234,267	237,143	243,027	247,211	260,967	315,678	379,353	411,042
Net Primary Income from Abroad	98.n	−1,617	−1,929	−2,265	−2,910	−3,168	−3,249	−3,386	−5,077	−2,595	−14,340	−16,655	−14,275
Gross National Income (GNI)	99a	86,523	120,592	161,281	202,016	231,099	233,894	239,641	242,134	258,371	301,338	362,698	396,767
GDP Vol. 1983 Prices (Millions)	99b.p	262	258	273	286	299	291	287	277	246	252	281	300
GDP Volume (2000=100)	99bvp	91.4	90.1	95.1	99.9	104.4	101.5	100.0	96.6	86.0	87.8	98.2	104.7
GDP Deflator (2000=100)	99bip	39.7	56.0	70.8	84.4	92.3	96.2	100.0	105.3	124.9	147.9	158.9	161.6
						Millions: Midyear Estimates							
Population	99z	3.19	3.22	3.24	3.27	3.29	3.32	3.34	3.37	3.39	3.42	3.44	3.46

Vanuatu 846

		1994	1995	1996	1997	1998	1999	2000	2001	2002	2003	2004	2005
Exchange Rates		*Vatu per SDR: Unless Otherwise Indicated: End of Period*											
Official Rate	aa	163.62	169.07	159.28	167.73	182.73	176.90	186.07	184.41	181.05	166.15	165.44	160.55
		Vatu per US Dollar: End of Period (ae) Period Average (rf)											
Official Rate	ae	112.08	113.74	110.77	124.31	129.78	128.89	142.81	146.74	133.17	111.81	106.53	112.33
Official Rate	rf	116.41	112.11	111.72	115.87	127.52	129.08	137.64	145.31	139.20	122.19	111.79	109.25
Fund Position		*Millions of SDRs: Unless Otherwise Indicated: End of Period*											
Quota	2f.s	12.50	12.50	12.50	12.50	12.50	17.00	17.00	17.00	17.00	17.00	17.00	17.00
SDRs	1b.s	.22	.29	.36	.44	.53	.60	.70	.79	.84	.89	.93	.99
Reserve Position in the Fund	1c.s	2.49	2.49	2.49	2.50	2.50	2.50	2.50	2.50	2.50	2.50	2.50	2.50
Total Fund Cred.&Loans Outstg.	2tl	—	—	—	—	—	—	—	—	—	—	—	—
International Liquidity		*Millions of US Dollars Unless Otherwise Indicated: End of Period*											
Total Reserves minus Gold	1l.d	43.58	48.29	43.92	37.30	44.67	41.35	38.92	37.66	36.52	43.82	61.81	67.20
SDRs	1b.d	.31	.43	.52	.60	.74	.83	.91	.99	1.15	1.32	1.44	1.42
Reserve Position in the Fund	1c.d	3.63	3.70	3.58	3.37	3.51	3.43	3.25	3.14	3.39	3.71	3.88	3.57
Foreign Exchange	1d.d	39.63	44.16	39.82	33.34	40.41	37.10	34.76	33.53	31.98	38.79	56.49	62.21
Monetary Authorities	1dad	39.62	44.16	39.82	33.34	40.41	37.10	34.76	33.53	31.98	38.79	56.49	62.21
Government	1dbd	.01	—	—	—	—	—	—	—	—	—	—	—
Monetary Authorities: Other Liab.	4..d	.22	.04	.16	.04	.13	.18	.23	.52	.40	.18	.06	.44
Deposit Money Banks: Assets	7a.d	158.73	183.94	205.28	204.83	189.99	164.26	160.63	192.62	215.72	243.35	263.41	260.65
Liabilities	7b.d	26.54	32.05	28.42	47.97	25.01	33.92	26.15	28.47	65.22	65.00	64.76	63.58
Other Banking Insts.: Assets	7e.d	—	—	—	—	....	....	....	....	....	....	....	....
Liabilities	7f.d	6	4	4	4	....	....	....	....	....	....	....	....
Monetary Authorities		*Millions of Vatu: End of Period*											
Foreign Assets	11	4,883	5,491	4,865	4,638	5,796	5,331	5,728	5,642	4,960	4,826	6,566	7,546
Claims on Central Government	12a	307	420	408	898	1,221	1,401	1,442	1,151	1,241	1,471	1,418	1,185
Claims on Nonfin.Pub.Enterprises	12c	310	327	353	260	36	32	58	294	320	—	—	—
Claims on Private Sector	12d	76	95	108	124	130	148	143	155	172	180	150	124
Claims on Deposit Money Banks	12e	1	3	98	257	—	316	2	—	2	100	19	2
of which: Fgn.Currency Claims	12ex	1	3	2	1	—	—	2	—	2	—	19	2
Reserve Money	14	2,801	3,654	3,500	3,493	3,674	4,493	4,579	4,563	4,561	4,924	5,431	6,020
of which: Currency Outside DMBs	14a	1,351	1,566	1,571	1,662	2,042	1,936	1,834	1,941	1,916	2,108	2,490	2,691
Liabs. of Central Bank: Securities	16ac	—	—	—	—	1,233	297	99	446	324	99	1,069	589
Foreign Liabilities	16c	25	5	18	4	17	23	33	77	53	20	6	49
Central Government Deposits	16d	2,102	1,962	1,739	2,104	1,679	1,902	1,898	1,377	965	833	1,091	1,728
Capital Accounts	17a	740	641	654	672	686	698	709	724	729	792	673	680
Valuation Adjustment	17rv	134	236	87	64	61	49	32	10	39	—	—	—
Other Items (Net)	17r	† −224	−162	−166	−161	−169	−233	23	45	22	−91	−117	−211
Deposit Money Banks		*Millions of Vatu: End of Period*											
Reserves	20	1,397	2,033	1,829	1,742	1,238	2,215	2,547	2,496	2,563	2,720	2,805	3,247
Claims on Mon.Author.:Securities	20c	—	—	—	—	1,001	297	99	446	324	99	1,069	589
Foreign Assets	21	17,790	20,921	22,738	25,462	24,657	21,171	22,940	28,265	28,727	27,209	28,061	29,279
Claims on Central Government	22a	527	506	492	496	1,131	930	1,417	1,108	1,191	773	813	838
Claims on Local Government	22b	—	2	2	4	—	4	3	5	2	5	6	13
Claims on Nonfin.Pub.Enterprises	22c	105	62	30	134	108	53	100	28	15	16	29	27
Claims on Private Sector	22d	8,540	9,075	9,796	9,580	10,605	12,158	11,556	12,295	13,265	14,558	15,953	18,545
Claims on Other Financial Insts	22f	38	21	—	2								
Demand Deposits	24	4,339	4,690	4,880	4,941	5,368	5,296	6,051	5,974	9,608	10,067	10,243	11,349
Time, Savings,& Fgn.Currency Dep	25	19,443	22,225	24,879	24,645	27,626	24,377	25,686	27,643	23,485	22,553	25,415	28,523
of which: Nonreporting Bks' Deps	25e	—	—	—	—	—	—	—	—	—	—	—	—
Foreign Liabilities	26c	2,975	3,645	3,148	5,963	3,246	4,372	3,735	4,177	8,685	7,268	6,899	7,141
Central Government Deposits	26d	296	161	10	52	140	141	157	292	244	282	185	457
Credit from Monetary Authorities	26g	1	3	1	3	—	316	—	—	—	—	—	—
Capital Accounts	27a	1,726	1,698	2,142	1,350	2,468	2,734	3,550	4,266	4,129	5,222	6,279	5,734
Other Items (Net)	27r	−381	199	−174	464	−108	−409	−515	2,290	−64	−11	−284	−666
Monetary Survey		*Millions of Vatu: End of Period*											
Foreign Assets (Net)	31n	19,674	22,763	24,438	24,132	27,189	22,107	24,901	29,653	24,948	24,748	27,722	29,634
Domestic Credit	32	† 7,514	8,385	9,439	9,341	11,412	12,683	12,664	13,366	14,996	15,888	17,094	18,547
Claims on Central Govt. (Net)	32an	−1,564	−1,197	−849	−762	533	288	804	589	1,223	1,129	954	−162
Claims on Local Government	32b	—	2	2	4	—	4	3	5	2	5	6	13
Claims on Nonfin.Pub.Enterprises	32c	† 416	389	382	394	144	85	158	322	334	16	29	27
Claims on Private Sector	32d	8,616	9,170	9,904	9,703	10,735	12,306	11,699	12,451	13,437	14,738	16,103	18,669
Claims on Other Financial Insts	32f	† 46	21	—	2								
Money	34	5,728	6,306	6,528	6,642	7,600	7,616	8,082	8,041	11,606	12,271	12,869	14,123
Quasi-Money	35	19,443	22,225	24,879	24,645	27,626	24,377	25,686	27,643	23,485	22,553	25,415	28,523
Capital Accounts	37a	2,466	2,339	2,797	2,022	3,155	3,432	4,259	4,990	4,858	6,014	6,952	6,415
Other Items (Net)	37r	† −449	277	−327	163	221	−636	−462	2,344	−5	−202	−420	−879
Money plus Quasi-Money	35l	25,171	28,531	31,407	31,287	35,226	31,994	33,769	35,684	35,091	34,824	38,284	42,645
Money (National Definitions)		*Millions of Vatu: End of Period*											
Reserve Money	19mb	....	....	3,423	3,454	3,483	4,108	4,382	4,437	4,479	4,829	5,295	5,937
M1	59ma	....	....	4,224	4,483	4,967	4,898	4,933	5,085	5,665	5,872	6,557	7,425
M2	59mb	....	....	6,489	6,615	7,576	7,587	8,049	7,965	11,524	12,175	12,733	14,040
MV	59mba	....	....	10,937	10,801	12,084	11,269	11,334	11,429	12,910	13,682	15,818	18,737
M3	59mc	....	....	13,202	12,933	14,694	13,959	14,449	14,309	18,769	19,985	21,994	25,353
MF	59mca	....	....	20,430	20,459	23,118	20,696	22,401	24,179	22,098	21,047	22,329	23,825
M4	59md	....	....	31,368	31,260	35,202	31,965	33,735	35,608	35,008	34,728	38,148	42,562

Vanuatu 846

		1994	1995	1996	1997	1998	1999	2000	2001	2002	2003	2004	2005
Other Banking Institutions						*Millions of Vatu: End of Period*							
Cash	40	15	5	572	36	....	....	....	....	....	....	....	....
Foreign Assets	41	45	51	—	—	....	....	....	....	....	....	....	....
Claims on Central Government	42a	10	10	10	10	....	....	....	....	....	....	....	....
Claims on Private Sector	42d	598	691	40	548	....	....	....	....	....	....	....	....
Claims on Deposit Money Banks	42e	—	—	—	—	....	....	....	....	....	....	....	....
Time and Savings Deposits	45	—	—	—	—	....	....	....	....	....	....	....	....
Foreign Liabilities	46c	625	495	492	491	....	....	....	....	....	....	....	....
Capital Accounts	47a	450	535	535	535	....	....	....	....	....	....	....	....
Other Items (Net)	47r	−407	−273	−405	−432	....	....	....	....	....	....	....	....
Banking Survey						*Millions of Vatu: End of Period*							
Foreign Assets (Net)	51n	19,094	22,318	23,946	23,641	....	....	....	....	....	....	....	....
Domestic Credit	52	8,076	9,065	9,488	9,897	....	....	....	....	....	....	....	....
Claims on Central Govt. (Net)	52an	−1,554	−1,187	−839	−752	....	....	....	....	....	....	....	....
Claims on Nonfin.Pub.Enterprises	52c	† 416	389	382	394	....	....	....	....	....	....	....	....
Claims on Private Sector	52d	9,214	9,861	9,944	10,251	....	....	....	....	....	....	....	....
Liquid Liabilities	55l	25,156	28,526	30,835	31,251	....	....	....	....	....	....	....	....
Other Items (Net)	57r	† 2,014	2,857	2,599	2,287	....	....	....	....	....	....	....	....
Interest Rates						*Percent Per Annum*							
Discount Rate (End of Period)	60	....	....	....	....	7.00	7.00	7.00	6.50	6.50	6.50	6.50	6.25
Money Market Rate	60b	6.00	6.00	6.00	6.00	8.65	6.99	5.58	5.50	5.50	5.50	5.50	5.50
Deposit Rate	60l	5.06	3.00	4.50	3.73	3.29	1.60	1.27	1.25	1.00	1.21	1.71	2.00
Lending Rate	60p	16.00	10.50	10.50	10.50	10.96	10.29	9.85	8.81	7.41	5.90	7.61	7.47
Government Bond Yield	61	8.00	8.00	8.00	8.00	8.00	8.50	8.50	8.50	8.50	8.50	8.50	8.50
Prices						*Index Numbers (2000=100): Period Averages*							
Consumer Prices	64	87.3	† 89.3	90.1	92.6	95.7	97.6	100.0	103.7	105.7	108.9	110.4	....
Intl. Transactions & Positions						*Millions of Vatu*							
Exports	70	2,911	3,173	3,368	4,087	4,323	3,327	3,622	2,895	2,590	3,252	4,168	4,370
Imports, c.i.f.	71	10,404	10,659	10,888	10,888	11,957	12,608	11,957	13,118	12,433	12,703	14,306	15,294
Balance of Payments						*Millions of US Dollars: Minus Sign Indicates Debit*							
Current Account, n.i.e.	78ald	−19.78	−18.25	−26.94	−19.34	−9.41	−33.22	−13.65	−14.53	−39.36	−46.93	−52.34	−63.65
Goods: Exports f.o.b.	78aad	25.11	28.28	30.20	35.32	33.78	25.66	27.19	19.89	20.20	26.84	38.14	37.97
Goods: Imports f.o.b.	78abd	−74.68	−79.44	−81.11	−78.99	−76.23	−84.46	−76.94	−77.96	−78.44	−91.80	−112.99	−131.16
Trade Balance	78acd	−49.58	−51.16	−50.91	−43.67	−42.44	−58.80	−49.74	−58.07	−58.24	−64.96	−74.85	−93.19
Services: Credit	78add	78.14	81.65	92.75	87.79	113.95	114.80	129.81	119.26	83.78	99.08	111.52	127.75
Services: Debit	78aed	−33.44	−35.27	−36.50	−35.95	−56.97	−72.00	−70.15	−72.99	−50.51	−60.64	−65.60	−73.58
Balance on Goods & Services	78afd	−4.88	−4.78	5.34	8.16	14.55	−16.09	9.91	−11.80	−24.97	−26.53	−28.93	−39.01
Income: Credit	78agd	9.94	13.07	15.82	15.41	20.98	21.00	18.74	17.23	22.45	24.21	27.21	27.78
Income: Debit	78ahd	−47.36	−49.79	−47.55	−45.68	−29.26	−26.09	−31.71	−21.23	−33.99	−39.53	−45.87	−53.66
Balance on Gds, Serv. & Inc.	78aid	−42.30	−41.49	−26.39	−22.11	6.26	−21.18	−3.06	−15.80	−36.51	−41.85	−47.59	−64.89
Current Transfers, n.i.e.: Credit	78ajd	23.24	23.81	22.39	21.77	15.55	18.72	27.41	39.53	5.92	4.82	5.26	7.39
Current Transfers: Debit	78akd	−.72	−.56	−22.94	−19.00	−31.22	−30.76	−38.00	−38.26	−8.77	−9.90	−10.02	−6.15
Capital Account, n.i.e.	78bcd	37.28	31.62	4.90	−5.46	−20.86	−49.72	−23.58	−16.03	−2.30	−4.65	−2.16	−3.58
Capital Account, n.i.e.: Credit	78bad	41.45	38.33	43.38	23.75	25.44	23.94	31.88	46.07	10.59	10.45	12.59	11.57
Capital Account: Debit	78bbd	−4.17	−6.71	−38.48	−29.21	−46.29	−73.66	−55.46	−62.10	−12.89	−15.10	−14.75	−15.15
Financial Account, n.i.e.	78bjd	−13.41	25.30	20.88	−16.73	17.37	56.17	19.33	12.75	51.74	47.74	83.31	63.37
Direct Investment Abroad	78bdd	—	—	....	....	....	....	....	....	−.57	−.67	−.78	−.77
Dir. Invest. in Rep. Econ., n.i.e.	78bed	29.79	31.04	32.73	30.23	20.38	13.40	20.26	18.00	14.32	18.14	19.98	13.40
Portfolio Investment Assets	78bfd	—	—	....	....	3.45	−1.01	.69	−4.33	−.33	2.11	.21	−1.06
Equity Securities	78bkd	—	—	....	....	....	....	....	....	....	....	....	....
Debt Securities	78bld	—	—	....	....	....	....	....	....	−.33	2.11	.21	−1.06
Portfolio Investment Liab., n.i.e.	78bgd	—	—	....	....	....	....	....	....	—	—	....	....
Equity Securities	78bmd	—	—	....	....	....	....	....	....	....	....	....	....
Debt Securities	78bnd	—	—	....	....	....	....	....	....	—	—	—	—
Financial Derivatives Assets	78bwd	....	....	....	....	....	....	....	....	....	....	....	....
Financial Derivatives Liabilities	78bxd	....	....	....	....	....	....	....	....	....	....	....	....
Other Investment Assets	78bhd	−45.47	−1.59	−16.63	−23.53	5.12	29.63	−13.55	−11.41	20.10	58.11	20.06	59.52
Monetary Authorities	78bod	....	....	....	....	....	....	....	....	24.26	8.13	29.28	11.91
General Government	78bpd	−.45	−.30	−.39	−.46	....	....	....	....	....	....	....	....
Banks	78bqd	10.60	−2.18	−16.25	−23.07	5.89	27.05	−13.10	−14.81	−22.39	11.55	−7.18	−10.89
Other Sectors	78brd	−55.62	.89	....	....	−.77	2.59	−.45	3.40	18.23	38.43	−2.04	58.51
Other Investment Liab., n.i.e.	78bid	2.27	−4.15	4.78	−23.43	−11.58	14.15	11.93	10.48	18.23	−29.95	43.83	−7.72
Monetary Authorities	78bsd	−.05	.18	−.12	.12	−.11	1.30	−.03	.53	−.17	−.32	−.14	.40
General Government	78btd	2.17	2.21	.45	.68	10.52	5.12	16.36	3.20	....	−.91	−2.61	−1.03
Banks	78bud	.16	−6.54	4.46	−24.23	−20.91	8.73	−4.79	3.05	34.11	−8.69	−6.76	12.17
Other Sectors	78bvd	—	—	....	....	−1.09	−1.01	.39	3.70	−15.35	−20.03	53.34	−19.25
Net Errors and Omissions	78cad	−10.21	−33.38	−4.14	39.37	6.01	3.57	−.88	7.55	−28.29	−5.44	−33.78	−5.51
Overall Balance	78cbd	−6.12	5.30	−5.30	−2.16	−6.89	−23.19	−18.77	−10.27	−18.20	−9.29	−4.98	−9.37
Reserves and Related Items	79dad	6.12	−5.30	5.30	2.16	6.89	23.19	18.77	10.27	18.18	9.29	4.98	9.37
Reserve Assets	79dbd	4.86	−5.30	5.30	2.16	−8.06	3.48	.87	.62	4.66	−2.99	−14.86	−8.97
Use of Fund Credit and Loans	79dcd	—	....	....	....	....	....	....	....	....	....	....	....
Exceptional Financing	79ded	1.26	....	....	....	14.95	19.71	17.90	9.64	13.52	12.27	19.85	18.34

Vanuatu 846

		1994	1995	1996	1997	1998	1999	2000	2001	2002	2003	2004	2005
International Investment Position						*Millions of US Dollars*							
Assets...............................	79aad	....	....	....	....	237.57	264.79	....	....	458.94	503.20	....	....
Direct Investment Abroad..............	79abd	....	....	....	....	—	—	....	....	9.33	11.84	....	....
Portfolio Investment.....................	79acd	....	....	....	....	2.93	4.42	....	....	11.79	12.19	....	....
Equity Securities...........................	79add	....	....	....	....	2.00	3.49	....	....	—	—	....	....
Debt Securities.........................	79aed	....	....	....	....	.92	.93	....	....	11.79	12.19	....	....
Financial Derivatives.....................	79ald	....	....	....	....	—	—	....	....	—	—	....	....
Other Investment.......................	79afd	....	....	....	....	189.99	219.01	....	....	401.30	435.10	....	....
Monetary Authorities..................	79agd	....	....	....	....	—	—	....	....	....	....		
General Government..................	79ahd	....	....	....	....	—	—	....	....	—	—		
Banks......................................	79aid	....	....	....	....	189.99	164.26	....	....	....	....		
Other Sectors............................	79ajd	....	....	....	....	—	54.74	....	....	412.04	442.66		
Reserve Assets.............................	79akd	....	....	....	....	44.65	41.36	....	....	36.52	44.07	....	....
Liabilities................................	79lad	....	....	....	....	265.14	280.72	....	....	483.14	578.92	....	....
Dir. Invest. in Rep. Economy..........	79lbd	....	....	....	....	47.62	66.53	....	....	108.88	149.45		
Portfolio Investment.....................	79lcd	....	....	....	....	—	—	....	....	—	—		
Equity Securities........................	79ldd	....	....	....	....	....	....	....	....	—	—	....	....
Debt Securities.........................	79led	....	....	....	....	....	....	....	....	—	—		
Financial Derivatives.....................	79lld	....	....	....	....	—	—	....	....	—	—		
Other Investment.......................	79lfd	....	....	....	....	217.52	214.19	....	....	374.27	429.47		
Monetary Authorities..................	79lgd	....	....	....	....	.18	1.70	....	....	....	....		
General Government..................	79lhd	....	....	....	....	51.93	56.98	....	....	....	....		
Banks......................................	79lid	....	....	....	....	162.17	153.25	....	....	....	....		
Other Sectors............................	79ljd	....	....	....	....	3.25	2.27	....	....	....	....		
National Accounts							*Millions of Vatu*						
Househ.Cons.Expend.,incl.NPISHs....	96f	12,286	12,777	....	17,473	18,399	18,727	19,376	19,407	20,035	21,085	....	....
Government Consumption Expend...	91f	6,903	6,916	....	6,161	6,751	7,462	7,787	7,688	7,582	7,707	....	....
Gross Fixed Capital Formation..........	93e	6,618	8,128	....	5,343	5,606	6,418	7,181	6,880	6,943	6,756	....	....
Changes in Inventories....................	93i	580	570	....	242	129	152	275	−65	−15	−42	....	....
Exports of Goods and Services..........	90c	11,796	12,041	....	15,459	14,145	12,930	14,491	13,734	13,891	14,786	....	....
Imports of Goods and Services (-).....	98c	14,278	14,603	....	14,945	17,543	18,630	19,087	20,119	19,200	19,829	....	....
Gross Domestic Product (GDP)........	99b	24,962	26,633	27,393	29,650	32,423	32,399	33,662	34,148	32,712	33,724	35,437	36,270
Net Primary Income from Abroad.....	98.n	−3,021	−2,792	−2,027	−1,342	−1,055	−657	−1,784	−669	−704	−1,416	....	....
Gross National Income (GNI)...........	99a	21,941	23,841	25,366	28,308	33,239	32,094	33,177	33,436	31,863	32,341	....	....
GDP Volume 1983 Prices.................	99b.p	14,024	14,469	15,733	16,505	17,216	16,668	17,113	16,650	15,832	16,216	....	....
GDP Volume (2000=100)................	99bvp	81.9	84.5	91.9	96.4	100.6	97.4	100.0	97.3	92.5	94.8	....	....
GDP Deflator (2000=100)...............	99bip	90.5	93.6	88.5	91.3	95.7	98.8	100.0	104.3	105.0	105.7	....	....
						Millions: Midyear Estimates							
Population.............................	99z	.17	.17	.18	.18	.18	.19	.19	.20	.20	.20	.21	.21

Venezuela, República Bolivariana de 299

		1994	1995	1996	1997	1998	1999	2000	2001	2002	2003	2004	2005
Exchange Rates						*Bolivares per SDR: End of Period*							
Official Rate	aa	† 248.175	431.082	685.188	680.359	794.833	889.730	911.711	958.885	1,905.027	2,374.580	2,978.673	3,068.643
					Bolivares per US Dollar: End of Period (ae) Period Average (rf)								
Official Rate	ae	† 170.000	290.000	476.500	504.250	564.500	648.250	699.750	763.000	1,401.250	1,598.000	1,918.000	2,147.000
Official Rate	rf	† 148.503	176.843	417.333	488.635	547.556	605.717	679.960	723.666	1,160.953	1,606.962	1,891.333	2,089.750
					Index Numbers (2000=100): Period Averages								
Market Rate	ahx	477.0	388.9	170.4	139.3	124.4	112.4	100.0	94.0	61.5	42.3	36.0	32.6
Nominal Effective Exchange Rate	nec	371.2	302.1	136.7	117.2	111.3	106.5	100.0	98.2	65.8	44.4	36.4	31.9
Real Effective Exchange Rate	rec	51.7	64.7	53.8	68.3	84.1	95.9	100.0	106.5	83.6	72.4	70.1	69.0
Fund Position						*Millions of SDRs: End of Period*							
Quota	2f.s	1,951	1,951	1,951	1,951	1,951	2,659	2,659	2,659	2,659	2,659	2,659	2,659
SDRs	1b.s	317	255	317	135	74	93	28	8	8	7	5	3
Reserve Position in the Fund	1c.s	145	145	145	145	145	322	322	322	322	322	322	322
of which: Outstg.Fund Borrowing	2c	—	—	—	—	—	—	—	—	—	—	—	—
Total Fund Cred.&Loans Outstg	2tl	1,810	1,506	1,527	1,199	870	540	156	—	—	—	—	—
International Liquidity					*Millions of US Dollars Unless Otherwise Indicated: End of Period*								
Total Reserves minus Gold	1l.d	8,067	6,283	11,788	14,378	11,920	12,277	13,088	9,239	8,487	16,035	18,375	23,919
SDRs	1b.d	463	380	456	183	104	127	36	10	11	10	9	5
Reserve Position in the Fund	1c.d	212	215	208	196	204	442	419	405	438	478	500	460
Foreign Exchange	1d.d	7,393	5,688	11,124	14,000	11,612	11,708	12,633	8,825	8,038	15,546	17,867	23,454
Gold (Million Fine Troy Ounces)	1ad	11.46	11.46	11.46	11.46	9.76	9.76	10.24	10.94	10.56	11.47	11.49	11.48
Gold (National Valuation)	1and	3,440	3,440	3,440	3,440	2,929	2,887	2,794	3,056	3,515	4,632	5,122	5,718
Monetary Authorities: Other Liab.	4..d	2,142	1,784	1,875	1,006	270	228	214	194	159	140	367	305
Deposit Money Banks: Assets	7a.d	1,133	647	794	767	859	1,192	1,159	976	1,096	1,146	1,625	1,354
Liabilities	7b.d	261	181	212	209	170	131	316	433	228	101	53	72
Other Banking Insts.: Assets	7e.d	32	23	40	37	67	8	18	5	6	2	6	3
Liabilities	7f.d	1	—	—	—	—	—	—	—	1	—	—	—
Monetary Authorities						*Billions of Bolivares: End of Period*							
Foreign Assets	11	1,951	2,814	† 7,242	9,610	8,851	9,863	11,149	9,460	16,938	33,154	45,185	63,746
Claims on Central Government	12a	632	1,038	† 1,649	1,096	1,007	1,057	1,106	1,045	1,657	1,115	1,160	2,619
Claims on Nonfin.Pub.Enterprises	12c	10	22	† 10	1	1	1	1	1	1	1	1	1
Claims on Nonbank Pub. Fin. Inst.	12cg	813	1,355	† 1,373	1,384	1,386	1,386	1,390	1,389	1,392	1,388	6	4
Claims on Deposit Money Banks	12e	19	26	† 11	10	1	1	18	43	36	1	1	3
Claims on Other Banking Insts.	12f	1	1	† —	—	1	1	1	—	—	—	—	—
Reserve Money	14	707	931	† 1,852	3,221	3,809	5,065	5,816	6,515	7,783	11,460	16,649	23,345
of which: Currency Outside DMBs	14a	279	355	† 567	987	1,235	1,817	1,998	2,286	3,796	4,778	6,506	8,926
Time, Savings,& Fgn.Currency Dep.	15	16	22	† 20	37	16	13	11	11	16	27	29	85
Liabs. of Central Bank: Securities	16ac	745	609	† 1,659	1,803	1,580	896	1	1	392	7,552	7,064	30,314
Foreign Liabilities	16c	811	1,166	† 1,936	1,320	843	628	291	148	222	224	702	654
Central Government Deposits	16d	223	192	† 991	1,739	728	685	2,119	1,082	786	3,614	8,322	8,399
Liab. to Nonbank Pub. Fin. Insts.	16dg	60	70	† 98	16	11	3	12	17	29	644	543	424
Capital Accounts	17a	312	326	† 2,250	3,278	4,232	4,849	3,898	3,919	10,293	10,700	13,049	15,735
Other Items (Net)	17r	552	1,940	† 1,478	686	28	170	1,515	244	502	1,437	−6	−12,582
Deposit Money Banks						*Billions of Bolivares: End of Period*							
Reserves	20	400	484	† 1,078	1,875	2,392	2,921	3,566	4,031	3,827	6,004	9,103	12,748
Claims on Mon.Author.:Securities	20c	354	252	† 1,044	783	802	391	—	—	381	7,468	6,746	10,432
Foreign Assets	21	193	188	† 377	386	484	772	810	744	1,532	1,828	3,113	2,903
Claims on Central Government	22a	441	840	† 722	765	778	1,220	2,511	2,905	4,364	5,373	9,524	10,067
Claims on State and Local Govts.	22b	1	5	† 1	—	—	14	27	—	—	—	—	—
Claims on Nonfin.Pub.Enterprises	22c	137	180	† 8	8	3	16	89	3	—	1	—	—
Claims on Nonbank Pub. Fin. Inst.	22cg	....	....	294	56	32	45	22	—	—	—	—	—
Claims on Private Sector	22d	798	1,185	† 2,392	5,288	6,022	6,655	8,351	10,310	10,407	11,494	22,850	38,717
Claims on Other Banking Insts.	22f	1	—	† 47	46	113	145	314	60	211	130	332	127
Claims on Nonbank Financial Insts.	22g	11	13	† 25	46	57	180	410	130	119	379	600	999
Demand Deposits	24	666	903	† 2,010	3,616	3,684	4,212	5,743	6,822	7,030	13,651	20,037	32,394
Time, Savings,& Fgn.Currency Dep.	25	1,532	2,079	† 2,406	3,432	4,509	5,247	6,325	7,270	8,191	11,139	16,445	25,398
Money Market Instruments	26aa	....	....	32	64	15	51	95	104	81	45	156	312
Bonds	26ab	....	....	17	1	3	9	11	28	7	14	10	7
Restricted Deposits	26b	....	....	48	63	68	95	169	227	259	306	439	619
Foreign Liabilities	26c	44	53	† 101	105	96	85	221	330	318	161	101	155
Central Government Deposits	26d	47	58	† 271	465	493	866	1,523	1,278	1,237	2,479	4,433	6,999
Liab. to Nonbank Pub. Fin. Insts.	26dg	106	13	† 42	52	53	109	139	64	87	89	2,948	1,606
Credit from Monetary Authorities	26g	18	26	† 1	—	—	13	41	84	972	22	41	88
Liabilities to Other Banking Insts.	26i	31	22	† 208	288	284	267	400	298	95	53	311	201
Liab. to Nonbank Financial Insts.	26j	....	....	39	106	195	161	164	296	253	204	391	402
Capital Accounts	27a	91	330	† 849	1,272	1,666	1,877	2,365	2,937	3,864	5,175	7,050	9,354
Other Items (Net)	27r	−201	−339	† −36	−208	−382	−632	−1,095	−1,555	−1,554	−660	−91	−1,540

Venezuela, República Bolivariana de   299

		1994	1995	1996	1997	1998	1999	2000	2001	2002	2003	2004	2005
Monetary Survey						*Billions of Bolivares: End of Period*							
Foreign Assets (Net).....................	31n	1,288	1,782	† 5,583	8,570	8,397	9,923	11,447	9,726	17,930	34,597	47,495	65,841
Domestic Credit.............................	32	2,574	4,388	† 5,259	6,486	8,179	9,169	10,579	13,484	16,127	13,788	21,719	37,137
Claims on Central Govt. (Net).......	32an	803	1,628	† 1,109	−343	564	727	−24	1,590	3,998	394	−2,071	−2,711
Claims on State and Local Govts....	32b	1	5	† 1	—	—	14	27	—	—	—	—	—
Claims on Nonfin.Pub.Enterprises..	32c	147	202	† 18	9	3	17	89	4	1	1	1	1
Claims on Nonbank Pub.Fin.Inst.....	32cg	813	1,355	† 1,667	1,441	1,418	1,431	1,412	1,389	1,392	1,388	6	4
Claims on Private Sector...............	32d	798	1,185	† 2,392	5,288	6,022	6,655	8,351	10,311	10,407	11,495	22,851	38,718
Claims on Other Banking Insts......	32f	2	1	† 48	46	114	146	315	60	211	130	332	127
Claims on Nonbank Financial Inst..	32g	11	13	† 25	46	57	180	410	130	119	379	600	999
Money...	34	974	1,344	† 2,778	4,918	5,149	6,413	8,037	9,287	10,973	19,056	27,927	42,922
Quasi-Money....................................	35	1,549	2,101	† 2,426	3,468	4,525	5,260	6,337	7,282	8,207	11,166	16,475	25,482
Money Market Instruments..............	36aa	....	....	32	64	15	51	95	104	81	45	156	312
Bonds..	36ab	....	....	17	1	3	9	11	28	7	14	10	7
Liabs. of Central Bank: Securities......	36ac	391	357	† 615	1,020	778	505	1	1	11	84	318	19,882
Restricted Deposits.........................	36b	....	....	48	63	68	95	169	227	259	306	439	619
Liab. to Nonbank Pub. Fin. Insts.......	36dg	166	84	† 140	67	63	113	151	81	117	733	3,491	2,030
Liabilities to Other Banking Insts......	36i	31	22	† 208	288	284	267	400	298	95	53	311	201
Liab. to Nonbank Financial Insts.......	36j	....	....	39	106	195	161	164	296	253	204	391	402
Capital Accounts.............................	37a	402	656	† 3,099	4,549	5,898	6,727	6,263	6,856	14,157	15,875	20,099	25,089
Other Items (Net)............................	37r	350	1,606	† 1,440	513	−403	−508	399	−1,250	−103	849	−401	−13,968
Money plus Quasi-Money.................	35l	2,523	3,445	† 5,204	8,386	9,674	11,673	14,374	16,569	19,181	30,222	44,402	68,404
Other Banking Institutions						*Billions of Bolivares: End of Period*							
Reserves..	40	23	28	† 38	87	96	211	299	95	73	91	181	246
Claims on Mon.Author.:Securities....	40c	1	2	† 39	40	23	9	—	—	6	15	14	302
Foreign Assets.................................	41	5	7	† 19	19	38	5	13	4	8	4	11	7
Claims on Central Government........	42a	104	88	† 25	18	23	97	238	63	101	274	446	230
Claims on Nonfin.Pub.Enterprises....	42c	2	—	† 28	5	2	—	—	—	—	—	—	—
Claims on Nonbank Pub. Fin. Inst....	42cg	....	....	16	11	5	5	5	—	—	—	—	—
Claims on Private Sector.................	42d	326	431	† 402	897	1,007	1,426	1,581	527	355	279	504	1,207
Claims on Deposit Money Banks......	42e	47	45	† 110	102	138	172	139	107	81	126	64	224
Claims on Nonbank Financial Insts...	42g	....	....	4	8	7	22	41	19	72	16	23	25
Demand Deposits..............................	44	13	16	† 30	47	110	156	277	92	109	136	280	690
Time, Savings,& Fgn.Currency Dep....	45	461	558	† 300	613	686	1,019	1,156	260	266	353	605	802
Money Market Instruments..............	46aa	....	....	5	—	—	—	1	13	—	—	—	—
Bonds..	46ab	8	7	† 1	1	19	50	49	29	16	3	2	—
Restricted Deposits.........................	46b	....	....	—	1	1	2	4	1	1	2	2	3
Foreign Liabilities............................	46c	....	....	† —	—	—	—	—	—	1	—	—	—
Central Government Deposits...........	46d	1	1	† 13	41	31	192	438	5	6	13	15	27
Liab. to Nonbank Pub. Fin. Insts......	46dg	1	—	† 2	3	1	4	9	1	38	81	81	81
Credit from Monetary Authorities.....	46g	1	—	† —	—	—	—	—	—	5	3	—	20
Credit from Deposit Money Banks.....	46h	8	7	† 42	115	118	111	71	80	100	77	11	33
Liab. to Nonbank Financial Insts.......	46j	....	....	10	21	8	50	89	13	11	8	6	22
Capital Accounts.............................	47a	64	77	† 174	199	243	296	363	112	87	103	124	96
Other Items (Net)............................	47r	−48	−68	† 103	146	123	67	−139	209	55	26	117	464
Banking Survey						*Billions of Bolivares: End of Period*							
Foreign Assets (Net).......................	51n	1,293	1,789	† 5,602	8,589	8,434	9,928	11,460	9,730	17,937	34,601	47,506	65,848
Domestic Credit.............................	52	3,004	4,905	† 5,673	7,339	9,079	10,382	11,692	14,029	16,437	14,214	22,346	38,444
Claims on Central Govt. (Net)........	52an	906	1,715	† 1,120	−366	557	632	−224	1,648	4,092	656	−1,639	−2,509
Claims on State and Local Govts....	52b	1	5	† 1	—	—	14	27	—	—	—	—	—
Claims on Nonfin.Pub.Enterprises...	52c	148	202	† 45	14	6	17	89	4	1	1	1	1
Claims on Nonbank Pub.Fin.Insts...	52cg	813	1,355	† 1,683	1,451	1,423	1,436	1,417	1,390	1,392	1,388	6	4
Claims on Private Sector...............	52d	1,124	1,615	† 2,794	6,185	7,029	8,081	9,932	10,838	10,762	11,774	23,355	39,924
Claims on Nonbank Financial Inst..	52g	11	13	† 29	54	64	202	450	149	190	395	623	1,025
Liquid Liabilities..............................	55l	2,974	3,992	† 5,496	8,960	10,374	12,638	15,508	16,826	19,483	30,619	45,106	69,651
Money Market Instruments..............	56aa	....	....	37	64	15	51	96	117	81	45	156	312
Bonds..	56ab	8	7	† 18	1	22	59	59	57	23	17	12	7
Liabs. of Central Bank: Securities......	56ac	389	355	† 576	980	755	496	1	1	4	69	304	19,580
Restricted Deposits.........................	56b	....	....	48	64	69	97	172	228	260	308	440	622
Liab. to Nonbank Pub. Fin. Insts......	56dg	166	84	† 142	70	64	116	160	82	155	813	3,571	2,110
Liab. to Nonbank Financial Insts.......	56j	....	....	49	126	203	210	254	309	264	213	398	424
Capital Accounts.............................	57a	466	734	† 3,274	4,748	6,141	7,023	6,626	6,969	14,244	15,978	20,224	25,186
Other Items (Net)............................	57r	293	1,522	† 1,635	914	−130	−381	277	−830	−140	753	−358	−13,600
Interest Rates						*Percent Per Annum*							
Discount Rate (End of Period)...........	60	48.00	49.00	45.00	45.00	60.00	38.00	38.00	37.00	40.00	28.50	28.50	28.50
Money Market Rate.........................	60b	....	....	16.70	12.47	18.58	7.48	8.14	13.33	28.87	13.23	4.38	2.62
Savings Rate...................................	60k	29.11	22.17	19.53	7.59	12.34	8.15	3.17	2.66	3.86	6.24	4.47	6.38
Deposit Rate...................................	60l	39.02	24.72	27.58	14.70	34.84	21.28	16.30	15.51	29.00	17.21	12.60	11.63
Lending Rate...................................	60p	54.66	39.74	39.41	23.69	46.35	32.13	25.20	22.45	36.58	25.19	18.50	16.81
Government Bond Yield....................	61	54.73	53.38	49.09	25.41	47.88	† 31.12	21.03	22.12	38.51	32.15	15.57	12.93
Prices, Production, Labor						*Index Numbers (2000=100): Period Averages*							
Industrial Share Prices.....................	62	† 23.0	24.5	73.6	130.8	79.2	76.5	100.0	112.6	100.1	208.5	418.5	360.4
Prices: Home & Import Goods..........	63	14.7	23.2	47.1	61.2	74.7	86.8	† 100.0	115.5	158.6	240.1	313.4	369.7
Home Goods.....................	63a	13.8	22.1	44.1	58.5	72.7	85.6	† 100.0	124.1	164.7	247.3	323.9	387.9
Consumer Prices..............................	64	10.7	17.1	34.2	51.3	69.6	† 86.1	100.0	112.5	137.8	180.6	219.9	255.0
Crude Petroleum Production.............	66aa	83.0	92.4	95.7	103.8	104.8	94.3	100.0	98.9	....	....	....	....
						Number in Thousands: Period Averages							
Labor Force.......................................	67d	8,027	8,545	....	9,507				11,105	11,674	....	....	....
Employment......................................	67e	7,626	7,667	7,819	8,287	8,711	8,717	8,822	9,405	9,699	9,759	10,234	....
Unemployment..................................	67c	687	875	1,043	1,061	1,093	1,526	1,424	1,436	1,823	2,142	1,841	1,469
Unemployment Rate (%)..................	67r	8.7	10.3	11.8	11.4	11.2	14.9	13.9	13.2	15.8	18.0	15.3	12.2

		1994	1995	1996	1997	1998	1999	2000	2001	2002	2003	2004	2005
Intl. Transactions & Positions							*Billions of Bolivares*						
Exports....................................	70	2,409.8	3,332.6	9,803.1	10,295.6	9,393.5	12,751.4	21,450.8	18,199.7	30,758.1	38,875.1 †	13,280.6	16,017.0
Petroleum............................	70a	1,751.6	2,444.8	7,844.8	8,853.1	6,557.6	9,954.5	18,102.6	14,495.3	22,497.0	30,153.6	—	—
Crude Petroleum.................	70aa	1,197.8	1,641.7	5,346.6	5,934.9	4,220.1	6,592.4	12,305.2	10,114.9	15,978.7	22,307.8	—	....
Imports, c.i.f...........................	71	1,324.0	2,202.0	4,179.9	7,145.5	8,604.0	8,380.5	10,964.0	13,221.1	14,594.9	14,835.1	31,647.4	50,981.8
Imports, f.o.b..........................	71.v	1,192.8	1,983.8	3,765.7	6,437.3	7,751.3	7,550.0	9,877.5	11,910.9	13,148.5	13,364.9	28,770.4	46,347.1
							Millions of US Dollars						
Exports................................	70..d	16,089	18,457	23,060	21,624	17,193	20,190	31,413	25,353	25,890	23,990	33,994	51,859
Petroleum............................	70a.d	11,473	13,739	18,520	18,186	12,021	16,295	26,485	20,122	18,839	18,552	26,829	38,971
Imports, f.o.b.........................	71.vd	8,277	11,396	8,901	13,159	14,250	12,670	14,606	16,507	11,678	8,339	15,163	21,843
Volume of Exports							*2000=100*						
Petroleum............................	72a	82.5	90.8	97.3	107.5	109.6	98.6	100.0	96.9	....	....	....	....
Crude Petroleum.................	72aa	84.5	92.2	98.9	110.3	112.8	96.0	100.0	103.0	....	....	....	....
Refined Pretroleum..............	72ab	78.4	87.8	93.9	101.7	103.0	104.0	100.0	84.3	....	....	....	....
Import Prices (Wholesale)...............	76.x	18.0	27.1	58.0	70.7	81.7	91.0	† 100.0	111.2	170.8	265.2	342.4	385.8
Balance of Payments							*Millions of US Dollars: Minus Sign Indicates Debit*						
Current Account, n.i.e....................	78ald	2,541	2,014	8,914	3,732	–4,432	2,112	11,853	1,983	7,599	11,448	13,830	25,359
Goods: Exports f.o.b......................	78aad	16,105	19,082	23,707	23,871	17,707	20,963	33,529	26,667	26,781	27,170	38,748	55,487
Goods: Imports f.o.b.....................	78abd	–8,480	–12,069	–9,937	–14,917	–16,755	–14,492	–16,865	–19,211	–13,360	–10,687	–17,318	–23,955
Trade Balance...........................	78acd	7,625	7,013	13,770	8,954	952	6,471	16,664	7,456	13,421	16,483	21,430	31,532
Services: Credit.......................	78add	1,576	1,671	1,573	1,314	1,423	1,352	1,182	1,376	1,013	878	1,098	1,334
Services: Debit.........................	78aed	–4,672	–4,836	–4,842	–3,922	–4,072	–4,191	–4,435	–4,681	–3,922	–3,522	–4,724	–5,416
Balance on Goods & Services.......	78afd	4,529	3,848	10,501	6,346	–1,697	3,632	13,411	4,151	10,512	13,839	17,804	27,450
Income: Credit...........................	78agd	1,626	1,867	1,579	2,421	2,479	2,272	3,049	2,603	1,474	1,729	1,564	4,152
Income: Debit...........................	78ahd	–3,530	–3,810	–3,304	–4,938	–5,013	–3,725	–4,437	–4,623	–4,230	–4,140	–5,449	–6,136
Balance on Gds, Serv. & Inc......	78aid	2,625	1,905	8,776	3,829	–4,231	2,179	12,023	2,131	7,756	11,428	13,919	25,466
Current Transfers, n.i.e.: Credit......	78ajd	606	413	526	233	169	203	261	356	288	257	180	213
Current Transfers: Debit.................	78akd	–690	–304	–388	–330	–370	–270	–431	–504	–445	–237	–269	–320
Capital Account, n.i.e..................	78bcd	—	—	—	—	—	—	—	—	—	—	—	—
Capital Account, n.i.e.: Credit........	78bad	—	—	—	—	—	—	—	—	—	—	—	—
Capital Account: Debit.................	78bbd	—	—	—	—	—	—	—	—	—	—	—	—
Financial Account, n.i.e...................	78bjd	–3,204	–2,964	–1,784	879	2,689	–516	–2,969	–211	–9,246	–4,942	–8,716	–16,172
Direct Investment Abroad...............	78bdd	–358	–91	–507	–557	–1,043	–872	–521	–204	–1,026	–1,318	348	–1,460
Dir. Invest. in Rep. Econ., n.i.e.......	78bed	813	985	2,183	6,202	4,985	2,890	4,701	3,683	782	2,659	1,518	2,957
Portfolio Investment Assets............	78bfd	–22	–14	–41	–1,651	470	248	–954	397	–1,354	–812	–1,090	–641
Equity Securities.....................	78bkd	10	–3	–11	–47	–240	72	13	138	–164	–222	5	–172
Debt Securities.......................	78bld	–32	–11	–30	–1,604	710	176	–967	259	–1,190	–590	–1,095	–469
Portfolio Investment Liab., n.i.e......	78bgd	275	–787	780	911	306	1,857	–2,180	710	–956	–143	–853	3,378
Equity Securities.....................	78bmd	585	270	1,318	1,444	187	417	–574	31	–5	97	–170	114
Debt Securities.......................	78bnd	–310	–1,057	–538	–533	119	1,440	–1,606	679	–951	–240	–683	3,264
Financial Derivatives Assets...........	78bwd	....	....	—	—	—	—	—	—	—	—	—	—
Financial Derivatives Liabilities.......	78bxd	—	—	—	—	—	—	—	—	—	—	—	—
Other Investment Assets...............	78bhd	–4,173	–661	–1,592	–3,748	–3,325	–4,788	–4,839	–3,919	–7,169	–4,328	–8,004	–18,851
Monetary Authorities...................	78bod	—	—	—	–2	28	128	18	42	22	11	13	–19
General Government.................	78bpd	–27	240	57	–264	391	64	–228	–1,016	65	–718	–1,047	–7,317
Banks...................................	78bqd	–932	216	–53	–17	–182	–262	–50	267	–32	46	15	–88
Other Sectors.........................	78brd	–3,214	–1,117	–1,596	–3,465	–3,562	–4,718	–4,579	–3,212	–7,224	–3,667	–6,985	–11,427
Other Investment Liab., n.i.e..........	78bid	261	–2,396	–2,607	–278	1,296	149	824	–878	477	–1,000	–635	–1,555
Monetary Authorities.................	78bsd	–51	–317	–289	–430	–561	–24	8	18	–4	19	250	–24
General Government.................	78btd	128	–262	–543	162	986	272	36	–1	170	298	–605	–491
Banks...................................	78bud	–77	52	153	36	–69	–34	197	122	–257	–141	1	82
Other Sectors.........................	78bvd	261	–1,869	–1,928	–46	940	–65	583	–1,017	568	–1,176	–281	–1,122
Net Errors and Omissions................	78cad	–281	–494	–892	–1,517	–1,662	–538	–2,926	–3,601	–2,781	–1,052	–2,959	–3,762
Overall Balance......................	78cbd	–944	–1,444	6,238	3,094	–3,405	1,058	5,958	–1,829	–4,428	5,454	2,155	5,425
Reserves and Related Items..............	79dad	944	1,444	–6,238	–3,094	3,405	–1,058	–5,958	1,829	4,428	–5,454	–2,155	–5,425
Reserve Assets.............................	79dbd	1,145	1,907	–6,271	–2,643	3,853	–608	–5,449	2,027	4,428	–5,454	–2,155	–5,425
Use of Fund Credit and Loans........	79dcd	–201	–463	33	–452	–448	–450	–508	–198				
Exceptional Financing...................	79ded	—	—	—	—	—	—	—					
International Investment Position							*Millions of US Dollars*						
Assets..	79aad	46,634	45,944	41,216	49,537	50,051	55,792	67,931	70,064	75,513	88,316	99,777	124,891
Direct Investment Abroad..............	79abd	3,124	3,427	4,595	5,209	6,176	7,143	7,676	7,894	8,732	9,548	9,204	10,665
Portfolio Investment......................	79acd	1,796	1,530	1,986	3,646	3,406	2,784	4,057	3,836	5,405	6,596	7,636	7,435
Equity Securities......................	79add	—	—	43	113	385	260	245	101	262	538	534	744
Debt Securities........................	79aed	1,796	1,530	1,943	3,533	3,021	2,524	3,812	3,735	5,143	6,058	7,102	6,691
Financial Derivatives.....................	79ald	—	—	—	—	—	—	—	—	—	—	—	—
Other Investment.........................	79afd	28,955	30,391	17,862	21,669	25,019	29,835	34,707	39,812	46,516	50,805	58,730	76,423
Monetary Authorities...................	79agd	—	—	205	340	313	186	167	125	106	96	84	103
General Government.................	79ahd	812	874	1,401	1,658	1,272	1,216	1,430	2,449	2,285	2,967	4,018	9,640
Banks...................................	79aid	3,774	3,586	188	240	443	703	753	485	517	471	456	1,057
Other Sectors.........................	79ajd	24,369	25,931	16,068	19,431	22,991	27,730	32,357	36,753	43,608	47,271	54,172	65,623
Reserve Assets...........................	79akd	12,759	10,596	16,773	19,013	15,450	16,030	21,491	18,522	14,860	21,367	24,207	30,368
Liabilities....................................	79lad	51,730	49,250	56,284	62,341	61,866	67,160	69,595	71,885	72,471	78,552	84,066	88,205
Dir. Invest. in Rep. Economy...........	79lbd	5,872	6,772	18,124	24,694	28,915	31,470	35,480	39,074	39,007	41,902	43,575	46,237
Portfolio Investment......................	79lcd	22,844	22,555	20,506	21,146	15,367	18,349	16,557	16,322	15,850	19,175	22,864	25,539
Equity Securities......................	79lld	1,184	1,060	2,488	3,882	1,623	2,185	1,706	1,301	948	1,713	1,812	1,172
Debt Securities........................	79led	21,660	21,495	18,018	17,264	13,744	16,164	14,851	15,021	14,902	17,462	21,052	24,367
Financial Derivatives.....................	79lld	—	—	—	—	—	—	—	—	—	—	—	—
Other Investment.........................	79lfd	23,014	19,923	17,654	16,501	17,584	17,341	17,558	16,489	17,614	17,475	17,627	16,429
Monetary Authorities...................	79lgd	4,246	3,525	2,271	2,275	1,316	810	278	93	75	86	338	315
General Government.................	79lhd	8,454	8,009	3,960	3,978	5,055	5,362	5,367	5,352	5,698	6,409	6,018	5,844
Banks...................................	79lid	1,394	1,451	294	328	261	226	423	545	290	149	149	231
Other Sectors.........................	79ljd	8,920	6,938	11,129	9,920	10,952	10,943	11,490	10,499	11,551	10,831	11,122	10,039

Venezuela, República Bolivariana de   299

		1994	1995	1996	1997	1998	1999	2000	2001	2002	2003	2004	2005
Government Finance							*Billions of Bolivares: Year Ending December 31*						
Deficit (-) or Surplus.........................	80	† −485.9	−493.8	456.5	955.5	−1,967.6	−999.8	−1,361.1	−3,941.1	....	....	....	....
Revenue...	81	† 1,575.1	2,242.6	5,767.8	10,241.0	9,157.1	11,251.8	16,873.5	19,326.5	....	....	....	....
Grants Received...........................	81z	—	—	—	—	—	—	—	—	....	....	....	621
Expenditure................................	82	1,666.3	2,541.5	4,964.2	8,894.3	11,014.0	12,170.0	17,860.2	22,883.8	....	....	....	....
Lending Minus Repayments............	83	394.6	195.0	347.1	391.2	110.6	81.7	374.4	383.8	....	....	....	....
Financing													
Net Borrowing.............................	84	485.9	493.8	−456.5	−955.5	1,967.6	999.8	1,361.1	3,941.1	....	....	....	....
Domestic......................	84a	530.6	476.2	−301.7	−1,359.9	1,378.4	1,623.4	3,207.4	3,640.4	....	....	....	....
Foreign.........................	85a	−44.8	17.7	−154.8	404.4	589.2	−623.6	−1,846.2	300.7	....	....	....	....
Use of Cash Balances....................	87	....	....	....	....	....	....	....	....	....	....	....	....
National Accounts							*Billions of Bolivares*						
Househ.Cons.Expend.,incl.NPISHs....	96f	6,077.1	9,507.7	18,618.0	21,610.1	28,822.6	34,071.6	41,220.7	48,838.8	57,740.1	73,483.7	103,303.9	....
Government Consumption Expend...	91f	627.0	974.8	1,475.6	5,675.8	6,735.6	7,309.5	9,917.0	12,663.4	14,027.2	17,288.3	26,233.2	....
Gross Fixed Capital Formation..........	93e	1,528.4	2,255.6	4,645.8	10,686.2	14,289.5	14,067.3	16,740.9	21,391.6	23,644.4	20,943.6	36,430.5	....
Changes in Inventories....................	93i	−300.3	223.4	227.6	920.5	1,044.6	1,669.0	2,512.2	3,090.0	−826.6	−58.6	6,957.8	....
Exports of Goods and Services..........	90c	2,677.5	3,709.8	10,748.9	12,272.2	10,463.0	13,596.9	23,693.0	20,222.3	32,819.6	45,344.7	74,956.8	....
Imports of Goods and Services (-).....	98c	1,934.5	2,985.7	6,278.3	9,221.6	11,342.4	11,369.6	14,428.0	17,260.5	19,564.5	22,784.4	41,756.8	....
Gross Domestic Product (GDP)........	99b	8,675.2	13,685.7	29,437.7	41,943.2	50,013.0	59,344.6	79,655.7	88,945.6	107,840.2	134,217.3	206,125.4	....
Net Primary Income from Abroad.....	98.n	−274.6	−322.9	−665.7	−1,203.8	−1,366.8	−887.4	−947.5	−1,469.0	−3,191.7	−3,887.5	−6,162.2	....
Gross National Income (GNI)...........	99a	8,400.6	13,362.8	28,772.0	40,739.4	48,646.1	58,457.2	78,708.2	87,476.6	104,648.5	130,329.9	199,963.2	....
Consumption of Fixed Capital..........	99cf	625.8	927.7	1,884.4	2,309.3	3,034.7	3,544.3	4,499.8	5,367.0	7,113.0	8,284.6	12,676.7	....
GDP Volume 1984 Prices.................	99b.p	545.1	566.6	565.5	601.5	602.6	565.9	584.2	600.5	547.2	....	....	....
GDP Volume (2000=100)...............	99bvp	92.7	96.3	96.1	† 102.3	102.6	96.4	100.0	103.4	94.2	87.0	102.0	....
GDP Deflator (2000=100)...............	99bip	11.8	17.8	38.4	51.5	61.2	77.2	100.0	108.0	143.7	193.8	253.6	....
							Millions: Midyear Estimates						
Population................................	99z	21.62	22.09	22.55	23.02	23.49	23.95	24.42	24.88	25.35	25.82	26.28	26.75

Vietnam 582

		1994	1995	1996	1997	1998	1999	2000	2001	2002	2003	2004	2005
Exchange Rates						*Dong per SDR: End of Period*							
Market Rate....................	aa	16,133	16,374	16,032	16,585	19,558	19,254	18,910	18,957	20,941	23,249	24,502	22,748
						Dong per US Dollar: End of Period (ae) Period Average (rf)							
Market Rate....................	ae	11,051	11,015	11,149	12,292	13,890	14,028	14,514	15,084	15,403	15,646	15,777	15,916
Market Rate....................	rf	10,966	11,038	11,033	11,683	13,268	13,943	14,168	14,725	15,280	15,510	....	15,859
Fund Position						*Millions of SDRs: End of Period*							
Quota.........................	2f.s	241.6	241.6	241.6	241.6	241.6	329.1	329.1	329.1	329.1	329.1	329.1	329.1
SDRs..........................	1b.s	11.0	2.2	11.9	9.4	1.8	1.1	.3	11.6	—	1.5	.3	.6
Reserve Position in the Fund...........	1c.s	—	—	—	—	—	—	—	—	—	—	—	—
Total Fund Cred.&Loans Outstg........	2tl	193.4	253.8	374.6	335.3	277.9	258.7	242.6	291.2	280.2	227.9	178.6	142.3
International Liquidity					*Millions of US Dollars Unless Otherwise Indicated: End of Period*								
Total Reserves minus Gold.............	1l.d	....	1,323.7	1,735.9	1,985.9	2,002.3	3,326.1	3,416.5	3,674.6	4,121.1	6,224.2	7,041.5	9,050.9
SDRs.......................	1b.d	16.1	3.3	17.1	12.7	2.5	1.5	.3	14.6	—	2.2	.5	.9
Reserve Position in the Fund.........	1c.d	—	—	—	—	—	—	—	—	—	—	—	—
Foreign Exchange..................	1d.d	....	1,320.4	1,718.8	1,973.1	1,999.7	3,324.7	3,416.2	3,660.0	4,121.0	6,222.0	7,041.0	9,050.0
Gold (Market Valuation).................	1and	....	55.4	77.9	112.3	98.2	97.3	93.1	90.6	110.8	135.0	144.6	165.9
Monetary Authorities: Other Liab.....	4..d	....	377.1	537.3	507.8	505.5	513.5	487.6	535.9	557.4	537.8	486.0	391.3
Deposit Money Banks: Assets...........	7a.d	....	864.3	976.0	973.3	1,320.5	2,119.0	4,221.8	5,261.4	4,589.2	3,264.2	3,746.5	4,639.1
Liabilities....................	7b.d	....	865.0	985.5	868.7	679.0	664.7	682.6	679.6	640.1	684.8	1,197.8	1,457.7
Monetary Authorities						*Billions of Dong: End of Period*							
Foreign Assets..........................	11	....	15,153	20,031	25,633	29,147	48,004	50,934	56,586	65,177	99,460	113,367	146,675
Claims on General Government.......	12a	....	9,593	12,576	13,382	16,658	11,289	11,732	12,421	15,130	15,223	21,005	16,952
Claims on Banking Institutions.........	12e	....	6,779	7,693	6,776	6,521	10,312	14,234	17,776	19,182	13,565	14,400	11,024
Reserve Money.......................	14	....	26,343	31,633	35,599	38,687	58,220	72,759	84,945	95,502	121,633	141,165	174,505
of which: Currency Outside DMBs..	14a	....	19,370	22,639	25,101	26,965	41,254	52,208	66,320	74,263	90,584	109,097	131,179
Foreign Liabilities.......................	16c	....	4,154	5,991	6,241	7,022	7,203	7,077	8,083	8,585	8,414	7,668	6,227
General Government Deposits..........	16d	....	6,575	7,383	9,348	10,340	11,089	7,410	4,390	4,005	4,553	9,729	9,079
Capital Accounts.........................	17a	....	1,378	1,568	3,512	8,201	8,201	10,015	12,008	12,736	15,919	18,584	18,543
Other Items (Net).........................	17r	....	−6,791	−6,245	−7,938	−10,611	−15,475	−20,361	−22,644	−21,338	−22,271	−28,373	−33,702
Banking Institutions						*Billions of Dong: End of Period*							
Reserves.................................	20	....	7,409	9,323	9,451	9,920	16,881	20,390	18,426	20,166	30,778	31,646	42,961
Foreign Assets..........................	21	....	9,520	10,881	11,964	18,342	29,725	61,276	79,364	70,687	51,071	59,109	73,836
Claims on General Government........	22a	....	4,372	2,031	3,492	5,332	6,358	8,246	10,258	17,566	34,169	17,307	56,230
Claims on Rest of Economy..............	22d	....	18,199	23,942	31,220	34,889	112,730	155,720	189,103	231,078	296,737	420,046	552,667
Demand Deposits.......................	24	....	6,870	10,213	14,682	18,241	27,106	38,781	46,089	51,066	66,441	88,891	110,823
Time and Savings Deposits................	25a	....	9,622	12,445	15,194	20,091	36,191	47,462	60,251	77,387	133,617	182,408	261,269
Foreign Currency Deposits................	25b	....	8,924	11,042	15,611	22,098	40,919	58,543	78,187	81,428	87,418	115,050	145,303
Bonds & Money Mkt. Instruments....	26a	....	5,490	5,635	7,703	10,890	10,865	18,842	21,012	35,262	26,265	26,530	31,048
Restricted Deposits.......................	26b	....	2,138	2,117	3,080	2,830	4,059	7,045	7,923	9,744	7,899	10,369	10,782
Foreign Liabilities.........................	26c	....	9,528	10,987	10,678	9,432	9,324	9,908	10,251	9,860	10,715	18,898	23,201
General Government Deposits..........	26d	....	3,321	2,795	3,127	4,974	3,606	13,052	16,187	19,848	23,805	32,201	33,656
Credit from Central Bank................	26g	....	5,793	6,133	5,565	4,249	11,576	14,427	17,753	19,250	14,491	16,679	20,943
Capital Accounts.........................	27a	....	8,166	7,984	9,798	13,172	22,033	24,801	26,962	34,684	46,986	59,411	71,920
Other Items (Net).........................	27r	....	6,688	5,735	3,655	2,246	15	12,772	12,537	967	−4,881	−22,331	16,749
Banking Survey						*Billions of Dong: End of Period*							
Foreign Assets (Net).....................	31n	....	10,992	13,934	20,679	31,036	61,201	95,225	117,616	117,419	131,402	145,910	191,083
Domestic Credit..........................	32	....	22,268	28,370	35,620	41,566	115,682	155,236	191,204	239,921	317,771	416,428	583,114
Claims on General Govt. (Net).......	32an	....	4,069	4,428	4,400	6,677	2,952	−484	2,102	8,843	21,034	−3,618	30,447
Claims on Rest of Economy...........	32d	....	18,199	23,942	31,220	34,889	112,730	155,720	189,103	231,078	296,737	420,046	552,667
Money...................................	34	....	26,736	33,439	39,972	45,207	68,360	90,989	112,408	125,329	157,025	197,989	242,002
Quasi-Money.............................	35	....	18,546	23,487	30,805	42,189	77,110	106,005	138,437	158,815	221,035	297,459	406,572
Bonds & Money Mkt. Instruments....	36a	....	5,490	5,635	7,703	10,890	10,865	18,842	21,012	35,262	26,265	26,530	31,048
Restricted Deposits........................	36b	....	2,138	2,117	3,080	2,830	4,059	7,045	7,923	9,744	7,899	10,369	10,782
Capital Accounts.........................	37a	....	9,544	9,552	13,310	21,374	30,601	34,816	38,970	47,420	62,904	77,995	90,463
Other Items (Net).........................	37r	....	−1,525	−2,398	−4,447	−8,835	−14,111	−7,236	−9,932	−19,229	−25,955	−48,004	−6,669
Money plus Quasi-Money.................	35l	....	45,283	56,926	70,777	87,396	145,470	196,994	250,846	284,144	378,060	495,447	648,574
Interest Rates						*Percent Per Annum*							
Refinancing Rate (End of Period)......	60	....	....	18.90	10.80	12.00	6.00	6.00	4.80	4.80	5.00	5.00	5.00
Treasury Bill Rate.........................	60c	....	....	....	....	....	....	5.42	5.49	5.92	5.83	....	6.13
Deposit Rate..............................	60l	....	....	....	8.51	9.23	7.37	3.65	5.30	6.45	6.62	....	7.15
Lending Rate..............................	60p	....	....	20.10	14.42	14.40	12.70	10.55	9.42	9.06	9.48	....	11.03
Prices						*Index Numbers (2000=100): Period Averages*							
Consumer Prices...........................	64	....	83.5	88.3	91.1	97.7	101.7	100.0	99.6	103.4	106.6	114.9	124.4
Intl. Transactions & Positions						*Billions of Dong*							
Exports...................................	70..d	....	....	7,256	9,185	9,361	11,540	14,449	15,100	16,530	20,176	25,625	31,625
Imports, c.i.f...............................	71..d	....	....	11,144	11,592	11,500	11,742	15,638	15,999	19,000	24,863	31,091	36,476

Vietnam 582

2006, International Monetary Fund : *International Financial Statistics Yearbook*

		1994	1995	1996	1997	1998	1999	2000	2001	2002	2003	2004	2005
Balance of Payments				*Millions of US Dollars: Minus Sign Indicates Debit*									
Current Account, n.i.e.	78ald	....	....	−2,020	−1,528	−1,074	1,177	1,106	682	−604	−1,878	−926	....
Goods: Exports f.o.b.	78aad	....	....	7,255	9,185	9,361	11,540	14,448	15,027	16,706	20,176	26,503	....
Goods: Imports f.o.b.	78abd	....	....	−10,030	−10,432	−10,350	−10,568	−14,073	−14,546	−17,760	−22,704	−28,759	....
Trade Balance	78acd	....	....	−2,775	−1,247	−989	972	375	481	−1,054	−2,528	−2,256	....
Services: Credit	78add	....	....	2,243	2,530	2,616	2,493	2,702	2,810	2,948	3,272	3,867	....
Services: Debit	78aed	....	....	−2,304	−3,153	−3,146	−3,040	−3,252	−3,382	−3,698	−4,050	−4,739	....
Balance on Goods & Services	78afd	....	....	−2,836	−1,870	−1,519	425	−175	−91	−1,804	−3,306	−3,128	....
Income: Credit	78agd	....	....	140	136	127	142	331	318	167	125	188	....
Income: Debit	78ahd	....	....	−524	−679	−804	−571	−782	−795	−888	−936	−1,079	....
Balance on Gds. Serv. & Inc.	78aid	....	....	−3,220	−2,413	−2,196	−4	−626	−568	−2,525	−4,117	−4,019	....
Current Transfers, n.i.e.: Credit	78ajd	....	....	1,200	885	1,122	1,181	1,732	1,250	1,921	2,239	3,093	....
Current Transfers: Debit	78akd	....	....	—	—	—	—	—	—	—	—	—	....
Capital Account, n.i.e.	78bcd	....	....	—	—	—	—	—	—	—	....	....	....
Capital Account, n.i.e.: Credit	78bad	....	....	—	—	—	—	—	—	—	....	....	....
Capital Account: Debit	78bbd	....	....	—	—	—	—	—	—	—	....	....	....
Financial Account, n.i.e.	78bjd	....	....	2,909	2,125	1,646	1,058	−316	371	2,090	3,279	2,807	....
Direct Investment Abroad	78bdd	....	....	—	—	—	—	—	—	—	....	....	....
Dir. Invest. in Rep. Econ., n.i.e.	78bed	....	....	2,395	2,220	1,671	1,412	1,298	1,300	1,400	1,450	1,610	....
Portfolio Investment Assets	78bfd	....	....	....	....	....	....	....	....	....	....	....	....
Equity Securities	78bkd	....	....	....	....	....	....	....	....	....	....	....	....
Debt Securities	78bld	....	....	....	....	....	....	....	....	....	....	....	....
Portfolio Investment Liab., n.i.e.	78bgd	....	....	....	....	....	....	....	....	....	....	....	....
Equity Securities	78bmd	....	....	....	....	....	....	....	....	....	....	....	....
Debt Securities	78bnd	....	....	....	....	....	....	....	....	....	....	....	....
Financial Derivatives Assets	78bwd	....	....	—	—	—	—	—	—	—	....	....	....
Financial Derivatives Liabilities	78bxd	....	....	....	....	....	....	....	....	....	....	....	....
Other Investment Assets	78bhd	....	....	−33	−112	−537	−786	−2,089	−1,197	624	1,372	35	....
Monetary Authorities	78bod	....	....	....	....	....	....	....	....	....	....	....	....
General Government	78bpd	....	....	....	....	....	....	....	....	....	....	....	....
Banks	78bqd	....	....	−33	−112	−537	−786	−2,089	−1,197	624	1,372	35	....
Other Sectors	78brd	....	....	....	....	....	....	....	....	....	....	....	....
Other Investment Liab., n.i.e.	78bid	....	....	547	17	512	432	475	268	66	457	1,162	....
Monetary Authorities	78bsd	....	....	—	—	—	—	—	—	—	—	—	....
General Government	78btd	....	....	....	....	....	....	....	....	....	....	....	....
Banks	78bud	....	....	....	....	....	....	....	....	....	....	....	....
Other Sectors	78bvd	....	....	547	17	512	432	475	268	66	457	1,162	....
Net Errors and Omissions	78cad	....	....	−611	−269	−535	−925	−680	−847	−1,038	745	−946	....
Overall Balance	78cbd	....	....	278	328	37	1,310	110	206	448	2,146	935	....
Reserves and Related Items	79dad	....	....	−278	−328	−37	−1,310	−110	−206	−448	−2,146	−935	....
Reserve Assets	79dbd	....	....	−453	−274	41	−1,284	−89	−267	−435	−2,099	−808	....
Use of Fund Credit and Loans	79dcd	....	....	175	−54	−78	−26	−21	61	−13	−74	−73	....
Exceptional Financing	79ded	....	....	—	—	—	—	—	—	—	26	−54	....
Government Finance				*Billions of Dong: Year Ending December 31*									
Deficit (-) or Surplus	80	−2,530	−1,219	−502	−5,397	−454	−6,328	−12,402	−14,130	....	....	....	....
Total Revenue and Grants	81y	42,125	53,370	62,387	65,352	72,965	78,489	90,749	103,050	....	....	....	....
Revenue	81	40,925	51,750	60,844	62,766	70,822	76,128	88,721	97,750	....	....	....	....
Grants	81z	1,200	1,620	1,543	2,586	2,143	2,361	2,028p	5,300f	....	....	....	....
Exp. & Lending Minus Repay	82z	44,655	54,589	62,889	70,749	73,419	84,817	103,151	117,180	....	....	....	....
Expenditure	82	44,655	54,589	62,889	70,749	73,419	84,817	103,151	117,180	....	....	....	....
Lending Minus Repayments	83	—	—	—	—	—	—	—	—	....	....	....	....
Total Financing	80h	2,530	1,219	502	5,397	454	6,328	12,402	14,130	....	....	....	....
Domestic Financing	84a	2,330	2,709	552	5,206	−2,814	1,491	6,110	9,086	....	....	....	....
Foreign Financing	85a	200	−1,490	−50	191	3,268	4,837	6,292	5,044	....	....	....	....
National Accounts							*Billions of Dong*						
Hous Cons.Expend.,incl.NPISHs	96f	133,299	168,492	202,509	225,084	255,921	274,553	293,507	312,144	348,747	406,451	465,506	533,141
Government Consumption Expend	91f	14,738	18,741	22,722	25,500	27,523	27,137	28,346	30,463	33,390	38,770	45,715	51,652
Gross Fixed Capital Formation	93e	43,325	58,187	71,597	83,734	97,551	102,799	122,101	140,301	166,828	204,608	237,868	277,647
Changes in Inventories	93i	2,153	3,944	4,853	5,020	7,324	7,704	8,670	9,732	11,155	12,826	15,818	19,453
Exports of Goods and Services	90c	60,725	75,106	111,177	135,180	161,910	199,836	243,049	262,846	304,262	363,735	470,216	578,373
Imports of Goods and Services (-)	98c	77,591	95,925	141,016	160,706	188,281	211,254	253,927	273,828	331,946	415,023	524,216	613,842
Gross Domestic Product (GDP)	99b	178,534	228,892	272,037	313,624	361,016	399,942	441,646	481,295	535,762	613,443	713,071	837,858
Net Primary Income from Abroad	98.n	−4,517.0	−2,501.0	−4,300.0	−5,748.0	−6,648.0	−5,328.0	−6,327.0	−6,440.0	−8,375.0	−9,755.0	−11,165.0	....
Gross National Income (GNI)	99a	174,017	226,391	267,736	308,675	354,368	394,614	435,319	474,855	527,387	603,688	701,906	....
GDP Volume 1994 Prices	99b.p	178,534	195,567	213,832	231,264	244,596	256,269	273,666	292,535	313,247	336,243	362,093	392,989
GDP Volume (2000=100)	99bvp	65.2	71.5	78.1	84.5	89.4	93.6	100.0	106.9	114.5	122.9	132.3	143.6
GDP Deflator (2000=100)	99bip	62.0	72.5	78.8	84.0	91.5	96.7	100.0	101.9	106.0	113.0	122.0	132.1
							Millions: Midyear Estimates						
Population	99z	71.88	73.16	74.36	75.48	76.55	77.60	78.67	† 79.77	80.88	82.00	83.12	84.24

		1994	1995	1996	1997	1998	1999	2000	2001	2002	2003	2004	2005
Exchange Rates							*Francs per SDR: End of Period*						
Official Rate	aa	† 780.44	728.38	753.06	807.94	791.61	896.19	918.49	935.39	850.37	771.76	747.90	794.73
							Francs per US Dollar: End of Period (ae) Period Average (rf)						
Official Rate	ae	† 534.60	490.00	523.70	598.81	562.21	652.95	704.95	744.31	625.50	519.36	481.58	556.04
Official Rate	rf	† 555.20	499.15	511.55	583.67	589.95	615.70	711.98	733.04	696.99	581.20	528.28	527.47
Fund Position							*Millions of SDRs: End of Period*						
Quota	2f.s	628.6	628.6	628.6	628.6	628.6	855.8	855.8	855.8	855.8	855.8	855.8	855.8
SDRs	1b.s	6.9	10.2	5.8	2.3	1.3	6.6	2.2	8.1	8.9	10.9	6.4	2.5
Reserve Position in the Fund	1c.s	28.1	28.2	28.3	28.5	28.5	28.6	28.7	28.9	29.0	29.3	29.5	29.8
Total Fund Cred.&Loans Outstg	2tl	686.9	836.0	920.6	938.1	1,076.0	1,068.3	1,031.3	984.6	949.0	824.4	655.9	535.5
International Liquidity						*Millions of US Dollars Unless Otherwise Indicated: End of Period*							
Total Reserves minus Gold	1l.d	....	2,538.6	2,739.8	2,868.4	3,164.3	2,932.1	3,283.9	3,780.5	5,454.9	6,728.8	7,248.8	6,172.7
SDRs	1b.d	10.1	15.2	8.3	3.1	1.9	9.1	2.8	10.2	12.2	16.2	10.0	3.5
Reserve Position in the Fund	1c.d	41.0	41.9	40.7	38.4	40.2	39.3	37.4	36.3	39.5	43.5	45.8	42.6
Foreign Exchange	1d.d	....	2,481.5	2,690.7	2,826.9	3,122.3	2,883.7	3,243.6	3,734.0	5,403.2	6,669.0	7,193.1	6,126.5
Gold (Million Fine Troy Ounces)	1ad	....	.801	.859	.902	.959	1.012	1.058	1.117	1.172	1.172	1.173	1.173
Gold (National Valuation)	1and	....	308.3	322.8	276.1	281.4	298.9	284.4	310.6	377.8	458.4	508.3	567.4
Monetary Authorities: Other Liab	4..d	313.1	264.1	256.5	252.9	242.0	239.9	203.6	144.1	220.3	276.6	379.9	226.1
Deposit Money Banks: Assets	7a.d	571.1	813.5	746.7	649.1	722.1	801.0	682.4	655.7	811.6	825.0	921.2	891.1
Liabilities	7b.d	461.2	641.1	527.9	438.7	565.4	659.7	478.3	438.8	405.9	507.0	601.8	628.2
Monetary Authorities							*Billions of Francs: End of Period*						
Foreign Assets	11	....	1,388	1,586	1,865	1,920	2,082	2,493	3,011	3,632	3,702	3,702	3,710
Claims on Central Government	12a	....	940	976	1,122	1,283	1,295	1,228	1,262	1,248	1,131	972	870
Claims on Deposit Money Banks	12e	....	150	146	159	179	123	91	43	16	2	1	11
Claims on Other Financial Insts	12f	....	13	16	15	17	16	14	11	9	6	1	1
Reserve Money	14	....	1,251	1,284	1,428	1,534	1,589	1,773	2,194	2,647	2,596	2,633	2,730
of which: Currency Outside DMBs	14a	....	1,018	1,060	1,217	1,305	1,361	1,465	1,703	2,010	1,848	1,797	2,036
Foreign Liabilities	16c	....	738	828	909	988	1,114	1,091	1,028	945	780	673	551
Central Government Deposits	16d	....	158	231	325	352	328	252	343	392	430	415	332
Other Items (Net)	17r	....	344	381	499	523	485	710	762	921	1,035	955	977
Deposit Money Banks							*Billions of Francs: End of Period*						
Reserves	20	....	177	178	188	175	198	280	392	534	700	829	651
Foreign Assets	21	....	399	391	389	406	523	481	488	508	428	444	495
Claims on Central Government	22a	....	724	827	807	824	805	699	705	719	776	846	877
Claims on Private Sector	22d	....	1,819	1,998	2,204	2,377	2,407	2,665	2,835	3,010	3,223	3,501	3,893
Claims on Other Financial Insts	22f	....	3	—	—	—	—	—	—	—	—	—	—
Demand Deposits	24	....	1,028	1,108	1,137	1,245	1,303	1,378	1,488	1,686	1,899	2,066	2,159
Time Deposits	25	....	995	1,101	1,157	1,090	1,160	1,264	1,369	1,598	1,718	1,910	2,044
Foreign Liabilities	26c	....	255	227	239	295	391	304	288	213	222	248	305
Long-Term Foreign Liabilities	26cl	....	59	49	24	23	40	33	39	41	41	42	44
Central Government Deposits	26d	....	524	624	599	663	606	706	765	778	778	765	758
Credit from Monetary Authorities	26g	....	162	148	159	180	114	96	44	16	2	4	12
Other Items (Net)	27r	....	98	136	274	285	320	343	426	439	468	585	594
Monetary Survey							*Billions of Francs: End of Period*						
Foreign Assets (Net)	31n	....	793	922	1,105	1,043	1,101	1,579	2,183	2,982	3,129	3,224	3,349
Domestic Credit	32	....	2,831	2,978	3,243	3,501	3,608	3,670	3,727	3,839	3,957	4,175	4,603
Claims on Central Govt. (Net)	32an	....	971	935	992	1,081	1,157	974	854	797	710	659	691
Claims on Private Sector	32d	....	1,844	2,028	2,236	2,404	2,435	2,682	2,862	3,033	3,241	3,515	3,911
Claims on Other Financial Insts	32f	....	16	16	15	17	16	14	11	9	6	1	1
Money	34	....	2,101	2,229	2,415	2,607	2,721	2,896	3,281	3,775	3,816	3,913	4,261
Quasi-Money	35	....	995	1,101	1,157	1,090	1,160	1,264	1,369	1,598	1,718	1,910	2,044
Long-Term Foreign Liabilities	36cl	....	59	49	24	23	40	33	39	41	41	42	44
Other Items (Net)	37r	....	469	521	752	825	788	1,056	1,222	1,407	1,511	1,534	1,603
Money plus Quasi-Money	35l	....	3,096	3,330	3,573	3,697	3,881	4,160	4,650	5,374	5,534	5,823	6,305
Interest Rates							*Percent Per Annum*						
Bank Rate (End of Period)	60	....	6.00	6.00	6.00	6.00	6.00	6.00	6.00	6.00	4.50	4.00	4.00
Money Market Rate	60b	....	4.95	4.95	4.95	4.95	4.95	4.95	4.95	4.95	4.95	4.95	4.95
Deposit Rate	60l	....	3.50	3.50	3.50	3.50	3.50	3.50	3.50	3.50	3.50	3.50	3.50
Prices							*Index Numbers (2000=100): Period Averages*						
Share Price Index	62	....	....	....	....	....	112.4	100.0	89.0	92.3	93.5	106.9	141.3
Consumer Prices	64	79.2	88.8	91.8	94.6	98.1	98.3	100.0	104.0	107.1	108.5	109.1	114.7
National Accounts							*Billions of Francs*						
Househ.Cons.Expend.,incl.NPISHs	96f	....	8,856.6	9,576.0	10,541.1	11,380.3	11,889.7	12,280.6	13,328.2	13,246.8	....	....	....
Government Consumption Expend	91f	....	2,576.3	2,880.7	3,016.1	3,740.8	3,769.4	3,779.9	3,940.5	4,354.0	....	....	....
Gross Fixed Capital Formation	93e	....	1,947.2	2,214.7	2,525.8	2,889.6	2,919.3	2,733.1	3,049.4	3,228.3	....	....	....
Changes in Inventories	93i	....	288.7	−13.6	86.2	−199.4	−62.5	209.6	78.9	−195.6	....	....	....
Exports of Goods and Services	90c	....	3,896.6	4,414.2	4,964.5	5,194.4	5,410.5	5,623.8	6,162.3	7,126.9	....	....	....
Imports of Goods and Services(-)	98c	....	4,463.8	4,649.2	5,063.1	5,459.4	5,762.6	6,263.4	6,814.8	7,038.3	....	....	....
Gross Domestic Product (GDP)	99b	....	13,101.5	14,422.7	16,070.0	17,546.4	18,163.8	18,363.7	19,744.6	20,722.2	....	....	....

West Bank and Gaza   487

		1994	1995	1996	1997	1998	1999	2000	2001	2002	2003	2004	2005
Exchange Rates						*US Dollars per SDR: End of Period (sa)*							
Market Rate....................	sa	1.45985	1.48649	1.43796	1.34925	1.40803	1.37251	1.30291	1.25673	1.35952	1.48597	1.55301	1.42927
Monetary Authorities						*Millions of US Dollars: End of Period*							
Foreign Assets....................	11	....	....	....	....	181.97	184.48	275.45	259.14	273.64	374.09	401.47	375.82
Claims on Central Government........	12a	....	....	....	....	14.10	15.94	13.98	16.04	18.02	13.76	7.91	7.36
Claims on Deposit Money Banks......	12e	....	....	....	....	95.59	146.28	111.82	96.66	103.59	130.68	158.18	201.58
Bankers Deposits....................	14c	....	....	....	....	266.37	321.38	372.28	338.91	357.18	479.01	530.04	539.55
Demand Deposits....................	14d	....	....	....	....	—	—	—	—	—	—	—	—
Foreign Liabilities....................	16c	....	....	....	....	—	—	—	—	—	—	—	—
Central Government Deposits..........	16d	....	....	....	....	—	—	—	—	—	—	—	—
Capital Accounts....................	17a	....	....	....	....	24.95	27.42	31.48	32.41	33.87	32.18	36.97	45.70
Other Items (Net)....................	17r	....	....	....	....	.33	−2.27	−2.51	.54	4.20	7.04	.56	−.49
Deposit Money Banks						*Millions of US Dollars: End of Period*							
Reserves....................	20	....	....	177.30	248.00	271.40	335.76	383.52	346.40	357.22	482.45	541.52	558.56
Foreign Assets....................	21	....	....	1,393.70	1,643.00	1,776.90	2,160.85	2,347.42	2,372.81	2,515.80	2,538.06	2,620.89	2,664.17
Claims on Central Government........	22a	....	....	18.63	58.00	81.63	92.03	328.87	296.87	133.83	224.95	383.30	565.19
Claims on Local Government..........	22b	....	....	—	—	.01	—	—	9.17	4.36	6.85	3.35	6.07
Claims on Nonfin.Pub.Enterprises.....	22c	....	....	8.62	10.00	6.76	6.19	87.80	62.86	6.61	23.18	33.88	26.24
Claims on Private Sector..................	22d	....	....	408.84	563.00	733.40	912.59	926.93	860.00	859.28	860.78	1,064.13	1,356.13
Demand Deposits....................	24	....	....	552.04	562.00	614.61	685.69	815.07	761.09	779.72	1,050.77	1,213.91	1,323.48
Time and Savings Deposits..............	25	....	....	1,093.10	1,329.00	1,634.72	1,985.41	2,522.39	2,461.03	2,298.34	2,300.49	2,282.51	2,308.48
Foreign Liabilities....................	26c	....	....	105.15	265.00	289.83	373.26	310.20	303.30	221.52	117.36	132.82	193.50
Central Government Deposits..........	26d	....	....	62.31	176.00	136.28	156.83	119.56	116.77	191.37	206.55	371.08	471.91
Credit from Monetary Authorities.....	26g	....	....	100.45	125.00	97.61	143.43	118.52	88.38	104.74	112.04	146.49	172.16
Capital Accounts....................	27a	....	....	144.22	229.00	265.18	304.78	343.31	369.09	383.01	467.96	568.45	830.86
Other Items (Net)....................	27r	....	....	−50.19	−164.00	−168.12	−141.98	−154.50	−151.56	−101.60	−118.11	−68.20	−124.04
Monetary Survey						*Millions of US Dollars: End of Period*							
Foreign Assets (Net)....................	31n	....	....	....	....	1,669.04	1,972.07	2,312.67	2,328.65	2,567.92	2,794.79	2,889.54	2,846.49
Domestic Credit....................	32	....	....	....	....	699.63	870.17	1,238.03	1,128.16	830.73	922.97	1,121.49	1,489.07
Claims on Central Govt. (Net)........	32an	....	....	....	....	−40.55	−48.86	223.29	196.13	−39.52	32.16	20.13	100.64
Claims on Local Government..........	32b	....	....	....	....	.01	—	—	9.17	4.36	6.85	3.35	6.07
Claims on Nonfin.Pub.Enterprises...	32c	....	....	....	....	6.76	6.19	87.80	62.86	6.61	23.18	33.88	26.24
Claims on Private Sector..............	32d	....	....	....	....	733.40	912.84	926.93	860.00	859.28	860.78	1,064.13	1,356.13
Deposit Money....................	34	....	....	....	....	614.61	685.69	815.07	761.09	779.72	1,050.77	1,213.91	1,323.48
Quasi-Money....................	35	....	....	....	....	1,634.72	1,985.41	2,522.39	2,461.03	2,298.34	2,300.49	2,282.51	2,308.48
Capital Accounts....................	37a	....	....	....	....	290.13	332.20	374.79	401.50	416.88	500.14	605.42	876.55
Other Items (Net)....................	37r	....	....	....	....	−170.80	−161.48	−161.55	−166.79	−96.29	−133.15	−90.81	−172.96
Interest Rates						*Percent Per Annum*							
Deposit Rate....................	60l	....	....	....	....	....	....	....	1.48	.89	.74	1.12	2.24
Lending Rate....................	60p	....	....	....	....	....	....	....	8.36	7.97	7.56	6.92	7.34
Prices and Labor						*Index Numbers (2000=100): Period Averages*							
Consumer Prices....................	64	....	....	81.5	87.3	92.2	97.3	100.0	101.2	107.0	111.7	115.1	119.1
						Number in Thousands: Period Averages							
Labor Force....................	67d	....	....	....	....	631	672	696	685	710	....	795	....
Employment....................	67e	....	....	429	481	549	588	597	505	477	565	578	....
Unemployment....................	67c	....	....	132	121	92	79	99	171	218	194	212	....
Unemployment Rate (%)..................	67r	....	....	23.8	20.3	14.4	11.8	14.1	25.2	31.2	25.4	26.7	....
						Millions: Midyear Estimates							
Population.................	99z	2.51	2.61	2.71	2.82	2.93	3.04	3.15	3.26	3.37	3.48	3.59	3.70

Yemen, Republic of   474

		1994	1995	1996	1997	1998	1999	2000	2001	2002	2003	2004	2005
Exchange Rates					*Rial per SDR: End of Period*								
Market Rate	aa	17.533	† 74.384	† 182.492	176.023	199.447	218.366	215.749	217.754	243.368	273.879	288.658	278.822
						Rial per US Dollar: End of Period (ae) Period Average (rf)							
Market Rate	ae	12.010	† 50.040	† 126.910	130.460	141.650	159.100	165.590	173.270	179.010	184.310	185.870	195.080
Market Rate	rf	12.010	† 40.839	† 94.157	129.281	135.882	155.718	161.718	168.672	175.625	183.448	184.776	191.509
Fund Position					*Millions of SDRs: End of Period*								
Quota	2f.s	176.5	176.5	176.5	176.5	176.5	243.5	243.5	243.5	243.5	243.5	243.5	243.5
SDRs	1b.s	33.5	37.0	33.3	124.1	131.6	128.5	65.0	14.7	33.0	3.3	33.0	13.2
Reserve Position in the Fund	1c.s	—	—	—	—	—	—	—	—	—	—	—	—
Total Fund Cred.&Loans Outstg	2tl	—	—	84.0	185.4	238.4	297.6	243.5	297.3	283.8	270.1	242.2	204.5
International Liquidity					*Millions of US Dollars Unless Otherwise Indicated: End of Period*								
Total Reserves minus Gold	1l.d	254.8	619.0	1,017.2	1,203.1	995.5	1,471.5	2,900.3	3,658.1	4,410.5	4,986.9	5,664.8	6,115.4
SDRs	1b.d	48.9	55.0	47.9	167.4	185.2	176.3	84.6	18.5	44.9	4.9	51.3	18.8
Reserve Position in the Fund	1c.d	—	—	—	—	—	—	—	—	—	—	—	—
Foreign Exchange	1d.d	205.9	564.0	969.3	1,035.7	810.3	1,295.1	2,815.6	3,639.6	4,365.6	4,982.0	5,613.5	6,096.6
Gold (Million Fine Troy Ounces)	1ad	.050	.050	.050	.050	.050	.050	.050	.050	.050	.050	.050	.050
Gold (National Valuation)	1and	2.6	2.6	18.6	18.5	15.3	15.3	14.4	14.6	18.4	21.9	23.4	27.2
Deposit Money Banks: Assets	7a.d	477.2	861.1	334.5	455.9	457.9	446.2	624.1	695.5	849.0	862.3	888.4	875.3
Liabilities	7b.d	548.1	479.1	209.8	60.8	50.2	45.6	56.5	26.9	18.7	21.7	52.6	61.5
Monetary Authorities					*Millions of Rial: End of Period*								
Foreign Assets	11	4,292	31,108	131,459	159,892	143,257	† 237,502	482,436	636,331	792,193	923,080	1,057,038	1,198,238
Claims on Central Government	12a	180,586	209,342	199,058	171,234	196,702	† 159,621	17,913	2,082	686	206	2,606	982
Claims on Nonfin.Pub.Enterprises	12c	57	—	10	50	1,108	† 9,026	1,821	1,540	1,513	1,650	1,767	1,854
Claims on Deposit Money Banks	12e	40	94	54	49	—	—	—	—	—	—	—	—
Reserve Money	14	147,585	176,756	189,030	165,443	184,002	222,245	253,255	288,694	315,140	381,668	436,649	529,882
of which: Currency Outside Banks	14a	111,006	129,114	120,477	126,904	139,668	166,924	197,123	212,795	239,329	268,813	297,939	330,620
Other Liab. to Dep. Money Banks	14n	....	....	....	....	....	5,659	5,865	41,933	46,807	39,429	33,490	17,230
Time, Savings,& Fgn.Currency Dep	15	3,881	9,440	19,966	22,193	18,978	11,932	18,531	22,112	20,267	31,902	23,040	38,537
Restricted Deposits	16b	....	....	....	....	....	8,388	7,935	19,858	15,090	42,623	39,184	47,795
Foreign Liabilities	16c	2,053	11,323	43,931	66,613	84,138	† 101,159	89,094	100,821	103,187	108,094	95,795	85,226
Central Government Deposits	16d	18,294	27,011	41,003	46,106	18,171	† 26,095	79,708	106,488	195,311	158,199	225,906	273,820
Capital Accounts	17a	1,100	2,738	5,835	5,673	6,323	† 35,201	24,592	65,636	91,451	143,224	180,888	199,295
Other Items (Net)	17r	12,023	13,182	30,762	24,846	29,458	† −4,526	23,190	−5,589	7,138	19,796	26,458	9,289
Deposit Money Banks					*Millions of Rial: End of Period*								
Reserves	20	32,879	44,055	59,903	28,052	35,714	43,631	45,545	50,647	55,710	87,593	112,679	152,886
Other Claims on Monetary Author	20n	....	....	....	....	....	5,659	5,865	31,790	46,207	38,779	31,440	16,630
Foreign Assets	21	5,731	43,088	42,453	59,472	64,857	70,991	103,340	120,511	151,981	158,925	165,128	170,756
Claims on Central Government	22a	336	1,295	6,963	34,873	36,267	39,972	63,173	54,814	75,215	112,467	158,680	180,205
Claims on Nonfin.Pub.Enterprises	22c	3,401	11,011	2,237	1,641	317	649	474	674	1,066	1,303	1,943	3,179
Claims on Private Sector	22d	14,143	23,865	22,358	34,380	45,957	62,426	75,747	95,318	108,949	137,553	183,611	222,648
Demand Deposits	24	25,390	22,985	27,353	28,875	31,490	29,649	41,004	49,458	49,819	56,346	69,628	69,368
Time, Savings,& Fgn.Currency Dep	25	19,359	71,956	88,640	106,272	130,753	155,981	204,053	252,725	328,914	405,096	485,199	547,200
Restricted Deposits	26b	1,210	1,977	3,661	3,540	3,684	4,185	4,692	5,064	9,034	12,909	18,495	21,309
Foreign Liabilities	26c	6,582	23,973	26,624	7,932	7,114	7,248	9,358	4,652	3,351	3,991	9,774	11,995
Central Government Deposits	26d	1,863	1,127	171	474	52	30	46	62	38	101	219	83
Credit from Monetary Authorities	26g	14	4	5	26	23	32	—	—	—	—	—	288
Capital Accounts	27a	2,829	4,601	6,669	10,762	17,615	† 22,688	23,439	28,074	32,724	36,424	48,127	62,933
Other Items (Net)	27r	−745	−3,305	−19,203	564	−7,597	† 3,515	11,552	13,718	15,249	21,754	22,040	33,129
Monetary Survey					*Millions of Rial: End of Period*								
Foreign Assets (Net)	31n	1,388	38,900	103,358	144,820	116,863	† 200,086	487,324	651,369	837,637	969,920	1,116,598	1,271,773
Domestic Credit	32	178,365	217,375	189,453	195,598	262,128	† 245,568	79,373	47,878	−7,921	94,879	122,482	134,966
Claims on Central Govt. (Net)	32an	160,765	182,499	164,848	159,527	214,746	† 173,468	1,331	−49,654	−119,449	−45,627	−64,839	−92,715
Claims on Nonfin.Pub.Enterprises	32c	3,457	11,011	2,247	1,691	1,425	† 9,674	2,295	2,214	2,579	2,953	3,710	5,033
Claims on Private Sector	32d	14,143	23,865	22,358	34,380	45,957	62,426	75,747	95,318	108,949	137,553	183,611	222,648
Money	34	139,590	164,019	156,579	166,384	179,927	207,197	247,248	283,149	306,450	347,465	390,541	442,464
Quasi-Money	35	23,239	81,396	108,605	128,465	149,731	167,913	222,585	274,836	349,181	436,997	508,239	585,737
Restricted Deposits	36b	1,210	1,977	3,661	3,540	3,684	† 12,573	12,627	24,922	24,123	55,532	57,679	69,104
Capital Accounts	37a	3,929	7,339	12,504	16,434	23,938	† 57,889	48,030	93,711	124,176	179,648	229,016	262,228
Other Items (Net)	37r	11,784	1,544	11,461	25,292	21,712	† 87	36,208	22,628	25,786	45,156	53,604	47,206
Money plus Quasi-Money	35l	162,829	245,415	265,184	294,849	329,658	375,109	469,833	557,985	655,631	784,463	898,781	1,028,200
Interest Rates					*Percent Per Annum*								
Discount Rate	60	....	27	29	15	20	19	16	15	13	....	....	....
Treasury Bill Rate	60c	....	....	25	16	13	21	14	13	12	13	14	15
Deposit Rate	60l	....	....	24	15	11	18	14	13	13	13	13	13
Lending Rate	60p	....	....	31	23	15	24	20	18	18	18	19	18
Prices					*Index Numbers (2000=100): Period Averages*								
Consumer Prices	64	40.1	62.2	81.3	83.0	88.0	95.6	100.0	111.9	125.6	139.2	....	....
Intl. Transactions & Positions					*Millions of Rial*								
Exports	70	11,216	79,434	251,830	323,716	203,480	380,010	659,609	569,007	575,102	684,908	....	....
Imports, c.i.f	71	25,070	64,591	191,862	260,331	294,510	312,749	375,783	415,899	487,730	674,128	....	....

Yemen, Republic of   474

		1994	1995	1996	1997	1998	1999	2000	2001	2002	2003	2004	2005
Balance of Payments					*Millions of US Dollars: Minus Sign Indicates Debit*								
Current Account, n.i.e.	78ald	178.3	143.7	38.8	−68.8	−472.2	358.2	1,336.6	667.1	538.2	148.7	224.6	1,215.1
Goods: Exports f.o.b.	78aad	1,796.2	1,980.1	2,262.7	2,274.0	1,503.7	2,478.3	3,797.2	3,366.9	3,620.7	3,934.3	4,675.7	6,379.8
Goods: Imports f.o.b.	78abd	−1,522.0	−1,831.5	−2,293.5	−2,406.5	−2,288.8	−2,120.5	−2,484.4	−2,600.4	−2,932.0	−3,557.4	−3,858.6	−4,124.1
Trade Balance	78acd	274.2	148.6	−30.8	−132.5	−785.1	357.8	1,312.8	766.4	688.7	376.9	817.1	2,255.7
Services: Credit	78add	148.0	179.4	185.7	207.6	174.4	183.2	210.9	166.4	166.2	317.7	369.7	372.1
Services: Debit	78aed	−704.3	−639.3	−555.4	−677.4	−692.9	−718.7	−809.4	−847.8	−934.8	−1,003.6	−1,059.4	−1,161.2
Balance on Goods & Services	78afd	−282.1	−311.3	−400.5	−602.3	−1,303.6	−177.6	714.2	85.1	−79.9	−308.9	127.3	1,466.7
Income: Credit	78agd	22.0	37.4	46.8	69.6	69.0	56.7	149.6	178.5	135.0	98.9	103.6	178.2
Income: Debit	78ahd	−553.9	−598.4	−680.7	−670.6	−413.4	−752.3	−926.7	−869.4	−900.6	−1,008.3	−1,450.1	−1,835.4
Balance on Gds, Serv. & Inc.	78aid	−814.0	−872.3	−1,034.4	−1,203.3	−1,648.0	−873.2	−62.9	−605.8	−845.6	−1,218.3	−1,219.1	−190.6
Current Transfers, n.i.e.: Credit	78ajd	1,062.3	1,080.5	1,140.1	1,177.6	1,223.5	1,262.1	1,471.9	1,344.4	1,456.8	1,442.1	1,493.1	1,458.4
Current Transfers: Debit	78akd	−70.0	−64.5	−66.9	−43.1	−47.7	−30.7	−72.4	−71.4	−73.1	−75.0	−49.4	−52.8
Capital Account, n.i.e.	78bcd	....	....	....	4,236.2	2.2	1.5	338.9	49.5	—	5.5	163.3	202.3
Capital Account, n.i.e.: Credit	78bad	....	....	....	4,236.2	2.2	1.5	338.9	49.5	—	5.5	163.3	202.3
Capital Account: Debit	78bbd					—	—	—	—	—	—	—	—
Financial Account, n.i.e.	78bjd	−710.7	−858.4	−367.8	−197.6	−418.0	−415.1	−376.2	−53.5	−156.8	19.7	−68.6	−569.5
Direct Investment Abroad	78bdd	....	....	....	....							....	....
Dir. Invest. in Rep. Econ., n.i.e.	78bed	15.8	−217.7	−60.1	−138.5	−219.4	−307.6	6.4	155.1	114.3	−89.1	143.6	−265.6
Portfolio Investment Assets	78bfd	2.8	−3.1	.9	5.0	4.9	4.1	.1	−1.4	−5.8	−.4	−6.4	−14.2
Equity Securities	78bkd	2.8	−3.1	.9	5.0	4.9	4.1	.1	−1.4	−5.8	−.4	−6.4	−14.2
Debt Securities	78bld	....	....	....	....	—	—	—	—	—	—	—	—
Portfolio Investment Liab., n.i.e.	78bgd	....	....	....	....	—	—	—	—	—	—	—	—
Equity Securities	78bmd	....	....	....	....	—	—	—	—	—	—	—	—
Debt Securities	78bnd	....	....	....	....	—	—	—	—	—	—	—	—
Financial Derivatives Assets	78bwd	....	....	....	....	....	....	....	....	....	....	....	....
Financial Derivatives Liabilities	78bxd	....	....	....	....	....	....	....	....	....	....	....	....
Other Investment Assets	78bhd	−130.9	158.8	24.0	196.3	60.1	−110.1	−177.9	5.6	−124.5	49.1	−25.4	−81.6
Monetary Authorities	78bod	....	....	....	....	—	—	—	—	—	—	....	....
General Government	78bpd	1.3	−32.5	−63.7	63.5	70.7	−119.4	—	75.6	−57.6	—	−5.7	−109.0
Banks	78bqd	67.8	141.3	7.7	−122.3	−10.6	9.3	−177.9	−70.0	−147.7	−12.8	−19.7	27.4
Other Sectors	78brd	−200.0	50.0	80.0	255.1	—	—	—	—	80.8	61.9	—	—
Other Investment Liab., n.i.e.	78bid	−598.4	−796.4	−332.6	−260.4	−263.6	−1.5	−204.8	−212.8	−140.8	60.2	−180.4	−208.0
Monetary Authorities	78bsd	61.1	4.4	−.6	34.3	−3.0	−23.7	−8.1	−11.5	−22.4	−10.9	−45.7	5.4
General Government	78btd	−656.6	−626.1	−353.2	−145.7	−250.5	27.1	−207.7	−171.6	−110.3	68.1	−165.6	−222.3
Banks	78bud	−1.4	−174.7	21.2	−149.0	−10.1	−4.9	11.0	−29.7	−8.1	2.9	30.9	8.9
Other Sectors	78bvd	−1.5											
Net Errors and Omissions	78cad	−189.2	186.5	−107.0	48.4	307.0	129.4	295.1	−110.0	43.3	156.4	53.3	−414.1
Overall Balance	78cbd	−721.6	−528.2	−436.0	4,018.2	−580.9	74.0	1,594.4	553.2	424.7	330.3	372.5	433.8
Reserves and Related Items	79dad	721.6	528.2	436.0	−4,018.2	580.9	−74.0	−1,594.4	−553.2	−424.7	−330.3	−372.5	−433.8
Reserve Assets	79dbd	−207.9	−263.1	−415.7	−192.7	210.9	−482.2	−1,429.4	−761.3	−556.9	−326.3	−532.3	−713.4
Use of Fund Credit and Loans	79dcd	—	—	122.5	139.4	72.3	79.5	−71.0	69.0	−17.2	−19.3	−41.2	−55.8
Exceptional Financing	79ded	929.5	791.3	729.3	−3,964.9	297.7	328.7	−94.0	139.1	149.4	15.3	201.0	335.4
International Investment Position						*Millions of US Dollars*							
Assets	79aad	....	....	....	....	1,484.0	2,067.5	3,686.8	4,441.7	5,405.6	6,020.7	6,744.8	....
Direct Investment Abroad	79abd	....	....	....	....	—	—	—	—	—	—	—	....
Portfolio Investment	79acd	....	....	....	....	4.5	.4	.3	1.7	7.5	7.9	14.4	....
Equity Securities	79add	....	....	....	....	4.5	.4	.3	1.7	7.5	7.9	14.4	....
Debt Securities	79aed	....	....	....	....	—	—	—	—	—	—	—	....
Financial Derivatives	79ald	....	....	....	....	—	—	—	—	—	—	—	....
Other Investment	79afd	....	....	....	....	466.3	576.5	772.9	767.3	972.5	1,004.3	1,043.2	....
Monetary Authorities	79agd	....	....	....	....	—	—	—	—	—	—	—	....
General Government	79ahd	....	....	....	....	12.0	131.4	149.1	73.5	131.0	149.9	155.6	....
Banks	79aid	....	....	....	....	454.3	445.1	623.8	693.8	841.5	854.4	874.1	....
Other Sectors	79ajd	....	....	....	....							13.5	....
Reserve Assets	79akd	....	....	....	....	1,013.2	1,490.6	2,913.6	3,672.7	4,425.6	5,008.5	5,687.2	....
Liabilities	79lad	....	....	....	....	6,077.9	6,305.5	6,372.9	6,006.5	6,092.8	6,543.6	6,825.2	....
Dir. Invest. in Rep. Economy	79lbd	....	....	....	....	1,088.6	993.2	843.0	998.1	1,112.4	1,010.7	1,248.9	....
Portfolio Investment	79lcd	....	....	....	....	—	—	—	—	—	—	—	....
Equity Securities	79ldd	....	....	....	....	—	—	—	—	—	—	—	....
Debt Securities	79led	....	....	....	....	—	—	—	—	—	—	—	....
Financial Derivatives	79lld	....	....	....	....	—	—	—	—	—	—	—	....
Other Investment	79lfd	....	....	....	....	4,989.3	5,312.3	5,529.9	5,008.4	4,980.3	5,532.9	5,576.3	....
Monetary Authorities	79lgd	....	....	....	....	624.6	664.0	538.0	596.3	576.4	586.5	515.4	....
General Government	79lhd	....	....	....	....	4,314.4	4,602.9	4,935.3	4,385.2	4,385.2	4,924.8	5,006.4	....
Banks	79lid	....	....	....	....	50.3	45.4	56.5	26.9	18.7	21.7	52.6	....
Other Sectors	79ljd	....	....	....	....	—	—	—	—	—	—	1.9	....
Government Finance						*Millions of Rial: Year Ending December 31*							
Deficit (-) or Surplus	80	−44,788	−24,907	−17,428	−13,588	−19,116f	−40,278f	....	....	....	....	....	....
Revenue	81	41,384	89,646	216,053	287,347	300,791f	279,418f	....	....	....	....	....	....
Grants Received	81z	856	1,620	1,870	4,639	5,480f	4,219f	....	....	....	....	....	....
Expenditure	82	85,875	111,128	215,738	290,571	309,942f	310,702f	....	....	....	....	....	....
Lending Minus Repayments	83	1,153	5,045	19,613	15,003	15,445f	13,213f	....	....	....	....	....	....
Financing													
Domestic	84a	43,838	25,976	11,860	2,696p	−7,750f	25,283f	....	....	....	....	....	....
Foreign	85a	950	−1,069	5,568	16,572p	26,866f	14,995f	....	....	....	....	....	....

Yemen, Republic of   474

National Accounts		1994	1995	1996	1997	1998	1999	2000	2001	2002	2003	2004	2005
							Millions of Rial						
Househ.Cons.Expend.,incl.NPISHs....	96f	244,753	431,346	531,423	618,701	620,429	765,695p	965,294p	1,105,217p	1,258,531p	1,551,942p	....	....
Government Consumption Expend...	91f	57,585	74,017	97,458	116,832	124,473	156,273p	193,322p	219,124p	244,560p	267,147p	....	....
Gross Fixed Capital Formation.........	93e	58,267	106,227	158,016	191,666	267,810	265,371p	251,684p	263,994p	277,593p	330,988p	....	....
Changes in Inventories....................	93i	6,123	6,486	12,863	29,549	8,655	13,122p	12,590p	13,894p	14,610p	19,541p	....	....
Exports of Goods and Services.........	90c	42,091	115,957	285,587	320,822	228,025	414,527p	645,230p	596,006p	659,824p	647,138p	....	....
Imports of Goods and Services (-).....	98c	98,218	217,390	351,795	398,686	405,152	442,194p	528,485p	582,290p	651,728p	735,112p	....	....
Gross Domestic Product (GDP)........	99b	310,601	516,643	733,552	878,884	844,240	1,172,794p	1,539,635p	1,615,945p	1,803,390p	2,081,644p	....	....
Net Primary Income from Abroad.....	98.n	−6,388	−22,535	−72,365	−77,697	−23,846	−74,262p	−125,746p	−113,566p	−130,484p	−113,898p	....	....
Gross National Income (GNI)............	99a	304,213	494,108	661,187	801,187	820,394	1,098,532p	1,413,889p	1,502,379p	1,672,906p	1,967,746p	....	....
GDP Volume 1990 Prices.................	99b.p	147,106	165,040	178,293	189,450	202,393	207,320p	216,970p	227,086p	235,943p	245,411p	....	....
GDP Volume (2000=100)...............	99bvp	67.8	76.1	82.2	87.3	93.3	95.6	100.0	104.7	108.7	113.1	....	....
GDP Deflator (2000=100)...............	99bip	29.8	44.1	58.0	65.4	58.8	79.7	100.0	100.3	107.7	119.5	....	....
							Millions: Midyear Estimates						
Population.................................	99z	† 14.60	15.22	15.80	16.34	16.86	17.39	17.94	18.51	19.09	19.70	20.33	20.97

Zambia 754

		1994	1995	1996	1997	1998	1999	2000	2001	2002	2003	2004	2005
Exchange Rates					*Kwacha per SDR: End of Period*								
Official Rate	aa	993.10	1,421.28	1,844.46	1,908.97	3,236.95	3,612.71	5,417.28	4,813.78	5,892.70	6,903.04	7,409.89	5,015.28
					Kwacha per US Dollar: End of Period (ae) Period Average (rf)								
Official Rate	ae	680.27	956.13	1,282.69	1,414.84	2,298.92	2,632.19	4,157.83	3,830.40	4,334.40	4,645.48	4,771.31	3,508.98
Official Rate	rf	669.37	864.12	1,207.90	1,314.50	1,862.07	2,388.02	3,110.84	3,610.94	4,398.60	4,733.27	4,778.88	4,463.50
					Index Numbers (2000=100): Period Averages								
Official Rate	ahx	408.0	357.9	255.9	233.3	167.1	128.5	100.0	85.3	71.6	64.8	64.1	68.8
Nominal Effective Exchange Rate	nec	315.2	231.9	181.6	177.4	142.3	118.2	100.0	97.3	85.4	70.8	69.0	78.6
Real Effective Exchange Rate	rec	87.1	83.4	90.1	104.3	98.7	99.2	100.0	112.0	110.9	101.7	107.8	134.8
Fund Position					*Millions of SDRs: End of Period*								
Quota	2f.s	270.3	363.5	363.5	363.5	363.5	489.1	489.1	489.1	489.1	489.1	489.1	489.1
SDRs	1b.s	—	8.2	1.4	.8	.6	.1	17.1	53.3	51.7	.3	16.0	11.0
Reserve Position in the Fund	1c.s	—	—	—	—	—	—	—	—	—	—	—	—
Total Fund Cred.&Loans Outstg.	2tl	551.2	833.4	833.4	843.4	843.4	853.4	873.4	781.6	746.6	577.9	573.3	413.6
International Liquidity					*Millions of US Dollars Unless Otherwise Indicated: End of Period*								
Total Reserves minus Gold	1l.d	268.1	222.7	222.7	239.1	69.4	45.4	244.8	183.4	535.1	247.7	337.1	559.8
SDRs	1b.d	—	12.1	2.0	1.1	.8	.1	22.3	66.9	70.3	.5	24.8	15.7
Reserve Position in the Fund	1c.d	—	—	—	—	—	—	—	—	—	—	—	—
Foreign Exchange	1d.d	268.1	210.5	220.7	238.0	68.6	45.3	222.5	116.5	464.8	247.2	312.2	544.0
Gold (Million Fine Troy Ounces)	1ad	....	....	—	—	—	—	—	—	—	—	—	—
Gold (National Valuation)	1and	....	....	—	—	—	—	—	—	—	—	—	—
Monetary Authorities: Other Liab.	4..d	736.0	160.0	151.7	114.4	69.7	52.4	37.0	69.1	160.6	146.1	51.1	36.6
Banking Institutions: Assets	7a.d	84.3	121.8	148.6	158.8	198.9	201.4	239.5	233.3	293.5	235.3	334.0	343.5
Liabilities	7b.d	15.6	9.8	11.2	13.5	29.2	34.9	25.9	24.5	26.0	35.0	42.9	141.9
Monetary Authorities					*Billions of Kwacha: End of Period*								
Foreign Assets	11	213.7	† 208.1	268.4	338.4	103.0	211.2	336.8	† 432.6	1,337.2	† 1,192.2	1,500.0	1,584.6
Claims on Central Government	12a	1,114.7	† 2,017.5	2,636.7	2,659.5	4,670.2	5,584.5	8,605.1	† 7,816.2	9,320.4	† 9,322.7	6,563.5	4,291.9
Claims on State and Local Govts.	12b	....	....	....	....	....	....	....	—	—	† —	—	—
Claims on Nonfin.Pub.Enterprises	12c	9.1	† 1.2	1.3	1.3	5.3	7.9	69.2	† 195.0	30.5	† 60.8	60.9	90.3
Claims on Private Sector	12d	4.4	† 14.0	23.6	25.1	30.7	31.4	35.7	† 42.6	50.9	† 29.4	30.9	38.8
Claims on Banking Institutions	12e	—	† 121.8	157.2	164.9	161.4	120.9	82.4	† 77.5	112.2	† 125.1	73.7	102.4
Claims on Nonbank Financial Insts.	12g	—	† —	—	—	—	—	—	† —	—	—	—	—
Reserve Money	14	151.4	† 129.2	175.0	259.3	303.0	389.2	597.0	† 847.9	1,212.3	† 1,446.2	1,913.4	2,023.5
of which: Currency Outside Banks	14a	56.3	† 77.8	106.3	136.7	† 169.7	212.2	287.8	† 372.8	421.1	† 590.7	727.0	752.5
Other Liabs. to Banking Insts.	14n	....	....	....	....	....	....	....	26.8	53.2	† —	3.9	9.3
Time, Savings,& Fgn.Currency Dep.	15	....	† 1.5	2.3	.7	.8	1.6	2.2	† —	—	.1	.3	.2
Liabs. of Central Bank: Securities	16ac	....	....	....	....	....	....	....	—	—	† —	—	5.3
Restricted Deposits	16b	....	....	....	....	....	....	....	—	—	† —	—	—
Foreign Liabilities	16c	1,048.1	† 1,337.6	1,731.8	1,771.9	2,890.4	3,221.2	4,885.6	† 4,027.0	5,095.3	† 4,667.8	4,491.7	2,202.9
Central Government Deposits	16d	173.6	† 545.4	895.6	955.0	1,351.6	2,011.9	2,975.3	† 3,112.4	3,642.8	† 4,359.3	816.0	1,242.3
Liab. to Nonbank Financial Insts.	16j	....	....	....	....	....	....	....	—	—	† —	—	—
Capital Accounts	17a	−52.7	† 172.5	211.1	300.9	304.7	440.9	1,023.7	† 937.5	418.2	† 645.3	725.8	207.2
Other Items (Net)	17r	21.6	† 176.3	71.4	−98.6	120.1	−108.8	−354.6	† −387.8	429.5	† −388.4	277.8	417.4
Banking Institutions					*Billions of Kwacha: End of Period*								
Reserves	20	96.1	34.6	62.8	87.8	† 134.7	175.6	322.7	† 476.3	732.6	† 768.1	1,111.4	1,488.2
Claims on Mon.Author.: Securities	20c	....	....	....	....	....	....	....	—	—	† —	—	—
Other Claims on Monetary Author.	20n	....	....	....	....	....	....	....	—	—	† —	—	—
Foreign Assets	21	57.4	116.5	190.7	224.6	† 457.3	530.2	995.7	† 893.6	1,272.1	† 1,093.2	1,593.8	1,205.3
Claims on Central Government	22a	84.7	202.8	216.4	222.7	† 153.0	231.6	356.7	† 731.8	1,216.6	† 1,833.6	1,824.6	2,104.3
Claims on State and Local Govts.	22b	—	—	—	—	† 2.6	.4	.4	† .4	—	† .6	.5	1.2
Claims on Nonfin.Pub.Enterprises	22c	16.8	35.6	49.7	40.9	† 119.1	248.9	289.7	† 240.5	61.3	† 60.8	113.4	133.3
Claims on Private Sector	22d	136.0	240.0	350.2	386.1	† 392.7	522.0	825.5	† 916.1	977.4	† 1,357.5	2,060.7	2,428.1
Claims on Nonbank Financial Insts.	22g	—	—	—	—	† 2.7	1.4	.5	† .4	9.7	† 10.4	.6	16.1
Demand Deposits	24	83.8	140.2	163.1	217.2	† 243.7	299.0	472.0	† 521.9	725.3	† 899.6	1,104.8	1,338.3
Time, Savings, & Fgn.Currency Dep.	25	191.0	287.6	423.4	515.6	† 679.0	883.3	1,651.0	† 1,653.0	2,226.7	† 2,731.7	3,740.3	3,589.4
Money Market Instruments	26aa	14.9	23.3	31.1	29.8	† 11.8	9.9	34.6	† —	—	† —	—	—
Restricted Deposits	26b	—	—	—	—	† —	—	—	† 42.9	46.7	† 46.7	46.7	46.7
Foreign Liabilities	26c	10.6	9.3	14.4	19.1	† 67.1	91.8	107.7	† 93.7	112.6	† 162.8	204.9	497.9
Central Government Deposits	26d	12.4	44.6	57.7	63.6	† 61.3	125.2	43.2	† 270.5	387.2	† 458.7	718.7	713.8
Credit from Monetary Authorities	26g	2.7	60.2	86.6	82.5	† 21.4	78.5	39.1	† 30.3	23.1	† 32.9	39.4	121.7
Liab. to Nonbank Financial Insts.	26j	....	....	....	....	....	....	....	74.9	99.1	† 110.9	64.6	101.7
Capital Accounts	27a	58.5	74.5	112.7	138.1	† 227.8	297.2	448.6	† 387.9	570.7	† 560.8	638.2	931.2
Other Items (Net)	27r	17.0	−10.1	−19.2	−103.8	† −50.1	−74.7	−4.9	† 184.2	78.3	† 120.0	147.5	35.8
Banking Survey					*Billions of Kwacha: End of Period*								
Foreign Assets (Net)	31n	−787.6	† −1,022.4	−1,287.1	−1,228.0	† −2,397.2	−2,571.6	−3,660.9	† −2,794.4	−2,598.6	† −2,545.2	−1,602.8	89.1
Domestic Credit	32	1,179.7	† 1,921.1	2,324.6	2,316.9	† 3,963.3	4,491.3	7,164.4	† 6,560.1	7,636.8	† 7,857.8	9,120.3	7,148.0
Claims on Central Govt. (Net)	32an	1,013.4	† 1,630.3	1,899.7	1,863.6	† 3,410.2	3,679.1	5,943.4	† 5,165.1	6,507.0	† 6,338.3	6,853.4	4,440.1
Claims on State and Local Govts.	32b	—	† —	—	—	† 2.6	.4	.4	† .4	—	† .6	.5	1.2
Claims on Nonfin.Pub.Enterprises	32c	25.9	† 36.9	51.0	42.2	† 124.4	256.9	358.8	† 435.5	91.8	† 121.7	174.3	223.6
Claims on Private Sector	32d	140.4	† 254.0	373.8	411.1	† 423.5	553.5	861.3	† 958.7	1,028.3	† 1,386.8	2,091.6	2,466.9
Claims on Nonbank Financial Inst.	32g	—	† —	—	—	† 2.7	1.4	.5	† .4	9.7	† 10.4	.6	16.1
Money	34	141.0	† 227.1	271.1	355.2	† 414.9	513.0	775.9	† 929.6	1,157.8	† 1,498.1	1,841.0	2,099.7
Quasi-Money	35	191.0	† 289.1	425.7	516.3	† 679.8	884.9	1,653.2	† 1,653.0	2,226.7	† 2,731.7	3,740.5	3,589.6
Money Market Instruments	36aa	14.9	† 23.3	31.1	29.8	† 11.8	9.9	34.6	† —	—	† —	—	5.3
Liabs. of Central Bank: Securities	36ac	....	....	....	....	† —	—	—	—	† 42.9	46.7	† 46.7	46.7	46.7
Restricted Deposits	36b	—	† —	—	—	† —	—	—	† 42.9	46.7	† 46.7	46.7	46.7
Liab. to Nonbank Financial Insts.	36j	....	....	....	....	....	....	....	74.9	99.1	† 110.9	64.6	101.7
Capital Accounts	37a	5.8	† 247.0	323.8	439.1	† 532.5	738.1	1,472.3	† 1,325.4	988.9	† 1,206.1	1,364.0	1,138.4
Other Items (Net)	37r	39.4	† 112.3	−14.3	−251.4	† −73.0	−226.2	−432.4	† −260.2	519.0	† −281.0	460.7	255.7
Money plus Quasi-Money	35l	332.0	† 516.2	696.9	871.5	† 1,094.7	1,397.9	2,429.1	† 2,582.6	3,384.5	† 4,229.8	5,581.5	5,689.4

Zambia 754

		1994	1995	1996	1997	1998	1999	2000	2001	2002	2003	2004	2005
Money (National Definitions)					*Billions of Kwacha: End of Period*								
Monetary Base	19ma	....	....	....	382.9	409.4	390.8	599.2	873.5	1,264.9	1,442.3	1,908.2	2,269.4
M1	59ma	....	....	....	382.9	409.4	513.8	795.3	1,036.6	1,328.3	1,513.8	1,860.4	2,165.9
M2	59mb	....	....	....	889.7	1,049.5	1,352.0	2,404.6	2,718.6	3,515.2	4,189.9	5,302.9	5,500.3
M3	59mc	....	....	....	901.3	1,080.2	1,396.9	2,446.4	2,747.4	3,606.2	4,268.4	5,639.4	5,782.6
Interest Rates						*Percent Per Annum*							
Discount Rate (End of Period)	60	20.50	40.20	47.00	17.70	....	32.93	25.67	40.10	27.87	14.35	16.68	14.81
Treasury Bill Rate	60c	74.21	39.81	52.78	29.48	24.94	36.19	31.37	44.28	34.54	29.97	12.60	16.32
Savings Rate	60k	44.21	25.01	31.14	24.95	7.42	10.43	10.18	9.52	8.54	7.89	6.41	5.73
Deposit Rate	60l	46.14	30.24	42.13	34.48	13.08	20.27	20.24	23.41	23.33	21.95	11.51	11.19
Lending Rate	60p	70.56	45.53	53.78	46.69	31.80	40.52	38.80	46.23	45.20	40.57	30.73	28.21
Prices and Production					*Index Numbers (2000=100): Period Averages*								
Share Prices	62	....	....	....	75.3	78.0	75.5	100.0	121.5	134.1	157.8	243.6	429.9
Wholesale Prices (1995=100)	63	58.1	100.0	....	....	....	....	....	....	....	....	....	....
Consumer Prices	64	20.9	28.2	40.4	50.3	62.6	79.3	100.0	121.4	148.4	180.1	212.5	251.4
Cons.Prices (Low Inc.Househ)(1995	64a	73.6	100.0	143.8	....	....	....	....	....	....	....	....	....
Industrial Production (1995=100)	66	107.0	100.0	....	....	....	....	....	....	....	....	....	....
Mining Production (1990=100)	66zx	76.8	....	....	....	....	....	....	....	....	....	....	....
Intl. Transactions & Positions						*Billions of Kwacha*							
Exports	70	706.5	891.8	1,252.5	1,202.6	1,921.7	2,538.5	2,071.8	3,556.8	4,088.5	4,642.1	6,984.2	7,677.2
Imports, c.i.f.	71	446.0	597.6	1,008.9	1,076.7	2,048.3	1,963.0	3,089.1	4,719.5	5,510.0	7,448.3	9,639.7	12,274.6
Balance of Payments					*Millions of US Dollars: Minus Sign Indicates Debit*								
Current Account, n.i.e.	78ald	....	....	....	−383	−573	−447	−584	....	....	....	....	....
Goods: Exports f.o.b.	78aad	....	....	....	1,110	818	772	757	....	....	....	....	....
Goods: Imports f.o.b.	78abd	....	....	....	−1,056	−971	−870	−978	....	....	....	....	....
Trade Balance	78acd	....	....	....	54	−153	−98	−221	....	....	....	....	....
Services: Credit	78add	....	....	....	112	102	107	114	....	....	....	....	....
Services: Debit	78aed	....	....	....	−282	−282	−306	−340	....	....	....	....	....
Balance on Goods & Services	78afd	....	....	....	−115	−332	−297	−447	....	....	....	....	....
Income: Credit	78agd	....	....	....	47	44	44	46	....	....	....	....	....
Income: Debit	78ahd	....	....	....	−296	−258	−178	−166	....	....	....	....	....
Balance on Gds, Serv. & Inc	78aid	....	....	....	−364	−546	−431	−566	....	....	....	....	....
Current Transfers, n.i.e.: Credit	78ajd	....	....	....	—	—	—	—	....	....	....	....	....
Current Transfers: Debit	78akd	....	....	....	−19	−27	−16	−18	....	....	....	....	....
Capital Account, n.i.e.	78bcd	....	....	....	—	203	196	153	....	....	....	....	....
Capital Account, n.i.e.: Credit	78bad	....	....	....	—	203	196	153	....	....	....	....	....
Capital Account: Debit	78bbd	....	....	....	—	—	—	—	....	....	....	....	....
Financial Account, n.i.e.	78bjd	....	....	....	−324	−264	−174	−274	....	....	....	....	....
Direct Investment Abroad	78bdd	....	....	....	....	....	....	....	....	....	....	....	....
Dir. Invest. in Rep. Econ., n.i.e.	78bed	....	....	....	207	198	162	122	....	....	....	....	....
Portfolio Investment Assets	78bfd	....	....	....	—	—	—	—	....	....	....	....	....
Equity Securities	78bkd	....	....	....	....	....	....	....	....	....	....	....	....
Debt Securities	78bld	....	....	....	....	....	....	....	....	....	....	....	....
Portfolio Investment Liab., n.i.e.	78bgd	....	....	....	1	1	13	−1	....	....	....	....	....
Equity Securities	78bmd	....	....	....	1	1	13	−1	....	....	....	....	....
Debt Securities	78bnd	....	....	....	....	....	....	....	....	....	....	....	....
Financial Derivatives Assets	78bwd	....	....	....	....	....	....	....	....	....	....	....	....
Financial Derivatives Liabilities	78bxd	....	....	....	....	....	....	....	....	....	....	....	....
Other Investment Assets	78bhd	....	....	....	−24	−40	−2	−85	....	....	....	....	....
Monetary Authorities	78bod	....	....	....	....	....	....	....	....	....	....	....	....
General Government	78bpd	....	....	....	....	....	....	....	....	....	....	....	....
Banks	78bqd	....	....	....	−24	−40	−2	−85	....	....	....	....	....
Other Sectors	78brd	....	....	....	....	....	....	....	....	....	....	....	....
Other Investment Liab., n.i.e.	78bid	....	....	....	−508	−422	−347	−309	....	....	....	....	....
Monetary Authorities	78bsd	....	....	....	—	—	—	−7	....	....	....	....	....
General Government	78btd	....	....	....	−192	−136	−259	−290	....	....	....	....	....
Banks	78bud	....	....	....	19	−2	—	—	....	....	....	....	....
Other Sectors	78bvd	....	....	....	−335	−284	−88	−12	....	....	....	....	....
Net Errors and Omissions	78cad	....	....	....	−225	−37	−229	185	....	....	....	....	....
Overall Balance	78cbd	....	....	....	−932	−671	−654	−520	....	....	....	....	....
Reserves and Related Items	79dad	....	....	....	932	671	654	520	....	....	....	....	....
Reserve Assets	79dbd	....	....	....	−25	194	−1	−90	....	....	....	....	....
Use of Fund Credit and Loans	79dcd	....	....	....	14	—	14	26	....	....	....	....	....
Exceptional Financing	79ded	....	....	....	944	477	642	584	....	....	....	....	....
Government Finance					*Billions of Kwacha: Year Ending December 31*								
Deficit (-) or Surplus	80	−27.4	−136.9	−96.2	−488.5	−330.4p	−275.4f	....	....	....	....	....	....
Revenue	81	502.8	600.7	745.3	957.0	1,097.6p	1,430.4f	....	....	....	....	....	....
Grants Received	81z	.6	5.6	25.4	4.7	432.7	414.2	....	....	....	....	....	....
Expenditure	82	492.2	727.5	842.7	1,313.6	1,717.1p	1,874.3f	....	....	....	....	....	....
Lending Minus Repayments	83	38.6	15.7	24.2	136.6	143.6p	245.7f	....	....	....	....	....	....
Financing													
Net Borrowing: Domestic	84a	−46.5	−351.4	−91.2	−283.9	50.2	....	....	....	....	....	....	....
Net Borrowing: Foreign	85a	73.9	488.3	187.4	772.4	280.2	....	....	....	....	....	....	....
Use of Cash Balances	87	−674.3	....	....	....	....	....	....	....	....	....	....	....
Debt: Domestic	88a	149.9	238.8	265.8	303.2	212.8p	....	....	....	....	....	....	....
Debt: Foreign	89a	3,502.4	4,869.4	7,378.7	8,185.9	10,408.4p	....	....	....	....	....	....	....

Zambia 754

		1994	1995	1996	1997	1998	1999	2000	2001	2002	2003	2004	2005
National Accounts							*Billions of Kwacha*						
Househ.Cons.Expend.,incl.NPISHs....	96f	1,780.8	2,169.4	3,020.2	3,761.1	4,840.7	6,599.3	8,278.0	9,177.0	11,280.0	13,576.0	....	....
Government Consumption Expend...	91f	293.6	464.0	721.6	898.0	951.5	965.6	960.6	1,686.7	2,109.4	2,981.2	....	....
Gross Fixed Capital Formation..........	93e	253.6	373.4	444.3	671.7	893.1	1,196.1	1,736.3	2,454.6	3,517.1	5,055.3	....	....
Changes in Inventories....................	93i	−69.0	104.8	63.1	77.3	95.0	117.1	144.3	177.8	219.1	270.0	....	....
Exports of Goods and Services..........	90c	806.5	1,082.3	1,237.4	1,548.3	1,610.1	1,674.4	2,121.0	3,537.2	3,849.9	4,190.2	....	....
Imports of Goods and Services (-).....	98c	824.9	1,195.0	1,535.7	1,815.4	2,361.9	3,072.9	3,165.6	3,900.6	4,715.0	5,695.7	....	....
Gross Domestic Product (GDP).........	99b	2,240.7	2,999.0	3,951.0	5,141.0	6,028.6	7,479.5	10,074.6	13,132.7	16,260.4	20,377.1	....	....
Net Primary Income from Abroad.....	98.n	69.0	−104.9	−13.2	−72.9	....	....	....	....	....	....	....	....
Gross National Income (GNI)............	99a	2,309.7	2,893.4	3,956.3	5,082.9	....	....	....	....	....	....	....	....
Net National Income.....................	99e	1,518.0	2,227.4	3,396.4	....	....	....	....	....	....	....	....	....
GDP Vol. 1977 Prices (Billions).........	99b.p	2.241	2.190	2.332	2.414	....	....	....	....	....	....	....	....
GDP Volume (1995=100)...............	99bvp	102.3	100.0	106.5	110.2	....	....	....	....	....	....	....	....
GDP Deflator (1995=100)...............	99bip	73.0	100.0	123.7	155.5	....	....	....	....	....	....	....	....
						Millions: Midyear Estimates							
Population...............................	99z	9.33	9.56	9.79	10.03	10.26	10.49	10.70	10.91	11.10	11.29	11.48	11.67

		1994	1995	1996	1997	1998	1999	2000	2001	2002	2003	2004	2005
Exchange Rates						_Zimbabwe dollars per SDR: End of Period_							
Official Rate	aa	12	14	16	25	53	52	72	69	75	1,224	8,898	111,432
						Zimbabwe dollars per US Dollar: End of Period (ae) Period Average (rf)							
Official Rate	ae	8	9	11	19	37	38	55	55	55	824	5,729	77,965
Official Rate	rf	8	9	10	12	24	38	44	55	55	697	5,069	22,364
Fund Position						_Millions of SDRs: End of Period_							
Quota	2f.s	261.3	261.3	261.3	261.3	261.3	353.4	353.4	353.4	353.4	353.4	353.4	353.4
SDRs	1b.s	—	.5	6.8	.2	.3	.8	.2	—	—	—	—	—
Reserve Position in the Fund	1c.s	.1	.1	.1	.1	.2	.3	.3	.3	.3	.3	.3	.3
Total Fund Cred.&Loans Outstg	2tl	257.5	310.0	304.1	285.5	289.2	268.8	215.4	208.4	206.1	202.9	188.8	77.3
International Liquidity					_Millions of US Dollars Unless Otherwise Indicated: End of Period_								
Total Reserves minus Gold	1l.d	405.3	595.5	598.8	160.1	130.8	268.0	193.1	64.7	83.4	....	....	....
SDRs	1b.d	.1	.8	9.8	.3	.4	1.1	.2	—	—	—	—	—
Reserve Position in the Fund	1c.d	.1	.1	.2	.2	.3	.4	.4	.4	.4	.5	.5	.5
Foreign Exchange	1d.d	405.1	594.6	588.9	159.6	130.1	266.5	192.5	64.3	82.9	....	....	....
Gold (Million Fine Troy Ounces)	1ad	.47	.76	.64	.77	.62	.73	.47	.20	.14	....	....	....
Gold (National Valuation)	1and	89.7	139.7	117.2	56.0	82.6	105.4	45.4	27.5	22.7	....	....	....
Monetary Authorities: Other Liab.	4..d	76.1	36.5	28.5	224.6	335.6	229.9	99.5	59.0	82.9	119.7	292.6	248.1
Deposit Money Banks: Assets	7a.d	321.3	275.0	299.8	314.7	179.3	156.9	163.4	146.0	230.6	219.0	147.9	180.7
Liabilities	7b.d	579.3	814.4	827.8	623.8	458.3	245.0	169.2	126.6	186.6	97.0	103.9	49.9
Other Banking Insts.: Assets	7e.d	1.0	3.9	6.4	1.3	.6	1.4	1.1	.7	—	—	—	—
Liabilities	7f.d	.2	17.0	15.4	6.8	2.4	2.6	4.0	3.0	1.8	.9	.7	—
Monetary Authorities						_Billions of Zimbabwe Dollars: End of Period_							
Foreign Assets	11	4.2	6.7	7.7	4.0	7.9	14.2	13.1	5.2	5.8	89.6	1,634.4	9,378.0
Claims on Central Government	12a	7.1	13.6	22.8	30.5	47.5	58.7	98.7	38.6	66.7	499.3	2,542.2	28,326.4
Claims on Nonfin.Pub.Enterprises	12c	.1	.1	.2	.2	.7	.7	.7	2.0	.6	.1	.1	988.6
Claims on Private Sector	12d	.2	.2	.3	.4	.8	1.1	2.0	2.3	2.7	7.2	35.6	3,443.7
Claims on Deposit Money Banks	12e	.4	1.3	1.3	1.4	4.4	3.2	8.1	26.6	62.8	423.7	3,249.7	3,483.1
Reserve Money	14	3.6	3.7	6.2	8.5	11.1	17.8	20.6	54.7	148.2	733.5	2,329.5	12,908.5
of which: Currency Outside DMBs	14a	1.5	1.8	2.4	3.6	4.5	7.3	9.9	25.6	79.7	441.7	1,655.9	9,875.8
Liabs.of the Central Bank:Securities	16ac	2.1	.9	—	—	—	—	—	—	—	—	732.3	4,926.9
Foreign Liabilities	16c	3.8	4.6	5.0	11.3	27.8	22.8	20.9	17.7	20.0	347.0	3,356.5	27,955.8
Central Government Deposits	16d	3.3	14.7	22.8	18.0	26.1	43.8	80.1	—	9.6	—	393.9	3,118.7
Capital Accounts	17a	.7	.9	.8	.8	1.0	2.0	1.9	5.0	6.3	12.5	1.9	1.1
Other Items (Net)	17r	−1.4	−2.9	−2.5	−2.3	−4.6	−8.4	−1.0	−2.7	−45.5	−73.1	648.0	−3,291.3
Deposit Money Banks						_Billions of Zimbabwe Dollars: End of Period_							
Reserves	20	2.0	1.8	3.6	4.3	6.0	10.1	9.7	30.6	88.7	610.6	3,904.0	17,413.9
Claims on Mon.Author.:Securities	20c	2.1	.6	—	—	—	—	—	—	—	—	732.3	4,926.9
Foreign Assets	21	2.7	2.6	3.2	5.9	6.7	6.0	9.0	8.0	12.7	180.4	847.6	14,091.8
Claims on Central Government	22a	1.0	6.0	7.1	7.1	6.7	11.2	30.9	56.6	108.5	167.3	3,560.6	20,223.2
Claims on Local Government	22b	—	—	—	.1	.2	.3	.4	.4	.7	1.5	31.7	74.2
Claims on Nonfin.Pub.Enterprises	22c	.7	.6	1.0	1.1	1.8	2.6	7.5	17.4	47.1	227.3	435.4	677.0
Claims on Private Sector	22d	11.7	15.1	18.1	27.1	36.8	41.4	62.0	101.2	293.4	2,116.6	4,981.0	15,793.4
Claims on Other Banking Insts	22f	—	.2	.3	.9	.1	1.5	1.9	2.1	10.4	22.4	52.9	96.0
Claims on Nonbank Financial Insts	22g	.1	—	.1	—	.2	.1	.7	6.0	6.2	52.5	102.8	86.6
Demand Deposits	24	5.8	9.4	11.3	17.1	21.4	27.8	44.2	106.0	275.4	1,636.4	5,148.2	34,048.0
Time, Savings,& Fgn.Currency Dep	25	5.8	5.2	8.1	9.8	8.3	11.5	25.0	49.2	172.3	717.1	2,377.3	13,678.4
Money Market Instruments	26aa	.7	.5	.3	.9	1.3	2.5	4.1	16.7	18.7	145.1	380.5	1,516.6
Foreign Liabilities	26c	4.9	7.6	9.0	11.6	17.1	9.3	9.3	7.0	10.3	79.9	595.3	3,887.3
Central Government Deposits	26d	.4	.7	1.1	1.8	1.7	2.0	5.3	6.7	23.6	53.7	267.0	1,106.5
Credit from Monetary Authorities	26g	.4	1.3	1.3	1.0	3.8	2.6	7.9	7.8	50.1	439.9	3,460.3	5,643.6
Capital Accounts	27a	1.9	2.1	2.5	4.4	6.4	9.5	15.2	31.4	79.9	406.2	1,964.1	10,175.9
Other Items (Net)	27r	.4	.2	−.1	—	−1.3	7.8	11.3	−2.4	−62.6	−99.6	455.5	3,326.6
Monetary Survey						_Billions of Zimbabwe Dollars: End of Period_							
Foreign Assets (Net)	31n	−1.8	−3.0	−3.1	−13.0	−30.2	−12.0	−8.1	−11.4	−11.7	−156.9	−1,469.8	−8,373.3
Domestic Credit	32	17.2	20.5	26.0	47.6	67.2	71.8	119.5	219.9	503.0	3,040.6	11,081.3	65,483.8
Claims on Central Govt. (Net)	32an	4.3	4.2	6.1	17.9	26.5	24.2	44.2	88.5	142.0	612.9	5,441.9	44,324.4
Claims on Local Government	32b	—	—	—	.1	.2	.3	.4	.4	.7	1.5	31.7	74.2
Claims on Nonfin.Pub.Enterprises	32c	.9	.8	1.1	1.3	2.5	3.3	8.2	19.4	47.7	227.4	435.5	1,665.5
Claims on Private Sector	32d	11.9	15.3	18.4	27.5	37.6	42.5	64.1	103.4	296.0	2,123.8	5,016.6	19,237.1
Claims on Other Banking Insts	32f	—	.2	.3	.9	.1	1.5	1.9	2.1	10.4	22.4	52.9	96.0
Claims on Nonbank Financial Inst	32g	.1	—	.1	—	.2	.1	.7	6.0	6.2	52.5	102.8	86.6
Money	34	7.4	11.3	13.9	21.3	26.3	35.5	54.4	132.1	356.6	2,086.7	6,856.6	44,746.2
Quasi-Money	35	5.8	5.2	8.1	9.8	8.3	11.5	25.0	49.2	172.3	717.1	2,377.3	13,678.4
Money Market Instruments	36aa	.7	.5	.3	.9	1.3	2.5	4.1	16.7	18.7	145.1	380.5	1,516.6
Liabs.of the Central Bank:Securities	36ac	—	.3	—	—	—	—	—	—	—	—	—	—
Capital Accounts	37a	2.6	—	3.3	5.3	7.5	11.5	17.1	36.5	86.2	418.7	1,966.0	10,177.1
Other Items (Net)	37r	−1.0	−2.7	−2.7	−2.7	−6.4	−1.2	10.8	−26.0	−142.5	−483.8	−1,968.9	−13,007.9
Money plus Quasi-Money	35l	13.1	16.5	22.0	31.1	34.6	47.0	79.4	181.3	529.0	2,803.8	9,233.9	58,424.6
Other Banking Institutions						_Billions of Zimbabwe Dollars: End of Period_							
Reserves	40	.9	3.6	4.5	7.5	4.7	5.1	12.3	21.3	50.2	150.3	511.5	2,347.9
Foreign Assets	41	—	—	.1	—	—	.1	.1	—	—	—	—	—
Claims on Central Government	42a	2.8	4.0	4.4	3.7	4.1	9.2	18.5	18.2	12.7	17.4	472.8	4,390.2
Claims on Local Government	42b	—	.1	.3	.4	.4	.4	.5	.4	.4	.4	.4	6.8
Claims on Nonfin.Pub.Enterprises	42c	.4	2.1	.6	.9	1.1	1.5	1.7	2.0	2.2	1.6	8.1	3.3
Claims on Private Sector	42d	4.0	5.6	8.3	12.4	15.0	16.1	16.5	25.4	65.7	154.3	287.5	1,085.1
Claims on Nonbank Financial Insts	42g	—	—	2.5	.7	—	—	—	—	.1	2.6	1.6	18.2
Time, Savings,& Fgn.Currency Dep	45	9.3	14.9	20.7	26.0	24.0	28.5	43.5	57.4	120.3	348.0	1,105.7	6,834.0
Money Market Instruments	46aa	.4	.5	.5	1.4	2.7	1.9	1.6	4.9	15.2	5.3	33.1	13.7
Foreign Liabilities	46c	—	.2	.2	.1	.1	.1	.2	.2	.1	.8	4.2	—
Credit from Deposit Money Banks	46h	—	.1	.1	.4	.3	.9	.4	1.3	3.4	10.2	12.7	—
Capital Accounts	47a	.7	1.0	1.5	2.1	2.0	4.0	7.5	9.3	15.4	65.6	256.9	2,470.3
Other Items (Net)	47r	−2.3	−1.3	−2.3	−4.4	−3.9	−3.1	−3.7	−5.6	−23.2	−103.2	−130.9	−1,466.6

Zimbabwe   698

		1994	1995	1996	1997	1998	1999	2000	2001	2002	2003	2004	2005
Banking Survey					*Billions of Zimbabwe Dollars: End of Period*								
Foreign Assets (Net)	51n	−1.8	−3.1	−3.2	−13.2	−30.3	−12.0	−8.3	−11.6	−11.8	−157.7	−1,473.9	−8,373.3
Domestic Credit	52	24.5	32.1	41.7	64.9	87.7	97.6	154.7	263.8	573.8	3,194.5	11,798.7	70,891.3
Claims on Central Govt. (Net)	52an	7.1	8.2	10.5	21.6	30.6	33.4	62.7	106.7	154.7	630.3	5,914.6	48,714.6
Claims on Local Government	52b	.1	.1	.3	.5	.7	.7	.8	.9	1.1	1.9	32.1	81.0
Claims on Nonfin.Pub.Enterprises	52c	1.3	2.9	1.7	2.1	3.6	4.8	9.9	21.4	50.0	229.1	443.6	1,668.8
Claims on Private Sector	52d	16.0	20.9	26.7	39.9	52.6	58.5	80.6	128.8	361.7	2,278.1	5,304.1	20,322.2
Claims on Nonbank Financial Inst.	52g	.1	—	2.5	.8	.2	.1	.7	6.0	6.3	55.1	104.3	104.8
Liquid Liabilities	55l	21.6	27.8	38.2	49.6	53.9	70.4	110.6	217.4	599.1	3,001.5	9,828.1	62,910.7
Money Market Instruments	56aa	1.1	1.0	.8	2.2	4.0	4.4	5.7	21.6	33.9	150.4	413.6	1,530.4
Liabs.of the Central Bank:Securities	56ac	—	.3	—	—	—	—	—	—	—	—	—	—
Capital Accounts	57a	3.3	4.0	4.8	7.4	9.5	15.5	24.5	45.7	101.7	484.3	2,222.9	12,647.3
Other Items (Net)	57r	−3.2	−4.0	−5.2	−7.6	−10.0	−4.8	5.6	−32.4	−172.7	−599.3	−2,140.0	−14,570.5
Interest Rates						*Percent Per Annum*							
Bank Rate (End of Period)	60	29.50	29.50	27.00	31.50	† 39.50	74.41	57.84	57.20	29.65	300.00	110.00	540.00
Money Market Rate	60b	30.90	29.64	26.18	25.15	37.22	53.13	64.98	21.52	32.35	110.05	129.58	....
Treasury Bill Rate	60c	29.22	27.98	24.53	22.07	32.78	50.48	64.78	17.60	28.51	52.72	125.68	185.11
Deposit Rate	60l	26.75	25.92	21.58	18.60	29.06	38.51	50.17	13.95	18.38	35.92	103.21	91.08
Lending Rate	60p	34.86	34.73	34.23	32.55	42.06	55.39	68.21	38.02	36.48	97.29	278.92	235.68
Prices, Production, Labor					*Index Numbers (2000=100): Period Averages*								
Consumer Prices	64	17.4	21.3	25.9	30.7	40.5	64.2	100.0	176.7	424.3	....	....	....
Manufacturing Prod.(1995=100)	66ey	115.8	100.0	103.6	106.9	....	....	....	....	....	....	....	....
					Number in Thousands: Period Averages								
Labor Force	67d	....	....	....	4,921		4,963						
Employment	67e	1,264	1,240	1,273	1,323	1,349	1,316	1,237	1,184	1,071	....	....	....
Intl. Transactions & Positions						*Billions of Zimbabwe Dollars*							
Exports	70	15.4	18.4	24.2	29.0	50.0	72.3	85.5	66.4	76.9	976.4	7,704.4	33,321.8
Imports, c.i.f.	71	18.3	23.0	38.2	37.6	64.0	81.4	82.8	94.4	96.4	1,192.6	11,166.3	61,500.0
Imports, f.o.b.	71.v	15.9	20.0	....									
Balance of Payments					*Millions of US Dollars: Minus Sign Indicates Debit*								
Current Account, n.i.e.	78ald	−424.9	....	....	....	....	....	....	....	....	....	....	....
Goods: Exports f.o.b.	78aad	1,961.1	....	....	....	....	....	....	....	....	....	....	....
Goods: Imports f.o.b.	78abd	−1,803.5	....	....	....	....	....	....	....	....	....	....	....
Trade Balance	78acd	157.6	....	....	....	....	....	....	....	....	....	....	....
Services: Credit	78add	383.2	....	....	....	....	....	....	....	....	....	....	....
Services: Debit	78aed	−711.7	....	....	....	....	....	....	....	....	....	....	....
Balance on Goods & Services	78afd	−170.9	....	....	....	....	....	....	....	....	....	....	....
Income: Credit	78agd	27.5	....	....	....	....	....	....	....	....	....	....	....
Income: Debit	78ahd	−321.2	....	....	....	....	....	....	....	....	....	....	....
Balance on Gds, Serv. & Inc.	78aid	−464.5	....	....	....	....	....	....	....	....	....	....	....
Current Transfers, n.i.e.: Credit	78ajd	69.4	....	....	....	....	....	....	....	....	....	....	....
Current Transfers: Debit	78akd	−29.8	....	....	....	....	....	....	....	....	....	....	....
Capital Account, n.i.e.	78bcd	284.4	....	....	....	....	....	....	....	....	....	....	....
Capital Account, n.i.e.: Credit	78bad	285.4	....	....	....	....	....	....	....	....	....	....	....
Capital Account: Debit	78bbd	−1.0	....	....	....	....	....	....	....	....	....	....	....
Financial Account, n.i.e.	78bjd	−25.5	....	....	....	....	....	....	....	....	....	....	....
Direct Investment Abroad	78bdd	−4.7	....	....	....	....	....	....	....	....	....	....	....
Dir. Invest. in Rep. Econ., n.i.e.	78bed	34.7	....	....	....	....	....	....	....	....	....	....	....
Portfolio Investment Assets	78bfd	—	....	....	....	....	....	....	....	....	....	....	....
Equity Securities	78bkd	—	....	....	....	....	....	....	....	....	....	....	....
Debt Securities	78bld	—	....	....	....	....	....	....	....	....	....	....	....
Portfolio Investment Liab., n.i.e.	78bgd	50.2	....	....	....	....	....	....	....	....	....	....	....
Equity Securities	78bmd	56.9	....	....	....	....	....	....	....	....	....	....	....
Debt Securities	78bnd	−6.7	....	....	....	....	....	....	....	....	....	....	....
Financial Derivatives Assets	78bwd	—	....	....	....	....	....	....	....	....	....	....	....
Financial Derivatives Liabilities	78bxd	—	....	....	....	....	....	....	....	....	....	....	....
Other Investment Assets	78bhd	−260.3	....	....	....	....	....	....	....	....	....	....	....
Monetary Authorities	78bod	—	....	....	....	....	....	....	....	....	....	....	....
General Government	78bpd	—	....	....	....	....	....	....	....	....	....	....	....
Banks	78bqd	−260.3	....	....	....	....	....	....	....	....	....	....	....
Other Sectors	78brd	—	....	....	....	....	....	....	....	....	....	....	....
Other Investment Liab., n.i.e.	78bid	154.7	....	....	....	....	....	....	....	....	....	....	....
Monetary Authorities	78bsd	−109.9	....	....	....	....	....	....	....	....	....	....	....
General Government	78btd	62.0	....	....	....	....	....	....	....	....	....	....	....
Banks	78bud	—	....	....	....	....	....	....	....	....	....	....	....
Other Sectors	78bvd	202.6	....	....	....	....	....	....	....	....	....	....	....
Net Errors and Omissions	78cad	80.2	....	....	....	....	....	....	....	....	....	....	....
Overall Balance	78cbd	−85.8	....	....	....	....	....	....	....	....	....	....	....
Reserves and Related Items	79dad	85.8	....	....	....	....	....	....	....	....	....	....	....
Reserve Assets	79dbd	12.9	....	....	....	....	....	....	....	....	....	....	....
Use of Fund Credit and Loans	79dcd	72.8	....	....	....	....	....	....	....	....	....	....	....
Exceptional Financing	79ded	....	....	....	....	....	....	....	....	....	....	....	....

Zimbabwe   698

		1994	1995	1996	1997	1998	1999	2000	2001	2002	2003	2004	2005
Government Finance					*Millions of Zimbabwe Dollars: Year Ending June 30*								
Deficit (-) or Surplus	80	−2,092	−5,791	−5,147	−5,077	....	....	....	....	....	....	....	....
Total Revenue and Grants	81y	13,699	18,687	23,811	31,126	....	....	....	....	....	....	....	....
Revenue	81	12,776	16,998	22,808	30,670	....	....	....	....	....	....	....	....
Grants	81z	923	1,690	1,003	456	....	....	....	....	....	....	....	....
Exp. & Lending Minus Repay	82z	15,790	24,479	28,958	36,202	....	....	....	....	....	....	....	....
Expenditure	82	14,538	22,000	29,691	36,454	....	....	....	....	....	....	....	....
Lending Minus Repayments	83	1,252	2,479	−733	−252	....	....	....	....	....	....	....	....
Total Financing	80h	2,092	5,791	5,147	5,077	....	....	....	....	....	....	....	....
Domestic	84a	1,733	4,802	3,973	5,168	....	....	....	....	....	....	....	....
Foreign	85a	359	990	1,175	−91	....	....	....	....	....	....	....	....
Total Debt by Residence	88	31,131	47,503	53,201	59,303	....	....	....	....	....	....	....	....
Domestic	88a	12,875	24,671	31,407	30,371	....	....	....	....	....	....	....	....
Foreign	89a	18,257	22,832	21,793	28,932	....	....	....	....	....	....	....	....
National Accounts						*Billions of Zimbabwe Dollars*							
Househ.Cons.Expend.,incl.NPISHs	96f	32	40	55	76	94	162	242	572	1,410	4,292	17,713	....
Government Consumption Expend	91f	9	11	14	17	23	31	46	99	216	924	5,015	5,414
Gross Fixed Capital Formation	93e	12	12	16	19	30	33	45	66	121	549	3,047	....
Changes in Inventories	93i	4	−3	—	—	—	3	6	−12	−32	−125	−625	....
Exports of Goods and Services	90c	19	24	31	38	62	106	118	100	89	1,294	8,587	32,001
Imports of Goods and Services (-)	98c	21	25	31	46	65	102	119	124	129	1,552	10,481	40,653
Gross Domestic Product (GDP)	99b	56	62	86	102	144	228	329	709	1,698	5,519	23,802	129,533
Net Primary Income from Abroad	98.n	−2	−3	−3	−5	−9	−9	−11	−12	−9	−7	....	....
Gross National Income (GNI)	99a	53	59	84	103	140	221	303	541	1,119	4,373	14,457	....
GDP Volume 1990 Prices	99b.p	23	23	25	26	27	26	24	23	22	20	19	....
GDP Volume (2000=100)	99bvp	96.5	96.7	106.8	109.7	112.7	108.5	100.0	97.5	93.2	83.5	80.1	....
GDP Deflator (2000=100)	99bip	17.7	19.4	24.4	28.3	38.8	64.1	100.0	221.3	554.1	2,011.4	9,042.0	....
						Millions: Midyear Estimates							
Population	99z	11.61	11.82	12.01	12.19	12.34	12.48	12.60	12.70	12.79	12.86	12.94	13.01

2006, International Monetary Fund : *International Financial Statistics Yearbook*

Notes

Notes

Notes